时 代 汉 英 词 典

TIMES
CHINESE-ENGLISH
DICTIONARY

DATE DUE

时代汉英词典

TIMES
CHINESE-ENGLISH
DICTIONARY

北京外国语学院英语系《汉英词典》编写组编

联邦出版社词典组改编

《汉英词典》编辑人员

主　　编	吴景荣
副主编	王佐良　刘世沐　危东亚　王　殷
编　　委	应曼蓉　王晋熙　高厚堃　郑荣成
	吴千之　庄绎传　赵慕昂　林　易
	林学洪　王桂林
英语顾问	大卫·柯鲁克
英语编辑	杜秉洲　陈文伯　王绍坊　张　志
	王　泭　刘国云　杨光慈　吕　霞
	章士法
汉语编辑	刘　沐　马耀徽　钟尚钧　林杏光
	陈敦荃
科技编辑	关品枢　王雪华　梁友德　方廷钰

联邦出版社·商务印书馆

©1980 Federal Publications (S) Pte Ltd

by

ngapore 536196

.com.sg/fpl

Ltd.

Shau Kei Wan, Hong Kong.

Original edition under the title
The Chinese-English Dictionary
first published 1979 by
The Commercial Press (Hong Kong) Ltd.

原版《汉英词典》由
香港鲗鱼涌芬街2号D侨英大厦五楼
商务印书馆（香港）有限公司出版
此改编版由
新加坡536196邮区新工业路1号
联邦出版（新）私人有限公司暨
香港鲗鱼涌芬街2号D侨英大厦五楼
商务印书馆（香港）有限公司联合出版
©1980联邦出版（新）私人有限公司

Reprinted 1980, 1982, 1983, 1984, 1985, 1986, 1987, 1988, 1989,
1990, 1991 (thrice), 1992, 1993, 1994 (twice), 1995 (twice), 1996,
1997, 1998

ISBN 98101 3906 3

Printed by Percetakan Warisan Sdn Bhd

出版说明

　　《时代汉英词典》是根据1979年出版的《汉英词典》改编的。原书由北京外国语学院英语系编写；先后参加编写、修改等工作的中外专家有五十多人。

　　为了适合广大读者的需要，新加坡联邦出版社和香港商务印书馆合作，将原书改编成为一部中型词典，称为《时代汉英词典》。

　　《时代汉英词典》保留了《汉英词典》的特色和精华，只删去了原书里冷僻单字、词条和具有强烈地方色彩的例句。此外，改编本还特别标出汉语中最常用的二千个单字。经过改编后，这部《时代汉英词典》将成为各阶层读者、教师、学生和翻译工作者不可缺少的汉英工具书。它内容较新又切合实用，也可供外国人士学习和使用汉语时参考。

　　《时代汉英词典》收汉语单字条目五千多，其中包括极少数的音变字。收入的多字条目四万余，连同合成词、词化短语及例证等达八万余。

　　本词典的编写，在汉语方面，以现代汉语为主；在英语方面，以现代英语为规范。词语释义力求准确、简明，例证力求实用；英译尽可能反映汉语的语体特点。

　　词典正文的单字和多字条目按汉语拼音顺序排列。正文前附有部首检字；书末附有汉语拼音方案，汉语拼音和威妥玛(Wade)式拼法音节表等附录。

FOREWORD

The *Times Chinese-English Dictionary* is an adaptation of *The Chinese-English Dictionary*. The original edition, published in 1979, was compiled and edited by the Beijing Foreign Languages Institute. Over fifty specialists, both Chinese and non-Chinese, took part in this lexicographical work of unprecedented dimensions.

This edition, which is a joint effort of Federal Publications, Singapore, and The Commercial Press, Hongkong, aims to meet the different requirements of a wider range of dictionary users. This is the first medium-sized, comprehensive Chinese-English Dictionary to be published locally.

This DICTIONARY incorporates the special features and approach of the original edition. Only rare words, unfamiliar allusions and strongly localised illustrative examples have been deleted. The 2,000 most frequently used Chinese characters are asterisked.

The adaptation of this DICTIONARY is an attempt to provide the learners and users of the Chinese language with a reference book comparatively new in content and more suited to practical use. It will be an indispensable linguistic tool for general readers, teachers, students and translators. It will also be useful for foreigners learning or working in the Chinese language.

There are over 5,000 single-character entries, including a small number of characters with variant tones, besides over 40,000 compound-character entries and over 40,000 compound words, set phrases and examples.

Emphasis was placed on using modern Chinese, and modern English was taken as the basis of all English translations. Care has been taken to ensure that definitions of words and expressions are clear and precise, and the examples practical.

All entries are arranged in alphabetical order according to the Chinese Phonetic System. A Radical Index has been placed before the text of the DICTIONARY for the convenience of the user. There are six appendices, including the Scheme for the Chinese Phonetic Alphabet and the Chinese Phonetic Alphabet and Wade System.

目　录
Contents

目　录
Contents

用 法 说 明

一 条目安排

1. 本词典所收条目分单字条目和多字条目。前者用大字排印，后者加鱼尾号"【 】"。

2. 单字条目按汉语拼音字母顺序排列。同音异调的汉字按声调顺序排列。同音同调的汉字，按笔划多少排列。单字右上角的星号（＊）代表最常用的二千个汉字。

3. 多字条目按第一个字分列于单字条目之下。同一单字条目下的多字条目不止一条时，按第二个字的汉语拼音字母顺序和笔划多少排列。第二个字相同时，按第三个字排列，依此类推。

4. 汉字字形相同而音或调不同者，分立条目。如："呆"ái 和"呆"dāi

5. 汉字字形及字音相同而意义不同者，作为同一条目的不同义项处理。

6. 轻声字一般紧接在同形的非轻声字后面。如："家"jia 排在"家"jiā 之后。但是，"了"le、"着"zhe 等轻声字排在去声音节之后。

7. 在同一单字条目下，多字条目意义相同，仅在用字上略有差异，一般只收录其中较常见者。在该条最后，加"又作…"。如：【差之毫厘，谬以千里】… 又作"差之毫厘，失之千里"。

二 注 音

1. 条目用汉语拼音字母注音。

2. 声调一般只注原调，不注变调。

3. 轻声不加调号。如：【喇叭】lǎba。

4. 多字条目的注音中，音节界限有可能混淆时，加隔音号"'"。如：【海鸥】hǎi'ōu；【阴暗】yīn'àn。

5. 专有名词和姓氏的注音，第一个字母大写。根据国名、地名、人名等命名的普通事物名称，第一个字母小写。

三 释义和例证

1. 专业条目一般注明所属专业或学科名称。名称或其略语，放在尖括号"〈 〉"内。凡日常生活中习见或汉字本身能表明所属专业或学科，不致引起误解者，不另加注释。

2. 一般条目根据需要注明修辞特征和六种虚词（副词、介词、连词、助词、叹词、象声词）及部分量词的词类，所用略语也放在尖括号"〈 〉"内。

3. 有关语法特征、使用范围、内容涵义等方面的简略汉语说明，放在方括号"〔 〕"内。凡英语中无适当对应词语或概念不完全符合者，酌用此类注释。如：

吧…〈助〉①〔在句末表示商量、提议、请求、命令〕：我们走～。Let's go.

【关于】…〈介〉〔引进某种行为或事物的关系者，组成介词结构〕about; on; with regard to; concerning

4. 条目如系简称，一般注出全称。如：

干… ②〈简〉（干部）

5. 条目一般用对应的英语释义；无适当对应词语时，用英语解释。同一义项下有两个或两个以上的英语释义时，用分号";"隔开。一个条目有两个或两个以上不同意义时，分立义项，用①②③等数码标出顺序；某一义项需再细分时，用ⓐⓑⓒ等字母标出顺序。如：

家… ① family; household… ② home… ③ a person or family engaged in a certain trade… ④ a specialist in a certain field…

把… ⑦〈量〉ⓐ〔用于有柄的器具〕：一～刀 a knife… ⓑ〔指一手抓起的数量〕：一～米 a handful of rice

6. 如英语对应词语的含义比汉语条目广泛或一词多义，则在圆括号"（ ）"内用英语作限定性说明。如：

嫁… ① (of a woman) marry

【机舱】… ① engine room (of a ship) ② passenger compartment (of an aircraft); cabin

【历次】… all previous (occasions, etc.)

7. 某些条目在英语释义后，根据需要，就有关背景、典故或其他方面加补充性说明，放在圆括号"（ ）"内或用逗号","隔开。如：

【嫦娥】… the goddess of the moon (the lady in the legend who swallowed elixir stolen from her husband and flew to the moon)

8. 某些专业条目在英语释义后，加拉丁语学名或符号。

9. 条目释义（或注释）后，根据需要，收入词、词组或句子作为例证。例证前面加冒号"："。例证中与本条目相同的部分，用代字号"～"表示。例证英语译文不止一个时，如果是词或词组，用分号"；"隔开；如果是句子，则用"或"字隔开。例证与例证之间，用斜线号"/"隔开。如：

【程度】…: 在很大（一定）～上 to a great (certain) extent/ 在不同～上 in varying degrees

【电话】…: 有你的～。There's a phone call for you. 或 You're wanted on the phone.

10. 例证中如有可以替换的部分，这部分及其译文都用圆括号"（　）"括出。如：

界…: 动(植、矿)物～ the animal (vegetable, mineral) kingdom

【工程】…: 土木(机械、电机、采矿)～ civil (mechanical, electrical, mining) engineering

11. 条目释义或例证译文中，如有可以省略的部分，用圆括号"（　）"括出。如：

户…: 存～ (bank) depositor

12. 条目释义或例证译文中，如有可以替换的英语词语时，也用圆括号"（　）"括出，另加"或"字。如：

【改观】… change the appearance (或 face) of

搞…: ～运动 carry on a movement (或 campaign)

13. 如条目释义或例证译文不止一个，适用范围各不相同，则在释义或译文前，用汉语加限定性说明，也放在圆括号"（　）"内。如：

【国会】… parliament; （美）Congress; （日）the Diet

【来历】…: ～不明（指事物）of unknown origin; （指人）of dubious background or of questionable antecedents

【陛下】…（直接称呼）Your Majesty; （间接称呼）His or Her Majesty

14. 在条目释义和例证译文中，出现某些专有名词或比较特殊的词语时，用汉语酌加注释。

15. 某些条目释义或例证译文后，加英文缩写。如：

【背面】…: 请阅～ please turn over (P.T.O.)

16. 在某些成语、谚语、习语及其他词语的条目释义或例证译文之后，加点明实质的补充性说明，用破折号"—"隔开。如：

【画蛇添足】… draw a snake and add feet to it — ruin the effect by adding sth. superfluous

【并蒂莲】… twin lotus flowers on one stalk — a devoted married couple

17. 中国人名、地名以及某些中国特有事物的名称，按汉语拼音方案音译。如：

亩… *mu*, a unit of area (= 0.0667 hectares): ～产量 per *mu* yield

四　合成词和词化短语

以多字条目领头的大多数合成词和词化短语，不按义项分列，而按汉语拼音字母顺序，集中排列在该条目释义或例证之后，前加一菱形号"◇"，其他符号的用法与例证部分相同。如数量较多，则另起一行排列。专业词语也酌加专业或学科注释。如：

【玻璃】… ① glass: 雕花～ cut glass/ 彩色～ stained glass/ 泡沫～ cellular glass ② <口> nylon; plastic

◇ ～杯 glass; tumbler

Guide to the Use of the Dictionary

I. Arrangement of Entries

1. All entries are divided into single-character and compound-character entries. The former are set in large, boldface type, the latter are placed in boldface square brackets " 【 】 "

2. Single-character entries are listed in strict alphabetical order. Characters with the same pronunciation but different tone are arranged according to tone. Characters with both the same pronunciation and tone are arranged according to number of strokes. The asterisk (*) at the right hand corner of a single-character entry is used to indicate 2000 most frequently used Chinese words.

3. Compound-character entries are arranged by first character under the respective single-character entries. Where there is more than one compound-character entry under a single-character entry, listing is done according to the alphabetical order of the second character in the compound. If the second character is the same in the two entries then listing is done according to the third character, and so on.

4. Separate entries are made for characters that are the same but have two or more pronunciations or different tones. For example:

"呆" ái 和 "呆" dāi。

5. Characters with the same form and pronunciation but with different meanings are dealt with in subentries in the same single-character entry.

6. Characters with no tone are listed after characters with the same form which have tones. Thus "家" jia is listed after "家" jiā , However, "了" le, "着" zhe , and other characters without tones are listed after characters with a fourth tone (去声).

7. In listing character-compounds that have slightly different usages, only the more common form is given. Variant forms are placed at the end of the entry with the words "also read" ("又作") preceding them. Thus: (差之毫厘，谬以千里)－chā

zhī haólí, miù yǐ qiānlǐ (an error the breadth of a single hair can lead you a thousand li astray), 又作"差之毫厘，失之千里"。

II. Phonetics

1. All entries are recorded in Chinese Phonetics (hanyupinyin).

2. Tonal changes within compound words are not generally marked.

3. Characters with no tones have no marking. Thus: (喇叭) lǎba .

4. An apostrophe (') is used to separate syllables in compound-character entries that may be confused. Thus : 【海鸥】 hǎi'ōu; 【阴暗】 yīn'àn.

5. The first letter of special names and surnames is capitalized. Common objects named after countries, places or people are not capitalized.

III. Definitions and Examples

1. Specialized entries generally note the names of the specialty or science to which they refer. These names or their abbreviations are put in angle brackets " 〈 〉 ". All specialized or scientific terms that are in common use, or whose relation to a specialized field or science is obvious from the Chinese characters, are not separately annotated.

2. Annotations explaining figures of speech, parts of speech (such as adverbs, prepositions, conjunctions, auxiliaries, exclamations and onomatopes) and some classifiers are also placed in angle brackets " 〈 〉 "

3. Explanations of the peculiarities of Chinese grammar, the scope of use of certain words or phrases or their implication are put in square brackets " 〔 〕 ". All words without an equivalent word, words or expression in English are annotated in this way. Thus:

吧…〈助〉①〔在句末表示商量、提议、请求、命令〕:我们走～。Let's go.

【关于】…〈介〉〔引进某种行为或事物的关系者,组成介词结构〕about; on; with regard to; concerning

4. If an entry is an abbreviation, the full word is put in brackets after it. Thus:

干… ②〈简〉(干部)

5. Entries generally use equivalent English definitions. Words and expressions that do not have an appropriate English definitions are explained in English. When two or more explanations are necessary, a semicolon ";" is used to divide them. The different meanings of an entry are listed numerically①②③. When finer divisions are required, ⓐⓑⓒ and so on are used. Thus:

家… ① family; household… ② home… ③ a person or family engaged in a certain trade… ④ a specialist in a certain field…

把… ⑦〈量〉 ⓐ〔用于有柄的器具〕: 一～刀 a knife… ⓑ〔指一手抓起的数量〕: 一～米 a handful of rice

6. An explanation is made in English in brackets when an English equivalent has a wider meaning or different meanings than the Chinese. Thus:

嫁… ① (of a woman) marry

【机舱】… ① engine room (of a ship) ② passenger compartment (of an aircraft); cabin

【历次】… all previous (occasions, etc.)

7. Where necessary, further explanations of the background or origin of a term or name are made in English in brackets or marked off by a comma. Thus:

【嫦娥】… the goddess of the moon (the lady in the legend who swallowed elixir stolen from her husband and flew to the moon)

8. Latin or scientific symbols are put in brackets after the English definition where applicable.

9. Where necessary, examples of usage have been given after the definition or explanation of a word or expression. All examples are preceded by a colon ":", and the word or words in the examples that are the same as the entry are represented by a wave line "～". When there is more than one English translation for an example then they are divided by a semicolon ";". If, however, the different translation is an independent sentence, the division is marked by the word "or" ("或"). Examples themselves are divided by a vergule "/". Thus:

【程度】…: 在很大(一定)～上 to a great (certain) extent/在不同～上 in varying degrees

【电话】…: 有你的～。There's a phone call for you. 或 You're wanted on the phone.

10. If there are sections of the example that can be substituted by another word or words, then the word or words are placed in brackets in both the Chinese and in the English. Thus:

界…: 动(植、矿)物～ the animal (vegetable, mineral) kingdom

【工程】…: 土木(机械、电机、采矿)～ civil (mechanical, electrical, mining) engineering

11. If deletions of a word or words can be made in the definitions of the entries or the translations of the examples then these are marked by brackets "( )" Thus:

户…: 存～ (bank) depositor

12. If there are English words or phrases that can replace other words or phrases in the definitions or examples, these are put in brackets and the word "or" ("或") is put before it. Thus:

【改观】… change the appearance (或 face) of

搞…: ～运动 carry on a movement (或 campaign)

13. If there are more than one English definition or example, then a Chinese explanation is placed in brackets in front of the English definition or example. Thus:

【国会】… parliament; (美) Congress; (日) the Diet

【来历】…: ～不明 (指事物) of unknown origin; (指人) of dubious background or of questionable antecedents

【陛下】… (直接称呼) Your Majesty; (间接称呼) His or Her Majesty

14. If there are specialized names or words in the English definitions or examples, an explanation is made in Chinese.

15. English abbreviations are added in brackets after the English definitions or translation of examples. Thus:

【背面】…: 请阅～ please turn over (P.T.O.)

16. Additional explanations of definitions or examples of four-character idioms, proverbs, idiomatic usage or other expressions are placed after a dash "—". Thus:

【画蛇添足】… draw a snake and add feet to it — ruin the effect by adding sth. superfluous

【并蒂莲】… twin lotus flowers on one stalk — a devoted married couple

17. All Chinese personal names, place names, and the names of things peculiar to China are spelt

in the Chinese Phonetic Alphabet (hanyupinyin). Thus:

亩… *mu*, a unit of area (= 0.0667 hectares): ~ 产量 per *mu* yield

IV. Compound Words and Set Phrases

The majority of compound words and set phrases that are preceded by compound-character entries are listed according to alphabetical (Chinese Phonetic Alphabet) order after the definitions or examples of their respective entries and are preceded by a diamond " ◇ " All other symbols used in these listings are the same as those used in the examples. If there are many compound words or set phrases, they are listed on a separate line. Specialized or scientific annotations are added to specialized words and phrases. Thus:

【玻璃】… ① glass: 雕花 ~ cut glass/ 彩色~ stained glass/ 泡沫~ cellular glass ② 〈口〉 nylon; plastic

◇ ~杯 glass; tumbler

略 语 表

（按汉语拼音字母顺序排列）

Table of Abbreviations

〈贬〉	贬义	derogatory sense		〈摄〉	摄影	cinematography
〈测〉	测绘	mapping		〈生〉	生物	biology
〈地〉	地质学；地理学	geology; geography		〈生化〉	生物化学	bio-chemistry
〈电〉	电学；电工	electricity; electrical engineering		〈生理〉	生理学；解剖学	physiology; anatomy
〈动〉	动物；动物学	animal; zoology		〈史〉	历史	history
〈法〉	法律	law		〈书〉	文言书面语	literary language
〈方〉	方言	dialect		〈数〉	数学	mathematics
〈纺〉	纺织印染	textile and dyeing		〈水〉	水利	irrigation
〈讽〉	讽刺语	satirical term		〈叹〉	叹词	exclamation
〈副〉	副词	adverb		〈套〉	套语	polite formula
〈工美〉	工艺美术	arts and crafts		〈体〉	体育	sports
〈化〉	化学；化工	chemistry; chemical industry		〈天〉	天文学	astronomy
〈化纤〉	化学纤维	chemical fibre		〈外〉	外交	diplomacy
〈环保〉	环境保护	environmental protection		〈婉〉	婉辞	euphemism
〈机〉	机械	machinery		〈微〉	微生物	microbiology
〈简〉	简称	abbreviation		〈无〉	无线电	radio
〈建〉	建筑	construction		〈物〉	物理学	physics
〈交〉	交通运输	transportation		〈象〉	象声词	onomatope
〈教〉	教育	education		〈心〉	心理学	psychology
〈介〉	介词	preposition		〈讯〉	电信	telecommunications
〈经〉	经济	economics		〈谚〉	谚语	proverb
〈敬〉	敬辞	polite expression		〈药〉	药物；药物学	pharmaceutical; pharmacology
〈旧〉	旧时用语	archaic expression		〈冶〉	冶金	metallurgy
〈剧〉	戏剧	drama		〈医〉	医学	medicine
〈军〉	军事	military		〈印〉	印刷	printing
〈口〉	口语	colloquial		〈邮〉	邮政	postal service
〈矿〉	矿物；矿业	mineral; mining		〈渔〉	渔业	fishery
〈连〉	连词	conjunction		〈字航〉	宇宙航行	astronavigation
〈量〉	量词	classifier		〈语〉	语言学	linguistics
〈林〉	林业	forestry		〈原〉	原子能	atomic energy
〈逻〉	逻辑学	logic		〈乐〉	音乐	music
〈骂〉	骂人的话	abusive language		〈哲〉	哲学	philosophy
〈牧〉	畜牧业	animal husbandry		〈植〉	植物；植物学	botanical; botany
〈农〉	农业	agriculture		〈纸〉	造纸	papermaking
〈气〉	气象学	meteorology		〈助〉	助词	auxiliary word
〈谦〉	谦辞	self-depreciatory expression		〈自〉	自动控制	automatic control
〈商〉	商业	commerce		〈宗〉	宗教	religion
				〈尊〉	尊称	respectful form of address

部 首 检 字
Radical Index

（一） 部首目录

部首左边的号码表示部首的次序

一 画	35 又	70 彐（彑⺕）	105 中	140 业	175 缶	209 鱼
1 丶	36 廴	71 弓	106 贝	141 目	176 耒	**九 画**
2 一	37 厶	72 己（巳）	107 见	142 田	177 舌	210 音
3 丨	38 凵	73 女	108 父	143 由	178 竹（⺮）	211 革
4 丿	39 匕	74 子（孑）	109 气	144 申	179 臼	212 是
5 乛	**三 画**	75 马	110 牛（牜）	145 罒	180 自	213 骨
6 乛	40 氵	76 幺	111 手	146 皿	181 血	214 香
7 乙（乛乚）	41 忄	77 纟（糸）	112 毛	147 钅	182 舟	215 鬼
二 画	42 丬（爿）	78 巛	113 攵	148 矢	183 羽	216 食
8 冫	43 亡	79 小（⺌）	114 片	149 禾	184 艮（⻌）	**十 画**
9 亠	44 广	**四 画**	115 斤	150 白	**七 画**	217 高
10 讠	45 丷	80 灬	116 爪（爫）	151 瓜	185 言	218 鬲
11 二	46 门	81 心	117 尺	152 鸟	186 辛	219 影
12 十	47 辶	82 斗	118 月	153 皮	187 辰	**十一画**
13 厂	48 工	83 火	119 殳	154 癶	188 麦	220 麻
14 ナ	49 土（士）	84 文	120 欠	155 矛	189 走	221 鹿
15 匚	50 卄	85 方	121 风	156 疋	190 赤	**十二画**
16 卜（⺊）	51 廾	86 户	122 氏	**六 画**	191 豆	222 黑
17 刂	52 大	87 礻	123 比	157 羊（⺶⺷）	192 束	**十三画**
18 冂	53 尢	88 王	124 屮	158 关	193 酉	223 鼓
19 冂	54 寸	89 主	125 水	159 米	194 豕	224 鼠
20 ⺈	55 扌	90 天（夭）	**五 画**	160 齐	195 里	**十四画**
21 亻	56 弋	91 韦	126 立	161 衣	196 足	225 鼻
22 厂	57 巾	92 耂	127 疒	162 亦	197 釆	
23 人（入）	58 口	93 廿（卄）	128 穴	163 耳	198 豸	226 余类
24 八（丷）	59 囗	94 木	129 衤	164 臣	199 谷	
25 乂	60 山	95 不	130 夫	165 戈	200 身	
26 勹	61 巾	96 犬	131 玉	166 西（覀）	201 角	
27 刀（⺈）	62 彳	97 歹	132 示	167 束	**八 画**	
28 力	63 彡	98 瓦	133 去	168 亚	202 青	
29 儿	64 夕	99 牙	134 业	169 而	203 卓	
30 几（凡）	65 夂	100 车	135 甘	170 页	204 雨	
31 ㄱ	66 丸	101 戈	136 石	171 至	205 非	
32 卩	67 尸	102 止	137 龙	172 光	206 齿	
33 阝（在左）	68 饣	103 日	138 戊	173 虍	207 隹	
34 阝（在右）	69 孑	104 曰	139 ⺍	174 虫	208 金	

（二）检字表

字右边的号码指词典正文的页码

甲 173
电 80
曲 307
曲 308
曳 466
冒 248
冕 254

(105) 中部
中 531
中 533
忠 532
贵 136
盅 532

(106) 贝部
贝 13
二画
则 506
三画
财 31
四画
贮 538
贤 426
贬 18
败 7
货 162
贩 99
贪 370
贫 283
购 127
贯 133
五画
贱 178
贴 384
贷 69
贸 248
贺 146
贻 472
费 104
六画
资 544
账 504
贼 115
赂 507
贿 160
赃 530
赊 544
赈 234
赆 239
七画
赈 519
赊 332
八画
赔 277
赋 113
赌 87
赎 354
赐 59
十画
赚 540
赘 542
赙 113
十二画
赠 508
赝 461
赞 504

十三画
赡 328

(107) 见部
见 177
觅 427
规 135
览 220
觉 184
觉 202
觊 382
觎 171
觐 493
觑 193
觑 309

(108) 父部
父 112
爷 465
爸 6
斧 111
釜 111
爹 82

(109) 气部
气 291
四画
氛 106
五画
氢 302
六画
氧 462
氨 479
八画
氯 240

(110) 牛(牜)部
牛 270
二画
牝 283
三画
牡 261
四画
牧 262
物 417
五画
牯 129
牲 339
六画
特 375
犄 418
七画
犁 225
八画
犊 87
犄 166
十画
犒 208
十一画
犟 225

(111) 手部
手 350

拜 7
挈 299
挚 530
拿 263
挛 367
挲 42
摩 304
攀 275

(112) 毛部
毛 248
毡 509
毫 142
毽 372
毯 179
氅 40

(113) 攵部
二画
收 349
三画
改 115
五画
政 523
故 129
六画
效 435
七画
救 334
教 183
敕 185
敚 198
敛 17
敝 229
敏 256
敢 117
八画
敦 90
散 324
敬 196
敞 40
九画
数 354
数 355
十一画
敷 109

(114) 片部
片 280
片 281
版 8
牍 275
牒 82
牖 490

(115) 斤部
斤 189
斥 48
欣 440
所 367
断 88
斯 361
新 440
斮 544

(116) 爪(爫)部
爪 514
爪 538
三画
妥 397
孚 110
四画
受 351
觅 252
爬 321
爰 274
五画
爱 496
六画
爲 2
舀 464
奚 418
八画
舜 359
十画
爵 109
十三画
爵 203

(117) 尺部
尺 48
尽 190
尽 191
昼 534
咫 528

(118) 月部
月 499
二画
肋 223
肌 165
三画
肝 117
肛 118
肚 87
肚 87
肘 534
肠 39
四画
肪 101
肮 4
育 494
肤 109
肺 104
肢 525
胧 542
肾 337
肿 532
服 110
服 112
胀 513
朋 278
股 129
胁 437
肥 103
五画
胖 275
胖 276
脉 246

脉 260
背 13
胡 151
胚 277
胧 237
胪 239
胆 70
胛 173
胜 339
胞 10
胝 525
胎 369
胫 196
六画
脊 168
脊 169
朔 360
脒 519
胼 281
脑 265
胶 183
脐 289
脏 504
脏 504
朗 221
胰 472
胱 134
胭 457
脓 270
脸 215
脆 61
胳 120
胸 445
脂 525
七画
脱 396
脚 184
脯 23
脖 111
脯 287
豚 396
脸 229
八画
腌 111
脾 466
腔 296
腕 402
期 288
腊 218
腊 419
腌 457
腴 382
腴 492
脾 280
九画
腠 483
腾 376
腈 376
腻 268
腩 265
腥 442
腮 323
腼 254
腰 463
腹 113
腺 428
腿 395
十画

膀 9
膀 276
膈 122
膜 258
膊 24
膂 240
十一画
膝 376
膝 419
膛 373
十二画
膳 328
膨 278
十三画
臌 477
臆 327
臃 484
臊 251
臌 325
臂 14
臀 17
臀 396

(119) 殳部
殴 273
段 88
殷 457
殿 479
毁 159
殿 81
毅 477

(120) 欠部
欠 296
三画
欢 492
四画
欧 273
七画
欷 419
欸 93
欸 93
欸 93
欸 93
八画
款 215
欺 288
九画
歇 436
歃 326
十画
歌 296
十一画
歉 121
十一画
歙 448

(121) 风部
风 107
飓 201
飘 282

(122) 氏部
氏 345
昏 160

(123) 比部
比 15
毕 17
皆 185
毙 17
琵 280

(124) 聿部
肃 228
肃 364
肆 363
肇 516

(125) 水部
水 357
氽 64
沓 369
浆 180
淼 255

(126) 立部
立 227
一画
产 38
三画
妾 299
四画
亲 299
亲 304
竖 355
飒 323
五画
站 511
竞 196
七画
童 389
竣 204
八画
靖 196
九画
竭 187
端 88

(127) 疒部
疔 231
二画
疔 231
三画
疟 272
疠 120
疚 198
疡 461
四画
疮 56
疫 476
疯 108
疤 5
五画
疴 209
疯病 22

症 521
症 523
疾 168
疹 519
疼 376
疲 280
痉 196
六画
痒 462
痔 530
疵 472
疣 58
痊 310
痕 147
七画
痧 326
痣 530
痘 86
痨 221
痦 280
痢 228
痪 156
痛 390
八画
痰 371
痹 61
痱 104
瘫 244
痼 130
痴 47
痿 494
九画
瘩 68
瘟 409
瘦 352
瘠 168
瘤 237
瘛 371
十画
瘪 513
瘪 311
瘫 480
十二画
癌 1
十三画
瘰 477
癞 219
癣 280
十四画
癣 451
十六画
癫 79
十八画
癯 308

(128) 穴部
穴 451
二画
穷 304
究 197
三画
空 211
空 212
帘 228

A

ā

阿 * ā 〈方〉〔用于小名、姓、排行或亲属名称前〕: ～宝 A Bao/ ～唐 A Tang; Tang/ ～大 the eldest/ ～哥 elder brother/ ～爹 dad/ ～婆 granny
另见 ē
【阿飞】āfēi a youth given to rowdy behaviour and queer dress; Teddy boy
【阿Q】·Ā Kiū 或 Ā Qiū A Q, the main character in Lu Xun's *The True Story of A Q* (《阿Q正传》), a backward peasant who interprets his defeats as moral victories
【阿门】āmén 〈宗〉amen
【阿姨】āyí ①〈方〉one's mother's sister; auntie ② a child's form of address for any woman of its mother's generation; auntie ③ nurse (in a family)

啊 ā 〈叹〉〔表示惊异或赞叹〕: ～! 庄稼长得真好哇! Oh, what a wonderful crop!

á

啊 á 〈叹〉〔表示追问或要求再说一遍〕: ～? 你说什么? Eh? 或 Pardon?/ ～, 你明儿倒是去不去呀? Well, are you going tomorrow or not?

ǎ

啊 ǎ 〈叹〉〔表示惊疑〕: ～! 这条铁路只用两年就修成啦? What! This railway took only two years to build?

à

啊 à 〈叹〉①〔表示应诺, 音较短〕: ～, 我就来。All right, I'm coming. ②〔表示明白过来, 音较长〕: ～, 原来是你! Ah, so it's you.

a

啊 * a 〈助〉①〔用于句末, 表示赞叹、肯定、嘱咐等语气〕: 多好的天儿～! What a fine day!/ 这次参观收获不小～! What a lot of things we've learned during this visit!/ 你这话说得～。What you say is quite true./ 你可要小心～! Do be careful! ②〔用于句末, 表示疑问的语气〕: 这消息是真的～? Is this really true? ③〔用于句中, 稍作停顿, 让人注意下面的话〕: 你～, 老这样下去可不行! Look! You can't go on like this. ④〔用于列举的事项之后〕: 茄子～、黄瓜～、洋白菜～、番茄～, 各种蔬菜摆满了货架。The shelves were filled with all sorts of vegetables — eggplants, cucumbers, cabbages, tomatoes.

āi

哎 āi 〈叹〉〔表示惊讶、提醒或不满意〕: ～! 是老刘啊! Why, it's Lao Liu!/ ～, 大伙儿来喝口水吧! Hey, come and have a drink of water, everyone!/ ～, 别把凳子碰倒了! Look out! Don't knock the stool over./ ～, 你怎么不早跟我说呢? But why didn't you tell me sooner?
【哎呀】āiyā 〈叹〉〔表示惊叹〕: ～! 我把钥匙弄断了。Damn, I've broken the key!/ ～! 这水真甜哪! Ah, this water is really sweet!/ ～! 好久不见面哪! So we meet again./ ～, 好大的雨呀! My God! It's raining like hell! 或 It's pouring!
【哎哟】āiyō 〈叹〉〔表示惊讶、痛苦等〕: ～, 壶漏啦! Hey, the kettle leaks!/ ～, 真烫。Ouch! (或 Ow!) It's hot.

哀 * āi ① grief; sorrow: 喜怒～乐 joy, anger, grief and happiness — the gamut of human feeling/ ～哭 wail ② mourning: 志～ express one's mourning for the deceased ③ pity: 乞～告怜 piteously beg for help
【哀愁】āichóu sad; sorrowful
【哀悼】āidào grieve (或 mourn) over sb.'s death; lament sb.'s death: 向死者家属表示深切的～ express one's heartfelt condolences to the family of the deceased
【哀怜】āilián feel compassion for; pity
【哀求】āiqiú entreat; implore: 苦苦～ piteously entreat
【哀叹】āitàn lament; bewail; bemoan
【哀痛】āitòng grief; deep sorrow

埃 āi dust

挨 āi ① get close to; be next to: ～着窗口坐 sit by the window/ 那两家铺子紧～着。The two shops are next to each other. ② in sequence; by turns: ～门～户给小孩打 预防针 go frøm door to door to give children inoculations/ 还没～到我吧? It isn't my turn yet, is it?
另见 ái

唉 * āi 〈叹〉①〔答应的声音〕: 快开门去。——～。Open the door, quick. —Right./ 小王! ——～! I say, Xiao Wang! —Yes? ②〔叹息的声音〕 alas
另见 ài
【唉声叹气】āishēng-tànqì heave deep sighs; sigh in despair; moan and groan: 不要受了一点挫折就～。Don't moan and groan because of a little setback.

ái

呆 ái
另见 dāi
【呆板】áibǎn stiff; rigid; inflexible; stereotyped: 动作～ stiff and awkward movements/ ～的公式 a rigid formula/ 这篇文章写得太～。This article is rather hackneyed.

挨 ái ① suffer; endure: ～饿 suffer from hunger; go hungry/ ～骂 get a scolding; get a dressing down/ ～淋 be caught in the rain/ ～批评 be criticized ② drag out: ～日子 suffer day after day; drag out a miserable existence ③ delay; stall; play for time: 别～时间了。Stop dawdling. 或 Quit stalling./ 为什么非要～到下个月不可? Why must we put it off till next month?
另见 āi
【挨打】áidǎ take a beating; get a thrashing; come under attack: 处于波动～的地位 be passive and vulnerable to attack

皑 ái 〈书〉pure white; snow white
【皑皑】ái'ái pure white: 白雪～ an expanse of white snow/ ～的雪山 a snowcapped mountain

癌 * ái 〈医〉cancer; carcinoma: 肝(肺、胃)～ cancer of the liver (lung, stomach)
【癌症】áizhèng 〈医〉cancer

ǎi

矮 * ǎi ① short (of stature): 他比他哥哥～一头。He's a head shorter than his brother. ② løw: ～墙 a low wall/ ～一级 a grade lower
【矮胖】ǎipàng short and stout; dumpy; roly-poly
【矮小】ǎixiǎo short and small; low and small; undersized:

身材～ short and slight in figure/ ～的房屋 a small, low house

【矮子】ǎizi a short person; dwarf

嗳 ǎi 〈叹〉〔表示不同意或否定〕: ～，别客气啦。Come on. Don't be so polite./ ～，你搞混啦。No, no, you're all mixed up.

另见 ài

蔼 ǎi friendly; amiable

【蔼然可亲】ǎirán kěqīn kindly; amiable; affable

ài

艾 ài 〈书〉end; stop: 方兴未～ be just unfolding.

另见 yì

唉 ài 〈叹〉〔表示伤感或惋惜〕: ～，要是老张在这儿该多好啊！Oh, if only Lao Zhang were here./ ～，谁能想到啊！Well, who'd have thought of that?/ ～，真可惜！What a pity!

另见 āi

爱* ài ①love; affection: ～祖国 love one's country/ 母～ maternal love/ 他们俩相～已经多年。They have been in love for a number of years./ 她～上了大草原。She's fallen in love with the grasslands. ②like; be fond of; keen on: ～游泳 be fond of swimming ③cherish; treasure; hold dear; take good care of ④be apt to; be in the habit of: ～发脾气 be apt to lose one's temper; be short-tempered / 铁～生锈。Iron rusts easily.

【爱不释手】ài bù shìshǒu fondle admiringly

【爱戴】àidài love and esteem: 受到人民的～ enjoy the love and esteem of the people; enjoy popular support

【爱国】àiguó love one's country; be patriotic: ～心 patriotic feeling; patriotism/ ～者 patriot/ ～主义 patriotism

【爱好】àihào ①love; like; be fond of; be keen on: ～和平 love peace; be peace-loving ②interest; hobby: 你在文娱方面有什么～? What kind of recreation do you go in for?

【爱护】àihù cherish; treasure; take good care of / ～公物 take good care of public property/ ～儿童 take good care of children; bring up children with loving care

【爱恋】àiliàn be in love with; feel deeply attached to: 对乡土的～ attachment to one's native soil

【爱面子】ài miànzi be concerned about face-saving; be sensitive about one's reputation

【爱莫能助】ài mò néng zhù willing to help but unable to do so

【爱慕】àimù adore; admire: 相互～ adore each other/ ～虚荣 be vain

【爱情】àiqíng love (between man and woman)

【爱人】àiren ①husband or wife ②sweetheart

【爱惜】àixī cherish; treasure; use sparingly

【爱憎】ài-zēng love and hate: ～分明 be clear about what to love and what to hate

碍* ài hinder; obstruct; be in the way of: 在这儿呆着吧，你～不着我。Stay where you are. You're not in my way./ 有～团结 be harmful (或 detrimental) to unity/ ～于情面 for fear of hurting sb.'s feelings; just to spare sb.'s feelings

【碍事】àishì ①be in the way: 这桌子放在门口太～了。This table is too close to the door, it gets in the way. ②be of consequence; matter: 这不～。It doesn't matter. 或 It's of no consequence./ 受了点凉，不～。It's just a slight cold, nothing serious.

【碍手碍脚】àishǒu-àijiǎo be in the way; be a hindrance

【碍眼】àiyǎn be unpleasant to look at; offend the eye; be an eyesore

嗳 ài 〈叹〉〔表示悔恨、懊恼〕: ～，早知道就好了。Oh! If only I'd known earlier.

另见 ǎi

ān

安* ān ①peaceful; quiet; tranquil; calm: ～睡 sleep peacefully/ 心神不～ feel uneasy or perturbed ②set (sb.'s mind) at ease; calm: ～神 (或 soothe) the nerves ③rest content; be satisfied: ～于现状 be content with things as they are; be satisfied with the existing state of affairs ④safe; secure; in good health: ～抵东京 arrive in Tokyo safely (或 safe and sound)/ 居～思危 mindful of possible danger in time of peace/ 欠～〈书〉be slightly indisposed; be unwell ⑤place in a suitable position; find a place for: 把我～在哪儿都行。I'll be happy with any job I'm assigned to. ⑥install; fix; fit: ～电灯 install electric lights／～窗玻璃 put in a windowpane/ 门上～锁 fit a lock on the door/ 村里～了广播喇叭。Loudspeakers have been set up in the village. ⑦bring (a charge against sb.); give (sb. a nickname): ～罪名 bring charges against ⑧harbour (an intention): ～坏心 harbour evil intentions/ 他们～的是什么心? What are they up to? ⑨〈书〉where: 其故～在? Wherein lies the cause? ⑩〈书〉how: ～能袖手旁观? How can one stand by and do nothing?

【安步当车】ān bù dàng chē walk over leisurely instead of riding in a carriage; walk rather than ride

【安定】āndìng ①stable; quiet; settled: ～团结 stability and unity/ ～的生活 a stable (或 settled) life/ 职业～ security of employment; job security ②stabilize; maintain: ～社会秩序 maintain social order/ ～人心 reassure the public; set people's minds at rest

【安顿】āndùn ①find a place for; help settle down; arrange for: 先把朋友们～好。First let's help the friends to settle in./ 家里都～好了吗? Have you got everything settled at home? ②undisturbed; peaceful: 病人吃了药，睡觉～多了。The patient slept much better after taking the medicine.

【安放】ānfàng lay; place; put in a certain place: 烈士墓前～着花圈。Wreaths were laid at the martyr's tomb./ 把仪器～好。Put the instruments in their proper places.

【安分】ānfèn not go beyond one's bounds; be law-abiding

【安分守己】ānfèn-shǒujǐ abide by the law and behave oneself; know one's place

【安抚】ānfǔ 〈书〉placate; pacify; appease

【安好】ānhǎo safe and sound; well: 全家～，请勿挂念。You will be pleased to know that everyone in the family is well.

【安家落户】ānjiā-luòhù make one's home in a place; settle: 他们已经在农村～。They have settled in the countryside.

【安静】ānjìng quiet; peaceful: 病人需要～。The patient needs peace and quiet./ 保持～。Keep quiet!

【安居乐业】ānjū-lèyè live and work in peace and contentment

【安康】ānkāng good health: 祝您～ wishing you the best of health

【安乐】ānlè peace and happiness ◇ ～窝 cosy nest/ ～椅 easy chair

【安眠】ānmián sleep peacefully ◇ ～药 sleeping pill (或 tablet)

【安宁】ānníng ①peaceful; tranquil: 确保两国边境～ ensure tranquillity on the border of the two countries ②calm; composed; free from worry: 心里很不～ feel rather worried

【安排】ānpái arrange; plan; fix up: 为外宾～参观游览 arrange visits and sightseeing trips for foreign guests/ ～本年度的生产 plan this year's production

【安全】ānquán safe; secure: ～到达 arrive safely/ ～第一 safety first/ 交通～ traffic safety/ 保证～生产 ensure safety in production/ ～行车 safe driving ◇ ～玻璃 safety glass/ ～操作 safe operation/ ～措施 safety measures (或 precautions)/ ～带 safety belt (或 strap); seat belt/ ～岛〈交〉safety (或 pedestrian) island/ ～阀 safety valve/ ～感 sense of security

【安然】ānrán ①safely: ～脱险 be out of danger/ ～无恙 safe and sound; (escape) unscathed ②peacefully; at rest: ～入睡 go to sleep peacefully

【安如磐石】ān rú pánshí as solid as a rock

【安适】ānshì quiet and comfortable: ～的生活 a quiet and

comfortable life; a life of ease and comfort

【安土重迁】 ān tǔ zhòng qiān hate to leave a place where one has lived long; be attached to one's native land and unwilling to leave it

【安危】 ān-wēi safety and danger; safety: 不顾个人～ heedless of one's personal safety

【安慰】 ānwèi comfort; console: ～他几句 say a few words to comfort him; give him a few words of comfort

【安稳】 ānwěn smooth and steady: 船走得很～。 The boat sailed smoothly./ 睡得很～ sleep peacefully (或 soundly)

【安息】 ānxī ① rest; go to sleep ② rest in peace

【安闲】 ānxián peaceful and carefree; leisurely: ～自在 leisurely and carefree/ ～的心情 a relaxed mood

【安详】 ānxiáng serene; composed; unruffled: 举止～ behave with composure

【安心】 ānxīn ① feel at ease; be relieved; set one's mind at rest: 春播还没完成,大家都安不下心来。 None of us could feel at ease until the spring sowing was finished./ 听到这个消息,她就～了。 She was relieved at the news./ 希望你～休养。 You just get better and don't worry. ② keep one's mind on sth.: ～工作 keep one's mind on one's work; work contentedly

【安逸】 ānyì easy and comfortable; easy: ～的生活 an easy life/ 贪图～ seek an easy life; love comfort

【安葬】 ānzàng bury (the dead)

【安置】 ānzhì find a place for; help settle down; arrange for: 把行李～好 put the luggage in the right place

【安装】 ānzhuāng install; erect; fix; mount: ～电话 install a telephone/ 机器 install machinery/ ～扩音器 set up a microphone/ ～蒸馏塔 erect a distillation column/ 推进器的叶片已经～好了。 The propeller blade has been mounted.

谙 ān 〈书〉 know well: 素～水性 be a skilful swimmer

庵 ān ①〈书〉 hut: 草～ a thatched hut ② nunnery; Buddhist convent

鞍 ān saddle

àn

岸* àn ① bank; shore; coast: 江～ the bank of a river; a river bank/ 海～ coast; seashore/ 上～ go ashore ② 〈书〉 lofty: 傲～ haughty

按 àn ① press; push down: ～电钮 press (或 push) a button/ ～门铃 ring a doorbell/ ～手印 put one's thumbprint (on a document, etc.) ② leave aside; shelve: ～下此事不提 leave this aside for the moment ③ restrain; control: ～不住心头怒火 be unable to restrain (或 control) one's anger ④ keep one's hand on; keep a tight grip on: ～住操纵杆 keep a tight grip on the control lever ⑤ according to; in accordance with; in the light of: ～姓氏笔划为序 in the order of the number of strokes in the surnames/ ～我的意见 in my opinion ⑥ 〈书〉 check; refer to: 有原文可～。 There's the original to refer to. ⑦ note: 编者～ editor's note

【按兵不动】 àn bīng bù dòng not throw the troops into battle; bide one's time; take no action: 大家都动起来了,你怎么还～呢? Everybody else has started work. Why do you sit there doing nothing?

【按部就班】 ànbù-jiùbān follow the prescribed order; keep to conventional ways of doing things

【按理】 ànlǐ according to reason; in the ordinary course of events; normally: 这种病～不该有并发症。 Normally there are no complications with this illness

【按摩】 ànmó 〈医〉 massage

【按钮】 ànniǔ push button ◇ ～控制 push-button control; dash control

【按期】 ànqī on schedule; on time: ～交货 deliver goods on schedule/ ～出版 come out on time

【按时】 ànshí on time; on schedule: ～到达 arrive on time

【按图索骥】 àn tú suǒ jì look for a steed with the aid of its picture — try to locate sth. by following up a clue

【按照】 ànzhào according to; in accordance with; in the light of; on the basis of: ～贡献大小,分别给以奖励 award people according to their contributions

案* àn ① table; desk: 条～ a long narrow table ② case; law case: 办～ handle a case/ 破～ clear up (或 solve) a criminal case ③ record; file: 有～可查 be on record (或 file)/ 备～ have a statement placed on record ④ a plan submitted for consideration; proposal: 提～ proposal; motion/ 决议草～ a draft resolution

【案件】 ànjiàn law case; case: 刑事～ a criminal case

【案情】 ànqíng details of a case; case: 了解～ investigate the details of a case

暗* àn ① dark; dim; dull: 天色渐～。 It's getting dark./ 灯光很～。 The light is rather dim./ ～紫色 dull purple/ ～绿 dark green ② hidden; secret: 我们在明处,敌人在～,要提高警惕。 We're in the open while the enemy is hidden; we must be vigilant./ 明人不做～事。 A person who is aboveboard does nothing underhand. ③ unclear; hazy: 对情况若明若～ have only a vague idea of the situation

【暗暗】 àn'àn secretly; inwardly; to oneself: ～跟踪 secretly follow sb./ ～吃了一惊 be startled but not show it

【暗藏】 àncáng hide; conceal: ～枪枝 conceal firearms; illegally possess firearms

【暗淡】 àndàn dim; faint; dismal; gloomy: ～的颜色 a dull colour/ ～的景象 a dismal picture/ 屋里灯光～。 The room is dimly lit.

【暗地里】 àndìlǐ secretly; inwardly; on the sly: ～捣鬼 secretly make trouble/ 我们～替他高兴。 We inwardly rejoiced for him.

【暗害】 ànhài ① kill secretly ② stab in the back

【暗号】 ànhào secret signal (或 sign); countersign; cipher

【暗疾】 ànjí unmentionable disease; a disease one is ashamed of

【暗箭】 ànjiàn an arrow shot from hiding; attack by a hidden enemy; a stab in the back: ～伤人 stab sb. in the back; injure sb. by underhand means

【暗流】 ànliú undercurrent

【暗杀】 ànshā assassinate

【暗伤】 ànshāng ① internal (或 invisible) injury ② internal (或 invisible) damage

【暗示】 ànshì ① drop a hint; hint; suggest: 他～要我走开。 He hinted that he wanted me to leave./ 她没有懂我的～。 She didn't take my hint. ② 〈心〉 suggestion

【暗室】 ànshì 〈摄〉 darkroom

【暗算】 ànsuàn plot against: 遭人～ fall a prey to a plot

【暗探】 àntàn secret agent; detective

【暗无天日】 àn wú tiānrì complete darkness; total absence of justice

【暗笑】 ànxiào laugh in (或 up) one's sleeve; snigger; snicker

【暗影】 ànyǐng ① shadow ② 〈天〉 umbra

【暗语】 ànyǔ code word

【暗中】 ànzhōng ① in the dark: ～摸索 grope in the dark ② in secret; on the sly; surreptitiously: ～操纵 pull strings from behind the scenes/ ～支持 give secret support to/ ～串通 collude with; conspire

【暗自】 ànzì inwardly; to oneself; secretly: ～庆幸 congratulate oneself; consider oneself lucky

黯 àn dim; gloomy

【黯淡】 àndàn 见“暗淡” àndàn

【黯然】 ànrán 〈书〉 ① dim; faint: ～失色 be overshadowed; be eclipsed; pale into insignificance ② dejected; low-spirited; downcast: ～神伤 feel dejected (或 depressed)

āng

肮 * āng
【肮脏】 āngzāng dirty; filthy: ～的阴沟 a filthy sewer/ ～的勾当 dirty work; a foul deed/ ～的政治交易 a dirty political deal

áng

昂 áng ① hold (one's head) high: ～首挺胸 hold up one's head and throw out one's chest; chin up and chest out ② high; soaring
【昂昂】 áng'áng high-spirited; brave-looking: 雄赳赳, 气～ fearless and militant
【昂贵】 ángguì expensive; costly
【昂然】 ángrán upright and unafraid
【昂首阔步】 ángshǒu-kuòbù stride forward with one's chin up; stride proudly ahead

àng

盎 àng an ancient vessel with a big belly and a small mouth
【盎然】 àngrán abundant; full; overflowing; exuberant: 趣味～ full of interest/ 生机～ overflowing with vigour; exuberant/ 春意～。 Spring is in the air.

āo

凹 * āo concave; hollow; sunken; dented: ～凸不平 full of bumps and holes; uneven
【凹度】 āodù concavity
【凹面镜】 āomiànjìng concave mirror
【凹透镜】 āotòujìng concave lens
【凹陷】 āoxiàn hollow; sunken; depressed: 双颊～ sunken (或 hollow) cheeks/ 地面～。 The ground caved in.

áo

遨 áo stroll; saunter
【遨游】 áoyóu roam; travel: 人造卫星～太空。 Satellites are travelling through space.
熬 áo ① boil; stew; decoct: ～粥 cook gruel/ ～药 decoct medicinal herbs ② endure; hold out: ～过苦难的岁月 go through years of suffering and privation
【熬夜】 áoyè stay up late or all night

翱 áo 〈书〉 take wing
【翱翔】 áoxiáng hover; soar: 海鸥在惊涛骇浪上～。 Seagulls hover over the surging waves./ 长空的女飞行员 women pilots soaring in the skies ◇ ～飞行 soaring flight/ ～机 sailplane; soaring glider

ǎo

拗 ǎo 〈方〉 bend so as to break: 把甘蔗～断 break a piece of sugarcane in two
另见 ào; niù

ào

拗 ào
另见 ǎo; niù
【拗口】 àokǒu hard to pronounce; awkward-sounding ◇ ～令 tongue twister

傲 * ào ① proud; haughty ② refuse to yield to; brave; defy: 红梅～雪凌霜开。 Braving snow and frost, the plum trees blossomed defiantly.
【傲慢】 àomàn arrogant; haughty: 态度～ adopt an arrogant attitude; put on airs
【傲气】 àoqì air of arrogance; haughtiness: ～十足 full of arrogance; extremely haughty
【傲然】 àorán loftily; proudly; unyieldingly: ～挺立的山峰 a mountain peak towering proudly into the skies

奥 ào profound; abstruse; difficult to understand
【奥秘】 àomì profound mystery: 探索宇宙的～ probe the mysteries of the universe
【奥妙】 àomiào profound; subtle; secret: 神奇～ mysterious and profound/ ～无穷 extremely subtle/ 不难明白其中的～。 It's not difficult to see what's behind it./ 其中定有～。 There must be more to it than meets the eye.

澳 ào 〔多用于地名〕 an inlet of the sea; bay: 三都～ Sandu Bay
懊 ào ① regretful; remorseful ② annoyed; vexed
【懊悔】 àohuǐ feel remorse; repent; regret: 我～不该错怪了她。 I regretted having blamed her unjustly.
【懊恼】 àonǎo annoyed; vexed; upset: 他工作没做好, 心里很～。 He was quite upset at not having done his work well.

B

bā

八* bā eight

【注意】"八"字在第四声(去声)字前念第二声(阳平),如"八月" báyuè,"八岁" básuì。本词典为简便起见,条目中的"八"字,都注第一声(阴平)。

【八宝】 bābǎo eight treasures (choice ingredients of certain special dishes) ◇ ~菜 eight-treasure pickles; assorted soy-sauce pickles/ ~饭 eight-treasure rice pudding (steamed glutinous rice with bean paste, lotus seeds, preserved fruit, etc.)

【八成】 bāchéng ①eighty per cent: ~新 eighty per cent new; practically new/ 事情有了~啦。It's almost as good as settled. 或 There's a fair chance of success. ②most probably; most likely: ~他不来了。Most probably he isn't coming.

【八面玲珑】 bāmiàn línglóng be smooth and slick (in establishing social relations)

【八月】 bāyuè ① August ② the eighth month of the lunar year; the eighth moon ◇ ~节 the Mid-Autumn Festival (15th day of the 8th lunar month)

【八字】 bāzì ① character 八: ~还没见一撇儿。Not even the first stroke of the character 八 is in sight — there's not the slightest sign of anything happening yet. ② Eight Characters (in four pairs, indicating the year, month, day and hour of a person's birth, each pair consisting of one Heavenly Stem and one Earthly Branch, formerly used in fortune-telling) ◇ ~步 a measured gait with the toes pointing outwards/ ~脚 splayfoot

巴* bā ① hope earnestly; wait anxiously: ~望 look forward to ② cling to; stick to: 爬山虎~在墙上。The ivy clings to the wall./ 粥~锅了。The porridge has stuck to the pot. ③ be close to; be next to: 前不~村,后不着店 with no village ahead and no inn behind — stranded in an uninhabited area

【巴不得】 bābude 〈口〉 be only too anxious (to do sth.); eagerly look forward to; earnestly wish: 他~立刻回到工作岗位。He is only too anxious to get back to work right away./ 我~天快晴。I wish it would clear up soon.

【巴结】 bājie fawn on; curry favour with; make up to

【巴掌】 bāzhang palm; hand: 拍~ clap hands/ 打他一~ give him a slap/ 一个~拍不响。One hand alone can't clap — it takes two to make a quarrel.

扒 bā ① hold on to; cling to: 孩子们~着窗台看游行队伍。Holding on to the window sill, the children watched the parade. ② dig up; rake; pull down: ~土 rake earth/ ~了旧房盖新房 pull down the old house to build a new one in its place/ 城墙~了个豁口。A breach was made in the city wall. ③ push aside: ~开芦苇 push aside the reeds

芭* bā

【芭蕉】 bājiāo 〈植〉 *bajiao* banana

【芭蕾舞】 bāléiwǔ ballet ◇ ~女演员 ballerina/ ~设计 choreography/ ~演员 ballet dancer

吧 bā ①〈象〉: ~的一声,弦断了。The string broke with a snap./ ~~两声枪响。Crack! Crack! Two shots rang out. ②〈口〉 draw on (或 pull at) one's pipe, etc. 另见 ba

疤 bā scar

【疤痕】 bāhén scar

笆 bā basketry

bá

拔* bá ① pull out; pull up: ~草 pull up weeds; weed/ ~麦子 harvest wheat (by pulling it up)/ ~牙 pull out (或 extract) a tooth/ ~剑 draw one's sword/ 把剥削根子全~掉 remove the roots of exploitation ② suck out; draw: 把火~一~。Put a chimney on the stove to make the fire draw. ③ choose; select; pick: 选~ select (from candidates) ④ lift; raise: ~起嗓子直嚷 shout at the top of one's voice ⑤ stand out among; surpass: 出类~萃 stand out among one's fellows; be out of the common run

【拔除】 báchú pull out; remove: ~敌军哨所 wipe out an enemy sentry post

【拔海】 báhǎi elevation (above sea level): ~五千米 at an elevation of 5,000 metres; 5,000 metres above sea level

【拔河】 báhé ·〈体〉 tug-of-war

【拔苗助长】 bá miáo zhù zhǎng try to help the shoots grow by pulling them upward — spoil things by excessive enthusiasm

【拔腿】 bátuǐ 〔多用于〕: ~就跑 start running away at once; immediately take to one's heels/ ~就追 give instant chase

跋 bá ① cross mountains: ~山涉水 scale mountains and ford streams; travel across mountains and rivers ② postscript

【跋涉】 báshè trudge; trek: 长途~ trudge over a long distance; trek a long way; make a long and difficult journey

bǎ

把* bǎ ① hold; grasp: ~住栏杆 hold on to a railing ② handle (of a pushcart, etc.): 自行车~ the handlebar of a bicycle ③ bundle; bunch: 草~ a bundle of straw ④ 〈量〉 ⓐ 〔用于有柄的器具〕: 一~刀 a knife/ 一~茶壶 a teapot/ 一~椅子 a chair ⓑ 〔指一手抓起的数量〕: 一~米 a handful of rice/ 一~花 a bunch of flowers ⓒ 〔用于某些抽象事物〕: 有一~年纪 be getting on in years/ 有~力气 be quite strong/ 加一~劲 make an extra effort; put on a spurt ⓓ 〔用于手的动作〕: 拉他一~ give him a tug; give (或 lend) him a hand ⑤ about; or so: 个~月 about a month; a month or so/ 百~人 some hundred people ⑥ 〈介〉 ⓐ〔宾语是后面动词的受事者,整个格式有处置的意思〕: ~衣服洗洗 wash the clothes/ ~头一扭 toss one's head/ ~方便让给别人,~困难留给自己 take difficulties on oneself and leave what is easy to others/ ~水搅浑 muddy the water; create confusion ⓑ 〔宾语后面接"忙""累""急""气"等词,加上表示结果的补语,整个格式有致使的意思〕: 这一趟可~他累坏了。That trip really tired him out. 另见 bà

【把柄】 bǎbǐng handle: 给人抓住~ give sb. a handle (against oneself)

【把持】 bǎchí control; dominate; monopolize: ~一切 monopolize everything/ ~一部分权力 seize a certain amount of power

【把舵】 bǎduò hold the rudder; hold (或take, be at) the helm; steer

【把风】 bǎfēng keep watch (for one's partners in a clandestine activity); be on the lookout

【把守】 bǎshǒu guard: ~城门 guard a city gate/ 分兵~ divide up one's forces for defence

【把手】 bǎshou handle; grip; knob

【把握】 bǎwò ① hold; grasp: 透过现象,~本质 see through

the phenomena to grasp the essence/ ～时机 seize the opportunity; seize the right time ② assurance; certainty: 没有成功的～ have no certainty of success/ 他很有～地回答所有的问题。 He answered all the questions with assurance./ 做这项工作,他很有～。 He's quite sure he can do this job.

【把戏】 bǎxì ① acrobatics; jugglery ② cheap trick; game: 要鬼～ play dirty tricks

【把兄弟】 bǎxiōngdì sworn brothers

靶 bǎ target: 打～ shooting (或 target) practice

【靶场】 bǎchǎng shooting range; range

【靶子】 bǎzi target

bà

把* bà ① grip; handle: 茶壶～儿 the handle of a teapot/, 枪～儿 rifle butt ② stem (of a leaf, flower or fruit)

另见 bǎ

坝 bà ① dam ② dyke; embankment

爸 bà pa; dad; father

【爸爸】 bàba papa; dad; father

罢 bà ① stop; cease: 欲～不能 try to stop but cannot; cannot refrain from carrying on ② dismiss: ～职 remove from office; dismiss ③ finish: 说～,他就走了。 With these words he left.

【罢黜】 bàchù〈书〉 ① dismiss from office ② ban; reject

【罢工】 bàgōng strike; go on strike

【罢官】 bàguān dismiss from office

【罢教】 bàjiào teachers' strike

【罢课】 bàkè students' strike

【罢了】 bàle〈助〉[用在句末,有"仅此而已"的意思]: 这没有什么,我不过做了我应该做的事～。 It's nothing. I've only done what I ought to do./ 你就是不想去～。 You just don't want to go, that's all.

【罢了】 bàliǎo [表示容忍,有勉强放过暂不深究的意思]: 他不肯也～,连个回信也不给。 I wouldn't have minded his refusing, but he didn't even answer my letter.

【罢论】 bàlùn abandoned idea: 此事已作～。 The idea has already been dropped.

【罢市】 bàshì shopkeepers' strike

【罢手】 bàshǒu give up: 不试验成功,我们决不～。 We will never stop until the experiment succeeds.

【罢休】 bàxiū give up; let the matter drop: 不达目的,决不～。 We'll not stop until we reach our goal.

霸* bà ① chief of feudal princes; overlord ② tyrant; despot; bully: 恶～ local tyrant (或 despot) ③ hegemonist power; hegemony

【霸道】 bàdao ① overbearing; high-handed ② (of liquor, medicine, etc.) strong; potent

【霸权】 bàquán hegemony; supremacy ◇ ～主义 hegemonism

【霸占】 bàzhàn forcibly occupy; seize: ～别国领土 forcibly occupy the territory of another country

ba

叭* ba 见"喇叭" lǎba

吧* ba〈助〉①[在句末表示商量、提议、请求、命令]: 咱们走～。 Let's go./ 你好好儿想想～ Just think it over. ②[在句末表示同意或认可]: 明天就明天～。 All right, let's make it tomorrow. ③[在句末表示疑问或不肯定]: 他会来～? He'll come, won't he?/ 他好象是这么说的～。 That's what he said, it seems. ④[在句中表示停顿,带假设的语气]: 打～,打不下去,跑～,跑不了,敌人只好投降。 Unable to fight on

or to escape, the enemy were forced to surrender.

另见 bā

bái

白* bái ① white: 几根～发 a few white (或 grey) hairs/ 皮肤～ have a fair complexion ② clear: 真相大～。 Everything is clear now. 或 The whole truth has come out. ③ pure; plain; blank: ～开水 plain boiled water/ 一纸～纸 a blank sheet of paper ④ in vain; for nothing: ～忙了半天 go to a lot of trouble for nothing/ ～跑一趟 make a fruitless trip/ 烈士们的鲜血没有～流。 The martyrs did not shed their blood in vain. ⑤ free of charge; gratis: ～送 give away free (of charge)/ ～给我也不要。 I wouldn't take it even as a gift. ⑥ (of a Chinese character) wrongly written or mispronounced: 念～字 mispronounce a character ⑦ spoken part in opera, etc.: 独～ soliloquy; monologue/ 对～ dialogue ⑧ state; explain: 自～ confessions

【白白】 báibái in vain; to no purpose; for nothing: 不要让时光～过去。 Don't let time slip by.

【白布】 báibù plain white cloth; calico

【白菜】 báicài Chinese cabbage

【白痴】 báichī ① idiocy ② idiot

【白饭】 báifàn plain cooked rice; rice with nothing to go with it

【白费】 báifèi waste: ～力气 (唇舌) waste one's energy (breath)/ ～心思 bother one's head for nothing

【白话】 báihuà vernacular ◇ ～诗 free verse written in the vernacular/ ～文 writings in the vernacular

【白金】 báijīn platinum

【白卷】 báijuàn blank examination paper: 交～ hand in a blank examination paper; hand in an examination paper unanswered

【白开水】 báikāishuǐ plain boiled water

【白茫茫】 báimángmáng (of mist, snow, floodwater, etc.) a vast expanse of whiteness: 下了一场大雪,田野上一一片。 After the heavy snow, the fields were a vast expanse of whiteness.

【白米】 báimǐ (polished) rice ◇ ～饭 (cooked) rice

【白日做梦】 báirì zuòmèng daydream; indulge in wishful thinking

【白色】 báisè white (colour)

【白手起家】 báishǒu qǐjiā build up from nothing; start from scratch

【白糖】 báitáng (refined) white sugar

【白天】 báitiān daytime; day

【白头】 báitóu hoary head; old age

【白头偕老】 báitóu xiélǎo live to ripe old age in conjugal bliss; remain a devoted couple to the end of their lives

【白熊】 báixióng polar bear; white bear

【白血病】 báixuèbìng leukaemia

【白血球】 báixuèqiú〈生理〉 white blood cell; leucocyte

【白眼】 báiyǎn supercilious look: ～看人 treat people superciliously; look upon people with disdain/ 遭人～ be treated with disdain

【白蚁】 báiyǐ termite; white ant

【白银】 báiyín silver

【白纸黑字】 báizhǐ-hēizì (written) in black and white

【白种】 báizhǒng the white race

【白昼】 báizhòu daytime

【白字】 báizì wrongly written or mispronounced character: ～连篇 pages and pages of wrongly written characters

bǎi

百* bǎi ① hundred ② numerous; all kinds of: ～花盛开 a hundred flowers in bloom/ ～忙之中 in the midst of pressing affairs; despite many claims on one's time/ ～问不厌, ～拿不烦 (of a shop assistant) patiently answer any questions the customers ask and show them any goods they want to see

【百般】 bǎibān in a hundred and one ways; in every possible way; by every means: ～咒骂 abuse in every possible way; heap abuse on/ ～抵赖 try by every means to deny/ ～刁难 create all sorts of obstacles; put up innumerable obstacles/ ～奉承 flatter sedulously/ ～照顾 show sb. every consideration

【百倍】 bǎibèi a hundredfold; a hundred times: 展望未来，信心～ look to the future with full confidence

【百步穿杨】 bǎi bù chuān yáng shoot an arrow through a willow leaf a hundred paces away; shoot with great precision

【百尺竿头，更进一步】 bǎi chǐ gāntóu, gèng jìn yī bù make still further progress

【百发百中】 bǎifā-bǎizhòng a hundred shots, a hundred bull's-eyes; every shot hits the target; shoot with unfailing accuracy; be a crack shot

【百废俱兴】 bǎi fèi jù xīng all neglected tasks are being undertaken — full-scale reconstruction is under way

【百分比】 bǎifēnbǐ percentage: 按～计算 in terms of percentage

【百分率】 bǎifēnlǜ percentage; per cent

【百分数】 bǎifēnshù percentage

【百分之百】 bǎifēn zhī bǎi a hundred per cent; out and out; absolutely: 有～的把握 be a hundred per cent sure; be absolutely certain/ 这是～的谎话! That's an out-and-out lie!

【百合】 bǎihé 〈植〉 lily

【百花齐放，百家争鸣】 bǎihuā qífàng, bǎijiā zhēngmíng let a hundred flowers blossom and a hundred schools of thought contend

【百货】 bǎihuò general merchandise: 日用～ articles of daily use ◇ ～商店 department store; general store

【百科全书】 bǎikē quánshū encyclopaedia

【百孔千疮】 bǎikǒng-qiānchuāng riddled with gaping wounds; afflicted with all ills

【百年】 bǎinián ① a hundred years; a century: ～不遇的大水灾 the biggest flood in a century ② lifetime: ～之后〈婉〉 when sb. has passed away; after sb.'s death ◇ ～纪念 centenary; centennial

【百年大计】 bǎinián dàjì a project of vital and lasting importance: 基本建设是～，要求质量第一。 Capital construction projects, which are to last for generations, call for good quality above everything else.

【百思不解】 bǎi sī bù jiě remain puzzled after pondering over sth. a hundred times; remain perplexed despite much thought

【百听不厌】 bǎi tīng bù yàn worth hearing a hundred times: 这个故事～。 You never get tired of hearing this story.

【百万】 bǎiwàn million: ～雄师 a million bold warriors ◇ ～吨级 megaton/ ～富翁 millionaire

【百闻不如一见】 bǎi wén bùrú yī jiàn it is better to see once than hear a hundred times; seeing for oneself is a hundred times better than hearing from others

【百无一失】 bǎi wú yī shī no danger of anything going wrong; no risk at all

【百姓】 bǎixìng common people

【百叶窗】 bǎiyèchuāng shutter; blind; jalousie

【百依百顺】 bǎiyī-bǎishùn docile and obedient; all obedience

【百战百胜】 bǎizhàn-bǎishèng fight a hundred battles, win a hundred victories; emerge victorious in every battle; be ever-victorious

【百折不挠】 bǎi zhé bù náo keep on fighting in spite of all setbacks; be undaunted by repeated setbacks; be indomitable 又作"百折不回"

【百足之虫，死而不僵】 bǎi zú zhī chóng, sǐ ér bù jiāng a centipede does not topple over even when dead; a centipede dies but never falls down; old institutions die hard

佰 bǎi hundred (used for the numeral 百 on cheques, etc. to avoid mistakes or alterations)

柏* bǎi cypress

【柏树】 bǎishù cypress

【柏油】 bǎiyóu pitch; tar; asphalt

捭 bǎi 见"纵横捭阖" zònghéng-bǎihé

摆* bǎi ① put; place; arrange: 把药瓶～在架子上 put the medicine bottles on the shelf/ 把碗筷～好 set (或 lay) the table/ 各种标本～了一桌子。The table was loaded with all kinds of specimens ② put on; assume: ～威风 give oneself airs; put on airs/ ～出一副吓人的架势 assume an intimidating posture/ ～老资格 flaunt one's seniority; put on the airs of a veteran ③ sway; wave: 他～～手叫我走开。He waved me away. ④〈物〉 pendulum

【摆布】 bǎibu order about; manipulate: 任人～ allow oneself to be ordered about; be at the mercy of others

【摆动】 bǎidòng swing; sway: 柳条迎风～。The willows swayed in the breeze./ 指示针来回～。The pointer flickered.

【摆渡】 bǎidù ferry

【摆架子】 bǎi jiàzi put on airs; assume great airs

【摆阔】 bǎikuò parade one's wealth; be ostentatious and extravagant

【摆门面】 bǎi ménmiàn keep up appearances

【摆设】 bǎishè furnish and decorate (a room): 屋里～得很雅致。The room is tastefully furnished.

【摆脱】 bǎituō cast off; shake off; break away from; free (或 extricate) oneself from: ～困境 extricate oneself from a predicament

bài

败* bài ① be defeated; lose: ～军之将 a defeated general/ ～下阵来 lose a battle/ 主队以二比三～于客队。The home team lost to the visitors 2 to 3. ② defeat; beat: 大～侵略军 inflict a severe defeat on the invading troops ③ fail: 成～ success or failure ④ spoil: 事情可能～在他手里。He may spoil the whole show. ⑤ counteract: ～毒 counteract a toxin ⑥ decay; wither: 枯枝～叶 dead twigs and withered leaves

【败坏】 bàihuài ruin; corrupt; undermine: ～名誉 discredit; defame/ 道德～ morally degenerate/～风俗 corrupt morals; exert a bad moral influence/ ～社会风气 corrupt social values

【败家子】 bàijiāzǐ spendthrift; wastrel; prodigal

【败局】 bàijú lost game; losing battle

【败类】 bàilèi scum of a community; degenerate: 民族～ scum of a nation

【败露】 bàilù (of a plot, etc.) fall through and stand exposed: 阴谋终于～。In the end the conspiracy was brought to light.

【败落】 bàiluò decline (in wealth and position): 这部小说反映了一个封建家庭的～。This novel reflects the decline of a feudal family.

【败诉】 bàisù lose a lawsuit

【败退】 bàituì retreat in defeat: 敌军节节～。Again and again the enemy retreated in defeat.

【败仗】 bàizhàng lost battle; defeat: 打～ be defeated in battle; suffer a defeat

拜* bài ① do obeisance: ～佛 prostrate oneself before the image of Buddha; worship Buddha ② make a courtesy call: 回～ pay a return visit ③ acknowledge sb. as one's master, godfather, etc. ④〈敬〉〔用于动词之前〕: ～读大作 I have the pleasure of perusing your work/ ～～谢 express one's thanks

【拜别】 bàibié 〈敬〉 take leave of

【拜倒】 bàidǎo prostrate oneself; fall on one's knees; grovel

【拜访】 bàifǎng　pay a visit; call on: 正式～ formal visit/专诚～ make a special trip to call on sb.

【拜会】 bàihuì 〔多用于外交场合〕pay an official call; call on: 告别～ farewell call/ 礼节性～ courtesy call/ 私人～ personal visit (或 call)

【拜见】 bàijiàn ① pay a formal visit; call to pay respects ② meet one's senior or superior

【拜金主义】 bàijīnzhǔyì　money worship

【拜年】 bàinián　pay a New Year call; wish sb. a Happy New Year

【拜寿】 bàishòu　congratulate an elderly person on his birthday; offer birthday felicitations

【拜托】 bàituō 〈敬〉request sb. to do sth.: ～您带个信给他。Would you be kind enough to take a message to him?

稗 bài ① barnyard grass ② 〈书〉insignificant; unofficial

【稗官野史】 bàiguān-yěshǐ　books containing anecdotes

bān

班* bān ① class; team: 学习～ study class/ 作业～ work team ② shift; duty: 三～倒 work in three shifts/ 上夜～ be on night shift/ 轮～护理病人 take turns tending the sick ③ 〈军〉squad ④ 〈量〉 ⓐ 〔用于人群〕这～青年人真了不起。They're a fine bunch of young people. ⓑ 〔用于定时开行的交通运输工具〕搭下一～火车 take the next train/ 末～车 last bus, train, etc. (of the day)/ 一号公共汽车每隔三分钟就有一～。There's a Number One bus every three minutes. ⑤ regularly-run; regular; scheduled: ～机 regular air service

【班次】 bāncì ① order of classes or grades at school: 在学校时，她～比我高。At school she was in a higher class than me. ② number of runs or flights: 增加货车～ increase the number of runs of freight trains

【班级】 bānjí　classes and grades in school

【班门弄斧】 Bān mén nòng fǔ　show off one's proficiency with the axe before Lu Ban (鲁班) the master carpenter— display one's slight skill before an expert

【班长】 bānzhǎng ① class monitor ② 〈军〉squad leader ③ (work) team leader

【班主任】 bānzhǔrèn　a teacher in charge of a class

般 bān sort; kind; way: 百～ in every possible way/ 这～ such; this kind of/ 暴风雨～的掌声 stormy (或 thunderous) applause/ 兄弟～的情谊 fraternal feelings

颁 bān promulgate; issue

【颁布】 bānbù　promulgate; issue; publish: ～法令 promulgate (或 issue) a decree

【颁发】 bānfā ① issue; promulgate: ～嘉奖令 issue an order of commendation ② award: ～奖章 award a medal

斑 bān ① spot; speck; speckle; stripe: 油～ oil stains; grease spots ② spotted; striped

【斑白】 bānbái　grizzled; greying: 两鬓～ greying at the temples

【斑斑】 bānbān　full of stains or spots: 血迹～ bloodstained

【斑驳】 bānbó 〈书〉mottled; motley

【斑点】 bāndiǎn　spot; stain; speckle

【斑马】 bānmǎ　zebra

【斑纹】 bānwén　stripe; streak

搬* bān ① take away; move; remove: 把桌子～走 take the table away ② move (house): 他早就～走了。He moved out long ago.

【搬家】 bānjiā　move (house): 我们下星期～。We're moving next week.

【搬弄】 bānnòng ① move sth. about; fiddle with: 别～枪栓。Don't fiddle with the rifle bolt. ② show off; display: ～学问 show off one's erudition

【搬弄是非】 bānnòng shìfēi　sow discord; tell tales; make mischief

【搬运】 bānyùn　carry; transport: ～货物 transport goods ◇ ～工人 (车站等) porter; (码头) docker

bǎn

板* bǎn ① board; plank; plate: 切菜～ chopping block/ 混凝土～ concrete slab/ 玻璃～ plate glass; glass top (of a desk)/钢～ steel plate ② shutter: 上～儿 put up the shutters ③ (乒乓球) hat; (板羽球) battledore ④ stop smiling; look serious: ～起面孔 put on a stern expression/ ～着脸 keep a straight face

【板凳】 bǎndèng　wooden bench or stool

版* bǎn ① printing plate (或 block): 铜～ copperplate/ 制～ plate making ② edition: 初～ first edition/ 绝～ out of print ③ page (of a newspaper): 头～新闻 front-page news

【版本】 bǎnběn　edition

【版次】 bǎncì　the order in which editions are printed

【版画】 bǎnhuà　a picture printed from an engraved or etched plate; print

【版刻】 bǎnkè　carving; engraving

【版权】 bǎnquán　copyright: ～所有 all rights reserved ◇ ～页 copyright page; colophon

【版图】 bǎntú　domain; territory: ～辽阔 vast in territory

bàn

办* bàn ① do; handle; manage; tackle; attend to: 大～农业 go in for agriculture in a big way/这点事她一个人～得了。She can handle (或 tackle) this by herself./ 我有点事得一一～。I have something to attend to. ② set up; run: 新～了一所中学。A new secondary school has been set up. ③ buy a fair amount of; get sth. ready: ～年货 do New Year shopping; do shopping for the Spring Festival/ ～酒席 prepare a feast ④ punish (by law); bring to justice: 严～ punish severely

【办案】 bàn'àn　handle a case

【办报】 bànbào　run a newspaper

【办到】 bàndào　get sth. done; accomplish: 原来认为办不到的事，现在～了。What was thought impossible has now been done./ 时代不同了，男女都一样。男人能～的事情，女人也能办得到。Times have changed, and today men and women are equal. Whatever men can accomplish, women can too.

【办法】 bànfǎ　way; means; measure: 找出克服困难的～ find a way to overcome a difficulty/ 用切实的～来改进我们的工作 adopt effective measures to improve our work

【办公】 bàngōng　handle official business; work (usu. in an office) ◇ ～费 administrative expenses/ ～时间 office hours/ ～室 office/ ～厅 general office/ ～桌 desk; bureau

【办理】 bànlǐ　handle; conduct; transact: ～进出口业务 handle imports and exports/ ～手续 go through the formalities (或 procedure)/ 这些事情你可以酌办。You may handle these matters as you see fit.

【办事】 bànshì　handle affairs; work: ～公正 be fair and just in handling affairs/ ～认真 be conscientious in one's work/ 按原则～ act according to principles ◇ ～处 office; agency/ ～机构 administrative body; working body/ ～员 office worker/ ～组 administrative group

半* bàn ① half; semi-: ～小时 half an hour/ 一个～月 a month and a half; one and a half months/ ～年 six months/ 增加一倍～ increase by 150%/ ～机械化 semi-mechanized ② in the middle; halfway: ～夜 midnight/ 山腰 halfway up a hill ③ very little; the least bit: 他连～句话都不说。He wouldn't breathe a word. ④ partly; about half: ~开玩笑地说 say sth. half jokingly/ 房门~开着。The door was left half open./ 给打了个~死 be beaten within an inch of one's life

【半百】 bànbǎi　fifty (years of age): 年近~ getting on for fifty; approaching fifty

【半…半…】 bàn...bàn...　〔分别用在意义相反的两个词或词素前面，表示相对的两种性质或状态同时存在〕半文半白 half literary, half vernacular/ 半饥半饱 underfed/ 半推半就 yield with a show of reluctance/ 半心半意 half-hearted/ 半信半疑 half-believing, half-doubting; not quite convinced/ 半真半假 half-genuine, half-sham; partly true, partly false/ 半嗔半喜 half-annoyed, half-pleased

【半辈子】 bànbèizi　half a lifetime

【半…不…】 bàn...bù...　〔意思和"半…半…"相同〕: 半生不熟 half cooked/ 半死不活 half-dead; more dead than alive/ 半新不旧 no longer new; showing signs of wear

【半导体】 bàndǎotǐ　semiconductor

【半岛】 bàndǎo　peninsula

【半点】 bàndiǎn　the least bit: 没有一慌张 not the least bit flurried/ 原则问题~也不能动摇。One should never waver on matters of principle.

【半工半读】 bàngōng-bàndú　part work, part study; work-study programme

【半公开】 bàngōngkāi　semi-overt; more or less open

【半官方】 bànguānfāng　semi-official: 据~人士称 according to semi-official sources

【半价】 bànjià　half price: ~出售 sell at half price

【半斤八两】 bànjīn-bāliǎng　six of one and half a dozen of the other — not much to choose between the two

【半决赛】 bànjuésài　〈体〉semifinals

【半空中】 bànkōngzhōng　in mid air; in the air: 悬在~ hang in midair

【半路】 bànlù　halfway; midway; on the way: 走到~，天就黑了。We had got only halfway when it began to get dark./ ~上遇到熟人 run into a friend on the way

【半路出家】 bànlù chūjiā　become a monk or nun late in life — switch to a job one was not trained for

【半票】 bànpiào　half-price ticket; half fare

【半瓶醋】 bànpíngcù　dabbler; smatterer

【半旗】 bànqí　half-mast: 下~ fly a flag at half-mast

【半球】 bànqiú　hemisphere: 东~ the Eastern Hemisphere/ 北~ the Northern Hemisphere

【半生】 bànshēng　half a lifetime: 前~ first half of one's life

【半身不遂】 bànshēn bùsuí　〈医〉hemiplegia

【半数】 bànshù　half the number; half: ~以上 more than half

【半天】 bàntiān　① half of the day: 前~ morning/ 后~ afternoon ② a long time; quite a while: 他~说不出话来。He remained tongue-tied for a long time.

【半透明】 bàntòumíng　translucent; semitransparent ◇ ~体 〈物〉translucent body/ ~纸 onionskin

【半途】 bàntú　halfway; midway: 拆伙 part company halfway

【半途而废】 bàntú ér fèi　give up halfway; leave sth. unfinished

【半夜】 bànyè　midnight; in the middle of the night: 会议一直开到~。The meeting went on far into the night.

【半夜三更】 bànyè-sāngēng　in the depth of night; late at night: ~的，你起来干什么? Why are you getting up at this time of night?

【半月刊】 bànyuèkān　semimonthly; fortnightly

扮* bàn　① be dressed up as; play the part of; disguise oneself as: 他在戏里~一位老贫农。In the opera he plays the part of an old poor peasant./ 侦察员~作一个商人。The scout disguised himself as a merchant. ② put on (an expression): ~鬼脸 make grimaces; make faces

【扮相】 bànxiàng　the appearance of an actor or actress in costume and makeup

【扮演】 bànyǎn　play the part of; act

【扮装】 bànzhuāng　makeup

伴* bàn　① companion; partner: 旅~ a travelling com-panion/ 作~ keep sb. company ② accompany

【伴唱】 bànchàng　① vocal accompaniment ② accompany (a singer)

【伴侣】 bànlǚ　companion; mate; partner

【伴随】 bànsuí　accompany; follow

【伴奏】 bànzòu　accompany (with musical instruments): 钢琴~ piano accompaniment/ 手风琴~: 张小芳 Accompanied on the accordion by Zhang Xiaofang ◇ ~者 accompanist

拌 bàn　mix: ~匀 mix thoroughly/ ~饲料 mix fodder/ ~鸡丝 shredded chicken salad

【拌和】 bànhuo　mix and stir; blend

【拌嘴】 bànzuǐ　bicker; squabble; quarrel

绊 bàn　(cause to) stumble; trip: ~手~脚 be in the way/ 他被树根~了一下。He stumbled over the root of a tree./ 差点儿~了我一交。I tripped and almost fell.

【绊脚石】 bànjiǎoshí　stumbling block; obstacle

瓣 bàn　① petal ② segment or section (of a tangerine, etc.); clove (of garlic)

bāng

邦* bāng　nation; state; country: 邻~ a neighbouring country

【邦交】 bāngjiāo　relations between two countries; diplomatic relations: 建立(断绝, 恢复)~ establish (sever, resume) diplomatic relations

帮 bāng　① help; assist: 互~互学 help each other and learn from each other/ ~他搬行李 help him with his luggage/ 她今天要~医生做手术。She's going to assist the doctor in an operation today./ 你能~我们弄点白菜吗? Could you get some cabbage seeds for us? ② side (of a boat, truck, etc.); upper (of a shoe) ③ outer leaf (of cabbage, etc.) ④ gang; band; clique: 匪~ bandit gang ⑤ 〈量〉〔用于人〕: 来了一~孩子。Here comes a group of children.

【帮忙】 bāngmáng　help; give (或 lend) a hand; do a favour; do a good turn: 帮大忙 be a big help; give a lot of help/ 来找人~ come for help/ 请你帮个忙。Will you give me a hand?/ 他帮过我们的忙。He once did us a good turn.

【帮派】 bāngpài　faction ◇ ~体系 factionalist setup

【帮手】 bāngshou　helper; assistant

【帮凶】 bāngxiōng　accomplice; accessary

【帮助】 bāngzhù　help; assist: 没有多大~ be of little help; not be much help/ 他~我学外文。He helped me learn a foreign language./ 希望你多给我~。I hope you will give me as much help as you can.

bǎng

绑* bǎng　① bind; tie: ~个三脚架 tie three sticks together to make a tripod ② bind sb.'s hands behind him; truss up

【绑匪】 bǎngfěi　kidnapper

【绑架】 bǎngjià　kidnap

【绑票】 bǎngpiào　kidnap (for ransom)

榜* bǎng　① a list of names posted up: 光荣~ honour roll/ 发~ publish the list of successful candidates ② announcement; notice

【榜样】 bǎngyàng　example; model

膀* bǎng　① upper arm; arm ② shoulder: ~阔腰圆 broad-shouldered and solidly-built; hefty; husky ③ wing (of a bird)
另见 páng

【膀臂】 bǎngbì　① 〈方〉upper arm; arm ② reliable helper; right-hand man

bàng

蚌* bàng　freshwater mussel; clam

谤　bàng　〈书〉slander; defame; vilify

傍* bàng　draw near; be close to: 船~了岸 The boat drew alongside the bank./ 依山~水 be situated at the foot of a hill and beside a stream
【傍晚】bàngwǎn　toward evening; at nightfall; at dusk

棒* bàng　① stick; club; cudgel: 垒球~ softball bat ② 〈口〉good; fine; excellent; strong: 字写得~ write a good hand
【棒球】bàngqiú　baseball ◇ ~场 baseball field
【棒子】bàngzi　stick; club; cudgel

磅 bàng　① pound ② scales: 把行李搁在~上看有多重。Put the luggage on the scales and see how much it weighs. ③ weigh: ~体重 weigh oneself or sb. on the scales 另见 páng
【磅秤】bàngchèng　platform scale; platform balance

镑 bàng　pound (a currency)

bāo

包* bāo　① wrap: 把东西~起来 wrap things up/ 头上~着一条白毛巾 with a white towel wrapped round one's head/ ~书 wrap up a book in a piece of paper; put a jacket (或 cover) on a book/ ~饺子 make dumplings/ 纸~不住火。You can't wrap fire in paper. ② bundle; package; pack; packet; parcel: 邮~ postal parcel (或 packet) ③ bag; sack: 书~ satchel; school bag ④ 〈量〉〔用于成包的东西〕一大~衣服 a big bundle of clothes/ 一~香烟 a packet (或 pack) of cigarettes/ 两~大米 two sacks of rice/ 一~棉纱 a bale of cotton yarn ⑤ protuberance; swelling; lump: 脑门上碰了个~ have (或 get) a bump on one's forehead/ 腿上起了个~ have a swelling in the leg ⑥ surround; encircle; envelop: 浓雾~住了群山。The hills were enveloped in dense fog. ⑦ include; contain: 无所不~ all-inclusive; all-embracing ⑧ undertake the whole thing: 这事由我~了吧。Just leave it all to me. ⑨ assure; guarantee: ~你满意。You'll like it, I assure you. 或 Satisfaction guaranteed. ⑩ hire; charter: ~一只船 hire (或 charter) a boat/ ~机 a chartered plane
【包办】bāobàn　① take care of everything concerning a job: 这件事你一个人~了吧。You'd better do the whole job yourself. ② run the whole show; monopolize everything: ~代替 take on what ought to be done by others; run things all by oneself without consulting others ◇ ~婚姻 arranged marriage
【包庇】bāobì　shield; harbour; cover up: 互相~ shield each other/ ~坏人坏事 harbour evildoers and cover up their evil deeds
【包藏】bāocáng　contain; harbour; conceal: 大海~着许多秘密。The sea contains many mysteries./ ~祸心 harbour evil intentions (或 malicious intent)
【包饭】bāofàn　get or supply meals at a fixed rate; board: 在附近的饭馆里~ board at a nearby restaurant
【包袱】bāofú　① cloth-wrapper ② a bundle wrapped in cloth
【包工】bāogōng　① undertake to perform work within a time limit and according to specifications; contract for a job ② contractor ◇ ~头 labour contractor
【包管】bāoguǎn　assure; guarantee: 这件活三天完成,~没问

题。We'll finish this job in three days without fail./ ~退换。Merchandise will be exchanged if found unsatisfactory.
【包裹】bāoguǒ　① wrap up; bind up ② bundle; package; parcel: 邮政~ postal parcel (或 packet)
【包含】bāohán　contain; embody; include: 他的建议~不少合理的因素。His proposal contains much that is reasonable.
【包涵】bāohan　〈套〉excuse; forgive; bear with: 我唱得不好,请多多~。Excuse (me for) my poor singing.
【包括】bāokuò　include; consist of; comprise; incorporate: 房租每月四百元,水电费~在内。 The rent is $400 a month, including water and electricity.
【包揽】bāolǎn　undertake the whole thing; take on everything: 这样多的事,一个人~不了。No one person can take on so much work./ ~诉讼 engage in pettifoggery
【包罗】bāoluó　include; cover; embrace: 民间艺术~甚广。Folk art covers a wide range.
【包罗万象】bāoluó wànxiàng　all-embracing; all-inclusive
【包围】bāowéi　surround; encircle
【包销】bāoxiāo　① have exclusive selling rights ② be the sole agent for a production unit or a firm
【包扎】bāozā　wrap up; bind up; pack: ~伤口 bind up (或 dress) a wound/ 待运的自行车已经~好了。The bicycles to be transported are packed.
【包治百病】bāozhì bǎibìng　guarantee to cure all diseases: ~的药方 remedy for all ills; panacea; cure-all
【包装】bāozhuāng　pack; package
【包子】bāozi　steamed stuffed bun
【包租】bāozū　〈旧〉① rent land or a house for subletting ② fixed rent for farmland (to be paid no matter how bad the harvest might be)

胞* bāo　① afterbirth ② born of the same parents: ~兄弟 full (或 blood) brothers

剥* bāo　shell; peel; skin: ~花生 shell peanuts/ ~香蕉 peel a banana / ~兔皮 skin a rabbit 另见 bō

褒 bāo　praise; honour; commend
【褒贬】bāo-biǎn　pass judgment on; appraise: ~人物 pass judgment on people/ 不加~ make no comment, complimentary or otherwise; neither praise nor censure
【褒奖】bāojiǎng　praise and honour; commend and award
【褒扬】bāoyáng　praise; commend

báo

雹 báo　hail
【雹子】báozi　hail; hailstone

薄* báo　① thin; flimsy: ~纸 thin paper/ 复写用的~纸 flimsy ② weak; light: 酒味很~。This is a light wine. ③ lacking in warmth; cold: 待他不~ treat him quite well ④ infertile; poor: ~地 poor land 另见 bó; bò

bǎo

宝* bǎo　① treasure: 粮食是~中之~。Grain is the treasure of treasures. ② precious; treasured: ~刀 a treasured sword ③ 〈敬〉〔旧时用于称别人的家眷等〕: ~眷 your wife and children; your family
【宝宝】bǎobǎo　〔对小孩的爱称〕darling; baby
【宝贝】bǎobèi　① treasured object; treasure ② darling; baby ③ cowry: 虎斑~ tiger cowry ④ 〈讽〉good-for-nothing or queer character: 这人真是个~! What a fellow!
【宝贵】bǎoguì　① valuable; precious: ~意见 valuable suggestion/ ~经验 valuable experience/ ~文物 precious cultural relics ② value; treasure; set store by: 世间一切事物中,人是第一个可~的。 Of all things in the world, people are the most precious.

【宝剑】 bǎojiàn a double-edged sword

【宝库】 bǎokù treasure-house: 中国医药学是一个伟大的~。 Chinese medicine and pharmacology are a great treasure-house.

【宝石】 bǎoshí precious stone; gem

【宝物】 bǎowù treasure

【宝藏】 bǎozàng precious (mineral) deposits: 发掘地下~ unearth buried treasure; tap mineral resources

【宝座】 bǎozuò throne

饱* bǎo ① have eaten one's fill; be full: 吃~喝足 eat and drink one's fill/ 我~了，一点也吃不下了。 I've had enough. I can't eat any more./ ~汉不知饿汉饥。 〈谚〉 The well-fed don't know how the starving suffer. ② full; plump: 谷粒很~。 The grains are quite plump. ③ fully; to the full: ~尝旧社会的辛酸 taste to the full the bitterness of life in the old society/ ~览海岛的美丽风光 drink in the beauty of the island scenery/ 她的眼眶里~含着幸福的热泪。 Her eyes filled with tears of joy. ④ satisfy: 一~眼福 have the opportunity to feast one's eyes on sth.; enjoy to the full watching a scene, show, etc.

【饱和】 bǎohé saturation

【饱经风霜】 bǎo jīng fēngshuāng weather-beaten; having experienced the hardships of life: ~的面容 a weather-worn face

【饱满】 bǎomǎn full; plump: 颗粒~的小麦 plump-eared wheat/ 精神~ full of vigour; energetic

【饱学】 bǎoxué learned; erudite; scholarly: ~之士 an erudite person; a learned scholar; a man of learning

保* bǎo ① protect; defend: ~家卫国 protect our homes and defend our country ② keep; maintain; preserve: 这种热水瓶能~暖二十四小时。 This kind of thermos flask keeps water hot for 24 hours./ ~水~肥 preserve moisture and fertility (in the soil) ③ guarantee; ensure: ~质~量 guarantee both quality and quantity ④ stand guarantor (或 surety) for sb.. ⑤ guarantor: 作~ stand guarantor (或 surety) for sb.

【保安】 bǎo'ān ① ensure public security ② ensure safety (for workers engaged in production) ◇ ~措施 security measures/ ~人员 security personnel

【保镖】 bǎobiāo bodyguard

【保藏】 bǎocáng keep in store; preserve: 食品~ food preservation

【保持】 bǎochí keep; maintain; preserve: ~安静 keep quiet/ ~冷静的头脑 keep a cool head; keep cool/~中立 remain neutral; maintain neutrality/~警惕 maintain vigilance

【保存】 bǎocún preserve; conserve; keep: ~实力 preserve one's strength; conserve one's forces

【保单】 bǎodān guarantee slip

【保管】 bǎoguǎn ① take care of: 负责~农具 take care of farm tools/ 图书~工作 the care of library books ② certainly; surely: 他~不知道。 He certainly doesn't know. ◇ ~费 storage charges; storage fee/ ~室 storeroom/ ~员 storeman; storekeeper

【保护】 bǎohù protect; safeguard: ~环境，防止污染 protect the environment against pollution/ ~人民的利益 safeguard the people's interests/ ~现场 keep intact the scene of a crime or accident/ 体操运动员都学会了互相~和自我~。 The gymnasts have all learnt to protect each other and themselves against injuries.

【保健】 bǎojiàn health protection; health care: 妇幼~ maternal and child hygiene; mother and child care

【保留】 bǎoliú ① continue to have; retain: 无~地同意 agree unreservedly (或 without reservation)/ 持~意见 have reservations/ 票给你~到明天中午。 We'll reserve the ticket for you till tomorrow noon./ 有意见都谈出来，不要~。 Don't hold back anything you want to say.

【保密】 bǎomì maintain secrecy; keep sth. secret: 这事绝对~。 This must be kept absolutely secret. 或 This is strictly confidential.

【保姆】 bǎomǔ ① (children's) nurse ② housekeeper

【保全】 bǎoquán ① save from damage; preserve: 由于战士们的抢救，这一批物资终于~了。 Thanks to the soldiers' rescue operations, the supplies were finally saved./ ~面子 save face ② maintain; keep in good repair

【保释】 bǎoshì 〈法〉 release on bail; bail: 准予 (不准)~ accept (refuse) bail

【保守】 bǎoshǒu ① guard; keep ② conservative: ~观点 conservative point of view/ 思想~ conservative ideas (或 thinking)

【保卫】 bǎowèi defend; safeguard: ~祖国 defend one's country/ ~国家主权和领土完整 safeguard state sovereignty and territorial integrity

【保险】 bǎoxiǎn ① insurance: 人寿(海损)~ life (maritime) insurance ② safe: 骑车太快可不~。 It's not safe to cycle too fast./ 你还是带上雨衣吧，~一点儿。 You'd better take your raincoat just to be on the safe side. ③ be sure; be bound to: 他明天~会来。 He is sure to come tomorrow./ ~能行 It's bound to work.

【保养】 bǎoyǎng ① take good care of (或 conserve) one's health ② maintain; keep in good repair: 机器~ maintenance (或 upkeep) of machinery/ 这条路~得很好。 This road is in good repair. ◇ ~费 maintenance cost; upkeep

【保佑】 bǎoyòu bless and protect: 我们相信人定胜天，不靠老天~。 We believe in man's conquest of nature and don't rely on blessings from heaven.

【保障】 bǎozhàng ensure; guarantee; safeguard: ~人民言论自由 guarantee freedom of speech for the people

【保证】 bǎozhèng pledge; guarantee; assure; ensure: ~完成任务 pledge (或 guarantee) to fulfil a task/ ~不再发生类似事件 guarantee against the occurrence of similar incidents

【保证金】 bǎozhèngjīn ① earnest money; cash deposit ② 〈法〉 bail

【保证人】 bǎozhèngrén 〈法〉 ① guarantor ② bail

【保重】 bǎozhòng 〔用于希望别人注意身体〕 take care of oneself: 多多~。 Take good care of yourself. 或 Look after yourself.

堡 bǎo fort; fortress

【堡垒】 bǎolěi fort; fortress; stronghold; blockhouse: ~是最容易从内部攻破的。 The easiest way to capture a fortress is from within.

报* bào ① report; announce; declare: ~火警 report a fire/ ~上级批准 report (或 submit) sth. to the higher authorities for approval ② reply; respond; reciprocate: ~友人书 a (letter in) reply to a friend/ ~以热烈的掌声 respond with warm applause ③ recompense; requite: 无以为~ be unable to repay a kindness/ 以怨~德 requite kindness with ingratitude; return evil for good ④ newspaper ⑤ periodical; journal: 画~ pictorial/ 周~ weekly/ 学~ college journal ⑥ bulletin; report: 喜~ report of success, a happy event, etc.; glad tidings; good news/ 战~ war bulletin ⑦ telegram; cable: 发~ transmit (或 send) a telegram

【报案】 bào'àn report a case to the security authorities

【报仇】 bàochóu revenge; avenge

【报酬】 bàochóu reward; remuneration; pay: 不计~ not concerned about pay; irrespective of remuneration

【报答】 bàodá repay; requite

【报到】 bàodào report for duty; check in; register: 向部里~ report for duty at the ministry/ 向大会秘书处~ check in at the secretariat of the congress/ 新生已开始~。 The new students have started registering.

【报道】 bàodào ① report (news); cover: ~考古新发现 report new archaeological finds/ ~会议情况 cover the conference/ 据~ it is reported that/ 各报都在第一版~了这条消息。 This was front-paged in all the papers. ② news report; story

【报恩】 bào'ēn pay a debt of gratitude

【报复】 bàofù make reprisals; retaliate: 图谋～ nurse thoughts of revenge ◇ ～性打击 vindictive blow; retaliatory strike

【报告】 bàogào ① report; make known: 向上级～ report to the higher authorities/ 向大家一个消息。 Here's a piece of good news for us all./ 现在～新闻。 Here is the news./ ② report; speech; talk; lecture: 作～ give a talk or lecture/ 总结～ summing-up report

【报馆】 bàoguǎn newspaper office

【报国】 bàoguó dedicate oneself to the service of one's country

【报界】 bàojiè the press; journalistic circles; the journalists: 向～发表谈话 make a statement to the press

【报警】 bàojǐng ① report (an incident) to the police ② give an alarm: 鸣钟～ sound the alarm bell

【报刊】 bàokān newspapers and periodicals; the press

【报名】 bàomíng enter one's name; sign up: ～参加百米赛跑 enter one's name for the 100-metre dash

【报社】 bàoshè general office of a newspaper; newspaper office

【报失】 bàoshī report the loss of sth. to the authorities concerned

【报摊】 bàotān news-stand; news stall

【报喜】 bàoxǐ announce good news; report success: ～不报忧 report only the good news and not the bad; hold back unpleasant information

【报应】 bàoyìng <宗> retribution; judgment

【报章】 bàozhāng newspapers ◇ ～杂志 newspapers and magazines

【报帐】 bàozhàng render an account; submit an expense account; apply for reimbursement: 修理费用可以～。 Costs of repairs may be reimbursed.

【报纸】 bàozhǐ ① newspaper ② newsprint ◇ ～夹 newspaper holder

刨 bào ① plane sth. down; plane: ～木板 plane a board ② plane; planer; planing machine
另见 páo

抱* bào ① hold or carry in the arms; embrace; hug: 把小孩子～起来 take a child in one's arms/ 不要～住错误观点不放。 Don't stick to your wrong views. ② have one's first child or grandchild: 她快～孙子了。 She'll soon be a grandmother. ③ adopt (a child): 他的女儿是～的。 His daughter is adopted. ④ <方> hang together: ～成一团 gang up; hang together ⑤ cherish; harbour: 很大希望 entertain high hopes/ ～正确的态度 adopt (或 take) a correct attitude/ 不～幻想 cherish no illusions

【抱病】 bàobìng be ill; be in bad health: ～工作 go on working in spite of ill health

【抱不平】 bào bùpíng be outraged by an injustice (done to another person): 打～ defend sb. against an injustice

【抱残守缺】 bàocán-shǒuquē cherish the outmoded and preserve the outworn — be conservative

【抱佛脚】 bào fójiǎo clasp Buddha's feet — profess devotion only when in trouble; make a hasty last-minute effort: 平时不烧香,急来～ never burn incense when all is well but clasp Buddha's feet when in distress; do nothing until the last minute

【抱负】 bàofù aspiration; ambition: 很有～ have high aspirations; cherish high ambitions

【抱歉】 bàoqiàn be sorry; feel apologetic; regret: 叫你久等了,很～。 Very sorry to have kept you waiting.

【抱头鼠窜】 bàotóu shǔcuàn cover the head and sneak away like a rat; scurry (或 scamper) off like a frightened rat

【抱头痛哭】 bàotóu tòngkū weep in each other's arms; cry on each other's shoulder

【抱怨】 bàoyuàn complain; grumble: 不要总是～别人对你

帮助不够。 Don't always complain that you haven't been given enough help.

豹* bào leopard; panther

鲍 Bào

【鲍鱼】 bàoyú ① abalone ② <书> salted fish: 如入～之肆,久而不闻其臭。 It's like staying in a fish market and getting used to the stink — long exposure to a bad environment accustoms one to evil ways.

暴* bào ① sudden and violent: ～雷 violent thunderclaps/ ～饮～食 eat and drink too much at one meal ② cruel; savage; fierce: 残～ brutal ③ short-tempered; hot-tempered: 脾气～ have a hot temper ④ stick out; stand out; bulge: 急得头上的青筋都～出来了 be so agitated that the veins on one's forehead stand out

【暴病】 bàobìng sudden attack of a serious illness: 得～ be suddenly seized with a severe illness

【暴跌】 bàodiē steep fall (in price); slump

【暴动】 bàodòng insurrection; rebellion

【暴发】 bàofā ① break out: 山洪～。 Torrents of water rushed down the mountain. ② suddenly become rich or important; get rich quick

【暴风】 bàofēng ① storm wind ② storm

【暴风雪】 bàofēngxuě snowstorm; blizzard

【暴风雨】 bàofēngyǔ rainstorm; storm; tempest: ～般的掌声 thunderous applause

【暴君】 bàojūn tyrant; despot

【暴力】 bàolì violence; force

【暴露】 bàolù expose; reveal; lay bare: ～思想 lay bare one's thoughts/ ～目标 give away one's position/ ～无遗 be thoroughly exposed/ 在光天化日之下 be exposed to the light of day

【暴乱】 bàoluàn riot; rebellion; revolt

【暴怒】 bàonù violent rage; fury

【暴跳如雷】 bàotiào rú léi stamp with fury; fly into a rage

【暴徒】 bàotú ruffian; thug

【暴行】 bàoxíng savage act; outrage; atrocity

【暴雨】 bàoyǔ torrential rain; rainstorm

【暴躁】 bàozào irascible; irritable

【暴涨】 bàozhǎng (of floods, prices, etc.) rise suddenly and sharply: 河水～。 The river suddenly rose./ 物价～。 Prices soared (或 skyrocketed).

爆* bào ① explode; burst: 车胎～了。 The tyre's burst./ 子弹打在石头上,～起许多火星。 The bullet hit the rock and sent sparks flying from it. ② quick-fry; quick-boil: 油～肚儿 quick-fried tripe

【爆发】 bàofā erupt; burst out; break out: 火山～ volcanic eruption/ 战争～。 War broke out./ 人群中～出一片欢呼声。 The crowd burst into cheers.

【爆裂】 bàoliè burst; crack: 豌豆过熟就会～。 Pea pods burst open when overripe.

【爆破】 bàopò blow up; demolish; dynamite; blast: 连续～ successive demolitions

【爆炸】 bàozhà explode; blow up; detonate: 炸弹～了。 A bomb exploded./ 敌人的军火库～了。 The enemy ammunition dump blew up./ ～一个核装置 detonate a nuclear device/ ～性的局势 an explosive situation

【爆竹】 bàozhú firecracker: 放～ let off firecrackers/ ～没响。 The firecracker didn't go off.

bēi

杯 bēi ① cup: 茶～ teacup/ 一～茶 a cup of tea/ 玻璃～ glass ② (prize) cup; trophy: 银～ silver cup

【杯弓蛇影】 bēigōng-shéyǐng mistaking the reflection of a bow in the cup for a snake — extremely suspicious

卑 bēi ① low: 地势～湿 low-lying and damp ② inferior: ～不足道 not worth mentioning ③ <书> modest; humble: ～辞厚礼 humble words and handsome gifts

【卑鄙】 bēibǐ base; mean; contemptible; despicable: ～行为 a base (或 mean) action; sordid conduct; abject behaviour/ ～手段 contemptible means; dirty tricks/ ～勾当 a dirty deal

【卑躬屈节】 bēigōng-qūjié bow and scrape; cringe; act servilely (或 obsequiously)

【卑贱】 bēijiàn ① lowly ② mean and low

【卑劣】 bēiliè base; mean; despicable: ～行径 base conduct/ ～手法 a mean (或 despicable) trick

【卑微】 bēiwēi petty and low

背* bēi ① carry on the back: ～着孩子 carry a baby on one's back ② bear; shoulder: 我怕～不起这样的责任。I'm afraid I can't shoulder such a responsibility. 另见 bèi

【背负】 bēifù bear; carry on the back; have on one's shoulder

悲 bēi ① sad; sorrowful; melancholy: ～不自胜 be overcome with grief/ 处于可～的境地 be in a deplorable state; be in a sorry plight ② compassion: 慈～ compassionate; merciful

【悲哀】 bēi'āi grieved; sorrowful

【悲惨】 bēicǎn miserable; tragic: ～的遭遇 a tragic experience/ ～的过去 the bitter past

【悲愤】 bēifèn grief and indignation: ～填膺 be filled with grief and indignation

【悲观】 bēiguān pessimistic: ～情绪 pessimism/ 感到～失望 feel disheartened/ 持～看法 take a pessimistic (或 gloomy) view ◇ ～主义 pessimism

【悲欢离合】 bēi-huān-lí-hé joys and sorrows, partings and reunions — vicissitudes of life

【悲剧】 bēijù tragedy

【悲泣】 bēiqì weep with grief

【悲伤】 bēishāng sad; sorrowful

【悲叹】 bēitàn sigh mournfully; lament

【悲痛】 bēitòng grieved; sorrowful: 感到深切的～ be deeply grieved; be filled with deep sorrow/ 化～为力量 turn grief into strength

【悲喜交集】 bēi-xǐ jiāojí mixed feelings of grief and joy; grief and joy intermingled; joy tempered with sorrow

碑 bēi an upright stone tablet; stele: 英雄纪念～ the Monument to the Heroes/ 墓～ tombstone

纪念碑

běi

北* běi ① north: ～风 a north wind/ 城～ north of the city/ 华～ north China/ ～屋 a room with a southern exposure

【北极】 běijí ① the North Pole; the Arctic Pole ② the north magnetic pole ◇ ～熊 polar bear

【北京人】 Běijīngrén 〈考古〉 Peking Man (Sinanthropus pekinensis)

bèi

贝* bèi ① shellfish ② cowrie: 虎斑～ tiger cowrie

【贝壳】 bèiké shell

狈 bèi 见 "狼狈" lángbèi

备* bèi ① be equipped with; have: 各种农业机械无一不～ be equipped with all sorts of farm machinery ② prepare; get ready: 把料～齐 get all the materials ready ③ provide (或 prepare) against; take precautions against: 以～万一 prepare against all eventualities ④ equipment: 军

military equipment; armaments ⑤ fully; in every possible way: ～受虐待 be subjected to every kind of maltreatment/ 艰苦～尝 suffer untold hardships/ ～受欢迎 enjoy great popularity; be very popular

【备查】 bèichá for future reference: 所有重要文件都要存档～。All important documents should be kept on file for reference.

【备忘录】 bèiwànglù 〈外〉 memorandum; aide-memoire ② memorandum book

【备注】 bèizhù remarks ◇ ～栏 remarks column

背* bèi ① the back of the body: ～痛 backache ② the back of an object: 手～ the back of the hand/ 刀～儿 the back of a knife/ 椅～ the back of a chair ③ with the back towards: ～着太阳坐 sit with one's back to the sun/ ～山面海 with hills behind and the sea in front ④ turn away: 把脸～过去 turn one's face away ⑤ hide sth. from; do sth. behind sb.'s back: ～着人说话 talk behind sb.'s back/ 没有什么～人的事 have nothing to hide from anyone ⑥ recite from memory; learn by heart (或 rote): ～台词 speak one's lines ⑦ act contrary to; violate; break: ～约 violate an agreement; break one's promise; go back on one's word ⑧ out-of-the-way: ～街 back street; side street ⑨ hard of hearing: 耳朵有点～ be a bit hard of hearing 另见 bēi

【背道而驰】 bèi dào ér chí run in the opposite direction; run counter to

【背地里】 bèidìli behind sb.'s back; privately; on the sly

【背后】 bèihòu ① behind; at the back; in the rear: 门～ behind the door/ 房子～ at the back of the house/ 从～袭击敌人 attack the enemy from the rear ② behind. sb.'s back: 当面不说，～乱说 say nothing to people to their faces but gossip about them behind their backs/ ～搞鬼 plot (或 scheme) behind the scenes; play underhand tricks/ ～下毒手 stab in the back

【背井离乡】 bèijǐng-líxiāng leave one's native place (esp. against one's will)

【背景】 bèijǐng background; backdrop: 历史～ historical background (或 setting)

【背面】 bèimiàn the back; the reverse side; the wrong side: 信封的～ the back of an envelope/ 请阅～ please turn over (P.T.O.); see overleaf

【背叛】 bèipàn betray; forsake

【背弃】 bèiqì abandon; desert; renounce: ～原来的立场 abandon one's original stand/ ～自己的诺言 go back on one's word

【背书】 bèishū ① recite a lesson from memory; repeat a lesson ② 〈经〉 endorsement (on a cheque)

【背诵】 bèisòng recite; repeat from memory

【背心】 bèixīn a sleeveless garment

【背影】 bèiyǐng a view of sb.'s back; a figure viewed from behind: 凝望着他逐渐消失的～ gazing at his receding figure

【背约】 bèiyuē break an agreement; go back on one's word; fail to keep one's promise

被* bèi ① quilt: 棉～ cotton-wadded quilt ② 〈介〉〔在被动式里引进主动者〕: 他爸爸是～强盗害死的。His father was murdered by a robber. ③ 〈助〉〔用在动词前，表示主语是被动者〕: ～捕 be arrested; be under arrest/ ～选为主席 be elected chairman

【被单】 bèidān (bed) sheet ◇ ～布 sheeting

【被动】 bèidòng passive: 陷于～地位 land oneself in a passive position; be thrown into passivity/ 变～为主动 regain the initiative ◇ ～式 〈语〉 passive form/ ～语态 〈语〉 passive voice

【被俘】 bèifú be captured; be taken prisoner ◇ ～人员 captured personnel

【被告】 bèigào 〈法〉 defendant; the accused ◇ ～席 defendant's seat; dock

【被迫】 bèipò be compelled; be forced; be constrained: 敌人～放下武器。The enemy were compelled to lay down their arms.

倍* bèi ① times; -fold: 四~ four times; fourfold/ 二的五~是十。 Five times two is ten./ 十是五的两~。 Ten is twice as much as five./ 大一~ twice as big; twice the size/ 增长了五~ increase by 500%; register a 500% increase; be six times as much/ 战胜了两~于我的敌人。 We defeated an enemy outnumbering us two to one./ 产量成~增长。 Output has doubled and redoubled. ② double; twice as much: 勇气~增 with redoubled courage

【倍数】 bèishù <数> multiple

辈* bèi ① people of a certain kind; the like: 无能之~ people without ability ② generation: 他比我长(小)一~。 He's one generation my senior (junior)./ 他俩同一~儿 the latter part of one's life. ③ lifetime: 后半儿 the latter part of one's life

【辈分】 bèifen seniority in the family or clan; position in the family hierarchy

【辈子】 bèizi all one's life; lifetime

惫 bèi exhausted; fatigued

蓓 bèi

【蓓蕾】 bèilěi bud

bei

臂* bei 见 "胳臂" gēbei
另见 bì

bēn

奔 bēn ① run quickly: ~马 a galloping horse ② hurry; hasten; rush: ~赴前线 hurry to the front ③ flee: 东~西窜 flee in all directions
另见 bèn

【奔波】 bēnbō rush about; be busy running about: 两地~ shuttle back and forth between two places

【奔驰】 bēnchí run quickly; speed: 骏马在草原上~。 Sturdy steeds gallop on the grasslands.

【奔放】 bēnfàng bold and unrestrained; untrammelled: ~不羁的风格 a bold and flowing style/ 热情~ overflowing with enthusiasm

【奔流】 bēnliú ① flow at great speed; pour: ~入海 flow into the sea/ 铁水~ molten iron pouring out in a stream ② racing current

【奔命】 bēnmìng rush about on errands; be kept on the run: 疲于~ be tired out by too much running around; be kept constantly on the run
另见 bènmìng

【奔跑】 bēnpǎo run

【奔逃】 bēntáo flee; run away: 四散~ flee in all directions; flee helter-skelter; stampede

【奔腾】 bēnténg ① gallop: 犹如万马~ like ten thousand horses galloping ahead ② surge forward; roll on in waves

【奔走】 bēnzǒu ① run about; rush about; be busy running about: ~呼号 go around campaigning for a cause/ ~相告 run around spreading the news; lose no time in telling each other the news

běn

本* běn ① the root or stem of a plant: 水有源, 木有~。 A stream has its source; a tree has its root. ② foundation; basis; origin ③ capital; principal: 还~付息 pay back the capital (或 principal) plus interest/ 小本微利 have tiny funds and small earnings ④ original; native: ~意 original idea; real intention/我~想不去。 Originally I didn't want to go. ⑤ one's own; native: ~厂 this factory/~乡~土 native soil; home village ⑥ this; current; present: ~周(月) this week

(month); the current week (month)/~决议 this resolution ⑦ according to; based on: ~着政策办事 act according to policy/ 每句话都有所~。 Every statement is well-founded. ⑧ book: 帐~儿 account book/日记~ diary/照相~ photograph album ⑨ edition; version ⑩ <量>〔用于书籍、簿册等〕: 两~书 two books/这部电影有十二~。 This is a twelve-reel film.

【本地】 běndì this locality: ~风光 local colour/ ~口音 local accent/ ~货 local (或 native) goods/ 我是~人。 I'm a native of this place. (或 I was born here.

【本分】 běnfèn one's duty: 尽~ do one's duty (或 bit)/ 为人民服务是我们的~。 To serve the people is our duty.

【本国】 běnguó one's own country: ~资源 national resources ◇ ~语 native language; mother tongue

【本行】 běnháng one's line; one's own profession: 搞建筑是他的~。 Architecture is his line.

【本届】 běnjiè current; this year's: ~联合国大会 the current session of the U.N. General Assembly/ ~毕业生 this year's graduates

【本来】 běnlái ① original: ~的意思 original meaning (或 intention) ② at first: 大会~定星期五举行。 The meeting was originally fixed for Friday. ③ it goes without saying; of course: ~就该这样办。 Of course it should be handled that way./ 你~用不着着急。 You needn't have worried about it./ 这样的事~不应该发生。 Such a thing should never have been allowed to happen in the first place.

【本来面目】 běnlái miànmù true colours; true features

【本领】 běnlǐng skill; ability; capability: 组织生产的~ ability to organize production

【本末】 běn-mò ① the whole course of an event from beginning to end; ins and outs: 详述~ tell the whole story from beginning to end ② the fundamental and the incidental

【本末倒置】 běn mò dàozhì take the branch for the root; put the incidental before the fundamental; put the cart before the horse

【本能】 běnnéng instinct

【本钱】 běnqián capital

【本人】 běnrén ① I (me, myself) ② oneself; in person: 我想见校长~。 I'd like to see the principal himself./ 必须你~来。 You must come in person.

【本色】 běnsè true (或 inherent) qualities; distinctive character

【本身】 běnshēn itself; in itself

【本题】 běntí the subject under discussion; the point at issue: 请不要离开~。 Please keep (或 stick) to the point./ 这跟~无关。 This has nothing to do with the point at issue. 或 This is quite irrelevant.

【本土】 běntǔ ① one's native country (或 land) ② metropolitan territory

【本文】 běnwén ① this text, article, etc. ② the main body of a book

【本性】 běnxìng natural instincts (或 character, disposition); nature; inherent quality: ~难移。 It is difficult to alter one's character. 或 The leopard can't change his spots.

【本意】 běnyì original idea; real intention

【本源】 běnyuán origin; source

【本着】 běnzhe in line with; in conformity with; in the light of: ~我们一贯的立场 in line with our consistent stand/ ~为人民服务的精神 motivated by a desire to serve the people/ ~增进两国之间友好关系的愿望 actuated by a desire to promote friendly relations between our two countries/ ~平等互利、互通有无的原则 adhering to the principles of equality, mutual benefit and helping to meet each other's needs/ 办一切事业都要~节约的原则。 In running all enterprises we should observe the principle of frugality.

【本质】 běnzhì essence; nature; innate character; intrinsic quality: ~方面 an essential aspect

畚 běn <方> scoop up with a dustpan

【畚箕】 běnjī <方> ① a bamboo or wicker scoop ② dustpan

bèn

奔* bèn ① go straight towards; head for: 直～实验室 head straight for the laboratory
另见 bēn

【奔命】 bènmìng <口> be in a desperate hurry
另见 bēnmìng

笨 bèn ① stupid; dull; foolish: ～人 a stupid person; fool/ 脑子～ stupid; slow-witted ② clumsy; awkward: 他这人～手～脚。He is clumsy. 或 His fingers are all thumbs. ③ cumbersome; awkward; unwieldy: 这把锄头太～。This is an awkward hoe.

【笨蛋】 bèndàn <骂> fool; idiot

【笨口拙舌】 bènkǒu-zhuōshé awkward in speech

【笨重】 bènzhòng heavy; cumbersome; unwieldy: ～的家具 heavy (或 cumbersome) furniture/ 通过技术革新，我们车间摆脱了～的体力劳动。Through technical innovations, our workshop has got rid of heavy manual labour.

【笨拙】 bènzhuō clumsy; awkward; stupid: 动作～ clumsy (或 awkward) in movement/ ～的伎俩 stupid tricks

bēng

崩* bēng ① collapse: 山～ landslide; landslip ② burst: 把气球吹～了 burst a balloon/ 他们谈～了。Their negotiations broke down. ③ be hit by sth. bursting: 爆竹～了他的手。The firecracker went off in his hand.

【崩溃】 bēngkuì collapse; crumble; fall apart: / 敌军全线～。The enemy collapsed all along the line.

【崩裂】 bēngliè burst (或 break) apart; crack: 炸药轰隆一声,山石～。Boom! The dynamite sent the rocks flying.

绷 bēng ① stretch (或 draw) tight: 弓弦～得很紧。The bowstring is stretched taut.
另见 běng

【绷带】 bēngdài bandage

běng

绷 běng <口> ① [多用于]: ～着脸 look displeased; pull a long face ② strain oneself: 咬住牙～住劲 clench one's teeth and strain one's muscles
另见 bēng

bèng

迸 bèng spout; spurt; burst forth: 火星乱～ sparks flying in all directions/ 他怎么突然～出这句话来? What made him blurt out such a remark?

【迸发】 bèngfā burst forth; burst out: 大厅里～出一阵笑声。There was an outburst of laughter in the hall.

【迸裂】 bèngliè split; burst (open): 脑浆～ have one's brains dashed out

泵 bèng pump: 离心～ centrifugal pump/ 高扬程～ high lift pump

蹦 bèng leap; jump; spring: 他使劲一～就过了沟。With one powerful leap he crossed the ditch./ 这件事还没处理完,那件事又～出来了。One problem had scarcely been solved when another cropped up.

【蹦蹦跳跳】 bèngbèng-tiàotiào bouncing and vivacious

bī

逼* bī ① force; compel; drive: ～使对方采取守势 force one's opponent onto the defensive/ 敌人～我招供,他一

句话也不说。The enemy tried to force him to talk, but he wouldn't say a word. ② press for; extort: ～租 press for payment of rent ③ press on towards; press up to; close in on: 直～城下 press up to the city wall

【逼供】 bīgòng extort a confession

【逼近】 bījìn press on towards; close in on; approach; draw near: 我军已～运河。Our troops were pressing on towards the canal./ ～敌主力 close in on the main force of the enemy

【逼迫】 bīpò force; compel; coerce

【逼人】 bīrén pressing; threatening: 形势～。The situation spurs us on./ 寒气～。There is a cold nip in the air.

【逼上梁山】 bī shàng Liángshān be driven to join the Liang-shan Mountain rebels; be driven to revolt; be forced to do sth. desperate

【逼真】 bīzhēn ① lifelike; true to life: 这幅湘竹画得十分～。This painting of mottled bamboos is really true to life. ② distinctly; clearly: 听得～ hear distinctly

bí

荸 bí
【荸荠】 bíqi water chestnut (*Eleocharis tuberosa*)

鼻* bí nose

【鼻孔】 bíkǒng nostril

【鼻梁】 bíliáng bridge of the nose

【鼻塞】 bísè have a stuffy nose

【鼻涕】 bítì nasal mucus; snivel: 流～ have a running nose

【鼻息】 bíxī breath: 听见均匀的～声 hear sb.'s regular and even breathing/ 仰人～ be slavishly dependent on others

【鼻烟】 bíyān snuff ◇ ～盒 snuffbox/ ～壶 snuff bottle

【鼻子】 bízi nose: 高～ high-bridged nose; high nose/ 塌～ snub nose; pug nose/ 鹰钩～ aquiline nose; Roman nose/ 牵着～走 lead by the nose/ 他把这事说得有～有眼的。He made the story sound quite convincing./ 不要只顾～底下的小事。Don't get bogged down in trivial matters.

bǐ

匕 bǐ an ancient type of spoon
【匕首】 bǐshǒu dagger

比* bǐ ① compare; contrast: ～得上 can compare with; compare favourably with/ 想想过去的苦, ～～今天的甜 recall past bitterness and contrast it with present happiness/ 不～不知道,一～吓一跳。If you don't compare, you're in the dark; the moment you do, you get a start. ② emulate; compete; match: 我俩～～谁先跑到。Let's have a race and see who gets there first. ③ compare to ④ gesture; gesticulate: 连说带～ gesticulate as one talks ⑤ copy; model after: ～着旧衣裁新衣 pattern a new garment on an old one ⑥ <介> [用来比较性状和程度的差别]: 许多同学都～我干得好。Many classmates have done better than I. / 人民的生活一年～一年好。The life of the people is getting better and better each year. ⑦ ratio; proportion: 反～ inverse ratio (或 proportion)/ 这里小麦同水稻的年产量约为一与三之～。Here the annual yield of wheat and rice is in a ratio of about one to three. ⑧ to (in a score): 甲队以二～一胜乙队。Team A beat team B (by a score of) two to one./ 现在几～几? What's the score? ⑨ <书> close together; next to

【比比皆是】 bǐbǐ jiē shì can be found everywhere

【比方】 bǐfang analogy; instance: 打～ draw an analogy/ 拿盖房子作～ take for instance the building of a house/ 这不过是个～。This is only by way of analogy.

【比分】 bǐfēn <体> score: 场上～是三比二。The score is 3 to 2./ 双方～十分接近。It's a close game.

【比较】 bǐjiào ①compare; contrast: 把译文和原文～一下 check the translation against the original ②〈介〉〔用来比较性状和程度的差别〕～去年有显著的增长 show a marked increase over last year ③〈副〉fairly; comparatively; relatively; quite; rather: 两个都可以，不过这个～好一点儿。Either will do, but this one is a bit better./ 这里条件～艰苦。Conditions are rather tough here.

【比例】 bǐlì ①proportion: 正(反)～ direct (inverse) proportion/ 不合～ out of proportion/ 按～发展 develop in proportion ②scale: 按～绘制 be drawn to scale/ 这个模型是按准确的～做的。This model is made exactly to scale.

【比例尺】 bǐlìchǐ ①〈测〉scale: 这张地图的～是四十万分之一。The scale of the map is 1:400,000. ②architect's scale; engineer's scale

【比邻】 bǐlín ①neighbour; next-door neighbour ②near; next to: 跟车站～的那个工厂 the factory next to the railway station

【比率】 bǐlù ratio; rate

【比拟】 bǐnǐ ①compare; draw a parallel; match: 无可～ beyond compare; incomparable; matchless ②analogy; metaphor; comparison: 这种～是不恰当的。It is inappropriate to draw such a parallel.

【比如】 bǐrú for example; for instance; such as

【比赛】 bǐsài match; competition: 友谊第一，～第二。Friendship first, competition second./ 足球～ football match/ 自行车～ bicycle race/ 射击～ shooting contest/ 象棋～ chess tournament ◇ ～规则 rules of the game; rules of a contest/ ～项目 event

【比上不足，比下有余】 bǐ shàng bù zú, bǐ xià yǒu yú fall short of the best but be better than the worst; can pass muster

【比喻】 bǐyù metaphor; analogy; figure of speech: 这只是一个～的说法。This is just a figure of speech.

彼 bǐ ①that; those; the other; another: ～时 at that time/ 由此及～ proceed from one to the other ②the other party: 要知己知～。You must know both your opponent and yourself.

【彼岸】 bǐ'àn the other shore

【彼此】 bǐcǐ ①each other; one another: ～呼应 support each other; act in coordination with each other ②〈常叠用做答语，表示大家一样〉您辛苦啦!——～～! You must have taken a lot of trouble about it. — So must you!

【彼一时，此一时】 bǐ yīshí, cǐ yīshí that was one situation, and this is another — times have changed

笔 bǐ ①pen: 圆珠～ ball-point pen/ 蘸水～ pen/ 钢～ fountain pen/ 毛～ writing brush/ 下～ set (或 put) pen to paper ②technique of writing, calligraphy or drawing: 文～ style of writing ③write: 代～ write sth. for sb./ ～之于书 put down in black and white ④stroke; touch: "天"字有四～。The character 天 has four strokes./ 这里再添几～，情节就更生动了。Add a few touches here and the episode will be more lively./ 你给他写信时，替我带一～。Please remember me to him when you write. ⑤〈量〉〔用于款项、书画等〕一～钱 a sum of money; a fund/ 我们有三～帐要算。We have three scores to settle./ 写得一～好字 write a good hand

【笔调】 bǐdiào (of writing) tone; style: 讽刺的～ a satirical tone/ 他用通俗的～写了许多科学读物。He wrote many books on science in a popular style.

【笔法】 bǐfǎ technique of writing, calligraphy or drawing

【笔锋】 bǐfēng ①the tip of a writing brush ②vigour of style in writing; stroke; touch: ～犀利 write in an incisive style; wield a pointed pen

【笔杆】 bǐgǎn ①the shaft of a pen or writing brush; penholder ②要～〈口〉wield the pen

【笔画】 bǐhuà strokes of a Chinese character

【笔迹】 bǐjī a person's handwriting; hand: 对～ identify sb.'s handwriting

【笔记】 bǐjì ①take down (in writing) ②notes: 记～ take notes ③a type of literature consisting mainly of short sketches ◇ ～本 notebook/ ～小说 literary sketches; sketchbook

【笔尖】 bǐjiān ①nib; pen point ②the tip of a writing brush or pencil

【笔名】 bǐmíng pen name; pseudonym

【笔墨】 bǐmò pen and ink; words; writing: 我们激动的心情难以用～来形容。Words can hardly describe how excited we were./ 把无关紧要的话删去，不要浪费～。To save space leave out superfluous words and sentences. ◇ ～官司 written polemics (或 controversy); a battle of words

【笔试】 bǐshì written examination

【笔心】 bǐxīn ①pencil lead ②refill (for a ball-point pen)

【笔译】 bǐyì written translation

【笔战】 bǐzhàn written polemics

【笔者】 bǐzhě 〔多用于作者自称〕the author; the writer

【笔直】 bǐzhí perfectly straight; straight as a ramrod; bolt upright: ～的马路 straight avenues/ ～走 go straight on (或 ahead)/ 身子挺得～ stand straight as a ramrod; draw oneself up to one's full height

俾 bǐ 〈书〉in order to; so that: 对该项工程应予大力支持，～能按期完成。We should give this project every support so that it may be completed on schedule./ ～众周知 for the information of all; so as to make it known to everyone

鄙 bǐ ①low; mean; vulgar: 粗～ coarse; vulgar/ 卑～ mean; despicable ②〈谦〉my: ～意 my humble opinion; my idea ③〈书〉despise; disdain; scorn: 可～ despicable ④〈书〉an out-of-the-way place: 边～ remote districts

【鄙视】 bǐshì despise; disdain; look down upon

bì

币 bì money; currency: 外～ foreign currency/ 银～ silver coin

【币值】 bìzhí currency value

【币制】 bìzhì currency (或 monetary) system ◇ ～改革 currency (或 monetary) reform

必 bì ①certainly; surely; necessarily: 你们这次访问将增强两国人民之间的友谊。Your visit will certainly strengthen the friendship between our two peoples./ 骄兵～败。An army puffed up with pride is bound to lose. ②must; have to: ～读书目 a list of required reading

【必不可少】 bì bùkě shǎo absolutely necessary; indispensable; essential

【必得】 bìděi must; have to: 你～去一趟。You simply must go.

【必定】 bìdìng be bound to; be sure to: 明天我们～把图纸送到。We'll be sure to send you the blueprints tomorrow.

【必恭必敬】 bìgōng-bìjìng reverent and respectful; extremely deferential

【必然】 bìrán ①inevitable; certain: ～结果 inevitable outcome/ ～趋势 inexorable trend ②〈哲〉necessity

【必修课】 bìxiūkè a required (或 obligatory) course

【必须】 bìxū must; have to: ～指出 it must be pointed out that/ ～厉行节约。It is imperative to practise economy./ 学习～刻苦。Study demands diligence.

【必需】 bìxū essential; indispensable: 发展工业所～的原料 raw materials essential for industrial development/ 应该把国家建设资金用在最～的地方。Our national construction funds should be spent where they are most needed.

【必需品】 bìxūpǐn necessities; necessaries

【必要】 bìyào necessary; essential; indispensable: 没有～再讨论了。There's no need to discuss it any more.

闭 bì ①shut; close: ～上眼 close one's eyes/ ～口不谈 refuse to say anything about; avoid mentioning/ ～口无言 remain silent; be tongue-tied; be left speechless/ ～嘴 Hold your tongue! 或 Shut up! ②stop up; obstruct: ～住气 hold one's breath

【闭关政策】 bìguān zhèngcè closed-door policy

【闭关自守】 bìguān zì shǒu close the country to international intercourse

【闭门羹】 bìméngēng 〔多用于〕: 给以 ~ slam the door in sb.'s face/ 吃~ be denied entrance; find the door slammed in one's face

【闭门思过】 bì mén sī guò shut oneself up and ponder over one's mistakes: 有错误要在实践中改正，不要~。 When we have made a mistake, we should correct it in practice and not ponder over it in seclusion.

【闭门造车】 bì mén zào chē make a cart behind closed doors; work behind closed doors; divorce oneself from the masses and from reality and act blindly

【闭幕】 bìmù ① the curtain falls; lower the curtain: 在观众热烈掌声中~。 The curtain fell to the loud applause of the audience. ② close; conclude: 会议已胜利~。 The conference has come to a successful close. ◇ ~词 closing address (或 speech)/ ~式 closing ceremony

毕* bì ① finish; accomplish; conclude: 阅~请放回原处。 Please replace after reading. ② 〈书〉 fully; altogether; completely: 原形~露 show one's true colours

【毕恭毕敬】 bìgōng-bìjìng 见 "必恭必敬" bìgōng-bìjìng

【毕竟】 bìjìng 〈副〉 after all; all in all; when all is said and done; in the final analysis: 她的缺点同她的成绩相比，~是第二位的。 Compared with her achievements, her shortcomings are, after all, only secondary.

【毕生】 bìshēng all one's life; lifetime: ~事业 lifework; work of a lifetime

【毕业】 bìyè graduate; finish school ◇ ~班 graduating class/ ~典礼 graduation (ceremony); ~证书 diploma; graduation certificate

庇 bì shelter; protect; shield

【庇护】 bìhù shelter; shield; put under one's protection; take under one's wing ◇ ~权 right of asylum/ ~所 sanctuary; asylum

【庇佑】 bìyòu bless; prosper

陛 bì 〈书〉 a flight of steps leading to a palace hall

【陛下】 bìxià （直接称呼） Your Majesty; （间接称呼） His or Her Majesty

毙 bì ① die; get killed: 倒~ drop dead ② 〈口〉 kill or execute by shooting; shoot

【毙命】 bìmìng meet violent death; get killed: 两名匪徒当场~。 Two of the bandits were killed on the spot.

秘* bì 见 "便秘" biànbì
另见 mì

敝 bì ① 〈书〉 shabby; worn-out; ragged: ~衣 ragged clothing; shabby (或 worn-out) clothes ② 〈谦〉 my; our; this: ~处 my place/ ~校 my school/ ~姓陈。 My name is Chen.

【敝帚自珍】 bìzhǒu zì zhēn value one's own old broom — cherish sth. of little value simply because it is one's own

婢 bì slave girl; servant-girl

【婢女】 bìnǚ slave girl; servant-girl

愎 bì wilful; self-willed

裨 bì 〈书〉 benefit; advantage: 无~于事。 It won't help matters. 或 It won't do any good.

【裨益】 bìyì 〈书〉 benefit; advantage; profit: 大有~ be of great benefit

睥 bì

【睥睨】 bìnì 〈书〉 look at sb. disdainfully out of the corner of one's eye: ~一切 consider everyone and everything beneath one's notice; be overweening

辟 bì ① 〈书〉 monarch; sovereign: 复~ restore a monarchy; restoration ② 〈书〉 ward off; keep away
另见 pì

碧 bì ① 〈书〉 green jade ② bluish green; blue: ~海 the blue sea/ ~空 a clear blue sky; an azure sky/ ~草如茵 a carpet of green grass

【碧蓝】 bìlán dark blue

【碧绿】 bìlǜ dark green

蔽 bì cover; shelter; hide: ~风雨 shelter from the wind and rain/ 衣不~体 be dressed in rags; have nothing but rags on one's back

弊 bì ① fraud; abuse; malpractice: 舞~ practise fraud; engage in corrupt practices ② disadvantage; harm: 有利无~。 There are both advantages and disadvantages./ ~多利少。 The disadvantages outweigh the advantages.

【弊病】 bìbìng ① malady; evil; malpractice ② drawback; disadvantage: 这种做法~不少。 This method has quite a few drawbacks (或 disadvantages).

【弊端】 bìduān malpractice; abuse; corrupt practice

避* bì ① avoid; evade; shun: ~而不谈 evade the question; avoid the subject; keep silent about the matter/ ~而不答 avoid making a reply/ ~雨 seek shelter from the rain/ ~开敌人岗哨 keep clear of enemy sentries ② prevent; keep away; repel: ~蚊剂 mosquito repellent

【避风】 bìfēng ① take shelter from the wind ② lie low; stay away from trouble ◇ ~港 haven; harbour

【避雷针】 bìléizhēn lightning rod

【避免】 bìmiǎn avoid; refrain from; avert: ~错误 avoid mistakes/ ~轻率行动 refrain from any rash action/ 设法~了一场事故 succeed in averting an accident

【避难】 bìnàn take refuge; seek asylum ◇ ~港 port of refuge/ ~所 refuge; sanctuary; asylum; haven

【避实就虚】 bì shí jiù xū stay clear of the enemy's main force and strike at his weak points

【避暑】 bìshǔ ① be away for the summer holidays; spend a holiday at a summer resort ② prevent sunstroke ◇ ~胜地 summer resort

【避嫌】 bìxián avoid doing anything that may arouse suspicion; avoid arousing suspicion

【避孕】 bìyùn contraception

【避重就轻】 bì zhòng jiù qīng avoid the important and dwell on the trivial; keep silent about major charges while admitting minor ones

壁* bì ① wall ② sth. resembling a wall: 细胞~ cell wall ③ cliff: 峭~ a precipitous cliff; precipice ④ rampart; breastwork: 作~上观 watch the fighting from the ramparts — be an onlooker

【壁报】 bìbào wall newspaper

【壁橱】 bìchú a built-in wardrobe or cupboard; closet

【壁灯】 bìdēng wall lamp; bracket light

【壁虎】 bìhǔ 〈动〉 gecko; house lizard

【壁画】 bìhuà mural (painting); fresco: 敦煌~ the Dunhuang frescoes

【壁垒】 bìlěi rampart; barrier: 关税~ tariff wall/ 贸易~ trade barrier

臂* bì ① arm: 左~ the left arm/ 助一~之力 give sb. a hand ② upper arm
另见 bei

【臂膀】 bìbǎng arm

biān

边* biān ① side: 三角形的一~ one side of a triangle/ 街道两~ both sides of the street ② margin; edge; brim; rim: 每页~上都有批注。 There are notes in the margin on every page./ 湖~有座扬水站。 There is a pumping station on the edge of the lake./ 田~地头 edges of fields/ 碗~儿 the rim of a bowl/ 宽~草帽 a straw hat with a broad brim/ 衬衣的～ the hem of a shirt ③ border; frontier; boundary: 戍～ garrison a border region/～城 border (或 frontier) town/ ～寨 borderland village ④ limit; bound: 无～的大海 a boundless sea/这话可太没～儿了。That's just absurd. ⑤ by the side of; close by

边* biān 〔方位词后缀〕:这～ here/ 东～ in the east/ 左～ on the left/ 前～ in front/ 里～ inside

【边…边…】 biān…biān… 〔分别用在动词前,表示动作同时进行〕:边干边学 learn while working; learn on the job/ 边读边议 read sth. and discuss it as one goes along/ 边发展边巩固 expand while consolidating

【边际】 biānjì limit; bound; boundary: 漫无～ rambling; discursive/ 不着～ wide of the mark; not to the point; irrelevant

【边疆】 biānjiāng border area; borderland; frontier; frontier region

【边界】 biānjiè boundary; border: 划定～ delimit boundaries/ 标定～ demarcate boundaries/ 越过～ cross a boundary; cross the border

【边境】 biānjìng border; frontier: 封锁～ close the frontiers; seal off the borders

【边缘】 biānyuán ①edge; fringe; verge; brink; periphery ②marginal; borderline

编* biān ① weave; plait: ～柳条筐 weave wicker baskets/ ～辫子 plait one's hair ② organize; group; arrange: ～班 group into classes/ 把他～在我们组吧。Put him in our group. ③ edit; compile: ～教材 compile teaching material/ ～杂志 edit a magazine; work in the editorial department of a magazine ④ write; compose: ～剧本 write a play/ ～儿童歌曲 compose songs for children ⑤ fabricate; invent; make up; cook up: 这事儿是他～出来的。He made the whole thing up. ⑥ part of a book; book; volume: 上～ Book I; Volume I; Part I

【编次】 biāncì order of arrangement

【编导】 biāndǎo ① write and direct (a play, film, etc.): 这个话剧是由两位青年作家～的。The play was written and directed by two young writers. ②(戏剧) playwright-director; (舞剧) choreographer-director; (电影) scenarist-director

【编号】 biānhào ① number: 给树苗～ number the saplings ②serial number

【编辑】 biānjí ① edit; compile: ～图书索引 compile an index (of books) ② (assistant) editor; compiler: 总～ editor-in-chief ◇ ～部 editorial department/ ～人员 editorial staff/ ～委员会 editorial board

【编剧】 biānjù ① write a play, scenario, etc. ②(戏剧) playwright; (电影) screenwriter; scenarist

【编目】 biānmù ① make a catalogue; catalogue: 新到的图书正在～。The new books are being catalogued. ② catalogue; list ◇ ～部 cataloguing department/ ～员 cataloguer

【编排】 biānpái arrange; lay out: 文字和图片的～ the layout of pictures and articles/ 课文要按难易程度～。The texts should be graded in order of difficulty.

【编写】 biānxiě ①compile: ～教科书 compile a textbook ②write; compose: ～歌剧 compose an opera/ ～剧本 write a play

【编选】 biānxuǎn select and edit; compile

【编译】 biānyì translate and edit

【编印】 biānyìn compile and print; publish

【编造】 biānzào ① compile; draw up; work out: ～预算 draw up a budget/ ～表册 compile statistical tables ② fabricate; invent; concoct; make up; cook up: ～谎言 fabricate lies/ ～情节 falsify the details of an event; invent (或 make up) a story; create out of the imagination: 古代人民～的神话 myths invented by the ancients

【编者】 biānzhě editor; compiler ◇ ～按 editor's note; editorial note

【编织】 biānzhī weave; knit; plait; braid: ～地毯 weave a rug/ ～草席 weave a straw mat/ ～毛衣 knit a sweater

【编制】 biānzhì ①weave; plait; braid: ～竹器 weave bamboo articles ② work out; draw up: ～生产计划 work out a pro-

duction plan/ ～教学大纲 draw up a teaching programme ③authorized strength; establishment: 部队～ establishment (for army units)

【编著】 biānzhù compile; write

【编纂】 biānzuǎn compile: ～词典 compile a dictionary

蝙* biān

【蝙蝠】 biānfú bat

鞭 biān ① whip; lash ② an iron staff used as a weapon in ancient China ③ sth. resembling a whip: 教～ (teacher's) pointer ④ a string of small firecrackers ⑤〈书〉 flog; whip; lash: ～马 whip a horse

【鞭长莫及】 biān cháng mò jí beyond the reach of one's power (或 authority); too far away for one to be able to help

【鞭笞】 biānchī 〈书〉 flog; lash

【鞭打】 biāndǎ whip; lash; flog; thrash

【鞭炮】 biānpào ① firecrackers ② a string of small firecrackers

biǎn

贬 biǎn ① demote; relegate ② reduce; devalue: ～价出售 sell at a reduced price ③ censure; depreciate: ～得一钱不值 condemn as worthless

【贬低】 biǎndī belittle; depreciate; play down: ～其重要性 belittle the importance of sth./ 企图～这一文件的意义 try to play down the significance of the document

【贬值】 biǎnzhí 〈经〉 ① devalue; devaluate ② depreciate

扁* biǎn flat: 一只～盒子 a flat case; a shallow box/ ～体字 squat-shaped handwriting/ 纸箱子压～了。The cardboard box was crushed./ 别把人看～了。Don't underestimate people.
另见 piān

【扁担】 biǎndan carrying pole; shoulder pole: ～没扎,两头打塌。〈谚〉 When the carrying pole is not secured at both ends, its loads slip off — try to grab both but end up getting neither.

匾 biǎn ①a horizontal inscribed board ②a silk banner embroidered with words of praise: 绣金～ embroidering a silk banner with words of gold ③a big round shallow basket

【匾额】 biǎn'é a horizontal inscribed board

biàn

变* biàn ① change; become different: 情况～了。The situation has changed./ 人～,地～,产量～。When people change, the land changes and output changes too./ 多～的战术 varied tactics ② change into; become: 旱地～水田。Dry land has been turned into paddy fields. ③ transform; change; alter: ～害为利 turn bane into boon ④ an unexpected turn of events: 事～ incident / 政～ coup d'état

【变本加厉】 biàn běn jiā lì become aggravated; be further intensified

【变成】 biànchéng change into; turn into; become

【变动】 biàndòng change; alteration: 文字上作一些～ make some changes (或 alterations) in the wording/ 人事～ personnel changes

【变革】 biàngé transform; change: ～自然 transform nature/ 社会～ social change

【变更】 biàngēng change; alter; modify: 所有制方面的～ changes in the system of ownership/ ～作息时间 alter the daily timetable/ 我们的计划稍有～。We have modified our plan.

【变故】 biàngù an unforeseen event; accident; misfortune: 发生了～。Something quite unforeseen has happened.

【变卦】 biànguà go back on one's word; break an agreement: 昨天说得好好的，怎么~了？ Yesterday you agreed. What made you change your mind?

【变化】 biànhuà change; vary: 化学~ chemical change/ 气温的~ variations (或 fluctuations) of temperature/ 我家乡有了很大的~. Great changes have taken place in my home village./ 他发球~多端. He's always changing his way of serving./ 高山天气~无常. In high mountains the weather is changeable.

【变幻】 biànhuàn change irregularly; fluctuate: ~莫测 changeable; unpredictable/ 风云~ unexpected gathering of clouds; constant change of events

【变换】 biànhuàn vary; alternate: ~手法 vary one's tactics/ ~位置 shift one's position

【变节】 biànjié make a political recantation; turn one's coat ◇ ~分子 recanter; turncoat

【变脸】 biànliǎn suddenly turn hostile

【变乱】 biànluàn turmoil; social upheaval

【变卖】 biànmài sell off (one's property)

【变迁】 biànqiān changes; vicissitudes: 煤乡的~ changes in a coal-mining district

【变色】 biànsè ①change colour; discolour: 这种墨水不会~. This ink will not change colour./ 脸不~心不跳 one's face does not change colour, nor does one's heart beat faster — without a trace of fear. ②change countenance; become angry: 勃然~ suddenly change countenance

【变色龙】 biànsèlóng chameleon

【变态】 biàntài ①〈生〉 metamorphosis ②abnormal; anomalous

【变通】 biàntōng be flexible; accommodate (或 adapt) sth. to circumstances: ~办法 accommodation; adaptation/ 根据不同情况作适当的~ make appropriate adaptations in the light of specific conditions

【变戏法】 biàn xìfǎ perform conjuring tricks; conjure; juggle

【变相】 biànxiàng in disguised form; covert: ~体罚 corporal punishment in disguised form/ ~的剥削行为 a covert act of exploitation

【变心】 biànxīn cease to be faithful

【变形】 biànxíng be out of shape; become deformed: 这箱子压得~了. The box has been crushed out of shape./ 病人的脊椎骨已经~. The patient has a deformed spine.

便* biàn ①convenient; handy: 日夜服务,顾客称~. Customers find the 24-hour service very convenient. ②when an opportunity arises; when it is convenient: 悉听尊~ suit your own convenience/ 得~请来一趟. Come whenever it's convenient. ③informal; plain; ordinary: ~宴 an informal dinner/ ~装 ordinary (或 everyday) clothes ④relieve oneself; 小~ piss; urinate/ 大~ defecate 小~ piss or shit; urine or excrement: 粪~ excrement; night soil ⑥〈副〉〔表示事情发生或结束得早及某种情况带来的结果等〕: 天一亮她~下地去了. She went to the fields as soon as it was light.
另见 pián

【便秘】 biànbì 〈医〉constipation

【便当】 biàndang convenient; handy; easy: 房子里家具不多,收拾起来很~. There isn't too much furniture in the room. We can easily tidy it up.

【便道】 biàndào ①shortcut: 抄~走 take a shortcut ②pavement; sidewalk: 行人走~. Pedestrians walk on the pavement. ③makeshift road

【便饭】 biànfàn a simple meal; potluck: 跟我们一块儿吃顿~吧. Come along and take potluck with us.

【便服】 biànfú ①everyday clothes; informal dress ②civilian clothes

【便利】 biànlì ①convenient; easy: 交通~ have convenient communications; have good transport facilities; be conveniently located ②facilitate: 水库建成后大大~了农田灌溉. The completion of the reservoir greatly facilitated irrigation.

【便条】 biàntiáo (informal) note

【便衣】 biànyī ①civilian clothes; plain clothes: ~公安人员 plainclothes public security personnel; public security personnel in plain clothes ②plainclothesman

【便于】 biànyú easy to; convenient for: ~携带 easy to carry

遍* biàn ①all over; everywhere: 走~全省 have travelled all over the province/ 我们的朋友~天下. We have friends all over the world. ②〈量〉〔表示动作从开始到结束的整个过程〕:这本书我从头到尾看过两~. I've read the book twice from cover to cover./ 请再说一~. Please say it again.

【遍布】 biànbù be found everywhere; spread all over

【遍及】 biànjí extend (或 spread) all over

【遍体鳞伤】 biàntǐ línshāng covered all over with cuts and bruises; beaten black and blue; be a mass of bruises

辨* biàn differentiate; distinguish; discriminate: 不~真伪 fail to distinguish between truth and falsehood; be unable to tell the true from the false

【辨别】 biànbié differentiate; distinguish; discriminate: ~香花毒草 differentiate between fragrant flowers and poisonous weeds/ ~方向 take one's bearings

【辨认】 biànrèn identify; recognize: 他的笔迹容易~. His handwriting is easy to identify./ 相片已经模糊,不能~. The photo has faded beyond recognition.

【辨析】 biànxī differentiate and analyse; discriminate: 同义词~ synonym discrimination

辩* biàn argue; dispute; debate: 真理愈~愈明. The more truth is debated, the clearer it becomes.

【辩白】 biànbái offer an explanation; plead innocence; try to defend oneself

【辩驳】 biànbó dispute; refute: 无可~ beyond all dispute; indisputable; irrefutable

【辩才】 biàncái 〈书〉eloquence: 颇有~ be quite eloquent; have a silver tongue

【辩护】 biànhù ①speak in defence of; argue in favour of; defend: 不要替他~了. Don't try to defend him. ②〈法〉plead; defend: 为被告人~ plead for the accused/ 出庭~ (of a lawyer) defend a case in court/ 被告人有权获得~. The accused has the right to defence.

【辩论】 biànlùn argue; debate: ~个水落石出 argue the matter out ◇ ~会 a debate

辫* biàn plait; braid; pigtail: 梳小~儿 wear pigtails/ 蒜~ a braid of garlic

【辫子】 biànzi ①plait; braid; pigtail: 梳~ wear one's hair in braids ②a mistake or shortcoming that may be exploited by an opponent; handle: 揪~ seize on sb.'s mistake or shortcoming; capitalize on sb.'s vulnerable point

biāo

标* biāo ①mark; sign: 商~ trade mark/ 路~ road sign/ 音~ phonetic symbol ②put a mark, tag or label on; label: ~上号码 put a number on/ ~界 demarcate a boundary/ 商品都~了价格. Every article has a price tag on it. ③prize; award: 夺~ compete for the first prize; win the championship ④outward sign; symptom: 治~ seek temporary relief ⑤tender; bid: 招~ invite tenders/ 投~ make (或 put in) a tender

【标榜】 biāobǎng ①flaunt; advertise; parade: ~自由平等 flaunt the banner of liberty and equality ②boost; excessively praise: 互相~ boost each other; exchange excessive praise/ 自我~ blow one's own trumpet; sing one's own praises

【标本】 biāoběn ①specimen; sample: 昆虫~ insect specimen ②〈中医〉the root cause and symptoms of a disease: ~同治 treat a disease by looking into both its root cause and symptoms

【标点】 biāodiǎn ①punctuation ②punctuate ◇ ~符号 punctuation mark

【标记】 biāojì sign; mark; symbol: 探清地雷,作出~ locate the landmines and mark their location

【标价】 biāojià ①mark a price ②marked price

【标明】 biāomíng mark; indicate: 货箱上~"小心轻放". The

crate is marked "Handle with care"./ 在这幅地图上北京是用一颗红星～的。Beijing is indicated on the map by a red star.

【标枪】 biāoqiāng javelin: 掷～ javelin throw

【标题】 biāotí title; heading; headline; caption: 通栏大字～ banner headline; banner／小～ subheading; crosshead

【标新立异】 biāoxīn-lìyì start something new in order to be different; do something unconventional or unorthodox; create something new and original

【标语】 biāoyǔ slogan; poster: 张贴～ put up slogans (或 posters) ◇ ～牌 placard

【标志】 biāozhì ① sign; mark; symbol: 兴旺发达的～ a sign of vigour and prosperity ② indicate; mark; symbolize

【标准】 biāozhǔn standard; criterion: 合乎～ up to standard／ 按我们的～来看 by our standards／ 用高～要求自己 set high demands on oneself

彪 biāo 〈书〉 young tiger

【彪炳】 biāobǐng 〈书〉 shining; splendid: ～千古 shining through the ages／ ～显赫的历史功绩 splendid achievements in history

【彪形大汉】 biāoxíng dàhàn burly chap; husky fellow

镖 biāo a dartlike weapon

【镖客】 biāokè 〈旧〉 armed escort (of travellers or merchants' caravans)

biǎo

表* biǎo ① surface; outside; external: 由～及里 proceed from the outside to the inside ② show; express: 深～同情 show deep sympathy／ ～决心 express (或 declare) one's determination ③ model; example ④〈中医〉 administer medicine to bring out the cold ⑤ table; form; list: 时间～ timetable; schedule／ 登记～ registration form／ 价目～ price list ⑥ meter; gauge: 温度～ thermometer ⑦ watch: 手～ (wrist) watch ⑧ the relationship between the children or grandchildren of a brother and a sister or of sisters: ～兄 cousin 参见"姑表" gūbiǎo; "姨表" yíbiǎo ⑨ memorial to an emperor

【表白】 biǎobái vindicate: ～诚意 assert one's sincerity／ 我们看一个人，不是根据他的～，而是根据他的行动。We judge a person not by what he says but by what he does.

【表达】 biǎodá express; convey; voice: 我激动的心情难以用语言来～。Words can hardly express my excitement.

【表带】 biǎodài watchband; watch strap

【表格】 biǎogé form; table: 填写～ fill in a form

【表决】 biǎojué decide by vote; vote: 付～ put to the vote; take a vote／ 投票～ vote by ballot／ 举手～ vote by a show of hands／ 唱名～ vote by roll call; roll-call vote／ 口头～ voice vote／ 起立～ vote by sitting and standing／ ～通过 be voted through

【表决权】 biǎojuéquán right to vote; vote: 行使～ exercise the right to vote／ 有(无)～ have the right (no right) to vote

【表里】 biǎo-lǐ the outside and the inside; one's outward show and inner thoughts: ～不一 think in one way and behave in another／ ～如一 think and act in one and the same way

【表露】 biǎolù show; reveal: 他很着急,但并没有～出来。He was very worried, but didn't show it.

【表面】 biǎomiàn surface; face; outside; appearance: 地球的～ the surface of the earth／ 你不能只看事情的～。You must not look only at the surface of things./ 他那番话不过是～文章。He was merely paying lip service./ ～上气壮如牛,实际上胆小如鼠 outwardly fierce as a bull but inwardly timid as a mouse

【表面化】 biǎomiànhuà come to the surface; become apparent: 矛盾～了。The contradiction has become apparent.

【表明】 biǎomíng make known; make clear; state clearly; indicate: ～立场 make known one's position; declare one's stand

【表亲】 biǎoqīn ① cousin ② cousinship

【表情】 biǎoqíng ① express one's feelings ② expression: 面部～ facial expression／ ～不自然 look awkward; wear an unnatural expression

【表示】 biǎoshì show; express; indicate: ～关切 show concern／ ～愤慨 voice (或 express) one's indignation／ ～热烈欢迎 extend a warm welcome／ 友好的～ a manifestation of friendship; a friendly gesture／ 我们谨向你们～衷心的祝贺。We wish to convey to you our hearty congratulations.

【表现】 biǎoxiàn ① expression; manifestation ② show; display; manifest: ～出极大的勇敢和智慧 display immense courage and wisdom／ 他在工作中～很好。He is doing very well in his work./ 一贯～积极 be always active; always show great initiative ③ show off: 好～ like to show off ◇ ～手法 technique of expression／ ～形式 form of expression; manifestation

【表演】 biǎoyǎn ① perform; act; play: ～节目 give a performance; put on a show／ 她～得很好。She performed very well. ② performance; exhibition: 杂技～ acrobatic performance／ 体育～ sports exhibition／ 航空模型～ model planes exhibition ③ demonstrate: ～新操作方法 demonstrate new techniques of operation ◇ ～唱 singing with actions／ ～赛 exhibition match

【表扬】 biǎoyáng praise; commend: ～好人好事 praise good people and good deeds

裱 biǎo mount (a picture, etc.): 把画拿去～一下 have the painting mounted

biǎo

鳔 biǎo 〈动〉① swim bladder; air bladder ② fish glue

biē

鳖 biē soft-shelled turtle

bié

别* bié ① leave; part: ～故乡 leave one's native place／ 临～赠言 parting advice／ 久～重逢 meet after a long separation ② other; another: ～人 other people; others／ ～处 another place; elsewhere ③ difference; distinction: 天渊之～ a world of difference／ 性～ sex distinction; sex ④ differentiate; distinguish: ～其真伪 determine whether it's true or false ⑤ fasten with a pin or clip: 把表格～在一起 pin (或 clip) the forms together／ 胸前～着大红花 with a big red flower pinned on one's breast ⑥ stick in: 腰里～着旱烟袋 with a pipe stuck in one's belt ⑦ don't: ～忘了。Don't forget./ ～忙₁ No hurry. 或 Take your time./ ～管我,救火要紧₁ Don't bother about me! Put out the fire first. ⑧ [跟"是"字合用,表示揣测]: 约定的时间都过了,～是他不来了吧！It's past the appointed time. Maybe he isn't coming.

另见 biè

【别称】 biéchēng another name; alternative name: 湘是湖南的～。Xiang is another name for Hunan.

【别出心裁】 bié chū xīncái adopt an original approach; try to be different

【别号】 biéhào alias

【别具一格】 bié jù yī gé having a unique (或 distinctive) style: 这个舞蹈刚健清新, ~。 There is something unique about the liveliness and vigour of the dance.

【别开生面】 bié kāi shēngmiàn start something new (或 original); break a new path; break fresh ground: 一次~ 的现场会 an entirely new sort of on-the-spot meeting

【别离】 biélí take leave of; leave: ~家乡, 踏上征途 leave home and start on a long journey

【别名】 biémíng another name: 铁牛是拖拉机的~。 Iron-ox is another name for tractor.

【别人】 biéren other people; others; people: 认真考虑~的 意见 consider other people's suggestions seriously

【别树一帜】 bié shù yī zhì set up a new banner; found a new school of thought; have a style of one's own

【别墅】 biéshù villa

【别有天地】 bié yǒu tiān-dì a place of unique beauty; scenery of exceptional charm

【别有用心】 bié yǒu yòngxīn have ulterior motives; have an axe to grind

【别针】 biézhēn ① safety pin; pin ② brooch

【别字】 biézì wrongly written or mispronounced character: 读~ mispronounce a character/ 写~ write a character wrongly

蹩 bié 〈方〉 sprain (one's ankle or wrist)

【蹩脚】 biéjiǎo inferior; shoddy

biè

别* biè
另见 bié

【别扭】 bièniu ① awkward; uncomfortable; difficult: 她刚 来牧区的时候, 生活上感到有点~。 When she first came to this pastoral area, she found life here a bit difficult to get used to./ 这个人真~。 That chap is really difficult to deal with. ② cannot see eye to eye: 闹~ be at odds ③ (of speech or writing) unnatural; awkward: 这句话听起来有点 ~。 This sentence sounds a bit awkward.

bīn

宾* bīn guest: 贵~ distinguished guest/ 国~ state guest

【宾馆】 bīnguǎn guesthouse

【宾客】 bīnkè guests; visitors

【宾至如归】 bīn zhì rú guī guests feel at home (in a hotel, guesthouse, etc.); a home from home

彬 bīn

【彬彬有礼】 bīnbīn yǒu lǐ refined and courteous; urbane

傧 bīn

【傧相】 bīnxiàng attendant of the bride or bridegroom at a wedding: 男~ best man/ 女~ bridesmaid

滨 bīn ① bank; brink; shore: 海~ seashore/ 湖 ~ lakeshore; lakeside/ 湘江之~ on the banks of the Xiangjiang River ② be close to (the sea, a river, etc.); border on: ~海 border on the sea/ ~海地区 coastal region/ ~江公园 riverside park

缤 bīn

【缤纷】 bīnfēn 〈书〉 in riotous profusion: 五彩~ a riot of colour/ 落英~ petals falling in riotous profusion

濒 bīn ① be close to (the sea, a river, etc.); border on: 东~大海 face the sea on the east ② be on the brink of; be on the point of: ~死 on the brink (或 verge) of death; dying/ ~行 on the point of going

【濒临】 bīnlín be close to; border on; be on the verge of: ~黄海 border on the Huanghai Sea

【濒于】 bīnyú be on the brink of: ~破产 be on the brink of bankruptcy/ ~崩溃 verge on collapse/ ~绝境 face an impasse/ ~灭亡 near extinction

bìn

摈 bìn 〈书〉 discard; get rid of: ~而不用 reject/ ~诸 门外 shut (或 lock) sb. out

【摈斥】 bìnchì reject; dismiss: ~异己 dismiss those who hold different opinions

【摈除】 bìnchú discard; get rid of; dispense with: ~繁文 缛节 dispense with all unnecessary formalities

【摈弃】 bìnqì abandon; discard; cast away

殡 bìn ① lay a coffin in a memorial hall ② carry a coffin to the burial place

【殡车】 bìnchē hearse

【殡殓】 bìnliàn encoffin a corpse and carry it to the grave

【殡仪馆】 bìnyíguǎn the undertaker's; funeral parlour (或 home)

鬓 bìn temples; hair on the temples

【鬓发】 bìnfà hair on the temples: ~灰白 greying at the temples

【鬓角】 bìnjiǎo temples; hair on the temples

bīng

冰* bīng ① ice ② put on the ice; ice: 把那瓶啤酒~上。 Ice the bottle of beer. ③ feel cold: 这水~手。 This water is freezing cold.

【冰雹】 bīngbáo hail; hailstone

【冰场】 bīngchǎng skating (或 ice) rink; ice stadium; ice arena

【冰点】 bīngdiǎn 〈物〉 freezing point ◇ ~测定器 cryoscope

【冰冻】 bīngdòng freeze: ~三尺, 非一日之寒。 It takes more than one cold day for the river to freeze three feet deep — the trouble has been brewing for quite some time. ◇ ~季节 freezing season/ ~区 frost zone/ ~食物 frozen food

【冰淇淋】 bīngqílín ice cream

【冰山】 bīngshān iceberg

【冰释】 bīngshì 〈书〉 (of misgivings, misunderstandings, etc.) disappear; vanish; be dispelled: 涣然~ be instantly dispelled (或 removed)

【冰霜】 bīngshuāng ① moral integrity ② austerity: 凛若~ severe-looking

【冰糖】 bīngtáng crystal sugar; rock candy ◇ ~葫芦 candied haws on a stick

【冰天雪地】 bīngtiān-xuědì a world of ice and snow

【冰箱】 bīngxiāng icebox; refrigerator; freezer

【冰消瓦解】 bīngxiāo-wǎjiě melt like ice and break like tiles; disintegrate; dissolve

【冰鞋】 bīngxié skating boots; skates

兵* bīng ① weapons; arms: 坚甲利~ strong armour and sharp weapons ② soldier: 当~ be a soldier; serve (或 enlist) in the armed forces/ 新~ recruit/ 老~ seasoned soldier; veteran ③ rank-and-file soldier; private: 官~一致 unity between officers and men ④ army; troops ⑤ military ⑥ pawn, one of the pieces in Chinese chess

【兵变】 bīngbiàn mutiny

【兵船】 bīngchuán man-of-war; naval vessel; warship

【兵法】 bīngfǎ art of war; military strategy and tactics

【兵荒马乱】 bīnghuāng-mǎluàn turmoil and chaos of war

【兵舰】 bīngjiàn warship

【兵力】 bīnglì military strength; armed forces; troops: ~ 对比 relative military strength/ 分散~ disperse one's troops; spread one's forces too thin/ ~不足 be short of men (或 armed forces)/ ～转移 transfer of troops/ ～部署 troop disposition; battle array

【兵器】 bīngqì weaponry; weapons; arms

【兵强马壮】 bīngqiáng-mǎzhuàng strong soldiers and sturdy horses — a well-trained and powerful army

【兵士】 bīngshì ordinary soldier

【兵书】 bīngshū a book on the art of war

【兵役】 bīngyì military service: 服～ serve in the army; perform military service ◇ ～法 military service law/ ～制 system of military service

【兵营】 bīngyíng military camp; barracks

槟* bīng

【槟榔】 bīngláng areca; betel palm ◇ ～子 〈中药〉 betel (或 areca) nut

bǐng

丙* bǐng ①the third of the ten Heavenly Stems ②third: ～等 the third grade; grade C/ ～种维生素 vitamin C

秉 bǐng 〈书〉①grasp; hold: ～烛夜游 take an evening stroll with a lantern ②control; preside over: ～政 hold political power; be in power

【秉承】 bǐngchéng 〈书〉take (orders); receive (commands): ～其主子的旨意 act on the orders of one's master

【秉公】 bǐnggōng justly; impartially: ～办理 handle a matter impartially

炳 bǐng 〈书〉bright; splendid; remarkable: 彪～ shining; splendid

柄* bǐng ①handle: 刀～ the handle of a knife/ 斧～ the shaft of an axe; helve ②stem (of a flower, leaf or fruit) ③〈书〉power; authority

饼* bǐng ①a round flat cake: 月～ moon cake/ 烙～ unleavened pancake; flapjack ②sth. shaped like a cake: 豆～ soybean cake/ 铁～ 〈体〉discus

【饼干】 bǐnggān biscuit; cracker

屏 bǐng ①hold (one's breath) ②reject; get rid of; abandon
另见 píng

【屏除】 bǐngchú get rid of; dismiss; brush aside: ～杂念 dismiss distracting thoughts

【屏气】 bǐngqì hold one's breath

【屏弃】 bǐngqì discard; reject; throw away; abandon

【屏息】 bǐngxī hold one's breath: ～静听 listen with bated breath

禀 bǐng ①report (to one's superior); petition ②receive; be endowed with

【禀告】 bǐnggào report (to one's superior)

【禀性】 bǐngxìng natural disposition: ～纯厚 be simple and honest by nature

bìng

并* bìng ①combine; merge; incorporate: 把几个小厂～成一个大厂 combine several small factories into a big one ②simultaneously; equally; side by side: 两者～重 equal stress on; pay equal attention to ③〈连〉and: 我完全同意～拥护这个报告。 I fully agree with and endorse this report.

【并蒂莲】 bìngdìlián twin lotus flowers on one stalk — a devoted married couple

【并发】 bìngfā be complicated by; erupt simultaneously ◇ ～症 〈医〉complication

【并驾齐驱】 bìngjià-qíqū run neck and neck; keep abreast of (或 keep pace with, be on a par with) one another

【并肩】 bìngjiān shoulder to shoulder; side by side; abreast:

～作战 fight side by side/ 四人～而行。 The four of them walked abreast./ 互帮互学、～前进 help and learn from each other and advance together

【并立】 bìnglì exist side by side; exist simultaneously

【并列】 bìngliè stand side by side; be juxtaposed: ～第二名 be both runners-up/ ～第二的 place ～ ～分句 〈语〉coordinate clauses/ ～句 〈语〉compound sentence

【并排】 bìngpái side by side; abreast: 不要～骑车。Don't all cycle abreast.

【并且】 bìngqiě 〈连〉and; besides; moreover; furthermore: 任务艰巨，～时间紧迫。The task is difficult and, moreover, time is pressing./ 这本书内容好，～写得很生动。This book is sound in content and lively in style.

【并吞】 bìngtūn swallow up; annex; merge

【并重】 bìngzhòng lay equal stress on; pay equal attention to: 两者～ lay equal stress on both

病* bìng ①ill; sick: 生～ fall ill; be taken ill/ 他～了三天。He was ill for three days. ②disease: 心脏～ heart trouble; heart disease/ 流行～ epidemic disease ③fault; defect: 语～ ill-chosen expression/ 不足为～ can't count as a fault

【病床】 bìngchuáng ①hospital bed: 这所医院有三百张～。The hospital has three hundred beds. ②sickbed

【病从口入】 bìng cóng kǒu rù illness finds its way in by the mouth

【病倒】 bìngdǎo be down with an illness; be laid up

【病房】 bìngfáng ward (of a hospital); sickroom: 隔离～ isolation ward/ 内科～ medical ward

【病夫】 bìngfū sick man

【病根】 bìnggēn ①an incompletely cured illness; an old complaint ②the root cause of trouble: 他犯错误的～在于私心太重。His error stems from selfishness.

【病故】 bìnggù die of an illness

【病假】 bìngjià sick leave: 请～ ask for sick leave/ 休～ be on sick leave/ 给三天～ grant three days' sick leave ◇ ～条 certificate for sick leave

【病菌】 bìngjūn pathogenic bacteria; germs

【病况】 bìngkuàng state of an illness; patient's condition

【病魔】 bìngmó serious illness: ～缠身 be afflicted with a lingering disease

【病情】 bìngqíng state of an illness; patient's condition: 孩子的～有好转。The child's condition took a favourable turn. 或 The child's condition was improving. ◇ ～公报 medical bulletin

【病人】 bìngrén patient; invalid: 重～ a serious case

【病容】 bìngróng sickly look: 面带～ look ill; look unwell

【病入膏肓】 bìng rù gāohuāng the disease has attacked the vitals — beyond cure

【病势】 bìngshì degree of seriousness of an illness; patient's condition: 针灸以后，～略为减轻。The patient became a bit better after the acupuncture treatment.

【病痛】 bìngtòng slight illness; indisposition; ailment

【病危】 bìngwēi be critically ill; be terminally ill

【病愈】 bìngyù recover (from an illness)

【病院】 bìngyuàn a specialized hospital: 精神～ mental hospital/ 传染～ infectious diseases hospital; isolation hospital

【病症】 bìngzhèng disease; illness

【病状】 bìngzhuàng symptom (of a disease)

bō

波* bō ①wave: 微～ ripples ②〈物〉wave: 声(光、电)～ sound (light, electric) wave ③an unexpected turn of events: 风～ storm; disturbance

【波长】 bōcháng wavelength ◇ ～计 wavemeter; cymometer

【波荡】 bōdàng heave; surge: 海水～。The sea surges.

【波动】 bōdòng ①undulate; fluctuate: 物价～ price fluctuation/ 情绪～ in an anxious state of mind ②〈物〉wave motion

【波及】 bōjí spread to; involve; affect: 经济危机～整个世界。

The economic crisis affected the entire world.

【波澜】 bōlán great waves; billows

【波澜起伏】 bōlán qǐfú (of a piece of writing) with one climax following another

【波澜壮阔】 bōlán zhuàngkuò surging forward with great momentum; unfolding on a magnificent scale: 一首~、气势磅礴的史诗 an epic of magnificent sweep

【波浪】 bōlàng wave: ~式前进 advance wave upon wave

【波涛】 bōtāo great waves; billows: ~汹涌 roaring waves/ ~滚滚的大海 rolling seas

【波折】 bōzhé twists and turns: 事情发生了~。Events took an unexpected turn.

拨* bō ① move with hand, foot, stick, etc.; turn; stir; poke: ~火 poke a fire/ ~钟 set a clock/ ~电话号码 dial a telephone number/~转马头 turn the horse round ② set aside; assign; allocate: ~两间房子给我们 set aside two rooms for us

【拨款】 bōkuǎn ① allocate funds ② appropriation: 军事~ military appropriations/ 财政~ financial allocation

【拨弄】 bōnong ① move to and fro (with hand, foot, stick, etc.); fiddle with: ~算盘子儿 move the beads of an abacus/ ~火盆里的木炭 poke the charcoal in the brazier/ ~琴弦 pluck the strings of a fiddle ② stir up: ~是非 stir things up

玻* bō

【玻璃】 bōli ① glass: 雕花~ cut glass/ 彩色~ stained glass/ 泡沫~ cellular glass ② 〈口〉nylon; plastic ◇ ~杯 glass; tumbler/ ~厂 glassworks

剥* bō

另见 bāo

【剥夺】 bōduó deprive; expropriate; strip

【剥削】 bōxuē exploit: 消灭人~人的制度 abolish the system of exploitation of man by man

钵 bō ① earthen bowl ② alms bowl (of a Buddhist monk)

菠 bō

【菠菜】 bōcài spinach

【菠萝】 bōluó pineapple

播* bō ① sow; seed: 夏~ summer sowing/ 撒~ broadcast sowing

【播弄】 bōnong ① order sb. about ② stir up: ~是非 stir things up; stir up trouble; sow dissension

【播送】 bōsòng broadcast; transmit; beam: ~新闻 broadcast news/ ~电视节目 broadcast a T. V. programme

【播音】 bōyīn transmit; broadcast: 这次~到此结束。That concludes our programme for this transmission. ◇ ~室 broadcasting studio/ ~员 announcer

【播种】 bōzhǒng sow seeds; sow; seed ◇ ~机 seeder; planter; grain drill

bó

伯* bó ① father's elder brother; uncle ② the eldest of brothers ③ earl; count

【伯伯】 bóbo father's elder brother; uncle

【伯父】 bófù father's elder brother; uncle

【伯母】 bómǔ wife of father's elder brother; aunt

【伯仲】 bó-zhòng 〈书〉〔多用于〕: 相~ be much the same/ ~之间 almost on a par

【伯仲叔季】 bó-zhòng-shū-jì eldest, second, third and youngest of brothers; order of seniority among brothers

驳 bó ① refute; contradict; gainsay: 真理不怕人~。Truth fears no refutation. ② barge; lighter: 铁~ iron barge/ 油~ oil barge

【驳斥】 bóchì refute; denounce

【驳船】 bóchuán barge; lighter

【驳倒】 bódǎo demolish sb.'s argument; refute; outargue

【驳回】 bóhuí reject; turn down; overrule: ~上诉 reject an appeal/ 法院~了他的无理要求。The court overruled his unreasonable claim.

【驳运】 bóyùn transport by lighter; lighter ◇ ~费 lighterage

【驳杂】 bózá heterogeneous: 内容~ heterogeneous in content

泊* bó be at anchor; moor; berth: 停~ lie at anchor/ ~岸 anchor alongside the shore

另见 pō

帛 bó 〈书〉 silks: 布~ cottons and silks/ ~画 painting on silk/ ~书 (ancient) book copied on silk

勃 bó suddenly

【勃勃】 bóbó thriving; vigorous; exuberant: 生气~ full of vitality; alive with activity/ 兴致~ full of enthusiasm; in high spirits/ 野心~ driven by wild ambition; overweeningly ambitious

【勃发】 bófā ① thrive; prosper ② break out: 游兴~ be seized with a desire to travel

【勃然】 bórán agitatedly; excitedly: ~变色 agitatedly change colour; be visibly stung/ ~大怒 fly into a rage; flare up

【勃兴】 bóxīng rise suddenly; grow vigorously: 一个工业城市的~ the vigorous growth of an industrial town

钹 bó 〈乐〉cymbals

舶 bó oceangoing ship

脖 bó neck

博* bó ① rich; abundant; plentiful: 地大物~ vast in territory and rich in natural resources/ ~而不精 have wide but not expert knowledge; know something about everything ② win; gain: 聊~一笑 just for your entertainment

【博爱】 bó'ài universal fraternity (或 brotherhood); universal love

【博得】 bódé win; gain: ~同情 win sympathy/ ~全场喝采 draw loud applause from the audience; bring the house down/ ~好评 have a favourable reception

【博古通今】 bógǔ-tōngjīn conversant with things past and present — erudite and informed

【博览】 bólǎn read extensively: ~群书 well-read

【博览会】 bólǎnhuì (international) fair

【博取】 bóqǔ try to gain; court: ~同情 seek (或 enlist) sb.'s sympathy/ ~欢心 curry favour/ ~信任 try to win sb.'s confidence

【博士】 bóshì doctor: 哲学~ Doctor of Philosophy (Ph. D.)

【博闻强记】 bówén-qiángjì have wide learning and a retentive memory; have encyclopaedic knowledge

【博物】 bówù natural science ◇ ~学家 naturalist

【博物馆】 bówùguǎn museum: 历史~ the Museum of History

【博学】 bóxué learned; erudite: ~之士 learned scholar; erudite person

搏 bó ① wrestle; fight; combat; struggle: 肉~ hand-to-hand fight (或 combat) ② pounce on; pounce: 恶狼~羊。The wolf pounced on the sheep. ③ beat; throb: 脉~ pulse

【搏斗】 bódòu wrestle; fight; struggle: 与风浪~ battle with the winds and waves/ 生死的~ a life-and-death struggle

魄 bó 见"落泊(魄)" luòbó

另见 pò; tuò

箔 bó ① screen (of reeds, sorghum stalks, etc.): 苇～ reed screen ② bamboo tray for rearing silkworms ③ foil; tinsel: 金～ gold foil (或 leaf) ④ paper tinsel burnt as offerings to the dead

膊 bó arm: 赤～ bare to the waist

薄* bó ① slight; meagre; small: ～技 〈谦〉 my slight skill/ ～酬 small reward; meagre remuneration ② ungenerous; unkind; mean: ～待 treat ungenerously ③ frivolous; given to philandering ④ despise; belittle: 鄙～ despise/ 厚此～彼 favour one and slight the other ⑤ 〈书〉 approach; near: 日～西山。 The sun is setting behind the western hills.
另见 báo; bò
【薄利】 bólì small profits: ～多销 small profits but quick turnover
【薄命】 bómìng 〈旧〉 (usu. of women) born under an unlucky star; born unlucky
【薄暮】 bómù 〈书〉 dusk; twilight
【薄片】 bópiàn thin slice; thin section
【薄情】 bóqíng inconstant in love; fickle
【薄弱】 bóruò weak; frail: 意志～ weak-willed/ 能力～ lacking in ability/ 技术力量～ lack qualified technical personnel ◇ ～环节 weak link; vulnerable spot

礴 bó 见"磅礴" pángbó

bǒ

跛* bǒ lame: ～了一只脚 lame in one leg/ 一颠一～ walk with a limp; limp along
【跛子】 bǒzi lame person; cripple

簸 bǒ winnow with a fan; fan: ～谷 winnow away the chaff; fan the chaff
另见 bò

【簸荡】 bǒdàng roll; rock: 船～得很厉害。 The ship was rolling heavily.

bò

薄* bò
另见 báo; bó
【薄荷】 bòhe 〈植〉 field mint; peppermint
◇ ～醇 〈化〉 menthol; peppermint camphor/ ～糖 peppermint drops/ ～酮 menthone/ ～油 peppermint oil

簸 bò
另见 bǒ
【簸箕】 bòji ① dustpan ② winnowing fan ③ loop (of a fingerprint)

bo

卜* bo 见"萝卜" luóbo
另见 bǔ

bǔ

卜* bǔ ① divination; fortune-telling: ～卦 divine by the Eight Diagrams ② 〈书〉 foretell; predict: 生死未～

hard to tell whether the person is alive or not/ 胜败可～。 Victory or defeat can be predicted. 或 We can forecast the outcome. ③ 〈书〉 select; choose: ～居 choose a place for one's home/ 行期未～。 The date of departure remains undecided.
另见 bo

补* bǔ ① mend; patch; repair: ～衣服 mend (或 patch) clothes/ ～鞋 repair (或 mend) shoes/ ～袜子 darn socks/ ～车胎 mend a puncture/ 修桥～路 build bridges and repair roads ② fill; supply; make up for: 弥～损失 make up for a loss/ 把漏了的字～上 supply the missing words/ 我们还得～两个人。 We have two vacancies to be filled. 或 We need two more people. ③ nourish: ～血 enrich the blood/ ～身体 build up one's health (with nourishing food or tonics) ④ 〈书〉 benefit; use; help: 不无小～ not be without some advantage; be of some help/ 无～于事 not help matters
【补白】 bǔbái filler (in a newspaper or magazine)
【补偿】 bǔcháng compensate; make up: ～所受的损失 compensate sb. for a loss/ 差额 make up a deficiency/ ～费 compensation
【补充】 bǔchōng replenish; supplement; complement; add: ～人力 replenish manpower/ ～兵员 fill up (an army unit) to full strength; replace losses/ ～库存 replenish the stock/ ～两点意见 have two points to add/ 互相～ complement each other; be mutually complementary ② additional; complementary; supplementary
◇ ～读物 supplementary reading material/ ～规定 additional regulations/ ～说明 additional remarks
【补给】 bǔjǐ 〈军〉 supply
◇ ～点 supply point/ ～品 supplies/ ～线 supply line/ ～站 depot
【补救】 bǔjiù remedy: ～办法 remedial measure; remedy/ 无可～ be past (或 beyond) remedy; irremediable; irreparable
【补考】 bǔkǎo make-up examination
【补课】 bǔkè make up a missed lesson: 教师给学生～。 The teacher helped his pupils make up the lessons they had missed.
【补习】 bǔxí take lessons after school or work ◇ ～学校 continuation school
【补选】 bǔxuǎn by-election
【补牙】 bǔyá 〈医〉 fill a tooth; have a tooth stopped
【补养】 bǔyǎng take a tonic or nourishing food to build up one's health
【补药】 bǔyào tonic
【补助】 bǔzhù subsidy; allowance
【补足】 bǔzú bring up to full strength; make up a deficiency; fill (a vacancy, gap, etc.)

捕* bǔ catch; seize; arrest: ～鱼 catch fish/ 被～ be arrested; be under arrest
【捕风捉影】 bǔfēng-zhuōyǐng chase the wind and clutch at shadows — make groundless accusations; speak or act on hearsay evidence
【捕获】 bǔhuò catch; capture; seize: 当场～ catch sb. red-handed
【捕食】 bǔshí catch and feed on; prey on: 蜻蜓～蚊蝇。 The dragonfly feeds on mosquitoes and flies.
【捕鼠器】 bǔshǔqì mousetrap
【捕鱼】 bǔyú catch fish; fish: 出海～ go fishing on the sea
【捕捉】 bǔzhuō catch; seize: ～昆虫 catch insects/ ～战机 seize the opportunity for battle; seize the right moment to strike/ ～镜头 seize the right moment to get a good shot (或 to take a picture)

哺 bǔ ① feed (a baby); nurse ② 〈书〉 the food in one's mouth
【哺乳】 bǔrǔ breast-feed; suckle; nurse
◇ ～动物 mammal
【哺养】 bǔyǎng 〈书〉 feed; rear
【哺育】 bǔyù ① feed: ～雏鸟 (of mother birds) feed little birds ② nurture; foster

bù

不 * bù 〈副〉①〔表示否定〕: ~严重 not serious/ ~必要 unnecessary/ ~正确 incorrect/ ~合法 illegal/ ~可能 impossible/ ~规则 irregular/ ~小心 careless/ 拿~动 find sth. too heavy to carry/ 睡~好 not sleep well/ 她~走了。She's not going. 或 She's decided to stay./ 互~侵犯 mutual nonaggression ②〔单用,表示否定对方的话〕: 他知道吧。—— ~,他不知道。He knows, doesn't he? — No, he doesn't./ 他不知道吧。—— ~,他知道。He doesn't know, does he? — Yes, he does. ③〔用在句末表示疑问〕: 你明儿来~? Are you coming tomorrow? ④〔在"不"字前后,叠用相同的词,前面常加"什么",表示不在乎或不相干〕: 什么难学~难学,我保证学会。No matter how hard it is, I'll learn how to do it. ⑤〔跟"就"搭用,表示选择〕他这会儿~是在车间就是在实验室。He's either in the workshop or in the laboratory.

〔注意〕"不"字在第四声(去声)字前念第二声(阳平),如"不必"búbì;"不是"búshì。本词典为简便起见,条目中的"不"字,都注第四声。

【不安】 bù'ān ①intranquil; unpeaceful; unstable: 世界局势动荡~。The world situation is characterized by turbulence and intranquility. ②uneasy; disturbed; restless: 坐立~ restless; on pins and needles/ 听了这消息我心里很~。I was rather disturbed by the news./ 老来麻烦您,真是~。I'm sorry to trouble you so often.

【不白之冤】 bù bái zhī yuān unrighted wrong; unredressed injustice

【不败之地】 bù bài zhī dì invincible position: 立于~ be in an invincible position

【不备】 bùbèi unprepared; off guard: 乘其~ catch sb. off guard/ 伺其~ watch for a chance to take sb. by surprise

【不必】 bùbì 〈副〉need not; not have to: ~担心(惊慌) There is no need to worry (panic)./ 你~去了。You don't have to go now.

【不避艰险】 bù bì jiānxiǎn shrink (或 flinch) from no difficulty or danger; make light of difficulties and dangers

【不便】 bùbiàn ①inconvenient; inappropriate; unsuitable: 交通~ have poor transport facilities; not be conveniently located/ 给治疗带来~ hamper medical treatment/ 在场的人很多,~同他长谈。With so many people around, it wasn't convenient to have a long talk with him./ 如果对你没有什么~的话,我想把时间提早一点。I'd like to make it earlier, if that's not inconvenient to you. ②〈口〉short of cash: 手头~ be short of cash; be hard up

【不…不…】 bù … bù … ①〔用于意思相同或相近的词或词素之前,表示否定,稍显强调〕: 不骄不躁 not conceited or rash; free from arrogance and rashness/ 不慌不忙 unhurried; calm; leisurely/ 不声不响 quiet; silent/ 不理不睬 ignore; take no notice of ②〔用于意思相对的词或词素之间,表示"既不…又不…"〕: 不大不小 neither too big nor too small; just right/ 不多不少 not too much and not too little; just right/ 不死不活 neither dead nor alive; lifeless; lethargic/ 不上不下 suspended in mid air; in a fix/ 不盈不亏 break even ③〔用于意思相对的词或词素之前,表示"如不…就不…"〕: 不破不立,不塞不流,不止不行。There is no construction without destruction, no flowing without damming and no motion without rest.

【不测】 bùcè accident; mishap; contingency: 以防~ be prepared for any contingency/ 如有~ if anything untoward should happen/ 险遭~ have a narrow escape

【不曾】 bùcéng never (have done sth.): 我~到过那里。I have never been there.

【不成】 bùchéng ①won't do: 只说不做,那是~的。Mere talk and no action won't do. ②〔助〕〔用在句末,表示揣度或反问的语气,前面常有"难道""莫非"等词相呼应〕: 难道就这样算了~? How can we let it go at that?/ 莫非起重机不到,大家就坐等~? Are we going to sit back and do nothing until the cranes arrive?

【不成材】 bùchéngcái good-for-nothing; worthless; ne'er-do-well 又作"不成器"

【不齿】 bùchǐ 〈书〉despise; hold in contempt: 为人民所~ held in contempt by the people

【不耻下问】 bù chǐ xià wèn not feel ashamed to ask and learn from one's subordinates

【不出所料】 bù chū suǒ liào as expected: ~,敌人果然自投罗网。As was expected, the enemy walked right into the trap.

【不揣冒昧】 bù chuǎi màomèi 〈套〉venture to; presume to; take the liberty of

【不辞而别】 bù cí ér bié leave without saying good-bye

【不辞辛苦】 bù cí xīnkǔ make nothing of hardships

【不错】 bùcuò ①correct; right: 一点儿~ perfectly correct; quite right ②〔单用,表示肯定对方的话〕: ~,他是这么说的。Yes, that's what he said. ③〈口〉not bad; pretty good: 庄稼长得挺~。The crops are doing quite well./ 这本小说~。This novel is pretty good.

【不打不相识】 bù dǎ bù xiāngshí 〈谚〉from an exchange of blows friendship grows; no discord, no concord

【不打自招】 bù dǎ zì zhāo confess without being pressed; make a confession without duress

【不大】 bùdà ①not very; not too: ~好 not very good/ ~清楚 not too clear ②not often: 他最近~来。He hasn't been coming around much recently.

【不待说】 bùdài shuō needless to say; it goes without saying

【不单】 bùdān ①not the only ②not merely; not simply

【不但】 bùdàn 〔连〕not only: 我们的产品~要求数量多,而且要求质量好。In production, we demand not only quantity but also quality.

【不当】 bùdàng unsuitable; improper; inappropriate: 处理~ not be handled properly/ 措词~ wrong choice of words

【不倒翁】 bùdǎowēng tumbler; roly-poly

【不道德】 bùdàodé immoral

【不得】 bùdé must not; may not; not be allowed: ~将参考书携出阅览室。Reference books may not be taken out of the reading room.

【不得】 bude 〔用在动词后面,表示不可以或不能够〕: 去~ must not go/ 马虎~ mustn't (或 can't afford to) be careless/ 这件事你做~。You must never do this.

【不得不】 bùdé bù have no choice (或 option) but to; cannot but; have to: 铁证如山,那个坏家伙~低头认罪。Confronted with ironclad evidence the scoundrel had to plead guilty.

【不得而知】 bùdé ér zhī unknown; unable to find out: 作者是谁,~。The name of the author is unknown./ 情况如何,~。We are unable to find out how the situation stands.

【不得了】 bùdéliǎo ①desperately serious; disastrous: 没有什么~的事。There's nothing really serious./ 成绩不夸跑不了,缺点不找~。If we don't speak of our achievements, they won't run away. If we don't find out our faults, we'll be in a bad way. ②〔用在"得"后作补语〕extremely; exceedingly: 高兴得~ be extremely happy; be wild with joy/ 坏得~ couldn't be worse; be very bad

【不得人心】 bù dé rénxīn not enjoy popular support; be unpopular

【不得要领】 bù dé yàolǐng fail to grasp the main points: 他讲了半天我还是~ He talked at great length, but I just couldn't see what he was driving at.

【不得已】 bùdéyǐ act against one's will; have no alternative but to; have to: ~而求其次 have to be content with the second best/ 实在~,她只好请几天假。She had no alternative but to ask for a few days' leave./ 非万~不要用这种药。Don't take this medicine unless it's absolutely necessary.

【不登大雅之堂】 bù dēng dàyǎ zhī táng 〈书〉not appeal to refined taste; be unrefined; be unpresentable

【不等】 bùděng vary; differ: 数量~ vary in amount/ 大小~ differ (或 vary) in size/每包的重量从三公斤到十公斤~。The packages vary in weight from 3 to 10 kg.

【不定】 bùdìng ①〔副〕〔表示不肯定〕: 他一天~来多少次。He comes I don't know how many times a day./ 我明天还~去不去呢。It's not at all certain whether I'll go tomorrow./ 事情还~怎样呢。It's hard to predict how things will turn out. ②indefinite

【不动产】 bùdòngchǎn real estate; immovable property; immovables

【不动声色】 bù dòng shēngsè maintain one's composure; stay calm and collected; not turn a hair; not bat an eyelid

【不断】 bùduàn unceasing; uninterrupted; continuous; constant: 促进生产力的~发展 promote the uninterrupted (或 continuous) growth of the productive forces/ 人类社会总是~进步的。Human society makes unceasing progress.

【不对】 bùduì ① incorrect; wrong: 这样做~ It's wrong to act like that. ②〔单用，表示否定对方的话〕: ~，我没有那么说。No, I didn't say that. ③ amiss; abnormal; queer: 这机器声音~。The machine makes a queer noise./ 她今天神色有点~。She doesn't quite look her usual self today.

【不二法门】 bù èr fǎmén the one and only way; the only proper course to take

【不乏】 bùfá〈书〉there is no lack of: ~先例。There is no lack of precedents./ ~其人。Such people are not rare.

【不法】 bùfǎ lawless; illegal; unlawful: ~之徒 a lawless person/ ~行为 unlawful practice; an illegal act

【不凡】 bùfán out of the ordinary; out of the common run: 自命~ consider oneself a person of no ordinary talent; have an unduly high opinion of oneself

【不妨】 bùfáng there is no harm in; might as well: 你~现在就告诉她。You might as well tell him right now./ ~一试。There is no harm in trying./ 你~同他联系一下。You might get in touch with him.

【不费吹灰之力】 bù fèi chuī huī zhī lì as easy as blowing off dust — not needing the slightest effort

【不分彼此】 bù fēn bǐ-cǐ make no distinction between what's one's own and what's another's; share everything; be on very intimate terms

【不分青红皂白】 bù fēn qīng-hóng-zào-bái indiscriminately

【不分胜负】 bù fēn shèng-fù tie; draw; come out even: 一场~的比赛 a drawn game/ 两队~。The two teams tied. 或 The two teams came out even.

【不服】 bù fú refuse to obey (或 comply); refuse to accept as final; remain unconvinced by; not give in to: ~输 refuse to take defeat lying down/ ~罪 not admit one's guilt; plead not guilty/ ~老 refuse to give in to old age/ ~指导 refuse to obey instructions/ ~裁判 refuse to accept the referee's ruling/ 对朋友们的批评表示~ express disagreement with the criticism of one's friends

【不服水土】 bù fú shuǐtǔ (of a stranger) not accustomed to the climate of a new place; not acclimatized

【不符】 bùfú not agree (或 tally, square) with; not conform to; be inconsistent with: 言行~ deeds not matching words/ 名实~ have an undeserved reputation/ 与事实~ be inconsistent (或 at variance) with the facts/ 他说话前后~ What he said was self-contradictory. 或 What he said didn't hang together.

【不干不净】 bùgān-bùjìng unclean; filthy: 嘴里~ be foul-mouthed

【不干涉】 bù gānshè noninterference; nonintervention ◇ ~政策 policy of noninterference (或 nonintervention)

【不甘】 bùgān unreconciled to; not resigned to; unwilling: ~落后 unwilling to lag behind/ ~示弱 not to be outdone

【不甘心】 bù gānxīn not reconciled to; not resigned to

【不敢当】 bùgǎndāng〈谦〉〔表示承当不起对方的招待、夸奖等〕: I really don't deserve this; you flatter me

【不公】 bùgōng unjust; unfair: 办事~ be unfair in handling matters

【不攻自破】 bù gōng zì pò collapse of itself: 这种谣言在事实面前将~。Facts will eventually scotch these rumours.

【不恭】 bùgōng disrespectful: 言词~ use disrespectful language/ 却之~ it would be disrespectful to decline (a gift, an invitation, etc.)

【不共戴天】 bù gòng dài tiān will not live under the same sky (with one's enemy) — absolutely irreconcilable: ~的敌人 sworn enemy/ ~之仇 inveterate hatred

【不苟】 bùgǒu not lax; not casual; careful; conscientious: 工作一丝~ work most conscientiously/ ~言笑 serious in speech and manner

【不够】 bùgòu not enough; insufficient; inadequate: 我做得

很~。I haven't done nearly enough./ 他们人力~。They haven't enough manpower./ 分析~深入。The analysis lacks depth./ 准备~ be inadequately prepared

【不顾】 bùgù in spite of; regardless of: ~后果 regardless of the consequences/ ~事实 fly in the face of the facts; have no regard for the truth/ ~大局 show no consideration for the general interest; ignore the larger issues/ ~信义 be guilty of bad faith

【不管】 bùguǎn no matter (what, how, etc.); regardless of: ~结果如何 whatever the consequences/ ~怎样 in any case; anyway

【不管三七二十一】 bù guǎn sān qī èrshí yī casting all caution to the winds; regardless of the consequences; recklessly

【不轨】 bùguǐ against the law or discipline: 图谋~ engage in conspiratorial activities

【不过】 bùguò ①〔用在形容词性的词组或双音形容词后面，表示程度最高〕那就再好~了! It couldn't be better! 或 That would be superb! ②〈副〉merely; only; no more than: 她参军的时候~十七岁。She was only seventeen when she joined the army. ③〈连〉but; however; only: 病人精神还不错，~胃口不大好。The patient feels pretty well, but he hasn't much of an appetite.

【不过意】 bù guòyì be sorry; feel apologetic: 叫您受累了，真~。I'm terribly sorry to have given you such a lot of trouble.

【不含糊】 bù hánhu〈口〉① unambiguous; unequivocal; explicit: 以毫~的语言作出回答 answer in clear and unequivocal terms; answer in explicit language/ 在原则问题上绝~ stand firm on matters of principle ② not ordinary; really good: 他那手乒乓球可~。He is a very good table-tennis player./ 他这活儿做得真~。He's really made a good job of it.

【不寒而栗】 bù hán ér lì shiver all over though not cold; tremble with fear; shudder

【不好惹】 bù hǎorě not to be trifled with; not to be pushed around; stand no nonsense

【不好意思】 bù hǎoyìsi ① feel embarrassed; be ill at ease: 她被夸得~了。She felt embarrassed by so much praise. ② find it embarrassing (to do sth.): ~推辞 find it difficult to refuse/ ~再问 hesitate to ask again

【不合】 bùhé not conform to; be unsuited to; be out of keeping with: ~规定 not conform to the rules/ ~当前的需要 be unsuited to present needs/ ~客观情况 be out of keeping with the objective conditions/ ~标准 not up to the (required) standard; below the mark/ 脾气~ be temperamentally incompatible/ ~她的口味 not be to her taste; not appeal to her/ ~时宜 be out of keeping with the times; be incompatible with present needs

【不和】 bùhé ① not get along well; be on bad terms; be at odds ② discord: 制造~ sow discord

【不怀好意】 bù huái hǎoyì harbour evil designs; harbour malicious intentions

【不欢而散】 bùhuān ér sàn part on bad terms; (of a meeting, etc.) break up in discord

【不会】 bùhuì ① be unlikely; will not (act, happen, etc.): 她~不知道。It's not likely that she doesn't know./ 人~多的。There won't be too many people. ② have not learned to; be unable to: 我~抽烟。I don't smoke. ③〔表示责备语气〕你就~打个电话问一问? Couldn't you have phoned up and asked?

【不羁】 bùjī〈书〉unruly; uninhibited

【不及】 bùjí ① not as good as; inferior to: 我学习~他刻苦。I don't study as hard as he does. ② find it too late: 躲避~ too late to dodge/ 后悔~ too late for regrets

【不计其数】 bù jì qí shù countless; innumerable

【不假思索】 bù jiǎ sīsuǒ without thinking; without hesitation; readily; offhand 又作"不加思索"

【不简单】 bù jiǎndān ① not simple; rather complicated: 这事，需要进一步调查。The matter is not so simple; it requires further investigation. ② remarkable; marvellous: 他有这么大的进步真~。It's remarkable he's made such good progress.

【不见】 bùjiàn not see; not meet: 好久~。Haven't seen

you for a long time./ 这孩子一年一, 长这么高了。It's only a year since I last saw the child and he's grown so tall./ 我们两点钟在大门口碰头, ～不散。Let's meet at the gate around two o'clock and not leave without seeing each other.

【不见得】 bù jiànde not necessarily; not likely: ～对 not necessarily correct/ 他今晚～会来。He's not likely to come tonight.

【不见经传】 bù jiàn jīngzhuàn not to be found in the classics — not authoritative; unknown: 此人名～。He was not a well-known figure. 或 He was a nobody.

【不见了】 bùjiànle disappear; be missing: 我的钢笔～。My pen's disappeared.

【不结盟】 bùjiéméng nonalignment ◇ ～国家 nonaligned countries/ ～政策 nonalignment policy

【不解】 bùjiě ① not understand: ～其意 not understand what he means/ 迷惑～ be puzzled; be bewildered/ ～之谜 an unsolved riddle; enigma; mystery ② indissoluble: ～之缘 an indissoluble bond

【不禁】 bùjīn can't help (doing sth.); can't refrain from: ～哑然失笑 can't help laughing

【不仅】 bùjǐn ① not the only one: 这～是我一个人的看法。I'm not the only one who holds this view. ② not only: ～如此 not only that; nor is this all; moreover

【不近人情】 bù jìn rénqíng not amenable to reason; unreasonable

【不景气】 bù jǐngqì ① <经> depression; recession; slump ② depressing state

【不胫而走】 bù jìng ér zǒu get round fast; spread like wildfire

【不久】 bùjiǔ ① soon; before long: 水库～就能完工。The reservoir will soon be completed. ② not long after; soon after: 插完秧～就下了一场雨。It rained soon after we had transplanted the rice seedlings.

【不拘】 bùjū not stick to; not confine oneself to: ～小节 not bother about small matters; not be punctilious/ 字数～。No limit is set on the length (for an article).

【不拘一格】 bùjū yī gé not stick to one pattern

【不倦】 bùjuàn tireless; untiring; indefatigable: 诲人～ be tireless in teaching; teach with tireless zeal

【不堪】 bùkān ① cannot bear; cannot stand: ～回首 cannot bear to look back; find it unbearable to recall/ ～设想 dreadful to contemplate/ ～入耳 intolerable to the ear; revolting; disgusting/ ～一击 cannot withstand a single blow; collapse at the first blow ② utterly; extremely: 疲惫～ extremely tired; exhausted; dog-tired/ 狼狈～ be in an extremely awkward position; be in a sorry plight/ 穿得破烂～ be dressed in rags

【不亢不卑】 bùkàng-bùbēi neither haughty nor humble; neither overbearing nor servile; neither supercilious nor obsequious 又作"不卑不亢"

【不可】 bùkě ① cannot; must not: 两者～偏废。Neither can be neglected./ ～一概而论 must not make sweeping generalizations/ ～剥夺的权利 an inalienable right/ ～抗拒的历史潮流 an irresistible historical trend ②[与"非"搭配, 表示必须或一定] 今天这个会很重要, 我非去～。Today's meeting is very important. I simply must go.

【不可多得】 bùkě duō dé hard to come by; rare: ～的佳作 a rare specimen of good writing

【不可告人】 bùkě gào rén not to be divulged; hidden: ～的动机 ulterior motives/ ～的勾当 a sinister trick

【不可救药】 bùkě jiù yào incurable; incorrigible; beyond cure; hopeless

【不可开交】 bùkě kāijiāo [只做"得"后的补语, 表示无法摆脱或结束] 忙得～ be up to one's eyes in work; be awfully (或 terribly) busy/ 打得～ be locked in a fierce struggle/ 争得～ be engaged in a heated argument

【不可理喻】 bùkě lǐyù be impervious to reason; won't listen to reason

【不可磨灭】 bùkě mómiè indelible: ～的印象 indelible impressions/ ～的贡献 an indelible contribution/ ～的功绩 everlasting merit

【不可胜数】 bùkě shèngshǔ countless; innumerable: 缴获的

武器装备～。The military equipment captured was beyond counting.

【不可收拾】 bùkě shōushi irremediable; unmanageable; out of hand; hopeless

【不可思议】 bùkě sīyì inconceivable; unimaginable

【不可同日而语】 bùkě tóngrì ér yǔ cannot be mentioned in the same breath

【不可一世】 bùkě yīshì consider oneself unexcelled in the world; be insufferably arrogant

【不客气】 bù kèqi ① impolite; rude; blunt: 说句～的话 to put it bluntly/ 你再这样, 我可就要～了。If you go on like this, I won't be so easy on you. ② <套>[回答别人的感谢] you're welcome; don't mention it; not at all ③ <套>[感谢别人的好意] please don't bother; I'll help myself

【不快】 bùkuài ① be unhappy; be displeased; be in low spirits ② be indisposed; feel under the weather; be out of sorts

【不愧】 bùkuì be worthy of; deserve to be called; prove oneself to be

【不劳而获】 bù láo ér huò reap without sowing; profit by other people's toil

【不理】 bùlǐ refuse to acknowledge; pay no attention to; take no notice of; ignore: 见了人～ cut sb. dead/ 别～他, 要帮助他。Don't ignore him; help him./ 我才～那些闲话呢。I don't pay attention to such gossip.

【不利】 bùlì ① unfavourable; disadvantageous; harmful; detrimental: 化～因素为有利因素 turn unfavourable factors into favourable ones ② unsuccessful: 首战～ lose the first battle

【不良】 bùliáng bad; harmful; unhealthy: ～倾向 harmful trends; ～现象 unhealthy tendencies/ ～影响 harmful (或 adverse) effects/ 存心～ harbour evil intentions; have ulterior motives

【不了】 bùliǎo [多用于动词加"个"之后] without end: 一天到晚忙个～ busy from morning till night/ 大雨下个～。The rain kept pouring down.

【不了了之】 bùliǎo liǎo zhī settle a matter by leaving it unsettled; end up with nothing definite

【不料】 bùliào unexpectedly; to one's surprise: 早上天气还好好的, ～下午竟下起雨来了。It was so fine this morning. Who would have thought it would rain in the afternoon!

【不灵】 bùlíng not work; be ineffective: 这机器～了。The machine doesn't work./ 老太太手脚有点～了。The old lady has trouble moving about.

【不露声色】 bù lù shēngsè not show one's feelings, intentions, etc.

【不伦不类】 bùlún-bùlèi neither fish nor fowl; nondescript: ～的比喻 an inappropriate metaphor; a far-fetched analogy

【不论】 bùlùn <连>[下文多用"都""总"等副词跟它呼应] no matter (what, who, how, etc.); whether... or...; regardless of: ～性别年龄 regardless (或 irrespective) of sex and age

【不满】 bùmǎn resentful; discontented; dissatisfied: 心怀～ nurse a grievance

【不毛之地】 bù máo zhī dì barren land; desert

【不免】 bùmiǎn unavoidable: 这段路太窄, 交通有时～堵塞。This section of the road is so narrow that there are bound to be traffic jams now and then.

【不妙】 bùmiào (of a turn of events) not too encouraging; far from good; anything but reassuring

【不名一文】 bù míng yī wén without a penny to one's name; penniless; stony-broke

【不名誉】 bùmíngyù disreputable; disgraceful

【不明】 bùmíng ① not clear; unknown: 失踪的渔船至今下落～。The whereabouts of the missing fishing boat is still unknown./ ～国籍的飞机 a plane of unidentified nationality; an unidentified aircraft ② fail to understand: ～事理 lack common sense/ ～是非 confuse right and wrong/ ～真相 be unaware of the truth; be ignorant of the facts

【不谋而合】 bù móu ér hé agree without prior consultation; happen to hold the same view: 我们的意见～。Our views happened to coincide.

【不能】 bùnéng cannot; must not; should not: 我们决不一见成绩就自满起来。We must not become complacent the moment we have some success.

【不能不】 **bùnéng bù** have to; cannot but: 表示惋惜 cannot but express regret/ ~指出 it must be pointed out that/ 我们~提到某些历史事实。We cannot very well avoid mentioning certain historical facts.

【不偏不倚】 **bùpiān-bùyǐ** even-handed; impartial; unbiased

【不平】 **bùpíng** ① injustice; unfairness; wrong; grievance ② indignant; resentful: 愤愤~ very indignant; deeply resentful/ 消除心中的~ allay one's resentment

【不平则鸣】 **bùpíng zé míng** where there is injustice, there will be an outcry; man will cry out against injustice

【不期而遇】 **bù qī ér yù** meet by chance; have a chance encounter

【不巧】 **bùqiǎo** unfortunately; as luck would have it: 我到那儿，~他刚走。As luck would have it, he had just left when I arrived.

【不切实际】 **bùqiè shíjì** unrealistic; unpractical; impracticable: ~的计划 an impracticable plan/ ~的幻想 unrealistic notions; fanciful ideas

【不屈】 **bùqū** unyielding; unbending: 坚强~ iron-willed and unyielding

【不屈不挠】 **bùqū-bùnáo** unyielding; indomitable

【不然】 **bùrán** ① not so: 其实~。Actually this is not so. ②〔用在句子开头，表示否定对方的话〕no: ~，事情没有那样简单。No, it's not as simple as that. ③〈连〉or else; otherwise; if not: 我得早点去，~就赶不上火车了。I've got to leave a bit early, otherwise I'll miss the train./ 要去就别迟到，~，就甭去了。Either be there on time, or don't go at all.

【不人道】 **bùréndào** inhuman

【不仁】 **bùrén** ① not benevolent; heartless: 为富~ in the pursuit of riches there is no benevolence; the heartless rich ② numb: 麻木~ insensitive; apathetic

【不忍】 **bùrěn** cannot bear to: ~坐视 cannot bear to stand idly by

【不日】 **bùrì** 〈书〉within the next few days; in a few days' time

【不容】 **bùróng** not tolerate; not allow; not brook: ~外国干涉 tolerate no foreign interference/ ~耽搁 allow of no delay/ ~置喙 not allow others to butt in; brook no intervention

【不如】 **bùrú** ① not equal to; not as good as; inferior to: 论手巧，一般人都~她。Few can equal (或 compare with) her in manual dexterity. ② it would be better to: 我看~派老王去。I think it would be better to send Lao Wang instead.

【不入虎穴，焉得虎子】 **bù rù hǔxué, yān dé hǔzǐ** how can you catch tiger cubs without entering the tiger's lair; nothing venture, nothing gain (或 have)

【不三不四】 **bùsān-bùsì** ① dubious; shady: ~的人 a person of dubious (或 shady) character ② neither one thing nor the other; neither fish nor fowl; nondescript: 自己生造的 ~的词句 nondescript expressions of one's own coinage/ 说些~的话 make frivolous remarks

【不善】 **bùshàn** ① bad; ill: 来意~ come with ill intent/ 处理~ not handle properly; mishandle ② not good at: ~管理 not good at managing things

【不胜】 **bùshèng** ① cannot bear (或 stand); be unequal to: 体力~ be physically unequal to (a task); be physically incapable of coping with (a job)/ ~其烦 be pestered beyond endurance ②〔前后重叠同一动词，表示不能做或做不完〕防~防 be difficult or impossible to prevent (或 ward off) ③〔用于感情方面〕very; extremely: ~遗憾 be very sorry; much to one's regret/ ~感激 be very much obliged; be deeply grateful

【不胜枚举】 **bùshèng méi jǔ** too numerous to mention individually (或 one by one)

【不识时务】 **bù shí shíwù** ① show no understanding of the times ② be insensible

【不识抬举】 **bù shí táijǔ** fail to appreciate sb.'s kindness; not know how to appreciate favours

【不时】 **bùshí** ① frequently; often ② at any time

【不时之需】 **bùshí zhī xū** a possible period of want or need:

以备~ for emergency needs; to provide against a rainy day

【不是】 **bùshi** fault; blame: 落个~ get blamed in the end/ 这就是你的~了。It's your fault. 或 You're to blame.

【不适】 **bùshì** unwell; indisposed; out of sorts: 胃部~ have a stomach upset/ 略感~ feel a bit unwell

【不爽】 **bùshuǎng** ① not well; out of sorts; in a bad mood ② without discrepancy; accurate: 丝毫~ not deviate a hair's breadth; be perfectly accurate; be right in every detail/ 屡试~。It comes out right every time.

【不死心】 **bù sǐxīn** unwilling to give up; unresigned: 敌人失败了，还~。The enemy is not reconciled to his defeat.

【不送】 **bùsòng** 〈套〉don't bother to see me out

【不速之客】 **bù sù zhī kè** uninvited (或 unexpected) guest

【不遂】 **bùsuì** 〈书〉fail; fail to materialize

【不通】 **bùtōng** ① be obstructed; be blocked up; be impassable: 管子~。The pipe is blocked./ 此路~。Not a Through Road./ 电话~。The line's dead./ 想~ cannot figure out why; remain unconvinced/ 行~ won't work ② not make sense; be illogical; be ungrammatical: 文章写得~。The article is badly written.

【不同】 **bùtóng** not alike; different; distinct: 在~的程度上 to varying degrees

【不同凡响】 **bùtóng fánxiǎng** outstanding; out of the ordinary; out of the common run

【不透明】 **bù tòumíng** opaque
◇ ~色 body colour/ ~体 opaque body/ ~性 opacity

【不透气】 **bù tòuqì** airtight

【不透水】 **bù tòushuǐ** waterproof; watertight; impermeable

【不妥】 **bùtuǒ** not proper; inappropriate: 这样处理，恐怕~。I'm afraid this isn't the proper way to handle the case./ 没有调查研究就作决定是~的。It's not right to make a decision without investigation and study./ 觉得有些~ feel that something is amiss

【不外】 **bùwài** not beyond the scope of; nothing more than: ~两种可能。There are only two possibilities.

【不闻不问】 **bùwén-bùwèn** not bother to ask questions or listen to what's said; show no interest in sth.; be indifferent to sth.: 同学们有困难我们不能~。We can't remain indifferent when any classmate is in difficulty.

【不问】 **bù wèn** ① pay no attention to; disregard; ignore: ~年龄大小 irrespective of age/ ~事实真相 ignore the facts/ ~是非曲直 make no distinction between right and wrong; not look into the rights and wrongs of the case ② let go unpunished; let off: 胁从~。Those who acted under duress shall go unpunished.

【不务正业】 **bù wù zhèngyè** ① not engage in honest work ② ignore one's proper occupation; not attend to one's proper duties

【不惜】 **bùxī** ① not stint; not spare: ~工本 spare neither labour nor money; spare no expense/ ~一切代价 at all costs; at any cost ② not hesitate (to do sth.): not scruple (to do sth.): 为国家~牺牲自己的一切 not hesitate to sacrifice one's all for the country

【不暇】 **bùxiá** have no time (for sth.); be too busy (to do sth.): ~顾及 be too busy to attend to sth.

【不相干】 **bù xiānggān** be irrelevant; have nothing to do with: ~的话 irrelevant remarks/ 那件事跟你~。That has nothing to do with you.

【不相容】 **bù xiāngróng** incompatible: 水火~ incompatible as fire and water; mutually antagonistic

【不相上下】 **bù xiāng shàng-xià** equally matched; about the same: 能力~ of about the same ability; equally able/ 这两种水稻都是良种，产量~。Both rice seeds are good strains and will give about the same yield.

【不详】 **bùxiáng** 〈书〉① not in detail: 言之~ not be given in detail; be stated too briefly ② not quite clear: 历史情况~。Little is known about the historical background.

【不祥】 **bùxiáng** ominous; inauspicious: ~之兆 an ill omen

【不像话】 **bù xiànghuà** ① unreasonable: 要你们自己掏钱做~了。It would be unreasonable for you to pay out of your own pockets. ② shocking; outrageous: 这种行为真~。Such behaviour is really shocking.

【不像样】 **bù xiàngyàng** ① in no shape to be seen; unpresentable: 这活儿～,拿不出手。This is a shoddy piece of work, it's hardly presentable. ②〔用在"得"后作补语〕beyond recognition: 瘦～ extremely thin; worn to a mere shadow/ 破得～ worn to shreds

【不肖】 bùxiào 〈书〉unworthy: ～子孙 unworthy descendants

【不行】 bùxíng ① won't do; be out of the question ② be no good; not work: 这个方法～。This method just doesn't work./ 他干这种工作身体～。He is physically unfit for this kind of work. ③〔用于"得"后作补语〕awfully; extremely: 高兴得～ awfully happy

【不行了】 bùxíngle on the point of death; dying: 病人怕～。The patient won't pull through, I'm afraid.

【不省人事】 bù xǐng rénshì be unconscious; be in a coma

【不幸】 bùxìng ① misfortune; adversity: 遭～ meet with a misfortune ② unfortunate; sad: ～的消息 sad news ③ unfortunately: ～而言中。The prediction has unfortunately come true./ 他～以身殉职。To our great sorrow he died at his post.

【不休】 bùxiū 〔用做补语〕endlessly; ceaselessly: 争论～ argue endlessly; keep on arguing

【不修边幅】 bù xiū biānfú not care about one's appearance; be slovenly

【不朽】 bùxiǔ immortal: ～的著作 an immortal masterpiece/ ～的功勋 immortal deeds

【不锈钢】 bùxiùgāng stainless steel

【不虚此行】 bù xū cǐ xíng the trip has not been made in vain; the trip has been well worthwhile; it's been a worthwhile trip

【不许】 bùxǔ ① not allow; must not: ～说谎。You mustn't tell lies./ 熄灯后～说话。No talking after lights out. ②〔用于反问句〕can't: 何必非等我,你就～自己去吗? Why wait for me? Can't you go yourself?

【不雅观】 bù yǎguān offensive to the eye; unbecoming

【不言而喻】 bù yán ér yù it goes without saying; it is self-evident

【不厌】 bùyàn not mind doing sth.; not tire of; not object to: ～其烦 not mind taking all the trouble; take great pains; be very patient/ ～其详 go into minute details; dwell at great length

【不要】 bùyào don't: ～麻痹大意。Don't slacken your vigilance./ ～总是以为自己对。Don't think you are always right.

【不要紧】 bù yàojǐn ① unimportant; not serious: 有点伤风,～。Just a slight cold, nothing serious. ② it doesn't matter; never mind: 路远也～,我们可以骑车去。It doesn't matter how far it is; we can go by bike. ③ it looks all right, but: 你这一嚷～,把大家都吵醒了。You may think it's all right for you to shout, but you've woken everybody up.

【不要脸】 bù yàoliǎn 〈骂〉have no sense of shame; shameless: 只有～的人才能做出这样～的事。Only those who have no sense of shame can do such shameful things./ 真～! What a nerve!

【不一】 bùyī vary; differ: 质量～ vary in quality/ 长短～ differ in length

【不一而足】 bùyī'érzú by no means an isolated case; numerous: 凡此种种～。Similar cases are numerous.

【不依】 bùyī ① not comply; not go along with: 我们劝他休息,他怎么也不～。We advised him to have a rest, but he simply wouldn't hear of it. ② not let off easily; not let sb. get away with it: 你要是再这样,我可～你。If you do this again, I won't let you off so easily.

【不宜】 bùyí not suitable; inadvisable: ～操之过急。It's no good being overhasty./ 这一点～过分强调。It's inadvisable to overemphasize this point./ 这种土壤～种花生。This kind of soil is not suitable for growing peanuts.

【不遗余力】 bù yí yúlì spare no pains (或 effort); do one's utmost

【不已】 bùyǐ endlessly; incessantly: 赞叹～ praise again and again

【不以为然】 bù yǐ wéi rán object to; take exception to; not approve

【不义之财】 bùyì zhī cái ill-gotten wealth (或 gains)

【不亦乐乎】 bùyìlèhū 〔用在"得"后作补语〕extremely; awfully: 忙得～ awfully (或 terribly) busy

【不翼而飞】 bù yì ér fēi ① disappear without trace; vanish all of a sudden ② spread fast: spread like wildfire

【不用】 bùyòng need not: ～着急。You needn't worry. 或 There is no need to worry./ ～说 it goes without saying; needless to say

【不由自主】 bù yóu zìzhǔ can't help; involuntarily: ～地流下了眼泪 couldn't help shedding tears; couldn't hold back one's tears

【不远千里】 bù yuǎn qiān lǐ make light of travelling a thousand li; go to the trouble of travelling a long distance

【不约而同】 bù yuē ér tóng take the same action or view without prior consultation; happen to coincide: 她一讲完,大家一都鼓起掌来。Spontaneous applause broke out as soon as she finished speaking./ 他们都～地提出了这个问题。They all raised the question as if by prior agreement.

【不在】 bùzài not be in; be out: 你找老王吗? 他～。Are you looking for Lao Wang? He's out.

【不在乎】 bùzàihu not mind; not care: 满～ not care a pin

【不在意】 bù zàiyì ① pay no attention to; take no notice of; not mind: 别人背后议论,他毫～。He doesn't care at all what people say behind his back. ② negligent; careless: 人家托你的事,你别～。When people ask you to do something, you should take it seriously.

【不择手段】 bù zé shǒuduàn by fair means or foul; by hook or by crook; unscrupulously

【不怎么】 bù zěnme not very; not particularly: 这块地～大。This plot isn't very big./ 我～想去。I'm not particularly keen on going.

【不怎么样】 bù zěnmeyàng not up to much; very indifferent: 这幅画画得～。This isn't much of a painting.

【不争气】 bù zhēngqì be disappointing; fail to live up to expectations: 他这个人真～。This chap has let us down./ 我这腿～,最后一圈跑不动了。My legs failed me and I wasn't able to run the last lap.

【不知不觉】 bùzhī-bùjué unconsciously; unwittingly: ～已过了三个月。Three months had passed before we knew it.

【不知好歹】 bù zhī hǎo-dǎi not know what's good for one

【不知死活】 bù zhī sǐ-huó act recklessly

【不知所措】 bù zhī suǒ cuò be at a loss; be at one's wits' end

【不知所云】 bù zhī suǒ yún not know what sb. is driving at; be unintelligible: 这篇文章写得太乱,使人看了～。This is such a chaotic piece of writing that it is practically unintelligible.

【不知天高地厚】 bù zhī tiāngāo-dìhòu not know the immensity of heaven and earth — have an exaggerated opinion of one's abilities

【不值】 bùzhí not worth: ～一文 not worth a penny; worthless/ ～一驳 not worth refuting/ ～识者一笑 beneath the contempt of the discerning/ 我看～那么多。I don't think it's worth that much.

【不止】 bùzhǐ ① incessantly; without end: 树欲静而风～。The tree craves calm but the wind will not drop. ② more than; not limited to: 他恐怕～六十岁了。He is probably over sixty.

【不只】 bùzhǐ not only; not merely

【不至于】 bùzhìyú cannot go so far; be unlikely: 他～连这一点道理也不明白。He must have more sense than that./ 如果你事先作好准备,也～那么被动。If you had prepared in advance, you wouldn't be in such an awkward position.

【不治之症】 bùzhì zhī zhèng incurable disease

【不置可否】 bù zhì kě-fǒu decline to comment; not express an opinion; be noncommittal; hedge: 你是负责人,你怎么能对这个问题～? You are in charge of the job. How could you evade the issue?

【不中用】 bù zhōngyòng unfit for anything; no good; useless: 这铁锨～,我去换一把吧。This spade is no good. I'll go and get another one.

【不中意】 bù zhòngyì not to one's liking

【不准】 bùzhǔn not allow; forbid; prohibit: 此处～吸烟。 Smoking is not allowed here. 或 No Smoking!/ ～停车! No parking!/ ～入内。No admittance.

【不着边际】 bù zhuó biānjì not to the point; wide of the mark; neither here nor there; irrelevant: ～的长篇大论 a long rambling talk/ 他越讲越～。The more he talked, the further he strayed from the point.

【不自量】 bù zìliàng not take a proper measure of oneself; overrate one's own abilities: 蚍蜉撼大树，可笑～ ridiculously overrate oneself like an ant trying to topple a giant tree

【不足】 bùzú ① not enough; insufficient; inadequate: 资源～ inadequate resources/ 给养～ be short of supplies/ 人手～ be shorthanded; be understaffed/ 估计～ underestimate/ 信心～ lack confidence/ ～之处 deficiency; inadequacy/ ～一千 less than a thousand/ ～以引起人们的注意 not enough to attract attention ② not worth: ～道 inconsiderable; of no consequence/ ～为奇 not at all surprising/ ～挂齿 not worth mentioning; nothing to speak of ③ cannot; should not: ～为凭 not to be taken as evidence

【不足为训】 bù zú wéi xùn not to be taken as an example; not an example to be followed; not to be taken as authoritative: 书本上讲的也有～的。What is taught in books is not always authoritative.

【不做声】 bù zuòshēng keep silent; not say a word

布 bù ① cloth: ～鞋 cloth shoes/ 花～ cotton prints ② declare; announce; publish; proclaim: 公～于众 make known to the public; make public ③ spread; disseminate: 控制疾病传～ check the spread of disease ④ dispose; arrange; deploy: ～好阵势 deploy the troops in battle formation/ ～下天罗地网 cast an escape-proof net

【布告】 bùgào notice; bulletin; proclamation: 张贴～ paste up a notice ◇ ～栏 notice board; bulletin board

【布谷鸟】 bùgǔniǎo cuckoo

【布景】 bùjǐng ① composition (of a painting) ② 〈剧〉 setting ◇ ～设计师 set designer

【布匹】 bùpǐ cloth; piece goods ◇～染色 piece dyeing

【布置】 bùzhì ① fix up; arrange; decorate: ～会场 fix up a place for a meeting/ ～展品 arrange exhibits/ 礼堂～得很漂亮。The auditorium was beautifully decorated. ② assign; make arrangements for; give instructions about: ～工作 assign work; give instructions about an assignment

步 bù ① step; pace: 只有几～路了。It's only a few steps away./ 快～走 walk at a quick pace/ 大～前进 advance with big strides ② stage; step: 下一～怎么办? What's the next step (或 move)?/ 这只好一～一～地去做。This will have to be done step by step. ③ condition; situation; state: 事情怎么发展到这一～? How did things get into such a state? ④ walk; go on foot: 学～ learn to walk/ 散～ take a walk ⑤ 〈书〉 tread: ～其后尘 follow in sb.'s footsteps ⑥ an old unit for measurement of length, equivalent to 5 chi (尺) ⑦ pace off: ～测二十米的距离 pace off a distance of 20 metres

【步兵】 bùbīng ① infantry; foot ② infantryman; foot soldier

【步步】 bùbù step by step; at every step: ～进逼 press forward steadily

【步步为营】 bùbù wéi yíng advance gradually and entrench oneself at every step; consolidate at every step

【步伐】 bùfá step; pace: 加快～ quicken one's steps (或 pace)/ ～整齐 (march) in step/ 跟上时代的～ keep pace with the times

【步法】 bùfǎ 〈体〉〈舞蹈〉 footwork

【步行】 bùxíng go on foot; walk

【步骤】 bùzhòu step; move; measure: 有计划有～地进行工作 carry on the work step by step in a planned way/ 采取适当的～ take proper steps/ 这是增产的一个具体～。This is a practical move to increase production.

怖 bù fear; be afraid of: 恐～ terror; horror/ 可～ horrible; frightful

部 bù ① part; section: 分为三～ divide into three parts (或 sections)/ 南～ the southern part ② unit; ministry; department; board: 国防～ the Ministry of Defence/ 编辑～ editorial board (或 office) ③ 〈量〉: 一～电影 a film/ 两～机器 two machines/ 一～好作品 a fine work of literature

【部队】 bùduì ① army; armed forces ② troops; force; unit: 通讯兵～ signal troops

【部分】 bùfen part; section; share: 我们看问题，不但要看到～,而且要看到全体。In approaching a problem we should see the whole as well as the parts./ 他完成了自己的那一～工作以后,又去帮助别人。After finishing his share of the work he went to help the others./ 我们一地改变了原计划。We've altered the original plan to some extent.

【部落】 bùluò tribe ◇ ～社会 tribal society

【部门】 bùmén department; branch: 政府各～ various government departments/ 主管～ the department responsible for the work

【部首】 bùshǒu 〈语〉 radicals by which characters are arranged in traditional Chinese dictionaries

【部属】 bùshǔ ① 见"部下" ② affiliated to a ministry: ～机构 organizations affiliated to the ministry

【部下】 bùxià ① troops under one's command ② subordinate

【部长】 bùzhǎng minister; head of a department

埠 bù ① wharf; pier ② port: 本～ this port/ 外～ other ports/ 商～ a commercial (或 trading) port

簿 bù book: 练习～ exercise book/ 账～ account book/ 登记～ register

【簿册】 bùcè books for taking notes or keeping accounts

【簿籍】 bùjí account books, registers, records, etc.

【簿记】 bùjì bookkeeping: 复(单)式～ double-entry (single-entry) bookkeeping

【簿子】 bùzi notebook; book

C

cā

擦* cā ① rub: ~伤了膝盖 rub the skin off one's knee; graze one's knee/ ~根火柴 strike a match/ 没关系,就~破了一点皮。Nothing serious. Just a scratch. ② wipe: ~桌子 wipe the table/ ~地板 mop (或 scrub) the floor/ ~汗 wipe the sweat away/ ~背 scrub one's or sb.'s back/ ~枪 clean a gun/ ~皮鞋 polish shoes ③ spread on; put on: 给伤口~碘酒 apply iodine to a wound/ ~粉 powder one's face ④ brush; shave: ~肩而过 brush past sb./ 飞机~着山顶飞过去。The plane shaved the hilltops. ⑤ scrape (into shreds): 把萝卜~成丝儿 shred turnips

cāi

猜* cāi ① guess; conjecture; speculate: 你~谁来了? Guess who's here./ 他准~不着 He's sure to guess wrong./ 这个谜语真难~。This riddle is really difficult to solve. ② suspect: 我~他和这件事有点牵连。I suspect that he is more or less involved in the affair.

【猜测】 cāicè　guess; conjecture; surmise: 那都是~。That's pure guesswork. 或 That's all guesswork./ 考古新发现否定了过去对这个问题的~。The new archaeological finds have disproved previous conjectures on this subject.

【猜忌】 cāijì　be suspicious and jealous of

【猜谜儿】 cāimèir　① guess a riddle ② guess: 快说吧,别让我们~了。Now out with it. Don't keep us guessing.

【猜拳】 cāiquán　a finger-guessing game; mora

【猜想】 cāixiǎng　suppose; guess; suspect: 我~他病了。I suspect he is ill.

【猜疑】 cāiyí　harbour suspicions; be suspicious; have misgivings

cái

才* cái ① ability; talent; gift: 德~兼备 have both ability and political integrity ② capable person: 人~ a person of talent; talent ③ people of a certain type: 奴~ flunkey ④〈副〉ⓐ〔表示事情刚发生,或发生得晚〕: 比赛~开始。The match has just started./ 怎么,~来了就走? Why leave so soon? You've only just arrived./ 你怎么~来? Why are you so late? ⓑ〔表示事情取决于某种条件〕: 我们只有依靠你们~有力量。Only by relying on all of you can we become strong./ 老马总要把办公室打扫干净~走。Lao Ma never leaves the office until he has given it a good cleaning./ 非要等起重机来了~能装运吗? Must we wait till the crane arrives before we start loading? ⓒ〔表示对比之下数量小,次数少等〕: 他到外国去的时候~十四岁。He was only fourteen when he went overseas. ⓓ〔表示强调〕: 麦子长得~好呢! The wheat is coming along fine./ 他要是不知道~怪呢! It would be strange if he didn't know.

【才干】 cáigàn　ability; competence

【才华】 cáihuá　literary or artistic talent: 他是一位很有~的作家。He is a gifted writer.

【才略】 cáilüè　ability and sagacity (in political and military affairs)

【才能】 cáinéng　ability; talent

【才气】 cáiqì　literary talent: ~横溢 brim with talent; have superb talent

【才识】 cáishí　ability and insight: ~过人 be gifted with talent and insight far beyond the average person

【才疏学浅】 cáishū-xuéqiǎn〈谦〉have little talent and less learning

【才思】 cáisī〈书〉imaginative power; creativeness: ~敏捷 have a facile imagination

【才学】 cáixué　talent and learning; scholarship

【才智】 cáizhì　ability and wisdom

【才子】 cáizǐ　gifted scholar: ~佳人 gifted scholars and beautiful ladies (in Chinese romances)

材* cái ① timber: 木~ timber; lumber ② material: 教~ teaching material/ 钢~ steel products/ 就地取~ obtain material from local sources; draw on local resources ③ ability; talent; aptitude: 因~施教 teach students in accordance with their aptitude ④ capable person: 人~难得 a person of rare talent ⑤ coffin

【材料】 cáiliào　① material: 建筑~ building material/ 原~ raw material ② data; material: 学习~ material for study/ 档案~ archival material/ 调查~ survey data; findings/ 搜集~ gather material; collect data/ 熟悉一下~ acquaint oneself with the facts/ 根据现有~还不能得出肯定的结论。We cannot draw any definite conclusion from the available data. ③ makings; stuff: 她不是演戏的~。She hasn't the makings of an actress.

财* cái　wealth; money

【财宝】 cáibǎo　money and valuables

【财产】 cáichǎn　property: 公共~ public property/ 国家~ state property/ 保护人民的生命~ protect the life and property of the people ◇ ~权 property right/ ~税 property tax

【财阀】 cáifá　financial magnate; plutocrat; tycoon

【财富】 cáifù　wealth; riches: 自然~ natural wealth/ 精神~ spiritual wealth

【财力】 cáilì　financial resources (或 capacity)

【财迷】 cáimí　moneygrubber; miser

【财神】 cáishén　the God of Wealth

【财团】 cáituán　financial group: 国际~ consortium

【财务】 cáiwù　financial affairs ◇ ~报告 financial statement (或 report)/ ~科 finance section/ ~行政 financial administration

【财物】 cáiwù　property; belongings: 个人~ personal effects

【财源】 cáiyuán　financial resources; source of revenue

【财政】 cáizhèng　(public) finance: ~金融危机 financial and monetary crisis/ ~收支平衡 balance of revenue and expenditure ◇ ~部 the Ministry of Finance/ ~赤字 financial deficits/ ~机关 financial organ (或 administration); fiscal organ (或 administration)/ ~年度 financial (或 fiscal) year/ ~收入 revenue/ ~政策 financial (或 fiscal) policy/ ~支出 expenditure

【财主】 cáizhu　rich man; moneybags

裁* cái ① cut (paper, cloth, etc.) into parts: 把一张纸~成条儿 cut a sheet of paper into strips/ ~件新衣服 cut out a new garment/ 这块料子可以~两套衣服。Two suits can be cut out of this piece of material. ② reduce; cut down; dismiss ③ judge; decide ④ check; sanction: 经济制~ economic sanction ⑤ mental planning: 别出心~ adopt an original approach; try to be different

【裁定】 cáidìng〈法〉ruling

【裁断】 cáiduàn　consider and decide

【裁夺】 cáiduó　consider and decide

【裁缝】 cáiféng　tailor; dressmaker

【裁减】 cáijiǎn　reduce; cut down: ~机关工作人员 reduce (或 cut down) the staff of an organization/ ~军备 reduction of armaments

【裁剪】 cáijiǎn　cut out: ~衣服 cut out garments

【裁决】 cáijué　ruling; adjudication: 依法~ adjudicate according to law/ 会议主席作出了~。A ruling was given by the chairman.

【裁军】 cáijūn　disarmament

【裁判】 cáipàn ⑴〈法〉judgment ⑵〈体〉act as referee; referee ⑶〈体〉referee; umpire; judge

【裁员】 cáiyuán cut down by the number of persons employed; reduce the staff; retrench

cǎi

采* cǎi ① pick; pluck; gather: ~茶 pick tea/ ~药 gather medicinal herbs/ ~珍珠 dive for pearls ② mine; extract: ~煤 mine coal/ ~油 extract oil ③ adopt; select: ~取一系列措施 adopt a series of measures ④ complexion; spirit: 兴高~烈 in high spirits

【采访】 cǎifǎng (of a reporter) gather material; cover: ~新闻 gather news; cover/ ~全国运动会消息 cover the National Games/ 向一位名演员进行~ interview a famous actor

【采购】 cǎigòu make purchases for an organization or enterprise; purchase: ~建筑材料 purchase building materials

【采集】 cǎijí gather; collect: ~标本 collect specimens/ 原始部落靠渔猎~为生。 Primitive tribes lived by fishing, hunting and gathering.

【采矿】 cǎikuàng mining: 露天~ opencut (或 opencast) mining/ 地下~ underground mining ◇ ~工程 mining engineering

【采纳】 cǎinà accept; adopt: ~建议 accept suggestions

【采取】 cǎiqǔ adopt; take: ~紧急措施 take emergency measures/ ~主动 take the initiative/ ~攻势 take the offensive/ ~一项新政策 adopt a new policy/ ~说服教育的办法 use the method of persuasion and education/ ~拖延战术 employ stalling tactics/ ~强制手段 resort to compulsion

【采用】 cǎiyòng adopt; use; employ: ~新技术 adopt new techniques

【采油】 cǎiyóu 〈石油〉oil extraction; oil recovery

【采摘】 cǎizhāi pluck; pick: ~苹果 pick apples

彩* cǎi ① colour: 五~ of different colours; multicoloured/ ~云 rosy clouds ② coloured silk; variegated silk: 张灯结~ decorate with lanterns and coloured ribbons ③ applause; cheer: 喝~ acclaim; cheer/ ~声 acclamation; applause ④ variety; splendour: 丰富多~ rich and colourful; rich and varied ⑤ prize: 中~ win a prize (in a lottery, etc.) ⑥ blood from a wound: 挂~ be wounded in battle

【彩虹】 cǎihóng rainbow

【彩排】 cǎipái dress rehearsal

【彩票】 cǎipiào lottery ticket

【彩旗】 cǎiqí coloured flag; bunting

【彩色】 cǎisè multicolour; colour: ~缤纷 a riot of colour ◇ ~电视 colour television/ ~胶片 colour film/ ~铅笔 colour pencil; crayon/ ~印刷 colour printing/ ~影片 colour film

睬 cǎi pay attention to; take notice of: 不要~他。 Take no notice of him. 或 Ignore him.

踩 cǎi step on; trample: 当心~坏了庄稼。 Mind you don't tread on the crops./ 一切困难~脚下 trample all difficulties underfoot; surmount all difficulties

cài

菜* cài ① vegetable; greens: 种~ grow vegetables/ 咸~ pickles ② (non-staple) food: 上街买~ go to the market to buy food ③ dish; course: ~肉 meat dish/ 素~ vegetable dish/ 一道~ a course/ 川~ Sichuan dishes/ Sichuan cuisine/ 做~ prepare the dishes; do the cooking

【菜场】 càichǎng food market

【菜单】 càidān menu; bill of fare

【菜刀】 càidāo kitchen knife

【菜豆】 càidòu kidney bean

【菜花】 càihuā ① cauliflower ② rape flower

【菜圃】 càipǔ vegetable garden; vegetable farm

【菜畦】 càiqí small sections of a vegetable plot; vegetable bed

【菜色】 càisè famished (或 emaciated) look: 面有~ look famished

【菜市】 càishì food market

【菜蔬】 càishū ① vegetables; greens ② dishes at a meal

【菜摊】 càitān vegetable stall

【菜肴】 càiyáo cooked food (usu. meat dishes)

【菜油】 càiyóu rapeseed oil; rape oil

【菜园】 càiyuán vegetable garden; vegetable farm

蔡 Cài a surname

cān

参* cān ① join; enter; take part in: ~战 enter a war ② refer; consult: ~阅 see; consult; compare ③ call to pay one's respects to: ~谒士陵园 pay homage at the mausoleum of the martyred heroes ④ impeach an official before the emperor
另见 cēn; shēn

【参半】 cānbàn half; half-and-half: 疑信~ half believing, half doubting/ 毁誉~ get both praise and blame; be as much praised as blamed

【参观】 cānguān visit; look around: ~工厂 visit a factory/ ~名胜古迹 go on sightseeing trips to scenic spots and historical monuments/ ~游览 visit places of interest; go sightseeing/ 欢迎~。 Visitors are welcome. ◇ ~团 visiting group

【参加】 cānjiā ① join; attend; take part in: ~会议 attend a meeting/ ~会谈 take part in talks ② give (advice, suggestion, etc.): 这件事你也来~点儿意见吧。 Come and give us your view on the matter, won't you?

【参看】 cānkàn ① see (also): ~下面注释 see note below/ ~第二十二页 see page 22 ② consult: 他~了不少有关书刊。 He consulted a number of relevant books and periodicals. ③ read sth. for reference: 学习时事可以~这篇文章。 In studying current affairs you might read this article for reference.

【参考】 cānkǎo ① consult; refer to: ~历史文献 consult historical documents ② reference: 仅供~ for reference only ◇ ~书 reference book/ ~书目 a list of reference books; bibliography/ ~资料 reference material

【参谋】 cānmóu ① staff officer ② give advice: 这事可以让老张给你~一下。 You might ask Lao Zhang for advice on this matter. ◇ ~长 chief of staff

【参议员】 cānyìyuán senator

【参议院】 cānyìyuàn senate

【参与】 cānyù participate in; have a hand in: ~其事 have a hand in the matter/ ~制订规划 participate in the drawing up of a plan

【参赞】 cānzàn counsellor: 商务~ commercial counsellor/ 文化~ cultural attaché

【参战】 cānzhàn enter a war; take part in a war ◇ ~国 belligerent state

【参照】 cānzhào consult; refer to: 我们~原文作了必要的修改。 We consulted the original and made some necessary changes./ 这个句子要~上下文来译。 We can't translate this sentence without reference to the context./ ~具体情况作出适当安排。 Make proper arrangements in the light of the specific situation.

餐* cān ① eat: 聚~ dine together/ 野~ go on a picnic; picnic ② food; meal: 中~ Chinese food/ 西~ Western food/ 午~ lunch ③ regular meal: 一日三~ three meals a day

【餐巾】 cānjīn table napkin ◇ ~纸 napkin paper; paper napkin

【餐具】 cānjù tableware; dinner service (或 set)

【餐厅】 cāntīng ① dining room (或 hall) ② restaurant

cán

残* cán ① incomplete; deficient: ～稿 an incomplete manuscript ② remnant; remaining: ～敌 remnants of the enemy forces/ ～冬 the last days of winter ③ injure; damage: 身～志不～ broken in health but not in spirit ④ savage; barbarous; ferocious: 凶～ cruel

【残暴】 cánbào cruel and ferocious; ruthless; brutal; savage

【残兵败将】 cánbīng-bàijiàng remnants of a routed army

【残存】 cáncún remnant; remaining; surviving: 大熊猫是一种～的古动物。The giant panda is one of the surviving ancient animals.

【残废】 cánfèi maimed; crippled; disabled

【残羹剩饭】 cángēng-shèngfàn remains of a meal; leftovers; crumbs from the table

【残骸】 cánhái remains; wreckage: 敌机～ the wreckage of an enemy plane

【残害】 cánhài cruelly injure or kill: ～肢体 cause bodily injury/ 侵略者到处～老百姓。Wherever they went, the invaders slaughtered the local people.

【残迹】 cánjī a remaining trace, sign, etc.; vestiges

【残局】 cánjú ① the final phase of a game of chess ② the situation after the failure of an undertaking or after social unrest: 收拾～ clear up the mess; pick up the pieces

【残酷】 cánkù cruel; brutal; ruthless: ～的剥削 cruel (或 ruthless) exploitation

【残留】 cánliú remain; be left over

【残年】 cánnián ① the last days of the year ② the evening of life; declining years: 风烛～ old and ailing like a candle guttering in the wind

【残破】 cánpò broken; dilapidated: 有些器皿在出土时已经～。Some utensils were in a state of decay when they were unearthed.

【残缺】 cánquē incomplete; fragmentary: 一套～不全的茶具 an incomplete tea set/ 迄今仍未发现竹简～的部分。The missing parts of the inscribed bamboo slips have not yet been discovered.

【残忍】 cánrěn cruel; ruthless

【残杀】 cánshā murder; massacre; slaughter

【残生】 cánshēng one's remaining years

【残阳】 cányáng the setting sun

【残余】 cányú remnants; remains; survivals; vestiges: 封建～ survivals of feudalism/ ～势力 remaining (或 surviving)

【残照】 cánzhào the setting sun: 西风～ the sun setting in the wild west wind

蚕 cán silkworm: 家～ Chinese silkworm/ 野～ wild silkworm/ 养～ raise silkworms; silkworm breeding; sericulture

【蚕蛾】 cán'é silk moth

【蚕茧】 cánjiǎn silkworm cocoon

【蚕眠】 cánmián the inactive state of the silkworm before it sheds its skin

【蚕食】 cánshí nibble ◇ ～政策 the policy of "nibbling" at another country's territory

惭* cán feel ashamed: 大言不～ be shamelessly boastful; brazenly brag

【惭愧】 cánkuì be ashamed: 我没有完成任务, 感到很～。I feel quite ashamed that I have not fulfilled the task.

cǎn

惨* cǎn ① miserable; pitiful; tragic: ～不忍睹 too horrible to look at/ ～遭不幸 die a tragic death ② cruel; savage: ～无人道 inhuman; brutal ③ to a serious degree; disastrously: 敌人愈是捣乱, 就失败得愈～。The more trouble the enemy makes, the worse will be his defeat.

【惨白】 cǎnbái pale: 脸色～ look deathly pale

【惨败】 cǎnbài crushing (或 disastrous) defeat

【惨淡经营】 cǎndàn jīngyíng keep (an enterprise, etc.) going by painstaking effort; take great pains to carry on one's work under difficult circumstances

【惨祸】 cǎnhuò horrible disaster; frightful calamity

【惨剧】 cǎnjù tragedy; calamity

【惨绝人寰】 cǎn jué rénhuán tragic beyond compare in this human world; extremely tragic: ～的暴行 atrocity of unparalleled savagery

【惨杀】 cǎnshā massacre; murder

【惨死】 cǎnsǐ die a tragic death

【惨痛】 cǎntòng deeply grieved; painful; bitter: ～的教训 a bitter lesson

【惨重】 cǎnzhòng heavy; grievous; disastrous: 损失～ suffer heavy (或 grievous) losses/ ～失败 a disastrous defeat/ 伤亡～ suffer heavy casualties

càn

灿 càn

【灿烂】 cànlàn magnificent; splendid; resplendent; bright: ～的阳光 the bright sun; brilliant sunshine/ ～的民族文化 splendid national culture/ 我国前途光辉～。Our country's prospects are magnificent.

粲 càn 〈书〉① bright; beaming ② smile: 以博一～ just for your amusement

【粲然】 cànrán ① bright; beaming ② smiling broadly: ～一笑 give a beaming smile; grin with delight

cāng

仓 cāng storehouse; warehouse: 谷～ barn/ 粮食满～。The granary is bursting with grain.

【仓促】 cāngcù hurriedly; hastily; all of a sudden: 走得～ leave in a hurry/ ～应战 accept battle in haste/ 不要～下结论。Don't jump to conclusions. 又作 "仓猝" "仓卒"

【仓皇】 cānghuáng in a flurry; in panic: ～失措 be scared out of one's wits; be panic-stricken/ ～逃窜 flee in confusion; flee in panic; flee helter-skelter/ ～退却 retreat in haste

【仓库】 cāngkù warehouse; storehouse; depository: 清理～ take stock; check warehouse stocks ◇ ～保管员 warehouseman

沧 cāng (of the sea) dark blue

【沧海】 cānghǎi the blue sea; the sea

【沧海桑田】 cānghǎi-sāngtián seas change into mulberry fields and mulberry fields into seas — time brings great changes to the world

【沧海一粟】 cānghǎi yī sù a drop in the ocean: 个人的力量和群众的力量相比, 不过是～。The strength of an individual, as compared with that of the masses, is but a drop in the ocean.

【沧桑】 cāngsāng ["沧海桑田"的略语]: 饱经～ have experienced many vicissitudes of life

苍* cāng ① dark green: ～松 green pines ② blue: ～天 the blue sky ③ grey; ashy: ～髯 a grey beard

【苍白】 cāngbái pale; pallid; wan: 脸色～ look pale/ ～无力 weak and feeble

【苍苍】 cāngcāng ① grey: 两鬓～ greying at the temples ② vast and hazy

【苍翠】 cāngcuì dark green; verdant: ～的山峦 verdant hills

【苍劲】 cāngjìng ① old and strong: ～挺拔的青松 hardy, old pines ② (of calligraphy or painting) vigorous; bold: 笔力～ (write or paint) in bold, vigorous strokes

【苍老】 cānglǎo ① old; aged: 他显得～了。He looks old. ② (of calligraphy or painting) vigorous; forceful

【苍凉】 cāngliáng desolate; bleak: 过去这一带满目～, 现在却有了无数的工厂。Numerous factories have sprung up in this once desolate area.

【苍茫】 cāngmáng ① vast; boundless: ~大地 boundless land ② indistinct: 暮色~ deepening shades of dusk/ 一片~的海天景色 a vast expanse of sea and sky
【苍天】 cāngtiān ① the blue sky ② Heaven
【苍鹰】 cāngyīng goshawk
【苍蝇】 cāngyíng fly ◇ ~拍子 flyswatter

舱 cāng ① cabin: 客~ (passenger) cabin/ 货~ hold ② <宇航> module: 指挥~ command moduie
【舱面】 cāngmiàn deck ◇ ~货 deck cargo
【舱室】 cāngshì cabin
【舱位】 cāngwèi ① cabin seat or berth ② shipping space

cáng

藏 cáng ① hide; conceal: 这人肚子里~不住话。This chap can't keep anything to himself. ② store; lay by 另见 zàng
【藏垢纳污】 cánggòu-nàwū shelter evil people and countenance evil practices: ~之地 a sink of iniquity
【藏匿】 cángnì conceal; hide; go into hiding
【藏身】 cángshēn hide oneself; go into hiding: 无处~ no place to hide/ ~之处 hiding-place; hideout
【藏书】 cángshū ① collect books ② a collection of books; library
【藏头露尾】 cángtóu-lùwěi show the tail but hide the head tell part of the truth but not all of it
【藏拙】 cángzhuō hide one's inadequacy by keeping quiet

cāo

糙 cāo rough; coarse: ~纸 rough paper/ 这活儿做得太~。This is very slipshod work.
【糙米】 cāomǐ brown rice; unpolished rice

操 cāo ① grasp; hold: ~刀 hold a sword, cleaver, etc. in one's hand/ ~胜算 find success within one's grasp; be sure to win ② act; do; operate: ~之过急 act with undue haste/ 重~旧业 resume one's old profession; take up one's old trade again ③ speak (a language or dialect): ~本地口音 speak with a local accent/ ~着一口流利的英语 speak fluent English ④ drill; exercise: 战士们在上~。The soldiers are drilling./ 大家去做~吧。Let's go and do exercises. ⑤ conduct; behaviour: 节~ one's moral principles; personal integrity
【操场】 cāochǎng playground; sports ground; drill ground
【操劳】 cāoláo ① work hard: ~过度 overwork (或 strain) oneself; 终年为公司~ work hard for the company all the year round ② take care; look after: 这事请您多~。Would you mind looking after this?
【操练】 cāoliàn drill; practice
【操守】 cāoshǒu personal integrity
【操心】 cāoxīn ① worry about; trouble about; take pains: 这件事,你不必~了。You needn't worry about it. ② rack one's brains
【操行】 cāoxíng behaviour or conduct of a student
【操演】 cāoyǎn demonstration; drill
【操纵】 cāozòng ① operate; control: 培养~新机器的工人 train workers to operate new machines/ 无线电~ radio control ② rig; manipulate: ~市场 rig the market/ ~表决机器 tamper with the voting machine; manipulate the voting/ 幕后~ manipulate from behind the scenes; pull strings
【操作】 cāozuò operate; manipulate: 避免~上的疏忽 avoid carelessness in manipulation/ 在老师傅的指导下,青年徒工很快就学会独立~了。 Guided by the master workers, the young apprentices quickly learned to operate the machines.

cáo

曹 cáo <书> people of the same kind: 尔~ all of you; you

嘈 cáo noise; din
【嘈杂】 cáozá noisy: 人声~ a hubbub of voices

cǎo

草 cǎo ① grass; straw: ~绳 straw rope ② careless; hasty; rough: 字写得很。The handwriting is very sloppy. ③ draft: 起~文件 draft a document ④ 见"草书" ⑤ <口> female (of certain domestic animals or fowls): ~驴 jenny ass/ ~鸡 hen
【草案】 cǎo'àn draft (of a plan, law, etc.): 决议~ a draft resolution
【草草】 cǎocǎo carelessly; hastily: ~地看过一遍 read through roughly; give a cursory reading; skim through/ ~收场 hastily wind up the matter/ ~了事 get through with sth. any old way
【草创】 cǎochuàng start (an enterprise, etc.): ~时期 initial (或 pioneering) stage
【草丛】 cǎocóng a thick growth of grass
【草地】 cǎodì ① grassland; meadow ② lawn
【草稿】 cǎogǎo rough draft; draft
【草菇】 cǎogū straw mushroom
【草菅人命】 cǎojiān rénmìng treat human life as if it were not worth a straw; act with utter disregard for human life
【草莓】 cǎoméi strawberry
【草木皆兵】 cǎo mù jiē bīng every bush and tree looks like an enemy — a state of extreme nervousness
【草拟】 cǎonǐ draw up; draft: ~一个计划 draft a plan
【草棚】 cǎopéng thatched shack; straw shed
【草书】 cǎoshū (in Chinese calligraphy) characters executed swiftly and with strokes flowing together; cursive hand
【草率】 cǎoshuài careless; perfunctory; rash: 不宜~从事 should not take any hasty action
【草图】 cǎotú sketch (map); draft
【草席】 cǎoxí straw mat
【草鞋】 cǎoxié straw sandals: ~没样,边打边像。Straw sandals need no last; the shape comes with the weaving — work things out as you go along.
【草药】 cǎoyào medicinal herbs
【草原】 cǎoyuán grasslands; prairie
【草纸】 cǎozhǐ ① rough straw paper ② toilet paper

cè

册 cè ① volume; book: 这部书一共六~。This book is in six volumes./ 装订成~ bind into book form/ 画~ an album of paintings ② <量> copy: 这本书已销售十万~。100,000 copies of the book have been sold.
【册子】 cèzi book; volume: 小~ pamphlet; booklet; brochure

厕 cè lavatory; toilet; washroom; W.C.: 公~ public lavatory/ 男~ men's (room, toilet)/ 女~ women's (room, toilet)
【厕所】 cèsuǒ lavatory; toilet; W.C.

侧 cè ① side: 左(右)~ the left (right) side/ 公路两~种着杨树。 Poplars are planted on both sides of the highway. ② incline; lean: ~耳细听 incline the head and listen attentively; prick up one's ears/ ~着身子睡 sleep on one's side
【侧击】 cèjī flank attack
【侧门】 cèmén side door; side entrance
【侧面】 cèmiàn side; aspect; flank: 从~进攻敌人 make a flank attack on the enemy/ 从~了解 find out from indirect sources
【侧目】 cèmù sidelong glance: ~而视 look askance at sb. (with fear or indignation)
【侧身】 cèshēn on one's side; sideways: ~匍匐前进 crawl ahead on one's side
【侧影】 cèyǐng silhouette; profile

【侧重】 cèzhòng lay particular emphasis on: 他～宣传工作。His job is to pay particular attention to propaganda work.

测* cè ①survey; fathom; measure: ～雨量 gauge (或 measure) rainfall/ 中国测绘工作者精确～得珠穆朗玛峰海拔高程为八千八百四十八点一三米。Chinese cartographers determined the exact height of Mount Qomolangma to be 8,848.13 metres above sea level. ② conjecture; infer: 变化莫～ unpredictable; constantly changing

【测定】 cèdìng determine: ～船只的方位 take a ship's bearings/ 放射性碳素～年代 radiocarbon dating/ 示踪～ tracer determination

【测度】 cèduó estimate; infer: 根据风向～，今天不会下雨。Judging by the direction of the wind, it won't rain today.

【测绘】 cèhuì survey and drawing; mapping
◇ ～板 plotting board/ ～部队 mapping unit; topographic troops/ ～飞机 air-mapping plane/ ～员 surveyor; cartographer

【测量】 cèliáng survey; measure; gauge: ～地形 survey the topography/ 大地～ geodetic survey/ 航空～ aerial survey; air survey
◇ ～队 survey party/ ～学 surveying/ ～仪表 instrumentation/ ～仪器 surveying instrument/ ～员 surveyor

【测验】 cèyàn test: 算术～ arithmetic test (或 quiz)/ ～机械性能 test the performance of a machine

【测字】 cèzì fortune-telling by analysing the component parts of a Chinese character; glyphomancy

恻 cè sorrowful; sad; 凄～ sad; grieved

【恻隐】 cèyǐn compassion; pity: ～之心 sense of pity

策* cè ① plan; scheme; strategy: 决～ policy making ② whip: ～马前进 whip a horse on ③ bamboo or wooden slips used for writing on in ancient China ④ a type of essay in ancient China: ～论 discourse on politics

【策动】 cèdòng instigate; engineer; stir up: 阴谋～政变 plot to stage a *coup d'état*

【策划】 cèhuà plan; plot; scheme; engineer: ～阴谋 hatch a plot/ 幕后～ plot behind the scenes

【策励】 cèlì encourage; spur on: 时时刻刻～自己 constantly spur oneself ahead

【策略】 cèlüè ①tactics: 研究对敌斗争的～ study the tactics of our struggle against the enemy ②tactful: 这个提法不～。It's not tactful to couch the statement in such terms.

cēn

参* cēn
另见 cān; shēn

【参差】 cēncī irregular; uneven:～不齐 uneven; not uniform

cén

岑 cén 〈书〉 high hill

涔 cén 〈书〉 rainwater in puddles

【涔涔】 céncén 〈书〉 dripping; streaming: 汗～下 sweat streaming down; dripping with sweat

céng

层* céng ①layer; tier; stratum: 一～油漆 a coat of paint/ 一～薄冰 a thin sheet (或 layer) of ice ②storey; floor: 五～大楼 a five-storey building/ 我住在一～。I live on the ground floor (美: first floor)./ 他住在二～。He lives on the first floor (美: second floor). ③a component part in a sequence: 他这话还有一～意思。What he said has further implications.

【层层】 céngcéng layer upon layer; ring upon ring; tier upon tier: ～梯田 tier upon tier of terraced fields/ ～包围 surround ring upon ring/ ～设防 set up successive lines of

defence; erect defensive works in depth/ ～把关 check at each level

【层出不穷】 céng chū bù qióng emerge in an endless stream

【层次】 céngcì ①administrative levels: 减少～，精简人员 simplify the administrative structure and reduce the staff ② arrangement of ideas (in writing or speech): 这篇文章～不清。This article lacks unity and coherence.

曾* céng 〈副〉〔表示有过某些行为或情况〕: 几年前我～见过她一面。I met her once several years ago./ 我未～听说过这样的事。I've never heard of such a thing.
另见 zēng

【曾几何时】 céng jǐ hé shí before long; not long after: 猖獗一时的社会党徒，～，遭到了彻底消灭。The secret society members were on the rampage for a time, but before long they were completely wiped out.

【曾经】 céngjīng 〈副〉〔表示有过某些行为或情况〕: 她～参加过石油大会战。She has taken part in a major battle for oil.

chā

叉* chā ①fork: 钢～ (steel) fork/ 干草～ hayfork; pitchfork/ 餐～ (table) fork ②work with a fork; fork: ～草上垛 fork hay onto a stack/ ～鱼 spear fish ③cross: 在每个错别字上打个～ put a cross above each wrongly written word
另见 chǎ

【叉腰】 chāyāo akimbo: 双手～ with arms akimbo

【叉子】 chāzi fork: 粪～ dung fork

杈 chā wooden fork; hayfork; pitchfork
另见 chà

差* chā ①difference; dissimilarity: 时～ time difference ②mistake: 偏～ deviation ③〈数〉 difference
另见 chà; chāi; cī

【差别】 chābié difference; disparity: 年龄～ disparity in age/ 数(质)量上的～ quantitative (qualitative) difference/ 二者之间～很大。There is a world of difference between the two.

【差错】 chācuò ①mistake; error; slip: 工作认真负责，就会少出～。If we work conscientiously, we won't make many mistakes./ 这笔账目里有～。There's an accounting error in this entry./ 几个月来这部机器一直运转正常，没有出过～。This machine has been running without a hitch for months. ② mishap; accident: 万一这孩子出了～怎么办? What if anything should happen to the child?

【差强人意】 chā qiáng rényì just passable

【差异】 chāyì difference; divergence; discrepancy; diversity: 这两个地区气候～很大。These two regions differ greatly in climate.

【差之毫厘，谬以千里】 chā zhī háolí, miù yǐ qiānlǐ an error the breadth of a single hair can lead you a thousand *li* astray 又作"差之毫厘，失之千里"

插* chā ①stick in; insert: 把插头～上 insert the plug in a socket; plug in/ 把双手～在口袋里 put one's hands in one's pockets/ 把门～上 bolt the door/ 山峰高～入云 peaks penetrating into the clouds/ 把旗～上峰顶 plant a flag on the mountain top/ 似尖刀直～敌人心脏 like a dagger stuck into the enemy's heart ②interpose; insert: 这本书再版时～入了新的一章。A new chapter is included in the second edition./ 他说个没完，别人半句话也～不进。He talked on and on and nobody else could get a word in edgeways.

【插班】 chābān join a class in the middle of the course

【插翅难飞】 chā chì nán fēi unable to escape even if given wings

【插曲】 chāqǔ ①〈乐〉 interlude ② songs in a film or play ③episode; interlude: 双方谈判中的一个～ an episode in the negotiations between the two parties

【插身】 chāshēn ① squeeze in; edge in: 很难～ difficult to squeeze in ② take part in; get involved in: 他不想～在这场纠纷中间。 He doesn't want to get involved in this dispute. 或 He's trying to keep out of this quarrel.

【插手】 chāshǒu ① take part; lend a hand: 人够多了，您就不用～了。 You don't have to join in, there are more than enough people on the job already./ 想帮忙又插不上手 be ready to help but not know how to ② have a hand in; poke one's nose into; meddle in: 想不到她会插上一手。 We never thought she would poke her nose into this.

【插头】 chātóu 〈电〉 plug: 三脚～ three-pin plug

【插图】 chātú illustration; plate: 书中有几幅彩色～。 The book has several colour plates. ◇ ～本 illustrated edition

【插足】 chāzú ① put one's foot in: 这儿几乎没有～的地方。 There's not even standing room. ② participate (in some activity)

【插嘴】 chāzuǐ interrupt; chip in: 插不上嘴 cannot get a word in edgeways

喳 chā
　　另见 zhā
【喳喳】 chāchā whispering sound
【喳喳】 chācha whisper: 她在她妈妈耳边～了两句。 She whispered a few words in her mother's ear.

chá

茶* chá ① tea: 沏～ make tea/ 浓（淡）～ strong (weak) tea/ 红（绿）～ black (green) tea ② certain kinds of drink or liquid food: 杏仁～ almond paste
【茶杯】 chábēi teacup
【茶匙】 cháchí teaspoon
【茶点】 chádiǎn tea and pastries; refreshments
【茶壶】 cháhú teapot
【茶会】 cháhuì tea party
【茶几】 chájī tea table; teapoy; side table
【茶具】 chájù tea set; tea-things; tea service
【茶盘】 chápán tea tray; teaboard
【茶钱】 cháqián ① payment for tea (in a teahouse) ② 〈旧〉 tip
【茶色】 chásè dark brown
【茶树】 cháshù tea tree
【茶水】 cháshuǐ tea or boiled water (supplied to walkers, trippers, etc.)
【茶叶】 cháyè tea; tea-leaves
【茶余酒后】 cháyú-jiǔhòu over a cup of tea or after a few glasses of wine — at one's leisure
【茶园】 cháyuán ① tea plantation ② a place where tea and soft drinks are served; tea garden
【茶座】 cházuò ① teahouse ② seats in a teahouse or tea garden

查* chá ① check; examine: ～卫生 make a public health and sanitation check (或 inspection)/ ～血 have a blood test ② look into; investigate: ～一～事故的原因 find out the cause of an accident/ ～个水落石出 get to the bottom of a matter; investigate sth. thoroughly ③ look up; consult: ～字典 look up a word in the dictionary; consult a dictionary/ ～资料 read up the literature (on a special subject)/ ～档案 look into the archives
【查办】 chábàn investigate and deal with accordingly: 撤职～ dismiss a person and have him prosecuted
【查点】 chádiǎn check the number or amount of; make an inventory of: ～人数 check the number of people present; check the attendance/ ～存货 make an inventory of the goods in stock; take stock
【查对】 cháduì check; verify: ～材料 check the data/ ～原文 check against the original (text, manuscript, etc.)/ ～

数字 verify the figures/ ～无误 examined and found correct; verified
【查房】 cháfáng (of doctors) make (或 go) the rounds of the wards
【查访】 cháfǎng go around and make inquiries; investigate
【查看】 chákàn look over; examine: ～帐目 examine the accounts/ ～水情 look into the water (或 flood) situation/ ～机器运转的情况 see how the machine is working
【查考】 chákǎo examine; do research on; try to ascertain: ～中国古时有关地震的全部文献 study all available literature about earthquakes in ancient China/ 一批新出土文物的年代 try to ascertain the date of a new lot of unearthed relics
【查明】 chámíng prove through investigation; find out; ascertain: ～事实真相 find out the truth; ascertain the facts/ 现已～ it has been established that; investigation reveals that
【查票】 chápiào examine (或 check) tickets
【查清】 cháqīng make a thorough investigation of; check up on: ～某人的来历 find out sb.'s background; check up on sb./ ～一件事情的来龙去脉 find out how sth. started and developed
【查收】 cháshōu 〔多用于书信〕 please find: 寄上样品两种，请～。 Please find two samples enclosed herewith.
【查问】 cháwèn question; interrogate: ～证人 interrogate a witness/ ～口令 challenge (for a password)
【查无实据】 chá wú shíjù investigation reveals no evidence (against the suspect)
【查询】 cháxún inquire about: ～地址 inquire sb.'s address/ ～行李下落 inquire about (the whereabouts of) the luggage
【查验】 cháyàn check; examine: ～护照 examine a passport
【查阅】 cháyuè consult; look up: ～技术资料 consult technical data; look up technical literature
【查帐】 cházhàng check (或 audit, examine) accounts
【查照】 cházhào 〔旧时公文用语〕 please note: 希～办理。 Please note and take appropriate action.
【查证】 cházhèng investigate and verify; check: ～属实 be checked and found to be true; be verified

搽* chá put (powder, ointment, etc.) on the skin; apply: ～雪花膏 put on vanishing cream/ ～药 apply ointment, lotion, etc./ ～粉 powder

察* chá examine; look into; scrutinize: ～其言，观其行 examine his words and watch his deeds; check what he says against what he does
【察觉】 chájué be conscious of; become aware of; perceive
【察看】 chákàn watch; look carefully at; observe: ～风向 watch which way the wind is blowing/ ～地形 survey the terrain/ ～杀虫药的治虫效果 check the effectiveness of the insecticide/ ～四周的动静 peer in all directions to see if anything is afoot

chǎ

叉 chǎ part so as to form a fork; fork: ～着腿站着 stand with one's legs apart
　　另见 chā

chà

杈 chà branch (of a tree)
　　另见 chā
【杈子】 chàzi branch: 树～ a branch of a tree

岔 chà ① branch off; fork: 这条路过了桥就分～了。 The road forks on the other side of the bridge./ ～路 branch road/ 三～路口 a fork in the road; a junction of three roads ② turn off: 自行车下了公路～上了小道。 The cyclist turned off the highway onto a side road.
【岔开】 chàkāi ① branch off; diverge: 线路在这儿～了。 The

line branches here. ② diverge to (another topic); change (the subject of conversation): 两个人正要争吵，我给～了。A quarrel was starting between the two of them, but I headed it off. ③ stagger: 把休假日～ stagger the days of rest

【岔口】 chàkǒu fork (in a road): 他们把他送到～。They saw him to a fork in the road.

【岔路】 chàlù branch road; byroad; side road 又作 "岔道儿"

【岔子】 chàzi ① accident; trouble: 拖拉机出了什么～? What's wrong with the tractor?/ 他开了好几年卡车，从没有出过～。He has been driving a truck for years and never had an accident./ 你放心吧，出不了～。Don't worry, everything will be all right. ② 见 "岔路"

诧 chà be surprised

【诧异】 chàyì be surprised; be astonished: ～的神色 a surprised look/ 听了这个突如其来的消息，我们都十分～。We were all astonished at the unexpected news.

衩 chà vent (或 slit) in the sides of a garment

刹 chà Buddhist temple (或 monastery)
另见 shā

【刹那】 chànà instant; split second: 一～ in an instant; in a flash; in the twinkling of an eye

差* chà ① differ from; fall short of ② wrong: 这你可说～了。You're wrong there. ③ wanting; short of: 一个月～两天 two days less than a month/ ～七天不到一年 seven days short of a year/ ～十分四点 ten minutes (to) four/ ～两个人 two people short/ 我还～你两块钱。I still owe you $2 / 还差一道工序。There's still one more step in the process./ 木料还～多少?——～不了多少了。How much more timber is needed? — Not much. ④ not up to standard; poor: 成绩不算太～。The results are by no means poor./ 这个街道工厂设备～，可是产品并不～。The neighbourhood factory's equipment is not up to much, but its products are not at all bad.
另见 chā; chāi; cī

【差不多】 chàbuduō ① almost; nearly: ～五点了。It's nearly five o'clock./ 这座大楼～快完工了。The building is nearing completion. ② about the same; similar: 他们俩高矮～。They two are about the same height./ 这两种观点～。These two views are similar. ③ just about right (或enough); not far off; not bad: 我们应该力争上游，而不应该有 "～" 的思想。We should aim high and not think "That's good enough".

【差点儿】 chàdiǎnr ① not quite up to the mark; not good enough: 她的技术还～。Her technique is not quite up to the mark./ 这块布质量挺好，就是颜色～。The quality of this cloth is fine, but the colour is not quite right. The cloth is quite good except for the colour. ② [副] [表示某种事情接近实现或勉强实现] almost; nearly; on the verge of: ～没赶上车 very nearly miss the bus/ 这盘棋他～赢了。He nearly won the chess game./ ～ (没) 哭出来 be on the verge of tears/ ～ (没) 触电 narrowly escape getting a shock

【差劲】 chàjìn no good; disappointing: 这条路坑坑洼洼的，太～了。The road is no good, it's rough and full of holes./ 真～，麦子刚上场就下起雨来了! Too bad! We'd just got the wheat to the threshing ground when it started to rain.

chāi

拆* chāi ① tear open; take apart: ～信 open a letter/ ～机器 disassemble a machine; take a machine apart; strip a machine/ 把这个组～了 break up the group ② pull down; dismantle: ～房子 pull down a house/ ～桥 dismantle a bridge/ ～帐蓬 strike tents/ 把旧毛衣～了重新织一下 unravel an old sweater and reknit it

【拆除】 chāichú demolish; dismantle; remove: ～城墙 remove (或 demolish) a city wall/ ～障碍物 remove obstacles/

～军事基地 dismantle military bases

【拆穿】 chāichuān expose; unmask: ～骗局 expose a fraud/ ～西洋镜 strip off the camouflage; expose sb.'s tricks

【拆东墙，补西墙】 chāi dōngqiáng, bǔ xīqiáng tear down the east wall to repair the west wall — resort to a makeshift solution

【拆毁】 chāihuǐ demolish; pull down: 侵略军强行～民房。The invading troops tore down the people's houses.

【拆伙】 chāihuǒ dissolve a partnership; part company

【拆开】 chāikāi take apart; open; separate: 把机器～ disassemble a machine/ 这两个字构成一个词，不能～。The two characters form a single word, they cannot be separated.

【拆散】 chāisàn break up (a marriage, family, etc.)

【拆台】 chāitái cut the ground (或 pull the rug) from under sb.'s feet; pull away a prop: 工作要互相支持，不要互相～。Our work calls for mutual support. We shouldn't counteract each other's efforts./ 你一定来，可别拆我的台。Be sure to come. Don't let me down.

【拆线】 chāixiàn 〈医〉 take out stitches

钗 chāi hairpin (formerly worn by women for adornment)

差* chāi ① send on an errand; dispatch: ～人去送封信 send a letter by messenger/ 派他去办件事 send (或 dispatch) him on an errand/ 因公出～ be away on official business ② errand; job: 兼～ hold more than one job concurrently
另见 chā; chà; cī

【差遣】 chāiqiǎn send sb. on an errand or mission; dispatch; assign: 听候～ await assignment; be at sb.'s disposal

【差使】 chāishǐ send; assign; appoint

【差事】 chāishi errand; assignment: 给你们一件～。Here's a job for you.

chái

柴* chái firewood

【柴草】 cháicǎo firewood; faggot

【柴火】 cháihuo firewood; faggot

【柴米油盐】 chái-mǐ-yóu-yán fuel, rice, oil and salt — chief daily necessities

【柴油】 cháiyóu diesel oil ◇ ～机车 diesel locomotive

【柴油机】 cháiyóujī diesel engine: 船用～ marine diesel engine/ 陆用～ stationary diesel engine

豺 chái jackal

【豺狼】 cháiláng jackals and wolves — cruel and evil people

chān

搀 chān ① help by the arm; support sb. with one's hand: 把老大娘～进屋 help the old lady into the room/ ～着他点。Help him along. ② mix: 往沙子里～石灰 mix lime into sand/ 油和水～不到一块儿。Oil and water do not mix.

【搀扶】 chānfú support sb. with one's hand

【搀杂】 chānzá mix; mingle: 别把这两种菜籽～在一起。Don't mix up the two kinds of vegetable seeds.

chán

单 chán
另见 dān

【单于】 chányú chief of the Xiongnu (匈奴) in ancient China

婵 chán
【婵娟】 chánjuān 〈书〉① lovely (used in ancient writings to describe women) ② the moon

谗 chán slander; backbite
【谗害】 chánhài calumniate or slander sb. in order to have him persecuted; frame sb. up
【谗言】 chányán slanderous talk; calumny

馋 chán greedy; gluttonous: 嘴～ greedy; fond of good food/ 看见下棋他就～得慌。His fingers itch at the sight of a game of chess.
【馋涎欲滴】 chánxián yù dī mouth drooling with greed: 使他～ make his mouth water
【馋嘴】 chánzuǐ gluttonous

孱 chán frail; weak
【孱弱】 chánruò frail (of physique); delicate (in health)

禅 chán 〈佛教〉① prolonged and intense contemplation; deep meditation; dhyana: 坐～ sit in meditation ② Buddhist: ～堂 a room in a Buddhist monastery set apart for meditation; meditation room/ ～杖 Buddhist monk's staff
另见 shàn

缠 chán ① twine; wind: ～线轴 wind thread onto a reel/ 他手上～着绷带。His hand was bandaged. ② tangle; tie up; pester: 这两股线～在一起了。The two threads got tangled up./ 他被事情～住了, 没能来。He couldn't come because he was tied up./ 干吗老～着我？Why do you keep worrying me?
【缠绵】 chánmián ① lingering: ～病榻 be bedridden with a lingering disease/ 乡思～ be tormented by nostalgia ② touching; moving
【缠绵悱恻】 chánmián-fěicè (of writing) exceedingly sentimental
【缠绕】 chánrào ① twine; bind; wind: 大树上～着藤萝。There is a wisteria twining round the big tree. ② worry; harass

蝉 chán cicada
【蝉联】 chánlián continue to hold a post or title: 多次～全国冠军 win the national championship several times running

潺 chán
【潺潺】 chánchán 〈象〉 murmur; babble; purl: ～流水 a murmuring stream
【潺湲】 chányuán 〈书〉 flow slowly: 秋水～。Gently flow the autumn streams.

蟾 chán
【蟾蜍】 chánchú 〈书〉① toad ② the fabled toad in the moon ③ the moon

chǎn

产* chǎn ① give birth to; be delivered of: 助～ midwifery/ 熊猫每胎～仔一、二只。Pandas have only one or two young at a birth. ② produce; yield: ～油 produce oil; oil-producing/ ～棉区 cotton-producing area/ 水稻亩～超千斤。The per *mu* yield of rice is over 1,000 *jin*. ③ product; produce: 土特～ local and special products ④

property; estate: 房地～ real estate; real property/ 家～ family possessions
【产地】 chǎndì place of production (或 origin); producing area: 甘蔗～ a sugarcane growing area/ 原料～ sources of raw materials/ 金丝猴～ the native haunt of the golden monkey
【产儿】 chǎn'ér newborn baby
【产房】 chǎnfáng delivery room
【产妇】 chǎnfù lying-in woman
【产假】 chǎnjià maternity leave
【产量】 chǎnliàng output; yield: 煤～ output of coal
【产卵】 chǎnluǎn （鸟、家禽）lay eggs; （鱼、蛙）spawn; （昆虫）oviposit
【产品】 chǎnpǐn product; produce: 农～ farm produce/ 畜～ livestock products/ 工业～ industrial products
【产前】 chǎnqián antenatal: ～检查 antenatal examination
【产生】 chǎnshēng ① produce; engender: ～好的结果 produce good results/ ～很大的影响 exert a great influence/ 实践使我们的认识～了新的飞跃。Practice brings about a new leap in our knowledge. ② emerge; come into being
【产物】 chǎnwù outcome; result; product
【产业】 chǎnyè ① estate; property ② industrial

谄 chǎn flatter; fawn on
【谄媚】 chǎnmèi flatter; fawn on; toady
【谄上欺下】 chǎnshàng-qīxià be servile to one's superiors and tyrannical to one's subordinates; fawn on those above and bully those below
【谄笑】 chǎnxiào ingratiating smile
【谄谀】 chǎnyú flatter

铲* chǎn ① shovel: 煤～ coal shovel/ 锅～ slice ② lift or move with a shovel; shovel: 煤～ shovel coal/ 把地～平 scrape the ground even; level the ground with a shovel or spade
【铲除】 chǎnchú root out; uproot; eradicate: ～毒草 uproot poisonous weeds

阐 chǎn explain
【阐发】 chǎnfā elucidate
【阐明】 chǎnmíng expound; clarify: ～观点 clarify one's views/ 支持声明中所～的正义立场 support the just stand expounded in the statement
【阐释】 chǎnshì explain; expound; interpret: 她对各项规定作了明确的～。She gave a clear explanation of each of the rules and regulations.
【阐述】 chǎnshù expound; elaborate; set forth: 各方～了自己对这一问题的立场。Each side set forth its position on this question.
【阐扬】 chǎnyáng expound and propagate

chàn

忏 chàn repent
【忏悔】 chànhuǐ ① repent; be penitent ② 〈宗〉 confess (one's sins)

颤 chàn quiver; tremble; vibrate: 他激动得说话声音都发～了。He was so overcome with emotion that his voice quivered.
另见 zhàn
【颤动】 chàndòng vibrate; quiver: 声带～ vibration of the vocal chords/ 树叶在微风中～。The leaves quivered in the breeze.
【颤抖】 chàndǒu shake; tremble; quiver; shiver: 冻得全身～ shiver all over with cold/ 吓得两腿～ shake in one's shoes

chāng

伥 chāng 见“为虎作伥” wèi hǔ zuò chāng

昌* chāng prosperous; flourishing
【昌明】 chāngmíng flourishing; thriving; well-developed: 科学～。 Science is flourishing.
【昌盛】 chāngshèng prosperous: 建设一个繁荣～的国家 build a prosperous country

猖 chāng
【猖獗】 chāngjué be rampant; run wild: 这个地区过去风沙～。 The area used to be struck by raging sandstorms.
【猖狂】 chāngkuáng savage; furious: ～的挑衅 reckless provocation/. ～的攻击 a furious attack

娼 chāng prostitute
【娼妓】 chāngjì prostitute; streetwalker

鲳 chāng
【鲳鱼】 chāngyú silvery pomfret; butterfish

cháng

长* cháng ① long: 这条河很～。 This is a long river./ 夏季昼～夜短。 In summer the days are long and the nights short. ② length: 南京长江大桥全～六千七百多米。 The overall length of the Changjiang River Bridge at Nanjing is more than 6,700 metres. ③ of long duration; lasting: 与世～辞 pass away ④ steadily; regularly ⑤ strong point; forte: 取人之～,补己之短 overcome one's shortcomings by learning from others' strong points/ 她～于绘画。 She is good at painting. 或 Painting is her forte. 另见 zhǎng
【长城】 Chángchéng ① the Great Wall ② impregnable bulwark

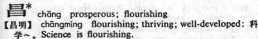

【长处】 chángchu good qualities; strong (或 good) points: 他有许多～。 He has many good qualities./ 有联系群众的～ have the strong point of maintaining close contact with the masses/ 国无论大小,都各有～和短处。 Every nation, big or small, has its strong and weak points.
【长此以往】 cháng cǐ yǐ wǎng if things go on like this; if things continue this way
【长存】 chángcún live forever
【长度】 chángdù length
【长短】 chángduǎn ① length: 这两条扁担～差不多。The two carrying poles are about the same length./ 这件上衣～不合适。This coat is not the right length. ② accident; mishap: 万一这孩子的母亲有个～,怎么办? What if anything should happen to the child's mother? ③ right and wrong; strong and weak points: 背地里议论别人～是不应该的。It is not right to gossip about a person behind his back.
【长方体】 chángfāngtǐ cuboid; rectangular parallelepiped
【长方形】 chángfāngxíng rectangle
【长江】 Chángjiāng the Changjiang (Yangtze) River: ～后浪推前浪,一代更比一代强。 As in the Changjiang River the waves behind drive on those before, so each new generation excels the last one.
【长颈鹿】 chángjǐnglù giraffe

【长久】 chángjiǔ for a long time; permanently: 他打算在这儿一住下去。He is thinking of living here permanently. 或 He is thinking of settling down here./ 不是～之计 not a permanent solution; just a makeshift arrangement
【长距离】 chángjùlí long distance: ～赛跑 a long-distance race
【长空】 chángkōng vast sky
【长裤】 chángkù trousers; slacks; pants
【长眠】 chángmián 〈婉〉 eternal sleep; death: ～地下 dead and buried
【长年】 chángnián all the year round: 筑路工人～奋战在风雪高原。 The road builders brave the wind and snow on the plateaus all the year round.
【长年累月】 chángnián-lěiyuè year in year out; over the years: 勘探队员～在各地寻找地下宝藏。 Year in year out, our prospectors travel far and wide, looking for mineral deposits./ ～没修理,墙上的灰泥都剥落了。 The plaster on the wall had peeled off through years of neglect.
【长袍】 chángpáo long gown; robe
【长跑】 chángpǎo long-distance race; long-distance running
【长篇大论】 chángpiān-dàlùn a lengthy speech or article
【长篇小说】 chángpiān xiǎoshuō novel
【长期】 chángqī over a long period of time; long-term: ～规划 a long-term plan/ 天气预报 a long-range weather forecast/ ～存在的问题 a long-standing problem/ ～无息贷款 a long-term loan without interest/ ～战争 a long-drawn-out war; a protracted war/ ～观点 a long-term view/ 作～打算 take a long view; make long-term plans
【长驱】 chángqū (of an army) make a long drive; push deep: ～千里 make a long drive of 1,000 li/ 我军～直入,所向披靡。Our army drove straight in, carrying everything before it.
【长舌】 chángshé fond of gossip
【长逝】 chángshì pass away; be gone forever
【长寿】 chángshòu long life; longevity: 祝您健康～。I wish you good health and a long life.
【长叹】 chángtàn deep sigh: ～一声 heave a deep sigh
【长途】 chángtú long-distance: ～跋涉 make a long, arduous journey
◇ ～奔袭 long-distance raid/ ～电话 long-distance (或 trunk) call/～飞行 long-range flight/ ～汽车 long-distance bus; coach/ ～运输 long-distance transport
【长物】 chángwù anything that may be spared; surplus: 别无～ have nothing other than daily necessities; have no valuable personal possessions
【长吁短叹】 chángxū-duǎntàn sighs and groans; moan and groan
【长远】 chángyuǎn long-term; long-range: ～的利益 long-term interests/ ～规划 a long-term (或 long-range) plan/ 从～的观点看问题 from a long-term point of view

场* cháng ① a level open space; threshing ground: 打～ threshing ② 〈量〉〔用于事情的经过〕: 一～大雨 a downpour/一～硬仗 a hard battle/ 大干一～ go in for sth. in a big way; go all out/ 害了一～病 be ill for a while 另见 chǎng

肠* cháng intestines: 大(小)～ large (small, ntestine
【肠胃】 cháng-wèi intestines and stomach; stomach; belly: ～不好 suffer from indigestion

尝* cháng ① taste; try the flavour of: ～～咸淡 have a taste and see if it's salty enough/ ～到甜头 become aware of the benefits of; come to know the good of/ 艰苦备～ have experienced all the hardships ② adv: 未～见过此人 have never seen the person/ 何～不想去,只是没时间。I meant to go, only I didn't have the time.
【尝试】 chángshì attempt; try: 他们为了增产,曾～过各种方法。 They have tried various things to increase production

常* cháng ① ordinary; common; normal: 人情之～ natural and normal/ 反～ unusual; abnormal/ 习以为～ be used (或 accustomed) to sth. ② constant; invariable: 冬夏～青 remain green throughout the year; evergreen ③ frequently; often; usually: ～来～往 exchange frequent visits; pay frequent calls/ 她～去听音乐会。She goes to concerts quite often./ 我们～见面。We see quite a lot of each other.

【常常】chángcháng frequently; often; usually; generally: 她～工作到深夜。She often works far into the night./ 年终时,人们～总结过去,展望将来。At the end of the year, people usually sum up their experience and make plans for the future.

【常规】chángguī ① convention; rule; common practice; routine: 按照～办事 follow the old routine/ 打破～ break with convention

【常见】chángjiàn common: 现在拖拉机在这里是很～的。Nowadays tractors are a common sight here.

【常例】chánglì common practice

【常绿树】chánglùshù evergreen (tree)

【常年】chángnián ① throughout the year; perennial: ～坚持体育锻炼 persist in physical training all the year round ② year in year out ③ average year: 这儿小麦～亩产五百斤。In this area the per mu yield of wheat for an average year is 500 jin.

【常青】chángqīng evergreen

【常情】chángqíng reason; sense: 按照～,他会提出这个问题同你讨论的。It stands to reason that he will take up the matter with you.

【常人】chángrén ordinary person; the man in the street

【常任】chángrèn permanent; standing: 安理会～理事国 permanent member of the Security Council ◇ ～代表 permanent delegate (或 representative)

【常识】chángshí ① general (或 elementary) knowledge: 卫生～ elementary knowledge of hygiene and sanitation/ 安全用电,在我们村已经成了～。How to use electricity safely has become general knowledge in our village. ② common sense: 天冷了要穿得暖一点儿,这是～。It's common sense to dress more warmly when it gets cold.

【常态】chángtài normality; normal behaviour or conditions: 一反～ contrary to one's normal behaviour; contrary to the way sb. usually behaves

【常务】chángwù day-to-day business; routine: 主持～ in charge of day-to-day business ◇ ～委员 member of the standing committee/ ～委员会 standing committee

【常言】chángyán saying: ～道 as the saying goes/ ～说得好 it is well said that

【常用】chángyòng in common use: ～词语 everyday expressions/ ～药材 medicinal herbs most in use

【常驻】chángzhù resident; permanent ◇ ～联合国代表 permanent representative to the United Nations

偿* cháng ① repay; compensate for: ～债 pay (或 discharge) a debt/ 补～损失 compensate for the loss ② meet; fulfil: 得～夙愿 have fulfilled one's long-cherished wish

【偿付】chángfù pay back; pay: 延期～ 〈法〉moratorium

【偿还】chánghuán repay; pay back: ～债务 pay a debt/ 如数～ pay back the exact amount

【偿命】chángmìng pay with one's life (for a murder); a life for a life

【偿清】chángqīng clear off: ～债务 clear off one's debts

裳 cháng skirt (worn in ancient China)
另见 shang

嫦 cháng

【嫦娥】Cháng'é the goddess of the moon (the lady in the legend who swallowed elixir stolen from her husband and flew to the moon)

chǎng

厂* chǎng ① factory; mill; plant; works: 鞋～ shoe factory/ 面粉～ flour mill/ 机床～ machine tool plant/

钢铁～ iron and steel works/ 制糖～ sugar refinery/ 造船～ shipyard ② yard; depot: 煤～ coal yard

【厂房】chǎngfáng ① factory building ② workshop

【厂商】chǎngshāng firm: 承包～ contractor

【厂长】chǎngzhǎng factory director

【厂址】chǎngzhǐ the site (或 location) of a factory: 选择～ choose a site for building a factory

【厂主】chǎngzhǔ factory owner; millowner

场* chǎng ① a place where people gather: 会～ meeting-place/ 战～ battlefield/ 篮球～ basketball court (或 pitch)/ 运动员人～ athletes enter the arena (或 sports field)/ 观众进～ spectators enter the stadium, etc. ② farm: 国营农～ state farm/ 养鸭～ duck farm/ 种马～ stud farm ③ stage: 出～ come on the stage; appear on the scene ④ 〈剧〉scene: 第二幕第三～ Act II, Scene iii ⑤ 〈量〉〔用于文娱体育活动〕: 一～电影 a film show/ 一～球赛 a match; a ball game/ 加演一～ give an extra performance or show/ 第二～两点开始。The second show starts at two. ⑥ 〈物〉field: 电(磁)～ electric (magnetic) field
另见 chǎng

【场地】chǎngdì space; place; site: 比赛～ competition arena; ground; court/ 施工～ construction site/ 由于～有限,他们只展出了部分产品。They displayed only a part of their products because space was limited.

【场合】chǎnghé occasion; situation: 外交～ a diplomatic occasion

【场面】chǎngmiàn ① scene (in drama, fiction, etc.); spectacle: 老工人讲家史的～很感人。The scene in which the old worker tells about his family's history is most moving./ 作者很善于描写大的～。The author is adept in depicting vast scenes. ② occasion; scene: 盛大的～ a grand occasion/ 热烈友好的～ a scene of warm friendship ③ appearance; front; façade: 撑～ keep up appearances

【场所】chǎngsuǒ place; arena: 公共～ a public place/ 娱乐～ place of recreation

敞 chǎng ① spacious: 宽～ spacious; roomy ② open; uncovered/ ～着门 leave the door open; with the door open/ ～着怀 with one's coat or shirt unbuttoned

【敞开】chǎngkāi open wide: 把门～ open the door wide/ ～思想 say what's in (或 on) one's mind; get things off one's chest

【敞亮】chǎngliàng ① light and spacious: 这间屋子很～。This room is light and spacious. ② clear (in one's thinking): 读了这篇社论,心里更～了。After I studied the editorial, things seemed much clearer.

氅 chǎng cloak: 大～ overcoat

chàng

怅 chàng disappointed; sorry: 走访不遇为～。Sorry not to have found you at home.

【怅然】chàngrán disappointed; upset: ～而返 come away disappointed

【怅惘】chàngwǎng distracted; listless

畅 chàng ① smooth; unimpeded: ～行无阻 pass unimpeded/ 流～ easy and smooth; fluent ② free; uninhibited: ～饮 drink one's fill

【畅达】chàngdá fluent; smooth: 译文～。The translation reads smoothly./ 交通～ have a good transport and communications network; be easily accessible

【畅快】chàngkuài free from inhibitions; carefree: 心情～ have ease of mind

【畅所欲言】chàng suǒ yù yán speak without any inhibitions; speak one's mind freely; speak out freely

【畅谈】chàngtán talk freely and to one's heart's content; speak glowingly of: ～国内外大好形势 speak glowingly of the excellent situation at home and abroad

【畅通】chàngtōng unimpeded; unblocked: 前面道路～无阻 open road ahead/ 这里过去是穷乡僻壤,现在铁路公路运

~了。 This formerly inaccessible place can now be reached by road and rail.

【畅销】 chàngxiāo be in great demand; sell well; have a ready market: 中国丝绸～国外。 Chinese silk fabrics sell well on foreign markets./ 秋天是毛织品～的季节。 Autumn is a lively season for the wool market. ◇ ～书 best seller

【畅游】 chàngyóu ① have a good`swim: ～长江 have a good swim in the Changjiang River ② enjoy a sightseeing tour: ～名胜古迹 enjoy a trip to places of historic interest

倡 chàng initiate; advocate: 首～ initiate; start

【倡导】 chàngdǎo initiate; propose: ～和平共处五项原则 initiate the principles of peaceful coexistence

【倡言】 chàngyán <书> propose; initiate

【倡议】 chàngyì propose: ～召开国际会议 propose the calling of an international conference/ 在他的～之下 at his suggestion/ 提出利用废料的～ put forward a proposal to make use of waste material

唱* chàng ① sing ② call; cry: 鸡～三遍。 The cock has crowed for the third time. ③ a song or a singing part of a Chinese opera

【唱对台戏】 chàng duìtáixì put on a rival show; enter into rivalry

【唱反调】 chàng fǎndiào sing a different tune; deliberately speak or act contrary to

【唱高调】 chàng gāodiào use high-flown words; affect a high moral tone

【唱歌】 chànggē sing (a song): 她很会～。 She is a good singer.

【唱和】 chànghè ① one singing a song and the others joining in the chorus: 此唱彼和。 When one starts singing, another joins in. ② one person writing a poem to which one or more other people reply, usu. using the same rhyme sequence

【唱机】 chàngjī gramophone; phonograph: 电～ record player

【唱片】 chàngpiàn gramophone (或 phonograph) record; disc: 放～ play a gramophone record/ 灌～ cut a disc

【唱戏】 chàngxì <口> act in an opera

chāo

抄* chāo ① copy; transcribe: 请把稿件～一下。 Please make a fair copy of the manuscript./ 照～原文 make a verbatim transcription of the original ② plagiarize; lift ③ search and confiscate; make a raid upon: ～土匪的老窝 destroy the bandits' den ④ go (或 walk) off with: 谁把我的字典～走了？ Who's gone off with my dictionary? ⑤ take a shortcut: ～到敌人前面 outstrip the enemy by taking a shortcut ⑥ fold (one's arms): ～着手站在一边 stand by with folded arms ⑦ grab; take up: ～起一把铁锹就干 take up a spade and plunge into the job

【抄本】 chāoběn hand-copied book; transcript: 《红楼梦》～ a handwritten copy of A Dream of Red Mansions

【抄录】 chāolù make a copy of; copy: 这段引文是从报上～来的。 This quotation is taken from a newspaper article.

【抄袭】 chāoxí ① plagiarize; lift: ～行为 (an act of) plagiarism ② borrow indiscriminately from other people's experience ③ launch a surprise attack on the enemy by making a detour

【抄写】 chāoxiě copy; transcribe ◇ ～员 copyist

吵* chāo
另见 chǎo

【吵吵】 chāochao make a row; kick up a racket: 一个一个说，别～。 Speak one at a time. Don't make such a row.

钞* chāo ① bank note; paper money: 现～ cash ② collected writings: 诗～ collected poems

【钞票】 chāopiào bank note; paper money; bill: 五元一张的～ a $5 bill/ ～纸 bank note paper

超* chāo ① exceed; surpass; overtake ② ultra-; super-; extra-: ～高温 superhigh temperature/ ～显微镜 ultra-microscope ③ transcend; go beyond

【超产】 chāochǎn overfulfil a production target (或 quota)

【超车】 chāochē overtake other cars on the road: 不准～! No overtaking!

【超出】 chāochū overstep; go beyond; exceed: ～范围 go beyond the scope (或 bounds)/ ～定额 exceed the quota/ ～预料 exceed one's expectations

【超等】 chāoděng of superior grade; extra fine: ～质量 extra good quality; superfine

【超度】 chāodù <宗> release souls from purgatory; expiate the sins of the dead

【超短裙】 chāoduǎnqún miniskirt

【超额】 chāo'é above quota: ～完成生产指标 overfulfil the production quota; surpass the production target ◇ ～利润 superprofit/ ～剩余价值 excess surplus value

【超过】 chāoguò outstrip; surpass; exceed: ～规定的速度 exceed the speed limit/ ～限度 go beyond the limit/ ～历史最高水平 top all previous records/ ～世界先进水平 surpass advanced world levels/ 有利条件～困难条件 The favourable conditions outweigh the difficulties./ 到会的代表已～百分之九十。 More than 90 per cent of the delegates to the conference have arrived.

【超级】 chāojí super ◇ ～大国 superpower/ ～公路 superhighway/ ～间谍 superspy/ ～商场 supermarket/ ～油轮 supertanker

【超龄】 chāolíng overage

【超群】 chāoqún head and shoulders above all others; preeminent: 武艺～ extremely skilful in martial arts

【超然物外】 chāorán wù wài hold aloof from the world; be above worldly considerations; stay away from the scene of contention

【超人】 chāorén ① be out of the common run: ～的记忆力 exceptionally good memory ② superman

【超速】 chāosù exceed the speed limit

【超脱】 chāotuō ① unconventional; original: 他的字，信笔写来，十分～。 His effortless calligraphy has an unconventional grace of its own. ② be detached; stand (或 hold, keep) aloof: ～现实是不可能的。 It's impossible to detach oneself from reality.

【超逸】 chāoyì unconventionally graceful; free and natural

【超音速】 chāoyīnsù supersonic speed ◇ ～喷气机 superjet/ ～战斗机 supersonic fighter-plane; supersonic fighter

【超越】 chāoyuè surmount; overstep; transcend; surpass: ～障碍 surmount an obstacle/ ～职权范围 go beyond one's terms of reference; overstep one's authority

【超重】 chāozhòng ① overload ② overweight: ～信件 overweight letter/ ～行李 excess luggage

【超重量级】 chāozhòngliàngjí <举重> super-heavyweight

【超自然】 chāozìrán supernatural

剿 chāo <书> plagiarize
另见 jiǎo

【剿袭】 chāoxí plagiarize

cháo

晁 Cháo a surname

巢 cháo nest: 鸟～ bird's nest/ 匪～ nest (或 den) of robbers; bandits' lair

【巢穴】 cháoxué lair; den; nest; hideout: 敌人的～ the enemy's lair

朝 cháo ① court; government: 上～ go to court/ 在～党 party in power; ruling party ② dynasty: 唐～ the Tang Dynasty/ 改～换代 dynastic changes ③ an emperor's reign: 康熙～ during the reign of Emperor Kangxi ④ have an audience with (a king, an emperor, etc.); make a pilgrimage to ⑤ facing; towards: 坐东～西 with a western exposure; facing west / 迈开大步～前走 march ahead with great strides/ ～敌人开火 fire at the enemy/ ～南走 go southward/ 这门～里开还是～外开? Does this door open inwards or outwards?

另见 zhāo

【朝拜】 cháobài pay respects to (a sovereign); pay religious homage to; worship

【朝代】 cháodài dynasty

【朝见】 cháojiàn have an audience with (a king, an emperor, etc.): 进宫～ be presented at court

【朝圣】 cháoshèng ＜宗＞ pilgrimage; hadj

【朝廷】 cháotíng ① royal or imperial court ② royal or imperial government

【朝野】 cháo-yě ① ＜旧＞ the court and the commonalty ② the government and the public

潮* cháo ① tide: 早～ morning tide/ 大(小)～ spring (neap) tide/ 涨(落)～了。 The tide is flowing (ebbing)./ 歌声如～ the sound of songs rising and falling like waves ② (social) upsurge; current; tide: 工～ workers' strike/ 思～ trend of thought ③ damp; moist: 火柴受～了。 The matches have got damp./ 雨季里东西容易返～。 In the rainy season things get damp easily.

【潮流】 cháoliú ① tide; tidal current ② trend: 历史～ historical trend/ 顺应世界之～ adapt oneself to (或 go along with) world trends

【潮气】 cháoqì moisture in the air; damp; humidity: 仓库里～太大,粮食就容易发霉。 The grain is liable to mildew when the humidity in the barn is too high.

【潮湿】 cháoshī moist; damp

【潮水】 cháoshuǐ tidewater; tidal water

【潮汐】 cháoxī morning and evening tides; tide ◇ ～表 tide table/ ～测站 tide station/ ～能 tidal energy

嘲 cháo ridicule; deride: 解～ try to explain things away when ridiculed/ 冷～热讽 freezing irony and burning satire

【嘲讽】 cháofěng sneer at; taunt

【嘲弄】 cháonòng mock; poke fun at: ～历史的人必将被历史所～。 Those who mock history will be mocked by history.

【嘲笑】 cháoxiào ridicule; deride; jeer at; laugh at

cháo

吵 chǎo ① make a noise: 别～! Don't make so much noise! 或 Be quiet!/ ～得慌 terribly noisy; 瞧,孩子被你们～醒了。 Look! You've woken the child with your noise./ 别～他。 Don't disturb him. ② quarrel; wrangle; squabble: 不要为一点小事就～起来。 Don't squabble over trifles./ ～翻了天 kick up a terrific row

另见 chāo

【吵架】 chǎojià quarrel; wrangle; have a row

【吵闹】 chǎonào ① wrangle; kick up a row ② din; hubbub: 院子里一片～声。 A hubbub was heard in the courtyard.

【吵嚷】 chǎorǎng make a racket; shout in confusion; clamour

【吵嘴】 chǎozuǐ quarrel; bicker

炒* chǎo stir-fry; fry; sauté: ～肉丝 stir-fried shredded pork/ ～黄瓜 sautéed cucumber/ ～鸡蛋 scrambled eggs/ 蛋～饭 rice fried with eggs/ 糖～栗子 chestnuts roasted in sand with brown sugar

【炒菜】 chǎocài ① stir-fry; sauté ② a fried dish ③ a dish cooked to order

【炒冷饭】 chǎo lěngfàn heat leftover rice — say or do the same old thing; rehash

【炒面】 chǎomiàn ① chow mein; fried noodles ② parched flour

chē

车* chē ① vehicle: 汽～ motor vehicle; automobile/ 火～ train/ 军用～ army vehicle ② wheeled machine or instrument: 纺～ spinning wheel/ 滑 ～ pulley/ 水～ waterwheel ③ machine: 开～ set the machine going; start the machine/ 停～ stop the machine/ 试～ trial (或 test) run ④ lathe; turn: ～机器零件 lathe a machine part/ ～光 smooth sth. on a lathe ⑤ lift water by waterwheel: 把河里的水～到稻田里 lift water from a river into paddy fields

另见 jū

【车道】 chēdào (traffic) lane

【车队】 chēduì motorcade

【车费】 chēfèi fare

【车祸】 chēhuò traffic (或 road) accident

【车辆】 chēliàng vehicle; car: 来往～ traffic

【车轮】 chēlún wheel (of a vehicle)

【车马费】 chēmǎfèi travel allowance

【车票】 chēpiào train or bus ticket; ticket

【车水马龙】 chēshuǐ-mǎlóng incessant stream of horses and carriages — heavy traffic: 门前～。 The courtyard is thronged with visitors.

【车胎】 chētāi tyre

【车厢】 chēxiāng railway carriage; railroad car

【车站】 chēzhàn station; depot; stop

【车照】 chēzhào licence (of a car, bicycle, etc.)

chě

扯 chě ① pull: 没等他说完,我～着他就走。 Without letting him finish what he had to say, I pulled him away./ ～着嗓子喊 shout at the top of one's voice/ 这是两个问题,不能往一块儿～。 These two questions should not be lumped together. ② tear: 把信～得粉碎 tear a letter to pieces/ ～下假面具 tear off the mask ③ buy (cloth, thread, etc.): ～点儿布 buy some cloth ④ chat; gossip: 我俩好好～一～。 Let's have a good chat./ ～家常 chat about everyday family affairs; chitchat/ 别～远了。 Don't wander from the subject. 或 Stick to the point.

【扯后腿】 chě hòutuǐ hold sb. back (from action); be a drag on sb.; be a hindrance to sb.

【扯谎】 chěhuǎng tell a lie; lie

chè

彻 chè thorough; penetrating: ～夜工作 work all night/ 透～的了解 thorough understanding/ 响～云霄 resounding across the skies

【彻底】 chèdǐ thorough; thoroughgoing: 进行～调查 make a thorough investigation

【彻骨】 chègǔ to the bone: 寒风～。 The bitter wind chills one to the bone.

【彻头彻尾】 chètóu-chèwěi out and out; through and through; downright: ～的骗局 a downright (或 sheer) fraud; deception from beginning to end/ ～的谎言 an absolute lie

【彻夜】 chèyè all night; all through the night: ～不眠 lie awake all night/ 工地上灯火～通明。 The lights were ablaze at the worksite all through the night.

掣 chè ① pull; tug ② draw: 他赶紧～回手去。 He quickly drew back his hand./ ～签 draw lots

【掣肘】 chèzhǒu hold sb. back by the elbow; impede; handicap: 这件事办得很顺利,没有人～。 As there was no one making things difficult for us, we settled the matter smoothly.

澈 chè (of water) clear; limpid

撤 chè ① remove; take away: 把障碍物～了 remove the barrier/ 把盘子、碗～了 clear away the dishes ② withdraw; evacuate: 向后～ withdraw; retreat/ 主动～出 withdraw on one's own initiative/ ～伤员 evacuate the wounded

【撤兵】 chèbīng withdraw troops
【撤除】 chèchú remove; dismantle: ～军事设施 dismantle military installations
【撤换】 chèhuàn dismiss and replace; recall; replace
【撤回】 chèhuí ① recall; withdraw: ～代表 recall a representative/ ～步哨 withdraw the guard ② revoke; retract; withdraw: ～起诉 withdraw charges; revoke a court action/ ～声明 retract a statement
【撤离】 chèlí withdraw from; leave; evacuate: ～阵地 abandon a position/ ～城市 evacuate a city
【撤退】 chètuì withdraw; pull out: ～方向 the line of withdrawal/ ～安全 make good one's retreat
【撤销】 chèxiāo cancel; rescind; revoke: ～其职务 dismiss a person from his post/ 一项决议 annul a decision/ ～处分 rescind (或 annul) a penalty/ 原计划 rescind the original plan/ ～命令 countermand an order/ ～法令 repeal a decree/ ～邀请 withdraw an invitation
【撤职】 chèzhí dismiss (或 discharge) sb. from his post; remove sb. from office: ～查办 discharge sb. from his post and prosecute him
【撤走】 chèzǒu withdraw

chēn

嗔 chēn ① be angry; be displeased: 生～ get angry ② be annoyed (with sb.): 他～着我说错了话。 He was annoyed with me for having said the wrong thing.
【嗔怪】 chēnguài blame; rebuke
【嗔怒】 chēnnù get angry
【嗔色】 chēnsè angry or sullen look: 微露～ look somewhat displeased

瞋 chēn 〈书〉 stare angrily; glare
【瞋目】 chēnmù stare angrily; glare: ～而视 stare at sb. angrily

chén

尘* chén ① dust; dirt: 一～不染 not stained with a particle of dust; spotless ② this world: ～俗 this mortal world
【尘埃】 chén'āi dust
【尘世】 chénshì 〈宗〉 this world; this mortal life
【尘土】 chéntǔ dust: 卡车过处，～飞扬。 The truck sped past raising a cloud of dust.
【尘嚣】 chénxiāo hubbub; uproar

臣* chén official under a feudal ruler; subject: 君～ the monarch and his subjects
【臣民】 chénmín subjects of a feudal ruler
【臣子】 chénzǐ official in feudal times

沉* chén ① sink: 船～了。 The boat has sunk./ ～底儿 sink to the bottom/ 月落星～。 The moon is down and the stars have set. ② [多指抽象事物] keep down; lower: ～下心来 settle down (to one's work, study, etc.); concentrate on one's work, study, etc.)/ 把心一～ put on a grave expression; pull a long face ③ deep; profound: 睡得很～ be in a deep sleep; be fast asleep; sleep like a log ④ heavy: 这只箱子真～! This trunk is heavy!/ 我头有点发～。 My head feels heavy (或 fuzzy).
【沉沉】 chénchén ① heavy: 穗子～地垂下来。 The ears hang heavy on the stalks. ② deep: ～入睡 sink into a deep sleep; 暮气～ lifeless; lethargic; apathetic/ 暮霭～。 Dusk is falling.
【沉淀】 chéndiàn sediment; precipitate: 墨水～了。 There is some sediment in the ink./ 水太浑浊，～一下再用。 The water is muddy; let it settle for a while.
【沉积】 chénjī 〈地〉 deposit: 陆(海)相～ continental (marine) deposit/ 泥沙～河底。 The silt is deposited in the riverbed.
【沉寂】 chénjì ① quiet; still: ～的深夜 in the still of (the)

night/ 傍晚，暴风雨已经过去，四周开始～下来。 By evening the storm had subsided and all was quiet again. ② no news: 消息～。 There has been no news whatsoever.
【沉静】 chénjìng ① quiet; calm: 夜深了，村子里～下来。 It was late at night, and all was quiet in the village. ② calm; serene; placid: ～的神色 a serene look/ 心情～ be in a placid mood
【沉沦】 chénlún sink into (vice, degradation, depravity, etc.)
【沉闷】 chénmèn ① (of weather, atmosphere, etc.) oppressive; depressing ② depressed; in low spirits: 心情～ feel depressed ③ not outgoing; withdrawn: 他这个人很～。 He's rather withdrawn.
【沉迷】 chénmí indulge; wallow: ～在幻想里 indulge in illusions
【沉湎】 chénmiǎn 〈书〉 wallow in; be given to: ～于酒 be given to heavy drinking
【沉没】 chénmò sink: 敌舰被鱼雷击中，立即～。 The enemy warship was torpedoed and sank at once.
【沉默】 chénmò ① reticent; taciturn; uncommunicative: ～寡言的人 a reticent person; a person of few words ② silent: 保持～ remain silent/ 他～了一会又继续说下去。 After a moment's silence he went on speaking.
【沉溺】 chénnì indulge; wallow: ～于声色 wallow in sensual pleasures
【沉睡】 chénshuì be sunk in sleep; be fast asleep
【沉思】 chénsī ponder; meditate; be lost in thought: 为这个问题，她坐在那里～了好久。 She sat there pondering over the problem for a long time.
【沉痛】 chéntòng ① deep feeling of grief or remorse: 怀着～的心情 be deeply grieved/ 表示～的哀悼 express profound condolences/ 他对自己的错误感到十分～。 He felt deep remorse for his error. ② deeply felt; bitter: 应该接受这个～的教训。 It is necessary to learn a lesson from this bitter experience.
【沉陷】 chénxiàn sink; cave in: 地震后路基～了。 The earthquake made the roadbed cave in.
【沉吟】 chényín mutter to oneself, unable to make up one's mind
【沉郁】 chényù depressed; gloomy
【沉重】 chénzhòng ① heavy: ～的脚步 heavy steps/ ～的打击 a heavy blow/ 心情～ with a heavy heart ② serious; critical: 病情～ critically ill
【沉住气】 chénzhùqì keep calm; keep cool; be steady: ～，等敌人靠近了再打。 Steady, don't fire till the enemy come closer./ 不要一听到不同意见就沉不住气。 Don't get excited the moment you hear a differing opinion.
【沉着】 chénzhuó cool-headed; composed; steady; calm: 勇敢～ brave and steady/ ～应战 meet the attack calmly
【沉醉】 chénzuì get drunk; become intoxicated: ～在节日的欢乐里 be intoxicated with the spirit of the festival

忱 chén 〈书〉 sincere feeling; true sentiment: 谢～ thankfulness/ 热～ zeal; warmheartedness

辰 chén ① celestial bodies: 星～ stars ② the fifth of the twelve Earthly Branches ③ any of the traditional twelve two-hour periods of the day 参见 "时辰" shíchen ④ time; day; occasion: 诞～ birthday

陈* chén ① lay out; put on display ② state; explain: 此事当另函详～。 The matter will be explained in detail in a separate letter. ③ old; stale
【陈兵】 chénbīng mass (或 deploy) troops: ～边境 mass troops along the border/ ～百万 deploy a million troops
【陈陈相因】 chén chén xiāng yīn follow a set routine; stay in the same old groove
【陈词滥调】 chéncí-làndiào hackneyed and stereotyped expressions; clichés
【陈腐】 chénfǔ old and decayed; stale; outworn: ～的词句 stale phrases
【陈规】 chénguī outmoded conventions: 打破～，大胆创造 break with outmoded conventions and make bold innovations

【陈规陋习】 chénguī-lòuxí outmoded conventions and bad customs; bad customs and habits
【陈货】 chénhuò old stock; shopworn goods
【陈迹】 chénjī a thing of the past
【陈酒】 chénjiǔ old wine; mellow wine
【陈旧】 chénjiù outmoded; obsolete; old-fashioned; out-of-date: ～的观点 an outmoded notion/ ～的设备 obsolete equipment/ ～的词语 obsolete words and expressions
【陈列】 chénliè display; set out; exhibit: 玻璃柜里～着各种矿物标本。 Ore specimens are on display in showcases. ◇ ～馆 exhibition hall/ ～柜 showcase/ ～品 exhibit/ ～室 exhibition room; showroom
【陈设】 chénshè ① display; set out: 屋子里～着几件工艺品。 There is some artware set out in the room. ② furnishings: 房间里的～朴素大方。 The room was furnished simply and in good taste.
【陈说】 chénshuō state; explain: ～利害 explain the advantages and disadvantages (of a situation, course of action, etc.)

晨* chén morning: 清～ early morning; dawn
【晨光】 chénguāng the light of the early morning sun; dawn: ～熹微 first faint rays of dawn
【晨曦】 chénxī first rays of the morning sun
【晨星】 chénxīng ① stars at dawn: 寥若～ as few as stars at dawn ②〈天〉 morning star

橙* chén
另见 chéng
【橙子】 chénzi orange

chèn

衬 chèn ① line; place sth. underneath: ～着驼绒的大衣 a fleece-lined overcoat/ ～上一层纸 put a piece of paper underneath/ 里面～一件背心 wear a vest underneath ② lining; liner: 领～ collar lining/ 袖～ cuff lining/ 钢～ steel liner/ 管～ liner tube ③ set off: 白雪～着红梅,景色十分美丽。 The red plum blossoms set off by the white snow were a beautiful sight.
【衬裤】 chènkù underpants; pants
【衬裙】 chènqún underskirt; petticoat
【衬衫】 chènshān shirt
【衬托】 chèntuō set off; serve as a foil to
【衬衣】 chènyī underclothes; shirt

称* chèn fit; match; suit: 颜色相～ well matched in colour
另见 chēng
【称身】 chènshēn fit: 这件衣服你穿了挺～的。 This coat fits you perfectly.
【称心】 chènxīn find sth. satisfactory; be gratified: 这辆自行车买得很～。 This bicycle is quite satisfactory — just the thing I want./ 这老人在年青时吃过很多苦, 晚年过得很～。 The old man who had suffered greatly in his youth spent his old age in contentment./ 这个问题解决得好, 双方都～如意。 The problem was solved to the satisfaction of both parties.
【称职】 chènzhí fill a post with credit; be competent

趁* chèn ① take advantage of; avail oneself of: 我想～这个机会讲几句话。 I'd like to take this opportunity to say a few words. ② while: ～他在这儿, 请他跟我们讲讲家乡的变化吧。 While he's here, let's ask him to tell us about the changes in our hometown./ 这面～热吃吧。 Eat the noodles while they are hot.
【趁便】 chènbiàn when it is convenient; at one's convenience: 你回去的时候, ～给我带个口信。 When you go back would you take a message for me?/ 我在回来的路上～去他家看了看。 I dropped in on him on my way home.
【趁火打劫】 chèn huǒ dǎ jié loot a burning house; take advantage of sb.'s misfortune to do him harm
【趁机】 chènjī seize the opportunity of the occasion; seize the

chance: ～捣乱 seize the opportunity to make trouble
【趁空】 chènkòng use one's spare time; avail oneself of leisure time
【趁热打铁】 chèn rè dǎtiě strike while the iron is hot
【趁势】 chènshì take advantage of a favourable situation: 他趁过对方后卫,～把球踢入球门。 He dribbled past the full-back and scored a goal.
【趁早】 chènzǎo as early as possible; before it is too late; at the first opportunity: 我们还是～把活干完, 免得雨淋。 We'd better finish the threshing as soon as possible, in case it rains./ 你脸色不好, ～去看看吧。 You don't look well. You'd better go and see a doctor right away.

讖 chèn 〈书〉 augury
【谶语】 chènyǔ a prophecy believed to have been fulfilled

chēng

称* chēng ① call: 自～ call (或 style) oneself ② name: 俗～ popular name/ 青藏高原素有世界屋脊之～。 The Qinghai-Xizang Plateau has long been known as the roof of the world. ③〈书〉 say; state: 连声～好 say "good, good" again and again/ 据外交部发言人～ according to the Foreign Ministry spokesman ④〈书〉 commend; praise: 这支部队以善于夜战著～。 This unit is famous for night fighting. ⑤ weigh: 用秤～一～
另见 chèn
【称霸】 chēngbà seek hegemony; dominate
【称号】 chēnghào title; name; designation: 她获得了先进工作者的～。 She has won the title of advanced worker.
【称呼】 chēnghu ① call; address: 我该怎么～她? What should I call her? 或 How should I address her? ② form of address
【称快】 chēngkuài express one's gratification: 拍手～ clap one's hands with satisfaction
【称赏】 chēngshǎng extol; speak highly of
【称颂】 chēngsòng praise; extol; eulogize: 人人～他的崇高品德。 Everyone extols his noble qualities.
【称谢】 chēngxiè express one's thanks; thank: ～不止 thank sb. again and again
【称兄道弟】 chēngxiōng-dàodì call each other brothers; be on intimate terms
【称雄】 chēngxióng hold sway over a region; rule the roost: 割据～ break away from central authority and exercise local power; set up separationist rule
【称许】 chēngxǔ praise; commendation: 他的工作博得广大群众的～。 His work won the praise of the broad masses.
【称赞】 chēngzàn praise; acclaim; commend

撑 chēng ① prop up; support: 他一手～起身子, 一手投弹。 He propped himself up on one hand and threw a grenade with the other./ 两手～着下巴 hold one's chin in one's hands ② push or move with a pole: ～船 pole a boat; punt ③ maintain; keep up: 他～不住, 笑了。 He could not help laughing./ 他连着打了两场球, 再打恐怕～不住劲儿了。 I'm afraid he won't be able to go on with another game; he's played two in a row already. ④ open; unfurl: ～伞 open an umbrella/ 把麻袋～开 hold open the sack ⑤ fill to the point of bursting: 我肚子有点～, I'm rather full./ 别装得太多, 把口袋～破了。 Don't stuff the sack too full or it'll burst.
【撑场面】 chēng chǎngmiàn keep up appearances 又作 "撑门面"
【撑持】 chēngchí prop up; shore up; sustain: ～局面 shore up a shaky situation
【撑竿跳高】 chēnggān tiàogāo pole vault; pole jump
【撑腰】 chēngyāo support; back up; bolster up: ～打气 bolster and pep up

瞠 chēng 〈书〉 stare
【瞠乎其后】 chēng hū qí hòu stare helplessly at the vanishing back of the runner ahead — despair of catching up
【瞠目结舌】 chēngmù-jiéshé stare tongue-tied (或 dumbfounded)

chéng

丞 chéng ① assist ② assistant officer (in ancient China): 县～ county magistrate's assistant

【丞相】 chéngxiàng prime minister (in ancient China)

成* chéng ① accomplish; succeed: 事～之后 after this is achieved ② become; turn into: 雪化～水。 Snow melts into water./ 磨～粉末 be ground into powder/ 绿树～荫。 The trees give welcome shade. /他～了水稻专家了。 He's become an expert on paddy rice. ③ achievement; result: 怎能坐享其～? How can one sit idle and enjoy the fruits of others' labour? ④ fully developed; fully grown: ～人 adult ⑤ established; ready-made: 既～事实 established fact; *fait accompli*/ 现～服装 ready-made clothes ⑥ in considerable numbers or amounts: ～千上万的人 tens of thousands of people/ ～排的新房 upon row of new houses/产量～倍增长。 Output has doubled and redoubled. ⑦ all right; O.K.: ～! 就这么办吧。 All right. Let's do it that way. 或 O.K. Go ahead./ 你不去可不～。 No, you must go. ⑧ able; capable: 说起庄稼活,他可真～! When it comes to farm work, he really knows his job. ⑨ one tenth: 增产两～ a 20% increase in output; output increased by 20 per cent

【成败】 chéng-bài success or failure: ～在此一举。 Success or failure hinges on this one action.

【成本】 chéngběn cost: 生产～ production cost/ 固定～ fixed cost/ 可变～ variable cost/ 直接(间接)～ direct (indirect) cost

【成材】 chéngcái ① grow into useful timber; grow to full size ② become a useful person: 不让孩子经风雨见世面,怎么能～呢? How can a child grow up to be useful if he is not allowed to face the world and brave the storm?

【成分】 chéngfèn composition; component part; ingredient: 化学～ chemical composition/ 肥料的～ the composition of a fertilizer

【成功】 chénggōng succeed; success: 大会开得很～。 The congress was a great success./ 试验～了吗? Did the experiment come off all right?/ 这项革新一定能够～。 The innovation is bound to be a success.

【成规】 chéngguī established practice; set rules; groove; rut: 墨守～ stick to conventions; get into a rut

【成果】 chéngguǒ achievement; fruit; gain; positive result: 科研～ achievements in scientific research/ 每一粒粮食都是辛勤劳动的～。 Every single grain is the fruit of hard work./ 会谈取得了一些～。 The talks have yielded some positive results.

【成婚】 chénghūn get married

【成绩】 chéngjì result; achievement; success: 取得了很大的～ have achieved great successes/ 在比赛中取得良好的～ get good results in a tournament/ 学习～优异 do exceedingly well in one's studies/ 在我们的工作中间～是主要的。 Our achievements are the main aspect of our work./ 他们的工作是有～的。 Their work has been fruitful. ◇ ～单 school report; report card

【成家】 chéngjiā ① (of a man) get married: 他才二十五岁,还没有～。 He's not married yet, he's only twenty-five./ ～立业 get married and start one's career

【成见】 chéngjiàn preconceived idea; prejudice: 消除～ dispel prejudices/ 固执～ prejudiced; biased; opinionated

【成交】 chéngjiāo strike a bargain; conclude a transaction; clinch a deal ◇ ～额 volume of business

【成就】 chéngjiù ① achievement; accomplishment; attainment; success: 取得很大的～ achieve great successes/ 他是一个很有～的科学家。 He is an accomplished scientist./ 剧本的艺术～ artistic merits of a play ② achieve; accomplish

【成立】 chénglì ① found; establish; set up: 举行～大会 hold an inaugural meeting ② betenable; hold water: 这个论点不能～。 That argument is untenable (或 does not hold water).

【成眠】 chéngmián 〈书〉 fall asleep; go to sleep: 夜不～ lie awake all night

【成名】 chéngmíng become famous; make a name for oneself

【成名成家】 chéngmíng-chéngjiā establish one's reputation as an authority

【成命】 chéngmìng order already issued: 收回～ countermand (或 retract) an order; revoke a command

【成年】 chéngnián ① grow up; come of age: 未～ be under age ② adult; grown-up: ～人 an adult; a grown-up ③ 〈口〉 year after year: 在外～ be away all year/ ～累月 year in year out; for years on end

【成批】 chéngpī group by group; in batches: ～的新钢材 batches of new-type steel products/ ～生产 serial production; mass production

【成品】 chéngpǐn end (或 finished) product

【成器】 chéngqì grow up to be a useful person

【成亲】 chéngqīn get married

【成全】 chéngquán help (sb. to achieve his aim)

【成群】 chéngqún in groups; in large numbers: 三五～ in threes and fours; in small groups/ ～结队 in crowds; in throngs/ ～的牛羊 herds of cattle and sheep/ ～的蜜蜂 swarms of bees/ ～的对虾 shoals of prawns

【成人】 chéngrén ① grow up; become full-grown: 长大～ be grown to manhood ② adult; grown-up ◇ ～教育 adult education

【成人之美】 chéng rén zhī měi help sb. to fulfil his wish; aid sb. in doing a good deed

【成事】 chéngshì accomplish sth.; succeed: ～不足,败事有余 unable to accomplish anything but liable to spoil everything

【成熟】 chéngshú ripe; mature: 桃子～了。 The peaches are ripe./ 时机～ The time is ripe./ ～的经验 ripe experience/ ～的意见 well-considered opinion

【成套】 chéngtào ① form a complete set: 这些仪器是～的, 不要拆散。 These instruments form a complete set. Don't separate them. ② whole (或 complete) set: ～设备 complete sets of equipment

【成天】 chéngtiān 〈口〉 all day long; all the time

【成为】 chéngwéi become; turn into: 她已经～一个出色的拖拉机手。 She's become an excellent tractor driver.

【成文】 chéngwén ① existing writings: 抄袭～ copy existing writings; follow a set pattern ② written ◇ ～法 written law; statute law

【成问题】 chéng wèntí be a problem; be open to question (或 doubt, objection): 雨再不停, 明天的比赛就要～了。 If the rain doesn't stop, I doubt if we can have the game tomorrow./ 这活干得这样粗, 真～。 The job has been done very carelessly; this is really serious.

【成效】 chéngxiào effect; result: ～显著 produce a marked effect; achieve remarkable success/ ～甚少 achieve little/ 初见～ win initial success/ 这种药连着吃下去一定会有～。 This medicine will be effective if you keep on taking it for a time./ 几年来家庭计划收到了巨大的～。 Family planning has had marked success during the last few years.

【成形】 chéngxíng take shape: 我们的计划开始～了。 Our plan is beginning to take shape.

【成性】 chéngxìng by nature; become sb.'s second nature: 帝国主义侵略～。 Imperialism is aggressive by nature./ 这家伙盗窃～。 Stealing has become that rascal's second nature.

【成因】 chéngyīn cause of formation; contributing factor

【成语】 chéngyǔ 〈语〉 set phrase; idiom: 《英语～词典》 *A Dictionary of English Idioms*

【成员】 chéngyuán member: 领导小组～ a member of the leading group ◇ ～国 member state (或 country)

【成长】 chéngzhǎng grow up; grow to maturity: 新栽的果树正在茁壮～。 The young fruit trees are growing well./ 关心年轻一代的健康～ take an active interest in the healthy growth of the younger generation

【成竹在胸】 chéngzhú zài xiōng 见 "胸有成竹" xiōng yǒu chénɡzhú

呈 chéng ① assume (form, colour, etc.): 叶～椭圆形。 The leaf is oval in shape. ② submit; present ③ petition; memorial

【呈报】 chéngbào submit a report; report a matter: ～上

级机关备案 report the matter to the higher level for the record

【呈递】 chéngdì present; submit: ~国书 present credentials (或 letter of credence)

【呈请】 chéngqǐng apply (to the higher authorities for consideration or approval)

【呈现】 chéngxiàn present (a certain appearance); appear; emerge

【呈献】 chéngxiàn respectfully present

诚*

chéng ① sincere; honest: 开~相见 treat sb. open-heartedly ② 〈书〉 really; actually; indeed: ~非易事 be by no means easy/ ~有此事。 There actually was such a thing.

【诚恳】 chéngkěn sincere

【诚然】 chéngrán true; indeed; to be sure: 旱情~是严重的,但是它吓不倒我们。 True, the drought is serious, but it can't scare us.

【诚实】 chéngshí honest: ~可靠 honest and dependable

【诚心】 chéngxīn sincere desire; wholeheartedness: 一片~ in all sincerity/ ~诚意 earnestly and sincerely

【诚意】 chéngyì good faith; sincerity: 表明~ show one's good faith/ 缺乏~ lack sincerity

【诚挚】 chéngzhì sincere; cordial: ~友好的气氛 a sincere and friendly atmosphere/ ~的谢意 heartfelt thanks/ ~的接待 a cordial reception

承*

chéng ① bear; hold; carry: 那木桥~得住这样重的卡车吗? Can that wooden bridge carry such heavy trucks? ② undertake; contract (to do a job): ~印 undertake the printing of/ ~制棉衣。 We accept orders for padded clothes. ③〈套〉 be indebted (to sb. for a kindness); be granted a favour: ~您过奖。 You flatter me. ④ continue; carry on: 继~ inherit; carry on

【承办】 chéngbàn undertake: ~土木工程 undertake civil engineering projects

【承包】 chéngbāo contract: ~桥梁工程 contract to build a bridge/ ~一万吨水泥的订货 contract for ten thousand tons of cement ◇ ~商 contractor

【承担】 chéngdān bear; undertake; assume: ~一切费用 bear all the costs/ ~由此而产生的一切严重后果 bear responsibility (或 be held responsible) for all the serious consequences arising therefrom/ ~新设备的全部安装任务 undertake to install all the new equipment

【承当】 chéngdāng take; bear: ~责任 bear the responsibility

【承继】 chéngjì ① be adopted as heir to one's uncle ② adopt one's brother's son (as one's heir)

【承接】 chéngjiē ① hold out a vessel to have liquid poured into it ② continue; carry on: ~上文 continued from the preceding paragraph

【承蒙】 chéngméng 〈套〉 be indebted (to sb. for a kindness); be granted a favour: ~热情招待,十分感激。I am very grateful to you for the cordial hospitality you accorded me.

【承诺】 chéngnuò promise to undertake; undertake to do sth: 双方~为进一步开展文化交流创造便利条件。Both sides undertake to facilitate further cultural exchanges.

【承认】 chéngrèn ① admit; acknowledge; recognize: ~错误 admit one's mistake; acknowledge one's fault/ 大家都~这个规划还很不完善。Everybody agreed that the plan was far from perfect. ② give diplomatic recognition; recognize

【承上启下】 chéngshàng-qǐxià form a connecting link between the preceding and the following (as in a piece of writing, etc.)

【承受】 chéngshòu ① bear; support; endure: 这桥能~很大的重量。The bridge can bear a tremendous weight./ 一种种考验 endure every kind of trial ② inherit (a legacy, etc.)

【承袭】 chéngxí ① adopt; follow (a tradition, etc.) ② inherit (a peerage, etc.)

【承先启后】 chéngxiān-qǐhòu inherit the past and usher in the future; serve as a link between past and future

城*

chéng ① city wall; wall: 长~ the Great Wall/ ~外 outside the city wall; outside the city ② city: 内(外)~ inner (outer) city/ 东~ the eastern part of the city

【城堡】 chéngbǎo castle

【城里】 chénglǐ inside the city; in town: ~人 city dwellers; townspeople

【城门】 chéngmén city gate

【城门失火,殃及池鱼】 chéngmén shīhuǒ, yāng jí chí yú when the city gate catches fire, the fish in the moat suffer — in a disturbance innocent bystanders get into trouble

【城市】 chéngshì town; city ◇ ~规划 city planning/ ~环境 urban environment/ ~建设 urban construction/ ~居民 city dwellers; urban population

【城镇】 chéngzhèn cities and towns

乘*

chéng ① ride: ~公共汽车 ride in a bus; go by bus/ ~出租汽车到火车站去 take a taxi to the railway station/ ~火车(飞机、海轮、船)旅行 travel by train (plane, ship, boat)/ 代表团~车前往宾馆。The delegation drove to the guesthouse. ② take advantage of; avail oneself of: ~夜出击 attack under cover of night/ ~敌不备 take the enemy unawares ③ 〈数〉 multiply: 五~三等于十五。Five times three is fifteen. 或 5 multiplied by 3 is 15.

另见 shèng

【乘便】 chéngbiàn when it is convenient; at one's convenience: 请你~把那本书带给我。Please bring me the book whenever it's convenient.

【乘法】 chéngfǎ 〈数〉 multiplication ◇ ~表 multiplication table

【乘风破浪】 chéngfēng-pòlàng ride the wind and cleave the waves; brave the wind and the waves

【乘机】 chéngjī seize the opportunity: ~反攻 seize the opportunity to counterattack

【乘客】 chéngkè passenger

【乘凉】 chéngliáng enjoy the cool; relax in a cool place

【乘人之危】 chéng rén zhī wēi take advantage of sb.'s precarious position

【乘胜】 chéngshèng exploit (或 follow up) a victory: ~追击 follow up a victory with hot pursuit/ ~前进 advance on the crest of a victory; push on in the flush of victory

【乘兴】 chéngxìng while one is in high spirits: ~作了一首诗 improvise a poem while in a joyful mood/ ~而来,兴尽而返 arrive in high spirits and depart after enjoying oneself to one's heart's content/ ~而来,败兴而归 set out cheerfully and return disappointed

【乘虚】 chéngxū take advantage of a weak point (或 an opening) in an opponent's defence; act when sb. is off guard: 在一营佯攻的时候,我们~而入,拿下了敌军司令部。While the first battalion created a diversion, we broke through and captured the enemy headquarters.

盛*

chéng ① fill; ladle: ~饭 fill a bowl with rice/ 把菜~出来 ladle food from the pot; dish out food/ ~汤 ladle out soup/ 缸里~满了酒。The crock is filled with wine. ② hold; contain: 这麻袋可以~一百公斤粮食。This sack can hold more than 100 kg of grain./ 这间屋子太小,~不了这么多东西。The room is too small to hold all these things./ 这个礼堂能~一千人。This hall is big enough for a thousand people.

另见 shèng

【盛器】 chéngqì vessel; receptacle

程*

chéng ① rule; regulation: 章~ rules; constitution/ 规~ rules ② order; procedure: 议~ agenda ③ journey; stage of a journey: 启~ set out on a journey/ 送他一~ accompany him part of the way/ 送了一~又一~ accompany (a guest, traveller, etc.) league after league before parting ④ distance: 行~ distance of travel/ 射~ range (of fire)

【程度】 chéngdù ① level; degree ② extent; degree: 在很大(一定)~上 to a great (certain) extent/ 在不同~上 in varying degrees

【程序】 chéngxù ① order; procedure; course; sequence: 工作~ working procedure/ 法律~ legal procedure/ ~事项 procedural matters/ ~问题 point of order

惩

chéng punish; penalize: 严~敢于入侵之敌 severely

punish any enemy that dares to intrude

【惩罚】 chéngfá punish; penalize: 受到一次严厉的～ pay a severe penalty/ 侵略者受到了应得的～。The aggressors got what they deserved.

【惩戒】 chéngjiè punish sb. to teach him a lesson; discipline sb. as a warning; take disciplinary action against: 吊销执照,以示～ revoke sb.'s licence as a punishment

【惩一儆百】 chéng yī jǐng bǎi punish one to warn a hundred; make an example of sb.

澄 chéng clear; transparent: ～空 a clear, cloudless sky
另见 dèng

【澄清】 chéngqīng ① clear; transparent: 湖水碧绿～。The water of the lake is green and clear. ② clear up; clarify: ～误会 clear up a misunderstanding/ ～事实 clarify some facts/ 要求～ demand clarification
另见 dèngqīng

橙* chéng ① orange ② orange colour: ～黄 orange (colour)
另见 chén

chěng

逞 chěng ① show off; flaunt: ～英雄 pose as a hero/ ～威风 show off one's strength or power; swagger about ② carry out (an evil design); succeed (in a scheme): 得～ succeed in one's schemes ③ indulge; give free rein to: ～性子 be wayward

【逞能】 chěngnéng show off one's skill or ability; parade one's ability: 他的缺点是好～。The trouble with him is that he likes to show off.

【逞强】 chěngqiáng flaunt one's superiority: ～好胜 parade one's superiority and strive to outshine others

【逞凶】 chěngxiōng act violently; act with murderous intent

骋 chěng 〈书〉① gallop: 驰～ gallop about; dash about ② give free rein to

chèng

秤* chèng balance; steelyard: 杆～ steelyard; lever scales/ 台～ platform balance (或 scale)

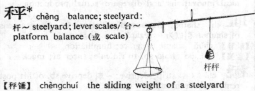

杆秤

【秤锤】 chèngchuí the sliding weight of a steelyard
【秤杆】 chènggǎn the arm (或 beam) of a steelyard
【秤盘】 chèngpán the pan of a steelyard

chī

吃* chī ① eat; take: ～苹果 eat an apple/ ～药 take medicine/ ～糖 have some sweets ② have one's meals; eat: ～馆子 eat in a restaurant; dine out/ ～食堂 have one's meals in the mess ③ live on (或 off): ～利钱 live on interest ④ annihilate; wipe out ⑤ exhaust; be a strain: 感到～力 feel the strain (of work, etc.); find a job difficult ⑥ absorb; soak up: 这种纸不～墨。This kind of paper does not absorb ink. ⑦ suffer; incur: 腿上～了一枪 get shot in the leg/ 连～败仗 suffer one defeat after another

【吃不下】 chībuxià not feel like eating; be unable to eat any more: 他不太舒服,～。He's not very well; he doesn't feel like eating./ 谢谢,我实在～了。Thanks, but I really can't eat any more. 或 Thanks, I've really had enough.

【吃不消】 chībuxiāo be unable to stand (exertion, fatigue, etc.): 走这么多的路恐怕你～。It may be too much for you

to walk such a long way./ 这文章写得又长又难懂,真让看的人～。No reader can put up with such a long and difficult article.

【吃醋】 chīcù be jealous (usu. of a rival in love)

【吃得下】 chīdexià be able to eat: 还有一点,你～吗? There's still a bit left. Can you eat some more?/ 她已经好多了,饭也～了。She's much better; she's got an appetite now.

【吃得消】 chīdexiāo be able to stand (exertion, fatigue, etc.): 再干一个夜班,我也完全～。I can easily stand working another night shift. 或 I'm certainly good for another night shift. 高空飞行,要身体结实才～。One needs a strong physique for high altitude flying.

【吃饭】 chīfàn ① eat; have a meal: 吃了饭再走吧! Don't go. Stay for dinner. ② keep alive; make a living: 靠打猎～ make a living by hunting

【吃喝玩乐】 chī-hē-wán-lè eat, drink and be merry — idle away one's time in pleasure-seeking

【吃惊】 chījīng be startled; be shocked; be amazed; be taken aback: 大吃一惊 be flabbergasted/他那坚强的毅力使人～。His will power is amazing.

【吃苦】 chīkǔ bear hardships: 耐劳 bear hardships and stand hard work/ ～在前,享乐在后 be the first to bear hardships and the last to enjoy comforts

【吃苦头】 chī kǔtou suffer: 蛮干是要～的。If you act rashly you'll suffer for it./ 要给敌人吃点苦头。We'll make the enemy suffer.

【吃亏】 chīkuī ① suffer losses; come to grief; get the worst of it: 有备才能无患,无备必定～。If one is prepared, one will be safe; if not, one will suffer. 或 Preparedness ensures security; unpreparedness invites disaster./ 有的人～,就在于不老实。Some people come to grief on account of their dishonesty.

【吃里扒外】 chīlǐ-páwài live off one person while secretly helping another

【吃力】 chīlì entail strenuous effort; be a strain: 他身体好,干这点儿活不算～。He's strong; this bit of work won't be too much for him./ ～不讨好的差使 a thankless task

【吃零嘴】 chī língzuǐ take snacks between meals; nibble between meals

【吃奶】 chīnǎi suck the breast: ～的孩子 sucking child; suckling/ 使尽～的力气 strain every muscle

【吃软不吃硬】 chīruǎn bù chīyìng be open to persuasion, but not to coercion

【吃水】 chīshuǐ ① drinking water:过去这里～很困难。It used to be difficult to get drinking water here. ② absorb water: 这块地不～。This plot of land absorbs little water./ 这种大米～。You need a lot of water in cooking this kind of rice.

【吃素】 chīsù abstain from eating meat; be a vegetarian

【吃闲饭】 chī xiánfàn lead an idle life; be a loafer or sponger

【吃香】 chīxiāng 〈口〉 be very popular; be much sought after; be well-liked: 这种花布在群众中很～。This kind of cotton print is very popular.

【吃斋】 chīzhāi practise abstinence from meat (as a religious exercise); be a vegetarian for religious reasons

【吃重】 chīzhòng arduous; strenuous: 这个任务很～。This is a hard job. 或 The task is arduous.

哧 chī 〈象〉: ～的一声斯下一块布来 rip off a piece of cloth with a sharp tearing sound/ ～～地笑 titter

笞 chī 〈书〉beat with a stick, cane, etc.: 鞭～ flog; whip

痴 chī ① silly; idiotic: 白～ idiot ② crazy about: 书～ bookworm ③〈方〉insane; mad: ～子 madman

【痴呆】 chīdāi dull-witted; stupid
【痴肥】 chīféi abnormally fat; obese
【痴迷】 chīmí infatuated; obsessed; crazy
【痴情】 chīqíng unreasoning passion; infatuation
【痴人说梦】 chīrén shuō mèng idiotic nonsense; lunatic ravings
【痴想】 chīxiǎng wishful thinking; illusion

【痴心】 chīxīn infatuation: 一片～ sheer infatuation
【痴心妄想】 chīxīn-wàngxiǎng wishful thinking; fond dream

嗤 chī sneer

【嗤笑】 chīxiào laugh at; sneer at
【嗤之以鼻】 chī zhī yǐ bí give a snort of contempt; despise

chí

池* chí ① pool; pond: 游泳～ swimming pool/ 养鱼～ fishpond ② an enclosed space with raised sides: 花～ flower bed/ 舞～ dance floor/ 乐～ orchestra pit ③ stalls (in a theatre): 一座 the stalls

【池塘】 chítáng pond; pool

弛 chí 〈书〉relax; slacken: 一张一～ tension alternating with relaxation

【弛缓】 chíhuǎn relax; calm down: 他听了这一番话,紧张的心情渐渐～下来。On hearing this he calmed down.

驰 chí ① speed; gallop: 一辆汽车飞～而过。A car sped past. ② spread: ～名 well-known ③ 〈书〉turn eagerly towards: 心～神往 let one's thoughts fly to (a place or person); long for

【驰骋】 chíchěng 〈书〉 gallop: ～在辽阔的原野上 gallop across the vast plain/ ～文坛 play an outstanding role in the literary world; bestride the literary stage
【驰名】 chímíng known far and wide; well-known; famous; renowned: 世界～的万里长城 the world-famous Great Wall
【驰援】 chíyuán rush to the rescue

迟* chí ① slow; tardy: ～于作复,歉甚。I'm sorry I have not been able to reply sooner. ② late: 对不起,来～了。I'm sorry I'm late.

【迟迟】 chíchí slow; tardy: ～不表态 not state one's position even after stalling for a long time/ 他为什么～不来? Why is he taking so long to come?
【迟到】 chídào be (或 come, arrive) late: ～五分钟 be five minutes late/ 上班从不～ never be late for work
【迟钝】 chídùn slow (in thought or action); obtuse: 反应～ be slow in reacting; react slowly
【迟缓】 chíhuǎn slow; tardy; sluggish: 进展～ make slow progress/ 行动～ act slowly/ 这件事要赶快办,不能～。This must be done at once. There must be no delay.
【迟慢】 chímàn slow; tardy
【迟暮】 chímù 〈书〉past one's prime; late in one's life
【迟误】 chíwù delay; procrastinate: 不得～ admit of no delay
【迟疑】 chíyí hesitate: ～不决 hesitate to make a decision; be irresolute; be undecided/ 毫不～地接受了任务 accept an assignment without hesitation
【迟早】 chízǎo sooner or later

持* chí ① hold; grasp: ～枪 hold a gun/ ～相反意见 hold a contrary opinion/ ～保留态度 have reservations/ ～不同政见者 dissident ② support; maintain: 支～ support; sustain; 维～ keep; maintain ③ manage; run: 主～ take charge of; manage/ 操～ manage; handle ④ oppose: 相～不下 be locked in stalemate

【持久】 chíjiǔ lasting; enduring; protracted: 作～打算 plan on a long-term basis
【持续】 chíxù continued; sustained: 生产～跃进 continued leap forward in production/ 使原油产量～稳定上升 keep up a steady increase in the output of crude oil/ 两国的文化交流已经～了一千多年。Cultural interchange between the two countries has gone on for more than a thousand years.
【持有】 chíyǒu hold: ～护照 hold a passport/ ～不同意见 hold differing views
【持之以恒】 chí zhī yǐ héng persevere: 刻苦学习,～ study assiduously and perseveringly

【持之有故】 chí zhī yǒu gù have sufficient grounds for one's views
【持重】 chízhòng prudent; cautious; discreet: 老成～ experienced and prudent

匙* chí spoon: 汤～ soup spoon/ 茶～ teaspoon
另见 shi

踟 chí

【踟蹰】 chíchú hesitate; waver: ～不前 hesitate to move forward

chǐ

尺* chǐ ① chi, a unit of length (=¹/₃ metre) ② rule; ruler: 折～ folding rule/ 丁字～ T-square ③ an instrument in the shape of a ruler: 计算～ slide rule/ 镇～ bronze paperweight

计算尺

【尺寸】 chǐcun measurement; dimensions; size: 衣服的～ measurements of a garment/ 量～ take sb.'s measurements/ 这块木板～正好。This board is just the right size
【尺度】 chǐdù yardstick; measure; scale
【尺码】 chǐmǎ size; measures: 你穿多大～的鞋子? What size shoes do you wear?

齿* chǐ ① tooth ② a tooth-like part of anything: 梳～儿 the teeth of a comb/ 锯～儿 the teeth of a saw ③ 〈书〉age: 稚～ very young ④ 〈书〉mention: 不足挂～ not worth mentioning

【齿轮】 chǐlún gear wheel; gear: 正～ spur gear/ 斜～ helical gear/ 伞～ bevel gear

侈 chǐ 〈书〉① wasteful; extravagant ② exaggerate

【侈谈】 chǐtán talk glibly about; prate about; prattle about: ～永久和平 prate about eternal peace/ 不能脱离生产实际去～技术革新。One should not prattle about technical innovations and disregard actual production.

耻* chǐ shame; disgrace; humiliation: 知～ have a sense of shame/ 引以为～ regard as a disgrace

【耻辱】 chǐrǔ shame; disgrace; humiliation
【耻笑】 chǐxiào hold sb. to ridicule; sneer at; mock

褫 chǐ 〈书〉strip; deprive: ～职 deprive sb. of his post; remove sb. from office

【褫夺】 chǐduó strip; deprive: ～公权 deprive sb. of civil rights

chì

叱 chì 〈书〉loudly rebuke; shout at: 怒～ shout angrily at sb.

【叱喝】 chìhè shout at; bawl at
【叱骂】 chìmà scold roundly; curse; abuse
【叱责】 chìzé scold; upbraid; rebuke
【叱咤风云】 chìzhà fēngyún commanding the wind and the clouds; shaking heaven and earth; all-powerful: ～的英雄气概 earthshaking heroism

斥 chì ① upbraid; scold; denounce; reprimand: 痛～ vehemently denounce ② repel; exclude; oust: ～逐 expel; oust; drive away/ 同电相～。Two like electric charges repel each other.

【斥骂】 chìmà reproach; upbraid; scold
【斥退】 chìtuì ① 〈旧〉dismiss sb. from his post ② 〈旧〉expel from a school ③ shout at sb. to go away

【斥责】 chìzé reprimand; rebuke; denounce: 厉声～ severely reprimand; excoriate

赤* chì ① red: 面红耳～ get red in the face; be flushed (with excitement, shame or shyness) ② loyal; sincere; single-hearted: ～心 loyalty; sincerity ③ bare: ～背 bare-backed/ ～身露体 naked

【赤诚】 chìchéng absolute sincerity: ～待人 treat people with absolute sincerity

【赤胆忠心】 chìdǎn-zhōngxīn utter devotion; wholeheartedness; loyalty: ～为人民 serve the people with utter devotion

【赤道】 chìdào ① the equator ② 〈天〉 the celestial equator

【赤脚】 chìjiǎo barefoot

【赤露】 chìlù bare: ～着胸口 with bared chest

【赤裸裸】 chìluǒluǒ ① without a stitch of clothing; stark-naked ② undisguised; naked; out-and-out: ～的勾结 undisguised collusion/ ～的强盗行径 plain robbery/ ～的侵略 naked aggression

【赤手空拳】 chìshǒu-kōngquán bare-handed; unarmed

【赤条条】 chìtiáotiáo have not a stitch on; be stark-naked

【赤字】 chìzì deficit: ～开支 deficit spending/ 财政 (贸易) ～ financial (trade) deficit/ 弥补～ make up (或 meet) a deficit

【赤足】 chìzú barefoot

炽 chì flaming; ablaze

【炽烈】 chìliè burning fiercely; flaming; blazing: 炉火～。 The stove is burning fiercely./ ～的气氛 a fervent atmosphere

【炽盛】 chìshèng flaming; ablaze; flourishing: 火势～。 The fire is blazing.

翅* chì ① wing ② shark's fin

【翅膀】 chìbǎng wing

啻 chì 〈书〉 only

chōng

冲* chōng ① pour boiling water on: ～茶 make tea ② rinse; flush: 把盘子～一～ rinse the plates/ 便后～水。 Flush the toilet after use./ 秧苗给大水～走了。 The seedlings were washed away by the flood. ③ charge; rush; dash: 向敌人～去 charge the enemy ④ clash; collide: ～突 conflict ⑤ thoroughfare; important place: 要～ hub

【冲冲】 chōngchōng in a state of excitement: 怒气～ in a great rage/ 兴～ bursting with enthusiasm; in high spirits

【冲淡】 chōngdàn ① dilute: 把溶液～ dilute the solution ② water down; weaken; play down

【冲动】 chōngdòng ① impulse: 出于一时～ act on impulse ② get excited; be impetuous: 他很容易～。 He easily gets excited.

【冲锋】 chōngfēng charge; assault: 打退敌人的～ beat back the enemy assault

【冲锋陷阵】 chōngfēng-xiànzhèn charge and shatter enemy positions; charge the enemy lines; charge forward

【冲服】 chōngfú take (medicine) after mixing it with water, wine, etc.

【冲昏头脑】 chōnghūn tóunǎo turn sb.'s head: 胜利～ dizzy with success

【冲击】 chōngjī lash; pound: 海浪～着礁石,飞起象珠子般的水花。 The waves lashed at the rocks, sending up pearly spray.

【冲口而出】 chōng kǒu ér chū say sth. unthinkingly; blurt sth. out

【冲垮】 chōngkuǎ burst; shatter: ～敌军防线 shatter the enemy lines

【冲力】 chōnglì impulsive force; momentum

【冲破】 chōngpò break through; breach: ～重重障碍 break through one barrier after another; surmount all obstacles/ ～敌军包围 break through the enemy encirclement/ ～传统观念的束缚 smash the bonds of tradition

【冲散】 chōngsàn break up; scatter; disperse: ～人群 disperse a crowd

【冲杀】 chōngshā charge; rush ahead

【冲晒】 chōngshài 〈摄〉 develop and print

【冲塌】 chōngtā (of floodwater, etc.) cause to collapse; burst: ～堤坝 burst dykes and dams/ ～房屋 dash against the houses and wash them away

【冲天】 chōngtiān towering; soaring: ～干劲 boundless enthusiasm/ 怒气～ in a towering rage

【冲突】 chōngtū conflict; clash: 武装～ an armed conflict/ 边境～ a border clash/利害～ conflict of interests/ 这两个会的时间～了。 The two meetings clash.

【冲洗】 chōngxǐ ① rinse; wash: 用消毒药水～伤口 wash a wound with a disinfectant ② 〈摄〉 develop

【冲撞】 chōngzhuàng ① collide; bump; ram: 渔船遭到敌舰的～。 The fishing boat was rammed by an enemy warship. ② give offence; offend: 我没想到这句话竟～了他。 I didn't expect him to take offence at that remark.

充* chōng ① sufficient; full: 供应～分 have ample supplies ② fill; charge: ～电 charge (a battery) ③ serve as; act as: ～向导 serve as a guide ④ pretend to be; pose as; pass sth. off as: ～内行 pretend to be an expert/ ～好汉 pose as a hero

【充斥】 chōngchì flood; congest; be full of

【充当】 chōngdāng serve as; act as; play the part of: ～翻译 act as interpreter

【充分】 chōngfèn full; ample; abundant: ～协商 full consultation/ ～证据 ample evidence/ 利用～ fully utilize; make full use of; turn to full account/ 我们有～理由相信这消息是可靠的。 We have every reason to believe that the news is true.

【充公】 chōnggōng confiscate

【充饥】 chōngjī allay (或 appease) one's hunger

【充满】 chōngmǎn full of; brimming with; permeated (或 imbued) with: 屋子里～着阳光。 The room is full of sunshine./ 大厅里～了孩子们的欢笑声 The hall resounded with the laughter of children./ ～热情的讲话 a speech brimming with warmth

【充沛】 chōngpèi plentiful; abundant; full of: 雨水～ abundant rainfall/ 精力～ full of vim and vigour; vigorous; energetic

【充其量】 chōngqíliàng at most; at best: 这点给养～只够维持三天。 The provisions can last three days at most./ ～十天就可以完成这项任务。 The job will be finished in ten days at most.

【充任】 chōngrèn fill the post of: hold the position of

【充塞】 chōngsè fill (up); cram

【充实】 chōngshí ① substantial; rich: 内容～ substantial in content ② substantiate; enrich; replenish: ～论据 substantiate one's argument/ ～库存 replenish the stocks

【充裕】 chōngyù abundant; ample; plentiful: 时间～ have ample (或 plenty of) time/ 经济～ well-off

【充足】 chōngzú adequate; sufficient; abundant; ample: 经费～ have sufficient (或 ample) funds/ 阳光～ full of sunshine; sunny

忡 chōng

【忡忡】 chōngchōng laden with anxiety; careworn: 忧心～ heavyhearted; deeply worried

舂 chōng pound; pestle: ～米 husk rice with mortar and pestle/ ～药 pound medicinal herbs in a mortar

憧 chōng

【憧憧】 chōngchōng flickering; moving: 树影～ flickering shadows of trees/ 人影～ shadows of people moving about

【憧憬】 chōngjǐng long for; look forward to

chóng

虫* chóng insect; worm

【虫害】 chónghài insect pest

重* chóng ① repeat; duplicate: 这两个例子～了。These two examples duplicate each other./ 书买～了。Two copies of the same book have been bought by mistake. ② again; once more: ～启战端 renew hostilities ③ layer: 越过万～山 climb over countless mountains
另见 zhòng

【重重】 chóngchóng layer upon layer; ring upon ring: 敌人陷入～包围之中。The enemy was encircled ring upon ring./ 克服～困难 overcome one difficulty after another; surmount numerous difficulties/ 受到～剥削 be fleeced right and left/ 顾虑～ full of misgivings

【重蹈覆辙】 chóng dǎo fùzhé follow the same old disastrous road

【重迭】 chóngdié one on top of another; overlapping: 山峦～ range upon range of mountains/ 精简～的行政机构 simplify overlapping administrative organizations

【重返】 chóngfǎn return: ～前线 go back to the front/ ～家园 return to one's homeland

【重犯】 chóngfàn repeat (an error or offence): 吸取教训,避免～错误 draw a lesson from past errors so as to prevent their recurrence

【重逢】 chóngféng meet again; have a reunion: 久别～ meet again after a long separation/ 旧友～ reunion of old friends

【重复】 chóngfù repeat; duplicate: 避免不必要的～ avoid unnecessary repetition/ 任何历史现象都不会是简单的～。No historical phenomenon is a mere repetition of the past.

【重婚】 chónghūn 〈法〉 bigamy

【重见天日】 chóng jiàn tiānrì once more see the light of day — be delivered from oppression or persecution

【重建】 chóngjiàn rebuild; reconstruct; reestablish; rehabilitate: 战后的～工作 postwar reconstruction/ ～家园 rehabilitate one's homeland; rebuild one's home village or town

【重起炉灶】 chóng qǐ lúzào begin all over again; make a fresh start

【重申】 chóngshēn reaffirm; reiterate; restate: ～前令 reaffirm an existing decree

【重施故技】 chóng shī gùjì play the same old trick; repeat a stock trick

【重孙】 chóngsūn great-grandson

【重孙女】 chóngsūnnǚ great-granddaughter

【重弹老调】 chóng tán lǎodiào harp on the same string; sing the same old tune

【重提】 chóngtí bring up again: 旧事～ bring up an old case; recall past events

【重围】 chóngwéi tight encirclement: 杀出～ break through a tight encirclement

【重温旧梦】 chóng wēn jiùmèng revive an old dream; relive an old experience

【重新】 chóngxīn 〈副〉 again; anew; afresh: ～做人 begin one's life anew; turn over a new leaf/ ～考虑 reconsider

【重修旧好】 chóng xiū jiùhǎo renew cordial relations; become reconciled; bury the hatchet

【重演】 chóngyǎn ① put on an old play, etc. ② recur; reenact; repeat: 历史的错误不许～。Past mistakes should not be repeated.

【重振军威】 chóng zhèn jūnwēi restore the prestige of an army; make an army's might felt once again

【重整旗鼓】 chóng zhěng qígǔ rally one's forces (after a defeat)

崇 chóng ① high; lofty; sublime: 山峻岭 high mountain ridges ② esteem; worship: ～洋迷外 worship and have blind faith in things foreign

【崇拜】 chóngbài worship; adore: ～偶像 worship of idols; idolatry

【崇奉】 chóngfèng believe in (a religion); worship

【崇高】 chónggāo lofty; sublime; high: ～的理想 a lofty ideal/ ～的威望 high prestige

【崇敬】 chóngjìng esteem; respect; revere: 怀着十分～的心情 cherish a feeling of great reverence for

【崇尚】 chóngshàng uphold; advocate: ～勤俭 advocate

industry and thrift

chǒng

宠 chǒng dote on; bestow favour on: 得～ find favour with sb.; be in sb.'s good graces/ 失～ fall out of favour/ 别把孩子～坏了。Don't spoil the child.

【宠爱】 chǒng'ài make a pet of sb.; dote on

【宠儿】 chǒng'ér pet; favourite

【宠信】 chǒngxìn be specially fond of and trust unduly (a subordinate)

chōu

抽* chōu ① take out (from in between): 从文件夹里～出一份申请书 take an application out of the file ② take (a part from a whole): 开会前请～时间把文件看一下。Try and find time to read the document before the meeting. ③ (of certain plants) put forth: ～枝 branch out; sprout/ 小树～出了嫩芽。The saplings are budding. ④ obtain by drawing, etc.: ～水 pump water/ ～血 draw blood (for a test or transfusion) ⑤ shrink: 这种布一洗就～。This cloth shrinks in the wash. ⑥ lash; whip; thrash

【抽筋】 chōujīn ① pull out a tendon ② 〈口〉 cramp: 腿～ have a cramp in the leg

【抽空】 chōukòng manage to find time: 他工作很忙,可是还～学习英语。Despite the pressure of work, he manages to find time to study English./ 抽不出空来 be unable to find time 又作"抽功夫"

【抽签】 chōuqiān draw (或 cast) lots

【抽身】 chōushēn leave (one's work); get away: 我七点钟以前恐怕抽不出身来。I'm afraid I'll be tied up until 7 o'clock. / I'm afraid I won't be free until 7 o'clock.

【抽水】 chōushuǐ draw (或 pump) water: 从河里～ pump water from a river
◇ ～机 water pump/ ～马桶 flush toilet; water closet/ ～站 pumping station

【抽税】 chōushuì levy a tax

【抽屉】 chōuti drawer

【抽象】 chōuxiàng abstract: ～的概念 an abstract concept/ 科学的～ scientific abstraction/ 不要这样～地谈问题。Don't speak in such abstract terms./ 从客观事物中～出正确的结论 draw a correct conclusion from objective facts

【抽烟】 chōuyān smoke (a cigarette or a pipe): 你～吗? Do you smoke?

【抽样】 chōuyàng 〈统计〉 sample; sampling: 随机～ random sampling

chóu

仇* chóu ① enemy; foe: 亲痛～快 sadden one's friends and gladden one's enemies ② hatred; enmity: 有～ have a score to settle/ 记～ nurse a grievance
另见 Qiú

【仇敌】 chóudí foe; enemy

【仇恨】 chóuhèn hatred; enmity; hostility: 满腔～ seething with hatred

【仇人】 chóurén personal enemy: ～相见,分外眼红。When enemies come face to face, their eyes blaze with hate.

【仇杀】 chóushā kill in revenge

【仇视】 chóushì regard as an enemy; look upon with hatred; be hostile to

惆 chóu

【惆怅】 chóuchàng disconsolate; melancholy

绸 chóu silk fabric; silk: ～伞 silk parasol

【绸缎】 chóuduàn silks and satins

【绸缪】 chóumóu ① sentimentally attached: 情意～ be head over heels in love ② 见 "未雨绸缪" wèi yǔ chóumóu

愁* chóu worry; be anxious: 不～吃,不～穿 not have

to worry about food and clothing/ 你别~，病人很快会好的。Don't worry. The patient will soon recover.

【愁肠】 chóucháng pent-up feelings of sadness: ~百结 weighed down with anxiety; with anxiety gnawing at one's heart

【愁苦】 chóukǔ anxiety; distress

【愁眉】 chóuméi knitted brows; worried look: ~不展 with a worried frown/ ~苦脸 have a worried look; pull a long face

【愁闷】 chóumèn feel gloomy; be in low spirits; be depressed

【愁容】 chóuróng worried look; anxious expression: ~满面 look extremely worried

稠 chóu ①thick: 粥很~。The porridge is very thick. ②dense: 地窄人~ small in area but densely populated

【稠密】 chóumì dense: 人烟~ densely populated; populous/ 交通网~ a dense communications network

酬 chóu ①〈书〉propose a toast; toast ②reward; payment: 稿~ payment for an article or book written ③friendly exchange ④fulfil; realize: 壮志未~ with one's lofty aspirations unrealized

【酬报】 chóubào requite; reward; repay; recompense

【酬答】 chóudá ①thank sb. with a gift ②respond with a poem or speech

【酬金】 chóujīn monetary reward; remuneration

【酬劳】 chóuláo recompense; reward

【酬谢】 chóuxiè thank sb. with a gift

【酬酢】 chóuzuò 〈书〉①exchange of toasts ②friendly intercourse

筹 chóu ①chip; counter: 竹~ bamboo chips ②prepare; plan: 统~ over-all planning/ ~款 raise money (或 funds)

【筹办】 chóubàn make preparations; make arrangements: 这次越野赛跑由我们厂负责~。Our factory is to make arrangements for the cross-country race.

【筹备】 chóubèi prepare; arrange: ~建校事宜 make preparations for the setting up of a school ◇ ~工作 preparatory work; preparations/ ~会议 preparatory (或 preliminary) meeting/ ~委员会 preparatory committee

【筹划】 chóuhuà plan and prepare: 这里正在~建设一座水力发电站。Plans are being drawn up to build a hydroelectric station here.

【筹建】 chóujiàn prepare to construct or establish sth.: 这个车间从去年开始~。Preparations were started last year for the construction of the workshop./ ~研究所 make preparations for the setting up of a research institute

【筹募】 chóumù collect (funds)

踌 chóu

【踌躇】 chóuchú hesitate; shilly-shally: ~不前 hesitate to move forward; hesitate to make a move

【踌躇满志】 chóuchú mǎn zhì enormously proud of one's success; smug; complacent

chǒu

丑* chǒu ①ugly; unsightly; hideous: 长得不~ not bad-looking ②disgraceful; shameful; scandalous: 出~ make a fool of oneself ③clown in Beijing opera, etc. ④the second of the twelve Earthly Branches

【丑八怪】 chǒubāguài 〈口〉a very ugly person

【丑恶】 chǒu'è ugly; repulsive; hideous: ~灵魂 an ugly soul/ ~面目 ugly features/ ~表演 a disgusting performance

【丑化】 chǒuhuà smear; uglify; defame; vilify

【丑角】 chǒujué clown; buffoon

【丑陋】 chǒulòu ugly

【丑事】 chǒushì scandal

【丑态】 chǒutài ugly (或 ludicrous) performance; buffoonery: ~百出 act like a buffoon; cut a contemptible figure

【丑闻】 chǒuwén scandal

chòu

臭* chòu ①smelly; foul; stinking: ~味 stink; offensive odour; foul smell/ ~鸡蛋 a rotten egg/ ~不可闻 give off an unbearable stink ②disgusting; disgraceful: 摆~架子 put on nauseating airs
另见 xiù

【臭虫】 chòuchóng bedbug

【臭骂】 chòumà curse roundly; scold angrily and abusively: 挨了一顿~ get a tongue-lashing; get a dressing down

【臭名远扬】 chòumíng yuǎn yáng notorious

【臭名昭著】 chòumíng zhāozhù of ill repute; notorious

【臭气】 chòuqì bad (或 offensive) smell; stink: ~熏天 stink

chū

出* chū ①go or come out: ~城 go out of town/ ~狱 be released from prison ②exceed; go beyond: ~月 after this month; next month/ 不~三年 within three years ③issue; put up: ~证明 issue a certificate/ ~考题 set the paper; set the examination questions/ ~主意 offer advice; supply ideas; make suggestions/ ~布告 put up a notice ④produce; turn out: 多~煤，~好煤 produce more coal and good coal, too/ 实践~真知。Genuine knowledge comes from practice./ 我们部队~过不少战斗英雄。Our unit has produced quite a few combat heroes. ⑤arise; happen: 这事~在三十年前。It happened thirty years ago./ 问题~在哪里 go wrong; go amiss/ 防止~事故 prevent accidents ⑥rise well (with cooking): 这种米~饭。This kind of rice rises well when it's cooked. ⑦put forth; vent: ~芽 put forth buds; sprout/ ~气 vent one's spleen/ ~疹子 have measles ⑧pay out; expend: 量入为~ keep expenditures within the limits of income; cut one's coat according to one's cloth/ 入不敷~ one's income falling short of one's expenditure; unable to make both ends meet ⑨a dramatic piece: 一~戏 an opera; a play

出 chu 〔用于动词之后，表示向外、显露或完成〕：从大厅里走~ come out of the hall/ 拿~证件 produce one's papers/ 派~代表团参加会议 send a delegation to attend a conference/ 看~问题 see where the problem lies; realize that there's something wrong/ 做~成绩 achieve (good) results

【出版】 chūbǎn come off the press; publish; come out: 这本书什么时候~? When will the book be published? ◇ ~社 publishing house/ ~物 publication/ ~自由 freedom of the press

【出殡】 chūbìn carry a coffin to the cemetery; hold a funeral procession

【出兵】 chūbīng dispatch troops

【出差】 chūchāi be away on official business; be on a business trip

【出产】 chūchǎn produce; manufacture: 江西景德镇~精美的瓷器。Jingdezhen in Jiangxi Province produces fine porcelain.

【出厂】 chūchǎng (of products) leave the factory ◇ ~价格 producer price; ex-factory price/ ~日期 date of production (或 manufacture)

【出场】 chūchǎng ①come on the stage; appear on the scene: 他们是今晚~的演员。They are the actors and actresses appearing tonight. ②enter the arena: ~的运动员名单 list of players for the match

【出超】 chūchāo favourable balance of trade

【出车】 chūchē ①dispatch a vehicle: 公共汽车早五点~。Bus service starts at 5 a.m. ②be out driving a vehicle: 老王~了。Lao Wang is out with the car.

【出丑】 chūchǒu make a fool of oneself; bring shame on oneself: 当众~ make a fool of oneself before others

【出处】 chūchù source (of a quotation or allusion): 注明~ indicate the source; give references

【出动】 chūdòng ①set out; start off ②send out; dispatch: ~军舰 dispatch warships

【出尔反尔】 chū ěr fǎn ěr go back on one's word; contradict oneself

【出发】 chūfā ①set out; start off: 巡回医疗队今晚就要~了。The mobile medical team is leaving tonight. ②start from; proceed from: 从长远的观点 ~ from a long-term point of view ◇ ~点 starting point; point of departure/ ~港 port of departure

【出风头】 chū fēngtou seek or be in the limelight: 喜欢~ like to be in the limelight; seek the limelight

【出阁】 chūgé (of a woman) get married; marry

【出轨】 chūguǐ ①be derailed; go off the rails ②overstep the bounds: ~行为 improper behaviour

【出国】 chūguó go abroad

【出海】 chūhǎi go to sea; put out to sea: ~捕鱼 go fishing on the sea

【出汗】 chūhàn perspire; sweat: 出一身汗 break into a sweat; sweat all over

【出乎意料】 chūhū yìliào exceeding one's expectations; contrary to one's expectations; unexpectedly: 试验结果~地好。The experiment turned out to be even more successful than was expected.

【出家】 chūjiā become a monk or nun

【出价】 chūjià offer a price; bid

【出嫁】 chūjià (of a woman) get married; marry

【出境】 chūjìng leave the country: 递解~ send out of the country under escort/ 驱逐~ deport/ 办理~手续 go through exit formalities ◇ ~登记 departure registration/ ~签证 exit visa/ ~许可证 exit permit

【出口】 chūkǒu ①speak; utter: ~伤人 speak bitingly ②exit: 会场的~ the exits of a conference hall ③export: ~大米 export rice

【出口成章】 chū kǒu chéng zhāng words flow from the mouth as from the pen of a master

【出来】 chūlai come out; emerge: 太阳~了。The sun has come out.

【出来】 chūlai ①〔用在动词后,表示动作由里向外朝着说话的人〕:从屋里走出一个人来。Someone came out of the room. ②〔用在动词后,表示动作完成或实现〕:他们终于把这种优质钢炼~了。They finally succeeded in making the high-grade steel. ③〔用在动词后,表示由隐蔽到显露〕:有什么困难说~,大家帮助解决。If you have any difficulty, just let us know and we'll help you out./ 我一眼就认出他来了。I recognized him the moment I saw him.

【出类拔萃】 chūlèi-bácuì stand out from one's fellows; be out of the common run: ~的人物 an outstanding figure

【出力】 chūlì put forth one's strength; exert oneself: 每人多出把力,任务就可以提前完成。If everyone puts in a bit more effort, the job will be finished ahead of time.

【出笼】 chūlóng come out of the steamer: 刚~的包子 hot stuffed buns just out of the steamer

【出路】 chūlù way out; outlet: 河道淤塞,水无~。The riverbed is silted up, so there's no outlet for the floodwater./ 给以生活~ provide sb. with the opportunity to earn a living

【出乱子】 chū luànzi go wrong; get into trouble

【出马】 chūmǎ go into action; take the field: 亲自~ take up the matter oneself; attend to the matter personally; take personal charge of the matter

【出卖】 chūmài ①offer for sale; sell ②sell out; betray: ~原则 barter away principles

【出毛病】 chū máobìng be or go out of order: 机器~了。The machine is out of order./ 汽车~了。Something has gone wrong with the car./ 一路上没出什么毛病。Nothing went wrong on the journey.

【出门】 chūmén be away from home; go on a journey; go out: 他刚~,一会儿就回来。He's just gone out, he'll be back soon.

【出面】 chūmiàn act in one's own capacity or on behalf of an organization; appear personally: ~调停 act as a mediator/ 部长亲自~向大使们说明情况。The minister personally explained the matter to the ambassadors./ 双方由民间团体~商谈贸易。Trade talks are to be held by non-governmental organizations of both sides./ 为什么你自己不~? Why didn't you take up the matter yourself?

【出名】 chūmíng famous; well-known: 哈密瓜~地甜。Hami melons are known for their sweetness.

【出没】 chūmò appear and disappear; haunt: ~无常 appear and disappear unexpectedly; come and go unpredictably

【出纳】 chūnà ①receive and pay out money or bills ②cashier; teller ③receive and lend books, etc. ◇ ~员 cashier; teller

【出品】 chūpǐn ①produce; manufacture; make

【出其不意】 chū qí bù yì take sb. by surprise; catch sb. unawares

【出奇】 chūqí unusually; extraordinarily: 今年夏天热得~。It's unusually hot this summer./ 那天清晨,大海~地宁静。The sea was extraordinarily calm that morning.

【出奇制胜】 chū qí zhì shèng defeat one's opponent by a surprise move

【出气】 chūqì give vent to one's anger; vent one's spleen ◇ ~筒 〈方〉 a person against whom sb.'s anger is wrongly vented; the undeserved target of sb.'s anger

【出去】 chūqu go out; get out: ~走走 go out for a walk/ 门口太拥挤,一时出不去。The exit is too crowded for us to get out yet.

【出让】 chūràng sell (one's own things): 自行车减价~ sell one's bicycle at a reduced price

【出人头地】 chū rén tóu dì rise head and shoulders above others; stand out among one's fellows

【出任】 chūrèn 〈书〉 take up the post of

【出入】 chūrù ①come in and go out: 骑自行车~请下车。Cyclists please dismount at the gate. ②discrepancy; divergence: 他说的和你说的有~。There's some discrepancy between your account and his./ 现款跟帐上的数目没有~。Cash on hand tallies with the figure in the accounts. ◇ ~证 pass (identifying a staff member, etc.)

【出色】 chūsè outstanding; remarkable; splendid: 干得很~ do a remarkable job; acquit oneself splendidly

【出身】 chūshēn ①family background: ~好 have a good background. ②one's previous experience or occupation: 工人~的技术员 a technician promoted from among the workers

【出神】 chūshén be spellbound; be in a trance; be lost in thought: 青年钢琴家的演奏使她听得~。She was held spellbound by the performance of the young pianist./ 他坐在那里~。He sat there, lost in thought.

【出神入化】 chūshén-rùhuà reach the acme of perfection; be superb: ~的表演艺术 superb performance

【出生】 chūshēng be born ◇ ~登记 registration of birth/ ~地 birthplace/ ~率 birthrate/ ~日期 date of birth/ ~证 birth certificate

【出生入死】 chūshēng-rùsǐ go through fire and water; brave untold dangers

【出使】 chūshǐ serve as an envoy abroad; be sent on a diplomatic mission

【出示】 chūshì show; produce: ~证件 produce one's papers

【出世】 chūshì ①come into the world; be born ②renounce the world; stand aloof from worldly affairs

【出事】 chūshì meet with a mishap; have an accident: 出了什么事? What's wrong? 或 What's happening?/ 放心吧,出不了事。Don't worry. Nothing will go wrong. ◇ ~地点 site of an accident

【出手】 chūshǒu ①get (hoarded goods, etc.) off one's hands; dispose of; sell: 货物已经~了。The goods have been disposed of. ②skill displayed in making opening moves: ~不凡 make skilful (或 masterly) opening moves (in wushu, chess, etc.) ③length of sleeve

【出售】 chūshòu offer for sale; sell

【出庭】 chūtíng appear in court: ~作证 appear in court as a witness

【出头】 chūtóu ①lift one's head; free oneself (from misery, persecution, etc.) ②appear in public; come forward: 救

唆犯自己不～，专唆使青少年干坏事。Abettors of crime put youngsters up to all sorts of evil while staying in the back ground themselves. ③〔用在整数之后〕a little over; odd: 他三十刚～。He's just a little over thirty./ 三百～ three hundred odd

【出头露面】chūtóu-lùmiàn appear in public; be in the lime-light: ～的人物 a public figure/ 喜欢～ fond of being in the limelight

【出土】chūtǔ ① be unearthed; be excavated: ～文物展览 exhibition of unearthed artifacts; exhibition of archaeo-logical finds ② come up out of the ground: 小苗刚～。The sprouts have just come up.

【出席】chūxí attend; be present: ～会议 attend a meeting/ ～宴会 be present at a banquet/ ～人数 number of per-sons present; attendance

【出息】chūxi promise; prospects; future: 满足于现状,不求上进是最没 ～ 的。To be content with things as they are and not strive to make progress is spineless and sterile. / 这个人真没～。This chap is a good-for-nothing.

【出险】chūxiǎn ① be or get out of danger ② be in danger; be threatened: 河堤～,全村的人都赶去抢修。When the dyke was in danger, the whole village rushed out to repair it.

【出现】chūxiàn appear; arise; emerge: 数百名手举鲜花的儿童 在运动场上。Several hundred children carrying bou-quets came out onto the sports ground.

【出血】chūxuè 〈医〉haemorrhage; bleeding: 大(内,胃)～ massive (internal, gastric) haemorrhage

【出巡】chūxún ① royal progress ② tour of inspection

【出言不逊】chūyán bù xùn make impertinent remarks; speak insolently

【出洋】chūyáng 〈旧〉go abroad: ～留学 go abroad to pur-sue one's studies; study abroad

【出洋相】chū yángxiàng make an exhibition of oneself

【出于】chūyú start from; proceed from; stem from: ～对工作的责任感 proceed from a sense of duty/ ～对朋友的关怀 out of concern for one's friends/ ～不可告人的目的 actuated by ulterior motives/ ～无奈 as it cannot be helped; there being no alternative/ ～自愿 on a voluntary basis; of one's own accord

【出众】chūzhòng be out of the ordinary; be outstanding: 人才～ a person of exceptional ability

【出走】chūzǒu leave; run away; flee: 仓卒～ leave in a hurry

【出租】chūzū hire; let: 游船按小时～。Rowboats for hire by the hour./ 房屋～。Houses to let.

初* chū ① at the beginning of; in the early part of: 年～ at the beginning of the year/ 夏 early summer/ 八月～ early in August; in early August ② first (in order): ～雪 first snow/ ～战 first battle/ ～五 the fifth day (of a lunar month) ③ for the first time: 感冒～起 with the first symptoms of a cold/ ～具规模 begin to take shape ④ elementary; rudimentary: ～级班 elementary course ⑤ original: ～愿 one's original intention/ 和好如～ become reconciled

【初版】chūbǎn first edition

【初步】chūbù initial; preliminary; tentative: ～设想(方案) a tentative idea (programme)/ ～估计 preliminary esti-mates/ 获得～成果 reap first fruits; get initial results

【初出茅庐】chū chū máolú just come out of one's thatched cottage — at the beginning of one's career; young and inexperienced: ～的作家 fledgling writer

【初次】chūcì the first time: ～见面 see sb. for the first time/ ～登台 appear for the first time on the stage; make one's début

【初等】chūděng elementary; primary ◇ ～教育 primary education/ ～数学 elementary mathematics

【初级】chūjí elementary; primary

【初露锋芒】chū lù fēngmáng display one's talent for the first time

【初期】chūqī initial stage; early days: 战争～ in the early days of the war

【初生之犊】chū shēng zhī dú newborn calf: ～不畏虎。

〈谚〉Newborn calves are not afraid of tigers — young people are fearless.

chú

除* chú ① get rid of; eliminate; remove: 为民～害 rid the people of a scourge/ 战天灾,～人祸 fight natural disasters and conquer human evils/ ～恶务尽 one must be thorough in exterminating an evil ② except: ～此而外 with the exception of this; excepting this ③ besides: ～水稻外,我们还种棉花和小麦。Besides rice, we grow cotton and wheat. ④ 〈数〉divide: 八～以四得二。8 divided by 4 is 2./ 二～六得三。2 goes into 6 three times./ 十能被五～尽。10 divides by 5. 或 5 goes into 10. ⑤ 〈书〉steps to a house; doorsteps: 洒扫庭～ sweep the courtyard

【除草】chúcǎo weeding ◇～机 weeder/ ～剂 weed killer

【除法】chúfǎ 〈数〉division

【除非】chúfēi 〈连〉①〔常跟 "才" "否则" "不然" 等合用, 表示唯一的条件〕only if; only when: ～在这里修个水库,才能解决灌溉问题。Only when a reservoir is built here can we solve our irrigation problem./ 若要人不知,～己莫为。If you don't want people to know, you'd better not do it. ②〔表示不计算在内〕unless: 他不会来,～他病了。He'll certainly come unless he is ill.

【除根】chúgēn dig up the roots; cure once and for all; root out: 斩草必须～。When you're weeding, you must dig up the roots./ 这病很难～。It's difficult to find a per-manent cure for this disease.

【除旧布新】chújiù-bùxīn get rid of the old to make way for the new; do away with the old and set up the new

【除了】chúle ① except: 那条山路,～这位老猎人,谁也不熟悉。Nobody knows the mountain path well except the old hunter. ② besides; in addition to

【除名】chúmíng remove sb.'s name from the rolls; take sb.'s name off the books; expunge sb.'s name from a list

【除外】chúwài except; not counting; not including: 展览会每天开放, 星期一～。The exhibition is open every day except Monday./ 一共五件行李, 药箱～。There are five pieces of luggage, not counting the medical kit.

【除夕】chúxī New Year's Eve

雏鸟 chú 见"雏" chú

厨* chú kitchen

【厨房】chúfáng kitchen ◇ ～用具 kitchen (或 cooking) uten-sils

【厨师】chúshī cook; chef

锄* chú ① hoe ② work with a hoe; hoe: ～玉米地 hoe the cornfields/ ～草 hoe up weeds; weed with a hoe ③ uproot; eliminate; wipe out

【锄头】chútou hoe

蜍 chú 见"蟾蜍" chánchú

雏 chú ① young (bird): ～燕 young swallow/ ～鸡 chicken ② nestling; fledgling

【雏鸟】chúniǎo nestling; fledgling

【雏儿】chúr 〈口〉a young, inexperienced person; fledg-ling

【雏形】chúxíng embryonic form; embryo

橱* chú cabinet; closet: 壁～ built-in cabinet/ 衣～ wardrobe/ 书～ bookcase/ 碗～ cupboard

【橱窗】chúchuāng ① show (或 display) window; show-case; shopwindow ② glass-fronted billboard

【橱柜】chúguì ① cupboard ② a cupboard that also serves as a table; sideboard

躇 chú 见"踌躇" chóuchú

蹰 chú 见"踟蹰" chíchú

chǔ

处* chǔ ① get along (with sb.): 容易相~ easy to get along with/ 他们俩一~得很好。They get along quite well./ 这个人不好~。This fellow is hard to get along with. ② be situated in; be in a certain condition ③ manage; handle; deal with: ~事 handle affairs; manage matters ④ punish; sentence: ~以两年徒刑 sentence sb. to two years' imprisonment
另见 chù

【处罚】chǔfá punish; penalize

【处分】chǔfèn take disciplinary action against; punish: 免予~ exempt sb. from punishment/ 按情节轻重予以~ punish a person according to the seriousness of his case/ 予以警告 give sb. disciplinary warning

【处境】chǔjìng unfavourable situation; plight: ~困难 be in a sorry plight; be in a predicament; be in a difficult situation/ ~危险 be in a dangerous (或 precarious) situation; be in peril

【处决】chǔjué put to death; execute: 依法~ put to death in accordance with the law

【处理】chǔlǐ handle; deal with; dispose of: 必须严加~ should be dealt with sternly/ ~国家大事 conduct state affairs/ ~日常事务 handle day-to-day work; deal with routine matters/ 我回去~一下家务就来。I'll go home and come back as soon as I'm through with my chores./ 垃圾~ garbage disposal

【处女】chǔnǚ virgin; maiden ◇ ~地 virgin land (或 soil)/ ~航 maiden voyage or flight/ ~作 maiden work; first effort

【处世】chǔshì conduct oneself in society

【处死】chǔsǐ put to death; execute

【处于】chǔyú be (in a certain condition): ~有利的地位 find oneself in an advantageous position/ ~平等地位 be on an equal footing/ ~优势 have the advantage/ ~高潮 be at high tide

【处之泰然】chǔ zhī tàirán take things calmly; remain unruffled

【处治】chǔzhì punish

【处置】chǔzhì ① handle; deal with; manage; dispose of: 妥善地~各种复杂情况 handle complex situations aptly/ ~失当 mismanage; mishandle ② punish

杵 chǔ ① pestle: ~臼 mortar and pestle . ② a stick used to pound clothes in washing

础* chǔ plinth: ~石 the stone base of a column;

储* chǔ store up: ~粮备荒 store up grain against natural disasters

【储备】chǔbèi ① store for future use; lay in; lay up: ~过冬饲料 lay up fodder for the winter/ ~粮食 store up grain; build up supplies of grain ② reserve: 黄金~ gold reserve/ 外汇~ foreign exchange reserve ◇ ~基金 reserve fund/ ~粮 grain reserves

【储藏】chǔcáng ① save and preserve; store; keep: 鲜果~ preservation (或 storage) of fresh fruit ② deposit ◇ ~量(矿) reserves/ ~室 storeroom

【储存】chǔcún lay in; lay up; store; stockpile: ~余粮 store up surplus grain/ ~战略物资 stockpile strategic materials

【储蓄】chǔxù save; deposit: 活期(定期)~ current (fixed) deposit/ 提倡~ encourage saving ◇ ~存款 savings deposit/ ~额 total savings deposits

【储油】chǔyóu 〈石油〉 oil storage

褚 Chǔ a surname

楚* chǔ ① clear; neat: 一清二~ perfectly clear ② 〈书〉 pang; suffering: 苦~ distress; suffering

【楚楚】chǔchǔ clear; tidy; neat: 衣冠~ immaculately dressed

chù

处* chù ① place: 住~ dwelling place; quarters/ 别~ another place; elsewhere/ 停车~ parking place (或 lot); car park ② point; part: 长~ strong point; forte/ 有相同之~ bear a resemblance; have something in common ③ 〈量〉: 几~人家 several homesteads/ 发现两~印刷错误 find two misprints ④ department; office: 人事~ personnel section/ 总务~ general affairs department/ 联络~ liaison office
另见 chǔ

【处处】chùchù everywhere; in all respects: ~严格要求自己 set strict demands on oneself in all respects

绌 chù 〈书〉 inadequate; insufficient: 相形见~ prove definitely inferior; pale by comparison

畜 chù domestic animal; livestock: ~群 a herd of livestock
另见 xù

【畜类】chùlèi domestic animals

【畜生】chùsheng ① domestic animal ② 〈骂〉 beast; dirty swine

触* chù ① touch; contact: 请勿~摸展品。Please don't touch the exhibits./ ~到痛处 touch a sore spot; touch sb. to the quick ② strike; hit: ~雷 strike (或 touch off) a mine ③ move sb.; stir up sb.'s feelings

【触电】chùdiàn get an electric shock: 小心~! Danger! Electricity! 或 Danger! Live wire!

【触动】chùdòng ① touch sth., moving it slightly: 他在暗中摸索着,忽然~了什么东西。Groping in the dark, he suddenly touched something./ 敌人的诽谤~不了我们一根毫毛。The enemy's slanders can't do us the slightest harm. ② move sb.; stir up sb.'s feelings: 有所~ be somewhat moved/ 这句话~了他的心事。That remark reminded him of something he'd had on his mind for a long time.

【触发】chùfā detonate by contact; touch off; spark; trigger

【触犯】chùfàn offend; violate; go against: ~法律 violate (或 break) the law/ 我什么地方~了你?What have I done to offend you?

【触及】chùjí touch: ~人们的灵魂 touch people to their very souls/ ~事物的本质 get to the essence of a matter

【触礁】chùjiāo run (up) on rocks; strike a reef (或 rock)

【触景生情】chù jǐng shēng qíng the sight strikes a chord in one's heart

【触觉】chùjué 〈生理〉 tactile (或 tactual) sensation; sense of touch ◇ ~器官 tactile organ

【触类旁通】chù lèi páng tōng grasp a typical example and you will grasp the whole category; comprehend by analogy

【触目】chùmù meet the eye: ~皆是 can be seen everywhere

【触目惊心】chùmù-jīngxīn startling; shocking

【触怒】chùnù make angry; infuriate; enrage

黜 chù 〈书〉 remove sb. from office; dismiss

【黜免】chùmiǎn 〈书〉 dismiss (a government official)

矗 chù 〈书〉 stand tall and upright

【矗立】chùlì stand tall and upright; tower over sth.

chuǎi

揣 chuǎi 〈书〉 estimate; surmise; conjecture

【揣测】chuǎicè guess; conjecture: 据我~,他已经离开香港了。My guess is that he's already left Hongkong.

【揣度】chuǎiduó estimate; appraise; conjecture: ~敌情 make an appraisal of the enemy's situation

【揣摩】chuǎimó　try to fathom; try to figure out: 我始终～不透他的用意。I simply couldn't figure out his intention.

chuān

川 * chuān ①river: 高山大～ high mountains and big rivers ②plain: 一马平～ a vast expanse of flat land; a great stretch of land

【川流不息】chuān liú bù xī flowing past in an endless stream; never-ending: 顾客～。Customers came in an endless stream. 或 Customers kept pouring in.

【川资】chuānzī travelling expenses

穿 chuān ①pierce through; penetrate: ～个窟窿 pierce (或 bore) a hole/ 看～ see through ②pass through; cross: ～过地道 pass through a tunnel/ ～过马路 cross a street/ 从人群中～过去 thread one's way through the crowd/ 飞机～云下降。The plane descended through the clouds./ 我们从操场～过去吧。Let's take the shortcut across the sports field. ③wear; put on; be dressed in: ～上工作服 put on work clothes/ ～灰大衣的那个客人 the guest in a grey overcoat/ 衣服～旧了。The clothes show signs of wear./ 这种鞋小点不要紧,一～就大了。It doesn't matter if the shoes feel a bit tight. They'll stretch with wearing./ ～得这么少,不冷吗? Aren't you cold with so little on?

【穿插】chuānchā ①alternate; do in turn: 施肥和锄草～进行 do manuring and weeding in turn ②weave in; insert: 他在报告中～了一些生动的例子。His talk was spiced with vivid examples. ③subplot; interlude; episode

【穿戴】chuāndài apparel; dress: ～整齐 be neatly dressed/ 不讲究～ not be particular about one's dress

【穿孔】chuānkǒng bore (或 punch) a hole; perforate ◇ ～机 punch; perforator/ ～卡片 punched card

穿孔机

【穿梭】chuānsuō shuttle back and forth ◇ ～轰炸 shuttle bombing

【穿越】chuānyuè pass through; cut across: 铁路～原始森林。The railway cuts through a primeval forest.

【穿针】chuānzhēn thread a needle

【穿针引线】chuānzhēn-yǐnxiàn act as a go-between

【穿着】chuānzhuó dress; apparel: ～朴素整洁 be plainly but neatly dressed

chuán

传 * chuán ①pass; pass on: ～球 pass a ball/ 此件请按名单顺序速～。Please pass on this document without delay, in the order of the name list. ②hand down: 家～秘方 a secret recipe handed down in the family ③pass on (knowledge, skill, etc.); impart; teach ④spread: 消息很快～开了。The news spread quickly. 或 The news soon got around./ 喜讯～来,欢声雷动。The glad tidings gave rise to thunderous cheers. ⑤transmit; conduct: ～热 transmit heat/ 铜～电。Copper conducts electricity. ⑥convey; express: 眉目～情 flash amorous glances ⑦summon: ～一个证人 summon a witness ⑧infect; be contagious: 小心别让你孩子～上流感。Mind that your children don't catch the flu. 另见 zhuàn

【传播】chuánbō ①disseminate; propagate; spread: ～知识 spread knowledge/ 制止病菌的～ check the spread of germs ②〈物〉propagation

【传布】chuánbù disseminate; spread

【传达】chuándá ①pass on (information, etc.); transmit; relay; communicate: ～命令 transmit an order/ 听～报告 hear a relayed report

【传单】chuándān leaflet; handbill

【传递】chuándì transmit; deliver; transfer: ～信件 deliver

mail/ ～信息 transmit messages

【传话】chuánhuà pass on a message

【传唤】chuánhuàn 〈法〉summon to court; subpoena

【传家宝】chuánjiābǎo ①family heirloom ②cherished tradition (或 heritage)

【传教】chuánjiào 〈宗〉do missionary work ◇ ～士 missionary

【传令】chuánlìng transmit (或 dispatch) orders: ～嘉奖 cite sb. in a dispatch

【传票】chuánpiào ①〈法〉(court) summons; subpoena: 发出～ issue a summons

【传染】chuánrǎn infect; be contagious: 接触～ contagion/ 空气～ infection through air/ 水～ waterborne infection/ 这病不～。This disease is not contagious (或 infectious). ◇ ～病 infectious (或 contagious) disease

【传神】chuánshén vivid; lifelike: ～之笔 a vivid touch (in writing or painting)

【传声器】chuánshēngqì microphone

【传声筒】chuánshēngtǒng ①megaphone; loud hailer ②one who parrots another; sb.'s mouthpiece

【传世】chuánshì be handed down from ancient times: ～珍宝 a treasure handed down from ancient times

【传授】chuánshòu pass on (knowledge, skill, etc.); impart; teach: ～技术 pass on (或 impart) one's technical skill/ 向青年～培育良种的经验 teach young people how to cultivate good strains of seed

【传说】chuánshuō ①it is said; they say: ～如此。So the story goes./ 这只不过是一而已。That's only hearsay. ②legend; tradition: 民间～ folklore; popular legend

【传诵】chuánsòng be on everybody's lips; be widely read: 为世人所～ be read with admiration by people all over the world

【传统】chuántǒng tradition: ～友谊 traditional (ties of) friendship/ ～观念 traditional ideas

【传闻】chuánwén ①it is said; they say ②hearsay; rumour; talk

【传言】chuányán ①hearsay; rumour: ～非虚。It's not just hearsay. ②pass on a message

【传扬】chuányáng spread (from mouth to mouth): ～四方 spread far and wide

【传真】chuánzhēn ①portraiture ②〈讯〉facsimile: 无线电～ radio facsimile; radiophotography ◇ ～电报 phototelegraph/ ～照片 radiophoto

【传种】chuánzhǒng propagate; reproduce

船 * chuán boat; ship: 上～ board a ship; go on board; embark/ 下～ disembark

【船舱】chuáncāng ①ship's hold ②cabin

【船队】chuánduì fleet; flotilla

【船票】chuánpiào steamer ticket: 预定～ book one's passage

【船期】chuánqī sailing date ◇ ～表 sailing schedule

【船首】chuánshǒu stem; bow; prow

【船尾】chuánwěi stern

【船位】chuánwèi ①accommodation (on a ship): 订～ book one's passage (on a ship) ②ship's position: 测定～ fix a ship's position (at sea); position finding

【船坞】chuánwù dock; shipyard: 浮～ floating dock/ 干～ dry (或 graving) dock

【船员】chuányuán (ship's) crew

【船长】chuánzhǎng captain; skipper

【船只】chuánzhī shipping; vessels: 往来～ shipping traffic/ 载货～ carrying vessels/ ～失事 shipwreck

chuǎn

喘 chuǎn ①breathe heavily; gasp for breath; pant ②〈医〉asthma

【喘气】 chuǎnqì ① breathe (deeply); pant; gasp: 喘不过气来 gasp for breath; be out of breath／喘粗气 puff and blow ② take a breather: 喘口气儿再干。Let's take a breather before we go on.

【喘息】 chuǎnxī ① pant; gasp for breath: 喘息未定 before regaining one's breath; before one has a chance to catch one's breath ② breather; breathing spell; respite: 乘胜追击，不让敌人有～的机会 follow up the victory with pursuit so as not to allow the enemy a breathing spell

chuàn

串 chuàn ① string together: 把鱼～起来 string the fish together ② conspire; gang up: ～骗 gang up and swindle sb. ③ get things mixed up: 电话～线 get the (telephone) lines crossed／(收音机)～台 get two or more (radio) stations at once／字印得太小，很容易看～行。The print is too small, you can easily miss (或 skip) a line. ④ 〈量〉〔用于连贯起来的东西〕string; bunch; cluster: 一～珠子 a string of beads／一～钥匙 a bunch of keys／一～葡萄 a cluster of grapes

【串通】 chuàntōng gang up; collaborate; collude: 两人～一气，互相包庇。Acting in collaboration, the two of them shielded each other.

chuāng

创* chuāng wound: 予以重～ inflict heavy casualties (on the enemy)／巨痛深 badly injured and in great pain — in deep distress
另见 chuàng

【创痕】 chuānghén scar

【创口】 chuāngkǒu wound; cut

【创伤】 chuāngshāng wound; trauma: 精神上的～ a mental scar; a traumatic experience／医治战争的～ heal the wounds of war

疮* chuāng ① sore; skin ulcer: 褥～ bedsore／头上长～，脚底流脓——坏透了 with boils on the head and feet running with pus — rotten from head to foot; rotten to the core ② wound: 刀～ a sword wound

【疮疤】 chuāngbā scar: 脸上的～ a scar on the face／揭他的～ pull the scab right off his sore — touch his sore spot／我们不能好了～忘了痛。We mustn't forget the pain after the wound is healed. 或 We mustn't forget the bitter past when we are relieved of our suffering.

【疮口】 chuāngkǒu the open part of a sore

【疮痍满目】 chuāngyí mǎnmù everywhere a scene of devastation meets the eye

窗* chuāng window

【窗玻璃】 chuāngbōli windowpane

【窗口】 chuāngkǒu ① window: 坐在～ sit at (或 by) the window ② wicket; window

【窗框】 chuāngkuàng window frame

【窗帘】 chuānglián (window) curtain

【窗明几净】 chuāngmíng-jījìng with bright windows and clean tables; bright and clean

chuáng

床* chuáng ① bed: 单人～ single bed／双人～ double bed／小孩～ child's cot; baby's crib／帆布～ camp bed; cot／折叠～ folding bed／卧病在～ take to one's bed; be laid up in bed ② sth. shaped like a bed: 车～ lathe／河～ riverbed ③ 〈量〉: 一～被 one quilt／两～铺盖 two sets of bedding

【床单】 chuángdān sheet

【床垫】 chuángdiàn mattress

【床架】 chuángjià bedstead

【床铺】 chuángpù bed

【床头】 chuángtóu the head of a bed; bedside ◇ ～灯 bedside lamp／～柜 bedside cupboard

【床位】 chuángwèi berth; bunk; bed

幢 chuáng ① pennant or streamer used in ancient China ② a stone pillar inscribed with Buddha's name or Buddhist scripture
另见 zhuàng

【幢幢】 chuángchuáng flickering; dancing: 人影～ shadows of people moving about

chuǎng

闯 chuǎng ① rush; dash; charge: ～进来 rush in; break in; force one's way in／横冲直～ charge about furiously; run amuck ② temper oneself (by battling through difficulties and dangers): 他这几年～出来了。He has hewed out his path in life during these past few years.／我们必须～出一条新路子。We must break a new path.

【闯祸】 chuǎnghuò get into trouble; bring disaster: 你～了！Look what you've done!／你开车要小心，千万别～。Drive carefully and be sure not to have an accident.

【闯江湖】 chuǎng jiānghú make a living wandering from place to place (as a fortune-teller, acrobat, quack doctor, etc.)

chuàng

创* chuàng start (doing sth.); achieve (sth. for the first time): 排万难，～高产 surmount all difficulties and achieve higher output／～记录 set a record／该厂钢产量～历史最高水平。The plant's steel output was an all-time high.
另见 chuāng

【创办】 chuàngbàn establish; set up: ～农具修理厂 set up a farm tool repair shop

【创见】 chuàngjiàn original idea: 有～的思想家 an original thinker

【创建】 chuàngjiàn found; establish

【创举】 chuàngjǔ pioneering work (或 undertaking): 伟大的～ a great beginning

【创刊】 chuàngkān start publication

【创立】 chuànglì found; originate: ～新学派 found a new academic school

【创设】 chuàngshè found; create; set up: ～一个新的研究所 set up a new research institute

【创始】 chuàngshǐ originate; initiate: 处在～阶段 be in the initial stage

【创新】 chuàngxīn bring forth new ideas; blaze new trails: 在艺术上不断～ constantly bring forth new ideas in the arts／勇于实践，大胆～。Be bold in putting things into practice and blazing new trails.

【创业】 chuàngyè start an undertaking; do pioneering work

【创造】 chuàngzào create; produce; bring about: ～有利条件 create favourable conditions／～优异成绩 produce excellent results／～奇迹 create miracles; work wonders; achieve prodigious feats ◇ ～力 creative power (或 ability)／～性 creativeness; creativity

【创制】 chuàngzhì formulate; institute; create: ～拼音文字 formulate an alphabetic system of writing

【创作】 chuàngzuò ① create; produce; write ② creative work; creation: 文艺～ literary and artistic creation／划时代的～ epoch-making creative work

chuī

吹* chuī ① blow; puff: ～火 blow a fire／把灯～灭 blow out the lamp／～一口气 give a puff／雨打风～ be exposed to the weather／门～开了。The door blew open.／什么风把你给～来了？What brings you here?／～起床号 sound the reveille ② play (wind instruments): ～

笛子 play the flute ③〈口〉boast; brag: 先别～，做出具体成绩来说说。Don't brag about what you're going to do. Get something done./ 自～自擂 blow one's own trumpet; ～得天花乱坠 boast in the most fantastic terms ④〈口〉break off; break up; fall through: 他们俩～了。That couple have broken up./ 原来的计划～了。The original plan has fallen through.

【吹吹打打】 chuīchuī-dǎdǎ beating drums and blowing trumpets; piping and drumming

【吹风】 chuīfēng ① be in a draught; catch a chill: 你病还没有好，不要～。Don't get in a draught, you aren't well yet. ② dry (hair, etc.) with a blower

【吹拂】 chuīfú sway; stir: 晨风～着垂柳。The morning breeze is swaying the weeping willows.

【吹鼓手】 chuīgǔshǒu trumpeter

【吹灰之力】 chuī huī zhī lì the effort needed to blow away a speck of dust; just a small effort: 不费～ as easy as blowing away dust; without the least effort

【吹冷风】 chuī lěngfēng blow a cold wind over; throw cold water on

【吹毛求疵】 chuī máo qiú cī find fault; pick holes; nitpick

【吹牛】 chuīniú boast; brag; talk big: ～拍马 boast and flatter

【吹捧】 chuīpěng flatter; laud to the skies; lavish praise on: 互相～ flatter each other

【吹嘘】 chuīxū lavish praise on oneself or others; boast: 自我～ self-praise

【吹奏】 chuīzòu play (wind instruments) ◇ ～乐 band music; wind music

炊 chuī cook a meal

chuí

垂* chuí ① hang down; droop; let fall: ～泪 shed tears; weep/ ～手站着 stand with one's hands at one's sides ②〈书〉bequeath to posterity; hand down: 功～竹帛 be recorded in history in letters of gold/ ～法后世 set an example for posterity ③〈书〉nearing; approaching: ～老 approaching old age; getting on in years ④〈书〉〈敬〉〔多用于称长辈、上级对自己的行动〕condescend: ～询 condescend to inquire/ ～念 show kind concern for (me)

【垂钓】 chuídiào fish with a hook and line; go angling

【垂暮】 chuímù 〈书〉dusk; towards sunset; just before sundown: ～之年 in old age

【垂青】 chuíqīng 〈书〉show appreciation for sb.; look upon sb. with favour

【垂死】 chuísǐ moribund; dying: ～挣扎 be in one's death throes; put up a last-ditch (或 deathbed) struggle

【垂头丧气】 chuítóu-sàngqì crestfallen; dejected

【垂危】 chuíwēi critically ill; at one's last gasp

【垂涎】 chuíxián drool; slaver; covet: ～三尺 spittle three feet long — drool with envy

【垂直】 chuízhí perpendicular; vertical: ～平面 vertical plane/ ～发射 vertical firing (或 launching)/ ～俯冲 steep dive; nose dive/ ～起飞 vertical takeoff/ 两线～相交。The two lines meet at right angles.

捶 chuí beat (with a stick or fist); thump; pound: ～背 pound sb.'s back (as in massage)/ ～鼓 beat a drum/ ～门 bang on the door

【捶打】 chuídǎ beat; thump: ～衣服 beat clothes (when washing them)

【捶胸顿足】 chuíxiōng-dùnzú beat one's breast and stamp one's feet (in deep sorrow, etc.)

槌 chuí mallet; beetle: 碾～ pestle/ 鼓～儿 drumstick

锤* chuí ① hammer: 铁～ iron hammer/ 大～ sledgehammer ② mace ③ hammer into shape

chūn

春* chūn ① spring: 温暖如～ as warm as spring ②

love; lust: ～情 stirrings of love ③ life; vitality: 枯木逢～。A withered tree comes to life again.

【春风】 chūnfēng spring breeze: 满面～ (a face) beaming with smiles

【春风化雨】 chūnfēng huà yǔ life-giving spring breeze and rain — salutary influence of education

【春风满面】 chūnfēng mǎnmiàn beaming with satisfaction; radiant with happiness

【春光】 chūnguāng sights and sounds of spring; spring scenery: ～明媚 a sunlit and enchanting scene of spring

【春季】 chūnjì spring; springtime

【春节】 Chūnjié the Spring Festival

【春梦】 chūnmèng spring dream; transient joy

【春色】 chūnsè spring scenery: 水乡～ spring in a waterside village/ ～满园 a garden full of the beauty of spring

chún

纯 chún ① pure; unmixed: ～毛 pure wool/ ～金 pure (或 solid) gold/ ～白 pure white/ ～黑 all black ② simple; pure and simple: ～属捏造 sheer fabrication ③ skilful; practised; well versed: 功夫不～ not skilful enough

【纯粹】 chúncuì pure; unadulterated: 一个～的人 a pure person/ ～是浪费时间 a sheer waste of time

【纯洁】 chúnjié pure; clean and honest

【纯净】 chúnjìng pure; clean

【纯利】 chúnlì net profit

【纯朴】 chúnpǔ honest; simple; unsophisticated: ～敦厚 simple and honest/ ～爽朗 honest and frank/ 文风～ simplicity of style

【纯熟】 chúnshú skilful; practised; well versed: 技术～ highly skilled

【纯真】 chúnzhēn pure; sincere: ～无邪 pure and innocent

【纯正】 chúnzhèng pure; unadulterated: 动机～ have pure motives

【纯种】 chúnzhǒng purebred: ～牛 purebred cattle; pedigree cattle

唇* chún lip: 上～ upper lip/ 下～ lower lip

【唇齿相依】 chún-chǐ xiāngyī be as close as lips and teeth; be closely related and mutually dependent

【唇膏】 chúngāo lipstick

【唇枪舌剑】 chúnqiāng-shéjiàn cross verbal swords; engage in a battle of words

【唇舌】 chúnshé words; argument: 费一番～ take a lot of explaining or arguing/ 徒费～ a waste of breath

【唇亡齿寒】 chúnwáng-chǐhán if the lips are gone, the teeth will be cold; if one (of two interdependent things) falls, the other is in danger; share a common lot

淳 chún 〈书〉pure; honest

【淳厚】 chúnhòu pure and honest; simple and kind

【淳朴】 chúnpǔ honest; simple; unsophisticated

醇 chún ①〈书〉mellow wine; good wine ②〈书〉pure; unmixed

【醇厚】 chúnhòu ① mellow; rich: 酒味～。The wine is (或 tastes) mellow. ② pure and honest; simple and kind

chǔn

蠢 chǔn ① stupid; foolish; dull; clumsy ②〈书〉wriggle

【蠢笨】 chǔnbèn clumsy; awkward; stupid

【蠢材】 chǔncái idiot; fool

【蠢蠢欲动】 chǔnchǔn yù dòng ready to start wriggling — ready to make trouble: 敌人又在～。The enemy is going to start something again.

【蠢动】 chǔndòng ① wriggle ② create disturbances; carry on disruptive activities

【蠢货】 chǔnhuò blockhead; dunce; idiot

【蠢人】 chǔnrén fool; blockhead

【蠢猪】 chǔnzhū idiot; stupid swine; ass

chuō

戳 chuō ① jab; poke; stab: 小心！你的竹竿儿别～了他的眼睛。Be careful! Don't jab his eye out with your bamboo pole./ 在纸上～了一个洞 poke a hole in the paper/ 一～就破 break at the slightest touch ② 〈方〉 sprain; blunt: 打排球～了手 sprain one's wrist while playing volleyball/ 钢笔尖儿～了。The nib is blunted. ③ 〈方〉 stand sth. on end: 把秫秸～起来 stand the bundle of sorghum stalks on end ④ 〈口〉 stamp; seal

【戳穿】 chuōchuān puncture; lay bare; expose; explode: ～谣言和诡辩 lay bare sb.'s lies and sophistry

【戳记】 chuōjì stamp; seal

【戳子】 chuōzi 〈口〉 stamp; seal: 在文件上盖个～ put a seal (或 stamp) on a document/ 橡皮～ rubber stamp

chuò

啜 chuò 〈书〉 ① sip; suck: ～茗 sip tea ② sob

【啜泣】 chuòqì sob

绰 chuò 〈书〉 ample; spacious: ～有余裕 enough and to spare

【绰绰有余】 chuòchuò yǒu yú more than sufficient; enough and to spare

【绰号】 chuòhào nickname

【绰约】 chuòyuē 〈书〉 (of a woman) graceful

辍 chuò 〈书〉 stop; cease: ～工 stop work/ 时作时～ on and off; by fits and starts

【辍笔】 chuòbǐ stop in the middle of writing or painting

【辍学】 chuòxué discontinue one's studies

龊 chuò 见"龌龊" wòchuò

cī

差 cī 见"参差" cēncī
另见 chā; chà; chāi

疵 cī flaw; defect; blemish: 小～ a trifling defect/ 无～ flawless; impeccable

【疵点】 cīdiǎn flaw; fault; defect

cí

词 cí ① 〈语〉 word; term: 贬义～ derogatory term/ 同义～ synonym ② speech; statement: 开幕～ opening speech/ 台～ lines of an opera or play/ 各执一～。Each holds to his own statement./ 我说了几句就没～儿了。After a few sentences I became tongue-tied. ③ cí, poetry written to certain tunes with strict tonal patterns and rhyme schemes, in fixed numbers of lines and words, originating in the Tang Dynasty (618-907) and fully developed in the Song Dynasty (960-1279)

【词不达意】 cí bù dá yì the words fail to convey the idea

【词典】 cídiǎn dictionary

【词汇】 cíhuì 〈语〉 vocabulary; words and phrases: 常用～ common words ◇ ～表 word list; vocabulary; glossary

【词句】 cíjù words and phrases; expressions

【词义】 cíyì 〈语〉 the meaning (或 sense) of a word

【词语】 cíyǔ words and expressions; terms

【词源】 cíyuán 〈语〉 the origin of a word; etymology

祠 cí ancestral temple: 宗～ clan hall

【祠堂】 cítáng ancestral hall (或 temple); memorial temple

瓷 cí porcelain; china: ～碗 china bowl/ 细～ fine china

【瓷雕】 cídiāo 〈工美〉 porcelain carving

【瓷漆】 cíqī enamel paint; enamel

【瓷器】 cíqì porcelain; chinaware: 薄胎～ eggshell china

【瓷砖】 cízhuān ceramic tile; glazed tile

辞 cí ① diction; phraseology: 修～ rhetoric ② a type of classical Chinese literature: 《楚～》 The Songs of Chu ③ a form of classical poetry: 《木兰～》 The Ballad of Mulan ④ take leave: 告～ take one's leave/ 不～而别 leave without saying good-bye ⑤ decline: 固～ firmly decline ⑥ dismiss; discharge ⑦ shirk: 不～劳苦 spare no effort; take pains

【辞别】 cíbié bid farewell; say good-bye; take one's leave

【辞典】 cídiǎn dictionary

【辞令】 cílìng language appropriate to the occasion: 外交～ diplomatic language/ 善于～ gifted with a silver tongue

【辞让】 círàng politely decline: 他～了一番，才在前排就座。After first politely declining, he eventually took a seat in the front row.

【辞退】 cítuì dismiss; discharge

【辞谢】 cíxiè politely decline; decline with thanks

【辞行】 cíxíng say good-bye (to one's friends, etc.) before setting out on a journey

【辞藻】 cízǎo flowery language; rhetoric; ornate diction: 堆砌～ string together ornate phrases

【辞章】 cízhāng ① poetry and prose; prose and verse ② art of writing; rhetoric

【辞职】 cízhí resign; hand in one's resignation

慈 cí ① kind; loving: 心～ tenderhearted; kindhearted ② 〈书〉 mother: 家～ my mother

【慈爱】 cí'ài love; affection; kindness

【慈悲】 cíbēi mercy; benevolence; pity: 发～ have pity; be merciful

【慈和】 cíhé kindly and amiable

【慈母】 címǔ loving mother; mother

【慈善】 císhàn charitable; benevolent; philanthropic ◇ ～机关 charitable institution (或 organization)/ ～家 philanthropist/ ～事业 charities; good works; philanthropy

【慈祥】 cíxiáng kindly: ～的面容 a kindly face

磁 cí ① 〈物〉 magnetism: 起～ magnetization/ 地～ terrestrial magnetism ② porcelain; china

【磁场】 cíchǎng 〈物〉 magnetic field

【磁带】 cídài (magnetic) tape ◇ ～录音机 tape recorder

【磁力】 cílì 〈物〉 magnetic force

【磁石】 císhí ① 〈矿〉 magnetite

【磁铁】 cítiě 〈物〉 magnet: 马蹄形～ horseshoe magnet/ 永久～ permanent magnet/ 电～ electromagnet ◇ ～矿 magnetite

【磁性】 cíxìng 〈物〉 magnetism; magnetic

【磁针】 cízhēn magnetic needle

雌 cí female

【雌花】 cíhuā 〈植〉 female (或 pistillate) flower

【雌黄】 cíhuáng ① 〈矿〉 orpiment ② 见"信口雌黄" xìnkǒu cíhuáng

【雌性】 cíxìng female

【雌雄】 cí-xióng ① male and female ② victory and defeat: 决一～ have a showdown; see who's master

cǐ

此 cǐ this: ～处 this place; here/ ～等 this kind; such as these/ 由～往南 go south from here

【此辈】 cǐbèi people of this type (或 ilk); such people: 勿与～来往。Don't associate with such people.

【此地】 cǐdì this place; here: ～人 local people

【此地无银三百两】 cǐdì wú yín sānbǎi liǎng No 300 taels of

silver buried here (the sign put up by the man in the folk tale over the place where he had hidden some money) — a guilty person gives himself away by conspicuously protesting his innocence; protest one's innocence too much

【此后】cǐhòu after this; hereafter; henceforth
【此刻】cǐkè this moment; now; at present
【此路不通】cǐ lù bù tōng dead end; blind alley: ~₁ (路牌) Not a Through Road.
【此起彼伏】cǐqǐ-bǐfú as one falls, another rises; rise one after another: 欢呼声~。 Loud cheers rang out continuously. 又作"此伏彼起"
【此时】cǐshí this moment; right now: ~此刻 at this very moment/ ~此地 here and now
【此外】cǐwài besides; in addition; moreover: ~,还要讨论一下分工问题。 In addition, we'll discuss the question of division of labour.
【此一时,彼一时】cǐ yīshí, bǐ yīshí this is one situation and that was another — times have changed

cì

次* cì ①order; sequence: 依~ in due order; in succession; one by one/ 席~ seating arrangement/ 车~ train number ②second; next: ~子 second son/ 日次 day ③second-rate; inferior: ~棉 poor quality cotton/ 真~ really no good; terrible ④<量>：三~ three times/ 首~ first time; first/ 二十一~列车 No. 21 train/ 进行几~会谈 hold several talks
【次等】cìděng second-class; second-rate; inferior
【次第】cìdì order; sequence ②one after another: ~入座 take seats one after another
【次数】cìshù number of times; frequency: ~不多 not very often/ 练习的~越多,熟练的程度越高。 The more you practise, the more skilful you'll become.
【次序】cìxù order; sequence: ~颠倒 not in the right order
【次要】cìyào less important; secondary; subordinate; minor: ~问题 secondary questions
【次之】cìzhī take second place: 该省矿藏,以锡最多,铜~。 Among the mineral deposits of the province, tin occupies first place; copper comes second.

伺 cì 另见 sì
【伺候】cìhou wait upon; serve: 难~ hard to please; fastidious

刺* cì ①thorn; splinter: 手上扎了个~ get a thorn (或 splinter) in one's hand/ 他说话总带~儿。 There's always a sting in his words. ②stab; prick: ~伤 stab and wound ③assassinate: 被~ be assassinated ④irritate; stimulate: ~鼻 irritate the nose; assail one's nostrils ⑤criticize: 讽~ satirize
【刺刺不休】cìcì bù xiū talk incessantly; chatter on and on
【刺刀】cìdāo bayonet: 上~! (口令) Fix bayonets!/ 下~! (口令) Unfix bayonets!

【刺耳】cì'ěr grating on the ear; jarring; ear-piercing; harsh: 这声音太~。 The sound is too piercing./ ~的话 harsh words; sarcastic remarks
【刺骨】cìgǔ piercing to the bones; piercing; biting: 寒风~。 The cold wind chills one to the bone.
【刺激】cìjī ①stimulate: 物质~ material incentive/ 强~ strong stimulus ②provoke; irritate; upset: 这一不幸的消息给了她很大的~。 She was badly upset by the sad news.
【刺客】cìkè <旧> assassin
【刺杀】cìshā ①assassinate ②<军> bayonet charge: 练~ practise bayonet fighting

【刺绣】cìxiù ①embroider ②embroidery ◇ ~品 embroidery
【刺眼】cìyǎn dazzling; offending to the eye: 亮得~ dazzlingly bright/ 打扮得~ be loudly dressed

赐 cì grant; favour; gift: 赏~ grant (或 bestow) a reward/ 请即~复。 Please favour me with an early reply./ 厚~受之有愧。 I feel unworthy of the precious gift you have bestowed on me.
【赐教】cìjiào <敬> condescend to teach; grant instruction: 不吝~ please favour (或 enlighten) me with your instructions; be so kind as to give me a reply
【赐予】cìyǔ grant; bestow

cōng

从* cōng 另见 cóng
【从容】cōngróng ①calm; unhurried; leisurely: ~不迫 calm and unhurried/ ~就义 go to one's death unflinchingly; meet one's death like a hero ②plentiful: 时间很~。 There's still plenty of time.

匆* cōng hastily; hurriedly
【匆匆】cōngcōng hurriedly: ~吃了一顿饭 take a hurried meal; hurry through a meal/ 行色~ be in a rush getting ready for a journey; be pressed for time on a journey
【匆促】cōngcù hastily; in a hurry: ~起程 set out hastily/ 时间~ be pressed for time
【匆忙】cōngmáng hastily; in a hurry: ~作出决定 make a hasty decision/ 临行~,未能向你告别。 I left in such a hurry that I didn't have time to say good-bye to you./ 他匆匆忙忙吃了几口东西,又回车间去了。 He bolted down a few mouthfuls of food and hurried back to the workshop.

葱 cōng ①onion; scallion: 大~ green Chinese onion/ 小~ shallot/ 洋~ onion ②green
【葱翠】cōngcuì fresh green; luxuriantly green: ~的竹林 a green bamboo grove
【葱绿】cōnglǜ pale yellowish green; light green; verdant: ~的田野 verdant fields/ 麦苗一片~。 The wheat shoots are a lush green.
【葱头】cōngtóu onion
【葱郁】cōngyù verdant; luxuriantly green: ~的松树林 a verdant pine wood

聪* cōng ①<书> faculty of hearing: 左耳失~ become deaf in the left ear ②acute hearing: 耳~目明 able to see and hear clearly
【聪慧】cōnghuì bright; intelligent
【聪明】cōngming intelligent; bright; clever: ~能干 bright and capable/ ~才智 intelligence and wisdom/ ~反被~误。 Clever people may be victims of their own cleverness. 或 Cleverness may overreach itself./ ~一世,糊涂一时 clever all one's life but stupid this once; smart as a rule, but this time a fool
【聪颖】cōngyǐng intelligent; bright; clever

cóng

从* cóng ①<介>〔表示起于或经过〕from; through: ~现在起 from now on/ ~这儿往西 go west from here; west of here/ ②<副>〔用在否定词前面〕ever: 她在成绩和荣誉面前从不骄傲。 Her head was never turned by achievements or honours./ ~不计较个人的名誉地位 never give any consideration to personal fame and position ③follow; comply with; obey: ~俗 follow the general custom; conform to custom/ ~命 comply with sb.'s wish; obey an order/ ~征 go on a military expedition ④join; be engaged in: ~军 join the army; enlist ⑤ in a certain manner or according to a certain principle ⑥ follower; attendant: 随~ attendant; retainer; retinue/ ~者如云 have

a large following ⑦ relationship between cousins, etc. of the same paternal grandfather, great-grandfather or a yet earlier common ancestor; of the same clan: ～兄 first, second or distant cousin of the same clan; cousin
另见　cōng

【从长计议】 cóng cháng jìyì　give the matter further thought and discuss it later

【从此】 cóngcǐ　from this time on; from now on; from then on; henceforth; thereupon

【从…到…】 cóng … dào … from… to…: 从上到下 from top to bottom; from the higher levels to the grass roots/ 从无到有 grow out of nothing/ 从早到晚 from dawn to dusk; from morning till night/ 从古到今 from ancient times to the present; from time immemorial

【从而】 cóng'ér 〈连〉 thus; thereby: 农业迅速发展，～为轻工业提供了充足的原料。 Agriculture has developed rapidly, thus providing light industry with ample raw materials.

【从简】 cóngjiǎn　conform to the principle of simplicity: 一切～ dispense with all unnecessary formalities

【从来】 cónglái　always; at all times; all along: 我～没有见过她。 I've never seen her before.

【从略】 cónglüè　be omitted: 此处引文～。 The quotation is omitted here.

【从前】 cóngqián　before; formerly; in the past: 我们村跟～大不一样了。 Our village is very different from what it was before./ ～，有一个老人，名叫“愚公”。 Once upon a time, there lived an old man called Yu Gong.

【从善如流】 cóng shàn rú liú　follow good advice as naturally as a river follows its course; readily accept good advice

【从事】 cóngshì ① go in for; be engaged in: ～科学研究工作 be engaged in scientific research/ ～文学创作 take up writing as a profession; be engaged in literary work/ ～技术革新 work on technical innovations ② deal with: 慎重～ act cautiously; steer a cautious course/ 军法～ deal with according to military law; court-martial

【从速】 cóngsù　as soon as possible; without delay: ～处理 deal with the matter as soon as possible; settle the matter quickly/ 存书无多，欲购～。 Only a few copies left. Buy now, while they last.

【从头】 cóngtóu ① from the beginning: ～儿做起 start from the very beginning ② anew; once again: ～儿再来 start afresh; start all over again

【从小】 cóngxiǎo　from childhood; as a child: 他～热爱劳动。 He has loved labour ever since he was a child.

【从中】 cóngzhōng　out of; from among; therefrom: ～渔利 profit from; cash in on/ ～调解 mediate between two sides/ ～吸取有益的教训 draw a salutary lesson from it

丛* cóng ① crowd together: ～生 grow thickly ② clump; thicket; grove: 草～ a patch of grass/ 树～ a clump of trees; grove ③ crowd; collection: 人～ a crowd of people/ 论～ a collection of essays; collected essays

【丛刊】 cóngkān　a series of books; collection

【丛林】 cónglín ① jungle; forest ② Buddhist monastery

【丛生】 cóngshēng ① (of plants) grow thickly: 荆棘～ be overgrown with brambles ② (of diseases, evils, etc.) break out: 百病～ all kinds of diseases and ailments breaking out

【丛书】 cóngshū　a series of books; collection: 知识青年自学～ school-leavers' self-study series

còu

凑 còu ① gather together; pool; collect: ～钱 pool money/ ～足人数 gather together enough people; get a quorum/ ～情况 pool information ② happen by chance; take advantage of: 正～上是个星期天。 It happened to be a Sunday./ ～空儿 try to find time (to do sth.) ③ move close to; press near: ～近точ儿。 Move closer, please.

【凑合】 còuhe ① gather together; collect; assemble: 昨天下班后大伙儿～在一起练歌。 Yesterday we gathered after work to practise singing. ② improvise: 请大家会前作好发

言准备，不要临时～。 Please prepare before coming to the meeting. Don't speak offhand. ③ make do: 我这件棉袄～～还能穿一冬。 I can make this padded jacket do for another winter./ 他没有学过会计，但还能～着记记帐。 He isn't a trained accountant, but he manages to keep simple accounts.

【凑集】 còují　gather together: ～图书以建立街道儿童阅览室 pool books to form a neighbourhood children's reading room

【凑巧】 còuqiǎo　luckily; fortunately; as luck would have it: 搬家的那一天，～赶上下雨。 As luck would have it, it rained the day we moved./ 真不～！ 他出去了。 What bad luck! He's not at home.

【凑热闹】 còu rènào ① join in the fun ② add trouble to: 我们够忙的，别再来～了。 We're busy enough as it is, don't give us more trouble.

【凑数】 còushù　make up the number or amount; serve as a stopgap

cū

粗* cū ① wide (in diameter); thick: ～绳 a thick rope/ 这棵树很～。 This tree has a thick trunk./ ～眉大眼 bushy eyebrows and big eyes ② coarse; crude; rough: ～沙 coarse sand; grit/ ～盐 crude salt/ ～黑的手 rough, work-soiled hands ③ gruff; husky: ～嗓子 a husky voice/ ～声大气 a deep, gruff voice ④ careless; negligent: ～中有细 usually careless, but quite sharp at times; crude in most matters, but subtle in some ⑤ rude; unrefined; vulgar: 说话很～ speak rudely; use coarse language ⑥ roughly; slightly: ～知一二 have a rough idea; know a little/ ～具规模 be roughly in shape

【粗暴】 cūbào　rude; rough; crude; brutal: ～态度 a rude attitude/ ～行为 crude behaviour

【粗笨】 cūbèn　clumsy; unwieldy: 动作～ clumsy/ ～的家具 unwieldy furniture

【粗鄙】 cūbǐ　vulgar; coarse: 言语～ vulgar in speech

【粗糙】 cūcāo　coarse; rough; crude: 皮肤～ rough skin/ 手工～ crudely made; of poor workmanship

【粗茶淡饭】 cūchá-dànfàn　plain tea and simple food; homely fare

【粗大】 cūdà ① thick; bulky: ～的手 big strong hands ② loud: ～的嗓门 a loud voice/ ～的鼾声 thunderous snoring

【粗犷】 cūguǎng ① rough; rude; boorish ② straightforward and uninhibited; bold and unconstrained; rugged

【粗话】 cūhuà　vulgar language

【粗活】 cūhuó　heavy manual labour; unskilled work

【粗劣】 cūliè　of poor quality; cheap; shoddy: ～的赝品 a cheap imitation

【粗陋】 cūlòu　coarse and crude: 这所房子盖得很～。 This is a crudely built house.

【粗鲁】 cūlǔ　rough; rude; boorish: 态度～ rude

【粗略】 cūlüè　rough; sketchy: ～估计 a rough estimate/ ～一看 on cursory examination

【粗浅】 cūqiǎn　superficial; shallow; simple: ～的体会 a superficial understanding/ ～的道理 a simple truth

【粗人】 cūrén　rough fellow; boor; unrefined person: 我是个～，说话直来直去，你可别见怪。 I'm a bit of a boor, so I hope you won't mind if I speak bluntly.

【粗率】 cūshuài　rough and careless; ill-considered: ～的决定 an ill-considered decision

【粗俗】 cūsú　vulgar; coarse: 说话～ use coarse or vulgar language

【粗细】 cūxì ① (degree of) thickness: 碗口～的钢管 steel tubes as big as the mouth of a bowl/ 这样～的沙子最合适。 Sand this fine will be just right. ② crudeness or fineness; degree of finish; quality of work: 庄稼长得好坏，也要看活的～。 Whether the crops grow well or badly depends also on how the work is done.

【粗线条】 cūxiàntiáo ① thick lines; rough outline: ～的描写 a rough sketch ② rough-and-ready; slapdash

【粗心】 cūxīn　careless; negligent; inadvertent: ～大意 negligent; careless; inadvertent

【粗野】 cūyě　rough; boorish; uncouth: 举止～ behave

boorishly/ 比赛中动作~ play rough

【粗枝大叶】 cūzhī-dàyè crude and careless; sloppy; slap-dash: ~的工作作风 a crude and careless style of work

【粗制滥造】 cūzhì-lànzào manufacture in a rough and slipshod way

【粗重】 cūzhòng ① (of voice, etc.) loud and jarring: ~的嗓音 a gruff voice/ ~的喘息声 loud breathing ② big and heavy; bulky: ~的钢管 big and heavy steel tubes ③ thick and heavy: ~眉毛浓黑 bushy black eyebrows ④ strenuous; heavy: ~的活计 heavy work; heavy manual labour

【粗壮】 cūzhuàng ① sturdy; thickset; brawny: ~的小伙子 a sturdy lad/ ~的胳臂 brawny arms ② thick and strong: ~的树干 a thick tree trunk ③ deep and resonant: 声音~ have a deep, resonant voice

cù

促* cù ① (of time) short; hurried; urgent: 气~ breathe quickly; be short of breath; pant ② urge; promote: 催~ urge; hurry ③ <书> close to; near: ~膝 sit knee to knee; sit close together

【促成】 cùchéng help to bring about; facilitate: ~双方取得协议 help to bring about an agreement between the two parties

【促进】 cùjìn promote; advance; accelerate: 互相~ help each other forward

【促使】 cùshǐ impel; urge; spur: 生产的发展~我们不断地钻研技术。 The development of production impels us continuously to study technique.

【促膝谈心】 cù xī tánxīn sit side by side and talk intimately; have a heart-to-heart talk

猝 cù <书> sudden; abrupt; unexpected: ~不及防 be taken by surprise

【猝然】 cùrán suddenly; abruptly; unexpectedly: ~决定 make a sudden decision

醋 cù ① vinegar ② jealousy (as in love affair): 吃~ feel jealous/ ~意 (feeling of) jealousy

簇 cù ①<书> form a cluster; pile up: 花团锦~ bouquets of flowers and piles of brocades — rich multicoloured decorations ②<量> cluster; bunch: 一~鲜花 a bunch of flowers/ 一~~灿烂的礼花 clusters of brilliant fireworks

【簇新】 cùxīn brand new

蹙 cù <书> ① pressed; cramped: 穷~ in dire straits ② knit (one's brows): ~额 knit one's brows; frown

蹴 cù <书> ① kick ② tread: 一~而就 reach the goal in one step; accomplish one's aim in one move

cuàn

窜 cuàn ① flee; scurry: 东逃西~ flee in all directions/ 鼠~ scurry like rats; run away like frightened rats ②<书> exile; expel ③ change (the wording in a text, manuscript, etc.); alter: 点~ make some alterations (in wording)

【窜改】 cuàngǎi alter; tamper with; falsify: ~原文 alter the original text/~记录 tamper with the minutes/ ~帐目 falsify accounts

【窜逃】 cuàntáo flee in disorder; scurry off

篡 cuàn usurp; seize: ~权 usurp power

【篡夺】 cuànduó usurp; seize

【篡改】 cuàngǎi distort; misrepresent; tamper with; falsify: ~历史 distort history

【篡位】 cuànwèi usurp the throne

cuī

崔 Cuī a surname

【崔巍】 cuīwēi <书> lofty; towering: 山势~。 The mountains stand tall and imposing.

【崔嵬】 cuīwéi <书> ① rocky mound ② high; towering

催* cuī ① urge; hurry; press: ~办 press sb. to do sth.; 扬鞭~马 urge one's horse on with a whip; whip one's horse on/ 去~他一下。 Go and hurry him up. ② hasten; expedite; speed up: 春风~绿。 The spring wind speeds the greening of the plants.

【催逼】 cuībī press (for payment of debt, etc.)

【催促】 cuīcù urge; hasten; press: 我们~她尽快来。 We urged her to come as soon as possible.

【催化】 cuīhuà <化> catalysis

【催泪弹】 cuīlèidàn tear bomb; tear-gas grenade

【催眠】 cuīmián lull (to sleep); hypnotize; mesmerize ◇ ~曲 lullaby; cradlesong/ ~术 hypnotism; mesmerism

摧 cuī break; destroy: ~折 break; snap/ 无坚不~ capable of destroying any stronghold; all-conquering

【摧残】 cuīcán wreck; destroy; devastate: ~身体 ruin one's health

【摧毁】 cuīhuǐ destroy; smash; wreck: ~敌人据点 destroy enemy strongholds

【摧枯拉朽】 cuīkū-lāxiǔ (as easy as) crushing dry weeds and smashing rotten wood

cuǐ

璀 cuǐ

【璀璨】 cuǐcàn <书> bright; resplendent: ~夺目 dazzling

cuì

脆 cuì ① fragile; brittle: 这纸太~。 This kind of paper is too fragile./ ~金属 brittle metal ② crisp: 这种梨又甜又~。 These pears are sweet and crisp. ③ (of voice) clear; crisp: 听她的嗓音多~! What a crisp voice she has!

【脆弱】 cuìruò fragile; frail; weak: 感情~ be easily upset

悴 cuì 见"憔悴" qiáocuì

萃 cuì <书> ① come together; assemble: 荟~ assemble ② a gathering of people or a collection of things: 出类拔~ outstanding

啐 cuì spit; expectorate: ~他一口 spit at him

瘁 cuì <书> overworked; tired: 心力交~ be physically and mentally tired

粹 cuì ① pure: ~白 pure white/ ~而不杂 pure and unadulterated ② essence; the best: 精~ essence; quintessence

翠 cuì ① emerald green; green: ~竹 green bamboos ② kingfisher: 点~ handicraft using kingfisher's feathers for ornament ③ jadeite: 珠~ pearls and jade jewellery

cūn

村* cūn ① village; hamlet ② rustic; boorish: ~野 boorish

【村落】 cūnluò village; hamlet

【村长】 cūnzhǎng village head

【村镇】 cūnzhèn villages and small towns

【村庄】 cūnzhuāng village; hamlet

cún

存* cún ① exist; live; survive: 父母均~。 Both parents are still living. ② store; keep: ~粮 store up grain/ 新

水库~了大量的水。 A large quantity of water is stored in the new reservoir. ③ accumulate; collect: 一下雨，洼地里就~了好些水。Whenever it rains, a lot of water accumulates in the low-lying land. ④ deposit: 把钱~在银行里 deposit money in a bank ⑤ leave with; check: 行李先~在这里,回头再来取。 Let's check our luggage here and come back for it later./ ~自行车 leave one's bicycle in a bicycle park ⑥ reserve; retain: 求同~异 seek common ground while reserving differences/ 他有什么说什么,肚子里~不住话。 He always says what he thinks; he can't hold anything back. ⑦ remain on balance; be in stock: 收支相抵,净~两千元。 The accounts show a surplus of $2,000 ⑧ cherish; harbour: ~着很大的希望 cherish high hopes/ 不~幻想 harbour no illusions

【存案】 cún'àn register with the proper authorities
【存储】 cúnchǔ 〈电子〉 memory; storage
【存档】 cúndàng keep in the archives; place on file; file
【存底儿】 cúndǐr keep the original draft; keep a file copy
【存放】 cúnfàng ①leave with; leave in sb.'s care: 我把箱子~在朋友那里了。 I've left my suitcase with a friend of mine. ② deposit (money)
【存根】 cúngēn counterfoil; stub: 支票~ cheque stub
【存户】 cúnhù depositor
【存货】 cúnhuò goods in stock; existing stock
【存款】 cúnkuǎn deposit; bank savings: 个人~ personal savings account/ 活期~ current deposit; demand deposit/ 定期~ fixed deposit; time deposit
【存亡】 cún-wáng live or die; survive or perish
【存心】 cúnxīn ① cherish certain intentions: ~不良 cherish evil designs (或 intentions)/ 他说这番话,不知安什么心。 It's hard to say what his intentions were in saying that. ② intentionally; deliberately; on purpose: 我不是~这么做的。 I didn't do it on purpose.
【存疑】 cúnyí leave a question open; leave a matter for future consideration: 这件事情暂时~吧。 Let's put this matter aside for the time being.
【存在】 cúnzài exist; be

cǔn

忖 cǔn turn over in one's mind; ponder; speculate
【忖度】 cǔnduó speculate; conjecture; surmise
【忖量】 cǔnliàng ① think over; turn over in one's mind: 她~了半天,还拿不定主意。 She turned the matter over in her mind for a long while but still could not come to a decision. ② conjecture; guess: 我一边走,一边~着他说的那番话的意思。 As I walked along I kept wondering what he really meant.

cùn

寸* cùn ①cun, a unit of length (= ¹/₃ decimetre) ② very little; very short; small: ~进 a little progress/ ~功 small contribution; meagre achievement/ ~草不留 leave not even a blade of grass; be devastated/ ~土必争 fight for every inch of land
【寸步】 cùnbù a tiny step; a single step: ~不离 follow sb. closely; keep close to/ ~不让 refuse to yield an inch
【寸金难买寸光阴】 cùn jīn nán mǎi cùn guāngyīn 〈谚〉 money can't buy time; time is more precious than gold
【寸心】 cùnxīn feelings: 聊表~ as a small token of my feelings; just to show my appreciation
【寸阴】 cùnyīn 〈书〉 time indicated by a shadow moving a cun — a very short time

cuō

搓 cuō rub with the hands: ~手取暖 rub one's hands together to warm them/ 麻绳 make cord by twisting hemp fibres between the palms/ 这件上衣太脏了,洗时要多~~。 This jacket is very dirty; give it a good scrubbing.

【搓球】 cuōqiú 〈乒乓球〉 chop: 一板一板地把球搓过去 return every shot with a chop
【搓手顿脚】 cuōshǒu-dùnjiǎo wring one's hands and stamp one's feet — get anxious and impatient

磋 cuō consult
【磋商】 cuōshāng consult; exchange views: 与各有关部门进行~ hold consultations with all departments concerned

撮 cuō ①〈书〉 gather; bring together ② scoop up (with a dustpan or shovel): ~走一簸箕土 scoop up a dustpan of dirt ③〈方〉 take up with the fingers: ~一点盐 take a pinch of salt ④ extract; summarize: ~要 make extracts ⑤ cuo, a unit of capacity (= 1 millilitre) ⑥〈量〉 pinch: 一~盐 a pinch of salt
另见 zuǒ
【撮合】 cuōhe make a match; act as go-between
【撮弄】 cuōnòng ① make fun of; play a trick on; tease ② abet; instigate; incite

蹉 cuō
【蹉跎】 cuōtuó waste time: ~岁月 let time slip by without accomplishing anything; idle away one's time/ 一再~ let one opportunity after another slip away

cuò

挫 cuò ①defeat; frustrate: 受~ suffer a setback ② subdue; lower: ~敌人的锐气,长自己的威风 deflate the enemy's arrogance and boost our own morale/ ~其锋芒 blunt the edge of one's advance
【挫败】 cuòbài frustrate; foil; defeat: 遭到严重的~ suffer a serious defeat
【挫伤】 cuòshāng ①〈医〉 contusion; bruise ② dampen; blunt; discourage
【挫折】 cuòzhé setback; reverse: 遭受~ suffer setbacks (或 reverses)

厝 cuò 〈书〉 ① lay; place ② place a coffin in a temporary shelter pending burial
【厝火积薪】 cuò huǒ jī xīn put a fire under a pile of faggots — a hidden danger

措 cuò ① arrange; manage; handle: 惊慌失~ be seized with panic; be frightened out of one's wits/ 不知所~ be at a loss what to do; be at one's wit's end ② make plans: 筹~款项 raise funds
【措辞】 cuòcí wording; diction: ~不当 inappropriate wording/ ~严厉 couched in harsh terms/ ~强硬 strongly worded
【措施】 cuòshī measure; step: 采取重大~ adopt an important measure/ 十分指标,十二分~。 If the target is ten, take measures to achieve twelve — make ample preparations to guarantee success.
【措手不及】 cuò shǒu bù jí be caught unprepared; be caught unawares: 打他个~ make a surprise attack on them

锉 cuò ① file: 方~ square file/ 圆~ round file/ 木~ (wood) rasp ② make smooth with a file; file: ~光 file sth. smooth
【锉刀】 cuòdāo file

错* cuò ① interlocked and jagged; intricate; complex: 犬牙交~ jigsaw-like; interlocking ② grind; rub: ~牙 grind one's teeth (in one's sleep) ③ alternate; stagger: 这两个会不能同时开,得~一下。 We can't hold the two meetings at the same time; we must stagger them. ④

wrong; mistaken; erroneous: 你弄～了。You've got it wrong./ 拿～东西 take sth. by mistake ⑤ fault; demerit: 这是他的～,不怨你。You are not to blame; it is his fault. ⑥〔用于否定式〕bad; poor: 今年的收成～不了。This year's harvest is sure to be good./ 他们感情不～。They are on good terms. ⑦＜书＞ inlay or plate with gold, silver, etc. ⑧＜书＞ grindstone for polishing jade: 他山之石,可以为～。Stones from other hills may serve to polish the jade of this one — advice from others may help one overcome one's shortcomings.

【错爱】cuò'ài ＜谦＞ undeserved kindness

【错别字】cuò-biézì wrongly written or mispronounced characters

【错处】cuòchu fault; demerit

【错怪】cuòguài blame sb. wrongly

【错过】cuòguò miss; let slip: ～机会 miss an opportunity/ ～这趟汽车,今天就走不成了。If we miss this bus, we won't be able to go today.

【错觉】cuòjué illusion; misconception; wrong impression: 这样会给人造成～。This will give people a false impression.

【错乱】cuòluàn in disorder; in confusion; deranged: 颠倒 ～ topsy-turvy/ 精神～ mentally deranged; insane

【错误】cuòwù ① wrong; mistaken; erroneous: ～思想 wrong thinking; a mistaken idea/ ～的结论 wrong conclusion/ ～路线 an erroneous line ② mistake; error; blunder: 犯～ make a mistake; commit an error/ ～百出 riddled with errors; full of mistakes

【错杂】cuòzá mixed; heterogeneous; jumbled; of mixed content

【错字】cuòzì ① wrongly written character ② misprint

【错综复杂】cuòzōng-fùzá intricate; complex: 这部小说的情节～,引人入胜。The plot of the novel is intricate and fascinating.

D

dā

搭* dā ① put up; build: ～一个临时舞台 put up a makeshift stage/ ～桥 build a bridge/ ～帐篷 pitch a tent ② hang over; put over: 把洗好的衣服～在绳上 hang the washing on a line/ 他肩膀上～着一块毛巾。He had a towel over his shoulder. ③ come into contact; join: 两根电线～上了。The two wires are touching./ ～上关系 strike up a relationship with; establish contact with/ 前言不～后语 speak incoherently; mumble disconnected phrases ④ throw in more (people, money, etc.); add: 你忙不过来,给你一个人吧。You're terribly busy. We'll send someone to help you. ⑤ lift sth. together: 帮我把这包大米～上卡车。Help me lift the bag of rice onto the truck./ 我们俩把这筐土～走。Let's carry this basket of earth away. ⑥ take (a ship, plane, etc.); travel (或 go) by: ～轮船去上海 go to Shanghai by boat/ ～飞机 go by plane/ ～长途汽车 travel by coach/ ～他们的车走 get a lift in their car

【搭乘】 dāchéng travel by (plane, car, ship, etc.)

【搭档】 dādàng ① cooperate; work together: 我俩～吧。Let us two team up. ② partner: 老～ old partner; old workmate

【搭伙】 dāhuǒ ① join as partner: 他们明天去参观故宫,我也想～去。They're going to visit the Palace Museum tomorrow and I'd like to join them. ② eat regularly in (a mess, etc.): 我们都在厂里食堂～。We all eat in the factory canteen.

【搭救】 dājiù rescue; go to the rescue of

【搭客】 dākè 〈方〉 take on passengers

【搭腔】 dāqiāng ① answer; respond: 我问了两遍,没人～。I repeated my question, but nobody answered. ② talk to each other: 以前他俩合不来,彼此不～。In the past the two did not get on at all well; they weren't even on speaking terms.

【搭讪】 dāshàn strike up a conversation with sb.; say something to smooth over an embarrassing situation: 他很尴尬,～着走开了。Feeling embarrassed, he muttered a few words and walked off.

答* dā
另见 dá

【答应】 dāying ① answer; reply; respond: 敲了半天门没人～。I knocked again and again but there was no answer. ② agree; promise; comply with: 我们请他来参加座谈会,他已经～了。We asked him to attend our discussion, and he agreed to come./ 他～八点半到。He promised to be here at 8:30.

dá

打* dá 〈量〉 dozen: 一～铅笔 a dozen pencils/ 论～出售 sell by the dozen
另见 dǎ

达 dá ① extend: 这里铁路四通八～。Here you find railways extending in all directions./ 这是开往泰国的直～火车。This is a through train to Thailand. ② reach; attain; amount to: 我们不～目的决不罢休。We will never cease our efforts until we achieve our aim./ 听众鼓掌～两分钟之久。The audience applauded for two whole minutes. ③ understand thoroughly: 通情～理 be understanding and reasonable; be sensible ④ express; communicate: 上级的重要指示要立即下～。Important directives from the higher authorities should be handed down immediately. ⑤ eminent; distinguished: ～官 ranking official

【达成】 dáchéng reach (agreement): 双方就会议议程～协议。The two parties reached agreement on the agenda of the meeting./ ～交易 strike a bargain

【达旦】 dádàn until dawn: 通宵～ all through the night

【达到】 dádào achieve; attain; reach: ～目的 achieve (或 attain) the goal/ ～高潮 reach a high tide; come to a climax/ ～世界先进水平 come up to advanced world standards/ 货物运输量～四千万吨。The volume of freight handled will amount to 40 million tons.

【达观】 dáguān take things philosophically

【达官贵人】 dáguān-guìrén high officials and noble lords; VIPs

【达意】 dáyì express (或 convey) one's ideas: 词不～。The words fail to convey the idea./ 抒情～ express one's thoughts and feelings

沓 dá 〈量〉 pile (of paper, etc.); pad: 一～报纸 a pile of newspapers/ 一～信纸 a pad of letter paper/ 一～钞票 a wad of bank notes
另见 tà

答* dá ① answer; reply; respond: ～非所问 an irrelevant answer ② return (a visit, etc.); reciprocate: ～礼 return a salute
另见 dā

【答案】 dá'àn answer; solution; key: 找不到问题的～ find no solution to the problem/ 练习的～ key to an exercise

【答辩】 dábiàn reply (to a charge, query or an argument): 保留公开～的权利 reserve the right of public reply

【答词】 dácí thank-you speech; answering speech; reply

【答复】 dáfù answer; reply: ～他的询问 reply to his inquiry

【答话】 dáhuà 〔多用于否定句〕 answer; reply: 你怎么不～? Why don't you answer?

【答谢】 dáxiè express appreciation (for sb.'s kindness or hospitality); acknowledge ◇ ～宴会 a return banquet

dǎ

打* dǎ ① strike; hit; knock: ～门 knock at the door/ 锣～鼓 beat gongs and drums/ ～稻子 thresh rice ② break; smash: 窗玻璃～了。The windowpane is broken. ③ fight; attack: ～硬仗 fight a hard battle/ 你们～得好。You're putting up a good fight. ④ mix; stir; beat: ～鸡蛋 beat eggs ⑤ raise; hoist: ～伞 hold up an umbrella/ ～起精神来 raise one's spirits; cheer up ⑥ send; dispatch; project: ～电报 send a telegram/ ～电话 make a phone call/ ～信号 signal; give a signal. ⑦ gather; collect; reap: ～柴 gather firewood ⑧ catch; hunt: ～鱼 catch fish/ ～野鸭 go duck-hunting. ⑨ play: ～篮球 play basketball/ ～扑克 play cards/ ～秋千 have a swing ⑩〔表示身体上的某些动作〕: ～个跟斗 turn (或 do) a somersault/ ～手势 make a gesture; gesticulate/ ～喷嚏 sneeze ⑪ adopt; use: ～个比方 draw an analogy
另见 dá

【打靶】 dǎbǎ target (或 shooting) practice ◇ ～场 target range

【打败】 dǎbài ① defeat; beat; worst ② suffer a defeat; be defeated

【打扮】 dǎbàn dress up; make up; deck out: 孩子们～得象春天的花朵一样。The gaily-dressed children looked like spring flowers.

【打抱不平】 dǎ bàobùpíng take up the cudgels for the injured party; defend sb. against an injustice

【打草惊蛇】 dǎ cǎo jīng shé beat the grass and frighten away the snake — act rashly and alert the enemy

【打岔】 dǎchà interrupt; cut in: 他们在谈正经事儿,别～。Don't interrupt them; they're talking business.

【打成一片】 dǎchéng yīpiàn become one with; identify oneself with; merge with

【打倒】 dǎdǎo overthrow

【打得火热】 dǎde huǒrè be on terms of intimacy; be as thick as thieves

【打点】 dǎdian get (luggage, etc.) ready

【打掉】 dǎdiào destroy; knock out; wipe out

【打动】 dǎdòng move; touch: ~了他的心。 He was moved (或 touched) by these words.

【打赌】 dǎdǔ bet; wager: 我敢~他明天准来。 I bet he'll come tomorrow.

【打断】 dǎduàn ① break: 我爸爸的腿是被强盗~的。 It was the robber who broke my father's leg. ② interrupt; cut short: ~思路 interrupt sb.'s train of thought/ 别~他,让他说完。 Don't cut him short; let him finish./ 他的讲话不时被热烈的掌声~。 His speech was punctuated with warm applause.

【打耳光】 dǎ ěrguāng box sb.'s ears; slap sb. in the face

【打发】 dǎfa ① send; dispatch: 赶快~人去请医生。 Send for a doctor at once. ② dismiss; send away: 他把孩子们~走了,坐下来工作。 He sent the children away and sat down to work. ③ while away (one's time)

【打嗝儿】 dǎgér 〈口〉 ① hiccup ② belch; burp

【打躬作揖】 dǎgōng-zuòyī fold the hands and make deep bows; do obeisance; beg humbly

【打鼓】 dǎgǔ ① beat a drum ② feel uncertain (或 nervous): 心里直~ feel extremely diffident

【打官腔】 dǎ guānqiāng talk like a bureaucrat; stall with official jargon

【打官司】 dǎ guānsi ① go to court (或 law); engage in a lawsuit ② 〈口〉 squabble: 打不完的官司 endless squabbles

【打滚】 dǎgǔn roll about: 小驴子在地上~。 The little donkey rolled on the ground./ 疼得直~ writhe with pain

【打哈哈】 dǎ hāha make fun; crack a joke: 别拿我~。Don't make fun of me./ 这是正经事,可别~。 This is a serious matter; let's not joke about it.

【打哈欠】 dǎ hāqian yawn

【打火】 dǎhuǒ strike sparks from a flint; strike a light ◇ ~机 lighter

【打击】 dǎjī hit; strike; attack: ~投机倒把活动 crack down on speculation and profiteering/ ~歪风 take strong measures against unhealthy tendencies/~报复 retaliate/ 狠狠~敌人 strike relentless blows at the enemy

【打家劫舍】 dǎjiā-jiéshè loot; plunder

【打架】 dǎjià come to blows; fight; scuffle

【打交道】 dǎ jiāodao come into (或 make) contact with; have dealings with: 两个厂经常~。 The two factories maintain frequent contacts./ 我没跟他打过交道。 I've never had any dealings with him.

【打搅】 dǎjiǎo disturb; trouble: 人家正在工作,别去~他了。 He's working. Don't disturb him./ 对不起,~您了! Sorry to have bothered you./ ~您一下。 May I trouble you a minute?

【打劫】 dǎjié rob; plunder; loot: 趁火~ loot a burning house

【打结】 dǎjié tie a knot

【打开】 dǎkāi ① open; unfold: 把门~ open the door/ ~盖子 take off the lid/ ~包袱 untie a bundle/ ~缺口 make a breach/ ~眼界 widen one's horizon ② turn on; switch on: ~收音机(电灯) turn on the radio (light)

【打开天窗说亮话】 dǎkāi tiānchuāng shuō liànghuà frankly speaking; let's not mince matters

【打瞌睡】 dǎ kēshuì doze off; nod

【打捞】 dǎlāo get out of the water; salvage: ~沉船 salvage a sunken ship/ ~尸体 retrieve a corpse from the water

【打量】 dǎliang ① measure with the eye; look sb. up and down; size up: 门卫上下~着那个陌生人。 The sentry looked the stranger up and down. ② think; suppose; reckon: 你~她这点事都干不了? Do you think she can't do a little job like that?

【打猎】 dǎliè go hunting

【打落水狗】 dǎ luòshuǐgǒu beat a drowning dog — completely crush a defeated enemy

【打屁股】 dǎ pìgu ① beat on the buttocks; spank ② 〈口〉 take sb. to task

【打破】 dǎpò break; smash: ~僵局 break a deadlock; find a way out of a stalemate/ ~记录 break a record/ ~界线 break down barriers/ ~平衡 upset a balance/

【打破沙锅问到底】 dǎpò shāguō wèn dàodǐ insist on getting to the bottom of the matter

【打气】 dǎqì ① inflate; pump up: 给车胎~ inflate (或pump up) a tyre ② bolster up (或 boost) the morale; encourage; cheer up ◇ ~筒 inflater; tyre pump

【打趣】 dǎqù banter; tease; make fun of

【打圈子】 dǎ quānzi circle: 飞机在机场上空~。 The plane circled over the airfield./ 不要在枝节问题上~。 Don't get bogged down in minor issues.

【打扫】 dǎsǎo sweep; clean: ~房间 clean a room/ ~垃圾 sweep away rubbish/ ~战场 clean up the battlefield/ 把院子~干净 sweep the courtyard clean

【打手】 dǎshou hired roughneck (或 thug); hatchet man

【打算】 dǎsuàn plan; intend: 代表团~去日本访问。 The delegation plans to visit Japan./ 他~当教师。 He intends to become a teacher./ 作最坏的~ be prepared for the worst/ 各有各的~。 Each has a plan of his own. 或 Each has his own calculations.

【打算盘】 dǎ suànpan calculate on an abacus; calculate: 打小算盘 be calculating; be petty and scheming/ 打错算盘 miscalculate

【打碎】 dǎsuì break into pieces; smash; destroy: 玻璃杯~了。 The glass is smashed to pieces.

【打胎】 dǎtāi have an (induced) abortion

【打听】 dǎting ask about; inquire about: 跟您~一件事。 I'd like to ask you about something.

【打通】 dǎtōng get through; open up: 电话打不通 be unable to get through (on the telephone)/ 两家的院墙~了。 An opening has been made in the wall between the two courtyards./ ~思想 straighten out sb.'s thinking; talk sb. round

【打头阵】 dǎ tóuzhèn fight in the van; spearhead the attack; take the lead

【打退堂鼓】 dǎ tuìtánggǔ beat a retreat; back out: 不能遇到点困难就~呀。 You can't back out the moment you run up against a little difficulty.

【打消】 dǎxiāo give up (an idea, etc.); dispel (a doubt, etc.): 她~了春节回家的念头。 She gave up the idea of going home for the Spring Festival./ ~顾虑 dispel misgivings

【打游击】 dǎ yóujī ① fight as a guerrilla: 上山~ join the guerrillas in the mountains; wage guerrilla warfare in the mountains ② 〈口〉 work (eat, sleep, etc.) at no fixed place

【打圆场】 dǎ yuánchǎng mediate a dispute; smooth things over

【打仗】 dǎzhàng fight; go to war; make war

【打招呼】 dǎ zhāohu ① greet sb.; say hello ② notify; let sb. know: 你什么时候去东京,给我打个招呼。 When you go to Tokyo, please let me know. ③ warn; remind: 事先已跟他们打过招呼了。 I've already warned them.

【打折扣】 dǎ zhékòu ① sell at a discount; give a discount ② fall short of a requirement or promise: 说到做到,不~ carry out one's pledge to the letter

【打针】 dǎzhēn give or have an injection

【打肿脸充胖子】 dǎzhǒng liǎn chōng pàngzi slap one's face until it's swollen in an effort to look imposing — puff oneself up to one's own cost

【打主意】 dǎ zhǔyì ① think of a plan; evolve an idea: 打定主意 make up one's mind/ 打错主意 miscalculate; make a wrong decision ② try to obtain; seek: 他们正在打你的主意,要你帮忙呢。 They are thinking of asking you to help.

【打桩】 dǎzhuāng pile driving; piling ◇ ~机 pile driver

【打字】 dǎzì typewrite; type ◇ ~带 typewriter ribbon/~稿 typescript/ ~机 typewriter/ ~员 typist/ ~纸 typing-paper

【打坐】 dǎzuò (of a Buddhist or Taoist monk) sit in meditation

dà

大* dà ① big; large; great: ~城市 a big city/ ~英雄 the great hero/ 这张照片~得~。The picture isn't large enough. ② heavy (rain, etc.); strong (wind, etc.) ③ loud: 声音太~ too loud/ 收音机开~一点。Turn the radio up a bit louder. ④ general; main; major: ~路 main road; highway/ ~问题 major issue; big problem/ ~手术 major operation/ ~反攻 general counteroffensive ⑤ size: 那间屋子有这间两个~。That room is twice the size of this one./ 你穿多~的鞋? What size shoes do you wear? ⑥ age: 你的孩子多~了? How old is your child? ⑦ greatly; fully: ~吃一惊 be greatly surprised; be quite taken aback ⑧ in a big way; on a big (或 large) scale; with all-out efforts; vigorously: ~搞农田水利 go all out with irrigation and water conservancy ⑨ eldest: ~哥 eldest brother ⑩〈敬〉your: ~札 your letter/ ~作 your writing ⑪〔用在时间或节日前表示强调〕: ~白天 in broad daylight/ ~清早 early in the morning
　　　另见　dài

【大白】 dàbái　come out; become known: 真相已~于天下。The truth has become known to all.

【大败】 dàbài ① defeat utterly; put to rout: ~敌军 inflict a crushing defeat on the enemy ② suffer a crushing defeat

【大半】 dàbàn ① more than half; greater part; most: 一天的~时间 most of the day/ 突击队的队员~是青年人。Most of the members of this shock team are young. ② very likely; most probably: 他~不来了。Most probably he isn't coming.

【大本营】 dàběnyíng ① supreme headquarters ② base camp: 登山队~ the base camp of a mountaineering expedition

【大便】 dàbiàn ① defecate; have a bowel movement; shit: ~不通 (suffer from) constipation ② stool; human excrement; shit; faeces: 去化验~ have one's stool examined

【大辩论】 dàbiànlùn great (或 mass) debate

【大不了】 dàbuliǎo ① at the worst; if the worst comes to the worst: ~我们走着回去。If the worst comes to the worst, we'll walk back. ②〔多用于否定式〕alarming; serious: 划破点皮, 没有什么~的。It's nothing serious, just a scratch.

【大材小用】 dàcái xiǎo yòng put fine timber to petty use; use talented people for trivial tasks; waste one's talent on a petty job

【大吹大擂】 dàchuī-dàlèi make a great fanfare; make a big noise

【大慈大悲】 dàcí-dàbēi 〔佛教用语, 现多用于讽刺〕infinitely merciful

【大打出手】 dà dǎ chūshǒu strike violently; attack brutally

【大大】 dàdà greatly; enormously: 生产效率~提高。Productivity has risen greatly. 今年的棉花产量~超过了去年。This year's cotton production exceeded last year's by a big margin.

【大…大…】 dà…dà… 〔分别用在名词、动词或形容词的前面, 表示规模大、程度深〕: 大鱼大肉 plenty of meat and fish; rich food/ 大红大绿 loud colours/ 大吵大闹 kick up a row; make a scene/ 大吃大喝 eat and drink extravagantly

【大胆】 dàdǎn bold; daring; audacious: ~的革新 a bold innovation

【大刀】 dàdāo broadsword

【大刀阔斧】 dàdāo-kuòfǔ bold and resolute; drastic

【大道理】 dàdàolǐ major principle; general principle; great truth: 这些~人人都懂, 真正做到可不容易啊! These general principles are widely known, but it isn't easy to live up to them./ 小道理要服从~。Minor principles should be subordinated to major ones.

【大敌】 dàdí formidable enemy; archenemy: ~当前 faced with a formidable foe

【大抵】 dàdǐ generally speaking; in the main; on the whole

【大地】 dàdì earth; mother earth: ~回春 Spring returns to the earth. 或 Spring is here again./ 走遍祖国~ travel all over the land

【大典】 dàdiǎn ① grand ceremony: 开国~ the ceremony to proclaim the founding of a state ② a body of classical writings; canon

【大都】 dàdū for the most part; mostly: 这些诗歌~是学生们写的。Most of these poems were written by students

【大多】 dàduō for the most part; mostly: 出席大会的代表~是科学工作者。The representatives present at the meeting are mostly scientists.

【大多数】 dàduōshù great majority; vast majority; the bulk: 团结~ unite with the great majority/ 人口的~ the bulk of the population

【大而无当】 dà ér wú dàng large but impractical; unwieldy: ~的计划 a grandiose but impractical plan

【大发雷霆】 dà fā léitíng be furious; fly into a rage; bawl at sb. angrily

【大方】 dàfāng ① generous; liberal ② natural and poised; easy; unaffected: 举止~ have an easy manner; have poise; carry oneself with ease and confidence ③ in good taste; tasteful: 这种料子的颜色和花样很~。The pattern and colour of this fabric are in good taste.

【大风】 dàfēng ①〈气〉fresh gale ② gale; strong wind: 外面刮着~。There's a gale blowing. 或 It's blowing hard.

【大风大浪】 dàfēng-dàlàng wind and waves; great storms

【大腹便便】 dàfù piánpián potbellied; big-bellied

【大概】 dàgài ① general idea; broad outline: 我只知道个~。I have only a general idea. ② general; rough; approximate: 作一个~的分析 make a general analysis/ ~的数字 an approximate figure/ ~的估计 a rough estimate ③ probably; most likely; presumably: 会议~要延期。The meeting will probably be postponed.

【大纲】 dàgāng outline: 世界史~ an outline history of the world

【大哥】 dàgē ① eldest brother ② elder brother (a polite form of address for a man about one's own age)

【大公无私】 dàgōng-wúsī ① selfless; unselfish ② perfectly impartial

【大功】 dàgōng great merit; extraordinary service: 立了~ have performed exceptionally meritorious services

【大功告成】 dàgōng gàochéng (of a project, work, etc.) be accomplished; be crowned with success

【大规模】 dàguīmó large-scale; extensive; massive; mass: ~生产 large-scale production/ ~兴修水利 launch a large-scale (或 extensive) water conservancy project

【大过】 dàguò serious offence: 记~一次 record a serious mistake

【大海捞针】 dàhǎi lāo zhēn fish for a needle in the ocean; look for a needle in a haystack

【大喊大叫】 dàhǎn-dàjiào shout at the top of one's voice

【大汉】 dàhàn big (或 hefty, burly) fellow

【大好】 dàhǎo very good; excellent: 形势~。The situation is very good./ ~河山 beautiful rivers and mountains of a country; one's beloved motherland/ ~时机 opportune moment; golden opportunity; finest hour

【大号】 dàhào ① large size: ~的鞋 large-size shoes ②〈乐〉tuba; bass horn ③〈敬〉your (given) name

【大亨】 dàhēng big shot; bigwig; magnate

【大红】 dàhóng bright red; scarlet

【大后年】 dàhòunián three years from now

【大后天】 dàhòutiān three days from now

【大话】 dàhuà big (或 tall) talk; boast; bragging: 说~ talk big; brag

【大会】 dàhuì ① plenary session; general membership meeting ② mass meeting; mass rally

【大伙儿】 dàhuǒr 〈口〉we all; you all; everybody

【大惑不解】 dà huò bù jiě be extremely puzzled; be unable to make head or tail of sth.

【大计】 dàjì a major programme of lasting importance; a matter of fundamental importance: 百年~ a matter of fundamental importance for generations to come: a major project affecting future generations/ 共商~ discuss matters of vital importance

【大家】 dàjiā ① great master; authority: 书法~ a great master of calligraphy; a noted calligrapher ② all; everybody: ~的事~管。Everybody's business should be every body's responsibility.

【大家庭】 dàjiātíng big family; community

【大教堂】 dàjiàotáng cathedral

【大街】 dàjiē main street; street

【大捷】 dàjié great victory

【大姐】 dàjiě ①eldest sister ②elder sister (a polite form of address for a woman about one's own age)

【大惊小怪】 dàjīng-xiǎoguài be surprised or alarmed at sth. perfectly normal; make a fuss: 有什么值得~的? What's there to be surprised at?

【大局】 dàjú overall (或 general, whole) situation: 顾全~ take the whole situation into account; take the interests of the whole into account/ 事关~。It's an issue that concerns the overall situation./ ~已定。The outcome is a foregone conclusion.

【大举】 dàjǔ carry out (a military operation) on a large scale: ~进攻 mount a large-scale offensive; attack in force

【大楷】 dàkǎi ①regular script in big characters, as used in Chinese calligraphy exercises ②block letters; blockwriting

【大考】 dàkǎo end-of-term examination; final exam

【大快人心】 dà kuài rénxīn (of the punishment of an evil-doer) affording general satisfaction; most gratifying to the people; to the immense satisfaction of the people

【大理石】 dàlǐshí marble

【大力】 dàlì energetically; vigorously: ~支援农业 give energetic support to agriculture/ ~发展教育事业 devote major efforts to developing education

【大力士】 dàlìshì a man of unusual strength

【大量】 dàliàng ①a large number; a great quantity: 为国家积累~资金 accumulate large funds for the state/ ~生产拖拉机 mass-produce tractors/ ~杀伤敌人 inflict heavy casualties on the enemy/ 收集~科学资料 collect a vast amount of scientific data/ ~财富 enormous wealth; large fortune/ ~事实 a host of facts/ ~库存 huge stocks ②generous; magnanimous: 宽宏~ magnanimous; large-minded

【大陆】 dàlù continent; mainland

【大略】 dàlüè ①general idea; broad outline: 我只知道个~。I have only a general idea. ②generally; roughly; approximately: ~相同 roughly the same/ 时间不多了,你~说说吧。There isn't much time left. Could you speak just briefly?

【大麻】 dàmá ①hemp ②marijuana

【大名】 dàmíng ①one's formal personal name ②〈敬〉your (given) name

【大名鼎鼎】 dàmíng dǐngdǐng famous; celebrated; well-known

【大模大样】 dàmú-dàyàng in an ostentatious manner; with a swagger

【大拇指】 dàmuzhǐ 〈口〉thumb: 竖起~叫好 hold up one's thumb in approval

【大难】 dànàn catastrophe; disaster: ~临头 be faced with imminent disaster

【大逆不道】 dà nì bù dào treason and heresy; worst offence; greatest outrage

【大炮】 dàpào ①artillery; big gun; cannon ②〈口〉one who speaks boastfully or forcefully; one who noisily overstates things

【大批】 dàpī ①large quantities (或 numbers, amounts) of: ~轻工业品运往农村。Large quantities of light industrial products are transported to the countryside.

【大气】 dàqì ①〈气〉atmosphere; air ②heavy breathing: 跑得直喘~ breathe heavily from running/ 吓得连~也不敢出 catch (或 hold) one's breath in fear

【大器晚成】 dàqì wǎn chéng great minds mature slowly

【大千世界】 dàqiān shìjiè 〈佛教〉the boundless universe

【大庆】 dàqìng ①grand celebration of an important event; great occasion: 十年~ the festive occasion of the 10th anniversary ②〈敬〉〔用于老年人〕birthday: 七十~ seventieth birthday

【大权】 dàquán power over major issues; authority: ~在握 hold power in one's hands/ ~独揽 centralize power in one man's hands ·to deal with major issues; arrogate all authority to oneself/ ~旁落。Power has fallen into the hands of others.

【大人】 dàrén 〈敬〉〔旧时多用于书信〕:父亲~ Dear Father

【大人】 dàren ①adult; grown-up ②〈旧〉(直接称呼) Your Excellency; (间接称呼) His Excellency

【大人物】 dàrénwù important person; great personage; big shot; VIP

【大扫除】 dàsǎochú general cleaning; thorough cleanup: 节日~ thorough cleanup before a holiday

【大嫂】 dàsǎo ①eldest brother's wife; sister-in-law ②elder sister (a polite form of address for a woman about one's own age)

【大厦】 dàshà large building; mansion

【大赦】 dàshè amnesty; general pardon

【大声疾呼】 dàshēng jíhū raise a cry of warning; loudly appeal to the public

【大失所望】 dà shī suǒ wàng greatly disappointed; to one's great disappointment

【大师】 dàshī ①great master; master: 国画~ a great master of traditional Chinese painting ②〈佛教〉Great Master, a courtesy title used to address a Buddhist monk

【大师傅】 dàshīfu cook; chef

【大使】 dàshǐ ambassador: 特命全权~ ambassador extraordinary and plenipotentiary ◇ ~馆 embassy/ ~级会谈 talks at ambassadorial level; ambassadorial talks/ ~衔 ambassadorial rank

【大事】 dàshì ①great (或 major) event; important matter; major issue: 头等~ a matter of prime (或 paramount) importance/ 关心国家~ concern oneself with affairs of state/ 当前国际政治中的一件~ a major event in current international politics/ 完成了一桩~ have accomplished an important task ②overall (或 general) situation: ~不好。A disaster is imminent. ③in a big way: ~渲染 enormously exaggerate; play up ◇ ~记 chronicle of events

【大事化小,小事化了】 dàshì huà xiǎo, xiǎoshì huà liǎo turn big problems into small problems and small problems into no problem at all

【大势】 dàshì general trend of events: ~所趋,人心所向 the trend of the times and the desire of the people; the general trend and popular feeling/ ~已去。The game is as good as lost. 或 Not much can be done about it now.

【大肆】 dàsì without restraint; wantonly: ~攻击 wantonly vilify; launch an unbridled (或 all-out) attack against/ ~鼓吹 noisily advocate/ ~宣扬 indulge in unbridled propaganda/ for; give enormous publicity to

【大…特…】 dà...tè... 〔分别用在同一个词前面,表示规模大,程度深〕:大错特错 make a gross error; be grievously mistaken/ 大书特书 record in letters of gold; write volumes about

【大提琴】 dàtíqín violoncello; cello

【大体】 dàtǐ ①cardinal principle; general interest: 识~, 顾大局 have the cardinal principles in mind and take the overall situation into account ②roughly; more or less; on the whole; by and large; for the most part: ~相同 more or less alike; about the same/ 收支~平衡。Income and expenditure roughly balance./ 我~上同意你的看法。On the whole I agree with you.

【大厅】 dàtīng hall

【大庭广众】 dàtíng-guǎngzhòng (before) a big crowd; (on) a public occasion: ~之中 in public; on a public occasion

【大同小异】 dàtóng-xiǎoyì largely identical but with minor differences; alike except for slight differences; very much the same

【大头针】 dàtóuzhēn pin

【大团圆】 dàtuányuán ①happy reunion ②happy ending

【大腿】 dàtuǐ thigh

【大王】 dàwáng king; magnate: 煤油~ oil king; oil magnate

【大无畏】 dàwúwèi dauntless; utterly fearless; indomitable: ~的英雄气概 dauntless heroism

【大喜】 dàxǐ 〈口〉great rejoicing: 在这~的日子里 in these days of great rejoicing

【大喜过望】 dàxǐ guò wàng be delighted that things are better than one expected; be overjoyed

【大显身手】 dà xiǎn shēnshǒu display one's skill to the full; give full play to one's abilities; distinguish oneself; give a good account of oneself

【大显神通】 dà xiǎn shéntōng give full play to one's remarkable skill (或 abilities)

【大小】 dàxiǎo ①big or small: ~水库十座 ten reservoirs

of varying sizes ② size: 这双鞋我穿上~正合适。These shoes are just my size. ③ degree of seniority: 说话没个~ speak impolitely to elderly people ④ adults and children: 全家~五口。There are five people in the family altogether.

【大写】 dàxiě ① the capital form of a Chinese numeral: ~金额 amount in words ② capitalization: ~字母 capital letter

【大兴】 dàxīng go in for sth. in a big way: ~土木 go in for large-scale construction

【大型】 dàxíng large-scale; large: ~企业 large enterprise/ ~彩色记录片 full-length colour documentary film

【大选】 dàxuǎn general election

【大学】 dàxué ① university; college ~生 university (或 college) student

【大雪】 dàxuě ① heavy snow

【大牙】 dàyá ① molar ② front tooth: 你这样会叫人笑掉~的。That would only make you a laughingstock.

【大雅】 dàyǎ 〈书〉 elegance; refinement; good taste: 不登~之堂 not appeal to refined taste; not in good taste

【大言不惭】 dàyán bù cán brag unblushingly; talk big

【大摇大摆】 dàyáo-dàbǎi strutting; swaggering

【大要】 dàyào main points; gist: 文章的~ the gist of an article

【大衣】 dàyī overcoat; topcoat

【大义】 dàyì cardinal principles of righteousness; righteous cause: 深明~ be deeply conscious of the righteousness of a cause

【大义凛然】 dàyì lǐnrán inspiring awe by upholding justice

【大义灭亲】 dàyì miè qīn place righteousness above family loyalty

【大意】 dàyì general idea; main points; gist; tenor: 段落~ the gist of a paragraph/ 把他讲话的~记下来就行了。Just jot down the main ideas (或 points) of what he says.

【大意】 dàyi careless; negligent; inattentive: 千万不可粗心~ never on any account be negligent

【大有可为】 dà yǒu kě wéi be. well worth doing; have bright prospects: 淡水养鱼~。There are bright prospects for freshwater fish farming.

【大有人在】 dà yǒu rén zài there are plenty of such people; such people are by no means rare

【大有文章】 dà yǒu wénzhāng there's something behind all this; there's more to it than meets the eye

【大有作为】 dà yǒu zuòwéi there is plenty of scope for one's talents; be able to develop one's ability to the full:

【大雨】 dàyǔ heavy rain: ~如注。The rain came down in sheets.

【大约】 dàyuē 〈副〉 ① approximately; about: ~一小时的路程。It's about an hour's journey. ② probably: 他~是到车间去了。He has probably gone to the workshop.

【大张旗鼓】 dà zhāng qí-gǔ on a grand scale; in a big way

【大丈夫】 dàzhàngfu 〈旧〉 true man; real man; man

【大志】 dàzhì high aim; lofty aim; exalted ambition; high aspirations

【大致】 dàzhì roughly; approximately; more or less: ~相同 roughly the same/ 这项工程~两年可以完工。This project will take about two years to complete.

【大智若愚】 dàzhì ruò yú a man of great wisdom often appears slow-witted

【大众】 dàzhòng the masses; the people; the public; the broad masses of the people ◇ ~歌曲 popular songs/ 文艺 art and literature for the masses; popular literature

【大众化】 dàzhònghuà popular; in a popular style: ~的饭菜 popular low-priced dishes/ 语言~ use the language of the ordinary people

【大主教】 dàzhǔjiào archbishop

【大专院校】 dà-zhuān yuàn-xiào universities and colleges; institutions of higher education

【大自然】 dàzìrán nature: 征服~ conquer nature

【大宗】 dàzōng ① a large amount (或 quantity): ~款项 a large amount of money; large sums ② staple: 本地出产以棉花为~。Cotton is the staple crop here.

da

瘩 da 见"疙瘩" gēda

dāi

呆* dāi ① slow-witted; dull: ~头~脑 dull-looking ② blank; wooden: ~~地望着 stare at sth. blankly/ 吓得发~ be stupefied; be scared stiff; be dumbstruck ③ stay: ~在家里 stay at home
另见 ái

【呆若木鸡】 dāi ruò mùjī dumb as a wooden chicken; dumbstruck; transfixed (with fear or amazement)

【呆帐】 dāizhàng bad debt

【呆滞】 dāizhì ① dull: 两眼~无神 with a dull look in one's eyes ② idle: 避免资金~ prevent capital from lying idle

【呆子】 dāizi idiot; simpleton; blockhead

待 dāi 〈口〉 stay: 他在广州~了三天。He stayed in Guangzhou for three days.
另见 dài

dǎi

歹* dǎi bad; evil; vicious: 为非作~ do evil

【歹徒】 dǎitú scoundrel; ruffian; evildoer

逮 dǎi capture; catch: 猫~老鼠。Cats catch mice.
另见 dài

dài

大* dài
另见 dà

【大夫】 dàifu 〈口〉 doctor; physician

代* dài ① take the place of; be in place of: 主任不在时由老王~。Lao Wang acts for the director during his absence./ ~人受过 suffer for the faults of another; bear the blame for somebody else/ 请~我向他致意。Please give him my regards. ② acting: ~部长 acting minister ③ historical period: 古~ ancient times/ 汉~ the Han Dynasty ④ 〈地〉 era: 古生~ the Palaeozoic Era ⑤ generation: ~~相传 pass on (或 hand down) from generation to generation/ 一~新人在成长。A generation of people of a new type is growing up.

【代办】 dàibàn ① do sth. for sb.; act on sb.'s behalf: 这件事请你~吧。Could you do this for me? 或 Could you act on my behalf? ② 〈外〉 chargé d'affaires

【代笔】 dàibǐ write on sb.'s behalf

【代表】 dàibiǎo ① deputy; delegate; representative: 双方~ representatives from both sides/ 常驻~ permanent representative (或 delegate) ② represent; stand for: 这三个人~三种不同性格。These three persons represent three different types of character./ ~时代精神 embody the spirit of the era ③ on behalf of; in the name of: ~我国政府表示衷心的感谢 express heartfelt thanks on behalf of our government/ ~全厂工人讲话 speak in the name of the workers of the factory
◇ ~权 representation/ ~人物 representative figure (或 personage); typical representative; leading exponent/ ~团 delegation; mission; deputation/ ~资格 qualifications of a representative/ ~作 representative work

【代步】 dàibù 〈书〉 ride instead of walk

【代价】 dàijià price; cost: 不惜任何~ prepared to pay any price; at any cost; at all costs

【代课】 dàikè take over a class for an absent teacher

【代劳】 dàiláo do sth. for sb.; take trouble on sb.'s behalf: 这事请你老李~吧。Will you do this for us, Lao Li?

【代理】 dàilǐ ①act on behalf of someone in a responsible position: ～厂长 acting manager of a factory ②act as agent (或 proxy, procurator)
【代理人】 dàilǐrén ①agent; deputy; proxy
【代名词】 dàimíngcí ①〈语〉pronoun ②synonym: 诸葛亮在民间传说中成了智慧的～. Zhuge Liang is a synonym for wisdom in folklore.
【代售】 dàishòu be commissioned to sell sth. (usu. as a sideline)
【代替】 dàitì replace; substitute for; take the place of:
【代销】 dàixiāo sell goods (for the state) on a commission basis; be commissioned to sell sth. (usu. as a sideline); act as a commission agent
【代言人】 dàiyánrén spokesman; mouthpiece

带* dài ①belt; girdle; ribbon; band; tape: 皮～ leather belt/ 丝～ silk ribbon/ 录音～ recording tape/ 腰～ waist band/ 鞋～ shoelaces; shoestrings ②tyre: 自行车～ bicycle tyre ③zone; area; belt: 热～ the torrid zone/ 绿化地～ greenbelt ④take; bring; carry: 我可以～多少行李? How much luggage can I take?/ 别忘了～雨衣. Don't forget to take your raincoat along./ 我没有～钱. I haven't any money on me. ⑤do sth. incidentally: 上街时给～点茶叶来. When you go out, get me some tea./ 你在信上给我～一笔, 问你父亲好. Remember me to your father in your letter./ 你出去请把门～上。 Please pull the door to when you go out. ⑥bear; have: ～有时代的特点 bear the imprint of the times/ 面～笑容 wear a smile/ 说话别～刺儿. Don't be sarcastic./ 一项～根本性的措施 a measure of fundamental importance ⑦having sth. attached; simultaneous: ～叶的橘子 tangerines with their leaves on/ 这几个茶杯是一碟儿的. There are saucers to go with these cups./ 连说～笑地走进来 enter laughing and talking ⑧lead; head: ～队 lead (或 be the leader of) a group of people/ ～兵 lead (或 be in command of) troops ⑨look after; bring up; raise: ～孩子 look after children/ 他是由一位贫农大娘～大的. He was brought up by a poor peasant woman.
【带领】 dàilǐng lead; guide
【带路】 dàilù show (或 lead) the way; act as a guide: 老猎户给我们～. The old hunter acted as our guide. ◇ ～人 guide
【带头】 dàitóu take the lead; be the first; take the initiative; set an example: ～冲锋 lead the charge/ 起～作用 play a leading role/ ～发言 be the first to speak; break the ice
【带孝】 dàixiào wear mourning for a parent, relative, etc.; be in mourning
【带子】 dàizi belt; girdle; ribbon; band; tape

殆 dài 〈书〉①danger: 危～ in great danger ②nearly; almost: 敌人伤亡～尽. The enemy were practically wiped out.

待* dài ①treat; deal with: ～人诚恳 treat people sincerely; be sincere with people/ 宽～俘虏 treat prisoners of war leniently ②entertain: ～客 entertain a guest ③wait for; await: ～机 await an opportunity; bide one's time/ 尚～解决的问题 a problem awaiting solution; an outstanding issue/ 有～改进 have yet to be improved ④need: 自不～言. This goes without saying. 或 This is taken for granted. ⑤going to; about to: 我正～出门, 有人来了. I was about to go out when someone came.
另见 dāi
【待价而沽】 dài jià ér gū wait for the right price to sell; wait for the highest bid
【待考】 dàikǎo need checking; remain to be verified
【待命】 dàimìng await orders: ～出发 await orders to set off/ 原地～ stay where one is, pending orders; stand by
【待人接物】 dàirén-jiēwù the way one gets along with people
【待续】 dàixù to be continued
【待遇】 dàiyù ①treatment ②remuneration; pay; wages; salary: 优厚～ excellent pay and conditions

贷 dài ①loan: 农～ agricultural loans ②borrow or lend: 向银行～款 get a bank loan/ 银行～给公司大量款项. The bank granted a large loan to the company. ③shift

(responsibility); shirk: 责无旁～ be one's unshirkable responsibility; be duty-bound ④pardon; forgive: 严惩不～ punish without mercy
【贷方】 dàifāng 〈簿记〉credit side; credit
【贷款】 dàikuǎn ①provide (或 grant) a loan; extend credit to; make an advance to ②loan; credit: 无息～ interest-free loans/ 未偿～ outstanding loans

怠 dài idle; remiss; slack
【怠惰】 dàiduò idle; lazy; indolent
【怠工】 dàigōng slow down; go slow
【怠慢】 dàimàn ①cold-shoulder; slight: 不要～了客人. See that none of the guests are neglected. ②〈套〉〔表示招待不周〕: ～了! I'm afraid I have been a poor host.

袋* dài ①bag; sack; pocket; pouch: 旅行～ travelling bag/ 邮～ mailbag/ 工具～ tool kit/ 衣～ pocket ②〈量〉: 一～面粉 a sack of flour
【袋鼠】 dàishǔ kangaroo

【袋装】 dàizhuāng in bags ◇ ～奶粉 milk powder in bags
【袋子】 dàizi sack; bag

逮 dài 〈书〉reach: 力有未～ beyond one's reach (或 power)
另见 dǎi
【逮捕】 dàibǔ arrest; take into custody: ～法办 arrest and deal with according to law; bring to justice ◇ ～证 arrest warrant

戴* dài ①put on; wear: ～上手套 put on one's gloves/ ～眼镜 wear glasses ②respect; honour: 爱～ love and respect ③(Dài) a surname
【戴孝】 dàixiào wear mourning for a parent, relative, etc.; be in mourning
【戴罪立功】 dàizuì lìgōng atone for one's crimes by doing good deeds; redeem oneself by good service

黛 dài a black pigment used by women in ancient times to paint their eyebrows
【黛绿】 dàilù 〈书〉dark green

dān

丹* dān ①red
【丹田】 dāntián the pubic region: ～之气 deep breath controlled by the diaphragm
【丹心】 dānxīn a loyal heart; loyalty

单* dān ①one; single: ～扇门 single-leaf door/ ～丝不成线, 独木不成林. One strand of silk doesn't make a thread; one tree doesn't make a forest. ②odd: ～日 odd-numbered days/ ～只袜子 an odd sock ③singly; alone: ～人独马 single-handed/ 把这几件东西～放在一个地方. Keep these things in a separate place. ④only; alone: 不～只不要～凭热情去工作. Don't work by enthusiasm alone. ⑤simple: 简～ simple; plain ⑥thin; weak ⑦unlined (clothing) ⑧sheet: 床～ bed sheet ⑨bill; list: 名～ name list/ 菜～ menu; bill of fare/ 价目～ price list
另见 chán
【单薄】 dānbó ①(of clothing) thin: 穿得～ be thinly clad ②thin and weak; frail: 身体～ have a poor physique ③insubstantial; flimsy; thin: 论据～ a feeble argument
【单程】 dānchéng one way ◇ ～车票 one-way (或 single) ticket
【单纯】 dānchún ①simple; pure: 问题决不象我们当初想象的那么～. The problem is by no means as simple as we first thought. ②alone; purely; merely: 不～追求数量 not concentrate on quantity alone
【单打】 dāndǎ 〈体〉singles: 男子(女子)～ men's (women's)

singles/ 少年男子（女子）~ boys' (girls') singles/ 她只参加 ~。She's only playing in the singles.

【单单】 dāndān only; alone: 别人都来了，~他没来。He's the only one absent. Everybody else is here. 或 Everybody has come except him.

【单刀直入】 dāndāo zhí rù come straight to the point; speak out without beating about the bush

【单调】 dāndiào monotonous; dull; drab: 声音~ in a monotonous tone/ 色彩~ dull colouring/ 昨天的节目比较~。Yesterday's programme was rather dull.

【单独】 dāndú alone; by oneself; on one's own; single-handed; independent: ~一个人干不了这个活儿。Nobody can do this job alone (或 by himself)./ 采取~行动 take independent action/ 她~住一间屋子。She has a room to herself./ 我要和他~谈一谈。I want to have a talk with him alone.

【单方面】 dānfāngmiàn one-sided; unilateral: ~撕毁协定 unilaterally tear up an agreement

【单杠】 dāngàng 〈体〉① horizontal bar ② horizontal bar gymnastics

【单据】 dānjù documents attesting to the giving or receiving of money, goods, etc., such as receipts, bills, vouchers and invoices: 货运~ shipping documents

【单枪匹马】 dānqiāng-pǐmǎ single-handed; all by oneself; alone

【单人床】 dānrénchuáng single bed

【单人舞】 dānrénwǔ solo dance: 跳~ dance a solo

【单日】 dānrì odd-numbered days (of the month)

【单色】 dānsè monochromatic

【单身】 dānshēn ① unmarried; single ② not be with one's family; live alone: ~在外 live alone away from home ◇ ~汉 bachelor/ ~宿舍 quarters for single men or women; bachelor quarters

【单数】 dānshù ① odd number ② 〈语〉singular number

【单位】 dānwèi ① unit (as a standard of measurement): 长度~ a unit of length/ 货币~ monetary unit/ ~面积产量 yield per unit area/ 以秒为~计算时间 measure time by the second ② unit (as an organization, department, division, section, etc.): 行政~ administrative unit/ 生产~ production unit

【单相思】 dānxiāngsī unrequited love

【单向】 dānxiàng one-way; unidirectional ◇ ~电路 one-way circuit/ ~交通 one-way traffic

【单项】 dānxiàng 〈体〉individual event ◇ ~比赛 individual competition

【单行线】 dānxíngxiàn one-way road

【单一】 dānyī single; unitary

【单元】 dānyuán unit: 运算~ arithmetic unit

【单子】 dānzi ① list; bill; form: 开个~ make out a list/ 菜~ bill of fare; menu/ 填写~ fill in a form ② bed sheet

【单字】 dānzì individual character; separate word

担* dān ① carry on a shoulder pole: ~水 carry water (with a shoulder pole and buckets) ② take on; undertake: 我们把任务~起来。Let's take on the job./ 不怕~风险 ready to face any danger; not be afraid of running risks
另见 dàn

【担保】 dānbǎo assure; guarantee; vouch for: 这事交给她办，~错不了。I assure you that she can be trusted to do the work well. 或 I'll vouch for her as the best person for the job./ 出口信贷~ export credit guarantees ◇ ~人 guarantor

【担当】 dāndāng take on; undertake; assume: ~重任 take on heavy responsibilities

【担负】 dānfù bear; shoulder; take on; be charged with: ~责任 shoulder responsibility/ ~费用 bear an expense/ ~领导工作 hold a leading post

【担任】 dānrèn assume the office of; hold the post of: ~工会主席 be the chairman of a trade union

【担心】 dānxīn worry; feel anxious: ~她的健康 worry about her health/ 快给老大娘写信，免得她~。Write to the old lady at once so as to set her mind at rest.

【担忧】 dānyōu worry; be anxious: 不要为我的身体~。Don't worry about my health.

耽 dān 见"虎视眈眈" hǔ shì dāndān

耽 dān ① delay ② 〈书〉abandon oneself to; indulge in: ~乐 indulge in pleasure

【耽搁】 dānge ① stop over; stay: 我不打算在这里~多久。I won't be here for long. ② delay: 毫不~ without delay/ 不得~ admit of no delay/ 一分钟也不能~。Not a single minute is to be lost.

【耽误】 dānwù delay; hold up: ~了整个工程 hold up (或 delay) the whole project/ ~功夫 waste time/ 把~的时间夺回来 make up for lost time/ 她从不为个人事情~生产。She never allows her private affairs to interfere with production.

dǎn

胆* dǎn ① gallbladder ② courage; guts; bravery: 壮~ boost sb.'s courage ③ a bladder-like inner container: 热水瓶~ the glass liner of a vacuum flask/ 球~ the rubber bladder of a ball

【胆大】 dǎndà bold; audacious: ~心细 bold but cautious/ ~包天 audacious in the extreme/ ~妄为 reckless

【胆敢】 dǎngǎn dare; have the audacity to: 敌人~来侵犯，就坚决消灭它。If the enemy dare to invade us, we'll resolutely wipe them out.

【胆寒】 dǎnhán be terrified; be struck with terror

【胆量】 dǎnliàng courage; guts; pluck; spunk: 很有~ have plenty of guts (或 spunk)

【胆略】 dǎnlüè courage and resourcefulness: ~过人 have unusual courage and resourcefulness

【胆怯】 dǎnqiè timid; cowardly

【胆识】 dǎnshí courage and insight

【胆小】 dǎnxiǎo timid; cowardly: ~如鼠 as timid as a mouse; chicken-hearted ◇ ~鬼 coward

【胆战心惊】 dǎnzhàn-xīnjīng tremble with fear; be terror-stricken: 使人~ strike terror into sb.; be terrifying

【胆子】 dǎnzi courage; nerve: 放开~ pluck up courage; stop being afraid/ 好大的~! What a nerve!

dàn

石 dàn dan, a unit of dry measure for grain (= 1 hectolitre)
另见 shí

旦* dàn ① 〈书〉dawn; daybreak ② day: 元~ New Year's Day ③ the female character type in Beijing opera, etc.

【旦夕】 dànxī 〈书〉this morning or evening — in a short while: 危在~ in imminent danger/ ~之间 in a day's time; overnight

但* dàn ① 〈连〉but; yet; still; nevertheless: 他早已年过六十，~毫不见老。He's well over sixty, but he doesn't look at all old. ② only; merely: 在辽阔的原野上，~见麦浪随风起伏。On the vast fields, one sees nothing but the wheat billowing in the wind.

【但是】 dànshì 〈连〉but; yet; still; nevertheless

【但愿】 dànyuàn if only; I wish: ~天气赶快放晴。If only it would clear up soon!/ ~如此。I wish it were true! 或 Let's hope so.

担* dàn ① dan, a unit of weight (=50 kilograms) ② a carrying pole and the loads on it; load; burden 〈量〉〔用于成担的东西〕：一~水 two buckets of water(carried on a shoulder pole)
另见 dān

【担子】 dànzi a carrying pole and the loads on it; load; burden: ~拣重的挑 ready to shoulder the heaviest loads

诞* dàn ① birth ② birthday ③ absurd; fantastic: 荒~ fantastic

【诞辰】 dànchén birthday
【诞生】 dànshēng be born; come into being; emerge

淡* dàn ①thin; light: ～酒 light wine/ 云～风轻. The clouds are pale and a light breeze is blowing. ②tasteless; weak: ～茶 weak tea/ ～而无味 tasteless; insipid/ 这个菜太～. This dish is not salty enough. ③light; pale: ～黄 light yellow/ ～紫 pale purple; lilac ④indifferent: ～然处之 treat with indifference/ ～～地答应了一声 answer drily ⑤slack; dull: 生意清～. Business is slack. ⑥〈方〉meaningless; trivial: 扯～ talk nonsense
【淡泊】 dànbó not seek fame and wealth
【淡薄】 dànbó ①thin; light: 朝雾渐渐地～了. The morning mist gradually thinned. ②become indifferent; flag: 他对象棋的兴趣逐渐～了. His interest in chess has begun to flag. ③faint; dim; hazy: 时间隔得太久, 印象也就～了. With the passage of time, these impressions became dim.
【淡季】 dànjì slack (或 dull, off) season
【淡漠】 dànmò ①indifferent; apathetic; nonchalant ②faint; dim; hazy: 这件事我脑子里已很～了. The event has left only faint memories in my mind.
【淡水】 dànshuǐ fresh water
◇ ～湖 freshwater lake/ ～养鱼 freshwater fish-farming/ ～鱼 freshwater fish
【淡忘】 dànwàng fade from one's memory

蛋* dàn ①egg ②an egg-shaped thing: 泥～儿 mud ball
【蛋白】 dànbái ①egg white; albumen ②protein
【蛋白质】 dànbáizhì protein
【蛋糕】 dàngāo cake
【蛋黄】 dànhuáng yolk
【蛋壳】 dànké eggshell

弹* dàn ①ball; pellet ②bullet; bomb: 燃烧～ incendiary bomb/ ～尽粮绝 run out of ammunition and food supplies
另见 tán
【弹弓】 dàngōng catapult; slingshot
【弹药】 dànyào ammunition
◇ ～库 ammunition depot (或 storehouse)/ ～手 ammunition man (或 bearer)/ ～所 ammunition supply (或 refilling) point/ ～箱 ammunition chest; cartridge box
【弹子】 dànzi ① a pellet shot from a slingshot ②marble: 打～ play marbles ③〈方〉billiards ◇ ～房 billiard room

dāng

当* dāng ①equal: 实力相～ well-matched in strength ②ought; should; must: 能省的就省, ～用的还是得用. Save what you can, but use what you must. ③in sb.'s presence; to sb.'s face: ～着大家谈一谈. Speak out in the presence of everyone. ④just at (a time or place): ～时 at that time/ ～场 on the spot ⑤work as; serve as; be: 选他～组长 elect him group leader ⑥bear; accept; deserve: 我可～不起这样的夸奖. I just don't deserve such praise. ⑦direct; manage; be in charge of: ～家 manage household affairs ⑧〈象〉[金属器物撞击声]: ～～的钟声 the tolling of a bell; the ding-dong of bells
另见 dàng
【当兵】 dāngbīng be a soldier; serve in the army
【当场】 dāngchǎng on the spot; then and there: ～拒绝他们的要求 turn down their request on the spot/ 他～表演了这种新的操作方法. He gave a demonstration of the new technique then and there./ ～抓住 catch red-handed (或 in the act)
【当场出彩】 dāngchǎng chūcǎi ①make a spectacle of oneself ②give the whole show away on the spot
【当初】 dāngchū originally; at the outset; in the first place; at that time: ～打算在这儿盖一座大楼. It was originally planned to put up a big building here./ ～这儿是一片荒芜, 如今工厂林立. Factories now stand where there used to be a wilderness./ 我～怎么对你讲的? What did I tell you, eh?/ ～你就不该这么做. You should never have acted the way

you did in the first place./ 早知今日, 何必～? If I had known it would come to this, I would have acted differently.
【当代】 dāngdài the present age; the contemporary era
【当道】 dāngdào ①blocking the way: 别在～站着. Don't stand in the way. ②〈贬〉be in power; hold sway: 坏人～, 好人受害. When evildoers are in power, good people suffer.
【当地】 dāngdì at the place in question; in the locality; local/ ～人民 local people/ ～时间 local time
【当机立断】 dāng jī lì duàn decide promptly and opportunely; make a prompt decision
【当家】 dāngjiā manage (household) affairs
【当家作主】 dāngjiā zuòzhǔ be master in one's own house; be the master of one's own affairs (或 destiny)
【当今】 dāngjīn now; at present; nowadays: ～之世 in the world of today; at the present time
【当局】 dāngjú the authorities: 政府(学校)～ the government (school) authorities
【当局者迷,旁观者清】 dāngjúzhě mí, pángguānzhě qīng the spectators see the chess game better than the players; the onlooker sees most of the game
【当空】 dāngkōng high above in the sky: 明月～. A bright moon is shining in the sky.
【当面】 dāngmiàn to sb.'s face; in sb.'s presence: ～撒谎 tell a barefaced lie/ ～弄清楚 straighten things out face to face/ ～说好话, 背后下毒手 say nice things to sb.'s face, then stab him in the back/ 信是我～交给主任的. I handed the letter to the director personally.
【当年】 dāngnián ①in those years (或 days): ～家里穷, 无力抚养孩子. In those years we were too poor to bring up our children properly./ 想～, 这里还没有火车呢! Well, in those days there was no railway here./ 他的精力不减～. He is as energetic as ever. ③the prime of life: 他正在～. He is in his prime.
【当前】 dāngqián ①before one; facing one: 大敌～. A formidable enemy stands before us. ②present; current: ～的中心任务 the central task at present/ ～世界的主要倾向 the main trend in the world today/ ～利益 immediate interests/ ～的国际形势 the current (或 present) international situation
【当权】 dāngquán be in power; hold power ◇ ～派 person in power; people in authority
【当然】 dāngrán ①as it should be; only natural: 理所～. That is just as it should be. 或 That's only natural. ②without doubt; certainly; of course; to be sure: 朋友有困难～要帮助. It goes without saying that we should help a friend in difficulty. ③natural: ～同盟军 natural ally
【当仁不让】 dāng rén bù ràng not pass on to others what one is called upon to do; not decline to shoulder a responsibility
【当时】 dāngshí then; at that time: ～我并不知道. I didn't know then.
另见 dàngshí
【当事人】 dāngshìrén ①〈法〉party (to a lawsuit); litigant ②person (或 party) concerned; interested parties
【当头】 dāngtóu ①right overhead; right on sb.'s head; head on: 烈日～照. The hot sun is shining right overhead./ 给他一瓢冷水 pour cold water on him/ ～一棒 a head-on blow ②imminent; be confronting: 那时候正是国难～, 爱国青年都纷纷到抗敌前线去. The country was in imminent danger, and large numbers of patriotic young people left for the front to fight the enemy.
【当务之急】 dāng wù zhī jí a pressing matter of the moment; a task of top priority; urgent matter
【当下】 dāngxià instantly; immediately; at once: 我一听这话, ～就警惕起来了. Hearing this, I was instantly on the alert.
【当先】 dāngxiān in the van; in the front ranks; at the head: 奋勇～ fight bravely in the van/ 一马～ gallop at the head — take the lead
【当心】 dāngxīn take care; be careful; look out: ～别把试管打碎了. Take care not to break the test tube./ ～别踩了庄稼. Be careful not to step on the crops./ ～! 汽车来了.

Look out! There's a car coming. 或 Mind that car./ ～路滑。Watch your step. The road is slippery.

【当选】 dāngxuǎn be elected

【当政】 dāngzhèng be in power; be in office

【当之无愧】 dāng zhī wúkuì fully deserve (a title, an honour, etc.); be worthy of

【当中】 dāngzhōng ① in the middle; in the centre: 河～水流最急。The current is swiftest in the middle of the river./ 坐在主席台～ be seated in the centre of the rostrum ② among

【当众】 dāngzhòng in the presence of all; in public: ～认错 acknowledge one's mistakes in public/ ～出丑 make an exhibition of oneself

珰 dāng 见"玎珰" dīngdāng

dǎng

挡* dǎng ① keep off; ward off; block: ～雨 keep off the rain; shelter one from the rain/ ～风 shelter sth. from (或 keep out) the wind/ 防护林带～住了风沙。The shelterbelt kept the sand in check./ 喝一口～～夜里的寒气。Have a drop. It'll ward off the cold of the night. ② block; get in the way of: ～路 be (或 get) in the way/ ～光 be (或 get) in the light/ 山高～不住太阳。The highest mountains can't shut out the sun./ 绝不能让私利～住了眼睛。Never be blinded by private interests. ③ fender; blind: 炉～儿 (fire) fender; fire screen/ 窗～子 window blind (或 shade) ④〈汽车〉gear: 前进(倒)～ forward (reverse) gear/ 高速 (低速)～ top (bottom) gear

【挡驾】 dǎngjià〈婉〉turn away a visitor with some excuse; decline to receive a guest

【挡箭牌】 dǎngjiànpái ① shield ② excuse; pretext

党* dǎng ① political party; party ② clique; faction; gang: 死～ sworn follower ③〈书〉be partial to; take sides with: ～同伐异 defend those who belong to one's own faction and attack those who don't ④〈书〉kinsfolk; relatives: 父～ father's kinsfolk

【党费】 dǎngfèi party membership dues

【党纲】 dǎnggāng party programme

【党籍】 dǎngjí party membership: 开除～ expel from the party

【党纪】 dǎngjì party discipline

【党魁】 dǎngkuí〈贬〉party chieftain (或 chief, boss)

【党派】 dǎngpài political parties and groups; party groupings: ～关系 party affiliation

【党同伐异】 dǎng tóng fá yì defend those who belong to one's own faction and attack those who don't; be narrowly partisan

【党徒】 dǎngtú〈贬〉① member of a clique or a secret society ② henchman

【党羽】 dǎngyǔ〈贬〉members of a clique; adherents; henchmen

【党员】 dǎngyuán party member ◇ ～大会 general membership meeting of a party organization; meeting of all party members

dàng

当* dàng ① proper; right: 用词不～ inappropriate choice of words ② match; equal to: 他一个人能～两个人用。He can do the work of two persons put together. ③ treat as; regard as; take for: 不要把支流～主流。Don't take minor aspects for major ones. ④ think: 我～你不知道。I thought you didn't know. ⑤ that very (day, etc.): ～月 the same month; that very month ⑥ pawn: ～衣服 pawn one's clothes; put one's clothes in pawn ⑦ sth. pawned; pawn;

pledge: 赎～ take sth. out of pledge; redeem sth. pawned

另见 dāng

【当票】 dàngpiào pawn ticket

【当铺】 dàngpù pawnshop ◇ ～老板 pawnbroker

【当日】 dàngrì the same day; that very day: ～有效 good for the date of issue only

【当时】 dàngshí right away; at once; immediately: 他一接到电报, ～就赶回去了。He hurried back the moment he received the telegram.

另见 dāngshí

【当天】 dàngtiān the same day; that very day: 你可以～来回。You can go and come back on the same day./ ～的事～做完。Today's work must be done today.

【当真】 dàngzhēn ① take seriously: 我只是开个玩笑, 何必～呢? I was only joking. Why take it seriously? ② really true; really: 这话～? Is it really true?/ 他说要来, ～来了。He said he would come and, sure enough, he did.

【当做】 dàngzuò treat as; regard as; look upon as

荡 dàng ① swing; sway; wave: ～秋千 play on a swing/ ～桨 pull on the oars ② loaf: 游～ loaf about ③ rinse: 冲～ rinse out; wash away ④ clear away; sweep off: 扫～ mopping up; mopping-up operation/ ～平 wipe out; quell ⑤ loose in morals: 放～ dissolute; dissipated/ 淫～ lustful; lascivious

【荡然无存】 dàngrán wú cún〈书〉all gone; nothing left

【荡漾】 dàngyàng ripple; undulate: 湖水～。There were ripples on the lake./ 歌声～。The song rose and fell like waves./ 金黄的小麦在微风中～。The golden wheat rippled in the breeze.

档 dàng ① shelves (for files); pigeonholes: 把文件归～ file a document; place a document on file ② files; archives: 查～ consult the files ③ crosspiece (of a table, etc.) ④ grade: 高(低)～商品 high-grade (low-grade) goods

【档案】 dàng'àn files; archives; record; dossier

dāo

刀* dāo ① knife; sword ② sth. shaped like a knife: 冰～ ice skates ③〈量〉one hundred sheets (of paper)

【刀叉】 dāo-chā knife and fork

【刀锋】 dāofēng the point or edge of a knife

【刀光剑影】 dāoguāng-jiànyǐng the glint and flash of cold steel

【刀口】 dāokǒu ① the edge of a knife ② where a thing can be put to best use; the crucial point; the right spot: 把劲儿使在～上 bring efforts to bear on the right spot/ 钱要花在～上。Use your money where it's needed most. ③ cut; incision

【刀片】 dāopiàn ① razor blade ②〈机〉(tool) bit; blade

【刀山火海】 dāoshān-huǒhǎi a mountain of swords and a sea of flames; most dangerous places; most severe trials

叨 dāo 另见 tāo

【叨唠】 dāolao talk on and on; chatter away: 他～了半天, 人都不爱听。He chattered for a long time and bored everybody. 又作"叨叨"

dǎo

导* dǎo ① lead; guide ② transmit; conduct: ～电 transmit electric current; conduct electricity ③ instruct; teach; give guidance to: 教～ teach; instruct

【导弹】 dǎodàn guided missile

【导火线】 dǎohuǒxiàn ① (blasting) fuse ② a small incident that touches off a big one: 战争的～ an incident that touches off a war

【导师】 dǎoshī ① tutor; teacher ② guide of a great cause; teacher

【导言】 dǎoyán introduction (to a piece of writing); introductory remarks

【导演】 dǎoyǎn ①direct (a film, play, etc.) ②director

【导游】 dǎoyóu ①conduct a sightseeing tour ②guidebook ◇ ~图 tourist map

【导源】 dǎoyuán ①(of a river) have its source: 黄河~于青海。The Huanghe River rises in Qinghai Province. ②originate; derive: 认识~于实践。Knowledge derives from practice.

【导致】 dǎozhì lead to; bring about; result in; cause

岛* dǎo island

【岛国】 dǎoguó country consisting of one or more islands; island country

【岛屿】 dǎoyǔ islands and islets; islands

倒* dǎo ①fall; topple: 摔~ fall over/ 风把树刮~了。The gale uprooted the tree./ 我~在床上就睡着了。I threw myself down on the bed and fell asleep immediately./ 一边~ lean to one side ②collapse; fail: 内阁~了。The cabinet collapsed. ③close down; go bankrupt ④(of voice) become hoarse: 他的嗓子~了。He has lost his voice. ⑤change; exchange: ~车 change trains or buses/ ~肩 shift a burden from one shoulder to the other/ 你们俩把座位~一~下。Will you two please swop (或 change) seats? ⑥move around: 地方太小，~不开身。There is no room to move around. 另见 dào

【倒闭】 dǎobì close down; go bankrupt; go into liquidation: 企业~ bankruptcy of an enterprise

【倒换】 dǎohuàn ①rotate; take turns: 几种作物~着种 rotate several crops/ ~着护伤员 take turns looking after the wounded ②rearrange (sequence, order, etc.); replace

【倒霉】 dǎoméi have bad luck; be out of luck; be down on one's luck: 真~，赶到车站车刚开走。What lousy luck! When I reached the station, the train had just left. 又作 "倒楣"

【倒塌】 dǎotā collapse; topple down

【倒台】 dǎotái fall from power; downfall

捣 dǎo ①pound with a pestle, etc.; beat; smash: ~药 pound medicine in a mortar/ ~米 husk rice with a pestle and mortar/ ~衣 beat clothes (in washing)/ 直~匪巢 drive straight on to the bandits' den ②harass; disturb

【捣蛋】 dǎodàn make trouble: 调皮~ be mischievous

【捣鬼】 dǎoguǐ play tricks; do mischief

【捣毁】 dǎohuǐ smash up; demolish; destroy: ~敌军据点 destroy enemy strongpoints

【捣乱】 dǎoluàn make trouble; create a disturbance: 权叔忙着呢，你别~。Uncle's busy. Don't disturb him.

【捣碎】 dǎosuì pound to pieces

祷* dǎo ①pray ②[旧时书信用语] ask earnestly; beg

【祷告】 dǎogào pray; say one's prayers

蹈* dǎo ①<书> tread; step: 赴汤~火 go through fire and water—defy all difficulties and dangers/ 循规~矩 not step out of bounds; toe the line; stick to convention ②skip; trip: 舞~ dance

dào

到* dào ①arrive; reach: 火车~站了。The train has arrived at the station./ ~了多少人？How many people were present?/ ~ˌ (点名时的回答) Here! ②go to; leave for ③up until; up to: 从星期三~星期五 from Wednesday to Friday/ ~目前为止 up to the present; until now; so far ④[用作动词的补语，表示动作有结果]: 办~ can be done/ 说~做~ be as good as one's word/ 想不~你来了。I didn't expect you would come. ⑤thoughtful; considerate: 不~之处请原谅。Please excuse me if I have been inconsiderate in any way.

【到场】 dàochǎng be present; show up; turn up

【到处】 dàochù at all places; everywhere: 侵略者~挨打。

The invaders were attacked wherever they went./ 烟头不要~乱扔。Don't drop cigarette ends about.

【到达】 dàodá arrive; get to; reach: 代表团于今晨~广州。The delegation arrived in Guangzhou this morning.

【到底】 dàodǐ ①to the end; to the finish: 打~ fight to the finish ②<副> at last; in the end; finally: 新方法~试验成功了。The new method has finally proved to be a success. ③<副>[用于问句，加强语气]: 你~是什么意思？What on earth do you mean? ④<副> after all; in the final analysis: 他~是新手，干活还不熟练。After all, he's new to the work and isn't very skilful at it yet.

【到顶】 dàodǐng reach the summit (或 peak, limit); cannot be improved

【到会】 dàohuì be present at a meeting; attend a meeting: ~人数很多。There was a large attendance.

【到家】 dàojiā reach a very high level; be perfect; be excellent: 这活儿做得很~。This is excellent workmanship./ 他这笔字写得还不~。His calligraphy is far from perfect.

【到来】 dàolái arrival; advent

【到期】 dàoqī become due; mature; expire: 这本书已经~了。This book is due for return./ 这张票据什么时候~？When does this bill mature (或 become due)?/ 签证下月~。The visa expires next month. ◇ ~日 date due

【到手】 dàoshǒu in one's hands; in one's possession: 眼看要~的粮食，决不能让洪水冲走。The grain is nearly in our hands. We mustn't allow the flood to carry it away.

【到头】 dàotóu to the end; at an end: 这条街走~就有一个邮局。There's a post office at the end of the street.

【到头来】 dàotóulai <副> in the end; finally: 不老实的人~总是要栽跟头的。Dishonest people are bound to come a cropper in the end.

倒* dào ①upside down; inverted; inverse; reverse: 次序~了。The order is reversed./ 小孩把画挂~了。The child hung the picture upside down. ②move backward; turn upside down: 火车~回去了。The train backed up. ③pour; tip: ~一杯茶 pour a cup of tea/ ~垃圾 tip (或 dump) rubbish/ 他把一肚子冤屈都~了出来。He poured out all his grievances. ④<副> ⓐ[表示跟意料相反]: 本想省事，~费事了。We wanted to save ourselves trouble but actually we gave ourselves more./ 你还有什么要说的，我~要听听。I'd like to hear what else you've got to say. ⓑ[表示事情不是那样]: 你说得~容易，做起来可不容易。It's easy for you to say that, but it's not so easy to do. 或 That's easier said than done. ⓒ[表示让步]: 我跟他认识~认识，就是不太熟。I know him, but not very well. ⓓ[表示催促或追问]: 你~去不去呀！Do you want to go or don't you? 另见 dǎo

【倒彩】 dàocǎi booing; hooting; catcall: 喝~ make catcalls; boo and hoot

【倒车】 dàochē back a car: 开历史~ turn back the wheel of history; put the clock back

【倒立】 dàolì ①stand upside down: 宝塔的影子~在水里。The pagoda is reflected upside down in the water. ②<体> handstand

【倒数】 dàoshǔ count backwards: ~第三行 the third line from the bottom

【倒退】 dàotuì go backwards; fall back

【倒行逆施】 dàoxíng-nìshī go against the historical trend; try to put the clock back

【倒悬】 dàoxuán <书> hang by the feet—be in sore straits

【倒因为果】 dào yīn wéi guǒ reverse cause and effect; take cause for effect

【倒影】 dàoyǐng inverted image; inverted reflection in water

【倒置】 dàozhì place upside down; invert: 轻重~ place the unimportant before the important

【倒转】 dàozhuǎn ①turn the other way round; reverse: ~来说，也是这样。The same is true the other way round. ②<方> contrary to reason or one's expectation: 你把事情搞糟了，~来怪我。You messed up the whole thing yourself and now you put the blame on me.

悼 dào mourn; grieve: 哀~死者 mourn for the dead

【悼词】 dàocí memorial speech

【悼念】 dàoniàn mourn; grieve over: 沉痛～ mourn with deep grief

盗* dào ① steal; rob ② thief; robber

【盗匪】 dàofěi bandits; robbers: 肃清～ exterminate banditry

【盗窃】 dàoqiè steal: ～国家机密 steal state secrets ◇ ～犯 thief/ ～罪 〈法〉 larceny

【盗取】 dàoqǔ steal; embezzle

【盗用】 dàoyòng embezzle; usurp: ～公款 embezzle public funds/ ～名义 usurp a name

【盗贼】 dàozéi robbers; bandits

道* dào ① road; way; path: 山间小～ a mountain path ② channel; course ③ way; method: 养生之～ the way to keep fit/ 以其人之～，还治其人之身 deal with a man as he deals with you; pay sb. back in his own coin ④ doctrine; principle ⑤ Taoism; Taoist: ～观 a Taoist temple/ 老～ a Taoist priest ⑥ superstitious sect: 会一门 superstitious sects and secret societies ⑦ line: 画一条斜儿 draw a slanting line ⑧〔量〕 @〔用于某些长条的东西〕: 一～河 a river/ 万～金光 myriads of golden rays/ 一～缝儿 a crack ⓑ〔用于门、墙等〕: 两一门 two successive doors/ 三～防线 three lines of defence ⓒ〔用于命令、题目等〕: 一～命令 an order/ 出五～题 set five questions (for an examination, etc.) ⓓ〔表示"次"〕: 上四～菜 serve four courses/ 省一～手续 save one step in the process ⑨ say; talk; speak: 能说会～ have a glib tongue; have the gift of the gab/ 常言～ as the saying goes ⑩ think; suppose: 我～是老周呢，原来是你。So it's you! I thought it was Lao Zhou.

【道不拾遗】 dào bù shí yí no one pockets anything found on the road — honesty prevails throughout society

【道德】 dàodé morals; morality; ethics: ～品质 moral character/ 旧～观念 old moral concepts/ 体育～ sportsmanship/ ～败坏 degenerate

【道贺】 dàohè congratulate

【道具】 dàojù 〔剧〕 stage property; prop

【道理】 dàoli ① principle; truth; hows and whys: 讲清深耕细作的～ explain the principles of deep ploughing and intensive cultivation/ 言语不多～深。The words were few, but they contained profound truth. ② reason; argument; sense: 你的话很有～。What you said is quite reasonable (或 right)./ 讲不出一点～ unable to come up with any convincing argument; unable to justify oneself in any way

【道路】 dàolù road; way; path: ～泥泞。The road is muddy./ 走前人没有走过的～ break paths none have explored before

【道貌岸然】 dàomào ànrán pose as a person of high morals; be sanctimonious

【道破】 dàopò point out frankly; lay bare; reveal: 一语～其中奥秘 lay bare its secret with one remark

【道歉】 dàoqiàn apologize; make an apology

【道听途说】 dàotīng-túshuō hearsay; rumour; gossip

【道喜】 dàoxǐ congratulate sb. on a happy occasion

【道谢】 dàoxiè express one's thanks; thank

【道学】 dàoxué ① a Confucian school of philosophy of the Song Dynasty (960-1279); Neo-Confucianism ② affectedly moral: 假～ canting moralist; hypocrite ◇ ～先生 Confucian moralist

【道义】 dàoyì morality and justice: ～上的支持 moral support

稻* dào rice; paddy

【稻田】 dàotián (rice) paddy; rice field; paddy field

dé

得* dé ① get; obtain; gain: 取～经验 gain experience/ ～了结核病 have (或 contract) tuberculosis/ 今天的幸福生活～来不易。The happy life we have today was not easily won. ② (of a calculation) result in: 二三～六。Twice three is six. ③ fit; proper: ～用 fit for use; handy ④ 〈书〉 satisfied; complacent: 自～ pleased with oneself; self-satisfied ⑤ 〈口〉 be finished; be ready: 饭～了。Dinner is ready. ⑥ 〈口〉〔表示同意或禁止〕: ～，就这么办。All right! Just go ahead./ ～，别再说了。That's enough. Let it go at that. ⑦ 〈口〉〔用于情况变坏时，表示无可奈何〕: ～，又错了！Look! I've got it wrong again! ⑧〔用在别的动词前，表示许可〕: 这笔钱非经批准不～动用。This fund may not be drawn on without permission.

另见 de; děi

【得便】 débiàn when it's convenient: 这几样东西，请你～捎给他。Please take these things to him whenever it's convenient.

【得不偿失】 dé bù cháng shī the loss outweighs the gain; the game is not worth the candle: 不打～的消耗战。Avoid battles of attrition in which we lose more than we gain.

【得逞】 déchěng 〈贬〉 have one's way; prevail; succeed

【得宠】 déchǒng 〈贬〉 find favour with sb.; be in sb.'s good graces

【得出】 déchū reach (a conclusion); obtain (a result)

【得寸进尺】 dé cùn jìn chǐ reach out for a yard after taking an inch; give him an inch and he'll take an ell; be insatiable

【得当】 dédàng apt; appropriate; proper; suitable: 安排～ be properly arranged/ 措词～ aptly worded; appropriate wording

【得到】 dédào get; obtain; gain; receive: ～及时治疗 get timely medical treatment

【得法】 défǎ do sth. in the proper way; get the knack: 管理～ be properly managed/ 讲授不甚～ not teach in the right (或 proper) way

【得分】 défēn score: 客队的六号～最多。Player No. 6 of the visiting team scored the most points./ 连得四分 in a row four points in a row

【得过且过】 dé guò qiě guò muddle along; drift along

【得计】 déjì succeed in one's scheme: 自以为～ think oneself clever

【得奖】 déjiǎng win (或 be awarded) a prize ◇ ～人 prize-winner

【得空】 dékòng have leisure; be free: 老想来看你，总不～。I've been meaning to come and see you but haven't had the time.

【得力】 délì ① benefit from; get help from: ～于平时勤学苦练 profit from diligent study and practice/ 我得他的力很不小。I benefited a lot from his help. ② capable; competent: ～助手 capable assistant; right-hand man/ 办事～ do things efficiently

【得胜】 déshèng win a victory; triumph: ～归来 return in triumph; return with flying colours

【得失】 dé-shī ① gain and loss; success and failure: ～相当 gains and losses balance each other; break even/ 从不计较个人～ never give a thought to personal gain or loss ② advantages and disadvantages; merits and demerits: 两种办法各有～。Each of the two methods has its advantages and disadvantages.

【得势】 déshì ① be in power ② get the upper hand; be in the ascendant

【得手】 déshǒu go smoothly; come off; do fine; succeed: 歼敌左翼，～后，迅速扩大战果 wipe out the enemy's left flank and, this accomplished, swiftly exploit the victory

【得体】 détǐ befitting one's position or suited to the occasion; appropriate: 讲话～ speak in appropriate terms

【得天独厚】 dé tiān dú hòu be richly endowed by nature; abound in gifts of nature; enjoy exceptional advantages

【得心应手】 déxīn-yìngshǒu ① with facility; with high proficiency ② serviceable; handy

【得以】 déyǐ so that... can (或 may)...

【得益】 déyì benefit; profit: 读者的意见使他～不少。He benefits considerably from the readers' comments.

【得意】 déyì proud of oneself; pleased with oneself; complacent: ～扬扬 be immensely proud; look triumphant

【得意忘形】 déyì wàngxíng get dizzy with success; have one's head turned by success

【得志】 dézhì achieve one's ambition; have a successful career: 少年～ enjoy success when young/ 小人～ villains holding sway

【得罪】 dézuì offend; displease: 不怕~人 not be afraid of giving offence

德＊ dé ① virtue; morals; moral character: 品~ moral character ② heart; mind: 同心同~ be of one heart and one mind ③ kindness; favour: 以怨报~ return evil for good; repay kindness with ingratitude; bite the hand that feeds you

【德高望重】 dégāo-wàngzhòng be of noble character and high prestige; enjoy high prestige and command universal respect

【德行】 déxíng moral integrity; moral conduct

【德育】 déyù moral education

【德政】 dézhèng benevolent rule

【德治】 dézhì rule of virtue

de

地＊ de 〔用在状语的后面〕: 实事求是~处理问题 handle problems in a practical and realistic way/ 天渐渐~冷了。The weather is getting cold.
另见 dì

的＊ de ① 〔用在定语的后面〕: 铁~纪律 iron discipline/ 我~母亲 my mother ② 〔用来造成没有中心词的"的"字结构〕: 赶大车~ a carter/我爱吃辣~. I like hot (或 peppery) food./菊花开了, 有红~, 有黄~. The chrysanthemums are in bloom; some are red and some yellow./ 他说他~, 我干我~. Let him say what he likes; I'll just get on with my work./ 火车上看书~看书, 聊天~聊天. On the train some people were reading and some were chatting. ③〔用在谓语动词后面, 强调动作的施事者、时间、地点等〕: 是我打~稿子, 他上~色. I made the sketch; he filled in the colours./ 他是昨天进~城. He went to town yesterday./ 我是在车站打~票. I bought the ticket at the station. ④〔用在陈述句末尾, 表示肯定的语气〕: 你们这两天真够辛苦~. You've really been working hard the past few days. ⑤〈口〉〔用在两个数量词中间, 表示相乘或相加〕: 这间屋子是五米~三米, 合十五平方米. This room is five metres by three, or fifteen square metres.
另见 dí; dì

【的话】 dehuà 〈助〉〔用在表示假设的分句后面, 引起下文〕: 如果你有事~, 就不要来了. Don't come if you're busy.

得＊ de ①〔用在动词后面, 表示能够或可以〕: 我们可粗心不~. We can't afford to be careless./ 她去~, 我为什么去不~! If she can go, why can't I? ②〔用在动词和补语中间, 表示可能〕: 我拿~动. I can carry it./ 那办~到. That can be done. ③〔用在动词或形容词后面, 连接表示程度或结果的补语〕: 写~非常好 very well written/ 唱~不好 not sing well/ 冷~打哆嗦 shiver with cold/ 笑~肚子痛 laugh till one's sides split
另见 dé; děi

děi

得＊ děi 〈口〉 ① need: 这个工程~三个月才能完. This project will take three months to complete. ② must; have to: 有错误就~批评. Wherever mistakes occur, they must be criticized. ③〔表示揣测的必然〕: 要不快走, 我们就~迟到了. We'll be late if we don't hurry.
另见 dé; de

dēng

灯＊ dēng ① lamp; lantern; light: 煤油~ kerosene lamp/ 电~ electric light/ 宫~ palace lantern ② valve; tube: 五~收音机 a five-valve radio set ③ burner: 酒精~ alcohol burner; spirit lamp

【灯彩】 dēngcǎi ① coloured-lantern making ② coloured lanterns (formerly used on the stage)

【灯光】 dēngguāng ① the light of a lamp; lamplight ② (stage) lighting: ~渐暗 lights slowly dim; lights fade to dark/ 舞台~ stage lights; lighting ◇ ~球场 floodlit (或 illuminated) court, field, etc.

【灯红酒绿】 dēnghóng-jiǔlǜ red lanterns and green wine — scene of debauchery

【灯火】 dēnghuǒ lights: ~辉煌 brilliantly illuminated; ablaze with lights ◇ ~管制 blackout

【灯节】 Dēngjié the Lantern Festival (15th of the first lunar month)

【灯笼】 dēnglong lantern

【灯泡】 dēngpào 〈口〉 (electric) bulb; light bulb: 螺口(卡口)~ screw (bayonet) socket bulb/ 乳白~ opal bulb

【灯丝】 dēngsī filament (in a light bulb or valve)

【灯塔】 dēngtǎ lighthouse; beacon

【灯罩】 dēngzhào (电灯) lampshade; (油灯) lamp-chimney

登＊ dēng ① ascend; mount; scale (a height): ~岸 go ashore/ ~上讲台 mount the platform/ ~上峰顶 reach the summit ② publish; record; enter: ~帐 enter an item in an account book/~广告 advertise (in a newspaper)/ 他的名字~上了光荣榜. His name appeared on the honour roll. ③ be gathered and taken to the threshing ground: 五谷丰~ reap a bumper grain harvest

【登报】 dēngbào publish in the newspaper: ~声明 make a statement in the newspaper

【登场】 dēngchǎng come on stage ◇ ~人物 characters in a play; dramatis personae

【登峰造极】 dēngfēng-zàojí reach the peak of perfection; have a very high level (of scholastic attainment or technical skill); reach the limit

【登高】 dēnggāo ascend a height: ~远眺 ascend a height to enjoy a distant view

【登记】 dēngjì register; check in; enter one's name: 结婚~ marriage registration/ 向有关部门~ register with the proper authorities/ 在旅馆~住宿 check in at a hotel ◇ ~簿 register; registry/ ~处 registration (或 registry) office

【登陆】 dēnglù land; disembark ◇ ~部队 landing force/ ~场 beachhead/ ~地点 debarkation (或 landing) point/ ~舰(艇) landing ship (boat)

【登门】 dēngmén call at sb.'s house: ~拜访 pay sb. a visit

【登山】 dēngshān 〈体〉 mountain-climbing; mountaineering ◇ ~队 mountaineering party (或 expedition)/ ~运动 mountaineering/ ~运动员 mountaineer

【登台】 dēngtái mount a platform; go up on the stage: 想~表演 strive to take the stage and perform

【登堂入室】 dēngtáng-rùshì pass through the hall into the inner chamber — reach a higher level in one's studies or become more proficient in one's profession

【登载】 dēngzǎi publish (in newspapers or magazines); carry: 各报在显著位置~了这条消息. The newspapers gave prominent coverage to the news.

děng

等＊ děng ① class; grade; rank: 分为三~ classify into three grades/ 一~品 top quality goods ② equal: 长短相~ be equal in length ③ wait; await: ~车 wait for a train, bus, etc./ ~上级批准 await approval by the higher authorities/ 请~一下. Would you mind waiting a minute, please./ 别~我吃饭. Don't wait dinner for me. ④ when; till: ~我做完再走. Stay till I'm through. ⑤〈助〉〔用在人称代词或指人的名词后面, 表示复数〕: 我~ we ⑥〈助〉and so on; and so forth; etc.: 购置书籍、纸张、文具~ buy books, stationery and so on ⑦〈助〉〔列举后煞尾〕: 长江、黄河、黑龙江、珠江~四大河流 the four large rivers — the Changjiang, the Huanghe, the Heilongjiang and the Zhujiang

【等待】 děngdài wait; await: ～时机 await a favourable opportunity; wait for a chance; bide one's time/ 抓紧时间, 不要～。Don't waste time. Go ahead.

【等到】 děngdào by the time; when

【等等】 děngděng and so on; and so on and so forth; etc.

【等而下之】 děng ér xià zhī from that grade down; lower down: 最好的尚且如此, ～的就不必说了。Even the best of the bunch is not worth much, to say nothing of those lower down.

【等高线】 děnggāoxiàn 〈地〉 contour (line) ◇ ～地图 contour map

【等号】 děnghào 〈数〉 equal-sign; equality sign

【等候】 děnghòu wait; await; expect: ～命令 wait for instructions; await orders

【等级】 děngjí ① grade; rank: 棉花按～收购 pay for cotton according to its grade ② order and degree; social estate; social stratum

【等量齐观】 děngliàng-qíguān equate; put on a par: 这两部小说差得太远了, 怎么能～呢? There is a world of difference between these two novels. How can you equate one with the other?

【等式】 děngshì 〈数〉 equality

【等同】 děngtóng equate; be equal: 你不能把现象和本质～起来。You must not equate the appearance with the essence.

【等闲】 děngxián ① ordinary; unimportant: ～视之 regard as unimportant; treat lightly (或 casually) ② aimlessly; thoughtlessly: 大好时光, 不可～度过。Don't fritter away your precious time.

【等于】 děngyú equal to; equivalent to: 一公里～二华里。One kilometre is equal to two li./ 三加二～五。Three plus two is five./ 我们厂去年的产量～一九六五年的五倍。Last year our factory produced five times as much as in 1965. ② amount to; be tantamount to: 这～拒绝执行命令。This is tantamount to refusal to carry out orders./ 抓而不紧, ～不抓。Not to grasp firmly is not to grasp at all.

dèng

邓 Dèng a surname

凳 dèng stool; bench: 方～ square stool/ 长～ bench

澄 dèng (of a liquid) settle
另见 chéng

【澄清】 dèngqīng (of a liquid) settle; become clear: 这水太浑, 等～了再用。This water is too muddy. Wait till it has settled before you use it.
另见 chéngqīng

瞪 dèng open (one's eyes) wide; stare; glare: 我生气地～了他一眼。I gave him an angry stare.

【瞪眼】 dèngyǎn ① open one's eyes wide; stare; glare: 干～ look on helplessly/ 别瞪着眼叫敌人溜了。Don't let the enemy get away from right under your nose. ② glower and glare at sb.; get angry with sb.: 你怎么老爱跟人～? Why are you always glowering at people?

dī

低* dī ① low: ～水位 low water level/ ～声 in a low voice/ ～年级学生 students of the junior years (或 lower grades)/ 我比他～一年级。I am one grade below him. ② let droop; hang down: ～头 hang one's head

【低潮】 dīcháo low tide; low ebb: 处于～ be at a low tide; be at a low ebb

【低沉】 dīchén ① overcast; lowering: ～的天空 an overcast sky ② (of voice) low and deep ③ low-spirited; downcast

【低地】 dīdì lowland

【低调】 dīdiào low-key

【低估】 dīgū underestimate; underrate

【低级】 dījí ① elementary; rudimentary; lower ② vulgar; low: ～趣味 vulgar interests; bad taste

【低贱】 dījiàn low and degrading; humble

【低空】 dīkōng low altitude; low level ◇ ～飞行 low-altitude (或 low-level) flying/ ～轰炸 low-level bombing/ ～扫射 low-level strafing; ground strafing

【低廉】 dīlián cheap; low: 物价～。Prices are low.

【低劣】 dīliè inferior; low-grade

【低落】 dīluò low; downcast: 情绪～ be low-spirited

【低能】 dīnéng mental deficiency; feeble-mindedness ◇ ～儿 imbecile; retarded child

【低人一等】 dī rén yī děng inferior to others

【低三下四】 dīsān-xiàsì ① lowly; mean; humble ② servile; obsequious; cringing

【低声】 dīshēng in a low voice; under one's breath; with bated breath

【低声下气】 dīshēng-xiàqì soft-spoken and submissive; meek and subservient

【低头】 dītóu ① lower (或 bow, hang) one's head: ～认罪 hang one's head and admit one's guilt; plead guilty/ ～哀 bow one's head in silent mourning ② yield; submit: 决不向困难～ never bow to difficulties

【低微】 dīwēi ① (of a voice or sound) low: ～的呻吟 low groans ② lowly; humble

【低息】 dīxī low interest

【低下】 dīxià (of status or living standards) low; lowly: 经济地位～ be of low economic status

堤* dī dyke; embankment

【堤岸】 dī'àn embankment

【堤坝】 dībà dykes and dams

【堤防】 dīfáng dyke; embankment: 加固～ strengthen the dykes ◇ ～工程 dyke building; embankment project

提* dī
另见 tí

【提防】 dīfang take precautions against; be on guard against; beware of: ～坏人破坏 guard against sabotage by bad elements

滴* dī ① drip: 他脸上的汗水直往下～。Sweat kept dripping from his face./ 往承里～油 put a few drops of lubricating oil in the bearings; oil the bearings/ ～药 put drops in one's eyes ② 〈量〉 drop: 一～水 a drop of water

【滴虫】 dīchóng trichomonad ◇ ～病 trichomoniasis

【滴答】 dīdā 〈象〉 tick; ticktack; ticktock: 夜很静, 只有钟摆～～地响。The night was very quiet except for the ticktack of the clock./ 发报机滴滴答答不停地发出电报。The transmitter ticked (或 tapped) out message after message./ 雨～～地下个不停。The rain kept pitter-pattering.

嘀 dī
另见 dí

【嘀嗒】 dīdā tick; ticktack; ticktock

dí

狄 Dí a surname

的* dí
另见 de; dì

【的确】 díquè indeed; really: 我～不知道。I really don't know.

荻 dí a kind of reed

敌* dí ① enemy; foe: 劲～ a formidable enemy; a foe worthy of one's steel; a worthy opponent/ ～机 an enemy plane ② oppose; fight; resist: 以寡～众 fight against heavy odds/ 所向无～ carry all (或 everything) before one; be all-conquering

【敌对】 díduì hostile; antagonistic: ~行为 a hostile act/ ~行动 hostilities/~分子 a hostile element/~情绪 hostility; enmity/~双方 opposing sides; parties to hostilities

【敌国】 díguó enemy state

【敌军】 díjūn enemy troops; the enemy; hostile forces

【敌忾】 díkài hatred towards the enemy

【敌情】 díqíng the enemy's situation: 侦察~ make a reconnaissance of the enemy's situation/ ~的变化 changes on the enemy's side/ ~严重。Enemy activities present a serious threat.

【敌人】 dírén enemy; foe

【敌视】 díshì be hostile (或 antagonistic) to; adopt a hostile attitude towards

【敌手】 díshǒu ①match; opponent; adversary ②enemy hands: 落入~ fall into enemy hands

【敌意】 díyì hostility; enmity; animosity

涤 dí <书> wash; cleanse

【涤除】 díchú wash away; do away with; eliminate: ~旧习 do away with old customs

笛* dí ①bamboo flute ②whistle: 汽~ steam whistle

【笛子】 dízi dizi, bamboo flute

嘀 dí
另见 dí

【嘀咕】 dígu ①whisper; talk in whispers: 两个女孩子嘀嘀咕咕地不知谈些什么。The two girls were talking in whispers. I couldn't hear a word. ②have misgivings about sth.; have sth. on one's mind: 我心里直~这件事。It's been on my mind all the while.

嫡* dí ①of or by the wife (as distinguished from a concubine under the feudal-patriarchal system): ~长子 the wife's eldest son ②of lineal descent; closely related

【嫡传】 díchuán handed down in a direct line from the master

【嫡派】 dípài ①见"嫡系" ②disciples taught by the master himself

【嫡亲】 díqīn blood relations; close paternal relations: ~弟兄 blood brothers; whole brothers

【嫡系】 díxì ①direct line of descent ②one's own clique

dǐ

诋 dǐ <书> slander; defame

【诋毁】 dǐhuǐ slander; vilify; calumniate; defame

邸 dǐ the residence of a high official: 官~ official residence

底* dǐ ①bottom; base: 井~ the bottom of a well/ ~价 base price ②the heart of a matter; ins and outs: 这一下就露了~儿了。And so the whole thing came out. / 心里没~ feel unsure of sth./ 刨根问~ get to the bottom of sth.; get to the root of things ③rough draft ④a copy kept as a record: 留个~儿 keep a copy on file; duplicate and file (a letter, etc.) ⑤end: 年~ the end of a year ⑥ground; background; foundation: 白~红花 red flowers on a white background ⑦<书> end up with; come to: 终~于成 succeed in the end

【底本】 dǐběn ①a copy for the record or for reproduction; master copy ②a text against which other texts are checked

【底层】 dǐcéng ①<建> (英) ground floor; (美) first floor ②bottom; the lowest rung

【底稿】 dǐgǎo draft; manuscript

【底片】 dǐpiàn negative; photographic plate

【底细】 dǐxì ins and outs; exact details: 我们不了解这件事的~。We don't know the ins and outs of the matter.

【底下】 dǐxia ①under; below; beneath: 树~ under the tree/ 手~工作多 have one's hands full/ 笔~不错 write well ②next; later; afterwards: 他们~说的话我就听不清了。I didn't catch what they said next./ ~再交换意见吧。We can exchange views after the meeting.

【底蕴】 dǐyùn <书> inside information; details

【底子】 dǐzi ①bottom; base: 鞋~ the sole of a shoe ②foundation: ~薄 have a poor foundation to start with/ 他的英文~好。He has a good grounding in English. ③rough draft or sketch: 画画儿要先打个~。When drawing a picture, first make a rough sketch. ④a copy kept as a record: 发出的文件要留个~。Keep a copy of each document sent out. ⑤remnant: 货~ remnants of stock

抵* dǐ ①support; sustain; prop: 用手~着下巴颏儿 prop one's chin in one's hands/ 用东西把门~住,别让风刮开。Prop something against the door so that it won't blow open. ②resist; withstand: ~住来自外面的压力 withstand the pressure from outside ③compensate for; make good: ~命 pay with one's life (for a murder, etc.); a life for a life ④mortgage: 用房屋做~ mortgage a house ⑤balance; set off: 收支相~。Income balances expenditure. ⑥be equal to: 干活他一个能~我们两个。He can do the work of two of us. ⑦<书> reach; arrive at

【抵偿】 dǐcháng compensate for; make good; give sth. by way of payment for

【抵触】 dǐchù conflict; contradict: 在个人利益和集体利益有~的时候,应服从集体利益。When individual and collective interests conflict, those of the collective should prevail./ 与法律相~ contravene (或 go against) the law

【抵达】 dǐdá arrive; reach

【抵挡】 dǐdǎng keep out; ward off; check; withstand: ~风寒 keep out the wind and the cold/ ~洪水 keep the flood in check

【抵当】 dǐhuàn substitute for; take the place of

【抵抗】 dǐkàng resist; stand up to: 奋起~ rise in resistance/ 增强对疾病的~力 build up one's resistance to disease

【抵赖】 dǐlài deny; disavow: 不容~ brook no denial/ 事实是~不了的。Denying the facts is futile. 或 Facts cannot be denied.

【抵消】 dǐxiāo offset; cancel out; counteract: ~影响 offset an influence/ ~药物的作用 counteract the effect of a medicine

【抵押】 dǐyā mortgage: 以某物作~ raise a mortgage on sth.; leave sth. as a pledge ◇ ~放款 mortgage loan; secured loan/ ~品 security; pledge

【抵御】 dǐyù resist; withstand: ~侵略 resist aggression/ ~自然灾害 withstand natural calamities/ 建立防风林带~风沙的侵袭 build a shelter belt against sandstorms

【抵债】 dǐzhài pay a debt in kind or by labour

【抵制】 dǐzhì resist; boycott

砥 dǐ <书> whetstone

【砥砺】 dǐlì ①temper: ~意志 temper one's will ②encourage: 互相~ encourage each other

dì

地* dì ①the earth ②land; soil: 山~ hilly land/ 盐碱~ saline and alkaline land (或 soil) ③fields: 下~干活儿 go and work in the fields/ 麦~ wheat field ④ground; floor: 水泥~ cement floor ⑤place; locality: 每到一~ wherever one goes/~处山区 be located in a mountain area ⑥position; situation: 立于不败之~ be in an invincible position ⑦background; ground: 一块白~黑字的木牌 a board with black characters on a white background/白~红花的大碗 a big white bowl with a pattern of red flowers on it 另见 de

【地板】 dìbǎn ①floor board ②floor: 水泥~ cement floor

【地表】 dìbiǎo the earth's surface

【地步】 dìbù ①condition; plight: 你怎么闹到这样的~?How did you get into such a mess?/ 事情到了不可收拾的~。The situation got out of hand. ②extent: 发展到公开对抗的~ develop to the point of an open clash/ 兴奋到不能入睡的~ be so excited that one can't get to sleep ③room for action: 留~ leave room for manoeuvre; have some leeway; give oneself elbowroom

【地产】 dìchǎn landed estate; landed property; real estate

【地大物博】 dìdà-wùbó vast territory and abundant resources; a big country abounding in natural wealth

【地带】 dìdài district; region; zone; belt: 沙漠(森林)~ a desert (forest) region/ 危险~ a danger zone/ 无人~ no man's land

【地道】 dìdào tunnel

【地点】 dìdiǎn place; site; locale: 开会~ place for a meeting; venue/ 故事发生的~ the locale (或 scene) of a story/ 在这里建个百货商店,一倒适中。This would be a suitable site for a new department store.

【地洞】 dìdòng a hole in the ground; burrow

【地段】 dìduàn a sector (或 section) of an area

【地对地导弹】 dì duì dì dǎodàn ground-to-ground (guided) missile; surface-to-surface missile

【地对空导弹】 dì duì kōng dǎodàn ground-to-air (guided) missile; surface-to-air missile

【地方】 dìfāng ① locality (as distinct from the central administration) ◇ ~病 endemic disease/ ~观念 localistic way of thinking; localism/ ~军 local forces; regional troops ~时间 local time/ ~税 local taxes/ ~戏 local opera; local drama/ ~志 local chronicles; annals of local history

【地方】 dìfang ① place; space; room: 你是什么~人?Where are you from?/ 这张桌子太占~。That desk takes up too much space./ 我这个~有点疼。I've got a pain here. ② part; respect: 你说的话有对的~,也有不对的~。What you say is partly right and partly wrong.

【地基】 dìjī ① ground ② foundation

【地雷】 dìléi (land) mine: 埋~ plant (或 lay) mines/ 防坦克~ antitank mine ◇ ~场 minefield

【地理】 dìlǐ ① geographical features of a place: 熟悉~民情 be familiar with the place and its people ② geography: 自然(经济)~ physical (economic) geography ◇ ~发现 geographical discovery/ ~分布 geographical distribution/ ~环境 geographical conditions/ ~特点 geographical features/ ~位置 geographical position/ ~学 geography/ ~学家 geographer

【地利】 dìlì ① favourable geographical position; topographical advantages ② land productivity

【地面】 dìmiàn ① the earth's surface; ground: 高出~两米 two metres above ground level ② <建> ground; floor: 水磨石~ terrazzo floor/ ~砖 <建> floor tile

【地名】 dìmíng place name ◇ ~辞典 dictionary of place names; gazetteer

【地盘】 dìpán territory under one's control; domain: 军阀互相争夺~。The warlords competed for spheres of influence.

【地皮】 dìpí ① land for building ② ground: 雨停了,~还没有干。The ground is still wet after the rain.

【地平线】 dìpíngxiàn horizon

【地契】 dìqì title deed for land

【地勤】 dìqín <航空> ground service ◇ ~人员 ground crew; ground personnel

【地球】 dìqiú the earth; the globe ◇ ~卫星 earth satellite/ ~物理学 geophysics/ ~仪 (terrestrial) globe

地球仪

【地区】 dìqū ① area; district; region: 北京~ the Beijing area/ 多山~ a mountainous district/ 这个~最适宜种小麦。This area is most suitable for growing wheat.

【地势】 dìshì physical features of a place; relief; terrain; topography: ~险要。The terrain is strategically situated and difficult of access.

【地毯】 dìtǎn carpet; rug

【地头蛇】 dìtóushé a snake in its old haunts — local villain (或 bully)

【地图】 dìtú map ◇ ~集 atlas

【地位】 dìwèi ① position; standing; place; status: 政治~ political position (或 standing)/ 国际~ international standing/ 经济~ economic status/ 社会~ social position (或 status)/ ~平等 equal in status; on an equal footing/ 一定的历史~ a proper or definite place in history ② place (as occupied by a person or thing)

【地下】 dìxià ① underground; subterranean: ~仓库 underground storehouse ② secret (activity); underground: 转入~ go underground/ 搞~工作 do underground work ◇ ~室 basement; cellar/ ~水 groundwater/ ~水位 groundwater level; water table/ ~铁道 underground (railway); tube; subway

【地下】 dìxia on the ground: 掉在~ fall on the ground/ 从~捡起 pick up from the ground

【地心】 dìxīn <地> the earth's core ◇ ~引力 terrestrial gravity; gravity

【地形】 dìxíng topography; terrain: ~优越 enjoy topographical advantages ◇ ~测量 topographic survey/ ~图 topographic map; relief map/ ~学 topography

【地狱】 dìyù hell; inferno

【地域】 dìyù region; district: ~辽阔 vast in territory ◇ ~观念 regionalism

【地震】 dìzhèn earthquake; seism: 这次~为七点一级。The shock was of 7.1 magnitude.

【地址】 dìzhǐ address: 回信~ return address

【地质】 dìzhì geology ◇ ~学 geology/ ~学家 geologist

【地主】 dìzhǔ ① landlord ② host: 尽~之谊 perform the duties of the host

【地租】 dìzū land rent; ground rent; rent

弟* dì ① younger brother ② 〔男性朋友相互间的谦称,多用于旧时书信中〕I

【弟弟】 dìdi younger brother; brother

【弟妇】 dìfù younger brother's wife; sister-in-law

【弟妹】 dìmèi ① younger brother and sister ② <口> younger brother's wife; sister-in-law

【弟兄】 dìxiong brothers: 亲~ blood brothers/ 他就~一个。He is the only son of the family.

【弟子】 dìzǐ disciple; pupil; follower

的* dì target; bull's-eye
另见 de; dí

帝* dì ① <宗> the Supreme Being: 玉皇大~ the Jade Emperor (supreme ruler of Heaven in Taoism)/ 上~ God ② emperor: 称~ proclaim oneself emperor

【帝国】 dìguó empire

【帝国主义】 dìguózhǔyì imperialism ◇ ~分子 imperialist element; imperialist/ ~者 imperialist

【帝王】 dìwáng emperor; monarch

递 dì ① hand over; pass; give: 把报~给我。Hand me the paper, please./ ~眼色 tip sb. the wink; wink at sb./ 给他~个口信 take a message to him ② successively; in the proper order: ~升 promote to the next rank

【递交】 dìjiāo hand over; present; submit: ~国书 (of an ambassador) present one's credentials

【递解】 dìjiè <旧> escort (a criminal) from one place to another: ~回籍 send (a convict, etc.) to his native place under escort

【递送】 dìsòng send; deliver: ~情报 send out (或 pass on) information/ ~信件 deliver letters

【递增】 dìzēng increase progressively; increase by degrees: 产量平均每年~百分之十五。The output increased at an average rate of 15 per cent a year. 或 The output showed a yearly average increase of 15 per cent.

第* dì ① 〔用在数词前面,表示次序〕: ~一 the first ② <书> grades into which successful candidates in the imperial examinations were placed: 及(落)~ pass (fail) in the imperial examinations ③ <旧> the residence of a high official

【第二世界】 dì'èr shìjiè the second world (composed of developed countries other than the two superpowers)

【第三世界】 dìsān shìjiè the third world (composed of the developing countries in Asia, Africa, Latin America and elsewhere)

【第三者】 dìsānzhě a third party (to a dispute, etc.)

【第五纵队】 dìwǔ zòngduì fifth column

【第一】　dìyī　first; primary; foremost: 做～等的工作 do first-rate work/ ～号种子选手 No.1 seeded player/ 获得～名 win first place; get a first; win a championship/ 他跑百米得了～。He came in first in the 100-metre dash.

【第一世界】　dìyī shìjiè　the first world (composed of the two superpowers, the Soviet Union and the United States)

蒂　dì　the base of a fruit

缔　dì　form (a friendship); conclude (a treaty)

【缔交】　dìjiāo ① establish diplomatic relations ② form (或 contract) a friendship

【缔结】　dìjié　conclude; establish: ～条约 conclude a treaty/ ～邦交 establish diplomatic relations

【缔约】　dìyuē　conclude (或 sign) a treaty: ～双方 both contracting parties ◇ ～国 signatory (state) to a treaty; party to a treaty; (high) contracting party

【缔造】　dìzào　found; create

diān

颠　diān ① crown (of the head) ② top; summit: 山～ mountain top/ 塔～ the top of a pagoda ③ jolt; bump: 路不平,卡车～得厉害。As the road was rough, the truck jolted badly. ④ fall; turn over; topple down: ～覆 overturn; subvert ⑤ 〈方〉 run; go away: 整天跑跑～～ be on the go all day long/ 对不起,我得～儿了。Sorry, I've got to be on my way.

【颠簸】　diānbǒ　jolt; bump; toss: 卡车在土路上～着前进。The truck bumped along the dirt road./ 风更大了,船身～起来。As the wind grew stronger, the boat was tossed about by the waves.

【颠倒】　diāndǎo ① put (或 turn) upside down; transpose; reverse; invert: 这一头朝下,别放～了。This is the top; don't put it upside down./ 把这两个字～过来句子就顺了。Transpose these two words and the sentence will read right./ 主次～ reverse the order of importance ② confused; disordered: 神魂～ be in a confused state of mind; be infatuated

【颠倒黑白】　diāndǎo hēi-bái　confound black and white; confuse right and wrong; stand facts on their heads

【颠倒是非】　diāndǎo shì-fēi　confound right and wrong; confuse truth and falsehood; turn things upside down

【颠覆】　diānfù　overturn; subvert

【颠来倒去】　diānlái-dǎoqù　over and over: 说那么点事,他～地说个没完。It was just a small matter but he kept harping on it./ 如果一篇文章～总是那么几个词,人家就不愿看。No one cares to read an article that merely rings the changes on a few terms.

【颠沛流离】　diānpèi-liúlí　drift from place to place, homeless and miserable; wander about in a desperate plight; lead a vagrant life

【颠扑不破】　diānpū bù pò　be able to withstand heavy battering; irrefutable; indisputable: ～的真理 irrefutable truth

【颠三倒四】　diānsān-dǎosì　incoherent; disorderly; confused

巅　diān　mountain peak; summit: 泰山之～ the summit of Taishan Mountain

癫　diān　mentally deranged; insane

【癫狂】　diānkuáng ① demented; mad; insane ② frivolous

diǎn

典＊　diǎn ① standard; law; canon ② standard work of scholarship: 词～ dictionary/ 药～ pharmacopoeia ③ allusion; literary quotation: 用～ use allusions ④ ceremony; 盛～ a grand ceremony (或 occasion) ⑤ mortgage

【典当】　diǎndàng　mortgage; pawn

【典范】　diǎnfàn　model; example; paragon

【典故】　diǎngù　allusion; literary quotation

【典籍】　diǎnjí　ancient codes and records; ancient books and records: 先秦～ pre-Qin books and records

【典礼】　diǎnlǐ　ceremony; celebration

【典型】　diǎnxíng ① typical case (或 example); model; type: 抓～ grasp typical cases ② typical; representative: ～人物 a typical character/ ～事例 a typical instance (或 case)/ ～的中国村庄 a representative Chinese village

【典押】　diǎnyā　mortgage; pawn

【典雅】　diǎnyǎ　(of diction, etc.) refined; elegant

【典章】　diǎnzhāng　institutions; decrees and regulations

点＊　diǎn ① drop (of liquid): 雨～ raindrops ② spot; dot; speck: 墨～ ink spots/ 污～ stain ③ dot stroke (in Chinese characters) ④ 〈数〉 point: 基准～ datum point (或 mark)/ 两线的交～ the point of intersection of two lines ⑤ decimal point; point: 三～五 three point five (3.5) ⑥ a little; a bit; some: 给我～纸。Give me some paper, will you?/ 读～鲁迅 read some of Lu Xun's works/ 他今天好～了。He's feeling a bit better today./ 人的认识一～也不能离开实践。Human knowledge can in no way be separated from practice. ⑦ 〈量〉〔用于事项〕: 我有几～不成熟的想法。I have some tentative suggestions. ⑧ place; point: 突破一～ make a breakthrough at one point/ 沸～ boiling point/ 居民～ residential area/ 以～带面 promote work in all areas by drawing upon experience gained at key points ⑨ aspect; feature: 特～ characteristic feature/ 从这一上去看 viewed from this aspect/ 对这一～没人怀疑。Nobody has any doubt about it. ⑩ put a dot: ～三个点表示省略 put three dots to show that something has been omitted ⑪ touch on very briefly; skim: 蜻蜓～水 dragonflies skimming (over) the water/ 他用篙一～就把船撑开了。He pushed the boat off with a shove of the pole./ 她发言时～了这件事。She touched on the matter in her speech. ⑫ drip: ～眼药 put drops in the eyes ⑬ sow in holes; dibble: ～豆子 dibble beans ⑭ check one by one: 请你把钱～一～。Please check and see if the money is right./ ～货 check over goods; take stock ⑮ select; choose: ～菜 order dishes (in a restaurant) ⑯ hint; point out: 一～就明白了。He quickly took the hint. ⑰ light; burn; kindle: ～灯 light a lamp/ 他是火爆性子,一～就着。He's got a fiery temper and flares up at the slightest provocation. ⑱ o'clock: 上午九～钟 nine o'clock in the morning/ 现在几～了? What time is it now? ⑲ appointed time: 误～ behind time; delayed; late/ 到～了,我们开会吧。It's time. Let's start the meeting. ⑳ refreshments: 茶～ tea and cake; tea/ 早～ breakfast

【点菜】　diǎncài　choose dishes from a menu; order dishes (in a restaurant)

【点火】　diǎnhuǒ ① light a fire ② ignition ③ stir up trouble

【点名】　diǎnmíng ① call the roll: 晚～ evening roll call ② mention sb. by name: 他～要你去。He named you as the one he wanted./ ～攻击 attack sb. by name ◇ ～册 roll book; roll

【点明】　diǎnmíng　point out; put one's finger on: ～问题所在 put one's finger on the cause of the trouble

【点破】　diǎnpò　bring sth. out into the open; lay bare; point out bluntly: 我没有～他的真实意图。I didn't point out what he was really after.

【点燃】　diǎnrán　light; kindle; ignite: ～火把 light a torch

【点收】　diǎnshōu　check and accept: 按清单～货物 acknowledge receipt of goods after checking them against a list

【点数】　diǎnshù　check the number (of pieces, etc.); count

【点头】　diǎntóu　nod one's head, nod: ～同意 nod assent/ ～打招呼 nod to sb. (as a greeting)/ ～示意 signal by nodding/ ～之交 nodding (或 bowing) acquaintance/ 他已经～了。He's already given the go-ahead.

【点心】　diǎnxin　light refreshments; pastry

【点缀】　diǎnzhuì ① embellish; ornament; adorn: 几株红梅把雪后的园林～得格外美丽。Embellished with the red blossoms of the plum trees, the garden looked more beautiful than ever after the snow. ② use sth. merely for show

碘　diǎn　〈化〉 iodine (I)

diàn

电* diàn ① electricity ② give or get an electric shock: 电门有毛病，～了我一下。 There was something wrong with the switch and I got a shock. ③ telegram; cable: 急～ urgent telegram/ ～上级请示 telegraph the higher authorities for instructions/ ～复 reply by telegraph/ ～贺 telegraph one's congratulations to sb.; cable a message of congratulations

【电报】 diànbào telegram; cable: 无线～ radiotelegram/ 有线～ wire telegram/ 打～ send a telegram/ 打～让他回来 wire him to come back

【电表】 diànbiǎo ① any meter for measuring electricity, such as ammeter or voltmeter ② kilowatt-hour meter; watt-hour meter; electric meter

【电冰箱】 diànbīngxiāng (electric) refrigerator; fridge; freezer

【电波】 diànbō electric wave

【电唱机】 diànchàngjī electric gramophone (或 phonograph); record player

【电车】 diànchē ① tram; tramcar; streetcar ② trolleybus; trolley

【电池】 diànchí (electric) cell; battery: 干～ dry cell/ 太阳能～ solar cell ◇ ～组 battery

【电传打字电报机】 diànchuán dǎzì diànbàojī teletypewriter; teleprinter

【电磁】 diàncí electromagnetism

【电灯】 diàndēng electric lamp; electric light: 偏僻的山村现在有了～。 Electric light has now reached remote mountain villages. ◇ ～泡 electric (light) bulb

【电动】 diàndòng motor-driven; power-driven; power-operated; electric

【电话】 diànhuà ① telephone; phone: 无线～ radio (或 wireless) telephone/ 自动～ automatic telephone/ 市内～ local call/ 请别把～挂上。 Hold the line, please./ 他把～挂了。 He's hung up./ ② phone call: 打～ make a phone call; phone sb.; call (或 ring) sb. up; give sb. a ring/ 他正在打～。 He's on the phone./ 有你的～。 There's a phone call for you. 或 You're wanted on the phone. ◇ ～簿 telephone directory (或 book)/ ～分机 extension (telephone)/ ～号码 telephone number/ ～机 telephone (set)/ ～间 telephone box (或 booth, kiosk); call box/ ～交换台 telephone exchange (或 switchboard)/ ～局 telephone office (或 exchange)/ ～用户 telephone subscriber

【电缆】 diànlǎn electric cable; cable

【电力】 diànlì electric power; power ◇ ～工程 electric power project/ ～工业 power industry/ ～供应 supply of electricity/ ～机械 electrical power equipment/ ～网 power network/ ～系统 power system/ ～线 power line; electric line of force/ ～消耗 power consumption

【电铃】 diànlíng electric bell

【电流】 diànliú electric current

【电炉】 diànlú ①（家用）electric stove; hot plate ②（工业用）electric furnace

【电码】 diànmǎ (telegraphic) code: 莫尔斯～ Morse code ◇ ～本 code book

【电鳗】 diànmán 〈动〉electric eel

电鳗

【电门】 diànmén (electric) switch

【电钮】 diànniǔ push button; button: 按～ press (或 push) a button

【电气】 diànqì electric ◇ ～机车 electric locomotive/ ～设备 electrical equipment

【电器】 diànqì electrical equipment (或 appliance)

【电热】 diànrè electric heat; electrothermal ◇ ～丝 heating wire

【电扇】 diànshàn electric fan

【电视】 diànshì television; TV: 看～ watch television/ 彩色（黑白，立体）～ colour (black-and-white, stereoscopic) television ◇ ～电话 video telephone; video-phone/ ～电影 telec-

ine/ ～发射机 television transmitter/ 广播 television broadcasting; telecasting; videocast/ ～讲座 telecourse/ ～接收机 television receiver; television set/ ～台 television station

【电台】 diàntái ① transmitter-receiver; transceiver ② broadcasting (或 radio) station

【电梯】 diàntī lift; elevator ◇ ～司机 lift operator; elevator runner

【电筒】 diàntǒng (electric) torch; flashlight

【电线】 diànxiàn (electric) wire ◇ ～杆子 (wire) pole

【电信】 diànxìn telecommunications ◇ ～局 telecommunication bureau/ ～业务 telecommunication service

【电讯】 diànxùn ① (telegraphic) dispatch: 世界各地发来的～ dispatches from all parts of the world ② telecommunications ◇ ～设备 telecommunication equipment

【电影】 diànyǐng film; movie; motion picture: 有声(无声)～ sound (silent) film/ 彩色(黑白)～ colour (black-and-white) film/ 立体～ three-dimensional film; stereoscopic film

【电灶】 diànzào electric cooking stove (或 range)

【电子】 diànzǐ electron: 热～ thermal electron/ 正～ positron/ 负～ negatron ◇ ～计算机 electronic computer

佃 diàn rent land (from a landlord)

【佃户】 diànhù tenant (farmer)

【佃农】 diànnóng tenant-peasant; tenant farmer

甸 diàn 〔多用于地名〕 pasture

店* diàn ① shop; store: 服装～ clothing store/ 书～ bookshop; bookstore/ 文具～ stationer's ② inn: 住～ stop at an inn

【店铺】 diànpù shop; store

【店员】 diànyuán shop assistant; salesclerk; clerk; salesman or saleswoman

玷 diàn ① a flaw in a piece of jade ② blemish; disgrace

【玷辱】 diànrǔ bring disgrace on; be a disgrace to

【玷污】 diànwū stain; sully; tarnish

垫 diàn ① put sth. under sth. else to raise it or make it level; fill up; pad: ～路 repair a road by filling the holes/ 桌子腿底下～点儿纸就平了。 Put a wad of paper under the leg of the table to make it level. ② pad; cushion: 椅～ chair cushion/ 鞋～ inner sole; insole/ 床～ mattress ③ pay for sb. and expect to be repaid later: 你先给我～上，以后再还你。 Would you mind paying for me? I'll pay you back later.

【垫付】 diànfù pay for sb. and expect to be repaid later

【垫脚石】 diànjiǎoshí stepping-stone

【垫款】 diànkuǎn money advanced for sb. to be paid back later

【垫平】 diànpíng level up: 把篮球场～ level a basketball court

【垫子】 diànzi mat; pad; cushion: 擦鞋～ doormat/ 体操～ gym mat/ 沙发～ sofa cushion/ 弹簧～ spring mattress/ 茶杯～ teacup mat; coaster

惦 diàn remember with concern; be concerned about; keep thinking about: 我一直～着这件事。 I've been thinking about that all the time.

【惦记】 diànjì remember with concern; be concerned about; keep thinking about: 她老～着给孩子打件毛衣。 She's always thinking of knitting a sweater for her child.

【惦念】 diànniàn keep thinking about; be anxious about; worry about: 我一切都好，请您不要～。 Everything's fine with me. Don't worry.

奠 diàn ① establish; settle ② make offerings to the spirits of the dead

【奠定】 diàndìng establish; settle: ～基础 lay a foundation

【奠都】 diàndū establish (或 found) a capital

【奠基】 diànjī lay a foundation ◇ ～礼 foundation stone laying ceremony/ ～人 founder/ ~石 foundation stone; cornerstone

殿 diàn ① hall; palace; temple ② at the rear
【殿后】 diànhòu bring up the rear
【殿军】 diànjūn ① rearguard ② a person who comes last in a contest or last among the winners; the last of the successful candidates
【殿下】 diànxià （直接称呼）Your Highness; （间接称呼）His or Her Highness

靛 diàn ① indigo ② indigo-blue
【靛蓝】 diànlán indigo
【靛青】 diànqīng ① indigo-blue ② 〈方〉 indigo

diāo

刁 diāo tricky; artful; sly
【刁滑】 diāohuá cunning; crafty; artful
【刁难】 diāonàn create difficulties; make things difficult: 故意~ deliberately make things difficult for others/ 百般~ create obstructions of every description; raise all manner of difficulties; put up innumerable obstacles

凋 diāo wither: 苍松翠柏,常绿不~。The pine and the cypress remain green all the year round.
【凋零】 diāolíng withered, fallen and scattered about
【凋落】 diāoluò wither and fall
【凋谢】 diāoxiè ① wither and fall ② die of old age: 老成~ the passing away of worthy old people

貂 diāo marten
【貂皮】 diāopí fur or pelt of marten; marten
【貂裘】 diāoqiú marten coat

碉 diāo
【碉堡】 diāobǎo pillbox; blockhouse
【碉楼】 diāolóu watchtower

雕 diāo ① carve; engrave: 石~ stone carving/ 瓷~ carved porcelain/ 浮~ relief ② 〈动〉 vulture
【雕虫小技】 diāo chóng xiǎojì insignificant skill (esp. in writing); the trifling skill of a scribe; literary skill of no high order
【雕花】 diāohuā ① carve patterns or designs on woodwork ② carving: ~家具 carved furniture
【雕刻】 diāokè carve; engrave: 玉石~ jade carving ◇ ~刀 carving tool; burin/ ~品 carving/ ~工艺 artistic carving
【雕梁画栋】 diāoliáng-huàdòng carved beams and painted rafters -- a richly ornamented building
【雕漆】 diāoqī 〈工美〉 carved lacquerware
【雕砌】 diāoqì write in a laboured and ornate style
【雕塑】 diāosù sculpture
【雕像】 diāoxiàng statue: 大理石~ marble statue/ 半身~ bust/ 小~ statuette
【雕琢】 diāozhuó ① cut and polish (jade, etc.); carve ② write in an ornate style

diào

吊* diào ① hang; suspend: 门前~着两盏红灯。There were two red lanterns hanging over the door./ ~打 hang up and beat sb. ② lift up or let down with a rope, etc.: 把和好的水泥~上去。Hoist up the mixed cement. ③ condole; mourn: ~丧 pay a condolence call ④ put in a fur lining: ~皮袄 line a coat with fur ⑤ revoke; withdraw: ~销 revoke (a licence, etc.) ⑥〈旧〉 a string of 1,000 cash ⑦ crane: 塔~ tower crane
【吊车】 diàochē crane; hoist
【吊灯】 diàodēng pendent lamp
【吊儿郎当】 diào'erlángdāng careless and casual; slovenly
【吊桥】 diàoqiáo ① suspension bridge ② drawbridge

【吊丧】 diàosāng visit the bereaved to offer one's condolences; pay a condolence call
【吊死】 diàosǐ hang by the neck; hang oneself
【吊销】 diàoxiāo revoke: ~驾驶执照 revoke a driving licence/ ~护照 withdraw a passport
【吊唁】 diàoyàn condole; offer one's condolences: ~函电 messages of condolence

钓* diào fish with a hook and line; angle
【钓饵】 diào'ěr bait
【钓竿】 diàogān fishing rod
【钓钩】 diàogōu fishhook
【钓具】 diàojù fishing tackle
【钓鱼】 diàoyú angle; go fishing

调* diào ① transfer; shift; move: 她~到这个小组来了。She has been transferred to this group. ② accent: 这人说话带山东~儿。This person speaks with a Shandong accent. ③〈乐〉 key ④ air; tune; melody ⑤〈语〉 tone; tune: 升~ rising tone (或 tune)/ 降~ falling tone (或 tune)
另见 tiáo
【调兵遣将】 diàobīng-qiǎnjiàng move troops; deploy forces
【调拨】 diàobō allocate and transfer (goods or funds); allot: ~款项购置图书 allocate funds for books
【调查】 diàochá investigate; inquire into; look into; survey: 作社会~ make a social investigation/ ~原因 investigate the cause/ 农村~ rural survey ◇ ~报告 findings report/ ~会 fact-finding meeting/ ~提纲 outline for investigation; questionnaire/ ~团 fact-finding mission
【调动】 diàodòng ① transfer; shift: ~工作 transfer sb. to another post ② move (troops); manoeuvre; muster: ~十万军队,一千辆坦克 muster a hundred thousand troops and a thousand tanks/ 部队~频繁。There have been numerous troop movements. ③ bring into play; arouse; mobilize: ~一切积极因素 bring every positive factor into play
【调号】 diàohào 〈语〉 tone mark
【调虎离山】 diào hǔ lí shān lure the tiger out of the mountains -- lure the enemy away from his base
【调换】 diàohuàn exchange; change; swop
【调回】 diàohuí recall (troops, etc.)
【调集】 diàojí assemble; muster: ~兵力 assemble forces/ ~二十个师 concentrate twenty divisions
【调派】 diàopài send; assign
【调遣】 diàoqiǎn dispatch; assign: ~军队 dispatch troops/ 听从~ be ready to accept an assignment
【调任】 diàorèn be transferred to another post: 他已~车间主任。He has been transferred to be head of a workshop.
【调用】 diàoyòng transfer (under a unified plan)
【调职】 diàozhí be transferred to another post
【调子】 diàozi tune; melody: 这个~倒挺热的。The tune is quite familiar.

掉* diào ① fall; drop; shed; come off: ~下几滴眼泪 shed a few tears/ 被击伤的敌机~在海里了。The damaged enemy plane dropped into the sea./ 镐头~了。The pick-head has come off. ② lose; be missing: 我把钥匙~了。I've lost my key./ 这本书~了两页。Two pages are missing from the book./ 他害了一场大病,体重~了十公斤。During his serious illness he lost over 10 kg. ③ fall behind: 他脚上打了泡,~在后面了。He got blisters on his feet, so he lagged behind. ④ change; exchange: ~座位 change (或 exchange) seats; swop places with sb. ⑤ turn: 把车头~过来 turn the car round ⑥〔用在某些动词后,表示动作的完成〕: 洗~ wash out/ 扔~ throw away/ 擦~ wipe off/ 改~坏习气 correct bad habits
【掉包】 diàobāo stealthily substitute one thing for another
【掉队】 diàoduì drop out (或 off); fall behind: 在三天的急行军中没有一个人~的。No one dropped out in the three days' forced march.
【掉换】 diàohuàn exchange; change; swop: 我们俩的上班时间~一下好吗? Would you mind swopping shifts with me?/ ~工作 be assigned a new job; be transferred to another

post

【掉色】 diàoshǎi lose colour; fade: 这种料子不~。 This material won't fade. 或 This material is colourfast.

【掉头】 diàotóu turn round; turn about: 这地方太窄, 汽车不好~。 The place is too narrow for the truck to turn around./ 敌人见势不妙,~就跑。 Seeing that the situation was getting hot for them, the enemy turned tail and fled.

【掉以轻心】 diào yǐ qīngxīn lower one's guard; treat sth. lightly: 虎狼在前, 我们决不可~。 With wolves and tigers pacing before us, we must not lower our guard.

【掉转】 diàozhuǎn turn round: ~身子 turn round/ ~枪口 turn one's gun (against one's superiors or old associates)

diē

爹 * diē 〈口〉 father; dad; daddy; pa: ~娘 father and mother; mum and dad; ma and pa; parents

【爹爹】 diēdie 〈方〉 father; dad; daddy; pa

跌 * diē ① fall; tumble: 他一伤了。 He fell down and injured himself. ② drop; fall: 物价下~。 Prices have dropped.

【跌打损伤】 diē-dǎ sǔnshāng injuries from falls, fractures, contusions and strains

【跌倒】 diēdǎo fall; tumble: 在哪儿~就从哪儿爬起来。 Pick yourself up from where you fell — correct your mistake where you made it.

【跌跌撞撞】 diēdiēzhuàngzhuàng dodder along; stagger along

【跌价】 diējià go down in price: 收音机~了。 The prices of radio sets have gone down.

【跌交】 diējiāo ① trip (或 stumble) and fall; fall: 跌了一交 have a fall ② make a mistake; meet with a setback

【跌落】 diēluò fall; drop

dié

迭 dié ① alternate; change ② repeatedly; again and again: ~挫强敌 inflict repeated reverses on a formidable enemy

【迭次】 diécì repeatedly; again and again: ~磋商 repeatedly consult each other

【迭起】 diéqǐ occur repeatedly; happen frequently

谍 dié ① espionage ② intelligence agent; spy

【谍报】 diébào information obtained through espionage; intelligence report; intelligence ◇ ~员 intelligence agent; spy

堞 dié battlements

喋 dié

【喋喋不休】 diédié bù xiū chatter away; rattle on, talk endlessly

【喋血】 diéxuè bloodshed; bloodbath

牒 dié an official document or note; certificate: 最后通~ ultimatum

叠 dié ① pile up; repeat: 层峦~嶂 peaks rising one higher than another ② fold: 把信~好 fold the letter/ ~被子 fold up a quilt

【叠床架屋】 diéchuáng-jiàwū pile one bed upon another or build one house on top of another — needless duplication: 这样~,文章就太罗嗦了。 So much needless repetition makes the article long-winded.

【叠罗汉】 dié luóhàn 〈体〉 pyramid

碟 * dié small plate; small dish: 一~炒黄豆 a dish of fried soya beans

【碟子】 diézi small dish; small plate

蝶 * dié butterfly

【蝶泳】 diéyǒng butterfly stroke

dīng

丁 * dīng ① man: 壮~ able-bodied man/ 成~ reach manhood ② members of a family; population: 添~ have a baby born into the family/ ~口 population ③ a person engaged in a certain occupation: 园~ gardener ④ the fourth of the ten Heavenly Stems ⑤ fourth: ~等 the fourth grade; grade D/ ~种维生素 vitamin D ⑥ small cubes of meat or vegetable; cubes: 黄瓜~ diced cucumber

【丁当】 dīngdāng 〈象〉 ding-dong; jingle; clatter: 碟子碗碰得丁丁当当的。 The dishes and bowls slid together with a clatter.

【丁宁】 dīngníng urge again and again; warn; exhort:

仃 dīng 见 "伶仃" língdīng

叮 dīng ① sting; bite: 腿上叫蚊子~了一下 get a mosquito bite on the leg ② say or ask again to make sure: 我~了他一句,他才说了真话。 I asked him again, and at last he came out with the truth.

【叮当】 dīngdāng 见 "丁当" dīngdāng

【叮咛】 dīngníng 见 "丁宁" dīngníng

【叮嘱】 dīngzhǔ urge again and again; warn; exhort

玎 dīng

【玎珰】 dīngdāng 见 "丁当" dīngdāng

【玎玲】 dīnglíng 〈象〉〔多形容玉石撞击声〕 clink; jingle; tinkle

盯 dīng fix one's eyes on; gaze at; stare at: 他两眼~着雷达荧光屏。 His eyes were fixed on the radar screen./ ~住这个坏蛋。 Keep a close watch on the scoundrel.

【盯梢】 dīngshāo shadow sb.; tail sb.

钉 * dīng ① nail; tack ② follow closely; tail: 紧紧~住敌长机 keep on the tail of the enemy's lead plane ③ urge; press: 你要~着他吃药,别让他忘了。 You must remind him to take his medicine, in case he forgets. ④ 见 "盯" dīng
另见 dìng

【钉人】 dīngrén 〈体〉 watch (或 mark) an opponent in a game ◇ ~防守 man-for-man (或 man-to-man) defence

【钉子】 dīngzi ① nail ② snag: 碰~ hit (或 strike, run against) a snag; meet with a rebuff

dǐng

顶 * dǐng ① the crown of the head: 秃~ be bald ② top: 山~ mountaintop; hilltop; peak/ 屋~ roof ③ carry on the head ④ gore; butt: 这牛爱~人。 This bull gores people. ⑤ go against: ~风雪,战严寒 face blizzards and brave severe cold ⑥ push from below or behind; push up; prop up: 嫩芽把土~起来了。 The sprouts have pushed up the earth./ 用千斤顶把汽车~起来 jack up a car ⑦ retort; turn down: 我~了他几句。 I said a few words to him in retort./ 把抗议~回去 reject a protest ⑧ cope with; stand up to: 负担虽重,他们两个也~下来了。 The load was heavy, but the two of them coped with it all right. ⑨ take the place of; substitute; replace: ~别人的名字 assume sb. else's name ⑩ equal; be equivalent to: 一台收割机能~几十个人。 One harvester can do the work of scores of people. ⑪〈量〉〔用于某些有顶的东西〕: 一~帽子 a cap; a hat/ 一~帐子 a mosquito net ⑫ very; most; extremely: ~有用 very useful/ ~小的那个孩子 the youngest (或 smallest) child

【顶点】 dǐngdiǎn ① apex; zenith; acme; pinnacle ②〈数〉vertex; apex

【顶端】 dǐngduān top; peak; apex

【顶多】 dǐngduō at (the) most; at best

【顶峰】 dǐngfēng peak; summit; pinnacle

【顶呱呱】 dǐngguāguā tip-top; first-rate; excellent

【顶尖】 dǐngjiān ① tip ②〈机〉centre: 死~ dead centre

【顶少】 dǐngshǎo at least

【顶替】 dǐngtì take sb.'s place; replace: 他走了谁来～他？ Who's going to take his place after he leaves?

【顶天立地】 dǐngtiān-lìdì of gigantic stature; of indomitable spirit: 做一个～的英雄汉 be a hero of indomitable spirit

【顶头】 dǐngtóu ① coming directly towards one: ～风 head wind ② top; end: 这条巷子的～有个公用电话。 There is a public telephone (booth) at the end of this lane.

【顶头上司】 dǐngtóu shàngsi one's immediate (或 direct) superior

【顶住】 dǐngzhù withstand; stand up to; hold out against: ～压力 withstand pressure/ ～逆流 stand up against an adverse current/ ～风浪 weather a storm

【顶撞】 dǐngzhuàng contradict (one's elder or superior)

【顶嘴】 dǐngzuǐ reply defiantly; answer back; talk back

酊 dǐng 见"酩酊大醉" mǐngdǐng dàzuì

鼎 dǐng an ancient cooking vessel with two loop handles and three or four legs: 三足～ tripod/ 四足～ quadripod

【鼎鼎大名】 dǐngdǐng dàmíng a great reputation

【鼎力】 dǐnglì 〈套〉 your kind effort: 多蒙～协助,无任感激。 We are extremely grateful to you for the trouble you have taken on our behalf.

【鼎立】 dǐnglì (of three antagonists confronting one another) stand like the three legs of a tripod; tripartite confrontation; tripartite balance of forces

【鼎盛】 dǐngshèng in a period of great prosperity; at the height of power and splendour: 春秋～ in the prime of manhood

【鼎足】 dǐngzú the three legs of a tripod — three rival powers: ～之势 a situation of tripartite confrontation

dìng

订* dìng ① conclude; draw up; agree on: ～条约 conclude a treaty/ ～合同 enter into (或 make) a contract/ ～计划 draw up (或 work out) a plan/ ～日期 fix (或 agree on) a date/ ～生产指标 set a production target ② subscribe to (a newspaper, etc.); book (seats, tickets, etc.); order (merchandise, etc.) ③ make corrections; revise: 修～ revise ④ staple together

【订单】 dìngdān order for goods; order form

【订费】 dìngfèi subscription (rate)

【订购】 dìnggòu order (goods); place an order for sth.

【订户】 dìnghù ① subscriber (to a newspaper or periodical) ② a person or household with a standing order for milk, etc.

【订婚】 dìnghūn be engaged (to be married); be betrothed

【订货】 dìnghuò order goods; place an order for goods

【订立】 dìnglì conclude (a treaty, agreement, etc.); make (a contract, etc.)

【订书机】 dìngshūjī stapler; stapling-machine

【订阅】 dìngyuè subscribe to (a newspaper, periodical, etc.)

【订正】 dìngzhèng make corrections; emend: ～了第一版中的错误。 Corrections have been made to the first edition.

钉 dìng ① nail: ～马掌 nail on horseshoes/ ～钉子 drive in a nail/ 把窗子～死 nail up a window ② sew on: ～扣子 sew a button on 另见 dīng

定* dìng ① calm; stable: 心神不～ be ill at ease; feel restless/ 天下大～。 General stability has been achieved in the country. ② decide; fix; set: 开会时间～在明天上午。 The meeting is fixed for tomorrow morning./ 代表团～于今日离京去。 The delegation is due to leave Beijing today./ ～方针 decide on a policy/ ～计划 make a plan ③ fixed; settled; established: ～数 fixed number/ ～评 accepted opinion ④ subscribe to (a newspaper, etc.); book (seats, tickets, etc.); order (merchandise, etc.) ⑤ 〈书〉 surely; certainly; definitely: ～可取胜 be sure to win

【定案】 dìng'àn ① decide on (或 pass) a verdict; reach a conclusion on a case ② verdict; final decision

【定单】 dìngdān order for goods; order form

【定都】 dìngdū choose a site for the capital; establish a capital: ～北京 make Beijing the capital; decide on Beijing as the capital

【定夺】 dìngduó make a final decision; decide: 讨论后再行～。 We won't make any decision until after the discussion.

【定额】 dìng'é quota; norm: 生产～ production quota

【定稿】 dìnggǎo ① finalize a manuscript, text, etc. ② final version or text

【定购】 dìnggòu ① order (goods); place an order for sth.

【定规】 dìngguī ① established rule or practice; set pattern: 并无～。 There's no hard and fast rule. ② 〈方〉 be bent on; be determined

【定婚】 dìnghūn be engaged (to be married); be betrothed

【定货】 dìnghuò order goods; place an order for goods

【定价】 dìngjià ① fix a price ② fixed price; list price

【定睛】 dìngjīng fix one's eyes upon: ～细看 look fixedly and scrutinize

【定居】 dìngjū settle down

【定局】 dìngjú ① foregone conclusion; inevitable outcome: 今年丰收已成～。 It's a foregone conclusion that we'll have a bumper harvest this year. ② settle finally: 事情还没有～,明天可以再议。 The matter isn't settled yet. We can take it up again tomorrow.

【定理】 dìnglǐ theorem: 基本～ fundamental theorem

【定量】 dìngliàng ① fixed quantity; ration ② determine the amounts of the components of a substance

【定律】 dìnglǜ law: 万有引力～ the law of universal gravitation

【定论】 dìnglùn final conclusion: 这个问题尚无～。 No final conclusion has yet been reached on this matter. 或 This is still an open question.

【定期】 dìngqī ① fix (或 set) a date ② regular; at regular intervals; periodical: ～体格检查 regular physical checkups/ ～轮换 rotate at regular intervals/ ～汇报工作 regularly report back on one's work/ ～刊物 periodical publication; periodical/ 不～刊物 nonperiodic publication ◇ ～存款 fixed deposit; time deposit

【定钱】 dìngqian deposit; earnest (money)

【定亲】 dìngqīn engagement (arranged by parents); betrothal

【定神】 dìngshén ① collect oneself; compose oneself; pull oneself together ② concentrate one's attention: 听见有人叫我,一看原来是小李。 I heard someone calling me and, looking hard, saw that it was Xiao Li.

【定时炸弹】 dìngshí zhàdàn time bomb

【定型】 dìngxíng finalize the design; fall into a pattern: 这种插秧机正在试制,尚未～。 This type of rice transplanter is being trial-produced; the design hasn't been finalized.

【定义】 dìngyì definition: 下～ give a definition; define

【定制】 dìngzhì have sth. made to order; have sth. custommade: ～家具 have furniture made to order/ 欢迎选购和～。 Orders for ready-made or custom-made articles are welcome.

【定罪】 dìngzuì declare sb. guilty; convict sb. (of a crime)

【定做】 dìngzuò have sth. made to order (或 measure): ～的衣服 tailor-made clothes; clothes made to measure/ 这双鞋是～的。 This pair of shoes was made to order.

diū

丢* diū ① lose; mislay: 这套书～了一本。 There's a book missing from the set./ 我把钳子～哪儿了？ Where have I left my pliers? ② throw; cast; toss: 把菜帮子～给小兔吃 throw the outer leaves to the rabbit ③ put (或 lay) aside: ～在脑后 let sth. pass out of one's mind; clean forget; completely ignore/ 只有这件事～不开。 That's the one thing that keeps worrying me. 或 That's my only worry.

【丢掉】 diūdiào ① lose: 我～了一支笔。 I've lost my pen. ② throw away; cast away; discard

【丢脸】 diūliǎn lose face; be disgraced: 这不是～的事。 There's nothing to be ashamed of.

【丢弃】 diūqì abandon; discard; give up

【丢失】 diūshī lose

【丢眼色】 diū yǎnsè wink at sb.; tip sb. the wink

dōng

东* dōng ① east: 城～ east of the city/ ～城 the eastern part of the city/ ～郊 eastern suburbs ② master; owner: 房～ landlord ③ host: 做～ stand treat; stand host; play the host

【东奔西跑】 dōngbēn-xīpǎo run around here and there; bustle about; rush about (或 around)

【东道】 dōngdào one who treats sb. to a meal; host: 做～ play the host; stand treat ◇ ～国 host country/ ～主 host

【东方】 dōngfāng ① the east: ～欲晓。 Dawn is breaking. ② (Dōngfāng) the East; the Orient

【东风】 dōngfēng east wind

【东拉西扯】 dōnglā-xīchě drag in all sorts of irrelevant matters; talk at random; ramble

【东鳞西爪】 dōnglín-xīzhǎo odds and ends; bits and pieces; fragments

【东南】 dōngnán southeast

【东拼西凑】 dōngpīn-xīcòu scrape together; knock together: 那篇文章是～的。 That article is scissors-and-paste work.

【东山再起】 dōngshān zài qǐ stage a comeback

【东施效颦】 Dōngshī xiào pín Dong Shi, an ugly woman, knitting her brows in imitation of the famous beauty Xi Shi (西施), only to make herself uglier — blind imitation with ludicrous effect

【东西】 dōng-xī ① east and west ② from east to west: 这地方～三里,南北五里。 This district is three li across from east to west and five li from north to south.

【东西】 dōngxi ① thing: 他收拾好～就走了。 He packed his things and left./ 一成不变的～是没有的。 Nothing is immutable./ 她买～去了。 She's out shopping./ 分析形势要注意全局性的～。 In analysing a situation, pay attention to things that concern the situation as a whole. ② 〔指人或动物,多含喜爱或厌恶的感情〕 thing; creature: 这小～真可爱。 What a sweet little thing!/ 真不是～! What a despicable creature!

【东…西…】 dōng … xī … here … there: 东一锤子,西一棒子 hammer here and batter there; act or speak haphazardly/ 东一个,西一个 (of things) be scattered here and there/ 东一句,西一句 talk incoherently

【东张西望】 dōngzhāng-xīwàng gaze (或 peer) around

冬* dōng winter

【冬菇】 dōnggū dried mushrooms (picked in winter)

【冬季】 dōngjì winter

【冬眠】 dōngmián 〈生〉 winter sleep; hibernation

【冬天】 dōngtiān winter

【冬装】 dōngzhuāng winter dress (或 clothes)

dǒng

董 dǒng ① 〈书〉 direct; superintend; supervise: ～其成 supervise the project until its completion ② director; trustee

【董事】 dǒngshì director; trustee ◇ ～会 (企业) board of directors; (学校等) board of trustees/ ～长 chairman of the board

懂* dǒng understand; know: ～英语 know English/ ～礼貌 have good manners/ 不要不～装～。 Don't pretend to know (或 understand) when you don't.

【懂得】 dǒngde understand; know; grasp

【懂事】 dǒngshì sensible; intelligent: ～的孩子 a sensible child/ 你怎么这样不～? How can you be so thoughtless?

dòng

动* dòng ① move; stir: 他扭了腰,～不了。 He's strained his back and can't move./ 微风吹～树叶。 A breeze stirred the leaves./ 这东西一个人拿不～。 No one can carry that single-handed./ 别～ Don't move. ② act; get moving ③ change; alter: 这句话只要～一两个字就顺了。 Just change one or two words and the sentence will read smoothly. ④ use: ～脑筋 use one's head ⑤ touch (one's heart); arouse: ～了公愤 have aroused public indignation/ ～感情 be carried away by emotion; get worked up/ ～肝火 flare up/ 不为甜言蜜语所～ not be swayed by fine words ⑥ 〈方〉 〔多用于否定式〕 eat or drink: 不～荤腥 never touch meat or fish; be a vegetarian

【动笔】 dòngbǐ take up the pen; start writing: 他最近很少～。 He hasn't done much writing recently./ 想清楚了再～。 Think it all out before you start writing.

【动兵】 dòngbīng send out troops to fight

【动不动】 dòngbudòng easily; frequently; at every turn: ～就感冒 catch cold easily/ ～就发脾气 be apt to lose one's temper; often get into a temper

【动产】 dòngchǎn movable property; movables; personal property

【动词】 dòngcí 〈语〉 verb ◇ ～不定式 infinitive

【动荡】 dòngdàng turbulence; upheaval; unrest: ～的局势 a turbulent situation

【动工】 dònggōng begin construction; start building

【动火】 dònghuǒ 〈口〉 get angry; flare up

【动机】 dòngjī motive; intention: 出于自私的～ be actuated by selfish motives/ ～不纯 have impure motives/ 他的～是好的。 His intentions are good. 或 He means well.

【动静】 dòngjing ① the sound of sth. astir: 屋子里静悄悄的,一点～也没有。 It was quiet in the room; nothing was stirring. ② movement; activity: 发现可疑～ spot something suspicious/ 一有～就来报告。 Report as soon as anything happens.

【动力】 dònglì ① motive power; power ② motive (或 driving) force; impetus: 社会发展的～ the motive force of the development of society

【动乱】 dòngluàn turmoil; disturbance; upheaval; turbulence: ～时期 a time of turmoil; a time of storm and stress/ 社会～ social upheaval/ ～年代 years of upheaval

【动怒】 dòngnù lose one's temper; flare up

【动气】 dòngqì 〈口〉 take offence; get angry

【动情】 dòngqíng ① get worked up; become excited ② become enamoured; have one's (sexual) passions aroused

【动人】 dòngrén moving; touching: ～的情景 a moving scene/ ～的事迹 stirring deeds

【动容】 dòngróng 〈书〉 change countenance; be visibly moved

【动身】 dòngshēn go (或 set out) on a journey; leave (for a distant place)

【动手】 dòngshǒu ① start work; get to work: 早点儿～,早点儿完成。 The sooner we start, the sooner we finish./ ～修建一座高炉 start building a blast furnace/ 大家一干了起来。 Everyone set to work. ② touch; handle: 爱护展品,请勿～。 Please don't touch the exhibits. ③ raise a hand to strike; hit out: 谁先动的手? Who struck the first blow?

【动手术】 dòngshǒushù ① perform an operation; operate on sb. ② have an operation; be operated on

【动态】 dòngtài trends; developments: 科技新～ recent developments in science and technology/ 了解敌军的～ find out about enemy troop movements/ 油井～ behaviour (或 performance) of an oil well

【动弹】 dòngtan move; stir: 车里太挤,～不得。 The bus was so crowded that nobody could move./ 机器～不了。 The machine has stopped.

【动听】 dòngtīng interesting or pleasant to listen to: 他能把极平常的事儿说得很～。 He can make ordinary things sound interesting./ 她唱得很～。 She sings beautifully.

【动土】 dòngtǔ break ground; start building

【动武】 dòngwǔ use force; start a fight; come to blows

【动物】 dòngwù animal

◇ ～油 animal oil/ ～园 zoological garden; zoo

【动向】 dòngxiàng trend; tendency: 新～ new trends/ 密切注意敌人～。 Keep a close watch on the enemy's movements.

【动心】 dòngxīn one's mind is perturbed; one's desire, enthusiasm or interest is aroused

【动刑】 dòngxíng subject sb. to torture; torture

【动摇】 dòngyáo shake; vacillate; waver

【动议】 dòngyì motion: 紧急～ an urgent motion/ 提出一项～ put forward a motion

【动用】 dòngyòng put to use; employ; draw on: ～大量人力 employ a tremendous amount of manpower/ ～库存 draw on stock

【动员】 dòngyuán mobilize; arouse: 整个医院都～起来, 抢救伤员。 The whole hospital was galvanized into action to save the wounded.

【动辄】 dòngzhé 〈书〉 easily; frequently; at every turn: ～发怒 fly into a rage on the slightest provocation/ ～得咎 be frequently taken to task; be blamed for whatever one does

【动作】 dòngzuò ① movement; motion; action: ～敏捷(缓慢) quick (slow) in one's movements/ 优美的舞蹈～ graceful dance movements ② act; start moving: 且看他下一步如何～。 Let's see how he acts next.

冻* dòng ① freeze: ～肉 frozen meat/ 不能让这些白菜～坏。 We mustn't let the cabbages be damaged by frost. ② jelly: 肉～儿 jellied meat ③ feel very cold; freeze; be frostbitten: 多穿些, 别～着了。 Put on more clothes so you don't catch cold./ 她手都～了。 Her hands were frostbitten.

【冻冰】 dòngbīng freeze: 河上～了。 The river is frozen.

【冻僵】 dòngjiāng frozen stiff; numb with cold

【冻结】 dòngjié ① freeze; congeal (of wages, prices, etc.) freeze: 工资～ wage freeze/ ～的资产 frozen assets

【冻死】 dòngsǐ freeze to death; freeze and perish; die of frost

【冻土】 dòngtǔ frozen earth (或 ground, soil) ◇ ～学 cryopedology

洞* dòng ① hole; cavity: 衬衣破了一个～ have a hole in one's shirt/ 山～ mountain cave/ 城门～儿 archway of a city gate ② penetratingly; thoroughly: ～见症结 see clearly the crux of the matter; get to the heart of the problem

【洞察】 dòngchá see clearly; have an insight into: ～是非 see clearly the rights and wrongs of the case/ ～一切 have a keen insight into matters

【洞彻】 dòngchè understand thoroughly; see clearly

【洞达】 dòngdá understand thoroughly: ～事理 be sensible

【洞房】 dòngfáng bridal (或 nuptial) chamber: ～花烛 wedding festivities; wedding

【洞若观火】 dòng ruò guān huǒ see sth. as clearly as a blazing fire

【洞悉】 dòngxī know clearly; understand thoroughly

【洞晓】 dòngxiǎo have a clear knowledge of: ～其中利弊 have a clear understanding of the advantages and disadvantages

【洞穴】 dòngxué cave; cavern

恫 dòng fear

【恫吓】 dònghè threaten; intimidate: 虚声～ bluff; bluster

栋 dòng ① 〈书〉 ridgepole ② 〈量〉 一～楼房 a building

【栋梁】 dòngliáng ridgepole and beam — pillar of the state

dōu

都* dōu 〈副〉 ① all: 大家～到了吗? Is everybody here? ② 〔跟"是"字合用, 说明理由〕 ～是你不好, 害得我们迟到了。 It was all because of you that we were late. ③ even: 今天天气真怪, 中午比早晨～冷。 Strange weather we're having

today. It's even colder at noon than it was early in the morning. ④ already: 他～八十岁了, 身子骨还那么硬朗。 He's already eighty but still going strong.

另见 dū

兜 dōu ① pocket; bag: 裤～儿 trouser pocket/ 网～儿 string bag ② wrap up in a piece of cloth, etc.: 用毛巾～着几个鸡蛋 carry a few eggs wrapped up in a towel ③ move round: 我们乘车在城里～了一圈。 We went for a drive around in town. ④ canvass; solicit: ～售 peddle ⑤ take upon oneself; take responsibility for sth.: 没关系, 出了问题我～着。 Don't worry. If anything goes wrong, I'll take responsibility for it.

【兜风】 dōufēng ① catch the wind: 帆破了, 兜不住风。 The sails are torn; they won't catch the wind. ② 〈方〉 go for a drive, ride or sail; go for a spin

【兜揽】 dōulǎn ① canvass; solicit: ～生意 solicit custom; drum up trade ② take upon oneself (sb. else's work, etc.)

【兜圈子】 dōu quānzi ① go around in circles; circle: 飞机在森林上空～。 The aeroplane circled over the forest. ② beat about the bush

【兜售】 dōushòu peddle; hawk

dǒu

斗* dǒu ① dou, a unit of dry measure for grain (=1 decalitre) ② a dou measure ③ an object shaped like a cup or dipper: 烟～ (tobacco) pipe/ 漏～ funnel ④ whorl (of a fingerprint)

另见 dòu

【斗胆】 dǒudǎn 〈谦〉 make bold; venture: 我～说一句, 这件事您做错了。 May I make bold to suggest that you were wrong to do so.

【斗室】 dǒushì 〈书〉 a small room

抖* dǒu ① tremble; shiver; quiver: 浑身直～ tremble all over/ 冷得发～ shiver with cold/ 气得发～ quiver with anger ② shake; jerk: 把衣服上的雪～掉 shake the snow off one's clothes/ ～一～缰绳 give the reins a jerk/ ～开棉被 spread the quilt with a flick ③ rouse; stir up: ～起精神 pluck up one's spirits

【抖动】 dǒudòng shake; tremble; vibrate

【抖擞】 dǒusǒu enliven; rouse: ～精神 brace up; pull oneself together/ 精神～ full of energy; full of beans

【抖威风】 dǒu wēifēng throw one's weight about

陡 dǒu ① steep; precipitous: 山～路险。 The hill is steep, and the climb is dangerous. ② suddenly; abruptly: 天气～变。 The weather changed suddenly.

【陡立】 dǒulì rise steeply

【陡峭】 dǒuqiào precipitous

【陡然】 dǒurán suddenly; unexpectedly: ～下降 fall suddenly

蚪 dǒu 见"蝌蚪" kēdǒu

dòu

斗* dòu ① fight; tussle: 拳～ fist fight; fisticuffs ② struggle against; denounce ③ contest with; contend with: 孤狸再狡猾也～不过好猎手。 The craftiest fox can't escape the skilled hunter. ④ make animals fight (as a game): ～牛 bullfight

另见 dǒu

【斗鸡】 dòujī ① gamecock ② cockfighting

【斗气】 dòuqì quarrel or contend with sb. on account of a personal grudge

【斗争】 dòuzhēng ① struggle; fight; combat ② strive for; fight for

【斗志】 dòuzhì will to fight; fighting will: ～昂扬 have high morale

【斗智】 dòuzhì battle of wits

豆* dòu ① legumes; pulses; beans; peas: 蚕~ broad beans/ 豌~ peas/ 扁~ hyacinth beans ② an ancient stemmed cup or bowl
【豆腐】 dòufu bean curd
【豆荚】 dòujiá pod
【豆浆】 dòujiāng soya-bean milk
【豆蔻】 dòukòu 〈植〉 round cardamom (Amomum cardamomum)
【豆沙】 dòushā sweetened bean paste
【豆芽儿】 dòuyár bean sprouts
【豆油】 dòuyóu soya-bean oil
【豆汁】 dòuzhī a fermented drink made from ground beans

逗 dòu ① tease; play with: ~孩子玩 play with a child ② provoke (laughter, etc.); amuse: 这小女孩~人喜欢。She's a charming little girl.
【逗号】 dòuhào comma (,)
【逗留】 dòuliú stay; stop: 他们中途在巴黎~了几天。They stopped over in Paris for several days
【逗弄】 dòunong tease; kid; make fun of: 他~你呢。He's kidding you.
【逗引】 dòuyǐn tease

痘* dòu ① smallpox ② smallpox pustule
【痘苗】 dòumiáo (bovine) vaccine

dū

都* dū ① capital ② big city; metropolis
另见 dōu
【都城】 dūchéng capital
【都会】 dūhuì city; metropolis
【都市】 dūshì city; metropolis

督 dū superintend and direct: ~战 supervise operations
【督察】 dūchá superintend; supervise
【督促】 dūcù supervise and urge: ~大家及时归还工具 urge everybody to return the tools on time
【督学】 dūxué educational inspector

嘟 dū ① 〈象〉 toot; honk: 汽车喇叭~~响。The car tooted. ② 〈方〉 pout: ~起了嘴 pout

dú

毒* dú ① poison; toxin: 服~ take poison ② narcotics: 吸~ take drugs/ 贩~ traffic in drugs ③ poisonous; noxious; poisoned: ~蜘蛛 poisonous spider/ 有~气体 noxious gas/ ~箭 a poisoned arrow ④ kill with poison; poison ⑤ malicious; cruel; fierce: 那时太阳正~，晒得他汗珠直往下滚。The sun was at its fiercest and beads of sweat kept rolling down his face./ ~打 beat up
【毒草】 dúcǎo poisonous weeds
【毒害】 dúhài poison (sb.'s mind)
【毒计】 dújì venomous scheme; deadly trap
【毒剂】 dújì toxic; toxicant
【毒辣】 dúlà sinister; diabolic
【毒瘤】 dúliú malignant tumour; cancer
【毒品】 dúpǐn narcotic drugs; narcotics
【毒气】 dúqì poisonous (或 poison) gas ◇ ~弹 gas shell; gas bomb/ ~室 gas chamber
【毒杀】 dúshā kill with poison
【毒蛇】 dúshé poisonous (或 venomous) snake; viper
【毒手】 dúshǒu violent treachery; murderous scheme: 下~ resort to violent treachery; lay murderous hands on sb.
【毒死】 dúsǐ kill with poison; poison
【毒素】 dúsù ① 〈生〉 toxin ② poison
【毒物】 dúwù poisonous substance; poison
【毒刑】 dúxíng cruel corporal punishment; horrible torture
【毒性】 dúxìng toxicity; poisonousness
【毒牙】 dúyá poison (或 venom) fang
【毒药】 dúyào poison; toxicant

【毒液】 dúyè venom

独* dú ① only; single: ~子 only son/ 大家都到了，有他还没来。He's the only one who isn't here yet. ② alone; by oneself; in solitude: ~居 live a solitary existence/ ~坐 sit alone ③ old people without offspring; the childless
【独霸】 dúbà dominate exclusively; monopolize: ~一方 lord it over a district; be a local despot
【独白】 dúbái soliloquy; monologue
【独裁】 dúcái dictatorship; autocratic rule ◇ ~者 autocrat; dictator/ ~政治 autocracy
【独唱】 dúchàng (vocal) solo ◇ ~会 recital (of a vocalist)
【独出心裁】 dú chū xīncái show originality; be original
【独创】 dúchuàng original creation: ~一格 create a style all one's own ◇ ~精神 creative spirit/ ~性 originality
【独当一面】 dú dāng yī miàn take charge of a department or locality: 他成长很快，已经可以~了。He's matured quickly. He can now take charge of the whole locality.
【独到】 dúdào original: ~的见解 original view/ ~之处 originality
【独断】 dúduàn arbitrary; dictatorial
【独断独行】 dúduàn-dúxíng make arbitrary decisions and take peremptory actions; act arbitrarily
【独角戏】 dújiǎoxì monodrama; one-man show: 唱~ put on a one-man show; go it alone
【独具匠心】 dú jù jiàngxīn show ingenuity; have originality
【独具只眼】 dú jù zhī yǎn be able to see what others cannot; have exceptional insight
【独揽】 dúlǎn arrogate; monopolize: ~大权 arrogate all powers to oneself
【独力】 dúlì by one's own efforts; on one's own: ~经营 manage affairs on one's own
【独立】 dúlì ① stand alone: ~山巅的苍松 a pine tree standing alone on a mountain peak ② independence: 宣布~ proclaim independence ③ independent; on one's own: ~营(团、师) independent battalion (regiment, division)/ ~分析问题和解决问题的能力 ability to analyse and solve problems on one's own
【独立性】 dúlìxìng independent character; independence: 闹~ assert one's "independence" — refuse to obey the leadership
【独立自主】 dúlì-zìzhǔ maintain independence and keep the initiative in one's own hands; act independently and with the initiative in one's own hands
【独木不成林】 dú mù bù chéng lín one tree does not make a forest — one person alone cannot accomplish much
【独木难支】 dú mù nán zhī one log cannot prop up a tottering building — one person alone cannot save the situation
【独木桥】 dúmùqiáo ① single-plank (或 single-log) bridge ② difficult path
【独木舟】 dúmùzhōu dugout canoe
【独幕剧】 dúmùjù one-act play
【独善其身】 dú shàn qí shēn pay attention to one's own moral uplift without thought of others
【独身】 dúshēn ① separated from one's family: ~在外 away from home and family ② unmarried; single ◇ ~主义 celibacy
【独生女】 dúshēngnǚ only daughter
【独生子】 dúshēngzǐ only son
【独树一帜】 dú shù yī zhì fly one's own colours — develop a school of one's own
【独特】 dútè unique; distinctive: ~的风格 a unique style
【独眼龙】 dúyǎnlóng a person blind in one eye; one-eyed person
【独一无二】 dúyī-wú'èr unique; unparalleled; unmatched
【独占】 dúzhàn have sth. all to oneself; monopolize
【独占鳌头】 dú zhàn áotóu come out first; head the list of successful candidates; be the champion
【独自】 dúzì alone; by oneself
【独奏】 dúzòu (instrumental) solo: 钢琴~ piano solo ◇ ~会 recital (of an instrumentalist)

dú

读* dú ① read; read aloud: 这部小说值得一~。This novel is worth reading. ② attend school: ~完大学 finish college
【读本】 dúběn reader; textbook: 汉语~ a Chinese reader
【读书】 dúshū ① read; study: 她~很用功。She studies hard. ② attend school
【读物】 dúwù reading matter (或 material): 儿童~ children's books/ 通俗~ popular literature
【读音】 dúyīn pronunciation
【读者】 dúzhě reader ◇ ~来信 readers' letters; letters to the editor

渎 dú 〈书〉① show disrespect or contempt: 亵~ blaspheme; profane ② ditch; drain
【渎职】 dúzhí malfeasance; dereliction of duty

犊 dú calf

牍 dú ① wooden tablets or slips for writing (in ancient times) ② documents; archives; correspondence

黩 dú ① blacken; defile ② act wantonly
【黩武】 dúwǔ militaristic; warlike; bellicose: 穷兵~ engage in unjust military ventures ◇ ~主义 militarism/ ~主义者 militarist

dǔ

肚 dǔ tripe: 拌~丝儿 slices of tripe and cucumber in soy sauce
另见 dù
【肚子】 dǔzi tripe
另见 dùzi

笃 dǔ ① sincere; earnest ② (of an illness) serious; critical: 病~ be dangerously ill; be in a critical condition; be terminally ill
【笃厚】 dǔhòu sincere and magnanimous
【笃实】 dǔshí ① honest and sincere ② solid; sound: 学问~ sound scholarship
【笃信】 dǔxìn sincerely believe in; be a devout believer in
【笃学】 dǔxué diligent in study; devoted to study; studious

堵 dǔ ① stop up; block up: 把老鼠洞~死 stop up mouseholes/ 别~着门! Don't stand in the doorway! ② stifled; suffocated; oppressed: 胸口~得慌 feel suffocated; feel a tightness in the chest/ 心里一~得难受 have a load on one's mind ③〈书〉wall: 观者如~。There was a crowd of spectators. ④〈量〉: 一~墙 a wall
【堵塞】 dǔsè stop up; block up: 交通~ traffic jam/ ~漏洞 stop up a loophole; plug a hole
【堵嘴】 dǔzuǐ gag sb.; silence sb.

赌* dǔ ① gamble: 禁~ ban gambling ② bet: 打~ make a bet; bet
【赌本】 dǔběn money to gamble with
【赌博】 dǔbó gambling
【赌场】 dǔchǎng gambling house
【赌棍】 dǔgùn hardened (或 professional) gambler
【赌窟】 dǔkū gambling-den
【赌气】 dǔqì feel wronged and act rashly: 他觉得受了委屈,一~就走了。Feeling he had been wronged, he went off in a fit of pique.
【赌钱】 dǔqián gamble
【赌徒】 dǔtú gambler
【赌咒】 dǔzhòu take an oath; swear
【赌注】 dǔzhù stake

睹 dǔ see: 目~ see with one's own eyes; be an eyewitness to
【睹物思人】 dǔ wù sī rén seeing the thing one thinks of the person — the thing reminds one of its owner

dù

杜 dù ① birch-leaf pear ② shut out; stop; prevent: ~门谢客 close one's door to visitors/ 以~流弊 so as to put an end to abuses
【杜鹃】 dùjuān 〈动〉cuckoo
【杜绝】 dùjué stop; put an end to: ~弊端 stop all corrupt practices/ ~浪费 put an end to waste
【杜撰】 dùzhuàn fabricate; make up: 他讲的是真有其事,不是~的。The story he told is true, not made up.

肚* dù belly; abdomen; stomach
另见 dǔ
【肚皮】 dùpí 〈方〉belly
【肚脐】 dùqí navel; belly button
【肚子】 dùzi belly; abdomen: ~痛 have a stomachache; suffer from abdominal pain/ 笑得~痛 laugh till one's sides split/ 一~气 absolutely exasperated; full of pent-up anger
另见 dǔzi

妒 dù be jealous (或 envious) of; envy
【妒忌】 dùjì be jealous (或 envious) of; envy

度* dù ① linear measure ② degree of intensity: 硬~ hardness/ 湿~ humidity ③ a unit of measurement for angles, temperature, etc.; degree: 直角为九十~。A right angle is an angle of 90 degrees./ 北纬三十八~ latitude 38° N./ 水的沸点是摄氏一百~。The boiling point of water is 100 degrees centigrade./ 您的眼镜多少~? What's the strength of the lenses of your glasses? ④〈电〉kilowatt-hour (kwh) ⑤ limit; extent; degree: 劳累过~ be overworked/ 将玻璃管加热,以能弯曲为~。Heat the glass tube to the point that it can bend./ 长短适~ be the right length ⑥ tolerance; magnanimity: 大~包容 regard with kindly tolerance; be magnanimous ⑦ consideration: 把生死置之~外 give no thought to personal safety ⑧〈量〉occasion; time: 再~ a second time; once more/ 一年一~ once a year ⑨ spend; pass: 在农村~过童年 spend one's childhood in the countryside/ 欢~节日 joyously celebrate a festival
另见 duó
【度假】 dùjià spend one's holidays (或 vacation)
【度量】 dùliàng tolerance; magnanimity: ~大 broad-minded; magnanimous/ ~小 narrow-minded
【度量衡】 dùliànghéng length, capacity and weight; weights and measures
【度日】 dùrì subsist (in hardship); eke out an existence: 过去他靠什么~的? What did he do for a living in the old days?
【度日如年】 dù rì rú nián one day seems like a year; days wear on like years
【度数】 dùshu number of degrees; reading: 那个表上的~是多少? What does that meter read?

渡* dù ① cross (a river, the sea, etc.): ~河 cross a river/ 飞~太平洋 fly (across) the Pacific ② tide over; pull through: ~过难关 tide over a difficulty; pull through ③ ferry (people, goods, etc.) across ④〔多用于地名〕ferry crossing
【渡船】 dùchuán ferryboat; ferry
【渡口】 dùkǒu ferry

镀 dù plating: 电~ electroplating; galvanizing/ ~镍 nickel-plating/ ~铝钢 aluminium-plated steel
【镀金】 dùjīn ① gold-plating; gilding ② get gilded (formerly said of students who went abroad to study in order to enhance their social status)
【镀锡】 dùxī tin-plating; tinning
【镀银】 dùyín silver-plating; silvering

蠹 dù a kind of insect that eats into books, clothing, etc.; moth: 书~ bookworm
【蠹虫】 dùchóng ① 见"蠹" ② a harmful person; vermin
【蠹鱼】 dùyú silverfish; fish moth

duān

端* duān ① end; extremity: 两~ both ends/ 岛的南~ the southern tip (或 end) of the island ② beginning: 开~ beginning ③ point; item: 举其一~ for instance; just to mention one example ④ reason; cause: 无~ without rhyme or reason; unwarranted/ 借~ use sth. as a pretext ⑤ upright; proper: ~坐 sit up straight/ 品行不~ improper behaviour; misconduct ⑥ hold sth. level with both hands; carry: ~盘子 carry a tray/~饭上菜 serve a meal/ ~进两杯茶来 bring in two cups of tea

【端倪】 duānní clue; inkling: 略有~ have an inkling of the matter

【端午节】 Duānwǔjié the Dragon Boat Festival (the 5th day of the 5th lunar month)

【端详】 duānxiáng ① details: 细说~ give a full and detailed account; give full particulars ② dignified and serene: 举止~ behave with serene dignity

【端详】 duānxiang look sb. up and down

【端绪】 duānxù inkling; clue: 我们谈了半天,仍然毫无~。 We talked the matter over for quite some time but didn't get anywhere.

【端正】 duānzhèng ① upright; regular: 五官~ have regular features/ 把画像端端正正地挂起来 hang the portrait straight ② proper; correct: 品行~ correct in behaviour ③ rectify; correct: ~思想 correct one's thinking; straighten out one's ideas/ ~学习态度 take a correct attitude towards study

【端庄】 duānzhuāng dignified; sedate

duǎn

短* duǎn ① short; brief: 这条路最~。 This is the shortest way./ 冬季日~夜长。 In winter the days are short and the nights long./ 我给他写了封~信。 I dropped him a few lines./ 开个~会 have a brief meeting ② lack; owe: 理~ lack sound argument/ ~斤缺两 give short measure/ 一个月~两天 two days short of a month; a month less two days/ 别人都来了,就~他一个。 All the others are here; he's the only one missing. ③ weak point; fault: 揭人的~儿 pick on sb.'s weakness/ 说长道~ gossip

【短兵相接】 duǎnbīng xiāng jiē fight at close quarters; engage in hand-to-hand fight (或 close combat)

【短不了】 duǎnbuliǎo ① cannot do without: 人~水。 Man cannot do without water. ② cannot avoid; have to: 以后~还要请你帮忙。 Most likely I'll have to ask you for help again.

【短程】 duǎnchéng short distance; short range

【短处】 duǎnchu shortcoming; failing; fault; weakness

【短促】 duǎncù of very short duration; very brief: 呼吸~ be short of breath; gasp; pant

【短见】 duǎnjiàn ① shortsighted view ② suicide: 寻~ attempt suicide; commit suicide

【短距离】 duǎnjùlí short distance ◇ ~赛跑 short-distance run; dash; sprint

【短裤】 duǎnkù shorts

【短命】 duǎnmìng die young; be short-lived

【短跑】 duǎnpǎo dash; sprint ◇ ~运动员 dash man; sprinter

【短篇小说】 duǎnpiān xiǎoshuō short story

【短片】 duǎnpiàn 〈电影〉 short film; short

【短评】 duǎnpíng short commentary; brief comment

【短期】 duǎnqī short-term: 在~内 in a short time; in a brief space of time

【短浅】 duǎnqiǎn narrow and shallow: 目光~ shortsighted/ 见识~ lacking knowledge and experience; shallow

【短欠】 duǎnqiàn ① owe; be in arrears ② be short of

【短枪】 duǎnqiāng short arm; handgun

【短缺】 duǎnquē shortage

【短视】 duǎnshì ① nearsightedness; myopia ② lack foresight; be shortsighted

【短途】 duǎntú short distance

【短袜】 duǎnwà socks

【短小】 duǎnxiǎo short and small; short; small: 身材~ of small stature/ ~的序幕 a brief prologue

【短小精悍】 duǎnxiǎo jīnghàn ① not of imposing stature but strong and capable ② (of a piece of writing) short and pithy; terse and forceful

【短暂】 duǎnzàn of short duration; transient; brief: 她的一生是~而光荣的一生。 Her life was short but glorious.

duàn

段* duàn ①〈量〉 section; segment; part: 一~铁路 a section of railway/ 一~衣料 a length of dress material/ 这~历史 this phase of history/ 一~时间 a period of time/ 边界东~ the eastern sector of the boundary ② paragraph; passage

【段落】 duànluò ① paragraph: 这篇文章~清楚。 This article is well paragraphed. ② phase; stage: 第一期工程已经告一~。 The first phase of the project has been completed.

断* duàn ① break; snap: 喀嚓一声,~成两截 break in two with a snap/ 他给小提琴调弦的时候,E 弦~了。 When he was tuning his violin, the E string snapped. ② break off; cut off; stop: ~水 cut off the water supply/ ~敌退路 cut off the enemy's retreat/ 与指挥部的联系~了 lose contact with headquarters ③ give up; abstain from: ~烟 give up (或 quit) smoking ④ judge; decide: 当机立~ decide promptly and opportunely; make a prompt decision ⑤〈书〉〈副〉〔只用于否定式〕 absolutely; decidedly: ~不可信 absolutely incredible/ ~无此理 absolutely untenable (或 unreasonable); the height of absurdity

【断案】 duàn'àn ① settle a lawsuit ②〈逻〉 conclusion (of a syllogism)

【断编残简】 duànbiān-cánjiǎn stray fragments of text 又作 "断简残编"

【断肠】 duàncháng heartbroken

【断炊】 duànchuī run out of rice and fuel; can't keep the pot boiling; go hungry

【断代】 duàndài division of history into periods ◇ ~史 dynastic history

【断定】 duàndìng conclude; form a judgment; decide; determine: 我们有理由可以~,会议推迟了。 We may reasonably conclude that the meeting has been postponed./ 他~机器出了毛病了。 He came to the conclusion that the machine was out of order.

【断断续续】 duànduànxùxù off and on; intermittently: ~读过四年书 had four years of schooling off and on/ ~地说 speak disjointedly

【断根】 duàngēn be completely cured; effect a permanent cure

【断后】 duànhòu ① bring up the rear; cover a retreat ② have no progeny

【断交】 duànjiāo ① break off a friendship ② sever (或 break off) diplomatic relations

【断绝】 duànjué break off; cut off; sever: ~外交关系 sever (或 break off) diplomatic relations/ ~交通 stop traffic

【断奶】 duànnǎi weaning

【断气】 duànqì ① breathe one's last; die ② cut off the gas

【断然】 duànrán ① absolutely; flatly; categorically: ~不能接受 absolutely inacceptable/ ~拒绝 flatly refuse/ ~否认 categorically deny ② resolute; drastic: 采取~措施 take drastic measures

【断送】 duànsòng forfeit (one's life, future, etc.); ruin

【断头台】 duàntóutái guillotine

【断线风筝】 duànxiàn fēngzheng a kite with a broken string — a person or thing gone beyond recall

【断言】 duànyán say (或 state) with certainty; assert categorically; affirm

【断语】 duànyǔ conclusion; judgment: 遽下~ jump to conclusions

【断垣残壁】 duànyuán-cánbì (a desolate scene of) broken walls; debris

【断章取义】 duàn zhāng qǔ yì quote out of context; garble a statement, etc.

【断肢再植】 duànzhī zàizhí 〈医〉 replantation of a severed limb

【断子绝孙】 duànzǐ-juésūn 〈骂〉 may you die without sons; may you be the last of your line

缎 duàn satin

煅 duàn ① forge: ~铁 forge iron

锻* duàn forge

【锻接】 duànjiē forge welding

【锻炼】 duànliàn ① take exercise; have physical training: 每天~半小时 take half an hour's exercise every day/ ~身体, 保卫祖国 build up a good physique to defend the country/ 在大江大海中游泳, 既可以~身体, 又可以~意志. Swimming in big rivers and seas helps to build up both physical strength and willpower. ② temper; steel; toughen

duī

堆* duī ① pile up; heap up; stack: 把麦秸~在场上 stack the wheat-stalks on the threshing ground/ 桌上~满了书. The desk was piled with books./ 粮食~满仓, 果子~成山. Storehouses are bursting with grain, and fruit is piled high on the ground. ② heap; pile; stack: 柴火~ a pile (或 stack) of firewood/ 土~ mound/ 粪~ manure (或 dung) heap; dunghill/ 草~ haystack ③ 〈量〉 heap; pile; crowd: 一~垃圾 a garbage (或 rubbish) heap/ 一~人 a crowd of people ④〔多用于地名〕hillock; mound

【堆放】 duīfàng pile up; stack: 库房里~着许多农具. A lot of farm tools are piled in the storehouse.

【堆积】 duījī ① pile up; heap up: 工地上建筑材料~如山. Building materials are piled up mountain-high on the construction site. ②〈地〉accumulation

【堆砌】 duīqì ① load one's writing with fancy phrases ② pile up (hewn rocks, etc. to build sth.)

duì

队* duì ① a row of people; line: 排成两~ fall into two lines ② team; group: 篮球~ basketball team/ 军乐~ military band

【队旗】 duìqí 〈体〉 team pennant: 互赠~ exchange team pennants

【队伍】 duìwǔ ① troops ② ranks; contingent: 游行~ contingents of marchers; procession; parade

【队形】 duìxíng formation: 成战斗~ in battle formation/ 以密集(散开)~前进 advance in close (open) order ◇ ~变换 evolution

【队员】 duìyuán team member

【队长】 duìzhǎng ① 〈体〉 captain ② team leader

对* duì ① answer; reply: 无言以~ have nothing to say in reply ② treat; cope with; counter: 刀~刀, 枪~枪 sword against sword and spear against spear/ ~事不~人 concern oneself with facts and not with individuals/ 上海队~北京队 the Shanghai team versus the Beijing team ③ be trained on; be directed at: 枪口~着敌人 train the gun on the enemy/ 她的话不是~着你的. What she said was not directed at you. ④ mutual; face to face: ~骂 call each other names/ ~坐 sit facing each other/ ~饮 (two people) have a drink together ⑤ opposite; opposing: ~岸 the opposite bank; the other side of the river ⑥ bring (two things) into contact; fit one into the other: ~暗号 exchange code words ⑦ compare; check; identify: ~笔迹 identify the handwriting/ ~号码 check numbers ⑧ set; adjust: ~准 set one's watch; synchronize watches/ ~好望远镜的距离 adjust the focus of a telescope ⑨ right; correct: 猜~了 guess right/~, 就这么办. All right, just go ahead./ 他今天神色不~. He doesn't look himself today. ⑩ mix; add: 茶太浓了, 给我~点儿水. Add some water to

the tea, it's too strong for me. ⑪ antithetical couplet; couplet: 喜~ wedding couplet ⑫ 〈量〉 pair; couple: 一~花瓶 a pair of vases/ 一~夫妇 a married couple ⑬ 〈介〉〔引进对象或事物的关系者〕: ~这个问题的不同意见 different views on this question/ ~青少年的教育工作 educational work among young people

【对白】 duìbái dialogue

【对半】 duìbàn half-and-half; fifty-fifty: ~儿分 divide half-and-half; go halves

【对比】 duìbǐ ① contrast; balance: 今昔~ contrast the present with the past/ 构成鲜明的~ form a sharp contrast ② ratio: 双方人数~是一对四. The ratio between the two sides (或 parties) is one to four.

【对不起】 duìbuqǐ ① 〈套〉 I'm sorry; sorry; excuse me; pardon me; I beg your pardon: ~, 给你添麻烦了. Sorry to have given you so much trouble./ ~, 是我的错. Pardon me. It was my fault./ ~, 我得走了. Excuse me, but I'll have to go now./ ~, 请你再讲一遍好吗? I beg your pardon, but would you repeat what you said? 或 I beg your pardon? ② let sb. down; be unworthy of; do a disservice to; be unfair to 又作"对不住"

【对策】 duìcè the way to deal with a situation; countermeasure; countermove

【对称】 duìchèn symmetry

【对答】 duìdá answer; reply: ~如流 answer fluently; answer the questions without any hitch

【对待】 duìdài treat; approach; handle

【对得起】 duìdeqǐ not let sb. down; treat sb. fairly; be worthy of 又作"对得住"

【对调】 duìdiào exchange; swop: ~工作 exchange jobs/ ~座位 exchange (或 swop) seats

【对方】 duìfāng the other (或 opposite) side; the other party

【对付】 duìfu ① deal with; cope with; counter; tackle: 沉着机智地~敌人 deal with the enemy calmly and resourcefully

【对话】 duìhuà dialogue: 两国政府已开始~. The two governments have opened a dialogue.

【对抗】 duìkàng ① antagonism; confrontation: 两国之间的~ confrontation between two states ② resist; oppose ◇ ~赛 〈体〉 dual meet

【对垒】 duìlěi stand facing each other, ready for battle; be pitted against each other: 两军~ two armies pitted against each other

【对立】 duìlì oppose; set sth. against; be antagonistic to: 两条~的路线 two sharply contrasting lines; two diametrically opposed lines

【对联】 duìlián antithetical couplet (written on scrolls, etc.)

【对面】 duìmiàn ① opposite: 他家就在我家~. His house is opposite mine. ② right in front ③ face to face: 这事儿得他们本人~儿谈. They should talk about this face to face. 他俩~坐着. The two of them sat facing each other.

【对内】 duìnèi internal; domestic; at home ◇ ~政策 domestic (或 internal) policy

【对牛弹琴】 duì niú tánqín play the lute to a cow—choose the wrong audience

【对手】 duìshǒu ① opponent; adversary ② match; equal: 他不是你的~ He's no match for you.

【对台戏】 duìtáixì rival show: 唱~ put on a rival show

【对头】 duìtou ① enemy: 死~ sworn enemy ② opponent; adversary

【对外】 duìwài external; foreign ◇ ~工作 external work; work in the field of external relations/ ~关系 external (或 foreign) relations/ ~援助 aid to foreign countries/ ~政策 external (或 foreign) policy

【对外贸易】 duìwài màoyì foreign trade: ~逆差 foreign trade deficit; unfavourable balance of trade/ ~顺差 foreign trade surplus; favourable balance of trade

【对象】 duìxiàng ① target; object: 研究~ an object of study/ 这本书的~是中学生. This book is intended for middle school students./ 讲话或写文章要看~. One should not speak or write without considering one's audience. ② boy or girl friend: 找~ look for a partner in marriage

【对消】 duìxiāo offset; cancel each other out

【对于】 duìyú 〈介〉〔引进对象或事物的关系者〕: ~每个具体

问题要进行具体分析。We should make a concrete analysis of each specific question.

【对照】 duìzhào contrast; compare: 形成鲜明的～ form a sharp contrast/ ～原文修改译文 check the translation against the original and make corrections/ 英汉～读本 an English-Chinese bilingual textbook

【对折】 duìzhé 50% discount

【对证】 duìzhèng verify; check: ～事实 verify the facts

【对症下药】 duì zhèng xià yào suit the medicine to the illness; suit the remedy to the case

【对质】 duìzhì confrontation (in court): 让被告与原告～ confront the accused with his accuser

【对峙】 duìzhì stand facing each other; confront each other: 两山～。The two mountains stand facing each other./ 武装～ military confrontation

【对准】 duìzhǔn ① aim at: 把枪口～敌人 aim a gun at the enemy ② 〈机〉 alignment: 轴～ shaft alignment

兑 duì ① exchange; convert ② add (water, etc.): 这酒是～了水的。The wine has been watered.

【兑付】 duìfù cash (a cheque, etc.)

【兑换】 duìhuàn exchange; convert
◇ ～率 rate of exchange

【兑现】 duìxiàn ① cash (a cheque, etc.) ② honour (a commitment, etc.); fulfil; make good: 他们的声明是不准备～的。They had no intention of carrying out what they had publicly undertaken to do./ 说话不～ not live up to one's promise; fail to make good one's promise

dūn

吨* dūn ton (t.)

敦 dūn honest; sincere: ～请 cordially invite; earnestly request

【敦促】 dūncù urge; press: ～他早日启程 urge him to start on his journey early

【敦厚】 dūnhòu honest and sincere

【敦睦】 dūnmù promote friendly relations

墩 dūn ① mound: 土～ mound ② a block of stone or wood: 树～ stump/ 桥～ pier (of a bridge)

蹲* dūn ① squat on the heels: 两人一下就聊起来了。Squatting down, the two of them started to have a chat. ② stay: 他在实验室里一～就是好几个小时。He would stay for hours at a stretch in the laboratory.

dǔn

盹 dǔn doze: 打～儿 doze off

dùn

沌 dùn 见"混沌" hùndùn

囤 dùn a grain bin
另见 tún

炖 dùn ① stew: ～鸡 stewed chicken/ 清～ boil sth. in its own soup without soy sauce ② warm sth. by putting the container in hot water: ～酒 warm (up) wine

盾* dùn shield

【盾牌】 dùnpái ① shield ② pretext; excuse

钝 dùn ① blunt; dull: 刀～了。The knife is blunt. ② stupid; dull-witted: 迟～ dull-witted; slow

顿* dùn ① pause: 他～了一下，又接着往下说。After a short pause, he went on. ② (in Chinese calligraphy) pause in writing in order to reinforce the beginning or ending of a stroke ③ arrange; settle: 安～ arrange for; help settle down ④ touch the ground (with one's head) ⑤ stamp (one's foot) ⑥ suddenly; immediately: ～悟 suddenly realize the truth, etc.; attain enlightenment ⑦ 〈量〉: 一天三～饭 three meals a day/ 说了他一～ give him a dressing down ⑧ fatigued; tired: 劳～ tired out; exhausted

【顿挫】 dùncuò pause and transition in rhythm or melody: 抑扬～ modulation in tone

【顿号】 dùnhào a slight-pause mark used to set off items in a series (、)

【顿开茅塞】 dùn kāi máo sè suddenly see the light

【顿时】 dùnshí immediately; at once; forthwith: 喜讯传来，人们～欢呼起来。People broke into cheers as soon as they heard the good news.

【顿足捶胸】 dùnzú-chuíxiōng stamp one's foot and beat one's breast

遁 dùn escape; flee; fly

【遁词】 dùncí subterfuge; quibble

duō

多* duō ① many; much; more: 要办的事情很～。There are many things to attend to./ 请你～～帮助。Please give me all the help you can. ② more than the correct or required number; too many: 这个句子～了一个字。There is one word too many in this sentence./ 我在那里～住了几天。I stayed there a few days longer. ③ excessive; too much: ～疑 oversensitive; oversuspicious; given to suspicion ④ more; over; odd: 三个～月 more than three months; three months and more/ 六十～岁 over sixty years old/ 全书一千～页。It's a book of 1,000-odd pages. ⑤ much more; far more: 病人今天好～了。The patient is much better today. ⑥ 〈副〉〔表示程度〕他～大年纪了？How old is he?/ 看她～精神！Look how energetic she is!/ 给我一根绳子，～长都行。Give me a piece of rope; any length will do./ 有～大劲使～大劲。Use all your strength.

【多半】 duōbàn ① the greater part; most: 这支足球队的成员～是工人。Most of the members of this football team are workers. ② probably; most likely: 他这会儿还不来，～不来了。Since he hasn't come yet, he probably isn't coming.

【多边】 duōbiān multilateral: ～会谈 multilateral talks/ ～贸易 multilateral trade/ ～条约 multilateral treaty

【多变】 duōbiàn changeable; changeful; varied: ～的气候 a changeable climate/ ～的战术 varied tactics

【多才多艺】 duōcái-duōyì versatile; gifted in many ways

【多愁善感】 duōchóu-shàngǎn sentimental

【多此一举】 duō cǐ yī jǔ make an unnecessary move: 何必～? Why have the trouble to do that?

【多次】 duōcì many times; time and again; repeatedly; on many occasions: 她曾～访问日本。She's visited Japan many times.

【多多益善】 duōduō yì shàn the more the better

【多方】 duōfāng in many ways; in every way: ～设法 try all possible means; make every effort/ ～协助 render all manner of help

【多方面】 duōfāngmiàn many-sided; in many ways:

【多亏】 duōkuī thanks to; luckily: ～你的帮助 thanks to your help/ ～你给我们带路。We were lucky to have you as our guide.

【多么】 duōme 〈副〉〔表示程度〕how; what: ～新鲜的水果啊！How fresh the fruit is! 或 What fresh fruit!/ 这是～高尚的精神！What a noble spirit this is!/ 不管天～冷，他都坚持户外锻炼。However cold it was, he never stopped taking outdoor exercise.

【多谋善断】 duōmóu-shànduàn resourceful and decisive; sagacious and resolute

【多幕剧】 duōmùjù a play of many acts; a full-length drama

【多少】 duōshǎo ① number; amount: ～不等 vary in amount or number ② somewhat; more or less; to some extent: ～有点失望 feel somewhat disappointed/ 他讲的

有点道理。There's something in what he says.

【多少】 duōshao ① how many; how much: 这一班有～学生？ How many pupils are there in this class?/ 这药我每次吃～？ How much of the medicine do I take each time?/ 这里的粮食产量是～？ What is the yield of grain here? ② 〔表示不定的数量〕：我跟你说过不知一次了。I've told you I don't know how many times./ 我知道一说。I'll tell all I know./ 不论有一困难，都不能阻止我们前进。No matter what the difficulties, nothing can stop our advance.

【多时】 duōshí a long time: 等候～ have waited a long time

【多事】 duōshì ① meddlesome: 怪我～。I shouldn't have poked my nose into this. 或 I shouldn't have interfered. ② eventful: ～之秋 an eventful period or year; troubled times

【多数】 duōshù majority; most: 绝大～ an overwhelming majority/ 微弱的～ a small majority/ 必要的～ the requisite majority/ 三分之二的～ a two-thirds majority/ 我们是～。We are in the majority./ 少数服从～。The minority is subordinate to the majority.
◇ ～表决 decision by majority/ ～票 majority vote

【多谢】 duōxiè 〈套〉 many thanks; thanks a lot

【多心】 duōxīn oversensitive; suspicious

【多样化】 duōyànghuà diversify; make varied: 使农作物～ diversify the crops/ ～的艺术风格 a variety of artistic styles

【多余】 duōyú unnecessary; surplus; superfluous; uncalled-for: 删掉～的词语 cut out superfluous words and phrases/ 事实证明我们的担心是～的。Facts proved that our worries were uncalled-for.

【多嘴】 duōzuǐ speak out of turn; shoot off one's mouth: ～多舌 gossipy and meddlesome; long-tongued/ 要不是他～，事情也不至于搞僵。If he hadn't shot his mouth off, things wouldn't have been so awkward./ 你不了解情况，别～! You don't know the facts, so keep your mouth shut!

咄 duō

【咄咄逼人】 duōduō bī rén overbearing; aggressive
【咄咄怪事】 duōduō guàishì monstrous absurdity

哆 duō

【哆嗦】 duōsuo tremble; shiver: 气得直～ tremble with rage/ 冷得打～ shiver with cold

duó

夺* duó ① take by force; seize; wrest: 从暴徒手上～下刀子 wrest a knife from a hooligan/ ～印 seize the seal — seize power ② force one's way: ～门而出 force open the door and rush out; force one's way out/ 眼泪～眶而出。Tears started from one's eyes. ③ contend for; compete for; strive for: ～得冠军 carry off the first prize ④ deprive: 剥～ deprive ⑤ 〈书〉 decide: 定～ make a final decision ⑥ 〈书〉 omission (in a text): 讹～ errors and omissions

【夺回】 duóhuí recapture; retake; seize back: ～阵地 recapture a position/ ～一局 win a game (after losing one or more); pull up by a game/ ～失去的时间 make up for lost time

【夺目】 duómù dazzle the eyes: 光彩～ with dazzling brightness; brilliant; resplendent

【夺取】 duóqǔ ① capture; seize; wrest: ～敌人的据点 capture an enemy stronghold/ ～主动权 seize the initiative ② strive for

【夺权】 duóquán seize power; take over power

度* duó 〈书〉 surmise; estimate
另见 dù

【度德量力】 duódé-liànglì estimate one's own moral and material strength; make an appraisal of one's own position

踱 duó pace; stroll: ～来～去 pace to and fro; pace up and down/ ～方步 walk with measured tread

duǒ

朵* duǒ 〈量〉: 一～花 a flower/ 一～云 a cloud
【朵儿】 duǒr flower

垛 duǒ ① buttress ② battlements

躲* duǒ ① hide (oneself): ～进深山老林 hide in a mountain forest ② avoid; dodge: 你怎么老～着他？ Why do you keep avoiding him?/ 车来了，快～开! Look out! A truck's coming! Get out of the way./ ～雨 take shelter from the rain

【躲避】 duǒbì ① hide (oneself) ② avoid; elude; dodge
【躲藏】 duǒcáng hide (或 conceal) oneself; go into hiding
【躲懒】 duǒlǎn shy away from work; shirk
【躲闪】 duǒshǎn dodge; evade: 小王～不及，和我撞了个满怀。It was too late for Xiao Wang to dodge and I bumped into him./ 躲躲闪闪 be evasive; hedge; equivocate
【躲债】 duǒzhài avoid a creditor

duò

剁 duò chop; cut: 把柳条～成三段 chop a willow branch into three pieces/ ～肉馅 chop up (或 mince) meat

舵 duò rudder; helm

【舵轮】 duòlún steering wheel
【舵手】 duòshǒu steersman; helmsman

堕 duò fall; sink: ～地 fall on the ground

【堕落】 duòluò degenerate; sink low: 走上～、犯罪的道路 embark on the road of degeneration and crime/

【堕入】 duòrù sink (或 lapse) into; land oneself in: ～陷阱 fall into a trap

【堕胎】 duòtāi ① induced abortion ② have an (induced) abortion

惰* duò lazy; indolent: 懒～ lazy

【惰性】 duòxìng inertia

跺 duò stamp (one's foot): 气得直～脚 stamp one's foot with fury

E

ē

阿 ē play up to; pander to: ~其所好 pander to sb.'s whims
另见 ā
【阿弥陀佛】 Ēmítuófó 〈佛教〉① Amitabha; Amitāyus ② may Buddha preserve us; merciful Buddha
【阿谀】 ēyú fawn on; flatter

婀 ē
【婀娜】 ēnuó (of a woman's bearing) graceful

é

讹 é ① erroneous; mistaken: ~字 wrong words (in a text)/ 以~传~ spread an error or a falsehood ② extort; blackmail; bluff: ~人 blackmail sb.; bluff sb.
【讹传】 échuán false (或 unfounded) rumour
【讹误】 éwù error (in a text)
【讹诈】 ézhà extort under false pretences; blackmail: ~钱财 extort money under false pretences

俄 é very soon; presently; suddenly: ~而日出。Presently the sun emerged.

峨 é 〈书〉 high: 巍~ towering; lofty

娥 é pretty young woman: 宫~ palace maid; maid of honour
【娥眉】 éméi ① delicate eyebrows ② beautiful woman

鹅* é goose
【鹅黄】 éhuáng light yellow
【鹅卵石】 éluǎnshí cobblestone; cobble
【鹅毛】 émáo goose feather: 下了一场~大雪。Snow fell in big flakes.
【鹅绒】 éróng goose down

蛾 é moth
【蛾眉】 éméi 见"娥眉" éméi

额* é ① forehead ② a horizontal tablet ③ a specified number or amount: 贸易~ volume of trade/ 超~ above quota
【额定】 édìng specified (number or amount); rated: ~的人数 the maximum number of persons allowed; the stipulated number of personnel
【额手称庆】 éshǒu chēng qìng put one's hand on one's forehead in jubilation; be overjoyed
【额外】 éwài extra; additional; added: ~开支 extra expenses/ ~收入 additional income/ ~负担 added burden

ě

恶 ě
另见 è; wù
【恶心】 ěxin ① feel like vomiting; feel nauseated; feel sick ② nauseating; disgusting

è

厄 è 〈书〉 ① strategic point: 险~ a strategic pass ②

adversity; disaster; hardship: 遭~ meet with disaster ③ be in distress; be stranded: 渔船~于风暴。The fishing boat was caught in a storm.
【厄运】 èyùn adversity; misfortune

扼 è 〈书〉 ① clutch; grip: ~住他的咽喉 clutch at his throat ② guard; control
【扼杀】 èshā strangle; smother; throttle: ~在摇篮里 strangle in the cradle/ 在萌芽状态中~ nip in the bud
【扼守】 èshǒu hold (a strategic point); guard
【扼死】 èsǐ strangle; throttle
【扼要】 èyào to the point: 简明~ brief and to the point/ 请~说明。Please explain the main points briefly.

呃 è
【呃逆】 ènì 〈医〉 hiccup

轭 è yoke

垩 è chalk

恶* è ① evil; vice; wickedness: 无~不作 stop at nothing in doing evil/ 罪大~极 guilty of the most heinous crimes ② fierce; ferocious: 一场~战 a fierce battle/ ~骂 vicious abuse/ ~狗 a ferocious (或 vicious) dog; cur ③ bad; evil; wicked: ~行 evil (或 wicked) conduct/ ~势力 evil force
另见 ě; wù
【恶霸】 èbà local tyrant (或 despot)
【恶报】 èbào retribution for evildoing; judgment
【恶臭】 èchòu foul smell; stench
【恶毒】 èdú vicious; malicious; venomous: ~的诬蔑 venomous slander/ ~攻击 viciously attack
【恶贯满盈】 è guàn mǎnyíng have committed countless crimes and deserve to come to judgment; face retribution for a life of crime
【恶棍】 ègùn ruffian; scoundrel; bully
【恶果】 èguǒ evil consequence; disastrous effect
【恶狠狠】 èhěnhěn fierce; ferocious: ~地瞪了他一眼 give him a ferocious stare
【恶化】 èhuà worsen; deteriorate; take a turn for the worse: 他的病情~了。His condition has worsened./ 两国关系不断~。The relations between the two countries have steadily deteriorated.
【恶劣】 èliè odious; abominable; disgusting: ~作风 abominable (或 dirty) behaviour/ ~行径 disgusting conduct/ ~手段 mean (或 dirty) tricks/ ~环境 adverse circumstances/ ~气候 harsh climate; vile weather/ 品质~ unprincipled; base/ 影响~ make a very bad impression/ 作案的情节十分~。The way in which the crime was committed was absolutely vile.
【恶魔】 èmó demon; devil; evil spirit
【恶人】 èrén evil person; vile creature; villain: ~先告状。The villain sues his victim before he himself is prosecuted. 或 The guilty party files the suit.
【恶习】 èxí bad (或 pernicious) habit: 染上~ contract a bad habit; fall into evil ways
【恶性】 èxìng malignant; pernicious; vicious: ~贫血 pernicious anaemia/ ~通货膨胀 galloping (或 runaway) inflation/ ~循环 vicious circle/ ~肿瘤 malignant tumour
【恶意】 èyì evil (或 ill) intentions; ill will; malice: ~攻击 malicious attack/ 并无~ bear no ill will
【恶作剧】 èzuòjù practical joke; prank; mischief

饿* è ① hungry: 挨~ go hungry ② starve: 别~着小猪。Don't starve the piglets.
【饿虎扑食】 èhǔ pū shí like a hungry tiger pouncing on its prey

愕 è stunned; astounded
【愕然】 èrán stunned; astounded: ~四顾 look around in astonishment/ 消息传来，大家为之~。Everyone was stunned by the news.

遏 è check; hold back: 怒不可~ be in a towering rage; be overcome with indignation; boil with anger
【遏止】 èzhǐ check; hold back
【遏制】 èzhì keep within limits; contain: ~愤怒的情绪 check one's anger

鹗 è osprey; fish hawk; sea eagle

颚 è ①jaw: 上(下)~ upper (lower) jaw ②palate
【颚骨】 ègǔ jawbone

噩 è shocking; upsetting
【噩耗】 èhào sad news of the death of one's beloved: ~传来，犹如晴天霹雳。The grievous news came like a bolt from the blue.
【噩梦】 èmèng frightening (或 horrible) dream; nightmare

鳄* è crocodile; alligator
【鳄鱼】 èyú crocodile; alligator: ~的眼泪 crocodile tears

欸 ē 〈叹〉〔表示招呼〕: ~，你快来! Hey! Come over here.
另见 é; ě; è

欸 é 或 éi 〈叹〉〔表示诧异〕: ~，他怎么走了! Why, he's gone!
另见 ē; ě; è

欸 ě 或 ěi 〈叹〉〔表示不以为然〕: ~，你这话可不对呀! Now, you can't say that.
另见 ē; é; è

欸 è 或 èi 〈叹〉〔表示答应或同意〕: ~，我这就来! Yes, I'll come in a minute. 或 Coming./ ~，就这么办! All right. That's settled.
另见 ē; é; ě

ēn

恩* ēn kindness; favour; grace: 施~ bestow favours/ 报~ requite a kindness; pay a debt of gratitude
【恩爱】 ēn'ài conjugal love ◇ ~夫妻 an affectionate couple
【恩赐】 ēncì ①bestow (favours, charity, etc.) ②favour; charity
【恩德】 ēndé favour; kindness; grace
【恩典】 ēndiǎn favour; grace
【恩惠】 ēnhuì favour; kindness; grace; bounty
【恩将仇报】 ēn jiāng chóu bào requite kindness with enmity
【恩情】 ēnqíng loving-kindness
【恩人】 ēnrén benefactor
【恩怨】 ēn-yuàn ①feeling of gratitude or resentment ②resentment; grievance; old scores: 不计较个人~ not allow oneself to be swayed by personal feelings
【恩泽】 ēnzé 〈旧〉 bounties bestowed by a monarch or an official

ér

儿* ér ①child: 小~ little child ②youngster; youth: 英雄~女 young heroes and heroines ③son: 他有一~一女。He has a son and a daughter. ④male: ~马〈口〉stallion ⑤〔后缀〕: 小猫~ kitten
【儿歌】 érgē children's song; nursery rhymes
【儿科】 érkē (department of) paediatrics ◇ ~医生 paediatrician
【儿女】 ér-nǚ ①sons and daughters; children: 都已长大成人。The children have all grown up. ②young man and woman (in love): ~情长 be immersed in love
【儿孙】 ér-sūn children and grandchildren; descendants; posterity
【儿童】 értóng children
【儿媳妇儿】 érxífur daughter-in-law
【儿戏】 érxì trifling matter: 这样重要的工作可不能当~。You shouldn't regard such important work as a trifling matter.
【儿子】 érzi son

而* ér 〈连〉 ①〔连接语意相承的成分〕: 伟大~艰巨的任务 a great and arduous task/ 战~胜之 fight and defeat the enemy ②〔连接肯定和否定互相补充的成分〕: 华~不实 flashy without substance/ 有其名~无其实 in name but not in reality/ 他们的错误在于只看到事情的支流，~没有看到事情的主流。Their mistake is that they see only the nonessentials but not the essence of the matter. ③〔连接语意相反的成分，表示转折〕: 大~无当 large but impractical; unwieldy ④〔连接事理上前后相因的成分〕: 疗效因人~异。The effect of the treatment varies with different individuals. ⑤〔表示"到"的意思〕: 由南~北 from south to north/ 自远~近 approach from a distance/ 一~再，再~三 again and again; time and again ⑥〔把表示时间或方式的成分连接到动词上面〕: 匆匆~来 come hastening/ 盘旋~上 spiral up
【而后】 érhòu after that; then: 先小组酝酿~由大会讨论。First exchange ideas in small groups and then hold a general discussion.
【而今】 érjīn now; at the present time
【而且】 érqiě 〈连〉 ①〔表示平列〕: 这屋子很宽敞，~光线充足。The room is spacious and bright. ②〔表示进一层〕: 农民不但战胜了灾害，~获得了丰收。The farmers not only overcame the effects of the natural adversity but won a bumper harvest.
【而已】 éryǐ 〈助〉 that is all; nothing more: 如此~，岂有他哉! That's all there is to it!

ěr

尔 ěr 〈书〉 ①you ②like that; so: 果~ if so/ 不过~~ just middling ③that: ~日 that day/ ~时 at that time ④〔形容词后缀〕: 率~而对 give a hasty reply; reply without thinking

耳* ěr ①ear: 外(中、内)~ the outer (middle, inner) ear ②any ear-like thing; ear of a utensil: 银~ tremella/ 鼎~ ears of a tripod ③on both sides; flanking; side: ~房 side rooms/ ~门 side doors ④〈书〉〈助〉 only; just: 距此不过五里~。It's only five li from here.
【耳背】 ěrbèi hard of hearing
【耳边风】 ěrbiānfēng a puff of wind passing the ear — unheeded advice: 当作~ let sth. in at one ear and out the other; turn a deaf ear to sth.
【耳聪目明】 ěrcōng-mùmíng ①(of old people) have good ears and eyes; can hear and see well ②have a thorough grasp of the situation
【耳朵】 ěrduo ear: ~尖 have sharp ears/ ~软 credulous; easily influenced; susceptible to flattery

【耳光】 ěrguāng a slap on the face; a box on the ear: 打～ slap sb.'s face; box sb.'s ear

【耳环】 ěrhuán earrings

【耳机】 ěrjī earphone

【耳孔】 ěrkǒng earhole

【耳目】 ěrmù ① what one sees and hears; knowledge; information: ～所及 from what one sees and hears; from what one knows/ ～闭塞 ill-informed ② one who spies for sb. else: ～众多 eyes and ears everywhere; too many people around

【耳目一新】 ěr-mù yī xīn find everything fresh and new:

【耳濡目染】 ěrrú-mùrǎn be imperceptibly influenced by what one constantly sees and hears

【耳屎】 ěrshǐ 〈口〉earwax

【耳熟】 ěrshú familiar to the ear

【耳提面命】 ěrtí-miànmìng pour (或 din) exhortations into sb.'s ear; give earnest exhortations

【耳闻】 ěrwén hear of (或 about): 这事曾经～，详细情况不很清楚。I've heard about it, but I don't know the details./ ～不如目见。Seeing for oneself is better than hearing from others.

【耳闻目睹】 ěrwén-mùdǔ what one sees and hears

【耳语】 ěryǔ whisper in sb.'s ear; whisper

迩 ěr 〈书〉near: 名闻遐～ be known far and near

饵 ěr ① cakes; pastry: 果～ candies and cakes; confectionery ② bait ③〈书〉entice: ～以重利 use great wealth as a bait; entice sb. with prospects of great wealth

一* èr ① two: ～两茶叶 two *liang* of tea/ ～～得四。Twice two is four. ～层楼〈英〉first floor; 〈美〉second floor/ 一百～ a hundred and twenty/ 三千～ three thousand two hundred/ ～者必居其一 either one or the other ② different: ～心 disloyalty; half-heartedness

【二重唱】 èrchóngchàng 〈乐〉(vocal) duet

【二重性】 èrchóngxìng dual character (或 nature); duality

【二重奏】 èrchóngzòu 〈乐〉(instrumental) duet

【二等】 èrděng second-class; second-rate
◇ ～舱 second-class cabin/ ～功 Merit Citation Class II; second-class merit/ ～奖 second prize/ ～秘书〈外〉Second Secretary

【二房东】 èrfángdōng sublessor (of a room or house); sub-landlord

【二十四史】 èrshí sì shǐ ① the Twenty-Four Histories (dynastic histories from remote antiquity till the Ming Dynasty) ② a long intricate story: 一部～，不知从何说起。It's such a long and complicated story, I hardly know where to start.

【二心】 èrxīn disloyalty; halfheartedness

【二月】 èryuè ① February ② the second month of the lunar year; the second moon

贰 èr two (used for the numeral 二 on cheques, banknotes, etc. to avoid mistakes or alterations)

【贰臣】 èrchén an official who retains his position after capitulating to the new dynasty; turncoat official

【贰心】 èrxīn 见"二心" èrxīn

F

fā

发* fā ① send out; issue; deliver; distribute: ～电报 send a telegram/ ～货 deliver goods/ ～传单 distribute leaflets/ ～信号 give a signal/ ～工资 pay out wages ② utter; express: 有五个会员在会上～了言。 Five members spoke at the meeting. ③ discharge; shoot; emit: 万箭齐～。 Ten thousand arrows shot at once./ ～光～热 emit light and heat ④ develop; expand: ～育 growth; development ⑤ (of foodstuffs) rise or expand when fermented or soaked: 面～起来了。 The dough has risen./ ～豆芽 raise bean sprouts; sprout beans ⑥ come or bring into existence: ～电 generate electricity/ 旧病复～ have an attack of a recurrent sickness; have a recurrence of an old illness; have a relapse ⑦ open up; discover; expose: ～现 find; discover/ 揭～ expose ⑧ get into a certain state; become: 树叶开始～黄。 The leaves are beginning to turn yellow./ 脸色～白 lose colour; become pale/ 肉～臭了。 The meat smells a bit off. 或 The meat smells bad. ⑨ show one's feeling: ～怒 get angry/ ～笑 laugh ⑩ feel; have a feeling: 有点～冷 feel a bit chilly/ 嘴里～苦 have a bitter taste in the mouth/ ～麻 tingle/ ～痒 itch ⑪ start; set out; begin an undertaking: 车船齐～。 All the boats and carts started off at the same time./ 朝～夕至 set off in the morning and arrive in the evening ⑫ 〈量〉: 一～炮弹 one shell/ 两百～子弹 two hundred rounds of ammunition; two hundred cartridges
另见 fà

【发榜】 fābǎng publish a list of successful candidates or applicants

【发报】 fābào transmit messages by radio, telegraphy, etc. ◇ ～机 transmitter

【发表】 fābiǎo publish; issue: ～文章 publish an article/ ～声明 issue (或 make) a statement/ ～意见 express an opinion; state one's views/ ～演说 make (或 deliver) a speech/ ～社论 carry an editorial

【发布】 fābù issue; release: ～命令 issue orders/ ～新闻 release news

【发财】 fācái get rich; make a fortune; make a pile

【发愁】 fāchóu worry; be anxious: 不要为这事～。 Don't worry about it.

【发出】 fāchū issue; send out; give out: ～指示 issue a directive/ ～警告 send out a warning/ ～阵阵清香 send forth wafts of delicate fragrance/ ～警报 sound the alarm

【发达】 fādá developed; flourishing: 肌肉～ have well-developed muscles/ 工商业很～。 Industry and commerce are flourishing. ◇ ～国家 developed country

【发呆】 fādāi stare blankly; be in a daze; be in a trance: 他话也不说，坐在那里～。 He said nothing but sat there staring blankly. 或 He said nothing but sat there as if in a trance.

【发电】 fādiàn generate electricity (或 electric power) ◇ ～量 generated energy; electric energy production/ ～站 power station

【发电厂】 fādiànchǎng power plant; power station: 水力(火力)～ hydraulic (thermal) power plant/ 地热～ geothermal power plant/ 原子能～ atomic power plant ◇ ～容量 station capacity

【发电机】 fādiànjī generator; dynamo

【发动】 fādòng ① start; launch: ～机器 start a machine; set a machine going/ ～战争 launch (或 unleash) a war ② call into action; mobilize; arouse: ～群众 arouse the masses to action; mobilize the masses ◇ ～机 engine; motor

【发抖】 fādǒu shiver; shake; tremble: 冷得～ shiver (或 shake) with cold/ 吓得～ tremble with fear; shake in one's shoes

【发奋】 fāfèn ① work energetically ② 见"发愤"

【发愤】 fāfèn make a firm resolution; make a determined effort: ～工作 put all one's energies into one's work/ ～图强 work with a will to make the country strong/ ～忘食 be so immersed in work as to forget one's meals

【发疯】 fāfēng go mad; go crazy; become insane; be out of one's mind: 发酒疯 be roaring drunk

【发福】 fāfú grow stout; put on weight

【发稿】 fāgǎo ① distribute news dispatches ② send manuscripts to the press

【发给】 fāgěi issue; distribute; grant: ～护照 issue a passport

【发光】 fāguāng ① give out light; shine; be luminous: 群星闪闪～。 The stars twinkled./ 有一分热，发一分光 give as much light as the heat can produce -- do one's best, however little it may be

【发号施令】 fāhào-shīlìng issue orders; order people about

【发狠】 fāhěn ① make a determined effort: 他们一～，三天的任务一天就完成了。 With a determined effort, they finished the three-day task in a single day. ② be angry

【发还】 fāhuán return sth. (usu. to one's subordinate); give (或 send) back: 把作业～给学生 return the homework to the pupils/ 把计划～原单位去讨论修改 send the plan back where it came from for discussion and revision

【发慌】 fāhuāng feel nervous; get flustered; get flurried: 她虽是第一次当众讲话，却一点都不～。 She didn't feel a bit nervous though it was the first time she'd spoken in public.

【发挥】 fāhuī ① bring into play; give play to; give free rein to: ～专长 give full play to sb.'s professional knowledge or skill/ ～想象力 give the rein to one's imagination ② develop (an idea, a theme, etc.); elaborate: 这一论点有待进一步～。 This point needs further elaboration.

【发昏】 fāhūn ① feel giddy (或 dizzy): 我的头有点儿～。 I feel a bit giddy. ② lose one's head; become confused: 你～啦! Are you out of your mind?

【发火】 fāhuǒ ① catch fire; ignite ② detonate; go off: 他打了一枪，没有～。 He pulled the trigger but the gun didn't go off. ③ get angry; flare up; lose one's temper

【发迹】 fājī (of a poor man) gain fame and fortune; rise to power and position

【发觉】 fājué find; detect; discover: 错误一经～，就应改正。 Mistakes should be corrected as soon as they are discovered.

【发掘】 fājué excavate; unearth; explore: ～古墓 excavate an ancient tomb/ ～文物 unearth cultural relics/ ～人才 seek gifted (或 talented) people

【发刊词】 fākāncí foreword (或 introduction) to a periodical

【发狂】 fākuáng go mad; go crazy

【发冷】 fālěng feel cold (或 chilly)

【发愣】 fālèng 〈口〉 stare blankly; be in a daze; be in a trance

【发亮】 fāliàng shine: 把机器擦得～ polish the machine till it shines

【发落】 fāluò deal with (an offender): 从轻～ deal with sb. leniently

【发霉】 fāméi go mouldy; become mildewed

【发明】 fāmíng ① invent: 印刷术是中国首先～的。 Printing was first invented by the Chinese. ② invention: 最新～ the latest invention ③ 〈书〉 expound ◇ ～权 inventor's patent right

【发难】 fānàn rise in revolt; launch an attack

【发胖】 fāpàng put on (或 gain) weight; get fat

【发脾气】 fā píqi lose one's temper; get angry: 有理慢慢儿说，何必～。 Speak calmly if you think you're in the right; there's no need to get angry.

【发票】 fāpiào bill; receipt: 开～ make out a bill; write a receipt

【发起】 fāqǐ ① initiate; sponsor: 这次会议是由十四个国家～的。The meeting was sponsored by 14 countries. ② start; launch: ～反攻 launch a counterattack ◇ ～国 sponsor nation/ ～人 initiator; sponsor

【发球】 fāqiú serve a ball: 该谁～? Whose service is it?/ 换～! Change service!/ 他～发得好。He has a very good serve.

【发热】 fārè ① give out heat; generate heat ② have (或 run) a fever: 我好象有点儿～. I feel as if I'm running a fever. ③ be hotheaded

【发人深省】 fā rén shēn xǐng set people thinking; call for deep thought; provide food for thought

【发轫】 fārèn 〈书〉 set sth. afoot; commence an undertaking

【发散】 fāsàn ① (of rays, etc.) diverge

【发烧】 fāshāo have (或 run) a fever; have (或 run) a temperature

【发射】 fāshè ① launch; project; discharge; shoot; fire:～导弹 launch (或 project) a guided missile/ ～人造卫星 launch a man-made satellite/ ～炮弹 fire shells ② 〈物〉 transmit; emit

【发生】 fāshēng happen; occur; take place: ～了意外。Something unexpected happened / 那里～了强烈地震。A violent earthquake occurred there./ ～了巨大的变化。Tremendous changes have taken place./ ～新的困难。New difficulties cropped up (或 arose)./ 机器～故障。The machine broke down./ 故事～在一九六二年秋天。The story is set in the autumn of 1962.

【发誓】 fāshì vow; pledge; swear

【发售】 fāshòu sell; put on sale: 这些杂志在全国各地书店均有～。These magazines are sold at bookstores throughout the country./ 新的纪念邮票将于下星期～。The new commemorative stamps will be put on sale next week.

【发抒】 fāshū express; voice: ～己见 express one's personal views

【发送】 fāsòng ① transmit by radio: ～密码电报 trànsmit a coded message ② dispatch (letters, etc.)

【发酸】 fāsuān ① turn sour: 牛奶～了。The milk has turned sour. ② ache slightly: 腰有点～ have a slight backache

【发问】 fāwèn ask (或 put, pose, raise) a question

【发现】 fāxiàn find; discover: ～一些线索 find some clues/ ～问题，解决问题 discover problems and solve them/～敌炮艇一艘 spot an enemy gunboat 我没有～什么情况。I didn't notice anything.

【发祥地】 fāxiángdì place of origin; birthplace: 中国古代文化的～ the birthplace of China's ancient culture

【发笑】 fāxiào laugh: 令人～ make one laugh; provoke laughter; be ridiculous

【发泄】 fāxiè give vent to; let off: ～个人情绪 give vent to one's personal feelings/ ～不满 air (或 express) one's grievances

【发信】 fāxìn post a letter ◇ ～人 addresser

【发行】 fāxíng (of currency, bonds, books, etc.) issue; publish; distribute; put on sale: ～纸币 issue paper money/ ～书刊 publish books and magazines/ ～影片 release a film/ 由新华书店～ distributed by Xinhua Bookstore/ 将在全国各地～ will be put on sale throughout the country ◇ ～银行 bank of issue/ ～者 publisher

【发芽】 fāyá germinate; sprout: 种子还没有～。The seeds haven't sprouted (或 come up) yet.

【发言】 fāyán speak; make a statement or speech; take the floor: 他在会上～了吗? Did he speak at the meeting?/ 要求～ ask to be heard; ask for the floor/ 他的～很精彩。He made a brilliant speech. ◇ ～稿 the text of a statement or speech

【发言权】 fāyánquán right to speak: 我们对这事当然有～。Of course we have a say in this matter./ 他们对这个问题最有～。They are best qualified to speak on this question.

【发言人】 fāyánrén spokesman: 政府～ government spokesman

【发炎】 fāyán 〈医〉 inflammation: 伤口～了。The wound has become inflamed.

【发扬】 fāyáng develop; carry on (或 forward): ～民主作风 develop a democratic style of work

【发扬光大】 fāyáng guāngdà carry forward; develop; enhance

【发音】 fāyīn pronunciation; enunciation; articulation: 这个字怎么～? How do you pronounce this word?/ 这字母不～。This letter is silent (或 not pronounced)./ 她～清晰。She enunciates her words clearly./ 他～不清楚。His articulation is poor.

【发育】 fāyù growth; development: ～健全 physically well developed/ 婴儿～情况良好。The baby is coming on well.

【发源】 fāyuán rise; originate: 长江～于青海。The Changjiang River rises in Qinghai Province. ◇ ～地 place of origin; source; birthplace

【发晕】 fāyùn feel dizzy (或 giddy)

【发展】 fāzhǎn develop; expand; grow: ～经济，保障供给。Develop the economy and ensure supplies

【发展中国家】 fāzhǎnzhōng guójiā developing country

【发胀】 fāzhàng swell: 肚子～ feel bloated/ 头脑～ have a swelled head

【发作】 fāzuò ① break out; show effect: 她的心脏病又～了。She's had another heart attack. 酒性开始～。The liquor began to show its effect. ② have a fit of anger; flare up: 他有些生气,但当着大家的面不好～。He was angry, but with everybody present, he kept his temper under control.

fá

乏* fá ① lack: 不～其人。There's no lack of such people./ 回天～术 unable to save the situation ② tired; weary: 走～了 be tired from a long walk

【乏味】 fáwèi dull; insipid; drab; tasteless: 语言～ dull (或 drab) language

伐 fá ① fell; cut down: ～了几棵树 cut down a few trees ② send an expedition against; strike; attack: 讨～ send a punitive expedition

【伐木】 fámù lumbering; felling; cutting ◇ ～工 lumberman/ ～业 lumbering

【伐区】 fáqū 〈林〉 cutting (或 felling) area

罚* fá punish; penalize: ～不当罪 be unduly punished/ 赏～分明 be fair in meting out rewards or punishments

【罚出场】 fá chūchǎng 〈体〉 be ordered off the field for foul play; foul out

【罚金】 fájīn fine; forfeit: 处以～ impose a fine on sb.; fine sb.

【罚酒】 fájiǔ be made to drink as a forfeit

【罚款】 fákuǎn ① impose a fine or forfeit ② fine; forfeit; penalty ◇ ～条款 penalty clause

【罚球】 fáqiú (篮球) penalty shot; (足球) penalty kick

阀 fá a powerful person or family: 军～ warlord/ 财～ financial magnate; plutocrat

筏 fá raft: 橡皮～ rubber raft

【筏道】 fádào log chute; logway

【筏子】 fázi raft

fǎ

法* fǎ ① law: 守～ observe the law; be law-abiding/ 违～ break the law ② method; way; mode: 教～ teaching method/ 表达～ mode of expression ③ follow; model after: 效～ take as model; follow ④ standard; model: ～书 model calligraphy ⑤ Legalists; the Legalist School ⑥ Buddhist doctrine; the dharma ⑦ magic arts: 戏～ conjuring tricks

【法案】 fǎ'àn proposed law; bill

【法办】 fǎbàn deal with according to law; punish by law; bring to justice

【法宝】 fǎbǎo a magic weapon: 战胜敌人的～ magic weapon for defeating the enemy

【法典】 fǎdiǎn code; statute book

【法定】 fǎdìng legal; statutory

【法定人数】 fǎdìng rénshù quorum: 已足～。We have a quorum now.

【法官】 fǎguān judge; justice

【法规】 fǎguī laws and regulations

【法力】 fǎlì supernatural power

【法令】 fǎlìng laws and decrees; decree: 政府～ government decree

【法律】 fǎlǜ law; statute
◇ ～保护 legal protection/ ～承认 de jure recognition/ ～地位 legal status/ ～根据 legal basis/ ～顾问 legal adviser

【法术】 fǎshù magic arts

【法庭】 fǎtíng court; tribunal: 军事～ military tribunal; court-martial

【法统】 fǎtǒng legally constituted authority

【法网】 fǎwǎng the net of justice; the arm of the law

【法院】 fǎyuàn court of justice; law court; court

【法则】 fǎzé rule; law: 自然～ law of nature

【法治】 fǎzhì rule by law

【法制】 fǎzhì legal system; legal institutions; legality

【法子】 fǎzi way; method: 我们得想个～解决这个问题。We'll have to think of a way to solve the problem. 或 We must find a way out.

砝 fǎ

【砝码】 fǎmǎ weight (used on a balance)

fà

发* fà hair: 理～ haircut
另见 fā

【发型】 fàxíng hair style; hairdo; coiffure

【发油】 fàyóu hair oil

fān

帆* fān sail: ～樯林立 a forest of masts

【帆布】 fānbù canvas
◇ ～包 canvas bag; kit bag/ ～床 cot; campbed/ ～篷 canvas roof; awning

【帆船】 fānchuán sailing boat (或 ship); junk

番 fān 〈量〉〔表示"种""回""次"〕: 别有一～天地 like stepping into a fairyland; an altogether different world/ 三～五次 time and again/ 费了一～功夫 put in a lot of effort

【番茄】 fānqié tomato ◇ ～酱 tomato ketchup/ ～汁 tomato juice

【番薯】 fānshǔ 〈方〉 sweet potato

藩 fān

【藩篱】 fānlí hedge; fence

【藩属】 fānshǔ vassal state

翻* fān ① turn over (或 up): ～谷子 turn over the grain (to dry)/ 船～了。The ship capsized. 或 The ship turned turtle./ 车～了。The cart turned over./ 把饼一个儿再烙一会儿，Turn the cake over and bake it some more./ 碰～ knock over ② cross; get over: ～过山头 cross a mountaintop/ ～墙 climb over a wall ③ rummage; search: 抽屉我都～了一遍了，还是找不到。I rummaged all the drawers, but still couldn't find it./ ～参考书 look through reference works ④ translate: ～把英文～成中文 translate the English into Chinese/ ～电报 decode a telegram ⑤ reverse: ～案 reverse a verdict ⑥ 〈口〉 fall out; break up: 他们闹～了。They quarrelled and split up. 或 They fell out.

【翻案】 fān'àn reverse a (correct) verdict

【翻白眼】 fān báiyǎn show the whites of one's eyes (as from emotion or illness)

【翻版】 fānbǎn reprint; reproduction; refurbished version

【翻覆】 fānfù overturn; turn upside down

【翻滚】 fāngǔn roll; toss; tumble: 白浪～。The waves rolled and foamed.

【翻江倒海】 fānjiāng-dǎohǎi overturning rivers and seas — overwhelming; stupendous; terrific: 以～之势 with the momentum of an avalanche

【翻来复去】 fānlái-fùqù ① toss and turn; toss from side to side: 他在床上～睡不着。He tossed and turned in bed, unable to sleep. ② again and again; repeatedly: 这种话，她～不知说过多少遍了。This is what she has been saying over and over again — I don't know how many times.

【翻脸】 fānliǎn fall out; suddenly turn hostile: ～不认人 turn against a friend/ ～无情 turn against a friend and show him no mercy; be treacherous and ruthless

【翻山越岭】 fānshān-yuèlǐng cross over mountain after mountain; tramp over hill and dale

【翻身】 fānshēn ① turn over: 他翻了个身又睡着了。He turned over in bed and fell asleep again./ 一～从床上爬起来 roll off the bed ② free oneself; stand up

【翻腾】 fānteng ① seethe; rise; churn: 波浪～ seething (或 turbulent) waves ② turn sth. over and over: 几个箱子都～遍了也没有找到。I rummaged through all the boxes but still could not find it.

【翻天覆地】 fāntiān-fùdì earth-shaking; world-shaking: ～的变化 an earth-shaking change/ ～的时代 an earth-shaking era

【翻箱倒柜】 fānxiāng-dǎoguì rummage through chests and cupboards; ransack boxes and chests

【翻新】 fānxīn renovate; recondition; make over: 旧大衣可以～。Old overcoats can be reconditioned./ ～车胎 retread a tyre/ 花样～ (the same old thing) in a new guise

【翻译】 fānyì ① translate; interpret: 请你替我～一下好吗？ Would you mind translating (或 interpreting) for me?/ ～电码 decode; decipher ② translator; interpreter ◇ ～本 translation/ ～片 dubbed film

【翻印】 fānyìn reprint; reproduce

【翻阅】 fānyuè browse; look over; glance over; leaf through: ～报章杂志 look over newspapers and magazines/ ～目录 glance through a catalogue

【翻云覆雨】 fānyún-fùyǔ produce clouds with one turn of the hand and rain with another — given to playing tricks; shifty

fán

凡* fán ① commonplace; ordinary: 非～ extraordinary ② this mortal world; the earth: 天仙下～ a celestial beauty come down to earth ③ every; any; all

【凡例】 fánlì notes on the use of a book, etc.; guide to the use of a book, etc.

【凡人】 fánrén ① ordinary person ② mortal

【凡事】 fánshì everything: ～应用脑筋好好想一想，We should always use our brains and think everything over carefully.

【凡是】 fánshì every; any; all: ～正义的事业都是不可战胜的。A just cause is invincible.

烦* fán ① be vexed; be irritated; be annoyed: 心～ feel vexed/ 真～人! How annoying!/ 你～什么? What are you getting so annoyed about? ② be tired of: 厌～ be fed up with ③ superfluous and confusing: 要言不～ giving the essentials in simple language; pithy; terse ④ trouble: ～交某人 please forward this to so-and-so/ ～您给她捎个信儿。May I trouble you to pass on a message to her?

【烦劳】 fánláo trouble: ～您带几本书给他。Would you mind taking a few books to him?

【烦闷】 fánmèn be unhappy; be worried: 你干吗这样～? Why are you so worried?/ 他一上午都没说话，心里一定很～。There must be something on his mind, he's been so quiet the whole morning.

【烦恼】 fánnǎo be vexed; be worried: 自寻~ worry over for nothing; bring vexation on oneself/ 何必为这些小事~? Why should you fret over such trifles?

【烦扰】 fánrǎo ① bother; disturb ② feel disturbed

【烦琐】 fánsuǒ loaded down with trivial details: ~的手续 overelaborate procedure; tedious formalities/ ~的考证 pedantic textual criticism; overelaborate research

【烦嚣】 fánxiāo noisy and annoying

【烦躁】 fánzào be fidgety; be agitated: 某些动物~不安可能是地震临震前的预兆。Agitated activity by certain animals may be a sign of an impending earthquake.

蕃 fán ① luxuriant; growing in abundance: ~茂 luxuriant; lush ② multiply; proliferate: ~衍 multiply; increase gradually in number or quantity

樊 fán <书> fence

【樊篱】 fánlí ① fence ② barriers; restriction: 冲破~ break down barriers; cast off trammels

【樊笼】 fánlóng bird cage — place or condition of confinement

繁* fán ① in great numbers; numerous; manifold: ~星满天 a starry sky/ 头绪纷~ have too many things to attend to; have too many irons in the fire/ 删~就简 simplify by weeding out superfluities; reduce to bare essentials ② propagate; multiply

【繁多】 fánduō various: 花样~ of all shapes and colours

【繁复】 fánfù heavy and complicated: 有了计算机,~的计算工作在几秒钟之内就可以完成。A computer does complicated calculations in a few seconds.

【繁华】 fánhuá flourishing; bustling; busy: 城里最~的地区 the busiest section of town; the downtown district

【繁忙】 fánmáng busy: ~的收获季节 the busy harvest season/ 工作~ be very busy with one's work; be busily engaged

【繁茂】 fánmào lush; luxuriant: 草木~ a lush growth of trees and grass/ 枝叶~ with luxuriant foliage

【繁密】 fánmì dense: 林木~ densely wooded

【繁难】 fánnán hard to tackle; troublesome

【繁荣】 fánróng ① flourishing; prosperous; booming: ~富强 rich, strong and prosperous/ 物价稳定,市场~。Prices are stable and the market is brisk. ② make sth. prosper: ~经济 bring about a prosperous economy; promote economic prosperity

【繁荣昌盛】 fánróng-chāngshèng thriving and prosperous: 祖国日益~。Our country is thriving and prospering day by day./ 祝贵国~,人民幸福。We wish your country prosperity and her people happiness.

【繁盛】 fánshèng thriving; flourishing; prosperous: 这个城市越来越~了。The city is becoming more and more prosperous.

【繁体字】 fántǐzì the original complex form of a simplified Chinese character

【繁文缛节】 fánwén-rùjié unnecessary and overelaborate formalities: red tape

【繁衍】 fányǎn <书> multiply; increase gradually in number or quantity

【繁育】 fányù breed: ~优良品种 breed good strains

【繁杂】 fánzá many and diverse; miscellaneous: ~的日常事务 daily chores of all sorts

【繁殖】 fánzhí <生> breed; reproduce; propagate: 自我~ self-reproduction; autosynthesis/ ~牲畜 breed livestock/ 靠种子~的植物 plants which propagate themselves by seeds

【繁重】 fánzhòng heavy; strenuous; onerous: ~的劳动 strenuous labour/ 任务~。The tasks are arduous.

fǎn

反* fǎn ① turn over: 易如~掌 as easy as turning one's hand over/ ~败为胜 turn defeat into victory; turn the tide ② in an opposite direction; in reverse; inside out: ~而 the reverse side/ ~绑着双手 with one's hands tied behind one's back/ ~其道而行之 act in a diametrically opposite way; do exactly the opposite/ 适得其~。The result is just the contrary./ 穿~了袜子 have one's socks on inside out/ ~科学 contrary to science ③ on the contrary; instead: 这样做不但于事无补,~会把事情弄糟。This won't do any good; on the contrary, it will make things even worse. ④ return; counter: ~问 counter with a question; ask in retort/ ~击 strike back; counterattack ⑤ revolt; rebel: ~叛 revolt; rebel ⑥ oppose; combat:~间谍 counterespionage

【反驳】 fǎnbó refute; retort

【反常】 fǎncháng unusual; abnormal; perverse; strange: 最近天气有点儿~。The weather is a bit unusual these days./ 他昨天的表现有点儿~。His behaviour yesterday was a bit strange.

【反潮流】 fǎn cháoliú go against the tide

【反唇相讥】 fǎn chún xiāng jī answer back sarcastically

【反对】 fǎnduì oppose; be against; fight; combat: ~贪污浪费 fight against corruption and waste/ 有~意见吗? Any objection?
◇ ~党 opposition party; the Opposition/ ~派 opposition faction/ ~票 dissenting vote; negative vote

【反而】 fǎn'ér <连> on the contrary; instead: 困难吓不倒我们,~激起我们更大的干劲。We were not cowed by difficulties. On the contrary, they inspired us to greater efforts.

【反复】 fǎnfù repeatedly; again and again; over and over again: ~解释 explain over and over again/ ~思考 think a lot about sth.; turn sth. over in one's mind again and again/ ~辩论 argue back and forth

【反复无常】 fǎnfù wú cháng changeable; fickle; capricious: 这个人~,很不可靠。This fellow is always chopping and changing; he's very unreliable.

【反感】 fǎngǎn be disgusted with; be averse to; dislike; take unkindly to: 我对他的话很~。I'm disgusted with what he said./ 对这种人极其~ have a strong aversion to such people; feel a repugnance to such people

【反攻】 fǎngōng counteroffensive; counterattack

【反躬自问】 fǎngōng zìwèn examine oneself; examine one's conscience

【反顾】 fǎngù <书> look back: 义无~ be duty-bound not to turn back

【反光】 fǎnguāng ① reflect light: 白墙~,屋里显得很敞亮。With the white walls reflecting the light, the room looks bright and spacious. ② reflection of light ◇ ~灯 reflector lamp/ ~镜 reflector

【反过来】 fǎnguolai ① conversely; the other way round: ~也是一样。It's the same the other way round./ 这话~说就不一定对。The converse of this statement may not be true. ② in turn

【反话】 fǎnhuà irony

【反悔】 fǎnhuǐ go back on one's word (或 promise): 一言为定,决不~。I give you my word and I'll never go back on it.

【反击】 fǎnjī strike back; beat back; counterattack: 自卫~ counterattack in self-defence/ 对敌人的挑衅给予有力的~ answer the enemy's provocation with a vigorous counter blow

【反间】 fǎnjiàn sow distrust or dissension among one's enemies; set one's enemies at odds (by spreading rumours, etc.) ◇ ~计 stratagem of sowing distrust or discord among one's enemies

【反建议】 fǎnjiànyì counterproposal

【反抗】 fǎnkàng revolt; resist: ~精神 spirit of revolt; rebellious spirit

【反面】 fǎnmiàn ① reverse side; wrong side; back: 唱片的~ the reverse side of a disc/ 料子的~ the wrong side of the cloth/ 我们必须学会全面地看问题,不但要看到事物的正面,也要看到它的~。We must learn to look at problems from all sides, seeing the reverse as well as the obverse side of things. ② opposite; negative side: 走向~ change (或 turn) into one's opposite/ ~的教训 a lesson learnt from negative (或 bitter) experience; wisdom won from hard knocks

【反目】 fǎnmù fall out (esp. between husband and wife)

【反派】 fǎnpài villain (in drama, etc.); negative character: 演～人物 act the part of the villain; play a negative role

【反叛】 fǎnpàn revolt; rebel

【反求诸己】 fǎn qiú zhū jǐ seek the cause in oneself (instead of in sb. else)

【反手】 fǎnshǒu ＜体＞ backhand: ～抽球 backhand drive

【反胃】 fǎnwèi gastric disorder causing nausea

【反问】 fǎnwèn ①ask (a question) in reply ②＜语＞ rhetorical question

【反响】 fǎnxiǎng repercussion; echo; reverberation: 在世界上引起广泛的～ evoke worldwide repercussions/ 在很多人心中引起～ find an echo in the hearts of many people

【反省】 fǎnxǐng introspection; self-questioning; self-examination

【反咬一口】 fǎnyǎo yī kǒu trump up a countercharge against one's accuser; make a false countercharge

【反义词】 fǎnyìcí ＜语＞ antonym

【反应】 fǎnyìng ①reaction: 过敏～＜医＞ allergic reaction/ 阳性(阴性)～ positive (negative) reaction/ 你打了针以后有什么～? Have you had a reaction to your injection? ②response; repercussion; reaction: ～不一。Reactions vary./ ～冷淡。The response was far from warm./ 作出～ make a response/ 这位青年科学家的研究报告在科学界引起了强烈的～。The young scientist's research paper evoked strong repercussions in scientific circles.

【反映】 fǎnyìng ①reflect; mirror: ～新时代的特点 mirror the features of our new age ②report; make known: 向上级～ report to the higher level/ 向他～学生们的意见 let him know the students' opinions/ 我将经常向你～进度。I'll keep you informed of the progress made.

【反正】 fǎnzheng ＜副＞ anyway; anyhow; in any case: ～得去一个人,就让我去吧! Since someone has to go anyway, let me go./ 不管怎么样,～工作不能停。Come what may, the work must go on./ 不管晴天雨天,～我们去支援。We'll go and give a hand, rain or shine.

返* fǎn return: ～伦敦 return to London/ 流连忘～ linger on without any thought of leaving/ 一去不复～ gone forever; gone never to return

【返航】 fǎnháng return to base or port: 在～途中 on the homebound voyage or flight

【返回】 fǎnhuí return; come or go back: ～原地 return to the starting point/ ～港口 put back to port/ 使人造地球卫星～地面 recover a man-made earth satellite

【返老还童】 fǎnlǎo-huántóng recover one's youthful vigour; feel rejuvenated

fàn

犯* fàn ①violate; offend (against law, etc.): ～纪律 violate discipline/ ～忌讳 offend a person's sensitivity; touch a person's sore spot ②attack; assail; work against: 人不～我,我不～人;人若～我,我必～人。We will not attack unless we are attacked; if we are attacked, we will certainly counterattack. ③criminal: 战～ war criminal/ 杀人～ murderer ④have a recurrence of (an old illness); revert to (a bad habit): 他又～了哮喘病。He's got another attack of asthma./ ～脾气 get angry; fly into a temper; be in a bad temper ⑤commit (a mistake, crime, etc.): ～错误 make a mistake

【犯案】 fàn'àn ＜旧＞ be found out and brought to justice

【犯病】 fànbìng have an attack of one's old illness

【犯不着】 fànbuzháo ＜口＞ not worthwhile: 在枝节问题上～花这么多时间。It isn't worthwhile spending so much time on minor problems.

【犯得着】 fàndezháo 〔多用于反问〕is it worthwhile: 为这么点小事～和他吵吗? Is it worthwhile quarrelling with him over such a trifling matter?

【犯法】 fànfǎ violate (或 break) the law ◇ ～行为 offence against the law

【犯规】 fànguī ①break the rules ②＜体＞ foul: 侵人～ personal foul ◇ ～者＜体＞ offender

【犯忌】 fànjì violate a taboo

【犯禁】 fànjìn violate a ban (或 prohibition)

【犯人】 fànrén prisoner; convict

【犯上】 fànshàng go against one's superiors

【犯嫌疑】 fàn xiányí arouse suspicion; come under suspicion

【犯罪】 fànzuì commit a crime (或 an offence) ◇ ～分子 offender; criminal/ ～行为 criminal offence

泛 fàn ①＜书＞ float: ～舟西湖 go boating on the West Lake ②be suffused with: 脸上～出红晕 with one's cheeks suffused with blushes/ 她的脸色黑里～红。She has a fanned and glowing face. ③flood; inundate ④extensive; general; nonspecific: 广～ wide; extensive/ 空～ containing nothing but generalities

【泛称】 fànchēng general term

【泛泛】 fànfàn general; not deepgoing: ～而谈 talk in generalities/ ～之交 casual acquaintance

【泛光灯】 fànguāngdēng floodlight

【泛滥】 fànlàn ①be in flood; overflow; inundate: 河水～。The river was in flood. 或 The river overflowed its banks. ②spread unchecked: ～成灾 run rampant; run wild; be swamped by sth.

【泛指】 fànzhǐ make a general reference; be used in a general sense: 他的发言是～一般情况,不是针对某一个人的。His statement refers to people in general, not to anyone in particular.

饭* fàn ①cooked rice or other cereals: 米～ (cooked) rice/ 小米～ (cooked) millet ②meal: 一天三顿饱～ three square meals a day/ ～前洗手。Wash your hands before meals.

【饭菜】 fàncài ①meal; repast: ～可口,服务周到 tasty food and good service ②dishes to go with rice, steamed buns, etc.

【饭店】 fàndiàn ①hotel ②＜方＞ restaurant

【饭馆】 fànguǎn restaurant

【饭锅】 fànguō pot for cooking rice; rice cooker

【饭来张口,衣来伸手】 fàn lái zhāngkǒu, yī lái shēnshǒu have only to open one's mouth to be fed and hold out one's hands to be dressed — lead an easy life, with everything provided; be waited on hand and foot

【饭量】 fànliàng appetite: ～很大 have an enormous appetite; be a big eater/ 她的～比你小多了。She eats much less than you do.

【饭厅】 fàntīng dining hall; dining room; mess hall

【饭桶】 fàntǒng ①rice bucket ②big eater ③fathead; good-for-nothing

【饭碗】 fànwǎn ①rice bowl ②job; means of livelihood: 丢～ lose one's job

【饭桌】 fànzhuō dining table

范* fàn ①＜书＞ pattern ②model; example; pattern: 典～ example/ 示～ demonstrate ③limits: 就～ submit

【范本】 fànběn model for calligraphy or painting

【范畴】 fànchóu category

【范例】 fànlì example; model: 这是厉行节约的一个出色的～。This is an outstanding example of strict economy.

【范围】 fànwéi scope; limits; range: ～狭小 limited in scope/ 国家管辖～ the limits of national jurisdiction/ 在法律许可～内 within the limits permitted by law/ 在协定规定的～内 within the framework of the agreement/ 实际控制～ the extent of actual control/ 势力～ sphere of influence/ 这不属于我们研究的～。This is outside the range of our study.

【范文】 fànwén model essay

贩* fàn ①buy to resell: ～牲口 buy and sell draught animals/ ～毒 traffic in narcotics ②dealer; monger; pedlar: 小～ vendor; pedlar

【贩卖】 fànmài traffic; peddle; sell: ～皮货 be in the fur trade/ ～军火 traffic in arms

【贩运】 fànyùn transport goods for sale; traffic

【贩子】 fànzi　dealer; monger: 马~ horse dealer/ 鱼~ fish-monger/ 战争~ warmonger

梵 fàn　Buddhist: ~宫 Buddhist temple
【梵文】 Fànwén　Sanskrit

fāng

方* fāng ① square: ~桌 square table/ 五米见~ five metres square ②〈数〉involution; power: 二的四次~是十六。The fourth power of 2 is 16./ 二的三次~是八。The cube of 2 is 8. ③〈量〉short for square metre or cubic metre: 一~木材 a cubic metre of lumber/ 土石~ cubic metres of earth or stone work/ 铺地板十五~ lay 15 square metres of wooden floor ④ upright; honest: 品行~正 have an upright character ⑤ direction: 东~ the east/ 前~ the front/ 四面八~ in all directions ⑥ side; party: 我~ our side/ 双~ both sides (或 parties) ⑦ place; region; locality: 远~ a faraway (或 remote) place/ ~音 local accent ⑧ method; way: 千~百计 in a hundred and one ways; by every means possible/ 多~ in various ways/ 领导有~ exercise good leadership ⑨ prescription: 处~ make out a prescription ⑩〈副〉just; at the time when: 年~二十 be just twenty years old/ ~今 at present; nowadays
【方案】 fāng'àn　scheme; plan; programme: 提出初步~ put forward a preliminary plan
【方便】 fāngbiàn ① convenient: 为了~起见 for convenience' sake/ ~人民 make things convenient for the people/ 什么时候~,什么时候来。Drop in whenever it's convenient./ 这儿说话不~。It's not convenient to talk here. 或 This isn't the right place to talk./ 交通~ have a good transport service/ 把~让给别人,把困难留给自己 take the difficulties on oneself and make things easy for others ②〈口〉go to the lavatory: 你要不要~一下? Do you want to use the lavatory (或 wash your hands)? ③〈婉〉have money to spare or lend: 手头不~ have little money to spare
【方步】 fāngbù　measured steps: 迈~ walk with measured steps
【方才】 fāngcái　just now: ~我到他家去了。I went to his place just now./ 她~还在这儿。She was here just a moment ago.
【方寸】 fāngcùn〈书〉heart: ~已乱 with one's heart troubled and confused; with one's mind in a turmoil; greatly agitated
【方法】 fāngfǎ　method; way; means: 用各种~ in all sorts of ways; by every means/ 用某种~ by some means or other; one way or another
【方块字】 fāngkuàizì　Chinese characters
【方括号】 fāngkuòhào　square brackets ([　])
【方略】 fānglüè　general plan
【方面】 fāngmiàn　respect; aspect; side; field: 在这~ in this respect (或 connection)
【方式】 fāngshì　way; fashion; pattern: 生活~ way (或 mode) of life; life-style
【方位】 fāngwèi　position; bearing; direction; points of the compass
【方向】 fāngxiàng　direction; orientation: 朝这个~ in this direction
【方兴未艾】 fāngxīng-wèi'ài　be just unfolding; be in the ascendant: 这场文化运动~。The cultural movement is now in the ascendant.
【方形】 fāngxíng　square
【方言】 fāngyán〈语〉dialect
【方圆】 fāngyuán ① circumference: 那个湖~八公里。The lake has a circumference of 8 km. ② neighbourhood: ~左近的人谁不知道他。Who in the neighbourhood doesn't know him?
【方针】 fāngzhēn　policy; guiding principle: 基本~ fundamental policy (或 principle)/ ~政策 general and specific policies/ 文艺~ guiding principles for literature and art
【方正】 fāngzhèng ① upright and foursquare: 字要写得~。In writing, make the characters square and upright. ②

straightforward; upright; righteous: 他为人~。He is an upright man.

坊* fāng ① lane (usu. as part of a street name) ②见 "牌坊" páifāng
【坊本】 fāngběn　block-printed edition prepared by a book-shop
【坊间】 fāngjiān ① on the street stalls ② in the bookshops

芳* fāng ① sweet-smelling; fragrant: ~草 fragrant grass ② good (name or reputation); virtuous: 流~百世 leave a good name to posterity
【芳香】 fāngxiāng　fragrant; aromatic

妨* fāng〔用于否定与疑问〕harm: 试试又何~? What harm is there in trying?/ 不~早点动身。There's no harm in leaving a little earlier./ 不~同他再谈一次。We might as well have another talk with him.
另见 fáng

fáng

防* fáng ① guard against; provide against: 预~ prevent sth. from happening; take precautions/ 以~万一 be prepared for all contingencies; be ready for any eventuality ② defend: 国~ national defence/ 边~ frontier defence/ ~身 defend oneself ③ dyke; embankment
【防备】 fángbèi　guard against; take precautions against: ~敌人突然袭击 be prepared for surprise attacks by the enemy/ 采取措施~发生事故 take precautions against accidents
【防波堤】 fángbōdī　breakwater; mole
【防不胜防】 fáng bùshèng fáng　impossible to defend effectively; very hard to guard against: 他的球路多变,打得对手~。His opponent couldn't stand up to his varied and fast-changing tactics.
【防潮】 fángcháo ① dampproof; moistureproof ② protection against the tide: ~堰堤 tidal barrage
【防弹】 fángdàn　bulletproof; shellproof ◇ ~背心 bullet-proof vest/ ~玻璃 bulletproof glass
【防盗】 fángdào　guard against theft; take precautions against burglars
【防毒】 fángdú　gas defence ◇ ~面具 gas mask
【防范】 fángfàn　be on guard; keep a lookout
【防风林】 fángfēnglín　windbreak (forest)
【防辐射】 fáng fúshè　radiation protection
【防腐】 fángfǔ　antiseptic; anticorrosive ◇ ~材料 antirot material/ ~剂 preservative; antiseptic
【防护】 fánghù　protect; shelter ◇ ~堤 (protection) embankment/ ~林 shelter-forest
【防患未然】 fáng huàn wèi rán　take preventive measures; provide against possible trouble
【防火】 fánghuǒ　fire prevention; fireproof
【防空】 fángkōng　air defence; antiaircraft ◇ ~部队 air defence forces/ ~导弹 air defence missile; interceptor missile/ ~壕 air-raid dugout/ ~警报 air defence warning/ ~演习 air defence exercise (或 practice); air-raid drill
【防空洞】 fángkōngdòng ① air-raid shelter ② a hideout for evildoers ③ a cover for wrong thoughts
【防守】 fángshǒu　defend; guard
【防暑】 fángshǔ　heatstroke (或 sunstroke) prevention ◇ ~药 heatstroke preventive
【防水】 fángshuǐ　waterproof ◇ ~表 waterproof watch
【防卫】 fángwèi　defend
【防务】 fángwù　matters pertaining to defence; defence
【防线】 fángxiàn　line of defence
【防锈】 fángxiù　antirust ◇ ~剂 rust inhibitor; antirusting agent/ ~漆 antirust paint

【防疫】 fángyì epidemic prevention ◇ ~站 epidemic prevention station/ ~针 (prophylactic) inoculation

【防御】 fángyù defence: 积极（消极）~ active (passive) defence/ 纵深~ defence in depth/ 加强~力量 strengthen defence capabilities/ 由~转入进攻 go over from the defensive to the offensive/ 迫使敌人转入~地位 force the enemy onto the defensive/ ~国家外部敌人的颠覆和侵略 guard against subversion and aggression by external enemies

【防灾】 fángzāi take precautions against natural calamities

【防震】 fángzhèn ① take precautions against earthquakes: ~措施 precautions against earthquakes ② shockproof; quakeproof

【防止】 fángzhǐ prevent; guard against; forestall; avoid ~浪费人力 avoid waste of manpower/ ~骄傲自满 guard against conceit and complacency

妨* fáng hinder; hamper; impede; obstruct
另见 fǎng

【妨碍】 fáng'ài hinder; hamper; impede; obstruct: ~团结 hinder unity/ ~生产的发展 hamper the growth of production/ ~工作 hinder one's work/ ~交通 block traffic/ 这不~我们按期动工。This won't stop us from starting the work on the project on time./ 这不应~我们两国之间良好关系的发展。This should not present an obstacle to the development of good relations between our two countries.

【妨害】 fánghài impair; jeopardize; be harmful to: ~健康 be harmful to one's health

房* fáng ① house: 平~ single-storey house/ 楼~ a building of two or more storeys/ 草~ thatched cottage/ 洗澡~ bathhouse ② room: 客~ guest room/ 书~ study/ 病~ sickroom; ward ③ a house-like structure: 蜂~ beehive

【房产】 fángchǎn house property

【房顶】 fángdǐng roof

【房东】 fángdōng the owner of the house one lives in; landlord or landlady

【房间】 fángjiān room: 一套~ a suite; an apartment; a flat

【房客】 fángkè tenant (of a room or house); lodger

【房契】 fángqì title deed (for a house)

【房事】 fángshì sexual intercourse (between a married couple)

【房屋】 fángwū houses; buildings

【房主】 fángzhǔ house-owner

【房子】 fángzi ① house; building ② room

【房租】 fángzū rent (for a house, flat, etc.)

肪 fáng 见"脂肪" zhīfáng

fǎng

访* fǎng ① visit; call on: ~友 call on a friend/ 互~ exchange visits ② seek by inquiry or search; try to get: ~求民间丹方 search for folk remedies

【访查】 fǎngchá go about making inquiries; investigate

【访问】 fǎngwèn visit; call on; interview: 正式（非正式）~ an official (unofficial) visit/ ~亲友 call on friends and relatives

仿* fǎng ① imitate; copy ② resemble; be like: 相~ be very much alike; be similar

【仿佛】 fǎngfú ① seem; as if: 这事他~已经知道了。He seems to know about it already. ② be more or less the same; be alike: 这两个人的年纪相~。These two persons are about the same age.

【仿古】 fǎnggǔ modelled after an antique; in the style of the ancients: ~青铜器 an imitation of an ancient bronze

【仿效】 fǎngxiào imitate; follow the example of: 她是个好榜样，我们应当~她。We ought to follow her good example.

【仿造】 fǎngzào copy; be modelled on

【仿照】 fǎngzhào imitate; follow: 这个办法很好，各地可以~办理。This is a good method. It might well be adopted by other localities.

【仿制】 fǎngzhì copy; be modelled on ◇ ~品 imitation; replica; copy

纺* fǎng ① spin: 把棉花~成纱 spin cotton into yarn ② a thin silk cloth

【纺车】 fǎngchē spinning wheel

【纺绸】 fǎngchóu a soft plain-weave silk fabric

【纺纱】 fǎngshā spinning ◇ ~工人 spinner/ ~机 spinning machine

【纺丝】 fǎngsī 〈化纤〉 spinning

【纺织】 fǎngzhī spinning and weaving ◇ ~厂 textile mill/ ~工人 textile worker/ ~工业 textile industry/ ~品 textile; fabric

fàng

放* fàng ① let go; set free; release: 不~他走 won't let him go/ 抓住绳子不~ won't let go of the rope/ 把俘虏~了 release the captives/ 把游泳池里的水~掉 let the water out of the swimming pool ② let off; give out: ~枪 fire a gun/ ~焰火 set off fireworks/ ~风筝 fly a kite ③ put out to pasture: ~牛 put cattle out to pasture; pasture (或 graze) cattle/ ~鸭 tend ducks ④ let oneself go; give way to: ~声歌唱 sing heartily/ ~声大哭 cry loudly and bitterly ⑤ lend (money) for interest: ~债 lend money at (a certain rate of) interest/ ~高利贷 practise usury ⑥ let out; expand; make larger, longer, etc.: 把裤腰~一寸 let the trousers out an inch at the waist/ 把上衣~长一点 lower the hemline of the jacket a little ⑦ blossom; open: 百花齐~ a hundred flowers in bloom/ 心花怒~ be wild with joy ⑧ put in; add: 菜里多~点酱油。Put a bit more soy sauce in the food (或 dish). ⑨ put; place: 把书~在桌子上。Put the book on the table./ 把人民利益~在个人利益之上 place the interests of the people above personal interests ⑩ leave alone; lay aside: 这事不急，先~一~。It's not an urgent matter. Let's lay it aside for the moment. ⑪ send away: 流~ send into exile ⑫ readjust (attitude, behaviour, etc.) to a certain extent: ~老实点儿 You behave yourself!/ ~明白些。Be sensible./ 脚步~轻些。Tread softly./ 把速度~慢些儿。Slow down a little. ⑬ show: ~电影 show a film/ ~幻灯 show slides/ ~电视 turn on the TV

【放长线，钓大鱼】 fàng chángxiàn, diào dàyú throw a long line to catch a big fish—adopt a long-term plan to secure sth. big

【放出】 fàngchū give out; let out; emit: ~光和热 give out light and heat/ ~清香 exude a delicate fragrance

【放大】 fàngdà enlarge; magnify; amplify: 把照片~ make enlargements of a photograph; have a photograph enlarged ◇ ~镜 magnifying glass; magnifier

【放胆】 fàngdǎn act boldly and with confidence

【放诞】 fàngdàn wild in speech and behaviour

【放荡】 fàngdàng ① dissolute; dissipated ② unconventional: ~不羁 unconventional and unrestrained

【放工】 fànggōng (of workers) knock off

【放过】 fàngguò let off; let slip: 我们决不冤枉一个好人，也决不~一个坏人。We will never wrong a single good person nor let off a single bad one./ 这是个好机会，不要~。Don't let slip this good opportunity.

【放虎归山】 fàng hǔ guī shān 见 "纵虎归山" zòng hǔ guī shān

【放火】 fànghuǒ ① set fire to; set on fire; commit arson ② create disturbances ◇ ~犯 arsonist

【放假】 fàngjià have a holiday or vacation; have a day off: 你们什么时候放假? When is your vacation?

【放宽】 fàngkuān relax restrictions; relax: ~尺度 relax the requirements/ ~期限 extend a time limit/ ~条件 soften the terms

【放屁】 fàngpì ① break wind; fart ② 〈骂〉 talk nonsense:

~! Shit! 或 What crap!

【放弃】 fàngqì abandon; give up; renounce: ~原来计划 abandon the original plan/ ~表决权 abstain from voting/ ~原则 forsake one's principles

【放任】 fàngrèn ① not interfere; let alone: ~自流 let things drift (或 slide) ② noninterference; *laissez-faire*: 采取~态度 take a *laissez-faire* attitude

【放哨】 fàngshào stand sentry (或 sentinel); be on sentry go: 在门口~ be posted as a sentry in front of the house

【放射】 fàngshè radiate: 初升的太阳~出万道金光。The rising sun radiated myriads of golden rays.
◇ ~病 radiation sickness/ ~疗法 radiotherapy/ ~现象 〈物〉 radioactivity/ ~线 radioactive rays

【放射性】 fàngshèxìng 〈物〉 radioactivity

【放生】 fàngshēng ① free captive animals ② (of Buddhists) buy captive fish or birds and set them free

【放手】 fàngshǒu ① let go; let go one's hold: 你抓紧,我要~了。Hold tight. I'm going to let go. ② have a free hand; go all out: 让他们~工作 give them a free hand in their work/我们信得过你,你~干吧。We trust you. Just go ahead boldly with your work.

【放肆】 fàngsì unbridled; wanton: ~的行为 unbridled behaviour/ 胆敢如此~! How dare you take such liberties!/ ~诬蔑 wantonly vilify/ 极为~ throw all restraint to the winds

【放松】 fàngsōng relax; slacken; loosen: ~肌肉 relax one's muscles/ ~警惕 relax one's vigilance

【放下】 fàngxià lay down; put down: ~手头的工作 put aside the work on hand/ 命令敌军~武器 order the enemy to lay down their arms

【放下屠刀,立地成佛】 fàngxià túdāo, lì dì chéng fó a butcher becomes a Buddha the moment he drops his cleaver — a wrongdoer achieves salvation as soon as he gives up evil

【放心】 fàngxīn set one's mind at rest; be at ease; rest assured; feel relieved: 昨天她来了电报,我们才~。We were worried about her until her telegram came yesterday./ 你~,一切都会安排好的。You can rest assured that everything will be all right./ 对他不大~ not quite trust him/ ~不下 be kept in suspense; feel anxious

【放学】 fàngxué ① classes are over: 他们学校下午五点~。Their school closes at five p.m.

【放眼】 fàngyǎn take a broad view; scan widely: 胸怀祖国 ~世界 have the whole country in mind and the whole world in view

【放映】 fàngyìng show; project: ~电影 show a film; have a film show

【放置】 fàngzhì lay up; lay aside: ~不用 lay up (machinery, equipment, etc.); lie idle

【放逐】 fàngzhú send into exile; exile; banish

【放纵】 fàngzòng ① let sb. have his own way; connive at; indulge: 你太~孩子了。You are too indulgent with your children. ② self-indulgent; undisciplined

fēi

飞* fēi ① fly; flit: 鹰~得高。Eagles fly high./ 乘专机 ~往加拿大 fly to Canada by special plane/ 从东京直 ~香港 make a nonstop flight from Tokyo to Hongkong/ 蜜蜂在花丛中~来~去。Bees are flitting from flower to flower. ② hover or flutter in the air: ~弯 a hovering kite/ ~絮 willow catkins flying in the air ③ swiftly: ~奔 dash; tear along/ 他沿着大路~跑。He flew down the road. ④ unexpected; accidental: ~来横祸 unexpected disaster ⑤ unfounded; groundless: 流言~语 rumours and slanders

【飞驰】 fēichí speed along: 火车~而过。A train sped by.

【飞虫】 fēichóng winged insect

【飞船】 fēichuán airship; dirigible

【飞弹】 fēidàn ① missile ② stray bullet

【飞短流长】 fēiduǎn-liúcháng spread embroidered stories and malicious gossip

【飞蛾投火】 fēi'é tóu huǒ a moth darting into a flame — bringing destruction upon oneself; seeking one's own doom

【飞黄腾达】 fēihuáng téngdá make rapid advances in one's career; have a meteoric rise

【飞机】 fēijī aircraft; aeroplane; plane: 垂直起落~ vertical takeoff and landing aircraft (VTOL)/ 短距起落~ short takeoff and landing aircraft (STOL)
◇ ~场 airfield; airport/ ~库 hangar/ ~制造业 aviation industry; aircraft industry

【飞溅】 fēijiàn splash: 浪花~到甲板上。The waves splashed on the deck./ 钢花~ sparks flying off molten steel

【飞快】 fēikuài very fast; at lightning speed: 以~的速度前进 forge ahead at full speed

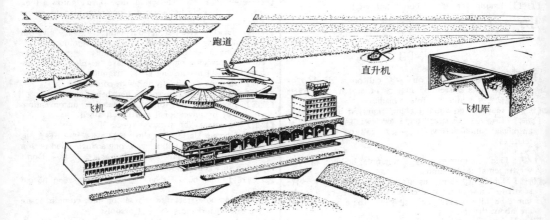

跑道　飞机　直升机　飞机库

【飞毛腿】fēimáotuǐ ① fleet-footed ② fleet-footed runner
【飞禽走兽】fēiqín-zǒushòu birds and beasts
【飞速】fēisù at full speed: 列车在～前进。The train is running at full speed.
【飞腾】fēiténg fly swiftly upward; soar
【飞艇】fēitǐng airship; dirigible
【飞舞】fēiwǔ dance in the air; flutter: 雪花～。Snowflakes are dancing in the air./ 蝴蝶在花丛中～。Butterflies fluttered about among the flowers.
【飞翔】fēixiáng circle in the air; hover: 象雄鹰在空中～ hovering in the air like an eagle
【飞行】fēixíng flight; flying ◇ ～员 pilot; aviator; flyer
【飞檐走壁】fēiyán-zǒubì (of swordsmen, etc., in old Chinese novels) leap onto roofs and vault over walls
【飞扬】fēiyáng fly upward; rise: 尘土～ clouds of dust flying up/ 到处～着欢乐的歌声。Songs of joy were floating in the air.
【飞扬跋扈】fēiyáng-báhù arrogant and domineering
【飞鱼】fēiyú <动> flying fish
【飞跃】fēiyuè leap: 英国的石油工业正～地发展。Britain's oil industry is developing by leaps and bounds.
【飞贼】fēizéi ① a burglar who makes his way into a house over walls and roofs ② an intruding enemy airman; air marauder (或 pirate)
【飞涨】fēizhǎng (of prices, etc.) soar; shoot up; skyrocket: 物价～。Prices were skyrocketing.

妃 fēi ① imperial concubine ② the wife of a prince
【妃子】fēizi imperial concubine

非* fēi ① wrong; evildoing: 分清是～ distinguish between right and wrong/ 为～作歹 do evil ② not conform to; run counter to: ～分 overstepping one's bounds; assuming; presumptuous ③ censure; blame: 未可厚～ not altogether inexcusable; excusable ④ not; no: ～所问 give an irrelevant answer/ ～笔墨所能形容 no words can adequately describe; beggar description/ ～比寻常 unusual; out of the ordinary/难道～你去处理这件事不成? Are you really the only one who can handle the matter? ⑥<口> have got to; simply must: 不行,我～去! No, I simply must go.
【非…不可】fēi...bùkě ① must; have to: 我非参加这次登山活动不可。I simply must join this mountaineering expedition. ② will inevitably; be bound to: 一味蛮干的人非碰壁不可。One who acts rashly and arbitrarily is bound to come to grief.
【非常】fēicháng ① extraordinary; unusual; special: ～会议 extraordinary session/ ～支出 a special expenditure/ ～措施 emergency measures/ ～时期 unusual times ② very; extremely; highly: ～必要 highly necessary/ ～重要 extremely important/ ～精彩 simply marvellous/ ～清楚 perfectly clear/ ～重视 attach great importance to/ ～抱歉 awfully (或 terribly) sorry
【非但】fēidàn not only: 他～自己干得好,还肯帮助别人。He not only does his own work well, but is also ready to help others.
【非得】fēiděi have got to; must: 干这活儿～仔细才行。You've got to be careful when you do this job./ 这病～马上开刀不可。This disease calls for an immediate operation.
【非法】fēifǎ illegal; unlawful; illicit: ～活动 unlawful (或 illegal) activities/ ～收入 illicit income/ 被宣布为～ be outlawed; be declared illegal; be illegalized
【非凡】fēifán outstanding; extraordinary; uncommon: ～的成就 outstanding achievements; extraordinary successes/ 热闹～ bustling with activity
【非…非…】fēi...fēi... neither... nor...: 非亲非故 neither relative nor friend; neither kith nor kin
【非分】fēifèn overstepping one's bounds; assuming; presumptuous: ～的要求 presumptuous demands/ ～之想 inordinate ambitions
【非公莫入】fēi gōng mò rù no admittance except on business
【非官方】fēiguānfāng unofficial

【非驴非马】fēilú-fēimǎ neither ass nor horse; neither fish, flesh, nor fowl
【非卖品】fēimàipǐn (articles) not for sale
【非命】fēimìng [多用于]:死于～ die a violent death
【非人】fēirén ①<书> not the right person: 所用～ choose the wrong person for a job ② inhuman: ～待遇 inhuman treatment
【非同小可】fēi tóng xiǎokě no small (或 trivial) matter
【非议】fēiyì [多用于否定式] reproach; censure: 无可～ beyond (或 above) reproach; irreproachable
【非正式】fēizhèngshì unofficial; informal: ～译文 unofficial translation/ ～访问 unofficial (或 informal) visit/ ～会议 informal meeting
【非正统】fēizhèngtǒng unorthodox

啡* fēi 见"咖啡" kāfēi; "吗啡" mǎfēi

绯 fēi red
【绯红】fēihóng bright red; crimson: 脸羞得～ blush with shame/ ～的晚霞 rosy evening clouds

扉 fēi door leaf
【扉页】fēiyè <印> title page

蜚 fēi
【蜚短流长】fēiduǎn-liúcháng 见"飞短流长" fēiduǎn-liúcháng
【蜚声】fēishēng <书> make a name; become famous: 我国的工艺美术品～海外。China's arts and crafts enjoy a high reputation abroad.
【蜚语】fēiyǔ rumours; gossip: 散布流言～ spread rumours

霏 fēi
【霏霏】fēifēi <书> falling thick and fast: 雨雪～。It was sleeting hard.

féi

肥* féi ① fat: ～猪 a big porker/ 这肉太～了。The meat is too fat. ② fertile; rich: 这里的地～极了。The soil here is extremely fertile. ③ fertilize: ～田 fertilize the soil ④ fertilizer; manure: 化～ chemical fertilizer
【肥大】féidà ① loose; large: ～的衣服 a loose garment ② fat; plump; corpulent: ～的鲤鱼 a fat carp
【肥厚】féihòu plump; fleshy: 果肉～。The pulp is full and fleshy.
【肥料】féiliào fertilizer; manure: 有机～ organic fertilizer/ 细菌～ bacterial fertilizer
【肥美】féiměi ① fertile; rich: ～的土地 rich soil; fertile land ② luxuriant; plump; fat: 水草～牛羊壮 rich pastures and thriving herds/ ～的北京鸭 fat Beijing ducks
【肥胖】féipàng fat; corpulent
【肥缺】féiquē <旧> lucrative post
【肥硕】féishuò ① (of fruit) big and fleshy ② (of limbs and body) large and firm-fleshed
【肥沃】féiwò fertile; rich
【肥皂】féizào soap ◇ ～粉 soap powder/ ～泡 soap bubble/ ～片 soap flakes/ ～水 soapsuds
【肥壮】féizhuàng stout and strong: 牛羊～ thriving herds of sheep and cattle

fěi

诽 fěi slander
【诽谤】fěibàng slander; calumniate; libel

匪* fěi ① bandit; brigand; robber ②<书> not: 获益～浅 reap no little benefit
【匪巢】fěicháo bandits' lair
【匪患】fěihuàn the evil of banditry; banditry
【匪窟】fěikū bandits' lair
【匪首】fěishǒu bandit chieftain
【匪徒】fěitú gangster; bandit
【匪夷所思】fěi yí suǒ sī unimaginably queer; fantastic

悱 fěi 〈书〉be at a loss for words
【悱恻】 fěicè 〈书〉laden with sorrow; sad at heart: 缠绵~ exceedingly sentimental; extremely sad

菲 fěi 〈书〉〔多用作谦词〕poor; humble; unworthy: ~ 酌 a simple meal/ ~材 my humble talent/ ~仪 my small (或 unworthy) gift
【菲薄】 fěibó ① humble; poor: ~的礼物 a small gift ② belittle; despise: 不可骄傲自满，也不可妄自~。Neither be conceited nor excessively humble.

斐 fěi
【斐然】 fěirán 〈书〉striking; brilliant: ~成章 show striking literary merit/ 成绩~ (achieve) splendid results

翡 fěi
【翡翠】 fěicuì ① jadeite ② 〈动〉halcyon

fèi

吠* fèi bark; yap
【吠形吠声】 fèixíng-fèishēng when one dog barks at a shadow all the others join in — slavishly echo others 又作"吠影吠声"

沸* fèi boil: ~水 boiling water
【沸点】 fèidiǎn 〈物〉boiling point
【沸沸扬扬】 fèifèiyángyáng bubbling with noise; in a hubbub: 大家~地嚷起来。A hubbub arose with everybody taking part./ 消息~地传开了。The news spread like wildfire.
【沸腾】 fèiténg ① 〈物〉boiling; ebullition ② seethe with excitement; boil over: 热血~ one's blood boils/ 工地上一片~。The construction site was seething with excitement.

废* fèi ① give up; abandon; abolish; abrogate: 半途而~ give up halfway/不以人~言 not reject an opinion because of the speaker ② waste; disused: ~热 waste heat/ ~棉 cotton waste/ ~油 used oil/ ~井 a disused well/ ~矿 an abandoned mine
【废弛】 fèichí ① (of a law, custom, etc.) cease to be binding ② (of discipline, etc.) become lax
【废除】 fèichú abolish; abrogate; annul; repeal: ~一切不平等条约 abrogate all unequal treaties/ ~烦琐的礼节 do away with tedious formalities
【废黜】 fèichù dethrone; depose
【废话】 fèihuà superfluous words; nonsense; rubbish: 我说的也可能是~,不过还是请你再考虑考虑。What I said may seem superfluous, but I do hope you'll give it a little more thought./ ~! 我还不知道? You're wasting your breath! Do you think I don't know that?/ 少~! No more nonsense!/ ~连篇 pages of nonsense; reams of rubbish
【废料】 fèiliào waste material; waste; scrap ◇ ~堆 scrap heap; waste heap
【废票】 fèipiào ① invalidated ticket ② invalidated ballot
【废气】 fèiqì waste gas or steam
【废弃】 fèiqì discard; abandon; cast aside: ~陈规旧习 discard outdated regulations and customs
【废寝忘食】 fèiqǐn-wàngshí (so absorbed or occupied as to) forget food and sleep
【废铁】 fèitiě scrap iron
【废物】 fèiwù ① waste material; trash: ~利用 make use of waste material; convert waste into useful material ② good-for-nothing
【废墟】 fèixū ruins
【废渣】 fèizhā waste residue
【废止】 fèizhǐ abolish; annul; put an end to: ~注入式教学法 abolish the cramming method of teaching
【废纸】 fèizhǐ waste paper: 不要乱扔~。Don't litter the place with waste paper./ 他们的那个条约不过是一张~而已。That treaty of theirs is a mere scrap of paper.
【废置】 fèizhì put aside as useless

狒 fèi
【狒狒】 fèifèi 〈动〉baboon

肺* fèi lungs
【肺癌】 fèi'ái carcinoma of the lungs; lung cancer
【肺病】 fèibìng pulmonary tuberculosis (TB)
【肺腑】 fèifǔ the bottom of one's heart: 出自~ straight from the heart; from the depths of one's heart/ ~之言 words from the bottom of one's heart/ 感人~ move one deeply; touch one to the depths of one's soul
【肺痨】 fèiláo consumption; tuberculosis
【肺炎】 fèiyán pneumonia
【肺脏】 fèizàng lungs

费* fèi ① fee; dues; expenses; charge: 学~ tuition (或 schooling) fees; tuition/ 会~ membership dues/ 生活~ living expenses/ 水电~ charges for water and electricity/ 报~ subscription for a newspaper/ 车~ fare/ 免~ free of charge ② cost; spend; expend: 买这部电影机~了我们不少钱。This projector cost us a lot of money./ 他为了改革钻头~了不少时间。He spent a lot of time trying to improve the drill bits./ 我们~了两个钟头才把屋子打扫干净。It took us two hours to clean the room. ③ wasteful; consuming too much; expending sth. too quickly: 这种锅炉~煤。This kind of boiler consumes too much coal.
【费工】 fèigōng take a lot of work; require a lot of labour: 这种房子抗震性能好,又不太~。This kind of house stands up to earthquakes well and isn't too hard to build.
【费工夫】 fèi gōngfu take time and energy; be time-consuming: 这种牙雕很~。This kind of ivory carving is time-consuming.
【费解】 fèijiě hard to understand; obscure; unintelligible: 这段文章实在~。This passage is really hard to understand.
【费尽心机】 fèijìn xīnjī rack one's brains in scheming
【费劲】 fèijìn need or use great effort; be strenuous: 安装这台机器真~。It really took a lot of effort to install this machine./ 这山越往上爬越~。The higher we went up the mountain, the more strenuous the climb became./ 他看英文参考书不~。He can read reference books in English without difficulty.
【费力】 fèilì need or use great effort; be strenuous: ~不好 do a hard but thankless job
【费钱】 fèiqián cost a lot; be costly: 修这样的水电站不很~。It doesn't cost much to build hydroelectric stations of this kind.
【费神】 fèishén 〈套〉may I trouble you (to do sth.); would you (doing sth.): 这篇稿子您~看看。Would you mind going over this article for us?
【费时】 fèishí take time; be time-consuming
【费事】 fèishì give or take a lot of trouble: 别给我们烧水了,太~了。——一点儿也不~。Don't bother to boil any water for us. — Oh, it's no trouble at all./ 他费了不少事才把材料找齐。He went to a lot of trouble to find all the necessary materials.
【费心】 fèixīn ① give a lot of care; take a lot of trouble: 她为这些孩子可费了不少心。She devoted a lot of care to these children. ② 〈套〉may I trouble you (to do sth.); would you (doing sth.): 您见到他时,~把这封信交给他。Will you be so kind as to give him this letter when you see him?
【费用】 fèiyòng cost; expenses: 生产~ production cost/ 生活~ cost of living; living expenses/ 这笔~由我们负担。We'll bear the expenses.

痱 fèi
【痱子】 fèizi 〈医〉prickly heat ◇ ~粉 prickly-heat powder

fēn

分* fēn ① divide; separate; part: 一年~四季。The year is divided into four seasons./ 难舍难~ cannot bear to

part from each other/ ~阶段实行 carry out stage by stage/ ~组讨论 hold discussions in groups/ 这药~三次吃。 This medicine is to be taken in three separate doses./ 这里的树木大致~为三类。 The trees grown here fall roughly into three categories. ② distribute; assign; allot: 音乐会的票都已经~完了。 The tickets for the concert have all been distributed./ 把这个任务~给我们排吧。 Assign (或 Give) this task to our platoon, please. ③ distinguish; differentiate: 是非不~ make no distinction between right and wrong ④ branch (of an organization): ~店 branch (of a shop) ⑤ fraction: 三~之二 two-thirds/ 二~之一 half ⑥ one-tenth: 七~成绩，三~错误 70 per cent achievements, 30 per cent mistakes/ 有十~把握 be hundred-percent sure ⑦ minute (=1/60 of an hour): 这个电影要演两小时十~。 This film lasts two hours and ten minutes./ 六点十~起床 get up at ten past six ⑧ minute (=1/60 of a degree): 东经129度15~ 129 degrees 15 minutes (129° 15′) east longitude/ 成36度30~角 form an angle of 36 degrees 30 minutes (36°30′) ⑨ point; mark: 甲队罚球连得二~。 Team A scored two successive points by free throws. ⑩ 〔指利率〕: 月利一~ 1% interest a month/ 年利一~ 10% interest a year
另见 fèn

【分辨】 fēnbiàn ① distinguish; differentiate: ~真假 distinguish truth from falsehood

【分辩】 fēnbiàn defend oneself (against a charge); offer an explanation: 不容~ allowing no explanation to be offered

【分别】 fēnbié ① part; leave each other: 他们~不久又见面了。 They met again after a short separation. ② distinguish; differentiate: ~善恶 distinguish good from evil/ ~轻重缓急 differentiate the important from the less important and the urgent from the less urgent; do things in order of importance and urgency ③ difference: 两者之间没有任何~。 There is no difference between the two. ④ respectively; separately: 他们~代表本国政府在协定上签了字。 They signed the agreement on behalf of their respective governments.

【分布】 fēnbù be distributed (over an area); be dispersed; be scattered

【分寸】 fēncun proper limits for speech or action; sense of propriety: 他说话很有~。 He knows what to say and what not to say./ 不知~ lack tact; have no sense of propriety

【分担】 fēndān share responsibility for: ~费用 shoulder part of the expenses; share the expenses/ 提倡男女~家务劳动。 Men and women are encouraged to share household duties.

【分道扬镳】 fēndào yángbiāo separate and go different ways; part company, each going his own way

【分等】 fēnděng grade; classify: 产品按质~ grade products according to quality/ 商品~论价 grade commodities and fix prices accordingly; fix prices according to the different grades of commodities

【分而治之】 fēn ér zhì zhī divide and rule

【分发】 fēnfā distribute; hand out; issue: 把学习材料~给同学们 hand out study materials to the students/ 给优胜者~奖品 distribute prizes to the winners/ ~证件 issue certificates individually

【分隔】 fēngé separate; divide: 把一间房~成两间 partition a room into two

【分工】 fēngōng divide the work; division of labour: ~合作 share out the work and cooperate with one another/ ~负责 division of labour with individual responsibility/ 我们怎么~? How shall we divide up the work?

【分管】 fēnguǎn be assigned personal responsibility for; be put in charge of

【分行】 fēnháng branch (of a bank): 国内~ home (或 domestic) branch/ 国外~ overseas branch

【分毫】 fēnháo fraction; iota: 不差~ without the slightest error; just right

【分号】 fēnhào ① semicolon (;) ② branch (of a firm, etc.)

【分红】 fēnhóng share out bonus; draw extra dividends (或 profits)

【分级】 fēnjí grade; classify: 这几筐苹果还没~。 These baskets of apples have not been graded yet.

【分家】 fēnjiā divide up family property and live apart; break up the family and live apart

【分解】 fēnjiě ① resolve; decompose; break down: 水可以~为氢和氧。 Water can be resolved (或 decomposed) into hydrogen and oxygen./ 力的~ resolution of force ② 〔章回小说用语〕 recount; disclose: 欲知后事如何,且听下回~。 But as to what happened thereafter, that will be disclosed in the ensuing chapter.

【分界】 fēnjiè ① have as the boundary; be demarcated by: 这两个县以运河~。 The two counties have the canal as their common boundary. ② dividing line; line of demarcation

【分界线】 fēnjièxiàn line of demarcation; boundary: 军事~ a military demarcation line

【分居】 fēnjū (of members of a family) live apart: 他们~两处。 They live in two separate places.

【分开】 fēnkāi separate; part: 弟兄俩~已经三年了。 It is three years since the two brothers parted./ 把好的和坏的~ sort out the good ones from the bad/ 这两个问题我们~来谈。 Let's discuss the two problems separately.

【分类】 fēnlèi classify: 把这些资料加以~ classify the data

【分离】 fēnlí separate; sever: 从空气中把氮~出来 separate nitrogen from air

【分裂】 fēnliè split; divide; break up

【分门别类】 fēnmén-biélèi put into different categories; classify

【分娩】 fēnmiǎn childbirth; parturition

【分秒必争】 fēn-miǎo bì zhēng seize every minute and second; every second counts; not a second is to be lost

【分明】 fēnmíng ① clearly demarcated; sharply contoured; distinct: 爱憎~ be clear about what to love and what to hate; know clearly whom to love and whom to hate/ 这件事情是非~, 无可争辩。 The rights and wrongs of the case are perfectly clear and admit of no dispute. ② clearly; plainly; evidently: ~是强盗,却要装圣贤。 He is obviously a gangster, but he pretends to be a saint.

【分派】 fēnpài assign (to different persons); apportion: 队长给各个组都~了任务。 The team leader has assigned tasks to all the groups.

【分配】 fēnpèi ① distribute; allot; assign: ~土地 distribute land/ ~住房 allot dwelling houses/ 服从组织~ accept the job that the organization assigns to one

【分批】 fēnpī in batches; in turn: ~轮流参加训练班 go to a training course in turn

【分期】 fēnqī by stages: ~实行 implement by stages/ ~分批 by stages and in groups; group after group at different times ◇ ~付款 payment by instalments; hire purchase; instalment plan

【分歧】 fēnqí difference; divergence: 意见~ divergence of views; differences of opinion/ 原则~ a difference in principle/ 制造~ sow discord; create dissension/ 消除~ iron out differences/ 在这个问题上我们的看法有~。 Our views are divergent on this question.

【分清】 fēnqīng distinguish; draw a clear distinction between; draw a clear line of demarcation between

【分散】 fēnsàn disperse; scatter; decentralize: ~注意力 divert one's attention; take sb.'s mind off sth.

【分身】 fēnshēn spare time from one's main work to attend to sth. else: 他实在太忙,无法~。 He is really too busy to attend to anything else.

【分神】 fēnshén give some attention to: 请~照顾一下这孩子。 Would you mind keeping an eye on the child?

【分手】 fēnshǒu part company; say good-bye: 我们是在车站~的。 We said good-bye to each other at the station.

【分数】 fēnshù ① 〈数〉 fraction ② mark; grade

【分水岭】 fēnshuǐlǐng ① 〈地〉 watershed; divide ② line of demarcation; watershed

【分送】 fēnsòng send; distribute: 把学习材料~给各组。 Distribute the study materials to all the groups.

【分摊】 fēntān share: ~费用 share the expenses

【分庭抗礼】 fēntíng-kànglǐ stand up to sb. as an equal; make rival claims as an equal; act independently and defiantly

【分头】 fēntóu ① separately; severally: 这事我们～去做吧。 Let's go about the work separately. ② parted hair

【分文】 fēnwén a single cent (或 penny): ～不取 not take (或 charge) a single cent; free of charge

【分析】 fēnxī analyse: 培养～问题和解决问题的能力 cultivate the ability to analyse and solve problems/ 善于～形势 be proficient in sizing up a situation

【分享】 fēnxiǎng share (joy, rights, etc.); partake of: ～胜利的喜悦 share the joys of victory

【分晓】 fēnxiǎo ① outcome; solution: 此事明天 就见～。 We'll know the outcome of the whole affair tomorrow. ② see or understand clearly: 问个～ inquire about and get to the bottom of a matter ③〔多用于否定式〕 reason: 没～的话 unreasonable remarks

【分心】 fēnxīn divert (或 distract) one's attention: 她工作起来,什么事也不能使她～。 Nothing can divert her attention once she starts working.

【分忧】 fēnyōu share sb.'s cares and burdens; help sb. to get over a difficulty

【分赃】 fēnzāng divide the spoils; share the booty (或 loot)

【分子】 fēnzǐ 〈数〉 numerator (in a fraction)

【分组】 fēnzǔ divide into groups: ～讨论 discuss in groups; group discussion

芬* fēn sweet smell; fragrance
【芬芳】 fēnfāng ① sweet-smelling; fragrant ② fragrance

吩* fēn
【吩咐】 fēnfu tell; instruct: 张叔叔～我好生照看小马驹。 Uncle Zhang told me to take good care of the foal.

纷* fēn ① confused; tangled; disorderly ② many and various; profuse; numerous: 大雪～飞。 The snow flakes were falling thick and fast. 或 It was snowing hard.

【纷繁】 fēnfán numerous and complicated: 头绪～ have too many things to take care of; be highly complicated/ 从～的现象中抓住本质的东西 grasp the essentials from a variety of phenomena; sort out the essentials from a mass of detail

【纷纷】 fēnfēn ① one after another; in succession: ～要求入伍 volunteer to join the army one after another /世界各地～来电祝贺我国国庆。 Telegrams congratulating us on our National Day poured in from every part of the world. ② numerous and confused: 敌军～逃窜。 The enemy troops fled pell-mell.

【纷乱】 fēnluàn numerous and disorderly; helter-skelter; chaotic: ～的脚步声 hurried footsteps/ ～的局面 a state of chaos

【纷扰】 fēnrǎo confusion; turmoil: 内心的～使他无法入睡。 His mind was in such a turmoil that he couldn't get to sleep.

【纷纭】 fēnyún diverse and confused: 众说～。 Opinions are widely divided.

【纷争】 fēnzhēng dispute; wrangle: ～不已 endless dispute

【纷至沓来】 fēnzhì-tàlái come in a continuous stream; come thick and fast; keep pouring in

氛 fēn atmosphere

fén

坟* fén grave; tomb
【坟地】 féndì graveyard; cemetery
【坟墓】 fénmù grave; tomb

焚 fén burn: ～香 burn incense/ 玩火者必自～。 He who plays with fire will get burned.
【焚化】 fénhuà incinerate; cremate ◇ ～炉 incinerator; cremator
【焚毁】 fénhuǐ destroy by fire; burn down
【焚烧】 fénshāo burn; set on fire

fěn

粉* fěn ① powder: 磨成～ grind into powder; pulverize/ 奶～ powdered milk/ 面～ flour/ 爽身～ talcum powder/ 漂白～ bleaching powder ② noodles or vermicelli made from bean or sweet potato starch ③ white: ～墙 whitewashed wall ④ pink: ～色 pink colour ⑤ 〈方〉 whitewash: 墙刚～过。 The wall has just been whitewashed.

【粉笔】 fěnbǐ chalk
【粉红】 fěnhóng pink
【粉末】 fěnmò powder ◇ ～冶金 powder metallurgy
【粉墨登场】 fěnmò dēngchǎng make oneself up and go on stage; embark upon a political venture
【粉墙】 fěnqiáng ① whitewash a wall ② whitewashed wall
【粉身碎骨】 fěnshēn-suìgǔ have one's body smashed to pieces; die the most cruel death
【粉饰】 fěnshì gloss over; whitewash: ～太平 present a false picture of peace and prosperity
【粉刷】 fěnshuā ① whitewash 〈方〉 plaster
【粉碎】 fěnsuì ① smash; shatter; crush: ～经济封锁 smash an economic blockade/ ～军事进攻 shatter a military attack ② broken to pieces: 茶杯摔得～。 The cup was smashed to pieces.

fèn

分* fèn ① component: 盐～ salt content ② what is within one's rights or duty: 本～ one's duty/ 过～ exceeding what is proper; going too far; excessive 另见 fēn

【分量】 fènliang weight: 给足～ give full measure/ ～给不足 give short measure/ 这个铺盖卷没多少～,我拿得动。 This bedding roll isn't heavy at all, I can manage it./ 掂掂这个问题的～ consider the significance of the question; weigh the matter carefully/ 他这话说得很有～。 What he said should not be taken lightly. 或 What he has said carries a lot of weight.

【分内】 fènnèi one's job (或 duty)

【分外】 fènwài ① particularly; especially: ～高兴 particularly happy/ ～香 especially fragrant/ 老友重逢～亲。 Meeting again after a long separation, old friends are drawn to each other more closely than ever. ② not one's job (或 duty)

【分子】 fènzǐ member; element: 知识～ intellectual

份* fèn ① share; portion: 股～ stock; share/ 为建设国家出一～力 do one's bit in nation building ② 〈量〉: 一～儿礼 a gift/复写三～ make three carbon copies/ 共两～,每～都用汉语和英语写成,两种文本具有同等效力 done in duplicate, in the Chinese and English languages, both texts being equally authentic

奋* fèn ① exert oneself; act vigorously: 振～ rouse oneself ② raise; lift: ～臂一呼 raise one's hand and issue a rousing call

【奋不顾身】 fèn bù gù shēn dash ahead regardless of one's safety: 他～地抢救遇险朋友。 Completely disregarding his own safety, he rushed to rescue the friends in danger.

【奋斗】 fèndòu struggle; fight; strive: ～目标 the objective of a struggle

【奋发】 fènfā • rouse oneself; exert oneself

【奋发图强】 fènfā túqiáng go all out to make the country strong; work hard for the prosperity of the country

【奋力】 fènlì do all one can; spare no effort: 骑兵战士冲入敌群,～杀。 The cavalrymen charged into the enemy ranks, slashing furiously.

【奋勉】 fènmiǎn make a determined effort

【奋起】 fènqǐ rise with force and spirit; rise: ～抗敌 rise against the enemy/ ～自卫 rise in self-defence/ ～直追 do all one can to catch up

【奋勇】 fènyǒng summon up all one's courage and energy: ～前进 advance bravely; forge ahead courageously

【奋战】 fènzhàn fight bravely: ～到底 fight to the bitter end/ ～七天 fight for seven days on end; work without a letup for seven days

忿 fèn 见"愤" fèn

粪* fèn ① excrement; faeces; dung; droppings ② 〈书〉 apply manure: ～田 manure the fields

【粪便】 fènbiàn excrement and urine; night soil ◇ ～检查 stool examination

【粪池】 fènchí manure pit

【粪堆】 fènduī dunghill; manure pile (或 heap)

【粪桶】 fèntǒng night-soil bucket; manure bucket

【粪土】 fèntǔ dung and dirt; muck

愤* fèn indignation; anger; resentment: 公～ public indignation/ ～然离去 leave in anger; walk off in a huff

【愤愤不平】 fènfèn bùpíng be indignant; feel aggrieved; be resentful

【愤恨】 fènhèn indignantly resent; detest

【愤激】 fènjī excited and indignant; roused

【愤慨】 fènkǎi (righteous) indignation: 表示～ express one's indignation

【愤懑】 fènmèn depressed and discontented; resentful

【愤怒】 fènnù indignation; anger; wrath: ～的烈火在胸中燃烧 burn with anger; boil with rage

【愤世嫉俗】 fènshì-jísú detest the world and its ways

fēng

丰* fēng ① abundant; plentiful: ～收 a bumper harvest ② great: ～功伟绩 great achievements ③ fine-looking; handsome

【丰富】 fēngfù ① rich; abundant; plentiful: 资源～ rich in natural resources/ 积累～的资料 accumulate a wealth of data ② enrich: ～自己的生活经验 enrich one's experience of life

【丰富多彩】 fēngfù duōcǎi rich and varied; rich and colourful: ～的节日活动 varied and colourful festival activities/ 演出了～的节目 present a varied and interesting programme/ ～的传统出口商品 a rich array of traditional products for export

【丰功伟绩】 fēnggōng-wěijī great achievements; signal contributions

【丰厚】 fēnghòu ① thick: 绒毛～ rich and thick fur ② rich and generous: ～的礼品 generous gifts

【丰满】 fēngmǎn ① plentiful: 粮仓～。 The granaries are full. ② full and round; well-developed; full-grown: ～的脸盘儿 a chubby (或 plump) face/ 羽毛～ full-fledged

【丰茂】 fēngmào luxuriant; lush

【丰美】 fēngměi lush: 水草～ lush pasture

【丰年】 fēngnián bumper harvest year; good year

【丰饶】 fēngráo rich and fertile: ～的草原 fertile grassland

【丰润】 fēngrùn plump and smooth-skinned

【丰盛】 fēngshèng rich; sumptuous: ～的酒席 a sumptuous feast

【丰收】 fēngshōu bumper harvest: 连年～ bumper harvests for years running/ ～在望。 A good harvest is in sight.

【丰硕】 fēngshuò plentiful and substantial; rich: 取得～的成果 reap rich fruits; score great successes

【丰衣足食】 fēngyī-zúshí have ample food and clothing; be well-fed and well-clothed: 过着～的生活 live a life of plenty

【丰盈】 fēngyíng ① have a full figure ② plentiful

【丰裕】 fēngyù well provided for; in plenty: 生活～ live in plenty; be comfortably off

【丰足】 fēngzú abundant; plentiful: 衣食～ have plenty of food and clothing

风* fēng ① wind: ～里来,雨里去 come in the wind and go in the rain; carry out one's task even in the teeth of wind and rain ② put out to dry or air: ～干 air-dry ③ winnow: 晒干～净 sun-dried and well winnowed ④ style; practice; custom: 文～ style of writing/ 节约成～.

Thrift has become the prevailing practice./ 纠正不正之～ correct unhealthy tendencies ⑤ scene; view: ～景 scenery; landscape ⑥ news; information: 走～ leak news/ 闻～而动 act without delay upon hearing sth.

【风暴】 fēngbào windstorm; storm; tempest: 海上～ a storm at sea

【风波】 fēngbō disturbance: ～迭起。 Disturbances arose repeatedly./ 平地起～ a storm out of nowhere

【风采】 fēngcǎi elegant demeanour; graceful bearing

【风餐露宿】 fēngcān-lùsù eat in the wind and sleep in the dew — endure the hardships of an arduous journey or fieldwork

【风潮】 fēngcháo agitation; unrest: 闹～ agitate (for reform, etc.)

【风车】 fēngchē ① windmill ② winnower ③ pinwheel

【风尘】 fēngchén ① travel fatigue: 满面～ travel-stained ② hardships or uncertainties in an unstable society: 沦落～ be driven to prostitution

【风尘仆仆】 fēngchén púpú endure the hardships of a long journey; be travel-stained; be travel-worn and weary

【风驰电掣】 fēngchí-diànchè swift as the wind and quick as lightning

【风吹草动】 fēngchuī-cǎodòng the rustle of leaves in the wind — a sign of disturbance or trouble: 不要一有～,就惊慌失措。 Don't fly into a panic at the mere rustle of leaves in the wind.

【风度】 fēngdù demeanour; bearing: 有～ have poise/ ～大方 have an easy manner

【风格】 fēnggé style: 散文的～ prose style

【风光】 fēngguāng scene; view; sight: 北国～ a typical northern scene/ 好～ a wonderful sight

【风寒】 fēnghán chill; cold: 只是受了点儿～。 It's nothing but a chill./ 经常洗冷水澡可以抵御～. Taking cold baths regularly can heighten one's resistance to colds.

【风和日暖】 fēnghé-rìnuǎn bright sunshine and gentle breeze; warm and sunny weather

【风花雪月】 fēng-huā-xuě-yuè wind, flowers, snow and moon — referring originally to the subject matter typical of certain types of feudal literary works and later to the effete and sentimental writings of the exploiting classes

【风化】 fēnghuà ① morals and manners; decency: 有伤～ an offence against decency ② 〈化〉 efflorescence ③ 〈地〉 weathering

【风纪】 fēngjì conduct and discipline; discipline

【风景】 fēngjǐng scenery; landscape: 欣赏～ admire the scenery/ 以～优美著称 famous for its scenic beauty ◇ ～画 landscape painting/ ～林 scenic forest/ ～区 scenic spot

【风卷残云】 fēng juǎn cányún a strong wind scattering the last clouds — make a clean sweep of sth.

【风浪】 fēnglàng stormy waves; storm: ～大,船颠簸得很利害。 There was a heavy sea and the ship tossed terribly./ 久经～ have weathered many a storm

【风力】 fēnglì ① wind-force ② wind power

【风凉】 fēngliáng cool

【风凉话】 fēngliánghuà irresponsible and sarcastic remarks: 说～ make sarcastic comments

【风流】 fēngliú ① distinguished and admirable: ～人物 truly great men ② talented in letters and unconventional in life style ③ dissolute; loose

【风流云散】 fēngliú-yúnsàn blown apart by the wind and scattered like the clouds — (of old companions) separated and scattered

【风马牛不相及】 fēng mǎ-niú bù xiāng jí have absolutely nothing to do with each other; be totally unrelated

【风靡】 fēngmǐ fashionable: ～一时 become fashionable for a time; be all the rage at the time

【风平浪静】 fēngpíng-làngjìng the wind has subsided and the waves have calmed down; calm and tranquil

【风起云涌】 fēngqǐ-yúnyǒng like a rising wind and scudding clouds; rolling on with full force

【风气】 fēngqì general mood; atmosphere; common (或 established) practice

【风琴】 fēngqín organ

【风情】 fēngqíng amorous feelings; flirtatious expressions: 卖弄～ play the coquette; coquette

【风趣】 fēngqù humour; wit: 他是一个很有～的人。He is a man of charm and wit./ 她说话很有～。She is a witty talker.

【风骚】 fēngsāo ①〈书〉literary excellence ② coquettish

【风沙】 fēngshā sand blown by the wind: 这里春天～很大。It's very windy and dusty here in spring.

【风扇】 fēngshàn electric fan

【风尚】 fēngshàng prevailing custom (或 practice, habit): 勤俭节约的新～ a new habit of diligence and frugality

【风声】 fēngshēng rumour: 听到～ get wind of sth./ ～很紧。The situation is getting tense./ 防止走漏～ prevent leakage of information

【风声鹤唳】 fēngshēng-hèlì the sound of the wind and the cry of cranes — a fleeing army's suspicion of danger at the slightest sound

【风湿】 fēngshī 〈医〉rheumatism

【风霜】 fēngshuāng wind and frost — hardships of a journey or of one's life: 饱经～ weather-beaten; having had one's fill of hardships

【风水】 fēngshui the location of a house or tomb, supposed to have an influence on the fortune of a family; geomantic omen: 看～ practise geomancy ◇ ～先生 geomancer

【风俗】 fēngsú custom

【风速】 fēngsù wind speed; wind velocity

【风调雨顺】 fēngtiáo-yǔshùn good weather for the crops; favourable weather

【风头】 fēngtou ① the trend of events (as affecting a person): 避避～ lie low until sth. blows over ② the publicity one receives: 出～ be in the limelight

【风土】 fēngtǔ natural conditions and social customs of a place: ～人情 local conditions and customs

【风味】 fēngwèi special flavour; local colour (或 flavour): 别有～ have a distinctive flavour; 家乡～ the pleasing taste of the cooking of one's native place; local flavour

【风险】 fēngxiǎn risk; hazard: 冒～ take risks

【风向】 fēngxiàng wind direction

【风行】 fēngxíng be in fashion (或 vogue); be popular: ～一时 be popular for a while; be all the rage for a time

【风雅】 fēngyǎ ① literary pursuits ② elegant; refined: 举止～ have refined manners

【风言风语】 fēngyán-fēngyǔ groundless talk; slanderous gossip

【风雨】 fēngyǔ wind and rain; the elements; trials and hardships

【风雨飘摇】 fēng-yǔ piāoyáo swaying in the midst of a raging storm; precarious; tottering

【风雨同舟】 fēng-yǔ tóng zhōu in the same storm-tossed boat — stand together through thick and thin

【风雨无阻】 fēng-yǔ wú zǔ stopped by neither wind nor rain — regardless of the weather; rain or shine

【风云】 fēngyún wind and cloud — a stormy or unstable situation: ～突变。There is a sudden change in the situation./ ～变幻 a changeable situation

【风云人物】 fēngyún rénwù man of the hour

【风韵】 fēngyùn graceful bearing; charm

【风灾】 fēngzāi disaster caused by a windstorm: 遭受～ be hit by a windstorm

【风筝】 fēngzheng kite: 放～ fly a kite

【风烛残年】 fēngzhú cánnián old and ailing like a candle guttering in the wind

【风姿】 fēngzī graceful bearing; charm

枫 fēng 〈植〉① Chinese sweet gum ② maple

疯* fēng ① mad; insane; crazy ② (of a plant, grain crop, etc.) spindle

【疯癫】 fēngdiān insane; mad

【疯疯癫癫】 fēngfēngdiāndiān be mentally deranged; act like a lunatic; be flighty

【疯狗】 fēnggǒu mad dog; rabid dog

【疯狂】 fēngkuáng ① insane ② frenzied; unbridled: ～咒骂 frenzied vilification/ ～反扑 a desperate counterattack/ ～掠夺 unbridled plunder/ ～叫嚣 frenzied clamouring

【疯人院】 fēngrényuàn madhouse; lunatic asylum

【疯子】 fēngzi lunatic; madman

封* fēng ① seal: 把信～上 seal a letter/ ～门 seal up a door/ 大雪纷飞,江河冰～。A heavy snow is falling, and the rivers and streams have frozen over. ② bank (a fire): 炉子～了吗? Have you banked up the fire? ③ envelope: 信～ envelope ④〈量〉: 一～信 a letter ⑤ confer (a title, territory, etc.) upon: 分～ grant titles and territories to the nobles/ ～王 make sb. a prince

【封闭】 fēngbì ① seal: 用蜡～瓶口 seal a bottle with wax ② seal off; close: ～机场 close an airport

【封建】 fēngjiàn feudalism: 反～ anti-feudal/ 头脑～ feudal minded ◇ ～社会 feudal society/ ～主 feudal lord

【封口】 fēngkǒu ① seal: 这封信还没～。The letter hasn't been sealed yet. ② heal: 腿上的伤已经～了。The leg wound has healed. ③ say sth. definitive so as to prevent further discussion

【封面】 fēngmiàn ① the title page of a thread-bound book ② the front and back cover of a book ③ front cover

【封山】 fēngshān seal (或 close) a mountain pass: 大雪～。Heavy snow has sealed the mountain passes.

【封锁】 fēngsuǒ blockade; block; seal off: ～港口 blockade a port/ ～边境 close the border/ ～消息 block the passage of information/ 经济～ economic blockade ◇ ～线 blockade line; blockade

【封套】 fēngtào big envelope (for holding documents, books, etc.)

【封条】 fēngtiáo a strip of paper used for sealing (doors, drawers, etc.); paper strip seal

峰* fēng ① peak; summit: 山～ mountain peak/ 攀登科学高～ scale the heights of science/ 浪～ the crest of a wave ② hump: 驼～ camel's hump

烽 fēng beacon

【烽火】 fēnghuǒ ① beacon-fire (used to give border alarm in ancient China); beacon ② flames of war: ～连天 flames of battle raging everywhere ◇ ～台 beacon tower

锋* fēng ① the sharp point or cutting edge of a sword, etc. ② van: 先～ vanguard

【锋利】 fēnglì ① sharp; keen: ～的钢刀 a sharp knife ② incisive; sharp; poignant: ～泼辣的笔调 a sharp and pungent style

【锋芒】 fēngmáng ① cutting edge; spearhead: 斗争的～ the spearhead of struggle/ ～所向 target of attack ② talent displayed; abilities: 不露～ refrain from showing one's ability; be able but modest/ ～逼人 display one's talent in an aggressive manner

【锋芒毕露】 fēngmáng bìlù make a showy display of one's abilities

蜂* fēng ① wasp ② bee: 蜜～ honeybee/ 养～场 apiary; bee yard ③ in swarms: ～聚 gather in swarms; swarm together/ ～起 rise in swarms

【蜂巢】 fēngcháo honeycomb

【蜂刺】 fēngcì the sting of a bee or wasp

【蜂毒】 fēngdú bee venom

【蜂房】 fēngfáng any of the six-sided wax cells in a honeycomb

【蜂蜜】 fēngmì honey

【蜂王】 fēngwáng ① queen bee ② queen wasp

【蜂窝】 fēngwō ① honeycomb ② a honeycomb-like thing

【蜂拥】 fēngyōng swarm; flock: ～而来 come swarming; swarm forward

蜂巢

féng

冯 Féng a surname

逢* féng meet; come upon: 久别重～ meet again after a long separation/ ～人便问 ask whoever happens to come one's way/ 山开路，遇水搭桥 cut paths through mountains and build bridges across rivers/ ～双(单)日开放 open on even (odd) days of the month
【逢场作戏】 féng chǎng zuò xì join in the fun on occasion
【逢年过节】 féng nián guò jié on New Year's Day or other festivals
【逢凶化吉】 féng xiōng huà jí turn ill luck into good
【逢迎】 féngyíng make up to; fawn on; curry favour with: 阿谀～ flatter and toady

缝* féng stitch; sew: ～被子 stitch a quilt/ ～扣子 sew on a button
另见 fèng
【缝补】 féngbǔ sew and mend
【缝合】 fénghé 〈医〉suture; sew up: ～伤口 sew up (或 suture) a wound
【缝纫】 féngrèn sewing; tailoring ◇ ～机 sewing machine

fěng

讽 fěng ① satirize; mock: 冷嘲热～ burning satire and freezing irony ②〈书〉chant; intone
【讽刺】 fěngcì satirize; mock: 这是一部～封建文人的作品。This is a satire on feudal scholars. ◇ ～画 satirical drawing; caricature; cartoon/ ～诗 satirical poem/ ～小品 satirical essay
【讽喻】 fěngyù parable; allegory

fèng

凤 fèng phoenix
【凤凰】 fènghuáng phoenix
【凤梨】 fènglí pineapple
【凤毛麟角】 fèngmáo-línjiǎo (precious and rare as) phoenix feathers and unicorn horns; rarity of rarities

凤凰

奉* fèng ① give or present with respect: 双手～上 present respectfully with both hands/ ～上新书一册。I am forwarding you a new book. ② receive (orders, etc.): ～上级指示，暂停开放 temporarily closed on orders from above ③ esteem; revere: ～为典范 look upon as a model ④ believe in: 信～伊斯兰教 believe in Islam ⑤ wait upon; attend to: 侍～老人 attend to aged parents or grandparents
【奉承】 fèngcheng flatter; fawn upon; toady ◇ ～话 flattery
【奉告】 fènggào let sb. know; inform: 详情容后～。I'll give you the details later./ 无可～。No comment.
【奉公守法】 fènggōng-shǒufǎ be law-abiding
【奉还】 fènghuán 〈敬〉return sth. with thanks
【奉命】 fèngmìng receive orders; act under orders: ～出发 receive orders to set off•
【奉陪】 fèngpéi keep sb. company: 恕不～。Sorry, I won't be able to keep you company
【奉劝】 fèngquàn may I offer a piece of advice
【奉若神明】 fèng ruò shénmíng worship sb. or sth.; make a fetish of sth.
【奉送】 fèngsòng offer as a gift; give away free
【奉献】 fèngxiàn offer as a tribute; present with all respect
【奉养】 fèngyǎng support and wait upon (one's parents, etc.)

俸 fèng pay; salary
【俸禄】 fènglù 〈旧〉an official's salary

缝* fèng ① seam: 无～钢管 seamless steel tube ② crack; crevice; fissure: 院墙上裂了一道～儿。There is a crack in the courtyard wall.
另见 féng

【缝隙】 fèngxì chink; crack; crevice

fó

佛* fó ① Buddha ② Buddhism: 信～ believe in Buddhism ③ image of Buddha: 铜～ a bronze statue of Buddha
另见 fú
【佛法】 fófǎ ① Buddha dharma; Buddhist doctrine ② power of Buddha
【佛教】 Fójiào Buddhism ◇ ～徒 Buddhist
【佛经】 Fójīng Buddhist Scripture; Buddhist sutra
【佛门】 Fómén Buddhism ◇ ～弟子 followers of Buddhism; Buddhists
【佛象】 fóxiàng figure (或 image) of Buddha
【佛学】 Fóxué Buddhism

fǒu

否 fǒu ① negate; deny: ～认 deny ②〈书〉nay; no: 这是妥当的办法吗，～。Is that the right way to do it? No. ③〈书〉〔用在句尾表示询问〕: 知其事～? Do you know anything about it? ④〔用于"是否""能否""可否"中〕: 明日能～出发，需视天气而定。Whether or not we can start off tomorrow will depend on the weather.
另见 pǐ
【否定】 fǒudìng ① negate; deny: 事实～了他的看法。Facts have refuted his views. ② negative: ～的答复 a negative answer; an answer in the negative
【否决】 fǒujué vote down; veto; overrule: 提案被大会～了。The motion was voted down at the assembly. 或 The assembly rejected the motion. ◇ ～权 veto power; veto
【否认】 fǒurèn deny; repudiate: 我们断然～这种无理指责。We categorically reject this groundless charge.
【否则】 fǒuzé 〈连〉otherwise; if not; or else: 快点走,～要迟到了。Hurry up, or we'll be late.

fū

夫* fū ① husband ② man: 匹～ ordinary man/ 一～当关,万～莫开。If one man guards the pass, ten thousand are unable to get through. ③〈旧〉a person engaged in manual labour: 船～ boatman/ 樵～ woodcutter
【夫妇】 fū-fù husband and wife: 新婚～ newly married couple; newlyweds
【夫妻】 fū-qī man and wife
【夫人】 fūren Lady; Madame; Mrs.: 某某～ Madame So-and-so/ 各国使节和～ foreign diplomatic envoys and their wives
【夫子】 fūzǐ ① an ancient form of address to a Confucian scholar or to a master by his disciples ② pedant: 迂～ a pedantic old fogey

肤 fū skin
【肤泛】 fūfàn superficial; shallow: ～之论 shallow views
【肤浅】 fūqiǎn superficial; shallow: 我对这个问题的认识很～。I have only a superficial understanding of the problem.
【肤色】 fūsè colour of skin: 不同国度、不同～的运动员欢聚一堂。Players from different lands and of different colours were gathered happily in the same hall.

孵* fū hatch; brood; incubate: ～小鸡 hatch chickens
【孵化】 fūhuà hatching; incubation: 人工～ artificial incubation ◇ ～场 hatchery
【孵卵】 fūluǎn hatch; brood; incubate ◇ ～鸡 brooding hen/ ～期 incubation period/ ～器 incubator

敷 fū ① apply (powder, ointment, etc.): 外～ for external application ② spread; lay out: ～设 lay (pipes, etc.) ③ be sufficient for: 入不～出 unable to make ends meet

【敷设】fūshè lay: ～管道 lay pipelines/ ～铁轨 lay a railway track

【敷衍】fūyǎn elaborate; expound 又作"敷演"

【敷衍】fūyan be perfunctory; go through the motions: 她办事认真，从不～了事。She is very conscientious and never does her work perfunctorily./ 他～了几句就走了。He made a few casual remarks and left.

【敷衍了事】fūyan liǎoshì muddle through one's work

【敷衍塞责】fūyan-sèzé perform one's duty in a perfunctory manner

fú

弗 fú <书> not: 自愧～如 feel ashamed of one's inferiority

伏* fú ① bend over: ～案读书 bend over one's desk reading ② lie prostrate: ～地不动 lie still on the ground with one's face downward ③ subside; go down: 此～彼起 down here, up there ④ hide: 昼～夜出 hide by day and come out at night/ 设～ lay an ambush ⑤ hot season; dog days ⑥ admit (defeat or guilt) ⑦ <电> volt

【伏笔】fúbǐ a hint foreshadowing later developments in a story, essay, etc.; foreshadowing

【伏兵】fúbīng (troops in) ambush

【伏击】fújī ambush: 遭～ fall into an ambush

【伏贴】fútiē fit perfectly: 这身衣服穿着很～。This suit fits perfectly.

扶* fú ① support with the hand; place a hand on sb. or sth. for support: ～着栏杆上楼 walk upstairs with one's hand on the banisters/ 你～着点梯子，我上去。Hold the ladder while I climb up. ② help sb. up; straighten sth. up: ～苗 straighten up the seedlings/ 护士～起伤员，给他换药。The nurse propped up the wounded soldier and changed the dressing on his wound. ③ help; relieve: 救死～伤 heal the wounded and rescue the dying

【扶病】fúbìng in spite of illness: ～出席 be present in spite of illness

【扶持】fúchí help sustain; give aid to; help sb. to stand or walk; support: 疾病相～。When one is ill, the others take good care of him./ 伤员们互相～着练习走路。Leaning on each other for support, the wounded men practised walking./ 荷花虽好，也要绿叶～。For all its beauty the lotus needs its green leaves to set it off.

【扶老携幼】fúlǎo-xiéyòu holding the old by the arm and the young by the hand; bringing along the old and the young

【扶手】fúshou ① handrail; rail; banisters ② armrest ◇～椅 armchair

【扶养】fúyǎng provide for; foster; bring up: ～成人 bring up (a child)

【扶摇直上】fúyáo zhí shàng soar on the wings of a cyclone; rise steeply; skyrocket

【扶植】fúzhí foster; prop up

【扶助】fúzhù help; assist; support: ～老弱 help the old and the weak

芙 fú

【芙蕖】fúqú <书> lotus

【芙蓉】fúróng <植> ① cottonrose hibiscus ② lotus

芙蓉

孚 fú inspire confidence in sb.: 深～众望 enjoy great popularity; enjoy high prestige

佛* fú 见"仿佛" fǎngfú
另见 fó

拂 fú ① stroke: 春风～面 a spring breeze stroking the face ② whisk; flick: ～去桌上的尘土 whisk the dust off a desk ③ go against (sb.'s wishes): 不忍～其意 not have

the heart to go against sb.'s wishes; not wish to refuse sb.

【拂晓】fúxiǎo before dawn: ～前发起总攻 start the general offensive before dawn

【拂袖而去】fú xiù ér qù leave with a flick of one's sleeve — go off in a huff

服* fú ① clothes; dress: 工作～ work clothes ② take (medicine): 日～三次，每次两片。To be taken three times a day, two (tablets) each time. ③ serve: ～兵役 serve in the army; perform military service/ ～刑 serve a sentence ④ be convinced; obey: 你说得有道理，我～了。What you've said is reasonable. I'm convinced./ 以理～人 convince people by force of argument/ 不～指导 refuse to obey directions ⑤ be accustomed to: 不～水土 not accustomed to the climate; not acclimatized
另见 fù

【服从】fúcóng obey; submit (oneself) to; be subordinated to: ～命令 obey orders/ 少数～多数。The minority should submit to the majority. 或 The minority is subordinate to the majority.

【服毒】fúdú take poison

【服气】fúqì be convinced: 他批评得对，你别不～。His criticism is justified. You shouldn't take it amiss.

【服丧】fúsāng be in mourning (for the death of a kinsman, etc.)

【服饰】fúshì dress and personal adornment; dress

【服侍】fúshì wait upon; attend: ～病人 attend the sick

【服输】fúshū admit (或 acknowledge) defeat

【服务】fúwù give service to; be in the service of; serve: 为人民～。Serve the people./ 提高～质量 improve one's service/ ～周到 provide good service

【服刑】fúxíng serve a sentence: ～期满 complete a term of imprisonment

【服役】fúyì ① be on active service; enlist in the army: ～期间 during one's term of military service; during the period of enlistment/ ～期满 complete one's term of service ② do corvée labour

【服用】fúyòng take (medicine)

【服装】fúzhuāng dress; clothing; costume: ～整齐 be neatly dressed/ 民族～ national costume/ 她负责保管这出戏的～。She's the wardrobe mistress of this play. ◇～厂 clothing factory/ ～商店 clothes shop; clothing store/ ～设计 dress designing; costume designing

【服罪】fúzuì plead guilty; admit one's guilt

俘 fú ① capture; take prisoner: 敌军长被～。The enemy army commander was taken prisoner. ② prisoner of war; captive: 遣～ repatriate prisoners of war

【俘获】fúhuò ① capture: ～敌军一千多人 capture over 1,000 enemy troops

【俘虏】fúlǔ ① capture; take prisoner ② captive; captured personnel; prisoner of war (P.O.W.)

浮* fú ① float: 木头～在水上。Wood floats on water./ 潜水员～上来了。The diver has merged./她脸上～起了笑容。A faint smile played on her face. ② on the surface; superficial: ～土 dust on the surface ③ hollow; inflated: ～名 bubble reputation ④ excessive; surplus: ～额 surplus number/ 人～于事 be overstaffed

【浮标】fúbiāo buoy

【浮沉】fúchén now sink, now emerge; drift along: 与世～ follow the trend; swim with the tide

【浮荡】fúdàng float in the air: 歌声在空中～。The air resounded with singing.

【浮雕】fúdiāo relief (sculpture): ～群像 a relief sculpture of a group of people

【浮动】fúdòng ① float; drift: 树叶在水面上～。Leaves floated on the water. ② be unsteady; fluctuate

【浮泛】fúfàn ① <书> float about: 轻舟～ a light boat gliding past ② reveal; display: 她的脸上～着愉快的神情。Her face beamed with joy. ③ superficial; too abstract: 他的发言内容～。His speech was superficial and full of generalities.

【浮光掠影】fúguāng-lüèyǐng skimming over the surface; hasty and casual; cursory

【浮华】 fúhuá showy; ostentatious; flashy: 文辞～ florid language; an ornate style/ ～的生活 a showy and luxurious life

【浮夸】 fúkuā be boastful; exaggerate: ～作风 proneness to boasting and exaggeration

【浮力】 fúlì 〈物〉 buoyancy

【浮码头】 fúmǎtou floating pier

【浮浅】 fúqiǎn superficial; shallow

【浮现】 fúxiàn appear before one's eyes: 往事～在我眼前。 Scenes of the past rose before my eyes. 或 The past came back to my mind.

【浮想】 fúxiǎng thoughts or recollections flashing across one's mind: ～联翩 thoughts thronging one's mind

【浮云】 fúyún floating clouds

袱 fú 见"包袱" bāofu

符* fú ① a tally issued by a ruler to generals, envoys, etc., as credentials in ancient China ② symbol: 音～ musical notes ③ tally with; accord with: 与事实不～ not tally with the facts ④ magic figures drawn by Taoist priests to invoke or expel spirits and bring good or ill fortune

【符号】 fúhào ① symbol; mark: 注音～ phonetic symbol/ 标点～ punctuation mark/ 代数～ algebraic symbol/ 文字是记录语言的～。 The written word is a symbol for recording human speech. ② insignia

【符合】 fúhé accord with; tally with; conform to; be in keeping with: ～要求 accord with the demands/ ～实际情况 tally with the actual situation; conform to reality

【符咒】 fúzhòu Taoist magic figures or incantations

匐 fú 见"匍匐" púfú

幅* fú ① width of cloth: 单(双)～床单 single-(double-)width bed sheet ② size: 大～照片 a large-sized photo ③〈量〉〔用于布帛、呢绒、图画等〕: 一～画 a picture; a painting

【幅度】 fúdù range; scope; extent: 病人血压变化的～不大。 The patient's blood pressure fluctuates within a narrow range./ 粮食产量大～增长。 There was a big increase in grain production. 或 Grain output increased by a big margin.

【幅员】 fúyuán the area of a country's territory; the size of a country: ～辽阔的国家 a country with a vast territory

福* fú good fortune; blessing; happiness: 造～人类 promote the well-being of mankind; benefit mankind/ 你可不能身在～中不知～啊! Don't take your good fortune for granted.

【福利】 fúlì material benefits; well-being; welfare: 为人民谋～ work for the well-being of the people ◇ ～费 welfare funds/ ～国家 welfare state/ ～设施 welfare facilities/ ～事业 welfare projects (或 services)

【福气】 fúqi happy lot; good fortune

【福星】 fúxīng lucky star; mascot

【福音】 fúyīn ①〈基督教〉 Gospel ② glad tidings

辐 fú spoke: 轮～ the spoke of a wheel

【辐射】 fúshè 〈物〉 radiation

蝠* fú 〈动〉 bat

fǔ

甫 fǔ ①〈书〉just; only: 年～二十 have just reached the age of twenty ② one's courtesy name: 台～ your name

抚 fǔ ① comfort; console: 安～ placate; appease; pacify ② nurture; foster: ～养 foster; raise; bring up ③ stroke: ～琴〈书〉play the zither

【抚爱】 fǔ'ài caress; fondle

【抚今追昔】 fǔjīn-zhuīxī recall the past and compare it with the present; reflect on the past in the light of the present

【抚摩】 fǔmó stroke

【抚弄】 fǔnòng stroke; fondle

【抚慰】 fǔwèi comfort; console; soothe: ～灾区人民 console the people in afflicted areas

【抚恤】 fǔxù comfort and compensate a bereaved family ◇ ～金 pension for the disabled or for the family of the deceased

【抚养】 fǔyǎng foster; raise; bring up

【抚育】 fǔyù foster; nurture; tend

府* fǔ ① seat of government; government office: 首～ capital ② official residence; mansion: 总统～ presidential palace ③〈敬〉your home: 贵～ your home

【府第】 fǔdì mansion; mansion house

【府上】 fǔshang 〈敬〉① your home; your family ② your native place

斧* fǔ ① axe; hatchet

【斧头】 fǔtou axe; hatchet

【斧正】 fǔzhèng (please) make corrections

釜 fǔ a kind of cauldron used in ancient China

【釜底抽薪】 fǔ dǐ chōu xīn take away the firewood from under the cauldron — take a drastic measure to deal with a situation

【釜底游鱼】 fǔ dǐ yóuyú a fish swimming in the bottom of a cauldron — a person whose fate is sealed

俯 fǔ ① bow (one's head): ～视 overlook

【俯冲】 fǔchōng 〈航空〉dive ◇ ～轰炸 dive bombing

【俯瞰】 fǔkàn look down at; overlook: 从飞机上～海面 look down on the sea from a plane ◇ ～摄影 crane (或 boom) shot

【俯拾即是】 fǔ shí jí shì can be found everywhere; be extremely common: 这类事例～。 Such instances are extremely common.

【俯视】 fǔshì look down at; overlook

【俯首】 fǔshǒu bow one's head (in submission): ～就范 meekly submit; surrender without a struggle/ ～帖耳 be docile and obedient; be all obedience; be servile/ ～听命 obey submissively

【俯仰】 fǔ-yǎng a bending or lifting of the head — a simple move or action: 随人～ be at sb.'s beck and call

脯 fǔ ① dried meat: 鹿～ dried venison ② preserved fruit: 桃～ preserved peaches 另见 pú

辅 fǔ assist; complement; supplement: 相～相成 complement each other

【辅币】 fǔbì fractional currency (或 money): 硬～ subsidiary coin; minor coin

【辅导】 fǔdǎo give guidance in study or training; coach: 学习这篇文章,你给我们～～好不好? Could you give us some guidance in studying this article? 个别～ individual coaching (或 tutorial)

【辅助】 fǔzhù ① assist ② supplementary; auxiliary; subsidiary

腑 fǔ 见"脏腑" zàngfǔ

腐* fǔ ① rotten; putrid; stale; corroded: 流水不～。 Running water is never stale./ ～肉 rotten meat ② bean curd

【腐败】 fǔbài ① rotten; putrid; decayed: ～的食物 putrid food ② corrupt; rotten: ～无能 corrupt and incompetent

【腐化】 fǔhuà ① degenerate; corrupt; dissolute; depraved: ～堕落 morally degenerate/ 生活～ lead a dissolute (或 dissipated) life ② rot; decay ◇ ～分子 degenerate; a depraved person

【腐烂】 fǔlàn ① decomposed; putrid ② corrupt; rotten

【腐蚀】 fǔshí ① corrode; etch ② corrupt; corrode

【腐朽】 fǔxiǔ ① rotten; decayed: 这些木材已经～了。 The timber has rotted. ② decadent; degenerate

fù

父* fù ①father ②male relative of a senior generation: 伯～ one's father's elder brother; uncle/ 祖～ grandfather
【父老】 fùlǎo elders (of a country or district): ～兄弟 elders and brethren
【父母】 fù-mǔ father and mother; parents
【父亲】 fùqin father
【父权制】 fùquánzhì patriarchy
【父系】 fùxì paternal line; the father's side of the family ◇ ～亲属 relatives on the paternal side
【父兄】 fù-xiōng ①father and elder brothers ②head of a family

讣 fù obituary
【讣告】 fùgào ① announce sb.'s death ② obituary (notice)
【讣闻】 fùwén obituary (notice)

付* fù ①hand (或 turn) over to; commit to: 交～审讯 hand over to the law; commit to trial/ ～表决 put to the vote/ ～诸实施 put into effect/ ～之一笑 dismiss with a laugh ②pay: ～税 pay taxes
【付出】 fùchū pay; expend: ～代价 pay a price
【付款】 fùkuǎn pay a sum of money: 货到～ cash on delivery (C.O.D.)/ 凭单～ cash against documents ◇ ～办法 methods of payment/ ～凭证 payment voucher/ ～人 payer; drawee
【付清】 fùqīng pay in full; pay off; clear (a bill): 一次～ pay off in one lump sum
【付托】 fùtuō put sth. in sb.'s charge; entrust: ～得人 have entrusted the matter to the right person/ ～重任 charge sb. with a heavy responsibility
【付印】 fùyìn ①send to the press ②turn over to the printing shop (after proofreading)
【付邮】 fùyóu take to the post; post
【付帐】 fùzhàng pay a bill
【付之一炬】 fù zhī yī jù commit to the flames
【付诸东流】 fù zhū dōngliú thrown into the eastward flowing stream — all one's efforts wasted; irrevocably lost

负* fù ①carry on the back or shoulder; shoulder; bear: ～薪 carry firewood on one's back/ 如释重～ feel as if relieved of a heavy load; feel greatly relieved/ 身～重任 shoulder an important task/ ～主要责任 assume the main responsibility ②have at one's back; rely on: ～险固守 put up a stubborn defence by relying on one's strategic position ③suffer; ～屈 suffer an injustice; be wronged/ ～伤 get wounded ④enjoy: 久～盛名 have long enjoyed a good reputation ⑤owe: ～债 be in debt ⑥fail in one's duty, obligation, etc.; betray: ～约 break a promise; 忘恩～义 lose (a battle, game, etc.); be defeated: 一比二～于对方 lose the match 1:2/ 该队以二胜一～的成绩取得小组第二名。 The team finished second in its group with two wins and one defeat./ 不分胜～ end in a draw; end in a tie; break even ⑧<数> minus; negative: ～一点五 minus one point five (-1.5)/ ～号 negative sign ⑨<电> negative
【负担】 fùdān ①bear (a burden); shoulder: 旅费由东道国～。 All the travelling expenses will be borne by the host country. ②burden; load; encumbrance: 财政～ financial burden/ 家庭～ family burden (esp. financial)/ 工作～ load of work; work load/ 思想～ a load on one's mind; mental burden/ 减轻学生～ lighten the students' load/ 解除精神～ free one's mind of encumbrances
【负荆请罪】 fùjīng qǐngzuì proffer a birch and ask for a flogging — offer a humble apology
【负疚】 fùjiù <书> feel apologetic; have a guilty conscience
【负片】 fùpiàn <摄> negative
【负气】 fùqì do sth. in a fit of pique:～而去 leave angrily out of spite
【负伤】 fùshāng be wounded; be injured: 光荣～ be wounded in action

【负隅顽抗】 fùyú wánkàng (of an enemy or a robber) fight stubbornly with one's back to the wall; put up a desperate struggle
【负约】 fùyuē break a promise; go back on one's word
【负载】 fùzài <电> load: 高峰～ peak load/ 工作～ operating load ◇ ～调整 load regulation
【负责】 fùzé ① be responsible for; be in charge of: 由此产生的一切后果由你方～。 Your side will be held responsible for all the consequences arising therefrom./ 他～保卫工作。 He is in charge of security affairs. ② conscientious: 她对工作很～。 She is very conscientious in her work.
【负债】 fùzhài be in debt; incur debts: ～累累 be heavily in debt; be up to one's eyes in debt/ 资产与～ assets and liabilities

妇* fù ① woman: ～孺 women and children ② married woman: 少～ young married woman ③ wife: 夫～ husband and wife
【妇科】 fùkē (department of) gynaecology ◇ ～医生 gynaecologist
【妇女】 fùnǚ woman
【妇人】 fùrén married woman

附* fù ①add; attach; enclose: ～上一笔 add a word or two (in a letter, etc.)/ ～表 attached list or chart/ ～寄一张照片 enclosed herewith a photo ②get close to; be near: ～在耳边低声说话 whisper in sb.'s ear ③agree to: ～议 second a motion
【附带】 fùdài ① in passing: ～说一下 mention in passing; by the way; incidentally ② attach: 我们提供的援助不～任何条件。 The aid we provide has no strings attached.
【附耳】 fù'ěr move close to sb.'s ear: ～低语 whisper in sb.'s ear
【附和】 fùhè echo; chime in with: ～别人的意见 echo other people's views/ 随声～ chime in with others
【附会】 fùhuì draw wrong conclusions by false analogy; strain one's interpretation: 穿凿～ give strained interpretations and draw farfetched analogies
【附加】 fùjiā ①add; attach: 文件后面～两项说明。 The document has two explanatory notes attached to it. ② additional; attached; appended
【附件】 fùjiàn ①appendix; annex: 作为调查报告的～ as an appendix to the investigation report ②enclosure
【附近】 fùjìn ①nearby; neighbouring: ～地区 nearby regions/ ～的城市 neighbouring (或 adjacent) towns ②close to; in the vicinity of: 住在工厂～ live close to the factory/ ～有没有邮局？ Is there a post office near here?
【附录】 fùlù appendix
【附上】 fùshàng enclosed herewith: 随信～商品目录一份。 A catalogue of commodities is enclosed herewith./ ～样稿一份,请查收。 Enclosed please find a set of sample sheets.
【附设】 fùshè have as an attached institution: 这个学院～一所中学。 There is a middle school attached to the institute./ 这个商店～了一个早晚服务部。 This store has set up an after-hours department.
【附属】 fùshǔ subsidiary; auxiliary; attached; affiliated: 医学院～医院 a hospital attached to a medical college ◇ ～国 dependency/ ～机构 subsidiary body/ ～品 accessory; appendage
【附图】 fùtú attached map or drawing; figure: 见～一。 See Figure 1.
【附言】 fùyán postscript (P.S.)
【附议】 fùyì second a motion; support a proposal: 我～! I second that!
【附庸】 fùyōng dependency; vassal; appendage
【附注】 fùzhù notes appended to a book, etc.; annotations
【附着】 fùzhuó adhere to; stick to: 这种病菌～在病人使用过的东西上。 This germ is found on things used by the patients

服 fù <量> [用于中药] dose: 一～药 a dose of medicine
另见 fú

驸 fù
【驸马】 fùmǎ emperor's son-in-law

赴 fù go to; attend: ～约 keep an appointment/ ～宴 attend a banquet

【赴难】 fùnàn go to the aid of one's country; go to help save the country from danger

【赴任】 fùrèn go to one's post; be on the way to one's post

【赴汤蹈火】 fùtāng-dǎohuǒ go through fire and water

复 fù ① duplicate: ～本 a duplicate ② compound; complex: ～姓 compound surname; two-character surname/ ～光谱 complex spectrum ③ turn round; turn over: 翻来～去睡不着 toss in bed, unable to sleep ④ answer; reply: 请即电～ Cable reply immediately. ⑤ recover; resume: 祝早日康～ Best wishes for an early recovery./ ～职 resume one's post ⑥ revenge: 报～ retaliate; take revenge ⑦ again: 周而～始 go round and begin again/ 一去不～返 gone never to return

【复仇】 fùchóu revenge; avenge: ～心理 vindictiveness; a desire for revenge

【复电】 fùdiàn telegram in reply (to one received)

【复发】 fùfā have a relapse; recur: 旧病～ have an attack of an old illness; have a relapse

【复工】 fùgōng return to work (after a strike or layoff)

【复古】 fùgǔ restore ancient ways; return to the ancients

【复合】 fùhé compound; complex; composite ◇ ～词〈语〉 compound (word)

【复活】 fùhuó ① bring back to life; revive ②〈基督教〉Resurrection ◇ ～节 Easter

【复交】 fùjiāo 〈外〉 reestablish (或 resume) diplomatic relations

【复刊】 fùkān resume publication

【复课】 fùkè resume classes

【复述】 fùshù ① repeat: ～命令 repeat an order ② retell (in language learning): 把故事～一遍 retell a story

【复苏】 fùsū ① ①come back to life or consciousness; resuscitate ② recovery

【复习】 fùxí review; revise: ～功课 review (或 revise) lessons

【复写】 fùxiě make carbon copies; duplicate ◇ ～纸 carbon paper

【复信】 fùxìn ① write a letter in reply ② letter in reply; reply

【复兴】 fùxīng revive; resurge; rejuvenate: 民族～ national rejuvenation/ 文艺～ the Renaissance

【复姓】 fùxìng compound surname; two-character surname

【复印】 fùyìn 〈印〉 duplicate ◇ ～机 duplicator; duplicating machine/ ～纸 duplicating paper

【复原】 fùyuán ① recover from an illness; be restored to health: 他身体已经～了。 He's already recovered. ② restore; rehabilitate

【复杂】 fùzá complicated; complex: 情况～。 The situation is complicated./ 故事情节～。 The story is very complicated./ ～的心情 mixed feelings/ 使问题～化 make things complicated; complicate matters

【复职】 fùzhí resume one's post; be reinstated

【复制】 fùzhì duplicate; reproduce; make a copy of ◇ ～模型 reconstructed model/ ～片 duplicated film; copy of a film/ ～品 replica; reproduction

副 fù ① deputy; assistant; vice-: ～主席 vice-chairman/ ～总理 vice-premier/ ～部长 vice-minister/ ～领事 vice-consul/ ～书记 deputy secretary/ ～秘书长 deputy secretary-general/ ～主任 deputy director/ ～司令员 assistant commanding officer (或 commandant)/ ～教授 associate professor/ (飞机) ～驾驶员 copilot ② auxiliary; subsidiary; secondary: ～泵 auxiliary pump ③ correspond to; fit: 名不～实。 The name falls short of the reality. ④〈量〉〔用于成套的东西或用于面部表情〕: 一～手套 a pair of gloves/ 装出一～笑脸 put on a false smile; assume a smiling face

【副本】 fùběn duplicate; transcript; copy

【副标题】 fùbiāotí subheading; subtitle

【副产品】 fùchǎnpǐn by-product

【副词】 fùcí 〈语〉 ① (in Chinese grammar) adverbial word, any of a class of words that are used mainly to modify a verb or an adjective ② (in English grammar) adverb

【副刊】 fùkān supplement: 文学～ literary supplement

【副手】 fùshǒu assistant

【副署】 fùshǔ countersign

【副业】 fùyè sideline; side occupation: ～生产 sideline (或 supplementary, subsidiary) production/ 家庭～ household sideline production

【副作用】 fùzuòyòng side effect; by-effect: 麻醉药物的～ side effects from the use of anaesthetics

富 fù rich; wealthy; abundant: ～日子当穷日子过。 Be thrifty even in days of abundance./ ～于养分 be rich in nutrition/ ～于创造性 be highly creative

【富国强兵】 fù guó qiáng bīng make one's country rich and build up its military power

【富贵】 fùguì riches and honour; wealth and rank

【富豪】 fùháo rich and powerful people

【富丽堂皇】 fùlì tánghuáng sumptuous; gorgeous; splendid

【富强】 fùqiáng prosperous and strong: 使国家更加繁荣～ make our country more prosperous and powerful

【富饶】 fùráo richly endowed; fertile; abundant: 美丽～的国家 a beautiful and richly endowed country/ ～的土地 fertile land

【富庶】 fùshù rich and populous

【富翁】 fùwēng man of wealth

【富有】 fùyǒu ① rich; wealthy ② rich in; full of: ～经验 rich in experience; very experienced/ ～代表性 typical/ 是～生命力的 be full of vitality

【富裕】 fùyù prosperous; well-to-do; well-off

【富余】 fùyu have more than needed; have enough and to spare: 粮食有～ have a surplus of grain/ 我们还～两张票。 We have two tickets to spare.

【富足】 fùzú plentiful; abundant; rich

赋 fù ① bestow on; endow with; vest with: 秉～ natural endowments ② tax: 田～ land tax ③ fu, descriptive prose interspersed with verse ④ compose (a poem): ～诗一首 compose a poem

【赋税】 fùshuì taxes

【赋闲】 fùxián (of an official, etc.) be unemployed

傅 fù ① teach; instruct ② teacher; instructor ③ lay on; apply: ～彩 lay on colours/ ～粉 put powder on; powder (the face, etc.)

腹 fù belly; abdomen; stomach

【腹背受敌】 fù-bèi shòu dí be attacked front and rear

【腹地】 fùdì hinterland

【腹稿】 fùgǎo a draft worked out in one's mind; mental notes

【腹痛】 fùtòng abdominal pain

【腹泻】 fùxiè diarrhoea

【腹心】 fùxīn ① true thoughts and feelings: 敢布～ venture to air some of my views ② 见"心腹" xīnfù ①

缚 fù tie up; bind fast: 手无～鸡之力 lack the strength to truss a chicken — physically very weak

赙 fù

【赙仪】 fùyí 〈书〉 a gift to a bereaved family

蝮 fù

【蝮蛇】 fùshé Pallas pit viper

覆 fù 〈书〉① cover ② overturn; upset: ～舟 capsized boat/ 前车之～,后车之鉴。The overturned cart ahead is a warning to the cart behind.

【覆巢无完卵】 fù cháo wú wánluǎn when the nest is overturned no egg stays unbroken — in a great disaster no one can escape unscathed

【覆盖】 fùgài ① cover: 积雪～着地面。The ground is covered with snow. ② plant cover; vegetation

【覆灭】 fùmiè destruction; complete collapse

【覆没】 fùmò ①〈书〉capsize and sink ② be overwhelmed; be annihilated: 敌人全军～。The enemy's whole army was destroyed.

【覆水难收】 fù shuǐ nán shōu spilt water can't be gathered up — what is done can't be undone

【覆亡】 fùwáng fall (of an empire, nation, etc.)

【覆辙】 fùzhé the track of an overturned cart: 重蹈～ take the same disastrous road

馥 fù 〈书〉fragrance

【馥郁】 fùyù 〈书〉strong fragrance; heavy perfume: ～的花香 the strong scent of flowers

fu

咐 fu 见"吩咐" fēnfu; "嘱咐" zhǔfu

G

gā

咖* gā
另见 kā
【咖喱】 gālí　curry: ～牛肉 beef curry ◇ ～粉 curry powder

嘎 gā
【嘎嘎】 gāgā　〈象〉〔鸭叫声〕quack
【嘎吱】 gāzhī　〈象〉〔物体受压力而发出的声音,多叠用〕creak: 行李压得扁担～～直响。The shoulder pole creaked under the weight of the luggage.

gà

尬 gà　见"尴尬" gāngà

gāi

该* gāi ① ought to; should: 这事你早就～办了! You ought to have done it long ago./ 本来如此。That's just as it should be./ 这会儿～开了。The meeting is long overdue./ ～干的都干了。All that needs to be done has been done./ 我们～走了。It's time we were leaving. ② be sb.'s turn to do sth.: 这一回～我了吧! It's my turn now, isn't it?/ 下一个～谁发言? Who's the next speaker? ③ deserve: 他～受到表扬。He deserves to be commended./ ～谁叫他不守纪律。It serves him right, he shouldn't have broken the rules. ④ most likely; probably; ought to; should: 再走一个钟头就～到了。We ought to (或 should) be able to get there in another hour./ 你明年春天再来,水库就～完工了。When you come again next spring, the reservoir will have been completed. ⑤〔用在感叹句中加强语气〕: 她的责任～有多重啊! How heavy her responsibilities are!/ 要是水泵今天就运到,～多好哇! If only the pump could arrive today! ⑥ owe: 我不～他钱。I don't owe him any money./ 没带钱不要紧,先～着吧。It doesn't matter if you haven't brought any money with you. You can have it on credit. ⑦〔多用于公文〕this; that; the said; the above-mentioned: ～厂 this (或 the said) factory/ ～校 that (或 the above-mentioned) school/ ～项工作 the job (或 work) in question
【该当】 gāidāng ① deserve: ～何罪? What punishment do you think you deserve? ② should: 集体的事,我们～尽力。It's for the collective and we should do our best.
【该死】 gāisǐ　〈口〉〔表示厌恶或愤恨的话〕: ～的天气! What wretched weather!/ 这牛又在吃麦子啦!真～! That damned cow's eating the wheat again!/ ～! 我又忘了带钥匙了。Oh, no! I've forgotten my key again.

赅 gāi　〈书〉complete; full: 言简意～ terse but comprehensive

gǎi

改* gǎi ① change; transform: 几年没来,这儿完全～样了。I've been away for only a few years, but the place has completely changed./ ～洼地为稻田 transform waterlogged land into paddy fields ② alter; revise: ～灶节煤 make alterations in an oven so that it will burn less coal/ 请把这条裤子～短一些。Please have this pair of trousers shortened./ 这个戏已经～了好多次了。The play has been revised many times. ③ correct; rectify; put right: ～作业 correct students' homework or papers ④〔后接动词〕switch over to (doing sth. else): ～种水稻 switch over to growing rice,
【改编】 gǎibiān ① adapt; rearrange; revise: 这支歌已～成小提琴曲。The music of the song has been rearranged (或 adapted) for the violin./ 经过～,戏的主题更突出了。The theme of the play stands out even more clearly now that it's been revised./ 根据这本小说～的剧本 a stage version of the novel ② reorganize; redesignate: 把七个师～为六个师 reorganize seven divisions into six
【改变】 gǎibiàn　change; alter; transform: ～主意 change one's mind/ 人们的精神面貌～了。People's spiritual complexion has changed
【改朝换代】 gǎicháo-huàndài　change of dynasty or regime; dynastic changes
【改道】 gǎidào ① change one's route: 他们决定～先去巴黎。They decided to change their route and go to Paris first. ② (of a river) change its course: 历史上,黄河曾多次～。The Huanghe River has changed its course many times over the centuries.
【改掉】 gǎidiào　give up; drop: ～坏习惯 give up bad habits
【改动】 gǎidòng　change; alter; modify: 文字上作少许～ make a few changes in wording
【改恶从善】 gǎi'è-cóngshàn　abandon evil and do good; turn over a new leaf; mend one's ways
【改革】 gǎigé　reform: 土地(或 agrarian)～ land reform/ 文字～ reform of a writing system/ 工具～ improvement of tools
【改观】 gǎiguān　change the appearance (或 face) of: 第二次世界大战后,世界的面貌大大～了。The face of the world has changed greatly since the Second World War./ 这一胜利使战争形势为之～。This victory changed the complexion of the war./ 昔日荒山已经大为～。The barren hills of yesterday have changed considerably.
【改过】 gǎiguò　mend one's ways; correct one's mistakes: ～自新 correct one's errors and make a fresh start; mend one's ways; turn over a new leaf
【改行】 gǎiháng　change one's profession (或 occupation, trade)
【改换】 gǎihuàn　change over to; change: ～一套新的做法 change over to new ways; adopt a new approach/ ～日期 change the date/ ～名称 rename
【改嫁】 gǎijià　(of a woman) remarry
【改建】 gǎijiàn　reconstruct; rebuild
【改进】 gǎijìn　improve; make better: ～工作作风 improve one's work style/ 有～就好。If you've improved, that's good.
【改口】 gǎikǒu　withdraw or modify one's previous remark; correct oneself: 他发现自己说错了,连忙～。He corrected himself as soon as he found he had made a mistake./ 他原来是那么说的,现在～了。That's what he said first, but he's changed it now.
【改良】 gǎiliáng ① improve; ameliorate: ～土壤 improve (或 ameliorate) the soil/ ～家畜品种 improve the breed of domestic animals ② reform ◇ ～派 reformists
【改期】 gǎiqī　change the date: 会议～举行。The meeting has been postponed.
【改日】 gǎirì　another day; some other day: 我们～再商量吧! Let's talk it over another day. 又作"改天"
【改善】 gǎishàn　improve; ameliorate: ～劳动条件 improve working conditions/ 两国关系有所～。The relations between the two countries have shown some improvement
【改头换面】 gǎitóu-huànmiàn　〈贬〉change the appearance; dish up in a new form
【改弦易辙】 gǎixián-yìzhé　change one's course; strike out on a new path
【改邪归正】 gǎixié-guīzhèng　give up evil and return to good; turn over a new leaf
【改写】 gǎixiě　rewrite; adapt: 经过～,文章生动多了。Rewriting has livened up the article

【改正】gǎizhèng　correct; amend; put right: ～错误 correct one's mistakes

【改组】gǎizǔ　reorganize; reshuffle: ～管理机构 reorganize the management/ ～内阁 reshuffle the cabinet

gài

丏* gài 〈书〉① beg ② beggar

芥 gài　另见 jiè
【芥菜】gàicài 〈植〉leaf mustard　另见 jiècài
【芥蓝】gàilán 〈植〉cabbage mustard

钙 gài 〈化〉calcium (Ca)

盖* gài ① lid; cover: 茶壶～ teapot lid/ 轴承～ 〈机〉 bearing cap (或 cover)/ 引擎～ bonnet (或 hood) of an engine ② shell (of a tortoise, crab, etc.) ③ canopy: 亭亭 如～ (of a tree) stand towering with a canopy of leaves ④ cover: 用塑料薄膜～住秧苗 cover the seedlings with plastic sheeting/ 箱子没～严。The lid of the box hasn't been put on right. 或 The box isn't closed properly./ 他昨天晚上没～好，着凉了。He didn't cover himself up well last night and now he's got a cold. ⑤ affix (a seal) ⑥ build: ～新房 build new houses

【盖棺论定】gài guān lùn dìng　final judgment can be passed on a person only when the lid is laid on his coffin

【盖世】gàishì　unparalleled; matchless; peerless: ～英雄 peerless hero/ ～无双 unparalleled anywhere in the world

【盖章】gàizhāng　affix one's seal; seal; stamp: 由本人签字～ to be signed and sealed by the recipient or applicant

【盖子】gàizi　① lid; cover; cap; top: 水壶～ the lid of a kettle/ 瓶～ bottle top

溉 gài 见"灌溉" guàngài

概 gài ① general; approximate: ～而论之 generally speaking ② without exception; all: ～莫能外 admit of no exception whatsoever/ ～不追究 no action will be taken (against sb. for his past offences)/ 药品售出，～ 不退换。Once medicines leave the store they may not be returned. ③ the manner of carrying oneself; deportment: 气～ mettle; spirit

【概观】gàiguān　general survey

【概况】gàikuàng　general situation; survey: 《非洲～》A Survey of Africa/ 我把这里的～介绍一下。I'll give a brief account of how things are in this place.

【概括】gàikuò　① summarize; generalize; epitomize: 这部小说的优点～起来有以下几方面。The good points of the novel may be summarized as follows./ ～起来说 to sum up/ 高度的艺术～ a highly artistic condensation ② briefly; in broad outline: ～地说 to put it briefly/ 请把你的看法～地讲一讲。Please give your views in broad outline.

【概括性】gàikuòxìng　generality: 最后这段话～很强。The last paragraph is a succinct summary.

【概略】gàilüè　outline; summary: 这只是故事的～。This is only an outline of the story.

【概论】gàilùn 〔多用于书名〕outline; introduction: 《地质学～》An Introduction to Geology

【概念】gàiniàn　concept; conception; notion; idea: 基本～ fundamental conception; basic concept

【概要】gàiyào 〔多用于书名〕essentials; outline: 《汉语语法～》Essentials of Chinese Grammar

gān

干* gān ① 〈古〉shield ② 〈书〉offend: ～犯 offend have to do with; be concerned with; be implicated in: 与你何～? What has this to do with you?/ 这事与我无～。It has nothing to do with me. 或 It's none of my business.

④ dry: 这天气洗衣服～得慢。The washing dries slowly in this weather./ 池塘快～了。The pond is running dry./ 口 ～ thirsty/ 油漆未～。Wet paint. ⑤ dried food: 豆腐～儿 dried bean curd/ 萝卜～儿 dried radish/ 牛肉～儿 dried beef; jerked beef ⑥ empty; hollow; dry: 外强中～ outwardly strong but inwardly weak/ ～号 cry aloud but shed no tears; affected wailing ⑦ taken into nominal kinship: ～儿子 (nominally) adopted son ⑧ (do sth.) for nothing; futilely: 他们上午不来，我们别～等了。They're not coming this morning. Let's not waste time waiting for them.
另见 gàn

【干巴巴】gānbābā　dull and dry; insipid; dryasdust; dull as ditchwater: ～的土地 parched land/ 文章写得～的。The article is dull.

【干杯】gānbēi　drink a toast: 我提议为两国人民的友谊～! I now propose a toast to the friendship between our two peoples — to our friendship!/ 为朋友们的健康～! Here's to the health of our friends — to your health!/ 老王，～! Lao Wang, cheers!

【干脆】gāncuì　① clear-cut; straightforward: 他回答得很～。His answer was clear-cut and straightforward. 或 He gave a clear-cut reply./ 我～跟你说吧。I'll be frank with you./ 一点嘛! Make it snappy! 或 Be quick about it! ② simply; just; altogether: 你～说"行"还是"不行"。Just say yes or no./ 她～不承认有这回事。She simply denied that such a thing had ever happened.

【干戈】gāngē　weapons of war; arms; war: 动～ take up arms; go to war

【干果】gānguǒ　① dry fruit (e.g. nuts) ② dried fruit

【干旱】gānhàn　(of weather or soil) arid; dry

【干净】gānjìng　① clean; neat and tidy: 把院子扫～ sweep the yard clean/ 屋子收拾得挺～。The room is neat and tidy./ 干干净净过春节 give every place a thorough cleaning for the Spring Festival ② completely; totally: 把谷子扬～ winnow the grain thoroughly/ 忘得干干净净 have completely forgotten; clean forgot

【干净利落】gānjìng-lìluo　neat and tidy; neat; efficient: 这一仗打得～。The battle was neatly won./ 他办事～。He's very efficient.

【干咳】gānké　dry cough

【干枯】gānkū　dried-up; withered; shrivelled; wizened: ～的树木 withered trees/ ～的皮肤 wizened skin/ 小河～了。The stream has dried up.

【干粮】gānliang　solid food (prepared for a journey); field rations; rations for a journey: 明天郊游，请自带～。Bring your own food on tomorrow's outing. ◇ ～袋 haversack; ration bag

【干扰】gānrǎo　① disturb; interfere; obstruct: 把收音机开小点儿，别～人家。Turn down the radio, or you'll disturb people. ② 〈电〉interference; jam

【干涉】gānshè　① interfere; intervene; meddle: 外来～ external interference/ 武装～ armed intervention/ 互不～内政 noninterference in each other's internal affairs ② 〈物〉 interference: 相长(相消)～ constructive (destructive) interference

【干洗】gānxǐ　dry-clean; dry cleaning

【干笑】gānxiào　hollow laugh

【干薪】gānxīn　salary drawn for a sinecure: 领～ hold a sinecure

【干预】gānyù　intervene; interpose; meddle: 这是你们内部的事情，我们不便～。This is your internal affair; it is not for us to interfere.

【干燥】gānzào　① dry; arid: 气候～ arid climate/ 大便～ constipated; costive ② dull; uninteresting: ～无味 dryasdust; dull

【干着急】gānzháojí　be anxious but unable to do anything

甘* gān ① sweet; pleasant: ～泉 sweet spring water ② willingly; of one's own accord: 不～落后 unwilling to lag behind

【甘拜下风】gān bài xiàfēng　candidly admit defeat (in friendly competition, etc.)

【甘苦】gānkǔ　① sweetness and bitterness; weal and woe

同甘共苦 share the joys and sorrows ② hardships and difficulties experienced in work: 没有搞过这种工作，就不知道其中的～。You don't know how difficult the job is, unless you have done it yourself.

【甘心】 gānxīn ① willingly; readily: ～情愿 willingly and gladly ② be reconciled to; resign oneself to; be content with

【甘休】 gānxiū be willing to give up: 试验不成功，决不～。We won't give up until the experiment succeeds.

【甘愿】 gānyuàn willingly; readily

【甘蔗】 gānzhe sugarcane: ～没有两头甜。A sugarcane is never sweet at both ends — you can't have it both ways.

杆 gān pole; staff: 旗～ flagstaff; flagpole/ 电线～ pole (for telephone or electric power lines, etc.)
另见 gǎn

【杆子】 gānzi pole

肝* gān liver

【肝癌】 gān'ái 〈医〉cancer of the liver

【肝胆】 gāndǎn ① liver and gall: ～俱裂 overwhelmed by grief or terror; heart-broken or terror-stricken ② heroic spirit; courage: ～过人 unsurpassed in valour ③ openheartedness; sincerity: ～相照 show utter devotion to (a friend, etc.)

【肝火】 gānhuǒ irascibility: 动～ get worked up; fly into a rage/ ～旺 hot-tempered; irascible

【肝脑涂地】 gān-nǎo tú dì (ready to) die the cruelest death

柑* gān mandarin orange

【柑橘】 gānjú ① oranges and tangerines ② citrus ◇ ～酱 marmalade

【柑子】 gānzi mandarin orange

竿* gān pole; rod: 竹～ bamboo pole/ 钓鱼～ fishing rod

【竿子】 gānzi bamboo pole: 一～插到底 carry (a task or directive) right down to the grass-roots level

尴 gān

【尴尬】 gāngà awkward; embarrassed: 处境～ in an awkward position; in a dilemma/ 样子十分～ look very much embarrassed

gǎn

杆 gǎn ① the shaft or arm of sth.: 秤～ the arm of a steelyard/ 钢笔～儿 penholder/ 枪～ the barrel of a rifle/ 保险～ 〈机〉bumper bar/ 调整～ 〈机〉adjusting rod ② 〈量〉〔用于有杆的器物〕: 一～秤 a steelyard/ 一～枪 a rifle/ 一～旗 a flag
另见 gān

赶* gǎn ① catch up with; overtake: ～先进 catch up with the advanced/ 后进的也～上来了。Those who lagged behind have caught up./ 要说摘棉花，可谁也～不上她。Nobody can keep up with her in picking cotton./ 她已经～到大伙儿前头去了。She's shot ahead of all the rest of us. ② try to catch; make a dash for; rush for: ～头班车 catch the first bus/ 火车七点三十分开，我们～得及吗？The train leaves at 7:30. Can we make it? ③ hurry (或 rush) through: ～任务 rush through one's job/ ～前不～后。It's better to hurry at the beginning than to do things in a rush at the last moment./ 他连夜～写了一份报告。He dashed off a report that very night./ ～调了一个团到灾区去帮助救灾。A regiment was rushed to the stricken area to help with relief work. ④ drive: 大车～ drive a cart/ 把羊～到山上去放 drive the sheep up the hill to graze ⑤ drive away; expel: 把敌人～走 drive the enemy away; throw out the enemy

【赶紧】 gǎnjǐn lose no time; hasten: ～刹车 quickly put on the brakes/ ～解释 hasten to explain/ 发现情况，～报告。If you find anything unusual, report at once./ 他～吃了饭就上工地去了。He had a hurried meal and made for the construction site.

【赶尽杀绝】 gǎnjìn-shājué spare none; be ruthless

【赶快】 gǎnkuài at once; quickly: ～跟我走。Come along with me 'at once./ ～把这块地收完。Let's finish reaping this plot quickly./ ～! Be quick! 或 Hurry up!

【赶路】 gǎnlù hurry on with one's journey: 快休息吧，明天一早还要～呢。Let's go to bed right away. We must push on with our journey early tomorrow morning./ 赶了一天路，累了吧？Aren't you tired after such a hard day's journey?

【赶忙】 gǎnmáng hurry; hasten; make haste: 趁还没熄灯，他～把最后两页书看完。He hurried through the last two pages before lights-out./ 他～道歉。He hastened to apologize.

【赶上】 gǎnshàng ① overtake; catch up with; keep pace with: ～先进单位 catch up with the advanced units/ ～时代的发展 keep abreast of the times/ 我们的认识常常赶不上形势的发展。Our knowledge often fails to keep pace with the march of events. ② run into (a situation); be in time for: 我到美国那天正～过国庆。It happened to be National Day when I arrived in America

【赶时髦】 gǎn shímáo follow the fashion; try to be in the swim

敢* gǎn ① bold; courageous; daring: 果～ courageous and resolute; daring ② dare: 要～想、～说、～干。We should dare to think, dare to speak and dare to act. ③ have the confidence to; be certain: 我不～说他究竟哪一天来。I'm not sure just what day he will come. ④ 〈书〉make bold; venture: ～问 I venture to ask; may I ask

【敢怒而不敢言】 gǎn nù ér bùgǎn yán be forced to keep one's resentment to oneself; suppress one's rage; choke with silent fury

【敢死队】 gǎnsǐduì 〈旧〉dare-to-die corps

【敢于】 gǎnyú dare to; be bold in; have the courage to

感* gǎn ① feel; sense: 身体略～不适 not feel very well; be under the weather; be out of sorts/ 他～到自己错了。He sensed that he himself was wrong./ 她对草原上的一切都～到新鲜。She found everything on the grasslands new and attractive. ② move; touch; affect: ～人 touching; moving/ ～激; be obliged: 请早日寄下为～。I should be grateful if you would send it to me at an early date. ④ 〈中医〉be affected: 外～风寒 be affected by the cold; have a cold ⑤ sense; feeling: 责任～ sense of responsibility/ 民族自豪～ sense of national pride/ 读后～ reaction to (或 impressions of) a book or an article/ 给人以一种新鲜～ engender a feeling of freshness

【感触】 gǎnchù thoughts and feelings; feelings: 深有～地说 say with deep feeling

【感动】 gǎndòng move; touch: ～得流下眼泪 be moved to tears

【感恩】 gǎn'ēn feel grateful; be thankful: ～图报 be grateful to sb. and seek ways to return his kindness/ ～戴德 be deeply grateful

【感化】 gǎnhuà help (a misguided or erring person) to change by persuasion, setting an example, etc.

【感怀】 gǎnhuái ① recall with emotion: ～往事 recall past events with deep feeling ② reflections; thoughts; recollections: ～思 thoughts on the Spring Festival

【感激】 gǎnjī feel grateful; be thankful; feel indebted: ～涕零 shed grateful tears; be moved to tears of gratitude/ 不胜～ be deeply grateful; feel very much indebted

【感觉】 gǎnjué ① sense perception; sensation; feeling: 个人的～。Personal feeling. ② feel; perceive; become aware of: 你～怎么样？How do you feel now?/ 他～到了问题的严重性。He became aware of the seriousness of the matter.

【感慨】 gǎnkǎi sigh with emotion: ～万端 all sorts of feelings well up in one's mind

【感冒】 gǎnmào common cold: 患～ catch cold; have a cold

【感情】 gǎnqíng ① emotion; feeling; sentiment: 动～ be carried away by one's emotions; get worked up/ 伤～ hurt sb.'s feelings/ 思想～开始发生变化 experience a change in one's thoughts and feelings ② affection; attachment; love: 我们对故乡的一草一木都怀有深厚的～。We cherish a deep affection for every tree and bush in our home town

【感情用事】 gǎnqíng yòngshì be swayed by one's emotions; act impetuously

【感染】 gǎnrǎn ① infect: 细菌～ bacterial infection/ 手术后～ postoperative infection ② influence; infect; affect: 诗人的激情～了每一个读者。The poet's passion affected all his readers./ 艺术～力 artistic appeal (或 power)

【感伤】 gǎnshāng sad; sorrowful; sentimental

【感受】 gǎnshòu ① be affected by: ～风寒 be affected by the cold; catch cold ②experience; feel: 这次去伦敦参观～很深。My visit to London made a deep impression on me.

【感叹】 gǎntàn sigh with feeling ◇ ～词 interjection; exclamation/ ～号 exclamation mark; exclamation point (!)/ ～句 exclamatory sentence

【感想】 gǎnxiǎng impressions; reflections; thoughts: 请你谈谈看了这部影片后的～。Please tell us your impressions of the film. 或 Tell us what you think of the film.

【感谢】 gǎnxiè thank; be grateful: 表示衷心的～ express heartfelt thanks/ 非常～你的帮助。Thank you very much for your help. ◇ ～信 letter of thanks

橄 gǎn

【橄榄】 gǎnlǎn <植> ① Chinese olive (Canarium album); the fruit of the canary tree ② olive

gàn

干* gàn ① trunk; main part: 树～ tree-trunk; trunk/ 骨～ backbone; hard core; mainstay ② <简> (干部) cadre ③ do; work: 叫我 ～什么都行。I'll do any job I may be assigned to ④ fight; strike: ～到底 fight to the bitter end 另见 gān

【干部】 gànbù cadre: 各级领导～ leading cadres at all levels

【干才】 gàncái ① ability; capability ②capable (或 able) person

【干掉】 gàndiào <口> kill; get rid of; put sb. out of the way: 先～敌人的哨兵。Get rid of the enemy sentry first.

【干活】 gànhuó work; work on a job: ～去吧。Let's get to work./ 他们都在～呢。They are all at work. 或 They are all on the job./ 今儿你干什么活啊？What's your job for today?

【干劲】 gànjìn drive; vigour; enthusiasm: 鼓～ rouse one's enthusiasm/ ～十足 be full of vigour (或 drive)

【干练】 gànliàn capable and experienced

【干吗】 gànmá <口> ① why on earth; whatever for: ～这么大规矩？Why all this formality? ② what to do: 今儿下午～？What are we going to do this afternoon?/ 你想～？What are you up to?

【干什么】 gàn shénme 见"干吗"

【干事】 gànshi a secretary (或 clerical worker) in charge of sth.: 文娱～ person in charge of recreational activities

gāng

冈 gāng ridge (of a hill)

扛* gāng ① lift with both hands ② <方> (of two or more people) carry together 另见 káng

刚* gāng ①firm; strong; indomitable: 她的舞蹈柔中有～ There is strength as well as grace in her dancing.②<副> just; exactly: 这双鞋大小～合适。This pair of shoes is just the right size. 或 This pair of shoes fits perfectly. ③<副> barely; only just ④ <副> only a short while ago; just: 她～走。She has just gone./ 她～来过。She was here just now.

【刚愎自用】 gāngbì zìyòng self-willed; headstrong; opinionated

【刚才】 gāngcái just now; a moment ago: 别把～跟你说的

事忘了。Don't forget what I told you just now./ 他～还说要去呢。He was saying only a moment ago that he wanted to go.

【刚刚】 gānggāng <副> ①just; only; exactly: 上次讨论到现在～一个月。It's only a month since the last discussion./ 那时候天～亮。It was just beginning to get light. ②a moment ago; just now: 报纸～到。The newspaper came just now.

【刚好】 gānghǎo ①just; exactly: 我们～赶上末班车。We just managed to catch the last bus./ 你们来得～。You've come in the nick of time. ②happen to; it so happened that: 他们两人～编在一个组里。The two of them happened to be in the same group.

【刚劲】 gāngjìng bold; vigorous; sturdy: 笔力～ write in a bold hand/ ～的松枝 sturdy boughs of a pine

【刚…就…】 gāng…jiù… 〔表示两件事紧接〕as soon as; no sooner than; immediately: 他刚开完会回来,就下地干活去了。As soon as he got back from the conference, he went to work in the fields.

【刚强】 gāngqiáng firm; staunch; unyielding

【刚巧】 gāngqiǎo 见"刚好"②

【刚毅】 gāngyì resolute and steadfast: 在危机中表现得非常～和机智 display both fortitude and resourcefulness in the crisis

【刚正】 gāngzhèng upright; honourable; principled: ～不阿 upright and never stooping to flattery

【刚直】 gāngzhí upright and outspoken

纲 gāng ① the headrope of a fishing net ② key link; guiding principle ③ outline; programme: 党章总～ the general programme of a party constitution

【纲领】 gānglǐng programme; guiding principle: 最低(高)～ minimum (maximum) programme

【纲目】 gāngmù 〔多用于书名〕detailed outline (of a subject); outline

【纲要】 gāngyào ① outline; sketch: 他把意见写成～,准备在会上发言。He made an outline of his views and got ready to present them at the meeting. ② essentials; compendium: 《英语语法～》 Essentials of English Grammar

肛 gāng anus

【肛门】 gāngmén anus

缸* gāng vat; jar; crock: 水～ water vat/ 一～咸菜 a jar of salted vegetables/ 金鱼～ goldfish bowl

钢* gāng steel: 炼～ steelmaking/ 不锈～ stainless steel

【钢板】 gāngbǎn ①steel plate; plate: 锅炉～ boiler plate/ 造船～ ship plate ② spring (of a motorcar, etc.) ③ stencil steel board

【钢笔】 gāngbǐ pen; fountain pen

【钢骨水泥】 gānggǔ shuǐní reinforced concrete

【钢管】 gāngguǎn steel tube (或 pipe): 无缝～ seamless steel tube/ 焊接～ welded steel pipe

【钢盔】 gāngkuī (steel) helmet

【钢琴】 gāngqín piano: 弹～ play the piano/ 大～ grand piano/ 竖式～ upright piano ◇ ～家 pianist

【钢丝】 gāngsī (steel) wire: 走～ <杂技> walk the wire; walk the tightrope; high-wire walking

【钢铁】 gāngtiě iron and steel; steel: ～意志 iron will

gǎng

岗* gǎng ①hillock; mound: ～峦起伏 undulating hills ②ridge; welt; wale ③ sentry; post: 站～ stand sentry; keep guard/ 布～ post a sentinel/ 下～ come off sentry duty

【岗位】 gǎngwèi post; station: 战斗～ fighting post; battle station/ 坚守～ stand fast at one's post; stick to one's guns/ 走上新的～ take up a new post; take on a new job

港* gǎng ①port; harbour: 天然～ natural harbour/ 停靠～ port of call

【港口】 gǎngkǒu port; harbour: 沿海~ coastal port

gàng

杠 gàng ① thick stick; stout carrying pole ② <体> bar: 单~ horizontal bar/ 双~ parallel bars ③ thick line (drawn beside or under words in reading, correcting papers, etc.) ④ cross out; delete: 她把草稿中不必要的词句都~掉了。 She crossed out all the superfluous words and phrases in the draft.

【杠杆】 gànggǎn lever
◇ ~臂 lever arm/ ~原理 lever principle/ ~率 leverage

gāo

高* gāo ① tall; high: 她比小红~一头。 She's a head taller than Xiao Hong./ 坝~四十米。 The dam is 40 metres high (或 in height)./ 这片地中间~起一块。 There is a mound in the middle of the field. ② of a high level or degree; above the average: ~年级 higher (或 senior) grades/ ~质量 high (或 good) quality/ ~招 masterstroke/ 他的思想境界比我~。 He has nobler thoughts than I./ 这主意真~! What a brilliant idea! ③ loud: 嗓门儿~ have a loud voice/ ~喊 shout loudly; raise a cry ④ high-priced; dear; expensive: 要价太~ ask too high a price ⑤ <敬> your: ~见 your opinion

【高矮】 gāo'ǎi height: 这两棵树~差不多。 The two trees are about the same height.
【高昂】 gāo'áng ① hold high (one's head, etc.) ② high; elated; exalted: 情绪~ be in high spirits ③ dear; expensive; exorbitant
【高傲】 gāo'ào supercilious; arrogant; haughty
【高不成,低不就】 gāo bù chéng, dī bù jiù ① be unfit for a higher post but unwilling to take a lower one ② can't have one's heart's desire but won't stoop to less
【高不可攀】 gāo bùkě pān too high to reach; unattainable
【高才生】 gāocáishēng a brilliant (或 outstanding) student
【高产】 gāochǎn high yield; high production
◇ ~品种 high-yield variety/ ~田 high-yield field/ ~作物 high-yield crop; highly productive crop
【高超】 gāochāo superb; excellent: 技艺~ superb skill
【高潮】 gāocháo ① high tide; high water ② upsurge; climax; high tide: 全剧的~ the climax of the play
【高大】 gāodà ① tall and big; tall: 身材~ be of great stature/ ~的建筑物 tall buildings ② lofty
【高等】 gāoděng higher
◇ ~哺乳动物 higher mammal/ ~教育 higher education/ ~数学 higher mathematics/ ~院校 institutions of higher learning; colleges and universities
【高低】 gāodī ① height: 山崖的~ the height of a cliff/ 声调的~ the pitch of a voice ② relative superiority or inferiority: 争个~ vie with each other to see who is better/ 难分~ hard to tell which is better ③ sense of propriety; discretion: 不知~ not know what's proper; have no sense of propriety
【高地】 gāodì highland; upland; elevation: ~田 an upland field
【高调】 gāodiào lofty tone; high-sounding words: 唱~ mouth high-sounding words; say fine-sounding things
【高度】 gāodù ① altitude; height: 飞行~ flying altitude/ 山的~ the height of a mountain ② a high degree of; highly: ~赞扬 pay high tribute to; speak highly of
【高尔夫球】 gāo'ěrfūqiú ① golf ② golf ball ◇ ~场 golf course; golf links
【高峰】 gāofēng peak; summit; height: 珠穆朗玛峰是世界第一~。 Mount Qomolangma is the world's highest peak./ 攀登科学的~ scale the heights of science

【高高在上】 gāogāo zài shàng stand high above the masses; be far removed from the masses and reality
【高个儿】 gāogèr a tall person 又作"高个子"
【高跟鞋】 gāogēnxié high-heeled shoes
【高官厚禄】 gāoguān-hòulù high position and handsome salary; high posts with salaries to match
【高贵】 gāoguì ① noble; high: ~品质 noble quality ② highly privileged; elitist
【高级】 gāojí ① senior; high-ranking; high-level; high: ~参谋 senior staff officer/ ~官员 high-ranking official/ 最~会议 summit meeting ② high-grade; high-quality; advanced: ~染料 high-grade dyestuff/ ~墨水 high-quality ink/ ~读本 advanced reader/ 这个旅馆真~! This hotel is really first-class.
【高价】 gāojià high price: ~收买 buy over at a high price/ ~货物 expensive goods
【高架桥】 gāojiàqiáo viaduct
【高架铁道】 gāojià tiědào overhead railway; elevated railway
【高见】 gāojiàn <敬> your brilliant idea; your opinion: 有何~? What do you think about it?/ 不知~以为何如? I wonder if you would be kind enough to enlighten us on this matter.
【高洁】 gāojié noble and unsullied
【高峻】 gāojùn high and steep
【高亢】 gāokàng loud and sonorous; resounding: ~的歌声 sonorous singing
【高空】 gāokōng high altitude; upper air
【高栏】 gāolán <体> high hurdles
【高利贷】 gāolìdài usury; usurious loan: 放~ practise usury/ ~者 usurer; loan shark/ ~资本 usurer's capital
【高龄】 gāolíng advanced age; venerable age: 八十~ the advanced age of 80
【高楼大厦】 gāolóu-dàshà high buildings and large mansions
【高论】 gāolùn <敬> enlightening remarks; brilliant views
【高迈】 gāomài advanced in years
【高帽子】 gāomàozi ① tall paper hat (worn as a sign of humiliation) ② flattery
【高妙】 gāomiào ingenious; masterly: 手艺~ masterly craftsmanship
【高明】 gāomíng brilliant; wise: 他这一手一点也不~。 This move of his is not at all clever./ 另请~。 Find someone better qualified (than myself).
【高攀】 gāopān make friends or claim ties of kinship with someone of a higher social position
【高强】 gāoqiáng excel in; be master of: 武艺~ excel in martial arts
【高跷】 gāoqiāo stilts: 踩~ walk on stilts
【高球】 gāoqiú <体> high ball; lob: 放~ lob
【高人一等】 gāo rén yī děng a cut above other people: 他老以为自己~。 He always thinks he's a cut above others.
【高僧】 gāosēng eminent monk
【高尚】 gāoshàng noble; lofty: ~的人 a noble-minded person/ ~的理想 lofty ideals
【高烧】 gāoshāo high fever: 发~ have (或 run) a high fever
【高射炮】 gāoshèpào antiaircraft gun (或 artillery)
【高深】 gāoshēn advanced; profound; recondite: 莫测~ unfathomable
【高视阔步】 gāoshì-kuòbù carry oneself proudly; strut; prance
【高手】 gāoshǒu past master; master-hand; ace: 象棋~ master (Chinese) chess player
【高寿】 gāoshòu ① longevity; long life ② <敬> your venerable age: 老大爷,您今年~? May I ask how old you are, Grandpa?
【高耸】 gāosǒng stand tall and erect; tower: ~入云 reach to the sky; tower into the clouds/ ~的纪念碑 a towering monument
【高速】 gāosù high speed: ~前进 advance at high speed/ ~发展 develop by leaps and bounds; develop at top speed/ ~转弯很危险。 It's dangerous to turn a corner at high speed. ◇ ~公路 expressway

【高谈阔论】 gāotán-kuòlùn indulge in loud and empty talk; talk volubly or bombastically; harangue
【高温】 gāowēn high temperature
【高兴】 gāoxìng ① glad; happy; cheerful: 小强高高兴兴地上学去了。 Xiao Qiang cheerfully went off to school./ 快把这消息告诉你爷爷，叫他老人家也～～。 Tell Grandpa the good news, so that he can share our joy./ 他们～得太早了。 They rejoiced too soon. ② be willing to; be happy to: 你不～去就别去了。 You needn't go if you don't feel like it.
【高血压】 gāoxuèyā 〈医〉 hypertension; high blood pressure
【高原】 gāoyuán plateau; highland; tableland
【高瞻远瞩】 gāozhān-yuǎnzhǔ stand high and see far; take a broad and long-term view; show great foresight
【高涨】 gāozhǎng rise; upsurge; run high
【高足】 gāozú 〈敬〉 your brilliant disciple; your pupil
【高祖】 gāozǔ (paternal) great-great-grandfather
【高祖母】 gāozǔmǔ (paternal) great-great-grandmother

羔 gāo lamb; kid; fawn
【羔羊】 gāoyáng lamb; kid

膏* gāo ① fat; grease; oil: 春雨如～。 Rain in spring is as precious as oil. ② paste; cream; ointment: 牙～ toothpaste/ 雪花～ vanishing cream/ 软～ ointment
【膏药】 gāoyao plaster: 贴～ apply a plaster to

睾 gāo
【睾丸】 gāowán 〈生理〉 testis; testicle

糕* gāo cake; pudding: 年～ New Year cake (made of glutinous rice)/ 蛋～ cake (enriched with eggs)

篙 gāo punt-pole

gǎo

杲 gǎo 〈书〉 bright

搞 gǎo ① do; carry on; be engaged in: ～调查研究 do some investigation and study/ ～运动 carry on a movement (或 campaign)/ ～生产 engage in production/ ～阴谋诡计的人注定要失败。 Those who go in for intrigues and conspiracy are doomed to failure./ 他是～建筑的。 He's in building. ② make; produce; work out: ～个计划 draw up a plan ③ set up; start; organize: 我们打算在这里～个发电站。 We're thinking of putting up a power station here. ④ get; get hold of; secure: 你去给我们～点吃的来。 Go and get us something to eat. ⑤〔后面接补语〕 produce a certain effect or result; cause to become: 把事情～糟了 make a mess of things/ 把问题～清楚 get a clear understanding of the question/ 别把机器～坏了。 Don't break the machine./ 我把你们的名字～混了。 I've mixed up your names.
【搞好】 gǎohǎo make a good job of; do well: ～团结 strengthen unity
【搞鬼】 gǎoguǐ play tricks; be up to some mischief: 提防敌人暗中～。 Beware of the enemy's tricks.

槁 gǎo withered
【槁木死灰】 gǎomù-sǐhuī dead trees and cold ashes — complete apathy

稿* gǎo ①〈书〉 stalk of grain; straw ② draft; sketch: 初～ first draft/ 先打个～儿再画 make a sketch before painting ③ manuscript; original text: 遗～ literary remains; posthumous papers/ 定～ finalize a text/ 来～ contributed article; contribution
【稿本】 gǎoběn manuscript
【稿费】 gǎofèi payment for an article or book written; contribution fee; author's remuneration
【稿件】 gǎojiàn manuscript; contribution
【稿纸】 gǎozhǐ squared or lined paper for making drafts or copying manuscripts

gào

告* gào ① tell; inform; notify: 何时启程,盼～。 Please inform me of your date of departure. ② accuse; go to law against; bring an action against ③ ask for; request; solicit: ～假 ask for leave ④ declare; announce: 不～而别 go away without taking leave; leave without saying good-bye/ 自～奋勇 volunteer to do sth. ⑤〔宣布或表示某种情况的实现〕: 一段落 come to the end of a stage; be brought to a temporary close/ 大功～成。 The task is at last accomplished.
【告别】 gàobié ① leave; part from: 我们～了这个地方,继续向前进。 We left the place and went on with our journey./ 他把信交给了队长,就匆匆～了。 He hurried off after giving the letter to the team leader. ② bid farewell to; say good-bye to: 挥手～ wave farewell/ 我向你～来了。 I've come to say good-bye to you./ 向遗体～ pay one's last respects to the deceased
◇ ～词 farewell speech; valediction/ ～宴会 farewell banquet/ ～仪式 farewell ceremony
【告吹】 gàochuī fizzle out; fail
【告辞】 gàocí take leave (of one's host)
【告发】 gàofā report (an offender); inform against; lodge an accusation against
【告急】 gàojí ① be in an emergency: 洪水猛涨,大坝～。 The dam was in danger because of the rising flood. ② report an emergency; ask for emergency help
【告假】 gàojià ask for leave
【告捷】 gàojié ① win victory: 首战～ win in the very first battle or game ② report a victory
【告诫】 gàojiè warn; admonish; exhort: 师长经常～我们要提高警惕。 The division commander constantly exhorted us to heighten our vigilance.
【告警】 gàojǐng ① report an emergency ② give (或 sound) an alarm
【告老】 gàolǎo retire on account of age: ～还乡 retire on account of old age and return to one's native place
【告密】 gàomì inform against sb. ◇ ～者 informer
【告示】 gàoshi official notice; bulletin; placard
【告诉】 gàosu tell; let know: ～他们别等了。 Tell them not to wait./ 有什么消息,～我一声。 Let me know if there's any news.
【告退】 gàotuì ask for leave to withdraw from a meeting, etc.
【告知】 gàozhī inform; notify
【告状】 gàozhuàng ① go to law against sb.; bring a lawsuit against sb. ② lodge a complaint against sb. with his superior

gē

戈 gē dagger-axe (an ancient weapon)
疙 gē
【疙瘩】 gēda a swelling on the skin; pimple; lump
咯 gē
另见 lo
【咯噔】 gēdēng 〈象〉 click: ～～的皮靴声 the click of boots (on a floor)
【咯咯】 gēgē 〈象〉①〔形容母鸡叫声〕 cluck; chuckle; cackle ②〔形容笑声〕 chuckle; titter
【咯吱】 gēzhī 〈象〉 creak; groan: 扁担压得～～地直响。 The carrying pole creaked under the load.

哥* gē (elder) brother

胳 gē
【胳臂】 gēbei arm
【胳膊】 gēbo arm

鸽* gē pigeon; dove: 家～ pigeon/ 野～ wild pigeon; dove/ 通信～ carrier (或 homing) pigeon

【鸽子】 gēzi pigeon; dove ◇ ～笼 dovecote; pigeon house; loft

割* gē cut: ～麦子 cut (或 reap) wheat/ ～草 cut grass; mow

【割爱】 gē'ài give up what one treasures; part with some cherished possession: 忍痛～ part reluctantly with what one treasures

【割草机】 gēcǎojī mower

【割除】 gēchú cut off; cut out; excise

【割地】 gēdì cede territory

【割断】 gēduàn sever; cut off: ～联系 sever relations

【割鸡焉用牛刀】 gē jī yān yòng niúdāo why use an ox-cleaver to kill a chicken; why break a butterfly on the wheel

【割胶】 gējiāo rubber tapping

【割让】 gēràng cede: ～领土 cession of territory

搁 gē ①put: 把箱子～在行李架上。Put the suitcase on the luggage-rack./ 汤里～点盐。Put some salt in the soup./ 把东西～在这儿吧。Just leave your things here./ 这屋子太热，种子～不住。This room is too hot; the seeds won't keep. ②put aside; leave over; shelve: 这件事得～一～再办。We'll have to put the matter aside for the time being.

【搁浅】 gēqiǎn run aground; be stranded; reach a deadlock: 船～了。The ship got stranded (或 ran aground)./ 谈判～了。The negotiations have come to a deadlock.

【搁置】 gēzhì shelve; lay aside; pigeonhole: ～一项动议 shelve a motion

歌* gē ①song ②sing: 纵情高～ sing loudly and without constraint

【歌唱】 gēchàng sing ◇ ～家 singer; vocalist

【歌词】 gēcí words of a song

【歌功颂德】 gēgōng-sòngdé eulogize sb.'s virtues and achievements; sing the praises of sb.

【歌喉】 gēhóu (singer's) voice; singing voice: ～婉转 sing in a beautiful voice

【歌剧】 gējù opera: 小～ operetta

【歌谱】 gēpǔ music of a song

【歌曲】 gēqǔ song

【歌手】 gēshǒu singer; vocalist

【歌颂】 gēsòng sing the praises of; extol; eulogize

【歌舞】 gēwǔ song and dance ◇ ～剧 song and dance drama/ ～团 song and dance ensemble (或 troupe)

【歌舞升平】 gēwǔ shēngpíng sing and dance to extol the good times — put on a false show of peace and prosperity

【歌谣】 gēyáo ballad; folk song; nursery rhyme

【歌咏】 gēyǒng singing ◇ ～比赛 singing contest/ ～队 singing group; chorus

gé

革* gé ①leather; hide: ～制品 leather goods/ ～履 leather shoes/ 制～厂 tannery ②change; transform: 洗心～面 turn over a new leaf ③remove from office; expel

【革除】 géchú ①abolish; get rid of: ～陈规陋习 abolish outmoded regulations and irrational practices ②expel; dismiss; remove from office

【革命】 gémìng revolution

【革新】 géxīn innovation: 技术～ technological innovation/ 传统的手工艺技术不断～。Traditional handicraft techniques are being steadily improved.

【革职】 gézhí remove from office; cashier

阁 gé ①pavilion (usu. two-storeyed) ②cabinet: 组～ form a cabinet/ 倒～ bring down a cabinet

【阁楼】 gélóu attic; loft; garret

【阁下】 géxià 〈敬〉(直接称呼) Your Excellency; (间接称呼) His or Her Excellency: 大使～ Your Excellency Mr. Ambassador; His Excellency the Ambassador

【阁员】 géyuán member of the cabinet

格* gé ①squares formed by crossed lines; check: 在纸上方～儿 square off the paper ②division (horizontal or otherwise): 横～纸 ruled paper/ 四～儿的书架 a bookcase with four shelves/ 每服一小～。Dose: one measure each time. ③standard; pattern; style: 合～ up to standard/ 别具一～ have a style of its own

【格调】 gédiào ①(literary or artistic) style: ～豪放 a vigorous and flowing style ②〈书〉one's style of work as well as one's moral quality

【格斗】 gédòu grapple; wrestle; fistfight

【格格不入】 gégé bù rù incompatible with; out of tune with; out of one's element; like a square peg in a round hole

【格律】 gélù rules and forms of classical poetic composition (with respect to tonal pattern, rhyme scheme, etc.)

【格杀勿论】 géshā wùlùn kill on the spot with the authority of the law

【格式】 géshì format; pattern: 公文～ the format of an official document

【格外】 géwài 〈副〉especially; all the more: 雪地上骑车要～小心。You've got to be especially careful when you cycle on snow.

【格言】 géyán maxim; motto; aphorism

【格子】 gézi check; chequer ◇ ～布 checked fabric; check

葛 gé 〈植〉kudzu vine
另见 gě

蛤 gé clam
另见 há

隔* gé ①separate; partition; stand or lie between: 把一间屋～成两间 partition a room into two/ 龟蛇二山～江相望。Tortoise and Snake Hills face each other across the river./ ～一座山就是水库。The reservoir is just on the other side of the hill. ② at a distance from; after or at an interval of: 相～千里 be a thousand li away from each other/ 每棵树苗要～开五米。The saplings should be five metres apart./ 你～两天再来吧。Come back in two days' time./ ～两周去一次 go there every third week/ 请～行写。Please write on every other line./ ～四小时服一次。To be taken once every four hours.

【隔岸观火】 gé àn guān huǒ watch a fire from the other side of the river — look on at sb.'s trouble with indifference

【隔壁】 gébì next door: ～邻居 next-door neighbour/ 住在～ live next door/ ～第二间 next door but one

【隔断】 géduàn cut off; separate; obstruct: 洪水把村子同市区的交通～了。The flood cut the village off from the town.

【隔阂】 géhé ①estrangement; misunderstanding ②barrier: 语言的～ language barrier

【隔绝】 géjué completely cut off; isolated: 和外界～ be cut off from the outside world/ 他走了以后就与我们音信～了。He has never been heard of since he left us.

【隔离】 gélí keep apart; isolate; segregate: 种族～ racial segregation/ 病人已经～了一周。The patient has been in isolation for a week. ◇ ～病房 isolation ward

【隔膜】 gémó ①lack of mutual understanding: 他们之间有些～。They are rather estranged from each other. ②unfamiliar with: 我对那里的情况很～。I know very little about the situation. there.

【隔墙有耳】 gé qiáng yǒu ěr walls have ears; beware of eavesdroppers

【隔声】 géshēng 〈建〉sound insulation ◇ ～板 sound insulating board/ ～材料 sound insulator

【隔靴搔痒】 gé xuē sāoyǎng scratch an itch from outside one's boot — attempt an ineffective solution

【隔夜】 géyè of the previous night: 把～的菜热一热 warm up last night's leftovers

嗝 gé ① belch ② hiccup

膈 gé diaphragm

【膈膜】 gémó diaphragm

骼 gé 见"骨骼" gǔgé

gě

个 gě 见"自个儿" zìgěr
另见 gè

葛 Gě a surname
另见 gé

gè

个* gè ①〈量〉ⓐ〔多用于没有专用量词的名词〕: 三～苹果 three apples/ 一～故事 a story/ 两～星期 two weeks; a fortnight/ 一～心眼儿 be of one mind/ 第五～年头 the fifth year ⓑ〔用于约数的前面〕: 这点活儿用～两三天就干完了。This bit of work can easily be finished in a couple of days. ⓒ〔用于带宾语的动词后面〕: 洗～澡 have a bath/ 睡～好觉 have a good sleep/ he was quite good at handling a plough and driving a cart. ⓓ〔用于动词和补语之间〕: 忙～不停 be as busy as a bee ② individual
另见 gě

【个别】 gèbié ① individual; specific: ～辅导 individual coaching/ ～照顾 special consideration for individual cases ② very few; one or two; exceptional: 只有一～人请假。Only one or two people asked for leave./ 这是极其～的事例。Such instances are very rare./ 这是～情况。These are isolated cases.

【个个】 gègè each and every one; all

【个人】 gèrén ① individual (person): 用他～的名义 in his own name ② I: ～认为 in my opinion

【个性】 gèxìng individual character; individuality; personality: 共性和～ the general and specific character of sth./ 这孩子～很强。The boy has a strong character.

【个子】 gèzi height; stature; build: 高～ a tall person/ 小～ a small fellow; a short person

各* gè each; every; various; different: 全国～地 in all parts of the country/ ～不相让 neither being ready to give way; each trying to outdo the other/ ～不相同 have nothing in common with each other.

【各半】 gèbàn half and half; fifty-fifty: 成败的可能性～ The chances of success are fifty-fifty.

【各奔前程】 gè bèn qiánchéng each pursues his own course; each goes his own way

【各别】 gèbié ① distinct; different: ～对待 treat differently; treat each on its (his, etc.) own merits ②〈方〉out of the ordinary; peculiar: 这只闹钟式样很～。This alarm clock is quite unusual-looking. ③ odd; eccentric; funny: 这个人真～! What an odd chap! 或 What a funny fellow!

【各持己见】 gè chí jǐjiàn each sticks to his own view

【各得其所】 gè dé qí suǒ each is in his proper place; each is properly provided for; each has a role to play

【各…各…】 gè…gè… ① each … his own…. 分了工, 就各干各的去吧。Now that the work has been divided up, let each one get on with his job./ 各吹各的号, 各唱各的调 Each blows his own bugle and sings his own tune — each does things in his own way./ 各就各位! 〈军〉Man your posts! 〈体〉On your marks! ② all kinds of; all: 各行各业 all trades and professions; all walks of life/ 各式各样的农具 farm tools of all kinds

【各个】 gègè ① each; every; various ② one by one; separately: ～击破 destroy (或 crush) one by one/ ～解决 piecemeal solution

【各界】 gèjiè all walks of life; all circles: ～人士 personalities of various circles

【各人】 gèrén each one; everyone: ～自扫门前雪, 不管他人瓦上霜。〈俗〉Each one sweeps the snow from his own doorstep and doesn't bother about the frost on his neighbour's roof—selfish

【各色】 gèsè of all kinds; of every description; assorted: 商店里～货物, 一应俱全。The shop is well stocked with goods of all kinds.

【各抒己见】 gè shū jǐjiàn each airs his own views

【各位】 gèwèi ① everybody (a term of address): ～请注意! Attention please, everybody. ② every: ～代表 fellow delegates

【各行其是】 gè xíng qí shì each does what he thinks is right; each goes his own way

【各有千秋】 gè yǒu qiānqiū each has something to recommend him; each has his strong points

【各有所长】 gè yǒu suǒ cháng each has his own strong points

【各有所好】 gè yǒu suǒ hào each has his likes and dislikes; each follows his own bent

【各执一词】 gè zhí yī cí each sticks to his own version or argument

【各自】 gèzì each; respective: 孩子们帮老人挑完了水, 就～回家了。After carrying water for the old man, the children went home./ 既要～努力, 也要彼此帮助。There must be both individual effort and mutual help.

【各自为政】 gèzì wéi zhèng each does things in his own way

gěi

给* gěi ① give; grant: ～他一个星期的假 grant him a week's leave/ 这本书是～你的。This book is for you. ②〔用在动词后面, 表示交付〕: 信已经交～他了。I've handed the letter to him./ 把锤子递～我。Pass me the hammer./ 我把钥匙留～你。I'll leave the key with you. ③〔表示行为的对象或有关事物〕for; for the benefit of: 她～旅客送水倒茶。She brought drinking water and tea for the passengers./ 医生～孩子们种牛痘。The doctor vaccinated the children. ④ let; allow: ～我看一看。Let me have a look. ⑤〔表示被动, 相当于"被"〕: 衣服～汗水湿透了。Clothes were soaked with sweat. ⑥〈助〉〔常与前面"叫""让""把"相呼应, 以加强语气〕: 把纸收起来, 别叫风～刮散了。Put away all the paper. Don't let it get blown about./ 我差点儿把这事～忘了。I almost forgot that.
另见 jǐ

【给以】 gěiyǐ〔多用于抽象事物〕give; grant: ～充分的重视 pay ample attention to/ ～适当照顾 show due consideration for

gēn

根* gēn ① root (of a plant): 连～拔 pull up by the root ②〈数〉root: 平方～ square root ③〈化〉radical: 酸～ acid radical ④ root; foot; base: 舌～ the root of the tongue/ 城墙～ the foot (或 base) of a city wall ⑤ cause; origin; source; root: 祸～ the root of trouble or disaster ⑥ thoroughly; completely: ～除 completely do away with; eradicate ⑦〈量〉〔用于细长的东西〕: 一～火柴 a match/ 一～小绳子 a piece of string

【根本】 gēnběn ① basic; fundamental; essential; cardinal: ～原因 basic reason; root cause/ ～原则 cardinal principle ②〔多用于否定〕at all; simply: 我～就不赞成你的主张。I don't agree with you at all. ③ radically; thoroughly: 问题已经得到～解决。The problem has been settled once and for all.

【根除】 gēnchú thoroughly do away with; eradicate; root out; eliminate: ～水患 eliminate the scourge of floods

【根底】 gēndǐ ① foundation: ～浅 have a shaky foundation/ 他的英文～很好。He has a solid foundation in English. ② cause; root: 追问～ inquire into the cause of the matter/ 你了解这个人的～吗? Do you know that fellow's background?

【根基】gēnjī foundation; basis: 打好～ lay a solid foundation

【根究】gēnjiū make a thorough investigation of; get to the bottom of; probe into: ～缘由 probe into the cause

【根据】gēnjù ① on the basis of; according to; in the light of; in line with: ～天气预报 according to the weather forecast/ ～具体情况 in the light of specific conditions/ ～两国人民的利益和愿望 in accordance (或 conformity) with the interests and desire of the peoples of the two countries/ ～公报的精神 in the spirit of the *communiqué*/ ～同名小说拍摄的影片 a film based on the novel of the same title ② basis; grounds; foundation: 说话要有～。One should avoid making assertions without good grounds./ 毫无～ utterly groundless ◇ ～地 base area; base

【根绝】gēnjué stamp out; eradicate; exterminate: ～血吸虫病 stamp out snail fever/ ～事故 eliminate accidents

【根深蒂固】gēnshēn-dìgù deep-rooted; ingrained; inveterate: ～的偏见 deep-rooted (或 ingrained) prejudice

【根深叶茂】gēnshēn-yèmào have deep roots and luxuriant leaves — be well established and vigorously developing

【根由】gēnyóu cause; origin

【根源】gēnyuán source; origin; root

【根治】gēnzhì effect a radical cure; cure once and for all; bring under permanent control: ～支气管炎 effect a radical cure of bronchitis

跟* gēn ① heel: 鞋后～ the heel of a shoe ② follow: ～我来。Come along with me. ③ 〈介〉〔表示 "和" "同"〕: 有事要～父母商量。Consult your parents when a problem crops up. ④ 〈介〉〔表示 "向" "对"〕: 快～大伙说说。Tell us all about it. ⑤ 〈介〉〔引进比较的对象〕: 今天的活儿～往常一样。Our job today is the same as before. ⑥ 〈连〉and: 种子～农药都准备好了。The seeds and the pesticide are both ready.

【跟前】gēnqián in front of; close to; near: 他把我叫到～又讲了几句。He told me to come closer and said a few words more.

【跟上】gēnshang keep pace with; catch up with; keep abreast of: 快～! Close up!

【跟随】gēnsuí follow

【跟头】gēntou ① fall: 摔～ have a fall ② somersault: 翻个～ turn a somersault

【跟着】gēnzhe follow; in the wake of: 我们听完报告～就讨论。We held a discussion right after the speech.

【跟踪】gēnzōng follow the tracks of: 雪地～ follow sb.'s tracks in the snow/ ～追击 go in hot pursuit of/ ～敌舰 shadow the enemy warships

gēng

更* gēng ① change; replace: 除旧～新 replace the old with the new ② 〈书〉experience: 少不～事 young and inexperienced ③ one of the five two-hour periods into which the night was formerly divided; watch: 打～ beat the watches/ 三～半夜 in the dead of night
另见 gèng

【更动】gēngdòng change; alter: 人事～ personnel changes/ 图案已有所～。The design has been altered.

【更改】gēnggǎi change; alter: 由于天气恶劣,飞机不得不～航线。Owing to bad weather the plane had to change its course./ 不可～的决定 an unalterable decision

【更换】gēnghuàn change; replace: ～位置 change places/ 农展馆的展品常有～。The exhibits in the agricultural exhibition keep changing.

【更深人静】gēngshēn-rénjìng deep is the night and all is quiet: 在～的时候 at dead of night; in the quiet of the night

【更生】gēngshēng regenerate; revive: 自力～ regeneration through one's own efforts; self-reliance

【更新】gēngxīn renew; replace: 设备～ renewal of equipment/ 万象～。Everything takes on a new look.

【更衣】gēngyī change one's clothes ◇ ～室 changeroom; locker room

【更正】gēngzhèng make corrections (of errors in statements or newspaper articles)

庚 gēng ① the seventh of the ten Heavenly Stems ② age: 同～ of the same age

耕* gēng plough; till: 春～ spring ploughing/ 深～ deep ploughing

【耕畜】gēngchù farm animal

【耕地】gēngdì ① plough; till ② cultivated land: ～面积 area under cultivation; cultivated area

【耕具】gēngjù tillage implements

【耕牛】gēngniú farm cattle

【耕耘】gēngyún ploughing and weeding; cultivation: 一分～,一分收获。The more ploughing and weeding, the better the crop.

【耕种】gēngzhòng till; cultivate

【耕作】gēngzuò tillage; cultivation; farming ◇ ～方法 methods of cultivation; farming methods

羹 gēng a thick soup: 鸡蛋～ egg custard (usu. salty)/ 分得一杯～ take a share of the spoils or profits

【羹匙】gēngchí soup spoon; tablespoon

gěng

耿 gěng ① 〈书〉bright ② dedicated ③ honest and just; upright ④ (Gěng) a surname

【耿耿】gěnggěng ① devoted; dedicated: 忠心～为人民 be dedicated heart and soul to the people ② have sth. on one's mind; be troubled: ～不寐 lose sleep over sth./ ～于怀 brood on (an injury, one's neglected duty, etc.); take sth. to heart

【耿直】gěngzhí honest and frank; upright: 秉性～ be upright by nature

哽 gěng choke (with emotion); feel a lump in one's throat

【哽咽】gěngyè choke with sobs

梗 gěng ① stalk; stem: 荷～ lotus stem/ 菠菜～儿 spinach stalk ② a slender piece of wood or metal: 火柴～ matchstick ③ straighten: ～着脖子 straighten up one's neck ④ obstruct; block: 从中作～ place obstacles in the way; put a spoke in sb.'s wheel

【梗概】gěnggài broad outline; main idea; gist: 故事的～ the gist of a story; synopsis

【梗直】gěngzhí honest and frank; upright

【梗阻】gěngzǔ block; obstruct; hamper: 横加～ unreasonably obstruct/ 山川～ be separated by mountains and rivers; be far away from each other

鲠 gěng ① 〈书〉fishbone ② (of a fishbone) get stuck in one's throat

【鲠直】gěngzhí honest and frank; upright

gèng

更* gèng 〈副〉① more; still more; even more: 团结起来,争取～大的胜利! Unite to win still greater victories! ② further; furthermore; what is more: ～进一步 go a step further
另见 gēng

【更加】gèngjiā 〈副〉more; still more; even more: 问题～复杂了。The problem became even more complicated.

gōng

工* gōng ① worker; workman; the working class: 女～

woman worker/ 矿～ miner/ ～欲善其事，必先利其器。A workman must first sharpen his tools if he is to do his work well. ② work; labour: 上～ go to work/ 既省料又省～ save both material and labour ③ (construction) project: 动～ begin a project/ 竣～ complete a project ④ industry: 化～ chemical industry ⑤ skill; craftsmanship: 唱～ (art of) singing/ 做～ acting ⑥ be versed in; be good at: ～诗善画 be well versed in painting and poetry

【工厂】gōngchǎng factory; mill; plant; works: 铁～ iron works ◇ ～区 factory district

【工场】gōngchǎng workshop

【工潮】gōngcháo workers' demonstration or protest movement; strike movement

【工程】gōngchéng engineering; project: 土木（机械、电机、采矿）～ civil (mechanical, electrical, mining) engineering/ 水利～ water conservancy project/ 浩大 a gigantic project; a tremendous amount of work ◇ ～师 engineer

【工地】gōngdì building site; construction site

【工夫】gōngfu ① time: 他三天～就学会了滑冰。It took him only three days to learn to skate./ 她去了没多大～就回来了。She didn't take long to get there and come back./ 明天有～再来吧。Come again tomorrow if you have time. ② workmanship; skill; art: 练～ (of actors, athletes, etc.) practise/ 这位杂技演员可真有～! The acrobat's skill is really superb! ③ work; labour; effort: 花了好大～ put in a lot of work/ 只要～深，铁杵磨成针。<谚> If you work at it hard enough, you can grind an iron rod into a needle.

【工会】gōnghuì trade union; labour union

【工匠】gōngjiàng craftsman; artisan

【工具】gōngjù tool; means; instrument; implement: 木工～ carpenter's tools/ 生产～ implements of production/ 运输～ means of transport

【工力】gōnglì skill; craftsmanship: ～深厚 remarkable craftsmanship/ 颇见～ show the hand of a master

【工钱】gōngqián ① money paid for odd jobs; charge for a service: 做这套衣服要多少～? How much should I pay for having the suit made? ② <口> wages; pay

【工人】gōngrén worker; workman: 产业～ industrial worker

【工商界】gōng-shāngjiè industrial and commercial circles; business circles

【工商业】gōng-shāngyè industry and commerce: 私营～ privately owned industrial and commercial enterprises ◇ ～者 industrialists and businessmen (或 merchants)

【工头】gōngtóu foreman; overseer

【工业】gōngyè industry: 轻（重）～ light (heavy) industry

【工艺】gōngyì technology; craft: 手～ handicraft

【工友】gōngyǒu ①fellow worker ②a manual worker such as janitor, cleaner, etc. in a school or government office

【工整】gōngzhěng carefully and neatly done: 字迹～ neatly lettered

【工资】gōngzī wages; pay: 基本～ basic wages/ 附加～ supplementary wages/ 货币～ money wages

【工作】gōngzuò work; job: 努力～ work hard/ 分配～ assign jobs (或 work)/ 他是做消防～的。He works in the fire brigade.

【工作者】gōngzuòzhě worker: 教育～ educational worker/ 文艺～ literary and art workers; writers and artists/ 美术～ art worker; artist/ 音乐～ musician/ 新闻～ journalist

弓* gōng ① bow: ～箭 bow and arrow ② anything bow-shaped ③ wooden land-measuring dividers ④ bend; arch; bow: ～着背 arch one's back; bend low

公* gōng ① public; state-owned; collective ② common; general: ～分母 common denominator ③ metric: ～里 kilometre ④ make public: ～之于世 make known to the world; reveal to the public ⑤ equitable; impartial; fair; just: 秉～办理 handle affairs equitably or impartially; be evenhanded ⑥ public affairs; official business: ～余 after work/ 因～外出 be away on official business ⑦ duke ⑧〔旧时对中年以上男子的尊称〕: 张～ the revered Mr.

Zhang ⑨ husband's father; father-in-law: ～说～有理，婆说婆有理。Each says he is right. 或 Both parties claim to be in the right. ⑩ male (animal): ～牛 bull/ ～鸡 cock; rooster

【公安】gōng'ān public security

【公报】gōngbào communiqué; bulletin: 联合～ joint communiqué/ 新闻～ press communiqué/ 政府～ (government) bulletin

【公报私仇】gōng bào sīchóu avenge a personal wrong in the name of public interests; abuse public power to retaliate on a personal enemy

【公布】gōngbù promulgate; announce; publish; make public: ～法令 promulgate a decree/ ～罪状 announce sb.'s crimes/ ～名单 publish a name list

【公道】gōngdào justice: 主持～ uphold justice

【公道】gōngdao fair; just; reasonable; impartial: 说句～话 to be fair; in fairness to sb./ 价钱～。The price is reasonable./ 办事～ be evenhanded; be impartial

【公德】gōngdé social morality; social ethics: 有～心 be public-spirited

【公敌】gōngdí public enemy: 人民～ an enemy of the people; a public enemy

【公断】gōngduàn arbitration

【公而忘私】gōng ér wàng sī so devoted to public service as to forget one's own interests; selfless

【公愤】gōngfèn public indignation; popular anger: 引起～ arouse public indignation

【公干】gōnggàn business: 有何～? What important business brings you here?

【公告】gōnggào announcement; proclamation

【公共】gōnggòng public; common; communal ◇ ～财产 public property/ ～厕所 public conveniences; public latrine/ ～场所 public places/ ～建筑 public buildings/ ～食堂 canteen; mess/ ～卫生 public health (或 hygiene)/ ～秩序 public order

【公共汽车】gōnggòng qìchē bus ◇ ～线路 bus line/ ～站 bus stop

【公公】gōnggong ① husband's father; father-in-law ② <方> grandfather ③ <尊> grandpa; grandad

【公海】gōnghǎi high seas

【公函】gōnghán official letter

【公祭】gōngjì public memorial ceremony

【公家】gōngjia <口> the state; the public; the organization

【公开】gōngkāi ① open; overt; public: ～的秘密 an open secret/ ～的场合 a public occasion/ ② make public; make known to the public: 把事情～出去 make the matter known to the public ◇ ～化 come out into the open; be brought into the open/ ～信 open letter

【公款】gōngkuǎn public money (或 fund)

【公历】gōnglì ① the Gregorian calendar ② 见“公元”

【公立】gōnglì established and maintained by the government; public

【公路】gōnglù highway; road: 高速～ express highway; expressway ◇ ～工程 highway engineering/ ～交通 highway communication (或 traffic)

【公论】gōnglùn public opinion; verdict of the masses: 是非自有～。Public opinion will decide which is right and which is wrong. 或 Public opinion is the best judge.

【公民】gōngmín citizen ◇ ～权 civil rights; citizenship; citizen's rights

【公平】gōngpíng fair; just; impartial; equitable: ～合理 fair and reasonable/ 买卖～ be fair in buying and selling; buy and sell at reasonable prices/ ～交易 fair deal/ ～的协议 an equitable agreement/ 太不～了。It's grossly unfair.

【公婆】gōng-pó husband's father and mother; parents-in-law

【公然】gōngrán <贬> openly; undisguisedly; brazenly: ～撕毁协议 brazenly tear up an agreement

【公认】gōngrèn generally acknowledged (或 recognized); (universally) accepted; established: ～的领袖 acknowledged leader/ ～的国际关系原则 generally recognized principles governing international relations/ ～的国际法准则 established principles of international law

【公使】 gōngshǐ envoy; minister ◇ ～馆 legation

【公式】 gōngshì formula

【公式化】 gōngshìhuà ① formulism (in art and literature) ② formulistic; stereotyped

【公事】 gōngshì public affairs; official business (或 duties): 还是～要紧。Public affairs should come first./ 我还有很多 ～要办。I still have a lot of official duties to attend to. ◇ ～包 briefcase; portfolio

【公事公办】 gōngshì gōng bàn do official business according to official principles; not let personal considerations interfere with one's execution of public duty

【公司】 gōngsī company; corporation: 钢铁～ iron and steel company/ 进出口～ import and export corporation

【公推】 gōngtuī recommend by general acclaim

【公文】 gōngwén official document

【公务】 gōngwù public affairs; official business

【公物】 gōngwù public property

【公益】 gōngyì public good; public welfare: 热心～ public-spirited

【公营】 gōngyíng publicly-owned; publicly-operated; public ◇ ～经济 the public sector of the economy; public economy/ ～企业 public enterprise

【公用】 gōngyòng for public use; public; communal ◇ ～电话 public telephone/ ～事业 public utilities

【公寓】 gōngyù ① flats; apartment house ② <旧> lodging house

【公元】 gōngyuán the Christian era: ～一二〇〇年 A. D. 1200/ ～前二二一年 221 B. C.

【公园】 gōngyuán park

【公约】 gōngyuē convention; pact: 北大西洋～ the North Atlantic Treaty

【公债】 gōngzhài (government) bonds

【公正】 gōngzhèng just; fair; impartial; fair-minded: ～的舆论 fair-minded public opinion

【公证】 gōngzhèng notarization ◇ ～人 notary public; notary

【公职】 gōngzhí public office; public employment: 担任～ hold public office

【公制】 gōngzhì the metric system ◇ ～尺寸 metric size

【公众】 gōngzhòng the public

【公主】 gōngzhǔ princess

【公子】 gōngzǐ son of a feudal prince or high official

【公子哥儿】 gōngzǐgēr a pampered son of a wealthy or influential family

功* gōng ① meritorious service (或 deed); merit; exploit: 立大～ render outstanding service/ 二等～ Merit Citation Class II/ ～大于过 one's achievements outweigh one's errors ② achievement; result: 事半～倍 yield twice the result with half the effort/ 劳而无～ work hard but to no avail ③ skill: 练～ do exercises in gymnastics, acrobatics, etc.; practise one's skill/ ～到自然成。Constant effort yields sure success. ④ <物> work: 机械～ mechanical work

【功败垂成】 gōng bài chuí chéng fail in a great undertaking on the verge of success; suffer defeat when victory is within one's grasp

【功臣】 gōngchén a person who has rendered outstanding service:不要以～自居。Don't give yourself the airs of a hero.

【功德】 gōngdé ① merits and virtues ② <佛教> charitable and pious deeds; benefaction; beneficence; works: ～无量 boundless beneficence

【功夫】 gōngfu 见"工夫" gōngfu

【功绩】 gōngjī merits and achievements; contribution

【功课】 gōngkè schoolwork; homework: 做～ do homework

【功亏一篑】 gōng kuī yī kuì fail to build a mound for want of one final basket of earth — fall short of success for lack of a final effort

【功劳】 gōngláo contribution; meritorious service; credit: 她的～可不小啊! She has certainly made no small contri-

bution! 或 She has rendered great service.

【功利】 gōnglì utility; material gain ◇ ～主义 utilitarianism/ ～主义者 utilitarian

【功名】 gōngmíng scholarly honour or official rank (in feudal times)

【功能】 gōngnéng function: ～锻炼 functional training/ ～性障碍 functional disorder/ 肝～正常。The liver is functioning normally.

【功效】 gōngxiào efficacy; effect

【功勋】 gōngxūn exploit; meritorious service

【功用】 gōngyòng function; use

红 gōng 见"女红" nǚgōng
另见 hóng

攻* gōng ① attack; take the offensive: ～入敌阵 storm into the enemy position/ 主～方向 the main direction of the offensive/ 全～型选手 an all-out attack player ② accuse; charge: 群起而～之。Everyone points an accusing finger at him. ③ study; specialize in: 他专～考古学。He specializes in archaeology.

【攻打】 gōngdǎ attack; assault

【攻读】 gōngdú ① assiduously study; diligently study ② specialize in

【攻击】 gōngjī ① attack; assault; launch an offensive: 发起总～ launch a general offensive ② accuse; charge; vilify: 恶毒～ viciously attack/ 无端的～ groundless charges/ 人身～ personal attack

【攻克】 gōngkè capture; take: ～敌军据点 capture an enemy stronghold/ ～技术难关 surmount (或 overcome) a technical difficulty; solve a difficult technical problem

【攻破】 gōngpò make a breakthrough; breach: ～敌军防线 break through (或 penetrate) the enemy defence lines/ 正义的事业是任何敌人也攻不破的。A just cause is invincible before any enemy.

【攻其不备】 gōng qí bù bèi strike where or when the enemy is unprepared; take sb. by surprise; catch sb. unawares

【攻取】 gōngqǔ storm and capture; attack and seize

【攻势】 gōngshì offensive: 采取～ take the offensive/ 政治～ political offensive/ 客队～凌厉。The visiting team maintained a powerful offensive.

【攻守同盟】 gōng-shǒu tóngméng ① offensive and defensive alliance; military alliance ② an agreement between partners in crime not to give each other away; a pact to shield each other

【攻无不克】 gōng wú bù kè all-conquering; ever-victorious

【攻下】 gōngxià capture; take; overcome: ～这一关,其他问题就好办了。Once this difficulty is overcome, other problems will be easy to solve.

【攻陷】 gōngxiàn capture; storm: 夺回被敌军～的城镇 recapture towns from enemy hands

【攻占】 gōngzhàn attack and occupy; storm and capture

供* gōng ① supply; feed: ～不上 run out; be in short supply/ 你～砖,我来砌。You pass the bricks to me, and I'll lay them. ② for (the use or convenience of): 仅～参考 for your reference only
另见 gòng

【供不应求】 gōng bù yìng qiú supply falls short of demand; demand exceeds supply

【供电】 gōngdiàn power supply

【供给】 gōngjǐ supply; provide; furnish: 原料由国家～。Raw materials are provided by the state.

【供求】 gōng-qiú supply and demand: ～关系 the relation between supply and demand/ ～平衡 balance between supply and demand

【供养】 gōngyǎng provide for (one's parents or elders); support
另见 gòngyǎng

【供应】 gōngyìng supply: 医药品～ medical supplies/ 市场～ supply of commodities; market supplies ◇ ～点 supply centre/ ～线 supply line

宫* gōng ① palace ② temple (used in a name)

【宫殿】gōngdiàn palace ◇ ~式建筑 palatial architecture

【宫女】gōngnǚ a maid in an imperial palace; maid of honour

【宫廷】gōngtíng ① palace ② royal or imperial court; court ◇ ~政变 palace coup; coup

【宫刑】gōngxíng castration (a punishment in ancient China)

恭* gōng respectful; reverent

【恭贺】gōnghè congratulate: ~新禧 Happy New Year

【恭候】gōnghòu 〈敬〉await respectfully: ~光临。We request the pleasure of your company.

【恭谨】gōngjǐn respectful and cautious

【恭敬】gōngjìng respectful: 恭恭敬敬地向老师学习 learn respectfully from the teacher

【恭顺】gōngshùn respectful and submissive

【恭维】gōngwei flatter; compliment ◇ ~话 flattery; compliments 又作"恭惟"

【恭喜】gōngxǐ 〈套〉congratulations

蚣 gōng 见"蜈蚣" wúgong

躬* gōng ①〈书〉personally: ~行实践 practise what one preaches/ ~逢其盛 be present in person on the grand occasion ② bend forward; bow: ~身 bend at the waist

【躬亲】gōngqīn attend to personally: 事必~ attend to everything personally

龚 Gōng a surname

gǒng

巩 gǒng consolidate

【巩固】gǒnggù ① consolidate; strengthen; solidify: ~阵地 consolidate a position ② consolidated; strong; solid; stable: ~的国防 strong national defence

拱* gǒng ① cup one hand in the other before the chest ② surround: 众星~月。A myriad of stars surround the moon. ③ hump up; arch: 猫~了~腰。The cat arched its back. ④〈建〉arch: ~道 archway

拱道

【拱手】gǒngshǒu ① make an obeisance by cupping one hand in the other before one's chest ② submissively: ~让人 surrender sth. submissively; hand over sth. on a silver platter

gòng

共* gòng ① common; general: ~性 general character ② share: 同呼吸，~命运 share a common fate; throw in one's lot with sb. ③ doing the same thing; together: 各族人民的代表~聚一堂，商讨国家大事。Representatives of different nationalities gather in the same hall to discuss affairs of state. ④ altogether; in all; all told

【共产主义】gòngchǎnzhǔyì communism

【共处】gòngchǔ coexist

【共存】gòngcún coexist

【共管】gòngguǎn 〈外〉condominium

【共和】gònghé republicanism; republic ◇ ~国 republic

【共计】gòngjì amount to; add up to; total: 参观展览会的~二十万人。Altogether 200,000 people visited the exhibition.

【共勉】gòngmiǎn mutual encouragement: 愿~之。Let us encourage each other in our endeavours.

【共鸣】gòngmíng ①〈物〉resonance ② sympathetic response: 引起~ arouse sympathy; strike a sympathetic chord

【共事】gòngshì work together (at the same organization); be fellow workers: ~多年 have been colleagues for many years

【共通】gòngtōng applicable to both or all: 这两者之间有~的道理。The same argument applies to both cases.

【共同】gòngtóng ① common: ~语言 common language/ ~敌人 common enemy/ ~关心的问题 matters of common concern; issues of common interest/有~之处 have something in common ② together; jointly: ~努力 make joint efforts ◇ ~点 common ground/ ~纲领 common programme/ ~市场 the Common Market

【共享】gòngxiǎng enjoy together; share: ~胜利的喜悦 share the joys of victory

贡* gòng ① tribute: 进~ pay tribute (to an imperial court) ② (Gòng) a surname

【贡品】gòngpǐn articles of tribute; tribute

【贡献】gòngxiàn contribute; dedicate; devote

供 gòng ① lay (offerings) ② offerings ③ confess; own up: 据该犯~称 as was confessed by the culprit/ 他~出了主犯的名字。He gave the name of the chief culprit. ④ confession; deposition: 口~ oral confession 另见 gōng

【供词】gòngcí a statement made under examination; confession

【供奉】gòngfèng enshrine and worship; consecrate

【供品】gòngpǐn offerings

【供认】gòngrèn confess: ~不讳 confess everything; candidly confess

【供养】gòngyǎng make offerings to; offer sacrifices to; enshrine and worship; consecrate 另见 gōngyǎng

gōu

勾* gōu ① cancel; cross out; strike out; tick off: 把他的名字~掉 cross out his name; strike his name off the register/ ~了这笔帐 cancel the debt/ 把重要的项目一~出来 tick off the important items ② delineate; draw: ~出一个轮廓 draw an outline ③ fill up the joints of brickwork with mortar or cement; point: ~墙缝 point a brick wall ④ induce; evoke; call to mind: 这件事~起了我对童年的回忆。This evoked memories of my childhood. ⑤ collude with; gang up with: 他们这帮人怎么~上的？How did these people come to gang up? 另见 gòu

【勾搭】gōuda ① gang up with: 这十个坏家伙~上了。The ten scoundrels ganged up./ 那家伙跟投机倒把分子勾勾搭搭。That fellow works hand in glove with speculators. ② seduce

【勾结】gōujié collude with; collaborate with; gang up with

【勾通】gōutōng collude with; work hand in glove with

【勾销】gōuxiāo liquidate; write off; strike out: ~债务 liquidate a debt/ 一笔~ write off at one stroke

【勾心斗角】gōuxīn-dòujiǎo 见"钩心斗角" gōuxīn-dòujiǎo

【勾引】gōuyǐn tempt; entice; seduce

沟* gōu ① ditch; channel; trench: 排水~ drainage ditch; drain/ 交通~ communication trench ② groove; rut; furrow: 拖拉机在泥路上轧出两道~。The tractor made ruts in the dirt road./ 开一~播种 make furrows for sowing

【沟渠】gōuqú irrigation canals and ditches: 田野上~纵横。The fields are crisscrossed by irrigation canals and ditches.

【沟通】gōutōng link up: ~南方各省的新铁路 the new railways that link up the southern provinces/ ~两大洋的河 an interoceanic canal/ 早在两千年前，著名的"丝绸之路"就~了中国和西亚各国的文化。As far back as 2,000 years ago, the famous Silk Road facilitated the flow of culture between China and the countries of West Asia.

钩* gōu ① hook: 钓鱼~ fishhook/ 挂衣~ clothes-hook ② hook stroke (in Chinese characters) ③ check mark; tick ④ secure with a hook; hook: 杂技演员用脚~住绳圈儿. The acrobat hooked his foot into a loop./ 他的袖子给钉子~住了. His sleeve caught on a nail./ 他把掉到井里的水桶~上来了. He fished up the bucket which had dropped into the well. ⑤ sew with large stitches: ~贴边 sew on an edging ⑥ crochet: ~花边 crochet lace

【钩心斗角】 gōuxīn-dòujiǎo intrigue against each other; jockey for position

gǒu

苟 gǒu careless; negligent; indifferent (to right or wrong): 一丝不~ be not the least bit negligent; be scrupulous about every detail; be conscientious and meticulous

【苟且】 gǒuqiě ① drift along; be resigned to circumstances: ~偷生 drag out an ignoble existence ② perfunctorily; carelessly: ~了事 dispose of sth. perfunctorily ③ illicit (sexual relations); improper

【苟全】 gǒuquán preserve (one's own life) at all costs: 他为了~一性命,无耻地向敌人屈膝投降了. To save his skin, he shamefully threw himself at the feet of the enemy.

【苟同】 gǒutóng 〔用于否定句〕 agree without giving serious thought; readily subscribe to (sb.'s view): 不敢~ beg to differ; cannot agree

【苟延残喘】 gǒuyán-cánchuǎn be on one's last legs; linger on in a steadily worsening condition

狗* gǒu ① dog ② 〈骂〉 damned; cursed

【狗胆包天】 gǒudǎn bāo tiān monstrous audacity

【狗急跳墙】 gǒu jí tiào qiáng a cornered beast will do something desperate

【狗拿耗子,多管闲事】 gǒu ná hàozi, duō guǎn xiánshì a dog trying to catch mice — too meddlesome; poke one's nose into other people's business

【狗屁】 gǒupì 〈骂〉 horseshit; rubbish; nonsense: ~不通 unreadable rubbish; mere trash

【狗腿子】 gǒutuǐzi 〈口〉 hired thug; lackey; henchman

【狗熊】 gǒuxióng ① black bear ② coward

【狗血喷头】 gǒuxuè pēn tóu 〔多用于〕: 骂得~ let loose a stream of abuse against sb.; pour out a flood of invective against sb.

【狗眼看人低】 gǒuyǎn kàn rén dī be damned snobbish; act like a snob

【狗咬吕洞宾】 gǒu yǎo Lǚ Dòngbīn snarl and snap at Lü Dongbin (one of the eight immortals in Chinese mythology) — mistake a good man for a bad one

【狗仗人势】 gǒu zhàng rén shì 〈骂〉 like a dog threatening people on the strength of its master's power — be a bully under the protection of a powerful person

【狗嘴里吐不出象牙】 gǒuzuǐli tǔbuchū xiàngyá a dog's mouth emits no ivory; a filthy mouth can't utter decent language; what can you expect from a dog but a bark

gòu

勾 gòu
另见 gōu

【勾当】 gòudang 〈贬〉 business; deal: 罪恶~ criminal activities/ 肮脏~ a dirty deal

构* gòu ① construct; form; compose: ~词 form a word ② fabricate; make up: 虚~ fabrication ③ literary composition: 佳~ a good piece of writing

【构成】 gòuchéng constitute; form; compose; make up: ~威胁 constitute (或 pose) a threat/ ~部分 component part

【构思】 gòusī ① (of writers or artists) work out the plot of a literary work or the composition of a painting: 故事的~相当巧妙. The plot of the story is ingeniously conceived. ② conception: 大胆的~ boldness of conception

【构图】 gòutú 〈美术〉 composition (of a picture)

【构陷】 gòuxiàn make a false charge against sb.; frame sb. up

【构造】 gòuzào structure; construction: 人体~ the structure of the human body/ 这种机器~简单, 使用方便. This machine is simple in construction and easy to handle.

购* gòu purchase; buy: ~粮 purchase grain/ 赊~ buy on credit

【购货单】 gòuhuòdān order form; order

【购买】 gòumǎi purchase; buy ◇ ~力 purchasing power

【购置】 gòuzhì purchase (durables): ~农具 purchase farm implements

诟 gòu 〈书〉 ① shame; humiliation ② revile; talk abusively

【诟病】 gòubìng 〈书〉 denounce; castigate: 为世~ become an object of public denunciation

【诟骂】 gòumà revile; abuse; vilify

垢 gòu ① 〈书〉 dirty; filthy: 蓬头~面 with dishevelled hair and a dirty face ② dirt; filth: 油~ grease stain/ 牙~ dental calculus ③ 〈书〉 disgrace; humiliation: 含~忍辱 endure humiliation and insult; (be forced to) swallow insults

够* gòu ① enough; sufficient; adequate: 这几个图钉~不~? Will these drawing pins be enough?/ 你们那里人力~不~? Have you got enough manpower? ② quite; rather; really: 这儿的土~肥的. The soil here is quite fertile./ 今天你们可~辛苦了. You've really done a hard day's work.

【够本】 gòuběn make enough money to cover the cost; break even

【够劲儿】 gòujìnr 〈口〉 ① (of an onerous task, etc.) almost too much to cope with: 他一个人担任那么多工作,真~. He really has a tough job having to attend to so many things. ② strong (in taste, strength, etc.): 这辣椒真~. This pepper is really hot./ 这茅台酒真~. This maotai is certainly powerful stuff.

【够朋友】 gòu péngyou deserve to be called a true friend; be a friend indeed

【够受的】 gòushòude quite an ordeal; hard to bear: 累得~ be dog-tired/ 他这一跤摔得真~. He had a really bad fall.

【够数】 gòushù sufficient in quantity; enough: 你领的镰刀不~. You didn't get enough sickles to go round.

【够味儿】 gòuwèir 〈口〉 just the right flavour; just the thing; quite satisfactory: 最后这两句你唱得真~! The way you sang the last two lines was just superb!

【够意思】 gòu yìsi ① really something; terrific: 这场球赛可真~. That was really a terrific game. ② generous; really kind: 不~ unfriendly; ungrateful

媾 gòu 〈书〉 ① wed: 婚~ marriage ② reach agreement: ~和 make peace ③ coition: 交~ copulate

【媾和】 gòuhé make peace: 单独~ make peace without consulting one's allies; make a separate peace

gū

估 gū estimate; appraise

【估计】 gūjì estimate; appraise; reckon: ~错误 miscalculate/ 清醒地~当前的形势 make a clearheaded appraisal of the present situation/ 我~他会来. I reckon he will come./ 这种可能性我们必须~到. We must take that possibility into account. 或 That is a possibility to be reckoned with./ ~今年又是一个丰收年. It looks as if there'll be another good harvest this year.

【估价】 gūjià ① appraise; evaluate: 对历史人物的~ evaluation of historical personages/ 对自己要有正确的~. One must have a correct estimate of oneself. ② 〈经〉 appraised price

【估量】 gūliáng appraise; estimate; assess: 不可～的损失 an immeasurable loss

沽 gū ① buy: ～酒 buy wine ② sell: 待价而～ wait to sell at a good price; wait for the highest bid
【沽名钓誉】 gūmíng-diàoyù fish for fame and compliments

咕 gū 〈象〉(of hens, etc.) cluck; (of turtledoves, etc.) coo
【咕咚】 gūdōng 〈象〉thud; splash; plump: 大石头一一声掉到水里去了。 The rock fell into the water with a splash.
【咕嘟】 gūdū 〈象〉bubble; gurgle: 泉水～～地往外冒。 The spring kept bubbling up./ 他端起一碗水, ～～地喝了下去。 He took up a bowl of water and gulped it down.
【咕隆】 gūlōng 〈象〉rumble; rattle; roll: 远处雷声～～地响。 Thunder rumbled in the distance./ 行李车在月台上～～地跑着。 The luggage trolley rattled along the platform.
【咕噜】 gūlū 〈象〉rumble; roll: 肚子～～直响 one's stomach keeps rumbling/ 粗大的圆木～～地从山坡上滚下来。 Large logs came rolling down the slope.
【咕哝】 gūnong murmur; mutter; grumble: 他在～些什么? What is he muttering about?

呱 gū
另见 guā
【呱呱】 gūgū 〈书〉the cry of a baby: ～坠地 (of a baby) come into the world with a cry; be born
另见 guāguā

孤 gū ① (of a child) fatherless; orphaned ② solitary; isolated; alone: ～雁 a solitary wild goose/ ～岛 an isolated island ③ I (used by feudal princes)
【孤傲】 gū'ào proud and aloof: 去掉～习气 rid oneself of aloofness and arrogance
【孤本】 gūběn the only copy extant; the only existing copy
【孤单】 gūdān ① alone: 孤孤单单一个人 all alone; all by oneself; a lone soul ② lonely; friendless
【孤独】 gūdú lonely; solitary: 过着～的生活 live in solitude
【孤儿】 gū'ér orphan
【孤芳自赏】 gūfāng zì shǎng a solitary flower in love with its own fragrance; a lone soul admiring his own purity; indulge in self-admiration
【孤寂】 gūjì lonely
【孤家寡人】 gūjiā-guǎrén a person in solitary splendour; a person who has no mass support; a loner
【孤苦伶仃】 gūkǔ-língdīng orphaned and helpless; friendless and wretched
【孤立】 gūlì ① isolated: 处境～ find oneself in an isolated position/ ～无援 isolated and cut off from help/ 任何事物都不是～地存在着的。 Nothing exists in isolation. ② isolate: ～敌人 isolate the enemy ◇ ～主义 isolationism
【孤零零】 gūlínglíng solitary; lone; all alone
【孤陋寡闻】 gūlòu-guǎwén ignorant and ill-informed
【孤僻】 gūpì unsociable and eccentric: 性情～ of an uncommunicative and eccentric disposition
【孤掌难鸣】 gūzhǎng nán míng it's impossible to clap with one hand; it's difficult to achieve anything without support
【孤注一掷】 gūzhù yī zhì stake everything on a single throw; risk everything on a single venture; put all one's eggs in one basket

姑* gū ① father's sister; aunt ② husband's sister; sister-in-law ③ 〈书〉husband's mother; mother-in-law ④ nun: 尼～ Buddhist nun/ 道～ Taoist nun ⑤ 〈书〉tentatively; for the time being
【姑表】 gūbiǎo the relationship between the children of a brother and a sister; cousinship: ～兄弟 cousins (the father of one and the mother of the other being brother and sister)
【姑夫】 gūfu the husband of one's father's sister; uncle 又作"姑父"
【姑姑】 gūgu 〈口〉father's sister; aunt

【姑母】 gūmǔ father's sister (married); aunt 又作"姑妈"
【姑娘】 gūniang ① girl ② 〈口〉daughter
【姑且】 gūqiě 〈副〉tentatively; for the moment: ～不谈 leave sth. aside for the moment/ 你～试一试。 Have a try, anyhow. 或 Suppose you give it a try.
【姑嫂】 gū-sǎo a woman and her brother's wife; sisters-in-law
【姑妄听之】 gū wàng tīng zhī see no harm in hearing what sb. has to say
【姑妄言之】 gū wàng yán zhī tell sb. sth. for what it's worth
【姑息】 gūxī appease; indulge; tolerate: 不应该～他的错误。 We shouldn't be indulgent towards his mistakes.

菇 gū mushroom

辜 gū guilt; crime: 无～ guiltless; innocent/ 死有余～。 Even death would not expiate all his crimes.
【辜负】 gūfù let down; fail to live up to; be unworthy of; disappoint: 我们决不～你的期望。 We will never let you down. 或 We'll certainly live up to your expectations

gú

骨* gú bone
另见 gǔ
【骨头】 gútou ① bone ② character; a person of a certain character: 懒～ lazybones/ 软～ a spineless creature

gǔ

古* gǔ ancient; age-old; palaeo-: ～时候 in ancient times; in olden days/ ～画 ancient painting/ ～瓷 old china
【古板】 gǔbǎn old-fashioned and inflexible
【古代】 gǔdài ancient times; antiquity: ～文化 ancient civilization ◇ ～史 ancient history
【古典】 gǔdiǎn ① classical allusion ② classical ◇ ～文学 classical literature/ ～音乐 classical music/ ～主义 classicism/ ～作品 classic
【古董】 gǔdǒng ① antique; curio ② old fogey ◇ ～鉴赏家 connoisseur of curios
【古风】 gǔfēng ① ancient customs; antiquities
【古怪】 gǔguài eccentric; odd; strange: ～脾气 eccentric character/ 样子～ odd-looking
【古话】 gǔhuà old saying: ～说, 有志者事竟成。 As the old saying goes, where there's a will there's a way.
【古迹】 gǔjì historic site; place of historic interest
【古籍】 gǔjí ancient books
【古今中外】 gǔ-jīn Zhōng-wài ancient and modern, Chinese and foreign; at all times and in all countries: ～, 概莫能外。 There is no exception to this in modern or ancient times, in China or elsewhere.
【古旧】 gǔjiù antiquated; archaic: ～词语 archaic words and expressions; archaisms
【古老】 gǔlǎo ancient; age-old: ～的传说 legend
【古朴】 gǔpǔ (of art, architecture, etc.) simple and unsophisticated; of primitive simplicity
【古人】 gǔrén the ancients; our forefathers
【古色古香】 gǔsè-gǔxiāng antique; quaint
【古书】 gǔshū ancient books
【古玩】 gǔwán antique; curio
【古往今来】 gǔwǎng-jīnlái through the ages; of all ages; since time immemorial
【古为今用】 gǔ wéi jīn yòng make the past serve the present
【古文】 gǔwén ① prose written in the classical literary style; ancient Chinese prose ② Chinese script before the Qin Dynasty (221-207 B.C.)
【古文字】 gǔwénzì ancient writing
【古物】 gǔwù ancient objects; antiquities ◇ ～陈列馆 museum of antiquities

古稀】 gǔxī seventy years of age: 年近～ getting on for seventy

古雅】 gǔyǎ of classic beauty and in elegant taste; of classic elegance

古语】 gǔyǔ ① archaism ② old saying

古装】 gǔzhuāng ancient cóstume

谷* gǔ ① valley; gorge: 深～ a deep valley; gorge ② cereal; grain: ～类作物 cereal crops ③ millet ④ 〈方〉 unhusked rice

谷物】 gǔwù cereal; grain

股* gǔ ① thigh ② section (of an office, enterprise, etc.): 人事～ personnel section ③ strand; ply: 三～的绳子 a rope of three strands/ 三～的毛线 three-ply wool ④ one of several equal parts; share in a company: 分～ divide into equal parts/ 优先～ preference shares; preferred stock ⑤ 〈量〉 ⓐ 〔用于成条的东西〕: 一～线 a skein of thread/ 一～泉水 a stream of spring water/ 两～道 two roads (或 paths, tracks) ⓑ 〔用于气体、气味、力气〕: 一～香味 a whiff of fragrance/ 一～热气 a stream (或 puff) of hot air/ 一～劲 a burst of energy ⓒ 〈贬〉〔用于成批的人〕: 两～土匪 two gangs of bandits/ 一～敌军 a horde of enemy soldiers; .an enemy detachment

股本】 gǔběn capital stock

股东】 gǔdōng shareholder; stockholder

股份】 gǔfèn share; stock

股金】 gǔjīn money paid for shares (in a partnership or cooperative)

股票】 gǔpiào share certificate; share; stock ◇ ～行市 current prices of stocks; quotations on the stock exchange/ ～交易 buying and selling of stocks/ ～交易所 stock exchange/ ～经纪人 stockbroker; stockjobber/ ～市场 stock market

股息】 gǔxī dividend

股子】 gǔzi ① share ② 〈量〉〔用于力量、气味等〕: 这小伙子有一～使不完的劲。The youngster just doesn't know what it is to be tired.

枯】 gǔ bull

枯牛】 gǔniú bull

骨* gǔ ① bone ② skeleton; framework: 钢～水泥 reinforced concrete ③ character; spirit: 傲～ lofty and unyielding character/ 媚～ obsequiousness 另见 gú

骨干】 gǔgàn ① 〈生理〉 diaphysis ② backbone; mainstay: 起～作用 be a mainstay/ 科技队伍中的～力量 the backbone of the scientific and technological contingents

骨鲠在喉】 gǔ gěng zài hóu have a fishbone caught in one's throat: 如～，不吐不快 feel as if one has a fishbone in one's throat and cannot rest until one has spat it out; have an opinion one cannot suppress

骨灰】 gǔhuī ① bone ash ② ashes of the dead

骨架】 gǔjià skeleton; framework: 房屋的～ the framework of a house/ 小说的～已经有了。The framework of the novel has been worked out.

骨气】 gǔqì strength of character; moral integrity; backbone: 我们是有～的。We have backbone./ 有～的人 a man of integrity

骨肉】 gǔròu flesh and blood; kindred: 亲生～ one's own flesh and blood/ ～兄弟 blood brothers; one's own brothers/ ～相连 as closely linked as flesh and blood/ ～之亲 blood relations/ ～情谊 kindred feelings; feelings of kinship/ ～团聚 a family reunion

骨瘦如柴】 gǔ shòu rú chái thin as a lath; worn to a shadow; a mere skeleton; a bag of bones

贾】 gǔ ① merchant ② engage in trade 另见 jiǎ

蛊】 gǔ a legendary venomous insect

蛊惑】 gǔhuò poison and bewitch: ～人心 confuse and poison people's minds; resort to demagogy

鹄】 gǔ 〈书〉 target (in archery): 中～ hit the target 另见 hú

鼓* gǔ ① drum: 打～ beat a drum/ ～声 drumbeats ② beat; strike; sound: ～瑟 play the se (an ancient Chinese plucked instrument)/ ～掌 clap one's hands/ ～其如簧之舌 talk glibly ③ blow with bellows, etc.: ～风 work a bellows ④ rouse; agitate; pluck up: ～起勇气 pluck up (或 muster) one's courage ⑤ bulge; swell: 把口袋装得～～的 fill one's pockets till they bulge/ ～着嘴 pout

鼓吹】 gǔchuī ① advocate ② 〈贬〉 preach; advertise; play up

鼓动】 gǔdòng ① agitate; arouse: 做宣传～工作 conduct propaganda and agitation/ ～群众 arouse the masses ② instigate; incite: 这些坏事是谁～你干的? Who put you up to all these dirty tricks?

鼓励】 gǔlì encourage; urge

鼓手】 gǔshǒu drummer

鼓舞】 gǔwǔ inspire; hearten: 在大好形势～下 inspired by the very good situation/ ～人心的消息 most heartening news

鼓乐】 gǔyuè strains of music accompanied by drumbeats: ～齐鸣,万众欢腾。The cheers of the jubilant crowds mingled with crescendos of music.

鼓噪】 gǔzào make an uproar; raise a hubbub; clamour: ～一时 make a great to-do about sth. for a time

鼓掌】 gǔzhǎng clap one's hands; applaud: 热烈～ warmly applaud/ ～通过 approve by acclamation

瞽】 gǔ 〈书〉 blind: ～者 blind person

gù

固* gù ① solid; firm: 加～ make sth. more solid; strengthen; reinforce/ 本～枝荣。When the root is firm, the branches flourish. ② firmly; resolutely: ～辞 resolutely refuse; firmly decline ③ solidify; consolidate; strengthen: ～堤 strengthen the dyke ④ 〈书〉 originally; in the first place; as a matter of course: ～当如此。It is just as it should be. ⑤ 〈书〉 admittedly; no doubt: 乘车～可,乘船亦无不可。Admittedly we can make the journey by train, but there is no harm in our travelling by boat.

固定】 gùdìng ① fixed; regular: 电台的～节目 a regular (或 scheduled) radio programme/ ～的作战线 fixed battle lines/ 不要用～眼光看问题。Don't take a static view of things. ② fix; regularize: 把灯泡～在车床上 fix the lampstand on the lathe/ 把业务学习时间～下来 set a regular time for vocational study

固然】 gùrán 〈副〉 ①〔表示承认某个事实,引起下文转折〕 no doubt; it is true; true: 这里条件～艰苦些,但正是我们锻炼的好地方。True, conditions are tougher here, but that gives us a chance to temper ourselves./ 这样办～稳当些,可就是要慢一些。No doubt it would be safer to do it that way, but it would be slower. ②〔表示承认甲事实,也不否认乙事实〕of course; admittedly: 他能来～很好,不来也没关系。If he can come, of course that'll be fine, but if he can't, it doesn't matter.

固若金汤】 gù ruò jīn tāng strongly fortified; impregnable

固守】 gùshǒu defend tenaciously; be firmly entrenched in: ～阵地 tenaciously defend one's position/ ～老一套的办法 stick to the old ways

固有】 gùyǒu intrinsic; inherent; innate: ～的属性 intrinsic attributes

固执】 gùzhí ① obstinate; stubborn ② persist in; cling to: ～己见 stubbornly adhere to one's opinions

故* gù ① incident; happening: 事～ accident/ 变～ unforeseen event; misfortune ② reason; cause: 无～缺勤 be absent without reason (或 cause)/ 托～离开 make an excuse and leave/ 该生不知何～缺席。The reason for the student's absence remains unknown. ③ on purpose; intentionally: 明知～犯 wilfully violate (a law or rule)/

作镇静 pretend to be calm; ～作惊讶 put on a show of surprise; feign surprise ④ hence; therefore; consequently; for this reason: 无私～能无畏。Fearlessness stems from selflessness. ⑤ former; old: ～址 site (of an ancient monument, etc.)/ 黄河～道 the old course of the Huanghe River ⑥ friend; acquaintance: 非亲非～ neither relative nor friend; a perfect stranger ⑦ die: 病～ die of illness

【故步自封】 gù bù zì fēng stand still and refuse to make progress; be complacent and conservative

【故伎】 gùjì stock trick; old tactics: ～重演 play the same old trick

【故居】 gùjū former residence (或 home)

【故里】 gùlǐ native place

【故弄玄虚】 gù nòng xuánxū purposely turn simple things into mysteries; be deliberately mystifying

【故事】 gùshi ① story; tale: 民间～ folktale; folk story ② plot: 这部小说～性很强。The novel has an interesting plot.

【故态复萌】 gùtài fù méng slip back into one's old ways

【故土】 gùtǔ native land

【故乡】 gùxiāng native place; hometown; birthplace

【故意】 gùyì intentionally; wilfully; deliberately; on purpose: ～刁难 place obstacles in sb.'s way/ 天气好象～和我们作对似的。It looks as if the weather was purposely making trouble for us./ 对不起,我不是～的。I'm sorry, I didn't do it on purpose. 或 I'm sorry, I didn't mean it.

【故障】 gùzhàng hitch; breakdown; stoppage; trouble: 排除～ fix a breakdown; clear a stoppage/ 发动机出了～。The engine has broken down. 或 The engine is out of order./ 出了什么～? What's gone wrong?

【故纸堆】 gùzhǐduī a heap of musty old books or papers

顾* gù ① turn round and look at; look at: 环～四周 look around/ 相～一笑 smile at each other knowingly ② attend to; take into consideration: 兼～ give consideration to both/ 不～个人安危 not give a thought to one's safety/ 医生一不得吃饭就去抢救病人。The doctor immediately attended to the emergency case without stopping for a meal./ 这么多事你一个人～得过来吗? You've got so many things to attend to. Can you manage all by yourself? ③ visit; call on: 三～茅庐 call on sb. repeatedly (to enlist his help, etc.)

【顾此失彼】 gùcǐ-shībǐ attend to one thing and lose sight of another; have too many things to take care of at the same time

【顾及】 gùjí take into account; attend to; give consideration to: 无暇～ have no time to attend to the matter/ 事前应该一事后的效果。Before taking an action, one should consider what effect it may have./ ～可能产生的后果 take the possible consequences into account

【顾忌】 gùjì scruple; misgiving: 毫无～ without scruple; have no scruples/ 不能不有所～ have to think twice (before doing sth.); be unable to overcome certain misgivings

【顾客】 gùkè customer; shopper; client

【顾虑】 gùlù misgiving; apprehension; worry: 打消～ dispel one's misgivings (或 worries)/ ～重重 be full of worries; have no end of misgivings/ 你不必有任何～。You needn't have any misgivings whatsoever./ 他毫无～地谈出了自己的想法。He spoke his mind without the slightest hesitancy.

【顾名思义】 gù míng sī yì seeing the name of a thing one thinks of its function; just as its name implies; as the term suggests

【顾前不顾后】 gù qián bù gù hòu drive ahead without considering the consequences; act rashly

【顾全】 gùquán show consideration for and take care to preserve: ～大局 take the interests of the whole into account; take the situation as a whole into consideration/ ～面子 spare sb.'s feelings

【顾问】 gùwèn adviser; consultant ◇ ～委员会 consultative (或 advisory) committee

【顾影自怜】 gù yǐng zì lián ① look at one's reflection and admire oneself ② look at one's shadow and lament one's lot

【顾主】 gùzhǔ customer; client; patron

雇 gù hire; employ: ～船 hire a boat

【雇工】 gùgōng ① hire labour; hire hands ② hired labourer (或 hand, worker)

【雇佣】 gùyōng employ; hire

【雇员】 gùyuán employee

【雇主】 gùzhǔ employer

痼 gù chronic; inveterate

【痼疾】 gùjí chronic (或 obstinate) illness

锢 gù ① plug with molten metal; run metal into crack ② 〈书〉 hold in custody; imprison

guā

瓜* guā melon, gourd, etc.: 冬～ white gourd/ 西～ watermelon

【瓜分】 guāfēn carve up; divide up; partition: ～别国领土 carve up the territory of another country

【瓜葛】 guāgé connection; implication; association: 他跟投机分子有～。He's got mixed up with speculators.

【瓜熟蒂落】 guāshú-dìluò when a melon is ripe it falls of its stem — things will be easily settled when conditions are ripe

【瓜田李下】 guātián-lǐxià in a melon patch or under a plum tree — in suspicious circumstances or surroundings: 瓜田不纳履,李下不正冠。Don't pull on your shoe in a melon patch; don't adjust your cap under a plum tree — don't do anything to arouse suspicion.

【瓜子】 guāzǐ melon seeds ◇ ～脸 oval face

呱 guā
另见 gū

【呱呱】 guāguā 〈象〉 (of ducks) quack; (of frogs) croak (of crows) caw
另见 gūgū

【呱呱叫】 guāguājiào 〈口〉 tiptop; top-notch

刮* guā ① scrape: ～锅子 scrape a pot clean/ ～鱼鳞 scale a fish/ ～胡子 shave the beard/ 就～破一点皮 It's only a scratch. ② plunder; fleece; extort: ～来的财富 extorted wealth ③ blow: ～大风了。It's blowing hard. There's a gale blowing./ 把～倒的树苗扶起来 straighten up the saplings that have been blown down

【刮脸】 guāliǎn shave (the face) ◇ ～刀 razor

【刮脸皮】 guā liǎnpí 〈方〉 rub the forefinger against one's own cheek (to indicate scorn for sb.); point the finger of scorn at sb.

【刮目相看】 guāmù xiāng kàn look at sb. with new eyes treat sb. with increased respect

guǎ

剐 guǎ ① cut to pieces (a form of capital punishment in ancient times); dismember: 千刀万～ be cut to pieces/ 舍得一身～,敢把皇帝拉下马。He who fears not being cut to pieces dares to unhorse the emperor. ③ cut; slit: 手上～了个口子 cut one's hand

寡 guǎ ① few; scant: 沉默～言 uncommunicative; taciturn/ 以～敌众 pit a few against many; fight against heavy odds/ 失道～助。An unjust cause finds scant support. ② tasteless: 清汤～水 watery soup; something insipid ③ widowed: 鳏～ widowers and widows/ 守～ live in widowhood

【寡不敌众】 guǎ bù dí zhòng be hopelessly outnumbered

【寡妇】 guǎfù widow

【寡廉鲜耻】 guǎlián-xiǎnchǐ lost to shame; shameless

【寡人】 guǎrén I, the sovereign; we (used by a royal person in proclamations instead of I)

guà

卦 guà divinatory symbols: 占~ divination

挂* guà ① hang; put up: 把地图~在墙上 put (或 hang) the map up on the wall/ 天上~着一轮明月。A bright moon hung in the sky. ② hitch; get caught: 她的衣服给钉子~住了。Her dress got caught on a nail. ③ ring off: 她已经把电话~了。She's hung up./ 你先别~，等我查一下。Hold the line while I find out. ④ <方> call (或 phone, ring) up; put sb. through to: 我呆会儿再给他~电话。I'll ring him up again./ 请给我~拖拉机站，Give me the tractor station, please. 或 Please put me through to the tractor station. ⑤ <方> be concerned about: 时刻把国家的利益~在心上 always have, the welfare of the nation at heart/ 他总是~着队上的病。He's very worried about the team leader's illness.

挂彩 guàcǎi ① decorate with coloured silk festoons; decorate for festive occasions ② be wounded in action

挂齿 guàchǐ mention: 区区小事，何足~。Such a trifling matter is not worth mentioning.

挂号 guàhào ① register (at a hospital, etc.): 请排队~。Please queue up to register. ② send by registered mail: 你这封信要不要~? Do you want to have this letter registered? ◇ ~处 registration office/ ~费 registration fee/ ~信 registered letter (或 mail)

挂怀 guàhuái have sth. weighing on one's mind; be concerned (或 worried) about

挂虑 guàlǜ be anxious about; worry about

挂名 guàmíng titular; nominal; only in name

挂念 guàniàn worry about sb. who is absent; miss: 十分~ miss sb. very much

挂牌 guàpái <旧> hang out one's shingle; put up one's brass plate

挂图 guàtú ① wall map ② hanging chart

挂羊头，卖狗肉 guà yáng tóu, mài gǒu ròu hang up a sheep's head and sell dogmeat — try to palm off sth. inferior to what it purports to be

挂一漏万 guà yī lòu wàn for one thing cited, ten thousand may have been left out — the list is far from complete

guāi

乖* guāi ① well-behaved (child); good: 真是个~孩子。There's a dear. ② clever; shrewd; alert: 学~了 become a little wiser ③ <书> perverse; contrary to reason: 有~常理 run counter to reason

乖乖 guāiguāi ① well-behaved; obedient: 孩子们都~儿地坐着听老师讲故事。The children all sat quietly listening to the teacher telling stories. ② little dear; darling

乖戾 guāilì perverse (behaviour); disagreeable (character)

乖谬 guāimiù absurd; abnormal

乖僻 guāipì eccentric; odd

乖巧 guāiqiǎo ① clever ② cute; lovely

掴 guāi slap; smack: ~耳光 box sb.'s ears; slap sb. on the face
另见 guó

guǎi

拐 guǎi ① turn: ~过墙角 turn the corner of a house/ ~进一条胡同 turn into an alley/ 往左~ turn to the left/ 前面走不通了，我们~回去吧。We can't get through here, let's turn back. ② limp: 一~一~地走 limp along; walk with a limp ③ crutch: 走路架着双~ walk with crutches ④ abduct; kidnap ⑤ swindle; make off with: ~款潜逃 abscond with funds

拐骗 guǎipiàn ① abduct ② swindle: ~钱财 swindle money (out of sb.)

拐弯 guǎiwān ① turn a corner; turn: ~要慢行。Slow down when turning a corner./ 往前走向左一一~就到了。Go straight ahead, turn left and you'll be there./ 在河水~的地方 at the river bend ② turn round; pursue a new course: 他思想一时还拐不过弯来。He hasn't straightened out his ideas yet.

拐弯抹角 guǎiwān-mòjiǎo talk in a roundabout way; beat about the bush: 说话不要~。Get to the point. Don't beat about the bush.

拐杖 guǎizhàng walking stick

guài

怪* guài ① strange; odd; queer; bewildering: 你说~不~? Isn't this strange?/ ~现象 something quite unusual/ 出~题 set queer (或 odd) questions (in an examination) ② find sth. strange; wonder at: 那有什么可~的? Is that anything to be surprised at? ③ quite; rather: 箱子~沉的。The suitcase is rather heavy./ 瞧，这些葡萄~水灵的。Look, how fresh and juicy those grapes are. ④ monster; demon; evil being: 鬼~ demons, ghosts and goblins; forces of evil ⑤ blame: 不能~他们。They're not to blame. 或 It's not their fault./ ~我没讲清楚。I'm to blame for not having made it clearer.

怪不得 guàibude ① no wonder; so that's why; that explains why: ~多一张票，小张把她的让出来了。So that's why (或 No wonder) there's an extra ticket. Xiao Zhang has given hers up. ② not to blame: 这事~他。He's not to blame for this.

怪诞 guàidàn weird; strange: ~不经 weird and uncanny; fantastic

怪话 guàihuà cynical remark; grumble; complaint: 说~ make cynical remarks

怪里怪气 guàiliguàiqì eccentric; peculiar; queer: ~的人 an eccentric fellow

怪模怪样 guàimú-guàiyàng queer-looking; grotesque

怪僻 guàipì eccentric: 性情~ eccentric

怪声怪气 guàishēng-guàiqì (speak in a) strange voice or affected manner

怪物 guàiwu ① monster; monstrosity; freak ② an eccentric person

怪异 guàiyì monstrous; strange; unusual

guān

关* guān ① shut; close: 请随手~门。Please close the door behind you./ 这扇门~不上。The door won't shut. ② turn off: ~收音机 turn (或 switch) off the radio/ ~电灯 turn off the light ③ lock up; put in: ~进监狱 lock up (in prison); put behind bars/ 别把孩子们成天~在屋里。Don't keep the children inside all day. ④ close down ⑤ pass: 把~ guard the pass; check ⑥ customhouse ⑦ barrier; critical juncture: 技术难~ technical barriers ⑧ concern; involve: 这不~他的事。That doesn't concern him./ 这些意见至~重要。These ideas are of extreme importance.

关闭 guānbì ① close; shut: ~门窗 close the doors and windows ② (of a shop or factory) close down; shut down

关怀 guānhuái show loving care for; show solicitude for: ~备至 show the utmost solicitude

关键 guānjiàn hinge; key; crux: 问题的~ the crux (或 heart) of the matter; the key to the question/ ~的一年 a year of crucial importance/ ~时刻 a critical (或 crucial) moment/ ~在于要有决心和信心。What counts is determination and confidence.

关节 guānjié ① <生理> joint ② key (或 crucial) links; links: 应该注意那些涉及全局的重要~。Attention should be centred on the links that have a bearing on the situation as a whole.

关口 guānkǒu ① strategic pass ② juncture

关联 guānlián be related; be connected: 国民经济各部门是互相~互相依存的。The various branches of the national economy are interrelated and interdependent./ 数学和天文学是互相~的科学. Mathematics and astronomy are cognate sciences.

【关门】 guānmén ① close: 展览馆六点半~. The exhibition centre closes at 6:30. ② slam the door on sth.; refuse discussion or consideration: 对方在谈判中还没有~. The other side hasn't yet slammed the door on further negotiations./ 采取~态度 adopt a closed-door attitude ③ behind closed doors: 我们不能~办报. We must not run a newspaper behind closed doors.

【关切】 guānqiè be deeply concerned; show one's concern over: 表示严重~ show grave concern over/ 获悉贵国遭受地震,我们极为~. We are deeply concerned at the news that your country has been struck by an earthquake.

【关税】 guānshuì customs duty; tariff: 保护~ protective tariff/ 特惠~ preferential tariff

【关头】 guāntóu juncture; moment: 紧要~ a critical moment

【关系】 guānxi ① relation; relationship: 外交~ diplomatic relations/ 两国间的友好合作~ friendly relations and cooperation between the two countries ② bearing; impact; significance: 这一点对今后工作~重大. This has an important bearing on our future work./ 你上午去还是下午去,~不大. It won't make much difference whether you go in the morning or in the afternoon. ③〔泛指原因条多与"由于""因为"连用〕: 由于时间~, 就谈到这里吧. Since time is limited, I'll have to stop here. ④ concern; affect; have a bearing on / 交通运输是~到工农业生产的重要部门. Transport and communications play a very important part in industrial and agricultural production.

【关心】 guānxīn be concerned with; be interested in: 我们要~国家大事. We should concern ourselves with affairs of state./ 双方共同~的问题 matters of interest to both sides

【关于】 guānyú 〈介〉〔引进某种行为或事物的关系者, 组成介词结构〕 about; on; with regard to; concerning: ~修改联合公报稿的具体建议 specific proposals with regard to the rewording of the draft joint communiqué/ ~保护森林的若干规定 regulations concerning the protection of forests

【关照】 guānzhào ① look after; keep an eye on: 我走后, 这里的工作就靠你多~了. When I'm gone, you'll have to look after the work here./ 感谢你的~. Thank you for the trouble you've taken on my behalf. ② notify by word of mouth: 你走的时候请~一声. Please let me know when you're ready to go.

【关注】 guānzhù follow with interest; pay close attention to; show solicitude for: 我们对这个地区的情况十分~. We follow with interest the development of the situation in this area. 或 We're paying a good deal of attention to what's going on in this area.

观*

guān ① look at; watch; observe: 登泰山, ~日出 ascend Taishan Mountain to see the sunrise/ 从轻处理, 以~后效 deal with it leniently and see how he behaves in future ② sight; view: 奇~ wonderful sight (或 spectacle)/ 外~ outward appearance ③ outlook; view; concept: 世界~ world outlook
另见 guàn

【观测】 guāncè observe: ~气象 make weather observations/ ~气球 balloon observation

【观察】 guānchá observe; watch; survey: ~地形 survey the terrain/ ~动静 watch what is going on ◇ ~机 observation aircraft/ ~家 observer/ ~所 observation post/ ~员 observer

【观点】 guāndiǎn point of view; viewpoint; standpoint: 阐明~ explain one's position

【观感】 guāngǎn impressions

【观光】 guānguāng go sightseeing; visit; tour ◇ ~团 sightseeing party; visiting group/ ~者 sightseer

【观看】 guānkàn watch; view: ~排球比赛 watch a volleyball match

【观礼】 guānlǐ attend a celebration or ceremony: 国庆~代表 a representative attending National Day celebrations

◇ ~台 reviewing stand; visitors' stand

【观摩】 guānmó inspect and learn from each other's work; view and emulate ◇ ~演出 performance before fellow artists for the purpose of discussion and emulation

【观念】 guānniàn sense; idea; concept: 组织~ sense of organization

【观赏】 guānshǎng view and admire; enjoy the sight of ◇ ~植物 ornamental (或 decorative) plant

【观望】 guānwàng wait and see; look on (from the sidelines): 采取~态度 take a wait-and-see attitude

【观象台】 guānxiàngtái 〈天〉 observatory

【观音】 Guānyīn 〈佛教〉 Avalokitesvara; Guanyin (a Bodhisattva) 又作"观世音"

【观瞻】 guānzhān the appearance of a place and the impressions it leaves; sight; view: 有碍~ be unsightly; be repugnant to the eye; offend the eye

【观众】 guānzhòng spectator; viewer; audience

官*

guān ① government official; officer; officeholder: ~兵一致 unity between officers and men ②〈旧〉 government-owned; government-sponsored; official; public: ~办 run by the government; operated by official bodies ③ organ: 感~ sense organ

【官场】 guānchǎng 〈旧〉 officialdom; official circles

【官邸】 guāndǐ official residence; official mansion: 大使~ ambassador's residence

【官方】 guānfāng of or by the government; official: ~人士 official quarters/ ~消息 news from government sources; official sources/ 以~身分 in an official capacity

【官架子】 guānjiàzi the airs of an official; bureaucratic airs

【官阶】 guānjiē official rank

【官吏】 guānlì 〈旧〉 government officials

【官僚】 guānliáo bureaucrat: 封建~ feudal bureaucrat/ 清除~习气 get rid of bureaucratic practices/ 这人真~! What a bureaucrat that fellow is!

【官僚主义】 guānliáozhǔyì bureaucracy ◇ ~者 bureaucrat/ ~作风 bureaucratic style of work; bureaucratic way of doing things

【官能】 guānnéng (organic) function; sense: 视、听、嗅、味、触这五种~ the five senses of sight, hearing, smell, taste and touch

【官腔】 guānqiāng bureaucratic tone; official jargon: 打~ speak in a bureaucratic tone; stall with official jargon

【官司】 guānsi 〈口〉 lawsuit: 和人打~ go to law against sb.

【官衔】 guānxián official title

【官样文章】 guānyàng wénzhāng mere formalities; officialese

【官员】 guānyuán official: 外交~ diplomatic official

【官职】 guānzhí government post; official position

冠*

guān ① hat: 免~照片 bare-headed photo/ 衣~整齐 be neatly dressed ② corona: 树~ the crown of a tree/ 花~ corolla/ 牙~ the crown of a tooth ③ crest; comb: 鸡~ cock's comb; crest
另见 guàn

【冠冕】 guānmiǎn royal crown; official hat

【冠冕堂皇】 guānmiǎn tánghuáng highfalutin; high-sounding: ~的理由 high-sounding excuses

棺*

guān coffin

【棺材】 guāncai coffin

鳏

guān wifeless; widowered

【鳏夫】 guānfū 〈书〉 an old wifeless man; bachelor or widower

【鳏寡孤独】 guān-guǎ-gū-dú widowers, widows, orphans and the childless — those who have no kith and kin and cannot support themselves

guǎn

馆*

guǎn ① accommodation for guests: 旅~ hotel/ 宾~ guesthouse ② embassy, legation or consulate: 办理大

~事宜 arrange for the setting up of an embassy ⑦ (of service trades) shop: 理发~ barbershop/ 茶~ teahouse/ 饭~ restaurant/ 照相~ photo studio ④ a place for cultural activities: 博物~ museum/ 展览~ exhibition hall/ 文化~ cultural centre/ 美术~ art gallery/ 体育~ gymnasium /图书~ library

管 * guǎn ① tube; pipe: 钢~ steel tube/ 血~ blood vessel/ 输油~ oil pipeline ② wind instrument: 单簧~ clarinet/ 铜~乐器 brass wind ③ 〈量〉〔用于细长圆筒形的东西〕: 一~毛笔 a writing brush/ 一~牙膏 a tube of toothpaste ④〈电子〉valve; tube: 电子~ electron tube ⑤ manage; run; be in charge of: ~伙食 be in charge of the mess/ ~家务 run the house; keep house/ 他把仓库~得井井有条。He keeps the warehouse in good order./ 每个工人~好几台机器。Each worker minds (或 tends) several machines. ⑥ subject sb. to discipline: 孩子要~，但更要引导。Children need discipline, but they need guidance even more. ⑦ bother about; mind: ~得宽 make everything one's own business/ 别~我！Don't bother about me.

【管保】 guǎnbǎo ① guarantee; assure: 我~你吃了这药就好。I guarantee that if you take this medicine, you'll soon get well. ② certainly; surely: 他~不知道。I'm sure he doesn't know.

【管道】 guǎndào pipeline; piping; conduit; tubing: 煤气~ gas piping/ ~安装 piping erection

【管风琴】 guǎnfēngqín 〈乐〉 pipe organ; organ

【管家】 guǎnjia ①〈旧〉steward; butler ② manager; housekeeper

【管见】 guǎnjiàn 〈谦〉 my humble opinion; my limited understanding: 容陈~。Let me state my humble opinion.

【管教】 guǎnjiào 〈方〉 certainly; assuredly; surely: 听他的话，~没错。Surely you won't go wrong if you follow his advice.

【管教】 guǎnjiào subject sb. to discipline

【管窥】 guǎnkuī look at sth. through a bamboo tube — have a restricted view: ~ in my humble opinion

【管窥蠡测】 guǎnkuī-lícè look at the sky through a bamboo tube and measure the sea with a calabash — restricted in vision and shallow in understanding

【管理】 guǎnlǐ manage; run; administer; supervise: ~生产 manage production/ 加强企业~ strengthen the administration (或 management) of enterprises ◇ ~处 administrative (或 management) office/ ~费 management expenses; costs of administration/ ~人员 administrative (或 managerial) personnel/ ~委员会 management committee; board of management/ ~员 a person managing some aspect of daily work within an organization

【管事】 guǎnshì ① run affairs; be in charge: 这里谁~? Who's in charge here?

【管束】 guǎnshù restrain; check; control: 严加~ keep sb. under strict control

【管辖】 guǎnxiá have jurisdiction over; administer: 在~范围之内 come within the jurisdiction of

【管弦乐】 guǎnxiányuè orchestral music ◇ ~队 orchestra/ ~法 orchestration

【管押】 guǎnyā take sb. into custody; keep in custody; detain

【管乐队】 guǎnyuèduì wind band; band

【管乐器】 guǎnyuèqì wind instrument

【管制】 guǎnzhì ① control: 军事~ military control/ 外汇~ foreign exchange control ② put under surveillance

【管中窥豹】 guǎnzhōng kuī bào look at a leopard through a bamboo tube — have a limited view of sth.

【管中窥豹，可见一斑】 guǎnzhōng kuī bào, kě jiàn yī bān look at one spot on a leopard and you can visualize the whole animal; conjure up the whole thing through seeing a part of it

guàn

观 * guàn Taoist temple
另见 guān

贯 guàn ① pass through; pierce: 纵~两省的铁路 a railway passing through two provinces from north to south/ 学~古今 well versed in both ancient and modern learning ② be linked together; follow in a continuous line: 鱼~而入 file in ③ birthplace; native place: 籍~ the place of one's birth or origin

【贯彻】 guànchè carry out (或 through); implement; put into effect

【贯通】 guàntōng ① have a thorough knowledge of; be well versed in: ~中西医学 have a thorough knowledge of both Western and traditional Chinese medicine/ 豁然~ suddenly see the light ② link up; thread together: 这条铁路已全线~。The whole railway line has been joined up.

【贯注】 guànzhù ① concentrate on; be absorbed in: 把精力~在教育工作上 concentrate one's energy on·educational work/ 全神~ be wholly absorbed; be rapt ② be connected in meaning or feeling: 这两句是一气~下来的。These two sentences are closely connected. 或 These two sentences hang together.

冠 * guàn ①〈书〉put on a hat ② precede; crown with ③ first place; the best: 这里的棉花产量为全国之~。This area ranks first in the whole country for cotton output.
另见 guān

【冠军】 guànjūn champion

惯 * guàn ① be used to; be in the habit of: 劳动~了，闲着就不舒服。When you are used to physical labour, you feel uncomfortable if you're idle./ 这里空气比较稀薄，~了就好了。The air is rather thin here, but you'll get used to it in time. ② indulge; spoil: 别把孩子~坏了。Don't spoil the child.

【惯例】 guànlì convention; usual practice: 国际~ international practice

【惯用】 guànyòng ① habitually practise; consistently use ② habitual; customary: ~伎俩 customary tactics; old tricks/ ~手法 habitual practice

盥 guàn 〈书〉wash (the hands or face)

【盥漱】 guànshù wash one's face and rinse one's mouth

【盥洗】 guànxǐ wash one's hands and face ◇ ~室 washroom

灌 guàn ① irrigate: 冬~ winter irrigation/ 引水~田 channel water to irrigate the fields ② fill; pour: 暖瓶都~满了。The thermos flasks have all been filled./ ~药 pour medicine down the throat/ 冷风往屋里直~。The cold air poured into the room./ ~醉 get sb. drunk

【灌唱片】 guàn chàngpiàn make a gramophone record; cut a disc

【灌溉】 guàngài irrigate: 提水~ irrigation by pumping ◇ ~面积 irrigated area/ ~渠 irrigation canal/ ~网 irrigation network/ ~系统 irrigation system

【灌输】 guànshū instil into; inculcate; imbue with

【灌音】 guànyīn have one's voice recorded

鹳 guàn stork

罐 * guàn jar; pot; tin: 一~苹果酱 a jar of apple jam/ 茶叶~ tea caddy/ 水~ water pitcher

【罐头】 guàntou tin; can: ~牛肉 tinned (或 canned) beef ◇ ~食品 tinned (或 canned) food

【罐子】 guànzi pot; jar; pitcher; jug

guāng

光 * guāng ① light; ray: 日~ sunlight/ 爱克斯~ X ray ② brightness; lustre: 红~满面 one's face aglow (with health, etc.)/ 两眼无~ dull-eyed ③ honour; glory: 为国家争~ win honour for one's country; bring credit to one's country/ 脸上无~ feel ashamed ④ scenery: 春~ sights and sounds of spring; spring scene ⑤ smooth; glossy;

polished: 这种纸两面～。This kind of paper is smooth on both sides./ 把工件磨～ polish the workpiece ⑥ used up; nothing left: 墨水用～了。The ink's used up./ ～ wipe out the enemy ⑦ bare; naked: ～着头 be bareheaded/ ～着膀子 be stripped to the waist ⑧ solely; only; merely; alone

【光彩】 guāngcǎi lustre; splendour; radiance: ～夺目 dazzlingly brilliant/ ～绚丽的贝雕吸引了许多观众。The brilliant lustre of the shell carving attracted many visitors.

【光顾】 guānggù 〔商业的敬辞〕patronize: 如蒙～,无任欢迎。Your patronage is cordially invited.

【光怪陆离】 guāngguài-lùlí grotesque in shape and gaudy in colour; bizarre and motley: ～的广告 grotesque and gaudy advertisements

【光棍儿】 guānggùnr unmarried man; bachelor

【光棍】 guānggùn ruffian; hoodlum

【光滑】 guānghuá smooth; glossy; sleek

【光辉】 guānghuī radiance; brilliance; glory

【光洁】 guāngjié bright and clean

【光景】 guāngjǐng ① scene ② circumstances; conditions ③ about; around: 离这儿有十里～。It's about 10 li away from here. ④ very probably; quite likely: 今天太闷热,～是要下雨。The weather is stifling. It looks like rain.

【光亮】 guāngliàng bright; luminous; shiny

【光临】 guānglín <敬> presence (of a guest, etc.): 敬请～。Your presence is cordially requested./ 欢迎你们～指导。We welcome you and would appreciate your advice.

【光溜溜】 guāngliūliū ① smooth; slippery: ～的大理石地面 a smooth marble floor ② bare; naked: 孩子们脱得～的在河里游泳。The children stripped off their clothes and swam naked in the river.

【光芒】 guāngmáng rays of light; brilliant rays; radiance: 旭日东升,～四射。The morning sun rises in the east, shedding its rays in all directions

【光芒万丈】 guāngmáng wàn zhàng shining with boundless radiance; gloriously radiant; resplendent

【光明】 guāngmíng ① light: 黑暗中的一线～ a streak of light in the darkness ② bright; promising: 世界的前途是～的。The future of the world is bright. ③ guileless: ～磊落 open and aboveboard

【光荣】 guāngróng honour; glory; credit: ～称号 a title of honour/ ～使者 an honoured envoy/ ～传统 a glorious tradition

【光润】 guāngrùn (of skin) smooth

【光天化日】 guāngtiān-huàrì broad daylight; the light of day: 把敌人的阴谋暴露在～之下 expose the enemy's plot to the light of day

【光头】 guāngtóu ① bareheaded ② shaven head; shavenheaded: 剃～ have one's head shaved

【光秃秃】 guāngtūtū bare; bald: ～的山坡 bare hillsides/ ～的树枝 naked branches

【光线】 guāngxiàn light; ray: 别在～不好的地方看书。Don't read in a poor light.

【光耀】 guāngyào ① brilliant light; brilliance: ～夺目 dazzling ② glorious; honourable

【光阴】 guāngyīn time: ～似箭。Time flies like an arrow. 或 How time flies.

【光泽】 guāngzé lustre; gloss; sheen

【光宗耀祖】 guāngzōng-yàozǔ bring honour to one's ancestors

胱 guāng 见"膀胱" pángguāng

guǎng

广* guǎng ① wide; vast; extensive: 地～人稀 a vast and thinly populated area/ 见多识～ have wide experience and extensive knowledge/ 我们县这次改造农田,面积之～是前所未有的。Such extensive improvement of farmland is unprecedented in our county./ 丰收不忘～积粮。When we reap a good harvest, we must make a point of storing grain everywhere. ② numerous: 在大庭～众之中 before a

large audience; in public ③ expand; spread: 以～流传 so that it may spread far and wide

【广播】 guǎngbō broadcast; be on the air: 实况～ live broadcast; live transmissions over the radio or television/ 开始(停止)～ go on (off) the air
◇ ～电台 broadcasting (或 radio) station/ ～稿 broadcast script/ ～讲话 broadcast speech; radio talk/ ～节目 broadcast programme/ ～剧 radio play/ ～员 (radio) announcer

【广博】 guǎngbó (of a person's knowledge) extensive; wide: 知识～ have extensive knowledge; erudite

【广场】 guǎngchǎng public square; square

【广大】 guǎngdà ① vast; wide; extensive: 幅员～ vast in territory/ 地区～ vast areas; extensive regions/ ～农村 the vast countryside; extensive rural areas ② large-scale; widespread ③ numerous: ～人民群众 the broad masses of the people/ ～读者 the reading public

【广而言之】 guǎng ér yán zhī speaking generally; in a general sense

【广泛】 guǎngfàn extensive; wide-ranging; widespread: ～的兴趣 wide interests/ ～而深入的影响 a widespread and profound influence

【广告】 guǎnggào advertisement: 做～ advertise
◇ ～画 poster/ ～栏 advertisement column/ ～牌 billboard/ ～色 poster colour

【广开言路】 guǎng kāi yánlù encourage the free airing of views

【广阔】 guǎngkuò vast; wide; broad: ～的国土 a vast country/ ～的前景 broad prospects/ 交游～ have a wide acquaintance; have a large circle of friends/ ～天地,大有作为 a vast world where much can be accomplished; a vast field for using one's talents

【广义】 guǎngyì broad sense: ～地说 in a broad sense; broadly speaking

犷 guǎng <书> rustic; uncouth; boorish

【犷悍】 guǎnghàn tough and intrepid

guàng

逛 guàng stroll; ramble; roam: 到郊外～～ go for a walk in the suburbs/ ～大街 go window-shopping; stroll around the streets

guī

归* guī ① go back to; return: ～期 date of return/ 无家可～ be homeless ② give back; return sth. to: 物～原主 return (或 restore) a thing to its rightful owner ③ converge; come together: 把性质相同的问题～为一类 group together problems of a similar nature ④ turn over to; put in sb.'s charge: 消防工作～我们管。We are in charge of fire fighting. ⑤ 〔用在重叠动词之间,表示不相干或无结果〕: 玩笑～玩笑,事情可得认真去办。It's all right to crack jokes but you must do your job seriously.

【归案】 guī'àn bring to justice: 缉拿～ arrest and bring to justice

【归并】 guībìng incorporate into; merge into: 这个厂后来～到另一个工厂里去了。This factory was later incorporated into another one.

【归程】 guīchéng return journey

【归档】 guīdàng place on file; file

【归队】 guīduì ① rejoin one's unit: 他的伤已经好了,可以～了。Now that his wound has healed, he can go back to his unit. ② return to the profession one was trained for

【归附】 guīfù submit to the authority of another: ～国法 obey the law of the state

【归根结底】 guīgēn-jiédǐ in the final analysis

【归功于】 guīgōng yú give the credit to; attribute the success to

【归还】 guīhuán　return; revert: 向图书馆借书要按时~。 Books borrowed from the library should be returned on time.

【归结】 guījié　① sum up; put in a nutshell　② end (of a story, etc.)

【归咎】 guījiù　impute to; attribute a fault to; put the blame on: 不要把你的错误都~于客观原因。 Don't attribute all your mistakes to objective causes.

【归类】 guīlèi　sort out; classify

【归纳】 guīnà　induce; conclude; sum up: 请你把这篇文章的大意~一下。 Will you please sum up the main ideas of this article?/ 这是他从大量事实中~出来的结论。 This is a conclusion which he has drawn from numerous facts. ◇ ~法 inductive method; induction

【归入】 guīrù　classify; include: 这些问题可一~一类。 These questions may be included in the same category.

【归顺】 guīshùn　come over and pledge allegiance

【归宿】 guīsù　a home to return to

【归天】 guītiān　〈旧〉 pass away; die

【归途】 guītú　homeward journey; one's way home

【归向】 guīxiàng　turn towards (the righteous side); incline to: 人心~ the inclination of the hearts of the people

【归心似箭】 guīxīn sì jiàn　with one's heart set on speeding home; impatient to get back; anxious to return

【归罪】 guīzuì　put the blame on; impute to

圭　guī　an elongated pointed tablet of jade held in the hands by ancient rulers on ceremonial occasions

龟* guī　tortoise; turtle
另见 jūn

【龟甲】 guījiǎ　tortoise-shell

【龟缩】 guīsuō　huddle up like a turtle drawing in its head and legs; withdraw into passive defence; hole up: 敌人一在几个孤立的据点里。 The enemy was holed up in a few isolated strongholds.

规* guī　① compasses; dividers: 一个圆~ a pair of compasses　② regulation; rule: 校~ school regulations　③ admonish; advise: ~劝 admonish　④ plan; map out: ~划 plan

【规程】 guīchéng　rules; regulations: 操作~ rules of operation

【规定】 guīdìng　① stipulate; provide: 法律~的措施 measures provided for by law/ 宪法~妇女享有与男子完全相同的权利。 The Constitution stipulates that women enjoy exactly the same rights as men.　② fix; set; formulate: 在~的时间内 within the fixed time/ ~的指标 a set quota/ ~的表格 prescribed forms/ 在~的地点集合 assemble at an assigned spot

【规范】 guīfàn　standard; norm: 合乎~ conform to the standard/ 这个词的用法不~。 This is not the normal way of using the word. ◇ ~化 standardization

【规格】 guīgé　specifications; standards; norms: 统一的~ unified standards/ 不合~ not be up to standard; fall short of specifications ◇ ~化 standardization

【规矩】 guīju　① rule; established practice　② well-behaved; well-disciplined: 守~ abide by the rules; behave oneself/ 没~ have no manners; be impolite/ 规规矩矩 well-behaved; law-abiding/ 他的字写得很~。 His handwriting shows care and training.

【规律】 guīlǜ　law; regular pattern: 客观~ objective law/ 生活有~ live a regular life ~性 regularity

【规模】 guīmó　scale; scope; dimensions: ~宏大 broad in scale (或 scope)/ ~空前的盛会 a grand gathering of unprecedented size

【规劝】 guīquàn　admonish; advise: 好意~ give well-meaning advice

【规约】 guīyuē　stipulations of an agreement

【规则】 guīzé　① rule; regulation: 交通~ traffic regulations　② regular: 这条河流的水道原来很不~。 The course of this river used to be quite irregular.

【规章】 guīzhāng　rules; regulations: ~制度 rules and regulations

皈　guī

【皈依】 guīyī　〈宗〉 ① the ceremony of proclaiming sb. a Buddhist　② be converted to Buddhism or some other religion

闺　guī　boudoir

【闺房】 guīfáng　boudoir

【闺女】 guīnü　① girl; maiden　② 〈口〉 daughter

瑰* guī　〈书〉 rare; marvellous

【瑰宝】 guībǎo　rarity; treasure; gem

【瑰丽】 guīlì　surpassingly beautiful; magnificent

guǐ

轨* guǐ　① rail; track: 单(双)~ single (double) track/ 出~ be derailed　② course; path: 常~ normal practice/ 走上正~ get onto the right path

【轨道】 guǐdào　① track: 地铁~ underground railway track　② orbit; trajectory: 人造卫星已进入~。 The man-made satellite is now in orbit.　③ course; path: 工作已走上~。 The work has got onto the right track.

诡　guǐ　① deceitful; tricky; cunning　② 〈书〉 weird; eerie

【诡辩】 guǐbiàn　sophistry; sophism; quibbling: ~改变不了事实。 Sophistry won't alter facts.

【诡计】 guǐjì　crafty plot; cunning scheme; trick; ruse: ~多端 have a whole bag of tricks; be very crafty

【诡秘】 guǐmì　surreptitious; secretive: 行踪~ surreptitious in one's movements

【诡诈】 guǐzhà　crafty; cunning; treacherous

鬼* guǐ　① ghost; spirit; apparition: 不信~,不信神 believe in neither ghosts nor gods　② 〈骂〉: 懒~ lazy bones/ 胆小~ coward/ 酒~ drunkard　③ stealthy; surreptitious　④ sinister plot; dirty trick: 心里有~ have a guilty conscience/ 这里边有~。 There's some dirty work going on here. 或 I smell a rat.　⑤ terrible; damnable: ~天气 terrible weather/ ~地方 a damnable place

【鬼斧神工】 guǐfǔ-shéngōng　uncanny workmanship; superlative craftsmanship

【鬼怪】 guǐguài　ghosts and monsters; monsters of all kinds; forces of evil

【鬼鬼祟祟】 guǐguǐsuìsuì　sneaking; furtive; stealthy: 这家伙~的,想干什么? What's that fellow up to, sneaking around like that?

【鬼话】 guǐhuà　lie: ~连篇 a pack of lies

【鬼魂】 guǐhún　ghost; spirit; apparition

【鬼混】 guǐhùn　lead an aimless or irregular existence; fool around: 和不三不四的人~ hang around with shady characters

【鬼哭狼嚎】 guǐkū-lángháo　wail like ghosts and howl like wolves; set up wild shrieks and howls

【鬼脸】 guǐliǎn　① funny face; wry face; grimace: 做~ make a wry face; make faces; make grimaces　② mask used as a toy

【鬼门关】 guǐménguān　the gate of hell; danger spot; a trying moment

【鬼迷心窍】 guǐ mí xīnqiào　be possessed; be obsessed

【鬼神】 guǐshén　ghosts and gods; spirits; supernatural beings

【鬼使神差】 guǐshǐ-shénchāi　doings of ghosts and gods — unexpected happenings; a curious coincidence

【鬼胎】 guǐtāi　sinister design; ulterior motive: 心怀~ harbour sinister designs

【鬼头鬼脑】 guǐtóu-guǐnǎo　thievish; stealthy; furtive: 有两个人~地从山洞里钻了出来。 Two people sneaked out of the cave.

【鬼蜮】 guǐyù　evil spirit; demon; treacherous person: ~伎俩 devilish stratagem; evil tactics

【鬼主意】 guǐzhǔyì　evil plan; wicked idea

晷 guǐ ①〈书〉a shadow cast by the sun ②〈书〉time: 余~ spare time ③ sundial

guì

刽 guì cut off; chop off
【刽子手】guìzishǒu ① executioner; headsman ② slaughterer; butcher

柜* guì cupboard; cabinet: 碗~ kitchen cupboard/ 书~ bookcase/ 衣~ wardrobe
【柜台】guìtái counter; bar: 站~ serve behind the counter
【柜子】guìzi cupboard; cabinet

贵* guì ① expensive; costly; dear: 这本书不~。This book is not expensive. ② highly valued; valuable; precious: 兵~精,不~多。Troops are valued for their quality, not their number./ 春雨~如油, Rain in spring is as precious as oil. ③ of high rank; noble ④〈敬〉your: ~国 your country/ ~姓? May I ask your name?
【贵宾】guìbīn honoured guest; distinguished guest ◇ ~席 seats for distinguished guests; distinguished visitors' gallery/ ~休息室 reserved lounge (for honoured guests)
【贵妃】guìfēi highest-ranking imperial concubine
【贵重】guìzhòng valuable; precious: ~物品 valuables/ ~药品 costly (或 expensive) medicines
【贵族】guìzú noble; aristocrat: 封建~ feudal nobles

桂 guì ① cassiabarktree ② laurel; bay tree ③ sweet-scented osmanthus
【桂冠】guìguān laurel (as an emblem of victory or distinction)
【桂花】guìhuā〈植〉sweet-scented osmanthus ◇ ~酒 wine fermented with osmanthus flowers

跪* guì kneel; go down on one's knees
【跪拜】guìbài worship on bended knees; kowtow
【跪倒】guìdǎo throw oneself on one's knees; prostrate oneself; grovel.

gǔn

滚* gǔn ① roll; trundle: ~铁环 trundle a hoop/ 一块石头从山坡上~下来。A stone came rolling down the slope./ 从马背上~下来 tumble from a horse/ 汗珠不停地从她脸上~下来。Drops of sweat coursed (或·trickled) down her face. ② get away; beat it: ~出去! Get out of here! ③〈方〉boil: 水~了。The water is boiling. ④ bind; trim: 袖口上~一条边儿 bind the cuffs/ 裙子上~花边 trim the skirt with lace
【滚蛋】gǔndàn〈骂〉beat it; scram
【滚瓜烂熟】gǔnguā lànshú (recite, etc.) fluently; (know sth.) pat: 背得~ have memorized sth. thoroughly; have sth. pat
【滚滚】gǔngǔn roll; billow; surge: ~的浓烟 billowing smoke

gùn

棍* gùn ① rod; stick ② scoundrel; rascal: 恶~ ruffian; rascal/ 赌~ gambler
【棍棒】gùnbàng ① club; cudgel; bludgeon ② a stick or staff used in gymnastics
【棍子】gùnzi rod; stick

guō

郭 guō the outer wall of a city

聒 guō noisy

【聒耳】guō'ěr grate on one's ears
【聒噪】guōzào〈方〉noisy; clamorous

锅* guō pot, pan, boiler, cauldron, etc.: 沙~ clay pot/ 炒菜~ frying pan/ 两口大~ two cauldrons

guó

国* guó ① country; state; nation: 全~各地 all over the country/ ~营 state-run/ 收归~有 be nationalized; be taken over by the state ② of the state; national: ~旗 national flag
【国宝】guóbǎo national treasure
【国宾】guóbīn state guest ◇ ~馆 state guesthouse
【国策】guócè the basic policy of a state; national policy
【国耻】guóchǐ national humiliation
【国粹】guócuì the quintessence of a nation's culture
【国都】guódū national capital; capital
【国法】guófǎ the law of the land; national law; law
【国防】guófáng national defence
【国歌】guógē national anthem
【国画】guóhuà traditional Chinese painting
【国徽】guóhuī national emblem
【国会】guóhuì parliament; (美) Congress; (日) the Diet
【国籍】guójí nationality: 双重~ dual nationality/ 选择~ choose one's nationality/ ~不明的飞机 unidentified aircraft
【国计民生】guójì-mínshēng the national economy and the people's livelihood
【国际】guójì international: ~地位 international status (或 standing)/ ~形势 the international (或 world) situation/ ~影响 international repercussions; impact abroad/ 带有~性 have an international character
【国家】guójiā country; state; nation
【国教】guójiào state religion
【国界】guójiè national boundaries
【国境】guójìng territory: 偷越~ cross the border illegally ◇ ~线 boundary line
【国君】guójūn monarch
【国库】guókù national (或 state) treasury; exchequer
【国力】guólì national power (或 strength, might): ~雄厚 have solid national strength
【国立】guólì〈旧〉state-maintained; state-run ◇ ~大学 national university
【国民】guómín national ◇ ~经济 national economy/ ~生产总值 gross national product (GNP)/ ~收入 national income
【国难】guónàn national calamity (caused by foreign aggression)
【国内】guónèi internal; domestic; home: ~市场 domestic (或 home) market/ ~贸易 domestic trade/ ~新闻 home news
【国旗】guóqí national flag
【国情】guóqíng the condition (或 state) of a country; national conditions ◇ ~咨文 (美) State of the Union Message
【国庆】guóqìng National Day
【国人】guórén〈书〉compatriots; fellow countrymen; countrymen
【国手】guóshǒu national champion (in chess, etc.); grand master
【国书】guóshū letter of credence; credentials
【国土】guótǔ territory; land: 神圣~ our sacred land/ 捍卫每一寸~ defend every inch of our territory
【国外】guówài external; overseas; abroad: ~事务 external affairs/ ~来信 letter from abroad/ ~市场 overseas (或 foreign) market
【国王】guówáng king
【国营】guóyíng state-operated; state-run ◇ ~工商业 state-operated industry and commerce
【国有化】guóyǒuhuà nationalization
【国葬】guózàng state funeral
【国债】guózhài national debt

国 guó 见"掴" guāi

国 guó 见"巾帼" jīnguó

guǒ

果* guǒ ① fruit: 开花结~ blossom and bear fruit ② result; consequence: 恶~ a disastrous result; dire consequences ③ resolute; determined: 行必~ be resolute in action ④ really; as expected; sure enough: ~不出所料 just as one expected ⑤ if indeed; if really: ~能如此 if things can really turn out that way; if that is so

果断】 guǒduàn resolute; decisive: 办事~ handle affairs in a decisive manner/ ~地作出决定 resolutely make a decision

果腹】 guǒfù fill the stomach; satisfy one's hunger

果敢】 guǒgǎn courageous and resolute: 采取~的行动 take resolute action/ 她~地跳入水中, 救起溺水的孩子 Without hesitation, she leapt into the water and saved the drowning child.

果酱】 guǒjiàng jam

果皮】 guǒpí the skin of fruit; peel; rind

果品】 guǒpǐn fruit: 干鲜~ fresh and dried fruit

果然】 guǒrán <副> really; as expected; sure enough: ~名不虚传 a really well-deserved reputation/ 敌人~中了我们的埋伏 Just as we expected, the enemy were caught in our ambush.

果实】 guǒshí ⑴ fruit: ~累累 fruit growing in close clusters; fruit hanging heavy on the trees ⑵ gains; fruits: 劳动~ fruits of labour

果树】 guǒshù fruit tree

果园】 guǒyuán orchard

果真】 guǒzhēn ① 见"果然" ② <连> if indeed; if really: ~如此, 我就放心了。 If this is really true, it'll take a load off my mind.

果汁】 guǒzhī fruit juice

果子】 guǒzi fruit

裹 guǒ bind; wrap: 把伤口~好 bind up (或 bandage) the wound/ 头上~着毛巾 have one's head wrapped in a towel; wear a towel turban

裹足不前】 guǒ zú bù qián hesitate to move forward

guò

过* guò ⑴ cross; pass: 野营部队要从咱们村~。 The troops will be passing through our village on their camping trip. ② across; past; through; over: 汽艇穿~激流, 绕~险滩。 The motorboat cut across swift currents and skirted dangerous reefs. ③ spend (time); pass (time): 假期~得怎样? How did you spend your holiday? ④ after; past: ~了好几个月我才收到他的信。 Several months passed before I heard from him./ ~了夏至, 天就开始变短。 The days get shorter after the Summer Solstice./ 我~两天再来。 I'll come again in a couple of days. ⑤ exceed; go beyond/ 小心别坐~了站。 Be sure you don't go past your station./ 雪深~膝。 The snow is more than knee-deep. ⑥ excessively; unduly: 雨水~多 excessive rainfall; too much rain/ ~早 too early; premature ⑦ fault; mistake: 勇于改~ be bold in correcting one's mistakes/ 记~ put a person's error on record ⑧〔用在动词后, 跟"得"或"不"连用, 表示胜过或通过〕: 要比跑, 我们谁也比不~他。 None of us can run as fast as he can./ 这样的大学生, 我们信得~。 We have confidence in college students of this sort./ 小伙子们干起活来, 个个赛(得)~小老虎。 The lads threw themselves into the work with more vigour than young tigers.

另见 guo

过

guo ⑴〔用在动词后, 表示完毕〕: 我吃~午饭就去。 I'll

go right after lunch./ 桃花都已经开~了。 The peach blossoms are over. ②〔用在动词后面, 表示行为曾经发生, 但并未继续到现在〕: 你去~韶山吗? Have you ever been to Shaoshan?

另见 guò

【过半数】 guòbànshù more than half; majority: 这个工厂~的职工是妇女。 More than half the workers and staff members in this mill are women.

【过不去】 guòbuqù ① cannot get through; be unable to get by; be impassable: 前面正在修路, ~。 As the road ahead is under repair, you can't get through. ② be hard on; make it difficult for; embarrass: 我们批评你, 并不是跟你~。 We didn't mean to be hard on you when we criticized you. ③ feel sorry: 费了你这么多时间, 我心里真~。 I'm sorry for having taken up so much of your time.

【过程】 guòchéng course; process: 在讨论~中 in the course of the discussion/ 缩短制作~ shorten the process of manufacture

【过错】 guòcuò fault; mistake: 这不是你的~。 That's not your fault.

【过得去】 guòdeqù ① be able to pass; can get through: 卡车从这儿~吗? Can the truck get through here? ② passable; tolerable; so-so; not too bad: 我身体还~。 My health is not too bad./ 干工作可不能满足于~。 No one should be satisfied with just doing a passable job. ③〔多用于反问〕feel at ease: 叫你一趟一趟地跑, 我怎么~呢? I'm terribly sorry to have kept you on the go like this.

【过度】 guòdù excessive; undue; over-: 饮酒~对身体有害。 Excessive drinking is harmful to the health./ ~兴奋 be overexcited/ ~疲劳 be overtired

【过渡】 guòdù transition; interim

【过渡时期】 guòdù shíqī transition period

【过分】 guòfèn excessive; undue; over-: ~的要求 excessive demands/ ~强调 put undue stress on; overemphasize/ 敬得太~ go too far; overdo sth.

【过关】 guòguān ① pass a barrier; go through an ordeal ② pass a test; reach a standard

【过河拆桥】 guò hé chāi qiáo remove the bridge after crossing the river — drop one's benefactor as soon as his help is not required; kick down the ladder

【过后】 guòhòu afterwards; later: 他起初同意, ~又翻悔了。 At first he agreed, but later he backed out.

【过活】 guòhuó make a living; live

【过火】 guòhuǒ go too far; go to extremes; overdo: ~的行动 excesses/ 这话说得太~了。 It's going too far to say that.

【过继】 guòjì ① adopt a young relative ② have one's child adopted by a relative

【过奖】 guòjiǎng <谦> overpraise; undeserved compliment: 您~了。 You flatter me.

【过节】 guòjié celebrate a festival

【过境】 guòjìng pass through the territory of a country; be in transit ◇ ~签证 transit visa

【过来】 guòlái〔用在动词后, 多跟"得"或"不"连用, 表示时间、能力、数量充分或不足〕: 孩子多了照顾不~ If you have too many children, you won't be able to take good care of them all./ 你一个人忙得~吗? Can you manage by yourself?

【过来】 guòlái come over; come up: 快~! Come over here, quick!/ 一个人~向我打听去火车站的路。 A person came up and asked me the way to the railway station.

【过来】 guòlai ①〔用在动词后, 表示来到自己所在的地方〕: 把被敌人占领的阵地夺~ recapture the position seized by the enemy ②〔用在动词后, 表示使正面对着自己〕: 把柴火翻~晒晒。 Turn the firewood over and sun it./ 请你转~让我量量胸围。 Please turn round and let me measure your chest. ③〔用在动词后, 表示回到原来的、正常的状态〕: 醒~ wake up; sober up; come to/ 喘不过气来 be out of breath/ 他终于觉悟~了。 At last he saw the light.

【过来人】 guòláirén a person who has had the experience: 作为~, 我可以讲讲我的体会。 As one who has had experience in this respect, let me tell you how I feel about it./ 要知水深浅, 须问~。 He knows the water best who has waded through it.

【过量】 guòliàng excessive; over-: 饮食～ excessive eating and drinking/ 这药千万不能服～。 Whatever happens, never take an overdose of this medicine.

【过路】 guòlù pass by on one's way ◇ ～人 passerby

【过忠】 guòlù be overanxious; worry overmuch; worry unnecessarily: 问题会得到解决的,你不必～。 The problem wil be solved. You needn't be overanxious.

【过滤】 guòlù filter; filtrate

【过敏】 guòmǐn 〈医〉 allergy

【过目】 guòmù look over (papers, lists, etc.) so as to check or approve: 名单已经排好,请您～。 Here's the list for you to go over.

【过目成诵】 guòmù chéng sòng be able to recite sth. after reading it over once; have a photographic (或 very reten tive) memory

【过年】 guònián celebrate the New Year; spend the New Year: 他今年回家～。 He'll be home for the New Year holiday./ 快～了。 It'll soon be New Year.

【过期】 guòqī exceed the time limit; be overdue: 你借的书已经～。 The book you borrowed is overdue./ ～作废 in valid after the specified date

【过谦】 guòqiān too modest: 这件事你办最合适,不必～了。 You are the best person for the job. Don't be so modest.

【过去】 guòqù in or of the past; formerly; previously: 不了解～的苦,就不知道今天的甜。 If you don't know the bitterness of the past, you won't appreciate the happiness of the present./ 这个地方～流行的一些疾病已经基本消除。 Diseases formerly prevalent here have mostly been eradicated./ ～的荒山现如今成了果园。 The once desolate slopes have been turned into orchards./ 他比～胖多了。 He's much fatter than he used to be.

【过去】 guòqu go over; pass by: 你在这里等着, 我～看看。 You wait here, I'll go over and see./ 一辆公共汽车刚～。 A bus has just passed by.

【过去】 guòqu ①〔用在动词后,表示离开或经过自己所在的地方〕: 向敌人阵地冲～ charge at the enemy position/ 一只燕子飞～了。 A swallow flew past. ②〔用在动词后,表示使反面对着自己〕: 先别把这一页翻～。 Don't turn over the page yet. ③〔用在动词后,表示失去原来的、正常的状态〕: 病人晕～了。 The patient has fainted. ④〔用在动词后,表示通过〕: 企图蒙混～ try to get by under false pretences

【过人】 guòrén surpass; excel: 精力～ surpass many others in energy/ 勇气～ excel in courage/ ～的记忆力 a remarkable memory/ ～之处 the things one excels in; one's forte

【过日子】 guò rìzi live; get along: 勤俭～ live industriously

and frugally/ 挺会～ can manage to get along quite we

【过剩】 guòshèng excess; surplus: 生产～ overproductio 资本～ surplus of capital/ 商品～ a glut of goods

【过失】 guòshī fault; slip; error

【过时】 guòshí ① out-of-date; outmoded; obsolete; an quated; out of fashion: ～的设备 outmoded (或 obsolet equipment/ ～的观念 antiquated ideas ② past the appoi ed time: 校车六点开车,～不候。 The school bus leaves six sharp and won't wait.

【过手】 guòshǒu take in and give out (money, etc.); rece and distribute; handle: 银钱～,当面点清。 Count the mo ey on the spot./ 他～信件千千万,但没有错过一件。 He ha dled thousands and thousands of letters without making single mistake.

【过堂】 guòtáng appear in court to be tried

【过头】 guòtóu go beyond the limit; overdo: 菜煮～了。 T food is overcooked./ 批评他是可以的,不过你说得～了。 was all right to criticize him, but you overdid it./ 聪明 be too clever by half

【过往】 guòwǎng ① come and go: ～的行人 pedestri traffic/ ～的车辆 vehicular traffic ② have friendly in course with; associate with

【过问】 guòwèn concern oneself with; take an interest bother about: 亲自～ take up a matter personally; take personal interest in a matter/ 无人～ not be attended by anybody; be nobody's business/ 这事你不必～了。 Y needn't bother about this.

【过夜】 guòyè pass the night; put up for the night; st overnight

【过意不去】 guòyì bùqù feel apologetic; feel sorry: 这事 你添不少麻烦,真～。 I'm very sorry to have put you to much trouble.

【过瘾】 guòyǐn satisfy a craving; enjoy oneself to the fu do sth. to one's heart's content: 今天我一口气游了两千 真～。 Today I really swam to my heart's content. I c 2,000 metres at a stretch.

【过犹不及】 guò yóu bù jí going too far is as bad as n going far enough

【过于】 guòyú 〈副〉 too; unduly; excessively: ～劳累 ove tired/ 你不必～为我们担心。 You needn't worry too mu about us.

【过帐】 guòzhàng transfer items (as from a daybook to ledger); post

【过重】 guòzhòng overweight

H

hā

哈* hā ① breathe out (with the mouth open): 眼镜上一点儿气再擦。 Breathe on your glasses before wiping them. ②〈象〉〔形容笑声，大多叠用〕：～～大笑 laugh heartily; roar with laughter ③〈叹〉〔表示得意或满意，大多叠用〕：～～，我猜着了。 Aha, I've got (或 guessed) it./ ～～，小鬼，这下子可跑不了啦。 Aha, you can't get away from me this time, you little devil.
另见 hà

【哈欠】 hāqian　yawn: 打～ give a yawn

há

蛤 há
另见 gé
【蛤蟆】 háma ① frog ② toad

hǎ

哈 hǎ
另见 hā
【哈巴狗】 hǎbagǒu　Pekinese (a breed of dog)

hāi

咳* hāi 〈叹〉〔表示伤感、后悔或惊异〕：～，我怎么这么糊涂！ Damn it! How stupid I was!/ ～，真有这种怪事儿！ What! That's really strange!
另见 ké

嗨 hāi
【嗨哟】 hāiyō 〈叹〉: heave ho; yo-heave-ho; yo-ho

hái

还* hái 〈副〉① still; yet: ～有一些问题要解决。 Some problems have yet to be solved. ② even more; still more: 今年的收成比去年～要好。 This year's harvest is even better than last year's. ③ also; too ④ passably; fairly: 屋子不大，收拾得倒～干净。 The room is small, but it's kept quite tidy. ⑤ even: 你跑那么快～赶不上他，何况我呢？ If a good runner like you can't catch up with him, how can I? ⑥〔用以加强语气〕：这～了得！ This is the limit! 或 This is simply atrocious!/ 那～用说！ That goes without saying.
另见 huán

【还好】 háihǎo ① not bad; passable: 你今天感觉怎样？——～。 How are you feeling today? — Not so bad. ② fortunately: ～，这场大水没有把堤坝冲坏。 Fortunately, the flood did not break the dyke.

【还是】 háishi ①〈副〉 still; nevertheless; all the same: 尽管下着大雨，农夫们～坚持插完了秧。 It was raining hard. Nevertheless, the farmers went on working in the fields until they finished transplanting the rice-seedlings. ② had better: 天冷了，你～多穿点儿吧。 It's getting cold, you'd better put on more clothes. ③ or: 你去，～他去？ Are you going or is he?/ 我们是上午去，～下午去？ Shall we go in the morning or in the afternoon？ ④〈副〉〔表示对某事物没想到如此，而居然如此〕：我没想到这事儿～真难办。 I didn't expect it to be so difficult.

孩* hái child: 小女～儿 a little girl

【孩提】 háití 〈书〉 early childhood; infancy

【孩子】 háizi ① child: 男～ boy/ 女～ girl ② son or daughter; children: 她有两个～。 She has two children.

【孩子气】 háiziqì childishness: 你已经十六啦，别这么～！ You shouldn't be so childish, you're sixteen now!

骸 hái ① bones of the body; skeleton: 四肢百～ all the limbs and bones ② body: 形～ the human body/ 病～ ailing body/ 遗～ (dead) body; corpse; remains

【骸骨】 háigǔ human bones; skeleton

hǎi

海* hǎi ① sea or big lake: 出～ put out to sea ② a great number of people or things coming together: 人～ a sea of people; crowds of people/ 林～ a vast stretch of forest ③ extra large; of great capacity: ～碗 a very big bowl

【海岸】 hǎi'àn seacoast; coast; seashore

【海拔】 hǎibá height above sea level; elevation: ～四千米 4,000 metres above sea level; with an elevation of 4,000 metres

【海豹】 hǎibào seal

【海滨】 hǎibīn seashore; seaside:. ～疗养院 a seaside sanatorium

【海产】 hǎichǎn marine products

海豹

【海潮】 hǎicháo (sea) tide

【海程】 hǎichéng distance travelled by sea; voyage

【海胆】 hǎidǎn 〈动〉 sea urchin

【海岛】 hǎidǎo island (in the sea)

【海盗】 hǎidào pirate; sea rover ◇ ～船 pirate (ship); sea rover/ ～行为 piracy

【海堤】 hǎidī sea wall

【海底】 hǎidǐ the bottom of the sea; seabed; sea floor ◇ ～采矿 undersea mining; offshore mining/ ～电报 submarine telegraph; cablegram/ ～电缆 submarine cable/ ～油田 offshore oilfield/ ～资源 seabed resources; submarine resources

【海底捞月】 hǎidǐ lāo yuè try to fish out the moon from the bottom of the sea — strive for the impossible or illusory: ～一场空 be as futile as fishing for the moon in the sea

【海底捞针】 hǎidǐ lāo zhēn fish for a needle in the ocean; look for a needle in a haystack

【海防】 hǎifáng coast defence

【海风】 hǎifēng sea breeze; sea wind

【海港】 hǎigǎng seaport; harbour ◇ ～设备 harbour installations

【海狗】 hǎigǒu fur seal; ursine seal

【海关】 hǎiguān customhouse; customs ◇ ～人员 customs officer/ ～手续 customs formalities/ ～税则 customs tariff

【海关检查】 hǎiguān jiǎnchá customs inspection (或 examination): 通过～ go through customs ◇ ～站 customs inspection post

【海角】 hǎijiǎo cape; promontory

【海景】 hǎijǐng seascape

【海军】 hǎijūn navy ◇ ～基地 naval base

【海口】 hǎikǒu ① seaport ②〔多用于〕: 夸～ boast about what one can do; talk big

【海枯石烂】 hǎikū-shílàn (even if) the seas run dry and the rocks crumble: ～心不变。 The sea may run dry and the rocks may crumble, but our hearts will always remain loyal.

【海阔天空】 hǎikuò-tiānkōng as boundless as the sea and sky; unrestrained and far-ranging: ～地聊个没完 have a rambling chat about everything under the sun

【海狸】 hǎilí beaver

【海量】hǎiliàng ①〈敬〉magnanimity: 对不住的地方，望您～包涵。I hope you will be magnanimous enough to excuse any incorrect behaviour on my part. ② great capacity for liquor: 您是～，再来一杯。Have another one. You can hold your liquor.

【海流】hǎiliú ocean current

【海路】hǎilù sea route; sea-lane; seaway: 走～ travel by sea

【海轮】hǎilún seagoing (或 oceangoing) vessel

【海洛因】hǎiluòyīn heroin

【海马】hǎimǎ sea horse

【海绵】hǎimián ① sponge ② foam rubber or plastic; sponge ◇～垫 foam-rubber cushion

【海鸥】hǎi'ōu sea gull

【海平面】hǎipíngmiàn sea level

【海上】hǎishàng at sea; on the sea: ～风暴 a storm at sea

【海市蜃楼】hǎishì shènlóu mirage

【海誓山盟】hǎishì-shānméng (make) a solemn pledge of love

【海水】hǎishuǐ seawater; brine; the sea: ～不可斗量。The sea cannot be measured with a bushel — great minds cannot be fathomed.

【海滩】hǎitān seabeach; beach

【海豚】hǎitún 〈动〉dolphin

【海外】hǎiwài overseas; abroad

【海湾】hǎiwān bay; gulf

海豚

【海峡】hǎixiá strait; channel: 台湾～ the Taiwan Straits/ 英吉利～ the English Channel

【海鲜】hǎixiān seafood

【海象】hǎixiàng walrus; morse

【海啸】hǎixiào tsunami; seismic sea wave

【海星】hǎixīng 〈动〉starfish; sea star

【海洋】hǎiyáng seas and oceans; ocean

【海域】hǎiyù sea area; maritime space: 南海～ Nanhai Sea waters

【海员】hǎiyuán seaman; sailor; mariner

【海运】hǎiyùn sea transportation; ocean shipping

【海藻】hǎizǎo marine alga; seaweed

【海战】hǎizhàn sea warfare; naval battle

【海蜇】hǎizhé jellyfish

hài

亥 hài the last of the twelve Earthly Branches

【亥时】hàishí the period of the day from 9 p.m. to 11 p.m.

骇 hài be astonished; be shocked

【骇人听闻】hài rén tīngwén shocking; appalling: ～的暴行 horrifying atrocities

【骇异】hàiyì be shocked; be astonished

害* hài ① evil; harm; calamity: 为民除～ rid the people of a scourge/ 多利少 more disadvantages than advantages; more harm than good/ 灾～ calamity; disaster ② harmful; destructive; injurious: ～鸟 harmful bird ③ do harm to; impair; cause trouble to: ～人不浅 do people great harm/ 你把地址搞错了，～得我白跑了。You gave me the wrong address and made me go all that way for nothing. ④ kill; murder: 遇～ be murdered ⑤ contract (an illness); suffer from: ～了一场大病 have a serious attack of illness/ ～了急性病 suffer from an acute illness ⑥ feel (ashamed, afraid, etc.)

【害虫】hàichóng injurious (或 destructive) insect

【害处】hàichu harm: 吸烟过多对身体有～。Excessive smoking is harmful to one's health.

【害怕】hàipà be afraid; be scared: 没有什么可～的。There's nothing to be afraid of./ ～得要命 be scared to death; be mortally afraid

【害群之马】hài qún zhī mǎ an evil member of the herd; one who brings disgrace on his group; black sheep

【害人虫】hàirénchóng an evil creature; pest; vermin

【害臊】hàisào 〈口〉feel ashamed; be bashful: 替他～ be ashamed of him/ 真不～。You've got some nerve!

【害羞】hàixiū be bashful; be shy: 她是第一次当众讲话，有些～。This was the first time she had spoken before many people, so she was a bit shy.

嗐 hài 〈叹〉〔表示伤感或惋惜〕～，想不到他病得这么重。Oh, I didn't know he was so seriously ill.

hān

酣 hān (drink, etc.) to one's heart's content: 酒～耳热 heated with wine/ 半～ half drunk/ ～歌 sing to one's heart's content

【酣睡】hānshuì sleep soundly; be fast asleep

【酣饮】hānyǐn drink to the full; carouse

【酣战】hānzhàn hard-fought battle: 两军～ two armies locked in fierce battle

【酣醉】hānzuì be dead drunk

憨 hān ① foolish; silly: ～痴 idiotic ② straightforward; naive; ingenuous: ～态可掬 charmingly naive

【憨笑】hānxiào smile fatuously; simper

【憨直】hānzhí honest and straightforward

鼾 hān snore

【鼾声】hānshēng sound of snoring: ～如雷 snore thunderously

【鼾睡】hānshuì sound, snoring sleep

hán

汗 hán 见"可汗" kèhán
另见 hàn

含* hán ① keep in the mouth: 嘴里～着止咳糖 with a cough drop in one's mouth/ 此丸宜～服。This pill is to be sucked, not swallowed. ② contain: ～多种矿物 contain several kinds of minerals/ ～泪 with tears in one's eyes/ ～硫污水 sulphur-bearing waste water/ 这种梨的水分很多。These pears are very juicy./ ～沙量 silt content ③ nurse; cherish; harbour: ～恨 nurse one's hatred

【含垢忍辱】hángòu-rěnrǔ endure contempt and insults; bear shame and humiliation

【含糊】hánhu ① ambiguous; vague: ～不清 ambiguous and vague/ ～其词 talk ambiguously/ 在原则问题上不能～。One must not be vague on matters of principle. ② careless; perfunctory: 这事一点儿也不能～。We'll have to handle the matter with meticulous care.

【含混】hánhùn indistinct; ambiguous: 言词～，令人费解 speak so ambiguously as to be barely intelligible

【含量】hánliàng content: 牛奶的乳糖～ the lactose content of the milk

【含怒】hánnù in anger

【含情脉脉】hánqíng mòmò (soft eyes) exuding tenderness and love

【含沙射影】hán shā shè yǐng attack by innuendo; make insinuations: 采用～的卑劣手法 resort to insinuation/ 恶语中伤 vilify sb. with insidious language

【含笑】hánxiào have a smile on one's face: ～点头 nod with a smile

【含辛茹苦】hánxīn-rúkǔ endure all kinds of hardships; put up with hardships

【含羞】hánxiū with a shy look; bashfully

【含蓄】hánxù ① contain; embody ② implicit; veiled: ～的批评 implicit criticism ③ reserved

【含血喷人】hán xuè pēn rén make slanderous accusations

【含义】hányì meaning; implication: 这个词用在不同场合有不同的～。The meaning of this word varies with different contexts./ 这句话～深刻。This remark has profound implications.

【含冤】hányuān suffer a wrong: ～死去 die uncleared of a false charge

【含怨】hányuàn bear a grudge; nurse a grievance

函 hán letter: 公~ official letter/ ~复 reply by letter / ~告 inform by letter

【函购】 hángòu purchase by mail; mail order ◇ ~部 mail-order department

【函件】 hánjiàn letters; correspondence

【函授】 hánshòu teach by correspondence; give a correspondence course ◇ ~部 correspondence department (of a school)/ ~学校 correspondence school

函 hán contain

【涵养】 hányǎng ① ability to control oneself; self-restraint: 很有~ know how to exercise self-control ② conserve: 用造林来~水源 conserve water through afforestation

【涵义】 hányì 见"含义" hányì

寒* hán ① cold: 天~地冻。 The weather is cold and the ground is frozen./ 受了一点~ catch a slight cold ② tremble (with fear): 胆~ be terrified ③ poor; needy: 贫~ in indigent circumstances; poverty-stricken ④ 〈谦〉 humble: ~舍 my humble home

【寒风】 hánfēng cold wind: ~刺骨。 The cold wind chilled one to the bone.

【寒噤】 hánjìn shiver (with cold or fear): 他打了个~。 A shiver ran over his body. 或 A chill shot through him.

【寒苦】 hánkǔ destitute; poverty-stricken

【寒来暑往】 hánlái-shǔwǎng as summer goes and winter comes; with the passage of time

【寒冷】 hánlěng cold; frigid: ~的气候 a cold climate

【寒毛】 hánmáo fine hair on the human body

【寒气】 hánqì cold air; cold draught; cold: ~逼人。 There is a nip in the air.

【寒暑表】 hánshǔbiǎo thermometer

【寒酸】 hánsuān (of a poor scholar in the old days) miserable and shabby

【寒微】 hánwēi 〈书〉 of low station; of humble origin

【寒心】 hánxīn be bitterly disappointed: 令人~ bitterly disappointing

【寒暄】 hánxuān exchange of conventional greetings; exchange of amenities (或 compliments): 她同客人~了几句。 She exchanged a few words of greeting with the guests.

【寒衣】 hányī winter clothing

【寒意】 hányì a nip (或 chill) in the air: 初春季节仍有~。 It's spring but there's still a chill in the air.

【寒战】 hánzhàn shiver (with cold or fear) 又作"寒颤"

韩 Hán a surname

hǎn

罕 hǎn rarely; seldom: ~闻 seldom heard of

【罕见】 hǎnjiàn seldom seen; rare: 一场~的洪水 an exceptionally serious flood

喊 hǎn ① shout; cry out; yell: ~口号 shout slogans/ 把嗓子~哑了 shout oneself hoarse/ ~救命 cry "Help! Help!" ② call (a person): 你走以前~他一声。 Give him a shout before you go.

【喊叫】 hǎnjiào shout; cry out

【喊冤叫屈】 hǎnyuān-jiàoqū cry out about one's grievances; complain loudly about an alleged injustice

hàn

汉* Hàn ① the Han Dynasty (206 B.C.-A.D. 220) ② The Han nationality ③ Chinese (language): ~ 英词典 a Chinese-English dictionary ④ (hàn) man: 老~ an old man/ 大~ a big fellow

【汉学】 Hànxué ① the Han school of classical philology ② Sinology ◇ ~家 Sinologist

【汉语】 Hànyǔ Chinese (language) ◇ ~拼音方案 the Scheme for the Chinese Phonetic Alphabet/ ~拼音字母 the Chinese phonetic alphabet

【汉字】 Hànzì Chinese character ◇ ~改革 reform of Chinese characters/ ~简化方案 the Scheme for Simplifying Chinese Characters/ ~注音 phonetic annotation of Chinese characters

汗* hàn sweat; perspiration: 出~ sweat; perspire/ ~如雨下 dripping with perspiration 另见 hán

【汗斑】 hànbān sweat stain

【汗流浃背】 hàn liú jiā bèi streaming with sweat (from fear or physical exertion)

【汗马功劳】 hàn mǎ gōngláo ① distinctions won in battle; war exploits: 立下了~ perform deeds of valour in battle ② one's contributions in work

【汗毛】 hànmáo fine hair on the human body

【汗牛充栋】 hàn niú chōng dòng enough books to make the ox carrying them sweat or to fill a house to the rafters — an immense number of books

【汗青】 hànqīng ① sweating green bamboo strips — completion of a literary undertaking (reference to the ancient practice of drying green bamboo strips on the fire before writing on them) ② historical records; chronicles; annals: 人生自古谁无死,留取丹心照~。 What man was ever immune from death? Let me but leave a loyal heart shining in the pages of history.

【汗衫】 hànshān undershirt; T-shirt

旱* hàn ① dry spell; drought: 抗~ combat drought/ 久~的禾苗逢甘雨。 A sweet rain falls on the parched seedlings. ② dryland: ~稻 dry rice ③ on land: ~路 overland route

【旱稻】 hàndào upland rice; dry rice

【旱地】 hàndì nonirrigated farmland; dry land

【旱季】 hànjì dry season

【旱灾】 hànzāi drought

悍 hàn ① brave; bold: 一员~将 a brave warrior ② fierce; ferocious: 凶~ fierce and tough; ferocious

【悍然】 hànrán outrageously; brazenly; flagrantly: ~入侵 outrageously invade/ ~撕毁协议 flagrantly scrap an agreement/ ~不顾 in flagrant defiance of

捍 hàn defend; guard

【捍卫】 hànwèi defend; guard; protect

焊 hàn weld; solder: 气~ gas welding

【焊缝】 hànfèng welding seam; weld line

【焊工】 hàngōng ① welding; soldering ② welder; solderer

【焊接】 hànjiē welding; soldering

颔 hàn 〈书〉 ① chin ② nod

【颔首】 hànshǒu 〈书〉 nod: ~微笑 nod smilingly

憾 hàn regret: 引以为~ deem it regrettable

【憾事】 hànshì a matter for regret

撼 hàn shake

【撼动】 hàndòng shake; vibrate

翰 hàn 〈书〉 ① writing brush: 挥~ wield one's writing brush; write (with a brush) ② writing: 华~ 〈敬〉 your letter

【翰墨】 hànmò 〈书〉 brush and ink — writing, painting, or calligraphy

瀚 hàn 〈书〉 vast

【瀚海】 hànhǎi 〈书〉 big desert

háng

行* háng ① line; row: 排成两~ fall into two lines/ 杨柳成~ lined with rows of willows ② seniority among brothers and sisters: 你~几? —— 我~三。Where do you come among your brothers and sisters? — I'm the third. ③ trade; profession; line of business: 各~各业 all trades and professions; different walks of life/ 改~ change one's profession/ 他干哪~? What's his line?/ 干一~爱一~ love whatever job one takes up ④ business firm: 拍卖~ auctioneer's/ 银~ bank ⑤〈量〉: 一~树 a row of trees/ 四~诗句 four lines of verse
另见 xíng

【行规】 hángguī 〈旧〉 guild regulations
【行话】 hánghuà jargon; cant
【行家】 hángjia expert; connoisseur
【行列】 hángliè ranks: 排成整齐的~ be drawn up in orderly ranks
【行情】 hángqíng quotations (on the market); prices ◇ ~表 quotations list
【行业】 hángyè trade; profession; industry: 服务~ service trades ◇ ~语 jargon; cant

吭 háng throat: 引~高歌 sing lustily
另见 kēng

航* háng ① boat; ship ② navigate (by water or air): 夜~ night navigation/ 首~ maiden voyage or flight/ 民~ civil aviation
【航程】 hángchéng voyage; passage; range
【航道】 hángdào channel; lane; course: 主~ the main channel/ 重要的国际~ an important international sea-lane
【航海】 hánghǎi navigation ◇ ~法规 navigation law/ ~罗盘 mariner's compass
【航空】 hángkōng aviation: 民用~ civil aviation ◇ ~公司 airline company; airways/ ~货运 airfreight/ ~母舰 aircraft carrier/ ~邮件 airmail
【航路】 hánglù air or sea route
【航速】 hángsù speed of a ship or plane
【航图】 hángtú chart
【航线】 hángxiàn air or shipping line; route; course: 内河~ inland navigation line
【航向】 hángxiàng course (of a ship or plane): 改变~ change course
【航行】 hángxíng ① navigate by water; sail: 内河~ inland navigation ② navigate by air; fly: 空中~ aerial navigation
【航运】 hángyùn shipping ◇ ~保险 shipping insurance/ ~公司 shipping company

háo

号* háo ① howl; yell: 北风怒~。A north wind is howling. ② wail: 哀~ cry piteously; wail
另见 hào
【号哭】 háokū wail
【号叫】 háojiào howl; yell
【号啕】 háotáo cry loudly; wail: ~大哭 cry one's eyes out

蚝 háo oyster
【蚝油】 háoyóu oyster sauce

毫* háo ① fine long hair: 羊~笔 a writing brush made of goat's hair ② writing brush: 挥~ wield one's writing brush; write or draw a picture (with a brush) ③〔用于否定式〕 in the least; at all: ~不足怪 not at all surprising/ ~不动摇 not waver in the least; be unswerving/ ~无道理 utterly unjustifiable; for no reason whatsoever/ ~无顾忌 free from all inhibitions ④ milli-: ~米 millimetre/ ~升 millilitre
【毫发】 háofà 〈书〉〔多用于否定式〕 a hair; the least bit; the slightest: ~不爽 not deviate a hair's breadth; be

perfectly accurate
【毫厘】 háolí the least bit; an iota: ~不差 without the slightest error; just right
【毫毛】 háomáo soft hair on the body: 敌人的诬蔑无损于我们一根~。The slanders of the enemy can't harm a single hair of our head.
【毫米】 háomǐ millimetre (mm.)
【毫无二致】 háo wú èr zhì without the slightest difference; just the same; identical

豪 háo ① a person of extraordinary powers or endowments: 文~ a literary giant ② bold and unconstrained; forthright; unrestrained: ~气 heroic spirit/ ~饮 unrestrained (或 heavy) drinking/ ~雨 torrential rain ③ despotic; bullying: 土~ local despot/ 巧取~夺 take away by force or trickery
【豪放】 háofàng bold and unconstrained: ~的性格 a bold and uninhibited character
【豪富】 háofù ① powerful and wealthy ② the rich and powerful
【豪横】 háohèng despotic; bullying
【豪华】 háohuá luxurious; sumptuous: ~的饭店 a luxury hotel
【豪杰】 háojié person of exceptional ability; hero
【豪举】 háojǔ ① bold move ② munificent act
【豪迈】 háomài bold and generous; heroic: ~的誓言 a bold pledge/ ~的气概 heroic spirit/ ~地说 say with pride/ 以~的步伐跨入新的一年 stride into the new year with pride and confidence
【豪门】 háomén rich and powerful family; wealthy and influential clan
【豪情】 háoqíng lofty sentiments: ~满怀 full of pride and enthusiasm/ ~壮志 lofty sentiments and aspirations
【豪爽】 háoshuǎng straightforward; forthright
【豪言壮语】 háoyán-zhuàngyǔ brave (或 proud) words
【豪壮】 háozhuàng grand and heroic: ~的事业 a grand and heroic cause/ ~的声音 a firm, strong voice

壕 háo ① moat ② trench: 掘~ dig trenches; dig in 防空~ air-raid dugout

嚎 háo howl; wail: 狼~ the howl of a wolf
【嚎啕】 háotáo cry loudly; wail

hǎo

好* hǎo ① good; fine; nice: ~看 good-looking; pleasant to the eye; beautiful/ ~儿子 a worthy (或 fine) son ② friendly; kind: ~朋友 great (或 good) friend/ 他们对我真~。They are really kind to me./ 这两个孩子又~了。The two children have become friends again. ③ be in good health; get well: 我的病~了。I'm well (或 all right) now./ 你~! Hello! ④〔用在动词后,表示完成〕工具都准备~了。The tools are ready./ 坐~吧,要开会了。Take your seats please. The meeting is going to begin. ⑤〔表示赞同、结束、不满等语气〕: ~,就这么办。O.K., it's settled./ ~,不要再说了。All right, no need to say any more./ ~,这下可麻烦了。Well, we're in for trouble now. ⑥ be easy (to do); be convenient: 这个问题~回答。This question is easy to answer./ 这本书可不~买。This book is not easily available./ 暖瓶放在这儿~拿。It's handy to have the thermos here. ⑦ so as to; so that: 今儿早点睡,明儿早起赶火车。Let's turn in early, so as to get up early tomorrow to catch the train./ 把她的地址告诉我,我~去找她。Tell me her address so that I can go and see her. ⑧〔表示程度深、数量多、时间久等〕: ~冷啊! How cold it is!/ ~大的工程! What a huge project!/ ~几个月 several months/ ~半天 quite a while ⑨〔用在形容词前面问数量或程度〕: 火车站离这儿~远! How far is the railway station from here? ⑩〈方〉 may; can; should: 我~进来吗! May I come in?/ 时间不早了,你~走了。It's getting late. You ought to get going. ⑪〔用于套语〕: ~走! Goodbye!
另见 hào

【好办】hǎobàn easy to handle: 这事不～。This is no easy matter. 或 This is rather a headache./ 这件事～。That can be easily arranged.

【好比】hǎobǐ can be compared to; may be likened to; be just like

【好不】hǎobù 〈副〉〔表示程度深，并带感叹语气〕: 人来人往，～热闹! What a busy place, with so many people coming and going./ 他们见了面，～欢喜。How happy they were to see each other./ 他～容易才挤到台前。He had a hard time squeezing through the crowd to get up to the platform.

【好吃】hǎochī good to eat; tasty; delicious

【好处】hǎochu ① good; benefit; advantage: 你每天做点户外运动会有～。Some outdoor exercises every day will do you good. ② gain; profit: 敌人从这里捞不到任何～。The enemy can gain nothing from this./ 别上他的当!他给你这点～是为了拉拢你。Don't fall into his trap. He's given you this to win you over.

【好歹】hǎodǎi ① good and bad; what's good and what's bad: 不知～ unable to tell what's good or bad for one; not appreciate a favour ② mishap; disaster: 万一她有个～,这可怎么办? What if something should happen to her? ③ in any case; at any rate; anyhow: ～试试看。Let's try, anyhow./ 他要是在这里,～也能拿个主意。If he were here he would give us some advice./ ～no matter in what way; anyhow: 别再做什么了,～吃点儿就得了。Don't cook us anything more. We'll have whatever there is.

【好端端】hǎoduānduān in perfectly good condition; when everything is all right: ～的,怎么生起气来了? Why are you angry when everything is perfectly all right?

【好多】hǎoduō a good many; a good deal; a lot of: 她上街买了～东西。She went shopping and bought quite a few things.

【好感】hǎogǎn good opinion; favourable impression: 对他有～ be well disposed towards him; have a good opinion of him/ 给人～ make a good impression on people

【好过】hǎoguò have an easy time; be in easy circumstances: 这几年她家的日子越来越～了。Her family have had an easier and easier time these last few years.

【好汉】hǎohàn brave man; true man; hero: ～做～当。A true man has the courage to accept the consequences of his own actions.

【好好儿】hǎohǎor ① in perfectly good condition; when everything is all right: 电话刚才还是～的,怎么这会坏了? Why isn't the phone working now? It was all right a moment ago./ ～的一支笔,叫他给弄折了。He broke a perfectly good pen./ 那棵百年的老树,至今还长得～的。That hundred-year-old tree is still growing well./ 你～地跟他说,别生气。Talk to him nicely. Don't get angry. ② all out; to one's heart's content: ～想一想。Think it over carefully./ 把这房间～打扫一下。Give the room a thorough cleaning./ 我得～谢谢他。I'll really have to thank him./ 我俩～聊一聊。Let's have a good talk.

【好好先生】hǎohǎo xiānsheng one who tries not to offend anybody

【好话】hǎohuà ① a good word; word of praise: 给他说句～ put in a good word for him/ 不要听了一些～就沾沾自喜。Don't become complacent when you hear a few words of praise. ② fine words: ～说尽,坏事做绝 say every fine word and do every foul deed

【好家伙】hǎojiāhuo 〈叹〉〔表示惊讶或赞叹〕good god; good lord; good heavens: ～,他们一天足足走了一百公里! Good lord, they walked a hundred kilometres in a day!

【好景不长】hǎojǐng bù cháng good times don't last long

【好看】hǎokàn ① good-looking; nice: 你戴那顶帽子很～。That hat looks nice on you. ② interesting: 这本小说很～。This novel is very interesting. ③ honoured; proud: 儿子立了功,我这做娘的脸上也～。My son has won distinction; as his mother, I share the honour. ④ in an embarrassing situation; on the spot: 等着吧,有他的～。You can be sure he'll soon find himself on the spot./ 让我上台表演,这不是要我的～吗? Me, on the stage? Do you want to make a fool of myself?

【好评】hǎopíng favourable comment; high opinion: 对他颇有～ have a rather high opinion of him /博得读者～ be well received by the readers

【好球】hǎoqiú well played; good shot; bravo

【好人】hǎorén ① good (或 fine) person: ～好事 good people and good deeds; fine people and fine deeds ② a healthy person ③ a person who tries to get along with everyone (often at the expense of principle)

【好日子】hǎorìzi ① auspicious day ② wedding day ③ good days; happy life: 过～ live a happy life; live well; live in happiness

【好容易】hǎoróngyì with great difficulty; have a hard time (doing sth.): 他们～才找到我这儿。They had a hard time finding my place. 又作"好不容易"

【好声好气】hǎoshēng-hǎoqì 〈口〉in a kindly manner; gently

【好事】hǎoshì ① good deed; good turn: 为群众做～ do people good turns ② 〈旧〉an act of charity; good works 另见 hàoshì

【好事多磨】hǎoshì duō mó ① the road to happiness is strewn with setbacks ② the course of true love never did run smooth

【好手】hǎoshǒu good hand; past master: 做针线活儿,她可是把～。She is adept at needlework.

【好受】hǎoshòu feel better; feel more comfortable: 我吃了药以后～多了。I felt much better after taking the medicine./ 白天太热,夜里还～一点。It's terribly hot during the day but a bit better at night./ 你别说了,他心里正不～呢! Don't say anything more; he's feeling bad enough as it is.

【好说】hǎoshuō 〈套〉〔用在别人向自己致谢或恭维自己时,表示不敢当〕: ～,～! 您太夸奖了。It's very good of you to say so, but I don't deserve such praise. 或 You flatter me. I wish I could deserve such compliments.

【好似】hǎosì seem; be like: 大坝～铜墙铁壁,顶住了洪水的冲击。Like an iron bastion, the dam withstood the rushing floodwaters.

【好听】hǎotīng pleasant to hear: ～的话 fine words/ 这支歌很～。This is a very pleasant song./ 他说的比唱的还～。His glib talk sounds as sweet as a song.

【好戏】hǎoxì ① good play ② 〈讽〉great fun: 这回可有～看了。We're going to see some fun!

【好象】hǎoxiàng seem; be like: 他们～是多年的老朋友了。They seem to have been close friends for many years./ ～要下雨。It looks like rain./ 她们俩处得～亲姐妹一样。The two of them were as intimate as sisters.

【好笑】hǎoxiào laughable; funny; ridiculous: 有什么～的? What's so funny? /又好气又～ be annoying and amusing at the same time

【好些】hǎoxiē quite a lot; a good deal of

【好心】hǎoxīn good intention: 一片～ with the best of intentions /～当作驴肝肺 take sb.'s goodwill for ill intent

【好一个】hǎoyīge what a: ～正人君子! An honourable man, indeed!

【好意】hǎoyì good intention; kindness: ～相劝 give well-intentioned advice/ 谢谢您的～。Thank you for your kindness.

【好意思】hǎoyìsi 〔多用在反问句中〕have the nerve: 做了这种事,亏他还～说呢! Fancy his doing that sort of thing and then having the nerve to talk about it!

【好在】hǎozài fortunately; luckily: ～他伤势不重。Luckily he was not very seriously wounded. /我可以再去一趟,～路不远。Luckily it's not very far. I can easily go there again.

【好转】hǎozhuǎn take a turn for the better; take a favourable turn; improve: 形势～。The situation took a favourable turn./ 病情～。The patient is on the mend.

hào

号* hào ① name: 国～ the name of a dynasty/ 绰～ nickname ② assumed name; alternative name ③ business house: 银～ banking house/ 分～ branch (of a firm, etc.) ④ mark; sign; signal: 问～ question mark/ 加～ plus sign/ 举火为～ light a beacon/ ～房子 mark out

houses (as billets, etc.) ⑤ number: 五~楼 Building No. 5/ 编~ serial number ⑥ size: 大(中,小)~ large (medium, small) size/ 这鞋小了两~。These shoes are two sizes too small. ⑦ date: 今天几~？—— 十三~。What date is it today? — The 13th. ⑧ order: 发~施令 issue orders ⑨〈乐〉any brass-wind instrument: 军~ bugle/ 小~ trumpet ⑩ anything used as a horn: 螺~ conch-shell trumpet; conch
另见 háo

【号称】hàochēng ①be known as: 美国~天府之国。America is known as a land of plenty. ②claim to be: ~五十万大军 an army claiming to be half a million strong
【号令】hàolìng　verbal command; order
【号码】hàomǎ　number: 电话~ telephone number
【号召】hàozhào　call; appeal

耗 hào ①consume; cost: ~了不少粮食 have consumed much grain/~资百万 cost a million dollars/ 锅里的水快~干了。The pot is boiling dry. ②waste time; dawdle: 别~着了,快走吧。Stop dawdling and get going. ③bad news: 噩~ the sad news of the death of one's beloved
【耗费】hàofèi　consume; expend: ~时间,金钱 expend time and money
【耗竭】hàojié　exhaust; use up: 人力~ be drained of manpower
【耗尽】hàojìn　exhaust; use up: ~心血 exhaust all one's energies/ ~体力 use up all one's strength
【耗损】hàosǔn　consume; waste; lose: 减少水果在运输中的~ reduce the wastage of fruit in transit
【耗子】hàozi　〈方〉mouse; rat

好* hào ①like; love; be fond of: 虚心~学 be modest and eager to learn/ ~表现 like to show off/ ~管闲事 meddlesome; officious ②be liable to: ~晕船 be liable to seasickness; be a bad sailor/ ~伤风 be subject to colds
另见 hǎo

【好吃懒做】hàochī-lǎnzuò　be fond of eating and averse to work; be gluttonous and lazy
【好大喜功】hàodà-xǐgōng　crave for greatness and success; have a fondness for the grandiose
【好高骛远】hàogāo-wùyuǎn　reach for what is beyond one's grasp; aim too high; bite off more than one can chew 又作"好高鹜远"
【好客】hàokè　be hospitable; keep open house
【好奇】hàoqí　be curious; be full of curiosity ◇ ~心 curiosity
【好强】hàoqiáng　eager to do well in everything
【好胜】hàoshèng　seek to do others down
【好事】hàoshì　meddlesome; officious ◇ ~之徒 busybody
另见 hǎoshì
【好恶】hào-wù　likes and dislikes; taste: 翻译时不应根据自己的~改变原文意思。In doing translation, one should not alter the meaning of the original to suit one's own taste.
【好逸恶劳】hàoyì-wùláo　love ease and hate work
【好战】hàozhàn　bellicose; warlike ◇ ~分子 bellicose (或 warlike) elements

浩 hào　great; vast; grand
【浩大】hàodà　very great; huge; vast: ~的工程 a huge (或 vast) project/ 声势~的示威游行 a gigantic (或 huge, mammoth) demonstration
【浩荡】hàodàng　vast and mighty: ~的长江 the mighty Changjiang River/ 石油工人浩浩荡荡开进了新油田。Oil workers gathered in force at the new oil field.
【浩繁】hàofán　vast and numerous: 卷帙~ a voluminous work; a vast collection of books/ ~的开支 heavy expenditure
【浩瀚】hàohàn　vast: ~的沙漠 a vast expanse of desert/ 典籍~ a vast accumulation of ancient literature
【浩劫】hàojié　great calamity; catastrophe: 空前~ an unheard-of calamity
【浩气】hàoqì　noble spirit: ~长存 imperishable noble spirit
【浩如烟海】hào rú yānhǎi　(of data, etc.) vast as the open sea; tremendous amount of; voluminous

【浩叹】hàotàn　heave a deep sigh; sigh deeply

皓 hào ①white: ~齿 white teeth ②bright; luminous: ~月当空。A bright moon hung in the sky.

hē

呵 hē ①breathe out (with the mouth open): ~手 breathe on one's hands (to warm them)/ ~一口气 give puff ②scold: ~责 scold sb. severely; give sb. a dressing
【呵斥】hēchì　berate; excoriate
【呵呵】hēhē　〈象〉: ~大笑 laugh loudly; roar with laughter
【呵欠】hēqiàn　yawn

喝* hē ①drink: ~茶 drink tea/ ~汤 drink soup ② drink alcoholic liquor: 爱~两盅 be fond of drinking/ ~醉了 be drunk
另见 hè
【喝西北风】hē xīběifēng　drink the northwest wind — have nothing to eat

嗬 hē 〈叹〉〔表示惊讶〕ah; oh: ~,这小伙子真棒！Oh, what a fine young chap!

hé

禾 hé　standing grain (esp. rice)
【禾苗】hémiáo　seedlings of cereal crops

合* hé ①close; shut: ~上眼 close one's eyes/ 笑得~不拢嘴 grin from ear to ear ②join; combine: ~力 combined strength; joint effort ③whole: ~家团聚 a reunion of the whole family ④suit; agree: ~口口 suit one's taste; be to one's taste/ ~得来 get along well/ 正~我意 It suits me fine. ⑤be equal to; add up to: 这件上衣连工带料~多少钱？How much will this coat cost, including material and tailoring? ⑥〈书〉proper: 理~声明。I deem it appropriate to make a statement.
【合抱】hébào　(of a tree, etc.) so big that one can just get one's arms around: ~之木,生于毫末。A huge tree grows from a tiny seedling. 或 Great oaks from little acorns grow.
【合璧】hébì　(of two different things) combine harmoniously; match well: 中西~ a good combination of Chinese and Western elements
【合并】hébìng　merge; amalgamate: 五个组~为两个组了 The five groups have merged into two./ 这三个提议~讨论。The three proposals will be discussed together.
【合唱】héchàng　chorus: 混声~ mixed chorus ◇ ~曲 chorus/ ~团 chorus/ ~团指挥 chorus master
【合成】héchéng　compose; compound: 由两部分~ be composed of two parts
【合法】héfǎ　legal; lawful; legitimate; rightful: 唯一~政府 the sole legal government
【合格】hégé　qualified; up to standard: ~的司机 a qualified driver/ 产品~。The product is up to standard./ 我们保证质量~。We can vouch for the quality. ◇ ~证 certificate of inspection; certificate of quality
【合股】hégǔ　pool capital; form a partnership ②〈纺〉plying: ~线 ply (或 plied) yarn
【合乎】héhū　conform with (或 to); correspond to; accord with; tally with: ~人民的利益 conform with the interests of the people/ ~实际 conform to the actual situation/ ~事实 tally with the facts/~逻辑 logical/~情理 reasonable; sensible
【合伙】héhuǒ　form a partnership: ~经营 run a business in partnership
【合击】héjī　make a joint attack on: 分进~ concerted attack by converging columns
【合计】héjì　amount to; add up to; total: 这两项开支~一千元。The cost of the two items amounts to $1,000./ 把这一栏的数字~一下。Add up the figures in this column

【合计】 héjì ① think over; figure out: 他心里老～这件事。He kept thinking it over. ② consult: 大家～～该怎么办。Let's put our heads together and see what's to be done.

【合理】 hélǐ rational; reasonable; equitable: ～分工 rational division of labour/ ～利用资源 put resources to rational use; make rational use of resources/ ～的价格 a reasonable (或 equitable) price/ ～解决两国之间的争端 equitable settlement of the issues between the two countries

【合力】 hélì ① join forces; pool efforts: ～修建水库 pool efforts to build a reservoir

【合谋】 hémóu ① conspire; plot together ② 〈法〉 conspiracy

【合情合理】 héqíng-hélǐ fair and reasonable; fair and sensible: 这个建议～。The proposal is fair and reasonable.

【合群】 héqún ① get on well with others ② be gregarious

【合身】 héshēn fit: 这件上衣很～。This jacket fits well.

【合十】 héshí put the palms together (a Buddhist greeting)

【合适】 héshì suitable; appropriate; becoming; right: 这双鞋我穿着正～。These shoes fit me beautifully./ 星期五对我最～。Friday suits me best./ 你这样说不～。It's not right (或 suitable) for you to say so./ 这个词用在这里不～。This isn't the right word to use here. 又作"合式"

【合算】 hésuàn ① paying; worthwhile ② reckon up

【合同】 hétong contract: 签订～ sign a contract/ 撕毁～ tear up a contract

【合意】 héyì suit; be to one's liking (或 taste)

【合营】 héyíng jointly owned; jointly operated

【合影】 héyǐng group photo (或 picture): ～留念 have a group photo taken to mark the occasion

【合辙】 hézhé ① in rhyme ② in agreement: 两人一说就～。The moment they started talking they found themselves in complete agreement.

【合著】 hézhù write in collaboration with; coauthor

【合奏】 hézòu instrumental ensemble

【合作】 hézuò cooperate; collaborate; work together: 互相～ cooperate with each other/ 这幅画是他们～的。This painting is their joint work.
◇ ～社 co-operative; co-op

何*

【何】 hé 〈书〉 ① 〔表示疑问〕: ～人 who/ ～时 what time; when/ ～处 what place; where/ ～往 whither/ 从～而来？Where from? ② 〔表示反问〕: ～济于事？Of what avail is it?/ 有～不可？Why not?

【何必】 hébì there is no need; why: ～去那么早。There is no need to go so early./ 开个玩笑嘛，～当真呢？I was only joking. Why take it so seriously?

【何不】 hébù why not: ～早说？Why didn't you say so earlier?

【何尝】 hécháng 〔用于反问，表示未曾或并不〕: 我～不想去，只是没工夫罢了。Not that I don't want to go; I just haven't got the time./ 他这样的态度，～有解决问题的诚意呢？If that's his attitude, how can you say he sincerely wants the question settled?

【何等】 héděng ① what kind: 你知道他是～人物？Do you know what kind of person he is? ② 〔用于感叹语气，表示不同寻常〕: 这是～高超的技术！What consummate skill!

【何妨】 héfāng why not; might as well: ～一试？Why not have a try? 或 You might as well have a try.

【何苦】 hékǔ why bother; is it worth the trouble: 你～在这些小事上伤脑筋？Why bother your head about such trifles?/ 冒着这么大的雨去看电影，～呢？Going to the movies in this rain — is it worth it?

【何况】 hékuàng 〈连〉 much less; let alone: 这根木头连小伙子都抬不动，～老人呢？The log is too heavy even for a young fellow to lift, let alone an old man.

【何乐而不为】 hé lè ér bù wéi what is there against it

【何去何从】 héqù-hécóng what course to follow: ～，速作抉择。What course to follow — that is a question you must quickly decide for yourselves.

【何如】 hérú ① how about: 请君一试，～？How about you having a try? ② wouldn't it be better: 与其强攻，～智取。It would be better to use strategy than to attack by force.

【何谓】 héwèi 〈书〉 what is meant by; what is the meaning of

【何以】 héyǐ how; why: ～自解？How are you to explain yourself?/ ～见得？What makes you think so?

【何在】 hézài where: 困难～？Wherein lies the difficulty?/ 原因～？What is the reason for it?

【何止】 hézhǐ far more than: 例子～这些。There are far more instances than we have just enumerated.

河*

【河】 hé river

【河岸】 hé'àn river bank

【河床】 héchuáng riverbed

【河道】 hédào river course

【河谷】 hégǔ river valley

【河口】 hékǒu river mouth; stream outlet ◇ ～湾 estuary

【河流】 héliú rivers

【河马】 hémǎ hippopotamus; hippo

【河渠】 héqú rivers and canals; waterways: ～纵横 be crisscrossed by rivers and canals

【河山】 héshān rivers and mountains; land; territory: 锦绣～ a land of enchanting beauty

【河源】 héyuán river head (或 source)

【河运】 héyùn river transport

和*

【和】 hé ① gentle; mild; kind: 风～日暖 bright sunshine and gentle breeze ② harmonious; on good terms: 兄弟不～ brothers on bad terms with each other ③ peace: 讲～ make peace ④ 〈体〉 draw; tie: 那盘棋～了。That game of chess ended in a draw. ⑤ together with: ～衣而卧 sleep with one's clothes on; sleep in one's clothes ⑥ 〈介〉 〔表示相关、比较等〕: ～这件事没有关系 have nothing to do with the matter; bear no relation to it/ 他～我一样高。He's the same height as I. ⑦ 〈连〉 and: 工人～农民 workers and peasants ⑧ 〈数〉 sum: 两数之～ the sum of the two numbers
另见 hè

【和蔼】 hé'ǎi kindly; affable; amiable: ～可亲 affable; genial/ 态度～ amiable

【和畅】 héchàng (of a wind) gentle and pleasant: 惠风～ a gentle and pleasant breeze

【和风】 héfēng ① soft (或 gentle) breeze: ～拂面 a gentle breeze caressing one's face/ ～丽日 a gentle breeze and a bright sun; fine weather ② 〈气〉 moderate breeze

【和风细雨】 héfēng-xìyǔ like a gentle breeze and a mild rain

【和好】 héhǎo become reconciled: 他们吵过架，现在～了。They had a quarrel but have made it up now./ ～如初 be on good terms again; restore good relations

【和缓】 héhuǎn ① gentle; mild: 水流～ gentle flow of a stream/ 态度～ adopt a mild attitude ② ease up; relax: ～一下气氛 relieve the tension a little

【和会】 héhuì peace conference

【和解】 héjiě become reconciled: 采取～的态度 adopt a conciliatory attitude

【和局】 héjú drawn game; tie

【和睦】 hémù harmony; concord; amity: ～相处 live in harmony/ 民族～ national concord/ 家庭～ family harmony; domestic peace/ 友好～关系 friendly and harmonious relations

【和暖】 hénuǎn pleasantly warm; genial: 天气～ warm, genial weather

【和盘托出】 hé pán tuōchū reveal everything; make a clean breast of everything: 把自己的想法～ reveal everything on one's mind

【和平】 hépíng peace: ～倡议 peace proposals/ ～利用原子能 peaceful utilization of atomic energy; use of atomic energy for peaceful purposes/ ～解决边界争端 peaceful settlement of a boundary dispute

【和平共处】 hépíng gòngchǔ peaceful coexistence

【和棋】 héqí a draw in chess or other board games

【和气】 héqì gentle; kind; amiable: 说话～ speak politely (或 gently); be soft-spoken/ 伤了～ hurt sb.'s feelings/ 和和气气 polite and amiable

【和善】 héshàn kind and gentle; genial

【和尚】 héshang Buddhist monk

【和事老】 héshìlǎo peacemaker (esp. one who is more concerned with stopping the bickering than settling the issue)

【和谈】 hétán peace talks

【和谐】 héxié harmonious: ~的气氛 a harmonious atmosphere/ 音调~ in perfect harmony; melodious; tuneful

【和颜悦色】 héyán-yuèsè with a kind and pleasant countenance

【和约】 héyuē peace treaty

【和衷共济】 hézhōng-gòngjì work together with one heart (in times of difficulty)

劾 hé expose sb.'s misdeeds or crimes: 弹~ impeach

阂 hé cut off from; not in communication with: 隔~ misunderstanding; estrangement

荷* hé lotus
另见 hè

【荷包】 hébao ①small bag (for carrying money and odds and ends); pouch ②pocket (in a garment) ◇ ~蛋 fried eggs

【荷花】 héhuā lotus

核 hé ①pit; stone: 桃~ peach-pit; peach-stone/ 无~葡萄干 seedless raisins ②nucleus: 细胞~ cell nucleus/ 原子~ atomic nucleus/ 大国 nuclear power ③examine; check: ~准 check and approve; ratify

【核定】 hédìng check and ratify; appraise and decide

【核对】 héduì check: ~数字 check figures/ ~帐单 check a bill/ ~事实 check the facts

【核试验】 héshìyàn nuclear test: 大气层(高空,地下)~ atmospheric (high-altitude, underground) nuclear test

【核算】 hésuàn business accounting: 成本~ cost accounting

【核桃】 hétao walnut

【核武器】 héwǔqì nuclear weapon ◇ ~储备 stockpiling of nuclear weapons; nuclear weapons stockpile

【核销】 héxiāo cancel after verification

【核心】 héxīn nucleus; core; kernel

【核战争】 hézhànzhēng nuclear war (或 warfare)

涸 hé 〈书〉 dry up

【涸辙之鲋】 hé zhé zhī fù a fish trapped in a dry rut — a person in a desperate situation

盒* hé box; case: 一~火柴 a box of matches/ 铅笔~ pencil case; pencil box

【盒子】 hézi box; case; casket

颌 hé 〈书〉 jaw: 上(下)~ the upper (lower) jaw

阖 hé 〈书〉 ①entire; whole: ~城 the whole town/ ~家 the whole family ②shut; close: ~户 close the door

hè

吓* hè ①threaten; intimidate ②〈叹〉〔表示不满〕: ~, 怎么能干这种事呢? Tut-tut, how could you do that?
另见 xià

和* hè ①join in the singing: 一唱百~。When one starts singing, all the others join in. ②compose a poem in reply: 奉~一首 write a poem in reply (to one sent by a friend, etc., using the same rhyme sequence)
另见 hé•

贺* hè congratulate

【贺词】 hècí speech (或 message) of congratulation; congratulations; greetings

【贺电】 hèdiàn message of congratulation; congratulatory telegram

【贺礼】 hèlǐ gift (as a token of congratulation)

【贺年】 hènián extend New Year greetings or pay a New Year call ◇ ~片 New Year card

【贺喜】 hèxǐ congratulate sb. on a happy occasion (e.g. a wedding, the birth of a child, etc.)

【贺信】 hèxìn congratulatory letter; letter of congratulation

荷* hè 〈书〉①carry on one's shoulder or back: ~锄 carry a hoe on one's shoulder/ ~枪实弹 carry a loaded rifle ②burden; responsibility: 肩负重~ shoulder heavy responsibilities ③〔多用于书信〕grateful; obliged: 无任感~。I'll be very much obliged./ 请早日示复为~。An early reply will be appreciated.
另见 hé

喝* hè shout loudly: ~问 shout a question to/ 大~一声 give a loud shout
另见 hē

【喝彩】 hècǎi acclaim; cheer: 齐声~ cheer in chorus; cheer with one accord/ 博得全场~ bring the house down

【喝倒彩】 hè dàocǎi make catcalls; hoot; boo

【喝令】 hèlìng shout an order (或 command)

褐 hè ①〈书〉coarse cloth or clothing ②brown

赫 hè ①conspicuous; grand: 显~ distinguished and influential; illustrious ②〈电〉hertz: 千~ kilohertz/ 兆~ megahertz

【赫赫】 hèhè illustrious; very impressive: ~战功 illustrious military exploits; brilliant military success/ ~有名的人物 an illustrious personage

【赫然】 hèrán ①impressively; awesomely: 一只猛虎~出现在山坡上。To his consternation, a fierce tiger suddenly appeared on the mountain slope. ②terribly (angry): ~震怒 get into a terrible temper; fly into a violent rage

鹤 hè crane

【鹤发童颜】 hèfà-tóngyán white hair and ruddy complexion; healthy in old age; hale and hearty

【鹤立鸡群】 hè lì jīqún like a crane standing among chickens — stand head and shoulders above others

壑 hè gully; big pool: 千山万~ innumerable mountains and valleys

hēi

黑* hēi ①black: ~发 black hair ②dark: 天~了。It's dark.

【黑暗】 hēi'àn dark: ~的角落 a dark corner

【黑白】 hēi-bái black and white; right and wrong: ~分明 with black and white sharply contrasted; in sharp contrast/ 颠倒~ confound black and white; confuse right and wrong ◇ ~电视 black-and-white television/ ~片 〈电影〉black-and-white film

【黑板】 hēibǎn blackboard

【黑货】 hēihuò ①smuggled goods; contraband ②sinister stuff; trash

【黑名单】 hēimíngdān blacklist

【黑幕】 hēimù inside story of a plot, shady deal, etc.: 揭穿~ expose a sinister project; tell the inside story of a plot, etc.

【黑啤酒】 hēipíjiǔ dark beer; stout

【黑漆漆】 hēiqīqī pitch-dark

【黑人】 hēirén Black people; Black; Negro: 美国~ Afro-American; Black American

【黑色】 hēisè black

【黑色人种】 hēisè rénzhǒng the black race

【黑市】 hēishì black market

【黑手】 hēishǒu a vicious person manipulating sb. or sth. from behind the scenes; evil backstage manipulator

【黑心】 hēixīn black heart; evil mind
【黑猩猩】 hēixīngxīng chimpanzee
【黑压压】 hēiyāyā a dense or dark mass of: 广场上～地挤满了人。 The square was thronged with a dense crowd./ 远处～的一片，看不清是些什么东西。 One couldn't make out what the dark mass was from a distance.
【黑眼镜】 hēiyǎnjìng sunglasses
【黑油油】 hēiyōuyōu jet-black; shiny black: ～的头发 shiny black hair
【黑黝黝】 hēiyōuyōu ① shiny black ② dim; dark: 四周～的。 It's dark all around.

嘿 hēi 〈叹〉hey: ～! 快走吧! Hey, hurry up!

hén

痕* hén mark; trace: 刀～ a mark or scar left by a knife-cut/ 泪～ tear stains/ 伤～ a scar from a wound
【痕迹】 hénjī mark; trace; vestige: 轮子的～ wheel tracks

hěn

很* hěn 〈副〉very; quite; awfully: 好得～ very good/ ～满意 feel very satisfied; feel quite pleased/ ～有道理 contain much truth; be quite correct

狠 hěn ① ruthless; relentless: 凶～ ferocious and ruthless/ 比豺狼还～ more savage than a wolf ② suppress (one's feelings); harden (the heart) ③ firm; resolute
【狠毒】 hěndú vicious; venomous: 用心～ with vicious intent
【狠心】 hěnxīn cruel-hearted; heartless

hèn

恨* hèn ① hate: ～之入骨 hate sb. to the very marrow of one's bones/ ～得咬牙切齿 grind one's teeth with hatred/ 怀～在心 nurse hatred in one's heart ② regret: 遗～ eternal regret
【恨不得】 hènbude how one wishes one could; one would if one could; itch to: 我～一把把敌机揍下来。 How I wished I could bring the enemy plane down with one burst./ 他～马上投入战斗。 He itched to plunge into the battle.
【恨事】 hènshì a matter for regret

hēng

亨 hēng go smoothly
【亨通】 hēngtōng go smoothly; be prosperous: 万事～。 Everything is going smoothly.

哼 hēng ① groan; snort: 痛得直～～ groan with pain/ 轻蔑地～了一声 give a snort of contempt ② hum; croon: 他一边走,一边～着曲子。 He was humming a tune as he walked along./ ～着歌子哄孩子睡觉 croon the baby to sleep
另见 hng

héng

恒* héng ① permanent; lasting: 永～ eternal; everlasting ② perseverance: 持之以～ persevere in (doing sth.) ③ usual; common; constant: ～言 common saying

【恒河沙数】 Hénghé shā shù as numerous as the sands of the Ganges; innumerable; countless
【恒心】 héngxīn perseverance; constancy of purpose: 你要是没有～可学不好。 Unless you persevere with a subject you can't hope to master it.

横 héng ① horizontal; transverse: 纵～ vertical and horizontal/ 人行～道 (pedestrians') street crossing ② across; sideways: ～写 write words sideways/ ～渡太平洋的飞行 a trans-Pacific flight/ 车间里～挂着一幅大标语。 A huge streamer was hung across the workshop. ③ move crosswise; traverse: ～刀跃马 gallop ahead with sword drawn/ 这条铁路～贯五省。 The railway traverses five provinces. ④ unrestrainedly; turbulently: 江河～溢 turbulent waters overflowing their banks/ 老泪～流 tears flowing from aged eyes ⑤ violently; fiercely; flagrantly: ～加阻挠 wilfully obstruct/ ～加干涉 flagrantly interfere
另见 hèng
【横冲直撞】 héngchōng-zhízhuàng push one's way by shoving or bumping; jostle and elbow one's way; dash around madly; barge about
【横断面】 héngduànmiàn cross (或 transverse) section
【横跨】 héngkuà stretch over or across: 一道彩虹～天际。 A rainbow arched across the sky.
【横眉】 héngméi frown; scowl: ～怒目 face others with frowning brows and angry eyes; dart fierce looks of hate/ ～冷对千夫指,俯首甘为孺子牛。 Fierce-browed, I coolly defy a thousand pointing fingers, Head-bowed, like a willing ox I serve the children.
【横剖面】 héngpōumiàn cross section
【横七竖八】 héngqī-shùbā in disorder; at sixes and sevens; higgledy-piggledy: 院子里～地堆放着许多东西。 The yard was cluttered up with all sorts of things.
【横切】 héngqiē crosscut ◇ ～锯 crosscut (saw)/ ～面 cross section
【横肉】 héngròu 〔多用于〕: 一脸～ look ugly and ferocious
【横扫】 héngsǎo sweep away; make a clean sweep of: ～千军如卷席 rolling back the enemy as we would a mat
【横生】 héngshēng ① grow wild: 蔓草～ be overgrown with weeds ② be overflowing with; be full of: 妙趣～ be full of wit and humour ③ happen unexpectedly
【横生枝节】 héngshēng zhījié ① side issues or new problems unexpectedly crop up ② raise obstacles; deliberately complicate an issue
【横竖】 héngshù 〈口〉in any case; anyway: ～我要去的, 不用给他打电话。 No need to ring him up. I'll be going there anyway.
【横心】 héngxīn steel one's heart; become desperate: 横下一条心 resolve to do sth. in desperation
【横行】 héngxíng run wild; run amuck; be on a rampage: ～一时 run wild for a time
【横行霸道】 héngxíng-bàdào ride roughshod; play the tyrant; tyrannize; domineer
【横征暴敛】 héngzhēng-bàoliǎn extort excessive taxes and levies; levy exorbitant taxes

衡 héng ① the graduated arm of a steelyard ② weighing apparatus ③ weigh; measure; judge: ～情度理 considering the circumstances and judging by common sense; all things considered
【衡量】 héngliáng weigh; measure; judge: ～得失 weigh up the gains and losses/ 请你～一下这件事该怎么办。 Will you please consider what to do about it?
【衡器】 héngqì weighing apparatus

hèng

横* hèng ① harsh and unreasonable; perverse: ～话 harsh, unreasonable words/ 发～ act in an unreasonable (或 brutal) way ② unexpected: ～事 an untoward accident
另见 héng
【横暴】 hèngbào perverse and violent

【横财】 hèngcái ill-gotten wealth (或 gains): 发~ get rich by foul means

【横祸】 hènghuò unexpected calamity; sudden misfortune

【横死】 hèngsǐ die a violent death; meet with a sudden death

hng

哼 hng 〈叹〉〔表示不满或怀疑〕humph: ~. 谁信你的! Humph! Who believes what you say?
另见 hēng

hōng

轰* hōng ①〈象〉bang; boom: ~的一声, 敌人的碉堡给炸飞了。The enemy pillbox was blown up with a bang./ ~! ~! ~! 一连串爆破声震越山谷。Boom! Boom! Boom! A series of explosions shook the valley. ② rumble; bombard; explode: 雷~电闪。Thunder rumbled and lightning flashed./ 万炮齐~ ten thousand cannons booming ③ shoo away; drive off: ~麻雀 shoo away the sparrows/ ~下台 hoot sb. off the platform; oust sb. from office or power/ 把他~出去。Throw him out.

【轰动】 hōngdòng cause a sensation; make a stir: ~全国 cause a sensation throughout the country/ ~一时 create a furore/ 全场~ make a stir in the audience (或 in the hall)

【轰轰烈烈】 hōnghōnglièliè on a grand and spectacular scale; vigorous; dynamic

【轰击】 hōngjī shell; bombard: ~敌人阵地 shell enemy positions

【轰隆】 hōnglōng 〈象〉rumble; roll: 雷声~~地响, Thunder rumbled./ ~的机器声 the hum of machines

【轰然】 hōngrán with a loud crash (或 bang)

【轰炸】 hōngzhà bomb
◇ ~机 bomber

哄 hōng ①〈象〉roars of laughter ② hubbub
另见 hǒng; hòng

【哄传】 hōngchuán (of rumours) circulate widely: 这个消息不久就~开了。It was not long before the news was widely circulated.

【哄动】 hōngdòng cause a sensation; make a stir

【哄然】 hōngrán boisterous; uproarious: ~大笑 burst into uproarious laughter

【哄堂大笑】 hōngtáng dàxiào the whole room rocking with laughter

烘* hōng dry or warm by the fire: ~手 warm one's hands at the fire/ 把湿衣服一~一~ dry wet clothes by the fire/ ~面包 bake bread

【烘烤】 hōngkǎo toast; bake

hóng

弘 hóng ① great; grand; magnificent ② enlarge; expand

【弘大】 hóngdà grand

红* hóng ① red: ~墙 a red ochre wall/ 他的眼睛都熬~了。His eyes became bloodshot from lack of sleep./ 脸上~一阵白一阵 flush and turn pale by turns ② red cloth, bunting, etc. used on festive occasions: 披~ wear red sashes or cloth as a sign of honour, festivity, etc./ 挂~ hang up red festoons ③ symbol of success: 开门~ get off to a good start ④ bonus; dividend: 分~ distribute or draw dividends
另见 gōng

【红榜】 hóngbǎng honour roll (或 board)

【红宝石】 hóngbǎoshí ruby

【红尘】 hóngchén 〈旧〉the world of mortals; human society: 看破~ see through the vanity of the world; be disillusioned with this human world

【红光满面】 hóngguāng mǎnmiàn one's face glowing with health; in ruddy health

【红利】 hónglì bonus; extra dividend

【红脸】 hóngliǎn ① blush: 这小孩跟生人说话爱~。This child often blushes when speaking to strangers. ② flush with anger; get angry: 他俩从来没有红过脸。There has never been a cross word between the two of them. ③ red face, face painting in Beijing opera, etc., traditionally for the heroic or the honest

【红绿灯】 hónglǜdēng traffic light; traffic signal

【红人】 hóngrén a favourite with sb. in power; fair-haired boy

【红润】 hóngrùn ruddy; rosy: 脸色~ ruddy complexion; rosy cheeks

【红色】 hóngsè red

【红烧】 hóngshāo braise in soy sauce: ~肉 pork braised in brown sauce

【红十字会】 Hóngshízìhuì the Red Cross

【红衣主教】 hóngyī zhǔjiào 〈天主教〉cardinal

【红运】 hóngyùn good luck

【红晕】 hóngyùn blush; flush: 脸上泛出~ one's face blushing scarlet

【红肿】 hóngzhǒng red and swollen

宏 hóng great; grand; magnificent

【宏大】 hóngdà grand; great: 规模~ on a grand scale/ ~的志愿 great aspirations

【宏观】 hóngguān 〈物〉macroscopic ◇ ~结构 macrostructure/ ~世界 macrocosm

【宏论】 hónglùn informed opinion; intelligent view

【宏图】 hóngtú great plan; grand prospect: 发展国民经济的~ great plans for developing the national economy

【宏伟】 hóngwěi magnificent; grand

【宏愿】 hóngyuàn great aspirations; noble ambition

【宏旨】 hóngzhǐ main theme; leading idea of an article: 无关~ insignificant

泓 hóng ① (of water) deep ②〈量〉: 一~清泉 a clear spring/ 一~秋水 an expanse of limpid water in autumn

洪* hóng ① big; vast: ~涛 big waves ② flood: 防~ control or prevent flood

【洪大】 hóngdà loud: ~的回声 resounding echoes

【洪亮】 hóngliàng loud and clear; sonorous: 嗓音~ a sonorous voice

【洪量】 hóngliàng ① magnanimity; generosity ② great capacity for liquor

【洪流】 hóngliú mighty torrent; powerful current: 时代的~ the powerful current of the times

【洪炉】 hónglú great furnace

【洪水】 hóngshuǐ flood; floodwater ◇ ~位 flood level

【洪水猛兽】 hóngshuǐ-měngshòu fierce floods and savage beasts — great scourges

【洪钟】 hóngzhōng 〈书〉large bell: 声如~ have a stentorian (或 sonorous) voice

虹 hóng rainbow

【虹吸管】 hóngxīguǎn siphon

鸿 hóng ① swan goose ②〈书〉letter: 远方来~ a letter from afar ③ great; grand: ~图 great plans; grand prospects

【鸿沟】 hónggōu wide gap; chasm: 不可逾越的~ an unbridgeable gap; an impassable chasm

【鸿鹄之志】 hónghú zhī zhì lofty ambition; high aspirations

【鸿毛】 hóngmáo 〈书〉a goose feather — something very light or insignificant

hǒng

哄 hǒng ① fool; humbug: 你这是~我, 我不信。You're

kidding me; I don't believe it. ② coax; humour: ～孩子吃药 coax a child to take medicine/ 她很会～孩子。She knows how to handle children. 或 She has a way with children.

另见 hōng; hòng

【哄骗】hǒngpiàn cheat; humbug; hoodwink

hòng

讧 hòng 见"内讧" nèihòng

哄 hòng uproar; horseplay: 一～而散 break up in an uproar

另见 hōng; hǒng

hōu

齁 hōu
【齁声】hōushēng the sound of snoring; snore

hóu

侯 hóu ① marquis ② a nobleman or a high official: ～门似海。The mansions of the nobility were inaccessible to the common man.

喉* hóu larynx; throat
【喉咙】hóulóng throat: ～痛 have a sore throat
【喉舌】hóushé mouthpiece: 人民的～ the mouthpiece of the people

猴* hóu ① monkey ② clever boy; smart chap
【猴子】hóuzi monkey

hǒu

吼 hǒu roar; howl: 狮～ the roar of a lion/ 远方传来大炮的～声。Guns rumbled in the distance.

hòu

后* hòu ① behind; back; rear: 屋～ behind (或 at the back of) a house/ ～排 back row/ 敌～ the enemy's rear/ ～五名 the last five (persons) ② after; afterwards; later: 课～ after class/ 不久以～ soon afterwards; before long ③ offspring: 无～ without male offspring; without issue ④ empress; queen

【后半】hòubàn latter half; second half: ～场球赛 the second half of the game
◇ ～生 the latter half of one's life/ ～天 afternoon/ ～夜 the second half of the night; the small hours

【后备】hòubèi reserve: 留有～ keep sth. in reserve
◇ ～部队 reserve units/ ～基金 reserve fund/ ～力量 reserve forces

【后备军】hòubèijūn ① reserves ② reserve force: 产业～ industrial reserve army; industrial reserve; reserve army of labour

【后辈】hòubèi ① younger generation ② posterity

【后步】hòubù room for manoeuvre: 留～ leave sufficient room for manoeuvre

【后尘】hòuchén ＜书＞〔多用于〕: 步人～ follow in sb.'s footsteps

【后代】hòudài ① later periods (in history); later ages ② later generations; descendants; posterity: 为～着想 for the sake of future generations; in the interest of future generations

【后盾】hòudùn backing; backup force: 坚强的～ powerful backing

【后方】hòufāng rear: ～工作 rear-area work; work in the rear

【后跟】hòugēn heel (of a shoe or sock)

【后顾】hòugù ① turn back (to take care of sth.): 无暇～ have no time to look after things one has left behind/ ～之忧 fear of disturbance in the rear; trouble back at home ② look back (on the past): ～与前瞻 look back to the past and ahead into the future

【后果】hòuguǒ consequence; aftermath: 承担～ accept the consequences/ ～不堪设想。The consequences would be too ghastly to contemplate. 或 The consequences would be disastrous./ 检查制度不严, 会造成严重的～。A lax checking system may have serious consequences.

【后患】hòuhuàn future trouble: 根除～ dig up the root of (或 remove the cause of) future trouble/ ～无穷 no end of trouble for the future

【后悔】hòuhuǐ regret; repent: ～不已 be overcome with regret/ ～莫及 too late to repent

【后会有期】hòuhuì yǒu qī we'll meet again some day

【后记】hòujì postscript

【后继】hòujì succeed; carry on

【后来】hòulái afterwards; later: ～怎么样? What happened afterwards?/ ～的情况好多了。Things got much better later on. ◇ ～人 successors

【后来居上】hòu lái jū shàng the latecomers surpass the old-timers

【后路】hòulù ① communication lines to the rear; route of retreat: 抄敌人～ attack the enemy from the rear/ 切断敌人～ cut off the enemy's route of retreat ② room for manoeuvre; a way of escape: 留条～ leave oneself a way of escape; leave oneself a way out

【后门】hòumén ① back door (或 gate): 大院的～ the back gate of a compound ② backdoor (或 backstairs) influence: 走～儿 get in by the "back door"; get sth. done through pull

【后面】hòumian ① at the back; in the rear; behind: ～还有座位。There are vacant seats at the back. ② later: 这个问题我～还要讲。I'll come back to this question later.

【后年】hòunián the year after next

【后娘】hòuniáng ＜口＞ stepmother

【后排】hòupái back row: ～座位 back row seats

【后期】hòuqī later stage; later period: 十九世纪四十年代～ the late 1840s

【后起】hòuqǐ (of people of talent) of new arrivals; of the younger generation: ～的乒坛好手 the younger generation of crack table-tennis players/ ～青年作家 budding young writers/ ～之秀 an up-and-coming youngster; a promising young person

【后勤】hòuqín rear service; logistics

【后人】hòurén ① later generations ② posterity; descendants

【后任】hòurèn successor

【后身】hòushēn ① the back of a person: 我只看见个～, 认不清是谁。I couldn't make out who he was as I only saw his back. ② the back of a garment: 这件衬衫的～太长了。The back of the shirt is too long.

【后生可畏】hòushēng kě wèi a youth is to be regarded with respect — the younger generation will surpass the older

【后世】hòushì ① later ages ② later generations ◇ ～子孙 descendants; posterity

【后事】hòushì ① 〔多见于章回小说〕 what happened afterwards: 欲知～如何, 且听下回分解。If you want to know what happened afterwards, read the next chapter. ② funeral affairs: 料理～ make arrangements for a funeral

【后台】hòutái ① backstage ② backstage supporter; behind-the-scenes backer: ～很硬 have very strong backing ◇ ～老板 backstage boss

【后天】hòutiān ① day after tomorrow: 大～ three days from today ② postnatal; acquired: 知识是～获得的,不是先天就有的。Knowledge is acquired, not innate.

【后退】hòutuì draw back; fall back; retreat: 遇到困难决不～ never shrink from difficulties

【后裔】hòuyì descendant; offspring

【后影】hòuyǐng the shape of a person or thing as seen from the back

【后援】 hòuyuán reinforcements; backup force; backing

【后院】 hòuyuàn backyard

【后者】 hòuzhě the latter

【后肢】 hòuzhī 〈动〉 hind legs

【后座议员】 hòuzuò yìyuán backbencher

厚*

hòu ① thick: ～木板 a thick plank/ ～棉衣 a heavy padded coat/ 一呎～的雪 snow one ·foot deep ② deep; profound: 深情～谊 profound friendship ③ kind; magnanimous: 忠～ honest and kind ④ large; generous: ～利 large profits/ ～礼 generous gifts ⑤ rich or strong in flavour: 酒味很～。 The wine tastes strong./ ～味 rich (或 greasy) food ⑥ favour; stress: ～此薄彼 favour one and be prejudiced against the other

【厚薄】 hòubó thickness: ～合适 It's just the right thickness.

【厚道】 hòudao honest and kind

【厚度】 hòudù thickness

【厚古薄今】 hòu gǔ bó jīn stress the past, not the present

【厚今薄古】 hòu jīn bó gǔ stress the present, not the past

【厚脸皮】 hòuliǎnpí thick-skinned; brazen; cheeky: 厚着脸皮说 have the nerve to say

【厚望】 hòuwàng great expectations: 不负～ live up to sb.'s expectations; not let sb. down

【厚颜无耻】 hòuyán-wúchǐ impudent; brazen; shameless

【厚意】 hòuyì kind thought; kindness: 多谢你的～。 Thank you for your kindness.

逅

hòu 见 "邂逅" xièhòu

候*

hòu ① wait; await: 请稍～一会儿。 Please wait a moment./ ～领 to be kept until claimed ② inquire after: 致～ send one's regards ③ time; season: 时～ time/ 季～ season ④ condition; state: 症～ symptom

【候补】 hòubǔ be a candidate (for a vacancy); be an alternate

【候车室】 hòuchēshì waiting room (in a railway or bus station)

【候机室】 hòujīshì airport lounge or waiting room

【候教】 hòujiào 〈动〉 await your instructions

【候审】 hòushěn 〈法〉 await trial

【候选人】 hòuxuǎnrén candidate: 提出～ nominate candidates ◇ ～名单 list of candidates/ ～资格 qualifications for standing for election

【候诊】 hòuzhěn wait to see the doctor ◇ ～室 waiting room (in a hospital)

hū

乎

hū 〈书〉〈助〉〔表示疑问或揣度〕: 一之为甚,其可再～? Once is more than enough. How can you do it again?/ 成败之机,其在斯～? Does not success or failure hinge on this? ②〈动词后缀〉: 合～客观规律 conform to an objective law/ 出～意料 exceed one's expectations; be beyond one's expectations/ 超～寻常 be out of the ordinary ③〔形容词或副词后缀〕: 巍巍～ towering; lofty/ 确～重要 very important indeed

呼*

hū ① breathe out; exhale: ～出二氧化碳 exhale carbon dioxide ② shout; cry out: ～口号 shout slogans ③ call: 直～其名 address sb. disrespectfully (by name)/ ～之即来 have sb. at one's beck and call ④ 〈象〉: 北风～～地吹。 A north wind is whistling.

【呼风唤雨】 hūfēng-huànyǔ ① summon wind and rain — control the forces of nature ② stir up trouble

【呼喊】 hūhǎn call out; shout

【呼号】 hūháo wail; cry out in distress: 奔走～ go around crying for help

【呼号】 hūhào ①〈讯〉 call sign; call letters ② catchword (of an organization)

【呼唤】 hūhuàn call; shout to

【呼叫】 hūjiào ① call out; shout ②〈讯〉 call ◇ ～灯 calling lamp/ ～信号 calling signal

【呼救】 hūjiù call for help

【呼声】 hūshēng cry; voice: 群众的～ the voice of the masses/ 世界舆论的强大～ the powerful voice of world opinion

【呼天抢地】 hūtiān-qiāngdì lament to heaven and knock one's head on earth — utter cries of anguish

【呼吸】 hūxī breathe; respire: ～新鲜空气 have a breath of fresh air/ ～急促 be short of breath/ ～困难 breathe with difficulty; lose one's breath

【呼啸】 hūxiào whistle; scream; whizz: 子弹～而过。 A bullet whizzed past./ 寒风～。 A cold wind is whistling.

【呼应】 hūyìng echo; work in concert with: 遥相～ echo each other over a distance; echo from afar

【呼吁】 hūyù appeal; call on: ～团结 appeal for unity ◇ ～书 letter of appeal; appeal

【呼之欲出】 hū zhī yù chū seem ready to come out at one's call (said of lifelike figures in pictures or characters in novels) — be vividly portrayed

忽*

hū ① neglect; overlook; ignore ② suddenly: ～发奇想 suddenly have a strange idea

【忽而】 hū'ér now..., now...: ～哭,～笑 cry and laugh by turns/ ～主张这个, ～主张那个 advocate one thing today and another tomorrow

【忽...忽...】 hū...hū... now..., now...: 情绪忽高忽低 be in high spirits one moment and in low spirits the next; be subject to sudden changes of mood/ 天气忽冷忽热。 The weather is cold one minute and hot the next./ 镜头忽远忽近。 Sometimes there are long shots, sometimes close-ups./ 灯光忽明忽暗。 The lights keep flickering.

【忽略】 hūlüè neglect; overlook; lose sight of

【忽然】 hūrán suddenly; all of a sudden

【忽视】 hūshì ignore; overlook; neglect: 不可～的力量 a force not to be ignored; a force to be reckoned with/ 不应～困难。 We should not overlook the difficulties./ 不要强调一面而～另一面。 Don't stress one aspect to the neglect of another.

糊

hū plaster: 用灰把墙缝～上 plaster up cracks in the wall/ ～一层泥 spread a layer of mud
另见 hú; hù

hú

囫

hú

【囫囵】 húlún whole: ～吞下 swallow sth. whole

【囫囵吞枣】 húlún tūn zǎo swallow dates whole — lap up information without digesting it; read without understanding

狐*

hú fox

【狐臭】 húchòu body odour; bromhidrosis

【狐假虎威】 hú jiǎ hǔ wēi the fox borrows the tiger's terror (by walking in the latter's company) — bully people by flaunting one's powerful connections

【狐狸】 húli fox ◇ ～精 fox spirit — seductive woman

【狐狸尾巴】 húli wěiba fox's tail — something that gives away a person's real character or evil intentions; cloven hoof: ～总是要露出来的。 A fox cannot hide its tail. 或 The devil can't hide his cloven hoof./ 抓住阴谋家的～ seize hold of the evidence which gives the conspirator away

【狐群狗党】 húqún-gǒudǎng a pack of rogues; a gang of scoundrels

【狐疑】 húyí doubt; suspicion: 满腹～ be full of misgivings; be very suspicious

弧

hú 〈数〉 arc

【弧度】 húdù 〈数〉 radian

【弧形】 húxíng arc; curve

胡* hú ①〈副〉recklessly; wantonly; outrageously: ～吹 boast outrageously; talk big/ ～编 recklessly concoct ②〈连〉why: ～不归? Why not return? ③ moustache, beard or whiskers

【胡扯】 húchě talk nonsense: ～! Nonsense! 或 That's a lie!

【胡蜂】 húfēng wasp; hornet

【胡搞】 húgǎo ① mess things up; meddle with sth. ② carry on an affair with sb.; be promiscuous

【胡话】 húhuà ravings; wild talk: 烧得直说～ be delirious from fever

【胡椒】 hújiāo pepper

【胡搅】 hújiǎo ① pester sb.; be mischievous ② argue tediously and vexatiously; wrangle: ～蛮缠 harass sb. with unreasonable demands; pester sb. endlessly

【胡来】 húlái ① mess things up; fool with sth.: 你要是不会修就别～. If you don't know how to repair it, don't fool with it (或 mess it up). ② run wild; make trouble

【胡乱】 húluàn carelessly; casually; at random: ～吃了点饭 eat a hasty meal; grab a quick bite/ ～写了几行 scribble a few lines/ ～猜测 make wild guesses

【胡萝卜】 húluóbo carrot

【胡闹】 húnào run wild; be mischievous

【胡说】 húshuō ① talk nonsense; drivel ② nonsense

【胡说八道】 húshuō-bādào ① talk nonsense ② sheer nonsense; rubbish

【胡思乱想】 húsī-luànxiǎng imagine things; go off into wild flights of fancy; let one's imagination run away with one

【胡须】 húxū beard, moustache or whiskers

【胡言乱语】 húyán-luànyǔ talk nonsense; rave

【胡诌】 húzhōu fabricate wild tales; cook up: ～了一大堆理由 cook up a lot of excuses

【胡子】 húzi beard, moustache or whiskers

【胡作非为】 húzuò-fēiwéi act wildly in defiance of the law or public opinion; commit all kinds of outrages

壶* hú ① kettle; pot: 水～ kettle/ 茶～ teapot/ 油～ oil can ② bottle; flask: 行军～ water bottle; canteen/ 暖～ thermos bottle (或 flask)

湖* hú lake

【湖滨】 húbīn lakeside

【湖泊】 húpō lakes

【湖色】 húsè light green

葫 hú

【葫芦】 húlu bottle gourd; calabash: 他的～里到底卖的是什么药? What has he got up his sleeve?

猢 hú

【猢狲】 húsūn macaque: 树倒～散. When the tree falls, the monkeys scatter — when the boss falls from power, his lackeys disperse.

餬* hú

【餬口】 húkǒu keep body and soul together; eke out one's livelihood

鹄 hú swan

另见 gǔ

【鹄候】 húhòu 〈书〉await respectfully; expect: ～回音. I am awaiting your reply.

瑚 hú 见"珊瑚" shānhú

糊 hú ① paste: 将面粉加水调成～状 mix flour and water into a paste ② (of food) burnt

另见 hū; hù

【糊涂】 hútu muddled; confused; bewildered: ～观念 a muddled idea/ 别装～. Don't play the fool./ 他越想越～. The more he thought the more confused he became./ 这个人糊里～的, 管帐不行. That chap's no good for book-keeping, he's so muddleheaded./ 我真～, 把信忘在家里了. How careless of me to have left the letter at home. ◇ ～虫

blunderer; bungler/ ～帐 chaotic accounts; a mess

蝴* hú

【蝴蝶】 húdié butterfly

hǔ

虎* hǔ ① tiger: 小～ a tiger cub ② brave; vigorous: ～将 brave general/ ～～有生气 be full of vigour

【虎口】 hǔkǒu tiger's mouth — jaws of death: 把朋友救出～ save one's friend from the jaws of death / ～拔牙 pull a tooth from the tiger's mouth — dare the greatest danger; beard the lion in his den/ ～余生 survive a disaster; have a narrow escape

【虎视眈眈】 hǔshì-dāndān glare like a tiger eyeing its prey; eye covetously

【虎头蛇尾】 hǔtóu-shéwěi in like a lion, out like a lamb; fine start and poor finish

【虎穴】 hǔxué tiger's den: ～追踪 track the tiger to its lair

浒 hǔ waterside

唬 hǔ 〈口〉bluff: 别让～人。Quit bluffing./ 她没被～住。She wasn't intimidated.

琥 hǔ

【琥珀】 hǔpò amber

hù

户* hù ① door: 足不出～ never step out of doors; confine oneself within doors/ ～外活动 outdoor activities ② household; family: 全村共三十～. There are thirty households in the village./ 家家～～ each and every family ③ (bank) account: 存～ (bank) depositor

【户口】 hùkǒu (bank) account: 开～ open an account

互* hù mutual; each other: ～不干涉内政 noninterference in each other's internal affairs/ ～为条件 mutually conditional; interdependent/ ～通情报 exchange information; keep each other informed/ ～派常驻使节 exchange resident envoys; mutually accredit resident envoys

【互不侵犯条约】 hù bù qīnfàn tiáoyuē nonaggression treaty (或 pact)

【互访】 hùfǎng exchange visits: 两国体育代表团的～ exchange of sports delegations between two countries

【互…互…】 hù…hù… mutual; each other: 互勉互助 encourage and help each other/ 互教互学 teach and learn from each other; teach each other/ 互谅互让 mutual understanding and (mutual) accommodation

【互换】 hùhuàn exchange: ～批准书 exchange instruments of ratification

【互惠】 hùhuì mutually beneficial; reciprocal: 在～的基础上 on a mutually beneficial basis/ 贸易～ reciprocity in trade ◇ ～待遇 reciprocal treatment/ ～关税 mutually preferential tariff/ ～条约 reciprocal treaty

【互相】 hùxiāng 〈副〉mutual; each other: ～依存 depend on each other for existence; be interdependent/ ～排斥 be mutually exclusive/ ～配合 work in coordination/ ～利用 each using the other for his own ends/ ～掣肘 hold each other back/ ～勾结 work in collusion

【互助】 hùzhù help each other: ～合作 mutual aid and co-operation

护* hù ① protect; guard; shield: ～林 protect a forest/ ～厂 guard a factory/ 在敌机扫射时,她用自己的身子～住伤员. She shielded the wounded soldier from the strafing of the enemy plane with her own body. ② be partial to; shield from censure: 别～着自己的孩子. Don't be partial to your own child.

【护持】 hùchí shield and sustain

【护短】 hùduǎn shield a shortcoming or fault

【护航】 hùháng escort; convoy: 由五艘军舰～ be convoyed by five warships; have an escort of five warships ◇ ～部队 escort force/ ～飞机 escort aircraft/ ～舰 convoy ship

【护理】 hùlǐ nurse; tend and protect: ～伤病员 nurse the sick and the wounded/ 重病～组 a team of nurses in charge of serious cases ◇ ～人员 nursing staff

【护身符】 hùshēnfú ① amulet; protective talisman ② a person or thing that protects one from punishment or censure; shield

【护士】 hùshi (hospital) nurse ◇ ～学校 nurses' school/ ～长 head nurse

【护送】 hùsòng escort; convoy: ～伤病员去后方医院 escort wounded men to a rear hospital/ ～救灾物资 convoy vehicles bringing relief to a disaster-stricken area

【护卫】 hùwèi ① protect; guard ② 〈旧〉 bodyguard ◇ ～舰 escort vessel; corvette

【护养】 hùyǎng ① cultivate; nurse; rear: ～秧苗 cultivate seedlings; nurse young plants/ ～仔猪 rear (或 look after) piglets ② maintain: ～公路 maintain a highway

【护照】 hùzhào passport: 外交～ diplomatic passport/ 公务～ service passport

扈 hù 〈书〉 retinue

【扈从】 hùcóng 〈书〉 retinue; retainer

糊 hù paste: 辣椒～ chilli paste/ 玉米～ (cornmeal) mush
另见 hū; hú

【糊弄】 hùnòng ① 〈方〉 fool; deceive; palm sth. off on: 你别～我。 Don't try to fool me. ② go through the motions; be slipshod in work: 这可是细活,不能瞎～。 This is a delicate job. It mustn't be done carelessly.

huā

化 huā spend; expend: ～钱 spend money; cost money/ ～工夫 spend time; take time
另见 huà

花* huā ① flower; blossom; bloom: 种～儿 cultivate (或 grow) flowers ② anything resembling a flower: 雪～ snowflakes/ 浪～ spray ③ fireworks: 放～ let off fireworks ④ pattern; design: 她织的～儿真好看。 The pattern she knitted is really beautiful./ 这被面的～儿很大方。 The design on this quilt cover is quite elegant. ⑤ multicoloured; coloured; variegated: ～衣服 bright-coloured clothes/ ～蝴蝶 variegated butterfly/ 小～狗 spotted puppy/ 布染～了。 The cloth is dyed unevenly. ⑥ blurred; dim: 看书看得眼睛都～了 read until the print looks blurred ⑦ fancy; florid; flowery; showy: 你的字太～了。 Your handwriting is too fancy. ⑧ spend; expend: ～了不少钱 spend a lot of money/ ～时间 take a lot of time; be time-consuming

【花白】 huābái grey; grizzled: 头发～ with grey (或 grizzled) hair; grey-haired

【花斑】 huābān piebald: ～马 a piebald horse

【花瓣】 huābàn petal

【花边】 huābiān ① decorative border: 瓶口上有一道～。 There is a floral border round the mouth of the vase. ② lace: ～装饰 lace trimmings/ 在衣服上镶一条～ trim a dress with lace ③ 〈印〉 fancy borders in printing

【花布】 huābù cotton print; print

【花草】 huācǎo flowers and plants

【花车】 huāchē festooned vehicle; float

【花丛】 huācóng flowering shrubs; flowers in clusters

【花灯】 huādēng festive lantern (as displayed on the Lantern Festival)

【花朵】 huāduǒ flower

【花房】 huāfáng greenhouse

【花费】 huāfèi spend; expend; cost: ～金钱 spend money (on a project,etc.)/ ～时间 spend time; take time/ ～心血 take pains

【花费】 huāfèi money spent; expenditure; expenses

【花好月圆】 huāhǎo-yuèyuán 〔旧时多用作新婚的颂词〕 blooming flowers and full moon — perfect conjugal bliss

【花红】 huāhóng ① 〈植〉 Chinese pear-leaved crabapple ② bonus

【花花公子】 huāhuā gōngzǐ dandy; coxcomb; fop

【花花绿绿】 huāhuālǜlǜ brightly coloured; colourful: 穿得～的 be colourfully dressed/ ～的招贴画 poster in colour

【花花世界】 huāhuā shìjiè 〈贬〉 the dazzling human world with its myriad temptations; this mortal world

【花环】 huāhuán garland; floral hoop

【花卉】 huāhuì ① flowers and plants ② 〈美术〉 painting of flowers and plants in traditional Chinese style ◇ ～画 flower-and-plant painting

【花甲】 huājiǎ a cycle of sixty years: 年逾～ over sixty years old

【花篮】 huālán ① a basket of flowers ② gaily decorated basket

【花蕾】 huālěi (flower) bud

【花柳病】 huāliǔbìng venereal disease (V.D.)

【花木】 huāmù flowers and trees (in parks or gardens)

【花鸟】 huāniǎo 〈美术〉 painting of flowers and birds in traditional Chinese style ◇ ～画 flower-and-bird painting

【花盆】 huāpén flowerpot

【花瓶】 huāpíng flower vase; vase

【花圃】 huāpǔ flower nursery

【花腔】 huāqiāng ① florid ornamentation in Chinese opera singing; coloratura ② guileful talk: 耍～ speak guilefully

【花圈】 huāquān (floral) wreath

【花色】 huāsè ① design and colour: 这布的～很好看。 This cloth is beautiful in both design and colour. ② (of merchandise) variety of designs, sizes, colours, etc.: 新的～ latest designs/ ～繁多 a great variety

【花生】 huāshēng peanut; groundnut

【花饰】 huāshì ornamental design

【花束】 huāshù a bunch of flowers; bouquet

【花坛】 huātán (raised) flower bed; flower terrace

【花天酒地】 huātiān-jiǔdì indulge in dissipation; lead a life of debauchery

【花团锦簇】 huātuán-jǐncù bouquets of flowers and piles of silks — rich multicoloured decorations

【花纹】 huāwén decorative pattern; figure: 各种～的地毯 carpets of different patterns/ 这些瓷盘的～很别致。 These porcelain plates have rather original designs on them.

【花絮】 huāxù titbits (of news); interesting sidelights: 运动会～ sidelights on the sports meet

【花言巧语】 huāyán-qiǎoyǔ sweet words; blandishments

【花样】 huāyàng ① pattern; variety: ～多 a great variety/ ～翻新 the same old thing in a new guise ② trick: 玩～ play tricks ◇ ～滑冰 〈体〉 figure skating

【花园】 huāyuán flower garden; garden

【花招】 huāzhāo ① showy movement in wushu (武术); flourish ② trick; game: 别耍～! None of your little tricks.

【花枝招展】 huāzhī zhāozhǎn (of women) be gorgeously dressed

哗 huā 〈象〉: 铁门～的一声拉上了。 The iron gate was pulled to with a clang./ 溪水～～地流。 The stream went gurgling on.
另见 huá

【哗啦】 huālā 〈象〉: 风吹得树叶～～地响。 The leaves rustled in the wind./ 墙～一声倒了。 The wall fell with a crash./ 雨～～地下个不停。 The rain kept pouring down.

huá

划* huá ① paddle; row: ～船 paddle (或 row) a boat; go boating ② be to one's profit; pay: 这么好的地,种饲料～不来。 It doesn't pay to grow feed crops on such good soil. ③ scratch; cut the surface of: 她手～破了。 Her hands were scratched./ ～玻璃 cut a piece of glass/ ～火柴 strike

a match/ 几道闪电~破长空。Flashes of lightning streaked across the sky.
另见 huà

【划算】 huásuàn ① calculate; weigh: ~来, ~去 carefully weigh the pros and cons ② be to one's profit; pay: ~不~, 不能只从本单位的利益考虑。One mustn't consider whether or not it pays simply from the standpoint of one's own unit.

华* huá ① magnificent; splendid: ~屋 magnificent house ② prosperous; flourishing: 繁~ flourishing; bustling ③ best part; cream: 精~ the cream; the best part ④ flashy; extravagant: 奢~ extravagant; luxurious/ 朴实无~ simple and unadorned ⑤ grizzled; grey: ~发 grey hair ⑥ 〈敬〉 your: ~翰 your esteemed letter/ ~诞 your birthday
另见 Huà

【华灯】 huádēng colourfully decorated lantern; light: ~初上 the evening lights are lit
【华而不实】 huá ér bù shí ① flashy and without substance ② superficially clever
【华贵】 huáguì luxurious; sumptuous; costly: ~的地毯 luxurious carpet
【华丽】 huálì magnificent; resplendent; gorgeous: ~的宫殿 a magnificent palace/ 服饰~ gorgeously dressed and richly ornamented/ ~的词藻 flowery language
【华美】 huáměi magnificent; resplendent; gorgeous
【华裔】 Huáyì foreign citizen of Chinese origin

哗 huá noise; clamour: 寂静无~ silent and still; very quiet
另见 huā

【哗变】 huábiàn mutiny
【哗然】 huárán in an uproar; in commotion: 举座~。The audience burst into an uproar./ 舆论~。There was a public outcry.
【哗笑】 huáxiào uproarious laughter
【哗众取宠】 huá zhòng qǔ chǒng try to please the public with claptrap

滑* huá ① slippery; smooth: 又圆又~的小石子 smooth, round pebbles/ 路~。The road is slippery. ② slip; slide: ~了一跤 slip and fall ③ cunning; crafty; slippery: 又奸又~ mean and crafty
【滑板】 huábǎn 〈机〉 slide
【滑冰】 huábīng ice-skating; skating ◇ ~场 skating rink
【滑道】 huádào chute; slide
【滑稽】 huájī ① funny; amusing; comical: 滑天下之大稽 be the biggest joke in the world; be the object of universal ridicule ② 〈曲艺〉 comic talk ◇ ~戏 farce
【滑溜】 huáliu 〈口〉 slick; smooth; slippery
【滑润】 huárùn smooth; well-lubricated
【滑头】 huátóu ① slippery fellow; sly customer ② slippery; shifty; slick: ~滑脑 crafty; artful; slick
【滑翔】 huáxiáng glide ◇ ~机 glider; sailplane
【滑行】 huáxíng slide; coast: 冰上~ slide on the ice/ ~下坡 coast down a slope/ 飞机在跑道上~。The plane taxied along the runway.
【滑雪】 huáxuě skiing

◇ ~板 skis/ ~鞋 ski boots/ ~杖 ski pole (或 stick)

猾 huá cunning; crafty; sly

huà

化* huà ① change; turn; transform: ~害为利 turn harm into good; turn a disadvantage into an advantage/ ~公为私 appropriate public property ② convert; influence: 潜

移默~ exert a subtle influence on sb.'s character, thinking, etc. ③ melt; dissolve: 雪~了。The snow has melted./ 用水~开 dissolve in water/ ~冻 thawing ④ digest: ~食 help digestion ⑤ burn up: 焚~ burn up; incinerate/ 火~ cremate ⑥ 〈简〉〈化学〉 chemistry ⑦ 〔后缀, 加在名词或形容词之后构成动词〕 -ize; -ify: 工业~ industrialize/ 现代~ modernize/ 简~ simplify ⑧ (of Buddhist monks or Taoist priests) beg alms: ~斋 beg a (vegetarian) meal
另见 huā

【化名】 huàmíng (use an) assumed name; alias
【化身】 huàshēn incarnation; embodiment: 智慧和勇敢的~ the embodiment of wisdom and courage/ 魔鬼的~ the devil incarnate
【化为乌有】 huà wéi wūyǒu melt into thin air; vanish; come to naught
【化险为夷】 huà xiǎn wéi yí turn danger into safety; head off a disaster
【化学】 huàxué chemistry: 应用~ applied chemistry/ 理论~ theoretical chemistry
【化验】 huàyàn chemical examination; laboratory test ◇ ~单 laboratory test report/ ~室 laboratory/ ~员 laboratory technician (或 assistant)
【化缘】 huàyuán 〈宗〉 (of Buddhist monks or Taoist priests) beg alms
【化整为零】 huà zhěng wéi líng break up the whole into parts
【化妆】 huàzhuāng put on makeup; make up ◇ ~品 cosmetics
【化装】 huàzhuāng ① (of actors) make up ② disguise oneself: ~侦察 go reconnoitring in disguise ◇ ~师 makeup man/ ~室 dressing room

戈划* huà ① delimit; differentiate: ~界 delimit a boundary/ ~分 determine class status ② transfer; assign: ~款 transfer money ③ plan: 筹~ plan and prepare ④ draw; mark; delineate: ~线 draw a line/ ~十字 mark sth. with a cross/ ~掉一个字 cross out a word ⑤ stroke (of a Chinese character)
另见 huá

【划定】 huàdìng delimit; designate: ~捕鱼区 delimit fishing areas/ ~边界 delimit a boundary line/ 在~的区域内游泳 swim in the designated areas
【划分】 huàfēn ① divide: ~行政区域 divide a country into administrative areas ② differentiate
【划归】 huàguī put under (sb.'s administration, etc.); incorporate into: 这个企业已~地方管理。The enterprise has been put under local administration./ 这个县已经~另一个省了。That county has now been incorporated into another province.
【划清】 huàqīng draw a clear line of demarcation; make a clear distinction: ~是非界限 make a clear distinction between right and wrong/ 跟他~界线 make a clean break with him
【划时代】 huàshídài epoch-making: 具有~的意义 have epoch-making significance/ ~的宣言 a declaration that is a landmark in history; an epoch-making declaration
【划一】 huàyī standardized; uniform: 整齐~ uniform
【划一不二】 huà yī bù èr fixed; unalterable; rigid: 价钱~ fixed price (not subject to bargaining)/ 写文章没有~的公式。There's no hard and fast rule for writing.

华* Huà a surname
另见 huá

话* huà ① word; talk: 说几句~ say a few words/ 留~ leave a message; leave word ② talk about; speak about: ~家常 chitchat; exchange small talk/ 忆苦思甜~今昔 talk about the happiness of today in contrast with the misery of the past/ ~不投机半句多。When the conversation gets disagreeable, to say one word more is a waste of breath.
【话本】 huàběn script for story-telling (in Song and Yuan folk literature); text of a story
【话别】 huàbié say a few parting words; say good-bye

【话柄】 huàbǐng subject for ridicule; handle 又作"话把儿"

【话旧】 huàjiù talk over old times; reminisce

【话剧】 huàjù modern drama; stage play ◇ ～团 modern drama troupe; theatrical company

【话里有话】 huàlǐ yǒu huà the words mean more than they say; there's more to it than what is said

【话题】 huàtí subject of a talk; topic of conversation: 转～ change the subject

【话筒】 huàtǒng ① microphone ② telephone transmitter ③ megaphone

【话头】 huàtóu thread of discourse: 打断～ interrupt sb.; cut sb. short/ 拾起～ take up the thread of a conversation

【话匣子】 huàxiázi 〈方〉 ① gramophone ② radio receiving set ③ chatterbox: 这人是个～. That fellow is a chatterbox./ 他打开～就没个完. Once he opens his mouth, he never stops.

画* huà ① draw; paint: ～画儿 draw a picture/ ～圈儿 draw (或 describe) a circle/ ～一张草图 make a sketch ② drawing; painting; picture: 年～ New Year picture/ 油～ oil painting ③ be decorated with paintings or pictures: ～栋雕梁 painted pillars and carved beams (of a magnificent building) ④ stroke (of a Chinese character): "人"字两～. The character 人 is made up of two strokes.

【画板】 huàbǎn drawing board

【画报】 huàbào illustrated magazine or newspaper; pictorial

【画笔】 huàbǐ painting brush; brush

【画饼充饥】 huà bǐng chōng jī draw cakes to allay hunger feed on illusions

【画布】 huàbù canvas (for painting)

【画册】 huàcè an album of paintings; picture album

【画地为牢】 huà dì wéi láo draw a circle on the ground to serve as a prison — restrict sb.'s activities to a designated area or sphere

【画法】 huàfǎ technique of painting or drawing: ～新颖 a novel technique in painting or drawing

【画舫】 huàfǎng gaily-painted pleasure-boat

【画幅】 huàfú ① picture; painting ② size of a picture: ～虽然不大,所表现的天地却十分广阔.The picture is small but it shows broad vistas.

【画稿】 huàgǎo rough sketch (for a painting)

【画虎类狗】 huà hǔ lèi gǒu try to draw a tiger and end up with the likeness of a dog — make a poor imitation 又作"画虎不成反类犬"

【画家】 huàjiā painter; artist

【画架】 huàjià easel

【画匠】 huàjiàng ① artisan-painter ②〈旧〉 inferior painter

【画境】 huàjìng picturesque scene: 如入～ feel as though one were in a landscape painting

【画具】 huàjù painter's paraphernalia

【画卷】 huàjuàn picture scroll

【画刊】 huàkān ① pictorial section of a newspaper ② pictorial

【画廊】 huàláng ① painted corridor ② (picture) gallery

【画龙点睛】 huà lóng diǎn jīng ① bring the painted dragon to life by putting in the pupils of its eyes — add the touch that brings a work of art to life; add the finishing touch ② add a word or two to clinch the point

【画面】 huàmiàn ① general appearance of a picture; tableau ②〈电影〉 frame

【画蛇添足】 huà shé tiān zú draw a snake and add feet to it — ruin the effect by adding sth. superfluous

【画师】 huàshī painter

【画室】 huàshì studio

【画图】 huàtú ① draw designs, maps, etc. ② picture

【画像】 huàxiàng ① draw a portrait; portray: 给孩子画个像 draw a portrait of the child/ 让人～ sit for one's portrait ② portrait; portrayal: 巨幅～ huge portrait/ 自～ self-portrait

【画押】 huàyā make one's cross (或 mark); sign

【画页】 huàyè page with illustrations (in a book or magazine), plate

【画展】 huàzhǎn art exhibition; exhibition of paintings

huái

怀* huái ① bosom: 小孩儿在妈妈的～里睡着了. The baby fell asleep in its mother's arms. ② mind: 襟～坦白 frank and open-minded ③ keep in mind; cherish: ～着真诚的愿望 cherish sincere hopes/ ～着深厚的感情 with deep feelings/ 不～好意 harbour evil designs ④ think of; yearn for: ～友 think of a friend/ ～乡 yearn for one's native place; be homesick ⑤ conceive (a child): ～了孩子 become pregnant; be with child

【怀抱】 huáibào ① bosom: 回到祖国的～ return to the embrace of one's homeland/ 投入敌人的～ throw oneself into the arms of the enemy ② cherish: ～远大的理想 cherish lofty ideals

【怀古】 huáigǔ meditate on the past; reflect on an ancient event

【怀恨】 huáihèn nurse hatred; harbour resentment

【怀旧】 huáijiù remember past times or old acquaintances (usu. with kindly thoughts)

【怀恋】 huáiliàn think fondly of (past times, old friends, etc.); look back nostalgically

【怀念】 huáiniàn cherish the memory of; think of: ～远方的友人 think of an absent friend who is far away

【怀胎】 huáitāi be pregnant

【怀想】 huáixiǎng think about with affection (a faraway person, place, etc.); yearn for

【怀疑】 huáiyí doubt; suspect: 引起～ raise doubts; arouse suspicion/ 消除～ dispel doubts; clear up suspicion/ 受到～ come under suspicion/ ～他的动机 suspect his motives/ ～有埋伏 suspect an ambush/ 我～他别有用心. I suspect that he has ulterior motives./ 持～态度 take a sceptical attitude

【怀孕】 huáiyùn be pregnant: ～五个月了 be five months pregnant; be five months gone ◇ ～期 period of pregnancy; gestation period

徊 huái 见"徘徊" páihuái

淮 Huái the Huaihe River

槐 huái Chinese scholartree

huài

坏* huài ① bad: ～习惯 bad habit/ ～透了 downright bad; rotten to the core/ ～书 a bad (或 harmful) book/ ～天气 foul weather ② go bad; spoil; ruin: 鱼～了. The fish has gone bad./ 他身体～了. His health has broken down./ 他胃口～了. He has lost his appetite. ③ badly; awfully; very: 吓～了 be badly scared/ 气～了 be beside oneself with rage/ 乐～了 be wild with joy/ 累～了 be dead tired; be dog-tired ④ evil idea; dirty trick: 使～ play a dirty trick/ 一肚子～ full of tricks

【坏处】 huàichu harm; disadvantage: 一点～也没有. There's no harm in it at all. 或 There's nothing bad about it./ 从～着想,往好处努力. Prepare for the worst; strive for the best.

【坏蛋】 huàidàn 〈口〉 bad egg; scoundrel; bastard

【坏东西】 huàidōngxi bastard; scoundrel; rogue

【坏话】 huàihuà ① malicious remarks; vicious talk: 讲别人～ speak ill of others ② unpleasant words: 好话～都要让人讲完. One should let others finish what they have to say whether it sounds pleasant or unpleasant.

【坏人】 huàirén bad person; evildoer; scoundrel

【坏事】 huàishì ① bad thing; evil deed ② ruin sth.; make things worse: 急躁只能～. Impetuosity will only make things worse./ ～了! Something terrible has happened.

【坏心眼儿】 huàixīnyǎnr 〈口〉 evil intention; ill will

huān

欢* huān joyous; merry; jubilant: ～跃 jump for joy/

~唱 sing merrily

【欢畅】 huānchàng thoroughly delighted; elated

【欢度】 huāndù spend (an occasion) joyfully: ~佳节 celebrate a festival with jubilation

【欢呼】 huānhū hail; cheer; acclaim

【欢聚】 huānjù happy get-together; happy reunion: ~一堂 happily gather under the same roof

【欢快】 huānkuài cheerful and light-hearted; lively: ~的曲调 a lively melody/ 随着音乐~地跳舞 dance cheerfully to the music

【欢乐】 huānlè happy; joyous; gay: ~的人群 happy crowds/ ~的景象 a scene of great joy/ 给节日增添了~气氛 add to the gaiety of the festival

【欢庆】 huānqìng celebrate joyously

【欢声雷动】 huānshēng léidòng cheers resound like rolls of thunder: 全场~。 The audience broke into deafening cheers.

【欢送】 huānsòng see off; send off

【欢腾】 huānténg great rejoicing; jubilation: 喜讯传来,举国~。 There was nationwide rejoicing at the good news./ 广场上一片~。 The square was astir with jubilant crowds

【欢天喜地】 huāntiān-xǐdì with boundless joy; wild with joy; overjoyed: ~地迎接国庆 greet National Day with boundless joy

【欢喜】 huānxǐ ① joyful; happy; delighted: 满心~ be filled with joy/ 欢欢喜喜过春节 spend a joyful Spring Festival ② like; be fond of; delight in: 她一拉手风琴。 She likes to play the accordion.

【欢笑】 huānxiào laugh heartily

【欢心】 huānxīn favour; liking; love: 想博取~ try to win sb.'s favour

【欢欣鼓舞】 huānxīn-gǔwǔ be filled with exultation; be elated: 捷报传来,全国人民无不~。 The good tidings filled the whole nation with joy. 或 The good tidings elated the whole nation.

【欢迎】 huānyíng welcome; greet: ~大家批评。 Criticisms are welcome./ 夹道~ line the streets to give sb. a welcome/ 到机场~贵宾 meet distinguished guests at the airport ◇ ~词 welcoming speech; address of welcome/ ~会 a party (或 meeting) to welcome sb.

huán

还* huán ① go (或 come) back: ~家 return home ② give back; return; repay: 这几本是到期要~的书。 These books are due for return./ 下个月~你钱。 I'll pay you back next month. ③ give or do sth. in return 另见 hái

【还本】 huánběn repayment of principal (或 capital): ~付息 repay capital with interest

【还击】 huánjī fight back; return fire; counterattack: 进行自卫~ fight in self-defence/ ~敌人 hit back at the enemy

【还价】 huánjià counter-offer; counter-bid

【还礼】 huánlǐ ① return a salute ② present a gift in return

【还清】 huánqīng pay off: ~债务 pay off one's debts

【还手】 huánshǒu strike (或 hit) back

【还俗】 huánsú (of Buddhist monks and nuns or Taoist priests) resume secular life

【还乡】 huánxiāng return to one's native place

【还愿】 huányuàn ① redeem a vow to a god ② fulfil one's promise: 说话要算数,不能光许愿不~。 You should do what you say; you can't go on making promises and not keeping them.

【还债】 huánzhài pay one's debt; repay a debt

【还嘴】 huánzuǐ 〈口〉 answer (或 talk) back; retort

环* huán ① ring; hoop: 耳~ earring ② link: 一~套一~ all linked with one another; wheels within wheels/ 最薄弱的一~ the weakest link ③ surround; encircle; hem in: 四面~山 be surrounded (或 hemmed in) by mountains

【环抱】 huánbào surround; encircle; hem in: 群山~的村庄 a village nestling among the hills

【环顾】 huángù 〈书〉 look about (或 round): ~四周 look

all round/ ~国际局势 take stock of the world situation

【环节】 huánjié link: 主要~ a key link/ 生产~ links in the production chain

【环境】 huánjìng environment; surroundings; circumstances: 换换~ have a change of environment/ 在艰苦的~中成长 grow up under tough conditions/ ~顺利 under favourable circumstances/ 如~许可 if circumstances permit ◇ ~保护 environmental protection/ ~改良 environmental improvement/ ~卫生 environmental sanitation; general sanitation/ ~污染 pollution of the environment

【环球】 huánqiú ① round the world: ~旅行 travel round the world; a round-the-world tour ② the earth; the whole world

【环绕】 huánrào surround; encircle; revolve around: 大院的四周,绿树~。 The compound is surrounded by trees./ 月亮~着地球转动。 The moon revolves around the earth./ ~着中心任务 centre around the main task

寰 huán extensive region: 人~ the world of man

【寰球】 huánqiú the earth; the whole world 又作"环球"

huǎn

缓 huǎn ① slow; unhurried: ~流 flow slowly/ ~步而行 walk unhurriedly/ ~不济急。 Slow action cannot save a critical situation. ② delay; postpone; put off: ~办 postpone doing sth./ ~口气 have a respite/ 这事~几天再说。 Let's put it off for a couple of days. ③ not tense; relaxed ④ recuperate; revive; come to: 过了好一阵他才~过来。 It was a long time before he came to.

【缓兵之计】 huǎn bīng zhī jì stratagem to gain a respite; stalling tactics

【缓冲】 huǎnchōng ① buffer; cushion: 弹性~ elastic buffer/ 起~的作用 produce a cushioning effect; absorb the shock/ ~的余地 leeway; room for manoeuvre ② 〈化〉 buffer ◇ ~地带 buffer zone/ ~国 buffer state

【缓和】 huǎnhé ① relax; ease up; mitigate; alleviate: 风势渐趋~。 The wind is subsiding./ ~紧张局势 relax the tension

【缓急】 huǎnjí ① pressing or otherwise; of greater or lesser urgency: 分别轻重~ do things in order of importance and urgency ② emergency: ~相助 give mutual help in an emergency; help each other in case of need

【缓慢】 huǎnmàn slow: 行动~ slow in action; slowmoving/ 进展~ make slow progress

【缓期】 huǎnqī postpone a deadline; suspend: ~付款 delay (或 defer) payment/ 判处死刑,~二年执行 condemned to death with the sentence suspended for two years; sentenced to death with a two-year reprieve

【缓气】 huǎnqì get a breathing space; have a respite; take a breather

【缓刑】 huǎnxíng 〈法〉 temporary suspension of the execution of a sentence; reprieve; probation: ~二年 two years' probation

【缓役】 huǎnyì 〈军〉 deferment (of service)

huàn

幻 huàn ① unreal; imaginary; illusory: 虚~ unreal; illusory; visionary ② magical; changeable: 变~ change irregularly; fluctuate

【幻灯】 huàndēng ① slide show: 放~ show slides/ 看~ watch a slide show ② slide projector ◇ ~机 slide projector

【幻景】 huànjǐng illusion; mirage

【幻境】 huànjìng dreamland; fairyland

【幻觉】 huànjué 〈心〉 hallucination

【幻梦】 huànmèng illusion; dream

【幻灭】 huànmiè vanish into thin air: 他的希望~了。 His hopes were dashed.

【幻术】 huànshù magic; conjuring

【幻想】huànxiǎng illusion; fancy; fantasy: 抱有～ cherish illusions/ 丢掉～ cast away illusions/ 沉湎于～ indulge in fantasy; be lost in reverie/ 把～看作现实 regard one's fantasies as reality

【幻象】huànxiàng mirage; phantom; phantasm

【幻影】huànyǐng unreal image

宦 huàn ①official ②eunuch

【宦官】huànguān eunuch

【宦海】huànhǎi 〈旧〉officialdom; official circles

【宦途】huàntú 〈旧〉official career

涣 huàn melt; vanish

【涣然】huànrán melt away; disappear; vanish: 他的疑虑～冰释。His misgivings have all vanished.

【涣散】huànsàn lax; slack: 纪律～ be lax in discipline/ ～斗志 sap sb.'s morale (或 fighting will)

换* huàn ①exchange; barter; trade: 以兽皮～工业品 exchange (或 barter) furs for industrial products/ 用鲜血来的教训 a lesson paid for in blood ②change: ～衣服 change one's clothes/ 带一套～洗的衣服。Take along a change of clothes./ 乘火车 change to a train/ ～句话说 in other words/ 出去走一下，～～脑筋。Let's go for a walk and give our minds a rest.

【换班】huànbān ①change shifts ②relieve a person on duty ③〈军〉changing of the guard

【换车】huànchē change trains or buses

【换岗】huàngǎng relieve a sentry (或 guard)

【换工】huàngōng exchange labour

【换钱】huànqián ①change money (或 bills) ②sell

【换取】huànqǔ exchange (或 barter) sth. for; get in return: 用工业品～农产品 exchange (或 barter) industrial products for farm produce/ ～外汇 gain foreign exchange

【换算】huànsuàn conversion ◇ ～表 conversion table

【换汤不换药】huàn tāng bù huàn yào the same medicine differently prepared; the same old stuff with a different label; a change in form but not in content (或 essence)

唤 huàn call out; call; shout

【唤起】huànqǐ ①arouse: ～民众 arouse the masses of the people ②call; recall: 有必要～人们注意这个事实。It is necessary to call attention to this fact./ ～对往事的回忆 evoke past memories

【唤醒】huànxǐng wake up; awaken: ～人民 arouse the people

焕 huàn shining; glowing

【焕发】huànfā shine; glow; irradiate: 容光～ one's face glowing with health/ ～精神，努力工作 call forth all one's vigour and work with redoubled efforts

【焕然一新】huànrán yī xīn take on an entirely new look (或 aspect); look brand-new: 这个老港经过改造和建设，面貌～。After renovation and reconstruction this old port has changed beyond recognition.

患* huàn ①trouble; peril; disaster: 防～于未然 take preventive measures; provide against possible trouble/ 有备无～。Preparedness averts peril. ②anxiety; worry: 何～之有。There's no need to worry. ③contract; suffer from: ～病 suffer from an illness; fall ill; be ill

【患处】huànchù affected part (of a patient's body)

【患得患失】huàndé-huànshī worry about personal gains and losses; be swayed by considerations of gain and loss

【患难】huànnàn trials and tribulations; adversity; trouble: ～之交 friend in adversity; tested friend/ ～与共 go through thick and thin together

【患者】huànzhě sufferer; patient: 结核病～ a person suffering from tuberculosis; a TB patient

瘓 huàn 见"瘫痪" tānhuàn

豢 huàn

【豢养】huànyǎng feed; groom; keep

huāng

肓 huāng 见"病入膏肓" bìng rù gāohuāng

荒* huāng ①waste: 地～了。The land lies waste. ②wasteland; uncultivated land: 垦～ open up (或 reclaim) wasteland ③desolate; barren: ～村 deserted village/ ～岛 desert (或 uninhabited) island/ ～山 barren hill ④famine; crop failure: 储粮备～ store up grain against natural disasters ⑤neglect; be out of practice: 别把功课～了。Don't neglect your lessons./ 好久不下棋～了。It's a long time since I played chess. I'm out of practice./ 他的英语丢～了。His English is rusty. ⑥shortage; scarcity: 房～ housing shortage/ 水～ water shortage

【荒诞】huāngdàn fantastic; absurd; incredible: ～的想法 a fantastic idea/ ～的情节 an incredible plot/ ～无稽之谈 a tall story; a preposterous statement/ 不经 preposterous; fantastic

【荒地】huāngdì wasteland; uncultivated (或 undeveloped) land

【荒废】huāngfèi ①leave uncultivated; lie waste ②fall into disuse (或 disrepair): ～了的水渠又利用起来了。The irrigation canals that fell into disrepair are in use again. ③neglect; be out of practice: ～学业 neglect one's studies

【荒郊】huāngjiāo desolate place outside a town; wilderness

【荒凉】huāngliáng bleak and desolate; wild: 一片～ a scene of desolation/ 过去这里是～的穷山沟。This used to be a bleak and barren gully./ ～的景色 wild scenery

【荒乱】huāngluàn in great disorder; in turmoil

【荒谬】huāngmiù absurd; preposterous: ～的说法 an absurd formulation/ ～绝伦 absolutely preposterous; utterly absurd

【荒年】huāngnián famine (或 lean) year

【荒僻】huāngpì desolate and out-of-the-way

【荒唐】huāngtang ①absurd; fantastic; preposterous: ～可笑 ridiculous; absurd/ ～透顶 absolutely ridiculous; preposterous ②dissipated; loose; intemperate

【荒无人烟】huāng wú rényān desolate and uninhabited: ～的地带 a region with no sign of human habitation

【荒芜】huāngwú lie waste; go out of cultivation

【荒野】huāngyě wilderness; the wilds

【荒淫】huāngyín dissolute; licentious; debauched: ～无耻 dissipated and unashamed

慌 huāng flurried; flustered; confused: 沉住气，别～! Keep calm! Don't panic!/ ～了手脚 be alarmed and confused; be flurried/ ～了神儿 be scared out of one's wits/ ～作一团 be thrown into utter confusion

慌* huang 〈口〉〔用做补语，前面加"得"〕awfully; unbearably: 心里闷得～ be bored beyond endurance/ 累得～ be tired out; be dog-tired; be played out

【慌乱】huāngluàn flurried; alarmed and bewildered: 作好充分准备，免得临时～ make ample preparations so as not to be in a rush at the last moment

【慌忙】huāngmáng in a great rush; in a flurry; hurriedly: ～赶到现场 rush to the spot/ 不慌不忙 unhurriedly; calmly

【慌张】huāngzhang flurried; flustered; confused: 神色～ look flurried/ 为什么这样慌慌张张的? Why are you so flustered?

huáng

皇* huáng emperor; sovereign: 女～ empress

【皇帝】huángdì emperor

【皇宫】huánggōng (imperial) palace

【皇冠】huángguān imperial crown

【皇后】huánghòu empress

【皇家】huángjiā imperial family (或 house)

【皇权】huángquán imperial power (或 authority)

【皇上】huángshang ①the emperor; the throne; the reigning sovereign ② (直接称呼) Your Majesty; (间接称呼) His Majesty

【皇室】huángshì imperial family (或 house)

【皇太后】huángtàihòu empress dowager

【皇太子】huángtàizǐ crown prince

【皇族】huángzú people of imperial lineage; imperial kinsmen

黄* huáng yellow; sallow: 脸色发～ a sallow face

【黄道吉日】huángdào jírì propitious (或 auspicious) date; lucky day

【黄豆】huángdòu soya bean; soybean

【黄蜂】huángfēng wasp

【黄瓜】huángguā cucumber

【黄昏】huánghūn dusk

【黄金】huángjīn gold ◇ ～储备 gold reserve (或 stock)/ ～时代 golden age/ ～市场 gold market

【黄粱美梦】huángliáng měimèng Golden Millet Dream (from the story of a poor scholar who dreamt that he had become a high official but awoke to find only the pot of millet still cooking on the fire); pipe dream

【黄毛丫头】huángmáo yātou a chit of a girl; a silly little girl

【黄色】huángsè ① yellow ② decadent; obscene; pornographic ◇ ～电影 pornographic movie; sex film/ ～书刊 pornographic books and periodicals

【黄色人种】huángsè rénzhǒng the yellow race

凰 huáng 见 "凤凰" fènghuáng

隍 huáng dry moat outside a city wall

惶 huáng fear; anxiety; trepidation: ～悚 sudden fear; fright

【惶惶】huánghuáng in a state of anxiety; on tenterhooks; alarmed: ～不可终日 be in a constant state of anxiety; be on tenterhooks

【惶惑】huánghuò perplexed and alarmed; apprehensive: ～不安 perplexed and uneasy

【惶恐】huángkǒng terrified: ～万状 be seized with fear; be frightened out of one's senses

徨 huáng 见 "彷徨" pánghuáng

煌 huáng bright; brilliant: 明星～～。The stars are sparkling.

潢 huáng 见 "装潢" zhuānghuáng

蝗 huáng locust: ～灾 plague of locusts

【蝗虫】huángchóng locust

磺 huáng sulphur

簧 huáng ① 〈乐〉 reed ② spring: 闹钟的～断了。The main spring of the alarm clock is broken.

huǎng

恍 huǎng ① all of a sudden; suddenly ② [与"如""若"等字连用] seem; as if: ～如梦境 as if in a dream

【恍惚】huǎnghū ① in a trance; absentminded: 精神～ be in a trance ② dimly; faintly; seemingly: 我～听见他进屋去了。I was faintly aware that he entered the room.

【恍然大悟】huǎngrán dàwù suddenly see the light; suddenly realize what has happened: 经他一指点, 我才～, 原来是我错了。When he dropped the hint, it suddenly dawned on me that I was wrong.

晃 huǎng ① dazzle: 亮得～眼 dazzlingly bright/ 明～～的刺刀 a shining bayonet ② flash past: 窗外有个人影儿

一～就不见了。A figure flashed past the window./ 一～半个月过去了。A fortnight passed in a flash.

另见 huàng

谎* huǎng lie; falsehood

【谎报】huǎngbào lie about sth.; give false information; start a canard: ～年龄 lie about one's age/ ～军情 make a false report about the military situation

【谎话】huǎnghuà lie; falsehood: 说～ tell a lie; lie

【谎言】huǎngyán lie; falsehood

幌 huǎng

【幌子】huǎngzi ① shop sign; signboard ② pretence; cover; front: 打着"援助"的～ under the pretence of aid; in the guise of aid/ 骗人的～ a facade; a front

huàng

晃 huàng shake; sway: 他～～手说: "不去了"。With a sweep of his hand he said, "I won't go."

另见 huǎng

【晃荡】huàngdang rock; shake; sway: 小船在江面上～。The small boat is rocking on the river./ 桶里水很满, 一～就出来了。The bucket was so full that it overflowed at the slightest motion./ 风吹得马灯不停地～。The barn lantern kept swaying in the wind./ 一瓶子不响, 半瓶子～。The half-filled bottle sloshes, the full bottle remains still — the dabbler in knowledge chatters away, the wise man stays silent

【晃动】huàngdòng rock; sway: 别～这船。Don't rock the boat./ 车轮有点～。The wheels wobble a bit.

huī

灰* huī ① ash: 飞～ fly ash/ 草木～ plant ash (as fertilizer) ② dust: 积了厚厚的一层～ accumulate a thick layer of dust ③ lime; (lime) mortar: ～墙 plastered wall/ 和～ mix mortar ④ grey: ～马 a grey horse ⑤ disheartened; discouraged: 心～意懒 feel disheartened

【灰暗】huī'àn murky grey; gloomy: ～的天空 a gloomy (或 murky grey) sky

【灰白】huībái greyish white; ashen; pale: ～的鬓发 greying temples/ 脸色～ look pale

【灰尘】huīchén dust; dirt: 大风过后, 桌上落了一层～。After the wind, there was a layer of dust on the desk./ 掸掉桌上的～ dust the table

【灰色】huīsè ① grey; ashy ② pessimistic; gloomy: ～人生观 a pessimistic (或 grey) outlook on life ③ obscure; ambiguous

【灰心】huīxīn lose heart; be discouraged: ～丧气 be utterly disheartened/ 成功不骄傲, 失败不～。When you succeed don't get conceited; when you fail don't be dejected.

诙 huī

【诙谐】huīxié humorous; jocular

恢* huī extensive; vast

【恢复】huīfù ① resume; renew: ～邦交 resume diplomatic relations/ ～正常 return to normal ② recover; regain: ～健康 recover one's health/ ～知觉 recover consciousness; come to ③ restore; reinstate; rehabilitate

【恢恢】huīhuī 〈书〉 extensive; vast: 天网～, 疏而不漏。The net of Heaven has large meshes, but it lets nothing through.

挥* huī ① wave; wield: ～刀 wield a sword/ ～笔 wield the brush; put pen to paper ② wipe off: ～泪 wipe away tears; wipe one's eyes/ ～汗如雨 drip with sweat ③ command (an army): ～师南下 command an army to march south ④ scatter; disperse

【挥动】huīdòng brandish; wave: ～大棒 brandish a big stick/ ～旗子 wave a flag/ ～拳头 shake one's fist

【挥毫】huīháo 〈书〉 wield one's writing brush; write or draw a picture (with a brush)

【挥霍】 huīhuò spend freely; squander: ～无度 spend without restraint

【挥金如土】 huī jīn rú tǔ throw money about like dirt; spend money like water

【挥手】 huīshǒu wave one's hand; wave: ～致意 wave greetings to; wave to sb. in acknowledgment/ ～告别 wave farewell; wave good-bye to sb.

【挥舞】 huīwǔ wave; wield; brandish: ～花束表示欢迎 wave bouquets in welcome/ ～指挥棒 brandish the baton — order sb. about

晖 huī sunshine; sunlight

辉* huī ①brightness; splendour ②shine: 与日月同～ shine for ever like the sun and the moon

【辉煌】 huīhuáng brilliant; splendid; glorious: ～的战果 a brilliant military victory/ ～的文化 splendid civilization/ 灯火～ brilliantly illuminated; ablaze with lights

【辉映】 huīyìng shine; reflect: 湖光山色,交相～。 The lake and the hills add radiance and beauty to each other.

麾 huī 〈书〉①standard of a commander (used in ancient times) ②command: ～军前进 command an army to march forward

【麾下】 huīxià 〈书〉①〈敬〉general; commander; your excellency ②those under one's command

徽 huī emblem; badge; insignia: 国～ national emblem/ 校～ school badge/ 帽～ cap insignia

【徽号】 huīhào title of honour

【徽章】 huīzhāng badge; insignia

huí

回* huí ①circle; wind: 迂～ winding; circuitous; roundabout/ 峰～路转 The path winds along mountain ridges. ②return; go back: 到原地 return to where one came from ③turn round:～过身来 turn round ④answer; reply: 这～信 send a letter in reply; write back ⑤〈量〉chapter: 这部小说共一百一十二。 This novel has 112 chapters. ⑥〈量〉〔用于事情、动作的次数〕来过一～ have been here once/ 完全是两～事 two entirely different matters/ 一～生,二～熟。First time strangers, second time friends.

【回拜】 huíbài pay a return visit

【回报】 huíbào ①report back on what has been done. ②repay; requite; reciprocate: ～他的盛情 repay him for his hospitality or kindness ③retaliate; get one's own back

【回避】 huíbì evade; dodge; avoid (meeting sb.): ～要害问题 evade (或 sidestep) the crucial question/ ～困难 dodge difficulties

【回驳】 huíbó refute

【回程】 huíchéng ①return trip ②〈机〉return (或 back) stroke

【回春】 huíchūn ①return of spring: 大地～。 Spring returns to the earth. 或 Spring is here again. ②bring back to life: ～灵药 a miraculous cure; a wonderful remedy

【回答】 huídá answer; reply; response: 从理论上～了这个问题 furnish a theoretical answer to this question/ 事实是对造谣者最有力的～。 Facts are the most powerful rebuff to rumourmongers.

【回荡】 huídàng resound; reverberate: 欢呼声在山谷间～。 Shouts of joy reverberated in the valleys.

【回电】 huídiàn wire back: 请即～。 Wire reply immediately.

【回访】 huífǎng pay a return visit

【回复】 huífù reply (to a letter)

【回顾】 huígù look back; review: 一九七七年的～ 1977 in retrospect

【回光返照】 huíguāng fǎnzhào ①the last radiance of the setting sun — momentary recovery of consciousness just before death ②a sudden spurt of activity prior to collapse

【回合】 huíhé round; bout: 第一个～的胜利 a first-round victory

【回话】 huíhuà reply; answer: 请你给他带个～。 Please take a message to him by way of reply.

【回击】 huíjī fight back; return fire; counterattack: 给以有力的～ strike a powerful counterblow; hit back hard

【回教】 Huíjiào Islam

【回敬】 huíjìng return a compliment; do or give sth. in return: ～一杯 drink a toast in return/ ～一拳 return a blow

【回扣】 huíkòu sales commission

【回来】 huílai return; come back; be back: 他马上就～。 He'll be back in a minute.

【回来】 huílai 〔用在动词后,表示到原来的地方来〕back: 跑～ run back/ 把借出去的书要～。 Recall the books on loan.

【回礼】 huílǐ ①return a salute ②send a present in return; present a gift in return

【回请】 huíqǐng return hospitality; give a return banquet

【回去】 huíqu return; go back; be back: 他离开家乡十年,从未～过。 He has never been back to his birthplace since he left it ten years ago.

【回去】 huíqu 〔用在动词后,表示到原来的地方去〕back: 请把这封信给他退～。 Please return the letter to him.

【回升】 huíshēng rise again (after a fall); pick up: 气温～。 The temperature has gone up again./ 指数～。 The index is picking up.

【回生】 huíshēng bring back to life: 起死～ bring the dying back to life

【回声】 huíshēng echo

【回手】 huíshǒu ①turn round and stretch out one's hand: 他走出了屋子,～把门带上。 He went out of the room and closed the door behind him. ②hit back; return a blow

【回首】 huíshǒu ①turn one's head; turn round ②〈书〉look back; recollect

【回条】 huítiáo a short note acknowledging receipt of sth.; receipt

【回帖】 huítiě a money order receipt to be signed and returned to the sender

【回头】 huítóu ①turn one's head; turn round ②repent: 及早～ repent before it is too late ③〈口〉later: ～再谈。 We'll talk it over later./ ～见! See you later!

【回头是岸】 huítóu shì àn repent and be saved: 希望劝说他们发出善心,～是不可能的。 It is impossible to persuade them to show kindness of heart and to turn from their evil ways.

【回味】 huíwèi ①aftertaste ②call sth. to mind and ponder over it: ～他说的话 ponder over what he has said

【回乡】 huíxiāng return to one's home village

【回响】 huíxiǎng reverberate; echo; resound: 雷声在山谷里激起了～。 Thunder reverberated in the valley./ 他的亲切教导仍在我的耳边～。 His earnest instructions still ring in my ears.

【回想】 huíxiǎng think back; recollect; recall

【回心转意】 huíxīn-zhuǎnyì change one's views; come around

【回信】 huíxìn ①write in reply; write back: 我回了他一封信。 I wrote him a reply./ 望早日～。 I'm looking forward to hearing from you soon. ②a letter in reply ③a verbal message in reply; reply: 事情办妥了,我给你个～儿。 I'll let you know when I'm through with it.

【回旋】 huíxuán ①circle round: 飞机在上空～。 The aeroplane is circling overhead. ②(room for) manoeuvre: 这件事还有～余地。 The whole thing is not final. 或 It's still possible to make changes.

【回忆】 huíyì call to mind; recollect; recall: ～对比 recall the past and contrast it with the present/ 战争年代的～ reminiscences of the war years/ 童年的～ recollections of childhood; childhood memories ◇ ～录 reminiscences; memoirs; recollections

【回音】 huíyīn ①echo ②reply: 立候～ hoping for an immediate reply

【回转】 huízhuàn turn round

【回嘴】 huízuǐ answer (或 talk) back; retort

洄 huí 〈书〉(of water) whirl

茴 huí

【茴香】 huíxiāng 〈植〉①fennel ②aniseed

蛔 huí
【蛔虫】huíchóng roundworm; ascarid ◇ ~病 roundworm disease; ascariasis

huǐ

悔* huǐ regret; repent
【悔不当初】huǐ bù dāngchū regret having done sth.: 早知今日，~。 If I'd known then what was going to happen, I wouldn't have done as I did.
【悔改】huǐgǎi repent and mend one's ways: 毫无~之意 have no intention of mending one's ways; show no sign of repentance
【悔过】huǐguò repent one's error; be repentant: 有~表示 show signs of repentance/ ~自新 repent and turn over a new leaf; repent and make a fresh start ◇ ~书 a written statement of repentance
【悔恨】huǐhèn regret deeply; be bitterly remorseful
【悔悟】huǐwù realize one's error and show repentance
【悔之无及】huǐ zhī wú jí too late to repent; too late to regret
【悔罪】huǐzuì show repentance; show penitence

毁* huǐ ① destroy; ruin; damage: ~于一旦 be destroyed in a moment/ 这场电子把庄稼~了。 The hailstorm ruined the crops. ② burn up: 焚~ destroy by fire; burn down ③ defame; slander
【毁谤】huǐbàng slander; malign; calumniate: 这纯系~。 This is slander, pure and simple.
【毁坏】huǐhuài destroy; damage
【毁灭】huǐmiè destroy; exterminate: 给侵略者以~性打击 deal the aggressors a crushing (或 devastating) blow
【毁弃】huǐqì scrap; annul
【毁伤】huǐshāng injure; hurt; damage
【毁损】huǐsǔn damage; impair
【毁誉】huǐ-yù praise or blame; praise or condemnation: 不计~ be indifferent to people's praise or blame/ ~参半 (of a person) get both praise and censure; (of a book, etc.) have a mixed reception
【毁约】huǐyuē ① break one's promise ② scrap a contract or treaty

huì

汇 huì ① converge: ~成巨流 converge into a mighty torrent ② gather together: ~印成书 have (articles on a given subject) collected and published in book form ③ things collected; assemblage; collection: 词~ vocabulary ④ remit: 给家里~钱 remit money to one's family/ 电~ telegraphic transfer
【汇报】huìbào report; give an account of: ~工作 report to sb. on one's work/ ~调查结果 report the findings of an investigation
【汇编】huìbiān compilation; collection; corpus: 资料~工作 compilation of reference material/ 文件~ a collection of documents/ 语言学研究资料~ a corpus of philological data
【汇兑】huìduì remittance
【汇费】huìfèi remittance fee 又作"汇水"
【汇合】huìhé converge; join: 这两条河在什么地方~? Where do the two rivers join?/ ~成一支巨大的力量 unite to form a gigantic force/ 五条支流的~口 the confluence of five tributaries
【汇集】huìjí ① collect; compile: ~材料 collect all relevant data ② come together; converge; assemble
【汇款】huìkuǎn ① remit money; make a remittance ② remittance: 收到一笔~ receive a remittance/ 邮政~ postal remittance ◇ ~单 money order/ ~人 remitter
【汇率】huìlǜ exchange rate: 固定~ fixed (exchange) rate/ 浮动~ floating (exchange) rate
【汇票】huìpiào draft; bill of exchange; money order: 银

行~ bank draft/ 邮政~ postal money order

卉 huì (various kinds of) grass: 奇花异~ rare flowers and grasses

会* huì ① get together; assemble: 明晨七时在门口~齐。 We'll assemble at the gate at 7 o'clock tomorrow morning. ② meet; see: 昨天我没有~着他。 I didn't see him yesterday. ③ meeting; gathering; party; get-together; conference: 晚上有个全组~。 There's going to be a meeting of the whole group tonight./ 欢迎~ welcoming party/ 欢送~ send-off party ④ association; society; union: 帮~ secret society/ 工~ trade union ⑤ 〈旧〉 a temple fair: 赶~ go to a fair ⑥ an association of people who regularly contribute to a common fund and draw from it by turns ⑦ chief city; capital: 都~ city; metropolis/ 省~ provincial capital ⑧ opportunity; occasion: 适逢其~ happen to be present on the occasion ⑨ understand; grasp: 误~ misunderstand ⑩ can; be able to: ~滑冰 can skate/ ~英文 know English ⑪ be good at: ~修各种钟表 be skilful in repairing all kinds of clocks and watches/ 很~这一套 be a past master of this sort of game ⑫ be likely to; be sure to ⑬ 〈口〉 a moment: 我去一~儿就回来。 I'll be back in a moment.
另见 kuài
【会场】huìchǎng meeting-place; conference (或 assembly) hall
【会费】huìfèi membership dues
【会馆】huìguǎn 〈旧〉 guild hall; provincial or county guild
【会合】huìhé join; meet; converge; assemble: 两军~后继续前进。 The two armies joined forces and marched on.
【会合点】huìhédiǎn 〈军〉 meeting point; rallying point; rendezvous
【会话】huìhuà conversation (as in a language course)
【会籍】huìjí membership (of an association)
【会见】huìjiàn meet with (esp. a foreign visitor)
【会客】huìkè receive a visitor (或 guest): ~时间 the time for receiving visitors; visiting hours/ 现在开会, 不~。 No visitors. Meeting in progress. ◇ ~室 reception room
【会面】huìmiàn meet: 我约定了星期天和他~。 I have an appointment to meet him on Sunday.
【会期】huìqī ① the time fixed for a conference; the date (或 time) of a meeting ② the duration of a meeting: ~定为三天。 The meeting is scheduled to last three days.
【会儿】huìr 〈口〉 moment: 一~ a little while/ 等~。 Wait a moment./ 用不了多大~。 It won't be a minute. 或 It won't take long.
【会商】huìshāng hold a conference or consultation: ~解决办法 consult to find a solution
【会谈】huìtán talks: 双边~ bilateral talks ◇ ~纪要 minutes of talks; notes on talks; summary of a conversation
【会堂】huìtáng assembly hall; hall
【会同】huìtóng (handle an affair) jointly with other organizations concerned
【会晤】huìwù meet: 两国外长定期~。 The foreign ministers of the two countries meet regularly.
【会心】huìxīn understanding; knowing: ~的微笑 an understanding smile/ 露出~的表情 with a knowing look
【会议】huìyì meeting; conference: 正式~ official meeting/ 全体~ plenary session ◇ ~地点 meeting-place; venue/ ~日程表 the daily agenda of a conference/ ~室 meeting (或 conference) room; council chamber/ ~厅 conference (或 assembly) hall
【会意】huìyì understanding; knowing
【会员】huìyuán member: 正式~ full (或 full-fledged) member/ ~人数 membership ◇ ~国 member state (或 nation)/ ~证 membership card/ ~资格 the status of a member; membership
【会章】huìzhāng ① the constitution (或 statutes) of an association, society, etc. ② the emblem of an association, society, etc.
【会长】huìzhǎng the president of an association or society
【会址】huìzhǐ ① the site of an association or society ② the site of a conference or meeting

讳

讳 huì ① avoid as taboo: 直言不~ speak bluntly; call a spade a spade ② forbidden word; taboo: 犯了他的~了. Something was said that happened to be taboo with him. ③〈旧〉the name, regarded as taboo, of a deceased emperor or head of a family
【讳疾忌医】 huìjí-jìyī hide one's sickness for fear of treatment — conceal one's fault for fear of criticism
【讳莫如深】 huì mò rú shēn closely guard a secret; not breathe a word to a soul; not utter a single word about sth.
【讳言】 huìyán dare not or would not speak up: 毫不~ make no attempt to conceal the truth; confess freely/ 无可~ there's no denying the fact

荟

荟 huì 〈书〉luxuriant growth (of plants)
【荟萃】 huìcuì (of distinguished people or exquisite objects) gather together; assemble: 人才~ a galaxy of talent/ ~一堂 gather together in one hall

绘

绘 huì paint; draw
【绘画】 huìhuà drawing; painting
【绘声绘色】 huìshēng-huìsè vivid; lively: ~的描述 a vivid description (或 portraiture) 又作"绘影绘声"; "绘声绘影"

贿

贿 huì bribe; bribe
【贿赂】 huìlù ① bribe ② bribery
【贿买】 huìmǎi buy over; suborn
【贿选】 huìxuǎn practise bribery at an election; get elected by bribery

彗

彗 huì 〈书〉broom
【彗星】 huìxīng 〈天〉comet

晦

晦 huì ① the last day of a lunar month ② dark; obscure ③ night
【晦暗】 huì'àn dark and gloomy
【晦气】 huìqì unlucky: 自认~ be resigned to one's bad luck
【晦涩】 huìsè hard to understand; obscure: ~的语言 obscure language (in poetry, drama, etc.)

秽

秽 huì ① dirty: 污~ filthy ② ugly; abominable: ~行 abominable behaviour
【秽土】 huìtǔ rubbish; refuse; dirt
【秽闻】 huìwén 〈书〉ill repute (referring to sexual behaviour); reputation for immorality

惠

惠 huì ① favour; kindness; benefit: 小恩小~ small favours/ 受~ receive kindness (或 favour); be favoured/ 互~ mutual benefit ②〈敬〉〔用于对方对待自己的行动〕: ~鉴 be kind enough to read (the following letter)/ ~书 your letter
【惠存】 huìcún 〈敬〉please keep (this photograph, book, etc. as a souvenir); to so-and-so
【惠顾】 huìgù 〈敬〉your patronage
【惠临】 huìlín 〈敬〉your gracious presence: 敬请~. Your presence is requested.

喙

喙 huì ① beak or snout ② mouth: 百~莫辩. A hundred mouths can't explain it away./ 不容置~ not allow others to butt in; brook no intervention

慧

慧 huì intelligent; bright: 智~ wisdom; intelligence
【慧心】 huìxīn wisdom
【慧眼】 huìyǎn ①〈佛教〉a mind which perceives both past and future ② mental discernment (或 perception); insight; acumen

hūn

昏

昏 hūn ① dusk: 晨~ at dawn and dusk ② dark; dim ③ confused; muddled: 利令智~ be blinded by lust for gain/ 以其~~,使人昭昭,是不行的. Those in the dark are in no position to light the way for others. ④ lose consciousness; faint: ~倒 fall into a swoon; go off into a faint; fall unconscious
【昏暗】 hūn'àn dim; dusky: ~的灯光 a dim light
【昏沉】 hūnchén ① murky: 暮色~ murky twilight ② dazed; befuddled: 我昨晚没睡好,头脑昏昏沉沉的. I feel in a daze because I didn't sleep well last night.
【昏黑】 hūnhēi dusky; dark
【昏花】 hūnhuā dim-sighted: 老眼~ dim-sighted from old age
【昏黄】 hūnhuáng pale yellow; faint; dim: 月色~ faint moonlight/ ~的灯光 a dim light
【昏昏欲睡】 hūnhūn yù shuì drowsy; sleepy
【昏君】 hūnjūn a fatuous and self-indulgent ruler
【昏乱】 hūnluàn dazed and confused; befuddled
【昏迷】 hūnmí stupor; coma: 处于~状态 be in a state of unconsciousness; be in a coma/ ~不醒 remain unconscious
【昏睡】 hūnshuì lethargic sleep; lethargy
【昏天黑地】 hūntiān-hēidì ① pitch-dark ② dizzy: 我只觉得一阵~,随即失去了知觉. I suddenly felt dizzy and then fell unconscious. ③ perverted; decadent: ~的生活 a dissipated life ④ dark rule and social disorder
【昏头昏脑】 hūntóu-hūnnǎo ① addleheaded; muddleheaded ② absentminded; forgetful
【昏眩】 hūnxuàn dizzy; giddy
【昏庸】 hūnyōng fatuous; muddleheaded; stupid

荤

荤 hūn meat or fish: ~菜 meat dishes/ 她不吃~. She doesn't eat meat. 或 She's a vegetarian.

婚

婚 hūn ① wed; marry ② marriage; wedding
【婚嫁】 hūnjià marriage
【婚礼】 hūnlǐ wedding ceremony; wedding
【婚期】 hūnqī wedding day
【婚事】 hūnshì marriage; wedding
【婚姻】 hūnyīn marriage; matrimony: ~自由 freedom of marriage/ 美满的~ a happy marriage/ ~纠纷 matrimonial dispute/ ~状况 marital status
【婚约】 hūnyuē marriage contract; engagement: 解除~ break off one's engagement

阍

阍 hūn 〈书〉① tend or guard a gate: 司~ gatekeeper; janitor ② palace gate
【阍者】 hūnzhě 〈书〉gatekeeper; janitor

hún

浑

浑 hún ① muddy; turbid: ~水 muddy water ② foolish; stupid ③ simple and natural; unsophisticated ④ whole; all over
【浑蛋】 húndàn 〈骂〉blackguard; wretch; scoundrel; bastard; skunk
【浑厚】 húnhòu ① simple and honest ② (of writing, painting, etc.) simple and vigorous: 笔力~ (of handwriting) bold and vigorous strokes
【浑浑噩噩】 húnhún'è'è ignorant; simple-minded; muddleheaded
【浑然一体】 húnrán yī tǐ one integrated mass; a unified entity; an integral whole
【浑身】 húnshēn from head to foot; all over: 吓得~发抖 tremble all over with fear/ ~疼痛 aching all over/ ~是劲 brimming with energy; bursting with energy/ ~是胆 be every inch a hero; be the very embodiment of valour
【浑水摸鱼】 húnshuǐ mō yú fish in troubled waters
【浑圆】 húnyuán perfectly round
【浑浊】 húnzhuó muddy; turbid

混 hún
另见 hùn

【混蛋】 húndàn 见"浑蛋" húndàn

馄 hún
【馄饨】 húntun won ton; dumpling soup

魂* hún
① soul ② mood; spirit: 神～不定 be distracted; have the jitters ③ the lofty spirit of a nation: 民族～ national spirit

【魂不附体】 hún bù fù tǐ as if the soul had left the body: 吓得～ be scared out of one's wits

【魂灵】 húnlíng 〈口〉 soul

【魂魄】 húnpò soul

hùn

诨 hùn
joke; jest: 打～ make gags

【诨名】 hùnmíng nickname

混* hùn
① mix; confuse: ～在一起 mix things up/ 这是两码事,不要搞～了。 They're two entirely different matters; don't mix them up. ② pass for; pass off as: 鱼目～珠 pass off fish eyes as pearls — pass off the sham as genuine ③ muddle along; drift along: ～日子 drift along aimlessly ④ get along with sb.: 同他们～得很熟 be quite familiar with them ⑤ thoughtlessly; recklessly; irresponsibly: ～出主意 put forward irresponsible suggestions

另见 hún

【混充】 hùnchōng pass oneself off as; palm sth. off as

【混沌】 hùndùn ① Chaos (the primeval state of the universe according to folklore): ～初开 when earth was first separated from heaven ② innocent as a child

【混合】 hùnhé mix; blend; mingle

【混进】 hùnjìn infiltrate; sneak into; worm one's way into

【混乱】 hùnluàn confusion; chaos: 敌军陷于～。 The enemy were thrown into confusion./ 思想～ ideological confusion

【混凝土】 hùnníngtǔ concrete ◇ ～搅拌机 concrete mixer

【混世魔王】 hùn shì mówáng fiend in human shape; devil incarnate

【混水摸鱼】 hùnshuǐ mō yú fish in troubled waters

【混为一谈】 hùn wéi yī tán lump (或 jumble) together; confuse sth. with sth. else

【混淆】 hùnxiáo obscure; blur; confuse; mix up: ～是非 confuse right and wrong/ ～视听 mislead the public; confuse public opinion

【混血儿】 hùnxuè'ér a person of mixed blood; half-breed

【混杂】 hùnzá mix; mingle: 不要把不同的种子～在一起。 Don't mix up different kinds of seeds.

【混战】 hùnzhàn tangled warfare: 军阀～ tangled warfare among warlords; tangled fighting between warlords

【混帐】 hùnzhàng 〈骂〉 scoundrel; bastard; son of a bitch ◇ ～话 impudent remark

【混浊】 hùnzhuó muddy; turbid: ～的水 turbid water/ ～的空气 foul (或 stale) air

huō

豁 huō
① slit; break; crack: 墙上～了一个口子。 There is a breach in the wall. ② give up; sacrifice: ～出三天时间,也要把它做好。 Even if it takes us three days, we must get the job done.

另见 huò

huó

活* huó
① live: 她～到八十岁。 She lived to be eighty./ ～到老,学到老。 One is never too old to learn. ② alive; living: 在他～着的时候 during his lifetime/ ～捉 capture alive/ ～老虎 a live tiger/ ～字典 a walking dictionary ③ save (the life of a person): ～人无算 (of a good doctor, etc.) save countless lives ④ vivid; lively: 脑子很～ have a quick mind ⑤ movable; moving: ～水 flowing water ⑥ exactly; simply: ～像 look exactly like; be the spit and image of ⑦ work: 干～儿 work/ 重～儿 heavy work/ 针线～儿 needlework ⑧ product: 这批～儿做得好。 This batch of products is well made.

【活动】 huódòng ① move about; exercise: 站起来～～ stand up and move around/ 一下筋骨 limber up the joints; limber oneself up ② shaky; unsteady: 这把椅子直～。 The chair is rickety./ 这颗牙～了。 This tooth's loose. ③ movable; mobile; flexible: 口气有点～ sound less adamant; begin to relent a little ④ activity; manoeuvre: 户外～ outdoor activities/ 政治～ political activities/ 从事科学～ go in for scientific pursuits ⑤ use personal influence or irregular means: 替他～～ put in a word for him; use one's influence on his behalf

【活佛】 huófó 〈宗〉 Living Buddha

【活该】 huógāi 〈口〉 serve sb. right: 这家伙落得如此下场,～。 The fellow got what he deserved.

【活活】 huóhuó while still alive: ～烧死 be burnt alive

【活见鬼】 huójiànguǐ it's sheer fantasy; you're imagining things

【活结】 huójié a knot that can be undone by a pull; slipknot

【活口】 huókǒu ① a survivor of a murder attempt ② a prisoner who can furnish information

【活力】 huólì vigour; vitality; energy: 充满着青春的～ be brimming with youthful vigour

【活灵活现】 huólíng-huóxiàn vivid; lifelike: 说得～ give a vivid description; make it come to life 又作"活龙活现"

【活埋】 huómái bury alive

【活门】 huómén 〈机〉 valve

【活泼】 huópo lively; vivacious; vivid: 天真～的孩子 lively children/ 文字～ written in a lively style

【活塞】 huósāi 〈机〉 piston

【活生生】 huóshēngshēng ① real; living: ～的例子 a living example ② while still alive

【活受罪】 huóshòuzuì 〈口〉 have a hell of a life

【活现】 huóxiàn appear vividly; come alive

【活像】 huóxiàng look exactly like; be the spit and image of; be an exact replica of: 这孩子长得～他父亲。 The child is the very spit (或 image) of his father.

【活页】 huóyè loose-leaf ◇ ～笔记本 loose-leaf notebook/ ～夹 loose-leaf binder; spring binder/ ～文选 loose-leaf selections/ ～纸 paper for a loose-leaf notebook

【活跃】 huóyuè ① brisk; active; dynamic. 市场～。 Business is brisk./ 人是生产力中最～的因素。 Man is the most active factor among the productive forces. ② enliven; animate; invigorate: ～文娱生活 liven up cultural and recreational activities/ ～会场气氛 enliven the atmosphere of the meeting

huǒ

火* huǒ
① fire: 生～ make a fire/ 这屋里有～。 There's a fire in the room. ② firearms; ammunition ③ fiery: ～红 red as fire; flaming ④ urgent; pressing: ～速回电。 Cable reply immediately. ⑤ anger; temper: 心火～起 flare up in anger/ 你怎么这么大的～儿? Why are you in such a temper?/ 他～儿了。 He flared up.

【火把】 huǒbǎ torch

【火并】 huǒbìng open fight between factions

【火柴】 huǒchái match ◇ ～盒 matchbox

【火场】 huǒchǎng the scene of a fire

【火车】 huǒchē train

【火车头】 huǒchētóu (railway) engine; locomotive

【火攻】 huǒgōng fire attack (using fire as a weapon against enemy personnel and installations)

【火光】 huǒguāng flame; blaze: ～冲天 The flames lit up the sky.

【火锅】huǒguō chafing dish

【火海】huǒhǎi a sea of fire: 刀山敢上，～敢闯 dare to climb a mountain of swords and plunge into a sea of flames — ready to undergo the most severe trials

【火候】huǒhou ① duration and degree of heating, cooking, smelting, etc.: 烧窑得看～. In operating a kiln you must pay attention to temperature control./ 这鸭子烤得正到～. This roast duck is done to a turn. ② level of attainment: 他的书法到了～. He has matured as a calligrapher.

【火花】huǒhuā spark: ～四溅 sparks flying off in all directions ◇ ～塞 〈机〉 sparking plug; spark plug; ignition plug

【火化】huǒhuà cremation

【火鸡】huǒjī turkey

【火急】huǒjí urgent; pressing: 十万～ most urgent

【火箭】huǒjiàn rocket: 发射～ fire (或 launch) a rocket ◇ ～部队 rocket troops/ ～弹 rocket projectile; rocket shell/ ～发射场 rocket launching site/ ～发射台 rocket launching pad; rocket mount/ ～技术 rocketry/ ～炮 rocket gun/ ～筒 rocket launcher (或 projector); bazooka

【火警】huǒjǐng fire alarm

【火炬】huǒjù torch

【火坑】huǒkēng fiery pit; pit of hell; abyss of suffering: 跳出～ escape from the living hell

【火辣辣】huǒlālā burning: ～的太阳 a scorching sun/ 疼得～的 a searing pain/ 脸上觉得～的 feel one's cheeks burning (as with shame)/ 心里～的 burning with anxiety

【火力】huǒlì 〈军〉 firepower; fire: 发扬～ make full use of firepower

【火炉】huǒlú (heating) stove

【火盆】huǒpén fire pan; brazier

【火漆】huǒqī sealing wax

【火气】huǒqì anger; temper: ～很大 have a bad temper

【火热】huǒrè ① burning hot; fervent; fiery: ～的太阳 a burning sun/ ～的心 a fervent heart ② intimate: 打得～ carry on intimately with; be as thick as thieves

【火山】huǒshān volcano: ～喷发 volcanic eruption/ 活(死)～ active (extinct) volcano/ 休眠～ dormant volcano

【火伤】huǒshāng burn (caused by fire)

【火上加油】huǒshàng jiā yóu pour oil on the fire; add fuel to the flames

【火烧火燎】huǒshāo-huǒliǎo ① feeling terribly hot ② restless with anxiety

【火烧眉毛】huǒ shāo méimao the fire is singeing the eyebrows — a desperate situation; a matter of the utmost urgency

【火石】huǒshí flint

【火树银花】huǒshù-yínhuā fiery trees and silver flowers — a display of fireworks and a sea of lanterns (on a festival night)

【火速】huǒsù at top speed; posthaste: 任务十分紧急，必须～完成. It's an urgent task and must be completed at once./ ～增援 rush up reinforcements

【火腿】huǒtuǐ ham

【火险】huǒxiǎn fire insurance

【火星】huǒxīng ① spark: ～迸发 a shower of sparks ② 〈天〉 Mars

【火性】huǒxìng 〈口〉 bad temper; hot temper

【火焰】huǒyàn flame

【火药】huǒyào gunpowder; powder ◇ ～库 powder magazine

【火药味】huǒyàowèi the smell of gunpowder: 这是一篇充满～的声明. This statement has a strong smell of gunpowder.

【火油】huǒyóu 〈方〉 kerosene

【火灾】huǒzāi fire (as a disaster); conflagration

【火葬】huǒzàng cremation ◇ ～场 crematorium; crematory

【火中取栗】huǒzhōng qǔ lì pull sb.'s chestnuts out of the fire; be a cat's-paw

【火烛】huǒzhú things that may cause a fire: 小心～! Be careful about fires!

伙* huǒ ① mess; board; meals: 包～ get or supply meals at a fixed rate; board/ 在学校人～ board at school ② partner; mate ③ partnership; company: 合～ enter into partnership/ 中途拆～ part company halfway ④ 〈量〉 group; crowd; band: 三个一群，五个一～ in small groups; in knots; in twos and threes/ 一～强盗 a band of robbers ⑤ combine; join: ～买 club together to buy sth.

【伙伴】huǒbàn partner; companion: 我小时候的～ a childhood pal of mine

【伙计】huǒji ① partner ② 〈口〉 fellow; mate: ～，上哪儿去? Where are you going, mate? ③ 〈旧〉 salesman; salesclerk; shop assistant

【伙食】huǒshí mess; food; meals: 管理～ handle messing arrangements

夥 huǒ 〈书〉 much; a great deal; many; numerous: 获益甚～ have derived much benefit

huò

或* huò ① 〈副〉 perhaps; maybe; probably: 代表团明晨～可到达. The delegation may arrive tomorrow morning. ② 〈连〉 or; either... or...: 这块地可以种高粱～玉米. We can grow sorghum or maize on this plot. ③ 〈书〉 someone; some people: ～日someone says; some say

【或...或...】huò...huò... 〈连〉 either... or...; or: 或明或暗 either overt or covert/ 或大或小 big or small/ 或迟或早 sooner or later/ 或多或少 more or less; to a greater or lesser extent; in varying degrees

【或然】huòrán probable

【或许】huòxǔ 〈副〉 perhaps; maybe: 他～没有赶上火车. Perhaps he has missed the train./ 她～能来. She might be able to come.

【或者】huòzhě ① 〈副〉 perhaps; maybe: 快点走，～还赶得上他. Be quick, we may catch up with him yet. ② 〈连〉 or; either... or...: 请你把这本书交给小王～小李. Please give this book to either Xiao Wang or Xiao Li.

货* huò ① goods; commodity: 送～上门 sell goods at the customers' doors ② money: 通～ currency ③ 〈骂〉: 蠢～ blockhead; idiot ④ 〈书〉 sell

【货币】huòbì money; currency: 储备～ reserve currency/ 周转～ vehicle currency/ 自由兑换～ convertible currency ◇ ～单位 monetary unit

【货币贬值】huòbì biǎnzhí ① (currency) devaluation ② (currency) depreciation

【货币升值】huòbì shēngzhí ① (currency) revaluation ② (currency) appreciation

【货车】huòchē ① goods train; freight train ② goods van (或 wagon); freight car (或 wagon) ③ lorry; truck

【货船】huòchuán freighter; cargo ship; cargo vessel: 定期～ cargo liner

【货单】huòdān manifest; waybill; shipping list

【货到付款】huò dào fù kuǎn cash on delivery (COD)

【货机】huòjī 〈航空〉 cargo aircraft (或 plane); air freighter

【货价】huòjià commodity price; price of goods

【货品】huòpǐn kinds or types of goods

【货色】huòsè ① goods: ～齐全. Goods of every description are available./ 上等～ first-class goods; quality goods

【货摊】huòtān stall; stand

【货物】huòwù goods; commodity; merchandise

【货箱】huòxiāng packing box

【货源】huòyuán source of goods; supply of goods: ～充足 an ample supply of goods/ 开辟～ find (或 open up) new sources of goods

【货运】huòyùn freight transport

【货栈】huòzhàn warehouse

【货真价实】huòzhēn-jiàshí ① genuine goods at a fair price ② through and through; out-and-out; dyed-in-the-wool

获 huò ① capture; catch: 捕～ capture ② obtain; win; reap: ～一等奖 win the first prize/ ～救 be rescued/ ～利 make a profit; reap profits/ 喜～丰收 happily reap a bumper harvest/ 不劳而~ enjoy the fruits of other people's labour; reap without sowing

【获得】 huòdé gain; obtain; acquire; win; achieve: ~解放 achieve emancipation; win liberation/ ~独立 gain independence/ ~巨大的成绩 achieve great success/ ~知识 acquire knowledge/ ~好评 win acclaim; earn favourable comment

【获胜】 huòshèng win victory; be victorious; triumph

【获悉】 huòxī <书> learn (of an event)

祸* huò ① misfortune; disaster; calamity: 车~ traffic accident; road accident ② bring disaster upon; ruin

【祸不单行】 huò bù dān xíng misfortunes never come singly

【祸端】 huòduān <书> the source of the disaster; the cause of ruin

【祸根】 huògēn the root of the trouble; the cause of ruin; bane

【祸国殃民】 huòguó-yāngmín bring calamity to the country and the people

【祸害】 huòhài ① disaster; curse; scourge ② damage; destroy: 防止野猪~庄稼, Don't let the boars damage the crops.

【祸患】 huòhuàn disaster; calamity

【祸事】 huòshì disaster; calamity; mishap

【祸首】 huòshǒu chief culprit (或 offender)

惑 huò ① be puzzled; be bewildered: 大~不解 be greatly puzzled ② delude; mislead: 造谣~众 fabricate rumours to mislead people

霍* huò suddenly; quickly

【霍地】 huòdì <副> suddenly: ~立起身来 suddenly stand up; spring to one's feet

【霍霍】 huòhuò ① <象>: ~的磨刀声 the scrape, scrape of a sword being sharpened ② flash: 电光~。 The lightning flashed.

【霍乱】 huòluàn <医> cholera

【霍然】 huòrán ① <副> suddenly; quickly: 手电筒一~亮 Suddenly somebody flashed an electric torch. ② <书> (of an illness) be cured quickly: 数日之后, 定当~。 You will be restored to health in a matter of days.

豁 huò ① clear; open; open-minded; generous: ~达大度 open-minded and magnanimous ② exempt; remit: ~免 exempt; remit

另见 huō

【豁亮】 huòliàng roomy and bright: 这屋子又干净, 又~。 The room is clean, bright and spacious.

【豁免】 huòmiǎn exempt (from taxes or from customs inspection, etc.); remit: ~捐税 exempt sb. from taxes; remit taxes/ 外交~权 diplomatic immunity

【豁然贯通】 huòrán guàntōng suddenly see the whole thing in a clear light

【豁然开朗】 huòrán kāilǎng suddenly see the light; be suddenly enlightened

J

jī

几 * jī ① a small table: 茶~儿 tea table; teapoy ② 〈书〉 nearly; almost; practically: 到会者~三千人。Nearly 3,000 people came to the meeting.
另见 jǐ

【几乎】 jīhū nearly; almost; practically: 他~一夜没睡。He lay awake almost the whole night. / 她干得飞快, ~谁也赶不上她。She worked so fast that hardly anyone could keep up with her. / 水电站~全部完工。The hydroelectric station is as good as completed. / 故乡变化太大了, 我~认不出来了。My home town had changed so much that I could hardly recognize it.

讥 * jī ridicule; mock; satirize
【讥刺】 jīcì 〈书〉 ridicule; satirize
【讥讽】 jīfěng ridicule; satirize
【讥诮】 jīqiào 〈书〉 sneer at; deride
【讥笑】 jīxiào ridicule; jeer; sneer at; deride: 他毫不理睬某些人的~, 继续进行试验。Completely ignoring some people's sneers, he went on with his experiments.

击 * jī ① beat; hit; strike: ~鼓 beat a drum/ ~掌 clap one's hands ② attack; assault: 声东~西 feint in the east and attack in the west ③ come in contact with; bump into: 撞~ collide with; ram
【击败】 jībài defeat; beat; vanquish: 以三比一~了对手 beat one's opponent 3 to 1
【击毙】 jībì shoot dead: 四名匪徒当场~。Four bandits were shot dead on the spot.
【击沉】 jīchén bombard and sink; send (a ship) to the bottom: ~敌舰三艘 sink three enemy warships
【击穿】 jīchuān 〈电〉 puncture; breakdown
【击毁】 jīhuǐ smash; wreck; shatter; destroy: ~坦克二十四辆 destroy 24 tanks
【击溃】 jīkuì rout; put to flight
【击落】 jīluò shoot down; bring down; down: ~敌机七架 bring down seven enemy planes
【击破】 jīpò break up; destroy; rout: 各个~ destroy (enemy forces) one by one
【击伤】 jīshāng wound (a person); damage (a plane, tank, etc.)
【击退】 jītuì beat back; repel; repulse: ~敌军几次进攻 repulse several enemy assaults
【击中】 jīzhòng hit: ~目标 hit the target/ ~要害 hit sb.'s vital point

叽 * jī 〈象〉: 小鸟~~叫。Little birds chirp.
【叽咕】 jīgu talk in a low voice; whisper; mutter: 他们俩叽叽咕咕地说些什么? What are those two whispering to each other about?
【叽叽嘎嘎】 jījigāgā 〈象〉〔形容说笑声等〕: 大家~地笑起来。Everybody started cackling. / 这门老~响。This door always creaks.
【叽叽喳喳】 jījizhāzhā 〈象〉 chirp; twitter: 麻雀在外面~地叫。Sparrows are twittering outside. / 别~的了, 干点正经事吧。Stop jabbering and get down to business.
【叽里咕噜】 jīligūlū 〈象〉 ①〔形容说话别人听不清楚或听不懂〕gabble; jabber: 他们~地说了半天。They gabbled away for a long time. ②〔形容物体滚动的声音〕: 石块~滚下山去。Rocks went tumbling down the hill.

饥 * jī ① be hungry; starve; famish ② famine; crop failure: 大~之年 a year of great famine
【饥不择食】 jī bù zé shí a hungry person is not choosy about his food

【饥肠】 jīcháng 〈书〉 empty stomach: ~辘辘 one's stomach rumbling with hunger
【饥饿】 jī'è hunger; starvation: 挣扎在~线上 struggle along on the verge of starvation
【饥寒交迫】 jī-hán jiāopò suffer hunger and cold; live in hunger and cold; be poverty-stricken
【饥荒】 jīhuang ① famine; crop failure ② 〈口〉 be hard up; be short of money
【饥馑】 jījǐn famine; crop failure
【饥民】 jīmín famine victim; famine refugee

圾 * jī 见"垃圾" lājī

机 * jī ① machine; engine: 挖泥~ dredging machine; dredge/ 内燃~ internal-combustion engine ② aircraft; aeroplane; plane: 客~ passenger plane ③ crucial point; pivot; key link: 转~ a turning point; a turn for the better ④ chance; occasion; opportunity: 趁~ take advantage of the occasion; seize the opportunity (或 chance)/ 见~行事 do as one sees fit; use one's discretion/ ~不可失, 时不再来。Don't let slip an opportunity; it may never come again. 或 Opportunity knocks but once. ⑤ organic: 有~体 organism/ 无~化学 inorganic chemistry ⑥ flexible; quick-witted: ~巧 adroit; ingenious
【机舱】 jīcāng ① engine room (of a ship) ② passenger compartment (of an aircraft); cabin
【机场】 jīchǎng airport; airfield; aerodrome: 国际~ international airport/ 简易~ airstrip/ 军用~ military airfield
【机断】 jīduàn act on one's own judgment in an emergency: ~行事 act promptly at one's own discretion
【机房】 jīfáng ① generator or motor room ② engine room (of a ship)
【机工】 jīgōng mechanic; machinist
【机构】 jīgòu ①〈机〉 mechanism: 传动~ transmission mechanism/ 分离~ disengaging mechanism ② organization; setup: 政府~ government organization/ 宣传~ propaganda organ/ 工厂的管理~ the administrative setup of a factory ③ the internal structure of an organization: 调整~ adjust the organizational structure
【机关】 jīguān ①〈机〉 mechanism; gear: 起动~ starting gear ② machine-operated: ~布景 machine-operated stage scenery ③ office; organ; body: 领导~ leading bodies/ 文化教育~ cultural and educational institutions/ 公安~ public security organs ④ stratagem; scheme; intrigue: 识破~ see through a trick
【机会】 jīhuì chance; opportunity: 错过(抓住)~ lose (seize) a chance/ 千载一时的好~ a golden opportunity; the chance of a lifetime/ 我愿借此~ 向你们表示衷心的感谢。I wish to avail myself of this opportunity to extend to you my heartfelt thanks.
【机会主义】 jīhuìzhǔyì opportunism: ~者 opportunist
【机件】 jījiàn 〈机〉 parts; works: 钟表的~ the works of a clock or watch
【机警】 jījǐng alert; sharp-witted; vigilant
【机灵】 jīling clever; smart; sharp; intelligent: 这孩子怪~的。This child's very smart./ 她有一双~的大眼睛。She has large, intelligent eyes./ 这个人办事挺~的。This chap manages things quite cleverly. ◇ ~鬼儿 a clever child
【机密】 jīmì ① secret; classified; confidential: ~文件 classified papers; confidential documents ② secret: 严守国家的~ strictly guard state secrets
【机敏】 jīmǐn alert and resourceful: 她在紧急关头总是沉着~。She is calm and resourceful in an emergency.
【机谋】 jīmóu 〈书〉 stratagem; artifice; scheme
【机能】 jīnéng 〈生〉 function
【机器】 jīqì machine; machinery; apparatus: ~保养 machine maintenance/ 安装新~ install new machinery/ 国家~ state apparatus (或 machine)

【机械】 jīxiè ① machinery; machine; mechanism: ～故障 mechanical failure (或 breakdown) ② mechanical; inflexible; rigid: 别人的经验不能～地照搬。 Other people's experience should not be applied mechanically.

【机械化】 jīxièhuà mechanize: 农业～ mechanization of agriculture; mechanization of farm work ◇ ～部队 mechanized force (或 troops, unit)

【机要】 jīyào confidential ◇ ～部门 departments in charge of confidential or important work/ ～工作 confidential work/ ～秘书 confidential secretary

【机宜】 jīyí principles of action; guidelines: 面授～ brief sb. on how to act

【机遇】 jīyù 〈书〉 favourable circumstances; opportunity

【机缘】 jīyuán good luck; lucky chance: ～凑巧 as luck would have it; by chance; by a lucky coincidence

【机长】 jīzhǎng aircraft (或 crew) commander

【机智】 jīzhì quick-witted; resourceful: ～勇敢的侦察兵 brave and resourceful scouts

肌 jī muscle; flesh

【肌肤】 jīfū 〈书〉 (human) skin

【肌肉】 jīròu muscle: ～发达 muscular

鸡 jī chicken: 公～ cock; rooster/ 母～ hen/ 雏～ chick; chicken/ ～鸣而起 rise at cockcrow

【鸡蛋】 jīdàn (hen's) egg ◇ ～糕 (sponge) cake

【鸡蛋里挑骨头】 jīdànli tiāo gútou look for a bone in an egg; look for a flaw where there is none; find fault; nitpick

【鸡蛋碰石头】 jīdàn pèng shítou like an egg striking a rock — attack sb. far stronger than oneself

【鸡肋】 jīlèi 〈书〉 chicken ribs — things of little value or interest: 味同～ taste like chicken ribs — be of little or no value

【鸡零狗碎】 jīlíng-gǒusuì in bits and pieces; fragmentary

【鸡毛】 jīmáo chicken feather: 拿着～当令箭 take a chicken feather for a warrant to give commands; treat one's superior's casual remark as an order and make a big fuss about it

【鸡毛蒜皮】 jīmáo-suànpí chicken feathers and garlic skins; trifles; trivialities: 这是～的事,不值得计较。 This is a trivial matter; it's not worth arguing about.

【鸡鸣狗盗】 jīmíng-gǒudào (ability to) crow like a cock and snatch like a dog — small tricks: ～之徒 people who know small tricks

【鸡皮疙瘩】 jīpí gēda gooseflesh: 冻得我直起～。 It was so cold I was gooseflesh all over./ 想起那可怕的情景,我浑身都起～。 The thought of the horrible scene made my flesh creep.

【鸡犬不惊】 jī-quǎn bù jīng even fowls and dogs are not disturbed — excellent army discipline; peace and tranquility

【鸡犬不留】 jī-quǎn bù liú even fowls and dogs are not spared — ruthless mass slaughter

【鸡犬不宁】 jī-quǎn bù níng even fowls and dogs are not left in peace — general turmoil

【鸡肉】 jīròu chicken (as food)

【鸡尾酒】 jīwěijiǔ cocktail ◇ ～会 cocktail party

奇 jī ① odd (number): ～数 odd number ② 〈书〉 a fractional amount (over that mentioned in a round number); odd lots: 五十有～ fifty odd
另见 qí

奇数 jīshù 〈数〉 odd number

迹 jī ① mark; trace: 足～ footmark; footprint/ 血～ bloodstain ② remains; ruins; vestige: 古城墙的遗～ the ruins of an old city wall/ 陈～ a thing of the past ③ an outward sign; indication: ～近剽窃 an act verging on plagiarism

【迹象】 jīxiàng sign; indication: 这是一种不寻常的～。 This is an unusual sign./ 有～表明两国将改善关系。 There are indications that the two countries are going to improve their relations.

唧 jī spurt; squirt: ～了我一身水。 The water squirted all over me.

【唧咕】 jīgu 见 "叽咕" jīgu

【唧唧】 jījī 〈象〉形容虫叫声 chirp: 蟋蟀在草丛里～地叫。 Crickets are chirping in the grass.

【唧唧喳喳】 jījizhāzhā 见 "叽叽喳喳" jījizhāzhā

【唧哝】 jīnong talk in a low voice; whisper

【唧筒】 jītǒng pump

积 jī ① amass; store up; accumulate: ～谷防荒 store up grain against a lean year/ 一长期工作的经验 accumulate experience of work over a long period/ 小胜为大胜。 Many small victories add up to a big one. ② long-standing; long-pending; age-old: ～案 a long-pending case ③ 〈数〉 product: 求～ find the product by multiplication

【积弊】 jībì age-old malpractice; long-standing abuse

【积存】 jīcún store up; lay up; stockpile: ～的物资 goods in stock

【积极】 jījí ① positive: 调动一切～因素 mobilize all positive factors/ 作出～贡献 make positive contributions ② active; energetic; vigorous: ～工作 work hard; work with all one's energy/ 采取～措施 adopt vigorous measures

【积极分子】 jījífènzǐ activist; active element; enthusiast

【积极性】 jījíxìng zeal; initiative; enthusiasm

【积久】 jījiǔ accumulate in the course of time: ～成习 form a habit or custom through long-repeated practice

【积聚】 jījù gather; accumulate; build up

【积劳成疾】 jī láo chéng jí 〈书〉 break down from constant overwork

【积累】 jīlěi accumulate: ～了丰富的经验 have accumulated a wealth of experience

【积木】 jīmù building blocks; toy bricks

【积欠】 jīqiàn ① have one's debts piling up ② outstanding debts; arrears: 还清～ clear up all outstanding debts

【积少成多】 jī shǎo chéng duō many a little makes a mickle

【积习】 jīxí old habit; long-standing practice: ～难除。 It is difficult to get rid of deep-rooted habits. 或 Old habits die hard.

【积蓄】 jīxù ① put aside; save; accumulate: ～力量 accumulate strength ② savings: 月月有～ save some money every month

【积怨】 jīyuàn accumulated rancour; piled-up grievances: ～甚多 have incurred widespread resentment; have many complaints against one

屐 jī ① clogs ② shoes in general: 草～ straw sandals

姬 jī ① a complimentary term for women used in ancient China ② a name used in ancient China for a concubine ③ 〈旧〉 a professional female singer: 歌～ singing girl; female entertainer

勣 jī achievement; accomplishment; merit

基 jī ① base; foundation: 坝～ the base of a dam/ 路～ roadbed; bed/ 房～ foundations (of a building)/ 奠～ lay a foundation ② basic; key; primary; cardinal: ～调 keynote/ ～数 cardinal number

【基本】 jīběn ① basic; fundamental; elementary: ～原则 basic principles/ ～观点 basic concept/ ～知识 elementary (或 rudimentary) knowledge ② main; essential: ～条件 main conditions ③ basically; in the main; on the whole; by and large: 这部电影～上是好的。 This film is good on the whole.

【基层】 jīcéng basic level; primary level; grass-roots unit: 深入～ go down to the grass-roots units

【基础】 jīchǔ foundation; base; basis: 打～ lay a foundation/ 物质～ material base/ 理论～ theoretical basis/ 经济～ economic base (或 basis)

【基地】 jīdì base: 军事～ military base/ 导弹～ missile base/ 工业～ industrial base/ 原料～ source of raw materials

【基点】jīdiǎn ① basic point; starting point; centre: 建立科研~ set up scientific research centres/ 分析问题是解决问题的~。The analysis of a problem is the starting point for its solution.

【基督】Jīdū〈宗〉Christ ◇ ~教 Christianity; the Christian religion/ ~教女青年会 the Young Women's Christian Association (Y.W.C.A.)/ ~教青年会 the .Young Men's Christian Association (Y.M.C.A.)/ ~徒 Christian

【基金】jījīn fund: 积累(消费)~ accumulation (consumption) fund ◇ ~会 foundation

【基石】jīshí foundation stone; cornerstone

【基于】jīyú·because of; in view of: ~目前这种情况, 我们不得不修改原来的计划。In view of the present situation, we'll have to revise our original plan./ ~以上理由, 我不赞同他的意见。For the above-mentioned reasons, I cannot agree with him.

绩* jī ① twist hempen thread ② achievement; accomplishment; merit: 战~ military achievement (或 exploit)/ 功~ merits and achievements; contributions

犄 jī

【犄角】jījiǎo corner: 桌子~ the corner of a table/ 屋子~里有一个衣架。A clothes tree stands in a corner of the room.

【犄角】jījiao horn: 牛~ ox horn/ 鹿~ antler

缉 jī seize; arrest

【缉捕】jībǔ seize; arrest

【缉拿】jīná seize; arrest; apprehend: ~凶手 apprehend the murderer/ ~归案 bring (a criminal) to justice

【缉私】jīsī seize smugglers or smuggled goods; suppress smuggling ◇ ~船 anti-smuggling patrol boat; coast guard vessel/ ~人员 anti-contraband personnel

畸 jī ① lopsided; unbalanced: ~轻~重 attach too much weight to this and too little weight to that; lopsided; now too much, now too little ② irregular; abnormal

【畸变】jībiàn〈物〉distortion

【畸形】jīxíng ①〈医〉deformity; malformation: 先天~ congenital malformation/ 肢体发育~ have deformed limbs ② lopsided; unbalanced; abnormal: ~发展 lopsided development/~现象 abnormal phenomenon

箕 jī ① dustpan ② winnowing basket; winnowing fan ③ loop (of a fingerprint)

【箕斗】jīdǒu〈矿〉skip

稽 jī ① check; examine; investigate: 有案可~ be on record; be verifiable ②〈书〉delay; procrastinate: ~延时日 be considerably delayed
另见 qǐ

【稽查】jīchá ① check (to prevent smuggling, tax evasion, etc.) ② an official engaged in such work; customs officer

【稽核】jīhé check; examine: ~账目 audit accounts

【稽考】jīkǎo〈书〉ascertain; verify: 无可~ be unverifiable

【稽留】jīliú〈书〉delay; detain: 因事~ be detained by business

激* jī ① swash; surge; dash: 海水冲击礁石, ~起高高的浪花。Swashing against the rocks, the breakers sent up a fountain of spray. ② arouse; stimulate; excite: ~起我们学习科学技术的热情 arouse our enthusiasm for studying science and technology/ ~于义愤 be stirred by righteous indignation ③ sharp; fierce; violent: ~战 fierce fighting ④ fall ill from getting wet: 他叫雨~着了。He caught a chill from getting wet in the rain.

【激昂】jī'áng excited and indignant; roused: 群情~。Public feeling was aroused (或 ran high)./ 会场上响起~的口号声。The meeting hall resounded with outbursts of militant slogans.

【激变】jībiàn violent change; cataclysm

【激荡】jīdàng agitate; surge; rage: 海水~。The sea surged./ 心潮~ thoughts surging in one's mind

【激动】jīdòng excite; stir; agitate: 情绪~ be excited; ge worked up/ 令人~的场面 an inspiring scene/ ~人心的讲话 a stirring (或 rousing) speech/ ~得流下眼泪 be moved to tears

【激发】jīfā arouse; stimulate; set off

【激奋】jīfèn be roused to action

【激愤】jīfèn' wrathful; indignant: 心情~ be filled with indignation

【激光】jīguāng〈物〉laser

【激将法】jījiàngfǎ prodding (或 goading) sb. into action (as by ridicule, sarcasm, etc.)

【激进】jījìn radical ◇ ~派 radicals

【激励】jīlì encourage; impel; urge

【激烈】jīliè intense; sharp; fierce; acute: ~的冲突 sharp conflict/~的争论 heated argument/一场~的比赛 a closely fought game; a gruelling match/ 争吵得很~ quarrel bitterly/ 这一仗打得很~。It was a fierce fight.

【激流】jīliú torrent; rapids; turbulent current: 闯过~ shoot the rapids

【激怒】jīnù enrage; infuriate; exasperate: 种族主义者的暴行~了人民。The atrocities committed by the racists enraged the people.

【激起】jīqǐ arouse; evoke; stir up: ~公愤 arouse public indignation/ ~强烈的反抗 evoke strong opposition/ ~全世界人民的愤怒 incur the wrath of the people of the whole world/ ~了一场风波 cause a commotion

【激切】jīqiè〈书〉impassioned; vehement: 言辞~ impassioned language

【激情】jīqíng intense emotion; fervour; passion; enthusiasm

【激赏】jīshǎng〈书〉highly appreciate; greatly admire

【激扬】jīyáng ① drain away the mud and bring in fresh water; drive out evil and usher in good ② encourage; urge: ~士气 boost the morale

【激增】jīzēng increase sharply; soar; shoot up: 化肥的产量~。The output of chemical fertilizer has soared./ 经济危机加剧, 失业人数~。With the deepening of the economic crisis, unemployment shot up.

羁 jī〈书〉① bridle; headstall: 无~之马 a horse without a bridle ② control; restrain: 放荡不~ unconventional and uninhibited ③ stay; delay; detain: 事务~身 be detained by one's duties

【羁绊】jībàn〈书〉trammels; fetters; yoke: 挣脱旧思想的~ break the fetters of old ideas; smash the shackles of convention

【羁留】jīliú stay; stop over

【羁旅】jīlǚ〈书〉stay long in a strange land; live in a strange land

jí

及* jí ① reach; come up to: 目力所~ as far as the eye can reach/ 水深~腰 The water came up to one's waist (或 was waist-deep)./ 由此~彼 proceed from one point to another/ 力所能~ within one's power/ 这辆自行车不~那辆好。This bike is not so good as that one. ② in time for: ~时 timely; in time ③〈连〉连接并列名词或名词性词组. 连接的成分中主要的放在"及"之前: 地里种着小麦、油菜~其他作物。The fields are under wheat, rape and other crops.

【及格】jígé pass a test, examination, etc.; pass

【及时】jíshí ① timely; in time; seasonable: 要~下种, Sowing must be done in good time./ 这场雪很~。This snow has come at the right time. ② promptly; without delay: ~纠正错误 correct a mistake promptly/ ~汇报 report without delay ◇ ~雨 timely rain

【及早】jízǎo at an early date; as soon as possible; before it is too late: ~回头 repent before it is too late; mend one's ways without delay/ 有病要~治。When you are ill, see the doctor as soon as possible.

汲 jí draw (water): 从井里~水 draw water from a well

【汲汲】 jíjí 〈书〉 anxious; avid: ~于个人名利 crave personal fame and gain

【汲取】 jíqǔ draw; derive

吉 jí ①lucky; auspicious; propitious: 万事大~。All is well.

【吉利】 jílì lucky; auspicious; propitious

【吉普车】 jípǔchē jeep

【吉期】 jíqī 〈旧〉 wedding day

【吉庆】 jíqìng auspicious; propitious; happy

【吉祥】 jíxiáng lucky; auspicious; propitious

【吉凶】 jí-xiōng good or ill luck: ~未卜。No one knows how it will turn out.

【吉兆】 jízhào good omen; propitious sign

岌 jí 〈书〉 (of a mountain) lofty; towering

【岌岌】 jíjí 〈书〉 precarious: ~可危 in imminent danger/ ~不可终日 live in constant fear; live precariously

级 jí ①level; rank; grade: 各~at all levels/甲~产品 first-class products ②any of the yearly divisions of a school course; grade; class; form: 同一不同班 be in different classes of the same grade ③step: 石~ stone steps ④〈量〉 step; stage: 十几~台阶 a flight of a dozen steps/多~火箭 multistage rocket ⑤〈语〉 degree: 比较~ the comparative degree/最高~ the superlative degree

【级别】 jíbié rank; level; grade; scale

极 jí ①the utmost point; extreme: 无所不用其~ go to any extreme; stop at nothing/ 愚蠢之~ be the height of folly/ ~而言之 talk in extreme terms ②pole: 北(南)~ the North (South) Pole ③〈副〉 extremely; exceedingly: ~为重要 of the utmost importance/ 高兴~了 extremely happy/ ~少数 a tiny minority; only a few; a handful/ 给予~大的注意 give maximum attention to; pay very close attention to/ ~尽招摇撞骗之能事 bluff and swindle right and left

【极点】 jídiǎn the limit; the extreme; the utmost: 感动到了~ be extremely moved/ 蛮横无理到了~ reach the height of truculence

【极度】 jídù extreme; exceeding; to the utmost: ~疲劳 be extremely tired; be overcome with fatigue/ ~兴奋 be elated

【极端】 jíduān ①extreme: 走~ go to extremes ②extreme; exceeding: ~仇视 show extreme hatred for/ ~困难 exceedingly difficult/ ~贫困 in dire poverty/ ~腐败 rotten to the core/ 对工作~负责任 have a boundless sense of responsibility in one's work

【极乐世界】 jílè shìjiè 〈佛教〉 Sukhavati; Pure Land; Western Paradise

【极力】 jílì do one's utmost; spare no effort: ~避免发生事故 do one's utmost (或 best) to avoid accidents/ ~劝阻 try very hard to dissuade sb. from doing sth./ ~吹捧 laud sb. to the skies/ ~鼓吹 vigorously publicize (an erroneous theory, etc.); clamorously advocate/ ~扩大 expand to the maximum/ ~缩小 reduce to the minimum; minimize

【极其】 jíqí 〈副〉 most; extremely; exceedingly: 一项~光荣的任务 a most glorious task

【极权主义】 jíquánzhǔyì totalitarianism

【极盛】 jíshèng heyday; zenith; acme: 在古埃及文明的~时期 at the height of ancient Egyptian civilization/ 在他精力~的时候 in his prime of life/ 唐朝是中国旧诗的~时期。The Tang Dynasty was the golden age of classical Chinese poetry.

【极限】 jíxiàn ①the limit; the maximum: 达到了~ reach the limit

【极刑】 jíxíng capital punishment; the death penalty

即 jí ①approach; reach; be near: 可望而不可~ within sight but beyond reach ②assume; undertake: ~位 ascend the throne ③at present; in the immediate future: ~日 this or that very day/ 成功在~。Success is in sight. ④prompted by the occasion: ~兴 impromptu ⑤〈书〉 be; mean; namely: 春节~农历新年。The Spring Festival is the lunar New Year./ 非此~彼。It must be either this or

that ⑥〈书〉promptly; at once: 闻过~改 correct one's mistake as soon as it is pointed out/ 招之~来 be on call at any hour ⑦〈书〉 even; even if

【即将】 jíjiāng be about to; be on the point of: 比赛~开始。The match is about to begin./ 水电站~竣工。The hydroelectric station is nearing completion./ 国庆节~来临。It will soon be National Day.

【即景生情】 jíjǐng shēng qíng the scene brings back memories; the scene touches a chord in one's heart

【即刻】 jíkè at once; immediately; instantly

【即日】 jírì 〈书〉 ①this or that very day: 本条例自~起施行。The regulations come into force as of today. ②within the next few days: 本片~放映。The film will be shown within a few days.

【即时】 jíshí immediately; forthwith

【即使】 jíshǐ 〈连〉 even; even if; even though: ~我们的工作得到了极其伟大的成绩,也没有任何值得骄傲自大的理由。Even if we achieve gigantic successes in our work, there is no reason whatsoever to be conceited and arrogant.

【即位】 jíwèi ascend the throne

【即席】 jíxí 〈书〉 ①impromptu; extemporaneous: ~赋诗一首 compose a poem impromptu; improvise a poem/ ~讲话 speak impromptu; make an impromptu (或 extemporaneous) speech ②take one's seat (at a dinner table, etc.)

亟 jí 〈书〉 urgently; anxiously; earnestly: ~盼 earnestly hope/ ~欲 desire most ardently; want very much/ ~待解决的重大问题 important problems demanding prompt solution/ ~须纠正 must be speedily put right

佶 jí 〈书〉 robust and sturdy

【佶屈聱牙】 jíqū áoyá full of difficult, unpronounceable words

急 jí ①impatient; anxious: ~着要出发 be impatient to set out ②worry: 你怎么来得这么晚,真把人~死啦! Why are you so late? We were worried to death about you. ③irritated; annoyed; nettled: 我没想到他真~了。I didn't expect him to get angry. ④fast; rapid; violent: 水流很~。The current is swift. 或 It's a strong current./ 雨下得正~。It's raining hard./ ~病 acute disease ⑤urgent; pressing: 事情很~,必须立即处理。The matter is pressing (或 urgent) and must be dealt with at once./ 他走得很~。He left in a hurry. ⑥urgency; emergency: 应~ meet an emergency ⑦be eager to help: ~人之难 be eager to help those in need

【急不可待】 jí bùkě dài too impatient to wait; extremely anxious

【急促】 jícù ①hurried; rapid: ~的脚步声 hurried footsteps/ ~的枪声 rapid gunfire/ 呼吸~ be short of breath/ 脉搏~ have a short, quick pulse ②(of time) short; pressing: 时间很~,别再犹豫了。Time is running short. Stop hesitating (或 dithering).

【急电】 jídiàn urgent telegram; urgent cable

【急风暴雨】 jífēng-bàoyǔ violent storm; hurricane; tempest: 经历过~的考验 have stood the test of violent storms/ 这场运动如~,势不可挡。This movement carried all before it like a hurricane.

【急公好义】 jígōng-hàoyì zealous for the common weal; public-spirited

【急功近利】 jígōng-jìnlì eager for quick success and instant benefit

【急件】 jíjiàn urgent document or dispatch

【急进】 jíjìn radical

【急救】 jíjiù first aid; emergency treatment ◇ ~包 first-aid dressing/ ~人员 first-aid personnel/ ~药品 first-aid medicine/ ~箱 first-aid kit/ ~站 first-aid station

【急剧】 jíjù rapid; sharp; sudden: ~的变化 rapid change/ ~上升 steep rise/ ~下降 sudden drop; sharp decline/ ~转折 abrupt turn

【急遽】 jíjù rapid; sharp; sudden

【急流】 jíliú ①torrent; rapid stream; rapids: 闯过~险滩

sweep over rapids and shoals ② 〈气〉jet stream; jet flow

【急流勇进】jíliú yǒng jìn　forge ahead against a swift current; press on in the teeth of difficulties

【急流勇退】jíliú yǒng tuì　resolutely retire at the height of one's official career

【急忙】jímáng　in a hurry; in haste; hurriedly; hastily: 你干吗这样急急忙忙的? Why are you in such a hurry?/ 她背起药箱,～朝病人家里跑去。She flung the medical kit over her shoulder and hastily set out for the patient's home.

【急难】jínàn　〈书〉① misfortune; grave danger ② be anxious to help (those in grave danger)

【急迫】jípò　urgent; pressing; imperative: 这是当前最～的任务。This is the most pressing task at present./ 事情很～,得赶快处理。The matter is urgent and something's got to be done about it at once.

【急起直追】jíqǐ-zhízhuī　rouse oneself to catch up

【急切】jíqiè　① eager; impatient: 用～的目光注视着 gaze intently at sb. or sth./ ～地盼望 eagerly look forward to; wait impatiently for ② in a hurry; in haste: ～难办 hard to do in a hurry/ ～间找不着适当的人 cannot find the right person at such short notice

【急如星火】jí rú xīnghuǒ　extremely pressing; most urgent; posthaste: 灾区需用医药,～。Medical aid must be sent to the stricken area posthaste.

【急速】jísù　very fast; at high speed; rapidly: 汽车～地向前行驶。The car was running at high speed./ 他的病情～恶化。His condition rapidly worsened./ 情况～变化。The situation changed quickly.

【急湍】jítuān　swift current

【急弯】jíwān　sharp turn: 拐了个～ made a sharp turn/ 前有～,行车小心。Sharp turn ahead. Drive carefully.

【急务】jíwù　urgent task: 有～在身 have some urgent task on hand

【急性子】jíxìngzi　① of impatient disposition; impetuous ② an impetuous person

【急需】jíxū　① be badly in need of: ～帮助 be in need of immediate help/ 提供～的资金 provide much-needed funds ② urgent need: 以应～ meet a crying need

【急用】jíyòng　urgent need: 节约储蓄,以备～ practise economy and save money against a rainy day/ 请把材料赶紧送来,有～。Please send us the material at once; it's urgently needed.

【急于】jíyú　eager; anxious; impatient: ～完成任务 eager to fulfil a task/ ～表态 impatient to state one's position/ ～求成 overanxious for quick results; impatient for success/ 没准备好, 就不要～开会。Don't call the meeting till we're ready.

【急躁】jízào　① irritable; irascible ② impetuous; rash; impatient: 防止～情绪 guard against impetuosity/ 产生～情绪 give way to impatience

【急诊】jízhěn　emergency call; emergency treatment ◇ ～病人 emergency case/ ～室 emergency ward

【急智】jízhì　nimbleness of mind in dealing with emergencies; quick-wittedness

【急中生智】jízhōng shēng zhì　suddenly hit upon a way out of a predicament; show resourcefulness in an emergency

【急转直下】jízhuǎn-zhíxià　(of the march of events, etc.) take a sudden turn and then develop rapidly

疾* jí ① disease; sickness; illness: 痼～ a stubborn illness/ 眼～ eye trouble ② suffering; pain; difficulty: ～苦 sufferings; hardships ③ hate: 疾恶如仇 hate evil like an enemy ④ fast; quick: ～驰而过 speed past

【疾病】jíbìng　disease; illness: 防治～ prevention and treatment of disease

【疾风】jífēng　① strong wind; gale ② 〈气〉moderate gale

【疾风劲草】jífēng jìngcǎo　the force of the wind tests the strength of the grass — strength of character is tested in a crisis 又作"疾风知劲草"

【疾苦】jíkǔ　sufferings; hardships: 关心人民的～ be concerned about the weal and woe of the people

【疾言厉色】jíyán-lìsè　harsh words and stern looks: 他对人很和气,从不～。He is affable and is never brusque with people.

脊 jí
另见 jǐ
【脊梁】jíliang　back (of the human body)

棘 jí ① sour jujube ② thorn bushes; brambles ③ 〈动〉spine; spina

【棘手】jíshǒu　thorny; troublesome; knotty: ～的问题 a knotty problem/ 这件事情很～。This is a sticky business.

殛 jí 〈书〉kill: 雷～ be struck dead by lightning

集* jí ① gather; collect: 聚～ gather together/ 大门口～了一大堆人。A crowd gathered at the gate./ 各家之长 incorporate the strong points of different schools ② country fair; market: 赶～ go to a country fair; go to market ③ collection; anthology: 诗～ a collection of poems/ 画～ an album of paintings ④ volume; part: 这些文章分三～出版。These articles will be published in three volumes./ 这部影片分上、下两～。This film is in two parts.

【集大成】jí dàchéng　be a comprehensive expression of; be an agglomeration of; epitomize: 他是这一学派思想的～者。He epitomized the thought of this school.

【集合】jíhé　gather; assemble; muster; call together: ～! (口令) Fall in!/ 紧急～ emergency muster/ ～地点 assembly place; rendezvous/ 命令全排战士～。Order the whole platoon to fall in./ 民兵～好了。The militiamen have already lined up.

【集会】jíhuì　assembly; rally; gathering; meeting: ～结社自由 freedom of assembly and association/ 举行群众～ hold a mass rally

【集结】jíjié　mass; concentrate; build up: ～军队 mass troops; concentrate forces/ ～力量 build up strength/ ～待命 assemble and await orders

【集锦】jíjǐn　a collection of choice specimens: 儿童画～ outstanding examples of children's drawings

【集聚】jíjù　gather; collect; assemble

【集刊】jíkān　collected papers (of an academic institution)

【集权】jíquán　centralization of state power

【集散地】jísàndì　collecting and distributing centre; distributing centre

【集思广益】jísī-guǎngyì　draw on collective wisdom and absorb all useful ideas; pool the wisdom of the masses

【集体】jítǐ　collective: ～的智慧 collective wisdom

【集团】jítuán　group; clique; circle; bloc: 军事～ a military bloc/ 小～ a small clique ◇ ～军 group army

【集训】jíxùn　assemble for training

【集腋成裘】jí yè chéng qiú　the finest fragments of fox fur, sewn together, will make a robe — many a little makes a mickle

【集邮】jíyóu　stamp collecting; philately ◇ ～簿 stamp-album/ ～者 stamp-collector; philatelist

【集中】jízhōng　concentrate; centralize; focus; amass; put together: ～精力 concentrate one's energy/ ～火力 concentrate fire (on a target)/ ～目标 concentrate on the same target/ ～大量财富 amass vast fortunes/ ～注意力 focus one's attention on ◇ ～管理 centralized management/ ～轰炸 mass bombing/ ～营 concentration camp

【集子】jízi　collection; collected works; anthology

楫 jí 〈书〉oar

辑 jí ① collect; compile; edit: 编～ edit; compile ② part; volume; division: 新闻简报第一～ Newsreel No. 1

【辑录】jílù　compile

【辑要】jíyào　summary; abstract

嫉 jí ① be jealous; be envious ② hate

【嫉妒】jídù　be jealous of; envy

【嫉恨】jíhèn　envy and hate; hate out of jealousy

瘠 jí 〈书〉① lean; thin and weak ② barren; poor; lean: ～土 poor soil; barren land

【瘠薄】 jíbó barren; unproductive: ～的山坡地 barren land on a mountain slope

藉 jí 见"狼藉" lángjí

籍* jí ① book; record: 古～ ancient books ② registry; roll: 户～ household register; population register ③ native place; home town; birthplace: 回～ return to one's native place/ 祖～ the land of one's ancestors ④ membership: 党～ party membership/ 国～ nationality

【籍贯】 jíguàn the place of one's birth or origin; native place

jǐ

几* jǐ ① how many: ～天可以完工？How many days will it take to finish the work?/ ～点钟了？What's the time? 或 What time is it?/ 你～号？What's your number?/ 离这儿有～里地？How far is it from here? ② a few; several; some: 说～句话 say a few words/ 过～天 in a couple of days/ ～十 tens; dozens; scores/ ～万 several hundred million; hundreds of millions/ 十～岁的孩子 teenager/ 二十～个人 twenty odd people/ 相差无～ not much difference
　另见 jī

【几分】 jǐfēn a bit; somewhat; rather: 有～醉意 a bit merry; a bit tipsy/ 让他～ humour him a little/ 她说的有～道理。There's something in what she said./ 对他的意图我有～怀疑。I'm somewhat suspicious of his intentions.

【几何】 jǐhé ①〈书〉how much; how many: 不知尚有～ be uncertain how much is left or how many are left ②〈数〉geometry

【几时】 jǐshí what time; when: 你们～走？What time are you leaving?/ 不知～我们能再见面！Who knows when we'll meet again?

【几许】 jǐxǔ〈书〉how much; how many: 不知～ No one can tell how much.

己* jǐ oneself; one's own; personal: 舍～为公 make personal sacrifices for the public good/ 引为～任 regard as one's (own) duty/ 各抒～见。Each airs his own views.

纪 Jǐ a surname
　另见 jì

济 jǐ
　另见 jì

【济济】 jǐjǐ (of people) many; numerous: 人才～ an abundance of capable people; a galaxy of talent

挤* jǐ ① squeeze; press: 把水～掉 squeeze the water out/ ～时间 try and find time to do sth.; find time ② jostle; push against: ～进去 force (或 elbow, shoulder, push) one's way in; squeeze in/ ～上前去 push to the front/ 别～。Don't push./ 人们互相～来～去。People jostled each other. ③ crowd; pack; cram: 做一团 pressed close together; packed like sardines/ 小屋～不下那么多人。It's impossible to pack so many people into the small room./ 礼堂已经～满了。The assembly hall is filled to capacity./ 几件事～在一块儿了。Several matters have cropped up at the same time.

【挤眉弄眼】 jǐméi-nòngyǎn make eyes; wink

【挤奶】 jǐnǎi milk (a cow, etc.) ◇～机 milking machine; milker

给* jǐ ① supply; provide: 这支部队粮食全部自～。This army unit produces all its own food grain. ② ample; well provided for: 家～户足。Every household is well provided for.
　另见 gěi

【给予】 jǐyǔ〈书〉give; render: ～支持 give support to/ ～协助 render assistance to/ ～正式承认 give official recognition to/ ～很高的评价 have a very high opinion of; appreciate highly/ ～同情 show sympathy for/ ～适当

纪律处分 take appropriate disciplinary measures against sb.

脊 jǐ ① spine; backbone ② ridge: 山～ the ridge of a hill or mountain/ 屋～ the ridge of a roof
　另见 jí

【脊背】 jǐbèi back (of a human being or any other vertebrate)

【脊髓】 jǐsuǐ spinal cord

【脊柱】 jǐzhù spinal column; vertebral column; backbone; spine

【脊椎】 jǐzhuī vertebra ◇～动物 vertebrate/ ～骨 vertebra; spine

jì

计* jì ① count; compute; calculate; number: 不～其数 countless; innumerable/ 数以万～ by the tens of thousands; numbering tens of thousands/ 工作不～时间 ready to work longer hours than required; not mind working extra hours/ 不～报酬 not be concerned about pay/ 大小拖拉机～二十台。The tractors, light and heavy, numbered twenty in all. 或 There were twenty light and heavy tractors in all. ② meter; gauge: 雨量～ rain gauge ③ idea; ruse; stratagem: 退敌之～ a stratagem to repulse the enemy/ 中～ fall into a trap/ 作归～ plan to go home/ 他们一～不成，又生一～。Their first ruse having failed, they tried another./ 为长远～ from a long-term point of view

【计策】 jìcè stratagem; plan

【计划】 jìhuà ① plan; project; programme: 切实可行的～ a feasible (或 workable) plan/ 宏伟的～ a magnificent project/ 河流开发～ a river development programme/ 有～地进行 proceed in a planned way ② map out; plan: ～好了再动手干。Map it out before you start./ 我们下周出发。We plan to leave next week.
◇～供应 planned supply/ ～经济 planned economy/ ～生产 planned production/ ～生育 family planning; birth control

【计件】 jìjiàn reckon by the piece ◇～工资 piece rate wage/ ～工作 piecework

【计较】 jìjiào ① haggle over; fuss about: ～小事 be too particular about trifles/ 他不～个人得失。He gives no thought to personal gains or losses. ② argue; dispute: 我不同你～，等你气平了再说。I won't argue with you now. Let's talk it over when you've calmed down. ③ think over; plan: 先安排一周的活儿，以后再作～。We'll arrange a week's work first and think about the rest afterwards.

【计量】 jìliàng measure; calculate; estimate: 不可～ inestimable

【计谋】 jìmóu scheme; stratagem

【计时】 jìshí reckon by time ◇～工资 payment by the hour; time wage/ ～工作 timework

【计数】 jìshù count

【计算】 jìsuàn ① count; compute; calculate: ～出席人数 count the number of people present/ ～产值 calculate the output value ② consideration; planning: 做事不能没个～。We shouldn't do anything without a plan. ◇～尺 slide rule

【计算机】 jìsuànjī computer; calculating machine: 机械～ mechanical computer/ 电子～ electronic computer

【计议】 jìyì deliberate; talk over; consult: 从长～ take one's time in coming to a decision; think sth. over carefully/ 二人～已定。The two of them settled on a scheme.

记* jì ① remember; bear in mind; commit to memory: ～错了 remember wrongly/ ～不清 cannot recall exactly; remember vaguely/ 死～硬背 learn by rote/ 我们要～住这个教训。We must keep this lesson in mind. ② write (或 put, take) down; record: ～在笔记本上 write it down in a notebook/ 把结果～下来 record the results/ ～下电话号码 jot down the telephone number ③ notes; record: 游～ travel notes/ 大事～ a chronicle of events ④ mark; sign: 暗～儿 secret mark ⑤ birthmark: 他左腿有块～。There is a birthmark on his left leg. ⑥ 〈方〉〈量〉：一～耳光 a slap in the face

【记仇】 jìchóu bear grudges; harbour bitter resentment: 他可不～。He's not the sort of person to bear a grudge.

【记得】 jìde remember: ～他的模样儿 remember what he looked like/ 我完全记不得了。I simply don't remember it./ 你～住这些数字吗? Can you carry all these figures in your head?

【记分】 jìfēn ① keep the score; record the points (in a game) ② register a student's marks ③ record workpoints

【记功】 jìgōng cite sb. for meritorious service; record a merit

【记挂】 jìguà 〈方〉 be concerned about; keep thinking about; miss

【记过】 jìguò record a demerit

【记号】 jìhao mark; sign: 做个～ make a sign; mark out

【记恨】 jìhèn bear grudges

【记录】 jìlù ① take notes; keep the minutes; record: 把发言的主要内容一下来 note down the main points of the speeches ② minutes; notes; record: 会议～ the minutes of a meeting/ 会谈～ a transcript of talks/ 正式～ official record/ 逐字～ verbatim record/ 摘要～ summary record/ 列入会议～ place on record in the minutes; minute ③ note-taker: 这次讨论请你做～好吗? Would you take the minutes of the discussion? ④ record: 创～ set a record; chalk up a record/ 打破～ break a record/ 世界～ world record ◇ ～本 minute book/ ～片 〈电影〉 documentary film; documentary

【记取】 jìqǔ remember; bear in mind: ～这个教训 bear firmly in mind this lesson

【记事】 jìshì ① keep a record of events; make a memorandum: 刻木结绳～ keep records by notching wood or tying knots ② account; record of events; chronicles

【记述】 jìshù record and narrate: 该书前言～了作者生平。The preface of the book includes an account of the author's life.

【记诵】 jìsòng commit to memory and be able to recite; learn by heart

【记性】 jìxing memory: ～好 have a good memory/ ～坏 have a poor (或 short) memory

【记叙】 jìxù narrate: ◇ ～文 narration; narrative

【记忆】 jìyì ① remember; recall: 就我～所及 so far as I can remember ② memory: 你们的深情厚谊将永远留在我们的～中。Your warm friendship will always remain in our memory.

【记忆力】 jìyìlì the faculty of memory; memory: ～衰退 one's memory is failing/ ～强(弱) have a good (poor) memory

【记忆犹新】 jìyì yóu xīn remain fresh in one's memory

【记载】 jìzǎi ① put down in writing; record: 详细地～事情经过 record the incident in detail/ 有文字～的历史 recorded history ② record; account: 地方志中有关于这次旱灾的～。There is an account of this drought in the local chronicles.

【记帐】 jìzhàng ① keep accounts ② charge to an account

【记者】 jìzhě reporter; correspondent; newsman; journalist: 新闻～ newspaper reporter; newsman/ 随军～ war correspondent/ 特派～ special correspondent

【记住】 jìzhu remember; learn by heart; bear in mind: 把这首诗～ learn the poem by heart

纪* jì ① discipline: 军～ military discipline/ 违法乱～ break the law and violate discipline ② put down in writing; record: ～事 chronicle ③ age; epoch: 中世～ the Middle Ages/ 世～ century
另见 Jǐ

【纪录】 jìlù 见"记录" jìlù

【纪律】 jìlǜ discipline: 遵守～ keep discipline; observe discipline/ 劳动～ labour discipline; labour regulations/ 无～现象 indiscipline/ 加强～性 heighten one's sense of discipline/ ～严明 highly disciplined/ 给予～处分 take disciplinary measures against sb.

【纪念】 jìniàn ① commemorate; mark: 值得～的日子 a

memorable day/ ～活动 commemorative activities/ 举行～大会 hold a commemoration meeting ② souvenir; keepsake; memento: 留个～ keep sth. as a souvenir/给你这张照片留个～。Have this picture for a souvenir. ③ commemoration day; anniversary: 十周年～ the tenth anniversary ◇ ～册 autograph book; autograph album/ ～品 souvenir; keepsake; memento/ ～日 commemoration day/ ～塔 memorial tower; monument/ ～邮票 commemorative stamp/ ～章 souvenir badge

【纪念碑】 jìniànbēi monument; memorial

【纪念馆】 jìniànguǎn memorial hall; museum in memory of sb.

【纪念堂】 jìniàntáng memorial hall; commemoration hall

【纪要】 jìyào summary of minutes; summary: 会谈～ summary of conversations (或 talks)/ 座谈会～ summary of a forum or panel discussion

【纪元】 jìyuán ① the beginning of an era (e.g. an emperor's reign); epoch; era: 开辟了世界历史的新～ usher in a new era in world history

伎 jì ① skill; ability; trick: 故～重演 be up to one's old tricks again; play the same old trick ② a professional female dancer or singer in ancient China

【伎俩】 jìliǎng trick; intrigue; manoeuvre

技* jì skill; ability; trick: 绝～ unique skill/ 一～之长 what one is skilled in; skill/ 使敌人无所施其～ make it impossible for the enemy to play any tricks

【技工】 jìgōng ① 〈简〉(技术工人) skilled worker ② mechanic; technician

【技能】 jìnéng technical ability; mastery of a skill or technique: 生产～ skill in production

【技巧】 jìqiǎo skill; technique; craftsmanship: 写作～ writing technique/ 艺术～ artistry/ 精湛的玉雕～ superb skill in jade carving

【技师】 jìshī technician

【技术】 jìshù technology; skill; technique: 科学～ science and technology/ 提高～水平 increase technical competence/ ～要求很高 demand high-level technology/ 重大～改革 key technological transformations ◇ ～工人 skilled worker

【技术性】 jìshùxìng technical; of a technical nature: ～问题 technical matters/ 这工作～很强。This job is highly technical.

【技术员】 jìshùyuán technician: 农业～ agronomist

【技艺】 jìyì skill; artistry: ～精湛 highly skilled; masterly

系 jì tie; fasten; do up; button up: ～鞋带 tie shoe laces/ 把衣服扣子～上 button up a jacket
另见 xì

忌 jì ① be jealous of; envy: ～才 be jealous of other people's talent; resent people more able than oneself/ ～恨 envy and hate ② fear; dread; scruple: 横行无～ ride roughshod; run amuck ③ avoid; shun; abstain from: ～生冷 avoid cold and uncooked food/ 研究问题，～带主观性、片面性和表面性。In studying a problem, we must shun subjectivity, one-sidedness and superficiality. ④ quit; give up: ～酒 give up alcohol; abstain from wine/ ～烟 quit smoking

【忌辰】 jìchén the anniversary of the death of a parent, ancestor, or anyone held in esteem

【忌惮】 jìdàn dread; fear; scruple: 肆无～ stopping at nothing; unscrupulous

【忌妒】 jìdu be jealous of; envy

【忌讳】 jìhuì ① taboo: 犯～ violate (或 break) a taboo ② avoid as taboo: 老张～人家叫他的外号。Lao Zhang resents being called by his nickname.

【忌口】 jìkǒu avoid certain food (as when one is ill); be on a diet

际* jì ① border; boundary; edge: 水～ the edge of a body of water; waterside/ 天～ horizon/ 无边无～ boundless ② between; among; inter-: 春夏之～ between spring and summer/ 国~ international; between nations/ 校~比赛 interschool matches; intercollegiate games ③ inside: 脑~ in one's head (或 mind) ④ occasion; time: 在代表大会召开之~ on the occasion of the convening of the congress; 临别之~ at the time of parting ⑤ on the occasion of: ~此盛会 on the occasion of this grand gathering ⑥ one's lot; circumstances: 遭~ vicissitudes in one's life; one's lot

【际遇】 jìyù 〈书〉favourable or unfavourable turns in life; spells of good or bad fortune

妓 jì prostitute
【妓女】 jìnǚ prostitute
【妓院】 jìyuàn brothel

季* jì ① season: 一年四~ the four seasons of the year; all the year round/ 雨~ rainy season; wet season ② the yield of a product in one season; crop: 由种一~改为种两~ reap two crops a year instead of one ③ the last month of a season: ~春 the last month of spring
【季度】 jìdù quarter (of a year): ~报告 a quarterly report/ 第一~生产指标 the production quota for the first quarter
【季风】 jìfēng 〈气〉monsoon ◇ ~气候 monsoon climate/ ~雨 monsoon rain 又作"季候风"
【季节】 jìjié season: 农忙~ a busy farming season/ 收获~ harvest season; harvest time
【季节性】 jìjiéxìng seasonal ◇ ~工作 seasonal work; seasonal jobs
【季刊】 jìkān quarterly publication; quarterly

剂 jì ① a pharmaceutical or other chemical preparation: 针~ injection/ 丸~ pill; bolus/ 片~ tablet/ 麻醉~ narcotic; anaesthetic/ 防腐制~ preservative; antiseptic/ 干燥~ drying agent; desiccant ②〈量〉〔用于汤药〕: 一~中药 a dose of Chinese herbal medicine

济 jì ① cross a river: 同舟共~ people in the same boat help each other; pull together to tide over difficulties ② aid; relieve; help: ~人之急 relieve sb. in need/ 扶危~困 help the distressed and succour those in peril/ 无~于事 not help matters; be of no help 另见 jǐ
【济事】 jìshì 〔多用于否定〕 be of help (或 use): 空谈不~。 Empty talk doesn't help matters.

既* jì ① already: 澉洗~毕 having performed one's ablutions/ ~得权利 vested right ②〈连〉since; as; now that: ~来之, 则安之。 Since we are here, we may as well stay and make the best of it. ③〈连〉与"且""又""也"等副词连用〕 both...and; as well as: 这间屋子~宽敞, 又亮堂。 The room is both light and spacious./ ~不实用, 又不美观 neither useful nor attractive
【既成事实】 jìchéng shìshí accomplished fact; fait accompli: 造成~ present a fait accompli; make sth. an accomplished fact/ 承认~ accept a fait accompli
【既然】 jìrán 〈连〉since; as; now that: ~如此 since it is so; such being the case; under these circumstances/ 你~表示了决心, 就应该见之于行动。 Now that you have expressed your determination, you should act.
【既往不咎】 jìwǎng bù jiù forgive sb.'s past misdeeds; let bygones be bygones

觊 jì
【觊觎】 jìyú 〈书〉covet; cast greedy eyes on: ~别国领土 covet another country's territory

继* jì ① continue; succeed; follow: ~踵 follow close on sb.'s heels/ ~位 succeed to the throne/ 前赴后~ advance wave upon wave ② then; afterwards: 初感头晕, 又又呕吐 feel dizzy and then begin to vomit
【继承】 jìchéng inherit; carry on: ~财产 inherit property/ ~优良传统 carry forward the good traditions
【继承权】 jìchéngquán right of succession; right of inheritance: 剥夺~ disinherit sb.

【继承人】 jìchéngrén heir; successor; inheritor: 直系~ lineal successor/ 王位~ successor to the throne/ 法定~ heir at law; legal heir
【继父】 jìfù stepfather
【继母】 jìmǔ stepmother
【继配】 jìpèi 〈旧〉second wife (taken after the death of one's first wife) 又作"继室"
【继任】 jìrèn succeed sb. in a post: ~首相 succeed sb. as prime minister
【继续】 jìxù continue; go on: ~工作 continue working/ ~有效 remain valid; remain in force/ ~执政 continue in office; remain in power/ 会议~到深夜。 The meeting went on till late at night./ 有些问题仍需~研究。 Some problems require further study./ 他们第二天又~会谈。 They resumed the talks the next day

寄* jì ① send; post; mail: ~信 post a letter; mail a letter/ ~包裹 send a parcel by post/ ~钱 remit money ② entrust; deposit; place: ~希望于人民 place hopes on the people ③ depend on; attach oneself to: ~食 live with a relative, etc. (because of one's straitened circumstances) ④〈旧〉adopted: ~儿 adopted son
【寄存】 jìcún deposit; leave with; check: 把大衣~在衣帽间 check one's overcoat at the cloakroom/ 行李~处 left-luggage office; checkroom
【寄放】 jìfàng leave with; leave in the care of: 把箱子~在朋友家里 leave a suitcase with a friend
【寄件人】 jìjiànrén sender
【寄居】 jìjū live away from home: 从小~在舅父家里 live from childhood with one's uncle
【寄卖】 jìmài consign for sale on commission; put up for sale in a secondhand shop: 把自行车放在委托商店里~ put a bicycle on sale in a secondhand shop
【寄人篱下】 jì rén líxià live under another's roof; depend on sb. for a living
【寄生】 jìshēng 〈生〉① parasitism ② parasitic: ~生活 parasitic life
【寄生虫】 jìshēngchóng parasite
【寄售】 jìshòu 见"寄卖"
【寄宿】 jìsù ① lodge: ~在朋友家里 lodge (或 put up) at a friend's house ② (of students) board ◇ ~生 resident student; boarder/ ~学校 boarding school; residential college
【寄托】 jìtuō ① entrust to the care of sb.; leave with sb.: 把孩子~在邻居家里 entrust one's child to the care of a neighbour ② place (hope, etc.) on; find sustenance in: 精神有所~ have spiritual sustenance
【寄信人】 jìxìnrén sender
【寄养】 jìyǎng entrust one's child to the care of sb.; ask sb. to bring up one's child
【寄予】 jìyǔ ① place (hope, etc.) on ② show; give; express: ~深切的同情 show heartfelt sympathy to
【寄语】 jìyǔ 〈书〉send word: ~亲人报喜讯。 Send our dear ones the happy news.

寂* jì ① quiet; still; silent: 万籁俱~。 All is quiet and still. ② lonely; lonesome; solitary: 枯~ bored and lonely
【寂静】 jìjìng quiet; still; silent: 在~的深夜里 in the still of the night/ ~的山村, 顿时沸腾起来。 The quiet mountain village suddenly became astir./ 一阵阵号子声, 打破了森林的~。 Work songs broke the silence of the forest.
【寂寥】 jìliáo 〈书〉solitary; lonesome
【寂寞】 jìmò lonely; lonesome: 我在这里又交了新朋友, 一点也不~。 I don't feel lonely as I've made new friends here.
【寂然】 jìrán 〈书〉silent; still

悸 jì 〈书〉(of the heart) throb with terror; palpitate: 惊~ palpitate with terror/ 心有余~ have a lingering fear

祭 jì ① hold a memorial ceremony for ② offer a sacrifice to: ~天 offer a sacrifice to Heaven; worship Heaven ③ wield: ~起法宝 wield a magic wand
【祭奠】 jìdiàn hold a memorial ceremony for
【祭礼】 jìlǐ ① sacrificial rites ② memorial ceremony ③ sacrificial offerings

【祭品】jìpǐn　sacrificial offerings; oblation

【祭坛】jìtán　sacrificial altar

【祭文】jìwén　funeral oration; elegiac address

霁　jì　〈书〉① cease raining or snowing; clear up after rain or snow: 雪～. It's stopped snowing and is clearing up./ ～月 an unclouded moon; the moon in a cloudless sky ② calm down after being angry: ～颜 calm down after a fit of anger; appear mollified

暨　jì　〈书〉① and ② up to; till: ～今 up till now

稷　jì　① millet ② the god of grains worshipped by ancient emperors

髻　jì　hair worn in a bun or coil

冀　jì　〈书〉hope; long for; look forward to: 希～ hope for; look forward to/ ～其成功 look forward to the success of sb. or sth.

骥　jì　〈书〉a thoroughbred horse

jiā

加*　jiā　① add; plus: 二～三等于五. Two plus three makes five. 或 Two and three is five. ② increase; augment: ～工资 increase (或 raise) sb.'s wages ③ put in; add; append: 汤里～点盐 put some salt in the soup/ ～注解 append notes to/ 给人～上种种罪名 level all sorts of charges against sb./ 给自己～上新的头衔 confer a new title on oneself ④〔表示施以某种动作〕大～赞扬 praise highly; lavish praise on/ 不～考虑 not consider at all

【加班】jiābān　work overtime; work an extra shift: ～加点 work extra shifts or extra hours; put in extra hours ◇～费 overtime pay

【加倍】jiābèi　double; redouble: ～努力 redouble one's efforts/ ～警惕 redouble one's vigilance/ ～注意 be doubly careful/ 明年产量可能～. The output may double next year.

【加工】jiāgōng　process: 食品～ food processing/ ～中草药 process medicinal herbs/ 这篇文章需要～. This article needs polishing.

【加害】jiāhài　injure; do harm to: ～于人 do harm to sb.; do sb. an injury

【加紧】jiājǐn　step up; speed up; intensify: ～生产 step up production/ ～准备 speed up preparation

【加劲】jiājìn　put more energy into; make a greater effort: ～把劲儿! Put your back into it!

【加剧】jiājù　aggravate; intensify; exacerbate: ～紧张局势 aggravate tension/ 病势～. The patient's condition has taken a turn for the worse.

【加快】jiākuài　quicken; speed up; accelerate; pick up speed: ～步子 quicken one's step/ ～农业机械化的进程 speed up farm mechanization/ 火车～了速度. The train picked up speed.

【加宽】jiākuān　broaden; widen: ～路面 widen the road

【加冕】jiāmiǎn　coronation

【加强】jiāqiáng　strengthen; enhance; augment; reinforce

【加热】jiārè　heating ◇～炉 heating furnace/ ～器 heating apparatus; heater

【加入】jiārù　① add; mix; put in ② join; accede to

【加深】jiāshēn　deepen: ～河道 deepen the channel of a river/ ～理解 get a deeper understanding

【加速】jiāsù　quicken; speed up; accelerate; expedite: 队伍～前进. The contingent quickened its advance./ ～发展工业 speed up the development of industry

【加以】jiāyǐ　①〔表示如何对待或处理前面提到的事物〕原计划须～修改. It is necessary to revise the original plan./ 有问题要及时～解决. Problems should be resolved in good time. ②〈连〉in addition; moreover: 这种鞋结实耐穿, ～价格便宜, 很受群众欢迎. These shoes are very popular.

They're sturdy and, what's more, they're cheap.

【加意】jiāyì　with special care; with close attention: ～保护 protect with special care/ ～提防 be particularly watchful

【加油】jiāyóu　① oil; lubricate: 这台机器该～了. This machine needs oiling. ② refuel: 飞机要在上海降落～. The plane will land in Shanghai for refuelling./ 空中（或 air）~ in-flight (或 air) refuelling ③ make an extra effort: ～干 work with added vigour/ ～! ～! Come on! Come on!/ 观众为运动员～. The spectators cheered the players on.

【加重】jiāzhòng　① make or become heavier; increase the weight of: ～任务 add to one's tasks ② make or become more serious; aggravate: ～危机 aggravate the crisis/ 病情～. The patient's condition worsened.

夹*　jiā　① press from both sides; place in between: 把相片～在书里 put the photos in between the leaves of a book/ 用钳子把烧红的铁～住 grip a piece of red-hot iron with a pair of tongs/ 用筷子～菜 pick up food with chopsticks/ ～着皮包 carry a briefcase under one's arm/ 他～在我们两人中间. He was sandwiched between the two of us./ 我的手指头被门～了一下. My fingers got squeezed in the door./ 鞋子～脚. The shoe pinches./ 敌军～起尾巴逃跑了. The enemy troops ran away with their tails between their legs./ 无论什么时候, 都要谦虚谨慎, 把尾巴～紧一些. We must always be modest and prudent and must, so to speak, tuck our tails between our legs. ② mix; mingle; intersperse: ～在人群里 mingle with the crowd/ ～叙～议 narration interspersed with comments/ 狂风～着暴雨 a violent wind accompanied by a torrential rain ③ clip, clamp, folder, etc.: 纸～ paper clip/ 发～ hairpin/ 文件～ folder

【夹板】jiābǎn　boards for pressing sth. or holding things together

【夹带】jiādài　① carry secretly; smuggle: 邮寄包裹不能～信件. Don't put letters into a parcel. ② notes smuggled into an examination hall

【夹道】jiādào　① a narrow lane; passageway ② line both sides of the street: ～欢迎贵宾 line the street to welcome a distinguished guest

【夹缝】jiāfèng　a narrow space between two adjacent things; crack; crevice

【夹攻】jiāgōng　attack from both sides; converging attack; pincer attack: 受到两面～ be under a pincer attack; be caught in a two-way squeeze/ 前后～ attack from the front and the rear simultaneously

【夹七夹八】jiāqī-jiābā　incoherent; confused; cluttered (with irrelevant remarks): 他～地说了许多话, 我也没听懂是什么意思. He rambled on at great length but I couldn't make head or tail of what he said.

【夹杂】jiāzá　be mixed up with; be mingled with: 脱粒机的轰鸣声～着年轻人的欢笑声 The droning of the threshers intermingled with youthful laughter./ 他说话～着南方口音. He speaks with a slight southern accent./ 文章里～着不少生造的词语. The article is cluttered up with unclear coined expressions.

【夹子】jiāzi　① clip; tongs: 弹簧～ spring clip/ 点心～ cake tongs/ 衣服～ clothes-peg; clothespin ② folder; wallet: 文件～ folder; binder/ 皮～ wallet; pocketbook

佳*　jiā　good; fine; beautiful: ～景 fine landscape; beautiful view/ 成绩甚～ achieve very good results/ ～宾 a welcome guest/ ～肴 delicacies/ 身体欠～ not feel well; be indisposed

【佳话】jiāhuà　a deed praised far and wide; a story on everybody's lips; a much-told tale: 两国运动员互相帮助的事become一时传为～. Everybody was telling the story of how the athletes of the two countries helped each other.

【佳节】jiājié　happy festival time; festival: 中秋～ the joyous Mid-Autumn Festival/ 欢度国庆～ celebrate the joyous festival of National Day

【佳境】jiājìng　〈书〉the most enjoyable or pleasant stage: 渐入～ become more and more delightful

【佳句】jiājù　beautiful line (in a poem); well-turned phrase

【佳偶】 jiā'ǒu 〈书〉a happily married couple

【佳期】 jiāqī wedding (或 nuptial) day

【佳人】 jiārén 〈书〉beautiful woman

【佳音】 jiāyīn welcome news; good tidings; favourable reply: 静候～. I am awaiting the news of your success.

【佳作】 jiāzuò a fine piece of writing; an excellent work

枷 jiā cangue

【枷锁】 jiāsuǒ yoke; chains; shackles; fetters: 精神～ spiritual shackles

浃 jiā 见"汗流浃背" hàn liú jiā bèi

家* jiā ① family; household: 他全～都是工人。 They're all workers in his family./ 张～和王～ the Zhangs and the Wangs /～事 family matters; domestic affairs ② home: 回～ go home/ 不在～ not be in; be out/ 上我～去吧. Come to my place. ③ a person or family engaged in a certain trade: 船～ boatman/ 渔～ fisherman's family ④ a specialist in a certain field: 科学～ scientist/ 政治～ statesman/ 文学～ a man of letters; writer/ 画～ painter ⑤ a school of thought; school: 法～ the Legalist School ⑥ 〈谦〉〔用于对别人称比自己辈分高或年纪大的亲属〕: ～父 my father/ ～兄 my elder brother ⑦ domestic; tame: ～兔 rabbit ⑧〔量〕〔用来计算家庭或企业〕: 三～商店 three shops/ 一～电影院 a cinema/ 两～人家 two families

家 jia 〈口〉〔后缀, 用在名词后, 表示属于哪一类人〕: 小孩子～别插嘴! You kids shouldn't interrupt!/ 现在姑娘也会开飞机啦! Nowadays girls pilot planes, too!

【家产】 jiāchǎn family property

【家常】 jiācháng the daily life of a family; domestic trivia: 拉～ engage in small talk ◇ ～话 small talk; chitchat

【家常便饭】 jiācháng biànfàn ① homely food; simple meal ② common occurrence; routine; all in the day's work

【家丑】 jiāchǒu family scandal; the skeleton in the cupboard (或 closet): ～不可外扬. Domestic shame should not be made public. 或 Don't wash your dirty linen in public.

【家畜】 jiāchù domestic animal; livestock

【家传】 jiāchuán handed down from the older generations of the family ◇ ～秘方 a secret recipe handed down in the family

【家道】 jiādào family financial situation: ～小康 be comfortably off

【家法】 jiāfǎ ① domestic discipline exercised by the head of a feudal household ② a rod for punishing children or servants in a feudal household

【家伙】 jiāhuo 〈口〉① tool; utensil; weapon: 这把～挺好使. This is a very handy tool. ② fellow; guy: 小～ little chap; kid/ 那个～是谁? Who's that fellow?

【家计】 jiājì 〈书〉family livelihood

【家家户户】 jiājiā-hùhù each and every family; every household: 做到～有余粮 ensure that every household has surplus grain

【家教】 jiājiào family education; upbringing: 没有～ not properly brought up; ill-bred/ ～严 be strict with one's children

【家境】 jiājìng family financial situation; family circumstances: ～困难 with one's family in straitened circumstances/ ～好 come from a well-to-do family

【家具】 jiāju furniture: 几件～ several pieces of furniture/ 一套～ a set of furniture

【家眷】 jiājuàn ① wife and children; one's family ② wife

【家破人亡】 jiāpò-rénwáng with one's family broken up, some gone away, some dead

【家谱】 jiāpǔ family tree; genealogical tree; genealogy

【家禽】 jiāqín domestic fowl; poultry

【家史】 jiāshǐ family history

【家书】 jiāshū ① a letter home ② a letter from home

【家属】 jiāshǔ family members; (family) dependents

【家庭】 jiātíng family; household ◇ ～背景 family background/ ～成员 family members/ ～出身 class status of one's family; family origin/ ～负

担 family responsibilities/ ～妇女 housewife/ ～副业 household sideline production/ ～观念 attachment to one's family/ ～教师 private teacher; tutor/ ～教育 family education; home education/ ～纠纷 family quarrel; domestic discord/ ～生活 home life; family life/ ～作业 homework

【家徒四壁】 jiā tú sì bì have nothing but the bare walls in one's house — be utterly destitute

【家务】 jiāwù household duties ◇ ～劳动 housework; household chores

【家乡】 jiāxiāng hometown; native place ◇ ～话 native dialect

【家小】 jiāxiǎo 〈口〉wife and children

【家信】 jiāxìn a letter to or from one's family

【家用】 jiāyòng family expenses; housekeeping money

【家喻户晓】 jiāyù-hùxiǎo widely known; known to all: 做到～ make known to every household

【家园】 jiāyuán home; homeland: 重建～ rebuild one's homeland; rebuild one's village or town

【家长】 jiāzhǎng ① the head of a family; patriarch ② the parent or guardian of a child: 学校里明天开～会. There will be a parents' meeting in our school tomorrow.

袈 jiā

【袈裟】 jiāshā kasaya, a patchwork outer vestment worn by a Buddhist monk

傢 jiā

【傢伙】 jiāhuo 见"家伙" jiāhuo

【傢具】 jiāju 见"家具" jiāju

嘉 jiā ① good; fine: ～宾 honoured guest; welcome guest ② praise; commend: 精神可～ a praiseworthy spirit

【嘉奖】 jiājiǎng commend; cite: 传令～全连指战员 cite the officers and men of the company for their meritorious service ◇ ～令 citation

【嘉勉】 jiāmiǎn 〈书〉praise and encourage

【嘉许】 jiāxǔ 〈书〉praise; approve

jiá

荚 jiá pod: 结～ bear pods; pod

戛 jiá 〈书〉knock gently; tap

【戛戛】 jiájiá 〈书〉① difficult; hard going ② original: ～独造 have great originality

【戛然】 jiárán 〈书〉①〈象〉〔多形容嘹亮的鸟声〕: ～长鸣 long and loud cries ②〔多用于〕: ～而止 (of a sound) stop abruptly

颊 jiá cheek: 两～红润 with rosy cheeks

jiǎ

甲* jiǎ ① first: ～级 first rate; / 桂林山水～天下. The mountains and waters of Guilin are the finest under heaven. ②〔用作代称〕: 某～与某乙 Mr. A and Mr. B/ ～方和乙方 the first party and the second party/ ～队和乙队 team A and team B ③ shell; carapace: 龟～ tortoise shell ④ nail: 手指～ fingernail ⑤ armour: 装～车 armoured car

【甲板】 jiǎbǎn deck

【甲骨文】 jiǎgǔwén inscriptions on bones or tortoise shells of the Shang Dynasty (c. 16th—11th century B.C.)

岬 jiǎ ① cape; promontory ② a narrow passage between mountains

【岬角】 jiǎjiǎo cape; promontory

胛 jiǎ

【胛骨】 jiǎgǔ 〈生理〉shoulder blade

贾 Jiǎ a surname

另见 gǔ

假 * jiǎ ① false; fake; sham; phoney; artificial: 以～乱真 create confusion by passing off the spurious as genuine ② borrow; avail oneself of: 久～不归 keep putting off returning sth. one has borrowed; appropriate sth. borrowed for one's own use ③ if; suppose: ～令 in case 另见 jià

【假扮】 jiǎbàn disguise oneself as; dress up as

【假充】 jiǎchōng pretend to be; pose as: ～内行 pretend to be an expert

【假道学】 jiǎdàoxué a sanctimonious person; hypocrite

【假定】 jiǎdìng ① suppose; assume; grant; presume: ～有这么一回事真的发生了／～这是真的，也影响不了大局。Even if this is the case, it will not affect the whole situation. ② hypothesis

【假发】 jiǎfà wig

【假公济私】 jiǎ gōng jì sī use public office for private gain; jobbery

【假花】 jiǎhuā artificial flower

【假话】 jiǎhuà lie; falsehood: 说～ tell lies

【假借】 jiǎjiè make use of: ～外力 make use of outside forces／～名义 under the guise of; in the name of; under false pretences

【假冒】 jiǎmào pass oneself off as; palm off (a fake as genuine): 谨防～ Beware of imitations.

【假寐】 jiǎmèi 〈书〉 catnap; doze

【假面具】 jiǎmiànjù mask; false front

【假名】 jiǎmíng pseudonym

【假仁假义】 jiǎrén-jiǎyì pretended benevolence and righteousness; hypocrisy

【假如】 jiǎrú if; supposing; in case: ～明天开会，准备工作来得及吗？Supposing we hold the meeting tomorrow, will there be enough time to prepare?／～我忘了，请提醒我一下。Remind me in case I forget.

【假若】 jiǎruò if; supposing; in case

【假山】 jiǎshān rockery

【假设】 jiǎshè ① suppose; assume; grant; presume ② hypothesis: 科学～ a scientific hypothesis

【假使】 jiǎshǐ if; in case; in the event that: ～他不同意，那就作罢。If he disagrees, let the matter drop.

【假手】 jiǎshǒu do sth. through sb. else; make a cat's-paw of sb.: ～于人 make sb. else do the work

【假说】 jiǎshuō hypothesis

【假死】 jiǎsǐ ① 〈医〉 suspended animation ② 〈动〉 play dead; feign death; play possum

【假托】 jiǎtuō ① on the pretext of: ～有病 on the pretext of illness ② under sb. else's name: 这篇文章不是他写的，是别人～他的名义发表的。He didn't write the essay; somebody else did, and published it under his name. ③ by means of; through the medium of: 人们～披着羊皮的狼的故事说明要警惕伪装的敌人。The story of the wolf in sheep's clothing is a fable intended to teach people to be on guard against enemies in disguise.

【假想】 jiǎxiǎng ① imagination; hypothesis; supposition ② imaginary; hypothetical; fictitious: 这个故事里的人物都是～的。The characters in this story are all fictitious. ◇ ～敌 〈军〉 imaginary enemy

【假象】 jiǎxiàng false appearance: 制造～ create a false impression; put up a false front／不要被～所迷惑。Don't be misled by appearances.

【假惺惺】 jiǎxīngxīng hypocritically; unctuously: ～地表示愿意支持 hypocritically express willingness to support／～地宣称 declare unctuously

【假牙】 jiǎyá dental prosthesis; false tooth; denture

【假眼】 jiǎyǎn ocular prosthesis; artificial eye; glass eye

【假意】 jiǎyì ① unction; insincerity; hypocrisy ② pretend; put on: ～奉承 cheap flattery

【假造】 jiǎzào ① forge; counterfeit: ～证件 forge a certificate／这张钞票是～的。This banknote is a forgery. 或 This is a forged banknote. ② invent; fabricate: ～理由 invent an excuse／～罪名 cook up a false charge against; frame up

【假装】 jiǎzhuāng pretend; feign; simulate; make believe

价 * jià ① price: 减～ reduce the price/要～ ask a price ② value: 等～交换 exchange of equal values／估～ estimate the value of; evaluate

【价格】 jiàgé price: 批发(零售)～ wholesale (retail) price／标明～ mark (goods) with a price tag; have goods clearly priced

【价目】 jiàmù marked price; price ◇～表 price list

【价钱】 jiàqian price: 讲～ bargain／～公道 a fair (或 decent, reasonable) price

【价值】 jiàzhí ① 〈经〉 value: 剩余～ surplus value／使用～ use value ② worth; value: ～五百万元的设备 five million dollars worth of equipment／～五百万元的设备 equipment worth (或 valued at) five million dollars／毫无～ completely worthless／这些资料对我们很有～。This data is of great value to us.

【价值连城】 jià zhí liánchéng worth several cities — invaluable; priceless

驾 * jià ① harness; draw (a cart, etc.): ～牲口耕地 harness cattle to plough the fields／那匹马没～过车。That horse has never been harnessed to a cart. ② drive (a vehicle); pilot (a plane); sail (a boat) ③〔原指车辆, 借用于对人的敬辞〕: 大～ your good self

【驾临】 jiàlín 〈敬〉 your arrival; your esteemed presence: 恭候～。Your presence is requested.

【驾轻就熟】 jiàqīng-jiùshú drive a light carriage on a familiar road; be able to handle a job with ease because one has had previous experience; do a familiar job with ease

【驾驶】 jiàshǐ drive (a vehicle); pilot (a ship or plane): ～拖拉机 drive a tractor

【驾驭】 jiàyù ① drive (a cart, horse, etc.): 这匹马不好～。This horse is hard to control. ② control; master: ～形势 have the situation well in hand／～自然 tame nature

架 * jià ① frame; rack; shelf; stand: 房～ the frame of a house／行李～ luggage-rack／工具～ tool rack／衣儿～ clothes hanger／衣帽～ clothes tree／书～ bookshelf／黄瓜～ cucumber trellis／钢～桥 steel-framed bridge ② put up; erect: ～桥 put up (或 build) a bridge／～电话线 set up telephone lines／～枪 stack rifles／～起机枪 mount a machine gun ③ fend off; ward off; withstand: 他一刀砍来, 我拿起～住。I fended off his sword thrust with my spear. ④ support; prop; help: ～着伤员走路 help a wounded soldier to walk／～着拐走 walk on crutches／他扭了脚脖子, 我们只得把他～回去。He sprained his ankle and had to be helped home. ⑤ kidnap; take sb. away forcibly: 强行～走 carry sb. away by force; kidnap ⑥ fight; quarrel: 劝～ step in and patch up a quarrel; mediate between quarrelling parties ⑦〈量〉: 一～收音机 a radio set／几百～飞机 several hundred planes

【架子】 jiàzi ① frame; stand; rack; shelf: 脸盆～ washstand ② framework; skeleton; outline: 写文章要先搭好～。Make an outline before you start writing.／把新机构的～搭起来 set up the framework of the new organization ③ airs; haughty manner: 摆～ put on airs／没有～ be modest and unassuming; be easy of approach／放下～ get down from one's high horse ④ posture; stance: 他拉开～, 打起了太极拳。He adopted a stance and began to do *Taiji* shadowboxing.

假 * jià ① holiday; vacation: 暑～ summer vacation ② leave of absence; furlough: 事～ leave of absence to attend to personal affairs／病～ sick leave／休～ be on leave; be on furlough／请～ ask for leave／超～ overstay one's leave of absence 另见 jiǎ

【假期】 jiàqī ① vacation ② period of leave

【假日】 jiàrì holiday; day off

嫁 * jià ① (of a woman) marry: ～人 get married／～女儿 marry off a daughter ② shift; transfer

【嫁祸于人】 jià huò yú rén shift the misfortune onto sb. else; put the blame on sb. else
【嫁娶】 jiàqǔ marriage
【嫁妆】 jiàzhuāng dowry; trousseau

稼 jià ① sow (grain): 耕～ ploughing and sowing; farm work ② cereals; crops: 庄～ crops; standing grain

jiān

尖* jiān ① point; tip; top: 针～ the point of a needle or pin; pinpoint/ 铅笔～ the tip of a pencil/ 指～ fingertip/ 塔～ the pinnacle of a pagoda ② pointed; tapering: ～下巴 a pointed chin/ 把铅笔削尖 sharpen a pencil ③ shrill; piercing: ～声～气 in a shrill voice/ ～叫 scream ④ sharp; acute: 耳朵～ have sharp ears; be sharp-eared/ 眼～have sharp eyes; be sharp-eyed/ 鼻子～ have an acute (或 sharp) sense of smell ⑤ the best of its kind; the pick of the bunch; the cream of the crop: 拔～儿的 top-notch; the pick of the bunch
【尖端】 jiānduān ① pointed end; acme; peak: 标枪的～ the point of a javelin ② most advanced; sophisticated
【尖刻】 jiānkè acrimonious; caustic; biting: 说话～ speak with biting sarcasm
【尖利】 jiānlì ① sharp; keen; cutting: ～的钢刀 a sharp knife/ ～的叫声 a shrill cry
【尖锐】 jiānruì ① sharp-pointed ② penetrating; incisive; sharp; keen: ～的批评 incisive (或 sharp) criticism/ ～地指出 point out sharply/ 他看问题很～ He sees things with a keen (或 sharp) eye. ③ shrill; piercing: ～的哨声 the shrill sound of a whistle ④ intense; acute; sharp: ～的思想斗争 sharp mental conflicts/ ～对立 be diametrically opposed to each other ◇ ～化 sharpen; intensify; become more acute
【尖酸】 jiānsuān acrid; acrimonious; tart: ～刻薄 tart and mean; bitterly sarcastic

奸* jiān ① wicked; evil; treacherous: ～计 an evil plot ② traitor: 内～ a secret enemy agent within one's ranks; hidden traitor/ 锄～ eliminate traitors ③ <口> self-seeking and wily: 这个人才～哪,总想占便宜。He's a self-seeker; he's always on the make. ④ illicit sexual relations: 通～ have illicit sexual relations; commit adultery
【奸臣】 jiānchén treacherous court official
【奸猾】 jiānhuá treacherous; crafty; deceitful
【奸佞】 jiānnìng <书> ① crafty and fawning ② crafty sycophant
【奸商】 jiānshāng unscrupulous merchant; profiteer
【奸污】 jiānwū rape or seduce
【奸细】 jiānxi spy; enemy agent
【奸险】 jiānxiǎn wicked and crafty; treacherous; malicious
【奸笑】 jiānxiào sinister (或 villainous) smile
【奸邪】 jiānxié <书> ① crafty and evil; treacherous ② a crafty and evil person
【奸雄】 jiānxióng a person who achieves high position by unscrupulous scheming; arch-careerist
【奸淫】 jiānyín ① illicit sexual relations; adultery ② rape or seduce: ～掳掠 rape and loot
【奸贼】 jiānzéi traitor; conspirator
【奸诈】 jiānzhà fraudulent; crafty; treacherous

间* jiān ① between; among: 同志之～ among comrades ② within a definite time or space: 世～ (in) the world/ 田～ (in) the fields/ 晚～ (in the) evening; (at) night ③ room: 里～ inner room/ 衣帽～ cloakroom ④ <量>: 一～卧室 a bedroom/ 三～门面 a three-bay shop front 另见 jiàn
【间不容发】 jiān bù róng fà not a hair's breadth in between—the situation is extremely critical

歼 jiān annihilate; wipe out; destroy: ～敌五千 annihilate 5,000 enemy troops

【歼灭】 jiānmiè annihilate; wipe out; destroy: ～敌人有生力量 wipe out the enemy's effective strength ◇ ～射击 annihilation fire/ ～战 war or battle of annihilation

坚* jiān ① hard; solid; firm; strong: ～冰 solid ice/ hard ice/ 身残志～ broken in body but firm in spirit ② a heavily fortified point; fortification; stronghold: 攻～ storm strongholds ③ firmly; steadfastly; resolutely: ～信 firmly believe/ ～拒 flatly refuse/ ～称 state insistently; insist
【坚不可摧】 jiān bùkě cuī indestructible; impregnable
【坚持】 jiānchí persist in; persevere in; uphold; insist on; stick to; adhere to: ～原则 adhere (或 stick) to principle/ ～真理 hold firmly to the truth/ ～上次会议上提出的条件 insist on the terms put forward at the previous session/ ～己见 hold on to one's own views/ ～错误 persist in one's errors/ 再～一会儿 hold out a little longer
【坚持不懈】 jiānchí bù xiè unremitting: 作～的努力 make unremitting efforts
【坚持不渝】 jiānchí bù yú persistent; persevering; unremitting
【坚定】 jiāndìng ① firm; staunch; steadfast: ～不移 firm and unshakable; unswerving; unflinching/ ～的步伐 firm strides/ ～的立场 a firm stand/ ～的意志 constancy of purpose ② strengthen: ～了攀登科学技术新高峰的决心 strengthen one's resolve to scale new heights of science and technology
【坚固】 jiāngù firm; solid; sturdy; strong: ～耐用 sturdy and durable/ ～的工事 strong fortifications/ 这座桥造得很～。This bridge is very solidly built.
【坚决】 jiānjué firm; resolute; determined: ～支持 firmly support; stand firmly by/ ～反对 resolutely oppose/ ～完成任务! We'll carry out the task without fail!/ 他很～。He stood firm. 或 He was determined./ 采取～措施 take resolute measures
【坚强】 jiānqiáng strong; firm; staunch: ～的决心 strong determination
【坚忍】 jiānrěn steadfast and persevering (in face of difficulties)
【坚韧】 jiānrèn ① tough and tensile ② firm and tenacious: 运动员在比赛中表现出～的斗志。The athletes displayed great tenacity throughout the contest.
【坚韧不拔】 jiānrèn bù bá firm and indomitable; persistent and dauntless
【坚如磐石】 jiān rú pánshí solid as a rock; rock-firm
【坚实】 jiānshí solid; substantial: ～的基础 a solid foundation/ 迈出～的步子 make solid progress/ 这条公路～平整。This is a smooth, strongly built highway.
【坚守】 jiānshǒu stick to; hold fast to; stand fast: ～岗位 stand fast at one's post/ ～阵地 hold fast to one's position; hold one's ground
【坚毅】 jiānyì firm and persistent; with unswerving determination; with inflexible will
【坚硬】 jiānyìng hard; solid: ～的岩石 solid rock
【坚贞】 jiānzhēn faithful; constant
【坚贞不屈】 jiānzhēn bù qū remain faithful and unyielding

肩* jiān ① shoulder: 并～战斗 fight shoulder to shoulder ② take on; undertake; shoulder; bear: 身～重任 shoulder heavy responsibilities
【肩膀】 jiānbǎng shoulder
【肩负】 jiānfù take on; undertake; shoulder; bear: 我们～人民的希望。The people place their hopes on us.

艰* jiān difficult; hard
【艰巨】 jiānjù arduous; formidable: 一项光荣而～的任务 a glorious but arduous task/ 付出～的劳动 make tremendous efforts/ 这个工程非常～。This is a formidable project.
【艰苦】 jiānkǔ arduous; difficult; hard; tough: ～的生活 hard life/ ～的斗争 arduous struggle/ ～朴素 hard work and plain living
【艰难】 jiānnán difficult; hard: 行动～ walk with difficulty/ 生活～ live in straitened circumstances/ 克服～困苦 overcome difficulties and hardships/ 经过无数～曲折 go through countless difficulties and setbacks/ ～险阻 difficulties and obstacles

【艰涩】 jiānsè involved and abstruse; intricate and obscure: 文词～ involved and abstruse writing
【艰深】 jiānshēn difficult to understand; abstruse
【艰危】 jiānwēi difficulties and dangers (confronting a nation)
【艰险】 jiānxiǎn hardships and dangers: 不避～ brave hardships and dangers
【艰辛】 jiānxīn hardships: 历尽～ experience all kinds of hardships

兼 jiān ①double; twice: ～旬 twenty days ②simultaneously; concurrently: ～管 be concurrently in charge of; also look after/ ～而有之 have both at the same time ③ hold two or more jobs concurrently: 身～数职 hold several posts simultaneously
【兼备】 jiānbèi have both... and...: 德才～ have both political integrity and ability; combine ability with political integrity
【兼并】 jiānbìng annex (territory, property, etc.)
【兼程】 jiānchéng travel at double speed: ～前进 advance at the double/ 日夜～ travel day and night
【兼顾】 jiāngù give consideration to (或 take account of) two or more things
【兼课】 jiānkè ①do some teaching in addition to one's main occupation ②hold two or more teaching jobs concurrently
【兼任】 jiānrèn hold a concurrent post
【兼收并蓄】 jiānshōu-bìngxù incorporate things of diverse nature; take in everything
【兼职】 jiānzhí ①hold two or more posts concurrently: ～过多 hold too many posts at the same time ②concurrent post; part-time job: 辞去～ resign one's concurrent job

监 jiān ①supervise; inspect; watch ②prison; jail 另见 jiàn
【监察】 jiānchá supervise; control
【监督】 jiāndū ①supervise; superintend; control ②supervisor
【监犯】 jiānfàn prisoner; convict
【监工】 jiāngōng ①supervise work; oversee ②overseer; supervisor
【监护】 jiānhù 〈法〉 guardianship ◇ ～人 guardian
【监禁】 jiānjìn take into custody; imprison; put in jail (或 prison)
【监考】 jiānkǎo invigilate ◇ ～人 invigilator
【监牢】 jiānláo prison; jail
【监视】 jiānshì keep watch on; keep a lookout over: ～敌人的行动 keep watch on the movements of the enemy
【监守】 jiānshǒu have custody of; guard; take care of
【监狱】 jiānyù prison; jail

笺 jiān 〈书〉①writing paper: 信～ letter paper ②letter ③annotation; commentary
【笺注】 jiānzhù 〈书〉 notes and commentary on ancient texts

菅 jiān 〈植〉 villous themeda (Themeda gigantea var. villosa)

缄 jiān seal; close: 信封上写着"刘～"。On the envelope is written: "from Liu".
【缄口】 jiānkǒu 〈书〉 keep one's mouth shut; hold one's tongue; say nothing
【缄默】 jiānmò keep silent; be reticent

煎 jiān ①fry in shallow oil: ～鸡蛋 fried eggs ②simmer in water; decoct: ～药 decoct medicinal herbs
【煎熬】 jiān'áo suffering; torture; torment
【煎饼】 jiānbing thin pancake made of millet flour, etc.

jiǎn

拣 jiǎn ① choose; select; pick out: 把最好的番茄一出 pick out the best tomatoes/ 担子～重的挑 choose the heavy loads to carry; volunteer to undertake difficult tasks/ ～要紧的说。Say what you think is most urgent. ② 见"捡" jiǎn
【拣选】 jiǎnxuǎn select; choose

茧 jiǎn ①cocoon: 蚕～ silkworm cocoon ②callus: 老～ thick callus

柬 jiǎn card; note; letter: 请～ invitation card
【柬帖】 jiǎntiě note; short letter

俭 jiǎn thrifty; frugal: 省吃～用 eat sparingly and spend frugally; be economical in everyday spending
【俭朴】 jiǎnpǔ thrifty and simple; economical: 生活～ lead a thrifty and simple life/ 衣着～ dress simply
【俭省】 jiǎnshěng economical; thrifty: 过日子～ live a frugal life; live economically

捡 jiǎn pick up; collect; gather: ～麦穗 pick up ears of wheat; glean a wheat field/ ～煤核儿 pick out unburnt coal from cinders/ ～粪 collect manure/ ～柴火 gather firewood/ ～到一支钢笔 find a fountain pen

检 jiǎn ①check up; inspect; examine: ～定 examine and determine ②restrain oneself; be careful in one's conduct: 行为不～ depart from correct conduct
【检查】 jiǎnchá ①check up; inspect; examine: ～工作 check up on work/ ～质量 check on the quality of sth./ ～护照 inspect sb.'s passport/ ～行李 inspect (或 examine) sb.'s luggage/ ～身体 have a physical examination; have a health check/ 新闻～ press censorship
【检点】 jiǎndiǎn ①examine; check: ～一下行李，看是不是都齐了。Check the luggage and see if everything is there. ② be cautious (about what one says or does): 言行有失～ be careless about one's words and acts; be indiscreet in one's speech and conduct/ 病人对饮食要多加～。Sick people should be careful about their diet.
【检举】 jiǎnjǔ report (an offence) to the authorities; inform against (an offender)
【检讨】 jiǎntǎo self-criticism: 作～ make a self-criticism/ ～自己的错误 examine one's mistakes
【检验】 jiǎnyàn test; examine; inspect: 严格～产品质量 strictly examine the quality of the products/ 商品～ commodity inspection
【检疫】 jiǎnyì quarantine
【检阅】 jiǎnyuè review (troops, etc.); inspect: ～仪仗队 review a guard of honour/ 对科研新成果的一次～ a review of recent achievements in scientific research ◇ ～台 reviewing stand

剪 jiǎn ①scissors; shears; clippers ②cut (with scissors); clip; trim: 别把头发～得太短了。Don't cut the hair too short./ ～指甲 trim one's nails/ ～羊毛 shear a sheep ③ wipe out; exterminate: ～除 wipe out; annihilate
【剪报】 jiǎnbào newspaper cutting (或 clipping)
【剪裁】 jiǎncái ①cut out (a garment); tailor ②cut out unwanted material (from a piece of writing); prune: 写文章要下一番～的工夫。In writing an essay one must do a lot of pruning.
【剪彩】 jiǎncǎi cut the ribbon at an opening ceremony: 展览会～ cut the ribbon at the opening of an exhibition
【剪除】 jiǎnchú wipe out; annihilate; exterminate
【剪刀】 jiǎndāo scissors; shears
【剪辑】 jiǎnjí ①〈电影〉 montage; film editing: 电影～机 motion-picture editing machine ②editing and rearrangement: 话剧录音～ highlights of a live recording of a play
【剪接】 jiǎnjiē montage; film editing
【剪票】 jiǎnpiào punch a ticket
【剪贴】 jiǎntiē ①clip and paste (sth. out of a newspaper, etc.) in a scrapbook or on cards ②cutting out (as schoolchildren's activity) ◇ ～簿 scrapbook

减* jiǎn ①subtract: 九～四得五。Nine minus four is five. 或 Four from nine is five. ②reduce; decrease; cut: ～半 reduce by half/ 工作热情有增无～ work with ever increasing zeal/ 他人虽老了,干劲却不～当年。Old as he is, he works just as hard as he did in his younger days.

【减产】 jiǎnchǎn reduction of output; drop in production

【减低】 jiǎndī reduce; lower; bring down; cut: ～速度 lower (或 slacken) speed; slow down/ 耗煤率～了百分之五。Consumption of coal went down by 5%.

【减缓】 jiǎnhuǎn retard; slow down: ～进程 slow down the pace (或 progress)

【减价】 jiǎnjià reduce the price; mark down: ～出售 sell at a reduced price/ ～一成 be marked down by 10%

【减轻】 jiǎnqīng lighten; ease; alleviate; mitigate: ～国家的负担 lighten the burden on the state/ ～劳动强度 reduce labour intensity/ ～病人的痛苦 alleviate (或 ease) a patient's suffering/ ～处分 mitigate a punishment

【减弱】 jiǎnruò weaken; abate: 体力大大～ be much weakened physically/ 风势～了。The wind has subsided.

【减少】 jiǎnshǎo reduce; decrease; lessen; cut down: ～非生产性开支 reduce nonproductive expenditure

【减速】 jiǎnsù slow down; decelerate; retard

【减缩】 jiǎnsuō reduce; cut down; retrench: ～开支 reduce expenditure

【减退】 jiǎntuì drop; go down: 视力(记忆力)～。One's eyesight (memory) is failing./ 雨后炎热～了许多。After the rain, the heat abated considerably.

【减刑】 jiǎnxíng 〈法〉reduce a penalty; commute (或 mitigate) a sentence

硷 jiǎn 见"碱" jiǎn

睑 jiǎn eyelid

简* jiǎn ①simple; simplified; brief: 从～conform to the principle of simplicity/ ～而言之 in brief; in short; to put it in a nutshell ②bamboo slips (used for writing on in ancient times) ③letter: 书～ letters; correspondence ④〈书〉select; choose: ～拔 select and promote

【简报】 jiǎnbào bulletin; brief report: 会议～ conference bulletin; brief reports on conference proceedings

【简编】 jiǎnbiān 〔多用于书名〕short course; concise edition

【简便】 jiǎnbiàn simple and convenient; handy: ～的方法 a simple and convenient method; a handy way/ 操作～ easy to operate

【简称】 jiǎnchēng ①the abbreviated form of a name; abbreviation ②be called sth. for short

【简单】 jiǎndān ①simple; uncomplicated: ～明了 simple and clear; concise and explicit/ 这机器构造～。The machine is simple in structure. ②〔多用于否定式〕commonplace; ordinary: 她的枪法那么准,真不～。 What a marvel to be able to shoot with such accuracy./ 这家伙鬼点子特多,可不～。This fellow is no simpleton. He is full of tricks. ③oversimplified; casual: ～粗暴 do things in an oversimplified and crude way/ 头脑～ simple-minded; seeing things too simply/ ～地看问题 take a naïve view; oversimplify a problem/ 不能用～的方法去解决这个问题。This matter cannot be settled in a summary fashion./ 这篇文章我只是～地看了看。I only skimmed through this article.

【简短】 jiǎnduǎn brief: 他的发言～有力。His speech was brief and forceful.

【简化】 jiǎnhuà simplify: ～工序 simplify working processes

【简洁】 jiǎnjié succinct; terse; pithy: ～生动的语言 terse and lively language/ 文笔～ written in a pithy style

【简介】 jiǎnjiè brief introduction; synopsis; summarized account: 剧情～ the synopsis of a drama

【简历】 jiǎnlì biographical notes; *curriculum vitae*; *résumé*

【简练】 jiǎnliàn terse; succinct; pithy: 内容丰富,文字～ rich in content and succinct in style

【简陋】 jiǎnlòu simple and crude: 设备～ simple and crude equipment

【简略】 jiǎnlüè simple (in content); brief; sketchy: 他提供的材料过于～。The material he supplied is too sketchy.

【简慢】 jiǎnmàn negligent (in attending to one's guest)

【简明】 jiǎnmíng simple and clear; concise: ～扼要 brief and to the point ◇ ～新闻 news in brief

【简朴】 jiǎnpǔ simple and unadorned; plain: 生活～ a simple and frugal life; plain living/ ～的语言 plain language

【简体字】 jiǎntǐzì simplified Chinese character

【简写】 jiǎnxiě ①write a Chinese character in simplified form ②simplify a book for beginners ◇ ～本 simplified edition

【简讯】 jiǎnxùn news in brief

【简要】 jiǎnyào concise and to the point; brief: ～的介绍 a brief introduction; briefing

【简易】 jiǎnyì ①simple and easy: ～的办法 a simple and easy method ②simply constructed; simply equipped; unsophisticated

【简直】 jiǎnzhí 〈副〉simply; at all: 我～不能想象有这种事。I simply couldn't imagine such a thing./ 这个星期～没有一个好天。We've had no fine weather at all this week./ ～是浪费时间。It's a sheer waste of time./ 跟新的一样好 as good as new

碱 jiǎn ①alkali ②soda: 纯～ soda (ash)/ 洗涤～ washing soda

【碱性】 jiǎnxìng basicity; alkalinity

见* jiàn ①see; catch sight of: 所～所闻 what one sees and hears/ 只～一个人影闪过墙角 catch sight of sb. turning the corner ②meet with; be exposed to: 这种药怕～光。This medicine is not to be exposed to daylight. 冰～热就化。Ice melts with heat./ ～困难就上, ～荣誉就让 dash forward where there are difficulties to overcome and draw back when honours are to be conferred; take the difficulties for oneself and leave the honours to others ③show evidence of; appear to be: 并不～瘦 not seem to be any thinner/ 病已～轻。The patient's condition has improved./ ～之于行动 be translated into action ④refer to; see; vide: ～第三十六页 see page 36/ ～上 see above; *vide supra*/ ～下 see below; *vide infra*/ ～前 see before; *vide ante*/ ～后 see after; *vide post* ⑤meet; call on; see: 你～到他了没有? Did you meet him?/ 我不想～他。I don't wish to see him./ 明天下午天要来～你。She'll call on you this afternoon. ⑥view; opinion: 依我之～ in my opinion; to my mind ⑦〈书〉〈助〉〔用在动词前面表示被动或表示对我怎么样〕: ～责 be blamed/ ～弃 be rejected; be discarded/ 即希～告。Hope to be informed immediately.
另见 xiàn

【见报】 jiànbào appear in the newspapers

【见不得】 jiànbude ①not to be exposed to; unable to stand: ～阳光 not to be exposed to the sunlight ②not fit to be seen or revealed: ～人 shameful; scandalous

【见长】 jiàncháng be good at; be expert in: 她以写作～。She is good at writing.

【见得】 jiànde 〔只用于否定式或疑问式〕seem; appear: 这片稻子不～比那片差。This plot of paddy doesn't seem to be any worse than that one./ 明天不～会下雨。It doesn't look as if it's going to rain tomorrow./ 怎么～他来不了? How do you know he can't come?/ 何以～? How so?

【见地】 jiàndì insight; judgment: 很有～ have keen insight; show sound judgment

【见多识广】 jiànduō-shíguǎng experienced and knowledgeable

【见风使舵】 jiàn fēng shǐ duò trim one's sails

【见怪】 jiànguài mind; take offence: 菜做得不好,请不要～。I hope you won't mind my poor cooking./ 批评得不对,可别～。Don't take offence if my criticism is incorrect.

【见怪不怪,其怪自败】 jiàn guài bù guài, qí guài zì bài face the fearful with no fears, and its fearfulness disappears

【见鬼】 jiànguǐ ①fantastic; preposterous; absurd: 种庄稼不除草不是～吗? Isn't it absurd to plant crops and not weed the fields?/ 手套怎么不见了? 真～! That's funny! What have I done with my gloves? ②go to hell

【见机】 jiànjī　as the opportunity arises; as befits the occasion; according to circumstances: ～行事 act according to circumstances; do as one sees fit

【见教】 jiànjiào　〈套〉favour me with your advice; instruct me: 有何～? Is there something you want to see me about?

【见解】 jiànjiě　view; opinion; understanding: 抱有不同～ hold different views/ 一篇很有～的文章 an article with original ideas/ 对这个问题他没有提出任何新的～。He didn't put forward any new ideas on the subject./ 这只是我个人的～。That's just my own opinion.

【见谅】 jiànliàng　〈书〉excuse me; forgive me: 务希～。I sincerely hope you'll excuse me.

【见猎心喜】 jiàn liè xīn xǐ　thrill to see one's favourite sport and itch to have a go

【见面】 jiànmiàn　meet; see: 他俩经常～。They see a lot of each other.

【见仁见智】 jiànrén-jiànzhì　different people, different views; opinions differ

【见世面】 jiàn shìmiàn　see the world; enrich one's experience: 经风雨,～ face the world and brave the storm; see life and stand its tests/ 这回到化工厂去参观,可见了世面了。The trip to the chemical works was a real eye-opener.

【见识】 jiànshi　① widen one's knowledge; enrich one's experience: 到各处走走,～～也是好的。It's not a bad idea to go around a bit and gain experience. ② experience; knowledge; sensibleness: 很～ widen one's knowledge; broaden one's horizons/ 他～很广。He's a man of wide experience./ 他那样对待你是不对的,你别和他一般～。He's behaved badly towards you, but a sensible person like you shouldn't want to take him up on it.

【见树不见林】 jiàn shù bù jiàn lín　not see the wood for the trees

【见所未见】 jiàn suǒ wèi jiàn　① see what one has never seen before ② never seen before; unprecedented

【见外】 jiànwài　regard sb. as an outsider: 你对我这样客气,倒有点～了。Please don't go to so much trouble about me, or I'll feel I'm being treated as a stranger./ 到了我这儿可别～。Just make yourself at home.

【见闻】 jiànwén　what one sees and hears; knowledge; information: 增长～ add to one's knowledge/ ～广 well-informed; knowledgeable

【见习】 jiànxí　learn on the job; be on probation

【见效】 jiànxiào　become effective; produce the desired result: 这药吃下去就～。This medicine produces an instant effect.

【见笑】 jiànxiào　① laugh at (me or us): 我刚开始学,您可别～。Now don't laugh at me. I'm only a beginner. ② incur ridicule (by one's poor performance): 写得不好,～,～。Excuse my poor writing.

【见义勇为】 jiàn yì yǒng wéi　ready to take up the cudgels for a just cause

【见异思迁】 jiàn yì sī qiān　change one's mind the moment one sees something new; be inconstant or irresolute

【见证】 jiànzhèng　witness; testimony ◇ ～人 eyewitness; witness

件* jiàn　① 〈量〉: 一～衬衫 a shirt/ 一～事 a matter; a thing/ 一～工作 a piece of work; a job/ 三～行李 three pieces of luggage ② 〔指可以一一计算的事物〕: 工～ workpiece/ 锻～ forged piece; forging/ 案～ (law) case ③ letter; correspondence; paper; document: 来～ a communication, document, etc. received/ 密～ confidential (或 classified) documents; secret papers

间 jiàn　① space in between; opening: 乘～ seize an opportunity; 亲密无～ closely united; on intimate terms ② separate: 黑白相～ chequered with black and white/ 晴～多云 fine with occasional clouds ③ sow discord: 离～ sow discord; drive a wedge between　　　另见 jiān

【间谍】 jiàndié　spy ◇ ～飞机 spy plane/ ～活动 espionage/ ～网 espionage network/ ～卫星 spy satellite

【间断】 jiànduàn　be disconnected; be interrupted: 他坚持锻炼,几年来从不～。He has kept up physical training for several years without interruption.

【间隔】 jiàngé　interval; intermission: 两次会议～才二十天。There was an interval of only twenty days between the two conferences./ 每两行树苗～三米。There is a space of three metres between each two rows of saplings./ 幼苗～匀整。The seedlings are evenly spaced.

【间或】 jiànhuò　occasionally; now and then; sometimes; once in a while

【间接】 jiànjiē　indirect; secondhand: 这消息我是～听来的。I heard the news indirectly.

建* jiàn　① build; construct; erect: ～电站 build a power station/ 新厂房已经～成。The new factory building has been completed./ ～桥工地 the construction site of the bridge/ 重～家园 rebuild one's homeland ② establish; set up: ～新功 make new contributions ③ propose; advocate: 我～一个议。I'd like to make a suggestion.

【建都】 jiàndū　found a capital; make (a place) the capital

【建国】 jiànguó　① found (或 establish) a state ② build up a country: 勤俭～ build up our country through diligence and frugality/ ～宏图 a grand project for national reconstruction

【建交】 jiànjiāo　establish diplomatic relations

【建军】 jiànjūn　① found an army ② army building

【建立】 jiànlì　build; establish; set up; found: ～外交关系 establish diplomatic relations

【建设】 jiànshè　build; construct

【建设性】 jiànshèxìng　constructive: ～的意见 constructive suggestions/ 起～的作用 play a constructive role

【建树】 jiànshù　make a contribution; contribute: 对发展体育事业有所～ contribute to the development of physical culture/ 人类认识史上的重大～ major attainments in the history of human knowledge

【建议】 jiànyì　① propose; suggest; recommend: 他们～休会。They propose that the meeting be adjourned./ 我～你多做点户外运动。I suggest you should have more outdoor exercise. ② proposal; suggestion; recommendation: 反～ counterproposal/ 合理化～ rationalization proposal

【建造】 jiànzào　build; construct; make

【建筑】 jiànzhù　① build; construct; erect: ～桥梁 construct a bridge/ ～高楼 erect a tall building/ ～铁路 build a railway ② building; structure; edifice: 古老的～ an ancient building/ 宏伟的～ a magnificent structure ③ architecture: 他是学现代～的。His speciality is modern architecture.

饯 jiàn　give a farewell dinner

【饯别】 jiànbié　give a farewell dinner: ～友人 give a friend a farewell dinner

【饯行】 jiànxíng　give a farewell dinner

剑* jiàn　sword; sabre: ～柄 the handle of a sword; hilt/ ～鞘 scabbard

【剑拔弩张】 jiànbá-nǔzhāng　with swords drawn and bows bent; at daggers drawn

荐 jiàn　① recommend ② 〈书〉grass; straw ③ 〈书〉straw mat

【荐举】 jiànjǔ　propose sb. for an office; recommend

贱* jiàn　① low-priced; inexpensive; cheap: ～卖 sell cheap ② lowly; humble: 贫～ poor and lowly ③ low-down; base; despicable: 下～ low-down; base ④ 〈谦〉my: ～恙 my illness

【贱骨头】 jiàngútou　〈骂〉miserable (或 contemptible) wretch

涧 jiàn　ravine; gully

舰 jiàn　warship; naval vessel; man-of-war

【舰队】 jiànduì　fleet; naval force

【舰艇】 jiàntǐng　naval ships and boats; naval vessels

【舰长】 jiànzhǎng　captain (of a warship)

【舰只】 jiànzhī warships; naval vessels: 海军~ naval vessels

监* jiàn an imperial office: 国子~ the Imperial College, the highest educational administration in feudal China 另见 jiān

健* jiàn ① healthy; strong ② strengthen; toughen; invigorate: ~胃 be good for the stomach/ ~脾 invigorate the function of the spleen ③ be strong in; be good at: ~谈 be a good talker
【健步】 jiànbù walk with vigorous strides: ~如飞 walk as if on wings; walk fast and vigorously
【健儿】 jiàn'ér ① valiant fighter ② good athlete: 乒坛~ skilful ping-pong players
【健将】 jiànjiàng master sportsman; top-notch player: 运动~ master sportsman/ 足球~ top-notch footballer
【健康】 jiànkāng ① health; physique: ~状况 state of health; physical condition/ 人民的~水平有了很大提高。The general level of the people's health has markedly improved. ② healthy; sound: 身体~ be in good health/ 祝你~! I wish you good health./ 运动正在~地发展。The movement is developing healthily./ 情况基本上是~的。The situation is basically sound. ◇ ~证明书 health certificate
【健美】 jiànměi strong and handsome; vigorous and graceful: ~的体操表演 a vigorous and graceful performance of callisthenics
【健全】 jiànquán ① sound; perfect: 身心~ sound in mind and body/ 头脑~的人 a person in his or her right mind ② strengthen; amplify; perfect: ~合理的规章制度 amplify necessary rules and regulations
【健身房】 jiànshēnfáng gymnasium; gym
【健谈】 jiàntán be a good talker; be a brilliant conversationalist
【健忘】 jiànwàng forgetful; having a bad memory ◇ ~症 amnesia
【健旺】 jiànwàng healthy and vigorous
【健在】 jiànzài 〈书〉 (of a person of advanced age) be still living and in good health

【健壮】 jiànzhuàng healthy and strong; robust: ~的小伙子 a robust young man

谏 jiàn 〈书〉 remonstrate with (one's superior or friend); expostulate with; admonish: ~止 plead with sb. not to do sth.; admonish against sth.

渐* jiàn gradually; by degrees: 天气~冷。The weather is getting cold.
【渐渐】 jiànjiàn 〈副〉 gradually; by degrees; little by little: 路上的行人~少了。The number of pedestrians gradually dwindled./ 雨~小了。The rain is beginning to let up.
【渐进】 jiànjìn advance gradually; progress step by step: 循序~ advance gradually in due order

溅 jiàn splash; spatter: ~一身泥 be spattered with mud/ 钢花四~ sparks of molten steel flying in all directions

践 jiàn ① trample; tread ② act on; carry out: ~诺 keep one's promise (或 word)
【践踏】 jiàntà tread on; trample underfoot: 请勿~草地。Keep off the grass.
【践约】 jiànyuē keep a promise; keep an appointment

毽 jiàn shuttlecock
【毽子】 jiànzi shuttlecock: 踢~ kick the shuttlecock (as a game)

鉴 jiàn ① ancient bronze mirror ② reflect; mirror: 水清可~ so clear that you can see your reflection in it. ③ warning; object lesson: 引以为~ take warning from it ④ inspect; scrutinize; examine: 请~核。Please examine. ⑤〔旧时书信套语，表示请对方看信〕 某先生台~ Dear Mr. so-and-so: May I draw your attention to the following.
【鉴别】 jiànbié distinguish; differentiate; discriminate: 有比较才能~。Only by comparing can one distinguish./ ~香花和毒草 distinguish fragrant flowers from poisonous weeds/ ~文物 make an appraisal of a cultural relic

【鉴定】 jiàndìng ①appraisal (of a person's strong and weak points): 毕业～ graduation appraisal ②appraise; identify; authenticate; determine: ～产品质量 appraise the quality of a product/ ～文物年代 determine the date of a cultural relic

【鉴戒】 jiànjiè warning; object lesson: 我们应当把这次挫折引为～。 We should take warning from this setback.

【鉴赏】 jiànshǎng appreciate: ～能力 ability to appreciate (painting, music, etc.); connoisseurship/ 对音乐颇有～力 have a good ear for music

【鉴于】 jiànyú in view of; seeing that: ～上述情况，我们提出以下建议。 In view of the above-mentioned facts, we wish to make the following proposals.

键 jiàn ①〈机〉key: 轴～ shaft key ②key (of a typewriter, piano, etc.)

【键盘】 jiànpán keyboard; fingerboard ◇ ～乐器 keyboard instrument

僭 jiàn 〈书〉overstep one's authority: ～越 overstep one's authority

箭 jiàn arrow
【箭靶子】 jiànbǎzi target for archery
【箭步】 jiànbù a sudden big stride forward
【箭在弦上】 jiàn zài xián shàng like an arrow on the bowstring — there can be no turning back

jiāng

江 jiāng river
【江河日下】 jiāng-hé rì xià go from bad to worse; be on the decline
【江湖】 jiānghú ①rivers and lakes ②all corners of the country: 流落～ live a vagabond life
【江湖】 jiānghu ①itinerant entertainers, quacks, etc. ②trade of such people ◇～骗子 swindler; charlatan/ ～医生 quack; mountebank/ ～艺人 itinerant entertainer
【江山】 jiāngshān ①rivers and mountains; land; landscape: ～如画 a picturesque landscape; beautiful scenery/ ～易改，本性难移。 It's easy to change rivers and mountains but hard to change a person's nature. ②country; state power: 打～ fight to win state power/ 坐～ rule the country
【江洋大盗】 jiāngyáng dàdào an infamous robber or pirate

将 jiāng ①〈书〉support; take; bring: ～幼弟而归 bring home one's little brother/ ～而之去 go off supporting each other ②take care of (one's health): ～养 rest; recuperate ③do sth.; handle (a matter): 慎重～事 handle a matter with care ④〈象棋〉check ⑤put sb. on the spot: 我们这一问可把他～住了。 Our question certainly put him on the spot. ⑥incite sb. to action; challenge; prod: 他已拿定主意不参加比赛了，你再～他也没用。 It's no use egging him on; he's made up his mind not to join in the tournament. ⑦〈介〉〔引进所凭借的工具、材料、方法等，意思跟"用"相同〕 with; by means of; by: ～功折罪 expiate one's crime by good deeds ⑧〈介〉〔宾语是后面动词的受事者，整个格式有处置的意思〕: ～他请来 invite him to come over ⑨be going to; be about to; will; shall: 船～启碇。 The ship is about to weigh anchor./ 我们～制定一个长远规划。 We are going to draw up a long-range plan./ ～欲取之；必先与之。 Give in order to take./ 必～取得更大胜利 be certain to win still greater victories ⑩〔叠用，表示"又"且"的意思〕: ～信～疑 half believing, half doubting ⑪〈助〉〔用在动词和表示趋向的补语之间〕: 唱～起来 start to sing/ 传～出去 (of news, etc.) spread abroad/ 赶～上去 hurry to catch up
另见 jiàng
【将错就错】 jiāng cuò jiù cuò leave a mistake uncorrected make the best of it
【将功补过】 jiāng gōng bǔ guò make amends for one's faults by good deeds

【将功赎罪】 jiāng gōng shú zuì atone for a crime by good deeds; expiate one's crime by good deeds
【将计就计】 jiāng jì jiù jì turn sb.'s trick against him; beat sb. at his own game
【将近】 jiāngjìn close to; nearly; almost: ～一百人 close to a hundred people/ ～完成 almost completed
【将就】 jiāngjiu make do with; make the best of; put up with: 这件大衣稍微短一点，你～着穿吧。 This coat may be a bit too short for you, but perhaps you could make do with it.
【将军】 jiāngjūn ①general ②〈象棋〉check ③put sb. on the spot; embarrass; challenge: 他们要我唱歌，这可将了我一军。 They embarrassed me by calling on me to sing.
【将来】 jiānglái future: 在不远的～ in the not too distant future; before long/ 在可以预见的～ in the foreseeable future
【将要】 jiāngyào be going to; will; shall: 他一到伦敦去工作。 He's going to work in London.

姜 jiāng ginger

浆 jiāng ①thick liquid: 糖～ syrup/ 纸～ pulp ②starch: ～衣服 starch clothes

僵 jiāng ①stiff; numb: 他的脚冻～了。 His feet were numb with cold. ②deadlocked: 他把事情搞～了。 He's brought things to a deadlock.
【僵持】 jiāngchí (of both parties) refuse to budge: 双方～好久。 For quite some time, neither party was willing to budge from its original position.
【僵化】 jiānghuà become rigid; ossify: 思想～ a rigid (或 ossified) way of thinking
【僵局】 jiāngjú deadlock; impasse; stalemate: 打破～ break a deadlock/ 谈判陷入～。 The negotiations have reached an impasse.
【僵尸】 jiāngshī corpse: 政治～ a political mummy
【僵死】 jiāngsǐ dead; ossified
【僵硬】 jiāngyìng ①stiff: 觉得四肢～ feel stiff in the limbs ②rigid; inflexible: ～的公式 a rigid formula

缰 jiāng reins; halter
【缰绳】 jiāngsheng reins; halter

疆 jiāng boundary; border
【疆场】 jiāngchǎng battlefield
【疆界】 jiāngjiè boundary; border
【疆土】 jiāngtǔ territory
【疆域】 jiāngyù territory; domain

jiǎng

讲 jiǎng ①speak; say; tell: ～英语 speak English/ ～故事 tell stories/ 给孩子们～村史 tell the children about the history of the village/ ～几句话 say a few words/ ～几点意见 make a few remarks/ ～的是一套，做的是另一套 say one thing and do another ②explain; make clear; interpret: 把道理～清楚 state the reasons clearly/ 我来～～今天开会的目的。 Let me explain the purpose of today's meeting./ 这本书是～气象的。 This is a book about meteorology./ 这个字有几个～法。 This word may be interpreted in different ways. ③discuss; negotiate: ～条件 negotiate the terms; insist on the fulfilment of certain conditions ④stress; pay attention to; be particular about: ～卫生 pay attention to hygiene/ ～质量 stress quality/ ～排场 go in for ostentation and extravagance; go in for showy display; be ostentatious ⑤as far as sth. is concerned; when it comes to; as to; as regards: ～干劲，谁也比不上她。 When it comes to drive, she's got more than any of us.
【讲稿】 jiǎnggǎo the draft or text of a speech; lecture notes
【讲和】 jiǎnghé make peace; settle a dispute; become reconciled

【讲话】 jiǎnghuà ① speak; talk; address: 对着话筒~ speak into a microphone/ 他在会上讲了话。He spoke at the meeting. 或 He addressed the meeting. ② speech; talk: 鼓舞人心的~ an inspiring speech ③ [多用于书名] guide; introduction: 《政治经济学~》 A Guide to Political Economy

【讲价】 jiǎngjià bargain; haggle over the price

【讲解】 jiǎngjiě explain

【讲究】 jiǎngjiu ① be particular about; pay attention to; stress; strive for: 不~吃穿 not be too fastidious about one's food or clothing/ ~卫生，减少疾病 pay attention to hygiene and reduce the incidence of disease/ ~实际效果 stress practical results/ 写文章一定要~逻辑。In writing one must have regard for logic. ② exquisite; tasteful: 宾馆布置得很。。The guesthouse is tastefully furnished. ③ careful study: 翻译技巧大有~。The art of translation calls for careful study. 或 Translation is quite an art.

【讲课】 jiǎngkè teach; lecture

【讲理】 jiǎnglǐ ① reason with sb.; argue: 我们跟他~去。Let's go and argue it out with him. ② listen (或 be amenable) to reason; be reasonable; be sensible: 蛮不~ be utterly unreasonable; be impervious to reason

【讲明】 jiǎngmíng explain; make clear; state explicitly: ~我们的立场 explain (或 state) our stand

【讲评】 jiǎngpíng comment on and appraise: ~学生的作业 comment on the students' work

【讲情】 jiǎngqíng intercede; plead for sb.

【讲求】 jiǎngqiú be particular about; pay attention to; stress; strive for: ~效率 strive for efficiency

【讲师】 jiǎngshī lecturer

【讲授】 jiǎngshòu lecture; instruct; teach ◇ ~提纲 an outline for a lecture; teaching notes

【讲述】 jiǎngshù tell about; give an account of; narrate; relate: ~自己的家史 tell (或 relate) one's family history

【讲台】 jiǎngtái platform; dais; rostrum

【讲坛】 jiǎngtán ① platform; rostrum ② forum

【讲堂】 jiǎngtáng lecture room; classroom

【讲演】 jiǎngyǎn lecture; speech

【讲义】 jiǎngyì (mimeographed or printed) teaching materials

【讲座】 jiǎngzuò a course of lectures: 英语广播~ English lessons over the radio; English by radio

奖*
jiǎng ① encourage; praise; reward: ~许 praise; give encouragement to/ 有功者~。Those who have gained merit will be rewarded. ② award; prize; reward: 发~ give awards; give prizes/ 得~ win a prize

【奖杯】 jiǎngbēi cup (as a prize)

【奖金】 jiǎngjīn money award; bonus; premium

【奖励】 jiǎnglì encourage and reward; award; reward: ~模范工作者 give awards to model workers/ 物质~ material reward/ ~发明创造 encourage innovations by giving awards

【奖品】 jiǎngpǐn prize; award; trophy

【奖券】 jiǎngquàn lottery ticket

【奖赏】 jiǎngshǎng award; reward

【奖学金】 jiǎngxuéjīn scholarship; exhibition

【奖掖】 jiǎngyè <书> reward and promote; encourage by promoting and rewarding

【奖章】 jiǎngzhāng medal; decoration

【奖状】 jiǎngzhuàng certificate of merit

桨*
jiǎng oar

蒋
Jiǎng a surname

jiàng

匠*
jiàng craftsman; artisan: 能工巧~ skilled craftsmen/ 铁~ blacksmith/ 石~ stonemason

【匠人】 jiàngrén artisan; craftsman

【匠心】 jiàngxīn <书> ingenuity; craftsmanship: 独具~ show ingenuity; have great originality

降*
jiàng fall; drop; lower: ~雨 a fall of rain; rainfall/ ~价 lower prices/ 温度~到摄氏零下十度。The temperature dropped to minus ten degrees centigrade.
另见 xiáng

【降低】 jiàngdī reduce; cut down; drop; lower: ~生产成本 reduce production costs/ ~原料消耗 cut down the consumption of raw materials/ 价格~了，但质量并未~。The price is lower, but the quality is the same.

【降级】 jiàngjí ① reduce to a lower rank; demote ② send (a student) to a lower grade

【降临】 jiànglín <书> befall; arrive; come: 夜色~。Night fell.

【降落】 jiàngluò descend; land: 大型飞机的起飞和~ the take-off and landing of big aircraft/ 强迫~ forced landing/ 垂直~ vertical landing ◇ ~场 landing field/ ~辅助设备 landing aid/ ~伞 parachute/ ~设备 landing equipment

【降旗】 jiàngqí lower a flag

【降生】 jiàngshēng <书> (of the founder of a religion, etc.) be born

将*
jiàng ① general ② commander in chief, the chief piece in Chinese chess ③ <书> command; lead: ~兵 command troops
另见 jiāng

【将官】 jiàngguān <口> high-ranking military officer; general

【将领】 jiànglǐng high-ranking military officer; general

【将士】 jiàngshì <书> officers and men

强*
jiàng stubborn; unyielding: 倔~ unbending; unyielding
另见 qiáng; qiǎng

【强嘴】 jiàngzuǐ reply defiantly; answer back; talk back

酱*
jiàng ① a thick sauce made from soya beans, flour, etc. ② cooked or pickled in soy sauce: ~肉 pork cooked in soy sauce; braised pork seasoned with soy sauce ③ sauce; paste; jam: 苹果~ apple jam/ 番茄~ tomato sauce; ketchup

【酱油】 jiàngyóu soy sauce; soy

【酱园】 jiàngyuán a shop making and selling sauce, pickles, etc.; sauce and pickle shop

jiāo

交*
jiāo ① hand over; give up; deliver: ~还 give back; return/ 把任务~给我们实验室吧。Assign the task to our laboratory. ② (of places or periods of time) meet; join: 井冈山位于四县之~。The Jinggang Mountains stand where the boundaries of four counties meet./ 春夏之~ when spring is changing into summer ③ reach (a certain hour or season): ~冬以后 when winter has set in/ ~了好运气 have good luck ④ cross; intersect: 圆周内两直径必相~。Any two diameters of a circle intersect each other. ⑤ associate with: ~朋友 make friends ⑥ friend; acquaintance; friendship; relationship: 一面之~ a passing (或 casual) acquaintance/ 知~ bosom friend/ 建~ establish diplomatic relations/ 绝~ sever relations; break off relations ⑦ have sexual intercourse ⑧ mate; breed: 杂~ crossbreed ⑨ mutual; reciprocal; each other: ~换 exchange ⑩ together; simultaneous: 内外~困 be beset with difficulties at home and abroad ⑪ business transaction; deal; bargain: 成~ strike a bargain; conclude a transaction; clinch a deal ⑫ fall: 他脚一滑，摔了一大~。He slipped and fell heavily.

【交白卷】 jiāo báijuàn ① hand in a blank examination paper ② completely fail to accomplish a task: 我们得把情况摸清楚，要不回去就得~。We must find out exactly how things stand here, or we'll have nothing to report.

【交兵】 jiāobīng <书> (of two or more parties) be at war; wage war

【交叉】 jiāochā ① intersect; cross; crisscross: 两条铁路在此～。The two railways cross here. ② overlapping: 两个提案中～的部分 the overlapping parts of the two proposals ③ alternate; stagger: ～进行 do alternately ◇ ～点 intersect

【交差】 jiāochāi report to the leadership after accomplishing a task: 你不开收据，我们回去怎么～? If you don't give us a receipt, how are we going to account for it?

【交出】 jiāochū surrender; hand over: ～武器 surrender one's weapons

【交错】 jiāocuò interlock; crisscross: 沟渠～。Ditches and canals crisscross.

【交代】 jiāodài ① hand over: ～工作 hand over work to one's successor; brief one's successor on handing over work ② explain; make clear; brief; tell: ～政策 explain policy/ ～任务 assign and explain a task; brief sb. on his task/ 作者对此未作进一步～。The author makes no further reference to this. ③ account for; justify oneself: 这个问题你怎么～? How are you going to account for this?/ ～不过去 be unable to justify an action ④ confess: ～罪行 confess a crime/ 彻底～ make a clean breast of 又作"交待"

【交锋】 jiāofēng cross swords; engage in a battle or contest: 敌人不敢和我们正面～。The enemy didn't dare to risk a frontal engagement with us./ 第一次大～ the first great trial of strength

【交付】 jiāofù ① pay: ～租金 pay rent ② hand over; deliver; consign: ～表决 put to the vote/ 新建的楼房已经～使用。The new building has been made available to the users.

【交媾】 jiāogòu sexual intercourse

【交好】 jiāohǎo (of people or states) be on friendly terms

【交换】 jiāohuàn exchange; swop: ～意见 exchange views; compare notes/ ～场地〈体〉change of courts, goals or ends/ 商品～ exchange of commodities/ 用小麦～大米 barter wheat for rice

【交货】 jiāohuò delivery: 即期～ prompt delivery/ 近期～ near delivery/ 远期～ forward delivery/ 分批～ partial delivery

【交集】 jiāojí (of different feelings) be mixed; occur simultaneously: 悲喜～ mixed feelings of grief and joy; joy and sorrow intermingled

【交际】 jiāojì social intercourse; communication: 语言是人们～的工具。Language is the means by which people communicate with each other./ 他不善于～。He is not a good mixer./ 她～很广。She has a large circle of acquaintances. ◇ ～花 social butterfly/ ～舞 ballroom dancing; social dancing

【交加】 jiāojiā〈书〉(of two things) accompany each other; occur simultaneously: 雷电～ lightning accompanied by peals of thunder; there was thunder and lightning/ 风雪～ a raging snowstorm/ 悔恨～ regret mingled with self-reproach/ 贫病～ be plagued by both poverty and illness

【交接】 jiāojiē ① join; connect: 夏秋～的季节 when summer is changing into autumn ② hand over and take over: ～班 relief of a shift ③ associate with: 他所～的朋友 the people he associates with; the friends he has made ◇ ～手续(仪式) handing over procedure (ceremony)

【交界】 jiāojiè (of two or more places) have a common boundary: 三省～的地方 a place where three provinces meet; the juncture of three provinces

【交卷】 jiāojuàn ① hand in an examination paper ② fulfil one's task; carry out an assignment

【交流】 jiāoliú ① exchange; interflow; interchange: ～经验 exchange experience; draw on each other's experience/ 城乡物资～ flow of goods and materials between city and country/ 国际文化～ international cultural exchange/ 经济和技术～ economic and technical interchange

【交纳】 jiāonà pay (to the state or an organization); hand in: ～会费 pay membership dues

【交配】 jiāopèi mating; copulation ◇ ～期 mating season

【交情】 jiāoqing friendship; friendly relations: 老～ long-standing friendship/ 讲～ do things for the sake of friend-ship/ 他们两人～不错。The two of them are on very good terms.

【交融】 jiāoróng blend; mingle: 水乳～ blend as well as milk and water; be in perfect harmony

【交涉】 jiāoshè negotiate; make representations: 办～ carry on negotiations with; take up a matter with/ 口头～ verbal representations/ 向有关方面进行过多次～ have made many representations to the quarters concerned; have more than once approached the departments concerned/ 经过～，问题解决了。The problem was solved through negotiations.

【交手】 jiāoshǒu fight hand to hand; be engaged in a hand-to-hand fight; come to grips

【交谈】 jiāotán talk with each other; converse; chat: 自由～ a freewheeling conversation/ 他们就广泛的问题进行了友好的～。They had a friendly conversation on a wide range of subjects.

【交替】 jiāotì ① supersede; replace: 新旧～。The new replaces the old. ② alternately; in turn: ～演奏两国乐曲 play music of the two countries alternately

【交通】 jiāotōng ① traffic; communications: 公路～ highway traffic/ 陆上～ land traffic/ 市区～ urban traffic/ ～便利 have transport facilities/ 妨碍～ interfere with the traffic ② liaison; liaison man
◇ ～安全 traffic safety/ ～标线 traffic marking/ ～标志 traffic sign/ ～部 the Ministry of Communications/ ～干线 main line of communication; main communications artery/ ～规则 traffic regulations/ ～警 traffic police/ ～量 volume of traffic/ ～事故 traffic (或 road) accident/ ～网 network of communication lines/ ～信号 traffic signal/ ～阻塞 traffic jam (或 block)

【交头接耳】 jiāotóu-jiē'ěr speak in each other's ears; whisper to each other

【交往】 jiāowǎng association; contact: 我和他～，得益不少。I have gained a lot by associating with him./ 在同各国人民的～中，我们学习到不少有用的东西。In our contacts with people of other countries, we have learned many useful things.

【交恶】 jiāowù fall foul of each other; become enemies

【交响乐】 jiāoxiǎngyuè〈乐〉symphony; symphonic music ◇ ～队 symphony orchestra; philharmonic orchestra

【交椅】 jiāoyǐ ① an ancient folding chair ② armchair: 坐第二把～ occupy the second highest post; be second in command

【交易】 jiāoyì business; deal; trade; transaction: 现款～ cash transaction/ 赊帐～ credit transaction/ 做成一笔～ make a deal/ 商品～会 trade fair; commodities fair

【交易所】 jiāoyìsuǒ exchange: 证券～ stock exchange/ 商品～ commodity exchange

【交谊】 jiāoyì〈书〉friendship; friendly relations

【交游】 jiāoyóu〈书〉make friends: ～甚广 have a large circle of friends

【交战】 jiāozhàn be at war; fight; wage war: ～状态 state of war; belligerency/ ～的一方 a belligerent/ ～双方 the two belligerent parties ◇ ～国 belligerent countries (或 states, nations)

【交帐】 jiāozhàng ① hand over the accounts ② account for: 把小孩冻坏了，我们怎么向他母亲～? If the child catches a chill, what are we going to say to its mother?

【交织】 jiāozhī interweave; intertwine; mingle: 惊异和喜悦的感情～在一起。Joy mingled with surprise.

郊* jiāo suburbs; outskirts

【郊区】 jiāoqū suburban district; suburbs; outskirts

【郊外】 jiāowài the countryside around a city; outskirts

【郊游】 jiāoyóu outing; excursion

浇* jiāo ① pour liquid on; sprinkle water on: 大雨～得他全身都湿透了。He was drenched with rain. ② irrigate; water: ～花 water flowers

【浇灌】 jiāoguàn ① water; irrigate ② pour: ～混凝土 pour concrete

娇* jiāo ① tender; lovely; charming: 嫩红～绿 tender

blossoms and delicate leaves ② fragile; frail; delicate: 这孩子身体太～。The child's health is fragile. ③ squeamish; finicky: 她才走二公里就叫苦，未免太～了。She started grumbling after walking only 2 km. She's really too soft. ④ pamper; spoil: 别把你的小女儿～坏了！Don't pamper your little daughter.

【娇滴滴】jiāodīdī delicately pretty; affectedly sweet

【娇惯】jiāoguàn pamper; coddle; spoil: ～孩子 pamper a child

【娇媚】jiāomèi ① coquettish ② sweet and charming

【娇嫩】jiāonèn ① tender and lovely ② fragile; delicate: ～的幼苗 delicate seedlings/ ～的身子 delicate health

【娇气】jiāoqì ① fragile; delicate: 这种菜太～，我们这儿种不了。This kind of vegetable's too delicate to grow here./ 你的身子太～了，淋这么几滴雨就感冒。You're really too delicate, catching cold from just a few drops of rain. ② squeamish; finicky: 粗粮细粮一样吃，别那么～。Coarse grain is just as good as fine. Don't be so finicky./ 去掉～ get rid of squeamishness

【娇生惯养】jiāoshēng-guànyǎng pampered since childhood

【娇小玲珑】jiāoxiǎo línglóng delicate and exquisite

【娇艳】jiāoyàn delicate and charming; tender and beautiful: ～的桃花 delicate and charming peach blossoms

【娇纵】jiāozòng indulge (a child); pamper; spoil

骄* jiāo proud; arrogant; conceited: ～兵必败。An army puffed up with pride is bound to lose./ 胜不～，败不馁 not be dizzy with success, nor discouraged by failure

【骄傲】jiāo'ào ① arrogant; conceited: ～自大 swollen with pride; conceited and arrogant/ 我们永远不～，不能翘尾巴。We should never become arrogant and cocky. ② be proud; take pride in: 老科学家为青年同事的成就感到～。The old scientist takes pride in the achievements of his young colleagues.

【骄横】jiāohèng arrogant and imperious; overbearing

【骄矜】jiāojīn 〈书〉self-important; proud; haughty: 他为人谦逊，毫无～之态。He is modest, and never puts on airs.

【骄气】jiāoqì overbearing airs; arrogance

【骄奢淫逸】jiāoshē-yínyì lordly, luxury-loving, loose-living and idle; wallowing in luxury and pleasure; extravagant and dissipated

【骄纵】jiāozòng arrogant and wilful

胶* jiāo ① glue; gum ② stick with glue; glue ③ gluey; sticky; gummy ④ rubber

【胶布】jiāobù ① rubberized fabric ② 〈口〉adhesive plaster ◇ ～带 〈电〉rubberized tape; adhesive tape

【胶合】jiāohé glue together; veneer ◇ ～板 plywood; veneer board

【胶结】jiāojié glued; cemented ◇ ～材料 cementing material/ ～剂 cementing agent

【胶卷】jiāojuǎn roll film; film

【胶片】jiāopiàn film

【胶鞋】jiāoxié ① rubber overshoes; galoshes; rubbers ② rubber-soled shoes; tennis shoes; sneakers

教* jiāo teach; instruct: 互～互学 teach and learn from each other/ 她～我们做实验。She taught us how to conduct experiments.
另见 jiào

【教书】jiāoshū teach school; teach: 在小学～ teach in a primary school/ ～育人 impart knowledge and educate people

蛟 jiāo flood dragon, a mythical creature capable of invoking storms and floods

【蛟龙】jiāolóng 见"蛟"

焦 jiāo ① burnt; scorched; charred: 饼烤～了。The pancake is burnt./ 树被烧～了。The trees are charred. ② coke: 炼～ coking ③ worried; anxious: 心～ worried

【焦点】jiāodiǎn ① 〈物〉focal point; focus ② central issue; point at issue: 这就是问题的～。That is the heart of the matter./ 争论的 ～ the point at issue

【焦黑】jiāohēi burned black

【焦黄】jiāohuáng sallow; brown: 脸色～ a sallow face

【焦急】jiāojí anxious; worried: 大家都在～地等着他。Everyone is waiting anxiously for him.

【焦枯】jiāokū shrivelled; dried up; withered

【焦虑】jiāolù feel anxious; have worries and misgivings

【焦头烂额】jiāotóu-làn'é badly battered; in a terrible fix: 敌军被打得～，狼狈逃窜。Badly battered, the enemy fled in utter confusion.

【焦土】jiāotǔ scorched earth — ravages of war ◇ ～政策 scorched earth policy

椒* jiāo any of several hot spice plants: 辣～ chili; red pepper; 胡～ pepper

鲛 jiāo shark

蕉* jiāo any of several broadleaf plants: 香～ banana

礁 jiāo reef: 触～ strike a reef; run up on a rock

【礁石】jiāoshí reef; rock

jiáo

嚼 jiáo masticate; chew; munch: 细～慢咽 chew carefully and swallow slowly; chew one's food well before swallowing it
另见 jué

【嚼舌】jiáoshé ① wag one's tongue; chatter; gossip: 别在背后～。Don't gossip behind people's backs. ② argue meaninglessly; squabble: 没功夫跟你～。I've got no time to argue with you. 又作"嚼舌头""嚼舌根"

jiǎo

角* jiǎo ① horn: 牛～ ox horn/ 鹿～ antler ② bugle; horn: 号～ bugle ③ sth. in the shape of a horn: 非洲之～ the Horn of Africa ④ corner: 墙～ corner (of a wall)/ 眼～ corner of the eye ⑤ 〈数〉angle: 锐（钝）～ acute (obtuse) angle/ 直～ right angle ⑥ promontory; headland: 好望～ the Cape of Good Hope
另见 jué

【角度】jiǎodù ① 〈数〉angle: 撑条和横梁之间～太大。The brace is at too big an angle with the beam. ② point of view; angle: 从各个～来研究问题 examine the matter from various angles

【角落】jiǎoluò corner; nook: 在院子的一个～里 in a corner of the courtyard/ 找遍每一个～ search every nook and cranny; search high and low

侥 jiǎo

【侥幸】jiǎoxìng lucky; by luck; by a fluke: ～取胜 gain victory by sheer good luck; win by a fluke/ ～心理 the idea of leaving things to chance; trusting to luck

佼 jiǎo 〈书〉handsome; beautiful

【佼佼】jiǎojiǎo 〈书〉above average; outstanding

狡* jiǎo crafty; foxy; cunning: ～计 crafty trick; ruse

【狡辩】jiǎobiàn quibble; indulge in sophistry

【狡猾】jiǎohuá sly; crafty; cunning; tricky

【狡赖】jiǎolài deny (by resorting to sophistry): 证据确凿，不容～。It's no use denying it, the evidence is conclusive.

【狡黠】jiǎoxiá 〈书〉sly; crafty; cunning

【狡诈】jiǎozhà deceitful; crafty; cunning

绞 jiǎo ① twist; wring; entangle: 把几股铁丝～在一起 twist several strands of wire together/ 把衣服～干 wring out wet clothes/ 心如刀～ feel as if a knife were being twisted in one's heart/ 尽脑汁 rack one's brains/ 许

多问题～在一起，闹不清楚。With so many things mixed up it's hard to make out what's what. ② wind: ～动辘轳 wind a windlass ③ hang by the neck
【绞刑】jiǎoxíng　death by hanging

饺 jiǎo　dumpling: 蒸～ steamed dumplings
【饺子】jiǎozi　dumpling (with meat and vegetable stuffing)

皎 jiǎo　clear and bright: ～月当空。A bright moon hung in the sky.
【皎皎】jiǎojiǎo　very clear and bright; glistening white: ～者易污。The immaculate stains easily. 或 The immaculate is easily sullied.
【皎洁】jiǎojié　(of moonlight) bright and clear

脚* jiǎo　① foot: 赤～ barefoot ② base; foot: 墙～ the foot of a wall/ 山～ the foot of a hill ③ 〈方〉 leg
【脚步】jiǎobù　step; pace: 加快～ quicken one's pace ◇ ～声 footfall; footsteps
【脚跟】jiǎogēn　heel: 站稳～ stand firm; gain a firm foothold
【脚尖】jiǎojiān　the tip of a toe; tiptoe: 踮着～走 walk on tiptoe
【脚力】jiǎolì　strength of one's legs: 他一天能走一百公里，～真好。He's really got strong legs to be able to walk 100 km a day.
【脚踏车】jiǎotàchē　〈方〉 bicycle
【脚踏两只船】jiǎo tà liǎng zhī chuán　straddle two boats—have a foot in either camp
【脚踏实地】jiǎo tà shídì　have one's feet planted on solid ground — earnest and down-to-earth: 既要有远大的理想，又要～地干 have both an ambitious goal and a down-to-earth style of work
【脚印】jiǎoyìn　footprint; footmark; track: 侦察兵在雪地上发现了可疑的～。The scouts discovered suspicious footprints in the snow.
【脚指甲】jiǎozhǐjiɑ　toenail
【脚趾】jiǎozhǐ　toe
【脚注】jiǎozhù　footnote

矫 jiǎo　① rectify; straighten out; correct ② strong; brave: ～若游龙 as powerful as a flying dragon; as strong and brave as a lion ③ pretend; feign; dissemble: ～命 counterfeit an order; issue false orders
【矫健】jiǎojiàn　strong and vigorous: ～的步伐 vigorous strides
【矫捷】jiǎojié　vigorous and nimble; brisk
【矫揉造作】jiǎoróu zàozuò　affected; artificial: ～的姿态 affected manners
【矫枉过正】jiǎo wǎng guò zhèng　exceed the proper limits in righting a wrong; overcorrect
【矫正】jiǎozhèng　correct; put right; rectify: ～发音 correct sb.'s pronunciation mistakes/ ～偏差 correct a deviation/ ～口吃 correct a stammer/ ～视力 correct defects of vision

搅 jiǎo　① stir; mix: 把粥～一～ give the porridge a stir ② disturb; annoy: 她在工作，别～她。She's working. Don't disturb her.
【搅动】jiǎodòng　mix; stir: 拿棍子～灰浆 stir the plaster with a stick
【搅混】jiǎohun　〈口〉 mix; blend; mingle
【搅和】jiǎohuo　① mix; blend; mingle: 这是两码事，别～在一起。They are two different matters. Don't mix them up. ② mess up; spoil: 事情都让他～糟了。He's messed everything up. 或 He's made a mess of everything.
【搅乱】jiǎoluàn　confuse; throw into disorder: 警惕敌人～我们的阵线 be on the alert and not let the enemy create confusion in our ranks

剿 jiǎo　send armed forces to suppress; put down: ～匪 suppress bandits
另见 chāo
【剿灭】jiǎomiè　exterminate; wipe out

缴* jiǎo　① pay; hand over; hand in: ～税 pay taxes/ 上～ turn over (或 in) to the higher authorities ② capture: 他们～了三挺机枪。They captured three machine guns./ ～枪不杀! Lay down your arms and we'll spare your lives!
【缴获】jiǎohuò　capture; seize: ～很多战利品 seize a lot of booty/ 一切～要归公。Turn in everything captured.
【缴纳】jiǎonà　见 "交纳" jiāonà
【缴械】jiǎoxiè　① disarm ② surrender one's weapons; lay down one's arms: ～投降 lay down one's arms and surrender

jiào

叫* jiào　① cry; shout: 大～一声 give a loud cry; shout; cry out loudly/ 狗～ bark/ 羊～ bleat/ 汽笛在～。The steam whistle is blowing. ② call; greet: 外边有人～你。Somebody outside is calling you./ 你的电话～通了。Your call has been put through./ 这孩子腼腆，不爱～人。The child is shy and doesn't like to greet people. ③ hire; order: ～一个出租汽车 hire (或 call) a taxi/ ～二百公斤煤 order 200 kg of coal/ ～菜 order dishes (at a restaurant) ④ name; call: 人们～他小张。People call him Xiao Zhang./ 他～什么名儿? What's his name?/ 这棉花长得真～棒。That's what I call a really good crop of cotton./ 这能～虚心接受批评么? Can this be called readiness to accept criticism? ⑤ ask; order: ～他进来么? Shall I ask him (to come) in?/ 医生～他卧床休息。The doctor ordered her to stay in bed. ⑥ 〈介〉〔用在被动式里引进主动者〕～你猜对了。You've guessed right./ 你～雨淋了吗? Did you get wet?
【叫喊】jiàohǎn　shout; yell; howl
【叫好】jiàohǎo　applaud; shout "Bravo!"; shout "Well done!"
【叫唤】jiàohuan　cry out; call out: 疼得直～ cry out with pain/ 咬紧牙关, 一声也不～ clench one's teeth and not utter a sound
【叫苦】jiàokǔ　complain of hardship or suffering; moan and groan: 暗暗～ groan inwardly/ ～不迭 pour out endless grievances
【叫骂】jiàomà　shout curses
【叫卖】jiàomài　cry one's wares; peddle; hawk: 沿街～ hawk one's wares in the streets
【叫门】jiàomén　call at the door to be let in
【叫屈】jiàoqū　complain of being wronged; protest against an injustice
【叫嚷】jiàorǎng　shout; howl; clamour
【叫嚣】jiàoxiāo　clamour; raise a hue and cry: 发出战争～ clamour for war/ 大肆～ raise a terrific hue and cry; raise a hullabaloo
【叫醒】jiàoxǐng　wake up; awaken
【叫座】jiàozuò　draw a large audience; draw well; appeal to the audience
【叫做】jiàozuò　be called; be known as: 这种机器～起重机。This machine is called a crane.

觉* jiào　sleep: 睡一～ have a sleep/ 午～ midday nap
另见 jué

校* jiào　check; proofread; collate
另见 xiào
【校订】jiàodìng　check against the authoritative text
【校对】jiàoduì　① proofread; proof ② proofreader ③ check against a standard; calibrate: 一切计量器都必须～合格才可以出厂。All measuring instruments must be calibrated before leaving the factory.
【校样】jiàoyàng　proof sheet; proof: 已看完～ have read the proofs
【校阅】jiàoyuè　read and revise
【校正】jiàozhèng　proofread and correct; rectify: ～错字 correct misprints

较* jiào　① compare: 工作～前更为努力 work even

harder than before/ ～一～劲儿 have a trial of strength ②comparatively; relatively; fairly; quite; rather: ～好 fairly good; quite good/ ～差 relatively poor/ 有～大的进步 have made considerable progress ③ clear; obvious; marked: 二者～然不同。There is a marked difference between the two. ④ dispute: 锱铢必～ quibble over every penny; dispute over every trifle

【较量】 jiàoliàng ① measure one's strength with; have a contest; have a trial (或 test) of strength: 经过反复的～ after repeated trials of strength ② haggle; argue; dispute

轿 jiào sedan (chair)

【轿车】 jiàochē ① 〈旧〉 (horse-drawn) carriage ② bus or car: 大～ bus; coach/ 小～ car; limousine; sedan

【轿子】 jiàozi sedan (chair)

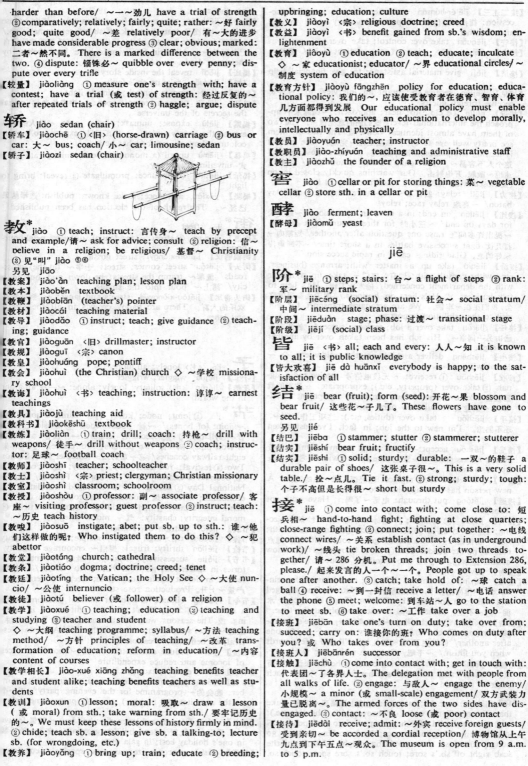

教* jiào ① teach; instruct: 言传身～ teach by precept and example/请～ ask for advice; consult ② religion: 信～ believe in a religion; be religious/ 基督～ Christianity ③ "见"叫" jiào ⑤⑥

另见 jiào

【教案】 jiào'àn teaching plan; lesson plan

【教本】 jiàoběn textbook

【教鞭】 jiàobiān (teacher's) pointer

【教材】 jiàocái teaching material

【教导】 jiàodǎo ① instruct; teach; give guidance ② teaching; guidance

【教官】 jiàoguān 〈旧〉 drillmaster; instructor

【教规】 jiàoguī 〈宗〉 canon

【教皇】 jiàohuáng pope; pontiff

【教会】 jiàohuì (the Christian) church ◇ ～学校 missionary school

【教诲】 jiàohuì 〈书〉 teaching; instruction: 谆谆～ earnest teachings

【教具】 jiàojù teaching aid

【教科书】 jiàokēshū textbook

【教练】 jiàoliàn ① train; drill; coach: 持枪～ drill with weapons/ 徒手～ drill without weapons ② coach; instructor: 足球～ football coach

【教师】 jiàoshī teacher; schoolteacher

【教士】 jiàoshì 〈宗〉 priest; clergyman; Christian missionary

【教室】 jiàoshì classroom; schoolroom

【教授】 jiàoshòu ① professor: 副～ associate professor; 客座～ visiting professor; guest professor ② instruct; teach: ～历史 teach history

【教唆】 jiàosuō instigate; abet; put sb. up to sth.: 谁～他们这样做的呢? Who instigated them to do this? ◇ ～犯 abettor

【教堂】 jiàotáng church; cathedral

【教条】 jiàotiáo dogma; doctrine; creed; tenet

【教廷】 jiàotíng the Vatican; the Holy See ◇ ～大使 nuncio/ ～公使 internuncio

【教徒】 jiàotú believer (或 follower) of a religion

【教学】 jiàoxué ① teaching; education ② teaching and studying ③ teacher and student ◇ ～大纲 teaching programme; syllabus/ ～方法 teaching method/ ～方针 principles of teaching/ ～改革 transformation of education; reform in education/ ～内容 content of courses

【教学相长】 jiào-xué xiāng zhǎng teaching benefits teacher and student alike; teaching benefits teachers as well as students

【教训】 jiàoxun ① lesson; moral: 吸取～ draw a lesson (或 moral) from sth.; take warning from sth./ 要牢记历史的～ We must keep these lessons of history firmly in mind. ② chide; teach sb. a lesson; give sb. a talking-to; lecture sb. (for wrongdoing, etc.)

【教养】 jiàoyǎng ① bring up; train; educate ② breeding;

upbringing; education; culture

【教义】 jiàoyì 〈宗〉 religious doctrine; creed

【教益】 jiàoyì 〈书〉 benefit gained from sb.'s wisdom; enlightenment

【教育】 jiàoyù ① education ② teach; educate; inculcate ◇ ～家 educationist; educator/ ～界 educational circles/ ～制度 system of education

【教育方针】 jiàoyù fāngzhēn policy for education; educational policy: 我们的～, 应该使受教育者在德育、智育、体育几方面都得到发展 Our educational policy must enable everyone who receives an education to develop morally, intellectually and physically

【教员】 jiàoyuán teacher; instructor

【教职员】 jiào-zhíyuán teaching and administrative staff

【教主】 jiàozhǔ the founder of a religion

窖 jiào ① cellar or pit for storing things: 菜～ vegetable cellar ② store sth. in a cellar or pit

酵 jiào ferment; leaven

【酵母】 jiàomǔ yeast

jiē

阶* jiē ① steps; stairs: 台～ a flight of steps ② rank: 军～ military rank

【阶层】 jiēcéng (social) stratum: 社会～ social stratum/ 中间～ intermediate stratum

【阶段】 jiēduàn stage; phase: 过渡～ transitional stage

【阶级】 jiējí (social) class

皆 jiē 〈书〉 all; each and every: 人人～知 it is known to all; it is public knowledge

【皆大欢喜】 jiē dà huānxǐ everybody is happy; to the satisfaction of all

结* jiē bear (fruit); form (seed): 开花～果 blossom and bear fruit/ 这些花～子儿了。These flowers have gone to seed.

另见 jié

【结巴】 jiēba ① stammer; stutter ② stammerer; stutterer

【结实】 jiēshí bear fruit; fructify

【结实】 jiēshi ① solid; sturdy; durable: 一双～的鞋子 a durable pair of shoes/ 这张桌子很～ This is a very solid table./ 拴～点儿。Tie it fast. ② strong; sturdy; tough: 个子不高但是长得很～ short but sturdy

接* jiē ① come into contact with; come close to: 短兵相～ hand-to-hand fight; fighting at close quarters; close-range fighting ② connect; join; put together: ～电线 connect wires/ ～关系 establish contact (as in underground work)/ ～线头 tie broken threads; join two threads together/ 请～286 分机。Put me through to Extension 286, please./ 起来发言的人一个～一个。People got up to speak one after another. ③ catch; take hold of: ～球 catch a ball ④ receive: ～到一封信 receive a letter/ ～电话 answer the phone ⑤ meet; welcome: 到车站～人 go to the station to meet sb. ⑥ take over: ～工作 take over a job

【接班】 jiēbān take one's turn on duty; take over from; succeed; carry on: 谁接你的班? Who comes on duty after you? 或 Who takes over from you?

【接班人】 jiēbānrén successor

【接触】 jiēchù ① come into contact with; get in touch with: 代表团一了各界人士。The delegation met with people from all walks of life. ② engage: 与敌人～ engage the enemy/ 小规模～ a minor (或 small-scale) engagement/ 双方武装力量已脱离～。The armed forces of the two sides have disengaged. ③ contact: ～不良 loose (或 poor) contact

【接待】 jiēdài receive; admit: ～外宾 receive foreign guests/ 受到亲切～ be accorded a cordial reception/ 博物馆从上午九点到下午五点～观众。The museum is open from 9 a.m. to 5 p.m.

【接二连三】 jiē'èr-liánsān one after another; in quick succession: 捷报～地传来。Reports of victory came in one after another.

【接管】 jiēguǎn take over control; take over

【接合】 jiēhé ＜机＞ joint: 气密～ airtight joint/ 螺栓～ bolted joint

【接济】 jiējì give material assistance to; give financial help to

【接见】 jiējiàn receive sb.; grant an interview to: ～外宾 receive foreign guests

【接近】 jiējìn be close to; near; approach: ～国际水平 approach the international level/ 他们俩的意见很～。The two of them have almost identical views. 或 The two of them see pretty well eye to eye./ 该项工程～完成。The project is nearing completion./ 比分很～。It was a close game./ 这个人不易～。That chap's rather standoffish./ 我舰飞速逼～敌舰,开炮射击。Our warships quickly closed in on (或 closed with) the enemy vessel and opened fire.

【接力】 jiēlì relay: 四百米～ 400-metre relay ◇ ～棒 relay baton/ ～赛跑 relay race; relay

【接连】 jiēlián on end; in a row; in succession: ～好几天 for days on end/ ～三小时 for three hours at a stretch/ ～提出许多问题 raise one question after another/ 短期内～打几仗 fight successive battles in a short time/ ～不断地传来好消息。Glad tidings came in rapid succession.

【接洽】 jiēqià take up a matter with; arrange (business, etc.) with; consult with: 同有关部门～ take up a matter with the department concerned/ 他来～工作。He's here to talk business. 或 He's here on business./ 明天去参观展览会,我们正在～车辆。We are arranging transport for our visit to the exhibition tomorrow.

【接任】 jiērèn take over a job; replace; succeed: 他的职务已由另一同事～。His job has been taken over by another colleague

【接生】 jiēshēng deliver a child; practise midwifery ◇ ～员 midwife

【接收】 jiēshōu ① receive: ～无线电信号 receive radio signals ② take over (property, etc.); expropriate: ～敌军的武器装备 take over the enemy's arms and equipment ③ admit: ～新党员 recruit new party members

【接手】 jiēshǒu take over (duties, etc.): 这项工作我刚～还不熟悉。I'm new to the job; in fact, I've just taken over.

【接受】 jiēshòu accept: ～邀请 accept an invitation/ ～任务 accept an assignment/～意见 take sb.'s advice/～考验 face up to a test

【接替】 jiētì take over; replace: 已经派人来～他的工作。A new person has been appointed to take over his work.

【接通】 jiētōng put through: 电话～了吗? Have you got through?

【接头】 jiētóu ① connect; join; joint ② ＜纺＞＜纱条＞ piecing; ＜经纱＞ tying-in ③ ＜口＞ contact; get in touch with; meet: 我找谁～? Who shall I get in touch with?/ ～地点 contact point; rendezvous ④ have knowledge of; know about: 这事我不～。I know nothing about it.

【接吻】 jiēwěn kiss

【接应】 jiēyìng ① come to sb.'s aid; coordinate with; reinforce: 一排冲上去了,二排随后～。Platoon One charged and was soon followed by Platoon Two. ② supply: 水泥一时～不上。Cement was in short supply at the time.

【接着】 jiēzhe ① catch: 给你一个苹果,～! Here's an apple for you. Catch! ② follow; carry on: 一个～一个 one after another/ 你说完了,我～说几句。I'll add a few words when you finish./ ～干吧。Carry on with your work.

【接踵】 jiēzhǒng ＜书＞ following on sb.'s heels: 来访者～而至。Visitors came one after another./ 摩肩～ jostle each other in a crowd

揭 jiē ① tear off; take off: 把墙上那幅画～下来。Take that picture off the wall. ② uncover; lift (the lid, etc.): ～盖子 take the lid off sth.; bring sth. into the open/ 不开锅 have nothing in the pot; have nothing to eat; go hungry ③ expose; show up; bring to light:～人疮疤 pull the scab right off sb.'s sore; touch sb.'s sore spot; touch sb.

on the raw

【揭穿】 jiēchuān expose; lay bare; show up: ～谎言 expose a lie/ ～假面具 tear the mask off sb.'s face; unmask sb./ ～阴谋 lay bare an evil plot/ 他们的一切好话都已被他们自己的行动～。All their fine words have been belied by their own deeds.

【揭底】 jiēdǐ reveal the inside story

【揭短】 jiēduǎn rake up sb.'s faults

【揭发】 jiēfā expose; unmask; bring to light

【揭开】 jiēkāi uncover; reveal; open: ～宇宙的奥秘 reveal the secrets of the universe

【揭露】 jiēlù expose; unmask; ferret out: ～敌人的阴谋 expose the enemy's plot/ ～其真面目 expose sb.'s true colours; show sb. up for what he is

【揭幕】 jiēmù unveil (a monument, etc.); inaugurate ◇ ～式 unveiling ceremony

【揭示】 jiēshì ① announce; promulgate ② reveal; bring to light

【揭晓】 jiēxiǎo announce; make known; publish: 选举结果已经～。The result of the election has been published.

街* jiē street

【街道】 jiēdào ① street ② residential district; neighbourhood

【街谈巷议】 jiētán-xiàngyì street gossip

【街头】 jiētóu street corner; street: 十字～ (at the) crossroads/ 流落～ tramp the streets; be down and out in a city/ 涌上～ pour into the streets

【街头巷尾】 jiētóu-xiàngwěi streets and lanes: ～,到处都是欢乐的人群。There are happy crowds in all the streets and lanes.

jié

孑 jié ＜书＞ lonely; all alone

【孑孓】 jiéjué wiggler; wriggler

【孑然】 jiérán ＜书＞ solitary; lonely; alone: ～一身 all alone in the world

节* jié ① joint; node; knot: 竹～ bamboo joint/ 骨～ joint (of bones)/ ～材 nodal wood ② division; part 音～ syllable ③ ＜量＞ section; length: 一～铁管 a length of iron pipe/ 两～课 two periods; two classes/ 八～车厢 eight railway coaches/ 第一章第二～ Chapter One, Section Two ④ festival; red-letter day; holiday: 过～ celebrate (或 observe) a festival/ 春～ the Spring Festival/ 国庆～ National Day ⑤ abridge: ～译 abridged translation ⑥ economize; save: ～煤 economize on coal; save coal ⑦ item: 细～ details/ 生活小～ trifling personal matters ⑧ moral integrity; chastity: 气～ moral integrity

【节哀】 jié'āi restrain one's grief

【节操】 jiécāo ＜书＞ high moral principle; moral integrity

【节俭】 jiéjiǎn thrifty; frugal: 提倡～ encourage frugality

【节节】 jiéjié successively; steadily: ～胜利 win many victories in succession; go from victory to victory/ ～败退 retreat in defeat again and again; keep on retreating/ 产量～上升。Production rose steadily.

【节令】 jiélìng climate and other natural phenomena of a season: ～不等人。Don't miss the right season in farming. 或 The seasons wait for no man./ 中秋节吃点月饼,应应～。Let's eat moon cakes at the Mid-Autumn Festival, as befits the occasion.

【节流】 jiéliú reduce expenditure: 开源～ broaden sources of income and reduce expenditure

【节录】 jiélù extract; excerpt

【节目】 jiémù programme; item (on a programme); number: 晚会的～ programme for the evening party/ 下一个～ the next item (或 number) ◇ ～单 programme; playbill

【节日】 jiérì festival; red-letter day; holiday: ～气氛 festive air/ 致以～的祝贺 extend holiday greetings/ 穿上～的盛装 in one's holiday best; in gala dress

【节省】 jiéshěng economize; save; use sparingly; cut down

on: ～时间 save time/ ～篇幅 save space/ ～人力物力 use manpower and material resources sparingly/ 财政的支出，应该根据～的方针。Thrift should be the guiding principle in our government expenditure.

【节外生枝】jiéwài shēng zhī ① side issues or new problems crop up unexpectedly ② raise obstacles; deliberately complicate an issue: 快要达成协议时, 对方又～。An agreement was about to be reached when the other side raised new issues.

【节衣缩食】jiéyī-suōshí economize on food and clothing; live frugally

【节育】jiéyù birth control

【节约】jiéyuē practise thrift; economize; save: ～粮食 save on food/ ～用电 economize on electricity/ ～开支 cut down expenses; retrench (expenditure)/ 厉行～ practise strict economy

【节制】jiézhì ① control; check; be moderate in: ～饮食 be moderate in eating and drinking ② temperance; abstinence

【节奏】jiézòu rhythm: ～明快 lively rhythm/ 有～地鼓掌 clap hands rhythmically

劫* jié ⟨书⟩ ① rob; plunder; raid: 打～ rob; loot ② coerce; compel ③ calamity; disaster; misfortune: 浩～ a great calamity/ ～后余生 be a survivor of a disaster

【劫持】jiéchí kidnap; hold under duress; hijack: ～飞机 hijack an aeroplane ◇ ～者 hijacker

【劫夺】jiéduó seize (a person or his property) by force

【劫掠】jiélüè plunder; loot

杰 jié ① outstanding; prominent ② outstanding person; hero

【杰出】jiéchū outstanding; remarkable; prominent: ～贡献 a brilliant contribution

【杰作】jiézuò masterpiece

诘 jié ⟨书⟩ closely question; interrogate

【诘问】jiéwèn ⟨书⟩ closely question; interrogate; cross-examine

【诘责】jiézé ⟨书⟩ censure; rebuke; denounce

洁* jié clean: 整～ clean and tidy; clean and neat

【洁白】jiébái spotlessly white; pure white

【洁净】jiéjìng clean; spotless

【洁身自好】jié shēn zì hào ① refuse to be contaminated by evil influence; preserve one's purity ② mind one's own business in order to keep out of trouble

拮 jié

【拮据】jiéjū in straitened circumstances; short of money; hard up

结* jié ① tie; knit; knot; weave: ～网 weave a net ② knot: 打～ tie a knot/ 活～ slipknot/ 死～ fast knot/ 蝴蝶～ bowknot ③ congeal; form; forge; cement: 牛奶上面～了一层皮。A skin has formed on the milk./ ～痂 form a scab; scab ④ settle; conclude: ～帐 settle accounts
另见 jié

【结拜】jiébài ⟨旧⟩ become sworn brothers or sisters

【结伴】jiébàn go with: ～而行 go or travel in a group

【结冰】jiébīng freeze; ice up; ice over

【结成】jiéchéng form: ～同盟 form an alliance; become allies/ ～一伙 gang up; band together

【结仇】jiéchóu start a feud; become enemies

【结存】jiécún ① cash on hand; balance ② goods on hand; inventory

【结党营私】jiédǎng-yíngsī form a clique to pursue selfish interests

【结构】jiégòu ① structure; composition; construction: 经济～ economic structure/ 原子～ atomic structure/ 这篇文章～严密。This article is compact and well organized. ② ⟨建⟩ structure; construction: 钢～ steel structure

【结果】jiéguǒ ① result; outcome: 必然～ inevitable result/ 会谈的～ the outcome of the talks/ 这样瞎吵下去不会有

什么～。Squabbling like this won't get you anywhere./ 经过一番争论, 他还是让步了。After a heated argument he finally gave in. ② kill; finish off

【结合】jiéhé ① combine; unite; integrate; link: 理论与实践相～ combine theory with practice ② be united in wedlock

【结核】jiéhé ⟨医⟩ tuberculosis: 肺～ pulmonary tuberculosis

【结婚】jiéhūn marry; get married ◇ ～登记 marriage registration/ ～证书 marriage certificate; marriage lines

【结集】jiéjí ① concentrate; mass: ～兵力 concentrate troops ② collect articles, etc. into a volume: ～付印 compile a collection of writings and send it to the press

【结交】jiéjiāo make friends with; associate with: 他～的朋友大多是青年工人。He associates mostly with young workers.

【结晶】jiéjīng ① crystallize ② crystal: 盐～ salt crystals ③ crystallization: 劳动的～ the fruit of labour

【结局】jiéjú final result; outcome; ending: 小说的～ the ending of a novel

【结论】jiélùn ① ⟨逻⟩ conclusion (of a syllogism) ② conclusion; verdict: 得出～ draw (或 come to, reach) a conclusion/ 不要忙于下～。Don't jump to conclusions./ 对某人的历史作～ reach a conclusion on sb.'s personal history; pass (official) judgment on sb.'s history/ 这是否可行, 还不能下～。Whether this is feasible is still an open question.

【结盟】jiéméng form an alliance; ally; align

【结亲】jiéqīn ① ⟨口⟩ marry; get married ② (of two families) become related by marriage

【结清】jiéqīng settle; square up: ～帐目 square accounts (with sb.)

【结识】jiéshí get acquainted with sb.; get to know sb.: ～了很多新朋友 have made a lot of new friends

【结束】jiéshù end; finish; conclude; wind up; close: ～讲话 wind up a speech/ ～战争状态 terminate the state of war

【结尾】jiéwěi ① ending; winding-up stage: ～工程 the winding-up work of a project/ 文章的～很有力量。The article has a forceful ending.

【结缘】jiéyuán form ties (of affection, friendship, etc.); become attached to: 他从小就和音乐结了缘。He developed a liking for music even as a boy.

【结怨】jiéyuàn contract enmity; incur hatred

【结帐】jiézhàng settle (或 square) accounts; balance the books

捷* jié ① victory; triumph: 大～ a great victory/ 报～ announce a victory/ 首战告～ be victorious in the first battle; win the first battle ② prompt; nimble; quick: 敏～ quick; nimble; agile

【捷报】jiébào news of victory; report of a success: ～频传。News of victory keeps pouring in.

【捷径】jiéjìng shortcut: 走～ take a shortcut

【捷足先登】jiézú xiān dēng the swift-footed arrive first; the race is to the swiftest: 他们一, 把最艰巨的任务抢走了。They grabbed the most difficult task before the others had a chance to.

睫 jié eyelash; lash

【睫毛】jiémáo eyelash; lash

竭 jié exhaust; use up

【竭诚】jiéchéng wholeheartedly; with all one's heart: ～拥护 give wholehearted support

【竭尽】jiéjìn use up; exhaust: ～全力 spare no effort; do one's utmost; do all one can/ ～造谣诬蔑之能事 stop at nothing in spreading lies and slanders

【竭力】jiélì do one's utmost; use every ounce of one's energy: ～支持 give all-out support/ ～反对 actively oppose/ ～鼓吹 boost with all one's might; energetically advocate/ ～抗拒 stubbornly resist

截 jié ① cut; sever: ～成两段 cut in two ② ⟨量⟩ section; chunk; length: 一～儿木头 a log/ 他话说了半～儿，又缩回去了。He broke off half way and said no more. ③ stop; check; stem: 把惊马～住 stop a bolting horse/ ～流 dam a river/ ～球 intercept a pass ④ by (a specified time); up to: ～至八月底 up to the end of August

【截长补短】jié cháng bǔ duǎn take from the long to add to the short; draw on the strength of each to offset the weakness of the other

【截断】jiéduàn ① cut off; block: ～敌人的退路 cut off the enemy's retreat/ ～河流 dam a river ② cut short; interrupt: 电话铃声～了他的话。 He was interrupted by the telephone.

【截然】jiérán sharply; completely: ～对立 be diametrically opposed/ ～不同 poles apart; completely different; different as black and white/ 同他们以前的谈话～相反 completely contradict their previous statement/ 两者不能～分开。 No hard and fast line can be drawn between the two.

【截止】jiézhǐ ① end; close: 登记已经～了。 Registration has closed./ 申请到本月二十日～。 The 20th of this month is the closing day for applications.

【截至】jiézhǐ by (a specified time); up to: ～本月底 by the end of this month/ ～目前为止 up to now

jiě

姐*

jiě ① elder sister; sister ② a general term for young women

【姐夫】jiěfu elder sister's husband; brother-in-law
【姐姐】jiějie elder sister; sister
【姐妹】jiěmèi ① sisters: 她没有～，只有一个哥哥。 She has a brother but no sisters. ② brothers and sisters

解*

jiě ① separate; divide: ～剖 dissect/ 溶～ dissolve/ 瓦～ disintegrate ② untie; undo: ～缆 untie the mooring rope/ ～鞋带 undo shoelaces/ ～扣儿 unbutton ③ allay; dispel; dismiss: ～热 allay a fever/ ～惑 dispel (或 remove) doubts/ ～油腻 cut the grease of a rich meal (as with a cup of tea, etc.) ④ explain; interpret; solve: 注～ (explanatory) notes; annotation/ 新～ a new interpretation/ ～题 solve a (mathematical, etc.) problem ⑤ understand; comprehend: 费～ hard to understand; obscure/ 令人不～ puzzling; incomprehensible ⑥ relieve oneself: 小～ go to the lavatory (to urinate)/ 大～ go to the lavatory (to defecate) ⑦〈数〉 solution: 求～ find the solution 另见 jiè

【解嘲】jiěcháo try to explain things away when ridiculed: 自我～ find excuses to console oneself

【解除】jiěchú remove; relieve; get rid of: ～职务 remove sb. from his post; relieve sb. of his office/ ～合同 terminate a contract/ ～武装 disarm/ ～禁令 lift a ban/ ～警报 sound the all clear/ ～婚约 renounce an engagement/ ～思想负担 have a load taken off one's mind; be relieved of a mental burden/ ～顾虑 free one's mind of apprehensions/ 旱象已经～。 The dry spell is over.

【解答】jiědá answer; explain: ～疑难问题 answer difficult questions

【解冻】jiědòng ① thaw; unfreeze: ～季节 thawing season ② unfreeze (funds, assets, etc.)

【解放】jiěfàng liberate; emancipate: ～思想 emancipate the mind; free oneself from old ideas

【解雇】jiěgù discharge; dismiss; fire
【解禁】jiějìn lift a ban
【解救】jiějiù save; rescue; deliver

【解决】jiějué ① solve; resolve; settle: ～争端 settle a dispute/ ～困难 overcome a difficulty; find a way out of a difficulty/ ～问题 solve a problem; settle a question (或 an issue); work out a solution/ 很快地～战斗 bring a battle to a quick decision ② dispose of; finish off: 这一仗把敌人全～了。 In that battle we finished off all the enemy troops.

【解开】jiěkāi untie; undo: ～头巾 untie a kerchief/ ～上衣 unbutton one's jacket/ ～这个谜 find a clue to the mystery

【解渴】jiěkě quench one's thirst: 这西瓜真～。 This watermelon really quenches your thirst.

【解铃系铃】jiělíng-xìlíng let him who tied the bell on the tiger take it off — whoever started the trouble should end it 又作 "解铃还是系铃人"

【解闷】jiěmèn divert oneself (from boredom)

【解聘】jiěpìn dismiss an employee (usu. at the expiration of a contract)

【解剖】jiěpōu dissect

【解散】jiěsàn ① dismiss: 队伍～后，战士们都在操场上休息。 After they were dismissed, the soldiers had a rest on the drill ground./ ～！（口令）Dismiss! ② dissolve; disband: ～组织 disband an organization

【解释】jiěshì explain; expound; interpret: ～一个新词 explain a new word/对这件事你作何～？ How do you account for this?/ 这是误会，～一下就行了。 This is a misunderstanding. A little explanation will clear it up.

【解数】jiěshù skill; art: 使出浑身～ bring all one's skill into play

【解说】jiěshuō explain orally; comment: 向观众～这种拖拉机的构造和性能 explain to the visitors the structure and performance of this type of tractor

【解脱】jiětuō free (或 extricate) oneself: 从困境中～出来 extricate oneself from a predicament/ 陷人不可～的危机 land oneself in an inextricable crisis

【解围】jiěwéi ① force an enemy to raise a siege; rescue sb. from a siege ② help sb. out of a predicament; save sb. from embarrassment: 他们拿我开玩笑，你怎么不来给我～？ Why didn't you come to my rescue when they were making fun of me?

【解约】jiěyuē terminate an agreement; cancel (或 rescind) a contract

jiè

介*

jiè ① be situated between; interpose: 这座山～于两县之间。 The mountain lies between two counties. ② take seriously; take to heart; mind: ～意 take offence; mind ③〈书〉upright: 耿～ honest and frank; upright ④ armour: ～胄之士 men in armour; ancient warriors ⑤ shell

【介词】jiècí〈语〉preposition

【介人】jièrù intervene; interpose; get involved: 不～无原则争论 not get involved in unprincipled disputes

【介绍】jièshào ① introduce; present: 让我～一下，这就是张教授。 Allow me to introduce Prof Zhang. / 作自我～ introduce oneself/ ～对象 introduce sb. to a potential marriage partner; find sb. a boy or girl friend/ ～灭虫方法是去年才～到我们县来的。 This method of pest control was introduced into our county only last year. ② recommend; suggest: 我给你～一本书。 I'll recommend you a book. ③ let know; brief: ～情况 brief sb. on the situation; put sb. in the picture; fill sb. in/ ～经验 pass on experience ◇ ～信 letter of introduction; reference

【介绍人】jièshàorén one who introduces or recommends sb.; sponsor

【介意】jièyì〔多用于否定词后〕take offence; mind: 我是开玩笑，你可别～呀。 I was only joking. I hope you won't take offence./ 即使有些批评过头了，他也不～。 He didn't mind even when some criticisms were excessive.

芥

jiè mustard 另见 gài

【芥菜】jiècài leaf mustard 另见 gàicài

【芥蒂】jièdì〈书〉ill feeling; unpleasantness; grudge: 心存～ bear a grudge

戒*

jiè ① guard against: 力～浮夸 strictly avoid boasting and exaggeration ② exhort; admonish; warn: 引以为～ take warning from sth.; take sth. as an object lesson ③ give up; drop; stop: ～烟 give up smoking/ ～酒 stop drinking/ ～荤腥 go on a vegetarian diet ④〈宗〉Buddhist monastic discipline: 受～ attain the full status of a monk or nun ⑤ (finger) ring: 钻～ diamond ring

【戒备】 jièbèi　guard; take precautions; be on the alert: ～森严 be heavily guarded/ 处于～状态 be on the alert

【戒除】 jièchú　give up; drop; stop: ～恶习 give up a bad habit

【戒骄戒躁】 jièjiāo-jièzào　guard against arrogance and rashness; be on guard against conceit and impetuosity

【戒律】 jièlǜ　<宗> religious discipline; commandment 又作 "戒条"

【戒心】 jièxīn　vigilance; wariness: 对某人怀有～ be on one's guard against someone; keep a wary eye on someone

【戒严】 jièyán　enforce martial law; impose a curfew; cordon off an area: 宣布～ proclaim martial law

【戒指】 jièzhi　(finger) ring

届 jiè ① fall due: ～期 when the day comes; on the appointed date ②<量>〔用于定期会议、毕业的班级等〕:本～联大 the present session of the U.N. General Assembly/ ～毕业生 this year's graduates

【届满】 jièmǎn　at the expiration of one's term of office: 任期～。 The term of office has expired.

【届时】 jièshí　when the time comes; at the appointed time; on the occasion: 大桥下月竣工，～将举行通车典礼。 There will be an opening ceremony next month when the bridge is completed./ ～务请出席。 Your presence is requested for the occasion.

诫 jiè ① warn; admonish: 告～ give warning; admonish ②<宗> commandment: 十～ the Ten Commandments

界 jiè ① boundary: 国～ the boundary of a country; national boundary ② scope; extent: 眼～ field of vision/ 外～ external world ③ circles: 新闻～ press circles/ 各～人民 all sections of the people; people of all walks of life ④ primary division; kingdom: 动(植、矿)物～ the animal (vegetable, mineral) kingdom

【界限】 jièxiàn ① demarcation line; dividing line; limits; bounds ② limit; end

【界线】 jièxiàn ① boundary line ② 见"界限"①

借 jiè ① borrow: 跟人～钱 borrow money from sb. ② lend: 把自行车～给我骑一下好吗？ Could you lend me your bicycle? ③ make use of; take advantage of (an opportunity, etc.): 火～风势, 越烧越旺。 Fanned by the wind, the fire burned more and more furiously./ 部队～月光急速前进。 The troops marched swiftly forward by the light of the moon. ④ use as a pretext

【借贷】 jièdài ① borrow or lend money ② debit and credit sides

【借刀杀人】 jiè dāo shā rén　murder with a borrowed knife — make use of another person to get rid of an adversary

【借方】 jièfāng　<簿记> debit; debit side

【借古讽今】 jiè gǔ fěng jīn　use the past to disparage the present

【借故】 jiègù　find an excuse: ～推托 find an excuse to refuse/ 他～走了。 He found an excuse and left.

【借花献佛】 jiè huā xiàn fó　present Buddha with borrowed flowers — borrow sth. to make a gift of it

【借火】 jièhuǒ　ask for a light: 劳驾, 借个火儿。 Excuse me. Would you mind giving me a light?

【借鉴】 jièjiàn　use for reference; draw lessons from; draw on the experience of: 他们的做法有许多值得我们～的地方。 There's much in their method that we can make use of./ ～外国的经验 use the experience of other countries for reference 又作"借镜"

【借据】 jièjù　receipt for a loan (IOU)

【借口】 jièkǒu ① use as an excuse (或 pretext): 别拿忙做～而放松学习。 Don't slacken your study on the excuse of being too busy. ② excuse; pretext: 找～ find an excuse (或 pretext)/ 制造～ invent an excuse; cook up a pretext

【借款】 jièkuǎn ① borrow or lend money; ask for or offer a loan ② loan

【借题发挥】 jiè tí fāhuī　make use of the subject under discussion to put over one's own ideas; seize on an incident to exaggerate matters

【借条】 jiètiáo　receipt for a loan (IOU)

【借问】 jièwèn　<敬> may I ask

【借用】 jièyòng ① borrow; have the loan of: ～一下你的铅笔。 May I use your pencil? ② use sth. for another purpose: ～一句古诗表达自己的心情 quote a line from classical poetry to express one's feelings

【借债】 jièzhài　borrow money; raise (或 contract) a loan: ～度日 live by borrowing

【借支】 jièzhī　ask for an advance on one's pay

【借重】 jièzhòng　rely on for support; enlist sb.'s help: 以后要～您的地方还多着呢。 We'll need a lot more of your help in the future.

【借助】 jièzhù　have the aid of; draw support from: ～望远镜观察天体 observe the celestial bodies with the aid of a telescope

解 jiè send under guard
另见 jiě

【解送】 jièsòng　send under guard

jīn

巾 jīn　a piece of cloth (as used for a towel, scarf, kerchief, etc.): 手～ (face) towel/ 围～ scarf/ 餐～ napkin

【巾帼】 jīnguó ① ancient woman's headdress ② woman ◇ ～英雄 heroine

今 jīn ① modern; present-day: ～人 moderns; contemporaries; people of our era ② today: ～明两天 today and tomorrow/ ～晚 tonight; this evening ③ this (year): ～冬 this (coming) winter ④ now; the present: 至～ to date; until now; up to now/ 从～以后 from now on; henceforth/ ～胜于昔。 The present is superior to the past.

【今后】 jīnhòu　from now on; in the days to come; henceforth; hereafter; in future: ～的十年内 in the next decade; in the coming ten years/ ～的任务 the tasks ahead/ 希望～两国人民之间有更多的交往。 We hope from now on there will be more exchanges between our two peoples.

【今年】 jīnnián　this year

【今日】 jīnrì ① today ② present; now

【今生】 jīnshēng　this life

【今世】 jīnshì ① this life ② this age; the contemporary age

【今天】 jīntiān ① today: 一年前的～ a year ago today ② the present; now

【今昔】 jīn-xī　the present and the past; today and yesterday

【今译】 jīnyì　modern translation; modern-language version: 古诗～ ancient poems rendered into modern Chinese

【今朝】 jīnzhāo　<书> today; the present; now

斤 jīn　jin, a unit of weight (=1/2 kilogram)

【斤斤计较】 jīnjīn jìjiào　haggle over every ounce; be calculating: ～个人得失 be preoccupied with one's personal gains and losses

金 jīn ① metals: 合～ alloy/ 五～店 hardware store ② money: 现～ cash; ready money ③ ancient metal percussion instruments: ～鼓齐鸣。 All the gongs and drums are beating. ④ gold (Au): ～银财宝 gold, silver and other treasures/ 镀～ gild ⑤ golden: 红底～字 golden characters on a red background

【金笔】 jīnbǐ　(quality) fountain pen

【金币】 jīnbì　gold coin

【金碧辉煌】 jīnbì-huīhuáng　(of a building, etc.) looking splendid in green and gold; resplendent and magnificent

【金箔】 jīnbó　goldleaf; gold foil

【金不换】 jīnbuhuàn　not to be exchanged even for gold; invaluable; priceless: 浪子回头～。 A prodigal who returns is more precious than gold.

【金蝉脱壳】 jīnchán tuō qiào　slip out of a predicament like a cicada sloughing its skin; escape by cunning manoeuvring

【金城汤池】 jīnchéng-tāngchí　ramparts of metal and a moat of boiling water — impregnable fortress

【金刚石】 jīngāngshí　diamond

【金刚钻】 jīngāngzuàn　diamond ◇ ～钻头 diamond bit

【金工】 jīngōng　metalworking; metal processing ◇ ～机械 metalworking machinery

【金黄】 jīnhuáng　golden yellow; golden: 菜花一片～ a vast stretch of golden rape flowers

【金婚】 jīnhūn　golden wedding

【金科玉律】 jīnkē-yùlǜ　golden rule and precious precept: 奉为～ accept as infallible law

【金块】 jīnkuài　gold bullion

【金缕玉衣】 jīnlǚ yùyī　〈考古〉 jade clothes sewn with gold thread

【金器】 jīnqì　gold vessel

【金钱】 jīnqián　money

【金融】 jīnróng　finance; banking ◇ ～寡头 financial oligarch (或 magnate)/ ～机关 financial institution/ ～界 financial circles/ ～市场 money (或 financial) market/ ～中心 financial (或 banking) centre

【金色】 jīnsè　golden: ～的朝阳 golden rays of the morning sun; golden dawn

【金石】 jīnshí　① 〈书〉 metal and stone — a symbol of hardness and strength: 精诚所至，～为开。 No difficulty is insurmountable if one sets one's mind on it. ② inscriptions on ancient bronzes and stone tablets

【金属】 jīnshǔ　metal: 黑色～ ferrous metal/ 有色～ nonferrous metal

【金条】 jīntiáo　gold bar

【金鱼】 jīnyú　goldfish

【金玉】 jīnyù　〈书〉 gold and jade; precious stone and metals; treasures: ～良言 golden saying; invaluable advice/ ～其外，败絮其中 rubbish coated in gold and jade; fair without, foul within

【金字塔】 jīnzìtǎ　pyramid

【金字招牌】 jīnzì zhāopái　① gold-lettered signboard ② a vainglorious title

津* jīn　① ferry crossing; ford: ～渡 a ferry crossing ② saliva: 生～止渴 help produce saliva and slake thirst ③ sweat: 遍体生～ perspire all over ④ moist; damp

【津津乐道】 jīnjīn lè dào　take delight in talking about; dwell upon with great relish

【津津有味】 jīnjīn yǒu wèi　with relish; with gusto; with keen pleasure: 吃得～ eat with great relish/ 饲养员～地讲着每头牲口的习性。 The stockman takes keen pleasure in talking about the habits of each of his draught animals./ 这个故事他们听得～。 They listened to the story with great interest.

【津贴】 jīntiē　subsidy; allowance

矜 jīn　① pity; sympathize with: ～恤 show sympathy and consideration for ② self-important; conceited: 骄～之气 arrogant airs ③ restrained; reserved: ～重 reserved and dignified

【矜持】 jīnchí　restrained; reserved: 举止～ have a reserved manner

【矜夸】 jīnkuā　conceited and boastful

筋 jīn　① muscle ② 〈口〉 tendon; sinew ③ 〈口〉 veins that stand out under the skin: 她的手背上露着青～。 The veins stand out on the back of her hands. ④ anything resembling a tendon or vein: 叶～ ribs of a leaf/ 钢～ reinforcing steel; steel reinforcement/ 这菜～多嚼不烂。 The greens are full of fibres that you can't chew.

【筋斗】 jīndǒu　① somersault: 翻～ turn a somersault ② fall; tumble (over): 摔了个～ fall; have a fall; tumble over

【筋骨】 jīngǔ　bones and muscles

【筋疲力尽】 jīnpí-lìjìn　exhausted; played out; worn out; tired out

禁* jīn　① bear; stand; endure: 这布～洗吗？ Will this cloth stand a lot of washing?/ 这鞋～穿。 These shoes are durable. ② contain (或 restrain) oneself: 不～流下眼泪 cannot hold back one's tears
另见 jìn

【禁不起】 jīnbuqǐ　be unable to stand (tests, trials, etc.): ～严峻考验 fail to stand rigorous tests

【禁不住】 jīnbuzhù　① be unable to bear or endure: 这种植物～冻。 This plant can't stand frost./ 你怎么这样～批评? How is it that you can't stand a little bit of criticism? ② can't help (doing sth.); can't refrain from: ～笑了起来 can't help laughing; burst out laughing

【禁得起】 jīndeqǐ　be able to stand (tests, trials, etc.): ～艰苦环境的考验 be able to stand the test of hardships

【禁得住】 jīndezhù　be able to bear or endure: 河上的冰已经～人走了。 The ice on the river is thick enough to walk on.

襟 jīn　① front of a garment ② brothers-in-law whose wives are sisters: ～兄 husband of one's wife's elder sister; brother-in-law

jǐn

仅 jǐn　〈副〉 only; merely; barely: ～次于 second only to/ 世所～见 have no parallel anywhere/ ～一人缺席。 Only one is absent.

【仅仅】 jǐnjǐn　〈副〉 only; merely; barely: 这～是开始。 This is only the beginning./ 这座桥～半年就完工了。 This bridge was built in the short space of six months.

尽 jǐn　① to the greatest extent: ～早 as early as possible; at the earliest possible date ② within the limits of: ～着三天把事情办好。 Get the job done in three days at the outside./ ～着一百块钱花。 Don't spend more than $100. ③ give priority to: ～着年纪大的坐。 Let the older people sit down first. ④〔用在表示方位的词前面，跟"最"相同〕 at the furthest end of: ～北边 the northernmost end, etc./ ～底下 at the very bottom/ 他家住在村子～西头。 He lives at the western end of the village. ⑤ 〈方〉 keep on doing sth.: 他衣服都叫汗湿透了，还～着干呢。 He was wet through with sweat, but he kept on working./ 这些日子～下雨。 We're having an awful lot of rain these days.
另见 jìn

【尽管】 jǐnguǎn　① 〈副〉 feel free to; not hesitate to: 有什么问题～问。 If you have any questions, don't hesitate to ask them./ 你～拿吧。 You're welcome to it. 或 Take as much as you like./ 场院的活儿有我们，你～放心吧。 Don't worry. We'll attend to all the work on the threshing ground. ② 〈连〉 though; even though; in spite of; despite: ～旱情严重，今年的小麦还是丰收了。 Despite the serious drought the wheat harvest this year was good.

【尽可能】 jǐnkěnéng　as far as possible; to the best of one's ability: ～早点儿来 come as early as possible

【尽快】 jǐnkuài　as quickly (或 soon, early) as possible: 请～答复。 Please reply at your earliest convenience.

【尽量】 jǐnliàng　to the best of one's ability; as far as possible: ～采用先进技术 make the widest possible use of advanced technology/ 请大家～发表意见。 Please voice your opinions as fully as possible.
另见 jìnliàng

紧* jǐn　① tight; taut; close: 把绳子拉～ pull the rope taut/ 把螺丝拧～ tighten the screw/ ～握手中枪 hold the gun tight in one's hands/ 这双鞋太～。 These shoes are too tight. 或 These shoes pinch./ 他住在我的～隔壁。 He lives right next door to me./ 日程安排得很～。 The programme is packed./ 一个胜利～接着一个胜利。 One victory followed another in quick succession./ 全国人民团结～。 The whole nation is closely united. ② tighten: ～一～背包带 tighten the knapsack straps ③ urgent; pressing;

tense: 任务～。The task is urgent./ 风声～。Things are tense./ 雨下得正～。It was raining hard./ 枪声越来越～。The firing got heavier and heavier. ④ strict; stringent: 管得～ exercise strict control; be strict with ⑤ hard up; short of money: 手头～ be short of money; be hard up/ 银根～。Money is tight.

【紧逼】 jǐnbī press hard; close in on: 步步～ press on at every stage

【紧凑】 jǐncòu compact; terse; well-knit: 这个工厂布局～。The factory is compactly laid out./ 影片情节～。The film has a well-knit plot./ 会议开得很～。It was a well-organized meeting./ 活动安排得很～ have a tight schedule

【紧跟】 jǐngēn follow closely; keep in step with: ～时代的步伐 keep in step with the times/ ～形势 keep abreast of the situation

【紧急】 jǐnjí urgent; pressing; critical: 发出～呼吁 issue an urgent appeal/ 情况～。The situation is critical./ ～行动 起来 act promptly; take immediate action
◇ ～措施 emergency measures/ ～法令 emergency act/ ～会议 emergency meeting/ ～任务 urgent task/ ～信号 emergency (或 distress) signal/ ～状态 state of emergency/ ～着陆 emergency landing

【紧紧】 jǐnjǐn closely; firmly; tightly: ～相连 closely linked/ ～盯着 watch closely; stare fixedly; gaze steadfastly

【紧锣密鼓】 jǐnluó-mìgǔ wildly beating gongs and drums — intense publicity campaign in preparation for some sinister undertaking, etc.

【紧密】 jǐnmì close together; inseparable

【紧迫】 jǐnpò pressing; urgent; imminent: 时间～ be pressed for time/ 我有更～的事情要做。I have more pressing things to attend to.

【紧缩】 jǐnsuō reduce; retrench; tighten: ～编制 reduce staff/ ～开支 cut down expenses; retrench; curtail outlay/ ～包围圈 tighten the ring of encirclement

【紧要】 jǐnyào critical; crucial; vital: ～关头 critical moment (或 juncture); crucial moment/ 无关～ of no consequence; of no importance/ 这一点十分～。That's an extremely important point. 或 That's a vital point.

【紧张】 jǐnzhāng ① nervous; keyed up: 神情～ look nervous/ 慢慢讲，别～。Speak slowly and don't be nervous./ 试验到了关键时刻,大家都～起来。Everybody was keyed up as the experiment reached a crucial point. ② tense; intense; strained: ～局势 a tense situation/ ～气氛 a tense atmosphere/ 两国关系～。Relations between the two countries are strained./ ～而有秩序 的工作 intense but orderly work/ 这场比赛真～! What an exciting game!/ 工程正在～地进行。Construction was in full swing.

锦 jǐn ① brocade ② bright and beautiful: 霞～ rose-tinted clouds/ 前程似～ splendid prospects; glorious future

【锦标】 jǐnbiāo prize; trophy; title

【锦标赛】 jǐnbiāosài championship contest; championships: 世界乒乓球～ the World Table Tennis Championships

【锦缎】 jǐnduàn brocade

【锦囊妙计】 jǐnnáng miàojì instructions for dealing with an emergency; wise counsel

【锦旗】 jǐnqí silk banner (as an award or a gift)

【锦上添花】 jǐnshàng tiān huā add flowers to the brocade —— make perfection still more perfect

【锦绣】 jǐnxiù as beautiful as brocade; beautiful; splendid: ～山河 a land of charm and beauty; a beautiful land/ ～前程 glorious future

谨 jǐn ① careful; cautious; circumspect: ～记在心 bear in mind/ ～守规则 strictly adhere to the rules ② solemnly; sincerely: ～致谢意。Please accept my sincere thanks./ 我～代表全体职工, 向你们表示热烈的欢迎。On behalf of the staff and workers, I wish to extend to you our warmest welcome.

【谨防】 jǐnfáng guard against; beware of: ～扒手。Beware of pickpockets.

【谨慎】 jǐnshèn prudent; careful; cautious; circumspect: 谦

虚～ modest and prudent/ 说话～ be guarded in one's speech/ ～从事 act with caution

【谨严】 jǐnyán careful and precise: 治学～ careful and exact scholarship/ 文章结构～。The article is compact and carefully constructed.

【谨言慎行】 jǐnyán-shènxíng speak and act cautiously; be discreet in word and deed

馑 jǐn 见"饥馑" jījǐn

jìn

尽* jìn ① exhausted; finished: 取之不～ inexhaustible/ 无穷无～ endless ② to the utmost: 用～气力 exert oneself to the utmost ③ use up; exhaust: 一言难～。It can't be expressed in a few words. 或 It's a long story./ 一饮而～ empty a glass at one gulp; drain the cup with one gulp ④ try one's best; put to the best use: ～责任 do one's duty; discharge one's responsibility/ ～最大努力 do one's best; exert one's utmost effort/ 人～ 其才, 物～ 其用 make the best possible use of men and material ⑤ all; exhaustive: 工具已～数交回。All the tools have been handed in./ 不可～信 not to be believed word for word; to be taken with a grain of salt/ ～收眼底 have a panoramic view
另见 jǐn

【尽力】 jìnlì do all one can; try one's best: ～而为 do one's best; do everything in one's power

【尽量】 jìnliàng (drink or eat) to the full
另见 jǐnliàng

【尽情】 jìnqíng to one's heart's content; as much as one likes: ～欢呼 cheer heartily/ ～歌唱 sing to one's heart's content

【尽人皆知】 jìn rén jiē zhī be known to all; be common knowledge

【尽人事】 jìn rénshì do what one can (to save a dying person, etc.); do all that is humanly possible (though with little hope of success)

【尽善尽美】 jìnshàn-jìnměi the acme of perfection; perfect

【尽是】 jìnshì full of; all; without exception: 这儿原来～石头。This place used to be full of boulders./ 这里展出的～新产品。All the exhibits here are new products./ 一路上～去参加庆祝活动的人群。There was a continuous stream of people going to the celebrations.

【尽头】 jìntóu end: 路的～ the end of the road

【尽心】 jìnxīn with all one's heart: ～竭力 (do sth.) with all one's heart and all one's might/ 医护人员～照看受伤的工人。The doctors and nurses did their utmost to tend the injured workers./ 这些年青人干活可～呢。These young people are really conscientious in their work.

【尽兴】 jìnxìng to one's heart's content; enjoy oneself to the full: ～而归 return after thoroughly enjoying oneself

【尽义务】 jìn yìwù do one's duty; fulfil one's obligation

【尽职】 jìnzhí fulfil one's duty: 他工作一向很～。He has always been a conscientious worker.

进* jìn ① advance; move forward; move ahead: 不～则退。Move forward, or you'll fall behind. ② enter; come or go into; get into: ～屋 enter a house or room/ ～大学 enter college/ ～工厂当学徒 start work in a factory as an apprentice/ ～医院 be sent to hospital; be hospitalized/ 请～! Come in!/ 火车～站了。The train is pulling in. ③ receive: ～款 income/ 这家商店前几天刚～了一批货。This shop laid in a new stock of goods just a few days ago. ④ eat; drink; take: 共～晚餐 have supper together/ 滴水不～ not take even a drop of water — unable to eat or drink ⑤ submit; present: ～一言 give a word of advice ⑥〔用在动词后,表示到里面〕into; in: 走～车间 walk into the workshop

【进逼】 jìnbī close in on; advance on; press on towards: 步步～ steadily close in

【进步】 jìnbù ① advance; progress; improve: 世界是在～的。 The world is progressing. 或 The world moves ahead./ 今年我们农场各方面的工作都有了很大的～。 Great advances have been made in every field of work on our farm this year./ 你的发音很有～。 Your pronunciation has greatly improved. ② (politically) progressive: 思想～ have progressive ideas

【进出】 jìnchū ① pass in and out: 这儿进进出出的人真多。 What a lot of people are coming in and out of here./ 车辆由此～。 Vehicles this way! ② (business) turnover: 这个商店每天有好几千元的～。 This store has a daily turnover of several thousand dollars.

【进出口】 jìn-chūkǒu ① imports and exports ② exits and entrances; exit ◇ ～公司 import and export corporation/ ～贸易 import and export trade; foreign trade/ ～业务 imports and exports

【进度】 jìndù ① rate of progress (或 advance): 加快～ quicken the pace (或 tempo) ② planned speed; schedule: 我们已按照～完成了这道工序。 We have finished this part of the process according to plan. ◇ ～报告 progress report/ ～表 progress chart

【进攻】 jìngōng attack; assault; offensive: 做好～准备 get ready to take the offensive/ 发起全面～ launch an all-out offensive

【进贡】 jìngòng pay tribute (to a suzerain or emperor)

【进化】 jìnhuà evolution

【进见】 jìnjiàn call on (sb. holding high office); have an audience with

【进军】 jìnjūn march; advance: 向西北～ march into the Northwest/ 吹响～的号角 sound the bugle to advance; sound the advance

【进口】 jìnkǒu ① enter port ② import ③ entrance

【进来】 jìnlái come (或 get) in; enter: 让他～。 Let him in.

【进来】 jìnlai 〔用在动词后，表示到里面来〕: 她气喘吁吁地走～，浑身湿透了。 She came in panting and soaked to the skin.

【进取】 jìnqǔ keep forging ahead; be eager to make progress; be enterprising: 永远保持谦虚和～的精神 always remain modest and keep forging ahead ◇ ～心 enterprising spirit; initiative; gumption; push

【进去】 jìnqu go in; get in; enter: 你～看看，我在门口等着。 Go in and have a look, and I'll wait for you at the gate.

【进去】 jìnqu 〔用在动词后，表示到里面去〕: 把桌子搬～ move the table in/ 冲～ rush in

【进入】 jìnrù enter; get into: ～阵地 get into position/ ～决赛阶段 enter the finals

【进食】 jìnshí take food; have one's meal

【进退】 jìn-tuì ① advance and retreat: ～自如 free to advance or retreat (in a battle or game); have room for manoeuvre/ ～两难 difficult to advance or to retreat — in a dilemma/ ～维谷 caught in a dilemma ② sense of propriety: 不知～ have no sense of propriety

【进行】 jìnxíng ① be in progress; be underway; go on: 工作～得怎么样？ How are you getting on with your work?/ 勘探工作已经在～。 Prospecting is already in progress./ 手术～了六个小时。 The operation lasted six hours./ 大会明天继续～。 The conference continues tomorrow. ② carry on; carry out; conduct: ～实地调查 make on-the-spot investigations/ ～科学实验 engage in scientific experiment/ ～核试验 conduct a nuclear test/ ～动员 mobilize; make a mobilization speech/ ～表决 put a question to the vote

【进修】 jìnxiū engage in advanced studies; take a refresher course: 在职～ in-service training; on-the-job training/ 教师的业务～ teachers' vocational studies ◇ ～班 class for advanced studies/ ～生 graduate student

【进一步】 jìnyíbù go a step further; further: ～发展我们两国之间的友好合作关系 further develop the friendly relations and cooperation between our two countries

【进展】 jìnzhǎn make progress; make headway: ～神速 advance at a miraculous pace/ 工程～很顺利。 The project

is making good progress. 或 Construction is proceeding smoothly./ 事情～如何？ How are things going?/ 谈判毫无～。 The talks have made no headway.

近* jìn ① near; close: 靠～些。 Come closer./ ～在咫尺 be close at hand; be well within one's reach/ 歌声由远而～。 The singing came closer and closer./ 他讲课总是由～及远，由浅入深。 His lectures always proceed from the close to the distant and from the elementary to the profound./ 离国庆节很～了。 National Day is drawing near. 或 It'll soon be National Day./ ～几年来 in recent years/ ～一百年史 the history of the last hundred years/ ～在眼前 right before one's eyes; imminent ② approaching; approximately; close to: 年～六十 approaching sixty; getting on for sixty/ 观众～万人。 There were nearly 10,000 spectators. ③ intimate; closely related: 两家走得挺～。 The two families are on intimate terms. ④ easy to understand: 浅～ simple and easy to understand/ 言～旨远 simple in language but profound in meaning

【近便】 jìnbian close and convenient: 我们找个～的饭馆吃点吧。 Let's have a snack at the nearest restaurant./ 来回挺～的,不用搭车。 It's no distance at all. There's no need to take a bus.

【近代】 jìndài modern times ◇ ～史 modern history

【近海】 jìnhǎi coastal waters; inshore; offshore: 我国～有丰富的水产资源。 Our country has rich inshore aquatic resources. ◇ ～渔业 inshore fishing

【近乎】 jìnhu close to; little short of: ～谬误的论点 an argument little short of being ridiculous; an argument bordering on the absurd

【近郊】 jìnjiāo outskirts of a city; suburbs; environs

【近景】 jìnjǐng 〈摄〉 close shot

【近况】 jìnkuàng recent developments; how things stand 中东～ recent developments in the Middle East/ 多日不见来信,不知～如何？ I haven't heard from you for a long time. How are things with you?

【近来】 jìnlái recently; of late; lately

【近邻】 jìnlín near neighbour

【近路】 jìnlù shortcut: 走～ take a shortcut

【近期】 jìnqī in the near future: ～内无大雨。 There won't be heavy rain in the coming few days.

【近亲】 jìnqīn close relative; near relation

【近日】 jìnrì ① recently; in the past few days ② within the next few days

【近视】 jìnshì myopia; nearsightedness; shortsightedness: 政治上的～ political myopia ◇ ～眼镜 spectacles for nearsighted persons

【近视眼】 jìnshìyǎn myopia; nearsightedness; shortsightedness: 他是～。 He is shortsighted (或 nearsighted).

【近水楼台先得月】 jìn shuǐ lóutái xiān dé yuè a waterfront pavilion gets the moonlight first — the advantage of being in a favoured position

【近似】 jìnsì approximate; similar

【近于】 jìnyú bordering on; little short of: ～荒唐 little short of preposterous; bordering on the absurd

【近朱者赤,近墨者黑】 jìn zhū zhě chì, jìn mò zhě hēi he who stays near vermilion gets stained red, and he who stays near ink gets stained black — one takes on the colour of one's company

劲* jìn ① strength; energy: 用～ put forth strength/ 加把～,不然你要落后了。 Put on a spurt, or you'll fall behind./ 她仿佛有使不完的～。 She seems to have inexhaustible energy. 或 She's a live wire./ 我烧是退了,可身上还是没～儿。 My temperature is down, but I'm still feeling weak. ② vigour; spirit; drive; zeal ③ air; manner: 瞧他那高兴～儿。 See how happy he looks.

另见 jìng

浸* jìn soak; steep; immerse: 把衣服放在肥皂水里～一会儿再洗。 Soak the clothes in soapy water for a while before you wash them.

【浸透】 jìntòu soak; saturate; steep; infuse: 汗水～了他的衣裳。 His clothes were soaked with sweat.

烬 jìn cinder: 灰~ ashes; cinders

晋 jìn ① enter; advance: ~见 have an audience with ② promote: 加官~爵 be promoted to a higher office and rank

【晋级】 jìnjí rise in rank; be promoted

【晋见】 jìnjiàn call on (sb. holding high office); have an audience with

【晋升】 jìnshēng promote to a higher office

【晋谒】 jìnyè <书> call on (sb. holding high office); have an audience with

禁* jìn ① prohibit; forbid; ban: 严~烟火。 Smoking and lighting fires strictly forbidden (或 prohibited)./ ~赌 suppress gambling/ 解~ lift a ban; remove a ban ② imprison; detain: 监~ imprison ③ what is forbidden by law or custom; a taboo: 入国问~ on entering a country ask about its taboos; 违~品 contraband (goods) ④ forbidden area: 宫~ the imperial palace
另见 jīn

【禁闭】 jìnbì confinement (as a punishment): 关~ be placed in confinement

【禁地】 jìndì forbidden area; restricted area; out-of-bounds area

【禁忌】 jìnjì ① taboo ② avoid; abstain from: ~辛辣油腻 abstain from peppery or greasy food

【禁绝】 jìnjué totally prohibit; completely ban

【禁例】 jìnlì prohibitory regulations; prohibitions

【禁令】 jìnlìng prohibition; ban

【禁区】 jìnqū ① forbidden zone; restricted zone: 空中~ <军> restricted airspace/ 那里是~，不准过去。 You can't go there. That place is out-of-bounds. ②(wildlife or plant) preserve; reserve; natural park ③<足球> penalty area ④ <篮球> restricted area

【禁书】 jìnshū banned book

【禁运】 jìnyùn embargo

【禁止】 jìnzhǐ prohibit; ban; forbid: ~砍伐树木。 Felling trees is forbidden./ ~入内。 No admittance./ ~停车。 No parking./ ~通行。 No thoroughfare. 或 Closed to traffic./ ~倒垃圾。 No garbage here./ ~招贴。 Post no bills.

觐 jìn ① present oneself before (a monarch) ② go on a pilgrimage

【觐见】 jìnjiàn present oneself before (a monarch); go to court; have an audience with

噤 jìn ① keep silent ② shiver: 寒~ shiver with cold

【噤若寒蝉】 jìn ruò hánchán as silent as a cicada in cold weather — keep quiet out of fear

jīng

泾 Jīng short for the Jinghe River

【泾渭分明】 Jīng-Wèi fēnmíng as different as the waters of the Jinghe and the Weihe — entirely different

京* jīng the capital of a country: 进~ go to the capital

【京剧】 jīngjù Beijing opera 又作"京戏"

茎* jīng stem (of a plant); stalk

经* jīng ①<纺> warp ②<中医> channels ③<地> longitude: 东(西)~ east (west) longitude ④ manage; deal in; engage in: ~商 engage in trade ⑤ constant; regular: ~常 regular; frequent/ 不~之谈 preposterous statement; cock-and-bull story ⑥ scripture; canon; classics: 佛~ Buddhist sutra; Buddhist scripture; 圣~ the Holy Bible/ 各有一本难念的~。 Each has his own hard nut to crack. 或 Each has his own trouble. ⑦ menses; menstruation ⑧ pass through; undergo: 途~上海 pass through Shanghai/ 身~百战 have fought many battles;

be a veteran of many wars/ ~卡拉奇回国 return home via (或 by way of) Karachi ⑨ as a result of; after; through: ~商定 it has been decided through consultation that/ ~某人建议 upon sb.'s proposal/ ~检查，产品质量合格。 Examination confirmed that the quality of the products was up to specification. ⑩ stand; bear; endure: ~得起时间的考验 can stand the test of time

【经常】 jīngcháng ① day-to-day; everyday; daily: ~工作 day-to-day work/ ~开支 running expenses ② frequently; constantly: 这类问题是~发生的。 This kind of problem frequently crops up. 或 This sort of thing is a common occurrence./ 他~上图书馆去。 He goes to the library regularly.

【经典】 jīngdiǎn ① classics ② scriptures: 佛教~ Buddhist scriptures ③ classical

【经费】 jīngfèi funds; outlay

【经风雨，见世面】 jīng fēngyǔ, jiàn shìmiàn face the world and brave the storm

【经过】 jīngguò ① pass; go through; undergo ② as a result of; after; through: ~充分讨论,大家取得了一致意见。 After thorough discussion unanimity was achieved. ③ process; course: 事件的全部~ the whole course of the incident; the whole process from beginning to end/ 事情的~是这样的。 This is how it happened.

【经纪】 jīngjì ① manage (a business) ② manager; broker

【经纪人】 jīngjìrén broker; middleman; agent: 房地产~ estate agent

【经济】 jīngjì ① economy
◇ ~部门 branches of the economy; economic departments/ ~成分 sector of the economy; economic sector/ ~命脉 economic lifeline; economic arteries; key branches of the economy/ ~危机 economic crisis/ ~学 economics/ ~学家 economist

【经久】 jīngjiǔ ① prolonged: ~不息的掌声 prolonged applause ② durable: ~耐用 durable; able to stand wear and tear

【经理】 jīnglǐ ① handle; manage ② manager; director

【经历】 jīnglì ① go through; undergo; experience ② experience: 他这人~多,见识广。 He's a man of wide knowledge and experience.

【经年累月】 jīngnián-lěiyuè for years; year in year out

【经商】 jīngshāng engage in trade; be in business

【经史子集】 jīng-shǐ-zǐ-jí Confucian classics, history, philosophy and belles-lettres — the four traditional categories of Chinese writings

【经手】 jīngshǒu handle; deal with: ~公款 handle public money/ 这件事是他~的。 He's the one who handled this matter. ◇ ~人 person handling a transaction, particular job, etc.

【经受】 jīngshòu undergo; experience; withstand; stand; weather: ~了各种考验 experience all sorts of trials; stand up to all tests; withstand all trials and tribulations

【经售】 jīngshòu sell on commission; deal in; distribute; sell

【经书】 jīngshū Confucian classics

【经销】 jīngxiāo sell on commission; deal in; distribute; sell ◇ ~处 agency

【经心】 jīngxīn careful; mindful; conscientious: ~搜集各种资料 take great care to collect all kinds of data/ 漫不~ careless; casual; negligent/ 干什么工作都要~。 One should be conscientious in any kind of work.

【经验】 jīngyàn ① experience: 交流~ exchange experience/ 介绍~ pass on one's experience/ ~丰富 have rich experience; be very experienced/ ~不足 lack experience; not be sufficiently experienced/ ~之谈 remark made by one who has had experience; the wise remark of an experienced person

【经意】 jīngyì careful; mindful: 他不~把茶杯碰倒了。 He inadvertently knocked over a cup.

【经营】 jīngyíng manage; run; engage in: 发展多种~ promote a diversified economy/ 改善~管理 improve management and administration/ 苦心~ take great pains to build up (an enterprise, etc.)

【经传】jīngzhuàn ① Confucian classics and commentaries on them; Confucian canon ② classical works; classics: 名不见～ not well-known; a mere nobody

荆
jīng chaste tree; vitex
【荆棘】jīngjí thistles and thorns; brambles; thorny undergrowth

旌
jīng an ancient type of banner hoisted on a feather-decked mast
【旌旗】jīngqí banners and flags

惊*
jīng ① start; be frightened: 听到大坝出现险情, 她心里一～。 She started at the news that the dyke was in danger./ ～呆了 be stupefied ② surprise; shock; alarm: 一声～雷 a sudden clap of thunder ③ shy; stampede: 马一了。 The horse shied./ 大雷雨～了牛群。 The thunderstorm stampeded the cattle.
【惊诧】jīngchà <书> surprised; amazed; astonished
【惊动】jīngdòng alarm; alert; disturb: 枪声～了森林中的鸟兽。 The report of a gun startled the birds and animals in the forest./ 注意隐蔽, 不要～敌人。 Take good cover and don't alert the enemy./ 别为这么点儿小事～他。 Don't trouble him about such a trifling matter.
【惊弓之鸟】jīng gōng zhī niǎo a bird startled by the mere twang of a bow-string; a badly frightened person
【惊呼】jīnghū cry out in alarm
【惊慌】jīnghuāng alarmed; scared; panic-stricken: ～不安 jittery; nervy/ ～失措 frightened out of one's wits; panic-stricken/ ～的神色 frightened looks/ 没有半点～ not in the least scared/ ～地叫了起来 cry out in alarm/ 不必～。 Don't panic. 或 There's no cause for alarm. 又作"惊惶"
【惊魂未定】jīnghún wèi dìng not yet recovered from a fright; still badly shaken
【惊叫】jīngjiào cry in fear; scream
【惊恐】jīngkǒng alarmed and panicky; terrified; panic-stricken; seized with terror: ～万状 in a great panic; convulsed with fear/ ～失色 pale with fear
【惊奇】jīngqí wonder; be surprised; be amazed
【惊人】jīngrén astonishing; amazing; alarming: ～的成就 astonishing (或 amazing) achievements/ ～的毅力 amazing willpower
【惊叹】jīngtàn wonder at; marvel at; exclaim (with admiration): 这些精美的牙雕, 使大家～不已。 The exquisite ivory carvings won everybody's admiration. ◇ ～号 exclamation mark (!)
【惊涛骇浪】jīngtāo-hàilàng ① terrifying waves; stormy sea ② a situation or life full of perils
【惊天动地】jīngtiān-dòngdì shaking heaven and earth; earthshaking; world-shaking: ～的事业 earthshaking undertaking
【惊悉】jīngxī be shocked to learn: ～某人不幸逝世 be distressed to learn of the passing away of sb.
【惊喜】jīngxǐ pleasantly surprised: ～地叫了起来 call out in happy astonishment
【惊吓】jīngxià frighten; scare: 这孩子受了～, 睡得不安稳。 The child has had a shock and isn't sleeping well.
【惊险】jīngxiǎn alarmingly dangerous; breathtaking; thrilling: ～动作 astounding feat/ ～的表演 breathtaking performance/ ～的场面 thrilling scene ◇ ～小说 thriller
【惊心动魄】jīngxīn-dòngpò soul-stirring; profoundly affecting
【惊醒】jīngxǐng ① wake up with a start ② rouse suddenly from sleep; awaken: 一声巨响把他从睡梦中～。 He was awakened by a terrific bang.
【惊醒】jīngxǐng sleep lightly; be a light sleeper: 他睡觉很～, 有点响动都知道。 He's a very light sleeper; any little noise disturbs him.
【惊讶】jīngyà surprised; amazed; astonished; astounded
【惊疑】jīngyí surprised and bewildered
【惊异】jīngyì surprised; amazed; astonished; astounded

菁
jīng ① lush ② essence; cream
【菁华】jīnghuá essence; cream; quintessence

【菁菁】jīngjīng <书> lush; luxuriant

晶*
jīng ① brilliant; glittering: 亮～～ shining; glittering ② quartz; (rock) crystal ③ any crystalline substance

睛*
jīng eyeball: 定～一看 give sth. or sb. a good look/ 目不转～地看着 gaze fixedly

精*
jīng ① refined; picked; choice: ～盐 refined salt/ ～金 fine gold/ ～白米 polished white rice ② essence; extract: 去粗取～ discard the dross and select the essence/ ～讲多练 teach only the essential and ensure plenty of practice/ 鱼肝油～ cod-liver oil extract ③ perfect; excellent: ～良 excellent; superior; of the best quality ④ meticulous; fine; precise: ～收细打 careful reaping and threshing/ 这花瓶工艺很～。 This vase is a piece of exquisite workmanship. ⑤ smart; sharp; clever; shrewd: 这小鬼真～。 That's a really smart kid./ 小算盘打得～ be selfish and calculating ⑥ skilled; conversant; proficient: ～于绘画 skilled in painting ⑦ energy; spirit: 聚～会神 concentrate one's attention; be all attention ⑧ sperm; semen; seed: 受～ fertilization ⑨ goblin; spirit; demon: 白骨～ White Bone Demon/ 害人～ ogre; mischief-maker
【精兵】jīngbīng picked troops; crack troops
【精彩】jīngcǎi brilliant; splendid; wonderful: ～的表演 a brilliant performance/ 发言中最～的地方 most interesting parts of a speech/ 这场球打得真～。 This is an exciting game.
【精诚】jīngchéng <书> absolute sincerity; good faith
【精萃】jīngcuì cream; pick: 世界乒坛的～ the pick of the world's table-tennis players
【精粹】jīngcuì succinct; pithy; terse
【精打细算】jīngdǎ-xìsuàn careful calculation and strict budgeting
【精雕细刻】jīngdiāo-xìkè work at sth. with the care and precision of a sculptor; work at sth. with great care
【精读】jīngdú ① read carefully and thoroughly ② intensive reading
【精干】jīnggàn (of a body of troops, etc.) small in number but highly trained; crack
【精光】jīngguāng with nothing left: 刚插的秧苗被洪水冲得～。 Every one of the newly planted seedlings was washed away by the flood.
【精悍】jīnghàn ① capable and vigorous ② pithy and poignant
【精华】jīnghuá cream; essence; quintessence: 民族文化的～ the cream of our national culture/ 去其糟粕, 取其～ discard the dross and select the essence
【精简】jīngjiǎn retrench; simplify; cut; reduce: ～节约 simplify administration and practise economy/ ～开支 cut expenses; retrench
【精力】jīnglì energy; vigour; vim: ～充沛 very energetic; full of vigour
【精练】jīngliàn concise; succinct; terse: 语言～ succinct language
【精炼】jīngliàn ① <冶> refine; purify: 火法～ fire refining/ 真空～ vacuum refining ② 见"精练"
【精良】jīngliáng excellent; superior; of the best quality: 制作～ of excellent workmanship/ 装备～ well-equipped
【精灵】jīnglíng ① spirit; demon ② <方> (of a child) clever; smart; intelligent
【精美】jīngměi exquisite; elegant: ～的刺绣 elegant embroidery/ 包装～ beautifully packaged
【精密】jīngmì precise; accurate: ～的观察 accurate (或 close) observation
【精明】jīngmíng astute; shrewd; sagacious: ～的政治家 an astute statesman/ ～的小伙子 a bright young fellow
【精明强干】jīngmíng qiánggàn intelligent and capable; able and efficient
【精疲力竭】jīngpí-lìjié exhausted; worn out; tired out; spent
【精辟】jīngpì penetrating; incisive: 进行～的分析 make a penetrating analysis/ ～的论述 a brilliant exposition

【精巧】 jīngqiǎo exquisite; ingenious: ～的牙雕 exquisite ivory carving/ 构造～ ingeniously constructed

【精确】 jīngquè accurate; exact; precise: ～的统计 accurate statistics/ 下一个～的定义 give a precise definition

【精锐】 jīngruì crack; picked: ～部队 crack troops; picked troops

【精深】 jīngshēn profound: 博大～ have both extensive knowledge and profound scholarship/ ～的理论 a comprehensive and profound theory

【精神】 jīngshén ① spirit; mind; consciousness: 国际主义～ the spirit of internationalism/ 崇高的～ noble spirit/ 作好～准备 be mentally prepared/ 给予～上的支持 give moral support/ ～上的负担 a load on one's mind/ 空虚 be spiritually barren ② essence; gist; spirit: 传达文件的～ convey (或 pass on) the gist of a document/ 领会社论的～ try to understand the thrust of an editorial/ 贯彻代表大会的～ act in the spirit of the congress/ 译者没有体会原文的～。The translator failed to capture the spirit of the original.

【精神】 jīngshen ① vigour; vitality; drive: ～饱满 full of vigour (或 vitality); energetic/ 没有～ listless; languid/ 振作～ bestir oneself; summon up one's energy; get up steam ② lively; spirited; vigorous: 他穿上军装显得格外～。The army uniform made him look especially impressive./ 那孩子大大的眼睛,怪～的。That child with the big eyes is certainly full of life.

【精神病】 jīngshénbìng mental disease; mental disorder; psychosis

【精通】 jīngtōng be proficient in; have a good command of; master: ～业务 be proficient in professional work/ 英语 have a good command of English

【精细】 jīngxì meticulous; fine; careful: 手工十分～ show fine workmanship/ ～的计算 careful calculation/ 考虑问题很～ think matters over carefully; be circumspect/ 这件上衣做工～。This jacket is well-tailored.

【精心】 jīngxīn meticulously; painstakingly; elaborately: ～护理 nurse with the best of care/ ～设计、～施工 be meticulous in design and construction; painstakingly design and carefully construct/ ～策划的阴谋 a carefully calculated plot; an elaborately planned conspiracy/ ～炮制 elaborately cook up

【精选】 jīngxuǎn ①〈矿〉concentration ② carefully chosen; choice: 用～的原料制成 made of choice material

【精益求精】 jīng yì qiú jīng constantly improve sth.; keep improving: 对技术～ constantly improve one's skill/ 这首诗他还在反复推敲。～。He's still trying to polish and improve the poem.

【精湛】 jīngzhàn consummate; exquisite: ～的技巧 consummate skill; superb technique/ 工艺～ exquisite workmanship; perfect craftsmanship

【精致】 jīngzhì fine; exquisite; delicate: ～的丝织品 fine silks

【精装】 jīngzhuāng (of books) clothbound; hardback; hardcover ◇ ～本 de luxe edition

【精壮】 jīngzhuàng able-bodied; strong

兢 jīng

【兢兢业业】 jīngjīngyèyè cautious and conscientious

鲸 jīng whale

jǐng

井* jǐng ① well: 打～ sink a well; drill a well ② sth. in the shape of a well: 矿～ pit; mine/ 油～ oil well ③ neat; orderly

【井底之蛙】 jǐngdǐ zhī wā a frog in a well — a person with a very limited outlook

【井井有条】 jǐngjǐng yǒu tiáo in perfect order; shipshape; methodical: ～地工作 work methodically/ 各种仪器、工具摆得～。All the instruments and tools are kept in perfect order.

【井然】 jǐngrán 〈书〉orderly; neat and tidy; shipshape; methodical: 秩序～ in good order

【井水不犯河水】 jǐngshuǐ bù fàn héshuǐ well water does not intrude into river water — I'll mind my own business, you mind yours

阱 jǐng trap; pitfall; pit

颈 jǐng neck

【颈项】 jǐngxiàng neck

景* jǐng ① view; scenery; scene: 外～ exterior view/ 西湖美～ the enchanting scenery of the West Lake/ 雪～ a snow scene ② situation; condition: 好～不长。Good times do not last long. ③ scenery (of a play or film): 换～ change of scenery ④ scene (of a play): 第三幕第一～ Act III, scene 1 ⑤ admire; revere; respect: ～慕 esteem; revere

【景观】 jǐngguān 〈地〉landscape: 自然～ natural landscape

【景况】 jǐngkuàng situation; circumstances: 她家的～越来越好了。Things are getting easier and easier for her family.

【景气】 jǐngqì prosperity; boom: 不～ depression; slump

【景色】 jǐngsè scenery; view; scene; landscape: 深秋～ a late autumn scene/ 南方～ southern landscape/ 海上看日出,～特别美丽。At sea one can get a particularly beautiful view of the sunrise.

【景物】 jǐngwù scenery: ～宜人 delightful scenery

【景象】 jǐngxiàng scene; sight; picture: 一派丰收～ one vast panorama of bumper crops

【景仰】 jǐngyǎng respect and admire; hold in deep respect: 怀着无限～的心情 with boundless respect and admiration

【景遇】 jǐngyù 〈书〉circumstances; one's lot

【景致】 jǐngzhì view; scenery; scene: 从塔顶可以看到全城的～。The tower commands a view of the whole town./ 一下雪,这里的～就更美了。This place looks even more beautiful after a fall of snow.

儆 jǐng warn; admonish: 惩一～百 punish one to warn a hundred; make an example of sb.

警* jǐng ① alert; vigilant: ～醒 be a light sleeper ② warn; alarm: ～告 warn ③ alarm: 火～ fire alarm ④〈简〉(警察) police

【警报】 jǐngbào alarm; warning; alert: 拉～ sound the alarm (或 siren)/ 解除空袭～ all clear/ 台风～ a typhoon warning/ 战斗～ combat alert

【警备】 jǐngbèi guard; garrison ◇ ～区 garrison command/ ～司令部 garrison headquarters

【警察】 jǐngchá police; policeman: 女～ policewoman

【警笛】 jǐngdí ① police whistle ② siren

【警告】 jǐnggào ① warn; caution; admonish: 对敌人的军事挑衅提出严重～ issue a serious warning to the enemy against their military provocations/ 我们一再～他不要跟那种人来往。We repeatedly admonished him not to associate with that sort of people. ② warning (as a disciplinary measure): 给予～处分 give sb. a disciplinary warning ◇ ～信号 〈交〉warning signal

【警戒】 jǐngjiè ① warn; admonish ② be on the alert against; guard against; keep a close watch on: 采取～措施 take precautionary measures/ 沿公路放出～ post guards along the highway

【警句】 jǐngjù aphorism; epigram

【警觉】 jǐngjué vigilance; alertness: 引起～ arouse vigilance

【警犬】 jǐngquǎn police dog

【警惕】 jǐngtì be on guard against; watch out for; be vigilant: 保持高度～ maintain sharp vigilance ◇ ～性 vigilance

【警卫】jǐngwèi (security) guard
◇ ～室 guardroom/ ～团 guards regiment/ ～员 body-guard
【警钟】jǐngzhōng alarm bell

jìng

劲* jìng strong; powerful; sturdy: ～松 sturdy pines
另见 jìn
【劲敌】jìngdí formidable adversary; strong opponent
【劲旅】jìnglǚ strong contingent; crack force: 这个厂的篮球队可算是全市的一支～。This factory's basketball team is one of the strongest in the city.

净* jìng ①clean: ～水 clean water/ 擦～ wipe sth. clean/ 这件裤子没洗～。This jacket hasn't been properly washed. ②completely: 用～ use up ③only; merely; nothing but: ～说不干 all talk, no action/ 这几天～刮大风。It's been very windy these last few days./ 别～打岔。Don't keep interrupting./ 桌上～是中草药的标本。There is nothing on the desk but specimens of medicinal herbs. ④net: ～收入 net income/ ～出口 net export/ ～进口 net import
【净化】jìnghuà purify: 水的～ purification of water ◇ ～塔 purifying column
【净尽】jìngjìn completely; utterly: 消灭～ utterly annihilate
【净利】jìnglì net profit
【净值】jìngzhí net worth; net value: 出口～ net export value/ 进口～ net import value
【净重】jìngzhòng net weight

径* jìng ①footpath; path; track: 曲～ a winding path ②way; means: 捷～ an easy way; shortcut ③<副> directly; straightaway: ～行办理 deal with the matter straightaway ④diameter: 半～ radius
【径赛】jìngsài <体> track events
【径庭】jìngtíng <书> very unlike: 大相～ entirely different; poles apart
【径直】jìngzhí <副> straight; directly; straightaway: 登山队员～向主峰进发。
【径自】jìngzì <副> without leave; without consulting anyone: 会没开完,他～走了。He left abruptly in the middle of the meeting.

胫 jìng <生理> shin
【胫骨】jìnggǔ shin bone; tibia

痉 jìng
【痉挛】jìngluán convulsion; spasm

竞* jìng compete; contest; vie: 百里江面,千帆～发。A thousand boats set sail on a long stretch of the river.
【竞渡】jìngdù ①boat race ②swimming race
【竞技】jìngjì sports; athletics ◇ ～场 arena
【竞赛】jìngsài contest; competition; emulation; race
【竞选】jìngxuǎn enter into an election contest; campaign for (office); run for: ～总统 run for the presidency
【竞争】jìngzhēng compete: 自由～ free competition ◇ ～价格 competitive price/ ～性 competitiveness
【竞走】jìngzǒu heel-and-toe walking race

竟* jìng ①finish; complete: 未～之业 unaccomplished cause; unfinished task ②throughout; whole: ～夜 the whole night; throughout the night ③in the end; eventually: 有志者事～成。Where there's a will there's a way. ④<副> [表示有点出于意料之外] unexpectedly; actually: 这么陡的峭壁,谁知他～爬上去了。Who would have expected that he could climb up that steep cliff? ⑤<副> go so far as to; go to the length of; have the impudence (或 effrontery) to
【竟敢】jìnggǎn have the audacity; have the impertinence;

dare: 敌人～如此嚣张,我们不能不予以回击。When the enemy is on the rampage like this, we've got to hit back.
【竟然】jìngrán <副> ①unexpectedly; to one's surprise; actually: 这样宏伟的建筑,～只用十个月的时间就完成了。To think that such a magnificent building was completed in ten months!/ 想不到他们～把一座荒山变成了花果山。Who would have thought that they could turn a barren hill into an orchard? ②go so far as to; go to the length of; have the impudence (或 effrontery) to: ～不顾事实 go so far as to disregard the facts

敬* jìng ①respect: 尊～ respect; esteem; honour/ 致～ pay one's respects; salute ②respectfully: ～请光临 request the honour of your presence ③offer politely: ～烟 offer a cigarette/ ～茶 serve tea/ ～你一杯! To your health!
【敬爱】jìng'ài respect and love
【敬而远之】jìng ér yuǎn zhī stay at a respectful distance from sb.
【敬奉】jìngfèng ①piously worship ②offer respectfully; present politely
【敬酒】jìngjiǔ propose a toast; toast
【敬酒不吃吃罚酒】jìngjiǔ bù chī chī fájiǔ refuse a toast only to drink a forfeit — submit to sb.'s pressure after first turning down his request; be constrained to do what one at first declined
【敬礼】jìnglǐ ①salute; give a salute ②extend one's greetings ③<敬> 〔用于书信结尾〕此致～ with high respect; with best wishes
【敬佩】jìngpèi esteem; admire: 大家以～的目光望着他。Everybody looked at him admiringly.
【敬挽】jìngwǎn 〔用于挽联、花圈等的落款〕with deep condolences from sb.
【敬畏】jìngwèi hold in awe and veneration; revere
【敬仰】jìngyǎng revere; venerate: 深受人民的爱戴和～ command deep love and reverence among the people
【敬意】jìngyì respect; tribute: 表示衷心的～ extend one's heartfelt respects; pay sincere tribute
【敬重】jìngzhòng deeply respect; revere; honour

靖 jìng ①peace; tranquillity ②pacify: ～乱 put down a rebellion

境* jìng ①border; boundary: 国～ national boundary/ 在本省～内 within the boundaries of this province/ 越～ cross the border illegally ②place; area; territory: 敌～ enemy territory/ 如入无人之～ like entering an unpeopled land — meeting no resistance ③condition; situation; circumstances: 困～ difficult position; predicament
【境地】jìngdì condition; circumstances: 处于狼狈的～ be in a sorry plight; be in a predicament/ 陷入完全孤立的～ land oneself in utter isolation
【境界】jìngjiè ①boundary ②extent reached; plane attained; state; realm: 达到崇高的思想～ attain a lofty realm of thought/ 理想～ ideal state; ideal
【境况】jìngkuàng condition; circumstances: ～不佳 in straitened circumstances
【境遇】jìngyù circumstances; one's lot: 极困难的～ extremely adverse circumstances

静* jìng still; quiet; calm: 风平浪～ calm and tranquil/ 夜深人～ in the still of the night; at the dead of night/ 请～一～。Please be quiet.
【静默】jìngmò ①become silent: 会场上又是一阵～。Another spell of silence fell upon the meeting room. ②mourn in silence; observe silence
【静穆】jìngmù solemn and quiet
【静悄悄】jìngqiāoqiāo very quiet: 屋里～的。It was very quiet in the room.
【静养】jìngyǎng rest quietly to recuperate; convalesce: 希望你安心～。I hope you'll set aside your worries and have a good rest.
【静止】jìngzhǐ static; motionless; at a standstill: 相对～的状态 a state of relative rest/ 生活永远不是～的。Life is never at a standstill.

【静坐】 jìngzuò ① sit quietly ② sit still as a form of therapy ◇ ～罢工 sit-down (strike)/ ～示威 sit-in (demonstration); sit-down (protest)

镜* jìng ① looking glass; mirror: 铜～ bronze mirror/ 湖平如～。 The lake is as smooth as a mirror. ② lens; glass: 放大～ magnifying glass; magnifier

【镜框】 jìngkuàng ① picture frame ② spectacles frame
【镜片】 jìngpiàn lens
【镜台】 jìngtái dressing table
【镜头】 jìngtóu ① camera lens: 远摄～ telephoto lens/ 可变焦距～ zoom lens/广角～ wide-angle lens ② shot; scene: 特技～ special effect shot; trick shot
【镜子】 jìngzi ① mirror; looking glass ② <口> glasses; spectacles

jiǒng

迥 jiǒng <书> ① far away ② widely different: 他病前病后～若两人。 He doesn't look like the same person after his illness.
【迥然】 jiǒngrán far apart; widely different: ～不同 utterly different; not in the least alike

炯 jiǒng bright; shining
【炯炯】 jiǒngjiǒng <书> (of eyes) bright; shining: 他的一双眼睛～有神。 He has a pair of bright piercing eyes.

窘 jiǒng ① in straitened circumstances; hard up: 他一度生活很～。 He was rather hard up for a time. ② awkward; embarrassed; ill at ease: 露出一态 show signs of embarrassment ③ embarrass; disconcert: 这个问题～得他无言可答。 The question embarrassed him so much that he was quite at a loss for an answer.
【窘境】 jiǒngjìng awkward situation; predicament; plight
【窘迫】 jiǒngpò ① poverty-stricken; very poor: 生活～ live in poverty ② hard pressed; embarrassed; in a predicament: 处境～ find oneself in a predicament

jiū

纠* jiū ① entangle: ～缠 get entangled (或 bogged down) ② gather together: ～合一伙流氓 get together (或 round up) a bunch of hoodlums ③ correct; rectify: ～偏 rectify a deviation
【纠察】 jiūchá ① maintain order at a public gathering ② picket ◇ ～队 pickets/ ～线 picket line
【纠缠】 jiūchán ① get entangled; be in a tangle: ～不清 too tangled up to unravel/ 防止在枝节问题上～不休 avoid endless quibbling over side issues/ 完成侦察任务要紧, 不要与敌人～。 Be sure to accomplish your scouting mission; don't get tied down by the enemy. ② nag; worry; pester: 他忙着呢, 别～他了。 He's busy. Stop pestering him.
【纠纷】 jiūfēn dispute; issue: 无原则～ an unprincipled dispute/ 国与国之间的～ disputes between countries/ 调解～ mediate an issue
【纠葛】 jiūgé entanglement; dispute: 他们之间发生了一点～。 There's a dispute between them.
【纠集】 jiūjí <贬> get together; muster: ～一批打手 gather together a bunch of thugs/ ～残部 muster the remaining forces
【纠正】 jiūzhèng correct; put right; redress: ～错误 correct a mistake; redress an error/ ～姿势 correct sb.'s posture/ ～不正之风 check unhealthy tendencies/ 问题处理不当的, 应予～。 Cases which have not been handled properly should be put right.

究* jiū ① study carefully; go into; investigate: 深～ go deeply into a matter; get to the bottom of a matter/ ～其根源 trace sth. to its source ② <书> actually; really; after all: ～应如何办理? How should this really be dealt with?/ ～系何因, 尚待深查。 The actual cause awaits further investigation.
【究办】 jiūbàn investigate and deal with: 依法～ investigate and deal with according to law
【究竟】 jiūjìng ① outcome; what actually happened: 大家都想知道个～。 Everybody wants to know what actually happened./ 不管什么事, 他总爱问个～。 He always likes to get to the heart of a matter, whatever it may be. ② <副> 〔用于问句, 表示追究〕 actually; exactly: 明天的会～谁去参加? Who is actually going to the meeting tomorrow?/ 你们～要什么? What exactly do you want?/ 这～是什么意思? Whatever does this mean?/ 他～上哪儿去了? Where on earth is he? ③ <副> 〔表示毕竟, 到底〕 after all; in the end: 他～经验丰富, 让他负责这项工作最合适。 After all, he is very experienced, so it is only suitable to put him in charge of the job.

鸠 jiū turtledove: 绿～ green pigeon

赳 jiū
【赳赳】 jiūjiū valiant; gallant: 雄～ valiant; gallant

揪 jiū ① hold tight; seize: ～住一个小偷 grab a thief/ 他承认了错误, 就不要再～住不放。 Now that he has admitted his mistake, we should not keep picking on him. ② pull; tug; drag: 别那么使劲～绳子。 Don't pull so hard at the rope.

啾 jiū
【啾啾】 jiūjiū <象> 〔形容许多小鸟一起叫的声音〕 chirps

jiǔ

九* jiǔ nine
【九牛二虎之力】 jiǔ niú èr hǔ zhī lì the strength of nine bulls and two tigers — tremendous effort: 我们费了～才找到这种矿石。 We found this ore only after great effort.
【九牛一毛】 jiǔ niú yī máo a single hair out of nine ox hides — a drop in the ocean
【九泉】 jiǔquán <书> grave; the nether world: ～之下 in the nether regions; after death
【九死一生】 jiǔ sǐ yī shēng a narrow escape from death
【九天】 jiǔtiān the Ninth Heaven; the highest of heavens
【九霄云外】 jiǔxiāo yúnwài beyond the highest heavens: 把个人安危抛到～ cast personal safety to the winds; totally disregard one's safety
【九月】 jiǔyuè ① September ② the ninth month of the lunar year; the ninth moon

久* jiǔ ① for a long time; long: 很～以前 long ago/ ～别重逢 meet after a long separation ② of a specified duration: 两个月之～ for as long as two months/ 来了有多～? How long have you been here?
【久而久之】 jiǔ ér jiǔ zhī in the course of time; as time passes: 只要你注意搜集, ～, 资料就丰富了。 If you keep on collecting, in time you'll have a wealth of data.
【久旱逢甘雨】 jiǔ hàn féng gānyǔ have a welcome rain after a long drought — have a long-felt need satisfied
【久久】 jiǔjiǔ for a long, long time
【久违】 jiǔwéi <套> how long it is since we last met; I haven't seen you for ages
【久仰】 jiǔyǎng <套> I've long been looking forward to meeting you; I'm very pleased to meet you
【久远】 jiǔyuǎn far back; ages ago; remote: 年代～ of the remote past; age-old; time-honoured

灸 jiǔ <中医> moxibustion

韭 jiǔ fragrant-flowered garlic; (Chinese) chives: 青～ young chives; chive seedlings
【韭菜】 jiǔcài fragrant-flowered garlic; (Chinese) chives

酒* jiǔ alcoholic drink; wine; liquor; spirits
【酒吧间】 jiǔbājiān bar; barroom

【酒菜】 jiǔcài food and drink; food to go with wine or liquor

【酒厂】 jiǔchǎng brewery; winery; distillery

【酒店】 jiǔdiàn wineshop; public house

【酒馆】 jiǔguǎn public house

【酒鬼】 jiǔguǐ ① drunkard; sot ② toper; wine bibber

【酒会】 jiǔhuì cocktail party

【酒家】 jiǔjiā wineshop; restaurant

【酒量】 jiǔliàng capacity for liquor: 他～很大。He's a heavy drinker. 或 He can hold a lot of liquor.

【酒肉朋友】 jiǔròu péngyou wine-and-meat friends; fair-weather friends

【酒徒】 jiǔtú wine bibber

【酒窝】 jiǔwō dimple

【酒席】 jiǔxí feast

【酒意】 jiǔyì a tipsy feeling: 已有几分～ be slightly tipsy; be mellow

jiù

旧* jiù ① past; bygone; old: ～社会 the old society/ ～思想 old way of thinking; timeworn ideas/ ～事重提 bring up a matter of the past/ ～的传统观念 outdated conventional ideas ② used; worn; old:～衣服 used (或 old) clothes/ 买～的 buy sth. secondhand ③ former; onetime: ～都 former capital ④ old friendship; old friend: 故～ old acquaintances

【旧病复发】 jiùbìng fù fā have a recurrence of an old illness; have a relapse

【旧地重游】 jiùdì chóng yóu revisit a once familiar place

【旧恶】 jiù'è old grievance; old wrong: 不念～ forgive an old wrong

【旧货】 jiùhuò secondhand goods; junk: 我买的是～。I bought it secondhand. ◇ ～店 secondhand shop; junk shop/ ～市场 flea market

【旧交】 jiùjiāo old acquaintance

【旧时】 jiùshí old times; old days

【旧式】 jiùshì old type: ～文人 old-type scholars

【旧书】 jiùshū ① secondhand book; used (或 old) book ② books by ancient writers

【旧址】 jiùzhǐ site (of a former organization, building, etc.): 农会～ the site of the former peasant association/ 这是我们机关的～。Here's where our organization used to be.

臼 jiù ① mortar: 石～ stone mortar ② any mortar-shaped thing ③ joint (of bones): 脱～ dislocation (of joints)

【臼齿】 jiùchǐ molar

疚 jiù 〈书〉 remorse: 感到内～ have a guilty conscience

咎 jiù ① fault; blame: 归～于人 lay the blame on sb. else ② censure; punish; blame: 既往不～ forgive sb.'s past misdeeds; let bygones be bygones

【咎由自取】 jiù yóu zì qǔ have only oneself to blame

柩 jiù a coffin with a corpse in it

【柩车】 jiùchē hearse

救* jiù ① rescue; save; salvage: 他跳进急流，把孩子～了出来。He jumped into the torrent and rescued the child from drowning./ 病人得～了。The patient was saved./ 呼～ call out for help; send out SOS signals ② help; relieve; succour

【救兵】 jiùbīng relief troops; reinforcements

【救护】 jiùhù relieve a sick or injured person; give first-aid; rescue: ～伤员 give first-aid to the wounded/ 奋勇～战友 valiantly go to the rescue of one's comrade-in-arms ◇ ～车 ambulance

【救活】 jiùhuó bring sb. back to life

【救火】 jiùhuǒ fire fighting ◇ ～车 fire engine/ ～队 fire brigade/ ～队员 fireman; fire fighter

【救急】 jiùjí help sb. to cope with an emergency; help meet an urgent need: 你们支援我们这些材料,可真～了。You gave us this material just when we needed it most.

【救济】 jiùjì relieve; succour: ～灾区人民 provide relief to the people in a disaster area/ 社会～事业 social relief facilities

【救苦救难】 jiùkǔ-jiùnàn help the needy and relieve the distressed

【救命】 jiùmìng save sb.'s life: ～! Help! ◇ ～稻草 a straw to clutch at/ ～恩人 saviour

【救生】 jiùshēng lifesaving ◇ ～带 life belt/ ～筏 life raft/ ～圈 life buoy/ ～设备 lifesaving appliance; life preserver/ ～艇 lifeboat/ ～衣 life jacket/ ～员 lifeguard; lifesaver

【救世主】 jiùshìzhǔ 〈基督教〉 the Saviour; the Redeemer

【救亡】 jiùwáng save the nation from extinction: ～图存 save the nation from subjugation and ensure its survival ◇ ～运动 national salvation movement

【救星】 jiùxīng liberator; emancipator

【救援】 jiùyuán rescue; come to sb.'s help

【救灾】 jiùzāi provide disaster relief; send relief to a disaster area; help the people tide over a natural disaster

【救治】 jiùzhì bring a patient out of danger; treat and cure: 大批医务人员奔赴灾区～伤病员。Large numbers of medical workers hurried to the disaster area to give treatment to the sick and wounded.

【救助】 jiùzhù help sb. in danger or difficulty; succour

厩 jiù stable; cattle-shed; pen

就* jiù ① come near; move towards: 大家～拢来烤火取暖。They all moved towards the fire to get warm./ ～着路灯下棋 play chess by the light of a street lamp ② undertake; engage in; enter upon: ～学 go to school/ ～席 take one's seat; be seated at the table ③ accomplish; make: 功成业～ (of a person's career) be crowned with success ④ concerning; on: ～我所知 so far as I know/ 双方～共同关心的问题进行了会谈。The two sides held talks on questions of common interest. ⑤〈副〉 at once; right away: 我这～去。I'll be going right away. ⑥〈副〉 as early as; already ⑦〈副〉 as soon as; right after: 说干～干 act without delay ⑧〈副〉〔表示在某种条件或情况下自然会怎样〕: 不经过艰苦奋斗,～不能胜利。We cannot be victorious without arduous struggle. ⑨〈副〉〔放在两个相同的成分之间,表示容忍〕: 丢了～丢了吧,以后小心点。If it's lost, it's lost. Just be more careful from now on. ⑩〈副〉〔表示原来或早已是这样〕: 我～料到他会等我们的。I knew he'd be waiting for us./ 我～不懂法语。I never said I knew any French. ⑪〈副〉 only; merely; just: ～这一本了,看完请马上还。This is the only copy left. Please return it as soon as you finish reading it./ ～等你一个了。You're the only one we're waiting for./ 我～要几张纸。I just want a few sheets of paper. ⑫〈副〉〔表示坚决〕: 我～不信我们妇女干不了这一行。I just wouldn't believe that we women couldn't do this sort of work./ 他～不肯歇一歇。He simply refused to take a rest. ⑬〈副〉 exactly; precisely: 我～要这只。This is the one I want./ 医务室～在这儿。This is where the clinic is.

【就此】 jiùcǐ at this point; here and now; thus: 讨论～结束。The discussion was thus brought to a close./ 工作虽然有了一点成绩,但不能～松懈下来。It's true that we have accomplished something, but this doesn't mean we can let up now.

【就地】 jiùdì on the spot: ～解决问题 settle the problem on the spot

【就地取材】 jiùdì qǔcái use local materials; draw on local resources

【就范】 jiùfàn submit; give in: 迫使～ compel sb. to submit/ 不肯～ refuse to submit to control; refuse to give in

【就近】 jiùjìn (do or get sth.) nearby; in the neighbourhood; without having to go far: ～找个住处 find accommodation in the neighbourhood

【就寝】 jiùqǐn 〈书〉 retire for the night; go to bed

【就任】 jiùrèn take up one's post; take office

【就事论事】jiù shì lùn shì consider sth. as it stands: 我不清楚这件事的背景,只能～地谈谈。As I don't know the whole background, I can only judge the case as it stands.

【就是】jiùshì ①〖用在句末表示肯定,多加"了"〗: 放心吧, 我照办～了。Don't worry. I promise to do just as you say. ② quite right; exactly; precisely: ～嘛, 我是这么想的。Precisely. That's just what I had in mind. ③〈连〉〖下半句常用"也"呼应〗even if; even: ～天塌下来我们也顶得住。Even if the sky falls, we'll be able to hold it up.

【就是说】jiùshìshuō that is to say; in other words; namely

【就算】jiùsuàn 〈口〉even if; granted that: ～你工作干得不错,也不应该骄傲吧。Granted you have not done badly, still there is no reason to be conceited.

【就位】jiùwèi take one's place

【就绪】jiùxù be in order; be ready: 一切都已～。Everything is ready (或 in order)./ 准备工作已经大致～。The preparations are more or less completed.

【就要】jiùyào be about to; be going to; be on the point of: 火车～开了。The train is about to start. 或 The train is starting in a minute.

【就业】jiùyè obtain employment; take up an occupation; get a job: 充分～ full employment/ ～不足 underemployment

【就职】jiùzhí assume office: 宣誓～ take the oath of office; be sworn in ◇ ～典礼 inaugural ceremony; inauguration/ ～演说 inaugural speech

【就座】jiùzuò take one's seat; be seated: 在主席台前列～的有… seated in the front row on the rostrum were…/ 贵宾们依次～。The honoured guests took their seats in due order.

舅* jiù ① mother's brother; uncle ② wife's brother; brother-in-law ③〈书〉husband's father

【舅父】jiùfù mother's brother; uncle
【舅舅】jiùjiu 〈口〉见"舅父"
【舅妈】jiùmā 〈口〉见"舅母"
【舅母】jiùmǔ wife of mother's brother; aunt
【舅子】jiùzi 〈口〉wife's brother; brother-in-law

鹫 jiù vulture

jū

车* jū chariot, one of the pieces in Chinese chess
另见 chē

拘 jū ① arrest; detain ② restrain; restrict; limit; constrain: 无～无束 unconstrained; free and easy/ 长短不～ with no limit on the length ③ inflexible: ～泥 be a stickler for (form, etc.); rigidly adhere to (formalities, etc.)

【拘捕】jūbǔ arrest
【拘谨】jūjǐn overcautious; reserved: 初次见面时,他有些～,不大爱说话。At the first meeting he was rather reserved and withdrawn.
【拘禁】jūjìn take into custody
【拘礼】jūlǐ be punctilious; stand on ceremony: 熟不～ be too familiar with each other to stand on ceremony
【拘留】jūliú detain; hold in custody; intern ◇ ～所 house of detention; lockup
【拘泥】jūnì be a stickler for (form, etc.); rigidly adhere to (formalities, etc.): ～于形式 rigidly adhere to form; be formalistic/ ～于细节 be very punctilious
【拘束】jūshù ① restrain; restrict: 不要～孩子们的正当活动。Don't restrict the proper activities of children. ② constrained; awkward; ill at ease: 在生人面前显得～ look ill at ease in the presence of strangers/ 不要～。Make yourself at home.
【拘押】jūyā take into custody

狙 jū
【狙击】jūjī snipe ◇ ～手 sniper/ ～战 sniping action

居* jū ① reside; dwell; live: 侨～国外 reside abroad/

穴～ live in caves ② residence; house: 故～ former residence/ 迁～ move house; change one's residence ③ be (in a certain position); occupy (a place): ～中 be in the middle/ ～世界首位 occupy first place in the world; rank first in the world/ 身～要职 hold an important post ④ claim; assert: ～以专家自～ claim to be an expert; be a self-styled expert ⑤ store up; lay by: 囤积～奇 hoarding and profiteering ⑥ stay put; be at a standstill: 岁月不～。Time marches on.

【居安思危】jū ān sī wēi be prepared for danger in times of peace; be vigilant in peace time
【居多】jūduō be in the majority
【居高临下】jū gāo lín xià occupy a commanding position (或 height)
【居功】jūgōng claim credit for oneself: ～自傲 claim credit for oneself and become arrogant
【居间】jūjiān (mediate) between two parties: ～调停 mediate between two parties; act as mediator ◇ ～人 intermediary; mediator
【居留】jūliú reside: 长期～ permanent residence ◇ ～权 right of residence/ ～证 residence permit
【居民】jūmín resident; inhabitant
【居然】jūrán 〈副〉① unexpectedly; to one's surprise: 这么重的担子,他一挑就走了十公里。Who would have thought he could carry such a heavy load for 10 km? ② go so far as to; have the impudence (或 effrontery) to: ～当面撒谎 go so far as to tell a bare-faced lie/ 你怎么～相信这种谣言? How could you believe such a rumour?
【居心】jūxīn harbour (evil) intentions: ～不良 harbour evil intentions/ 他们～何在? What are they up to?
【居中】jūzhōng ① (mediate) between two parties: ～斡旋 mediate between disputants ② be placed in the middle: 小标题一律～。Subheads should be placed in the middle of the column. 或 Centre the subheads.
【居住】jūzhù live; reside; dwell: 他家一直～在乡下。His family have always lived in the country.

掬 jū hold with both hands: 以手～水 scoop up some water with one's hands/ 笑容可～ radiant with smiles/ 憨态可～ charmingly naive

据 jū 见"拮据" jié jū
另见 jù

鞠* jū rear; bring up: ～养 bring up

【鞠躬】jūgōng ① bow: ～致谢 bow one's thanks/ 深深地鞠一个躬 make a deep bow; bow low ②〈书〉in a discreet and scrupulous manner
【鞠躬尽瘁】jūgōng jìn cuì bend oneself to a task and exert oneself to the utmost; spare no effort in the performance of one's duty: ～,死而后已 bend one's back to the task until one's dying day; give one's all till one's heart stops beating

jú

局* jú ① chessboard ② game; set; innings: 第一～(乒乓球等) the first game; the first set/ (板球、棒球、垒球) the first innings/ 下一～棋 play a game of chess ③ situation; state of affairs: 战～ the war situation/ 全～ the overall situation; the situation as a whole ④ largeness or smallness of mind; extent of one's tolerance of others: 度量大 be large-minded; be tolerant/ ～量不能容物 not tolerant of others ⑤ ruse; trap: 骗～ fraud; trap; swindle ⑥ limit; confine ⑦ part; portion ⑧ office; bureau: 邮～ post office/ 电话～ telephone exchange ⑨ shop: 书～ publishing house

【局部】júbù part: ～必须服从全局。The part must be subordinated to the whole./ 不能只顾～和眼前。One mustn't be concerned only with the partial and the immediate.

【局促】júcù ① narrow; cramped: 这地方～,走动不便。This place is rather cramped; there's little room for free movement. ②〈方〉(of time) short: 三天太～,恐怕办不成。I'm afraid three days is not long enough for us to get it done. ③ feel or show constraint: ~不安 ill at ease

【局面】 júmiàn aspect; phase; situation: 出现了崭新的~。 Things have taken on a new aspect./ 打开~ open up a new prospect; make a breakthrough

【局势】 júshì situation: 国际~ the international situation/ 紧张~ a tense situation; tension

【局外人】 júwàirén outsider

【局限】 júxiàn limit; confine: 颇有~ be rather limited (in outlook, etc.); have many limitations/ 他的报告不~于教学法问题。His talk wasn't confined to teaching methods. ◇ ~性 limitations

桔
jú 见"橘" jú

菊*
jú chrysanthemum

【菊花】 júhuā chrysanthemum

橘
jú tangerine; mandarin orange

【橘汁】 júzhī orange juice

【橘子】 júzi tangerine

jǔ

沮
jǔ ①<书> stop; prevent: ~其成行 stop sb. from going ② turn gloomy; turn glum

【沮丧】 jǔsàng dejected; depressed; dispirited; disheartened: 敌人士气~。 The enemy's morale is low.

咀
jǔ chew

【咀嚼】 jǔjué ① masticate; chew ② mull over; ruminate; chew the cud

举*
jǔ ① lift; raise; hold up: ~杯 raise one's glass (to propose a toast) ② act; deed; move: 壮~ a heroic undertaking/ 一~一动 every act and every move; every action ③ start: ~义 rise in revolt ④ elect; choose: 公~他当代表 choose him as representative ⑤ cite; enumerate: 我可以~出好几件事来说明。 I can cite quite a few instances to illustrate./ ~不胜~ too numerous to mention

【举办】 jǔbàn conduct; hold; run: ~训练班 conduct a training course/ ~音乐会 give a concert

【举动】 jǔdòng movement; move; act; activity: ~缓慢 slow in movement/ 轻率的~ a rash act

【举凡】 jǔfán <书> ranging from...to...; all...such as

【举国】 jǔguó the whole nation: ~欢腾。 The whole nation is jubilant./ ~上下团结一致。 There is solid unity throughout the nation./ 得到~一致的支持 enjoy nationwide support/ ~一致的愿望 the unanimous aspiration of the nation

【举火】 jǔhuǒ <书> ① light a fire: ~为号 light a beacon ② light a kitchen fire; light a stove

【举例】 jǔlì give an example: ~说明 illustrate with examples

【举目】 jǔmù <书> raise the eyes; look: ~四望 look round/ ~远眺 look into the distance/ ~无亲 have no one to turn to (for help); be a stranger in a strange land

【举棋不定】 jǔ qí bù dìng hesitate about (或 over) what move to make; be unable to make up one's mind; vacillate; shilly-shally

【举世】 jǔshì throughout the world; universally: ~皆知 known to all/ ~公认 universally acknowledged/ ~瞩目 attract worldwide attention; become the focus of world attention/ ~闻名 of world renown; world-famous/ ~无双 unrivalled; matchless

【举手】 jǔshǒu raise (或 put up) one's hand or hands: 赞成的请~。 Those in favour please put up their hands./ 举起手来! Hands up! ◇ ~表决 vote by a show of hands/ ~礼 hand salute

【举行】 jǔxíng hold (a meeting, ceremony, etc.): ~会谈 hold talks/ ~宴会 give (或 host) a banquet

【举一反三】 jǔ yī fǎn sān draw inferences about other cases from one instance

【举止】 jǔzhǐ bearing; manner; mien: ~庄重 deport oneself in a dignified manner; carry oneself with dignity/ ~大方 have poise; have an easy manner; be gentle of mien

【举重】 jǔzhòng weight lifting

【举足轻重】 jǔ zú qīng-zhòng hold the balance; prove decisive: 一支~的力量 a decisive force/ 处于~的地位 occupy a decisive position

矩
龃
jǔ ① carpenter's square; square ② rules; regulations

jǔ

【龃龉】 jǔyǔ <书> the upper and lower teeth not meeting properly — disagreement; discord

jù

巨*
jù huge; tremendous; gigantic: ~款 a huge sum of money/ 山村~变 tremendous changes in a mountain village/ ~幅标语 a huge poster/ ~型运输机 a giant transport plane

【巨擘】 jùbò ① thumb ② authority in a certain field

【巨大】 jùdà huge; tremendous; enormous; gigantic; immense: ~的胜利 a tremendous victory/ ~的力量 tremendous force; immense strength/ ~的工程 a giant project/ ~的规模 a massive scale/ 做出~的努力 make gigantic efforts

【巨额】 jù'é a huge sum: ~投资 huge investments/ ~利润 enormous profits/ ~赤字 huge financial deficits

【巨匠】 jùjiàng <书> great master; consummate craftsman

【巨流】 jùliú a mighty current: 汇成一股~ converge into a mighty current

【巨轮】 jùlún ① a large wheel: 历史的~ the wheel of history ② a large ship: 远洋~ a large oceangoing ship

【巨人】 jùrén giant; colossus

【巨头】 jùtóu magnate; tycoon: 金融~ financial magnate

【巨细】 jù-xì big and small: 事无~ all matters, big and small

【巨星】 jùxīng <天> giant star; giant

【巨著】 jùzhù monumental work: 历史~ a magnum opus of historic significance

句*
jù ① sentence ②<量>: 两~诗 two lines of verse/ 我来说几~。 Let me say a few words./ 一~话也没说 not utter a word

【句子】 jùzi sentence

拒
jù ① resist; repel: ~敌 resist the enemy; keep the enemy at bay ② refuse; reject: ~不接受 refuse to accept

【拒捕】 jùbǔ resist arrest

【拒付】 jùfù refuse payment; dishonour (a cheque)

【拒绝】 jùjué ① refuse: ~参加 refuse to participate/ ~发表意见 refuse to comment ② reject; turn down; decline: ~无理要求 turn down (或 reject) unreasonable demands/ ~别人的批评 reject other people's criticism

苣
jù 见"莴苣" wōju

具*
jù ① utensil; tool; implement: 农~ farm tool (或 implement); agricultural implement ②<书><量>: 一~座钟 a desk clock/ 一~尸体 a corpse ③ possess; have: 初~规模 have begun to take shape ④<书> provide; furnish: 谨~薄礼 allow me to present to you this trifling gift

【具备】 jùbèi possess; have; be provided with

【具名】 jùmíng put one's name to a document, etc.; affix one's signature

【具体】 jùtǐ concrete; specific; particular

【具体而微】 jù tǐ ér wēi small but complete; miniature

【具有】 jùyǒu possess; have; be provided with: 这场运动~深远的历史意义。 The resent movement has profound historical significance.

炬 jù ① torch ② fire: 付之一～ be burnt down; be committed to the flames

钜 jù 〈书〉① hard iron ② hook ③ great; huge

俱 jù all; complete: 罪证～在。All the evidence of the crime is available.
【俱乐部】 jùlèbù club
【俱全】 jùquán complete in all varieties: 日用百货一应～。Goods for daily use are available in all varieties.

剧* jù ① theatrical work; drama; play; opera: 独幕～ one-act play/ 粤～ Guangdong opera/ 广播～ radio play ② acute; severe; intense: ～痛 a severe pain/ ～变 a violent (或 drastic) change/ 产量～增 a sharp increase in output/ 病势加～。The patient's condition is getting worse.
【剧本】 jùběn ① drama; play ② script; (电影) scenario
【剧场】 jùchǎng theatre
【剧烈】 jùliè violent; acute; severe; fierce: ～运动 strenuous exercise/ ～的斗争 a fierce struggle/ ～的对抗 acute antagonism/ ～的社会变动 radical social changes
【剧情】 jùqíng the story (或 plot) of a play or opera: ～简介 synopsis
【剧团】 jùtuán theatrical company; opera troupe; troupe
【剧院】 jùyuàn theatre
【剧照】 jùzhào stage photo; still
【剧中人】 jùzhōngrén characters in a play or opera; *dramatis personae*
【剧作家】 jùzuòjiā playwright; dramatist

倨 jù 〈书〉haughty; arrogant

惧 jù fear; dread: 毫无所～ not cowed in the least; fearless/ 千难万险何所～？ What is there to fear even if untold hardships lie ahead?
【惧怕】 jùpà fear; dread
【惧色】 jùsè a look of fear: 面无～ look undaunted

据* jù ① occupy; seize: ～为己有 take forcible possession of; appropriate ② rely on; depend on: ～险固守 take advantage of a natural barrier to put up a strong defence ③ according to; on the grounds of: ～报道 according to (press) reports; it is reported that/ ～我看 as I see it; in my opinion/ ～我所知 as far as I know/ ～实报告 report the facts; give a factual report/ ～理力争 argue strongly on just grounds/ 只有充分了解具体情况，才能～以定出正确的政策。Correct policies can be formulated only on the basis of a thorough understanding of the actual situation. ④ evidence; certificate: 查无实～。Investigation reveals no evidence (against the suspect).
另见 jū
【据传】 jùchuán a story is going around that; rumour has it that
【据此】 jùcǐ on these grounds; in view of the above; accordingly
【据点】 jùdiǎn strongpoint; fortified point; stronghold
【据守】 jùshǒu guard; be entrenched in: ～交通要道 guard vital lines of communication; be entrenched in communication centres/ 掘壕～ dig in; entrench oneself
【据说】 jùshuō it is said; they say; allegedly: ～他在那里干得不错。They say he is doing quite well there./ 这场事故～是由于疏忽造成的。The accident was allegedly due to negligence.
【据悉】 jùxī it is reported

距* jù ① distance: 行～ the distance between rows of plants ② be apart (或 away) from; be at a distance from: 两地相一十公里。The two places are 10 km apart./～今已有十年。That was ten years ago. ③ spur (of a cock, etc.)
【距离】 jùlí ① distance: 保持一个～ keep one's distance; keep at a distance ② be apart (或 away) from; be at a distance from: ～车站十五公里 15 km from the station

飓 jù
【飓风】 jùfēng hurricane

锯* jù ① saw: 手～ handsaw/ 圆～ circular saw ② cut with a saw; saw: ～木头 saw wood
【锯木厂】 jùmùchǎng sawmill; lumber-mill

聚 jù assemble; gather; get together: 大家～在一起商量商量。Let's get together and talk it over.
【聚宝盆】 jùbǎopén treasure bowl — a place rich in natural resources
【聚餐】 jùcān dine together (usu. on festive occasions); have a dinner party
【聚光灯】 jùguāngdēng spotlight
【聚合】 jùhé get together
【聚会】 jùhuì ① get together; meet: 老朋友一在一起，格外亲热。The meeting of the old friends was extremely cordial. ② get-together
【聚积】 jùjī accumulate; collect; build up
【聚集】 jùjí gather; assemble; collect: 机场上一着数千人，为代表团送行。Thousands of people gathered at the airport to see the delegation off.
【聚精会神】 jùjīng-huìshén concentrate one's attention; be all attention: ～地工作 concentrate on one's work; be intent on one's work/ ～地听 listen with rapt attention
【聚居】 jùjū inhabit a region (as an ethnic group); live in a compact community: 少数民族～的地区 regions where minority nationalities live in compact communities
【聚首】 jùshǒu 〈书〉gather; meet: ～一堂 gather together

踞 jù ① crouch; squat ② sit

遽 jù ① hurriedly; hastily: ～下结论 pass judgment hastily ② frightened; alarmed
【遽然】 jùrán 〈书〉suddenly; abruptly: ～变色 suddenly change countenance

juān

涓 juān 〈书〉a tiny stream
【涓滴】 juāndī 〈书〉a tiny drop; dribble; driblet: ～归公 turn in every cent of public money

捐* juān ① relinquish; abandon ② contribute; donate; subscribe: ～钱 contribute money/ 募～ solicit contributions; appeal for donations ③ tax: 上～ pay a tax
【捐款】 juānkuǎn ① contribute money ② contribution; donation; subscription
【捐躯】 juānqū sacrifice one's life; lay down one's life: 为国～ lay down one's life for one's country
【捐税】 juānshuì taxes and levies
【捐献】 juānxiàn contribute (to an organization); donate; present: 他把全部藏书～给图书馆。He presented his whole collection of books to the library.
【捐赠】 juānzèng contribute (as a gift); donate; present
【捐助】 juānzhù offer (financial or material assistance); contribute; donate

娟 juān 〈书〉beautiful; graceful
【娟秀】 juānxiù 〈书〉beautiful; graceful: 字迹～ beautiful handwriting; a graceful hand

鹃 juān 见"杜鹃" dùjuān

镌 juān 〈书〉engrave: ～碑 engrave a stone tablet
【镌刻】 juānkè 〈书〉engrave

juǎn

卷* juǎn ① roll up: 把竹帘子～起来 roll up the bamboo screen/ ～起袖子就干 roll up one's sleeves and pitch in ② sweep off; carry along: 一个大浪把小船～走了。A huge

wave swept the boat away./ 汽车飞驰而过，～起一阵尘土。A car sped past, raising a cloud of dust. ③cylindrical mass of sth.; roll: 花～儿 fancy-shaped (或 plaited, twisted) steamed roll/ 铺盖～儿 bedding roll ④<量> roll; spool; reel: 一～手纸 a roll of toilet paper/ 一～软片 a roll of film
另见 juàn

【卷入】 juǎnrù be drawn into; be involved in: ～漩涡 be drawn into a whirlpool/ 一场纠纷 be involved in a dispute

【卷逃】 juǎntáo abscond with valuables

【卷土重来】 juǎn tǔ chóng lái stage a comeback

【卷烟】 juǎnyān ①cigarette ②cigar

juàn

卷* juàn ①book: 手不释～ always have a book in one's hand; be a diligent reader ②volume: 第三～ Volume III/ 该图书馆藏书十万。This library has 100,000 volumes. ③examination paper: 交～ hand in an examination paper ④file; dossier: 查～ look through the files
另见 juǎn

【卷轴】 juànzhóu <书> scroll

【卷子】 juànzi examination paper: 看～ mark examination papers

倦* juàn weary; tired: 面有～容 look tired/ 毫无～意 not feel in the least tired

绢 juàn thin, tough silk

隽 juàn

【隽永】 juànyǒng <书> meaningful: 语颇～, 耐人寻味。The remarks are meaningful and thought-provoking.

眷 juàn ①family dependant: 女～ female members of a family ②<书> have tender feeling for

【眷恋】 juànliàn <书> be sentimentally attached to (a person or place)

【眷念】 juànniàn <书> think fondly of; feel nostalgic about

【眷属】 juànshǔ family dependants

juē

撅 juē stick up: ～着尾巴 sticking up the tail/ ～嘴 pout (one's lips)

jué

孑 jué 见"孑孓" jiéjué

决* jué ①decide; determine: 犹豫不～ hesitate; be unable to reach a decision; be in a state of indecision/ ～一胜负 fight it out ②〔用在否定词前面〕 definitely; certainly; under any circumstances: ～非恶意 be entirely without malice; bear no ill will whatsoever/ ～不退让 will under no circumstances give in/ ～不达目的, 誓不罢休。We'll never give up until the goal is reached. ③execute a person: 枪～ execute by shooting ④(of a dyke, etc.) be breached; burst

【决策】 juécè ①make policy; make a strategic decision ②policy decision; decision of strategic importance: 战略～ strategic decision ◇ ～机构 policy-making body/ ～人 policymaker

【决定】 juédìng ①decide; resolve: 一时～不了 cannot make up one's mind for the moment; be unable to come to a decision for the moment ②decision; resolution: 通过一项～ pass a resolution ③determine; decide: ～性胜利 a decisive victory

【决定权】 juédìngquán power to make decisions: 有最后～ have the final say

【决斗】 juédòu ①duel ②decisive struggle

【决断】 juéduàn ①make a decision ②resolve; decisiveness; resolution

【决裂】 juéliè break with; rupture

【决然】 juérán <书> ①resolutely; determinedly ②definitely; unquestionably; undoubtedly: 搞阴谋的人～没有好下场。Those who engage in conspiracies are bound to come to no good end.

【决赛】 juésài <体> finals: 半～ semifinals

【决胜】 juéshèng decide the issue of the battle; determine the victory

【决死】 juésǐ life-and-death: ～的斗争 a life-and-death struggle; a last-ditch fight

【决心】 juéxīn determination: 下定～ make up one's mind; be resolute; be determined/ 有～, 有信心 have both determination and confidence/ ～改正错误 be determined to correct one's mistake

【决一雌雄】 jué yī cí-xióng fight to see who is the stronger; fight it out

【决议】 juéyì resolution ◇ ～(草)案 draft resolution

【决意】 juéyì have one's mind made up; be determined: 他～要走。He's made up his mind to quit.

【决战】 juézhàn decisive battle; decisive engagement

诀 jué ①rhymed formula: 十六字～ the sixteen-character formula ②knack; tricks of the trade: 秘～ secret of success; key to success ③bid farewell; part: 永～ part never to meet again; part for ever

【诀别】 juébié bid farewell; part

【诀窍】 juéqiào secret of success; tricks of the trade; knack: 你这么快就做得了, 有什么～啊？ You finished your job really fast. What's the secret of it?/ 你掌握了～就容易了。It's easy once you've got the knack of it. 或 It's simple if you know the trick.

抉 jué <书> pick out; single out

【抉择】 juézé <书> choose: 作出～ make one's choice

角* jué ①role; part; character: 主～ leading (或 principal) role; main character ②type of role (in traditional Chinese drama): 旦～ female role/ 丑～ clown ③actor or actress: 名～ a famous actor or actress ④contend; wrestle: ～斗 wrestle/ 口～ quarrel; bicker ⑤an ancient, three-legged wine cup
另见 jiǎo

【角色】 juésè ①role; part: 她在这部电影里演哪个～? What part does she play in that film?/ 扮演了不光彩的～ play a contemptible role ②type of role (in traditional Chinese drama)

【角逐】 juézhú contend; tussle; enter into rivalry: 超级大国～的场所 an arena of fierce rivalry between the superpowers

觉* jué ①sense; feel: 听～ sense of hearing/ 下过这场雪, 就～出冷来了。After the snow it is really cold./ 身上～着不舒服 not feel well ②wake (up); awake: 如梦初～ as if waking from a dream ③become aware; become awakened
另见 jiào

【觉察】 juéchá detect; become aware of; perceive: 敌人没有～出我侦察排的行动。The enemy didn't detect our scouting platoon's movements./ 她～到这里面有问题。She sensed there was something wrong.

【觉得】 juéde ①feel: 一点儿也不～累 not feel tired at all ②think; feel: 我～应该先跟他商量一下。I think we should consult him first./ 我～他这几天情绪不好。I have a feeling that he's been in low spirits these last few days./ 你～这个计划怎么样? What do you think of the plan?

【觉悟】 juéwù ①consciousness; awareness; understanding ②come to understand; become aware of

【觉醒】 juéxǐng awaken

绝* jué ①cut off; sever: ～其后路 cut off his retreat/ 掌声不～ prolonged applause ②exhausted; used up; finished: 弹尽粮～ have run out of ammunition and provisions/ 法子都想～了. All possible ways have been tried. 或 All possibilities have been exhausted. ③ desperate; hopeless: ～境 hopeless situation; impasse ④ unique; superb; matchless: 她发的那球真～. Her serve was a beauty. ⑤ extremely; most: ～大的错误 an egregious error; a grievous fault/ ～大多数 most; the overwhelming majority/ ～好的机会 an excellent opportunity/ ～早 extremely early ⑥〔用在否定词前〕 absolutely; in the least; by any means; on any account: ～无此意 have absolutely no such intentions/ ～非偶然 by no means fortuitous

【绝版】 juébǎn out of print
【绝笔】 juébǐ ① last words written before one's death ② the last work of an author or painter
【绝唱】 juéchàng the peak of poetic perfection: 堪称千古～ rank as a poetic masterpiece through the ages
【绝处逢生】 juéchù féng shēng be unexpectedly rescued from a desperate situation
【绝代】 juédài 〈书〉 unique among one's contemporaries; peerless: 才华～ unrivalled talent
【绝顶】 juédǐng extremely; utterly: ～聪明 extremely intelligent/ ～愚蠢的行为 the height of folly
【绝对】 juéduì ① absolute: ～优势 absolute predominance; overwhelming superiority ② absolutely; perfectly; definitely: ～可靠 absolutely reliable
【绝后】 juéhòu ① without offspring (或 issue) ② never to be seen again: 空前～ never known before and never to occur again; unique
【绝迹】 juéjì disappear; vanish; be stamped out
【绝技】 juéjì unique skill; consummate skill
【绝交】 juéjiāo break off relations (as between friends or countries)
【绝境】 juéjìng hopeless situation; impasse; blind alley; cul-de-sac: 濒于～ face an impasse
【绝口】 juékǒu ①〔只用在"不"字后〕 stop talking: 赞不～ give unstinted praise; praise profusely/ 骂不～ heap endless abuse upon; pour out unceasing abuse ② keep one's mouth shut: ～不提 never say a single word about; avoid all mention of
【绝路】 juélù road to ruin; blind alley; impasse: 自寻～ court destruction; bring ruin upon oneself
【绝伦】 juélún unsurpassed; unequalled; peerless; matchless: 精美～ exquisite beyond compare; superb/ 荒谬～ utterly absurd; utterly preposterous
【绝妙】 juémiào extremely clever; ingenious; excellent; perfect: ～的一招 a masterstroke
【绝色】 juésè 〈书〉 (of a woman) exceedingly beautiful; of unrivalled beauty
【绝食】 juéshí fast; go on a hunger strike
【绝望】 juéwàng give up all hope; despair: ～情绪 feeling of despair/ ～的挣扎 desperate struggle
【绝无仅有】 juéwú-jǐnyǒu the only one of its kind; unique
【绝育】 juéyù 〈医〉 sterilization
【绝招】 juézhāo ① unique skill ② unexpected tricky move (as a last resort)
【绝症】 juézhèng incurable disease; fatal illness
【绝种】 juézhǒng (of a species) become extinct; die out

倔 jué
【倔强】 juéjiàng stubborn; unbending

掘 jué dig: ～井 dig a well/ 自～坟墓 dig one's own grave

崛 jué 〈书〉 rise abruptly
【崛起】 juéqǐ ① (of a mountain, etc.) rise abruptly; suddenly appear on the horizon ② rise (as a political force): 太平军～于广西金田村. The Taipings rose in revolt at Jintian Village, Guangxi.

厥 jué faint; lose consciousness; fall into a coma: 昏～ fall to the ground in a faint

谲 jué 〈书〉 cheat; swindle

【谲诈】 juézhà cunning; crafty

蕨 jué 〈植〉 brake (fern)

獗 jué 见"猖獗" chāngjué

爵 jué ① the rank of nobility; peerage: 封～ confer a title (of nobility) upon ② an ancient wine vessel with three legs and a loop handle
【爵士】 juéshì ① knight ② Sir: 约翰·史密斯～ Sir John Smith
【爵士音乐】 juéshì yīnyuè jazz
【爵位】 juéwèi the rank (或 title) of nobility

蹶 jué ① fall ② suffer a setback: 一～不振 collapse after one setback; never recover from a setback

矍 jué
【矍铄】 juéshuò 〈书〉 hale and hearty

嚼 jué masticate; chew
另见 jiáo

攫 jué seize; grab: ～为己有 seize possession of; appropriate
【攫取】 juéqǔ seize; grab

jūn

军* jūn ① armed forces; army; troops: 参～ join the army ② army: 全歼敌人一个～ wipe out an enemy army
【军备】 jūnbèi armament; arms: ～扩充 engage in arms expansion ◇ ～竞赛 armament (或 arms) race
【军部】 jūnbù army headquarters
【军操】 jūncāo military drill
【军车】 jūnchē military vehicle
【军队】 jūnduì armed forces; army; troops
【军阀】 jūnfá warlord
【军法】 jūnfǎ military criminal code; military law
【军方】 jūnfāng the military
【军费】 jūnfèi military expenditure
【军服】 jūnfú military uniform; uniform
【军港】 jūngǎng naval port
【军官】 jūnguān officer
【军火】 jūnhuǒ munitions; arms and ammunition ◇ ～工业 munitions industry; armament industry/ ～舰 ammunition ship/ ～库 arsenal/ ～商 munitions merchant; arms dealer; merchant of death
【军机】 jūnjī ① military plan: 贻误～ delay or frustrate the fulfilment of a military plan ② military secret: 泄漏～ leak a military secret
【军纪】 jūnjì military discipline
【军舰】 jūnjiàn warship; naval vessel
【军阶】 jūnjiē (military) rank; grade
【军礼】 jūnlǐ military salute
【军力】 jūnlì military strength
【军粮】 jūnliáng army provisions; grain for the army ◇ ～库 military grain depot; army granary
【军令】 jūnlìng military orders: 颁布～ issue a military order
【军旗】 jūnqí army flag; colours; ensign
【军情】 jūnqíng military (或 war) situation: 刺探～ spy on the military movements; collect military information
【军人】 jūnrén soldier; serviceman; armyman
【军师】 jūnshī military counsellor; army adviser
【军士】 jūnshì noncommissioned officer (NCO)
【军事】 jūnshì military affairs ◇ ～表演 display of military skills

【军衔】 jūnxián military rank
【军校】 jūnxiào military school; military academy
【军械】 jūnxiè ordnance; armament
　◇ ～处 ordnance department/ ～库 ordnance depot; arms depot; armoury/ ～员 armourer
【军心】 jūnxīn soldiers' morale: 动摇～ shake the army's morale/ ～大振。The morale of the troops has been greatly raised.
【军训】 jūnxùn military training
【军医】 jūnyī medical officer; military surgeon
【军营】 jūnyíng military camp; barracks
【军用】 jūnyòng for military use; military
　◇ ～地图 military map/ ～飞机 warplane; military aircraft/ ～列车 military train/ ～物资 military supplies; *matériel*
【军援】 jūnyuán military aid
【军职】 jūnzhí official post in the army; military appointment

均 jūn ① equal; even: 劳逸不～ uneven allocation of work ② without exception; all: 各项准备工作～已就绪。All the preparatory work has been completed.
【均等】 jūnděng equal; impartial; fair
【均分】 jūnfēn divide equally; share out equally
【均衡】 jūnhéng balanced; proportionate; harmonious
【均势】 jūnshì balance of power; equilibrium of forces; equilibrium; parity
【均匀】 jūnyún even; well-distributed: ～的呼吸 even breathing/ ～撒播 even broadcasting of seeds/ 今年的雨水很～。Rainfall has been fairly well-distributed this year.

君 jūn ① monarch; sovereign; supreme ruler ② gentleman; Mr.: 诸～ gentlemen/ 张刘二～ Messrs. Zhang and Liu
【君权】 jūnquán monarchical power
【君主】 jūnzhǔ monarch; sovereign
　◇ ～国 monarchical state; monarchy/ ～立宪 constitutional monarchy/ ～制 monarchy/ ～专制 autocratic monarchy; absolute monarchy
【君子】 jūnzǐ a man of noble character; gentleman: 伪～ hypocrite/ 正人～ a man of moral integrity/ ～成人之美。

A gentleman is always ready to help others attain their aims./ 以小人之心度～之腹 gauge the heart of a gentleman with one's own mean measure
　◇ ～协定 gentlemen's agreement

龟 jūn
　另见 guī
【龟裂】 jūnliè ① (of parched earth) be full of cracks ② (of skin) chap

钧 jūn 〈敬〉 you; your: ～座 Your Excellency

菌 jūn ① fungus ② bacterium
　另见 jùn

jùn

俊 jùn ① handsome; pretty: 这小伙子长得挺～的。That lad is very handsome./ 这孩子长得多～哪! What a pretty little child! ② a person of outstanding talent
【俊杰】 jùnjié a person of outstanding talent; hero
【俊美】 jùnměi pretty

郡 jùn 〈史〉 prefecture

峻 jùn ① (of mountains) high: 高山～岭 high mountains/ 险～ precipitous ② harsh; severe; stern: 严刑～法 harsh law and severe punishment
【峻峭】 jùnqiào high and steep

骏 jùn fine horse; steed
【骏马】 jùnmǎ fine horse; steed

菌 jùn mushroom
　另见 jūn

竣 jùn complete; finish: 告～ have been completed
【竣工】 jùngōng (of a project) be completed: 这座大楼已提前～。The building has been completed ahead of schedule.

K

kā

咖[*] kā
另见 gā
【咖啡】 kāfēi coffee ◇ ~馆 café/ ~色 coffee (colour)

喀 kā 〈象〉 noise made in coughing or vomiting
【喀嚓】 kāchā 〈象〉 crack; snap: ~一声,树枝断了。 The branch broke with a crack. 或 The branch snapped.

kǎ

卡[*] kǎ block; check: ~住通往海港的公路 block the road to the seaport/ 会计及时~住了这笔不必要的开支。The accountant checked this unnecessary spending in good time.
【卡车】 kǎchē lorry; truck
【卡片】 kǎpiàn card

kāi

开[*] kāi ① open: ~锁 open a lock; unlock ② make an opening; open up; reclaim: 墙上~个窗口 make a window in the wall ③ open out; come loose: 花都~了。The flowers are all open./ 扣儿~了。The knot has come untied. ④ thaw; become navigable: 等河~了坐船走。 Wait until the river is open and then go by boat. ⑤ lift (a ban,restriction, etc.): ~禁 lift a ban ⑥ start; operate: ~机器 operate a machine/ ~拖拉机 drive a tractor/ ~灯 turn on a light/ ~飞机 fly (或 pilot) an airplane/ 火车就要~了。The train is about to start. ⑦ (of troops, etc.) set out; move: 军队正~往前线。The troops are moving to the front. ⑧ set up; run: ~工厂 set up a factory/ ~茶馆 run a teahouse ⑨ begin; start: ~拍 start shooting (a film) ⑩ hold (a meeting, exhibition, etc.): ~运动会 hold an athletic meet ⑪ make a list of; write out: 把你需要领的工具~个单子。Make a list of the tools you need. ⑫ pay (wages, fares, etc.) ⑬ boil: 水~了。The water is boiling. ⑭ percentage: 大家认为他的功过是三七~。The general assessment of his work is 70% achievements and 30% mistakes. ⑮ 〈印〉 division of standard size printing paper: 四~ quarto/ 八~ octavo ⑯ carat: 十四~金 14-carat gold ⑰ 〔用在动词后,表示扩大或扩展〕 消息传~了。The news has got about./ 这支歌儿流行~了。The song has become very popular.

开 kāi ① 〔用在动词后,表示离开或分开〕躲~ get out of the way/ 把门开~。Open the door. ③ 〔用在动词后,表示容得下〕这间屋子大,五十个人也坐~了。This room is big enough to seat 50 people.
【开拔】 kāibá (of troops) move; set out
【开办】 kāibàn open; set up; start: ~训练班 start a training course
【开采】 kāicǎi mine; extract; exploit: ~煤炭 mine coal/ ~石油 recover petroleum/ ~天然气 tap (或 extract) natural gas
【开场】 kāichǎng begin: 他们到剧院时,戏已经~了。The play had already begun when they got to the theatre.
【开场白】 kāichǎngbái ① prologue (of a play) ② opening (或 introductory) remarks
【开车】 kāichē ① drive or start a car, train, etc.: ~的时候精神要集中。You should concentrate your attention when driving. /快~了,大家上车吧。The bus is going to start. Hurry up, everybody. ② set a machine going
【开诚布公】 kāichéng-bùgōng speak frankly and sincerely

【开除】 kāichú expel; discharge
【开船】 kāichuán set sail; sail
【开创】 kāichuàng start; initiate
【开刀】 kāidāo ① 〈口〉 perform or have an operation; operate or be operated on: 给病人~ operate on a patient/ 他得了阑尾炎,~了。He had an operation for appendicitis. ② behead; decapitate ③ make sb. the first target of attack: 拿某人~ make an example of sb.
【开导】 kāidǎo help sb. to see what is right or sensible; help sb. to straighten out his wrong or muddled thinking; enlighten: 他一时想不通,你~开导他吗? He hasn't come round yet. Could you try and straighten him out?
【开倒车】 kāi dàochē turn the clock back; turn back the wheel of history
【开动】 kāidòng ① start; set in motion: ~机器 start a machine/ 宣传机器 set the propaganda machine in motion/ ~脑筋 use one's brains ② move; march: 队伍休息了一会儿又~了。The troops were on the move again after a short rest.
【开端】 kāiduān beginning; start: 良好的~ a good beginning /两国关系新的~ a new turn in the relations between the two countries
【开恩】 kāi'ēn show mercy; bestow favours
【开发】 kāifā develop; open up; exploit: ~山区 develop mountain areas/ ~油田 open up oilfields/ ~自然资源 exploit natural resources
【开饭】 kāifàn serve a meal: ~了。The meal's ready. 或 Time to eat!
【开放】 kāifàng ① come into bloom ② lift a ban, restriction, etc. ③ open to traffic or public use: 新建的港口已向外轮~。The new port has been opened to foreign ships. ④ be open (to the public): 星期日图书馆照常~。The library is open on Sundays as well as on weekdays.
【开工】 kāigōng ① (of a factory, etc.) go into operation: ~不足 be operating under capacity / 新厂~了。The new factory has gone into operation. ② (of work on a construction project, etc.) start: 水库工程~了。Construction of the reservoir has started.
【开关】 kāiguān 〈电〉 switch
【开国】 kāiguó found a state ◇ ~大典 founding ceremony (of a state)
【开航】 kāiháng ① become open for navigation: 又一条新航线~了。Another new air route has been opened up. / 运河~了。The canal is now open. ② set sail: 去武汉的船上午八点~。 The boat for Wuhan sails at 8 a.m.
【开花】 kāihuā blossom; bloom; flower: 木兰要~了。The magnolias are beginning to blossom./ 心里乐开了花 burst with joy; feel elated
【开花结果】 kāihuā-jiēguǒ blossom and bear fruit — yield positive results
【开化】 kāihuà become civilized
【开怀】 kāihuái to one's heart's content: ~畅饮 drink (alcohol) to one's heart's content; go on a drinking spree
【开会】 kāihuì hold or attend a meeting: 我要~去。I'm going to a meeting./ 他正在~。He's at a meeting./ 现在~。Let's start the meeting.
【开火】 kāihuǒ open fire: ~! (口令) Fire!
【开阔】 kāihuò ① open and clear: 雾气一散,四处都显得十分~。With the lifting of the mist, the view opened up. ② (of one's mental outlook) broadened: 听了报告,他的心里更~了。The report widened his horizons.
【开戒】 kāijiè break an abstinence (from smoking, drinking, etc.)
【开禁】 kāijìn lift a ban
【开卷】 kāijuàn open a book; read: ~有益。Reading is always profitable.
【开课】 kāikè ① school begins ② (chiefly in college) give a course; teach a subject: 开一门光合作用课 give a course

in photosynthesis / 朱教授这学期给研究生 ～。 Professor Zhu will give lectures to the research students this term.

【开垦】 kāikěn　open up (或 reclaim) wasteland; bring under cultivation: ～荒山 bring barren hills under cultivation

【开口】 kāikǒu　① open one's mouth; start to talk: 难以～ find it difficult to bring the matter up/ 没等我～，他就抢先替我说了。 Before I could open my mouth, he hastened to speak on my behalf. ② put the first edge on a knife

【开快车】 kāi kuàichē　① step on the gas; open the throttle ②(of a machine) speed up ③ hurry through one's work; make short work of a job

【开矿】 kāikuàng　open up a mine; exploit a mine

【开阔】 kāikuò　① open; wide: ～的广场 an open square ② tolerant: 心胸～ broad-minded; unprejudiced ③ widen: ～眼界 broaden one's outlook (或 horizons)

【开朗】 kāilǎng　① open and clear: 豁然～ suddenly see the light ② sanguine; optimistic: 性情～ of a sanguine disposition; always cheerful

【开例】 kāilì　create a precedent

【开路】 kāilù　open a way; blaze a trail: 逢山～，遇水搭桥 cut paths through the mountains and build bridges across the rivers ◇ ～先锋 pathbreaker; trail-blazer; pioneer

【开门】 kāimén　open the door: 有人敲门，快～去。 Somebody's knocking at the door. Quick, go and open it.

【开门见山】 kāimén jiàn shān　come straight to the point

【开门揖盗】 kāimén yī dào　open the door to robbers; invite disaster by letting in evildoers

【开明】 kāimíng　enlightened ◇ ～人士 enlightened persons

【开幕】 kāimù　① the curtain rises: 戏已经～了。 The opera has begun. ② open; inaugurate: 展览会明天～。 The exhibition will open tomorrow./ 大会今天上午～了。 The conference was inaugurated this morning. ◇ ～词 opening speech (或 address)/ ～式 opening ceremony

【开炮】 kāipào　① open fire with artillery; fire ② fire criticism at sb.

【开辟】 kāipì　open up; start: ～航线 open an air or sea route/ ～专栏 start a special column/ ～财源 tap new financial resources

【开启】 kāiqǐ　open: 自动～ open automatically

【开枪】 kāiqiāng　fire with a rifle, pistol, etc.; shoot: ～射击 open fire/ ～还击 return fire

【开腔】 kāiqiāng　begin to speak; open one's mouth: 他半天不～。 For a long time he didn't utter a word. 或 He kept silent for a long while.

【开球】 kāiqiú　〈足球〉 kick off

【开山祖师】 kāishān zǔshī　the founder of a religious sect or a school of thought

【开设】 kāishè　① open (a shop, factory, etc.) ② offer (a course in college, etc.)

【开始】 kāishǐ　① begin; start: 今天从第五课～。 Today we'll begin with Lesson 5./ ～讨论实质性问题 come to substantive questions/ ～生效 take effect; come into effect (或 force) ② initial stage; beginning; outset

【开市】 kāishì　①(of a shop) reopen after a cessation of business ② the first transaction of a day's business

【开水】 kāishuǐ　① boiling water ② boiled water

【开天辟地】 kāitiān-pìdì　① when heaven was separated from earth — the creation of the world ② since the beginning of history

【开庭】 kāitíng　〈法〉 open a court session; call the court to order

【开通】 kāitōng　remove obstacles from; dredge; clear: ～河道 dredge a river /坚冰已经打破,航道已经～。 The ice has been broken; the road is open.

【开通】 kāitong　open-minded; liberal; enlightened

【开头】 kāitóu　begin; start: 我们的学习刚～。 We've only just begun our study./ 请你先开个头儿。 Would you make a start?/ 万事～难。 The first step is always difficult. 这篇文章～讲了我国当前的形势。 The article begins with an account of the current situation in our country./ 你从一～就错了。 You've been wrong from the start.

【开脱】 kāituō　absolve; exonerate: ～罪责 absolve sb. from

guilt or blame/ 替某人～ plead for sb.

【开玩笑】 kāi wánxiào　crack a joke; joke; make fun of: 他是跟你～呢,你别当真。 He was only joking. Don't take it seriously./ 这可不是～的事情。 This is no joke.

【开胃】 kāiwèi　whet (或 stimulate) the appetite

【开小差】 kāi xiǎochāi　①(of a soldier) desert ② be absent-minded: 思想～ be woolgathering

【开销】 kāixiāo　① pay expenses: 我带的钱够一路～的。 I've brought enough money with me to cover the expenses of the trip. ② expense: 日常的～ daily expenses; running expenses/ 住在这儿～不大。 Living is cheap here.

【开心】 kāixīn　① feel happy; rejoice: 他们去高原玩得很～。 They went on a trip to the highland and enjoyed it very much. ② amuse oneself at sb.'s expense; make fun of sb.: 别拿这老汉～了。 Don't amuse yourself at the old man's expense.

【开学】 kāixué　school opens; term begins

【开颜】 kāiyán　smile; beam

【开眼】 kāiyǎn　open one's eyes; widen one's view (或 horizons); broaden one's mind: 这个展览会真叫人～。 The exhibition is a real eye-opener.

【开演】 kāiyǎn　(of a play, movie, etc.) begin: 今晚节目七点三十分～。 The performance begins at 7:30 this evening.

【开夜车】 kāi yèchē　work late into the night; put in extra time at night; burn the midnight oil

【开源节流】 kāiyuán jiéliú　broaden sources of income and reduce expenditure; increase income and decrease expenditure

【开战】 kāizhàn　① make war; open hostilities ② battle (against nature, conservative forces, etc.)

【开张】 kāizhāng　① open a business; begin doing business: 重打锣鼓另～ reopen a business to the beating of gongs and drums; start all over again ② the first transaction of a day's business

【开仗】 kāizhàng　make war; open hostilities

【开支】 kāizhī　① pay (expenses): 这笔钱厂里不能～。 The factory shouldn't foot this bill. ② expenses; expenditure; spending: 节省～ cut down expenses; retrench/ 军费～ military spending

【开宗明义】 kāizōng-míngyì　make clear the purpose and main theme from the very beginning: ～第一章 in the first

【开足马力】 kāizú mǎlì　put into high gear; go full steam ahead; open the throttle

揩　kāi　wipe: 把桌子～干净 wipe the table clean

【揩油】 kāiyóu　get petty advantages at the expense of other people or the state; scrounge

kǎi

凯　kǎi　① triumphant strains ② triumphant; victorious

【凯歌】 kǎigē　a song of triumph; paean: ～阵阵,喜报频传。 Songs of triumph are heard all round and good news keeps pouring in.

【凯旋】 kǎixuán　triumphant return: 大军～归来。 The army returned in triumph.

铠　kǎi

【铠甲】 kǎijiǎ　(a suit of) armour

慨　kǎi　① indignant ② deeply touched: 感～ sigh with emotion ③ generous: ～允 consent readily; kindly promise

【慨然】 kǎirán　① with deep feeling: ～长叹 heave a sigh of regret ② generously: ～相赠 give generously

【慨叹】 kǎitàn　sigh with regret

楷　kǎi　① model; pattern ② (in Chinese calligraphy) regular script: 小～ regular script in small characters/ 大～ regular script in big characters

【楷模】 kǎimó　model; pattern

【楷书】 kǎishū　(in Chinese calligraphy) regular script

【楷体】 kǎitǐ　① 见"楷书" ② block letter

kài

忾 kài 见"敌忾" díkài

kān

刊 kān ① print; publish: 停~ suspend or stop publication (of a newspaper, etc.) ② periodical; publication: 报~ newspapers and magazines/ 周~ weekly (publication) ③ delete or correct: ~误 correct errors in printing

【刊登】 kāndēng publish in a newspaper or magazine; carry: ~广告 print an advertisement; advertise

【刊物】 kānwù publication: 定期~ periodical (publication)

【刊载】 kānzǎi publish (in a newspaper or magazine); carry: 报纸上~了几篇有关激光技术的文章。 The newspaper carried a few articles about laser technique.

看* kān ① look after; take care of; tend: ~孩子 look after children/ ~瓜 keep watch in the melon fields/ ~牛 tend cattle/他病很重, 得有人~着。 He is seriously ill and needs someone to look after him./ 她一个人~两台机器。 She minds two machines all by herself. ② keep under surveillance: ~住他, 别让这坏家伙跑了! Keep an eye on that rascal. Don't let him run away.
另见 kàn

【看管】 kānguǎn ① look after; attend to: 留个人~行李。 Someone will stay here to look after the luggage. ② guard; watch: ~犯人 guard prisoners

【看护】 kānhù ① nurse: ~病人 nurse the sick ② 〈旧〉 hospital nurse

【看家】 kānjiā ① look after the house; mind the house ② outstanding (ability); special (skill) ◇ ~本领 one's special skill

【看门】 kānmén ① guard the entrance; act as doorkeeper ② look after the house

【看守】 kānshǒu ① watch; guard: ~仓库 guard a storehouse/ ~犯人 guard prisoners ② turnkey; warder

勘 kān ① read and correct the text of; collate ② investigate; survey

【勘测】 kāncè survey

【勘察】 kānchá reconnaissance

【勘探】 kāntàn exploration; prospecting

【勘误】 kānwù correct errors in printing ◇ ~表 errata; corrigenda

龛 kān niche; shrine

堪 kān ① may; can: ~称佳作 may be rated as a good piece of writing or a fine work of art/ ~当重任 be capable of shouldering important tasks; can fill a position of great responsibility ② bear; endure: 不~一击 cannot withstand a single blow; collapse at the first blow

戡 kān suppress: ~平叛乱 suppress (或 put down) a rebellion

kǎn

坎 kǎn ① bank; ridge: 田~儿 a raised path through fields ②〈书〉 pit; hole

【坎坷】 kǎnkě ① bumpy; rough: ~不平的道路 a rough and bumpy road ②〈书〉 full of frustrations: ~一生 a lifetime of frustrations

侃 kǎn

【侃侃而谈】 kǎnkǎn ér tán speak with fervour and assurance

砍* kǎn cut; chop; hack: 把树枝~下来 cut (或 lop) off a branch/ ~柴 cut firewood/ 把树~倒 fell a tree

【砍伐】 kǎnfá fell (trees)

【砍头】 kǎntóu chop off the head; behead

槛 kǎn threshold

kàn

看* kàn ① see; look at; watch: ~电影 see a film; go to the movies/ ~戏 go to the theatre; see a play, an opera, etc./ ~电视 watch TV/ ~球赛 watch a ball game ② read: ~报 read a newspaper/ ~书 read (a book) ③ think; consider: ~她这个人可靠吗? Do you think she's reliable?/ 你对这件事怎么~? What's your view on this matter?/ 比较全面地~问题 try and look at (或 approach) problems from all angles/ ~清形势 make a correct appraisal of the situation ④ look upon; regard: 把国家的利益~得高于一切 put the interests of the nation above all else ⑤ treat (a patient or an illness): 李医生把她的肺炎~好了。 Dr. Li has cured her of pneumonia. ⑥ look after: ~顾 look after; take care of/ 她在幼儿园照~孩子。 She looks after children in the kindergarten. ⑦ call on; visit; see: 我有空去~你。 I'll drop in on you when I have time. ⑧ depend on: 明天是不是去钓鱼, 得~天气。 Whether we'll go fishing tomorrow will depend on the weather. ⑨ mind; watch out: 别跑这么快! ~摔着! Don't run so fast! Mind you don't fall. ⑩〔用在动词或动词结构后面, 表示试一试〕: 试试~ have a try/ 等一等~ wait and see/ 尝尝~。 Just taste this.
另见 kān

【看病】 kànbìng ① (of a doctor) see a patient: 医生出去~去了。 The doctor's gone to see a patient./ 王医生~很认真。 Dr. Wang handles his cases with great care./ 哪位是给你~的医生? Who is your doctor? ② (of a patient) see (或 consult) a doctor: 明天我要~去。 I'm going to see a doctor tomorrow.

【看不惯】 kànbuguàn cannot bear the sight of; frown upon: 这种浪费现象我们~。 We hate to see such waste.

【看不起】 kànbuqǐ look down upon; scorn; despise: 对于落后的人们, 我们不应当~他们, 而是要帮助他们。 We shouldn't look down upon backward people, we should help them.

【看成】 kànchéng look upon as; regard as: 你把我~什么人了? What do you take me for?

【看出】 kànchū make out; see: ~问题在那里 see where the trouble is/ 看不出真假 cannot tell whether it is genuine or fake

【看穿】 kànchuān see through: 观众立即~了他的诡计。 The spectators at once saw through his trick.

【看待】 kàndài look upon; regard; treat

【看得起】 kàndeqǐ have a good opinion of; think highly of

【看法】 kànfǎ a way of looking at a thing; view: 对这个问题有两种不同的~。 There are two different views on this question.

【看风使舵】 kàn fēng shǐ duò trim one's sails

【看见】 kànjian catch sight of; see: 你~老张了吗? Did you see Lao Zhang?/ 他们航行了二十天, 才~陆地。 They sighted land after being at sea for twenty days.

【看来】 kànlái it seems (或 appears); it looks as if: 这活儿~今天可以做完。 It looks as if we'll be able to finish this job today./ 他还没有拿定主意。 Evidently he has not made up his mind yet.

【看破】 kànpò see through: ~那些卑劣勾当 see through those base tricks/ ~红尘 be disillusioned with the mortal world

【看齐】 kànqí ① dress: 向右(左)~! Dress right (left), dress! ② keep up with; emulate

【看轻】 kànqīng underestimate; look down upon: 我们不应~自己的力量。 We must not underestimate our own strength.

【看上】 kànshang take a fancy to; settle on: ~一位姑娘 take a fancy to a girl

【看台】 kàntái 〈体〉 bleachers; stand

【看透】 kàntòu ① understand thoroughly: 这一着棋我看不透。I don't quite understand this move. ② see through: 这个人我～了，没有什么真才实学。I've seen through him: he's not a man of real learning.

【看头】 kàntou 〈口〉 sth. worth seeing or reading: 这个展览会没什么～。There is nothing much to see in the exhibition. /这部小说很有～。This novel is well worth reading.

【看图识字】 kàn tú shí zì learn to read with the aid of pictures

【看中】 kànzhòng take a fancy to; settle on: 这些布你～了哪块？Which piece of cloth have you settled on?

【看重】 kànzhòng regard as important; value; set store by: 不要只～书本知识，还要在实践中学习。We must not consider that book knowledge alone is important; we should also learn through practice./ ～友谊 set store by the ties of friendship

【看做】 kànzuò look upon as; regard as: 你把次要问题～主要问题了。You have taken a minor question for a major one.

瞰 kàn look down from a height; overlook: 鸟～ get a bird's-eye view

kāng

康* kāng well-being; health

【康复】 kāngfù restored to health; recovered: 祝您早日～。Hope you'll soon be well again. 或 I wish you a speedy recovery.

【康健】 kāngjiàn healthy; in good health

【康乐】 kānglè peace and happiness

慷 kāng

【慷慨】 kāngkǎi ① vehement; fervent: ～陈词 present one's views vehemently ② generous; liberal: ～解囊 help sb. generously with money /慷他人之慨 be generous at other people's expense

【慷慨激昂】 kāngkǎi jī'áng impassioned; vehement: 他讲得～,非常感人。His impassioned speech was very moving.

【慷慨就义】 kāngkǎi jiùyì go to one's death like a hero; die a martyr's death

糠 kāng chaff; bran; husk

káng

扛* káng carry on the shoulder; shoulder: ～着锄头 carry a hoe on one's shoulder/ ～枪 shoulder a gun; bear arms 另见 gāng

kàng

亢 kàng ① high; haughty: 高～ loud and sonorous; resounding/ 不～不卑 neither supercilious nor obsequious ② excessive; extreme

【亢奋】 kàngfèn stimulated; excited

【亢旱】 kànghàn severe drought

伉 kàng

【伉俪】 kànglì 〈书〉 married couple; husband and wife

抗* kàng ① resist; combat; fight: ～灾 fight natural calamities ② refuse; defy: ～捐～税 refuse to pay levies and taxes ③ contend with; be a match for: 分庭～礼 stand up to sb. as an equal

【抗击】 kàngjī resist; beat back: ～侵略者 resist the aggressors

【抗拒】 kàngjù resist; defy

【抗命】 kàngmìng defy orders; disobey

【抗议】 kàngyì protest: 提出～ lodge a protest

kǎo

考* kǎo ① give or take an examination, test or quiz: 我～～你。I'll give you a quiz. 或 Let me quiz you./ 你的数学～得怎么样？How did you do in the maths test (或 quiz)?/ 应～ sit for (或 take) an examination/ ～上大学 be admitted to a university ② check; inspect ③ study; investigate; verify: 待～ remain to be verified

【考查】 kǎochá examine; check: ～学生成绩 check students' work

【考察】 kǎochá ① inspect; make an on-the-spot investigation: ～水利工程 investigate water conservancy projects/ 出国～ go abroad on a tour of investigation ② observe and study

【考场】 kǎochǎng examination hall or room

【考订】 kǎodìng examine and correct; do textual research

【考古】 kǎogǔ ① engage in archaeological studies ② archaeology ◇ ～学 archaeology/ ～学家 archaeologist

【考核】 kǎohé examine; check; assess (sb.'s proficiency): 定期～ routine check

【考究】 kǎojiu ① observe and study; investigate: 这问题很值得～。We need to go into the matter seriously. 或 This problem merits serious attention. ② fastidious; particular: 穿衣服不必过于～。One need not be too particular about dress. ③ exquisite; fine: 这本画册装订得很～。This album is beautifully bound.

【考据】 kǎojù textual criticism; textual research

【考卷】 kǎojuàn examination paper

【考虑】 kǎolù think over; consider: 让我～一下再答复你。Let me think it over before I give you an answer./ 这方面的情况你～了吗？Have you taken this aspect of the matter into account?/ 计划～不周。The plan has not been carefully thought out./ 不～个人得失 disregard personal gains and losses/ 给予同情的～ give sympathetic consideration to

【考取】 kǎoqǔ pass an entrance examination; be admitted to school or college (after an examination)

【考生】 kǎoshēng candidate for an entrance examination; examinee

【考试】 kǎoshì examination; test

【考题】 kǎotí examination questions; examination paper: 出～ set an examination paper; set examination questions

【考验】 kǎoyàn test; trial: 经受了严峻的～ have stood a severe test

【考证】 kǎozhèng textual criticism; textual research

拷 kǎo flog; beat; torture

【拷贝】 kǎobèi 〈电影〉 copy ◇ ～纸 copy (或 copying) paper

【拷打】 kǎodǎ flog; beat; torture: 严刑～ subject sb. to severe torture

【拷问】 kǎowèn torture sb. during interrogation; interrogate with torture

烤* kǎo ① bake; roast; toast: ～白薯 baked sweet potatoes/ ～馒头 toasted steamed bun/ 把湿衣裳～干 dry wet clothes by a fire ② scorching: 这炉子太～人。This stove is really scorching.

【烤面包】 kǎomiànbāo toast: 一片～ a slice of toast

【烤肉】 kǎoròu roast meat; roast ◇ ～叉 spit; skewer

【烤鸭】 kǎoyā roast duck: 北京～ roast Beijing duck

kào

铐 kào ① handcuffs ② put handcuffs on; handcuff: 把犯人～起来 handcuff the criminal

犒 kào reward with food and drink

【犒劳】 kàolao reward with food and drink

【犒赏】 kàoshǎng reward a victorious army, etc. with bounties

靠* kào ① lean against; lean on: 把梯子～在墙上 lean a ladder against a wall/ 背～背坐着 sit back to back ② keep to; get near; come up to: 车辆一律~左走。 All vehicles should keep to the left./ 船已经~码头了。 The ship has docked. ③ near; by: 疗养院~海。 The sanatorium stands by the sea./ ~山吃山，~水吃水 those living on a mountain live off the mountain, those living near the water live off the water — make use of local resources ④ depend on; rely on: 他家里~他维持生活。 His family depended on him for support. ⑤ trust: 可~ reliable; trustworthy

【靠岸】 kào'àn pull in to shore; draw alongside
【靠背】 kàobèi back (of a chair)
【靠边】 kàobiān keep to the side: ~儿！~儿！ Out of the way, please! 或 Mind your backs, please!/ 行人~走。 Pedestrians keep to the side of the road.
【靠不住】 kàobuzhù unreliable; undependable; untrustworthy: 这话~。 This story cannot be relied upon.
【靠得住】 kàodezhù reliable; dependable; trustworthy: 这消息~吗? Is the information reliable?
【靠拢】 kàolǒng draw close; close up: 向前~！ Close ranks!
【靠山】 kàoshan backer; patron; backing
【靠手】 kàoshǒu armrest

kē

苛 kē severe; exacting: ~待 treat harshly; be hard upon
【苛捐杂税】 kējuān-záshuì exorbitant taxes and levies
【苛刻】 kēkè harsh: ~的条件 harsh terms
【苛求】 kēqiú make excessive demands; be overcritical
【苛责】 kēzé criticize severely; excoriate
【苛政】 kēzhèng harsh (或 oppressive) government; tyranny: ~猛于虎。 Tyranny is fiercer than a tiger.

柯 kē ① <书> stalk or branch ② <书> axe-handle; helve
科* kē ① a branch of academic or vocational study: 文~ the humanities; the liberal arts/ 理~ the sciences/ 眼~ department of ophthalmology ② a division or subdivision of an administrative unit; section: 财务~ finance section/ 卫生~ health section; clinic ③ <生> family: 猫~动物 animals of the cat family
【科技】 kējì science and technology
【科目】 kēmù ① subject (in a curriculum); course ② headings in an account book
【科学】 kēxué science; scientific knowledge
  ◇ ~工作者 scientific worker; scientist/ ~幻想小说 science fiction/ ~家 scientist/ ~实验 scientific experiment/ ~文献 scientific literature/ ~研究 scientific research/ ~仪器 scientific instruments (或 apparatus)
【科学技术】 kēxué-jìshù science and technology: ~是生产力。 Science and technology are part of the productive forces.
【科学院】 kēxuéyuàn academy of sciences

疴 kē <书> illness: 沉~ severe and lingering illness
棵* kē <量>: 一~树 a tree/ 一~大白菜 a (head of) Chinese cabbage
颏 kē chin
窠 kē nest; burrow
【窠臼】 kējiù <书> set pattern (usu. of writing or artistic creation): 不落~ show originality; be unconventional
颗* kē <量>: 一~珠子 a pearl/ 一~黄豆 a soya bean
【颗粒】 kēlì ① anything small and roundish (as a bean, pearl, etc.); pellet ② grain
磕 kē knock (against sth. hard): 摔了一跤，脸上~破了皮 fall and graze one's face/ 碗边儿~掉了一块 chip the edge of a bowl
【磕头】 kētóu kowtow
【磕头碰脑】 kētóu-pèngnǎo bump against things on every side (as in a room full of furniture); push and bump against one another (as in a crowd)

瞌 kē
【瞌睡】 kēshuì sleepy; drowsy: 打~ doze off; nod; have a nap/ 一宿没睡，白天~得很。 I'm terribly sleepy today, I didn't sleep a wink last night.
蝌* kē
【蝌蚪】 kēdǒu tadpole

ké

壳* ké ① shell: 鸡蛋~ egg shell/ 核桃~ walnut shell
  另见 qiào
咳* ké cough
  另见 hāi
【咳嗽】 késou cough

kě

可* kě ① approve: 不置~否 decline to comment; be noncommittal ② can; may: 由此~见 thus it can be seen that; this proves/ 今秋~望丰收。 We expect a good harvest this autumn. ③ need (doing); be worth (doing): 没有什么~担心的。 There is nothing to worry about./ ~爱 lovable/~靠 reliable ④ <副> [用于加强语气]: ~别忘了。 Mind you don't forget it. 或 Be sure to remember it./ 你~来了! So you're here at last!/ ~不是吗? That's just the way it is. 或 Exactly./ 有人这么说，~谁见过呢? So they say, but who has ever seen it? ⑤ <副> [表示疑问]: 你~曾跟他谈过这个问题? Did you ever talk it over with him?
  另见 kè
【可爱】 kě'ài lovable; likable; lovely: ~的祖国 my beloved country/ 多么~的孩子! What lovely children!
【可悲】 kěbēi sad; lamentable
【可鄙】 kěbǐ contemptible; despicable; mean: 行为~ act contemptibly
【可乘之机】 kě chéng zhī jī an opportunity that can be exploited to sb.'s advantage: 不给敌人以~ give the enemy no opportunity
【可耻】 kěchǐ shameful; disgraceful; ignominious: ~的失败 ignominious defeat/ 以爱学习为光荣，以不学习为~ It is praiseworthy to love study, and shameful to neglect it.
【可歌可泣】 kěgē-kěqì move one to song and tears: ~的英雄事迹 heroic and moving deeds/ ~的斗争 an epic struggle
【可观】 kěguān considerable; impressive; sizable: 这个数目相当~。 This is a considerable figure.
【可贵】 kěguì valuable; praiseworthy; commendable: ~的品质 fine qualities/ 这种积极性和热情是很~的。 Such initiative and enthusiasm are highly commendable.
【可恨】 kěhèn hateful; detestable; abominable
【可见】 kějiàn it is thus clear (或 evident, obvious) that
【可敬】 kějìng worthy of respect; respected
【可靠】 kěkào reliable; dependable; trustworthy: ~消息 reliable information/ 这个人很~。 This person is reliable (或 trustworthy). ◇ ~性 reliability
【可可】 kěkě cocoa
【可口】 kěkǒu good to eat; nice; tasty; palatable: 这菜很~。 This dish is very tasty.
【可怜】 kělián ① pitiful; pitiable; poor: 装出一付~相 put on a pitiable face ② have pity on; pity: 他这是自作自受，没人~他。 Nobody feels sorry for him; he's got what he deserves. ③ meagre; wretched; miserable; pitiful: 这一带雨水少得~。 There's terribly little rainfall in this area. 或 The rainfall is pitifully low in this area. ◇ ~虫 pitiful creature; wretch
【可能】 kěnéng ① possible; probable: 提前一个月交工是完全~的。 It's entirely possible to complete the project and hand it over one month ahead of time. ② probably; maybe: 他~不知道。 He probably doesn't know./ 她今天~会再来的。 Maybe she'll pop in again today. ③ possibility: 事情发展有两种~。 The matter may develop in two possible directions. ◇ ~性 possibility

【可怕】 kěpà fearful; frightful; terrible; terrifying: 真～! How dreadful!/ 困难再大也没什么～的。However great the difficulties, there's nothing to be afraid of.

【可欺】 kěqī ① gullible; easily duped ② easily cowed or bullied: 不要把我方的克制看做是软弱。Do not take our restraint for a sign of weakness.

【可气】 kěqì annoying; exasperating: 这孩子刚换的衣服就弄脏了,真～! The child just changed his clothes and now he's got them dirty again. How annoying!

【可取】 kěqǔ desirable: 双方认为增进两国人民之间的了解是～的。Both sides consider it desirable to further the understanding between the two peoples./ 这个方案有～之处。This plan has something to recommend it.

【可是】 kěshì 〈连〉but; yet; however: 他们劳动了一天,虽然很累,～都很愉快。They were tired out after the day's work, but they all felt happy.

【可望而不可即】 kě wàng ér bùkě jí within sight but beyond reach; unattainable; inaccessible

【可谓】 kěwèi one may well say; it may be said; it may be called

【可恶】 kěwù hateful; abominable; detestable: 这些虫真～! What a curse those worms are!

【可惜】 kěxī it's a pity; it's too bad: ～我去晚了一步,最精彩的节目已经演过了。What a pity I was just too late for the best item on the programme./ 这手套还没破,扔了多～。The gloves aren't worn out yet. It would be a pity to throw them away.

【可喜】 kěxǐ gratifying; heartening: ～的成就 gratifying achievements/ 取得了～的进展 have made encouraging progress

【可笑】 kěxiào laughable; ridiculous; ludicrous; funny: 简直～! It's simply ridiculous!/ ～不自量 ridiculously overrate oneself; make oneself ridiculous by overestimating one's ability

【可疑】 kěyí suspicious; dubious; questionable: 形迹～ look suspicious ◇ ～分子 a suspect; a suspicious character

【可以】 kěyǐ ① can; may: 人类는～征服自然的。Man can conquer nature./ 问题一定会搞清楚的,你～放心。Don't worry. Things will be straightened out in the end./ 你～走了。You may go. ② 〈口〉passable; pretty good; not bad: 这篇文章写得还～。This article is pretty good./ 她的英语还～。Her English is not at all bad.

【可有可无】 kěyǒu-kěwú not essential; not indispensable

坷 kě 见"坎坷" kǎnkě

渴* kě ① thirsty: 这里有开水,～了请随便喝。Here's some boiled water. Have a drink whenever you're thirsty. ② yearningly: ～念 yearn for

【渴望】 kěwàng . thirst for; long for; yearn for

---

kè

可 kě 另见 kě

【可汗】 kèhán 〈史〉khan

克* kè ① can; be able to: 不～分身 be unable to leave what one is doing at the moment; can't get away ② restrain: ～制 exercise restraint ③ overcome; subdue; capture (a city, etc.): 连～名城 capture one important city after another/ 战无不胜,攻无不～ be invincible; carry all before one ④ digest: ～食 help one's digestion ⑤ set a time limit: ～期完工 set a date for completing the work ⑥ gram (g.)

【克敌制胜】 kèdí-zhìshèng vanquish (或 conquer) the enemy

【克服】 kèfú ① surmount; overcome; conquer: ～困难 surmount a difficulty/ ～私心杂念 overcome selfish considerations

【克复】 kèfù retake; recapture; recover: ～失地 recover lost territory

【克己奉公】 kèjǐ-fènggōng wholehearted devotion to public duty; work selflessly for the public interest

【克制】 kèzhì restrain; exercise restraint: ～自己的感情 restrain one's passion/ 表现很大的～ exercise great restraint

刻* kè ① carve; engrave; cut: ～图章 engrave a seal/ ～蜡版 cut stencils/ 木～ woodcut ② a quarter (of an hour): 五点一～ a quarter past five ③ moment: 此～ at the moment ④ cutting; penetrating: 尖～ acrimonious; biting; sarcastic ⑤ in the highest degree: 深～ penetrating; profound ⑥ set a time limit

【刻板】 kèbǎn ① cut blocks for printing ② mechanical; stiff; inflexible: ～地照抄 copy mechanically

【刻版】 kèbǎn cut blocks for printing

【刻本】 kèběn block-printed edition

【刻薄】 kèbó unkind; harsh; mean: 说～话 speak unkindly; make caustic remarks/ 待人～ treat people meanly

【刻不容缓】 kè bùróng huǎn brook no delay; demand immediate attention; be of great urgency

【刻毒】 kèdú venomous; spiteful: ～的语言 venomed remarks

【刻骨】 kègǔ deeply ingrained; deep-rooted: ～仇恨 inveterate hatred; deep-seated hatred

【刻骨铭心】 kègǔ-míngxīn be engraved on one's bones and heart; remember with gratitude to the end of one's life

【刻花】 kèhuā engraved designs; carved designs

【刻画】 kèhuà depict; portray: ～英雄人物的形象 portray heroic characters

【刻苦】 kèkǔ ① assiduous; hardworking; painstaking: ～钻研 study assiduously ② simple and frugal: 生活～ lead a simple and frugal life

【刻意】 kèyì painstakingly; sedulously: ～求工 sedulously strive for perfection

【刻舟求剑】 kè zhōu qiú jiàn cut a mark on the side of one's boat to indicate the place where one's sword has dropped into the river— take measures without regard to changes in circumstances

【刻字】 kèzì carve (或 engrave) characters on a seal, etc.

客* kè ① visitor; guest ② traveller; passenger: ～舱 passenger cabin ③ travelling merchant ④ customer: 房～ boarder; lodger ⑤ settle or live in a strange place; be a stranger: 作～他乡 live in a strange land ⑥ a person engaged in some particular pursuit: 政～ politician/ 刺～ assassin ⑦ objective: ～观 objective

【客船】 kèchuán passenger ship (或 boat)

【客串】 kèchuàn (of an amateur singer, actor, etc.) play a part in a professional performance; be a guest performer

【客房】 kèfáng guest room

【客观】 kèguān objective

【客机】 kèjī passenger plane; airliner

【客满】 kèmǎn (of theatre tickets, etc.) sold out; full house

【客气】 kèqi ① polite; courteous: 他对人很～。He is very polite to people./ 双方～了一番,就开始谈正事。After a few words of courtesy, they got down to business./ 别～。(对来客) Please don't stand on ceremony. 或 Make yourself at home. (对主人) Please don't bother. ② modest: 您太～了。You are being too modest.

【客人】 kèrén ① visitor; guest ② guest (at a hotel, etc.)

【客套】 kètào polite formula; civilities: 我们是老朋友,用不着讲～。As old friends we don't need to stand on ceremony./ 他们～了几句,就坐下了。After an exchange of greetings, they took their seats.

【客厅】 kètīng drawing room; parlour

【客栈】 kèzhàn inn

恪 kè scrupulously and respectfully

【恪守】 kèshǒu scrupulously abide by (a treaty, promise, etc.)

课* kè ① subject; course: 主～ the main subject/ 必修～ required courses ② class: 上～ go to class/ 一节物理～ a class in physics/ 讲(听)～ give (attend) a lecture ③ 〈量〉lesson: 第一～ Lesson One/ 这本教科书共有二十五～。This textbook contains 25 lessons. ④ tax ⑤ levy: ～以重税 levy heavy taxes

【课本】kèběn　textbook
【课程】kèchéng　course; curriculum ◇ ～表 school time-table
【课堂】kètáng　classroom; schoolroom
【课题】kètí ① a question for study or discussion ② problem; task: 提出新的～ pose a new problem; set a new task
【课外】kèwài　extracurricular; outside class; after school ◇ ～辅导 instruction after class/ ～活动 extracurricular activities/ ～阅读 outside reading/ ～作业 homework
【课文】kèwén　text
【课余】kèyú　after school; after class: 利用～时间进行义务劳动 do voluntary labour after school

嗑 kè　crack sth. between the teeth: ～瓜子儿 crack melon seeds

kěn

肯* kěn ① agree; consent: 我劝说了半天，他才～了。 He did not agree until I had talked to him for a long time./ 首～ nod assent ② be willing to; be ready to: ～干 be willing to do hard work/ ～虚心接受意见 be ready to listen to criticism with an open mind/ 青年人最～学习。 Young people are most eager to learn.
【肯定】kěndìng ① affirm; confirm; approve; regard as positive: 对于我们的工作的看法，～一切或者否定一切，都是片面性的。 In the appraisal of our work, it is one-sided to affirm everything or to negate everything. ② positive; affirmative: ～的判断 a positive assessment/ 他的回答是～的。 His answer is in the affirmative. ③ definite; sure: 请给我一个～的答复。 Please give me a definite answer./ 他今天来不来，我不能～。 I'm not sure whether he will come today. ④ certainly; undoubtedly; definitely: ～按时送到 guarantee delivery on time

垦 kěn　cultivate (land); reclaim (wasteland)
【垦荒】kěnhuāng　reclaim wasteland; bring wasteland under cultivation; open up virgin soil

恳* kěn ① earnestly; sincerely: ～谈 talk earnestly ② request; beseech; entreat: 敬～ respectfully request
【恳切】kěnqiè　earnest; sincere: 言词～ speak in an earnest tone/ ～希望 earnestly (或 sincerely) hope
【恳请】kěnqǐng　earnestly request: ～协助。 Your assistance is earnestly requested.
【恳求】kěnqiú　implore; entreat; beseech
【恳挚】kěnzhì 〈书〉earnest; sincere: 情意～ show sincere feeling/ 词意～ express oneself earnestly

啃 kěn　gnaw; nibble: ～骨头 gnaw a bone/ ～书本 delve into books

kēng

坑 kēng ① hole; pit; hollow: 泥～ mud puddle/ 水～ puddle/ 粪～ manure pit/一个萝卜一个～ one radish, one hole — each has his own task, and there is nobody to spare ② tunnel; pit: 矿～ pit ③ bury alive

吭 kēng　utter a sound or a word: 他坐在旁边一声不～。 He sat there without saying a word.
另见 háng

【吭声】kēngshēng　utter a sound or a word: 你为什么不～？ Why do you keep silent?

铿 kēng 〈象〉clang; clatter: 拖拉机走在路上～～地响。 Tractors clattered along the road.
【铿锵】kēngqiāng　ring; clang: 这首诗读起来～有力。 This poem is sonorous and forceful.

kōng

空* kōng ① empty; hollow; void: ～箱子 an empty box/ 把抽屉腾～ empty out a drawer/ 这棵树被虫子蛀～了。 This tree has been eaten hollow by worms./ 屋里～无一人。 There isn't a single soul in the house. ② sky; air: 晴～ a clear sky ③ for nothing; in vain: ～跑一趟 make a journey for nothing/ ～忙 make fruitless efforts
另见 kòng
【空城计】kōngchéngjì　empty-city stratagem (bluffing the enemy by opening the gates of a weakly defended city); presenting a bold front to conceal a weak defence
【空荡荡】kōngdàngdàng　empty; deserted: 农忙季节，人都下地了，村子里显得～的。 In the busy season the village looked deserted when the peasants had gone to the fields.
【空洞】kōngdòng ① cavity: 肺～ pulmonary cavity ② empty; hollow; devoid of content: ～的理论 empty theory/ ～的词句 empty phraseology/ ～无物 utter lack of substance; devoid of content
【空泛】kōngfàn　vague and general; not specific: ～的议论 vague and general opinions; generalities
【空防】kōngfáng　air defence
【空话】kōnghuà　empty talk; idle talk; hollow words: 说～ indulge in idle talk/ ～连篇 pages and pages of empty verbiage
【空欢喜】kōnghuānxǐ　rejoice too soon; be or feel let down
【空间】kōngjiān　space: 外层～ outer space
【空降】kōngjiàng　airborne: ～兵 airborne force/ 降落地点 landing area
【空军】kōngjūn　air force ◇ ～部队 air (force) unit/ ～基地 air base
【空空如也】kōngkōng rú yě　absolutely empty
【空口说白话】kōngkǒu shuō báihuà　make empty promises
【空口无凭】kōngkǒu wú píng　a mere verbal statement is no guarantee: ～，立字为证。 Words of mouth being no guarantee, a written statement is hereby given.
【空旷】kōngkuàng　open; spacious: ～的原野 an expanse of open country; champaign
【空阔】kōngkuò　open; spacious: 水天～ a vast expanse of water and sky
【空论】kōnglùn　empty talk
【空气】kōngqì ① air: 呼吸新鲜～ breathe fresh air/ 湿～ moist air ② atmosphere: ～紧张 a tense atmosphere
【空前】kōngqián　unprecedented
【空前绝后】kōngqián-juéhòu　unprecedented and unrepeatable; unique
【空手】kōngshǒu　empty-handed
【空谈】kōngtán ① indulge in empty talk ② empty talk; idle talk; prattle
【空头】kōngtóu ① (on the stock exchange) bear; short-seller ② nominal; phony
【空头支票】kōngtóu zhīpiào ① dud (或 rubber) cheque; bad cheque ② empty promise; lip service
【空袭】kōngxí　air raid; air attack
【空想】kōngxiǎng　idle dream; fantasy: 别～了，还是从实际出发吧。 Stop daydreaming. Be realistic. ◇ ～家 dreamer; visionary
【空虚】kōngxū　hollow; void: 生活～ lead a life devoid of meaning/ 思想～ lack mental or spiritual ballast; be impractical in one's thinking/ 敌人后方～。 The enemy rear is weakly defended.
【空穴来风】kōngxué lái fēng　an empty hole invites the wind — weakness lends wings to rumours
【空运】kōngyùn　air transport; airlift: ～救灾物资 airlift relief supplies (to a stricken area)
【空战】kōngzhàn　air battle; aerial combat
【空中】kōngzhōng　in the sky; in the air; aerial; overhead ◇ ～补给 air-supply; air-resupply/ ～待战 air alert/ ～飞人 〈杂技〉flying trapeze/ ～加油 air refueling; inflight refueling
【空中楼阁】kōngzhōng lóugé　castles in the air

kǒng

孔* kǒng hole; opening; aperture: 钥匙~ keyhole/ 十七~桥 a seventeen-arched bridge

【孔道】 kǒngdào a narrow passage providing the only means of access to a certain place; pass

【孔洞】 kǒngdòng opening or hole in a utensil, etc.

【孔雀】 kǒngquè peacock

恐* kǒng ① fear; dread: 惊~ be alarmed ② terrify; intimidate: ~吓 threaten; intimidate ③ I'm afraid: 消息~不可靠。 I'm afraid the information is not reliable./ ~另有原因。 There may be some other reason for it.

【恐怖】 kǒngbù terror: 白色~ White terror ◇ ~分子 terrorist/ ~统治 reign of terror/ ~主义 terrorism

【恐吓】 kǒnghè threaten; intimidate ◇ ~信 blackmailing letter; threatening letter

【恐慌】 kǒnghuāng panic: ~万状 panic-stricken/ 使敌人感到~ throw the enemy into a panic; strike terror into the enemy

【恐惧】 kǒngjù fear; dread: ~不安 be frightened and restless

【恐龙】 kǒnglóng 〈古生物〉 dinosaur

【恐怕】 kǒngpà 〈副〉① I'm afraid: 这样做~，~不行。 I'm afraid this won't work. ② perhaps; I think: 他走了~有十天了。 It's ten days now, I think, since he left./ ~要下雨。 It looks like rain.

kòng

空* kòng ① leave empty or blank: 请把前面一排座位~出来。 Please leave the front row of seats vacant./ 每段开头要~两格。 Leave two blank spaces at the beginning of each paragraph. ② unoccupied; vacant: ~房 a vacant room/ 车厢里~得很。 There are many vacant seats in the carriage. ③ empty space: 各行之间多留点~儿。 Leave a little more space between the rows. ④ free time; spare time: 有~儿时我去看你。 Come over when you have time./ 今天没~，改日再谈吧。 I'm busy today. Let's talk about it some other day.
另见 kōng

【空白】 kòngbái blank space: 版面上那块~可以补一篇短文。 We can fill up that space with a short article./ 填补科学技术上的~ fill the gaps in science and technology ◇ ~表格 blank form/ ~支票 blank cheque

【空地】 kòngdì vacant lot; open ground; open space: 我们把砖卸在那边~上吧。 Let's leave the bricks on the open ground over there.

【空额】 kòng'é vacancy: ~已经补上。 The vacancy has already been filled.

【空格】 kònggé blank space (on a form)

【空缺】 kòngquē vacant position; vacancy

【空隙】 kòngxì space; gap; interval: 铁轨接头的地方都有一定的~。 There is a specified gap at every rail joint.

【空暇】 kòngxiá free time; spare time; leisure

【空闲】 kòngxián ① idle; free: 我们车间里的机器没有一台是~的。 None of the machines in our workshop are idle./ 等你~的时候，我俩谈谈心。 Let's have a heart-to-heart talk when you're free. ② free time; spare time; leisure: 战士们一有~时间就练习投弹。 The soldiers practise grenade-throwing whenever they have some spare time.

控* kòng ① accuse; charge: 指~ accuse ② control; dominate: 遥~ remote control; telecontrol ③ turn a (container) upside down to let the liquid trickle out: 把瓶子先~一~再装油。 Turn the bottle upside down to empty it before you fill it with oil.

【控告】 kònggào charge; accuse; complain: 向法院提出~ file charges in court/向国家机关提出~ lodge complaints with organs of state

【控诉】 kòngsù accuse; denounce

【控制】 kòngzhì control; dominate; command: ~局面 have the situation under control/ ~险要 command a strategic position/ 她~不住自己的感情。 She lost control of her feelings./ ~地面沉降 bring surface subsidence under control

kǒu

口* kǒu ① mouth ② opening; entrance; mouth: 胡同~ the entrance of an alley/ 河~ the mouth of a river; estuary/ 入~ entrance/ 出~ exit/ 瓶~ the mouth of a bottle/ 枪~ the muzzle of a gun/ 信箱的~儿 the slit of a letter box ③ a gateway of the Great Wall (often used in place names, e.g. 张家~ Zhangjiakou) ④ cut; hole: 伤~ wound; cut/ 衣服撕了个~儿 tear a hole in one's jacket/ 茶碗缺了个~儿。 The rim of the teacup is chipped. ⑤〈量〉：一~井 a well/ 三~猪 three pigs/ 他家五~人。 There are five people in his family.

【口才】 kǒucái eloquence: 他很有~。 He is an eloquent speaker.

【口吃】 kǒuchī stutter; stammer: 他说话有点~。 He speaks with a slight stutter.

【口齿】 kǒuchǐ ① enunciation: ~清楚 have clear enunciation ② ability to speak: ~伶俐 be clever and fluent

【口臭】 kǒuchòu halitosis; bad breath

【口服】 kǒufú ① profess to be convinced: ~心不服 pretend to be convinced/ 心服~ be sincerely convinced ② take orally: 不得~ not to be taken orally

【口福】 kǒufú gourmet's luck; the luck to get sth. very nice to eat

【口供】 kǒugòng a statement made by the accused under examination

【口号】 kǒuhào slogan; watchword: 呼~ shout slogans

【口红】 kǒuhóng lipstick

【口惠】 kǒuhuì lip service; empty promise: ~而实不至 make a promise and not keep it; pay lip service

【口角】 kǒujiǎo corner of the mouth ◇ ~炎 perlèche
另见 kǒujué

【口角】 kǒujué quarrel; bicker; wrangle
另见 kǒujiǎo

【口渴】 kǒukě thirsty

【口口声声】 kǒukoushēngshēng say again and again; keep on saying: 他~说不知道。 He kept on pleading ignorance.

【口令】 kǒulìng ① word of command ② password; watchword; countersign: ~问答 challenge and reply

【口蜜腹剑】 kǒumì-fùjiàn honey-mouthed and dagger-hearted; honey on one's lips and murder in one's heart; hypocritical and malignant

【口气】 kǒuqì ① tone; note: 严肃的~ a serious tone/ 改变~ change one's tone/ 他说话有埋怨的~。 There was a note of complaint in what he said./ ~强硬的声明 a strongly worded statement ② manner of speaking: 他的~真不小。 He talked big. ③ what is actually meant; implication: 听他的~，好象感到为难。 Judging by the way he spoke, he seemed to be in an awkward situation.

【口琴】 kǒuqín mouth organ; harmonica

【口若悬河】 kǒu ruò xuán hé let loose a flood of eloquence; be eloquent

【口哨儿】 kǒushàor whistling sound through rounded lips: 吹~ whistle (through rounded lips)

【口舌】 kǒushé ① quarrel; dispute ② talking round: 费了很大的~才把他说服。 It took a lot of talking to convince him./ 不必费~了。 You might as well save your breath.

【口试】 kǒushì oral examination; oral test

【口是心非】 kǒushì-xīnfēi say yes and mean no; say one thing and mean another

【口授】 kǒushòu ① oral instruction ② dictate: 他写的这封信是他父亲~的。 The letter he wrote was dictated by his father.

【口述】 kǒushù oral account

【口水】 kǒushuǐ saliva: 流~ slobber

【口头】 kǒutóu oral: ~通知 notify orally/~上赞成，实际上反对 agree in words but oppose in deeds

【口头禅】 kǒutóuchán pet phrase 又作"口头语"
【口味】 kǒuwèi ① a person's taste: 合～ suit one's taste/ 不合～ not be to one's taste/ 各人～不同。 Tastes differ. ② the flavour or taste of food: 这些菜都是湖南～。 These are all Hunanese dishes.
【口吻】 kǒuwěn ①〈动〉muzzle; snout ② tone; note: 玩笑的～ jocular tone
【口香糖】 kǒuxiāngtáng chewing gum
【口信】 kǒuxìn oral message
【口译】 kǒuyì oral interpretation
【口音】 kǒuyīn 〈语〉oral speech sounds
【口音】 kǒuyīn ① voice: 她一听是她儿子的～，就赶紧出来了。 Recognizing her son's voice, she hurried out. ② accent: 说话带广东～ speak with a Guangdong accent
【口语】 kǒuyǔ spoken language
【口诛笔伐】 kǒuzhū-bǐfá condemn both in speech and in writing

kòu

叩 kòu ① knock: ～门 knock at a door ② kowtow
【叩头】 kòutóu kowtow

扣* kòu ① button up; buckle: 把衣服～上 button (up) one's coat/ 把皮带～上 buckle a belt/ 把门～上 latch the door/ ～扣子 do up the buttons ② place a cup, bowl, etc. upside down; cover with an inverted cup, bowl, etc.: 把缸～过来。 Turn the vat upside down./ 用碗把菜～上，免得凉了。 Cover the food with a bowl to keep it from getting cold. ③ detain; take into custody; arrest: 他违反交通规则，交通警～了他的自行车。 The policeman took away his bike because he had violated traffic regulations. ④ deduct: ～工资 deduct a part of sb.'s pay ⑤ discount: 打九～ give a 10 per cent discount ⑥ knot; button; buckle: 系个～儿 tie (或make) a knot ⑦ smash (the ball)
【扣除】 kòuchú deduct: ～各种费用后，收入超过万元。 After deducting costs, the income was more than $10,000
【扣留】 kòuliú detain; arrest; hold in custody: 把走私犯～起来 detain the smuggler/ ～行车执照 suspend a driving licence
【扣人心弦】 kòu rén xīnxián exciting; thrilling: 一场～的比赛 an exciting match
【扣压】 kòuyā withhold; pigeonhole: ～稿件 withhold a manuscript from publication
【扣押】 kòuyā ① detain; hold in custody ②〈法〉distrain

寇 kòu ① bandit; invader; enemy: 海～ pirate/ 敌～ the (invading) enemy ② invade: 入～ invade (a country)

kū

枯* kū ① (of a plant, etc.) withered: ～草 withered grass/ ～叶 dead leaves ② (of a well, river, etc.) dried up: ～井 a dry well ③ dull; uninteresting: ～坐 sit in boredom
【枯肠】 kūcháng 〈书〉impoverished mind: 搜索～ rack one's brains (for ideas or expressions)
【枯槁】 kūgǎo ① withered ② haggard: 形容～ look haggard
【枯黄】 kūhuáng withered and yellow: 树叶逐渐～了。 The leaves are beginning to turn yellow.
【枯竭】 kūjié dried up; exhausted: 水源～。 The source has dried up./ 财源～。 Financial resources were exhausted.
【枯木逢春】 kūmù féng chūn spring comes to the withered tree — get a new lease of life
【枯涩】 kūsè dull and heavy: 文字～ a dull and heavy style
【枯瘦】 kūshòu emaciated; skinny
【枯水】 kūshuǐ low water ◇ ～期 dry season
【枯萎】 kūwěi withered
【枯燥】 kūzào dull and dry; uninteresting: ～无味 dry as dust

哭* kū cry; weep: 放声大～ cry loudly; cry unrestrainedly/ ～了起来 burst into tears
【哭哭啼啼】 kūkūtítí endlessly weep and wail
【哭泣】 kūqì cry; weep; sob
【哭丧着脸】 kūsangzhe liǎn put on (或 wear) a long face; go around with a long face
【哭诉】 kūsù complain tearfully
【哭笑不得】 kū-xiào bude not know whether to laugh or to cry; find sth. both funny and annoying

窟 kū ① hole; cave: 石～ cave; grotto ② den: 匪～ a robbers' den/ 赌～ a gambling-den
【窟窿】 kūlong ① hole; cavity: 耗子～ rat-hole/ 鞋底磨了个～ have worn a hole in the sole of one's shoe ② deficit; debt

骷 kū
【骷髅】 kūlóu ① human skeleton ② human skull; death's-head

kǔ

苦* kǔ ① bitter: 这药～极了。 This medicine tastes very bitter. ② hardship; suffering; pain: ～里生，甜里长 be born in misery but brought up in happiness ③ cause sb. suffering; give sb. a hard time: 这事可～了他了。 This matter really gave him a hard time. ④ suffer from; be troubled by: ～旱 suffer from drought ⑤ painstakingly; doing one's utmost: 勤学～练 study and train hard/ ～劝 earnestly advise (或 exhort)/ ～～哀求 entreat piteously; implore urgently
【苦差】 kǔchāi hard and unprofitable job
【苦楚】 kǔchǔ suffering; misery; distress
【苦处】 kǔchu suffering; hardship; difficulty
【苦干】 kǔgàn work hard: ～精神 hard-working spirit/ ～加巧干 work hard and skilfully; work hard and use one's brain
【苦工】 kǔgōng hard (manual) work; hard labour
【苦功】 kǔgōng hard work; painstaking effort: 语言这东西，不是随便可以学好的，非下～不可。 The mastery of language is not easy and requires painstaking effort./ 下～学习 study hard
【苦瓜】 kǔguā ①〈植〉balsam pear ② bitter gourd
【苦海】 kǔhǎi sea of bitterness; abyss of misery: ～无边，回头是岸。 The sea of bitterness has no bounds, repent and the shore is at hand.
【苦寒】 kǔhán bitter cold
【苦尽甘来】 kǔjìn-gānlái when bitterness is finished, sweetness begins — after suffering comes happiness
【苦口】 kǔkǒu ① (admonish) in earnest: ～相劝 earnestly advise (或 exhort) ② bitter to the taste: 这些话都是～良药。 The advice may be bitter medicine, but it will do good.
【苦口婆心】 kǔkǒu-póxīn urge sb. time and again with good intentions
【苦力】 kǔlì 〈旧〉coolie
【苦闷】 kǔmèn depressed; dejected; feeling low
【苦难】 kǔnàn suffering; misery; distress
【苦恼】 kǔnǎo vexed; worried: 受到一点挫折用不着～。 You shouldn't feel vexed just because of a few setbacks.
【苦肉计】 kǔròujì the ruse of inflicting an injury on oneself to win the confidence of the enemy
【苦涩】 kǔsè ① bitter and astringent ② pained; agonized; anguished: ～的表情 a pained look
【苦痛】 kǔtòng pain; suffering
【苦头】 kǔtou suffering: 他在监狱里吃尽了～。 He endured untold sufferings in the prison.
【苦笑】 kǔxiào forced smile; wry smile
【苦心】 kǔxīn trouble taken; pains: 煞费～ take great pains/ ～经营 painstakingly build up (an enterprise, etc.)
【苦心孤诣】 kǔxīn gūyì make extraordinarily painstaking efforts

【苦役】 kǔyì 〈法〉 hard labour; penal servitude
【苦于】 kǔyú suffer from (a disadvantage): ～不识字 handicapped by illiteracy/ ～时间紧 hard pressed for time
【苦战】 kǔzhàn wage an arduous struggle; struggle hard
【苦衷】 kǔzhōng difficulties that one is reluctant to discuss or mention: 应该体谅他的～。 Allowance must be made for his difficulties./ 难言的～ feelings of pain or embarrassment which are hard to mention

kù

库 kù warehouse; storehouse: 粮食已经入～。 The grain is already in the granary./ 汽车～ garage/ 军械～ armoury
【库藏】 kùcáng have in storage: ～图书三十万册。 There are 300,000 books in the library.
【库存】 kùcún stock; reserve: 有大量～ have a large stock of goods/ ～物资 goods kept in stock; reserve of materials
【库房】 kùfáng storehouse; storeroom

裤* kù trousers; pants: 短～ shorts
【裤子】 kùzi trousers; pants

酷 kù ① cruel; oppressive: ～吏 an oppressive (feudal) official ② very; extremely: ～寒 bitter cold/ ～似 be the very image of; be exactly like/ ～爱 ardently love
【酷烈】 kùliè cruel; fierce: ～的太阳 the scorching sun
【酷热】 kùrè extremely hot (weather): 天气～ a sweltering hot day
【酷刑】 kùxíng cruel (或 savage) torture

kuā

夸* kuā ① exaggerate; overstate; boast: ～口 boast; brag ② praise: 人人都～她爱劳动。 Everyone praised her for her love of labour./ 成绩不～跑不了，缺点不找不得了。 Merits uncited will not vanish; shortcomings undiscovered may prove disastrous.
【夸大】 kuādà exaggerate; overstate; magnify: ～困难 exaggerate the difficulties/ ～敌情 overestimate the enemy/ 原来的数字被～了。 The original figures were inflated.
【夸大其词】 kuādà qí cí make an overstatement; exaggerate
【夸奖】 kuājiǎng praise; commend: 工人师傅～他进步很快。 The master worker praised him for his rapid progress.
【夸口】 kuākǒu boast; brag; talk big
【夸耀】 kuāyào brag about; show off; flaunt: 她从不～自己。 She never brags./ ～他的见识 show off his knowledge and experience
【夸赞】 kuāzàn speak highly of; commend; praise
【夸张】 kuāzhāng ① exaggerate; overstate: 你这样说未免太～了。 I'm afraid you've been exaggerating. 或 I'm afraid you've overstated the case./ ～的语言 inflated language; exaggerations/ 艺术～ artistic exaggeration ② 〈语〉 hyperbole

kuǎ

垮 kuǎ collapse; fall; break down: 这堵墙要～了。 The wall's going to collapse./ 我身体结实，累不～。 I'm very strong; no amount of hard work can wear me down./ 洪水冲～了堤坝。 The flood waters burst the dyke./ 打～敌人 put the enemy to rout
【垮台】 kuǎtái collapse; fall from power

kuà

跨 kuà ① step; stride: ～进大门 step into a doorway/ 向前～一步 take a step forward/ ～过小沟 stride over a ditch/ 欢欣鼓舞地～入了新的一年 stride into the new year in high spirits ② bestride; straddle: ～上战马 mount (或 bestride) a war-horse/ 横～长江的大桥 a gigantic bridge spanning the Changjiang River. ③ cut across; go beyond: 亚洲地～寒、温、热三带。 Asia extends across the frigid, temperate and tropical zones.
【跨国公司】 kuàguó gōngsī transnational corporation
【跨越】 kuàyuè stride across; leap over; cut across: ～几个历史阶段 leap over several historical stages of development/ ～障碍 surmount an obstacle

kuài

会 kuài 另见 huì
【会计】 kuàijì ① accounting ② bookkeeper; accountant ◇ ～年度 financial (或 fiscal) year

快* kuài ① fast; quick; rapid: 请别说得那么～。 Please don't speak so fast./ 我的表～五分。 My watch is five minutes fast./ 他进步很～。 He has made rapid progress./ 大干一～ race against time and go all out ② speed: 这车能跑多～？ How fast can this car go? ③ hurry up; make haste: ～上车吧！ Hurry up and get on the bus!/ ～跟我走。 Quick, come with me. ④ soon; before long: 他～回来了。 He'll be back soon./ 我来了～两年了。 It is nearly two years since I came here./ 春节～到了。 The Spring Festival is drawing near. ⑤ quick-witted; ingenious: 他脑子～。 He's quick-witted. 或 He understands things quickly. ⑥ sharp: ～刀 a sharp knife ⑦ straightforward; forthright; plainspoken: 心直口～ straightforward and outspoken/ ～人～语 straightforward talk from a straightforward person ⑧ pleased; happy; gratified: 心中不～ feel unhappy/ 拍手称～ clap and cheer/ 大～人心 to the immense satisfaction of the people
【快餐】 kuàicān quick meal; snack
【快车】 kuàichē express train or bus: 特别～ special express
【快刀斩乱麻】 kuàidāo zhǎn luànmá cut a tangled skein of jute with a sharp knife; cut the Gordian knot
【快递】 kuàidì express delivery ◇ ～邮件 express mail
【快干】 kuàigān quick-drying ◇ ～漆 quick-drying paint
【快感】 kuàigǎn pleasant sensation; delight
【快活】 kuàihuo happy; merry; cheerful: 孩子们～地打雪仗。 The children were enjoying a snowball fight.
【快乐】 kuàilè happy; joyful; cheerful: ～的童年生活 a happy childhood/ 节日过得很～。 The festival was spent joyfully.
【快马加鞭】 kuàimǎ jiā biān spur on the flying horse — at top speed; posthaste
【快慢】 kuài-màn speed: 这些按钮是管～的。 These buttons control the speed.
【快事】 kuàishì a happening that gives great satisfaction or pleasure; delight: 引为～ recall (an event) with great satisfaction/ 生平一大～ one of the most delightful experiences in one's life
【快手】 kuàishǒu quick worker; deft hand
【快速】 kuàisù fast; quick; high-speed
【快艇】 kuàitǐng speedboat; motor boat; mosquito boat
【快慰】 kuàiwèi feel pleased with and derive comfort from sth.; be pleased: 我们都为她的进步感到～。 We are all pleased with the progress she has made.
【快信】 kuàixìn express letter
【快意】 kuàiyì pleased; satisfied; comfortable
【快嘴】 kuàizuǐ one who readily voices his thoughts; one who is quick to articulate his ideas

块* kuài ① piece; lump; chunk: 糖～儿 fruit drops; lumps of sugar/ 把肉切成～儿 cut the meat into cubes ② 〈量〉 〔用于块状或某些片状的东西〕: 两～肥皂 two cakes of soap/ 一～面包 a piece of bread/ 一～手表 a wrist watch/ 一～试验田 an experimental plot

侩 kuài middleman

脍 kuài <书> meat chopped into small pieces; minced meat
【脍炙人口】 kuàizhì rénkǒu (of a piece of good writing, etc.) win universal praise; enjoy great popularity: 一首～的古诗 an oft-quoted and widely loved ancient poem

筷* kuài chopsticks
【筷子】 kuàizi chopsticks: 火～ fire-tongs; tongs

kuān

宽* kuān ① wide; broad: ～肩膀 broad-shouldered/ ～边草帽 broad-brimmed straw hat/ 眼界～ have a broad outlook ② width; breadth: 这条河有一里～. This river is one li wide. ③ relax; relieve: 听说他的病情并不严重，我们的心就～多了. We were greatly relieved to learn that his condition was not serious./ 把心放～一点. Don't worry. 或 Don't take it too hard. ④ extend: 限期能再～几天吗? Can the deadline be extended a few more days? ⑤ generous; lenient: 从～处理 treat with leniency/ 严以律己，～以待人 be strict with oneself and lenient with others ⑥ comfortably off; well-off: 他手头比过去～多了. He's much better off than before.
【宽畅】 kuānchàng free from worry; happy
【宽敞】 kuānchang spacious; roomy; commodious: ～的房子 a commodious house
【宽绰】 kuānchuo ① spacious; commodious: 这间屋子很～. The room is spacious. ② relax; relieve: 听了他的话，我心里～多了. I felt greatly relieved to hear what he said. 或 I felt a big load taken off my mind when I heard what he said. ③ comfortably off; well-off
【宽大】 kuāndà ① spacious; roomy: ～的候车室 a spacious waiting room ② lenient; magnanimous: 受到～处理 be dealt with leniently; be accorded lenient treatment; receive clemency/ ～为怀 be magnanimous or lenient (with an offender)
【宽待】 kuāndài treat with leniency; be lenient in dealing with: ～俘虏 give lenient treatment to prisoners of war; treat prisoners of war leniently
【宽度】 kuāndù width; breadth: 领海～ the extent of the territorial sea
【宽广】 kuānguǎng broad; extensive; vast: ～的田野 a broad expanse of country/ 心胸～ broad-minded
【宽宏大量】 kuānhóng-dàliàng large-minded; magnanimous
【宽厚】 kuānhòu generous: 待人～ be generous to people
【宽旷】 kuānkuàng extensive; vast: ～的草原 extensive grasslands
【宽阔】 kuānkuò broad; wide: ～的林荫道 a broad (或 wide) avenue/ ～的胸怀 broad-mindedness
【宽饶】 kuānráo forgive; show mercy; give quarter
【宽容】 kuānróng tolerant; lenient
【宽恕】 kuānshù forgive: 请求～ ask for forgiveness
【宽慰】 kuānwèi comfort; console: ～她几句. Say something to comfort her./ 这样一想，我心里才～了些. This thought brought me a little comfort.
【宽限】 kuānxiàn extend a time limit: ～一星期 give a week's grace/ 请～几天. Please extend the deadline a few days.
【宽心】 kuānxīn feel relieved: 说几句～话 say a few reassuring words
【宽衣】 kuānyī <敬> take off your coat: 请～. Do take off your coat.
【宽银幕】 kuānyínmù wide screen ◇ ～电影 wide-screen film
【宽裕】 kuānyù well-to-do; comfortably off; ample: 经济～ in easy circumstances; well-off/ 时间很～. There's plenty of time yet.
【宽窄】 kuānzhǎi width; breadth; size: 这块布做窗帘，～正合适. This piece of cloth is just the right size for a curtain.

kuǎn

款* kuǎn ① sincere: ～曲 heartfelt feelings ② receive with hospitality; entertain ③ section of an article in a legal document, etc.; paragraph: 根据该条约的第六条第二～ according to Article 6, Section 2 of the Treaty ④ a sum of money; fund: 公～ public funds/ 筹～ raise funds/ 汇～ remit money ⑤ the name of sender or recipient inscribed on a painting or a piece of calligraphy presented as a gift ⑥ <书> leisurely; slow: ～步 with deliberate steps
【款待】 kuǎndài treat cordially; entertain: ～客人 entertain guests/ 感谢你对我们的盛情～. Thank you for the hospitality you have shown us.
【款式】 kuǎnshì pattern; style; design
【款项】 kuǎnxiàng a sum of money; fund

kuāng

匡 kuāng ① rectify; correct: ～谬 correct mistakes ② <书> assist; save: ～我不逮 help me to overcome my shortcomings
【匡正】 kuāngzhèng rectify; correct

诓 kuāng deceive; hoax: 我哪能～你? How could I deceive you?
【诓骗】 kuāngpiàn deceive; hoax; dupe

框 kuāng ① frame; circle ② <方> draw a frame round: 用红线把标题～起来 frame the heading in red 另见 kuàng
【框框】 kuāngkuang ① frame; circle ② restriction; convention; set pattern: 条条～ regulations and restrictions/ 突破旧～的限制 throw convention to the winds

筐 kuāng basket
【筐子】 kuāngzi small basket

kuáng

狂* kuáng ① mad; crazy: 发～ go mad ② violent: 雨骤风～. The wind blew hard and the rain came down in sheets./ 股票价格～跌. The stocks slumped. ③ wild; unrestrained: ～奔的马 a bolting horse/ 欣喜若～ be wild (或 beside oneself) with joy ④ arrogant; overbearing
【狂暴】 kuángbào violent; wild: ～的山洪 raging mountain torrents
【狂放】 kuángfàng unruly or unrestrained
【狂吠】 kuángfèi bark furiously; howl
【狂风】 kuángfēng ① <气> whole gale ② fierce wind: ～呼啸. The wind howled./ ～暴雨 a violent storm
【狂欢】 kuánghuān revelry; carnival
【狂热】 kuángrè fanaticism: ～的军备竞赛 feverish armament race/ ～的信徒 a fanatical follower; fanatic; zealot ◇ ～性 fanaticism
【狂人】 kuángrén madman; maniac: ～呓语 ravings of a madman
【狂妄】 kuángwàng wildly arrogant; presumptuous: ～自大 arrogant and conceited/ ～的野心 a wild ambition
【狂喜】 kuángxǐ wild with joy
【狂笑】 kuángxiào laugh wildly; laugh boisterously
【狂言】 kuángyán ravings; wild language: 口出～ talk wildly

诳 kuáng
【诳语】 kuángyǔ lies; falsehood

kuàng

况 kuàng ① condition; situation: 近~如何? How have you been recently? ② compare: 以古~今 draw parallels from history ③ <书> moreover; besides
【况且】 kuàngqiě <连> moreover; besides; in addition

旷 kuàng ① vast; spacious: 地~人稀 a vast territory with a sparse population ② free from worries and petty ideas: 心~神怡 carefree and happy ③ neglect ④ loose-fitting: 这身衣服她穿着太~了。 The dress sits loosely on her.
【旷达】 kuàngdá broad-minded; bighearted
【旷废】 kuàngfèi neglect: ~学业 neglect one's studies
【旷工】 kuànggōng stay away from work without leave or good reason
【旷课】 kuàngkè be absent from school without leave; cut school: 旷一堂课 cut a class
【旷野】 kuàngyě wilderness
【旷职】 kuàngzhí be absent from duty without leave or good reason

矿* kuàng ① ore (或 mineral) deposit: 报~ report where deposits are found ② ore: 铁~ iron ore ③ mine: 煤~ coal mine; colliery/ 他在~上工作。 He works at the mine.
【矿藏】 kuàngcáng mineral resources
【矿层】 kuàngcéng ore bed; ore horizon; seam
【矿产】 kuàngchǎn mineral products; minerals
【矿工】 kuànggōng miner
【矿泉】 kuàngquán mineral spring ◇ ~水 mineral water
【矿石】 kuàngshí ore

框 kuàng frame; case: 门~ door frame/ 窗~ window frame; window case/ 镜~儿 picture frame/ 眼镜~儿 rims (of spectacles)/ 无~眼镜 rimless spectacles
另见 kuāng
【框架】 kuàngjià <建> frame
【框子】 kuàngzi frame: 眼镜~ rims (of spectacles)

眶 kuàng the socket of the eye: 热泪盈~ one's eyes filling with tears/ 眼泪夺~而出 tears starting from one's eyes

kuī

亏* kuī ① lose (money, etc.); have a deficit: ~了二万元 have a deficit of $20,000; have lost $20,000/ 盈~ profit and loss ② deficient; short: 理~ be in the wrong ③ treat unfairly: 你放心吧, ~不了你。 Don't worry, we won't be unfair to you./ 人不~地,地不~人。 The land won't fail people as long as people don't fail the land. ④ fortunately; luckily; thanks to: ~他提醒了我,要不我早忘了。 Luckily he reminded me; otherwise I'd have forgotten all about it. ⑤〔反说,表示讥讽〕: ~他说得出口! And he had the nerve to say so! ⑥ (of the moon) wane
【亏本】 kuīběn lose money in business; lose one's capital: ~生意 a losing proposition
【亏待】 kuīdài treat unfairly; treat shabbily
【亏得】 kuīde ① fortunately; luckily; thanks to: ~大家帮忙,我们才按时把这活干完。 Thanks to everybody's help, we finished the job on time. ②〔反说,表示讥讽〕: ~你长这么大,那么点事儿都不懂。 Fancy a big boy like you not understanding such a simple thing!
【亏空】 kuīkong ① be in debt ② debt; deficit: 拉~ get into debt/ 弥补~ meet (或 make up) a deficit; make up (for) a loss
【亏欠】 kuīqiàn have a deficit; be in arrears
【亏蚀】 kuīshí ① eclipse of the sun or moon ② lose (money) in business
【亏损】 kuīsǔn ① loss; deficit: 企业~ loss incurred in an enterprise ② general debility

【亏心】 kuīxīn have a guilty conscience ◇ ~事 a deed that troubles (或 weighs on) one's conscience

盔 kuī helmet
【盔甲】 kuījiǎ a suit of armour

窥 kuī peep; spy
【窥测】 kuīcè spy out: ~方向,以求一逞 spy out the land in order to accomplish one's schemes; see which way the wind blows in order to achieve one's evil ends/ ~时机 bide one's time
【窥见】 kuījiàn get (或 catch) a glimpse of; detect: 从一个人的生活作风可以~他的思想意识。 We can get a hint of a person's ideology from his life style.
【窥视】 kuīshì peep at; spy on
【窥伺】 kuīsì lie in wait for; be on watch for
【窥探】 kuītàn spy upon; pry about: ~军事秘密 pry into military secrets

kuí

奎 kuí
【奎宁】 kuíníng <药> quinine

隗 Kuí a surname

逵 kuí <书> thoroughfare

馗 kuí 见"逵" kuí

葵 kuí certain herbaceous plants with big flowers: 向日~ sunflower

魁 kuí ① chief; head: 罪~ chief criminal; arch-criminal ② of stalwart build
【魁首】 kuíshǒu a person who is head and shoulders above others; the brightest and best: 文章~ outstanding writer of the day
【魁伟】 kuíwěi big and tall
【魁梧】 kuíwú big and tall; stalwart

睽 kuí
【睽睽】 kuíkuí stare; gaze: 众目~之下 in the public eye

蝰 kuí
【蝰蛇】 kuíshé viper

kuǐ

傀 kuǐ
【傀儡】 kuǐlěi puppet ◇ ~戏 puppet show; puppet play/ ~政府 puppet government/ ~政权 puppet regime

kuì

匮 kuì <书> deficient
【匮乏】 kuìfá <书> short (of supplies); deficient

溃 kuì ① (of a dyke or dam) burst: 千里之堤,~于蚁穴。 One ant hole may cause the collapse of a thousand-*li* dyke. ② break through (an encirclement): ~围南奔 break through the encirclement and head south ③ be routed: 一触即~ be routed at the first encounter/ ~不成军 be utterly routed ④ fester; ulcerate
【溃败】 kuìbài be defeated; be routed
【溃决】 kuìjué (of a dyke or dam) burst
【溃灭】 kuìmiè crumble and fall
【溃散】 kuìsàn be defeated and dispersed
【溃逃】 kuìtáo escape in disorder; fly pell-mell; flee helter-skelter

【溃退】 kuìtuì beat a precipitate retreat

【溃疡】 kuìyáng 〈医〉ulcer: 胃～ gastric ulcer

馈 kuì make a present of: ～送 present (a gift); make a present of sth.

【馈赠】 kuìzèng present (a gift); make a present of sth.

喟 kuì 〈书〉sigh

【喟然长叹】 kuìrán chángtàn 〈书〉sigh deeply; heave a deep sigh

愧* kuì ashamed; conscience-stricken: 问心无～ have a clear conscience; have nothing on one's conscience/ 于心有～ have a guilty conscience; have something on one's conscience; feel ashamed

【愧恨】 kuìhèn ashamed and remorseful; remorseful: ～交集 overcome with shame and remorse/ 内心深自～ feel bitterly remorseful

【愧色】 kuìsè a look of shame: 面有～ look ashamed/ 毫无～ look unashamed (或 unabashed)

聩 kuì 〈书〉deaf; hard of hearing: 振聋发～ rouse the deaf and awaken the unhearing

篑 kuì 〈书〉basket for holding earth: 功亏一～ fail to build a mound for want of the last basket of earth — fall short of success for want of a final effort

kūn

坤 kūn female; feminine: ～表 woman's watch

昆 kūn ① elder brother ② 〈书〉offspring: 后～ descendants; children

【昆虫】 kūnchóng insect

kǔn

捆 kǔn ① tie; bind; bundle up: ～行李 tie up one's baggage/ ～谷草 bundle up millet stalks/ 把他～起来 tie him up/ ～住手脚 bound hand and foot ② 〈量〉bundle: 一～柴禾 a bundle of firewood

【捆绑】 kǔnbǎng truss up; bind; tie up

【捆扎】 kǔnzā tie up; bundle up

kùn

困 kùn ① be stranded; be hard pressed: 为病所～ be afflicted with illness ② surround; pin down: 把敌人～死在据点里 bottle up the enemy in his stronghold ③ tired: ～乏 tired; fatigued ④ sleepy: 你～了就睡吧。 Go to bed if you feel sleepy.

【困乏】 kùnfá tired; fatigued

【困惑】 kùnhuò perplexed; puzzled: ～不解 feel puzzled

【困境】 kùnjìng difficult position; predicament; straits: 陷于～ fall into dire straits; find oneself in a tight corner; land oneself in a fix/ 摆脱～ extricate oneself from a difficult position

【困窘】 kùnjiǒng in straitened circumstances; in a difficult position; embarrassed

【困倦】 kùnjuàn sleepy

【困苦】 kùnkǔ (live) in privation: 艰难～ difficulties and hardships

【困难】 kùnnan ① difficulty: 情况十分～。 Conditions are very difficult./ ～重重 be beset with difficulties ② financial difficulties; straitened circumstances: 生活～ live in straitened circumstances

【困扰】 kùnrǎo perplex; puzzle: 为一个难题所～ be puzzled by a difficult question

【困守】 kùnshǒu defend against a siege; stand a siege: ～孤城 be entrenched in a beseiged city

kuò

扩* kuò expand; enlarge; extend

【扩充】 kuòchōng expand; strengthen; augment: ～实力 expand (military or political) forces/ ～军备 arms (或 armaments) expansion/ ～设备 augment the equipment

【扩大】 kuòdà enlarge; expand; extend: ～战果 exploit the victory/ ～眼界 widen one's outlook; broaden one's horizons

【扩建】 kuòjiàn extend (a factory, mine, etc.) ◇ ～工程 extension (project)

【扩散】 kuòsàn spread; diffuse: 不让废气～ prevent the diffusion of waste gas/ 病菌～ proliferation of germs/ 癌～ proliferation of cancer; spread of cancer

【扩音器】 kuòyīnqì ① megaphone ② audio amplifier

【扩展】 kuòzhǎn expand; spread; extend; develop

【扩张】 kuòzhāng expand; enlarge; extend; spread: 对外～ expansionism; foreign aggrandizement/ ～野心 expansionist ambitions/ 领土～ territorial expansion (或 aggrandizement)

括* kuò ① draw together (muscles, etc.); contract ② include

【括号】 kuòhào brackets ([], (), <>)

【括弧】 kuòhú parentheses

阔* kuò ① wide; broad; vast ② wealthy; rich

【阔别】 kuòbié long separated; long parted: ～多年的朋友 long-separated friends

【阔步】 kuòbù take big strides: ～前进 advance with giant strides/ 昂首～ stride forward with one's chin up; stride proudly ahead

【阔绰】 kuòchuò ostentatious; liberal with money: ～的生活 an extravagant life

【阔老】 kuòlǎo rich man 又作"阔佬"

【阔气】 kuòqi luxurious; extravagant; lavish: 花钱～ spend lavishly/ 摆～ display (或 parade) one's wealth

廓 kuò ① wide; extensive ② outline

L

lā

拉* lā ① pull; draw; tug; drag: ~弓 draw a bow/ ~风箱 work the bellows/ 把车~过来。Pull the cart over here./ ② play (certain musical instruments): ~小提琴 (手风琴) play the violin (accordion) ③ drag out; draw out; ④ draw in; win over; canvass: ~选票 canvass votes; canvass/ ~买卖 tout; canvass orders ⑤ empty the bowels: 又吐又~ suffer from vomiting and diarrhoea

【拉丁文】 Lādīngwén Latin (language)

【拉丁字母】 Lādīng zìmǔ the Latin alphabet; the Roman alphabet

【拉肚子】 lā dùzi suffer from diarrhoea; have loose bowels

【拉关系】 lā guānxi 〔多含贬义〕try to establish a relationship with sb.; cotton up to: 拉亲戚关系 claim kinship

【拉后腿】 lā hòutuǐ hold sb. back; be a drag on sb.

【拉交情】 lā jiāoqing try to form ties with; cotton up to

【拉开】 lākāi ① pull open; draw back: ~抽屉 open the drawer/ ~窗帘 draw back the curtain/ ~枪栓 pull back the bolt (of a rifle)/ ~嗓门就唱 start singing when asked to without making a fuss ② increase the distance between; space out: 不要~距离! Close up!/ 比分逐渐~了。The gap between the scores gradually widened./ 把比分~到十六比八 pull away to 16—8; increase the lead to 16—8

【拉拉扯扯】 lālāchěchě ① pull (或 drag) sb. about ② exchange flattery and favours

【拉拉队】 lālāduì cheering squad; rooters

【拉链】 lāliàn zip fastener; zipper

【拉拢】 lālong draw sb. over to one's side; rope in: 不要受坏人~。Don't get roped in by bad people.

【拉平】 lāpíng bring to the same level; even up: 双方比分渐渐~。The score gradually evened up.

【拉下水】 lāxia shuǐ drag sb. into the mire; make an accomplice of sb.; corrupt sb.

【拉杂】 lāzá rambling; jumbled; ill-organized: 这篇文章写得太~。This article is very badly organized./ 我拉拉杂杂地就谈这些吧。I think I'll stop my rambling talk here.

垃 lā

【垃圾】 lājī rubbish; garbage; refuse: ~处理 garbage disposal/ 焚化~ refuse incineration/ 清除~ remove refuse ◇ ~箱 dustbin; ash can; garbage can

【垃圾堆】 lājīduī rubbish heap; refuse dump; garbage heap

lǎ

喇* lǎ

【喇叭】 lǎba ① 〈乐〉a popular name for *suona* (唢呐), a woodwind instrument ② 〈乐〉 brass-wind instruments in general or any of these instruments ③ loudspeaker ◇ ~花 (white-edged) morning glory/ ~口 bell (of a wind instrument)/ ~裤 flared trousers; bell-bottoms/ ~筒 megaphone

là

腊 là ① the ancient practice of offering sacrifices to the gods in the twelfth month of the lunar year, hence the term "sacrificial" for the twelfth moon: ~尽残冬 towards the end of the (lunar) year ② cured (fish, meat, etc., generally done in the twelfth moon)
另见 xī

【腊肠】 làcháng sausage

【腊肉】 làròu cured meat; bacon

【腊味】 làwèi cured meat, fish, etc.

【腊月】 làyuè the twelfth month of the lunar year; the twelfth moon

辣* là ① peppery; hot ② (of smell or taste) burn; bite; sting: 切葱头~眼睛。When you slice an onion it makes your eyes sting./ ~得舌头发麻。The hot taste burns the tongue. ③ vicious; ruthless: 心毒手~ vicious and ruthless

【辣酱】 làjiàng thick chilli sauce

【辣椒】 làjiāo hot pepper; chilli ◇ ~粉 chilli powder

【辣手】 làshǒu ① ruthless method; vicious device ② 〈方〉vicious; ruthless ③ 〈口〉thorny; troublesome; knotty: 这件事真~。That's really a knotty problem. 或 That's a real hot potato.

蜡 là ① wax ② candle: 点一支~ light a candle ③ polish: 地板~ floor wax; floor polish

【蜡笔】 làbǐ wax crayon ◇ ~画 crayon drawing

【蜡纸】 làzhǐ ① wax paper ② stencil paper; stencil: 刻~ cut a stencil

【蜡烛】 làzhú (wax) candle

la

啦 la 〈助〉〔"了" le 和"啊" a 的合音,表示感叹、疑问等语气〕: 他早来~! Why, he's been here a long time!/ 二组跟我们挑战~。Look! Group B has sent us a challenge./ 这回我可亲眼看见~! This time I've actually seen it for myself./ 她真来~? Has she really come?

lái

来* lái ① come; arrive: 你~啦! Hello! 或 So you're here already./ 他什么时候~? When is he coming?/ 外宾还没有~。The foreign guests have not arrived yet./ 电~啦! The electricity is on!/ 我们都是~自五湖四海。We hail from all corners of the country./ ~函 incoming letter; your letter/ ~稿 a contribution received by an editor ② crop up; take place: 问题一~就设法解决 try to solve a problem as soon as it crops up/ 雷阵雨马上就要~了。A thunder shower is coming up. ③〔做某个动作,代替意义更具体的动词〕: 你歇歇,让我~。You take a rest. Let me do it./ (指请人吃东西)再~一点吧! Would you like a little more?/ 我自己~吧。(指吃东西) I'll help myself. 或 (指做事) Let me do it myself./ ~一个动员。Let's get mobilized./ ~一个一百八十度的大转弯 make an about face; make a 180-degree turn/ 我们去打棒球,你~不~? We're going to play baseball. Do you want to join in?/ (请演员表演)再~一个! Encore! ④〔跟"得"或"不"连用,表示可能或不可能〕: 坡太陡,车子上不~。The car can't come up, the slope is so steep./ 他们俩很合得~。The two of them get along very well./ 你的稿子今天出得~吗? Will you be able to finish your article today? ⑤〔用在动词前面,表示要做某件事〕: 请你~想办法。Will you please read the paper to us?/ 大家~想办法。Let's pool our ideas and see what to do. 或 Let's put our heads together and see how to do it. ⑥〔用在动词或动词结构后面,表示来做某件事〕: 他回村看望乡亲们。He's come back to the village to see us folks./ 我们报喜~了。We've brought you good news. ⑦〔用在动词前面,表示后面部分是目的〕: 你能用什么方法~帮助他呢? How are you going to help him? ⑧ future; coming; next: ~年 the coming year; next year ⑨ ever since: 别~无恙乎! How have you been since I saw you last?/ 十多天~ for the last ten days and more/ 两千年~ over the past 2,000 years ⑩〔用在"十"

"百""千"等数词或数量词后面，表示概数〕about; around: 二十~个 around twenty/ 两米~高 about two metres high/ 五十~岁 about fifty (years old) ⑪〔用在"一""二""三"等数词后面，列举理由〕: 一~…，二~… in the first place.../ 我好久没去看他，一~路太远，二~没工夫。I haven't been to see him for a long time now. For one thing, he lives too far away; for another, I've been rather busy.

来 lái ①〔用在动词后面，表示动作朝着说话人所在的地方〕: 过~! Come over here!/ 拿把锯。Bring me a saw./ 象潮水般涌~ surge towards us like a rising tide/ 寄~许多宝贵意见 send in many valuable suggestions ②〔用在动词后面，表示动作的结果〕: 一觉醒~ wake up after a sound sleep/ 信笔写~ write down one's ideas as they come to mind/ 说~话长。It's a long story.

【来宾】 láibīn guest; visitor ◇ ~席 seats for guests

【来不及】 lái bu jí there's not enough time (to do sth.); it's too late (to do sth.): 今天我们一~去看他了。There's no time for us to go and see him today./ 写信已经~了，还是给他打个电报吧。It's too late to reach him by letter. Better send a telegram.

【来到】 láidào arrive; come: 雨季~了。The rainy season has set in./ 你们终于~了。So here you are at last.

【来得】 láide 〈口〉① competent; equal to: 样样农活她都~。She can cope with any kind of farmwork. ② emerge (from a comparison) as; come out as: 海水比淡水重，因此压力也~大。Sea water is heavier than freshwater, so its pressure is greater, too.

【来得及】 láidejí there's still time; be able to do sth. in time; be able to make it: 赶快去，还~。Go at once while there's still time./ 春耕前把拖拉机修好，~吗? Can you get the tractor repaired in time for the spring ploughing?/ 我把车开快点还~。We can make it if I drive a bit faster.

【来电】 láidiàn ① incoming telegram; your telegram; your message: 三月十七日~悉。Your message of March 17 received. ② send a telegram here: 请~告知。Please inform me by telegram.

【来回】 láihuí ① make a round trip; make a return journey: ~有多远? How far is it there and back?/ 打个~儿make a round trip ② back and forth; to and fro: 织布机上梭子~地飞动。The shuttle flies back and forth on the loom./ 在房间里~走动 pace up and down the room/ ~摇摆 oscillate; vacillate ◇ ~飞行 round-trip flight/ ~票 return ticket; round-trip ticket

【来客】 láikè guest; visitor

【来历】 láilì origin; source; antecedents; background; past history: 查明~ trace to the source; ascertain a person's antecedents/ ~不明(指事物) of unknown origin; (指人) of dubious background or of questionable antecedents/ 提起这把手术刀可大有~。Talking of this scalpel, there is a long history to it.

【来临】 láilín arrive; come; approach: 每当春天~，这里是一片绿油油的庄稼。When spring comes, this place is an expanse of lush green crops.

【来龙去脉】 láilóng-qùmài origin and development; cause and effect: 弄清事情的~ find out the cause and effect of the incident/ 请你把事情的~跟我们讲一遍。Please tell us the whole story from beginning to end.

【来路】 láilu origin; antecedents: ~不正 (指物) of questionable origin; (指人) of dubious background/ ~不明的飞机 unidentified aircraft

【来年】 láinián the coming year; next year

【…来…去】 …lái…qù 〔用在同一个动词或两个同义的动词后面，表示动作的不断反复〕back and forth; over and over again: 飞来飞去 fly back and forth/ 挑来挑去 pick and choose/ 考虑来考虑去 turn sth. over and over again in one's mind/ 翻来复去睡不着 toss and turn in bed

【来人】 láirén bearer; messenger: 收条请交~带回。Please give the receipt to the bearer.

【来日方长】 láirì fāng cháng there will be ample time; there will be time for that

【来生】 láishēng next life 又作"来世"

【来势】 láishì the force with which sth. breaks out; oncom-

ing force: 这场雨~很猛。The rainstorm broke with tremendous force./ ~汹汹 bear down menacingly

【来头】 láitou ① connections; backing: ~不小 have powerful backing ② the motive force (sb.'s words, etc.); cause: 他这些话是有~的，是冲着我们说的。He didn't say all that without cause; it was directed against us. ③ the force with which sth. breaks out

【来往】 láiwǎng come and go: 街上~的人很多。There are many people coming and going on the streets./ 翻修路面，禁止车辆~。Road under repair. No thoroughfare./ ~的信件 correspondence

【来往】 láiwang dealings; contact; intercourse: 我跟他从来没有任何~。I've never had any dealings with him.

【来信】 láixìn ① send a letter here: 到了那里就~。Write to us as soon as you get there./ 他好久没~了。I haven't heard from him for a long time. ② incoming letter: 十日~收到。I have received your letter of the 10th.

【来意】 láiyì one's purpose in coming: 说明~ make clear what one has come for

【来由】 láiyóu reason; cause: 没~ without rhyme or reason

【来源】 láiyuán ① source; origin: 经济~ source of income ② originate; stem from

【来者不拒】 láizhě bù jù refuse nobody; refuse nobody's request or offer

【来者不善，善者不来】 láizhě bù shàn, shànzhě bù lái ① he who has come is surely strong or he'd never have come along ② he who has come, comes with ill intent, certainly not on virtue bent

【来之不易】 lái zhī bù yì it has not come easily; hard-earned: 我们的胜利~。Our victory was hard-won.

徕 lái 见"招徕" zhāolái

lài

睐 lài 〈书〉look at; glance; squint

赖 lài ① rely; depend: 完成任务，还有~于大家的努力。Getting the job done depends on everyone's efforts./ ~以生存的条件 conditions on which persons or things rely (或 depend) for existence ② hang on in a place; drag out one's stay in a place; hold on to 'a place: ~着不走 hang on and refuse to clear out ③ deny one's error or responsibility; go back on one's word: ~是~不掉的。It's no good trying to deny it. 或 You simply can't deny it. ④ blame sb. wrongly; put the blame on sb. else: 自己错了还~别人，这就不对了。It's not right to blame others for one's own mistake. ⑤〈口〉blame: 这事全~我。I'm entirely to blame for that.

【赖债】 làizhài repudiate a debt

【赖帐】 làizhàng ① repudiate a debt ② go back on one's word

癞 lài ①〈医〉leprosy ②〈方〉favus of the scalp

【癞蛤蟆】 làiháma toad: ~想吃天鹅肉 a toad lusting after a swan's flesh — aspiring after sth. one is not worthy of

籁 lài ① an ancient musical pipe ② sound; noise: 万~俱寂。Silence reigns supreme. 或 All is quiet and still.

lán

兰 lán orchid

【兰花】 lánhuā cymbidium; orchid

拦 lán bar; block; hold back: ~住去路 block the way/ 他刚要说话，被他哥哥~住了。He was about to speak when he was stopped by his brother.

【拦挡】 lándǎng block; obstruct

【拦截】 lánjié intercept: ~增援的敌人 intercept enemy reinforcements

【拦路】 lánlù block the way: ~抢劫 waylay; hold up

【拦路虎】 lánlùhǔ obstacle; stumbling block

【拦腰】 lányāo by the waist; round the middle: ～抱住 seize round the middle; clasp sb. by the waist/ 大坝把河水～截断。 The dam cut the river in the middle.

【拦阻】 lánzǔ block; hold back; obstruct

栏* lán ① fence; railing; balustrade; hurdle: 凭～ lean on a railing/ 跨～赛跑 hurdle race; the hurdles ② pen; shed: 牛～ cowshed ③ column: 备注～ remarks column/ 布告～ bulletin board; notice board

【栏杆】·lángān railing; banisters; balustrade

婪 lán 见"贪婪" tānlán

阑 lán ① late: 夜～人静 in the stillness of the night ② railing; balustrade

【阑干】 lángān ① <书> crisscross; athwart ② railing; banisters; balustrade

【阑珊】 lánshān <书> coming to an end; waning: 春意～。 Spring is waning.

蓝* lán ① blue ② indigo plant

【蓝宝石】 lánbǎoshí sapphire

【蓝本】 lánběn ① writing upon which later work is based; chief source ② original version (of a literary work)

【蓝靛】 lándiàn indigo

【蓝皮书】 lánpíshū blue book

【蓝图】 lántú blueprint

褴 lán

【褴褛】 lánlǚ ragged; shabby: 衣衫～ shabbily dressed; out at elbows; in rags

篮* lán ① basket ② <篮球> goal; basket: 投～ shoot a basket; shoot

【篮球】 lánqiú basketball
◇ ～场 basketball court/ ～队 basketball team/ ～架 basketball stands

【篮子】 lánzi basket

lǎn

览 lǎn ① look at; see; view: 游～ go sightseeing; tour/ 一～无余 take in everything at a glance ② read: 博～ read extensively; 浏～ glance over; skim through (或 over)

揽 lǎn ① pull sb. into one's arms; take into one's arms: 母亲把孩子～在怀里。 The mother clasped the child to her bosom. ② fasten with a rope, etc.: 用绳子～上 put a rope around sth. ③ take on; take upon oneself; canvass: 他把责任都～到自己身上。 He took all the responsibility on himself./ ～买卖 canvass business orders ④ grasp; monopolize: 包～ monopolize; undertake the whole thing/ ～权 arrogate power to oneself

缆 lǎn ① hawser; mooring rope; cable: 解～ cast off; set sail/ 新船砍～下水。 The new ship cut her cable and slipped into the water. ② thick rope; cable: 电～ power cable; cable

【缆车】 lǎnchē cable car ◇ ～铁道 cable railway

榄 lǎn 见"橄榄" gǎnlǎn

懒* lǎn ① lazy; indolent; slothful: 趄～ disinclined to move about; lazy about paying visits/ 人勤地不～。 Where the tiller is tireless the land is fertile. ② sluggish; languid: 身上发～ feel sluggish

【懒得】 lǎnde not feel like (doing sth.); not be in the mood to; be disinclined to: 天太热,我～出去。 It's too hot. I don't feel like going out.

【懒惰】 lǎnduò lazy

【懒散】 lǎnsǎn sluggish; negligent; indolent: 不要这样～,振作起来。 Don't be so sluggish. Pull yourself together.

【懒洋洋】 lǎnyāngyāng languid; listless

làn

烂* làn ① sodden; mashed; pappy: 连下了三天雨,地上都是～泥。 It's rained for three days on end and the ground is sodden./ 牛肉烧得很～。 The beef is very tender 或 The beef melts in your mouth./ 豆子煮～了。 The beans are now soft enough to eat. ② rot; fester: 这样的阴湿天要防止～秧。 In such wet weather we must prevent the seedlings from rotting. ③ worn-out: 衣服穿～了。 The clothes are worn-out

【烂漫】 lànmàn ① bright-coloured; brilliant: 山花～ bright mountain flowers in full bloom ② unaffected: 天真～ naive; innocent

【烂泥】 lànní mud; slush

【烂熟】 lànshú ① thoroughly cooked ② know sth. thoroughly: 台词背得～ learn one's lines thoroughly

【烂醉】 lànzuì dead drunk: ～如泥 be dead drunk; be as drunk as a lord

滥 làn ① overflow; flood ② excessive; indiscriminate: ～施轰炸 indiscriminate bombing; wanton bombing

【滥调】 làndiào hackneyed tune; worn-out tune: 陈词～ hackneyed and stereotyped expressions; clichés

【滥用】 lànyòng abuse; misuse; use indiscriminately: ～职权 abuse one's power/ ～经费 squander funds/ 不要～成语典故。 We should not use proverbs and allusions indiscriminately.

【滥竽充数】 lànyú chōng shù pass oneself off as one of the players in an ensemble — be there just to make up the number (used of incompetent people or inferior goods)

láng

郎 láng ① an ancient official title ② 〔用于对男子的称呼〕: 令～ your son/ 新～ bridegroom/ 货～ street vendor ③〔女子称丈夫或情人〕 my darling

狼 láng wolf

【狼狈】 lángbèi in a difficult position; in a tight corner: ～不堪 in an extremely awkward position; in a sorry plight; in sore straits/ ～逃窜 flee in panic; flee helter-skelter/ 陷于～境地 find oneself in a fix; be caught in a dilemma (或 quandary)/ 显出一副～相 cut a sorry figure/ 傀儡政权的处境极为孤立和～。 The puppet regime was extremely isolated and in dire straits./ 打得敌人十分～。 The enemy was badly battered.

【狼狈为奸】 lángbèi wéi jiān act in collusion (或 cahoots) with each other

【狼藉】 lángjí <书> in disorder; scattered about in a mess: 杯盘～ wine cups and dishes lying about in disorder after a feast/ 声名～ notorious; in disrepute; discredited

【狼吞虎咽】 lángtūn-hǔyàn gobble up; wolf down; devour ravenously

【狼心狗肺】 lángxīn-gǒufèi ① rapacious as a wolf and savage as a cur; cruel and unscrupulous; brutal and cold-blooded ② ungrateful

廊* láng porch; corridor; veranda: 回～ winding corridor

琅 láng

【琅琅】 lángláng <象>: ～的读书声 the sound of reading aloud

榔* láng 见"槟榔" bīngláng

银 láng
【铛铛】 lángdāng ①〈书〉 iron chains: ~入狱 be chained and thrown into prison ② clank; clang

螂 láng
见 "螳螂" tángláng; "蟑螂" zhāngláng

lǎng

朗* lǎng
① light; bright: 天~气清。The sky is clear and bright. ② loud and clear

【朗读】 lǎngdú read aloud; read loudly and clearly

【朗朗】 lǎnglǎng ①〈象〉 the sound of reading aloud ② bright; light

【朗诵】 lǎngsòng read aloud with expression; recite; declaim

làng

浪* làng
① wave; billow; breaker: 白~滔天 white breakers leaping skywards/ 麦~起伏 wheat rippling in the wind ② unrestrained; dissolute: 放~ dissolute; dissipated

【浪潮】 làngcháo tide; wave: 罢工~ a wave of strikes

【浪荡】 làngdàng ① loiter about; loaf about ② dissolute; dissipated

【浪费】 làngfèi waste; squander; be extravagant: 反对~ combat waste/ ~时间 waste time; fritter away one's time

【浪漫】 làngmàn romantic ◇ ~主义 romanticism

【浪头】 làngtou 〈口〉 ① wave ② trend: 赶~ follow the trend

【浪子】 làngzǐ prodigal; loafer; wastrel

lāo

捞 lāo
① drag for; dredge up; fish for; scoop up from the water: 在河里~水草 dredge up water plants from the river/ ~鱼 net fish; catch fish ② get by improper means; gain: 他们能从这里~到什么好处呢？ What good can they get from this?

【捞本】 lāoběn win back lost wagers; recover one's losses

láo

牢* láo
①〈书〉 pen; fold: 家~ pigpen ② sacrifice: 太~ sacrificial ox ③ prison; jail: 坐~ be in prison ④ firm; fast; durable: 绳子没系~。The rope hasn't been tied fast.

【牢不可破】 láo bùkě pò unbreakable; indestructible: ~的友谊 unbreakable friendship

【牢固】 láogù firm; secure: 地基很~。The foundations are very firm.

【牢记】 láojì keep firmly in mind; remember well

【牢牢】 láoláo firmly; safely

【牢笼】 láolóng cage; bonds ② trap; snare: 陷入~ fall into a trap; be entrapped

【牢骚】 láosāo discontent; grievance; complaint: 满腹~ be querulous; be full of grievances/ 发~ grumble

【牢狱】 láoyù prison; jail

劳* láo
① work; labour: 多~多得 more pay for more work ② put sb. to the trouble of: ~你帮个忙。Will you please do me a favour (或 give me a hand)? ③ fatigue; toil: 积~成疾 break down from constant overwork ④ meritorious deed; service: 汗马之~ distinctions won in battle; war exploits ⑤ express one's appreciation (to the performer of a task); reward: ~军 bring greetings and gifts to army units

【劳动】 láodòng ① work; labour: 不~者不得食。He who does not work, neither shall he eat./ 大家的~热情很高。Everyone worked with great enthusiasm. ② physical labour; manual labour

【劳动力】 láodònglì ① labour (或 work) force; labour: 调剂~ adjust the use of the labour force/ ~调配 allocation of the labour force/ ~不足 short of manpower; shorthanded ② capacity for physical labour: 丧失~ lose one's ability to work; be rendered unfit for physical labour; be incapacitated; be disabled ③ able-bodied person: 全~和半~ able-bodied and semi-able-bodied (farm) workers/ 他年青力壮,是个强~。He's young and strong; he can do heavy work.

【劳而无功】 láo ér wú gōng work hard but to no avail; work fruitlessly

【劳工】 láogōng 〈旧〉 labourer; worker ◇ ~运动 labour movement

【劳驾】 láojià 〈套〉 (要求让路等) excuse me; (要求别人做事) may I trouble you: ~替我带个信儿。Would you mind taking a message for me?

【劳苦】 láokǔ toil; hard work: 不辞~ spare no pains/ ~大众 toiling masses; labouring people/ ~功高 have worked hard and performed a valuable service

【劳累】 láolèi tired; run-down; overworked

【劳力】 láolì labour; labour force: ~可能紧张一些,但我们一定努力完成任务。We may be a little short of labour, but we'll do our best to fulfil the task./ 合理安排~ rational allocation of labour

【劳碌】 láolù work hard; toil

【劳民伤财】 láomín-shāngcái tire the people and drain the treasury; waste money and manpower

【劳神】 láoshén be a tax on (one's mind); bother; trouble: 你现在身体不好,不要过于~。You're in poor health, so don't overtax yourself./ ~替我照顾一下孩子。Please keep an eye on my child.

【劳心】 láoxīn work with one's mind or brains

【劳燕分飞】 láo-yàn fēn fēi be like birds flying in different directions; part; separate

【劳资】 láo-zī labour and capital ◇ ~关系 relations between labour and capital; labour-capital relations

唠 láo
【唠叨】 láodao chatter; be garrulous: 唠唠叨叨说个不停 chatter interminably

痨 láo
consumptive disease; tuberculosis; consumption: 肺~ pulmonary tuberculosis

【痨病】 láobìng 〈中医〉 tuberculosis; TB

lǎo

老* lǎo
① old; aged: 活到~,学到~。Learn, and work as long as you live. ② old people: 扶~携幼 bringing along the old and the young ③ of long standing; old: ~朋友 an old friend ④ outdated: ~式 old-fashioned; outmoded; outdated ⑤ tough; overgrown: 肉太~。The meat is too tough./ 菠菜不收就~了。The spinach will be overgrown if we don't cut it now./ 青菜不要炒得太~。Don't overcook the greens. ⑥ (of colour) dark: 这件上衣颜色太~了。This jacket is too dark. ⑦ for a long time: ~没见你啊。I haven't seen you for ages. ⑧ always (doing sth.): 他住院期间~惦念着儿女们。He was always thinking of his children when he was in hospital. ⑨ very: ~早 very early/ ~远 far away ⑩〈口〉 the youngest: 闺女my youngest daughter ⑪〔前缀, 用于称人, 排列次序, 某些动, 植物名〕: ~王 Lao Wang/ ~二 the second child or brother/ 玉米 maize/ ~虎 tiger

【老百姓】 lǎobǎixìng 〈口〉 common people; ordinary people; civilians: 这些故事~很欢迎。These stories are popular with the man in the street.

【老板】 lǎobǎn shopkeeper; proprietor; boss ◇ ~娘 shopkeeper's wife; proprietress

【老辈】 lǎobèi one's elders; old folks

【老伯】 lǎobó 〈尊〉 uncle

【老伯伯】 lǎobóbo 〈尊〉 granddad

【老成】 lǎochéng experienced; steady: 少年~ young but steady; old head on young shoulders/ ~持重 experienced and prudent

【老处女】 lǎochǔnǚ old maid; spinster

【老粗】 lǎocū 〔多用作谦辞〕 uneducated person; rough and ready chap

【老搭档】 lǎodādàng old partner; old workmate

【老大】 lǎodà ①〈书〉 old: 少壮不努力,~徒伤悲。 If one does not exert oneself in youth, one will regret it in old age. 或 Laziness in youth means sorrow in old age. ② eldest child (in a family) ③〈方〉 master of a sailing vessel ④ greatly; very: 心里~不高兴 feel very annoyed

【老当益壮】 lǎo dāng yì zhuàng old but vigorous

【老弟】 lǎodì (a familiar form of address to a man much younger than oneself) young man; young fellow; my boy

【老调】 lǎodiào hackneyed theme; platitude: ~重弹 harp on the same string; play the same old tune

【老公公】 lǎogōnggong 〈方〉 ① grandpa ② husband's father; father-in-law

【老古董】 lǎogǔdǒng ① old-fashioned article; antique ② old fogey

【老规矩】 lǎoguīju old rules and regulations; convention; established custom or practice

【老狐狸】 lǎohúli ① old fox ② crafty scoundrel

【老虎】 lǎohǔ tiger

【老话】 lǎohuà ① old saying; saying; adage: 正如中国~说的 as the Chinese saying goes ② remarks about the old days

【老奸巨猾】 lǎojiān-jùhuá a past master of machination and manoeuvre; a crafty old scoundrel; a wily old fox

【老将】 lǎojiàng veteran; old-timer: ~出马,一个顶俩。 When a veteran goes into action, he can do the job of two.

【老交情】 lǎojiāoqing long-standing friendship; an old friend

【老老实实】 lǎolǎoshíshí honestly; conscientiously; in earnest

【老练】 lǎoliàn seasoned; experienced: 他比起过去来已经~得多了。 He's much more experienced and capable now than before./ 她办事很~。 She is experienced and works with a sure hand.

【老马识途】 lǎomǎ shí tú an old horse knows the way; an old hand is a good guide

【老迈】 lǎomài aged; senile

【老毛病】 lǎomáobìng old trouble; old weakness: 这是我的~,一到冬天就咳。 My cough is an old trouble. I get it every winter./ 粗心大意是他的~。 Carelessness is an old weakness of his.

【老谋深算】 lǎomóu-shēnsuàn circumspect and farseeing; experienced and astute

【老年】 lǎonián old age ◇ ~人 old people; the aged

【老牛破车】 lǎoniú-pòchē an old ox pulling a rickety cart —— making slow progress

【老牌】 lǎopái old brand

【老婆婆】 lǎopópo 〈方〉 ① granny ② husband's mother; mother-in-law

【老气横秋】 lǎoqì héngqiū ① arrogant on account of one's seniority ② lacking in youthful vigour

【老前辈】 lǎoqiánbèi one's senior; one's elder

【老人】 lǎorén ① old man or woman; the aged; the old ② one's aged parents or grandparents

【老人家】 lǎorenjia ① a respectful form of address for an old person: 你~今年多大年纪了? How old are you, granddad (grandma)? ② parent: ~都好吗? How are your parents?

【老弱】 lǎo-ruò the old and weak

【老弱病残】 lǎo-ruò-bìng-cán the old, weak, sick and disabled

【老弱残兵】 lǎoruò-cánbīng remaining troops made up of the old and weak; those who on account of old age, illness, etc. are no longer active or efficient in work

【老生常谈】 lǎoshēng chángtán commonplace; platitude

【老师】 lǎoshī teacher

【老实】 lǎoshí ① honest; frank: 做~人,说~话,办~事 be an honest person, honest in word and honest in deed/ ~说我很不赞成这个意见。 To be frank, I don't like the idea at all./ ~回答我的问题。 Give me a straight answer./ ~交待 come clean; own up; make a clean breast of ② well-behaved; good: 放~点! Behave yourself! 或 None of your tricks!/ 这孩子可~了。 The child is as good as gold. ③〈婉〉 simpleminded; naive; easily taken in

【老手】 lǎoshǒu old hand; old stager; veteran: 干这一行他是~。 He is an old hand at the trade.

【老鼠】 lǎoshǔ mouse; rat: ~过街,人人喊打。 When a rat runs across the street, everybody cries, "Kill it!" (said of a person or thing hated by everyone)

【老态龙钟】 lǎotài lóngzhōng senile; doddering

【老套】 lǎotào old stuff; old ways: 报纸要办得生动,切忌死板~。 A newspaper should be lively and should avoid hackneyed stuff.

【老天爷】 lǎotiānyé God; Heavens: 我的~! My goodness! 或 Good Heavens! 或 Good Gracious!

【老顽固】 lǎowángu old stick-in-the-mud; old diehard

【老翁】 lǎowēng old man; greybeard

【老小】 lǎo-xiǎo grown-ups and children; one's family: 一家~ the whole family

【老兄】 lǎoxiōng (a familiar form of address between male friends) brother; man; old chap

【老羞成怒】 lǎo xiū chéng nù fly into a rage out of shame; be shamed into anger

【老朽】 lǎoxiǔ decrepit and behind the times; old and useless

【老眼光】 lǎoyǎnguāng old ways of looking at things; old views: 不能以~看新事物。 One mustn't judge new things by old standards.

【老爷】 lǎoye ① master; bureaucrat; lord: 做官当~ act as lords and masters/ 采取~式的态度 adopt a bureaucratic attitude ②〈方〉 (maternal) grandfather; grandpa

【老一辈】 lǎoyībèi older generation

【老一套】 lǎoyītào the same old stuff; the same old story: 他们的所谓新建议无非是~。 Their so-called new proposal is nothing but the same old stuff./ 改变~的做法 change outmoded methods

【老鹰】 lǎoyīng black-eared kite; hawk; eagle

【老于世故】 lǎoyú shìgù versed in the ways of the world; worldly-wise

【老帐】 lǎozhàng old debts; long-standing debts: ~未清,又欠新帐。 While old debts are still unpaid, new ones are incurred./ 翻~ bring up old scores

【老资格】 lǎozīge old-timer; veteran

【老子】 lǎozi ①〈口〉 father ② 〔气忿或开玩笑的场合下的自称〕: ~不吃你这一套! I'll have none of your nonsense!/ ~天下第一 regard oneself as No. 1 authority under heaven; think oneself the wisest person in the world

佬 lǎo 〈贬〉 man; guy; fellow: 阔~ a rich guy

姥 lǎo

【姥姥】 lǎolao 〈方〉 (maternal) grandmother; grandma

lào

烙 lào ① brand; iron: 给马~上印记 brand a horse/ ~衣服 iron clothes ② bake in a pan: ~两张饼 bake a couple of cakes

【烙印】 làoyìn brand

落* lào
另见 luò

【落色】 làoshǎi discolour; fade

酪 lào ① junket ② thick fruit juice; fruit jelly

lè

乐* lè ① happy; cheerful; joyful: 我心里~开了花。 My heart swelled with happiness (或 was filled with joy)./

人为～ find pleasure in helping others ② be glad to; find pleasure in; enjoy: ～此不疲 always enjoy it; never be bored with it ③〈方〉laugh; be amused: 他说的笑话把大家逗～了。His joke amused everyone./ 你～什么呀？What are you laughing at? 或 What's the joke?

另见 yuè

【乐不可支】lè bùkě zhī overwhelmed with joy; overjoyed

【乐得】lèdé readily take the opportunity to; be only too glad to: 既然如此，我们～在这儿多呆几天。In that case, we'll be only too glad to spend a few more days here.

【乐观】lèguān optimistic; hopeful; sanguine: ～的看法 an optimistic view/ ～的报道 a sanguine report/ 对前途很～ be optimistic about the future; be sanguine about the future/ 事情的发展是很可～的。The prospects are very bright. ◇ ～主义 optimism/ ～主义者 optimist

【乐极生悲】lè jí shēng bēi extreme joy begets sorrow

【乐趣】lèqù delight; pleasure; joy: 工作中的～ delight in work/ 生活中的～ joys of life

【乐事】lèshì pleasure; delight: 以助人为～ find pleasure in helping others

【乐天】lètiān carefree; happy-go-lucky

【乐土】lètǔ land of happiness; paradise

【乐意】lèyì ① be willing to; be ready to: ～帮忙 be willing to help ② pleased; happy: 他听了这话有点不～。He seemed somewhat displeased with that remark.

【乐园】lèyuán paradise: 人间～ earthly paradise; paradise on earth/ 儿童～ children's playground

勒 lè ① rein in: ～马 rein in the horse ② force; coerce: ～交 force sb. to hand sth. over ③〈书〉carve; engrave: ～碑 carve on a stone tablet

【勒索】lèsuǒ extort; blackmail: ～钱财 extort money from sb.

le

了 le 〈助〉①〔用在动词或形容词后面表示动作或变化已经完成的〕: 我等～半天他还没来。I've been waiting a long time, but he still hasn't turned up./ 水位已经低～两米。The water level has fallen by two metres./ 你先去，我下～班就去。You go ahead. I'll go right after work. ②〔用在句子的末尾或句中停顿的地方，表示肯定，表示出现新的情况，表示催促或劝止〕: 下雨～。It's started raining./ 是我错～。I was wrong./ 她开头不想来，后来还是来～。At first she didn't want to come, but she came in the end./ 你早来一天就见着他～。You would have seen him if you'd come a day sooner./ 走～，走～，不能再等～。Let's go. We can't wait any longer./ 别说话～！Stop talking!

另见 liǎo; liào

lēi

勒 lēi tie or strap sth. tight: 带子太松了，再～一～。The strap is too loose. Tighten it up a bit.

擂 lēi hit; beat: ～了一拳 give sb. a punch

另见 léi; lèi

léi

累 léi

另见 lěi; lèi

【累累】léiléi ① clusters of; heaps of: 果实～ fruit hanging in clusters; fruit hanging heavy ② haggard; gaunt: ～若丧家之犬 wretched as a stray cur

另见 lěi

【累赘】léizhui ① burdensome; cumbersome ② wordy; verbose: 这个句子太～。That's a clumsy, involved sentence. ③ encumbrance; burden; nuisance: 行李带的多了，是个～。Too much luggage is a nuisance.

雷 léi ① thunder ② mine: 布～ lay mines/ 扫～ sweep mines

【雷达】léidá radar: 全景～ panoramic radar

【雷电】léidiàn thunder and lightning: ～交作 lightning accompanied by peals of thunder

【雷动】léidòng thunderous: 欢声～ thunderous cheers

【雷击】léijī be struck by lightning

【雷厉风行】léilì-fēngxíng (in carrying out policies, etc.) with the power of a thunderbolt and the speed of lightning; vigorously and speedily; resolutely

【雷鸣】léimíng thunderous; thundery: ～般的掌声 thunderous applause

【雷声】léishēng thunderclap; thunder: ～隆隆 the rumble (或 roll) of thunder

【雷声大，雨点小】léishēng dà, yǔdiǎn xiǎo loud thunder but small raindrops; much said but little done

【雷霆】léitíng ① thunderclap; thunderbolt ② thunder-like power or rage; wrath: 大发～ fly into a rage

【雷霆万钧】léitíng wàn jūn as powerful as a thunderbolt: 以～之力 with the force of a thunderbolt

【雷同】léitóng ① echoing what others have said ② duplicate; identical

擂 léi pestle; pound

另见 lēi; lèi

lěi

垒 lěi ① build by piling up bricks, stones, earth, etc.: ～一道墙 build a wall ② rampart ③〈棒、垒球〉base

【垒球】lěiqiú softball ◇ ～棒 softball bat

累 lěi ① pile up; accumulate: 日积月～ accumulate day by day and month by month/ 成千上万 thousands upon thousands ② continuous; repeated; running: 奋战～日 carry on the fight for several days running/ ～戒不改 refuse to mend one's ways despite repeated warnings ③ involve: 连～ involve; implicate; get sb. into trouble ④同"垒"①

另见 léi; lèi

【累积】lěijī accumulate: 头八个月完成的工程量～起来，已达到全年任务的百分之九十。The work done in the first eight months amounts to ninety per cent of the year's quota.

【累及】lěijí implicate; involve; drag in: ～无辜 involve the innocent

【累计】lěijì ① add up ② accumulative total; grand total

【累累】lěilěi ① again and again; many times ② innumerable; countless: 罪行～ have a long criminal record; commit countless crimes

【累卵】lěiluǎn a stack of eggs — liable to collapse any moment; precarious: 危如～ as precarious as a stack of eggs; in an extremely precarious situation

【累年】lěinián for years in succession; year after year

【累世】lěishì for many generations; generation after generation

磊

【磊落】lěiluò open and upright: 胸怀～ openhearted and upright/ 光明～ open and aboveboard

蕾 lěi flower bud; bud

儡 lěi 见"傀儡"kuǐlěi

lèi

肋 lèi ① rib ② costal region: 两～ both sides of the chest

泪 lèi tear; teardrop: 她哭得～人儿一样。She was all tears.

【泪痕】lèihén　tear stains: 满脸~ a face bathed in tears/~斑斑 tear-stained
【泪水】lèishuǐ　tear; teardrop
【泪汪汪】lèiwāngwāng　(eyes) brimming with tears
【泪眼】lèiyǎn　tearful eyes: ~模糊 eyes blurred by tears
【泪珠】lèizhū　teardrop

类* lèi　① kind; type; class; category: 同~ be of a kind; belong to the same category/ 这是另一~问题。This is another kind of problem./ 诸如此~ things like that; and suchlike; and what not ② resemble; be similar to: 画虎不成反~犬 try to draw a tiger but end up with the likeness of a dog — attempt something too ambitious and end in failure/ ~乎神话 sound like a fairy tale
【类别】lèibié　classification; category: 土壤的~ classification of soil/ 属于不同的~ belong to different categories
【类似】lèisì　similar; analogous: 保证不再发生~事件 guarantee against the occurrence of similar incidents
【类推】lèituī　analogize; reason by analogy: 照此~ on the analogy of this
【类型】lèixíng　type

累* lèi　① tired; fatigued; weary: ~坏了 tired out; worn out; exhausted/ 不怕苦, 不怕~ fear neither hardship nor fatigue ② tire; strain; wear out: ~活 tiring work; heavy work/ 看小字~眼睛。Reading small print strains the eyes. ③ work hard; toil: 你~了一天, 该休息了。You've been working hard all day. You need a rest.
　另见 lěi; lěi

擂 lèi　① beat (a drum) ② 见"擂台"
　另见 lēi; lěi
【擂台】lèitái　ring (for martial contests); arena: 摆~ give an open challenge / 打~ take up the challenge

léng

棱 léng　① arris; edge: 桌子~儿 edges of a table/ 见~见角 angular ② corrugation; ridge: 搓板的~儿 ridges of a washboard

lěng

冷* lěng　① cold: ~天 the cold season; cold days/ 你~不~? Do you feel cold? ② cold in manner; frosty: ~若冰霜 frosty in manner ③〈方〉cool: ~一下再吃。Let it cool off before you eat it. ④ unfrequented; deserted; out-of-the-way: 星星~清清的。The house looked deserted. ⑤ strange; rare: ~字 a rarely used word; an unfamiliar word ⑥ shot from hiding: ~枪 a sniper's shot
【冷板凳】lěngbǎndèng　cold bench — an indifferent post or a cold reception: 坐~ hold a title without any obligations of office; be kept waiting long for an assignment or an audience with a VIP
【冷冰冰】lěngbīngbīng　ice cold; icy; frosty: ~的脸色 cold expression; frosty looks/ ~的态度 icy manners
【冷不防】lěngbufáng　unawares; suddenly; by surprise: 打他一个~ take him unawares; catch him off guard
【冷藏】lěngcáng　refrigeration; cold storage
【冷场】lěngchǎng　① awkward silence on the stage when an actor enters late or forgets his lines ② awkward silence at a meeting
【冷嘲热讽】lěngcháo-rèfěng　freezing irony and burning satire
【冷淡】lěngdàn　① cheerless; desolate ② cold; indifferent: 反映~ a cold response/ 对倡议表示~ show indifference towards a proposal/ ~的态度 a frigid manner ③ treat coldly; cold-shoulder; slight
【冷冻】lěngdòng　freezing
【冷宫】lěnggōng　cold palace — a place to which disfavoured queens and concubines were banished; limbo: 被打入~ be consigned to limbo

【冷汗】lěnghàn　cold sweat: 出~ be in a cold sweat; break out in a cold sweat
【冷货】lěnghuò　goods not much in demand; dull goods
【冷箭】lěngjiàn　an arrow shot from hiding; sniper's shot: 放~ make a sneak attack
【冷静】lěngjìng　sober; calm: 头脑~ sober-minded; level-headed; cool-headed/ 保持~ keep calm
【冷觉】lěngjué　〈生理〉sensation of cold; sense of cold
【冷酷】lěngkù　unfeeling; callous; grim: ~无情 unfeeling; cold-blooded/ 谎言掩盖不住~的现实。Lies cannot cover up grim reality.
【冷冷清清】lěnglěngqīngqīng　cold and cheerless; desolate: 对待朋友要满腔热忱, 不能~, 漠不关心。We should be warm towards our friends, not cold and indifferent./ 不要只靠少数人~地做工作。Do not rely entirely on a handful of people working in quiet isolation./ 会议开得~。The meeting was very dull.
【冷落】lěngluò　① unfrequented; desolate: 狭窄~的小巷 an unfrequented narrow alley ② treat coldly; cold-shoulder; leave out in the cold: ~了客人 leave a guest out in the cold
【冷门】lěngmén　① a profession, trade or branch of learning that receives little attention ② an unexpected winner; dark horse: 那次比赛爆出了个~。The contest produced an unexpected winner. ◇ ~货 goods not much in demand; dull goods
【冷漠】lěngmò　cold and detached; unconcerned; indifferent
【冷暖】lěngnuǎn　changes in temperature: 注意~ be careful about changes of temperature; take care of oneself
【冷盘】lěngpán　cold dish; hors d'oeuvres
【冷僻】lěngpì　① deserted; out-of-the-way ② rare; unfamiliar: ~的字眼 rarely used words/ ~的典故 unfamiliar allusions
【冷气】lěngqì　air conditioning: 这个剧院有~设备。The theatre is air-conditioned. ◇ ~机 air conditioner
【冷清】lěngqīng　cold and cheerless; desolate; lonely; deserted
【冷却】lěngquè　cooling
【冷食】lěngshí　cold drinks and snacks ◇ ~部 cold drink and snack counter
【冷水】lěngshuǐ　① cold water: 泼~ throw cold water on; dampen sb.'s enthusiasm ② unboiled water ◇ ~浴 cold bath
【冷笑】lěngxiào　sneer; laugh grimly; grin with dissatisfaction, helplessness, bitterness, etc.
【冷血动物】lěngxuè dòngwù　① cold-blooded animal ② an unfeeling person; a coldhearted person
【冷言冷语】lěngyán-lěngyǔ　sarcastic comments; ironical remarks
【冷眼】lěngyǎn　① cool detachment ② cold shoulder
【冷眼旁观】lěngyǎn pángguān　① look on coldly; stay aloof ② look on with a critical eye
【冷战】lěngzhàn　cold war
【冷战】lěngzhan　〈口〉shiver: 打~ shiver with cold

lèng

愣 lèng　① distracted; stupefied; blank: 发~ stare blankly; look distracted/ 他~了半天没说话。For a long while he remained speechless./ 听到这消息他~住了。He was struck dumb by the news. ②〈口〉rash; reckless; foolhardy: ~小子 rash young fellow; young hothead
【愣头愣脑】lèngtóu-lèngnǎo　rash; impetuous; reckless

lí

厘 lí　① li, a unit of length (=1/3 millimetre) ② li, a unit of weight (=0.05 grams) ③ li, a unit of area (=0.666 square metres)
【厘定】lídìng　collate and stipulate (rules and regulations, etc.)

【厘米】 límǐ　centimetre

离* lí ① leave; part from; be away from: 她～家已经三年了。She's been away from home for three years. ② off; away; from: 车站～这儿三十公里。The railway station is 30 km from here./ ～国庆节只有十天了。National Day is only ten days away. ③ without; independent of: 发展工业～不了钢铁。Industry cannot develop without steel.

【离别】 líbié part (for a longish period); leave; bid farewell: 我～故乡已经两年了。It's two years since I left my hometown.

【离婚】 líhūn divorce

【离间】 líjiàn sow discord; drive a wedge between; set one party against another

【离境】 líjìng leave a country or place ◇ ～签证 exit visa/ ～许可证 exit permit

【离开】 líkāi leave; depart from; deviate from:～本题 stray from the subject; digress

【离奇】 líqí odd; fantastic; bizarre: ～的谎言 a fantastic lie/ 这事儿很～。This is a very odd business.

【离任】 lírèn leave one's post: ～回国 leave one's post for home/ 即将～的大使 the outgoing ambassador

【离散】 lísàn dispersed; scattered about; separated from one another

【离题】 lítí digress from the subject; stray from the point: 发言不要～。Please keep to the subject.

【离乡背井】 líxiāng-bèijǐng 见"背井离乡" bèijǐng-líxiāng

狸* lí racoon dog

骊* lí <书> black horse

梨* lí pear

犁* lí ① plough ② work with a plough; plough: 地已经～了两遍。The fields have been ploughed twice.

喱* lí 见"咖喱" gālí

漓* lí 见"淋漓" línlí

璃* lí 见"玻璃" bōli; "琉璃" liúli

犛* lí yak

黎* lí <书> multitude; host: ～庶 the multitude

【黎明】 límíng dawn; daybreak

罹* lí <书> suffer from; meet with: ～病 suffer from a disease; fall ill

【罹难】 línàn <书> ① die in a disaster or an accident ② be murdered

篱* lí hedge; fence: 竹～茅舍 thatched cottage with bamboo fence/ 树～ hedge; hedgerow

【篱笆】 líba bamboo or twig fence: ～墙 wattled wall

蠡* lí <书> ① calabash shell serving as a dipper; dipper ② seashell

【蠡测】 lícè <书> measure the sea with an oyster shell — have a shallow understanding of a person or subject

lǐ

礼* lǐ ① ceremony; rite: 丧～ funeral ceremony; funeral/ 婚～ wedding ② courtesy; etiquette; manners: 行～ (give a) salute/ 彬彬有～ refined and courteous; urbane/ 失～行为 breach of etiquette; discourtesy ③ gift; present: 送～ give a present; send a gift

【礼拜】 lǐbài ① <宗> religious service: 做～ go to church; be at church ② <口> week: 下～ next week ③ <口> day of the week: 今天～几₁ What day is it today? ④ <口> Sunday: 今儿个～。Today is Sunday.

◇ ～寺 <伊斯兰教> mosque/ ～堂 <基督教> church/ ～天 <口> Sunday

【礼宾司】 Lǐbīnsī the Department of Protocol; the Protocol Department ◇ ～司长 Director of the Protocol Department; Chief of Protocol

【礼服】 lǐfú ceremonial robe or dress; full dress; formal attire

【礼教】 lǐjiào the Confucian ethical code

【礼节】 lǐjié courtesy; etiquette; protocol; ceremony: ～性拜访 a courtesy call/ 这是～上所需要的。This is required by protocol. 或 This is demanded by etiquette./ 社交～ social etiquette

【礼貌】 lǐmào courtesy; politeness; manners: 有～ courteous; polite/ 没～ have no manners; be impolite

【礼炮】 lǐpào salvo; (gun) salute: 鸣～二十一响。A 21-gun salute was fired.

【礼品】 lǐpǐn gift; present ◇ （商店）～部 gift and souvenir department or counter

【礼轻人意重】 lǐ qīng rényì zhòng the gift is trifling but the feeling is profound; it's nothing much, but it's the thought that counts

【礼让】 lǐràng give precedence to sb. out of courtesy or thoughtfulness; comity: 国际～ the comity of nations/ 中速行驶，安全～。Drive at moderate speed; yield right of way for safety's sake.

【礼尚往来】 lǐ shàng wǎng-lái ① courtesy demands reciprocity ② deal with a man as he deals with you; pay a man back in his own coin

【礼俗】 lǐsú etiquette and custom

【礼堂】 lǐtáng assembly hall; auditorium

【礼物】 lǐwù gift; present

【礼仪】 lǐyí etiquette; rite; protocol

【礼遇】 lǐyù courteous reception: 受到～ be accorded courteous reception

李* lǐ plum

【李代桃僵】 lǐ dài táo jiāng ① substitute one thing for another; substitute this for that ② sacrifice oneself for another person

【李子】 lǐzi plum

里* lǐ ① lining; inside: 衣服～儿 the lining of a garment/ 这面是～儿，那面是面儿。This is the back, that is the front. ② inner: ～间 inner room ③ neighbourhood: 邻～ people of the neighbourhood ④ <书> hometown; native place: 返～ return to one's hometown ⑤ lǐ, a Chinese unit of length (=1/2 kilometre)

里* lǐ ① in; inside: 手～ in one's hands/ 小提箱～ in (或 inside) the suitcase ② 〔附在"这""那""哪"等字后边表示地点〕: 这～ here/ 那～ there

【里边】 lǐbian inside; in; within: 壁橱～ inside the cupboard/ 他一年～没有请过一次假。He has not once asked for leave during the whole year./ 这～有问题。There is something wrong here. 或 Something is wrong here.

【里程】 lǐchéng ① mileage ② course of development; course

【里程碑】 lǐchéngbēi milestone: 历史的～ a milestone in history

【里里外外】 lǐlǐwàiwài inside and outside: 屋子～都打扫得很干净。The house has been given a thorough cleaning inside and out./ 一把手 competent in all one does, both inside and outside the house

【里面】 lǐmiàn inside; interior: 宿舍～清洁豁亮。It's clean and bright inside the dormitory.

【里头】 lǐtou inside; interior

【里应外合】 lǐyìng-wàihé act from inside in coordination with forces attacking from outside; collaborate from within with forces from without

俚* lǐ vulgar

【俚俗】 lǐsú vulgar; unrefined; uncultured

【俚语】 lǐyǔ slang

娌* lǐ 见"妯娌" zhóuli

理* lǐ

① texture; grain (in wood, skin, etc.): 纹~ texture; grain/ 肌~ skin texture ② reason; logic; truth: 是他没~。He's the one who's been unreasonable./ 不可~喻 will not listen to reason; be impervious to reason/ 他讲的句句是~。There is truth in every word he says./ 当如此。That's just as it should be. ③ natural science, esp. physics: ~工科 science and engineering/ 数~化 mathematics, physics and chemistry ④ manage; run: ~家 keep house; manage family affairs/ 有要事待~ have important business to attend to ⑤ put in order; tidy up: ~东西 put things in order ⑥〔多用于否定句〕pay attention to; acknowledge: 置之不~ pay no attention to sth.; brush sth. aside/ 爱~不~ look cold and indifferent; be stand-offish

【理财】lǐcái manage money matters; conduct financial transactions

【理睬】lǐcǎi 〔多用于否定句〕pay attention to; show interest in: 没人~这事。Nobody pays any attention to this matter./ 不予~ ignore; turn a deaf ear to; pay no heed to

【理发】lǐfà haircut; hairdressing: 我去~。I'm going to have a haircut. 或（指女子）I'm going to have my hair done.

【理会】lǐhuì ① understand; comprehend: 不难~ not difficult to understand ②〔多用于否定句〕take notice of; pay attention to: 叫了他好几声,他都没~。We called him several times, but he took no notice of us.

【理解】lǐjiě understand; comprehend: 你的意思我完全~。I understand you completely. 或 I see perfectly well what you mean./ 加深~ deepen one's comprehension; acquire a better understanding/ 不可~ incomprehensible; beyond one's comprehension

【理解力】lǐjiělì faculty of understanding; understanding; comprehension: ~强 have good understanding (或 comprehension)

【理科】lǐkē ① science department in a college ② science (as a school subject)

【理亏】lǐkuī be in the wrong: 自知~ know that one is in the wrong; realize that justice is not on one's side

【理亏心虚】lǐkuī-xīnxū feel apprehensive because one is not on solid ground

【理论】lǐlùn theory: 在~上 in terms of theory; on the theoretical plane; theoretically

【理屈词穷】lǐqū-cíqióng fall silent on finding oneself bested in argument; be unable to advance any further arguments to justify oneself

【理事】lǐshì member of a council; director: 常任~国 permanent member state of a council ◇ ~会 council; board of directors

【理所当然】lǐ suǒ dāngrán of course; naturally: 他们的荒谬提案~地被否决了。Their absurd proposal was of course rejected.

【理想】lǐxiǎng ideal: 这天气出去郊游太~了。This is ideal weather for an outing.

【理性】lǐxìng reason: 失去~ lose one's reason

【理应】lǐyīng ought to; should: ~归公 ought to be handed over to the state or collective

【理由】lǐyóu reason; ground; argument: 有充分~相信 have every reason to believe/ 没有~抱怨 have no grounds for complaint/ 他提出的~不能成立。His argument is untenable./ 他想找~为自己的错误辩解。He tried to find an excuse for his error.

【理直气壮】lǐzhí-qìzhuàng with justice on one's side, one is bold and assured: ~地回答 reply with perfect assurance/ ~地予以驳斥 justly and forcefully refute

【理智】lǐzhì reason; intellect: 丧失~ lose one's reason; lose one's senses

鲤 lǐ carp
【鲤鱼】lǐyú carp

lì

力* lì

① power; strength; ability: 人~ manpower/ 物~ material resources/ 兵~ military strength; military capabilities/ 能~ ability; capability/ 视~ power of vision/ 魄~ drive and decisiveness; boldness ②〈物〉force: 磁~ magnetic force ③ physical strength: 大~士 a man of great strength/ ~不能支 unable to stand the strain any longer; too weak to stay on one's feet ④ do all one can; make every effort: ~谏 try all one can to remonstrate/ 办事不~ not do one's best in one's work; not pull one's weight

【力不从心】lì bù cóng xīn ability falling short of one's wishes; ability not equal to one's ambition

【力不胜任】lì bù shèngrèn be unequal to one's task

【力戒】lìjiè strictly avoid; do everything possible to avoid; guard against: ~临战分散兵力 strictly avoid the dispersal of forces before an engagement/ ~浪费 do everything possible to avoid waste/ ~骄傲 guard against arrogance

【力量】lìliàng ① physical strength ② power; force: 国防~ defence capability

【力排众议】lì pái zhòngyì prevail over all dissenting views

【力气】lìqi physical strength; effort: 他很有~。He is a man of great strength.

【力求】lìqiú make every effort to; do one's best to; strive to: 文字~精炼。Strive to be concise in writing./ 我们~取得一致意见。We'll do our best to reach an identity of views.

【力所能及】lì suǒ néng jí in one's power: 在~的范围内 within one's power

【力图】lìtú try hard to; strive to: ~否认 try hard to deny/ ~摆脱困境 strive to get out of a predicament

【力挽狂澜】lì wǎn kuánglán make vigorous efforts to turn the tide

【力争】lìzhēng ① work hard for; do all one can to: ~主动 do all one can to gain the initiative/ ~更大的丰收 work hard for a still bigger harvest/ ~少花钱, 多办事 strive by every means to spend less and accomplish more ② argue strongly; contend vigorously: 据理~ argue strongly on just grounds

历* lì

① go through; undergo; experience: ~尽艰辛 have gone through all kinds of hardships and difficulties ② all previous (occasions, sessions, etc.) ③ covering all; one by one: ~访各有关部门 have visited the departments concerned one by one ④ calendar: 阴（阳）~ lunar (solar) calendar

【历程】lìchéng course: 回顾战斗的~ look back on the course of the struggle

【历次】lìcì all previous (occasions, etc.): 在~比赛中她都取得了优异的成绩。She has done well in all past contests.

【历代】lìdài successive dynasties; past dynasties: ~封建王朝 the feudal dynasties of past ages/ ~名画 famous paintings through the ages

【历届】lìjiè all previous (sessions, governments, etc.): ~毕业生 graduates of all previous years

【历来】lìlái always; constantly; all through the ages: ~如此。This has always been the case./ ~认为 have invariably insisted; have consistently held; have always maintained

【历历】lìlì distinctly; clearly: ~在目 come clearly into view; leap up vividly before the eyes/ 往事~在心头。Past events remain fresh in my memory./ 湖水清澈, 游鱼~可数。The water of the lake was so clear that every fish could be seen distinctly.

【历年】lìnián over the years: ~的积蓄 savings over the years

【历任】lìrèn ① have successively held the posts of; have served successively as: 他~连长、营长、团长、师长等职。He successively held the posts of company, battalion, regiment and division commander. ② successive

【历时】lìshí last (a period of time); take (a period of time): 手术~三小时。The operation lasted three hours.

【历史】 lìshǐ history; past records: ~上 in history; down the ages
◇ ~博物馆 history (或 historical) museum/ ~潮流 the tide of history; historical trend/ ~地图 historical map or atlas/ ~剧 historical play/ ~人物 historical personage; historical figure/ ~问题 question of a political nature in sb.'s history/ ~小说 historical novel/ ~学家 historian

立* lì ① stand: 起~ stand up ② erect; set up: 把梯子~起来 set up the ladder/ ~界桩 erect boundary markers ③ upright; erect; vertical ④ found; establish; set up: ~国 found a state/ ~合同 sign a contract ⑤ exist; live: 自~ be on one's feet ⑥ immediate; instantaneous: ~见功效 produce immediate results; feel the effect immediately/ ~候回音。An immediate reply is requested. 或 Awaiting your prompt reply.
【立案】 lì'àn ① register; put on record ② 〈法〉 place a case on file for investigation and prosecution
【立场】 lìchǎng position; stand; standpoint: 阐明我们对这一问题的~ make clear our position on this question
【立法】 lìfǎ legislation ◇ ~机关 legislative body; legislature/ ~权 legislative power
【立方】 lìfāng ① 〈数〉 cube: 二的~ the cube of 2; 2³ 〈简〉（立方体）cube ② 〈量〉 cubic metre
◇ ~根 〈数〉 cube root/ ~厘米 cubic centimetre/ ~米 cubic metre/ ~体 cube
【立竿见影】 lì gān jiàn yǐng set up a pole and see its shadow — get instant results
【立功】 lìgōng render meritorious service; do a deed of merit; win honour; make contributions: 立大功 render outstanding service/ 立新功 make new contributions/ ~赎罪 perform meritorious services to atone for one's crimes
【立即】 lìjí 〈副〉 immediately; at once; promptly: ~照办 carry out promptly/ 判处死刑，~执行 be sentenced to death and executed immediately
【立刻】 lìkè 〈副〉 immediately; at once; right away: 我~就去。I'll go right away.
【立誓】 lìshì take an oath; vow
【立体】 lìtǐ ① three-dimensional; stereoscopic ② 〈数〉 solid
【立宪】 lìxiàn constitutionalism: 君主~ constitutional monarchy/ ~政体 constitutional government; constitutionalism
【立言】 lìyán expound one's ideas in writing; achieve glory by writing
【立意】 lìyì ① be determined; make up one's mind ② conception; approach: 这幅画~新颖。This painting shows an interesting new approach.
【立正】 lìzhèng stand at attention: ~！（口令）Attention!
【立志】 lìzhì resolve; be determined: ~改革 be determined to carry out reforms; be resolved to institute reforms
【立锥之地】 lì zhuī zhī dì a place to stick an awl — a tiny bit of land: 无~ not possess a speck of land
【立足】 lìzú ① have a foothold somewhere: 获得~之地 gain a foothold ② base oneself upon: ~于独立自主和自力更生 be based on independence and self-reliance
【立足点】 lìzúdiǎn ① foothold; footing: 找不到~ be unable to find a foothold ② standpoint; stand

厉* lì ① strict; rigorous: ~禁 strictly forbid ② stern; severe: ~声 in a stern voice
【厉兵秣马】 lìbīng-mòmǎ sharpen the weapons and feed the horses — get ready for battle
【厉害】 lìhai 见"利害" lìhai
【厉行】 lìxíng strictly enforce; rigorously enforce; make great efforts to carry out: ~节约 practise strict economy

吏 lì official; mandarin

沥 lì ① drip; trickle: 滴~ patter ② drop: 余~ last drops
【沥青】 lìqīng pitch; asphalt; bitumen

丽* lì beautiful: ~人 a beauty/ 风和日~。The wind is gentle and the sun radiant. 或 The weather is glorious.

励* lì encourage
【励精图治】 lì jīng tú zhì (usu. of a feudal ruler) rouse oneself for vigorous efforts to make the country prosperous

利* lì ① sharp: ~刃 a sharp sword or blade/ ~爪 sharp claws ② favourable: 形势对他们不~。The situation is unfavourable to them. ③ advantage; benefit: 有~有弊。There are both advantages and disadvantages. ④ profit; interest: 连本带~ both principal and interest; profit as well as capital ⑤ do good to; benefit: ~己~人 benefit other people as well as oneself/ 毫不~己，专门~人 be utterly devoted to others without any thought of self
【利弊】 lì-bì advantages and disadvantages; pros and cons: 权衡~ weigh the advantages and disadvantages
【利害】 lì-hài advantages and disadvantages; gains and losses: 不计~ regardless of gains or losses/ ~冲突 conflict of interests/ 有共同的~关系 have common interests
【利害】 lìhai terrible; formidable: 这几天热得~。It's been terribly hot these few days./ 这着棋十分~。That's a devastating move. / 他这张嘴~了。He has a sharp tongue./ 给敌人点~ teach the enemy a lesson
【利令智昏】 lì lìng zhì hūn be blinded by lust for gain
【利率】 lìlǜ 〈经〉 rate of interest; interest rate
【利落】 lìluo ① agile; nimble; dexterous: 动作~ agile movements/ 手脚~ dexterous; deft/ 说话不~ speak slowly and indistinctly ② neat; orderly: 他做事干净~。He is a neat worker. ③ settled; finished: 事情已经办~了。The matter is all settled.
【利器】 lìqì ① sharp weapon ② good tool; efficient instrument
【利钱】 lìqian interest
【利权】 lìquán ① economic rights ② financial power
【利润】 lìrùn profit ◇ ~率 profit margin; profit rate/ ~税 profits tax
【利息】 lìxī interest ◇ ~回扣 interest rebate
【利益】 lìyì interest; benefit; profit: 为大多数人谋~ work for the interests of the vast majority of people/ 使人民群众得到~ benefit the masses of the people
【利用】 lìyòng ① use; utilize; make use of: ~废料 make use of scrap material; turn scrap material to good account/ 充分~最新科学技术成就 make full use of the latest achievements in science and technology ② take advantage of; exploit: ~职权 take advantage of one's position and power; exploit one's office/ 受人~ be made use of; be a cat's-paw
【利诱】 lìyòu lure by promise of gain
【利欲熏心】 lì yù xūn xīn be blinded by greed; be obsessed with the desire for gain; be overcome by covetousness

呖 lì
【呖呖】 lìlì 〈象〉〔形容鸟类清脆的叫声〕莺声~ warbling of the oriole

戾 lì ① crime; sin ② perverse; unreasonable

例* lì ① example; instance: 举~ give an example; cite an instance ② precedent: 破~ break all precedents; make an exception/ 援~ quote (或 follow) a precedent ③ case; instance: 患这种病的三十三~中，二十一~有显著好转。Out of the 33 cases of this disease, 21 showed marked progress. ④ rule; regulation: 旧~ an old rule/ 不在此~。That is an exception. ⑤ regular; routine
【例假】 lìjià ① official holiday; legal holiday ② 〈婉〉 menstrual period; period
【例句】 lìjù illustrative sentence; example sentence
【例如】 lìrú for instance; for example (e.g.); such as
【例题】 lìtí example
【例外】 lìwài exception: 毫无~ without exception
【例行公事】 lìxíng gōngshì ① routine; routine business ② mere formality
【例证】 lìzhèng illustration; example; case in point
【例子】 lìzi example; case; instance

隶 lì ①be subordinate to; be under ②a person in servitude: 奴～ slave ③见"隶书"
【隶书】 lìshū official script, an ancient style of calligraphy current in the Han Dynasty (206 B.C.—A.D. 220), simplified from *xiaozhuan* (小篆)
【隶属】 lìshǔ be subordinate to; be under the jurisdiction or command of: 局部～于全局。The part is subordinate to the whole.

荔 lì
【荔枝】 lìzhī litchi

荔枝

俐 lì 见"伶俐" línglì

俪 lì ①pair; couple ②husband and wife; married couple

莉 lì 见"茉莉" mòlì

莅 lì 〈书〉arrive; be present: ～场 be present on the occasion/ ～会 be present at a meeting
【莅临】 lìlín 〈书〉arrive; be present: 敬请～指导。Your presence and guidance are requested.

砺 lì 〈书〉①whetstone ②whet; sharpen

栗 lì 〈植〉①chestnut ②tremble; shudder: 不寒而～ tremble with fear ③(Lì) a surname

粒 lì ①grain; granule; pellet: 砂～儿 grains of sand ②〈量〉〔用于粒状物〕: 一～米 a grain of rice/ 三～子弹 three bullets/ 每服五～ dosage: 5 pills each time

笠 lì a large bamboo or straw hat with a conical crown and broad brim

唳 lì cry (of a crane)

雳 lì 见"霹雳" pīlì

痢 lì dysentery
【痢疾】 lìji dysentery

li

哩 li 〈方〉〈助〉〔跟"呢"相同，但只用于非疑问句〕: 天还早着～! It's still early.

liǎ

俩 liǎ 〈口〉①two: 我～ we two; both of us; the two of us
另见 liǎng

lián

连* lián ①link; join; connect: 把零散的土地～成一片 join together scattered pieces of land/ 天～水，水～天。The sky and the water seem to merge./ 这两句话～不起来。The two sentences are disconnected. 或 The two sentences don't hang together. ②in succession; one after another; repeatedly: ～发三封电报 send three telegrams in succession/ ～挫强手 defeat strong opponents one after another/ ～战皆捷 win a series of victories; win battle after battle ③including: ～你一共十个人。There'll be ten people, including you. ④even: ～小孩也参加了跑步运动。Even children joined in the jog.
【连带】 liándài related: 人的作风和思想是有～关系的。A person's work style is related to his ideology.

【连…带…】 lián…dài… ①〔表示前后两项包括在一起〕and; as well as: 连老带小一共二十三个人。There are altogether 23, including the old people and children. ②〔表示两种动作差不多同时发生〕and; while: 连说带比划 talking and gesticulating/ 连蹦带跳 hopping and skipping
【连贯】 liánguàn ①link up; piece together; hang together/把各种材料～起来考虑 piece together various kinds of data and ponder over them ②coherent; consistent: 文章写得很不～。This article is rather incoherent. ◇ ～性 coherence; continuity
【连环】 liánhuán chain of rings ◇ ～画 a book (usu. for children) with a story told in pictures; picture-story book
【连接】 liánjiē join; link: 把两条铁路线～起来 link up the two railway lines
【连累】 liánlěi implicate; involve; get sb. into trouble
【连连】 liánlián 〈口〉repeatedly; again and again: ～点头 nod again and again (to show agreement, etc.)
【连忙】 liánmáng promptly; at once: 他一道歉。He hastened to apologize.
【连绵】 liánmián continuous; unbroken; uninterrupted: 阴雨～。There was an unbroken spell of wet weather./ ～起伏的山峦 rolling hills
【连年】 liánnián in successive years; in consecutive years; for years running; for years on end: 战胜～干旱 conquer successive years of drought/ ～丰收 reap rich harvests for many years running/ 产量～上升。Output increases year after year.
【连篇】 liánpiān ①throughout a piece of writing; page after page: 空话～ pages and pages of empty verbiage ②one article after another; a multitude of articles
【连篇累牍】 liánpiān-lěidú lengthy and tedious; at great length: ～地发表文章 publish one article after another
【连任】 liánrèn be reappointed or reelected consecutively; renew one's term of office/ ～部长 be reappointed minister
【连日】 liánrì for days on end; day after day: ～来 for the last few days/ ～刮大风。It blew hard for several days running.
【连同】 liántóng together with; along with: 图纸～清单一并送去。Send the blueprints along with the inventory.
【连续】 liánxù continuous; successive; in a row; running: ～作战 continuous fighting; successive battles; consecutive operations/ ～爆破 continuous demolition/ ～十五年丰收 reap bumper harvests for fifteen years in succession/ ～工作八个小时 work eight hours at a stretch/ ～六年未出事故。There have been no accidents for six years running.
【连夜】 liányè the same night; that very night: 他们～立起了井架。They got the derrick into place before the night was out.
【连用】 liányòng use consecutively; use together: 这两个词不能～。These two words do not go together.
【连载】 liánzǎi publish in instalments; serialize: 长篇～ serial (of a novel, etc.)
【连珠炮】 liánzhūpào continuous firing; drumfire: 说话象～ chatter away like a machine gun/ 象～似地向他提问 bombard him with questions; fire questions at him

奁 lián a toilet case used by women in ancient China

帘 lián ①flag as shop sign: 酒～ wineshop sign ②curtain: 窗～ window curtain

怜* lián ①sympathize with; pity: 同病相～。Fellow sufferers sympathize with each other. ②见"怜爱"
【怜爱】 lián'ài love tenderly; have tender affection for
【怜悯】 liánmǐn pity; take pity on; have compassion for
【怜惜】 liánxī take pity on; have pity for: 决不～恶人。We should never take pity on evil people.

涟 lián 〈书〉①ripples ②continual flow (of tears)
【涟漪】 liányī 〈书〉ripples

莲* lián 〈植〉lotus
【莲花】 liánhuā lotus flower; lotus
【莲子】 liánzǐ lotus seed

梿* lián 见"榴梿" liúlián

联* lián ① ally oneself with; unite; join ② antithetical couplet: 春～ Spring Festival couplets

【联邦】 liánbāng federation; union; commonwealth: 英～ the British Commonwealth of Nations ◇ ～调查局 the (U.S.) Federal Bureau of Investigation (FBI)

【联播】 liánbō radio hookup; broadcast over a radio network ◇ ～节目时间 network time

【联合】 liánhé ① unite; ally: ～一切可能～的力量 ally oneself with all forces that can be allied with ② alliance; union; coalition ③ joint; combined: ～举办 jointly organize or sponsor

【联合国】 Liánhéguó the United Nations (U.N.) ◇ ～安全理事会 the United Nations Security Council/ ～大会 the United Nations General Assembly/ ～秘书处 the United Nations Secretariat

【联合会】 liánhéhuì federation; union

【联欢】 liánhuān have a get-together: 节日～ gala celebrations ◇ ～会 get-together/ ～节 festival/ ～晚会 (evening) party

【联接】 liánjiē 见"连接" liánjiē

【联结】 liánjié bind; tie; join

【联络】 liánluò ① get in touch with; come into contact with: ～感情 make friendly contacts ② contact; liaison

【联盟】 liánméng alliance; coalition; league; union

【联名】 liánmíng jointly signed; jointly: ～发起 jointly initiate; jointly sponsor/ ～上书 submit a joint letter

【联赛】 liánsài 〈体〉 league matches: 足球～ league football matches

【联系】 liánxì ① contact; touch; connection; relation: 取得～ get in touch with; establish contact with/ 保持～ keep in contact (或 touch) with/ 有广泛的社会～ have wide social connections/ 事物的内(外)部～ the internal (external) relations of things ② integrate; relate; link; get in touch with: 理论～实际 integrate theory with practice; apply theory to reality 把两件事～起来看就清楚了。Relate the two problems to each other and you'll understand them clearly./ 看电影的问题，找俱乐部～。As for movies, please get in touch with the club.

【联想】 liánxiǎng associate; connect in the mind

廉 lián ① honest and clean ② low-priced; inexpensive; cheap: 价～物美 good and cheap ③ (Lián) a surname

【廉耻】 liánchǐ sense of honour; sense of shame

【廉价】 liánjià low-priced; cheap: ～书 a cheap book/ ～买进 buy cheap/ ～出售 sell at a low price; sell cheap ◇ ～部 bargain counter/ ～劳动力 cheap labour/ ～品 cheap goods; bargain

【廉洁】 liánjié honest: ～奉公 be honest in performing one's official duties

镰 lián sickle

【镰刀】 liándāo sickle

liǎn

敛 liǎn ① hold back; restrain: ～足 hold back from going; check one's steps ② collect: 横征暴～ extort heavy taxes and levies

【敛迹】 liǎnjī temporarily desist from one's evil ways; lie low

脸* liǎn face; countenance: 笑～ a smiling face/ 丢～ lose face/ 不要～ shameless/ 没～见人 too ashamed to face anyone/ 撕破了～ put aside all considerations of face; not spare sb.'s sensibilities

【脸红】 liǎnhóng ① blush with shame; blush ② flush with anger; get excited; get worked up

【脸面】 liǎnmiàn face; self-respect; sb.'s feelings: 看我的～，不要生他的气了。For my sake, don't get angry with him.

【脸皮】 liǎnpí face; cheek: ～厚 thick-skinned; shameless/ ～薄 thin-skinned; shy; sensitive/ 居然有～说出这种话来 have the cheek (或 nerve) to say such things

【脸色】 liǎnsè ① complexion; look: ～红润 a ruddy complexion/ 他这几天～不好。He doesn't look well these days. ② facial expression: 一看他的～，我就知道有了好消息。I could see from the expression on his face that there was good news.

liàn

练* liàn ① white silk: 江平如～。The river lies as smooth as silk. ② boil and scour raw silk: ～漂〈纺〉scouring and bleaching ③ practise; train; drill: ～跑 practise running/ ～字 practise calligraphy/ ～节目 rehearse/ ～单杠 train (或 practise) on the horizontal bar/ ～气功 do breathing exercises/ ～好本领 perfect one's skill/ ～好身体 do exercises to build up one's physique (或 health) ④ experienced; skilled; seasoned: 老～ experienced and assured

【练兵】 liànbīng troop training; training

【练球】 liànqiú practise a ball game: 主队和客队在一起～。The home team and the visitors are practising together./ 赛前～ warm-up (before a match); knockup

【练武】 liànwǔ do weapon practice; practise martial arts

【练习】 liànxí ① practise: ～射击 practise marksmanship/ ～写文章 practise writing ② exercise: 做～ do exercises/ 算术～ arithmetic exercises ◇ ～簿 exercise-book/ ～题 problems of an exercise; exercises

炼* liàn ① smelt; refine: ～铅 smelt lead/ ～糖 refine sugar ② temper (a metal) with fire: 真金不怕火～。True gold does not fear the test of fire.

【炼乳】 liànrǔ condensed milk

【炼油】 liànyóu ① oil refining ② extract oil by heat ③ heat edible oil ◇ ～厂〈石油〉(oil) refinery

恋 liàn ① love: 初～ be in love for the first time; first love ② long for; feel attached to: ～家 reluctant to be away from home

【恋爱】 liàn'ài love: 谈～ be in love; have a love affair

【恋恋不舍】 liànliàn bù shě be reluctant to part with; hate to see sb. go

殓 liàn put a body into a coffin; encoffin

链 liàn ① chain: 铁～ iron chain/ 表～ watch chain ② cable length

liáng

良* liáng ① good; fine: ～将 a good general; an able general/ ～工 a skilled worker/ ～马 a fine horse ② good people: 除暴安～ get rid of bullies and bring peace to good people ③〈书〉very; very much: 获益～多 benefit a great deal

【良材】 liángcái ① good timber ② able person

【良策】 liángcè good plan; sound strategy

【良辰美景】 liángchén-měijǐng beautiful scene on a bright day

【良方】 liángfāng ① effective prescription; good recipe ② good plan; sound strategy

【良好】 liánghǎo good; well: ～的愿望 good intentions/ 自我感觉～ feel fine/ ～的比赛风格 fine sportsmanship/ 为双方会谈创造～的气氛 create a favourable atmosphere for bilateral talks/ 打下～的基础 lay a sound foundation/ 水稻长势～。The rice is coming on splendidly./ 手术经过～。The operation came off well./ 财政贸易情况～。Finance and trade are in a good state.

【良机】 liángjī 〈书〉good (或 golden) opportunity: 莫失～。Don't let this good opportunity slip.

【良久】 liángjiǔ ＜书＞ a good while; a long time
【良师益友】 liángshī-yìyǒu good teacher and helpful friend
【良心】 liángxīn conscience: ～上感到不安 have an uneasy conscience/ 说句～话 to be fair; in all fairness/ 有～的人 people with a conscience; good-hearted people/ 没～ conscienceless; ungrateful; heartless
【良药苦口】 liángyào kǔ kǒu good medicine tastes bitter: ～利于病,忠言逆耳利于行。Just as bitter medicine cures sickness, so unpalatable advice benefits conduct.
【良莠不齐】 liáng-yǒu bù qí the good and the bad are intermingled

凉 liáng ① cool; cold: ～风 cool breeze/ 饭～了。The food's got cold. ② discouraged; disappointed: 他一听这消息就～了半截。His heart sank at the news.
另见 liàng

【凉快】 liángkuai ① nice and cool; pleasantly cool: 这里～，坐下来歇会儿。It's nice and cool here. Let's sit down and have a rest. ② cool oneself; cool off: 我们到树荫下面去一下吧！Let's sit in the shade and cool off a bit.
【凉棚】 liángpéng mat-awning; mat shelter
【凉伞】 liángsǎn sunshade; parasol
【凉爽】 liángshuǎng nice and cool; pleasantly cool: ～的秋天 pleasantly cool autumn days
【凉水】 liángshuǐ ① cold water ② unboiled water
【凉台】 liángtái balcony; veranda
【凉亭】 liángtíng wayside pavilion; summer house; kiosk
【凉鞋】 liángxié sandals

梁 liáng ① roof beam: 架～ set a roof beam in place/ 横～ cross beam ② bridge: 桥～ bridge ③ ridge: 山～ mountain ridge
【梁上君子】 liángshàng jūnzǐ gentleman on the beam — burglar; thief

量 liáng measure: ～地 measure land; measure a piece of ground/ 用斗～米 mete out rice with a *dou* measure/ ～身材 take sb.'s measurements/ ～尺寸 take sb.'s measurements/ ～体温 take sb.'s temperature
另见 liàng

粱 liáng ＜书＞ ① a fine strain of millet ② fine grain; choice food

粮 liáng ① grain; food; provisions: ～棉双丰收 a bumper harvest of grain and cotton/ 要～有～，要人有人 have both provisions and manpower ready/ 弹尽～绝 run out of ammunition and food ② grain tax paid in kind
【粮仓】 liángcāng granary; barn
【粮草】 liángcǎo army provisions; rations and forage (或 fodder)
【粮食】 liángshi grain; cereals; food

liǎng

两 liǎng ①〔用于量词和"半"前面，也可用于"千""万""亿"前面〕two: ～匹马 two horses/ ～个半月 two and a half months/～亿二千万 two hundred and twenty million ② both (sides); either (side): ～鬓斑白 greying at the temples/ ～利 benefit both; be good for both sides/ 势不～立 irreconcilably hostile to each other; mutually exclusive ③ a few; some: 我想讲～句。I'd like to say a few words./ 这事过～天再说。Let's leave it for a couple of days. ④ *liang*, a unit of weight (＝50 grams) ⑤ ＜旧＞ tael, a unit of weight for silver
【两败俱伤】 liǎng bài jù shāng both sides suffer (或 lose); neither side gains
【两半儿】 liǎngbànr two halves; in half; in two: 碟子摔成～了。The dish is broken in two./ 把苹果切成～ cut an apple in half
【两边】 liǎngbiān ① both sides; both directions; both places: 沟的～种着豆子。Beans were grown on both sides of the ditch./ 人群向～散开。The crowd dispersed in both direc-

tions./ 老祖母常常～走动，看望两个孙女儿。Grandma is always going back and forth, visiting her two granddaughters. ② both parties; both sides: ～讨好 try to please both sides/ ～都说好了，明儿下午赛球。The two teams have agreed to play the match tomorrow afternoon.
【两回事】 liǎng huí shì two entirely different things; two different matters: 严格要求和求全责备是～。Being strict and being a nit-picker are two entirely different things.
【两极】 liǎngjí ① the two poles of the earth ② ＜物＞ the two poles (of a magnet or an electric battery)
【两口子】 liǎngkǒuzi ＜口＞ husband and wife; couple: 小～过得挺和美。The young couple get along quite happily. 又作"两口儿"
【两面】 liǎngmiàn ① two sides; both sides; two aspects; both aspects: 这张纸～都写满了字。Both sides of the paper were covered with writing./ 问题的～我们都要看到。We should see both aspects of the problem. ② having a dual (或 double) character; dual; double: ～性 dual character/ ～手法 double-faced tactics; double-dealing; double game
【两面夹攻】 liǎngmiàn jiāgōng make a pincer attack: 受到～ be caught in cross fire; be caught in a pincer attack
【两难】 liǎngnán face a difficult choice; be in a dilemma: 进退～ can neither advance nor retreat; be in a dilemma
【两旁】 liǎngpáng both sides; either side: 大街～挤满了欢迎的人群。The streets were lined with welcoming crowds.
【两栖】 liǎngqī ＜军＞ amphibious
◇ ～部队 amphibious forces; amphibious units/ ～动物 amphibious animal; amphibian
【两全】 liǎngquán be satisfactory to both parties; have regard for both sides: ～的办法 measures satisfactory to both sides (或 in both respects)
【两全其美】 liǎngquán qí měi satisfy both sides; satisfy rival claims
【两头】 liǎngtóu ① both ends; either end: ～尖 pointed at both ends/ ～儿跑 go back and forth between two places ② both parties; both sides: ～说情 intercede between two parties/ ～为难 find it hard to please either party; find it difficult to satisfy two conflicting demands/ ～落空 fall between two stools
【两下子】 liǎngxiàzi a few tricks of the trade: 要做好工作，光靠这～是不够的。If we are to do good work, we can't rely on just these few tricks of the trade./ 你真有～！You really are smart!
【两相情愿】 liǎng xiāng qíngyuàn both parties are willing
【两小无猜】 liǎng xiǎo wú cāi (of a boy and a girl) be innocent playmates
【两袖清风】 liǎng xiù qīngfēng ＜旧＞ (of an official) have clean hands; remain uncorrupted
【两样】 liǎngyàng different: ～做法，两种结果。Two different methods, two different results./ 有什么～？What's the difference?
【两用】 liǎngyòng dual purpose
【两院制】 liǎngyuànzhì two-chamber system; bicameral system; bicameralism
【两造】 liǎngzào ① ＜法＞ both parties in a lawsuit; both plaintiff and defendant ② ＜方＞ two crops: 改一年～为一年三造 change from two crops a year to three

俩 liǎng 见"伎俩" jìliǎng
另见 liǎ

魉 liǎng 见"魍魉" wǎngliǎng

liàng

亮 liàng ① bright; light: 那个灯泡很～。That electric bulb is very bright./ 天～了。It's light already./ 地板擦得真～。The floor has been scrubbed clean and shiny. ② shine: 屋子里～着灯光。Lights were shining in the room./ 他把手电筒～了一下。He flashed the torch on for a second. ③ loud and clear: 她的嗓子真～。She has a resonant voice./ ～起嗓子 lift one's voice ④ enlightened: 你这一说，

我心里头～了。I find what you say most enlightening.

【亮度】liàngdù 〈物〉brightness; brilliance: 星的～ the brightness of a star

【亮光】liàngguāng light: 一道～ a shaft of light ◇ ～漆 polish lacquer

【亮晶晶】liàngjīngjīng glittering; sparkling; glistening: ～的星星 glittering stars/ ～的露珠 glistening dewdrops

【亮相】liàngxiàng ①(of Beijing opera, dancing, etc.) strike a pose on the stage ②declare one's position; state one's views

凉 liàng make or become cool: 把开水～一～再喝。Let the water cool before you drink it.
另见 liáng

谅* liàng ①forgive; understand: 本着互～互让的精神 in the spirit of mutual understanding and mutual accommodation/ 尚希见～。I hope you will excuse me. ②I think; I suppose; I expect: 前信～已收到。I expect you have received my last letter./ ～他也不会这样做。I don't think he'd do that./ ～必如此。I think it must be so. 或 Presumably it is so.

【谅解】liàngjiě understand; make allowance for: 互相～ mutual understanding/ 达成～ reach an understanding

辆* liàng 〈量〉〔用于车〕: 一～公共汽车 a bus/ 三～大车 three carts

晾 liàng ①dry in the air; air: 草垫子该～一～了。The straw mattress needs to be aired. ②dry in the sun; sun: ～衣服 sun clothes; hang out the washing to dry/ 海滩上～着渔网。Fishnets are spread out on the beach to dry.

【晾干】liànggān dry by airing: 草药已经～了。The medicinal herbs are dry now.

量* liàng ①capacity: 酒～ capacity for liquor/ 他饭～大。He's a big eater. ②quantity; amount; volume: 保质保～ guarantee both quantity and quality/ 工业产～ the volume of industrial output ③estimate; measure: ～力 estimate one's own strength or ability (and act accordingly)
另见 liáng

【量才录用】liàng cái lùyòng give sb. work suited to his abilities; assign jobs to people according to their abilities

【量词】liàngcí 〈语〉classifier (as 个, 只, 次, 阵) ; measure word

【量力】liànglì estimate one's own strength or ability (and act accordingly): 不自～ overrate one's ability; overreach oneself

【量力而行】liànglì ér xíng do what one is capable of; act according to one's capability

【量入为出】liàng rù wéi chū keep expenditures within the limits of income; live within one's mean

【量体裁衣】liàng tǐ cái yī cut the garment according to the figure — act according to actual circumstances

踉 liàng

【踉跄】liàngqiàng stagger: ～而行 stagger along

liáo

辽 liáo ①distant; faraway

【辽阔】liáokuò vast; extensive: ～的土地 a vast expanse of land; vast territory

【辽远】liáoyuǎn distant; faraway: ～的边疆 distant frontier regions

疗* liáo treat; cure: 治～ treat (a patient); give medical care to/ 诊～ make a diagnosis and give treatment

【疗法】liáofǎ therapy; treatment: 化学～ chemotherapy/ 新针～ new acupuncture therapy

【疗养】liáoyǎng recuperate; convalesce ◇ ～院 sanatorium; convalescent hospital (或 home)

聊 liáo ①merely; just: ～表谢意 just a token of gratitude; just to show my appreciation ②a little; slightly: ～胜于无。It's better than nothing. ③〈口〉chat: 晚饭后我们～～。Let's have a chat after supper.

【聊备一格】liáo bèi yī gé may serve as a specimen

【聊天儿】liáotiānr 〈口〉chat

【聊以自慰】liáo yǐ zì wèi just to console oneself

寥 liáo ①few; scanty: ～～可数 just a sprinkling ②silent; deserted: 寂～ deserted and lonely

【寥廓】liáokuò boundless; vast: ～的天空 the boundless sky

【寥寥无几】liáoliáo wú jǐ very few

【寥落】liáoluò few and far between; sparse; scattered: 疏星～ only a few solitary stars twinkling in the sky

【寥若晨星】liáo ruò chénxīng as sparse as the morning stars; few and far between

僚 liáo ①official: 官～ official; bureaucrat ②an associate in office: 同～ colleague

寮 liáo small house; hut: 僧～ a monk's cell (或 hut)/ 茶～酒肆 teahouses and wineshops

【寮棚】liáopéng shed; hut

撩 liáo ①tease; tantalize ②provoke; stir up
另见 liào

【撩乱】liáoluàn 见"缭乱" liáoluàn

嘹 liáo

【嘹亮】liáoliàng resonant; loud and clear: 歌声～。The singing is loud and clear./ ～的号角 a clarion call

獠 liáo

【獠牙】liáoyá long, sharp, protruding teeth: 青面～ be green-faced and long-toothed; have fiendish features

缭 liáo ①entangled ②sew with slanting stitches: ～贴边 stitch a hem; hem

【缭乱】liáoluàn confused; in a turmoil: 心绪～ in a confused state of mind/ 眼花～ be dazzled

【缭绕】liáorào curl up; wind around: 炊烟～ smoke curling up from kitchen chimneys/ 歌声～。The song lingered in the air.

燎 liáo burn

【燎原】liáoyuán set the prairie ablaze: ～烈火 a blazing prairie fire

liǎo

了* liǎo ①know clearly; understand: 明～ understand ②end; finish; settle; dispose of: 没完没～ endless/ 未～之事 unfinished task; an unsettled matter/ 好吧! 这事儿就这样～啦。All right, so that's that. ③〔放在动词之后, 与"得""不"连用, 表示可能〕办得～ can manage it / 受不～ cannot stand sth./ 你来得～来不～? Will you be able to come? ④〈书〉〔多用于否定〕entirely: ～无惧色 not show a trace of fear; look completely undaunted
另见 le

【了不得】liǎobude ①terrific; extraordinary: 一下子歼灭敌人两个师, 真～! It's really terrific to have wiped out two enemy divisions at one blow./ 一件～的大事 a matter of the utmost importance/ 高兴得～ extremely happy ②terrible; awful: 可～啦, 他昏过去了! Good God! He's fainted./ 危险是有的, 但并不是那么～。There was danger, but it wasn't so serious.

【了不起】liǎobuqǐ amazing; terrific; extraordinary: ～的成就 an amazing achievement

【了得】liǎode 〔用于句尾, 常跟在"还"字后面, 表示情况严重〕哎呀! 这还～! Oh! How outrageous (或 terrible, awful)!/

过去要是遇到这样的大旱，那还～！ How terrible such a drought would have been in the past!

【了结】 liǎojié finish; settle; wind up; bring to an end: ～一场纠纷 settle a dispute; end a conflict

【了解】 liǎojiě ① understand; comprehend: ～事物发展的规律 understand the laws of development of things/ ～会议的重要意义 grasp the significance of the conference/ 增进两国人民之间的～ promote understanding between the two peoples/ 部长对钻井队工人的思想和生活都很～。 The minister has an intimate understanding of how the workers of the drilling teams live and work and what they think. ② find out; acquaint oneself with: 我们必须设法～全部情况。 We must try to find out about the whole situation./ ～国内外技术发展状况 keep abreast of current developments in technology at home and abroad

【了了】 liǎoliǎo 〈书〉 know clearly: 不甚～ not be too clear (about sth.); not know much (about sth.)/ 为仇为友，～分明。 It is perfectly clear who are our friends and who are our foes.

【了却】 liǎoquè settle; solve: 这就～了我的一桩心事。 That settled a matter which had been weighing on my mind.

【了然】 liǎorán understand; be clear: 一目～ be clear at a glance

【了如指掌】 liǎo rú zhǐ zhǎng know sth. like the palm of one's hand; have sth. at one's fingertips: 他对这一带的地形～。 He knows the terrain of this locality like the back of his hand.

【了事】 liǎoshì dispose of a matter; get sth. over: 草草～ get through sth. in a careless or perfunctory way; rush through sth.

潦 liǎo

【潦草】 liǎocǎo ① (of handwriting) hasty and careless; illegible ② sloppy; slovenly: 干活儿～ work in a slipshod way

【潦倒】 liǎodǎo be frustrated: 穷愁～ be penniless and frustrated; be down and out

liào

了* liào watch from a height or a distance
另见 le; liǎo

【了望】 liàowàng watch from a height or a distance; keep a lookout: 用望远镜～敌军阵地 look at the enemy's position through field glasses ◇ ～台 observation tower; lookout tower

料* liào ① expect; anticipate: 不出所～ as was expected/ ～定敌军会有行动 anticipate movements on the part of the enemy ② material; stuff: 原～ raw material/ 燃～ fuel/ ～备足了没有! Have we got enough material? ③ (grain) feed: 多给牲口加点～。 Put more grain in the fodder. ④〈多含贬义〉 makings; stuff: 我不是唱歌的～。 I haven't got the makings of a singer./ 他这块～，干不了大事儿。 A person like him can't do anything big.

【料到】 liàodào foresee; expect: 没～他会来。 We didn't expect him to come./ 我们克服了许多没有～的困难。 We overcame many unforeseen difficulties.

【料理】 liàolǐ arrange; manage; attend to; take care of: ～家务 manage household affairs/ ～后事 make arrangements for a funeral/ 孩子们已能自己～生活。 The children can take care of themselves now.

【料事如神】 liào shì rú shén predict like a prophet; foretell with miraculous accuracy

【料想】 liàoxiǎng expect; think; presume: 真是～不到的事情！ Who would have thought that would happen!

【料子】 liàozi ① material for making clothes ② 〈方〉 woollen fabric: ～裤 trousers made of woollen fabric

廖 Liào a surname

镣 liào fetters

【镣铐】 liàokào fetters and handcuffs; shackles; irons; chains: 戴上～ be shackled; be in chains

liě

咧 liě

【咧嘴】 liězuǐ grin: 疼得直～ grin with pain/ 他咧着嘴笑。 His face broadened into a grin.

liè

列* liè ① arrange; line up: 排～成行 arrange in a row or column/ ～队欢迎 line up to welcome sb./ ～出理由 set out one's reasons (for sth.)/ ～表 arrange (facts, figures, etc.) in tables or columns; tabulate/ 入甲等 be classified as first-rate; be rated as class A ② list; enter in a list: 代表姓名～后。 Listed below are the names of the delegates./ ～入议程 be placed on the agenda/ 名～前茅 be among the best of the successful candidates ③ row; file; rank: 站在最前～ stand in the forefront ④ 〈量〉〈用于成行列的事物〉: 一～火车 a train ⑤ kind; sort: 不在讨论之～ not among the subjects to be discussed ⑥ various; each and every: ～国 various countries

【列举】 lièjǔ enumerate; list: ～大量事实 cite numerous facts/ 计划中～了各种具体办法。 Various concrete measures were enumerated in the plan.

【列强】 lièqiáng big powers

【列席】 lièxí attend (a meeting) as a nonvoting delegate ◇ ～代表 delegate without the right to vote; nonvoting delegate

劣* liè bad; inferior; of low quality: 难分优～ very hard to tell which is better

【劣等】 lièděng of inferior quality; low-grade; poor

【劣根性】 lièqēnxìng deep-rooted bad habits

【劣马】 lièmǎ ① inferior horse; nag ② vicious horse; fiery steed

【劣势】 lièshì inferior strength or position: 敌军已处于绝对～。 The enemy forces were reduced to absolute inferiority.

【劣质】 lièzhì of poor (或 low) quality; inferior: ～煤 inferior coal; faulty coal

【劣种】 lièzhǒng inferior strain (或 breed, stock)

冽 liè 〈书〉 cold: 凛～ piercingly cold

烈* liè ① strong; violent; intense: ～酒 a strong drink/ ～焰 a roaring blaze ② staunch; upright; stern: 刚～ fiery and forthright; upright and unyielding ③ sacrificing oneself for a just cause: 先～ martyr/ 壮～牺牲 die heroically; die a heroic death

【烈度】 lièdù intensity: 地震～ earthquake intensity

【烈风】 lièfēng 〈气〉 strong gale

【烈火】 lièhuǒ raging fire; raging flames

【烈火见真金】 lièhuǒ jiàn zhēnjīn pure gold proves its worth in a blazing fire—people of worth show their mettle during trials and tribulations

【烈日】 lièrì burning sun; scorching sun: ～当空 with the scorching sun directly overhead

【烈士】 lièshì ① martyr: 革命～ revolutionary martyrs ② a person of high endeavour: ～暮年，壮心不已。 The heart of a hero in his old age is as stout as ever. 或 A noble-hearted man retains his high aspirations even in old age. ◇ ～纪念碑 a monument to martyrs/ ～墓 the grave of a martyr

【烈性】 lièxìng ① spirited: ～汉子 a man of character ② strong: ～酒 a strong (或 stiff) drink; hard liquor; spirits/ ～毒药 deadly poison/ ～炸药 high explosive

【烈性子】 lièxìngzi ① fiery disposition ② spitfire

捩 liè twist; turn: 转～点 turning point

猎 *　liè hunt: ~虎 tiger hunting/ 从事渔~ engage in fishing and hunting

【猎场】 lièchǎng hunting ground; hunting field

【猎狗】 liègǒu hunting dog; hound

【猎奇】 lièqí hunt for novelty; seek novelty

【猎枪】 lièqiāng shotgun; fowling piece; hunting rifle

【猎取】 lièqǔ ① hunt: 原始社会的人用粗糙的石器~野兽。Primitive man hunted wild animals with crude stone implements. ② pursue; seek; hunt for: ~个人名利 pursue personal fame and gain/ ~廉价的声誉 make a bid for cheap popularity

【猎人】 lièrén hunter; huntsman

裂 *　liè split; crack; rend: 分~ split; break up/ ~成两半 be rent in two/ 杯子~了。The cup's cracked./ 他的手冻~了。His hands are chapped by the cold.

【裂缝】 lièfèng rift; crevice; crack; fissure: 墙上的~ crevices in a wall

【裂痕】 lièhén rift; crack; fissure: 这块玻璃有一道~。There is a crack in the glass.

【裂开】 lièkāi split open; rend

【裂口】 lièkǒu ① breach; gap; split ② <地> vent ◇ ~火山锥 breached cone

lín

邻 *　lín ① neighbour: 近~ a close neighbour ② neighbouring; near; adjacent: ~县 a neighbouring county/ ~座 an adjacent seat

【邻邦】 línbāng neighbouring country: 我们两国历来是友好的~。Our two countries have always been good neighbours.

【邻接】 línjiē border on; be next to; be contiguous to; adjoin: 西班牙~法国西南部。Spain borders on the southwest of France./ 化肥厂~农机厂。The chemical fertilizer plant adjoins the farm machinery plant.

【邻近】 línjìn near; close to; adjacent to: ~没有医院。There's no hospital in the neighbourhood.

【邻居】 línjū neighbour: 隔壁~.a next-door neighbour

【邻里】 línlǐ ① neighbourhood ② people of the neighbourhood; neighbours

【邻舍】 línshè <方> neighbour

林 *　lín ① forest; woods; grove: 松~ pine forest/ 竹~ bamboo grove ② circles: 艺~ art circles ③ forestry

【林立】 línlì stand in great numbers (like trees in a forest): 港口樯橹~。There is a forest of masts in the harbour.

【林木】 línmù ① forest; woods: ~葱郁 densely wooded ② <林> forest tree

【林荫道】 línyīndào boulevard; avenue

临 *　lín ① face; overlook: ~街的窗子 a window overlooking the street/ 东~大海 border on the sea in the east/ 如~大敌 as if confronted with a formidable enemy ② be present: 亲~指导 come personally to give guidance/ 双喜~门。A double blessing has descended upon the house. ③ on the point of; just before; be about to: ~行 on the point of leaving; on the eve of departure/ ~睡 just before going to bed; at bedtime/ ~刑 just before execution ④ copy (a model of calligraphy or painting): ~画 copy a painting/ ~帖 practise calligraphy after a model

【临本】 línběn copy (of a painting, etc.)

【临别】 línbié at parting; just before parting: ~赠言 words of advice at parting; parting advice/ 作为~纪念 as a parting souvenir

【临产】 línchǎn about to give birth; parturient ◇ ~阵痛 labour pains; birth pangs

【临床】 línchuáng <医> clinical: 有丰富的~经验 have rich clinical experience

【临到】 líndào ① just before; on the point of: ~开会, 她还在准备发言。She was still preparing her speech when

the meeting began. ② befall; happen to: 这事如果~你的头上, 你怎么办? What would you do if it happened to you?

【临机】 línjī <书> as the occasion requires: ~应变 adapt to changing circumstances; cope with any contingency

【临近】 línjìn close to; close on: ~黎明 close on daybreak

【临盆】 línpén be giving birth to a child; be confined; be in labour

【临时】 línshí ① at the time when sth. happens: 事先作好准备, 免得~忙乱。Arrange everything in advance so that you won't be in a rush at the last moment. ② temporary; provisional; for a short time: ~工作人员 a temporary member of the staff/ ~凑合 make do for the moment/ ~办法 a temporary arrangement; makeshift measures

【临时抱佛脚】 línshí bào fójiǎo embrace Buddha's feet in one's hour of need; seek help at the last moment; make a frantic last-minute effort

【临死】 línsǐ on one's deathbed

【临头】 líntóu befall; happen: 大祸~。Disaster is imminent./ 事到~, 我们要冷静。Now that the critical moment has come, we must keep cool.

【临危】 línwēi ① be dying (from illness) ② facing death or deadly peril; in the hour of danger: ~不惧 face danger fearlessly; betray no fear in an hour of danger

【临行】 línxíng before leaving; on departure: ~匆匆, 不及告别。I left in such a hurry that I didn't have time to say goodbye.

【临渊羡鱼】 lín yuān xiàn yú stand on the edge of a pool and idly long for fish: ~, 不如退而结网。It's better to go back and make a net than to stand by the pond and long for fish — one should take practical steps to achieve one's aims.

【临阵磨枪】 línzhèn mó qiāng sharpen one's spear only before going into battle — start to prepare only at the last moment

【临阵脱逃】 línzhèn tuōtáo desert on the eve of a battle; sneak away at a critical juncture

【临终】 línzhōng approaching one's end; immediately before one's death; on one's deathbed: ~遗言 deathbed testament; last words

淋 *　lín pour; drench: 日晒雨~ sun-scorched and rain-drenched; exposed to the elements/ 浑身都~湿了 be drenched from head to foot

【淋漓】 línlí ① dripping wet: 大汗~ dripping with sweat/ 鲜血~ dripping with blood ② (of a piece of writing or a speech) free from inhibition: 痛快~ impassioned and forceful

【淋漓尽致】 línlí jìn zhì incisively and vividly; thoroughly: 刻画得~ portray most vividly/ 揭露得~ make a most telling exposure/ 他这番表演, 真可谓~。He put on an act, which showed him up completely.

【淋淋】 línlín dripping: 湿~的衣服 dripping clothes

【淋浴】 línyù shower bath; shower

琳 lín <书> beautiful jade

【琳琅】 línláng beautiful jade; gem

【琳琅满目】 línláng mǎnmù a superb collection of beautiful things; a feast for the eyes: 展品~, 美不胜收。One is dazzled by the endless array of beautiful exhibits. 或 The exhibition is a feast for the eyes.

遴 lín

【遴选】 línxuǎn <书> select sb. for a post; select; choose

嶙 lín

【嶙峋】 línxún <书> ① (of mountain rocks, cliffs, etc.) jagged; rugged; craggy: 怪石~ jagged rocks of grotesque shapes ② (of a person) bony; thin

霖 lín continuous heavy rain: 甘~ good soaking rain; timely rain

【霖雨】 línyǔ continuous heavy rain

lín

鳞 lín ① scale(of fish, etc.) ② like the scales of a fish: 遍体~伤 be covered with bruises or injuries; be a mass of bruises

【鳞次栉比】 líncì-zhìbǐ (of houses, etc.) row upon row of: 码头上新建的仓库~。 Row upon row of newly built warehouses line the docks.

【鳞甲】 línjiǎ scale and shell (of reptiles and arthropods)

【鳞片】 línpiàn ① scale (of fish, etc.) ② 〈植〉 bud scale

麟 lín 见"麒麟" qílín

lǐn

凛 lǐn ① cold ② strict; stern; severe: ~遵 strictly abide by ③ afraid; apprehensive: ~于远行 be afraid of going on a long journey

【凛凛】 lǐnlǐn ① cold: 寒风~ a piercing wind ② stern; awe-inspiring: 威风~ majestic-looking; awe-inspiring

【凛然】 lǐnrán stern; awe-inspiring: 正气~ awe-inspiring righteousness/ 态度~ stern in manner

lìn

吝 lìn stingy; mean; closefisted

【吝啬】 lìnsè stingy; niggardly; miserly; mean ◇ ~鬼 miser; niggard; skinflint

【吝惜】 lìnxī grudge; stint: 不~自己的力量 spare no effort; stint no effort

赁 lìn rent; hire: 房屋出~ house to let/ ~费 rent; rental

躏 lìn 见"蹂躏" róulìn

líng

〇 líng zero: 三~六号 No. 306 (number three-oh-six)/ 一九八~年 1980 (nineteen eighty)

伶 líng 〈旧〉 actor or actress

【伶仃】 língdīng left alone without help; lonely: 孤苦~ alone and uncared for

【伶俐】 línglì clever; bright; quick-witted: 这孩子真~! What a clever child!

【伶牙俐齿】 língyá-lìchǐ have the gift of the gab; have a glib tongue

灵 líng ① quick; clever; sharp: 耳朵很~ have sharp ears/ 心~手巧 quick-witted and nimble-fingered; clever and deft ② efficacious; effective: ~药 an effective remedy/ 我们试了一下,果然很~。 We tried it out and it really worked. ③ spirit; intelligence: 心~ the mind; the soul/ 英~ the spirit of the brave departed ④ fairy; sprite; elf: ~怪 elf; goblin ⑤ (remains) of the deceased; bier: 守~ stand as guards at the bier; keep vigil beside the bier/ ~前摆着花圈。 Wreaths were laid in front of the coffin.

【灵车】 língchē hearse

【灵丹妙药】 língdān-miàoyào miraculous cure; panacea

【灵感】 línggǎn inspiration

【灵魂】 línghún soul; spirit: ~深处 in one's innermost soul; in the depth of one's soul/ 出卖~ sell one's soul (to the enemy, etc.)

【灵活】 línghuó ① nimble; agile; quick: 手脚~ dexterous and quick in action/ 脑筋~ be quick-witted; have a supple mind ② flexible; elastic: ~机动的战略战术 flexible strategy and tactics ◇ ~性 flexibility; adaptability; mobility

【灵机】 língjī sudden inspiration; brainwave: 她~一动,想出了一个好办法。 She had a brainwave and found a good solution.

【灵柩】 língjiù a coffin containing a corpse; bier

【灵敏】 língmǐn sensitive; keen; agile; acute: ~的嗅觉 an acute sense of smell/ 这架仪器很~。 This instrument is highly sensitive.

【灵巧】 língqiǎo dexterous; nimble; skilful; ingenious: 一双~的手 a pair of clever hands/ 做得真~。 It's really ingeniously made./ 她的体操动作准确而~。 Her movements in callisthenics were precise and nimble.

【灵通】 língtōng having quick access to information; well-informed: 消息~人士 well-informed sources

【灵性】 língxìng intelligence (of animals): 这匹马很有~,能领会主人的意图。 This horse is very intelligent. He can sense what the rider wants.

【灵验】 língyàn ① efficacious; effective: 这药非常~。 This medicine is highly efficacious. ② (of a prediction, etc.) accurate; right: 天气预报果然~。 The weather forecast turned out to be accurate.

囹 líng

【囹圄】 língyǔ 〈书〉 jail; prison: 身入~ be behind prison bars; be thrown into prison

玲 líng

【玲珑】 línglóng ① (of things) ingeniously and delicately wrought; exquisite: 小巧~ small and exquisite ② (of people) clever and nimble: 娇小~ petite and dainty

凌 líng ① insult: 盛气~人 arrogant and aggressive ② approach: ~晨 before dawn ③ rise high; tower aloft: ~霄 reach the clouds ④ 〈方〉 ice: 冰~ icicle

【凌晨】 língchén in the small hours; before dawn: 七月三日~ in the small hours of July 3/ 火车将于明日~四时半到达。 The train arrives at half past four tomorrow morning.

【凌驾】 língjià place oneself above; override: ~一切 overriding; predominant

【凌空】 língkōng be high up in the air; soar or tower aloft: 铁路桥~飞架两山之间。 High up in the air, a railway bridge spans the valley./ 飞机~而过。 The plane streaked across the sky.

【凌厉】 línglì swift and fierce: 攻势~ a swift and fierce attack

【凌乱】 língluàn in disorder; in a mess: ~不堪 in a fearful mess; in a state of utter confusion

【凌辱】 língrǔ insult; humiliate: 受到~ be humiliated; suffer humiliation

【凌云】 língyún 〈书〉 reach the clouds; soar to the skies: 壮志~ (cherish) high aspirations

铃* líng ① bell: 门~ door bell ② anything in the shape of a bell: 哑~ dumbbell ③ boll; bud: 棉~ cotton boll

陵 líng ① hill; mound: ~谷 hills and valleys ② imperial tomb; mausoleum: 中山~ the Sun Yat-sen Mausoleum

【陵墓】 língmù mausoleum; tomb

羚 líng antelope

【羚羊】 língyáng antelope; gazelle: 大~ oryx ◇ ~角 〈中药〉 antelope's horn

聆 líng 〈书〉 listen; hear: ~教 hear your words of wisdom

【聆听】 língtīng listen (respectfully)

菱 líng 〈植〉 ling; water chestnut; water caltrop

【菱形】 língxíng rhombus; lozenge

翎 líng plume; tail feather; quill: 孔雀~ peacock plumes; peacock feathers

绫 líng a silk fabric resembling satin but thinner; damask silk: ~罗绸缎 silks and satins

零＊ líng ① zero sign (0); nought: 五~六号 No. 506 (number five-oh-six)/ ~点一三 0.03 (point nought three) ②〔放在两个数量之间，表示较大的量之下附有较小的量〕: 一年一三天 a year and three days/一块一五分 one dollar and five cents ③ odd; with a little extra: 年纪六十有~ a little more than sixty years old/ 到会人数五百挂~儿。 Five hundred odd were present at the meeting. ④ nought; zero; nil: 一减一等于~。 One minus one leaves nought (或 zero)./ 我在这方面的知识几乎等于~。 My knowledge of the subject is practically nil. ⑤ zero (on a thermometer): 摄氏下十度 10 degrees below zero centigrade; minus ten degrees centigrade ⑥ fractional; part: 化整为~ break up the whole into parts ⑦ wither and fall: 凋~ withered, fallen and scattered about ⑧ 〈体〉 nil; love: 一比一 no score; love all/ 上半场的比分是二比~。 The score at half-time was two-nil (或 two-nothing).

【零吃】língchī 〈口〉 between-meal nibble
【零度】língdù zero: 气温降到~。 The (atomospheric) temperature has fallen to zero./ ~以下 below zero; sub-zero
【零工】línggōng ① odd job; short-term hired labour: 打~ do odd jobs ② odd-job man; casual labourer
【零件】língjiàn spare parts; spares
【零落】língluò ① withered and fallen: 草木~ bare trees and withered grass ② decayed: 凄凉~ a desolate scene ③ scattered; sporadic: ~的枪声 sporadic shooting; scattered reports of gunfire
【零卖】língmài ① retail; sell retail ② sell by the piece or in small quantities: 这些茶具成套出售,不~。 These tea things are sold by the set, not separately.
【零钱】língqián ① small change: 劳驾,把这十块钱换成~。 Please give me small change for this ten dollar note. ② pocket money
【零散】língsan scattered: 桌子上~地放着几本书。 Several books lie scattered on the desk./ 把~的情况凑到一块儿 piece together scraps of information
【零时】língshí zero hour
【零食】língshí between-meal nibbles; snacks: 吃~ nibble between meals
【零售】língshòu retail; sell retail
◇ ~店 retail shop; retail store/ ~额 turnover (from retail trade)/ ~价格 retail price/ ~网 retail network/ ~总额 total volume of retail sales
【零数】língshù remainder; fractional amount
【零碎】língsuì ① scrappy; fragmentary; piecemeal: ~活儿 odd jobs/ ~东西 odds and ends/我们收集的材料还是~的。 The material we have collected is still fragmentary./ 他每天有很多~事要办。 Every day he has all sorts of things to attend to. ② odds and ends; oddments; bits and pieces: 她正在拾掇~儿。 She is tidying up the odds and ends.
【零星】língxīng ① fragmentary; odd; piecemeal: ~材料 fragmentary material/ ~土地 odd pieces of land/ 一些零零星星的消息 some odd scraps of news ② scattered; sporadic: ~小雨 occasional drizzles; scattered showers/ ~战斗 sporadic fighting
【零用】língyòng ① small incidental expenses ② pocket money
◇ ~费 petty cash/ ~钱 pocket money

龄＊ líng ① age; years: 年~ age/ 高~ advanced in years/ 学~儿童 school-age children ② length of time; duration: 工~ length of service; number of years worked; years of service

líng

岭 líng ① mountain range: 大(小)兴安~ the Greater (Lesser) Xing'an Mountains ② mountain; ridge: 翻山越~ cross over mountain after mountain/ 崇山峻~ high mountain ridges

领＊ lǐng ① neck: 引~而望 crane one's neck for a look; eagerly look forward to ② collar; neckband: 把大衣儿翻起来 turn up one's coat collar/ 尖~儿 V-shaped collar ③ outline; main point: 要~ main points; essentials ④ 〈量〉: 一~席 a mat ⑤ lead; usher: ~兵打仗 lead troops into battle/ 把客人~到餐厅去 usher the guests into the dining hall/ ~我们参观学校 show us round the school ⑥ have jurisdiction over; be in possession of: ~土 territory ⑦ receive; draw; get: ~奖 receive a prize (或 an award)/ ~养老金 draw one's pension ⑧ understand; comprehend; grasp: 心~神会 understand tacitly; readily take a hint

【领班】lǐngbān 〈旧〉 gaffer; foreman
【领唱】lǐngchàng ① lead a chorus ② leading singer (of a chorus)
【领带】lǐngdài necktie; tie ◇ ~扣针 tiepin
【领导】lǐngdǎo ① lead; exercise leadership: 担任~工作 shoulder the responsibility of leadership; hold a leading position ② leadership
【领队】lǐngduì ① lead a group ② the leader of a group, sports team, etc.
【领港】lǐnggǎng ① pilot a ship into or out of a harbour; pilot ② (harbour) pilot
【领海】lǐnghǎi territorial waters; territorial sea
【领航】lǐngháng ① navigate; pilot ② navigator; pilot ◇ ~飞机 pathfinder aircraft/ ~设备 navigation equipment/ ~员 navigator
【领会】lǐnghuì understand; comprehend; grasp: ~文件的精神 grasp the essence of a document
【领教】lǐngjiào ① 〈套〉〔用于接受人的教益或欣赏人的表演时〕 thanks; much obliged: ~你说得很对,~~ You're quite right. Thanks for your advice. ② ask advice: 你有什么新的看法? 我想~~。 Have you some new ideas on the subject? If so, I'd very much like to hear them. ③〈讽〉 experience; encounter: 他们的伎俩,我们早就~过了。 We've had experience of their tricks.
【领结】lǐngjié bow tie
【领巾】lǐngjīn scarf; neckerchief: 红~ red scarf
【领空】lǐngkōng territorial sky(或 air); territorial air space
【领口】lǐngkǒu ① collarband; neckband: 这件毛衣~太小。 The neckband of the sweater is too small. ② the place where the two ends of a collar meet
【领款】lǐngkuǎn draw money
◇ ~人 payee
【领路】lǐnglù lead the way
【领略】lǐnglüè have a taste of; realize; appreciate: ~川菜风味 taste Sichuan dishes
【领情】lǐngqíng feel grateful to sb.; appreciate the kindness: 朋友们的好意,我十分~。 I'm very grateful to you friends for your kindness./ 你的心意我~,但是礼物不能收。 I appreciate your kindness but I can't accept your gift.
【领取】lǐngqǔ draw; receive: ~工资 draw one's pay/ ~办公用品 get stationery for use in the office/ ~出入证 receive one's pass
【领事】lǐngshì 〈外〉 consul: 总~ consul general/ 副~ vice-consul/ 代理~ pro-consul
◇ ~裁判权 consular jurisdiction/ ~处 consular section/ ~馆 consulate/ ~条例 consular act
【领受】lǐngshòu accept (kindness, etc.); receive: 她怀着激动的心情~了朋友的慰问。 She was deeply moved by her friends' comforting words.
【领土】lǐngtǔ territory: 保卫国家的~完整 safeguard a country's territorial integrity
【领悟】lǐngwù comprehend; grasp
【领先】lǐngxiān be in the lead; lead: 遥遥~ hold a safe lead/ 客队~五分。 The visiting team led by five points./ 前半场球赛二比一,法国队~。 The score at half-time stood at 2:1 in favour of the French Team./ 她~登上了山顶。 She was the first to reach the top of the hill
【领袖】lǐngxiù leader
【领养】lǐngyǎng adopt (a child)
【领域】lǐngyù ① territory; domain; realm ② field; sphere;

domain; realm: 社会科学～ the domain of the social sciences

lìng

另* lìng other; another; separate: ～想办法 try to find some other way/ ～有打算 have other plans/ ～搞一套 do what suits oneself; go one's own way/ ～立户口 open another (或 a separate) bank account/ 从一个极端跳到另一个极端 jump from one extreme to another/ ～行安排 make separate arrangements/ 会议改期,时间～行通知。The meeting is postponed till further notice.

【另寄】lìngjì post separately; post under separate cover 又作"另邮"

【另起炉灶】lìng qǐ lúzào set up a separate kitchen — make a fresh start; start all over again

【另请高明】lìng qǐng gāomíng find someone better qualified (than myself)

【另外】lìngwài in addition; moreover; besides

【另眼相看】lìng yǎn xiāng kàn ① regard (或 look up to) sb. with special respect ② view sb. in a new, more favourable light; see sb. in a new light

令* lìng ① command; order; decree: 下～ issue an order/ 法～ laws and decrees ② make; cause: ～人满意 satisfactory; satisfying/ ～人鼓舞 heartening; inspiring; encouraging/ ～人深思 make one ponder; provide food for thought/ ～人作呕 make one sick; nauseating; revolting ③ season: 当～ in season/ 夏～时ãng summer time ④ an ancient official title: 县～ county magistrate ⑤〈书〉good; excellent: ～名 good name; reputation ⑥〈敬〉your: ～尊 your father/ ～堂 your mother/ ～爱 your daughter/ ～郎 your son ⑦ drinking game: 行酒～ play a drinking game

liū

溜 liū ① slide; glide: 从山坡上～下来 slide down a slope ② smooth: ～光 very smooth/ 滑～ slippery ③ sneak off; slip away: ～掉 sneak off; slip away/ 从后门～出去 slip out through the back door

【溜冰】liūbīng ① skating ②〈方〉roller-skating ◇ ～场 skating rink

【溜达】liūda〈口〉stroll; saunter; go for a walk: 他在河边来回～。He sauntered up and down the river bank./ 吃完饭出去～～吧。Let's go for a stroll after the meal.

【溜之大吉】liū zhī dàjí make oneself scarce; sneak away; slink off

liú

刘 Liú a surname

浏 liú〈书〉① (of water) clear; limpid ② (of wind) swift

【浏览】liúlǎn glance over; skim through; browse: 这本书我只一过一遍。I've only skimmed through (或 glanced over) the book./ ～各种报章杂志 browse among newspapers and magazines

流* liú ① flow: 江水东～。The river flows east./ 农村人口～入城市 flow of rural population into urban areas/ 伤口～脓。The wound is festering./ ～鼻涕 have a running nose/ ～涎 water at the mouth; slaver; slobber/ ～汗 perspire; sweat/ ～泪 shed tears ② moving from place to place; drifting; wandering: ～民 refugees ③ spread; circulate: ～传甚广 spread far and wide ④ change for the worse; degenerate: ～于形式 become a mere formality ⑤ banish; send into exile ⑥ stream of water: 中～ midstream/ 河～ river/ 逆～而上 sail against the current ⑦ sth. resembling a stream of water; current: 气～ air current/ 电～ electric current ⑧ class; rate; grade: 第一～作品 a first-rate (literary) work

【流弊】liúbì corrupt practices; abuses

【流产】liúchǎn ①〈医〉abortion; miscarriage: 人工～ induced abortion/ 习惯性～ habitual abortion ② miscarry; fall through: 他的计划～了。His project miscarried.

【流畅】liúchàng easy and smooth: 文笔～ write with ease and grace/ 这篇文章读起来很～。The essay reads very smoothly.

【流传】liúchuán spread; circulate; hand down: 古代～来的寓言 fables handed down from ancient times

【流弹】liúdàn stray bullet

【流动】liúdòng ① flow: 溪水缓缓地～。The brook flowed sluggishly. ② going from place to place; on the move; mobile: 放映队常年在农村～。Film projection teams are always on the move in the countryside.

【流毒】liúdú ① exert a pernicious (或 baneful) influence: ～甚广 exert a widespread pernicious influence ② pernicious influence; baneful influence

【流芳百世】liúfāng bǎishì leave a good name for a hundred generations; leave a reputation which will go down to posterity

【流放】liúfàng ① banish; send into exile ② float (logs) downstream

【流浪】liúlàng roam about; lead a vagrant life: ～街头 roam the streets ◇ ～儿 waif; street urchin/ ～汉 tramp; vagrant

【流离失所】liúlí shī suǒ become destitute and homeless; be forced to leave home and wander about

【流利】liúlì fluent; smooth: 文章写得～ The article reads smoothly./ 她说一口～的英语。She speaks fluent English.

【流连忘返】liúlián wàng fǎn enjoy oneself so much as to forget to go home; linger on, forgetting to return

【流露】liúlù reveal; betray; show unintentionally: 真情的～ a revelation of one's true feelings

【流落】liúluò wander about destitute: ～他乡 wander destitute far from home

【流氓】liúmáng ① rogue; hoodlum; hooligan; gangster ② immoral (或 indecent) behaviour; hooliganism; indecency: 耍～ behave like a hoodlum; take liberties with women; act indecently

【流年】liúnián〈书〉① fleeting time: 似水～ time passing swiftly like flowing water ② (in fortune-telling) prediction of a person's luck in a given year: ～不利 an unlucky year

【流派】liúpài school; sect: 学术～ schools of thought

【流沙】liúshā drift sand; quicksand; shifting sand

【流失】liúshī run off; be washed away: 水土～ loss of water and erosion of soil; soil erosion/ 黄金储备～ drain on gold reserves/ 堵住管道的漏洞,不让石油～ stop up the leaks in the pipe so that no oil will seep through

【流逝】liúshì (of time) pass; elapse: 随着时间的～ with the passage of time

【流通】liútōng circulate: 空气(货币、商品)～ circulation of air (money, commodities)

【流亡】liúwáng be forced to leave one's native land; go into exile ◇ ～政府 government-in-exile

【流星】liúxīng ①〈天〉meteor; shooting star ② an ancient weapon, composed of two iron balls fixed on a long iron chain ③〈杂技〉meteors: 火～ fire-meteors/ 水～ water-meteors

【流行】liúxíng prevalent; popular; fashionable; in vogue: 这是当时～的论调。This argument was prevalent at the time./ 这个民歌在北部很～。This folk song is very popular in the north.

【流行病】liúxíngbìng epidemic disease

【流行性】liúxíngxìng〈医〉epidemic ◇ ～感冒 influenza; flu

【流血】liúxuè bleed; shed blood

【流言】liúyán rumour; gossip: 散布～ spread rumours/ 飞语 rumours and slanders

【流域】 liúyù valley; river basin; drainage area: 黄河～ the Huanghe River valley (或 basin) ◇ ～面积 drainage area

留* liú ① remain; stay: 你～在原地。Stay where you are./ 会后支部书记～一下。Will branch secretaries please remain after the meeting. ② ask sb. to stay; keep sb. where he is: 他们一定要～我们吃午饭。They pressed us to stay for lunch./ 那我就不～你了。In that case I won't keep you any longer. ③ reserve; keep; save: ～座位 reserve a seat for sb./ ～饭 save food for sb./ ～作储备粮 set aside some grain for reserve/ 这本书是我给你～着的。I've kept this book for you. ④ let grow; grow; wear: ～胡子 grow a beard (或 moustache)/ ～小辫儿 wear plaits; wear one's hair in plaits/ ～短头发 wear one's hair short; have short hair; have bobbed hair ⑤ accept; take: 把礼物～下 accept a present ⑥ leave: 给她～个条 leave a note for her/ 这次参观给我们～下了深刻的印象。The visit made a deep impression on us.
【留班】 liúbān 〈口〉(of pupils, etc.) fail to go up to the next grade; stay down
【留步】 liúbù 〈套〉don't bother to see me out; don't bother to come any further
【留存】 liúcún ① preserve; keep: 此稿～ keep this copy on file ② remain; be extant
【留得青山在, 不愁没柴烧】 liúdé qīngshān zài, bù chóu méi chái shāo as long as the green mountains are there, one need not worry about firewood
【留后路】 liú hòulù keep a way open for retreat; leave a way out: 给自己留条后路 leave oneself a way out; leave oneself an option
【留话】 liúhuà leave a message; leave word
【留级】 liújí (of pupils, etc.) fail to go up to the next grade (或 year); repeat the year's work; stay down
【留恋】 liúliàn ① be reluctant to leave (a place); can't bear to part (from sb. or with sth.): 临毕业时, 同学们对学校都十分～。As their graduation day drew near, the students felt reluctant to leave their school. ② recall with nostalgia: ～过去 yearn for the past
【留念】 liúniàn accept or keep as a souvenir
【留情】 liúqíng show mercy or forgiveness: 对敌人毫不～ show the enemy no mercy; give the enemy no quarter
【留任】 liúrèn retain a post; remain (或 continue) in office
【留神】 liúshén be careful; take care: 过马路要～。Be careful when you cross the street./ ～, 汽车来了! Mind the car!
【留守】 liúshǒu stay behind to take care of things; stay behind for garrison or liaison duty (after the main force has left)
【留宿】 liúsù ① put up a guest for the night ② stay overnight; put up for the night
【留心】 liúxīn be careful; take care: ～别写错了。Mind you don't write it wrong./ ～听讲 listen attentively to a lecture
【留学】 liúxué study abroad ◇ ～生 student studying abroad; return student
【留言】 liúyán leave one's comments; leave a message
【留意】 liúyì be careful; look out; keep one's eyes open: 这是个细致活, 稍不～就会出错。This is a delicate job. If you let your mind wander for a single moment, you'll do it wrong.
【留影】 liúyǐng take a photo as a memento; have a picture taken as a souvenir
【留用】 liúyòng continue to employ; keep on
【留余地】 liú yúdì allow for unforeseen circumstances; leave some leeway: 我们订计划时要留有余地。When drawing up a plan, we should allow for unforeseen circumstances.

琉 liú
【琉璃】 liúlí coloured glaze ◇ ～塔 glazed pagoda/ ～瓦 glazed tile

硫 liú 〈化〉sulphur (S)
【硫磺】 liúhuáng 〈化〉sulphur ◇ ～泉 〈地〉sulphur spring 又作"硫黄"

馏 liú 见"蒸馏" zhēngliú

榴* liú pomegranate
【榴弹】 liúdàn 〈军〉high explosive shell
【榴莲】 liúlián 〈植〉durian 亦作"榴梿"

瘤 liú tumour: 毒～ malignant tumour

liǔ

柳 liǔ willow

liù

六* liù six:
【六边形】 liùbiānxíng hexagon
【六亲】 liùqīn the six relations (father, mother, elder brothers, younger brothers, wife, children); one's kin: ～不认 refuse to have anything to do with all one's relatives and friends
【六神无主】 liù shén wú zhǔ all six vital organs failing to function — in a state of stupefaction
【六月】 liùyuè ① June ② the sixth month of the lunar year; the sixth moon

陆 liù six (used for the numeral 六 on cheques, etc. to avoid mistakes or alterations) 另见 lù

遛 liù ① saunter; stroll: 出去～～. Let's go for a stroll.

lo

咯 lo 〈助〉〔用于句末, 语气比"了"(le) 较重〕: 当然～ of course; needless to say 另见 gē

lóng

龙* lóng ① dragon ② imperial: ～袍 imperial robe ③ a huge extinct reptile: 恐～ dinosaur
【龙船】 lóngchuán dragon boat
【龙飞凤舞】 lóngfēi-fèngwǔ like dragons flying and phoenixes dancing — lively and vigorous flourishes in calligraphy
【龙潭虎穴】 lóngtán-hǔxué dragon's pool and tiger's den — a danger spot
【龙虾】 lóngxiā lobster
【龙眼】 lóngyǎn 〈植〉longan
【龙争虎斗】 lóngzhēng-hǔdòu a fierce struggle between two evenly-matched opponents
【龙钟】 lóngzhōng 〈书〉decrepit; senile: 老态～ senile; doddering
【龙舟】 lóngzhōu dragon boat: ～竞渡 dragon-boat regatta; dragon-boat race

咙 lóng 见 "喉咙" hóulóng

珑 lóng 见 "玲珑" línglóng

昽 lóng 见 "曚昽" ménglóng

胧 lóng 见 "朦胧" ménglóng

眬 lóng 见 "矇眬" ménglóng

聋* lóng deaf; hard of hearing
【聋哑】 lóngyǎ deaf and dumb; deaf-mute
◇. ~人 deaf-mute/ ~学校 school for deaf-mutes
【聋子】 lóngzi a deaf person

笼* lóng ① cage; coop: 鸟~ birdcage/ 鸡~ chicken coop ② basket; container ③ (food) steamer: 刚出~的肉包子 meat-filled buns fresh from the food steamer 另见 lǒng
【笼子】 lóngzi ① cage; coop ② basket; container

隆 lóng ① grand ② prosperous; thriving ③ intense; deep: ~情厚谊 profound sentiments of friendship ④ swell; bulge: 他碰得前额~起一个大包。He got a bad bump on his forehead.
【隆隆】 lónglóng ⟨象⟩ rumble: 雷声(炮声)~ the rumble of thunder (gunfire)
【隆重】 lóngzhòng grand; solemn; ceremonious: ~的典礼 a grand ceremony/ 受到~的接待 be accorded a grand reception; be given a red carpet reception/ 代表大会于昨日~开幕。The congress was solemnly opened yesterday.

窿 lóng 见 "窟窿" kūlong

lǒng

垄 lǒng ridge (in a field)
【垄断】 lǒngduàn monopolize: ~市场 monopolize (或 corner) the market

拢 lǒng ① approach; reach: ~岸 come alongside the shore

笼 lǒng ① envelop; cover: 烟~雾罩 be enveloped (或 hidden) in mist ② a large box or chest; trunk 另见 lóng
【笼络】 lǒngluò win sb. over by any means; draw over; rope in: ~人心 try to win people's support by hook or by crook
【笼统】 lǒngtǒng general; sweeping: 他的话说得很~。He spoke in very general terms./ 这么说未免太~了。That statement is rather too sweeping.
【笼罩】 lǒngzhào envelop; shroud: 晨雾~在湖面上。The lake is shrouded in morning mist.

lóu

喽 lóu
【喽罗】 lóuluo ① the rank and file of a band of outlaws ② underling; lackey

楼* lóu ① a storied building: 办公~ office building ② storey; floor: 一~ (英) ground floor/ (美) first floor/ 二~ (英) first floor; (美) second floor ③ superstructure: 城~ city-gate tower
【楼板】 lóubǎn floor; floorslab
【楼房】 lóufáng a building of two or more storeys
【楼上】 lóushàng upstairs: ~住的是一位退休老工人。A retired worker lives upstairs.
【楼梯】 lóutī stairs; staircase
【楼下】 lóuxià downstairs: ~的房间 a downstairs room; a room on the floor below

髅 lóu 见 "骷髅" kūlóu

lǒu

搂 lǒu hold in one's arms; hug; embrace
【搂抱】 lǒubào hug; embrace; cuddle

篓 lǒu basket: 字纸~ wastepaper basket; wastebasket
【篓子】 lǒuzi basket

lòu

陋 lòu ① plain; ugly: 丑~ ugly ② humble; mean: ~室 a humble room/ ~巷 a mean alley ③ vulgar; corrupt; undesirable: ~习 corrupt customs; bad habits ④ (of knowledge) scanty; limited; shallow: 浅~ shallow; superficial
【陋规】 lòuguī objectionable practices
【陋俗】 lòusú undesirable customs
【陋习】 lòuxí corrupt customs; bad habits

漏* lòu ① leak: 水壶~了。The kettle leaks./ ~雨了。The rain is leaking in./ 那个管子~煤气。That gas pipe leaks. ② water clock; hourglass: ~尽更残。The night is waning. ③ divulge; leak: 走~消息 leak information ④ be missing; leave out: ~了一行。A line is missing./ 这一项可千万不能~掉。Be sure to leave out this item.
【漏报】 lòubào fail to report sth.; fail to declare (dutiable goods)
【漏电】 lòudiàn leakage of electricity
【漏洞】 lòudòng ① leak: 检查一下管道有没有~ check and see if there is any leak in the pipe ② flaw; hole; loophole: 他的话前后矛盾,~百出。What he says is inconsistent and full of holes./ 严格制度,堵塞~ tighten the rules and stop up all loopholes
【漏风】 lòufēng ① air leak: 这个风箱~。This bellows is not airtight. ② speak indistinctly through having one or more front teeth missing ③ (of information, secrets) leak out
【漏光】 lòuguāng light leak: 这个照相机~。The camera has a light leak.
【漏税】 lòushuì evade payment of a tax; evade taxation
【漏网】 lòuwǎng slip through the net; escape unpunished: 四面包围敌人,力求全歼,不使~。Encircle the enemy forces completely, strive to wipe them out thoroughly and do not let any escape from the net.

露* lòu ⟨口⟩ reveal; show 另见 lù
【露脸】 lòuliǎn look good as a result of receiving honour or praise
【露马脚】 lòu mǎjiǎo give oneself away; let the cat out of the bag
【露面】 lòumiàn show one's face; make (或 put in) an appearance; appear or reappear on public occasions
【露一手】 lòu yīshǒu make an exhibition of one's abilities or skills; show off

lū

噜 lū 见 "咕噜" gūlū

lú

卢 Lú a surname

庐 lú hut; cottage
【庐山真面目】 Lúshān zhēnmiànmù what Lushan Mountain really looks like — the truth about a person or a matter

芦 lú ⟨植⟩ reed

炉* lú ① stove; furnace: 围~烤火 sit round a fire to get warm ② ⟨量⟩ heat: 一~钢 a heat of steel
【炉火纯青】 lúhuǒ chúnqīng pure blue flame — high degree of technical or professional proficiency: 他的山水画达到了~的地步。He attained perfection in landscape painting.

【炉灶】lúzào kitchen range; cooking range: 另起～ make a fresh start
【炉子】lúzi stove; oven; furnace

胪 lú ＜书＞ set out; display; exhibit
【胪列】lúliè ＜书＞ enumerate; list

轳 lú 见"辘轳" lùlu

lǔ

卤 lǔ ①bittern ②＜化＞ halogen ③stew (whole chickens or ducks, large cuts of meat, etc.) in soy sauce: ～鸡 pot-stewed chicken ④thick gravy used as a sauce for noodles, etc.: 打～面 noodles served with thick gravy
【卤味】lǔwèi pot-stewed fowl, meat, etc. served cold

虏 lǔ ①take prisoner ②captive; prisoner of war
【虏获】lǔhuò ①capture ②men and arms captured

掳 lǔ carry off; capture
【掳掠】lǔlüè pillage; loot: 奸淫～,无恶不作 rape and pillage and commit all kinds of atrocities

鲁 lǔ ①stupid; dull ②rash; rough; rude
【鲁钝】lǔdùn dull-witted; obtuse; stupid
【鲁莽】lǔmǎng crude and rash; rash: ～行事 act rashly; act without thought

橹 lǔ scull; sweep

lù

陆* lù land: 水～交通 land and water communications
另见 liù
【陆地】lùdì dry land; land
【陆军】lùjūn ground force; land force; army
【陆路】lùlù land route: 走～ travel by land/ ～交通 overland communication; land communication
【陆续】lùxù one after another; in succession: 代表们～到达。The delegates arrived one after another.
【陆运】lùyùn land transportation
【陆战队】lùzhànduì ＜军＞ marine corps; marines

录* lù ①record; write down; copy: 抄～ copy down/ 记～在案 put on record ②employ; hire: 收～ employ; take sb. on the staff ③tape-record: 报告已经～下来了。The speech has been tape-recorded. ④record; register; collection: 语～ quotation; a book of quotations/ 回忆～ memoirs; reminiscences
【录取】lùqǔ enroll; recruit; admit: ～新学员五百名 enroll 500 students
【录音】lùyīn sound recording: 实况～ on-the-spot recording; live-recording/ 磁带～ tape recording/ 放～ play back the recording ◇ ～机 (tape) recorder
【录用】lùyòng employ; take sb. on the staff: 量才～ give a person employment commensurate with his abilities

赂 lù 见"贿赂" huìlù

鹿 lù deer: 公～ stag; buck/ 母～ doe/ 小～ fawn
【鹿肉】lùròu venison
【鹿死谁手】lù sǐ shuí shǒu at whose hand will the deer die — who will win the prize; who will gain supremacy: ～,尚难逆料。It's still hard to tell who will emerge victorious.

绿* lù
另见 lǜ
【绿林好汉】lùlín hǎohàn ①heroes of the greenwood; forest outlaws ②a band of bandits entrenched in a mountain stronghold; brigands

禄 lù official's salary in feudal China; emolument: 高官厚～ high position and handsome salary

碌* lù ①commonplace; mediocre ②busy
【碌碌】lùlù ①mediocre; commonplace: ～无能 incompetent; devoid of ability ②busy with miscellaneous work: 忙忙～ busy going about one's work; as busy as a bee

路* lù ①road; path; way: 大～ broad road; highway/ 小～ path; trail ②journey; distance: 走很远的～ walk a long distance; make a long journey/ 一小时走十二里～ cover 12 li an hour ③way; means: 生～ means of livelihood; a way out ④sequence; line; logic: 理～ line of reasoning/ 思～ train of thought ⑤region; district: 外～人 nonlocal people ⑥route
【路不拾遗】lù bù shí yí no one picks up and pockets anything lost on the road — descriptive of a high moral standard in society
【路程】lùchéng distance travelled; journey: 三天～ a three days' journey
【路灯】lùdēng street lamp; road lamp
【路费】lùfèi travelling expenses
【路过】lùguò pass by or through (a place): 他每次～总要来看望他的老朋友。Every time he passes by, he drops in to see his old friends.
【路口】lùkǒu crossing; intersection: 三岔～ a fork in a road/ 十字～ crossroads
【路面】lùmiàn road surface; pavement: 柔(刚)性～ flexible (rigid) pavement
【路牌】lùpái street nameplate
【路人】lùrén passerby; stranger: 视若～ treat sb. like a stranger
【路上】lùshàng ①on the road ②on the way; en route: ～不要耽搁。Don't waste any time on the way./ 由于～的种种耽搁,我们比原计划迟到了两天。Owing to various delays en route, we arrived two days behind schedule.
【路途】lùtú ①road; path: 他熟悉这一带的～。He knows the roads in this district quite well. ②way; journey: ～遥远 a long way to go; far away
【路线】lùxiàn ①itinerary: 旅行的～ the route of a journey/ 参观～图 visitors' itinerary ②line
【路遥知马力】lù yáo zhī mǎlì distance tests a horse's stamina: ～,日久见人心。As distance tests a horse's strength, so time reveals a person's heart./ ～,事久见人心。As a long road tests a horse's strength, so a long task proves a person's heart.
【路障】lùzhàng roadblock

辘 lù
【辘轳】lùlu windlass; winch
【辘辘】lùlù ＜象＞ rumble: 车轮的～声 the rumbling of cart wheels/ 饥肠～ so hungry that one's stomach rumbles; one's stomach growling from hunger; famished

戮 lù ①kill; slay: 杀～ slaughter ②＜书＞ unite; join: ～力 join hands
【戮力同心】lùlì tóngxīn ＜书＞ unite in a concerted effort; make concerted efforts

麓 lù ＜书＞ the foot of a hill or mountain

露* lù ①dew ②beverage distilled from flowers, fruit or leaves; syrup: 果子～ fruit syrup ③show; reveal; betray: 不～声色 not betray one's feelings or intentions/ ～出原形 reveal one's true colours; betray oneself
另见 lòu
【露骨】lùgǔ thinly veiled; undisguised; barefaced: 说得十分～ speak undisguisedly; speak in no equivocal terms/
【露水】lùshui dew
【露宿】lùsù sleep in the open
【露天】lùtiān in the open (air); outdoors: 今晚电影在～演。The film will be shown in the open air tonight. ◇ ～堆栈 open-air repository; open-air depot/ ～剧场 open-air theatre/ ～开采 opencast mining / ～矿 opencut; open-

cast; open-pit; strip mine/ ～煤矿 opencut coal mine

【露头角】 lù tóujiǎo (of a young person) beginning to show ability or talent; budding: 参加会议的，有不少是初～的新作家。Present at the meeting were a number of budding writers.

【露营】 lùyíng camp (out); encamp; bivouac

lú

驴 lú donkey; ass

闾 lú ①〈书〉the gate of (或 entrance to) an alley: 倚～而望 waiting at the entrance to the alley (for the return of one's son) ② alleys and lanes; neighbourhood

榈 lú 见 "棕榈" zōnglú

lǚ

吕 lǚ a surname

侣 lǚ companion; associate: 作～ companion; partner/ 情～ lovers

旅 *lǚ ① travel; stay away from home ②〈军〉brigade ③ troops; force: 军～之事 military affairs/ 劲～ a powerful army; a crack force

【旅伴】 lǚbàn travelling companion; fellow traveller

【旅程】 lǚchéng route; itinerary

【旅店】 lǚdiàn inn

【旅费】 lǚfèi travelling expenses

【旅馆】 lǚguǎn hotel

【旅居】 lǚjū reside abroad; sojourn

【旅客】 lǚkè hotel guest; traveller; passenger: 过往～ travellers passing through; transients ◇～登记簿 hotel register

【旅社】 lǚshè hotel

【旅途】 lǚtú journey; trip: ～见闻 what one sees and hears during a trip; traveller's notes

【旅行】 lǚxíng travel; journey; tour: 作长途～ make a long journey

【旅游】 lǚyóu tour; tourism: ～事业 tourist trade; tourism

捋 lǚ smooth out with the fingers; stroke: ～胡子 stroke one's beard/ 把纸～平 smooth out a piece of paper 另见 luō

铝 lǚ 〈化〉aluminium (Al)

偻 lǚ ① crooked (back): 伛～ humpback(ed); hunchback(ed)

屡 lǚ repeatedly; time and again: ～战～胜 have fought many battles and won every one of them; score one victory after another

【屡次】 lǚcì time and again; repeatedly: ～打破全国纪录 repeatedly break the national record

【屡次三番】 lǚcì-sānfān again and again; over and over again; many times: 我～提醒他要谨慎。I've reminded him over and over again that he should be cautious.

【屡见不鲜】 lǚ jiàn bù xiān common occurrence; nothing new

【屡教不改】 lǚ jiào bù gǎi refuse to mend one's ways despite repeated admonition

【屡试不爽】 lǚ shì bù shuǎng put to repeated tests and proved right; time-tested: 这种新农药杀虫效果良好，～。This new insecticide has proved effective every time it is used.

缕 lǚ ① thread ②〈量〉wisp; strand; lock: 一～烟 a wisp of smoke/ 一～麻 a strand of hemp ③ detailed; in detail: ～陈 state in detail

【缕缕】 lǚlǚ continuously: 村中炊烟～上升。Wisps of smoke rose continuously from the village chimneys.

膂 lǚ 〈书〉backbone

【膂力】 lǚlì muscular strength; physical strength; brawn: ～过人 possessing extraordinary physical strength

履 lǚ ① shoe: 革～ leather shoes ② tread on; walk on: 如～薄冰 as if walking on thin ice ③ footstep: 步～艰难 walk with difficulty; hobble along ④ carry out; honour; fulfil: ～约 honour an agreement; keep an appointment

【履历】 lǚlì personal details (of education and work experience); antecedents; *curriculum vitae*

【履行】 lǚxíng perform; fulfil; carry out: ～职责 do one's duty/ ～诺言 keep one's word; fulfil (或 carry out) one's promise

lù

律 *lǜ ① law; statute; rule ②〈书〉restrain; keep under control: 严以～己 be strict with oneself; exercise strict self-discipline

【律师】 lǜshī lawyer; (英) barrister; (英) solicitor; (美) attorney

虑 lǜ ① consider; ponder; think over: 深思熟～ careful consideration (或 deliberation) ② concern; anxiety; worry: 不足为～ give no cause for anxiety/ 过～ worry overmuch; be overanxious

率 lǜ rate; proportion; ratio: 人口增长～ the rate of population increase/ 废品～ the rate (或 proportion) of rejects 另见 shuài

绿 lǜ green: ～叶 green leaves/ ～油油的秧苗 green and lush seedlings 另见 lù

【绿宝石】 lǜbǎoshí emerald

【绿茶】 lǜchá green tea

【绿灯】 lǜdēng ①〈交〉green light ② permission to go ahead with some project; green light: 开～ give the green light to

【绿豆】 lǜdòu mung bean; green gram ◇～芽 mung bean sprouts

【绿洲】 lǜzhōu oasis

氯 lǜ 〈化〉chlorine (Cl)

滤 lǜ strain; filter: 过～ filter

【滤器】 lǜqì filter

luán

峦 luán 〈书〉① low but steep and pointed hill ② mountains in a range

孪 luán twin

【孪生】 luánshēng twin: ～姐妹 twin sisters

挛 luán contraction: 拘～ contraction/ 痉～ spasm; convulsions

【挛缩】 luánsuō contracture

鸾 luán a mythical bird like the phoenix

【鸾凤】 luánfèng husband and wife: ～和鸣 be blessed with conjugal felicity; be a happy couple

脔 luán 〈书〉a small slice of meat

【脔割】 luángē 〈书〉slice up; carve up

銮 luán a small tinkling bell

luǎn

卵* luǎn ovum; egg; spawn
【卵白】 luǎnbái 〈动〉 white of an egg; albumen
【卵黄】 luǎnhuáng 〈动〉 yolk
【卵生】 luǎnshēng 〈动〉 oviparity
【卵石】 luǎnshí cobble; pebble; shingle
【卵子】 luǎnzǐ 〈生〉 ovum; egg

luàn

乱* luàn ① in disorder; in a mess; in confusion: 屋里很~，请你把它收拾一下。The room is in a mess; please tidy it up./ 这篇稿子太~，是不是给抄一下？The manuscript's too messy. How about copying it out?/ 这里太~，找个安静点的地方谈谈。It's too noisy here; let's find a quieter place to chat. ② disorder; upheaval; chaos; riot; unrest; turmoil: 内~ internal unrest/ 叛~ armed rebellion; mutiny ③ confuse; mix up; jumble: 扰~ create confusion; disturb; harass/ 各种木料~堆在一起。Logs and planks of all shapes and sizes were jumbled together. ④ confused (state of mind); in a turmoil: 我心里很~。My mind is in a turmoil. ⑤ indiscriminate; random; arbitrary: ~来 act recklessly/~作决定 make an arbitrary decision/ ~讲一气 speak indiscreetly; make irresponsible remarks/ ~花钱 spend money extravagantly/ ~说~动 be unruly in word or deed ⑥ promiscuous sexual behaviour; promiscuity
【乱兵】 luànbīng ① mutinous soldiers ② totally undisciplined troops
【乱哄哄】 luànhōnghōng in noisy disorder; in a hubbub; tumultuous; in an uproar: 大家听到这个消息，~地议论起来。The news set them arguing heatedly among themselves.
【乱伦】 luànlún commit incest
【乱七八糟】 luànqībāzāo at sixes and sevens; in a mess; in a muddle
【乱世】 luànshì troubled times; turbulent days
【乱说】 luànshuō speak carelessly; make irresponsible remarks; gossip: 当面不说，背后~ gossip behind people's backs but say nothing to their faces
【乱糟糟】 luànzāozāo ① chaotic; in a mess: 屋子里~的。The room is in a mess. ② confused; perturbed: 心里~的 feel very perturbed
【乱真】 luànzhēn ① (of fakes) look genuine: 以假~ pass off a fake as genuine ② 〈物〉 spurious: ~放电 spurious discharge/ ~脉冲 spurious pulse
【乱子】 luànzi disturbance; trouble; disorder: 闹~ create a disturbance; cause trouble

lüè

掠 lüè ① plunder; pillage; sack ② sweep past; brush past; graze; skim over: 凉风~面。A cool breeze brushed my face./ 探照灯~过夜空。The searchlights swept the night sky./ 燕子~水而过。The swallows skimmed over the water./ 她嘴角上~过一丝微笑。A faint smile flickered across her lips
【掠夺】 lüèduó plunder; rob; pillage
【掠美】 lüèměi claim credit due to others: 这是她的高见，我不敢~。It was her idea. I can't claim credit for it. 又作「掠人之美」
【掠取】 lüèqǔ seize; grab; plunder

略* lüè ① brief; sketchy; simple/ ~述大意 give a brief account ② slightly; a little; somewhat: ~加修改 make some slight changes; edit slightly/ ~有所闻 have heard a little about the matter/ ~有出入 vary slightly; there's a slight discrepancy ③ summary; brief account; outline: 史~ outline history; brief history/ 事~ a short biographical account ④ omit; delete; leave out: 从~ be

omitted/ ~去不提 make no mention of; leave out altogether ⑤ strategy; plan; scheme: 方~ overall plan/ 策~ tactics; 雄才大~ (a person of) great talent and bold vision; (a statesman or general of) rare gifts and bold strategy ⑥ capture; seize: 攻城~地 attack cities and seize territories
【略见一斑】 lüè jiàn yī bān catch a glimpse of; get a rough idea of
【略略】 lüèlüè slightly; briefly: 关于那个问题他只~说了几句。He touched only briefly on that question.
【略胜一筹】 lüè shèng yī chóu a notch (或 cut) above; slightly better
【略图】 lüètú sketch map; sketch
【略微】 lüèwēi slightly; a little; somewhat: ~有点感冒 have a slight cold; have a touch of flu
【略语】 lüèyǔ 〈语〉 abbreviation; shortening
【略知一二】 lüè zhī yī-èr have a smattering of; know something about

lūn

抡 lūn brandish; swing: ~刀 brandish a sword/ ~起大铁锤 swing a sledgehammer

lún

伦 lún ① human relations, esp. as conceived by feudal ethics ② logic; order ③ peer; match: 绝~ peerless; matchless
【伦比】 lúnbǐ 〈书〉 rival; equal: 无与~ unrivalled; unequalled; peerless
【伦常】 lúncháng feudal order of importance or seniority in human relationships
【伦次】 lúncì coherence; logical sequence: 语无~ speak incoherently; babble like an idiot
【伦理】 lúnlǐ ethics; moral principles ◇~学 ethics

沦 lún ① sink: 沉~ sink into depravity, etc. ② fall; be reduced to: ~于敌手 fall into enemy hands/ ~为殖民地 be reduced to the status of a colony
【沦落】 lúnluò fall low; come down in the world; be reduced to poverty: ~街头 be driven onto the streets (to become a tramp, beggar or prostitute)
【沦亡】 lúnwáng (of a country) be annexed (或 subjugated)
【沦陷】 lúnxiàn (of territory, etc.) be occupied by the enemy; fall into enemy hands ◇~区 enemy-occupied area

囵 lún 见 "囫囵" húlún

纶 lún ① black silk ribbon ② fishing line ③ synthetic fibre: 锦~ polyamide fibre/ 涤~ polyester fibre

轮* lún ① wheel: 齿~ gear wheel/ 三~摩托 motor tricycle ② sth. resembling a wheel; disc; ring: 月~ the moon/ 光~ halo/ 年~〈植〉 annual ring ③ steamboat; steamer: 江~ river steamer ④ take turns: ~值 on duty by turns/ 下一个轮到你。It will be your turn next. ⑤ 〈量〉：一~红日 a red sun/ 一~明月 a bright moon ⑥〈量〉round: 第一~比赛 the first round of the match/ 新的一~会谈 a new round of talks
【轮班】 lúnbān in shifts; in relays; in rotation
【轮唱】 lúnchàng 〈乐〉 round
【轮船】 lúnchuán steamer; steamship; steamboat
【轮换】 lúnhuàn rotate; take turns
【轮回】 lúnhuí 〈佛教〉 samsara; transmigration
【轮廓】 lúnkuò outline; contour; rough sketch: 先画个~，再画细部。Draw an outline before you fill in the details./ 夜幕降临了，但厂房还能看见个~。Night fell, but the outline of the factory buildings was still discernible. 或 The factory buildings were silhouetted against the growing darkness./ 听了汇报后，新来的经理对这个公司的情况有了个~。After hearing the reports from below, the newly-appointed manager got a general picture of the situation in the company.

【轮流】 lúnliú take turns; do sth. in turn: 他俩～值夜班。 They work on night shifts in turn.
【轮胎】 lúntāi tyre: 防滑～ antiskid tyre; nonskid tyre/ 双层～ two ply tyre/ 翻制～ retreaded tyre
【轮椅】 lúnyǐ wheelchair
【轮轴】 lúnzhóu ①〈物〉 wheel and axle ② wheel axle
【轮转】 lúnzhuàn rotate
【轮子】 lúnzi wheel

lùn

论* lùn ① discuss; talk about; discourse: 讨～ discuss/ 就事～事 talk about a matter in isolation; deal with a matter on its merits ② view; opinion; statement: 高～ your brilliant views; your wise counsel/ 舆～ public opinion/ 立～ argument; line of reasoning/ 持平之～ unbiased views ③ dissertation; essay ④ theory: 进化～ the theory of evolution ⑤ mention regard; consider: 相提并～ mention; in the same breath/ 又当别～ should be regarded as a different matter ⑥ decide on; determine: 按质～价 determine the price according to the quality ⑦ by; in terms of
【论点】 lùndiǎn argument; thesis: 这篇文章～鲜明。 The argument set forth in the article is clear-cut.
【论调】 lùndiào 〔常含贬义〕 view; argument: 这种～是错误的。 Such views are erroneous.
【论断】 lùnduàn inference; judgment; thesis: 作出～ draw an inference
【论功行赏】 lùn gōng xíng shǎng dispense rewards or honours according to merit; award people according to their contributions
【论据】 lùnjù grounds of argument; argument: ～不足 insufficient grounds/ 有力的～ strong argument; valid reasons
【论理】 lùnlǐ normally; as things should be ◇ ～学 logic
【论述】 lùnshù discuss; expound: 精辟的～ brilliant exposition
【论说】 lùnshuō exposition and argumentation: ～文 argumentation
【论坛】 lùntán forum; tribune
【论题】 lùntí 〈逻〉 proposition
【论文】 lùnwén thesis; dissertation; treatise; paper: 学术～ an academic thesis (或 paper)/ 科学～ a scientific treatise
【论证】 lùnzhèng ① demonstration; proof: 无可辩驳的～ irrefutable proof ② expound and prove
【论著】 lùnzhù treatise; work; book

luō

罗 luō
另见 luó
【罗嗦】 luōsuo ① long-winded; wordy: 他说话太～。 He's far too long-winded./ 我再～几句。 Let me say just another word or two. 或 Bear with me a little longer. ② over-elaborate; troublesome: 这些手续真～。 All these formalities are overelaborate. 又作"罗唆"

捋 luō rub one's palm along (sth. long)
另见 lǚ
【捋虎须】 luō hǔxū stroke a tiger's whiskers — do sth. very daring; run great risks

luó

罗* luó ① a net for catching birds: ～网 net; trap ② catch birds with a net: 门可～雀 you can catch sparrows on the doorstep — visitors are few and far between ③ collect; gather together ④ display; spread out: 星～棋布 spread out like stars in the sky or chessmen on the chessboard ⑤ sieve; sift: ～面 sift flour ⑥ a kind of

silk gauze: ～扇 silk gauze fan ⑦〈量〉 twelve dozen; a gross
另见 luō
【罗列】 luóliè ① spread out; set out: 厂房～在山坡上。 Factory buildings spread out over the hillside. ② enumerate: 光～事实还不够，必须加以分析。 It's not enough just to enumerate the facts. You've got to analyse them, too.
【罗马数字】 Luómǎ shùzì Roman numerals
【罗盘】 luópán compass
【罗网】 luówǎng net; trap: 自投～ walk right into the trap
【罗致】 luózhì enlist the services of; secure sb. in one's employment; collect; gather together: ～人材 enlist the services of able people

偻 luó 见"偻儸" lóuluo

萝* luó trailing plants: 藤～ Chinese wistaria
【萝卜】 luóbo radish

猡 luó 见"猪猡" zhūluó

逻 luó patrol: 巡～ patrol
【逻辑】 luóji logic: ～上的错误 an error in logic/ 数理～ mathematical logic/ 合乎～ logical/ 按照这种～ according to that kind of reasoning/ 这是什么～? What sort of logic is that?

锣* luó gong
【锣鼓】 luógǔ ① gong and drum: 喧天 a deafening sound of gongs and drums ② traditional percussion instruments ③ ensemble of such instruments with gongs and drums playing the main part

箩* luó a square-bottomed bamboo basket
【箩筐】 luókuāng a large bamboo or wicker basket

骡 luó mule

螺 luó ① spiral shell; snail: 马蹄～ top shell/ 田～ field snail ② whorl (in fingerprint)
【螺钉】 luódīng screw: 木～ wood screw; screwnail
【螺丝】 luósī 〈口〉 screw ◇ ～板牙 screw die; threading die/ ～刀 screwdriver/ ～钉 screw/ ～扣 thread (of a screw)/ ～母 (screw) nut; ～起子 screwdriver
【螺旋】 luóxuán ① spiral; helix: ～式发展 spiral development; developing in spirals ②〈物〉 screw ◇ ～线 helix; helical line; spiral/ ～钻 spiral drill; (screw) auger
【螺旋桨】 luóxuánjiǎng 〈机〉 (screw) propeller; screw: 飞机～ airscrew; aircraft propeller

luǒ

裸 luǒ bare; naked; exposed: 赤～～ stark-naked; undisguised
【裸露】 luǒlù uncovered; exposed: ～的煤层 exposed coal seam
【裸体】 luǒtǐ naked; nude

luò

络* luò ① sth. resembling a net: 橘～ tangerine pith/ 丝瓜～ loofah ②〈中医〉 subsidiary channels in the human body through which vital energy, blood and nutriment circulate ③ hold sth. in place with a net: 她头上～着一个发网。 She kept her hair in place with a net. ④ twine; wind: ～纱 winding yarn; spooling
【络绎不绝】 luòyì bù jué in an endless stream: 参观展览会的人～。 A continuous stream of visitors came to the exhibition.

骆* luò a white horse with a black mane, mentioned in ancient Chinese books

【骆驼】luòtuo camel: 单峰~ dromedary; one-humped camel/ 双峰~ Bactrian camel; two-humped camel/ 无峰~ llama

【骆驼队】luòtuoduì camel train; caravan

落*

luò ① fall; drop: 有些棉桃~在地上了。Some cotton bolls have fallen on the ground. ② go down; set: 潮水~了。The tide is low (或 out)./ 太阳~山了。The sun has set. ③ lower: 把帘子~下来 lower the blinds ④ decline; come down; sink: 衰~ decline; go downhill/ 没~ be on the downgrade/ ~到这步田地 come to such a pass ⑤ lag behind; fall behind: 领导不应当~在群众运动的后头。The leadership should never lag behind the mass movement. ⑥ leave behind; stay behind: 不~痕迹 leave no trace ⑦ whereabouts: 下~ whereabouts ⑧ settlement: 村~ a small village; hamlet ⑨ fall onto; rest with: 突袭的任务~在他们肩上。The task of making a surprise attack fell on them.

另见 lào

【落笔】luòbǐ start to write or draw; put pen to paper

【落泊(魄)】luòbó be in dire straits; be down and out

【落成】luòchéng completion (of a building, etc.) ◇~典礼 inauguration ceremony (for a building, etc.)

【落得】luòde get; end in: ~一场空 come to nothing; end up in smoke

【落地】luòdì ① fall to the ground: 人头~ be killed or beheaded ② (of babies) be born: 呱呱~ come into the world with a cry; be born

【落发】luòfà shave one's head—become a Buddhist monk or nun

【落后】luòhòu ① fall behind; lag behind: 思想~于现实的事是常有的。It often happens that thinking lags behind reality./ 上半场主队~一分。The home team trailed by one point at half time. ② backward: 改变山区~面貌 put an end to the backwardness of the mountainous areas ◇~地区 backward areas; less developed areas

【落户】luòhù settle: 在农村~ settle in the countryside

【落花流水】luòhuā-liúshuǐ like fallen flowers carried away by the flowing water; utterly routed: 敌人被打得~。The enemy was utterly routed.

【落花有意，流水无情】luòhuā yǒu yì, liúshuǐ wú qíng shedding petals, the waterside flower pines for love, while the heartless brook babbles on — unrequited love

【落荒而逃】luòhuāng ér táo take to the wilds — be defeated and flee the battlefield; take to flight

【落价】luòjià fall (或 drop) in price: 收音机~了。The price of radios has gone down.

【落脚】luòjiǎo stay (for a time); stop over; put up: 找个地方~ find a place to stay/ 在客店~ put up at an inn ◇~处 temporary lodging

【落井下石】luò jǐng xià shí drop stones on someone who has fallen into a well — hit a person when he's down

【落空】luòkōng come to nothing; fail; fall through: 两头~ fall between two stools/ 希望~ fail to attain one's hope/ 这事有~的危险。There is a danger that nothing will come of it.

【落落大方】luòluò dàfāng natural and graceful

【落难】luònàn meet with misfortune; be in distress

【落日】luòrì setting sun

【落水狗】luòshuǐgǒu dog in the water: 痛打~ flog the cur that's fallen into the water — be merciless with bad people even if they're down

【落汤鸡】luòtāngjī like a drenched chicken; like a drowned rat; soaked through; drenched and bedraggled

【落网】luòwǎng (of a criminal) fall into the net — be caught; be captured: 主犯已经~。The chief criminal has been caught.

【落伍】luòwǔ fall behind the ranks; straggle; drop behind; drop out

【落选】luòxuǎn fail to be chosen (或 elected); lose an election

【落叶】luòyè ① fallen leaves ② <植> deciduous leaf ◇~树 deciduous tree/ ~松 larch

M

mā

妈* mā 〈口〉① ma; mum; mummy; mother ② a form of address for a married woman one generation one's senior: 姑~ (paternal) aunt/ 姨~ (maternal) aunt/ 大~ aunt (a form of address for one's father's elder brother's wife or for any elderly married woman)
【妈妈】 māma 〈口〉 ma; mum; mummy; mother

抹* mā ① wipe: ~桌子 wipe a table clean/ 一把脸 wipe one's face ② rub sth. down; slip sth. off: 把帽子 ~下来 slip one's cap off/ ~不下脸来 find it difficult to be strict with sb. (for fear of hurting his feelings)
另见 mǒ
【抹布】 mābù rag (to wipe things with)

má

吗 má 〈方〉 what: 下午干~？ What are we going to do this afternoon?
另见 mǎ; ma

麻* má ① a general term for hemp, flax, etc. ② sesame: ~糖 sesame candy ③ rough; coarse: 这种纸一面光,一面~。 This paper is smooth on one side and rough on the other. ④ pocked; pockmarked; pitted; spotty: ~脸 a pockmarked face/ 铸件上有~点。 There are pits in the casting. ⑤ have pins and needles; tingle: 腿发~ have pins and needles in one's legs/ 针灸医生问病人~不~。 The acupuncturist asked the patient if he felt a tingling sensation. ⑥ anaesthesia: 针~ acupuncture anaesthesia
【麻痹】 mábì ① 〈医〉 paralysis: 小儿~ infantile paralysis; poliomyelitis; polio/ 面部神经~ facial paralysis ② benumb; lull; blunt: ~人们的斗志 lull (或 blunt) people's fighting will ③ lower one's guard; slacken one's vigilance: ~大意 lower one's guard and become careless; be off one's guard
【麻布】 mábù ① gunny (cloth); sackcloth; burlap; hessian ② linen
【麻袋】 mádài gunny-bag; gunnysack; sack
【麻烦】 máfan ① troublesome; inconvenient: 这事要是太~, 你就别管了。 —— 一点也不~。 Don't bother if it's too much trouble. — No trouble at all./ 这下可~了, 我把钥匙锁在屋里了。 What a nuisance. I've locked my key in the room./ 服务周到, 不怕~ spare no pains to give good service/ 自找~ ask for trouble ② put sth. to trouble; trouble sb.; bother: 对不起, ~你了。 Sorry to have put you to so much trouble./ 这点小事不要去~他了。 Don't bother him with such trifles.
【麻风】 máfēng 〈医〉 leprosy ◇ ~病人 leper
【麻将】 májiàng mahjong ◇ ~牌 mahjong pieces; mahjong tiles
【麻木】 mámù ① numb ② apathetic; insensitive
【麻木不仁】 mámù bùrén apathetic; insensitive; unfeeling
【麻雀】 máquè (house) sparrow
【麻雀虽小, 五脏俱全】 máquè suī xiǎo, wǔzàng jù quán the sparrow may be small but it has all the vital organs — small but complete
【麻绳】 máshéng rope made of hemp, flax, jute, etc.
【麻油】 máyóu sesame oil
【麻疹】 mázhěn 〈医〉 measles
【麻醉】 mázuì ① 〈医〉 anaesthesia; narcosis: 全身(局部、脊髓)~ general (local, spinal) anaesthesia/ 针刺~ acupuncture anaesthesia ② anaesthetize; poison ◇ ~剂 anaesthetic; narcotic/ ~品 narcotic; drug/ ~师 anaesthetist

麻 má
【麻痹】 mábì 见"麻痹" mábì
【麻风】 máfēng 见"麻风" máfēng
【麻疹】 mázhěn 见"麻疹" mázhěn

蟆 má 见"蛤蟆" háma

mǎ

马* mǎ ① horse: 母~ mare/ 种~ stallion; stud/ 小~ pony ② horse, one of the pieces in Chinese chess
【马鞍】 mǎ'ān saddle
【马不停蹄】 mǎ bù tíng tí without a stop; nonstop: 部队~地赶到了目的地。 The troops rushed to their destination without a single halt.
【马车】 mǎchē ① (horse-drawn) carriage ② cart
【马到成功】 mǎ dào chénggōng win success immediately upon arrival; gain an immediate victory; win instant success
【马后炮】 mǎhòupào belated action or advice; belated effort: 我这个建议也许是~。 My suggestion may already be too late./ 事情都做完了, 你才说要帮忙, 这不是~吗？ You come and offer to help when the work's all done. Isn't that a bit late?
【马虎】 mǎhu careless; casual: ~了事 get it done in a slapdash manner/ 他这个人做事比较~。 He's a rather careless fellow./ 这是个大事, 不能~过去。 This is a serious matter. It shouldn't be done just any old way.
【马鲛鱼】 mǎjiāoyú Spanish mackerel
【马脚】 mǎjiǎo sth. that gives the game away: 露出~ show the cloven hoof; give oneself away
【马厩】 mǎjiù stable
【马拉松】 mǎlāsōng marathon ◇ ~赛跑 marathon race; marathon
【马力】 mǎlì 〈物〉 horsepower (h.p.): 开足~ at full speed; at full steam
【马铃薯】 mǎlíngshǔ potato
【马路】 mǎlù road; street; avenue
【马马虎虎】 mǎmǎhūhū ① careless; casual: 他的信我只是~地看了一下。 I merely glanced over his letter./ 产品出厂要严格检查, ~可不行。 Products must be strictly, not perfunctorily, inspected before they leave the factory. ② fair; not so bad: 这种牌子的香烟怎么样？ —— ~, 你来一支试试。 How's this brand of cigarettes? — Not so bad. Try one. ③ not very good; just passable; so-so: 你的游泳技术怎么样？ —— ~, 游不远。 Are you a good swimmer? — Just so-so. I can't swim far.
【马匹】 mǎpǐ horses
【马前卒】 mǎqiánzú ① pawn ② cat's-paw
【马上】 mǎshàng at once; immediately; straight away; right away: 我们~就动手。 We'll start working straight away./ 你~就走吗？ Are you leaving right away?/ 我~就回来。 I won't be a minute. 或 I'll be back in a minute.
【马首是瞻】 mǎshǒu shì zhān take the head of the general's horse as guide — follow sb.'s lead
【马戏】 mǎxì circus ◇ ~团 circus troupe

吗 mǎ
另见 má; ma
【吗啡】 mǎfēi 〈药〉 morphine

玛 mǎ
【玛瑙】 mǎnǎo agate

码* mǎ ① a sign or thing indicating number: 页~ page number/ 价~ marked price/ 筹~ counter; chip ② 〔计

一件事或一类的事]: 一~事 the same thing/ 两~事 two different things ③ <口> pile up; stack: ~砖 stack bricks ④ yard (yd.)

【码头】 mǎtou ① wharf; dock; quay; pier ② <方> port city; commercial and transportation centre: 跑~ travel from port to port as a trader; be a travelling merchant ◇ ~费 wharfage; dockage/ ~工人 docker; stevedore; longshoreman

蚂* mǎ

【蚂蚁】 mǎyǐ ant

【蚂蚁搬泰山】 mǎyǐ bān Tàishān ants can move Mount Taishan — the united efforts of the masses can accomplish mighty projects

mà

骂* mà ① abuse; curse; swear; call names: ~人 swear (at people)/ ~不绝口 pour out a stream of abuse; curse unceasingly/ ~人话 abusive language; swearword; curse ② condemn; rebuke; reprove; scold: 这样铺张浪费, 没有一个人不~。 Such extravagance is an object of general condemnation./ 把孩子~了一顿 give one's child a scolding (或 dressing down)

【骂街】 màjiē shout abuses in the street; call people names in public: 泼妇~ like a shrew shouting abuses in the street

ma

吗* ma <助> ①〔用在句末, 表示疑问〕: 下午有会~? Is there a meeting this afternoon?/ 你找我有事~? Is there something you want to see me about? ②〔用在句中停顿处, 点出话题〕: 特殊情况~, 还得特殊对待。 Special cases, of course, need special consideration.
另见 má; mǎ

嘛* ma <助>〔表示道理显而易见〕: 这也不能怪他, 头一回做~。 He's not to blame. After all, it was the first time he'd done it./ 这件事他是知道的~。 He's well aware of it.

mái

埋* mái cover up (with earth, snow, etc.); bury: 雪把这口井一起来了。 The well is buried in snow./ ~地雷 lay a mine
另见 mán

【埋藏】 máicáng lie hidden in the earth; bury: 这一带地下~着丰富的矿产。 There are rich mineral deposits in this region.

【埋伏】 máifu ① ambush: 设下~ lay an ambush/ 中~ fall into an ambush ② hide; lie low

【埋没】 máimò ① bury; cover up (with earth, snow, etc.): 泥石流~了整个村庄。 The mud-rock flow submerged the whole village. ② neglect; stifle: ~人材 stifle real talents/ 瞧, 这儿有重要的资料, 差点给~了。 Look, here's some important source material we almost overlooked.

【埋头】 máitóu immerse oneself in; be engrossed in: ~苦干 quietly immerse oneself in hard work; quietly put one's shoulder to the wheel/ ~读书 bury oneself in books/ ~业务 engross oneself in vocational work

【埋葬】 máizàng bury

mǎi

买* mǎi buy; purchase: 公司~了几台拖拉机。 The company has bought several tractors./ 这是人家送的, 不是~的。 It is a present, not a purchase./ ~东西 buy things; go shopping/ ~得起 can afford/ ~不起 cannot afford

【买方】 mǎifāng the buying party (of a contract, etc.); buyer

【买价】 mǎijià buying price

【买空卖空】 mǎikōng-màikōng speculate (in stocks, etc.)

【买卖】 mǎimai ① buying and selling; business; deal; transaction: 做成一笔~ make a deal/ ~兴隆。 The business is brisk./ 今天~怎么样? How was business today? ② (private) shop

【买通】 mǎitōng bribe; buy over; buy off

【买主】 mǎizhǔ buyer; customer

mài

迈* mài ① step; stride: ~过门槛 step over the threshold/ ~着矫健的步伐 walk with vigorous strides/ ~开双脚, 到基层去。 Get yourself moving and go down to the grass roots. ② advanced in years; old: 年~ aged

【迈步】 màibù take a step; make a step; step forward: ~向讲台 step up to the platform/ 迈出第一步 make the first step

【迈进】 màijìn stride forward; forge ahead; advance with big strides

麦* mài ① a general term for wheat, barley, etc. ② wheat

【麦克风】 màikèfēng microphone; mike

【麦片】 màipiàn oatmeal

【麦子】 màizi wheat

卖* mài ① sell: ~得快 sell well/ ~不出去 not sell well ② betray: ~友 betray one's friend ③ exert to the utmost; not spare: ~劲儿 exert all one's strength; spare no effort ④ show off: ~乖 show off one's cleverness

【卖唱】 màichàng sing for a living

【卖方】 màifāng the selling party (of a contract, etc.); seller

【卖关子】 mài guānzi stop a story at a climax to keep the listeners in suspense; keep people guessing: 结果怎么样呢? 快说吧, 别~了。 How did it end? Come on! Don't keep us guessing.

【卖国】 màiguó betray one's country; turn traitor to one's country: ~求荣 seek power and wealth by betraying one's country; turn traitor for personal gain

【卖价】 màijià selling price

【卖力】 màilì exert all one's strength; spare no effort; do all one can

【卖力气】 mài lìqi ① exert all one's strength; exert oneself to the utmost; do one's very best ② live by the sweat of one's brow; make a living by manual labour

【卖命】 màimìng ① work oneself to the bone for sb.: 地主逼着长工们为他~。 The landlord forced the farm labourers to work themselves to the bone. ② die (unworthily) for

【卖弄】 màinong show off; parade: ~学问 show off one's learning; parade one's knowledge/ ~小聪明 show off one's smartness

【卖身】 màishēn ① sell oneself or a member of one's family ② sell one's body; sell one's soul ◇ ~契 an indenture by which one sells oneself or a member of one's family

【卖身投靠】 màishēn tóukào barter away one's honour for sb.'s patronage; basely offer to serve some reactionary bigwig

【卖艺】 màiyì make a living as a performer: 在街头~ be a street-performer

【卖淫】 màiyín prostitution

【卖主】 màizhǔ seller

【卖座】 màizuò (of a theatre, etc.) draw large audiences; (of a restaurant, etc.) attract large numbers of customers:

那出戏可～啦。That play drew large audiences. 或 That play was a great draw.

脉 mài ① <生理> arteries and veins ② <简>(脉搏) pulse: 号～ feel sb.'s pulse ③ vein: 叶～ veins in a leaf/ 矿～ ore vein; mineral vein
另见 mò

【脉搏】màibó pulse: 他的～每分钟一百次。The beat of his pulse was a hundred./ 这部小说扣捏了我们时代的～。The novel throbs with the pulse of our times. ◇ ～计 sphygmometer

【脉络】màiluò ① <中医> a general name for arteries and veins ② vein (of a leaf, etc.) ③ thread of thought; sequence of ideas: 这篇文章结构严谨,～分明。This article is closely knit and presents its ideas in a clear, logical way.

mān

颟頁 mān
【颟顸】mānhan muddleheaded and careless

mán

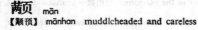
埋* mán
另见 mái
【埋怨】mányuàn blame; complain; grumble: 这场球打输了,大家找点原因,不要互相～。Instead of blaming one another for losing the game, let's find out what exactly went wrong.

蛮 mán ① rough; fierce; reckless; unreasoning: 野～ savage/ ～劲 sheer animal strength ② an ancient name for southern nationalities ③ <方> quite; pretty: 这电影～好。This is quite a good film. 或 This is a pretty good film.
【蛮不讲理】mán bù jiǎnglǐ be impervious to reason; persist in being unreasonable
【蛮干】mángàn act rashly; act recklessly; be foolhardy: 要苦干加巧干,不要～。We should work hard and intelligently, not blindly./ 那纯粹是～。That's downright foolhardy.
【蛮横】mánhèng rude and unreasonable; arbitrary; peremptory: ～无理的要求 peremptory demands/ ～地拒绝合理建议 arbitrarily reject reasonable proposals

馒 mán
【馒头】mántou steamed bun; steamed bread

瞒 mán hide the truth from: 不～你说 to tell you the truth
【瞒哄】mánhǒng deceive; pull the wool over sb.'s eyes
【瞒上欺下】mán shàng qī xià deceive those above and bully those below
【瞒天过海】mán tiān guò hǎi cross the sea by a trick — practise deception

鳗 mán eel

mǎn

满* mǎn ① full; filled; packed: 这两个抽屉都～了。Both drawers are full./ 屋里坐～了人。The room was packed with people./ 果树～山坡。The slope was covered with fruit trees./ 欢声笑语～山村。The mountain village rang with cheers and laughter./ ～～一卡车煤 a full truckload of coal/ ～头大汗 one's face streaming with sweat ② fill; meet: 再给你～一上一杯。Let me fill your glass once more. ③ expire; reach the limit: 年～十八的青年 young people who have reached the age of 18/ 他的服役期还没～。His

term of service hasn't expired yet./ 她到农村去还不～一年。It isn't a year yet since she went to live in the countryside./ 假期已～。The holidays are over. ④ completely; entirely; perfectly: ～不是那么回事。That wasn't the way it was at all./ 我～以为他会同意的。I had counted on him to agree with me. ⑤ satisfied: 不～ dissatisfied; discontented ⑥ complacent; conceited: 反骄破～ combat arrogance and complacence
【满不在乎】mǎn bù zàihu not worry at all; not care in the least; give (或 take) no heed: 别人都替他着急,他却～。Everybody was anxious about him, but he wasn't worried at all.
【满城风雨】mǎn chéng fēngyǔ (become) the talk of the town: 闹得～ create a sensation; create a scandal
【满额】mǎn'é fulfil the (enrolment, etc.) quota: 我校今年招生已～。Our school has already fulfilled its enrolment quota for this year.
【满分】mǎnfēn full marks
【满腹】mǎnfù have one's mind filled with: ～牢骚 full of grievances; full of resentment/ ～狐疑 filled with suspicion; extremely suspicious
【满怀】mǎnhuái ① have one's heart filled with; be imbued with: ～胜利的信心 fully confident of victory; with full confidence in victory ②〔多用于〕撞了个～ bump right into sb.
【满口】mǎnkǒu (speak) unreservedly; profusely; glibly: ～称赞 praise unreservedly (或 profusely)/ ～答应 readily promise/ ～谎言 spout lies
【满门】mǎnmén the whole family
【满面】mǎnmiàn have one's face covered with: 泪流～ tears streaming down one's cheeks/ ～笑容 grinning from ear to ear; be all smiles/ ～红光 glowing with health/ ～春风 beaming with satisfaction; radiant with happiness
【满目】mǎnmù meet the eye on every side: ～荒凉 A scene of desolation met the eye on every side.
【满目疮痍】mǎnmù chuāngyí 见"疮痍满目" chuāngyí mǎnmù
【满腔】mǎnqiāng have one's bosom filled with: ～仇恨 burning with hatred/ ～怒火 filled with rage/ ～热忱 filled with ardour and sincerity/ ～热情地接待顾客 attend to customers enthusiastically
【满身】mǎnshēn have one's body covered with; be covered all over with: ～油泥 covered all over with grime/ ～是汗 sweat all over
【满天】mǎntiān all over the sky: ～星斗 a star-studded sky/ 乌云～。The sky is overcast with dark clouds./ 鹅毛大雪～飞。The snow is falling thick and heavy.
【满眼】mǎnyǎn ① have one's eyes filled with: ～红丝 with bloodshot eyes ② meet the eye on every side: ～的山花 mountain flowers greeting the eye everywhere
【满意】mǎnyì satisfied; pleased: 双方对会谈的结果表示～。Both sides expressed satisfaction with the results of the talks./ 大家对他的工作很～。Everyone was pleased with his work.
【满月】mǎnyuè ① full moon ② a baby's completion of its first month of life: 孩子明天就～了。The baby will be a month old tomorrow.
【满载】mǎnzài loaded to capacity; fully loaded; laden with: 一辆～木材的卡车 a truck fully loaded with timber/ 一艘～煤炭的货船 a freighter laden with coal
【满载而归】mǎnzài ér guī come back with fruitful results; return from a rewarding journey
【满招损,谦受益】mǎn zhāo sǔn, qiān shòu yì one loses by pride and gains by modesty
【满足】mǎnzú ① satisfied; content; contented: ～于现状 be satisfied with the existing state of affairs; be content with things as they are/ 不～于已经取得的成绩 not rest content with one's achievements; not rest on one's laurels/ 学习的敌人是自己的～。Complacency is the enemy of study. ② satisfy; meet: ～人民的需要 satisfy (或 meet) the needs of the people/ 我们将尽可能地～你们的要求。We'll do our best to meet your demands.
【满座】mǎnzuò capacity audience; capacity house; full house: 这个剧演了一个月,场场～。The play ran for a month to capacity audiences.

màn

曼 màn ①graceful: 轻歌～舞 soft music and graceful dances ②prolonged; long-drawn-out: ～延 draw out (in length)

谩 màn disrespectful; rude
【谩骂】 mànmà hurl invectives; fling abuses; rail: ～决不是战斗。To hurl abuse is no way to fight.

漫 màn ①overflow; brim over; flood; inundate: 池塘的水～出来了。The pool overflowed its banks./ 水不深, 只～过我脚面。The water wasn't deep. It only came up to my ankles. ②all over the place; everywhere: ～江碧透。The whole stream was emerald green. ③free; unrestrained; casual: ～无目标 aimless; at random/ ～无止境 know no bounds; be without limit
【漫笔】 mànbǐ informal essay; literary notes
【漫不经心】 màn bù jīngxīn careless; casual; negligent
【漫步】 mànbù stroll; ramble; roam
【漫长】 màncháng very long; endless: ～的海岸线 a long coastline/ 在～的岁月中 during the long years; over the years
【漫画】 mànhuà caricature; cartoon
【漫山遍野】 mànshān-biànyě all over the mountains and plains; over hill and dale
【漫谈】 màntán (have an) informal discussion: 听完报告我们～一下吧。After we've heard the report, we'll talk about it.
【漫天】 màntiān ①filling the whole sky; all over the sky: ～大雾 a dense fog obscuring the sky/ ～大雪 whirling snow ②boundless; limitless: ～大谎 a monstrous lie/ ～要价 ask (或 demand) an exorbitant price
【漫无边际】 màn wú biānjì ①boundless ②straying far from the subject; rambling; discursive
【漫游】 mànyóu go on a pleasure trip; roam; wander: ～西湖 go boating on or roam around the West Lake

蔓 màn
【蔓延】 mànyán spread; extend: 火势～很快。The fire spread quickly.

慢* màn ①slow: 反应～ be slow to react/ ～下来 slow down/ 我的表～一分钟。My watch is one minute slow./ 这钟一天～十秒。This clock loses ten seconds a day. ②postpone; defer: 且～! Hold on a moment. 或 Just a moment!/ 这事先一点儿告诉她。Don't tell her about this yet. ③supercilious; rude: 做～ arrogant; haughty/ 言语骄～ use arrogant language
【慢镜头】 mànjìngtóu ⟨电影⟩ slow motion
【慢慢】 mànmàn slowly; gradually: 火车～地驶进了车站。Slowly the train pulled into the station./ ～来。Take your time. 或 Don't be in a rush./ 他～会想通的。He'll come round by and by.
【慢条斯理】 màntiáo-sīlǐ leisurely; unhurriedly: 他说话做事总是～的。He always speaks slowly and acts unhurriedly.
【慢性】 mànxìng chronic: ～病 chronic disease
【慢性子】 mànxìngzi ①phlegmatic temperament ②slow-poke; slow coach
【慢走】 mànzǒu ①don't go yet; stay; wait a minute ②⟨套⟩〔用于送别时〕good-bye; take care

幔 màn curtain; screen: 布～ cotton curtain
【幔帐】 mànzhàng curtain; screen; canopy

máng

忙* máng ①busy; fully occupied: 你在～什么呢? What are you busy with (或 at)?/ 这两天～不? Are you busy these days?/ 我一个人～不过来。I can't manage all this by myself./ 不要～于小事而忽略大事。Don't immerse yourself in minor matters to the neglect of major ones. ②hurry; hasten; make haste: ～从里屋出来 come hurrying out of the inner room; hasten out of the inner room/ ～着去开会 be in a hurry to go to a meeting/ 你～什么, 再坐一会儿吧。What's the hurry? Stay a bit longer./ 别～于下结论。Don't jump to conclusions.
【忙里偷闲】 mánglǐ tōuxián snatch a little leisure from a busy life
【忙碌】 mánglù be busy; bustle about: 为了全厂工人的生活, 她成天～不停。She's busy all day looking after the daily life of the workers in the factory.
【忙乱】 mángluàn be in a rush and a muddle; tackle a job in a hasty and disorderly manner: 要克服～现象。Don't work in a rush and get into a muddle.
【忙人】 mángrén busy person

芒 máng awn; beard; arista
【芒刺在背】 mángcì zài bèi feel prickles down one's back—feel nervous and uneasy

杧* máng
【杧果】 mángguǒ ⟨植⟩ mango

盲* máng blind
【盲肠】 mángcháng ⟨生理⟩ caecum
【盲从】 mángcóng follow blindly
【盲动】 mángdòng act blindly; act rashly
【盲目】 mángmù blind: ～崇拜 worship blindly/ ～乐观 be unrealistically optimistic/ 人口的～增长 unchecked growth of the population
【盲人】 mángrén blind person
【盲人摸象】 mángrén mō xiàng like the blind men trying to size up the elephant — take a part for the whole
【盲人瞎马】 mángrén xiāmǎ a blind man on a blind horse — rushing headlong to disaster
【盲文】 mángwén braille
【盲哑教育】 máng-yǎ jiàoyù education for the blind and the deaf-mute

氓 máng 见"流氓" liúmáng

茫 máng ①boundless and indistinct ②ignorant; in the dark
【茫茫】 mángmáng boundless and indistinct; vast: ～大海 a vast sea/ ～草原 the boundless grasslands
【茫然】 mángrán ignorant; in the dark; at a loss: ～无知 be utterly ignorant; be in the dark/ ～不知所措 be at a loss what to do; be at sea/ 显出～的神情 look blank
【茫无头绪】 máng wú tóuxù (of a thing) be confused like a tangle of flax; (of a person) not know where to begin

mǎng

莽 mǎng ①rank grass ②rash
【莽莽】 mǎngmǎng ①luxuriant; rank ②(of fields, plains, etc.) vast; boundless
【莽撞】 mǎngzhuàng crude and impetuous; rash: ～的小伙子 a young harum-scarum

蟒 mǎng boa; python
【蟒蛇】 mǎngshé boa; python

māo

猫* māo cat: 雄～ tomcat/ 小～ kitten/ ～叫 mewing; purring

【猫哭老鼠】 māo kū lǎoshǔ the cat weeping over the dead mouse — shed crocodile tears
【猫头鹰】 māotóuyīng owl

máo

毛* máo ① hair; feather; down: 腋～ armpit hairs/ 羽～ feather/ 桃子上的～ the down of a peach ②wool: ～毯 woollen blanket/ ～袜 woollen stockings/ ～裤 long woollen underwear ③ mildew: 长～ become mildewed; be covered with mildew ④ semifinished: ～坯 semifinished product ⑤ gross: ～利 gross profit ⑥ little; small: ～孩子 a small child; a mere child ⑦ careless; crude; rash: ～头～脑 rash; impetuous ⑧ panicky; scared; flurried: 心里直发～ feel scared; be panic-stricken/ 吓～了 be in a flurry of alarm ⑨〈口〉(of currency) be no longer worth its face value; depreciate
【毛笔】 máobǐ writing brush
【毛病】 máobìng ① trouble; mishap; breakdown: 发动机出了～。There's some trouble with the engine./ 这架收音机有点～。There's something wrong with the radio. ② defect; shortcoming; fault; mistake: 他的～是性急。He's impetuous — that's the trouble with him
【毛虫】 máochóng caterpillar 又作"毛毛虫"
【毛发】 máofà hair (on the human body and head)
【毛骨悚然】 máogǔ sǒngrán with one's hair standing on end — absolutely terrified: 令人～ send cold shivers down one's spine; make sb.'s hair stand on end; be bloodcurdling
【毛巾】 máojīn towel ◇ ～被 towelling coverlet/ ～布 towelling/ ～架 towel rail or rack
【毛孔】 máokǒng 〈生理〉pore
【毛毛雨】 máomaoyǔ drizzle
【毛皮】 máopí fur
【毛茸茸】 máorōngróng hairy; downy
【毛手毛脚】 máoshǒu-máojiǎo careless (in handling things)
【毛遂自荐】 Máo Suì zì jiàn offer one's services as Mao Sui (of the Warring States Period) did — volunteer one's services
【毛毯】 máotǎn woollen blanket
【毛线】 máoxiàn knitting wool ◇ ～针 knitting needle
【毛衣】 máoyī woollen sweater; sweater; woolly
【毛毡】 máozhān felt
【毛织品】 máozhīpǐn ① wool fabric; woollens ② woollen knitwear

矛* máo lance; pike; spear
【矛盾】 máodùn contradictory: 自相～ self-contradictory/ ～百出 full of contradictions
【矛头】 máotóu spearhead: ～所向 the target of attack

茅* máo 〈植〉cogongrass
【茅草】 máocǎo 〈植〉cogongrass ◇ ～棚 thatched shed; thatched shack
【茅庐】 máolú thatched cottage
【茅塞顿开】 máo sè dùn kāi suddenly see the light
【茅舍】 máoshè 〈书〉thatched cottage
【茅屋】 máowū thatched cottage

锚 máo anchor: 抛～ drop anchor; cast anchor/ 起～ weigh anchor

髦 máo 见"时髦" shímáo

蝥 máo an insect destructive of the roots of seedlings
【蝥贼】 máozéi a person harmful to the country and people; pest

mǎo

卯 mǎo the fourth of the twelve Earthly Branches
【卯时】 mǎoshí the period of the day from 5 a.m. to 7 a.m.

mào

茂 mào ① luxuriant; exuberant; profuse: 根深叶～ deep roots and exuberant foliage ② rich and splendid: 图文并～。The picture and its accompanying essay are both excellent.
【茂密】 màomì (of grass or trees) dense; thick: ～的森林 a dense forest
【茂盛】 màoshèng luxuriant; exuberant; flourishing: 庄稼长得很～。The crops are growing luxuriantly.

冒* mào ① emit; send out (或 up, forth); give off: ～泡 send up bubbles; be bubbling/ ～气 give off steam; be steaming/ 泥浆从地下～出来。Mud oozed from underground./烟囱里～着白烟。White smoke rose from the chimneys./ 他脑门上直～汗。Sweat kept oozing out from his forehead. ② risk; brave: 小李～着生命危险抢救国家财产。Xiao Li risked his life to save state property./～雨 braving the rain; in spite of the rain/ ～风险 run risks/～着风浪出海 put to sea in spite of wind and wave; venture out on a stormy sea ③ falsely (claim, etc.); fraudulently: 那人～称是连长的亲戚。The man falsely claimed to be a relative of the company commander.
【冒充】 màochōng pretend to be (sb. or sth. else); pass sb. or sth. off as: ～内行 pretend to be an expert; pose as an expert
【冒渎】 màodú 〈书〉bother or annoy a superior
【冒犯】 màofàn offend; affront: 谁知道这一句话竟～了他? Who would have thought that the remark would offend him?
【冒号】 màohào colon (:)
【冒火】 màohuǒ burn with anger; get angry; flare up
【冒昧】 màomèi 〈谦〉make bold; venture; take the liberty: ～陈辞 make bold to express my views; venture an opinion/ 不揣～ may I take the liberty to; I venture to
【冒名】 màomíng go under sb. else's name; assume another's name: ～顶替 take another's place by assuming his name
【冒牌】 màopái a counterfeit of a well-known trade mark; imitation; fake ◇ ～货 imitation; fake
【冒失】 màoshi rash; abrupt: 说话～ speak without due consideration/ 这样冒冒失失去找他可不好。It's not appropriate to drop in on him so casually. ◇ ～鬼 harum-scarum
【冒天下之大不韪】 mào tiānxià zhī dà bùwěi defy world opinion; risk universal condemnation; fly in the face of the will of the people
【冒险】 màoxiǎn take a risk; take chances: 戴上安全帽再下去,不要～。Wear your safety helmet when you go down. Don't take any chances./ 小分队～穿过敌人的封锁线。The detachment ventured a thrust through the enemy blockade./ 军事～ military adventure ◇ ～家 adventurer/ ～政策 adventurist policy

贸 mào trade: 外～ foreign trade
【贸然】 màorán rashly; hastily; without careful consideration: ～下结论 draw a hasty conclusion; jump to a conclusion
【贸易】 màoyì trade: 和别国进行～ trade with foreign countries; do business with other countries/ 对外～ foreign trade / 国内～ domestic trade/ 国际～ international trade

帽* mào ① headgear; hat; cap: 草～ straw hat/ 军服～ service cap/ 安全～ safety helmet ② cap-like cover for sth.: 笔～儿 the cap of a pen/ 螺钉～ screw cap

【帽徽】mòohuī insignia (或 badge) on a cap
【帽子】mòozi headgear; hat; cap

貌* mào looks; appearance: 美~ good looks/山村新~ the new look of a mountain village/ 人不可~相。Never judge people by their appearance.
【貌合神离】mòohé-shénlí (of two persons or parties) seemingly in harmony but actually at variance
【貌似】mòosì seemingly; in appearance: ~强大 seemingly powerful; outwardly strong/ ~公正 seemingly impartial

me

么* me ①〔后缀〕: 什~ what/ 多~ how/ 怎~ why; how/ 这~ such; so; in this way ②〔歌词中的衬字〕五月的花儿红呀~红似火。Red as fire are the flowers that bloom in May.

méi

没* méi 见"没有" 另见 mò
【没错儿】méicuòr ① I'm quite sure; you can rest assured: ~,准是小王告诉他的。I'm quite sure it was Xiao Wang who told him about it./ ~,就是他干的。There's no doubt about it. He's the one that did it. ② can't go wrong: 照说明书做,准保~。Just follow the directions. You can't go wrong.
【没法子】méi fǎzi can do nothing about it; can't help it
【没关系】méi guānxi it doesn't matter; it's nothing; that's all right; never mind
【没精打采】méijīng-dǎcǎi listless; in low spirits; out of sorts; lackadaisical
【没…没…】méi…méi… ①〔用在两个同义词前面,强调没有〕: 没完没了 endless; without end/ 没羞没臊 shameless; have no sense of shame ②〔用在两个反义词前面,表示应区别而未区别〕: 没轻没重 tactless/ 没大没小 impolite (to an elder); impertinent; impudent
【没命】méimìng ① lose one's life; die: 要不是医生及时赶到,这小孩就~了。The child would have died if the doctor hadn't come in time. ② recklessly; desperately; like mad; for all one's worth: 敌兵~地逃跑。The enemy soldiers ran off as fast as their legs could carry them.
【没趣】méiqù feel put out; feel snubbed: 没有人理他,他觉得~,只好走了。Very much put out by their indifference, he slunk off./ 自讨~ ask for a snub
【没什么】méi shénme it doesn't matter; it's nothing; that's all right; never mind: 你怎么了? ——~,有点头疼。What's the matter with you? — Just a bit of a headache; nothing serious.
【没事儿】méishìr ① have nothing to do; be free; be at a loose end: 今晚~,我想去看电影。I've got nothing to do this evening. I think I'll go to the film. ② it doesn't matter; it's nothing; that's all right; never mind: 唷,踩了你的脚了。——~。Sorry to have stepped on your toe. — That's all right./ 外边乱哄哄的,出了什么事儿? ——~,就几个孩子起哄。What's all that noise outside? — It's nothing. Only some kids making a row.
【没事找事】méishì zhǎoshì ① ask for trouble; ask for it ② try hard to find fault; cavil
【没有】méiyǒu ① not have: there is not; be without: 屋里~人。There·isn't anyone in the room./ ② not so… as: 这项试验~我们预料的那样顺利。The experiment didn't go as smoothly as we had expected. ③ less than: 他来了还~三天就走了。He was less than three days. 或 He wasn't here even three days. ④〔副〕〔表示"已然""曾经"的否定〕: 他回来没有? ——还~呢。Has he come back yet? — No, not yet. 昨天我~见到他。I didn't see him yesterday.

玫* méi
【玫瑰】méigui 〈植〉rugosa rose; rose

枚* méi 〈量〉〔多用于形体小的东西〕: 三~纪念章 three badges/ 一~古币 an ancient coin

眉* méi ① eyebrow; brow ② the top margin of a page
【眉笔】méibǐ eyebrow pencil
【眉飞色舞】méifēi-sèwǔ with dancing eyebrows and radiant face—enraptured; exultant
【眉睫】méijié (as close to the eye as) the eyebrows and eyelashes: 迫在~ urgent; imminent
【眉开眼笑】méikāi-yǎnxiào be all smiles; beam with joy
【眉来眼去】méilái-yǎnqù make eyes at each other; flirt with each other
【眉毛】méimao eyebrow; brow
【眉目】méimù ① features; looks: ~清秀 have delicate features ② logic; sequence of ideas: 这篇文章~清楚。The article is clear and well-organized.
【眉目】méimu prospect of a solution; sign of a positive outcome: 你托我办的事已经有点~了。About that job you asked me to do, I'm beginning to get somewhere with it. 或 I'm getting on with what you asked me to do./ 计划有了~。The plan is beginning to take shape.
【眉批】méipī notes and commentary at the top of a page
【眉清目秀】méiqīng-mùxiù have delicate features
【眉梢】méishāo the tip of the brow: 喜上~ look very happy
【眉头】méitóu brows: 皱~ knit the brows; frown/ ~一皱,计上心来。Knit the brows and a stratagem comes to mind.

莓 méi certain kinds of berries: 草~ strawberry

梅* méi plum
【梅毒】méidú 〈医〉syphilis
【梅花】méihuā ① plum blossom ②〈方〉wintersweet

媒 méi ① matchmaker; go-between: 做~ act as a matchmaker ② intermediary
【媒介】méijiè intermediary; medium; vehicle: 空气是传播声音的~。Air is a medium of sound./ 传染疾病的~ vehicle of disease; vector
【媒婆】méipó 〈旧〉woman matchmaker
【媒人】méirén matchmaker; go-between

煤* méi coal: 粉~ fine coal/ 块~ lump coal/ 原~ raw coal
【煤矿】méikuàng coal mine; colliery ◇ ~工人 coal miner
【煤气】méiqì coal gas; gas: 你们家烧~吗? Do you use a gas stove at home? ◇ ~厂 gasworks; gashouse/ ~灯 gas lamp; gas light/ ~管 gas pipe
【煤炭】méitàn coal
【煤烟】méiyān ① smoke from burning coal ② soot ◇ ~污染 smoke pollution
【煤油】méiyóu kerosene; paraffin ◇ ~灯 kerosene lamp/ ~炉 kerosene stove

霉 méi mould; mildew: 发~ go mouldy; mildew

měi

每* měi ① every; each; per: 节约~一分钱 save every penny/ ~星期五 every Friday/ ~四小时服一次 to be taken once every four hours/ ~人一把铁锹 a spade for each person/ 以~小时四十公里的速度行驶 drive at (a speed of) forty kilometres an hour/ ~时~刻 all the time; at all times/ ~年的平均产量 average yearly yield; average output per annum ② often: 春秋佳日,~作郊游。We often go for an outing in the country on fine days in spring and autumn.

【每当】 měidāng whenever; every time: ～我想起童年的悲惨遭遇，心情总是很不平静。Whenever I recall the misery of my childhood, my mind is in a turmoil.

【每逢佳节倍思亲】 měiféng jiājié bèi sī qīn on festive occasions more than ever we think of our dear ones far away

【每况愈下】 měi kuàng yù xià steadily deteriorate; go from bad to worse

【每每】 měiměi often: 他给青年讲村史，～一谈就是好几个钟头。When he talked to the young people about the history of the village, he would often go on for hours.

美* měi ① beautiful; pretty: 风景多～啊! What beautiful scenery!/ 真、善、～ the true, the good and the beautiful ② very satisfactory; good: ～酒 good wine/ 价廉物～ good and inexpensive/ 日子过得挺～ live quite happily

【美不胜收】 měi bùshèng shōu so many beautiful things that one simply can't take them all in

【美称】 měichēng laudatory title; good name: 四川向有天府之国的～。Sichuan has always enjoyed the reputation of being a "Heavenly Land of Plenty".

【美德】 měidé virtue; moral excellence

【美感】 měigǎn aesthetic feeling; aesthetic perception; sense of beauty

【美观】 měiguān pleasing to the eye; beautiful; artistic: 房间布置得很～。The room is artistically decorated.

【美好】 měihǎo fine; happy; glorious: ～的日子 happy days; a happy life/ ～的将来 a glorious future/ ～的回忆 happy memories/ ～的远景 magnificent prospects

【美化】 měihuà beautify; prettify; embellish: ～环境 beautify the environment/ 竭力～自己 try hard to prettify oneself

【美景】 měijǐng beautiful scenery (或 landscape)

【美丽】 měilì beautiful: ～富饶的国家 a beautiful and richly-endowed country

【美满】 měimǎn happy; perfectly satisfactory: ～的生活 a happy life/ ～婚姻 a happy marriage; conjugal happiness

【美梦】 měimèng fond dream

【美妙】 měimiào beautiful; splendid; wonderful: ～的青春 the wonderful days of one's youth/ ～的诗句 beautiful verse

【美名】 měimíng good name; good reputation: 英雄～天下扬。A hero's good name spreads far and wide.

【美其名曰】 měi qí míng yuē call it by the fine-sounding name of

【美人】 měirén beautiful woman; beauty ◇ ～计 use of a woman to ensnare a man; sex-trap

【美容】 měiróng ① improve (a woman's) looks ② cosmetology ◇ ～院 beauty parlour

【美术】 měishù ① the fine arts; art: 工艺～ industrial arts; arts and crafts ② painting

【美谈】 měitán a story passed on with approval; 传为～ be told from mouth to mouth with general approval

【美味】 měiwèi ① delicious food; delicacy ② delicious; dainty: ～小吃 dainty snacks

【美学】 měixué aesthetics

【美言】 měiyán put in a good word for sb.

【美中不足】 měi zhōng bù zú a blemish in an otherwise perfect thing; a fly in the ointment

mèi

妹* mèi younger sister; sister

【妹夫】 mèifu younger sister's husband; brother-in-law

【妹妹】 mèimei younger sister; sister

昧 mèi ① have hazy notions about; be ignorant of: 素～平生 have never made sb.'s acquaintance ② hide; conceal: 拾金不～ not pocket the money one has picked up/ ～着良心 (do evil) against one's conscience

【昧心】 mèixīn (do evil) against one's conscience

寐 mèi 〈书〉 sleep

谜 mèi

另见 mí

【谜儿】 mèir 〈口〉 riddle: 猜～ guess a riddle

媚 mèi ① fawn on; curry favour with; flatter; toady to: ～敌 curry favour with (或 toady to) the enemy ② charming; fascinating; enchanting: ～人的景色 enchanting scenery

【媚外】 mèiwài fawn on (或 toady to) foreign powers: 崇洋～ worship foreign things and fawn on foreign powers

魅 mèi evil spirit; demon

【魅力】 mèilì glamour; charm; enchantment; fascination: 艺术～ artistic charm

mēn

闷* mēn ① stuffy; close: 开开窗吧，屋里太～了。Open the windows. The air here is too close. ② cover tightly: ～一会儿，茶味就出来了。Let the tea draw for a while and the flavour will come out./ 你有什么事就说吧，别～在心里。Speak out. Don't just brood over things. ③ 〈方〉 (of a sound) muffled: 说话～声～气 speak in a muffled voice; won't come out with a clear statement ④ shut oneself or sb. indoors: 别老～在屋里。Don't shut yourself indoors all day.

另见 mèn

【闷气】 mēnqì stuffy; close

【闷热】 mēnrè hot and suffocating; sultry; muggy

【闷声不响】 mēnshēng bù xiǎng remain silent

mén

门* mén ① entrance; door; gate: 请走南～。Please use the south entrance./ 前(后)～ front (back) door/ 校～ school gate/ 炉～ stove door ② valve; switch: 气～ air valve/ 电～ switch ③ way to do sth.; knack: 我到钢厂劳动了一段时间，对炼钢摸着点～儿了。After working in the steel mill for a while I got an inkling of how steel is made. ④ family: 豪～ wealthy and influential family ⑤ (religious) sect; school (of thought): 佛～ Buddhism ⑥ class; category: 分～别类 divide into different categories / 脊椎动物～ Vertebrata ⑦ 〈量〉: 一～大炮 a piece of artillery; a cannon; a gun/ 两～功课 two subjects; two courses

【门齿】 ménchǐ front tooth; incisor

【门当户对】 méndāng-hùduì be well-matched in social and economic status (for marriage)

【门第】 méndì 〈旧〉 family status

【门户】 ménhù ① door: ～紧闭 with the doors tightly shut ② gateway; important passageway: 天津港是北京通往海洋的～。The port of Tianjin is Beijing's gateway to the sea. ③ faction; sect: ～之见 sectarian bias; sectarianism ④ family status

【门槛】 ménkǎn threshold

【门可罗雀】 mén kě luó què you can catch sparrows on the doorstep — where visitors are few and far between

【门口】 ménkǒu entrance; doorway: 在～等候 wait at the door (或 gate)/ 走过学校～ walk past the school entrance/ 把客人送到～ see the guest to the door

【门框】 ménkuàng doorframe

【门联】 ménlián scrolls pasted on either side of the door forming a couplet; gatepost couplet

【门路】 ménlu ① knack; way: 摸到一些～ have learned the ropes; know one's way around/ 广开饲料～，发展养猪事业 tap new sources of feed to boost pig farming ② social connections (for securing jobs, etc.); pull: 找～ solicit help from potential backers

【门面】 ménmian ① the façade of a shop; shop front: 三间～ a three-bay shop front ② appearance; façade: 装点

keep up appearances; put up a facade; put on a front; do some window dressing ◇～话 formal and insincere remarks; lip service

【门牌】 ménpái ① (house) number plate ② house number: 你家～几号? What's the number of your house?

【门票】 ménpiào entrance ticket; admission ticket: 不收～ admission free

【门神】 ménshén door-god (whose pictures were often pasted on the front door of a house as a talisman in old China)

【门生】 ménshēng pupil; disciple

【门市】 ménshì retail sales ◇～部 retail department; sales department; salesroom

【门庭若市】 mén-tíng ruò shì the courtyard is as crowded as a marketplace — a much visited house

【门徒】 méntú disciple; follower; adherent

【门外汉】 ménwàihàn layman; the uninitiated

【门牙】 ményá front tooth; incisor

【门诊】 ménzhěn outpatient service
◇～病人 outpatient; clinic patient/ ～部 clinic; outpatient department/ ～时间 consulting hours

扪 mén <书> touch; stroke

【扪心自问】 ménxīn zìwèn examine one's conscience

mèn

闷* mèn ① bored; depressed; in low spirits: 你一个人在这儿多～得慌,跟我们出去走走吧! Don't you feel bored staying here all alone? Why not come out with us for a walk? ② tightly closed; sealed
另见 mēn

【闷葫芦】 mènhúlu enigma; puzzle; riddle: 这几句没头没脑的话真把人揣进～里了。 These abrupt remarks were really a puzzle to everyone.

【闷闷不乐】 mènmèn bù lè depressed; in low spirits

焖 mèn boil in a covered pot over a slow fire; braise: ～饭 cook rice over a slow fire/ ～牛肉 braised beef

懑 mèn 见"愤懑" fènmèn

men

们* men 〔用在代词或指人的名词后面, 表示复数〕: 他～ they/ 人～ people

mēng

蒙* mēng ① cheat; deceive; dupe: ～我! You're kidding me! ② make a wild guess: ～对了 make a lucky guess ③ unconscious; senseless: 给打～了 be knocked senseless; be stunned by a blow/ 他觉得脑袋发～。 He felt his head swimming.
另见 méng

【蒙骗】 mēngpiàn deceive; cheat; hoodwink; delude

méng

萌 méng sprout; shoot forth; bud; germinate

【萌芽】 méngyá ① sprout; germinate; shoot; bud ② rudiment; shoot; seed; germ: 处于～状态 in the embryonic stage; in the bud

蒙* méng ① cover: ～上一层灰尘 be covered with a layer of dust/ ～住眼睛 be blindfolded/ ～头睡大觉 tuck oneself in and sleep like a log ② receive; meet with: ～

大力协助,十分感谢。 Thank you very much for your kind help. ③ ignorant; illiterate: 启～ enlighten
另见 mēng

【蒙蔽】 méngbì hoodwink; deceive; hide the truth from; pull the wool over sb.'s eyes

【蒙蒙】 méngméng drizzly; misty: ～细雨 a fine drizzle/ 烟雾～ misty

【蒙难】 méngnàn (of a revolutionary) be confronted by danger; fall into the clutches of the enemy

【蒙受】 méngshòu suffer; sustain: ～损失 sustain a loss/ ～耻辱 be subjected to humiliation; be humiliated

【蒙在鼓里】 méng zài gǔlǐ be kept inside a drum — be kept in the dark

盟 méng ① alliance: 结～ form an alliance ② league ③ sworn (brothers)
另见 míng

【盟邦】 méngbāng allied country; ally

【盟国】 méngguó allied country; ally

【盟军】 méngjūn allied forces

【盟友】 méngyǒu ally

【盟约】 méngyuē oath of alliance; treaty of alliance

【盟主】 méngzhǔ the leader (或 chief) of an alliance

濛 méng

【濛濛】 méngméng 见"蒙蒙" méngméng

獴 méng <动> mongoose

檬 méng 见"柠檬" níngméng

曚 méng

【曚昽】 ménglóng <书> dim daylight

朦 méng

【朦胧】 ménglóng ① dim moonlight; hazy moonlight ② obscure; dim; hazy: ～的景色 a hazy view

矇 méng

【矇眬】 ménglóng half asleep; drowsy; somnolent: 睡眼～ eyes heavy with sleep; drowsy/ ～睡去 doze off/ 他中他仿佛听见有人敲门。 While he was half asleep, he seemed to hear a knock on the door.

měng

猛* měng ① fierce; violent; energetic; vigorous: ～将 a valiant general/ ～虎 a fierce tiger/ 产量～增 a sharp increase in output/ 穷追～打 hotly pursue and fiercely attack/ 用力过～ use too much strength; overexert oneself/ 在背上击一～拳 give sb. a powerful shove in the back ② suddenly; abruptly: ～地往前一跳 suddenly jump forward/ ～吃一惊 be startled

【猛不防】 měngbufáng by surprise; unexpectedly; unawares: ～后面有人推了他一下。 Suddenly someone gave him a push from behind.

【猛进】 měngjìn push ahead vigorously: 突飞～ advance by leaps and bounds

【猛力】 měnglì vigorously; with sudden force: ～扣杀 smash with all one's strength/ 把手榴弹一～甩 throw a grenade with all one's might

【猛烈】 měngliè fierce; vigorous; violent: 发动～的进攻 wage a vigorous offensive/ ～的炮火 heavy shellfire/ 风势～。 There was a fierce wind.

【猛然】 měngrán suddenly; abruptly: 我～想起来了。 In a flash I remembered./ ～一拉 pull with a jerk

【猛兽】 měngshòu beast of prey

蜢 měng 见"蚱蜢" zhàměng

懵 měng muddled; ignorant

【懵懂】 měngdǒng muddled; ignorant

mèng

孟 mèng ① the first month (of a season) ② eldest (brother)

梦* mèng dream
【梦话】 mènghuà ① words uttered in one's sleep; somniloquy: 昨晚我听见你说～。 I heard you talk in your sleep last night. ② daydream; nonsense
【梦幻】 mènghuàn illusion; dream; reverie: ～般的境界 a dreamlike world; dreamland
【梦幻泡影】 mènghuàn-pàoyǐng pipe dream; bubble; illusion
【梦见】 mèngjiàn see in a dream; dream about: 他～自己又回到了部队。 He dreamt that he was back in the army.
【梦境】 mèngjìng dreamland; dreamworld; dream: 如入～ feel as if one were in a dream
【梦寐】 mèngmèi dream; sleep: ～难忘 be unable to forget sth. even in one's dreams
【梦寐以求】 mèngmèi yǐ qiú crave sth. so that one even dreams about it; long (或 yearn) for sth. day and night
【梦乡】 mèngxiāng dreamland: 进入～ go off to dreamland; fall asleep
【梦想】 mèngxiǎng ① dream of; vainly hope ② fond dream; earnest wish
【梦游症】 mèngyóuzhèng somnambulism; sleepwalking 又作"梦行症"

mī

咪 mī
【咪咪】 mīmī ① 〈象〉 mew; miaow ② smilingly: 笑～ be all smiles; be wreathed in smiles

眯 mī ① narrow (one's eyes): ～着眼睛笑 narrow one's eyes into a smile/ ～着眼瞧 squint at ② 〈方〉 take a nap: ～一会儿 take a short nap; have forty winks

mí

弥 mí ① full; overflowing: ～漫 fill the air ② cover; fill: ～缝 plug up holes; gloss over faults ③ more: 欲盖～彰 try to cover sth. up only to make it more conspicuous
【弥补】 míbǔ make up; remedy; make good: ～损失 make up for (或 make good) a loss/ ～赤字 make up (或 meet) a deficit/ ～缺陷 remedy a defect/ 学习别人的优点，～自己的不足 learn from other people's strong points to counteract one's own weaknesses
【弥漫】 mímàn fill the air; spread all over the place: 烟雾～ heavy with smoke; smoke-laden; (of a place) be enveloped in mist
【弥撒】 mísa 〈天主教〉 Mass
【弥天大谎】 mítiān dàhuǎng monstrous (或 thundering, outrageous) lie
【弥天大罪】 mítiān dàzuì monstrous crime; heinous crime

迷* mí ① be confused; be lost: ～了方向 lose one's bearings; get lost ② be fascinated by; be crazy about: 她对游泳着了～。 She was crazy about swimming. ③ fan; enthusiast; fiend: 乒乓球～ a table tennis fan (或 enthusiast)/ 棋～ a chess fiend/ 官～ a person who craves office ④ confuse; perplex; fascinate; enchant: ～人的景色 scenery of enchanting beauty/ 财～心窍 be befuddled by a craving for wealth; be obsessed by lust for money
【迷宫】 mígōng labyrinth; maze
【迷糊】 míhu ① misted; blurred; dimmed: 这么多花布我都看～了。 I was simply dazzled by all these cotton prints.

② dazed; confused; muddled: 睡～了 dazed with sleep/ 他这个人有点～。 He's somewhat muddleheaded.
【迷魂汤】 míhúntāng sth. intended to turn sb.'s head; magic potion: 灌～ try to ensnare sb. with honeyed words
【迷魂阵】 míhúnzhèn a scheme for confusing or bewildering sb.; maze; trap: 摆～ lay out a scheme to bewitch sb.; set a trap
【迷惑】 míhuo puzzle; confuse; perplex; baffle: 感到～不解 feel puzzled; feel perplexed
【迷恋】 míliàn be infatuated with; madly cling to
【迷路】 mílù lose one's way: get lost
【迷茫】 mímáng ① vast and hazy: 大雪纷飞，原野一片～。 The vast plain was obscured by the falling flakes of snow. ② confused; perplexed; dazed: 他脸上显出～的神情。 There was a confused look on his face.
【迷失】 míshī lose (one's way, etc.): ～方向 lose one's bearings; get lost
【迷途】 mítú ① lose one's way ② wrong path: 走入～ go astray
【迷信】 míxìn ① superstition; superstitious belief; blind faith; blind worship ② have blind faith in; make a fetish of

谜* mí ① riddle; conundrum: 猜～ guess a riddle ② enigma; mystery; puzzle: 不解之～ unfathomable enigma; insoluble mystery (或 puzzle)/ 这件事到现在还是个～。 The affair remains a mystery to this day.
另见 mèi
【谜底】 mídǐ ① answer (或 solution) to a riddle ② truth
【谜语】 míyǔ riddle; conundrum

糜 mí ① gruel ② rotten ③ wasteful; extravagant
【糜费】 mífèi waste: ～钱财 waste money
【糜烂】 mílàn rotten to the core; dissipated; debauched: 生活～ lead a fast life

麋 mí elk

靡 mí waste: 奢～ wasteful; extravagant
另见 mǐ
【靡费】 mífèi waste; spend extravagantly

mǐ

米* mǐ ① rice ② shelled or husked seed: 花生～ peanut seed; peanut kernel
【米粉】 mǐfěn ① ground rice; rice flour: ～肉 pork steamed with ground glutinous rice ② rice-flour noodles
【米酒】 mǐjiǔ rice wine
【米糠】 mǐkāng rice bran
【米粒】 mǐlì grain of rice
【米色】 mǐsè cream-coloured
【米汤】 mǐtang ① water in which rice has been cooked ② thin rice or millet gruel; rice water

靡 mǐ ① blown away by the wind: 所向披～ send the enemy fleeing helter-skelter; carry all before one ② 〈书〉 no; not: ～日不思 not a day passes without one's thinking of sth. or sb.
另见 mí
【靡靡之音】 mǐmǐ zhī yīn decadent music

mì

泌 mì secrete

觅 mì look for; hunt for; seek: 鸟雀经常在这里～食。 Birds often look for food here.

秘* mì ① secret: ～事 a secret ② keep sth. secret; hold sth. back: ～而不宣 keep sth. secret; not let anyone

into a secret ⑧ 〈简〉(使馆秘书) secretary: 一～ First Secretary
另见 bì

【秘本】 mìběn treasured private copy of a rare book

【秘方】 mìfāng secret recipe: 祖传～ a secret recipe handed down from generation to generation

【秘诀】 mìjué secret (of success): 成功的～ the secret of (或 key to) one's success

【秘密】 mìmì secret; clandestine; confidential: ～会议 secret meeting; closed-door session/ ～活动 clandestine activities/ ～文件 secret papers; confidential document/ 探索海底～ explore the secrets of the ocean bed

【秘史】 mìshǐ secret history (as of a feudal dynasty); inside story

【秘书】 mìshū secretary: 机要～ confidential secretary/ 私人～ private secretary ◇～处 secretariat/ ～长 secretary-general

密* mì ① close; dense; thick: ～林 thick (或 dense) forest/ ～不透风 airtight/ 枪声很～。 There was the sound of intensive gunfire./ 这两行苗栽得太～了。 These two rows of seedlings are planted too close together. ② intimate; close: ～友 close friend; bosom friend ③ fine; meticulous: 周～ carefully considered; meticulous ④ secret: 绝～ top secret; strictly confidential/ ～通声息 secretly communicate with each other

【密闭】 mìbì airtight; hermetic

【密布】 mìbù densely covered: 阴云～。 The sky is overcast. 或 Dark clouds are gathering./ 礁石～ thick with reefs

【密电】 mìdiàn ① cipher telegram ② secretly telegraph sb. ◇～码 cipher code

【密度】 mìdù ① density; thickness: 人口～ population density/ 兵力～ density of troops/ 火力～ density (或 volume) of fire ② 〈物〉density

【密封】 mìfēng seal up: ～的文件 sealed documents

【密集】 mìjí concentrated; crowded together: 人口～ densely populated; thickly populated

【密件】 mìjiàn a confidential paper or letter; classified matter; classified material

【密锣紧鼓】 mìluó-jǐngǔ 见 "紧锣密鼓" jǐnluó-mìgǔ

【密码】 mìmǎ cipher; cipher code; secret code ◇～电报 cipher telegram/ ～机 cipher machine; cryptograph

【密密麻麻】 mìmìmámá close and numerous; thickly dotted: 笔记本上写满了～的小字。 The notebook was filled with small, closely-written characters.

【密谋】 mìmóu conspire; plot; scheme

【密切】 mìqiè ① close; intimate: ～配合 act in close coordination/ ～相关 be closely related ② carefully; intently; closely: ～注视 pay close attention to; watch closely

【密商】 mìshāng hold private counsel; hold secret talks

【密室】 mìshì a room used for secret purposes: 策划于～ plot behind closed doors

【密谈】 mìtán secret (或 confidential, private) talk; talk behind closed doors

【密探】 mìtàn secret agent; spy

【密友】 mìyǒu close (或 fast) friend; bosom friend

【密约】 mìyuē secret agreement; secret treaty

蜜* mì ① honey ② honeyed; sweet

【蜜蜂】 mìfēng honeybee; bee

【蜜柑】 mìgān mandarin orange; tangerine orange

【蜜月】 mìyuè honeymoon

mián

眠* mián ① sleep: 不～之夜 a sleepless night; a white night ② dormancy: 冬～ hibernate

绵* mián ① silk floss ② continuous ③ soft

【绵薄】 miánbó 〈谦〉(my) meagre strength; humble effort: 愿尽～ I'll do what little I can.

【绵绵】 miánmián continuous; unbroken: 秋雨～。 The autumn rain goes on and on.

【绵延】 miányán be continuous; stretch long and unbroken

【绵羊】 miányáng sheep

【绵纸】 miánzhǐ tissue paper

棉* mián ① a general term for cotton and kapok ② cotton: ～纺织品 cotton textiles ③ cotton-padded; quilted: ～大衣 cotton-padded overcoat/ ～衣 cotton-padded clothes

【棉花】 miánhua cotton

【棉衣】 miányī cotton-padded clothes

【棉织品】 miánzhīpǐn cotton goods; cotton textiles; cotton fabrics

miǎn

免* miǎn ① excuse sb. from sth.; exempt; dispense with: ～试 be excused from an examination/ ～服兵役 be exempt from military service/ 互相～办签证协议 mutual exemption of visas agreement/ 这些手续就～了。 We'll dispense with the formalities. ② remove from office; dismiss; relieve: 任～事项 appointments and removals/ 他工作太多,得给他～掉几项。 He's got too much to do. He should be relieved of some of his jobs. ③ avoid; avert; escape: 事先做好准备,以～临时忙乱。 Get prepared beforehand to avoid being rushed when the work starts./ ～于受灾 avert a disaster ④ not allowed: 闲人～进。 No admittance except on business.

【免不了】 miǎnbuliǎo be unavoidable; be bound to be: 在前进的道路上,～会有困难。 There are bound to be difficulties in the course of our advance.

【免除】 miǎnchú ① prevent; avoid: 兴修水利,～水旱灾害 build irrigation works to prevent droughts and floods ② remit; excuse; exempt; relieve: ～债务 remit a debt/ ～一项任务 excuse sb. from a task; relieve sb. of a task

【免得】 miǎnde so as not to; so as to avoid: 多问几句,～走错路。 Make some more inquiries so that you won't go the wrong way./ 我再说明一下,～引起误会。 To avoid any misunderstanding, let me explain once again./ 你要是能去最好,～他跑一趟。 It would be best if you could go. It would save him a trip.

【免费】 miǎnfèi free of charge; free; gratis: ～医疗 free medical care/ ～入场 admission free; be admitted gratis

【免税】 miǎnshuì ① exempt from taxation ② tax-free; duty-free ◇～货物 duty-free goods

【免役】 miǎnyì exempt from service

【免职】 miǎnzhí remove sb. from office; relieve sb. of his post

【免罪】 miǎnzuì exempt from punishment

勉* miǎn ① exert oneself; strive: ～力为之 exert oneself to the utmost; do one's best ② encourage; urge; exhort: 互～ encourage one another/ 自～ spur oneself on ③ strive to do what is beyond one's power: ～为其难 undertake to do a difficult job as best one can

【勉励】 miǎnlì encourage; urge

【勉强】 miǎnqiǎng ① manage with an effort; do with difficulty: 病人～喝了点粥。 With an effort the patient ate some gruel. ② reluctantly; grudgingly: ～同意 reluctantly agree/ ～地笑了笑 force a smile/ 他接受了我们的建议,但是很～。 He accepted our suggestion, but rather grudgingly. ③ force sb. to do sth.: 要是他不愿意去,就不要～他。 If he doesn't want to go, don't force him to. ④ inadequate; unconvincing; strained; farfetched: 你的理由很～。 The reason you give is rather unconvincing. ⑤ barely enough: 草料～够牲口吃一天。 There's just enough cattle fodder for one day's feed./～维持生活 eke out a bare living; scrape along

娩 miǎn childbirth; delivery; parturition

冕 miǎn crown: 加~礼 coronation

湎 miǎn 见"沉湎" chénmiǎn

缅 miǎn remote; far back
【缅怀】 miǎnhuái cherish the memory of; recall: ~往事 recall past events
【缅想】 miǎnxiǎng think of (past events); recall

腼 miǎn
【腼腆】 miǎntian shy; bashful: 这孩子见了生人有点~。The child is shy with strangers.

miàn

面* miàn ① face: ~带笑容 with a smile on one's face/ ~无惧色 not look at all afraid ② face (a certain direction): 这房子~南坐北。The house faces south. ③ surface; top; face: 桌~ the top of a table; tabletop/ 水~ the surface of the water/ 路~ road surface/ 钟~ clock face; dial ④ personally; directly: ~告 tell sb. personally/ ~交 deliver personally; hand-deliver ⑤ the right side; cover; outside: 书~儿破了。The cover of the book is torn. ⑥ ⟨数⟩ surface ⑦ an entire area (as opposed to particular points) ⑧ side; aspect: 四~包围敌人 surround the enemy on all sides/ 这只是问题的一~。This is only one aspect of the question. ⑨ extent; range; scale; scope ⑩ 〔方位词后缀〕: 前~ in front/ 左~ on the left/ 外~ outside ⑪ ⟨量⟩〔多用于扁平的物件〕: 一~镜子 a mirror/ 两~旗子 two flags ⑫ wheat flour; flour ⑬ powder ⑭ noodles
【面包】 miànbāo bread
【面不改色】 miàn bù gǎisè not change colour; remain calm; without turning a hair; without batting an eyelid
【面辞】 miàncí go to say good-bye to sb.; take leave of sb.
【面对】 miànduì face; confront: ~现实 face reality; be realistic/ ~危险情况, 镇定自若 remain calm in the face of danger/ ~这一派大好形势, 怎能不欢欣鼓舞？Who wouldn't be happy to see such a good situation？
【面对面】 miàn duì miàn facing each other; face-to-face; vis-à-vis: ~地坐着 sit face-to-face; sit vis-à-vis
【面粉】 miànfěn wheat flour; flour ◇ ~厂 flour mill
【面红耳赤】 miànhóng-ěrchì be red in the face; be flushed: 争得~ argue until everyone is red in the face; have a heated argument/ 羞得~ flush with shame or shyness
【面黄肌瘦】 miànhuáng-jīshòu sallow and emaciated; lean and haggard
【面积】 miànjī area: 中国~约为九百六十万平方公里。The area of China is about 9.6 million square kilometres./ 棉花种植的~ the acreage under cotton/ 展览会~为三千平方米。The exhibition covers a floor space of 3,000 square metres.
【面颊】 miànjiá cheek
【面具】 miànjù mask: 防毒~ gas mask
【面孔】 miànkǒng face: 严肃的~ a stern face/ 板起~ put on a stern expression
【面临】 miànlín be faced with; be confronted with; be up against: ~一场严重的危机 be faced with a serious crisis
【面貌】 miànmào ① face; features: 他俩的~十分相似。The two of them look very much alike. ② appearance (of things); look; aspect: 精神~ mental outlook/ 一新 take on a new look (或 aspect)
【面面俱到】 miànmiàn jù dào attend to each and every aspect of a matter
【面面相觑】 miànmiàn xiāng qù look at each other in blank dismay; gaze at each other in speechless despair
【面目】 miànmù ① face; features; visage: ~可憎 repulsive in appearance ② appearance (of things); look; aspect: ~全非 be changed or distorted beyond recognition/ 还其本来~ reveal sth. in its true colours/ 政治~不清 of dubious political background ③ self-respect; honour; sense of shame; face: 愧无~见人 feel too ashamed to face people

【面目一新】 miànmù yī xīn take on an entirely new look; present a completely new appearance; assume a new aspect
【面庞】 miànpáng contours of the face; face: 圆圆的~ a round face
【面洽】 miànqià discuss with sb. face to face; take up a matter with sb. personally
【面前】 miànqián in (the) face of; in front of; before: 困难~不动摇 not waver in the face of difficulties/ 在凶恶的敌人~, 他没有丝毫怯懦的表现。He did not show the slightest timidity before the ferocious enemy.
【面容】 miànróng facial features; face: ~消瘦 look emaciated
【面如土色】 miàn rú tǔsè look ashen; look pale: 吓得~ turn pale with fright
【面色】 miànsè ① complexion: ~苍白 look pale/ ~红润 have rosy cheeks; be ruddy-cheeked ② facial expression: ~忧郁 have a melancholy look; look worried
【面纱】 miànshā veil
【面善】 miànshàn look familiar
【面商】 miànshāng discuss with sb. face to face; consult personally
【面食】 miànshi cooked wheaten food
【面授机宜】 miàn shòu jīyí personally instruct sb. on the line of action to pursue; give confidential briefing
【面熟】 miànshú look familiar: 这人看着~, 就是想不起来是谁。That person looks familiar but I simply can't place him.
【面谈】 miàntán speak to sb. face to face; take up a matter with sb. personally
【面条】 miàntiáo noodles
【面无人色】 miàn wú rénsè look ghastly pale
【面向】 miànxiàng turn one's face to; turn in the direction of; face
【面谢】 miànxiè thank sb. in person
【面值】 miànzhí ① par value; face value; nominal value ② denomination
【面子】 miànzi ① outer part; outside; face: 大衣的~ the outside of an overcoat ② reputation; prestige; face: 丢~ lose face/ 保全~ save face/ 爱~ be concerned about face-saving/ 撕破~ cast aside all considerations of face; not spare sb.'s sensibilities/ 有~ enjoy due respect/ 给~ show due respect for sb.'s feelings

miáo

苗* miáo ① young plant; seedling: 麦~儿 wheat seedling ② the young of some animals: 鱼~ fry ③ vaccine: 牛痘~ (bovine) vaccine ④ sth. resembling a young plant: 火~儿 flame
【苗条】 miáotiao (of a woman) slender; slim
【苗头】 miáotou symptom of a trend; suggestion of a new development: 要注意不良倾向的~。Watch out for symptoms of unhealthy tendencies./ 他一看~不对就溜了。He slipped off when he saw what was going to happen.
【苗裔】 miáoyì ⟨书⟩ progeny; descendants; offspring

描 miáo ① trace; copy: ~图样 trace designs; copy designs ② touch up; retouch: 练毛笔字, 一笔是一笔, 不要~。In practising Chinese calligraphy, write with a sure hand — don't retouch.
【描画】 miáohuà draw; paint; depict; describe: ~出美好的前景 paint a bright future/ 漓江美景难以用语言来~。The beauty of the scenery along the Lijiang River defies description.
【描绘】 miáohuì depict; describe; portray
【描摹】 miáomó depict; portray; delineate
【描述】 miáoshù describe: 详细~事情的经过 describe what happened in great detail
【描图】 miáotú tracing ◇ ~员 tracer/ ~纸 tracing paper
【描写】 miáoxiě describe; depict; portray: ~一位优秀国家的成长过程 describe how he grew up to be an outstanding painter

瞄 miáo concentrate one's gaze on; take aim: ~得准，打得狠 take good aim and hit hard
【瞄准】 miáozhǔn take aim; aim; train on; lay; sight: 练习 ~ practise aiming/ ~靶心 aim at the bull's-eye

miǎo

杪 miǎo ① the tip of a twig: 树~ tree top ② end (of a year, month or season): 岁~ the end of the year; year-end

秒* miǎo second (=1/60 of a minute)
【秒表】 miǎobiǎo stopwatch; chronograph
【秒针】 miǎozhēn second hand (of a clock or watch)

渺 miǎo ① (of an expanse of water) vast ② distant and indistinct; vague: ~无人迹 remote and uninhabited/ ~若烟云 as vague as mist ③ tiny; insignificant: ~不足道 insignificant; negligible; not worth mentioning
【渺茫】 miǎománg ① distant and indistinct; vague: 他走后音信~。We haven't heard from him since he left. ② uncertain: 前途~ have an uncertain future/ 希望~ have slim hopes (of success)
【渺小】 miǎoxiǎo tiny; negligible; insignificant; paltry: 个人的力量是~的。The strength of an individual is insignificant.

淼 miǎo 〈书〉 (of an expanse of water) vast

缈 miǎo 见"缥缈" piāomiǎo

邈 miǎo 〈书〉 far away; remote

藐 miǎo ① small; petty ③ slight; despise: 言者谆谆，听者~~。The words were earnest but they fell on deaf ears.
【藐视】 miǎoshì despise; look down upon
【藐小】 miǎoxiǎo tiny; negligible; insignificant; paltry

miào

妙* miào ① wonderful; excellent; fine: 这主意真~。That's an excellent idea./ ~不可言 too wonderful for words; most intriguing/ 绝~的讽刺 a supreme irony ② ingenious; clever; subtle: 深得其中之~ have got the trick of it; fully appreciate its subtlety/ 他回答得很~。He made a clever answer.
【妙计】 miàojì excellent plan; brilliant scheme
【妙趣横生】 miàoqù héngshēng full of wit and humour; very witty
【妙手回春】 miàoshǒu huí chūn (of a doctor) effect a miraculous cure and bring the dying back to life
【妙用】 miàoyòng magical effect: 小小银针,大有~。A tiny acupuncture needle can work wonders.
【妙语】 miàoyǔ witty remark; witticism

庙* miào temple; shrine
【庙宇】 miàoyǔ temple

miè

灭* miè ① (of a light, fire, etc.) go out: 火~了。The fire has gone out./ 灯突然~了。All of a sudden the lights went out. ② extinguish; put out; turn off: ~火 put out a fire; extinguish a fire/ 节约用电,人走灯~。Save electricity — turn off the lights when you leave. ③ submerge; drown: ~顶 be drowned ④ destroy; exterminate; wipe out: ~蝇 kill flies
【灭顶】 mièdǐng be drowned
【灭火】 mièhuǒ ① put out a fire; extinguish a fire ② cut out

an engine ◇ ~剂 fire-extinguishing chemical (或 agent)/ ~器 fire extinguisher
【灭迹】 mièjī destroy the evidence (of one's evildoing)
【灭绝】 mièjué become extinct: 现已~的动物 extinct animals
【灭口】 mièkǒu (of a hidden criminal) do away with a witness or accomplice
【灭亡】 mièwáng be destroyed; become extinct; die out: 自取~ court destruction

蔑 miè 〈书〉 ① slight; disdain: 轻~ disdain ② nothing; none: ~以复加 could not be surpassed; reach the limit ③ smear: 诬~ slander; vilify
【蔑视】 mièshì despise; show contempt for; scorn

mín

民* mín ① the people: 为~除害 rid the people of a scourge ② a member of a nationality: 回~ a Hui ③ a person of a certain occupation: 农~ peasant/ 渔~ fisherman/ 牧~ herdsman ④ of the people; folk: ~歌 folk song ⑤ civilian: 军~联防 joint defence by army and civilians/ ~船 a junk or small boat for civilian use
【民办】 mínbàn run by the local people: ~公助 run by the local people and subsidized by the state
【民兵】 mínbīng ① people's militia; militia ② militiaman
【民不聊生】 mín bù liáo shēng the people have no means of livelihood; the masses live in dire poverty
【民愤】 mínfèn popular indignation; the people's wrath: ~极大 have earned the bitter hatred of the people; have incurred the greatest popular indignation
【民歌】 míngē folk song
【民航】 mínháng 〈简〉 (民用航空) civil aviation ◇ ~机 civil aircraft; civil airplane
【民间】 mínjiān ① among the people; popular; folk: 这个故事长久地在~流传。For generations the story has circulated among the people./ ~疾苦 hardships of the people ② nongovernmental; people-to-people: ~来往 nongovernmental contact; people-to-people exchange ◇~传说 popular legend; folk legend; folklore/ ~故事 folktale; folk story/ ~文学 folk literature/ ~舞蹈 folk dance/ ~艺术 folk art/ ~音乐 folk music
【民情】 mínqíng ① condition of the people: 熟悉地理~ be familiar with the place and the people ② feelings of the people; public feeling
【民权】 mínquán civil rights; civil liberties; democratic rights
【民生】 mínshēng the people's livelihood: 国计~ the national economy and the people's livelihood/ ~凋敝。The people lived in destitution.
【民事】 mínshì 〈法〉 relating to civil law; civil ◇~案件 civil case
【民俗】 mínsú folk custom; folkways
【民心】 mínxīn popular feelings; common aspiration of the people: ~所向 where the popular will inclines; (what conforms to) the common aspiration of the people/ 深得~ enjoy the ardent support of the people
【民谣】 mínyáo folk rhyme (esp. of the topical and political type)
【民意】 mínyì the will of the people; popular will ◇~测验 public opinion poll; poll
【民用】 mínyòng for civil use; civil ◇~航空 civil aviation/ ~机场 civil airport
【民众】 mínzhòng the masses of the people; the common people; the populace: 唤起~ arouse the masses ◇~团体 people's organization; mass organization
【民主】 mínzhǔ ① democracy; democratic rights: 党内~ inner-party democracy ② democratic: 他作风~。He has a democratic work-style.
【民族】 mínzú nation; nationality: 中华~ the Chinese nation; 被压迫~ oppressed nations/ 少数~ minority nationality; national minority/ ~复兴 revival of nationhood; national rejuvenation

◇～意识 national consciousness/ ～英雄 national hero/ ～主义 nationalism

mǐn

皿 mǐn 见"器皿" qìmǐn

闵 Mǐn a surname

泯 mǐn vanish; die out: 永存不～ be everlasting; be immortal
【泯灭】mǐnmiè die out; disappear; vanish: 难以～的印象 an indelible impression
【泯没】mǐnmò vanish; sink into oblivion; become lost

抿 mǐn ① smooth (hair, etc.) with a wet brush ② close lightly; furl; tuck: ～着嘴笑 smile with closed lips; compress one's lips to smile

闽 Mǐn another name for Fujian Province

悯 mǐn ① commiserate; pity: 其情可～。His case deserves sympathy. ② 〈书〉sorrow

敏* mǐn quick; nimble; agile
【敏感】mǐngǎn sensitive; susceptible: 政治～ political sensitivity/ 他对机器里不正常的声音非常～。His ears are highly sensitive to any unusual sound in the machine.
【敏捷】mǐnjié quick; nimble; agile: 动作～ be quick in movement/ 守门员～地跃向右方, 救出了险球。The goalkeeper leapt nimbly to the right and saved the goal.
【敏锐】mǐnruì sharp; acute; keen: 目光～ have sharp eyes; be sharp-eyed/ 听觉～ have good (或 sharp) ears/ 嗅觉～ have a keen sense of smell/ ～的政治眼光 keen political insight

míng

名* míng ① name: 地～ place name/ 一种～为九二〇的生长激素 a growth hormone known as 920/ 他～叫张南。His name is Zhang Nan. 或 He is called Zhang Nan. ② given name: 这位朋友姓李～大刚。This friend's surname is Li and his given name, Dagang. ③ fame; reputation; renown: 不为～,不为利 seek neither fame nor gain/ ～闻中外 well known both at home and abroad ④ famous; celebrated; well-known; noted: ～厨师 a famous cook/ ～诗人 a noted poet/ ～句 a well-known phrase; a much `quoted line ⑤ express; describe: 不可～状 indescribable; nondescript ⑥〈量〉〔用于人〕:十二～战士 twelve soldiers/ 得第一～ come in first; win first place
【名不副实】míng bù fù shí the name falls short of the reality; be sth. more in name than in reality; be unworthy of the name or title: 一个～的军事学家 not a military expert in the real sense of the term 又作"名不符实"
【名不虚传】míng bù xūchuán have a well-deserved reputation; deserve the reputation one enjoys; live up to one's reputation
【名册】míngcè register; roll: 学生～ students' register; students' roll
【名产】míngchǎn famous product
【名称】míngchēng name (of a thing or organization)
【名垂青史】míng chuí qīngshǐ go down in history; be crowned with eternal glory
【名词】míngcí ①〈语〉noun; substantive ② term; phrase: 化学～ chemical term/ 新一儿 new expression; vogue word
【名次】míngcì position in a name list; place in a competition: 我们参加这次运动会不是为了争～。We haven't come to this sports meet just to compete for places./ 按比赛成绩排列～ arrange the names of contestants in the order of their results
【名存实亡】míngcún-shíwáng cease to exist except in name; exist in name only

【名单】míngdān name list: 候选人～ list of candidates/ 入伍～ list of recruits
【名额】míng'é the number of people assigned or allowed; quota of people: 代表～ the number of deputies to be elected or sent/ 招生～ the number of students to be enrolled; planned enrolment figure/ 今年的征兵～已满。This year's enlistment quota has already been filled./ 由于～有限, 这次参观不能人人都去。Since the number of people allowed is limited, not everyone can go on this visit.
【名分】míngfèn 〈旧〉a person's status
【名副其实】míng fù qí shí the name matches the reality; be sth. in reality as well as in name; be worthy of the name: 这真是～的奇迹。That's a veritable miracle. 又作"名符其实"
【名贵】míngguì famous and precious; rare: ～药材 rare medicinal herbs/ ～的字画 priceless scrolls of calligraphy and painting
【名家】míngjiā a person of academic or artistic distinction; famous expert; master
【名将】míngjiàng famous general; great soldier: 足球～ a football hero (或 star)
【名利】mínglì fame and gain; fame and wealth ◇ ～思想 desire for personal fame and gain
【名列前茅】míng liè qiánmáo be among the best of the successful candidates
【名流】míngliú distinguished personages; celebrities
【名落孙山】míng luò Sūn Shān fall behind Sun Shan (who was last on the list of successful candidates) — fail in a competitive examination
【名目】míngmù names of things; items: ～繁多 a multitude of names (或 items); names of every description/ 巧立～ invent all kinds of names (as pretexts for exorbitant taxes or to pad an expense account)
【名牌】míngpái ① famous brand: ～香烟 a famous brand of cigarettes ② nameplate; name tag
【名片】míngpiàn visiting card; calling card: 留下～ leave one's card
【名气】míngqi 〈口〉reputation; fame; name: 有点～ enjoy some reputation; be quite well-known; have made a name for oneself
【名人】míngrén famous person; eminent person; celebrity; notable
【名山大川】míngshān-dàchuān famous mountains and great rivers
【名声】míngshēng reputation; repute; renown: ～很坏 have an unsavoury reputation; be held in ill repute; be notorious/ 享有好～ enjoy a good reputation; be held in high repute
【名胜】míngshèng a place famous for its scenery or historical relics; scenic spot ◇ ～古迹 places of historic interest and scenic beauty; scenic spots and historical sites
【名手】míngshǒu a famous artist, player, etc.
【名堂】míngtang ① variety; item: 别看他们只是个业余文工团.演出的～可多啦!It's true they're only an amateur troupe, but they have an amazingly large repertoire./ 这个环家伙又在搞什么～? What's that villain up to now? ② result; achievement: 依靠集体力量,一定能搞出～来。As long as we rely on collective effort we can certainly achieve something./ 问了他半天也没问出个～。I questioned him for a long time but couldn't get anything out of him.
【名望】míngwàng fame and prestige; good reputation; renown: 有～的医生 a famous doctor
【名位】míngwèi fame and position
【名下】míngxià under sb.'s name; belonging or related to sb.: 这笔帐就记在我～吧。Charge these expenses to my account.
【名言】míngyán well-known saying; celebrated dictum; famous remark
【名义】míngyì ① name: 假借～ under false pretences ②〔后面多带"上"字〕nominal; titular; in name: ～上裁军, 实际上扩军 disarmament in name, armament in reality
【名誉】míngyù ① fame; reputation: 闹～地位 be out for fame and position/ ～好 have a good reputation; be of

high repute; be held in high esteem ② honorary ◇ ~会员 honorary member/ ~主席 honorary chairman; honorary president

【名噪一时】 míng zào yī shí gain considerable fame among one's contemporaries

【名正言顺】 míngzhèng-yánshùn come within one's jurisdiction; be perfectly justifiable

【名著】 míngzhù famous book; famous work: 文学~ a famous literary work; a literary masterpiece

【名字】 míngzi ① (given) name ② name: 这种花的~很特别。 This flower has a peculiar name.

明* míng ① bright; brilliant; light: ~月 a bright moon/ 灯火通~ be brightly lit; be brilliantly illuminated/ 天已微~。 Day is breaking. ② clear; distinct: 是非愈辩愈~。 As the debate progressed, it became clearer and clearer which side was right./ 情况不~。 The situation is not clear./ 去向不~ whereabouts unknown/ 指~出路 point the way out ③ open; overt; explicit: ~一套暗一套 act one way in the open and another way in secret/ 我对你~说了吧。 I'll be frank with you. ④ sharp-eyed; clear-sighted: 耳聪目~ have sharp ears and eyes/ 眼~手快 quick of eye and deft of hand ⑤ aboveboard; honest: ~人不做暗事。 An honest man doesn't do anything underhand. ⑥ sight: 双目失~ go blind in both eyes/ 复~ regain one's sight ⑦ understand; know: 不~真相 not know the facts; be ignorant of the actual situation ⑧ immediately following in time: ~年 next year/ ~晚 tomorrow evening

【明白】 míngbai ① clear; obvious; plain: 他讲得~易懂。 He spoke clearly and simply./ 这个问题很~。 The matter is quite clear. ② frank; unequivocal; explicit: 你还是跟他讲~了好。 It would be best to be frank with him./ 他~表示不赞成这个提议。 He stated clearly that he didn't agree with the proposal. ③ sensible; reasonable: ~人 a sensible person ④ understand; realize; know: ~事理 know what's what; have good sense/ 我不~你的意思。 I don't see what you mean./ 我忽然~了。 The truth suddenly dawned on me.

【明辨是非】 míng biàn shì-fēi make a clear distinction between right and wrong

【明察暗访】 míngchá-ànfǎng observe publicly and investigate privately; conduct a thorough investigation

【明察秋毫】 míng chá qiūháo have eyes sharp enough to perceive an animal's autumn hair — be perceptive of the minutest detail: ~之末, 而不见舆薪 be sharp-sighted enough to perceive the tip of an animal's autumn hair but unable to see a cartload of firewood — see the minute details but miss the major issue

【明澈】 míngchè bright and limpid; transparent: ~的眼睛 bright and limpid eyes/ 湖水~如镜。 The lake is like a mirror.

【明净】 míngjìng bright and clean; clear and bright: ~的橱窗 a bright and clean shop window

【明来暗往】 mínglái-ànwǎng have overt and covert contacts with sb.

【明朗】 mínglǎng ① bright and clear: ~的月色 bright moonlight/ ~的天空 a clear sky ② clear; obvious: 局势逐渐~。 The situation is becoming clear./ 态度~ take a clear-cut position; adopt a unequivocal attitude ③ forthright; bright and cheerful: ~的性格 an open and forthright character/ 这幅画色调~。 This picture is painted in bright, warm colours.

【明亮】 míngliàng ① light; well-lit; bright: 宽敞而~的厂房 bright and spacious workshops/ 会议大厅里灯光~。 The conference hall is brightly lit. ② bright; shining: ~的眼睛 bright eyes ③ become clear

【明了】 míngliǎo ① understand; be clear about: ~体力劳动的重要性 understand the importance of manual labour/ 不~实际情况, 就不能做出正确的判断。 You can't form a correct judgment without a clear understanding of the actual situation. ② clear; plain: 简单~ simple and clear

【明媚】 míngmèi bright and beautiful; radiant and enchanting: 春光~ a radiant and enchanting spring scene

【明明】 míngmíng ＜副＞ obviously; plainly; undoubtedly: 这事~是他干的嘛; This is obviously his doing. 或 There can be no doubt that it was he who did it.

【明目张胆】 míngmù-zhāngdǎn brazenly; flagrantly: ~地进行武装干涉 brazenly commit an act of armed intervention

【明年】 míngnián next year

【明枪易躲, 暗箭难防】 míngqiāng yì duǒ, ànjiàn nán fáng it is easy to dodge a spear in the open, but hard to guard against an arrow shot from hiding

【明确】 míngquè ① clear and definite; clear-cut; explicit; unequivocal: ~的目标 a clear aim/ ~的立场 a clear-cut stand/ ~的答复 a definite answer ② make clear; make definite: 这篇社论进一步~了当前的中心任务。 The editorial further defined the key task for the present period.

【明日】 míngrì ① tomorrow ② the near future

【明日黄花】 míngrì huánghuā overblown blossoms — things that are stale and no longer of interest

【明天】 míngtiān ① tomorrow ② the near future: 光辉灿烂的~ a bright future

【明文】 míngwén (of laws, regulations, etc.) proclaimed in writing: ~规定 stipulate in explicit terms; expressly provide

【明晰】 míngxī distinct; clear: 雷达荧光屏上出现了~的图像。 A distinct blip appeared on the radar screen.

【明显】 míngxiǎn obvious; evident; distinct: ~的优势 clear superiority/ ~的改进 distinct improvement/ ~的成效 tangible result/ 目标~。 The target is quite clear./ 这显然是一个借口。 This is evidently a pretext.

【明信片】 míngxìnpiàn postcard

【明星】 míngxīng star: 电影~ film star; movie star

【明修栈道, 暗度陈仓】 míng xiū zhàndào, àn dù Chéncāng pretend to prepare to advance along one path while secretly going along another; do one thing under cover of another

【明眼人】 míngyǎnrén a person with a discerning eye; a person of good sense

【明喻】 míngyù simile

【明哲保身】 míng zhé bǎo shēn be worldly wise and play safe

【明争暗斗】 míngzhēng-àndòu both open strife and veiled struggle

【明证】 míngzhèng clear proof

【明知】 míngzhī know perfectly well; be fully aware: ~山有虎, 偏向虎山行 go deep into the mountains, knowing well that there are tigers there — go on undeterred by the dangers ahead

【明知故犯】 míngzhī-gùfàn knowingly violate (discipline, etc.); deliberately break (a rule, etc.); do sth. one knows is wrong

【明知故问】 míngzhī-gùwèn ask while knowing the answer

【明智】 míngzhì sensible; sagacious; wise: 表现出~的态度 show a sensible attitude/ 他这样决定是~的。 It was wise of him to make that decision.

【明珠】 míngzhū bright pearl; jewel

鸣* míng ① the cry of birds, animals or insects: 鸡~ the crow of a cock/ 秋虫夜~ autumn insects chirping at night ② ring; sound: 耳~ ringing in the ears/ ~笛 blow a whistle/ ~鼓 beat a drum/ ~枪示警 fire a warning shot/ ~礼炮二十一响 fire a 21-gun salute/ 钟~三下。 The clock struck three. ③ express; voice; air: ~谢 express one's thanks formally/ ~不平 complain of unfairness; cry out against an injustice/ 自~得意 be very pleased with oneself; preen oneself

【鸣禽】 míngqín songbird; singing bird

【鸣冤叫屈】 míngyuān-jiàoqū complain and call for redress; voice grievances

茗 míng ① tender tea leaves ② tea: 品~ sip tea (to judge its quality); sample tea

冥 míng ① dark; obscure: 幽~ dark hell; the nether world ② deep; profound: ~思 be deep in thought ③ dull; stupid: ~顽 thickheaded; stupid ④ underworld; the

nether world: ～府 the nether world
【冥思苦想】 míngsī-kǔxiǎng think long and hard; cudgel one's brains
【冥顽】 míngwán ＜书＞ thickheaded, stupid: ～不灵 impenetrably thickheaded
【冥王星】 míngwángxīng ＜天＞ Pluto
【冥想】 míngxiǎng deep thought; meditation: 苦思～ think long and hard; cudgel one's brains

铭 míng ① inscription: 墓志～ inscription on the memorial tablet within a tomb/ 座右～ motto ② engrave: ～诸肺腑 engrave on one's mind (或 memory); bear firmly in mind
【铭感】 mínggǎn be deeply grateful: ～终身 remain deeply grateful for the rest of one's life
【铭记】 míngjì engrave on one's mind; always remember
【铭刻】 míngkè ① inscription ② engrave on one's mind; always remember

盟 míng
另见 méng
【盟誓】 míngshì take an oath; make a pledge

瞑 míng
【瞑目】 míngmù close one's eyes in death — die content: 死不～ die discontent; die with everlasting regret

mǐng

酩 mǐng
【酩酊大醉】 mǐngdǐng dàzuì be dead drunk

mìng

命* mìng ① life: 逃～ run for one's life/ ～在旦夕 be on the verge of death ② lot; fate; destiny ③ order; command: 待～ await orders ④ assign (a name, title, etc.): ～题 assign a topic; set a question
【命案】 mìng'àn a case involving the killing of a person; homicide case
【命根子】 mìnggēnzi one's very life; lifeblood
【命令】 mìnglìng order; command: 下～ issue an order/ 服从～ obey orders/ ～式的口气 a commanding tone
【命脉】 mìngmài lifeblood; lifeline: 经济～ economic lifelines/ 水利是农业的～。 Irrigation is the lifeblood of agriculture.
【命名】 mìngmíng name (sb. or sth.)
【命题】 mìngtí ① assign a topic; set a question: ～作文 assign a subject for composition ② ＜数＞ proposition: ～演算 propositional calculus ③ ＜逻＞ proposition
【命途多舛】 mìngtú duō chuǎn suffer many a setback during one's life
【命运】 mìngyùn destiny; fate; lot: 悲惨的～ a tragic lot
【命中】 mìngzhòng hit the target (或 mark); score a hit: 她第一枪就～靶心。 Her first shot hit the bull's-eye. ◇ ～率 percentage of hits

miù

谬 miù wrong; false; erroneous; mistaken: ～见 a wrong view/ ～传 a false report/ 大～不然 be grossly mistaken
【谬论】 miùlùn fallacy; false (或 absurd) theory; falsehood

mō

摸* mō ① feel; stroke; touch: ～～刀口，看看快不快 feel the edge of a knife to see whether it is sharp/ 这衣料～着很软。 This material feels soft./ 她轻轻地～了～孩子的

头。 She gently stroked the child's head. ② feel for; grope for; fumble: 在黑暗中～着下楼 grope one's way down the stairs in the dark/ 从床底下～出一双鞋来 fish out a pair of shoes from under the bed/ ～敌人岗哨 steal up to an enemy sentinel in the dark and get rid of him ③ try to find out; feel out; sound out: 你去～～他对这个问题的看法。 Go and sound him out on this matter./ ～透了这匹马的脾气 get to know the horse well/ ～不着头脑 be unable to make head or tail of sth.
【摸索】 mōsuo ① grope; feel about; fumble: 在黑暗中～ grope (或 fumble) in the dark ② try to find out: ～种花生的规律 try to find out the laws (或 secret) of peanut growing

mó

摹 mó copy; trace: 临～ copy a model of calligraphy or painting
【摹本】 móběn facsimile; copy
【摹仿】 mófǎng 见"模仿" mófǎng
【摹刻】 mókè ① carve a reproduction of an inscription or painting ② a carved reproduction of an inscription or painting
【摹拟】 mónǐ imitate; simulate
【摹写】 móxiě ① copy ② imitate ③ describe; depict: ～人物情状 depict characters in various situations

模* mó ① pattern; standard: 楷～ model; paragon ② imitate ③ ＜简＞ (模范) model: 劳～ model worker
另见 mú
【模本】 móběn calligraphy or painting model
【模范】 mófàn an exemplary person or thing; model; fine example: 劳动～ model worker/ ～作用 exemplary role/ ～事迹 exemplary deeds
【模仿】 mófǎng imitate; copy; model oneself on: ～动物的叫声 imitate the cries of animals/ 这部机器是～英国一种新产品制造的。 This machine is modelled on one recently made in Britain.
【模糊】 móhu ① blurred; indistinct; dim; vague: 字迹～了。 The writing was blurred./ ～的景物 a hazy scene/ 只有～的印象 have only a vague idea of sth./ 她对这个问题还有一些～认识。 She still has some confused ideas about that question. ② blur; obscure; confuse; mix up: 泪水～了他的双眼。Tears blurred his eyes. 或 His eyes were dim with tears. 又作"模胡"
【模棱两可】 móléng liǎngkě equivocal; ambiguous: 采取～的态度 take an equivocal attitude/ ～的提法 an ambiguous formulation
【模拟】 mónǐ imitate; simulate
【模特儿】 mótèr ＜美术＞ model
【模型】 móxíng ① model: 船的～ a model of a ship; a model ship/ 原尺寸～ mock-up ② mould; matrix; pattern

膜 mó ① membrane: 细胞～ cell membrane/ 鼓～ tympanic membrane ② film; thin coating: 塑料薄～ plastic film/ 纸浆表面结了一层～。 A thin film formed on the surface of the pulp.
【膜拜】 móbài prostrate oneself (before an idol or person); worship: 顶礼～ prostrate oneself in worship; pay homage to

摩 mó ① rub; scrape; touch: 峻岭～天。 The high mountains seem to scrape the sky. ② mull over; study: 揣～ try to fathom
【摩擦】 mócā ① rub: 轴颈在轴承面上～。 The journal rubs against the bearing surface. ② ＜物＞ friction: ～生热。 Friction generates heat./ 滑动～ sliding friction/ 滚动～ rolling friction ③ clash (between two parties); friction: 制造～ create friction/ 与某人发生～ have a brush with sb. ◇ ～力 ＜物＞ frictional force; friction
【摩登】 módēng modern; fashionable

【摩肩接踵】 mójiān-jiēzhǒng jostle each other in a crowd: 那天街上人特别多,真是～,川流不息。 That day the street was jam-packed with people coming and going all the time.

【摩拳擦掌】 móquán-cāzhǎng rub one's fists and wipe one's palms — be eager for a fight; itch to have a go: 大家～, 恨不得马上投入战斗。 We all rolled up our sleeves, itching for the battle.

【摩挲】 mósuō stroke; caress

【摩天】 mótiān skyscraping ◇ ～楼 skyscraper

【摩托】 mótuō motor
◇ ～车 motorcycle; motor bicycle; motorbike/ ～船 motorboat/ ～化部队 motorized troops

磨* mó ① rub; wear: 他的脚上～了泡。 His feet were blistered from the rubbing./ 没关系,就～破了一点皮。 Nothing serious. Just a graze./ 袜子～破了。 The socks are worn into holes./ 鞋跟～平了。 The heels of the shoes are worn down./ 我劝了他半天,嘴皮都快～破了。 I talked till my jaws ached, trying to bring him around. ② grind; polish: ～剪子 grind scissors; sharpen scissors/ ～大理石 polish marble/ ～墨 rub an ink stick against an inkstone; make ink for writing with a brush ③ wear down; wear out: 他被这场病～得不成样子。 The illness has worn him down to a mere shadow of his former self.
另见 mò

【磨光】 móguāng polish ◇ ～玻璃 polished glass/ ～机 polishing machine; glazing machine

【磨耗】 móhào wear and tear

【磨练】 móliàn put oneself through the mill; temper oneself; steel oneself

【磨灭】 mómiè wear away; efface; obliterate: 建立不可～的功勋 perform meritorious deeds never to be obliterated/ 留下不可～的印象 leave an indelible impression

【磨损】 mósǔn wear and tear: 这台机器基本上没有什么～。 The machine shows scarcely any sign of wear and tear.

蘑 mó mushroom

【蘑菇】 mógu mushroom

魔* mó ① evil spirit; demon; devil; monster: 群～乱舞 a horde of demons dancing in riotous revelry/ 着了～似的 like one possessed ② magic; mystic: ～力 magic power

【魔怪】 móguài demons and monsters; fiends

【魔鬼】 móguǐ devil; demon; monster

【魔力】 mólì magic power; magic; charm

【魔术】 móshù magic; conjuring; sleight of hand ◇ ～演员 magician; conjurer

【魔王】 mówáng ① Prince of the Devils ② tyrant; despot; fiend

【魔掌】 mózhǎng devil's clutches; evil hands: 逃出敌人的～ escape from the clutches of the enemy

【魔杖】 mózhàng magic wand

【魔爪】 mózhǎo devil's talons; claws; tentacles: 侵略者的～ the tentacles of the aggressors

mǒ

抹* mǒ ① put on; apply; smear; plaster: ～点雪花膏 put on a little vanishing cream/ 面包上～点果酱 spread some jam on a piece of bread ② wipe: ～眼泪 wipe one's eyes; be weeping/ ～把脸 wipe one's face ③ cross (或 strike, blot) out; erase: 把这一行字～了。 Cross out this line./ ～掉磁带上的录音 erase the recording from a tape
另见 mā

【抹杀】 mǒshā blot out; obliterate; write off: 一笔～ write off at one stroke: deny completely 又作"抹煞"

【抹一鼻子灰】 mǒ yī bízi huī suffer a snub; meet with a rebuff

mò

末* mò ① tip; end: 秋毫之～ the tip of an animal's autumn hair ② nonessentials; minor details: 本～倒置 take the branch for the root; put the nonessentials before the essentials; put the cart before the horse ③ end; last stage: 周～ weekend/ 明～农民起义 the peasant uprisings towards the end of the Ming Dynasty/ 一学期的最～一天 the last day of a school term ④ powder; dust: 茶叶～儿 broken tea leaves; tea dust/ 锯～ sawdust

【末节】 mòjié minor details; nonessentials: 细枝～ minor details

【末了】 mòliǎo last; finally; in the end: 第五行～的那个字我不认识。 I don't know the last word of the fifth line./ 他～表示同意了大家的意见。 In the end he agreed with the others.

【末流】 mòliú the later and decadent stage of a school of thought, literature, etc.

【末路】 mòlù dead end; impasse

【末年】 mònián last years of a dynasty or reign

【末期】 mòqī last phase; final phase; last stage: 七十年代～ in the late seventies/ 第二次世界大战～ the last stage of the Second World War

【末日】 mòrì ① <基督教> doomsday; Day of Judgment; Judgment Day: ～审判 Last Judgment ② end; doom: 封建王朝的～ the end of a feudal dynasty

【末世】 mòshì last phase (of an age): 封建～ the last years of feudalism

【末尾】 mòwěi end: 信的～ at the end of the letter/ 一切结论产生于调查情况的～,而不是在它的先头。 Conclusions invariably come after investigation, and not before.

【末叶】 mòyè last years (of a century or dynasty): 十九世纪～ the end of the 19th century; the late 19th century

没* mò ① sink; submerge: 潜水艇很快就～入水中。 It was not long before the submarine submerged./ 迅速沉～ sink fast ② overflow; rise beyond: 洪水几乎～过了大坝。 The flood nearly overflowed the dam./ 水深～顶。 The water goes above a man's head./ 雪深～膝。 The snow was knee-deep. ③ disappear; hide: 出～ now appear, now disappear ④ confiscate; take possession of: ～收 confiscate ⑤ till the end: ～世 till the end of one's life ⑥ die
另见 méi

【没齿不忘】 mò chǐ bù wàng will never forget to the end of one's days; remember for the rest of one's life

【没落】 mòluò decline; wane

【没奈何】 mònàihé be utterly helpless; have no way out; have no alternative: 等了他好久也没来,～我只好一个人去了。 I waited for a long time, but he didn't show up, so I had to go alone.

【没收】 mòshōu confiscate; expropriate

沫 mò foam; froth: 啤酒～ froth on beer; the head on a glass of beer/ 肥皂～ soapsuds; lather/ 口吐白～ foam at the mouth

茉 mò

【茉莉】 mòli <植> jasmine ◇ ～花茶 jasmine tea

殁 mò <书> die: 病～ die of illness

陌* mò ① a path between fields (running east and west): 阡～纵横。 The paths crisscrossed in the fields. ② road: ～头杨柳 roadside willows

【陌路】 mòlù <书> stranger (whom one passes in the street): 视同～ treat like a stranger; cut sb. dead

【陌生】 mòshēng strange; unfamiliar: 对这些年青人来说, 养鹿是一件～的事情。 Breeding deer was something completely new for these young people./ 尽管我们初次见面, 但并不感到～。 Although this was only our first meeting, we didn't feel like strangers./ 在会场上我看到许多～的面孔。 I saw many unfamiliar faces at the meeting.
◇ ～人 stranger

脉 mò

另见 mài

【脉脉】 mòmò affectionately; lovingly; amorously: 她~地注视着远去的亲人。 She followed with loving eyes her dear one's departing figure./ 温情~ full of tender affection, sentimental

莫 mò

① 〈书〉 no one; nothing; none: ~之能御。 No one (或 Nothing) can resist it. ② no; not: ~知所措 not know what to do; be at a loss ② don't: 非公~入。 No admittance except on business./ ~性急。 Don't be impatient. 或 Take it easy.

【莫不】 mòbù there's no one who doesn't or isn't: 听到这胜利的消息, 各族人民~为之欢欣鼓舞。 People of all nationalities were jubilant on hearing the news of victory./ ~为之感动。 There was no one who was unmoved.

【莫测高深】 mò cè gāoshēn unfathomable; enigmatic

【莫大】 mòdà greatest; utmost: 感到~的光荣 feel greatly honoured/ ~的幸福 the greatest happiness/ ~的侮辱 a gross insult/ ~的愤慨 the utmost indignation

【莫非】 mòfēi 〈副〉 can it be that; is it possible that: 老沈今天没有来, ~又病了? Lao Shen is absent today. Can he be ill again?/ 听你的意思, ~是我错了不成? Do you mean to say that I'm in the wrong?

【莫过于】 mòguòyú nothing is more... than

【莫名其妙】 mò míng qí miào ① be unable to make head or tail of sth., be baffled: 他为什么讲这番话, 真叫人~。 It is quite baffling why he should have made such remarks. ② without rhyme or reason; inexplicable; odd: 她~地哭了起来。 Quite unaccountably she burst out crying. 又作 "莫明其妙"

【莫逆】 mònì very friendly; intimate: ~之交 bosom friends

【莫如】 mòrú would be better; might as well: 与其你去, ~他来。 It would be better for him to come than for you to go./ 她想既然来了, ~跟着进去看看。 Now that she'd come to the place, she thought she might as well go in with the others to have a look. 又作 "莫若"

【莫须有】 mòxūyǒu unwarranted; groundless; fabricated; trumped-up: ~的罪名 a fabricated charge; an unwarranted charge

【莫衷一是】 mò zhōng yī shì unable to agree or decide which is right: 众说纷纭, ~。 There are so many contradictory views that it is difficult to decide which is right. 或 As opinions vary, no decision can be reached.

秣 mò

① fodder ② feed animals

【秣马厉兵】 mòmǎ-lìbīng feed the horses and sharpen the weapons—make active preparations for war; prepare for battle

漠 mò

① desert ② indifferent; unconcerned: 冷~ cold and indifferent

【漠不关心】 mò bù guānxīn indifferent; unconcerned

【漠然】 mòrán indifferently; apathetically; with unconcern: ~置之 remain indifferent towards sth.; look on with unconcern

【漠视】 mòshì treat with indifference; ignore; overlook; pay no attention to: 不能~群众的意见。 The masses' opinions must not be treated with indifference.

寞 mò

lonely; deserted: 寂~ lonely

蓦 mò

suddenly

【蓦地】 mòdì suddenly; unexpectedly; all of a sudden

【蓦然】 mòrán suddenly: ~想起 suddenly remember

墨* mò

① China (或 Chinese) ink; ink stick ② ink: 油~ printing ink ③ handwriting or painting: 遗~ writing or painting left by the deceased ④ learning: 胸无点~ without any learning; unlettered ⑤ black; pitch-dark: 一个~黑的夜里 one pitch-dark night

【墨宝】 mòbǎo ① treasured scrolls of calligraphy or painting ⑤ 〈敬〉 your beautiful handwriting

【墨迹】 mòjī ① ink marks: ~未干 before the ink is dry ② sb.'s writing or painting: 这是鲁迅的~。 This is Lu Xun's calligraphy.

【墨守成规】 mò shǒu chéngguī stick to conventions; stay in a rut

【墨水】 mòshuǐ ① prepared Chinese ink ② ink ③ book learning: 他肚子里还有点~。 He's a bit of a scholar.

【墨鱼】 mòyú inkfish; cuttlefish

【墨汁】 mòzhī prepared Chinese ink

默* mò

① silent; tacit: ~不作声 keep silent ② write from memory: ~生字 write the new words from memory

【默哀】 mò'āi stand in silent tribute: 全体起立~。 All rose and stood in silent tribute./ ~三分钟 observe three minutes' silence

【默祷】 mòdǎo pray in silence; say a silent prayer

【默读】 mòdú read silently

【默默】 mòmò quietly; silently: ~无言 without saying a word; silently

【默默无闻】 mòmò wú wén unknown to the public; without attracting public attention: 一生~ remain obscure all one's life

【默契】 mòqì ① tacit agreement; tacit understanding: 互相~ have a tacit mutual understanding; coordinate by tacit agreement ② secret agreement: 关于这个问题双方普有~。 The two sides had a secret agreement on this question.

【默然】 mòrán silent; speechless: ~无语 fall silent; be speechless

【默认】 mòrèn give tacit consent to; tacitly approve; acquiesce in: ~现状 give tacit consent to the status quo

【默写】 mòxiě write from memory

【默许】 mòxǔ tacitly consent to; acquiesce in

磨* mò

① mill; millstones: 电~ electric mill ② grind; mill: ~麦子 grind wheat/ ~面 mill flour/ ~豆腐 grind soya beans to make bean curd

另见 mó

貘 mò

〈动〉 tapir

mōu

哞 mōu

〈象〉 〔形容牛叫的声音〕: moo; low; bellow

móu

牟 móu

try to gain; seek; obtain: ~利 seek profit

【牟取】 móuqǔ try to gain; seek; obtain: ~暴利 seek exorbitant profits

谋 móu

① stratagem; plan; scheme: 足智多~ wise and full of stratagems; resourceful/ 有勇无~ brave but not astute ② work for; seek; plot ③ consult: 不~而合 agree without previous consultation

【谋财害命】 móucái-hàimìng murder sb. for his money

【谋反】 móufǎn conspire against the state; plot a rebellion

【谋害】 móuhài ① plot to murder ② plot a frame-up against

【谋略】 móulüè astuteness and resourcefulness; strategy: 此人颇有~。 He is a man of resource and astuteness.

【谋求】 móuqiú seek; strive for; be in quest of: ~两国关系正常化 seek normalization of relations between the two countries

【谋取】 móuqǔ try to gain; seek; obtain: 不能为了~暂时的利益而牺牲原则。 We mustn't seek temporary gain at the expense of principle.

【谋杀】 móushā murder

【谋生】 móushēng seek a livelihood; make a living: ～的手段 a means of life

【谋士】 móushì adviser; counsellor

眸 móu pupil (of the eye); eye: 凝～ fix (或 focus) one's eyes on/ 明～皓齿 have shining eyes and white teeth; be comely

【眸子】 móuzi pupil (of the eye); eye

缪 móu 见"绸缪" chóumóu; "未雨绸缪" wèi yǔ chóumóu

mǒu

某* mǒu ① certain; some: ～日 at a certain date／ 张～ a certain person called Zhang／ ～些农产品 certain agricultural products／ 在～种程度上 to some (或 a certain) extent／ 在～种意义上 in a sense ②〔用来代替自己的名字〕: 我李～不是干这种事的人。Yours truly is not the sort of person to do a thing like that.

【某某】 mǒumǒu so-and-so: ～先生 Mister so-and-so／ ～学校 a certain school

【某人】 mǒurén ① a certain person ②〔用来代替自己的名字〕: 我王～从来不说假话。As for me, I've never told lies.

mú

模 mú mould; matrix; pattern: 铜～〈印〉matrix; (copper) mould 另见 mó

【模样】 múyàng ① appearance; look: 那人是什么～? What did that person look like?/ 这孩子的～象他妈妈。The child takes after his mother. ② approximately; about; around: 我等了有半小时～。I waited for about half an hour./ 那男的有三十岁～。The man was around thirty.

【模子】 múzi mould; matrix; pattern; die: 一个～里铸出来的 made out of the same mould; as like as two peas

mǔ

母* mǔ ① mother ② one's female elders: 伯～ aunt／ 祖～ grandmother ③ female (animal): ～鸡 hen／ ～狗 bitch／ ～马 mare／ ～狼 she-wolf／ ～象 female elephant／ ～狮 lioness ④ nut (so called because of the female screw thread): 螺～ nut ⑤ origin; parent: 失败是成功之～。Failure is the mother of success.

【母爱】 mǔ'ài mother love; maternal love

【母老虎】 mǔlǎohǔ ① tigress ② vixen; shrew; termagant

【母亲】 mǔqīn mother

【母系】 mǔxì ① maternal side ② matriarchal ◇ ～亲属 maternal relatives／ ～社会 matriarchal society

【母校】 mǔxiào one's old school; Alma Mater

【母性】 mǔxìng maternal instinct

【母语】 mǔyǔ ① mother tongue ② parent language; linguistic parent

亩 mǔ mu, a unit of area (=0.0667 hectares): ～产量 per mu yield

牡 mǔ male: ～牛 bull

【牡丹】 mǔdan tree peony; peony

拇 mǔ

【拇指】 mǔzhǐ ① thumb ② big toe

姆 mǔ 见"保姆" bǎomǔ

mù

木* mù ① tree: 伐～ fell trees／ 果～ fruit tree／ 独～不成林。One tree does not make a forest. ② timber; wood: 松～ pinewood ③ made of wood; wooden: ～制家具 wooden furniture／ ～箱 wooden box／ ～桥 wooden bridge ④ coffin: 行将就～ have one foot in the grave ⑤ numb; wooden: 两脚都冻～了。Both feet were numb with cold./ 舌头～了，什么味儿也尝不出来。My tongue has lost all its sense of taste./ ～头～脑 wooden-headed; dull-witted

【木板】 mùbǎn plank; board ◇ ～床 plank bed

【木材】 mùcái wood; timber; lumber ◇ ～厂 timber mill

【木柴】 mùchái firewood

【木工】 mùgōng ① woodwork; carpentry ② woodworker; carpenter: 细～ cabinetmaker; joiner

【木瓜】 mùguā 〈植〉① Chinese flowering quince ②〈方〉papaya

【木屐】 mùjī clogs

【木匠】 mùjiang carpenter

【木刻】 mùkè woodcut; wood engraving

【木料】 mùliào timber; lumber

【木马】 mùmǎ ①〈体〉vaulting horse; pommelled horse ② (children's) hobbyhorse; rocking horse

【木乃伊】 mùnǎiyī mummy

【木偶】 mù'ǒu ① wooden image; carved figure: 象～似地站着 stand as still as a carved figure ② puppet; marionette ◇ ～剧 puppet show; puppet play／ ～片 puppet film

【木片】 mùpiàn wood chip

【木器】 mùqì wooden furniture: wooden articles

【木然】 mùrán stupefied

【木头】 mùtou wood; log; timber

【木头人儿】 mùtourén woodenhead; blockhead; slow coach

【木屋】 mùwū log cabin

【木星】 mùxīng 〈天〉Jupiter

【木已成舟】 mù yǐ chéng zhōu the wood is already made into a boat — what is done cannot be undone

【木鱼】 mùyú wooden fish (a percussion instrument made of a hollow wooden block, originally used by Buddhist priests to beat rhythm when chanting scriptures)

目* mù ① eye: 双～失明 be blind in both eyes ②〈书〉look; regard: ～为奇迹 regard as a miracle ③ item: 细～ detailed items ④〈生〉order: 亚～ suborder ⑤ a list of things; catalogue; table of contents: 书～ book list

【目标】 mùbiāo ① objective; target: 命中～ hit the target (或 mark)／ 攻击～ target (或 objective) of attack／ 军事～ military objective; military target ② goal; aim; objective

【目不交睫】 mù bù jiāo jié not sleep a wink

【目不识丁】 mù bù shí dīng not know one's ABC; be totally illiterate

【目不暇接】 mù bù xiá jiē the eye cannot take it all in; there are too many things for the eye to take in 又作"目不暇给"

【目不转睛】 mù bù zhuǎn jīng look with fixed eyes; watch with the utmost concentration

【目次】 mùcì table of contents; contents

【目瞪口呆】 mùdèng-kǒudāi gaping; stupefied; dumbstruck: 吓得～ be struck dumb with fear

【目的】 mùdì purpose; aim; goal; objective; end: ～明确 have a definite purpose／ ～与手段 ends and means／ 怀着不可告人的～ harbour evil intentions; have ulterior motives ◇ ～地 destination

【目睹】 mùdǔ see with one's own eyes; witness

【目光】 mùguāng ① sight; vision; view: ～短浅 shortsighted／ ～锐利 sharp-eyed; sharp-sighted／ ～远大 farsighted; farseeing ② gaze; look: ～炯炯 flashing eyes／ 两人的～碰到一起。Their eyes met.

【目光如豆】 mùguāng rú dòu of narrow vision; shortsighted

【目光如炬】 mùguāng rú jù ① eyes blazing like torches blazing with anger ② looking ahead with wisdom; farsighted

【目击】 mùjī see with one's own eyes; witness ◇ ～者 eyewitness; witness

【目见】 mùjiàn see for oneself: 耳闻不如～。Seeing a thing for oneself is better than hearing about it.

【目空一切】 mù kōng yīqiè consider everybody and everything beneath one's notice; be supercilious

【目力】 mùlì eyesight; vision: ～好（不好）have good (poor) eyesight
【目录】 mùlù ① catalogue; list: 图书～ library catalogue/ 出口商品～ a catalogue of export commodities; export list ② table of contents; contents
【目前】 mùqián at present; at the moment: ～形势 the present (或 current) situation/ ～的生产能力 existing production capacity/ 到～为止 up till the present moment; up till now; so far; to date/ ～我还不能给你肯定的答复。I can't give you a definite answer at the moment.
【目送】 mùsòng follow sb. with one's eyes; watch sb. go; gaze after
【目无法纪】 mù wú fǎjì disregard (或 flout) law and discipline
【目下】 mùxià at present; now
【目眩】 mùxuàn dizzy; dazzled: 灯光强烈,令人～。The light is too dazzling.
【目中无人】 mùzhōng wú rén consider everyone beneath one's notice; be supercilious; be overweening

沐 mù wash one's hair
【沐猴而冠】 mùhóu ér guàn a monkey with a hat on — a worthless person in imposing attire
【沐浴】 mùyù ① have (或 take) a bath ② bathe; immerse: 百里油田～着金色的朝晖。The vast oilfield was bathed in the golden rays of the morning sun.

牧 mù herd; tend: ～马 herd horses/ ～羊 tend sheep
【牧草】 mùcǎo herbage; forage grass
【牧场】 mùchǎng grazing land; pastureland; pasture 又作"牧地"
【牧人】 mùrén herdsman
【牧师】 mùshī 〈基督教〉pastor; minister; clergyman
【牧童】 mùtóng shepherd boy; buffalo boy
【牧羊人】 mùyángrén shepherd
【牧业】 mùyè animal husbandry; stock raising

募 mù raise; collect; enlist; recruit: ～款 raise money/ ～兵 recruit soldiers
【募捐】 mùjuān solicit contributions; collect donations

墓 mù grave; tomb; mausoleum
【墓碑】 mùbēi tombstone; gravestone
【墓地】 mùdì graveyard; burial ground; cemetery
【墓穴】 mùxué coffin pit; open grave
【墓志】 mùzhì inscription on the memorial tablet within a tomb
【墓志铭】 mùzhìmíng inscription on the memorial tablet within a tomb; epitaph

幕 mù ① curtain; screen: ～启。The curtain rises./ ～落。The curtain falls. 或 Curtain./ 夜～ the veil of night ② act: 第一～ the first act; Act 1/ 一出三～五场的话剧 a play in three acts and five scenes
【幕后】 mùhòu behind the scenes; backstage: 退居～ retire backstage/ ～操纵 pull strings (或 wires) behind the scenes/ ～活动 behind-the-scenes activities; backstage manoeuvring/ ～交易 behind-the-scenes deal; backstage deal/ ～人物 wirepuller; backstage manipulator
【幕僚】 mùliáo ① aides and staff

睦 mù peaceful; harmonious
【睦邻】 mùlín good-neighbourliness ◇ ～关系 good-neighbourly relations/ ～政策 good-neighbour policy

慕 mù admire; yearn for: 爱～ love; adore/ 仰～ look up to with admiration/ ～名 out of admiration for a famous person

暮 mù ① dusk; evening; sunset: 薄～ dusk ② towards the end; late: ～春 late spring/ 岁～ the end of the year
【暮鼓晨钟】 mùgǔ-chénzhōng evening drum and morning bell in a monastery — timely exhortations to virtue and purity
【暮年】 mùnián declining years; old age; evening of one's life
【暮气】 mùqì lethargy; apathy: ～沉沉 lethargic; apathetic; lifeless
【暮色】 mùsè dusk; twilight; gloaming: ～苍茫 deepening dusk; spreading shades of dusk

穆 mù solemn; reverent: 肃～ solemn

N

ná

拿* ná ① hold; take: ~去 take it away/ ~来 bring it here/ 他手里~的是什么? What is he holding in his hand?/ 不~枪的敌人 enemies without guns ② seize; capture: ~下敌人的碉堡 capture the enemy's blockhouse ③ have a firm grasp of; be able to do; be sure of: 样样农活她都~得起来。 She can do every kind of farm work./ ~不准 not be sure; feel uncertain/ 这事儿~得稳吗? Are you sure of it? ④〈介〉〔引进所凭借的工具、材料、方法等〕: ~尺量 measure with a ruler/ ~事实证明 prove with facts; cite tacts to prove/我们不能~原则作交易。 We cannot barter away our principles./ ~几句话来概括 to sum up in a few words ⑤〈介〉〔引进所处置的对象〕: 别~他开玩笑。 Don't make fun of him. 或 Don't crack jokes at his expense./ 我简直~他没有办法。 I simply can't do anything with him.

【拿不出手】 nábuchū shǒu not be presentable: 我这笔字~。 My handwriting is not presentable.

【拿手】 náshǒu adept; expert; good at: 剪纸她很~。 She's good at making paper-cuts./ ~好戏 a game or trick one is good at

【拿主意】 ná zhǔyi make a decision; make up one's mind: 究竟去不去,你自己~吧。 You'd better decide for yourself whether to go or not./ 我的主意拿定了。 My mind is made up./ 她一直拿不定主意。 She's been wavering all along.

nǎ

哪* nǎ ① which; what: 我们这里有两位姓张的,您要见的是~一位? We've got two Zhangs here. Which one do you want to see?/ 你学的是~国语言? What foreign language are you studying? ②〔表示反问〕: 没有前辈的牺牲,~有今天的幸福生活? Without the sacrifices of the older generation, how could we have such a happy life today? 另见 něi

【哪个】 nǎge ① which: 你们是~班的? Which class are you in? ②〈方〉who: ~在打电话? Who's using the telephone?

【哪里】 nǎli ① where: 你~去? Where are you going? ② wherever; where: ~最艰苦就在~干 go and work where the work is hardest/ ~有压迫,~就有反抗。 Where there is oppression, there is resistance. ③〔用于反问,表示否定〕: 我~知道他费了那么大的劲? Little did I know what a great effort he'd made./ 你对我们帮助很大。—— ~,~。 You gave us a lot of help. — It was nothing.

【哪怕】 nǎpà 〈连〉even; even if; even though; no matter how: ~是一粒米也不应该浪费。 We should not waste even a single grain of rice./ ~是再大的困难我们也能克服。 However great the difficulties may be, we can overcome them.

【哪儿】 nǎr 〈口〉① where: 他上~去啦? Where has he gone? ② wherever; anywhere: ~需要,我就上~去。 I'll go wherever I'm needed./ ~都找不到他。 He is nowhere to be found. ③〔用于反问,表示否定〕: 我~知道他不吃牛肉。 How was I to know he didn't eat beef?

【哪些】 nǎxiē which; who; what: ~是你的? Which ones are yours?/ ~人出席这次会议? Who will attend the meeting?/ 你们讨论了~问题? What problems did you discuss?

【哪样】 nǎyàng what kind of: 你要~颜色的? What colour do you want?

nà

那* nà ① that: ~是我的过错。 That was my fault./ ~是谁? Who is that?/ ~是一九五八年的事。 That was in 1958. ②〈连〉then; in that case: 你要是跟我们一块走,~就得快点。 If you're coming with us, you must hurry./ ~我

们就不再等了。 In that case, we won't wait any longer.

【那个】 nàge ① that: ~孩子 that child/ ~根本谈不到。 That's out of the question./ ~你甭担心。 Don't you worry about that. ②〈口〉〔用在动词、形容词之前,表示夸张〕: 瞧他们干得~欢哪! See how they're throwing themselves into their work! ③〈口〉〔代替不便直说的话,含有婉转或诙谐的意味〕: 你刚才的脾气也太~了。 The way you lost your temper was a little too — you know what I mean.

【那里】 nàli that place; there: 我刚从~回来。 I've just come from there. 或 I've just been there./ ~气候怎么样? What's the weather like there?

【那么】 nàme ① like that; in that way: 你不该~做。 You shouldn't have done that. 或 You oughtn't to have acted the way you did./ 她不好意思~说。 It embarrassed her to say that./ 问题没有他所想象的~复杂。 The problem is not as complicated as he imagined. ②〔放在数量词前,表示估计〕about; or so: 再有~二三十个麻袋就够了。 Another twenty or thirty sacks will probably be enough. ③〈连〉then; in that case; such being the case: 既然这样不行,~你打算怎么办呢? Since that's impossible, what are you going to do? 又作"那末"

【那么点儿】 nàmediǎnr so little; so few: ~活儿,一天就可以干完了。 We can finish that little bit of work in a day.

【那儿】 nàr 〈口〉① 见"那里" ②〔用在"打""从""由"后面〕that time; then: 打~起,她就用心念书了。 She's been studying hard since then.

【那时】 nàshí at that time; then; in those days: 说时迟~快 in the twinkling of an eye; in an instant

【那些】 nàxiē those: ~水渠是一九五八年修成的。 Those irrigation channels were built in 1958.

【那样】 nàyàng of that kind; like that; such; so: 他~你~仔细。 He's not so careful as you are./ ~儿也好,先试试再说。 All right, let's try it out./ 这点小事你怎么就急得~儿了? Why let such trifles worry you so much?

呐 nà

【呐喊】 nàhǎn shout loudly; shout out: ~助威 shout encouragement; cheer

纳 nà ① receive; admit: 闭门不~ refuse to admit; shut sb. out ② accept: 采~ adopt ③ enjoy ④ pay; offer

【纳粹】 Nàcuì Nazi ◇ ~分子 Nazi/ ~主义 Nazism

【纳福】 nàfú (usu. of elderly people) enjoy a life of ease and comfort

【纳贿】 nàhuì ① take bribes ② offer bribes

【纳凉】 nàliáng enjoy the cool (in the open air)

【纳入】 nàrù bring (或 channel) into: ~正轨 put sth. on the right course/ ~国家计划 bring sth. into line with the state plan

【纳税】 nàshuì pay taxes ◇ ~人 taxpayer

捺 nà press down; restrain: ~着性子 control one's temper/ 勉强~住心头的怒火 barely manage to restrain one's anger

nǎi

乃 nǎi 〈书〉① be: 失败~成功之母。 Failure is the mother of success. ② so; therefore: 因山势高峻,~在山腰休息片时。 It was a steep climb, so we rested for a while halfway up the hill. ③ only then: 惟虚心~能进步。 You can make progress only if you are modest./ 今~知之,I didn't know it until now. ④ you; your: ~父 your father

奶* nǎi ① breasts ② milk ③ suckle; breast-feed: ~孩子 suckle (或 breast-feed) a baby

【奶茶】 nǎichá tea with milk

【奶粉】 nǎifěn milk powder; powdered milk; dried milk

【奶酪】 nǎilào　cheese
【奶妈】 nǎimā　wet nurse
【奶名】 nǎimíng　a child's pet name; infant name
【奶奶】 nǎinai　〈口〉① (paternal) grandmother; grandma ② a respecful form of address for an old woman
【奶牛】 nǎiniú　milch cow; milk cow; cow
【奶品】 nǎipǐn　milk products; dairy products
【奶瓶】 nǎipíng　feeding bottle; nursing bottle; baby's bottle
【奶头】 nǎitóu　〈口〉① nipple; teat ② nipple (of a feeding bottle)
【奶油】 nǎiyóu　cream
【奶罩】 nǎizhào　brassiere; bra

nài

奈 nài
【奈何】 nàihé　①〔反问〕how; to no avail: 民不畏死，～以死惧之。The people fear not death, why threaten them with it? 徒唤～ utter bootless cries/ 无可～ be utterly helpless ② do sth. to a person: 其奈我何？What can they do to me?

耐* nài　be able to bear or endure: 吃苦～劳 bear hardships and stand hard work/ ～穿 can stand wear and tear; be endurable/ 这种料子很～洗。This material washes well.
【耐烦】 nàifán　patient: 显出不～的样子 show signs of impatience
【耐寒】 nàihán　cold-resistant: 耐严寒 resistant to low temperature
【耐火】 nàihuǒ　fire-resistant; refractory
【耐久】 nàijiǔ　lasting long; durable
【耐力】 nàilì　endurance; staying power; stamina
【耐热】 nàirè　heat-resisting; heatproof ◇ ～合金 heat-resisting alloy/ ～性 heat resistance
【耐人寻味】 nài rén xúnwèi　afford food for thought: 他的话是很～的。What he said gives one much food for thought.
【耐心】 nàixīn　patient: 用～说服的方法 adopt the method of patient persuasion
【耐性】 nàixìng　patience; endurance
【耐用】 nàiyòng　durable: ～物品 durable goods; durables.

nán

男* nán　① man; male: ～病房 men's ward/ ～护士 male nurse/ ～主人公 hero/ ～学生 boy student/ ～佣人 manservant ② son; boy: 长～ one's eldest son ③ baron
【男厕所】 náncèsuǒ　① men's lavatory (或 toilet, room) ②〔用于公共厕所门上〕Gentlemen; Men; Gents
【男盗女娼】 nándào-nǚchāng　behave like thieves and whores; be out-and-out scoundrels
【男儿】 nán'ér　man: 好～ a fine man
【男方】 nánfāng　the bridegroom's or husband's side
【男高音】 nángāoyīn　〈乐〉tenor
【男孩】 nánhái　boy
【男家】 nánjiā　the bridegroom's or husband's family
【男女】 nán-nǚ　men and women: ～青年 young men and women/ ～老少 men and women, old and young/ ～同工同酬。Men and women get equal pay for equal work.
【男女平等】 nán-nǚ píngděng　equality of men and women; equality of the sexes
【男朋友】 nánpéngyou　boyfriend
【男人】 nánrén　① man ② menfolk
【男生】 nánshēng　man student; boy student; schoolboy
【男性】 nánxìng　① the male sex ② man
【男装】 nánzhuāng　men's clothing: 女扮～ a woman disguised as a man
【男子】 nánzǐ　man; male ◇ ～单(双)打 men's singles (doubles)/ ～团体赛 men's team event
【男子汉】 nánzǐhàn　man: 不象个～ not manly; not man enough

南* nán　south: ～风 a south wind/ 城～ south of

the city/ 大军～下 large contingents of the army advancing south
【南北】 nán-běi　① north and south ② from north to south: 这个水库～足有五公里。This reservoir extends a good 5 km from north to south.
【南部】 nánbù　southern part; south
【南方】 nánfāng　① south ② the southern part of the country, esp. the area south of the Changjiang River; the South: 住在～ live in the South/ ～风味 southern style; southern flavour ◇ ～话 southern dialect/ ～人 southerner
【南风】 nánfēng　south wind
【南瓜】 nánguā　pumpkin; cushaw
【南极】 nánjí　① the South Pole; the Antarctic Pole ② the south magnetic pole
【南柯一梦】 Nánkē yī mèng　Nanke dream (from the story of a man who dreamed that he became governor of Nanke in the Kingdom of the Ants); illusory joy; fond dream
【南腔北调】 nánqiāng-běidiào　(speak with) a mixed accent
【南洋】 Nányáng　① a general name used towards the end of the Qing Dynasty for the coastal provinces of Jiangsu, Zhejiang, Fujian and Guangdong ② an old name for the Malay Archipelago, the Malay Peninsula and Indonesia or for southeast Asia
【南辕北辙】 nányuán-běizhé　try to go south by driving the chariot north — act in a way that defeats one's purpose
【南征北战】 nánzhēng-běizhàn　fight north and south on many fronts

难* nán　① difficult; hard; troublesome: 这道题～解。This problem is hard to solve./ 路～走。The road is bad. 或 The going is hard. ② put sb. into a difficult position: 这问题一下子把我～住了。The question put me on the spot. ③ hardly possible: ～说 it's hard to say; you never can tell/ ～忘 unforgettable ④ bad; unpleasant: ～吃 taste bad; be unpalatable/ ～听 unpleasant to the ear
另见 nàn
【难保】 nánbǎo　one cannot say for sure: 今天～不下雨。You can't say for sure that it won't rain today.
【难产】 nánchǎn　①〈医〉difficult labour; dystocia ② (of a literary work, plan, etc.) be difficult of fulfilment; be slow in coming
【难处】 nánchǔ　hard to get along (或 on) with: 他只是脾气暴躁些，并不～。He's a bit quick-tempered, but not difficult to get along with.
【难处】 nánchu　difficulty; trouble: 他有他的～。He has his difficulties.
【难倒】 nándǎo　daunt; baffle; beat: 这个问题可把我～了。This problem baffles (或 beats) me.
【难道】 nándào　〈副〉〔用以加强反问语气〕：～你忘了自己的诺言吗？Can you have forgotten your promise?/ 这一点儿困难～我们还不能克服吗？Can't we overcome even such small difficulties?/ 这～还不明白吗？Isn't this perfectly clear?/ ～就罢了不成？How can we let the matter rest here?
【难得】 nándé　① hard to come by; rare: ～的好机会 a rare chance/ 这种草药很～。This medicinal herb is hard to come by./ 他在一年之内两次打破世界纪录，是十分～的。He's performed the rare feat of breaking a world record twice in one year. ② seldom; rarely: 我们～见面，你多待一会儿吧。Can't you stay a bit longer? We so seldom have a chance to get together.
【难怪】 nánguài　① no wonder: ～找不到人，都开会去了。No wonder you can't find anybody here; they're all away at a meeting. ② understandable; pardonable: 他不大了解情况，搞错了也～。You can hardly blame him for the mistake he made; he didn't know much about the situation.
【难关】 nánguān　difficulty; crisis: 渡过～ tide over a difficulty (或 crisis)/ 攻克技术～ break down a technical barrier; resolve key technical problems
【难过】 nánguò　① have a hard time ② feel sorry; feel bad; be grieved: 他听到朋友去世的消息，非常～。He was deeply grieved to learn that his friend had died.
【难解难分】 nánjiě-nánfēn　① be inextricably involved (in a dispute); be locked together (in a struggle): 两军厮杀，～。The

two opposing armies are locked in battle. ② be sentimentally attached to each other

【难堪】 nánkān ① intolerable; unbearable ② embarrassed: 感到~ feel very much embarrassed/ 处于~的境地 be in an extremely awkward (或 miserable) situation

【难看】 nánkàn ① ugly; unsightly: 这座楼房真~。 This building is ugly./ 他听到这个消息,脸色变得很~。 When he heard the news, his face took on a ghastly expression. ② shameful; embarrassing: 我们在音乐会上要是演奏不好, 那就太~了。 It would be a shame if we put on a bad performance at the concert.

【难免】 nánmiǎn hard to avoid: 犯错误是~的, 你认真改了就好了。 Mistakes are hard to avoid, but if you correct them conscientiously, things will be all right./ 人们的看法有时一带片面性。 Sometimes people can't help being one-sided in their views.

【难能可贵】 nán néng kě guì difficult of attainment, hence worthy of esteem; deserving praise for one's excellent performance or behaviour; estimable; commendable

【难色】 nánsè appear to be reluctant or embarrassed: 面有~ show signs of reluctance or embarrassment

【难上难】 nánshàngnán extremely difficult 又作"难上加难"

【难舍难分】 nánshě-nánfēn loath to part from each other

【难受】 nánshòu ① feel unwell; feel ill; suffer pain: 浑身疼得~ be aching all over ② feel unhappy; feel bad: 他知道事情做错了,心里很~。 He felt bad when he realized his error.

【难说】 nánshuō it's hard to say; you never can tell: 他什么时候回来还很~。 No one can tell when he will return.

【难题】 nántí difficult problem; a hard nut to crack; poser: 出~ set difficult questions/ 在这样干旱的地区种水稻可是一个~。 How to grow rice in such a dry area is a difficult problem.

【难听】 nántīng ① unpleasant to hear: 这个曲子真~。 This tune is not very pleasing to the ear. ② offensive; coarse: 你怎么骂人,多~! Why do you swear? It's really bad. ③ scandalous: 这事情说出去多~。 The story will create a scandal once it gets out.

【难忘】 nánwàng unforgettable; memorable: ~的一课 an unforgettable lesson/ ~的岁月 memorable years

【难为情】 nánwéiqíng ① ashamed; embarrassed; shy: 试验不成功也别~。 Don't feel ashamed if your experiment isn't a success./他听见别人这样夸他,感到很~。 He was very embarrassed to hear people speak so highly of him. ② embarrassing; disconcerting: 答应吧,办不到;不答应吧,又有点~。 It's not feasible to comply, but a bit embarrassing to refuse.

【难为】 nánwei ① embarrass; press: 她不会唱歌,就别~她了。 She can't sing. So don't press her to. ② be a tough job to: 在战争年代, 她一个人拉扯好几个孩子, 真~她了。 It was quite a job for her to bring up several children all by herself during the war.

【难闻】 nánwén smell unpleasant; smell bad

【难兄难弟】 nánxiōng-nándì 〈讽〉 two of a kind 另见 nànxiōng-nándì

【难言之隐】 nán yán zhī yǐn sth. which it would be awkward to disclose; sth. embarrassing to mention; a painful topic

【难以】 nányǐ difficult to: ~捉摸 difficult to pin down; elusive; unintelligible/ ~想象 unimaginable/ ~形容 indescribable; beyond description/ ~逆料 hard to predict (或 forecast)/ ~置信 hard to believe

喃 nán

【喃喃】 nánnán 〈象〉 mutter; murmur: ~自语 mutter to oneself

nǎn

赧 nǎn blushing

【赧然】 nǎnrán 〈书〉 blushing

【赧颜】 nǎnyán 〈书〉 blush; be shamefaced

腩 nǎn 见"牛腩" niúnǎn

nàn

难* nàn ① calamity; disaster; adversity: 逃~ flee from danger; be a refugee ② take to task; blame: 非~ blame; reproach 另见 nán

【难民】 nànmín refugee ◇ ~营 refugee camp

【难兄难弟】 nànxiōng-nàndì fellow sufferers 另见 nánxiōng-nándì

【难友】 nànyǒu fellow sufferer

náng

囊 náng ① bag; pocket: 药~ medicine bag/ 胶~ capsule ② anything shaped like a bag: 胆~ gallbladder

【囊空如洗】 náng kōng rú xǐ with empty pockets; penniless; broke

【囊括】 nángkuò include; embrace: ~四海 bring the whole country under imperial rule

【囊中物】 nángzhōngwù sth. which is in the bag — sth. certain of attainment

nǎng

曩 nǎng 〈书〉 former; past: ~时 in olden days; of yore

náo

挠 náo ① scratch: ~痒痒 scratch an itch ② hinder: 阻~ obstruct ③ yield; flinch: 不屈不~ indomitable; unyielding

nǎo

恼* nǎo ① angry; irritated; annoyed: ~恨 resent ② unhappy; worried: 烦~ vexed; worried

【恼恨】 nǎohèn resent; hate: 他的批评是为你好, 你可别~他。 You shouldn't resent his criticism. He meant well.

【恼火】 nǎohuǒ annoyed; irritated; vexed: 对于他那种听不进批评的态度,我们感到~。 We're annoyed at his not listening to criticism.

【恼怒】 nǎonù angry; indignant; furious

【恼人】 nǎorén irritating; annoying

【恼羞成怒】 nǎo-xiū chéng nù fly into a rage from shame; be shamed into anger

脑* nǎo 〈生理〉 brain: 大~ cerebrum/ 小~ cerebellum/ 用~过度 overtax one's brain

【脑袋】 nǎodai 〈口〉 head

【脑海】 nǎohǎi brain; mind: 多年前的旧事又重现在他的~里。 Memories of things long past flashed across his mind.

【脑浆】 nǎojiāng brains

【脑筋】 nǎojīn ① brains; mind; head: 动~ use one's brains (或 head)/ 你问老杨去。他~好,记得清。 Ask Lao Yang, he has a good memory. ② way of thinking; ideas: 旧~ a person who clings to old-fashioned ideas; an old fogey

【脑壳】 nǎoké ① skull ② 〈方〉 head

【脑满肠肥】 nǎomǎn-chángféi heavy-jowled and potbellied — the idle rich

【脑子】 nǎozi ① 〈口〉 brain ② brains; mind; head: 没~ have no brains/ 问题是复杂的,我们的~也要复杂一点。 The problems are complicated, and our brains must be a little complicated, too.

瑙 nǎo 见"玛瑙" mǎnǎo

nào

闹* nào ① noisy: 这屋里太～。This room is too noisy. ② make a noise; stir up trouble: 叫孩子们别～了。Tell the children to stop making a noise (或 fooling around)./ ～着玩儿 do sth. for fun; be joking/ 又哭又～ make a tearful scene ③ give vent (to one's anger, resentment, etc.): ～脾气 vent one's spleen; lose one's temper; be in a tantrum ④ suffer from; be troubled by: ～肚子 have diarrhoea/～虫灾 suffer from insect pests

【闹别扭】 nào bièniu be difficult with sb.; be at odds with sb.

【闹病】 nàobìng fall ill; be ill

【闹翻】 nàofān fall out with sb.

【闹风潮】 nào fēngcháo carry on agitation; stage strikes, demonstrations, etc.

【闹鬼】 nàoguǐ ① be haunted ② play tricks behind sb.'s back; use underhand means

【闹哄哄】 nàohōnghōng clamorous; noisy

【闹剧】 nàojù farce

【闹乱子】 nào luànzi cause trouble

【闹情绪】 nào qíngxù be disgruntled; be in low spirits

【闹市】 nàoshì busy streets; busy shopping centre; downtown area

【闹事】 nàoshì create a disturbance; make trouble

【闹笑话】 nào xiàohuà make a fool of oneself; make a stupid mistake: 不懂装懂就会～。If you pretend to know what you don't know, you'll only make a fool of yourself.

【闹意见】 nào yìjiàn be on bad terms because of a difference of opinion

【闹意气】 nào yìqì feel resentful because something is not to one's liking; sulk: 你有意见就提出来，不要～。If you have any complaint, don't just sulk; speak up.

【闹着玩儿】 nàozhe wánr joke: 他是跟你～的, 你别当真。He was joking. Don't take it seriously./ 这可不是～的事。This is no joking matter (或 no joke).

【闹钟】 nàozhōng alarm clock

ne

呢* ne 〈助〉① 〔用在疑问句的末尾〕: 我错在哪儿～? What have I done wrong?/ 他们两人都有任务了, 我～? They've both got something to do. What about me? ② 〔用在陈述句的末尾,表示确认事实〕: 远得很, 有好几千里地呢～。It's a long way off — thousands of li away. ③ 〔用在陈述句的末尾,表示动作或情况正在继续〕: 老张, 有人找你～。Lao Zhang, somebody is looking for you.

另见 ní

něi

哪 něi 〈口〉 which; what
另见 nǎ

馁 něi ① hungry; famished ② disheartened; dispirited: 气～ lose heart; be disheartened/ 胜不骄, 败不～ not become dizzy with success, nor be discouraged by failure

nèi

内* nèi ① inner; within; inside: 房子～外都很干净。The house is clean inside and out. ② one's wife or her relatives: ～弟 wife's younger brother; brother-in-law

【内部】 nèibù inside; internal; interior: ～联系 internal relations

【内地】 nèidì inland; interior; hinterland: ～城市 inland city/ 我国的～ the interior of our country

【内定】 nèidìng (of an official appointment) decided at the higher level but not officially announced

【内服】 nèifú 〈医〉 to be taken orally

【内阁】 nèigé cabinet: 影子～ shadow cabinet

【内功】 nèigōng exercises to benefit the internal organs

【内行】 nèiháng expert; adept: 种稻子很～ know a lot about growing rice/ 充～ pose as an expert/ 要说木匠活呀, 他可是～。When it comes to carpentry, he is quite a dab hand.

【内河】 nèihé inland river (或 waters, waterway) ◇ ～航行权 inland navigation rights/ ～运输 inland water transport

【内讧】 nèihòng internal conflict; internal strife; internal dissension

【内奸】 nèijiān a secret enemy agent within one's ranks; hidden traitor

【内疚】 nèijiù compunction; guilty conscience: 感到～ feel compunction; have qualms of conscience

【内科】 nèikē 〈医〉 (department of) internal medicine ◇ ～病房 medical ward/ ～医生 physician

【内陆】 nèilù inland; interior; landlocked ◇ ～国 landlocked country/ ～河 continental river/ ～盆地 interior (或 inland) basin

【内乱】 nèiluàn civil strife; internal disorder

【内幕】 nèimù what goes on behind the scenes; inside story

【内亲】 nèiqīn a relative on one's wife's side; in-law

【内勤】 nèiqín ① office staff ② internal or office work (as distinguished from work carried on mainly outside the office)

【内情】 nèiqíng inside information (或 story): 了解～ be an insider; be in the know

【内人】 nèiren my wife

【内容】 nèiróng content; substance: ～和形式的统一 unity of content and form/ 他的演说, 毫无～。His speech lacked substance (或 content)./ 这本书～丰富。This book has substantial content./ 这次谈话的～牵涉面很广。The talk covered a lot of ground./ ～提要 synopsis; résumé

【内外】 nèi-wài ① inside and outside; domestic and foreign: 长城～ both sides of the Great Wall／～夹攻 attack from both within and without／～交困 beset with difficulties both at home and abroad ② around; about: 五十年～ in about fifty years

【内详】 nèixiáng name and address of sender enclosed

【内向】 nèixiàng 〈心〉 introversion

【内销】 nèixiāo sold inside the country; for the domestic market

【内心】 nèixīn heart; innermost being: ～深处 in one's heart of hearts／ 他～很矛盾。He is torn by conflicting thoughts.

【内衣】 nèiyī underwear; underclothes

【内因】 nèiyīn 〈哲〉 internal cause

【内应】 nèiyìng a person operating from within in coordination with outside forces; a planted agent; a plant

【内忧外患】 nèiyōu-wàihuàn domestic trouble and foreign invasion

【内在】 nèizài inherent; intrinsic; internal

【内脏】 nèizàng internal organs; viscera

【内战】 nèizhàn civil war

【内政】 nèizhèng internal (或 domestic, home) affairs: 互不干涉～ noninterference in each other's internal affairs

【内助】 nèizhù 〈书〉 wife

nèn

嫩* nèn ① tender; delicate: ～叶 tender leaves/ 这肉炒得很～。This stir-fried meat is very tender./ 小孩子肉皮儿～。Young children have delicate skin./ 脸皮儿～ shy; bashful ② light: ～黄 light yellow/ ～绿 light green; soft green ③ inexperienced; unskilled: ～手 raw hand; new hand

【嫩色】 nènsè light colour; soft colour; pastel shade

néng

能* néng ① ability; capability; skill: 无～ lacking in ability; incompetent/ 一专多～ good at many things and expert in one ② 〈物〉 energy: 原子～ atomic energy/ 太阳～ solar energy/ 热～ thermal energy ③ able; capable: ～

人 able person ④ can; be able to; be capable of: 她一分钟~打七十个字。She can type 70 words a minute./ 他好多了,~下床了。He's much better and can get up now./ 我干这个工作~行吗? Am I really fit for the job?

【能干】nénggàn able; capable; competent: 他是个很~的人。He is a man of great ability./ 这些女电工真~。These women electricians really know their job.

【能够】nénggòu can; be able to; be capable of: ~独立工作 be able to work on one's own/ 他~说三种外国语。He can speak three foreign languages./ 这河的下游~行驶轮船。The lower reaches of the river are navigable for steamers.

【能力】nénglì ability; capacity; capability: ~强 have great ability; be very capable/ 培养学生的推理~ develop the students' reasoning capacity/ 分析问题和解决问题的~ ability to analyse and solve problems

【能量】néngliàng ①〈物〉energy: ~转化 conversion of energy ② capabilities: 他们人数很少,~很大。Though few in number, they have enormous capacity for manoeuvre.

【能…能…】néng...néng...〔表示"既能…又能"〕be good at offence and defence; be able to take the offensive or hold one's ground

【能事】néngshì〔常跟"尽"字配合〕what one is particularly good at: 竭尽挑拨离间之~ stop at nothing to sow discord

【能手】néngshǒu dab; expert; crackajack: 木刻~ a dab at wood engraving/ 技术革新~ a crackajack at technical innovation

【能说会道】néngshuō-huìdào have the gift of the gab; have a glib tongue

【能源】néngyuán the sources of energy; energy resources; energy: ~危机 energy crisis

【能者多劳】néngzhě duō láo able people should do more work (said as when asking sb. to perform a service or do extra work)

ńg

嗯 ńg 或 ń〈叹〉[表示疑问]: ~,你说什么? What? What did you say?
另见 ňg; ng

ňg

嗯 ňg 或 ň〈叹〉[表示出乎意外或不以为然]: ~,怎么又不见了? Hey! It's gone again./ ~, 你怎么还没去? What! Haven't you started yet?
另见 ńg; ng

ng

嗯 ng 或 ǹ〈叹〉[表示答应]: 他~了一声,就走了。He merely said, "H'm", and went away.
另见 ńg; ňg

nī

妮 nī
【妮子】nīzi〈方〉girl; lass 又作"妮儿"

ní

尼 * ní Buddhist nun
【尼姑】nígū Buddhist nun

泥 * ní ① mud; mire ② mashed vegetable or fruit: 枣~ jujube paste/ 土豆~ mashed potato/ 苹果~ applesauce
【泥垢】nígòu dirt; grime
【泥浆】níjiāng slurry; mud: 钻井~ drilling mud
【泥坑】níkēng mud pit; mire; morass: 陷在~里 get stuck in the mud

【泥泞】nínìng muddy; miry; ~的道路 a muddy road
【泥菩萨】nípúsà clay idol: ~过河,自身难保 like a clay idol fording a river — hardly able to save oneself (let alone anyone else)
【泥塑】nísù clay sculpture
【泥塘】nítáng mire; bog; morass
【泥土】nítǔ ① earth; soil: 春天的原野散发着~的芳香。In spring the fields give off the aroma of the earth. ② clay

呢 ní (cloth made of) wool; woollen cloth (for heavy clothing); heavy woollen cloth; wool coating or suiting: 制服~ uniform coating/ 格子~ woollen check
另见 ne
【呢绒】níróng woollen goods; wool fabric
【呢子】nízi woollen cloth (for heavy clothing); heavy woollen cloth; wool coating or suiting

怩 ní 见"忸怩"niǔní

倪 ní 见"端倪"duānní

霓 ní〈气〉secondary rainbow
【霓虹灯】níhóngdēng neon lamp; neon light; neon

nǐ

拟 nǐ ① draw up; draft: ~稿 make a draft/ ~一个方案 draw up a plan ② intend; plan: ~于下月前往香港 plan to go to Hong Kong next month ③ imitate: 模~ imitate; copy
【拟订】nǐdìng draw up; draft; work out: ~计划 draw up a plan; draft a plan/ ~具体办法 work out specific measures/ ~城市建设规划 map out a programme for municipal construction 又作"拟定"
【拟议】nǐyì ① proposal; recommendation: 事实证明他的~是正确的。Facts show that his recommendations were sound. ② draw up; draft: 小组一致通过了她所~的意见书。The group unanimously adopted the proposal she drew up.

你 * nǐ ① you (second person singular): ~爸爸 your father ② you (second person plural): ~方 your side; you/ ~校 your school ③〔泛指任何人〕you; one; anyone: 碰到这么一个人,~有什么办法? What can you do with a person like that?/ 三个人~看看我,我看看~,谁也没说话。The three of them kept looking at one another without saying a word./ ~一言,我一语,谈得很热闹。A lively conversation went on with everybody joining in.
【你好】nǐhǎo how do you do; how are you; hello
【你们】nǐmen you (second person plural)
【你死我活】nǐsǐ-wǒhuó life-and-death; mortal: ~的斗争 a life-and-death struggle/ 拼个~ fight to the bitter end
【你追我赶】nǐzhuī-wǒgǎn try to overtake each other in friendly emulation

旎 nǐ 见"旖旎"yǐnǐ

nì

逆 nì ① contrary; counter: ~风 contrary wind; head wind ② go against; disobey; defy: ~时代潮流而动 go against the trend of the times ③ traitor: ~产 traitor's property
【逆耳】nì'ěr grate on the ear; be unpleasant to the ear: ~的话 words or advice unpleasant to hear/ 忠言~。Good advice often jars on the ear.
【逆风】nìfēng ① against the wind: ~行舟 sail against the wind ② contrary wind; head wind
【逆境】nìjìng adverse circumstances; adversity
【逆来顺受】nì lái shùn shòu meekly submit to oppression, maltreatment, etc.; resign oneself to adversity
【逆流】nìliú adverse current; countercurrent

【逆水】 nìshuǐ against the current: ～行舟，不进则退。A boat sailing against the current must forge ahead or it will be driven back.

昵 nì close; intimate: 亲～ very intimate

匿 nì hide; conceal: 隐～ go into hiding; hide
【匿伏】 nìfú be in hiding; lurk
【匿迹】 nìjī go into hiding; stay in concealment: 销声～ be in hiding; disappear from the scene
【匿名】 nìmíng anonymous ◇ ～信 anonymous letter
【匿影藏形】 nìyǐng-cángxíng hide from public notice; conceal one's identity; lie low

溺 nì ① drown: ～死 be drowned ② be addicted to: ～于酒色 given over to wine and woman
【溺爱】 nì'ài spoil (a child); dote on (a child)

睨 nì 〈书〉 look askance

膩 nì ① greasy; oily: 这燉肉有点～。This stew is a bit greasy./ 汤太～了。The soup is too oily. ② be bored with; be tired of: 这些话我都听～了。I'm tired of listening to all this. ③ meticulous: 细～的描写 a minute description ④ dirt; grime: 尘～ dirt
【腻烦】 nìfan 〈口〉 ① be bored; be fed up: 这本书我看了多少遍都不觉得～。I never get bored reading and rereading this book. ② loathe; hate: 我最～说大话的人。I can't stand people who brag.

niān

拈 niān pick up (with the thumb and one or two fingers): 从罐子里～出一块糖 take a candy from the jar/ 信手～来 pick up at random

nián

年* nián ① year: 去～ last year/ ～复一～ year after year; year in year out ② annual; yearly: ～产量 annual output; annual yield ③ age: ～过六十 over sixty (years old) ④ New Year: 拜～ pay a New Year visit ⑤ a period in one's life: 童～ childhood ⑥ a period in history: 近～来 in recent years/ 明朝末～ towards the end of the Ming Dynasty ⑦ harvest: 丰～ rich harvest
【年报】 niánbào ① annual report; annual ② annals (of a learned society)
【年表】 niánbiǎo chronological table
【年初】 niánchū the beginning of the year: 去年～ at the beginning of last year
【年代】 niándài ① age; years; time: 战争～ during the war years/ ～久了，石碑上的字迹已经模糊了。The inscriptions on the stone tablet have become blurred with the passage of time./ 展出的古代文物都标明了～。The antiques on display are all marked with dates. ② a decade of a century: 八十～ the eighties/ 二十世纪七十～ the 1970s
【年底】 niándǐ the end of the year
【年度】 niándù year: 财政～ financial year; fiscal year/ ～计划 annual plan
【年份】 niánfen ① a particular year: 这两笔开支不在一个～。These two expenditures were not incurred in the same year. ② age; time: 这件瓷器的～比别件久。This piece of porcelain is older than that one.
【年富力强】 niánfù-lìqiáng in the prime of life; in one's prime
【年高德劭】 niángāo-déshào of venerable age and eminent virtue; venerable
【年糕】 niángāo New Year cake (made of glutinous rice flour)
【年关】 niánguān the end of the year (formerly time for settling accounts)
【年号】 niánhào the title of an emperor's reign

【年华】 niánhuá time; years: 虚度～ idle away one's time; waste one's life
【年货】 niánhuò special purchases for the Spring Festival: 办～ do Spring Festival shopping
【年级】 niánjí grade; year: 大学三～学生 third year university student/ 小学一～学生 first grade primary school pupil
【年纪】 niánjì age: 上了～ old; advanced in years/ ～轻 young
【年假】 niánjià ① New Year holidays ② annual leave
【年鉴】 niánjiàn yearbook; almanac
【年历】 niánlì a calendar with the whole year printed on one sheet; single-page calendar
【年利】 niánlì annual interest ◇ ～率 annual interest rate
【年龄】 niánlíng age: 从马的牙齿可以看出它的～。You can tell a horse's age from its teeth.
【年迈】 niánmài old; aged: ～力衰 old and infirm; senile
【年年】 niánnián every year; year after year
【年谱】 niánpǔ a chronicle of sb.'s life
【年青】 niánqīng young
【年轻】 niánqīng young: ～人 young people/ ～力壮 young and vigorous/ ～一代 the younger (或 rising) generation
【年深日久】 niánshēn-rìjiǔ with the passage of time; as the years go by: 河里的泥沙淤积在这里，～便成了沙洲。The bar was formed by the mud and sand deposited here over a long period of time.
【年岁】 niánsuì ① age: 上了～的人 a person who is getting on in years ② years: 因为～久远，当时的具体情况已记不清了。As it happened so many years ago, I don't remember the details.
【年头】 niántóu ① year ② years; long time: 她干这一行～了。She has been doing this sort of work for years. / 这些树不够～，还没成材呢。These trees need more time to grow into useful timber. ③ days; times: 那～ in those days ④ harvest: 今年～真好。This year's harvest is very good indeed.
【年息】 niánxī annual interest
【年限】 niánxiàn fixed number of years: 学习～ the number of years set for a course (of study)/ 工具使用～ the service life of a tool
【年夜】 niányè the eve of the lunar New Year
【年月】 niányue days; years
【年终】 niánzhōng the end of the year; year-end: ～结帐 year-end settlement of accounts/ ～评比 year-end appraisal of work

粘 nián 见"黏" nián
另见 zhān

黏 nián sticky; glutinous: ～米 glutinous rice/ 这浆糊不～。This paste is not sticky enough.
【黏附】 niánfù adhere ◇ ～力 adhesion
【黏合】 niánhé 〈化〉 bind; bond; adhere
【黏糊】 niánhu ① sticky; glutinous ② languid; slow-moving
【黏土】 niántǔ clay
【黏性】 niánxìng stickiness; viscidity; viscosity
【黏液】 niányè 〈生理〉 mucus
【黏着】 niánzhuó stick together; adhere

niǎn

捻 niǎn ① twist with the fingers: ～线 twist thread/ 把油灯～大些 turn up the wick (of a lamp) ② sth. made by twisting: 纸～儿 a paper spill/ 灯～儿 lampwick

辇 niǎn ① a man-drawn carriage used in ancient times ② imperial carriage

碾 niǎn ① roller ② grind or husk with a roller: ～米 husk rice ③ crush: ～得粉碎 be crushed to powder; be crushed to pieces; be pulverized ④ flatten

撵 niǎn drive out; oust: 把人～走 drive sb. away/ ～下台 oust from a leading position

niàn

廿 niàn twenty

念* niàn ① think of; miss: 我们老~着你。We miss you very much. ② thought; idea: 杂~ distracting thoughts ③ read aloud ④ study; attend school: ~书 read; study/ 他~过中学。He has been to middle school.
【念佛】 niànfó chant the name of Buddha; pray to Buddha
【念经】 niànjīng recite or chant scriptures
【念旧】 niànjiù ① keep old friendships in mind ② for old time's sake
【念念不忘】 niànniàn bù wàng bear in mind constantly
【念念有词】 niànniàn yǒu cí ① mutter incantations ② mumble
【念头】 niàntou thought; idea; intention: 当时他心中只有一个~, 就是为祖国增光。At that time he had only one thing in mind: to win credit for his country./ 你最好放弃这个~。You'd better give up the idea.

niáng

娘* niáng ① ma; mum; mother: 爹~ father and mother ② a form of address for an elderly married woman: 婶~ wife of one's father's younger brother; aunt/ 老大~ grandma ③ a young woman: 新~ bride
【娘家】 niángjia a married woman's parents' home

niàng

酿 niàng ① make (wine); brew (beer): ~酒 make wine ② make (honey): 蜜蜂~蜜。Bees make honey. ③ lead to; result in: ~祸 lead to disaster ④ wine: 佳~ good wine
【酿成】 niàngchéng lead to; bring on; breed: 小错不改往往~大错。Small mistakes left uncorrected will lead to big ones.
【酿酒】 niàngjiǔ make wine; brew beer ◇ ~厂 winery; brewery/ ~业 wine-making industry

niǎo

鸟 niǎo bird
【鸟粪】 niǎofèn ① birds' droppings ② guano
【鸟尽弓藏】 niǎojìn-gōngcáng cast aside the bow once the birds are gone — cast sb. aside when he has served his purpose
【鸟瞰】 niǎokàn ① get a bird's-eye view: ~全城 get a bird's-eye view of the city ② general survey of a subject; bird's-eye view
【鸟类】 niǎolèi birds
【鸟笼】 niǎolóng birdcage
【鸟枪】 niǎoqiāng ① fowling piece ② air gun
【鸟兽】 niǎo-shòu birds and beasts; fur and feather: 作~散 scatter like birds and beasts; flee helter-skelter; stampede
【鸟语花香】 niǎoyǔ-huāxiāng birds sing and flowers give forth their fragrance — characterizing a fine spring day

袅 niǎo slender and delicate
【袅袅】 niǎoniǎo ① curl upwards: 炊烟~。Smoke is curling upward from kitchen chimneys. ② wave in the wind: 垂杨~。Drooping willows are dancing in the wind. ③ linger: 余音~。The music lingered in the air long after the performance ended.
【袅娜】 niǎonuó slender and graceful; willowy

niào

尿 niào ① urine ② urinate; make water; pass water
【尿布】 niàobù diaper; napkin; nappy
【尿床】 niàochuáng wet the bed; bed-wetting
【尿盆】 niàopén chamber pot; urinal

niē

捏 niē ① hold between the fingers; pinch: 把米里的虫子~出来 pick the worms out of the rice ② knead with the fingers; mould: ~泥人儿 mould clay figurines ③ fabricate; make up: ~报 fake a report
【捏一把汗】 niē yī bǎ hàn be breathless with anxiety or tension: 看着他往悬崖上爬, 大家都~。Watching him climb up the precipice, everybody was breathless with anxiety.
【捏造】 niēzào fabricate; concoct; fake; trump up: ~事实 invent a story; make up a story/ ~罪名 trump up charges/ ~数字 conjure up figures/ 纯属~。That's sheer fabrication.

niè

聂 Niè a surname

啮 niè <书> gnaw
【啮齿动物】 nièchǐ dòngwù rodent

镍 niè <化> nickel (Ni): ~币 nickel coin; nickel/ ~箔 nickel foil

蹑 niè ① lighten (one's step); walk on tiptoe: 他~着脚走出病房。He tiptoed out of the ward. ② <书> follow: ~踪 follow along behind sb.; track ③ tread; step on; walk with: ~足其间 join (a profession); follow (a trade); associate with (a certain type of people)
【蹑手蹑脚】 nièshǒu-nièjiǎo walk gingerly; walk on tiptoe

孽 niè evil; sin: 作~ do evil/ 妖~ evildoer; monster
【孽障】 nièzhàng (a term of abuse formerly used by the elders of a clan cursing their juniors) evil creature; vile spawn

nín

您* nín <敬> you

níng

宁* níng peaceful; tranquil
另见 nìng
【宁静】 níngjìng peaceful; tranquil; quiet: ~的夜晚 a tranquil night/ 心里渐渐~下来 calm down gradually

拧 níng ① twist; wring: ~麻绳 twist hemp into rope/ 把衣服~干 wring out wet clothes/ 大家~成一股劲儿 pull together; make joint efforts ② pinch; tweak: ~了他一把 give him a pinch

狞 níng ferocious; hideous
【狞笑】 níngxiào grin hideously

柠 níng
【柠檬】 níngméng lemon ◇ ~水 lemonade; lemon squash

凝 níng ① congeal; curdle; coagulate ② with fixed attention: ~思 be lost in thought
【凝固】 nínggù solidify
【凝结】 níngjié coagulate; congeal; condense: 湖面上~了一层薄冰。A thin layer of ice formed over the lake.
【凝聚】 níngjù ① (of vapour) condense: 荷叶上~着晶莹的露珠。Glistening dewdrops have formed on the lotus leaves.
【凝练】 níngliàn concise; condensed; compact
【凝神】 níngshén with fixed (或 concentrated, rapt) attention: ~谛听 listen with rapt attention; listen attentively
【凝视】 níngshì gaze fixedly; stare

nìng

宁* nìng ① rather; would rather; better ② <书> could there be: 山之险峻，~有逾此? Could there be a mountain more precipitous than this?
另见 níng

【宁可】 nìngkě would rather; better: ~站着死，绝不跪着生 would rather die on one's feet than live on one's knees/ ~小心 一点。Better safe than sorry.

【宁肯】 nìngkěn would rather

【宁缺毋滥】 nìng quē wú làn rather go without than have something shoddy — put quality before quantity

【宁死不屈】 nìng sǐ bù qū rather die than submit (或 surrender)

【宁为玉碎,不为瓦全】 nìng wéi yù suì, bù wéi wǎ quán rather be a shattered vessel of jade than an unbroken piece of pottery — better to die in glory than live in dishonour

佞 nìng given to flattery: ~人 sycophant; toady

niū

妞 niū <口> girl

niú

牛* niú ox: 母~ cow/ 公~ bull

【牛刀小试】 niúdāo xiǎo shì a master hand's first small display

【牛痘】 niúdòu ① cowpox ② smallpox pustule; vaccine pustule: 种~ give or get smallpox vaccination

【牛鬼蛇神】 niúguǐ-shéshén monsters and demons — forces of evil; class enemies of all descriptions

【牛角尖】 niújiǎojiān the tip of a horn — an insignificant or insoluble problem 参见"钻牛角尖" zuān niújiǎojiān

【牛劲】 niújìn ① great strength; tremendous effort ② stubbornness; obstinacy; tenacity: 这小伙子有股~,干一件事就非干到底不行。The lad is strong-willed; once he starts doing something, he won't leave off until he's finished it.

【牛栏】 niúlán cattle pen

【牛马】 niúmǎ oxen and horses — beasts of burden

【牛奶】 niúnǎi milk ◇~场 dairy/ ~糖 toffee

【牛腩】 niúnǎn <方> sirloin; tenderloin

【牛排】 niúpái beefsteak

【牛脾气】 niúpíqì stubbornness; obstinacy; pigheadedness

【牛肉】 niúròu beef

【牛头不对马嘴】 niútóu bù duì mǎzuǐ horses' jaws don't match cows' heads — incongruous; irrelevant

【牛仔裤】 niúzǎikù close-fitting pants; jeans

niǔ

忸 niǔ

【忸怩】 niǔní blushing; bashful: ~作态 behave coyly; be affectedly shy

扭* niǔ ① turn round: 他~过头来看了一下。He looked over his shoulder. ② twist; wrench: 把树枝子一~断 twist a twig and break it/ 用力把门~开 wrench the door open ③ sprain; wrench: ~了筋 wrench a tendon; sprain a muscle/ ~了腰 sprain one's back ④ roll; swing: 他走路一~一~的。He walks with a rolling gait. ⑤ seize; grapple with: 两人~在一起。The two were grappling with each other.

【扭打】 niǔdǎ wrestle; grapple

【扭捏】 niǔnie be affectedly bashful: 有话快说，别扭扭捏捏的。Out with it. Don't be bashful.

【扭伤】 niǔshāng sprain; wrench: ~手腕 sprain one's wrist

【扭转】 niǔzhuǎn ① turn round: 他~身子,向车间走去。He turned round and made for the workshop. ② turn back;

reverse: ~局势 turn the tide; reverse a trend/ ~乾坤 bring about a radical change in the situation; reverse the course of events / ~被动局面 put an end to a passive state of affairs; regain the initiative

纽 niǔ ① handle; knob: 秤~ the lifting cord of a steelyard/ 印~ the knob (或 handle) of a seal ② button: 衣~ button ③ bond; tie

【纽扣】 niǔkòu button

niù

拗 niù stubborn; obstinate: 这老头子脾气很~。He is a difficult old fellow.
另见 ǎo; ào

【拗不过】 niùbuguò unable to dissuade; fail to talk sb. out of doing sth.: 他这个人脾气犟,你可~他。He is very obstinate; you won't be able to make him change his mind.

nóng

农* nóng ① agriculture; farming: 务~ go in for agriculture ② peasant; farmer: 菜~ vegetable grower

【农产品】 nóngchǎnpǐn agricultural products; farm produce

【农场】 nóngchǎng farm: 国营~ state farm

【农村】 nóngcūn rural area; countryside; village

【农夫】 nóngfū farmer

【农妇】 nóngfù <旧> peasant woman

【农户】 nónghù peasant household

【农家】 nóngjiā peasant family

【农具】 nóngjù farm implements; farm tools

【农历】 nónglì the traditional Chinese calendar; the lunar calendar

【农民】 nóngmín peasant; peasantry

【农田】 nóngtián farmland; cropland; cultivated land

【农业】 nóngyè agriculture; farming

【农作物】 nóngzuòwù crops

浓 nóng ① dense; thick; concentrated: ~烟 dense smoke; thick smoke/ ~墨 thick, dark ink/ ~茶 strong tea/ ~硫酸 concentrated sulphuric acid ② (of degree or extent) great; strong: 兴趣很~ take a great interest in sth./ 玫瑰花香味很~。The rose has a heavy fragrance.

【浓度】 nóngdù consistency; concentration; density: 矿浆~ pulp density

【浓厚】 nónghòu ① dense; thick: ~的云层 thick clouds ② strong; pronounced: ~的地方色彩 pronounced (或 marked) local colour

【浓眉】 nóngméi heavy (或 bushy, thick) eyebrows: ~大眼 heavy features

【浓密】 nóngmì dense; thick: ~的枝叶 thick foliage

【浓缩】 nóngsuō <化> concentrate; enrich

【浓艳】 nóngyàn rich and gaudy: 色彩~ in gaudy colours

【浓郁】 nóngyù strong; rich: 桂花发出~的香味。Osmanthus blossoms give off (或 exhale) a rich perfume./ 这些作品具有~的农村生活气息。These works have a strong flavour of rural life.

【浓重】 nóngzhòng dense; thick; strong: 雾越发~了。The fog became thicker still./ 他画的花卉,设色十分~。His paintings of flowers are distinguished by their rich colours.

脓 nóng pus

【脓包】 nóngbāo ① <医> pustule ② worthless fellow; good-for-nothing

nòng

弄* nòng ① play with; fool with: 小孩儿爱~沙土。Children like to play with sand./ 你别~闹钟了。Stop fooling with that alarm clock. ② do; manage; handle; get sb. or sth. into a specified condition: ~饭 prepare a meal; cook/ 你来不及了，我替你~吧。You haven't got enough time; let me do it for you./ 他这一说反把我~糊涂了。His explanation only made me feel more puzzled than ever./ 他把衣服~脏了。He got his clothes dirty./ 有些问题还需要~清楚。Certain questions have yet to be clarified./ ~得不好，就会前功尽弃。If we don't do a good job now, all the work we've done will be wasted. ③ get; fetch: 去~点水来。Go and get some water. ④ play: ~手段 play tricks

【弄错】 nòngcuò make a mistake; misunderstand: 你~了。You've got it wrong.

【弄好】 nònghǎo ① do well: 把事情~ do a good job ② finish doing sth.: 计划~了没有？Is the plan ready?

【弄坏】 nònghuài ruin; put out of order; make a mess of: 把事情~ make a mess of things

【弄假成真】 nòng jiǎ chéng zhēn what was make-believe has become reality

【弄僵】 nòngjiāng bring to a deadlock; deadlock

【弄巧成拙】 nòng qiǎo chéng zhuō try to be clever only to end up with a blunder; outsmart oneself

【弄清】 nòngqīng make clear; clarify; gain a clear idea of; understand fully: ~问题所在 get to the heart of the problem; clarify the point at issue/ ~情况 gain a clear idea of the situation; find out the real situation/ ~事实 set the facts straight/ ~是非 thrash out the rights and wrongs; distinguish right from wrong

【弄权】 nòngquán manipulate power for personal ends

【弄死】 nòngsǐ put to death; kill

【弄通】 nòngtōng get a good grasp of

【弄虚作假】 nòngxū-zuòjiǎ practise fraud; employ trickery; resort to deception

【弄糟】 nòngzāo make a mess of; mess up; bungle; spoil: 他一插手，就把事情全都~了。His meddling made a mess of everything.

nú

奴* nú ① bondservant; slave ② enslave

【奴才】 núcai flunkey; lackey: 〇 ~相 servile behaviour; servility; shameless fawning

【奴隶】 núlì slave

【奴仆】 núpú servant; lackey

【奴性】 núxìng servility; slavishness

【奴颜婢膝】 núyán-bìxī subservient; servile

【奴役】 núyì enslave; keep in bondage

驽 nú 〈书〉 ① inferior horse; jade ② (of a person) dull; incompetent

【驽钝】 núdùn 〈书〉 dull; stupid

【驽马】 númǎ 〈书〉 inferior horse; jade: ~千里. 功在不含. If a jade travels a thousand li, it's only through perseverance.

nǔ

努* nǔ ① put forth (strength); exert (effort): ~劲儿 put forth all one's strength ② protrude; bulge: ~着眼睛 with bulging eyes ③ injure oneself through overexertion: 箱子太沉，你别扛，看~着。Don't carry that heavy trunk, or you'll strain yourself.

【努力】 nǔlì make great efforts; try hard; exert oneself: ~工作 work hard/ ~发展生产 actively expand production/ 为实现科学技术现代化而~奋斗 exert oneself in the struggle for the modernization of science and technology/ 尽最大~ do one's utmost; do the best one can/ 大家再努一把力。Let's make still greater efforts./ 学好一门外语要作出极大的~。It takes great effort to master a foreign language.

【努嘴】 nǔzuǐ pout one's lips as a signal: 我向他努努嘴，让他先说。I pouted my lips at him, hinting that he should speak first.

弩 nǔ crossbow

【弩弓】 nǔgōng crossbow

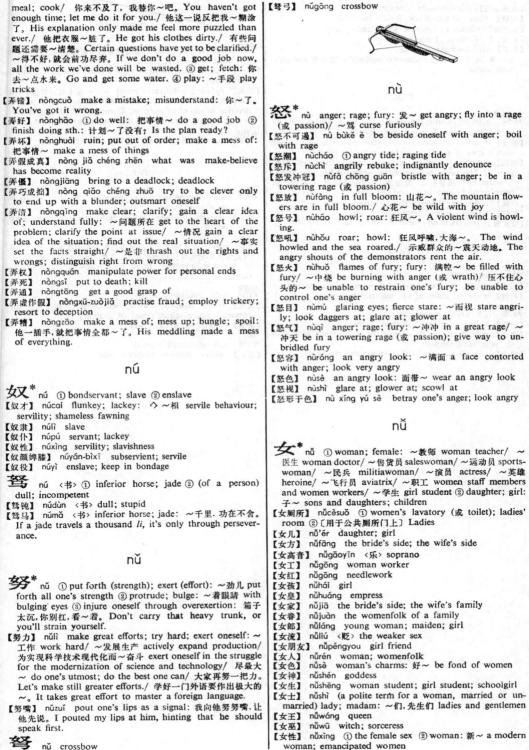

nù

怒* nù anger; rage; fury: 发~ get angry; fly into a rage (或 passion)/ ~骂 curse furiously

【怒不可遏】 nù bùkě è be beside oneself with anger; boil with rage

【怒潮】 nùcháo ① angry tide; raging tide

【怒斥】 nùchì angrily rebuke; indignantly denounce

【怒发冲冠】 nùfà chōng guān bristle with anger; be in a towering rage (或 passion)

【怒放】 nùfàng in full bloom: 山花~. The mountain flowers are in full bloom./ 心花~ be wild with joy

【怒号】 nùháo howl; roar: 狂风~. A violent wind is howling.

【怒吼】 nùhǒu roar; howl: 狂风呼啸,大海~。The wind howled and the sea roared./ 示威群众的~震天动地。The angry shouts of the demonstrators rent the air.

【怒火】 nùhuǒ flames of fury; fury: 满腔~ be filled with fury/ ~中烧 be burning with anger (或 wrath)/ 压不住心头的~ be unable to restrain one's fury; be unable to control one's anger

【怒目】 nùmù glaring eyes; fierce stare: ~而视 stare angrily; look daggers at; glare at; glower at

【怒气】 nùqì anger; rage; fury: ~冲冲 in a great rage/ ~冲天 be in a towering rage (或 passion); give way to unbridled fury

【怒容】 nùróng an angry look: ~满面 a face contorted with anger; look very angry

【怒色】 nùsè an angry look: 面带~ wear an angry look

【怒视】 nùshì glare at; glower at; scowl at

【怒形于色】 nù xíng yú sè betray one's anger; look angry

nǚ

女* nǚ ① woman; female: ~教师 woman teacher/ ~医生 woman doctor/ ~售货员 saleswoman/ ~运动员 sportswoman/ ~民兵 militiawoman/ ~演员 actress/ ~英雄 heroine/ ~飞行员 aviatrix/ ~职工 women staff members and women workers/ ~学生 girl student ② daughter; girl: 子~ sons and daughters; children

【女厕所】 nǚcèsuǒ ① women's lavatory (或 toilet); ladies' room ②〔用于公共厕所门上〕 Ladies

【女儿】 nǚ'ér daughter; girl

【女方】 nǚfāng the bride's side; the wife's side

【女高音】 nǚgāoyīn 〈乐〉 soprano

【女工】 nǚgōng woman worker

【女红】 nǚgōng needlework

【女孩】 nǚhái girl

【女皇】 nǚhuáng empress

【女家】 nǚjiā the bride's side; the wife's family

【女眷】 nǚjuàn the womenfolk of a family

【女郎】 nǚláng young woman; maiden; girl

【女流】 nǚliú 〈贬〉 the weaker sex

【女朋友】 nǚpéngyou girl friend

【女人】 nǚrén woman; womenfolk

【女色】 nǚsè woman's charms: 好~ be fond of women

【女神】 nǚshén goddess

【女生】 nǚshēng woman student; girl student; schoolgirl

【女士】 nǚshì (a polite term for a woman, married or unmarried) lady; madam: ~们,先生们 ladies and gentlemen

【女王】 nǚwáng queen

【女巫】 nǚwū witch; sorceress

【女性】 nǚxìng ① the female sex ② woman: 新~ a modern woman; emancipated women

【女修道院】 nǔxiūdàoyuàn convent
【女婿】 nǔxu ① son-in-law ② <口> husband
【女主角】 nǔzhǔjué feminine lead; leading lady
【女主人】 nǔzhǔren hostess
【女子】 nǔzǐ woman; female
◇~单(双)打 women's singles (doubles)/ ~团体赛 women's team event

nuǎn

暖* nuǎn ① warm; genial: 天~了。It's getting warm. ② warm up: ~~手 warm one's hands
【暖壶】 nuǎnhú ① thermos flask; thermos bottle ② a teapot with a cosy ③ metal or earthen hotwater bottle
【暖和】 nuǎnhuo ① warm; nice and warm: 炉子一着, 屋里就~了。The room became warm when the fire got going. ② warm up: 屋里有火, 快进来~~吧！There is a fire in here; come in and warm yourself up.
【暖瓶】 nuǎnpíng thermos flask; thermos bottle
【暖气】 nuǎnqì central heating
【暖水瓶】 nuǎnshuǐpíng thermos flask; thermos bottle

nüè

疟* nüè malaria
【疟疾】 nüèji malaria; ague: 恶性~ pernicious malaria
【疟蚊】 nüèwén malarial (或 malaria) mosquito

虐 nüè cruel; tyrannical
【虐待】 nüèdài maltreat; ill-treat; tyrannize
【虐杀】 nüèshā cause sb.'s death by maltreating him; kill sb. with maltreatment
【虐政】 nüèzhèng tyrannical government; tyranny

nuó

挪 nuó move; shift: 劳驾把桌子~到那边儿去。Move the table over there, please.
【挪借】 nuójiè borrow money for a short time; get a short-term loan
【挪用】 nuóyòng ① divert (funds): 不得~基本建设资金。The fund earmarked for capital construction is not to be diverted to any other purpose. ② misappropriate; embezzle: ~公款 misappropriation (或 embezzlement) of public funds

娜 nuó 见"婀娜" ēnuó; "袅娜" niǎonuó

nuò

诺 nuò ① promise: 许~ promise ② yes: ~~连声 keep on saying "yes"
【诺言】 nuòyán promise: 履行~ fulfil one's promise; keep one's word

喏 nuò <叹>〔表示让人注意自己所指示的事物〕: ~, 这不就是你的那把雨伞？There! Isn't that your umbrella?/ ~, 要这样挖, 才挖得快。Look, do it this way and you can dig faster.

懦 nuò cowardly; weak
【懦夫】 nuòfū coward; craven; weakling: ~懦汉思想 the coward's and sluggard's way of thinking
【懦弱】 nuòruò cowardly; weak

糯 nuò glutinous (cereal)
【糯米】 nuòmǐ polished glutinous rice

O

喔 ō 〈叹〉〔表示了解〕：～，原来是你！ Oh, so it's you!/ ～，原来你也这样想！ Oh, so you feel the same way!
另见 wō
【喔唷】 ōyō 〈叹〉〔表示惊讶、痛苦〕：～，这么大的西瓜！ Oh, what a big watermelon!/ ～，好疼！ Ouch, it hurts!

哦 ó 〈叹〉〔表示将信将疑〕：～！会有这样的事？ What! How can that be? 或 Is that really so?
另见 ò

哦 ò 〈叹〉〔表示领会、醒悟〕：～，我懂了。 Oh! I see. 或 Oh! Now I understand./ ～，我想起来了 Ah, I've got it./ ～！你是老王。 Ah, so you're Lao Wang.
另见 ó

区 Ōu a surname
另见 qū
讴 ōu ① sing ② folk songs; ballads
【讴歌】 ōugē sing the praises of; celebrate in song; eulogize
欧 Ōu short for Europe
【欧化】 ōuhuà Europeanize; westernize
殴 ōu beat up; hit: ～伤 beat and injure
【殴打】 ōudǎ beat up; hit: 互相～ come to blows; exchange blows

鸥 ōu gull: 海～ sea gull

呕* ǒu vomit; throw up
【呕吐】 ǒutù vomit; throw up; be sick: ～不止 keep vomiting
【呕心】 ǒuxīn exert one's utmost effort: ～之作 a work embodying one's utmost effort
【呕心沥血】 ǒuxīn-lìxuè shed one's heart's blood; take infinite pains; work one's heart out
【呕血】 ǒuxuè 〈医〉 haematemesis; spitting blood

偶* ǒu ① image; idol: 木～ wooden image; puppet ② even (number); in pairs: 无独有～. It is not a unique instance, but has its counterpart. ③ mate; spouse: 配～ spouse ④ by chance; by accident; once in a while; occasionally: ～遇 meet by chance
【偶尔】 ǒu'ěr once in a while; occasionally: 我们～见面。 We see each other once in a long while.
【偶犯】 ǒufàn ① casual offence ② casual offender
【偶合】 ǒuhé coincidence: 他们在这一点上见解一致完全是～. It is a mere coincidence that they see eye to eye on this point.
【偶然】 ǒurán accidental; fortuitous; chance: ～现象 accidental (或 fortuitous) phenomena/ ～遇见一个老朋友 run into an old acquaintance; meet an old friend by chance; come across an old friend
【偶数】 ǒushù 〈数〉 even number
【偶像】 ǒuxiàng image; idol ◇～崇拜 idolatry/ ～化 idolize

藕 ǒu 见"偶" ǒu③④
藕 ǒu lotus root
【藕断丝连】 ǒuduàn-sīlián the lotus root snaps but its fibres stay joined — apparently severed, actually still connected

P

pā

趴 pā ① lie on one's stomach; lie prone: ～在地上打靶 lie on the ground for target practice ② bend over; lean on: 他正～在桌子上画图。He was bending over the desk, drawing.

啪 pā 〈象〉〔形容放枪、拍掌等声音〕: ～～两声枪响。Bang, bang, went the gun.

【啪嚓】 pāchā 〈象〉〔形容东西落地、撞击或碰碎等声音〕: ～一声, 碗掉在地上碎了。The bowl dropped and broke with a crash.

葩 pā 〈书〉flower: 一朵艺术上的奇～ a wonderful work of art

pá

扒 pá ① gather up; rake up: 把枯树叶～在一起 rake together the dead leaves ② stew; braise: ～羊肉 stewed mutton／～鸡 braised chicken

【扒手】 páshǒu pickpocket

杷 pá 见"枇杷" pípá

爬 pá ① crawl; creep: 蛇正往洞里～。The snake is crawling into a hole. ② climb; clamber; scramble: ～树 (绳, 山) climb a tree (rope, mountain)／墙上～满了常春藤。The wall is covered all over with ivy.

【爬虫】 páchóng reptile

【爬行】 páxíng crawl; creep: 跟在别人后面一步一步地～ trail behind others at a snail's pace ◇～动物 reptile

【爬泳】 páyǒng 〈体〉the crawl

耙 pá ① rake: 木～ wooden rake ② make smooth with a rake; rake: 把地～平 rake the soil level

琶 pá 见"琵琶" pípá

pà

怕 pà ① fear; dread; be afraid of: 一不～苦, 二不～死 fear neither hardship nor death／不～疲劳 not be afraid of fatigue／不～任何困难 brave all difficulties ② I'm afraid; I suppose; perhaps: 事情～不这么简单。I'm afraid things are not so simple.／这个瓜～有三公斤吧。This melon weighs more than 3 kg, I should think.

【怕事】 pàshì be afraid of getting into trouble: 胆小～ timid and overcautious

【怕死】 pàsǐ fear (或 be afraid of) death

【怕羞】 pàxiū coy; shy; bashful

帕 pà handkerchief

pāi

拍 pāi ① clap, pat; beat: ～巴掌 clap one's hands／掉身上的土 pat one's clothes to get the dust off／～桌子大骂 strike the table and pour out a stream of abuse／～球 bounce a ball／～翅膀 flap wings; beat wings／惊涛～岸 mighty waves beating the shore ② bat; racket: 乒乓球～ ping-pong bat; table-tennis bat／苍蝇～儿 flyswatter 〈乐〉beat; time: 一小节四～ four beats in (或 to) a bar／

这歌是几～的↑ ——是4/4拍的。What time is the song in? — It's in four-four time. ④ take (a picture); shoot: ～照 take a picture／～电影 shoot (或 make) a film／这部小说已～成电影了。This novel has been made into a film. ⑤ send (a telegram, etc.): ～电报 send a telegram ⑥ 〈口〉flatter; fawn on: ～马 lick sb.'s boots; flatter

【拍案】 pāi'àn strike the table (in anger, surprise, admiration, etc.): ～而起 smite the table and rise to one's feet

【拍案叫绝】 pāi àn jiào jué thump the table and shout "bravo!": 精彩的表演令人～。We were overwhelmed with admiration for the superb performance.

【拍马屁】 pāi mǎpì 〈口〉lick sb.'s boots; flatter; soft-soap; fawn on

【拍卖】 pāimài ① auction ② selling off goods at reduced prices; sale

【拍摄】 pāishè take (a picture); shoot: ～一张照片 take a photo／～特写镜头 shoot a close-up／把舞剧～成电影 film a dance drama／在～外景 be on location

【拍手】 pāishǒu clap one's hands; applaud: ～叫好 clap and shout "bravo!"／～称快 clap and cheer (usu. on being avenged)

【拍照】 pāizhào take a picture; photograph

pái

排 pái ① arrange; put in order: ～座位 arrange seats／把课桌～整齐 put the desks in order／节目单已～好。The programme has been arranged. ② row; line: 前(后)～ front (back) row ③ 〈量〉〔用于成行列的东西〕row; line: 一～椅子 a row (或 line) of chairs ④ 〈军〉platoon ⑤ rehearse: ～戏 rehearse a play ⑥ raft: 竹(木)～ bamboo (timber) raft ⑦ exclude; eject; discharge: 把水～出去 drain the water away

【排场】 páichang ostentation and extravagance: 讲～ go in for ostentation and extravagance

【排斥】 páichì repel; exclude; reject: 同种电荷互相～。Two like electric charges repel one another.／～异己 exclude outsiders; discriminate against those who hold different views

【排除】 páichú get rid of; remove; eliminate: ～障碍 remove (或 get over) an obstacle／～故障 fix a breakdown／～私心杂念 get rid of all selfish ideas／不能～这种可能性 cannot rule out this possibility／下定决心, 不怕牺牲, ～万难, 去争取胜利。Be resolute, fear no sacrifice and surmount every difficulty to win victory.

【排队】 páiduì form a line; line up; queue up: ～买票 line up for tickets／～上车 queue up for a bus／～前进 march in a column

【排骨】 páigǔ spareribs: 糖醋～ spareribs in sweet-sour sauce

【排行】 páiháng seniority among brothers and sisters: 他～第三。He's the third child of the family.

【排挤】 páijǐ push aside; push out; squeeze out; elbow out: 拉拢一些人, ～一些人 draw some in, push others out／互相～ each trying to squeeze the other out

【排解】 páijiě mediate; reconcile: ～纠纷 mediate a dispute; reconcile a quarrel

【排练】 páiliàn rehearse: ～节目 have a rehearsal

【排列】 páiliè arrange; range; put in order: ～成行 arrange in a row (或 line, column)／按字母顺序～ arrange in alphabetical order

【排难解纷】 páinàn-jiěfēn mediate a dispute; pour oil on troubled waters

【排球】 páiqiú volleyball

【排山倒海】 páishān-dǎohǎi topple the mountains and overturn the seas: 以～之势 with the momentum of an avalanche; with the force of a landslide and the power of a tidal wave

【排水】 páishuǐ drain off (或 away) water ◇~工程 drainage works/ ~沟渠 escape canal/ ~管 drain pipe/ ~管道 drainage pipeline

【排水量】 páishuǐliàng ① displacement: ~两万二千吨的远洋轮船 an ocean-going liner of 22,000 tons displacement ② discharge capacity (of a spillway, etc.)

【排泄】 páixiè ① drain: ~不畅 drainage difficulty ② excrete ◇ ~器官 excretory organ/ ~物 excreta; excrement

【排演】 páiyǎn rehearse

【排印】 páiyìn typesetting and printing

【排字】 páizì composing; typesetting

徘 pái

【徘徊】 páihuái ① pace up and down ② hesitate; waver: ~歧路 hesitate at the crossroads

牌* pái ① plate; tablet: 门~儿 doorplate/ 车~儿 number plate (on a vehicle)/ (衣帽间等的)号码~ check/ 招~ shop sign; signboard/ 路~ signpost ② brand: 名~儿货 goods of a well-known brand ③ cards, dominoes, etc.: 一副扑克~ a pack of playing cards

【牌匾】 páibiǎn board (fixed to a wall or the lintel of a door)

【牌坊】 páifāng memorial archway (或 gateway)

【牌号】 páihào ① the name of a shop; shop sign ② trademark

【牌照】 páizhào license plate; license tag

【牌子】 páizi ① plate; sign: 存车~ tally (for parking a bicycle) ② brand; trademark: 老~ old brand; well-known brand

pǎi

迫 pǎi
另见 pò

【迫击炮】 pǎijīpào mortar ◇~弹 mortar projectile; mortar shell

pài

派* pài ① group; school; faction; clique: 党~ political parties and groups/ 学~ school of thought/ 左~ leftists/ 各~政治力量 the different political forces ② style; manner and air: 气~ bearing ③〈量〉④〔用于派别〕: 三~ 学者 scholars of three different schools ⑤〔用于景色、声音、语言等,前面用"一"字〕: 好一~北国风光! What magnificent northern scenery!/ 一~胡言! A pack of nonsense! ④ send; dispatch; assign; appoint: ~代表团出席大会 send a delegation to the conference/ ~他担任车间主任 appoint him head of the workshop/ ~兵 dispatch troops/ ~工作 set sb. a task/ ~勤务 assign fatigue duties

【派别】 pàibié group; school; faction: ~斗争 factional strife

【派遣】 pàiqiǎn send; dispatch: ~代表团 send a delegation/ ~驻外全权代表 dispatch a plenipotentiary (envoy) to a foreign country

【派头】 pàitóu style; manner: 他~真不小! He certainly puts on quite a show!

【派系】 pàixì factions (within a political party, etc.)

【派驻】 pàizhù 〈外〉 accredit: ~联合国的代表 a representative accredited to the United Nations

湃 pài 见"滂湃" pāngpài; "澎湃" péngpài

pān

潘 Pān a surname

攀 pān ① climb; clamber: ~着绳子往上爬 climb up a rope hand over hand ② seek connections in high places

【攀扯】 pānchě implicate (sb. in a crime)

【攀登】 pāndēng climb; clamber; scale: ~峭壁 climb up a cliff/ ~科学技术新高峰 scale new heights in science and technology

【攀龙附凤】 pānlóng-fùfèng play up to people of power and influence; put oneself under the patronage of a bigwig

【攀亲】 pānqīn ① claim kinship: ~道故 claim ties of blood or friendship ②〈方〉 arrange a match

pán

胖 pán 〈书〉 easy and comfortable: 心广体~ carefree and contented; fit and happy
另见 pàng

盘* pán ① tray; plate; dish: 茶~儿 tea tray ② sth. shaped like or used as a tray, plate, etc.: 磨~ millstone/ 棋~ chessboard ③〈旧〉 market quotation; current price ④ coil; wind; twist: 把绳子~起来 coil up the rope/ ~山小道 a winding mountain path ⑤ check; examine; interrogate: ~根究底 try to get to the heart of a matter ⑥〈体〉 game; set: 下一~棋 play a game of chess/ 以六比零胜了这一~ win the set in six straight games ⑦〈量〉: 一~香 a coil of incense/ 一~磨 a mill; a millstone/ 一~电线 a coil of wire/ 一~菜 a dish

【盘古】 Pángǔ Pan Gu, creator of the universe in Chinese mythology: 自从~开天地 since Pan Gu separated heaven and earth; since the beginning of the world

【盘桓】 pánhuán 〈书〉 stay; linger: ~终日 linger about all day long/

【盘诘】 pánjié 〈书〉 cross-examine; question

【盘踞】 pánjù illegally or forcibly occupy; be entrenched: 我军一举歼灭了~海岛的敌人。At one stroke our troops wiped out the enemy who were entrenched on the island.

【盘算】 pánsuan calculate; figure; plan: 我们~了一下,产量将增加百分之五。We figured that the output would increase by five per cent.

【盘梯】 pántī winding staircase; spiral staircase

【盘问】 pánwèn cross-examine; interrogate

【盘旋】 pánxuán ① spiral; circle; wheel: 车队沿山路~而上。The motorcade spiralled up the mountain./ 飞机~侦察。The aircraft circled for reconnaissance./ 雄鹰在空中~。Eagles were wheeling in the air./ 这件事在我脑子里~了好久。I've been turning this over in my mind for a long while. ② linger; stay: 他在暖房里~了半天才离开。He lingered in the greenhouse for some time before he left.

【盘子】 pánzi tray; plate; dish

磐 pán

【磐石】 pánshí huge rock: 坚如~ as solid as a rock/ ~般的团结 rocklike unity; monolithic unity

蹒 pán

【蹒跚】 pánshān walk haltingly; limp; hobble

蟠 pán coil; curl

【蟠桃】 pántáo ① flat peach ② peach of immortality in Chinese mythology

pàn

判* pàn ① distinguish; discriminate ② obviously (different): 前后~若两人 be quite a different person; be no longer one's old self/ 两个世界~然不同。The two worlds are markedly different. ③ judge; decide: ~案 decide a case/ ~卷子 mark examination papers ④ sentence; condemn: ~五年徒刑 be sentenced to five years' imprisonment

【判别】 pànbié differentiate; distinguish: ~真假 distinguish the true from the false

【判处】 pànchǔ sentence; condemn: ~死刑 sentence sb. to death

【判词】 pàncí 〈法〉 court verdict
【判定】 pàndìng judge; decide; determine
【判断】 pànduàn ① judge; decide; determine: ~是非 judge (或 decide) what is right and what is wrong/ ~情况 assess (或 size up) the situation/ 你~得很正确。Your judgment is sound./ 正确的~来源于周密的调查研究。Correct judgments stem from thorough investigation and study. ② 〈逻〉 judgment
【判决】 pànjué 〈法〉 court decision; judgment: ~有罪(无罪) pronounce sb. guilty (not guilty)
【判罪】 pànzuì declare guilty; convict

叛 pàn betray; rebel against: ~国 betray one's country; commit treason
【叛变】 pànbiàn betray one's country, party, etc.; turn traitor; turn renegade; defect: ~投敌 turn traitor and go over to the enemy
【叛军】 pànjūn rebel army; rebel forces; insurgent troops
【叛离】 pànlí betray; desert
【叛乱】 pànluàn armed rebellion: 煽动~ incite people to rise in rebellion
【叛逆】 pànnì ① rebel against; revolt against ② rebel: 封建礼教的~ a rebel against feudal ethics
【叛徒】 pàntú traitor; renegade; turncoat

盼* pàn ① hope for; long for; expect ② look: 左顾右~ glance right and left; look round
【盼望】 pànwàng hope for; long for; look forward to

畔 pàn ① side; bank: 河~ river bank; riverside/ 湖~ the shore of a lake ② the border of a field

pāng

乒* pāng 〈象〉[形容枪声、关门声、东西砸破声等] bang: 门~地一声关上了。The door banged shut.

滂 pāng
【滂湃】 pāngpài (of water) roaring and rushing

páng

彷 páng
【彷徨】 pánghuáng walk back and forth, not knowing which way to go; hesitate: ~歧途 hesitate at the crossroads

庞 páng ① huge ② innumerable and disordered ③ face: 面~ face
【庞大】 pángdà huge; enormous; colossal; gigantic: 机构~ an unwieldy organization/ 开支~ an enormous expenditure/ ~的正规军 a massive regular army
【庞然大物】 pángrán dàwù huge monster; colossus; giant
【庞杂】 pángzá numerous and jumbled: 议论~ numerous and jumbled views/ 机构~ cumbersome administrative structure

旁* páng ① side: 马路两~ both sides of the street/ 站在路~ stand by the roadside ② other; else: 还有~的建议吗? Any other suggestions?/ 他没说~的话。He didn't say anything else.
【旁白】 pángbái aside (in a play)
【旁边】 pángbiān side: 我坐在他~。I sat by his side./ ~有一棵树。There is a tree nearby.
【旁观】 pángguān look on; be an onlooker: 袖手~ look on with folded arms ◇~者 onlooker; bystander; spectator
【旁观者清】 pángguānzhě qīng the spectator sees most clearly; the onlooker sees the game best
【旁及】 pángjí take up (along with sth. more important): 他专攻历史, ~考古。He is an historian, but also takes an interest in archaeology.

【旁门】 pángmén side door
【旁敲侧击】 pángqiāo-cèjī attack by innuendo; make oblique references
【旁人】 pángrén other people
【旁若无人】 páng ruò wú rén act as if there was no one else present — self-assured or supercilious
【旁听】 pángtīng be a visitor at a meeting, in a school class, etc. ◇~生 auditor/ ~席 visitors' seats; public gallery
【旁征博引】 pángzhēng-bóyǐn quote copiously from many sources
【旁证】 pángzhèng circumstantial evidence; collateral evidence

膀 páng
另见 bǎng;
【膀胱】 pángguāng (urinary) bladder

磅 páng
另见 bàng
【磅礴】 pángbó ① boundless; majestic: 五岭逶迤腾细浪, 乌蒙~走泥丸。The Five Ridges wind like gentle ripples And the majestic Wumeng roll by, globules of clay. ② fill; permeate:

螃* páng
【螃蟹】 pángxiè crab

pàng

胖* pàng fat; stout; plump: 他~起来了。He's getting fat. 或 He's putting on weight.
另见 pán
【胖子】 pàngzi fat person; fatty

pāo

抛* pāo ① throw; toss; fling: ~球 throw (或 toss) a ball/ ~出一项欺骗性的提案 dish out (或 trot out) a phoney proposal ③ leave behind; cast aside: 跑到第三圈, 他已经把别人远远地~在后面了。On the third lap he left the other runners far behind.
【抛锚】 pāomáo ① drop anchor; cast anchor ② (of vehicles) break down: 汽车中途~了。The car broke down on the way.
【抛弃】 pāoqì abandon; forsake; cast aside: 被人民所~ be abandoned (或 spurned) by the people/ 我们决不会~真正的朋友。We shall never forsake (或 desert) our true friends.
【抛售】 pāoshòu sell (goods, shares, etc.) in big quantities, usu. in anticipation of or in order to bring about a fall in price
【抛头露面】 pāotóu-lùmiàn (of a woman in feudal society) show one's face in public
【抛掷】 pāozhì 〈书〉 throw; cast
【抛砖引玉】 pāozhuān-yǐnyù 〈谦〉 cast a brick to attract jade — offer a few commonplace remarks by way of introduction so that others may come up with valuable opinions

泡 pāo ① sth. puffy and soft: 豆腐~儿 beancurd puff ② spongy: 这木料发~。This wood is spongy. ③ 〈量〉[用于屎和尿]: 撒一~尿 make water; urinate; piss/ 拉一~屎 have a shit
另见 pào

páo

刨 páo ① dig; excavate: ~坑儿 dig a hole (或 pit)/ ~地 dig the ground/ ~白薯 dig (up) sweet potatoes ② 〈口〉 excluding; not counting; minus: 十五天~去五天, 只剩下十天了。Fifteen minus five — there are only ten days to go now.
另见 bào

庖 páo 〈书〉① kitchen ② cook: 名～ famous *chef*
【庖厨】 páochú 〈书〉 kitchen

咆 páo
【咆哮】 páoxiào roar; thunder: 黄河～。The Huanghe River roars on./ ～如雷 be in a thundering rage; roar with rage

炮 páo
另见 pào
【炮制】 páozhì 〈贬〉 concoct; cook up: 如法～ act after the same fashion; follow suit

袍* páo robe; gown
【袍子】 páozi robe; gown: 皮～ fur robe

pǎo

跑* pǎo ① run: 他～得很快。He can run very fast./ ～百米 run the 100-metre dash/ 火车在飞～。The train is racing along. ② run away; escape; flee: 车带～气了。Air is escaping from the tyre./ 汽油都～了。The gas has all evaporated. ③ 〈方〉 walk: 我们一了五公里路。We walked 5 km. ④ run about doing sth.; run errands: ～材料 run about collecting material or making inquiries/ ～买卖 be a commercial traveller/ 我～了好几家商店，才找到那种扳手。I had to run around to several shops to get that wrench./ 你这辆大车一天能～几个来回? How many round trips can your cart make in a day? ⑤ away; off: 吓～ frighten away/ 桌上的报纸叫风给刮～了。The newspaper blew off the table.
【跑步】 pǎobù run; march at the double: ～走!（口令）At the double, quick march! / ～前进!（口令）Double time!
【跑道】 pǎodào ① 〈航空〉 runway ② 〈体〉 track: 煤渣～ cinder track/ 塑料～ plastic track
【跑电】 pǎodiàn leakage of electricity
【跑江湖】 pǎo jiānghú wander about, making a living as an acrobat, fortuneteller, physiognomist, etc.
【跑马】 pǎomǎ ① have a ride on a horse ② horse race ◇ ～场 racecourse; the turf
【跑腿儿】 pǎotuǐr 〈口〉 run errands; do legwork: 我没干多少，就是跑跑腿儿。I didn't do much, just a bit of running around.
【跑鞋】 pǎoxié running shoes; track shoes

pào

泡 pào ① bubble: 肥皂～儿 soap bubbles/ 冒～儿 send up bubbles; rise in bubbles ② sth. shaped like a bubble: 手上起了～ get (或 raise) blisters on one's palm/ 电灯～ electric light bulb ③ steep; soak: 把种子放在温水里～一下 steep the seeds in lukewarm water/ 他是在苦水里～大的。He was brought up in bitter misery. ④ dawdle: 别瞎～了，快把工作做完! Stop dawdling and finish your work!
另见 pāo
【泡茶】 pàochá make tea
【泡饭】 pàofàn ① soak cooked rice in soup or water ② cooked rice reheated in boiling water; thick gruel (from recooked rice)
【泡沫】 pàomò foam; froth: 啤酒～ the head on a glass of beer
【泡影】 pàoyǐng visionary hope, plan, scheme, etc.; bubble: 化为～ vanish like soap bubbles; melt into thin air; go up in smoke; come to nothing

炮* pào ① big gun; cannon; artillery piece ② cannon, one of the pieces in Chinese chess
另见 páo
【炮兵】 pàobīng artillery; artillerymen ◇ ～部队 artillery (troops)
【炮弹】 pàodàn (artillery) shell
【炮轰】 pàohōng bombard; shell

【炮灰】 pàohuī cannon fodder
【炮火】 pàohuǒ artillery fire; gunfire
【炮击】 pàojī bombard; shell
【炮舰】 pàojiàn gunboat ◇ ～政策 gunboat policy/ ～外交 gunboat diplomacy
【炮声】 pàoshēng report (of a gun): ～隆隆 boom (或 roar) of guns
【炮手】 pàoshǒu gunner; artilleryman
【炮台】 pàotái fort; battery
【炮艇】 pàotǐng gunboat

pēi

呸 pēi 〈叹〉〔表示唾弃或斥责〕: pah; bah; pooh: ～! 胡说八道! Bah! That's nonsense!

胚 pēi 〈生〉 embryo
【胚胎】 pēitāi 〈生〉 embryo

péi

陪* péi accompany; keep sb. company: 我～你到农场去。I'll accompany you to the farm.
【陪伴】 péibàn accompany; keep sb. company
【陪衬】 péichèn ① serve as a contrast or foil; set off ② serve as a contrast or foil
【陪嫁】 péijià 〈方〉 dowry
【陪客】 péikè a guest invited to a dinner party to help entertain the guest of honour
【陪审】 péishěn 〈法〉 ① act (或 serve) as an assessor (in a law case) ② serve on a jury ◇ ～团 jury/ ～员 juror; juryman/ ～制 jury system
【陪送】 péisong 〈口〉 ① give a dowry to a daughter; dower ② dowry
【陪同】 péitóng accompany: ～前往参观 accompany sb. on a visit
【陪葬】 péizàng be buried with the dead

培* péi ① bank up with earth; earth up: 在玉米根上～点土 earth up the roots of maize ② cultivate; foster; train: ～干部 train cadres
【培养】 péiyǎng ① foster; train; develop: ～学生自学能力 foster the students' ability to study on their own
【培育】 péiyù cultivate; foster; breed: 小麦新品种 breed new varieties of wheat/ ～树苗 grow saplings
【培植】 péizhí cultivate; foster; train: ～中草药 cultivate medicinal herbs/ ～私人势力 build up one's personal influence

赔* péi ① compensate; pay for: 玻璃是我打碎的，由我～。I broke the glass, so I'll pay for it. ② stand a loss: ～钱 lose money in business transactions
【赔本】 péiběn sustain losses in business; run a business at a loss
【赔不是】 péi bùshi apologize
【赔偿】 péicháng compensate; pay for: ～损失 compensate (或 pay) for a loss; make good a loss/ 照价～ compensate according to the cost/ 保留要求～的权利 reserve the right to demand compensation for losses/ 战争～ war reparations ◇ ～费 damages/ ～协定 reparations agreement
【赔款】 péikuǎn ① pay an indemnity; pay reparations ② indemnity; reparations
【赔礼】 péilǐ offer (或 make) an apology; apologize
【赔笑】 péixiào smile obsequiously or apologetically
【赔罪】 péizuì apologize

裴 Péi a surname

pèi

沛 pèi copious; abundant: ～然降雨。A copious rain began to fall./ 精力充～ be full of energy

佩* pèi ① wear (at the waist, etc.): ～刀 wear a sword/ 腰～手枪 carry a pistol in one's belt ② an ornament worn as a pendant at the waist in ancient times: 玉～ jade pendant ③ admire: 他的精神十分可～。His spirit is altogether admirable.
【佩带】 pèidài wear: ～徽章 wear a badge
【佩服】 pèifu admire: 他机智勇敢,令人～。One must admire his resourcefulness and courage.

配* pèi ① join in marriage: 婚～ marry ② mate (animals): ～马 mate horses ③ compound; mix: ～颜色 mix colours (on a palette)/ ～药 make up a prescription ④ distribute according to plan; apportion: ～售 ration ⑤ find sth. to fit or replace sth. else: ～钥匙 have a key made to fit a lock/ ～零件 replace parts ⑥ match: 颜色不～。The colours don't match./ 粉红～浅蓝。Pink and light blue go well together./ 这段唱腔要用笛子来～。This passage is to be sung to the accompaniment of a bamboo flute. ⑦ deserve; be worthy of; be qualified: 她不～当一名代表。She is not qualified to be a representative.
【配备】 pèibèi ① allocate; provide; fit out: ～拖拉机 allocate tractors/ ～助手 provide assistants/ 这些舰艇～有大口径炮。These ships are fitted with large-calibre guns. ② outfit; equipment: 现代化的～ modern equipment
【配搭】 pèidā supplement; match; accompany: 这出戏,主角儿配角儿～得很整齐。Both the major and minor roles of the play are competently filled.
【配合】 pèihé coordinate; cooperate; concert: ～作战 coordination of military operations/ ～行动 take concerted action/ 起～作用 play a supporting role
【配给】 pèijǐ ration
【配件】 pèijiàn ① fittings (of a machine, etc.): 窗～ window fittings/ 管子～ pipe fittings ② a replacement
【配角】 pèijué ① appear with another leading player; costar ② supporting role; minor role
【配偶】 pèi'ǒu 〔多用于法令文件〕 spouse
【配色】 pèishǎi match colours; harmonize colours
【配药】 pèiyào make up a prescription
【配音】 pèiyīn dub (a film, etc.): 给外国电影～ dub foreign films in Chinese ◇～机 dubbing machine
【配乐】 pèiyuè dub in background music
【配制】 pèizhì compound; make up: ～药剂 compound medicines
【配种】 pèizhǒng 〈牧〉 breeding

辔 pèi bridle: 鞍～ saddle and bridle
【辔头】 pèitóu bridle

pēn

喷* pēn ① spurt; spout; gush: 喷泉向空中～水。The fountain spurted water into the air./ 石油从井口～了出来。Oil gushed from the well. ② spray; sprinkle: 给花～点水 sprinkle some water on the flowers/ 往果树上～农药 spray fruit trees with insecticide
另见 pèn
【喷饭】 pēnfàn laugh so hard as to spew one's food; split one's sides with laughter: 令人～ sidesplitting; screamingly funny
【喷漆】 pēnqī spray paint; spray lacquer ◇～枪 paint (spraying) gun
【喷气式】 pēnqìshì jet-propelled ◇～飞机 jet plane; jet aircraft; jet/ ～客机 jet airliner
【喷泉】 pēnquán fountain
【喷射】 pēnshè spray; spurt; jet: ～火焰 spurt flames
【喷水池】 pēnshuǐchí fountain
【喷嚏】 pēntì sneeze: 打～ sneeze

pén

盆* pén basin; tub; pot: 脸～ washbasin/ 澡～ bathtub/ 花～ flowerpot

【盆地】 péndì 〈地〉 basin: 柴达木～ the Qaidam Basin
【盆景】 pénjǐng 〈工美〉 potted landscape; miniature trees

pèn

喷 pèn
另见 pēn
【喷香】 pènxiāng fragrant; delicious: 饭菜～。The dishes smell delicious.

pēng

怦 pēng 〈象〉〔形容心跳〕: 他的心～～地跳。His heart thumped (或 went pit-a-pat).

抨 pēng
【抨击】 pēngjī attack (in speech or writing); assail; lash out at

砰 pēng 〈象〉〔形容撞击或重物落地的声音〕: ～的一声,门关上了。The door banged shut.

烹 pēng ① boil; cook: ～茶 brew tea; make tea ② fry quickly in hot oil and stir in sauce: ～对虾 quick-fried prawns in brown sauce
【烹饪】 pēngrèn cooking; culinary art: 擅长～ be good at cooking; be a good cook ◇～法 cookery; cuisine; recipe
【烹调】 pēngtiáo cook (dishes): 中国式～ Chinese cooking

澎 pēng splash; spatter
【澎湃】 pēngpài surge: 大海中波涛～。Waves surge in the sea.

péng

朋* péng friend: 良～ good friend/ 宾～满座。There was a houseful of guests. 或 Visitors filled all the seats.
【朋比为奸】 péngbǐ wéi jiān act in collusion with; conspire; collude; gang up
【朋党】 péngdǎng clique
【朋友】 péngyou ① friend ② boy friend or girl friend

棚* péng ① canopy or awning of reed mats, etc.: 凉～ awning ② shed; shack: 牲口～ livestock shed

彭 péng a surname

蓬 péng fluffy; dishevelled: ～着头 with dishevelled hair
【蓬勃】 péngbó vigorous; flourishing; full of vitality
【蓬松】 péngsōng fluffy; puffy: ～的头发 fluffy hair
【蓬头垢面】 péngtóu-gòumiàn with dishevelled hair and a dirty face; unkempt

鹏 péng roc
【鹏程万里】 péngchéng wànlǐ (make) a roc's flight of 10,000 li — have a bright future

篷 péng ① covering or awning on a car, boat, etc. ② sail (of a boat): 扯起～来 hoist the sails
【篷布】 péngbù tarpaulin: 用～把货物盖上 cover the goods with a tarpaulin

膨 péng
【膨大】 péngdà expand; inflate
【膨胀】 péngzhàng expand; swell; dilate; inflate: 金属受了热就会～。Metals expand when they are heated./ 通货～ inflation

pěng

捧* pěng ① hold or carry in both hands: ～着一个西瓜 hold a watermelon in both hands/ 她双手～着孩子的脸

She cupped the child's face in her hands./ 他～起水来喝了一大口。He scooped up some water with his hands and took a big mouthful. ②〈量〉〔用于能捧的东西〕：一～枣儿 a double handful of dates ③ boost; exalt; extol; flatter: 把某人～上天 praise sb. to the skies

【捧场】 pěngchǎng ① be a member of a *claque* ② boost; sing the praises of; flatter: 无原则的～ unprincipled praise

【捧腹】 pěngfù split (或 shake, burst) one's sides with laughter: 令人～ set people roaring with laughter; make one burst out laughing/ ～大笑 be convulsed with laughter

pèng

碰* pèng ① touch; bump: 这件精密仪器,你可别～。Mind you don't touch this precision instrument./ 把墨水瓶～翻了 knock the ink-bottle over/ 头～在门上 bump one's head against the door/ 在事实面前～得头破血流 butt one's head against a wall of hard facts ② meet; run into: 在街上～到一个熟人 run into an acquaintance in the street/ ～到困难 run up against difficulties/ 挖河没挖多深就～上了流沙。Before we'd got very far in digging the canal, we met with quicksand./ 我没～着他。I didn't see him. ③ take one's chance: ～～机会 take a chance

【碰壁】 pèngbì run up against a stone wall; be rebuffed: 到处～ run into snags and be foiled everywhere

【碰钉子】 pèng dīngzi meet with a rebuff: 碰了个软钉子 be tactfully rebuked; be mildly rebuffed

【碰见】 pèngjiàn meet unexpectedly; run into: 你猜我昨晚在体育馆～谁了？Who do you think I ran into at the stadium last night?

【碰巧】 pèngqiǎo by chance; by coincidence: 我～也在那儿。I happened to be there too. 或 It just so happened that I was there too.

【碰头】 pèngtóu meet and discuss; put (our, your, their) heads together: 决定下次～的时间 decide on the time of the next meeting/ 他们一～，很快就把问题解决了。They put their heads together and promptly solved the problem.

【碰一鼻子灰】 pèng yī bízi huī be snubbed; meet with a rebuff

【碰运气】 pèng yùnqì try one's luck; take a chance

【碰撞】 pèngzhuàng collide; run into: 一辆卡车从后面～了我们的汽车。A lorry ran into our car from behind.

pī

批* pī ① slap: ～烦 slap right at sb.'s face; box sb.'s ear ② criticize; refute ③ write instructions or comments on (a report from a subordinate, etc.): ～文件 write instructions on documents ④ wholesale: ～购 buy goods wholesale ⑤ 〈量〉 batch; lot; group: 新到的一～化肥 a new lot of chemical fertilizer

【批驳】 pībó ① veto an opinion or a request from a subordinate body ② refute; criticize; rebut: 逐点予以～ refute point by point

【批发】 pīfā ① wholesale ② (of an official document) be authorized for dispatch: 那份电报是由副部长～的。That telegram was authorized for dispatch by the vice-minister. ◇ ～部 wholesale department/ ～价格 wholesale price

【批改】 pīgǎi correct: ～作业 correct students' papers

【批判】 pīpàn criticize

【批评】 pīpíng ① criticize: ～缺点和错误 criticize shortcomings and mistakes ② criticism: ～与自我～ criticism and self-criticism

【批示】 pīshì written instructions or comments on a report, memorandum, etc. submitted by a subordinate

【批语】 pīyǔ ① remarks on a piece of writing ② 见"批示"

【批阅】 pīyuè read over (official papers); read and amend or comment on (writings, texts, etc.)

【批准】 pīzhǔn ratify; approve; sanction: ～条约 ratify a treaty/ 大会～了他的报告。The congress approved his report.

纰 pī (of cloth, thread, etc.) become unwoven or untwisted; be spoilt: 线～了。The thread came untwisted.

【纰漏】 pīlòu careless mistake; small accident; slip: 出了～ make a small error; make a slip

披 pī ① drape over one's shoulders; wrap around: ～着棉大衣 have a padded overcoat draped over one's shoulders/ ～上衣服 throw on some clothing/ ～上节日的盛装 be colourfully decorated for the festival/ 一只～着羊皮的狼 a wolf in sheep's clothing/ ～着合法的外衣,干着非法的勾当 carry on illegal activities under the cloak of legality ② open; unroll; spread out: ～卷 open a book

【披风】 pīfēng cloak

【披肝沥胆】 pīgān-lìdǎn ① open up one's heart; speak without reserve; be open and sincere ② be loyal and faithful

【披肩】 pījiān ① cape ② shawl

【披荆斩棘】 pījīng-zhǎnjí break through brambles and thorns — hack one's way through difficulties

【披露】 pīlù ① publish; announce: 这一消息已在报上～。The news has been published in the press. ② reveal; show; disclose: ～肝胆 open up one's heart; be openhearted

【披散】 pīsan (of hair, etc.) hang down loosely

【披沙拣金】 pī shā jiǎn jīn sort out the fine gold from the sand — get essentials from a large mass of material

【披头散发】 pītóu-sǎnfà with hair dishevelled; with hair in disarray

【披星戴月】 pīxīng-dàiyuè under the canopy of the moon and the stars — work or travel night and day

【披阅】 pīyuè open and read (a book); peruse: ～群书 peruse books of all sorts; read widely

砒 pī arsenic

【砒霜】 pīshuāng (white) arsenic

劈 pī ① split; chop; cleave: ～木柴 chop wood; split logs/ ～成两半 cleave sth. in two/ 这块木头好～。This log splits easily ② right against (one's face, etc.): 大浪把我们一面打来。Huge waves came crashing almost on top of us. ③ strike: 老树让雷～了。The old tree was struck by lightning. ④ 〈物〉 wedge
另见 pǐ

【劈里啪啦】 pīlipālā 〈象〉〔形容爆裂、拍打等的连续声音〕：鞭炮～地响。The firecrackers were crackling and spluttering./ 敌人～乱打了一阵枪,就跑了。The enemy fired off a few random shots and fled.

【劈脸】 pīliǎn right in the face: ～就是一巴掌 slap sb. on the face/ 一块石头～向他打来。A stone came hurtling towards his face.

【劈啪】 pīpā 〈象〉〔形容拍打或爆裂的声音〕：把鞭子抽得～响 crack a whip/ 孩子们劈劈啪啪地鼓起掌来。The children began to clap their hands.

噼 pī

【噼啪】 pīpā 见"劈啪"pīpā

霹 pī

【霹雷】 pīléi 〈口〉 thunderbolt; thunderclap

【霹雳】 pīlì thunderbolt; thunderclap: 晴天～ a bolt from the blue

pí

皮* pí ① skin: 猪～ pigskin/ 香蕉～ banana skin/ 树～ bark/ 土豆～ potato peel/ 西瓜～ watermelon rind/ 擦破一块～ scrape a bit of skin off ② leather; hide: ～靴 leather boots/ ～大衣 fur coat ③ cover; wrapper: 书～儿 book cover; jacket/ 饺～儿 cloth-wrapper ④ surface: 飘在水～儿上 float on the surface of the water ⑤ a broad, flat piece (of some thin material); sheet: 铁～ iron sheet/ 奶～儿 skin (on boiled milk) ⑥ become soft and soggy: 花生～了。The peanuts aren't crisp any more. ⑦ naughty: 这孩子真～! What a naughty child! ⑧ case-hardened: 他老挨

剋，都～了。He gets scolded so often that he no longer cares. ⑨ rubber: ～筋儿 rubber band; elastic band

【皮袄】 pí'ǎo fur-lined jacket

【皮包】 píbāo leather handbag; briefcase; portfolio

【皮包骨头】 pí bāo gútou skinny: 瘦得～ be only skin and bone

【皮鞭子】 píbiānzi leather-thonged whip

【皮带】 pídài ① leather belt ② ‹机› (driving) belt: 交叉～ cross belt/ 三角～ triangle belt

【皮蛋】 pídàn preserved egg

【皮肤】 pífū skin

【皮肤病】 pífūbìng skin disease

【皮革】 pígé leather; hide

【皮开肉绽】 píkāi-ròuzhàn the skin is torn and the flesh gapes open: 打得～ be bruised and lacerated (from flogging)

【皮毛】 pímáo ① fur ② smattering; superficial knowledge: 略知～ have only a superficial knowledge (of a subject)

【皮球】 píqiú rubber ball; ball

【皮箱】 píxiāng leather suitcase; leather trunk

【皮笑肉不笑】 pí xiào ròu bù xiào put on a false smile

【皮鞋】 píxié leather shoes ◇ ～油 shoe polish

【皮之不存，毛将焉附】 pí zhī bù cún, máo jiāng yān fù with the skin gone, what can the hair adhere to — a thing cannot exist without its basis

枇 pí

【枇杷】 pípa loquat

毗 pí adjoin; be adjacent to

【毗连】 pílián adjoin; border on; be adjacent to: ～地区 contiguous zone/ 又作"毗邻"

疲* pí tired; weary; exhausted: 精～力尽 completely exhausted; tired out

【疲惫】 píbèi tired out; exhausted: ～不堪 be in a state of utter exhaustion; be dog-tired

【疲乏】 pífá weary; tired: 感到～ feel weary

【疲倦】 píjuàn tired; weary

【疲劳】 píláo ① tired; fatigued; weary: 身心～ be weary in body and mind ② fatigue: 肌肉～ muscular fatigue

【疲于奔命】 píyú bēnmìng be kept constantly on the run; be tired out by too much running around; be weighed down with work: 使之～ tire sb. out by keeping him on the run

啤 pí

【啤酒】 píjiǔ beer: 生～ draught beer/ 黑～ porter; brown ale; stout ◇ ～厂 brewery

琵 pí

【琵琶】 pípa pipa, a plucked string instrument with a fretted fingerboard

脾* pí spleen

【脾气】 píqi ① temperament; disposition: ～很好 have a good temper/ 摸熟机器的～ get to know the characteristics of a machine ② bad temper: ～大 hot-tempered/ 发～ lose one's temper; flare up

【脾胃】 píwèi taste: 不合～ not suit one's taste; not be to one's liking/ 两人～相投。The two have similar likes and dislikes.

pǐ

匹* pǐ ① be equal to; be a match for: 世无其～ matchless; peerless ② ‹量› ⓐ〔用于马、骡等〕两～骡子 two mules/ 三～马 three horses ⓑ〔用于整卷的绸或布〕一～布 a bolt of cloth

【匹敌】 pǐdí be equal to; be well matched: 双方实力～。The two sides are well matched.

【匹夫】 pǐfū ① ordinary man: 国家兴亡，～有责。Every man has a share of responsibility for the fate of his country. ② an ignorant person: ～之勇 reckless courage; foolhardiness

仳 pǐ

【仳离】 pǐlí ‹书› ① (of husband and wife) be separated ② divorce one's spouse, esp. forsake one's wife

否 pǐ ① bad; wicked; evil ② censure: 臧～ pass judgment on (people)
另见 fǒu

【否极泰来】 pǐ jí tài lái out of the depth of misfortune comes bliss

痞 pǐ ① a lump in the abdomen ② ruffian; riffraff: 地～ local ruffian

劈* pǐ divide; split: 把绳子～成三股 split the rope into three strands
另见 pī

【劈柴】 pǐchai kindling; firewood

癖 pǐ addiction; weakness for: 嗜酒成～ be addicted to drinking

【癖好】 pǐhào favourite hobby; fondness for: 他有集邮的～。His favourite hobby is stamp collecting.

【癖性】 pǐxìng natural inclination; proclivity; propensity

pì

屁* pì wind (from bowels): 放～ break wind; fart

【屁股】 pìgu ① ‹口› buttocks; bottom; behind; backside: 拍拍～就走了 leave without a word of explanation; leave things in a mess ② ‹动› rump; haunch; hindquarters ③ end; butt: 香烟～ cigarette butt

【屁滚尿流】 pìgǔn-niàoliú 〔多用于〕: 吓得～ scare the shit out of sb., wet one's pants in terror; be frightened out of one's wits

【屁话】 pìhuà shit; nonsense; rubbish

辟 pì ① open up (territory, land, etc.); break (ground): 开～果园 lay out an orchard/ 另～专栏 start a new column (in a newspaper, etc.) ② penetrating; incisive: 精～ profound; incisive ③ refute; repudiate: ～谣 refute a rumour
另见 bì

【辟谣】 pìyáo refute a rumour

媲 pì

【媲美】 pìměi compare favourably with; rival

僻* pì ① out-of-the-way; secluded: ～巷 side lane/ 处一隅 live in a remote corner ② eccentric: 怪～ eccentric ③ rare: ～字 rare word

【僻静】 pìjìng secluded; lonely: ～的地方 a secluded place

【僻壤】 pìrǎng an out-of-the-way place

譬 pì example; analogy

【譬如】 pìrú for example; for instance; such as

【譬喻】 pìyù metaphor; simile; analogy; figure of speech

piān

片* piān
另见 piàn

【片子】 piānzi ① a roll of film ② film; movie ③ gramophone record; disc
另见 piànzi

扁* piān
另见 biǎn

【扁舟】 piānzhōu 〈书〉 small boat; skiff

偏* piān ① inclined to one side; slanting; leaning: 正东~北 east by north/ 中间~右 (take a position) right of centre/ 太阳~西了。The sun is to the west./ 这一枪打~了。That shot missed./ 这个指标~低。The target is on the low side. ② partial; prejudiced: ~爱 have partiality for sth.; show favouritism to sb. ③〈套〉〔表示先用或已用过茶饭等〕谢谢，我已经先~了，您请自己吃吧。Thank you, I've eaten already. You go ahead. ④〔副〕〔相当于"偏偏"〕: 他为什么~要那么做？Why must he do it that way?/ 他~不听。He simply wouldn't listen./ 不该她去，她~要去。She was not supposed to go but she insisted on going.

【偏爱】 piān'ài have partiality for sth.; show favouritism to sb.

【偏安】 piān'ān (of a feudal regime) be content to retain sovereignty over a part of the country: ~一隅 content to exercise sovereignty over a part of the country

【偏差】 piānchā deviation; error: ~减为一毫米。The deviation is reduced to one millimetre./ 纠正执行政策中的~ correct any deviations made in implementing a policy

【偏废】 piānfèi do one thing and neglect another; emphasize one thing at the expense of another: 二者不可~。Neither should be overemphasized at the expense of the other.

【偏护】 piānhù be partial to and side with: 不~任何一方 show no partiality to either side; be impartial; be unbiased

【偏激】 piānjī extreme: 意见~ hold extreme views/ 他这个人比较~。He tends to go to extremes.

【偏见】 piānjiàn prejudice; bias: 我对他没有~。I've no prejudice against him.

【偏旁】 piānpáng character components, basic structural parts of Chinese characters (as 亻 in 住，口 in 圈，匚 in 匪，令 in 领, etc.)

【偏僻】 piānpì remote; out-of-the-way: ~的山区 a remote mountainous district/ 地点~。It is an out-of-the-way place.

【偏偏】 piānpiān 〔副〕① 〔表示故意跟客观要求或客观情况相反〕: 我们劝他不要那样做，可他~不听。We tried to talk him out of it, but he just wouldn't listen. ②〔表示事实跟所希望或期待的恰恰相反〕: 他来找我，~我出差了。I happened to be away on business when he came to see me./ 事情的发展~同他的愿望相反。Things turned out just the opposite to what he wanted. ③〔表示范围，跟"单单"略同〕: 干吗~问他，Why ask him, of all people?/ 你为什么~不提这一点呢？Why did you choose to omit this point?

【偏巧】 piānqiǎo it so happened that; as luck would have it: 我们正找她，~她来了。We were looking for her when she turned up./ 我找他两次，~都不在家。I called at his house twice, but he happened to be out each time.

【偏向】 piānxiàng ① erroneous tendency; deviation: 纠正~ correct a deviation/ 反对单纯追求数量的~ oppose the tendency to concentrate on quantity alone ② be partial to

【偏心】 piānxīn partiality; bias: 她对小儿子有点儿~。She makes rather a favourite of her youngest son./ 他丝毫不~。He is free from any bias. 或 He's absolutely impartial.

【偏重】 piānzhòng lay particular stress on: 学习只~记忆而忽视理解是不行的。In studying one shouldn't stress memorization at the expense of comprehension.

翩 piān

【翩翩】 piānpiān ① lightly (dance, flutter, etc.): 蝴蝶在花丛中~飞舞。Butterflies are fluttering among the flowers. ②〈书〉 elegant: ~少年 an elegant young man

篇* piān ① a piece of writing: 不朽的诗~ an immortal poem ② sheet (of paper, etc.): 歌~儿 song sheet/ 单~油印材料 mimeographed sheets ③〈量〉〔用于纸张、书页、文章等〕: 三~儿纸 three sheets (或 pieces) of paper/ 一~文章 a piece of writing; an article/ 这本书缺了一~儿。One leaf is missing from this book.

【篇幅】 piānfu ① length (of a piece of writing): 这篇文章~不太长。This article is not very long. ② space (on a printed page): ~有限 have limited space/ 报纸用大量~报道了

这次会议的情况。The press gave the conference wide coverage.

【篇目】 piānmù table of contents; contents; list of articles

【篇章】 piānzhāng sections and chapters; writings: ~结构 structure of an article; composition

pián

便* pián
另见 biàn

【便宜】 piányi ① cheap: ~货 goods sold at bargain prices/ 价钱相当~。It's a real bargain. 或 It's quite cheap. ② small advantages; petty gains: 贪小~ out for small advantages; on the fiddle ③ let sb. off lightly: 这次~了他。This time we have let him off lightly.

骈 pián parallel; antithetical: ~句 parallel sentences

胼 pián

【胼胝】 piánzhī callosity; callus

piàn

片* piàn ① a flat, thin piece; slice; flake: 布~儿 small pieces of cloth/ 皂~ soap flakes/ 雪~ snowflakes/ 牛肉~ slices of beef/ 玻璃~儿 bits and pieces of glass/ 碎纸~儿 scraps of paper ② part of a place: 分~包干 divide up the work and assign a part to each individual or group ③ cut into slices: ~肉片儿 slice meat/ ~鱼片儿 flake a fish ④ incomplete; fragmentary; partial; brief: ~言 a few words ⑤〈量〉①〔用于成片的东西〕: 一~儿面包 a slice of bread/ 两~儿安眠药 two sleeping tablets ⑥〔用于地面和水面等〕: 一~土地 a stretch of land/ 一~草地 a tract of meadow/ 一~汪洋 a vast sheet (或 expanse) of water ⑥〔用于景色、气象、声音、心意等〕: 一~丰收景象 a vast countryside busy bringing in bumper crops/ 一~欢腾 a scene of great rejoicing/ 一~脚步声 a patter of footsteps/ 一~真心 in all sincerity
另见 piān

【片段】 piànduàn part; passage; extract; fragment: 谈话的~ parts (或 snatches) of a conversation/ 小说的一些~ certain passages of a novel/ 生活的~ an episode of sb.'s life; a slice of life/ ~的消息 bits of information/ ~的回忆 fragments of sb.'s reminiscences 又作"片断"

【片甲不存】 piàn jiǎ bù cún not a single armoured warrior remains — the army is completely wiped out: 杀得敌人~ wipe out the enemy to a man 又作"片甲不留"

【片刻】 piànkè a short while; an instant; a moment

【片面】 piànmiàn ① unilateral: ~撕毁协议 unilaterally tear up an agreement/ ~之词 an account given by one party only; one party's version of an event, etc.; one person's word against another's ② one-sided: ~观点 a lopsided (或 one-sided) view/ ~地看问题 take a one-sided approach to problems

【片瓦无存】 piàn wǎ wú cún not a single tile remains — be razed to the ground

【片言】 piànyán a few words; a phrase or two: ~可决 can be settled in a few words/ 挑出~只语 pick out a phrase or two

【片子】 piànzi ① flat, thin piece; slice; flake; scrap: 铁~ small pieces of sheetiron ② visiting card
另见 piānzi

骗* piàn ① deceive; fool; hoodwink: 受~ be taken in; be deceived/ 这种花招~不了人。Nobody will be fooled by such tricks. ② cheat; swindle: ~钱 cheat sb. out of his money

【骗局】 piànjú fraud; hoax; swindle: 政治~ a political fraud/ 事实证明，这不过是个大~。Facts show that this is nothing but a swindle.

【骗取】 piànqǔ gain sth. by cheating; cheat (或 trick, swindle) sb. out of sth.; defraud: ~财物 defraud sb. of his money and belongings/ ～信任 worm one's way into sb.'s confidence/ ～支持 fool sb. into giving his support/ ～选票 wangle votes/弄虚作假，～荣誉 seek honour through fraud and deception

【骗人】 piànrén deceive people: ～的空话 deceitful empty talk/ ～的幌子 a camouflage; a smokescreen/ ～的勾当 a fraudulent practice (或 deal)/ 他们的一切花言巧语都是～的, All their fine words are nothing but humbug.

【骗术】 piànshù deceitful trick; ruse; hoax: 施行～ perpetrate a fraud

【骗子】 piànzi swindler; impostor; cheat; trickster

piāo

剽 piāo ①rob: ～掠 plunder; loot ②nimble; swift
【剽悍】 piāohàn agile and brave; quick and fierce
【剽窃】 piāoqiè plagiarize; lift

漂* piāo float; drift: 树叶在水上～着。Leaves were floating on the water./ 小船顺流～去。The boat drifted down the stream./ ～洋过海 travel far away across the sea
另见 piǎo; piào

【漂泊】 piāobó lead a wandering life; drift: ～异乡 wander aimlessly in a strange land
【漂浮】 piāofú ①float: 湖面上～着几只小船。A few boats are floating on the lake. ②(of style of work) superficial; showy
【漂流】 piāoliú ①be driven by the current; drift about ②见"漂泊"

缥 piāo
【缥缈】 piāomiǎo dimly discernible; misty: 虚无～ visionary; illusory

飘 piāo wave to and fro; float (in the air); flutter: 旗～～。Flags are fluttering./ 稻花～香。The air was heavy with the aroma of the paddy fields./ 外面～着小雪。Outside it was snowing slightly./ 随风～来一阵阵花香。The scent of the flowers was wafted to us by the breeze.
【飘荡】 piāodàng drift; wave; flutter: 小船随波～。The boat was drifting with the tide./ 彩旗在风中～。Coloured flags were flapping in the wind.
【飘忽】 piāohū ①(of clouds) move swiftly; fleet ②mobile; uncertain: ～不定 drift from place to place
【飘零】 piāolíng ①faded and fallen ②wandering; adrift; homeless; forsaken
【飘飘然】 piāopiāorán smug; self-satisfied; complacent
【飘然】 piāorán floating in the air: 浮云～而过。Fleecy clouds floated past.
【飘洒】 piāosǎ float; drift: 天空～着雪花。Snowflakes were swirling in the air.
【飘扬】 piāoyáng wave; flutter; fly
【飘摇】 piāoyáo sway; shake; totter: 风雨～ buffeted by wind and rain; precarious; tottering
【飘逸】 piāoyì 〈书〉possessing natural grace; elegant: 神采～ have an elegant bearing

piáo

嫖 piáo visit prostitutes; go whoring

piǎo

漂* piǎo ①bleach ②rinse: 把衣服～干净 give the clothes a good rinse
另见 piāo; piào
【漂白】 piǎobái bleach: ～棉布 bleached cotton cloth ◇ ～粉 bleaching powder

瞟 piǎo look sidelong (或 askance) at; glance sideways at: ～了他一眼 cast a sidelong glance at him

piào

票* piào ①ticket: 火车～ train ticket/ 凭～入场。Admission by ticket only. ②ballot: 投～ cast a ballot; vote ③bank note; bill: 零～儿 notes of small denominations; change ④a person held for ransom by brigands; hostage: 绑～儿 kidnap (for ransom)
【票额】 piào'é the sum stated on a cheque or bill; denomination; face value
【票房】 piàofáng 〈口〉(车站等) booking office; (戏院等) box office ◇ ～价值 box-office value
【票根】 piàogēn counterfoil; stub
【票价】 piàojià the price of a ticket; admission fee; entrance fee: ～一元。Admission $1.
【票据】 piàojù ①bill; note: 应收(应付)～ bills receivable (payable)/ 即期～ a demand note/ 流通～ negotiable instruments; negotiable papers/ 到期未付～ overdue bill ②voucher; receipt
【票面】 piàomiàn face (或 par, nominal) value: 各种～的邮票 stamps of various denominations ◇ ～价值 face value; par (value)

漂* piào
另见 piāo; piǎo
【漂亮】 piàoliang ①handsome; good-looking; pretty; beautiful: ～的小伙子 a handsome young man/ ～的小姑娘 a pretty little girl/ ～的衣服 pretty dress; fine clothes/ 打扮得漂漂亮亮的 be smartly dressed/ ～的色彩 beautiful colours ②remarkable; brilliant; splendid; beautiful: 打一个～仗 fight a fine battle; win a brilliant victory/ 普通话说得很～ speak beautiful standard Chinese/ 守门员这个球救得真～。The goalie made a beautiful save. ◇ ～话 fine words; high-sounding words

骠 piào 〈书〉①(of horses) fast ②brave; valiant

piē

撇 piē cast aside; throw overboard; neglect: 不能只抓一头,把别的事都～在一旁。We should not just concentrate on one thing to the neglect of everything else.
另见 piě
【撇开】 piēkai leave aside; bypass: ～这个问题 bypass this issue/ 我们把次要问题～不谈了吧。Let's leave aside questions of minor importance.

瞥 piē shoot a glance at; dart a look at: 他刚要插嘴,妈妈～了他一眼。He was going to butt in when his mother darted a look of disapproval at him./ 《故宫一～》A Glimpse of the Imperial Palace
【瞥见】 piējiàn get a glimpse of; catch sight of: 在大街上无意中～了一位多年不见的老友。In the street I caught sight of an old friend whom I had not seen for years.

piě

撇 piě ①throw; fling; cast: ～手榴弹 throw hand grenades ②left-falling stroke (in Chinese characters) ③〈量〉: 两～浓眉,一双大眼 two bushy brows over a pair of big eyes
另见 piē
【撇嘴】 piězuǐ curl one's lip (in contempt, disbelief or disappointment); twitch one's mouth: 这女孩儿～要哭。The girl's mouth began to twitch; she was on the verge of tears.

pīn

拼* pīn ①put together; piece together: 把两块木板一起~ put two boards together side by side ②be ready to risk one's life (in fighting, work, etc.); go all out in work: ～到底 fight to the bitter end/ 不畏强手，敢打敢～ not fear a strong opponent but dare to stand up to him

【拼命】 pīnmìng ① risk one's life; defy death; go all out regardless of danger to one's life: ～精神 the death-defying spirit/ 被围困的敌人摆出一副～的架势 The encircled enemy seemed to be getting ready for a last-ditch stand. ② exerting the utmost strength; for all one is worth; with all one's might; desperately: ～奔跑 run for all one is worth/ ～工作 work with all one's might

【拼盘】 pīnpán assorted cold dishes; hors d'oeuvres

【拼死】 pīnsǐ risk one's life; defy death; fight desperately: ～挣扎 wage a desperate struggle

【拼写】 pīnxiě spell; transliterate: 照汉语拼音方案～汉字 transliterate Chinese characters into the Chinese Phonetic Alphabet

【拼音】 pīnyīn ① combine sounds into syllables ② spell; phoneticize ◇ ～文字 alphabetic (system of) writing/ ～字母 phonetic alphabet; phonetic letters

姘 pīn have illicit relations with

【姘居】 pīnjū live illicitly as husband and wife; cohabit

【姘头】 pīntou paramour

pín

贫* pín ① poor; impoverished: ～无立锥之地 utterly destitute; in extreme poverty ② inadequate; deficient: ～油国 oil-poor country ③ garrulous; loquacious: 他的嘴真～。 He is really too garrulous.

【贫病交迫】 pín-bìng jiāopò suffering from both poverty and sickness; sick as well as poor

【贫乏】 pínfá poor; short; lacking: ～煤炭资源的省份 provinces poor in coal deposits/ 经验～ lack experience/ 语言～ flat, monotonous language

【贫寒】 pínhán poor; poverty-stricken: ～人家 an impoverished family

【贫瘠】 pínjí barren; infertile; poor: ～的土壤 poor soil; impoverished soil

【贫贱】 pínjiàn poor and lowly; in straitened and humble circumstances

【贫苦】 pínkǔ poor; poverty-stricken; badly off

【贫困】 pínkùn poor; impoverished; in straitened circumstances: 生活～ live in poverty

【贫民】 pínmín poor people; pauper: 城市～ the urban poor ◇ ～窟 slum/ ～区 slum area; slum district

【贫穷】 pínqióng poor; needy; impoverished

【贫弱】 pínruò (of a country) poor and weak

频 pín frequently; repeatedly: 捷报～传。 Reports of new victories keep pouring in.

【频繁】 pínfán frequently; often: 两国人民之间交往～。 There are frequent contacts between the people of the two countries.

【频率】 pínlǜ 〈物〉 frequency: ～范围 frequency range

【频频】 pínpín again and again; repeatedly: ～举杯 propose repeated toasts/ ～招手 wave one's hand again and again

颦 pín 〈书〉 knit the brows

pǐn

品* pǐn ① article; product: 商～ commodity; merchandise/ 农产～ farm produce/ 工业～ industrial products ② grade; class; rank: 上～ highest grade; top grade ③ character; quality: 人～ moral quality; character/ ～学兼优 (of a student) of good character and scholarship ④ taste sth. with discrimination; sample; savour: ～茶 sample tea/ ～～味儿 savour the flavour

【品尝】 pǐncháng taste; sample; savour

【品德】 pǐndé moral character

【品格】 pǐngé ① one's character and morals ② quality and style (of literary or artistic works)

【品级】 pǐnjí ① official rank in feudal times ② grade (of products, commodities, etc.)

【品评】 pǐnpíng judge; comment on

【品头论足】 pǐntóu-lùnzú ① make frivolous remarks about a woman's appearance ② find fault; be overcritical

【品味】 pǐnwèi taste; savour

【品行】 pǐnxíng conduct; behaviour: ～端正 having good conduct; well-behaved/ ～不端 having bad conduct; ill-behaved

【品性】 pǐnxìng moral character

【品质】 pǐnzhì ① character; quality: 道德～ moral character ② quality (of commodities, etc.): ～优良 of the best quality

【品种】 pǐnzhǒng ① 〈生〉 breed; variety: 羊的优良～ improved breeds of sheep ② variety; assortment: 货物～齐全 have a good assortment of goods/ 增加花色～ increase the variety of colours and designs

pìn

牝 pìn female (of some birds and animals): ～马 mare/ ～牛 cow/ ～鸡 hen

聘 pìn engage: ～某人为顾问 engage sb. as a consultant/ 被～为名誉会长 be invited to be honorary chairman

【聘礼】 pìnlǐ betrothal gifts (from the bridegroom's to the bride's family); bride-price

【聘请】 pìnqǐng engage; invite: ～一位工程师担任技校兼职教师 get an engineer to act as a part-time teacher in the technical school

【聘任】 pìnrèn engage; appoint to a position

【聘书】 pìnshū letter of appointment; contract

pīng

乒* pīng ① 〈象〉: ～的一声枪响 the crack of a rifle or pistol ② table tennis; ping-pong: ～坛 table tennis circles

【乒乓】 pīngpāng ① 〈象〉: 雹子打在屋顶上～乱响。 Hailstones were rattling on the roofs. ② table tennis; ping-pong

【乒乓球】 pīngpāngqiú ① table tennis; ping-pong ② table tennis ball; ping-pong ball ◇ ～拍 table tennis bat/ ～台 table tennis table/ ～网 table tennis net

娉 pīng

【娉婷】 pīngtíng 〈书〉 (of a woman) have a graceful demeanour

píng

平* píng ① flat; level; even; smooth: 桌面不～。 The table is not level./ 把纸铺～ smooth out the paper/ 让病人躺～ help the patient to lie stretched out/ 把地～一～ level the ground ② be on the same level; be on a par; equal: 水涨得～了河岸 The water rose until it was level with the banks./ ～世界纪录 equal a world record ③ 〈体〉 make the same score; tie; draw: 双方打成十五～ The two teams tied at 15-15./ 这场足球最后踢～了。 The football game ended in a draw./ 场上比分是七～。 The score is now seven all. ④ equal; fair; impartial: ～分 divide equally/ 持～之论 a fair argument; an unbiased view ⑤ calm; peaceful; quiet: 海上风～浪静。 The sea was calm./ 经他一解释，老太太的气也就～了。 His explanation soothed the old woman's anger./ ～民愤 assuage popular indignation/ 为民～愤 redress the grievances of the people ⑥ put down; suppress: ～叛 put down a rebellion ⑦ average; common: ～日 on ordinary days ⑧ 〈语〉 见 "平声"

【平安】 píng'ān safe and sound; without mishap; well: ～到达目的地 arrive safe and sound; arrive without mishap/ ～无事。 All is well./ 全家～。 The whole family is well./ 一路～! Have a good trip! 或 Bon voyage!

【平白】 píngbái for no reason; gratuitously: ～挨一顿骂 get a scolding for no reason at all

【平辈】 píngbèi of the same generation

【平步青云】 píngbù qīngyún rapidly go up in the world; have a meteoric rise

【平常】 píngcháng ① ordinary; common: 这种现象很～. This sort of thing is quite a common occurrence. ② generally; usually; ordinarily; as a rule: ～我很少进城. I don't go to town much as a rule. / 这个词儿～很少用. This word is seldom used on ordinary occasions.

【平淡】 píngdàn flat; insipid; prosaic; pedestrian: ～无味的谈话 insipid (或 dull) conversation/ ～无奇的文章 pedestrian writing

【平等】 píngděng equality: ～待遇 equal treatment/ ～待人 treat others as equals/ 男女～ equality between the sexes/ ～互利 equality and mutual benefit/ ～协商 consultation on the basis of equality

【平地】 píngdì ① level the land (或 ground); rake the soil smooth ② level ground; flat ground

【平地风波】 píngdì fēngbō a sudden storm on a calm sea; a sudden, unexpected turn of events; unforeseen trouble

【平地一声雷】 píngdì yī shēng léi a sudden clap of thunder —— a sudden big change. e.g. a sudden rise in fame and position; an unexpected happy event

【平定】 píngdìng ① calm down: 他的情绪逐渐～下来. He gradually calmed down. ② suppress; put down: ～叛乱 put down a rebellion

【平凡】 píngfán ordinary; common: 在～的岗位上做出不～的成绩 achieve extraordinary successes at an ordinary post

【平分】 píngfēn divide equally; share and share alike; go halves; go fifty-fifty: ～土地 equal distribution of land/ 兵力 divide one's forces evenly ◇ ～线 〈数〉 bisector

【平分秋色】 píngfēn qiūsè (of two parties) have equal shares (of honour, power, glory, etc.)

【平复】 píngfù ① calm down; subside; be pacified: 风浪渐渐地～了. The storm gradually subsided./ 事态～. The situation has quietened. ② be cured; be healed: 伤口～了. The wound is healed.

【平和】 pínghé gentle; mild; moderate; placid: 性情～ be of gentle (或 mild) disposition/ ～的语气 mild (或 placid) tone/ 这种药药性～. This medicine is quite mild.

【平衡】 pínghéng balance; equilibrium: 收支～ balance between income and expenditure/ 失去～ lose one's balance; be in a state of imbalance/ 保持～ maintain one's equilibrium; keep one's balance

【平缓】 pínghuǎn ① gently: 地势～. The terrain slopes gently./ 水流～. The water flows gently. ② mild; placid; gentle: ～的语调 a mild tone

【平静】 píngjìng calm; quiet; tranquil: ～的夜晚 a quiet night/ ～的海面 a calm sea/ 他很激动,心情久久不能～. He was very excited, and it was long before he calmed down.

【平局】 píngjú draw; tie: 比赛最后打成～. The game ended in a draw./ 场上屡次出现～. The score was tied again and again./ 扳成～ equalize the score

【平均】 píngjūn ① average; mean: ～速度 average speed; mean velocity/ ～每年增长百分之五 increase by an average of 5% a year ② equally; share and share alike: ～分摊 share out equally ◇ ～利润 〈经〉 average profit/ ～寿命 average life span; life expectancy/ ～数 average; mean/ ～值 average value; mean value; mean

【平列】 píngliè place side by side; place on a par with each other

【平面】 píngmiàn 〈数〉 plane

【平面图】 píngmiàntú ① plan ② plane figure

【平民】 píngmín the common people; the populace

【平平】 píngpíng average; mediocre; indifferent: 成绩～. The results are about up to the average.

【平铺直叙】 píngpū-zhíxù ① tell in a simple, straightforward way ② speak or write in a dull, flat style

【平生】 píngshēng all one's life; one's whole life: ～的志愿 one's lifelong aspiration (或 wish)/ 艰苦朴素 live simply and work hard all one's life

【平声】 píngshēng 〈语〉 level tone, one of the four tones in classical Chinese, which has evolved into the high and level tone (阴平) and the rising tone (阳平) in modern standard pronunciation

【平时】 píngshí ① at ordinary times; in normal times: 他～住在厂里, 星期六才回家. Ordinarily he sleeps at the factory and goes home only on Saturdays. ② in peacetime

【平手】 píngshǒu draw: 两队打了个～. The two teams drew.

【平素】 píngsù usually: 他～就不爱说话. He's usually very quiet. 或 He is a man of few words.

【平坦】 píngtǎn (of land, etc.) level; even; smooth: 地势～ smooth terrain

【平稳】 píngwěn smooth and steady; smooth; stable: 我们的飞机飞得很～. We had a smooth flight./ 机器运转～. The machine runs smoothly./ 物价～. Prices are stable./ 病人的血压～. The patient's blood pressure is stable.

【平息】 píngxī ① calm down; quiet down; subside: 一场风波～了. The tumult has subsided. 或 The trouble is over./ 他的怒气～了. His anger has cooled. ② put down (a rebellion, etc.); suppress

【平心而论】 píngxīn ér lùn in all fairness; to give sb. his due: ～, 这出戏还算不错. In all fairness, it's not a bad play./ ～, 他工作还是比较认真的. To give him his due, he is quite a conscientious worker.

【平心静气】 píngxīn-jìngqì calmly; dispassionately: ～地讨论 calmly discuss

【平信】 píngxìn ① ordinary mail ② surface mail

【平行】 píngxíng ① of equal rank; on an equal footing; parallel: ～机关 units (或 organizations) of equal rank; parallel organizations ② simultaneous; parallel: ～作业 parallel operations/ 就各种问题举行～的会谈 hold simultaneous talks on different subjects ③ 〈数〉 parallel

【平易】 píngyì ① unassuming; amiable: ～近人 amiable and easy of approach ② (of a piece of writing) easy; plain

【平庸】 píngyōng mediocre; indifferent; commonplace: ～的作家 a mediocre writer/ 才能～ of limited ability

【平原】 píngyuán plain; flatlands

【平装】 píngzhuāng paperback; paper-cover; paperbound ◇ ～本 paperback (book); paperbound edition

评* píng ① comment; criticize; review: 博得好～ receive favourable comments; be well received/ 短～ brief commentary/ 书～ book review ② judge; appraise: 你来～谁说得对. Now you be the judge and say which of us is right.

【评定】 píngdìng pass judgment on; evaluate; assess: ～训练成绩 evaluate the results of training

【评断】 píngduàn judge; arbitrate: ～是非 judge between right and wrong; arbitrate a dispute

【评分】 píngfēn give a mark; mark (students' papers, etc.)

【评价】 píngjià appraise; evaluate: 高度～ set a high value on; speak highly of; highly appraise

【评奖】 píngjiǎng decide on awards through discussion

【评介】 píngjiè review (a new book, etc.): 新书～ book review

【评理】 pínglǐ ① judge between right and wrong; decide which side is right: 谁是谁非, 让大家来评个理. Let others judge who is right and who is wrong. ② reason things out; have it out: 我们得找他评评理. Let's go and have it out with him.

【评论】 pínglùn comment on; discuss; review: 小～ short comments ◇ ～家 critic; reviewer/ ～员 commentator

【评判】 píngpàn pass judgment on; judge: ～胜负 decide who is the winner; judge between contestants/ ～优劣 judge which is superior ◇ ～员 (体育, 演讲等) judge

【评语】 píngyǔ comment; remark

【评阅】 píngyuè read and appraise (sb.'s writing, etc.)

【评注】 píngzhù ① make commentary and annotation ② notes and commentary

坪 píng level ground: 草～ lawn; grassplot

苹* píng

【苹果】 píngguǒ apple
◇ ~脯 preserved apple/ ~干 dried apple slices/ ~酱 apple jam/ ~酒 cider; applejack/ ~绿 apple green/ ~园 apple orchard

凭 píng ① lean on; lean against: ~栏远眺 lean on a railing and gaze into the distance ② rely on; depend on: ~险抵抗 make use of a strategic vantage point to fight back ③ evidence; proof: 真~实据 ironclad evidence/ 口说无~。 Verbal statements are no guarantee. ④ go by; base on; take as the basis/ ~良心说 in all fairness/ ~票入场。 Admission by ticket only./ 你~什么得出这个结论? What do you base this conclusion on?

【凭单】 píngdān a certificate for drawing money, goods, etc.; voucher

【凭吊】 píngdiào visit (a historical site, etc.) and ponder on the past: ~古战场 pay a visit to an ancient battleground

【凭借】 píngjiè rely on; depend on: ~自己的力量 rely on one's own strength/ ~想象力 draw on one's imagination/ 人类的思维是~语言来进行的。 Man thinks in words.

【凭据】 píngjù evidence; proof

【凭空】 píngkōng out of the void; out of thin air; without foundation; groundless: 这完全是~捏造。 This is a sheer fabrication./ 他这种看法决不是~产生的。 His view is by no means without foundation.

【凭仗】 píngzhàng rely on; depend on: 他们~着顽强不屈的精神克服了重重困难。 They overcame all kinds of difficulties by dint of an indomitable spirit.

【凭证】 píngzhèng proof; evidence; certificate; voucher

屏 píng ① screen: 画~ painted screen ② a set of scrolls ③ shield sb. or sth.; screen
另见 bǐng

【屏风】 píngfēng screen

【屏幕】 píngmù 〈电子〉 screen: 电视~ telescreen; screen

【屏障】 píngzhàng protective screen: 燕山是北京的天然~。 The Yanshan Hills provide a natural defence for Beijing.

瓶* píng bottle; vase; jar; flask: 两~牛奶 two bottles of milk/ 热水~ thermos flask/ 花~ flower vase

【瓶装】 píngzhuāng bottled

【瓶子】 píngzi bottle

萍 píng duckweed

【萍水相逢】 píng-shuǐ xiāng féng (of strangers) meet by chance like patches of drifting duckweed

【萍踪】 píngzōng 〈书〉 tracks (或 whereabouts) of a wanderer

pō

泊* pō lake: 罗布~ Lop Nur/ 血~ pool of blood
另见 bó

坡* pō ① slope: 山~ a mountain slope; hillside/ 陡~ a steep slope/ 平~ a slight (或 gentle, gradual) slope ② sloping; slanting: 把板子~着放 put the board on a slant

【坡度】 pōdù slope; gradient: 有六十度~的一段山路 a mountain path with a slope of 60 degrees

泼* pō ① sprinkle; splash; spill: 先~点儿水再扫。 Sprinkle some water before you sweep. /互相~水 splash water on each other/ 这孩子把汤~了一地。 The boy spilt the soup on the floor./ 别把脏水~到院子里。 Don't throw the slops in the yard. ② rude and unreasonable; shrewish: 撒~ act hysterically and refuse to see reason

【泼妇】 pōfù shrew; vixen: ~骂街 like a shrew shouting abuse in the street

【泼辣】 pōla ① rude and unreasonable; shrewish ② pun-

gent; forceful: 文章写得很~。 The article is written in a pungent style.

【泼冷水】 pō lěngshuǐ pour (或 throw) cold water on; dampen the enthusiasm (或 spirits) of

颇 pō ① 〈书〉 inclined to one side; oblique: 偏~ biased; partial ② quite; rather; considerably: ~佳 quite good/ 影响~大 exert a considerable influence/ ~为费解 rather difficult to understand/ ~不以为然 highly disapprove of sth./ 他说的~有道理。 There is a lot of sense in what he says.

pó

婆* pó ① old woman ② a woman in a certain occupation: 媒~儿 woman matchmaker/ 收生~儿 midwife ③ husband's mother; mother-in-law

【婆家】 pójia husband's family

【婆婆】 pópo ① husband's mother; mother-in-law ② 〈方〉 grandmother

【婆婆妈妈】 pópomāmā ① womanishly fussy ② sentimental; mawkish; maudlin

【婆娑】 pósuō whirling; dancing: ~起舞 start dancing 杨柳~。 The willows dance in the breeze.

pǒ

叵 pǒ 〈书〉 impossible

【叵测】 pǒcè 〈贬〉 unfathomable; unpredictable: 居心~ with hidden intent/ 心怀~ harbour dark designs; nurse evil intentions

pò

迫* pò ① compel; force; press: 被~拿起武器 be compelled to take up arms/ ~敌投降 force the enemy to surrender/ ~于形势 under the stress of circumstances; under the pressure of events/ 为饥寒所~ be driven (to do sth.) by cold and hunger ② urgent; pressing: 从容不~ calm and unhurried ③ approach; go towards (或 near): ~近 get close to
另见 pǎi

【迫不得已】 pòbùdéyǐ have no alternative (but to); be forced (或 driven, compelled) to; (do sth.) against one's will

【迫不及待】 pò bùjí dài unable to hold oneself back; too impatient to wait: 他们错误估计形势, ~地跳了出来。 Miscalculating the situation, they rushed out into the open.

【迫害】 pòhài persecute: 政治~ political persecution/ 遭受~ suffer persecution; be subjected to persecution

【迫近】 pòjìn approach; get close to; draw near: ~敌人据点 close in on the enemy stronghold/ ~胜利 be nearing victory; come in sight of victory/ 行期~。 The day of departure is drawing near.

【迫切】 pòqiè urgent; pressing; imperative: ~的需要 an urgent need; a crying need/ ~的心情 eager desire; eagerness ◇ ~性 urgency

【迫使】 pòshǐ force; compel: ~敌人缴械投降 force the enemy to hand over their weapons and surrender/ ~对方处于守势 force (或 drive) one's opponent into a defensive position/ 事态的发展~他重新考虑自己的决定。 The march of events compelled him to reconsider his decision.

【迫在眉睫】 pò zài méijié ① extremely urgent ② imminent

破* pò ① broken; damaged; torn; worn-out: ~碗 a broken bowl/ ~衣服 worn-out (或 ragged, tattered) clothes/ ~房子 a dilapidated (或 tumbledown) house/ 我的手~了。 I've cut my hand. ② break; split; cleave; cut: ~成两半 break (或 split) into two/ ~浪前进 cleave (或 cut, plough) through the waves/ 把十元的票子~开 break a ten-dollar note ③ get rid of; destroy; break with: 大~天命观 eradicate the concept of the mandate of heaven/ ~旧俗, 立新风 break with outmoded customs and establish new ones/

~纪录 break a record ④ defeat; capture (a city, etc.): 大~敌军 inflict a crushing defeat on the enemy/ 城~之日 the day the city fell ⑤ expose the truth of; lay bare: 看~ see through/ 一语道~ get to the heart of the matter in a few words; puncture a fallacy with one remark ⑥ paltry; lousy: 这支~笔真气人！ This lousy pen really drives me mad!

【破案】 pò'àn solve (或 clear up) a case; crack a criminal case

【破冰船】 pòbīngchuán icebreaker: 原子~ atomic icebreaker

【破财】 pòcái suffer unexpected personal financial losses

【破产】 pòchǎn ① go bankrupt; become insolvent; become impoverished: ~地主 bankrupt landlords/ ~农民 impoverished peasants/ 银行~ bank failure ② come to naught; fall through; be bankrupt

【破除】 pòchú do away with; get rid of; eradicate; break with: ~迷信 do away with superstitions or blind faith; topple old idols/ ~情面 not spare anybody's feelings

【破费】 pòfèi 〈套〉 spend money; go to some expense: 你何必这么~呢？ Why must you go to this expense?/ 不要多~，随便吃点就行了。 Don't go to any expense. I'll enjoy whatever there is to eat.

【破釜沉舟】 pòfǔ-chénzhōu break the cauldrons and sink the boats (after crossing) — cut off all means of retreat; burn one's boats

【破坏】 pòhuài ① destroy; wreck: ~桥梁 destroy a bridge ② do great damage to: ~生产 sabotage production/ ~团结 disrupt unity; undermine unity/ ~边疆现状 disrupt the status quo along the boundary line/ ~名誉 damage sb.'s reputation/ 警惕敌人的~活动。 Guard against enemy sabotage. ③ change (a social system, custom, etc.) completely or violently; violate (an agreement, regulation, etc.); break: ~停战协定 violate an armistice agreement ⑤ decompose; destroy (the composition of a substance): 维生素 C 受热过度就会被~。 Vitamin C is destroyed when overheated. ◇ ~分子 saboteur/ ~力 destructive power/ ~性 destructiveness

【破获】 pòhuò unearth; uncover: ~一个特务组织 unearth (或 uncover) a spy ring

【破戒】 pòjiè ① break a religious precept ② break one's vow of abstinence

【破镜重圆】 pòjìng chóng yuán a broken mirror joined together — reunion of husband and wife after an enforced separation or rupture

【破旧】 pòjiù old and shabby; worn-out; dilapidated: 戴一顶~的草帽 wear a shabby straw hat/ ~的家具 old, disreputable furniture

【破旧立新】 pò jiù lì xīn destroy the old and establish the new

【破口大骂】 pòkǒu dàmà shout abuse; let loose a torrent of abuse

【破烂】 pòlàn ① tattered; ragged; worn-out: 一家~的小工厂 a small run-down factory ② 〈口〉 junk; scrap: 捡~ search a garbage heap for odds and ends ◇ ~货 worthless stuff; rubbish; trash

【破例】 pòlì break a rule; make an exception

【破裂】 pòliè .burst; split; rupture; crack: 血管~ rupture (或 breaking) of a blood vessel/ 谈判~了。 The negotiations broke down./ 他们两口子感情~了。 Their marriage has broken up.

【破落】 pòluò decline (in wealth and position); fall into reduced circumstances; be reduced to poverty: ~地主家庭 an impoverished landlord family ◇ ~户 a family which has gone down in the world

【破门】 pòmén ① burst (或 force) open the door: ~而入 force open a door ② 〈宗〉 excommunicate

【破灭】 pòmiè be shattered; fall through; evaporate: 他的幻想~了。 He was disillusioned./ 他的希望~了。 His hopes were shattered.

【破碎】 pòsuì tattered; broken: ~的玻璃 broken glass/ 这张帛画已经~了。 This painting on silk is in tatters.

【破损】 pòsǔn damaged; worn; torn: 这本书有几页已经~。 Some pages of the book are damaged.

【破题儿第一遭】 pò tír dìyī zāo the first time one ever does sth.; the first time ever: 登台演戏我还是~。 This is the first time (that) I've acted on the stage.

【破涕为笑】 pò tì wéi xiào smile through tears

【破天荒】 pòtiānhuāng occur for the first time; be unprecedented

【破土】 pòtǔ ① break ground (in starting a building project, etc.) ② start spring ploughing ③ (of a seedling) break through the soil

【破晓】 pòxiǎo dawn; daybreak: 天将~。 Day is breaking.

【破颜】 pòyán break into a smile

【破约】 pòyuē break one's promise

【破绽】 pòzhàn ① a burst seam ② flaw; weak point: 看出~ spot sb.'s weak point/ 他的论证~百出。 His argument is full of flaws.

粕 pò 〈书〉 dregs of rice

魄 pò ① soul: 魂飞~散 (be frightened) out of one's wits ② vigour; spirit: 气~ boldness of vision; spiriteness
另见 bó; tuò

【魄力】 pòlì daring and resolution; boldness: 工作有~ be bold and resolute in one's work

pōu

剖 pōu ① cut open; rip open: 把鱼肚子~开 cut open the belly of a fish ② analyse; examine; dissect: ~明事理 analyse the whys and wherefores

【剖白】 pōubái explain oneself; vindicate oneself: ~心迹 lay one's heart bare

【剖解】 pōujiě analyse; dissect: ~细密 make a minute analysis

【剖面】 pōumiàn section: 横~ cross section/ 纵~ longitudinal section/ ~图 sectional drawing; section

【剖视图】 pōushìtú cutaway view

【剖析】 pōuxī analyse; dissect: ~问题的实质 analyse the essence of the problem

pū

仆 pū fall forward; fall prostrate: 前~后继 one stepping into the breach as another falls
另见 pú

扑 pū ① throw oneself on; pounce on: 孩子一下子~到他妈的怀里去。 The child threw himself into his mother's arms./ 老虎向山羊~去。 The tiger sprang on the goat./ 一心~在集体事业上 devote oneself heart and soul to the cause of the group ② rush at; attack: 直~匪徒的巢穴 swoop down on the bandits' lair/ ~蝴蝶 catch butterflies ③ flap; flutter: 鸭子~着翅膀。 The duck flapped its wings. ④ 〈方〉 bend over: ~在桌上看地图 bend over a map on the desk

【扑鼻】 pūbí assail the nostrils: 香气~。 A sweet smell greeted us.

【扑哧】 pūchī 〈象〉〔形容笑声或水、气挤出的声音〕: ~一笑 titter; snigger/ ~一声，瓶子打开了。 The bottle opened with a fizz.

【扑打】 pūdǎ ① swat: ~蝗虫 swat locusts ② beat; pat: ~身上的尘土 dust off one's clothes

【扑粉】 pūfěn ① face powder; talcum powder ② apply powder

【扑救】 pūjiù put out a fire to save life and property

【扑克】 pūkè ① playing cards ② ~牌 poker

【扑空】 pūkōng fail to get or achieve what one wants; come away empty-handed: 昨天我去找他，又~了。 Yesterday I went to see him, but again he wasn't home.,

【扑面】 pūmiàn blow on (或 against) one's face: 春风~。 The spring wind caressed our faces.

【扑灭】 pūmiè ① stamp out; put out; extinguish: ～火灾 put out a fire ② exterminate; wipe out: ～蚊蝇 wipe out mosquitoes and flies

【扑朔迷离】 pūshuò mílí complicated and confusing

【扑通】 pūtōng ＜象＞ flop; thump; splash; pit-a-pat: ～一声,跌倒在地上 fall with a flop on the ground/ ～一声,掉进水里 fall into the water with a splash/ 她的心～～地跳。 Her heart went pit-a-pat.

铺* pū ① spread; extend; unfold: ～桌布 spread a table-cloth/ ～开。The movement is fully under way. ② pave; lay: 一条～砖的小路 a path paved with bricks/ ～铁轨 lay a railway track/ ～路面 surface a road/ ～平道路 pave the way
另见 pù

【铺陈】 pūchén narrate in detail; describe at great length; elaborate

【铺床】 pūchuáng make the bed

【铺地砖】 pūdìzhuān floor tile; paving tile

【铺砌】 pūqì ＜建＞ pave

【铺设】 pūshè lay; build: ～双轨 lay a double-track/ ～友谊之路 open up a path of friendship

【铺叙】 pūxù narrate in detail; elaborate

【铺展】 pūzhǎn spread out; sprawl

【铺张】 pūzhāng extravagant: 反对～浪费 oppose extravagance and waste

噗 pū ＜象＞ puff: ～,一口气吹灭了蜡烛 blow out a candle with one puff

【噗嗤】 pūchī 见"扑哧" pūchī

pú

仆* pú servant: 男～ manservant/ 女～ maidservant
另见 pū

【仆从】 púcóng footman; retainer; henchman ◇ ～国 vassal country

【仆仆风尘】 púpú fēngchén 见"风尘仆仆" fēngchén púpú

【仆人】 púrén (domestic) servant

匍 pú

【匍匐】 púfú ① crawl; creep: ～前进 crawl forward ② lie prostrate

菩 pú

【菩萨】 púsà ① Bodhisattva ② Buddha; Buddhist idol ③ a term applied to a kindhearted person: ～心肠 kind-hearted and merciful

脯 pú chest; breast
另见 fǔ

葡* pú

【葡萄】 pútao grape: 一串～ a bunch (或 cluster) of grapes

蒲 pú ＜植＞ cattail

璞 pú uncut jade

pǔ

朴* pǔ simple; plain

【朴实】 pǔshí ① simple; plain: ～无华 simple and un-adorned/ 文风～ simple style of writing ② sincere and honest; guileless: ～的工作作风 a down-to-earth style of work

【朴素】 pǔsù simple; plain: 衣着～ simply dressed

【朴直】 pǔzhí honest and straightforward: 文笔～ simple and straightforward writing

【朴质】 pǔzhì simple and unadorned; natural

圃 pǔ garden: 菜～ vegetable plot/ 苗～ seed plot; (seedling) nursery

普* pǔ general; universal: ～天下 all over the world; everywhere in the world

【普遍】 pǔbiàn universal; general; widespread; common: 有～意义 be of universal significance
◇ ～规律 universal law/ ～性 universality

【普及】 pǔjí ① popularize; disseminate; spread: ～与提高相结合 combine popularization with the raising of stand-ards/ ～文化科学知识 spread cultural and scientific know-ledge among the people/ ～中等教育 make secondary education universal ② universal; popular ◇ ～本 popular edition/ ～教育 universal education

【普天同庆】 pǔtiān tóng qìng the whole world or nation joins in the jubilation

【普通】 pǔtōng ordinary; common; average: ～一兵 an ordinary soldier; a soldier in the ranks; a rank-and-filer/ ～人 the average person; the man in the street/ 这是两所～的房子。 These are just two ordinary houses.
◇ ～法 common law/ ～话 putonghua; common speech (of the Chinese language): standard Chinese pro-nunciation

【普选】 pǔxuǎn general election ◇ ～权 universal suffrage

【普照】 pǔzhào illuminate all things: 阳光～大地。 The sun illuminates every corner of the land.

谱 pǔ ① table; chart; register: 家～ family tree; genealogy/ 食～ cookbook; menu ② manual; guide: 棋～ chess manual ③ music score; music: 乐～ music score; music/ 歌～ music of a song ④ set to music; compose (music）: 这首歌是谁的曲? Who is the composer of the song? ⑤ sth. to count on; a fair amount of confi-dence: 心里没个～儿 have nothing definite in mind/ 做事有～儿 do things with confidence; know what one is doing

【谱子】 pǔzi ＜口＞ music score; music

蹼 pǔ web (of the feet of ducks, frogs, etc.)

【蹼趾】 pǔzhǐ webbed toe

【蹼足】 pǔzú webfoot; palmate foot

pù

铺* pù ① shop; store ② plank bed
另见 pū

【铺面】 pùmiàn shop front

【铺位】 pùwèi bunk; berth

【铺子】 pùzi shop; store

瀑* pù waterfall

【瀑布】 pùbù waterfall; falls; cataract

曝 pù ＜书＞ expose to the sun

【曝光】 pùguāng ＜摄＞ exposure ◇ ～表 exposure meter/ ～宽容度 exposure latitude

【曝露】 pùlù ＜书＞ exposed to the open air

Q

qī

七 * qī seven

【注意】"七"字在第四声（去声）字前念第二声（阳平），如"七月"qíyuè；"七位"qíwèi。本词典为简便起见，条目中的"七"字，都注第一声（阴平）。

【七…八…】 qī…bā…〔嵌用动词或名词，表示多或多而杂乱〕：七扭八歪 crooked; uneven; disorderly; irregular/ 七折八扣 various deductions/ 七颠八倒 at sixes and sevens; all upside down; topsy-turvy/ 大家七手八脚一会儿就把院子打扫干净了。 With everybody lending a hand, the courtyard was soon swept clean.

【七零八落】 qīlíng-bāluò scattered here and there; in disorder: ～的几间草房 a few ramshackle huts scattered here and there/ 敌人被打得～，四散奔逃。 Badly battered, the enemy fled in disorder.

【七拼八凑】 qīpīn-bācòu piece together; knock together; rig up: 用碎布～做成一个枕套 make a pillowcase from odd pieces of cloth/ 我们这个小工厂是自己动手～搞起来的。 We rigged up this little factory with our own hands.

【七窍】 qīqiào the seven apertures in the human head, i.e. eyes, ears, nostrils and mouth

【七窍生烟】 qīqiào shēng yān fume with anger; foam with rage

【七情】 qīqíng the seven human emotions, namely, joy, anger, sorrow, fear, love, hate and desire

【七上八下】 qīshàng-bāxià be agitated; be perturbed: 他心里～的，不知怎么办才好。 He was so agitated that he didn't know what to do.

【七十二行】 qīshí èr háng all sorts of occupations; in every conceivable line of work

【七夕】 qīxī the seventh evening of the seventh moon (when according to legend the Cowherd 牛郎 and the Weaver Maid 织女 meet in Heaven)

【七月】 qīyuè ①July ②the seventh month of the lunar year; the seventh moon

【七嘴八舌】 qīzuǐ-bāshé lively discussion with everybody trying to get a word in; all talking at once: 方案一公布，大家就～地议论开了。 Publication of the draft plan touched off a lively discussion, with everybody eager to put in a word.

妻 * qī wife

【妻儿老小】 qī-ér lǎo-xiǎo a married man's entire family (parents, wife and children)

【妻离子散】 qīlí-zǐsàn breaking up or scattering of one's family

【妻子】 qī-zǐ wife and children

【妻子】 qīzi wife

柒 qī seven (used for the numeral 七 on cheques, etc., to avoid mistakes or alterations)

凄 qī ①chilly; cold: 风雨～～。 Cold, cold are the wind and the rain. ②bleak and desolate: ～清 lonely and sad ③sad; wretched; miserable: ～楚 miserable

【凄惨】 qīcǎn wretched; miserable; tragic

【凄风苦雨】 qīfēng-kǔyǔ wailing wind and weeping rain — wretched circumstances

【凄厉】 qīlì sad and shrill: ～的叫声 sad, shrill cries/ 风声～。 The wind was wailing.

【凄凉】 qīliáng dreary; desolate; miserable: 满目～ desolation all round/ 晚景～ lead a miserable and dreary life in old age

【凄切】 qīqiè plaintive; mournful

栖 qī ①(of birds) perch ②dwell; stay

【栖身】 qīshēn stay; sojourn: 无处～ have no place to stay

【栖息】 qīxī (of birds) perch; rest: 许多水鸟在岛上～。 A great number of water fowls dwell on the island. ◇ ～地 habitat

戚 * qī ①relative: 皇亲国～ relatives of an emperor ②sorrow; woe: 休～相关 share joys and sorrows; share weal and woe

期 * qī ①a period of time; phase; stage: 假～ vacation/ 学～ school term/ 潜伏～ incubation period/ 第一～工程 the first phase of the project ②scheduled time: 到～ fall due/ 限～ set a time limit (或 deadline) ③〈量〉用于分期的事物〕： 短训班办了三～。 The short-term training class has been run three times. ④make an appointment: 不～而遇 meet unexpectedly; meet by chance ⑤expect: ～待 expect; await

【期待】 qīdài expect; await; look forward to: 殷切地～你早日答复 eagerly await your early reply/ 我们一直～着这一天。 We've been looking forward to this day for a long time.

【期间】 qījiān time; period; course: 就在这～ during this time; in this very period/ 会议～ in the course of the conference; during the conference

【期刊】 qīkān periodical ◇ ～阅览室 periodical reading room

【期考】 qīkǎo end-of-term examination; terminal examination

【期满】 qīmǎn expire; run out; come to an end: 合同～ when the contract expires; on the expiration of the contract/ 服役～ complete one's term of (military) service

【期望】 qīwàng hope; expectation: 我们决不辜负人民的～。 We will never disappoint the people's expectations.

【期限】 qīxiàn alloted time; time limit; deadline: 规定一个～ set a deadline; fix a target date/ 延长～ extend the time limit/ 必须在规定的～内完成这项工作。 The work must be finished in the allotted time.

欺 * qī ①deceive: 自～～人 deceive oneself as well as others/ ～人之谈 deceitful words; deceptive talk ②bully; take advantage of: ～人太甚。 That's going too far./ 不要把我们的克制当作软弱可～。 Don't mistake our restraint for weakness or something you can take advantage of.

【欺负】 qīfu bully; treat sb. high-handedly: 大国不应当～小国。 Big nations should not bully small ones.

【欺凌】 qīlíng bully and humiliate: 受尽了～ be subjected to endless bullying and humiliation/ 决不任人～ never allow oneself to be trodden upon

【欺瞒】 qīmán hoodwink; dupe; pull the wool over sb.'s eyes

【欺骗】 qīpiàn deceive; cheat; dupe: ～世界舆论 befuddle world opinion/ 这只能～那些不明真相的人。 This can only deceive those who do not know the truth. 或 This can only mislead those who are not aware of the facts.

【欺软怕硬】 qīruǎn-pàyìng bully the weak and fear the strong

【欺上瞒下】 qīshàng-mánxià deceive one's superiors and delude one's subordinates

【欺世盗名】 qīshì-dàomíng gain fame by deceiving the public; angle for undeserved fame

【欺侮】 qīwǔ bully; treat sb. high-handedly

【欺压】 qīyā bully and oppress; ride roughshod over

【欺诈】 qīzhà cheat; swindle

漆 qī ①lacquer; paint: ～盘 lacquer tray ②coat with lacquer; paint: 把门～成深绿色 paint the door dark green/

把桌子再～一遍 give the table another coat of paint

【漆黑】 qīhēi pitch-dark; pitch-black

【漆黑一团】 qīhēi yī tuán ① pitch-dark: 把形势描绘成～ paint a dark picture of the situation ② be entirely ignorant of; be in the dark: 这个问题在他心中还是～。 He is still completely in the dark about the matter.

【漆器】 qīqì lacquerware; lacquerwork

嘁 qī

【嘁嘁喳喳】 qīqichāchā 〈象〉 chatter away; jabber

蹊 qī

另见 xī

【蹊跷】 qīqiāo odd; queer; fishy

qí

齐* qí ① neat; even; uniform: 整～ neat and tidy/ 把桌子摆～ arrange the tables in an orderly way/ 剪得很～ be evenly trimmed/ 长短不～ not of uniform length ② on a level with: 水涨得～了岸 The water has risen until it's on a level with the river banks./ 在～腰深的水里筑坝 stand waist-deep in water to build the dam/ 把玉米秆儿～着根儿砍断 cut the cornstalks right down to the roots ③ together; simultaneously: 男女老幼～动手。 Men and women, old and young, all pitched in./ 万炮～发。 All the batteries fired at once. ④ all ready; all present: 客人都～了。 The guests are all present./ 一切准备～了。 Everything is ready. ⑤ alike; similar: 人心～, 泰山移。 When people work with one mind, they can even remove Mount Taishan.

【齐备】 qíbèi all ready: 实验所需的东西都已～。 The things necessary for the experiment are all ready.

【齐名】 qímíng enjoy equal popularity; be equally famous

【齐全】 qíquán complete; all in readiness: 尺码～ have a complete range of sizes/ 登山队装备～。 The mountaineers are fully equipped./ 新建的工人住宅设备～。 The new workers' houses have all the necessary fittings./ 这商店虽然小, 货物却很～。 The shop, though small, has a satisfactory variety of goods.

【齐声】 qíshēng in chorus; in unison: ～回答 answer in chorus/ ～欢呼 cheer in unison

【齐心】 qíxīn be of one mind (或 heart): 群众～了, 一切事情就好办了。 When the masses are of one heart, everything becomes easy./ ～协力 work as one; make concerted efforts

祈* qí ① pray: ～年 pray for a good harvest ② entreat: 敬～指导。 We respectfully request your guidance.

【祈祷】 qídǎo pray; say one's prayers

【祈求】 qíqiú earnestly hope; pray for

【祈望】 qíwàng hope; wish

其* qí ① his (her; its; their): ～父 his father/ 各得～所。 Each is in his proper place. 或 Everyone is properly provided for. ② he (she, it, they): 不要让～自流。 Don't let things slide./ 促～早日实现 help bring it about at an early date ③ that; such: 正当～时 just at that time; at the opportune moment/ 不乏～人。 There is no lack of such people./ 如闻～声, 如见～人 (so vividly described that) you seem to see and hear the person ④〔虚指〕: 大请～客 invite many guests to dinner; entertain lavishly ⑤〔书〕〈助〉〔表示揣测、反诘或命令〕: ～奈我何? What can they do to me?/ 子～勉之! Exert yourself to the utmost!

【其次】 qícì ① next; secondly; then: 先看生产车间, ～再参观托儿所。 Let's see the workshop first and then the nursery. ② secondary: 内容是主要的, 形式还在～。 Content comes first, form second.

【其实】 qíshí 〈副〉 actually; in fact; as a matter of fact: ～情况不是那样。 Actually, that is not the case./ 这台机器看起来复杂, ～不难掌握。 This machine looks complicated, but it's really not difficult to operate.

【其他】 qítā other; else: 除了整地, ～活儿也需要人。 We need people for other jobs besides levelling the land./ 还有

什么～事情要我们做吗? Is there anything else you want us to do? 又作 "其它" (用于事物)

【其余】 qíyú the others; the rest; the remainder: ～的人马上就来。 The others will be here in a minute.

【其中】 qízhōng among (which, them, etc.); in (which, it, etc.): 乐在～ find pleasure in it/ 我们车间有五百人, ～妇女占百分之六十。 There are five hundred workers in our shop, and 60 per cent of them are women.

奇* qí ① strange; queer; rare: ～事 a strange affair; an unusual phenomenon/ ～花异木 exotic flowers and rare trees ② surprise; wonder; astonish: 这是不足为～的。 This is nothing to be surprised at.

另见 jī

【奇耻大辱】 qíchǐ-dàrǔ galling shame and humiliation; deep disgrace: 这真是～。 This is really galling and humiliating.

【奇功】 qígōng outstanding service: 屡建～ repeatedly perform outstanding service

【奇怪】 qíguài strange; surprising; odd: 陨石雨是一种自然现象, 没有什么可～的。 A meteorite shower is a natural phenomenon; there's nothing strange about it./ 真～, 他们至今还一无所知。 It's really surprising that they should still be in the dark.

【奇观】 qíguān marvellous spectacle; wonder: 自然界的～ a marvellous natural phenomenon

【奇货可居】 qíhuò kě jū hoard as a rare commodity

【奇迹】 qíjì miracle; wonder; marvel: 创造～ work wonders; accomplish wonders; perform miracles/ 医学上的～ a marvel of medical science

【奇景】 qíjǐng wonderful view; extraordinary sight: 冰峰～ a wonderful view of ice-capped peaks

【奇妙】 qímiào marvellous; wonderful; intriguing

【奇巧】 qíqiǎo (of art or handicraft) ingenious; exquisite

【奇谈】 qítán strange tale; absurd argument: 海外～ strange tales from over the seas

【奇特】 qítè peculiar; queer; singular

【奇文】 qíwén ① a remarkable piece of writing: ～共欣赏, 疑义相与析 A remarkable work should be shared and its subtleties discussed. ② queer writing

【奇闻】 qíwén sth. unheard-of; a thrilling, fantastic story: 千古～ an unheard-of fantastic story

【奇形怪状】 qíxíng-guàizhuàng grotesque or fantastic in shape or appearance: ～的钟乳石 stalactites of grotesque shapes

【奇异】 qíyì ① queer; strange; bizarre: ～的动物 rare animals ② curious: 他们都用～的眼光看着我。 They all looked at me with curious eyes.

【奇遇】 qíyù ① happy encounter; fortuitous meeting ② adventure

【奇装异服】 qízhuāng-yìfú exotic costume; bizarre dress; outlandish clothes

歧 qí ① fork; branch ② divergent; different

【歧路】 qílù branch road; forked road

【歧视】 qíshì discriminate against: 种族～ racial discrimination

【歧途】 qítú wrong road: 误入～ take the wrong road by mistake; go astray/ 被引入～ be led astray

耆 qí over sixty years of age; very old

【耆宿】 qísù venerated old people (of a community)

脐 qí ① 〈生理〉 navel; umbilicus ② the abdomen of a crab

【脐带】 qídài 〈生理〉 umbilical cord

畦 qí rectangular pieces of land in a field, separated by ridges, usu. for growing vegetables: 菜～ a vegetable bed

崎 qí

【崎岖】 qíqū rugged: ～不平 rugged and rough/ ～的山路 a rugged mountain path

骑*

qí ① ride (an animal or bicycle); sit on the back of: ～马 ride a horse; be on horseback/ ～车回家 go home by bicycle/ 善～射 excel in horsemanship and marksmanship

【骑兵】 qíbīng cavalryman; cavalry ◇ ～部队 mounted troops; cavalry unit

【骑虎难下】 qí hǔ nán xià ride a tiger and find it hard to get off — have no way to back down

【骑墙】 qíqiáng sit on the fence ◇ ～派 fence-sitter

【骑士】 qíshì knight; cavalier

【骑术】 qíshù horsemanship; equestrian skill

棋*

qí chess or any board game: 下一盘～ play a game of chess/ 象～ Chinese chess/ 国际象～ (international) chess

【棋逢对手】 qí féng duìshǒu meet one's match in a chess tournament; be well-matched in a contest 又作"棋逢敌手"

【棋迷】 qímí chess fan; chess enthusiast

【棋盘】 qípán chessboard; checkerboard

【棋谱】 qípǔ chess manual

【棋子】 qízǐ piece (in a board game); chessman

旗*

qí flag; banner; standard: 国～ national flag/ 队～ team pennant/ 锦～ brocade banner

【旗杆】 qígān flagpole; flag post

【旗鼓相当】 qí-gǔ xiāngdāng be well-matched: 这两个队～，打得十分激烈。 The two teams were well-matched, and the game was hotly contested./ ～的对手 an opponent worthy of one's steel

【旗号】 qíhào 〔多用于贬义〕 banner; flag

【旗舰】 qíjiàn flagship

【旗开得胜】 qí kāi déshèng win victory the moment one raises one's standard; win victory in the first battle; win speedy success

【旗袍】 qípáo a close-fitting woman's dress with high neck and slit skirt; cheongsam; a sheath with a slit skirt

【旗手】 qíshǒu standard-bearer

【旗帜】 qízhì ① banner; flag: 鲜红的～迎风飘扬。 Bright red banners are fluttering in the breeze. ② stand; colours: ～鲜明 have a clear-cut stand

鳍

qí <动> fin: 背～ dorsal fin/ 腹～ ventral fin; pelvic fin/ 尾～ caudal fin

麒

qí

【麒麟】 qílín kylin; (Chinese) unicorn

qǐ

乞

qǐ beg (for alms, etc.); supplicate: ～食 beg for food/ ～哀告怜 piteously beg for help

【乞丐】 qǐgài beggar

【乞怜】 qǐlián beg for pity (或 mercy): 摇尾～ be like a dog wagging its tail pitifully; abjectly beg for mercy

【乞求】 qǐqiú beg for; supplicate; implore: ～宽恕 beg for mercy (或 pardon)

【乞讨】 qǐtǎo beg; go begging: 沿街～ go begging from door to door

【乞降】 qǐxiáng beg to surrender

【乞援】 qǐyuán ask for assistance; beg for aid

岂

qǐ <书> <副> 〔表示反问〕: ～非白日做梦? Isn't that daydreaming?/ 这样做～不更实际些? Wouldn't that be more practical?

【岂但】 qǐdàn not only: ～青年人爱好运动，就连上了年纪的人也积极锻炼身体。 Not only are the young keen on sports, even elderly people are enthusiastic about physical training.

【岂敢】 qǐgǎn <套> you flatter me; I don't deserve such praise or honour

【岂能】 qǐnéng how could; how is it possible: ～不辞而别?

How could you leave without saying good-bye? 又作 "岂可"

【岂有此理】 qǐ yǒu cǐ lǐ preposterous; outrageous: 真是～! This is really outrageous!

企

qǐ ① stand on tiptoe ② anxiously expect sth.; look forward to

【企鹅】 qǐ'é penguin

【企求】 qǐqiú desire to gain; seek for; hanker after: 他一心只想把工作做好，从不～个人名利。 All he wanted was to do his job well; he never sought personal gain.

【企图】 qǐtú 〔多含贬义〕 attempt; try; seek: 敌军～突围，但未得逞。 The enemy failed in his attempt to effect a breakthrough.

【企望】 qǐwàng hope for; look forward to: 这是我们多年所～的。 This is what we have been looking forward to for years.

【企业】 qǐyè enterprise; business: 工矿～ factories, mines and other enterprises/ ～管理 business management ◇ ～家 entrepreneur; enterpriser

启*

qǐ ① open: ～门 open the door/ 幕～。 The curtain rises. ② start; initiate: ～行 start on a journey ③ enlighten; awaken: ～发 arouse; inspire; enlighten ④ <书> state; inform: 敬～者 I beg to state; I wish to inform you ⑤ <书> letter; note: 谢～ a note of thanks

【启程】 qǐchéng set out; start on a journey

【启齿】 qǐchǐ open one's mouth; start to talk about sth.: 难以～ find it difficult to bring the matter up

【启发】 qǐfā arouse; inspire; enlighten

【启航】 qǐháng set sail; weigh anchor: 这艘货轮什么时候～? When does the freighter set sail?

【启蒙】 qǐméng ① impart rudimentary knowledge to beginners; initiate: ～老师 the teacher who introduces one to a certain field of study/ ～课本 children's primer ② enlighten; free sb. from prejudice or superstition

【启示】 qǐshì enlightenment; inspiration; revelation: 从他的经验中得到很大～ gain a good deal of enlightenment from his experience; draw great inspiration from his experience

【启事】 qǐshì notice; announcement: 征稿～ a notice inviting contributions (to a magazine, newspaper, etc.)

【启用】 qǐyòng start using (an official seal, etc.)

杞

Qǐ a surname

【杞人忧天】 Qǐ rén yōu tiān like the man of Qi who was haunted by the fear that the sky might fall — entertain imaginary or groundless fears

起*

qǐ ① rise; get up; stand up: ～席 rise from the table/ 早睡早～ early to bed and early to rise ② remove; extract; pull: ～油 remove grease stains/ ～瓶塞 pull the cork from a bottle/ ～钉子 draw out a nail/ ～雷 clear mines/ 把画～下来 take down a picture ③ appear; raise: 脚上～水泡 get blisters on one's feet ④ rise; grow: ～风了。 The wind is rising./ ～疑心 become suspicious/ ～作用 take effect ⑤ draft; work out: ～稿子 work out (或 make) a draft/ ～草 draft ⑥ build; set up: ～一堵墙 build a wall/ ～伙 set up a mess ⑦ start; begin: 从今天～ starting from today

起*

qǐ ①〔用在动词后，表示动作的趋向〕: 拿～武器 take up arms/ 引～注意 draw one's attention ②〔用在动词后，常跟 "不""得"连用，表示力量够得上或够不上〕: 买不～ can't afford to buy/ 经得～时间的考验 can stand the test of time

【起笔】 qǐbǐ ① the first stroke of a Chinese character ② the start of each stroke in writing a Chinese character

【起草】 qǐcǎo draft; draw up: ～文件 draft (或 draw up) a document ◇ ～人 draftsman/ ～委员会 drafting committee

【起程】qǐchéng leave; set out; start on a journey: 日内～ leave in a day or two

【起初】qǐchū originally; at first; at the outset: 这个工厂～很小。The factory was originally very small./ 他一个字也不认识,现在已经能够写信了。At first he couldn't read and write, but now he can even carry on a correspondence.

【起床】qǐchuáng get up; get out of bed: 他们已经～了。They are already up.

【起点】qǐdiǎn starting point: 把成绩作为继续前进的新～ take achievements as starting points for further progress

【起飞】qǐfēi (of aircraft) take off

【起伏】qǐfú rise and fall; undulate: 凝望远处山峦～ gaze at the mountain ranges rising and falling in the distance/ 微风中麦浪～ a field of wheat undulating in the breeze

【起稿】qǐgǎo make a draft; draft

【起航】qǐháng set sail

【起火】qǐhuǒ ① fire breaking out ② cook meals: 在食堂吃饭比自己～方便多了。It's much more convenient to have meals in a mess hall than to do one's own cooking. ③ <方> get angry; flare up

【起家】qǐjiā build up; grow and thrive; make one's fortune, name, etc.: 白手～ build up from nothing; start from scratch

【起见】qǐjiàn 〔与"为"连用,表示目的〕for the purpose of; in order to: 为醒目～ in order to make it stand out clearly

【起劲】qǐjìn vigorously; energetically; enthusiastically: 干得很～ work very energetically

【起居】qǐjū daily life: ～有恒 lead a regular life

【起来】qǐlai ① stand up; sit up; rise to one's feet: 你～吃药吧。Sit up and take your medicine./ 有个小伙子～给老太太让了个座儿。A youngster stood up and offered his seat to the old lady. ② get up; get out of bed: 他们一～就下地了。They went to work in the fields as soon as they got up. ③ rise; arise; revolt: ～捍卫真理 come forward in defence of truth

【起来】qǐlai ①〔用在动词后,表示向上〕: 把孩子抱～ take a child up in one's arms/②〔用在动词或形容词后,表示动作或情况开始并且继续〕: 唱～ start to sing/ 他这句话使我们大笑～。This remark of his set us roaring with laughter./ 天气暖和～了。It's getting warm. ③〔用在动词后,表示动作完成或达到目的〕:合唱队组织～了。The chorus has been organized./ 想～了,这是杜甫的诗句。I've got it. It's a line from Du Fu. ④〔用在动词后,表示印象或看法〕: 看～要下雨。It looks like rain./ 听～颇有道理。It sounds quite reasonable./ 说～容易,做～难。It's easier said than done.

【起立】qǐlì stand up; rise to one's feet: ～欢迎 rise to welcome sb.

【起落】qǐluò rise and fall; up and down

【起码】qǐmǎ ① minimum; rudimentary; elementary: ～的要求 minimum requirements/ ～的知识 rudimentary knowledge; elementary knowledge/ 国际关系中最～的准则 the most rudimentary principles governing international relations/ 最～的生活必需品 the bare necessities of life ② at least: 这项工程～要到五月才能完成。This project can't be completed until May at the earliest.

【起跑】qǐpǎo <体> start of a race: 在跑道上练～ practise starts on a running track

【起色】qǐsè improvement; pickup: 她工作最近很有～。Recently there's been a great improvement in her work.

【起身】qǐshēn ① get up; get out of bed ② leave; set out; get off

【起死回生】qǐsǐ-huíshēng (of a doctor's skill) bring the dying back to life; snatch a patient from the jaws of death

【起诉】qǐsù <法> bring a suit (或 an action) against sb.; sue; prosecute ◇ ～人 suitor; prosecutor/ ～书 indictment; bill of complaint

【起头】qǐtóu ① start; originate: 这件事是谁起的头儿? Who started all this? ② at first; in the beginning: ～她答应来的,后来因为有别的事不能来了。At first she promised to come but then had another engagement and couldn't in the beginning. ③ beginning: 万事～难。Everything is hard in the beginning.

【起先】qǐxiān at first; in the beginning

【起行】qǐxíng start on a journey; set out

【起义】qǐyì uprising; insurrection; revolt: 农民～ a peasant uprising/ 敌军纷纷～投诚。Many enemy soldiers revolted and crossed over.

【起因】qǐyīn cause; origin: 调查事故的～ investigate the cause of the accident

【起用】qǐyòng reinstate (an official who has retired or been dismissed)

【起源】qǐyuán ① origin: 生命的～ the origin of life ② originate; stem from

【起运】qǐyùn start shipment: 货物业已～。The goods are on their way.

【起重机】qǐzhòngjī hoist; crane; derrick: ～的起重能力 the lifting (或 hoisting) capacity of a crane

绮 qǐ ① figured woven silk material; damask ② beautiful; gorgeous

【绮丽】qǐlì beautiful; gorgeous: 春天的西湖显得格外～。In spring the West Lake looks especially enchanting.

稽 qǐ
另见 jī

【稽首】qǐshǒu kotow; kowtow

qì

气 * qì ① gas: 沼～ marsh gas; methane/ 毒～ poisonous gas; poison gas ② air: 打开窗子透一透～ open the window to let in some fresh air ③ breath: 上～不接下～ be out of breath; gasp for breath/ 停下来歇口～ stop to catch one's breath ④ smell; odour: 香～扑鼻。A sweet smell assailed the nostrils./ 臭～ bad odour; foul smell ⑤ weather: 秋高～爽 fine autumn weather ⑥ airs; manner: 官～ bureaucratic airs/ 书生～十足 bookish in the extreme/ 表面上～壮如牛,实际上胆小如鼠 outwardly fierce as a bull, but inwardly timid as a mouse ⑦ spirit; morale: 鼓～ boost the morale; cheer on/ 朝～勃勃 vigorous; full of youthful vigour/ ～可鼓而不可泄。Morale should be boosted, not dampened. ⑧ make angry; enrage: 我故意～他一下。I was deliberately trying to annoy him. 或 I got him angry on purpose. ⑨ get angry; be enraged: ～得直哆嗦 tremble with rage/ 他说的是～话。He just said it to vent his anger. ⑩ bully; insult: 挨打受～ be bullied and beaten ⑪ <中医> vital energy; energy of life

【气昂昂】qì'áng'áng full of mettle; full of dash

【气冲冲】qìchōngchōng furious; beside oneself with rage

【气喘】qìchuǎn <医> asthma: 阵发性～ spasmodic asthma

【气度】qìdù tolerance; bearing

【气短】qìduǎn ① breathe hard; be short of breath; pant: 快爬到山顶时,大家都感到～。By the time we got near the top of the hill, we were all out of breath. ② lose heart; be discouraged: 失败并没有使他～。He was not discouraged by failure.

【气氛】qìfēn atmosphere: 会谈是在亲切友好的～中进行的。The talks were held in a cordial and friendly atmosphere./ 讨论会的～始终热烈。The atmosphere was lively throughout the discussion.

【气愤】qìfèn indignant; furious: 对于这种蛮横态度,大家无不感到～。Everybody was indignant at such an overbearing manner.

【气概】qìgài lofty quality; mettle; spirit: 英雄～ the heroic spirit

【气功】qìgōng qigong, a system of deep breathing exercises

【气管】qìguǎn windpipe; trachea

【气候】qìhòu ① climate: 大陆性～ continental climate/ 海洋性～ oceanic climate ② climate; situation: 政治～ political climate/ 成不了～ will not get anywhere

【气呼呼】qìhūhū in a huff; panting with rage

【气急败坏】qìjí bàihuài flustered and exasperated; utterly discomfited

【气节】qìjié integrity; moral courage

【气力】qìlì effort; energy; strength: 我们得费很大～去完成

这项工作。We'll have to exert great efforts to accomplish the task./ 这事需要花费～。This will take a lot of doing./ 他用出全身～向对手猛扑过去。 He pounced on the adversary with all his strength.

【气量】qìliàng tolerance: ～大 large-minded; magnanimous/ ～小 narrow-minded/ ～大的人对这点小事是不会介意的。Broad-minded people won't bother about such trifles.

【气流】qìliú ① air current; airflow; airstream ②〈语〉 breath

【气恼】qìnǎo get angry; take offence; be ruffled

【气馁】qìněi become dejected; be discouraged; lose heart: 他多次遇到挫折,但从不～。He never lost heart despite repeated setbacks.

【气派】qìpài manner; style; air: 东方～的建筑物 architecture of oriental style

【气泡】qìpào air bubble; bubble

【气魄】qìpò boldness of vision; breadth of spirit; daring:

【气枪】qìqiāng air gun; pneumatic gun: 玩具～ popgun

【气球】qìqiú balloon: 测风～ pilot balloon/ 定高～ constant-level balloon/ 彩色～ coloured balloon

【气色】qìsè complexion; colour: ～很好 have a rosy complexion; have a good colour/ ～不好 look pale; be off colour

【气势】qìshì momentum; imposing manner: ～雄伟的长城 the imposing Great Wall

【气势磅礴】qìshì pángbó of great momentum; powerful

【气势汹汹】qìshì xiōngxiōng fierce; truculent; overbearing: 看起来～,实际上十分虚弱 fierce in appearance but feeble in reality

【气态】qìtài〈物〉gaseous state

【气体】qìtǐ gas

【气味】qìwèi ① smell; odour; flavour: ～难闻。The smell is awful. ②〔多含贬义〕smack; taste: 有沙文主义～ smack of chauvinism

【气味相投】qìwèi xiāng tóu be birds of a feather; be two of a kind: 他们俩～。Both have lousy taste.

【气温】qìwēn〈气〉air temperature; atmospheric temperature

【气息】qìxī ① breath ② flavour; smell: 具有强烈的生活～ have the rich flavour of life

【气象】qìxiàng ①〈气〉meteorological phenomena ②〈气〉 meteorology ③ atmosphere; scene: 生气勃勃的新～ a new and dynamic atmosphere

【气象万千】qìxiàng wànqiān spectacular; majestic: 天都峰上看群山,～。From the top of Tiandu, one can see range after range of mountains unfolding in all their majesty.

【气吁吁】qìxūxū panting; gasping for breath

【气压】qìyā〈气〉atmospheric pressure; barometric pressure: 高～ high pressure ◇ ～表 barometer

【气质】qìzhì ① temperament; disposition ② qualities; makings

【气壮山河】qì zhuàng shānhé full of power and grandeur; magnificent: 一篇～的宣言 a magnificent manifesto

讫 qì ① settled; completed: 付～ paid/ 收～ received in full/ 验～ checked; examined ② end: 起～ the beginning and the end

迄 qì ① up to; till: ～今 up to now; to this day; so far ②〔用于"未"或"无"前〕so far; all along: ～无音信。We have received no information so far.

【迄今】qìjīn up to now; to this day; to date; so far: 他的态度～并无明显的转变。There has been no visible change in his attitude so far.

汽* qì vapour; steam

【汽车】qìchē automobile; motor vehicle; car ◇ ～吊 truck crane/ ～队 motor transport corps; fleet of cars (或 trucks)/ ～工业 auto industry/ ～库 garage/ ～修配厂 motor repair shop/ ～制造厂 automobile factory; motor works

【汽船】qìchuán steamship; steamer

【汽水】qìshuǐ aerated water; soft drink ; soda water

【汽艇】qìtǐng motorboat

【汽油】qìyóu petrol; gasoline; gas

弃* qì throw away; discard; abandon: ～之可惜 hesitate to discard sth.; be unwilling to throw away/ 敌军～城而逃。The enemy abandoned the city and fled.

【弃甲曳兵】qìjiǎ-yèbīng (of troops) throw away their armour and trail their weapons behind them; be routed; flee pell-mell

【弃旧图新】qì jiù tú xīn turn over a new leaf

【弃权】qìquán ① abstain from voting: 两票～ two abstentions ②〈体〉waive the right (to play); forfeit

【弃世】qìshì pass away; die

【弃婴】qìyīng ① abandon a baby ② foundling

【弃置】qìzhì discard; throw aside: ～不用 be discarded; lie idle

泣 qì ① weep; sob: ～诉 accuse while weeping; accuse amid tears/ ～不成声 choke with sobs ② tears: ～下如雨 shed tears like rain; weep copious tears

契 qì ①〈书〉engrave; carve ② contract; deed: 地～ title deed for land; land deed ③ agree; get along well: 默～ tacit agreement (或 understanding)

【契合】qìhé agree with; tally with; correspond to: 与进化论相～ agree with the theory of evolution

【契据】qìjù deed; contract; receipt

【契友】qìyǒu close friend; bosom friend

【契约】qìyuē contract; deed; charter: 租船～ contract of affreightment; charter party

砌 qì build by laying bricks or stones: ～砖 lay bricks/ ～墙 build a wall (with bricks, stones, etc.) ② step: 雕栏玉～ carved balustrades and marble steps

器* qì ① implement; utensil; ware: 漆～ lacquerware/ 瓷～ chinaware; china; porcelain/ 玉～ jade article/ 乐～ musical instrument/ 拾音～ pickup; adapter ② organ: 生殖～ reproductive organs; generative organs; genitals ③ capacity; talent: ～识 capability and judgment/ ～使 give sb. employment according to his ability

【器材】qìcái equipment; material: 照相～ photographic equipment/ 线路～ line materials

【器官】qìguān organ; apparatus: 发音～ organs of speech/ 消化～ digestive organs/ 呼吸～ respiratory apparatus

【器件】qìjiàn parts of an apparatus or appliance: 电子～ electronic device

【器具】qìjù utensil; implement; appliance: 日用～ household utensils; articles of daily use

【器量】qìliàng tolerance: ～小 narrow-minded; petty

【器皿】qìmǐn household utensils; containers esp. for use in the house

【器物】qìwù implements; utensils

【器械】qìxiè ① apparatus; appliance; instrument: 医疗～ medical appliances/ 体育～ sports apparatus/ 光学～ optical instrument ② weapon

【器重】qìzhòng〔上级对下级,长辈对晚辈〕think highly of; regard highly

憩 qì〈书〉rest

【憩息】qìxī〈书〉rest; have a rest

qiā

掐 qiā pinch; nip: 把杈子～掉 pinch off the side shoots/ 不要～花。Don't nip off the flowers.

qià

洽 qià ① be in harmony; agree: 融～ be in harmony/

意见不~ have different opinions; not see eye to eye ② consult; arrange with: ~商 make arrangements with; talk over with/ ~谈贸易事宜 hold trade talks

恰 * qià ① appropriate; proper ② just; exactly: ~到好处 just right/ ~似 exactly like

【恰当】 qiàdàng proper; suitable; fitting; appropriate: 用词~ use proper words/ 提出~的口号 propose a suitable slogan/ 采取~的措施 adopt appropriate measures

【恰好】 qiàhǎo just right; as luck would have it: 这块布~够做一件衬衣 This piece of cloth is just the right length for a shirt.

【恰恰】 qiàqià just; exactly; precisely: 这~是我想说的话。That's exactly what I wanted to say./ ~相反 just the opposite; exactly the reverse

【恰巧】 qiàqiǎo by chance; fortunately; as chance would have it: 那天~我也在那里。I happened to be there that day, too.

qiān

千 * qiān ① thousand: 成~上万 by the thousands and tens of thousands/ ~~万万 thousands upon thousands ② a great amount of; a great number of: 一条条建议 lots and lots of suggestions/ 一百年来的梦想 an age-old dream

【千变万化】 qiānbiàn-wànhuà ever changing

【千差万别】 qiānchā-wànbié differ in thousands of ways: 各地气候~。Climate varies from place to place./ 事物的~ the immense variety of things

【千锤百炼】 qiānchuí-bǎiliàn ① thoroughly tempered (或 steeled) ② (of literary works) be polished again and again; be revised and re-written many times; be highly finished

【千方百计】 qiānfāng-bǎijì in a thousand and one ways; by every possible means; by hook or by crook: ~挖掘潜力 try in every possible way to tap the potential/ ~掩盖错误 use all one's ingenuity to cover up one's mistakes

【千古】 qiāngǔ ① through the ages; eternal; for all time: 成为~罪人 stand condemned through the ages/ ~奇闻 a fantastic story; a forever strange tale/ ~遗恨 eternal regret ②〔用于挽联,花圈的上款〕: 某某先生~! Eternal repose to Mr. So-and-so!

【千金】 qiānjīn ① a thousand pieces of gold; a lot of money: ~难买 not to be had even for 1,000 pieces of gold; not to be bought with money/ 一掷~ spend money extravagantly; spend lavishly ②〈敬〉daughter (other than one's own)

【千钧一发】 qiān jūn yī fà 见"一发千钧" yī fà qiān jūn

【千里马】 qiānlǐmǎ a horse that covers a thousand li a day; a winged steed

【千里送鹅毛】 qiānlǐ sòng émáo a goose feather sent from a thousand li away: ~,礼轻情意重。The gift itself may be light as a goose feather; but sent from afar, it conveys deep feeling.

【千里迢迢】 qiānlǐ tiáotiáo thousands of li away; from afar; over a great distance

【千里眼】 qiānlǐyǎn ① farsighted person ②〈旧〉telescope; field glasses

【千里之行,始于足下】 qiānlǐ zhī xíng, shǐ yú zú xià a thousand-li journey is started by taking the first step

【千篇一律】 qiān piān yī lù stereotyped; following the same pattern: ~的论调 stereotyped views/ 那些文章~,没有什么新东西。Those articles repeat each other and contain nothing new.

【千奇百怪】 qiānqí-bǎiguài all kinds of strange things; an infinite variety of fantastic phenomena

【千秋】 qiānqiū ① a thousand years; centuries: ~万代 throughout the ages ②〈敬〉birthday (other than one's own)

【千丝万缕】 qiānsī-wànlǚ countless ties; a thousand and one links: 有着~的联系 have a thousand and one links; be tied in a hundred and one ways

【千头万绪】 qiāntóu-wànxù thousands of strands and loose ends; a multitude of things: 心里~,不知从何说起。There are so many thoughts welling up in my mind that I really don't know where to start.

【千万】 qiānwàn ① ten million; millions upon millions ②〔表示恳切丁宁〕: 到达后~来信。Be sure to write us when you get there./ ~要小心啊! Do be careful!/ 这事儿~不可掉以轻心。We must under no circumstances take this lightly.

【千…万…】 qiān...wàn...〔形容很多或表示强调〕: 千山万水 ten thousand crags and torrents; numerous mountains and rivers; a long and arduous journey/ 千难万险 numerous dangers and hazards/ 千军万马 thousands upon thousands of horses and soldiers — a powerful army; a mighty force/ 千刀万剐 hack sb. to pieces; give sb. a thousand cuts/ 千真万确 absolutely true/ 千丁宁万嘱咐 exhort sb. repeatedly

【千辛万苦】 qiānxīn-wànkǔ innumerable trials and tribulations; untold hardships: 地质勘探队历尽~,找到了不少新的矿藏。After innumerable hardships, the prospecting team discovered many new ores.

【千言万语】 qiānyán-wànyǔ thousands and thousands of words

【千载难逢】 qiān zǎi nán féng occurring only once in a thousand years; very rare: ~的机会 a golden opportunity; the chance of a lifetime

【千载一时】 qiān zǎi yī shí (of an opportunity) only once in a thousand years; golden

仟 qiān thousand (used for the numeral 千 on cheques, etc., to avoid mistakes or alterations)

阡 qiān〈书〉a footpath between fields, running north and south

【阡陌】 qiānmò crisscross footpaths between fields

迁 qiān ① move: ~往他处 move to another place ② change: 事过境~。The matter is all over, and the situation has changed.

【迁都】 qiāndū move the capital to another place

【迁就】 qiānjiù accommodate oneself to; yield to: ~姑息 excessively accommodating; overlenient/ 无原则的~ unprincipled accommodation/ 在小事情上互相~着点儿 give in a little to each other over small matters

【迁居】 qiānjū change one's dwelling place; move (house): ~外地 move away to another place

【迁怒】 qiānnù vent one's anger on sb. who's not to blame; take it out on sb.

【迁徙】 qiānxǐ move; migrate; change one's residence

【迁移】 qiānyí move; remove; migrate: 从城市~到农村 move from urban to rural areas

牵 * qiān lead along (by holding the hand, the halter, etc.); pull: ~牛下地 lead an ox to the fields/ 手~手 hand in hand

【牵肠挂肚】 qiāncháng-guàdù feel deep anxiety about; be very worried about

【牵扯】 qiānchě involve; implicate; drag in: 这事~很多人。A number of people have become involved in the matter.

【牵制】 qiānchè ① hold up; impede: 互相~ hold each other up/ 抓住主要问题,不要被枝节问题~住。Let's focus our attention on the main problem and not get bogged down in minor issues. ② pin down; check; contain

【牵动】 qiāndòng affect; influence: ~全局 affect the situation as a whole/ ~整个作战计划 affect the overall operational plan

【牵挂】 qiānguà worry; care: 没有~ free from care/ 好好工作,不要~家中老小。Do your work well and don't worry about us folks at home.

【牵累】 qiānlěi ① tie down: 受家务~ be tied down by household chores ② implicate; involve (in trouble)

【牵连】 qiānlián involve (in trouble); implicate; tie up with: 清查同这次破坏活动有~的人和事 investigate the individuals and incidents connected with the sabotage

【牵牛花】 qiānniúhuā (white-edged) morning glory

【牵强】 qiānqiǎng forced (interpretation, etc.); farfetched: 这些理由都很～。 These reasons are farfetched.

【牵强附会】 qiānqiǎng fùhuì draw a forced analogy; make a farfetched (或 irrelevant) comparison; give a strained interpretation

【牵涉】 qiānshè involve; drag in: 这项决定～很多部门。 This decision involves many departments./ 他的发言既然～到我，我就想讲几句。 Since he has dragged me into his speech, I'd like to say a few words.

【牵线】 qiānxiàn ① pull strings; pull wires; control from behind the scenes ② act as go-between ◇ ～人 wire-puller; go-between

【牵一发而动全身】 qiān yī fà ér dòng quánshēn pull one hair and the whole body is affected — a slight move in one part may affect the situation as a whole

【牵制】 qiānzhì pin down; tie up; check; contain: ～敌人 pin down the enemy/ 这对敌人是一种～。 This is a kind of check on the enemy. ◇ ～行动 containing action

悭 qiān
【悭吝】 qiānlìn stingy; miserly

铅* qiān ① lead (Pb) ② lead (in a pencil); black lead
【铅笔】 qiānbǐ pencil
◇ ～刀 small knife for sharpening pencils; pen-knife/ ～盒 pencil-case/ ～画 pencil drawing/ ～芯 lead (in a pencil); black lead
【铅球】 qiānqiú 〈体〉 shot: 推～ shot put; putting the shot
【铅印】 qiānyìn letterpress (或 relief, typographic) printing; stereotype
【铅字】 qiānzì 〈印〉 type; letter: 大号～ large type

谦 qiān modest: ～和 modest and amiable
【谦卑】 qiānbēi humble; modest
【谦辞】 qiāncí self-depreciatory expression
【谦恭】 qiāngōng modest and courteous
【谦谦君子】 qiān qiān jūnzǐ ① 〈旧〉 a modest, self-disciplined gentleman ② a hypocritically modest person
【谦让】 qiānràng modestly decline: 你做这工作再合适不过，不要～了。 You're just the person for the job. Don't decline out of modesty.
【谦虚】 qiānxū ① modest; self-effacing: ～谨慎 modest and prudent ② make modest remarks: 他～了一番，终于答应来做一次演讲。 After making a few modest remarks he finally agreed to come and give a talk.
【谦逊】 qiānxùn modest; unassuming

签* qiān ① sign; autograph: 请你～个字。 Please sign your name here. ② make brief comments on a document ③ bamboo slips used for divination or drawing lots: 抽～ draw lots ④ label; sticker: 标～ label; sticker/ 航空邮～ air mail sticker/ 书～ bookmarker ⑤ a slender pointed piece of bamboo or wood: 牙～ tooth pick ⑥ tack: 把袖口～上 tack on a cuff
【签到】 qiāndào register one's attendance at a meeting or at an office; sign in ◇ ～簿 attendance book/ ～处 sign-in desk
【签订】 qiāndìng conclude and sign (a treaty, etc.): ～条约 sign a treaty/ ～合同 sign a contract/ ～协定的各方 the parties signatory to the agreement
【签发】 qiānfā sign and issue (a document, certificate, etc.)
【签名】 qiānmíng sign one's name; autograph: ～盖章 sign and affix one's seal; set one's hand and seal to/ 亲笔～的照片 an autographed picture/ 来宾～簿 visitors' book ◇ ～运动 signature drive
【签收】 qiānshōu sign after receiving sth.: 挂号信须由收件人～。 A receipt for a registered letter is to be signed by

the recipient. 或 A registered letter must be signed for by the recipient.

【签署】 qiānshǔ sign: ～联合公报 sign a joint *communiqué*/ ～意见 write comments and sign one's name (on a document)
【签证】 qiānzhèng visa; visé: 入(出)境～ entry (exit) visa/ 过境～ transit visa/ 一次有效出入境～ entry-exit visa valid for a single journey/ 互免～ mutual exemption of visas
【签注】 qiānzhù attach a slip of paper to a document with comments on it; write comments on a document (for a superior to consider)
【签字】 qiānzì sign; affix one's signature: ～后立即生效 come into force upon signature

qián

前* qián ① front: ～院 front courtyard/ 楼～ in front of the building ② forward; ahead: 勇往直～ go bravely forward; forge ahead dauntlessly/ 往～看 look forward ③ ago; before: 日～ a few days ago; the other day/ 晚饭～ before supper ④ preceding: ～一阶段 the preceding stage/ 战～ prewar/ 史～ prehistory ⑤ former; formerly: ～校长 former principal of a school ⑥ first: 这次比赛的～六名 the first six places in this competition/ ～三排 the first three rows
【前半天】 qiánbàntiān forenoon; morning
【前半夜】 qiánbànyè the first half of the night (from nightfall to midnight)
【前辈】 qiánbèi senior (person); elder; the older generation: 他们都是我的～。 They are all my seniors.
【前臂】 qiánbì forearm
【前边】 qiánbian ① in front ② ahead ③ above; preceding
【前车之覆，后车之鉴】 qiánchē zhī fù, hòuchē zhī jiàn the overturned cart ahead is a warning to the carts behind
【前车之鉴】 qiánchē zhī jiàn warning taken from the overturned cart ahead; lessons drawn from others' mistakes: 这对我们是一个～。 This is a warning for us.
【前尘】 qiánchén 〈书〉 the past: 回首～ look back upon the past
【前程】 qiánchéng ① future; prospect: 锦绣～ a bright (或 rosy) future/ ～远大 have brilliant prospects ② 〈旧〉 career
【前导】 qiándǎo ① lead the way; march in front; precede ② a person who leads the way; guide: 以仪仗队为～ with the guard of honour marching at the head
【前额】 qián'é forehead
【前方】 qiánfāng ① ahead: 注视着～ look (或 gaze) ahead ② the front: 开赴～ be dispatched to the front
【前锋】 qiánfēng ① vanguard: 部队～已到达目的地。 The vanguard units have reached the destination. ② 〈体〉 forward
【前赴后继】 qiánfù-hòujì advance wave upon wave
【前功尽弃】 qiángōng jìn qì all that has been achieved is spoiled; all one's previous efforts are wasted
【前后】 qián-hòu ① around (a certain time); about: 十点～ around 10 o'clock/ 在1949年～ round about 1949/ 节～ around the Spring Festival ② from beginning to end; altogether: 这项工程，从动工到完成，～只用了十个月。 The entire project, from beginning to end, took only ten months./ 她～来过四次。 She has been here four times altogether. ③ in front and behind: 房子～都有树。 There are trees both in front and at the back of the house./ ～受敌 be attacked by the enemy both front and back; be caught between two fires/ ～左右 on all sides; all around
【前…后…】 qián…hòu… ① 〔表示两种事物或行为在空间或时间上一先一后〕: 前街后巷 front street and back lane/ 前思后想 think over again and again/ 前呼后拥 with many attendants crowding round/ 前倨后恭 be first supercilious and then deferential; change from arrogance to humility/ 前紧后松 be slack at the beginning and have to speed up towards the end ② 〔表示动作的向前向后〕: 前俯后仰 bend forwards and backwards
【前进】 qiánjìn advance; go forward; forge ahead: 继续～

continue to make progress/ 大踏步~ make big strides forward

【前景】 qiánjǐng ①<摄> foreground ② prospect; vista; perspective: 美好的~ good prospects; a bright future

【前例】 qiánlì precedent: 史无~ without precedent in history; unprecedented

【前列】 qiánliè front row (或 rank); forefront; van: 主席台~ the front row on the rostrum

【前轮】 qiánlún (车辆) front wheel; (飞机) nosewheel

【前门】 qiánmén front door

【前门拒虎，后门进狼】 qiánmén jù hǔ, hòumén jìn láng drive the tiger away from the front door and let a wolf in at the back — fend off one danger only to fall prey to another

【前面】 qiánmian ① in front; at the head; ahead: 在房子~ in front of the house/ 走在队伍~ march at the head of the column/ ~就是宿营地。 The campsite is right ahead./ 科学研究工作应当走在经济建设的~。 Scientific research should anticipate economic construction. ② above; preceding: ~提到的原则 the above-mentioned principle/ ~的一章 the preceding chapter

【前年】 qiánnián the year before last

【前怕狼，后怕虎】 qián pà láng, hòu pà hǔ fear wolves ahead and tigers behind — be full of fears: 我们如果~，就什么事情也做不成。 We'll never get anywhere if we are plagued by all sorts of fears.

【前排】 qiánpái front row: ~座位 front-row seats/ 在~就座 be seated in the front rows

【前仆后继】 qiánpū-hòujì no sooner has one fallen than another steps into the breach

【前期】 qiánqī earlier stage; early days

【前前后后】 qiánqiánhòuhòu the whole story; the ins and outs: 一件事情的~ the ins and outs of a matter

【前驱】 qiánqū forerunner; precursor; pioneer

【前人】 qiánrén forefathers; predecessors: ~总结的经验 experience summed up by our predecessors/ ~栽树，后人乘凉。 One generation plants the trees under whose shade another generation rests — profiting by the labour of one's forefathers.

【前任】 qiánrèn predecessor: ~书记 former secretary/ 他的~ his predecessor/ ~总统 ex-president

【前日】 qiánrì the day before yesterday

【前身】 qiánshēn predecessor

【前世】 qiánshì 〔迷信〕 previous existence 又作"前生"

【前事不忘，后事之师】 qiánshì bù wàng, hòushì zhī shī past experience, if not forgotten, is a guide for the future

【前所未闻】 qián suǒ wèi wén never heard of before: ~的奇迹 an unheard-of miracle

【前所未有】 qián suǒ wèi yǒu hitherto unknown; unprecedented: ~的盛况 an unprecedentedly grand occasion

【前台】 qiántái ① proscenium ② (on) the stage

【前提】 qiántí ①<逻> premise: 大(小)~ major (minor) premise ② prerequisite; presupposition: 必要的~ essential prerequisite

【前天】 qiántiān the day before yesterday: ~晚上 the night before last

【前途】 qiántú future; prospect: ~无量 have boundless prospects/ 你们的工作很有~。 Your work has a great future.

【前往】 qiánwǎng go to; leave for; proceed to: 代表团已动身一日内瓦。 The delegation has left for Geneva.

【前无古人】 qián wú gǔrén without parallel in history; unprecedented

【前夕】 qiánxī eve

【前线】 qiánxiàn front; frontline: 上~ go to the front/ 远离~ far from the frontline

【前言】 qiányán preface; foreword; introduction

【前言不搭后语】 qiányán bù dā hòuyǔ utter words that do not hang together; talk incoherently

【前仰后合】 qiányǎng-hòuhé rock (with laughter): 笑得~ rock (或 shake) with laughter

【前因后果】 qiányīn-hòuguǒ cause and effect; the entire process: 这件事情的~已经调查得清清楚楚。 The entire matter, its cause and effect, has been fully cleared up through investigation.

【前兆】 qiánzhào omen; forewarning; premonition: 地震的~ warning signs (或 indications) of an earthquake

【前者】 qiánzhě the former

【前奏】 qiánzòu prelude ◇ ~曲<乐> prelude

钳 qián ① pincers; pliers; tongs: 老虎~ pincer pliers/ 克丝~ combination pliers/ 火~ fire (或 coal) tongs/ 手~ hand vice ② grip (with pincers); clamp ③ restrain: ~口不言 keep one's mouth shut; keep mum

【钳制】 qiánzhì clamp down on; suppress: ~舆论 muzzle (或 gag) public opinion

【钳子】 qiánzi pliers; pincers; forceps

虔 qián pious; sincere

【虔诚】 qiánchéng pious; devout: ~的佛教徒 a pious adherent of Buddhism; devout Buddhist

【虔敬】 qiánjìng reverent

钱* qián ① copper coin; cash: 两个铜~ two coppers (或 cash) ② money: 挣~ make money/ 这个多少~? How much is this? ③ fund; sum: 这笔~是专为保健事业用的。 The fund is earmarked for public health services./ 买拖拉机的~ the wherewithal to buy tractors

【钱包】 qiánbāo wallet; purse

【钱币】 qiánbì coin

【钱财】 qiáncái wealth; money: 浪费~ waste of money

【钱柜】 qiánguì money-locker; money-box; till

掮 qián <方> carry on the shoulder

乾 qián <旧> male

【乾坤】 qiánkūn heaven and earth; the universe: 扭转~ bring about a radical change in the existing state of affairs; reverse the course of events

潜 qián ① latent; hidden: ~能 latent energy ② stealthily; secretly; on the sly

【潜藏】 qiáncáng hide; go into hiding

【潜伏】 qiánfú hide; conceal; lie low: ~特务 hidden enemy agent/ ~的疾病 an insidious disease/ ~着的危机 a latent crisis

【潜力】 qiánlì latent capacity; potential; potentiality: 有很大~ have great potentialities/ 充分发挥~ fully bring out latent potentialities; bring the potential into full play/ 挖掘~ exploit potentialities; tap potentials

【潜入】 qiánrù ① slip into; sneak into; steal in ② dive; submerge

【潜水】 qiánshuǐ go under water; dive

【潜水艇】 qiánshuǐtǐng submarine

【潜水员】 qiánshuǐyuán diver; frogman

【潜逃】 qiántáo abscond: 携公款~ abscond with public funds

【潜艇】 qiántǐng submarine

【潜心】 qiánxīn with great concentration: ~研究科学 apply oneself to scientific study with great concentration; devote oneself to the study of science

【潜行】 qiánxíng ① move under water ② move stealthily; slink

【潜移默化】 qiányí-mòhuà exert a subtle influence on sb.'s character, thinking, etc.; imperceptibly influence: 文艺对人们的思想起着~的作用。 Literature and art exert an imperceptible influence on people's thinking.

【潜意识】 qiányìshí the subconscious; subconsciousness

【潜泳】 qiányǒng underwater swimming

【潜在】 qiánzài latent; potential: ~的力量 latent power

黔 qián ①<书> black ② (Qián) another name for Guizhou Province

【黔驴技穷】 Qián lú jì qióng the proverbial donkey in

ancient Guizhou has exhausted its tricks
【黔驴之技】 Qián lǘ zhī jì tricks not to be feared; cheap tricks

qiǎn

浅* qiǎn ① shallow: ～水 shallow water; shoal water/ ～种 shallow sowing ② simple; easy: 这篇课文很～。 This lesson is very easy. ③ superficial: 对问题的认识很～ just have a superficial understanding of the problem ④ not intimate; not close: 交情很～ not on familiar terms ⑤ (of colour) light: ～蓝 light blue/ ～黄 pale yellow ⑥ not long in time: 相处的日子还～ have not been together long

【浅薄】 qiǎnbó shallow; superficial; meagre: 他的历史知识很～。 He has a very meagre knowledge of history.
【浅海】 qiǎnhǎi 〈地〉 shallow sea; epeiric sea; epicontinental sea ◇ ～水域 the shallow waters along the coast
【浅见】 qiǎnjiàn 〈谦〉 superficial view; humble opinion: 依我～ in my humble opinion
【浅近】 qiǎnjìn simple; plain; easy to understand: ～的文字 simple language
【浅陋】 qiǎnlòu meagre; mean: 学识～ have meagre knowledge
【浅色】 qiǎnsè light colour: ～的女衬衣 a light-coloured blouse
【浅释】 qiǎnshì simple explanation
【浅水池】 qiǎnshuǐchí the shallow end of a swimming pool; shallow pool
【浅说】 qiǎnshuō elementary introduction: 《无线电～》 An Elementary Introduction to Radio
【浅滩】 qiǎntān shoal; shallows
【浅显】 qiǎnxiǎn plain; easy to read and understand: ～的道理 a plain truth/ ～通俗的科学读物 simple popular scientific literature
【浅易】 qiǎnyì simple and easy: ～读物 easy readings

遣 qiǎn ① send; dispatch: 派～ dispatch/ 调兵～将 dispatch officers and men; move troops; deploy forces ② dispel; expel: ～闷 dispel boredom/ 消～ diversion; pastime
【遣词造句】 qiǎncí-zàojù choice of words and building of sentences; wording and phrasing
【遣返】 qiǎnfǎn repatriate: ～战俘 repatriate prisoners of war
【遣散】 qiǎnsàn disband; dismiss; send away
【遣送】 qiǎnsòng send back; repatriate: ～回国 repatriate/ ～出境 deport

谴 qiǎn
【谴责】 qiǎnzé condemn; denounce; censure

缱 qiǎn
【缱绻】 qiǎnquǎn 〈书〉 (of love between man and woman) deeply attached to each other: ～之情 deep attachment; sentimental attachment

qiàn

欠* qiàn ① owe; be behind with: ～债 owe a debt; run (或 get) into debt/ ～租 be behind with the rent/ ～情 owe sb. a debt of gratitude; be indebted to sb. ② not enough; lacking; wanting: ～佳 not good enough; not up to the mark/ 文字～通。 The writing is not altogether grammatical./ 这一屉馒头～火。 These buns haven't been steamed long enough./ 三天就～一个月了。 It's three days short of a month. ③ raise slightly (a part of the body): ～脚儿 slightly raise one's heels/ 他～了～身子又继续工作。 He rose slightly and then sat down to work again. ④ yawn: 呵～ yawn
【欠款】 qiànkuǎn money that is owing; arrears; balance due; debt

【欠缺】 qiànquē ① be deficient in; be short of: 我们的经验还很～。 We are still lacking in experience. ② shortcoming; deficiency: 我们的工作还有很多～。 There are still many shortcomings in our work.
【欠身】 qiànshēn raise oneself slightly; half rise from one's seat: 他～坐起，和客人打招呼。 He raised himself to a half-sitting position to greet the visitors. 或 He made an attempt to sit up as he greeted the visitors.
【欠妥】 qiàntuǒ not proper: 措词～ not properly worded
【欠帐】 qiànzhàng bills due; outstanding accounts

倩 qiàn 〈书〉 ① pretty; handsome ② ask sb. to do sth.: ～人执笔 ask sb. to write on one's behalf

堑 qiàn moat; chasm: 天～ natural chasm
【堑壕】 qiànháo 〈军〉 trench; entrenchment: ～工事 entrenchment works ◇ ～战 trench warfare

嵌 qiàn inlay; embed; set: 镶～螺钿的漆器 lacquerware inlaid with mother-of-pearl/ ～花的地面 a mosaic pavement

歉* qiàn ① apology: 道～ offer (或 make) an apology; apologize/ 抱～ be sorry ② crop failure: 以丰补～ make up for a crop failure with a bumper harvest
【歉年】 qiànnián lean year
【歉收】 qiànshōu crop failure; poor harvest: 因遭天灾而～ have a bad harvest due to natural disaster
【歉意】 qiànyì apology; regret: 表示～ offer an apology; express one's regret/ 谨致～。 Please accept my apologies.

qiāng

抢 qiāng 见"呼天抢地" hūtiān-qiāngdì
另见 qiǎng

呛 qiāng choke: 吃饭吃～了 choke over one's food/ 他喝得太猛，～着了。 He took a big gulp and almost choked.
另见 qiàng

枪* qiāng ① rifle; gun; firearm: 机～ machine gun/ ～架 rifle rack; gun rack/ 持～致敬， (口令) Present arms! ② spear: 红缨～ a red-tasselled spear
【枪毙】 qiāngbì execute by shooting
【枪弹】 qiāngdàn ① cartridge ② bullet
【枪法】 qiāngfǎ marksmanship: 她～高明。 She is a crack shot.
【枪林弹雨】 qiānglín-dànyǔ a hail of bullets: 冒着～冲锋陷阵 charge under a hail of bullets; charge under heavy fire
【枪炮】 qiāngpào firearms; arms; guns
【枪杀】 qiāngshā shoot dead
【枪伤】 qiāngshāng bullet wound
【枪声】 qiāngshēng report of a gun; shot; crack: 听到远处的～ hear shots in the distance
【枪手】 qiāngshǒu ① marksman; gunner: 神～ an expert marksman; a crack shot ② 〈旧〉 spearman

戕 qiāng kill: 自～ kill oneself; commit suicide

腔 qiāng ① cavity: 口(鼻)～ the oral (nasal) cavity/ 胸～ thoracic cavity/ 满～热情 full of enthusiasm ② tune; pitch: 高～ high pitched tune/ 唱走了～儿 sing out of tune/ 秦～ Shaanxi opera ③ accent: 他说话南～北调。 He speaks with a mixture of accents./ 澳洲～ Australian accent/ 学生～ schoolboy talk; classroom tone of a schoolboy ④ speech: 答～ answer/ 不开～ keep mum
【腔调】 qiāngdiào ① tune: 京剧的～ tunes of Beijing opera ② accent; intonation: 听他说话的～ 象是美国人。 Judging from his accent, he is probably from the United States.

锵 qiāng 〈象〉 clang; gong

镪 qiāng
【镪水】 qiāngshuǐ strong acid: 硝～ nitric acid

qiáng

强* qiáng ① strong; powerful: 身～体壮 strong and healthy/ 能力很～ very capable/ 责任心～ have a strong sense of responsibility/ ～敌 formidable enemy ② by force: ～取 take by force/ ～令执行 arbitrarily give orders to carry out sth. ③ better: 我们的劳动条件一年比一年～。 Our working conditions are getting better each year. ④ slightly more than; plus: 三分之一～ slightly more than one third

另见 jiàng; qiǎng

【强暴】 qiángbào ① violent; brutal: ～的行为 act of violence ② ferocious adversary: 不畏～ defy brute force

【强大】 qiángdà big and powerful; powerful; formidable

【强盗】 qiángdào robber; bandit: ～行为 banditry; robbery

【强调】 qiángdiào stress; emphasize; underline: 不适当地～情况特殊 lay undue stress on special circumstances/ 必须～产品质量。 Emphasis must be placed on the quality of the products.

【强度】 qiángdù intensity; strength: 劳动～ the intensity of labour/ 钢的～ the strength of the steel/ 抗震～ shock strength/ 辐射～ radiation intensity

【强固】 qiánggù strong; solid: ～的工事 strong fortifications/ ～的基础 a solid foundation

【强国】 qiángguó powerful nation; power

【强悍】 qiánghàn intrepid; doughty; valiant

【强横】 qiánghèng brutal and unreasonable; tyrannical

【强加】 qiángjiā impose; force: 不要～于人。 Don't force your views on others.

【强奸】 qiángjiān rape; violate: ～民意 defile public opinion

【强健】 qiángjiàn strong and healthy: 体魄～ be physically strong; have a strong constitution

【强将手下无弱兵】 qiángjiàng shǒuxià wú ruòbīng there are no poor soldiers under a good general

【强劲】 qiángjìng powerful; forceful: ～的海风 a strong wind blowing from the sea

【强烈】 qiángliè strong; intense; violent: ～的愿望 a strong desire/ ～的仇恨 intense hatred/ ～的对比 a striking contrast/ ～反对 strongly oppose/ ～谴责 vehemently condemn; vigorously denounce

【强弩之末】 qiángnǔ zhī mò an arrow at the end of its flight — a spent force

【强权】 qiángquán power; might: ～政治 power politics

【强行】 qiángxíng force: ～闯入 force one's way in/ ～登陆 force a landing/ ～通过一项议案 force through a bill

【强硬】 qiángyìng strong; tough; unyielding: 措词～的声明 a strongly worded statement/ 提出～抗议 lodge a strong protest/ ～路线 tough line; hard line/ ～的态度 an uncompromising stand ◇～派 hardliner

【强有力】 qiángyǒulì strong; vigorous; forceful: 采取～的行动 take vigorous action

【强制】 qiángzhì force; compel; coerce: ～劳动 forced labour/ ～手段 compulsory means; coercive measure/ ～执行 enforce/ ～机关 institutions of coercion/ ～性的命令 mandatory order

【强中自有强中手】 qiángzhōng zì yǒu qiángzhōng shǒu however strong you are, there's always someone stronger

【强壮】 qiángzhuàng strong; sturdy; robust ◇～剂〈药〉 roborant; tonic

墙* qiáng wall

【墙报】 qiángbào wall newspaper

【墙壁】 qiángbì wall

【墙脚】 qiángjiǎo ① the foot of a wall ② foundation: 挖～ cut the ground (from under sb.'s feet); undermine the foundation

【墙头】 qiángtóu the top of a wall ◇～草 grass on the top of a wall which sways with every wind — a person who bends with the wind

【墙纸】 qiángzhǐ 〈建〉 wall paper

蔷 qiáng

【蔷薇】 qiángwēi 〈植〉 rose

樯 qiáng 〈书〉 mast: 帆～如林 a forest of masts

qiǎng

抢* qiǎng ① rob; loot ② snatch; grab: 他把信～了过去。 He snatched away the letter. ③ vie for; scramble for: ～球 scramble for the ball/ ～干重活 vie with each other for the hardest job ④ rush: ～收 rush in the harvest

另见 qiāng

【抢渡】 qiǎngdù speedily cross (a river)

【抢夺】 qiǎngduó snatch; wrest; seize: ～胜利果实 seize the fruits of victory

【抢购】 qiǎnggòu rush to purchase: ～风潮 panic purchasing

【抢劫】 qiǎngjié rob; loot; plunder

【抢救】 qiǎngjiù rescue; save; salvage: ～国家财产 save state property/ ～水淹了的庄稼 salvage flooded crops/ ～病人 give emergency treatment to a patient; rescue a patient/ ～无效。 All rescue measures proved ineffectual. ◇～工作 rescue work/ ～组 rescue party

【抢掠】 qiǎnglüè loot; sack; plunder

【抢先】 qiǎngxiān try to be the first to do sth.; anticipate; forestall

强* qiǎng make an effort; strive: ～作镇静 make an effort to appear composed; try hard to keep one's composure/ ～不知以为知 pretend to know what one does not know

另见 jiàng; qiáng

【强逼】 qiǎngbī compel; force

【强辩】 qiǎngbiàn defend oneself by sophistry

【强词夺理】 qiǎngcí-duólǐ use lame arguments; resort to sophistry; reason fallaciously

【强迫】 qiǎngpò force; compel; coerce: ～命令 resort to coercion and commandism/ ～敌机降落 compel the enemy plane to land

【强求】 qiǎngqiú insist on; impose: 各地情况不同，不能一律。 No uniformity should be imposed since conditions vary from place to place.

【强人所难】 qiǎng rén suǒ nán try to make sb. do sth. which he won't or can't

【强使】 qiǎngshǐ force; compel

【强颜欢笑】 qiǎng yán huānxiào put on an air of cheerfulness; try to look happy when one is sad

襁 qiǎng

【襁褓】 qiǎngbǎo swaddling clothes: ～中 be in one's infancy

qiàng

呛 qiàng irritate (respiratory organs): 炸辣椒的味儿～鼻子。 The smell of red pepper being fried irritates the nose./ 烟把我～着了。 The smoke almost choked me.

另见 qiāng

跄 qiàng

【跄踉】 qiàngliàng stagger

qiāo

悄 qiāo

另见 qiǎo

【悄悄】 qiāoqiāo quietly; on the quiet: ～离开 leave quietly/ 他～儿地跟我全说了。 He told me everything on the quiet.

跷 qiāo ① lift up (a leg); hold up (a finger): ～着腿坐

着 sit with one's legs crossed ② on tiptoe: ~着脚走路 walk on tiptoe ③ stilts
【跷蹊】qiāoqi fishy; dubious
【跷跷板】qiāoqiāobǎn seesaw: 玩~ play on a seesaw

踽 qiāo 见"跷" qiāo

敲* qiāo ① knock; beat; strike: ~门 knock at the door/ ~警钟 sound the alarm/ 钟刚~过四点。The clock has just struck four./ ~锣打鼓迎新年 usher in the new year with drums and gongs; beat drums and gongs to greet the new year ② 〈口〉 overcharge; fleece sb.: 给~去五块钱 be stung for five dollars
【敲打】qiāoda beat; rap; tap: 锣鼓~得很热闹。Drums and gongs were beating boisterously.
【敲门砖】qiāoménzhuān a brick picked up to knock on the door and thrown away when it has served its purpose — a stepping-stone to success
【敲诈】qiāozhà extort; blackmail; racketeer: ~钱财 extort money

锹 qiāo spade: 挖一~深 dig a spade's depth; dig a spit deep/ 每一~煤 each shovelful of coal

橇 qiāo sledge; sled; sleigh

qiáo

乔 qiáo ① tall ② disguise
【乔迁】qiáoqiān 〔多用于祝贺〕move to a better place or have a promotion: ~之喜。Best wishes for your new home.
【乔装】qiáozhuāng disguise: ~成商人 disguise oneself as a merchant

侨* qiáo ① live abroad ② a person living abroad: 外~ ~ foreign residents; aliens
【侨居】qiáojū live abroad ◇ ~国 country of residence

桥* qiáo bridge
【桥梁】qiáoliáng bridge: 起~作用 play the role of a bridge; serve as a link/ 商业是联结生产同消费的~。Commerce is a bridge that links production with consumption.
【桥牌】qiáopái bridge (a card game): 打~ play bridge

翘 qiáo ① raise (one's head) ② become warped: 木板~了。The board has warped.
另见 qiào
【翘楚】qiáochǔ 〈书〉 an outstanding (或 talented) person: 医中~ an eminent physician
【翘首】qiáoshǒu 〈书〉 raise one's head and look: ~星空 look up at the starry sky

憔 qiáo
【憔悴】qiáocuì ① wan and sallow; thin and pallid ② (of plants) withered

樵 qiáo ① 〈书〉 gather firewood ② 〈方〉 firewood
【樵夫】qiáofū woodcutter; woodman

瞧* qiáo 〈口〉 look; see: 等着~吧。Wait and see./ ~书 read a book/ 东~西~ look about/ 你~着办吧。You can do as you see fit.
【瞧不起】qiáobuqǐ 〈口〉 look down upon; hold in contempt
【瞧不上眼】qiáobushàng yǎn 〈口〉 consider beneath one's notice; turn one's nose up at
【瞧得起】qiáodeqǐ 〈口〉 think much (或 highly) of sb.
【瞧见】qiáojiɑn 〈口〉 see; catch sight of

qiǎo

巧* qiǎo ① skilful; ingenious; clever: ~匠 a skilled (或

clever) workman/ 手~ clever with one's hands; dexterous ② cunning; deceitful; artful: ~言 cunning words; deceitful talk ③ opportunely; coincidentally; as it happens; as luck would have it: 来得真~ arrive at a most opportune moment/ 无~不成书。There is no story without coincidences./ 他偏~那天不在。As luck would have it, he was away that day.
【巧夺天工】qiǎo duó tiāngōng wonderful workmanship (或 superb craftsmanship) excelling nature
【巧妇难为无米之炊】qiǎofù nán wéi wú mǐ zhī chuī the cleverest housewife can't cook a meal without rice — one can't make bricks without straw
【巧合】qiǎohé coincidence
【巧计】qiǎojì clever device; artful scheme
【巧克力】qiǎokèlì chocolate
【巧立名目】qiǎo lì míngmù concoct various pretexts; invent all sorts of names: ~，搜刮民财 extort people's wealth under all sorts of pretexts
【巧妙】qiǎomiào ingenious; clever: ~的战术 ingenious tactics/ ~的手段 a clever move
【巧取豪夺】qiǎoqǔ-háoduó secure (sb.'s belongings, right, etc.) by force or trickery
【巧舌如簧】qiǎoshé rú huáng have a glib tongue
【巧手】qiǎoshǒu a dab hand
【巧遇】qiǎoyù chance encounter

悄 qiǎo ① quiet; silent ② 〈书〉 sad; worried; grieved
另见 qiāo
【悄然】qiǎorán ① sorrowfully; sadly: ~泪下 shed tears in sorrow; shed sad tears ② quietly; softly: ~离去 leave quietly
【悄声】qiǎoshēng quietly; in a low voice

愀 qiǎo
【愀然】qiǎorán 〈书〉 ① sorrowful-looking ② stern; grave-looking

qiào

壳* qiào shell; hard surface
另见 ké

俏 qiào ① pretty; smart; handsome: 打扮得真~ be smartly dressed ② sell well; be in great demand: ~货 goods in great demand
【俏丽】qiàolì handsome; pretty
【俏皮】qiàopi ① good-looking; smart ② lively and delightful; witty
【俏皮话】qiàopihuà ① witty remark; witticism; wisecrack ② sarcastic remark

窍 qiào ① aperture ② a key to sth.: 诀~ knack; trick of a trade
【窍门】qiàomén key (to a problem); knack: 找~ try to find the key to a problem; try to get the knack of doing sth.

峭 qiào ① high and steep; precipitous ② severe; stern
【峭拔】qiàobá ① high and steep ② vigorous: 笔锋~ have a vigorous style of writing
【峭壁】qiàobì cliff; precipice; steep
【峭立】qiàolì rise steeply

翘 qiào stick up; hold up; bend upwards; turn upwards
另见 qiáo
【翘尾巴】qiào wěiba be cocky; get stuck-up: 别一有成绩就~。Don't get cocky when you've achieved something.

撬 qiào prize; pry: 把箱子~开 prize (或 pry) open a box

鞘 qiào sheath; scabbard

qiē

切 qiē cut; slice: ~菜 cut up vegetables/ ~肉 slice meat
另见 qiè

【切除】 qiēchú 〈医〉 excision; resection: ~脂肪瘤 the resection (或 removal) of a lipoma/ 全(部分)~ total (partial) excision

【切磋】 qiēcuō learn from each other by exchanging views; compare notes: 比赛后两国篮球运动员聚在一起，~球艺。The basketball players of the two countries got together and swopped pointers after the match.

【切断】 qiēduàn cut off: ~敌人后路 cut off the enemy's retreat/ ~电源 cut off the electricity supply

【切面】 qiēmiàn ① 〈数〉 tangent plane ② section ③ cut noodles; machine-made noodles

【切片】 qiēpiàn cut into slices

【切纸机】 qiēzhǐjī paper cutting machine; paper cutter

qié

茄 qié eggplant; aubergine
【茄子】 qiézi eggplant; aubergine

qiě

且 qiě ①〈副〉 just; for the time being: 你~等一下。Just wait a little while./ 这事~放一下。Let the matter rest for the time being./ ~不说中文期刊，外文期刊也订了不少。Lots of periodicals in foreign languages have been subscribed to, not to mention those in Chinese. ②〈方〉〈副〉 for a long time: 这种钢笔~使呢。These fountain pens last a long time./ 他~来不了呢。He's a long time coming. ③〈书〉〈连〉 even: 死~不惧，况困难乎！Even death holds no fears for us, to say nothing of difficulties. ④〈书〉〈连〉 both... and...: 既高~大 both tall and heavy set; both high and wide

【且慢】 qiěmàn wait a moment; not go or do so soon: ~，听我把话说完。Wait a minute, let me finish what I have to say./ ~高兴！Don't rejoice too soon!

【且…且…】 qiě…qiě… while; as: 他们一路上且谈且走。All the way they talked as they walked.

qiè

切 qiè ① correspond to; be close to: 不~实际 not correspond to reality; unrealistic; impractical/ 译文不~原意。The translation does not quite correspond to the original. ② eager; anxious: 回国心~ be anxious to return to one's country ③ be sure to: ~勿迟延。Be sure not to delay./ ~不可自以为是。One should never be presumptuous and opinionated.
另见 qiē

【切齿】 qièchǐ gnash one's teeth: ~痛恨 gnash one's teeth in hatred

【切肤之痛】 qiè fū zhī tòng keenly felt pain

【切合】 qièhé suit; fit in with: 计划要~实际。Plans should be geared to actual circumstances./ ~人民的需要 fit in with the needs of the people

【切记】 qièjì be sure to keep in mind; must always remember

【切忌】 qièjì must guard against; avoid by all means: ~主观片面。Be careful to avoid being subjective and one-sided.

【切近】 qièjìn close to: 这样解释比较~作者原意。This interpretation seems to be closer to what is meant by the author.

【切切】 qièqiè ① be sure to: ~不可骄傲。Be sure not to become conceited. 或 Guard against arrogance by every

means. ②〔用于布告、条令等末尾〕: ~此布。This proclamation is hereby issued in all earnestness.

【切身】 qièshēn ① of immediate concern to oneself: ~利益 one's immediate or vital interests ② personal: ~体会 personal understanding; intimate knowledge

【切实】 qièshí ① feasible; practical; realistic: ~有效的办法 practical and effective measures/ ~可行的计划 a feasible (或 realistic) plan ② conscientiously; earnestly: ~改正错误 correct one's mistakes in real earnest/ 切切实实地工作 do one's job conscientiously

【切题】 qiètí keep to the point; be relevant to the subject: 写文章要~。When writing, keep to the subject.

【切诊】 qièzhěn 〈中医〉 pulse feeling and palpation, one of the four methods of diagnosis

妾 qiè concubine

怯 qiè timid; cowardly; nervous
【怯场】 qièchǎng have stage fright
【怯懦】 qiènuò timid and overcautious
【怯弱】 qièruò timid and weak-willed
【怯生】 qièshēng 〈方〉 shy with strangers
【怯阵】 qièzhèn ① feel nervous when going into battle; be battle-shy ② have stage fright

窃 qiè ① steal; pilfer: 行~ steal; practise theft/ ~案 larceny; burglary ② secretly; surreptitiously; furtively: ~笑 laugh secretly; laugh up one's sleeve/ ~~私议 exchange whispered comments ③ 〈谦〉〔指自己〕: ~以为 in my humble opinion; I presume

【窃国】 qièguó usurp state power ◇ ~大盗 arch usurper of state power

【窃据】 qièjù usurp; unjustly occupy: ~要职 usurp a high post; unjustly occupy a high post

【窃取】 qièqǔ usurp; steal; grab: ~机密情报 steal secret information

【窃听】 qiètīng eavesdrop; wiretap; bug ◇ ~器 tapping device; listening-in device; bug

【窃贼】 qièzéi thief; burglar; pilferer

挈 qiè ① take along: ~眷 take one's family along ② lift; raise; take up: 提纲~领 hold a net by the headrope or a coat by the collar — concentrate on the main points

惬 qiè 〈书〉 be satisfied
【惬意】 qièyì be pleased; be satisfied

箧 qiè 〈书〉 small suitcase: 藤~ wicker suitcase

锲 qiè 〈书〉 carve; engrave
【锲而不舍】 qiè ér bù shě keep on carving unflaggingly — work with perseverance: 学习要有~的精神。Study requires perseverance.

qīn

亲 qīn ① parent: 双~ parents ② blood relation; next of kin: ~兄弟 blood brother ③ relative: 近~ close relative; near kin/ 远~ distant relative ④ marriage; match: 说~ act as a matchmaker ⑤ bride: 迎~ (of the groom's family) send a party to escort the bride to the groom's home ⑥ close; intimate; dear: ~如一家 as dear to each other as members of one family ⑦ in person; oneself ⑧ kiss: 她~了~孩子的脸。She kissed the child on the cheek.
另见 qìng

【亲爱】 qīn'ài dear; beloved ~的祖国 one's beloved country

【亲笔】 qīnbǐ ① in one's own handwriting: 这信是他~写的。This letter is in his own hand. ② one's own handwriting: 这是他的~。This is his handwriting. ◇ ~签名 one's own signature; autograph/ ~信 a personal, handwritten message; an autograph letter

【亲近】 qīnjìn be close to; be on intimate terms with: 这

两人很～。Those two are on intimate terms./ 他对人热情诚恳,大家都愿意～他。As he is warmhearted and sincere, everyone wants to be friends with him.

【亲眷】 qīnjuàn 〈方〉one's relatives

【亲口】 qīnkǒu (say sth.) personally: 这是他～告诉我的。He told me this himself.

【亲密】 qīnmì close: intimate: ～的朋友 a close friend

【亲昵】 qīnnì very intimate: ～的称呼 an affectionate form of address

【亲戚】 qīnqī relative: 我在香港的～不多。I have very few relatives in Hong Kong.

【亲切】 qīnqiè cordial; kind: ～的关怀 kind attention; loving care/ ～的教导 kind guidance/ ～的谈话 a cordial conversation/ 他的话我们感到很～。What he said touched our hearts.

【亲热】 qīnrè affectionate; intimate; warmhearted: 我们都～地称她为大姐。We all affectionately refer to her as our elder sister./ ～地问长问短 make warmhearted inquiries (about sb.'s health, etc.)

【亲人】 qīnrén ① one's parents, spouse, children, etc.; one's family members: 他除母亲外, 没有别的～。His mother is the only other member of his family. ② dear ones; those dear to one

【亲善】 qīnshàn goodwill (between countries)

【亲身】 qīnshēn personal; firsthand: ～经历 personal experience; firsthand experience

【亲生】 qīnshēng one's own (children, parents): ～父母 one's own parents

【亲事】 qīnshì marriage

【亲手】 qīnshǒu with one's own hands; personally; oneself: 这些是他～种的树。Those are the trees he planted with his own hands./ 你～做一做。Do it yourself.

【亲属】 qīnshǔ kinsfolk; relatives

【亲痛仇快】 qīn tòng chóu kuài sadden one's own people and gladden the enemy

【亲王】 qīnwáng prince

【亲信】 qīnxìn trusted follower

【亲眼】 qīnyǎn with one's own eyes; personally: 这是我～看见的。I saw it with my own eyes.

【亲友】 qīnyǒu relatives and friends; kith and kin

【亲自】 qīnzì personally; in person; oneself: ～动手 personally take a hand in the work; do the job oneself/ ～拜访 make a personal call/ 你～去看看。Go and see for yourself./ 他～带领我们参观博物馆。He showed us round the museum himself.

【亲族】 qīnzú members of the same clan

【亲嘴】 qīnzuǐ kiss

侵* qīn　invade; intrude into; infringe upon

【侵犯】 qīnfàn encroach on; infringe upon; violate: ～人权 infringe upon human rights/ ～领土和主权 violate a country's territorial integrity and sovereignty

【侵害】 qīnhài encroach on; make inroads on: 建造防护林,减少风沙的～ build shelterbelts to reduce encroachments by sandstorms/ 防止蝗虫～农作物 prevent the inroads of locusts on the crops

【侵略】 qīnlüè aggression; invasion: ～别国 commit aggression against another country ◇ ～国 aggressor (nation)/ ～军 aggressor troops; invading army/ ～行为 act of aggression/ ～战争 war of aggression/ ～者 aggressor; invader

【侵扰】 qīnrǎo invade and harass: ～边境 harass a country's frontiers; make border raids

【侵入】 qīnrù invade; intrude into; make incursions into: ～领海 intrude into a country's territorial waters

【侵蚀】 qīnshí corrode; erode: 风雨的～ erosion by wind and rain

【侵吞】 qīntūn ① embezzle; misappropriate: ～公款 embezzle public funds/ ～社会财富 appropriate social property ② swallow up; annex: ～别国领土 annex another country's territory

【侵袭】 qīnxí make inroads on; invade and attack; hit: 台风～沿海地区。The typhoon hit the coastal areas.

【侵占】 qīnzhàn invade and occupy; seize: ～别国领土 invade and occupy another country's territory/ ～公有土地 seize public land

钦 qīn ① admire; respect ② by the emperor himself: ～定 (of a book, etc.) made by imperial order

【钦敬】 qīnjìng admire and respect

【钦佩】 qīnpèi admire; esteem: 表示～ express admiration for/ 他们坚持科学实验的精神令人～。Their persistence in scientific experiment commands admiration.

【钦仰】 qīnyǎng 〈书〉revere; venerate; esteem

qín

芹 qín
【芹菜】 qíncài celery

秦 Qín a surname

琴* qín ① a general name for certain musical instruments: 小提～ violin/ 钢～ piano/ 口～ harmonica ② qín, a seven-stringed plucked instrument in some ways similar to the zither

禽* qín birds: 鸣～ song birds/ 家～ (domestic) fowls; poultry

【禽兽】 qínshòu birds and beasts: 衣冠～ a beast in human clothing/ ～行为 brutish acts; bestial acts

勤* qín ① diligent; industrious; hardworking: ～学苦练 study diligently and train hard ② frequently; regularly: 衣服要～洗～换。Clothes should be changed and washed regularly./ 夏季雨水～。Rain is frequent in summer. ③ (of-fice, school, etc.) attendance: 值～ be on duty/ 考～ check on work attendance

【勤奋】 qínfèn diligent; assiduous; industrious: 学习～ be diligent in one's studies

【勤工俭学】 qíngōng-jiǎnxué part-work and part-study system; work-study programme

【勤俭】 qínjiǎn hardworking and thrifty: ～建国 build up the country through thrift and hard work

【勤恳】 qínkěn diligent and conscientious: 勤勤恳恳地为人民服务 be diligent and conscientious in serving the people

【勤快】 qínkuai 〈口〉diligent; hardworking: 她真～,一会儿也不闲着。She is diligent and keeps herself busy all the time.

【勤劳】 qínláo diligent; industrious; hardworking: ～的双手 an untiring pair of hands

【勤勉】 qínmiǎn diligent; assiduous: ～好学 diligent and eager to learn

擒 qín capture; catch; seize: 生～ capture alive/ ～贼先～王。To catch bandits, first catch the ringleader.

噙 qín hold in the mouth or the eyes: ～着烟袋 hold a pipe between one's lips/ ～着眼泪 eyes brimming with tears

qǐn

寝 qǐn ① sleep: 废～忘食 (so absorbed or occupied as to) forget about eating and sleeping ② bedroom: 就～ go to bed ③ coffin chamber: 陵～ imperial burial place; mausoleum

【寝食】 qǐn-shí sleeping and eating: ～不安 feel uneasy even when eating and sleeping; be worried waking or sleeping

【寝室】 qǐnshì bedroom; dormitory

qìn

沁 qìn ooze; seep; exude: 额上～出了汗珠。His forehead was oozing sweat.

【沁人心脾】 qìn rén xīn-pí gladdening the heart and refreshing the mind; mentally refreshing; refreshing

qīng

青* qīng ① blue or green: ~天 blue sky/ ~椒 green pepper ② black: ~布 black cloth ③ green grass; young crops: 踏~ walk on the green grass — go for an outing in early spring
【青菜】 qīngcài ① green vegetables; greens ② Chinese cabbage
【青草】 qīngcǎo green grass
【青出于蓝】 qīng chūyú lán indigo blue is extracted from the indigo plant (but is bluer than the plant it comes from) — the pupil surpasses the master
【青春】 qīngchūn youth; youthfulness: 把~献给祖国 dedicate one's youth to one's country/ 充满着~的活力 be bursting with youthful vigour ◇ ~期 puberty
【青葱】 qīngcōng verdant; fresh green: ~的竹林 a verdant grove of bamboo
【青翠】 qīngcuì verdant; fresh and green: 雨后, 垂柳显得格外~。The weeping willows looked fresher and greener after the rain.
【青黄不接】 qīng-huáng bù jiē when the new crop is still in the blade and the old one is all consumed — temporary shortage
【青睐】 qīnglài 〈书〉favour; good graces: 获得某人的~ find favour in sb.'s eyes; be in sb.'s good graces
【青面獠牙】 qīngmiàn-liáoyá green-faced and long-toothed — terrifying in appearance: 露出~的凶相 reveal the ferocious features of an ogre
【青年】 qīngnián youth; young people: ~时代 one's youth/ ~人 young people; youth/ ~学生 young students; student youth
【青山】 qīngshān green hill: 留得~在, 不愁没柴烧。As long as the green hills are there, one need not worry about firewood.
【青少年】 qīng-shàonián teen-agers; youngsters
【青史】 qīngshǐ annals of history: 永垂~ go down in the annals of history
【青苔】 qīngtái moss
【青天】 qīngtiān ① blue sky ② 〈旧〉a just judge; an upright magistrate
【青天霹雳】 qīngtiān pīlì 见 "晴天霹雳" qíngtiān pīlì
【青蛙】 qīngwā frog
【青云】 qīngyún high official position: ~直上 rapid advancement in one's career; meteoric rise

轻* qīng ① light: 油比水~。Oil is lighter than water./ ~武器 light arms; small arms ② small in number, degree, etc.: 年纪很~ be very young/ 他的病很~ His illness is not at all serious. ③ not important: 责任~ carry a light responsibility ④ gently; softly: 拿~放。Handle gently./ 病人睡着了, ~点儿! Be quiet! The patient is asleep. ⑤ rashly: ~信 readily believe ⑥ belittle; make light of: 掉以~心 take sth. lightly/ 文人相~的恶习 the evil practice of scholars disparaging one another
【轻便】 qīngbiàn light; portable: ~铁道 light railway
【轻薄】 qīngbó given to philandering; frivolous
【轻敌】 qīngdí take the enemy lightly; underestimate the enemy ◇ ~思想 tendency to take the enemy lightly
【轻而易举】 qīng ér yì jǔ easy to do: 这决不是~的事。It's certainly no easy job./ 不要以为~就可以把庄稼种好。Don't think you can do a good job in farming without making an effort.
【轻放】 qīngfàng put down gently: 易碎物品, 小心~! Fragile! Handle with care!
【轻风】 qīngfēng 〈气〉light breeze
【轻浮】 qīngfú frivolous; flighty; light: 举止~ behave frivolously/ ~的行为 frivolous conduct
【轻歌曼舞】 qīnggē-mànwǔ sing merrily and dance gracefully
【轻工业】 qīnggōngyè light industry

【轻举妄动】 qīngjǔ-wàngdòng act rashly; take reckless action: 不可~ make no move without careful thought
【轻快】 qīngkuài ① brisk; spry: 迈着~的步子 walk at a brisk pace ② lighthearted; lively: ~的曲调 lively tune
【轻狂】 qīngkuáng extremely frivolous
【轻慢】 qīngmàn treat sb. without proper respect; slight
【轻描淡写】 qīngmiáo-dànxiě touch on lightly; mention casually: 要认真检查自己的错误, 不要~。You should criticize your own faults earnestly, and not just touch on them lightly.
【轻蔑】 qīngmiè scornful; disdainful; contemptuous: ~的眼光 a disdainful look
【轻诺寡信】 qīngnuò-guǎxìn make promises easily but seldom keep them
【轻飘飘】 qīngpiāopiāo light; buoyant: 垂柳~地摆动。The branches of the drooping willows were swaying lightly./ 她高兴地走着, 脚底下~的。She tripped along joyfully as if treading on air.
【轻巧】 qīngqiǎo ① light and handy: 一架~的录音机 a handy tape recorder/ 你说得倒~。You talk as if it were a simple matter. ② dexterous; deft: 他操纵机器动作非常~。He operates the machine dexterously.
【轻轻】 qīngqīng lightly; gently: 把孩子~地放在床上 put the baby on the bed gently/ ~地说 speak in a soft voice
【轻取】 qīngqǔ beat easily; win an easy victory; win hands down: ~第一局 win the first game easily (或 without effort)
【轻柔】 qīngróu soft; gentle: ~的枝条 pliable twigs/ ~的声音 a gentle voice
【轻伤】 qīngshāng slight (或 minor) wound; flesh wound
【轻生】 qīngshēng make light of one's life — commit suicide
【轻声】 qīngshēng ① in a soft voice; softly: ~低语 speak softly; whisper ② 〈语〉(in Chinese pronunciation) light tone, unstressed syllable pronounced without its original pitch
【轻视】 qīngshì despise; look down on; underestimate
【轻手轻脚】 qīngshǒu-qīngjiǎo gently; softly: 护士出来进去都~, 怕惊醒病人。The nurse moved around very softly so as not to wake the patient.
【轻率】 qīngshuài rash; hasty; indiscreet: ~的态度 reckless attitude/ ~从事 act rashly/ 这样处理太~了。It was indiscreet of you to handle it that way.
【轻松】 qīngsōng light; relaxed: ~的工作 light work; soft job; cushy job/ ~愉快 happy and relaxed/ ~地打败了对手 beat one's opponent with ease
【轻佻】 qīngtiāo frivolous; skittish; giddy: 举止~ skittish behaviour
【轻微】 qīngwēi light; slight; trifling; to a small extent: ~的伤亡 light casualties/ ~的头痛 a slight headache/ ~的损失 a trifling loss
【轻信】 qīngxìn be credulous; readily place trust in; readily believe: 不要~谣言。Give no credence to rumours./ 重证据, 不能~口供。Lay stress on evidence and do not readily believe confessions.
【轻型】 qīngxíng light-duty; light: ~机械 light-duty machinery/ ~载重汽车 light truck; light-duty truck/ ~飞机 light aircraft
【轻易】 qīngyì ① easily: 胜利成果不是~得来的。The fruits of victory were not easily won. ② lightly; rashly: 不要~地下结论。Don't draw hasty conclusions. 或 Don't jump to conclusions./ 他不~发表意见。He does not express an opinion rashly.
【轻音乐】 qīngyīnyuè light music
【轻盈】 qīngyíng slim and graceful; lithe; lissom: 她的自由体操动作~优美。Her movements in free gymnastics are lithe and graceful./ 笑语~ talk and laugh merrily and lightheartedly.
【轻于鸿毛】 qīng yú hóngmáo lighter than a goose feather: 死或重于泰山, 有~。One's death may be weightier than Taishan Mountain or lighter than a feather.
【轻重】 qīng-zhòng ① weight: 这两只箱子~不一样。The two boxes do not weigh the same. ② degree of seriousness; relative importance: 工作应分~缓急 Work should be done in order of importance and urgency./ 此事无足~。

It's a matter of no consequence./ 根据病情～决定病人是否住院。Whether a patient is to be hospitalized depends on how serious the case is. ③ propriety: 这个人说话不知～。 That chap doesn't know the proper way to talk.

【轻重倒置】qīng-zhòng dàozhì put the trivial above the important

【轻装】qīngzhuāng light; with light packs: ～就道 travel light/ ～前进 march with light packs

【轻罪】qīngzuì 〈法〉misdemeanour; minor offence; minor crime: ～重判不对,重罪轻判也不对。 It is wrong to deal with a minor offence as if it were a major one and vice versa.

氢 qīng 〈化〉hydrogen (H)

【氢弹】qīngdàn hydrogen bomb ◇ ～头 hydrogen warhead; H-warhead

【氢气】qīngqì hydrogen ◇ ～球 hydrogen balloon

倾 qīng ① incline; lean; bend: 向左～ incline to the left/ 身子向前～ bend forward; lean forward ② deviation; tendency ③ collapse: 大厦将～ a great mansion on the point of collapse ④ overturn and pour out; empty: ～囊相助 empty one's purse to help; give generous financial support ⑤ do all one can; use up all one's resources: ～全力把工作做好 exert oneself to the utmost to do the work well

【倾巢】qīngcháo (of the enemy or bandits) turn out in full force: 敌军～而出。The enemy turned out in full strength.

【倾城倾国】qīngchéng-qīngguó (of a woman) lovely enough to cause the fall of a city or a state; exceedingly beautiful

【倾倒】qīngdǎo ① topple and fall; topple over ② greatly admire: 为之～ be infatuated with sb.; be overwhelmed with admiration for sb.

【倾倒】qīngdào tip; dump; empty; pour out: ～垃圾 dump rubbish

【倾覆】qīngfù overturn; topple; capsize

【倾家荡产】qīngjiā-dàngchǎn lose a family fortune

【倾慕】qīngmù have a strong admiration for; adore

【倾盆大雨】qīngpén dàyǔ heavy downpour; torrential rain; cloudburst: 赶上一场～ be caught in a downpour/ 下起了～。The rain was pelting down. 或 It was raining cats and dogs.

【倾诉】qīngsù pour out (one's heart, troubles, etc.): ～衷肠 pour out one's heart; reveal one's innermost feelings

【倾谈】qīngtán have a good, heart-to-heart talk

【倾听】qīngtīng listen attentively to; lend an attentive ear to: ～群众的意见 listen attentively to the views of the masses

【倾吐】qīngtǔ say what is on one's mind without reservation: ～衷情 unbosom oneself/ ～苦水 unburden oneself of one's grievances

【倾箱倒箧】qīngxiāng-dǎoqiè turn out all one's boxes and suitcases

【倾向】qīngxiàng ① tendency; trend; inclination; deviation: 政治～ political inclination/ 要注意一种～掩盖另一种～。 One must be alive to the possibility that one tendency may conceal another. ② be inclined to; prefer: 这两种方案我～于第一种。Of the two plans, I prefer the first.

【倾销】qīngxiāo dump: ～货物 dump goods

【倾斜】qīngxié tilt; incline; slope; slant: 中国地势大致从西北向东南～。Generally speaking, the terrain of China slopes from northwest to southeast./ 地面微微向南～。The land inclines gently to the south./ 这墙有点～。The wall is a little out of the perpendicular.

【倾泻】qīngxiè come down in torrents: 山水～而下,汇成洪流。Streams rushed down the mountain and converged into a torrent.

【倾心】qīngxīn ① admire; fall in love with: 一见～ fall in love at first sight ② cordial; heart-to-heart: ～交谈 have a heart-to-heart talk

【倾轧】qīngyà engage in internal strife; jostle against each other

【倾注】qīngzhù ① pour into: 几股山泉～到深潭里。Several mountain streams pour into the pool. ② throw (energy,

etc.) into: 把全部心血～到工作中去 throw all one's energy into one's work

卿 qīng ① a minister or a high official in ancient times ② an emperor's form of address for a minister ③ a term of endearment formerly used between husband and wife or among close friends

清* qīng ① unmixed; clear: ～汤 clear soup/ ～水 clear water ② distinct; clarified: 分～ make a clear distinction/ 说不～ hard to explain/ 数不～ countless/ 问～底细 make sure of every detail; get to the bottom of the matter ③ quiet: ～静 quiet ④ completely; thoroughly: 把帐还～ pay up what one owes ⑤ settle; clear up; clean up: 帐～了吗? Has the account been settled (或 cleared up)?/ ～政治、～思想、～组织、～经济 clean things up in the fields of politics, ideology, organization and economy ⑥ count: ～一～行李的件数 count the pieces of luggage and see how many there are

【清白】qīngbái pure; clean; stainless: 历史～ have a clean personal record/ ～无辜 innocent

【清茶】qīngchá ① green tea ② tea served without refreshments

【清偿】qīngcháng pay off; clear off: ～债务 pay off (或 clear off) debts

【清澈】qīngchè limpid; clear: ～的池塘 a limpid pool/ 湖水～见底。The lake water is so clear that you can see to the bottom.

【清晨】qīngchén early morning

【清除】qīngchú clear away; eliminate; get rid of: ～垃圾 clear away the rubbish/ ～障碍 remove obstacles

【清楚】qīngchu ① clear; distinct: 字迹～ written in a clear hand/ 发音～ a clear pronunciation/ 头脑～ a clear head/ 他的话说得不～。He didn't speak clearly. 或 What he said was ambiguous./ 把工作交代～ explain one's job clearly on handing it over/ 大是大非问题要彻底弄～。Major issues of principle must be thoroughly thrashed out. ② be clear about; understand: 这个问题你～不～? Do you understand this question or not?

【清脆】qīngcuì clear and melodious: ～的歌声 clear and melodious singing

【清单】qīngdān detailed list; detailed account: 货物～ a detailed list of goods; inventory

【清淡】qīngdàn ① light; weak; delicate: ～的绿茶 weak green tea/ ～的花香 the delicate fragrance of flowers ② not greasy or strongly flavoured; light: ～的食物 light food ③ dull; slack: 生意～。Business is slack.

【清道夫】qīngdàofū 〈旧〉scavenger; street cleaner; street sweeper

【清点】qīngdiǎn check; make an inventory; sort and count: ～物资 make an inventory of equipment and materials/ ～货物 take stock/ ～战利品 check and sort out spoils of war

【清风】qīngfēng cool breeze; refreshing breeze: ～徐来。A cool breeze blows gently.

【清高】qīnggāo aloof from politics and material pūrsuits: 自鸣～ profess to be above politics and worldly considerations

【清官】qīngguān 〈旧〉honest and upright official: ～难断家务事。Even an upright official finds it hard to settle a family quarrel.

【清规戒律】qīngguī jièlù ① regulations, taboos and commandments for Buddhists or Taoists ② restrictions and fetters: 过多的评头品足, 数不尽的～ endless carping and countless taboos

【清寒】qīnghán ① poor; in straitened circumstances: 家境～ come of an impoverished (或 poor) family ② cold and clear: 月色～ clear, cold moonlight

【清剿】qīngjiǎo clean up; suppress; eliminate: ～土匪 clean up bandits; suppress bandits

【清洁】qīngjié clean: 整齐～ clean and tidy/ 人人要注意卫生。Everybody should pay attention to sanitation and hygiene.

【清净】qīngjìng peace and quiet: 怕麻烦,图～ fear trouble

and seek peace and quiet

【清静】qīngjìng　quiet: 我们找个～的地方谈谈。Let's find a quiet place to chat.

【清蜡】qīnglà 〈石油〉paraffin removal

【清朗】qīnglǎng ① cool and bright: ～的天气 clear and bright weather ② clear and resounding

【清冷】qīnglěng ① chilly: 一个～的秋夜 a chilly autumn night ② deserted; desolate: 夜已深了，街上十分～。It was late at night and the streets were quite deserted.

【清理】qīnglǐ　put in order; check up; clear; sort out: 把房间～～ put the room in order; clean up the room/ ～物资 check up on equipment and materials/ ～债务 clear up debts/ ～仓库 take stock; make an inventory of warehouse stocks/ ～档案 put the archives in order; sort out documents

【清廉】qīnglián　honest and upright; free from corruption

【清凉】qīngliáng　cool and refreshing: ～饮料 cold drink; cooler

【清明】qīngmíng ① (Qīngmíng) Pure Brightness (5th solar term) ② clear and bright: 月色～ clear and bright moonlight ③ sober and calm: 神志～ be in full possession of one's faculties

【清贫】qīngpín (usu. of scholars in old days) be poor: 家境～ be a person of scanty means

【清瘦】qīngshòu 〈婉〉thin; lean; spare: 你病后略见～。You look rather thin after your illness.

【清爽】qīngshuǎng ① fresh and cool: 晚风吹来，十分～。The evening breeze is cooling and refreshing. ② relieved; relaxed: 事情解决了，我心里也～了。Now that the matter is settled, I feel relieved.

【清算】qīngsuàn ① clear (accounts); square ② settle accounts; expose and criticize

【清谈】qīngtán　idle talk; empty talk: ～不能解决问题。Idle talk solves no problems.

【清汤】qīngtāng　clear soup; light soup

【清晰】qīngxī　distinct; clear: 她发音～。Her pronunciation is clear./ 远山的轮廓～可见。The outlines of the distant hills are clearly discernible.

【清洗】qīngxǐ ① rinse; wash; clean: ～炊具 clean cooking utensils ② purge; comb out

【清闲】qīngxián　at leisure; idle: 他过不惯～的退休生活。He finds it difficult to get used to the idle life of retirement.

【清香】qīngxiāng　delicate fragrance; faint scent: 晨风吹来野花的～。The morning breeze carried with it the scent of wild flowers.

【清新】qīngxīn　pure and fresh; fresh: 雨后空气～。The air was pure and fresh after the rain./ 画报的版面～活泼。The layout of the pictorial is fresh and lively.

【清醒】qīngxǐng ① clear-headed; sober: 保持～的头脑 keep a clear (或 cool) head; keep sober-minded/ 我们对形势要有～的估计。We should make a sober estimate of the situation./ ② regain consciousness: 病人已经～过来。The patient has come to.

【清秀】qīngxiù　delicate and pretty: 面貌～ fine, delicate features/ 山水～ beautiful landscape

【清雅】qīngyǎ　elegant; refined: 风格～ in an elegant style

【清夜扪心】qīngyè mén xīn　examine one's conscience in the stillness of night

【清一色】qīngyísè ① all of one suit (in playing mahjong); flush ② all of the same colour; uniform; homogeneous: 运动员一色穿着红色运动服。The players were all dressed alike in red sports suits.

【清幽】qīngyōu (of a landscape) quiet and beautiful

【清早】qīngzǎo 〈口〉early in the morning; early morning

【清蒸】qīngzhēng　steamed in clear soup (usu. without soy sauce): ～鱼 steamed fish

蜻*　qīng

【蜻蜓】qīngtíng　dragonfly

【蜻蜓点水】qīngtíng diǎn shuǐ　like a dragonfly skimming the surface of the water —touch on sth. without going into it deeply: 做调查工作不能～，要深入实际。To make an investigation, one should go into matters deeply, not just scratch the surface.

qíng

情*　qíng ① feeling; affection; sentiment: 热～ enthusiasm/ 温～ tender sentiments ② love; passion: 谈～说爱 be courting; talk love/ ～欲 sexual passion ③ favour; kindness: 求～ ask for a favour; plead with sb. ④ situation; circumstances; condition: 军～ military situation/ 病～ patient's condition

【情报】qíngbào　intelligence; information: 科技～ scientific and technological information/ 搜集～ collect intelligence/ 刺探～ pry for information
◇ ～机关 intelligence agency/ ～人员 intelligence personnel; intelligence agent/ ～系统 intelligence channel

【情不自禁】qíng bù zì jìn　cannot refrain from; cannot help (doing sth.); be seized with a sudden impulse to: ～地流下泪来 cannot refrain from tears/ ～地笑起来 can't help laughing

【情操】qíngcāo　sentiment

【情敌】qíngdí　rival in love

【情调】qíngdiào　sentiment; emotional appeal

【情窦初开】qíngdòu chū kāi (of a young girl) first awakening (或 dawning) of love

【情分】qíngfèn　mutual affection: 朋友～ friendship/ 兄弟～ fraternity; brotherhood

【情夫】qíngfū　lover

【情妇】qíngfù　mistress

【情感】qínggǎn　emotion; feeling

【情歌】qínggē　love song

【情话】qínghuà　lovers' prattle

【情急智生】qíngjí zhì shēng　hit on a good idea in a moment of desperation

【情节】qíngjié ① plot: 这个剧本～很复杂。The play has a very complicated plot./ ～紧凑 a tightknit plot ② circumstances: 根据～轻重，分别予以处理。Each will be dealt with according to the seriousness of his case.

【情景】qíngjǐng　scene; sight; circumstances: 兴奋热烈的～ an exhilarating scene/ 感人的～ a moving sight

【情境】qíngjìng　circumstances; situation

【情况】qíngkuàng ① circumstances; situation; condition; state of affairs: 在这种～下 under these circumstances; such being the case/ 根据具体～ in accordance with specific conditions/ 在许多～下 in many cases/ 这种～必须改变。This state of affairs must change./ 现在～不同了。Now things are different./ 他们的～怎么样？ How do matters stand with them?/ 那得看～而定。That depends. 或 It all depends.

【情理】qínglǐ　reason; sense: 合乎～ be reasonable; stand to reason/ 不近～ unreasonable; irrational/ ～难容 incompatible with the accepted code of human conduct

【情侣】qínglǚ　sweethearts; lovers

【情面】qíngmian　feelings; sensibilities: 留～ spare sb.'s feelings/ 对以前的错误一定要揭发，不讲～。The mistakes of the past must be exposed without sparing anyone's sensibilities.

【情趣】qíngqù ① temperament and interest: 他们二人～相投。The two of them are temperamentally compatible (或 congenial). ② interest; appeal: 这首诗写得很有～。This poem is very charming.

【情人】qíngrén　sweetheart: ～眼里出西施。In the eye of the lover, his beloved is a beauty. 或 Beauty is in the eye of the beholder.

【情势】qíngshì　situation; circumstances; trend of events: ～危急。The situation is critical./ 对～作出估计 size up the situation

【情书】qíngshū　love letter

【情随事迁】qíng suí shì qiān　people's feelings change with the circumstances

【情态】 qíngtài spirit; mood: 生动地描绘了儿童的～ depict children's spirit vividly

【情同手足】 qíng tóng shǒuzú like brothers; with brotherly love for each other: 两国人民～。 Our two peoples are bound together by ties of fraternal friendship.

【情投意合】 qíngtóu-yìhé find each other congenial; hit it off perfectly

【情形】 qíngxing circumstances; situation; condition; state of affairs: 两地～大不相同。 Conditions in the two places differ greatly./ 大家看了这种～,非常气愤。 People felt indignant at this state of affairs./ 这是一方面的～。 This is one side of the picture.

【情绪】 qíngxù ① morale; feeling; mood; sentiments: ～高涨。Morale is high./ 防止急躁～ guard against rashness/ ～不高 be in low spirits ② depression; moodiness: 有点儿～ rather sulky/ 闹～ be in a fit of depression; be in low spirits; have a fit of the sulks

【情义】 qíngyì ties of friendship, comradeship, etc.

【情谊】 qíngyì friendly feelings; friendly sentiments

【情意】 qíngyì tender regards; affection; goodwill: 深厚的～ deep affection

【情由】 qíngyóu the hows and whys: 不问～ without asking about the circumstances or causes

【情有可原】 qíng yǒu kě yuán excusable; pardonable

【情欲】 qíngyù sexual passion; lust

【情愿】 qíngyuàn ① be willing to: 两相～ by mutual consent; both parties being willing ② would rather; prefer: 她～粉身碎骨,也不在敌人面前屈服。 She would rather be cut to pieces than yield to the enemy.

晴* qíng fine; clear: 天转～了。 It's clearing up.

【晴和】 qínghé warm and fine: 天气～。 It's a fine, warm day.

【晴空】 qíngkōng clear sky; cloudless sky: ～万里 a clear and boundless sky

【晴朗】 qínglǎng fine; sunny: 天气～。 It's a sunny day.

【晴天】 qíngtiān fine day; sunny day

【晴天霹雳】 qíngtiān pīlì a bolt from the blue

【晴雨表】 qíngyǔbiǎo weatherglass; barometer

擎 qíng prop up; hold up; lift up: 众～易举, When there are many people it's easy to lift a load. 或 Many hands make light work.

qǐng

顷 qǐng ① qing, a unit of area (＝6.6667 hectares): 碧波万～ a boundless expanse of blue water ② 〈书〉just; just now: ～接来信。 I have just received your letter. ③ 〈书〉a little while: 少～ after a while

【顷刻】 qǐngkè in a moment; in an instant; instantly: ～之间 in a twinkling; in no time/ ～瓦解 collapse instantly

请* qǐng ① request; ask: ～他进来。 Ask him in./ ～你多加指导。 It is hoped you will give us guidance./ ～人来修机器 get someone to repair the machine; get the machine repaired ② invite; engage: ～医生 send for a doctor/ ～总工程师来讲课 invite the chief engineer to give a lecture ③ 〈敬〉please: ～坐。 Won't you sit down? 或 Please be seated./ ～安静。 Be quiet, please./ ～速回信。 Please reply as soon as possible.

【请安】 qǐng'ān pay respects to sb.; wish sb. good health

【请便】 qǐngbiàn do as you wish; please yourself: 你要是想现在去,那就～吧。 Well, if you want to leave now, go ahead.

【请功】 qǐnggōng ask the higher level to record sb.'s meritorious deeds

【请假】 qǐngjià ask for leave: 请三天假 ask for three days' leave/ 她病假回家了。 She's gone home on sick leave. ◇ ～条 written request for leave (of absence)

【请柬】 qǐngjiǎn 〈书〉invitation card

【请见】 qǐngjiàn 〈书〉request an audience; ask for an interview

【请教】 qǐngjiào ask for advice; consult: 我们想～你几个问题。 We wish to consult you on a few questions./ 向老工人～ consult a veteran worker

【请君入瓮】 qǐng jūn rù wèng kindly step into the vat — try what you have devised against others

【请客】 qǐngkè stand treat; invite sb. to dinner; entertain guests; give a dinner party

【请命】 qǐngmìng plead on sb.'s behalf

【请求】 qǐngqiú ask; request: 宽恕 ask for forgiveness

【请示】 qǐngshì ask for(或 request) instructions: 事前～,事后报告 ask for instructions beforehand and submit reports afterwards

【请帖】 qǐngtiě invitation card; invitation: 发～ send out invitations

【请问】 qǐngwèn ① 〈敬〉[用于请对方回答问题]: excuse me; please: ～,到火车站怎么走? Excuse me, but could you tell me how to get to the station? ② we should like to ask; it may be asked; one may ask

【请勿】 qǐngwù please don't: 本室书籍～携出室外。 Please don't take the books out of this room./ ～吸烟。 No smoking./ ～入内。 No admittance./ ～践踏草地。 Keep off the lawn.

【请降】 qǐngxiáng beg to surrender

【请愿】 qǐngyuàn present a petition; petition ◇ ～书 petition

【请罪】 qǐngzuì admit one's error and ask for punishment; apologize

qìng

庆* qìng ① celebrate; congratulate: ～丰收 celebrate a bumper harvest ② occasion for celebration: 国～ National Day

【庆典】 qìngdiǎn celebration; a ceremony to celebrate: 盛大～ grand celebrations

【庆贺】 qìnghè congratulate; celebrate

【庆幸】 qìngxìng rejoice: 值得～的事 a matter for rejoicing/

【庆祝】 qìngzhù celebrate: ～国庆 celebrate National Day ◇ ～大会 celebration meeting

亲 qìng 另见 qīn

【亲家】 qìngjia ① parents of one's daughter-in-law or son-in-law ② relatives by marriage

磬 qìng 〈书〉use up; exhaust: 告～ be all used up; run out/ ～其所有 empty one's purse; offer all one has

【磬尽】 qìngjìn 〈书〉with nothing left; all used up

【磬竹难书】 qìng zhú nán shū (of crimes, etc.) too numerous to record: 这个恶霸罪行累累,～。 This local despot's crimes were too numerous to mention.

qióng

穷* qióng ① poor; poverty-stricken: ～山沟变成了米粮川。 The once poor mountain village has become a granary. ② limit; end: 无～无尽 endless; inexhaustible/ 技～ exhaust one's whole bag of tricks; come to the end of one's rope ③ thoroughly: ～究 make a thorough (或 exhaustive) inquiry ④ extremely: ～奢极侈 extremely extravagant and luxurious

【穷兵黩武】 qióngbīng-dúwǔ use all one's armed might to indulge in wars of aggression; wantonly engage in military aggression

【穷光蛋】 qióngguāngdàn 〈口〉pauper; poor wretch

【穷极无聊】 qióngjí wúliáo ① be utterly bored ② absolutely senseless; disgusting

【穷尽】 qióngjìn limit; end

【穷苦】 qióngkǔ poverty-stricken; impoverished

【穷困】 qióngkùn poverty-stricken; destitute; in straitened circumstances

【穷年累月】 qióngnián-lěiyuè for years on end; year after year

【穷人】 qióngrén poor people; the poor

【穷日子】 qióngrìzi days of poverty; straitened circumstances: 我们要把富日子当～过。We're well off now, but we should still live as if we were poor.

【穷奢极欲】 qióngshē-jíyù (indulge in) luxury and extravagance; (live a life of) wanton extravagance: 过着～的生活 wallow in luxury

【穷酸】 qióngsuān (of a scholar) poor and pedantic

【穷途末路】 qióngtú-mòlù cul-de-sac; dead end

【穷乡僻壤】 qióngxiāng-pìrǎng a remote, backward place

【穷凶极恶】 qióngxiōng-jí'è extremely vicious; utterly evil; atrocious; diabolical: ～的敌人 most vicious enemy/ 一副～的样子 with the look of a fiendish brute

【穷则思变】 qióng zé sī biàn poverty gives rise to a desire for change

【穷追】 qióngzhuī go in hot pursuit: ～猛打 vigorously pursue and fiercely maul

穹 qióng 〈书〉① vault; dome ② the sky

【穹苍】 qióngcāng 〈书〉 the vault of heaven; the firmament; the sky; the heavens

【穹形】 qióngxíng vaulted; arched: ～的屋顶 a vaulted roof

琼 qióng 〈书〉 fine jade: ～楼玉字 a richly decorated jade palace; a magnificent building/ ～阁 a jewelled palace

【琼脂】 qióngzhī agar-agar; agar

qiū

丘* qiū ① mound; hillock: 荒～ a barren hillock/ 沙～ a sand dune ② grave: 坟～ grave

【丘八】 qiūbā 〈旧〉 (a jocular term for) soldier

【丘陵】 qiūlíng hills: ～起伏 a chain of undulating hills ◇ ～地带 hilly country; hilly land

邱 Qiū a surname

秋* qiū ① autumn: 深～ late autumn/ ～风 autumn wind ② harvest time: 麦～ time for the wheat harvest ③ year: 千～万代 for thousands of years / 一日不见，如隔三～。One day apart seems like three years — miss sb. very much. ④〔多指不好的〕 a period of time: 多事之～ an eventful period; troubled times

【秋波】 qiūbō bright eyes of a beautiful woman: 送～ (of a woman) make eyes; ogle; cast amorous glances

【秋毫】 qiūháo autumn hair; newly-grown down; sth. so small as to be almost indiscernible

【秋毫无犯】 qiūháo wú fàn (of highly disciplined troops) not commit the slightest offence against the civilians; not encroach on the interests of the people to the slightest degree

【秋季】 qiūjì autumn ◇ ～作物 autumn crops

【秋千】 qiūqiān swing: 打～ have a swing

【秋色】 qiūsè autumn scenery: ～宜人 charming autumn scenery

【秋水】 qiūshuǐ autumn waters — limpid eyes (of a woman): 望穿～ gaze anxiously till one's eyes are worn out; eagerly look forward (to seeing a dear one)

【秋天】 qiūtiān autumn

蚯* qiū

【蚯蚓】 qiūyǐn earthworm

qiú

仇 Qiú a surname
另见 chóu

囚 qiú ① imprison: 被～ be thrown into prison ② prisoner; convict: 死～ a convict sentenced to death

【囚车】 qiúchē .prison van; prisoners' van

【囚犯】 qiúfàn prisoner; convict

【囚禁】 qiújìn imprison; put in jail; keep in captivity

【囚牢】 qiúláo prison; jail

【囚笼】 qiúlóng prisoner's cage

【囚室】 qiúshì prison cell

【囚首垢面】 qiúshǒu-gòumiàn with unkempt hair and dirty face

【囚徒】 qiútú convict; prisoner

求* qiú ① beg; request; entreat; beseech: ～你帮忙，行吗？May I ask you a favour?/ 有～于人 have to look to others for help ② strive for; seek; try: ～进步 strive for further progress/ ～得一致 try to achieve a consensus ③ demand: 供不应～。Supply falls short of demand.

【求爱】 qiú'ài pay court to; woo

【求和】 qiúhé sue for peace

【求婚】 qiúhūn make an offer of marriage; propose

【求见】 qiújiàn ask to see; request an interview; beg for an audience

【求教】 qiújiào ask for advice: 登门～ call on sb. for counsel; request advice

【求救】 qiújiù ask sb. to come to the rescue; cry for help: 发出～的信号 signal an SOS; send an SOS

【求乞】 qiúqǐ beg: 沿门～ go begging from door to door

【求亲】 qiúqīn seek a marriage alliance

【求情】 qiúqíng plead; intercede; ask for a favour; beg for leniency: 向他～ plead with him/ 为某人～ intercede for sb.; beg (for mercy) on sb.'s behalf

【求全】 qiúquán ① demand perfection: 不要～责备。We shouldn't demand perfection. 或 Don't nitpick. ② try to round sth. off: 委曲～ make concessions to achieve one's purpose

【求饶】 qiúráo beg for mercy; ask for pardon

【求人】 qiúrén ask for help

【求胜】 qiúshèng strive for victory: ～心切 be anxious to gain victory

【求实精神】 qiúshí jīngshén matter-of-fact attitude; realistic approach

【求降】 qiúxiáng beg to surrender; hang out (或 hoist) the white flag

【求学】 qiúxué ① go to school; attend school ② pursue one's studies; seek knowledge

【求援】 qiúyuán ask for help; request reinforcements

【求之不得】 qiú zhī bù dé all that one could wish for; most welcome: 这对他真是～的事情。This is just what he wants./ 这是～的好机会。This is a most welcome opportunity./ 给王师傅当徒弟，他是～。He was only too glad to be an apprentice to Master Worker Wang.

【求知】 qiúzhī seek knowledge ◇ ～欲 thirst (或 craving) for knowledge

【求助】 qiúzhù turn to sb. for help; seek help: 他理屈词穷，只好～于诡辩。As he had a weak case and could not defend himself, he had to resort to sophistry.

泅 qiú swim

【泅渡】 qiúdù swim across: 武装～ swim across with one's weapons; swim across fully armed

【泅水】 qiúshuǐ swim

酋 qiú ① chief of a tribe ② chieftain: 敌～ enemy chieftain/ 匪～ bandit chief

【酋长】 qiúzhǎng ① chief of a tribe ② sheik(h); emir

球* qiú ① sphere; globe ② ball: 传～ pass the ball/ 网～ tennis ③ the globe; the earth: 全～战略 global strategy/ 东半～ the Eastern Hemisphere ④ anything shaped like a ball: 雪～ snowball

【球场】 qiúchǎng a ground where ball games are played; (volleyball, basketball, tennis, badminton, etc.) court; (football, baseball, softball, etc.) field

【球队】 qiúduì (ball game) team

球类运动

网球

台球

垒球（棒球）

篮球

足球

排球

羽球

乒乓

【球类运动】qiúlèi yùndòng ball games
【球门】qiúmén 〈体〉goal ◇ ～柱 goalpost
【球迷】qiúmí (ball game) fan: 乒乓～ ping-pong fan
【球拍】qiúpāi ①(tennis, badminton, etc.) racket ②(ping-pong) bat
【球赛】qiúsài ball game; match
【球坛】qiútán the ball-playing world; ball-playing circles; ball-players: ～盛会 a grand gathering of (table tennis, etc.) players/ ～新手 a new player; a newcomer to the tournament
【球鞋】qiúxié gym shoes; tennis shoes; sneakers
【球形】qiúxíng spherical; globular; round
【球艺】qiúyì skills in playing a ball game; ball game skills

遒 qiú 〈书〉powerful; forceful
【遒劲】qiújìng 〈书〉powerful; vigorous: 笔力～ vigorous strokes in calligraphy/ 苍老～的古松 a sturdy old pine tree

裘 qiú 〈书〉fur coat: 狐～ a fox fur coat

qū

区* qū ①area; district; region: 山～ mountainous district/ 林～ forest/ 商业～ business section (of a city)/ 住宅～ residential quarters/ 风景～ scenic spot ②an administrative division: 自治～ autonomous region ③distinguish; classify; subdivide
另见 Ōu
【区别】qūbié ①distinguish; differentiate; make a distinction between: 把两者～开来 differentiate one from the other/ ～对待 deal with each case on its merits; deal with different things or people in different ways/ ～好坏 distinguish between good and bad ②difference: 这两个词在意义上没有～。There is no difference in meaning between the two words.
【区分】qūfēn differentiate; distinguish: 严格～两类不同性质的矛盾 strictly distinguish between the two different types of contradictions/～两个历史时代 mark off two historical epochs
【区划】qūhuà division into districts: 行政～ administrative divisions
【区区】qūqū trivial; trifling: ～小事,何足挂齿。Such a trifling thing is hardly worth mentioning.
【区域】qūyù region; area; district: ～间合作 inter-regional cooperation ◇ ～会议 regional conference; local conference
【区域性】qūyùxìng regional
◇ ～公约 regional convention/ ～同盟 regional alliance/ ～问题 a matter of regional significance/ ～战争 regional war

曲* qū ①bent; crooked: 弯腰～背 with one's back bent/ ～径通幽 a winding path leading to a secluded spot ②bend (of a river, etc.) ③wrong; unjustifiable: 是非～直 the rights and wrongs of a matter
另见 qǔ
【曲解】qūjiě (deliberately) misinterpret; twist: 这话意思很明确,不可能～。These remarks are so clear that there can be no room for misinterpretation./ 你～了他的意思。You've misrepresented his meaning.
【曲线】qūxiàn 〈数〉curve
◇ ～球〈棒、垒球〉curve ball/ ～图 diagram (of curves)/
【曲意逢迎】qūyì féngyíng go out of one's way to curry favour
【曲折】qūzhé ①tortuous; winding: 河道～。The river has a winding course / 前途是光明的,道路是～的。The road is tortuous, but the prospects are bright. ②complications: 这件事情里面还有不少～。There are many complications in this matter.
【曲直】qū-zhí right and wrong: ～不分 not distinguish between right and wrong

岖 qū 见"崎岖" qíqū

驱 qū ①drive (a horse, car, etc.): ～车前往 drive (in a vehicle) to a place ②expel; disperse: ～云防雹 disperse clouds to prevent a hailstorm ③run quickly: 驰～ gallop/ 并驾齐～ run neck and neck
【驱策】qūcè ①drive; whip on ②order about: 任人～ allow oneself to be ordered about
【驱除】qūchú drive out; get rid of
【驱遣】qūqiǎn ①〈书〉drive away; banish; expel ②order about; drive
【驱散】qūsàn disperse; dispel; break up: 阳光～了薄雾。The sun dispelled the mist.
【驱使】qūshǐ ①order about: 供～ be ordered about; be at sb.'s beck and call/ 奴隶主把奴隶当作牛马任意～。The slave owners drove their slaves as they drove their cattle. ②prompt; urge; spur on: 为好奇心所～ be prompted by curiosity
【驱逐】qūzhú drive out; expel; banish: ～侵略者 drive out the aggressors/ ～出境 deport; expel ◇ ～机 pursuit plane/ ～舰 destroyer

屈* qū ①bend; bow; crook: ～臂 crook one's arm ②subdue; submit: 宁死不～ would rather die than yield/ 不～不挠 indomitable; dauntless; unyielding ③wrong; injustice: 受～ be wronged/ 叫～ complain about an injustice/ ～死 be wronged and driven to death; be persecuted to death ④in the wrong: 理～ have a weak case
【屈从】qūcóng submit to; yield to
【屈打成招】qū dǎ chéng zhāo confess to false charges under torture
【屈服】qūfú surrender; yield; knuckle under: ～于外界的压力 yield to pressure from outside
【屈驾】qūjià 〈旧〉〈敬〉condescend (或 be kind enough) to make the journey: 明日请～来舍一叙。Would you be kind enough to come over to my place for a chat tomorrow?
【屈节】qūjié forfeit one's honour
【屈就】qūjiù 〈套〉condescend to take a post offered
【屈辱】qūrǔ humiliation; mortification
【屈膝】qūxī go down on one's knees; bend one's knees: ～投降 go down on one's knees in surrender; knuckle under
【屈心】qūxīn 〈口〉have a guilty conscience: 你做出这样的事~不~哪? Has your action never given you a twinge of conscience?/ 这种～的事我不干。I wouldn't do a mean thing like that.
【屈指】qūzhǐ count on one's fingers: ～已经八年啦。Come to think of it, eight years have already passed.
【屈指可数】qūzhǐ kě shǔ can be counted on one's fingers — very few

祛 qū dispel; remove; drive away: ～暑 drive away summer heat
【祛除】qūchú dispel; get rid of; drive out: ～疑虑 dispel one's misgivings/ ～邪魔 drive out (或 exorcize) evil spirits

躯 qū the human body: 血肉之～ mortal flesh and blood/ 为国捐～ lay down one's life for one's country
【躯壳】qūqiào the body (as opposed to the soul); outer form
【躯体】qūtǐ body

趋 qū ①hasten; hurry along: ～前 hasten forward/ 疾～而过 hurry past ②tend towards; tend to become: 大势所～ irresistible general trend/ 局势～于稳定。The situation is tending towards stability./ 他们的意见～于一致。They are reaching unanimity.
【趋奉】qūfèng toady to; fawn on
【趋附】qūfù ingratiate oneself with; curry favour with
【趋时】qūshí 〈书〉follow the fashion
【趋势】qūshì trend; tendency:他的病有进一步恶化的～。His condition is tending to deteriorate.
【趋向】qūxiàng ①tend to; incline to: 日益～好转 tend to improve with each passing day/ 这个工厂的生产管理制度逐步～完善。This factory is gradually perfecting its system of production management. ②trend; direction

【趋炎附势】 qūyán-fùshì curry favour with the powerful; play up to those in power

【趋之若鹜】 qū zhī ruò wù go after sth. like a flock of ducks; scramble for sth.

黢 qū black; dark: 黑~~ pitch-black; pitch-dark

【黢黑】 qūhēi pitch-black; pitch-dark

qú

劬 qú ① fatigued ② diligent; hardworking

【劬劳】 qúláo <书> fatigued; overworked

渠 qú canal; ditch; channel: 灌溉~ irrigation canal

【渠道】 qúdào ① irrigation ditch ② medium of communication; channel: 通过外交~ through diplomatic channels

癯 qú <书> thin; lean: 清~ thin

衢 qú <书> thoroughfare

qǔ

曲 qǔ ① qu, a type of verse for singing, which emerged in the Southern Song and Jin dynasties and became popular in the Yuan Dynasty ② song; tune; melody: 高歌一~ lustily sing a song/ 小~儿 ditty ③ music (of a song) 另见 qū

【曲调】 qǔdiào <乐> tune (of a song); melody

【曲高和寡】 qǔ gāo hè guǎ highbrow songs find few singers; too highbrow to be popular

【曲谱】 qǔpǔ ① music score of Chinese operas ② a collection of tunes of qu (曲) 参见"曲"①

【曲艺】 qǔyì quyi, folk art forms including ballad singing, story telling, comic dialogues, clapper talks, cross talks, etc.

【曲子】 qǔzi song; tune; melody

取 qǔ ① take; get; fetch: 她回去~行李去了。She's gone back to fetch her luggage./ 我来~自行车。I came to collect my bike./ 上银行~钱 go and draw some money from the bank/ ~之于民, 用之于民。What is taken from the people is used in the interests of the people. ② aim at; seek: ~乐 seek pleasure/ 自~灭亡 court destruction/ 信于人 win confidence ③ adopt; assume; choose: ~慎重态度 adopt a cautious attitude/ 给孩子~个名儿 choose a name for a child; give a name to a child/ 无不可~之处 not without something to recommend it/ 不足~ inadvisable; undesirable

【取材】 qǔcái draw materials: 就地~ make use of (或 draw on) local materials/ 这本小说~于炼钢工人的生活。This novel has drawn its material from the life of steel workers.

【取长补短】 qǔcháng-bǔduǎn learn from others' strong points to offset one's weaknesses

【取代】 qǔdài replace; substitute for; supersede; supplant

【取道】 qǔdào by way of; via: 代表团~巴黎回国。The delegation will come back by way of Paris.

【取得】 qǔdé gain; acquire; obtain: 通过实践~经验 gain experience through practice/ ~完全一致的意见 reach complete identity of views/ ~群众支持 enlist popular support/ ~圆满成功 be crowned with success; achieve complete success/ ~相当大的进展 make considerable headway

【取缔】 qǔdì outlaw; ban; suppress: ~投机倒把 ban speculation and profiteering

【取而代之】 qǔ ér dài zhī replace sb.; supersede sb.

【取法】 qǔfǎ take as one's model; follow the example of: ~乎上, 仅得乎中。Aim high or you'll fall below the average.

【取乐】 qǔlè seek pleasure; find amusement; amuse oneself; make merry: 饮酒~ drink and make merry

【取暖】 qǔnuǎn warm oneself (by a fire, etc.): 烤火~ warm oneself (或 keep warm) by the fire

【取巧】 qǔqiǎo resort to trickery to serve oneself: 投机~ resort to dubious shifts to further one's interests; be opportunistic

【取舍】 qǔshě accept or reject; make one's choice: 对技术资料进行分析后决定~ analyse the technical data and then decide which to use

【取胜】 qǔshèng win victory; score a success: 以多~ win victory through numerical superiority/ 侥幸~ gain a victory by sheer luck

【取消】 qǔxiāo cancel; call off; abolish: ~一次会议 cancel (或 call off) a meeting/ ~会员资格 deprive sb. of his membership/ ~决定 rescind a decision/ ~禁令 lift a ban

【取笑】 qǔxiào ridicule; make fun of; poke fun at

【取样】 qǔyàng sampling: 井壁~ <石油> wall sampling/ ~检查 take a sample to check

【取悦】 qǔyuè try to please; ingratiate oneself with sb.

【取之不尽, 用之不竭】 qǔ zhī bù jìn, yòng zhī bù jié inexhaustible

娶 qǔ marry (a woman); take to wife

【娶亲】 qǔqīn (of a man) get married

qù

去 qù ① go; leave: 谁~都一样。It makes no difference who goes./ 他~多久了? How long has he been away?/ 你~过巴黎没有? Have you ever been to Paris?/ 从曼谷~香港 leave Bangkok for Hongkong/ 给他~个电话。Give her a ring. 或 Call her up. ② remove; get rid of: ~皮 remove the peel or skin; peel/ ~掉官僚主义的工作作风 get rid of the bureaucratic style of work/ ~掉思想上的负担 get a load off one's mind ③ be apart from: 两地相~五十里。The two places are 50 li apart./ 今五十余年 more than fifty years ago ④ of last year: ~冬 last winter ⑤ [用在另一动词前表示要作某事]: 我们自己~想办法。We'll find a way out ourselves. ⑥ [用在动宾结构后表示去做某事] 他吃饭~了。He's gone to eat.

去 qu ① [用在动词后表示动作离开说话人所在地]: 上~ go up/ 进~ go in/ 把这个给他捎~ Take this and give it to him. ② [用在动词后表示动作的继续]: 信步走~ stroll along/ 让他说~。Let him talk. 或 Let him say what he likes.

【去处】 qùchù ① place to go; whereabouts: 有谁知道他的~? Who knows his whereabouts? ② place; site: 这是一个风景优美的~。This is a beautiful place.

【去粗取精】 qùcū-qǔjīng discard the dross and select the essential

【去垢剂】 qùgòujì <化> detergent

【去路】 qùlù the way along which one is going; outlet: 挡住敌人的~ block the enemy's way/ 给洪水找到~ find an outlet for the flood

【去年】 qùnián last year: ~十二月 last December/ ~此时 this time last year

【去声】 qùshēng <语> falling tone, one of the four tones in classical Chinese and the fourth tone in modern standard Chinese pronunciation

【去世】 qùshì (of grown-up people) die; pass away

【去伪存真】 qùwěi-cúnzhēn eliminate the false and retain the true

【去污粉】 qùwūfěn household cleanser; cleanser

【去向】 qùxiàng the direction in which sb. or sth. has gone: 不知~ be nowhere to be found

【去职】 qùzhí no longer hold the post

阒 qù quiet; still: ~无一人。All was quiet and not a soul was to be seen./ ~然无声 very quiet; absolutely still

趣 qù ① interest; delight: 有~ interesting; delightful; amusing ② interesting: ~事 an interesting episode ③ bent;

purport: 志~ aspirations and interests; bent/ 本书旨~ the purport of the book

【趣剧】 qùjù farce

【趣味】 qùwèi ① interest; delight: ~无穷 be of infinite interest; afford the greatest delight; be fascinating ② taste; liking; preference: 迎合低级~ cater to vulgar tastes

觑 qù ① look; gaze: 面面相~ gaze at each other in speechless despair; 偷偷地~了他一眼 steal a glance at him ② 〈口〉 narrow (one's eyes); squint: 他~着眼睛仔细地看一幅画。 He was studying a painting with narrowed eyes.

quān

悛 quān 〈书〉 repent; make amends: 怙恶不~ be steeped in evil and refuse to repent

圈* quān ① circle; ring: 画个~儿 draw a circle/ 包围~ ring of encirclement; encirclement/ 绕跑道跑两~ run around the track twice/ 这是他一千五百米赛跑的最后一~。 This is his last lap in the 1,500-metre race./ 我到外面转了一~。 I've been out for a walk./ 这话说得出~儿了。 That's really going too far. ② circle; group: 他不是~里人。 He doesn't belong to the inner circle. 或 He's not on the inside. ③ enclose; encircle: 用篱笆把菜园~起来 enclose the vegetable garden with a fence ④ mark with a circle: 把那个错字~了。 Mark the wrong word with a circle.

【圈套】 quāntao snare; trap: 落入~ fall into a trap; play into sb.'s hands

【圈子】 quānzi circle; ring: 围成一个~站着 stand in a circle/ 说话不要绕~。 Don't speak in a roundabout way. 或 Don't beat about the bush./ 走出家庭小~ come out of the narrow family circle/ 他的生活~很小。 He moves in a very small circle./ 搞小~不好。 A few banding together is no good.

quán

权* quán ① right: 选举~和被选举~ the right to vote and stand for election/ 在这个问题上没有发言~ not be entitled to speak on the matter; have no say in the matter ② power; authority: 当~ in power/ 越~ overstep one's authority/ 受~ be authorized (to do sth.) ③ advantageous position: 主动~ initiative/ 霸~ hegemony/ 制空~ mastery of the air ④ 〈书〉 counterpoise; weight (of a steelyard) ⑤ weigh: 权其轻重 weigh up one thing against another; weigh up the matter carefully ⑥ tentatively; for the time being: ~充 act temporarily as; serve as a stopgap for ⑦ expediency: 通~达变 adapt oneself to circumstances

【权变】 quánbiàn adaptability (或 flexibility) in tactics; tact

【权柄】 quánbǐng power; authority: 掌握~ be in power; be in the saddle

【权贵】 quánguì influential officials (in the old society); bigwigs

【权衡】 quánhéng weigh; balance: ~利弊 weigh the advantages and disadvantages; weigh the pros and cons

【权力】 quánlì power; authority: 国家~机关 organ of state power/ ~下放 delegate power to the lower levels/ 行使会议主席的~ exercise the functions of chairman of a conference; invoke the authority of chairman of a conference

【权利】 quánlì right: 劳动的~ the right to work/ 受教育的~ the right to education/ 政治~ political rights

【权谋】 quánmóu (political) tactics; trickery

【权能】 quánnéng powers and functions

【权且】 quánqiě for the time being; as a temporary measure: ~如此办理。 This is to be carried out as an interim measure.

【权势】 quánshì power and influence

【权术】 quánshù political trickery; shifts in politics: 玩弄~ play politics

【权威】 quánwēi ① authority; authoritativeness ② a person of authority; authority ◇ ~人士 authoritative person; authoritative sources

【权限】 quánxiàn limits of authority; jurisdiction; competence: 在法律规定的~内 within the limits of one's authority as prescribed by law/ 确定委员会的~ define the competence (或 terms of reference) of the committee

【权宜】 quányí expedient: ~之计 an expedient measure; makeshift (device)

【权益】 quányì rights and interests: 维护民族经济~ safeguard national economic rights and interests

全* quán ① complete: 不获~胜, 决不收兵。 We will never leave the field until complete victory is won./ 手稿已残缺不~。 The manuscript is no longer complete./ 人都来~了吗? Is everybody here? ② whole; entire; full; total: ~中国 the whole of China; all over China/ ~称 full name/ ~书共三卷。 The work is in three volumes. ③ entirely; completely: ~错了 completely wrong; all wrong/ ~怪我。 It's entirely my fault./ 我们一家~去了。 My whole family went. ④ make perfect or complete; keep intact: 两~其美 satisfy both sides

【全豹】 quánbào whole picture; overall situation: 未窥~ fail to see the whole picture; fail to grasp the overall situation 参见 "管中窥豹" guǎnzhōng kuī bào

【全部】 quánbù whole; complete; total; all: ~情况就这样。 That's all there is to it./ 公布这个月的~开支 make public the month's total expenditure/ 粮食~自给 be completely self-supporting in food grain

【全才】 quáncái a versatile person; all-rounder: 文武~ be versed in both civil and military affairs

【全场】 quánchǎng the whole audience; all those present: ~欢声雷动。 The audience broke out into thunderous cheers.

【全程】 quánchéng whole journey; whole course: 自行车比赛~一百二十公里。 The whole course of the bicycle race is 120 kilometres.

【全都】 quándōu all; without exception: 村里男女老少~出来欢迎贵客。 The whole village, men and women, old and young, turned out to welcome the distinguished visitors./ 去年栽的树~活了。 All the trees planted last year have survived.

【全份】 quánfèn complete set: ~表册 a complete set of lists and forms

【全副】 quánfù complete: ~武装 fully armed; in full battle array

【全国】 quánguó the whole nation (或 country); nationwide; countrywide; throughout the country: ~人民 the people of the whole country; the people throughout the country; the whole nation/ ~上下 the whole nation from the leadership to the masses/ ~人口普查 a nationwide census/ ~运动会 the national games/ ~冠军 national champion

【全国性】 quánguóxìng nationwide; countrywide; national: ~报纸 a national newspaper; a newspaper with a nationwide circulation

【全集】 quánjí complete works; collected works: 《鲁迅~》 The Complete Works of Lu Xun

【全家福】 quánjiāfú 〈方〉① a photograph of the whole family ② hotchpotch (as a dish)

【全景】 quánjǐng panorama; full view; whole scene: 西湖~ full view of the West Lake ◇ ~宽银幕电影 cinepanoramic/ ~摄影机 panoramic camera

【全局】 quánjú overall situation; situation as a whole: 影响~ affect the overall situation/ 胸有~ with the situation as a whole in mind

【全力】 quánlì with all one's strength; all-out; sparing no effort: ~支持 support with all one's strength; spare no effort to support; give all-out support/ 竭尽~ exert all one's strength; move heaven and earth; throw in one's whole might/ ~以赴 go all out; spare no effort

【全貌】 quánmào complete picture; full view: 弄清问题的~ try to get a complete picture of the problem/ 从这里可以看到大桥的~。 You can get a view of the whole bridge from here.

【全面】 quánmiàn overall; comprehensive; all-round: ~规

划 overall planning/ ～总结 comprehensive summing-up/ ～崩溃 total collapse; *débâcle*/ ～进攻 an all-out attack/ ～战争 a full-scale war

【全民】 quánmín the whole (或 entire) people; all the people

【全能】 quánnéng ＜体＞ all-round: ～运动员 all-round athlete; all-rounder/ ～冠军 all-round champion/ 获得女子～冠军 win the women's individual all-round title/ 五项～运动 pentathlon/ 十项～运动 decathlon

【全年】 quánnián annual; yearly: ～收入 annual income/ 平均温度 mean annual temperature/ ～雨量 yearly rainfall

【全盘】 quánpán overall; comprehensive; wholesale: ～考虑 give overall consideration to/ ～接受 total and uncritical acceptance/ ～否定 total repudiation

【全球】 quánqiú the whole world: ～战略 global strategy/ 在～范围内 on a global scale

【全权】 quánquán full powers; plenary powers: ～证书 full powers/ 特命～公使 envoy extraordinary and minister plenipotentiary/ 特命～大使 ambassador plenipotentiary and extraordinary/ ～代表 plenipotentiary

【全然】 quánrán completely; entirely: ～不了解情况 be completely ignorant of the situation/ ～不计后果 in utter disregard of the consequences/ ～不顾个人安危 give no thought to one's own safety

【全日制】 quánrìzhì full-time ◇ ～教育 full-time schooling/ ～学校 full-time school

【全身】 quánshēn the whole body; all over (the body): ～不适 general malaise/ ～发抖 shake all over/ ～湿透 be soaked to the skin/ ～是伤 be covered with cuts and bruises/ ～检查 a general physical checkup ◇ ～像 full-length picture

【全神贯注】 quánshén guànzhù be absorbed (或 engrossed) in; be preoccupied with: 她～地听着 She listened with rapt attention. 或 She was all ears.

【全盛】 quánshèng flourishing; in full bloom: ～时期 period of full bloom; prime; heyday

【全食】 quánshí ＜天＞ total eclipse ◇ ～带 path of total eclipse; belt (或 zone) of totality

【全数】 quánshù total number; whole amount: 我们已～付讫。 We have paid the whole amount.

【全套】 quántào complete set ◇ ～设备 a complete set of equipment

【全体】 quántǐ all; entire; whole: ～船员 the crew (of a ship); the ship's complement/ ～演员 the entire cast/ ～工作人员 the whole staff/ 开～会 meet in full session; hold a plenary session/ ～起立默哀 All rose to their feet in silent tribute./ ～起立, 长时间鼓掌。 There was a long standing ovation./ 内阁～辞职。 The cabinet resigned *en bloc*.

【全文】 quánwén full text: ～如下。 The full text follows./ ～发表 publish in full/ ～记录 verbatim record

【全线】 quánxiàn all fronts; the whole line; the entire length: 边界～ the entire length of the boundary/ ～出击 launch an attack on all fronts/ 敌人～崩溃。 The enemy was put to rout all along the line./ 这条铁路已～通车。 The whole railway line has been opened to traffic.

【全心全意】 quánxīn-quányì wholeheartedly; heart and soul: ～地为人民服务。 Serve the people wholeheartedly.

诠 quán

【诠释】 quánshì annotation; explanatory notes

【诠注】 quánzhù notes and commentary

泉* quán ① spring: 温～ hot spring/ 矿～ mineral spring/ 喷～ fountain ② an ancient term for coin: ～币 ancient coin

【泉水】 quánshuǐ spring water; spring

【泉源】 quányuán ① fountainhead; springhead; wellspring ② source: 智慧(力量)的～ source of wisdom (strength)

拳* quán ① fist: 挥～ shake one's fist ② ＜量＞: 打了一～ give a punch ③ boxing; pugilism: 练～ practise shadow boxing

【拳打脚踢】 quándǎ-jiǎotī cuff and kick; beat up

【拳击】 quánjī boxing; pugilism ◇ ～台 boxing ring/ ～运

动员 boxer; pugilist

【拳师】 quánshī boxing coach; pugilist

【拳头】 quántou fist

痊 quán recover from an illness

【痊愈】 quányù fully recover from an illness; be fully recovered: 她还没有～。 She's not recovered yet./ 希望你早日～。 I wish you a speedy recovery.

蜷 quán curl up; huddle up

【蜷伏】 quánfú curl up; huddle up; lie with the knees drawn up: 他喜欢～着睡觉。 He likes to sleep with his knees drawn up. 或 He likes to sleep curled up on his side.

【蜷曲】 quánqū curl; coil; twist: 一条蛇在草丛里～着。 A snake lay coiled in the grass./ 他把两腿～起来做了个前滚翻。 Drawing up his knees against his chest, he made a forward roll.

【蜷缩】 quánsuō roll up; huddle up; curl up: 刺猬一受到攻击就～成一团。 A hedgehog rolls itself into a ball when attacked.

鬈 quán curly; wavy: ～发 curly hair

【鬈曲】 quánqū ＜纺＞ crimp; crinkle; curl: ～羊毛 crimpy wool; crinkled wool

颧 quán cheekbone

【颧骨】 quángǔ cheekbone: ～突起 have prominent cheekbones

quǎn

犬 quǎn dog: 牧～ shepherd dog; sheep dog/ 猎～ hunting dog; hound/ 警～ police dog/ 鸡鸣～吠 the crowing of cocks and the barking of dogs — country sounds/ 丧家之～ a stray cur

【犬齿】 quǎnchǐ canine tooth

【犬马之劳】 quǎn-mǎ zhī láo serve like a dog or a horse: 效～ serve one's master faithfully; be at sb.'s beck and call

【犬牙】 quǎnyá ① canine tooth ② fang (of a dog)

【犬牙交错】 quǎnyá jiāocuò jigsaw-like; interlocking: 形成～的状态 form a jagged, interlocking pattern

绻 quǎn 见"缱绻" qiānquǎn

quàn

劝* quàn ① advise; urge; try to persuade: ～他戒烟 advise him to give up smoking/ ～他休息 urge him to take a rest/ 我～了他半天, 他就是不听。 I spent a long time trying to talk him round, but he just wouldn't listen. ② encourage: ～学 encourage learning

【劝导】 quàndǎo try to persuade; advise; induce: 耐心～ try patiently to talk sb. round

【劝告】 quàngào advise; urge; exhort: 医生～他注意休息。 The doctor advised him to have a good rest./ 她不顾我们的一再～。 She disregarded our repeated exhortations.

【劝架】 quànjià try to reconcile parties to a quarrel; try to stop people from fighting each other; mediate

【劝解】 quànjiě ① help sb. to get over his worries, etc.: 大家～了半天, 她才消气了。 It was some time before we succeeded in pacifying her. ② mediate; make peace between; bring people together: 他们吵架了, 你去～一下。 They've had a quarrel. You try and patch things up between them.

【劝戒】 quànjiè admonish; expostulate

【劝酒】 quànjiǔ urge sb. to drink (at a banquet)

【劝勉】 quànmiǎn advise and encourage: 互相～ help and encourage each other

【劝说】 quànshuō persuade; advise

【劝慰】 quànwèi console; soothe

【劝降】 quànxiáng induce to capitulate

【劝诱】 quànyòu induce; prevail upon

【劝阻】 quànzǔ dissuade sb. from; advise sb. not to: 你最好~他别那样干。 You'd better dissuade him from doing that./ ~无效 try in vain to talk sb. out of doing sth.

券* quàn certificate; ticket: 入场~ admission ticket/ 公债~ government bond

quē

缺* quē ① be short of; lack: ~人 be short of hands/ ~粮户 grain-deficient household/ 庄稼~肥~水就长不好。 Lacking manure and water, crops won't grow well./ 这种原料较~。 This kind of material is rather scarce./ 这本书缺两页。 Two pages are missing from this book./ 这些条件一不可。 Not a single one of these conditions can be dispensed with. ② incomplete; imperfect: 残~不全 incomplete; fragmentary/ 完美无~ flawless; perfect; impeccable ③ be absent: 人都到齐了, 一个不~。 No one is absent. Everybody's here. ④ vacancy; opening: 空~ vacancy; opening/ 补~ fill a vacancy

【缺德】 quēdé mean; wicked; villainous: 做~事 do sth. mean; play a mean trick/ 他这样做可真~。 It's wicked of him to act like that.

【缺点】 quēdiǎn shortcoming; defect; weakness; drawback: 克服工作中的~ overcome shortcomings in one's work/ 这种药的主要~是败胃。 The chief drawback of this medicine is that it spoils your appetite.

【缺乏】 quēfá be short of; lack; be wanting in: ~劳动力 be short of labour power/ ~经验 lack experience/ ~战斗力 have poor fighting capacity/ 资源~ be deficient in resources/ ~证据 want of proof

【缺货】 quēhuò be in short supply; be out of stock

【缺课】 quēkè be absent from school; miss a class: 缺了三课 miss three lessons/ 给一个因病~的学生补习功课 help a pupil who has missed some classes on account of illness

【缺口】 quēkǒu breach; gap: 篱笆上有个~。 There is a gap in the fence.

【缺勤】 quēqín absence from duty (或 work) ◇ ~率 absence rate

【缺少】 quēshǎo lack; be short of: ~零件 lack spare parts/ ~人手 be short of hands; be shorthanded/ 不可~的条件 indispensable conditions

【缺席】 quēxí absent (from a meeting, etc.): 因事~ be absent through being otherwise engaged/ 他这学期从没~过。 He has never been absent from class this term. ◇ ~判决 〈法〉 judgment by default/ ~审判 〈法〉 trial by default

【缺陷】 quēxiàn defect; drawback; flaw; blemish: 生理~ physical defect/ 这个计划有些~。 The plan has some shortcomings.

【缺嘴】 quēzuǐ 〈方〉 harelip

阙 quē 〈书〉 ① fault; error ② 见 "缺" quē
另见 què

【阙如】 quērú 〈书〉 be wanting

【阙疑】 quēyí leave the question open

qué

瘸 qué 〈口〉 be lame; limp: 左腿~了 be lame in the left leg/ 一步一~ walk with a limp

【瘸腿】 quétuǐ lame: ~的人 a lame person

【瘸子】 quézi 〈口〉 a lame person; cripple

què

却* què ① step back: 退~ go back; retreat ② drive back; repulse: ~敌 repulse the enemy ③ decline; refuse: 推~ decline; refuse ④〈副〉〔表示转折〕 but; yet; however; while: 她有许多话要说, 一时~什么也说不出来。 She had a lot to say, but at the time she was unable to utter a word. ⑤〔用在某些动词后, 表示动作的完成〕: 冷~ cool off/ 了~一个心愿 fulfil a wish

【却步】 quèbù step back (in fear or disgust); hang back: 望而~ shrink back at the sight (of sth. dangerous or disgusting)

【却之不恭】 què zhī bù gōng it would be impolite to decline: ~, 受之有愧。 To decline would be disrespectful but to accept is embarrassing.

雀* què sparrow

【雀斑】 quèbān freckle

【雀跃】 quèyuè jump for joy: 欢呼~ shout and jump for joy

确* què ① true; reliable; authentic: ~有其事。 It's a fact. 或 It really happened./ ~证 ironclad proof ② firmly: ~信 firmly believe

【确保】 quèbǎo ensure; guarantee: 安全生产 ensure safety in production/ ~质量 guarantee quality/ ~适时播种。 Be sure to do the sowing in good time.

【确定】 quèdìng ① define; fix: ~会议宗旨 define the aims of the conference/ ~开会的日期和地点 determine (或 fix) the time and place for a meeting/ ~行军路线 decide the route of the march/ ~作战方案 decide on a battle plan/ ~任务 set the tasks/ ~地层的年代 ascertain the ages of the strata/ ~领海宽度 delimit the extent of territorial waters ② definite: ~的答复 a definite reply/ ~不移的结论 an incontestable conclusion

【确乎】 quèhū really; indeed: ~有效 really effective

【确立】 quèlì establish

【确切】 quèqiè definite; exact; precise: ~的日期 an exact date/ ~的解释 a clear and unambiguous explanation/ 下个~的定义 give a precise definition

【确认】 quèrèn affirm; confirm; acknowledge: 与会各国~下述原则。 The participating countries affirm the following principles.

【确实】 quèshí ① true; reliable: ~的消息 reliable information ② really; indeed: 这~是个很好的建议。 This is really a very good suggestion./ 他~来过。 Yes, he did come.

【确信】 quèxìn firmly believe; be convinced; be sure: 我们~正义的事业一定会胜利。 We firmly believe that a just cause is bound to triumph.

【确凿】 quèzuò conclusive; authentic; irrefutable: ~的证据 conclusive evidence; absolute proof/ ~的事实 irrefutable facts

阙 què ① watchtower on either side of a palace gate ② imperial palace: 宫~ imperial palace
另见 quē

鹊 què magpie

【鹊巢鸠占】 què cháo jiū zhàn the turtledove occupies the magpie's nest — one person seizes another person's place, land, etc.

榷 què discuss: 商~ discuss; deliberate over

qún

裙* qún skirt: 绸~ silk skirt/ 衬~ slip; petticoat/ 围~ apron

【裙带】 qúndài connected through one's female relatives: 通过~关系 with the help of one's female relatives; through petticoat influence

【裙子】 qúnzi skirt

群* qún ① crowd; group: 人~ crowd/ 成~结队 in crowds; in flocks; in groups/ 鱼~ shoals of fish/ 建筑~ a building complex; a cluster of buildings/ ~山环抱 surrounded by hills/ ~起而攻之 rally together to attack sb. or sth.; rise up in struggle against sb. or sth. ②〈量〉 group; herd; flock: 一~小孩 a group of children/ 一~人

a crowd of people/ 一～牛 a herd of cattle/ 一～羊 a flock of sheep/ 一～狼 a pack of wolves/ 一～蜜蜂 a swarm of bees

【群策群力】 qúncè-qúnlì pool the wisdom and efforts of everyone

【群岛】 qúndǎo archipelago

【群芳】 qúnfāng beautiful and fragrant flowers: ～竞艳 flowers vying with each other in beauty

【群居】 qúnjū living in groups; gregarious; social ◇ ～动物 social animal/ ～昆虫 social insect

【群龙无首】 qún lóng wú shǒu a host of dragons without a head — a group without a leader

【群英会】 qúnyīnghuì gathering of heroes; conference of outstanding workers

【群众】 qúnzhòng the masses

麇 qún 〈书〉 flock together

【麇集】 qúnjí 〈书〉 swarm; flock together

R

rán

然* rán ① right; correct: 大谬不~ entirely wrong; absurd/ 不以为~ object to; not approve ② so; like that: 知其~，不知其所以~ know the hows but not the whys/ 不尽~ not exactly so; not exactly the case ③ 〈书〉〈连〉 but; nevertheless; however: 此事虽小，~亦不可忽视。This is a minor point, but it must not be overlooked. ④〔副词或形容词词后缀〕: 忽~ suddenly; all of a sudden/ 显~ obviously/ 巍立 tower majestically

【然而】 rán'ér 〈连〉 yet; but; however: 试验失败了多次，~他们并不灰心。Time after time they failed in the experiment, but they did not lose heart.

【然后】 ránhòu 〈副〉 then; after that; afterwards: 贵宾们将在巴黎停留一天，~飞往伦敦。The distinguished guests will stay in Paris for one day and then fly to London./ 我们先研究一下，~再决定。We'll consider the problem carefully before coming to any decision.

【然则】 ránzé 〈书〉〈连〉 in that case; then: ~如之何而可? Then, what is to be done?

燃* rán burn; ignite; light: 易~物品 combustibles; inflammables/ ~起一堆篝火 light a bonfire

【燃放】 ránfàng set off (fireworks, etc.): ~爆竹 set off firecrackers

【燃料】 ránliào fuel

【燃眉之急】 rán méi zhī jí as pressing as a fire singeing one's eyebrows — a matter of extreme urgency; a pressing need

【燃烧】 ránshāo ① burn; kindle: 干柴容易~。Dry wood burns easily./ 怒火~ burning with rage

rǎn

冉 rǎn 〈书〉 ① slowly ② (Rǎn) a surname

【冉冉】 rǎnrǎn 〈书〉 slowly; gradually: 一轮红日~升起。A red sun slowly rose.

苒 rǎn 见 "荏苒" rěnrǎn

染* rǎn ① dye: 把一块布~成绿色 dye a piece of cloth green ② catch (a disease); acquire (a bad habit, etc.); soil; contaminate: ~上了痢疾 have caught dysentery/ 污~ pollution/ 一尘不~ not soiled by a speck of dust; spotless/ 出污泥而不~ emerge unstained from the filth

【染病】 rǎnbìng catch (或 contract) an illness; be infected with a disease

【染料】 rǎnliào dyestuff; dye: 活性~ reactive dye

【染色】 rǎnsè dyeing; colouring

【染指】 rǎnzhǐ take a share of sth. one is not entitled to; encroach on: 妄图~别国资源 attempt to encroach on the resources of other countries

rāng

嚷 rāng
另见 rǎng

【嚷嚷】 rāngrang 〈口〉 ① shout; yell; make an uproar: 谁在那儿~? Who is shouting there?/ 屋里一片乱~。The room was in an uproar. ② make widely known: 这件事, 你可别~。Don't breathe a word about this.

rǎng

壤 rǎng ① soil: 沃~ fertile soil; rich soil ② earth: 天

~之别 be as far removed as heaven from earth; be vastly different/ 有霄~之别。There is a world of difference. ③ area: 穷乡僻~ a remote, backward place/ 接~ have a common border; be adjacent to each other

攘 rǎng 〈书〉 ① reject; resist: ~外 resist foreign aggression ② seize; grab ③ push up one's sleeves

嚷 rǎng shout; yell; make an uproar: 孩子们在~些什么? What are the children shouting about?/ 别~了! Stop yelling. 或 Don't make such a noise.
另见 rāng

ràng

让* ràng ① give way; give ground; yield; give up: 各相~。Neither is willing to give ground./ 寸步不~ refuse to yield an inch; not budge an inch/ 见困难就上, 见荣誉就~ dash towards difficulties and retreat from honours/ 你该~着弟弟一点。You ought to humour your younger brother a little./ 请~一~。Please step aside. 或 Excuse me./ 幸亏我~得快, 要不早给那辆自行车撞倒了。Luckily I dodged in time, or I'd have been knocked down by the bike. ② invite; offer: ~茶 offer sb. tea/ 把客人~进里屋 invite guests to the inner room ③ let; allow; make: ~我想一想。Let me think it over./ 医生不~她起来。The doctor told her to stay in bed./ 他~我把这个消息转告你。He told me to pass the message on to you./ 老板~学徒一天干十四小时的活。The boss made the apprentices work fourteen hours a day./ 对不起, ~你久等了。Sorry to have kept you waiting. ④ let sb. have sth. at a fair price: 我们按原价把这辆大车~给你们队。We can let your production team have this cart at cost price. ⑤ 〈介〉〔在被动式里引进主动者〕: 行李~雨淋湿了。The crops were washed away by the flood./ 行李~雨淋湿了。The luggage got wet in the rain.

【让步】 ràngbù make a concession; give in; give way; yield: 准备作出某些必要的~ be prepared to make some necessary concessions/ 不向无理要求~ not yield to any unreasonable demand

【让开】 ràngkāi get out of the way; step aside; make way

【让路】 rànglù make way for sb. or sth.; give way; give sb. the right of way: 大家让让路。Please get out of the way, everybody.

【让球】 ràngqiú concede points: 教练员让了小李五个球。The coach conceded Xiao Li five points.

【让位】 ràngwèi ① resign sovereign authority; abdicate ② offer (或 give up) one's seat to sb. ③ yield to; give way to; change into: 经过大家的努力, 困难的局面终于~于顺利的局面。As a result of collective effort, the difficult situation changed into a favourable one.

【让座】 ràngzuò ① offer (或 give up) one's seat to sb.: 他给一位抱孩子的妇女~。He offered his bus seat to a woman carrying a baby. ② invite guests to be seated

ráo

饶 ráo ① rich; plentiful: ~有风趣 full of wit and humour ② have mercy on; let sb. off; forgive: 求~ beg for mercy/ 下回可不能轻~了你。We won't let you off so easily next time.

【饶命】 ráomìng spare sb.'s life

【饶舌】 ráoshé ① too talkative; garrulous ② say more than is proper; shoot off one's mouth

【饶恕】 ráoshù forgive; pardon

【饶沃】 ráowò (of soil) fertile; rich

娆 ráo 见"妖娆" yāoráo

rǎo

扰 rǎo ① harass; trouble: 纷～ tumult; turmoil ② 〈套〉trespass on sb.'s hospitality: 叨～,叨～。Thank you for your hospitality./ 我～了他一顿饭。He kindly entertained me to dinner.

【扰乱】 rǎoluàn harass; disturb; create confusion: ～治安 disturb public order/ ～市场 disrupt the market/ ～军心 undermine the morale of an army/ ～视线 interfere with sb.'s view/ 谨防敌人～我们的阵线 guard against the enemy creating confusion within our ranks

【扰攘】 rǎorǎng hustle and bustle; noisy confusion; tumult: 干戈～ in the tumult of a raging war

绕 rǎo 见"围绕" wéirǎo; "环绕" huánrǎo; "缠绕" chánrǎo; "缭绕" liáorǎo

另见 rào

rào

绕* rào ① wind; coil: ～线 wind thread/ 把铁丝～成圈 coil wire; wind wire into a coil ② move round; circle; revolve: 地球～着太阳转。The earth moves (或 revolves) round the sun./ 运动员一场一周。The athletes marched around the arena./ 飞机在机场上空～圈。The plane circled over the airfield. ③ make a detour; bypass; go round: 道路施工,车辆～行。Detour. Road under repair./ ～过暗礁 bypass hidden reefs; steer clear of submerged rocks/ 货轮～过好望角,驶入大西洋。The freighter rounded the Cape of Good Hope and sailed into the Atlantic.

另见 rǎo

【绕道】 ràodào make a detour; go by a roundabout route: 前面有个水库,我们得～过去。There's a reservoir ahead. We'll have to make a detour./ 你不要一遇困难就～走。Don't always try to skirt round difficulties.

【绕口令】 ràokǒulìng tongue twister

【绕圈子】 rào quānzi ① circle; go round and round ② take a circuitous route; make a detour

rě

惹 rě ① invite or ask for (sth. undesirable): ～麻烦 ask for trouble; invite trouble/ ～是非 provoke a dispute; stir up trouble ② offend; provoke; tease: 我～不起他。I cannot afford to offend him./ 我可没～他呀! I said nothing to provoke him. 或 I did nothing to provoke him./ 他这个人是不好～的。He's not a man to be trifled with. ③ attract; cause: ～人注意 attract attention/ ～人讨厌 make a nuisance of oneself/ 他的话把大家～得哈哈大笑。His words set everybody roaring with laughter.

【惹火烧身】 rě huǒ shāo shēn stir a fire only to burn oneself — court disaster; ask for trouble

【惹祸】 rěhuò court disaster; stir up trouble: 这都是我惹的祸。It was I who started all the trouble.

【惹气】 rěqì get angry: 不值得为这点小事～。It's senseless to get angry over such a trifle.

【惹事】 rěshì stir up trouble

【惹是生非】 rěshì-shēngfēi provoke a dispute; stir up trouble

rè

热* rè ① heat: 传～ conduct heat ② hot: ～水 hot water ③ heat up; warm up; warm: 把汤～一～ heat up the soup ④ fever; temperature: 发～ have a fever; run a fever/ 先给他退～再说。First bring down his temperature. ⑤ ardent; warmhearted: ～望 ardently wish; fervently hope/ ～心肠 warmheartedness; ardour/ 采取不冷不～的态度 be

neither cold nor warm (towards sb.); take a lukewarm attitude ⑥ craze; fad: 乒乓～ intense popular interest in table tennis; ping-pong craze ⑦ envious; eager: 眼～ feel envious at the sight of sth. ⑧ in great demand; popular: ～货 goods in great demand; goods which sell well

【热爱】 rè'ài ardently love; have deep love (或 affection) for: ～自己的工作 love one's work

【热潮】 rècháo great mass fervour; upsurge: 生产～ a great upsurge in production/ 掀起群众性体育锻炼的～ unfold a vigorous mass campaign for sports and physical training

【热忱】 rèchén zeal; warmheartedness; enthusiasm and devotion

【热诚】 rèchéng warm and sincere; cordial: ～欢迎 cordially welcome/ ～地希望 sincerely hope

【热带】 rèdài the torrid zone; the tropics

◇ ～草原 savanna/ ～风暴 tropical storm/ ～鱼 tropical fish/ ～植物 tropical plants/ ～作物 tropical crops

【热度】 rèdù ① degree of heat; heat ② fever; temperature: 你～降下去了吗? Has your temperature come down?

【热锅上的蚂蚁】 règuōshàngde mǎyǐ ants on a hot pan: 急得像～一样 as restless as ants on a hot pan

【热烘烘】 rèhōnghōng very warm: 炉火烧旺,屋里～的。With the stove burning cheerfully, it's very warm in the room

【热辣辣】 rèlàlà burning hot; scorching: 太阳晒得人～的。The sun feels scorching./ 他听了大家的批评,觉得脸上～的。After hearing everybody's criticism, he felt his cheeks burning.

【热浪】 rèlàng 〈气〉heat wave; hot wave

【热恋】 rèliàn be passionately in love; be head over heels in love

【热量】 rèliàng 〈物〉quantity of heat

【热烈】 rèliè warm; enthusiastic; ardent: ～的祝贺 warm congratulations/ ～欢送 give sb. a warm send-off/ 进行～的讨论 have a lively discussion

【热流】 rèliú ① 〈气〉thermal current ② warm current: 我感到一股～传遍全身。I felt a warm current coursing through my body.

【热门】 rèmén in great demand; popular: ～货 goods in great demand; goods which sell well/ 赶～ follow a craze

【热闹】 rènao ① lively; bustling with noise and excitement: ～的菜市场 a food market bustling with activity; a busy food market/ 晚会很～。It was a very lively evening party. ② liven up; have a jolly time: 你说个笑话让大伙儿～吧。Tell us a joke to liven things up./ 那天他们聚在一起～了一番。That day they got together and had a jolly time. ③ a scene of bustle and excitement; a thrilling sight: 看～ watch the excitement; watch the fun

【热能】 rènéng 〈物〉heat (或 thermal) energy

【热气】 rèqì steam; heat: 壶里开始冒～了。The kettle's just on the boil.

【热气腾腾】 rèqì téngténg ① steaming hot: ～的馒头 steaming hot buns ② seething with activity

【热切】 rèqiè fervent; earnest: ～的愿望 earnest wish; fervent hope/ ～希望各位提出宝贵意见。We earnestly hope that you will give us your valuable criticisms and suggestions.

【热情】 rèqíng ① enthusiasm; zeal; warmth: 一封～洋溢的感谢信 an ebullient letter of thanks ② warm; fervent; enthusiastic; warmhearted: ～接待 warmly receive; give sb. a warm reception/ ～支持这个倡议 fervently (或 enthusiastically) support this proposal/ 对旅客非常～ be very warm towards the passengers

【热水袋】 rèshuǐdài hot-water bottle (或 bag)

【热水瓶】 rèshuǐpíng 〈口〉thermos bottle (或 flask); thermos; vacuum bottle (或 flask)

【热腾腾】 rètēngtēng steaming hot: ～的汤面 steaming hot noodles in soup

【热天】 rètiān hot weather; hot season; hot days

【热望】 rèwàng fervently hope; ardently wish

【热心】 rèxīn enthusiastic; ardent; earnest; warmhearted: ～集体福利事业 be enthusiastic in promoting public welfare/ ～为顾客服务 warmheartedly serve the customers/ ～科学 eager to promote science/ ～传授技术 make earnest

efforts to pass on one's skill

【热心肠】 rèxīncháng 〈口〉warmheartedness

【热血】 rèxuè warm blood — righteous ardour: ～沸腾 burning with righteous indignation/ ～青年 ardent youth

【热中】 rèzhōng ① hanker after; crave: ～于个人名利 hanker after personal fame and gain ② be fond of; be keen on: ～于溜冰 be very fond of skating

rén

人* rén ① human being; man; person; people: 男～ man/ 女～ woman/ 黄种～ the yellow race; yellow/ 非洲～ African/ 外国～ foreigner; foreign national/ 四川～ a native of Sichuan; Sichuanese/ ～对自然界的认识 man's knowledge of nature/ 消灭～剥削～的制度 abolish the system of exploitation of man by man/ 一个高尚的～ a noble-minded person/ 表扬好～好事 praise good people and good deeds/ 团结得象一个～ be united as one/ 昨天有三个～来找你 Three people came to see you yesterday./ 他～在那儿, 心可想着别的事。 He was there all right, but his mind was elsewhere./ 你一个～行吗？ Can you manage on your own?/ 这个座位有～吗？ Is this seat occupied (或 taken)? ② adult; grown-up: 长大成～ become a grown-up ③ a person engaged in a particular activity: 工～ worker/ 军～ soldier/ 主～ host ④ other people: 助～为乐 take pleasure in helping people/ 别小看～！ Don't look down on people! ⑤ personality; character: 他～很好。 He's a very nice man./ 为～公正 upright in character ⑥ state of one's health; how one feels: 这几天我～不大舒服。 I haven't been feeling well for several days./ 送到医院, ～已经昏迷过去了。 When the patient was taken to hospital, he had already lost consciousness. ⑦ everybody; each; all: ～手一册。 Everyone has a copy./ ～所共知 be known to all (或 everybody) ⑧ manpower; hand: 我们这里正缺～。 We are shorthanded at the moment.

【人不为己，天诛地灭】 rén bù wèi jǐ, tiānzhū-dìmiè unless a man looks out for himself, Heaven and Earth will destroy him; everyone for himself and the devil take the hindmost

【人才】 réncái ① a person of ability; a talented person; talent; qualified personnel: 难得的～ a person of extraordinary ability/ 科技～ qualified scientists and technicians/ ～辈出 people of talent coming forth in large numbers/ ～济济 a galaxy of talent ②〈口〉handsome appearance: 一表～ a man of striking appearance

【人称】 rénchēng 〈语〉person: 第一～ the first person/ 不定～ indefinite person ②～代词 personal pronoun

【人道】 réndào ① humanity; human sympathy ② human; humane: 不～ inhuman ◇ ～主义 humanitarianism

【人地生疏】 rén-dì shēngshū be unfamiliar with the place and the people; be a complete stranger

【人浮于事】 rén fú yú shì have more hands than needed; be overstaffed

【人格】 réngé ① personality; character; moral quality: ～高尚 have a noble character; have moral integrity ② human dignity ◇ ～化 personification

【人工】 réngōng ① man-made; artificial: ～湖 man-made lake/ ～降雨 artificial rainfall ② manual work; work done by hand: 抽水机坏了, 只好用～车水。 We had to move water by a chain pump because the electric pump had broken down. ③ manpower; man-day: 修建这条渠道不需要很多～。 It won't take a lot of manpower to construct this irrigation canal./ 修这所房子用了多少～？ How many man-days were put in on repairing the house?

【人海】 rénhǎi a sea of faces; a huge crowd (of people)

【人和】 rénhé support of the people; unity and coordination within one's own ranks

【人家】 rénjiā ① household: 村子里有多少～？ How many households are there in the village? ② family: 勤俭～ an industrious and frugal family 或 fiancé's family: 她有了～了。 She is engaged to be married.

【人家】 rénjia ①〔指自己或某人以外的人〕: ～能做到的, 我们也能做到。 If other people can do it, so can we. 或 What

other people can do we can do, too./ ～都这么说。 That's what everybody says. ②〔指某个人或某些人〕: 把信给～送去。 Take the letter to him ③〔指说话者本人〕: ～等你半天了。 I've been waiting for you for quite a while./ 把～吓了一大跳。 You gave me quite a fright.

【人间】 rénjiān man's world; the world: ～地狱 a hell on earth/ ～奇迹 a miracle

【人杰】 rénjié an outstanding personality

【人口】 rénkǒu ① population: ～稠密的地区 densely populated area; thickly inhabited district/ ～众多(稀少) have a very large (a sparse) population ② number of people in a family: 他们家～不多。 There aren't many people in their family.

◇ ～结构 population structure/ ～密度 density of population/ ～普查 census/ ～统计 vital statistics/ ～增长 population growth

【人类】 rénlèi mankind; humanity: ～起源 the origin of mankind; the origin of the human species

【人力】 rénlì manpower; labour power: ～资源 human resources

【人力车】 rénlìchē ① a two-wheeled vehicle drawn by man ②〈旧〉rickshaw

【人伦】 rénlún human relations (according to feudal ethics)

【人马】 rénmǎ forces; troops: 全部～已安全渡江。 All the troops have crossed the river safely./ 大队～随后就到。 The main force will arrive soon.

【人们】 rénmen people; men; the public: 草原上的～ people of the grasslands

【人面兽心】 rénmiàn-shòuxīn have the face of a man but the heart of a beast — a beast in human shape

【人民】 rénmín the people

【人命】 rénmìng human life: ～案子 a case of homicide or manslaughter/ ～关天。 A case involving human life is to be treated with the utmost care.

【人怕出名猪怕壮】 rén pà chūmíng zhū pà zhuàng fame portends trouble for men just as fattening does for pigs

【人品】 rénpǐn ① moral standing; moral quality; character: ～很好 be a person of excellent character ②〈口〉looks; bearing

【人情】 rénqíng ① human feelings; human sympathy; sensibilities: 不近～ not amenable to reason; unreasonable ② human relationship: ～练达 experienced in the ways of the world/ ～之常 natural and normal ③ favour: 做个～ do sb. a favour ④ gift; present: 送～ send gifts; make a gift of sth. ◇ ～味 human touch; human interest

【人情世故】 rénqíng-shìgù worldly wisdom: 不懂～ not know the ways of the world

【人权】 rénquán human rights; rights of man

【人权宣言】 Rénquán Xuānyán ①(法国) Declaration of the Rights of Man and of the Citizen (1789) ②(联合国) Declaration of Human Rights

【人群】 rénqún crowd; throng; multitude

【人人】 rénrén everybody; everyone

【人山人海】 rénshān-rénhǎi huge crowds of people; a sea of people: 广场上～。 The square was a sea of people.

【人身】 rénshēn living body of a human being; person ◇ ～安全 personal safety/ ～不可侵犯 inviolability of the person/ ～攻击 personal attack/ ～事故 personal injury caused by an accident/ ～自由 freedom of person; personal freedom

【人参】 rénshēn ginseng

【人生】 rénshēng life ◇ ～观 outlook on life/ ～哲学 philosophy of life

【人声】 rénshēng voice: 远处传来～。 Voices came from afar. 或 Voices were heard in the distance./ ～嘈杂 a confusion of voices/～鼎沸 a hubbub of voices

【人士】 rénshì personage; public figure: 爱国～ patriotic personage/ 友好～ friendly personality/ 官方～ official quarters/ 体育界～ figures in the sports world / 文艺界～ people of literary and art circles/ 消息灵通～ informed sources/ 知名～ well-known figures; celebrities

【人世】 rénshì this world; the world: ～沧桑 tremendous changes in the world/ 不在～ be no longer living; be no longer in the land of the living

【人事】 rénshì ① human affairs; occurrences in human life ② personnel matters: ～调动 transfer of personnel/ ～更迭 change of personnel ③ ways of the world: 不懂～ not know the ways of the world ④ consciousness of the outside world: 不省～ lose consciousness ⑤ what is humanly possible: 尽～ do what is humanly possible; do one's best
◇ ～处 personnel division/ ～档案 personal file (或 dossier)/ ～关系 organizational affiliation/ ～制度 personnel system

【人手】 rénshǒu manpower; hand: ～太少 short of hands; shorthanded

【人体】 réntǐ human body

【人同此心,心同此理】 rén tóng cǐ xīn, xīn tóng cǐ lǐ everybody feels the same about this

【人微言轻】 rénwēi-yánqīng the words of the lowly carry little weight

【人为】 rénwéi artificial; man-made: ～的障碍 an artificially imposed obstacle/ 这些困难完全是～的。 These difficulties were purely man-made.

【人为刀俎,我为鱼肉】 rén wéi dāo-zǔ, wǒ wéi yú-ròu be meat on sb.'s chopping block — be at sb.'s mercy

【人文科学】 rénwén kēxué the humanities; humane studies

【人文主义】 rénwénzhǔyì humanism

【人物】 rénwù ① figure; personage: 领袖～ a leading personage; a leading public figure/ 英雄～ a heroic figure; a hero or heroine/ 历史上的伟大～ great historic figures/ 大～ a big shot/ 小～ a nobody; a small potato/ 杰出的～ an outstanding personage ② person in literature; character: 典型～ typical character/ ～塑造 characterization ◇ ～表 characters (in a play or novel)/ ～画 figure painting

【人像】 rénxiàng portrait; image; figure ◇ ～靶 silhouette target

【人心】 rénxīn popular feeling; public feeling; the will of the people: 得～ have the support of the people; enjoy popular support/ 不得～ go against the will of the people; be unpopular/ ～丧尽 lose (或 forfeit) all popular sympathy/ 深入～ strike root in the hearts of the people/ 振奋～ boost popular morale/ 大快～ most gratifying to the people; to the great satisfaction of the people/ 收买～ curry favour with the public/ 这是～所向,大势所趋。 This accords with the will of the people and the general trend of events.

【人行道】 rénxíngdào pavement; sidewalk

【人性】 rénxìng human nature; humanity: 具体的～ human nature in the concrete/ 灭绝～ most barbarous; utterly inhuman

【人性】 rénxing normal human feelings; reason: 不通～ unfeeling and unreasonable

【人选】 rénxuǎn person selected; choice of persons: 物色适当～ try to find a suitable person (for a job)/ 决定秘书长的～ decide who is to be secretary-general

【人烟】 rényān signs of human habitation: ～稀少(稠密) be sparsely (densely) populated/ 没有～ uninhabited; without a trace of human habitation

【人言可畏】 rényán kě wèi gossip is a fearful thing

【人仰马翻】 rényǎng-mǎfān men and horses thrown off their feet — utterly routed

【人影儿】 rényǐngr ① the shadow of a human figure ② the trace of a person's presence; figure: 她看见一个～在黑暗中消失了。 She caught sight of a figure disappearing into the darkness./ 我等了半天,连个～也不见。 I waited a long time but not a soul turned up.

【人员】 rényuán personnel; staff: 全体～ the entire personnel; the whole staff

【人缘儿】 rényuánr relations with people; popularity: ～好

be very popular; enjoy great popularity

【人云亦云】 rén yún yì yún echo the views of others; parrot

【人造】 rénzào man-made; artificial; imitation
◇ ～宝石 imitation jewel/ ～冰 artificial ice/ ～革 imitation (或 artificial) leather; leatherette/ ～棉 staple rayon/ ～丝 artificial silk; rayon/ ～卫星 man-made satellite/ ～纤维 man-made fibre/ ～橡胶 artificial rubber; synthetic rubber/ ～羊毛 artificial wool

【人证】 rénzhèng 〈法〉 testimony of a witness ◇ ～物证 human testimony and material evidence

【人之常情】 rén zhī chángqíng the way of the world; what is natural and normal (in human relationships)

【人质】 rénzhì hostage

【人种】 rénzhǒng ethnic group; race

壬 rén the ninth of the ten Heavenly Stems

仁* rén ① benevolence; kindheartedness; humanity: ～政 policy of benevolence; benevolent government ② sensitive: 麻木不～ insensitive; apathetic ③ kernel: 核桃～ walnut kernel; walnut meat/ 花生～ shelled peanuts/ 虾～ shelled shrimps; shrimp meat

【仁爱】 rén'ài kindheartedness

【仁慈】 réncí benevolent; merciful; kind

【仁人志士】 rénrén-zhìshì people with lofty ideals

【仁兄】 rénxiōng 〔旧时敬词,多用于书信〕 my dear friend

【仁义道德】 rényì-dàodé humanity, justice and virtue; virtue and morality

【仁者见仁,智者见智】 rénzhě jiàn rén, zhìzhě jiàn zhì the benevolent see benevolence and the wise see wisdom — different people have different views

【仁政】 rénzhèng policy of benevolence; benevolent government

【仁至义尽】 rénzhì-yìjìn do everything called for by humanity and duty; do what is humanly possible to help; show extreme forbearance: 我们对这些人,真可谓做到了～。 We have really shown the utmost tolerance and patience towards these people.

rěn

忍* rěn ① bear; endure; tolerate; put up with: 他～着剧痛,继续工作。 He continued to work despite the intense pain./ ～饥挨饿 endure the torments of hunger/ ～着眼泪 hold back one's tears/ 是可～,孰不可～? If this can be tolerated, what cannot? ② be hardhearted enough to; have the heart to: 残～ cruel; ruthless/ 于心不～ not have the heart to

【忍不住】 rěnbuzhù unable to bear (或 endure); cannot help (doing sth.): 他痒得几乎～了。 The itching was almost more than he could stand./ 她～掉下了眼泪。 She couldn't hold back her tears.

【忍俊不禁】 rěnjùn bùjìn cannot help laughing

【忍耐】 rěnnài exercise patience; exercise restraint; restrain oneself

【忍气吞声】 rěnqì-tūnshēng swallow an insult; submit to humiliation

【忍让】 rěnràng exercise forbearance; be forbearing and conciliatory

【忍辱负重】 rěn rǔ fù zhòng endure humiliation in order to carry out an important mission

【忍受】 rěnshòu bear; endure; stand: ～艰难困苦 endure hardships/ 热得难以～ unbearably hot

【忍痛】 rěntòng very reluctantly: ～割爱 part reluctantly with what one treasures/ ～牺牲 reluctantly give up

【忍无可忍】 rěn wú kě rěn be driven beyond (the limits of) forbearance; come to the end of one's patience

【忍心】 rěnxīn have the heart to; be hardhearted enough to: 他不～拒绝他们的要求。 He didn't have the heart to (或 couldn't bear to) turn down their request.

荏 rén ① 〈书〉 weak; weak-kneed: 色厉内～ fierce of

mien but faint of heart; threatening in manner but cowardly at heart

【荏苒】 rěnrǎn ‹书› (of time) elapse quickly or imperceptibly; slip by: 光阴～，转瞬又是一年。Time slipped by and the year was soon over.

稔 rěn ‹书› ① harvest: 丰～ bumper harvest / 一年两～ two crops a year ② be familiar with sb.: ～知 know sb. quite well/ 素～ have long been familiar with sb.

rèn

刃 rèn ① the edge of a knife, sword, etc.; blade: 刀～ knife blade ② sword; knife: 利～ sharp sword/ 白～战 bayonet fighting ③ kill with a sword or knife: 手～ stab sb. to death; kill with one's own hand

认* rèn ① recognize; know; make out; identify: ～出某人 identify a person; recognize a person/ ～敌为友 take a foe for a friend/ 自己的东西,自己来～。Come and pick out your own things./ 他的字真难～。His handwriting is barely legible. 或 His handwriting is hard to read. ② enter into a certain relationship with; adopt: ～师傅 apprentice oneself to sb./ ～她作女儿 adopt her as a daughter ③ admit; recognize; own: 公～ be generally acknowledged (或 recognized)/ ～个不是 offer an apology; apologize/ 承～ admit; recognize/ 否～ deny ④ undertake to do sth.: ～捐五十元 undertake to contribute $50.

【认错】 rèncuò acknowledge a mistake; admit a fault; make an apology

【认得】 rènde know; recognize: 这地方我已经不～了。I can no longer recognize the place./ 你～回家的路吗？Can you find your way home?

【认定】 rèndìng ① firmly believe; maintain; hold ② set one's mind on: 既然～了目标,就要坚持不懈地干下去。Now that you've set your mind on the goal, you must go through with the task.

【认购】 rèngòu offer to buy; subscribe: ～公债 subscribe for bonds

【认可】 rènkě approve: 得到领导的～ be approved by the leadership

【认领】 rènlǐng claim: 拾得钱包一个, 希望失主前来～。Found a purse. Will the owner please come to claim it.

【认清】 rènqīng see clearly; recognize; get a clear understanding of: ～形势 get a clear understanding of the situation/ ～问题的性质 grasp the nature of the problem

【认识】 rènshi ① know; understand; recognize: 你在哪儿～她的？Where did you get to know her? ② understanding; knowledge; cognition: 感性(理性) perceptual (rational) knowledge/ 我们都谈了对这件事的～。We all said what we thought about the matter.

【认输】 rènshū admit defeat; throw in (或 up) the sponge; give up

【认为】 rènwéi think; consider; hold; deem: 大家～这个建议是可行的。All think (或 consider) this proposal feasible./ 你～怎样？What do you think of it?/ 这件事我们一有必要跟你们说清楚。We deem it neccessary to make this clear to you./ 你～这是真的吗？Do you believe it to be true?/ 我们～,国家不分大小,应该一律平等。We hold that all nations, big or small, should be equal.

【认贼作父】 rèn zéi zuò fù take the foe for one's father; regard the enemy as kith and kin

【认帐】 rènzhàng acknowledge a debt (或 an account); admit what one has said or done: 错了就要～。If you're wrong, you should admit it./ 自己说的话,怎么不～? How can you go back upon your word?

【认真】 rènzhēn ① conscientious; earnest; serious: 进行～的研究 make a serious study ② take seriously; take to heart: 我说着玩儿的,他就～了。I was only joking, but he took it to heart.

【认字】 rènzì know or learn how to read

【认罪】 rènzuì admit one's guilt; plead guilty

任* rèn ① appoint: 新～的厂长 the newly appointed director of the factory ② assume a post; take up a job: 他～教多年了。He has been a teacher for many years. ③ official post; office: 上～ take up an official post; assume office/ 离～ leave office/ 就～ assume office/ ～满 expiration of one's term of office/ ～内 during one's term (或 tenure) of office ④ ‹量› 〔用于担任官职的次数〕: 做过两～大使 have twice been ambassador ⑤ let; allow; give free rein to: ～其自流 let things run their course/ ～你挑选一个。Choose any one you like. ⑥ no matter (how, what, etc.): ～我们怎样劝说,他总不听。No matter how hard we tried to persuade him, he wouldn't listen.

【任便】 rènbiàn as you like; as you see fit: 你来不来～。You may come or not as you see fit.

【任何】 rènhé any; whichever; whatever: 我们能战胜～困难。We can overcome any difficulty./ 没有～理由拒绝这个建议。There's no reason whatsoever to turn down this suggestion.

【任劳任怨】 rènláo-rènyuàn work hard and not be upset by criticism; willingly bear the burden of office

【任免】 rèn-miǎn appoint and remove (或 dismiss)

【任命】 rènmìng appoint: ～他为校长 appoint him president (of the university)

【任凭】 rènpíng ① at one's convenience; at one's discretion: 这事不能～他一人决定。This shouldn't be left entirely to his discretion. ② no matter (how, what, etc.): ～问题多复杂, 我们也能搞清楚。We can solve the problem no matter how complicated it is./ 你怎样说,事实总是事实。Whatever you say, facts are facts./ ～什么挫折都不能使他动摇。No setbacks can make him waver.

【任期】 rènqī term of office; tenure of office

【任务】 rènwu assignment; mission; task; job: 接受～ receive (或 accept) an assignment/ 我们保证完成～。We guarantee to fulfil (或 complete) our mission./ 这个～就交给我吧! Give this job to me./ 担负艰巨的～ shoulder heavy responsibilities

【任性】 rènxìng wilful; self-willed; wayward; headstrong

【任意】 rènyì wantonly; arbitrarily; wilfully: ～诬蔑 wantonly vilify/ ～捏造事实 indulge in pure fabrication/ ～歪曲历史 wilfully distort history/ ～掠夺别国资源 wantonly plunder other countries' resources/ ～欺负别人 bully people at will

【任用】 rènyòng appoint; assign sb. to a post

【任职】 rènzhí hold a post; be in office: 在外交部～ work (或 hold a post) in the Ministry of Foreign Affairs/ 在～期间 during one's tenure of office

【任重道远】 rènzhòng-dàoyuǎn the burden is heavy and the road is long — shoulder heavy responsibilities

妊 rèn be pregnant

【妊妇】 rènfù pregnant woman

【妊娠】 rènshēn gestation; pregnancy: 输卵管～ tubal pregnancy ◇ ～期 gestational period

纫 rèn ① sew; stitch ② thread (a needle)

韧 rèn pliable but strong; tenacious; tough

【韧性】 rènxìng toughness; tenacity

轫 rèn 见"发轫" fārèn

饪 rèn 见"烹饪" pēngrèn

rēng

扔* rēng ① throw; toss; cast: ～手榴弹 throw a hand grenade/ ～球 throw (或 toss) a ball/ 敌机～了几颗炸弹。The enemy plane dropped a few bombs. ② throw away; cast aside: 把它～了吧。Throw it away./ 被～进历史的垃圾堆 be relegated to (或 tossed on to) the rubbish heap of history/ 这事他早就～在脖子后边了。He'd clean forgotten about it.

【扔下】 rēngxia abandon; put aside; leave behind: 敌人～武器逃跑了。The enemy dropped their weapons and took to their heels./ 这工作我不能～不管。I can't leave the work half-finished.

réng

仍 réng ① remain: 一～其旧 remain the same; follow the beaten track ② <副> still; yet: ～有效力 be still effective; be still in force/ ～未痊愈 have not yet recovered/ ～须努力 must continue to make efforts

【仍旧】 réngjiù ① remain the same ② <副> still; yet: 他虽然遇到许多挫折，可是意志～那样坚强。His determination remains as strong as ever despite all the setbacks he has encountered/ 他～是十年前的老样子。After ten years, he still looked the same./ 有些问题～没解决。Some problems remain to be solved.

【仍然】 réngrán <副> still; yet

rì

日 rì ① sun: ～出 sunrise/ ～落 sunset ② daytime; day: ～～夜夜 day and night; night and day ③ day: 今～ today/ 多～不见了,你好吗? Haven't seen you for a long time. How are you?/ 我们改～再谈。Let's talk about it some other time. ④ daily; every day; with each passing day: 产量～增。Output is going up every day./ 天气～暖。It's getting warmer and warmer./ 第三世界国家在国际事务中的作用～趋重要。The third world countries are playing an increasingly important role in world affairs. ⑤ time: 春～ springtime; spring/ 来～ the days to come; the future

【日班】 rìbān day shift: 上～ be on the day shift

【日报】 rìbào daily paper; daily

【日常】 rìcháng day-to-day; everyday; daily: ～工作 day-to-day work; routine duties/ ～生活 everyday life; daily life/ ～用语 words and expressions for everyday use

【日场】 rìchǎng day show; daytime performance; matinée

【日程】 rìchéng programme; schedule: 访问～ itinerary of a visit/ 工作～ work schedule; programme of work/ 提到～上来 place (或 put) sth. on the order of the day ◇ ～表 schedule

【日光】 rìguāng sunlight; sunbeam

【日光灯】 rìguāngdēng fluorescent lamp; daylight lamp

【日后】 rìhòu in the future; in days to come: 这东西～可能用得着。We may find it useful in future. 或 It may come in handy someday.

【日积月累】 rìjī-yuèlěi accumulate over a long period: 每天学一点,～也能学不少。Learn a little every day and in time you'll have learned a lot.

【日记】 rìjì diary: 记～ keep a diary/ 工作～ work diary; daily account of one's work ◇ ～本 diary

【日间】 rìjiān in the daytime; during the day

【日见】 rìjiàn with each passing day; day by day: ～好转 get better every day/ ～衰败 decline day by day

【日渐】 rìjiàn with each passing day; day by day: ～强壮 get stronger and stronger

【日久】 rìjiǔ with the passing of time; in (the) course of time: ～天长 in (the) course of time; as the years go by

【日久见人心】 rìjiǔ jiàn rénxīn time reveals a person's heart; it takes time to know a person

【日来】 rìlái recently; of late; in the past few days

【日理万机】 rì lǐ wànjī attend to numerous affairs of state every day; be occupied with a myriad of state affairs

【日历】 rìlì calendar ◇ ～表 calendar watch

【日暮途穷】 rìmù-túqióng the day is waning and the road is ending — approaching the end of one's days

【日内】 rìnèi in a few days; in a day or two; in a couple of days

【日期】 rìqī date: 起程的～定了吗? Has the departure date

been fixed?/ 信上的～是六月二日。The letter is dated June 2.

【日前】 rìqián a few days ago; the other day

【日趋】 rìqū with each passing day; gradually; day by day: 市场～繁荣。The market is becoming brisker day by day.

【日上三竿】 rì shàng sān gān the sun is three poles high — it's late in the morning (referring to getting up late)

【日食】 rìshí <天> solar eclipse: 日环食 annular eclipse/ 日偏食 partial solar eclipse/ 日全食 total solar eclipse

【日头】 rìtou <方> sun

【日新月异】 rìxīn-yuèyì change with each passing day

【日夜】 rì-yè day and night; night and day; round the clock: ～警惕地守卫着边疆 vigilantly guard the borders day and night/ 我们厂～三班倒。Our factory operates round the clock on three shifts.

【日以继夜】 rì yǐ jì yè night and day; round the clock

【日益】 rìyì increasingly; day by day: 矛盾～尖锐。The contradictions are becoming increasingly acute./ 我们的队伍～壮大。Our ranks are growing stronger day by day.

【日用】 rìyòng ① daily expenses ② of everyday use ◇ ～必需品 daily necessities; household necessities/ ～工业品 manufactured goods for daily use/ ～品 articles of everyday use

【日月如梭】 rì-yuè rú suō the sun and the moon move back and forth like a shuttle — time flies

【日子】 rìzi ① day; date: 这个～好不容易盼到了。The day we have been looking forward to has come at long last./ 定一个～ fix a date ② time: 他走了有些～了。He's been away for some time./ 这些～我校师生在工厂实习。The teachers and students of our school have been doing field work at a factory recently. ③ life; livelihood: 今天我们的～多幸福啊! How happy is our life today!/ 勤俭过～ lead an industrious and frugal life

róng

戎 róng <书> army; military affairs: 投笔从～ cast aside the pen to join the army; give up intellectual pursuits for a military career

【戎马】 róngmǎ <书> army horse: ～生涯 army life; military life

【戎装】 róngzhuāng <书> martial attire

荣 róng ① grow luxuriantly; flourish: 欣欣向～ flourishing; thriving; growing luxuriantly/ 春～冬枯 grow in spring and wither in winter ② honour; glory: 引以为～ take it as an honour/ ～立一等功 be cited for meritorious service, first class/ 以艰苦为～ take pride in working under difficult conditions/ 为人民而死,虽死犹～! It is a glorious thing to die for the people.

【荣归】 róngguī return in glory

【荣华富贵】 rónghuá-fùguì glory, splendour, wealth and rank; high position and great wealth

【荣获】 rónghuò have the honour to get or win: ～冠军 win the championship/ ～一枚奖章 be awarded a medal

【荣辱】 róng-rǔ honour or disgrace

【荣幸】 róngxìng be honoured: 我们应邀访问贵国,感到非常～。We feel greatly honoured by your invitation to visit your country./ 如蒙光临,不胜～。We shall be greatly honoured by your gracious presence./ 今天很～能参加你们的晚会。It is a great honour to be with you at this evening party.

【荣耀】 róngyào honour; glory

【荣誉】 róngyù honour; credit; glory: 为祖国赢得～ win honour for one's country/ 爱护集体的～ cherish the good name of the group ◇ ～感 sense of honour

茸 róng ① (of grass, etc.) fine and soft; downy ② young pilose antler

【茸茸】 róngróng (of grass, hair, etc.) fine, soft and thick; downy: 绿草～ a carpet of green grass

绒 róng ① fine hair; down: 鸭～ eiderdown ② cloth with a soft nap or pile on one or either side: 丝～ velvet/

灯芯~ corduroy/ 法兰~ flannel ③ fine floss for embroidery

【绒布】 róngbù flannelette; cotton flannel

【绒毛】 róngmáo ① fine hair; down; villus ② <纺> nap; pile

【绒线】 róngxiàn ① floss for embroidery ② <方> knitting wool ◇ ~刺绣 crewelwork/ ~衫 woollen sweater

【绒衣】 róngyī sweat shirt

容* róng ① hold; contain: 这个礼堂能~一千人. The auditorium can hold a thousand people./ 可~水三万多立方米的蓄水池 a reservoir with a capacity of over 30,000 cubic metres/ 这座大桥可~四辆卡车并列通行. The bridge can take four lorries abreast. ② tolerate: 宽~ be tolerant ③ permit; allow: 详情~后再告. Permit me to give the details later./ 此事不~耽搁. The matter allows of no delay./ 不~歪曲 brook no distortion/ 不~怀疑 admit of no doubt ④ facial expression: 笑~ a smiling face/ 怒~ an angry look ⑤ appearance; looks: 市~ the appearance (或 look) of a city/ 阵~ lineup; battle array

【容光焕发】 róngguāng huànfā one's face glowing with health

【容量】 róngliàng capacity

【容貌】 róngmào appearance; looks

【容纳】 róngnà hold; have a capacity of; accommodate: 首都体育馆能~一万八千观众. The Capital Stadium has a seating capacity of 18,000./ 他不能~不同意见. He can't tolerate dissenting views.

【容器】 róngqì container; vessel

【容忍】 róngrěn tolerate; put up with; condone: 我们不能~这种浪费现象. We cannot tolerate such waste.

【容身】 róngshēn shelter oneself: 无~之地. There is no place for one in society.

【容许】 róngxǔ ① tolerate; permit; allow: 情况不~我们再等待了. In such circumstances we can't afford to wait any longer./ 可以~你有三天的准备时间. You'll be allowed three days to prepare./ 我们决不~任何外来干涉. We will brook no outside interference. ② possibly; perhaps: 此类事件,十年前~有之. Such things might possibly have happened ten years ago.

【容貌】 róngyàn appearance; looks

【容易】 róngyì ① easy: 这台机床~操作. This lathe is easy to operate./ 说起来~做起来难. It's easier said than done./ 这种草药很~弄到. This medicinal herb is easy to come by. ② easily; likely; liable; apt: 他~生病. He often gets ill./ 这~引起误会. This is liable to cause misunderstanding./ 人们~把这两个问题混淆起来. People are apt to confuse the two issues.

嵘 róng 见 "峥嵘" zhēngróng

溶* róng dissolve: 樟脑~于酒精而不~于水. Camphor dissolves in alcohol, but not in water.

【溶化】 rónghuà dissolve: 盐在水里很快就~. Salt dissolves quickly in water.

【溶剂】 róngjì <化> solvent

【溶解】 róngjiě dissolve: 这种物质在水中不会~. This substance does not dissolve in water.

【溶液】 róngyè <化> solution: 实在~ real solution/ 当量~ normal solution

蓉 róng 见 "芙蓉" fúróng

熔* róng melt; fuse; smelt

【熔化】 rónghuà melt: 纯铁加热到摄氏 1,535 度就~. Pure iron melts at 1,535°C.

【熔解】 róngjiě <物> fuse; fusion ◇ ~热 heat of fusion

【熔炉】 rónglú ① smelting furnace ② crucible; furnace

榕 róng <植> small-fruited fig tree; banyan

融 róng ① melt; thaw: 春雪易~. Spring snow soon melts. ② blend; fuse; be in harmony: 水乳交~ blend as well as milk and water; be in perfect harmony

【融合】 rónghé mix together; fuse; merge: 铜与锡的~ the fusion of copper and tin

【融化】 rónghuà melt; thaw: 湖上的冰已经~了. The ice on the lake has already melted./ 雪已开始~. The snow is beginning to thaw.

【融会贯通】 rónghuì guàntōng achieve mastery through a comprehensive study of the subject

【融解】 róngjiě melt; thaw

【融洽】 róngqià harmonious; on friendly terms: 劳资关系很~. The relations between management and workers are harmonious.

【融融】 róngróng <书> ① happy and harmonious: 老朋友欢聚一堂,其乐~. When old friends meet, their happiness knows no bounds. ② warm: 春光~. Spring fills the air with warmth.

rǒng

冗 rǒng ① superfluous; redundant: ~词 superfluous words ② full of trivial details ③ busyness: 拨~ find time in the midst of one's work

【冗长】 rǒngcháng tediously long; lengthy; long-winded; prolix: ~的讲演 a long and tedious speech

【冗员】 rǒngyuán redundant personnel

【冗杂】 rǒngzá ① (of writing) lengthy and jumbled ② (of affairs) miscellaneous

róu

柔* róu ① soft; supple; flexible: ~枝嫩叶 supple twigs and tender leaves ② soften: ~麻 soften jute, hemp, etc. ③ gentle; yielding; mild: 温~ gentle and soft/ ~中有刚 firm but gentle

【柔道】 róudào judo

【柔和】 róuhé soft; gentle; mild: ~的光线 soft light/ ~的声音 a gentle (或 mild) voice; a soft sound/ 颜色~ a soft colour

【柔嫩】 róunèn tender; delicate: ~的幼芽 tender sprouts

【柔情】 róuqíng tender feelings; tenderness

【柔软】 róuruǎn soft; lithe: ~的垫子 a soft cushion/ ~的动作 lithe movements ◇ ~体操 callisthenics

【柔弱】 róuruò weak; delicate: 身体~ in delicate health; weak; frail

【柔顺】 róushùn gentle and agreeable; meek

揉 róu rub; knead: 别~眼睛. Don't rub your eyes./ ~一~腿 rub one's legs/ ~面 knead dough/ 把信~成一团 crumple a letter into a ball

【揉搓】 róucuo rub; knead

糅 róu mix; mingle

【糅合】 róuhé mix; form a mixture (usu. of things which don't blend well)

蹂 róu

【蹂躏】 róulìn trample on; ravage; make havoc of; devastate: ~别国主权 trample upon the sovereignty of other countries

ròu

肉* ròu ① meat; flesh: 瘦~ lean meat/ 肥~ fat meat; fat/ ~制品 meat products/ 猪~ pork/ 牛~ beef/ 羊~ mutton ② pulp; flesh (of fruit): 果~ pulp of fruit/ 桂圆~

【肉饼】 ròubǐng meat pie

【肉搏】 ròubó fight hand-to-hand ◇ ~战 hand-to-hand fight (或 combat); bayonet fighting

【肉店】 ròudiàn butcher's (shop)

【肉丁】 ròudīng diced meat: 辣子~ diced pork with hot pepper

【肉麻】 ròumá nauseating; sickening; disgusting: ~的吹捧 fulsome praise

【肉排】 ròupái steak
【肉皮】 ròupí pork skin
【肉片】 ròupiàn sliced meat
【肉色】 ròusè yellowish pink
【肉食】 ròushí carnivorous ◇ ~动物 carnivorous animal; carnivore
【肉身】 ròushēn meat
【肉丝】 ròusī shredded meat ◇ ~面 noodles with shredded meat
【肉松】 ròusōng dried meat floss
【肉汤】 ròutāng broth
【肉体】 ròutǐ the human body; flesh
【肉丸子】 ròuwánzi meatball
【肉刑】 ròuxíng corporal punishment
【肉眼】 ròuyǎn naked eye: ~看不到 be invisible to the naked eye
【肉欲】 ròuyù carnal desire
【肉汁】 ròuzhī gravy; (meat) juice

rú

如* rú ① in compliance with; according to: ~命 in compliance with your instructions ② like; as; as if: ~临大敌 as if faced with a formidable enemy/~你所说 as you've said ③〖用于否定〗 can compare with; be as good as: 我不~他。 I'm not as good as he is. 或 I can't compare with him. ④ for instance; such as; as: 唐朝有很多大诗人,如李白、杜甫、白居易等。The Tang Dynasty produced a host of great poets, such as Li Bai, Du Fu and Bai Juyi. ⑤〈连〉if: ~处理得当,问题不难解决。 The problem will not be difficult to solve, if properly handled. ⑥〈书〉go to: ~厕 go to the toilet
【如常】 rúcháng as usual: 一切~。 Things are as usual.
【如出一辙】 rú chū yī zhé be exactly the same as; be no different from; be cut from the same cloth
【如此】 rúcǐ so; such; in this way; like that: 似乎是~。 So it appears./ 理当~。 Rightly so./ ~重要的问题应呈报总经理批准。 Such an important problem should be submitted to the General Manager for approval./ 事已~,后悔也是枉然。 Now it's done, regrets are of no avail. 或 It's no use crying over spilt milk./ 情况就是~。 That's how things stand./ ~等等 and so on and so forth
【如此而已】 rúcǐ éryǐ that's what it all adds up to: ~,岂有他哉！ That's all there is to it!
【如次】 rúcì as follows: 其理由~。 The reasons are as follows.
【如堕五里雾中】 rú duò wǔlǐwù zhōng as if lost in a thick fog; utterly mystified
【如法炮制】 rú fǎ páozhì prepare herbal medicine by the prescribed method — follow a set pattern; follow suit
【如故】 rúgù ① as before: 依然~ remain the same as before; remain one's same old self ② like old friends: 一见~ feel like old friends at the first meeting; hit it off well right from the start
【如果】 rúguǒ 〈连〉if; in case; in the event of: 你~要来,请事先告诉我。 Let me know in advance if you're coming./ 我们~不加强学习,就会跟不上形势。 We can't keep abreast of the developing situation unless we study harder./ ~不是他指引,我们就迷路了。 If it weren't for him, we would have gone astray.
【如何】 rúhé how; what: 此事~办理？ How are we to handle this matter?/ 他不知~是好。 He didn't know what to do./ 这个电影你觉得~? How do you like the film? 或 What do you think of the film?
【如虎添翼】 rú hǔ tiān yì like a tiger that has grown wings — with might redoubled
【如火如荼】 rúhuǒ-rútú like a raging fire
【如获至宝】 rú huò zhìbǎo as if one had found a treasure
【如饥似渴】 rújī-sìkě as if thirsting or hungering for sth.; eagerly
【如胶似漆】 rújiāo-sìqī stick to each other like glue or lacquer; remain glued to each other; be deeply attached to each other
【如今】 rújīn nowadays; now

【如狼似虎】 rúláng-sìhǔ as ferocious as wolves and tigers; like cruel beasts of prey
【如雷贯耳】 rú léi guàn ěr reverberate like thunder: 久闻大名,~。 Your name has long resounded in my ears.
【如梦初醒】 rú mèng chū xǐng as if awakening from a dream
【如鸟兽散】 rú niǎo-shòu sàn flee helter-skelter; be utterly routed
【如期】 rúqī as scheduled; by the scheduled time; on schedule: 会议将~召开。 The conference will be convened as scheduled./ 任务已~完成。 The task has been accomplished according to schedule./ 货物已~运到。 The goods arrived on schedule.
【如日中天】 rú rì zhōngtiān like the sun at high noon; at the apex (或 zenith) of one's power, career, etc.
【如入无人之境】 rú rù wú rén zhī jìng like entering an unpeopled land — breaking all resistance
【如若】 rúruò 〈连〉if: ~不信,请拭目以待。 If you don't believe it, wait and see./ ~不然 if not; otherwise
【如上】 rúshàng as above: ~所述 as stated (或 mentioned) above
【如实】 rúshí strictly according to the facts; as things really are: ~地反映情况 report the situation accurately; reflect things as they really are
【如释重负】 rú shì zhòngfù as if relieved of a heavy load
【如数家珍】 rú shǔ jiāzhēn as if enumerating one's family valuables — very familiar with one's subject
【如数】 rúshù exactly the number or amount: ~偿还 pay back in full/ ~到齐 all present and correct
【如同】 rútóng like; as: 待我们~亲人一样 treat us like their kith and kin
【如下】 rúxià as follows: 这个计划的要点~。 The main points of the plan are as follows./ 全文~。 The full text follows./ 发表~声明 make the following statement
【如意】 rúyì ① as one wishes: 很难万事~。 You can't expect everything to turn out as you wish./ 称心~ after one's own heart ② rúyì, an S-shaped ornamental object, usu. made of jade, formerly a symbol of good luck
【如意算盘】 rúyì suànpan wishful thinking: 打~ indulge in wishful thinking /打乱了他的~ upset his smug calculations
【如影随形】 rú yǐng suí xíng like the shadow following the person — very closely associated with each other
【如鱼得水】 rú yú dé shuǐ feel just like fish in water; be in one's element
【如愿以偿】 rúyuàn yǐ cháng have one's wish fulfilled; achieve what one wishes
【如坐针毡】 rú zuò zhēnzhān feel as if sitting on a bed of nails; be on pins and needles; be on tenterhooks

茹 rú 〈书〉eat: ~素 be a vegetarian
【茹苦含辛】 rúkǔ-hánxīn 见"含辛茹苦" hánxīn-rúkǔ
【茹毛饮血】 rúmáo-yǐnxuè (of primitive man) eat birds and animals raw

儒 rú ① (Rú) Confucianism; Confucianist ②〈旧〉scholar; learned man: 腐~ pedantic scholar
【儒家】 Rújiā the Confucianists (a school of thought in the Spring and Autumn and Warring States Periods 770-221 B.C.); the Confucian school

濡 rú 〈书〉① immerse; moisten: ~笔 dip a writing brush in ink ② linger
【濡染】 rúrǎn immerse; imbue

孺 rú child: 妇~ women and children
【孺子】 rúzǐ 〈书〉child

蠕 rú wriggle; squirm
【蠕动】 rúdòng wriggle; squirm

rǔ

汝 rǔ 〈书〉you: ~辈 you people; you

乳 * rǔ ① breast ② milk: 炼～ condensed milk ③ any milk-like liquid: 豆～ bean milk ④ give birth to: 孳～‹书› breed; multiply ⑤ newborn (animal); sucking: ～猪 sucking pig; suckling pig

【乳白】 rǔbái milky white; cream colour

【乳齿】 rǔchǐ milk tooth; deciduous tooth

【乳臭未干】 rǔchòu wèi gān still smell of one's mother's milk — be young and inexperienced; be wet behind the ears

【乳房】 rǔfáng breast

【乳胶】 rǔjiāo ‹化› emulsion ◇ ～漆 emulsion paint; latex paint

【乳酪】 rǔlào cheese

【乳名】 rǔmíng infant name; child's pet name

【乳牛】 rǔniú dairy cattle; milch cow ◇ ～场 dairy farm

【乳头】 rǔtóu nipple; teat; mammilla

【乳罩】 rǔzhào brassière; bra

【乳汁】 rǔzhī milk

【乳制品】 rǔzhìpǐn dairy products ◇ ～工业 dairy industry

辱 * rǔ ① disgrace; dishonour: 奇耻大～ galling shame and humiliation; terrible disgrace ② bring disgrace (或 humiliation) to; insult: 丧权～国 humiliate the nation and forfeit its sovereignty

【辱骂】 rǔmà abuse; call sb. names; hurl insults

【辱命】 rǔmìng fail to accomplish a mission

rù

入 * rù ① enter: ～境 enter a country/ 长江流～东海。The Changjiang River empties into the Donghai Sea./ 投～更多人力 throw in more manpower/ ～议程 put on the agenda ② join; be admitted into; become a member of ③ income: 岁～ annual income/ ～不敷出 income falling short of expenditure; unable to make ends meet ④ conform to; agree with: ～时 fashionable; à la mode/ ～情～理 fair and reasonable

【入场】 rùchǎng entrance; admission: 凭票～。Admission by ticket only./ 运动员在乐曲声中列队～。The athletes marched into the arena to the sound of music. ◇ ～券 (admission) ticket

【入耳】 rù'ěr pleasant to the ear: 不～的话 unpleasant words/ 不堪～ (of language) offensive to the ear; obscene; vulgar

【入骨】 rùgǔ to the marrow: 恨之～ bitterly hate; bear a bitter hatred for sb. or sth.

【入伙】 rùhuǒ ① join a gang; join in partnership ② join a mess: 在我们食堂～ eat at our mess

【入境】 rùjìng enter a country ◇ ～登记 entrance registration/ ～签证 entry visa

【入境问俗】 rùjìng wèn sú on entering a country, inquire about its customs

【入口】 rùkǒu ① enter the mouth: 难于～ have a nasty taste; 不可～! Not to be taken orally! ② entrance: 车站～处 entrance to the station

【入殓】 rùliàn put a corpse in a coffin; encoffin

【入门】 rùmén ① cross the threshold; learn the rudiments of a subject: 学英语～并不难,学好可不容易。Rudimentary English is easy to acquire, but mastery of the language is quite difficult./ 他是我的～师傅。He is the master who initiated me into the craft./ 我还没～呢。I don't even know the ABC of the subject yet. ② elementary course; ABC: 《英语语法～》 Elementary English Grammar/ 《摄影～》 The ABC of Photography

【入迷】 rùmí be fascinated; be enchanted: 他们的精采表演使观众看得入了迷。The audience was fascinated by their superb performance./ 看书看～了 be engrossed in a book

【入木三分】 rù mù sān fēn ① written in a forceful hand ② penetrating; profound; keen

【入侵】 rùqīn invade; intrude; make an incursion; make inroads: 消灭一切敢于～的敌人 wipe out all enemies who dare to invade our country/ 再次～ make another intrusion/ ～飞机 the intruding aircraft/ 军事～ military incursion

【入神】 rùshén ① be entranced; be enthralled: 他越说越起劲,大家越听越～。As he talked with more and more gusto, we came more and more under his spell. ② superb; marvellous: 这幅画画得真是～。This picture is really superb. 或 This is a marvellous picture.

【入声】 rùshēng ‹语› entering tone, one of the four tones in classical Chinese pronunciation, still retained in certain dialects

【入手】 rùshǒu start with; begin with; proceed from; take as the point of departure: 解决问题要从调查研究～。To solve a problem, one has to start with investigation.

【入睡】 rùshuì go to sleep; fall asleep

【入土】 rùtǔ be buried; be interred: 快～了 have one foot in the grave

【入微】 rùwēi in every possible way; in a subtle way: 体贴～ show every possible consideration; be extremely thoughtful/ 细腻～的表演 an exquisite performance

【入伍】 rùwǔ enlist in the armed forces; join up

【入席】 rùxí take one's seat at a banquet, ceremony, etc.

【入选】 rùxuǎn be selected; be chosen

【入学】 rùxué ① start school: 我国儿童五、六岁～。In our country children start school at the age of five or six. ② enter a school: 新生后天～。The new students will enter school the day after tomorrow./ 从～到毕业 from entrance to graduation ◇ ～考试 entrance examination/ ～年龄 school age

【入眼】 rùyǎn pleasing to the eye: 看不～ not to one's liking

【入夜】 rùyè at nightfall: ～,工地上灯火通明。When night fell the construction site was ablaze with light.

【入狱】 rùyù be put in prison; be sent to jail

【入院】 rùyuàn be admitted to hospital; be hospitalized

【入赘】 rùzhuì marry into and live with one's bride's family

缛 rù elaborate; cumbersome: 繁文～节 unnecessary and overelaborate formalities; red tape

蓐 rù ‹书› straw mat or mattress

褥 rù cotton-padded mattress: 被～ bedding; bedclothes

【褥单】 rùdān bed sheet

【褥套】 rùtào ① bedding sack ② mattress cover

【褥子】 rùzi cotton-padded mattress

ruǎn

阮 ruǎn a surname

软 * ruǎn ① soft; flexible; supple; pliable: ～椅 soft chair/ 柳条很～。Willow twigs are pliable. ② soft; mild; gentle: ～语 soft words/ 你对他～了些。You've been a bit soft with him./ 他的话太～了。What he said was too mild. ③ weak; feeble: 两腿发～。One's legs feel like jelly./ 欺～怕硬 bully the weak and fear the strong ④ poor in quality, ability, etc.: 货色～ poor-quality goods/ 工夫～ inadequate skill ⑤ easily moved or influenced: 心～ tenderhearted

【软骨头】 ruǎngǔtou a weak-kneed person; a spineless person; a coward

【软和】 ruǎnhuo ‹口› ① soft: ～的褥子 a soft mattress ② gentle; kind; soft: 给老太太说几句～话儿 Say some kind words (或 Say something nice) to please the old lady

【软禁】 ruǎnjìn put (或 place) sb. under house arrest

【软绵绵】 ruǎnmiánmián ① soft: ～的枕头 a soft pillow/ 这支歌～的。This song is too sentimental. ② weak: 她病好了,但身体仍然～的。She is well now, but she still feels weak.

【软弱】 ruǎnruò weak; feeble; flabby: 他病后身体～。His illness has left him weak./ ～无能 weak and incompetent/ ～可欺 be weak and easy to bully

【软硬兼施】 ruǎn-yìng jiān shī　use both hard and soft tactics; couple threats with promises

ruǐ

蕊　ruǐ　stamen or pistil: 雄～ stamen/ 雌～ pistil

ruì

锐　ruì　① sharp; keen; acute: 尖～ pointed and sharp; sharp; acute ② vigour; fighting spirit: 养精蓄～ conserve strength and store up energy

【锐不可当】 ruì bùkě dāng　can't be held back; be irresistible: 以～之势 with irresistible force/ 我军攻势迅猛，～。Our attack was so swift and violent that nothing could hold it back.

【锐利】 ruìlì　sharp; keen: ～的匕首 a sharp dagger/ ～的武器 a sharp (或 powerful) weapon/ 目光～ sharp-eyed; sharp-sighted/ ～的攻势 a spirited attack/ ～的笔锋 a sharp pen; a vigorous style

【锐敏】 ruìmín　sensitive; keen: ～的嗅觉 a keen sense of smell

【锐气】 ruìqì　dash; drive: 表现了青年人的～ show the dashing spirit of young people/ 挫敌～ take the edge off the enemy's spirit

瑞　ruì　auspicious; lucky

睿　ruì　〈书〉 farsighted

【睿智】 ruìzhì　〈书〉 wise and farsighted

rùn

闰　rùn　〈天〉 intercalary

【闰年】 rùnnián　leap (或 intercalary) year

【闰月】 rùnyuè　intercalary month in the lunar calendar; leap month

润*　rùn　① moist; smooth; sleek: 湿～ moist/ 墨色很～ in dark full-bodied ink ② moisten; lubricate: ～一～嗓子 moisten one's throat ③ embellish; touch up ④ profit; benefit: 分～ share in the benefit (或 profit)

【润笔】 rùnbǐ　remuneration for a writer, painter or calligrapher

【润滑】 rùnhuá　lubricate ◇ ～系统 lubricating system; lubrication system/ ～油 lubricating oil; lubrication oil/ ～脂 (lubricating) grease

【润色】 rùnsè　polish (a piece of writing, etc.); touch up: 这篇文章需要～一下。This article needs polishing.

【润饰】 rùnshì　见 "润色"

ruò

润泽　rùnzé　① moist; smooth; sleek: 这匹马全身～有光。The horse's coat was sleek and glossy./ 雨后荷花显得更加～了。After the rain the lotus flowers looked fuller. ② moisten; lubricate: 用油～轮轴 oil the axle

ruò

若　ruò　① like; seem; as if: ～有所失 feel as if something were missing; look distracted/ ～有所思 seem lost in thought; look pensive/ ～～现 appear indistinctly ② 〈书〉〈连〉 if: 人不犯我，我不犯人；人～犯我，我必犯人。We will not attack unless we are attacked; if we are attacked, we will certainly counterattack. ③ 〈书〉 you: ～辈 people like you

【若非】 ruòfēi　if not; were it not for: ～亲身经历，岂知其中甘苦。You cannot appreciate the difficulty except through personal experience.

【若干】 ruògān　① a certain number or amount: ～年 a number of years/ ～次 several times/ ～地区 certain areas ② how many; how much: 共得～? How many in all? 或 What is the sum total?

【若即若离】 ruòjí-ruòlí　be neither friendly nor aloof; maintain a lukewarm relationship; keep sb. at arm's length

【若明若暗】 ruòmíng-ruò'àn　have an indistinct (或 blurred) picture of; have a hazy (或 vague) notion about

【若是】 ruòshì　〈连〉 if

【若无其事】 ruò wú qí shì　as if nothing had happened; calmly; casually: 发生这么大的事，你怎么还～? How can you remain indifferent when such an important thing has happened?

【若要人不知，除非己莫为】 ruò yào rén bù zhī, chúfēi jǐ mò wéi　if you don't want others to know about it, don't do it

偌　ruò　such; so

【偌大】 ruòdà　of such a size; so big: ～的地方 such a big place/ ～年纪 so old; so advanced in years

弱*　ruò　① weak; feeble: 他身体很～。He is very weak./ 由～变强 go from weakness to strength/ 他年纪虽老，干活并不～。Old as he is, he works energetically. ② young: ～老 old and young ③ inferior: 她的能力并不比别人～。She's no less capable than the others. ④ 〈书〉 lose (through death) ⑤ [接在分数或小数后面] a little less than: 三分之一～ a little less than one-third

【弱不禁风】 ruò bù jīn fēng　too weak to stand a gust of wind; extremely delicate; fragile

【弱点】 ruòdiǎn　weakness; weak point; failing

【弱肉强食】 ruòròu-qiángshí　the weak are the prey of the strong — the law of the jungle

【弱小】 ruòxiǎo　small and weak: ～民族 small and weak nations

S

sā

撒 sā ① cast; let go; let out: ~网 cast a net; pay out a net/ 把手~开 let go one's hold ② throw off all restraint; let oneself go: ~酒疯 be drunk and act crazy; be roaring drunk
另见 sǎ

【撒谎】 sāhuǎng <口> tell a lie; lie: 当面 ~ tell a barefaced lie; lie in one's teeth

【撒娇】 sājiāo act like a spoiled child

【撒尿】 sāniào <口> piss; pee

【撒手】 sāshǒu let go one's hold; let go: 你拿稳, 我~了。Hold it tight. I'll let go./ ~不管 wash one's hands of the business; refuse to have anything more to do with the matter

【撒野】 sāyě act wildly; behave atrociously

sǎ

洒* sǎ sprinkle; spray; spill; shed:

【洒泪】 sǎlèi shed tears: ~告别 take a tearful leave

【洒扫】 sǎsǎo sprinkle water and sweep the floor; sweep: 黎明即起, ~庭除。Rise at dawn and sweep the courtyard.

【洒脱】 sǎtuō free and easy

撒 sǎ ① scatter; sprinkle; spread: ~农药 dust crops with an insecticide ② spill; drop: 她把~在路上的麦粒儿扫到一块儿。She swept up the grains of wheat that had spilled on the ground.
另见 sā

sà

卅 sà thirty

飒 sà

【飒飒】 sàsà <象> sough; rustle: 秋风~。The autumn wind is soughing in the trees.

【飒爽】 sàshuǎng <书> of martial bearing; valiant: ~英姿 of valiant and heroic bearing; bright and brave

萨 Sà a surname

sāi

塞* sāi ① fill in; squeeze in; stuff: 箱子不太满, 还可以再~点东西。There is still room in the suitcase to squeeze a few more things in. 水管~住了。The waterpipe is clogged up. ② stopper: 软木~ cork
另见 sài; sè

【塞子】 sāizi stopper; cork; plug; spigot

腮 sāi cheek

鳃 sāi gill; branchia: ~盖 gill cover

sài

塞* sài a place of strategic importance: 边~ frontier fortress

另见 sāi; sè

【塞翁失马, 安知非福】 sàiwēng shī mǎ, ān zhī fēi fú when the old man on the frontier lost his mare, who could have guessed it was a blessing in disguise? —a loss may turn out to be a gain

赛 sài ① match; game; competition; contest: 足球~ football match (或 game)/ 田径 ~ track and field events ② be comparable to; surpass: 我这萝卜~梨。These radishes of mine taste as good as pears.

【赛车】 sàichē <体> ① cycle racing; motorcycle race; automobile race ② racing bicycle

【赛过】 sàiguò overtake; be better than; surpass; exceed: 此处风光~江南。The scenery here surpasses that south of the lower reaches of the Changjiang River.

【赛马】 sàimǎ horse race

【赛跑】 sàipǎo race: 长距离~ long-distance race/ 一百米~ 100-metre dash/ 越野~ cross-country race

【赛艇】 sàitǐng <体> ① rowing ② racing boat; shell

sān

三* sān ① three ② more than two; several; many: ~弯九转 (full of) twists and turns/ ~思 think again and again; think twice (about doing sth.)

【三部曲】 sānbùqǔ trilogy

【三岔路口】 sānchà lùkǒu a fork in the road; a junction of three roads

【三长两短】 sāncháng-liǎngduǎn unexpected misfortune; sth. unfortunate, esp. death: 万一他有个~ if anything untoward should happen to him; in case he should die

【三重】 sānchóng triple; threefold

【三从四德】 sāncóng sìdé the three obediences (to father before marriage, to husband after marriage, and to son after the death of husband) and the four virtues (morality, proper speech, modest manner and diligent work) — spiritual fetters imposed on women in feudal society

【三番五次】 sānfān-wǔcì again and again; time and again; over and over again; repeatedly

【三纲五常】 sāngāng wǔcháng the three cardinal guides (ruler guides subject, father guides son, and husband guides wife) and the five constant virtues (benevolence, righteousness, propriety, wisdom and fidelity) as specified in the feudal ethical code

【三个臭皮匠, 合成一个诸葛亮】 sān ge chòupíjiang, héchéng yīge Zhūgě Liàng three cobblers with their wits combined equal Zhuge Liang the master mind — the wisdom of the masses exceeds that of the wisest individual 又作"三个臭皮匠, 赛过诸葛亮"

【三顾茅庐】 sān gù máolú make three calls at the thatched cottage — repeatedly request sb. to take up a responsible post

【三合板】 sānhébǎn three-ply board; plywood

【三级跳远】 sān jí tiàoyuǎn <体> hop, step and jump; triple jump

【三角】 sānjiǎo ① triangle ② <数> trigonometry

【三脚架】 sānjiǎojià tripod

【三教九流】 sānjiào jiǔliú ① the three religions (Confucianism, Taoism and Buddhism) and the nine schools of thought (the Confucians, the Taoists, the Yin-Yang, the Legalists, the Logicians, the Mohists, the Political Strategists, the Eclectics and the Agriculturists) ② various religious sects and academic schools ③ <贬> people in various trades; people of all sorts

【三句话不离本行】 sān jù huà bù lí běnháng can hardly open one's mouth without talking shop; talk shop all the time

【三军】 sānjūn ①<旧> the army ② the three armed services

【三轮车】 sānlúnchē tricycle; pedicab

【三昧】 sānmèi ①<佛教> samadhi ② secret; knack: 深得其中~ master the secrets of an art

【三三两两】 sānsānliǎngliǎng in twos and threes

【三生有幸】 sānshēng yǒu xìng consider oneself most fortunate (to make sb.'s acquaintance, etc.)

【三十六计,走为上计】 sānshíliù jì, zǒu wéi shàngjì of the thirty-six stratagems, the best is running away — the best thing to do now is to quit 又作"三十六策,走为上策"

【三思而行】 sān sī ér xíng think thrice before you act; look before you leap

【...三...四】 ...sān...sì 〔表示杂乱〕: 颠三倒四 incoherently; without order/ 丢三落四 always be forgetting things ②〔表示重复〕: 推三阻四 decline with all sorts of excuses

【三头六臂】 sāntóu-liùbì (with) three heads and six arms — superhuman

【三位一体】 sān wèi yī tǐ ①<基督教> the Trinity ② trinity; three forming an organic whole; three in one

【三五成群】 sān-wǔ chéngqún in threes and fours; in knots

【三心二意】 sānxīn-èryì ① be of two minds; shilly-shally: 别~了,就这样办吧。Don't shilly-shally. Go right ahead. ② half-hearted: 为人民服务不能~。We must not serve the people half-heartedly.

【三言两语】 sānyán-liǎngyǔ in a few words; in one or two words: 这事不是~能说清楚的。The matter can't be explained in a few words.

【三月】 sānyuè ① March ② the third month of the lunar year; the third moon

叁 sān three (used for the numeral 三 on cheques, etc. to avoid mistakes or alterations)

sǎn

伞* sǎn ① umbrella ② sth. shaped like an umbrella: 降落~ parachute

【伞兵】 sǎnbīng paratrooper; parachuter ◇ ~部队 parachute troops; paratroops

散* sǎn ① come loose; fall apart; not hold together: 背包~了。The blanket roll has come loose./ 木箱~了。The wooden box fell apart./ 麦包~了。The sack of wheat has spilled. ② scattered ③<中药> medicine in powder form; medicinal powder 另见 sàn

【散光】 sǎnguāng astigmatism ◇ ~眼镜 astigmatic glasses

【散记】 sǎnjì random notes; sidelights

【散漫】 sǎnmàn ① undisciplined; careless and sloppy ② unorganized; scattered: 无组织的状态 a disorganized state of affairs

【散文】 sǎnwén prose

【散装】 sǎnzhuāng bulk; in bulk

sàn

散* sàn ① break up; disperse: 会还没有~。The meeting is not over yet./ 大家别走~了。Let's not get separated./ 今天星期六,早点~吧。It's Saturday today. Let's stop a bit earlier./ 乌云~了。Dark clouds dispersed. ② distribute; disseminate; give out: ~传单 give out handbills; distribute leaflets ③ dispel; let out: 请打开门窗~~烟。Please open the door and windows to let the smoke out. 另见 sǎn

【散播】 sànbō disseminate; spread

【散布】 sànbù spread; disseminate; scatter; diffuse: ~流言蜚语 spread slanderous rumours/ 在一望无际的原野上~着一座座井架。Derricks are scattered here and there on the boundless plain.

【散步】 sànbù take a walk; go for a walk; go for a stroll

【散场】 sànchǎng (of a theatre, cinema, etc.) empty after the show

【散发】 sànfā ① send out; send forth; diffuse; emit: 花儿~着清香。The flowers sent forth a delicate fragrance. ② distribute; issue; give out: ~传单 distribute leaflets/ 作为正式文件~ be circulated as an official document

【散会】 sànhuì (of a meeting) be over; break up: 宣布~ declare the meeting over/ 一直到中午才~。The meeting didn't end until noon.

【散伙】 sànhuǒ (of a group, body or organization) dissolve; disband

【散开】 sànkāi spread out or apart; disperse; scatter: 看热闹的群众~了。The crowd, which had gathered to watch the fun, dispersed.

【散失】 sànshī ① scatter and disappear; be lost; be missing: 防止图书~ prevent any loss of library books/ 有些古籍早已~。Some ancient works have long been lost./ ~的工具已经找到。The missing tools have been found. ② (of moisture, etc.) be lost; vaporize; dissipate

【散心】 sànxīn drive away one's cares; relieve boredom

sāng

丧* sāng funeral; mourning 另见 sàng

【丧服】 sāngfú mourning apparel

【丧礼】 sānglǐ obsequies; funeral

【丧事】 sāngshì funeral arrangements

【丧葬】 sāngzàng burial; funeral ◇ ~费 funeral expenses

【丧钟】 sāngzhōng funeral bell; death knell; knell

桑 sāng white mulberry; mulberry

sǎng

嗓 sǎng ① throat; larynx ② voice

【嗓门儿】 sǎngménr voice: 提高~ raise one's voice/ ~大 have a loud voice

【嗓子】 sǎngzi ① throat; larynx: ~疼 have a sore throat ② voice: 好~ have a good voice/ 他的~哑了。He's lost his voice.

sàng

丧* sàng lose 另见 sāng

【丧胆】 sàngdǎn be terror-stricken; be smitten with fear: 我军向前推进,敌人闻风~。The enemy trembled with fear on hearing of our advance.

【丧魂落魄】 sànghún-luòpò be driven to distraction: 吓得~ be scared out of one's wits; be frightened out of one's life

【丧家之犬】 sàng jiā zhī quǎn stray cur: 惶惶如~ as frightened as a stray cur

【丧尽天良】 sàngjìn tiānliáng utterly devoid of conscience; conscienceless; heartless

【丧命】 sàngmìng meet one's death; get killed 又作"丧身","丧生"

【丧偶】 sàng'ǒu <书> bereft of one's spouse, esp. one's wife

【丧权辱国】 sàngquán-rǔguó humiliate the nation and forfeit its sovereignty; surrender a country's sovereign rights under humiliating terms: ~的条约 a treaty of national betrayal and humiliation

【丧失】 sàngshī lose; forfeit: ~信心 lose confidence/ ~时机 miss the opportunity/ ~立场 depart from the correct stand/ ~会员资格 forfeit one's membership/ 睡眠和休息~了时间,却取得了明天工作的精力。Sleep and rest involve loss of time, but they provide energy for next day's work.

【丧心病狂】 sàng xīn bìng kuáng frenzied; unscrupulous;

perverse: ～地进行破坏活动 carry on frenzied wrecking activities

sāo

搔 sāo scratch: ～痒 scratch where it itches
【搔首】 sāoshǒu scratch one's head: ～脚踝 scratch one's head in hesitation; hesitate
【搔头弄姿】 sāotóu-nòngzī 〈书〉 (of a woman) stroke one's hair in coquetry; be coquettish

骚 sāo disturb; upset
【骚动】 sāodòng ① disturbance; commotion; ferment ② be in a tumult; become restless: 人群～起来。The crowd was in a tumult.
【骚乱】 sāoluàn disturbance; riot
【骚扰】 sāorǎo harass; molest: ～破坏活动 harassing and wrecking activities

缫 sāo reel silk from cocoons; reel
【缫丝】 sāosī silk reeling; filature ◇ ～厂 reeling mill; filature/ ～机 reeling machine; filature

sǎo

扫* sǎo ① sweep; clear away: ～雪 sweep away the snow/ ～清道路 clear the path; pave the way ② pass quickly along or over; sweep: 他向会场～了一眼。He swept his eyes over the meeting-place./ 探照灯光～过夜空。The searchlights swept across the night sky. ③ put all together: ～数归还 the whole amount returned
另见 sào
【扫除】 sǎochú ① cleaning; cleanup: 大～ general cleaning ② clear away; remove; wipe out: ～一切害人虫 sweep away all pests; away with all pests/ ～前进道路上的障碍 remove the obstacles on the road of advance/ ～文盲 eliminate (或 wipe out) illiteracy
【扫荡】 sǎodàng mop up: 粉碎敌人的～ smash the enemy's mopping-up operations
【扫地】 sǎodì ① sweep the floor ② (of honour, credibility, etc.) reach rock bottom; reach an all-time low; be dragged in the dust: 名誉～ be thoroughly discredited/ 威信～ be shorn of one's prestige
【扫墓】 sǎomù sweep a grave — pay respects to a dead person at his tomb
【扫兴】 sǎoxìng have one's spirits dampened; feel disappointed: 真叫人～! How disappointing!

嫂* sǎo ① elder brother's wife; sister-in-law ② sister (a form of address for a married woman about one's own age): 桂英～ Sister Guiying
【嫂嫂】 sǎosao 〈方〉 elder brother's wife; sister-in-law
【嫂子】 sǎozi 〈口〉 elder brother's wife; sister-in-law

sào

扫* sào
另见 sǎo
【扫帚】 sàozhou broom
【扫帚星】 sàozhouxīng 〈天〉 comet

臊 sào shy; bashful: 害～ be bashful/ ～得脸通红 blush scarlet

sè

色* sè ① colour: 红～ red/ 原～ primary colour ② look; countenance; expression: 满面喜～ beaming with joy ③ kind; description: 各～人等 people of every descrip-

tion; all kinds of people ④ scene; scenery: 湖光山～ a landscape of lakes and mountains ⑤ quality (of precious metals, goods, etc.): 成～好 of good quality ⑥ woman's looks: 姿～ good looks
另见 shǎi
【色彩】 sècǎi colour; hue; tint; shade: 地方～ local colour/ 文学～ literary flavour/ 感情～ emotional colouring
【色盲】 sèmáng 〈医〉 achromatopsia; colour blindness
【色情】 sèqíng pornographic; sexy ◇ 文学 pornography
【色泽】 sèzé colour and lustre: ～鲜明 bright and lustrous
【色纸】 sèzhǐ coloured paper

涩 sè ① puckery; astringent: 这柿子～不～? Are these persimmons puckery? ② unsmooth; hard-going: 推子发～了,该上点油了。This pair of hair-clippers doesn't work smoothly. It needs oiling. ③ obscure; difficult: 文句艰～ make difficult reading

啬 sè stingy; miserly

塞* sè
另见 sāi; sài
【塞责】 sèzé not do one's job conscientiously: 敷衍～ perform one's duty in a perfunctory manner

瑟 sè 〈乐〉 se, a twenty-five-stringed plucked instrument, somewhat similar to the zither

sēn

森 sēn ① full of trees ② 〈书〉 multitudinous; in multitudes: ～罗万象 myriads of things; everything under the sun ③ dark; gloomy: 阴～ gloomy; grim
【森林】 sēnlín forest
【森严】 sēnyán stern; strict; forbidding: 壁垒～ strongly fortified/ 戒备～ heavily guarded/ 门禁～ with the entrance carefully guarded/ 等级～ be rigidly stratified; form a strict hierarchy

sēng

僧 sēng Buddhist monk; monk
【僧多粥少】 sēng duō zhōu shǎo 见 "粥少僧多" zhōu shǎo sēng duō
【僧侣】 sēnglǚ monks and priests; clergy
【僧尼】 sēng-ní Buddhist monks and nuns

shā

杀* shā ① kill; slaughter: ～人放火, 无恶不作 commit murder, arson and every crime imaginable ② fight; go into battle: ～出重围 fight one's way out of a heavy encirclement ③ weaken; reduce; abate: ～～敌人的威风 deflate the enemy's arrogance/ 风势稍～。The wind abated. ④ 〈方〉 smart: 碘酒涂在伤口上真～得慌。Iodine smarts when it is put on a cut. ⑤ take off; counteract: 白菜馅里放点盐～一～水 put some salt in the chopped cabbage to draw out the water ⑥ in the extreme; exceedingly: 笑～人 absolutely ridiculous; terribly funny/ 闷～人 bored to death
【杀虫剂】 shāchóngjì 〈农〉 insecticide; pesticide
【杀敌】 shādí fight the enemy; engage in battle: 苦练杀敌本领 practise hard to master combat skills/ 英勇～ be brave in battle; fight heroically
【杀风景】 shā fēngjǐng spoil the fun; be a wet blanket
【杀害】 shāhài murder; kill
【杀鸡取卵】 shā jī qǔ luǎn kill the hen to get the eggs; kill the goose that lays the golden eggs
【杀鸡吓猴】 shā jī xià hóu kill the chicken to frighten the

monkey — punish someone as a warning to others

【杀菌】shājūn　disinfect; sterilize ◇ ～剂 germicide; bacte"
ricide

【杀戮】shālù　massacre; slaughter: 惨遭～ be massacred in
cold blood

【杀气】shāqì ① murderous look: ～腾腾 with a murderous
look on one's face; be out to kill ② vent one's ill feeling:
你有委屈就说出来，不该拿别人～. Get it off your chest if
you feel you've been wronged. Don't take it out on
others.

【杀人】shārén　kill a person; murder ◇ ～犯 murderer;
manslayer; homicide

【杀人不见血】shārén bù jiàn xiě　kill without spilling
blood; kill by subtle means

【杀人不眨眼】shārén bù zhǎyǎn　kill without batting an
eyelid; kill without blinking an eye

【杀人如麻】shārén rú má　kill people like flies

【杀人越货】shārén yuè huò　kill a person and seize his
goods

【杀伤】shāshāng　kill and wound; inflict casualties on:
大批敌军 take a heavy toll of enemy troops／ 这种炮弹～
力很强. This is a powerful antipersonnel shell. ◇ ～弹
fragmentation bomb; antipersonnel shell

【杀身成仁】shā shēn chéng rén　die to achieve virtue — die
for a just cause

【杀身之祸】shā shēn zhī huò　a fatal disaster

【杀头】shātóu　behead; decapitate

【杀一儆百】shā yī jǐng bǎi　execute one as a warning to a
hundred

沙* shā ① sand ② granulated; powdered: 豆～ bean
paste ③ (of voice) hoarse; husky

【沙场】shāchǎng　battlefield; battleground

【沙袋】shādài　sandbag

【沙丁鱼】shādīngyú　sardine

【沙发】shāfā　sofa; settee: 单人～ upholstered (或 padded)
armchair

【沙里淘金】shālǐ táo jīn　wash grains of gold out of the
sands — extract the essential from a large mass of material;
get small returns for great effort

【沙漠】shāmò　desert: 塔克拉玛干～ the Taklamakan Desert

【沙滩】shātān　sandy beach

【沙文主义】shāwénzhǔyì　chauvinism

【沙哑】shāyǎ　hoarse; husky; raucous: 声音～ have a
husky voice

【沙眼】shāyǎn　trachoma

纱* shā ① yarn: 棉～ cotton yarn／ ～厂 cotton mill ②
gauze; sheer: 铁～ wire gauze

【纱布】shābù　gauze

【纱线】shāxiàn　yarn

杉 shā 〈植〉China fir
另见 shān

刹 shā　put on the brakes; stop; check: 把车～住 stop
(或 brake) a car／ ～住歪风 check an unhealthy tendency
另见 chà

【刹车】shāchē ① stop a vehicle by applying the brakes;
put on the brakes ② stop a machine by cutting off the
power; turn off a machine ③ brake

砂 shā　sand; grit

痧 shā　〈中医〉acute diseases such as cholera and sunstroke

【痧子】shāzi　〈方〉measles

裟 shā　见"袈裟" jiāshā

煞 shā ① stop; halt; check; bring to a close: ～住脚
stop short／ 文章写到这里还～不住. The article can't very
well end here. ② tighten: ～一～腰带 tighten one's belt
③ 见"杀" shā ③④⑥

另见 shà

【煞车】shāchē ① 见"刹车" shāchē ② firmly fasten a load
(on a vehicle); lash down

鲨 shā　shark

【鲨鱼】shāyú　shark

shǎ

傻* shǎ ① stupid; muddleheaded: 你真～，他这点意思都
听不出来. How stupid you were. You should have known
what he was driving at./ 装～ act dumb; pretend not to
know／ 吓～了 be dumbfounded; be stunned／ 你别～乎乎
的,事情没有那么简单. Don't be naive. The matter is not
so simple. ② think or act mechanically: 别一个劲儿～干,
要讲究方法. Don't just keep slogging away. Pay attention
to method.

【傻瓜】shǎguā　fool; blockhead; simpleton

【傻头傻脑】shǎtóu-shǎnǎo ① foolish-looking ② muddleheaded

【傻笑】shǎxiào　laugh foolishly; giggle; smirk

【傻子】shǎzi　fool; blockhead; simpleton

shà

厦* shà　a tall building; mansion: 高楼大～ tall buildings and great mansions
另见 xià

歃 shà　〈书〉suck

【歃血】shàxuè　smear the blood of a sacrifice on the
mouth — an ancient form of swearing an oath

煞 shà ① evil spirit; goblin ② very
另见 shā

【煞费苦心】shà fèi kǔxīn　cudgel one's brains; take great
pains: ～地寻找借口 cudgel one's brains to find an excuse／
他们为了攻克技术难关,可真是～。They took great pains to
solve the difficult technical problem.

【煞有介事】shà yǒu jiè shì　make a great show of being in
earnest; pretend to be serious (about doing sth.)

霎 shà　a very short time; moment; instant: 一～ in a
moment

【霎时间】shàshíjiān　in a twinkling; in a split second; in a
jiffy

shāi

筛 shāi ① sieve; sifter; screen ② sift; sieve; screen;
riddle: ～面 sieve flour; sift flour／ ～煤 screen coal／ ～砂
砾 riddle gravel／ ～煤渣 sift cinders

shǎi

色 shǎi　〈口〉colour: 这布掉～吗? Will this cloth fade?
另见 sè

【色子】shǎizi　dice: 掷～ play dice

shài

晒* shài ① (of the sun) shine upon: 日～雨淋 be exposed to the sun and rain/ 这里～得慌. There's too much sun here. ② dry in the sun; bask: ～粮食 dry grain in the sun/ ～被子 air a quilt/ 他的脸～黑了. His face is tanned./ 让孩子们尽量多～～太阳. Take the children out to get as much sun as possible.

shān

山* shān ① hill; mountain ② anything resembling a mountain: 冰～ iceberg ③ bushes in which silkworms spin cocoons: 蚕上～了. The silkworms have gone into the bushes to spin their cocoons.
【山崩】 shānbēng　landslide; landslip
【山川】 shānchuān　mountains and rivers — land; landscape
【山村】 shāncūn　mountain village
【山地】 shāndì　① mountainous region; hilly area; hilly country ② fields on a hill
【山顶】 shāndǐng　the summit (或 top) of a mountain; hilltop
【山洞】 shāndòng　cave; cavern
【山峰】 shānfēng　mountain peak
【山冈】 shāngāng　low hill; hillock
【山高水低】 shāngāo-shuǐdī　unexpected misfortune; sth. unfortunate, esp. death
【山歌】 shāngē　folk song (sung in the fields during or after work)
【山沟】 shāngōu　gully; ravine; (mountain) valley
【山谷】 shāngǔ　mountain valley
【山河】 shānhé　mountains and rivers — the land of a country: 祖国的锦绣～ our beautiful land
【山脚】 shānjiǎo　the foot of a hill
【山口】 shānkǒu　mountain pass; pass
【山林】 shānlín　mountain forest; wooded mountain: ～地区 mountain and forest region; wooded and hilly lands
【山岭】 shānlǐng　mountain ridge
【山麓】 shānlù　the foot of a mountain ◇ ～丘陵 foothills
【山峦】 shānluán　chain of mountains; multipeaked mountain: ～起伏 undulating hills
【山脉】 shānmài　mountain range; mountain chain
【山盟海誓】 shānméng-hǎishì　(make) a solemn pledge of love
【山明水秀】 shānmíng-shuǐxiù　green hills and clear waters — picturesque scenery　又作"山清水秀"
【山坡】 shānpō　hillside; mountain slope
【山穷水尽】 shānqióng-shuǐjìn　where the mountains and the rivers end — at the end of one's rope (或 tether, resources)
【山区】 shānqū　mountain area
【山泉】 shānquán　mountain spring
【山水】 shānshuǐ　① water from a mountain ② mountains and rivers; scenery with hills and waters: ～相连 be linked by common mountains and rivers ③〈美术〉 traditional Chinese painting of mountains and waters; landscape ◇～画 mountains-and-waters painting; landscape painting
【山羊】 shānyáng　① goat ②〈体〉 buck ◇ ～胡子 goatee/ ～绒 cashmere
【山腰】 shānyāo　half way up the mountain
【山雨欲来风满楼】 shānyǔ yù lái fēng mǎn lóu　the wind sweeping through the tower heralds a rising storm in the mountains; the rising wind forebodes the coming storm
【山岳】 shānyuè　lofty mountains ◇ ～冰川 mountain glacier; alpine glacier/ ～地区 mountainous region
【山珍海味】 shānzhēn-hǎiwèi　delicacies from land and sea; dainties of every kind　又作"山珍海错"

杉 shān〈植〉China fir
另见 shā

删* shān　delete; leave out: 这一段可以～去. This paragraph can be left out./ ～掉不必要的细节 cut out the unnecessary details
【删除】 shānchú　delete; strike (或 cut, cross) out
【删繁就简】 shānfán-jiùjiǎn　simplify sth. by cutting out the superfluous
【删改】 shāngǎi　delete and change; revise: 稿子几经～才定下来. The draft was revised several times before it was finalized.
【删节】 shānjié　abridge; abbreviate: 本报略有～ slightly abridged by our editorial staff ◇ ～本 abridged edition; abbreviated version/ ～号 ellipsis; suspension points; ellipsis dots (……) (...)

衫 shān　unlined upper garment: 衬～ shirt/ 汗～ undershirt

姗 shān
【姗姗来迟】 shānshān lái chí　be slow in coming; be late

珊 shān
【珊瑚】 shānhú　coral
◇ ～虫 coral polyp; coral insect/ ～岛 coral island/ ～礁 coral reef

舢* shān
【舢板】 shānbǎn　sampan

扇 shān　① fan: ～火 fan a fire/ ～子 fan oneself; use a fan ② incite; instigate; fan up; stir up: ～阴风 fan up an evil wind; secretly stir up trouble
另见 shàn
【扇动】 shāndòng　① fan; flap: ～翅膀 flap the wings ② instigate; incite; stir up; whip up: ～无政府主义 incite anarchism
【扇风点火】 shānfēng-diǎnhuǒ　fan the flames; inflame and agitate people; stir up trouble
【扇惑】 shānhuò　incite; agitate: ～人心 agitate people by demagogy

蹒 shān　见"蹒跚" pánshān

煽 shān　见"扇" shān②

潸 shān　〈书〉 in tears; tearfully: ～然泪下 tears trickling down one's cheeks

膻 shān　the smell of mutton: 这羊肉不～. This mutton hasn't got a strong smell.

shǎn

闪* shǎn　① dodge; get out of the way: 往旁边一～ dodge swiftly to one side; jump out of the way ② twist; sprain: ～了腰 sprain one's back ③ lightning: 打～ flashes of lightning ④ flash; sparkle; shine: 远处灯光一～. There was a flash of light in the distance. 一～而过 flash past; streak past/ 这时我脑子里一过一个念头. At this moment an idea flashed through my mind. ⑤ leave behind: 你去的时候叫我一声, 可别把我～下. Please call for me when you go; don't leave me behind.
【闪避】 shǎnbì　dodge; sidestep
【闪电】 shǎndiàn　lightning ◇ ～战 lightning war; blitzkrieg; blitz
【闪光】 shǎnguāng　① flash of light: 流星像一道～, 划破黑夜的长空. With a flash, the meteor shot across the night sky. ② gleam; glisten; glitter: 露珠在晨曦中～. Dewdrops glistened in the morning light. ◇ ～灯〈摄〉 flash lamp; photoflash
【闪开】 shǎnkāi　get out of the way; jump aside; dodge: 车来了, 快～! Look out! There's a bus coming.
【闪闪】 shǎnshǎn　sparkle; glisten; glitter: ～的星星 sparkling stars/ ～发光 sparkle; glitter/ 天空中电光～. Lightning flashed in the sky.

【闪烁】 shǎnshuò ①twinkle; glimmer; glisten: 远处～着灯光。 Lights glimmered in the distance./ 她的眼睛里～着喜悦的泪花。 Her eyes glistened with tears of joy. ②evasive; vague; noncommittal: ～其词 speak evasively; hedge/ 他闪闪烁烁,不做肯定的答复。 He hummed and hawed, giving no definite reply. 或 He was evasive and noncommittal.

【闪耀】 shǎnyào glitter; shine; radiate: 繁星～ glittering stars/ 他两眼～着刚毅的光芒。 His eyes flashed with resolution.

陕 Shǎn short for Shaanxi Province

睒 shǎn blink; twinkle: 这孩子一～眼就不见了。 The boy vanished in the twinkling of an eye.

shàn

讪 shàn ①mock; ridicule ②embarrassed; awkward; shamefaced: ～～地走开 walk away looking embarrassed
【讪笑】 shànxiào ridicule; mock; deride

扇* shàn ①fan: 电～ electric fan ②leaf: 门～ door leaf/ 八～屏风 eight-leaf screen/ 隔～partition ③〈量〉〔用于门窗等〕: 一～门 a door
另见 shān
【扇形】 shànxíng ①fan-shaped ②〈数〉sector ◇ ～齿轮 〈机〉sector (或 segment) gear
【扇子】 shànzi fan

善* shàn ①good: 心怀不～ harbour ill intent/ 改恶从～ give up evil and return to good; mend one's ways ②satisfactory; good: ～策 a wise policy; the best policy ③make a success of; perfect: 工欲～其事,必先利其器。 A workman must sharpen his tools if he is to do his work well. ④kind; friendly: 友～ be friendly; be kind and helpful ⑤be good at; be expert (或 adept) in: 不～经管 not good at management/ ～破～立 be good at destroying the old and establishing the new/ 勇敢～战 be brave and skilful in battle/ ～观风色 quick to see which way the wind blows — very shrewd ⑥properly: 自保重 take good care of yourself/ ～为说辞 put in a good word for sb. ⑦be apt to: ～变 be apt to change; be changeable/ ～忘 be forgetful; have a short memory
【善本】 shànběn reliable text; good edition: ～书 rare book
【善后】 shànhòu deal with problems arising from an accident, etc.: 处理这次火灾的～ deal with the aftermath of the fire
【善举】 shànjǔ 〈书〉philanthropic act or project
【善良】 shànliáng good and honest; kindhearted: ～的人们 good and honest people; people of goodwill/ ～愿望 the best of intentions; 心地～ kindhearted
【善人】 shànrén philanthropist; charitable person; well-doer
【善始善终】 shànshǐ-shànzhōng start well and end well; do well from start to finish; see sth. through
【善心】 shànxīn mercy; benevolence
【善意】 shànyì goodwill; good intentions: 出于～ out of goodwill; with the best intentions/ ～的批评 well-meaning criticism
【善有善报,恶有恶报】 shàn yǒu shànbào, è yǒu èbào good will be rewarded with good, and evil with evil
【善于】 shànyú be good at; be adept in: ～歌舞 be good at singing and dancing
【善终】 shànzhōng die a natural death; die in one's bed

禅 shàn
另见 chán
【禅让】 shànràng abdicate and hand over the crown to another person

缮 shàn ①repair; mend: 房屋修～ house repairing ②copy; write out: ～清 make a fair copy

【缮写】 shànxiě write out; copy

擅 shàn ①arrogate to oneself; do sth. on one's own authority: ～权 monopolize power; usurp power/ ～作主张 make a decision without authorization ②be good at; be expert in: 不～辞令 lack facility in polite or tactful speech
【擅长】 shàncháng be good at; be expert in; be skilled in: 他～侧泳。 He has a good sidestroke.
【擅离职守】 shàn lí zhíshǒu be absent from one's post without leave; leave one's post without permission
【擅自】 shànzì do sth. without authorization: 不得～修改操作规程。 No unauthorized changes may be made in the rules of operation./ ～行动 act presumptuously

膳 shàn meals; board: 在食堂用～ have one's meals at the mess
【膳费】 shànfèi board expenses
【膳食】 shànshí meals; food
【膳宿】 shàn-sù board and lodging

赡 shàn ①support; provide for: ～家养口 support a family ②〈书〉sufficient; abundant
【赡养】 shànyǎng support; provide for: ～父母 support one's parents ◇ (离婚后付给对方的) ～费 alimony

shāng

伤* shāng ①wound; injury: 刀～ a knife wound/ 轻～ a slight injury/ 烫～ a scald/ 满身是～ be covered with cuts and bruises/ ～好了。 The wound has healed. ②injure; hurt: 被汽车撞～ be knocked down and injured by a car/ 摔～ fall and hurt oneself/ ～感情 hurt sb.'s feelings ③be distressed: 哀～ sad/ sorrowful ④get sick of sth.; develop an aversion to sth.: 这孩子吃糖吃～了。 The child has got sick of eating sweets. ⑤be harmful to; hinder: 无～大雅 involving no major principle; not matter much/ 有～国体 discredit one's country
【伤疤】 shāngbā scar
【伤兵】 shāngbīng wounded soldier
【伤风】 shāngfēng catch cold; have a cold
【伤风败俗】 shāngfēng-bàisú offend public decency; corrupt public morals
【伤感】 shānggǎn sick at heart; sentimental
【伤害】 shānghài injure; harm; hurt: 不要～益鸟。 Don't harm beneficial birds./ 饮酒过多会～身体。 Excessive drinking is harmful to the health./ ～自尊心 injure (或 hurt) one's pride; hurt one's self-respect
【伤痕】 shānghén scar; bruise
【伤口】 shāngkǒu wound; cut: 洗～ bathe a wound
【伤脑筋】 shāngnǎojīn knotty; troublesome; bothersome: ～的问题 a knotty problem; headache/ 老下雨,真～。 It's a nuisance the way it keeps on raining.
【伤神】 shāngshén overtax one's nerves; be nerve-racking
【伤势】 shāngshì the condition of an injury (或 wound): ～很重 be seriously wounded (或 injured)
【伤亡】 shāng-wáng injuries and deaths; casualties: ～惨重 suffer heavy casualties
【伤心】 shāngxīn sad; grieved; broken-hearted: ～落泪 shed sad tears; weep in grief/ 别为这事～。 Don't let it grieve you./ 丈夫有泪不轻弹,只因未到～处。 A man does not easily shed tears until his heart is broken. ◇～事 old sore; painful memory; grief
【伤心惨目】 shāngxīn-cǎnmù too ghastly to look at; tragic (scene)

商* shāng ①discuss; consult: 有要事相～。 I have important matters to discuss with you. ②trade; commerce; business: 经～ engage in trade; be in business/ 通～ have trade relations ③merchant; trader; businessman; dealer: 私～ businessman/ 盐～ salt dealer/ 奸～ profiteer ④〈数〉quotient

【商标】shāngbiāo trade mark ◇ ~注册 trade mark registration

【商埠】shāngbù 〈旧〉commercial (或 trading) port

【商场】shāngchǎng market; bazaar

【商船】shāngchuán merchant ship; merchantman

【商店】shāngdiàn shop; store

【商定】shāngdìng decide through consultation; agree: 经~ it has been decided through consultation that/ 已~的条款 the provisions already agreed upon/ 双方~建立大使级外交关系。The two sides have agreed to establish diplomatic relations at ambassadorial level.

【商港】shānggǎng commercial port

【商贾】shānggǔ 〈书〉merchants

【商行】shāngháng trading company; commercial firm

【商号】shānghào shop; store; business establishment

【商会】shānghuì chamber of commerce

【商界】shāngjiè business circles; commercial circles

【商量】shāngliang consult; discuss; talk over: 这事好~。That can be settled through discussion.

【商品】shāngpǐn commodity; goods; merchandise

【商洽】shāngqià arrange with sb.; take up (a matter) with sb.

【商情】shāngqíng market conditions ◇ ~预测 business forecasting

【商榷】shāngquè discuss; deliberate: 这一点值得~。This point is open to question./ 提出几点意见，与诸位~。Here are a few points I wish to discuss with you.

【商人】shāngrén businessman; merchant; trader

【商谈】shāngtán exchange views; confer; discuss; negotiate: ~递交国书事宜 discuss matters relating to the presentation of credentials/ 望贵方即指派代表前来~。We hope that you will appoint representatives to come here for the negotiations.

【商讨】shāngtǎo discuss; deliberate over: 就发展两国关系进行有益的~ hold useful discussions on developing relations between the two countries

【商务】shāngwù commercial affairs; business affairs ◇ ~参赞 commercial counsellor/ ~处 commercial counsellor's office/ ~代表 commercial representative; trade representative

【商业】shāngyè commerce; trade; business ◇ ~部门 commercial departments/ ~惯例 business practice/ ~机构 business organization; commercial undertaking/ ~区 business quarter; commercial district; business district/ ~网 commercial network; network of trading establishments/ ~信贷 commercial credit/ ~银行 commercial bank/ ~中心 commercial centre; trading centre; shopping centre/ ~资本 commercial capital; merchant capital

【商议】shāngyì confer; discuss

shǎng

上* shǎng 〈语〉见"上声"shàngshēng
另见 shàng; shang

晌 shǎng ①part of the day: 前半~儿 morning/ 晚半~儿 dusk ②〈方〉noon: 歇~ take a midday nap or rest

【晌午】shǎngwu 〈口〉midday; noon: ~饭 midday meal; lunch

赏* shǎng ①grant (或 bestow) a reward; award: 国王~给那个士兵一匹马。The king awarded the soldier a horse. ②reward; award: 有~有罚。Duly mete out rewards and punishments. ③admire; enjoy; appreciate: ~月 admire the full moon; enjoy looking at the moon/ 奇文共~ share the pleasure of reading a rare piece of writing

【赏赐】shǎngcì grant (或 bestow) a reward; award: 把奴隶~给贵族 award slaves to aristocrats/ 得到很多~ be given a handsome reward

【赏罚】shǎng-fá rewards and punishments: ~严明 be strict and fair in meting out rewards and punishments

【赏光】shǎngguāng 〈套〉〔用于请对方接受邀请〕: 务请~ request the pleasure of your company

【赏鉴】shǎngjiàn appreciate (a work of art)

【赏金】shǎngjīn money reward; pecuniary reward

【赏识】shǎngshí recognize the worth of; appreciate: 主编很~他这篇文章。The editor in chief thinks highly of this article of his.

【赏玩】shǎngwán admire the beauty of sth.; delight in; enjoy: ~山景 enjoy mountain scenery/ ~古董 delight in antiques

【赏心悦目】shǎngxīn-yuèmù find the scenery pleasing to both the eye and the mind

shàng

上* shàng ①upper; up; upward: ~铺 upper berth/ 这头朝~ this side up/ 往~看 look up; look upward ②higher; superior; better: 中~水平 above the average; better than the average/ 这个词是旧时下对~的称呼。This word was used in the old days to address one's superiors. ③first (part); preceding; previous: ~册 the first volume; Volume One; Book One/ ~集 the first part; Part One; Volume One/ ~半夜 the first half of the night; before midnight/ 二十世纪~半叶 the first half of the twentieth century/ ~星期三 last Wednesday/ ~一季度 the previous quarter/ ~一段 the preceding (或 above, foregoing) paragraph ④the emperor: ~谕 imperial decree ⑤〈乐〉a note of the scale in gongchepu (工尺谱), corresponding to 1 in numbered musical notation ⑥go up; mount; board; get on: ~坡 go up a slope/ ~山 go up a hill; go uphill/ ~公共汽车 get on a bus/ ~自行车 get on a bike/ ~飞机 board a plane/ ~船 go aboard a ship; go on board/ ~岸 go ashore; go on shore; land/ ~楼 go upstairs/ 逆流而~ go upstream; go against the current ⑦go to; leave for: 你~哪儿去? Where are you going? ⑧submit; send in; present: 李小红谨~ Yours respectfully Li Xiaohong ⑨forge ahead; go ahead: 快~,投篮! Go ahead. Quick! Shoot!/ 有条件要~,没有条件创造条件也要~。When the conditions exist, go ahead; when they don't, create them and go ahead. ⑩〈剧〉appear on the stage; enter: 二战士~。Enter left two soldiers. ⑪〈体〉enter the court or field: 换人: 三号下,四号~。Substitution: Player No. 4 for No. 3./ 这一盘你~。You play this game. ⑫fill; supply; serve: 给水箱~水 fill the tank with water/ 一连~了好几道菜。Several courses were served in succession. ⑬place sth. in position; set; fix: ~刀具 fix a cutting tool/ ~梁 set the roof beams in place/ 行李还没~架。The luggage has not been put on the rack yet. ⑭apply; paint; smear: ~药膏 apply ointment/ ~肥 spread manure/ 给门~漆 paint the door/ 给机器~油 oil (或 grease) the machine ⑮be put on record; be carried(in a publication) ⑯wind; screw; tighten: 表该~了。The watch needs winding./ 螺丝没有~紧。The screw hasn't been tightened./ 门没~锁。The door isn't locked. ⑰be engaged (in work, study, etc.) at a fixed time: 我今天~中班。I'm on the middle shift today./ 她的大女儿在~大学。Her eldest daughter is now in college. ⑱up to; as many as: ~百人 up to a hundred people/~万 as many as ten thousand ⑲〈语〉见"上声"
另见 shǎng; shang

上* shang ①〔用在动词后,表示由低处向高处〕: 爬~河堤 climb up to the top of the dyke/ 登~山顶 reach the summit/ 踏~非洲的土地 set foot on African soil/ 对敌人的新仇旧恨,一齐涌~心头。Hatred of the enemy, for old and new wrongs, welled up in his heart. ②〔用在动词后,表示达到目的〕: 锁~门 lock the door; lock up/ 穿~外衣 put on a coat/ 当~会计 become an accountant/ 没吃~饭 be too late for the meal/ 你跟他接~头了吗? Have you got in touch with him? ③〔用在动词后,表示开始并继续〕: 她爱~了草原。She's fallen in love with the grasslands./ 他拿起一把铁就干~了。He seized a shovel and set to. ④〔用在名词后,表示位置、范围或方面〕: 会~ at the meeting/ 报

~说的 what is reported in the newspapers/ 事实~ in fact; in reality; actually/ 理论~ in theory; theoretically 另见 shǎng; shàng

【上班】 shàngbān go to work; start work; be on duty: 她~去了。She's gone to work./ 下午不~。We'll take the afternoon off. 或 No work this afternoon./ 我们每天早上八点钟~。We start work at 8 every morning. ◇ ~时间 work hours; office hours

【上半场】 shàngbànchǎng first half (of a game): ~比分多少? What was the score at half time?

【上半响】 shàngbànshǎng forenoon; morning

【上半身】 shàngbànshēn the upper part of the body; above the waist

【上半夜】 shàngbànyè before midnight

【上辈】 shàngbèi ① ancestors ② the elder generation of one's family; one's elders

【上臂】 shàngbì the upper arm

【上边】 shàngbian 见"上面"

【上宾】 shàngbīn distinguished guest; guest of honour

【上苍】 shàngcāng Heaven; God

【上策】 shàngcè the best plan; the best way out; the best thing to do

【上层】 shàngcéng upper strata; upper levels ◇ ~分子 members of the upper strata; upper-class elements/ ~人士 upper circles/ ~社会 upper classes of society; upper-class society

【上场】 shàngchǎng ① 〈剧〉 appear on the stage; enter: 战士甲~。Enter Soldier A. ② 〈体〉 enter the court or field; join in a contest: 双方运动员都已经~。Players of both teams have entered the court./ 今天该谁~? Who's playing today?

【上床】 shàngchuáng go to bed

【上达】 shàngdá reach the higher authorities: 下情~ make the situation at the lower level known to the higher authorities

【上代】 shàngdài the previous generation; former generations

【上当】 shàngdàng be taken in; be fooled; be duped: 这回我可不~啦! I won't be taken in this time./ 走这条路可~了, 尽是水坑。We're fools to have chosen this path; it's full of puddles./ 不要上坏人的当。Don't let yourself be fooled by evil people.

【上等】 shàngděng first-class; first-rate; superior: ~货 first-class goods/ ~料子 high-quality material

【上帝】 Shàngdì God

【上吊】 shàngdiào hang oneself

【上方宝剑】 shàngfāng bǎojiàn the imperial sword (a symbol of high authority, investing the bearer with discretionary powers)

【上告】 shànggào complain to the higher authorities or appeal to a higher court

【上工】 shànggōng go to work; start work: 夜班十点钟~。The night shift starts at 10.

【上钩】 shànggōu rise to the bait; swallow the bait; get hooked

【上古】 shànggǔ ancient times; remote ages ◇ ~史 ancient history

【上轨道】 shàng guǐdào get on the right track; begin to work smoothly: 生产已~。Production is proceeding smoothly.

【上好】 shànghǎo first-class; best-quality; tip-top: ~烟叶 best-quality tobacco

【上级】 shàngjí higher level; higher authorities

【上届】 shàngjiè previous term or session; last

【上进】 shàngjìn go forward; make progress: 不求~ not strive to make progress ◇ ~心 the desire to do better; the urge for improvement

【上课】 shàngkè ① attend class; go to class: 你昨天怎么没来? Why didn't you come to class yesterday?/ 今天下午我们不~。We have no classes this afternoon. ② conduct a class; give a lesson (或 lecture): 学校八点开始~。Classes begin at 8.

【上空】 shàngkōng in the sky; overhead

【上口】 shàngkǒu ① be able to read aloud fluently: 孩子们把这首诗念了又念, 现在都能琅琅~了。The children have read the poem several times, and can all recite it quite fluently now. ② be suitable for reading aloud; make smooth reading: 这段文字太艰深,不易~。The passage is too difficult and doesn't lend itself to reading aloud.

【上来】 shànglai come up:游了半天了,快~歇会儿吧。You've been swimming a long time now. Come out and have a rest.

【上来】 shanglai ①〔用在动词后, 表示由低处到高处或由远处到近处来〕: 部队从两路增援~。Reinforcements arrived by two routes./ 外国朋友围~要他们签名留念。The foreign friends gathered around them and asked for their autographs. ②〔用在动词后, 表示成功〕: 这个问题你答得~吗? Can you answer this question?/ 看他面熟, 名字可叫不~。I know his face but I can't recall his name./ 等我爬到山顶的时候, 气都快喘不~了。By the time I got to the top of the hill, I was quite out of breath.

【上梁】 shàngliáng ① (of bicycles) cross bar; top tube ② (of buildings) upper beam: ~不正下梁歪。If the upper beam is not straight, the lower ones will go aslant — when those above behave unworthily, those below will do the same.

【上列】 shàngliè the above-listed; the above: ~各项 the items listed above; the above-listed items

【上流】 shàngliú ① upper reaches (of a river) ② belonging to the upper circles; upper-class: ~社会 high society; polite society

【上路】 shànglù set out on a journey; start off

【上门】 shàngmén ① come or go to see sb.; call; drop in; visit: 他好久没~了。It's a long time since he last called./ 送货~ deliver goods to the doorstep ② shut the door (或 lock up) for the night; bolt the door

【上面】 shàngmian ① above; over; on top of; on the surface of: 飞机在云层~飞行。The plane flew above the clouds./ 粉墙~挂着大幅标语。Large streamers bearing slogans were hanging on the white wall./ 你的行李袋就在我的箱子~。Your bag is on top of my suitcase./ ~就是琉璃塔了。Further up is the glazed-tile pagoda./ 大桥~走汽车, 下面走火车。The upper deck of the bridge is for motor vehicles, the lower deck for trains./ 运河~架了一座桥。A bridge has been built across the canal. ② above-mentioned; aforesaid; foregoing: ~所举的例子 the above-mentioned example/ ~这几条理由 the aforesaid reasons/ ~几个发言 the speeches you've just heard; the previous speeches ③ the higher authorities; the higher-ups: ~有指示。There are instructions from above. ④ aspect; respect; regard: 他在外文~下了很多功夫。He has put a lot of effort into his study of foreign languages.

【上年纪】 shàng niánji be getting on in years

【上品】 shàngpǐn highest grade; top grade

【上气不接下气】 shàngqì bù jiē xiàqì gasp for breath; be out of breath

【上去】 shàngqu go up: 登着梯子~ go up (on) a ladder/ 车来了,我们~吧。Here comes the bus. Let's get on.

【上去】 shangqu 〔用在动词后, 表示由低到高, 或由近及远, 或由主体向对象〕: 爬~ climb up/ 把大车推~ push the cart up

【上任】 shàngrèn take up an official post; assume office

【上上】 shàngshàng ① the very best: ~策 the best plan ② before last: ~星期 the week before last

【上身】 shàngshēn ① the upper part of the body: 光着~ be stripped to the waist/ 他~穿一件土布衬衫。He's wearing a shirt of handwoven cloth. ② upper outer garment; shirt; blouse; jacket: 姑娘们穿着白~, 花裙子。The girls are wearing white blouses and bright-coloured skirts.

【上升】 shàngshēng rise; go up; ascend: 气温~。The temperature is going up./ 生产持续~。Production is rising steadily./ 一缕炊烟袅袅~。A wisp of smoke is curling up from the kitchen chimney.

【上声】 shàngshēng 或 shǎngshēng 〈语〉 falling-rising tone, one of the four tones in classical Chinese and the third tone in modern standard Chinese pronunciation

【上乘】 shàngchéng ① 〈佛教〉 Mahayana; Great Vehicle ② a literary or artistic work of a high order

【上市】 shàngshì go (或 appear) on the market: 番茄大量～。There are plenty of tomatoes on the market./ 这是刚～的苹果。These apples have just come in.

【上述】 shàngshù above-mentioned; aforementioned; aforesaid: 严格遵守～原则 strictly abide by the above-mentioned principles/ 达到～目标 achieve the aforementioned objectives

【上司】 shàngsi superior; boss: 顶头～ one's immediate superior

【上诉】 shàngsù 〈法〉appeal (to a higher court): 提出～ lodge an appeal

【上算】 shàngsuàn paying; worthwhile: 烧煤气比烧煤～。It's more economical to use gas than coal.

【上台】 shàngtái ① go up onto the platform; appear on the stage: 她～演奏了两支钢琴曲子。She went up onto the platform and played two piano pieces. ② assume power; come (或 rise) to power

【上体】 shàngtǐ 〈书〉the upper part of the body

【上天】 shàngtiān ① Heaven; Providence; God ② go up to the sky; fly sky-high

【上天无路,入地无门】 shàng tiān wú lù, rù dì wú mén there is no road to heaven and no door into the earth — no way of escape; in desperate straits

【上文】 shàngwén foregoing paragraphs or chapters; preceding part of the text: 见～ see above

【上午】 shàngwǔ forenoon; morning

【上下】 shàng-xià ① high and low; old and young: 全军～ the whole army, officers and men alike/ ～通气 full communication between the higher and lower levels/ ～一条心。The leadership and the rank and file are of one mind./ 举国～一片欢腾。The whole nation is jubilant./ 全家上上下下都很高兴。All members of the family, old and young, are very pleased. ② from top to bottom; up and down: ～打量 look sb. up and down; scrutinize sb. from head to foot/ 这个水塔～有五十米。The water tower is fifty metres high. ③ go up and down: 山上修了公路, 汽车～很方便。With the completion of the highway up the mountain, cars can easily go up and down. ④ relative superiority or inferiority: 不相～ equally matched; about the same ⑤ 〔用在数量词后面〕about; or so; or thereabouts: 四十岁～ about forty years old; forty or so

【上下其手】 shàng-xià qí shǒu practise fraud; league together for some evil end

【上下文】 shàng-xiàwén context

【上行下效】 shàng xíng xià xiào those in subordinate positions will follow the example set by their superiors; if a leader sets a bad example, it will be followed by his subordinates; those below follow the (usu. bad) example of those above

【上学】 shàngxué go to school; attend school; be at school: 上过几年学 have been to school for a few years; have had a few years' schooling/ 这孩子～了没有? Is the child at school?

【上演】 shàngyǎn put on the stage; perform: 国庆节将～几个新戏。Several new plays will be performed on National Day.

【上衣】 shàngyī upper outer garment; jacket

【上议院】 shàngyìyuàn upper house; the House of Lords (of Britain)

【上瘾】 shàngyǐn be addicted (to sth.); get into the habit (of doing sth.): 他抽烟抽上了瘾。He's got into the habit of smoking./ 这种药吃多了会～。This medicine is habit-forming.

【上映】 shàngyìng show (a film); screen: 近来有几部新片～。A number of new films have been shown recently.

【上游】 shàngyóu ① upper reaches (of a river) ② advanced position: 力争～ aim high; strive for the best/ ～无止境。One can always aim higher.

【上涨】 shàngzhǎng rise; go up: 河水～。The river has risen./ 物价～。The prices are going up.

【上阵】 shàngzhèn go into battle; pitch into the work: 男女老少齐～。Men and women, old and young, all pitched into the work./ 今晚比赛谁～? Who's going to play in tonight's match?

【上肢】 shàngzhī upper limbs

【上座】 shàngzuò seat of honour

尚* shàng ① 〈书〉〈副〉still; yet: 一息～存 as long as one lives; so long as there is still breath left in one/ ～待进一步讨论 pending further discussion/ 为时～早。It is still too early. 或 The time is not yet ripe./ 此事～未解决。The matter remains to be settled. 或 The problem is not resolved as yet. ② esteem; value; set great store by: 崇～ uphold; advocate/ ～武 set great store by martial qualities; emphasize military affairs

【尚且】 shàngqiě 〈连〉〔提出程度更甚的事例作为衬托, 下文常用 "何况" 等呼应, 表示进一层的意思〕even: 大人～举不起来, 何况小孩子。Even grown-ups can't lift it, to say nothing of children./ 你～不行, 更不用说我了。If you can't do it, how can I?

shang

裳 shang 见 "衣裳" yīshang
另见 cháng

shāo

烧* shāo ① burn: 干柴好～。Wood burns better (或 more easily) when dry./ 把这些废纸～掉吧。Let's burn up all this waste paper./ 侵略军到处～杀抢掠。The invaders burned, killed and looted wherever they went./ 把帽子～了一个洞 burn a hole in one's hat ② cook; bake; heat: ～饭 cook food; prepare a meal/ ～一点水 heat up some water/ 水～开了。The water is boiling./ ～炭 make charcoal/ ～砖 bake (或 fire) bricks ③ stew after frying or fry after stewing: ～茄子 stewed eggplant/ 红～肉 pork stewed in soy sauce ④ roast: ～鸡 roast chicken ⑤ run a fever; have a temperature: 病人～得厉害。The patient's running a high fever. 或 The patient has a high temperature. ⑥ fever: ～退了。The fever is down.

【烧火】 shāohuǒ make a fire; light a fire; tend the kitchen fire

【烧卖】 shāomai 〈食品〉a steamed dumpling with the dough gathered at the top 又作 烧麦

【烧香】 shāoxiāng burn joss sticks (before an idol)

【烧灼】 shāozhuó burn; scorch; singe

捎 shāo take along sth. to or for sb.; bring to sb.: 请把这张报～给她。Take this paper to her, please./ 我给你孩子～来一点花生。I've brought your children some peanuts./ ～个口信 take a message to sb./ 替我给大家～个好。Please give my regards to everybody.

梢 shāo tip; the thin end of a twig, etc.: 鞭～ whiplash/ 树～ the top of a tree/ 辫子～ the end of a plait

【梢头】 shāotóu ① the tip of a branch ② 〈林〉top log

稍 shāo 〈副〉a little; a bit; slightly; a trifle: ～加修改 make slight changes; make a few alterations/ ～胜一筹 just a little better/ 这大衣～长了一点。The coat is a bit too long./ 请～等一会儿。Please wait a moment. 或 Just a moment, please./ ～事休息后又继续开会。The meeting continued after a short interval.

【稍微】 shāowēi 〈副〉a little; a bit; slightly; a trifle: ～掘点盐 put in a little salt/ 今天～有点冷。It's rather chilly today./ ～有点惊慌 be a trifle alarmed/ 这种颜色比那种深一点。This colour is just a shade darker than that one.

【稍息】 shāoxī 〈军〉stand at ease: ～! (口令) At ease!

【稍许】 shāoxǔ 见 "稍微"

sháo

勺 sháo ① spoon; ladle: 长柄～ ladle; dipper ② sháo,

an old unit of capacity (=1 centilitre)
【勺子】 sháozi ladle; scoop

芍 sháo
【芍药】 sháoyao 〈植〉 Chinese herbaceous peony

韶 sháo 〈书〉 splendid; beautiful
【韶光】 sháoguāng 〈书〉 ① beautiful springtime ② glorious youth 又作"韶华"

sháo

少* sháo ① few; little; less: 以～胜多 defeat the many with the few/ ～花钱，多办事。Get more done on less money./ ～走弯路 avoid detours/ ～吃多餐 have many meals but little food at each/ 最近我们很～见到他。We've seen very little of him lately./ 现在我工作中困难～些了。Now I meet with fewer difficulties in my work./ 七比九一二。Seven is two less than nine. ② be short; lack: 我们还～两把椅子。We're still two chairs short./ 缺医～药 be short of doctors and medicine/ 我们～一个好的守门员。We lack a good goalkeeper./ 帐算错了，～一块钱。This account is wrong; we're one *yuan* short. ③ lose; be missing: 看看～不～人。See if anyone is missing./ 这里肯定～了一个字。Surely, there's a word missing here./ 羊群里～了几只羊。A few sheep have been lost from the flock. ④ a little while; a moment: 请～候。Wait a moment, please. ⑤ stop; quit: ～废话！Stop talking rubbish!/ ～来这一套。Cut it out. 或 Quit that!/ ～给我装蒜！Stop pretending!
另见 shào
【少安毋躁】 shǎo ān wú zào don't be impatient, wait for a while
【少不得】 shǎobude cannot do without; cannot dispense with: 学科学，参考书是～的。Reference books are indispensable in scientific studies./ 这事～还要麻烦您。We may have to trouble you again about this.
【少不了】 shǎobuliǎo ① cannot do without; cannot dispense with: 这次比赛～你。We can't do without you for this match. ② be bound to; be unavoidable: 准备仓促，演出～会有缺点。The performance has been arranged at short notice, so it's bound to have shortcomings. ③ considerable: 困难看来～。It looks as if there are going to be a lot of difficulties.
【少而精】 shǎo ér jīng smaller quantity, better quality; fewer but better: 教学内容要～。Teaching content should be concise.
【少见多怪】 shǎojiàn-duōguài consider sth. remarkable simply because one has not seen it before; comment excitedly on a commonplace thing (out of ignorance or inexperience): 用不着～。There's nothing to be surprised at./ 也许是我～。Maybe it was all due to my own ignorance.
【少刻】 shǎokè after a little while; a moment later
【少量】 shǎoliàng a small amount; a little; a few
【少陪】 shǎopéi 〈套〉 if you'll excuse me; I'm afraid I must be going now
【少顷】 shǎoqǐng 〈书〉 after a short while; after a few moments; presently
【少数】 shǎoshù small number; few; minority: ～人 a small number of people; a few people; the minority/ 他们是～。They are in the minority./ ～服从多数。The minority is subordinate to the majority.

【少数民族】 shǎoshù mínzú minority nationality; national minority
【少许】 shǎoxǔ 〈书〉 a little; a few; a modicum

shào

少* shào ① young: 男女老～ men and women, old and young ② son of a rich family; young master: 阔～ a profligate son of the rich/ 恶～ young ruffian
另见 shǎo
【少妇】 shàofù young married woman
【少奶奶】 shàonǎinai 〈旧〉 ① young mistress of the house ② your daughter-in-law
【少年】 shàonián ① early youth (from ten to sixteen) ② boy or girl of that age; juvenile ◇ ～单打 boys' and girls' singles/ ～读物 juvenile books; books for young people/ ～犯罪 juvenile delinquency
【少年老成】 shàonián lǎochéng ① an old head on young shoulders ② a young person lacking in vigour and drive
【少女】 shàonǚ young girl
【少爷】 shàoye 〈旧〉 ① young master of the house: ～脾气 behaviour of a spoilt boy ② your son
【少壮】 shàozhuàng young and vigorous: ～不努力，老大徒伤悲。If one does not exert oneself in youth, one will regret it in old age. 或 Laziness in youth spells regret in old age.

邵 Shào a surname

劭 shào 〈书〉 ① encourage; urge; exhort ② excellent; admirable: 年高德～ of venerable age and eminent virtue; venerable

绍* shào carry on; continue

哨 shào ① sentry post; post: 岗～ sentry post/ 观察～ observation post/ 放～ be on sentry duty; stand guard; stand sentry ② (of birds) warble; chirp ③ whistle: 吹～ blow a whistle
【哨兵】 shàobīng sentry; guard
【哨所】 shàosuǒ sentry post; post: 前沿～ forward post; outpost
【哨子】 shàozi whistle

shē

奢 shē ① luxurious; extravagant: 穷～极欲 (indulge in) luxury and extravagance ② excessive; inordinate; extravagant: ～望 extravagant hopes
【奢侈】 shēchǐ luxurious; extravagant; wasteful: 生活～ live in luxury ◇ ～品 luxury goods; luxuries
【奢华】 shēhuá luxurious; sumptuous; extravagant: 陈设～ be luxuriously furnished
【奢靡】 shēmí extravagant; wasteful
【奢望】 shēwàng extravagant hopes; wild wishes

赊 shē buy or sell on credit
【赊欠】 shēqiàn buy or sell on credit; give or get credit

shé

舌* shé ① tongue (of a human being or animal) ② sth. shaped like a tongue: 火～ tongues of flame
【舌头】 shétou tongue
【舌战】 shézhàn have a verbal battle with; argue heatedly: 一场～ a heated dispute; a battle royal

折 shé ① break; snap: 扁担～了。The shoulder pole broke./ 他们太使劲，把绳子拉～了。They pulled the rope

so hard that it snapped. ② lose money in business
另见 zhé

【折本】 shéběn lose money in business: ~生意 a losing business; a bad bargain

【折耗】 shéhào damage (to goods during transit, storage, etc.); loss

余 Shé a surname

蛇* shé snake; serpent
另见 yí

【蛇蝎】 shéxiē snakes and scorpions — vicious people: 毒如~ as vicious as a viper

【蛇行】 shéxíng 〈书〉 move with the body on the ground; crawl

【蛇形】 shéxíng snakelike; S-shaped

【蛇足】 shézú feet added to a snake by an ignorant artist — sth. superfluous 参见 "画蛇添足" huà shé tiān zú

shě

舍* shě ① give up; abandon: ~此别无他法。There is no other way than this. 或 This is the only way. ② give alms; dispense charity
另见 shè

【舍本逐末】 shěběn-zhúmò attend to trifles to the neglect of essentials

【舍不得】 shěbude hate to part with or use; grudge: 他是队里的好管家，~乱花一分钱。He is our team's good manager and hates to waste a single cent. / 他~穿那套新衣服。He begrudged wearing his new suit. 或 He was reluctant to wear his new suit.

【舍得】 shěde be willing to part with; not grudge: 练字必须~下功夫。To acquire good handwriting one mustn't begrudge time spent on practice.

【舍己为人】 shě jǐ wèi rén sacrifice one's own interests for the sake of others

【舍近求远】 shějìn-qiúyuǎn seek far and wide for what lies close at hand

【舍命】 shěmìng risk one's life; sacrifice oneself

【舍弃】 shěqì give up; abandon

【舍身】 shěshēn give one's life; sacrifice oneself: ~救人 give one's life to rescue sb.; sacrifice oneself to save others

【舍生取义】 shě shēng qǔ yì lay down one's life for a just cause

【舍死忘生】 shěsǐ-wàngshēng disregard one's own safety; risk one's life

shè

设* shè ① set up; establish; found: 指挥所~在前沿阵地上。The command post was set up in a forward position./ 部下面~六个司。Under the ministry there are six departments./ 我们这个市，下面~十个区。Our municipality is divided into ten districts. ② work out: ~计陷害 plot a frame-up; frame ③ 〈数〉 given; suppose; if: ~长方形的宽是 x 米。Suppose the width of a rectangle is x metres./ ~x=1 Given: x=1 ④ 〈书〉 if; in case: ~有困难，当助一臂之力。You can count on me to help in case of difficulty.

【设备】 shèbèi equipment; installation; facilities: 冶金~ metallurgical equipment/ 电气~ electrical installations/ 交通运输~ facilities for transport and communication/ 旅馆~齐全。The hotel is well appointed.

【设法】 shèfǎ think of a way; try; do what one can: 我们乐队正在~找个小提琴手。Our orchestra is trying to find a violinist.

【设防】 shèfáng set up defences; fortify; garrison: 层层~ set up defences in depth ◇ ~地带 fortified zone

【设计】 shèjì design; plan: 建筑~ architectural design/ 舞台~ stage design/ ~一座厂房 make designs for a factory building/ ~一种新机器 design a new machine/ ~一座水

坝 project a dam/ ~版面 lay out a printed page

【设立】 shèlì establish; set up; found: ~新的机构 set up a new organization

【设若】 shèruò if; suppose; provided

【设身处地】 shèshēn-chǔdì put oneself in sb. else's position; be considerate: 服务员事事~为旅客着想。The attendants look at everything from the passengers' angle and take care of their every need.

【设施】 shèshī installation; facilities: 防洪~ flood control installations/ 军事~ military installations/ 医疗~ medical facilities/ 集体福利~ collective welfare institutions

【设使】 shèshǐ if; suppose; in case

【设想】 shèxiǎng ① imagine; envisage; conceive; assume: 不堪~ too ghastly (或 dreadful) to contemplate/ 从最坏的可能来~ anticipate the worst; prepare for the worst ② tentative plan; tentative idea: 这些只是我们的初步~。Those are just our tentative ideas. ③ have consideration for: 多为青少年~ give much thought to the needs of the younger generation

【设宴】 shèyàn give a banquet; fête: ~招待贵宾 give a banquet in honour of the distinguished visitors; fête the distinguished guests

【设置】 shèzhì set up; put up; install: ~专门机构 set up a special organization/ 给会议~重重障碍 place all sorts of obstacles before the conference/ 课程~ courses offered in a college or school; curriculum

社 shè organized body; agency; society: 通讯~ news agency/ 合作~ cooperative/ 报~ newspaper office/ 出版~ publishing house

【社会】 shèhuì society: 人类~ human society

【社会工作】 shèhuì gōngzuò work, in addition to one's regular job, done for the collective

【社会关系】 shèhuì guānxì ① human relations in society; social relations ② one's social connections

【社会学】 shèhuìxué sociology ◇ ~家 sociologist

【社会主义】 shèhuìzhǔyì socialism

【社稷】 shèjì the god of the land and the god of grain — the state; the country

【社交】 shèjiāo social intercourse; social contact

【社论】 shèlùn editorial; leading article; leader

【社评】 shèpíng 〈旧〉 editorial

【社团】 shètuán mass organizations

【社员】 shèyuán ① a member of a society, etc.: 合作社~ cooperative member ② commune member ◇ ~大会 general meeting of commune members

舍 shè ① house; shed; hut: 牛~ cowshed/ 茅~ thatched hut/ 校~ school buildings ② 〈谦〉〔用于对别人称比自己辈分低或年纪小的亲属〕: ~弟 my younger brother/ ~侄 my nephew
另见 shě

【舍利】 shèlì 〈佛教〉 Buddhist relics ◇ ~塔 stupa; pagoda for Buddhist relics; Buddhist shrine

【舍亲】 shèqīn 〈谦〉 my relative

【舍下】 shèxià 〈谦〉 my humble abode; my house

涉 shè ① wade; ford: ~水过河 wade across a river; ford a stream/ 远~重洋 travel all the way from across the oceans ② go through; experience: ~险 go through dangers/ ~世不深 have scanty experience of life; have seen little of the world ③ involve

【涉及】 shèjí involve; relate to; touch upon: 双方的分歧~一些重大原则性问题。The differences between the two sides involve major matters of principle.

【涉猎】 shèliè do desultory reading; read cursorily: 有的书必须精读，有的只要稍加~即可。Some books are for intensive study and some are for cursory reading.

【涉禽】 shèqín 〈动〉 wading bird; wader

【涉讼】 shèsòng be involved in a lawsuit

【涉嫌】 shèxián be suspected of being involved; be a suspect

【涉足】 shèzú 〈书〉 set foot in: ~其间 set foot there

射* shè

① shoot; fire: ~箭 shoot an arrow/ 速~ rapid fire/ 扫~ strafe/ 能骑善~ be a good horseman as well as a crack shot; be known for one's equestrian skill and marksmanship/ ~进一球 kick the ball into the goal; score a goal/ 炮弹~中了敌人坦克。The shell hit the enemy tank. ② discharge in a jet: 喷~ spout; spurt; jet/ 注~ inject ③ send out (light, heat, etc.): 反~ reflect/ 光芒四~ radiate brilliant light/ 探照灯~出一道道强光。The searchlights projected powerful beams of light. ④ allude to sth. or sb.; insinuate: 影~ insinuate

【射程】 shèchéng range (of fire): 有效~ effective range
【射击】 shèjī ① shoot; fire: 向敌人~ fire at the enemy ② 〈体〉shooting
【射箭】 shèjiàn ① shoot an arrow ② 〈体〉archery ◇ ~手 archer
【射手】 shèshǒu shooter; marksman: 机枪~ machine gunner

赦 shè

remit (a punishment); pardon: 大~ general pardon; amnesty/ 特~ special pardon

【赦免】 shèmiǎn remit (a punishment); pardon
【赦罪】 shèzuì absolve sb. from guilt; pardon sb.

摄 shè

① absorb; assimilate ② take a photograph of; shoot: 下几个珍贵的镜头 take some superb shots ③ conserve (one's health) ④ act for: ~理 hold (an office) in an acting capacity

【摄取】 shèqǔ ① absorb; assimilate; take in: ~营养 absorb nourishment ② take a photograph of; shoot: ~镜头 shoot a scene
【摄影】 shèyǐng ① take a photograph: ~留念 have a souvenir photograph taken/ 航空~ aerial photography/ 红外~ infrared photography ② shoot a film; film: 全景 (内景,外景)~ panoramic (interior, exterior) shooting ◇ ~记者 press photographer; cameraman/ ~棚 film studio/ ~师 photographer; cameraman/ ~室 photographic studio; photo studio/ ~展览 photographic exhibition; photo exhibition
【摄影机】 shèyǐngjī camera: 电影~ cinecamera; cinematograph/ 立体~ stereoscopic camera
【摄制】 shèzhì 〈电影〉produce ◇ ~组 production unit

慑 shè

〈书〉fear; be awed

【慑服】 shèfú ① submit because of fear; succumb ② cow sb. into submission

麝 shè

① musk deer ② musk

【麝牛】 shèniú musk-ox
【麝鼠】 shèshǔ muskrat
【麝香】 shèxiāng musk

shéi

谁 shéi 见 "谁" shuí

shēn

申* shēn

① state; express; explain: 重~前令 reiterate the previous order ② the ninth of the twelve Earthly Branches

【申辩】 shēnbiàn defend oneself; explain oneself; argue (或 plead) one's case: 允许~ allow sb. to argue his case/ 被告有权~。The accused has the right to defend himself.
【申斥】 shēnchì rebuke (usu. one's subordinates); reprimand
【申明】 shēnmíng declare; avow: ~自己的立场 state one's position
【申请】 shēnqǐng apply for: ~入(出)境签证 apply for an entry (exit) visa ◇ ~国 applicant country/ ~人 applicant/ ~书 (written) application
【申述】 shēnshù state; explain in detail: ~立场 state one's position/ ~来意 explain the purpose of one's visit/ ~自己的观点 expound one's views/ 谨~如下 have the honour to state the following/ 作进一步的~ make further observations
【申说】 shēnshuō state (reasons)
【申诉】 shēnsù appeal: 向上级提出~ appeal to the higher authorities/ 不服判决,提出~ appeal against a legal decision
【申讨】 shēntǎo openly condemn; denounce
【申谢】 shēnxiè acknowledge one's indebtedness; express one's gratitude
【申冤】 shēnyuān ① redress an injustice; right a wrong ② appeal for redress of a wrong

伸* shēn

stretch; extend: ~胳臂 stretch one's arms/ ~大拇指 hold up one's thumb/ 两臂平~ extend (或 stretch, spread) one's arms horizontally/ 跳水时腿要~直。When you dive you must keep your legs straight./ 不要把头~出窗外。Don't put (或 stick) your head out of the window (of a bus, etc.).

【伸懒腰】 shēn lǎnyāo stretch oneself
【伸手】 shēnshǒu ① stretch (或 hold) out one's hand: 他~去拿碗。He reached for the bowl./ ~不见五指 so dark that you can't see your hand in front of you; pitch dark ② ask for help, etc.: ~派 a person who is in the habit of asking the higher level for help/ 尽管遭了水灾,他们却没有向国家~要一分钱。Although hit by the flood, they did not ask for a single copper from the state.
【伸缩】 shēnsuō ① stretch out and draw back; expand and contract; lengthen and shorten: 这架照像机的镜头可以前后~。The lens of this camera can be pulled back and forth. ② flexible; elastic; adjustable: 这些规定~性很大。These regulations are quite elastic (或 flexible)./ 没有~余地 leave one no latitude
【伸腿】 shēntuǐ ① stretch one's legs ② step in (to gain an advantage) ③ 〈口〉kick the bucket; turn up one's toes
【伸腰】 shēnyāo straighten one's back; straighten oneself up
【伸冤】 shēnyuān 见 "申冤" shēnyuān
【伸展】 shēnzhǎn spread; extend; stretch: 草原一直~到遥远的天边。The prairie stretches to the distant horizon.
【伸张】 shēnzhāng uphold; promote: ~正气,打击歪风 promote healthy tendencies and combat unhealthy ones

身* shēn

① body: ~心 body and mind/ 这套衣服挺合~。This suit fits perfectly./ 转过~去 turn round/ ~负重伤 be seriously injured (或 wounded) ② life: 以~殉职 die a martyr at one's post ③ oneself; personally: 以~作则 set a good example with one's own conduct/ 你~为组长,应当负起责任来。As group leader, you should take charge. ④ one's moral character and conduct: 修~ cultivate one's mind ⑤ the main part of a structure; body: 汽车车~ the body of a motor car/ 机~ fuselage/ 树~ trunk/ 船~ the body of a ship; hull ⑥ 〈量〉〔用于衣服〕suit: 一~新衣服 a new suit

【身败名裂】 shēnbài-míngliè lose all standing and reputation; bring disgrace and ruin upon oneself; be utterly discredited
【身边】 shēnbiān ① at (或 by) one's side: 老人把全家人叫到~。The old man summoned the whole family to his side. ② (have sth.) on one; with one: ~没带钱 have no money on one / 她~总是带着药箱。She never goes anywhere without her medical kit.
【身不由己】 shēn bù yóu jǐ involuntarily; in spite of oneself: 车子突然一停,他~地向前一扑。When the bus came to a sudden stop, he jerked forward involuntarily.
【身材】 shēncái stature; figure: ~矮小 short and slight of stature/ ~苗条 have a slender (或 slim) figure/ ~魁梧 of great height and powerful build; tall and sturdy
【身长】 shēncháng ① height (of a person) ② length (of a garment from shoulder to hemline)
【身段】 shēnduàn ① (woman's) figure ② (dancer's) posture

【身分】 shēnfen ① status; capacity; identity: 不合～ incompatible with one's status／ ～不明 of unknown identity; unidentified／ 暴露～ reveal one's identity／ 以官方（私人，个人）～发言 speak in an official (a private, a personal) capacity ② dignity: 有失～ be beneath one's dignity ◇ ～证 identity card; identification card 又作“身份”

【身高】 shēngāo height (of a person): 他一米八。 He is 180 centimetres in height.

【身故】 shēngù die: 因病～ die of an illness

【身后】 shēnhòu after one's death

【身价】 shēnjià ① social status: 突然～百倍 have a sudden rise in social status ② the selling price of a slave

【身教】 shēnjiào teach others by one's own example: ～胜于言教。 Example is better than precept.

【身经百战】 shēn jīng bǎi zhàn have fought a hundred battles: ～的老战士 a veteran who has fought countless battles; a battle-tested veteran; a seasoned fighter

【身临其境】 shēn lín qí jìng be personally on the scene: 这个场面写得很生动，使人有～之感。 The scene is so vividly portrayed that the reader feels as if he is participating.

【身强力壮】 shēnqiáng-lìzhuàng (of a person) strong; tough; sturdy

【身躯】 shēnqū body; stature: 健壮的～ a sound body／ 高大 tall of stature

【身上】 shēnshang ① on one's body: ～穿一件白衬衫 wear a white shirt／ 我～不舒服。 I'm not feeling well.／ 希望寄托在青年人～。 Our hopes are placed on the young people. ② (have sth.) on one; with one: ～没带笔 I haven't got a pen with me.／ ～有零钱吗？ Have you got any change on you?

【身世】 shēnshì one's life experience; one's lot: ～凄凉 have had a sad life

【身手】 shēnshǒu skill; talent: 大显～ fully display one's talents; exhibit one's skill

【身受】 shēnshòu experience (personally): 感同～。 I shall count it as a personal favour.

【身体】 shēntǐ ① body: 保持～平衡 keep one's balance ② health: 注意～ look after one's health／ ～非常健康 be in excellent health

【身体力行】 shēntǐ-lìxíng earnestly practise what one advocates

【身外之物】 shēn wài zhī wù external things; mere worldly possessions

【身先士卒】 shēn xiān shìzú lead one's men in a charge; charge at the head of one's men

【身心】 shēn-xīn body and mind: ～健康 sound in body and mind; physically and mentally healthy／ 受到摧残 be physically injured and mentally affected

【身影】 shēnyǐng a person's silhouette; form; figure: 一个高大的～ a tall figure

【身孕】 shēnyùn pregnancy: 她有了三个月的～。 She is three months pregnant.

【身在福中不知福】 shēn zài fú zhōng bù zhī fú growing up in happiness, one often fails to appreciate what happiness really means; not appreciate the happy life one enjoys

【身子】 shēnzi 〈口〉 ① body: 光着～ be naked／ ～不大舒服 not feel well ② pregnancy: 有了七个月的～ be seven months pregnant

呻 shēn

【呻吟】 shēnyín groan; moan: 伤员的～ the moans of the wounded／ 无病～ moan and groan without being ill; make a fuss about an imaginary illness

绅 shēn gentry: 土豪劣～ local tyrants and evil gentry

【绅士】 shēnshì gentleman; gentry

参 shēn ginseng

另见 cān; cēn

莘 shēn

【莘莘】 shēnshēn 〈书〉 numerous: ～学子 a great number of disciples; large numbers of students

娠 shēn 见“妊娠” rènshēn

深 shēn ① deep: 一口～井 a deep well／ 测量水～ sound the depth of the water／ 雪～过膝 knee-deep snow／ 林～苔滑。 The forest is thick and the moss is slippery. ② difficult; profound: 由浅入～ from the easy to the difficult／ 这本书给孩子看太～了。 The book is too difficult for children. ③ thoroughgoing; penetrating; profound: 问题想得～ think deeply about a question／ 功夫～ have put in a great deal of effort／这个问题我没同他～谈。 I didn't go deeply into the matter with him. ④ close; intimate: 交情～ be on intimate terms ⑤ dark; deep: ～蓝 dark blue／ ～红 deep red; crimson／ 颜色太～。 The colour is too dark (或 deep). ⑥ late: ～秋 late autumn／ 夜～了。 It was late at night. ⑦ very; greatly; deeply: ～恐 be very much afraid／ ～知 know very well; be fully (或 keenly) aware／ ～感 feel deeply; feel keenly／ ～信 be deeply convinced; firmly believe／ ～受感动 be deeply moved; be greatly touched／ ～表同情 show deep (或 profound) sympathy／ ～得人心 enjoy immense popular support

【深奥】 shēn'ào abstruse; profound; recondite: ～的哲理 abstruse philosophy; a profound truth

【深藏若虚】 shēn cáng ruò xū be modest about one's talent or learning; not be given to boasting or showing off

【深长】 shēncháng profound: 意味～ pregnant with meaning; significant

【深沉】 shēnchén ① dark; deep: 暮色～。 The dusk is deepening. ② (of sound or voice) deep; heavy; dull: 大提琴～的音调 the deep notes of a cello／ ～的夯土声 the dull sound of earth being tamped ③ concealing one's real feelings: 这人很～。 He's a deep one.

【深仇大恨】 shēnchóu-dàhèn bitter and deep-seated hatred; profound hatred

【深处】 shēnchù depths; recesses: 在密林～ in the depths (或 recesses) of the forest／ 在内心～ in the depth (或 innermost recesses) of one's heart／ 在灵魂～ in one's innermost soul／ 在思想～ in one's heart of hearts

【深度】 shēndù ① degree of depth; depth: 测量河水的～ sound the depth of the river ② profundity; depth: 他的发言缺乏～。 His speech lacks depth.

【深更半夜】 shēngēng-bànyè at dead of night; in the depth (或 dead) of night; in the middle of the night

【深海】 shēnhǎi deep sea ◇ ～鱼 deep-sea fish／ ～资源 deep-sea resources

【深厚】 shēnhòu ① deep; profound ② solid; deepseated: ～的基础 a solid foundation

【深呼吸】 shēnhūxī deep breathing

【深究】 shēnjiū go into (a matter) seriously; get to the bottom of (a matter): 对这些小事不必～。 These are small matters and you don't have to go into them seriously.

【深居简出】 shēnjū-jiǎnchū live in the seclusion of one's own home; live a secluded life

【深刻】 shēnkè deep; profound; deepgoing: ～地阐明 expound profoundly／ 给某人留下～的印象 make a deep impression on sb.／ 受到一次～的教育 learn a profound lesson

【深谋远虑】 shēnmóu-yuǎnlǜ think deeply and plan carefully; be circumspect and farsighted

【深浅】 shēnqiǎn ① depth: 你去打听一下这河的～，看能不能蹚水过去。 Go and find out how deep the river is and whether we can wade across. ② proper limits (for speech or action); sense of propriety: 说话没～ speak without thought and often inappropriately ③ shade (of colour): 颜色～不同 of different shades

【深切】 shēnqiè heartfelt; deep; profound: ～的同情 deep sympathy／ ～关怀 be deeply concerned about; show profound concern for／ ～怀念 dearly cherish the memory of／ 表示～的哀悼 express one's heartfelt condolences (to the deceased's family); express one's profound grief (at sb.'s death)

【深情】 shēnqíng deep feeling; deep love: ～厚谊 profound sentiments of friendship

【深入】 shēnrù ① go deep into; penetrate into: ～实际 go

deep into the realities of life/ ~敌后 penetrate far behind enemy lines/ ~基层 go down to the grass-roots units/ ~群众 immerse oneself (或 go deep) among the masses; go into the midst of the common people ② thorough; deepgoing: ~进行调查研究 make a thorough investigation and study

【深入浅出】 shēnrù-qiǎnchū explain the profound in simple terms

【深山】 shēnshān remote mountains: ~老林 remote, thickly forested mountains

【深深】 shēnshēn profoundly; deeply; keenly

【深水】 shēnshuǐ deepwater ◇ ~港 deepwater port/ ~码头 deepwater wharf/ ~炸弹 depth charge; depth bomb

【深思】 shēnsī think deeply about; ponder deeply over: 这难道不值得~吗? Is this not worth pondering? 或 Does this not call for deep thought?/ 这个问题值得我们~。 This matter gives us much food for thought.

【深思熟虑】 shēnsī-shúlǜ careful consideration

【深邃】 shēnsuì ① deep: ~的山谷 a deep valley ② profound; abstruse; recondite: 寓意~ have a profound message

【深恶痛绝】 shēnwù-tòngjué hate bitterly; abhor; detest

【深夜】 shēnyè late at night; in the small hours of the morning: 工作到~ work late into the night

【深渊】 shēnyuān abyss: 苦难的~ the abyss of suffering (或 misery)

【深远】 shēnyuǎn profound and lasting; far-reaching: 具有~的历史意义 have profound historic significance

【深造】 shēnzào take a more advanced course of study or training; pursue advanced studies

shén

什* shén
另见 shí

【什么】 shénme ①〔表示疑问〕 ⓐ〔单用, 问事物〕 他说~, What did he say? ⓑ〔用在名词前面, 问人或事物〕 他是~人? Who is he?/ 那是~颜色? What colour is it?/ 他~时候走? When will he leave? ②〔虚指, 表示不肯定的事物〕 我饿了, 想吃点儿~。 I'm hungry. I'd like to have a bite./ 好象出了~事儿。 It seems something is amiss. ③〔任指〕 ⓐ〔用在 "也" 或 "都" 前面, 表示所说的范围之内没有例外〕 他~也不怕。 He is afraid of nothing./ ~用处也没有 be quite worthless/ 只要认真学, ~都能学会。 If you study conscientiously, you can learn anything. ⓑ〔两个 "什么" 前后照应, 表示由前者决定后者〕 想~就说~。 Just say what's on your mind. ④〔表示惊讶或不满〕 ~! 没有水? What! (或 What's that?) No water?/ ~! 九点了, 车还没来! What's happened! 9 o'clock and the bus hasn't come yet! ⑤〔表示责难〕 你笑~? 你这~! 你说~! 装~哑巴! Speak! Stop playing dumb. ⑥〔表示不同意对方刚说的某一句话〕 ~不懂! 装糊涂就是了。 What do you mean—not understand? You're just pretending. ⑦〔用在几个并列成分前面, 表示列举不尽〕 ~乒乓球啊, 羽毛球啊, 篮球啊, 排球啊, 他都会。 He can play table tennis, badminton, basketball, volleyball, anything.

神* shén ① god; deity; divinity ② supernatural; magical: ~效 magical effect; miraculous effect/ 用兵如~ direct military operations with miraculous skill ③ spirit; mind: 凝~ concentrate (或 focus) one's attention/ 走~ be absentminded/ 耗~ take up one's energy/ 闭目养~ close one's eyes and rest one's mind/ 他双目炯炯有~。 He has a pair of bright piercing eyes. ④ expression; look: 眼~ expression in the eyes

【神不知, 鬼不觉】 shén bù zhī, guǐ bù jué unknown to god or ghost — (do sth.) without anybody knowing it; in great secrecy

【神采】 shéncǎi expression; look: ~奕奕 glowing with health and radiating vigour

【神出鬼没】 shénchū-guǐmò come and go like a shadow; appear and disappear mysteriously

【神怪】 shén-guài gods and spirits

【神乎其神】 shén hū qí shén fantastic; wonderful; miraculous: 吹得~ laud sth. or sb. to the skies

【神话】 shénhuà mythology; myth; fairy tale

【神魂】 shénhún state of mind; mind: ~不定 be deeply perturbed/ ~颠倒 be infatuated

【神机妙算】 shénjī-miàosuàn wonderful foresight (in military operations, etc.)

【神经】 shénjīng nerve: 脑 (感觉, 交感) ~ cranial (sensory, sympathetic) nerve/ ~紧张 be nervous

【神经病】 shénjīngbìng ① neuropathy ② mental disorder: 这家伙有点~。 That chap's not quite right in the head.

【神经过敏】 shénjīng guòmǐn ① neuroticism ② neurotic; oversensitive

【神力】 shénlì superhuman strength; extraordinary power

【神灵】 shénlíng gods; deities; divinities

【神秘】 shénmì mysterious; mystical: ~人物 a mysterious person; a person shrouded in mystery

【神妙】 shénmiào wonderful; marvellous; ingenious: ~的笔法 wonderful style of writing; ingenious brushwork

【神明】 shénmíng gods; deities; divinities: 奉若~ worship sb. or sth.; make a fetish of sth.

【神女】 shénnǚ ① goddess ② <旧> prostitute

【神奇】 shénqí magical; mystical; miraculous: ~的效果 miraculous effect; magical effect/ 这些古代传说都为人们渲染上一层~的色彩。 Through the ages, these legends have acquired an element of mystery and wonder.

【神气】 shénqì ① expression; air; manner: 他脸上显出得意的~。 He had an air of complacency./ 他说话的~特别象他爸爸。 He is very much like his father in the way he speaks. ② spirited; vigorous ③ putting on airs; cocky; overweening: ~十足 putting on grand airs; very arrogant/ 啊! 他倒~起来了。 Humph! What airs he gives himself!/ 你~什么? What makes you think you're so wonderful? 或 You've got nothing to be cocky about.

【神气活现】 shénqì huóxiàn very cocky; as proud as a peacock

【神枪手】 shénqiāngshǒu crack shot; expert marksman; sharpshooter

【神情】 shénqíng expression; look: 露出愉快的~ look happy; wear a happy expression

【神色】 shénsè expression; look: ~不对 look queer/ ~慌张 look flustered/ ~自若 be perfectly calm and collected; show composure and presence of mind

【神圣】 shénshèng sacred; holy: ~职责 sacred duty/ ~权利 sacred right/ 我国领土不可侵犯。 Our territory is sacred and inviolable.

【神思】 shénsī state of mind; mental state: ~不定 be distracted

【神似】 shénsì be alike in spirit; be an excellent likeness: 不仅形似, 而且~ be alike not only in appearance but also in spirit/ 他画的奔马, 栩栩如生, 极其~。 The galloping horses he paints are extremely lifelike.

【神速】 shénsù marvellously quick; with amazing speed: 收效~ yield marvellously quick results/ ~地向前挺进 advance with lightning speed/ 兵贵~。 Speed is precious in war.

【神算】 shénsuàn miraculous foresight; marvellous prediction

【神态】 shéntài expression; manner; bearing; mien: ~悠闲 look perfectly relaxed/ 看她的~象个舞蹈演员。 From the way she carries herself she must be a dancer.

【神通】 shéntōng remarkable ability; magical power: ~广大 be infinitely resourceful/ 大显~ display one's prowess; give full play to one's ability

【神童】 shéntóng child prodigy

【神往】 shénwǎng be carried away; be rapt; be charmed: 令人~的西湖景色 the enchanting scenery of the West Lake

【神仙】 shénxian supernatural being; celestial being; immortal

【神像】 shénxiàng the picture or statue of a god or Buddha

【神学】 shénxué <宗> theology

【神医】 shényī highly skilled doctor; miracle-working doctor

【神异】 shényì ① gods and spirits ② magical; mystical; miraculous

【神勇】 shényǒng extraordinarily brave

【神韵】 shényùn romantic charm (in literature and art)

【神志】 shénzhì consciousness; senses; mind: ~清醒 be in one's right mind; remain fully conscious/ ~昏迷 lose consciousness; be in a state of delirium

shěn

沈 Shěn a surname

审 * shěn ① careful: ~视 look closely at; gaze at; examine ② examine; go over: ~稿 go over a manuscript or draft ③ interrogate; try: ~案 try a case; 公~ put sb. on public trial ④ 〈书〉 know: 未~其详 not know the details ⑤ 〈书〉 indeed; really: ~如其言。 What he says is indeed true.

【审查】 shěnchá examine; investigate: ~属实。 The fact was established after investigation.

【审订】 shěndìng examine and revise: ~教材 revise teaching materials

【审定】 shěndìng examine and approve: 计划已由委员会~。 The plan has been examined and approved by the committee.

【审核】 shěnhé examine and verify: ~预算 examine and approve a budget/ 这些数字必须加以~。 These figures will have to be verified.

【审理】 shěnlǐ 〈法〉 try; hear: ~案件 try a case; hear a case

【审美】 shěnměi appreciation of the beautiful

【审判】 shěnpàn bring to trial; try

【审慎】 shěnshèn cautious; careful; circumspect: ~从事 steer a cautious course/ ~地考虑问题 think over a problem carefully/ 处理这个问题必须~。 The matter has to be handled with circumspection.

【审问】 shěnwèn interrogate; question: 正在进行~。 The interrogation is going on.

【审讯】 shěnxùn 〈法〉 interrogate; try: ~俘虏 interrogate prisoners of war/ 送交军事法庭~ hand over to a military tribunal for interrogation

【审阅】 shěnyuè check and approve: 此讲话记录未经本人~。 These notes of the speech have not been checked and approved by the speaker./ ~稿件 go over a manuscript

哂 shěn 〈书〉 smile

【哂纳】 shěnnà 〈套〉 kindly accept (this small gift)

婶 * shěn ① wife of father's younger brother; aunt ② a form of address to a woman about one's mother's age; aunt; auntie: 张大~ Aunt Zhang

【婶母】 shěnmǔ wife of father's younger brother; aunt

shèn

肾 shèn 〈生理〉 kidney

【肾脏】 shènzàng kidney

甚 * shèn ① very; extremely: 知者~少。 Very few people know about it./ ~为痛快 find it most satisfying ② more than: 他的病情恶化, 日~一日。 His condition got worse and worse. 或 His condition steadily deteriorated.

【甚而】 shèn'ér 〈连〉 even; (go) so far as to

【甚或】 shènhuò 〈书〉 〈连〉 even; (go) so far as to; so much so that

【甚嚣尘上】 shèn xiāo chén shàng cause a temporary clamour

【甚至】 shènzhì 〈连〉 even; (go) so far as to; so much so that: ~不惜承担最大的牺牲 not flinch from even the greatest sacrifices

渗 shèn ooze; seep: 包扎伤口的绷带上~出了血。 Blood oozed out of the dressing.

【渗漏】 shènlòu seepage; leakage

【渗入】 shènrù ① permeate; seep into: ~地下 permeate the ground; seep into the ground ② (of influence, etc.) penetrate; infiltrate

【渗透】 shèntòu ① 〈物〉 osmosis ② permeate; seep: 雨水~了泥土。 The rain permeated the soil. ③ infiltrate: 经济~ economic infiltration

慎 * shèn careful; cautious: 谨小~微 overcautious

【慎重】 shènzhòng cautious; careful; prudent; discreet: 采取~的态度 adopt a prudent policy/ 处理这件事必须~。 The matter has to be handled with great care./ 经过~考虑, 我们决定延期开会。 After careful consideration we decided to postpone the meeting.

蜃 shèn 〈动〉 clam

【蜃景】 shènjǐng 〈气〉 mirage

shēng

升 * shēng ① rise; hoist; go up; ascend: 太阳~。 The sun is rising. ② promote: 被提~到领导岗位 be promoted to positions of leadership ③ litre (l.): 一~啤酒 a litre of beer

【升班】 shēngbān go up (one grade in school)

【升格】 shēnggé promote; upgrade: 将外交关系~为大使级 upgrade diplomatic relations to ambassadorial level/ 将各自外交代表由公使~为大使 promote the status of their respective diplomatic representatives from Minister to Ambassador

【升官发财】 shēngguān-fācái win promotion and get rich; (be out for) power and money

【升级】 shēngjí ① go up (one grade, etc.) ② escalate: 战争~ escalation (of a war)

【升平】 shēngpíng peace: ~世界 peaceful world; peaceful life

【升旗】 shēngqí hoist (或 raise) a flag ◇ ~典礼 flag-raising ceremony

【升堂入室】 shēngtáng-rùshì pass through the hall into the inner chamber — have profound scholarship; become highly proficient in one's profession

【升学】 shēngxué go to a school of a higher grade; enter a higher school ◇ ~率 proportion of students entering schools of a higher grade

【升值】 shēngzhí 〈经〉 ① revalue ② appreciate

生 * shēng ① give birth to; bear: 新~儿 newborn baby/ ~孩子 give birth to a child ② grow: ~根 take root/ ~芽 sprout/ 新~力量 newly rising (或 emerging) forces ③ existence; life: 一~ all one's life; one's lifetime/ 起死回~ raise sb. from the dead; bring sb. back to life ④ livelihood: 谋~ earn one's livelihood; make a living ⑤ living: ~物 living things ⑥ get; have: ~冻疮 get chilblains ⑦ light (a fire): ~炉子 light a stove ⑧ unripe; green: ~的苹果 a green apple/ 这些桃子还是~的。 The peaches are not ripe yet. ⑨ raw; uncooked: ~肉 raw meat/ 黄瓜可以~吃。 Cucumbers can be eaten raw. ⑩ unprocessed; unrefined; crude: ~铁 pig iron/ ~皮 raw hide; (untanned) hide ⑪ unfamiliar; unacquainted; strange: ~词 new word/ 人地~不熟 a stranger in a strange place/ 刚到这里, 工作很~。 I've only just come here. I'm still not familiar with the work./ 这个小孩认~。 The child is shy with strangers. ⑫ stiff; mechanical: ~凑 mechanically put together (disconnected words and phrases); arbitrarily dish up (unrelated facts) ⑬ 〔用在少数表示感情、感觉的词的前面〕 very: ~怕 for fear that/ ~疼 very painful/ 黄瓜可以~吃。 ⑭ pupil; student: 新型的师~关系 teacher-student relations of a new type ⑮ the male character type in Beijing opera, etc. ⑯ 〔某些指人的名词后缀〕: 医~ doctor

【生搬硬套】 shēngbān-yìngtào copy mechanically in disregard of specific conditions; apply or copy mechanically

【生病】 shēngbìng fall ill

【生菜】 shēngcài 〈植〉 romaine lettuce; cos lettuce

【生产】 shēngchǎn ① produce; manufacture: 很多工厂～农业机械。Many factories produce farm machinery./ 这个车间～螺丝钉。This shop manufactures screws./ 这个工厂已开始～。The plant has gone into operation./ 坚守～岗位 stick to one's post on the production front ② give birth to a child: 她快～了。She'll be having her baby soon. 或 She's expecting her baby soon.

【生辰】 shēngchén birthday

【生存】 shēngcún subsist; exist; live: 鱼离开了水是不能～的。Fish cannot live without water. ◇ ～竞争 struggle for existence

【生动】 shēngdòng lively; vivid: ～的描写 lively description

【生动活泼】 shēngdòng huópō lively; vivid and vigorous: ～的语言 vivid language/ 这次会开得～。It was a lively meeting.

【生根】 shēnggēn take root; strike root

【生花妙笔】 shēnghuā miàobǐ (straight from) a gifted pen; (written with) a graphic pen

【生活】 shēnghuó ① life: 日常～ daily life/ 政治～ political life ② live: 一个人脱离了社会就不能～下去。One cannot live cut off from society. ③ livelihood: ～困难 be badly off ◇ ～必需品 necessaries of life; daily necessities/ ～补助 extra allowance for living expenses/ ～方式 way of life; life style/ ～费用 living expenses; cost of living/ ～福利 welfare; welfare benefits/ ～环境 surroundings; environment/ ～经验 experience of life/ ～来源 source of income/ ～能力 〈生〉 viability/ ～水平 living standard/ ～条件 living conditions/ ～习惯 habits and customs/ ～细节 trifling matters of everyday life; domestic trivia/ ～用品 articles for daily use

【生机】 shēngjī ① lease of life: 一线～ a slim chance of survival; a gleam of hope ② life; vitality: 春天来了，田野里充满了～。Spring has come and the fields are full of life.

【生计】 shēngjì means of livelihood; livelihood: 另谋～ try to find some other means of livelihood

【生老病死】 shēng-lǎo-bìng-sǐ birth, age, illness and death

【生离死别】 shēnglí-sǐbié part never to meet again; part for ever

【生理】 shēnglǐ physiology

【生力军】 shēnglìjūn ① fresh troops ② fresh activists; new force: 文艺战线上的一支～ a vital new force on the art and literary front

【生灵涂炭】 shēnglíng túdàn the people are plunged into an abyss of misery

【生龙活虎】 shēnglóng-huóhǔ doughty as a dragon and lively as a tiger; brimming (或 bursting) with energy; full of vim and vigour: 小伙子干起活来真是～。When the lads work, they do it with furious energy.

【生路】 shēnglù means of livelihood; way out: 另谋～ try to find another job; look for a new means of livelihood/ 杀出一条～ fight one's way out (of an encirclement)

【生米煮成熟饭】 shēngmǐ zhǔchéng shúfàn the rice is cooked — what's done can't be undone

【生命】 shēngmìng life

【生命力】 shēngmìnglì life-force; vitality: 具有强大的～ have great vitality

【生怕】 shēngpà for fear that; so as not to; lest: 她轻轻地走进卧室，～惊醒了孩子。She went into the bedroom softly so as not to wake her child.

【生僻】 shēngpì uncommon; rare: ～的字眼 rarely used words

【生平】 shēngpíng all one's life: ～事迹 one's life story/ 作者～简介 a brief account of the author's life; a biographical note on the author

【生气】 shēngqì ① take offence; get angry ② life; vitality: ～勃勃 dynamic; vigorous; full of vitality/ 青年是整个社会力量中的一部分最积极最有～的力量。Young people are the most active and dynamic force in society.

【生前】 shēngqián before one's death; during one's lifetime: ～愿望 unrealized wish (of a person who has passed away)

【生擒】 shēngqín capture (alive)

【生人】 shēngrén stranger

【生日】 shēngrì birthday

【生色】 shēngsè add colour to; add lustre to; give added significance to: 老师们的演出，为英语晚会～不少。The teachers' performance made the English evening more enjoyable.

【生身父母】 shēngshēn fù-mǔ one's own parents

【生事】 shēngshì make trouble; create a disturbance: 造谣～ spread rumours and make trouble

【生手】 shēngshǒu sb. new to a job

【生疏】 shēngshū ① not familiar: 人地～ be unfamiliar with the place and the people/ 我对这个地方并不算～。I'm no stranger here./ 我对这项工作很～。I don't know much about the job. ② out of practice; rusty: 他的英文有点～了。His English is getting rusty. ③ not as close as before: 多年不来往，我们的关系～了。We haven't been in touch with each other for years, so we're not as close as we used to be.

【生死】 shēng-sǐ life and death: ～关头 a moment when one's fate hangs in the balance/ ～存亡的斗争 a life-and-death struggle/ ～攸关的问题 a matter of life and death; a matter of vital importance

【生吞活剥】 shēngtūn-huóbō swallow sth. raw and whole — accept sth. uncritically

【生物】 shēngwù living things; living beings; organisms: 超显微镜～ ultramicroscopic organisms/ 浮游～ plankton; 寄生～ parasites

【生息】 shēngxī ① bear interest ② 〈书〉 live; grow; propagate: 休养～ recuperate and multiply; rest and build up one's strength/ 自古以来，我们的祖先就劳动、～、繁殖在这块土地上。From ancient times our forefathers have laboured, lived and multiplied on this land. ◇ ～资本 interest-bearing capital

【生肖】 shēngxiào any of the twelve animals, representing the twelve Earthly Branches, used to symbolize the year in which a person is born

【生效】 shēngxiào go into effect; become effective: 签字后立即～ become effective immediately upon signature/ 自签字之日起～ go into effect from the date of signature/ 在互换批准书以后立即～ come into force immediately on exchange of the instruments of ratification

【生性】 shēngxìng natural disposition

【生锈】 shēngxiù get rusty: 经常擦油，以免～。Oil it regularly to prevent rust.

【生涯】 shēngyá career; profession: 舞台～ a stage career/ 操笔墨～ write for a living

【生意】 shēngyì tendency to grow; life and vitality: ～盎然 full of life/ 春天的大地一片蓬勃的～。Spring has filled the earth with life and vitality.

【生意】 shēngyi business; trade: 做～ do business/ 做成一笔～ make a deal; strike a bargain/ ～兴隆。Trade is brisk. 或 Business is booming. ◇ ～经 the knack of doing business; shrewd business sense

【生硬】 shēngyìng stiff; rigid; harsh: 态度～ be stiff in manner

【生育】 shēngyù give birth to; bear: ～子女 bear children/ 不能～ be unable to have children; be sterile/ 她已过了～年龄。She is past her child-bearing age.

【生造】 shēngzào coin (words and expressions): 不要～谁也不懂的词语。Do not coin words and expressions that nobody can understand. ◇ ～词 coinage

【生长】 shēngzhǎng ① grow: 小麦～良好。The wheat is growing well. 或 The wheat is doing fine. ② grow up; be brought up

【生殖】 shēngzhí reproduction ◇ ～器官 reproductive organs; genitals/ ～系统 reproductive system

【生字】 shēngzì new word ◇ ～表 (a list of) new words

声* shēng ① sound; voice: 脚步～ the sound of footsteps/ 小～说话 speak in a low voice ② make a sound: 不～

不响 not utter a word; keep quiet ③ initial consonant (of a Chinese syllable): 双～ alliteration ④ tone: 四～ the four tones in classical and modern Chinese ⑤〈量〉: 我喊了他两～。 I called him twice. ⑥ reputation: ～誉 reputation; fame; prestige

【声辩】 shēngbiàn argue; justify; explain away

【声称】 shēngchēng profess; claim; assert: ～已打破僵局 claim to have broken the deadlock

【声带】 shēngdài ①〈生理〉 vocal cords ②〈电影〉 sound track

【声调】 shēngdiào ① tone; note: ～激昂 in an impassioned tone/ ～低沉 in a low, sad voice ②〈语〉 the tone of a Chinese character 参见"四声" sìshēng

【声东击西】 shēng dōng jī xī make a feint to the east and attack in the west

【声价】 shēngjià reputation: ～甚高 (of a person) be held in high repute; be held in high esteem

【声浪】 shēnglàng voice; clamour: 抗议的～ a wave of protest

【声泪俱下】 shēng-lèi jù xià shedding tears while speaking; in a tearful voice: 他一地诉说了自己的不幸遭遇。 Tears streamed down his cheeks as he recounted his unhappy experience.

【声名】 shēngmíng reputation: ～狼藉 have a bad name; be notorious

【声明】 shēngmíng ① state; declare; announce: 庄严～ solemnly state ② statement; declaration: 联合～ joint statement

【声母】 shēngmǔ 〈语〉 initial consonant (of a Chinese syllable)

【声气】 shēngqì ① information: 互通～ exchange information; keep in contact with each other ②〈方〉 voice; tone: 小声小气地 in a low voice; in undertones

【声色】 shēng-sè ① voice and countenance: 不动～ maintain one's composure; stay calm and collected ②〈书〉 woman and song

【声色俱厉】 shēng-sè jù lì stern in voice and countenance

【声势】 shēngshì impetus; momentum: 虚张～ make a show of strength; bluff and bluster/ ～浩大 great in strength and impetus; mammoth (demonstration, etc.)

【声嘶力竭】 shēngsī-lìjié shout oneself hoarse; shout oneself blue in the face

【声速】 shēngsù 〈物〉 velocity of sound

【声讨】 shēngtǎo denounce; condemn

【声望】 shēngwàng popularity; prestige: 在群众中有很高的～ enjoy great prestige among the masses

【声威】 shēngwēi renown; prestige: ～大震 gain great fame and high prestige

【声息】 shēngxī ①〔多用于否定〕 sound; noise: 没有一点～。 Not a sound is heard. ② information: ～相闻 keep in touch with each other

【声响】 shēngxiǎng sound; noise: 这发动机～太大。 This motor makes too much noise./ 瀑布奔泻，发出巨大的～。 The waterfall came down with a rush and a roar.

【声言】 shēngyán profess; claim; declare

【声音】 shēngyīn sound; voice

【声誉】 shēngyù reputation; fame; prestige: 维护国家的～ defend the honour of one's country/ 在国内外享有很高的～ enjoy great prestige both at home and abroad

【声援】 shēngyuán express support for; support

【声张】 shēngzhāng make public; disclose: 不要～。 Don't breathe a word of it to anyone.

牲* shēng ① domestic animal ② animal sacrifice

【牲畜】 shēngchù livestock; domestic animals ◇ ～车〈铁道〉 livestock wagon; stock wagon; stock car

【牲口】 shēngkou draught animals; beasts of burden ◇ 贩子 cattle dealer/ ～棚 stock barn; livestock shed

笙 shēng 〈乐〉 sheng, a reed pipe wind instrument

【笙歌】 shēnggē 〈书〉 playing and singing

甥* shēng sister's son; nephew

【甥女】 shēngnǚ sister's daughter; niece

绳* shéng ① rope; cord; string: 麻～ hemp rope/ 钢丝～ steel cable; wire rope ② restrict; restrain: ～以纪律 enforce discipline upon sb.

【绳索】 shéngsuǒ rope; cord

【绳梯】 shéngtī rope ladder

【绳子】 shéngzi cord; rope; string

省* shěng ① economize; save: ～着点用 use sparingly/ ～时间 save time/ ～掉不少麻烦 save a lot of trouble/ 能～的就～ economize wherever possible ② omit; leave out: 这两个字不能～。 These two words cannot be omitted./ ～一道工序 eliminate one step from the process ③ province 另见 xǐng

【省城】 shěngchéng provincial capital

【省吃俭用】 shěngchī-jiǎnyòng live frugally

【省得】 shěngde so as to save (或 avoid): 你就住在这儿吧，～天天来回跑。 Better stay here to avoid having to go back and forth every day./ 到了就来信，～我挂念。 Send me a letter as soon as you arrive so that I won't worry.

【省份】 shěngfèn province

【省会】 shěnghuì provincial capital

【省界】 shěngjiè provincial boundaries

【省力】 shěnglì save effort; save labour: 这种耕作方法～不少。 This method of farming saves a lot of labour.

【省略】 shěnglüè leave out; omit: 与主题关系不大的段落可以～。 The irrelevant paragraphs can be omitted./ 这个句子的主语～了。 The subject of the sentence is understood. ◇ ～号 ellipsis; suspension points; ellipsis dots (……)(...)/ ～句〈语〉 elliptical sentence

【省钱】 shěngqián save money; be economical: 每月省点钱 save some money each month

【省事】 shěngshì save trouble; simplify matters: 这样可以省很多事。 We can make it much simpler this way./ 在食堂里吃饭～。 It's more convenient to eat in the canteen.

圣* shèng ① sage; saint ② holy; sacred: 神～领土 sacred territory ③ emperor: ～上 His or Her Majesty

【圣餐】 shèngcān 〈宗〉 Holy Communion

【圣诞】 shèngdàn the birthday of Jesus Christ ◇ ～老人 Santa Claus/ ～树 Christmas tree

【圣诞节】 Shèngdànjié Christmas Day: ～前夜 Christmas Eve

【圣地】 shèngdì ①〈宗〉 the Holy Land (或 City) ② sacred place; shrine

【圣经】 Shèngjīng the Holy Bible; the Bible; Holy Writ

【圣母】 shèngmǔ ① a female deity; goddess ② the (Blessed) Virgin Mary; Madonna

【圣人】 shèngrén sage; wise man

【圣贤】 shèngxián sages and men of virtue: 古语说："人非～，孰能无过?" As the old saying goes, "Men are not saints, how can they be free from faults?"

【圣旨】 shèngzhǐ imperial edict

胜* shèng ① victory; success: 得～ win (victory)/ 力争每战必～ try our best to ensure victory in every battle/ 战而～之 fight to win/ 我队以四～两负一平的成绩获得亚军。 Our team finished second with two wins, two defeats and one tie./ ～不骄,败不馁 not dizzy with success, nor discouraged by failure ② surpass; be superior to; get the better of: 事实～于雄辩。 Facts speak louder than words./ 聊～于

无 better than nothing ③ superb; wonderful; lovely: ～景 wonderful scenery ④ be equal to; can bear: 力不能～ beyond one's ability/ 数不～数 too numerous to count; countless

【胜败】 shèng-bài victory or defeat; success or failure

【胜地】 shèngdì famous scenic spot: 避暑～ summer resort

【胜负】 shèng-fù victory or defeat; success or failure: 战争的～ the outcome of a war/ ～未定。Victory hangs in the balance./ 这场比赛～已定。The outcome of the game is a foregone conclusion./ 比赛的～是暂时的,友谊是永久的。To win or lose in a match is temporary while friendship between the contestants is lasting.

【胜迹】 shèngjī famous historical site

【胜利】 shènglì ① victory; triumph: 充满了～的信心 fully confident of victory/ ～果实 fruits of victory/ 敢于斗争,敢于～ dare to struggle and dare to win ② successfully; triumphantly: ～完成任务 successfully carry out one's task ◇ ～者 victor; winner

【胜券】 shèngquàn confidence in victory: 操～ be sure to win

【胜任】 shèngrèn competent; qualified; equal to: ～工作 be competent at a job; prove equal to the task/ ～愉快 be fully competent; be well qualified

【胜似】 shèngsì be better than; surpass

【胜诉】 shèngsù win a lawsuit (或 court case)

【胜算】 shèngsuàn 〈书〉 a stratagem which ensures success: 操～ be sure of success

【胜仗】 shèngzhàng victorious battle; victory: 打～ win a battle; score a victory

乘 shèng 〈史〉 a war chariot drawn by four horses: 千～之国 a state with a thousand chariots
另见 chéng

盛* shèng ① flourishing; prosperous: 桃花～开。The peach trees are in full bloom. 或 The peach blossoms are out./ 兴～ flourish ② vigorous, energetic: 火势很～。The fire is raging./ 年轻气～ young and aggressive ③ magnificent; grand: ～举 a grand occasion (或 event) ④ abundant, plentiful: ～意 great kindness ⑤ popular; common; widespread: ～传 be widely known; be widely rumoured ⑥ greatly; deeply: ～夸 praise highly
另见 chéng

【盛产】 shèngchǎn abound in; teem with: ～煤铁 abound in coal and iron/ ～石油 be rich in oil/ ～鱼蟹 teem with fish and crabs

【盛大】 shèngdà grand; magnificent: ～欢迎 a rousing welcome/ ～招待会 a grand reception/ ～游行 a mammoth parade

【盛典】 shèngdiǎn grand ceremony

【盛会】 shènghuì distinguished gathering; grand meeting: 团结友谊的～ a grand gathering of unity and friendship/ 体育～ a magnificent sports meet

【盛极一时】 shèngjí yīshí be in fashion for a time; be all the rage at the moment

【盛况】 shèngkuàng grand occasion; spectacular event: ～空前 an exceptionally grand occasion

【盛名】 shèngmíng great reputation: ～之下,其实难副。It is hard to live up to a great reputation.

【盛气凌人】 shèngqì líng rén domineering; arrogant; overbearing: ～的样子 imperious bearing

【盛情】 shèngqíng great kindness; boundless hospitality: ～难却。It would be ungracious not to accept your invitation./ 受到～款待 be accorded lavish hospitality

【盛世】 shèngshì flourishing age; heyday: 太平～ times of peace and prosperity; piping times of peace

【盛事】 shèngshì grand occasion; great event

【盛暑】 shèngshǔ sweltering summer heat; very hot weather; the dog days

【盛衰】 shèng-shuāi prosperity and decline; rise and fall; ups and downs

【盛衰荣辱】 shèng-shuāi róng-rǔ prosperity and decline, glory and humiliation; rise and fall; ups and downs; vicissitudes of life

【盛夏】 shèngxià the height of summer; midsummer

【盛行】 shèngxíng be current (或 rife, rampant); be in vogue: ～一时 be in vogue for a time; prevail for a time

【盛宴】 shèngyàn grand banquet; sumptuous dinner 又作 "盛筵"

【盛意】 shèngyì great kindness; generosity

【盛誉】 shèngyù great fame; high reputation: 中国丝绸在世界上素有～。Chinese silk has long been famous all over the world.

【盛赞】 shèngzàn highly praise; speak of sb. in glowing terms

【盛装】 shèngzhuāng splendid attire; rich dress: 穿着节日的～ be dressed in one's holiday best

剩* shèng surplus; remnant: ～货 surplus goods/ ～菜～饭 leftovers/ 所～无几。There is not much left.

【剩下】 shèngxia be left (over); remain: ～多少? How much is left (over)?/ ～的敌军已经被我们消灭了。We have wiped out the remaining enemy troops.

【剩余】 shèngyú surplus; remainder: 收支相抵,略有～。The reckoning up of revenue and expenditure shows a small surplus.

shī

尸* shī corpse; dead body; remains: 死～ dead body; corpse/ 兽～ carcass

【尸骨】 shīgǔ skeleton 又作 "尸骸"

【尸横遍野】 shī héng biànyě a field littered with corpses

【尸身】 shīshēn corpse; dead body; remains 又作 "尸首"

【尸体】 shītǐ corpse; dead body; remains ◇ ～解剖 autopsy; postmortem (examination)

失* shī ① lose: ～而复得 lost and found again/ 迷～方向 lose one's bearings ② miss; let slip: 坐～良机 let slip a good opportunity; lose a good chance ③ fail to achieve one's end: 大～所望 be greatly disappointed ④ mishap; defect; mistake: 唯恐有～ fear that there may be some mishap/ ～之于烦琐 have the defect of being too detailed ⑤ deviate from the normal: ～色 turn pale ⑥ break (a promise); go back on (one's word): ～信 break one's promise

【失败】 shībài ① be defeated; lose (a war, etc.): 遭到了可耻的～ meet with ignominious defeat ② fail: ～是成功之母。Failure is the mother of success. ◇ ～情绪 defeatist sentiments/ ～主义 defeatism

【失策】 shīcè unwise; inexpedient: 这样做非常～。It was a very unwise move.

【失察】 shīchá neglect one's supervisory duties

【失常】 shīcháng not normal; odd: 举止～ act oddly/ 精神～ be distraught; not be in one's right mind

【失宠】 shīchǒng fall into disfavour; be out of favour; be in disgrace

【失传】 shīchuán not be handed down from past generations; be lost: 一种～的艺术 a lost art

【失措】 shīcuò lose one's presence of mind; lose one's head: 惊慌～ be panic-stricken

【失当】 shīdàng improper; inappropriate: 这个问题处理～。This problem was not properly handled.

【失地】 shīdì lost territory: 收复～ recover lost territory

【失掉】 shīdiào ① lose: ～联系 lose contact with/ ～权力 be stripped of power/ ～民心 lose popular support ② miss: ～机会 miss a chance

【失和】 shīhé fail to keep on good terms; become estranged

【失魂落魄】 shīhún-luòpò driven to distraction: 吓得～ be scared out of one's wits; be frightened out of one's life

【失火】 shīhuǒ catch fire; be on fire

【失脚】 shījiǎo lose one's footing; slip: ～跌倒 lose one's footing (或 balance) and fall

【失节】 shījié ① forfeit one's integrity; be disloyal ② (of a woman, according to feudal morality) lose one's chastity

【失敬】 shījìng 〈套〉 sorry I didn't recognize you; sorry

【失口】 shīkǒu a slip of the tongue

【失礼】 shīlǐ breach of etiquette; impoliteness; discourtesy

【失利】 shīlì suffer a setback (或 defeat): 军事上的～ military reverses/ 在这场乒乓球比赛中我方第一盘～。Our side lost the first game of the table-tennis match.

【失恋】 shīliàn be disappointed in a love affair

【失灵】 shīlíng (of a machine, instrument, etc.) not work or not work properly; be out of order: 开关～了。The switch is out of order.

【失落】 shīluò lose

【失眠】 shīmián (suffer from) insomnia: 病人昨夜～。The patient had a sleepless night last night.

【失明】 shīmíng lose one's sight; go blind: 双目～ lose the sight of both eyes

【失陪】 shīpéi ＜套＞ excuse me, but I must be leaving now

【失窃】 shīqiè have things stolen; suffer loss by theft

【失去】 shīqù lose: ～知觉 lose consciousness/ ～信心 lose confidence/ ～时效 be no longer effective; cease to be in force

【失散】 shīsàn be separated from and lose touch with each other; be scattered

【失色】 shīsè ① turn pale: 大惊～ turn pale with fright ② be eclipsed; be outshone: 黯然～ be cast into the shade; be eclipsed; pale into insignificance

【失神】 shīshén ① inattentive; absent-minded ② out of sorts; in low spirits

【失声】 shīshēng ① cry out involuntarily ② lose one's voice: 痛哭～ be choked with tears

【失实】 shīshí inconsistent with the facts: 传闻～。The rumour was unfounded.

【失势】 shīshì lose power and influence; fall into disgrace

【失事】 shīshì (have an) accident: 飞机～ aviation accident; aeroplane crash

【失手】 shīshǒu accidentally drop: 他一～打碎了一个茶杯。He accidentally dropped a cup and broke it.

【失守】 shīshǒu fall: 城市～ the fall of a city

【失算】 shīsuàn miscalculate; misjudge; be injudicious

【失态】 shītài forget oneself: 酒后～ forget oneself in one's cups

【失调】 shītiáo ① imbalance; dislocation: 供求～ imbalance of supply and demand/ 经济～ economic dislocation/ 雨水～ abnormal rainfall ② lack of proper care (after an illness, etc.): 产后～ lack of proper care after childbirth

【失望】 shīwàng ① lose hope ② disappointed: 感到～ be disappointed/ 令人～ disappointing

【失物】 shīwù lost article; lost property

【失误】 shīwù 〔多指打球、下棋〕fault; muff: 接球～ muff a ball/ 由于发球～而丢了几分 lose several points through serving faults

【失陷】 shīxiàn (of cities, territory, etc.) fall; fall into enemy hands

【失效】 shīxiào ① lose efficacy; lose effectiveness; cease to be effective: 这药已～了。The medicine no longer has any effect./ 使水雷～ deactivate mines ② (of a treaty, an agreement, etc.) be no longer in force; become invalid: 自动～ automatically cease to be in force

【失笑】 shīxiào laugh in spite of oneself; cannot help laughing

【失信】 shīxìn break one's promise; go back on one's word

【失修】 shīxiū (of houses, etc.) be in bad repair; fall into disrepair: 年久～ have long been out of repair; have been neglected for years

【失学】 shīxué be deprived of education; be unable to go to school; be obliged to discontinue one's studies

【失血】 shīxuè lose blood: ～过多 excessive loss of blood

【失言】 shīyán make an indiscreet remark: 酒后～ make an indiscreet remark under the influence of alcohol

【失业】 shīyè lose one's job; be out of work; be unemployed ◇ ～率 rate of unemployment/ ～者 the unemployed; the jobless

【失意】 shīyì have one's aspirations, plans, etc. thwarted; be frustrated; be disappointed

【失迎】 shīyíng ＜套＞ fail to meet (a guest): ～, ～! Excuse me for not meeting you at the gate./ 昨天～了, 很抱歉。Sorry I was out when you called yesterday.

【失约】 shīyuē fail to keep an appointment

【失真】 shīzhēn (of voice, images, etc.) lack fidelity; not be true to the original

【失之东隅,收之桑榆】 shī zhī dōngyú, shōu zhī sāngyú lose at sunrise and gain at sunset — make up on the roundabouts what you lose on the swings

【失之交臂】 shī zhī jiāo bì just miss the person or opportunity: 机会难得, 幸勿～。Don't let slip such a golden opportunity.

【失职】 shīzhí neglect one's duty; dereliction of duty

【失主】 shīzhǔ owner of lost property

【失踪】 shīzōng be missing: 伤亡之外, 尚有多人～。In addition to the killed and wounded, many were missing.

【失足】 shīzú ① lose one's footing; slip: ～落水 slip and fall into the water ② take a wrong step in life: 一～成千古恨。One false step brings everlasting grief.

师* shī ① teacher; master: 提倡尊～爱生 advocate students respecting teachers and teachers cherishing students ② model; example: 前事不忘, 后事之～。Lessons learned from the past can guide one in the future. ③ a person skilled in a certain profession: 工程～ engineer/ 理发～ barber /技～ technician ④ of one's master or teacher: ～母 the wife of one's teacher or master ⑤ division: 步兵～ infantry division ⑥ troops; army: 正义之～ an army fighting for a just cause

【师表】 shībiǎo ＜书＞ a person of exemplary virtue: 为人～ be worthy of the name of teacher; be a paragon of virtue and learning

【师出无名】 shī chū wú míng dispatch troops without just cause

【师弟】 shīdì ① junior fellow apprentice ② the son of one's master (younger than oneself) ③ father's apprentice (younger than oneself)

【师法】 shīfǎ ① model oneself after (a great master); imitate ② knowledge or technique handed down by one's master

【师范】 shīfàn ① teacher-training; pedagogical: ～学院 teachers college; teachers training college ② normal school

【师父】 shīfu ① 见"师傅" ② a polite form of address to a monk or nun

【师傅】 shīfu master worker (a qualified worker as distinct from an apprentice)

【师兄】 shīxiōng ① senior fellow apprentice ② the son of one's master (older than oneself) ③ father's apprentice (older than oneself)

【师长】 shīzhǎng ① ＜尊＞ teacher ② ＜军＞ division commander

【师资】 shīzī persons qualified to teach; teachers: ～不足 shortage of teachers/ 培训～ train teachers

虱* shī louse

【虱子】 shīzi louse

诗* shī poetry; verse; poem

【诗歌】 shīgē poems and songs; poetry: ～朗诵 recitation of poems; poetry readings

【诗集】 shījí collection of poems; poetry anthology

【诗句】 shījù verse; line

【诗篇】 shīpiān ① poem ② inspiring story: 我们时代的壮丽～ a magnificent epic of our era

【诗人】 shīrén poet

【诗兴】 shīxìng urge for poetic creation; poetic inspiration; poetic mood: ～大发 feel a strong urge to write poetry; be in an exalted, poetic mood

【诗意】 shīyì poetic quality or flavour: 饶有～ rich in poetic flavour; very poetic

【诗韵】 shīyùn ① rhyme (in poetry) ② rhyming dictionary

狮* shī lion

【狮身人面像】 shīshēn-rénmiànxiàng sphinx

【狮子】 shīzi　lion

【狮子搏兔】 shīzi bó tù　not stint the strength of a lion in wrestling with a rabbit — go all out even when fighting a small enemy or tackling a minor problem

【狮子舞】 shīziwǔ　lion dance

施 shī ① execute; carry out: 无所～其技 no chance (for sb.) to play his tricks/ 他们一计不成，又一计。Their first ruse having failed, they tried another. ② bestow; grant; hand out: ～恩 bestow favour ③ exert; impose: ～压力 exert pressure ④ use; apply: ～底肥 apply fertilizer to the subsoil

【施放】 shīfàng　discharge; fire: ～催泪弹 fire tear-gas shells/ ～烟幕 lay a smokescreen

【施工】 shīgōng　construction: 桥梁正在～。The bridge is under construction.

【施加】 shījiā　exert; bring to bear on: ～压力 bring pressure to bear on sb.; put pressure on sb./ ～影响 exert one's influence on sb.

【施礼】 shīlǐ　salute

【施舍】 shīshě　give alms; give in charity

【施威】 shīwēi　exhibit one's power; show severity

【施行】 shīxíng　① put in force; execute; apply: 本条例自公布之日起～。These regulations come into force upon promulgation. ② perform: ～手术 perform a surgical operation/ ～急救 administer first aid

【施与】 shīyǔ　grant; bestow

【施展】 shīzhǎn　put to good use; give free play to: ～本领 put one's ability to good use; give full play to one's talent/ ～出种种威逼利诱的伎俩 resort to all kinds of threats and inducements/ ～阴谋诡计 carry out plots and schemes

【施政】 shīzhèng　administration ◇ ～纲领 administrative programme

【施主】 shīzhǔ　① alms giver; benefactor ② <物> donor

湿 shī　wet; damp; humid: 小心点，别～了衣裳。Be careful! Don't get your clothes wet./ 别穿那双袜子，还～着呢。Don't wear those socks, they're still damp.

【湿度】 shīdù　humidity

【湿淋淋】 shīlínlín　dripping wet; drenched: 身上浇得～的 get dripping (或 soaking, sopping) wet; be soaked to the skin/ ～的衣服 sopping wet clothes

【湿漉漉】 shīlùlù　wet; damp

【湿气】 shīqì　moisture; dampness

【湿热】 shīrè　damp and hot

【湿润】 shīrùn　moist: ～的土壤 damp soil/ 空气～ humid air/ 她眼睛～了。Her eyes were moist with tears.

【湿透】 shītòu　wet through; drenched: 汗水～了他的衣服。His clothes are drenched with sweat.

嘘 shī <叹> 〔表示制止、驱逐等〕: ～，别作声! Sh (或 Hush)! Keep quiet!
另见 xū

shí

十 shí　① ten: ～倍 ten times; tenfold/ ～个指头有长短。Fingers are unequal in length — you can't expect everybody to be the same. ② topmost: ～成 100 per cent

【十八般武艺】 shíbā bān wǔyì　skill in wielding the 18 kinds of weapons — skill in various types of combat: ～，样样精通 be skilful in using each and every one of the 18 weapons; be versatile

【十恶不赦】 shí è bù shè　guilty of unpardonable evil; unpardonably wicked

【十二分】 shí'èrfēn　more than 100 per cent; extremely: 感到～的满意 be more than satisfied

【十二月】 shí'èryuè　① December ② the twelfth month of the lunar year; the twelfth moon

【十分】 shífēn <副> very; fully; utterly; extremely: ～高兴 be very pleased; be elated/ ～难过 feel very sorry; feel very bad/ ～宝贵 most valuable/ ～有害 extremely harmful/ ～注意 pay close (或 the closest) attention to/ ～仇视 harbour intense hatred for/ ～猖狂 be on a rampage

【十进制】 shíjìnzhì <数> the decimal system

【十拿九稳】 shíná-jiǔwěn　90 per cent sure; practically certain; in the bag: 这事情，我们是～了。We have the matter well in hand.

【十年九不遇】 shí nián jiǔ bù yù　not occur once in ten years; be very rare: 这样大的洪水真是～。A flood of this sort is really unprecedented.

【十年树木，百年树人】 shí nián shù mù, bǎi nián shù rén <谚> it takes ten years to grow trees, but a hundred to rear people

【十全十美】 shíquán-shíměi　be perfect in every way; be the acme of perfection; leave nothing to be desired

【十室九空】 shí shì jiǔ kōng　nine houses out of ten are deserted — a scene of desolation after a plague or war when the population is decimated

【十万八千里】 shíwàn bāqiān lǐ　a distance of one hundred and eight thousand li; poles apart: 离题～ miles away from the subject; completely off the point

【十万火急】 shíwàn huǒjí　① posthaste ② Most Urgent (as a mark on dispatches)

【十项全能运动】 shí xiàng quánnéng yùndòng <体> decathlon

【十一月】 shíyīyuè　① November ② the eleventh month of the lunar year; the eleventh moon

【十月】 shíyuè　① October ② the tenth month of the lunar year; the tenth moon

【十之八九】 shí zhī bā-jiǔ　in eight or nine cases out of ten; most likely: ～他是这样。Most likely there is some misunderstanding on his part. 又作"十有八九"

【十字架】 shízìjià　cross

【十字街头】 shízì jiētóu　crisscross streets; busy city streets

【十字路口】 shízì lùkǒu　crossroads: 徘徊在～ hesitate at the crossroads

【十足】 shízú　100 per cent; out-and-out; sheer; downright: 干劲～ full of energy/ ～的强权政治 100％ (或 naked) power politics

什 shí　① assorted; varied; miscellaneous ② <书> 〔多用于分数或倍数〕ten: ～一 one tenth/ ～百 tenfold or hundredfold
另见 shén

【什锦】 shíjǐn <食品> assorted; mixed: ～饼干 assorted biscuits/ ～奶糖 assorted toffees

石 shí　① stone; rock ② stone inscription: 金～ inscriptions on ancient bronzes and stone tablets
另见 dàn

【石斑鱼】 shíbānyú　grouper

【石板】 shíbǎn <建> slabstone; flagstone; flag

【石碑】 shíbēi　stone tablet; stele

【石壁】 shíbì　cliff; precipice

【石沉大海】 shí chén dàhǎi　like a stone dropped into the sea — disappear forever

【石雕】 shídiāo　① stone carving ② carved stone

【石膏】 shígāo　gypsum; plaster stone: 熟～ plaster; plaster of Paris/ 生～ plaster stone

【石灰】 shíhuī　lime: 生～ quick lime/ 熟～ slaked lime

【石匠】 shíjiang　stonemason; mason

【石刻】 shíkè　① carved stone ② stone inscription

【石窟】 shíkū　rock cave; grotto: 龙门～ the Longmen Grottoes (in Luoyang)

【石块】 shíkuài　stone, rock

【石榴】 shíliu <植> pomegranate

【石棉】 shímián　asbestos

【石破天惊】 shípò-tiānjīng　earth-shattering and heaven-battering; remarkably original and forceful (music, writing, etc.)

【石器】 shíqì　① stone implement; stone artifact ② stone vessel; stoneware ◇ ～时代 the Stone Age

【石头】 shítou　stone; rock: 心里好象一块～落了地 feel as though a load has been taken off one's mind

【石英】 shíyīng　quartz

【石油】 shíyóu petroleum; oil ◇ ～产品 petroleum products/ ～地质学 petroleum geology/ ～工业 oil industry; petroleum industry/ ～管路 petroleum pipeline/ ～化工厂 petrochemical works/ ～勘探 petroleum prospecting

【石油化学】 shíyóu huàxué petrochemistry ◇ ～产品 petroleum chemicals

【石油气】 shíyóuqì petroleum gas: 液化～ liquefied petroleum gas (LPG)

【石子】 shízǐ cobblestone; cobble; pebble

识* shí ① know: 一字不～ not know a single character — absolutely illiterate ② knowledge: 学～ learning; knowledge
另见 zhì

【识别】 shíbié distinguish; discern; spot

【识货】 shíhuò know all about the goods; be able to tell good from bad; know what's what: 不怕不～,就怕货比货。 Don't worry about not knowing much about the goods; just compare and you will see which is better. 或 Don't fear it won't be appreciated; it stands up well to comparison.

【识破】 shípò see through; penetrate: ～骗局 see through a fraud

【识趣】 shíqù know how to behave in a delicate situation

【识时务者为俊杰】 shí shíwù zhě wéi jùnjié whosoever understands the times is a great man

【识途老马】 shí tú lǎomǎ an old horse which knows the way — a person of rich experience; a wise old bird

【识相】 shíxiàng 〈方〉 be sensible; be tactful: 你还是～点, 赶快走吧。 You'd better be sensible and quit.

【识字】 shízì learn to read; become literate

时* shí ① time; times; days: 古～ ancient times/ 当～ at that time; in those days ② fixed time: 按～上班 get to work on time/ 准～到站 arrive at the station on time ③ hour: 报～ announce the hour; give the time signal/ 上午八～ at 8 o'clock in the morning; at 8 a.m. ④ season: 四～ the four seasons/ ～菜 delicacies of the season ⑤ current; present: ～下 at present ⑥ opportunity; chance: 失～ lose the opportunity; miss the chance/ 待～而动 bide one's time ⑦ now and then; occasionally; from time to time: ～有出现 occur now and then/ ～…now…now…; sometimes…sometimes…: ～断～续 on and off/ ～起～伏 now rise, now fall; have ups and downs/ 心情～喜～忧 have changing moods, now gay, now gloomy/ 镜头～远～近 sometimes long shots and sometimes close-ups ⑨ 〈语〉 tense: 过去～ the past tense

【时差】 shíchā time difference

【时常】 shícháng often; frequently

【时辰】 shíchen one of the 12 two-hour periods into which the day was traditionally divided, each being given the name of one of the 12 Earthly Branches

【时代】 shídài ① times; age; era; epoch: ～潮流 the tendency of the day; the trend of the times/ ～的需要 the needs of the times/ 开创一个新～ usher in a new era/ 反映我们一代的面貌 reflect the features of our age ② a period in one's life: 青年～ youth

【时而】 shí'ér ① from time to time; sometimes: 天上～飘过几片薄薄的白云。 Every now and then fleecy clouds floated across the sky. ② ～now…now…; sometimes…sometimes…: 这天气变化无常,～晴天,～下雨! What changeable weather, fine one moment, raining the next!

【时分】 shífēn time: 黄昏～ at dusk; at twilight

【时光】 shíguāng ① time: ～不早了。 It's getting late. ② times; years; days

【时候】 shíhou ① (the duration of) time: 你写这篇文章用了多少～? How much time did you spend writing this article?/ 农忙的～ a busy farming season ② (a point in) time; moment: 现在是什么～了? What time is it?/ 就在这～ just at this moment

【时机】 shíjī opportune moment; an opportune moment: 等待～ wait for an opportunity; bide one's time/ ～的选择 choice of the right moment; timing/ ～一到 when the opportunity arises; at the opportune moment/ ～不成熟。 Conditions are not yet ripe. 或 The time is not yet ripe.

【时价】 shíjià current price

【时间】 shíjiān ① (the concept of) time: ～与空间 time and space ② (the duration of) time: 这项工程需要多少～? How long will it take to finish this project?/ ～紧,任务重。 Time is pressing and the task heavy./ ～到了。 Time! 或 Time's up./ 办公～ office hours/ 不给敌人喘息的～ give the enemy no breathing space/ ～掌握得好 beautiful timing ③ (a point in) time: 现在的～是四点五分。 The time now is five minutes past four. ◇ ～表 timetable; schedule

【时间性】 shíjiānxìng timeliness: 新闻报导的～强。 News reports must be timely./ 这项任务～强。 This task must be fulfilled on time.

【时节】 shíjié season: 春耕～ the season for spring ploughing/ 清明～ at or around the Qing Ming festival

【时局】 shíjú the current political situation

【时刻】 shíkè ① time; hour; moment: 欢乐的～ a time of rejoicing/ 幸福的～ a happy moment/ 关键～ a critical moment ② constantly; always: ～准备保卫祖国 be ready to defend the country at any moment

【时令】 shílìng season: ～不正 unseasonable weather/ ～已交初秋。 It is already early autumn. ◇ ～病 seasonal disease

【时髦】 shímáo fashionable; stylish; in vogue: ～的服装 fashionable clothes/ 赶～ follow the fashion

【时期】 shíqī period

【时区】 shíqū time zone

【时尚】 shíshàng fashion; fad

【时时】 shíshí often; constantly: ～想到 often recall or think about/ ～处处严格要求自己 be strict with oneself in all matters

【时势】 shíshì the current situation; the trend of the times; the way things are going: ～造英雄。 The times produce their heroes.

【时事】 shíshì current events; current affairs ◇ ～报告 report on current events/ ～述评 current events survey

【时速】 shísù speed per hour

【时务】 shíwù current affairs; the trend of the times: 不识～ show no understanding of the times

【时鲜】 shíxiān (of vegetables, fruits, etc.) in season: ～果品 fresh fruits

【时限】 shíxiàn time limit

【时效】 shíxiào ① effectiveness for a given period of time ② 〈法〉 prescription ③ ageing

【时样】 shíyàng the latest fashion

【时宜】 shíyí what is appropriate to the occasion: 不合～ be not appropriate to the occasion; be inappropriate; be out of keeping with the times

【时疫】 shíyì epidemic

【时运】 shíyùn luck; fortune: ～不济 have bad luck; down on one's luck

【时针】 shízhēn ① hands of a clock or watch ② hour hand

【时至今日】 shí zhì jīnrì at this late hour

【时钟】 shízhōng clock

【时装】 shízhuāng fashionable dress; the latest fashion

实* shí ① solid: 里面是～的。 It's solid. ② true; real; honest: ～心眼儿 honest and sincere/ ～有其事。 It's a fact. ③ reality; fact: 名不副～ The name falls short of the reality. ④ fruit; seed: 开花结～ blossom and bear fruit

【实弹】 shídàn 〈军〉 live shell; live ammunition ◇ ～射击 firing practice; range practice/ ～演习 practice with live ammunition

【实地】 shídì on the spot: ～考察 on-the-spot investigation/ ～了解施工情况 learn on the spot how construction is proceeding

【实话】 shíhuà truth: 说～ to tell the truth/ ～实说 not mince words; not beat about the bush

【实惠】 shíhuì ① material benefit: 从中得到～ really benefit from it ② substantial; solid: 让顾客吃到经济～的饭菜 serve the customers inexpensive but substantial meals

【实际】 shíjì ① reality; practice: 理论和～统一 the unity of

theory and practice/ 客观～ objective reality/ 从～出发 proceed from actual conditions; be realistic/ ～上 in fact; in reality; actually ② practical; realistic: ～经验 practical experience/ 你这种想法不～。 This idea of yours is unrealistic. ③ real; actual; concrete: ～的例子 a concrete instance/ ～情况 the actual situation; reality/ ～生活水平 the real standard of living

【实价】 shíjià actual price

【实践】 shíjiàn ① practice: ～出真知。 Genuine knowledge comes from practice. ② put into practice; carry out; live up to: ～诺言 keep one's word; make good one's promise

【实据】 shíjù substantial evidence; substantial proof: 真凭～ ironclad evidence

【实况】 shíkuàng what is actually happening: 电视转播群众大会 televise a mass rally; live telecast of a mass rally ◇ ～录音 on-the-spot recording; live recording/ ～转播 live broadcast; live telecast

【实力】 shílì actual strength; strength: 部队的～ the actual strength of the armed forces/ 军事～ military strength/ ～相当 match each other in strength; be well matched in strength

【实例】 shílì living example; example

【实情】 shíqíng the true state of affairs; the actual situation; truth

【实权】 shíquán real power

【实施】 shíshī put into effect; implement; carry out: 协定的条款正在付诸～。 The provisions of the agreement are being put into effect./ 检查政策的～情况 check up on the implementation of the policy/ 监督宪法的～ supervise the enforcement of the constitution

【实事求是】 shíshì qiú shì seek truth from facts; be practical and realistic: ～的工作作风 a practical and realistic style of work/ ～的批评 criticism based on facts/ ～地拟定生产指标 set realistic production targets

【实物】 shíwù ① material object ② in kind

【实习】 shíxí practice; fieldwork; field trip: 去煤矿～ go on a field trip to a coal mine/ 进行教学～ do practice teaching ◇ ～工厂 factory attached to a school/ ～生 trainee/ ～医生 intern

【实现】 shíxiàn realize; achieve; bring about: 为～我们的宏伟目标而奋斗 work hard to achieve our lofty goal/ strive for the realization of our lofty goal/ ～优质高产 attain top quality and high output

【实效】 shíxiào actual effect; substantial results: 注重～ emphasize practical results/ 如果这方法确有～，就应该推广，If the method proves to be really effective, it should be popularized.

【实心】 shíxīn ① sincere: ～实意 honest and sincere ② solid: 这种车胎是～的。 These tyres are solid.

【实行】 shíxíng put into practice (或 effect); carry out; practise; implement: ～精兵简政的政策 put into effect the policy of better staff and simpler administration

【实学】 shíxué real learning; sound scholarship

【实验】 shíyàn experiment; test: 做～ do (或 carry out) an experiment; make a test ◇ ～室 laboratory

【实业】 shíyè industry and commerce; industry ◇ ～家 industrialist

【实用】 shíyòng practical; pragmatic; functional: 既美观，又～ not only beautiful, but also practical/ ～美术 applied fine arts

【实用主义】 shíyòngzhǔyì 〈哲〉 pragmatism ◇ ～者 pragmatist

【实在】 shízài ① true; real; honest; dependable: ～的本事 real ability/ 心眼儿～ honest; trustworthy ② indeed; really; honestly: ～太好了 very good indeed/ 我～不知道。 I really don't know. ③ in fact; as a matter of fact: 他装懂，～并没懂。 He pretends to understand, but as a matter of fact he doesn't.

【实在】 shízai 〈方〉 (of work) well-done; done carefully: 工作做得很～。 The work is well-done.

【实质】 shízhì substance; essence: 问题的～ the crux of the matter; the central point at issue/ ～性条款 substantive

provision/ ～上 in substance; in essence; essentially; virtually

拾* shí ① pick up (from the ground); collect: ～柴 collect firewood/ ～麦穗 glean (stray ears of) wheat ② ten (used for the numeral 十 on cheques, banknotes, etc. to avoid mistakes or alterations)

【拾荒】 shíhuāng glean and collect scraps (to eke out an existence)

【拾金不昧】 shí jīn bù mèi not pocket the money one picks up

【拾取】 shíqǔ pick up; collect

【拾人牙慧】 shí rén yáhuì pick up phrases from sb. and pass them off as one's own

【拾遗】 shíyí ① appropriate lost property: 路不～。 No one pockets anything found on the road. ② make good omissions: ～补阙 make good omissions and deficiencies

食* shí ① eat: 不劳动者不得～。 He who does not work, neither shall he eat. ② meal; food: 废寝忘～ (be so engrossed as to) forget food and sleep/ 主～ staple food ③ feed: 猪～ pig feed/ ～油 edible oil; cooking oil ⑤ eclipse: 日～ solar eclipse/ 月～ lunar eclipse

【食古不化】 shí gǔ bù huà swallow ancient learning without digesting it; be pedantic

【食粮】 shíliáng grain; food: 精神～ spiritual food

【食量】 shíliàng capacity for eating; appetite

【食品】 shípǐn foodstuff; food; provisions: 罐头～ tinned (或 canned) food ◇ ～部 food department/ ～厂 bakery and confectionery; food products factory/ ～工业 food industry

【食谱】 shípǔ recipes; cookbook

【食宿】 shí-sù board and lodging

【食堂】 shítáng dining room; mess hall; canteen

【食糖】 shítáng sugar

【食物】 shíwù food; eatables; edibles

【食言】 shíyán go back on one's word; break one's promise: ～而肥 fail to make good one's promise; break faith with sb.

【食盐】 shíyán table salt; salt

【食用】 shíyòng edible: ～植物油 edible vegetable oil

【食油】 shíyóu edible oil; cooking oil

【食欲】 shíyù appetite: ～不振 have a jaded appetite; have a poor appetite/ 促进～ stimulate (或 whet) the appetite; be appetizing

【食指】 shízhǐ index finger; forefinger

蚀 shí ① lose: 亏～ lose (money) in business ② erode; corrode: 风雨～ erosion by wind and rain/ 锈能～铁。 Rust corrodes iron. ③ 见"食" shí ⑤

【蚀本】 shíběn lose one's capital: ～生意 a business running at a loss; a losing proposition; an unprofitable venture (或 undertaking)

shǐ

史* shǐ ① history: 现代～ contemporary history/ 编年～ annals/ 断代～ dynastic history/ 国际关系～ history of international relations/ 有～以来 since the beginning of recorded history

【史册】 shǐcè history; annals: 载入～ go down in history

【史官】 shǐguān official historian; historiographer

【史迹】 shǐjī historical site or relics

【史料】 shǐliào historical data; historical materials

【史前】 shǐqián prehistoric: ～时代 prehistoric age (或 times) ◇ ～学〈考古〉 prehistory

【史诗】 shǐshī epic

【史实】 shǐshí historical facts

【史书】 shǐshū history; historical records: 据～记载 according to historical records

【史无前例】 shǐ wú qiánlì without precedent in history; unprecedented

史学】 shǐxué the science of history; historical science; historiography ◇ ～家 historian; historiographer

矢 shǐ ① arrow: 飞～ flying arrow ② vow; swear: ～志不移 vow to adhere to one's chosen course

矢口否认】 shǐkǒu fǒurèn flatly deny

豕 shǐ 〈书〉pig

使* shǐ ① send; tell sb. to do sth.: ～人去打听消息 send sb. to make inquiries ② use; employ; apply: ～化肥 use chemical fertilizer/ 这支笔很好～。This pen writes well./ 心往一处想,劲往一处～ with everyone's thoughts and efforts directed towards one goal ③ make; cause; enable: 虚心～人进步,骄傲～人落后。Modesty helps one to go forward, conceit makes one lag behind./ ～青少年在 德、智、体几方面都得到发展 enable the youth to develop morally, intellectually and physically/ 修改原计划～之适合于新的情况 revise the original plan so as to gear it to the need of the new situation/ 帮助朋友克服缺点,～他们能够大踏步前进 help friends to overcome their shortcomings so that they can advance with great strides ④ envoy; messenger: 特～ special envoy/ 出～国外 be accredited to a certain country; be sent abroad as an envoy/ 信～ courier; messenger ⑤ if; supposing: 纵～ even if; even though

使不得】 shǐbude ① cannot be used; useless; unserviceable: 这笔尖坏了,～了。This nib's broken — it can't be used. ② impermissible; undesirable: 你病刚好,干这种重活可～。You've just been ill, you mustn't do such heavy work.

使出】 shǐchū use one's; exert: ～全副本领 use all one's resources/ ～浑身解数 use all one's skill/ ～最后一点力气 expend one's last bit of strength

使得】 shǐde ① can be used; usable: 这台汽筒～使不得？Does this pump work all right? ② workable; feasible: 这个主意倒～。That's rather a good idea. ③ make; cause; render: ～家喻户晓 make known to everyone

使馆】 shǐguǎn diplomatic mission; embassy

使唤】 shǐhuan ① order about: 爱～人 be in the habit of ordering people about; be bossy ② 〈口〉use; handle: 这些新式农具～起来很方便。These new farm implements are easy to use (or handle)./ 这匹马不听生人～。This horse won't obey a stranger.

使节】 shǐjié diplomatic envoy; envoy

使劲】 shǐjìn exert all one's strength: ～干活 work hard/ ～蹬车 pedal (a bicycle) furiously/ ～划桨 strain at the oars/ 有使不完的劲 have inexhaustible energy/ 再使把劲 put in more effort; put on another spurt

使命】 shǐmìng mission

使女】 shǐnǚ maidservant; housemaid; chambermaid; maid

使性子】 shǐ xìngzi get angry; lose one's temper

使眼色】 shǐ yǎnsè tip sb. the wink; wink

使用】 shǐyòng make use of; use; employ; apply: 我国各民族都有～自己的语言的自由。Every nationality in our country has the freedom to use its own language./ 灵活地～兵力 flexible employment of forces/ 新机器已开始～。The new machine has been put into operation./ ～种种手段 resort to every possible means/ ～方便 be easy to operate

使者】 shǐzhě emissary; envoy; messenger

始* shǐ ① beginning; start: 自～至终 from beginning to end; from start to finish/ 不知～于何时 not know exactly when this came into being/ ～而不解,继而恍然。At first I didn't catch on; then I suddenly saw the light. ② 〈书〉〈副〉only then; not ... until: 群众大会结束后,广场～能通行。Traffic cannot pass through the square until the mass meeting is over.

始末】 shǐ-mò beginning and end — the whole story: 事情的～ the whole story

始业】 shǐyè the beginning of the school year: 秋季～。The school year begins in autumn.

始终】 shǐzhōng from beginning to end; from start to finish; all along; throughout: 会谈～在友好的气氛中进行。The talks proceeded in a friendly atmosphere from beginning to end.

始终不渝】 shǐzhōng bù_yú unswerving; steadfast

始终如一】 shǐzhōng rú yī constant; consistent; persistent

始祖】 shǐzǔ first ancestor; earliest ancestor

驶 shǐ ① sail; drive: ～入港口 sail into the harbour/ 火车～出车站。The train pulled out of the station. ② (of a vehicle, etc.) speed: 疾～而过 speed by; fly past

屎 shǐ ① excrement; faeces; dung; droppings: 鸡～ chicken droppings/ 牛～ cow dung/ 拉～ empty the bowels; shit ② secretion (of the eye, ear, etc.): 耳～ earwax

shì

士* shì ① bachelor (in ancient China) ② a social stratum in ancient China, between senior officials (大夫) and the common people (庶民) ③ scholar ④ noncommissioned officer: 上～(英) staff sergeant; (美) sergeant first class/ 中～ sergeant/ 下～ corporal ⑤ a person trained in a certain field: 护～ nurse ⑥ (commendable) person: 勇～ brave fighter; warrior/ 烈～ martyr ⑦ bodyguard, one of the pieces in Chinese chess

士兵】 shìbīng rank-and-file soldiers; privates

士大夫】 shìdàfū literati and officialdom (in feudal China)

士女】 shìnǚ ① young men and women ② 见"仕女" shìnǚ

士气】 shìqì morale: 鼓舞～ boost morale/ 我军～高昂。Our army's morale is high.

士卒】 shìzú soldiers; privates: 身先～ (of an officer) fight at the head of his men; lead the charge

氏 shì ① family name; surname: 张～兄弟 the Zhang brothers ② née: 李王～ Mrs. Li, née Wang ③ 〈对名人专家的称呼〉: 陈～定理 Chen's theorem/ 摄～温度计 Celsius thermometer

氏族】 shìzú clan

市* shì ① market: 米～ rice market/ 上～ be on the market; be in season ② city; municipality: ～中心 the heart of the city; city centre; downtown

市场】 shìchǎng marketplace; market; bazaar: 国内外～ domestic and foreign markets/ ～供应充足。There is an ample supply of commodities. / ～繁荣。The market is brisk.

市集】 shìjí ① fair ② small town

市价】 shìjià market price

市郊】 shìjiāo suburb; outskirts

市井】 shìjǐng 〈书〉marketplace; town: ～小人 philistine

市侩】 shìkuài sordid merchant: ～习气 sordid merchants' ways; philistinism

市面】 shìmiàn market conditions; business: ～繁荣。Trade is flourishing. 或 Business is brisk./ ～萧条。Business is slack.

市民】 shìmín residents of a city; townspeople

市区】 shìqū city proper; urban district

市容】 shìróng the appearance of a city: 保持～整洁 keep the city clean and tidy/ 参观～ go sight-seeing in the city; have a look around the city

市长】 shìzhǎng mayor

市镇】 shìzhèn small towns; towns

示* shì show; notify; instruct: 出～证件 produce one's papers/ 暗～ hint; drop a hint/ 告～ notice/ 请～ ask for instructions/ ～悉。Your letter has been received. 或 Yours to hand.

示范】 shìfàn set an example; demonstrate: 起～作用 play an exemplary role

示警】 shìjǐng give a warning; warn: 鸣锣～ give a warning by beating a gong

示例】 shìlì give typical examples; give a demonstration

示弱】 shìruò give the impression of weakness; take sth. lying down: 不甘～ not to be outdone

示威】 shìwēi ① demonstrate; hold a demonstration ② put

on a show of force; display one's strength ◇ ~游行 demonstration; parade; march

【示意】 shìyì signal; hint; motion: ~他出去 motion to him to go out/ 以目~ give a hint with the eyes; tip sb. the wink

世* shì ① lifetime; life: 今生今~ this present life ② generation: ~谊 friendship spanning many generations ③ age; era: 当今之~ at present; nowadays ④ world: 举~闻名 well known all over the world; world-famous ⑤ <地> epoch: 古新~ the Palaeocene Epoch

【世仇】 shìchóu ① family feud ② bitter enemy (in a family feud)

【世传】 shìchuán be handed down through generations

【世代】 shìdài ① for generations; from generation to generation; generation after generation: ~相传 pass on from generation to generation/ 他家~务农。 He comes from a long line of farmers. ② <生> generation

【世故】 shìgù the ways of the world: 老于~ versed in the ways of the world; worldly-wise/ 人情~ worldly wisdom

【世故】 shìgu worldly-wise: 这人相当~。 This chap is rather a smooth character.

【世纪】 shìjì century

【世交】 shìjiāo ① friendship spanning two or more generations ② old family friends

【世界】 shìjiè world
◇ ~博览会 World's Fair/ ~大事 world events/ ~观 world outlook/ ~冠军 world champion/ ~纪录 world record/ ~时 <天> universal time/ ~语 Esperanto/ ~主义 cosmopolitanism

【世界大战】 shìjiè dàzhàn world war: 第一次~ the First World War (1914-1918); World War I/ 第二次~ the Second World War (1939-1945); World War II

【世面】 shìmiàn various aspects of society; society; world; life: 见过~ have seen the world; have experienced life/ 经风雨,见~ face the world and brave the storm

【世人】 shìrén common people

【世上】 shìshang in the world; on earth: ~无难事,只怕有心人。 Nothing in the world is difficult for one who sets his mind on it.

【世事】 shìshì affairs of human life

【世俗】 shìsú ① common customs: ~之见 common views ② secular; worldly

【世态】 shìtài the ways of the world: ~人情 the ways of the world/ ~炎凉 inconstancy of human relationships

【世外桃源】 shìwài táoyuán the Land of Peach Blossoms — a fictitious land of peace, away from the turmoil of the world; a haven of peace

【世袭】 shìxí hereditary: ~财产 hereditary property; patrimony/ ~制度 the hereditary system

【世系】 shìxì pedigree; genealogy

仕 shì ① be an official; fill an office: 学而优则~。 A good scholar will make an official — a Confucian doctrine. ② bodyguard, one of the pieces in Chinese chess

【仕女】 shìnǚ <美术> traditional Chinese painting of beautiful women

【仕途】 shìtú <书> official career

式* shì ① type; style: 新~ new type; new style ② pattern; form: 程~ pattern; form to be copied ③ ceremony; ritual: 开幕~ opening ceremony ④ formula: 分子~ molecular formula

【式样】 shìyàng style; type; model: 各种~的服装 clothes in different styles/ 不同~的房屋 houses of different designs/ 各种~的车床 lathes of various models/ 美观~ graceful-looking; stylish

似* shì
另见 sì

【似的】 shìde <助> 〔用在名词、代词或动词后面，表示跟某种事物或情况相似〕: 象雪~那么白 as white as snow/ 他仿佛睡着了~。 He seems to be asleep./ 这孩子乐得什么~。 The child is as happy as a lark.

试* shì ① try; test: ~一~ have a try/ ~穿 try on (a garment, shoes, etc.)/ ~跳 (田径) trial jump; (跳水) trial dive/ ~~绳子结实不结实 test the strength of a rope/ ~产 trial production ② examination; test: 口~ oral examination

【试办】 shìbàn run an enterprise, etc. as an experiment; run a pilot scheme

【试场】 shìchǎng examination hall (或 room)

【试车】 shìchē <机> test run; trial run

【试飞】 shìfēi test flight; trial flight ◇ ~驾驶员 test pilot

【试管】 shìguǎn <化> test tube

【试航】 shìháng ① trial trip; trial voyage or flight; shakedown cruise or flight ② shake down (a ship or an aeroplane)

【试金石】 shìjīnshí touchstone

【试卷】 shìjuàn examination paper; test paper

【试探】 shìtàn sound out; feel out; probe; explore: ~一下他对这个问题的看法 sound him out about the question

【试题】 shìtí examination questions; test questions

【试图】 shìtú attempt; try

【试问】 shìwèn we should like to ask; it may well be asked; may we ask

【试想】 shìxiǎng 〔用于委婉的质问〕just think: ~你这样干下去会有好结果吗？ Just think. Will it do you any good if you go on like this?

【试行】 shìxíng try out: 先~,再推广 first try out, then popularize/ 由上级批准~ be ratified by the higher authorities for trial implementation

【试演】 shìyǎn trial performance (of plays, operas, etc.)

【试验】 shìyàn trial; experiment; test: 水力~ hydraulic test/ 进行反坦克武器~ try out antitank weapons ◇ ~场 proving ground; testing ground/ ~农场 experimental farm/ ~田 experimental plot; experimental field/ ~性工厂 pilot plant

【试样】 shìyàng (test) sample

【试映】 shìyìng <电影> preview

【试用】 shìyòng ① try out ② on probation ◇ ~本 edition put out to solicit comments; trial edition/ ~品 trial products/ ~期 probation period/ ~人员 person on probation; probationer

势* shì ① power; force; influence: 权~ (a person's) power and influence/ 仗~欺人 bully people on the strength of one's powerful connections ② momentum; tendency: 来~甚猛 come with tremendous force/ 以排山倒海之~ with the momentum of an avalanche ③ the outward appearance of a natural object: 地~ physical features of the land; terrain/ 山~ the lie of a mountain ④ situation; state of affairs; circumstances: ~难从命。 Circumstances make it difficult for me to comply with your request./ ~所必然 inevitably; as a matter of course ⑤ sign; gesture: 作手~ make a sign with the hand/ 摆姿~ pose ⑥ male genitals: 去~ castration

【势必】 shìbì certainly will; be bound to: 饮酒过度,~影响健康。 Excessive drinking will undoubtedly affect one's health.

【势不当】 shì bùkě dāng irresistible

【势不两立】 shì bù liǎng lì mutually exclusive; extremely antagonistic; irreconcilable

【势均力敌】 shìjūn-lìdí match each other in strength: 双方~。 The two sides are evenly matched./ 一场~的比赛 a close contest

【势力】 shìlì force; power; influence: ~范围 sphere of influence

【势利】 shìlì snobbish: ~小人 snob

【势利眼】 shìlìyǎn ① snobbish attitude; snobbishness ② snob

【势如破竹】 shì rú pò zhú like splitting a bamboo; like a hot knife cutting through butter; with irresistible force: ~,所向披靡 smash all enemy resistance and advance victoriously everywhere

【势头】 shìtóu ① impetus; momentum: 风的~越来越大。 It blew harder and harder. ② <口> tendency; the look of things: 他见～不对,转身就走。Sensing that the odds were against him, he immediately turned back. 【势在必行】 shì zài bì xíng be imperative (under the circumstances)

事* shì ① matter; affair; thing; business: 国家大～ affairs of state/ 把坏～变成好～ turn a bad thing into a good one/ ～非经过不知难。You never know how hard a task is until you have done it yourself.② trouble; accident: 出～ have an accident/平安无～。All is well./ 惹～ make trouble; stir up trouble/ 省了不少～ save a lot of trouble ③ job; work: 有～大家做。We should all share the work./ 找～ look for a job ④ responsibility; involvement: 这件案子里还有他的～呢。He was involved in the case too. ⑤ wait upon; serve: ～父母 wait upon one's parents ⑥ be engaged in: 不～生产 lead an idle life/ 无所～～ doing nothing; loafing
【事半功倍】 shì bàn gōng bèi get twice the result with half the effort
【事倍功半】 shì bèi gōng bàn get half the result with twice the effort
【事必躬亲】 shì bì gōng qīn see (或 attend) to everything oneself; take care of every single thing personally
【事变】 shìbiàn ① incident: 七七～ the July 7 Incident of 1937 ② emergency; exigency: 准备应付可能的突然～ be prepared against all possible emergencies ③ the course of events; events: 研究周围～的联系 look into the relations of events occurring around one
【事不宜迟】 shì bù yí chí one must lose no time in doing it; we must attend to the matter immediately; the matter brooks no delay
【事出有因】 shì chū yǒu yīn there is good reason for it; it is by no means accidental
【事到临头】 shì dào líntóu when things come to a head; when the situation becomes critical; at the last moment
【事端】 shìduān disturbance; incident: 挑起～ provoke incidents/ 制造～ create disturbances
【事故】 shìgù accident; mishap: 防止发生～ try to avert accidents/ 责任～ accident arising from sb.'s negligence
【事过境迁】 shìguò-jìngqiān the affair is over and the situation has changed; the incident is over and the circumstances are different
【事后】 shìhòu after the event; afterwards: 不要老是只作～的批评。Don't get into the habit of criticizing only after the event.
【事迹】 shìjī deed; achievement: 英雄～ heroic deeds
【事假】 shìjià leave of absence (to attend to private affairs); compassionate leave: 请两小时～ ask for two hours leave of absence
【事件】 shìjiàn incident; event: 流血～ bloody incident/ 二十世纪最大的～ the greatest event in the 20th century
【事理】 shìlǐ reason; logic: 明白～ be reasonable; be sensible
【事例】 shìlì example; instance: 典型～ a typical case
【事略】 shìlüè biographical sketch; short biographical account
【事前】 shìqián before the event; in advance; beforehand
【事情】 shìqing affair; matter; thing; business: 急待解决的～ affairs to be settled right away/ 大家的～大家管。Public business is everybody's business./ ～的真相 the truth of the matter; the facts of the case/ ～也真巧 as luck would have it/ ～是这样的。It happened like this.
【事实】 shìshí fact: 与～不符 not tally with the facts/ ～俱在。The facts are all there./ ～恰恰相反。The facts are just the opposite./ ～或 The opposite is the case./ ～如此。This is how things are (或 stand).
【事实上】 shìshíshang in fact; in reality; as a matter of fact; actually: ～的承认 de facto recognition/ ～的停火 de facto cease-fire
【事事】 shìshì everything: ～都要从人民的利益出发。In whatever we do, our primary concern should be the interests of the people.
【事态】 shìtài state of affairs; situation: ～严重。The situation is serious./ ～在恶化。The situation is deteriorating./

～的发展,证明了我们的看法是完全正确的。The development of events entirely confirmed our view.
【事务】 shìwù ① work; routine: ～繁忙 have a lot (of work) to do ② general affairs
【事物】 shìwù thing; object
【事先】 shìxiān in advance; beforehand; prior: ～做好准备 get everything ready beforehand/ ～跟他们打个招呼。Notify them in advance./ ～磋商 prior (或 preliminary) consultations
【事项】 shìxiàng item; matter: 注意～ matters needing attention; points for attention
【事业】 shìyè ① cause; undertaking: 文化教育～ cultural and educational undertakings ② enterprise; facilities: 公用～ public utilities
【事宜】 shìyí 〔多用于公文、法令〕matters concerned; arrangements: 商谈有关建馆～ discuss matters relating to the establishment of the embassy
【事由】 shìyóu ① the origin of an incident; particulars of a matter ②〔公文用语〕main content
【事与愿违】 shì yǔ yuàn wéi things go contrary to one's wishes
【事在人为】 shì zài rén wéi it all depends on human effort

侍* shì wait upon; attend upon; serve: ～立一旁 stand at sb.'s side in attendance
【侍从】 shìcóng 〈旧〉attendants; retinue ◇ ～副官 aide-de-camp (A.D.C.); aide
【侍奉】 shìfèng wait upon; attend upon; serve
【侍候】 shìhòu wait upon; look after; attend
【侍女】 shìnǚ maidservant; maid
【侍卫】 shìwèi imperial bodyguard
【侍者】 shìzhě 〈书〉attendant; servant; waiter

视* shì ① look at: 注～ look at closely ② regard; look upon: ～为莫大光荣 regard as a great honour/ ～如仇敌 look upon sb. as one's enemy ③ inspect; watch: 巡～ go on an inspection tour; go around and inspect
【视察】 shìchá inspect: ～边防部队 inspect a frontier guard unit
【视而不见】 shì ér bù jiàn look but see not; turn a blind eye to: ～,听而不闻 look but see not, listen but hear not/ 这是事实,不能～。These are facts and you can't just ignore them.
【视觉】 shìjué 〈生理〉visual sense; vision; sense of sight
【视力】 shìlì vision; sight: ～测验 eyesight test/ ～好(差) have good (poor) eyesight ◇ ～表 visual chart
【视如敝屣】 shì rú bìxǐ regard as worn-out shoes; cast aside as worthless
【视若无睹】 shì ruò wú dǔ take no notice of what one sees; shut one's eyes to; turn a blind eye to; ignore
【视事】 shìshì (of officials) attend to business after assuming office; assume office
【视死如归】 shì sǐ rú guī look upon death as going home; look death calmly in the face; face death unflinchingly
【视听】 shì-tīng seeing and hearing; what is seen and heard: 混淆～ throw dust in people's eyes; confuse the public/ 以正～ so that the public may know the facts; so as to clarify matters to the public
【视同儿戏】 shì tóng érxì treat (a serious matter) as a trifle; trifle with
【视同路人】 shì tóng lùrén regard as a stranger
【视线】 shìxiàn line of vision; line of sight (in surveying)
【视野】 shìyě field of vision: 广阔的～ a wide field of vision

饰* shì ① decorations; ornaments: 服～ clothes and ornaments/ 窗～ window decorations ② adorn; dress up; polish; cover up: 把文章修～一下 polish a piece of writing/ 文过～非 cover up one's mistakes/ 拒谏～非 reject representations and gloss over errors ③ play the role of; act the part of; impersonate
【饰词】 shìcí excuse; pretext
【饰物】 shìwù ① articles for personal adornment; jewelry ② ornaments; decorations

室 shì room: 卧～ bedroom/ 会客～ reception room/ 办公～ office

【室内】 shìnèi indoor; interior: ～运动 indoor sport/ ～溜冰场 indoor skating rink/ ～游泳池 indoor swimming pool/ ～装饰 interior decoration

【室外】 shìwài outdoor; outside: ～活动 outdoor activities

恃 shì rely on; depend on: 有～无恐 secure in the knowledge that one has strong backing

【恃才傲物】 shì cái ào wù be inordinately proud of one's ability; be conceited and contemptuous

【恃强凌弱】 shì qiáng líng ruò use one's strength to bully the weak

拭 shì wipe away; wipe

【拭目以待】 shì mù yǐ dài wait and see

柿 shì persimmon

是 shì ① correct; right: 你说得～。What you said is right./ 似～而非 apparently right but actually wrong/ 实事求～ seek truth from facts ② yes; right: ～，我们一定完成任务。Right, we will fulfil the task. ③〔与"这""那"等连用，指前面提到的事物〕this; that: ～日天气晴朗。It was fine that day./ ～可忍,孰不可忍? If this can be tolerated, what cannot? ④〔表示两种事物同一,或后者说明前者〕: 我～一个学生。I am a student. ⑤〔联系两种事物,表示陈述的对象属于"是"后面所说的情况〕: 院子里～冬天,屋子里～春天。It was winter outdoors, but spring indoors. ⑥〔与"的"字相应,有分类的作用〕: 这艘轮船～日本制造的。This ship was made in Japan./ 我～来看老王的。I came to see Lao Wang. ⑦〔表示存在〕: 前面～一片稻田。There is a stretch of rice fields ahead./ 满身～汗 sweating all over ⑧〔表示承认所说的,再转入正意〕: 这东西旧～旧,可还能用。Yes, it's old, but it can still be used./ 诗～好诗,就是长了点。It is a good poem all right, but it's a bit too long. ⑨〔"是"前后用相同的名词或动词(两次以上),连用两个这样的格式,表示所说的几桩事物互不相干〕: 敌～敌,友～友,必须分清敌我的界限。A friend is a friend, a foe is a foe; one must be clearly distinguished from the other. ⑩〔表示适合〕: 这场雨下的不～地方。This rain has come at just the right time./ 工具放的不～地方。The tools are not put in the right place. ⑪〔表示"凡是""任何"〕: ～集体的事大家都要关心。Whatever concerns the collective concerns all of us./ ～重活,他都抢着干。When there's a tough job, he always rushes to do it. ⑫〔重读,表示坚决肯定〕: 他～不知道。He certainly doesn't know./ 天气～冷。It's really cold. ⑬〔用于问句〕: 你～坐火车,还～坐汽车? Are you going by train or bus?/ 你～累了不～? You're tired, aren't you? ⑭〔用在句首,加重语气〕: ～谁告诉你的? Who told you?

【是的】 shìde ① yes; right; that's it ② 见"似的" shìde

【是非】 shìfēi ① right and wrong: 问题～ a matter of right and wrong/ 明辨～ distinguish clearly between right and wrong/ ～自有公论。The public will judge the rights and wrongs of the case. ② quarrel; dispute: 搬弄～ tell tales; sow discord

【是非曲直】 shì-fēi qū-zhí rights and wrongs; truth and falsehood; merits and demerits: 不问～ not bother to look into the rights and wrongs of a case

【是否】 shìfǒu whether or not; whether; if: ～符合实际 whether or not it corresponds to reality/ 他～能来,还不一定。It's not certain whether he can come or not.

适 shì ① fit; suitable; proper: ～于儿童阅读的书籍 books suitable for children ② right; opportune: ～量 just the right amount/ ～逢休假。It happened to be a holiday. ③ comfortable; well: 舒～ comfortable/ 感到不～ not feel well ④ go; follow; pursue: 无所～从 not know what course to pursue; be at a loss what to do

【适当】 shìdàng suitable; proper; appropriate: ～的工作 suitable work/ ～的安排 proper arrangement/ ～调整 appropriate readjustment/ ～时机 an opportune moment;

the right moment/ 到～的时候 in due course

【适得其反】 shì dé qí fǎn run counter to one's desire; be just the opposite to what one wished: 多施肥能增产,但肥料过多会～。More fertilizer will raise the output, but too much will lead to just the opposite.

【适度】 shìdù appropriate measure; moderate degree: ～的体育活动有利于病人恢复健康。A moderate amount of physical exercise will help improve the patient's health.

【适逢其会】 shì féng qí huì happen to be present at the right moment

【适合】 shìhé suit; fit: ～当地情况 be suited to local conditions/ 他的口味 suit his taste; be to his taste/ 这类野生植物不～用作饲料。These wild plants are not fit for fodder.

【适可而止】 shìkě ér zhǐ stop before going too far; know when or where to stop; not overdo it

【适口】 shìkǒu agreeable to the taste; palatable

【适龄】 shìlíng of the right age: (入学)～儿童 children of school age/ (入伍)～青年 young people old enough to join the army

【适时】 shìshí at the right moment; in good time; timely: ～的号召 a timely call/ ～播种 begin sowing in good time/ ～召开经验交流会 call timely meetings to exchange experience

【适宜】 shìyí suitable; fit; appropriate: 他～做卫生工作。He's suitable for public health work./ 游泳对老年人也是～的。Swimming is good for old people too./ 这种土壤～种花生。This kind of soil is good for growing peanuts.

【适意】 shìyì agreeable; enjoyable; comfortable

【适应】 shìyìng suit; adapt; fit: ～时代的要求 keep abreast of the times/ ～环境 adapt oneself to circumstances

【适用】 shìyòng suit; be applicable: 这个新的种植法对我们这个地区很～。The new method of cultivation is suitable for our area.

【适者生存】 shìzhě shēngcún 〈生〉 survival of the fittest

【适值】 shìzhí just when: 昨日来访,～外出,憾甚。I called on you yesterday, but unfortunately you were out.

【适中】 shìzhōng ① moderate: 雨量～ moderate rainfall/ 大小～ moderate size ② well situated: 招待所地点～。The hostel is well situated.

逝 shì ① pass: 时光易～。Time passes quickly. ② die; pass away: 病～ die of illness

【逝世】 shìshì pass away; die

弑 shì 〈书〉 murder (one's sovereign or father)

释 shì ① explain; elucidate: ～义 explain the meaning (cf a word, etc.) ② clear up; dispel: 疑～ clear up (或 remove) doubts ③ let go; be relieved of: ～手 loosen one's grip; let go/ 如～重负 (feel) as if relieved of a heavy load ④ release; set free: 保～ set prisoners free; release prisoners ⑤〈简〉(释迦牟尼) Sakyamuni ⑥ Buddhism

【释放】 shìfàng ① release; set free: 刑满～ be released upon completion of a sentence ② 〈物〉 release: ～出能量 release energy

【释迦牟尼】 Shìjiāmóuní Sakyamuni, the founder of Buddhism

【释然】 shìrán 〈书〉 feel relieved; feel at ease

嗜 shì have a liking for; be addicted to: ～酒 be addicted to drink

【嗜好】 shìhào ① hobby ② addiction; habit

誓 shì ① swear; vow; pledge ② oath; vow: 发～ take an oath; swear

【誓不罢休】 shì bù bàxiū swear not to stop; swear not to rest: 不达目的,～。We'll never give up until we reach our goal. 又作"誓不甘休"

【誓不两立】 shì bù liǎng lì swear not to coexist with one's enemy; resolve to destroy the enemy or die in the attempt; be irreconcilable

【誓词】 shìcí oath; pledge

【誓死】 shìsǐ pledge one's life; dare to die: ~保卫祖国 pledge to fight to the death in defending one's country

【誓言】 shìyán oath; pledge: 履行~ fulfil a pledge

【誓约】 shìyuē vow; pledge; solemn promise

噬 shì bite: 吞~ swallow up/ 反~ make a false countercharge; hurl back an accusation

螫 shì sting

【螫针】 shìzhēn 〈动〉 sting; stinger

shi

匙* shi 见"钥匙" yàoshi

另见 chí

shōu

收* shōu ① receive; accept: ~发报 transmitting and receiving telegrams/ 请~下作为纪念。 Please accept this as a souvenir./ 学校今年又~了一批研究生。 The college has enrolled another group of research students this year./ 这本词典共收~词六万余条。 The dictionary contains over 60,000 entries. ② put away; take in: ~工具 put the tools away/ 洗的衣服~了没有? Have you brought in the washing? ③ collect: ~水电费 collect water and electricity bills/ ~税 collect taxes/ ~废品 collect scrap ④ money received; receipts; income: 税~ tax revenue ⑤ harvest; gather in: ~庄稼 harvest (或 gather in) crops/ 秋~ autumn harvest ⑥ close: 伤~口了。 The wound has healed. ⑦ bring to an end; stop: 时间不早了,今天就~了吧。 It's getting late. Let's call it a day. ⑧ restrain; control: 孩子玩得心都~不回来了。 The boy can't get his mind off play.

【收报机】 shōubàojī telegraphic or radiotelegraphic receiver

【收兵】 shōubīng withdraw (或 recall) troops; call off a battle: 不获全胜,决不~。 We will not withdraw our force till complete victory.

【收藏】 shōucáng collect; store up: ~古画 collect old paintings/ ~粮食 store up grain ◇ ~家 collector (of books, antiques, etc.)

【收场】 shōuchǎng ① wind up; end up; stop: 他的话匣子一打开, 就不容易~。 Once he opens his trap, he just never stops./ 这件事不好~。 It's hard to wind this matter up./ 草草~ wind up a matter hastily or perfunctorily/ 看他怎样~。 Let's wait and see how he's going to end it all. ② end; ending; denouement: 圆满的~ a happy ending

【收成】 shōucheng harvest; crop: 从来没有过的好~ a record harvest/ ~不好 poor harvests; crop failures

【收存】 shōucún receive and keep

【收到】 shōudào receive; get; achieve; obtain: ~一封信 receive a letter/ ~良好效果 achieve good results

【收发】 shōufā receive and dispatch

【收费】 shōufèi collect fees; charge

【收复】 shōufù recover; recapture: ~失地 recover lost territory/ ~城市 recapture a city

【收割】 shōugē reap; harvest; gather in: ~小麦 gather in the wheat/ ~机 harvester; reaper

【收工】 shōugōng stop work for the day; knock off; pack up: 该~了。 It's time to knock off./ 我们今天下午五点半~。 We stop work at 5:30 this afternoon.

【收购】 shōugòu purchase; buy: ~农副产品 purchase farm produce and sideline products

【收回】 shōuhuí ① take back; call in; regain; recall: ~发出的文件 recall the documents which have been issued/ ~借出的书籍 call in books lent/ ~主权 regain sovereignty/ ~贷款 recall loans/ ~投资 recoup capital outlay ② withdraw; countermand: ~建议 withdraw a proposal/ ~成命 countermand (或 retract) an order; revoke a command

【收货人】 shōuhuòrén consignee

【收获】 shōuhuò ① gather (或 bring) in the crops; harvest:

春天播种,秋天~ sow in spring and reap in autumn ② results; gains: 你们的艰苦劳动,一定会有~。 Your hard work will be duly rewarded.

【收集】 shōují collect; gather: ~民间验方 collect time-tested folk prescriptions/ ~废铁 collect scrap iron

【收件人】 shōujiànrén addressee; consignee

【收缴】 shōujiǎo take over; capture: ~敌人的武器 take over the enemy's arms

【收据】 shōujù receipt ◇ ~簿 receipt book

【收款人】 shōukuǎnrén payee

【收敛】 shōuliǎn ① weaken or disappear: 她的笑容突然~了。 Her smile suddenly disappeared. ② restrain oneself: 碰了钉子以后,他~些了。 He has pulled in his horns since that setback. ③ 〈数〉 convergence

【收殓】 shōuliàn lay a body in a coffin

【收留】 shōuliú take sb. in; have sb. in one's care

【收拢】 shōulǒng draw sth. in: 把网~ draw the net in

【收录】 shōulù ① 〈旧〉 employ; recruit; take on: ~几个职员 recruit some office workers ② include: 这篇文章已~在他的选集里。 This essay is included in his selected works. ③ listen in and take down; take down; record: ~新闻广播 take down the news from the radio; make a recording of the news broadcast

【收罗】 shōuluó collect; gather; enlist: ~人才 recruit qualified personnel/ ~资料 collect data

【收买】 shōumǎi ① purchase; buy in: ~旧书 buy used books ② buy over; bribe: ~人心 buy popular support

【收盘】 shōupán 〈经〉 closing quotation (on the exchange, etc.)

【收票员】 shōupiàoyuán ticket collector

【收起】 shōuqǐ pack up; cut out; stop: ~你们那一套高调吧! Cut out your high-sounding talk!/ ~你那套鬼把戏! None of your dirty tricks!/ 你这些空话还是~为好。 You'd better stop this empty talk.

【收讫】 shōuqì ① payment received; paid ② (on a bill of lading, an invoice, etc.) all the above goods received; received in full

【收清】 shōuqīng received in full

【收容】 shōuróng take in; accept; house: ~伤员 take in wounded soldiers/ ~难民 house refugees ◇ ~所 collecting post

【收入】 shōurù ① income; revenue; receipts; earnings; proceeds: 集体(个人)~ collective (personal) income/ 副业~ income from sideline occupations/ 财政~ state revenue ② take in; include: 修订版~许多新词语。 Many new words and phrases have been included in the revised edition.

【收拾】 shōushi ① put in order; tidy; clear away: 把工具~一下。 Put the tools in order./ ~屋子 tidy up the room/ ~床铺 make the bed/ ~碗筷 clear away the bowls and chopsticks; clear the table/ ~残局 clear up a messy situation ② get things ready; pack: ~药箱 get one's medical kit ready; pack one's medical kit/ ~行李 pack one's luggage; pack up one's things/ 我们赶紧~~走吧。 Let's get our things together at once and be off. ③ repair; mend: ~鞋子 mend shoes ④ 〈口〉 settle with; punish: 早晚我们要~这个坏蛋。 We'll settle with the scoundrel one of these days.

【收缩】 shōusuō contract; shrink: 金属遇冷就会~。 Metals contract as they become cool./ 这种布下水后要~。 This kind of cloth shrinks when it's washed.

【收摊儿】 shōutānr pack up the stall — wind up the day's business or the work on hand

【收条】 shōutiáo receipt

【收听】 shōutīng listen in: ~新闻广播 listen to the news broadcast/ 你的收音机能~多少电台? How many stations can you get on your radio set?

【收尾】 shōuwěi ① wind up: ~工作 winding up ② ending (of an article, etc.)

【收效】 shōuxiào yield results; produce effects; bear fruit: ~显著 bring notable results/ ~甚微 produce very little effect

【收信人】 shōuxìnrén the recipient of a letter; addressee

【收押】 shōuyā take into custody; detain

【收养】shōuyǎng take in and bring up; adopt: ～孤儿 adopt an orphan/ 爹妈死后,周伯伯就把我～下来了。After my parents died, Uncle Zhou took me in.

【收益】shōuyì income; profit; earnings; gains

【收音】shōuyīn ① (of radio) reception: ～情况良好。Reception is good. ② (of an auditorium, etc.) have good acoustics ◇ ～电唱两用机 radiogramophone

【收音机】shōuyīnjī radio (set); wireless (set): 便携式～ portable radio

【收支】shōu-zhī revenue and expenditure; income and expenses: ～平衡。Revenue and expenditure are balanced.

shǒu

手 * shǒu ① hand: ～把～地教 take a person in hand and teach him how to do a job/ ～织的毛衣 a hand-knitted woollen sweater ② have in one's hand; hold: 人～一册。Everyone has a copy. ③ handy; convenient: ～册 handbook ④ personally: ～植 personally plant (a tree, etc.) ⑤ a person doing or good at a certain job: 拖拉机～ tractor driver/ 机枪～ machine gunner/ 助～ assistant/ 多面～ all-rounder/ 能～ a skilled (或 good) hand; crackerjack ⑥ 〈量〉〔用于技能、本领〕: 他有一～好手艺。He's a real craftsman. 或 He's a master of his craft/ 他真有两～。He really knows his stuff.

【手背】shǒubèi the back of the hand

【手臂】shǒubei arm

【手笔】shǒubǐ ① sb.'s own handwriting or painting: 这一题词是鲁迅的～。This inscription is in Lu Xun's own handwriting. ② literary skill: 大～ a well-known writer; master

【手边】shǒubiān on hand; at hand

【手表】shǒubiǎo wrist watch

【手不释卷】shǒu bù shì juàn always have a book in one's hand; be very studious

【手册】shǒucè handbook; manual: 教师～ teacher's manual

【手抄本】shǒuchāoběn hand-written copy

【手电筒】shǒudiàntǒng electric torch; flashlight

【手段】shǒuduàn ① means; medium; measure; method: 达到目的的一种～ a means to an end/ 高压～ high-handed measures / 不择～ by fair means or foul; by hook or by crook; unscrupulously ② trick; artifice: 采用种种～ resort to all sorts of tricks; use every artifice

【手法】shǒufǎ ① skill; technique: 国画的传统～ traditional technique of Chinese painting/ 艺术表现～ means of artistic expression ② trick; gimmick: 贼喊捉贼的拙劣～ the clumsy trick of thief crying "stop thief"

【手风琴】shǒufēngqín accordion

【手稿】shǒugǎo original (或 holograph) manuscript; manuscript

【手工】shǒugōng ① handwork: 做～ do handwork/ ～费 payment for a piece of handwork ② by hand; manual: ～操作 done by hand; manual operations/ ～织的布 handwoven cloth/ ～制纸 handmade paper ③ 〈口〉 charge for a piece of handwork: 你这件上衣～多少? How much did you pay for the tailoring of this coat?

【手工业】shǒugōngyè handicraft industry; handicraft

【手工艺】shǒugōngyì handicraft art; handicraft ◇ ～工人 craftsman; artisan/ ～品 articles of handicraft art; handicrafts

【手迹】shǒujì sb.'s original handwriting or painting

【手疾眼快】shǒu jí yǎn kuài quick of eye and deft of hand

【手脚】shǒujiǎo ① movement of hands or feet; motion: ～利落 nimble; agile/ ～不干净 sticky-fingered; questionable in money matters ② 〈方〉 underhand method; trick: 一定是有人从中弄～。Someone must have juggled things.

【手巾】shǒujin towel

【手绢】shǒujuàn handkerchief

【手铐】shǒukào handcuffs: 带上～ be handcuffed

【手快】shǒukuài deft of hand: 眼明～ quick of eye and deft of hand

【手榴弹】shǒuliúdàn hand grenade; grenade

【手忙脚乱】shǒumáng-jiǎoluàn running around in circles; in a frantic rush; in a muddle

【手民】shǒumín 〈书〉 typesetter: ～之误 misprint; typographical error

【手摸】shǒumó fingerprint

【手帕】shǒupà 〈方〉 handkerchief

【手气】shǒuqì luck at gambling, card playing, etc.

【手枪】shǒuqiāng pistol

【手巧】shǒuqiǎo skilful with one's hands; deft; dexterous: 心灵～ clever and deft

【手勤】shǒuqín diligent; industrious; hardworking: 这徒弟～脚快。This apprentice is keen and quick in his work.

【手轻】shǒuqīng not use too much force; handle gently

【手软】shǒuruǎn be irresolute when firmness is needed; be softhearted

【手势】shǒushì gesture; sign; signal: 打～ make a gesture; gesticulate ◇ ～语 sign language

【手书】shǒushū ① write in one's own hand ② personal letter: 顷接～。I have just received your letter.

【手术】shǒushù surgical operation; operation: 大(小)～ major (minor) operation/ 动～ perform or undergo an operation ◇ ～室 operating room; operating theatre

【手套】shǒutào ① gloves; mittens ② baseball gloves; mitts

【手提】shǒutí portable ◇ ～包 handbag; bag/ ～打字机 portable typewriter/ ～箱 suitcase

【手头】shǒutóu ① right beside one; on hand; at hand: 放在～待用 place right beside one in case of need/ ～工作挺多 have a lot of work on hand; have one's hands full/ 这本书我倒是有,可惜不在～。I have a copy of the book, but unfortunately not with me. ② one's financial condition at the moment: ～紧 be short of money; be hard up/ ～宽裕 be in easy circumstances; be quite well off at the moment

【手腕】shǒuwàn artifice; finesse; stratagem: 耍～ play tricks; use artifices/ 政治～ political stratagem/ 外交～ diplomatic skill; diplomacy

【手纹】shǒuwén lines of the hand

【手无寸铁】shǒu wú cùn tiě bare-handed; unarmed; defenceless

【手无缚鸡之力】shǒu wú fù jī zhī lì lack the strength to truss up a chicken

【手舞足蹈】shǒuwǔ-zúdǎo dance for joy

【手下】shǒuxià ① under the leadership (或 guidance, direction) of; under: 在他～工作 work under him ② at hand: 东西不在～。I haven't got the thing with me. ③ at the hands of sb.: ～败将 one's vanquished foe; one's defeated opponent ④ one's financial condition at the moment

【手下留情】shǒuxià liú qíng show mercy; be lenient

【手心】shǒuxīn ① the palm of the hand ② control: 这事儿全操在他～里。He's got the matter in the palm of his hand.

【手续】shǒuxù procedures; formalities: 办～ go through formalities/ 行政～ administrative formalities/ 法律～ legal formalities/ ～不完备 have not completed the formalities/ ～费 service charge; commission

【手艺】shǒuyì ① craftsmanship; workmanship: ～高 be highly skilled ② handicraft; trade: 跟师傅学～ learn the trade from a master ◇ ～人 craftsman

【手淫】shǒuyín masturbation

【手印】shǒuyìn ① an impression of the hand ② thumb print; fingerprint

【手语】shǒuyǔ sign language; dactylology

【手札】shǒuzhá 〈书〉 personal letter

【手掌】shǒuzhǎng palm

【手杖】shǒuzhàng walking stick; stick

【手指甲】shǒuzhǐjia finger nail

【手指头】shǒuzhǐtou 〈口〉 finger

【手指】shǒuzhǐ finger

【手镯】shǒuzhuó bracelet

【手足】shǒuzú brothers: ～之情 brotherly affection

【手足无措】shǒu-zú wúcuò all in a fluster; at a loss what to do

守* shǒu ① guard; defend: 把～关口 guard the pass/ ～城 defend a city/ ～球门 keep goal/ ～住阵地 hold the position ② keep watch: ～着伤员 look after the wounded ③ observe; abide by: ～纪律 observe discipline/ ～规矩 behave well/ ～信用 keep one's promise; be as good as one's word/ ～着老一套 stick to the old practice

【守备】 shǒubèi perform garrison duty; be on garrison duty; garrison ◇ ～部队 garrison force; (holding) garrison

【守财奴】 shǒucáinú miser

【守成】 shǒuchéng 〈书〉 maintain the achievements of one's predecessors

【守法】 shǒufǎ abide by (或 observe) the law; be law-abiding

【守寡】 shǒuguǎ remain a widow; live in widowhood

【守候】 shǒuhòu ① wait for; expect: ～着前线的消息 wait for news from the front ② keep watch: ～在病人身旁 keep watch by the patient's bedside

【守护】 shǒuhù guard; defend ◇ ～神 〈宗〉 patron saint

【守节】 shǒujié (of a woman under feudalism) preserve chastity after the death of her husband; not remarry

【守旧】 shǒujiù adhere to past practices; stick to old ways; be conservative ◇ ～派 old liners

【守军】 shǒujūn defending troops; defenders

【守口如瓶】 shǒu kǒu rú píng keep one's mouth shut; breathe not a single word; be tight-mouthed

【守灵】 shǒulíng stand as guards at the bier; keep vigil beside the coffin

【守门】 shǒumén ① be on duty at the door or gate ② 〈体〉 keep goal ◇ ～员 goalkeeper

【守势】 shǒushì defensive: 采取～ be on the defensive

【守望】 shǒuwàng keep watch ◇ ～台 watchtower

【守望相助】 shǒuwàng xiāng zhù (of neighbouring villages) keep watch and help defend each other; give mutual help and protection

【守卫】 shǒuwèi guard; defend: 海防战士警惕地～着祖国的海疆。 The coastguardsmen vigilantly guard our territorial waters.

【守业】 shǒuyè maintain what has been achieved by one's forefathers or predecessors; safeguard one's heritage

【守夜】 shǒuyè keep watch at night; spend the night on watch

【守株待兔】 shǒu zhū dài tù stand by a stump waiting for more hares to come and dash themselves against it — trust to chance and windfalls

首* shǒu ① head: 昂～ hold one's head high/ 搔～ scratch one's head ② first: ～批 the first batch ③ leader; head; chief: 祸～ chief culprit ④ bring charges against sb.: 出～ inform against sb. ⑤ 〈量〉 〔用于诗歌〕 一～歌 a song/ 《唐诗三百～》 300 Tang Poems

【首倡】 shǒuchàng initiate; start

【首创】 shǒuchuàng initiate; originate; pioneer: ～精神 creative initiative; pioneering spirit

【首次】 shǒucì for the first time; first: ～航行 maiden (或 first) voyage/ ～公演 first (或 opening) performance; première

【首当其冲】 shǒu dāng qí chōng be the first to be affected (by a disaster, etc.); bear the brunt

【首都】 shǒudū capital (of a country)

【首级】 shǒují chopped-off head (in battle, etc.)

【首肯】 shǒukěn nod approval; nod assent; approve; consent

【首领】 shǒulǐng chieftain; leader; head

【首脑】 shǒunǎo head: 政府～ head of government ◇ ～会议 conference of heads of state or government; summit conference / ～人物 leading figure

【首屈一指】 shǒu qū yī zhǐ come first on the list; be second to none

【首任】 shǒurèn the first to be appointed to an office

【首饰】 shǒushì (woman's personal) ornaments; jewelry ◇ ～盒 jewel case

【首途】 shǒutú 〈书〉 set out on a journey; start a journey

【首尾】 shǒu-wěi ① the head and the tail; the beginning and the end: ～不能相顾。 The vanguard is cut off from the rear. ② from beginning to end: 我对这个问题的看法是～一贯的。 I have always been consistent in my views on this subject.

【首位】 shǒuwèi the first place: 放在～ put in the first place; place before everything else; give first priority to

【首席】 shǒuxí ① seat of honour: 坐～ be seated at the head of the table; be in the seat of honour ② chief ◇ ～代表 chief representative

【首先】 shǒuxiān ① first: ～发言 speak first/ ～到达工地 be the first to arrive at the construction site ② in the first place; first of all; above all

【首相】 shǒuxiàng prime minister

【首要】 shǒuyào of the first importance; first; chief: ～的事先办。 First things first./ ～任务 the most important task/ ～分子 major culprit; ringleader

【首战告捷】 shǒuzhàn gào jié ① win the first battle ② 〈体〉 score a victory in the first game

【首长】 shǒuzhǎng leading cadre; senior officer

shòu

寿* shòu ① longevity ② life; age: 长～ long life; longevity ③ birthday: 祝～ congratulate sb. on his birthday ④ 〈婉〉 for burial: ～木 coffin (prepared before one's death)

【寿辰】 shòuchén birthday (of an elderly person)

【寿礼】 shòulǐ birthday present (for an elderly person)

【寿面】 shòumiàn noodles eaten on one's birthday; birthday (或 longevity) noodles

【寿命】 shòumìng life-span; life: 平均～ average life-span (或 life expectancy)/ 机器～ service life of a machine/

【寿桃】 shòutáo ① peaches offered as a birthday present ② (peach-shaped) birthday cake

【寿星】 shòuxīng ① the god of longevity ② an elderly person whose birthday is being celebrated

【寿衣】 shòuyī graveclothes; shroud; cerements

【寿终正寝】 shòuzhōng-zhèngqǐn die in bed of old age; die a natural death

受* shòu ① receive; accept: ～教育 receive an education/ ～礼 accept gifts ② suffer; be subjected to: ～损失 suffer losses/ ～压迫 suffer oppression/ ～监督 be subjected to supervision/ ～法律制裁 be dealt with according to law ③ stand; endure; bear: ～不了 cannot bear; be unable to endure/ 真够～的。 This is really hard to put up with. 或 It's really unbearable. ④ 〈方〉 be pleasant: ～听 be pleasant to hear/ ～看 be pleasant to look at

【受宠若惊】 shòu chǒng ruò jīng be overwhelmed by an unexpected favour; feel extremely flattered

【受挫】 shòucuò be foiled; be baffled; be thwarted; suffer a setback

【受罚】 shòufá be punished

【受害】 shòuhài suffer injury; fall victim; be affected: ～不浅 suffer not a little; suffer a lot/ ～的一方 the aggrieved (或 injured) party

【受寒】 shòuhán catch a chill; catch cold

【受贿】 shòuhuì accept (或 take) bribes

【受奖】 shòujiǎng be rewarded: 立功者～。 Those who perform deeds of merit shall be rewarded.

【受戒】 shòujiè 〈佛教〉 be initiated into monkhood or nunhood

【受尽】 shòujìn suffer enough from; suffer all kinds of; have one's fill of

【受惊】 shòujīng be frightened; be startled

【受精】 shòujīng be fertilized: 体内(外)～ internal (external) fertilization/ 异体～ cross-fertilization/ 自体～ self-fertilization

【受窘】 shòujiǒng be embarrassed; be in an awkward position

【受苦】 shòukǔ suffer (hardships); have a rough time: ～难 live in misery; have one's fill of sufferings

【受累】 shòulěi get involved on account of sb. else

【受累】 shòulèi be put to much trouble; be inconvenienced: 他为了我们大家,可没少～。 He's been put to no little trouble for our sake./ 让您～了。 Sorry to have given you so much trouble.

【受凉】 shòuliáng catch cold

【受命】 shòumìng receive instructions

【受难】 shòunàn suffer calamities or disasters; be in distress: 战争～者 war victim

【受骗】 shòupiàn be deceived (或 fooled, cheated, taken in)

【受气】 shòuqì be bullied; suffer wrong ◇ ～包儿 a person whom anyone can vent his spite upon; one who always gets blamed (或 takes the rap)

【受权】 shòuquán be authorized

【受热】 shòurè ① be heated: 物体～则膨胀。 When matter is heated, it expands. ② be affected by the heat; have heatstroke (或 sunstroke)

【受辱】 shòurǔ be insulted; be disgraced; be humiliated

【受伤】 shòushāng be injured; be wounded; sustain an injury: 头部受重伤 sustain a severe head injury

【受审】 shòushěn stand trial; be tried; be on trial

【受托】 shòutuō be commissioned; be entrusted (with a task): 受朋友之托买一块手表 be asked to buy a watch for a friend

【受洗】 shòuxǐ 〈基督教〉 be baptized; receive baptism

【受降】 shòuxiáng accept a surrender

【受刑】 shòuxíng be tortured; be put to torture

【受训】 shòuxùn receive (或 undergo) training

【受益】 shòuyì profit by; benefit from; be benefited: 这本书使我～不浅。 This book has benefitted me a great deal. ◇ ～人〈法〉 beneficiary

【受用】 shòuyòng benefit from; profit by; enjoy: ～不尽 benefit from sth. all one's life

【受用】 shòuyong 〈方〉〔多用于否定〕 feel comfortable: 今天身体有点不～。 I feel a bit under the weather today.

【受援】 shòuyuán receive aid ◇ ～国 recipient country

【受孕】 shòuyùn become pregnant; be impregnated; conceive

【受罪】 shòuzuì endure hardships, tortures, rough conditions, etc.; have a hard time: 大热天穿这么厚的衣服,真～! It's really awful to be wearing such heavy clothes on a hot day like this.

狩 shòu 〈书〉 hunting (esp. in winter)

【狩猎】 shòuliè hunting

兽* shòu ① beast; animal: 野～ wild animal ② beastly; bestial: 人面～心 a beast in human shape

【兽类】 shòulèi beasts; animals

【兽王】 shòuwáng the king of beasts — the lion

【兽行】 shòuxíng brutal act; brutality

【兽性】 shòuxìng brutish nature; barbarity

【兽医】 shòuyī veterinary surgeon; veterinarian; vet ◇ ～学 veterinary medicine; veterinary science/ ～站 veterinary station

【兽欲】 shòuyù animal (或 bestial) desire

授 shòu ① award; vest; confer; give: ～旗 present (sb. with) a flag/ ～以全权 vest sb. with full authority ② teach; instruct: 函～ teach by correspondence; give a correspondence course

【授计】 shòujì confide a stratagem to sb.; tell sb. the plan of action

【授奖】 shòujiǎng award (或 give) a prize ◇ ～仪式 prize-giving ceremony

【授精】 shòujīng insemination: 人工～ artificial insemination

【授课】 shòukè give lessons; give instruction

【授命】 shòumìng ① give orders: ～组阁 authorize sb. to form a cabinet ②〈书〉 give (或 lay down) one's life

【授权】 shòuquán empower; authorize

【授受】 shòu-shòu grant and receive; give and accept: 私相～ give and accept in private; illegally pass things between individuals

【授勋】 shòuxūn confer orders or medals; award a decoration

【授意】 shòuyì incite (或 get) sb. to do sth.; inspire: 他这样干,是谁～的? Who got him to do that? 或 Who put him up to it?/ 我这封信是在老张～下写的。 It was Lao Zhang who gave me the idea of writing the letter. 或 I drafted the letter at Lao Zhang's suggestion.

【授予】 shòuyǔ confer; award

售* shòu ① sell: 出～ put on sale/ ～完 be sold out ② 〈书〉 make (one's plan, trick, etc.) work; carry out (intrigues): 以～其奸 achieve one's treacherous purpose

【售货】 shòuhuò sell goods ◇ ～机 vending machine

【售货员】 shòuhuòyuán shop assistant; salesclerk: 女～ saleswoman; salesgirl; shopgirl

【售价】 shòujià selling price; price

【售卖】 shòumài sell

【售票处】 shòupiàochù ticket office; (火车站) booking office; (剧院等) box office

【售票员】 shòupiàoyuán ticket seller; (公共汽车) conductor; (火车站) booking-office clerk; (剧院等) box-office clerk

绶 shòu

【绶带】 shòudài ribbon (attached to an official seal or a medal)

瘦* shòu ① thin; emaciated: 脸～ be thin in the face/ 面黄肌～ be sallow and emaciated ② lean: ～肉 lean meat ③ tight: 这件上衣腰身～了点。 The coat is a bit tight at the waist. ④ not fertile; poor: ～土薄田 poor soil and barren land

【瘦长】 shòucháng long and thin; tall and thin; lanky: 他是～个儿。 He's a tall, lean chap.

【瘦弱】 shòuruò thin and weak; emaciated

【瘦小】 shòuxiǎo thin and small: 身材～ slight of figure (或 stature)

【瘦削】 shòuxuē very thin; gaunt: ～的面孔 a haggard face

【瘦子】 shòuzi a lean (或 thin) person

shū

书* shū ① write: 振笔直～ take up the pen and write vigorously ② style of calligraphy; script: 楷～ regular script ③ book: 一本关于中国历史的新～ a new work on Chinese history ④ letter: 家～ a letter to or from home ⑤ document: 证～ certificate/ 国～ letter of credence; credentials/ 批准～ instrument of ratification/ 议定～ protocol

【书包】 shūbāo satchel; schoolbag

【书报】 shū-bào books and newspapers

【书本】 shūběn book: ～知识 book learning; book knowledge

【书橱】 shūchú bookcase

【书呆子】 shūdāizi pedant; bookworm

【书店】 shūdiàn bookshop; bookstore; bookseller's

【书法】 shūfǎ penmanship; calligraphy ◇ ～家 calligrapher

【书房】 shūfáng study

【书后】 shūhòu postscript (by the author or sb. else)

【书画】 shū-huà painting and calligraphy

【书籍】 shūjí books; works; literature: 军事～ military literature

【书记】 shūji ① secretary: 总～ general secretary ② clerk ◇ ～处 secretariat/ ～员〈法〉 clerk (of a court)

【书架】 shūjià bookshelf

【书局】 shūjú publishing house; press

【书刊】 shū-kān books and periodicals

【书面】 shūmiàn written; in written form; in writing: ～材料 written material/ ～通知 written notice/ ～答复 written reply; answer in writing/ ～声明 written statement ◇ ～语 written language; literary language

【书名】 shūmíng the title of a book; title ◇ ～号 punctuation marks used to enclose the title of a book or an article (《》)/ ～页 title page

【书目】 shūmù booklist; title catalogue: 参考~ a list of reference books; bibliography

【书皮】 shūpí book cover; jacket; dust cover; cover: 塑料~ plastic cover ◇ ~纸 paper for covering books

【书评】 shūpíng book review

【书签】 shūqiān ① a title label pasted on the cover of a Chinese-style thread-bound book ② bookmark

【书生】 shūshēng intellectual; scholar: ~之见 a pedantic view

【书生气】 shūshēngqì bookishness

【书摊】 shūtān bookstall; bookstand

【书套】 shūtào slipcase

【书写】 shūxiě write: ~标语 write slogans; letter posters ◇ ~规则 rules for writing/ ~纸 writing paper

【书信】 shūxìn letter; written message: 常有~往来 keep up a regular correspondence

【书页】 shūyè page

【书院】 shūyuàn academy of classical learning

【书札】 shūzhá 〈书〉 letters; correspondence

【书斋】 shūzhāi study

【书桌】 shūzhuō desk; writing desk

抒 shū express; give expression to; convey: 让大家各~己见。 Let everybody freely express his views.

【抒发】 shūfā express; voice; give expression to

【抒情】 shūqíng express (或 convey) one's emotion ◇ ~散文 lyric prose/ ~诗 lyric poetry; lyrics

【抒写】 shūxiě express; describe

枢 shū pivot; hub; centre: 神经中~ nerve centre

【枢纽】 shūniǔ pivot; hub; axis; key position: ~作用 a pivotal role/ 交通~ a hub of communications/ 水利~工程 a key water control (或 conservancy) project

叔* shū ① father's younger brother; uncle ② a form of address for a man about one's father's age; uncle: 刘大~ Uncle Liu ③ husband's younger brother

【叔伯】 shūbai relationship between cousins of the same grandfather or great-grandfather: ~兄弟 first or second cousins on the paternal side; cousins

【叔父】 shūfù father's younger brother; uncle

【叔母】 shūmǔ wife of father's younger brother; aunt

【叔叔】 shūshu 〈口〉 ① father's younger brother; uncle ② uncle (a child's form of address for any young man one generation its senior)

殊 shū ① different: 悬~ differ widely ② outstanding; special; remarkable: 待以~礼 receive sb. with unusual ceremony ③ very much; extremely; really: ~觉欣然 feel most regretful/ ~难相信 very difficult to believe; hardly credible/ ~深轸念 express deep solicitude; feel deeply concerned

【殊不知】 shūbùzhī little imagine; hardly realize

【殊死】 shūsǐ desperate; life-and-death: ~的搏斗 a life-and-death struggle/ 作~战 fight a last-ditch battle; put up a desperate fight

【殊途同归】 shū tú tóng guī reach the same goal by different routes

倏 shū swiftly

【倏忽】 shūhū swiftly; in the twinkling of an eye: ~不见 quickly disappear

淑 shū 〈书〉 kind and gentle; fair: ~女 a fair maiden

梳* shū ① comb: 木~ wooden comb ② comb one's hair, etc.

【梳理】 shūlǐ 〈纺〉 carding

【梳洗】 shūxǐ wash and dress ◇ ~用具 toilet articles

【梳妆】 shūzhuāng dress and make up: ~打扮 deck oneself out; dress smartly; be dressed up ◇ ~台 dressing table

【梳子】 shūzi comb

舒* shū ① stretch; unfold ② easy; leisurely: ~徐 leisurely; in no hurry

【舒畅】 shūchàng happy; entirely free from worry: 心情~ have ease of mind; feel happy

【舒服】 shūfu ① comfortable: 这把椅子坐着很~。 This chair is very comfortable. ② be well: 她今天不大~。 She isn't well today.

【舒卷】 shūjuǎn 〈书〉 roll back and forth: 白云~。 The white clouds mass and scatter.

【舒适】 shūshì comfortable; cosy; snug: ~的生活 a comfortable life/ 房间不大, 但很~。 The rooms are not big but they're very cosy./ 孩子们都~地睡在小床上。 All the children lay snug in their little beds.

【舒坦】 shūtan comfortable; at ease

【舒展】 shūzhǎn ① unfold; extend; smooth out: 荷叶~着, 发出清香。 The lotus leaves are unfolding, sending forth a delicate fragrance. ② limber up; stretch: ~一下筋骨 limber up one's muscles and joints

疏* shū ① dredge (a river, etc.) ② thin; sparse; scattered: ~林 sparse woods/ ~~的几根胡子 a sparse beard/ 几点~星 a few scattered stars ③ (of family or social relations) distant: 不分亲~ regardless of relationship (family or social) ④ not familiar with: 人地生~ be unfamiliar with the place and the people; be a complete stranger ⑤ neglect: ~于职守 negligent of one's duties/ ~于防范 neglect to take precautions ⑥ scanty: 才~学浅 have little talent and less learning/ 志大才~ have great ambition but little talent ⑦ disperse; scatter: 仗义~财 be generous in aiding needy people

【疏导】 shūdǎo dredge

【疏忽】 shūhu carelessness; negligence; oversight: ~大意就可能造成事故。 Carelessness is liable to cause accidents./ 我一时~, 搞错了。 I made the mistake through an oversight.

【疏浚】 shūjùn dredge: ~水道 dredge the waterways/ ~港口 dredge a harbour

【疏懒】 shūlǎn careless and lazy; indolent

【疏漏】 shūlòu careless omission; slip; oversight: 计划匆促拟成, 难免有~之处。 The plan was drawn up in haste, so there are bound to be oversights and omissions.

【疏落】 shūluò sparse; scattered: ~的村庄 scattered villages/ 河边疏疏落落有几棵柳树。 The river was sparsely lined with willow trees.

【疏密】 shūmì density; spacing: ~不匀 of uneven density/ 花木栽得~有致。 The flowers and trees are artistically spaced.

【疏散】 shūsàn ① sparse; scattered; dispersed: ~的村落 scattered villages ② evacuate: 我们要做好地震预报工作, 以便及时~人口。 We must do a good job of predicting earthquakes so that we can disperse the population in time.

【疏失】 shūshī careless mistake; remissness

【疏松】 shūsōng ① loose: 土质~。 The soil is porous. ② loosen: ~土壤 loosen the soil

【疏通】 shūtōng ① dredge: ~田间的排水沟 dredge the irrigation ditches in the fields ② mediate between two parties

【疏远】 shūyuǎn drift apart; become estranged

输* shū ① transport; convey: 油管把原油从油田直接~往港口。 The pipeline carries crude oil direct from the oil field to the harbour. ② 〈书〉 contribute money; donate: 慷慨~将 make liberal contributions ③ lose; be beaten: ~了一局 lose one game in the set

【输出】 shūchū ① export: 资本~ export of capital

【输电】 shūdiàn transmit electricity: 这个发电站已开始向山区~。 The power station has begun to transmit electricity to the mountain area.

【输入】 shūrù ① import: ~新思想 the influx of new ideas

【输送】 shūsòng carry; transport; convey: 卡车把物资~到边疆地区。 Commodities are transported to border areas by truck./ ~新鲜血液 infuse new blood

【输血】 shūxuè ① 〈医〉 blood transfusion ② give aid and support; bolster up; give sb. a shot in the arm ◇ ~者 blood donor

【输油管】 shūyóuguǎn petroleum pipeline

shū

蔬* shū vegetables: 布衣～食 coarse clothes and simple fare
【蔬菜】shūcài vegetables; greens; greenstuff ◇ ～栽培 vegetable growing; vegetable farming

shú

孰 shú 〈书〉① who; which: ～胜～负? Who wins and who loses?/ ～是～非? Which is right and which is wrong? ② what: 是可忍,～不可忍? If this can be tolerated, what cannot?

赎 shú ① redeem; ransom: 把东西～回来 redeem a pledge ② atone for (a crime)
【赎当】shúdàng redeem sth. pawned
【赎价】shújià ransom price; ransom
【赎金】shújīn ransom money; ransom
【赎身】shúshēn (of slaves, prostitutes) redeem (或 ransom) oneself; buy back one's freedom
【赎罪】shúzuì atone for one's crime: 立功～ perform meritorious services to atone for one's crime

塾 shú private (或 family) school: ～师 tutor of a private (或 family) school

熟* shú ① ripe: 番茄～了。 The tomatoes are ripe./ 一年两～ two crops a year ② cooked; done: ～肉 cooked meat/ 半生不～ half-cooked/ 饭已经～了。 The rice is done. ③ processed: ～铜 wrought copper/ ～皮子 tanned leather ④ familiar: 这口音听起来很～。 The voice sounds familiar. ⑤ skilled; experienced; practised: ～手 practised hand; old hand ⑥ deeply: ～睡 be in a deep sleep; be fast asleep
【熟谙】shú'ān 〈书〉be familiar with; be good at: ～水性 be an expert swimmer
【熟菜】shúcài cooked food; prepared food
【熟记】shújì learn by heart; memorize; commit to memory
【熟客】shúkè frequent visitor
【熟练】shúliàn skilled; practised; proficient: ～工人 skilled worker/ ～操纵机器 skilfully operate the machine/ 他枪法很～。 He's a good shot.
【熟路】shúlù familiar route; beaten track: 熟门～ a familiar road and a familiar door — things that one knows well 又作"熟道儿"
【熟能生巧】shú néng shēng qiǎo skill comes from practice; practice makes perfect
【熟人】shúrén acquaintance; friend
【熟食】shúshí prepared food; cooked food
【熟视无睹】shú shì wú dǔ pay no attention to a familiar sight; turn a blind eye to; ignore: 对不良倾向决不能～。 We must not turn a blind eye to unhealthy tendencies.
【熟识】shúshi be well acquainted with; know well: 我们交往不多,不太～。 We haven't met often and don't know each other very well.
【熟思】shúsī ponder deeply; consider carefully; deliberate
【熟悉】shúxī know sth. or sb. well; be familiar with; have an intimate knowledge of: ～内情 know the ins and outs of the matter; know the inside story of/ 用群众～的语言来写作 write in language familiar to the masses/ 你到了那里,要先～当地的情况。 When you get there, first of all familiarize yourself with the situation./ 他对各项生产数字很～。 He has the various production figures at his fingertips./ 他对这工作不～。 He is new to the task.
【熟习】shúxí be skilful at; have the knack of; be practised in: ～业务 be practised (或 well versed) in one's field of work/ ～蔬菜的栽培法 have the knack of growing vegetables
【熟语】shúyǔ 〈语〉idiom; idiomatic phrase
【熟知】shúzhī know very well; know intimately
【熟字】shúzì words already learned; familiar words

shǔ

黍 shǔ broomcorn millet (*Panicum miliaceum*)
【黍子】shǔzi 见"黍"

属* shǔ ① category: 金～ metals ② 〈生〉genus: 亚～ subgenus/ 小麦和燕麦是同科的,但不同～。 Wheat and oats are of the same family, but of different genera. ③ under; subordinate to: 所～单位和部门 subordinate units and departments ④ belong to: 马来西亚～热带气候。 Malaysia has a tropical climate. ⑤ family members; dependents: 军～ families of armymen ⑥ be: 查明～实 prove to be true after investigation/ 实～无理 be really unreasonable ⑦ be born in the year of (one of the twelve animals): 她比我小一岁,是～牛的。 She is one year younger than I am; she was born in the year of the ox. 参见 "生肖" shēngxiào
另见 zhǔ
【属地】shǔdì possession; dependency
【属国】shǔguó vassal state; dependent state
【属于】shǔyú belong to; be part of

暑 shǔ heat; hot weather: 盛～ at the height of the summer; very hot weather/ 中～ get sunstroke; get heatstroke; suffer heat exhaustion/ 寒来～往 as summer goes and winter comes; as time passes
【暑气】shǔqì summer heat; heat
【暑热】shǔrè hot summer weather
【暑天】shǔtiān hot summer days; dog days

署 shǔ ① a government office; office: 专员公～ prefectural commissioner's office ② make arrangements for; arrange: 部～春耕生产 make arrangements for the spring ploughing ③ handle by proxy; act as deputy: ～理部务 handle the ministry's affairs during the minister's absence ④ sign; put one's signature to: 签～协定 sign an agreement
【署名】shǔmíng sign; put one's signature to: 这条子没有～,不知是谁写的。 I don't know who wrote this note. It's unsigned. ◇ ～人 the undersigned/ ～文章 a signed article

数* shǔ ① count: 从一～到十 count from 1 to 10/ ～～看一行有多少棵苗。 Count and see how many seedlings there are in a row. ② be reckoned as exceptionally (good, bad, etc.): 全班～他最高。 He is the tallest in the class. ③ enumerate; list: 历～其罪 enumerate the crimes sb. has committed
另见 shù
【数不着】shǔbuzháo not count as outstanding, important, etc.: 论游泳技术,在我们厂里可～我。 I don't count as a good swimmer in our factory.
【数典忘祖】shǔ diǎn wàng zǔ give all the historical facts except those about one's own ancestors; forget one's own origins; be ignorant of the history of one's own country
【数一数二】shǔyī-shǔ'èr count as one of the very best; ranking very high: 他在我们连里是～的射手。 He is one of the best marksmen in our company.

蜀 Shǔ another name for Sichuan Province
【蜀犬吠日】Shǔ quǎn fèi rì in Sichuan dogs bark at the sun (because it's a rare sight in that misty region) — an ignorant person makes a fuss about something which he alone finds strange

鼠* shǔ mouse; rat
【鼠辈】shǔbèi mean creatures; scoundrels
【鼠窜】shǔcuàn scamper off like a rat; scurry away like frightened rats
【鼠目寸光】shǔmù cùn guāng a mouse can see only an inch; see only what is under one's nose; be shortsighted
【鼠窃狗偷】shǔqiè-gǒutōu filch like rats and snatch like dogs — play petty tricks on the sly

【鼠疫】 shǔyì the plague

薯 shǔ potato; yam: 白～ sweet potato/ 木～ cassava

曙 shǔ 〈书〉 daybreak; dawn
【曙光】 shǔguāng first light of morning; dawn: 胜利的～ the dawn of victory
【曙色】 shǔsè light of early dawn: 从窗口透进了灰白的～。The pale light of early dawn slanted in through the window.

shù

术* shù ① art; skill; technique: 医～ the art of healing; doctor's skill/ 美～ the fine arts/ 不学无～ have neither learning nor skill ② method; tactics: 战～ military tactics / 权～ political trickery
【术语】 shùyǔ technical terms; terminology: 军事～ military terms/ 医学～ medical terminology

戍 shù defend; garrison: ～边 garrison the frontiers

束* shù ① bind; tie: 腰～皮带 wear a belt round one's waist ②〈量〉bundle; bunch; sheaf: 一～鲜花 a bunch of flowers/ 一～稻草 a sheaf of straw ③ control; restrain: 无拘无～ without any restraint
【束缚】 shùfù tie; bind up; fetter: ～手脚 bind sb. hand and foot; tie sb.'s hands; hamper the initiative of/ ～生产力 fetter the productive forces/ 冲破旧思想的～ smash the trammels of old ideas
【束手】 shùshǒu have one's hands tied; be helpless: ～就擒 allow oneself to be seized without putting up a fight
【束手待毙】 shùshǒu dài bì fold one's hands and await destruction; helplessly wait for death; resign oneself to extinction
【束手无策】 shùshǒu wú cè be at a loss what to do; feel quite helpless; be at one's wit's end
【束之高阁】 shù zhī gāogé bundle sth. up and place it on the top shelf; lay aside and neglect; shelve; pigeonhole: 如果有了正确的理论，只是把它空谈一阵，～，并不实行，那么，这种理论再好也是没有意义的。If we have a correct theory but merely prate about it, pigeonhole it and do not put it into practice, then that theory, however good, is of no significance.

述 shù state; relate; narrate: 陈～意见 state one's views/ 略～其经过 relate briefly how it happened; give a brief account of the matter
【述说】 shùshuō state; recount; narrate
【述职】 shùzhí report on one's work; report: 大使已回国～。The ambassador has gone back for consultations.

树 shù ① tree: 苹果～ apple tree ② plant; cultivate: 十年～木，百年～人。It takes ten years to grow trees, but a hundred years to rear people. ③ set up; establish; uphold: 建～ achievement/ ～正气 uphold (或 foster) healthy tendencies/ ～雄心 have lofty ambitions; aim high
【树丛】 shùcóng grove; thicket
【树大招风】 shù dà zhāofēng 〈谚〉a tall tree catches the wind — a person in a high position is liable to be attacked
【树倒猢狲散】 shù dǎo húsūn sàn when the tree falls the monkeys scatter — when an influential person falls from power, his hangers-on disperse
【树敌】 shùdí make an enemy of sb.; set others against oneself; antagonize: ～太多 make too many enemies; antagonize too many people
【树干】 shùgàn tree trunk; trunk
【树高千丈，叶落归根】 shù gāo qiānzhàng, yè luò guī gēn a tree may grow a thousand zhang high, but its leaves fall back to the roots —— a person residing away from home eventually returns to his native soil
【树胶】 shùjiāo gum (of a tree)
【树立】 shùlì set up; establish: ～榜样 set an example

【树林】 shùlín woods; grove
【树苗】 shùmiáo sapling
【树木】 shùmù trees
【树皮】 shùpí bark
【树梢】 shùshāo the tip of a tree; treetop
【树阴】 shùyīn shade (of a tree) 又作"树荫"
【树枝】 shùzhī branch; twig

竖 shù ① vertical; upright; perpendicular: 画一条～线 draw a vertical line ② set upright; erect; stand: ～旗杆 erect a flagstaff/ 这杆子我～不起来。I can't get the pole to stand up. ③ vertical stroke (in Chinese characters): "王"字的写法是三横一～。The character 王 is composed of one vertical and three horizontal strokes.
【竖立】 shùlì erect; set upright; stand
【竖起】 shùqǐ hold up; erect: ～大拇指 hold up one's thumb in approval; thumbs up/ ～一面大旗 hoist a huge banner/ ～耳朵听 prick up one's ears
【竖琴】 shùqín 〈乐〉harp

恕 shù ① forgive; pardon; excuse: 宽～ forgive/ ～罪 pardon an offence; forgive a sin ②〈套〉excuse me; beg your pardon: ～不奉陪。Excuse me (for not keeping you company)./ ～难从命。We regret that we cannot comply with your wishes. ③ forbearance (as advocated by Confucius)

庶 shù ① multitudinous; numerous: 富～ rich and populous/ ～物 every kind of creature; all things ②〈旧〉of or by the concubine (as distinguished from the legal wife): ～出 be born of a concubine ③〈书〉so that; so as to: ～免误会 so as to avoid misunderstanding
【庶民】 shùmín 〈书〉the common people; the multitude
【庶务】 shùwù 〈旧〉① general affairs; business matters ② a person in charge of business matters

数* shù ① number; figure: 代表人～ the number of delegates/ ～以万计 number tens of thousands/ 心中有～ have a good idea of how things stand; know what's what ②〈数〉number: 无理～ irrational number/ ～域 number field/ ～系 number system ③〈语〉number: 单(复)～ singular (plural) number ④ several; a few: ～百人 several hundred people/ ～分钟后 a few minutes later ⑤ fate; destiny
另见 shǔ
【数额】 shù'é number; amount: 超出～ exceed the number fixed/ 不足规定～ fall short of the amount required
【数量】 shùliàng quantity; amount: ～和质量并重 stress both quantity and quality/ ～上的差别 quantitative difference/ ～上的增减 increase or decrease in quantity/ 在～上占优势 be superior in numbers; have numerical superiority
【数码】 shùmǎ ① numeral: 阿拉伯～ Arabic numerals/ 罗马～ Roman numerals ② number; amount
【数目】 shùmù number; amount
【数目字】 shùmùzì 见"数字"
【数学】 shùxué mathematics ◇ ～家 mathematician
【数字】 shùzì ① numeral; figure; digit: 阿拉伯～ Arabic numerals/ 天文～ astronomical figures ② quantity; amount: 不要单纯追求～。Don't just go after quantity. ◇ ～计算机 digital computer/ ～控制系统 numerical control system

漱* shù gargle; rinse
【漱口】 shùkǒu rinse the mouth; gargle: 用盐水～ gargle with salt water ◇ ～杯 a glass or mug for mouth-rinsing or teeth-cleaning; tooth glass/ ～剂 gargle

墅 shù villa

shuā

刷* shuā ①brush: 牙~ toothbrush/ 油漆~ paintbrush/ 板~ scrub brush ②brush; scrub: ~鞋 brush shoes/ ~锅 clean (或 scour) a pot ③daub; paste up: 用石灰浆~墙 whitewash a wall/ ~标语 paste up posters ④〈口〉eliminate; remove: 那个队直到半决赛才给~下来。That team was not eliminated until the semifinals. ⑤〈象〉〔形容迅速擦过去的声音〕swish; rustle: 玉米叶子被风吹得~~响。The corn leaves rustled in the wind.

【刷洗】shuāxǐ scrub: ~地板 scrub the floor

【刷新】shuāxīn ①renovate; refurbish: ~门面 repaint the front (of a shop, etc.); put up a new shopfront ②break: ~纪录 break (或 better) a record/ 一再~生产纪录 shatter the production records again and again

【刷牙】shuāyá brush (或 clean) one's teeth

【刷子】shuāzi brush; scrub

shuǎ

耍* shuǎ ①〈方〉play: 叫孩子们到院子里去~。Tell the children to go and play in the courtyard./ 这可不是~的! It's no joke! ②play with; flourish: ~刀 flourish a sword; give a performance of swordplay/ ~猴儿 put on a monkey show ③play (tricks): ~鬼把戏 play dirty tricks/ ~两面派 resort to double-dealing; be double-faced

【耍笔杆】shuǎ bǐgǎn wield a pen; be skilled in literary tricks: 他光会~，碰到实际问题就束手无策。He knows only how to wield a pen and is helpless in the face of practical problems.

【耍花招】shuǎ huāzhāo ①display showy movements in *wushu* (武术), etc. ②play (或 get up to) tricks: 别~了！None of your tricks!/ 你这是耍的什么花招？What are you up to? 或 What sort of game are you playing?/ 他又在~了。He is up to his tricks again.

【耍赖】shuǎlài act shamelessly; be perverse

【耍流氓】shuǎ liúmáng behave like a hoodlum; take liberties with women; act indecently

【耍弄】shuǎnòng make fun of; make a fool of; deceive

【耍脾气】shuǎ píqi get into a huff; put on a show of bad temper

【耍威风】shuǎ wēifēng make a show of authority; throw one's weight about; be overbearing

【耍无赖】shuǎ wúlài act shamelessly; be perverse

【耍笑】shuǎxiào ①joke; have fun ②make fun of; play a joke on sb.

shuāi

衰* shuāi decline; wane: 兴~ rise and decline/ 体力渐~ get weaker physically/ 懒则~。Laziness leads to debility.

【衰败】shuāibài decline; wane; be at a low ebb

【衰竭】shuāijié 〈医〉exhaustion; prostration: 心力~ heart failure

【衰老】shuāilǎo old and feeble; decrepit; senile

【衰落】shuāiluò decline; be on the wane; go downhill

【衰弱】shuāiruò weak; feeble: 久病之后身体~ be weak after a long illness/ 神经~ suffer from neurasthenia/ 攻势已经~。The offensive is losing momentum.

【衰颓】shuāituí weak and degenerate

【衰退】shuāituì fail; decline: 视力~ failing eyesight/ 记忆力~ be losing one's memory/ 经济~ economic recession

【衰亡】shuāiwáng become feeble and die; decline and fall; wither away

【衰微】shuāiwēi 〈书〉decline; wane

摔* shuāi ①fall; tumble; lose one's balance: 他~了好多次才学会骑自行车。He fell off many times before he learned to ride a bicycle. ②hurtle down; plunge: 飞机

~下来了。The plane plunged to the ground. ③cause to fall and break; break: 我不小心把玻璃杯~了。I accidentally broke a glass./ 他把腿~断了。He had a fall and broke his leg. ④cast; throw; fling: 把帽子往床上一~ throw one's cap onto the bed

【摔交】shuāijiāo ①tumble; trip and fall ②trip up; come a cropper; blunder ③〈体〉wrestling

shuǎi

甩 shuǎi ①move backward and forward; swing: ~胳膊 swing one's arms/ ~鞭子 crack a whip/ 小女孩一跑，辫子就来回~动。The girl's pigtails swing to and fro as she runs. ②throw; fling; toss: ~手榴弹 throw hand grenades ③leave sb. behind; throw off: ~掉尾巴 throw off a pursuer (或 a tail)/ ~掉包袱 cast off a burden; get a load off one's back/ 他加快速度，一会儿就把别的运动员都~在后头了。Quickening his pace, he soon left all the other runners behind.

【甩手】shuǎishǒu ①swing one's arms ②refuse to do; wash one's hands of: 这事该你负责，你可不能~不管。You can't wash your hands of this. It's your responsibility.

shuài

帅* shuài ①commander in chief: 统~ supreme commander/ 挂~ take command ②beautiful; graceful; smart: 他字写得真~。He writes a beautiful hand./ 他的双杠动作可~了！His movements on the parallel bars were very graceful. ③commander in chief, the chief piece in Chinese chess

率 shuài ①lead; command: ~师 command troops/ ~众前往 go (to a place) at the head of many people/ ②rash; hasty: 草~ careless; cursory/ 轻~ hasty ③frank; straightforward: 坦~ frank/ 直~ straightforward ④generally; usually: 大~如此。This is usually the case. 另见 lǜ

【率尔】shuài'ěr 〈书〉rashly; hastily: 不可~应战。We should not rashly accept battle.

【率领】shuàilǐng lead; head; command: ~代表团 lead (或 head) a delegation/ 这支部队由他~。This unit is under his command./ 连长~全连战士冲锋。The company commander led his men in the charge.

【率先】shuàixiān take the lead in doing sth.; be the first to do sth.

【率真】shuàizhēn forthright and sincere

蟀 shuài 见"蟋蟀"xīshuài

shuān

闩 shuān ①bolt; latch: 门~ door bolt ②fasten with a bolt or latch: 把门~好 bolt the door

拴 shuān tie; fasten: 把马~在树上 tie (或 tether) a horse to a tree/ ~绳子晒衣服 put up a clothes line/ 把船~住。Make the boat fast.

栓 shuān ①bolt; plug: 枪~ rifle bolt/ 消火~ fire hydrant; fireplug ②stopper; cork

shuàn

涮 shuàn ①rinse: 把衣服~一~。Rinse the clothes./

把这瓶子~一下。 Give this bottle a rinse. ② scald thin slices of meat in boiling water; instant-boil: ~羊肉 instant-boiled mutton

shuāng

双 * shuāng ① two; twin; both; dual: ~向交通 two-way traffic/ ~发动机飞机 twin-engined plane ②〈量〉〔用于成对的东西〕pair: 一~鞋 a pair of shoes ③ even: ~数 even numbers/~号座位 even-numbered seats ④ double; twofold: ~份 double the amount; twice as much

【双胞胎】shuāngbāotāi twins

【双边】 shuāngbiān bilateral: ~会谈 bilateral talks/ ~贸易 bilateral trade; two-way trade/ ~条约 bilateral treaty

【双层】 shuāngcéng double-deck; having two layers; of two thicknesses: ~桥 double-decker bridge/ ~床 double-decker (bed, bunk)/ ~火车 double-decker

【双重】 shuāngchóng double; dual; twofold: ~任务 double task; twofold task/ ~标准 double standard/ ~领导 dual leadership/ 起~作用 serve a dual purpose ◇ ~代表权〈外〉 dual representation/ ~国籍 dual nationality/ ~人格 dual personality

【双打】 shuāngdǎ 〈体〉 doubles: 男子(女子)~ men's (women's) doubles/ 男女混合~ mixed doubles

【双方】 shuāngfāng both sides; the two parties: 缔约国~ both signatory states; the contracting parties/ ~各执一词。 Each side persisted in its own views./ ~同意 by mutual consent

【双关】 shuāngguān having a double meaning: 一语~ a phrase with a double meaning ◇ ~语 pun

【双管】 shuāngguǎn double-barrelled: ~猎枪 double-barrelled shotgun

【双管齐下】 shuāng guǎn qí xià paint a picture with two brushes at the same time — work along both lines

【双轨】 shuāngguǐ 〈交〉 double track ◇ ~铁路 double-track railway

【双号】 shuānghào even numbers (of tickets, seats, etc.)

【双簧】 shuānghuáng 〈曲艺〉 a two-man act, with one speaking or singing while hiding behind the other who does the acting: 唱~ give a two-man comic show; collaborate

【双轮】 shuānglún 〈体〉 double round: 五十米~射箭 50-metre double round archery event

【双面】 shuāngmiàn two-sided; double-edged; double-faced; reversible: ~刀片 a double-edged razor blade

【双亲】 shuāngqīn (both) parents; father and mother

【双全】 shuāngquán complete in both respects; possessing both: 智勇~ possessing both wisdom and courage/ 文武~ be adept with both the pen and the sword

【双人床】 shuāngrénchuáng double bed

【双人舞】 shuāngrénwǔ dance for two people; *pas de deux*

【双日】 shuāngrì even-numbered days (of the month)

【双生】 shuāngshēng twin: ~姐妹 twin sisters/ ~兄弟 twin brothers/ ~子 twins

【双声】 shuāngshēng 〈语〉 a phrase consisting of two or more characters with the same initial consonant (as 方法 fāngfǎ); alliteration

【双手】 shuāngshǒu both hands: 我举~赞成。 I'm all for it.

【双双】 shuāngshuāng in pairs

【双筒望远镜】 shuāngtǒng wàngyuǎnjìng binoculars; field glasses

【双喜】 shuāngxǐ double happiness: ~临门。 A double blessing has descended upon the house.

【双月刊】 shuāngyuèkān bimonthly

【双周刊】 shuāngzhōukān biweekly; fortnightly

霜 shuāng ① frost ② frostlike powder: 糖~ frosting; icing/ 柿~ powder on the surface of a dried persimmon ③ white; hoar: ~鬓 grey (或 hoary) temples

孀 shuāng widow

【孀妇】 shuāngfù widow

【孀居】 shuāngjū be a widow; live in widowhood

shuǎng

爽 * shuǎng ① bright; clear; crisp: 秋高气~。 The autumn sky is clear and the air is crisp. ② frank; straightforward; openhearted: 豪~ straightforward; forthright ③ feel well: 身体不~ not feel well ④ deviate: 毫厘不~ not deviating a hair's breadth; without the slightest error

【爽口】 shuǎngkǒu tasty and refreshing

【爽快】 shuǎngkuai ① refreshed; comfortable: 洗完澡身上~多了 feel much refreshed after a bath ② frank; straightforward; outright: 为人~ be frank and straightforward/ 他~地说出了对我的看法。 He told me frankly what he thought of me. ③ with alacrity; readily: ~地答应帮忙 readily agree to help/ 办事~ work readily and briskly

【爽朗】 shuǎnglǎng ① bright and clear: 深秋的天空异常~。 In late autumn the sky is crystal clear. ② hearty; candid; frank and open; straightforward: ~的笑声 hearty laughter/ ~的性格 a frank and open personality

【爽身粉】 shuǎngshēnfěn talcum powder

【爽约】 shuǎngyuē 〈书〉 fail to keep an appointment; break an appointment

【爽直】 shuǎngzhí frank; straightforward; candid

shuí

谁 * shuí 或 shéi ① who: 他是~? Who is he?/ 这是~的意见? Whose idea is it?/ ~不说他好。 Who wouldn't speak well of him?/ 我是开玩笑,~知他竟当真了。 I was only joking; who would have thought he would take it seriously. ② someone; anyone: 有~能帮助我就好了! If only someone could help me!/ 大家比着干, ~都不甘落后。 Everyone was competing, and nobody wanted to lag behind./ 他们俩~也说不服~。 Neither of them could convince the other./ 大家看~合适就选~。 You may select whoever you think is suitable.

shuǐ

水 * shuǐ ① water: 淡~ fresh water/ 硬~ hard water ② river: 汉~ the Han River ③ a general term for rivers, lakes, seas, etc.; water: ~陆运输 land and water transportation/ ~上人家 boat dwellers/ ~平如镜。 The surface of the water is as smooth as a mirror. ④ a liquid: 墨~ ink/ 桔子~ orangeade

【水坝】 shuǐbà dam

【水表】 shuǐbiǎo water meter

【水兵】 shuǐbīng seaman; sailor; bluejacket

【水彩】 shuǐcǎi watercolour ◇ ~画 watercolour (painting)/ ~颜料 watercolours

【水草】 shuǐcǎo ① water and grass: ~丰美 (a place) with plenty of water and lush grass/ 逐~而居 (of nomads) live where there is water and grass; rove about seeking water and grass ② waterweeds; water plants

【水产】 shuǐchǎn aquatic product

【水池】 shuǐchí pond; pool; cistern

【水到渠成】 shuǐ dào qú chéng where water flows, a channel is formed — when conditions are ripe, success will come

【水道】 shuǐdào ① water course ② waterway; water route

【水稻】 shuǐdào paddy (rice); rice

【水滴石穿】 shuǐ dī shí chuān dripping water wears through rock — constant effort brings success

【水底电缆】 shuǐdǐ diànlǎn submarine cable; subaqueous cable

【水电】 shuǐ-diàn water and electricity: ~供应 water and electricity supply ◇ ~费 charges for water and electricity

【水电站】 shuǐdiànzhàn 〈简〉 (水力发电站) hydroelectric (power) station; hydropower station

【水痘】 shuǐdòu 〈医〉 varicella; chicken pox

【水分】 shuǐfèn moisture content: 吸收~ absorb moisture

【水沟】 shuǐgōu ditch; drain; gutter

【水管】 shuǐguǎn waterpipe
【水果】 shuǐguǒ fruit
◇ ～罐头 tinned (或 canned) fruit
【水壶】 shuǐhú ① kettle ② canteen ③ watering can
【水患】 shuǐhuàn flood; inundation
【水火】 shuǐ-huǒ ① fire and water — two things diametrically opposed to each other: ～不相容 be incompatible as fire and water ② extreme misery
【水火无情】 shuǐ-huǒ wúqíng floods and fires have no mercy for anybody
【水饺】 shuǐjiǎo boiled dumplings
【水晶】 shuǐjīng crystal; rock crystal
【水库】 shuǐkù reservoir
【水雷】 shuǐléi 〈军〉 (submarine) mine: 敷设～ lay mines (in water)/ ～密布的河道 a heavily mined river
【水力】 shuǐlì waterpower; hydraulic power
◇ ～发电 hydraulic electrogenerating/ ～发电站 hydroelectric (power) station; hydropower station/ ～开采 〈矿〉 hydraulic mining; hydraulicking
【水利】 shuǐlì ① water conservancy: ～设施 water conservancy facilities ② irrigation works; water conservancy project: 兴修～ build irrigation works
◇ ～工程 irrigation works; water conservancy project (或 works)
【水流】 shuǐliú ① rivers; streams; waters ② current; flow: ～湍急(迟缓) rapid (sluggish) flow; rushing current
【水龙头】 shuǐlóngtóu (water) tap; faucet; bibcock: 开(关) ～ turn on (off) the tap/ 用后将～关紧。Don't leave the tap running after use.
【水陆】 shuǐ-lù land and water: ～并进 proceed by both land and water; conduct a combined operation· by army and navy/ ～两用 amphibious
◇ ～交通线 land and water communication lines/ ～联运 water-land transshipment/ ～坦克 amphibious tank/ ～运输 transportation by land and water
【水路】 shuǐlù waterway; water route
【水落石出】 shuǐluò-shíchū when the water subsides the rocks emerge — the whole thing comes to light: 把事情辩个～ argue a matter out/ 我们一定要把这事弄个～。We must get to the bottom of this matter.
【水磨石】 shuǐmóshí 〈建〉 terrazzo
【水墨画】 shuǐmòhuà 〈美〉 ink and wash; wash painting: 中国～ Chinese ink and wash
【水母】 shuǐmǔ 〈动〉 jellyfish; medusa

【水泥】 shuǐní cement
【水牛】 shuǐniú (water) buffalo
【水泡】 shuǐpào ① bubble ② blister: 脚上打了～ get blisters on one's feet
【水疱】 shuǐpào blister
【水平】 shuǐpíng ① horizontal; level: ～梯田 level terraced field; level terrace ② standard; level: 生活～ living standard/ 文化～ standard of education; cultural level/ 认识～ level of one's understanding/ 赶超世界先进～ attain and surpass advanced world levels
【水汽】 shuǐqì vapour; steam; moisture
【水球】 shuǐqiú 〈体〉 water polo
【水渠】 shuǐqú ditch; canal
【水乳交融】 shuǐ-rǔ jiāoróng as well blended as milk and water — in complete harmony
【水上飞机】 shuǐshàng fēijī seaplane; hydroplane
【水上飞行】 shuǐshàng fēixíng overwater flight
【水上居民】 shuǐshàng jūmín boat dwellers
【水上运动】 shuǐshàng yùndòng 〈体〉 aquatic sports; water sports ◇ ～会 aquatic sports meet
【水蛇】 shuǐshé 〈动〉 water snake
【水深火热】 shuǐshēn-huǒrè deep water and scorching fire — an abyss of suffering; extreme misery
【水生植物】 shuǐshēng zhíwù water (或 aquatic) plant; hydrophyte

【水势】 shuǐshì the flow of water; rise and fall of floodwater: 密切注意～ keep a close eye on the flow of the water/ ～减退。The flood subsided (或 abated).
【水手】 shuǐshǒu seaman; sailor
【水塔】 shuǐtǎ water tower
【水潭】 shuǐtán puddle; pool
【水塘】 shuǐtáng pool; pond
【水田】 shuǐtián paddy field
【水桶】 shuǐtǒng pail; bucket
【水土】 shuǐtǔ ① water and soil: ～流失 soil erosion/ ～保持 water and soil conservation ② natural environment and climate: ～不服 unaccustomed to the climate of a new place; not acclimatized
【水汪汪】 shuǐwāngwāng (of children's or young women's eyes) bright and intelligent
【水位】 shuǐwèi water level: 高(低)～ high (low) water level/ 地下～ water table; groundwater level
【水系】 shuǐxì river system; hydrographic net
【水仙】 shuǐxiān 〈植〉 narcissus
【水险】 shuǐxiǎn marine insurance
【水乡】 shuǐxiāng a region of rivers and lakes
【水箱】 shuǐxiāng water tank
【水泄不通】 shuǐ xiè bù tōng not even a drop of water could trickle through; be watertight: 挤得～ be packed with people/ 围得～ be so closely besieged that not a drop of water could trickle through
【水星】 shuǐxīng 〈天〉 Mercury
【水性】 shuǐxìng ① ability in swimming: 这姑娘的～很好。This girl is a good swimmer. ② the depth, currents and other characteristics of a river, lake, etc.
【水压】 shuǐyā hydraulic (或 water) pressure
【水银】 shuǐyín 〈化〉 mercury; quicksilver
◇ ～灯 mercury-vapour lamp/ ～气压表 〈气〉 mercury (或 mercurial) barometer/ ～温度计 〈气〉 mercury (或 mercurial) thermometer/ ～柱 mercury column
【水有源，树有根】 shuǐ yǒu yuán, shù yǒu gēn every river has its source and every tree its roots — everything has its origin
【水域】 shuǐyù waters; water area; body of water: 内陆～ inland waters/ 国际～ an international body of water; international waters
【水源】 shuǐyuán ① the source of a river; headwaters; waterhead: 黄河的～ the headwaters of the Huanghe River ② source of water: 寻找～ seek new sources of water
【水运】 shuǐyùn water transport ◇ ～码头 a port handling river cargo
【水灾】 shuǐzāi flood; inundation
【水葬】 shuǐzàng water burial
【水闸】 shuǐzhá sluice; water gate
【水涨船高】 shuǐ zhǎng chuán gāo when the river rises the boat goes up — particular things improve with the improvement of the general situation
【水蒸汽】 shuǐzhēngqì steam; water vapour
【水中捞月】 shuǐzhōng lāo yuè fish for the moon in the water — make impractical or vain efforts
【水柱】 shuǐzhù water column
【水准】 shuǐzhǔn level; standard: 高（低）于一般～ above (below) average
【水族】 shuǐzú aquatic animals ◇ ～馆 aquarium

shuì

说 shuì try to persuade: 游～ go around urging rulers to adopt one's political views; peddle an idea; drum up support for a scheme or plan
另见 shuō

税* shuì tax; duty: 营业～ business tax/ 进口（出口）～ import (export) duty
【税额】 shuì'é the amount of tax to be paid
【税款】 shuìkuǎn tax payment; taxation
【税率】 shuìlǜ tax rate; rate of taxation; tariff rate

【税目】 shuìmù tax items; taxable items

【税收】 shuìshōu tax revenue ◇ ～政策 tax policy

【税务局】 shuìwùjú tax bureau

【税务员】 shuìwùyuán tax collector

【税则】 shuìzé tax regulations

【税制】 shuìzhì tax system; taxation: 累进～ progressive taxation

睡* shuì sleep: 他～着了。 He's asleep./ 一～就～到大天亮 sleep like a log till broad daylight

【睡觉】 shuìjiào sleep: 该～了。 It's time to go to bed./ 睡午觉 take a nap after lunch/ 睡懒觉 get up late; sleep in; sleep late/ 马上上床，好好地睡一觉。 Get straight into bed and have a good sleep.

【睡莲】 shuìlián 〈植〉 water lily

【睡梦】 shuìmèng sleep; slumber: 一阵敲门声把他从～中惊醒了。 He was roused from sleep by a heavy pounding on the door.

【睡眠】 shuìmián sleep: ～不足 not have enough sleep

【睡醒】 shuìxǐng wake up

【睡衣】 shuìyī night clothes; pajamas

【睡意】 shuìyì sleepiness; drowsiness: 有几分～ feel somewhat sleepy; be drowsy

shǔn

吮 shǔn suck

【吮吸】 shǔnxī suck

shùn

顺* shùn ① in the same direction as; with: ～流而下 go downstream/ ～时针方向 clockwise ② along: ～着这条道儿走。 Follow this road./ 水～着渠道流进地里。 Water runs along the channel to the fields. ③ arrange; put in order: 这篇文章还得～一～。 This essay needs polishing. ④ obey; yield to; act in submission to: 他不对嘛，怎么能～着他呢？ How can we do as he wishes when he's obviously wrong? ⑤ suitable; agreeable: 不～他的意 not fall in with his wishes ⑥ take the opportunity to: ～致最崇高的敬意。 I avail myself of this opportunity to renew to you the assurances of my highest consideration. ⑦ in sequence: 这些号码是一～的。 These are serial numbers.

【顺便】 shùnbiàn conveniently; in passing: 你～把这些学习材料带到课室去吧。 Please take this study material with you to the classroom./ 这一点现在～提一下，以后还会讲到。I mention this point now in passing and shall refer to it again./ ～说一句 by the way; incidentally

【顺畅】 shùnchàng smooth; unhindered: 病人的呼吸渐渐～了。 The patient is beginning to breathe more easily.

【顺次】 shùncì in order; in succession; in proper sequence: 按问题的轻重缓急～解决 dispose of the problems one by one in order of importance and urgency

【顺从】 shùncóng be obedient to; submit to; yield to

【顺耳】 shùn'ěr pleasing to the ear: 不要只爱听～的话。 You shouldn't just listen to what pleases you.

【顺风】 shùnfēng ① have a favourable wind; have a tail wind: ～行船 sail with the wind/ 一路～ a pleasant journey; bon voyage ② favourable wind; tail wind

【顺风耳】 shùnfēng'ěr ① a person in traditional Chinese novels who can hear voices a long way off ② a well-informed person

【顺风转舵】 shùn fēng zhuǎn duò trim one's sails; take one's cue from changing conditions

【顺口】 shùnkǒu ① read smoothly: 稿子经过这样一改，念起来就～多了。 After being touched up, the essay reads more smoothly. ② say offhandedly: 他当时不想想就～答应了。 He agreed without thinking.

【顺理成章】 shùn lǐ chéng zhāng to write well, you must follow a logical train of thought; to do some work well, you must follow a rational line: 这显然是～的。 This is undoubtedly logical.

【顺利】 shùnlì smoothly; successfully; without a hitch: 工作正在～进行。 The work is going on smoothly./ 会议进行得很～。 The meeting went off without a hitch./ 在～的情况下，要看到还会有困难。 When circumstances are favourable, we must not forget that there will still be difficulties.

【顺路】 shùnlù ① on the way: 我昨天回家时～去看了看李叔叔。 I dropped in at Uncle Li's on my way home yesterday. ② direct route: 到海洋公园这么走不～。 This is not the most direct route to the Ocean Park.

【顺势】 shùnshì take advantage of an opportunity (as provided by an opponent's reckless move)

【顺手】 shùnshǒu ① smoothly; without difficulty: 事情办得相当～。 It was done without a hitch./ 开始试验有时不很～，也是很自然的。 It is to be expected that an experiment will sometimes run into a snag at first. ② conveniently; without extra trouble: 出去时请～关上门。 Would you close the door when you go out? ③ do sth. as a natural sequence or simultaneously: 我们扫完院子，～把房间也扫一扫。 After sweeping the courtyard, we might as well clean the rooms. ④ handy; convenient and easy to use: 这把镰刀使起来挺～。 This sickle is very handy.

【顺手牵羊】 shùnshǒu qiān yáng lead away a goat in passing — pick up sth. on the sly; walk off with sth.

【顺水】 shùnshuǐ downstream; with the stream

【顺水人情】 shùnshuǐ rénqíng a favour done at little cost to oneself

【顺水推舟】 shùnshuǐ tuī zhōu push the boat along with the current — make use of an opportunity to gain one's end

【顺我者昌，逆我者亡】 shùn wǒ zhě chāng, nì wǒ zhě wáng those who submit will prosper, those who resist shall perish (said of the arbitrary, brutal rule of a tyrant)

【顺心】 shùnxīn satisfactory: 诸事～。 All is well./ 他父亲晚年过得挺～。 His father spent the evening of his life in happiness.

【顺序】 shùnxù ① sequence; order: 文物按年代～展出。 The cultural relics are displayed in chronological sequence./ 按字母～排列 in alphabetical order ② in proper order; in turn

【顺眼】 shùnyǎn pleasing to the eye: 看着不～ be offensive to the eye; be an eyesore

【顺应】 shùnyìng comply with; conform to: ～历史发展的潮流 conform to the historical trend of the times; go with the tide of historical development

舜 Shùn Shun, the name of a legendary monarch in ancient China

瞬 shùn wink; twinkling: 转～之间 in a twinkling

【瞬时】 shùnshí 〈物〉 instantaneous

【瞬息】 shùnxī twinkling: ～间 in the twinkling of an eye/ ～万变 undergoing a myriad changes in the twinkling of an eye; fast changing

shuō

说* shuō ① speak; talk; say: 请～慢一点儿。 Please speak more slowly./ ～得多做得少 talk much but do little/ 你～得很对。 What you say is quite true./ 那未免～得太轻了。 That's putting it too mildly./ 俗话～，"吃一堑，长一智"。 As the saying goes, "A fall into the pit, a gain in your wit." ② explain: 他一～了又，我还是不懂。 He explained and explained, but I still couldn't understand./ 我一～他就明白了。 I told him how and he caught on at once. ③ theory; teachings; doctrine: 著书立～ write books to expound a theory ④ scold: 他父亲～了他一顿。 His father gave him a scolding (或 talking-to).
另见 shuì

【说白】 shuōbái spoken parts in an opera

【说不得】 shuōbude ① unspeakable; unmentionable ② scandalous

【说不定】 shuōbudìng perhaps; maybe: ～她已经走了。 Maybe she's already left.

【说不过去】 shuō bu guòqù　cannot be justified or explained away: 条件这样好,再不增产,可~。 With such favourable conditions, we'll have no excuse if we fail to increase output.

【说不来】 shuōbùlái　cannot get along (with sb.): 我跟他~。 I don't see eye to eye with him.

【说不上】 shuōbùshàng　① cannot say; cannot tell: 他也~问题在哪儿。 He can't put his finger on what's wrong./ 我~他来不来。 I can't say whether he is coming or not. ② not worth mentioning: 这些材料~有什么史料价值。 These materials can't be said to have much value as historical records.

【说穿】 shuōchuān　tell what sth. really is; reveal; disclose: ~了,无非是想推卸责任。 To put it bluntly, this is shifting responsibility.

【说大话】 shuō dàhuà　brag; boast; talk big

【说到底】 shuōdàodǐ　in the final analysis; at bottom

【说到做到】 shuōdào zuòdào　do what one says; match one's deeds to one's words; live up to one's word

【说定】 shuōdìng　say

【说…道…】 shuō...dào...　〔分别嵌用相对或相类的形容词或数词〕: 说长道短 make captious comments/ 说三道四 make irresponsible remarks/ 说东道西 chatter away on a variety of things

【说得过去】 shuōde guòqù　justifiable; passable: 他的英语发音还~。 His English pronunciation is passable.

【说定】 shuōdìng　settle; agree on: 这件事基本上已经~了。 The matter is as good as settled.

【说法】 shuōfa　① way of saying a thing; wording; formulation: 换一个~ say it in another way/ 这个意思可以有两种~。 This idea can be formulated in two different ways. ② statement; version; argument: 那种~是不对的。 That's a false statement./ 关于那件事,各人~不同。 Different people have different versions of the incident./ 这种~是完全正确的。 This argument is very sound./ 照他的~去做。 Do as he says.

【说服】 shuōfú　persuade; convince; prevail on; talk sb. over: 要耐心~他。 Talk to him patiently to bring him round./ 她的话很有~力。 What she says is very convincing.

【说好】 shuōhǎo　come to an agreement or understanding: 我已经跟他~明天一块去看足球赛。 I've arranged to go with him to tomorrow's football match.

【说和】 shuōhe　mediate a settlement; compose a quarrel: 你去给他们~~。 Try to patch things up between them, will you?

【说话】 shuōhuà　① speak; talk; say: 他不爱~。 He doesn't like to talk./ 感动得说不出话来 be too moved to say anything / 还是让事实来~。 Let the facts speak for themselves./ 不算话 go back on one's word ② chat; talk: 我找他~儿去。 I'd like to have a chat with him. ③ gossip; talk: 你这样干,别人当然要~。 Considering what you've done, it's natural that people should be talking. ④

【说谎】 shuōhuǎng　tell a lie; lie

【说教】 shuōjiào　deliver a sermon; preach

【说客】 shuōkè　a person often sent to win sb. over or enlist his support through persuasion; a persuasive talker

【说来话长】 shuōlái huà cháng　it's a long story

【说理】 shuōlǐ　argue; reason things out: 我们找他~去。 Let's go and reason things out with him.

【说漏嘴】 shuōlòuzuǐ　inadvertently blurt out

【说媒】 shuōméi　act as matchmaker

【说明】 shuōmíng　① explain; illustrate; show: ~机器的用法 explain how a machine works/ 举例~ illustrate by examples/ ~理由 give reasons/ 代表团认为有必要~自己的立场。 The delegation deems it necessary to state its position./ 事实充分~这种做法是正确的。 The results show clearly that this procedure is correct. ② explanation; directions; caption: 图片下边附有~。 There is a caption under the picture. ◇ ~书 (a booklet of) directions; (technical) manual; synopsis (of a play or film)/ ~文 expository writing; exposition

【说亲】 shuōqīn　act as matchmaker

【说情】 shuōqíng　plead for mercy for sb.; intercede for sb.

【说妥】 shuōtuǒ　come to an agreement

【说项】 shuōxiàng　put in a good word for sb.; intercede for sb.

【说笑】 shuōxiào　chatting and laughing: 这时满屋子的人又说又笑,兴高采烈。 The room was then full of people chatting animatedly and laughing.

【说一不二】 shuō yī bù èr　mean what one says; stand by one's word: 老班长是~的,他答应的事一定能办到。 The old squad leader is a man of his word; he never makes a promise he cannot keep.

【说嘴】 shuōzuǐ　brag; boast: 我们谁也别~。 Let's not have any boasting.

shuò

烁 shuò　bright; shining: 闪~ twinkle; glimmer
【烁烁】 shuòshuò　glitter; sparkle

朔 shuò　① new moon ② the first day of the lunar month ③ north: ~风 north wind
【朔日】 shuòrì　the first day of the lunar month
【朔望】 shuò-wàng　the first and the fifteenth day of the lunar month; syzygy
【朔月】 shuòyuè　new moon

硕 shuò　large
【硕大无朋】 shuòdà wú péng　of unparalleled size; gigantic: 整个地球可以想象为一块~的磁石。 The earth may be thought of as a gigantic magnet.
【硕果】 shuòguǒ　rich fruits; great achievements
【硕果仅存】 shuòguǒ jǐn cún　rare survival
【硕士】 shuòshì　Master ◇ ~学位 Master's degree

sī

司* sī　① take charge of; attend to; manage: 各~其事。 Each attends to his own duties. ② department (under a ministry): 外交部礼宾~ the Protocol Department of the Ministry of Foreign Affairs
【司法】 sīfǎ　administration of justice; judicature ◇ ~部门 judicial departments; judiciary/ ~机关 judicial organs
【司机】 sījī　driver: 火车~ engine driver; locomotive engineer
【司空见惯】 sīkōng jiàn guàn　a common sight; a common occurrence
【司令】 sīlìng　commander; commanding officer ◇ ~部 headquarters; command
【司马昭之心,路人皆知】 Sīmǎ Zhāo zhī xīn, lùrén jiē zhī　Sima Zhao's ill intent is known to all — the villain's design is obvious
【司仪】 sīyí　master of ceremonies

丝* sī　① silk ② a threadlike thing: 蜘蛛~ cobweb/ 铜~ copper wire/ 钨~ tungsten filament/ 肉~ meat cut into slivers; shredded meat/ 一~亮光 a thread of light ③ a tiny bit; trace: 一~不差 not a bit of difference/ 她脸上没有一~笑容。 There isn't a trace of a smile on her face./ 一~风也没有。 There isn't a breath of air.
【丝绸】 sīchóu　silk cloth; silk ◇ ~之路 〈史〉 the Silk Road
【丝带】 sīdài　silk ribbon; silk braid; silk sash
【丝毫】 sīháo　〔一般用于否定句〕 the slightest amount or degree; a bit; a particle; a shred; an iota: 我们~不应当放松自己的斗志。 We must not, in the slightest degree, weaken our will to fight./ 拿不出~证据 cannot provide a shred of evidence/ ~不差 not err by a hair's breadth; tally in every detail; be just right
【丝网】 sīwǎng　〈印〉 silk screen
【丝线】 sīxiàn　silk thread (for sewing); silk yarn
【丝织品】 sīzhīpǐn　① silk fabrics ② silk knit goods

私* sī ① personal; private: ~信 personal (或 private) letter ② selfish: 无~ unselfish; selfless ③ secret; private: ~话 confidential talk

【私奔】 sībēn elopement

【私弊】 sībì corrupt practices

【私产】 sīchǎn private property

【私仇】 sīchóu personal enmity (或 grudge)

【私德】 sīdé personal morals

【私邸】 sīdǐ 〈旧〉 private residence (of a high-ranking official)

【私法】 sīfǎ 〈法〉 private law

【私房】 sīfang ① private savings: ~钱 private savings of a family member ② confidential: 谈~话 exchange confidences

【私愤】 sīfèn personal spite: 泄~ vent personal spite

【私货】 sīhuò smuggled goods; contraband goods

【私交】 sījiāo personal friendship

【私立】 sīlì 〈旧〉 privately run; private: ~学校 private school

【私利】 sīlì private (或 selfish) interests; personal gain: 图~ pursue private ends/ 不谋~ seek no personal gain

【私囊】 sīnáng private purse: 饱~ line one's pockets; feather one's nest

【私念】 sīniàn selfish motives (或 ideas)

【私情】 sīqíng personal relationships: 不徇~ not swayed by personal considerations

【私人】 sīrén ① private; personal: ~访问 private visit/ ~关系 personal relations ② one's own man: 任用~ fill a post with one's own man; practise nepotism
◇ ~代表 personal representative/ ~秘书 private secretary/ ~企业 private enterprise

【私生活】 sīshēnghuó private life

【私生子】 sīshēngzǐ illegitimate child; bastard

【私事】 sīshì private (或 personal) affairs

【私逃】 sītáo abscond

【私通】 sītōng ① have secret communication with: ~敌人 have secret communication with the enemy ② illicit intercourse; adultery

【私下】 sīxià in private; in secret: ~商议 discuss a matter in private

【私相授受】 sī xiāng shòu-shòu privately give and privately accept; make an illicit transfer: 不许拿公家的东西~。There must be no illicit transfer of public property.

【私心】 sīxīn selfish motives (或 ideas); selfishness: ~杂念 selfish ideas and personal considerations

【私刑】 sīxíng illegal punishment (meted out by a kangaroo court)

【私营】 sīyíng privately owned; privately operated; private: ~工商业 privately owned industrial and commercial enterprises/ ~企业 private enterprise

【私有】 sīyǒu privately owned; private: 绝不能把公家财产占为~。One should never make public property one's private possession.
◇ ~财产 private property

【私语】 sīyǔ ① whisper: 窃窃~ talk in whispers ② confidence

【私欲】 sīyù selfish desire

【私自】 sīzì privately; secretly; without permission: 本阅览室参考书不得~携出。No reference books are to be taken out of the reading room without permission.

咝 sī 〈象〉 〔形容炮弹、枪弹等飞过声〕 whistle: 子弹~~地从头顶上飞过。Bullets whistled overhead.

思* sī ① think; consider; deliberate: 多~ think more/ 前~后想 think over again and again ② think of; long for: ~亲 think of one's parents with affection ③ thought; thinking: 文~ train of thought in writing/ 哀~ mourning

【思潮】 sīcháo ① trend of thought; ideological trend: 无政府主义~ the anarchist trend of thought ② thoughts: ~起伏 disquieting thoughts surging in one's mind

【思忖】 sīcǔn 〈书〉 ponder; consider

【思考】 sīkǎo think deeply; ponder over; reflect on: ~问

题 ponder a problem/ 独立~ think things out for oneself; think independently

【思量】 sīliang consider; turn sth. over in one's mind

【思路】 sīlù train of thought; thinking: 打断~ interrupt one's train of thought/ 她的~很清楚。She thinks very clearly.

【思虑】 sīlù consider carefully; contemplate; deliberate

【思慕】 sīmù think of sb. with respect; admire

【思念】 sīniàn think of; long for; miss

【思索】 sīsuǒ think deeply; ponder: 用心~ do some hard thinking/ 周密地~ consider carefully/ 我一夜没睡着，反复~这个问题。I lay awake all night, turning the problem over and over in my mind.

【思维】 sīwéi 〈哲〉 thought; thinking

【思想】 sīxiǎng thought; thinking; idea; ideology: 政治~ political thought/ ~内容好 have good ideological content

【思绪】 sīxù ① train of thought; thinking: ~纷乱 a confused state of mind; a confused train of thought ② feeling: ~不宁 feel perturbed

斯 sī ① 〈书〉 this: ~时 at this moment/ ~人 this person/ 生于~，长于~ be born and brought up here ② 〈书〉 then; thus

【斯文】 sīwén refined; gentle: 他说话挺~的。He's a soft-spoken person.

厮 sī 〔多见于早期白话〕 ① male servant: 小~ page boy; page ② fellow; guy: 那~ that guy ③ with each other; together: ~混 fool (或 play) around together

【厮打】 sīdǎ come to blows; exchange blows; tussle

【厮杀】 sīshā fight at close quarters (with weapons)

撕* sī tear; rip: 把信~开 rip open a letter/ ~得粉碎 tear to shreds/ 从日历上~下一页 tear a page from the calendar/ ~下假面具 tear off the mask; unmask/ 上衣~了。The jacket is torn.

【撕毁】 sīhuǐ tear up; tear to shreds: ~协定 tear up an agreement; tear an agreement to shreds

嘶 sī 〈书〉 ① neigh: 人喊马~ men shouting and horses neighing ② hoarse: 声~力竭 hoarse and exhausted

【嘶哑】 sīyǎ hoarse: 他讲话过多，嗓子都~了。He has talked himself hoarse.

　　　　　　　sǐ

死* sǐ ① die: ~人 a dead person; the dead/ 打~ beat to death/ 一般的寂静 a deathly stillness ② to the death: ~战 fight to the death ③ extremely; to death: 高兴~了 be extremely happy/ 累~了 be tired to death; be dog-tired/ 渴得要~ be parched with thirst; be dying for a drink/ 甜~了 much too sweet/ 咸~ terribly salty/ 我差点没笑~。I just about died laughing. ④ implacable; deadly: ~对头 sworn enemy ⑤ fixed; rigid; inflexible: ~规矩 a rigid rule/ ~教条 lifeless dogma/ 窗子钉~了。The window has been nailed fast. ⑥ impassable; closed: 把漏洞堵~ plug the holes; stop up loopholes

【死板】 sǐbǎn rigid; inflexible; stiff: 办事~ work in a mechanical way/ ~的公式 stereotyped formula

【死不】 sǐbù would rather die than; stubbornly refuse to: ~认错 stubbornly refuse to admit one's mistake/ ~放手 cling (或 hold on, hang on) to sth. like grim death/ ~改悔(回头) absolutely unrepentant; incorrigible/ ~要脸 be dead to all feelings of shame; be utterly shameless

【死不瞑目】 sǐ bù míngmù not close one's eyes when one dies — die with a grievance or everlasting regret

【死党】 sǐdǎng sworn followers; diehard followers

【死敌】 sǐdí deadly enemy; mortal enemy; implacable foe

【死地】 sǐdì a fatal position; deathtrap: 置之~而后生 confront a person with the danger of death and he will fight to live/ 必欲置之~而后快 (hate sb. so much that one) cannot be happy with anything less than his death

【死读书】 sǐ dúshū study mechanically; be a bookworm

【死而后已】 sǐ érhòu yǐ until one's dying day; to the end of one's days: 他真是鞠躬尽瘁，～。 Of him it can be said that he gave his best, gave his all, till his heart ceased to beat.

【死鬼】 sǐguǐ 〔多用于骂人或开玩笑〕 devil: 你这个～，刚才跑到哪儿去了？ You devil! Where have you been all this while?

【死胡同】 sǐhútòng blind alley; dead end

【死灰复燃】 sǐhuī fù rán dying embers glowing again — resurgence; revival

【死活】 sǐhuó ① life or death; fate ②〈口〉 anyway; simply: 他～不让我去。 I wanted to go, but he simply wouldn't hear of it.

【死火山】 sǐhuǒshān extinct volcano

【死记硬背】 sǐjì-yìngbèi mechanical memorizing

【死寂】 sǐjì 〈书〉 deathly stillness: 夜深了，山谷里一片～。 As night wore on, a deathly silence filled the valley.

【死角】 sǐjiǎo ①〈军〉 dead angle; blind angle; dead space ② a spot as yet untouched by a political movement, etc.

【死结】 sǐjié fast knot

【死劲儿】 sǐjìnr 〈口〉 ① all one's strength; all one's might: 大家用～推，才把车子推出泥坑。 Using all their strength, they pushed the cart out of the mud. ② with all one's strength (或 might); with might and main; for all one's worth: ～跑 run for all one's worth/ ～盯住他 watch him closely

【死里逃生】 sǐlǐ táoshēng escape by the skin of one's teeth; have a narrow escape; barely escape with one's life

【死力】 sǐlì ① all one's strength: 出～ exert one's utmost effort ② with all one's strength: ～抵抗 resist with might and main; fight tooth and nail

【死路】 sǐlù ① blind alley ② the road to ruin (或 destruction)

【死马当作活马医】 sǐmǎ dàngzuò huómǎ yī doctor a dead horse as if it were still alive — not give up for lost; make every possible effort

【死命】 sǐmìng ① doom; death: 制敌于～ send the enemy to his doom ② desperately: ～挣扎 struggle desperately

【死难】 sǐnàn die in an accident or a political incident (esp. for a revolutionary cause): ～烈士 martyr

【死皮赖脸】 sǐpí-làiliǎn thick-skinned and hard to shake off; brazen-faced and unreasonable

【死棋】 sǐqí a dead piece in a game of chess — a hopeless case; a stupid move

【死囚】 sǐqiú a convict sentenced to death; a convict awaiting execution

【死去活来】 sǐqù-huólái half dead; half alive; hovering between life and death: 被打得～ be beaten half dead; be brutally beaten/ 哭得～ weep one's heart out

【死尸】 sǐshī corpse; dead body

【死守】 sǐshǒu ① defend to the death; defend to the last; make a last-ditch defence: ～阵地 defend the position to the last ② obstinately cling to; rigidly adhere to

【死水】 sǐshuǐ stagnant water

【死亡】 sǐwáng death; doom: 挣扎在～线上 struggle for existence on the verge of death; struggle to stave off starvation/ 把病人从～边缘抢救过来 snatch the patient from the jaws of death ◇ ～率 death rate; mortality

【死心】 sǐxīn drop the idea forever; have no more illusions about the matter: 你还是死了这条心吧。 You'd better give up the idea altogether.

【死心塌地】 sǐxīntādì be dead set; be hell-bent

【死心眼儿】 sǐxīnyǎnr ① stubborn; as obstinate as a mule ② a person with a one-track mind

【死刑】 sǐxíng 〈法〉 death penalty; death sentence; capital punishment

【死讯】 sǐxùn news of sb.'s death

【死硬】 sǐyìng ① stiff; inflexible ② very obstinate; die-hard ◇ ～派 diehards

【死有余辜】 sǐ yǒu yú gū even death would be too good for him; even death would not expiate all his crimes

【死于非命】 sǐ yú fēimìng die an unnatural (或 a violent) death

【死者】 sǐzhě the dead; the deceased; the departed

【死罪】 sǐzuì capital offence (或 crime)

sì

巳 sì the sixth of the twelve Earthly Branches
【巳时】 sìshí the period of the day from 9 a.m to 11 a.m.

四* sì four
【四边】 sìbiān (on) four sides: ～儿围着篱笆 with a fence running all round
【四边形】 sìbiānxíng quadrilateral
【四不象】 sìbùxiàng ①〈动〉 David's deer; mi-lu ② nondescript; neither fish nor fowl
【四处】 sìchù all around; in all directions; everywhere: ～逃窜 flee in all directions/ ～奔走 go hither and thither/ ～寻找 search high and low; look into every hole and corner
【四方】 sìfāng ① the four directions (north, south, east, west); all sides; all quarters: ～响应。 Response came from every quarter. ② square; cubic: 一个～的盒子 a square box/ 一块四四方方的木头 a wooden cube
【四分五裂】 sìfēn-wǔliè fall apart; be rent by disunity; be all split up; disintegrate: 敌人内部～。 The ranks of the enemy are all split up (或 disintegrating).
【四海】 sìhǎi the four seas; the whole country; the whole world: ～为家 make one's home wherever one is
【四季】 sìjì the four seasons
【四郊】 sìjiāo suburbs; outskirts
【四脚蛇】 sìjiǎoshé lizard
【四邻】 sìlín one's near neighbours
【四面】 sìmiàn (on) four sides; (on) all sides: ～受敌 exposed to enemy attacks on all sides/ ～出击 hit out in all directions/ ～包围敌人 completely encircle the enemy forces
【四面八方】 sìmiàn-bāfāng all directions; all quarters; all around; far and near: 治河大军从～奔向工地。 Hosts of river control workers rushed to the site from all directions.
【四面楚歌】 sìmiàn Chǔ gē be besieged on all sides; be utterly isolated
【四平八稳】 sìpíng-bāwěn ① very steady; well organized: 办事～ be dependable in work/ 文章写得～ The essay is well argued. ② lacking in initiative and overcautious
【四起】 sìqǐ rise from all directions: 歌声～。 Sounds of singing were heard from all around.
【四散】 sìsàn scatter (或 disperse) in all directions
【四舍五入】 sìshě-wǔrù 〈数〉 rounding (off); to the nearest whole number
【四声】 sìshēng 〈语〉 ① the four tones of classical Chinese phonetics ② the four tones of modern standard Chinese pronunciation
【四时】 sìshí the four seasons
【四书】 sìshū The Four Books, namely, *The Great Learning* (《大学》), *The Doctrine of the Mean* (《中庸》), *The Analects of Confucius* (《论语》) and *Mencius* (《孟子》)
【四通八达】 sìtōng-bādá extend in all directions: 公路～。 Highways radiate in all directions./ 全国交通运输～ Transport and communication lines link up all parts of the country.
【四围】 sìwéi all around: 这村子～都是菜地。 All around the village are vegetable fields.
【四野】 sìyě the surrounding country; a vast expanse of open ground: ～茫茫，寂静无声。 All is quiet on the vast expanse of open ground.
【四月】 sìyuè ① April ② the fourth month of the lunar year; the fourth moon
【四肢】 sìzhī the four limbs; arms and legs
【四周】 sìzhōu all around

寺* sì temple: 清真～ mosque
【寺院】 sìyuàn temple; monastery

似* sì ① similar; like: 这两本书内容相～。 These two

books are similar in content./ 骄阳～火。The sun was scorching hot. ②seem; appear: ～曾相识 seem to have met before ③〔表示超过〕: 日子一年胜～一年。Life has been getting better year by year.
另见 shì

【似…非…】 sì…fēi… 〔嵌用同一个单音词，表示又像又不像的意思〕: 似懂非懂 have only a hazy notion; not quite understand/ 她似笑非笑。There's a faint smile on her face./ 这东西似绸非绸，不知是什么料子。This looks like silk but it isn't — I don't know what it is.

【似乎】 sìhu it seems; as if; seemingly: 他的意思～另有所指。It seems he was referring to something else./ ～明天要起风。It looks as if it'll be windy tomorrow.

【似是而非】 sì shì ér fēi apparently right but actually wrong; specious: ～的说法 a specious argument

祀 sì 〈书〉offer sacrifices to the gods or the spirits of the dead

伺 sì watch; await
另见 cì

【伺机】 sìjī watch for one's chance: ～反扑 wait for an opportunity to stage a comeback/ ～而动 wait for the opportune moment to go into action

饲* sì raise; rear
【饲槽】 sìcáo feeding trough
【饲草】 sìcǎo forage grass
【饲料】 sìliào forage; fodder; feed: 猪～ pig feed
【饲养】 sìyǎng raise; rear: ～家禽 raise (或 rear) poultry/ ～牲畜 raise livestock

驷 sì
【驷马】 sìmǎ 〈书〉a team of four horses: 一言既出，～难追。Even four horses cannot take back what one has said — what has been said cannot be unsaid.

俟 sì 〈书〉wait: ～机进攻 wait for an opportunity to attack/ 一～准备就绪，即行公开展出。The exhibition will be opened as soon as everything is in order.

嗣 sì ①succeed; inherit: ～位 succeed to the throne ②heir; descendant: 后～ descendants
【嗣后】 sìhòu 〈书〉hereafter; subsequently; afterwards; later on

肆 sì ①wanton; unbridled: 大～攻击 wantonly vilify; launch an unbridled attack against ②four (used for the numeral 四 on cheques, etc. to avoid mistakes or alterations) ③〈书〉shop: 茶楼酒～ teahouses and wineshops
【肆虐】 sìnüè indulge in wanton massacre or persecution; wreak havoc
【肆无忌惮】 sì wú jìdàn unbridled; brazen; unscrupulous: ～地攻击 make unbridled attacks
【肆意】 sìyì wantonly; recklessly; wilfully: ～歪曲事实 wantonly distort the facts

sōng

松* sōng ①pine ②loose; slack: 这里的土质很～。The soil here is very loose./ 套～了。The harness has come loose./ 绳子太～了。The rope is too loose./ 把绳子再放～点儿。Give the rope more play. ③loosen; relax; slacken: ～～螺丝 loosen the screw a little bit/ 现在我们可以～一口气了。Now we can have a breathing spell. ④not hard up: 现在手头～些 be better off ⑤light and flaky; soft: 这点心～脆可口。The pastry is light and crisp./ 这种木料～，做家具不合适。The wood is too soft for making furniture. ⑥dried meat floss; dried minced meat: 猪肉～ dried minced pork
【松绑】 sōngbǎng untie a person

【松弛】 sōngchí ①limp; flabby; slack: 肌肉～ flaccid muscles/ ～一下肌肉 relax the muscles ②lax: 纪律～ lax discipline

【松紧】 sōngjǐn ①degree of tightness ②elasticity ◇ ～带 elastic cord; elastic

【松劲】 sōngjìn relax one's efforts; slacken (off): ～情绪 slack mood

【松快】 sōngkuai ①less crowded: 搬走一张桌子，屋里～多了。With a desk moved out, there's much more space in the room. ②relieved: 吃了药以后身上～多了。I feel much better after taking the medicine. ③relax: 干了一天活，～吧。After the day's work, let's relax a bit.

【松软】 sōngruǎn soft; spongy; loose: ～的表土 spongy topsoil

【松散】 sōngsǎn ①loose: 文章结构～。The article is loosely organized./ 掺点沙子使土质～一些。Add sand to make the soil more porous. ②inattentive

【松散】 sōngsan relax; take one's ease: 屋里太闷热，出去～～吧。It's too hot and stuffy in here. Let's go out for a breath of air.

【松手】 sōngshǒu loosen one's grip; let go

【松鼠】 sōngshǔ squirrel

【松树】 sōngshù pine tree; pine

【松土】 sōngtǔ 〈农〉loosen the soil; scarify the soil

【松懈】 sōngxiè relax; slacken; slack: ～斗志 relax one's will to fight/ 工作～ be slack in one's work

嵩 sōng (of mountains) high; lofty

sǒng

怂 sǒng
【怂恿】 sǒngyǒng instigate; incite; egg sb. on; abet

悚 sǒng
【悚然】 sǒngrán terrified; horrified: 毛骨～ with one's hair standing on end

耸 sǒng ①towering; lofty ②alarm; shock: 危言～听 exaggerate things just to frighten people
【耸动】 sǒngdòng ①shrug (one's shoulders) ②create a sensation: ～视听 create a sensation
【耸肩】 sǒngjiān shrug one's shoulders
【耸立】 sǒnglì tower aloft
【耸人听闻】 sǒng rén tīngwén deliberately exaggerate so as to create a sensation: ～的谣言 a sensational rumour/ 这不是～，而是铁的事实。This is not alarmist talk, but a hard fact.
【耸入云霄】 sǒng rù yúnxiāo tower to the skies: ～的高山 a high mountain towering to the skies

sòng

讼 sòng ①bring a case to court ②dispute; argue
【讼事】 sòngshì lawsuit; litigation

宋 Sòng ①the Song Dynasty (960-1279) ②the Song Dynasty (420 - 479), one of the Southern Dynasties

送* sòng ①deliver; carry: ～信 deliver a letter ②give as a present; give: 姐姐～我一本书。My sister gave me a book. ③see sb. off or out; accompany; escort: ～他回家 see her home/ 到车站～人 see sb. off at the station/ 把客人～到门口 see a guest to the door; walk a guest to the gate/ 我～你一段路。Let me walk with you part of the way./ ～孩子上学 take a child to school
【送殡】 sòngbìn attend a funeral; take part in a funeral procession
【送还】 sònghuán give back; return
【送货】 sònghuò deliver goods: ～上门 deliver goods to the door-step of a customer
【送交】 sòngjiāo deliver; hand over

【送旧迎新】sòngjiù-yíngxīn　see off the old and welcome the new; ring out the Old Year and ring in the New
【送客】sòngkè　see a visitor out
【送礼】sònglǐ　give sb. a present; present a gift to sb.: 请客～ give dinners or send gifts (in order to curry favour)
【送命】sòngmìng　lose one's life; get killed; go to one's doom
【送人情】sòng rénqíng　① do favours at no great cost to oneself ② 〈方〉 make a gift of sth.
【送死】sòngsǐ　〈口〉 court death
【送往迎来】sòngwǎng-yínglái　see off those who depart and welcome those who arrive; speed the parting guests and welcome the new arrivals: 负责～事宜 be in charge of arrangements for receiving and seeing off guests
【送行】sòngxíng　① see sb. off; wish sb. bon voyage ② give a send-off party
【送葬】sòngzàng　take part in a funeral procession
【送终】sòngzhōng　attend upon a dying parent or other senior member of one's family; bury a parent

诵　sòng　① read aloud; chant ② recite
【诵读】sòngdú　read aloud; chant

颂　sòng　① praise; extol; eulogize; laud: 歌～ sing the praises of ② song; ode; paean; eulogy
【颂词】sòngcí　① complimentary address; panegyric; eulogy ② a speech delivered by an ambassador on presentation of his credentials
【颂歌】sònggē　song; ode
【颂扬】sòngyáng　sing sb.'s praises; laud; extol; eulogize

sōu

搜　sōu　search
【搜捕】sōubǔ　track down and arrest
【搜查】sōuchá　search; ransack; rummage ◇ ～证 search warrant
【搜刮】sōuguā　extort; plunder; expropriate; fleece
【搜集】sōují　collect; gather: ～标本 collect specimens/ ～情报 gather information
【搜罗】sōuluó　collect; gather; recruit: ～大量史料 collect a large amount of historical data/ ～人才 recruit qualified persons; scout for talent
【搜求】sōuqiú　seek
【搜身】sōushēn　search the person; make a body search
【搜索】sōusuǒ　search for; hunt for; scout around: ～失踪船只 search for missing boats/ ～前进 advance and reconnoitre ◇ ～飞行 scouting flight
【搜索枯肠】sōusuǒ kūcháng　rack one's brains (for fresh ideas or apt expressions)
【搜寻】sōuxún　search for; look for; seek
【搜腰包】sōu yāobāo　search sb.'s pockets; search sb. for money and valuables

艘　sōu　〈量〉〔用于船只〕: 两～油船 two tankers

sǒu

叟　sǒu　old man

嗾　sǒu
【嗾使】sǒushǐ　instigate; abet

薮　sǒu　〈书〉① a shallow lake overgrown with wild plants ② a gathering place of fish or beasts; den; haunt

擞　sǒu　见"抖擞" dǒusǒu

sòu

嗽　sòu　cough

sū

苏　sū　revive; come to: 死而复～ come back to life
【苏打】sūdá　soda ◇ ～饼干 soda biscuit; soda cracker
【苏丹】sūdān　sultan
【苏醒】sūxǐng　revive; regain consciousness; come to; come round: 他昏迷了一个多小时才～过来。He remained unconscious for more than an hour before he came to.

酥　sū　① crisp; short: ～糖 crunchy candy/ 香～鸡 savoury and crisp chicken ② shortbread: 杏仁～ almond shortbread ③ (of a person's limbs) limp; weak; soft
【酥脆】sūcuì　crisp: ～的饼干 crisp (或 short) biscuit
【酥麻】sūmá　limp and numb: 两腿～ one's legs feel weak and numb
【酥软】sūruǎn　limp; weak; soft

稣　sū　revive; come to

sú

俗　sú　① custom; convention: 移风易～ break with old customs; bring about a change in morals and mores ② popular; common: ～话 common saying/ 通～ popular (language, style, etc.) ③ vulgar: 不可耐 unbearably vulgar ④ secular; lay: 僧～ monks and laymen; clergy and laity
【俗话】súhuà　common saying; proverb: ～说 as the saying goes
【俗名】súmíng　popular name; local name
【俗气】súqì　vulgar; in poor taste
【俗套】sútào　conventional pattern; convention: 不落～ conform to no conventional pattern
【俗语】súyǔ　common saying; folk adage

sù

夙　sù　〈书〉① early in the morning ② long-standing; old: ～志 long-cherished ambition
【夙兴夜寐】sùxīng-yèmèi　rise early and retire late — hard at work night and day
【夙愿】sùyuàn　long-cherished wish

诉*　sù　① tell; relate; inform: 告～ tell ② complain; accuse: 控～ accuse/ 倾～ pour out (one's feelings, troubles, etc.); unbosom oneself of; unburden oneself of ③ appeal to; resort to: 上～ appeal to a higher court/ ～诸武力 resort to force; appeal to arms
【诉苦】sùkǔ　vent one's grievances; pour out one's woes
【诉说】sùshuō　tell; relate; recount: ～苦难家史 relate the family's sufferings in the old society/ ～苦衷 recount one's worries and difficulties; tell one's troubles
【诉讼】sùsòng　〈法〉 lawsuit; litigation: 民刑～ civil and criminal lawsuits/ 对某人提出～ take (或 start) legal proceedings against sb./ 撤消～ withdraw an accusation; drop a lawsuit/ 提出离婚～ take (或 start) divorce proceedings
【诉状】sùzhuàng　〈法〉 plaint; indictment: 向法院提出～ file a plaint at court

肃*　sù　① respectful ② solemn: 严～ solemn; serious; grave
【肃静】sùjìng　solemn silence: 全场～无声。A solemn silence reigned.
【肃立】sùlì　stand as a mark of respect: 奏国歌时全场～。All stood as the band struck up the national anthem. 或 Everyone stood when the national anthem was played./ ～默哀 stand in silent mourning
【肃穆】sùmù　solemn and respectful
【肃清】sùqīng　eliminate; clean up; mop up: ～敌军残部

mop up the remnants of the enemy

【肃然起敬】sùrán qǐ jìng be filled with deep veneration: 使我 ~ call forth in me a feeling of profound respect

素* sù ① white: ~服 white clothing (as a sign of mourning) ② plain; simple; quiet: ~色 plain colour ③ vegetable: 吃~ be a vegetarian/ 三荤一~ three meat dishes and one vegetable dish ④ native: ~性 one's disposition; one's temperament ⑤ basic element; element: 色~ pigment/ 毒~ poison/ 维生~ vitamin ⑥ usually; habitually; always: 我与他~不相识。 I don't know him at all. 或 He's a perfect stranger to me.
【素材】sùcái source material (of literature and art); material: 搜集小说~ gather material for a novel
【素菜】sùcài vegetable dish
【素餐】sùcān ① vegetarian meal ② be a vegetarian ③ 〈书〉 not work for one's living: 尸位~ hold down a job without doing a stroke of work
【素净】sùjing plain and neat; quiet (colour): 一套~的蓝衣服 a plain blue suit/ 花色~ a pattern in quiet colours
【素酒】sùjiǔ ① wine served at a vegetarian feast ② 〈方〉 vegetarian feast
【素来】sùlái always; usually: 他~是严格遵守纪律的。 He always strictly observes discipline.
【素昧平生】sù mèi píngshēng have never met before: 一个~的人 a complete stranger/ 我同他~。 I have never had the honour of making his acquaintance. 或 I know nothing about him.
【素描】sùmiáo ① sketch ② literary sketch
【素朴】sùpǔ simple and unadorned
【素日】sùrì generally; usually: 他~不爱说话。 He is usually very quiet.
【素食】sùshí ① vegetarian diet ② be a vegetarian ◇ ~者 vegetarian
【素雅】sùyǎ simple but elegant; unadorned and in good taste: 衣着~ be tastefully dressed in a simple style
【素质】sùzhì quality: 提高部队的军政~ enhance the military and political quality of the troops

速* sù ① fast; rapid; quick; speedy: 收效甚~ produce quick results; have a speedy effect ② speed; velocity: 音~ velocity of sound ③ 〈书〉 invite: 不~之客 uninvited guest; gate-crasher
【速成】sùchéng speeded-up educational program ◇ ~班 accelerated course; crash course/ ~教学法 quick method of teaching/ ~识字法 quick method of achieving literacy
【速冻】sùdòng quick-freeze: ~水果（蔬菜） quick-frozen fresh fruits (vegetables)
【速度】sùdù ① 〈物〉 speed; velocity ② 〈乐〉 tempo ③ speed; rate; pace; tempo: 加快~ increase speed/ 生产~ the tempo of production/ 经济发展的~ the rate of economic development/ 工业化的~ the pace of industrialization
【速记】sùjì shorthand; stenography ◇ ~员 stenographer
【速决】sùjué quick decision: 速战~ fight a quick battle to force a quick decision
【速率】sùlù speed; rate: 冷却~ rate of cooling
【速效】sùxiào quick results
【速写】sùxiě ① sketch ② literary sketch

宿* sù ① lodge for the night; stay overnight: 借~ ask for a night's lodging ② 〈书〉 long-standing; old: ~志 long-cherished ambition ③ 〈书〉 veteran; old: ~将 veteran general
【宿命论】sùmìnglùn 〈哲〉 fatalism ◇ ~者 fatalist
【宿舍】sùshè hostel; living quarters; dormitory: 学生~ students' hostel (或 dormitory)/ 职工~ living quarters for staff and workers
【宿怨】sùyuàn old grudge; old scores
【宿愿】sùyuàn long-cherished wish

粟 sù millet

溯 sù ① go against the stream: ~流而上 go upstream ② trace back; recall: 回~往事 recall past events
【溯源】sùyuán trace to the source: 追本~ track down the origin; trace to the source

塑 sù model; mould: ~像 mould a statue/ 泥~ clay sculpture
【塑料】sùliào plastics: 通用~ general-purpose plastics
【塑像】sùxiàng statue
【塑造】sùzào ① model; mould: ~石膏像 mould (或 model) a plaster figure ② portray

簌 sù
【簌簌】sùsù ① 〈象〉 rustle: 风吹树叶~响。 The leaves are rustling in the wind. ② (tears) streaming down

suān

酸* suān ① 〈化〉 acid: 醋~ acetic acid ② sour; tart: ~梨 sour pear/ ~果 tart fruit/ 牛奶~了。 The milk has turned sour. ③ sick at heart; grieved; distressed: 大娘鼻子一~，流下泪来。 The old woman's nose twitched and she began to weep. ④ pedantic; impractical: ~秀才 impractical old scholar; priggish pedant ⑤ tingle; ache: 腰~背痛 have a pain in the back; have a backache
【酸溜溜】suānliūliū ① sour ② tingle; ache: 走了一天路，我的腿肚子~的。 My legs ached after I'd been walking all day. ③ sad; mournful
【酸梅】suānméi smoked plum; dark plum ◇ ~汤 sweet-sour plum juice
【酸牛奶】suānniúnǎi yoghurt; sour milk
【酸软】suānruǎn aching and limp
【酸甜苦辣】suān-tián-kǔ-là sour, sweet, bitter, hot — joys and sorrows of life
【酸痛】suāntòng ache: 浑身~ ache all over
【酸味】suānwèi tart flavour; acidity
【酸性】suānxìng 〈化〉 acidity

suàn

蒜 suàn garlic: 一辫~ a braid of garlic
【蒜头】suàntóu the head (或 bulb) of garlic

算* suàn ① calculate; reckon; compute; figure: ~~旅行的费用 calculate the cost of a journey/ 能写会~ good at writing and reckoning/ 请你~一~我该付多少钱? Please reckon up how much I must pay./ 他们~了一下，完成这项工程需要两年。 They figured it would take two years to finish the project. ② include; count: ~上你，一共有十个人。 There were ten people, including you./ 把我也~上。 Count me in. ③ plan; calculate: 失~ miscalculate; make an unwise decision/ 暗~ plot against sb. ④ think; suppose: 我~他今天该动身了。 I suppose he'll have started (或 be starting) today. ⑤ consider; regard as; count as: 他可以~一个车把势。 He can be counted as a carter./ 就~你对了，也不该那么说呀! Even if you are right, that's not the way to put it. ⑥ carry weight; count: 我一个人说的不~，还得大伙儿说。 It's not just what I say, but what we all say, that counts./ 你怎么刚说了又不~了! You just made a promise and now you've gone back on it!/ 这点困难~不了什么。 A little difficulty like this is nothing to us./ 世界上的事不应该由一两个国家说了~。 One or two powers should not have the final say on world affairs. ⑦ at long last; in the end; finally: 现在~把情况弄清楚了。 At long last we have got things clear. 或 We've finally sized up the situation./ 问题~解决了。 The problem is finally solved. ⑧ 〔后面跟 "了"〕 let it be; let it pass: ~了，别说了。 That's enough! Let it go at that. 或 Forget it./ 他不愿意去就~了吧，我们反正去。 If he doesn't want to go, he doesn't need to. We'll go anyway.

【算命】 suànmìng fortune-telling ◇ ～先生 fortune-teller

【算盘】 suànpan abacus: 打～ use an abacus/ 不要打个人小～。 Don't be so calculating.

【算是】 suànshì at last: 这一下你～猜着了。 At last you've guessed right./ 我们的计划～实现了。 At last our plan has materialized.

【算术】 suànshù arithmetic: 做～ do sums

【算数】 suànshù count; hold; stand: 个别情况不～。 Isolated instances do not count./ 这条规定仍然～。 This rule still holds (或 stands)./ 我们说话是～的。 We mean what we say.

【算学】 suànxué ① mathematics ② arithmetic

【算帐】 suànzhàng ① do (或 work out) accounts; balance the books; make out bills: ～算得快 be quick at accounts ② square (或 settle) accounts with sb.; get even with sb.: 以后再找这坏蛋～。 We'll get even with the scoundrel later. 或 We'll make the scoundrel pay for this.

suī

虽* suī 〈连〉 though; although; even if: 问题～小，但很典型。 The question is small but typical./ ～死犹荣 honoured though dead; have died a glorious death

【虽然】 suīrán 〈连〉 though; although

【虽说】 suīshuō 〈口〉〈连〉 though; although

【虽则】 suīzé 〈连〉 though; although

suí

绥 suí 〈书〉 ① peaceful ② pacify

【绥靖】 suíjìng pacify; appease ◇ ～政策 policy of appeasement

隋 Suí ① the Sui Dynasty (581-618) ② a surname

随* suí ① follow: ～我来。 Follow me. 或 Come along with me. ② comply with; adapt to: ～顺 yield and comply/只要你们做得对，我都～着。 So long as what you do is right, I'll go along with you. ③ let (sb. do as he likes): ～你的便。 Do as you please./ 去不去～你。 Whether you go or not is up to you. ④ along with (some other action): 请你～手把门带上。 Please close the door as you go out. 或 Please shut the door after you. ⑤ 〈方〉 look like; resemble: 她长得～她母亲。 She looks like her mother. 或 She takes after her mother.

【随笔】 suíbǐ informal essay; jottings

【随便】 suíbiàn ① casual; random; informal: ～闲谈 chat; chitchat/ ～说了几句 make some casual remarks/ 你怎么能这样～答应呢？ How could you agree so casually? ② do as one pleases: ～吃吧。 Help yourselves./ (主人对客人)请～吧。 Make yourself at home. ③ careless; slipshod: 说话～ not be careful about the way one talks ④ wanton; wilful; arbitrary: ～撕毁协议 wantonly tear up an agreement ⑤ anyhow; any: ～什么时候来都行。 Come any time you like.

【随波逐流】 suíbō-zhúliú drift with the tide (或 current)

【随处】 suíchù everywhere; anywhere

【随从】 suícóng ① accompany (one's superior); attend ② retinue; suite; *entourage*

【随带】 suídài ① going along with: 信外～书籍一包。 Accompanying the letter is a parcel of books. ② have sth. taken along with one: ～行李两件 two pieces of luggage which a passenger takes along with him

【随地】 suídì anywhere; everywhere: 不要～扔东西。 Don't litter.

【随风倒】 suífēngdǎo bend with the wind — be easily swayed (by whichever side has more power or influence)

【随风转舵】 suí fēng zhuǎn duò trim one's sails; take one's cue from changing conditions

【随和】 suíhe amiable; obliging: 脾气～ have an amiable disposition

【随后】 suíhòu 〈副〉 soon afterwards: 你先走，我～就去。 You go first. I'll follow. 或 You go ahead. I'll be there right away.

【随机应变】 suíjī-yìngbiàn adapt oneself to changing conditions; act according to circumstances

【随即】 suíjí immediately; presently

【随口】 suíkǒu speak thoughtlessly or casually; blurt out whatever comes into one's head: ～答应 say "yes" absent-mindedly; agree without thinking

【随人俯仰】 suí rén fǔ-yǎng be at sb.'s beck and call; follow sb. servilely

【随身】 suíshēn (carry) on one's person; (take) with one: 他～没有带钱。 He had no money on him./ 我～可以带几公斤行李？ How many kilograms of luggage can I take with me? ◇ ～行李 personal luggage

【随声附和】 suí shēng fùhè echo what others say; chime in with others

【随时】 suíshí ① at any time; at all times: ～准备歼灭入侵之敌 be ready at all times to wipe out any invader/ ～掌握工作进程 constantly have a grip on the progress of the work; always know clearly how the work is progressing/ 有了问题～向我报告。 Keep me informed of any problems that may arise. ② whenever necessary; as the occasion demands: ～纠正错误 correct mistakes as soon as they occur/ ～表扬好人好事 commend good people for their good deeds when the occasion arises

【随手】 suíshǒu conveniently; without extra trouble: 出门～关灯。 Turn the light off as you go out./ ～关门。 Shut the door after you.

【随俗】 suísú comply with convention; do as everybody else does

【随…随…】 suí … suí … 〔分别用在两个动词或动词性词组前面，表示后一动作紧接前一动作〕: 随叫随到 be on call at any hour/ 雪随下随化。 The snow melted as it fell.

【随同】 suítóng be in company with; be accompanying

【随乡入乡】 suí xiāng rù xiāng when in Rome do as the Romans do

【随心所欲】 suí xīn suǒ yù follow one's inclinations; have one's own way; do as one pleases

【随行人员】 suíxíng rényuán *entourage*; suite; party: 总统及其～ the President and his *entourage*

【随意】 suíyì at will; as one pleases

【随遇而安】 suí yù ér ān feel at home wherever one is; be able to adapt oneself to different circumstances

【随员】 suíyuán ① suite; retinue; *entourage* ② 〈外〉 attaché

【随葬物】 suízàngwù funerary objects; burial articles

【随着】 suízhe along with; in the wake of; in pace with: ～运动的深入 with the deepening of the movement/ ～时间

遂 suí 见"半身不遂" bànshēn bùsuí
另见 suì

suǐ

髓 suǐ 〈生理〉 marrow: 脊～ spinal marrow (或 cord)

suì

岁* suì ① year: ～末 the end of the year/ ～入 annual income/ ～出 annual expenditure/ 辞旧～，迎新年 ring out the Old Year and ring in the New ② year (of age): 三一女孩儿 a three-year-old girl; a little girl three years old/ 这匹马两～口。 This horse is two years old. ③ year (for crops): 歉～ lean year

【岁暮】 suìmù 〈书〉 the close of the year: ～天寒。 Cold weather sets in as the year draws to its close.

【岁首】 suìshǒu 〈书〉 the beginning of the year

【岁数】 suìshu 〈口〉 age; years

【岁修】 suìxiū annual repairs

【岁月】 suìyuè years: 艰苦斗争的～ years of arduous struggle/ ～不居。 Time and tide wait for no man.

祟 suì evil spirit; ghost: 作~ act like an evil spirit; haunt and plague

遂 suì ① satisfy; fulfil: ~愿 have one's wish fulfilled ② succeed: 所谋不~ fail in an attempt ③ <书> then; thereupon: 病人服药后腹痛~止。The patient's stomachache stopped after he took the medicine. 另见 suí

【遂心】 suìxīn after one's own heart; to one's liking: ~如意 perfectly satisfied

【遂意】 suìyì to one's liking

碎* suì ① break to pieces; smash: 碗打~了。The bowl is smashed to pieces. ② broken; fragmentary: ~玻璃 bits of broken glass/ ~布 oddments of cloth

【碎石】 suìshí <建> crushed stones; broken stones ◇ ~混凝土 <建> crushed stone concrete/ ~机 stone crusher/ ~路 broken stone road; macadam road

隧 suì
【隧道】 suìdào tunnel

燧 suì ① flint ② beacon fire

【燧石】 suìshí flint ◇ ~玻璃 flint glass

邃 suì <书> ① remote (in time or space): ~古 remote antiquity ② deep; profound: 精~ profound

穗 suì ① the ear of grain; spike: 麦~儿 the ear of wheat ② tassel; fringe

sūn

孙* sūn ① grandson ② generations below that of the grandchild: 曾~ great-grandson/ 玄~ great-great-grandson ③ second growth of plants: ~竹 new shoots of bamboo from the old stump

【孙女】 sūnnǚ granddaughter ◇ ~婿 granddaughter's husband; grandson-in-law

【孙媳妇】 sūnxífu grandson's wife; granddaughter-in-law

【孙子】 sūnzi grandson

狲 sūn 见"猢狲" húsūn

sǔn

笋 sǔn bamboo shoot
【笋干】 sǔngān dried bamboo shoots

损* sǔn ① decrease; lose: 增~ increase and decrease/ 亏~ loss ② harm; damage: 有益无~ can only do good, not harm/ ~公肥私 seek private gain at public expense; feather one's nest at public expense/ 以~人开始，以害己告终 begin with injuring others and end up ruining oneself/ 狂犬吠日，无~于太阳的光辉。A cur barking at the sun cannot detract from its glory. ③ <方> sarcastic; caustic; cutting: 他爱~人。He delights in making caustic remarks./ 说话别太~。Don't be so sarcastic. ④ <方> mean; shabby: 这法子真~。That's a mean trick.

【损害】 sǔnhài harm; damage; injure: ~庄稼 damage crops; be harmful to crops/ ~健康 impair one's health/ 光线不好，看书容易~视力。Reading in poor light is bad for one's eyes.

【损耗】 sǔnhào ① loss; wear and tear: 摩擦~ friction loss ② <商> wastage; spoilage

【损坏】 sǔnhuài damage; injure: ~公物要赔。Pay for public property you damage.

【损人利己】 sǔn rén lì jǐ harm others to benefit oneself; benefit oneself at the expense of others

【损伤】 sǔnshāng ① harm; damage; injure ② loss: 敌军兵力~很大。The enemy forces suffered heavy losses.

【损失】 sǔnshī ① lose: ~坦克五辆 lose five tanks ② loss; damage: 遭受重大~ suffer (或 sustain) heavy losses

【损益】 sǔnyì ① increase and decrease: 斟酌~ consider making necessary adjustments ② profit and loss; gains and losses: ~相抵。The gains offset the losses.

隼 sǔn <动> falcon

榫 sǔn tenon

suō

唆 suō instigate; abet: 教~ instigate; abet

【唆使】 suōshǐ instigate; abet ◇ ~者 instigator; abettor

挲 suō 见"摩挲" mósuō

梭 suō shuttle: 无~织机 shuttleless loom

【梭巡】 suōxún <书> move around to watch and guard; patrol

【梭子】 suōzi ① <纺> shuttle ② cartridge clip

蓑 suō
【蓑衣】 suōyī straw or palm-bark rain cape

缩* suō ① contract; shrink: 热胀冷~ expand with heat and contract with cold/ 这种布下水不~。This cloth won't shrink when it's washed. ② draw back; withdraw; recoil: 退~ flinch; shrink/ 他把身子一~。He shrank back (in shame, horror, etc.)./ 冷得~成一团 huddle oneself up with cold

【缩短】 suōduǎn shorten; curtail; cut down: ~学制 shorten the period of schooling/ ~距离 reduce the distance; narrow the gap/ ~战线 contract the front/ 把报告~一半 cut a report down to half its length/ 把停留时间~一天 cut short one's stay by one day

【缩减】 suōjiǎn reduce; cut: ~开支 reduce (或 cut) spending/ ~军费 cut back military expenditure

【缩手】 suōshǒu ① draw back one's hand ② shrink (from doing sth.)

【缩手缩脚】 suōshǒu-suōjiǎo ① shrink with cold ② be overcautious: 不要～。Don't be overcautious.

【缩水】 suōshuǐ (of cloth through wetting) shrink

【缩头缩脑】 suōtóu-suōnǎo ① be timid; be fainthearted ② shrink from responsibility

【缩小】 suōxiǎo reduce; lessen; narrow; shrink: ~范围 reduce the scope; narrow the range

【缩写】 suōxiě ① abbreviation ② abridge ◇ ~本 abridged edition (或 version)/ ~签字 initials

【缩印】 suōyìn reprint books in a reduced format

【缩影】 suōyǐng epitome; miniature

suŏ

所* suŏ ① place: 住~ dwelling place/ 各得其~ each in his proper place ② 〔用作机关或其他办事地方的名称〕: 研究~ research institute/ 诊疗~ clinic/ 指挥~ command post ③ <量> 〔用于房屋等〕: 一~房子 a house/ 两~学校 two schools/ 这~医院 this hospital ④ <助> ⓐ〔跟"为"或"被"合用，表示被动〕: 为人~笑 be laughed at/ 被表面现象~迷惑 be misled by outward appearances/ 深为他的忘我无私精神~感动 be deeply touched by his selfless spirit ⓑ〔跟动词连用，代表接受动作的事物〕: 各尽~能 from each according to his ability/ 闻~未闻 unheard-of/ 无~不为

stop at nothing (in doing evil) ⓒ〔跟动词连用,动词后再用接受动作的事物的词〕:我~认识的人 the people I know/ 大家~提的意见 the opinions various people put forward ⓓ〔跟动词连用,动词后再用"者"或"的"代表接受动作的事物〕:~见者广 have wide experience/ 这是我们~拥护的。This is what we support.

【所长】 suǒcháng what one is good at; one's strong point; one's forte

【所得】 suǒdé income; earnings; gains ◇ ~税 income tax

【所属】 suǒshǔ ① what is subordinate to one or under one's command : 教育部~单位 the organizations under the Ministry of Education

【所谓】 suǒwèi ① what is called ② so-called

【所向披靡】 suǒ xiàng pīmǐ (of troops) carry all before one; sweep away all obstacles

【所以】 suǒyǐ ①〈连〉〔表示因果关系〕so; therefore; as a result: 他有事,~没来。He hasn't come because he's got something else to do./ 我们之一一定会胜利,是因为我们的事业是正义的。The reason why we are bound to succeed is that our cause is just. ②〈口〉〔单独成句,表示"原因就在这里"〕: ~呀,要不然我怎么这么说呢? That's just the point, otherwise I wouldn't have said it. ③〔用于固定词组中作宾语,表示实在的情由或适宜的举动〕:忘其~ forget oneself

【所以然】 suǒyǐrán the reason why; the whys and wherefores: 知其然而不知其~ know that sth. is so but not why it is so; know what is done but not why it is done/ 他说了半天还是没说出个~来。He talked a lot but made you none the wiser.

【所有】 suǒyǒu ① own; possess ② possessions: 尽其~ give everything one has; give one's all ③ all: 把 的劲儿都使出来 exert all one's strength

【所在】 suǒzài place; location: 风景优美的~ a picturesque place; a scenic spot/ 这是我们的力量~。That is where our strength lies./ Herein lies our strength./ ~多有 be found almost everywhere ◇ ~地 location; seat; site

【所致】 suǒzhì be caused by; be the result of: 这次事故是由于疏忽~。The accident was the result of (或 was due to) negligence.

索 suǒ ① large rope: 绳~ rope/ 麻~ hempen rope/ 船~ ship's rigging/ 绞~ (the hangman's) noose/ 铁~桥 chain bridge ② search: 遍~不得 search high and low for sth. in vain ③ demand; ask; exact: ~价 ask a price; charge/ ~债 demand payment of a debt/ ~赔 claim damages ④〈书〉all alone; all by oneself: 离群~居 live all alone ⑤〈书〉dull; insipid

【索取】 suǒqǔ ask for; demand; exact; extort: ~样品 ask for a sample/ ~巨额赔款 extort a huge indemnity

【索然】 suǒrán dull; dry; insipid: ~寡味 flat and insipid

【索性】 suǒxìng〈副〉〔表示直截了当,干脆〕: 既然已经做了,~就把它做完。Since you have started the job, you might as well finish it./ 找了几个地方都没找着,~不再找了。It was nowhere to be found, so we simply gave it up for lost.

【索引】 suǒyǐn index: 卡片~ card index/ 书名~ title index/ 作者~ author index/ 标题~ subject index

唢 suǒ

【唢呐】 suǒnà *suona* horn, a woodwind instrument

琐 suǒ trivial; petty

【琐事】 suǒshì trifles; trivial matters: 家庭~ household affairs

【琐碎】 suǒsuì trifling; trivial

【琐闻】 suǒwén bits of news; scraps of information

【琐细】 suǒxì trifling; trivial

【琐屑】 suǒxiè〈书〉trifling; trivial

锁 * suǒ ① lock: 挂~ padlock/ 弹簧~ spring lock ② lock up: ~门 lock a door/ ~在保险箱里 be locked up in a safe/ 双眉紧~ with knitted brows ③ lockstitch: ~眼 do a lockstitch on a buttonhole/ ~边 lockstitch a border

【锁匠】 suǒjiang locksmith

【锁紧】 suǒjǐn〈机〉locking: 自~ self-locking

【锁链】 suǒliàn ① chain ② shackles; fetters; chains

SUO

嗦 suo 见"哆嗦" duōsuo;"罗嗦" luōsuo

T

tā

它* tā 〔称人以外的事物〕it: 这杯牛奶你喝了~。 Drink this glass of milk.

【它们】 tāmen 〔称一个以上的事物〕they

他* tā ①he: ~俩 the two of them/ ~家在农村。 His home is in the countryside. ②〔泛指,不分男性和女性〕: 从远处看不出~是男的还是女的。 You can't tell if it's a man or a woman from a distance. ③〔虚指,用在动词和数量词之间〕: 好好睡~一觉 have a good sleep/ 再读~一遍 read it a second time ④other; another; some other: 调往~处 be transferred to another place/ 留作~用 reserve for other uses/ 此人早已~去。 He has long since left.

【他妈的】 tāmāde 〈骂〉damn it; blast it; to hell with it

【他们】 tāmen 〔指人〕they: ~俩 the two of them

【他人】 tārén another person; other people; others

【他日】 tārì 〈书〉some other time (或 day); some day; later on

【他乡】 tāxiāng a place far away from home; an alien land: ~遇故知 run into an old friend in a distant land

她* tā she

【她们】 tāmen 〔指女性〕they

塌 tā ①collapse; fall down; cave in: 墙~了。 The wall collapsed./ 没什么好怕的,天不会~下来。 There's nothing to be afraid of. The sky won't fall down. ②sink; droop: 他病了好久,两腮都~下去了。 His cheeks were sunken after his long illness./ 鼻梁~ a flat nose/ 花儿晒~秧了。 The flowers drooped in the hot sun. ③calm down; settle down: ~下心去 set one's mind at ease; settle down to (work, etc.)

【塌实】 tāshi ①steady and sure; dependable: 工作~ be a steady worker; be steadfast in one's work ②free from anxiety; having peace of mind: 觉得~ have one's mind set at rest; feel secure about sth./ 睡得很~ enjoy a deep, quiet sleep; have a good, sound sleep/ 经过检查,发电机并没有毛病,我们心里就~了。 We felt relieved when the generator was checked and found in order.

【塌台】 tātái collapse; fall from power

【塌陷】 tāxiàn subside; sink; cave in: 这座房子的地基~了。 The foundations of this building have subsided.

踏* tā 另见 tà

【踏实】 tāshi 见"塌实" tāshi

tǎ

塔* tǎ ①Buddhist pagoda; pagoda ②tower: 水~ water tower/ 灯~ lighthouse; beacon

獭 tǎ otter: 水~ (common) otter/ 海~ sea otter/ 旱~ marmot

水獭

tà

拓 tà make rubbings from inscriptions, pictures, etc.

on stone tablets or bronze vessels

另见 tuò

沓 tà 〈书〉crowded; repeated: 杂~ numerous and disorderly/ 纷至~来 come thick and fast; keep pouring in

另见 dá

挞 tà 〈书〉flog; whip: 鞭~ flog; lash

榻 tà a long, narrow and low bed; couch: 竹~ bamboo couch/ 藤~ rattan (或 cane) couch/ 同~ sleep in the same bed; share a bed

踏 tà step on; tread; stamp: 把火~灭 tread out a fire/ ~平匪巢 smash the bandits' lair/ ~上贵国的土地 set foot on the soil of your country

另见 tā

【踏板】 tàbǎn ①treadle; footboard; footrest: 缝纫机~ the treadle of a sewing machine ②footstool (usu. placed beside a bed)

【踏步】 tàbù mark time

【踏破铁鞋无觅处,得来全不费工夫】 tàpò tiěxié wú mìchù, delái quán bù fèi gōngfu find sth. by chance after travelling far and wide in search of it

蹋 tà 见"糟蹋" zāota

tāi

胎* tāi ①foetus; embryo: ~形 the form of the foetus/ 怀~ become or be pregnant ②birth: 头~ first baby; firstborn/ 一~十五只小猪 fifteen piglets at a litter (或 one farrow) ③padding; stuffing; wadding: 棉花~ the cotton padding of a quilt, etc. ④roughcast (in the making of china, cloisonné, etc.) ⑤tyre: 内~ inner tube (of a tyre)/ 外~ outer cover (of a tyre); tyre

【胎盘】 tāipán 〈生理〉placenta

【胎生】 tāishēng 〈动〉viviparity ◇ ~动物 viviparous animal; vivipara

tái

台* tái ①platform; stage; terrace: 讲~ platform; rostrum/ 了望~ watch tower; lookout/ 检阅~ reviewing stand/ 舞~ stage/ 下不了~ unable to extricate oneself from an awkward position; unable to get off the spot ②stand; support: 灯~ lampstand/ 蜡~ candlestick/ 导弹发射~ missile launching pad ③anything shaped like a platform, stage or terrace: 灶~ the top of a kitchen range/ 窗~ windowsill ④table; desk: 写字~ (writing) desk/ 梳妆~ dressing table/ 工作~ (work) bench ⑤broadcasting station/ 电视~ television broadcasting station ⑥a special telephone service: 长途~ trunk call service; toll board; long distance/ 查号~ directory inquiries; information ⑦〈量〉: 一~戏 a theatrical performance/ 一~机车 a railway engine; a locomotive ⑧〔旧时称对方的敬辞〕: ~端 you/ ~命 your instructions

【台步】 táibù the gait of an actor or actress in Beijing opera, etc.

【台词】 táicí actor's lines

【台灯】 táidēng desk lamp; table lamp; reading lamp

【台风】 táifēng 〈气〉typhoon: 强~ violent typhoon

【台阶】 táijiē ①a flight of steps; steps leading up to a house, etc. ②chance to extricate oneself from an awkward position: 给他个~下吧。 Give him an out. ③〈矿〉bench:

上~ upper bench

【台球】 táiqiú ① billiards ② billiard ball

【台子】 táizi ①〈口〉 platform; stage ②〈方〉 table; desk ③ billiard table ④ ping-pong table

抬* tái ① lift; raise: ~手 raise one's hand/ 把桌子～起来 lift (up) the table/打击别人,～高自己 attack others so as to build up oneself ②(of two or more persons) carry: ～担架 carry a stretcher ③ 见"抬杠"

【抬杠】 táigàng 〈口〉 argue for the sake of arguing; bicker; wrangle: 他俩抬起杠来就没完。Those two can go on arguing for hours and hours.

【抬价】 táijià force up commodity prices

【抬举】 táiju praise or promote sb. to show favour; favour sb.: 不识～ not know how to appreciate favours

【抬头】 táitóu ① raise one's head: ～一看 look up ② gain ground; look up; rise

苔 tái 〈植〉 liver mosses

tái

太* tài ① highest; greatest; remotest: ～空 the firmament; outer space ② more or most senior: ～老伯 granduncle/ ～老师 father of one's teacher or teacher of one's father ③〈副〉 excessively; too; over: ～晚 too late/ 水～烫,没法喝。The water is too hot to drink./ 那～过分了。That's going too far./ 这～不象话了！This is simply outrageous! 或 This is the height of absurdity!/ 他～客气了,使大家感到很拘束。He was so polite everybody felt ill at ease. ④〈副〉〔用于赞叹〕extremely: 又见到您,～高兴了。I'm extremely glad to see you again./ ～感谢你了。Thanks a lot. 或 Thank you ever so much. ⑤〈副〉〔用于否定〕very: 不～好 not very good; not good enough

【太公钓鱼,愿者上钩】 Tàigōng diào yú, yuànzhě shàng gōu like the fish rising to Jiang Tai Gong's hookless and baitless line — a willing victim letting himself be caught

【太古】 tàigǔ remote antiquity

【太后】 tàihòu mother of an emperor; empress dowager; queen mother

【太极拳】 tàijíquán taijiquan, a kind of traditional Chinese shadow boxing: 打～ do taijiquan

【太监】 tàijiàn (court) eunuch

【太空】 tàikōng the firmament; outer space

【太平】 tàipíng peace and tranquility: ～盛世 piping times of peace/ ～无事。All is well. 或 Everything is all right.

【太上皇】 tàishànghuáng ① a title assumed by an emperor's father who abdicated in favour of his son ② overlord; supersovereign; backstage ruler

【太师椅】 tàishīyǐ an old-fashioned wooden armchair

【太岁】 tàisuì an ancient name for the planet Jupiter

【太岁头上动土】 tàisuì tóushang dòng tǔ provoke sb. far superior in power or strength

【太太】 tàitai 〈旧〉① Mrs.; madame: 王～ Mrs. Wang; Madame Wang ② the mistress of a household; madam; lady

【太阳】 tàiyáng ① the sun: 青年人朝气蓬勃,好象早晨八九点钟的～。Young people, full of vigour and vitality, are like the sun at eight or nine in the morning. ② sunshine; sunlight: 晒～ bask in the sun/ ～地儿 a place where there is sunshine; sunny spot/ 今天～很好。It's a lovely sunny day.

【太阳镜】 tàiyángjìng sunglasses

【太阳穴】 tàiyángxué the temples

【太医】 tàiyī imperial physician

【太阴】 tàiyīn ①〈方〉 the moon ②〈天〉 lunar ◇ ～历 lunar calendar/ ～年 lunar year/ ～月 lunar month; lunation

【太子】 tàizi crown prince

汰* tài discard; eliminate

态* tài ① form; appearance; condition: 形～ shape; morphology/ 姿～ posture; stance; gesture; attitude/ 事～的发展 the course of events; developments ②〈物〉state: 气～ gaseous state/ 液～ liquid state ③〈语〉voice: 主动语～ the active voice

【态度】 tàidu ① manner; bearing; how one conducts oneself: ～和蔼 amiable; kindly/ 耍～ lose one's temper; get into a huff/ 你这是什么～? What sort of an attitude is that? 或 Is this the way to behave?/ 他今天～有些异常。He is not his usual self today. ② attitude; approach: 劳动～ attitude towards labour/ 改变自己的～ change one's attitude; shift one's position

泰 tài ① safe; peaceful: 康～ in good health/ 国～民安。The country is prosperous and the people live in peace. ② extreme; most: ～西 the West; the Occident

【泰然】 tàirán calm; composed; self-possessed: ～处之 take sth. calmly; bear sth. with equanimity/ ～自若 behave with perfect composure; be self-possessed

【泰山】 Tàishān ① Mount Taishan; Taishan Mountain (a symbol of great weight or import): 人固有一死,或重于～,或轻于鸿毛。Though death befalls all men alike, it may be weightier than Mount Taishan or lighter than a feather./有眼不识～ have eyes but fail to see Mount Taishan; entertain an angel unawares ②〈旧〉 father-in-law

【泰山北斗】 tàishān běidǒu Mount Taishan and the Big Dipper (respectful epithet for a person of distinction)

【泰山压顶】 Tàishān yā dǐng bear down on one with the weight of Mount Taishan: ～不弯腰 bend one's head even if Mount Taishan topples on one; not give in to any pressure or difficulty

tān

坍 tān collapse; fall; tumble: 土墙～了。The earthern wall collapsed.

【坍塌】 tāntā cave in; collapse

【坍台】 tāntái 〈方〉① (of enterprises, etc.) collapse ② fall into disgrace; lose face

贪 tān ① corrupt; venal: ～官污吏 corrupt officials; venal officials ② have an insatiable desire for: ～财 be greedy for money/ ～得无厌 be insatiably avaricious/ ～杯 be too fond of drink; be a winebibber/ ～玩 be too fond of play/ ～大求全 go in for grandiose projects/ ～多嚼不烂 bite off more than one can chew ③ covet; hanker after

【贪婪】 tānlán 〈书〉 avaricious; greedy; rapacious: ～的目光 greedy eyes/ ～地掠夺别国的资源 rapaciously plunder the resources of other countries

【贪恋】 tānliàn be reluctant to part with; hate to leave; cling to: ～西湖景色 hate to leave the beautiful West Lake/ ～舒适的生活 be reluctant to give up ease and comfort

【贪便宜】 tān piányi anxious to get things on the cheap; keen on gaining petty advantages

【贪生怕死】 tānshēng-pàsǐ cravenly cling to life instead of braving death; care for nothing but saving one's skin; be mortally afraid of death

【贪天之功】 tān tiān zhī gōng arrogate to oneself the merits of others; claim credit for other people's achievements

【贪图】 tāntú seek; hanker after; covet: ～安逸 seek ease and comfort/ ～小利 covet small advantages; hanker after petty gains/ 警惕～享乐的情绪 guard against the tendency to seek pleasure

【贪污】 tānwū corruption; graft: ～盗窃 graft and embezzlement/ ～腐化 corruption and degeneration; corruption/ ～和浪费是极大的犯罪。Corruption and waste are very great crimes. ◇ ～分子 a person guilty of corruption; grafter; embezzler

【贪心】 tānxīn ① greed; avarice; rapacity ② greedy; avaricious; insatiable; voracious: ~不足 insatiably greedy

【贪小失大】 tān xiǎo shī dà covet a little and lose a lot; seek small gains but incur big losses

【贪赃】 tānzāng take bribes; practise graft: ~枉法 take bribes and bend the law; pervert justice for a bribe

【贪嘴】 tānzuǐ greedy (for food); gluttonous

滩 tān ① beach; sands: 海~ seabeach; beach/ 沙~ sand bank; sands ② shoal: 险~ dangerous shoals/ ~多水急 with many shoals and rapids

摊* tān ① spread out: 把豆子~开晒一晒 spread the beans out to dry in the sun/ 把事情~到桌面上来谈 put the problems on the table and thrash them out ② vendor's stand; booth; stall: 水果~儿 fruit stand; fruit stall/ 报~ newsstand; 收~儿 shut up shop; wind up the day's business ③ 〈量〉 〔用于摊开的糊状物〕: 一~稀泥 a mud puddle/ 一~血 a pool of blood

【摊牌】 tānpái lay one's cards on the table; show one's hand (或 cards); have a showdown: 迫使对方~ force one's opponent to show his hand; force a showdown

【摊子】 tānzi ① vendor's stand; booth; stall: 菜~ vegetable stall (或 stand) ② the structure of an organization; setup: ~ 铺得太大 do sth. on too large a scale

瘫 tān paralysis: 吓~了 be paralysed with fright

【瘫痪】 tānhuàn ① paralysis; palsy: ~病人 paralytic ② be paralysed; break down; be at a standstill: 交通运输陷于~。 Transportation was at a standstill.

【瘫软】 tānruǎn (of arms, legs, etc.) weak and limp

tán

坛 tán ① altar: 天~ the Temple of Heaven (in Beijing)/ 日~ the Altar to the Sun (in Beijing) ② a raised plot of land for planting flowers, etc.: 花~ (raised) flower bed ③ platform; forum: 讲~ speaker's platform ④ circles; world: 文~ the literary world; literary circles/ 棋~ chess circles ⑤ earthen jar; jug: 一~醋 a jar of vinegar/ 酒~ wine jug

【坛子】 tánzi earthen jar

昙 tán covered with clouds

【昙花】 tánhuā 〈植〉 broad-leaved epiphyllum (Epiphyllum oxypetalum)

【昙花一现】 tánhuā yī xiàn flower briefly as the broad-leaved epiphyllum; last briefly; be a flash in the pan: ~的人物 a transient figure

谈* tán ① talk; chat; discuss: 我们好好~~。 Let's have a good chat./ 我想同你们一一~文学创作问题。 I would like to discuss with you the question of creative writing./ ~得来 get along well ② what is said or talked about: 奇~ strange talk; fantastic tale/ 无稽之~ fantastic talk; sheer nonsense

【谈不到】 tánbudào out of the question: 没有政治上的独立，就~经济上的独立。 Without political independence, you can't begin to talk about economic independence. 又作 “谈不上”

【谈到】 tándào speak of; talk about; refer to: 他~我国工业发展的前景。 He talked about the prospects for industrial development in our country.

【谈锋】 tánfēng volubility; eloquence: ~甚健 talk volubly; be a good talker; have the gift of the gab

【谈何容易】 tán hé róngyì easier said than done; by no means easy

【谈虎色变】 tán hǔ sè biàn turn pale at the mention of a tiger; turn pale at the mere mention of something terrible

【谈话】 tánhuà ① conversation; talk; chat: 亲切友好的~ a cordial and friendly conversation ② statement: 发表书面~ make a written statement

【谈家常】 tán jiācháng talk about everyday matters; engage in small talk; chitchat

【谈论】 tánlùn discuss; talk about

【谈判】 tánpàn negotiations; talks: 举行~ hold talks; hold negotiations/ 开始~ enter into (或 open) negotiations with/ 贸易~ trade negotiations; trade talks/ 重开~ resume the talks/ ~中断。 The talks broke down. ◇ ~桌 conference table

【谈天】 tántiān chat; make conversation: ~说地 talk of everything under the sun

【谈吐】 tántǔ style of conversation

【谈笑风生】 tánxiào fēng shēng talk cheerfully and humorously

【谈笑自若】 tánxiào zìruò go on talking and laughing as if nothing had happened: 沉着镇静，~ go on talking and laughing without turning a hair

【谈心】 tánxīn heart-to-heart talk

弹* tán ① shoot (as with a catapult, etc.); send forth: ~石子 shoot pebbles with a catapult ② spring; leap: 跳 从篮板上~回来。 The ball rebounded from the backboard./ 从跳板上~起来 leap from the springboard ③ flick; flip: ~烟灰 flick the ash off a cigarette/ 把帽子上的灰尘 ~掉 flick the dust off a hat ④ fluff; tease: ~棉花 fluff (或 tease) cotton (with a bow) ⑤ play (a stringed musical instrument); pluck: ~钢琴 play the piano/ ~琵琶 pluck the pipa/ 老调重~ strike up a hackneyed tune; harp on the same old tune ⑥ elastic: ~性 elasticity ⑦ accuse; impeach: ~劾 impeach
另见 dàn

【弹劾】 tánhé impeach (a public official)

【弹簧】 tánhuáng spring: 回动~ return spring/ 保险~ relief spring ◇ ~秤 spring balance/ ~床 spring bed/ ~钢 spring steel/ ~锁 lock

【弹力】 tánlì elastic force; elasticity; resilience; spring: 失去~的橡皮圈 a perished rubber band

【弹跳】 tántiào bounce; spring: ~力好 have a lot of spring ◇ ~板 〈体〉 springboard

【弹性】 tánxìng elasticity; resilience; spring: 又软又有~的地毯 soft and springy carpets/ 这种毛~大，拉力强。 This wool possesses high resilience and tensile strength./ 球的~符合标准。 The balls reach the specifications for bounce.

【弹压】 tányā suppress; quell

【弹指】 tánzhǐ a snap of the fingers: ~之间 in a flash; in the twinkling of an eye; in an instant

【弹奏】 tánzòu play (a stringed musical instrument); pluck

覃 tán 〈书〉 deep: ~思 deep in thought

痰* tán phlegm; sputum

【痰盂】 tányú spittoon; cuspidor

谭 Tán a surname

潭 tán ① deep pool; pond: 一~死水 a pond of stagnant water/ 龙~虎穴 dragon's pool and tiger's den — a danger spot ② 〈方〉 pit; depression

檀 tán wingceltis

【檀板】 tánbǎn hardwood clappers

【檀香】 tánxiāng 〈植〉 white sandalwood; sandalwood ◇ ~木 sandalwood/ ~扇 sandalwood fan/ ~油 sandalwood oil

tǎn

忐 tǎn

【忐忑】 tǎntè perturbed; mentally disturbed: ~不安 uneasy; fidgety

坦* tǎn ① level; smooth: 平~ (of land, etc.) level; smooth ② calm; composed ③ open; candid

【坦白】 tǎnbái ① honest; frank; candid: ~对你说 to be frank with you; frankly speaking/ 襟怀~ honest and aboveboard ② confess; make a confession; own up (to):

彻底～交代 make a clean breast of (one's crimes)/ ～从宽,抗拒从严 leniency to those who confess their crimes and severity to those who refuse to

【坦荡】 tǎndàng ① (of a road, etc.) broad and level ② magnanimous; bighearted

【坦克】 tǎnkè tank

【坦然】 tǎnrán calm; unperturbed; having no misgivings: ～自若 calm and confident; completely at ease

【坦率】 tǎnshuài candid; frank; straightforward: 为人～ frank and open/ ～地交换意见 have a frank exchange of views

【坦途】 tǎntú level road; highway: 攀登科学高峰,既无捷径,又无～。There are neither shortcuts nor easy paths to the heights of science.

袒 tǎn ① leave (the upper part of the body) uncovered; be stripped to the waist or have one's shirt unbuttoned: ～胸露臂 (of a woman) exposing one's neck and shoulders; *décolleté* ② give unprincipled protection to; shield; shelter: 偏～ give unprincipled support to; be partial to

【袒护】 tǎnhù give unprincipled protection to; be partial to; shield: ～一方 be partial to one side/ 公然～ openly shield/ 你别～他。Don't make excuses for him.

毯 tǎn blanket; rug; carpet: 毛～ woollen blanket/ 绒～ flannelette blanket/ 地～ rug; carpet/ 挂～ tapestry

【毯子】 tǎnzi blanket

tàn

叹* tàn ① sigh: 长～一声 heave a deep sigh ② exclaim in admiration; acclaim; praise: 赞～ highly praise; sigh in admiration/ ～为奇迹 admire and praise sth. as a wonderful achievement

【叹词】 tàncí 〈语〉 interjection; exclamation

【叹服】 tànfú gasp in admiration: 令人～ compel (或 command) admiration

【叹气】 tànqì sigh; heave a sigh: 唉声～ sigh in despair

【叹赏】 tànshǎng admire; express admiration for

【叹为观止】 tàn wéi guān zhǐ acclaim (a work of art, etc.) as the acme of perfection

【叹息】 tànxī 〈书〉 heave a sigh; sigh

炭* tàn charcoal: 木～ charcoal/ 烧～ make charcoal

【炭笔】 tànbǐ charcoal pencil

【炭画】 tànhuà 〈美术〉 charcoal drawing; charcoal

【炭火】 tànhuǒ charcoal fire

探* tàn ① try to find out; explore; sound: 试～ sound out; put out a feeler/ ～路 explore the way ② scout; spy; detective: 敌～ enemy scout/ 侦～ detective ③ visit; pay a call on: ～亲访友 visit one's relatives and friends ④ stretch forward: 有人从门口一～进头来。Somebody popped his head in at the door./ 行车时不要～身窗外。Don't lean out of the window while the bus is in motion.

【探测】 tàncè survey; sound; probe: ～海底情况 survey the seabed/ ～水深 take soundings/ ～悬崖高度 gauge the height of a bluff ◇ ～器 sounder; probe; detector

【探访】 tànfǎng ① seek by inquiry or search: ～民间秘方 seek out secret medicinal recipes from among the people ② pay a visit to; visit

【探监】 tànjiān visit a prisoner

【探井】 tànjǐng ① 〈矿〉 prospect (或 test) pit; exploring (或 exploratory) shaft ② 〈石油〉 test well; exploratory well

【探究】 tànjiū make a thorough inquiry; probe into: ～原因 look into the causes

【探口气】 tàn kǒuqi ascertain (或 find out) sb.'s opinions or feelings; sound sb. out

【探明】 tànmíng ascertain; verify: 已～的煤储量 proven (或 known) coal deposits/ 新油田的含油层结构已经～。The oil-bearing structure of the new oilfield has been verified.

【探囊取物】 tàn náng qǔ wù like taking something out of one's pocket — as easy as winking; as easy as falling off a log

【探亲】 tànqīn go home to visit one's family or go to visit one's relatives: 到故乡～访友 return to one's homeland to visit one's relatives and friends ◇ ～假 home leave

【探求】 tànqiú seek; pursue; search after (或 for): ～真理 seek truth

【探视】 tànshì visit: ～病人 visit a patient ◇ ～时间 visiting hours (in a hospital)

【探索】 tànsuǒ explore; probe: ～宇宙的秘密 probe (或 explore) the secrets of the universe/ 星际～ interplanetary exploration/ ～事物的本质 probe into the essence of things/ ～真理 seek truth/ 对一些具体政策问题,应当继续考察和～。We must further investigate and study certain specific policies.

【探讨】 tàntǎo inquire into; probe into: 从不同角度对问题进行～ approach a subject from different angles/ 对针麻原理作进一步的～ go further into the principles governing acupuncture anaesthesia/ ～性的访问 an exploratory visit

【探听】 tàntīng try to find out; make inquiries: ～下落 inquire about the whereabouts of sb. or sth./ ～消息 make inquiries about sb. or sth.; fish for information/ ～人家的私事 pry into other people's private affairs/ ～虚实 try to find out about an opponent, adversary, etc.; try to ascertain the strength of the enemy

【探头探脑】 tàntóu-tànnǎo pop one's head in and look about

【探望】 tànwàng ① look about: 她不时向窗外～。She looked out the window every now and then. ② visit: 回国～亲友 return to one's home country to visit relatives and friends

【探问】 tànwèn ① make cautious inquiries about: 他们一再～此事。They inquired about the matter time and again. ② inquire after

【探悉】 tànxī ascertain; learn; find out: 从有关方面～ learn from those concerned

【探险】 tànxiǎn explore; make explorations; venture into the unknown: 到原始森林去～ explore a primeval forest ◇ ～队 exploring (或 exploration) party; expedition/ ～家 explorer

【探照灯】 tànzhàodēng searchlight: ～的灯光 searchlight beam

【探子】 tànzi ① scout ② a thin tube used to extract samples of food grains, etc.

碳 tàn 〈化〉 carbon (C)

【碳黑】 tànhēi 〈化〉 carbon black

tāng

汤* tāng ① hot water; boiling water: 温～浸种 hot-water treatment of seeds ② 〔多用于地名〕 hot springs ③ soup; broth: 清～ clear soup; *consommé*/ 鸡～ chicken soup/ 肉～ broth/ 姜～ ginger tea/ 三菜一～ soup and three other courses

【汤匙】 tāngchí tablespoon; soupspoon

【汤面】 tāngmiàn noodles in soup

【汤碗】 tāngwǎn soup bowl

【汤圆】 tāngyuán stuffed dumplings made of glutinous rice flour served in soup

蹚 tāng wade; ford: ～水过河 wade (across) a stream/ ～了一脚泥 get one's feet muddy through wading

táng

唐 Táng the Tang Dynasty (618-907): ～诗 Tang poetry

【唐人街】 Tángrénjiē Chinatown

【唐突】 tángtū brusque; rude; offensive: 出言～ make a blunt remark/ ～的行动 a presumptuous act

堂* táng ① the main room of a house ② a hall (或 room) for a specific purpose: 课～ class room/ 食～ dining hall/ 澡～ bathhouse ③ court of law; a principal hall in a *yamen*: 过～ have a hearing; be tried ④ relationship between cousins, etc. of the same paternal grandfather or great-grandfather; of the same clan: 兄 弟 cousins on the paternal side; cousins ⑤〈量〉: 一～家具 a set (或 suite) of furniture/ 每天上四～课 have four classes every day

【堂皇】 tánghuáng grand; stately; magnificent: 富丽～ beautiful and imposing; in majestic splendour; resplendent

【堂堂】 tángtáng ① dignified; impressive: 仪表～ dignified in appearance; impressive-looking ② (of a man) having high aspirations and boldness of vision ③ imposing; awe-inspiring; formidable: ～之阵 an imposing array of troops; awe-inspiring military strength

【堂堂正正】 tángtángzhèngzhèng ① impressive or dignified in personal appearance ② open and aboveboard

棠 táng
【棠棣】 tángdì〈植〉① Chinese bush cherry ② a kind of white poplar

塘* táng ① dyke; embankment: 河～ river embankment/ 海～ seawall ② pool; pond: 鱼～ fish pond ③ hot-water bathing pool: 澡～ bathhouse; public baths

搪 táng ① ward off; keep out: ～风 keep out the wind/ ～饥 allay one's hunger ② evade; do sth. perfunctorily: ～帐 put off a creditor

【搪塞】 tángsè stall sb. off; do sth. perfunctorily: ～他几句 stall him off with a vague answer/ ～差事 perform a duty perfunctorily

膛 táng ① thorax; chest: 胸～ chest/ 杀猪开～ slit a pig's throat and cut open its chest ② an enclosed space inside sth.; chamber: 炉～ stove chamber/ 枪～ bore (of a gun)/ 子弹上了～。The gun is loaded.

糖* táng ① sugar: 白～ refined sugar/ 砂～ granulated sugar; 红～ brown sugar; 冰～ crystal sugar; rock candy ② sugared; in syrup: ～姜 sugared ginger; ginger in syrup/ ～蒜 garlic in syrup; sweetened garlic ③ sweets; candy

【糖厂】 tángchǎng sugar refinery
【糖果】 tángguǒ sweets; candy; sweetmeats ◇ ～店 sweet shop; candy store; confectionery
【糖浆】 tángjiāng syrup
【糖精】 tángjīng saccharin; gluside
【糖尿病】 tángnlàobìng diabetes ◇ ～患者 diabetic
【糖水】 tángshuǐ syrup: ～桔子(荔枝) tangerines (lichees) in syrup
【糖衣】 tángyī sugarcoating: 这种药片有～。These pills are sugarcoated.

镗 táng〈机〉boring
【镗床】 tángchuáng〈机〉boring machine; boring lathe; borer: 坐标～ jig boring machine
【镗刀】 tángdāo〈机〉boring cutter; boring tool
【镗孔】 tángkǒng〈机〉bore hole; boring

螳 táng mantis
【螳臂当车】 táng bì dāng chē a mantis trying to stop a chariot — overrate oneself and try to hold back an overwhelmingly superior force
【螳螂】 tángláng〈动〉mantis
【螳螂捕蝉，黄雀在后】 tángláng bǔ chán, huángquè zài hòu the mantis stalks the cicada, unaware of the oriole behind — covet gains ahead without being aware of danger behind

tǎng

帑 tǎng〈书〉state treasury; funds in the state treasury: 公～ public funds

倘 tǎng〈连〉if; supposing; in case: ～有不测 in case of accidents; if anything untoward should happen
【倘若】 tǎngruò〈连〉if; supposing; in case: ～发现情况，立即报告。In case you find anything unusual, report immediately.
【倘使】 tǎngshǐ 见"倘若"

淌 tǎng drip; shed; trickle: ～眼泪 shed tears/ ～口水 let saliva dribble from the mouth; slaver; slobber/ 伤口～血。Blood trickled from the wound./ 他脸上～着汗水。Sweat was dripping from his face./ 木桶漏水，～了一地。The pail leaked, so water ran all over the place.

躺* tǎng lie; recline: ～下歇歇 lie down and rest a while/ 不要～在过去的成绩上睡大觉。Don't rest content with past achievements. 或 Don't rest on your laurels.
【躺倒】 tǎngdǎo lie down: ～不干 stay in bed — refuse to shoulder responsibilities any longer
【躺椅】 tǎngyǐ deck chair; sling chair

tàng

烫* tàng ① scald; burn: 让开水～着了 be scalded by boiling water/ ～了个泡 get a blister through being scalded (或 burnt)/ 热得～手 so hot that it burns (或 scalds) one's hand; scalding to the touch ② heat up in hot water; warm: ～酒 heat wine (by putting the container in hot water)/ ～澡 take a hot bath/ ～脚 bathe one's feet in hot water ③ very hot; scalding; boiling hot: 这汤真～! This soup is boiling hot! ④ iron; press: ～衣服 iron (或 press) clothes ⑤ perm; have one's hair permed: 冷～ cold wave/ 到理发店去～发 go to the hairdresser's for a perm
【烫发】 tàngfà give or have a permanent wave; perm
【烫金】 tàngjīn〈印〉gilding; bronzing: 布面～ cloth gilt
【烫伤】 tàngshāng〈医〉scald

趟 tàng ①〈量〉〔表示走动的次数〕: 到昆明去了一～ have been to Kunming once; have made a trip to Kunming/ 这辆卡车昨天往工地跑了三～。Yesterday the truck made three trips to the construction site.

tāo

叨 tāo be favoured with; get the benefit of
另见 dāo
【叨光】 tāoguāng〈套〉much obliged to you
【叨教】 tāojiào〈套〉many thanks for your advice
【叨扰】 tāorǎo〈套〉thank you for your hospitality

涛 tāo great waves; billows: 惊～骇浪 terrifying crashing waves/ 松～ the soughing of the wind in the pines

掏 tāo ① draw out; pull out; fish out: 从口袋里～出笔记本 pull a notebook from one's pocket; take a notebook out of one's pocket/ ～手枪 draw a pistol/ ～炉灰 clear the ashes from a stove/ ～鸟窝 take young birds or eggs out of a nest; go bird's-nesting/ ～耳朵 pick one's ears ② dig (a hole, etc.); hollow out; scoop out: 在墙上～一个洞 make a hole in the wall ③ steal from sb.'s pocket: 他的皮夹子被～了。He had his wallet stolen by a pickpocket.
【掏腰包】 tāo yāobāo〈口〉① pay out of one's own pocket; foot a bill: 这顿饭我～。This meal is on me. ② pick sb.'s pocket

滔 tāo inundate; flood
【滔滔】 tāotāo ① torrential; surging: 白浪～ whitecaps surging ② keeping up a constant flow of words: 口若悬河，～不绝 talk on and on in a flow of eloquence
【滔天】 tāotiān ① (of billows, etc.) dash to the skies: 波浪～ waves running high ② heinous; monstrous: ～罪行 monstrous crimes

韬 tāo 〈书〉① sheath or bow case ② hide; conceal ③ the art of war

【韬光养晦】 tāoguāng-yǎnghuì hide one's capacities and bide one's time

【韬晦】 tāohuì conceal one's true features or intentions; lie low

【韬略】 tāolüè military strategy

táo

逃* táo ① run away; escape; flee: ~出敌人监狱 escape from the enemy's prison/ 敌军望风而~. The enemy fled pell-mell before our army. ② evade; dodge; shirk; escape: ~债 dodge a creditor/ 罪责难~ cannot shirk responsibility for the crime

【逃奔】 táobèn run away to (another place)

【逃避】 táobì escape; evade; shirk: ~现实 try to escape reality/ ~责任 shirk responsibility

【逃兵】 táobīng army deserter; deserter

【逃窜】 táocuàn run away; flee in disorder: 敌军狼狈~. The enemy troops fled helter-skelter.

【逃遁】 táodùn flee; escape; evade: 仓皇~ flee in panic

【逃犯】 táofàn escaped criminal or convict

【逃荒】 táohuāng flee from famine; get away from a famine-stricken area

【逃命】 táomìng run (或 flee, fly) for one's life

【逃难】 táonàn flee from a calamity; be a refugee

【逃匿】 táonì escape and hide; go into hiding

【逃跑】 táopǎo run away; flee; take flight; take to one's heels

【逃散】 táosàn become separated in flight

【逃生】 táoshēng flee (或 run, fly) for one's life; escape with one's life: 死里~ barely escape with one's life; have a narrow escape; escape by the skin of one's teeth

【逃税】 táoshuì evade (或 dodge) a tax

【逃脱】 táotuō succeed in escaping; make good one's escape; get clear of: ~责任 succeed in evading responsibility

【逃亡】 táowáng become a fugitive; flee from home; go into exile

【逃学】 táoxué play truant; cut class

【逃逸】 táoyì 〈书〉 escape; run away; abscond

【逃之夭夭】 táo zhī yāoyāo decamp; make one's getaway; show a clean pair of heels

【逃走】 táozǒu run away; flee; take flight; take to one's heels

桃* táo peach

【桃符】 táofú ① peach wood charms against evil, hung on the gate on the lunar New Year's Eve in ancient times ② Spring Festival couplets

【桃脯】 táofǔ preserved peach

【桃红】 táohóng pink

【桃花】 táohuā peach blossom

【桃李】 táolǐ peaches and plums — one's pupils or disciples: ~满天下 have pupils everywhere

【桃树】 táoshù peach (tree)

【桃子】 táozi peach

陶* táo ① pottery; earthenware: ~俑 pottery figurine/ 彩~ painted pottery ② make pottery ③ cultivate; mould; educate: 熏~ exert a gradual, uplifting influence on; nurture ④ contented; happy: 乐~~ feel happy and contented

【陶瓷】 táocí pottery and porcelain; ceramics ◇ ~工 potter/ ~片 〈考古〉 potsherd/ ~学 ceramics/ ~业 ceramics; ceramic industry

【陶器】 táoqì pottery; earthenware

【陶然】 táorán happy and carefree

【陶冶】 táoyě ① make pottery and smelt metal ② exert a favourable influence (on a person's character, etc.); mould: ~性情 mould a person's temperament

【陶醉】 táozuì be intoxicated (with success, etc.); revel in:

自我~ be intoxicated with self-satisfaction/ 我们不能~于已取得的成绩. We mustn't let success go to our heads.

淘* táo ① wash in a pan or basket: ~米 wash rice ② clean out; dredge: ~阴沟 clean out a drain (或 sewer) ③ 〈方〉 naughty

【淘金】 táojīn 〈矿〉 panning

【淘气】 táoqì naughty; mischievous ◇ ~鬼 mischievous imp; a regular little mischief

【淘汰】 táotài ① eliminate through selection or competition: 他在第一轮比赛中就被~了. He was eliminated in the very first round. ② die out; fall into disuse: 这种机器已经~了. This kind of machine is already obsolete. ◇ ~赛 elimination series

萄* táo grapes: ~酒 grape wine

啕 táo 见"号啕" háotáo

tǎo

讨* tǎo ① send armed forces to suppress; send a punitive expedition against: ~平叛乱 put down a rebellion ② denounce; condemn: 声~ denounce ③ demand; ask for; beg for: ~帐 demand the payment of a debt; dun/ 去跟老张~点墨汁. Go and ask Lao Zhang for some Chinese ink. ④ marry (a woman): ~老婆 take a wife; get married ⑤ incur; invite: ~了个没趣儿 court a rebuff; ask for a snub/ 自~苦吃 bring trouble upon oneself; ask for trouble/ ~人喜欢 likable; cute ⑥ discuss; study: 商~ discuss

【讨伐】 tǎofá send armed forces to suppress; send a punitive expedition against

【讨饭】 tǎofàn beg for food; be a beggar

【讨好】 tǎohǎo ① ingratiate oneself with; fawn on; toady to; curry favour with ② 〔多用于否定〕 be rewarded with a fruitful result; have one's labour rewarded: 费力不~ put in much hard work, but get very little result; undertake a thankless task

【讨还】 tǎohuán get sth. back

【讨价】 tǎojià ask (或 name) a price

【讨价还价】 tǎojià-huánjià bargain; haggle

【讨教】 tǎojiào ask for advice

【讨论】 tǎolùn discuss; talk over: 参加~ join in the discussion

【讨论会】 tǎolùnhuì discussion; symposium: 科学~ science symposium

【讨便宜】 tǎo piányi seek undue advantage; try to gain sth. at the expense of others; look for a bargain

【讨乞】 tǎoqǐ beg alms; beg

【讨巧】 tǎoqiǎo act artfully to get what one wants; get the best for oneself at the least expense; choose the easy way out

【讨亲】 tǎoqīn 〈方〉 take a wife; get married

【讨情】 tǎoqíng 〈方〉 plead for sb.; beg sb. off: ~告饶 plead for leniency; beg for pardon

【讨饶】 tǎoráo beg for mercy; ask for forgiveness

【讨厌】 tǎoyàn ① disagreeable; disgusting; repugnant: ~的天气 abominable weather ② hard to handle; troublesome; nasty: 气管炎是很~的病. Tracheitis is a nasty illness. ③ dislike; loathe; be disgusted with: 工人们很~他那官僚架子. The workers detest his bureaucratic airs.

tào

套* tào ① sheath; case; cover; sleeve: 枕~ pillowcase; pillowslip/ 毛笔~ cap of a writing brush/ 椅~ slipcover for a chair/ 轴~ axle sleeve/ 手枪~ holster ② cover with; slip over; encase in: ~上一件毛衣 slip on a sweater/ 把枕套~上 put the pillow in the pillowcase ③ that which covers (other garments, etc.): ~袖 oversleeve/ ~鞋 over-

shoes ④ overlap; interlink: 一环～一环 one ring linked with another — a closely linked succession ⑤ the bend of a river or curve in a mountain range: 河～ the Great Bend of the Huanghe River ⑥ 〈方〉cotton padding (或 wadding); batting: 被～ cotton padding of a quilt; quilt padding ⑦ traces; harness: 牲口～ harness for a draught animal; 雇～ hire a draught animal and a plough/ 拉～ pull a plough or cart ⑧ harness (an animal); hitch up (an animal to a cart): 我去～牲口。I'll go and harness the beast. ⑨ knot; loop; noose: 栓个～儿 tie a knot; make a loop/ 活～儿 slipknot; running knot ⑩ put a ring, etc. round; tie: ～上救生圈 put on a life ring/ ～马 lasso a horse ⑪ model on (或 after); copy: 生搬硬～ apply mechanically; copy indiscriminately/ ～公式 apply a formula/ 这一段是从现成文章上～下来的。This passage is modelled on one in another article. ⑫ convention; formula: 客～ polite remarks; civilities; pleasantries/ 老一～ the same old stuff; stereotype ⑬ coax a secret out of sb.; pump sb. about sth.: 拿话～他 coax the secret out of him; trick him into telling the truth ⑭ try to win (sb.'s friendship): ～交情 try to get in good with sb. ⑮ 〈量〉set; suit; suite: 两～衣服 two suits of clothes. 一～房间 a flat
【套衫】tàoshān pullover
【套索】tàosuǒ lasso; noose
【套问】tàowèn find out by asking seemingly casual questions; tactfully sound sb. out
【套用】tàoyòng apply mechanically; use indiscriminately: 不能每处～这个公式。This formula cannot be applied indiscriminately.
【套语】tàoyǔ polite formula
【套子】tàozi ① sheath; case; cover: 照相机～ camera case/ 沙发～ sofa cover/ 唱片～ (gramophone) record sleeve ② conventional (或 stereotyped) remark; conventionality ③ 〈方〉cotton padding (或 wadding); batting

tè

忒 tè 〈书〉error; mistake: 差～ error

忑 tè 见"忐忑" tǎntè

特* tè ① special; particular; unusual; exceptional: ～使 special envoy/ 奇～ peculiar; quaint ② for a special purpose; specially: ～为此事而来 come specially for this purpose ③ secret agent; spy: 敌～ enemy agent/ 防～ guard against enemy agents ④ very; especially: 这个医生扎针～灵。That doctor is very good at giving needle treatment. ⑤ 〈书〉but; only: 不～如此 not only that
【特别】tèbié ① special; particular; out of the ordinary: 没什么～的地方 nothing out of the ordinary/ 他的口音很～。He has a peculiar accent. ② especially; particularly: 工作～努力 be especially hardworking/ 建设一支～能战斗的队伍 train a contingent of especially good fighters/ 质量～好 be of extra fine quality/ 这里最需要医务人员,～是外科医生。We're very much in need of medical workers, especially surgeons. ③ going out of one's way to (do sth.); specially: 老祖母～为伤员燉了一只鸡。Granny cooked a chicken especially for the wounded soldier. ◇ ～会议 special meeting; special session/ ～开支 special expenses/ ～快车 express train; express
【特产】tèchǎn special local product; speciality; specialty: 东北～ specialities (或 special local products) of the Northeast
【特长】tècháng what one is skilled in; strong point; speciality: 他有什么～? What is he skilled in?/ 绘画不是他的～。Painting is not his strong point./ 发挥每个人的～ give scope to everyone's special skill
【特出】tèchū outstanding; prominent; extraordinary: ～的成绩 outstanding achievements/ ～的作用 a prominent role
【特此】tècǐ 〔公文、书信用语〕: 定于明天上午八点在礼堂开会,～通知。It is hereby announced that there will be a meeting in the auditorium at 8 tomorrow morning.

【特大】tèdà especially (或 exceptionally) big; the most: ～喜讯 excellent news; most welcome news/ ～丰收 an exceptional bumper harvest
【特等】tèděng special grade (或 class); top grade ◇ ～舱 〈交〉stateroom; de luxe cabin
【特地】tèdì 〈副〉for a special purpose; specially
【特点】tèdiǎn characteristic; distinguishing feature; peculiarity; trait: 生理～ physiological characteristics/ 照顾妇女的～ pay attention to the special needs of women/ 这个厂的产品具有工艺精湛,经久耐用的～。The products of this factory are noted for their fine workmanship and durability.
【特定】tèdìng ① specially designated (或 appointed): ～的人选 a person specially designated for a post ② specific; specified; given: 在～的条件下 under given (或 specified) conditions/ 这种钢有～的用途。This kind of steel is used for special purposes.
【特工】tègōng secret service ◇ ～人员 special agent; secret service personnel
【特惠关税】tèhuì guānshuì preferential tariff
【特级】tèjí special grade (或 class); superfine: ～茉莉花茶 superfine jasmine tea
【特急】tèjí extra urgent ◇ ～电 extra urgent telegram; flash message
【特辑】tèjí ① special number (或 issue) of a periodical ② a special collection of short films
【特技】tèjì ① stunt; trick ② 〈电影〉special effects ◇ ～飞行 〈军〉stunt flying; aerobatics/ ～镜头 trick shot/ ～摄影 trick photography/ ～跳伞 trick parachuting
【特价】tèjià special offer; bargain price: ～出售 sell at a bargain price
【特刊】tèkān special issue (或 number); special: 国庆～ special National Day issue
【特快】tèkuài 〈交〉express
【特例】tèlì special case
【特命全权公使】tèmìng quánquán gōngshǐ envoy extraordinary and minister plenipotentiary
【特派】tèpài specially appointed ◇ ～记者 special correspondent; accredited journalist
【特遣部队】tèqiǎn bùduì task force
【特权】tèquán privilege; prerogative: ～地位 privileged position/ 外交～ diplomatic privileges/ 不把职权变～ not use one's power to seek privileges/ ～阶层 privileged stratum/ ～思想 the idea that prerogatives and privileges go with position; the "special privilege" mentality
【特色】tèsè characteristic; distinguishing feature (或 quality): 艺术～ artistic characteristics/ 富有民族～的歌舞节目 songs and dances with distinctive national features/ 象牙雕刻的传统～ the traditional features of ivory carving
【特设】tèshè ad hoc: ～委员会 ad hoc committee
【特赦】tèshè ① special pardon ② special amnesty: ～战犯 grant a special amnesty to war criminals ◇ ～令 decree (或 writ) of special pardon or amnesty
【特使】tèshǐ special envoy
【特殊】tèshū special; particular; peculiar; exceptional: ～条件下的～产物 a special product of special conditions/ ～情况 an exceptional case; special circumstances
【特殊性】tèshūxìng particularity; peculiarity; specific characteristics: 那个地区有它的～。That region has its specific characteristics.
【特为】tèwèi for a special purpose; specially; going out of one's way to (do sth.): 我～来请你们去帮忙。I've come specially to ask you for help.
【特务】tèwu special (或 secret) agent; spy ◇ ～活动 espionage/ ～机关 secret service; espionage agency/ ～组织 secret service; spy organization
【特效】tèxiào specially good effect; special efficacy ◇ ～药 specific drug; special; effective cure
【特写】tèxiě ① feature article or story; feature ② 〈电影〉close-up ◇ ～镜头 close-up (shot)
【特性】tèxìng specific property (或 characteristic)
【特许】tèxǔ special permission ◇ ～证书 special permit; letters patent

【特邀】 tèyāo specially invite ◇ ～代表 specially invited representative

【特异】 tèyì ① exceptionally good; excellent; superfine: 成绩～ an excellent record (或 performance); extraordinary results ② peculiar; distinctive: ～的风格 distinctive style

【特有】 tèyǒu peculiar; characteristic: 表现出青年～的热情 display the characteristic enthusiasm of youth/ 这是广东人～的一种说法。This is an expression peculiar to people from Guangdong.

【特约】 tèyuē engage by special arrangement ◇ ～稿 special contribution (to a publication)/ ～记者 special correspondent

【特征】 tèzhēng characteristic; feature; trait: 面部～ facial characteristics/ 地理～ geographical features/ 民族～ national traits

【特种】 tèzhǒng special type; particular kind

tēng

腾 tēng 〈象〉: 他～地一声跳到台上。He leaped on to the platform with a thump.
另见 téng

téng

疼* téng ① ache; pain; sore: 头～ have a headache/ 胃～ have a stomachache/ 嗓子～ have a sore throat/ 腿～ have a pain in the leg/ 浑身都～ be aching all over/ 你那个牙还～吗? Does your tooth still hurt? ② love dearly; be fond of; dote on: 奶奶最～小孙子。Granny dotes on her little grandson.

【疼爱】 téng'ài be very fond of; love dearly

【疼痛】 téngtòng pain; ache; soreness

誊 téng transcribe; copy out: 照底稿～一份 make a clean copy of the draft

【誊录】 ténglù transcribe; copy out: ～文稿 copy out a manuscript

【誊清】 téngqīng make a fair copy of ◇ ～稿 fair copy

【誊写】 téngxiě transcribe; copy out

腾 téng ① gallop; jump; prance: ～跃 prance/ ～身而过 jump over sth. ② rise; soar: 升～ rise; ascend/ 飞～ soar ③ make room; clear out; vacate: ～出自己的房子给客人住 vacate one's own room to put up a visitor ④〔用在某些动词后面，表示反复〕: 翻～ toss about; turn over and over/ 扑～ (of the heart) throb
另见 tēng

【腾贵】 téngguì (of prices) shoot up; soar; skyrocket

【腾空】 téngkōng soar; rise high into the air; rise to the sky: 五彩缤纷的礼花～而起。Colourful fireworks shot into the sky.

【腾腾】 téngténg steaming; seething: 热气～ steaming hot; seething with activity/ 烟雾～ hazy with smoke; smoke-laden/ 烈焰～ raging flames/ 杀气～ full of bellicosity; murderous-looking

【腾越】 téngyuè jump over: ～障碍 jump over obstacles

【腾云驾雾】 téngyún-jiàwù ① mount the clouds and ride the mist — speed across the sky ② feel giddy

滕 Téng a surname

藤 téng ① cane; rattan: ～制品 rattan work/ ～椅 cane chair; rattan chair/ ～盔 rattan helmet ② vine: 葡萄～ grape vine/ 西瓜～ watermelon vine

【藤条】 téngtiáo rattan

【藤子】 téngzi 〈口〉 vine

tī

体 tī
另见 tǐ

【体己】 tǐji ① intimate; confidential: ～话 things one says only to one's intimates ② 〈旧〉 private savings: ～钱 private savings of a family member

剔 tī ① clean with a pointed instrument; pick: ～骨头 pick a bone/ ～牙 pick one's teeth ② pick out and throw away; reject: 把烂梨～出去 pick out the rotten pears ③ rising stroke (in Chinese characters)

【剔除】 tīchú reject; get rid of: 吸取精华，～糟粕 absorb the essence and reject the dross

梯* tī ① ladder; steps; stairs: 楼～ staircase/ 电～ lift; elevator ② shaped like a staircase; terraced: ～田 terraced fields

【梯级】 tījí stair; step

【梯田】 tītián 〈农〉 terraced fields; terrace: 修～ build terraced fields; terrace mountain slopes

【梯形】 tīxíng ① ladder-shaped ② 〈数〉 (美) trapezoid; (英) trapezium

【梯子】 tīzi ladder; stepladder

踢* tī ① kick: ～开绊脚石 kick away a stumbling block/ 一脚把门～开 open the door with a kick; kick the door open/ 把凳子～翻 kick over a stool/ 小心这马～人! Be careful! This horse kicks. ② play (football); kick: ～足球 play football/ ～进一个球 kick (或 score) a goal/ 他～中锋。He plays centre forward.

【踢皮球】 tī píqiú ① kick a ball; play children's football ② kick sth. back and forth like a ball; pass the buck

tí

提* tí ① carry (in one's hand with the arm down): 手里～着篮子 carry a basket in one's hand ② lift; raise; promote: 这种自行车十分轻便，一只手就能～起来。This bicycle is very light. You can lift it with one hand./ 从井里～水 draw water from a well/ ～价 raise the price/ 把问题～到原则高度来分析 analyse a problem from the high plane of principle/ ～前 shift to an earlier time; move up a date: 会议日期～前了。The date of the meeting has been moved up. ③ put forward; bring up; raise: ～问题 ask a question/ ～意见 make a criticism; make comments or suggestions/ ～抗议 lodge a protest/ ～条件 put forward conditions/ ～要求 make demands/ ～方案 suggest (或 propose) plans ⑤ draw (或 take) out; extract: ～款 draw money/ ～炼 extract and purify; refine ⑥ mention; refer to; bring up: 别再～那件事了。Don't bring that up again.
另见 dī

【提案】 tí'àn motion; proposal; draft resolution ◇ ～国 sponsor country (of a resolution); sponsor

【提拔】 tíbá promote: ～某人担任领导工作 promote sb. to a position of leadership

【提包】 tíbāo handbag; shopping bag; bag; valise

【提倡】 tíchàng advocate; promote; encourage; recommend: ～晚婚和计划生育 advocate late marriage and family planning/ ～勤俭建国 spread the idea of building our country through diligence and thrift

【提出】 tíchū put forward; advance; pose; raise: ～建议 put forward a proposal; make a suggestion/ ～一种新的理论 advance a new theory/ ～程序问题 raise a point of order/ ～警告 give (或 serve) a warning/ ～抗议 lodge a protest/ 向自己～更高的要求 set a still higher demand on oneself

【提单】 tídān bill of lading (B/L): 直达～ direct bill of lading/ 联运～ through bill of lading

【提法】 tífǎ the way sth. is put; formulation; wording: 他们不同意你对这个问题的～。They take exception to the way you put the question./ 这是个新的～。This is a new formulation./ 这只是个～问题。This is just a matter of wording.

【提纲】 tígāng outline: 写发言～ make an outline for a speech

【提纲挈领】 tígāng-qièlǐng take a net by the headrope or a coat by the collar — concentrate on the main points; bring out the essentials: 我来~地谈一谈。 I'll just touch briefly on the essentials.

【提高】 tígāo raise; heighten; enhance; increase; improve: ~水位 raise the water level/ ~警惕 enhance (或 heighten) one's vigilance/ ~认识 deepen one's understanding/ ~勇气 pluck up one's courage/ ~部队的战斗力 increase the combat effectiveness of the troops/ ~工作效率 raise working efficiency/ ~单位面积产量 raise the per unit yield/ ~产品质量 improve the quality of products/ 人民生活水平逐年~ The living standards of the people rise year by year.

【提供】 tígōng provide; supply; furnish; offer: 为轻工业~原料 supply light industry with raw materials/ ~援助 give aid; provide assistance/ ~贷款 offer a loan/ ~新的证据 furnish fresh evidence/ 历史给我们~了有益的经验教训。 History affords us useful lessons.

【提货】 tíhuò pick up goods; take delivery of goods: 到火车站~ pick up goods at the railway station/ 请于三日内来车站~。 Please take delivery of the goods at the station within three days. ◇ ~单 bill of lading (B/L)

【提交】 tíjiāo submit (a problem, etc.) to; refer to: 将决议草案~大会讨论 submit the draft resolution to the congress for discussion

【提款】 tíkuǎn draw money (from a bank)

【提炼】 tíliàn extract and purify; abstract; refine: 从矿石中~金属 extract (或 abstract) metal from ore/ ~蔗糖 refine cane sugar

【提名】 tímíng nominate: ~某人为代表 nominate sb. for representative

【提起】 tíqǐ ① mention; speak of ② raise; arouse; brace up: ~精神 raise one's spirits; brace oneself up/ ~人们的注意 call (或 arouse) people's attention

【提前】 tíqián ① shift to an earlier date; move up (a date); advance: 总攻的时间~了。 The time for the general offensive has been moved up. ② in advance; ahead of time; beforehand: 明天要是割麦子，请~通知我们。 If we are going to cut wheat tomorrow, please notify us in advance./ ~两个月完成全年生产指标 meet the year's production target two months ahead of time/ ~释放战犯 release war criminals before their sentences expire/ ~召开大会 convene the congress before the due date

【提挈】 tíqiè 〈书〉① lead; take with one; marshal: ~全军 marshal all one's forces ② guide and support; give guidance and help to

【提琴】 tíqín the violin family: 小~ violin/ 中~ viola/ 大~ violoncello; cello/ 低音~ double bass; contrabass

小提琴　中提琴　大提琴

【提请】 tíqǐng submit sth. to: ~大会批准 submit to the congress for approval/ ~大家注意 call everybody's attention to sth.

【提取】 tíqǔ ① draw; pick up; collect: ~银行存款 draw money from a bank; withdraw bank deposits/ 到车站~行李 pick up (或 collect) one's luggage at the railway station ② extract; abstract; recover: 从油页岩中~石油 extract oil from shale/ 从废水中~有用物质 recover useful materials from waste water

【提神】 tíshén refresh oneself; give oneself a lift: 喝杯茶提神 refresh oneself with a cup of tea

【提审】 tíshěn ① bring (a prisoner) before the court; bring (sb. in custody) to trial; fetch (a detainee) for interrogation ② review (a case tried by a lower court)

【提升】 tíshēng ① promote: ~他当排长 promote him to be platoon leader ② hoist; elevate ◇ ~机 hoist; elevator

【提示】 tíshì point out; prompt: 请把学习重点向大家一下。 Please brief us on the main points to be studied./ 如果她忘了台词，你就给她~一下。 Prompt her if she forgets her lines.

【提问】 tíwèn put questions to; quiz: 回答老师的~ answer the teacher's questions

【提携】 tíxié ① lead (a child) by the hand ② guide and support; give guidance and help to

【提心吊胆】 tíxīn-diàodǎn have one's heart in one's mouth; be on tenterhooks

【提醒】 tíxǐng remind; warn; call attention to: 如果我忘了，请你~我一下。 Please remind me in case I should forget./ ~他早点儿来。 Remind him to come early./ 司机在这一带要低速行驶。 Warn the driver to drive slowly in this area.

【提要】 tíyào précis; summary; abstract; epitome; synopsis: 本书内容~ capsule summary (of the book)

【提议】 tíyì ① propose; suggest; move: 我~为两国人民的友谊干杯。 I propose a toast to the friendship between the peoples of the two countries./ 我~现在休会。 I move the meeting be adjourned. ② proposal; motion: 大会一致通过了他们的~。 The meeting unanimously adopted their proposal./ 根据会议主席的~ on the motion of the chairman of the meeting

【提早】 tízǎo shift to an earlier time; be earlier than planned or expected: 汛期~了。 The flood season is here earlier than expected./ ~出发 set out earlier than planned/ ~一声 notify in advance

【提制】 tízhì obtain through refining; distil; extract: 香草香精是从一种热带兰~出来的。 Vanilla is extracted from a tropical orchid.

啼 *

tí ① cry; weep aloud: 哭哭~~ weep and wail ② crow; caw: 鸡~。 Cocks crow./ 月落乌~。 The crows caw when the moon goes down.

【啼哭】 tíkū cry; wail

【啼笑皆非】 tí-xiào jiē fēi not know whether to laugh or cry

题 *

tí ① topic; subject; title; problem: 讨论~ topic for discussion/ 话~ subject of conversation/ 考~ examination questions/ 文不对~ wide of the mark; irrelevant; not to the point; stray from the subject; digress ② inscribe: ~诗 inscribe a poem (on a painting, fan, wall, etc.)/ 某某~ an inscription by so-and-so

【题跋】 tíbá ① preface and postscript ② short comments, annotations, etc. on a scroll (of painting or calligraphy)

【题材】 tícái subject matter; theme: ~范围 range of subjects/ 这是写小说的好~。 This is a good material for a novel.

【题词】 tící ① write a few words of encouragement, appreciation or commemoration ② inscription; dedication; foreword

【题解】 tíjiě ① explanatory notes on the title or background of a book ② key to exercises or problems: 《平面几何~》 Key to Exercises in Plane Geometry

【题名】 tímíng inscribe one's name; autograph: 在照片上~ autograph a photograph/ ~留念 give one's autograph as a memento

【题目】 tímù ① title; subject; topic

【题签】 tíqiān ① write the title of a book on a label to be stuck on the cover ② a label with the title of a book on it

【题字】 tízì ① inscribe ② inscription; autograph: 书上有作者亲笔~。 The book is autographed by the author.

蹄 *

tí hoof: 马~ horse's hoofs/ 燉猪~ stewed pig's trotters

【蹄子】 tízi ① 〈口〉 hoof ② 〈方〉 leg of pork

tǐ

体 *

tǐ ① body; part of the body: 人~构造 the structure of the human body/ ~重 (body) weight/ 肢~ limbs ② substance; state of a substance: 固~ solid ③ style; form: 文~ literary style; style of writing/ 旧~诗 old-style poems; classical poetry ④ personally do or experience sth.; put

oneself in another's position: 身～力行 earnestly practise what one advocates ⑤ system: 政～ system of government/ 国～ state system ⑥ <语> aspect (of a verb)
另见 tī

【体裁】 tǐcái types or forms of literature

【体操】 tǐcāo gymnastics: 徒手～ freestanding exercise/器械～ gymnastics on or with apparatus/ 自由～ floor (或 free) exercise

【体察】 tǐchá experience and observe: 虚心～情况 be ready to look into matters with an open mind; not be prejudiced in sizing up situations

【体罚】 tǐfá corporal (或 physical) punishment

【体格】 tǐgé physique; build: ～壮 of strong physique; of powerful build; of strong constitution ◇ ～检查 physical examination; health checkup

【体会】 tǐhuì know (或 learn) from experience; realize: 深有～ have an intimate knowledge of sth./ 谈谈我个人的～, I'll say a few words about my personal experience (或 understanding).

【体积】 tǐjī volume; bulk: ～大 bulky/ 容器的～ the volume of a container ◇ ～膨胀<物> volume expansion

【体力】 tǐlì physical (或 bodily) strength; physical power: 增强～ build up one's strength/ 消耗～ be a drain on one's (physical) strength; consume (或 sap) one's strength

【体力劳动】 tǐlì láodòng physical (或 manual) labour: 参加～ take part in (或 do) physical labour

【体例】 tǐlì stylistic rules and layout; style: 印刷～ style sheet; stylebook

【体谅】 tǐliang show understanding and sympathy for; make allowances for: 充分～人家的困难 make full allowances for their difficulties/ 她是很～人的。 She is quite understanding.

【体面】 tǐmian ① dignity; face: 有失～ be a loss of face/ 他并不认为干这些事就会有失～。 He did not consider it beneath his dignity to concern himself with these things./ 维持～ keep up appearances ②honourable; creditable: 不～的行为 disgraceful (或 disreputable) conduct ③ good-looking: 长得～ be handsome

【体念】 tǐniàn give sympathetic consideration to

【体魄】 tǐpò physique: 强壮的～ strong (或 powerful) physique; vigorous health/ 锻炼～ go in for physical training

【体式】 tǐshì ① form of characters or letters: 汉语拼音字母有手写体和印刷体两种。 There are two forms of the Chinese phonetic alphabet, the cursive and the printed. ② form of literary works: 词和律诗～不同。 Ci poems are different in form from lüshi poems.

【体态】 tǐtài posture; carriage: ～轻盈 a graceful carriage

【体贴】 tǐtiē show consideration for; give every care to: ～病人 show a patient every consideration/ 入微 look after with meticulous care; care for with great solicitude

【体统】 tǐtǒng decorum; propriety; decency: 不成～ most improper; downright outrageous/ 有失～ be disgraceful; be scandalous

【体味】 tǐwèi appreciate; savour: 仔细～这首诗的含义 savour the meaning of the poem

【体温】 tǐwēn (body) temperature: 给孩子量～。 Take the child's temperature./ 她的～在上升。 Her temperature is going up./ ～过低 hypothermia ◇ ～计 (clinical) thermometer

【体无完肤】 tǐ wú wán fū ① have cuts and bruises all over the body; be a mass of bruises: 被打得～ be beaten black and blue ② be thoroughly (或 scathingly) refuted

【体惜】 tǐxī understand and sympathize with

【体系】 tǐxì system; setup: 建成独立的、比较完整的工业～和国民经济～ complete an independent and fairly comprehensive industrial complex and economic system

【体现】 tǐxiàn embody; incarnate; reflect; give expression to: 这个提案～了发展中国家的利益和要求。 This proposal reflects the interests and demands of the developing countries.

【体形】 tǐxíng bodily form; build

【体型】 tǐxíng type of build or figure

【体恤】 tǐxù understand and sympathize with; show solici-

tude for

【体验】 tǐyàn learn through practice; learn through one's personal experience: ～生活 observe and learn from real life

【体育】 tǐyù physical culture; physical training; sports: 今天下午有一节～课。 We'll have an hour of PE this afternoon.
◇ ～场 stadium/ ～道德 sportsmanship/ ～锻炼 physical training/ ～馆 gymnasium; gym/ ～活动 sports activities/ ～课 physical education (PE)/ ～疗法 physical exercise therapy/ ～用品 sports goods; sports requisites

【体制】 tǐzhì system of organization; system: 国家～ state system

【体质】 tǐzhì physique; constitution: 他们的～都很好。 They all have good physique./ 各人的～不同, 对疾病的抵抗力也不同。 People's constitutions differ; so does their resistance to disease.

【体重】 tǐzhòng (body) weight: 增加～ put on weight; gain weight/ ～减轻 lose weight/ 她～六十公斤。 She weighs 60 kilograms.

tì

屉 tì a food steamer with several trays: steamer tray: ～帽 the lid (或 cover) of a steamer

【屉子】 tìzi ①(one of) a set of removable trays (in furniture or a utensil) ② <方> drawer

剃* tì shave: ～胡子 have a shave; shave oneself

【剃刀】 tìdāo razor

【剃度】 tìdù <佛教> tonsure

【剃头】 tìtóu ① have one's head shaved ② have one's hair cut; have a haircut

涕 tì ① tears: 痛哭流～ shed bitter tears; cry one's heart out/ 感激～零 be moved to tears of gratitude ② mucus of the nose; snivel

【涕泣】 tìqì <书> weep

悌 tì <书> love and respect for one's elder brother

惕 tì cautious; watchful: 警～ be on the alert; watch out

替* tì ① take the place of; replace; substitute for: 今天老王没来,谁～他? Lao Wang is absent today. Who'll take his place?/ 你歇会儿,我来～你。 Have a rest. I'll take over. ② for; on behalf of: ～别人买火车票 buy a train ticket for someone/ ～顾客着想 think about the interests of the customers/ 别～我担心。 Don't worry about me. ③ <书> decline: 兴～ rise and fall

【替代】 tìdài substitute for; replace; supersede: 用石油～煤 replace coal by petroleum; substitute petroleum for coal

【替工】 tìgōng ① work as a temporary substitute ② temporary substitute (worker): 找一个～ find a substitute; get a replacement

【替换】 tìhuan replace; substitute for; displace; take the place of: 教练决定让3号～8号。 The coach decided to replace player No. 8 by No. 3.

【替身】 tìshēn ① substitute; replacement; stand-in ② scapegoat

【替死鬼】 tìsǐguǐ <口> scapegoat; fall guy

【替罪羊】 tìzuìyáng scapegoat

嚏 tì <书> sneeze

【嚏喷】 tìpen sneeze

tiān

天* tiān ① sky; heaven: 明朗的～ a clear sky/ 太阳一出

满~红。The sky is aglow with the rising sun. ② overhead: ~桥 overline bridge; platform bridge ⑧ day: 每 ~ every day/ 前~ the day before yesterday/ 忙了一~ have had a busy day; have done a good day's work/ 夏天 ~长夜短。In summer the days are long and the nights short. ④ a period of time in a day: 五更~ around four in the morning/ ~不早啦。It's getting late. ⑤ season: 春 ~ spring/ 三伏~ the hottest days of summer; dog days ⑥ weather: 下雨~ wet (或 rainy) weather/ ~越来越冷了。 It's getting colder and colder./~大旱, 人大干。The heavens may bring drought, but we can go all out. ⑦ nature: ~ 灾 natural calamity ⑧ God; Heaven: 归~ go to heaven; die/~知道! God knows!/ 哪! Good Heavens!/ 谢~ 谢地! Thank Heaven!

【天边】 tiānbiān horizon; the ends of the earth; remotest places: ~的渔帆 the sails of the fishing boats that appear on the horizon/ 远在~, 近在眼前 seemingly far away, actually close at hand

【天不怕,地不怕】 tiān bù pà, dì bù pà fear neither Heaven nor Earth; fear nothing at all; nothing daunted

【天才】 tiāncái genius; talent; gift; endowment: 世界上不 存在什么生而知之的~。There is no such thing as a genius born with knowledge./ 这孩子有音乐~。The child has musical talent (或 a gift for music).

【天长地久】 tiāncháng-dìjiǔ enduring as the universe; everlasting and unchanging

【天长日久】 tiāncháng-rìjiǔ after a considerable period of time: 由于水的侵蚀,~就形成了一个大溶洞。As a result of prolonged water erosion, a huge cave was formed.

【天窗】 tiānchuāng 〈建〉 skylight

【天大】 tiāndà as large as the heavens; extremely big: ~的 好事 an excellent thing

【天底下】 tiāndǐxia 〈口〉 in the world; on earth: ~哪有这 种道理! Nobody on earth would reason that way. 或 How preposterous!

【天地】 tiāndì ① heaven and earth; world; universe: 炮声 震动~。The earth shook with the roar of guns. ② field of activity; scope of operation: 开辟科学研究的新~ open up a new field for scientific research/ 不要把自己关在办 公室的小~里。Don't confine yourself within the four walls of an office.

【天然气】 tiānránqì natural gas: 干~ dry gas; poor gas/ 湿~ wet gas; rich gas

【天壤】 tiānrǎng 〈书〉 heaven and earth: ~之别 as far apart as heaven and earth; worlds (或 poles) apart; a world of difference

【天日】 tiānrì the sky and the sun; light: 重见~ once more see the light of day — be delivered from oppression or persecution

【天色】 tiānsè colour of the sky; time of the day as shown by the colour of the sky; weather: ~已晚。It is getting dark./ ~突变。The weather suddenly changed./ 看~要晴。 It seems to be clearing up./ 看~怕要下雨。It looks like rain.

【天神】 tiānshén god; deity

【天生】 tiānshēng born; inborn; inherent; innate: 本事不 是~的,是锻炼出来的。Ability is not innate, but comes through practice./ 他~聋哑。He was born a deaf-mute.

【天时】 tiānshí ① weather; climate: ~不正 abnormal weather/ 庄稼活儿一定要趁~,早了晚了都不好。Farming should be done in season, neither too early nor too late. ② timeliness; opportunity

【天使】 tiānshǐ 〈宗〉 angel

【天书】 tiānshū a book from heaven: abstruse or illegible writing: 对我来说,这本书就跟~一样难懂。To me this book is as difficult as a book from heaven. 或 This book is all Greek to me./ 这封信字迹太潦草,象~似的。This letter is as illegible as hieroglyphics.

【天堂】 tiāntáng paradise; heaven

【天体】 tiāntǐ 〈天〉 celestial body

【天天】 tiāntiān every day; daily; day in, day out: ~ 锻炼身体 do physical training every day

【天庭】 tiāntíng the middle of the forehead

【天网恢恢,疏而不漏】 tiānwǎng huīhuī, shū ér bù lòu the net of Heaven has large meshes, but it lets nothing through; the mills of God grind slowly, but they grind exceeding small; justice has a long arm

【天文】 tiānwén astronomy ◇ ~台 (astronomical) observatory/ ~仪 astroscope

【天文学】 tiānwénxué astronomy ◇ ~家 astronomer

【天无绝人之路】 tiān wú jué rén zhī lù Heaven never seals off all the exits — there is always a way out

【天下】 tiānxià ① land under heaven — the world or China: ~大乱 great disorder under heaven; big upheaval throughout the world/ ~大治 great order across the land/ ~无 敌 all-conquering; invincible/ 打~坐~ conquer and rule the country/ ~奇闻 unheard-of absurdity ② rule; domination

【天下乌鸦一般黑】 tiānxià wūyā yībān hēi all crows are black — evil people are bad all over the world

【天仙】 tiānxiān ① goddess ② a beauty

【天险】 tiānxiǎn natural barrier: 此山向有 ~ 之称。This mountain has long been known as a natural barrier.

【天线】 tiānxiàn 〈无〉 aerial; antenna: 架设~ put up an aerial

【天象】 tiānxiàng astronomical phenomena; celestial phenomena: 观测~ observe the heavenly bodies; astronomical observation ◇ ~仪〈天〉 planetarium

【天晓得】 tiānxiǎode 〈口〉 God (或 Heaven) knows: ~他 在那儿待了多久。He stayed there God knows how long.

【天性】 tiānxìng natural instincts; nature

【天幸】 tiānxìng a providential escape; a close shave

【天旋地转】 tiānxuán-dìzhuàn (feel as if) the sky and earth were spinning round; very dizzy: 昏沉沉,只觉得~ feel faint and dizzy as if the earth were spinning round

【天涯】 tiānyá the end of the world; the remotest corner of the earth: 浪迹~ rove all over the world

【天涯海角】 tiānyá-hǎijiǎo the ends of the earth; the remotest corners of the earth

【天衣无缝】 tiānyī wú fèng a seamless heavenly robe — flawless: 这篇文章,论证严密,~。The article is close-knit and its argument flawless.

【天意】 tiānyì God's will; the will of Heaven: 事在人为, 不存在什么~。There is no such thing as the will of Heaven. It is man that decides everything.

【天有不测风云】 tiān yǒu bù cè fēng-yún a storm may arise from a clear sky; something unexpected may happen any time: ~,人有旦夕祸福。〈谚〉In nature there are unexpected storms and in life unpredictable vicissitudes.

【天渊】 tiānyuān 〈书〉 high heaven and deep sea; poles apart: 相去~ as far apart as the sky and the sea/ ~之别 a world of difference

【天灾】 tiānzāi natural disaster (或 calamity): 遭受~ suffer natural disasters

【天灾人祸】 tiānzāi-rénhuò natural and man-made calamities

【天造地设】 tiānzào-dìshè created by nature; heavenly; ideal: 这里山水秀丽,真是个~的游览区。This beautiful place is a heavenly tourist resort.

【天真】 tiānzhēn innocent; simple and unaffected; artless; naive: ~烂漫的儿童 innocent and artless children/ ~的 幻想 a naive delusion/ 你要相信这样的话,那就太~了。If you believe that sort of talk you're really naive.

【天之骄子】 tiān zhī jiāozǐ God's favoured one — an unusually lucky person

【天职】 tiānzhí bounden duty; vocation

【天诛地灭】 tiānzhū-dìmiè 〔咒骂或发誓用语〕 stand condemned by God: 我要是说谎,~! May heaven strike me down if I lie!

【天主教】 Tiānzhǔjiào Catholicism ◇ ~会 the Roman Catholic Church/ ~徒 Catholic

【天资】 tiānzī natural gift; talent; natural endowments

【天子】 tiānzǐ the Son of Heaven — the emperor

【天字第一号】 tiān zì dìyī hào the greatest in the world; par excellence

【天鹅】 tiān'é swan

【天鹅绒】 tiān'éróng velvet

【天翻地覆】 tiānfān-dìfù heaven and earth turning upside down: ~的变化 earthshaking (或 tremendous) changes

【天分】 tiānfèn special endowments; natural gift; talent: ~高 gifted; talented

【天府之国】 tiānfǔ zhī guó the land of plenty

【天赋】 tiānfù ① inborn; innate; endowed by nature ② natural gift; talent; endowments ◇ ~人权论 the theory of natural rights

【天干】 tiāngān the ten Heavenly Stems, used as serial numbers and also in combination with the twelve Earthly Branches to designate years, months, days and hours

【天高地厚】 tiāngāo-dìhòu ① (of kindness) profound; deep ② how high the sky and how deep the earth — immensity of the universe; complexity of things: 不知~ have an exaggerated opinion of one's abilities; not understand things

【天各一方】 tiān gè yī fāng (of a family or friends) live far apart from each other

【天公】 tiāngōng the ruler of heaven; God: ~不作美。Unfortunately, the weather let us down.

【天公地道】 tiāngōng-dìdào absolutely fair: 在我看来,她这样处理真是~。In my opinion, the way she disposed of the matter was truly fair and reasonable.

【天宫】 tiāngōng heavenly palace

【天光】 tiānguāng ① daylight; time of the day: ~不早了。It's getting late. ② 〈方〉 morning

【天国】 tiānguó the Kingdom of Heaven; paradise

【天河】 tiānhé 〈天〉 the Milky Way; the Galaxy

【天花】 tiānhuā 〈医〉 smallpox

【天花板】 tiānhuābǎn ceiling

【天花乱坠】 tiānhuā luàn zhuì as if it were raining flowers — give an extravagantly colourful description: 吹得~ give an extravagant account of; make a wild boast about

【天皇】 tiānhuáng the emperor of Japan; Mikado

【天昏地暗】 tiānhūn-dì'àn ① a murky sky over a dark earth; dark all round: 呼啸的西北风夹着黄沙,刮得~。A howling northwest wind swept by, carrying yellow dust that darkened the sky and obscured everything else. ② in a state of chaos and darkness: 当时军阀混战,真是~哪! In those years, with the warlords fighting among themselves, the country was plunged into chaos and darkness.

【天机】 tiānjī ① nature's mystery; something inexplicable ② God's design; secret: 泄漏~ give away a secret

【天极】 tiānjí 〈天〉 celestial pole

【天际】 tiānjì 〈书〉 horizon

【天经地义】 tiānjīng-dìyì unalterable principle — right and proper; perfectly justified

【天井】 tiānjǐng ① small yard; courtyard ② skylight

【天空】 tiānkōng the sky; the heavens

【天籁】 tiānlài 〈书〉 sounds of nature

【天理】 tiānlǐ ① heavenly principles — feudal ethics as propounded by the Song Confucianists ② justice: 是无~。That would be a gross injustice.

【天良】 tiānliáng conscience: 丧尽~ conscienceless

【天亮】 tiānliàng daybreak; dawn: ~以前赶到 get there before daybreak

【天伦】 tiānlún 〈书〉 the natural bonds and ethical relationships between members of a family: ~之乐 family happiness

【天罗地网】 tiānluó-dìwǎng nets above and snares below; tight encirclement: 布下~,使罪犯无路可逃 spread a dragnet so the criminals have no way to escape

【天马行空】 tiānmǎ xíng kōng a heavenly steed soaring across the skies — a powerful and unconstrained style

【天明】 tiānmíng daybreak; dawn

【天命】 tiānmìng God's will; the mandate of heaven; destiny; fate

【天幕】 tiānmù ① the canopy of the heavens ② backdrop (of a stage)

【天南地北】 tiānnán-dìběi ① far apart; poles apart: 他们哥儿俩~,见一次面不容易。The two brothers live so far apart they don't often get a chance to see each other. ② from different places or areas: 他们来自~,参加石油会战。They came from all over the country to take part in the battle for oil.

【天南海北】 tiānnán-hǎiběi ① all over the country ② discursive; rambling: ~地谈起来 start chattering away about this and that; start a bull session

【天年】 tiānnián natural span of life; one's allotted span: 尽其~ die a natural death; live one's full span

【天怒人怨】 tiānnù-rényuàn the wrath of God and the resentment of men; widespread indignation and discontent

【天平】 tiānpíng balance; scales

【天气】 tiānqì weather: ~要变。The weather is changing./ ~转晴。It's clearing up./ 不管~如何,也要继续施工。Construction will go on in all weathers. ◇ ~图 weather map; synoptic chart/ ~预报 weather forecast

【天堑】 tiānqiàn natural moat: 长江~ the natural moat of the Changjiang River

【天桥】 tiānqiáo overline bridge; platform bridge

【天穹】 tiānqióng the vault of heaven

【天球】 tiānqiú 〈天〉 celestial sphere

【天然】 tiānrán natural: ~财富 natural resources (或 wealth)/ ~景色 natural scenery/ ~障碍物 natural barrier; topographical barrier

添* tiān ① add; increase: 增~光彩 add lustre to/ ~煤 put in more coal; stoke/ ~衣服 put on more clothes/ ~设早晚服务部 set up an additional department for after-hours service/ 给你们~麻烦了。Sorry to have troubled you. ② 〈方〉 have a baby: 她最近~了个女孩儿。She recently had a daughter.

【添补】 tiānbu replenish; get more: 需要~机器零件 need a fresh supply of machine parts

【添丁】 tiāndīng have a baby (esp. a boy) born into the family

【添油加醋】 tiānyóu-jiācù add colour and emphasis to (a narration); add inflammatory details to (a story)

【添枝加叶】 tiānzhī-jiāyè embellish a story: 照我说的对他讲,可别~。Tell him exactly what I said and don't embroider./ 接着,他就~,甚至公开扯谎。Then he started to embellish and even lie outright.

【添置】 tiānzhì add to one's possessions; acquire: ~家俱 buy more furniture

tián

田* tián ① field; farmland; cropland: 犁~ plough a field/ 在~里劳动 work in the fields; work on the land/ 耕者有其~ land to the tiller/ 油~ oilfield/ 煤~ coalfield

【田地】 tiándì ① field; farmland; cropland ② wretched situation; plight: 真没想到事情会发展到这步~。I never dreamt things would come to such a pass./ 你怎么落到这步~! How did you get into such a plight?

【田鸡】 tiánjī frog

【田间】 tiánjiān field; farm

【田径】 tiánjìng 〈体〉 track and field ◇ ~队 track and field team/ ~赛 track and field meet/ ~赛项目 track and field events/ ~运动 track and field sports; athletics/ ~运动员 athlete

【田野】 tiányě field; open country: 广阔的~ a vast field; a vast expanse of farmland

【田园】 tiányuán fields and gardens; countryside: ~生活 idyllic life/ ~风光 rural scenery ◇ ~诗 idyll; pastoral poetry/ ~诗人 pastoral poet

【田庄】 tiánzhuāng country estate

田径

跳高

撑竿跳

跳远

铅球

跳栏

接力赛

铁饼

标枪

赛跑

恬 tián <书> ① quiet; tranquil; calm: ~适 quiet and comfortable ② not care at all; remain unperturbed

【恬不知耻】 tián bù zhī chǐ not feel ashamed; have no sense of shame; be shameless

【恬淡】 tiándàn indifferent to fame or gain

【恬静】 tiánjìng quiet; peaceful; tranquil

【恬然】 tiánrán <书> unperturbed; calm; nonchalant: 处之~ remain unruffled

甜* tián ① sweet; honeyed: 这西瓜好~哪! This watermelon is really sweet! ② sound: 睡得真~ have a sound (或 sweet) sleep; sleep soundly

【甜菜】 tiáncài ① beet: 糖~ sugar beet ② beetroot

【甜瓜】 tiánguā muskmelon

【甜美】 tiánměi ① sweet; luscious: 味道~ taste sweet; have a sweet taste/ ~多汁的桃儿 luscious and juicy peaches ② pleasant; refreshing: 睡了个~的午觉 have a refreshing nap after lunch

【甜蜜】 tiánmì sweet; happy: ~的回忆 happy (或 sweet) memories/ 孩子们笑得多么~! How merrily the children laughed!

【甜品】 tiánpǐn sweetmeats

【甜食】 tiánshí sweet food; sweetmeats: 他爱吃~。He has a sweet tooth. 或 He likes sweet things.

【甜水】 tiánshuǐ ① fresh water: 井~ fresh water well ② sugar water — happiness; comfort: 这孩子是在~里长大的。The child's grown up in happy times.

【甜丝丝】 tiánsīsī ① pleasantly sweet: 这个菜~儿的。This dish is sweet and delicious. ② quite pleased; gratified; happy: 心里感到~的 feel quite pleased (或 happy)

【甜头】 tiántou ① sweet taste; pleasant flavour ② good; benefit (as an inducement): 尝到~ get something out of it; draw benefit from it

【甜味】 tiánwèi sweet taste: 有点~ taste sweet; have a sweet taste

甜言蜜语 tiányán-mìyǔ sweet words and honeyed phrases; fine-sounding words

填* tián ① fill; stuff: 往坑里~土 fill a pit with earth/ ~枕芯 stuff a pillow/ 义愤~膺 be filled with righteous indignation ② write; fill in: ~表 fill in a form/ 别~错日期。Don't fill in the wrong date.

【填报】 tiánbào fill in a form and submit it to the leadership: 每周~工程进度 make a weekly progress report on a project

【填补】 tiánbǔ fill (a vacancy, gap, etc.): ~缺额 fill a vacancy/ ~亏空 make up a deficit/ ~科学技术领域的空白 fill in the gaps in the fields of science and technology

【填充】 tiánchōng ① fill up; stuff ② fill in the blanks (in a test paper)

【填空】 tiánkòng ① fill a vacant position; fill a vacancy ② 见"填空"②

【填平】 tiánpíng fill and level up: ~弹坑 fill up craters/ 搬倒土山~沟,大搞人造小平原 flatten hills to fill up gullies and create man-made plains

【填写】 tiánxiě fill in; write: ~表格 fill in a form/ 这里~你的姓名和住址。Please fill in the blanks here with your name and address.

【填鸭】 tiányā ① force-feed a duck ② force-fed duck ◇ ~式教学法 cramming (或 forced-feeding) method of teaching

tiǎn

忝 tiǎn <书><谦> be unworthy of the honour: ~在相知之列 having the honour, though I'm unworthy of it, to be counted among your acquaintances

殄 tiǎn extirpate; exterminate: 暴~天物 a reckless waste of grain, etc.

腆 tiǎn ① sumptuous; rich ② <方> protrude; thrust out: ~着胸脯 stick out one's chest

靦 tiǎn ① <书> ashamed: ~颜 shamefaced ② <口> brazen: ~着脸 brazen it out

舔 tiǎn lick; lap: ~~嘴唇 moisten one's lips with the tongue

tiāo

佻 tiāo 见"轻~" qīngtiāo

挑* tiāo ① choose; select; pick: ~最好的作种子 select the best for seeds/ ~毛病 pick faults; find fault/ 把那筐番茄~一~。pick over that basket of tomatoes ② carry (或 tote) on the shoulder with a pole; shoulder: ~着一担菜 carry two baskets of vegetables on a shoulder pole/ ~水 点苗种 carry (或 fetch) water for dibbling (seeds, young plants, etc.) ③ <量> 〔用于成挑儿的东西〕: 一~水 two buckets of water carried on a shoulder pole 另见 tiǎo

【挑肥拣瘦】 tiāoféi-jiǎnshòu <贬> pick the fat or choose the lean — choose whichever is to one's personal advantage

【挑夫】 tiāofū <旧> porter

【挑拣】 tiāojiǎn pick; pick and choose: 挑挑拣拣 be choosy/ 苹果都是好的,用不着~。 All the apples are good. There's no need to pick and choose.

【挑三拣四】 tiāosān-jiǎnsì pick and choose; be choosy

【挑剔】 tiāoti nitpick; be hypercritical; be fastidious: 总的来说,这个计划是好的,我们不应过于~。On the whole it's a good plan and we shouldn't nitpick.

【挑选】 tiāoxuǎn choose; select; pick out: ~和培养接班人 choose and train successors/ 百货商店有很多童装可供~。 The department store has a large choice of children's clothes.

【挑字眼儿】 tiāo zìyǎnr find fault with the choice of words

tiáo

条* tiáo ① twig: 柳~儿 willow twigs ② a long narrow piece; strip; slip: 布~ a strip of cloth/ ~石 a rectangular slab of stone/ 便~ a brief informal note/ 金~ gold bar ③ item; article: 逐~ item by item; point by point/ 这项条约的正文共八~。The main body of the treaty consists of eight articles. ④ order: 有~不紊 in perfect order; orderly ⑤ <量>: 两~鱼 two fish/ 三~船 three ships/ 一~大街 an avenue/ 一~肥皂 a bar of soap/ 一~香烟 a carton of cigarettes/ 一~裤子 a pair of trousers/ 两~新闻 two pieces (或 items) of news/ 四~建议 four proposals

【条分缕析】 tiáofēn-lǚxī make a careful and detailed analysis

【条幅】 tiáofú a vertically-hung scroll; scroll

【条件】 tiáojiàn ① condition; term; factor: 自然~ natural conditions/ 贸易~ terms of trade/ 利用有利的~ make use of the favourable factors/ 在目前~下 given the present conditions; under present circumstances ② requirement; prerequisite; qualification: 提出~ list the prerequisites; put forward the requirements

【条款】 tiáokuǎn clause; article; provision: 最惠国~ most-favoured-nation clause/ 法律~ legal provision

【条理】 tiáolǐ proper arrangement or presentation; orderliness; method: 她工作很有~。She is a methodical worker./ 这篇文章~清楚。The article is well-organized.

【条例】 tiáolì regulations; rules; ordinances

【条令】 tiáolìng <军> regulations

【条目】 tiáomù ① clauses and subclauses (in a formal document) ② entry (in a dictionary)

【条文】 tiáowén article; clause ◇ ~范例 standard clause

【条纹】 tiáowén stripe; streak ◇ ~布 striped cloth; stripe

【条约】 tiáoyuē treaty; pact: 互不侵犯~ mutual nonaggression treaty/ 多边~ multilateral pact

【条子】 tiáozi ① strip: 纸～ a narrow strip of paper; a slip of paper ② a brief informal note

迢 tiáo far; remote

【迢迢】 tiáotiáo far away; remote: 千里～ from a thousand *li* away; from afar

调* tiáo ① mix; adjust: ～匀 mix well/ ～弦 tune a stringed instrument ② suit well; fit in perfectly: 风～雨顺 good weather for the crops; propitious weather/ 饮食失～ ailment caused by an unbalanced or irregular diet ③ mediate; ～人 mediator; peacemaker ④ tease; provoke 另见 diào

【调羹】 tiáogēng spoon

【调和】 tiáohe ① be in harmonious proportion: 雨水～。 Rainfall is well distributed./ 这两种颜色配得很～。 These two colours blend well. ② mediate; reconcile: 从中～ mediate; act as mediator ③ compromise; make concessions

【调护】 tiáohù care of a patient during convalescence; nursing: 病人需要特别～。 The patient needs special care during his convalescence.

【调剂】 tiáojì ① make up (或 fill) a prescription ② adjust; regulate: ～劳动力 redistribute labour power/ ～生活 enliven one's life

【调节】 tiáojié regulate; adjust: ～室温 regulate the room temperature/ ～水流 regulate the flow of water/ 空气～ air conditioning

【调解】 tiáojiě mediate; make peace: ～家庭纠纷 mediate in (或 patch up) a family quarrel

【调理】 tiáoli ① nurse one's health; recuperate: 精心～ nurse with great care; careful nursing ② take care of; look after: ～牲口 look after livestock

【调料】 tiáoliào condiment; seasoning; flavouring

【调弄】 tiáonòng ① make fun of; tease ② arrange; adjust ③ instigate; stir up

【调配】 tiáopèi mix; blend: ～颜色 mix colours

【调皮】 tiáopí ① naughty; mischievous: ～的孩子 a naughty child/ ～捣蛋 mischievous ② unruly; tricky: ～的牲口 skittish beasts

【调情】 tiáoqíng flirt

【调色】 tiáoshǎi 〈美术〉 mix colours

【调唆】 tiáosuo incite; instigate

【调停】 tiáotíng mediate; intervene; act as an intermediary: 居间～ mediate (或 offer one's good offices) between two parties/ 对争端进行～ mediate (或 intervene in) a dispute

【调味】 tiáowèi flavour; season: 加点生姜～ flavour (或 season) food with some ginger ◇ ～品 flavouring; seasoning; condiment

【调戏】 tiáoxi take liberties with (a woman); assail (a woman) with obscenities

【调笑】 tiáoxiào make fun of; poke fun at; tease

【调养】 tiáoyǎng take good care of oneself (after an illness); build up one's health by rest and by taking nourishing food; be nursed back to health

【调音】 tiáoyīn 〈乐〉 tuning

【调整】 tiáozhěng adjust; regulate; revise: 工资～ adjustment of wages (usu. upwards)/ 价格readjust (或 modify) prices/ ～供求关系 regulate (或 readjust) supply and demand/ ～生产计划 revise production plans

【调治】 tiáozhì recuperate under medical treatment

笤 tiáo

【笤帚】 tiáozhou whisk broom

髫 tiáo 〈书〉 a child's hanging hair

【髫龄】 tiáolíng 〈书〉 childhood

tiǎo

挑* tiǎo ① push sth. up with a pole or stick; raise: 把帘子～起来 raise the curtain/ ～灯夜战 fight by torchlight; continue working by lamplight ② poke; pick: ～火 poke a fire/ ～刺 pick out a splinter/ ～破水泡 prick a blister with a needle/ 把问题～开来说吧。 Let's put all the cards on the table. ③ stir up; instigate: ～事 stir up trouble; sow discord ④ rising stroke (in Chinese characters) 另见 tiáo

【挑拨】 tiǎobō instigate; incite; sow discord: ～是非 foment discord/ ～民族关系 sow dissension among the various nationalities

【挑拨离间】 tiǎobō líjiàn sow dissension; foment discord; incite one against the other; drive a wedge between

【挑动】 tiǎodòng provoke; stir up; incite: ～内战 provoke civil war

【挑逗】 tiǎodòu provoke; tease; tantalize

【挑起】 tiǎoqǐ provoke; stir up; instigate: ～边境冲突 provoke a border conflict (或 clash)

【挑唆】 tiǎosuo incite; abet; instigate: 聲慇有人在背后～。 Beware of people stirring up trouble behind the scenes.

【挑衅】 tiǎoxìn provoke: 进行武装～ carry out armed provocation/ 故意～ deliberate provocation/ 提出～性的问题 raise provocative questions

【挑战】 tiǎozhàn ① throw down the gauntlet; challenge to battle: ～的口吻 a provocative tone/ 接受～ take up the gauntlet; accept a challenge ② challenge to a contest ◇ ～书 letter of challenge; challenge

窕 tiǎo 见"窈窕" yǎotiǎo

tiào

眺 tiào look into the distance from a high place: 远～ look far into the distance

【眺望】 tiàowàng look into the distance from a high place

跳* tiào ① jump; leap; spring; bounce: 高兴得～起来 jump for (或 with) joy/ ～下自行车 jump off a bicycle/ ～过一条沟 leap over a ditch/ 孩子们蹦～～地进了教室。 The children bounced into the classroom./ 他～过了二米的高度。 He cleared two metres in the high jump. ② move up and down; beat: 他激动得心直～。 His heart was throbbing with excitement./ 我眼皮老是～。 My eyelids keep twitching all the time./ 她的心～正常。 Her heartbeat is normal. ③ skip (over); make omissions: 从第一页～到第五页 jump from page one to page five/ ～过了三页 skip over three pages

【跳班】 tiàobān (of pupils) skip a grade

【跳板】 tiàobǎn ① gangplank ② springboard; diving board

【跳高】 tiàogāo 〈体〉 high jump: 撑竿～ pole vault; pole jump ◇ ～运动员 high jumper

【跳行】 tiàoháng ① skip a line (in reading or transcribing) ② change to a new occupation

【跳级】 tiàojí (of pupils) skip a grade

【跳脚】 tiàojiǎo stamp one's foot: 气得～ stamp with rage

【跳栏】 tiàolán 〈体〉 hurdle race; the hurdles

【跳梁小丑】 tiàoliáng xiǎochǒu a buffoon who performs antics; contemptible scoundrel

【跳伞】 tiàosǎn ① parachute; bale out ② 〈体〉 parachute jumping

【跳绳】 tiàoshéng rope skipping

【跳水】 tiàoshuǐ 〈体〉 dive: ～表演 diving exhibition/ 高(低)难度跳台～ variety (plain) high diving/ 跳板～ springboard diving/ 面对池反身～ reverse dive/ 向前（后）～ front (back) dive/ 面对板向内～ inward dive

【跳台】 tiàotái diving tower; diving platform

【跳舞】 tiàowǔ dance

【跳远】 tiàoyuǎn 〈体〉 long jump; broad jump: 三级～ hop, step and jump

【跳跃】 tiàoyuè jump; leap; bound

【跳蚤】 tiàozǎo flea

tiē

帖* tiē ① submissive; obedient: 服～ docile and obedient ② well-settled; well-placed: 办事妥～ manage things fittingly; handle matters well
另见 tiě; tiè

贴* tiē ① paste; stick; glue: ～邮票 stick on a stamp/ ～上胶布 stick on a piece of adhesive tape ② keep close to; nestle closely to: ～墙站着 stand against the wall/ 这孩子紧紧～在妈妈身边。The child was nestling closely to its mother. ④ 见 "帖"② tiē
【贴补】 tiēbǔ subsidize; help (out) financially: ～家用 help out with the family expenses
【贴金】 tiējīn ① cover with gold leaf (或 gold foil); gild ② touch up; prettify: 别往自己脸上～了。Don't put feathers in your own cap. 或 Don't go blowing your own trumpet.
【贴近】 tiējìn press close to; nestle up against: 那孩子～他身边,轻声说了几句话。The child nestled up against him and murmured a few words.
【贴切】 tiēqiè (of words) apt; suitable; appropriate; proper: 这个比喻很～。This metaphor is very appropriate./ 我找不到～的词儿来表达我的意思。I can't find suitable words to express what I mean./ 这样说不～。That's not the right word for it./ 措词～ aptly worded; well-put
【贴身】 tiēshēn next to the skin: ～衣服 underclothes; underclothing
【贴水】 tiēshuǐ 〈商〉agio
【贴题】 tiētí relevant; pertinent; to the point: 着墨不多,但是十分～ brief but very much to the point/ 你的话不～。What you say is irrelevant (或 beside the point).
【贴息】 tiēxī 〈商〉① pay interest in the form of a deduction when selling a bill of exchange, etc. ② interest so deducted; discount
【贴现】 tiēxiàn discount (on a promissory note)
【贴心】 tiēxīn intimate; close: ～朋友 a person one can confide in; bosom friend/ ～话 words spoken in confidence

tiě

帖* tiě ① invitation: 请～ invitation/ 谢～ card of thanks; thank-you note (或 card) ② note; card: 字～儿 brief note ③ 〈方〉〈量〉: 一～药 a dose (或 draught) of herbal medicine
另见 tiē; tiè

铁* tiě ① iron (Fe): 熟～ wrought iron/ 生～ pig iron; cast iron/ 废～ scrap iron/ ～工厂 ironworks/ 趁热打～。Strike while the iron is hot. ② arms; weapon: 手无寸～ completely unarmed; bare-handed ③ hard or strong as iron: ～拳 iron fist/ ～打的江山 unshakable state power ④ indisputable; unalterable: ～的事实 hard fact; ironclad evidence/ ～的纪律 iron discipline ⑤ resolve; determine: ～了心 be unshakable in one's determination
【铁案如山】 tiě'àn rú shān borne out by ironclad evidence
【铁板】 tiěbǎn iron plate; sheet iron
【铁笔】 tiěbǐ ① a cutting tool used in carving seals, etc. ② stylus for cutting stencils; stencil pen
【铁饼】 tiěbǐng 〈体〉① discus ② discus throw
【铁杵磨成针】 tiěchǔ móchéng zhēn an iron pestle can be ground down to a needle — perseverance will prevail; little strokes fell great oaks
【铁窗】 tiěchuāng ① a window with iron grating ② prison bars; prison: ～风味 prison life; life behind bars
【铁道】 tiědào railway; railroad: 地下～ underground (railway); tube; subway
【铁定】 tiědìng ironclad; fixed; unalterable: ～的事实 hard fact; ironclad evidence/ ～的局面 unalterable situation

【铁饭碗】 tiěfànwǎn iron rice bowl — a secure job
【铁工】 tiěgōng ① ironwork ② ironworker; blacksmith
【铁公鸡】 tiěgōngjī iron cock — a stingy person; miser
【铁观音】 tiěguānyīn a variety of oolong tea
【铁管】 tiěguǎn iron pipe; iron tube
【铁轨】 tiěguǐ rail
【铁汉】 tiěhàn man of iron (或 steel); man of iron will; a strong determined person
【铁甲】 tiějiǎ ① mail; armour ② 〈军〉armour for vessels, vehicles, etc. ◇ ～车 armoured car; armoured vehicle

【铁匠】 tiějiang blacksmith; ironsmith ◇ ～铺 smithy; blacksmith's shop
【铁军】 tiějūn iron army — invincible army
【铁矿】 tiěkuàng ① iron ore ② iron mine ◇ ～石 iron ore
【铁链】 tiěliàn iron chain; shackles
【铁路】 tiělù railway; railroad: ～运输 railway transportation; railway (或 rail) transport; shipping by rail/ 国际～联运 international railway through transport ◇ ～网 railway network/ ～线 railway line
【铁马】 tiěmǎ ① cavalry: 金戈～ shining spears and armoured horses — a symbol of war in ancient China ② tinkling pieces of metal hanging from the eaves of pagodas, temples, etc.
【铁门】 tiěmén ① iron gate ② grille
【铁面无私】 tiěmiàn wú sī impartial and incorruptible
【铁骑】 tiěqí 〈书〉cavalry
【铁器】 tiěqì ironware ◇ ～时代 the Iron Age
【铁青】 tiěqīng ashen; livid; ghastly pale: 气得脸色～ turn livid with rage
【铁人】 tiěrén iron man — a person of exceptional physical and moral strength
【铁石心肠】 tiěshí xīncháng be ironhearted; have a heart of stone; be hardhearted
【铁树】 tiěshù 〈植〉sago cycas (Cycas revoluta)
【铁树开花】 tiěshù kāi huā the iron tree in blossom — something seldom seen or hardly possible: 千年的铁树开了花,银针使得聋哑人说了话。Miraculously, like the thousand-year-old iron tree bursting into blossom, many deaf-mutes have regained their power of speech after acupuncture treatment.
【铁丝】 tiěsī iron wire
【铁丝网】 tiěsīwǎng ① wire netting; wire meshes ② wire entanglement: 有刺～ barbed wire entanglement
【铁索】 tiěsuǒ cable; iron chain ◇ ～吊车 cable car/ ～桥 chain bridge
【铁塔】 tiětǎ ① iron tower; iron pagoda ② 〈电〉pylon; transmission tower
【铁蹄】 tiětí iron heel — cruel oppression of the people
【铁桶】 tiětǒng metal pail (或 bucket); drum: 包围得～似的 be tightly encircled
【铁腕】 tiěwàn iron hand ◇ ～人物 an ironhanded (或 despotic, tyrannical) person; strong man
【铁屑】 tiěxiè (锉后的) iron tilings; (车削后的) iron chippings and shavings
【铁锈】 tiěxiù rust
【铁证】 tiězhèng ironclad proof; irrefutable evidence: ～如山 irrefutable, conclusive evidence

tiè

帖* tiè a book containing models of handwriting or painting for learners to copy: 习字～ a book of models of calligraphy for copying; calligraphy models/ 画～ a book of model paintings or drawings; painting models/ 碑～ a book of stone rubbings
另见 tiē; tiě

饕 tiè greedy for food

tīng

厅* tīng ① hall: 餐~ dining hall; restaurant/ (旅馆,剧场等的)休息~ lounge; *foyer*/ 会议~ conference hall/ 音乐~ concert hall ② office: 办公~ general office ③ a government department at the provincial level

听* tīng ① listen; hear: ~广播 listen to the radio/ 兼~则明,偏信则暗. Listen to both sides and you will be enlightened, heed only one side and you will be benighted./ 请~我讲完. Please hear me out./ 我~了会儿,什么也没~见. I listened for quite a while, but heard nothing. ② heed; obey: 我劝他别去,他不~. I advised him not to go,but he wouldn't listen./ 对批评~不进去 turn a deaf ear to criticism ③ 〈书〉 administer; manage: ~讼 administer justice; hear a case (in a law court) ④ allow; let: ~任摆布 allow oneself to be ordered about

【听便】 tīngbiàn as one pleases; please yourself: 去留~. You may go or stay as you please.

【听差】 tīngchāi 〈旧〉 manservant; office attendant

【听从】 tīngcóng obey; heed; comply with : ~吩咐 be at sb.'s beck and call; do sb.'s bidding/ ~劝告 accept sb.'s advice

【听而不闻】 tīng ér bù wén hear but pay no attention; turn a deaf ear to

【听候】 tīnghòu wait for (a decision, settlement, etc.); pending: ~分配 wait for one's assignment (to work)/ ~上级指示 pending further instructions from the higher authorities

【听话】 tīnghuà heed what an elder or superior says; be obedient

【听见】 tīngjiàn hear: 我~有人敲门. I heard a knock at the door./ 她说的什么你~了吗? Did you catch what she said?/ 说话的声音小得几乎听不见 speak in a scarcely audible voice

【听讲】 tīngjiǎng listen to a talk; attend a lecture: 一面~,一面记笔记 take notes while listening to a lecture

【听觉】 tīngjué 〈生理〉 sense of hearing

【听课】 tīngkè ① visit (或 sit in on) a class ② attend a lecture

【听力】 tīnglì ① hearing: 经过针刺恢复了~ regain one's hearing after receiving acupuncture treatment ② aural comprehension (in language teaching)

【听命】 tīngmìng take orders from; be at sb.'s command: 俯首~ be at sb.'s beck and call

【听凭】 tīngpíng allow; let (sb. do as he pleases): ~别人的摆布 be at the mercy of others

【听其言观其行】 tīng qí yán guān qí xíng listen to what a person says and watch what he does; judge people by their deeds, not just by their words

【听其自然】 tīng qí zìrán let things take their own course; let matters slide

【听起来】 tīngqǐlai sound; ring: 她的建议~还不错. Her proposal sounds good./ 他的话~不诚恳. What he said seemed insincere. 或 His words rang hollow.

【听取】 tīngqǔ listen to: ~工作报告 listen to a work report/ ~汇报 hear reports (from below); debrief

【听任】 tīngrèn allow; let (sb. do as he pleases): 不能~错误思想泛滥 never allow erroneous ideas to spread unchecked

【听说】 tīngshuō be told; hear of: 我~她到南方去了. I hear she has gone to the south./ 我们从来没~过这种事. We've never heard of such a thing./ 这只不过是~而已. This is only hearsay. 或 It's nothing but hearsay.

【听天由命】 tīngtiān-yóumìng submit to the will of Heaven; resign oneself to one's fate; trust to luck

【听筒】 tīngtǒng ① (telephone) receiver ② 〈电〉 headphone; earphone ③ 〈医〉 stethoscope

【听闻】 tīngwén 〈书〉 ① hear: 骇人~ appalling; shocking

② what one hears

【听写】 tīngxiě 〈教〉 dictation: 教师让学生~. The teacher gave the pupils (a piece of) dictation.

【听信】 tīngxìn ① wait for information: 今天开会就决定这件事儿, 你~吧. The matter will be decided at today's meeting and we'll let you know the result. ② believe what one hears; believe: 不要~这种谣言. Don't believe such rumours.

【听之任之】 tīngzhī-rènzhī let sth. (undesirable, evil, etc.) go unchecked; take a laissez-faire attitude; let matters drift: 对于损害国家利益的事情, 我们不能~. We cannot shut our eyes to things that harm the interests of the state.

【听众】 tīngzhòng audience; listeners

tíng

廷 tíng the court of a feudal ruler; the seat of a monarchical government: 清~ the Qing government

亭* tíng ① pavilion; kiosk: 八角~ octagonal pavilion/ 茶~ tea stall/ 书~ bookstall/ 报~ newsstand/ 邮~ postal kiosk/ 凉~ wayside pavilion; kiosk ②〈书〉 well-balanced; in the middle; even: ~午 midday; noon

【亭亭】 tíngtíng 〈书〉 erect; upright: ~玉立 (of a woman) slim and graceful; (of a tree, etc.) tall and erect

【亭匀】 tíngyún 〈书〉 ① (of the human figure) well-proportioned; well-balanced ② (of the rhythm of a melody) regular; balanced

【亭子】 tíngzi pavilion; kiosk

庭 tíng ① front courtyard; front yard ③ law court: 民(刑)~ a civil (criminal) court

【庭园】 tíngyuán flower garden; grounds

【庭院】 tíngyuàn courtyard

停* tíng ① stop; cease; halt; pause: 雨~了. The rain has stopped./ 她~了一会儿, 又接着讲下去. She paused a moment before going on with the story./ 我们一下来休息休息, 好吗? Let's stop and have a rest, shall we?/ 他不~地写 He kept on writing. ② stop over; stay: 我在石家庄~了三天. I stopped over at Shijiazhuang for three days. ③ (of cars) be parked; (of ships) lie at anchor: 汽车~在哪儿? Where can we park the car?/ 船~在江心. The ship anchored in the middle of the river. ④〈口〉 part (of a total); portion: 十~儿有九~儿是好的. Nine out of ten are good.

【停办】 tíngbàn close down 又作"停闭"

【停泊】 tíngbó anchor; berth: 这个码头可以~五十多艘轮船. The docks can berth over fifty vessels./ 你们的货船~在五号码头. Your cargo boat is berthed at No.5 wharf./ 港口里~着我国新造的一艘远洋巨轮. One of our new ocean-going ships is lying at anchor in the harbour. ◇ ~处 berth; anchorage; roads; roadstead

【停产】 tíngchǎn stop production

【停车】 tíngchē ① stop; pull up: 下一站~十分钟. At the next station we'll have a ten-minute stop. ② park: 此处不准~! No Parking! ③ (of a machine) stall; stop working: 机器~了, 得加点油. The machine's stalled. It needs oiling./ 三号车间~修理. No. 3 Workshop has stopped working to undergo repairs. ◇ ~场 car park; parking lot; parking area

【停当】 tíngdang ready; settled: 一切准备~. Everything's ready. 或 All set.

【停电】 tíngdiàn power cut; power failure

【停顿】 tíngdùn ① stop; halt; pause; be at a standstill: 陷于~状态 be at a standstill; stagnate ② pause (in speaking): 念到这里要~一下. When you've read up to here, you pause.

【停放】 tíngfàng park; place: 人行道上不准~自行车. Don't park bicycles on the pavement.

【停飞】 tíngfēi 〈军〉 grounding of aircraft

【停工】 tínggōng stop work; shut down: ~待料 work

being held up for lack of material

【停航】 tínghángsuspend air or shipping service: 班机因气候恶劣～。 The regular flight is suspended on account of bad weather.

【停火】 tínghuǒ cease fire: ～协议 cease-fire agreement

【停刊】 tíngkān stop publication (of a newspaper, magazine, etc.)

【停靠】 tíngkào (of a train) stop; (of a ship) berth: 六艘万吨货轮可以同时在这个码头～。 Six 10,000-ton freighters can berth at this dock. ◇ ～港 port of call

【停课】 tíngkè suspend classes: 那天学校～了。 Classes were suspended that day.

【停灵】 tínglíng keep a coffin in a temporary shelter before burial

【停留】 tíngliú stay for a time; stop; remain: 在巴黎～过夜 make an overnight stop at Paris/ 他在波恩作短暂～。 He had a brief stopover in Bonn./ 人类对自然界的认识不断发展,永远不会～在一个水平上。 Man's understanding of nature is developing all the time; it never remains at the same level.

【停水】 tíngshuǐ cut off the water supply; cut off the water: 明天上午八点至下午三点～。 There will be no water tomorrow from 8 a.m. to 3 p.m.

【停妥】 tíngtuǒ be well arranged; be in order: 事情已商议～。 The matter has been discussed and satisfactorily arranged.

【停息】 tíngxī stop; cease: 暴风雨～了。 The storm has subsided.

【停歇】 tíngxiē ① stop doing business; close down ② cease: 从上午八点工作到下午两点一直没有～ work from 8 a.m. until 2 p.m. without stopping (或 letup) ③ stop for a rest; rest: 队伍在小树林里～。 The troops rested in a grove.

【停学】 tíngxué ① stop going to school; drop out of school ② suspend sb. from school

【停业】 tíngyè stop doing business; wind up a business; close down: 修理内部,暂时～。 Closed temporarily for repairs.

【停战】 tíngzhàn armistice; truce; cessation of hostilities ◇ ～谈判 armistice talks (或 negotiations)/ ～协定 armistice; truce agreement

【停职】 tíngzhí suspend sb. from his duties

【停止】 tíngzhǐ stop; cease; halt; suspend; call off: ～工作 stop working/ ～营业 business suspended/ ～前进! Halt!/ ～敌对行动 cease hostilities/ ～供水 cut off the water supply; cut off the water/ ～广播 stop broadcasting; go off the air; close down/ ～罢工 call off a strike/ ～会籍 suspend sb.'s membership

【停滞】 tíngzhì stagnate; be at a standstill; bog down: 会谈～不前。 The negotiations have bogged down (或 have reached a stalemate).

蜓 * tíng 见 "蜻蜓" qīngtíng

婷 tíng graceful

霆 tíng thunderbolt

tǐng

挺 tǐng ① straight; erect; stiff: ～立 stand erect/ 直～～地躺着 lie stiff/ 笔～的衣服 well-pressed clothes ② stick out; straighten up (physically): ～胸 throw out one's chest; square one's shoulders/ ～起腰杆 straighten one's back; straighten up ③ endure; stand; hold out: 你～得住吗? Can you stand it?/ 他受了伤,还硬～。 Though wounded, he was still holding out. ④ very; rather; quite: ～好 very good/ 今天～冷。 It's rather (或 pretty, quite) cold today. ⑤ 〈量〉〔用于机关枪〕: 轻重机枪六十余～ over sixty heavy and light machine guns

【挺进】 tǐngjìn (of troops) boldly drive on; press onward; push forward: ～敌后 boldly drive into the areas behind

the enemy lines

【挺立】 tǐnglì stand upright; stand firm: 几棵青松～在山坡上。 Several pine trees stand erect on the hillside.

【挺身】 tǐngshēn straighten one's back: ～反抗 stand up and fight; stand up to (an enemy, reactionaries, etc.)

【挺身而出】 tǐng shēn ér chū step forward bravely; come out boldly

【挺秀】 tǐngxiù tall and graceful

铤 tǐng (run) quickly

【铤而走险】 tǐng ér zǒu xiǎn risk danger in desperation; make a reckless move

艇 tǐng a light boat: 汽～ steamboat/ 炮～ gunboat/ 登陆～ landing craft

tōng

通 * tōng ① open; through: 路～了。 The road is now open./ 管子是～的。 The pipe is not blocked./ 山洞打～了。 The tunnel has been driven through./ 电话打～了。 The call has been put through./ 这个主意行得～。 This idea will work. ② open up or clear out by poking or jabbing: 用铅丝～烟嘴儿 poke a piece of wire through a cigarette holder to clean it/ ～炉子 poke the fire ③ lead to; go to: 四～八达 extend in all directions; be linked by rail and road to various parts of the country/ 这趟列车直～泰国。 This train goes straight to Thailand. 或 This is a through train to Thailand. ④ connect; communicate: 两个房间是～着的。 The two rooms are connected (或 open into each other)./ 互～情报 exchange information/ 互～有无 each supplies what the other needs; supply each other's needs ⑤ notify; tell: 互～姓名 each telling his name to the other/ 给个电话 give sb. a ring; call (或 phone) sb. up ⑥ understand; know: 他～三种语言。 He knows three languages. ⑦ authority; expert: 日本～ an expert on Japan/ 中国～ an old China hand; Sinologue ⑧ logical; coherent: 文理不～ ungrammatical and incoherent (writing) ⑨ general; common: ～称 a general term ⑩ all; whole: ～身 the whole body/ ～观全局 take an overall view of the situation
另见 tòng

【通报】 tōngbào ① circulate a notice: ～表扬 (批评) circulate a notice of commendation (criticism) ② circular: 关于情况的～ a circular on the situation ③ bulletin; journal: 《科学～》 Science Bulletin/ 《经济～》 Economic Journal

【通病】 tōngbìng common failing

【通才】 tōngcái an all-round (或 versatile) person; a universal genius

【通常】 tōngcháng general; usual; normal: ～情况下 under normal conditions/ 我～六点钟起床。 I generally get up at six o'clock./ ～消息可靠人士 usually reliable sources

【通畅】 tōngchàng ① unobstructed; clear: 道路～。 The road is clear./ 血液循环～ free circulation of the blood/ 大便～ free movement (of the bowels)/ 保持运输～ keep transportation going ② easy and smooth: 文字～ smooth writing

【通车】 tōngchē ① (of a railway or highway) be open to traffic ② have transport service

【通称】 tōngchēng ① be generally called; be generally known as: 汞～水银。 Mercury is generally known as quicksilver. ② a general term

【通达】 tōngdá understand: ～人情 be understanding and considerate/ 见解～ hold sensible views; show good sense

【通道】 tōngdào thoroughfare; passageway; passage

【通敌】 tōngdí collude (或 collaborate) with the enemy; have illicit relations with the enemy

【通电】 tōngdiàn ① set up an electric circuit; electrify; energize: ～的铁丝网 electrified (或 live) wire entanglements ② circular (或 open) telegram: 大会～ the circular telegram of the conference/ ~全国 publish an open telegram to the nation

【通牒】 tōngdié diplomatic note: 最后~ ultimatum

【通风】 tōngfēng ① ventilate: 把窗子打开通通风。Open the windows to ventilate the room. 或 Open the windows to let in some fresh air./ ~降温 ventilation and cooling ② be well ventilated: 这屋里不~。This room is badly ventilated (或 is stuffy)./ 炉子不~。The stove doesn't draw well. ③ divulge information: ~报信 divulge secret information; tip sb. off

【通告】 tōnggào ① give public notice; announce ② public notice; announcement; circular

【通共】 tōnggòng in all; altogether; all told: 我们~十八个人。There are eighteen of us altogether.

【通过】 tōngguò ① pass through; get past; traverse: 电流~导线。Electricity passes through the wires./ 路太窄，汽车不能~。The road is too narrow for cars to get by./ 注意交通安全，一慢二看三~。Pay attention to traffic safety; slow down, look around and then go ahead./ 代表们~大厅进入会场。The delegates entered the assembly hall by way of the lobby. ② adopt; pass; carry: 提案已一致~。The motion was carried unanimously./ 以压倒多数~ be passed by an overwhelming majority/ 议案没~。The bill did not get through. ③ by means of; by way of; by; through: ~协商 取得一致 reach unanimity (或 a consensus) through consultation ④ ask the consent or approval of

【通航】 tōngháng be open to navigation or air traffic ◇ ~水域 navigable waters

【通好】 tōnghǎo <书> (of nations) have friendly relations

【通红】 tōnghóng very red; red through and through: 她羞得满脸~。She blushed scarlet with shyness./ 高炉照得满天~。The sky was aglow with the fires of the blast furnaces.

【通话】 tōnghuà ① converse ② communicate by telephone

【通婚】 tōnghūn be (或 become) related by marriage; intermarry

【通货】 tōnghuò <经> currency; current money ◇ ~膨胀 inflation/ ~收缩 deflation

【通缉】 tōngjī order the arrest of a criminal at large; list as wanted: 下~令 issue a wanted circular

【通奸】 tōngjiān commit adultery

【通力】 tōnglì concerted effort: ~合作 make a concerted (或 united) effort; give full cooperation to

【通例】 tōnglì general rule; usual practice: 星期天休息是学校的~。It is a general rule that schools close on Sundays.

【通亮】 tōngliàng well-illuminated; brightly lit: 照明弹照得满天~。Star shells lit up the sky.

【通令】 tōnglìng circular order; general order: ~各省 issue a general order to all provinces/ ~嘉奖 issue an order of commendation

【通路】 tōnglù thoroughfare; passageway; route: 将兵力集结于敌军必经的两侧 concentrate forces on both sides of the route the enemy is sure to take

【通论】 tōnglùn ① a well-rounded argument ② a general survey: 《地震学~》 *General Seismology*

【通明】 tōngmíng well-illuminated; brightly lit: 灯火~ be ablaze with lights; be brightly lit

【通年】 tōngnián throughout the year; all the year round

【通盘】 tōngpán overall; all-round; comprehensive: ~计划 overall planning/ ~估计 an all-round estimate/ ~安排 a comprehensive arrangement/ 把这个问题~研究一下 examine the question in its entirety

【通气】 tōngqì ① ventilate; aerate: 粘土结构紧，~性差。Clayey soils are tight and poorly aerated. ② be in touch (或 communication) with each other; keep each other informed: 各单位要经常~。The various units must keep in touch with each other.

【通窍】 tōngqiào understand things; be sensible or reasonable: 道理讲得很明白，可是他就是不~。The reason was explained to him clearly, but he couldn't see it.

【通情达理】 tōngqíng-dálǐ showing good sense; reasonable

【通衢】 tōngqú thoroughfare

【通权达变】 tōngquán-dábiàn act as the occasion requires; adapt oneself to circumstances

【通人】 tōngrén a person of wide knowledge and sound scholarship

【通融】 tōngróng stretch rules, get around regulations, etc., to accommodate sb.; make an exception in sb.'s favour: 这事可以~。We can make an exception in this case.

【通商】 tōngshāng (of nations) have trade relations: 订立~条约 conclude a trade treaty; sign a treaty of commerce ◇ ~口岸 trading port

【通身】 tōngshēn the whole body: ~是汗 sweat all over

【通史】 tōngshǐ comprehensive history; general history

【通书】 tōngshū almanac

【通顺】 tōngshùn clear and coherent; smooth: 文理~ coherent writing/ 这个句子不~。This sentence doesn't read smoothly.

【通俗】 tōngsú popular; common: ~易懂 easy to understand/ 拿一句~的话来讲 to use a common expression/ 用~的语言说明深刻的道理 expound a profound truth in simple language ◇ ~读物 books for popular consumption; popular literature/ ~化 popularization

【通天】 tōngtiān ① exceedingly high or great: ~的本事 exceptional ability; superhuman skill ② direct access to the highest authorities

【通通】 tōngtōng all; entirely; completely: ~拿去吧。Take away the lot. 或 Take them all./ ~卖完 completely sold out/ ~到了吗? Is everybody here? 或 Are we (you) all here?/ 一切魔鬼~都会被消灭。Monsters of all kinds shall be wiped out. 又作 "通统"

【通同】 tōngtóng collude; gang up: ~作弊 act fraudulently in collusion with sb.; gang up to cheat

【通宵】 tōngxiāo all night; the whole night; throughout the night: ~达旦 all night long/ 干了个~ work all night/ ~值班 on duty all night

【通晓】 tōngxiǎo thoroughly understand; be well versed in; be proficient in: ~几种文字 have a good command of several languages/ ~中国历史 have a good knowledge of Chinese history; be well versed in Chinese history

【通心粉】 tōngxīnfěn macaroni

【通信】 tōngxìn communicate by letter; correspond: 他经常跟我们~。He often writes to us./ 我们好久没有~了。We haven't corresponded for a long time.

【通行】 tōngxíng ① pass (或 go) through: 自由~ can pass freely; have free passage/ 道路泥泞,卡车无法~。The road was too muddy for trucks./ 没有特别通行证,一律不准~。Nobody is allowed through without a special pass./ 停止~ closed to traffic ② current; general: 这是全国~的办法。This is the current practice throughout the country./ 这项规定在一些地区仍然~。This regulation is still in force in some districts.

【通行证】 tōngxíngzhèng pass; permit; safe-conduct; laissez-passer: 边境~ border pass/ 军事~ military pass/ 临时~ provisional pass

【通讯】 tōngxùn ① communication: 无线电(或 wireless) communication/ 红外线~ infrared ray communication/ 微波~ microwave communication/ 激光~ laser communication ② news report; news dispatch; correspondence; newsletter: ~报导 news report; news dispatch; news story ◇ ~方法 means of communication/ ~设备 communication apparatus (或 equipment)/ ~卫星 communications satellite/ ~线路 communication line

【通讯录】 tōngxùnlù address book

【通讯社】 tōngxùnshè news agency; news (或 press) service

【通讯员】 tōngxùnyuán reporter; (press) correspondent

【通夜】 tōngyè all night; the whole night; throughout the night: ~不眠 lie awake all night

【通用】 tōngyòng ① in common use; current; general: 国际会议~的语言 languages used at international conferences/ 全国~教材 national textbooks ② interchangeable:

这两个字可以～。These two words are interchangeable.

【通则】tōngzé　general rule

【通知】tōngzhī ① notify; inform; give notice: 请马上～他。Please notify him immediately. 或 Please let him know at once./ 把我们的决定～他 inform him of our decision/ 将集合地点～大家 notify everyone of the place of assembly/ 预先～ give advance notice ② notice; circular: 发出～ send out (或 dispatch) a notice

【通知书】tōngzhīshū ① notice: 终止契约～ notice of termination of a treaty; notice of denunciation ②〈商〉advice note

tóng

同* tóng ① same; alike; similar: ～类（岁）the same kind (age)/ 异～ similarities and dissimilarities ② be the same as: "鎚"～"锤"。鎚 is the same as 锤。③ together; in common: 和工人～吃，～住，～劳动 eat, live and work together with the workers; live with the workers, eat the same food and join them in physical labour/ ～甘苦，共患难 share weal and woe ④〈介〉[引进动作的对象或比较的事物，跟"跟"相同]: 有事～他们商量。Consult with them when problems arise. ⑤〈介〉[表示替人做事，跟"给"相同]: 这封信我一直～你保存着。I've kept this letter for you all this time./ 别着急，我～你 想个办法。Don't worry. I'll find a way out for you. ⑥〈连〉[表示联合关系，跟"和"相同]: 我～你一起去。I'll go with you.

【同班】tóngbān ① in the same class: ～同学 classmate ② classmate

【同伴】tóngbàn　companion

【同胞】tóngbāo ① born of the same parents: ～兄弟（姐妹）full brothers (sisters) ② fellow countryman; compatriot

【同辈】tóngbèi　of the same generation

【同病相怜】tóng bìng xiāng lián　those who have the same illness sympathize with each other; fellow sufferers commiserate with each other

【同仇敌忾】tóngchóu-díkài　share a bitter hatred of the enemy

【同窗】tóngchuāng ① study in the same school ② schoolmate

【同床异梦】tóngchuáng-yìmèng　share the same bed but dream different dreams — be strange bedfellows

【同等】tóngděng　of the same class, rank, or status; on an equal basis (或 footing): ～重要 of equal importance/ ～对待 put on an equal footing

【同等学力】tóngděng xuélì　(have) the same educational level (as graduates or a certain grade of students)

【同房】tóngfáng ① of the same branch of a family ②〈婉〉(of husband and wife) sleep together; have sexual intercourse

【同甘共苦】tónggān-gòngkǔ　share weal and woe (或 comforts and hardships, joys and sorrows)

【同感】tónggǎn　the same feeling (或 impression): 老张认为这部小说的人物写得很成功，我也有～。Lao Zhang feels — and so do I — that the characters of this novel are very well drawn.

【同工同酬】tónggōng-tóngchóu　equal pay for equal work: 男女～。Men and women enjoy equal pay for equal work.

【同归于尽】tóng guī yú jìn　perish together; end in common ruin

【同行】tóngháng ① of the same trade or occupation ② a person of the same trade or occupation 另见 tóngxíng

【同化】tónghuà ① assimilate (ethnic groups) ②〈语〉assimilation ◇ ～政策 the policy of national assimilation (as pursued by reactionary rulers)/ ～作用〈生〉assimilation

【同伙】tónghuǒ ① work in partnership; collude (in doing evil) ② partner; confederate

【同居】tóngjū ① live together: 父母死后，他和叔父～。After his parents died, he lived with his uncle. ② cohabit

【同僚】tóngliáo〈旧〉colleague; fellow official

【同流合污】tóngliú-héwū　wallow in the mire with sb.; associate with an evil person: 跟他们～ go along with them in their evil deeds

【同路】tónglù　go the same way: 我俩～，一块儿走吧。Come along with me. I'm going that way too. ◇ ～人 fellow traveller

【同盟】tóngméng　alliance; league: 结成～ form (或 enter into) an alliance

【同名】tóngmíng　of the same name (或 title): 根据～小说摄制的电影 a film based on a novel of the same name/ 他与我～。He is my namesake.

【同谋】tóngmóu ① conspire (with sb.) ② confederate; accomplice ◇ ～犯 accomplice

【同年】tóngnián ① the same year: ～九月大桥竣工。The bridge was completed in September of the same year. ②〈方〉of the same age

【同期】tóngqī ① the corresponding period: 他们第一季度的钢产量超过了历史～的最高水平。Their steel output in the first quarter of the year was higher than their previous record for the period. ② the same term (in school, etc.): 我和他～毕业。I graduated the same time as he.

【同情】tóngqíng　sympathize with; show sympathy for: 博得～ win sympathy/ 我很～你。I heartily sympathize with you. 或 I have every sympathy for you. ◇ ～罢工 sympathetic strike; strike in sympathy/ ～心 sympathy; fellow feeling

【同人】tóngrén〈旧〉colleagues 又作"同仁"

【同上】tóngshàng　ditto; idem

【同时】tóngshí ① at the same time; simultaneously; meanwhile; in the meantime: ～发生 happen at the same time; coincide; concur/ ～存在 exist simultaneously; exist side by side; coexist/ 我们在加快工程进度的～，必须注意质量。While speeding up the work on the project, we must pay attention to ensuring its quality. ② moreover; besides; furthermore: 任务艰巨，～时间又很紧迫。The task is arduous; besides, there's not much time./ 造林可以保持水土，～也可以止住流沙。Afforestation conserves soil and water; it also checks drift sand.

【同事】tóngshì ① work in the same place; work together: 我们～已经多年。We've worked together for years. ② colleague; fellow worker: 老～ an old colleague

【同室操戈】tóng shì cāo gē　family members drawing swords on each other — internal strife; internecine feud

【同岁】tóngsuì　of the same age: 我们两人～。We two are the same age.

【同乡】tóngxiāng　a person from the same village, town or province; a fellow villager, townsman or provincial

【同心】tóngxīn ① concentric ② with one heart

【同心协力】tóngxīn-xiélì　work in full cooperation and with unity of purpose; work together with one heart; make concerted efforts

【同行】tóngxíng　travel together 另见 tóngháng

【同性】tóngxìng ① of the same sex: ～恋爱 homosexuality ② of the same nature or character: ～的电互相排斥。Two like electric charges repel each other.

【同姓】tóngxìng　of the same surname: 他与我～。He is my namesake.

【同学】tóngxué ① be in the same school; be a schoolmate of sb.: 我和他同过三年学。I studied in the same school with him for three years. ② fellow student; schoolmate ③ a form of address used in speaking to a student

【同样】tóngyàng　same; equal; similar: 用～的方法 use the same method/ ～情况下 under similar circumstances/ 他说英语和法语～流利。He speaks English and French with equal fluency.

【同业】tóngyè ① the same trade or business ② a person of the same trade or business ◇ ～公会 trade council; trade association; guild

【同一】tóngyī　same; identical: 向～目标前进 advance towards the same goal/ 抱～观点的人 those who hold identical views

【同义词】 tóngyìcí 〈语〉 synonym

【同意】 tóngyì agree; consent; approve: 我的意见你～吗? Do you agree with me?/ 他～这项建议。 He consented to the proposal.

【同音词】 tóngyīncí 〈语〉 homonym; homophone

【同志】 tóngzhì comrade

【同舟共济】 tóng zhōu gòng jì cross a river in the same boat — people in the same boat help each other

【同宗】 tóngzōng of the same clan; have common ancestry: 同姓不～ of the same surname, but not the same clan

彤
tóng 〈书〉 red

【彤云】 tóngyún 〈书〉 ① red clouds ② dark clouds

桐
tóng a general term for paulownia, phoenix tree and tung tree

【桐油】 tóngyóu tung oil ◇ ～树 tung tree

铜*
tóng copper (Cu): ～丝 copper wire/ ～像 bronze statue/ ～扣子 brass button

【铜板】 tóngbǎn 〈方〉 copper coin; copper

【铜版】 tóngbǎn 〈印〉 copperplate

【铜臭】 tóngchòu the stink of money — profits-before-everything mentality: 满身～ stinking (或 filthy) with money; filthy rich

【铜鼓】 tónggǔ 〈考古〉 bronze drum

【铜管乐队】 tóngguǎn yuèduì brass band

【铜器】 tóngqì bronze, brass or copper ware ◇ ～时代 the Bronze Age

【铜钱】 tóngqián copper cash

【铜墙铁壁】 tóngqiáng-tiěbì bastion of iron — impregnable fortress

【铜像】 tóngxiàng bronze statue

童*
tóng ① child: 顽～ naughty boy/ 牧～ cowherd; shepherd boy ② virgin: 男～ virgin boy/ ～女 maiden; virgin ③ bare; bald: ～山 bare hills

【童工】 tónggōng ① child labourer ② child labour

【童话】 tónghuà children's stories; fairy tales

【童年】 tóngnián childhood

【童仆】 tóngpú 〈书〉 houseboys; menservants; servants

【童山】 tóngshān bare hills: ～秃岭 bare hills and mountains

【童声】 tóngshēng child's voice ◇ ～合唱 children's chorus

【童心】 tóngxin (of an old man) childlike innocence; (of a young man) childishness; playfulness: ～未泯 still preserve traces of childishness or childlike innocence

【童养媳】 tóngyǎngxí a girl taken into the family as a daughter-in-law-to-be; child daughter-in-law; child bride

【童谣】 tóngyáo children's folk rhymes

【童贞】 tóngzhēn virginity; chastity

【童子】 tóngzǐ boy; lad

【童子鸡】 tóngzǐjī 〈方〉 young chicken; broiler

【童子军】 tóngzǐjūn boy scouts

瞳
tóng pupil (of the eye)

【瞳孔】 tóngkǒng 〈生理〉 pupil: 放大～ have one's pupils dilated

【瞳人】 tóngrén pupil (of the eye) 又作"瞳仁"

tǒng

统
tǒng ① interconnected system: 传～ tradition/ 系～ system/ 血～ blood relationship ② gather into one; unite: 由老李～管 be under Lao Li's overall leadership ③ all; together: 这些东西～归你了。 You have all these things at your disposal.

【统称】 tǒngchēng ① be called by a joint name: 武昌、汉口和汉阳常～为武汉。 The cities of Wuchang, Hankou and Hanyang are often referred to as Wuhan. ② a general designation

【统筹】 tǒngchóu plan as a whole: ～全局 take the whole situation into account and plan accordingly/ ～规划 overall planning

【统筹兼顾】 tǒngchóu-jiāngù unified planning with due consideration for all concerned; making overall plans and taking all factors into consideration: ～、全面安排的方针 the policy of overall consideration and all-round arrangement

【统共】 tǒnggòng altogether; in all: 我们小组～七个人。 There are altogether seven people in our group.

【统计】 tǒngjì ① statistics: 人口～ census; vital statistics/ 据不完全～ according to incomplete statistics (或 figures)/ 这些～数字很说明问题。 These statistics throw a lot of light on the matter. 或 These statistics are very eloquent. ② add up; count: ～出席人数 count up the number of people present (at a meeting, etc.)/ 将图书分类整理并加以～ have the books classified, arranged in order and counted ◇ ～数字 statistical figures; statistics/ ～学 statistics/ ～家 statistician/ ～员 statistician/ ～资料 statistical data

【统属】 tǒngshǔ subordination: 彼此不相～。 Neither is subordinate to the other.

【统帅】 tǒngshuài ① commander in chief; commander: 最高～ supreme commander ② command ◇ ～部 supreme command

【统率】 tǒngshuài command

【统统】 tǒngtǒng 〈副〉 all; completely; entirely: 把杂草除掉 get rid of all the weeds/ ～讲出来 make a clean breast of it

【统辖】 tǒngxiá have under one's command; exercise control over; govern

【统一】 tǒngyī ① unify; unite; integrate: ～思想 seek unity of thinking; reach a common understanding/ ～行动 seek unity of action; coordinate actions; act in unison/ 把理论同实践～起来 integrate theory with practice/ ～度量衡 standardize the system of weights and measures/ 大家的意见逐渐～了。 People gradually reached unanimity of opinion. 或 A consensus gradually emerged./ 秦始皇于公元前二二一年～中国。 The First Emperor of Qin unified China in 221 B.C. ② unified; unitary; centralized: ～领导 unified leadership

【统一战线】 tǒngyī zhànxiàn united front

【统治】 tǒngzhì rule; dominate ◇ ～阶级 ruling class/ ～者 ruler

【统制】 tǒngzhì control: 严格～军用物资 exercise strict control over military supplies/ 经济～ economic control

捅
tǒng ① poke; stab: 在硬纸盒上～个洞 poke a hole in the cardboard box/ 把炉子～～ give the fire a poke/ 刺刀～ stab with a bayonet/ ～马蜂窝 stir up a hornets' nest: bring a hornets' nest about one's ears/ 他用胳膊肘～了我一下。 He gave me a nudge. ② disclose; give away; let out: 谁把秘密给～出去了? Who gave away (或 let out) the secret?

桶*
tǒng ① tub; pail; bucket; keg; barrel: 水～ water bucket/ 汽油～ petrol drum/ 一～牛奶 a pail of milk/ 装啤酒 barrelled beer; draught beer ② 〈石油〉 barrel

筒*
tǒng ① a section of thick bamboo: 竹～ a thick bamboo tube ② a thick tube-shaped object: 笔～ brush pot/ 烟～ smokestack; chimney/ 邮～ pillar-box; mailbox ③ the tube-shaped part of an article of clothing: 袜～ the leg of a stocking/ 袖～儿 sleeve

【筒子】 tǒngzi tube or tube-shaped object: 竹～ bamboo tube/ 枪～ barrel of a gun

tòng

恸
tòng 〈书〉 deep sorrow; grief: ～哭 wail; cry one's heart out

通
tòng 〈量〉 〔用于动作〕: 说了他一～ give him a talking-to/ 摇鼓三～ three rolls of the drums 另见 tōng

痛 tòng ① ache; pain: 头～ (have a) headache/ 肚子～ (have a) stomachache/ 嗓子～ have a sore throat/ ～不～? Does it hurt? ② sadness; sorrow: 悲～ deep sorrow; grief ③ extremely; deeply; bitterly: ～饮 drink one's fill; drink to one's heart's content/ ～哭 cry bitterly/ ～骂 severely scold; roundly curse

【痛斥】 tòngchì bitterly attack; scathingly denounce: ～谬论 sharply denounce a fallacy

【痛楚】 tòngchǔ pain; anguish; suffering

【痛处】 tòngchù sore spot; tender spot: 触及～ touch sb.'s sore spot; touch sb. on the raw

【痛定思痛】 tòng dìng sī tòng recall a painful experience; draw a lesson from a bitter experience

【痛改前非】 tòng gǎi qiánfēi sincerely mend one's ways; thoroughly rectify one's errors

【痛感】 tònggǎn keenly feel: ～自己知识不足 keenly feel one's lack of knowledge

【痛恨】 tònghèn hate bitterly; utterly detest

【痛哭】 tòngkū cry (或 weep) bitterly; wail: ～一场 have a good cry/ ～流涕 weep bitterly; cry one's heart out/ ～失声 be choked with tears

【痛苦】 tòngkǔ pain; suffering; agony: 关心病人的～ be concerned about the sufferings of the patient/ 精神上的～ mental agony

【痛快】 tòngkuai ① very happy; delighted; joyful: 看见麦子堆成了山,心里真～ be delighted at the sight of a mountain of wheat/ 感到从来没有过的～ be filled with joy as never before/ 图一时的～ seek momentary gratification ② to one's heart's content; to one's great satisfaction: 喝个～ drink one's fill/ 玩个～ have a wonderful time/ 这个澡洗得真～ I had a very refreshing bath. ③ simple and direct; forthright; straightforward: 说话很～ speak simply and directly; not mince matters/ 她这人～,心里有什么就说什么。 She is frank and says what's on her mind./ 他一口地答应了。 He readily agreed.

【痛切】 tòngqiè with intense sorrow; most sorrowfully: ～反省 examine oneself with feelings of deep remorse

【痛恶】 tòngwù bitterly detest; abhor: 他的两面派行为令人～。 His double-dealing was disgusting.

【痛惜】 tòngxī deeply regret; deplore: 我们都为失去一个好朋友而感到～。 We all deeply regretted the loss of such a good friend.

【痛心】 tòngxīn pained; distressed; grieved: 这样浪费粮食令人～。 It is distressing to see food being wasted like this./ 他对自己的错误感到很～。 He keenly regretted his mistake.

【痛心疾首】 tòngxīn-jíshǒu with bitter hatred: 他～地说:"我上了这个坏家伙的当。" "I was duped by that villain!" he said bitterly.

【痛痒】 tòngyǎng ① sufferings; difficulties: ～相关 share a common lot/ 关心群众的～ be concerned with the well-being of the masses ② importance; consequence: 无关～ a matter of no consequence

tōu

偷 tōu ① steal; pilfer; make off with: 有人把我的雨衣～走了。 Someone has made off with my raincoat. ② stealthily; secretly; on the sly: ～看 steal a glance; peek; peep/ ～听 eavesdropping; bugging; tapping/ ～越封锁线 run a blockade; slip through a cordon ③ find (time): ～空 take time off (from work)

【偷安】 tōu'ān seek temporary ease: 苟且～ seek only temporary ease and comfort

【偷盗】 tōudào steal; pilfer

【偷工减料】 tōugōng-jiǎnliào do shoddy work and use inferior material; scamp work and stint material; jerry-build

【偷鸡不着蚀把米】 tōu jī buzháo shí bǎ mǐ try to steal a chicken only to end up losing the rice; go for wool and come back shorn

【偷空】 tōukòng take time off (from work to do sth. else); snatch a moment

【偷懒】 tōulǎn loaf on the job; be lazy

【偷梁换柱】 tōuliáng-huànzhù steal the beams and pillars and replace them with rotten timber — perpetrate a fraud

【偷漏】 tōulòu tax evasion

【偷窃】 tōuqiè steal; pilfer

【偷情】 tōuqíng carry on a clandestine love affair

【偷生】 tōushēng drag out an ignoble existence

【偷税】 tōushuì evade taxes

【偷天换日】 tōutiān-huànrì steal the sky and put up a sham sun — perpetrate a gigantic fraud

【偷偷】 tōutōu stealthily; secretly; covertly; on the sly (或 quiet): ～溜走 sneak away/ 他～瞧了一眼 steal a glance at/ ～告诉他 tell him on the quiet

【偷偷摸摸】 tōutōumōmō furtively; surreptitiously; covertly

【偷袭】 tōuxí sneak attack; sneak raid; surprise attack

【偷闲】 tōuxián snatch a moment of leisure: 忙里～ snatch a little leisure from a busy life; allow oneself a bit of time ② <方> loaf on the job; be idle

【偷眼】 tōuyǎn steal a glance; take a furtive glance: 他～看了一下母亲的神色。 He stole a glance at his mother's face.

【偷营】 tōuyíng make a surprise attack on an enemy camp; raid an enemy camp

【偷嘴】 tōuzuǐ take food on the sly

tóu

头 tóu ① head ② hair or hair style: 梳～ comb the hair/ 平～ crew cut/ 分～ parted hair ③ top; end: 山～ the top of a hill; hilltop/ 桥西～ the west end of a bridge/ 中间粗,两～儿细 be thick in the middle and thin at both ends; taper off at both ends ④ beginning or end: 从～儿讲起 tell the story from the very beginning/ 提个～儿 give sb. a lead/ 到～来 in the end; finally ⑤ remnant; end: 蜡～儿 candle end/ 铅笔～儿 pencil stub (或 stump)/ 烟～ cigarette end (或 stub, stump) ⑥ chief; head: 她是我们组的～儿。 She is the head of our group. ⑦ side; aspect: 他们是一～儿的。 They are on the same side./ 事情不能只顾一～。 We mustn't pay attention to only one aspect of the matter./ 两～落空 fall between two stools/ 既然决定了,就分～去办。 Now that a decision has been taken, let each one do his job ⑧ first: ～等 first-class/ ～胎 firstborn ⑨ leading: ～马 lead horse ⑩〔用在数量词前面〕first: ～一遍 the first time/ ～半场比赛 the first half of a game/ ～三天 the first three days ⑪〈方〉〔用在"年"或"天"前面〕previous; last: ～年 last year; the previous year/ ～天 the day before; the previous day ⑫〈方〉before; prior to: ～五点就得动身 have to start before (或 by) five ⑬〔量〕ⓐ〔用于牛、驴、骡、羊等家畜〕:三十～牛 thirty heads of cattle/ 两～骡子 two mules ⓑ〔用于蒜〕:一～蒜 a bulb of garlic

头 tóu ①〔名词后缀,接于名词、动词或形容词词根〕:木～ wood/ 看～ sth. worth seeing/ 甜～儿 a foretaste of sweetness; benefit ②〔方位词后缀〕:上～ above/ 下～ below

【头版】 tóubǎn front page (of a newspaper)

【头等】 tóuděng first-class; first-rate: ～大事 a matter of prime importance; a major event/ ～重要任务 a task of primary importance/ ～舱 first-class cabin

【头顶】 tóudǐng the top (或 crown) of the head

【头发】 tóufa hair (on the human head) ◇ ～夹子 hairpin

【头号】 tóuhào ① number one; size one: ～字 size one type/ ～敌人 number one enemy; archenemy ② first-rate; top quality: ～大米 top-grade rice

【头昏】 tóuhūn dizzy; giddy: 我～。 I feel dizzy. 或 My head is swimming.

【头角】 tóujiǎo brilliance (of a young person); talent: 初露～ begin to show ability or talent/ ～峥嵘 brilliant; very promising; outstanding

【头巾】 tóujīn scarf; kerchief

【头颅】 tóulú head: 抛～,洒热血 lay down one's life (for a just cause)

【头面人物】 tóumiàn rénwù prominent figure; bigwig; big shot

【头面】 tóumiàn woman's head-ornaments

【头目】 tóumù head of a gang; ringleader; chieftain: 小~ head of a small group in a gang

【头脑】 tóunǎo ① brains; mind: 她很有~。 She has plenty of brains./ 不用~ not use one's head/ ~简单 simple-minded/ ~清醒 clearheaded; sober-minded/ 有政治~ be politically-minded/ 有冷静的~ have a cool head ② main threads; clue: 摸不着~ cannot make head or tail of sth.

【…头…脑】 ...tóu...nǎo ①〔指脑筋〕昏头昏脑 muddleheaded; absentminded ②〔指首尾〕没头没脑 without rhyme or reason; abrupt

【头皮】 tóupí ① scalp: 搔~ scratch one's head/ 硬着~顶 住 toughen one's scalp and butt back; resist firmly ② dandruff; scurf

【头人】 tóurén tribal chief; headman

【头疼】 tóuténg (have a) headache

【头疼脑热】 tóuténg-nǎorè headache and slight fever; slight illness

【头痛】 tóutòng (have a) headache: ~得厉害 have a bad headache/ 这件事真让我~。 This business is a headache for me.

【头痛医头，脚痛医脚】 tóutòng yī tóu, jiǎotòng yī jiǎo treat the head when the head aches, treat the foot when the foot hurts — treat symptoms but not the disease

【头头是道】 tóutóu shì dào clear and logical; closely reasoned and well argued: 战争的学问, 有些人可以在书本上讲 得~,但打起仗来可不一定能取胜。 Some people may appear impressive when discoursing on military science in books, but when it comes to actual fighting, they may not win a battle.

【头衔】 tóuxián title

【头像】 tóuxiàng head (portrait or sculpture)

【头绪】 tóuxù main threads (of a complicated affair): ~ 太多 have too many things to attend to/ 茫无~ be in a hopeless tangle/ 理出个~来 get things into shape/ 事情渐 渐有了~。 Things are settling into shape.

【头油】 tóuyóu hair oil; pomade

【头晕】 tóuyūn dizzy; giddy

【头重脚轻】 tóuzhòng-jiǎoqīng top-heavy

【头子】 tóuzi chieftain; chief; boss

投*

投* tóu ① throw; fling; hurl: ~手榴弹 throw a hand grenade ② put in; drop: 把信~进邮筒 drop a letter into the pillar-box ③ throw oneself into (a river, well, etc. to commit suicide): ~井(河) drown oneself in a well (river) ④ project; cast: 树影~在窗户上。 The tree cast its shadow on the window./ 把眼光~到来访者身上 cast one's eyes on the visitor ⑤ send; deliver: ~书 deliver a letter ⑥ go to; join: ~军 join the army/ ~店 put up at an inn ⑦ fit in with; agree with; cater to: ~其所好 cater to sb.'s likes (或 tastes)/ 意气相~ find each other congenial

【投案】 tóu'àn give oneself up (或 surrender oneself) to the police

【投奔】 tóubèn go to (a friend or a place) for shelter: ~亲 戚 seek refuge with relatives; go to one's relatives for help

【投笔从戎】 tóu bǐ cóng róng throw aside the writing brush and join the army — renounce the pen for the sword

【投标】 tóubiāo submit a tender; enter a bid

【投产】 tóuchǎn go into operation; put into production: 这 个农具厂是去年~。 This farm implement factory went into operation last year.

【投诚】 tóuchéng (of enemy troops, rebels, bandits, etc.) surrender; cross over

【投弹】 tóudàn ① drop a bomb ② throw a hand grenade

【投敌】 tóudí go over to the enemy; defect to the enemy

【投递】 tóudì deliver: ~信件 deliver letters/ 无法~,退回原 letter Undeliverable, returned to sender./ 无法~的信 dead letter

【投放】 tóufàng ① throw in; put in: ~鱼饵 throw in the bait ② put (money) into circulation; put (goods) on the market

【投稿】 tóugǎo submit a piece of writing for publication; contribute (to a newspaper or magazine): 欢迎~。 Con-

tributions are welcome.

【投合】 tóuhé ① agree; get along: 他们俩脾气很~。 The two of them are quite congenial. ② cater to: ~顾客的口味 cater to the tastes of the customers

【投机】 tóujī ① congenial; agreeable: 谈得很~ talk very congenially; have a most agreeable chat ② speculate: ~ 倒把 engage in speculation and profiteering ③ seize a chance to seek private gain; be opportunistic: ~取巧 seize every chance to gain advantage by trickery; be opportunistic

◇ ~倒把分子 profiteer; speculator/ ~分子 opportunist; political speculator/ ~商 speculator; profiteer

【投井下石】 tóu jǐng xià shí 见 "落井下石" luò jǐng xià shí

【投考】 tóukǎo sign up for an examination: ~大学 sign up for a college entrance examination

【投靠】 tóukào go and seek refuge with sb.: ~亲友 go and seek refuge with one's relatives and friends

【投篮】 tóulán 〈篮球〉 shoot (a basket): 远(近)距离~ long (close-in) shot/ 跳起~ jump up and shoot/ ~不准 inaccurate shooting

【投票】 tóupiào vote; cast a vote: ~赞成 vote for; vote in favour of/ ~反对 vote against/ ~表决 decide by ballot/ ~记名 secret ballot/ 去投票处~ go to the polls

◇ ~日 polling day/ ~箱 ballot box/ ~站 polling booth (或 station); the polls

【投契】 tóuqì 〈书〉 see eye to eye; get along well; be congenial

【投亲】 tóuqīn go and live with relatives; seek refuge with relatives

【投入】 tóurù throw into; put into: ~战斗 throw (oneself, troops, etc.) into the battle/ ~生产 put into production; go into operation/ ~全部劳动力 throw in the whole labour force

【投射】 tóushè ① throw (a projectile, etc.); cast ② project (a ray of light); cast: 金色的阳光~到平静的海面上。 The sun cast its golden rays on the calm sea./ 周围的人都对他 ~出惊异的眼光。 All those around him looked at him with amazement.

【投身】 tóushēn throw oneself into

【投师】 tóushī seek instruction from a master: ~访友 learn from a master and call on friends to exchange knowledge or skills

【投鼠忌器】 tóu shǔ jì qì hesitate to pelt a rat for fear of smashing the dishes beside it; spare the rat to save the dishes — hold back from taking action against an evildoer for fear of involving good people

【投宿】 tóusù seek temporary lodging; put up for the night: ~客栈 put up at an inn for the night

【投胎】 tóutāi reincarnation

【投桃报李】 tóu táo bào lǐ give a plum in return for a peach — return present for present; exchange gifts

【投降】 tóuxiáng surrender; capitulate

【投效】 tóuxiào 〈书〉 go and offer one's services

【投掷】 tóuzhì throw; hurl: ~标枪(铁饼,手榴弹) throw a javelin (discus, hand grenade)

【投资】 tóuzī ① invest: ~工矿企业 invest in industrial and mining enterprises/ ~五万元 make an investment of 50,000 dollars ② money invested; investment

tòu

透* tòu ① penetrate; pass through; seep through: 阳光 ~过窗户照进来。 Sunlight came in through the windows./ 这双鞋不~水。 These shoes are waterproof./ ~过现象看本 质 see through the appearance to get at the essence ② tell secretly: ~消息 tell sb. news on the quiet/ 一个信儿 tip sb. off ③ fully; thoroughly; in a penetrating way: 挑熟 ~了。 The peaches are quite ripe./ 他的衣服湿~了。 His clothes are wet through./ 雨下~了。 It was a real good soaker./ 把道理说~了 have thoroughly explained one's reasons; have driven the point home/ 对问题了解得很

have an intimate knowledge of the subject; know the subject inside out/ 有意思～了 extremely interesting/ 他摸～了这台车床的脾气。He got to know this lathe very well. ④ appear; show: 他脸上～出幸福的微笑。A happy smile appeared on his face./ 白里～红 white touched with red。

【透彻】 tòuchè penetrating; thorough: 她把问题分析得很～。She made a penetrating analysis of the problem./ 有～的了解 have a thorough understanding/ 这一番话说得非常～。Those words really drove the point home.

【透顶】 tòudǐng 〈贬〉 thoroughly; downright; in the extreme; through and through: 腐败～ thoroughly corrupt; rotten to the core; decadent in the extreme

【透风】 tòufēng ①let in air; ventilate: 打开窗户透透风 open the window and let in some air/ 这门关不严,有点～。This door doesn't fit very tightly and the wind blows through. ②divulge a secret; leak: 这个人嘴很紧,一点风也不透。The man was closemouthed and didn't drop a hint.

【透镜】 tòujìng 〈物〉 lens: 凹(凸)～ concave (convex) lens

【透亮】 tòuliang ①bright; transparent: 这间房子又向阳,又～。This room is sunny and bright. ②perfectly clear: 经你这么一说,我心里就～了。Thanks to your explanation, it's clear to me now.

【透漏】 tòulòu divulge; leak; reveal: 消息～出去了。The news has leaked out.

【透露】 tòulù divulge; leak; disclose; reveal: ～风声 leak (或 disclose) information/ 真相～出来了。The truth has come to light (或 has come out)./ 她跟她娘～过这个意思。She said to her mother something to that effect.

【透明】 tòumíng transparent: 不～ opaque/ 半～ translucent/ ～的纱巾 diaphanous veil

【透气】 tòuqì ①ventilate: 屋子太闷了,打开窗子透透气。The room is too stuffy. Open the windows and let some air in. ②breathe freely: 透不过气来 feel suffocated

【透视】 tòushì perspective

【透支】 tòuzhī ①〈经〉overdraw; make an overdraft: ～的帐户 overdrawn account ②draw one's salary in advance

tū

凸* tū protruding; raised: ～花银瓶〈工美〉a silver vase with a raised floral design/ ～面 convex

【凸面镜】 tūmiànjìng 〈物〉 convex mirror

【凸透镜】 tūtòujìng 〈物〉 convex lens

秃 tū ①bald; bare: 他的头开始～了。He's getting bald./ ～山 bare (或 barren) hills/ ～树 bare trees; defoliated trees ②blunt; without a point: 铅笔～了。The pencil is blunt. ③incomplete; unsatisfactory: 这篇文章的结尾显得有点～。This article seems to end rather lamely.

【秃笔】 tūbǐ bald writing brush—poor writing ability; low skill at composition: 我这支～不行,得找个笔杆子。I'm no good at writing; you'll have to find someone who is./ 非我这支～所能形容 beyond the power of my poor pen

【秃顶】 tūdǐng bald

【秃鹫】 tūjiù cinereous vulture

【秃子】 tūzi baldhead

突* tū ①dash forward; charge: ～入敌阵 charge into enemy positions/ 狼奔豕～ tear about like wild beasts ②sudden; abrupt: 气温～降。The temperature suddenly dropped. ③projecting; sticking out ④〈书〉chimney: 灶～ chimney

【突出】 tūchū ①protruding; projecting; sticking out: 眼球～ bug-eyed/ ～的岩石 projecting rocks ②outstanding; prominent: ～的成绩 outstanding achievements/ 这个例子～地说明了他的态度是错误的。This is a glaring example of his wrong attitude./ 他的优点和缺点都很～。His virtues are as conspicuous as his defects. ③give prominence to; stress; highlight: 他的发言没有～重点。In his speech he failed to stress the main points./ 她老想～自己。She always tries to push herself forward. 或 She is very pushy.

【突飞猛进】 tūfēi-měngjìn advance by leaps and bounds; advance with seven-league strides; make giant strides

【突击】 tūjī ①make a sudden and violent attack; assault ②make a concentrated effort to finish a job quickly; do a crash job

【突破】 tūpò ①break through; make (或 effect) a breakthrough: ～防线 break through a defence line/ 医学上的～ a medical breakthrough ②surmount; break; top: 难关 break the back of a tough job

【突起】 tūqǐ ①break out; suddenly appear: 战事～。Hostilities broke out. ②rise high; tower: 奇峰～。Peaks tower magnificently.

【突然】 tūrán suddenly; abruptly; unexpectedly: ～停止 suddenly stop; stop (或 pull up) short/ ～哭起来 burst into tears/ ～袭击 surprise attack/ 准备对付一切～事变 prepare for all eventualities (或 contingencies)

【突如其来】 tū rú qí lái arise suddenly; come all of a sudden

【突突】 tūtū 〈象〉: 她的心～地跳。Her heart went pit-a-pat./ 汽艇～地驶入港口。The motorboat chugged its way into the harbour.

【突围】 tūwéi break out of an encirclement

【突兀】 tūwù ①lofty; towering: ～的山石 towering crags/ 怪峰～。A grotesque peak thrusts itself towards the sky. ②sudden; abrupt; unexpected: 事情来得这么～,使他简直不知所措。It all happened so suddenly he didn't know what to do.

【突袭】 tūxí surprise attack

tú

图* tú ①picture; drawing; chart; map: 制～ make a drawing or chart/ 蓝～ blueprint/ 草～ (rough) sketch; draft/ 地形～ topographic map/ 天气～ weather map; synoptic chart/ 插～ illustration; plate ②scheme; plan; attempt: 宏～ great plan/ 另作他～ find another way out; work out a different scheme ③pursue; seek: ～私 pursue private ends/ ～一时痛快 seek momentary satisfaction ④intention; intent

【图案】 tú'àn pattern; design: 装饰～ decorative pattern; ornamental design/ 几何～ geometrical pattern

【图板】 túbǎn drawing board

【图版】 túbǎn plate (for printing photos, maps, illustrations, etc.)

【图表】 túbiǎo chart; diagram; graph: 统计～ statistical chart (或 table)

【图钉】 túdīng drawing pin; thumbtack

【图画】 túhuà drawing; picture; painting ◇ ～文字〈语〉picture writing/ ～纸 drawing paper

【图鉴】 tújiàn illustrated (或 pictorial) handbook: 《中草药～》 Pictorial Handbook of Chinese Medicinal Herbs

【图解】 tújiě ①diagram; graph; figure: 用～说明 explain through diagrams ②〈数〉graphic solution ◇ ～法 graphic method

【图景】 tújǐng view; prospect: 展现出一幅壮丽的～ open up a magnificent prospect

【图例】 túlì legend (of a map, etc.); key

【图谋】 túmóu plot; scheme; conspire: ～不轨 hatch a sinister plot

【图片】 túpiàn picture; photograph: ～展览 photo (或 picture) exhibition/ ～说明 caption

【图穷匕首见】 tú qióng bǐshǒu xiàn when the map was unrolled, the dagger was revealed—the real intention is revealed in the end 又作"图穷匕见"

【图书】 túshū books: ～资料 books and reference materials ◇ ～馆 library/ ～馆管理员 librarian/ ～馆学 library science/ ～目录 catalogue of books; library catalogue

【图像】 túxiàng picture; image

【图形】 túxíng graph; figure: 几何～ geometric figure

【图样】 túyàng pattern; design; draft; drawing: 机器～

draft for a machine
【图章】 túzhāng seal; stamp

涂* tú ① spread on; apply; smear: ~漆 apply a coat of paint; paint/ ~点软膏 apply some ointment/ 给机器部件~油 smear machine parts with grease/ 木桩子上~了沥青。 The wooden stakes are coated with pitch. ② scribble; scrawl: 别在墙上乱~。 Don't scribble (或 scrawl) on the wall. ③ blot out; cross out: ~掉几个字 cross out a few words
【涂改】 túgǎi alter; ~无效 invalid if altered
【涂抹】 túmǒ ① daub; smear; paint ② scribble; scrawl: 信笔~ doodle
【涂饰】 túshì ① cover with paint, lacquer, colour wash, etc. ② daub (plaster, etc.) on a wall; whitewash
【涂炭】 tútàn ① utter misery; great affliction; misery and suffering 参见“生灵涂炭” shēnglíng tútàn
【涂鸦】 túyā 〔多用作谦辞〕 poor handwriting; scrawl; chicken tracks

荼 tú 〔见于古书〕 ① a bitter edible plant ② the white flower of reeds, etc.
【荼毒】 túdú ＜书＞ afflict with great suffering; torment: ~生灵 plunge the people into the depths of suffering

途* tú way; road; route: 沿~ along the way (或 road)/ ~中 on the way; en route/ 半~而废 give up halfway
【途程】 túchéng road; way; course
【途次】 túcì ＜书＞ stopover; travellers' lodging
【途经】 tújīng by way of; via
【途径】 tújìng way; channel: 寻找消除分歧的~ seek ways to eliminate differences/ 探索和平解决的~ explore avenues to a peaceful settlement/ 外交~ diplomatic channels

徒* tú ① on foot: ~涉 wade through; ford ② empty; bare: ~手 bare-handed; unarmed ③ merely; only: ~具形式 be a mere formality/ 不~无益,反而有害 not only useless, but harmful ④ in vain; to no avail: ~费唇舌 waste one's breath/ ~自惊扰 frighten oneself without reason; become needlessly alarmed ⑤ apprentice; pupil: 门~ pupil; disciple/ 学~ apprentice ⑥ follower; believer: 佛教~ Buddhist ⑦ ＜贬＞ person; fellow: 无耻之~ a shameless person/ 酒~ drunkard/ 赌~ gambler/ 歹~ rascal; evildoer; bandit/ 暴~ ruffian; thug ⑧ (prison) sentence; imprisonment
【徒步】 túbù on foot: ~旅行 travel on foot
【徒弟】 túdì apprentice; disciple
【徒劳】 túláo futile effort; fruitless labour: ~往返 make a futile journey; hurry back and forth for nothing
【徒劳无功】 túláo wú gōng make a futile effort; work to no avail
【徒然】 túrán in vain; for nothing; to no avail: ~耗费精力 waste one's energy (或 effort)
【徒手】 túshǒu bare-handed; unarmed
【徒孙】 túsūn disciple's disciple
【徒刑】 túxíng ＜法＞ imprisonment; (prison) sentence: 有期~ specified (prison) sentence/ 无期~ life imprisonment (或 sentence)/ 判三年~ sentence sb. to three years' imprisonment
【徒子徒孙】 túzǐ-túsūn ＜贬＞ disciples and followers; adherents; hangers-on and their spawn

屠* tú ① slaughter (animals for food) ② massacre; slaughter: ~城 massacre the inhabitants of a captured city
【屠刀】 túdāo butcher's knife
【屠夫】 túfū ① butcher ② a ruthless ruler
【屠户】 túhù butcher
【屠戮】 túlù ＜书＞ slaughter; massacre
【屠杀】 túshā massacre; butcher; slaughter
【屠宰】 túzǎi butcher; slaughter: ~牲畜 slaughter animals; butcher fat stock
◇ ~场 slaughterhouse

tǔ

土* tǔ ① soil; earth: ~坷拉 a lump of earth; clod/ 肥~ fertile (或 good) soil/ 瘠~ lean (或 poor) soil/ 用~把种子盖上 cover seeds with earth/ ~台 earthern platform/ ~路 dirt road/ 他鞋上都是~。 There's dirt all over his shoes. ② land; ground: 国~ a country's territory; land/ 领~ territory; domain ③ local; native: ~音 local accent/ ~产 local product ④ homemade; indigenous: ~办法 indigenous methods/ ~杂肥 farmyard manure ⑤ unrefined; unenlightened: ~里~气 rustic; uncouth; countrified ⑥ opium: 烟~ opium
【土包子】 tǔbāozi clodhopper; (country) bumpkin
【土崩瓦解】 tǔbēng-wǎjiě disintegrate; crumble; fall apart; collapse like a house of cards
【土产】 tǔchǎn local (或 native) product
【土地】 tǔdì ① land; soil: 肥沃的~ fertile land; good soil ② territory
【土地】 tǔdì local god of the land; village god ◇ ~庙 a tiny temple housing the village god
【土地改革】 tǔdì gǎigé land reform; agrarian reform
【土法】 tǔfǎ indigenous method; local method
【土匪】 tǔfěi bandit; brigand
【土话】 tǔhuà local, colloquial expressions; local dialect
【土皇帝】 tǔhuángdì local despot; local tyrant
【土货】 tǔhuò local product; native produce
【土木】 tǔmù building; construction: 大兴~ go in for large-scale building (或 construction) ◇ ~工程 civil engineering/ ~工程师 civil engineer
【土壤】 tǔrǎng soil: 多腐植质的~ humus-rich soil
【土人】 tǔrén aborigines
【土色】 tǔsè ashen; pale: 面如~ turn deadly pale
【土生土长】 tǔshēng-tǔzhǎng locally born and bred; born and brought up on one's native soil
【土音】 tǔyīn local accent
【土语】 tǔyǔ local, colloquial expressions; local dialect
【土著】 tǔzhù original inhabitants; aboriginals; aborigines
【土专家】 tǔzhuānjiā self-taught expert; local expert

吐* tǔ ① spit: ~核儿 spit out the pips, stone or pits/ ~痰 spit; expectorate/ ~舌头 put (或 stick) out one's tongue/ 蚕~丝。 Silkworms spin silk./ 机枪~着火舌。 The machine gun was spitting fire. ② say; tell; pour out: ~实 tell the truth/ ~字清楚 enunciate clearly/ ~怨气 vent one's grievances
另见 tù
【吐故纳新】 tǔ gù nà xīn get rid of the stale and take in the fresh
【吐露】 tǔlù reveal; tell: ~真情 unbosom oneself; tell the truth
【吐气】 tǔqì ① feel elated after unburdening oneself of resentment; feel elated and exultant: 扬眉~ blow off steam in rejoicing ② ＜语＞ aspirated
【吐弃】 tǔqì spurn; cast aside; reject

tù

吐* tù ① vomit; throw up: 恶心要~ feel sick; feel like vomiting (或 throwing up) ② give up unwillingly; disgorge: ~赃 disgorge ill-gotten gains
另见 tǔ
【吐沫】 tùmo saliva; spittle; spit
【吐血】 tùxiě spitting blood; haematemesis
【吐泻】 tù-xiè vomiting and diarrhoea

兔* tù hare; rabbit: 家~ rabbit/ 野~ hare
【兔死狗烹】 tù sǐ gǒu pēng the hounds are killed for food once all the hares are bagged — trusted aides are eliminated when they have outlived their usefulness

【兔死狐悲】 tù sǐ hú bēi the fox mourns the death of the hare — like grieves for like

【兔崽子】 tùzǎizi ⟨骂⟩ brat; bastard

【兔子】 tùzi hare; rabbit

【兔子不吃窝边草】 tùzi bù chī wōbiān cǎo a rabbit doesn't eat the grass near its own hole (so that it will be protected) — a villain doesn't harm his nextdoor neighbours

【兔子尾巴长不了】 tùzi wěiba chángbuliǎo ⟨贬⟩ the tail of a rabbit can't be long — won't last long

tuān

湍 tuān ⟨书⟩ ① (of a current) rapid; torrential ② rapids; rushing waters: 急～ a rushing current

【湍急】 tuānjí (of a current) rapid; torrential: 水流～。The current is swift.

【湍流】 tuānliú ⟨书⟩ swift current; rushing waters; torrent; rapids

tuán

团 tuán ① round; circular: ～扇 round fan ② sth. shaped like a ball: 缩成一～ curl up into a ball/ 汤～ boiled rice dumpling ③ roll sth. into a ball; roll: ～纸团儿 roll paper into a ball/ ～药丸 roll pills ④ unite; conglomerate ⑤ group; society; organization: 剧～ drama troupe/ 代表～ delegation; mission; deputation ⑥ ⟨军⟩ regiment ⑦ ⟨量⟩: 一～毛线 a ball of wool/ 一～面 a lump of dough

【团结】 tuánjié unite; rally: ～一致 unite as one/ ～对敌 unite to oppose the enemy; close ranks to fight the enemy/ 一切可以～的力量 unite with all the forces that can be united/ ～就是力量。Unity is strength.

【团聚】 tuánjù reunite: 全家～ family reunion

【团体】 tuántǐ organization; group; team: 群众～ mass organization ◇ ～操 group callisthenics/ ～冠军 team title/ ～票 group ticket/ ～赛 team competition

【团团】 tuántuán round and round; all round: ～围住 surround completely; encircle/ 忙得～转 be up to one's ears in work; run round in circles

【团员】 tuányuán member: 代表团～ a member of a delegation

【团圆】 tuányuán reunion: 全家～ family reunion ◇ ～饭 family reunion dinner

【团子】 tuánzi dumpling: 糯米～ dumpling made of glutinous rice/ 菜～ cornmeal dumpling with vegetable stuffing/ 饭～ rice ball

抟 tuán 见"团" tuán③

tuī

推 tuī ① push; shove: ～车 push a cart/ 把门一～ push (或 shove) the door open/ 把竹排一～进河里 shove (或 push) the bamboo raft into the river/ ～铅球 shot put; put the shot (或 weight)/ 把子弹一上膛 ram a cartridge into the rifle chamber ② turn a mill or grindstone; grind: ～磨 turn a millstone/ ～点白面 grind some wheat into flour ③ cut; pare: ～头 have a haircut or cut sb.'s hair (with clippers)/ 用刨子～光 make smooth with a plane; plane ④ push forward; promote; advance: 把运动～向高潮 push the movement to a climax ⑤ infer; deduce: 类～ reason by analogy ⑥ push away; shirk; shift: 不要把重担子～给人家。Don't shift burdensome tasks onto others. ⑦ put off; postpone: 这项工作得抓紧，不能老是往后～。We have to get on with this job, we can't put it off day after day. ⑧ elect; choose: ～他担任小组长 elect him group leader; choose him to be group leader ⑨ hold in esteem; praise highly: ～许 esteem and commend

【推本溯源】 tuīběn-sùyuán trace the origin; ascertain the cause

【推波助澜】 tuībō-zhùlán make a stormy sea stormier; add fuel to the flames

【推测】 tuīcè infer; conjecture; guess: 根据～ by inference/ 不过是～而已 mere guesswork; nothing but conjecture

【推陈出新】 tuī chén chū xīn weed through the old to bring forth the new: 百花齐放，～。Let a hundred flowers blossom; weed through the old to bring forth the new.

【推诚相见】 tuīchéng xiāngjiàn deal with sb. in good faith; treat sb. with sincerity

【推迟】 tuīchí put off; postpone; defer: ～作出决定 defer making a decision/ 这个会议～几天开。The meeting will be postponed for a few days.

【推斥】 tuīchì ⟨物⟩ repulsion ◇ ～力 repulsive force

【推崇】 tuīchóng hold in esteem; praise highly: ～备至 have the greatest esteem for

【推辞】 tuīcí decline (an appointment, invitation, etc.)

【推戴】 tuīdài support sb. assuming leadership

【推倒】 tuīdǎo ① push over; overturn: 把他一～在地 shove him to the ground ② repudiate; cancel; reverse: 这个计划不切实际，要～重来。The plan is not practical and has to be replaced with a new one./ 一切诬蔑不实之词，应予～。All slanders and libels should be repudiated.

【推动】 tuīdòng push forward; promote; give impetus to: ～工作 push the work forward; expedite the work/ ～社会向前发展 propel the society forward ◇ ～力 motive (或 driving) force

【推断】 tuīduàn infer; deduce: 经过周密的调查和分析才能作出正确的～。Correct inferences can be drawn only from careful investigation and analysis.

【推度】 tuīduó infer; conjecture; guess

【推翻】 tuīfān ① overthrow; overturn; topple ② repudiate; cancel; reverse: ～协议 repudiate an agreement/ ～原定计划 cancel the original plan

【推广】 tuīguǎng popularize; spread; extend

【推己及人】 tuī jǐ jí rén put oneself in the place of another; treat other people as you would yourself; be considerate

【推荐】 tuījiàn recommend: ～她去当拖拉机手 recommend her for training as a tractor driver/ 向青年～优秀的文学作品 recommend outstanding literary works to the youth

【推进】 tuījìn ① push on; carry forward; advance; give impetus to: 把两国之间的友好关系～到一个新阶段 carry the friendly relations between the two countries to a new stage ② ⟨军⟩ move forward; push; drive: 战线再次向前～。The battle-front has again moved forward.

【推究】 tuījiū examine; study: ～事理 study the whys and wherefores of things

【推举】 tuījǔ ① elect; choose: 大家～他到大会发言。They chose him to speak on their behalf at the meeting. ② ⟨举重⟩ clean and press; press: 一百三十七公斤 press 137 kilograms

【推理】 tuīlǐ ⟨逻⟩ inference; reasoning: 用～方法 by inference/ 类比～ reasoning from analogy

【推力】 tuīlì thrust: 螺旋桨～ propeller thrust/ 喷气发动机～ jet thrust

【推论】 tuīlùn inference; deduction; corollary

【推敲】 tuīqiāo weigh; deliberate: ～词句 weigh one's words; seek the right word/ 这个提法是经过反复～的。This formulation was worked out after repeated deliberation./ 他写的东西经得起～。His writings can stand close scrutiny.

【推求】 tuīqiú inquire into; ascertain: ～地面沉降的原因 inquire into the causes of surface subsidence

【推却】 tuīquè refuse; decline: 他要请我吃饭，我～了。I declined his invitation to dinner.

【推让】 tuīràng decline (a position, favour, etc. out of modesty)

【推三阻四】 tuīsān-zǔsì decline with all sorts of excuses; give the runaround

【推事】 tuīshì ⟨旧⟩ judge

【推算】 tuīsuàn calculate; reckon: 日食发生的时间可以～出

来。The time when a solar eclipse will occur can be calculated.

【推托】 tuītuō offer as an excuse (for not doing sth.); plead: 她~嗓子疼,不肯唱。Pleading a sore throat, she refused to sing.

【推脱】 tuītuō evade; shirk: ~责任 evade (或 shirk) responsibility

【推委】 tuīwěi shift responsibility onto others 又作"推诿"

【推想】 tuīxiǎng imagine; guess; reckon

【推销】 tuīxiāo promote sales; market; peddle: ~商品 promote the sale of goods ◇ ~员 salesman

【推卸】 tuīxiè shirk (responsibility): ~责任,委过于人 shirk responsibility and shift the blame onto others

【推心置腹】 tuīxīn-zhìfù repose full confidence in sb.; confide in sb.: ~地交换意见 have a confidential exchange of views

【推行】 tuīxíng carry out; pursue; practise: ~新的政策 pursue a new policy

【推选】 tuīxuǎn elect; choose

【推延】 tuīyán put off; postpone: 把讨论~到明天 put off the discussion till tomorrow

【推移】 tuīyí ①(of time) elapse; pass: 随着时间的~ with the lapse (或 passage) of time; as time goes on (或 by) ② (of a situation, etc.) develop; evolve

【推重】 tuīzhòng have a high regard for; hold in esteem: 《本草纲目》问世之后,深受人们的~。The Compendium of Materia Medica has been held in high esteem since it was first published.

tuí

颓 tuí ①ruined; dilapidated: ~垣断壁 crumbling walls and dilapidated houses ②declining; decadent: 衰~ weak and degenerate; on the decline/ ~风败俗 decadent (或 depraved) customs ③dejected; dispirited

【颓败】 tuíbài 〈书〉declining; decadent

【颓废】 tuífèi dispirited; decadent: ~情绪 decadent sentiments ◇ ~派 the decadent school; the decadents

【颓糜】 tuímǐ downcast; dejected; crestfallen

【颓然】 tuírán 〈书〉dejected; disappointed

【颓丧】 tuísàng dejected; dispirited; listless

【颓势】 tuíshì declining tendency: 挽回~ turn the tide in one's favour

【颓唐】 tuítáng dejected; dispirited

tuǐ

腿* tuǐ ①leg: 大~ thigh/ 小~ shank/ 前~ foreleg/ 后~ hindleg/ ~快 quick-footed; swift-footed/ ~勤 tireless in running around/ 盘~而坐 sit cross-legged ②a leglike support: 桌子(椅子)~ legs of a table (chair) ③ham: 云~ Yunnan ham

【腿脚】 tuǐjiǎo legs and feet — ability to walk: ~不灵便 have difficulty walking

【腿子】 tuǐzi 〈口〉hired thug; lackey; henchman

tuì

退* tuì ①move back; retreat: 他往后~了几步。He stepped back a few paces. 或 He backed up several steps./ 敌人已经~了。The enemy has retreated./ ~一步说 even if that is so; even so ②cause to move back; withdraw; remove: ~敌 repulse the enemy/ 把子弹~出来 remove a cartridge from the breech of a gun; unload a gun ③withdraw from; quit: ~党 withdraw from a political party ④ decline; recede; ebb: 潮水~了。The tide has receded. 或 The tide is on the ebb. ⑤fade: ~色 fade ⑥return; give back; refund: 把这份礼~掉。Return this gift./ ~货 return merchandise/ ~钱 refund ⑦cancel; break off: ~婚 break off an engagement

【退避】 tuìbì withdraw and keep off; keep out of the way

【退避三舍】 tuìbì sān shè retreat ninety li — give way to sb. to avoid a conflict

【退兵】 tuìbīng ① retreat; withdrawal: 传令~ order a retreat ② force the enemy to retreat: ~之计 a plan for repulsing the enemy

【退步】 tuìbù ① lag (或 fall) behind; retrogress: 这孩子功课~了。The boy's not doing so well in his studies as he used to ② room for manoeuvre; leeway: 留个~ leave some room for manoeuvre; leave some leeway

【退潮】 tuìcháo ebb tide; ebb

【退出】 tuìchū withdraw from; secede; quit: ~战斗 withdraw from action; break contact/ ~会场 walk out of a meeting/ ~组织 withdraw (或 resign) from an organization/ ~比赛 withdraw from a competition; scratch

【退化】 tuìhuà ①〈生〉degeneration ②degenerate; deteriorate; retrograde

【退还】 tuìhuán return: ~公物 return public property/ ~抗议照会 reject a protest note

【退换】 tuìhuàn exchange (或 replace) a purchase: 产品不合规格,保证~。Replacement is guaranteed if the products are not up to standard. 或 We undertake to replace any product not up to specifications.

【退回】 tuìhuí ①return; send (或 give) back: 无法投递,~原处。Undeliverable, returned to sender./ 原稿已经~。The manuscript has been sent back. ② go (或 turn) back: 道路不通,我们只得~。Finding the road impassable, we had to turn back.

【退伙】 tuìhuǒ cancel an arrangement to eat at a mess; withdraw from a mess

【退路】 tuìlù ① route of retreat: 切断敌军~ cut off the enemy's retreat ② room for manoeuvre; leeway: 留个~ leave some leeway

【退却】 tuìquè ①〈军〉retreat; withdraw: 战略~ strategic retreat ②hang back; shrink back; flinch

【退让】 tuìràng make a concession; yield; give in: 稍微~一点 give in a little/ 决不~ never yield an inch

【退色】 tuìshǎi fade: 这种布~吗? Will this cloth fade? 或 Is this cloth colourfast?

【退烧】 tuìshāo ① bring down (或 allay) a fever ② (of a person's temperature) come down: 他已经~了。His fever is gone. 或 His temperature has come down.

【退缩】 tuìsuō shrink back; flinch; cower: 在困难面前从不~ never flinch from difficulty

【退位】 tuìwèi give up the throne; abdicate

【退伍】 tuìwǔ retire or be discharged from active military service; be demobilized; leave the army ◇ ~军人 demobilized soldier; ex-serviceman; veteran

【退席】 tuìxí ①leave a banquet or a meeting ②walk out: ~以示抗议 walk out in protest

【退休】 tuìxiū retire ◇ ~工人 retired worker/ ~金 retirement pay; pension/ ~年龄 retirement age

【退学】 tuìxué leave school; discontinue one's schooling: 因病~ leave school owing to bad health/ 勒令~ order to quit school

【退押】 tuìyā ①return a deposit ② (of a landlord) return deposits to tenants in the land reform

【退役】 tuìyì retire or be released from military service (on completing the term of reserve) ◇ ~军官 retired officer/ ~军人 ex-serviceman

【退隐】 tuìyǐn 〈旧〉(of an official) retire from public life; go into retirement

【退职】 tuìzhí resign or be discharged from office; quit working

蜕 tuì ①slough off; exuviate; moult ②exuviae: 蛇~ snake slough

【蜕变】 tuìbiàn change qualitatively; transform; transmute

【蜕化】 tuìhuà ①slough off; exuviate ②degenerate

褪 tuì ①take off (clothes); shed (feathers): 小鸭~了黄毛。The ducklings have shed their yellow down. ② (of colour) fade

tūn

吞* tūn ① swallow; gulp down: 把药丸～下去 swallow the pills/ 一口～掉 gobble up in one go; devour in one gulp ② take possession of; annex: 独～ take exclusive possession of

【吞并】 tūnbìng　annex; gobble (或 swallow) up

【吞金】 tūnjīn　swallow gold (to commit suicide)

【吞没】 tūnmò　① embezzle; misappropriate: ～巨款 misappropriate a huge sum ② swallow up; engulf: 小船被波浪～了。 The little boat was engulfed in the waves.

【吞声】 tūnshēng　〈书〉 gulp down one's sobs; dare not cry out

【吞食】 tūnshí　swallow; devour: 大鱼～小鱼 Big fish eat small fish.

【吞噬】 tūnshì　swallow; gobble up; engulf: 白血球～细菌。 White corpuscles engulf bacteria./ 洪水～了整个村庄。 The flood waters engulfed the whole village.

【吞吞吐吐】 tūntūntǔtǔ　hesitate in speech; hem and haw

tún

屯 tún　① collect; store up: ～粮 store up grain/ ～聚 assemble; collect ② station (troops); quarter (troops): ～兵 station troops ③ village (often used in village names): 皇姑～ Huanggu Village

【屯扎】 túnzhā　station (troops); quarter (troops)

囤 tún　store up; hoard: ～货 store goods
另见 dùn

【囤积】 túnjī　hoard for speculation; corner (the market): ～小麦 corner the wheat market/ ～居奇 hoarding and cornering; hoarding and speculation

饨 tún　见"馄饨" húntun

豚 tún　① suckling pig ② pig

【豚鼠】 túnshǔ　guinea pig; cavy

臀 tún　buttocks

【臀部】 túnbù　buttocks: 在～打一针 give or have an injection in the buttock

tuō

托* tuō　① hold in the palm; support with the hand or palm: ～着盘子 hold a tray on one's palm/ 两手～腮 cup one's chin in one's hands ② sth. serving as a support: 枪～ the stock (或 butt) of a rifle, etc. ③ serve as a foil (或 contrast); set off: 衬～ make sth. stand out by contrast; set off ④ ask; entrust: ～人买书 ask sb. to buy books for one/ ～人照看孩子 leave a child in sb.'s care: 这事就～给她吧。 Let's leave the matter to her. ⑤ plead; give as a pretext: ～病 plead illness ⑥ rely upon; owe to: ～庇 rely upon one's elder or an influential person for protection

【托词】 tuōcí　① find a pretext; make an excuse: ～谢绝 decline on some pretext ② pretext; excuse; subterfuge: 他说他有事,不过是～。 He said he was busy, but that was just an excuse.

【托儿所】 tuō'érsuǒ　nursery; child-care centre; crèche

【托福】 tuōfú　〔套〕〔多用于回答别人的问候〕 thanks to you: 托您的福,我身体好多了。 I'm much better now, thank you.

【托付】 tuōfù　entrust; commit sth. to sb.'s care: 我们把这任务～给他了。 We have entrusted him with the task.

【托故】 tuōgù　give (或 find) a pretext; make an excuse: ～早退 leave early under some pretext

【托管】 tuōguǎn　trusteeship ◇ ～国 trustee/ ～理事会 Trusteeship Council/ ～领土 trust territory/ ～制度 trusteeship

【托梦】 tuōmèng　(of the ghost of one's kith and kin) appear in one's dream and make a request

【托名】 tuōmíng　do sth. in sb. else's name

【托盘】 tuōpán　(serving) tray

【托人情】 tuō rénqíng　ask an influential person to help arrange sth.; gain one's end through pull; seek the good offices of sb.

拖* tuō　① pull; drag; haul: 火车头～着十二个车皮。 The locomotive was pulling (或 drawing) twelve carriages./ 拖轮～着几条小船。 The tugboat was towing some small boats./ 把箱子从床底下～出来 drag (或 haul) a trunk out from under the bed/ ～着根竹竿 trail a bamboo pole along/ ～地板 mop the floor/ ～人下水 get sb. into hot water; get sb. into trouble/ 问题要彻底解决,不要～个尾巴。 The problem must be solved once for all, without leaving any loose ends. ② delay; drag on; procrastinate: 再～就太晚了。 Don't delay any more, or it'll be too late./ 这件工作～得太久了。 This work has been dragging on far too long.

【拖把】 tuōbǎ　mop

【拖车】 tuōchē　trailer

【拖船】 tuōchuán　tugboat; tug; towboat

【拖带】 tuōdài　traction; pulling; towing

【拖拉】 tuōlā　dilatory; slow; sluggish: 办事拖拖拉拉的 be dilatory in doing things/ ～作风 dilatory style of work/ 她工作从不～。 She never puts off her work.

【拖拉机】 tuōlājī　tractor: 手扶～ walking tractor ◇ ～厂 tractor plant/ ～手 tractor driver

【拖累】 tuōlěi　① encumber; be a burden on: 受家务～ be tied down by household chores/ 子女过多是个～。 Too many children are a burden. ② implicate; involve

【拖轮】 tuōlún　tugboat; tug; towboat

【拖泥带水】 tuōní-dàishuǐ　messy; sloppy; slovenly: 这篇文章写得～。 This article is sloppily written./ 办事要利落,不要～。 Do things neatly, not sloppily.

【拖欠】 tuōqiàn　be behind in payment; be in arrears; default: ～税款 be in arrears with tax payment

【拖网】 tuōwǎng　trawlnet; trawl; dragnet ◇ ～渔船 trawler

【拖鞋】 tuōxié　slippers

【拖延】 tuōyán　delay; put off; procrastinate: 期限快到,不能再～了。 The deadline is drawing near; we can't delay any more./ ～时间 play for time; stall (for time) ◇ ～战术 dilatory (或 delaying, stalling) tactics

脱* tuō　① (of hair, skin) shed; come off: 他脸晒～皮了。 His face is peeling because of sunburn./ 头发～光了 lose all one's hair; become bald ② take off; cast off: ～鞋(衣服) take off one's shoes (clothes) ③ escape from; get out of: ～险 escape danger ④ miss out (words): 这一行里～了三个字。 Three characters are missing in this line. ⑤ 〈书〉 neglect; slight

【脱班】 tuōbān　① be late for work ② (of a bus, train, etc.) be behind schedule

【脱稿】 tuōgǎo　(of a manuscript) be completed: 这本书已～,即可付印。 The book is completed and is ready for printing.

【脱轨】 tuōguǐ　derail: 火车～了。 The train was derailed.

【脱缰之马】 tuō jiāng zhī mǎ　a runaway horse — uncontrollable; running wild: 通货膨胀如～ runaway inflation/ 物价飞腾,有如～。 Prices were running wild.

【脱胶】 tuōjiāo　(of parts joined with gum or glue) come unglued; come unstuck: 这件橡皮雨衣～了。 The rubber of this raincoat has disintegrated.

【脱节】 tuōjié　come apart; be disjointed; be out of line with: 管子～了 Faultily welded piping is apt to come apart / 理论与实践不能～。 Theory must not be divorced from practice.

【脱臼】 tuōjiù　〈医〉 dislocation

【脱口而出】 tuō kǒu ér chū say sth. unwittingly; blurt out; let slip

【脱离】 tuōlí separate oneself from; break away from; be divorced from: ～实际 lose contact with reality; be divorced from reality/ 使双方武装力量～接触 disengage (或 separate) the armed forces of the two sides/ ～关系 break off relations; cut ties/ 病人～危险了。 The patient is out of danger.

【脱漏】 tuōlòu be left out; be omitted; be missing: 这里～了一行。 A line is missing here./ ～一针 drop a stitch (in knitting)

【脱落】 tuōluò drop; fall off (或 away); come off: 毛发～ lose (one's) hair/ 门的把手～了。 The door handle has come off./ 墙上油漆已经～了。 The paint on the wall has peeled off.

【脱毛】 tuōmáo lose hair or feathers; moult; shed: 那只骆驼刚脱了毛。 That camel has just shed.

【脱帽】 tuōmào take off (或 raise) one's hat (in respect): ～致敬 take off one's hat in salutation/ ～默哀 bare one's head and mourn in silence

【脱期】 tuōqī (of a periodical) fail to come out on time

【脱色】 tuōsè ① decolour; decolourize ② fade

【脱身】 tuōshēn get away; get free; extricate oneself: 我事情太多, 不能～。 I have so much to do that I just can't get away.

【脱手】 tuōshǒu ① slip out of the hand: 他用力一扔, 石块一飞了出去。 With a powerful fling he sent the stone flying. ② get off one's hands; dispose of; sell: 这些货不好～。 These goods are difficult to dispose of.

【脱水】 tuōshuǐ 〈医〉 deprivation (或 loss) of body fluids; dehydration

【脱俗】 tuōsú free from vulgarity; refined

【脱胎】 tuōtāi ① emerge from the womb of; be born out of

【脱胎换骨】 tuōtāi-huàngǔ be reborn; cast off one's old self; thoroughly remould oneself

【脱逃】 tuōtáo run away; escape; flee: 临阵～ flee from battle

【脱误】 tuōwù omissions and errors

【脱险】 tuōxiǎn escape (或 be out of) danger: 经过抢救, 孩子～了。 The child was out of danger after the emergency treatment.

【脱颖而出】 tuō yǐng ér chū the point of an awl sticking out through a bag — talent showing itself

tuó

驮 tuó carry (或 bear) on the back: 这头驴子能～三袋粮食。 This donkey can carry three sacks of grain.

【驮畜】 tuóchù pack animal

【驮马】 tuómǎ pack horse

陀 tuó

【陀螺】 tuóluó top: 抽～ whip a top

驼* tuó ① camel ② hunchbacked; humpbacked

【驼背】 tuóbèi ① hunchback; humpback ② hunchbacked; humpbacked

【驼峰】 tuófēng hump (of a camel)

【驼色】 tuósè the colour of camel's hair; light tan

【驼子】 tuózi 〈口〉 hunchback; humpback

沱 tuó 〈方〉 a small bay in a river (often used in place names)

鸵 tuó ostrich

【鸵鸟】 tuóniǎo ostrich
◇ ～政策 ostrich policy; ostrichism

跎 tuó 见 "蹉跎" cuōtuó

橐 tuó ① 〈书〉 a kind of bag ② 〈象〉: ～～的脚步声 the tread of footsteps

tuǒ

妥* tuǒ ① appropriate; proper: 欠～ not proper; not quite satisfactory/ 请～为保存。 Please look after it carefully./ 以上意见～否, 请指示。 Please indicate whether you consider the above views sound or not. ② 〔多用在动词后〕 ready; settled; finished: 款已备～。 The money is ready./ 事已办～。 The matter has been settled.

【妥当】 tuǒdàng appropriate; proper: 办得很～ well handled; quite well done

【妥善】 tuǒshàn appropriate; proper; well arranged: ～安排 make appropriate arrangements/ 问题比较复杂, 需要～处理。 The problem is rather complicated and needs careful and skilful handling.

【妥帖】 tuǒtiē appropriate; fitting; proper: 看来这段译文不十分～。 That doesn't seem to be an apt translation.

【妥协】 tuǒxié come to terms; compromise: 达成～ reach a compromise ◇ ～性 a tendency towards compromise (或 accommodation)

椭 tuǒ

【椭圆】 tuǒyuán 〈数〉 ellipse

tuò

拓 tuò open up; develop: 开～边远地区 open up the border regions
另见 tà

【拓荒】 tuòhuāng open up virgin soil; reclaim wasteland ◇ ～者 pioneer; pathbreaker; trailblazer

唾 tuò ① saliva; spittle ② spit

【唾骂】 tuòmà spit on and curse; revile

【唾沫】 tuòmo saliva; spittle

【唾弃】 tuòqì cast aside; spurn

【唾手可得】 tuò shǒu kě dé extremely easy to obtain

【唾液】 tuòyè saliva ◇ ～腺 salivary gland

魄 tuò 见 "落拓(魄)" luòtuò
另见 bó; pò

W

wā

洼 wā ① hollow; low-lying: 这地太~，不适于种棉花。This is low-lying land and not suitable for cotton. ② low-lying area; depression: 水~儿 a waterlogged depression
【洼地】 wādì depression; low-lying land
【洼陷】 wāxiàn (of ground) be sunken; be low-lying

挖* wā dig; excavate: ~井 dig (或 sink) a well/ ~隧道 excavate a tunnel/ ~防空洞 dig an air-raid shelter/ ~塘泥 scoop up sludge from a pond
【挖补】 wābǔ mend by replacing a damaged part
【挖掘】 wājué excavate; unearth: ~古物 excavate ancient relics/ ~地下宝藏 unearth buried treasure/ ~企业潜力 tap the latent power (或 potentialities) of an enterprise
【挖空心思】 wākōng xīnsī 〔多含贬义〕 rack one's brains: ~为自己辩护 rack one's brains trying to justify oneself
【挖苦】 wāku speak sarcastically or ironically: 那话是~我的。That was a dig at me. ◇ ~话 ironical remarks; verbal thrusts
【挖泥船】 wāníchuán dredger; dredge
【挖墙脚】 wā qiángjiǎo 〈口〉 undermine the foundation; cut the ground from under sb.'s feet

哇 wā 〈象〉〔形容呕吐声、哭声等〕: ~的一声哭了起来 burst out crying
另见 wa
【哇啦】 wālā 〈象〉 hullabaloo; uproar; din

蛙* wā frog
【蛙人】 wārén frogman
【蛙泳】 wāyǒng 〈体〉 breaststroke ◇ ~蹬腿 frog kick

wá

娃 wá baby; child
【娃娃】 wáwa baby; child: 胖~ a chubby child ◇ ~床 crib; cot

wǎ

瓦* wǎ ① tile: 无梭~ plain tile ② made of baked clay: ~器 earthenware ③ 〈电〉 watt
【瓦匠】 wǎjiang bricklayer; tiler; plasterer
【瓦解】 wǎjiě disintegrate; collapse; crumble: ~敌军 disintegrate the enemy forces/ 傀儡政权已经土崩~了。The puppet regime has collapsed./ 经过三个月战斗，敌军全线~。After three months' fighting the enemy front crumbled.
【瓦全】 wǎquán 见"宁为玉碎，不为瓦全" nìng wéi yù suì, bù wéi wǎ quán
【瓦斯】 wǎsī gas ◇ ~爆炸 gas explosion/ ~筒 gas cylinder
【瓦特】 wǎtè 〈电〉 watt ◇ ~计 wattmeter

wà

袜* wà socks; stockings; hose
【袜带】 wàdài suspenders; garters
【袜套】 wàtào socks; ankle socks
【袜子】 wàzi socks; stockings; hose

wa

哇 wa 〈助〉〔"啊"受到前一个字收音 u 或 ɑo 的影响而发生的变音〕: 你怎么还不走~? Why haven't you gone yet, eh?/ 你好~? Well, how are you?
另见 wā

wāi

歪* wāi ① askew; crooked; inclined; slanting: ~戴帽子 have one's hat on crooked/ 这堵墙有点~。This wall is a little out of the perpendicular./ 小女孩儿~着头聚精会神地听故事。The little girl listened attentively to the story with her head tilted to one side. ② devious; underhand; crooked: ~主意 evil ideas; devil's advice/ ~道理 false reasoning
【歪风】 wāifēng evil wind; unhealthy trend: ~邪气 evil winds and noxious influences; unhealthy trends and evil practices
【歪门邪道】 wāimén-xiédào 见"邪门歪道" xiémén-wāidào
【歪曲】 wāiqū distort; misrepresent; twist: ~事实 distort the facts/ ~作者原意 misrepresent the author's meaning/ ~别人的话 twist people's words
【歪诗】 wāishī inelegant verses; doggerel
【歪歪扭扭】 wāiwāiniǔniǔ crooked; askew; shapeless and twisted: 字写得~ write a poor hand; scrawl
【歪斜】 wāixié crooked; askew; aslant

wǎi

崴 wǎi ① rugged (mountain path) ② sprain; twist: 把脚~了 sprain one's ankle

wài

外* wài ① outer; outward; outside: ~屋 outer room/ 窗~ outside the window ② other: ~省 other provinces ③ foreign; external: ~商 foreign merchants/ 对~贸易 foreign trade; external trade ④ (relatives) of one's mother, sisters or daughters: ~孙 daughter's son; grandson ⑤ not of the same organization, class, etc.; not closely related: ~客 a guest who is not a relative/ 见~ regard sb. as an outsider/ 电话不~借。This telephone is not for public use. ⑥ besides; in addition; beyond: 此~ besides; into the bargain/ 预算~的开支 extra-budgetary expenditure ⑦ unofficial: ~传 unofficial biography
【外币】 wàibì foreign currency
【外边】 wàibian ① outside; out: 到~散步 go out for a walk/ 我们上~去谈,好不好? Let's go outside to talk, shall we? ② a place other than where one lives or works: 她儿子在~工作。Her son works somewhere away from home. ③ exterior; outside: 行李卷儿~再裹一层塑料布。Wrap a plastic sheet round the bedroll.
【外表】 wàibiǎo outward appearance; exterior; surface: ~美观 have a fine exterior; look nice/ 事物的~ the outward appearance of things/ 从~看人 judge people by appearances
【外宾】 wàibīn foreign guest (或 visitor)
【外部】 wàibù ① outside; external: 事物的~联系 external relations of things/ ~世界 the external world ② exterior; surface
【外埠】 wàibù towns or cities other than where one is
【外层空间】 wàicéng kōngjiān outer space
【外敌】 wàidí foreign enemy
【外地】 wàidì parts of the country other than where one is: 代表团将在首都访问三天，然后再到~游览。The delegation will pay a three-day visit to the capital before leaving for

other parts of the country.

【外调】 wàidiào transfer (materials or personnel) to other localities: ~物资 materials allocated for transfer to other places

【外公】 wàigōng 〈方〉 (maternal) grandfather

【外观】 wàiguān outward appearance; exterior: 这座大楼~很美。This is a fine-looking building.

【外国】 wàiguó foreign country: ~朋友 foreign friends/ 到 ~学习 go abroad to study ◇ ~人 foreigner/ ~语 foreign language

【外行】 wàiháng ⑴ layman; nonprofessional ⑵ lay; unprofessional: 种庄稼他可不~。He's no amateur in farming. ◇ ~话 lay language; a mere dabbler's opinion

【外号】 wàihào nickname

【外患】 wàihuàn foreign aggression: 内忧~ internal disturbance and foreign aggression

【外汇】 wàihuì foreign exchange ◇ ~储备 foreign exchange reserve/ ~兑换率 rate of exchange

【外货】 wàihuò foreign goods; imported goods

【外籍】 wàijí foreign nationality: ~工作人员 foreign personnel

【外加】 wàijiā more; additional; extra: 给你们十份报纸, ~三本小册子。Here you are — ten copies of the newspaper, plus three pamphlets.

【外间】 wàijiān ⑴ outer room ⑵ 〈书〉 the external world; outside circles

【外交】 wàijiāo diplomacy; foreign affairs: 建立大使级的~关系 establish diplomatic relations at ambassadorial level/ 通过~途径解决 be settled through diplomatic channels ◇ ~部 the Ministry of Foreign Affairs; the Foreign Ministry/ ~部长 Minister of (或 for) Foreign Affairs; Foreign Minister/ ~辞令 diplomatic language (或 parlance)/ ~代表机构 diplomatic mission/ ~官 diplomat/ ~惯例 diplomatic practice/ ~护照 diplomatic passport/ ~豁免权 diplomatic immunities/~机关 diplomatic establishment/ ~家 diplomat/ ~礼节 diplomatic protocol/ ~签证 diplomatic visa/ ~人员 diplomatic personnel/ ~使节 diplomatic envoy/ ~使团 diplomatic corps/ ~特权 diplomatic prerogatives (或 privileges)/ ~政策 foreign policy

【外界】 wàijiè ⑴ the external (或 outside) world: 对~的认识 knowledge of the external world ⑵ outside: 向~征求意见 solicit comments and suggestions from people outside one's organization/ 顶住~的种种压力 withstand all kinds of outside pressure

【外景】 wàijǐng outdoor scene; a scene shot on location; exterior: 拍摄~ film the exterior; shoot a scene on location

【外科】 wàikē 〈医〉 surgical department ◇ ~病房 surgical ward/ ~手术 surgical operation; surgery/ ~学 surgery/ ~医生 surgeon

【外壳】 wàiké outer covering (或 casing); shell; case: 热水瓶的~ the outer casing of a thermos flask

【外快】 wàikuài extra income

【外来】 wàilái outside; external; foreign: ~干涉 outside interference; foreign (或 external) intervention

【外力】 wàilì ⑴ outside force ⑵ 〈物〉 external force

【外流】 wàiliú outflow; drain: 美元~ dollar outflow/ 黄金~ gold bullion outflow

【外貌】 wàimào appearance; exterior; looks

【外面】 wàimiàn outward appearance; exterior; surface

【外面】 wàimian outside; out: 把椅子搬到~去 take the chair out/ 今天我们要在~吃饭。We'll eat (或dine) out today.

【外婆】 wàipó 〈方〉 (maternal) grandmother

【外戚】 wàiqī relatives of a king or emperor on the side of his mother or wife

【外强中干】 wàiqiáng-zhōnggān outwardly strong but inwardly weak; strong in appearance but weak in reality

【外侨】 wàiqiáo foreign national; alien

【外勤】 wàiqín ⑴ work done outside the office or in the field (as surveying, prospecting, news gathering, etc.) ⑵ field personnel

【外圈】 wàiquān 〈体〉 outer lane; outside lane

【外人】 wàirén ⑴ stranger; outsider: 别客气, 我又不是~。Don't stand on ceremony. I'm no stranger./ 不足为~道 not to be mentioned to outsiders/ 你说吧, 这里没~。Speak up. You're among friends. ⑵ foreigner; alien

【外伤】 wàishāng an injury or wound; trauma

【外甥】 wàisheng sister's son; nephew

【外甥女】 wàishengnǚ sister's daughter; niece

【外孙】 wàisūn daughter's son; grandson

【外孙女】 wàisūnnǚ daughter's daughter; granddaughter

【外胎】 wàitāi tyre (cover)

【外逃】 wàitáo ⑴ flee to some other place ⑵ flee the country

【外套】 wàitào ⑴ overcoat ⑵ loose coat; outer garment

【外头】 wàitou outside; out: 汽车在~。The car is outside./ 这事儿~全知道了。Even those on the outside know about it./ 夏天我常在~睡。In summer I often sleep outdoors.

【外围】 wàiwéi periphery: 首都~ the periphery of the capital ◇ ~防线 outer defence line/ ~组织 peripheral organization

【外文】 wàiwén foreign language

【外侮】 wàiwǔ foreign aggression; external aggression: 抵御~ resist foreign aggression

【外务】 wàiwù ⑴ matters outside one's job ⑵ foreign affairs; external affairs

【外乡】 wàixiāng another part of the country; some other place: ~口音 a nonlocal accent/ 他是~人。He is not from these parts.

【外向】 wàixiàng 〈心〉 extroversion

【外销】 wàixiāo for sale abroad or in another part of the country: ~产品 products for export; articles for sale in other areas

【外心】 wàixīn ⑴ unfaithful intentions (of husband or wife) ⑵ 〈数〉 circumcentre

【外形】 wàixíng appearance; external form; contour

【外姓】 wàixìng (people) not of the same surname

【外衣】 wàiyī ⑴ coat; jacket; outer clothing; outer garment ⑵ semblance; appearance; garb

【外因】 wàiyīn 〈哲〉 external cause

【外用】 wàiyòng 〈药〉 external use; external application: ~药水 lotion/ 只能~ for external use only

【外语】 wàiyǔ foreign language: ~教学 foreign language teaching/ ~学院 institute of foreign languages

【外援】 wàiyuán foreign aid; outside help; external assistance

【外在】 wàizài external; extrinsic: ~因素 external factor

【外债】 wàizhài external debt; foreign debt

【外长】 wàizhǎng 〈简〉 (外交部长) Minister of (或 for) Foreign affairs; Foreign Minister

【外罩】 wàizhào outer garment; dustcoat; overall

【外资】 wàizī foreign capital

【外族】 wàizú ⑴ people not of the same clan ⑵ foreigner; alien ⑶ other nationalities

【外祖父】 wàizǔfù (maternal) grandfather

【外祖母】 wàizǔmǔ (maternal) grandmother

wān

弯* wān ⑴ curved; tortuous; crooked: ~~的月牙儿 a crescent moon/ 累累的果实把树枝都压~了。Clusters of fruit weighed the branches down. ⑵ bend; flex: ~弓 bend a bow/ ~着腰插秧 bend over to transplant rice ⑶ turn; curve; bend: 拐~儿 go round curves; turn a corner

【弯路】 wānlù ⑴ crooked road; tortuous path ⑵ roundabout way; detour: 少走~ avoid detours/ 由于缺乏经验, 我们工作走了~。Owing to lack of experience we took a roundabout course in our work.

【弯曲】 wānqū winding; meandering; zigzag; crooked; curved: 一条~的山间小道 a winding mountain path/ 一根~的木棍 a crooked stick/ 小河弯弯曲曲地向东流去。The brook meanders eastwards.

剜 wān cut out; gouge out; scoop out: 把苹果烂的地

方～掉。Scoop out the rotten part of the apple.

【剜肉补疮】 wānròu-bǔchuāng　cut out a piece of one's flesh to cure a boil — resort to a remedy worse than the ailment; resort to a stopgap measure detrimental to long-term interests

湾* wān ① a bend in a stream: 河～ river bend ② gulf; bay: 渤海～ Bohai Bay/ 墨西哥～ the Gulf of Mexico ③ cast anchor; moor: 把船～在那边。Moor the boat over there.

蜿 wān
【蜿蜒】 wānyán ① (of snakes, etc.) wriggle ② wind; zigzag; meander: 小溪～流过田野。The stream winds through the fields.

豌 wān
【豌豆】 wāndòu　pea

wán

丸* wán ① ball; pellet: 泥～ mud ball ② pill; bolus: 每服两～ take two pills each time
【丸剂】 wánjì　pill
【丸药】 wányào　pill (或 bolus) of Chinese medicine
【丸子】 wánzi ① a round mass of food; ball: 肉～ meatball ② pill; bolus

纨 wán 〈书〉fine silk fabrics
【纨袴子弟】 wánkù zǐdì　profligate son of the rich; fop; dandy; playboy　又作"纨绔子弟"

完* wán ① intact; whole: ～好 in good condition; intact/ 覆巢之下无～卵。When a bird's nest is overturned no egg can remain intact. ② run out; use up: 我们的煤快烧～了。We're running out of coal./ 听～别人的话 hear sb. out/ 信纸用～。The writing pad is used up. ③ finish; complete; be over; be through: 我马上就～。I'll be through soon./ 会开～了。The meeting is over./ 下期续～ to be concluded in the next issue ④ pay: ～税 pay taxes
【完备】 wánbèi　complete; perfect: 一套～的工具 a complete set of tools/ 指出不～之处 point out the imperfections
【完毕】 wánbì　finish; complete; end: 第一期工程已经～。The first phase of the project has been completed./ 一切准备～。Everything is ready.
【完璧归赵】 wánbì guī Zhào　return the jade intact to the State of Zhao — return sth. to its owner in good condition
【完成】 wánchéng　accomplish; complete; fulfil; bring to success (或 fruition): ～任务 complete one's mission; accomplish a task; discharge one's duty/ ～国家计划 fulfil the state plan/ ～生产指标 hit the production target; fulfil the production quota
【完蛋】 wándàn 〈口〉be done for; be finished
【完稿】 wángǎo　finish a piece of writing; complete the manuscript
【完工】 wángōng　complete a project, etc.; finish doing sth.; get through: 这座桥一个月就～了。It took only one month to complete the bridge.
【完好】 wánhǎo　intact; whole; in good condition: ～无缺 intact; undamaged/ 货物已到,～无损。The goods have arrived in good condition.
【完婚】 wánhūn 〈书〉(of a man) get married; marry
【完结】 wánjié　end; be over; finish: 事情并没有～。This is not the end of the matter.
【完竣】 wánjùn (of a project, etc.) be completed
【完了】 wánliǎo　come to an end; be over
【完满】 wánmǎn　satisfactory; successful: 找个～的解决办法 seek a satisfactory solution/ 会议～结束。The meeting came to a satisfactory close.
【完美】 wánměi　perfect; consummate: ～无疵 perfect; flawless
【完全】 wánquán ① complete; whole: 他话没说～。He

didn't give a full picture. ② completely; fully; wholly; entirely; absolutely: ～错了 be completely wrong/ ～不同 be totally different; have nothing in common/ ～相反 be the exact opposite/ ～正确 perfectly right; absolutely correct/ 他～同意我们的意见。He fully agrees with us./ 她～不考虑个人得失。She gave no thought whatsoever to personal gain or loss.
【完人】 wánrén　perfect man
【完善】 wánshàn　perfect; consummate: 设备～ very well equipped/ 新生事物难免有不够～的地方。Imperfections are almost unavoidable in newborn things./ 我们厂的规章制度日益～。The rules and regulations of our factory are being perfected.
【完事】 wánshì　finish; get through; come to an end: 你～了没有? Have you finished (the job)?/ 他们校对到深夜才～。They didn't finish their proofreading until late at night.
【完整】 wánzhěng　complete; integrated; intact: ～的工业体系 an integrated (或 all-round, comprehensive) industrial system/ 维护领土～ safeguard territorial integrity/ 许多珍贵的历史文物～地保存下来了。Many precious historical relics have been preserved intact./ 没有经济上的独立,一个国家的独立是不～的。Without economic independence, no country can achieve complete independence.

玩* wán ① play; have fun; amuse oneself: ～儿牌 play cards/ 我们～儿盘棋好吗? Shall we have a game of chess?/ 孩子们都喜欢～儿。Children all love to play./ 我们在曼谷～了几天。We spent a few days enjoying ourselves in Bangkok./ 真好～儿! That's great fun!/ 他是说着～儿的。He only said it for fun. 或 He was only joking. ② employ; resort to: ～儿邪的 employ underhand means; not play fair/ ～手段 resort to crafty manoeuvres; play tricks ③ trifle with; treat lightly: ～法 trifle with the law ④ enjoy; appreciate: ～月 enjoy looking at the moon/ ～儿邮票 make a hobby of collecting stamps ⑤ object for appreciation: 古～ curio; antique
【玩忽】 wánhū　neglect; trifle with: ～职守 neglect (或 dereliction) of duty
【玩火】 wánhuǒ　play with fire
【玩火自焚】 wánhuǒ zì fén　he who plays with fire will get burnt; whoever plays with fire will perish by fire
【玩具】 wánjù　toy; plaything: ～汽车 toy car ◇ ～店 toyshop
【玩弄】 wánnòng ① dally with: ～女性 philander; dally with women ② play with; juggle with: ～词句 juggle with words; go in for rhetoric ③ resort to; employ: ～种种阴谋诡计 resort to all sorts of schemes and intrigues/ ～新花招 employ some new tricks/ ～两面派手法 engage in double-dealing
【玩赏】 wánshǎng　enjoy; take pleasure in: ～风景 enjoy (或 admire) the scenery
【玩世不恭】 wán shì bù gōng　be cynical
【玩耍】 wánshuǎ　play; have fun; amuse oneself
【玩味】 wánwèi　ponder; ruminate: 他的话很值得～。His words are worth pondering.
【玩物】 wánwù　plaything; toy
【玩物丧志】 wán wù sàng zhì　riding a hobby saps one's will to make progress; excessive attention to trivia saps the will
【玩笑】 wánxiào　joke; jest: 开～ play a joke (或 prank) on; make jests/ 他这是开～,你别认真。He's only joking; don't take him seriously.
【玩意儿】 wányìr 〈口〉① toy; plaything ② thing: 新鲜～ newfangled gadget/ 他手里拿的是什么～? What's that thing in his hand?/ 他是什么～! What kind of louse is he! 又作"玩艺儿"

顽* wán ① stupid; dense; insensate: ～石 hard rock; insensate stone ② stubborn; obstinate: ～敌 stubborn enemy; inveterate foe ③ naughty; mischievous
【顽钝】 wándùn　dull and obtuse; stupid; thickheaded
【顽固】 wángù ① obstinate; stubborn; headstrong: ～不化

incorrigibly obstinate/ ～地坚持错误立场 stubbornly cling to one's wrong position ② bitterly opposed to change: die-hard ◇ ～分子 diehard; die-hard element/ ～派 the diehards

【顽抗】 wánkàng stubbornly resist: 敌人再～就消灭它。If the enemy continues to resist stubbornly, wipe them out.

【顽皮】 wánpí naughty; mischievous

【顽强】 wánqiáng indomitable; staunch; tenacious: 同疾病进行～的斗争 carry on a tenacious struggle against illness

【顽石点头】 wánshí diǎntóu (be so persuasive as to make) the insensate stones nod in agreement

【顽童】 wántóng naughty child; urchin

【顽症】 wánzhèng chronic and stubborn disease; persistent ailment

wǎn

宛 wǎn ① winding; tortuous ② <书> as if: 音容～在 as if the person were still alive

【宛然】 wǎnrán as if: 这里山清水秀，～江南风景。The scenery here has great charm, reminding one of the land south of the Changjiang River.

【宛如】 wǎnrú just like

【宛延】 wǎnyán <书> meander

【宛转】 wǎnzhuǎn ① 见"辗转" zhǎnzhuǎn ② 见"婉转" wǎnzhuǎn

莞 wǎn

【莞尔】 wǎn'ěr <书> smile: 不觉～ cannot help smiling

挽 wǎn ① draw; pull: ～弓 draw a bow/ 手～着手 arm in arm ② roll up: ～起袖子 roll up one's sleeves ③ lament sb.'s death: ～诗 elegy ④ coil up

【挽歌】 wǎngē dirge; elegy

【挽回】 wǎnhuí retrieve; redeem: ～败局 retrieve a defeat/ ～面子 save face/ ～劣势 retrieve oneself from an inferior position; improve one's position/ ～损失 retrieve a loss/ ～影响 redeem (或 retrieve) one's reputation/ 无可～ irredeemable; irretrievable

【挽救】 wǎnjiù save; remedy; rescue: ～病人的生命 save the patient's life/ 想出一个有效的～办法 think out an effective remedy

【挽联】 wǎnlián elegiac couplet

【挽留】 wǎnliú urge (或 persuade) sb. to stay: 再三～ repeatedly urge to stay; press sb. to stay

惋 wǎn sigh

【惋惜】 wǎnxī feel sorry for sb. or about sth.; sympathize with

晚* wǎn ① evening; night: 今～ this evening; tonight ② far on in time; late: ～唐 the late Tang Dynasty/ 睡得～ go to bed late/ ～做总比不做好。Better late than never./ 现在去还不～。It's still not too late to go. ③ younger; junior

【晚安】 wǎn'ān <套> good night

【晚班】 wǎnbān night shift: 上～ be on the night shift

【晚报】 wǎnbào evening paper

【晚辈】 wǎnbèi the younger generation; one's juniors: 我是他的～。I am his junior by one generation.

【晚餐】 wǎncān supper; dinner

【晚场】 wǎnchǎng evening show; evening performance

【晚饭】 wǎnfàn supper; dinner

【晚会】 wǎnhuì an evening of entertainment; soirée; social evening; evening party: 除夕～ New Year's Eve entertainment

【晚婚】 wǎnhūn marry at a mature age

【晚间】 wǎnjiān (in the) evening; (at) night

【晚近】 wǎnjìn in recent years; during the past few years

【晚景】 wǎnjǐng ① evening scene ② one's circumstances in old age

【晚年】 wǎnnián old age; one's later (或 remaining) years: 过者幸福的～ spend one's remaining years in happiness

【晚期】 wǎnqī later period: ～作品 sb.'s later works; the works of sb.'s later period/ 十九世纪～ the late 19th century; the latter part of the 19th century/ 他的病已到～。His illness has reached an advanced stage.

【晚秋】 wǎnqiū late autumn; late in the autumn ◇ ～作物 late-autumn crops

【晚上】 wǎnshang (in the) evening; (at) night

【晚霞】 wǎnxiá sunset glow; sunset clouds

婉 wǎn ① gentle; gracious; tactful: ～商 consult with sb. tactfully (或 politely)/ ～顺 complaisant; obliging ② beautiful; graceful; elegant: ～丽 beautiful; lovely

【婉辞】 wǎncí ① gentle words; euphemism ② graciously decline; politely refuse

【婉言】 wǎnyán gentle words; tactful expressions: ～相劝 gently persuade; plead tactfully/ ～谢绝 graciously decline; politely refuse

【婉约】 wǎnyuē <书> graceful and restrained

【婉转】 wǎnzhuǎn ① mild and indirect; tactful: 措词～ put it tactfully/ 他那话虽然说得～，意见却很尖锐。His remark, for all its mildness, is nevertheless a sharp criticism. ② sweet and agreeable: 歌喉～ a sweet voice; sweet singing

挽 wǎn ① pull; draw: ～车 pull (或 draw) a cart or carriage ② lament sb.'s death

【挽歌】 wǎngē dirge; elegy

【挽联】 wǎnlián elegiac couplet

碗* wǎn bowl: 摆～筷 put out bowls and chopsticks for a meal; lay the table

wàn

万* wàn ① ten thousand ② a very great number; myriad: ～事～物 myriads of things; all nature/ ～里长空 vast clear skies ③ absolutely; by all means: ～不得已 out of absolute necessity; as a last resort

【万般】 wànbān ① all the different kinds ② utterly; extremely: ～无奈 have no alternative (but to)

【万变不离其宗】 wàn biàn bù lí qí zōng change ten thousand times without departing from the original aim or stand; remain essentially the same despite all apparent changes

【万端】 wànduān multifarious: 变化～ multifarious changes; kaleidoscopic changes/ 感慨～ all sorts of feelings welling up in one's mind

【万恶】 wàn'è extremely evil; absolutely vicious: ～之源 the root of all evil

【万方】 wànfāng ① all places ② extremely; incomparably: 仪态～ incomparably graceful

【万分】 wànfēn very much; extremely: ～感谢 thank you very much indeed/ ～抱歉 be extremely sorry/ ～高兴 be very happy; be highly pleased

【万古】 wàngǔ through the ages; eternally; forever: ～长存 last forever; be everlasting

【万古长青】 wàngǔ chángqīng remain fresh forever; be everlasting: 祝两国人民的友谊～！May the friendship between our two peoples last forever!

【万花筒】 wànhuātǒng kaleidoscope

【万家灯火】 wànjiā dēnghuǒ a myriad twinkling lights (of a city)

【万劫不复】 wànjié bù fù beyond redemption

【万金油】 wànjīnyóu ① a balm for treating headaches, scalds and other minor ailments ② Jack of all trades and master of none

【万籁俱寂】 wànlài jù jì all is quiet; silence reigns supreme

【万里长城】 Wànlǐ Chángchéng the Great Wall

【万马奔腾】 wànmǎ bēnténg ten thousand horses galloping ahead — going full steam ahead

【万难】 wànnán extremely difficult; utterly impossible: ～照办 impossible to do as requested/ ～同意 can by no means agree

【万难】 wànnán all difficulties: 排除～ surmount all difficulties

【万能】 wànnéng ① omnipotent; all-powerful ② universal; all-purpose

【万年】 wànnián ten thousand years; all ages; eternity: 遗臭～ leave a bad name for generations to come

【万年青】 wànniánqīng 〈植〉 evergreen

【万千】 wànqiān multifarious; myriad: 变化～ eternally changing; changing all the time/ 思绪～ myriads of thoughts welling up in one's mind

【万全】 wànquán perfectly sound; surefire: ～之计 a completely safe plan; a surefire plan

【万人空巷】 wànrén kōng xiàng the whole town turns out (to welcome sb. or celebrate some event)

【万世】 wànshì all ages; generation after generation

【万事】 wànshì all things; everything: ～起头难。 Everything's hard in the beginning.

【万事大吉】 wànshì dàjí everything is just fine; all's well with the world: 以为这次胜利了便～的思想是危险的。 It is a dangerous illusion to think that after this victory everything will go off without a hitch.

【万事亨通】 wànshì hēngtōng everything goes well

【万事俱备，只欠东风】 wànshì jù bèi, zhǐ qiàn dōngfēng everything is ready, and all that we need is an east wind — all is ready except what is crucial

【万事通】 wànshìtōng 〈讽〉 know-all

【万寿无疆】 wànshòu-wújiāng (wish sb.) a long life

【万水千山】 wànshuǐ-qiānshān ten thousand crags and torrents — the trials of a long journey

【万死】 wànsǐ die ten thousand deaths: 罪该～ deserve to die ten thousand deaths/ ～不辞 willing to risk any danger to do one's duty

【万岁】 wànsuì ① long live ② the emperor; （直接称呼） Your Majesty; （间接称呼） His Majesty

【万万】 wànwàn ① 〔用于否定〕 absolutely; wholly: 我～没有想到。 This idea never occurred to me./ 那是～不行的。 That's absolutely out of the question. 或 That won't do at all. ② hundred million

【万无一失】 wàn wú yī shī no danger of anything going wrong; no risk at all; perfectly safe; surefire

【万物】 wànwù all things on earth

【万象】 wànxiàng every phenomenon on earth; all manifestations of nature: 春回大地，～更新。 Spring comes round to the earth again and everything looks fresh and gay.

【万幸】 wànxìng very lucky （或 fortunate）; by sheer luck

【万一】 wànyī ① 〈连〉 just in case; if by any chance: ～有人找我,就请他留个条。 If by any chance somebody comes to see me, ask him to leave a message. ② contingency; eventuality: 防备～ be ready for all eventualities; be prepared for the worst ③ one ten thousandth; a very small percentage: 笔墨不能形容其～。 It simply beggars description.

【万应灵丹】 wànyìng língdān cure-all; panacea

【万有引力】 wànyǒu yǐnlì 〈物〉 (universal) gravitation ◇ ～定律 the law of universal gravitation

【万丈】 wànzhàng lofty or bottomless: ～深渊 a bottomless chasm; abyss/ 怒火～ a towering rage; a fit of violent anger/～高楼平地起。 Lofty towers are all built up from the ground. 或 Great oaks from little acorns grow.

【万众】 wànzhòng millions of people; the multitude: 喜讯传来,～欢腾。 Millions of people rejoiced at the happy news.

【万众一心】 wànzhòng-yīxīn millions of people all of one mind

【万状】 wànzhuàng in the extreme; extremely: 危险～ extremely dangerous/ 惊恐～ be frightened out of one's senses

【万紫千红】 wànzǐ-qiānhóng a riot （或 blaze） of colour: 百花盛开,～。 Flowers of all sorts are blooming in a riot of colour.

萬 wàn ten thousand (used for the numeral 万 on cheques, etc. to avoid mistakes or alterations)

腕 wàn wrist

wāng

汪 wāng ① (of liquid) collect; accumulate: 汤里～着油。 There are blobs of fat in the soup. ② 〈量〉〔用于液体〕: 一～雨水 a puddle of rainwater ③ 〈象〉 bark; bowwow

【汪汪】 wāngwāng ① tears welling up; tearful: 泪～的 with tearful eyes ② 〈象〉 bark; yap; bowwow: 狗～地叫。A dog is barking.

【汪洋】 wāngyáng (of a body of water) vast; boundless: 一片～ a vast expanse （或 body） of water

wáng

亡* wáng ① flee; run away: 出～ flee; live in exile ② lose; be gone: 唇～齿寒。 If the lips are gone, the teeth will feel cold. ③ die; perish: 阵～ die （或 fall） in battle ④ deceased: ～妻 deceased wife ⑤ conquer; subjugate

【亡故】 wánggù die; pass away; decease

【亡国】 wángguó ① subjugate a nation; let a state perish: ～灭种 national subjugation and genocide ② a conquered nation: ～之民 the people of a conquered nation ◇ ～奴 a slave of a foreign power; a slave without a country; a conquered people

【亡灵】 wánglíng the soul of a deceased person; ghost; spectre

【亡命】 wángmìng ① flee; seek refuge; go into exile ② desperate: ～之徒 desperado

【亡羊补牢】 wáng yáng bǔ láo mend the fold after a sheep is lost: ～,犹未为晚。 It is not too late to mend the fold even after some of the sheep have been lost.

王* wáng ① king; monarch: 国～ king ② 〈书〉 grand; great: ～父 grandfather

【王八】 wángba ① tortoise ② 〈骂〉 cuckold ◇ ～蛋 bastard; son of a bitch

【王朝】 wángcháo ① imperial court; royal court ② dynasty: 封建～ feudal dynasties

【王储】 wángchǔ crown prince

【王道】 wángdào kingly way; benevolent government

【王法】 wángfǎ the law of the land; the law

【王公】 wánggōng princes and dukes; the nobility: ～大臣 princes, dukes and ministers/ ～贵族 the nobility

【王宫】 wánggōng (imperial) palace

【王冠】 wángguān imperial crown; royal crown

【王国】 wángguó ① kingdom ② realm; domain: 从必然到自由～ from the realm of necessity to the realm of freedom/ 独立～ independent kingdom; private preserve

【王侯】 wánghóu princes and marquises; the nobility

【王后】 wánghòu queen consort; queen

【王牌】 wángpái trump card ◇ ～军 elite troops; crack units

【王室】 wángshì ① royal family ② imperial court; royal court

【王孙】 wángsūn prince's descendants; offspring of the nobility

【王位】 wángwèi throne: 继承～ succeed to the throne

【王子】 wángzǐ king's son; prince

【王族】 wángzú persons of royal lineage; imperial kinsmen

忘 wáng 另见 wàng

【忘八】 wángba 见"王八" wángba

wǎng

网* wǎng ① net: 鱼～ fishnet; fishing net/ 发～ hairnet/ 蜘蛛～ cobweb/ 电～ electrified barbed wire ② network: 铁路～ railway network/ 广播～ a network of broadcasting stations ③ catch with a net; net: ～着了一条鱼

net a fish ④ cover or enclose as with a net: 眼里～着红丝 have bloodshot eyes

【网开一面】 wǎng kāi yī miàn leave one side of the net open — give the wrongdoer a way out

【网罗】 wǎngluó ⑴ a net for catching fish or birds; trap ⑵ enlist the services of: ～人材 enlist able men

【网球】 wǎngqiú ① tennis ② tennis ball ◇ ～场 tennis court/ ～拍 tennis racket

枉 wǎng ① crooked: 矫～ straighten sth. crooked; right a wrong ② twist; pervert: ～法 pervert the law ③ treat unjustly; wrong: 冤～ wrong sb. (with false charges, etc.)/ ～死 be wronged and driven to death ④ in vain; to no avail: ～活了半辈子 have wasted half a lifetime

【枉法】 wǎngfǎ pervert the law: 贪赃～ take bribes and pervert the law

【枉费】 wǎngfèi waste; try in vain; be of no avail: ～唇舌 be a mere waste of breath/ ～心机 rack one's brains in vain; scheme without avail

【枉然】 wǎngrán futile; in vain; to no purpose

罔 wǎng 〈书〉 ① deceive: 欺～ deceive; cheat ② no; not: 置若～闻 take no heed of; turn a deaf ear to

往 wǎng ① go: 来来～～ coming and going ② in the direction of; toward: ～东走去 go in an eastward direction/ 这车开～伦敦。 The train is bound for London. ③ past; previous: ～事 the past
另见 wàng

【往常】 wǎngcháng habitually in the past; as one used to do formerly: 他～不这样。 He was not like that before./ 我们～都是天黑了才收工。 We used to go on working until it got dark.

【往返】 wǎngfǎn go there and back; journey to and fro: ～于成都、重庆之间 travel to and fro between Chengdu and Chongqing/ ～要多少时间？ How long does it take to go there and back?

【往复】 wǎngfù move back and forth; reciprocate: 循环～，以至无穷 repeat itself in endless cycles

【往还】 wǎnghuán contact; dealings; intercourse: 经常有书信 write to each other regularly; keep in contact by correspondence

【往来】 wǎnglái ① come and go ② contact; dealings; intercourse: 贸易～ trade contacts; commercial intercourse/ 友好～ exchange of friendly visits; friendly intercourse/ 他们俩～密切。 The two of them are in close contact. 或 They see a lot of each other. ◇ ～帐 current (或 open, running) account

【往年】 wǎngnián (in) former years

【往日】 wǎngrì (in) former days; (in) bygone days

【往事】 wǎngshì past events; the past: 回忆～ recollections of the past

【往往】 wǎngwǎng 〈副〉 often; frequently; more often than not: 这里春天～刮大风。 It often blows hard here in spring./ 有些人～只看到当前的、局部的、个人的利益。 Some people are prone to see only immediate, partial and personal interests.

【往昔】 wǎngxī in the past; in former times

惘 wǎng feel frustrated; feel disappointed

【惘然】 wǎngrán frustrated; disappointed: ～若失 feel lost

魍 wǎng

【魍魉】 wǎngliǎng demons and monsters

wàng

妄 wàng ① absurd; preposterous: 狂～ wildly arrogant ② presumptuous; rash: ～作主张 make a presumptuous decision/ ～加评论 make improper comments

【妄动】 wàngdòng rash (或 reckless, ill-considered) action: 轻举～ take rash action

【妄念】 wàngniàn wild fancy; improper thought

【妄求】 wàngqiú inappropriate request; presumptuous demand

【妄人】 wàngrén 〈书〉 an ignorant and presumptuous person

【妄图】 wàngtú try in vain; vainly attempt: ～打破一个缺口 vainly attempt to make a breach/ ～掩盖事实真相 try in vain to cover up the truth; vainly attempt to conceal the facts

【妄想】 wàngxiǎng vain hope; wishful thinking

【妄语】 wàngyǔ ① tell lies; talk nonsense ② wild talk; rant 又作 "妄言"

【妄自菲薄】 wàng zì fěibó improperly belittle oneself; unduly humble oneself; underestimate one's own capabilities

【妄自尊大】 wàng zì zūndà have too high an opinion of oneself; be overweening; be self-important

忘 wàng ① forget: 他把这事全～了。 He forgot all about it. 或 He clean forgot about the whole thing./ 饮水不～掘井人。 When you drink the water, think of those who dug the well. ② overlook; neglect: 不要只看到事物的一面而～了另一面。 Don't look at only one aspect of the thing and neglect the other./ 别～了给我打电话。 Don't forget to phone me./ 我～了拿笔记本。 I've left my notebook behind.
另见 wáng

【忘本】 wàngběn forget one's class origin; forget one's past suffering: 我们过上了幸福的生活，可不能～。 We must not forget our old sufferings, now that we are living happy lives.

【忘掉】 wàngdiào forget; let slip from one's mind: 我当时忙于工作，把这件事给～了。 I was so busy working it simply slipped my mind./ 我们把这件不愉快的事～吧。 Let's forget the unpleasantness.

【忘恩负义】 wàng'ēn-fùyì devoid of gratitude; ungrateful

【忘乎所以】 wàng hū suǒyǐ forget oneself: 头脑发热，～ be carried away by a sudden impulse; lose one's head in a moment of excitement/ 不要因为胜利而～。 Don't get swollen-headed because of victory. 又作 "忘其所以"

【忘怀】 wànghuái forget; dismiss from one's mind: 当时情景我久久不能～。 For a long time afterwards I could not get the scene out of my mind./ ～得失 not worried about personal gains or losses

【忘记】 wàngjì ① forget: 我永不会～我们初次见面的那一天。 I'll never forget the day we first met. ② overlook; neglect; forget: 不能～自己的责任。 One mustn't neglect one's duties./ 他紧张地工作，～了去吃晚饭。 He was working so hard that he forgot to go for supper.

【忘年交】 wàngniánjiāo ① friendship between generations ② good friends despite great difference in age

【忘情】 wàngqíng ① 〔常用于否定〕 be unruffled by emotion; be unmoved; be indifferent: 不能～ be still emotionally attached ② let oneself go: ～地歌唱 let oneself go and sing lustily

【忘却】 wàngquè forget

【忘我】 wàngwǒ oblivious of oneself; selfless: ～地工作 work selflessly; work untiringly/ ～的精神 spirit of selflessness

【忘形】 wàngxíng be beside oneself (with glee, etc.); have one's head turned: 得意～ get dizzy with success; have one's head turned by success

旺 wàng prosperous; flourishing; vigorous: 购销两～ Both purchasing and marketing are brisk./ 人畜两～ Both men and livestock are flourishing./ 屋中炉火烧得正～ There was a roaring fire in the room.

【旺季】 wàngjì peak period; busy season

【旺盛】 wàngshèng vigorous; exuberant: 士气～ have high morale/ ～的生命力 exuberant vitality/ 麦子长势～。 Wheat is growing luxuriantly.

【旺月】 wàngyuè busy month (in business)

往 wàng 〈介〉 to; toward: ～左拐 turn to the left/ ～南走 go southwards/ ～前看 look forward/ 劲～一处使 all

directing their efforts toward the same goal/ 水～低处流。 Water naturally flows downhill. 或 Water always finds its own level.
另见 wǎng

【往后】 wànghòu from now on; later on; in the future: ～我们要加倍努力。 From now on we'll redouble our efforts./ ～的日子会更好。 As time goes on we'll live an even better life.

望* wàng ① gaze into the distance; look over: 登山远～ climb a mountain and gaze far afield/ 放眼～去 look ahead as far as the eye can reach/ ～了他一眼 shoot a glance at him ② call on; visit: 拜～ call to pay one's respects/ 看～ call on; visit ③ hope; expect: ～速归。 Hoping you'll return as soon as possible./ ～回信。Awaiting your reply./ 丰收在～。 A bumper harvest is in sight. ④ reputation; prestige: 德高～重 be of noble character and high prestige ⑤ 〈介〉〔表示"对着""朝着"〕: ～我点点头 nod at me/ ～他笑了笑 smile at him ⑥ full moon ⑦ the 15th day of a lunar month: 既～ the 16th day of a lunar month

【望尘莫及】 wàng chén mò jí so far behind that one can only see the dust of the rider ahead; too far behind to catch up; too inferior to bear comparison
【望穿秋水】 wàngchuān qiūshuǐ 见"望眼欲穿"
【望而却步】 wàng ér quèbù shrink back at the sight of (sth. dangerous or difficult); flinch
【望而生畏】 wàng ér shēng wèi be terrified (或 awed) by the sight of sb. or sth.: 令人～ awe-inspiring; forbidding
【望风】 wàngfēng be on the lookout (while conducting secret activities); keep watch
【望风而逃】 wàng fēng ér táo flee at the mere sight of the oncoming force
【望风披靡】 wàng fēng pīmǐ flee pell-mell (或 helter-skelter) at the mere sight of the oncoming force: 我军所到之处,敌人～。 Wherever our troops went, the enemy fled pell-mell before them.
【望楼】 wànglóu watchtower; lookout tower
【望梅止渴】 wàng méi zhǐkě quench one's thirst by thinking of plums — console oneself with false hopes; feed on fancies
【望日】 wàngrì the 15th day of a lunar month
【望文生义】 wàng wén shēng yì take the words too literally; interpret without real understanding
【望眼欲穿】 wàng yǎn yù chuān anxiously gaze till one's eyes are strained; have long been looking forward with eager expectancy
【望洋兴叹】 wàng yáng xīngtàn lament one's littleness before the vast ocean — bemoan one's inadequacy in the face of a great task
【望远镜】 wàngyuǎnjìng telescope: 双筒～ binoculars; field glasses

双筒望远镜

望远镜

【望月】 wàngyuè full moon
【望族】 wàngzú 〈书〉 distinguished family; prominent family

wēi

危* wēi ① danger; peril: 居安思～ think of danger in times of peace ② endanger; imperil: ～及生命 endanger one's life ③ dying; dead: 病～ be critically ill; be dying ④ 〈书〉 high; precipitous: ～楼 a high tower/ ～崖 a precipitous cliff ⑤ 〈书〉 proper: 正襟～坐 sit up properly

【危殆】 wēidài 〈书〉 in great danger; in jeopardy; in a critical condition: 病势～ be dangerously ill; be critically ill

【危笃】 wēidǔ 〈书〉 critically ill; on the point of death
【危害】 wēihài harm; endanger; jeopardize: ～治安 jeopardize public security/ ～公共利益 harm the public interest ◇ ～性 harmfulness; perniciousness
【危机】 wēijī crisis: 经济～ economic crisis/ ～重重 bogged down in crises; crisis-ridden/ 四伏 beset with crises; crisis-ridden
【危急】 wēijí critical; in imminent danger; in a desperate situation: ～关头 critical juncture (或 time, moment)/ 情况十分～。 The situation is desperate./ 伤势～。 The wound may be fatal.
【危局】 wēijú a dangerous (或 critical, desperate) situation
【危惧】 wēijù worry and fear; be apprehensive
【危难】 wēinàn danger and disaster; calamity: 处于～之中 be in dire peril
【危如累卵】 wēi rú lěi luǎn as precarious as a pile of eggs; in a precarious situation
【危亡】 wēiwáng in peril; at stake: 民族～的时刻 when the nation's existence is in peril; when, the fate of the nation hangs in the balance
【危险】 wēixiǎn dangerous; perilous: 冒生命～ at the risk of one's life/ 脱离～ out of danger/ 有电,～! Danger! Electricity! ◇ ～地带 danger zone/ ～品 dangerous articles; dangerous goods/ ～人物 a dangerous person; a danger/ ～信号 danger signal
【危言耸听】 wēiyán sǒngtīng say frightening things just to raise an alarm; exaggerate things just to scare people: 这不是～,而是历史多次证明了的真理。 This is not alarmist talk; it is a truth repeatedly borne out by history.
【危在旦夕】 wēi zài dànxī on the verge of death or destruction: 生命～。 Death is expected at any moment./ 该城～。 The city may fall at any moment.

委 wēi
另见 wěi
【委蛇】 wēiyí ① 见"逶迤" wēiyí ② 见"虚与委蛇" xū yǔ wěiyí

威* wēi ① impressive strength; might; power: 军～ the might of an army; military prowess/ ～震四方 known far and wide for one's military prowess/ 示～ demonstrate one's strength ② by force

【威逼】 wēibī threaten by force; coerce; intimidate: ～利诱 alternate intimidation and bribery; combine threats with inducements
【威风】 wēifēng ① power and prestige: 灭敌人的～ puncture (或 deflate) the enemy's arrogance ② imposing; impressive; awe-inspiring
【威风凛凛】 wēifēng lǐnlǐn majestic-looking; awe-inspiring
【威风扫地】 wēifēng sǎodì with every shred of one's prestige swept away — completely discredited
【威吓】 wēihè intimidate; threaten; bully: 不顾敌人～ in defiance of the enemy's intimidation
【威力】 wēilì power; might
【威名】 wēimíng fame based on great strength or military exploits; prestige; renown
【威权】 wēiquán authority; power
【威慑】 wēishè terrorize with military force; deter ◇ ～力量 deterrent force; deterrent
【威士忌】 wēishìjì whisky
【威势】 wēishì power and influence
【威望】 wēiwàng prestige: 崇高的～ high prestige
【威武】 wēiwǔ ① might; force; power: ～不能屈 not to be subdued by force ② powerful; mighty: 雄壮 full of power and grandeur
【威胁】 wēixié threaten; menace; imperil: ～邻国的安全 threaten (或 menace) the security of a neighbouring country
【威信】 wēixìn prestige; popular trust
【威严】 wēiyán ① dignified; stately; majestic; awe-inspiring ② prestige; dignity: 保持～ keep up one's prestige
【威仪】 wēiyí impressive and dignified manner

逶 wēi

【逶迤】 wēiyí winding; meandering: ～的山路 a winding mountain path/ 这条铁路～在群山之中。The railway winds its way through the mountains.

偎 wēi

snuggle up to; lean close to

【偎抱】 wēibào hug; cuddle

【偎依】 wēiyī snuggle up to; lean close to: 孩子～在母亲的怀里。The child snuggled up in its mother's arms.

隈 wēi

〈书〉 ① river bend ② mountain recess

煨 wēi

① cook over a slow fire; stew; simmer: ～牛肉 stewed beef ② roast (sweet potatoes, etc.) in fresh cinders

微* wēi

① minute; tiny; 细～ minute; tiny/ 相差甚～。The difference is slight (或 negligible)./ ～火 slow fire/ ～云 thin clouds/ ～雨 drizzle ② profound; abstruse: 精～ subtle ③ decline: 衰～ on the decline

【微波】 wēibō 〈电子〉 microwave

【微薄】 wēibó meagre; scanty: 收入～ have a meagre income/ 尽我们～的力量。We'll exert what little strength we have. 或 We'll do what little we can.

【微不足道】 wēibùzúdào not worth mentioning; insignificant; inconsiderable; negligible

【微风】 wēifēng 〈气〉 gentle breeze

【微乎其微】 wēi hū qí wēi very little; next to nothing: 我一个人的力量是～的。On my own I can do very little.

【微贱】 wēijiàn humble; lowly

【微粒】 wēilì particle

【微量】 wēiliàng trace; micro-

【微茫】 wēimáng 〈书〉 blurred; hazy

【微妙】 wēimiào delicate; subtle: 关系～ subtle relations/ 谈判进入～阶段。The negotiations have entered a delicate stage.

【微末】 wēimò trifling; insignificant: ～的贡献 an insignificant contribution/ ～的成就 an achievement of minor importance

【微弱】 wēiruò faint; feeble; weak: 呼吸～ faint breath/ 光线～ faint light; glimmer/ 脉搏～ feeble pulse/ ～的声音 a thin voice/ ～的多数 a slender majority

【微微】 wēiwēi slight; faint: ～一笑 smile faintly

【微细】 wēixì very small; tiny: ～的血管 very small blood vessels

【微小】 wēixiǎo small; little: 极其～ infinitely small; infinitesimal/ ～的希望 slender hopes/ ～的进步 meagre progress

【微笑】 wēixiào smile

【微言大义】 wēiyán-dàyì sublime words with deep meaning

【微恙】 wēiyàng slight illness; indisposition

【微震】 wēizhèn ① slight shock ② 〈地〉〈物〉 microseism

薇 wēi

见"蔷薇" qiángwēi

巍 wēi

towering; lofty

【巍峨】 wēi'é towering; lofty: ～的群山 lofty mountains

【巍然】 wēirán towering; lofty; majestic; imposing: ～屹立 stand lofty and firm; stand rock-firm/ 大桥～横跨在江上。The bridge stands majestic astride the river.

【巍巍】 wēiwēi towering; lofty

wéi

为* wéi

① do; act: 敢作敢～ decisive and bold in action; act with daring/ 事在人～。Human effort is the decisive factor. ② act as; serve as: 选她～人民代表 elect her a people's deputy/ 以此～凭。This will serve as a proof./ 有诗～证。A poem testifies to that. ③ become: 变沙漠～良田 turn the desert into arable land/ 一分～二。One divides into two. ④ be; mean: 一公里～二华里。One kilometre is equivalent to two *li*. ⑤ 〈介〉〔跟"所"字合用,表示被动〕: ～人民所爱戴 be loved and respected by the people/ 不～表面现

象所迷惑 not be confused by superficial phenomena ⑥ 〈书〉〈助〉〔常跟"何"相应,表示疑问〕: 何以家～? What need have I of a home?

另见 wèi

【为非作歹】 wéifēi-zuòdǎi do evil; commit crimes; perpetrate outrages

【为富不仁】 wéi fù bù rén be rich and cruel; be one of the heartless rich

【为难】 wéinán ① feel embarrassed; feel awkward: ～的事 an awkward matter/ 使人～ embarrass sb.; put sb. in an awkward situation ② make things difficult for: 故意～ deliberately make things difficult for sb.

【为期】 wéiqī (to be completed) by a definite date: 以两周～ not to exceed two weeks/ 举办一个月的摄影展览 hold a photo exhibition lasting a month/ 会议～三天。The meeting is scheduled to last three days./ ～不远。The day is not far off.

【为人】 wéirén behave; conduct oneself: ～正直 be upright

【为生】 wéishēng make a living: 以狩猎～ make a living as a hunter

【为时过早】 wéi shí guò zǎo premature; too early; too soon: 现在下结论～。It's still too early to reach a conclusion.

【为首】 wéishǒu with sb. as the leader; headed (或 led) by: 以某某～的代表团 a delegation headed (或 led) by so-and-so

【为数】 wéishù amount to; number: ～不少 come up to a large number; amount to quite a lot/ ～不多 have only a small number

【为所欲为】 wéi suǒ yù wéi 〈贬〉 do as one pleases; do whatever one likes; have one's own way

【为伍】 wéiwǔ associate with: 羞与～ think it beneath one to associate with

【为限】 wéixiàn be within the limit of; not exceed: 费用以一百元～。The expenses shall not exceed 100 dollars

【为止】 wéizhǐ up to; till: 迄今～ up to now; so far/ 到去年年底～ up to the end of last year/ 一直等到他回来～ wait till he returns/ 今天的讨论到此～。That's all for today's discussion.

【为重】 wéizhòng attach most importance to: 以大局～ put the general interest first

【为主】 wéizhǔ give first place to; give priority to

圩 wéi

dyke; embankment: 筑～ build dykes

【圩田】 wéitián low-lying paddy fields surrounded with dykes

违 wéi

① disobey; violate: ～令 disobey orders/ ～警 violation of police regulations ② be separated: 久～了。I haven't seen you for ages.

【违碍】 wéi'ài taboo; prohibition

【违拗】 wéi'ào disobey; defy

【违背】 wéibèi violate; go against; run counter to: ～原则 violate a principle/ ～自己的诺言 go back on one's word/ ～历史事实 be contrary to the historical facts

【违法】 wéifǎ break the law; be illegal: ～乱纪 violate the law and discipline/ ～行为 illegal activities; unlawful practice/ ～失职 transgression of the law and neglect of duty

【违反】 wéifǎn violate; run counter to; transgress; infringe: ～交通规则 violate traffic regulations/ ～决议的精神 be contrary to the spirit of the resolution/ ～社会发展规律 go against the laws of social development

【违犯】 wéifàn violate; infringe; act contrary to: ～纪律 violation of discipline; breach of discipline

【违禁】 wéijìn violate a ban ◇ ～品 contraband (goods)

【违抗】 wéikàng disobey; defy: ～命令 disobey orders; act in defiance of orders/ ～上级 defy the higher leading body; defy one's superiors; be insubordinate

【违例】 wéilì 〈体〉 breach of rules

【违误】 wéiwù 〔公文用语〕disobey orders and cause delay: 迅速办理,不得～。This is to be acted upon without delay.

【违心】 wéixīn against one's will; contrary to one's convictions: ～之论 words uttered against one's conscience;

obviously insincere talk

【违约】 wéiyuē ① break a contract; violate a treaty ② break one's promise; break off an engagement

围* wéi ① enclose; surround: 用篱笆把菜园子～上 enclose the vegetable patch with a fence/ 团团～住 completely surround; encircle; besiege/ ～着炉子坐 sit around a fire/ ～着他问长问短 gather round him, asking all sorts of questions/ ～湖造田 (build dykes to) reclaim land from a lake; reclaim lake bottom land and plant it to crops ② all round; around: 四～都是山。There are mountains all round. ③〈量〉〔两手拇指和食指或两只胳膊合拢的长度〕: 树大十～ a tree trunk ten arm spans around

【围城】 wéichéng ① encircle (或 besiege) a city ② besieged city

【围攻】 wéigōng ① besiege; lay siege to: 停止～ abandon a siege ② jointly speak or write against sb.; jointly attack sb.: 遭到～ come under attack from all sides; be caught in a cross fire

【围击】 wéijī besiege; lay siege to

【围歼】 wéijiān surround and annihilate

【围剿】 wéijiǎo encircle and suppress

【围巾】 wéijīn muffler; scarf

【围困】 wéikùn besiege; hem in; pin down: 把敌人～在少数据点中 pin down the enemy in a few strongholds

【围拢】 wéilǒng crowd around

【围屏】 wéipíng 〈工美〉 (folding) screen

【围棋】 wéiqí weiqi, a game played with black and white pieces on a board of 361 crosses; go

【围墙】 wéiqiáng enclosure; enclosing wall

【围裙】 wéiqún apron

【围绕】 wéirǎo ① round; around: 月亮～着地球旋转。The moon revolves round the earth. ② centre of; revolve round

【围魏救赵】 wéi Wèi jiù Zhào besiege Wei to rescue Zhao — relieve the besieged by besieging the base of the besiegers

桅 wéi mast: 船～ mast/ ～顶 masthead

【桅灯】 wéidēng ① 〈航海〉 mast head light; range light ② barn lantern

【桅杆】 wéigān mast

【桅樯】 wéiqiáng mast

惟 wéi ① only; alone: ～你是问 You'll be held personally responsible. ② 〈书〉 but: 母已痊愈，一体力尚未恢复。Mother's well now, but she hasn't fully recovered her strength yet. ③ thinking; thought: 思～ thinking

【惟独】 wéidú only; alone: 人家都回家了，～她还在工作。She kept on working when all the others had gone home./ 他心里总是装着别人，～没有他自己。His thoughts always turn to other people; hardly ever does he think of himself.

【惟恐】 wéikǒng for fear that; lest: ～落后 for fear that one should lag behind/ ～天下不乱 desire to see the world plunged into chaos; crave nothing short of nationwide chaos; desire to stir up trouble/ 我几次提醒他，～他忘了。I reminded him several times lest he should forget.

【惟利是图】 wéi lì shì tú be bent solely on profit; be intent on nothing but profit; put profit-making first: ～的思想 profit-before-everything mentality

【惟妙惟肖】 wéimiào-wéixiào 见 "维妙维肖" wéimiào-wéixiào

【惟命是听】 wéi mìng shì tīng always do as one is told; be absolutely obedient 又作 "惟命是从"

【惟我独尊】 wéi wǒ dú zūn overweening; extremely conceited

【惟一】 wéiyī only; sole: ～可行的办法 the only feasible way/ ～合法的政府 the sole legitimate government/ ～出路 the only way out

【惟有】 wéiyǒu only; alone

唯 wéi only; alone
另见 wěi

【唯美主义】 wéiměizhǔyì aestheticism

【唯物论】 wéiwùlùn 〈哲〉 materialism

【唯物主义】 wéiwùzhǔyì 〈哲〉 materialism

【唯心论】 wéixīnlùn 〈哲〉 idealism

【唯心主义】 wéixīnzhǔyì 〈哲〉 idealism

维* wéi ① tie up; hold together: ～系 hold together; maintain ② maintain; safeguard; preserve: ～护 safeguard; defend; uphold ③ thinking; thought

【维持】 wéichí keep; maintain; preserve: ～秩序 keep order; maintain order/ ～现状 maintain the status quo; let things go on as they are/ ～生活 support oneself or one's family

【维护】 wéihù safeguard; defend; uphold: ～团结 uphold unity/ ～人民的利益 safeguard the people's interests/ ～国家主权 defend state sovereignty/ ～民族尊严 vindicate (或 defend) national honour

【维妙维肖】 wéimiào-wéixiào remarkably true to life; absolutely lifelike: 这幅画把儿童天真活泼的神态画得～。This picture catches the innocent vivacity of children.

【维生素】 wéishēngsù vitamin: 丁种～ vitamin D ◇ ～缺乏症 vitamin-deficiency; avitaminosis

【维他命】 wéitāmìng vitamin

【维修】 wéixiū keep in (good) repair; service; maintain: ～房屋 maintain houses and buildings/ ～汽车 service a car/ ～设备 maintenance (或 upkeep) of equipment/ ～得很好 be in good repair ◇ ～费 maintenance cost; upkeep/ ～工 maintenance worker

帷 wéi curtain

【帷幕】 wéimù heavy curtain 又作 "帷幔"

【帷幄】 wéiwò 〈书〉 army tent: 运筹～ devise strategies within a command tent

【帷子】 wéizi curtain: 床～ bed-curtain

嵬 wéi 〈书〉 lofty; towering

伪 wěi ① false; fake; bogus: ～证 false witness/ ～钞 counterfeit (或 forged) bank note/ ～科学 pseudoscience/ 去～存真 eliminate the false and retain the true ② puppet; collaborationist: ～政权 puppet regime

【伪币】 wěibì ① counterfeit money; counterfeit (或 forged) bank note; spurious coin ② money issued by a puppet government

【伪军】 wěijūn puppet army or soldier

【伪君子】 wěijūnzǐ hypocrite

【伪善】 wěishàn hypocritical: ～的言词 hypocritical words ◇ ～者 hypocrite

【伪书】 wěishū ancient books found to have been incorrectly dated, forged, or attributed to a wrong author; ancient books of dubious authenticity

【伪托】 wěituō forge ancient literary or art works, or pass off modern works as ancient ones

【伪造】 wěizào forge; falsify; fabricate; counterfeit: ～签名 forge a signature/ ～证件 forge a certificate/ ～帐目 falsify accounts/ ～历史 fabricate history; falsify history/ ～货币 counterfeit money; forge money/ ～的文件 spurious (或 fake, forged) document; pseudograph ◇ ～品 counterfeit; forgery/ ～罪 forgery

【伪装】 wěizhuāng ① pretend; feign: ～进步 pretend to be progressive/ ～中立 feign neutrality ② disguise; guise; mask: 假的就是假的，～应当剥去。Sham is sham, and the mask must be stripped off. ③ 〈军〉 camouflage: 高射炮已经用树枝～起来。The antiaircraft guns have been camouflaged with boughs of trees.

伟* wěi big; great: 身体魁～ tall and broad-shouldered; gigantic in stature; stalwart/ 雄～ magnificent/ ～力 mighty force

【伟大】 wěidà great; mighty: 生的～，死的光荣。A great life! A glorious death!/ ～的事业 a great undertaking/

~的政治力量 a mighty political force/ ～的胜利 a signal victory

【伟绩】 wěijī great feats; great exploits; brilliant achievements

【伟人】 wěirén a great man; a great personage: 当代的～ a great man of our time

【伟业】 wěiyè 〈书〉 great cause; exploit

苇 wěi reed

纬 wěi ① weft; woof ② 〈地〉 latitude: 北～四十度 forty degrees north latitude

【纬度】 wěidù 〈地〉 latitude: 高(低)～ high (low) latitudes

【纬线】 wěixiàn ① 〈地〉 parallel ② 〈纺〉 weft

尾 * wěi ① tail: 牛～ ox-tail ② end: 排～ a person standing at the end of a line ③ remaining part; remnant: 扫～工程 the final phase of a project ④ 〈量〉〔用于鱼〕: 两～鱼 two fish

【尾巴】 wěiba ① tail: 夹起～逃跑 run away with one's tail between one's legs/ 夹着～做人 behave oneself tuck one's tail between one's legs; pull one's head in/ 翘上了天 be very cocky ② tail-like part: 飞机～ the tail of a plane/ 彗星～ the tail of a comet ③ servile adherent; appendage ④ a person shadowing sb.: 甩掉～ throw off one's tail

【尾大不掉】 wěi dà bù diào ① leadership rendered ineffectual by recalcitrant subordinates ② (of an organization) too cumbersome to be effective

【尾灯】 wěidēng tail light; tail lamp

【尾声】 wěishēng ① 〈乐〉 coda ② epilogue: 序幕和～ prologue and epilogue ③ end: 会谈已接近～。 The talks are drawing to an end.

【尾数】 wěishù odd amount in addition to the round number (usually a credit balance)

【尾随】 wěisuí tail behind; tag along after; follow at sb.'s heels: 孩子们～着巡回演出队走了好远。 The kids followed the mobile cultural troupe for quite a distance.

【尾追】 wěizhuī in hot pursuit; hot on the trail of

炜 wěi 〈书〉 bright

玮 wěi 〈书〉 valuable; precious: ～宝 rare treasure

委 * wěi ① entrust; appoint: ～以重任 entrust sb. with an important task ② throw away; cast aside: ～弃 discard/ ～之于地 cast sth. upon the ground ③ shift: 过于人 put the blame on sb. else ④ indirect; roundabout: ～婉 mild and roundabout; tactful ⑤ 〈书〉 end: 原～ the beginning and the end ⑥ listless; dejected: ～靡 listless; dispirited ⑦ 〈书〉 actually; certainly: ～系实情。 This is the true story. ⑧ 〈简〉（委员）committee member: 常～ member of a standing committee
另见 wèi

【委靡】 wěimǐ listless; dispirited; dejected: 精神～ listless; dispirited and inert/ ～不振 dispirited; in low spirits; dejected and apathetic

【委派】 wěipài appoint; delegate; designate

【委曲】 wěiqū (of roads, rivers, etc.) winding; tortuous

【委曲求全】 wěiqū qiú quán compromise out of consideration for the general interest; stoop to compromise

【委屈】 wěiqu ① feel wronged; nurse a grievance: 诉～ pour out one's grievances (或 troubles) ② put sb. to great inconvenience: 你只好～一点。 You'll have to put up with it./ 对不起,～你了。 Sorry to have made you go through all this. 或 Sorry to have put you to such inconvenience.

【委任】 wěirèn appoint: ～某人为首席顾问 appoint sb. chief adviser
◇ ～书 certificate of appointment/ ～统治 mandate/ ～统治地 mandated territory/ ～状 certificate of appointment

【委实】 wěishí really; indeed: 我～不知道。 I really don't know./ ～不容易 by no means easy

【委托】 wěituō entrust; trust: ～他负责这项工作 entrust him

with responsibility for the work/ 队长～我主持今天的会议。 The team leader asked me to chair the meeting on his behalf./ 这事就～你了。 I leave this matter in your hands.

【委婉】 wěiwǎn mild and roundabout; tactful: ～的语气 a mild tone/ 他批评得很～。 He made his criticism very tactfully.

【委员】 wěiyuán committee member ◇ ～会 committee; commission; council

【委罪】 wěizuì put the blame on sb. else

娓 wěi

【娓娓】 wěiwěi (talk) tirelessly: ～不倦 talk tirelessly/ ～动听 speak with absorbing interest/ ～而谈 talk volubly

萎 wěi wither; wilt; fade

【萎缩】 wěisuō ① wither; shrivel ② (of a market, economy, etc.) shrink; sag ③ 〈医〉 atrophy: 肝～ hepatatrophy; atrophy of the liver/ 肌肉～ amyotrophy; muscular atrophy

【萎谢】 wěixiè wither; fade

唯 wěi 〈书〉 yea
另见 wéi

【唯唯诺诺】 wěiwěinuònuò be a yes-man; be obsequious

猥 wěi ① numerous; multifarious: ～杂 miscellaneous ② base; obscene; salacious; indecent

【猥贱】 wěijiàn lowly; humble

【猥劣】 wěiliè 〈书〉 abject; base; mean

【猥陋】 wěilòu 〈书〉 base; mean; despicable

【猥琐】 wěisuǒ of wretched appearance

【猥亵】 wěixiè ① obscene; salacious ② act indecently towards (a woman)

韪 wěi 见“冒天下之大不韪” mào tiānxià zhī dà bùwěi

wèi

卫 * wèi ① defend; guard; protect: 保家～国 protect our homes and defend our country/ 自～ self-defence

【卫兵】 wèibīng guard; bodyguard

【卫道】 wèidào defend traditional moral principles ◇ ～士 〈贬〉 apologist

【卫队】 wèiduì squad of bodyguards; armed escort ◇ ～长 captain of the guard

【卫护】 wèihù protect; guard

【卫生】 wèishēng hygiene; health; sanitation: 讲～ pay attention to hygiene/ 个人～ personal hygiene/ 工业～ industrial hygiene/ 公共～ public health/ 环境～ environmental sanitation/ 劳动～ labour hygiene/ 喝生水,不～。 Drinking unboiled water is bad for the health.

【卫星】 wèixīng ① satellite; moon: 木星有几个～? How many moons has the planet Jupiter? ② artificial satellite; man-made satellite: 气象～ weather satellite; meteorological satellite/ 通讯～ communications satellite ◇ ～城 satellite town/ ～国 satellite state; satellite country

为 * wèi ① 〈介〉〔表示行为的对象〕: ～什么人的问题,是一个根本的问题,原则的问题。 The question of "for whom?" is fundamental; it is a question of principle./ ～大多数人谋利益 work in the interests of the vast majority of people ② 〈介〉〔表示原因〕: ～胜利而欢呼 hail a victory ③ 〈介〉〔表示目的〕: ～方便起见 for the sake of convenience/ 不～名,不～利 seek no personal fame or gain/ 让我们～实现这一宏伟目标而共同努力。 Let us strive together to attain this splendid goal. ④ 〈介〉〔表示“对”“向”〕: 且～诸君言 Now I'll inform you about it. ⑤ 〈书〉 stand for; support
另见 wéi

【为此】 wèicǐ to this end; for this reason (或 purpose); in this connection: ～而作出种种努力 make every effort to that end/ ～,大会作出一项重要决定。 The conference made a very important decision in this connection./ 我们都～感到欢欣鼓舞。 We all feel delighted and encouraged by this./ ～，我们不能投票。For this reason we must abstain from voting.

【为何】 wèihé why; for what reason

【为虎傅翼】 wèi hǔ fù yì give wings to a tiger — assist an evildoer 又作"为虎添翼"

【为虎作伥】 wèi hǔ zuò chāng help a villain do evil

【为了】 wèile for; for the sake of; in order to

【为民请命】 wèi mín qǐngmìng plead in the name of the people; plead for the people: 打着～的幌子 pose as a spokesman of the people

【为人作嫁】 wèi rén zuò jià sewing sb. else's trousseau — doing work for others with no benefit to oneself

【为什么】 wèishénme why; why (或 how) is it that: ～犹豫不决呢? Why hesitate?/ ～不和我们商量呢? Why not consult us?

未* wèi ①have not; did not: 意犹～尽 have not given full expression to one's views/ 走访～遇。I called but you were out./ 尚～恢复健康 not yet recovered (from illness); not yet restored to health ②not: ～知可否 not know whether sth. can be done ③the eighth of the twelve Earthly Branches

【未必】 wèibì may not; not necessarily: 他～知道。He doesn't necessarily know./ 事情～会如此。Things may not necessarily turn out that way.

【未便】 wèibiàn not be in a position to; find it hard to: ～擅自处理 cannot do it without authorization/ ～立即答复 find it difficult to give an immediate reply

【未卜先知】 wèi bǔ xiān zhī foresee; have foresight

【未曾】 wèicéng have not; did not: ～听说过 never heard of it/ 历史上～有过的奇迹 a miracle unprecedented in history

【未尝】 wèicháng ①have not; did not: 她一夜～合眼。She didn't get a wink of sleep the whole night. ②〔用在否定词前面，表示委婉的肯定〕: 这～不是好主意。That might not be a bad idea./ 那样也～不可。That should be all right./ ～没有可取之处 not without its merits

【未成年】 wèichéngnián not yet of age; under age

【未定】 wèidìng uncertain; undecided; undefined: 行期～。The date of departure is not yet fixed. ◇ ～稿 draft/ ～界 undefined boundary; undemarcated boundary

【未敢苟同】 wèi gǎn gǒutóng 〈书〉 beg to differ; cannot agree: 你的意见，我～。I beg to differ. 或 Let's agree to differ.

【未婚】 wèihūn unmarried; single ◇ ～夫 fiancé/ ～妻 fiancée

【未决】 wèijué unsettled; outstanding: 悬而～的问题 an outstanding issue; an open (或 a pending) question/ 胜负～。The outcome (of the battle or contest) is not yet decided.

【未可】 wèikě cannot: ～乐观 give no cause for optimism; nothing to be optimistic about/ 前途～限量 have a brilliant future

【未可厚非】 wèi kě hòu fēi be not altogether inexcusable; give no cause for much criticism

【未来】 wèilái ①coming; approaching; next; future: ～的一年 the coming year; next year ②future; tomorrow: 美好的～ a glorious future/ ～是属于人民的。Tomorrow belongs to the people. ◇ ～派 futurism

【未老先衰】 wèi lǎo xiān shuāi prematurely senile; old before one's time

【未了】 wèiliǎo unfinished; outstanding: ～事宜 unfinished business/ ～的手续 formalities still to be complied with/ ～的债务 outstanding debts/ ～的心愿 an unfulfilled wish

【未免】 wèimiǎn rather; a bit too; truly: 这～太过份了。This is really going too far./ 他的话～太多。He's rather talkative./ 你这样作～操之过急。You were a bit too impetuous in doing that.

【未能】 wèinéng fail to; cannot: ～实现 fail to materialize/ 阴谋～得逞 be frustrated in one's plot/ 他们～取得预期的结果。They have failed to achieve the expected result.

【未时】 wèishí the period of the day from 1 p.m. to 3 p.m.

【未遂】 wèisuì not accomplished; abortive: 政变～。The coup d'état aborted. / 自杀～ an attempted suicide

【未完】 wèiwán unfinished: ～待续 to be continued

【未详】 wèixiáng unknown: 本书作者～。The author of the book is unknown./ 病因～。What brought on the illness is not clear.

【未雨绸缪】 wèi yǔ chóumóu repair the house before it rains; provide for a rainy day; take precautions

【未知量】 wèizhīliàng unknown quantity

【未知数】 wèizhīshù ①〈数〉unknown number ②unknown; uncertain: 这事能不能办成还是个～。It's still uncertain whether this can be arranged.

位* wèi ①place; location: 座～ seat ②position: 名～ fame and position ③throne: 即～ come to the throne/ 篡～ usurp the throne ④〈数〉place; figure; digit: 个～ unit's place/ 十～ ten's place/ 小数～ decimal place/ 计算到小数点后五～ calculate to five decimal places/ 四～数 four-figure number; four-digit number ⑤〈量〉〔用于人，含敬意〕: 各～代表! Fellow Delegates!/ 今天我们家要来几～朋友。We have some friends coming to see us today.

【位次】 wèicì precedence; seating arrangement

【位于】 wèiyú 〈书〉be located; be situated; lie: ～亚洲东部 be situated in the eastern part of Asia

【位置】 wèizhi ①seat; place: 请按指定的～坐。Will everybody please take his proper seat. ②place; position: 《红楼梦》在中国文学史上占有重要～。A Dream of the Red Mansions occupies an important place in the history of Chinese literature.

【位子】 wèizi seat; place

味* wèi ①taste; flavour: 甜～儿 a sweet taste ②smell; odour: 香～儿 a sweet smell; fragrance; aroma/ 臭～儿 an offensive (或 foul) smell; stench; stink ③interest: 语言无～ insipid language; colourless language ④distinguish the flavour of: 细～其言 ponder his words/ 玩～ ponder; ruminate ⑤〈量〉ingredient (of a Chinese medicine prescription): 这个方子共有七～药。The prescription specifies seven medicinal herbs. 或 Seven medicinal herbs are prescribed.

【味道】 wèidao taste; flavour: 这个菜～很好。This dish is delicious./ 心里有一股说不出的 ～ have an indescribable feeling/ 他的话里有点讽刺的～。There's a touch of irony in his remarks.

【味精】 wèijīng monosodium glutamate; gourmet powder

【味觉】 wèijué sense of taste

【味同嚼蜡】 wèi tóng jiáo là it is like chewing wax — insipid

畏 wèi ①fear: 大无～ fearless; dauntless/ 不～强敌 stand in no fear of a formidable enemy ②respect: 后生可～。Youth are to be regarded with respect.

【畏避】 wèibì avoid sth. out of fear; recoil from; flinch from

【畏忌】 wèijì have scruples; fear; dread

【畏惧】 wèijù fear; dread

【畏难】 wèinán be afraid of difficulty: ～情绪 fear of difficulty

【畏怯】 wèiqiè cowardly; timid; chickenhearted

【畏首畏尾】 wèishǒu-wèiwěi be full of misgivings; be overcautious

【畏缩】 wèisuō recoil; shrink; flinch: 在困难面前从不～ never shrink (或 flinch) from difficulty/ ～不前 recoil in fear; hesitate to press forward; hang back

【畏途】 wèitú 〈书〉a dangerous road — a perilous undertaking: 视为～ regard it as a dangerous road to take; be afraid to undertake it

【畏友】 wèiyǒu esteemed friend

【畏罪】 wèizuì dread punishment for one's crime: ～潜逃 abscond to avoid punishment/ ～自杀 commit suicide to escape punishment

胃* wèi stomach

【胃癌】 wèi'ái cancer of the stomach; gastric carcinoma

【胃病】 wèibìng stomach trouble; gastric disease

【胃口】 wèikǒu ① appetite: ～好 have a good appetite/ 没有～ have no appetite ② liking: 对～ to one's liking

【胃痛】 wèitòng stomachache; gastralgia

谓 wèi ① say: 或～ someone says/ 可～神速 may well be termed lightning speed ② call; name: 所～ so-called/ 此之～形式主义。 This is what is called formalism./ 何～平衡？ What is meant by equilibrium? ③ meaning; sense: 无～的话 senseless talk; twaddle

【谓语】 wèiyǔ 〈语〉 predicate

尉 wèi 见"尉官"
另见 yù

【尉官】 wèiguān a military officer above the rank of warrant officer and below that of major; a junior officer

遗 wèi 〈书〉 offer as a gift; make a present of sth.: ～之千金 present sb. with a generous gift of money
另见 yí

喂* wèi ① 〈叹〉[招呼的声音] hello; hey: ～，请接三一三号分机。 Hello, extension 313, please!/ ～，你的围巾快掉了。 Hey, your scarf is slipping off. ② feed: ～猪 feed pigs/ 给病人～饭 feed a patient

【喂奶】 wèinǎi breast-feed; suckle; nurse

【喂养】 wèiyǎng feed; raise; keep: ～家禽 keep fowls

渭 Wèi short for the Weihe River

猬 wèi 〈动〉 hedgehog

【猬集】 wèijí 〈书〉 (of matters) as numerous as the spines of a hedgehog: 诸事～ have too many things to attend to; have too many irons in the fire

蔚 wèi 〈书〉 ① luxuriant; grand ② colourful: 云蒸霞～。 The rosy clouds are slowly rising.

【蔚蓝】 wèilán azure; sky blue: ～的天空 a bright blue sky/ ～的海洋 the blue sea

【蔚然成风】 wèirán chéng fēng become common practice; become the order of the day

【蔚为大观】 wèi wéi dàguān present a splendid sight; afford a magnificent view: 展出的美术作品,～。 There's a splendid array of works of art on display.

慰* wèi ① console; comfort: ～勉 comfort and encourage ② be relieved: 知你平安到达,甚～。 I am greatly relieved to learn that you have arrived safely.

【慰劳】 wèiláo bring gifts to, or send one's best wishes to, in recognition of services rendered

【慰问】 wèiwèn express sympathy and solicitude for; extend one's regards to; convey greetings to; salute: 对灾区人民表示～ express sympathy and solicitude for the people of disaster areas

【慰唁】 wèiyàn condole with sb.

魏 Wèi a surname

wēn

温* wēn ① warm; lukewarm: ～水 lukewarm water ② temperature: 体～ temperature (of the body) ③ warm up: 把酒～一下 warm up the wine ④ review; revise: ～课 review (或 revise) one's lessons

【温饱】 wēnbǎo dress warmly and eat one's fill: 终年劳累,不得～ toil all the year round without enough to eat and wear

【温床】 wēnchuáng ① 〈农〉 hotbed ② breeding ground; hotbed

【温存】 wēncún ① attentive (usu. to a person of the opposite sex) ② gentle; kind

【温带】 wēndài temperate zone

【温度】 wēndù temperature: 室内（外）～ indoor (outdoor) temperature ◇～计 〈气〉 thermograph

【温度表】 wēndùbiǎo thermometer: 摄氏～ centigrade (或 Celsius) thermometer/ 华氏～ Fahrenheit thermometer

【温故知新】 wēngù-zhīxīn ① gain new insights through restudying old material ② reviewing the past helps one to understand the present

【温和】 wēnhé ① temperate; mild; moderate: 气候～ a temperate climate ② gentle; mild: 性情～ a gentle disposition/ 语气～ a mild tone ◇～派 moderates

【温厚】 wēnhòu gentle and kind; good-natured

【温暖】 wēnnuǎn warm: 天气～ warm weather

【温情】 wēnqíng ① tender feeling: ～脉脉 full of tender feeling ② too softhearted: 你对他太～了。 You're too lenient with him.

【温泉】 wēnquán hot spring

【温柔】 wēnróu gentle and soft

【温室】 wēnshì hothouse; greenhouse; glasshouse; conservatory: ～育苗 nurse young plants in hothouses

【温顺】 wēnshùn docile; meek: 象小羊一般～ as meek as a lamb

【温文尔雅】 wēnwén-ěryǎ gentle and cultivated

【温习】 wēnxí review; revise: ～功课 review one's lessons

【温煦】 wēnxù warm

【温血动物】 wēnxuè dòngwù warm-blooded animal

【温驯】 wēnxún (of animals) docile; meek; tame

瘟 wēn 〈中医〉 acute communicable diseases

【瘟病】 wēnbìng 〈中医〉 seasonal febrile diseases

【瘟神】 wēnshén god of plague

【瘟疫】 wēnyì pestilence

wén

文* wén ① character; script; writing: 钟鼎～ inscriptions on ancient bronze objects/ 《说～解字》 Analytical Dictionary of Characters ② language: 英～ the English language ③ literary composition; writing: ～如其人。 The writing mirrors the writer./ 情～并茂 excellent in both content and language ④ literary language: 半～半白 half literary and half vernacular ⑤ culture: ～物 cultural relic ⑥ formal ritual: 虚～ a mere formality ⑦ civilian; civil: ～职 civilian post ⑧ gentle; refined: ～野之分 the difference between crudeness and refinement ⑨ certain natural phenomena: 天～ astronomy/ 水～ hydrology ⑩ cover up; paint over: ～过饰非 conceal faults and gloss over wrongs ⑪〈量〉[用于旧时的铜钱] 一～钱 a cash/ 一～不值 not worth a farthing

【文本】 wénběn text; version: 本合同两种～同等有效。 Both texts of the contract are equally valid.

【文笔】 wénbǐ style of writing: ～流利 write in an easy and fluent style

【文不对题】 wén bù duì tí irrelevant to the subject; beside the point; wide of the mark

【文才】 wéncái literary talent; aptitude for writing

【文采】 wéncǎi ① rich and bright colours ② literary grace; literary talent: 这个人很有～。 This is a man of unusual literary talent.

【文辞】 wéncí diction; language: ～优美 exquisite diction; elegant language

【文从字顺】 wéncóng-zìshùn readable and fluent

【文牍】 wéndú official documents and correspondence ◇～主义 red tape

【文法】 wénfǎ grammar

【文房四宝】 wénfáng sìbǎo the four treasures of the study (writing brush, ink stick, ink slab and paper)

【文风】 wénfēng style of writing: 整顿～ rectify the style of writing

【文稿】 wéngǎo manuscript; draft

【文告】 wéngào proclamation; statement; message

【文工团】 wéngōngtuán song and dance ensemble; art troupe; cultural troupe

【文官】 wénguān civil official

【文过饰非】 wénguò-shìfēi conceal faults and gloss over wrongs; gloss over one's faults; cover up (或 explain away) one's errors

【文豪】 wénháo literary giant; great writer; eminent writer

【文化】 wénhuà ① civilization; culture: 中国～ Chinese civilization (或 culture)/ 仰韶～ the Yangshao Culture/ ～和思想阵地 positions on the cultural and ideological fronts ② education; culture; schooling; literacy: 学～ acquire an elementary education: acquire literacy; learn to read and write 她的～程度比我高。 She's better educated than I.

【文火】 wénhuǒ slow fire; gentle heat: ～焖四十分钟 simmer gently for forty minutes

【文集】 wénjí collected works

【文件】 wénjiàn documents; papers; instruments

【文教】 wénjiào 〈简〉(文化教育) culture and education ◇ ～界 cultural and educational circles/ ～事业 cultural and educational work; culture and education

【文静】 wénjìng gentle and quiet

【文具】 wénjù writing materials; stationery ～店 stationer's; stationery shop

【文科】 wénkē liberal arts

【文库】 wénkù a series of books issued in a single format by a publisher; library

【文理】 wénlǐ unity and coherence in writing: ～通顺 have unity and coherence; make smooth reading/ ～不通 illogical and ungrammatical

【文盲】 wénmáng an illiterate person: 扫除～ wipe out illiteracy

【文明】 wénmíng ① civilization; culture: 物质～ material civilization/ ～古国 a country with an ancient civilization ② civilized

【文墨】 wénmò writing: 粗通～ barely know the rudiments of writing

【文凭】 wénpíng diploma

【文人】 wénrén man of letters; scholar; literati: ～相轻。 Scholars tend to scorn each other.

【文弱】 wénruò gentle and frail-looking: ～书生 a frail scholar

【文身】 wénshēn 〈书〉tattoo

【文史】 wénshǐ literature and history

【文书】 wénshū ① document; official dispatch ② copy clerk

【文思】 wénsī the thread of ideas in writing; the train of thought in writing: ～敏捷 have a ready pen

【文坛】 wéntán the literary world (或 arena, circles); the world of letters

【文体】 wéntǐ type of writing; literary form; style

【文武】 wén-wǔ civil and military: ～官员 civil and military officials/ ～双全 be well versed in both polite letters and martial arts

【文物】 wénwù cultural relic; historical relic: ～保护 preservation of cultural relics; protection of historical relics

【文献】 wénxiàn document; literature: 历史～ historical documents

【文选】 wénxuǎn selected works; literary selections

【文学】 wénxué literature ◇ ～家 writer; man of letters; literati/ ～流派 schools of literature/ ～批评 literary criticism/ ～作品 literary works

【文学语言】 wénxué yǔyán ①〈语〉standard speech ② literary language

【文雅】 wényǎ elegant; refined; cultured; polished: 举止～ refined in manner

【文言】 wényán classical Chinese ◇ ～文 writings in classical Chinese; classical style of writing

【文艺】 wényì literature and art ◇ ～创作 literary and artistic creation/ ～作品 literary and artistic works/ ～复兴 the Renaissance

【文娱】 wényú cultural recreation; entertainment ◇ ～活动 recreational activities

【文责】 wénzé the responsibility an author should assume for his own writings; author's responsibility: ～自负。 The author takes sole responsibility for his views.

【文摘】 wénzhāi abstract; digest

【文章】 wénzhāng ① essay; article ② literary works; writings ③ hidden meaning; implied meaning: 话里有～。 There is an insinuation in that remark. 或 That's an insinuating remark./ 其中大有～。 There is a lot behind all this.

【文职】 wénzhí civilian post ◇ ～人员 nonmilitary personnel

【文质彬彬】 wénzhì bīnbīn gentle; suave

【文绉绉】 wénzhōuzhōu genteel: 说话～的 speak in an elegant manner

【文字】 wénzì ① characters; script; writing: 楔形～ cuneiform characters/ 拼音～ alphabetic writing ② written language: ～宣传 written propaganda/ ～游戏 play with words; juggle with terms/ 有～可考的历史 recorded history ③ writing (as regards form or style): ～清通 lucid writing

纹* wén lines; veins; grain: 脸上的皱～ lines on one's face; furrows/ 细～木 fine-grained wood

【纹理】 wénlǐ veins; grain: 有～的大理石 veined marble/ 这木头的～很好看。 This wood has a beautiful grain.

【纹丝不动】 wénsī bù dòng absolutely still: 没有一点风, 柳条儿～。 There wasn't a breath of wind and the willow twigs were absolutely still.

闻* wén ① hear: ～讯 hear the news/ 听而不～ listen but not hear; turn a deaf ear to ② news; story: 要～ important news ③ well-known; famous: ～人 well-known figure ④ reputation: 秽～ ill repute ⑤ smell: 你～～这是什么味儿? Smell this and see what it is.

【闻风而动】 wén fēng ér dòng immediately respond to a call; go into action without delay

【闻风丧胆】 wén fēng sàng dǎn become terror-stricken (或 panic-stricken, terrified) at the news

【闻过则喜】 wén guò zé xǐ feel happy when told of one's errors; be glad to have one's errors pointed out

【闻名】 wénmíng ① well-known; famous; renowned: ～全国 well-known throughout the country/ 世界～ world-famous; world-renowned ② be familiar with sb.'s name; know sb. by repute: ～不如见面。 Knowing a person by repute is not as good as seeing him in the flesh.

【闻人】 wénrén well-known figure; famous man; celebrity

【闻所未闻】 wén suǒ wèi wén unheard-of: 他们给我讲了很多～的事情。 They told me a lot of things I had never heard before.

蚊* wén mosquito

【蚊香】 wénxiāng mosquito-repellent incense

【蚊帐】 wénzhàng mosquito net ◇ ～纱 mosquito netting

【蚊子】 wénzi mosquito

wěn

刎 wěn cut one's throat: 自～ cut one's own throat

吻 wěn ① lips ② kiss ③ an animal's mouth

【吻合】 wěnhé be identical; coincide; tally: 意见～ have identical views/ 他讲的情况和我听到的～。 His account tallies with what I heard.

紊 wěn disorderly; confused

【紊流】 wěnliú 〈物〉turbulence; turbulent flow

【紊乱】 wěnluàn disorder; chaos; confusion: 秩序～ in a state of chaos/ 新陈代谢功能～ metabolic disorder

稳 wěn ① steady; firm: 把桌子放～ make the table steady/ 站～ stand steadily; stand firm/ 坐～ sit tight/ 她 做事很～。 She is steady and reliable in doing things./ 企图～住阵脚 try to maintain one's position; attempt to hold one's ground ② sure; certain: 这事你拿得～吗? Are you quite sure of it?/ 这场比赛他～赢。 He is certain to win the game.

【稳步】 wěnbù　with steady steps; steadily: ～前进 advance steadily; make steady progress/ 生产～上升。 Production is going up steadily.

【稳操左券】 wěn cāo zuǒquàn　have full assurance of success 又作"稳操胜券"

【稳当】 wěndang　reliable; secure; safe: ～的办法 a reliable method

【稳定】 wěndìng　① stable; steady: 物价～ Prices remain stable./ 情绪～ be in a calm, unruffled mood/ ～的多数 a stable majority/ 不～的国际金融市场 a shaky international monetary market ② stabilize; steady: ～物价 stabilize commodity prices; ～情绪 set sb.'s mind at rest; reassure sb.

【稳固】 wěngù　firm; stable: ～的基础 a firm (或 solid) foundation/ ～的政权 a stable government

【稳健】 wěnjiàn　firm; steady: 迈着～的步子 walk with firm steps/ 办事～ go about things steadily/ 他这个人很～。 He's a steady person. ◇ ～派 moderates

【稳如泰山】 wěn rú Tàishān　as stable as Mount Taishan

【稳妥】 wěntuǒ　safe; reliable: ～的计划 a safe plan/ 我看这样办更～。 I think it's safer to do it this way.

【稳扎稳打】 wěnzhā-wěndǎ　① go ahead steadily and strike sure blows ② go about things steadily and surely

【稳重】 wěnzhòng　steady; staid; sedate

wèn

问*　wèn　① ask; inquire: ～路 ask the way/ 不懂就～。 Ask when you don't know./ 我～他为什么要那样做。 I asked him why he did it./ 他在食堂～了一下开饭的时间。He inquired about the meal times at the canteen. ② ask after; inquire after: 他信里～起你。 He asks after you in his letter. ③ interrogate; examine: 审～ interrogate ④ hold responsible: 出了事唯你是～。 You'll be held responsible if anything goes wrong.

【问安】 wèn'ān　pay one's respects (usu. to elders); wish sb. good health

【问案】 wèn'àn　try (或 hear) a case

【问长问短】 wèncháng-wènduǎn　take the trouble to make detailed inquiries

【问答】 wèn-dá　questions and answers ◇ ～练习 question-and-answer drills

【问道于盲】 wèn dào yú máng　ask the way from a blind person — seek advice from one who can offer none

【问寒问暖】 wènhán-wènnuǎn　ask after sb.'s health with deep concern; be solicitous for sb.'s welfare

【问好】 wènhǎo　send one's regards to; say hello to: 请代我向你父亲～。 Please give my regards to your father. 或 Remember me to your father./ 他向您～。 He wished to be remembered to you.

【问号】 wènhào　① question mark; interrogation mark (或 point) (?) ② unknown factor; unsolved problem: 致癌的真正原因还是个～。 The exact cause of cancer is still unknown.

【问候】 wènhòu　send one's respects (或 regards) to; extend greetings to: 致以亲切的～ extend cordial greetings

【问津】 wènjīn　〈书〉〔多用于否定句〕 make inquiries (as about prices or the situation): 不敢～ not dare to make inquiries (as about prohibitively priced goods)/ 无人～ nobody cares to ask about sth.

【问世】 wènshì　be published; come out: 本书作者的一部新小说即将～。 A new novel by the same author will soon come out.

【问题】 wèntí　① question; problem; issue: 我提个～。 May I ask a question?/ 悬而未决的～ an outstanding issue/ 原则～ a question (或 matter) of principle/ 思想～ an ideological problem/ 关键～ a key problem/ ～的关键 the heart (或 crux) of the matter ② trouble; mishap: 那台车床出了～。 Something has gone wrong with that lathe./ 一路上没出～。 The trip went off without mishap. ◇ ～单 questionnaire

【问心无愧】 wèn xīn wú kuì　have a clear conscience; feel no qualms upon self-examination

【问心有愧】 wèn xīn yǒu kuì　feel a twinge of conscience; have a guilty conscience

【问讯】 wènxùn　inquire; ask ◇ ～处 inquiry office; information desk

【问罪】 wènzuì　denounce; condemn: 兴师～ send a punitive force against; denounce sb. publicly for his crimes or serious errors

wēng

翁*　wēng　① old man: 渔～ an old fisherman ② father ③ father-in-law: ～姑 a woman's parents-in-law/ ～婿 father-in-law and son-in-law

嗡　wēng　〈象〉 drone; buzz; hum: 蜜蜂～～地飞。 Bees are buzzing all around.

wèng

瓮　wèng　urn; earthen jar: 水～ water jar/ 菜～ a jar for pickling vegetables

【瓮中之鳖】 wèngzhōng zhī biē　a turtle in a jar — bottled up; trapped

【瓮中捉鳖】 wèngzhōng zhuō biē　catch a turtle in a jar — go after an easy prey

蕹　wèng

【蕹菜】 wèngcài　water spinach

wō

涡　wō　whirlpool; eddy: 水～ eddies of water

【涡流】 wōliú　the circular movement of a fluid; whirling fluid; eddy

【涡轮】 wōlún　turbine ◇ ～发电机 turbogenerator/ ～机 turbine/ ～螺旋桨发动机 turboprop (engine)/ ～喷气发动机 turbojet (engine)

【涡旋】 wōxuán　〈气〉 vortex: 大气～ atmospheric vortex

倭　Wō　an old name for Japan

【倭瓜】 wōguā　〈方〉 pumpkin; cushaw

【倭寇】 Wōkòu　〈史〉 Japanese pirates (operating in Chinese coastal waters from the fourteenth to the sixteenth century)

莴　wō

【莴苣】 wōju　lettuce

窝*　wō　① nest: 鸟～ bird's nest/ 鸡～ hencoop; roost; 蜂～ beehive ② lair; den: 贼～ thieves' den/ 土匪～ bandits' lair; bandits' nest ③ a hollow part of the human body; pit: 夹肢～ armpit/ 心～ the pit of the stomach ④ 〈方〉 place: 这炉子真碍事，给它挪个～儿。 The stove's in the way; let's move it to some other place./ 他就是不动～儿。 He refused to budge. ⑤ harbour; shelter: ～娼 harbour stolen goods ⑥ hold in; check: ～着一肚子火 be simmering with rage; be forced to bottle up one's anger ⑦ bend: 把铁丝～个圆圈 bend the wire into a circle/ 别把画片～了。 Be careful not to bend (或 crease) the picture. ⑧ 〈量〉〔用于动物〕 litter; brood: 一～十只小猪 ten piglets at a litter/ 一～小鸡 a brood of chickens

鸟窝

【窝藏】wōcáng harbour; shelter: ～罪犯 give shelter to (或 harbour) a criminal

【窝囊】wōnang ① feel vexed; be annoyed: 受～气 be subjected to petty annoyances/ 这事办得真～。 That's really botched it up. ② good-for-nothing; hopelessly stupid

喔 wō ＜象＞ cock's crow: ～～～! Cock-a-doodle-doo!
另见 ō

蜗* wō snail
【蜗牛】wōniú snail

wǒ

我* wǒ ① I ② we: ～方 our side; we/ ～军 our army ③〔"你""我"对举，表示泛指〕: 大家你帮～、～帮你，很快就把活儿干完了。 With each one giving the other a hand, they soon got the job done. ④ self: 自～牺牲 self-sacrifice/ 忘～的献身精神 selfless devotion
【我们】wǒmen we
【我行我素】wǒ xíng wǒ sù persist in one's old ways (no matter what others say); stick to one's old way of doing things

wò

沃 wò ① fertile; rich: ～土 fertile soil; rich soil/ ～野千里 a vast expanse of fertile land ② irrigate: ～田 irrigate farmland

卧* wò ① lie: 仰～ lie on one's back ② (of animals or birds) crouch; sit ③ for sleeping in: ～室 bedroom/ ～铺 sleeping berth ④ ＜方＞ poach (eggs)
【卧病】wòbìng be confined to bed; be laid up
【卧车】wòchē ① sleeping car; sleeping carriage; sleeper ② automobile; car; limousine; sedan
【卧床】wòchuáng lie in bed: 医生叫她～休息两天。 The doctor told her to stay in bed for a couple of days.
【卧倒】wòdǎo drop to the ground; take a prone (或 lying-down) position: ～!(口令) Lie down! 或 Hit the ground!
【卧房】wòfáng bedroom
【卧式】wòshì horizontal: ～镗床 horizontal boring machine/ ～发动机 horizontal engine
【卧室】wòshì bedroom
【卧榻】wòtà ＜书＞ bed
【卧薪尝胆】wò xīn cháng dǎn sleep on brushwood and taste gall — undergo self-imposed hardships so as to strengthen one's resolve to wipe out a national humiliation

握* wò hold; grasp: 紧～手中枪 hold one's gun with a firm grip
【握别】wòbié shake hands at parting; part: ～以来, 已逾三月。 It is more than three months since we parted.
【握力】wòlì the power of gripping; grip ◇ ～器 ＜体＞ spring-grip dumb-bells
【握拳】wòquán make a fist; clench one's fist
【握手】wòshǒu shake hands; clasp hands

幄 wò ＜书＞ tent

斡 wò
【斡旋】wòxuán ① mediate: 由于他从中～, 双方的争端得到了解决。 Through his mediation the dispute between the two parties was settled. ②＜法＞ good offices

龌 wò
【龌龊】wòchuò dirty; filthy: 卑鄙～ sordid; foul

wū

乌* wū ① crow ② black; dark: ～云 black clouds; dark

clouds ③＜书＞〔用于反问〕: ～足道哉? What's there worth mentioning about it?
【乌龟】wūguī ① tortoise ② cuckold ◇ ～壳 tortoiseshell
【乌合之众】wūhé zhī zhòng a disorderly band; a motley crowd; rabble; mob
【乌黑】wūhēi pitch-black; jet-black
【乌呼】wūhū 见"呜呼"
【乌亮】wūliàng glossy black; jet-black: ～的头发 dark, glossy hair; raven locks
【乌溜溜】wūliūliū (of eyes) dark and liquid: 一双～的眼睛 sparkling, black eyes
【乌七八糟】wūqībāzāo ① in a horrible mess; in great disorder ② obscene; dirty; filthy
【乌纱帽】wūshāmào ① black gauze cap (worn by feudal officials) ② official post: 丢～ be dismissed from office
【乌托邦】wūtuōbāng Utopia
【乌鸦】wūyā crow
【乌烟瘴气】wūyān-zhàngqì foul atmosphere; pestilential atmosphere: 搞得～ foul up
【乌有】wūyǒu ＜书＞ nothing; naught: 化为～ come to nothing (或 naught)
【乌云】wūyún black clouds; dark clouds: ～遮天。Black clouds blotted out the sky. 或 The sky was covered with dark clouds.
【乌贼】wūzéi ＜动＞ cuttlefish; inkfish

污* wū ① dirt; filth: 血～ blood stains ② dirty; filthy; foul: ～泥 mud; mire ③ corrupt: 贪官～吏 corrupt officials ④ defile; smear: 玷～ stain; sully; tarnish
【污点】wūdiǎn stain; spot; blemish; smirch
【污垢】wūgòu dirt; filth
【污秽】wūhuì ＜书＞ filthy; foul
【污迹】wūjī stain; smear; smudge
【污蔑】wūmiè ① 见"诬蔑" wūmiè ② defile; sully; tarnish
【污泥】wūní mud; mire; sludge
【污染】wūrǎn pollute; contaminate: 大气层～ atmosphere pollution/ 放射性～ radioactive contamination/ 环境～ environmental pollution/ 空气～ air pollution/ 水～ water contamination/ 噪音～ noise pollution
【污辱】wūrǔ ① humiliate; insult ② defile; sully; tarnish
【污水】wūshuǐ foul (或 polluted, waste) water; sewage; slops: 生活～ domestic sewage
【污浊】wūzhuó (of air, water, etc.) dirty; muddy; foul; filthy

邬 Wū a surname

巫* wū shaman; witch; wizard
【巫婆】wūpó witch; sorceress
【巫师】wūshī wizard; sorcerer
【巫术】wūshù witchcraft; sorcery
【巫医】wūyī witch doctor

呜* wū ＜象＞ toot; hoot; zoom: 轮船上的汽笛～～叫。The ship's whistle kept hooting./ 汽车～的一声飞驰而过。The car zoomed past.
【呜呼】wūhū ①＜书＞ alas; alack ② die: 一命～ give up the ghost
【呜呼哀哉】wūhū-āizāi ① alas ② dead and gone ③ all is lost
【呜咽】wūyè sob; whimper

诬 wū accuse falsely
【诬告】wūgào lodge a false accusation against; bring a false charge against; trump up a charge against ◇ ～案件 frame-up; trumped-up case
【诬害】wūhài injure by spreading false reports about; calumniate; malign
【诬赖】wūlài falsely incriminate: ～好人 incriminate innocent people
【诬蔑】wūmiè slander; vilify; calumniate; smear: 造谣～ rumourmongering and mudslinging; calumny and slander/ ～不实之词 slander and libel

【逐陷】 wūxiàn frame a case against; frame sb.

屋* wū ① house ② room: 里～ inner room
【屋顶】 wūdǐng roof; housetop ◇～花园 roof garden
【屋脊】 wūjǐ ridge (of a roof): 世界～ the roof of the world
【屋面】 wūmiàn 〈建〉 roofing: 瓦～ tile roofing ◇～板 roof boarding
【屋檐】 wūyán eaves
【屋宇】 wūyǔ house
【屋子】 wūzi room: 三间～ three rooms

wú

无* wú ① nothing; nil: 从～到有 grow out of nothing; start from scratch ② not have; there is not; without: ～一定计划 without a definite plan ③ not: ～碍大局 not affect the situation as a whole/ ～须乎着急。There's no need to get excited. ④ regardless of; no matter whether, what, etc.: 事～大小，都有人负责。Everything, big and small, is properly taken care of.
【无比】 wúbǐ incomparable; unparalleled; matchless: ～的优越性 incomparable (或 unparalleled) superiority/ ～的毅力 tremendous determination/ ～英勇 unrivalled in bravery/ ～愤怒 furiously indignant
【无边无际】 wúbiān-wújì boundless; limitless; vast: ～的大海 a boundless ocean/ ～的沙漠 a vast expanse of desert
【无病呻吟】 wú bìng shēnyín ① moan and groan without being ill; make a fuss about an imaginary illness ② adopt a sentimental pose
【无补】 wúbǔ of no help; of no avail: 这样恐怕～于事。That would be of no avail./ 空谈～于实际。Mere words won't help matters.
【无常】 wúcháng ① variable; changeable: 反复～ capricious; uncertain ②〈佛教〉impermanence
【无耻】 wúchǐ shameless; brazen; impudent: ～谰言 shameless slander/ ～之尤 brazen in the extreme; the height of shamelessness/ ～之徒 a person who has lost all sense of shame; a shameless person
【无出其右】 wú chū qí yòu second to none; matchless; unequalled
【无从】 wúcóng have no way (of doing sth.); not be in a position (to do sth.): 我们不了解情况，～答复这类问题。As we do not know the facts, we are in no position to answer such questions./ 心中千言万语，一时～说起 have a thousand things to say but not know where to begin
【无敌】 wúdí unmatched; invincible; unconquerable: ～于天下 unmatched anywhere in the world; invincible
【无底洞】 wúdǐdòng a bottomless pit (that can never be filled)
【无地自容】 wú dì zì róng can find no place to hide oneself for shame; feel too ashamed to show one's face; look for a hole to crawl into
【无的放矢】 wú dì fàng shǐ shoot an arrow without a target; shoot at random: 批评要有针对性，不要～。Criticism shouldn't be random shooting; it should be to the point.
【无动于衷】 wú dòng yú zhōng aloof and indifferent; unmoved; untouched; unconcerned: 对这种情况，我们不能～。We cannot remain indifferent in such a situation./ 他对我的忠告～。He turned a deaf ear to my advice.
【无独有偶】 wúdú-yǒu'ǒu 〔多含贬义〕it is not unique, but has its counterpart; not come singly but in pairs
【无度】 wúdù immoderate; excessive: 饮食～ excessive (或 immoderate) eating and drinking/ 挥霍～ squander wantonly
【无端】 wúduān for no reason: ～侮辱 a gratuitous insult
【无恶不作】 wú è bù zuò stop at nothing in doing evil; stop at no evil; commit all manner of crimes
【无法】 wúfǎ unable; incapable: ～应付 unable to cope with; at the end of one's resources/ ～形容 beyond description/ ～解脱的困境 an inextricable dilemma/ ～投递，退回原处。Undeliverable, returned to sender.

【无法无天】 wúfǎ-wútiān defy laws human and divine; become absolutely lawless; run wild
【无方】 wúfāng not in the proper way; in the wrong way; not knowing how: 经营～ mismanagement
【无妨】 wúfāng there's no harm; may (或 might) as well: 你～试一试。There's no harm in having a try.
【无非】 wúfēi nothing but; no more than; simply; only: 我想说的～是那么几句话。What I want to say is no more than (或 nothing but) this./ ～是好坏两种可能。There are only two possibilities, a good one and a bad one.
【无风】 wúfēng 〈气〉calm
【无风不起浪】 wú fēng bù qǐ làng there are no waves without wind; there's no smoke without fire
【无干】 wúgān have nothing to do with: 这事与你～。It has nothing to do with you. 或 It's none of your business./ 这全是我的过错，跟别人～。It was entirely my fault; nobody else had anything to do with it.
【无功受禄】 wú gōng shòu lù get a reward without deserving it
【无辜】 wúgū ① innocent ② an innocent person
【无故】 wúgù without cause or reason: 不得～缺席。Nobody may be absent without reason.
【无关】 wúguān have nothing to do with: 此事与他～。It has nothing to do with him./ 那也～大局。That does not matter very much./ ～紧要 of no importance; immaterial; ～痛痒的话 comment without any bite; irrelevant or pointless remarks
【无国籍】 wúguójí 〈外〉stateless ◇～者 a stateless person
【无花果】 wúhuāguǒ 〈植〉fig
【无话不谈】 wú huà bù tán keep no secrets from each other; be in each other's confidence
【无稽】 wújī unfounded; fantastic; absurd: ～之谈 fantastic talk; sheer nonsense
【无几】 wújǐ very few; very little; hardly any: 所剩～。There's very little left./ 两人的年岁相差～。The two are almost the same age.
【无计可施】 wú jì kě shī at one's wits' end; at the end of one's tether
【无济于事】 wú jì yú shì of no avail; to no effect
【无家可归】 wú jiā kě guī wander about without a home to go to; be homeless
【无价之宝】 wú jià zhī bǎo priceless treasure; invaluable asset
【无坚不摧】 wú jiān bù cuī overrun all fortifications; carry all before one; be all-conquering
【无间】 wújiàn 〈书〉① not keeping anything from each other; very close to each other: 亲密～的朋友 close friends; bosom friends ② continuously; without interruption: 坚持户外锻炼，寒暑～ keep on doing outdoor exercise all the year round
【无精打采】 wújīng-dǎcǎi listless; lackadaisical; in low spirits; out of sorts
【无拘束】 wújūshù unrestrained; unconstrained: 在～的气氛中 in an unconstrained atmosphere/ 大家～地发表意见，Everyone freely expressed his views. 又作“无拘无束”
【无可比拟】 wúkě bǐnǐ incomparable; unparalleled
【无可非议】 wúkě fēiyì blameless; beyond reproach; above criticism
【无可厚非】 wúkě hòufēi give no cause for much criticism
【无可讳言】 wúkě huìyán there is no hiding the fact: 这些都是～的事实。All these are indisputable facts.
【无可救药】 wúkě jiùyào incorrigible; incurable
【无可奈何】 wúkě nàihé have no way out; have no alternative
【无可无不可】 wúkě-wúbùkě not care one way or another: 我去也行，不去也行，～。I don't care whether I go or not.
【无可争辩】 wúkě zhēngbiàn indisputable; irrefutable
【无可置疑】 wúkě zhìyí indubitable; unquestionable
【无孔不入】 wú kǒng bù rù ① (of odours, ideas, etc.) all-pervasive ② (of persons) seize every opportunity (to do evil)
【无愧】 wúkuì feel no qualms; have a clear conscience: 问心～ feel no qualms upon self-examination
【无赖】 wúlài ① rascally; scoundrelly; blackguardly: 耍～

act shamelessly ② rascal

【无理】 wúlǐ unreasonable; unjustifiable: ～要求 unreasonable demands/ ～阻挠 unjustifiable obstruction/ ～指责 unwarranted accusations; groundless charges

【无理取闹】 wúlǐ qǔnào wilfully make trouble; be deliberately provocative

【无力】 wúlì ① lack strength; feel weak: 四肢～ feel weak in one's limbs ② unable; incapable; powerless: 一个人是～完成这项任务的。 One person alone can't accomplish this task. 或 No one can do this job single-handed.

【无量】 wúliàng measureless; immeasurable; boundless: 前途～ a boundless future

【无聊】 wúliáo ① bored ② senseless; silly; stupid: 不要讲这种～的话。 Don't make such silly remarks.

【无论】 wúlùn 〈连〉 no matter what, how, etc.; regardless of: ～发生什么情况,你都要保持冷静。 Keep calm, whatever happens.

【无论如何】 wúlùn rúhé in any case; at any rate; whatever happens; at all events: 你～得来一趟。 You've got to come, whatever happens. /我们～得把丢失的文件找到。 At all costs, we have to find the missing document./ ～,现在已经来不及了。 Anyhow, it's too late now./ 我们～不能急躁。 On no account must we be impetuous.

【无米之炊】 wú mǐ zhī chuī cook a meal without rice; make bricks without straw 参见 "巧妇难为无米之炊" qiǎo fù nán wéi wú mǐ zhī chuī

【无名】 wúmíng ① nameless; unknown ② indefinable; indescribable: ～的恐惧 an indefinable feeling of terror ◇ ～氏 an anonymous person/ ～小卒 a nobody/ ～英雄 an unknown hero/ ～指 the third finger; ring finger

【无奈】 wúnài ① cannot help but; have no alternative; have no choice: 他出于～,只得表示同意。 He had no choice but to agree. ② but; however: 他本想来的,～临时有会,来不了。 He had meant to come, but was prevented by an unexpected meeting.

【无能】 wúnéng incompetent; incapable: 软弱～ weak and incompetent

【无能为力】 wú néng wéi lì powerless; helpless; incapable of action: 人类对于自然界不是～的。 Man is not powerless before nature.

【无期徒刑】 wúqī túxíng life imprisonment: 判处～ be sentenced to imprisonment for life; be given a life sentence

【无情】 wúqíng merciless; ruthless; heartless: ～的打击 a merciless blow/ ～的事实 harsh reality; hard facts/ 水火～。 Fire and water have no mercy.

【无穷】 wúqióng infinite; endless; boundless; inexhaustible: ～的烦恼和忧虑 endless troubles and worries/ ～尽的智慧和力量 inexhaustible wisdom and power/ 言有尽而意～。 There's an end to the words, but not to their message.

【无权】 wúquán have no right: ～干预 have no right to interfere

【无人】 wúrén ① unmanned: ～火箭 unmanned rocket/ ～驾驶飞机 unmanned plane; pilotless plane; robot plane ② depopulated: ～区 a depopulated zone; no man's land

【无任】 wúrèn 〈书〉 extremely; immensely: ～感激 be deeply grateful

【无任所大使】 wúrènsuǒ dàshǐ ambassador-at-large

【无伤大雅】 wú shāng dàyǎ not affect the whole; not matter much

【无上】 wúshàng supreme; paramount; highest: ～权力 supreme power/ ～光荣 the highest honour

【无神论】 wúshénlùn atheism ◇ ～者 atheist

【无声】 wúshēng noiseless; silent

【无声无臭】 wúshēng-wúxiù unknown; obscure

【无时无刻】 wúshí-wúkè all the time; incessantly: 我们～不在想念你。 You are constantly in our thoughts.

【无事不登三宝殿】 wú shì bù dēng sānbǎodiàn never go to the temple for nothing; would not go to sb.'s place except on business, for help, etc.; I wouldn't come to you if I hadn't something to ask of you

【无事生非】 wú shì shēng fēi make trouble out of nothing; be deliberately provocative

【无数】 wúshù ① innumerable; countless: ～的事实 innu-

merable facts ② not know for certain; be uncertain: 这计划是否可行, 我心中～。 I'm not too sure whether the plan will work.

【无双】 wúshuāng unparalleled; unrivalled; matchless: 举世～ absolutely unrivalled

【无所不包】 wú suǒ bù bāo all-embracing; all-encompassing

【无所不能】 wú suǒ bù néng omnipotent

【无所不为】 wú suǒ bù wéi stop at nothing; do all manner of evil

【无所不用其极】 wú suǒ bù yòng qí jí resort to every conceivable means; stop at nothing; go to any length: 这个家伙造谣诽谤、挑拨离间, ～。 That scoundrel went all the way in rumourmongering, mudslinging and sowing dissension.

【无所不在】 wú suǒ bù zài omnipresent; ubiquitous

【无所不知】 wú suǒ bù zhī omniscient

【无所不至】 wú suǒ bù zhì ① penetrate everywhere: 细菌活动的范围很广, ～。 Bacteria are active practically everywhere. ② spare no pains (to do evil); be capable of anything; stop at nothing: 威胁利诱, ～ use intimidation, bribery and every other means

【无所措手足】 wú suǒ cuò shǒu-zú be at a loss as to what to do

【无所事事】 wú suǒ shì shì be occupied with nothing; have nothing to do; idle away one's time

【无所适从】 wú suǒ shì cóng not know what course to take; be at a loss as to what to do

【无所畏惧】 wú suǒ wèijù fearless; dauntless; undaunted

【无所谓】 wúsuǒwèi ① cannot be designated as; not deserve the name of: 这是随便说的, ～什么批评。 It was a passing remark; I didn't mean to criticize anybody. ② be indifferent; not matter: 采取～的态度 adopt an indifferent attitude/ 你替他着急,他自己却好象～似的。 You are worried about him, but he himself doesn't seem to care./ 他去不去～。 It makes no difference whether he goes or not.

【无所用心】 wú suǒ yòngxīn not give serious thought to anything: 饱食终日, ～ be sated with food and remain idle

【无所作为】 wú suǒ zuòwéi attempt nothing and accomplish nothing; be in a state of inertia: ～和骄傲自满的论点都是错误的。 Ideas of inertia and complacency are both wrong.

【无题】 wútí no title (used as a title for writings for which the author cannot find, or chooses not to give, a title)

【无条件】 wútiáojiàn unconditional; without preconditions: 建议～地立即举行谈判 propose that negotiations be held at once without preconditions ◇ ～投降 unconditional surrender

【无头案】 wútóu'àn a case without any clues; unsolved mystery

【无往不利】 wú wǎng bù lì go smoothly everywhere; oe ever successful

【无往不胜】 wú wǎng bù shèng ever-victorious; invincible

【无往不在】 wú wǎng bù zài present everywhere; omnipresent

【无妄之灾】 wú wàng zhī zāi unexpected calamity; undeserved ill turn

【无微不至】 wú wēi bù zhì meticulously; in every possible way

【无为】 wúwéi letting things take their own course (a Taoist concept of human conduct); inaction; inactivity: ～而治 govern by doing nothing that goes against nature

【无味】 wúwèi ① tasteless; unpalatable: 食之～, 弃之可惜 unappetizing and yet not bad enough to throw away ② dull; insipid; uninteresting: 枯燥～ dry as dust

【无畏】 wúwèi fearless; dauntless

【无谓】 wúwèi meaningless; pointless; senseless: ～的争吵 a pointless quarrel/ ～的牺牲 a meaningless (或 senseless) sacrifice

【无…无…】 wú...wú... 〔分别用在两个意义相同或相近的词或词素前面,强调没有〕: 无尽无休 incessant; endless/ 无穷无尽 inexhaustible; endless/ 无牵无挂 have no cares/ 无忧无虑 free from care; carefree/ 无依无靠 have no one to depend on; helpless/ 无影无踪 disappear completely; vanish

without a trace

【无息贷款】 wúxī-dàikuǎn　interest-free loan

【无隙可乘】 wú xì kě chéng　no crack to get in by; no loophole to exploit; no weakness to take advantage of: no chink in sb.'s armour: 他们时刻保持警惕，坏人～。They were always on the alert so that no opening was left for the enemy to exploit.

【无暇】 wúxiá　have no time; be too busy: ～他顾 have no time to attend to other things

【无限】 wúxiàn　infinite; limitless; boundless; immeasurable: ～光明的未来 a future of incomparable brightness

【无限期】 wúxiànqī　indefinite duration: ～罢工 a strike of indefinite duration/～休会 adjourn indefinitely

【无限制】 wúxiànzhì　unrestricted; unbridled; unlimited

【无线】 wúxiàn　wireless: ～电话 radiotelephone; radiophone/～电报 wireless telegram; radiotelegram

【无线电】 wúxiàndiàn　radio

【无效】 wúxiào　of (或 to) no avail; invalid; null and void: 医治～ fail to respond to medical treatment/ 宣布合同～ declare a contract invalid (或 null and void); invalidate (或 nullify) a contract/ 宣布选举～ nullify an election

【无懈可击】 wú xiè kě jī　with no chink in one's armour; unassailable; invulnerable: 这篇文章论证周密，～。The article is closely reasoned and the arguments are unassailable.

【无心】 wúxīn ① not be in the mood for: 他工作还没做完，～去看电影。He was in no mood to go to the film, as he hadn't finished his work. ② not intentionally; unwittingly; inadvertently: 他说这话是～的，你可别见怪。Don't take offence. He didn't say it intentionally./ 言者～，听者有意。A casual remark sounds deliberate to a suspicious listener. 或 A careless word may be important information to an attentive listener.

【无形】 wúxíng　invisible: ～的枷锁 invisible shackles

【无形中】 wúxíngzhōng　imperceptibly; virtually: 这～成了风气。This has imperceptibly become a common practice./ 他～成了我的助手。He's virtually become my assistant.

【无休止】 wúxiūzhǐ　ceaseless; endless: ～地争论 argue on and on

【无须】 wúxū　need not; not have to: ～顾虑 need not worry/～细说 It's unnecessary to go into details. 又作 "无须乎"

【无恙】 wúyàng 〈书〉in good health; well; safe: 安然～ safe and sound/ 别来～? I trust you've been in good health since we last met?

【无业游民】 wúyè yóumín　vagrant

【无疑】 wúyí　beyond doubt; undoubtedly: 这种行为～是错误的。Such conduct is undoubtedly wrong.

【无以复加】 wú yǐ fù jiā　in the extreme: 荒谬到了～的地步 be absurd in the extreme

【无异】 wúyì　not different from; the same as; as good as: 这件复制品几乎与原作～。The reproduction is almost as good as the original.

【无益】 wúyì　unprofitable; useless; no good

【无意】 wúyì ① have no intention (of doing sth.); not be inclined to: ～参加 have no intention of joining/ 于此不感兴趣 not keen on it ② inadvertently; unwittingly; accidentally: 他们在挖井时，～中发现了一些古代文物。While digging a well they accidentally unearthed some ancient relics.

【无意识】 wúyìshí　unconscious: ～的动作 an unconscious act (或 movement)

【无垠】 wúyín　boundless; vast: 一望～的草原 a boundless prairie

【无用】 wúyòng　useless; of no use

【无与伦比】 wú yǔ lúnbǐ　incomparable; unparalleled; unique; without equal: 他在地质学方面的贡献是～的。His contribution in the field of geology was unparalleled.

【无原则】 wúyuánzé　unprincipled: ～纠纷 an unprincipled dispute

【无缘无故】 wúyuán-wúgù　without cause or reason; for no reason at all: 世上决没有～的爱，也没有～的恨。There is absolutely no such thing in the world as love or hatred

without reason or cause.

【无源之水】 wú yuán zhī shuǐ　water without a source: 理论脱离实践，就成了～，无本之木。Theory divorced from practice would be like water without a source, or a tree without roots.

【无政府主义】 wúzhèngfǔzhǔyì　anarchism

【无知】 wúzhī　ignorant: ～妄说 ignorant nonsense/ 出于～ out of ignorance

【无止境】 wúzhǐjìng　have no limits; know no end: 科学的发展是～的。The development of science has no limits.

【无中生有】 wú zhōng shēng yǒu　purely fictitious; fabricated

【无足轻重】 wú zú qīng-zhòng　of little importance (或 consequence); insignificant: ～的人物 a nobody; a nonentity

【无罪】 wúzuì　innocent; not guilty: ～释放 set a person free with a verdict of "not guilty"/ 宣判～ acquit sb. of a crime

毋 wú 〈书〉〈副〉〔表示禁止或劝阻〕no; not: ～临渴而掘井。Don't wait till you are thirsty to dig a well./ ～令逃逸。You must not let him escape.

【毋宁】 wúnìng 〈副〉rather... (than); (not so much...) as: 与其固守，～出击。Better to strike out than to entrench oneself in defence.

【毋庸】 wúyōng　need not: ～讳言 no need for reticence

吾 wú 〈书〉I or we: ～辈 we/ ～国 my or our country

【吾侪】 wúchái 〈书〉we

【吾人】 wúrén 〈书〉we

芜 wú 〈书〉① overgrown with weeds: 荒～ lie waste ② grassland: 平～ open grassland ③ mixed and disorderly; miscellaneous: ～词 superfluous words

【芜菁】 wújīng 〈植〉turnip

【芜杂】 wúzá　mixed and disorderly; miscellaneous

吴 Wú　a surname

梧 wú

【梧桐】 wútóng 〈植〉Chinese parasol (tree)

蜈 wú

【蜈蚣】 wúgong 〈动〉centipede

鼯 wú

【鼯鼠】 wúshǔ 〈动〉flying squirrel

wǔ

五* wǔ　five: ～十 fifty/ ～倍 fivefold; quintuple/ ～分之一 one fifth/ ～十年代 the fifties

【五边形】 wǔbiānxíng　pentagon

【五彩】 wǔcǎi ① the five colours (blue, yellow, red, white and black) ② multicoloured: ～缤纷 colourful; blazing with colour

【五更】 wǔgēng ① the five watches (或 periods) of the night ② the fifth watch of the night; just before dawn: 起～，睡半夜 retire at midnight and rise before dawn

【五谷】 wǔgǔ ① the five cereals (rice, two kinds of millet, wheat and beans) ② food crops: ～丰登 an abundant harvest of all food crops

【五官】 wǔguān ① 〈中医〉the five sense organs (ears, eyes, lips, nose and tongue) ② facial features: ～端正 have regular features

【五光十色】 wǔguāng-shísè ① multicoloured; bright with many colours ② of great variety; of all kinds; multifarious

【五湖四海】 wǔhú-sìhǎi　all corners of the land

【五花八门】 wǔhuā-bāmén　multifarious; of a wide (或 rich) variety

【五金】 wǔjīn ① the five metals (gold, silver, copper, iron and tin) ② metals; hardware ◇ ～厂 hardware factory/ ～店 hardware store/ ～商 dealer in hardware; ironmonger

【五里雾】 wǔlǐwù thick fog: 如堕～中 as if lost in a thick fog; utterly mystified

【五内】 wǔnèi 〈书〉 viscera: ～俱焚 be rent with grief

【五年计划】 wǔnián jìhuà Five-Year Plan

【五十步笑百步】 wǔshí bù xiào bǎi bù one who retreats fifty paces mocks one who retreats a hundred — the pot calls the kettle black

【五体投地】 wǔ tǐ tóu dì prostrate oneself before sb. in admiration: 佩服得～ admire sb. from the bottom of one's heart; worship sb.

【五味】 wǔwèi ① the five flavours (sweet, sour, bitter, pungent and salty) ② all sorts of flavours

【五线谱】 wǔxiànpǔ 〈乐〉 staff; stave

【五香】 wǔxiāng ① the five spices (prickly ash, star aniseed, cinnamon, clove and fennel) ② spices ◇ ～豆 spiced beans

【五行】 wǔxíng the five elements (metal, wood, water, fire and earth, held by the ancients to compose the physical universe and later used in traditional Chinese medicine to explain various physiological and pathological phenomena)

【五颜六色】 wǔyán-liùsè of various colours; multicoloured; colourful

【五月】 wǔyuè ① May ② the fifth month of the lunar year; the fifth moon ◇ ～节 the Dragon Boat Festival (the 5th day of the 5th lunar month)

【五脏】 wǔzàng 〈中医〉 the five internal organs (heart, liver, spleen, lungs and kidneys) ◇ ～六腑 the vital organs of the human body

【五指】 wǔzhǐ the five fingers (thumb, index finger, middle finger, third finger and little finger)

午* wǔ ① noon; midday ② the seventh of the twelve Earthly Branches

【午饭】 wǔfàn midday meal; lunch

【午后】 wǔhòu afternoon

【午前】 wǔqián forenoon; before noon; morning

【午时】 wǔshí the period of the day from 11 a.m. to 1 p.m.

【午睡】 wǔshuì ① afternoon nap; noontime snooze ② take (或 have) a nap after lunch

【午夜】 wǔyè midnight

伍* wǔ ① five (used for the numeral 五 on cheques, banknotes, etc. to avoid mistakes or alterations) ② the basic five-man unit of the army in ancient China; army: 入～ join the army ③ company: 羞与为～ be ashamed of sb.'s company

妩 wǔ

【妩媚】 wǔmèi lovely; charming

忤 wǔ ① disobedient: ～逆 disobedient (to parents) ② uncongenial: 与人无～ bear no ill will against anybody

武* wǔ ① military: ～官 military officer ② connected with boxing skill, swordplay, etc. ③ valiant; fierce: 威～ martial-looking

【武备】 wǔbèi 〈书〉 defence preparations, specifically the condition of the armed forces and armaments

【武打】 wǔdǎ acrobatic fighting in Chinese opera or dance

【武斗】 wǔdòu resort to violence (in a debate, dispute, etc.)

【武断】 wǔduàn arbitrary decision; subjective assertion

【武功】 wǔgōng ① 〈书〉 military accomplishments ② 见 "武工"

【武官】 wǔguān ① military officer ② 〈外〉 military attaché: 海(空)军～ naval (air) attaché

【武力】 wǔlì ① force ② military force; armed might; armed strength; force of arms: ～镇压 armed suppression/ 诉诸 ～ resort to force

【武器】 wǔqì weapon; arms: 常规～ conventional weapons/ 轻～ small arms/ 核～ nuclear weapons/ 放下～ lay down one's arms/ 拿起～ take up arms/ ～装备 weaponry

【武士】 wǔshì ① palace guards in ancient times ② man of prowess; warrior; knight

【武士道】 wǔshìdào bushido

【武术】 wǔshù wushu, martial arts such as shadowboxing, swordplay, etc., formerly cultivated for self-defence, now a form of physical culture

【武艺】 wǔyì skill in wushu 参见 "武术"

【武装】 wǔzhuāng ① arms; military equipment; battle outfit: 全副～ (in) full battle gear ② armed forces: 人民～ the armed forces of the people/ 夺取政权 seizure of power by armed force ③ equip (或 supply) with arms; arm: ～到牙齿 be armed to the teeth ◇ ～部队 armed forces/ ～冲突 armed clash/ ～力量 armed power; armed forces

侮* wǔ insult; bully: 不可～ not to be bullied/ 外～ foreign aggression

【侮慢】 wǔmàn slight; treat disrespectfully

【侮辱】 wǔrǔ insult; humiliate; subject sb. to indignities

鹉 wǔ 见 "鹦鹉" yīngwǔ

舞* wǔ ① dance: 集体～ group dance/ 秧歌～ yangko dance/ 腰鼓～ drum dance/ 红绸～ red silk dance ② move about as in a dance: 手～足蹈 dance for joy/ 雪花～ snowflakes dancing in the air ③ dance with sth. in one's hands: ～剑 perform a sword-dance ④ flourish; wield; brandish: 挥～大棒 brandish the big stick/ 挥～指挥棒 wield the baton

【舞伴】 wǔbàn dancing partner

【舞弊】 wǔbì fraudulent practices; malpractices; irregularities; embezzlement: 我们在清查帐目时发现了他的～行为。 We discovered his irregularities while checking the accounts.

【舞厂】 wǔchǎng dance hall; ballroom

【舞蹈】 wǔdǎo dance

【舞动】 wǔdòng wave; brandish

【舞会】 wǔhuì dance; ball: 举行～ hold a dance

【舞弄】 wǔnòng wave; wield; brandish: ～刀枪 brandish swords and spears

【舞女】 wǔnǚ dancing girl; dance-hostess; taxi dancer

【舞曲】 wǔqǔ dance music; dance

【舞台】 wǔtái stage; arena: 政治～ political arena (或 scene, stage)/ 在国际～上 in the international arena

【舞厅】 wǔtīng ballroom; dance hall

【舞文弄墨】 wǔwén-nòngmò ① pervert the law by playing with legal phraseology ② engage in phrase-mongering

wù

兀 wù 〈书〉 ① rising to a height; towering ② bald

【兀鹫】 wùjiù 〈动〉 griffon vulture

【兀立】 wùlì stand upright

勿 wù 〈副〉〔表示禁止或劝阻〕: 请～吸烟 No Smoking/ ～谓言之不预也。 Do not say that you have not been forewarned. 或 Do not blame us for not having forewarned you.

戊 wù the fifth of the ten Heavenly Stems

务* wù ① affair; business: 公～ official business/ 任～ task; job/ 不急之～ business requiring no immediate attention; a matter of no great urgency ② be engaged in; devote one's efforts to: ～农 be engaged in agriculture; be a farmer/ 不～正业 not engage in honest work; not attend to one's proper duties ③ must; be sure to: ～使大家明了这一点。Be sure to make this point clear to everyone./ ～请光临指导。You are cordially invited to come and give guidance.

【务必】wùbì must; be sure to: 你～在本周内去看望他一次。Be sure to go and see him before the week is out.

【务实】wùshí deal with concrete matters relating to work

【务使】wùshǐ make sure; ensure

【务故】wùgù 见"务必"

【务虚】wùxū discuss principles or ideological guidelines

坞 wù ① a depressed place: 船～ dock/ 花～ sunken flower-bed ② 〈书〉 a fortified building; castle

物* wù ① thing; matter: 废～ waste matter/ 矿～ minerals/ 公～ public property/ 以～易～ barter/ 地大～博 vast territory and rich resources ② the outside world as distinct from oneself; other people: 待人接～ the way one gets along with people ③ content; substance: 言之无～ talk or writing devoid of substance

【物产】wùchǎn products; produce

【物故】wùgù 〈书〉 pass away; die

【物归原主】wù guī yuánzhǔ return sth. to its rightful owner

【物换星移】wùhuàn-xīngyí change of the seasons

【物极必反】wù jí bì fǎn things will develop in the opposite direction when they become extreme

【物价】wùjià (commodity) prices: ～稳定。Prices remain stable./ ～波动 price fluctuation/ ～飞涨。Prices skyrocketed. ◇ ～政策 pricing policy/ ～指数 price index

【物件】wùjiàn 〈方〉 thing; article

【物尽其用】wù jìn qí yòng make the best use of everything; let all things serve their proper purpose

【物理】wùlǐ ① innate laws of things ② physics

【物理学】wùlǐxué physics: 理论～ theoretical physics/ 应用～ applied physics/ 原子核～ nuclear physics ◇ ～家 physicist

【物力】wùlì material resources; *matériel*: 节约人力～ use manpower and material resources sparingly

【物品】wùpǐn article; goods: 贵重～ valuables/ 零星～ sundries; odds and ends

【物色】wùsè look for; seek out; choose: ～这方面的人才 look for qualified persons in this field

【物体】wùtǐ body; substance; object: 运动～ a body in motion/ 透明～ a transparent substance (或 object)

【物以类聚】wù yǐ lèi jù things of one kind come together; like attracts like; birds of a feather flock together

【物议】wùyì criticism from the people: 免遭～ so as to avoid public censure; so as not to incur criticism by the masses

【物证】wùzhèng material evidence

【物质】wùzhì matter: substance; material

【物资】wùzī goods and materials

误* wù ① mistake; error: 失～ error/ 笔～ a slip of the pen/ 经验主义把局部经验～认为普遍真理。Empiricism mistakes fragmentary experience for universal truth. ② miss: ～了火车 miss a train ③ harm: ～人子弟 harm the younger generation; lead young people astray/ 生产学习两不～。Neither production nor political study is to suffer. ④ by mistake; by accident: ～伤 accidentally injure

【误差】wùchā error: 平均～ mean error; average error

【误点】wùdiǎn late; overdue; behind schedule: 飞机～了。The plane is overdue (或 late)./ 火车～十分钟。The train was ten minutes late (或 behind schedule).

【误工】wùgōng ① delay one's work ② loss of working time

【误会】wùhuì ① misunderstand; mistake; misconstrue: 你～了我的意思。You've mistaken my meaning./ 你一定是搞～了。You must have misunderstood. 或 You must be mistaken. ② misunderstanding: 消除～ dispel (或 remove) misunderstanding

【误解】wùjiě ① misread; misunderstand: 你～了我的话。You misunderstood what I said. ② misunderstanding: 你亲自去和他谈谈,以免引起～。Go and talk to him yourself so that there will be no misunderstanding.

【误入歧途】wù rù qítú go astray; be misled

【误杀】wùshā 〈法〉 manslaughter

【误伤】wùshāng ① accidentally injure ② accidental injury

【误事】wùshì ① cause delay in work or business; hold things up ② bungle matters

悟* wù realize; awaken: ～出其中的道理 realize why it should be so

【悟性】wùxìng power of understanding; comprehension

恶* wù loathe; dislike; hate: 好～ likes and dislikes/ 可～ loathsome; hateful
另见 ě; è

晤 wù meet; interview; see

【晤面】wùmiàn meet; see

【晤谈】wùtán meet and talk; have a talk; interview

骛 wù go after; seek for: 好高～远 reach for what is beyond one's grasp; aim too high

雾* wù ① fog: 薄～ mist ② fine spray: 喷～器 sprayer

【雾气】wùqì fog; mist; vapour

寤 wù 〈书〉 awake

鹜 wù 〈书〉 duck

XĪ

夕 xī ① sunset: 朝发～至 start at daybreak and arrive at sunset ② evening; night: 除～ New Year's Eve/ 旦～ this morning or evening — in a short time/ 这些问题不是一朝一～能够解决的. These problems cannot be solved overnight.

【夕阳】 xīyáng the setting sun.
【夕照】 xīzhào the glow of the setting sun; evening glow: 满目青山一明. On all sides, verdant sunset-bathed hills greet the eye.

兮 xī 〈书〉〈助〉〔跟现代的"啊"相似〕: 大风起～云飞扬. A gale has risen and is sweeping the clouds across the sky.

汐 xī tide during the night; nighttide

西 xī ① west: ～屋 west room/ 太原以～ to the west of Taiyuan/ 往～去 head west ② (Xī) Occidental; Western: ～乐 Western music

【西北】 xīběi northwest ◇～风 northwest (或 northwesterly) wind
【西餐】 xīcān Western-style food
【西方】 xīfāng ① west ② (Xīfāng) the West; the Occident: ～国家 the Western countries
【西服】 xīfú Western-style clothes
【西瓜】 xīguā watermelon ◇～子 watermelon seed
【西南】 xīnán southwest ～风 southwest (或 southwesterly) wind
【西式】 xīshì Western style: ～点心 Western-style pastry
【西天】 xītiān 〈佛教〉 Western Paradise
【西洋】 Xīyáng the West; the Western world ◇～人 Westerner/ ～文学 Western literature
【西洋景】 xīyángjǐng ① peep show ② hanky-panky; trickery: 拆穿～ expose sb.'s tricks; strip off the camouflage 又作"西洋镜"
【西药】 xīyào Western medicine
【西医】 xīyī ① Western medicine (as distinguished from traditional Chinese medicine) ② a doctor trained in Western medicine
【西乐】 xīyuè Western music
【西装】 xīzhuāng Western-style clothes

吸 xī ① inhale; breathe in; draw: ～进新鲜空气 inhale fresh air/ 深深一一口气 draw a deep breath ② absorb; suck up: 用粉笔把墨水一干 blot ink with a piece of chalk/ 海绵一水. A sponge absorbs water. ③ attract; draw to oneself: 磁石一铁. A magnet attracts iron.

【吸尘器】 xīchénqì dust catcher; dust collector: 真空～ vacuum cleaner

真空吸尘器

【吸毒】 xīdú drug taking ◇～者 drug addict
【吸附】 xīfù 〈化〉 adsorption
【吸力】 xīlì suction; attraction: 相互～ mutual attraction/ 地心～ force of gravity
【吸墨纸】 xīmòzhǐ blotting paper
【吸取】 xīqǔ absorb; draw; assimilate: ～水分 absorb water/ ～精华 absorb the quintessence/ ～教训 draw a lesson
【吸热】 xīrè absorption of heat

【吸食】 xīshí suck; take in
【吸收】 xīshōu ① absorb; suck up; assimilate; imbibe; draw: ～养分 assimilate nutriment/ ～水分 suck up moisture/ ～知识 absorb (或 imbibe) knowledge ② recruit; enrol; admit
【吸吮】 xīshǔn suck; absorb
【吸血鬼】 xīxuèguǐ bloodsucker; vampire
【吸烟】 xīyān smoke
【吸引】 xīyǐn attract; draw; fascinate: ～注意力 attract attention/ 把敌人火力～过来 draw enemy fire on oneself/ 被工地热火朝天的场面一住了 be fascinated by the hustle and bustle of the construction site/ 这部电影对观众有～力. This film has a strong appeal to the audience.

希 xī ① hope: 敬～读者指正. It is hoped that the readers will kindly point out our errors./ ～准时到会. Please get to the meeting on time. ② rare; scarce; uncommon

【希罕】 xīhan ① rare; scarce; uncommon: 骆驼在南方是～的东西. Camels are a rare sight in the south. ② value as a rarity; cherish: 你～, 我还～呢. You may not cherish it, but I do./ 谁～你的臭钱？ Who cares about your lousy money?
【希冀】 xījì 〈书〉 hope for; wish for; aspire after
【希奇】 xīqí rare; strange; curious: 十月下雪在这儿不是什么～的事. Snow in October is nothing strange in this place.
【希图】 xītú harbour the intention of; try to; attempt to: ～蒙混过关 try to wangle; try to get by under false pretences/ ～年取暴利 go after quick profits
【希望】 xīwàng hope; wish; expect: 把～变成现实 turn hopes into reality/ 大有成功的～ promise high hopes of success; stand a very good chance of success/ 这就是朋友们对你的～. This is what your friends expect of you./ 那时候我们是多么～把水引到这儿来啊! How we wished then that the water over there could be diverted to our area!/ ～寄托在你们青年人身上. Our hope is placed on you young people.

昔 xī former times; the past: 今～对比 contrast the past with the present/ 今胜于～. The present is superior to the past.

【昔年】 xīnián 〈书〉 in former years
【昔日】 xīrì in former days (或 times): ～荒坡, 今日良田. The once barren hillsides are now good farmland.

析 xī ① divide; separate: 分崩离～ fall to pieces; come apart ② analyse; dissect; resolve: ～义 analyse the meaning (of a word, etc.)

【析疑】 xīyí 〈书〉 resolve a doubt; clear up a doubtful point

矽 xī 〈化〉 silicon (Si)

郗 Xī a surname

唏 xī 〈书〉 sob

【唏嘘】 xīxū 〈书〉 sob; sigh

奚 xī 〈书〉 why; how; where; what

【奚落】 xīluò scoff at; taunt; gibe

牺 xī 〈书〉 a beast of a uniform colour for sacrifice; sacrifice: ～牛 sacrificial ox

【牺牲】 xīshēng ① a beast slaughtered for sacrifice; sacrifice ② sacrifice oneself; die a martyr's death; lay down one's life: 英勇～ die a heroic death ③ sacrifice; give up; do sth. at the expense of: ～个人利益 sacrifice one's personal interests/ ～质量而去追求数量是错误的. It is wrong to sacrifice quality to quantity ◇～品 victim; prey

息* xī ① breath: 屏～ hold one's breath/ 一～尚存 so long as there is breath left in one/ 战斗到最后一～ fight to one's last breath ② news: 信～ news; message ③ cease; stop: 风止雨～。The wind has subsided and the rain stopped./ 经久不～的掌声 prolonged applause ④ rest: 按时作～ work and rest according to the timetable ⑤ grow; multiply: 蕃～ multiply greatly ⑥ interest: 年～ annual interest/ 无～贷款 interest-free loan ⑦〈书〉one's children

【息怒】xīnù cease to be angry; calm one's anger

【息事宁人】xīshì-níngrén ① patch up a quarrel and reconcile the parties concerned ② make concessions to avoid trouble; gloss things over to stay on good terms

【息息相关】xīxī xiāng guān be closely linked; be closely bound up

淅 xī〈书〉wash rice

【淅沥】xīlì〈象〉〔形容轻微的雨声等〕: 雨声～ the patter of rain

惜* xī ① cherish; value highly; care for tenderly: 爱～ cherish; treasure/ ～寸阴 value every bit of time; make good use of every moment ② spare; grudge; stint: ～指失掌 stint a finger only to lose the whole hand — try to save a little only to lose a lot/ 不～工本 spare neither labour nor money; spare no expense ③ have pity on sb.: ～惘～ feel sorry for

【惜别】xībié be reluctant to part; hate to see sb. go: 我们怀着～的心情, 送走了老朋友。We reluctantly parted with our old friends.

【惜力】xīlì be sparing of one's energy; not do one's best: 小张干活从不～。Xiao Zhang never spares himself in his work.

晞 xī〈书〉① dry: 晨露未～ before the dew is dry ② the first light of day; daybreak: 东方未～ before daybreak

欷 xī

【欷歔】xīxū〈书〉sob; sigh

悉 xī ① all; entirely: ～力 go all out; spare no effort ② know; learn; be informed of: 熟～ know very well/ 惊～ be shocked to learn/ 来函敬～。Your letter has come to hand.

【悉数】xīshǔ enumerate in full detail: 不可～ too many to enumerate

【悉数】xīshù〈书〉all; every single one: ～奉还 return all that has been borrowed or taken away

【悉心】xīxīn devote all one's attention; take the utmost care: ～研究 devote oneself to the study of sth./ ～照料病人 take the utmost care of the patient

晰 xī clear; distinct: 明～ clear; lucid/ 清～ distinct

翕 xī〈书〉① amiable and compliant ② furl; fold; shut: ～张 furl and unfurl; close and open

稀* xī ① rare; scarce; uncommon: 物以～为贵。When a thing is scarce, it is precious. ② sparse; scattered: 地广人～ a vast, sparsely populated area/ 月明星～。The moon is bright and the stars are few. ③ watery; thin: 粥太～了。This gruel is too thin./ 我想吃点儿～的。I'd like to have some liquid food.

【稀薄】xībó thin; rare: 山顶空气～。The air is thin on the top of the mountain.

【稀饭】xīfàn rice or millet gruel; porridge

【稀罕】xīhan 见"希罕"xīhan

【稀客】xīkè rare visitor

【稀烂】xīlàn ① completely mashed; pulpy: 肉煮得～。The meat was cooked to a pulp. ② smashed to pieces (或 smithereens); broken to bits

【稀里糊涂】xīlihútu not knowing what one is about; muddleheaded

【稀奇】xīqí 见"希奇"xīqí

【稀少】xīshǎo few; rare; scarce: 人口～ a sparse population/ 街上行人～。There were few people in the street.

【稀疏】xīshū few and scattered; few and far between; thin; sparse: ～的晨星 a few scattered morning stars/ ～的头发 thin hair; sparse hair/ ～的枪声 scattered shots; sporadic firing/ 林木～。The woods are sparse.

【稀松】xīsōng ① poor; sloppy: 这活儿干得～。This is sloppy work. ② unimportant; trivial: 别把这些～的事放在心里。Don't take such trivial matters to heart.

【稀有】xīyǒu rare; unusual

腊 xī〈书〉dried meat
另见 là

犀 xī rhinoceros

【犀角】xījiǎo rhinoceros horn

【犀利】xīlì sharp; incisive; trenchant: ～的目光 sharp eyes/ 谈锋～ incisive in conversation/ 文笔～ a trenchant pen

【犀鸟】xīniǎo hornbill

【犀牛】xīniú rhinoceros

犀牛

溪* xī small stream; brook; rivulet

【溪涧】xījiàn mountain stream

【溪流】xīliú brook; rivulet

锡* xī〈化〉tin (Sn)

【锡箔】xībó tinfoil paper (formerly used as funeral offerings)

【锡匠】xījiang tinsmith

【锡矿】xīkuàng tin ore

【锡纸】xīzhǐ silver paper; tinfoil

皙 xī〈书〉fair-skinned; light-complexioned

熄* xī extinguish; put out: ～灯 put out the light/ 火～了。The fire has gone out.

【熄灭】xīmiè go out; die out

熙 xī ① bright; sunny ② prosperous ③ gay; merry

【熙熙攘攘】xīxīrǎngrǎng bustling with activity; with people bustling about

蜥 xī

【蜥蜴】xīyì lizard

嘻* xī ①〈书〉〈叹〉〔表示惊叹〕: ～, 技至此乎! How wonderful! What superb skill! ②〈象〉〔形容笑声〕: ～～地笑 giggle

【嘻嘻哈哈】xīxīhāhā laughing and joking; laughing merrily; mirthful

膝 xī knee

【膝盖】xīgài knee ◇ ～骨 kneecap; patella

【膝关节】xīguānjié knee joint

嬉 xī〈方〉play; sport

【嬉皮士】xīpíshì hippy; hippie

【嬉皮笑脸】xīpí-xiàoliǎn grinning cheekily; smiling and grimacing

【嬉戏】xīxì〈书〉play; sport: 湖面上鸭群在～。Ducks are sporting on the lake.

【嬉笑】xīxiào be laughing and playing: 孩子们的～声 the happy laughter of children at play

熹 xī〈书〉dawn; brightness

【熹微】 xīwēi 〈书〉(of morning sunlight) dim; pale: 晨光 ~ the dim light (或 first faint rays) of dawn

蹊 xī 〈书〉footpath
另见 qī
【蹊径】 xījìng 〈书〉path; way

螅 xī
【蟋蟀】 xīshuài 〈动〉cricket

谿 xī 〈书〉见"溪" xī

曦 xī 〈书〉sunlight (usu. in early morning): 晨~ early morning sunlight

xí

习* xí ①practise; exercise; review: 自~ study by oneself/ 复~ review (one's lessons) ②get accustomed to; be used to; become familiar with: ~闻 often hear/ 不~水性 be not good at swimming ③habit; custom; usual practice: 积~ old habit; longstanding practice/ 陋~ bad custom
【习非成是】 xí fēi chéng shì accept what is wrong as right as one grows accustomed to it
【习惯】 xíguàn ①be accustomed to; be used to; be inured to: ~于过部队生活 be accustomed (或 inured) to army life/ 这样潮湿的天气我实在不~。I just can't get used to this damp weather. ②habit; custom; usual practice: 从小培养劳动~ cultivate the habit of doing manual labour from childhood/ 破除旧~ break down out-moded customs and establish new ones/ ~成自然。Once you form a habit, it comes natural to you. ◇ ~法 common law; customary law
【习见】 xíjiàn (of things) commonly seen: ~的现象 a common sight
【习气】 xíqì bad habit; bad practice: 官僚~ habitual prac-tice of bureaucracy; bad bureaucratic habits
【习染】 xírǎn 〈书〉①contract (a bad habit); fall into a bad habit of ②bad habit
【习尚】 xíshàng common practice; custom
【习俗】 xísú custom; convention
【习题】 xítí exercises (in school work)
【习习】 xíxí (of the wind) blow gently: 微风~。A gentle breeze is blowing.
【习性】 xíxìng habits and characteristics: 熊猫的~ the habits and characteristics of the giant panda
【习以为常】 xí yǐ wéi cháng be used to (或 accustomed) to sth.
【习用】 xíyòng habitually use
【习语】 xíyǔ idiom
【习字】 xízì practise penmanship; do exercises in calligra-phy ◇ ~帖 copybook; calligraphy model
【习作】 xízuò ①do exercises in composition ②an exercise in composition, drawing, etc.

席* xí ①mat: 草~ straw mat ②seat; place: 入~ take one's seat/ 来宾~ seats for visitors/ 该党在议会选举中失去了十五~。That party lost 15 seats in the parliamentary election. ③feast; banquet; dinner: ~间宾主频频举杯。Host and guests frequently raised their glasses during the feast. ④〈量〉: 一~酒 a banquet/ 一~话 a talk (with sb.); a conversation
【席不暇暖】 xí bù xiá nuǎn not sit long enough to warm the seat; be in a tearing hurry; be constantly on the go
【席次】 xícì the order of seats; seating arrangement; one's place among the seats arranged: 按指定~入座 take one's assigned seat; sit down in one's place
【席地】 xídì on the ground: ~而坐 sit on the ground
【席卷】 xíjuǎn ①roll up like a mat; carry everything with one; take away everything: ~而去 make off with every-thing that one can lay hands on ②sweep across; engulf:

暴风雪~大草原。A blizzard swept across the vast grass-lands.
【席位】 xíwèi seat (at a conference, in a legislative assem-bly, etc.)

袭 xí ①make a surprise attack on; raid: 夜~ night raid/ 偷~ surprise attack; sneak raid/ 花气~人。The fra-grance of flowers assails one's nose. ②follow the pattern of; carry on as before; carry on (an old tradition, etc.)/ 抄~ plagiarize ③〈书〉〈量〉〔用于成套的衣服〕: 衣一~ a suit of clothes
【袭击】 xíjī make a surprise attack on; surprise; raid: 敌军阵地遭到~ make a surprise attack on the enemy positions/ 沿海一带受到台风的~。The coastal areas were hit by a typhoon.
【袭取】 xíqǔ ①take by surprise ②见"袭用"
【袭扰】 xírǎo 〈军〉harassing attack
【袭用】 xíyòng take over (something that has long been used in the past): ~古方 take over an age-old recipe/ ~老谱 follow old practice

媳* xí daughter-in-law
【媳妇】 xífù ①son's wife; daughter-in-law ②the wife of a relative of the younger generation: 侄~ nephew's wife/ 孙~ grandson's wife

檄 xí 〈书〉①a call to arms (in ancient times) ②an-nounce or denounce in such a call
【檄文】 xíwén ①an official call to arms ②an official de-nunciation of the enemy

xǐ

洗* xǐ ①wash; bathe: ~衣服 wash clothes/ ~干净 wash sth. clean/ ~伤口 bathe a wound/ 碧空如~ a cloud-less blue sky ②〈宗〉baptize: 受~ receive baptism; be baptized ③redress; right: ~冤 right a wrong; redress a grievance ④kill and loot; sack: ~城 massacre the in-habitants of a captured city/ 血~ plunge (the inhabitants) in a bloodbath; massacre ⑤develop (a film) ⑥shuffle (cards, etc.)
【洗尘】 xǐchén give a dinner of welcome (to a visitor from afar)
【洗涤】 xǐdí wash; cleanse ◇ ~剂 detergent
【洗耳恭听】 xǐ ěr gōng tīng listen with respectful attention
【洗发剂】 xǐfàjì shampoo
【洗剂】 xǐjì 〈药〉lotion
【洗劫】 xǐjié loot; sack
【洗礼】 xǐlǐ ①〈宗〉baptism ②severe test: 炮火的~ the baptism of fire/ 受过战斗的~ have gone through (the test of) battle
【洗脸盆】 xǐliǎnpén washbasin; washbowl
【洗染店】 xǐrǎndiàn cleaners and dyers; laundering and dyeing shop
【洗手】 xǐshǒu ①(of a thief, bandit, etc.) stop doing evil and reform oneself ②wash one's hands of sth.
【洗刷】 xǐshuā ①wash and brush; scrub: ~地板 scrub the floor ②wash off; clear oneself of (opprobrium, stigma, guilt, etc.)
【洗头】 xǐtóu wash one's hair; shampoo
【洗心革面】 xǐxīn-gémiàn turn over a new leaf; thoroughly reform oneself
【洗雪】 xǐxuě wipe out (a disgrace); redress (a wrong)
【洗衣】 xǐyī wash clothes; do one's washing ◇ ~板 washboard/ ~店 laundry/ ~粉 washing powder/ ~机 washing machine; washer/ ~刷 wash brush
【洗澡】 xǐzǎo have (或 take) a bath; bathe
【洗濯】 xǐzhuó wash; cleanse

玺 xǐ imperial or royal seal

徙 xǐ move (from one place to another)

【徙居】 xǐjū　move house: ～内地 move up-country

喜* xǐ ① happy; delighted; pleased: 心中暗～ secretly feel pleased/ ～不自胜 be delighted beyond measure; be beside oneself with joy/ 笑在脸上,～在心里 with a smile on one's face and joy in one's heart/ ～获丰收 reap a bumper harvest ② happy event (esp. wedding); occasion for celebration: 报～ report good news/ 大～的日子 a day of great happiness; a joyful occasion; an occasion for celebration ③〈口〉 pregnancy: 有～ be expecting; be in the family way ④ be fond of; like; have an inclination for: ～读书 be fond of reading/ 猴子性～攀缘 Monkeys have a natural inclination for climbing.

【喜爱】 xǐ'ài　like; love; be fond of; be keen on: ～户外活动 be keen on outdoor activities/ 我们最～这首歌曲。We like this song best.

【喜冲冲】 xǐchōngchōng　look exhilarated; be in a joyful mood

【喜出望外】 xǐ chū wàng wài　be overjoyed (at an unexpected gain, good news, etc.); be pleasantly surprised

【喜好】 xǐhào　like; love; be fond of; be keen on: 她从小就～音乐。She's been a music lover since childhood.

【喜欢】 xǐhuan ① like; love; be fond of; be keen on: ～看电视 like watching TV/ 这孩子真讨人～。This is a lovable child./ 她最不～吹吹拍拍。She loathes boasting and flattery. ② happy; elated; filled with joy: 听到胜利的消息好不～ become elated at the news of victory

【喜酒】 xǐjiǔ ① wine drunk at a wedding feast ② wedding feast

【喜剧】 xǐjù　comedy ◇ ～演员 comedian

【喜怒无常】 xǐ-nù wú cháng　subject to changing moods

【喜气洋洋】 xǐqì yángyáng　full of joy; jubilant

【喜庆】 xǐqìng ① joyous; jubilant: 在这～的日子里 on this day of jubilation; on this happy occasion ② happy event

【喜鹊】 xǐque〈动〉magpie

【喜色】 xǐsè　happy expression; joyful look: 面有～ wear a happy expression

【喜事】 xǐshì ① happy event; joyous occasion ② wedding

【喜笑颜开】 xǐxiào-yánkāi　light up with pleasure; be wreathed in smiles

【喜新厌旧】 xǐxīn-yànjiù　love the new and loathe the old — be fickle in affection

【喜形于色】 xǐ xíng yú sè　be visibly pleased; light up with pleasure

【喜讯】 xǐxùn　happy news; good news; glad tidings

【喜洋洋】 xǐyángyáng　beaming with joy; radiant

【喜雨】 xǐyǔ　seasonable rain; a welcome fall of rain: 普降～ a widespread fall of seasonable rain; a seasonable fall of rain over a wide area

【喜悦】 xǐyuè　happy; joyous: 怀着万分～的心情 with a feeling of immeasurable joy

【喜滋滋】 xǐzīzī　feeling pleased; filled with joy

蒠 xǐ〈书〉fear; dread; be afraid: 畏～不前 be too timid to go ahead; hang back

屣 xǐ〈书〉shoe: 敝～ worn-out shoes

禧 xǐ　auspiciousness; happiness; jubilation: 恭贺新～. Happy New Year!

xì

戏* xì ① play; sport: 嬉～ sport; have fun/ 二龙～珠 two dragons playing with a pearl ② make fun of; joke: ～言 say something for fun; joke ③ drama; play; show: 京～ Beijing opera/ 马～ circus show (或 performance)/ 去看～ go to the theatre/ 这场～演得精彩。It was a wonderful performance./ 好～还在后头呢。The really interesting part of the show is yet to come.

【戏班】 xìbān　theatrical troupe (或 company)

【戏法】 xìfǎ　conjuring; juggling; tricks; magic: 变～ juggle; conjure; perform tricks/ ～人人会变,各有巧妙不同. Many are the magicians, but each has his own tricks.

【戏剧】 xìjù　drama; play; theatre: 现代～ modern drama; the modern theatre/ 一个富有～性的事件 a dramatic event ◇ ～家 dramatist/ ～界 theatrical circles/ ～评论 dramatic criticism

【戏迷】 xìmí　theatre fan

【戏弄】 xìnòng　make fun of; play tricks on; tease; kid

【戏曲】 xìqǔ ① traditional opera: 地方～ local operas ② singing parts in *chuanqi* (传奇) and *zaju* (杂剧)

【戏台】 xìtái〈口〉stage

【戏谑】 xìxuè　banter; crack jokes

【戏院】 xìyuàn　theatre

【戏装】 xìzhuāng　theatrical (或 stage) costume

系* xì ① system; series: 太阳～ the solar system/ 语～ (language) family/ 派～ faction ② department (in a college); faculty: 哲学～ the department of philosophy ③ tie; fasten: ～马 tether a horse ④ relate to; bear on: 名誉所～ have a direct bearing on one's reputation/ 成败～于此举 stand or fall by this ⑤ feel anxious; be concerned: ～念 feel concerned about ⑥〈书〉be: 纯～试验性质 be purely experimental in character
另见 jì

【系列】 xìliè　series; set: 一～的问题 a series of problems/ 一～政策 a whole set of policies/ 运载～ vehicle series

【系统】 xìtǒng ① system: 灌溉～ irrigation system/ 财贸～ departments of trade and finance and affiliated organizations/ 通过组织～ through organizational channels ② systematic: 作～的研究 make a systematic study/ ～地说明 explain in a systematic way ◇ ～化 systematize/ ～性 systematicness

细* xì ① thin; slender: ～铁丝 thin wire ② in small particles; fine: ～沙 fine sand/ 玉米面磨得很～. The corn flour has been ground very fine. ③ thin and soft: ～嗓子 a thready voice ④ fine; exquisite; delicate: ～瓷 fine porcelain (或 china)/ 这几件象牙雕刻做得真～! What exquisite (或 delicate) ivory carvings these are!/ 粗粮～作 make delicacies out of coarse food grain ⑤ careful; meticulous; detailed: ～看 examine carefully; scrutinize/ ～问 make detailed inquiries; ask about details/ 工作做得～ be meticulous in one's work ⑥ minute; trifling: ～节 minute detail/ 事无巨～ all matters, big and small/ 分工很～ have an elaborate division of labour

【细胞】 xìbāo　cell

【细长】 xìcháng　long and thin; tall and slender: ～的身材 a tall and slender figure

【细工】 xìgōng　fine workmanship

【细故】 xìgù　trivial matter; trifle

【细活】 xìhuó　a job requiring fine workmanship or meticulous care; skilled work

【细节】 xìjié　details; particulars: 讨论计划的～ discuss the details of a plan; go into the particulars of a plan/ 通过～描写来表现人物性格 portray a character through the description of detail

【细菌】 xìjūn　germ; bacterium ◇ ～肥料 bacterial fertilizer/ ～农药 bacterial pesticide/ ～武器 bacteriological (或 germ) weapon/ ～战 bacteriological (或 germ) warfare

【细毛】 xìmáo　fine, soft fur

【细毛羊】 xìmáoyáng　fine-wool sheep

【细密】 xìmì ① fine and closely woven; close: 质地～ of close texture/ 针脚～ in fine close stitches/ ～的纹理 a close grain ② meticulous; detailed: ～的分析 a detailed analysis

【细目】 xìmù ① detailed catalogue ② specific item; detail

【细嫩】 xìnèn　delicate; tender: ～的皮肤 delicate skin

【细腻】 xìnì ① fine and smooth ② exquisite; minute: ～的描写 a minute description/ ～的表演 an exquisite performance

【细巧】 xìqiǎo exquisite; dainty; delicate: ~的图案 an exquisite design

【细软】 xìruǎn jewelry, expensive clothing and other valuables

【细润】 xìrùn fine and glossy: 瓷质~。The porcelain is fine and glossy.

【细弱】 xìruò thin and delicate; slim and fragile: ~的身子 of slim and delicate build/ 声~ a feeble voice

【细声细气】 xìshēng-xìqì in a soft voice; soft-spoken

【细水长流】 xìshuǐ cháng liú ① economize to avoid running short ② go about sth. little by little without a letup

【细碎】 xìsuì in small, broken bits: ~的脚步声 the sound of light and hurried footsteps

【细微】 xìwēi slight; fine; subtle: ~的变化 slight (或 subtle) changes/ ~差别 a fine distinction; a subtle difference

【细小】 xìxiǎo very small; tiny; fine; trivial: ~的零件 small parts (of a machine)/ ~的雨点 tiny raindrops/ ~的事情 trivial matters

【细心】 xìxīn careful; attentive: ~观察 carefully observe/ ~护理伤员 nurse the wounded with care

【细雨】 xìyǔ drizzle; fine rain

【细则】 xìzé detailed rules and regulations

【细致】 xìzhì careful; meticulous: 她想得很~。She thought it out in detail./这活做得很~。This is a careful piece of work.

阋 xì 〈书〉quarrel; strife: 兄弟~于墙。Brothers quarrel at home.

隙 xì ① crack; chink; crevice: 墙~ a crack in the wall/ 云~ a rift in the clouds ② gap; interval: 农~ interval between busy seasons in farming ③ loophole; opportunity: 无~可乘 no loophole to take advantage of/ 乘~突围 seize an opportunity to break through the encirclement ④ discord; rift: 并无嫌~ bear no ill will (或 grudge)

【隙地】 xìdì unoccupied place; open space

xiā

呷 xiā 〈方〉sip: ~一口茶 take a sip of tea

虾 xiā shrimp: ~群 a shoal of shrimps/ 对~ prawn/ 龙~ lobster

【虾兵蟹将】 xiābīng-xièjiàng shrimp soldiers and crab generals — ineffective troops

【虾干】 xiāgān dried shrimps

【虾酱】 xiājiàng shrimp paste

【虾米】 xiāmǐ ① dried, shelled shrimps ②〈方〉small shrimps

【虾仁】 xiārén shelled fresh shrimps; shrimp meat

【虾油】 xiāyóu shrimp sauce

瞎 xiā ① blind: ~了一只眼 blind in one eye ② groundlessly; foolishly; to no purpose: ~讲 speak groundlessly/ ~花钱 spend money foolishly/ ~干 go it blind/ ~猜 make a wild guess/ ~费劲儿 make a vain effort

【瞎扯】 xiāchě ① talk irresponsibly; talk rubbish ② talk at random about anything under the sun; waffle; natter

【瞎话】 xiāhuà untruth; lie: 说~ tell a lie; lie

【瞎闹】 xiānào ① act senselessly; mess about ② fool around; be mischievous: 赶快做作业, 别~。Do your homework quickly and don't fool around.

【瞎说】 xiāshuō talk irresponsibly; talk rubbish

【瞎子】 xiāzi a blind person: ~摸鱼 a blind person groping for fish — act blindly/ ~点灯白费蜡 like lighting a candle for a blind person — a sheer waste

xiá

匣 xiá a small box (或 case); casket

【匣子】 xiázi a small box (或 case); casket

狎 xiá be improperly familiar with

【狎昵】 xiánì be improperly familiar with

侠 xiá

【侠客】 xiákè a person adept in martial arts and given to chivalrous conduct (in olden times)

【侠义】 xiáyì having a strong sense of justice and ready to help the weak; chivalrous

峡 xiá gorge: 三门~ the Sanmen Gorge/ 海~ strait

【峡谷】 xiágǔ gorge; canyon

狭 xiá narrow: 坡陡路~。The slope is steep and the path narrow.

【狭隘】 xiá'ài ① narrow: ~的山道 a narrow mountain path ② narrow and limited; parochial: ~的看法 a narrow view/ 心胸~ be narrow-minded ◇ ~民族主义 narrow (或 parochial) nationalism/ ~性 narrow-mindedness; parochialism

【狭长】 xiácháng long and narrow

【狭路相逢】 xiálù xiāng féng (of adversaries) meet face to face on a narrow path — come into unavoidable confrontation

【狭小】 xiáxiǎo narrow and small; narrow: ~的阁楼 a poky attic/ 气量~ be intolerant; be narrow-minded/ 走出~的圈子 step out of one's narrow circle

【狭义】 xiáyì narrow sense

【狭窄】 xiázhǎi ① narrow; cramped: ~的巷子 a narrow lane (或 alley) ② narrow and limited; narrow: 心地~ be narrow-minded/ 见识~ be limited in knowledge and narrow in experience

遐 xiá 〈书〉① far; distant ② lasting; long: ~龄 advanced age

【遐迩】 xiá'ěr 〈书〉far and near: ~闻名 be well-known far and near; enjoy widespread renown

【遐想】 xiáxiǎng reverie; daydream

瑕 xiá ① flaw in a piece of jade ② flaw; defect; shortcoming

【瑕不掩瑜】 xiá bù yǎn yú one flaw cannot obscure the splendour of the jade — the defects cannot obscure the virtues

【瑕疵】 xiácī flaw; blemish

【瑕瑜互见】 xiá-yú hù jiàn have defects as well as merits; have both strong and weak points

暇 xiá free time; leisure: 无~兼顾 be too busy to attend to other things/ 自顾不~ be unable even to fend for oneself (much less look after others); be busy enough with one's own affairs

辖 xiá ① linchpin ② have jurisdiction over; administer; govern: 省~市 a municipality (或 city) under the jurisdiction of the provincial government/ 下~四个兵团 have four army corps under its command

【辖区】 xiáqū area under one's jurisdiction

霞 xiá rosy clouds; morning or evening glow: 晚~ the glow of sunset; sunset clouds/ 彩~ (the many hues of) rosy clouds

【霞光】 xiáguāng rays of morning or evening sunlight: ~万道 a myriad of sun rays/ 彩云万朵, ~四射。Rays of sunlight shine through multihued clouds.

黠 xiá 〈书〉crafty; cunning

xià

下* xià ① below; down; under; underneath: 零~五度 five degrees below zero/ 上至司令员,~至普通战士 from the commander down to the rank and file/ 树~ under the tree/ 山~ at the foot of the hill ② lower; inferior: 分为上、中、三等 divided into three grades: the upper, the middle and the lower ③ next; latter; second: ~一班车 the next bus/ ~半月 the latter (或 second) half of the month/ ~半辈子 the latter half of one's life; the rest of one's life/ ~册 the last of two or three volumes ④ downward; down: 防止圆木~滑 prevent the logs from rolling down/ 物价~跌。Prices dropped./ 俘房敌师长以~六千人 capture 6,000 enemy troops from the division commander downward ⑤ 〔表示属于一定范围、情况、条件等〕: 国家在他的领导~ The country under his leadership 在这种情况~ in such circumstances/ 在朋友的帮助~ with the help of friends ⑥ 〔表示当某个时间或时节〕: 眼~ at the moment; at present/ 年~ during the lunar New Year ⑦ 〔用在数字后,表示方面或方位〕: 往四~一看 look all around/ 两~里都同意。Both sides have agreed. ⑧ descend; alight; get off: ~山 descend the mountain/ ~飞机 alight from a plane/ ~车 get off a car or bus/ ~床 get out of bed/ ~楼 descend the stairs; go or come downstairs; 顺流而~ sail downstream ⑨ (of rain, snow, etc.) fall: 雪~得很大。The snow is falling heavily. 或 It's snowing hard./ ~雨了。It's raining. ⑩ issue; deliver; send: ~命令 issue (或 give) orders/ ~请帖 send an invitation ⑪ go to: ~车间 go to the workshop/ ~馆子 go and eat in a restaurant; eat out ⑫ exit; leave: 从左边门儿~ exit from the left door/ 换人,四号~,三号上。Substitution, No.3 for No.4. ⑬ put in; cast: ~作料 put in the condiments/ ~网打鱼 cast a net to catch fish/ ~面条 cook noodles ⑭ take away (或 off); dismantle; unload: ~纱窗 take the screen window off/ 了俘房的枪 disarm the captured soldier/ 船上的货还没~完。The cargo hasn't all been unloaded yet. ⑮ form (an opinion, idea, etc.): ~结论 draw a conclusion/ ~决心 make a resolution; be determined/ ~定义 give a definition; define ⑯ apply; use: ~力气 put forth strength; make an effort; exert oneself/ 对症~药 prescribe the right remedy for an illness ⑰ (of animals) give birth to; lay: ~了一窝小猪 give birth to a litter of piglets/ ~蛋 lay eggs ⑱ capture; take: 连~数城 capture several cities in succession ⑲ give in: 双方相持不~。Neither side would give in (或 yield). ⑳ finish (work, etc.); leave off: ~夜班 come off night duty ㉑ 〔用于否定式〕 be less than: 不~一万人 no less than ten thousand people ㉒ 〔量〕〔用于动作的次数〕: 敲了三~门 give three knocks on the door/ 摇了几~旗子 wave the flag several times

下 xia ① 〔用在动词后,表示由高处到低处〕: 坐~ sit down/ 躺~ lie down/ 跑~山 run down a hill ② 〔用在动词后,表示有空间,能容纳〕: 这房间能坐~五十人。The room can hold (或 seat) fifty people./ 这么多菜我吃不~。I can't eat all this food. ③ 〔用在动词后,表示动作的完成或结果〕: 打~扎实的基础 lay a solid foundation/ 准备~必需的材料 prepare necessary material

【下巴】 xiàba ① the lower jaw ② chin
【下摆】 xiàbǎi ① the lower hem of a gown, jacket or skirt ② width of such a hem
【下班】 xiàbān come or go off work; knock off
【下半场】 xiàbànchǎng second half (of a game)
【下半旗】 xià bànqí fly a flag at half-mast
【下半夜】 xiàbànyè the time after midnight; the latter half of the night
【下辈】 xiàbèi ① future generations; offspring ② the younger generation of a family
【下笔】 xiàbǐ put pen to paper; begin to write or paint: 不知如何~ be at a loss as to how to begin writing or painting/ ~千言,离题万里。A thousand words from the pen in a stream, but ten thousand *li* away from the theme. — write quickly but stray from the theme

【下不为例】 xià bù wéi lì not to be taken as a precedent; not to be repeated: 就这一回,~。Just this once.
【下策】 xiàcè a bad plan; an unwise decision; the worst thing to do; a stupid move
【下层】 xiàcéng ① lower levels: 深入~ go to lower-level units; go down to the grass-roots level ② lower strata
【下场】 xiàchǎng ① 〈剧〉 go off stage; exit ② 〈体〉 leave the playing field
【下场】 xiàchang end; fate: 遭到可耻~ come to a disgraceful end; meet with an ignominious fate/ 搞阴谋诡计的人绝不会有好~。Those who plot and conspire will certainly come to no good end.
【下沉】 xiàchén sink; subside; submerge: 敌舰起火~。The enemy warship caught fire and sank./ 潜水艇逐渐~。The submarine gradually submerged./ 地基~。The foundations have subsided.
【下船】 xiàchuán go ashore; disembark
【下垂】 xiàchuí hang down; droop
【下达】 xiàdá make known (或 transmit) to lower levels: ~作战命令 issue orders of operation/任务已经~。The task has been assigned.
【下等】 xiàděng low-grade; inferior
【下碇】 xiàdìng cast anchor: 船在九江~。The ship anchored at Jiujiang.
【下毒手】 xià dúshǒu strike a vicious blow; lay murderous hands on sb.: 背后~ stab sb. in the back
【下颚】 xià'è the lower jaw; mandible
【下凡】 xiàfán (of gods or immortals) descend to the world
【下饭】 xiàfàn ① go with rice: 你这两个菜都不喜欢,拿什么~呀? If you don't like either of the two dishes, what are you going to have with your rice? ② go well with rice: 这个菜下酒不~。This dish goes well with wine, but not with rice.
【下风】 xiàfēng disadvantageous position: 占~ be at a disadvantage
【下工】 xiàgōng come or go off work; stop work; knock off
【下工夫】 xià gōngfu put in time and energy; concentrate one's efforts: 在技术革新上狠~ devote a lot of time and energy to technical innovation/ 你要学好一门外语就要舍得~。If you want to master a foreign language, you must put in a lot of effort.
【下跪】 xiàguì kneel down; go down on one's knees
【下海】 xiàhǎi go to sea; put out to sea: ~捕鱼 go fishing on the sea
【下怀】 xiàhuái one's heart's desire: 正中~ be exactly what one wants
【下级】 xiàjí ① lower level: ~服从上级。The lower level is subordinate to the higher level. ② subordinate: 帮助~解决工作中的问题 help one's subordinates to solve the problems they encounter in their work
【下贱】 xiàjiàn low; mean; degrading
【下降】 xiàjiàng descend; go or come down; drop; fall; decline: 飞机开始~。The plane began to descend./ 气温显著~。There was a marked drop in the temperature./ 药品价格平均~百分之三十七。The prices of medicines dropped 37% on an average./ 生产成本逐年~。Production costs come down every year./ 出生率~ a decline in the birth rate
【下脚】 xiàjiǎo get a foothold; plant one's foot: 没有~的地方 be unable to gain a footing (或 foothold); have nowhere to plant one's foot
【下界】 xiàjiè the world of mortals; the world of man
【下酒】 xiàjiǔ ① go with wine: 买点花生米~ buy some peanuts to go with the wine ② go well with wine: 这菜不~。This dish doesn't go very well with wine. ◇ ~菜 a dish that goes with wine
【下课】 xiàkè get out of class; finish class: ~后再去。Go there after class./ 现在~。The class is dismissed. 或 The class is over.
【下来】 xiàlái come down: 梯子不牢,快~! Come down at once! The ladder isn't steady.
【下来】 xiàlai ① 〔用在动词后,表示由高处向低处或由远处向近处来〕: 把树上的苹果都摘~。Pick all the apples off the

tree./ 溪水从山上流～。The stream flows down from the mountain. ②〔用在动词后，表示从过去继续到现在或过去从开始继续到最后〕: 古代流传～的寓言 fables handed down from ancient times/ 所有上夜校的人都坚持～了。All those who joined the evening classes went on with them to the end. ③〔用在动词后，表示动作的完成或结果〕: 风突然停了～。The wind dropped all of a sudden./ 剩的就这么些了。This is all that's left. ④〔用在形容词后面，表示程度继续增加〕: 他的声音慢慢低了～。His voice trailed off./ 天色渐渐黑～。It was getting darker and darker.

【下联】 xiàlián the second line of a couplet

【下列】 xiàliè listed below; following: 应注意～几点。Attention should be paid to the following points.

【下令】 xiàlìng give orders; order: 团长～紧急集合。The regiment commander ordered (或 gave orders for) an emergency muster.

【下流】 xiàliú ① lower reaches (of a river): 黄河～ the lower reaches of the Huanghe River ② low-down; mean; obscene; dirty: ～的谩骂 scurrilous attacks; coarse invectives/ ～的勾当 base acts/ ～的玩笑 dirty (或 obscene) jests; coarse jokes ◇ ～话 obscene (或 dirty, foul) language; obscenities

【下落】 xiàluò ① whereabouts: 打听某人的～ inquire about sb.'s whereabouts/ 有一件古物现在～不明。The whereabouts of one of the antiques is unknown. ② drop; fall: 气球～的地点 the place where the balloon has fallen

【下马威】 xiàmǎwēi severity shown by an official on assuming office: 给他个～ deal him a head-on blow at the first encounter

【下面】 xiàmian ① below; under; underneath: 大桥～ under the bridge/ 图表～的说明 the caption below the chart/ 褥子～铺着一领席。There is a mat underneath the mattress. ② next; following: ～该谁了？Who's next?/ 必须记住～几点。These points should be borne in mind./ 请老李谈谈。Now we'll ask Lao Li to say something. ③ lower level; subordinate: 细心倾听～的意见 listen carefully to the views of one's subordinates/ 了解～的情况 find out about how things are at the lower levels

【下品】 xiàpǐn low-grade; inferior

【下坡路】 xiàpōlù downhill path; downhill journey; decline: 走～ go downhill; be on the decline

【下棋】 xiàqí play chess; have a game of chess

【下情】 xiàqíng conditions at the lower levels; feelings or wishes of the masses: ～上达 make the situation at the lower levels known to the higher levels/ 不了解～ not know what is going on at the lower levels

【下去】 xiàqu ① go down; descend: ～看看是谁在楼下敲门。Go downstairs and see who's knocking at the door./ 到站了，快～。Here we are. let's get off at once. ② go on; continue: 你这样～要累垮的。If you go on like this you'll crack up.

【下去】 xiàqu ①〔用在动词后，表示由高处到低处或由近处向远处去〕: 洪水退～了。The flood has receded./ 把犯人带～ take the prisoner away/ 把敌人的火力压～ silence the enemy's fire ②〔用在动词后，表示从现在继续到将来〕: 坚持～ stick it out/ 她激动得说不～。She was so overcome with emotion that she couldn't go on./ 希望两国人民世世代代友好～。We hope the people of the two countries will remain friendly from generation to generation. ③〔用在形容词后，表示程度继续增加〕: 看来天气还会冷～。It seems it will get even colder.

【下身】 xiàshēn ① the lower part of the body ② private parts

【下乘】 xiàshèng literary or artistic work of low order; inferior work

【下手】 xiàshǒu ① put one's hand to; start; set about: set to: 不知从何～ not know where to start; not know how to set about a job ② right-hand seat: 坐在主宾的～ sit on the right hand of the chief guest

【下属】 xiàshǔ subordinate

【下水】 xiàshuǐ ① enter the water; be launched: 又一艘新船～了。Another new ship was launched. ② take to evildoing; fall into evil ways: 拖人～ involve sb. in evildoing;

entice (或 inveigle) sb. into evildoing ③ downriver; downstream: ～船 downriver boat ◇ ～典礼 launching ceremony

【下榻】 xiàtà 〈书〉 stay (at a place during a trip): ～于新侨饭店 stay at the Xinqiao Hotel

【下台】 xiàtái ① step down from the stage or platform ② fall out of power; leave office: 被赶～ be driven out of office; be thrown out ③〔多用于否定式〕get out of a predicament or an embarrassing situation: 没法～ be unable to back down with good grace/ 叫他下不了台 put him on the spot

【下体】 xiàtǐ 〈书〉 ① the lower part of the body ② private parts

【下同】 xiàtóng 〔多用于附注〕 similarly hereinafter; the same below

【下文】 xiàwén ① what follows in the passage, paragraph, article, etc.: ～再作阐述 be explained in the ensuing chapters or paragraphs ② later development; outcome; sequel: 申请书交上去两个星期了，还没有～。The application was handed in a couple of weeks ago, but so far there's been no reply./ 事情并没有就此结束，还有～哩。The matter didn't end there; there was a sequel to it.

【下午】 xiàwǔ afternoon

【下弦】 xiàxián 〈天〉 last (或 third) quarter ◇ ～月 the moon at the last (或 third) quarter

【下旬】 xiàxún the last ten-day period of a month

【下药】 xiàyào ① prescribe medicine: 对症～ prescribe the right remedy for an illness ② put in poison

【下野】 xiàyě (of a ruler) retire from the political arena; be forced to relinquish power

【下议院】 xiàyìyuàn ① lower house; lower chamber ② the House of Commons

【下意识】 xiàyìshí subconsciousness

【下游】 xiàyóu ① lower reaches (of a river) ② backward position: 甘居～ be resigned to being backward

【下狱】 xiàyù throw into prison; imprison

【下葬】 xiàzàng bury; inter

【下肢】 xiàzhī 〈生理〉 lower limbs; legs

吓* xià frighten; scare; intimidate: ～坏了 be terribly frightened; be overcome with fear/ ～破了胆 be scared out of one's wits/ 把我～一跳 give me a start (或 scare)/ 这种困难～不倒我们。Difficulties like this don't scare us. 另见 hè

【吓唬】 xiàhu 〈口〉 frighten; scare; intimidate

夏* xià ① summer ② (Xià) an ancient name for China: 华～ China ③ the Xia Dynasty (c. 21st—c. 16th century B.C.)

【夏季】 xiàjì summer

【夏历】 xiàlì the traditional Chinese calendar; the lunar calendar

【夏令】 xiàlìng ① summer; summertime ② summer weather: 春行～ summer weather in spring; exceptionally warm days in spring

【夏天】 xiàtiān summer

【夏衣】 xiàyī summer clothing; summer wear

厦 xià 另见 shà

【厦门】 Xiàmén Xiamen (Amoy)

罅 xià 〈书〉 crack; rift; chink: 云～ a rift in the clouds/ 石～ a crack in a rock

【罅漏】 xiàlòu 〈书〉 omission; shortcoming; deficiency: ～之处，有待订补。Shortcomings will be remedied in future editions.

【罅隙】 xiàxì 〈书〉 crack; rift; chink

xiān

仙* xiān celestial being; immortal

【仙丹】 xiāndān elixir of life

【仙姑】 xiāngū ① female immortal (或 celestial) ② sorceress
【仙鹤】 xiānhè red-crowned crane
【仙境】 xiānjìng fairyland; wonderland; paradise
【仙女】 xiānnǚ female celestial; fairy maiden
【仙人】 xiānrén celestial being; immortal
【仙人掌】 xiānrénzhǎng ‹植› cactus
【仙逝】 xiānshì ‹婉› pass away
【仙子】 xiānzǐ 见"仙女"

先* xiān ① earlier; before; first; in advance: ～人后己 put others before oneself; put other people's interest ahead of one's own/ 他比我～到。He arrived earlier than I did./ 我一说几句。Let me say a few words first./ 你一拟个提纲再写。Make an outline before you start writing./ 没有什么～于经验的知识。There is no knowledge prior to experience./你不必～付款。You don't have to pay in advance. ② elder generation; ancestor: 祖～ ancestor; forefather ③ deceased; late: ～父 my late father ④ ‹口› earlier on; before: 你 ～怎么不告诉我? Why didn't you tell me before?
【先辈】 xiānbèi elder generation; ancestors
【先导】 xiāndǎo guide; forerunner; precursor: 错误常常是正确的～。Error is often the precursor of what is correct.
【先睹为快】 xiān dǔ wéi kuài consider it a pleasure to be among the first to read (a poem, article, etc.)
【先发制人】 xiān fā zhì rén gain the initiative by striking first; forestall the enemy: 采取～的手段 take preemptive measures
【先锋】 xiānfēng vanguard; van: 打～ fight in the van; be a pioneer
【先后】 xiān-hòu ① early or late; priority; order: 这些事都该办,可也得有个～。All these matters should be tackled, but they should be taken up in order of priority. ② successively; one after another: 代表团～在北京、上海等地参观访问。The delegation first went to Beijing and afterwards to Shanghai and other places.
【先见之明】 xiān jiàn zhī míng prophetic vision; foresight
【先进】 xiānjìn advanced
【先决】 xiānjué prerequisite: ～条件 prerequisite; precondition
【先来后到】 xiānlái-hòudào in the order of arrival; first come, first served
【先礼后兵】 xiān lǐ hòu bīng take strong measures only after courteous ones fail; try peaceful means before resorting to force
【先例】 xiānlì precedent: 开～ set (或 create) a precedent/ 有～可援 have a precedent to go by
【先烈】 xiānliè martyr
【先期】 xiānqī earlier on; in advance: 代表团的部分团员已～到达。Some members of the delegation had arrived at an earlier date.
【先前】 xiānqián before; previously: 这孩子比～高多了。The child is much taller than before.
【先遣】 xiānqiǎn sent in advance ◇ ～部队 advance troops (或 force)/ ～队 advance party
【先驱】 xiānqū pioneer; forerunner; harbinger
【先人】 xiānrén ① ancestor; forefather ② my late father
【先入为主】 xiān rù wéi zhǔ first impressions are strongest; preconceived ideas keep a strong hold; be prejudiced
【先入之见】 xiān rù zhī jiàn preconception; preconceived idea; prejudice
【先声】 xiānshēng first signs; herald; harbinger
【先声夺人】 xiānshēng duó rén forestall one's opponent by a show of strength; overawe others by displaying one's strength
【先生】 xiānsheng ① teacher ② mister (Mr.); gentleman; sir: 总统～ Mr. President/ 女士们,～们 ladies and gentlemen ③ ‹方› doctor
【先世】 xiānshì forefathers; ancestors
【先天】 xiāntiān ① congenital; inborn: ～畸形 congenital malformation/ ～性心脏病 congenital heart disease/ ～不足 be congenitally deficient; suffer from an inherent shortage

【先头】 xiāntóu ① ahead; in front; in advance: ～部队 an advance party of soldiers; vanguard/ 走在最～ walk ahead of all other people ② before; formerly; in the past: 你～没说过这事。You didn't mention this before./ 她～已来过两次。She's been here twice already.
【先下手为强】 xiān xiàshǒu wéi qiáng he who strikes first gains the advantage; to take the initiative is to gain the upper hand: ～,后下手遭殃。‹谚› He who strikes first prevails, he who strikes late fails.
【先行】 xiānxíng ① go ahead of the rest; start off before the others: 兵马未动,粮草～ Food and fodder should go ahead of troops and horses. ② beforehand; in advance: ～通知 notify in advance/ 新产品将在本市～试销。The new products will first be put on trial sale in this city.
【先斩后奏】 xiān zhǎn hòu zòu execute the criminal first and report to the emperor afterwards — act first and report afterwards
【先兆】 xiānzhào omen; portent; sign; indication: 地震的～ indications of an impending earthquake/ 不祥的～ ill omen ◇ ～流产 threatened abortion
【先哲】 xiānzhé a great thinker of the past; sage
【先知】 xiānzhī a person of foresight ② ‹宗› prophet
【先知先觉】 xiānzhī-xiānjué ① a person of foresight ② having foresight

纤 xiān fine; minute: ～尘 fine dust
【纤巧】 xiānqiǎo dainty; delicate
【纤弱】 xiānruò slim and fragile; delicate
【纤维】 xiānwéi fibre; staple: 天然(合成、人造)～ natural (synthetic, man-made) fibre/ ～长度 fibre length; staple
【纤细】 xiānxì very thin; slender; fine; tenuous: ～的头发 fine hair/ ～的游丝 tenuous gossamer
【纤小】 xiānxiǎo fine; tenuous

掀 xiān lift (a cover, etc.): ～门帘 lift the door curtain/ ～掉盖子 take the lid off/ 把对手～翻在地 throw the opponent off his balance/ 在两国关系史上～开了新的一页 open a new chapter in the annals of relations between the two countries
【掀动】 xiāndòng lift; start; set in motion: 春风～了她的衣襟。The spring breeze lifted the edge of her blouse.
【掀起】 xiānqǐ ① lift; raise ② surge; cause to surge: 大海～了巨浪。Big waves surged on the sea. ③ set off (a movement, etc.); start

鲜* xiān ① fresh: ～奶 fresh milk/ ～蘑 fresh mushrooms ② bright-coloured; bright: 这块布颜色太～。This cloth is too bright. ③ delicious; tasty ④ delicacy: 时～ delicacies of the season ⑤ aquatic foods: 海～ seafood 另见 jiǎn
【鲜红】 xiānhóng bright red; scarlet
【鲜花】 xiānhuā fresh flowers; flowers
【鲜美】 xiānměi delicious; tasty
【鲜明】 xiānmíng ① (of colour) bright: 色彩～ in bright colours; bright-coloured ② clear-cut; distinct; distinctive: ～的对照 a striking (或 sharp) contrast/ ～的节奏 strongly accented rhythms/ 主题～ have a distinct theme/ 富有～的地方特色 be characterized by a distinctive local style or flavour
【鲜嫩】 xiānnèn fresh and tender
【鲜血】 xiānxuè blood
【鲜艳】 xiānyàn bright-coloured; gaily-coloured: 颜色～ in gay colours/ ～夺目 dazzlingly beautiful; resplendent/ 穿着～的民族服装 wearing bright national costume

xián

闲* xián ① not busy; idle; unoccupied: ～不住 refuse to stay idle; always keep oneself busy/ 不吃～饭 won't be an idler ② not in use; unoccupied; lying idle: ～房 unoccupied (或 vacant) room or house/ 别让机器～着! Don't let the machine stand idle./ 没有一辆车～着。There's not a single free vehicle. 或 All the vehicles are in use. ③ spare (或 free) time; leisure: 今天她不得~。 She has no time to spare today.

【闲扯】 xiánchě chat; engage in chitchat

【闲荡】 xiándàng saunter; stroll; loaf

【闲工夫】 xiángōngfu spare time; leisure

【闲逛】 xiánguàng saunter; stroll

【闲话】 xiánhuà ① digression: ~少说,书归正传。 Enough of this digression; let's return to our story. 或 However, to continue the story. ② complaint; gossip: 别让人说我们的~。 We mustn't give anyone cause for complaint./ 她可不爱说人~。 She's not fond of gossip. ③ 〈书〉 talk casually about; chat about: ~当年 chat about bygone days

【闲居】 xiánjū stay at home idle

【闲空】 xiánkòng free time; spare time; leisure

【闲聊】 xiánliáo chat

【闲气】 xiánqì anger about trifles: 我可没功夫生这份儿~。 I'm too busy to lose my temper over such a little thing. 或 I've no time to get angry about such a trivial matter.

【闲情逸致】 xiánqíng-yìzhì leisurely and carefree mood; leisure and mood for enjoyments

【闲人】 xiánrén ① an unoccupied person; idler: 现在正是农忙季节,村里一个~也没有。 It's the busy season and nobody in the village is idle. ② persons not concerned: ~免进。 No admittance except on business. 或 Admittance to staff only.

【闲事】 xiánshì ① a matter that does not concern one; other people's business: 爱管~ like to poke one's nose into other people's business/ 别管~! Mind your own business. 或 None of your business. ② unimportant matter

【闲适】 xiánshì leisurely and comfortable

【闲书】 xiánshū light reading

【闲谈】 xiántán chat; engage in chitchat

【闲暇】 xiánxiá leisure

【闲杂】 xiánzá without fixed duties: ~人员 people without fixed duties; miscellaneous personnel

贤* xián ① virtuous; worthy; able: 任人唯~ appoint people on their merits ② a worthy person; an able and virtuous person: 让~ relinquish one's post in favour of sb. better qualified ③ 〈敬〉〔旧时用于平辈或晚辈〕: ~弟 my worthy brother; your good self

【贤达】 xiándá prominent personage; worthy

【贤惠】 xiánhuì (of a woman) virtuous

【贤良】 xiánliáng (of a man) able and virtuous

【贤明】 xiánmíng wise and able; sagacious

【贤人】 xiánrén a person of virtue; worthy

弦 xián ① bowstring; string ② the string of a musical instrument ③ 〈方〉 spring (of a watch, etc.) ④ 〈数〉 chord

【弦外之音】 xián wài zhī yīn overtones; implication

【弦乐队】 xiányuèduì string orchestra (或 band)

【弦乐器】 xiányuèqì stringed instrument

涎 xián saliva

【涎皮赖脸】 xiánpí-làiliǎn brazenfaced; shameless and loathsome; cheeky

【涎水】 xiánshuǐ 〈方〉 saliva

咸 xián ① salted; salty: ~鱼 salt fish/ ~蛋 salted egg/ 菜太~了。 The dish is too salty. ② 〈书〉 all: ~受其益。 All benefited from it.

【咸菜】 xiáncài salted vegetables; pickles

【咸肉】 xiánròu salt meat; bacon

【咸水】 xiánshuǐ salt water ◇ ~湖 saltwater lake/ ~鱼 saltwater fish

娴 xián 〈书〉 ① refined ② adept; skilled: ~于辞令 be gifted with a silver tongue

【娴静】 xiánjìng gentle and refined

【娴熟】 xiánshú adept; skilled: 弓马~ adept in archery and horsemanship/ ~的技巧 consummate skill/ 她在平衡木上动作~。 She showed great skill in her exercises on the balance beam.

【娴雅】 xiányǎ (of a woman) refined; elegant

舷 xián the side of a ship; board: 左~ port/ 右~ starboard

【舷窗】 xiánchuāng porthole

【舷梯】 xiántī ① gangway ladder; accommodation ladder ② ramp

衔* xián ① hold in the mouth: ~着烟斗 have a pipe between one's teeth/ 燕子~泥筑窠。 Swallows carry bits of earth in their bills to build nests. ② harbour; bear: ~恨 harbour resentment; bear a grudge ③ rank; title: 大使~常驻代表 permanent representative with the rank of ambassador

【衔接】 xiánjiē link up; join: 大桥把两条公路~起来。 The bridge links up the two highways./ 使计划互相~ make the plans dovetail

嫌 xián ① suspicion: 避~ avoid suspicion/ 特~ a suspected enemy agent ② ill will; resentment; enmity; grudge: 前~尽释。 All previous ill will has been removed. 或 We have agreed to bury the hatchet. ③ dislike; mind; complain of: ~麻烦 not want to take the trouble; think it troublesome/ 大家都~他脾气太急。 Everybody disliked him because of his hot temper./ 你不~我们在这里抽烟吧? You don't mind us smoking here, do you? 这文章内容不错,只是文字略~罗唆。 The article is good in content, only it's a bit wordy.

【嫌弃】 xiánqì dislike and avoid; cold-shoulder

【嫌恶】 xiánwù detest; loathe

【嫌隙】 xiánxì feeling of animosity; enmity; ill will; grudge

【嫌疑】 xiányí suspicion: 有间谍~ be suspected of being a spy ◇ ~犯 suspect/ ~分子 suspected person; marked man

【嫌怨】 xiányuàn grudge; resentment; enmity

xiǎn

冼 Xiǎn a surname

险* xiǎn ① a place difficult of access; narrow pass; defile: 天~ natural barrier/ 无~可守 have no tenable defence position; be strategically indefensible ② danger; peril; risk: 遇~ meet with danger/ 脱~ be out of danger/ 冒~ run a risk ③ sinister; vicious; venomous: 阴~ sinister ④ by a hair's breadth; by inches; nearly: ~遭不来 come within an ace of death/ 好~哪! That was a near thing!

【险隘】 xiǎn'ài strategic pass; defile

【险恶】 xiǎn'è ① dangerous; perilous; ominous: 处境~ be in a perilous position/ 病情~ be dangerously ill ② sinister; vicious; malicious; treacherous: ~的用心 sinister (或 vicious) intentions; evil motives

【险峰】 xiǎnfēng perilous peak

【险境】 xiǎnjìng dangerous situation: 脱离~ be out of danger

【险峻】 xiǎnjùn dangerously steep; precipitous

【险区】 xiǎnqū danger zone

【险胜】 xiǎnshèng win by a narrow margin: 以二十一比十九~ win the game by the close score of 21-19

【险滩】 xiǎntān dangerous shoal; rapids

【险些】 xiǎnxiē narrowly (escape from sth. untoward); nearly: ~掉到水里 nearly fall into the water

【险要】 xiǎnyào strategically located and difficult of access

【险诈】 xiǎnzhà sinister and crafty

【险阻】 xiǎnzǔ (of roads) dangerous and difficult: 崎岖的山路 a dangerous and difficult mountain path/ 不畏艰难~ not be afraid of dangers and difficulties

显 xiǎn ① apparent; obvious; noticeable: 药的效果还不~。 The effect of the medicine is not yet noticeable.

② show; display; manifest: 深色衣服不～脏。Dark clothes do not show the dirt. ③ illustrious and influential

【显达】 xiǎndá illustrious and influential

【显得】 xiǎnde look; seem; appear: 他～有点紧张。He seems a bit nervous./ 屋子这么一布置，～宽敞多了。Arranged the way it is, the room looks much more spacious.

【显而易见】 xiǎn ér yì jiàn obviously; evidently; clearly

【显赫】 xiǎnhè illustrious; celebrated: ～的战功 illustrious war exploits/ 声势～ have a powerful influence/ ～的名声 great renown

【显见】 xiǎnjiàn obvious; self-evident; apparent: ～的理由 an obvious (或 apparent) reason

【显灵】 xiǎnlíng (of a ghost or spirit) make its presence or power felt

【显露】 xiǎnlù become visible; appear; manifest itself: 他脸上～出亲切的笑容。A genial smile appeared on his face./ 这次运动的深刻影响正在各个方面～出来。The profound influence of the movement is manifesting itself in every field.

【显明】 xiǎnmíng obvious; manifest; distinct; marked: ～的道理 an obvious truth/ ～的对照 a sharp contrast/ ～的特点 a distinct (或 marked) characteristic

【显然】 xiǎnrán obvious; evident; clear: 这～是另一码事。That's obviously quite another matter.

【显身手】 xiǎn shēnshǒu display one's talent or skill

【显圣】 xiǎnshèng (of the ghost of a saintly person) make its presence or power felt

【显示】 xiǎnshì show; display; demonstrate; manifest: ～力量 make a show of force; display one's strength

【显微镜】 xiǎnwēijìng microscope

【显现】 xiǎnxiàn manifest (或 reveal) oneself; appear; show: 雾气逐渐消失，重叠的山峦一层一层地～出来。As the mist lifted, the mountains revealed themselves one behind the other.

【显眼】 xiǎnyǎn conspicuous; showy: 穿得太～ be loudly (或 showily) dressed

【显要】 xiǎnyào ① powerful and influential: ～人物 an influential figure ② influential figure; important personage; VIP

【显影】 xiǎnyǐng 〈摄〉 develop ◇～机 developing machine/ ～剂 developer

【显著】 xiǎnzhù notable; marked; striking; remarkable; outstanding: 收效～ yield notable results/ 有～的进步 make marked progress/ 取得～的成就 achieve remarkable success/ ～的特征 outstanding characteristics/ 各报均以～地位刊载了这条消息。This news was prominently featured in all the papers.

鲜 xiǎn little; rare: ～见 rarely seen; seldom met with 另见 xiān

藓 xiǎn 〈植〉 moss

xiàn

见 xiàn appear; become visible 参见 "图穷匕首见" tú qióng bǐshǒu xiàn 另见 jiàn

县 xiàn county

【县长】 xiànzhǎng the head of a county; county magistrate

现* xiàn ① present; current; existing: ～阶段 the present stage/ ～况 the existing (或 present) situation ②(do sth.) in time of need; extempore: ～打白烧饼 sesame cakes just out of the oven/ 这点技术也是工作中～学的。What skill I have has been picked up on the job./ 他在晚会上～编了一首诗。He improvised a poem at the evening party. ③(of money) on hand: ～钱 ready money; cash ④ cash; ready money: 付～ pay cash ⑤ show; appear: 她脸上～出一丝笑容。A faint smile appeared on (或 crept over) her face.

【现场】 xiànchǎng ① scene (of an incident): 作案～ the scene of a crime/ 保护～ keep the scene (of a crime or accident) intact ② site; spot: 工作～ worksite/ 试验～ testing ground

【现成】 xiànchéng ready-made: 买～衣服 buy ready-made clothes; buy clothes off the peg/ 吃～的 eat whatever is ready or prepared by others

【现存】 xiàncún extant; in stock: ～的手稿 extant manuscripts/ ～物资 goods and materials in stock

【现代】 xiàndài ① modern times; the contemporary age ② modern; contemporary: ～交通工具 modern means of communication/ ～作家 modern (或 contemporary) writer/ ～题材 contemporary theme ◇～派 modernist school/ ～史 contemporary history

【现代化】 xiàndàihuà modernize: ～企业 modernized enterprise/ ～设备 sophisticated equipment

【现货】 xiànhuò 〈商〉 merchandise on hand; spots

【现今】 xiànjīn nowadays; these days

【现金】 xiànjīn ① ready money; cash ② cash reserve in a bank ◇～付款 cash payment; payment in cash/ ～交易 cash transaction/ ～帐 cash account; cash book/ ～支出 out-of-pocket expenses

【现款】 xiànkuǎn ready money; cash

【现钱】 xiànqián 〈口〉 ready money; cash

【现任】 xiànrèn ① at present hold the office of ② currently in office; incumbent

【现身说法】 xiàn shēn shuō fǎ advise sb. or explain sth. by using one's own experience as an example

【现时】 xiànshí now; at present

【现实】 xiànshí ① reality; actuality: 脱离～ be divorced from reality; be unrealistic/ 面对～ face the facts/ 理想变成了～。A dream has come true. ② real; actual: ～生活 real (或 actual) life/ ～意义 practical or immediate significance/ 采取～的态度 adopt a realistic attitude

【现实主义】 xiànshízhǔyì realism

【现世】 xiànshì ① this life ② lose face; be disgraced; bring shame on oneself

【现下】 xiànxià 〈口〉 now; at present

【现象】 xiànxiàng appearance (of things); phenomenon: 社会～ social phenomenon

【现行】 xiànxíng ① currently in effect; in force; in operation: ～法令 decrees in effect/ ～规章制度 rules and regulations in force/ ～政策 present policies ②(of a criminal) active

【现形】 xiànxíng reveal one's true features; betray oneself

【现役】 xiànyì ① active service; active duty: 服～ be on active service ② on active service; on active duty; active

【现有】 xiànyǒu now available; existing: ～材料 materials now available (或 on hand); available information

【现在】 xiànzài now; at present; today

【现状】 xiànzhuàng present (或 current) situation; *status quo*; existing state of affairs: 研究这个国家的历史和～ study the history and present condition of this country/ 改变(维持)～ change (maintain) the *status quo*/ 安于～ be content with things as they are

限* xiàn ① limit; bounds: 期～ time limit/ 以年底为～ set the end of the year as the deadline ② set a limit; limit; restrict: ～一个月完成 allow one month to finish sth./ 每人～购四张票。Each customer is limited to four tickets./ 人数不～。There is no restriction (或 limit) on the number of people./ 不要～得太死，要有点灵活性。Don't make rigid restrictions, allow a certain latitude.

【限定】 xiàndìng prescribe (或 set) a limit to; limit; restrict: ～时间完成 prescribe a time limit for fulfilment/ 参加这次讨论会的人数～为一百四十人。Participation in the discussion will be limited to 140.

【限度】 xiàndù limit; limitation: 超过～ go beyond (或 exceed) the limit/ 最大～地发挥人的主观能动性 bring people's subjective initiative into full play/ 把非生产性的开支减少到最低～ reduce nonproductive expenditures to a minimum/ 我们的忍耐是有～的。There is a limit to our patience.

【限额】 xiàn'é　norm; limit; quota

【限量】 xiànliàng　limit the quantity of; set bounds to: 前途不可～ have boundless prospects

【限令】 xiànlìng　order sb. to do sth. within a certain time: ～某人于四十八小时内离境 order sb. to leave the country within 48 hours; give sb. 48 hours' notice to leave the country

【限期】 xiànqī　① within a definite (或 set) time: ～报到 report for duty by the prescribed time/ ～撤退 withdraw within a stated time/ 这项工程～完成。This project must be completed within the specified time./ ② time limit; deadline: ～已满。The time limit has been reached./ 给他三天～ give him three days (to do sth.)

【限于】 xiànyú　be confined to; be limited to: ～篇幅，来电不能一一登载。As space is limited, it is impossible to publish all the messages we have received

【限制】 xiànzhì　place (或 impose) restrictions on; restrict; limit; confine: 年龄～ age limit/ 数量～ limit to a number or amount/ ～发言时间 restrict (或 limit) the time allowed for a speaker/ ～在必要的范围内 confine sth. within necessary limits/ 受健康状况的～ be handicapped by one's poor health.

【限制性】 xiànzhìxìng　restricted; restrictive: ～会议 restricted meeting

线*

xiàn　① thread; string; wire: 丝～ silk thread/ ～团 a ball of string; a reel of thread/ 铜～ copper wire ② made of cotton thread: ～衣 ～裤 cotton knitwear ③ 〈数〉line: 直～ straight line ④ sth. shaped like a line, thread, etc.: 光～ ray ⑤ route; line: 供应～ supply route (或 line)/ 航～ airline or shipping line/ 铁道～ railway line ⑥ demarcation line; boundary: 边界～ boundary line/ 军事分界～ military demarcation line/ 海岸～ coastline ⑦ (political) line ⑧ brink; verge: 在死亡～上 on the verge of death/ 在饥饿～上 on the brink of starvation ⑨ clue; thread: 案子的～儿断了。The clue could not be followed up. ⑩ 〈量〉[用于抽象事物，数词限用"一"]: 一～希望 a ray (或 gleam) of hope/ 一～光明 a gleam of light/ 一～生机 a slim chance of life

【线路】 xiànlù　① 〈电〉circuit; line: 电话～ telephone line

【线索】 xiànsuǒ　clue; thread: 破案的～ clues for solving a case/ 故事的～ threads of a story/ 为深入研究提供～ provide leads for further study

【线条】 xiàntiáo　① 〈美术〉line: 粗犷、雄浑的～ bold and vigorous lines ② lines: 这个陶俑～非常优美。The lines of this pottery figurine are very graceful.

【线头】 xiàntóu　① the end of a thread ② an odd piece of thread

【线装】 xiànzhuāng　traditional thread binding (of Chinese books) ◇ ～本 thread-bound edition/ ～书 thread-bound Chinese book

宪

xiàn　① statute ② constitution: 制～ draw up a constitution

【宪兵】 xiànbīng　military police; military policeman; gendarme ◇ ～队 gendarmerie; military police corps

【宪法】 xiànfǎ　constitution; charter: ～草案 draft constitution

【宪章】 xiànzhāng　charter: 联合国～ the United Nations Charter

【宪政】 xiànzhèng　constitutional government; constitutionalism

陷

xiàn　① pitfall; trap ② get stuck or bogged down: ～进泥里 get stuck in the mud/ ～在日常事务堆里 get bogged down in everyday routine/ ～于孤立 find oneself isolated ③ sink; cave in: 深～的两颊 sunken cheeks/地基下～。The foundations have sunk (或 caved in). ④ frame (up): ～人 frame sb. (up); incriminate sb. ⑤ (of a town, etc.) be captured; fail: 城～之日 the day the city fell ⑥ defect; deficiency: 缺～ defect; flaw

【陷害】 xiànhài　frame (up); make a false charge against:

～好人 frame up an innocent person/ 政治～ political frame-up

【陷阱】 xiànjǐng　pitfall; pit; trap: 布设～ lay a trap

【陷坑】 xiànkēng　pitfall; pit

【陷落】 xiànluò　① subside; sink in; cave in: 许多盆地都是因地壳～而形成的。Many basins were formed by the subsidence of the earth's crust. ② (of territory) fall into enemy hands

【陷入】 xiànrù　① sink (或 fall) into; land oneself in; be caught in; get bogged down in: ～被动地位 fall into a passive position/ ～重围 find oneself tightly encircled/ ～困境 land in a predicament; be put in a tight spot; be cornered/ ～无休止的争论 be bogged down in endless debates/ 谈判～僵局 The negotiations came to a deadlock. ② be lost in; be immersed in; be deep in: ～沉思 be lost in thought; be deep in meditation

馅

xiàn　filling; stuffing: 肉～儿 meat filling/ 饺子～儿 stuffing for dumplings

羡*

xiàn　admire; envy: 人人称～ be the admiration of everyone

【羡慕】 xiànmù　admire; envy: 她很～我有这样一个好老师。She envies me my good teacher.

献*

xiàn　① offer; present; dedicate; donate: 敬～花圈 lay a wreath ② show; put on; display　～殷勤 show sb. excessive attentions; pay one's addresses

【献宝】 xiànbǎo　① present a treasure ② offer a valuable piece of advice or one's valuable experience ③ show off what one treasures

【献策】 xiàncè　offer advice; make suggestions

【献丑】 xiànchǒu　〈谦〉[用于表演或写作时] show oneself up; show one's incompetence (或 inadequacy): 一定要我唱，就只好～了。Since you insist, I'll make a fool of myself and sing.

【献词】 xiàncí　congratulatory message: 新年～ New Year message

【献计】 xiànjì　offer advice; make suggestions: 在技术革新中人人～献策。Everyone suggested ways and means for technical innovation.

【献技】 xiànjì　show one's skill

【献礼】 xiànlǐ　present a gift

【献媚】 xiànmèi　try to ingratiate oneself with; make up to

【献旗】 xiànqí　present a banner

【献身】 xiànshēn　devote (或 dedicate) oneself to; give one's life for

腺

xiàn　gland: 汗(泪、唾液)～ sweat (lachrymal, salivary) gland

xiāng

乡*

xiāng　① country; countryside; village; rural area: 城～物资交流 flow of goods between town and country (或 urban and rural areas); exchange of goods between the city and the countryside ② native place; home village or town: 回～ return to one's native place/ 丝绸之～ the home of silk ③ township (a former rural administrative unit under the county)

【乡巴佬】 xiāngbalǎo　〈贬〉(country) bumpkin

【乡村】 xiāngcūn　village; countryside; rural area

【乡间】 xiāngjiān　village; country: ～小贩 village pedlar/ ～别墅 country villa

【乡里】 xiānglǐ　① home village or town ② fellow villager or townsman

【乡僻】 xiāngpì　far from town; out-of-the-way

【乡亲】 xiāngqīn　① a person from the same village or town; fellow villager or townsman ② local people; villagers; folks: 把粮食分给～们 distribute the grain among the villagers

【乡绅】 xiāngshēn　country gentleman; squire

【乡思】 xiāngsī　homesickness; nostalgia

【乡土】 xiāngtǔ ① native soil; home village ② of one's native land; local: ~风味 local flavour
【乡下】 xiāngxia 〈口〉 village; country; countryside: 他刚从~来。He's just come from the countryside. ◇ ~人 country folk; country cousin
【乡音】 xiāngyīn accent of one's native place; local accent
【乡镇】 xiāngzhèn ① villages and towns ② small towns

相*

xiāng ① each other; one another; mutually: 素不~识 not know each other/ ~距太远 too far apart ② 〔表示一方对另一方的动作〕: 实不~瞒 to tell you the truth/ 另眼~看 look upon sb. with special respect or concern; view sb. in a new, more favourable light ③ see for oneself (whether sb. or sth. is to one's liking): ~女婿 take a look at one's prospective son-in-law
另见 xiàng

【相安无事】 xiāng'ān wú shì live in peace with each other
【相帮】 xiāngbāng 〈方〉 help; aid
【相比】 xiāngbǐ compare: 二者不能~。There's no comparison between the two (of them).
【相差】 xiāngchà differ: 两者~无几。There's hardly any difference between the two.
【相称】 xiāngchèn match; suit: 这两种颜色配在一起很~。The two colours match very well./ 这头巾跟你的年龄不~。This kerchief doesn't suit a person of your age.
【相持】 xiāngchí be locked in a stalemate: 双方~不下。Neither side was ready to yield./ 战争处于~阶段。The war was at a stalemate.
【相处】 xiāngchǔ get along (with one another): 不好~ difficult to get along with/ ~得很好 get on well with each other/ 我们~时间不长，但已经结下了深厚的友谊。We've not been together long, but we've become close friends.
【相传】 xiāngchuán ① tradition has it that...; according to legend ② hand down or pass on from one to another: 世代~ hand down from generation to generation
【相当】 xiāngdāng ① match; balance; correspond to; be equal to; be commensurate with: 得失~。The gains balance the losses./ 他们俩年龄~。They are well-matched in age. 或 They're about the same age./ 水坝高达七十八米，~于二十层的大楼。The dam rises to a height of 78 metres, or the height of a 20-storey building. ② suitable; fit; appropriate: 他一时想不出~的字眼来。At the time he couldn't think of a suitable word for it./ 这个工作还没有找到~的人。We haven't found a fit person for the job yet. ③ quite; fairly; considerably: ~好 fairly good/ 演出~成功。The performance was quite a success.
【相得益彰】 xiāng dé yì zhāng each shining more brilliantly in the other's company; bring out the best in each other; complement each other
【相等】 xiāngděng be equal: 数量~ be equal in amount (或 quantity, number); be numerically equal/ 这两间房子的面积~。The two rooms have the same amount of floor space.
【相抵】 xiāngdǐ offset; balance; counterbalance: 收支~,尚余一百五十元。The accounts show a favourable balance of $150.
【相对】 xiāngduì ① opposite; face to face: ~而坐 sit opposite (或 facing) each other; sit face to face/ 两山遥遥~。The two hills stand opposite each other at a distance./ 美是与丑~的。Beauty is the opposite of ugliness. ② relative: 平衡是~的,不平衡是绝对的。Balance is relative, imbalance is absolute. ③ relatively; comparatively: ~稳定 relatively stable/ ~地说 comparatively speaking
【相对论】 xiāngduìlùn 〈物〉 the theory of relativity; relativity
【相反】 xiāngfǎn opposite; contrary: 朝~方向驶去 drive off in the opposite direction/ 结果与我们的愿望恰好~。The result turned out contrary to our expectations.
【相反相成】 xiāngfǎn-xiāngchéng (of two things) be both opposite and complementary to each other; oppose each other and yet also complement each other
【相仿】 xiāngfǎng similar; more or less the same: 内容~ be similar in content/ 年纪~ be about the same age

【相逢】 xiāngféng meet (by chance); come across
【相符】 xiāngfú conform to; tally (或 agree) with; correspond to (或 with): 报告与事实~。The report tallies with the facts.
【相辅而行】 xiāng fǔ ér xíng coordinate; go together
【相辅相成】 xiāngfǔ-xiāngchéng supplement each other; complement each other
【相干】 xiānggān 〔多用于否定句或疑问句〕 have to do with; be concerned with: 这件事与她有什么~? What has this to do with her?/ 这事与你不~。This has nothing to do with you.
【相隔】 xiānggé be separated by; be apart; be at a distance of: ~万里 be thousands of li apart; be a long way away from each other/ ~多年 after an interval of many years/ ~千山万水 be separated by numerous rivers and mountains/ 从我上次来到现在~不过三两个月,情况已经发生了很大的变化。It's only two or three months since my last visit here, but the situation has greatly changed.
【相关】 xiāngguān be interrelated: 体育事业和人民健康密切~。Physical culture has a direct bearing on the people's health.
【相好】 xiānghǎo ① be on intimate terms ② intimate friend ③ have an affair with ④ lover or mistress
【相互】 xiānghù mutual; reciprocal; each other: 增进~了解 promote mutual understanding/ ~影响 influence each other; interact/ ~关系 mutual relation; interrelation/ ~作用 interaction; interplay
【相继】 xiāngjì in succession; one after another: 代表们~发言。The delegates spoke in succession (或 one after another).
【相间】 xiāngjiàn alternate with: 黑白~ black alternating with white; in black and white check
【相交】 xiāngjiāo ① intersect: 直线 AB 与直线 CD ~于 E 点上。Line AB intersects line CD at E. ② make friends with: ~有年 have been friends for years
【相近】 xiāngjìn ① close; near: 地点~的两个学校 two neighbouring schools/ 比分~。The score was very close. ② be similar (或 close) to: 两人性格~。The two of them are similar in character.
【相距】 xiāngjù apart; at a distance of; away from: 两地~不到二里。The two places are less than two li apart./ 这两个桥墩之间~二十米。The distance between the two piers of the bridge is 20 metres.
【相连】 xiānglián be linked together; be joined: 两地有铁路~。The two places are linked by rail./ 两国山水~。The two countries are joined by common mountains and rivers.
【相劝】 xiāngquàn persuade; offer advice: 好意~ offer well-meaning advice
【相商】 xiāngshāng consult: 有要事~。I have something important to consult you about.
【相生相克】 xiāngshēng-xiāngkè mutual promotion and restraint between the five elements (a concept held by the ancients to explain natural phenomena and later used in traditional Chinese medicine, etc.)
【相识】 xiāngshí ① be acquainted with each other: 素不~ have never met; not be acquainted with each other ② acquaintance: 老~ an old acquaintance
【相思】 xiāngsī yearning between lovers; lovesickness: 单~ one-sided love; unrequited love ◇ ~病 lovesickness
【相似】 xiāngsì resemble; be similar; be alike: 面貌~ look alike
【相提并论】 xiāngtí-bìnglùn 〔多用于否定式〕 mention in the same breath; place on a par: 两者不能~。The two cannot be mentioned in the same breath.
【相通】 xiāngtōng communicate with each other; be interlinked: 这是两间~的屋子。These are two communicating rooms./ 这两个院子有门~。The two courtyards open onto each other./ 我们的心是~的。Our hearts beat in harmony.
【相同】 xiāngtóng identical; the same; alike: 我们在这个问题上观点~。We have identical (或 the same) views on this question./ 两者毫无~之处。The two have nothing in common.

【相投】 xiāngtóu be congenial; agree with each other: 兴趣 ～ have similar tastes and interests; find each other congenial

【相象】 xiāngxiàng resemble; be similar; be alike: 这两种花很～。 These two flowers are very much alike.

【相信】 xiāngxìn believe in; be convinced of; have faith in: ～真理 believe in truth/ ～自己的事业是正义的 be convinced of the justice of one's cause

【相形见绌】 xiāng xíng jiàn chù prove definitely inferior; pale by comparison; be outshone

【相沿成习】 xiāng yán chéng xí become a custom through long usage

【相依】 xiāngyī depend on each other; be interdependent: ～为命 depend on each other for survival/ 唇齿～ as close as lips and teeth; be closely related and mutually dependent

【相宜】 xiāngyí suitable; fitting; appropriate: 在那个场合你说这样的话是不～的。 What you said on that occasion was not appropriate./ 秋分前变最～。 The Autumnal Equinox is the best time for wheat-sowing.

【相应】 xiāngyìng corresponding; relevant: 随着工业的发展,对环境保护也采取了～的措施。 With the development of industry, appropriate measures have been taken to protect the environment./ 大会一致谴责这种侵略行为,并通过了～的决议。 The conference unanimously condemned this act of aggression and passed relevant resolutions.

【相映】 xiāngyìng set each other off; form a contrast: ～成趣 form a delightful contrast; contrast finely with each other

【相与】 xiāngyǔ ① get along with sb.; deal with sb.: 极难～ extremely difficult to get along with (或 a deal with) each other; together: ～大笑 have a good laugh together

【相约】 xiāngyuē agree (on meeting place, date, etc.); reach agreement; make an appointment

【相知】 xiāngzhī ① be well acquainted with each other; know each other well: ～有素 have known each other long ② bosom friend; great friend

【相左】 xiāngzuǒ 〈书〉① fail to meet each other ② conflict with each other; fail to agree; be at odds with

香* xiāng ① fragrant; sweet-smelling; aromatic; scented: 稻～千里 the fragrance of ripening rice spreading a thousand li/ 茉莉花～ the sweet scent of jasmines ② savoury; appetizing: 这饭菜～! This rice is really appetizing./ 炒什么菜啊!好～呀! Mmm! What's cooking? It smells delicious. ③ with relish; with good appetite: 吃得很～ eat with relish; enjoy the food/ 昨晚没睡好,吃饭不～。 I have no appetite because I didn't sleep well last night. ④ (sleep) soundly ⑤ popular; welcome perfume or spice: 麝～ musk; 檀～ sandalwood ⑦ incense; joss stick: 盘～ incense coil/ 蚊～ mosquito-repellent incense

【香案】 xiāng'àn a long altar on which incense burners are placed; incense burner table

【香槟酒】 xiāngbīnjiǔ champagne

【香肠】 xiāngcháng sausage

【香粉】 xiāngfěn face powder

【香馥馥】 xiāngfùfù strongly scented; richly fragrant

【香菇】 xiānggū Xianggu mushroom

【香花】 xiānghuā ① fragrant flower

【香火】 xiānghuǒ ① joss sticks and candles burning at a temple: ～甚盛 (of a temple) have many worshippers; attract a large number of pilgrims ② burning joss stick; burning incense: 用～点爆竹 light a firecracker with a burning joss stick

【香蕉】 xiāngjiāo banana

【香精】 xiāngjīng essence: 食用～ flavouring essence/ 合成～ compound essence ◇ ～油 essential oil

【香客】 xiāngkè pilgrim

【香料】 xiāngliào ① perfume ② spice ◇ ～厂 perfumery

【香炉】 xiānglú incense burner

【香喷喷】 xiāngpēnpēn ① sweet-smelling ② savoury; appetizing: 一碗～的炖肉 a bowl of savoury (pork) stew

【香气】 xiāngqì sweet smell; fragrance; aroma

【香水】 xiāngshuǐ perfume; scent

【香甜】 xiāngtián ① fragrant and sweet: ～的瓜果 sweet melons and fruits ② (sleep) soundly: 小伙子们劳动了一天,晚上睡得格外～。 The boys slept soundly after a day's work.

【香味】 xiāngwèi sweet smell; fragrance; scent; perfume

【香烟】 xiāngyān ① cigarette ② incense smoke: ～缭绕 coiling incense smoke ◇ ～盒 cigarette case/ ～头 cigarette butt (或 end)

【香油】 xiāngyóu sesame oil

【香皂】 xiāngzào perfumed (或 scented) soap; toilet soap

【香烛】 xiāngzhú joss sticks and candles (burned when offering sacrifices to gods or ancestors)

厢 xiāng ① wing (usu. of a one-storeyed house); wing-room: 一正两～ a central room with two wing-rooms ② railway carriage or compartment; (theatre) box: 车～ carriage/ 包～ box ③ the vicinity outside of a city gate: 城～ the city proper and areas just outside its gates ④ side: 一～情愿 one-sided wish; one's own wishful thinking/ 让开大路,占领两～ leave the high road alone and seize the land on both sides (as in mobile warfare)

【厢房】 xiāngfáng wing (usu. of a one-storeyed house); wing-room

湘 Xiāng ① short for the Xiangjiang River (in Hunan Province) ② another name for Hunan Province

箱* xiāng ① chest; box; case; trunk: 大木～ wooden trunk; chest/ 货～ packing box/ 书～ a box for books/ 皮～ leather suitcase/ 垃圾～ dustbin; garbage can; ash can ② anything in the shape of a box: 风～ bellows

【箱底】 xiāngdǐ ① the bottom of a chest ② valuables stowed away at the bottom of the chest; one's store of valuables

【箱子】 xiāngzi chest; box; case; trunk

襄 xiāng 〈书〉 assist; help: 共～义举 let everybody help to promote this worthy undertaking

【襄理】 xiānglǐ 〔旧时银行、企业用语〕 assistant manager

【襄助】 xiāngzhù assist

镶 xiāng ① inlay; set; mount: 金～玉嵌 inlaid with gold and jade/ ～宝石 set gems; mount precious stones/ 给窗子～玻璃 glaze a window ② rim; edge; border: 给裙子～花边 edge a skirt with lace

【镶嵌】 xiāngqiàn inlay; set; mount: ～银丝漆器 silver-inlaid lacquerware/ ～细工 inlaid work; marquetry; mosaic

【镶牙】 xiāngyá put in a false tooth; insert an artificial tooth

xiáng

详 xiáng ① detailed; minute: ～谈 speak in detail (或 at length); go into details ② details; particulars: ～见附录。 For details, see the appendix./ ～述自己的论点 elaborate one's thesis ③ know clearly: 作者生卒年月不～。 The author's dates are unknown.

【详尽】 xiángjìn detailed; exhaustive; thorough: ～的记录 a detailed record/ ～的调查 a thorough investigation/ 对问题进行～的研究 make an exhaustive study of a subject

【详密】 xiángmì elaborate; meticulous: ～的计划 a meticulous plan

【详明】 xiángmíng full and clear: ～的注解 full and clear annotations

【详情】 xiángqíng detailed information; details; particulars: ～后报。 Details to follow./ 请问办事处。 Please apply to the office for particulars.

【详实】 xiángshí full and accurate: ～的材料 full and accurate data (或 material)

【详图】 xiángtú detail (drawing): 发动机～ engine detail

【详细】 xiángxì detailed; minute: ~的报告 a detailed report/ ~了解情况 acquire detailed knowledge of the situation/ ~占有材料 collect all the available material; have all the relevant data at one's fingertips/ ~地描述 give a minute description/ 请说~点。 Please explain in greater detail.

降* xiáng ① surrender; capitulate: 宁死不~ rather die than surrender ② subdue; vanquish; tame: ~妖伏魔 vanquish demons and monsters
另见 jiàng
【降伏】 xiángfú subdue; vanquish; tame: ~劣马 break in a wild horse
【降服】 xiángfú yield; surrender
【降龙伏虎】 xiánglóng-fúhǔ subdue the dragon and tame the tiger — overcome powerful adversaries
【降顺】 xiángshùn 〈书〉 yield and pledge allegiance to

祥* xiáng auspicious; propitious; lucky
【祥瑞】 xiángruì auspicious sign; propitious omen

翔 xiáng circle in the air: 翱~ soar; hover
【翔实】 xiángshí full and accurate

xiǎng

享* xiǎng enjoy: 共~胜利的欢乐 share the joy of victory
【享福】 xiǎngfú enjoy a happy life; live in ease and comfort
【享乐】 xiǎnglè lead a life of pleasure; indulge in creature comforts
【享年】 xiǎngnián 〈敬〉 die at the age of
【享受】 xiǎngshòu ① enjoy: ~公费医疗 enjoy public health services ② enjoyment; treat: 贪图~ seek ease and comfort
【享用】 xiǎngyòng enjoy the use of; enjoy
【享有】 xiǎngyǒu enjoy (rights, prestige, etc.): ~崇高的威望 enjoy high prestige; be held in esteem/ 在我国, 妇女~同男子平等的权利。 Women in our country enjoy equal rights with men.

响* xiǎng ① sound; noise: 听不见~儿了。 No more sound was heard./ 一声炮~ the report of a cannon/ 两响的爆竹 double-bang firecrackers ② make a sound; sound; ring: ~锣 sound a gong/ 电话铃~了。 The telephone rang./ 全场一起暴风雨般的掌声。 A stormy applause broke out in the hall. 或 The hall resounded with stormy applause./ 扩音器不~了。 The loudspeaker's stopped working./ 他一声不~地走了。 He left without a word. ③ noisy; loud: 收音机开得太~了。 The radio's too loud (或 noisy). ④ echo: ~应 respond; answer
【响彻】 xiǎngchè resound (或 reverberate) through: 一曲云霄的凯歌 a song of triumph that resounds through the skies/ 炮声~山谷。 The roar of guns reverberated in the valley.
【响动】 xiǎngdòng sound of sth. astir: 夜很静, 一点~也没有。 The night was quiet, and there was no sound of anything astir.
【响亮】 xiǎngliàng loud and clear; resounding; resonant; sonorous: ~的回答 a loud and clear reply; an unequivocal reply/ ~的声音 a resounding voice/ 一记~的耳光 a heavy slap in the face; a smart box on the ear
【响声】 xiǎngshēng sound; noise: 沙沙的~ rustling sound
【响尾蛇】 xiǎngwěishé rattlesnake
【响应】 xiǎngyìng respond; answer

饷 xiǎng ①〈书〉 entertain (with food and drink) ②〈旧〉 pay (for soldiers, policemen, etc.): 月~ monthly pay

飨 xiǎng 〈书〉 provide dinner for; entertain: ~客 entertain a guest/ 以~读者 offer to the readers

想 xiǎng ① think: ~问题 think over a problem/ ~得真周到 have really thought of everything/ ~办法 think of a way; try to find a solution (或 way out)/ 让我~一~。 Let me think it over. 或 Let me see./ 也要~~困难。 We must also anticipate difficulties. ② suppose; reckon; consider; think: 我~他今天不会来。 I don't think he'll be coming today./ 我~我该走了。 I'm afraid I must be going now. ③ want to; would like to; feel like (doing sth.): 你~看足球赛吗? Do you want to see (或 feel like seeing) a football match?/ 我也~试试。 I'd also like to have a try. ④ remember with longing; miss: 你走了以后, 我们都很~你。 After you left, we all missed you.
【想必】 xiǎngbì presumably; most probably (或 likely): 这事~你知道。 You most probably know this./ 他没有答复, ~没有收到我的信。 No word from him yet; presumably he hasn't received my letter.
【想不到】 xiǎngbudào unexpected: 这真是~的事! This is something quite unexpected!/ ~家乡变化这么大。 I never expected my village would have changed so much./ 真~会在这儿见到你。 Fancy seeing you here!
【想不开】 xiǎngbukāi take things too hard; take a matter to heart: 别为这些小事~。 Don't take such small things to heart.
【想当然】 xiǎngdāngrán assume sth. as a matter of course; take for granted: 我们不能凭~办事。 We must not act on assumptions.
【想到】 xiǎngdào think of; call to mind: 忽然~一件重要的事情 suddenly think of something important/ 经常~人民的利益 always have the interests of the people at heart/ 我们没~你会来。 We didn't expect you (to come).
【想得到】 xiǎngdedào 〔多用于反问〕 think; imagine; expect: 谁~会出事故? Who would have thought there'd be an accident?
【想得开】 xiǎngdekāi not take to heart; take philosophically; try to look on the bright side of things: 这老太太真~了。 This old lady always looks on the bright side of things.
【想法】 xiǎngfǎ think of a way; do what one can; try: ~给大伙儿弄点水喝喝。 Try and get some drinking water for everyone.
【想法】 xiǎngfa idea; opinion; what one has in mind: 这个~不错。 This is a good idea./ 按我的~ in my opinion; to my mind/ 把你的~给大家说说。 Tell us what you have in mind.
【想方设法】 xiǎngfāng-shèfǎ do everything possible; try every means; try by hook or by crook
【想见】 xiǎngjiàn infer; gather: 从这些事情上, 你可以~他的为人。 From these instances you can gather what kind of person he is.
【想来】 xiǎnglái it may be assumed that; presumably: 他的话~不是没有根据的。 I suppose what he says is not groundless.
【想念】 xiǎngniàn remember with longing; long to see again; miss: 我们很~老大娘。 We all miss grandma very much.
【想起】 xiǎngqǐ remember; recall; think of; call to mind: 他看起来面熟, 可我一下子想不起他是谁。 He looked familiar to me but I couldn't immediately place him./ 我忽然忘了锁门了。 It suddenly occured to me that I had left the door unlocked.
【想入非非】 xiǎngrù fēifēi indulge in fantasy; allow one's fancy to run wild
【想通】 xiǎngtōng straighten out one's thinking; become convinced; come round: 我~了。 I've come round to the idea now./ 只要~了, 他就会积极地去干。 Once he's straightened out his thinking, he'll go all out on the job./ 你要是一时想不通, 还可以再想想。 Think the matter over again if you're still not convinced.
【想望】 xiǎngwàng desire; long for: 他从小就~着当一名教师。 He's longed to be a teacher ever since he was a child.
【想象】 xiǎngxiàng ① imagine; fancy; visualize: 难以~

hard to imagine (或 visualize)/ ～不到的困难 unimaginable difficulties ②〈心〉imagination ◇ ～力 imaginative power (或 faculty); imagination

鲞 xiǎng dried fish: 鳗～ dried eel

xiàng

向* xiàng ① direction: 风～ wind direction/ 人心所～ (the trend of) popular sentiment ② face; turn towards: 这间屋子～东。This room faces east./ 葵花朵朵～太阳。Sunflowers turn towards the sun. ③ take sb.'s part; side with; be partial to: ～理不～人 stand by what is right, not by a particular person; side with whoever is right ④〈介〉〔表示动作的方向〕: ～上级汇报工作 report to one's superior on one's work/ ～自然开战 wage a battle against nature ⑤ always; all along: ～无此例。There's no precedent for this.

【向背】xiàng-bèi support or oppose: 人心～ whether the people are for or against; the will of the people

【向导】xiàngdǎo guide

【向后】xiànghòu towards the back; backward: ～看 look back/ ～撤 withdraw/ ～转1(口令) About face! 或 About turn!/ ～转走1(口令) To the rear, march!

【向来】xiànglái always; all along: ～如此。It has always been so./ 我～不抽烟。I have never smoked.

【向前】xiàngqián forward; onward; ahead: 奋勇～ forge ahead/ 采取 ～看的态度 adopt a forward-looking attitude/ ～看1(口 令) Eyes front! 或 Ready, front!

【向日葵】xiàngrìkuí sunflower

【向上】xiàngshàng upward; up: 卡车沿着盘山公路～爬去。The trucks climbed the twisting mountain road./ 好好学习,天天～。Study well and make progress every day.

【向上爬】xiàngshàngpá be intent on personal advancement: 有～的思想 have the mentality of a careerist (或 social climber)

【向往】xiàngwǎng yearn for; look forward to: ～幸福的新生活 look forward to a happy new life

【向下】xiàngxià downward; down: 滑雪运动员飞快地～滑去。The skiers sped down the slope.

【向心力】xiàngxīnlì〈物〉centripetal force

【向阳】xiàngyáng ① exposed to the sun; sunny ② with a sunny usu. southern, exposure: 这间屋～。The room has a southern exposure.

【向右】xiàngyòu towards the right: ～转1 (口令) Right face! 或 Right turn!/～转走1(口令) By the right flank, march!

【向隅】xiàngyú〈书〉stand in a corner — be disappointed for lack of opportunity; feel left out

【向着】xiàngzhe ① turn towards; face: ～光明的未来前进 advance towards a bright future ②〈口〉take sb.'s part; side with; be partial to: 她说话在理,我就～她。I take her part because she's right./ 老奶奶～小孙女 Grandma favours her little granddaughter.

【向左】xiàngzuǒ towards the left: ～转1(口令) Left face! 或 Left turn!/ ～转走1(口令) By the left flank, march!

巷* xiàng lane; alley

【巷战】xiàngzhàn street fighting

项* xiàng ① nape (of the neck) ②〈量〉〔用于分项目的事物〕: 八～原则 eight principles/ 一～一～地进行解释 explain item by item/ 第五条第二款第三～ article 5, clause 2, item 3/ 还有一～工作要做。There is another job to do. ③ sum (of money): 进～ income/ 欠～ liabilities ④〈数〉term

【项背】xiàngbèi a person's back: ～相望 (walk) one after another in close succession/ 不可望其～ cannot hold a candle to sb.

【项链】xiàngliàn necklace

【项目】xiàngmù item: 出口～ goods for export; export items/ 基本建设～ capital construction project/ 援助～ aid project/ 训练～ training courses/ 田径～ track and field events

【项圈】xiàngquān necklet; necklace

【项庄舞剑,意在沛公】Xiàng Zhuāng wǔ jiàn, yì zài Pèigōng Xiang Zhuang performed the sword dance as a cover for his attempt on Liu Bang's life — act with a hidden motive

相 xiàng ① looks; appearance: 长～儿 a person's appearance/ 一副可怜 a pitiful appearance; a sorry figure/ 一脸凶～ a fierce look on one's face ② bearing; posture: 站没站～,坐没坐～ not know how to stand or sit properly/ 这孩子睡～不好。The child sleeps sprawled all over the bed. ③ look at and appraise: ～马 look at a horse to judge its worth/ 人不可以貌～。Never judge a person by his appearance. ④〈书〉assist ⑤〈书〉prime minister ⑥ ministers in Japanese government ⑦ photograph: 照个～ take a photo; have a photo taken ⑧ elephant, one of the pieces in Chinese chess
另见 xiāng

【相册】xiàngcè photo album

【相机】xiàngjī ① watch for an opportunity: ～行事 act as the occasion demands; do as one sees fit/ ～而动 wait for an opportunity to act; bide one's time ② camera

【相貌】xiàngmào facial features; looks; appearance: ～端正 have regular features

【相面】xiàngmiàn tell sb.'s fortune by reading his face; practise physiognomy

【相片】xiàngpiàn photograph; photo

【相声】xiàngsheng〈曲艺〉comic dialogue; cross talk: 说～ perform a comic dialogue

象* xiàng ① elephant ② appearance; shape; image: 万～更新。All things take on a new aspect. 或 Everything looks new and fresh. ③ imitate: ～声 onomatopoeia ④ be like; resemble; take after: 姐妹俩长得很～。The two sisters are very much alike./ 这孩子～他父亲。The child takes after its father./ ～猛虎下山一样向敌人扑去 charge at the enemy like tigers dashing down a mountain ⑤ look as if; seem: ～要下雨了。It looks like rain./ ～是有人在敲门。It sounds like somebody's knocking on the door. ⑥ such as; like ⑦ elephant, one of the pieces in Chinese chess

【象鼻】xiàngbí trunk

【象话】xiànghuà〔多用于否定或反问〕reasonable; proper; right: 大家都忙,就我在家休息,～吗? How can I take it easy at home when everybody else is so busy?/ 你发这么大脾气,～吗? Aren't you ashamed to fly into such a rage? 真不～! That's really the limit. 或 It's simply outrageous.

【象棋】xiàngqí (Chinese) chess

【象形】xiàngxíng〈语〉pictographic characters or pictographs, e.g. 日 (sun) and 月 (moon) — one of the six categories of Chinese characters (六书) ◇ ～文字 pictograph; hieroglyph/ ～字 pictographic character

【象牙】xiàngyá elephant's tusk; ivory: ～雕刻 ivory carving (或 sculpture)/ ～制品 ivories/ ～之塔 ivory tower

【象样】xiàngyàng up to the mark; presentable; decent; sound: 他的针线活还挺～的。His needlework is quite presentable./ 这屋里连张～的桌子也没有。There isn't even a decent table in this room./ 他提不出～的理由来解释他的行动。He couldn't give any sound reason for his action.

【象征】xiàngzhēng ① symbolize; signify; stand for ② symbol; emblem; token: 友谊的～ emblem (或 symbol) of friendship

【象征性】xiàngzhēngxìng symbolic; emblematic; token

像 xiàng ① likeness (of sb.); portrait; picture: 画～ portrait/ 铜～ bronze statue ②〈物〉image: 虚(实)～

virtual (real) image ③ 见"象" xiàng ④⑤⑩

橡 xiàng ① oak ② rubber tree
【橡胶】 xiàngjiāo rubber: 天然~ natural rubber/ 合成~ synthetic rubber/ 生~〈化〉 raw rubber; caoutchouc/ 海棉~ foam rubber ◇ ~轮胎 rubber tyre/ ~树 rubber tree/ ~种植园 rubber plantation
【橡皮】 xiàngpí ① rubber ② eraser; rubber

xiāo

枭 xiāo ① owlet ②〈书〉 fierce and ambitious: ~雄 a fierce and ambitious person; a formidable man
【枭首示众】 xiāoshǒu shìzhòng cut off a person's head and hang it up as a warning to all

削* xiāo ① pare (或 peel) with a knife: ~苹果 pare (或 peel) an apple/ ~铅笔 sharpen a pencil/ ~木头 whittle a piece of wood ②〈乒乓球〉 cut; chop: ~球 cut; chop 另见 .xuē

哓 xiāo
【哓哓不休】 xiāoxiāo bù xiū argue endlessly

骁 xiāo valiant; brave
【骁将】 xiāojiàng 〈书〉 valiant general
【骁勇】 xiāoyǒng 〈书〉 brave; valiant

哮 xiāo ① heavy breathing; wheeze ② roar; howl: 咆~ roar; thunder
【哮喘】 xiāochuǎn 〈医〉 asthma

消* xiāo ① disappear; vanish: 云~雾散。The clouds dispersed and the fog lifted./ 红肿已~。The swelling has gone down./ 他的气~了。He has cooled down. ② eliminate; dispel; remove: ~烟除尘 eliminate smoke and dust/ ~痰 reduce phlegm/ ~愁解闷 divert oneself from boredom; dispel depression or melancholy ③ pass the time in a leisurely way; while away (the time): ~夏 pass the summer in a leisurely way ④〈方〉[前面常有"不""只""何"等] need; take: 来回只~一个星期。It takes only a week to get there and back./ 不~说 needless to say; it goes without saying
【消沉】 xiāochén downhearted; low-spirited; dejected; depressed: 意志~ demoralized; despondent
【消除】 xiāochú eliminate; dispel; remove; clear up: ~分歧 eliminate (或 iron out) differences/ ~顾虑 dispel misgivings/ ~隐患 remove a hidden danger/ ~误会 clear up a misunderstanding
【消毒】 xiāodú disinfect; sterilize: 用酒精~ sterilize in (或 with) alcohol/ 用漂白粉~ disinfect with bleaching powder
【消防】 xiāofáng fire control; fire fighting; fire protection ◇ ~车 fire engine (或 truck)/ ~队 fire brigade/ ~人员 fire fighter/ ~设备 fire-fighting equipment/ ~水龙 fire hose/ ~演习 fire drill/ ~站 fire station
【消费】 xiāofèi consume ◇ ~合作社 consumers' cooperative/ ~品 consumer goods/ ~者 consumer
【消耗】 xiāohào consume; use up; deplete; expend: ~精力 consume one's energy/ ~大量武器弹药 expend large amounts of arms and ammunition/ ~敌人的有生力量 wear down the enemy's effective strength/ 人力物力的~ a drain on manpower and material resources ◇ ~战 war of attrition
【消化】 xiāohuà digest: 好~ digestible; easy to digest/ 帮助学生~所学的东西 help the students digest what they have learnt ◇ ~不良 indigestion; dyspepsia/ ~道 alimentary canal; digestive tract/ ~系统 digestive system
【消极】 xiāojí ① negative: ~因素 negative factor/ ~影响 negative influence ② passive; inactive: ~抵抗(御) pas-

sive resistance (defence)/ 态度~ take a passive attitude; remain inactive/ 情绪~ be dispirited/ ~怠工 be slack in work
【消解】 xiāojiě clear up; dispel
【消弭】 xiāomǐ put an end to; prevent: ~水患 prevent floods
【消灭】 xiāomiè ① perish; die out; pass away: 自行~ perish (或 die out) of itself/ 发生、发展和~的过程 the process of coming into being, developing and passing away ② eliminate; abolish; exterminate; wipe out: ~剥削制度 eliminate the system of exploitation/ ~病虫害 wipe out insect pests and plant diseases
【消磨】 xiāomó ① wear down; fritter away: ~志气 sap one's will/ ~精力 fritter away one's energy ② while (或 idle) away: ~岁月 while away the time/ ~时间 kill time; pass the time
【消气】 xiāoqì cool down; be mollified
【消遣】 xiāoqiǎn ① divert oneself; while away the time: 在火车上下棋~ beguile the train journey by playing chess ② pastime; diversion
【消融】 xiāoróng melt: 冰雪~ melting of ice and snow
【消散】 xiāosàn scatter and disappear; dissipate: 雾~了。The mist has lifted./ 他脸上的愁容~了。The worried expression has disappeared from his face.
【消失】 xiāoshī disappear; vanish; dissolve; die (或 fade) away: ~在浓雾中 disappear in the dense fog/ ~在人群中 be lost in a crowd
【消逝】 xiāoshì die (或 fade) away; vanish; elapse: 火车的隆隆声慢慢~了。The rumbling of the train slowly died away./ 随着时间的~ with the lapse of time
【消释】 xiāoshì clear up; dispel: ~疑虑 dispel misgivings/ 误会~了。The misunderstanding has been cleared up.
【消受】 xiāoshòu [多用于否定] enjoy: 无福~ not have the luck to enjoy; be unable to enjoy ② endure; bear
【消瘦】 xiāoshòu become thin (或 emaciated): 身体一天天~下去 be getting thinner every day/ 显得有点~ look a bit emaciated
【消损】 xiāosǔn wear and tear
【消亡】 xiāowáng wither away; die out
【消息】 xiāoxi ① news; information: 本地~ local news/ 头版~ a front-page story/ ~灵通人士 a well-informed source ② tidings; news: 杳无~ have not heard from sb. since; have had no news of sb or sth.
【消夜】 xiāoyè 〈方〉 ① midnight snack ② have a midnight snack
【消长】 xiāo-zhǎng growth and decline: 双方力量的~ growth and decline of the relative strength of the two sides
【消肿】 xiāozhǒng 〈医〉 subsidence of a swelling; detumescence

宵 xiāo night: 通~ all night; throughout the night
【宵禁】 xiāojìn curfew: 实行~ impose a curfew/ 解除~ lift a curfew

逍 xiāo
【逍遥】 xiāoyáo free and unfettered: ~自在 be leisurely and carefree
【逍遥法外】 xiāoyáo fǎ wài go scot-free; be (或 remain) at large

萧 xiāo ① desolate; dreary
【萧规曹随】 Xiāo guī Cáo suí Cao (a Han Dynasty prime minister) followed the rules set by Xiao (his predecessor) — follow established rules
【萧瑟】 xiāosè ① rustle in the air: 秋风~。The autumn wind is soughing. ② bleak; desolate
【萧疏】 xiāoshū ① desolate ② (of trees, leaves, etc.) sparse but graceful; thinly scattered
【萧索】 xiāosuǒ bleak and chilly; desolate
【萧条】 xiāotiáo ① desolate; bleak: 一片~的景象 a desolate scene on all sides ②〈经〉 depression: 经济~ economic depression; slump/ 生意~。Business is bad (或 slack).

【萧萧】 xiāoxiāo 〈书〉〈象〉：车辚辚，马～。Chariots rumble and roll; horses whinny and neigh./ 风～。The wind soughs and sighs.

硝 xiāo ① nitre; saltpetre ② 〈皮革〉 tawing

销* xiāo ① melt (metal) ② cancel; annul: 注～ write off; cancel ③ sell; market: 畅～ sell well/ 滞～ sell poorly/ 产～平衡 balance between production and marketing ④ expend; spend: 开～ expenditure

【销案】 xiāo'àn close a case

【销毁】 xiāohuǐ destroy by melting or burning: ～罪证 destroy incriminating evidence/ ～核武器 the destruction of nuclear weapons

【销魂】 xiāohún be overwhelmed with sorrow or joy; feel transported

【销假】 xiāojià report back after leave of absence

【销路】 xiāolù sale; market: ～很好 have a good sale; find a good market/ 没有～ find no sale (或 market)

【销声匿迹】 xiāoshēng-nìjī keep silent and lie low; disappear from the scene

【销售】 xiāoshòu sell; market ◇ ～价格 selling price/ ～量 sales volume/ ～税 sales tax/ ～总额 total (或 aggregate) sales

【销行】 xiāoxíng sell; be on sale: ～各地 be on sale everywhere/ ～百万册 have sold a million copies

【销帐】 xiāozhàng cancel or remove from an account; write off

潇 xiāo 〈书〉 (of water) deep and clear

【潇洒】 xiāosǎ natural and unrestrained

【潇潇】 xiāoxiāo ① whistling and pattering: 风雨～ the whistling of wind and pattering of rain ② drizzly

箫 xiāo xiao, a vertical bamboo flute

霄 xiāo ① clouds: 高入云～ towering into the clouds ② sky; heaven

【霄汉】 xiāohàn 〈书〉 the sky; the firmament

【霄壤】 xiāorǎng heaven and earth: 有～之别 be as far apart (或 as different) as heaven and earth

嚣 xiāo clamour; hubbub; din: 叫～ clamour

【嚣张】 xiāozhāng rampant; arrogant; aggressive: ～一时 run rampant (或 wild) for a time/ 气焰～ swollen with arrogance

xiáo

淆 xiáo confuse; mix: 混～ mix up; confuse; obscure/ ～惑 confuse; bewilder

【淆乱】 xiáoluàn confuse; befuddle: ～视听 befuddle the minds of the public

xiǎo

小* xiǎo ① small; little; petty; minor: ～姑娘 a little girl/ ～国 a small country/ ～问题 a minor question/ ～声说话 speak in a low voice/ 风～些了。The wind has dropped a little./ 鞋～了点儿。These shoes are a bit too tight. ② for a while; for a short time: ～坐 sit for a while/ ～住 stay for a few days ③ young: 一家老～ the whole family, old and young/ ～儿子 the youngest son/ 她比我～。She is younger than I am./ ～鸡 chick; chicken/ ～牛 calf/ ～狗 puppy/ ～猫 kitten ④ 〈谦〉[称自己或与自己有关的人或事物]: ～女 my daughter ⑤ [用于姓、名、排行等之前]: ～王 Little Wang; Xiao Wang

【小半】 xiǎobàn less than half; lesser (或 smaller) part

【小报】 xiǎobào small-sized newspaper; tabloid

【小辈】 xiǎobèi younger member of a family; junior

【小本经营】 xiǎoběn jīngyíng ① business with a small capital ② do business in a small way

【小便】 xiǎobiàn ① urinate; pass (或 make) water; empty one's bladder ② urine ◇ ～处(池) urinal

【小菜】 xiǎocài ① pickled vegetables; pickles ② 〈方〉 meat, fish and vegetable dishes; common dishes

【小册子】 xiǎocèzi booklet; pamphlet

【小产】 xiǎochǎn miscarriage; abortion

【小车】 xiǎochē ① wheelbarrow; handbarrow; handcart; pushcart ② sedan (car)

【小吃】 xiǎochī ① snack; refreshments ② cold dish; made dish ◇ ～部 snack counter; refreshment room/ ～店 snack bar; lunchroom

【小丑】 xiǎochǒu clown; buffoon: 扮演～角色 play the buffoon

【小丑跳梁】 xiǎochǒu tiàoliáng a contemptible wretch making trouble

【小聪明】 xiǎocōngming cleverness in trivial matters; petty trick: 耍～ play petty tricks

【小刀】 xiǎodāo ① small sword ② pocket knife

【小道理】 xiǎodàoli minor principle

【小调】 xiǎodiào ① ditty ② 〈乐〉 minor: A ～协奏曲 concerto in A minor

【小动作】 xiǎodòngzuò petty action; little trick (或 manoeuvre): 搞～ get up to little tricks

【小队】 xiǎoduì team; squad

【小恩小惠】 xiǎo'ēn-xiǎohuì petty (或 small) favours; economic sops (或 bait)

【小儿】 xiǎo'ér ① children ② 〈谦〉 my son

【小儿科】 xiǎo'érkē 〈医〉 (department of) paediatrics ◇ ～医生 paediatrician

【小贩】 xiǎofàn pedlar; vendor; hawker

【小费】 xiǎofèi tip; gratuity

【小腹】 xiǎofù underbelly; lower abdomen

【小个子】 xiǎogèzi little chap; small fellow

【小姑】 xiǎogū husband's younger sister; sister-in-law

【小广播】 xiǎoguǎngbō spreading of hearsay information; grapevine

【小鬼】 xiǎoguǐ ① imp; goblin ② little devil (a term of endearment in addressing a child)

【小孩儿】 xiǎoháir 〈口〉 child 又作“小孩子”

【小户】 xiǎohù ① small family ② family of limited means and without powerful connections

【小伙子】 xiǎohuǒzi 〈口〉 lad; young fellow (或 chap); youngster

【小集团】 xiǎojítuán clique; faction

【小轿车】 xiǎojiàochē sedan (car); limousine

【小节】 xiǎojié small matter; trifle: 生活～ matters concerning personal life/ 不拘～ not bother about small matters; not be punctilious

【小结】 xiǎojié ① brief (或 preliminary) summary; interim summary ② summarize briefly: ～一下前阶段的工作 summarize briefly the work done in the previous stage

【小解】 xiǎojiě urinate; pass (或 make) water

【小姐】 xiǎojie ① Miss ② young lady

【小舅子】 xiǎojiùzi 〈口〉 wife's younger brother; brother-in-law

【小楷】 xiǎokǎi regular script in small characters, as used in Chinese calligraphy exercises

【小看】 xiǎokàn 〈口〉 look down upon; belittle

【小康】 xiǎokāng comparatively well-off; comfortably off: ～之家 a comfortable family

【小老婆】 xiǎolǎopo concubine

【小两口】 xiǎoliǎngkǒu 〈口〉 young couple

【小麦】 xiǎomài wheat

【小名】 xiǎomíng pet name for a child; childhood name

【小拇指】 xiǎomuzhǐ 〈口〉 little finger

【小农】 xiǎonóng small farmer ◇ ～经济 small-scale peasant economy; small-scale farming by individual owners

【小朋友】 xiǎopéngyǒu ① children ② (form of address by an adult to a child) little boy or girl; child

【小便宜】 xiǎopiányi small gain; petty advantage: 贪～ go after petty advantages

【小品】 xiǎopǐn a short, simple literary or artistic creation; essay; sketch: 历史~ short historical essay/ 广播~ short piece for broadcasting ◇ ~文 familiar essay; essay

【小气】 xiǎoqi ① stingy; niggardly; mean ②〈方〉narrow-minded; petty

【小前提】 xiǎoqiántí 〈逻〉 minor premise

【小巧玲珑】 xiǎoqiǎo línglóng small and exquisite

【小圈子】 xiǎoquānzi small circle (或 set) of people; small coterie: 搞~ form a small coterie

【小人】 xiǎorén ①〈旧〉a person of low position ② a base (或 mean) person; villain; vile character: ~得志 villains holding sway

【小人物】 xiǎorénwù an unimportant person; a nobody; cipher; nonentity

【小时】 xiǎoshí hour

【小时候】 xiǎoshíhou 〈口〉 in one's childhood; when one was young: 这是他~的照片。 These are his childhood photos.

【小市民】 xiǎoshìmín urban petty bourgeois

【小事】 xiǎoshì trifle; petty thing; minor matter: 大事做不来, ~又不做 disdain minor assignments while being unequal to major ones

【小试锋芒】 xiǎo shì fēngmáng display only a small part of one's talent

【小手工业者】 xiǎoshǒugōngyèzhě small handicraftsman

【小手小脚】 xiǎoshǒu-xiǎojiǎo ① stingy; mean ② lacking boldness; timid; niggling

【小叔子】 xiǎoshūzi 〈口〉 husband's younger brother; brother-in-law

【小数】 xiǎoshù 〈数〉 decimal ◇ ~点 decimal point

【小说】 xiǎoshuō novel; fiction: 长篇~ novel/ 中篇~ medium-length novel; novelette/ 短篇~ short story ◇ ~家 novelist; writer of fiction

【小算盘】 xiǎosuànpan selfish calculations: ~打得精 be very calculating

【小提琴】 xiǎotíqín violin

【小提琴手】 xiǎotíqínshǒu violinist: 首席~ concertmaster

【小题大作】 xiǎo tí dà zuò make a fuss over a trifling matter; make a mountain out of a molehill

【小天地】 xiǎotiāndì one's own little world

【小艇】 xiǎotǐng small boat; skiff

【小偷】 xiǎotōu petty (或 sneak) thief; pilferer: ~小摸 pilfering

【小腿】 xiǎotuǐ shank

【小巫见大巫】 xiǎowū jiàn dàwū like a small sorcerer in the presence of a great one — feel dwarfed; pale into insignificance by comparison

【小五金】 xiǎowǔjīn metal fittings (e.g. nails, wires, hinges, bolts, locks, etc.); hardware

【小写】 xiǎoxiě ① the ordinary form of a Chinese numeral (e.g. 一，二，三，as against 壹，贰，叁) ② small letter

【小心】 xiǎoxīn take care; be careful; be cautious: ~火烛! Guard against fire!/ ~轻放! Handle with care!/ 过马路要~。 Be careful when crossing the street./ ~油漆! Mind the wet paint!

【小心眼儿】 xiǎoxīnyǎnr narrow-minded; petty

【小心翼翼】 xiǎoxīn yìyì with great care; cautiously

【小型】 xiǎoxíng small-sized; small-scale; miniature: ~企业 small enterprise/ ~运动会 a small-scale athletic meet

【小学】 xiǎoxué primary (或 elementary) school

【小学生】 xiǎoxuéshēng (primary school) pupil; schoolchild; schoolboy or schoolgirl

【小业主】 xiǎoyèzhǔ small (或 petty) proprietor

【小夜曲】 xiǎoyèqǔ 〈乐〉 serenade

【小姨子】 xiǎoyízi 〈口〉 wife's younger sister; sister-in-law

【小意思】 xiǎoyìsi small token of kindly feelings; mere trifle: 这是我的一点儿~，送给你做个纪念。 This is just a little keepsake for you.

【小引】 xiǎoyǐn introductory note; foreword

【小雨】 xiǎoyǔ light rain

【小月】 xiǎoyuè ① a solar month of 30 days ② a lunar month of 29 days

【小帐】 xiǎozhàng tip; gratuity

【小照】 xiǎozhào small-sized photograph

【小指】 xiǎozhǐ little finger or toe

【小传】 xiǎozhuàn brief biography; biographical sketch; profile

【小篆】 xiǎozhuàn an ancient style of calligraphy, adopted in the Qin Dynasty (221-207 B.C.) for the purpose of standardizing the script

【小子】 xiǎozi 〈口〉 ① boy: 他有两个孩子，一个闺女，一个~。 He has two children, one girl and one boy. ②〔含轻蔑意〕bloke; fellow; chap

【小组】 xiǎozǔ group: ~讨论 group discussion ◇ ~委员会 sub committee

晓* xiǎo ① dawn; daybreak: 拂~ foredawn/ ~行夜宿 (of a person on a journey) start at dawn and stop at dusk ② know: 谁个不知，哪个不~? There's not a person who doesn't know. ③ let sb. know; tell: ~以利害 warn sb. of the consequences

【晓得】 xiǎode know: 天~! God knows!

【晓示】 xiǎoshì tell explicitly; notify

【晓谕】 xiǎoyù 〈书〉 give explicit instructions (或 directions)

筱 xiǎo ①〈书〉 thin bamboo ② a substitute for 小 in a person's name

xiào

孝* xiào ① filial piety ② mourning: 带~ in mourning

【孝服】 xiàofú mourning (dress)

【孝敬】 xiàojìng give presents (to one's elders or superiors)

【孝顺】 xiàoshùn show filial obedience

【孝悌】 xiàotì filial piety and fraternal duty

【孝子】 xiàozǐ ① dutiful son ② son in mourning

【孝子贤孙】 xiàozǐ-xiánsūn worthy progeny; true son

肖 xiào resemble; be like: 维妙维~ absolutely lifelike

【肖像】 xiàoxiàng portrait; portraiture ◇ ~画 portrait-painting

效* xiào ① effect: 见~ produce an effect; prove effective ② imitate; follow the example of: 上行下~。 Those in subordinate positions will follow the example set by their superiors. ③ devote (one's energy or life) to; render (a service): ~死 ready to give one's life for a cause

【效法】 xiàofǎ follow the example of; model oneself on; learn from: 他治学严谨，值得~。 His meticulous scholarship is worthy of emulation.

【效果】 xiàoguǒ ① effect; result: ~不大 not be very effective; produce little effect/ 试验治虫药的~ test the effectiveness of the insecticide/ 取得良好的~ achieve good results ②〈剧〉 sound effects

【效劳】 xiàoláo work in the service of; work for: 乐于~ be glad to offer one's services

【效力】 xiàolì ① render a service; serve: 为国~ serve one's country ② effect: 这药很有~。 The medicine is efficacious./ 两种文本具有同等~。 Both texts (in two different languages) are equally authentic.

【效率】 xiàolǜ efficiency: ~高 efficient/ ~低 inefficient/ 这项革新使工作~提高五倍 The innovation raised efficiency fivefold.

【效命】 xiàomìng go all out to serve sb. regardless of the consequences: ~疆场 ready to lay down one's life on the battlefield

【效能】 xiàonéng efficacy; usefulness: 充分发挥水、肥的~ make the best possible use of irrigation and fertilizer

【效验】 xiàoyàn intended effect; desired result: 没有~ prove ineffective; fall flat/ 这种方法具有明显的~。 This method produces tangible results.

【效益】 xiàoyì beneficial result; benefit: 灌溉~ irrigation benefit

【效用】 xiàoyòng effectiveness; usefulness: 充分发挥水库的~ make full use of the reservoir

【效尤】 xiàoyóu knowingly follow the example of a wrongdoer: 以儆～ to warn others against following a bad example

【效忠】 xiàozhōng　pledge loyalty to; devote oneself heart and soul to

校*
xiào ① school: 夜～ night school ② field officer
另见 jiào

【校车】 xiàochē　school bus
【校风】 xiàofēng　school spirit:
【校官】 xiàoguān　field officer; field grade officer
【校规】 xiàoguī　school regulations
【校徽】 xiàohuī　school badge
【校刊】 xiàokān　school magazine; college journal
【校历】 xiàolì　school calendar
【校庆】 xiàoqìng　anniversary of the founding of a school or college
【校舍】 xiàoshè　schoolhouse; school building
【校外】 xiàowài　outside school; after school
【校务】 xiàowù　administrative affairs of a school or college
【校医】 xiàoyī　school doctor
【校友】 xiàoyǒu　alumnus or alumna
【校园】 xiàoyuán　campus; school yard
【校长】 xiàozhǎng　①(中小学) headmaster; principal ②(大专院校) president; chancellor
【校址】 xiàozhǐ　the location of a school or college

笑*
xiào ① smile; laugh: 微～ smile/ 真～死人 be terribly funny/ 小伙子被批准入伍,～得合不上嘴。The young man grinned from ear to ear when his application to join the army was approved. ② ridicule; laugh at: 叫人～掉大牙 ridiculous enough to make people laugh their heads off/ 他刚学,别～他。He's just started learning. Don't laugh at him.

【笑柄】 xiàobǐng　laughingstock; butt; joke: 这句话已成为～. That remark has become a standing joke.
【笑哈哈】 xiàohāhā　laughingly; with a laugh
【笑话】 xiàohua　① joke; jest: 说～ crack a joke/ 闹～ make a fool of oneself; make a funny mistake ② laugh at; ridicule: 他们看着看着我们的～,可到头来让人～的是他们自己。They had been waiting to have a good laugh at us, but in the end, the joke was on them.
【笑剧】 xiàojù　farce
【笑里藏刀】 xiàolǐ cáng dāo　hide a dagger in a smile — with murderous intent behind one's smiles
【笑脸】 xiàoliǎn　smiling face: ～相迎 greet sb. with a smile/ 陪～ meet rudeness with a flattering smile
【笑料】 xiàoliào　laughingstock; joke
【笑骂】 xiàomà　deride and taunt
【笑眯眯】 xiàomīmī　smilingly; with a smile on one's face: 他老是～。He's always smiling.
【笑面虎】 xiàomiànhǔ　smiling tiger — an outwardly kind but inwardly cruel person
【笑纳】 xiàonà　〈套〉 kindly accept (this small gift of mine)
【笑气】 xiàoqì　〈化〉 laughing gas; nitrous oxide
【笑容】 xiàoróng　smiling expression; smile: 慈祥的～ a kindly smile/ ～可掬 be radiant with smiles/ ～满面 be all smiles; have a broad smile on one's face/ 她脸上露出一丝～. A faint smile crept over her face.
【笑谈】 xiàotán　laughingstock; object of ridicule: 传为～ become a standing joke
【笑窝】 xiàowō　dimple
【笑嘻嘻】 xiàoxīxī　grinning; smiling broadly
【笑颜】 xiàoyán　smiling face
【笑靥】 xiàoyè　〈书〉 ① dimple ② smiling face
【笑逐颜开】 xiào zhú yán kāi　beam with smiles; be wreathed in smiles

啸
xiào ① whistle ② howl; roar: 虎～ the roar of a tiger
【啸聚】 xiàojù　〈书〉 band together; gang up: ～山林 go to the greenwood

些*
xiē 〔表示不定的数量〕: 这～ these/ 那么～ that much; that many/ 前～日子 a few days ago; sometime ago/ 买～东西 do some shopping/ 好～人 a lot of people/ 稍大～ a little bigger/ 好～了吗? Are you better?

【些微】 xiēwēi　slightly; a little; a bit: ～有点儿疼 hurt slightly; be a bit painful/ 这颜色～深了一点。The colour is a trifle too dark.

揳
xiē 〈方〉 drive (a wedge, nail, etc.): 在墙上～个钉子 drive (或 knock) a nail into the wall

楔
xiē
【楔形文字】 xiēxíng wénzì　cuneiform (characters); sphenogram

【楔子】 xiēzi　① wedge ② peg ③ prologue or interlude in Yuan Dynasty drama ④ prologue in some modern novels

歇
xiē ① have a rest: ～一会儿 have a short rest/ ～口气儿 stop for a breather; take (或 have) a breather ② stop (work, etc.); knock off: ～伏 stop work during the dog days/ ～会儿,喝杯茶。Let's knock off for a cup of tea.

【歇班】 xiēbān　be off duty; have time off: 今天小王～。 Xiao Wang is off duty today.
【歇工】 xiēgōng　stop work; knock off
【歇后语】 xiēhòuyǔ　a two-part allegorical saying, of which the first part, always stated, is descriptive, while the second part, sometimes unstated, carries the message, e.g. 泥菩萨过河——自身难保 a clay idol fording a river — hardly able to save oneself (let alone assist anyone else)
【歇脚】 xiējiǎo　stop on the way for a rest: 我们到那边荫凉地歇歇脚吧。Let's stop for a rest in the shade over there.
【歇凉】 xiēliáng　〈方〉 enjoy the cool in some shade; relax
【歇手】 xiēshǒu　stop doing sth.
【歇斯底里】 xiēsīdǐlǐ　hysteria: ～大发作 go into hysterics; become hysterical
【歇宿】 xiēsù　put up (somewhere) for the night; make an overnight stop
【歇息】 xiēxi　① have a rest ② go to bed; put up for the night
【歇业】 xiēyè　close a business; go out of business

蝎
xiē　scorpion
【蝎子】 xiēzi　scorpion

协*
xié ① joint; common: ～办 do sth. jointly ② assist

【协定】 xiédìng　① agreement; accord: 贸易～ trade agreement ② reach an agreement on sth.
【协会】 xiéhuì　association; society
【协理】 xiélǐ　assist in the management (of an enterprise, etc.)
【协力】 xiélì　unite efforts; join in a common effort: ～进攻 launch a joint assault

【协商】 xiéshāng　consult; talk things over: 民主~ democratic consultation/ ~一致的原则 the principle of reaching unanimity through consultation/ 需要和有关部门~。It's necessary to consult with the departments concerned. ◇ ~会议 consultative conference

【协调】 xiétiáo　coordinate; concert; harmonize; bring into line: 使我们的行动~起来 coordinate our activities/ 国民经济各部门的发展必须互相~。Development of the different branches of the national economy should be well coordinated./ 他的意见好象和大家不~。His opinions don't seem to be in tune with those of the others./ 体操运动员的动作~优美。The gymnast's movements are harmonious and graceful. ◇ ~委员会 coordination committee

【协同】 xiétóng　work in coordination with; cooperate with: 此事请~办理。Your cooperation is requested in influences that cause disease

【协议】 xiéyì　① agree on: 一致~的文件 a document unanimously agreed upon ② agreement: 达成~ reach an agreement/ 口头~ verbal agreement

【协约国】 Xiéyuēguó　the *Entente* countries (during World War I)

【协助】 xiézhù　assist; help; give assistance; provide help: 副总理~总理工作。The Vice-Premiers assist the Premier in his work.

【协奏曲】 xiézòuqǔ　〈乐〉concerto: 钢琴(小提琴)~ piano (violin) concerto

【协作】 xiézuò　cooperation; coordination; combined (或 joint) efforts: 双方~得很好。The two sides cooperated harmoniously.

邪

xié　① evil; heretical; irregular: 不信~ not believe in heresy; refuse to be taken in by fallacies/ 改~归正 give up one's evil ways and return to the right path; turn over a new leaf ② 〈中医〉 unhealthy environmental influences that cause disease

【邪道】 xiédào　evil ways; depraved life; vice: 走~ lead a depraved life; abandon oneself to evil ways

【邪恶】 xié'è　evil; wicked; vicious: ~的念头 wicked thoughts

【邪路】 xiélù　evil ways; vice: 个别人企图把运动引向~。Certain individuals tried to lead the movement astray.

【邪门儿】 xiéménr　〈方〉strange; odd; abnormal: 这天气真~,这时候还下雪。What strange weather — snowing at this time of the year!/ 真~,钥匙刚才还在这儿呢! That's strange! The key was·here just a minute ago.

【邪门歪道】 xiémén-wāidào　crooked ways (或 means); dishonest practices (或 methods)

【邪魔】 xiémó　evil spirit; demon

【邪念】 xiéniàn　evil thought; wicked idea: 他起了~。A wicked idea came into his head.

【邪气】 xiéqì　perverse trend; evil influence: 使正气上升,~下降 encourage healthy trends and check unhealthy ones

【邪说】 xiéshuō　heresy; heretical ideas; fallacy

【邪行】 xiéxíng　evil deeds

胁

xié　① the upper part of the side of the human body ②coerce; force: 裹~ force to take part; coerce/ 威~ threaten

【胁从】 xiécóng　be an accomplice under duress ◇ ~分子 reluctant (或 unwilling) follower; accomplice under duress

【胁肩谄笑】 xiéjiān chǎnxiào　cringe and smile obsequiously

【胁迫】 xiépò　coerce; force

挟

xié　① hold sth. under the arm: ~泰山以超北海 carry Taishan Mountain under one's arm and leap over the north sea — an impossibility ② coerce; force ·sb. to submit to one's will: 要~ coerce/ ~天子以令诸侯 have the emperor in one's power and order the dukes about in his name ③ harbour (resentment, etc.)

【挟持】 xiéchí　① seize sb. on both sides by the arms ② hold sb. under duress

【挟嫌】 xiéxián　〈书〉harbour resentment; bear a grudge: ~报复 bear resentment against sb. and retaliate

【挟制】 xiézhì　take advantage of sb.'s weakness to enforce obedience; force sb. to do one's bidding

谐

xié　① in harmony; in accord: 和~ harmonious ② 〈书〉come to an agreement; settle: 事~之后, 即可动身。We shall set out immediately once the matter is settled. ③ humorous: 诙~ humorous; jocular

【谐和】 xiéhé　harmonious; concordant

【谐谑】 xiéxuè　banter: 语带~ speak somewhat jokingly

偕

xié　together with; in the company of: ~行 travel together

【偕老】 xiélǎo　husband and wife grow old together

【偕同】 xiétóng　in the company of; accompanied by; along with

斜*

xié　oblique; slanting; inclined; tilted: ~圆锥〈数〉oblique cone/ 这根线~了。The line is slanting./ 柱子有点~。The pillar is a little tilted./ ~躺在沙发上 recline on a sofa/ 把桌子~过来 turn the table sideways/ ~着眼看人 cast sidelong glances at sb.; look sideways at sb.

【斜路】 xiélù　wrong path: 正路不走走~ turn from the right road and take the wrong one — give up an honest life for a dishonest one

【斜面】 xiémiàn　①〈数〉inclined plane

【斜坡】 xiépō　slope

【斜视】 xiéshì　①〈医〉strabismus ② look sideways; cast a sidelong glance: 目不~ not look sideways; refuse to be distracted

【斜阳】 xiéyáng　setting sun

携

xié　① carry; take along: ~眷 bring one's wife and children along/ ~款潜逃 abscond with funds/ ~械投诚 come over from the enemy's side bringing weapons ② take (或 hold) sb. by the hand: 让我们~起手来,共同前进。Let us join hands and advance together.

【携带】 xiédài　carry; take along: ~方便 be easy to carry about/ 随身~的物品 things carried on one's person/ 旅客每人可~行李二十公斤。Each passenger can take up to twenty kilograms of luggage.

【携手】 xiéshǒu　hand in hand: ~并进 go forward hand in hand

鞋*

xié　shoes

【鞋带】 xiédài　shoelace; shoestring

【鞋底】 xiédǐ　sole (of a shoe)

【鞋垫】 xiédiàn　shoe-pad; insole

【鞋跟】 xiégēn　heel (of a shoe)

【鞋匠】 xiéjiang　shoemaker; cobbler

【鞋扣】 xiékòu　shoe buckle

【鞋刷】 xiéshuā　shoe brush

【鞋样】 xiéyàng　shoe pattern; outline of sole

【鞋油】 xiéyóu　shoe polish (或 cream)

撷

xié　〈书〉pick; pluck

xiě

写*

xiě　① write: ~得一手好字 have good handwriting; write a good hand/ 这支笔不好~。This pen doesn't write well. ② compose; write: ~诗 compose a poem/ ~日记 make an entry in one's diary; keep a diary/ ~科学论文 write scientific papers; write theses on scientific subjects ③ describe; depict: ~景 describe the scenery/ ~一个英雄的成长过程 depict the growth of a hero ④ paint; draw: ~生 paint from life
另见 xiè

【写稿】 xiěgǎo　write for (或 contribute to) a magazine, etc.:

他经常为儿童刊物～。He is a regular contributor to children's magazines.
【写生】xiěshēng 〈美术〉paint from life; draw, paint or sketch from nature: 人物～ portrait from life ◇ ～画 sketch
【写实】xiěshí write or paint realistically
【写意】xiěyì 〈美术〉freehand brushwork in traditional Chinese painting (characterized by vivid expression and bold outline)
另见 xiěyì
【写照】xiězhào portrayal; portraiture
【写真】xiězhēn ① portray a person; draw a portrait ② portrait ③ describe sth. as it is
【写字台】xiězìtái writing desk; desk
【写作】xiězuò writing: 从事～ take up writing as one's career

血 xiě 〈口〉blood: ～的教训 a lesson paid for (或 written) in blood/ 流了一点～，不要紧。There was just a little bleeding. Nothing serious.
另见 xuè

xiè

写
另见 xiě
【写意】xièyì 〈方〉comfortable; enjoyable
另见 xiěyì

泻 xiè ① flow swiftly; rush down; pour out: 大江奔腾，一～千里。The (Changjiang) River rolls and roars on and on for a thousand li. ② have loose bowels; have diarrhoea: 上吐下～ suffer from vomiting and diarrhoea
【泻肚】xièdù have loose bowels; have diarrhoea
【泻药】xièyào laxative; cathartic; purgative

泄 xiè ① let out; discharge; release: 开闸～洪 open a sluice to release floodwater/ 象个～了气的皮球 like a deflated rubber ball — dejected ② let out (a secret); leak (news, secrets, etc.) ③ give vent to; vent: ～私愤 give vent to personal spite
【泄底】xièdǐ reveal or expose what is at the bottom of sth.
【泄劲】xièjìn lose heart; feel discouraged; be disheartened; slacken one's efforts: 他近来有点～。He has been a bit disheartened lately./ 继续努力,不要～! Keep at it, don't relax!
【泄漏】xièlòu leak; let out; divulge; give away: ～秘密 let out (或 divulge. give away) a secret/ 消息已～出去了。The news has leaked out.
【泄露】xièlù let out; reveal: 敌人无意中～了行动计划。The enemy unwittingly revealed their plan of action.
【泄密】xièmì divulge a secret; betray confidential matters
【泄气】xièqì ① lose heart; feel discouraged; be disheartened: 困难面前不～ keep one's end up in the face of difficulties/ 我不说那些～话。I shouldn't have made those discouraging (或 pessimistic) remarks. ② disappointing; frustrating; pathetic: 这么矮他都跳不过去,真～! He can't even jump that high. How pathetic!

卸 xiè ① unload; discharge; lay down: ～车 unload a vehicle/ ～担子 lay down a burden/ ～牲口 unhitch a draught animal ② remove; strip: ～零件 remove parts from a machine; strip a machine/ 把门～下来 lift a door off its hinges ③ get rid of; shirk: ～责 shirk the responsibility
【卸车】xièchē unload (goods, etc.) from a vehicle; unload
【卸货】xièhuò unload (或 discharge) cargo; unload: 从船上～ unload a ship; land goods from a ship
【卸任】xièrèn be relieved of one's office
【卸装】xièzhuāng remove stage makeup and costume

屑 xiè ① bits; scraps; crumbs: 纸～ scraps of paper/ 煤～ (coal) slack/ 金属～ metal filings/ 面包～ crumbs (of bread) ② trifling: 琐～ trifling; trivial ③〔多用于〕: 不～ disdain to do sth.

械 xiè ① tool; instrument: 机～ machine; mechanism ② weapon: 军～ weapons; arms; ordnance ③ 〈书〉fetters, shackles, etc.
【械斗】xièdòu fight with weapons between groups of people

谢 xiè ① thank: ～了又～ thank again and again/ 多～。Thanks a lot. ② 〈书〉make an apology; excuse oneself: ～过 apologize for having done sth. wrong/ ～病 excuse oneself on grounds of illness ③ decline: 敬～不敏 beg to be excused ④ (of flowers, leaves) wither
【谢忱】xièchén gratitude; thankfulness: 承蒙协助,谨致～。Allow us to express our thanks for your kindly help.
【谢词】xiècí thank-you speech
【谢绝】xièjué 〈婉〉refuse; decline: 婉言～ politely decline; politely refuse/ ～参观。Not open to visitors.
【谢幕】xièmù answer (或 respond to) a curtain call
【谢世】xièshì 〈书〉pass away; die
【谢天谢地】xiètiān-xièdì thank goodness; thank heaven: ～,你总算回来了! Thank goodness, you're back at last!
【谢帖】xiètiě a note of thanks; a thank-you note
【谢谢】xièxie thanks; thank you
【谢意】xièyì gratitude; thankfulness: 预致～ thank you in anticipation/ 谨致薄礼,聊表～。Please accept this gift and my gratitude.
【谢罪】xièzuì apologize for an offence; offer an apology

亵 xiè ① treat with irreverence; be disrespectful ② obscene; indecent
【亵渎】xièdú blaspheme; profane; pollute

榭 xiè a pavilion or house on a terrace: 水～ waterside pavilion/ 歌台舞～ halls for the performance of songs and dances

懈 xiè slack; lax: 松～ slacken; relax; let up/ 作不～的努力 make unremitting efforts
【懈怠】xièdài slack; sluggish: 学习上不可～。Don't slack off in your studies.

邂 xiè
【邂逅】xièhòu 〈书〉meet (a relative, friend, etc.) unexpectedly; run into sb.; meet by chance

蟹 xiè crab: 寄居～ hermit crab/ 沙～ ghost crab/ 梭子～ swimming crab

xīn

心 xīn ① the heart ② heart; mind; feeling; intention: 爱国～ patriotic feeling; patriotism/ 羞耻之～ sense of shame/ 伤人的～ wound (或 hurt) sb.'s feelings/ ～往一处想,劲往一处使 think and work with one heart and one mind/ 你的～是好的,但是事情办得不好。You meant well but you didn't handle the job well. 他人在这儿,～不在。He himself is here, but his thoughts are elsewhere. ③ centre; core: 手～ the hollow of the palm/ 核～ core; nucleus
【心爱】xīn'ài love; treasure: ～的人 one's beloved; loved one/ ～的东西 treasured (或 prized) possession
【心安理得】xīn'ān-lǐdé feel at ease and justified; have an easy conscience
【心病】xīnbìng ① worry; anxiety: 这事老惹着,一直是他的～。Not having this matter settled has always worried him. ② sore point; secret trouble
【心搏】xīnbó 〈生理〉heartbeat
【心不在焉】xīn bù zài yān absent-minded; inattentive; preoccupied (with sth. else): ～地听着 listen absent-mindedly

【心裁】 xīncái idea; conception; mental plan: 独出~ show originality; be original

【心肠】 xīncháng ① heart; intention: ~软 have a soft heart; be softhearted/ 好~ kindhearted/ 他真是个热~! He's a really warmhearted person! ② state of mind; mood

【心潮】 xīncháo a tidal surge of emotion; surging thoughts and emotions: ~澎湃 feel an upsurge of emotion/ ~翻滚 one's mind being in a tumult

【心慈手软】 xīncí-shǒuruǎn softhearted

【心胆俱裂】 xīn-dǎn jù liè be frightened out of one's wits; be terror-stricken: 吓得敌人~ strike terror into the enemy's hearts

【心得】 xīndé what one has learned from work, study, etc

【心地】 xīndì a person's mind, character, moral nature, etc.: ~坦白 candid; open/ ~单纯 simpleminded/ ~善良 good-natured; kindhearted

【心烦】 xīnfán be vexed; be perturbed: ~意乱 be terribly upset

【心服】 xīnfú be genuinely convinced; acknowledge (one's defeat, mistake, etc.) sincerely: ~口服 be sincerely convinced

【心腹】 xīnfù ① trusted subordinate; henchman; reliable agent ② confidential: 说~话 tell sb. sth. in strict confidence; confide in sb.; exchange confidences/ ~事 a secret in the depth of one's heart

【心腹之患】 xīnfù zhī huàn disease in one's vital organs — serious hidden trouble or danger

【心甘情愿】 xīngān-qíngyuàn be most willing to; be perfectly happy to

【心肝】 xīngān ① conscience: 没~ heartless ② darling; deary

【心广体胖】 xīnguǎng-tǐpán carefree and contented; fit and happy

【心寒】 xīnhán 〈方〉 be bitterly disappointed: 令人~ chill the heart; be bitterly disappointing

【心狠】 xīnhěn cruel; merciless: ~手辣 cruel and evil; wicked and merciless

【心花怒放】 xīnhuā nùfàng burst with joy; be wild with joy; be elated

【心怀】 xīnhuái ① harbour; entertain; cherish: ~叵测 harbour dark designs; have evil intentions/ ~不满 feel discontented; nurse a grievance/ ~鬼胎 entertain dark schemes; have ulterior motives ② intention; purpose ③ state of mind; mood

【心慌】 xīnhuāng ① be flustered; be nervous; get alarmed: ~意乱 be alarmed and nervous ② 〈方〉 (of the heart) palpitate

【心灰意懒】 xīnhuī-yìlǎn be disheartened; be downhearted

【心机】 xīnjī thinking; scheming: 枉费~ rack one's brains in vain; make futile efforts/ 费尽~ leave no stone unturned; try all ingenious ways; take great pains; cudgel one's brains

【心迹】 xīnjì the true state of one's mind; true motives or feelings: 表明~ lay bare one's true feelings

【心急】 xīnjí impatient; short-tempered: ~火燎 burning with impatience

【心计】 xīnjì calculation; scheming; planning: 工于~ adept at scheming; very calculating/ 这个年轻人做事很有~. This young chap does things intelligently.

【心焦】 xīnjiāo anxious; worried: 真叫人~啊! This is really worrying!/ 我们等得好~! How anxiously we waited!

【心惊胆战】 xīnjīng-dǎnzhàn tremble with fear; shake with fright

【心惊肉跳】 xīnjīng-ròutiào palpitate with anxiety and fear; be filled with apprehension

【心境】 xīnjìng state (或 frame) of mind; mental state; mood: ~不好 be in a bad mood/ ~非常愉快 be in a very happy mood

【心静】 xīnjìng calm: ~自然凉. So long as one keeps calm, one doesn't feel the heat too much.

【心坎】 xīnkǎn the bottom of one's heart: 我从~里感谢您. I thank you from the bottom of my heart./ 字字句句都说

到我~上. Each word struck a chord in my heart.

【心口如一】 xīn-kǒu rú yī say what one thinks; be frank and unreserved

【心旷神怡】 xīnkuàng-shényí relaxed and happy; carefree and joyous

【心理】 xīnlǐ psychology; mentality: 这位保育员很懂得孩子们的~. That kindergarten teacher understands the children's psychology very well./ 不要养成依赖别人的~. Don't get into the habit of depending on others./ 这是一般人的~. This is how ordinary people feel about it./ 他老说有心脏病,其实是~作用. He's always complaining of heart trouble; but it's only his imagination. ◇ ~病态 morbid state of mind/ ~学 psychology/ ~学家 psychologist/ ~战 psychological warfare

【心力】 xīnlì mental and physical efforts: 费尽~ make strenuous efforts/ ~交瘁 be mentally and physically exhausted

【心里】 xīnli in the heart; at heart; in (the) mind: ~发闷 feel constriction in the area of the heart/ ~不痛快 feel bad about sth./ 记在~ keep (或 bear) in mind/ ~有事 have sth. on one's mind

【心里话】 xīnlihuà one's innermost thoughts and feelings: 说出工人的~ give voice to the workers' innermost feelings/ 我看他没有说~. I don't think he has come out with what's on his mind./ 说~,我真不想去. To be honest, I just don't want to go.

【心灵】 xīnlíng ① clever; intelligent; quick-witted: ~手巧 clever and deft ② heart; soul; spirit: ~深处 deep in one's heart/ 在她幼小的~里 in her childish heart

【心领】 xīnlǐng 〈套〉 〔表示辞谢〕雅意~. I appreciate your kindness but must decline the offer.

【心领神会】 xīnlǐng-shénhuì understand tacitly; readily take a hint: 这个佣人对主人的意图~. The servant understood tacitly what his master wanted.

【心乱如麻】 xīn luàn rú má have one's mind as confused as a tangled skein; be utterly confused and disconcerted; be terribly upset

【心满意足】 xīnmǎn-yìzú be perfectly content (或 satisfied)

【心明眼亮】 xīnmíng-yǎnliàng see and think clearly; be sharp-eyed and clearheaded

【心目】 xīnmù ① mood; frame of mind: 以娱~ to amuse oneself ② memory: 动人情景犹在~. The moving scene remains (或 is still) fresh in our memories. ③ mind; mental view: 在某些人的~中 in some people's eyes

【心平气和】 xīnpíng-qìhé even-tempered and good-humoured; calm: ~地交换意见 exchange views calmly

【心窍】 xīnqiào capacity for clear thinking: 权迷~ be obsessed by a lust for power/ 他的话打开了我的~, 知道该怎么办了. What he said cleared up my thinking and then I knew what to do next.

【心情】 xīnqíng frame (或 state) of mind; mood: ~愉快 be in a cheerful frame (或 state) of mind; be in a good (或 happy) mood; have a light heart/ ~激动 be excited; be thrilled/ ~沉重 with a heavy heart/ ~舒畅 have ease of mind/ ~不一样,感受也不同. People in different frames of mind feel differently about things.

【心曲】 xīnqū 〈书〉 ① innermost being; mind: 乱我~ disturb my peace of mind ② sth. weighing on one's mind: 倾诉~ pour out one's secret concern (或 pent-up feelings); lay one's heart bare

【心如刀割】 xīn rú dāo gē feel as if a knife were piercing one's heart: 她听到这不幸的消息~. The sad news stabbed her to the heart.

【心软】 xīnruǎn be softhearted; be tenderhearted

【心神】 xīnshén mind; state of mind: ~不定 have no peace of mind; be distracted

【心声】 xīnshēng heartfelt wishes; aspirations; thinking: 表达人民的~ voice the aspirations of the people/ 言为~. One's words reflect one's thinking. 或 What the heart thinks the tongue says.

【心事】 xīnshì sth. weighing on one's mind; a load on one's mind; worry: ~重重 be laden with anxiety; be weighed down with care/ 了结一桩~ take a load off one's mind.

one's mind/ 她好象有什么～似的。She seems to have something on her mind.

【心术】 xīnshù intention; design. ～不正 harbour evil intentions (或 designs)

【心思】 xīnsi ① thought; idea: 坏～ a wicked idea/ 想～ ponder; contemplate/ 我猜不透他的～。I can't read his mind. 或 I can't figure out what's on his mind. ② thinking: 用～ do a lot of thinking; think hard/ 白费～ rack one's brains in vain; make futile efforts ③ state of mind; mood: 没有～去看戏 not be in the mood to see a play

【心酸】 xīnsuān be grieved; feel sad

【心算】 xīnsuàn mental arithmetic; doing sums in one's head

【心疼】 xīnténg ① love dearly: 这样惯孩子不是～他。Pampering a child like this is not loving him. ② feel sorry; be distressed: 这么浪费，叫人看了～。It makes one's heart ache to see such waste.

【心跳】 xīntiào palpitation

【心头】 xīntóu mind; heart: 记在～ bear (或 keep) in mind/ ～恨 rankling hatred/ 抑制不住的～的喜悦 be unable to conceal one's delight

【心无二用】 xīn wú èr yòng one cannot keep one's mind on two things at the same time; one should concentrate on one's work

【心细】 xīnxì careful; scrupulous: 胆大～ bold but cautious

【心弦】 xīnxián heartstrings: 动人～ tug at one's heartstrings

【心心相印】 xīn-xīn xiāng yìn have mutual affinity; be kindred spirits

【心胸】 xīnxiōng breadth of mind: ～开阔 broad-minded; unprejudiced/ ～狭窄 narrow-minded; intolerant

【心虚】 xīnxū ① afraid of being found out; with a guilty conscience: 做贼～ have a guilty conscience ② lacking in self-confidence; diffident

【心绪】 xīnxù state of mind: ～不宁 in a disturbed state of mind; in a flutter/ ～烦乱 emotionally upset; in an emotional turmoil

【心血】 xīnxuè painstaking care (或 effort): 费尽～ expend all one's energies/ 多年～的结晶 the fruit of many years' painstaking labour

【心血来潮】 xīnxuè lái cháo be prompted by a sudden impulse; be seized by a whim: ～，忘乎所以 forget oneself in an impulsive moment; be carried away by one's whims and act recklessly

【心眼儿】 xīnyǎnr ① heart; mind: ～小 oversensitive 看到孩子们这么幸福，大家从～里感到高兴。It warms the cockles of the heart to see the children so happy. ② intention: 没安好～ have bad intentions; be up to no good/ ～好 good-natured; kindhearted ③ intelligence; cleverness: 他～多，什么事都想得周到。He is alert and thoughtful./ 长点～，别受人家的骗。Smarten up and don't be taken in. ④ unfounded doubts; unnecessary misgivings: ～多 full of unnecessary misgivings; oversensitive

【心意】 xīnyì ① regard; kindly feelings: 这点礼物是我们大家的一点～。This little gift is a token of our regard. ② intention; purpose: 你们不了解他的～。You don't understand his intention.

【心硬】 xīnyìng hardhearted; stonyhearted; callous; unfeeling

【心有余而力不足】 xīn yǒu yú ér lì bùzú the spirit is willing, but the flesh is weak; unable to do what one wants very much to do

【心有余悸】 xīn yǒu yújì one's heart still fluttering with fear; have a lingering fear

【心猿意马】 xīnyuán-yìmǎ restless and whimsical; fanciful and fickle; capricious

【心愿】 xīnyuàn cherished desire; aspiration; wish; dream

【心悦诚服】 xīn yuè chéng fú feel a heartfelt admiration; be completely convinced: 他对你们的批评～。He fully accepted your criticism.

【心脏】 xīnzàng the heart ◇ ～病 heart disease

【心照】 xīnzhào understand without being told; have an understanding: ～不宣 have a tacit understanding

【心直口快】 xīnzhí-kǒukuài frank and outspoken

【心中有数】 xīnzhōng yǒu shù have a pretty good idea of; know fairly well; know what's what: 对计划执行情况～ have a pretty clear idea of how the plan is being carried out

【心醉】 xīnzuì be charmed; be enchanted; be fascinated

芯 xīn rush pith
另见 xìn

辛* xīn ① hot (in taste, flavour, etc.); pungent ② hard; laborious: 艰～ hardships ③ suffering: ～酸 sad; bitter ④ the eighth of the ten Heavenly Stems

【辛苦】 xīnkǔ ① hard; toilsome; laborious: 犁地这活儿很～。Ploughing is hard work. ② work hard; go to great trouble; go through hardships: 这事恐怕还得你～一趟。I'm afraid you'll have to take the trouble of going there to see about it./ 路上～了。You must have had a tiring journey. 或 Did you have a good trip?

【辛辣】 xīnlà pungent; hot; bitter: ～的味道 a sharp (或 pungent) flavour/ ～的讽刺 bitter irony; biting sarcasm

【辛劳】 xīnláo pains; toil: 日夜～ toil day and night/ 不辞～ spare no pains

【辛勤】 xīnqín industrious; hardworking: ～劳动 work hard; labour assiduously

【辛酸】 xīnsuān sad; bitter; miserable: ～泪 hot and bitter tears/ ～的往事 sad (或 poignant) memories

【辛辛苦苦】 xīnxīnkǔkǔ take a lot of trouble; take great pains; work laboriously: ～地收集技术革新的资料 take great pains in collecting data for technical innovation

欣* xīn glad; happy; joyful: 欢～ happy; joyful/ ～逢佳节 on the happy occasion of the festival

【欣然】 xīnrán 〈书〉 joyfully; with pleasure: ～接受 accept with pleasure/ ～同意 gladly consent; readily agree

【欣赏】 xīnshǎng appreciate; enjoy; admire: 音乐～ music appreciation/ ～风景 enjoy (或 admire) the scenery/ 我很～这个花园的格局。I admire the layout of this garden. 或 I like the way the garden is laid out.

【欣慰】 xīnwèi be gratified: 我们对实验的成功感到～。We were gratified at the success of the experiment./ 获悉你身体康复，至感～。I am relieved to learn that you have recovered from your illness.

【欣悉】 xīnxī be glad (或 happy) to learn

【欣喜】 xīnxǐ glad; joyful; happy: ～若狂 be wild with joy; go into raptures

【欣羡】 xīnxiàn 〈书〉 admire

【欣欣向荣】 xīnxīn xiàng róng thriving; flourishing; prosperous: 一派～的景象 a picture of prosperity/ 我国国民经济～。Our national economy is thriving.

【欣幸】 xīnxìng be glad and thankful

锌 xīn 〈化〉 zinc (Zn)

新* xīn ① new; fresh; up-to-date: ～社会 the new society/ ～技术 new (或 up-to-date) technique/ 最～消息 the latest news ② newly; freshly; recently: ～建的工厂 a newly built factory/～上油漆的门 a freshly-painted door/ 他是～来的。He's a new arrival. ③ recently married: ～人 newlywed

【新陈代谢】 xīn-chén dàixiè ① 〈生〉 metabolism: 生物都有～，有生长、繁殖和死亡。All living matter undergoes a process of metabolism: it grows, reproduces and perishes. ② the new superseding the old: ～是宇宙间普遍的永远不可抵抗的规律。The supersession of the old by the new is a general, eternal and inviolable law of the universe.

【新仇旧恨】 xīnchóu-jiùhèn new hatred piled on old; old scores and new

【新春】 xīnchūn the 10 or 20 days following Lunar New Year's Day

【新大陆】 Xīn Dàlù the New World — the Americas

【新房】 xīnfáng bridal chamber

【新妇】 xīnfù bride

【新官上任三把火】 xīnguān shàngrèn sān bǎ huǒ a new official applies strict measures; a new broom sweeps clean

【新婚】 xīnhūn newly-married: ～夫妇 newly-married couple; newlyweds

【新纪元】 xīnjìyuán new era; new epoch: 开创～ usher in a new epoch; open a new era

【新交】 xīnjiāo new acquaintance; new friend: 他与老王是～。 He and Lao Wang have become acquainted only recently.

【新教】 Xīnjiào ＜宗＞ Protestantism ◇ ～徒 Protestant

【新近】 xīnjìn recently; lately; in recent times

【新居】 xīnjū new home; new residence

【新来乍到】 xīnlái-zhàdào newly arrived: 我～，请多帮助。 I'm a newcomer here and would be glad to have your help.

【新郎】 xīnláng bridegroom

【新名词】 xīnmíngcí new term; new expression; vogue word; newfangled phrase: 满口～ mouthing newfangled phrases

【新年】 xīnnián New Year: ～好！ Happy New Year!／～献词 New Year message

【新娘】 xīnniáng bride

【新瓶装旧酒】 xīnpíng zhuāng jiùjiǔ old wine in a new bottle — the same old stuff with a new label

【新奇】 xīnqí strange; novel; new: ～的想法 a novel idea／他初到矿山时,处处觉得～。 When he first got to the mine, everything struck him as new.

【新人】 xīnrén ① people of a new type: ～新事 new people and new things ② new personality; new talent: 科学界涌现出了一批～。 A new batch of gifted people has emerged in the world of science. ③ newlywed, esp. the bride

【新生】 xīnshēng ① newborn; newly born: ～婴儿 newborn (baby) ② new life; rebirth; regeneration

【新生力量】 xīnshēng lìliàng newly emerging force; new rising force; new force

【新生事物】 xīnshēng shìwù newly emerging things; new things

【新诗】 xīnshī free verse written in the vernacular

【新石器时代】 Xīnshíqì Shídài the Neolithic Age; the New Stone Age

【新式】 xīnshì new type; latest type; new-style: ～农具 new types of farm implements; improved farm implements／～武器 modern weapons

【新手】 xīnshǒu new hand; raw recruit

【新闻】 xīnwén news: 头版～ front-page news (或 story)／简明～ news in brief ◇ ～处 office of information; information service／～稿 press (或 news) release／～工作者 journalist／～公报 press communiqué／～广播 newscast／～记者 newsman; newspaperman; reporter; journalist／～简报 news summary／～界 press circles; the press／～片 newsreel; news film

【新鲜】 xīnxiān ① fresh: 空气～ fresh air／～牛奶 fresh milk／鱼有点不～了。 The fish is slightly off.／尝个～ have a taste of what is just in season ② new; novel; strange: ～经验 new (或 fresh) experience／这话真～。 That's a strange thing to say.

【新兴】 xīnxīng new and developing; rising; burgeoning: ～工业城市 a developing industrial city／～的独立国家 newly independent countries／～势力 the rising forces; the forces in the ascendant

【新颖】 xīnyǐng new and original; novel: 题材～ original in choice of subject (或 theme)／式样～ in a novel style

【新约】 Xīnyuē ＜基督教＞ the New Testament

【新月】 xīnyuè ① crescent ② ＜天＞ new moon

【新装】 xīnzhuāng new clothes: 山村换～。 The mountain village takes on a new look.

薪* xīn ① firewood; faggot; fuel ② salary: 发～ pay out the salary

【薪俸】 xīnfèng salary; pay

【薪金】 xīnjīn salary; pay

【薪水】 xīnshuǐ salary; pay; wages

馨 xīn ＜书＞ strong and pervasive fragrance

【馨香】 xīnxiāng ＜书＞ ① fragrance ② smell of burning incense

【馨香祷祝】 xīnxiāng dǎozhù ① burn incense and pray to the gods ② earnestly pray for sth.; sincerely wish

xín

寻 xín
另见 xún

【寻短见】 xín duǎnjiàn commit suicide; take one's own life

【寻死】 xínsǐ ① try to commit suicide; attempt suicide ② commit suicide

【寻死觅活】 xínsǐ-mìhuó repeatedly attempt suicide (in order to threaten)

【寻思】 xínsi think sth. over; consider: 你～～这事该怎么办。 Think over what to do about it.

xìn

芯 xìn core: 岩～ core
另见 xīn

【芯子】 xìnzi ① fuse; wick: 蜡烛～ candle wick ② the forked tongue of a snake

信* xìn ① true: ～而有征 borne out by evidence ② confidence; trust; faith: 取～于民 win the people's confidence (或 trust)／失～ break faith (或 one's promise)／～得过 trustworthy ③ believe: 不～由你 believe it or not／～以为真 accept sth. as true ④ profess faith in; believe in: ～佛 profess Buddhism ⑤ at will; at random; without plan: ～步 walk aimlessly ⑥ sign; evidence: ～号 signal／印～ official seal ⑦ letter; mail: 公开～ an open letter／证明～ certificate; certification ⑧ message; word; information: 口～ a verbal message; an oral message／还没有～儿呢。 No news yet.／你到达后给我来个～儿。 Please send me word of your arrival. ⑨ fuse: 炸药～管 fuse in a blasting charge

【信步】 xìnbù take a leisurely walk; stroll; walk aimlessly

【信贷】 xìndài credit: 长期～ long-term credit

【信封】 xìnfēng envelope

【信奉】 xìnfèng believe in: ～基督教 be a Christian

【信服】 xìnfú completely accept; be convinced: 令人～的论据 convincing argument; argument that carries conviction

【信鸽】 xìngē carrier pigeon; homing pigeon; homer

【信号】 xìnhào signal

【信笺】 xìnjiān letter paper; writing paper

【信件】 xìnjiàn letters; mail

【信教】 xìnjiào profess a religion; be religious

【信口雌黄】 xìnkǒu cíhuáng make irresponsible remarks; wag one's tongue too freely

【信口开河】 xìnkǒu kāihé talk irresponsibly; wag one's tongue too freely; talk nonsense

【信赖】 xìnlài trust; count on; have faith in

【信念】 xìnniàn faith; belief; conviction

【信任】 xìnrèn trust; have confidence in: 得到人民的～ enjoy the trust (或 confidence) of the people ◇ ～投票 vote of confidence

【信赏必罚】 xìnshǎng-bìfá due rewards and punishments will be meted out without fail

【信实】 xìnshí trustworthy; honest; reliable

【信史】 xìnshǐ true (或 authentic) history; faithful historical account

【信使】 xìnshǐ courier; messenger: 外交～ diplomatic messenger ◇ ～证明书 courier's credentials

【信誓旦旦】 xìnshì dàndàn pledge in all sincerity and seriousness; vow solemnly

【信手拈来】 xìnshǒu niānlái have words, material, etc. at one's fingertips and write with facility

【信守】 xìnshǒu abide by; stand by: ～协议 abide (或 stand) by an agreement／～诺言 keep a promise; be as good as one's word／～不渝 be unswervingly faithful (to one's promise, etc.)

【信条】 xìntiáo article of creed (或 faith); creed; precept; tenet

【信筒】 xìntǒng pillar-box; mailbox

【信徒】 xìntú believer; disciple; follower; adherent; devotee: 佛教～ Buddhist

【信托】 xìntuō trust; entrust
◇ ～公司 trust company/ ～基金 trust fund

【信物】 xìnwù authenticating object; token; keepsake

【信箱】 xìnxiāng ① letter box; mailbox ② post-office box (P.O.B.)

【信心】 xìnxīn confidence; faith: 满怀～ full of confidence/ 有～提前完成任务 be confident of fulfilling a task ahead of schedule/ 我对这药～不大。 I haven't much faith in this medicine.

【信仰】 xìnyǎng faith; belief; conviction: 政治～ political conviction/ 宗教～ religious belief

【信义】 xìnyì good faith; faith: 有～ act in good faith/ 无～ be perfidious

【信用】 xìnyòng ① trustworthiness; credit: 讲～ keep one's word/ 失去～ lose one's credit ② 〈经〉 credit

【信誉】 xìnyù prestige; credit; reputation: 享有很高的国际～ enjoy high international prestige

【信札】 xìnzhá letters

【信纸】 xìnzhǐ letter paper; writing paper

衅 xìn quarrel; dispute: 寻～ pick a quarrel with sb./ 挑～ provoke

【衅端】 xìnduān 〈书〉 a cause for a quarrel or dispute

xīng

兴* xīng ① prosper; rise; prevail; become popular: ～衰 rise and decline; ups and downs/ 新社会不～这一套了。 We don't go in for that sort of thing in the new society. ② start; begin: ～工 start construction/ ～兵 send an army ③ encourage; promote: 大～调查研究之风 energetically encourage the practice of investigation and study ④ 〈书〉 get up; rise: 夙～夜寐 rise early and retire late —— work hard ⑤ 〈方〉〔通常用于否定〕 permit; allow: 不～胡说！ None of your nonsense!
另见 xìng

【兴办】 xīngbàn initiate; set up: ～福利事业 initiate welfare work

【兴奋】 xīngfèn ① be excited: 他～得睡不着觉。 He was too excited to fall asleep. ② 〈生理〉 excitation ◇ ～剂 excitant; stimulant/ ～性 excitability

【兴风作浪】 xīngfēng-zuòlàng stir up (或 make) trouble; fan the flames of disorder

【兴革】 xīnggé 〈书〉 initiation (of the new) and abolition (of the old); reforms

【兴建】 xīngjiàn build; construct: 正在～一座大坝。 A dam is now under construction./ 又～了一个化肥厂。 Another fertilizer plant has been built.

【兴利除弊】 xīnglì-chúbì promote what is beneficial and abolish what is harmful

【兴隆】 xīnglóng prosperous; thriving; flourishing; brisk: 生意～。 Business is brisk.

【兴起】 xīngqǐ rise; spring up; be on the upgrade: 激光是六十年代初期～的一门新科学。 Laser is a new branch of science which rose in the early 1960s.

【兴盛】 xīngshèng prosperous; flourishing; thriving; in the ascendant: 国家～ prosperity of the nation

【兴师】 xīngshī 〈书〉 send an army; dispatch troops

【兴师动众】 xīngshī-dòngzhòng move troops about and stir up the people —— drag in many people (to do sth.): 这点小事，用不着～。 It's only a small matter; you needn't make a fuss about it and drag in a lot of people.

【兴师问罪】 xīngshī wèn zuì send a punitive expedition against

【兴亡】 xīng-wáng rise and fall (of a nation)

【兴旺】 xīngwàng prosperous; flourishing; thriving: 青年人朝气蓬勃，正在～时期。 Young people, full of vitality,

are in the heyday of life.

【兴修】 xīngxiū start construction (on a large project); build: ～水利 build water conservancy projects

【兴妖作怪】 xīngyāo-zuòguài conjure up a host of demons to make trouble; stir up trouble

星* xīng ① star: ～空 starlit sky; starry sky ② heavenly body: 彗～ comet/ 卫～ satellite ③ bit; particle: 一～半点 a tiny bit/ 火～儿 spark

【星辰】 xīngchén stars

【星斗】 xīngdǒu stars: 满天～ a star-studded sky

【星号】 xīnghào asterisk (*)

【星河】 xīnghé 〈天〉 the Milky Way

【星火】 xīnghuǒ ① spark: ～燎原。 A single spark can start a prairie fire. ② shooting star; meteor: 急如～ most urgent

【星际】 xīngjì interplanetary; interstellar: ～飞行 interplanetary (或 space) flight

【星罗棋布】 xīngluó-qíbù scattered all over like stars in the sky or men on a chessboard; spread all over the place: 全国中小型水利工程～。 Small and medium-sized irrigation works spread all over the country.

【星期】 xīngqī ① week: 今天～几？ What day (of the week) is it today?/ 本～ this week/ 上～ last week/ 下～ next week ② Sunday: ～休息。 Sunday is a holiday. 或 Sunday is our day off.
◇ ～日(天) Sunday (Sun.)/ ～一 Monday (Mon.)/ ～二 Tuesday (Tues.)/ ～三 Wednesday (Wed.)/ ～四 Thursday (Thur.)/ ～五 Friday (Fri.)/ ～六 Saturday (Sat.)

【星球】 xīngqiú celestial (或 heavenly) body

【星散】 xīngsàn 〈书〉 (of one's family, friends, etc.) scattered about like the stars; scattered far and wide

【星系】 xīngxì 〈天〉 galaxy

【星星】 xīngxing tiny spot: 天空晴朗，一～云彩也没有。 The sky is clear and bright without a speck of cloud./ ～之火，可以燎原。 A single spark can start a prairie fire.

【星星】 xīngxing 〈口〉 star

【星星点点】 xīngxingdiǎndiǎn tiny spots; bits and pieces: 对于科学的最新成就我只是～知道一些。 I have only fragmentary knowledge of the latest scientific achievements.

【星夜】 xīngyè on a starlit (或 starry) night; by night: ～启程 set out by starlight; set out in great haste

【星移斗转】 xīngyí-dǒuzhuǎn change in the positions of the stars —— change of the seasons; passage of time

【星云】 xīngyún 〈天〉 nebula: 旋涡～ spiral nebula/ 银河～ galactic nebula/ 蟹状～ Crab Nebula/ 网状～ network nebula

【星占】 xīngzhān divine by astrology; cast a horoscope ◇ ～术 astrology

【星座】 xīngzuò 〈天〉 constellation

惺 xīng

【惺忪】 xīngsōng (of eyes) not yet fully open on waking up: 睡眼～ eyes still heavy with sleep; sleepy eyes

【惺惺】 xīngxīng ① clearheaded; awake ② wise; intelligent: ～惜～。 The wise appreciate one another. ③ 见"假惺惺" jiǎxīngxīng

【惺惺作态】 xīngxīng zuò tài be affected; simulate (friendship, innocence, etc.)

猩* xīng orangutan

【猩红】 xīnghóng scarlet: 血红 bloodred

【猩猩】 xīngxing 〈动〉 orangutan: 大～ gorilla/ 黑～ chimpanzee

腥* xīng ① raw meat or fish: 荤～ dishes of meat

or fish ② having the smell of fish, seafood, etc.

【腥臭】 xīngchòu stinking smell as of rotten fish, stench

【腥气】 xīngqì ① the smell of fish, seafood, etc. ② stinking; fishy

【腥味儿】 xīngwèir smelling of fish; fishy

xíng

刑* xíng ① punishment: 死~ capital punishment; the death penalty/ ~满释放 be released after serving a sentence ② torture; corporal punishment: 用~ put sb. to torture; torture

【刑场】 xíngchǎng execution ground

【刑罚】 xíngfá <法> penalty; punishment

【刑法】 xíngfǎ <法> penal code; criminal law

【刑法】 xíngfa corporal punishment; torture: 动了~ administer corporal punishment/ 受了~ suffer corporal punishment

【刑具】 xíngjù instruments of torture; implements of punishment

【刑律】 xínglǜ <法> criminal law: 触犯~ violate the criminal law

【刑期】 xíngqī <法> term of imprisonment; prison term

【刑事】 xíngshì <法> criminal; penal
◇ ~案件 criminal case/ ~处分 criminal sanction/ ~法庭 criminal court/ ~犯 criminal offender; criminal/ ~犯罪 criminal offence; crime

【刑讯】 xíngxùn <法> inquisition by torture: ~逼供 extort a confession by torture; subject sb. to the third degree

邢 Xíng a surname

行* xíng ① go: 步~ go on foot; walk/ 日~百里 cover a hundred li a day ② travel: ~程 route or distance of travel/非洲之~ a trip to Africa ③ temporary; makeshift: ~灶 makeshift cooking stove④ be current; prevail; circulate: 风~一时 be popular (或 in fashion) for a time; be all the rage/ 货币发~ monetary issue; issue of bank notes ⑤ do; perform; carry out; engage in: 实~ carry out; put into effect/ 简便易~ simple and easy to do/ ~窃 commit theft/ ~骗 practise deception; cheat ⑥〔用于双音动词前，表示进行某项活动〕: 另~安排 make other (或 separate) arrangements ⑦ behaviour; conduct: 品~ character; conduct/ 言~ words and deeds ⑧ all right; O. K.: 在快车道上骑车不~。 Cycling along the motorway is not allowed./ 你替我到邮局跑一趟，~吗？ ── ~! Would you run over to the post office for me? ── O. K.! ⑨ capable; competent: 老王，你真~! Lao Wang, you are really terrific (或 something great)!/ 你看他干这工作~吗？ Do you think he is up to it?/ 不要认为只有自己才~。 Don't think that you're the only capable one. ⑩ <书> soon: ~将完毕 soon to be completed
另见 háng

【行不通】 xíngbutōng won't do (或 work); get nowhere: 这个计划~。 This plan won't work./ 这样的作法是绝对~的。 This course of action will get us absolutely nowhere.

【行车】 xíngchē drive a vehicle

【行程】 xíngchéng route or distance of travel: ~一万多公里 travel over 10,000 kilometres

【行船】 xíngchuán sail a boat; navigate

【行刺】 xíngcì assassinate

【行动】 xíngdòng ① move (或 get) about: ~不便 have difficulty getting about/ ~缓慢 move slowly; be slow-moving ② act; take action: ~起来 go into action/ 按计划~。 Proceed according to plan. ③ action; operation: 军事~ military operations ◇ ~纲领 programme of action

【行方便】 xíng fāngbiàn make things convenient for sb.; be accommodating

【行宫】 xínggōng imperial palace for short stays away from the capital; temporary dwelling place of an emperor when away from the capital

【行好】 xínghǎo act charitably; be merciful (或 charitable)

【行贿】 xínghuì bribe; offer a bribe; resort to bribery

【行将】 xíngjiāng <书> about to; on the verge of: ~就道 about to set out on a journey

【行将就木】 xíngjiāng jiù mù be getting nearer and nearer the coffin — be fast approaching death; have one foot in the grave

【行劫】 xíngjié commit robbery; rob

【行进】 xíngjìn march forward; advance

【行经】 xíngjīng go (或 pass) by: 火车~山谷的时候，已是半夜了。 It was midnight when the train passed through Bangkok.

【行径】 xíngjìng act; action; move: 侵略~ act of aggression/ 野蛮~ barbarous act

【行军】 xíngjūn (of troops) march: 夜~ night march; march by night/ 急~ rapid march

【行乐】 xínglè <书> indulge in pleasures; seek amusement; make merry

【行礼】 xínglǐ salute

【行李】 xíngli luggage; baggage: 超重~ excess luggage/ 手提~ hand-luggage

【行猎】 xíngliè <书> hunt; go hunting

【行旅】 xínglǚ traveller; wayfarer: ~称便 travellers find it convenient

【行囊】 xíngnáng <书> travelling bag

【行期】 xíngqī date of departure: ~已近。 The date of departure is drawing near.

【行乞】 xíngqǐ beg one's bread; beg alms; beg

【行人】 xíngrén pedestrian: ~走便道。 Pedestrians, keep to the sidewalk (或 footpath)!

【行若无事】 xíng ruò wú shì behave as if nothing had happened

【行色】 xíngsè circumstances or style of departure: ~匆匆 in a hurry to go on a trip/ 以壮~ (give a grand send-off, etc.) to enable sb. to depart in style

【行善】 xíngshàn do good works

【行商】 xíngshāng itinerant trader; pedlar

【行尸走肉】 xíngshī-zǒuròu a walking corpse — one who vegetates; an utterly worthless person

【行使】 xíngshǐ exercise; perform: ~检察权 exercise procuratorial authority

【行驶】 xíngshǐ (of a vehicle, ship, etc.) go; ply; travel: 列车向南~。 The train is going south./ 汽车正以每小时八十公里的速度~着。 The car was doing eighty kilometres an hour.

【行事】 xíngshì ① act; handle matters: 按计划~ act according to plan ② behaviour; conduct

【行书】 xíngshū running hand (in Chinese calligraphy)

【行为】 xíngwéi action; behaviour; conduct: 正义的~ righteous action/ 不法~ illegal act

【行文】 xíngwén ① style or manner of writing: ~流畅 read smoothly ② (of a government office) send an official communication to other organizations

【行销】 xíngxiāo be on sale; sell: ~全国 be on sale throughout the country

【行星】 xíngxīng <天> planet

【行刑】 xíngxíng carry out a death sentence; execute

【行凶】 xíngxiōng commit physical assault or murder; do violence

【行医】 xíngyī practise medicine (usu. on one's own)

【行云流水】 xíngyún-liúshuǐ (of style of writing) like floating clouds and flowing water — natural and smooth: 他的文章如~，流畅自然。 He writes with natural grace.

【行政】 xíngzhèng administration

【行之有效】 xíng zhī yǒuxiào effective (in practice); effectual: ~的办法 effective measures

【行止】 xíngzhǐ <书> ① whereabouts: ~不明 whereabouts unknown/ ~无定 there's no telling where sb. is ② behaviour; conduct: ~有亏。 His conduct has some shortcomings.

【行装】 xíngzhuāng outfit for a journey; luggage: 整理~ pack (for a journey)

【行踪】 xíngzōng whereabouts; track: ~不定 be of uncertain whereabouts

【行走】 xíngzǒu walk: 起重机下，禁止~或停留。 Walking or

standing under the crane is prohibited./ 在崎岖的山路上 ~ walk on a rugged mountain path

形 * xíng ① form; shape: 不成~ shapeless; formless/ 方~ square ② body; entity: 有~ tangible/ 无~ intangible ③ appear; look: 喜~于色 look very pleased; beam with undisguised happiness ④ compare; contrast: 相~之 下 by comparison; by contrast

【形成】 xíngchéng take shape; form: ~鲜明的对比 form a sharp contrast/ ~风气 become a common practice/ 近代 自然科学是从有了实验科学之后才~的。 Modern natural science came into being only after the emergence of experimental science.

【形单影只】 xíngdān-yǐngzhī a solitary form, a single shadow — extremely lonely; solitary

【形骸】 xínghái 〈书〉 the human skeleton; the human body

【形迹】 xíngjī ① a person's movements and expression: 不露~ betray nothing in one's expression and movements/ ~可疑 of suspicious appearance; suspicious-looking ② formality: 不拘~ without formality; not standing on ceremony

【形容】 xíngróng ① 〈书〉 appearance; countenance: ~憔悴 looking wan; thin and pallid ② describe: 难以~ difficult to describe; beyond description

【形容词】 xíngróngcí 〈语〉 adjective

【形式】 xíngshì form; shape: 从思想内容到艺术~ both in ideological content and in artistic form

【形式上】 xíngshìshang in form; formal: ~的一致 formal unity/ ~的独立 nominal independence/ 在~保持外交关系 maintain formal diplomatic relations

【形势】 xíngshì ① terrain; topographical features: ~险要 strategically important terrain ② situation; circumstances: ~越来越好。 The situation is getting better and better./ ~ 逼人。 The situation is pressing. 或 The situation demands action./ ~发展的必然结果 the inevitable result of developing circumstances

【形似】 xíngsì be similar in form or appearance

【形态】 xíngtài form; shape; pattern: 社会经济~ social-economic formation; economic formation of society

【形体】 xíngtǐ ① shape (of a person's body); physique; body ② form and structure: 文字的~ form of the written character

【形象】 xíngxiàng image; form; figure

【形象思维】 xíngxiàng sīwéi thinking in (terms of) images: 诗是用~的。 Poetry conveys ideas by means of images.

【形形色色】 xíngxíngsèsè of every hue; of all shades; of all forms; of every description: of every hue/ ~的错误 思想 erroneous ideas of every description

【形影不离】 xíng-yǐng bù lí inseparable as body and shadow; always together

【形状】 xíngzhuàng form; appearance; shape

型 * xíng ① mould: 砂~ sand mould ② model; type; pattern: 新~ new model/ 血~ blood group

xǐng

省 * xǐng ① examine oneself critically: 反~ make a self-examination; introspect ② visit (esp. one's parents or elders) ③ become conscious; be aware: 不~人事 lose consciousness 另见 shěng

【省察】 xǐngchá examine oneself critically; examine one's thoughts and conduct

【省亲】 xǐngqīn pay a visit to one's parents or elders (living at another place)

【省视】 xǐngshì ① call upon; pay a visit to ② examine carefully; inspect

醒 * xǐng ① regain consciousness; sober up; come to:

酒醉未~ be drunk and not sobered up yet/ 他~过来了。 He's come to. ② wake up; be awake: 如梦初~ like awakening from a dream/ 他还~着呢。 He is still awake. ③ be clear in mind: 头脑清~ keep a cool head ④ be striking to the eye: ~眼 catch the eye

【醒豁】 xǐnghuò clear; explicit: 道理说得~。 The argument is clearly presented.

【醒酒】 xǐngjiǔ dispel the effects of alcohol; sober up

【醒目】 xǐngmù (of written words or pictures) catch the eye; attract attention; be striking: ~的标语 eye-catching slogans/ ~的标题 bold headlines

【醒悟】 xǐngwù come to realize (或 see) the truth, one's error, etc.; wake up to reality

擤 xǐng blow (one's nose): ~鼻涕 blow one's nose

xìng

兴 * xìng mood or desire to do sth.; interest; excitement: 游~ the mood for sight-seeing/ 酒~ excitement due to drinking/ 诗~ an exalted, poetic mood 另见 xīng

【兴冲冲】 xìngchōngchōng (do sth.) with joy and expedition; excitedly: 他~地跑进来,告诉我这个好消息。 He rushed into the room excitedly and told me the good news.

【兴高采烈】 xìnggāo-cǎiliè in high spirits; in great delight; jubilant: 人们~地参加祝捷大会。 People were jubilant at the victory celebration.

【兴会】 xìnghuì a sudden flash of inspiration; brain wave: 这首诗是乘一时的~写成的。 This poem was improvised on the spur of the moment.

【兴趣】 xìngqù interest: 我对下棋不感~。 I'm not interested in chess.

【兴味】 xìngwèi interest: ~索然 uninterested; bored stiff/ 青少年们~盎然地阅读各种新出版的小说。 Teen-agers read the newly-published novels with keen interest.

【兴致】 xìngzhì interest; mood to enjoy: ~勃勃 full of zest

杏 xìng apricot

【杏仁】 xìngrén apricot kernel; almond

性 * xìng ① nature; character; disposition: 本~ inherent character; nature ② property; quality: 药~ medicinal properties/ 酒~ alcoholic strength ③ 〈后缀,表示性质、范围或方式〉: 正确~ correctness/ 可能~ possibility/ 灵活~ flexibility ④ sex: 男 (女) ~ the male (female) sex/ ~行为 the sex act ⑤ 〈语〉 gender: 阳~ the masculine gender/ 阴~ the feminine gender/ 中~ the neuter gender

【性别】 xìngbié sexual distinction; sex

【性病】 xìngbìng venereal disease; V. D.

【性格】 xìnggé nature; disposition; temperament: ~开朗 have a bright and cheerful disposition

【性急】 xìngjí impatient; short-tempered

【性交】 xìngjiāo sexual intercourse

【性命】 xìngmìng life

【性命交关】 xìngmìng jiāoguān (a matter) of life and death; of vital importance 又作"性命攸关"

【性能】 xìngnéng function (of a machine, etc.); performance; property

【性器官】 xìngqìguān 〈生理〉 sexual organs; genitals

【性情】 xìngqíng disposition; temperament; temper: ~温柔 have a gentle disposition/ ~暴躁 have an irascible temperament; be short-tempered

【性欲】 xìngyù sexual desire (或 urge)

【性质】 xìngzhì quality; nature; character: 弄清问题的~ ascertain the nature of the problem

【性子】 xìngzi ① temper: 使~ get into a temper/ 这匹马的~ 很野。 This is a vicious horse. ② strength; potency: 这 药~平和。 This is a mild drug./ 这酒的~很烈。 This liquor is very strong.

幸* xìng ① good fortune: 有～ be lucky; have good fortune/ ～甚 very fortunate indeed ② rejoice: 庆～ congratulate oneself; rejoice ③ 〈书〉 I hope; I trust: ～勿推却。I hope that you will not refuse. 或 Pray do not refuse. ④ fortunately; luckily: ～未成灾。Fortunately it didn't cause a disaster. ⑤ 〈书〉 favour: 得～ gain favour/ ～臣 a favourite at court ⑥ (of a monarch) come; arrive: 巡～ imperial tour of inspection

【幸而】 xìng'ér luckily; fortunately

【幸福】 xìngfú ① happiness; well-being: 为人民谋～ work for the well-being of the people/ 祝你～。I wish you happiness. ② happy: ～的回忆 happy memories

【幸亏】 xìngkuī 〈副〉 fortunately; luckily: 我～走得早,才没叫雨淋了。Luckily I left early and wasn't caught in the rain.

【幸免】 xìngmiǎn escape by sheer luck; have a narrow escape: ～于难 escape death by sheer luck; escape death by a hair's breadth

【幸运】 xìngyùn ① good fortune; good luck ② fortunate; lucky ◇ ～儿 fortune's favourite; lucky fellow

【幸灾乐祸】 xìngzāi-lèhuò take pleasure in (或 gloat over) others' misfortune

姓* xìng surname; family (或 clan) name: 他～王。He is surnamed Wang. 或 His surname is Wang.

【姓名】 xìngmíng surname and personal name; full name

【姓氏】 xìngshì surname

悻 xìng

【悻悻】 xìngxìng angry; resentful: ～而去 go away angry; leave in a huff

xiōng

凶* xiōng ① inauspicious; ominous: ～兆 ill omen ② crop failure: ～年 a year of crop failure or famine; a bad year ③ fierce; ferocious: 这个人样子真～。This chap looks really fierce. ④ terrible; fearful: 病势很～ terribly ill/ 闹得太～了! What a terrific row! /这场雨来势很～。The rain came down with a vengeance. ⑤ act of violence; murder: 行～ commit physical assault or murder

【凶暴】 xiōngbào fierce and brutal

【凶残】 xiōngcán fierce and cruel; savage and cruel

【凶多吉少】 xiōngduō-jíshǎo bode ill rather than well; be fraught with grim possibilities

【凶恶】 xiōng'è fierce; ferocious; fiendish

【凶犯】 xiōngfàn one who has committed homicide or mayhem; murderer

【凶悍】 xiōnghàn fierce and tough

【凶耗】 xiōnghào news of sb.'s death

【凶狠】 xiōnghěn fierce and malicious

【凶横】 xiōnghèng fierce and arrogant

【凶猛】 xiōngměng violent; ferocious: 山洪来势～ The mountain torrents rushed down with a terrifying force.

【凶器】 xiōngqì tool or weapon for criminal purposes; lethal weapon

【凶杀】 xiōngshā homicide; murder: 这是一件～案。This is a case of murder.

【凶神】 xiōngshén demon; fiend

【凶神恶煞】 xiōngshén-èshà devils; fiends

【凶手】 xiōngshǒu murderer; assassin; assailant (who has caused injury to sb.)

【凶险】 xiōngxiǎn in a very dangerous state; critical: 病情～ dangerously ill; critically ill; in a critical condition

【凶相】 xiōngxiàng ferocious features; fierce look: ～毕露 look thoroughly ferocious; unleash all one's ferocity

【凶信】 xiōngxìn news of sb.'s death

【凶焰】 xiōngyàn ferocity; aggressive arrogance: ～万丈 extremely ferocious

【凶宅】 xiōngzhái haunted house; unlucky abode

【凶兆】 xiōngzhào ill omen; boding of evil

兄* xiōng ① elder brother: 胞～ elder brother of the same parents ② a courteous form of address between men

【兄弟】 xiōngdì ① brothers: 我们～三人 we three brothers ② fraternal; brotherly: ～党 fraternal parties/ ～般的团结 fraternal solidarity; brotherly unity

【兄弟】 xiōngdi 〈口〉 ① younger brother ② a familiar form of address for a man younger than oneself: 大～,这件事就托你了。And so, brother, I'll leave the matter in your hands. ③ your humble servant; I

【兄弟阋墙】 xiōngdì xì qiáng quarrel between brothers; internal dispute: 兄弟阋于墙,外御其侮。Brothers quarrelling at home join forces against attacks from without. 或 Internal disunity dissolves at the threat of external invasion.

【兄长】 xiōngzhǎng a respectful form of address for an elder brother or a man friend

匈 xiōng 〈书〉 见"胸" xiōng

汹 xiōng

【汹汹】 xiōngxiōng 〈书〉 ① the sound of roaring waves ② violent; truculent: 气势～ blustering and truculent ③ tumultuous; agitated: 议论～ tumultuous debate; heated discussion/ 群情～。Public feeling ran high. 或 Public opinion was deeply stirred.

【汹涌】 xiōngyǒng tempestuous; turbulent: 波涛～ turbulent waves

【汹涌澎湃】 xiōngyǒng péngpài surging; turbulent; tempestuous: ～的历史潮流 a tempestuous historical trend

胸* xiōng ① chest; bosom; thorax: 挺～ throw out one's chest/ 孩子把脸贴在母亲的～前。The child buried its face in its mother's bosom. ② mind; heart: ～怀祖国,放眼世界 have the whole country in mind and the whole world in view; keep at heart the interests of both one's own country and the whole world

【胸部】 xiōngbù chest; thorax

【胸怀】 xiōnghuái mind; heart: ～坦白 openhearted; frank

【胸襟】 xiōngjīn mind; breadth of mind: ～开阔 broad-minded; large-minded/ ～狭窄 narrow-minded; small-minded

【胸口】 xiōngkǒu the pit of the stomach

【胸脯】 xiōngpú chest: 挺起～ throw out one's chest/ 拍～保证 strike one's chest as a gesture of guarantee or reassurance

【胸腔】 xiōngqiāng thoracic cavity

【胸膛】 xiōngtáng chest: 挺起～ throw out one's chest

【胸围】 xiōngwéi chest measurement; bust

【胸无点墨】 xiōng wú diǎn mò unlearned; unlettered

【胸有成竹】 xiōng yǒu chéngzhú have a well-thought-out plan, strategem, etc.

【胸中有数】 xiōng yǒu shù have a good idea of how things stand

xióng

雄* xióng ① male: ～猫 male cat; tomcat ② grand; imposing: ～伟 imposing; magnificent ③ powerful; mighty: ～兵 a powerful army ④ a person or state having great power and influence: 英～ hero

【雄辩】 xióngbiàn convincing argument; eloquence: ～地证明 prove incontrovertibly; be eloquent proof of/ 事实胜于～。Facts speak louder than words.

【雄才大略】 xióngcái-dàlüè (a man of) great talent and bold vision; (a statesman ors general of) rare gifts and bold strategy

【雄厚】 xiónghòu rich; solid; abundant: ～的人力物力 rich human and material resources/ 资金～ abundant funds

【雄浑】 xiónghún vigorous and firm; forceful: ～的诗篇 powerful poetry/ 笔力～ vigour of strokes in calligraphy or drawing/ ～高亢的乐曲 resounding music

【雄鸡】 xióngjī cock; rooster
【雄健】 xióngjiàn robust; vigorous; powerful: ～的步伐 vigorous strides
【雄赳赳】 xióngjiūjiū valiantly; gallantly: ～，气昂昂 valiantly and spiritedly
【雄师】 xióngshī powerful army: 百万～ a million bold warriors; a mighty army one million strong
【雄图】 xióngtú great ambition; grandiose plan: ～大业 a grandiose and noble enterprise; a great cause
【雄伟】 xióngwěi grand; imposing; magnificent: 壮丽 grand; sublime
【雄心】 xióngxīn great ambition; lofty aspiration
【雄心壮志】 xióngxīn-zhuàngzhì lofty aspirations and great ideals: 树立～ set up high aims and lofty aspirations; set one's sights high
【雄壮】 xióngzhuàng full of power and grandeur; magnificent; majestic: ～的军乐 majestic martial music
【雄姿】 xióngzī majestic appearance; heroic posture: 我国喷气式战斗机编队飞行的～ the imposing sight of our jet fighters flying in formation

熊* xióng ① bear: 白～ polar bear/ 狗～ Asiatic black bear ② 〈方〉rebuke; upbraid; scold

【熊猫】 xióngmāo 〈动〉panda: 大～ giant panda/ 小～ (lesser) panda
【熊熊】 xióngxióng flaming; ablaze; raging
【熊掌】 xióngzhǎng bear's paw (as a rare delicacy)

xiū

休* xiū ① stop; cease: 争论不～ argue ceaselessly ② rest: ～大礼拜 have a day off every two weeks ③ 〈旧〉cast off one's wife and send her home ④ 〈副〉〔多见于早期白话〕don't: ～要胡言乱语 Don't talk nonsense. ⑤ 〈书〉good fortune: ～咎 good and bad fortune; weal and woe
【休会】 xiūhuì adjourn: 无限期～ adjourn indefinitely (或 sine die)/ 会议～一周。The meeting was adjourned for a week./ ～期间 between sessions; when the meeting stands adjourned/ 会议主席宣布～十分钟。The chairman of the meeting announced a ten-minute recess.
【休假】 xiūjià (of workers, students, etc.) have (或 take, go on) a holiday or vacation; (of soldiers, personnel working abroad, etc.) be on leave or furlough: ～一周 have a week's holiday/ 回国～ go home on furlough
【休眠】 xiūmián 〈生〉dormancy ◇ ～火山 dormant volcano
【休戚】 xiū-qī weal and woe; joys and sorrows: ～与共 share weal and woe; stand together through thick and thin/ ～相关，患难与共 be bound by a common cause and go through thick and thin together
【休息】 xiūxi have (或 take) a rest; rest
【休息】 xiūxi have (或 take) a rest; rest: ～一会儿 rest for a while; have a rest/ 幕间～ intermission; interval/ 课间～ break (between classes)/ ～一天 have (或 take) a day off/ 百货公司元旦不～。The department store is open as usual on New Year's Day. ◇ ～室 lounge; lobby; vestibule; foyer
【休想】 xiūxiǎng don't imagine that it's possible: 你～逃脱。Don't imagine you can get away.
【休学】 xiūxué suspend one's schooling without losing one's status as a student
【休养】 xiūyǎng recuperate; convalesce: ～所 sanatorium; rest home
【休养生息】 xiūyǎng shēngxī (of a nation) recuperate and multiply; rest and build up strength; rehabilitate
【休业】 xiūyè ① suspend business; be closed down: 今天

～。Closed today. ② (of a short-term course, etc.) come to an end; wind up
【休战】 xiūzhàn truce; cease-fire; armistice: ～状态 (state of) cease-fire
【休止】 xiūzhǐ stop; cease: 无～地争论 argue ceaselessly/ 这座火山已进入～状态。The volcano is inactive.

咻 xiū 〈书〉make a din
【咻咻】 xiūxiū 〈象〉〔喘气声或某些动物的叫声〕: ～地喘气 pant noisily/ 小鸭～地叫着。The ducklings are cheeping.

修* xiū ① embellish; decorate: 装～铺面 paint and decorate the front of a shop ② repair; mend; overhaul: ～收音机 repair a radio/ ～鞋 mend shoes ③ write; compile: ～史 write history/ ～县志 compile the historical and other records of a county ④ study; cultivate: 自～ study by oneself ⑤ build; construct: ～铁路 build a railway/ ～水库 construct a reservoir/ ～渠 dig irrigation ditches ⑥ trim; prune: ～指甲 trim (或 manicure) one's fingernails ⑦ 〈书〉long; tall and slender: 茂林～竹 dense forests and tall bamboos
【修补】 xiūbǔ ① mend; patch up; repair; revamp: ～渔网 mend fishing nets/ ～衣服 patch clothes/ ～篱笆 mend a fence ② 〈医〉repair
【修长】 xiūcháng tall and thin; slender: ～的身材 a slender figure
【修船厂】 xiūchuánchǎng shipyard; dockyard
【修辞】 xiūcí rhetoric
【修道】 xiūdào cultivate oneself according to a religious doctrine
【修道院】 xiūdàoyuàn 〈宗〉(男) monastery; (女) convent
【修订】 xiūdìng revise: ～条约 revise a treaty/ ～教学计划 revise a teaching plan ◇ ～本 revised edition
【修复】 xiūfù repair; restore; renovate: 这段铁路已～通车。This section of the railway has been repaired and reopened to traffic./ ～有历史意义的建筑物 renovate historic buildings
【修改】 xiūgǎi revise; modify; amend; alter: ～计划 revise a plan/ ～宪法 amend (或 revise) a constitution/ 对宣草案提出建设性的～意见 submit constructive amendments to the draft declaration
【修函】 xiūhán 〈书〉write a letter
【修好】 xiūhǎo ① 〈书〉foster cordial relations between states ② 〈方〉do good works
【修剪】 xiūjiǎn prune; trim; clip: ～果枝 prune fruit trees/ ～指甲 trim one's fingernails
【修建】 xiūjiàn build; construct; erect: ～机场 build an airport/ ～纪念碑 erect a monument/ ～桥梁 construct a bridge
【修浚】 xiūjùn dredge: ～河道 dredge a river
【修理】 xiūlǐ repair; mend; overhaul; fix: ～机器 repair (或 fix) a machine/ 正在～ be under repair/ 当场～ 立等可取。Repairs done while you wait. ◇ ～店 fix-it shop; repair shop/ ～行业 repairing trades
【修面】 xiūmiàn 〈方〉shave; have a shave ◇ ～膏 shaving cream/ ～刷 shaving brush
【修明】 xiūmíng 〈书〉(of a government) honest and enlightened
【修女】 xiūnǚ 〈宗〉nun (of the Roman Catholic and Greek Orthodox churches); sister: 当～ become a nun; enter a convent
【修配】 xiūpèi make repairs and supply replacements ◇ ～车间 repair and spare parts workshop
【修葺】 xiūqì repair; renovate: ～一新 take on a new look after renovation; be completely renovated
【修缮】 xiūshàn repair; renovate: ～房屋 repair houses
【修身】 xiūshēn cultivate one's moral character
【修士】 xiūshì 〈宗〉brother (of the Roman Catholic and Greek Orthodox churches); friar
【修饰】 xiūshì ① decorate; adorn; embellish ② make up and dress up ③ polish (a piece of writing) ④ 〈语〉qualify; modify
【修书】 xiūshū 〈旧〉① compile a book ② write a letter

【修行】 xiūxíng practise Buddhism or Taoism: 出家～ become a Buddhist or Taoist monk or nun

【修修补补】 xiūxiūbǔbǔ patch up; tinker

【修养】 xiūyǎng ① accomplishment; training; mastery: 有艺术～ be artistically accomplished ② self cultivation

【修业】 xiūyè study at school: ～年限 length of schooling/ ～证书 certificate showing courses attended

【修造】 xiūzào build as well as repair: ～轮船 build or repair ships

【修整】 xiūzhěng ① repair and maintain: ～农具 repair and maintain farm implements ② prune; trim: ～果树 prune fruit trees

【修正】 xiūzhèng revise; amend; correct: 坚持真理，～错误 uphold the truth and correct one's mistakes/ ～草案 a revised draft/ ～后的决议草案 the draft resolution as amended/ 提出对建议的一～意见 put forward amendments to the proposal ◇ ～案 amendment

【修枝】 xiūzhī 〈农〉 pruning ◇ ～剪 pruning scissors; pruning shears

【修筑】 xiūzhù build; construct; put up: ～公路 build highways/ ～工事 construct defences; build fortifications (或 defence works)/ ～堤坝 put up dykes

脩 xiū 见"修" xiū

羞* xiū ① shy; bashful: 害～ feel bashful/ ～红了脸 blush ② shame; disgrace: 遮～ conceal (或 hide) one's shame; 恼～成怒 get angry from shame ③ feel ashamed: ～与为伍 consider it beneath one (或 feel ashamed) to associate with sb. ④ 见"馐" xiū

【羞惭】 xiūcán be ashamed: 满面～ be shamefaced

【羞耻】 xiūchǐ sense of shame; shame: ～之心 sense of shame/ 真不知天下有～事 lose all sense of shame

【羞答答】 xiūdādā coy; shy; bashful 又作"羞羞答答"

【羞愤】 xiūfèn ashamed and resentful

【羞愧】 xiūkuì ashamed; abashed: ～难言 be ashamed beyond words/ ～地低着头 hang one's head for shame

【羞怯】 xiūqiè shy; timid; sheepish: ～得说不出话来 be too shy to utter a word

【羞人】 xiūrén feel embarrassed or ashamed: 羞死人 simply die of shame; feel terribly embarrassed

【羞辱】 xiūrǔ ① shame; dishonour; humiliation ② humiliate; put sb. to shame

【羞涩】 xiūsè shy; bashful; embarrassed

馐 xiū 〈书〉 delicacy; dainty: 珍～ a rare delicacy

xiǔ

朽 xiǔ ① rotten; decayed: 枯木～株 withered trees and rotten stumps ② senile: 老～ old and useless

【朽迈】 xiǔmài 〈书〉 old and weak; senile; decrepit

【朽木】 xiǔmù ① rotten wood or tree ② a hopeless case; a good-for-nothing

【朽木粪土】 xiǔmù-fèntǔ rotten wood and dirt; a worthless person; useless stuff

xiù

秀* xiù ① (of grain crops) put forth flowers or ears: ～穗 put forth ears ② elegant; beautiful: 眉清目～ having well-chiselled features; handsome/ 山清水～ beautiful hills and waters; lovely scenery ③ excellent: 优～ excellent; first-rate

【秀才】 xiùcái ① xiucai, one who passed the imperial examination at the county level in the Ming and Qing dynasties ② scholar; skilful writer

【秀丽】 xiùlì beautiful; handsome; pretty: 这个小姑娘长得很～。This little girl is very pretty.

【秀美】 xiùměi graceful; elegant: 书法～ beautiful handwriting

【秀气】 xiùqi ① delicate; elegant; fine: 眉眼生得～ have beautiful eyes ② (of manners) refined; urbane ③ delicate and well-made

岫 xiù 〈书〉 ① cave ② hill: 远～ a distant hill

袖* xiù ① sleeve: 长（短）～ long (short) sleeves ② tuck inside the sleeve: 他～着手，踱来踱去。He paced the floor, his hands tucked deep in his sleeves.

【袖口】 xiùkǒu cuff (of a sleeve): 衬衫～ wristband

【袖手旁观】 xiùshǒu pángguān look on (或 stand by) with folded arms; look on unconcerned: 看到损害国家财产的现象,不能～。We must not stand by with folded arms when people damage state property.

【袖珍】 xiùzhēn pocket-size; pocket: ～式半导体收音机 pocket-size transistor radio/ ～字典 pocket dictionary/ ～照相机 vest-pocket camera/ ～潜艇 midget submarine ◇ ～本 pocket edition

【袖子】 xiùzi sleeve

绣 xiù ① embroider: 在桌布上～花 embroider flowers on a tablecloth ② embroidery: 苏～ Suzhou embroidery

【绣花】 xiùhuā embroider; do embroidery ◇ ～被面 embroidered quilt cover/ ～丝线 floss silk/ ～鞋 embroidered shoes/ ～针 embroidery needle

【绣花枕头】 xiùhuā zhěntou ① a pillow with an embroidered case ② an outwardly attractive but worthless person

【绣球】 xiùqiú ① a ball made of strips of silk ② 〈植〉 big-leaf hydrangea

【绣像】 xiùxiàng ① tapestry (或 embroidered) portrait ② exquisitely drawn portrait

臭* xiù ① odour; smell: 纯空气是无色无～的。Pure air is colourless and odourless. ② 见"嗅" xiù
另见 chòu

【臭味相投】 xiùwèi xiāngtóu share the same rotten tastes habits, etc.; be two of a kind

锈* xiù ① rust ② become rusty: 门上的锁～住了。The lock on the door is rusty and won't open.

溴 xiù 〈化〉 bromine (Br)

【溴化物】 xiùhuàwù 〈化〉 bromide

嗅* xiù smell; scent; sniff: 警犬～来～去,终于找到了踪迹。The police dog scented about till he found the trail./ 我们对任何东西都要用鼻子～一～,鉴别其好坏。We should take a sniff at everything and distinguish the good from the bad.

【嗅觉】 xiùjué (sense of) smell; scent: ～很灵 have a keen sense of smell/ 政治～灵敏 be politically sharp

xū

戌 xū the eleventh of the twelve Earthly Branches

【戌时】 xūshí the period of the day from 7 p.m. to 9 p.m.

吁 xū 〈书〉 ① sigh: 长～短叹 sighs and groans; moan and groan ② 〈叹〉〔表示惊异〕: why; oh
另见 yù

【吁吁】 xūxū 〈象〉: 气喘～ pant; puff hard

胥 xū 〈书〉 ① petty official ② all; each and every: 万事～备。Everything is ready.

须* xū ① must; have to: 务～注意下列各项。Attention must be paid to the following./ ～作出很大努力 have to make a great effort ② 〈书〉 await: ～我片刻 wait a moment for me ③ beard; mustache: 留~ grow a beard ④ (动物) palpus; feeler; (植物) tassel

【须发】 xūfà beard and hair: ~皆白 white hair and beard

【须眉】 xūméi 〈书〉 beard and eyebrows — a man

【须要】 xūyào must; have to: 做这项工作~细心。 This work needs to be done carefully.

【须臾】 xūyú 〈书〉 moment; instant: ~之间, 雨过天晴。 In an instant the rain stopped and the sky cleared up./ ~不可离 cannot do without even for a moment

【须知】 xūzhī ① one should know that; it must be understood (或 borne in mind) that: ~胜利来之不易。 It must be borne in mind) that: the victory is hard-won. ② points for attention; notice: 游览~ tourist guide; information for tourists/ 旅客~ notice to travellers, passengers, etc.

虚 xū ① void; emptiness: 太~ the great void; the universe/ 乘~而入 infiltrate by taking advantage of the other side's unpreparedness; exploit a weak point ② empty; void; unoccupied: 座无~席。 There was no empty seat. 或 All seats were occupied. ③ diffident; timid; 胆~ timid; milk-livered/ 心里有点~ feel rather diffident ④ in vain: ~此行 have not made the trip in vain/ 箭不~发。 Not a single arrow missed its target. ⑤ false; nominal: ~名 false reputation/ 耳闻为~, 眼见为实。 What you hear about may be false; what you see is true. ⑥ humble; modest: 谦~ modest ⑦ weak; in poor health: 气~ lacking in vital energy; sapless/ 身体很~ be very weak physically ⑧ guiding principles; theory. 务~ discuss principles or ideological guidelines/ 以~带实。 Let correct ideology guide practical work.

【虚报】 xūbào make a false report: ~账目 cook accounts/ ~冒领 make a fraudulent application and claim

【虚词】 xūcí 〈语〉 function word; form word

【虚度】 xūdù spend time in vain; waste: ~光阴 fritter away one's time/ 我们不能让青春~。 We must not let our youth slip idly by.

【虚浮】 xūfú impractical; superficial: ~的计划 an impractical plan/ 作风~ have a superficial style of work

【虚构】 xūgòu fabricate: make up: ~的情节 a made-up story/ ~的人物 a fictitious character/ 纯属~ an out-and-out fabrication; a sheer fabrication

【虚汗】 xūhàn abnormal sweating due to general debility

【虚怀若谷】 xūhuái ruò gǔ have a mind as open as a valley; be very modest; be extremely open-minded

【虚幻】 xūhuàn unreal; illusory: ~的情景 a mere illusion

【虚假】 xūjiǎ false; sham: ~的安全感 a false sense of security/ ~的可能性 spurious possibility/ ~的友谊 hypocritical friendship/ 我感到他对人有点~。 I don't think he is quite honest with people.

【虚惊】 xūjīng false alarm: 受了一场~ be the victim of a false alarm

【虚夸】 xūkuā exaggerative; bombastic; boastful

【虚名】 xūmíng undeserved reputation

【虚拟】 xūnǐ invented; fictitious: 这个故事是~的。 This is a fictitious story.

【虚情假意】 xūqíng-jiǎyì false display of affection; hypocritical show of friendship

【虚荣】 xūróng vanity: 不慕~ not affected by vanity; not vain ◇ ~心 vanity

【虚弱】 xūruò ① in poor health; weak; debilitated: 病后身体很~ suffer from general debility after an illness; be very weak after an illness ② weak; feeble: 兵力~ weak in military strength/ ~的本质 inherent (或 intrinsic) weakness

【虚设】 xūshè nominal; existing in name only: 这个机构形同~。 That organization is but an empty shell.

【虚实】 xū-shí false or true — the actual situation (as of the opposing side): 探听~ try to find out about an opponent, etc.; try to ascertain the strength (of the enemy)

【虚数】 xūshù ① unreliable figure ② 〈数〉 imaginary number

【虚岁】 xūsuì nominal age (reckoned by the traditional method, i.e. considering a person one year old at birth and adding a year each lunar new year)

【虚妄】 xūwàng unfounded; fabricated; invented: ~的故事 a fabricated story

【虚伪】 xūwěi sham; false; hypocritical: 知识的问题是一个科学问题, 来不得半点~和骄傲。 Knowledge is a matter of science, and no dishonesty or conceit whatsoever is permissible.

【虚文】 xūwén ① rules and regulations that have become a dead letter; dead letter ② empty forms: ~浮礼 mere formalities; conventionalities

【虚无】 xūwú nihility; nothingness ◇ ~主义 nihilism/ ~主义者 nihilist

【虚无缥缈】 xūwú-piāomiǎo purely imaginary; entirely unreal; visionary; illusory

【虚线】 xūxiàn ① dotted line or line of dashes ② 〈数〉 imaginary line

【虚象】 xūxiàng 〈物〉 virtual image

【虚心】 xūxīn open-minded; modest: ~听取别人的意见 listen to people's criticisms with an open mind/ ~使人进步, 骄傲使人落后。 Modesty helps one to go forward, whereas conceit makes one lag behind.

【虚掩】 xūyǎn with the door left unlocked or unlatched

【虚应故事】 xū yìng gùshì do sth. perfunctorily as a mere matter of form or as a routine practice

【虚有其表】 xū yǒu qí biǎo look impressive but lack real worth; appear better than it is

【虚与委蛇】 xū yǔ wēiyí deal with sb. courteously but without sincerity; pretend politeness and compliance

【虚张声势】 xū zhāng shēngshì make an empty show of strength; bluff and bluster; be swashbuckling

【虚字】 xūzì empty word; function word; form word

需* xū ① need; want; require: 急~ need badly/ ~款甚巨 require a big sum of money ② necessaries; needs: 必~品 necessaries/ 军~ military supplies (或 requirements)

【需求】 xūqiú requirement; demand

【需要】 xūyào ① need; want; require; demand: 这所房子~修理。 The house wants repairing./ 这种情况~立即采取措施。 This situation requires (或 demands) immediate action. ② needs: 保证人民吃穿的基本~ ensure the people their basic needs in food and clothing

嘘 xū ① breathe out slowly ② utter a sigh ③ (of cooking fire, steam, etc.) come into contact with sth.; scald; burn ④〈叹〉sh; hush ⑤〈方〉hiss; boo: 把他~下台去 hiss (或 boo) him off the platform
另见 shī

【嘘寒问暖】 xūhán-wènnuǎn inquire after sb.'s well-being; be solicitous about sb.'s health

【嘘唏】 xūxī 〈书〉 sob

墟 xū ruins: 废~ ruins

歔 xū

【歔欷】 xūxī 〈书〉 sob: 暗自~ sob in secret

xú

徐 xú slowly; gently: 清风~来。 A refreshing breeze is blowing gently.

【徐步】 xúbù walk slowly (或 leisurely); stroll

【徐徐】 xúxú 〈书〉 slowly; gently

xǔ

许* xǔ ① praise: 赞~ praise; commend ② promise: 他~过我一张票。 He promised me a ticket. ③ allow; permit:

这项任务限三天完成，不～拖延。The task must be accomplished within three days and permits of no delay. ④ maybe; perhaps: 他今天没来，也～是生病了。He didn't come today, perhaps he's ill. ⑤ [表示约略的估计] 少～ somewhat; a little/ 年四十～ about forty years old ⑥ <书> place: 何～人？Where does the person come from?

【许多】 xǔduō many; much; a great deal of; a lot of: ～人 many people/ 积累了～经验 have accumulated much experience/ 我们有～工作要做。We have a lot of work to do.

【许久】 xǔjiǔ for a long time; for ages: 大家商量了～。We talked things over for a long time./ 我们～没有通信了。We have not corresponded for ages.

【许可】 xǔkě permit; allow: 凡是条件～的地方 wherever conditions permit

【许诺】 xǔnuò make a promise; promise

【许配】 xǔpèi (said of an arranged marriage) betroth a girl

【许愿】 xǔyuàn ① make a vow (to a god) ② promise sb. a reward

诩 xǔ <书> brag; boast: 自～为... style oneself...; boast that one is...

栩 xǔ

【栩栩】 xǔxǔ vivid; lively: ～如生 lifelike; to the life

xù

旭 xù <书> brilliance of the rising sun

【旭日】 xùrì the rising sun: ～东升 the sun rising in the eastern sky

序* xù ① order; sequence: 顺～ sequence/ 程～ procedure/ 井然有～ in perfect order ② arrange in order: ～齿 <书> arrange (seats, etc.) in order of age ③ introductory; initial: ～战 initial battle ④ preface: ～文 preface; foreword

【序跋】 xùbá preface and postscript

【序幕】 xùmù prologue; prelude

【序曲】 xùqǔ <乐> overture

【序数】 xùshù ordinal number; ordinal

【序文】 xùwén preface; foreword

【序言】 xùyán preface; foreword

恤 xù ① pity; sympathize: 体～ understand and sympathize with ② give relief; compensate: 抚～ comfort and compensate a disabled person or a bereaved family

【恤金】 xùjīn pension for a disabled person or the family of the deceased

叙 xù ① talk; chat: ～家常 chitchat ② narrate; recount; relate ③ assess; appraise: ～功 assess service and give credit for it ④ 见 "序"②④

【叙别】 xùbié have a farewell talk

【叙旧】 xùjiù talk about the old days

【叙事】 xùshì narrate; recount ◇ ～曲 <乐> ballade/ ～诗 narrative poem/ ～文 narrative; narrative prose

【叙述】 xùshù narrate; recount; relate

【叙说】 xùshuō tell; narrate

【叙谈】 xùtán chat; chitchat

【叙用】 xùyòng appoint (an official); employ

畜* xù raise (domestic animals)
另见 chù

【畜产】 xùchǎn livestock (或 animal) products

【畜牧】 xùmù raise (或 rear) livestock or poultry: 从事～ go in for animal husbandry ◇ ～场 animal farm; livestock (或 stock) farm/ ～业 animal (或 livestock) husbandry; livestock farming

【畜养】 xùyǎng raise (domestic animals)

酗 xù

【酗酒】 xùjiǔ excessive drinking: ～滋事 get drunk and

create a disturbance

绪 xù ① thread; order in sequence or arrangement: 头～ main threads (of a complicated affair); main lines/ 准备就～ be all set ② mental or emotional state: 心～不宁 be in a state of agitation ③ task; cause; undertaking: 续未竟之～ carry on an unfinished task; take up where another has left off

【绪论】 xùlùn introduction

【绪言】 xùyán introduction

续* xù ① continuous; successive ② continue; extend; join: 待～ to be continued/ ～会 extended session; follow-up meeting/ 这条绳子太短，再～上一截儿吧。This piece of string is too short. Join another piece on to it. ③ add; supply more: 壶要烧干了，赶快～水。The kettle (on the fire) is nearly dry. Put some more water in it, quick./ 炉子该～煤了。The fire needs more coal.

【续编】 xùbiān continuation (of a book); sequel

【续订】 xùdìng renew one's subscription to (a newspaper or magazine)

【续集】 xùjí continuation (of a book); sequel

【续假】 xùjià extend one's leave of absence; extend leave: ～一星期 have one's leave extended for another week

【续借】 xùjiè renew (a library book)

【续弦】 xùxián <旧> remarry after the death of one's wife

絮 xù ① (cotton) wadding ② sth. resembling cotton: 柳～ (willow) catkin ③ long-winded; garrulous

【絮叨】 xùdao long-winded; garrulous; wordy

婿* xù ① son-in-law ② husband: 夫～ husband/ 妹～ younger sister's husband

蓄 xù ① store up; save up: 这个水库能～多少水？How much water can this reservoir hold? ② grow: ～须 grow a beard/ ～发 wear one's hair long ③ entertain (ideas); harbour: ～念已久 have long entertained such ideas

【蓄电池】 xùdiànchí storage battery; accumulator ◇ ～车 battery car

【蓄积】 xùjī store up; save up: ～粮食 store up grain

【蓄谋】 xùmóu premeditate: ～已久 long premeditated/ ～迫害 harbour a design of persecuting sb.

【蓄水】 xùshuǐ retain (或 store) water: 在山坡上建池～ dig ponds on the slopes to store water/ 这水库能～二千万立方米。This reservoir has a storage capacity of 20 million cubic metres. ◇ ～池 cistern; reservoir/ ～工程 (water) storage project

【蓄意】 xùyì premeditated; deliberate: ～挑衅 premeditated provocation/ ～进行破坏 deliberately sabotage/ ～干涉别国内政 be bent on interfering in other countries' internal affairs

煦 xù <书> warm; balmy: 春风和～ a balmy spring breeze

xuān

轩 xuān ① <书> high; lofty ② a small room or veranda with windows ③ a high-fronted, curtained carriage used in ancient times ④ <书> window or door

【轩昂】 xuān'áng dignified; imposing: 气宇～ have an imposing appearance; have an impressive presence

【轩敞】 xuānchǎng spacious and bright

【轩然大波】 xuānrán dàbō a great disturbance; a mighty uproar

【轩轾】 xuān-zhì high or low; good or bad: 不分～ be equal; be on a par

宣 xuān ① declare; proclaim; announce: ～示 declare; make known publicly/ ～赦 proclaim a general amnesty/ ～旨 announce an imperial decree ② lead off (liquids); drain: ～泄洪水 drain off floodwater

【宣布】 xuānbù declare; proclaim; announce: ～独立 declare (或 proclaim) independence/ ～会议开始 declare a meeting open; call a meeting to order/ ～无效 declare sth. invalid (或 null and void)/ ～戒严 declare (或 proclaim) martial law/ ～一件事 make an announcement

【宣称】 xuānchēng assert; declare; profess

【宣传】 xuānchuán conduct propaganda; propagate; disseminate; give publicity to

【宣读】 xuāndú read out (in public)

【宣告】 xuāngào declare; proclaim: ～成立 proclaim the founding of (a state, organization, etc.)/ ～无效 declare sth. null and void/ ～破产 declare bankruptcy; go bankrupt

【宣判】 xuānpàn 〈法〉 pronounce judgment: ～有罪(无罪) pronounce sb. guilty (not guilty)

【宣誓】 xuānshì take (或 swear) an oath; make a vow; make a pledge: 庄严～ make a solemn vow/ ～就职 take an oath of office; be sworn in

【宣泄】 xuānxiè ① lead off (liquids); drain ② get sth. off one's chest; unbosom oneself

【宣言】 xuānyán declaration; manifesto

【宣扬】 xuānyáng publicise; propagate; advocate; advertise: ～好人好事 give publicity to good people and their good deeds

【宣战】 xuānzhàn declare (或 proclaim) war

【宣纸】 xuānzhǐ *Xuan* paper, a high quality paper made in Xuancheng (宣城), Anhui Province, esp. good for traditional Chinese painting and calligraphy

喧 xuān noisy: 锣鼓～天 a deafening sound of gongs and drums

【喧宾夺主】 xuān bīn duó zhǔ a presumptuous guest usurps the host's role; the secondary supersedes the primary

【喧哗】 xuānhuá confused noise; hubbub; uproar: 请勿～。 Quiet, please!/ 笑语～ uproarious talk and laughter/ 门外一阵～。 There was a hubbub outside the door.

【喧闹】 xuānnào noise and excitement; bustle; racket

【喧嚷】 xuānrǎng clamour; hubbub; din; racket: 人声～ a hubbub of voices; loud confused voices

【喧扰】 xuānrǎo noise and disturbance; tumult

【喧腾】 xuānténg noise and excitement; hubbub: 广场上一片～。 A hubbub filled the square.

【喧嚣】 xuānxiāo ① noisy: ～的车马声 the noise of dense traffic ② clamour; hullabaloo; din: ～鼓噪 make a clamour; stir up a commotion/ 诸如此类的论调～一时。 This sort of talk created quite a stir.

暄 xuān 〈书〉 warmth (of the sun): 负～ bask in the sunshine

xuán

玄 xuán ① black; dark: ～狐 a black fox ② profound; abstruse: ～理 a profound theory ③〈口〉 unreliable; incredible: 这话太～了。 That's a pretty tall story.

【玄妙】 xuánmiào mysterious; abstruse

【玄孙】 xuánsūn great-great-grandson

【玄虚】 xuánxū deceitful trick; mystery; 故弄～ purposely turn simple things into mysteries; be deliberately mystifying

【玄之又玄】 xuán zhī yòu xuán mystery of mysteries — extremely mysterious and abstruse

旋* xuán ① revolve; circle; spin: 觉得天～地转 feel as if heaven and earth were spinning round and round; feel one's head swim/ 一架飞机在空中盘～。 An airplane is circling in the sky. ② return; come back: 凯～ return in triumph/ ～里 return home ③ part of the scalp where the hair is whorled ④〈书〉 soon: 入场券～即发完。 All the tickets were soon distributed.
另见 xuàn

【旋律】 xuánlù 〈乐〉 melody

【旋绕】 xuánrǎo curl up; wind around: 炊烟～。 Smoke is curling up from the kitchen chimneys./ 他们的歌声在山谷中～。 Their songs reverberated throughout the valley.

【旋涡】 xuánwō whirlpool; vortex; eddy

【旋踵】 xuánzhǒng 〈书〉 in the brief time it takes to turn round on one's heel — in an instant: ～即逝 vanish before one has time to turn round; disappear in the twinkling of an eye

【旋转】 xuánzhuǎn revolve; gyrate; rotate; spin: 陀螺在～。 The top is spinning./ 地球绕地轴～,同时也围绕太阳～。 The earth revolves round the sun on its own axis./ 顺时针方向～ clockwise rotation/ 逆时针方向～ counterclockwise rotation

【旋转乾坤】 xuánzhuǎn qiánkūn effect a drastic change in nature or the established order of a country; be earthshaking

悬 xuán ① hang; suspend: ～灯结彩 hang up lanterns and festoons; adorn with lanterns and festoons ② outstanding; unresolved: ～而未决的问题 an outstanding question/ 这笔账～了好久了。 This account has remained unsettled for a long time. ③ feel anxious; be solicitous: ～念 be anxious about (sb. who is elsewhere) ④ imagine: ～拟 imagine; conjecture ⑤ far apart: ～隔 be separated by a great distance

【悬案】 xuán àn ① unsettled law case ② outstanding issue; unsettled question

【悬挂】 xuánguà hang; fly: 高大的建筑物上～着巨幅标语。 Huge streamers trailed from tall buildings.

【悬空】 xuánkōng ① hang in the air; suspend in midair: 这件事不能老～,要抓紧紧解决。 Let's deal with the matter now; it's hung in the air too long. ② be divorced from reality

【悬梁】 xuánliáng hang oneself from a beam: ～自尽 commit suicide by hanging oneself from a beam; hang oneself

【悬念】 xuánniàn ① 〈书〉 be concerned about (sb. who is elsewhere) ② audience involvement in a film or play; reader involvement in a piece of literature

【悬赏】 xuánshǎng offer (或 post) a reward: ～缉拿逃犯 offer a reward for the capture of a runaway criminal; set a price on a runaway criminal's head

【悬殊】 xuánshū great disparity; wide gap: 力量～ a great disparity in strength

【悬索桥】 xuánsuǒqiáo suspension bridge

【悬梯】 xuántī hanging ladder

【悬想】 xuánxiǎng imagine; fancy

【悬心吊胆】 xuánxīn-diàodǎn on tenterhooks; filled with anxiety or fear

【悬崖】 xuányá overhanging (或 steep) cliff; precipice: ～绝壁 sheer precipice and overhanging rocks

【悬崖勒马】 xuányá lè mǎ rein in at the brink of the precipice — wake up to and escape disaster at the last moment

xuǎn

选* xuǎn ① select; choose; pick: 挑～ pick and choose/ 比赛前～场地 choose sides before a contest ② elect: 普～ general election/ 我们～她当生产队长。 We elected her leader of our production team./ 入～ be chosen (或 selected); be elected ③ selections; anthology: 文～ an anthology of prose/ 诗～ selected poems/ 民歌～ selections of folk songs

【选拔】 xuǎnbá select; choose: ～运动员 select athletes ◇～赛 (selective) trials/ ～委员会 selection committee

【选本】 xuǎnběn anthology; selected works

【选材】 xuǎncái select (suitable) material

【选读】 xuǎndú selected readings: 文学～ selected readings in literature

【选购】 xuǎngòu pick out and buy; choose: 新到各种花布,欢迎～。 A new variety of cotton prints awaits your choice.

【选集】 xuǎnjí selected works (或 writings); selections; anthology

【选举】 xuǎnjǔ elect

【选举权】 xuǎnjǔquán the right to vote; franchise: 有～和被～ have the right to vote and to stand for election

【选民】 xuǎnmín (个人) voter; elector; (全体) constituency;

electorate

◇ ～榜 list of eligible voters/ ～登记 registration of voters/ ～名册 voting register

【选派】 xuǎnpài select; detail: ～代表参加会议 depute sb. to attend a conference; select sb. as representative to a conference

【选票】 xuǎnpiào vote; ballot

【选区】 xuǎnqū electoral (或 election) district; electoral ward; constituency

【选曲】 xuǎnqǔ selected songs (或 tunes)

【选取】 xuǎnqǔ select; choose

【选手】 xuǎnshǒu an athlete selected for a sports meet; (selected) contestant; player: 参加体操比赛的～有几百名。 There were hundreds of contestants in the gymnastics competition.

【选修】 xuǎnxiū take as an elective course: 我们班大部分同学～英语。 Most of the students of our class take English as an elective course. ◇ ～课 elective course

【选样】 xuǎnyàng sampling; sample

【选育】 xuǎnyù 〈农〉 seed selection; breeding: ～良种小麦 wheat variety development by selection

【选择】 xuǎnzé select; choose; opt: ～日期 choose a date/自然～ natural selection/ 没有～的余地 have no choice at all

烜

烜 xuǎn ① ablaze ② bright

【烜赫】 xuǎnhè of great renown and influence

癣

癣 xuǎn tinea; ringworm

xuàn

泫 xuàn drip; trickle

【泫然】 xuànrán (usu. of tears) fall; trickle

炫 xuàn 〈书〉 ① dazzle: 光彩～目 blindingly bright; dazzling splendour ② show off; display: 自～其能 show off one's ability

【炫示】 xuànshì show off; display

【炫耀】 xuànyào make a display of; show off; flaunt: ～力量 flaunt one's strength/ ～武力 make a show of force/ ～自己的学问 parade one's learning

绚 xuàn gorgeous

【绚烂】 xuànlàn splendid; gorgeous: ～的朝霞 gorgeous morning clouds/ ～的杜鹃花 splendid azaleas

【绚丽】 xuànlì gorgeous; magnificent: ～多彩 bright and colourful; gorgeous/ ～的景色 magnificent scenery

昡 xuàn sunshine; sunlight

眩 xuàn 〈书〉 ① dizzy; giddy: 头晕目～ feel dizzy ② dazzled; bewildered: ～于名利 dazzled by the prospect of fame and wealth; obsessed with a desire for fame and wealth

【眩晕】 xuànyùn 〈医〉 ① dizziness: 一阵～ a fit of dizziness ② vertigo

旋* xuàn ① whirl: ～风 whirlwind ② turn sth. on a lathe; lathe; pare: 把一根圆钢～成车轴 shape a round piece of steel into an axle

另见 xuán

【旋风】 xuànfēng whirlwind

渲 xuàn 〈书〉 wash (a piece of drawing paper) with watercolours

【渲染】 xuànrǎn ① apply colours to a drawing ② play up; exaggerate; pile it on: ～战争恐怖 play up the horrors of war/ 轻快的舞蹈给这场戏～了欢乐气氛。 The lively dance heightened the joyous atmosphere of the scene.

楦 xuàn ① shoe last ② hat block ③ shape with a last or block: ～鞋 last a shoe

xuē

削* xuē 〔专用于合成词〕 pare; whittle; cut: 剥～ exploit
另见 xiāo

【削壁】 xuēbì precipice; cliff

【削价】 xuējià cut prices; lower the price

【削减】 xuējiǎn cut (down); reduce; slash; whittle down: ～非生产性开支 cut down nonproductive expenditures; cut back on nonproductive spending

【削弱】 xuēruò weaken; cripple: ～敌人的力量 cripple (或 weaken) the enemy

【削足适履】 xuē zú shì lǚ cut the feet to fit the shoes; act in a Procrustean manner

靴 xuē boots: 马～ riding boots/ 雨～ rubber boots

【靴子】 xuēzi boots

薛 Xuē a surname

xué

穴 xué ① cave; den; hole: 洞～ cave/ 蚁～ ant hole/ 虎～ tiger's lair/ 匪～ bandits' den ② grave ③ 〈中医〉 acupuncture point; acupoint

【穴居】 xuéjū live in caves

【穴位】 xuéwèi 〈中医〉 acupuncture point; acupoint

学* xué ① study; learn: 跟人～绘画 take lessons in painting/ 把新技术～到手 master a new skill/ 你的功课～会了吗? Have you learned your lessons?/ 活到老，～到老。 Keep on learning as long as you live. ② imitate; mimic: 这孩子～他爸爸走路的样子。 The boy imitates his father's way of walking./ ～鸡叫 mimic the crowing of a cock ③ learning; knowledge: 才疏～浅 have little talent and less learning ④ subject of study; branch of learning: 数～ mathematics/ 文～ literature/ 政治经济～ political economy ⑤ school; college: 小～ primary school/ 中～ middle school/ 大～ college; university/ 上～ go to school

【学报】 xuébào learned journal; journal

【学潮】 xuécháo student strike; campus upheaval

【学而不厌】 xué ér bù yàn have an insatiable desire to learn

【学费】 xuéfèi tuition fee; tuition

【学分】 xuéfēn 〈教〉 credit ◇ ～制 the credit system

【学风】 xuéfēng style of study

【学府】 xuéfǔ seat of learning; institution of higher learning

【学好】 xuéhǎo learn from good examples; emulate good

【学会】 xuéhuì ① learn; master: 她～了游泳。 She's learned to swim. ② learned society; institute

【学籍】 xuéjí one's status as a student; one's name on the school roll: 保留～ retain one's status as a student/ 取消～ be struck off the school roll

【学究】 xuéjiū pedant ◇ ～气 pedantry

【学科】 xuékē branch of learning; course; subject; discipline

【学力】 xuélì knowledge; educational level; academic attainments: 具有同等～ have the same educational level (as school graduates)

【学历】 xuélì record of formal schooling

【学龄】 xuélíng school age: ～儿童 children of school age; school-age children/ ～前儿童 preschool children; preschoolers

【学名】 xuémíng ① scientific name (e.g. Latin name for plants, etc.) ② formal name used at school (as distinguished from pet name at home)

【学年】 xuénián school (或 academic) year ◇ ～考试 year-end examination

【学派】 xuépài school of thought; school

【学期】 xuéqī school term; term; semester

【学前教育】 xuéqián jiàoyù preschool education; infant

school education

【学舌】xuéshé ① mechanically repeat other people's words; parrot: 鹦鹉～ imitate mechanically; parrot ② 〈口〉 loose-tongued; gossipy

【学生】xuésheng ① student; pupil: 医科～ a medical student/ ～运动 student movement/ ～时代 school days ② disciple; follower ◇ ～会 student union; student association

【学识】xuéshí learning; knowledge; scholarly attainments: ～渊博 have great learning; be learned/ ～浅薄 have little learning

【学士】xuéshì ① scholar: 文人～ scholars; men of letters ② bachelor: 文～ Bachelor of Arts (B.A.)

【学术】xuéshù learning; science: ～领域 sphere of learning/ 国际～交流活动 international academic exchanges ◇ ～报告 learned report; academic report / ～界 academic circles/ ～论文 research paper; scientific paper; thesis/ ～团体 learned society/ ～研究 academic research

【学说】xuéshuō theory; doctrine: 达尔文的进化论～ Darwin's theory of evolution

【学堂】xuétáng 〈旧〉 school

【学徒】xuétú apprentice; trainee

【学位】xuéwèi academic degree; degree: 博士～ doctor's degree; doctorate/ 名誉～ honorary degree

【学问】xuéwen learning; knowledge; scholarship: 做～ engage in scholarship; do research/ ～高深的人 a man of great learning; an erudite scholar

【学无止境】xué wú zhǐjìng knowledge is infinite; there is no limit to knowledge

【学习】xuéxí study; learn; emulate: ～别人的长处,克服自己的弱点 emulate others' strong points and overcome one's own weaknesses

【学校】xuéxiào school; educational institution: 师范～ teachers' school; normal school/ 专业～ specialized school/ 高等～ institution of higher learning

【学业】xuéyè one's studies; school work

【学以致用】xué yǐ zhì yòng study for the purpose of application; study sth. in order to apply it

【学员】xuéyuán student (usu. of a college or a training course)

【学院】xuéyuàn college; academy; institute: 师范～ teachers training college/ 军事～ military institute/ 建筑工程～ institute of civil engineering/ 美术～ school of art/ 音乐～ conservatory (或 academy) of music

【学者】xuézhě scholar; learned man; man of learning

【学制】xuézhì ① educational (或 school) system

嗅 xué 〈方〉 laugh: 发～ make one laugh; excite laughter

【嗅头】xuétóu 〈方〉① words or act meant to amuse or to excite laughter: 这个丑角～真多。That clown is full of amusing tricks./ 卖弄～ play to the gallery ② tricks meant to deceive: 不要摆～! Don't try any tricks! 或 None of your tricks!

xuě

雪* xuě ① snow: 一场大～ a heavy fall of snow/ 路上积～很深。The roads are deep in snow. ② wipe out (a humiliation); avenge (a wrong): ～耻 avenge an insult; wipe out a humiliation/ 昭～ right a wrong; clear sb. of an unjust or unfounded charge; rehabilitate

【雪白】xuěbái snow-white; snowy white

【雪糕】xuěgāo 〈方〉 ice cream

【雪恨】xuěhèn wreak vengeance; avenge: 报仇～ avenge oneself; take revenge

【雪花】xuěhuā snowflake

【雪茄】xuějiā cigar

【雪亮】xuěliàng bright as snow; shiny: 把自行车擦得～ polish the bike till it has a good shine/ 灯光～ dazzling lamplight

【雪片】xuěpiàn snowflake: 贺电如～飞来。Messages of congratulation poured in.

【雪人】xuěrén snowman

【雪上加霜】xuě shàng jiā shuāng snow plus frost — one disaster after another

【雪冤】xuěyuān clear sb. of a false charge; redress a wrong

【雪中送炭】xuě zhōng sòng tàn send charcoal in snowy weather — provide timely help

鳕 xuě cod

xuè

血* xuè ① blood: 流～ shed blood/ 出～ bleed/ ～的教训 a lesson paid for with blood; a lesson written in blood ② related by blood: ～亲 blood relation
另见 xiě

【血案】xuè'àn murder case

【血本】xuèběn principal; original capital

【血管】xuèguǎn 〈生理〉 blood vessel

【血海】xuèhǎi a sea of blood: ～深仇 a huge debt of blood; intense and deep-seated hatred

【血汗】xuèhàn blood and sweat; sweat and toil: ～钱 money earned by hard toil

【血红】xuèhóng blood red

【血迹】xuèjī bloodstain: ～斑斑 bloodstained

【血口喷人】xuèkǒu pēn rén make unfounded and malicious attacks upon sb.; venomously slander

【血库】xuèkù 〈医〉 blood bank

【血泪】xuèlèi tears of blood: ～帐 debts of blood and tears/ ～斑斑的家史 family history of blood and tears

【血淋淋】xuèlínlín dripping with blood; bloody

【血泊】xuèpō pool of blood

【血气】xuèqì ① animal spirits; sap; vigour: ～方刚 full of sap ② courage and uprightness: 有～的青年 a courageous and upright youth

【血球】xuèqiú 〈生理〉 blood cell; blood corpuscle

【血肉】xuèròu flesh and blood: ～之躯 the human body; flesh and blood

【血肉相连】xuèròu xiānglián as close as flesh and blood

【血色】xuèsè redness of the skin; colour: 脸上几乎没有～ have little colour in the cheeks; look pale

【血书】xuèshū a letter (expressing one's determination, last wish, etc.) written in one's own blood

【血统】xuètǒng blood relationship; blood lineage; extraction: 德国～的美国人 Americans of German extraction

【血腥】xuèxīng reeking of blood; bloody; sanguinary: ～味 smell of blood/ ～ 统治 sanguinary (或 bloodstained) rule

【血型】xuèxíng 〈生理〉 blood group; blood type ◇ ～分类 typing of blood

【血性】xuèxìng courage and uprightness

【血压】xuèyā 〈生理〉 blood pressure: 高～ high blood pressure; hypertension/ 低～ low blood pressure; hypotension/ ～计 sphygmomanometer

【血液】xuèyè blood: 新鲜～ fresh blood/ 石油是工业的～。Petroleum is the lifeblood of industry.

【血印】xuèyìn bloodstain

【血缘】xuèyuán ties of blood; consanguinity; blood relationship

【血债】xuèzhài a debt of blood: ～累累 have heavy blood debts

【血战】xuèzhàn bloody (或 sanguinary) battle: ～到底 fight to the last drop of one's blood; fight to the bitter end

谑 xuè 〈书〉 crack a joke; banter; tease: 戏～ banter; tease/ ～而不虐 tease without embarrassing

xūn

勋 xūn merit; meritorious service; achievement: 功～ meritorious service; contribution

【勋绩】 xūnjī meritorious service; outstanding contribution

【勋爵】 xūnjué ① a feudal title of nobility conferred for meritorious service ② (英国) Lord

【勋劳】 xūnláo meritorious service: 卓著～ noted for meritorious service

【勋业】 xūnyè <书> meritorious service and great achievement

【勋章】 xūnzhāng medal; decoration

熏 xūn ① smoke; fumigate: 烟把厨房的墙壁～黑了。The kitchen walls were blackened by smoke./ 我被烟～得直流眼泪。The smoke brought tears to my eyes./ ～蚊子 smoke out mosquitoes/ ～房间 fumigate a room ② treat (meat, fish, etc.) with smoke; smoke: ～鱼 smoked fish

【熏染】 xūnrǎn exert a gradual, corrupting influence on

【熏陶】 xūntáo exert a gradual, uplifting influence on; nurture; edify: 起～作用 exert an edifying influence on

薰 xūn <书> ① a kind of sweet grass ② fragrance (of flowers, etc.) ⑶ 见"熏" xūn

曛 xūn ① dim glow of the setting sun ② dusk; nightfall

醺 xūn drunk: 醉～～的 dead drunk; tight/ 微～ tipsy

xún

旬 xún ① a period of ten days: ～日 ten days/ 兼～ twenty days/ 上(中、下)～ the first (second, last) ten days of a month/ 按～计算 calculate in ten-day periods ② a period of ten years in a person's age (applied only to old persons): 八～老母 80-year-old mother

驯 xún ① tame and docile: ～象 a tame elephant ② tame; domesticate: 善于～虎 good at taming tigers/ ～马 break in a horse

【驯服】 xúnfú ① docile; tame; tractable ② tame; break; domesticate: 这匹野马终于被～了。The wild horse was finally broken in./ ～洪水 bring a flood under control

【驯化】 xúnhuà domestication; taming: 鹿群经过～，可以放牧。Deer can be tamed and trained to go out to pasture.

【驯良】 xúnliáng tractable; docile; tame and gentle

【驯鹿】 xúnlù <动> reindeer

【驯顺】 xúnshùn tame and docile

【驯养】 xúnyǎng raise and train (animals); domesticate

寻* xún ① look for; search; seek: ～物 look for sth. lost/ ～欢作乐 seek pleasure ② an ancient measure of length, equal to about eight chi (尺)
另见 xín

【寻常】 xúncháng ordinary; usual; common: 不～ unusual; out of the ordinary/ 异乎～的冷 extraordinarily cold

【寻访】 xúnfǎng look for (sb. whose whereabouts is unknown); try to locate; make inquiries about

【寻根究底】 xúngēn-jiūdǐ get to the bottom of things; inquire deeply into

【寻机】 xúnjī look for an opportunity

【寻开心】 xún kāixīn <方> make fun of; joke

【寻觅】 xúnmì seek; look for

【寻求】 xúnqiú seek; explore; go in quest of: ～真理 seek truth/ ～打开僵局的途径 explore possible paths for ending the stalemate

【寻事生非】 xúnshì-shēngfēi seek a quarrel; make trouble

【寻味】 xúnwèi chew sth. over; ruminate; think over: 他这番话耐人～。What he has said affords much food for thought.

【寻衅】 xúnxìn pick a quarrel; provoke

【寻章摘句】 xúnzhāng-zhāijù cull phrases but not meaning; write in clichés without originality

【寻找】 xúnzhǎo seek; look for

巡* xún ① patrol; make one's rounds: ～夜 go on

night patrol ② <量>〔用于给 全座斟酒〕round of drinks: 酒过三～。The wine has gone round three times.

【巡捕】 xúnbǔ police or policeman (in former foreign concessions)

【巡查】 xúnchá go on a tour of inspection; make one's rounds

【巡航】 xúnháng cruise ～导弹 cruise missile

【巡回】 xúnhuí go the rounds; tour; make a circuit of: 剧团正在全国各地～演出。The theatrical troupe is touring the country.
◇ ～大使 roving ambassador

【巡礼】 xúnlǐ ① visit a sacred land; go on a pilgrimage ② tour; sight-seeing

【巡逻】 xúnluó go on patrol; patrol: 执行～任务 be on patrol duty; be on one's beat
◇ ～队 patrol party; patrol/ ～护卫舰 patrol escort/ ～艇 patrol boat/ ～线 patrol route

【巡视】 xúnshì make (or be on) an inspection tour; tour: ～各地 make an inspection tour of various places

【巡幸】 xúnxìng <旧> (of a monarch) go on an inspection tour

【巡洋舰】 xúnyángjiàn cruiser

【巡弋】 xúnyì (of warships) cruise

询* xún ask; inquire: 查～ make inquiries (about)

【询问】 xúnwèn ask about; inquire: ～我们学习情况 ask us about our studies/ ～病状 inquire about sb.'s illness

洵 xún <书> truly; indeed

峋 xún 见"嶙峋" línxún

浔 xún <书> waterside

荀 Xún a surname

循 xún follow; abide by: ～此前进 proceed along this line/ ～例 follow the usual practice; follow a precedent

【循规蹈矩】 xúnguī-dǎojǔ follow rules, orders, etc. docilely; conform to convention; toe the line

【循环】 xúnhuán circulate; cycle: ～不息 move in endless cycles/ 四季的～ the cycle of the seasons/ 血液～ blood circulation/ 恶性～ vicious circle

【循序】 xúnxù in proper order or sequence: ～渐进 follow in order and advance step by step; proceed in an orderly way and step by step

【循循善诱】 xúnxún shàn yòu be good at giving systematic guidance; teach with skill and patience

xùn

讯* xùn ① interrogate; question: 审～犯人 interrogate a prisoner ② message; dispatch: 电～ a telegraphic report; dispatch/ 消防队闻～赶到。On hearing the alarm the fire brigade rushed to the scene.

【讯问】 xùnwèn ① interrogate; question: ～被告人 interrogate the defendant ② ask about; inquire

训* xùn ① lecture; teach; train: ～他一顿 give him a lecture (或 a dressing down)/ 受～ undergo training ② standard; model; example: 不足为～ not fit to serve as a model

【训斥】 xùnchì reprimand; rebuke; dress down

【训词】 xùncí admonition; instructions

【训话】 xùnhuà <旧> (give) an admonitory talk to subordinates

【训诲】 xùnhuì <书> instruct; teach

【训诫】 xùnjiè ① admonish; advise ② rebuke; reprimand

【训练】 xùnliàn train; drill: ～部队 train troops/ 实战～ exercises under battle conditions/ ～有素的运动员 a well-trained athlete

【训练班】 xùnliànbān training class; training course: 养猪

~ a training course in pig-farming/ 短期~ short course
【训令】 xùnlìng 〈旧〉 instructions; order; directive

汛 xùn flood; high water: 秋~ autumn floods/ 防~ flood control/ ~情严重。 The flood (situation) is serious.

迅* xùn fast; swift

【迅即】 xùnjí immediately; at once: 此事望~处理。 It is hoped that immediate action will be taken on this matter.
【迅疾】 xùnjí swift; rapid
【迅捷】 xùnjié fast; agile; quick
【迅雷不及掩耳】 xùnléi bùjí yǎn ěr a sudden peal of thunder leaves no time for covering the ears; as sudden as lightning: 以~之势袭击敌人 fall on the enemy with the suddenness of a thunderbolt
【迅猛】 xùnměng swift and violent: 水势~异常。 The flood roared on, swift and violent.
【迅速】 xùnsù rapid; swift; speedy; prompt: 动作~ swift in action; quick-moving/ 工农业的~发展 rapid development of industry and agriculture/ ~取得成效 produce speedy results/ ~作出决定 come to a prompt decision

逊 xùn ① abdicate ② modest: 谦~ modest/ 出言不~ speak insolently ③ 〈书〉 inferior: 稍~一筹 be slightly inferior

【逊色】 xùnsè be inferior: 毫无~ be by no means inferior/ 其他玉雕跟这件相比大为~。 Other jade carvings pale beside this.
【逊位】 xùnwèi abdicate

徇 xùn ① 〈书〉 give in to; submit to; comply with ② 见 "殉" xùn ②

【徇情】 xùnqíng 〈书〉 act wrongly out of personal considerations; practise favouritism: ~枉法 bend the law for the benefit of relatives or friends
【徇私】 xùnsī 见 "徇情"

殉 xùn ① be buried alive with the dead ② sacrifice one's life for

【殉国】 xùnguó die (或 give one's life) for one's country
【殉难】 xùnnàn die (for a just cause or for one's country)
【殉葬】 xùnzàng be buried alive with the dead: ~的奴隶 slaves buried alive with their deceased masters ◇ ~品 funerary object; sacrificial object/ ~制度 institution of burying the living with the dead
【殉职】 xùnzhí die at one's post; die in the course of performing one's duty; die in line of duty

蕈 xùn 〈植〉 gill fungus

Y

yā

丫 yā bifurcation; fork
【丫杈】yāchà ① fork (of a tree); crotch ② crotched; forked
【丫鬟】yāhuan 〈旧〉slave girl; servant girl
【丫头】yātou ① 〈方〉girl ② 〈旧〉slave girl

压* yā ① press; push down; hold down; weigh down: ~扁 press flat; flatten/ ~碎 crush (to pieces)/ 用石头~住地图的四角 put a stone on each corner of the map to hold it down/ 果子把树枝~弯了。The fruit weighed the branches down. ② keep under control; control; keep under; quell: 喝点热水把咳嗽~一~ drink some hot water to ease a cough/ ~住阵脚 keep the troops in battle array; hold the line/ ~低嗓门 lower one's voice; speak under one's breath/ 强~住心头怒火 try hard to control one's anger; hold back one's rage/ 我们的重机枪~住了敌人的火力。Our heavy machine guns stilled the enemy's fire. ③ bring pressure to bear on; suppress; daunt; intimidate: 不受捧，不怕~ withstand both flattery and pressure/ 再大的自然灾害也~不垮我们。Even a greater natural calamity cannot daunt us. ④ pigeonhole; shelve: 这份公文~了不少时间。This document was pigeonholed for quite some time. ⑤ risk (money, etc.) on sth.; stake ⑥ pressure: 血~ blood pressure
另见 yà
【压倒】yādǎo overwhelm; overpower; prevail over: ~一切的任务 an overriding task/ 以~多数通过一项决议 pass a resolution by an overwhelming majority/ 困难压不倒我们。No difficulty can overwhelm us.
【压服】yāfú force (或 compel) sb. to submit: ~手段 coercive measure
【压价】yājià force prices down; demand a lower price: ~出售 undersell/ ~百分之二十五 force the price down by 25 per cent
【压惊】yājīng help sb. get over a shock (by entertaining him, etc.)
【压境】yājìng (of enemy troops) press on to the border: 大军~。A large enemy force is bearing down upon the border.
【压力】yālì ① 〈物〉pressure: 大气~ atmospheric (或 barometric) pressure/ 外界~ ambient pressure ② overwhelming force; pressure: 对某人施加~ bring pressure to bear on sb.
【压路机】yālùjī road roller; roller
【压迫】yāpò oppress; repress: ~者 oppressor
【压岁钱】yāsuìqián money given to children as a lunar New Year gift (in the old days)
【压缩】yāsuō compress; condense; reduce; cut down: ~开支 cut down (或 reduce) expenses; retrench/ 这篇文章可以~一下。The article can be cut down.
【压缩机】yāsuōjī compressor: 空气~ air compressor
【压抑】yāyì ① constrain; inhibit; depress; hold back: 心情~ feel constrained/ 这部影片气氛比较~。The film is rather depressing. ② oppressive; stifling: 胸口感到~ feel tight in the chest
【压韵】yāyùn rhyme: 这两句不~。These two lines don't rhyme.
【压榨】yāzhà ① press; squeeze: ~甘蔗 press sugar cane ② oppress and exploit; bleed
【压制】yāzhì suppress; stifle; inhibit: ~批评 suppress (或 muzzle) criticism/ ~不同意见 stifle differing opinions
【压轴子】yāzhòuzi ① present the last item but one on a theatrical programme ② present a theatrical performance as the last but one item on a programme: 明儿晚上拿《空城计》来~。Let's have *The Empty City Ruse* as the second major item for tomorrow evening's performance.

呀* yā ①〈叹〉〔表示惊异〕ah; oh: ~，下雪了！Oh, it's snowing! ②〈象〉creak: 门~的一声开了。The door opened with a creak.
另见 ya
押 yā ① give as security; mortgage; pawn; pledge: 以手表作~ leave one's watch as security ② detain; take into custody: 在~犯 criminal in custody ③ escort: ~车 escort goods on a train, truck, etc./ ~行李 escort luggage/ 把小偷~到派出所去 escort the thief to the police station/ ~下去！Take him away. ④ signature; mark in lieu of signature: 画~ mark (a document) in lieu of signature; sign
【押当】yādàng ① pawn sth. ② a small pawnshop
【押解】yājiè send (a criminal or captive) under escort; escort: ~出境 deport under escort
【押金】yājīn cash pledge; deposit
【押款】yākuǎn 〈商〉① borrow money on security ② a loan on security
【押送】yāsòng send under escort; escort
【押运】yāyùn escort (goods) in transportation

鸦* yā crow
【鸦片】yāpiàn opium
【鸦雀无声】yā-què wú shēng not even a crow or sparrow can be heard — silence reigns
桠 yā fork (of a tree)
【桠杈】yāchà ① fork (of a tree); crotch ② crotched; forked
鸭* yā duck: 母~ duck/ 公~ drake/ 小~ duckling
【鸭蛋】yādàn duck's egg
【鸭舌帽】yāshémào peaked cap

yá

牙* yá ① tooth ② tooth-like thing: 轮~ cog ③ ivory: ~筷 ivory chopsticks/ ~章 ivory seal
【牙齿】yáchǐ tooth
【牙床】yáchuáng ① 〈生理〉gum ② ivory-inlaid bed
【牙雕】yádiāo ivory carving
【牙膏】yágāo toothpaste
【牙关】yáguān mandibular joint: 咬紧~ clench (或 grit) one's teeth
【牙科】yáke 〈医〉(department of) dentistry ◇ ~医生 dentist; dental surgeon/ ~诊疗所 dental clinic
【牙签】yáqiān toothpick
【牙刷】yáshuā toothbrush
【牙痛】yátòng toothache
【牙牙】yáyá 〈象〉babble: ~学语 babble out one's first speech sounds; learn to speak
【牙医】yáyī dentist
【牙龈】yáyín 〈生理〉gum

芽* yá bud; sprout; shoot
涯 yá margin; limit: 一望无~ stretching beyond the horizon; boundless
崖 yá precipice; cliff
【崖壁】yábì precipice
睚 yá 〈书〉the corner of the eye
【睚眦】yázì 〈书〉① angry stare ② small grievance: ~必报 seek revenge for the smallest grievance

衙 yá
【衙门】yámen *yamen*, government office in feudal China: ~八字开，有理无钱莫进来。The *yamen* gate is open wide;

with right but no money, don't go inside.
【衙役】 yáyì *yamen* runner

yǎ

哑* yǎ ① mute; dumb ② hoarse; husky: ~嗓子 husky
(或 hoarse) voice/ 嗓子喊~了 shout oneself hoarse
【哑巴】 yǎba a dumb person; mute: ~吃黄连，有苦说不
出 be unable to express one's discomfort, like a dumb
person tasting bitter herbs; be compelled to suffer
in silence/ 今儿个怎么~了？Why are you so silent today？
或 Have you lost your tongue？
【哑剧】 yǎjù dumb show; pantomime
【哑口无言】 yǎkǒu wúyán be left without an argument; be
rendered speechless
【哑谜】 yǎmí puzzling remark; enigma; riddle: 别给我们打
~啦！Don't keep us guessing.
【哑然】 yǎrán 〈书〉① 〔多用于〕: ~无声。Silence reigns. ②
〔多用于〕: ~失笑 unable to stifle a laugh; can't help
laughing

雅 yǎ ① standard; proper; correct ② refined; elegant:
古~ of classic elegance ③ 〈敬〉〔用于对方的情意、举动〕:
~教 your esteemed opinion ④ a section in *The Book of
Songs* (《诗经》) consisting of dynastic hymns ⑤ 〈书〉ac-
quaintance; friendship: 无一日之~ not have the pleasure
of knowing sb.
【雅观】 yǎguān 〔多用于否定〕 refined (in manner, etc.); in
good taste: 很不~ most unseemly; rather unsightly
【雅量】 yǎliàng ① magnanimity; generosity ② great capacity for liquor
【雅俗共赏】 yǎ-sú gòng shǎng (of a work of art or literature) appeal to both the more and the less cultured; suit
both refined and popular tastes
【雅兴】 yǎxìng aesthetic mood: ~不浅 be really in an aesthetic mood; have a really keen interest in sth./ 无此~
not be in such a poetic mood; be in no mood for such
things
【雅意】 yǎyì 〈敬〉your kindness; your kind offer
【雅正】 yǎzhèng ① 〈书〉standard; correct ② upright; righteous ③ 〈套〉〔用于把自己的诗文书画送人时，表示请对方指
教〕would you kindly point out my inadequacies
【雅致】 yǎzhì refined; tasteful: 陈设~ tastefully furnished

yà

轧 yà ① roll; run over: 把路面~平 roll a road surface/
被车~伤 get run over and injured by a car/ ~碎 crush to
pieces/ ~棉花 gin cotton ② oust; squeeze out; push out:
倾~ engage in internal strife; jostle against each other
③ 〈象〉〔形容机器开动时发出的声音〕: 机声~~。The ma-
chine is clicking away.
另见 zhá

亚* yà ① inferior; second: 不~于人 second to none;
not inferior to anyone ② (Yà) short for Asia
【亚军】 yàjūn second place (in a sports contest); runner-up:
他在百米赛跑中得了~。He came second in the 100-metre
dash. 或 He was runner-up in the 100-metre dash.

压 yà
另见 yā
【压根儿】 yàgēnr 〈口〉〔多用于否定句〕 from the start; in
the first place; altogether: ~就不知道 have had no idea
from the start; not know anything about it/ 他全忘了,好
象~就没有这回事。He's clean forgotten about it, as if it
had never happened.

讶 yà 〈书〉be surprised; be astonished; wonder

迓 yà 〈书〉welcome; meet

揠 yà 〈书〉pull up; tug upward
【揠苗助长】 yà miáo zhù zhǎng try to help the shoots grow
by pulling them upward — spoil things by excessive enthusiasm

ya

呀* ya 〈助〉〔"啊"受前一字韵母 a, e, i, o, ü 的影响而发
生的变音〕: 她是谁~? Who is she?/ 快来~! Come here,
quick!
另见 yā

yān

咽 yān 〈生理〉pharynx
另见 yàn; yè
【咽喉】 yānhóu ① 〈生理〉pharynx and larynx; throat ②
strategic (或 vital) passage; key link: ~要地 key junction/
直布罗陀海峡是地中海通向大西洋的~。The Straits of
Gibraltar are the strategic passage between the Mediter-
ranean and the Atlantic.

恹 yān
【恹恹】 yānyān 〈书〉weak and weary through illness

烟* yān ① smoke ② mist; vapour: 云~ clouds and
mist ③ (of eyes) be irritated by smoke: 谁在这里生火啊？
都~得睁不开眼了。Who's lighting the stove here? I can't
even open my eyes for the smoke. ④ tobacco or cigarette:
烤~ flue-cured tobacco/ 抽支~ have a cigarette; have a
smoke/ 一袋~的功夫 time enough to smoke a pipeful of
tobacco ⑤ opium: 禁~ ban opium
【烟霭】 yān'ǎi 〈书〉mist and clouds
【烟波】 yānbō mist-covered waters:
~浩渺的太湖 the wide
expanse of misty Taihu Lake
【烟草】 yāncǎo tobacco

烟草

【烟囱】 yāncōng chimney; funnel; stovepipe
【烟斗】 yāndǒu (tobacco) pipe ◇ ~架 pipe rack/ ~丝
pipe tobacco
【烟鬼】 yānguǐ ① opium addict ② heavy smoker
【烟海】 yānhǎi a vast sea of fog — huge and voluminous:
浩如~ a tremendous amount (of data, etc.); voluminous/
如堕~ be lost in a fog
【烟盒】 yānhé cigarette case
【烟灰】 yānhuī tobacco or cigarette ash ◇ ~缸 ashtray
【烟火】 yānhuǒ ① smoke and fire: 动~ light a fire and
cook/ 严禁~! Smoking or lighting fires strictly forbidden.
② cooked food ◇ ~食 cooked food
【烟火】 yānhuo fireworks: 放~ let off fireworks; put on a
display of fireworks
【烟幕】 yānmù smoke screen ◇ ~弹 smoke shell; smoke
bomb
【烟农】 yānnóng tobacco grower
【烟丝】 yānsī cut tobacco; pipe tobacco
【烟筒】 yāntong chimney; funnel; stovepipe
【烟头】 yāntóu cigarette end (或 stub, butt, stump)
【烟土】 yāntǔ crude opium
【烟雾】 yānwù smoke; mist; vapour; smog: ~弥漫 full of
smoke/ ~笼罩着大地。The land is draped in a veil of
mist./ 厨房里一腾腾 The kitchen is filled with steam and
smoke.
【烟消云散】 yānxiāo-yúnsàn vanish like mist and smoke;
completely vanish
【烟叶】 yānyè tobacco leaf; leaf tobacco
【烟瘾】 yānyǐn a craving for tobacco: 他~可大了。He's a
heavy smoker. 或 He smokes like a chimney.

殷 yān ‹书› blackish red
另见 yīn
【殷红】 yānhóng blackish red; dark red

胭 yān
【胭脂】 yānzhī rouge

淹* yān ① flood; submerge; inundate: 修好河堤, 庄稼就不怕～了。When the river dike is completed, the crops will be safe from floods. ② be tingling from sweat ③ ‹书› wide: 学识～博 have a wide knowledge; be well-read; be learned
【淹没】 yānmò submerge; flood; inundate; drown: 被～的田地 inundated fields/ 他的讲话被欢呼声～了。His speech was drowned out by cheers.
【淹死】 yānsǐ drown

阉 yān castrate or spay: ～鸡 capon/ ～牛 bullock/ ～羊 wether/ ～猪 hog
【阉割】 yāngē ① castrate or spay ② deprive a theory, etc. of its essence; emasculate

焉 yān ‹书› ① here; herein: 她心不在～。Her mind is elsewhere. 或 She is absent-minded. ～罪莫大～。There is no greater crime than this. ②〔多用于反问〕how; why: ～能不去? How could I possibly not go?/ 不入虎穴,～得虎子? How can you catch tiger cubs without entering the tiger's lair? 或 Nothing venture, nothing have. ③〔表示只有在某种条件下才能怎样〕: 必知乱之所自起,～能治之。You have to know how the trouble arose before you can deal with it. ④ ‹助›: 有厚望存～ cherish high hopes for/ 少～,月出于东山之上。After a little while, the moon lifted itself above the eastern hills.

湮 yān ‹书› ① fall into oblivion; bury in oblivion ② clog up; stop
【湮灭】 yānmiè bury in oblivion; annihilate
【湮没】 yānmò ① fall into oblivion; be neglected; be forgotten: ～无闻 sink into oblivion; drift into obscurity

腌 yān preserve in salt; salt; pickle; cure: ～菜 pickled vegetables; pickles/ ～鱼 salted fish/ ～肉 salted meat; bacon

嫣 yān ‹书› handsome; beautiful
【嫣红】 yānhóng bright red
【嫣然】 yānrán ‹书› beautiful; sweet: ～一笑 give a winsome smile

yán

延* yán ① prolong; extend; protract: 蔓～ spread/ 苟～残喘 be on one's last legs; linger on in a steadily worsening condition ② postpone; delay: 大会遇雨顺～。In case of rain the mass meeting will be postponed till the first fine day. ③ engage; send for: ～医 send for a doctor
【延长】 yáncháng lengthen; prolong; extend: 输油管又～二百公里。The oil pipeline has been extended another 200 kilometres./ 会议～了三天。The conference was prolonged for three more days.
【延迟】 yánchí delay; defer; postpone: 展览会开幕的日期～了。The opening of the exhibition has been postponed.
【延宕】 yándàng procrastinate; delay; keep putting off
【延搁】 yángē procrastinate; delay
【延缓】 yánhuǎn delay; postpone; put off: ～工作进度 retard the progress of work/ 这个手术过～几天再做。The operation can be put off for a few days.
【延年益寿】 yánnián-yìshòu (of tonics, etc.) prolong life; promise longevity
【延聘】 yánpìn ‹书› engage; employ
【延期】 yánqī postpone; defer; put off: ～付款 defer payment/ 比赛因雨～。The game was put off on account of

rain./ 要求～十年偿还债务 demand a ten-year moratorium/ 办理签证～手续 have one's visa extended; extend a visa
【延请】 yánqǐng engage; employ; send for
【延伸】 yánshēn extend; stretch; elongate: 铁路一直～到海边。The railway line stretches right to the coast.
【延误】 yánwù incur loss through delay: ～时机 miss an opportunity because of a delay/ ～时日 lose time
【延续】 yánxù continue; go on; last: 不能让这种状况～下去。This state of affairs must not be allowed to continue./ 旱象～了半年之久。The drought lasted for as long as six months. ◇ ～性 continuity

言* yán ① speech; word: 发～ make a speech; take the floor/ 无～以对 have nothing to say in reply/ 有～在先 let it be clearly understood beforehand/ 一～不发 not utter a word ② say; talk; speak: 自～自语 talk to oneself/ ～明 state explicitly; clearly stipulate/ 妙在不～中。The best part lies in what is left unsaid./ 不幸而～中。The prophecy has unfortunately come true. ③ character; word: 全书近二十万～。It is a book of nearly 200,000 words.
【言必信, 行必果】 yán bì xìn, xíng bì guǒ promises must be kept and action must be resolute; always be true in word and resolute in deed
【言必有中】 yán bì yǒu zhòng whenever one speaks, one speaks to the point; whenever one says something one hits the nail on the head
【言不及义】 yán bù jí yì never talk about anything serious; talk frivolously
【言不由衷】 yán bù yóuzhōng speak insincerely; speak with one's tongue in one's cheek
【言传】 yánchuán explain in words: 只可意会, 不可～ only to be sensed, not explained
【言传身教】 yánchuán-shēnjiào teach by personal example as well as verbal instruction
【言词】 yáncí one's words; what one says: ～恳切 be sincere in what one says 又作 "言辞"
【言而无信】 yán ér wú xìn fail to keep faith; go back on one's word
【言归于好】 yán guī yú hǎo make it up with sb.; become reconciled
【言归正传】 yán guī zhèngzhuàn to come back to our story; to return to the subject
【言过其实】 yán guò qí shí exaggerate; overstate
【言和】 yánhé make peace; become reconciled; bury the hatchet: 握手～ shake hands and make it up
【言简意赅】 yánjiǎn-yìgāi concise and comprehensive; compendious
【言路】 yánlù channels through which criticisms and suggestions may be communicated to the leadership: 广开～ provide wide opportunities for airing views; encourage the free airing of views/ 堵塞～ stifle criticisms and suggestions
【言论】 yánlùn opinion on public affairs; expression of one's political views; speech: 我们的一切～和行动都应符合人民的利益。Everything we say and do must be in the interests of the people./ 我们看一个人, 不仅要听他的～, 还要看他的行动。We must judge a person not only by his words, but also by his deeds. ◇ ～自由 freedom of speech
【言人人殊】 yán rén rén shū different people give different views; each person offers a different version
【言谈】 yántán the way one speaks or what he says: ～举止 speech and deportment/ ～之间可以看出他很懂行。It's clear from the way he talks that he knows the subject well.
【言听计从】 yántīng-jìcóng always follow sb.'s advice; act upon whatever sb. says; have implicit faith in sb.
【言外之意】 yán wài zhī yì implication; what is actually meant: 体会到文章的～ read between the lines 又作 "言下之意"
【言为心声】 yán wéi xīnshēng words are the voice of the mind; what the heart thinks the tongue speaks
【言行】 yánxíng words and deeds; statements and actions: ～不一 one's deeds do not match (或 square with) one's words; one's actions are not in keeping with one's prom-

ises/ ～一致 be as good as one's word

【言犹在耳】 yán yóu zài ěr the words are still ringing (或 reverberating) in one's ears

【言语】 yányǔ spoken language; speech: ～和文字 spoken and written language/ ～粗鲁 speak rudely

【言语】 yányu 〈方〉speak; talk; answer: 他这个人不受～。 He is a man of few words./ 人家问你这事儿,你怎么不～? Why didn't you say something when people asked you about it?

【言者无罪,闻者足戒】 yánzhě wú zuì, wénzhě zú jiè blame not the speaker but be warned by his words

【言之成理】 yán zhī chéng lǐ sound reasonable; speak in a rational and convincing way

【言之无物】 yán zhī wú wù (of speech or writing) be devoid of substance; be just empty verbiage

【言之有据】 yán zhī yǒu jù speak on good grounds

严* yán ①tight: 把窗户关～了。 Shut the window tight./ 他的嘴很～。 He is tight-mouthed. ②strict; severe; stern; rigorous: ～以律己,宽以待人 be strict with oneself and broad-minded towards others/ ～加批驳 sternly refute/ ～是爱,松是害。 Strictness helps, indulgence spoils. ③〈旧〉 father: 家～ my father

【严办】 yánbàn deal with severely; punish with severity

【严惩】 yánchéng punish severely: ～不贷 punish severely without mercy; punish mercilessly/ ～入侵之敌 deal the invaders a crushing blow

【严词】 yáncí in strong terms; in stern words: ～谴责 denounce in strong terms; sternly condemn/ ～拒绝 give a stern rebuff; sternly refuse

【严冬】 yándōng severe winter

【严防】 yánfáng be strictly on guard against; take strict precautions against

【严格】 yángé strict; rigorous; rigid; stringent: ～履行协定条款 strictly implement the terms of the agreement/ ～训练,～要求 go in for rigorous training and set strict demands; train hard and strictly/ 作出～的规定 set rigid (或 stringent) rules/ ～规章制度 rigorously enforce rules and regulations/ ～说来 strictly speaking

【严寒】 yánhán severe cold; bitter cold

【严谨】 yánjǐn ①rigorous; strict: ～的科学态度 a rigorous scientific approach ②compact; well-knit: 文章结构～。 The essay is well-knit.

【严禁】 yánjìn strictly forbid (或 prohibit): ～体罚 strictly forbid corporal punishment

【严紧】 yánjǐn tight; close: 防守～ guard carefully

【严峻】 yánjùn stern; severe; rigorous; grim: ～的考验 a severe test; a rigorous test/ ～的态度 a stern (或 an uncompromising) attitude/ ～的局势 a grim situation

【严酷】 yánkù ①harsh; bitter; grim: ～的现实 harsh reality/ ～的教训 a bitter lesson ②cruel; ruthless

【严厉】 yánlì stern; severe: ～制裁 apply stern (或 severe) sanctions/ ～的批评 severe criticism/ ～声讨 sternly (或 strongly) denounce

【严密】 yánmì tight; close: ～封锁 impose a tight blockade/ ～监视 put under close surveillance; keep close watch over/ ～防范 take strict precautions against/ ～注视国际局势的发展 closely follow the development of world events/ ～组织 be well-organized

【严明】 yánmíng strict and impartial: 赏罚～ be strict and impartial in meting out rewards and punishments; give rewards and punishments impartially/ 纪律～ observe strict discipline; be highly disciplined

【严肃】 yánsù serious; solemn; earnest: ～地指出 point out in all earnestness/ ～的态度 a serious attitude/ ～的气氛 a solemn atmosphere

【严刑】 yánxíng cruel torture: ～拷打 cruelly torture; cruelly beat up

【严刑峻法】 yánxíng-jùnfǎ severe law; draconian law

【严阵以待】 yán zhèn yǐ dài be ready in full battle array; stand in combat readiness

【严整】 yánzhěng in neat formation: 军容～。 The troops are in gallant array.

【严正】 yánzhèng solemn and just; serious and principled; stern: ～立场 solemn and just stand/ 发表～声明 issue a solemn statement; solemnly declare/ ～警告 serve a stern warning

【严重】 yánzhòng serious; grave; critical: ～后果 serious (或 grave) consequences/ ～关头 critical juncture/ 病情～ be seriously ill/ 事态～。 The situation is grave./ 感到～不安 feel deeply disturbed/ 有～问题的人 a person guilty of a serious misdeed or a person with a dubious background/ 问题的～性在于 the gravity of the question lies in the fact that ◇ ～警告 serious warning

妍 yán 〈书〉beautiful: 百花争～。 A hundred flowers contend in beauty.

沿* yán ①along: ～着海岸航行 sail along the coast ②follow (a tradition, pattern, etc.): 世代相～ be handed down from generation to generation
另见 yàn

【沿岸】 yán'àn along the bank or coast; littoral or riparian: 长江～ along (the banks of) the Changjiang River/ 地中海～国家 the littoral countries of the Mediterranean/ 尼日尔河～国家 riparian states along the Niger

【沿革】 yángé the course of change and development; evolution: 社会风俗的～ the evolution of social customs

【沿海】 yánhǎi along the coast; coastal; littoral ◇ ～城市 coastal city/ ～岛屿 offshore islands/ ～地区 coastal areas; coastland/ ～国家 coastal state (或 country); littoral state (或 country)/ ～航船 coaster/ ～航行 coastal navigation; cabotage/ ～贸易 coasting trade; cabotage/ ～渔业 inshore fishing

【沿路】 yánlù along the road; on the way: 看到庄稼长势良好 see thriving crops along the way

【沿途】 yántú on the way; throughout a journey: 参观团～受到热情的接待。 The visiting group was warmly received throughout its journey.

【沿袭】 yánxí carry on as before; follow: ～陈规 follow convention

【沿线】 yánxiàn along the line: 铁路～的村镇 villages and towns along the railway line

【沿用】 yányòng continue to use (an old method, etc.): ～原来的名称 continue to use the old name

炎* yán ①scorching; burning hot: ～夏 hot summer ②inflammation: 嗓子发～ suffer from an inflammation of the throat/ 阑尾～ appendicitis

【炎热】 yánrè scorching; blazing; burning hot: 冒着～ braving the sweltering heat

【炎暑】 yánshǔ hot summer; sweltering summer days; dog days

【炎炎】 yányán scorching; sweltering; blazing: 赤日～ the scorching sun

【炎症】 yánzhèng inflammation

岩 yán ①rock ②cliff; crag

【岩洞】 yándòng grotto

【岩浆】 yánjiāng 〈地〉magma

【岩石】 yánshí rock

研* yán ①grind; pestle: ～成粉末 grind into fine powder/ ～墨 rub an ink stick on an inkslab (to prepare ink for brush writing) ②study: 钻～ study intensively

【研究】 yánjiū ①study; research: ～自然规律 study the laws of nature/ 科学～ scientific research ②consider; discuss; deliberate ◇ ～工作者 research worker/ ～生 postgraduate (student); graduate student/ ～所 research institute/ ～员 research fellow/ ～院 research institute; graduate school

【研磨】 yánmó ①grind; pestle ②abrade; polish

【研讨】 yántǎo deliberate; discuss

盐* yán salt: 精～ refined salt/ 正～ normal salt

【盐井】 yánjǐng salt well; brine pit

【盐矿】 yánkuàng salt mine

阎 yán 〈书〉 the gate of a lane

【阎罗】 Yánluó 〈宗〉 Yama

【阎王】 Yánwang ① Yama; King of Hell: 活~ living King of Hell; devil incarnate/ 见~ die ② an extremely cruel and violent person ◇ ~殿 the Palace of Hell/ ~账 usurious loan; shark's loan

筵 yán ①〈书〉 formerly, a bamboo mat spread on the floor for people to sit ② feast; banquet: 喜~ a wedding feast

【筵席】 yánxí ① seats arranged at a banquet ② feast; banquet

蜒 yán 见 "蜿蜒" wānyán

颜* yán ① face; countenance: 和~悦色 with a kind and pleasant countenance ② prestige; face: 无~见人 not have the face to appear in public ③ colour: 五~六色 of all colours; multicoloured; colourful

【颜料】 yánliào pigment; colour; dyestuff

【颜面】 yánmiàn ① face: ~神经 facial nerve ② prestige; face: 顾全~ save face/ ~扫地 lose face altogether; be thoroughly discredited

【颜色】 yánsè ① colour ② countenance; facial expression: 给他一点~看看 make it hot for him; teach him a lesson

【颜色】 yánshai 〈口〉 pigment; dyestuff

檐 yán ① eaves ② ledge; brim: 帽~儿 the visor of a cap; the brim of a hat

yǎn

奄 yǎn 〈书〉 ① cover; overspread ② all of a sudden; suddenly

【奄奄】 yǎnyǎn feeble breathing: 气息~ breathe feebly; be sinking fast; be dying/ ~一息 at one's last gasp; on the verge of death

俨 yǎn 〈书〉 majestic; solemn; dignified

【俨然】 yǎnrán 〈书〉 ① solemn; dignified: 望之~ look dignified ② neatly arranged: 屋舍~ houses set out in neat order ③ just like: 这孩子说起话来~是个大人。 This child speaks just like a grown-up./ ~以恩人自居 assume the airs of a benefactor

【俨如】 yǎnrú just like: ~白昼 as bright as day

衍 yǎn 〈书〉 ① spread out; develop; amplify ② redundant; superfluous

【衍变】 yǎnbiàn develop; evolve

【衍文】 yǎnwén redundancy due to misprinting or miscopying

掩* yǎn ① cover; hide: ~口而笑 hide one's smile/ ~鼻而过 pass by (sth. nauseating) holding one's nose ② shut; close: ~卷 close a book/ 虚~着门 with the door left unlocked or unlatched ③ 〈方〉 get squeezed (或 pinched) while shutting a door, lid, etc.: 小心门~了手。 Don't get your fingers caught in the door. ④ attack by surprise: ~袭 launch a surprise attack

【掩蔽】 yǎnbì screen; shelter; cover

【掩藏】 yǎncáng hide; conceal

【掩耳盗铃】 yǎn ěr dào líng plug one's ears while stealing a bell; deceive oneself; bury one's head in the sand

【掩盖】 yǎngài cover; conceal: 一个倾向~着另一个倾向。 One tendency conceals another./ 谎言~不了事实。 Lies cannot cover up (或 conceal) the facts.

【掩护】 yǎnhù screen; shield; cover: ~进攻 screen an advance

【掩埋】 yǎnmái bury

【掩人耳目】 yǎn rén ěr-mù deceive the public; hoodwink people

【掩饰】 yǎnshì cover up; gloss over; conceal: ~错误 gloss over (或 cover up) one's mistakes/ ~真实的意图 conceal one's true intentions/ ~不住内心的恐慌 be unable to hide (或 conceal) one's fears/ 毫不~自己的感情 make no secret of one's feelings

眼* yǎn ① eye: 亲~看见 see with one's own eyes ② look; glance: 瞪了他一~ give him a hard look/ 瞥了他一~ shoot a glance at him/ 一~就认出是她 recognize her at first glance ③ small hole; aperture: 针~ the eye of a needle/ 打个~ bore a hole/ 网~ mesh (of a net)

【眼巴巴】 yǎnbābā ① (expecting) eagerly; anxiously: 大家~地盼着他回来。 We were eagerly looking forward to his return. ② helplessly (watching sth. unpleasant happen)

【眼底下】 yǎndǐxia ① right before one's eyes ② at the moment: 先处理~的事。 Let's settle the business on hand first.

【眼福】 yǎnfú the good fortune of seeing sth. rare or beautiful: ~不浅 be lucky enough to see sth./ 一饱~ feast one's eyes on sth.

【眼高手低】 yǎngāo-shǒudī have grandiose aims but puny abilities; be fastidious but incompetent

【眼观六路，耳听八方】 yǎn guān liùlù, ěr tīng bāfāng have sharp eyes and keen ears — be observant and alert

【眼光】 yǎnguāng ① eye: 锐利的~ sharp eyes/ 大家的~都集中到他身上。 Everyone turned their eyes on him. ② sight; foresight; insight; vision: ~远大 farsighted/ ~短浅 short-sighted/ 政治~ political foresight/ 历史~ historical perspective/ 有~的政治家 a farsighted statesman/ 他开始用新的~来观察周围事物。 He began to view everything around him in a different light./ 不能用老~来看新事物。 One mustn't judge new things by old standards.

【眼红】 yǎnhóng ① covet; be envious; be jealous ② furious

【眼花】 yǎnhuā have dim eyesight; have blurred vision: 使人头晕~ make one's head swim; be dazzling/ 耳不聋眼不花 (of an old person) be neither hard of hearing nor dim-sighted

【眼花缭乱】 yǎnhuā liáoluàn be dazzled: 使人~的杂技表演 a dazzling display of acrobatics

【眼尖】 yǎnjiān be sharp-eyed; have sharp eyes

【眼角】 yǎnjiǎo the corner of the eye; canthus

【眼睫毛】 yǎnjiémáo 〈口〉 eyelash

【眼界】 yǎnjiè field of vision (或 view); outlook: 扩大~ widen one's field of vision; broaden one's horizon

【眼镜】 yǎnjìng glasses; spectacles: 戴~ wear glasses

【眼镜蛇】 yǎnjìngshé cobra

【眼睛】 yǎnjing eye

【眼看】 yǎnkàn ① soon; in a moment: 暴风雨~就要来了。 The storm will start any moment./ ~天就要亮了。 It'll be daylight soon. ② watch helplessly; look on passively: 我们哪能~着他走邪道不管呢? How can we sit idly by and watch him go astray?

【眼科】 yǎnkē 〈医〉 (department of) ophthalmology ◇ ~学 ophthalmology/ ~医生 oculist; ophthalmologist; eye doctor

【眼眶】 yǎnkuàng ① eye socket; orbit: 他~里含着热泪。 His eyes were filled with tears. ② rim of the eye

【眼泪】 yǎnlèi tears: ~汪汪 eyes brimming with tears

【眼力】 yǎnlì ① eyesight; vision: ~好(差) have good (poor) eyesight ② judgment; discrimination

【眼里】 yǎnli within one's vision; in one's eyes: ~没有群众 not take the masses into account/ 看在~，记在心里 bear in mind what one sees; see and heed/ ~有活 see where there's work to be done; know where one can be of use/ 在他~,我还是个孩子。 In his eyes, I'm only a child./ 这点困难她根本不放在~。 She thinks nothing of a difficulty like that.

【眼帘】 yǎnlián eye: 映入~ come into view; greet (或 meet)

the eye

【眼明手快】 yǎnmíng-shǒukuài quick of eye and deft of hand; sharp-eyed and quick-moving

【眼皮】 yǎnpí eyelid

【眼前】 yǎnqián ① before one's eyes: ~是一片碧绿的稻田。 Before our eyes was a stretch of green paddy fields. ② at the moment; at present; now: ~利益服从长远利益 subordinate immediate interests to long-term interests/ 不能只顾~，不管将来。 One must not think only of the present and neglect the future./ 胜利就在~。 Victory is at hand.

【眼球】 yǎnqiú eyeball

【眼圈】 yǎnquān ①eye socket; orbit: ~红了 be on the verge of tears ② rim of the eye

【眼热】 yǎnrè covet; be envious

【眼色】 yǎnsè hint given with the eyes; meaningful glance; wink: 使~ tip sb. the wink; wink at sb./ 看某人的~行事 take one's cue from sb.

【眼神】 yǎnshén ① expression in one's eyes ②〈方〉 eyesight: ~不济 have poor eyesight

【眼熟】 yǎnshú look familiar: 这人看着很~。 That person looks familiar.

【眼跳】 yǎntiào twitching of the eyelid

【眼下】 yǎnxià at the moment; at present; now: ~正是秋收大忙季节。 We're right in the middle of the autumn harvest rush.

【眼药】 yǎnyào medicament for the eyes; eye ointment or eyedrops

【眼睁睁】 yǎnzhēngzhēng (looking on) helplessly or unfeelingly: 咱不能~地看着庄稼被水淹了。 We can't just sit here and watch the crops being flooded.

【眼中钉】 yǎnzhōngdīng thorn in one's flesh (或 side)

【眼珠子】 yǎnzhūzi 〈口〉 eyeball

偃 yǎn 〈书〉① fall on one's back: ~卧 lie supine; lie on one's back ② lay down ③ desist; cease: ~武修文 desist from military activities and encourage culture and education

【偃旗息鼓】 yǎnqí-xīgǔ lower the banners and muffle the drums — cease all activities

演* yǎn ① develop; evolve: 愈~愈烈 grow in intensity ② deduce; elaborate: 推~ deduce ③ drill; practise: ~算 perform mathematical calculations ④ perform; play; act; put on

【演变】 yǎnbiàn develop; evolve: 从猿到人的~过程 evolution from ape to man

【演唱】 yǎnchàng sing (in a performance)

【演出】 yǎnchū perform; show; put on a show: 登台~ appear on the stage/ 首次~ first performance or show; première (of a play, film, etc.); début (of an actor or actress)

【演化】 yǎnhuà evolution

【演技】 yǎnjì acting

【演讲】 yǎnjiǎng give a lecture; make a speech; lecture

【演进】 yǎnjìn gradual progress; evolution

【演说】 yǎnshuō ① deliver a speech; make an address ② speech

【演算】 yǎnsuàn perform mathematical calculations

【演习】 yǎnxí manoeuvre; exercise; drill; practice: 军事~ military manoeuvre; war exercise

【演戏】 yǎnxì ① put on a play; act in a play ② playact; pretend: 别再~了。 Stop playacting.

【演义】 yǎnyì historical novel; historical romance: 《三国~》 The Romance of the Three Kingdoms

【演绎】 yǎnyì 〈逻〉 deduction ◇ ~法 the deductive method

【演员】 yǎnyuán actor or actress; performer ◇ ~表 cast

【演奏】 yǎnzòu give an instrumental performance; play a musical instrument (in a performance): ~琵琶 play the pipa

魇 yǎn have a nightmare

鼹 yǎn mole

【鼹鼠】 yǎnshǔ mole

yàn

厌* yàn ① be disgusted with; detest: ~弃 detest and reject ② be fed up with; be bored with; be tired of: 看~了 have seen more than enough of sth./ 吃~了 be sick of eating sth./ 不~其烦 not mind taking all the trouble ③ be satisfied: 贪得无~ be insatiably greedy

【厌烦】 yànfán be sick of; be fed up with

【厌倦】 yànjuàn be weary of; be tired of

【厌弃】 yànqì detest and reject

【厌世】 yànshì be world-weary; be pessimistic

【厌恶】 yànwù detest; abhor; abominate; be disgusted with

【厌战】 yànzhàn be weary of war; be war-weary ◇ ~情绪 war-weariness

沿 yàn water's edge; bank: 河~ riverside/ 沟~儿 edge of a ditch
另见 yán

砚 yàn inkstone; inkslab

【砚池】 yànchí inkstone; inkslab

【砚台】 yàntái inkstone; inkslab

咽 yàn swallow: 细嚼慢~ chew carefully and swallow slowly/ 他话到嘴边又~了回去。 He was on the point of saying something when he checked himself./ ~不下这口气 unable to stomach (或 take) an insult, etc., like that
另见 yān; yè

【咽气】 yànqì breathe one's last; die

彦 yàn 〈书〉 a man of virtue and ability

宴* yàn ① entertain at a banquet; fête: ~客 entertain guests at a banquet ② feast; banquet: 盛~ grand banquet; magnificent feast ③ ease and comfort

【宴会】 yànhuì banquet; feast; dinner party ◇ ~厅 banquet hall

【宴请】 yànqǐng entertain (to dinner); fête: ~贵宾 entertain the distinguished guests

【宴席】 yànxí banquet; feast

晏 yàn ① late: ~起 get up late ② ease and comfort

艳 yàn ① gorgeous; colourful; gaudy: 百花争~ Flowers blossom in a riot of colour./ 这布的花太~了。 The cloth is too gaudy. ② amorous: ~诗 love poem in a flowery style ③〈书〉 admire; envy: ~羡 admire; envy

【艳丽】 yànlì bright-coloured and beautiful; gorgeous: ~夺目 of dazzling beauty/ 词藻~ flowery diction/ 打扮得非常~ be gorgeously dressed

【艳阳天】 yànyángtiān bright spring day; bright sunny skies

唁 yàn extend condolences

【唁电】 yàndiàn telegram (或 cable) of condolence; message of condolence

【唁函】 yànhán letter (或 message) of condolence

验* yàn ① examine; check; test: ~护照 examine (或 check) a passport ② prove effective; produce the expected result: 应~ come true/ 屡试屡~ prove successful in every test

【验方】 yànfāng 〈中医〉 proved recipe

【验关】 yànguān customs examination

【验尸】 yànshī 〈法〉 postmortem; autopsy

【验收】 yànshōu check and accept; check before acceptance; check upon delivery: 逐项~ check item by item before acceptance/ 工程已由国家~。 The completed project has been checked and accepted by the government. ◇ ~单 receipt (issued after examination and acceptance of goods)/ ~试验 acceptance test

【验算】 yànsuàn 〈数〉 checking computations ◇ ~公式

check formula
【验血】 yànxiě blood test
【验证】 yànzhèng test and verify

谚 yàn proverb; saying; adage; saw
【谚语】 yànyǔ proverb; saying; adage; saw

焰 yàn flame; blaze: 烈～ blazing (或 raging) flames

雁 yàn wild goose

餍 yàn 〈书〉① have enough (food); be satiated ② satisfy

燕* yàn ① swallow: 家～ house swallow ② 见"宴" yàn
【燕尾服】 yànwěifú swallowtail; swallow-tailed coat; tailcoat; tails
【燕窝】 yànwō edible bird's nest
【燕子】 yànzi swallow

赝 yàn 〈书〉counterfeit; spurious; fake
【赝本】 yànběn spurious edition or copy
【赝币】 yànbì 〈书〉counterfeit coin
【赝品】 yànpǐn counterfeit; fake; sham

yāng

央* yāng ① entreat ② centre ③ 〈书〉end; finish: 夜未～。 The night is not yet spent.
【央告】 yānggào beg; ask earnestly
【央求】 yāngqiú beg; plead; implore: ～宽恕 beg for mercy

泱 yāng
【泱泱】 yāngyāng 〈书〉① (of waters) vast ② magnificent: ～大国 a great and proud country

殃 yāng ① calamity; disaster; misfortune: 遭～ meet with (或 suffer) disaster ② bring disaster to: 祸国～民 bring calamity to the country and the people

秧 yāng ① seedling; sprout: 黄瓜～儿 cucumber sprout ② rice seedling: 插～ transplant rice seedlings ③ vine: 白薯～ sweet potato vine ④ young; fry: 鱼～ young fish; fry; 猪～ piglets
【秧苗】 yāngmiáo rice shoot; rice seedling

鸯 yāng 见"鸳鸯" yuānyang

yáng

羊* yáng sheep: 绵～ sheep/ 山～ goat/ 母～ ewe/ 公～ ram/ 小～ lamb/ ～叫 baa; bleat
【羊肠小道】 yángcháng xiǎodào narrow winding trail; meandering footpath
【羊毫】 yángháo writing brush made of goat's hair
【羊毛】 yángmáo sheep's wool; fleece ◇ ～衫 woollen sweater; cardigan/ ～袜 woollen socks or stockings
【羊毛出在羊身上】 yángmáo chū zài yáng shēnshang after all, the wool still comes from the sheep's back — in the long run, whatever you're given, you pay for
【羊排】 yángpái mutton chop; lamb chop
【羊皮】 yángpí sheepskin: 披着～的狼 a wolf in sheep's clothing
【羊皮纸】 yángpízhǐ parchment
【羊群里头出骆驼】 yángqún lǐtou chū luòtuo stand out like a camel in a flock of sheep
【羊肉】 yángròu mutton: 烤～串 mutton cubes roasted on a skewer; kebab
【羊质虎皮】 yángzhì-hǔpí a sheep in a tiger's skin — outwardly strong, inwardly weak

阳* yáng ① (in Chinese philosophy, medicine, etc.)

yang, the masculine or positive principle in nature ② the sun ③ open; overt: 阴一套,～一套 act one way in public and another in private; be engaged in double-dealing ④ belonging to this world; concerned with living beings ⑤〈物〉positive: ～离子 positive ion; cation ⑥ male genitals
【阳电】 yángdiàn positive electricity
【阳奉阴违】 yángfèng-yīnwéi overtly agree but covertly oppose; comply in public but oppose in private; feign compliance
【阳关道】 yángguāndào broad road; thoroughfare: 你走你的～,我过我的独木桥。 You take the open road, I'll cross the log bridge — you go your way, I'll go mine.
【阳光】 yángguāng sunlight; sunshine: ～充足 full of sunlight; with plenty of sunshine (或 sun); sunny/ ～普照大地。 Sunlight floods the earth. 或 The sun illuminates every corner of the land.
【阳极】 yángjí 〈物〉positive pole; positive electrode; anode
【阳间】 yángjiān this world
【阳历】 yánglì solar calendar
【阳平】 yángpíng 〈语〉rising tone, the second of the four tones in modern standard Chinese pronunciation
【阳台】 yángtái balcony

扬* yáng ① raise: ～手 raise one's hand (and beckon)/ ～起灰尘 raise (或 kick up) a dust/ ～鞭催马 flourish the whip to urge on the horse; whip one's horse on ② winnow: ～谷去糠 winnow the chaff from the grain ③ spread; make known: 宣～ propagate; publicize
【扬长而去】 yángcháng ér qù stalk off; swagger off
【扬帆】 yángfān 〈书〉hoist the sails; set sail
【扬眉吐气】 yángméi-tǔqì feel proud and elated
【扬名】 yángmíng make a name for oneself; become famous: ～天下 become world-famous; become known throughout the country
【扬弃】 yángqì develop what is useful or healthy and discard what is not
【扬声器】 yángshēngqì loudspeaker: 高频～ tweeter/ 低频～ woofer
【扬言】 yángyán threaten (that one is going to take action): ～要进行报复 threaten to retaliate
【扬扬】 yángyáng triumphantly; complacently: 得意～ be immensely proud; look triumphant/ ～自得 be very pleased with oneself; be complacent

杨 yáng poplar
【杨柳】 yángliǔ ① poplar and willow ② willow
【杨桃】 yángtáo 〈植〉carambola

佯 yáng pretend; feign; sham: ～作不知 feign ignorance; pretend not to know/ ～死 feign death; play dead
【佯攻】 yánggōng 〈军〉feign (或 simulate) attack; make a feint
【佯言】 yángyán 〈书〉tell lies; lie

疡 yáng 〈医〉sore: 溃～ ulcer

洋* yáng ① vast; multitudinous ② ocean: 太平～ the Pacific Ocean ③ foreign: ～房 Western-style house ④ modern: ～办法 modern methods ⑤〈旧〉silver coin
【洋场】 yángchǎng metropolis infested with foreign adventurers (usu. referring to preliberation Shanghai): ～恶少 rich young bully in a metropolis (in old China)
【洋葱】 yángcōng onion
【洋服】 yángfú Western-style clothes
【洋灰】 yánghuī cement
【洋泾浜】 yángjīngbāng pidgin (English)
【洋里洋气】 yánglǐyángqì in an ostentatiously foreign style
【洋人】 yángrén foreigner
【洋相】 yángxiàng 〔多用于〕: 出～ make an exhibition of oneself
【洋洋】 yángyáng ① numerous; copious: ～万言 run to ten thousand words — be very lengthy ② 见"扬扬" yángyáng
【洋洋大观】 yángyáng dàguān spectacular; grandiose; im-

posing

【洋洋洒洒】 yángyángsǎsǎ voluminous; at great length: ~一大篇 a magnificent piece of writing

【洋溢】 yángyì be permeated with; brim with: 热情~的讲话 a speech brimming with warm feeling 宴会上~着团结友好的热烈气氛。The banquet was permeated with a warm atmosphere of unity and friendship.

yǎng

仰* yǎng ① face upward; ~着睡 sleep on one's back/ ~天大笑 laugh sardonically ② admire; respect; look up to: ~瞻 look at with reverence; pay one's respects to ③ rely on: ~给于人 rely on others for support

【仰慕】 yǎngmù admire; look up to

【仰人鼻息】 yǎng rén bíxī be dependent on the pleasure of others; be slavishly dependent

【仰望】 yǎngwàng ① look up at ② 〈书〉respectfully seek guidance or help from; look up to

【仰卧】 yǎngwò lie on one's back; lie supine ◇ ~起坐 〈体〉(do) sit-ups

【仰泳】 yǎngyǒng 〈体〉backstroke

【仰仗】 yǎngzhàng rely on; look to sb. for backing (或 support)

养* yǎng ① support; provide for: ~家 support a family ② raise; keep; grow: ~鸭 raise ducks/ ~鸟 keep pet birds/ ~花 grow flowers ③ give birth to: 她~了个儿子。She gave birth to a boy. ④ foster; adoptive: ~父(母) foster father (mother)/ ~子(女) adopted son (daughter) ⑤ form; acquire; cultivate: ~成良好的习惯 cultivate good habits ⑥ rest; convalesce; recuperate one's health; heal: ~身体 recuperate/ ~好伤 heal one's wounds ⑦ maintain; keep in good repair: ~路 maintain a road or railway

【养兵千日，用兵一时】 yǎng bīng qiānrì, yòng bīng yīshí maintain an army for a thousand days to use it for an hour

【养病】 yǎngbìng take rest and nourishment to regain one's health; recuperate: 他在家~呢。He's recuperating at home.

【养分】 yǎngfèn nutrient: 土壤~ soil nutrient

【养虎遗患】 yǎng hǔ yí huàn to rear a tiger is to court calamity — appeasement brings disaster

【养护】 yǎnghù ① maintain; conserve: 道路~ road maintenance/ 生物资源~ conservation of living resources ② curing: 混凝土~ concrete curing

【养活】 yǎnghuo 〈口〉① support; feed: ~一家子 support (或 feed) a family ② raise (animals) ③ give birth to: ~孩子 have a baby

【养鸡场】 yǎngjīchǎng chicken run; chicken farm

【养精蓄锐】 yǎngjīng-xùruì conserve strength and store up energy

【养老】 yǎnglǎo ① provide for the aged (usu. one's parents) ② live out one's life in retirement ◇ ~金 old-age pension

【养料】 yǎngliào nutriment; nourishment

【养神】 yǎngshén rest to attain mental tranquillity; repose: 闭目~ sit in repose with one's eyes closed

【养生】 yǎngshēng preserve one's health; keep in good health: ~之道 the way to keep in good health

【养鱼池】 yǎngyúchí fishpond

【养育】 yǎngyù bring up; rear: ~子女 bring up children

【养殖】 yǎngzhí breed (aquatics): ~海带 cultivate kelp

【养猪场】 yǎngzhūchǎng pig farm; piggery

【养尊处优】 yǎngzūn-chǔyōu enjoy high position and live in ease and comfort; live in clover

氧 yǎng 〈化〉oxygen (O)

【氧化】 yǎnghuà 〈化〉oxidize; oxidate

【氧气】 yǎngqì oxygen

痒* yǎng itch; tickle: 浑身发~ itch all over/ 搔到~处 scratch where it itches — hit the nail on the head/ 怕~ ticklish

【痒痒】 yǎngyang 〈口〉itch; tickle: 蚊子咬得腿上直~。The mosquito bites on my leg itch terribly.

yàng

怏 yàng

【怏怏】 yàngyàng disgruntled; sullen: ~不乐 unhappy about sth.; morose

恙 yàng 〈书〉ailment; illness: 无~ in good health/ 偶染微~ feel slightly indisposed

样* yàng ① appearance; shape: 这两支笔~儿差不多，色儿不一样。These two pens are alike except that they're different colours./ 几年没见，他还是那个~儿。It's years since I last saw him, but he still looks the same. ② sample; model; pattern: 鞋~ outline of a shoe; shoe pattern/ 校~ proof sheet ③ 〈量〉kind; type: 三~儿菜 three kinds of vegetables; three dishes/ 商品虽小，各~货物俱全。Small as it is, the shop stocks all kinds of wares.

【样本】 yàngběn ① sample book ② 〈印〉sample; specimen

【样品】 yàngpǐn sample (product); specimen

【样式】 yàngshì pattern; type; style; form: 各种~的羊毛衫 woollen sweaters in all styles

【样样】 yàngyàng every kind; each and every; all: 地里的活她~都会。She knows how to do every kind of farm work./ 这孩子德、智、体~都好。The child is developing in every way, morally, intellectually and physically.

【样子】 yàngzi ① appearance; shape: 这件大衣的~很好看。This coat is well cut./ 这活做得不象~。This job has been done too crudely. ② manner; air: 看他那高兴的~。How happy he looks!/ 装出一副公正的~ assume a righteous posture (或 manner, air) ③ sample; model; pattern: 衣服~ clothes pattern/ 做出~来 set an example ④ 〈口〉tendency; likelihood: 天象是要下雨的~。It looks like rain./ 看~这星期他来不了。It seems (或 looks as if) he won't be able to come this week.

漾 yàng ① ripple: 荡~ ripple; undulate ② brim over; overflow: 碗里的汤快~出来了。The soup in the bowl is brimming over./ 他脸上~出了笑容。His face broadened into a smile.

yāo

幺 yāo one (used for the numeral — orally)

夭 yāo ① die young ② 〈书〉tender; young: ~桃秾李 beautiful peach and plum blossoms — a beautiful young lady

【夭亡】 yāowáng die young

【夭折】 yāozhé ① die young ② come to a premature end: 谈判中途~。The negotiations came to a premature end.

吆 yāo

【吆喝】 yāohe ① cry out; call: 走的时候~一声。Give us a shout when it's time to leave. ② cry one's wares: 她头一次上街卖菜，不好意思~。The first time she went out selling vegetables, she was too shy to cry out for customers. ③ loudly urge on (an animal): 牲口不听~。The animal wouldn't obey its driver.

妖* yāo ① goblin; demon; evil spirit ② evil and fraudulent: ~术 sorcery; witchcraft; black art ③ bewitching; coquettish: 打扮得~里~气 (of a woman) be seductively dressed

【妖怪】 yāoguài monster; bogy; goblin; demon

【妖精】 yāojing ① evil spirit; demon ② alluring woman

【妖媚】 yāomèi seductively charming; bewitching
【妖魔】 yāomó evil spirit; demon
【妖魔鬼怪】 yāomó-guǐguài demons and ghosts; monsters of every description
【妖孽】 yāoniè ① person or event associated with evil or misfortune ② evildoer
【妖娆】 yāoráo 〈书〉 enchanting; fascinating
【妖人】 yāorén sorcerer; enchanter
【妖物】 yāowù evil spirit; monster
【妖言】 yāoyán heresy; fallacy: ～惑众 spread fallacies to deceive people
【妖艳】 yāoyàn pretty and coquettish
【妖冶】 yāoyě pretty and coquettish

要* yāo ① demand; ask ② force; coerce
另见

【要求】 yāoqiú ask; demand; require; claim: ～发言 ask to be heard; ask for the floor/ 严格～自己 set strict demands on oneself; be strict with oneself/ 达到质量～ fulfil quality requirements/ 提出领土～ make territorial claims/ ～赔偿 claim compensation/ 这项工作～精神高度集中。 This job calls for intense concentration.
【要挟】 yāoxié coerce; put pressure on; threaten: 对小国进行～ use coercion against small nations/ ～对方 put pressure on the other party

腰* yāo ① waist; small of the back: 齐～深 waist-deep; up to the waist/ 弯～ bend down; stoop/ ～酸腿疼 aching back and legs/ 扭了～ sprain one's back muscles/ 两手叉～ with one's hands on one's hips; akimbo/ 拦～抱住 seize sb. round the middle ② waist (of a garment): 裤～ waist of trousers ③ pocket: 我～里还有些钱。 I've still got some money in my pocket. ④ middle: 半山～ halfway up a mountain; on a hillside
【腰包】 yāobāo purse; pocket: 把钱装进自己的～ pocket the money
【腰部】 yāobù waist; small of the back
【腰带】 yāodài waistband; belt; girdle
【腰痛】 yāotòng lumbago
【腰子】 yāozi 〈口〉 kidney

邀* yāo ① invite; request: 应～出席 be present by invitation ② solicit; seek: ～准 seek approval; ask permission ③ intercept: ～击 intercept (the enemy); waylay
【邀功】 yāogōng 〈书〉 take credit for someone else's achievements: ～请赏 take credit and seek rewards for someone else's achievements
【邀集】 yāojí invite to meet together; call together: 今天～大家来开个座谈会。 You have been invited here today to hold a forum.
【邀请】 yāoqǐng invite: 发出～ send (或 extend) an invitation ◇ ～国 host country/ ～赛 〈体〉 invitational tournament

yáo

尧 Yáo Yao, a legendary monarch in ancient China
【尧舜】 Yáo-Shùn Yao and Shun, legendary monarchs in ancient China — ancient sages

肴 yáo meat and fish dishes
【肴馔】 yáozhuàn sumptuous courses at a meal

姚 Yáo a surname

窑 yáo ① kiln: 砖～ brickkiln ② (coal) pit: 小煤～ small coal pit ③ cave dwelling
【窑洞】 yáodòng cave dwelling

谣 yáo ① ballad; rhyme: 民～ popular verse; ballad/ 童～ children's rhyme ② rumour: 造～ cook up a story and spread it around; start a rumour/ 辟～ refute a rumour

【谣传】 yáochuán ① rumour; hearsay ② it is rumoured that; rumour has it that
【谣言】 yáoyán rumour; groundless allegation: 散布～ spread (或 circulate) rumours/ 戳穿～ give the lie to a rumour

遥 yáo 〈书〉 distant; remote; far: 千里之～ at a distance of a thousand li; a thousand li away
【遥控】 yáokòng remote control; telecontrol ◇ ～飞机 remote control aircraft; telecontrolled airplane
【遥望】 yáowàng look into the distance
【遥相呼应】 yáo xiāng hūyìng echo each other at a distance; coordinate with each other from afar
【遥遥】 yáoyáo far away; a long way off: ～领先 be far ahead; get a good lead/ ～相对 stand far apart facing each other/ ～无期 not (realizable, etc.) within the foreseeable future
【遥远】 yáoyuǎn distant; remote; faraway: ～的将来 the distant (或 remote) future/ ～的山村 a remote mountain village/ ～的边疆 remote frontiers/ 路途～ a long journey; a long way to go

摇* yáo shake; wave; rock; turn: ～铃 ring a bell/ ～扇子 wave a fan/ ～辘轳 turn a windlass/ ～船 row a boat/ ～橹 scull/ 小狗～着尾巴跑了。 The little dog ran off wagging its tail.
【摇摆】 yáobǎi sway; swing; rock; vacillate: 柳枝迎风～。 The branches of the willow trees swayed in the breeze./ 船身～。 The ship rocked./ 左右～ vacillate now to the left, now to the right ◇ ～舞 rock and roll
【摇唇鼓舌】 yáochún-gǔshé flap one's lips and beat one's tongue; wag one's tongue; engage in loose talk (to stir up trouble)
【摇荡】 yáodàng rock; sway
【摇动】 yáodòng ① wave; shake: 欢迎的群众～着花束。 The welcoming crowd waved their bouquets. ② sway; rock: 大树在狂风中～。 The big tree rocked in the strong wind.
【摇撼】 yáohàn give a violent shake to; shake to the root or foundation; rock
【摇晃】 yáohuang rock; sway; shake: 地震时大楼都～了。 The tall buildings shook during the earthquake./ 这椅子有点～。 The chair is a bit rickety (或 shaky)./ 他病了很久,走起路来摇摇晃晃。 He walked with faltering steps after a long illness.
【摇篮】 yáolán cradle: 古代文化的～ the cradle of ancient culture
【摇旗呐喊】 yáo qí nàhǎn wave flags and shout battle cries — bang the drum for sb.
【摇钱树】 yáoqiánshù a legendary tree that sheds coins when shaken — a ready source of money
【摇身一变】 yáo shēn yī biàn 〈贬〉 give oneself a shake and change into another form — suddenly change one's identity
【摇手】 yáoshǒu shake one's hand in admonition or disapproval
【摇头】 yáotóu shake one's head
【摇头摆尾】 yáotóu-bǎiwěi shake the head and wag the tail — assume an air of complacency or levity
【摇头晃脑】 yáotóu-huàngnǎo wag one's head — look pleased with oneself; assume an air of self-approbation or self-conceit
【摇尾乞怜】 yáo wěi qǐ lián wag the tail ingratiatingly — fawn
【摇摇欲坠】 yáoyáo yù zhuì tottering; crumbling; on the verge of collapse
【摇曳】 yáoyè flicker; sway: ～的灯光 flickering light/ 垂柳在微风中轻轻～。 The willow branches swayed gently in the breeze.
【摇椅】 yáoyǐ rocking chair

徭 yáo
【徭役】 yáoyì corvée

瑶 yáo 〈书〉 precious jade

yǎo

杳 yǎo 〈书〉 distant and out of sight: ～无踪迹 disappear without a trace; vanish
【杳如黄鹤】 yǎo rú huánghè disappear like the yellow crane — nowhere to be found
【杳无音信】 yǎo wú yīnxìn there has been no news whatsoever about sb.; have never been heard of since

咬* yǎo ① bite; snap at: ～不动 too tough to bite (或 chew)/ ～了一口 take a bite/ ～紧牙关 grit (或 clench) one's teeth; endure with dogged will/ 一口～定 assert emphatically; insist ② grip; bite: 这个旧螺母～不住扣儿了。 This old nut won't bite (或 grip). ③ (of a dog) bark: 鸡叫狗～ cocks crow and dogs bark ④ incriminate another person (usu. innocent) when blamed or interrogated: 反～一口 trump up a countercharge against one's accuser; make a false countercharge ⑤ pronounce; articulate: 这个字他～不准。 He can't pronounce this word correctly./ ～字清楚 clear articulation (或 enunciation)
【咬文嚼字】 yǎowén-jiáozì pay'excessive attention to wording
【咬牙】 yǎoyá ① grit (或 set, clench, gnash) one's teeth: 恨得直～ gnash one's teeth in hatred ② grind one's teeth (in sleep)
【咬牙切齿】 yǎoyá-qièchǐ gnash one's teeth: ～地咒骂 curse between one's teeth
【咬住】 yǎozhù ① bite into; grip with one's teeth ② grip; take firm hold of; refuse to let go of: 别老～我那句话不放。 Don't keep nagging me about that remark of mine.

窈 yǎo
【窈窕】 yǎotiǎo 〈书〉 ① (of a woman) gentle and graceful ② (of a palace, landscape, etc.) secluded

舀 yǎo ladle out; spoon up (或 out); scoop up: ～汤 ladle out soup
【舀子】 yǎozi dipper; ladle; scoop

yào

药* yào ① medicine; drug; remedy: 服～ take medicine/ 良～ good medicine; a good remedy/ 煎～ decoct herbal medicine ② certain chemicals: 火～ gunpowder/ 杀虫～ insecticide/ 耗子～ rat poison; ratsbane ③ 〈书〉 cure with medicine: 不可救～ incurable; incorrigible ④ kill with poison: ～老鼠 poison rats
【药材】 yàocái medicinal materials; crude drugs
【药草】 yàocǎo medicinal herbs
【药厂】 yàochǎng pharmaceutical factory
【药店】 yàodiàn drugstore; chemist's shop; pharmacy
【药方】 yàofāng prescription: 开～ write out a prescription
【药房】 yàofáng ① drugstore; chemist's shop; pharmacy ② hospital pharmacy; dispensary
【药费】 yàofèi expenses for medicine; charges for medicine
【药粉】 yàofěn (medicinal) powder
【药膏】 yàogāo ointment; salve
【药剂】 yàojì medicament; drug ◇ ～师 pharmacist; druggist/ ～学 pharmaceutics; pharmacy
【药酒】 yàojiǔ medicinal liquor
【药力】 yàolì efficacy of a drug (或 medicine): ～发作。 The drug is taking effect./ ～达不到。 The medicine was not potent enough to produce the desired effect.
【药片】 yàopiàn (medicinal) tablet
【药品】 yàopǐn medicines and chemical reagents
【药瓶】 yàopíng medicine bottle
【药铺】 yàopù herbal medicine shop
【药水】 yàoshuǐ ① liquid medicine; medicinal liquid ② lotion
【药丸】 yàowán pill: 大～ bolus

【药味】 yàowèi ① herbal medicines in a prescription ② flavour of a drug
【药物】 yàowù medicines; pharmaceuticals; medicaments
【药箱】 yàoxiāng medical kit; medicine-chest· 急救～ first-aid kit
【药性】 yàoxìng property of a medicine
【药皂】 yàozào medicated soap

要* yào ① important; essential: ～事 an important matter (或 affair)/ 择～记录 note down the essential points/ 上述规定希严格执行为～。 It is imperative that the above rules be strictly observed. ② want; ask for; wish; desire: 这双鞋我还～呢。 I want to keep these shoes./ 谁没有票，问他～。 Anyone without a ticket can ask her for one. ③ ask (或 want) sb. to do sth.: 老人家～我替他写封信。 The old man asked me to write a letter for him./ 班长～我们五点以前归队。 The squad leader told us to get back before five o'clock. ④ want to; wish to: 我还有几句话～说。 I'd like to say a few more words. ⑤ must; should: 这是～紧的事。 It is necessary (或 imperative, essential) ⑥ shall; will; be going to: ～下雨了。 It's going to rain. ⑦ need; take: 这项任务～十天才能完成。 It will take ten days to get the work done. ⑧ [表示估计，用于比较]: 你们比～比我们辛苦得多。 You must have had a much tougher time than we did. ⑨ 〈连〉 if; suppose; in case: 明天～下雨，我们就不去了。 If it rains tomorrow, we won't go./ 他～来不了呢？ Suppose he can't come?/ 我～赶不回来，你替我说一声。 In case I can't get back in time, please apologize for me. 另见 yāo
【要隘】 yào'ài strategic pass
【要不】 yàobù 〈连〉 otherwise; or else; or: 我得马上走，～就赶不上火车了。 I have to leave at once or I'll miss the train. 又作"要不然"
【要不得】 yàobude no good; intolerable: 这种自私行为～。 Such selfish acts are not to be tolerated.
【要不是】 yàobushi if it were not for; but for: ～他们勇敢地抢救国家财产，那损失可就大了。 If it weren't for their courage in rescuing the state property, the loss would have been enormous.
【要冲】 yàochōng communications centre (或 hub): 军事～ strategic point
【要道】 yàodào thoroughfare: 交通～ important line of communications; vital communications line
【要得】 yàodé 〈方〉 good; fine; desirable: 这个办法～! That's a good idea!
【要地】 yàodì important place; strategic point
【要点】 yàodiǎn ① main points; essentials; gist: 抓住～ grasp the main points/ 讲话的～ the gist of a speech ② key strongpoint: 战略～ strategic point
【要犯】 yàofàn important criminal
【要饭】 yàofàn beg (for food or money) ◇ ～的 beggar
【要害】 yàohài ① vital part; crucial point: ～部位 vital part/ ～部门 key department/ 回避～问题 evade the crucial question (或 issue)/ 击中～ hit home
【要好】 yàohǎo ① be on good terms; be close friends: 他们俩从小就很～。 The two of them have been close friends since childhood. ② eager to improve oneself; try hard to make progress: 这孩子很～。 The kid is eager to make progress.
【要价】 yàojià ask a price; charge: ～过高 demand an exorbitant price; ask too much/ 对方在谈判中～越来越高。 The other party demanded more and more in the negotiations.
【要件】 yàojiàn ① important document ② important condition
【要津】 yàojīn 〈书〉 key post: 位居～ hold a key post
【要紧】 yàojǐn ① important; essential: 随便做什么工作，～的是实事求是。 In whatever we do, the most important thing is to be realistic and down-to-earth./ 我有点～的事儿跟他商量。 I have something urgent to discuss with him. ② be critical; be serious; matter: 不～，你明天去也可以。 You can go tomorrow. It doesn't matter.
【要领】 yàolǐng ① main points; essentials; gist: 不得～ fail to grasp the main points; not see what sb. is driving at;

miss the point ② essentials (of an exercise in military or athletic training): 掌握～ grasp the essentials

【要略】yàolüè outline; summary

【要么】yàome ＜连＞ or; either...or...: 赶快给他发个电报，～挂个长途也行。Send him a telegram at once, or call him long-distance./ 他来，～我去，我们总得碰个头。Either he comes here or I go there; in any case we've got to see each other.

【要面子】yào miànzi be keen on face-saving; be anxious to keep up appearances

【要命】yàomìng ① drive sb. to his death; kill: 这样短的期限，要了我的命，也完成不了定额。I cannot fulfil the quota in such a short time even if I kill myself. ② confoundedly; extremely; awfully; terribly: 热得～ awfully hot ③ a nuisance: 真～，车胎又没气了。What an awful nuisance. The tyre's flat again.

【要强】yàoqiáng be eager to excel; be anxious to outdo others

【要人】yàorén very important person (V.I.P.); important personage

【要塞】yàosài fort; fortress; fortification

【要是】yàoshi if; suppose; in case: ～下雨怎么办？ What if it rains? 或 Suppose it rains?

【要素】yàosù essential factor; key element

【要闻】yàowén important news; front-page story

【要职】yàozhí important post: 身居～ hold an important post

【要旨】yàozhǐ main idea; gist

钥 yào
另见 yuè
【钥匙】yàoshi key: 一把～开一把锁 open different locks with different keys — use different methods to deal with different people or problems

曜 yào ＜书＞ ① sunlight ② shine; illuminate

耀* yào ① shine; illuminate; dazzle: 照～ shine upon; illuminate ② boast of; laud: 夸～ boast about ③ honour; credit

【耀武扬威】yàowǔ-yángwēi make a show of one's strength; swagger around

【耀眼】yàoyǎn dazzling: 车灯～。The headlights are dazzling.

yē

耶 yē
另见 yé
【耶稣】Yēsū ＜宗＞ Jesus
◇ ～会 the Society of Jesus; the Jesuits/ ～基督 Jesus Christ/ ～教 Protestantism

掖 yē tuck in; thrust in between: 把被角～好 tuck in the corner of the quilt/ 把纸条从门缝里～进去 slip a note under the door/ 腰里～着枪 with a pistol in one's belt
另见 yè

椰* yē ＜植＞ coconut palm; coconut tree; coco

【椰子】yēzi ① coconut palm; coconut tree; coco ② coconut
◇ ～肉 coconut meat/ ～糖 coconut candy/ ～汁 coconut milk

噎 yē ① choke: 慢点吃，留神别～着。Eat slowly. Be careful not to choke. ② ＜方＞ render sb. speechless by saying sth. blunt or rude; choke off: 他一句话就把她给～回去了。She was just going to say something when that one remark of his choked her off.

yé

爷* yé ① ＜方＞ father: ～娘 father and mother ② ＜方＞

grandfather ③ uncle (a respectful form of address for an elderly man) ④＜旧＞ a form of address for an official or rich man: 老～ sir; master; lord/ 少～ young master (of the house) ⑤ god: 老天～ God; Heaven

【爷爷】yéye ＜口＞ ① (paternal) grandfather ② grandpa (a respectful form of address for an old man)

耶 yé ＜书＞ ＜助＞〔表示疑问的语气〕: 是～非～? Is it or isn't it? 或 Yes or no?
另见 yē

揶 yé
【揶揄】yéyú ＜书＞ ridicule; deride

yě

也* yě ① ＜副＞ also; too; as well; either: 我妹妹～是售货员。My sister is a shop assistant too./ 你不去，我～不去。If you're not going, I'm not going either. ②＜副＞〔表示强调，常跟"再""一点""连"等字连用〕: 他病得一点～不吃饭。He is so ill that he doesn't feel like eating anything. ③＜副＞〔表示转折或让步，常跟上文的"虽然""即使"等呼应〕: 我即使干不了重活，～可以干点轻活嘛。If I can't do heavy work, I can still do some light work./ 你不说我～知道。You don't have to tell me. I know already. ④＜副＞〔表示委婉等语气〕: ～只好这样了。We'll have to leave it at that

【也罢】yěbà ①〔表示容忍或只得如此〕: 这次不去～，下次可一定要让我去。All right, I won't go this time but next time you must let me go. ② ＜助＞〔叠用，表示不以某种情况为条件〕whether...or...; no matter whether: 刮风～，下雪～，他都坚持长跑。He keeps up his long-distance running whether it's windy or snowy.

【也好】yěhǎo ① it may not be a bad idea; may as well: 说明一下～。Better give an explanation./ 让他们自己干一干，实践出真知嘛。We might as well let them do it themselves, since real knowledge comes from practice. ②〔叠用，表示不以某种情况为条件〕whether ... or ...; no matter whether

【也许】yěxǔ ＜副＞ perhaps; probably; maybe: 他～病了。Perhaps he's ill./ 我～来，～不来。I may or may not come.

【也...也...】yě...yě... ①〔表示并列〕: 操场上也有打球的，也有跑步的。Some of the people on the sports ground are playing ball games, some are running./ 他也不抽烟，也不喝酒。He neither smokes nor drinks. ②〔表示不以某种情况为条件〕: 天好我们也干，天不好我们也干。We never stop working, rain or shine./ 你去也得去，不去也得去。You've got to go, whether you want to or not./ 他左想也不是，右想也不是。He just couldn't make up his mind either way.

冶 yě ① smelt (metal) ② ＜书＞ seductively dressed or made up

【冶金】yějīn metallurgy ◇ ～工业 metallurgical industry/ ～学 metallurgy

【冶炼】yěliàn smelt

野* yě ① open country; the open: 田～ open fields ② limit; boundary: 分～ line of demarcation/ 视～ field of vision ③ not in power; out of office: 在～党 a party not in power/ 下～ be forced to relinquish power ④ wild; uncultivated; undomesticated; untamed: ～花 wild flower/ ～鸭 wild duck ⑤ rude; rough: 说话太～ use coarse language; speak rudely/ 动作太～ rough play ⑥ unrestrained; abandoned; unruly: 这孩子的心都玩～了。After the fun he's had during the holidays, the boy can't concentrate on his school work.

【野餐】yěcān picnic

【野草】yěcǎo weeds: ～丛生 be overgrown (或 choked) with weeds

【野地】yědì wild country; wilderness

【野果】yěguǒ wild fruit

【野火】yěhuǒ prairie fire; bush fire: ～烧不尽，春风吹又生。Not even a prairie fire can destroy the grass; it grows again when the spring breeze blows.

【野鸡】 yějī (ring-necked) pheasant
【野蛮】 yěmán ① uncivilized; savage ② barbarous; cruel; brutal
【野禽】 yěqín wild fowl
【野人】 yěrén savage
【野生】 yěshēng wild; uncultivated; feral ◇ ~动物 wild animal; wildlife/ ~植物 wild plant
【野史】 yěshǐ unofficial history
【野兽】 yěshòu wild beast; wild animal
【野兔】 yětù hare
【野外】 yěwài open country; field: 在~工作 do fieldwork
【野味】 yěwèi game (as food)
【野心】 yěxīn wild ambition; careerism: 侵略~ aggressive ambitions/ ~不死 cling to one's ambitious designs/ ~勃勃 be overweeningly ambitious; be obsessed with ambition ◇ ~家 careerist/ ~狼 a vicious wolf — a person of wicked ambition
【野性】 yěxìng wild nature; unruliness
【野战】 yězhàn <军> field operations
【野猪】 yězhū wild boar

yè

业* yè ① line of business; trade; industry: 各行各~ all trades and professions; different trades and callings; all walks of life/ 矿~ mining industry ② occupation; profession; employment; job: 失~ be out of a job; be unemployed ③ course of study: 结~ complete a course of study; graduate ④ cause; enterprise: 创~ start an enterprise; do pioneering work ⑤ estate; property: 家~ family property ⑥ engage in: ~农 engage in farming ⑦ already: 已核实 have already been verified
【业绩】 yèjī outstanding achievement
【业经】 yèjīng already: ~批准 have been approved
【业务】 yèwù vocational work; professional work; business: 恢复正常~ resume normal business
【业余】 yèyú sparetime; after-hours; amateur ◇ ~爱好 hobby/ ~爱好者 amateur
【业主】 yèzhǔ owner (of an enterprise or estate); proprietor

叶* yè ① leaf; foliage: 落~ fallen leaves ② leaf-like thing: 百~窗 shutter; blind/ 一~扁舟 a small boat ③ page; leaf ④ part of a historical period: 清朝末~ the closing period of the Qing Dynasty/ 二十世纪中~ the middle of the twentieth century; mid-20th century
【叶落归根】 yè luò guī gēn falling leaves settle on their roots — a person residing elsewhere finally returns to his ancestral home
【叶片】 yèpiàn <植> (leaf) blade
【叶子】 yèzi leaf

页* yè page; leaf: 活~ loose leaf/ 一本三百~的书 a book of three hundred pages/ 打开新的一~ open up a new chapter

曳 yè drag; haul; tug; tow

夜* yè night; evening: 冬天昼短~长。 In winter the days are short and the nights long./ 三天三~讲不完。 It would take days to tell it all.
【夜班】 yèbān night shift
【夜半】 yèbàn midnight
【夜叉】 yèchā ① <佛教> yaksha (a malevolent spirit) ② a hideous, ferocious person
【夜长梦多】 yècháng-mèngduō a long night is fraught with dreams — a long delay means many hitches
【夜场】 yèchǎng evening show

【夜车】 yèchē ① night train ② [多用于]: 开~ work deep into the night; burn the midnight oil
【夜工】 yègōng night work; night job: 打~ work at night; do a night job 又作"夜作"
【夜间】 yèjiān at night: ~行军 march by night; night march/ ~施工 carry on construction work at night ◇ ~演习 night exercise
【夜景】 yèjǐng night scene (或 view)
【夜阑人静】 yèlán-rénjìng in the dead of night; in the still (或 quiet) of the night
【夜郎自大】 Yèláng zìdà ludicrous conceit of the king of Yelang — parochial arrogance
【夜里】 yèli at night
【夜明珠】 yèmíngzhū a legendary luminous pearl
【夜幕】 yèmù curtain of night; gathering darkness: ~笼罩着大地。 The land is enveloped in a curtain of darkness./ ~降临。 Night has fallen.
【夜勤】 yèqín night duty
【夜色】 yèsè the dim light of night: 趁着~ by starlight or moonlight
【夜晚】 yèwǎn night
【夜校】 yèxiào night (或 evening) school
【夜以继日】 yè yǐ jì rì day and night; round the clock: 工程正在~地进行。 Work is going on day and night at the construction site.
【夜莺】 yèyīng nightingale
【夜游神】 yèyóushén the legendary god on patrol at night — a person who is up and about at night; night owl
【夜总会】 yèzǒnghuì nightclub

咽 yè 见"哽咽" gěngyè; "呜咽" wūyè 另见 yān; yàn

烨 yè <书> ① firelight or sunlight ② (of light) bright

晔 yè <书> (of light) bright

液* yè liquid; fluid; juice: 体~ body fluid/ 胃~ gastric juice
【液体】 yètǐ liquid

掖 yè ① support sb. by the arm ② help; assist; promote: 奖~ <书> encourage by rewarding and promoting 另见 yē

谒 yè <书> call on (a superior or an elder person); pay one's respects to: ~陵 pay homage at sb.'s mausoleum
【谒见】 yèjiàn call on (a superior or a senior in the clan hierarchy); have an audience with

腋 yè ① <生理> axilla; armpit ② <植> axil
【腋毛】 yèmáo armpit hair
【腋窝】 yèwō armpit

靥 yè dimple

yī

一* yī ① one: ~万~ eleven thousand/ 三千~ three thousand one hundred/ ~营~连 the First Company of the First Battalion/ 棉纺~厂 No. 1 Cotton Mill ② single; alone; only one: ~枪就命中目标 hit the target with a single shot/ 你~个人行吗? Can you manage all by yourself? ③ same: 意见不~。 Opinions differ./ ~根藤上的苦瓜 bitter gourds from the same vine — people with a similar bitter past ④ whole; all; throughout: ~冬 the whole winter; all winter; throughout the winter/ ~脸的土 one's face covered with dust/ ~屋子的人都欢腾起来。 Everybody in the room was overjoyed. ⑤ each; per; every time: 四个小组，~组五人 five groups with five people in each/ ~小时六十公里 at 60 kilometres per hour/ 大家~提起那艰苦创业的日子，总有说不完的话。 Every time we talk about the hard pioneering days, we have so much to say that we can't get it all out. ⑥ also; otherwise: 汞溴红～名红汞。Merbromin is also known as mercurochrome. ⑦ concentrated; wholehearted: ～心～意 heart and soul; wholeheartedly ⑧〔表示动作是一次或短暂的〕: 笑一笑 give a smile/ 歇一歇 have a rest/ 等一等 wait a bit/ 瞧一眼 take a look/ 咳一声 give a cough ⑨〔用在动词或动量词之前，表示先做某个动作，下文说明动作当时间紧接〕～跳跳了过去 get over in one jump/ 他一脚把球踢进了球门。He kicked the ball into the goal. 或 He kicked a goal./ 经他这么一说，大家又都有信心了。This explanation of his restored our confidence. ⑩〔与"就"即"等字相呼应，表示两事时间紧接〕once; as soon as: 一切好准备，就破土动工。Construction will begin as soon as preparations are completed. ⑪〈书〉〈助〉〔用于某些词前加强语气〕:事态之严重～至于此! To think that things should have come to such a pass!/ ～似瓮中捉鳖 be as easy as catching a turtle in a jar

〔注意〕在第四声(去声)字前念第二声(阳平)，如"一半" yíbàn; "一共" yígòng。在第一、二、三声(阴平、阳平、上声)字前念第四声(去声)，如"一天" yìtiān; "一年" yìnián; "一点" yìdiǎn。本词典为简便起见，条目中的"一"字，都注第一声(阴平)。

【一败涂地】yī bài tú dì suffer a crushing defeat

【一班人】yībānrén members of a squad — a small body of people working together

【一般】yībān ① same as; just like: 他们俩～高。The two of them are the same height./ 火车飞～地急去。The train flashed past like lightning. ② general; ordinary; common: ～工作人员 ordinary personnel; an ordinary member of the staff/ ～的做法 common practice/ ～说来 generally speaking

【一般见识】yībān jiànshi lower oneself to the same level as sb.: 别跟他～! You don't want to bother yourself arguing with a person like him.

【一半】yībàn one half; half; in part: ～以上 more than half/ 歉收～由于干旱，～由于虫灾。The crop failure was due in part to drought and in part to insect pests.

【一…半…】yī… bàn…〔分别用在同义词或近义词前，表示不多或不久〕: 这活儿一时半会儿完不了。This job can't be finished in a short while./ 我只听到一句半句的。What I heard was very fragmentary.

【一辈子】yībèizi all one's life; throughout one's life; as long as one lives; a lifetime: ～也忘不了。I won't forget as long as I live.

【一本万利】yī běn wàn lì a small investment brings a ten thousand-fold profit; make big profits with a small capital

【一本正经】yī běn zhèngjīng in all seriousness; in dead earnest: 装得～的样子 be sanctimonious

【一鼻孔出气】yī bíkǒng chūqì breathe through the same nostrils — sing the same tune

【一笔勾销】yī bǐ gōuxiāo write off at one stroke; cancel: 前帐～ cancel all debts

【一笔抹杀】yī bǐ mǒshā blot out at one stroke; condemn out of hand; totally negate: 这些成绩是不能～的。These achievements cannot be gainsaid.

【一臂之力】yī bì zhī lì a helping hand: 助我～ lend me a hand

【一边】yībiān ① one side: 这块木料只有～光滑。Only one side of this piece of wood is smooth. ②〔表示一个动作跟另一个动作同时进行〕at the same time; simultaneously: 他～往前走，～唱着歌儿。He sang as he strolled along./ ～喝茶，～聊天 chat over a cup of tea

【一边倒】yībiāndǎo ① lean to one side; side with sb. without reservation ② predominate; enjoy overwhelming superiority

【一并】yībìng〈副〉along with all the others; in the lump: 连同类似情况～考虑 to be considered together with all similar cases

【一病不起】yī bìng bù qǐ take to one's bed and never leave it again; fall ill and die

【一波未平，一波又起】yī bō wèi píng, yī bō yòu qǐ hardly has one wave subsided when another rises — one trouble follows another

【一…不…】yī… bù…①〔分别用在两个动词前面，表示动作或

情况一经发生就不改变〕: 一去不返 gone never to return/ 一定不易 unalterable ②〔分别用在一个名词和一个动词前面，表示强调或夸张〕:一字不漏 without missing a single word/ 一动不动 not move an inch; not stir; be perfectly still

【一不怕苦，二不怕死】yī bù pà kǔ, èr bù pà sǐ fear neither hardship nor death

【一不做，二不休】yī bù zuò, èr bù xiū carry the thing through, whatever the consequences; in for a penny, in for a pound

【一步登天】yī bù dēng tiān reach the sky in a single bound — attain the highest level in one step; have a meteoric rise

【一差二错】yīchā-èrcuò possible mistake or mishap: 万一有个～ just in case there is a slip somewhere; just in case of accidents

【一场空】yīchángkōng all in vain; futile: 竹篮打水～ as futile as drawing water with a bamboo basket

【一唱百和】yī chàng bǎi hè when one starts singing, all the others join in — (of a suggestion, etc.) meet with general approval

【一唱一和】yīchàng-yīhè sing a duet with sb.; sing the same tune; echo each other

【一朝天子一朝臣】yī cháo tiānzǐ yī cháo chén every new sovereign brings his own courtiers — a new chief brings in new aides

【一尘不染】yī chén bù rǎn not soiled by a speck of dust; spotless: 仪器上～。The apparatus is spotlessly clean.

【一成不变】yī chéng bù biàn immutable and frozen; invariable; unalterable: ～的东西是没有的。Nothing is immutable./ 没有～的规则。There is no hard and fast rule.

【一筹莫展】yī chóu mò zhǎn can find no way out; be at one's wits' end; be at the end of one's tether

【一触即发】yī chù jí fā may be triggered at any moment; be on the verge of breaking out: 武装冲突有～之势。Armed conflict may break out at any moment./ 形势～。It's an explosive situation.

【一触即溃】yī chù jí kuì collapse at the first encounter

【一次】yīcì once: 我只跟他见过一面。I've met him only once./ 机器～试运成功。The machine worked successfully on its first test run.

【一蹴而就】yī cù ér jiù accomplish in one move

【一旦】yīdàn ① in a single day; in a very short time: 毁于～ be destroyed in one day ② once; in case; now that: 他们多年相处，～分别，不免依依不舍。After being together for years, they can't bear to part from each other.

【一刀两断】yī dāo liǎng duàn sever at one blow — make a clean break

【一道】yīdào together; side by side; alongside: 我们～走吧。Let's go together./ 学校、家长和社会～担负起教育下一代的责任。School, parents and society share the responsibility of educating the younger generation.

【一得之愚】yī dé zhī yú〈谦〉my humble opinion

【一等】yīděng first-class; first-rate; top-grade ◇～功 Merit Citation, First Class/ ～秘书 First Secretary/ ～品 first-rate (或 top-quality) product

【一点儿】yīdiǎnr a bit; a little: ～也不累 not feel the least bit tired/ ～都不知道 have not the faintest idea/ ～用处也没有 utterly useless/ 这事我知道～ I know a little about it./ 壶里水只剩下这么～了。This is all the water that's left in the kettle./ 还有～希望。There is still a gleam of hope./ 这是我们的～心意。This is just a small token of our appreciation./ 桌上没有～灰尘。There isn't a speck of dust on the desk.

【一点一滴】yīdiǎn-yīdī every little bit: ～地积累资料 gather material bit by bit

【一定】yīdìng ① fixed; specified; definite; regular: 工人每个月都有～的生产指标。The workers have fixed monthly production quotas./ 按照～的规格进行生产 work according to specifications/ 勘探队员成天在野外作业，没有～的住处。The prospectors are always out in the field and never settle down in a fixed place./ 她一忙起来，吃饭睡觉都没有～的时间了。When she gets really busy, she doesn't keep regular hours for eating or sleeping. ② certainly; surely; necessarily: 我们的目的～要达到。我们的目的～能够达到。 Our goal must be attained. Our goal can unquestionably be attained./ 星期天～来啊！Be sure to come on Sunday. ③ given; particular; certain: 在～意义上 in a certain sense/ 在～程度上 to a certain degree/ 在～条件下 under given conditions ④ proper; fair; due: 具有～规模的工厂 a fair-sized factory/ 作出了～的贡献 have made some contributions/ 达到～水平 reach a fairly high level

【一定之规】 yīdìng zhī guī ① fixed pattern ② one's own way

【一动】 yīdòng easily; frequently; at every turn: 他～就生气。He takes offence easily.

【一度】 yīdù once; on one occasion; for a time: 一年～ once a year; yearly; annually/ 他因病～休学。He stopped going to school for a time on account of illness.

【一端】 yīduān one aspect (或 side) of the matter: 此其～。This is one aspect of the matter./ 各执～ each sticking to his own argument

【一…而…】 yī… ér… 〔分别用在两个动词前面，表示前一个动作很快产生了结果〕: 一怒而去 go away in a temper; leave in anger/ 一饮而尽 empty the glass at one gulp/ 一拥而上 rush up in a crowd/ 一掠而过 skim over

【一而再，再而三】 yī ér zài, zài ér sān again and again; time and again; repeatedly

【一二】 yī-èr one or two; just a few; just a little: 略知～ know a little about; have some idea about/ 邀请～知己 invite a few close friends

【一…二…】 yī…èr… 〔分别加在某些双音节形容词的两个词素前面，表示强调〕: 一清二白 perfectly clean; unimpeachable; spotless/ 一清二楚 perfectly clear; as clear as daylight; crystal clear

【一发千钧】 yī fà qiān jūn a hundredweight hanging by a hair — in imminent peril: 在这～的时刻 at this critical moment

【一帆风顺】 yī fān fēng shùn plain (或 smooth) sailing

【一反常态】 yī fǎn chángtài depart from one's normal behaviour; act out of character

【一方面】 yī fāngmiàn ① one side: 这只是事情的～。This is only one side of the matter. ②〔常叠用〕on the one hand…, on the other hand…; for one thing…, for another…: 他们一很想去医院看望班长，一又怕影响他休息。On the one hand they wanted very much to visit their squad leader in hospital; on the other hand, they didn't want to disturb his rest./ 这场球打输了，一是由于对方实力较强，另一也是因为我们没有配合好。We lost the game because, for one thing, our opponents were quite strong and, for another, our teamwork was poor.

【一夫多妻制】 yīfū-duōqīzhì polygyny; polygamy

【一夫一妻制】 yīfū-yīqīzhì monogyny; monogamy

【一概】 yīgài 〈副〉one and all; without exception; totally; categorically: ～拒绝 reject without exception/ ～排斥 totally exclude

【一概而论】 yīgài ér lùn 〔多用于否定〕treat (different matters) as the same: ～ not to be lumped together

【一干二净】 yīgān-èrjìng thoroughly; completely: 忘得～ clean (或 completely) forget/ 把自己洗刷得～ try to absolve oneself from all blame

【一共】 yīgòng altogether; in all; all told: ～二十个。There are twenty in all (或 all told)./ ～多少人？How many are there altogether?

【一股脑儿】 yīgūnǎor 〈方〉completely; lock, stock and barrel; root and branch 又作"一古脑儿"

【一鼓作气】 yī gǔ zuò qì press on to the finish without letup; get sth. done in one vigorous effort: 他们～爬上山顶。They pressed on without letup until they got to the top of the hill.

【一贯】 yīguàn consistent; persistent; all along: ～政策 consistent policy

【一国三公】 yī guó sān gōng a state with three rulers — divided leadership

【一哄而起】 yī hōng ér qǐ (of a group of people) be aroused to precipitate action; rush headlong into mass action

【一哄而散】 yī hòng ér sàn break up (或 disperse) in a hubbub

【一呼百诺】 yī hū bǎi nuò have hundreds at one's beck and call

【一呼百应】 yī hū bǎi yìng hundreds respond to a single call

【一晃】 yīhuǎng flash: 窗外有个人影，～就不见了。A figure flashed past the window.

【一晃】 yīhuàng (of time) pass in a flash: ～几年又过去了。Several years passed in a flash.

【一挥而就】 yī huī ér jiù a flourish of the pen and it's done; finish a piece of writing or a painting at one go

【一回生，二回熟】 yī huí shēng, èr huí shú ① first time strangers, second time friends; soon get to know each other ② first time awkward (或 clumsy), second time skilful; difficult at first, easy later on

【一回事】 yī huí shì ① one and the same (thing): 他们所说的是～。They were talking about the same thing. ② one thing: 主观愿望是一，实际情况又是一。Subjective wishes are one thing, objective reality is another.

【一会儿】 yīhuìr ① a little while: 我们歇～。Let's rest for a while. ② in a moment; presently: 我～就来。I'll be coming in a moment. 或 I won't be a minute./ ～地上积起了一层雪。Soon the ground was covered with a layer of snow. ③〔叠用在两个反义词前面，表示情况的交替〕now … now…; one moment… the next…: 天气～晴～阴。The weather is now clear, now cloudy./ 他～这么说，～那么说。He says one thing one moment and another thing the next.

【一己】 yījǐ oneself: ～之私 one's own selfish interests

【一技之长】 yī jì zhī cháng proficiency in a particular line (或 field); professional skill; speciality

【一见如故】 yī jiàn rú gù feel like old friends at the first meeting

【一见钟情】 yī jiàn zhōngqíng fall in love at first sight

【一箭双雕】 yī jiàn shuāng diāo shoot two hawks with one arrow; kill two birds with one stone

【一经】 yījīng 〈副〉〔表示只要经过某种步骤或行为〕as soon as; once: 错误～发现，就应立即纠正。Mistakes should be corrected as soon as detected.

【一…就…】 yī… jiù… 〔表示两事时间上前后紧接〕no sooner …than…; the moment…; as soon as; once: 这情况她一看就明白了。She took in the situation at a glance./ 他一接到通知就动身了。He started off as soon as he got the message.

【一举】 yījǔ with one action; at one stroke; at one fell swoop: ～歼灭来犯之敌 wipe out the invaders at one fell swoop/ ～成名 become famous overnight; achieve instant fame

【一举两得】 yī jǔ liǎng dé kill two birds with one stone

【一句话】 yī jù huà in a word; in short

【一蹶不振】 yī jué bù zhèn collapse after one setback; never be able to recover after a setback

【一刻千金】 yīkè qiānjīn every minute is precious

【一孔之见】 yī kǒng zhī jiàn a peephole view; a narrow view; a limited view

【一口】 yī kǒu ① a mouthful; a bite: 吸～气 draw a breath/ 吃不成个胖子 You can't build up your constitution on one mouthful. ② with certainty; readily; flatly: ～断定 arbitrarily assert; allege/ ～答应 readily agree; readily promise/ ～回绝 flatly refuse

【一口气】 yīkǒuqì ① one breath ② in one breath; without a break; at one go; at a stretch: ～干完 finish the work at one go/ ～跑了五千米 run 5,000 metres at a stretch

【一块儿】 yīkuàir ① at the same place: 在～工作 work at the same place ② together: ～去 go together

【一览】 yīlǎn general survey; bird's-eye view

【一览无余】 yī lǎn wú yú take in everything at a glance

【一劳永逸】 yī láo yǒng yì get sth. done once and for all: ～的解决办法 a solution that holds good for all time; a permanent solution

【一力】 yīlì do one's best; do all one can: ～成全 do one's best to help (sb. to achieve his aim)

【一连】 yīlián 〈副〉in a row; in succession; running: ～三年获得丰收 reap good harvests for three years in a row/ ～下了三天雨。It rained for three days running.

【一连串】 yīliánchuàn a succession of; a series of; a string

of; a chain of: ～的事件 a succession of events/ ～问题 a series of questions

【一了百了】 yī liǎo bǎi liǎo ① all troubles end when the main trouble ends ② death ends all one's troubles

【一鳞半爪】 yīlín-bànzhǎo odd bits; fragments: ～的情况 odd bits of information/ ～的知识 fragmentary knowledge

【一溜烟】 yīliùyān (run away) swiftly: 小汽车～开走了。The car sped off./ 他一～就没影几了。He disappeared in an instant (或 a flash).

【一路】 yīlù ① all the way; throughout the journey: ～上说说笑笑 chat cheerfully all the way/ ～多保重。Take care of yourself on the journey./ 一平安! Have a pleasant journey. 或 Have a good trip. 或 Bon voyage./ 客队～领先。The visiting team led from the beginning. ② of the same kind: ～货 one of a kind; birds of a feather ③ go the same way; take the same route: 我们是～吗? Are we going the same way?

【一律】 yīlù ① same; alike; uniform: ～对待 treat in the same way (或 equally)/ 不宜强求～。No rigid uniformity should be sought. ② all; without exception: 国家不分大小, 应该一平等。All countries, big or small, should be equal (或 on an equal footing).

【一落千丈】 yī luò qiānzhàng drop a thousand *zhang* in one fall — suffer a disastrous decline

【一马当先】 yī mǎ dāngxiān take the lead; be in the forefront

【一脉相承】 yī mài xiāng chéng come down in one continuous line; can be traced to the same origin

【一毛不拔】 yī máo bù bá unwilling to give up even a hair — very stingy

【一面】 yīmiàn ① one side; one aspect: 这座房子朝南的～有两个窗户。The house has two windows on the south side./ 这里的条件既有有利的～, 也有不利的～。The situation here has both favourable and unfavourable aspects. ②〔表示一个动作跟另一个动作同时进行〕at the same time; simultaneously: ～教, ～学 learn while teaching/ 他～说着, ～朝门口走去。So saying, he made for the door.

【一面之词】 yīmiàn zhī cí the statement of only one of the parties

【一面之交】 yī miàn zhī jiāo have met only once; be casually acquainted

【一鸣惊人】 yī míng jīng rén (of an obscure person) amaze the world with a single brilliant feat; set the world on fire

【一命呜呼】 yī mìng wūhū die; kick the bucket

【一模一样】 yīmú-yīyàng exactly alike; as like as two peas: 她长得跟她母亲～。She's the image of her mother.

【一目了然】 yī mù liǎorán be clear at a glance

【一目十行】 yī mù shí háng take in ten lines at a glance — read rapidly

【一年半载】 yīnián-bànzǎi a year or so; in about a year

【一年到头】 yī nián dào tóu throughout the year; all (the) year round

【一年四季】 yīnián-sìjì throughout (the four seasons of) the year; all the year round

【一年之计在于春】 yī nián zhī jì zàiyú chūn the whole year's work depends on a good start in spring

【一念之差】 yī niàn zhī chā a wrong decision made in a moment of weakness (with serious consequences); a momentary slip

【一诺千金】 yī nuò qiānjīn a promise that will be kept; that's a solemn promise

【一拍即合】 yī pāi jí hé fit in readily; chime in easily

【一盘散沙】 yī pán sǎnshā (like) a sheet of loose sand — in a state of disunity

【一偏】 yīpiān one-sided: ～之见 one-sided view

【一瞥】 yīpiē ① a quick glance: 就在这一～之间, 我看出了她非常激动。In a quick glance I noticed her agitation. ② a glimpse; a brief survey:《长城》一～ A Glimpse of the Great Wall

【一贫如洗】 yī pín rú xǐ penniless; in utter destitution

【一暴十寒】 yī pù shí hán work hard for one day and do nothing for ten — work by fits and starts

【一妻多夫制】 yīqī-duōfūzhì polyandry

【一齐】 yīqí 〈副〉 at the same time; simultaneously; in unison: ～鼓掌 clap hands in unison/ ～努力 make a con-

certed effort/ ～出动 go into action simultaneously/ 人和行李～到了。The luggage arrived at the same time as the passengers.

【一起】 yīqǐ ① in the same place: 住在～ live in the same place ② together; in company

【一气】 yīqì ① at one go; without a break; at a stretch: ～游了三千米 swim three thousand metres at a stretch ② of the same gang; hand in glove: 串通～ work hand in glove; collude ③ a spell; a fit: 瞎闹～ raise hell; kick up a row/ 胡吹～ tell tall stories

【一气呵成】 yīqì hē chéng ① (of an essay) form a coherent whole; make smooth reading ② get sth. done at one go; accomplish sth. without any interruption or letup

【一钱不值】 yī qián bù zhí not worth a penny; utterly worthless; mere trash

【一窍不通】 yī qiào bù tōng know nothing about (a subject); lack the slightest knowledge of; be utterly ignorant of

【一切】 yīqiè all; every; everything: 抓住一机会 seize every opportunity/ 把一献给祖国 give one's all to one's country

【一清早】 yīqīngzǎo early in the morning

【一丘之貉】 yī qiū zhī hé jackals from the same lair; birds of a feather

【一去不复返】 yī qù bù fù fǎn gone for ever; gone never to return

【一人得道, 鸡犬升天】 yī rén dé dào, jī-quǎn shēng tiān when a man attains the Tao (enlightenment and immortality), even his pets ascend to heaven — when a man gets to the top, all his friends and relations get there with him

【一任】 yīrèn 〈书〉 allow: 岂能～他胡作非为? How can we let him run amuck?

【一仍旧贯】 yī réng jiù guàn stick to the old practice; follow the old routine

【一日千里】 yīrì qiānlǐ a thousand *li* a day — at a tremendous pace; with giant strides

【一日三秋】 yīrì sānqiū one day (away from a dear one) seems like three years

【一如既往】 yī rú jìwǎng just as in the past; as before; as always

【一扫而光】 yī sǎo ér guāng make a clean sweep of; clear off; finish off; get rid of sth. lock, stock and barrel: 忧虑的心情～ rid oneself of all shadows of anxiety

【一色】 yīsè ① of the same colour: 水天～。The water and the sky are of one hue. ② of the same type; uniform: ～的瓦房 tiled houses of a uniform style

【一身】 yīshēn ① the whole body; all over the body: ～是泥 covered all over with mud/ ～是汗 be sweating all over ② a suit: ～新衣服 a new suit of clothes ③ a single person: 孑然～ solitary; all alone

【一身是胆】 yī shēn shì dǎn know no fear; be absolutely fearless

【一生】 yīshēng all one's life; throughout one's life

【一声不响】 yī shēng bù xiǎng not say a word; not utter a sound

【一失足成千古恨】 yī shīzú chéng qiāngǔ hèn a single slip may cause lasting sorrow; the error of a moment becomes the regret of a lifetime

【一时】 yīshí ① a period of time: 此～彼～。Times have changed. ② for a short while; temporary; momentary: 风行～ be popular for a while; be all the rage/ ～的多数 a temporary majority/ 为～的表面现象所迷惑 be misled by transient phenomena; be taken in by appearances/ 不凭～的热情 not rely on a moment's enthusiasm/ ～想不起来 can't recall offhand (或 for the moment)/ 看一个人不要光看他的～一事。Don't judge a person by a single act or a short period of his life. ③〔叠用〕now..., now...; one moment..., the next: 他的病～好, ～坏。He'd be better for a while and then have a relapse.

【一时一刻】 yīshí-yīkè 〔多用于否定〕for a single moment

【一事无成】 yī shì wú chéng accomplish nothing; get nowhere

【一视同仁】 yī shì tóng rén treat equally without discrimination

【一手】 yīshǒu ① proficiency; skill: 露～ show off one's

skill/ 业务上有～ be proficient in one's own line; know one's stuff/ 这个篮球队在防守上很有～。 This basketball team has a very strong defence. ② trick; move: 他这～可真毒辣! What a vicious trick he played! ③ single-handed; all by oneself; all alone: 这场争端是～挑起的。 The dispute was all started by them./ 小王是他叔叔～拉扯大的。 Xiao Wang was brought up all along by his uncle./ ～包办 keep everything in one's own hands; take everything on oneself

【一手遮天】 yī shǒu zhē tiān shut out the heavens with one hand — hide the truth from the masses; hoodwink the public

【一瞬】 yīshùn an instant; a flash; the twinkling of an eye: ～即逝 vanish in a flash

【一丝不苟】 yī sī bù gǒu not be the least bit negligent; be scrupulous about every detail; be conscientious and meticulous

【一丝不挂】 yī sī bù guà not have a stitch on; be stark-naked

【一丝一毫】 yīsī-yīháo a tiny bit; an iota; a trace: 没有～的差别 without the least difference

【一塌糊涂】 yītāhútú in a complete mess; in an awful (或 terrible) state: 他把事情弄得～。 He has made a mess of the job./ 屋子乱得～。 The room was a complete mess./ 为了一件小事争得～ make a fearful row over a mere trifle

【一体】 yītǐ ① an organic (或 integral) whole: 融成～ merge into an organic whole / all people concerned; to a man: 上述各项望～遵照。 It is expected that the above stipulations will be observed by all.

【一天】 yī tiān ① a day: ～二十四小时都有人值班。 There are people on duty round the clock. ② one day (in the past) ③ 〈方〉 the whole day; all (the) day; from morning till night: 忙碌了～ have been busy all day

【一天到晚】 yī tiān dào wǎn from morning till night; from dawn to dusk; all day long

【一条心】 yī tiáo xīn be of one mind; be at one

【一通百通】 yī tōng bǎi tōng grasp this one thing and you'll grasp everything; sort this one thing out and you'll sort out all the rest

【一同】 yītóng 〈副〉 together; at the same time and place: ～出发 set out together

【一统】 yītǒng unify (a country): ～天下 unify the whole country/ 大～ a unified domain

【一团和气】 yī tuán héqì keep on good terms with everyone at the expense of principle; keep on the right side of everyone

【一团漆黑】 yī tuán qīhēi pitch-dark —utterly hopeless: 把我们的工作描绘成～是完全错误的。 It is completely wrong to describe our work as an utter failure.

【一团糟】 yītuánzāo a complete mess; chaos

【一网打尽】 yī wǎng dǎjìn catch the whole lot in a dragnet; round up the whole gang at one fell swoop

【一往情深】 yīwǎng qíngshēn be passionately devoted; be head over heels in love

【一往无前】 yīwǎng wúqián press forward with indomitable will: ～的精神 indomitable spirit

【一望无际】 yī wàng wú jì stretch as far as the eye can see; stretch to the horizon: ～的大草原 a boundless stretch of grassland

【一味】 yīwèi 〈副〉 blindly: ～蛮干 persist in acting blindly/ ～地固执成见 stubbornly stick to one's own view/ ～迁就 make endless concessions; make one concession after another

【一文不名】 yī wén bù míng penniless

【一问三不知】 yī wèn sān bù zhī say "I don't know" to every question — not know a thing; be entirely ignorant

【一窝蜂】 yīwōfēng like a swarm of bees: 孩子们～似地奔向海滩。 The children swarmed towards the beach.

【一无是处】 yī wú shìchù without a single redeeming feature; devoid of any merit: 不要把他说得～。 Don't talk as if he had no saving graces.

【一无所长】 yī wú suǒcháng have no special skill; be Jack of all trades

【一无所有】 yī wú suǒyǒu not own a thing in the world;

not have a thing to one's name

【一无所知】 yī wú suǒzhī know nothing about; not have the least inkling of; be absolutely ignorant of

【一五一十】 yīwǔ-yīshí (narrate) systematically and in full detail

【一误再误】 yī wù zài wù ① make one error after another; keep on making mistakes ② make things worse by repeated delays: 你这病要即刻治，可能～了。 You should go and see a doctor at once. You mustn't put it off any more.

【一息尚存】 yī xī shàng cún so long as one still has a breath left; till one's last gasp

【一席话】 yī xí huà what one says during a conversation: 他的～打动了我的心。 What he said touched my heart./ 听君一席话，胜读十年书。 I profit more from one consultation with you than from ten years of reading.

【一系列】 yīxìliè a series of: ～措施 a series of measures/ ～问题 a whole series of questions/ ～的事件 a whole train of events

【一下】 yīxià ①〔用在动词前后,表示做一次或试着做〕 one time; once: 亲～孩子的脸 give the baby a kiss on the cheek/ 拍～他的肩膀 give him a pat on the shoulder/ ～打死两个苍蝇 kill two flies with one swat/ 让我想～。 Let me think a bit. 或 Let me see. / 打听～再说。 Better make some inquiries first./ 请等～。 Wait a minute, please./ 老鹰～就把小鸡叼走了。 The hawk snatched away the chick at one swoop. ② in a short while; all at once; all of a sudden: 灯～又亮了。 After a little while the lights went on again./ 这天气,～冷,～热。 Look at this weather. It's cold one moment and hot the next./ 天～阴了。 It became overcast all of a sudden./ 不能希望人们把旧观念～都清除掉。 One cannot expect people to get rid of their old ideas overnight.

【一线】 yīxiàn a ray of; a gleam of: ～希望 a gleam of hope/ ～光明 a ray of light

【一相情愿】 yī xiāng qíngyuàn one's own wishful thinking 又作 "一厢情愿"

【一向】 yīxiàng ① earlier on; lately: 前～雨水多。 There was quite a lot of rain earlier on./ 这～进步不小吧? You must have made a lot of progress lately. ② 〈副〉 consistently; all along

【一小撮】 yī xiǎocuō a handful

【一笑置之】 yī xiào zhì zhī dismiss with a laugh (或 smile); laugh off

【一些】 yīxiē 〈量〉 a number of; certain; some; a few; a little: 有～国家 some (或 a number of) countries/ 作～适当的调整 make certain appropriate readjustments/ 有～事情我还不明白。 There are a few things that still puzzle me。/ 只剩这～了,够吗? There's only this much left. Is it enough?/ 我想说的就这～。 That's all I wanted to say.

【一泻千里】 yī xiè qiānlǐ ① (of a river) rush down a thousand li — flow down vigorously ② (of a writer's style) bold and flowing

【一心】 yī xīn ① wholeheartedly; heart and soul

【一心一意】 yīxīn-yīyì heart and soul; wholeheartedly

【一星半点】 yīxīng-bàndiǎn a tiny bit; a very small amount: 这可是细活,不能有～差错。 This is a high precision job. There mustn't be the slightest slip.

【一行】 yīxíng a group travelling together; party: 总理及其～ the Premier and his party

【一言不发】 yī yán bù fā not say a word; keep one's mouth shut

【一言既出,驷马难追】 yī yán jì chū, sìmǎ nán zhuī a word once spoken cannot be overtaken even by a team of four horses — what is said cannot be unsaid

【一言难尽】 yī yán nán jìn it is hard to explain in a few words; it's a long story

【一言为定】 yī yán wéi dìng that's settled then

【一言以蔽之】 yī yán yǐ bì zhī to sum up in a word

【一样】 yīyàng the same; equally; alike; as...as...: ～耐用 equally durable; 他跑得他哥哥跑得～快。 He runs as fast as his brother./ 我买的伞和你的～。 The umbrella I've bought is the same as yours.

【一叶知秋】 yī yè zhī qiū the falling of one leaf heralds the autumn; it is a straw in the wind; a small sign can indicate a great trend

【一一】 yìyī one by one; one after another: ~检查 examine one by one/ 没时间~介绍 have no time to go into details or cover everything/ ~告别 say goodbye to everyone; bid farewell to all, one after another

【一……一……】 yī…yī… ①〔分别用在两个名词前面〕ⓐ〔表示整个〕:一生一世 one's whole life; all one's life ⓑ〔表示数量极少〕一言一行 every word and deed/ 一举一动 every act/ 一点一滴 every drop; every bit ②〔分别用在同类的动词前面,表示动作的连续〕:一蹦一跳 skipping and hopping ③〔分别用在相对的动词前面,表示动作协调配合或交替进行〕:一问一答 one asking and the other answering/ 一打一拉 strike and stroke alternately; hit and cajole by turns; alternate hard and soft tactics ④〔分别用在相反的方位词,形容词等前面,表示相反的方位或情况〕:一东一西 one east, one west; poles apart/ 一长一短 one short, one long

【一衣带水】 yī yī dài shuǐ a narrow strip of water: ~的邻邦 close neighbours separated only by a strip of water

【一意孤行】 yī yì gū xíng cling obstinately to one's course; act wilfully; be bent on having one's own way

【一语道破】 yī yǔ dàopò lay bare the truth with one penetrating remark; hit the nail on the head

【一语破的】 yī yǔ pò dì hit the mark with a single comment

【一月】 yīyuè January

【一再】 yízài time and again; again and again; repeatedly: ~宣称 declare time and again/ ~表示感谢 express one's gratitude again and again/ 一让再让 make one concession after another/ 一拖再拖 postpone again and again

【一早】 yìzǎo 〈口〉 early in the morning: 我明天~就告诉他。I'll let him know first thing tomorrow morning.

【一朝】 yìzhāo ① in one day: ~覆亡 collapse (或 be toppled) in one short day ② once: ~被蛇咬,十年怕井绳。Once bitten by a snake, one shies at a coiled rope for the next ten years — once bitten, twice shy.

【一朝一夕】 yìzhāo-yìxī in one morning or evening; overnight; in one day: 非~之功 not the work of a single day/ 不是~所能完成的 cannot be accomplished overnight

【一针见血】 yī zhēn jiàn xiě pierce to the truth with a single pertinent remark; hit the nail on the head: ~地指出 point out sharply

【一枕黄粱】 yī zhěn huángliáng Golden Millet Dream — a brief dream of grandeur

【一阵】 yízhèn a burst; a fit; a peal: ~掌声 a burst of applause/ ~咳嗽 a fit (或 spasm) of coughing/ ~笑声 peals of laughter/ ~狂风 a violent gust of wind; a blast (of wind)/ ~枪声 a burst of gunfire/ 脸上红~,白~ one's face turning now red, now pale

【一阵子】 yízhènzi a period of time; a spell: 这~尽下雨。We've had a spell of rainy weather.

【一知半解】 yìzhī-bànjiě have a smattering of knowledge; have scanty (或 half-baked) knowledge

【一直】 yìzhí ① straight ahead; keep straight on ②〈副〉 continuously; always; all along; all the way: 雪~下了两天两夜。 It snowed for two days and nights on end./ 我们~是同事。We've been colleagues all along./ 从年初起~到现在 from the beginning of the year right up to now; ever since the beginning of the year

【一纸空文】 yī zhǐ kōngwén a mere scrap of paper

【一致】 yízhì showing no difference; identical; unanimous; consistent: 观点~ hold identical views; be of the same view/ 步调~ march in step; act in unison/ 官兵~ unity between officers and men/ 取得完全~的意见 reach unanimity; reach a consensus/ 提案~通过。The resolution was adopted (或 carried) unanimously./ 举国上下,~努力。The whole nation is working together with one mind.

【一掷千金】 yī zhì qiānjīn ① stake a thousand pieces of gold on one throw ② throw away money like dirt; spend money like water

衣* yī ① clothing; clothes; garment: 丰~足食 have ample food and clothing/ 和~而睡 sleep in one's clothes/ 上~ jacket/ 毛~毛裤 woolen sweater and pants/ ~不蔽体 be dressed in rags ② coating; covering: 糖~ sugar coating

【衣钵】 yībō a Buddhist monk's mantle and alms bowl which he hands down to his favourite disciple; legacy

【衣橱】 yīchú wardrobe

【衣服】 yīfu clothing; clothes: 外边冷,多穿些~。It's cold outside. Put on more clothes.

【衣钩】 yīgōu clothes hook

【衣冠】 yīguān hat and clothes; dress: ~不整 be sloppily dressed

【衣冠楚楚】 yīguān chǔchǔ be immaculately dressed

【衣冠禽兽】 yīguān qínshòu a beast in human attire; brute

【衣柜】 yīguì wardrobe

【衣架】 yījià ① coat hanger; clothes-rack ② clothes tree; clothes stand

【衣锦还乡】 yī jǐn huán xiāng return to one's hometown in silken robes — return home after making good

【衣料】 yīliào material for clothing; dress material

【衣裳】 yīshang 〈口〉 clothing; clothes

【衣食住行】 yī-shí-zhù-xíng food, clothing, shelter and transportation — basic necessities of life

【衣物】 yīwù clothing and other articles of daily use

【衣箱】 yīxiāng suitcase; trunk

【衣着】 yīzhuó clothing, headgear and footwear: ~整洁 be neatly dressed

伊 yī he or she

【伊甸园】 yīdiànyuán 〈基督教〉 the Garden of Eden; paradise

【伊始】 yīshǐ beginning: 就职~ upon assuming office/ 下车~ as soon as one alights from the official carriage — on arrival at a new post

【伊斯兰教】 Yīsīlánjiào Islam; Islamism

医* yī ① doctor (of medicine) ② medical science; medical service; medicine: 行~ practise medicine ③ cure; treat: 把他的病~好 cure him of his illness

【医科】 yīkē medical courses in general; medicine

【医理】 yīlǐ principles of medical science; medical knowledge

【医疗】 yīliáo medical treatment

【医生】 yīshēng doctor; medical man: 内科~ physician/ 外科~ surgeon/ 实习~ intern

【医师】 yīshī (qualified) doctor

【医书】 yīshū 〔多指中医〕 medical book

【医术】 yīshù medical skill; art of healing

【医务】 yīwù medical matters
◇ ~工作者 medical worker/ ~人员 medical personnel (或 staff, workers); public health worker/ ~所 clinic

【医学】 yīxué medical science; medicine

【医药】 yīyào medicine ◇ ~常识 general medical knowledge/ ~费 medical expenses (或 costs)

【医院】 yīyuàn hospital

【医治】 yīzhì cure; treat; heal: ~无效 fail to respond to any medical treatment/ ~战争创伤 heal war wounds

依* yī ① depend on: 相~为命 depend on each other for existence; be bound by a common destiny ② comply with; listen to; yield to: 不能因为孩子小,就什么都~着他。You shouldn't comply with every wish of his just because he is a child./ 当初要是~了他们的主张,今天就不可能有这个水电站。If we had listened to them, this hydropower station would never have been built./ 你要是把这些资料弄丢了,我可不~你。If you lose these data, I'll never forgive you. ③ according to; in the light of; judging by: ~法惩办 punish according to law; deal with in accordance with the law; bring to justice/ ~我看 in my view; as I see it/ ~当时情况来说 in the light of the situation at the time; as matters then stood

【依此类推】 yī cǐ lèituī the rest may be deduced by analogy; and so on and so forth

【依次】 yīcì in proper order; successively: 他们~入座。They take their seats in proper order./ ~递补 fill vacancies in order of precedence/ ~说明下列问题 illustrate the following points in their given order

【依从】 yīcóng comply with; yield to: 她坚持要单独去,我只好~她了。 Since she insisted on going alone, I had to comply.

【依存】 yīcún depend on sb. or sth. for existence: 相互~ be interdependent

【依附】 yīfù depend on; attach oneself to; become an appendage to: ~权贵 attach oneself to bigwigs

【依旧】 yījiù as before; still: 书房的陈设~未变。 The study is furnished as it was before./ 他~是那个老样子。 He still looks his old self./ 山河~。 The landscape remains unchanged.

【依据】 yījù ① according to; in the light of; on the basis of; judging by: ~上述意见 in accordance with the above views ② basis; foundation: 提供科学~ provide scientific basis for sth./ 这些遗址是我们研究殷代文化的重要~。 These sites form an important basis for our study of the culture of the Yin Dynasty./ 当时我们没有什么蓝图可以作~。 We didn't have any blueprints to go by at that time.

【依靠】 yīkào ① rely on; depend on: ~自己的力量 depend on one's own strength ② something to fall back on; support; backing: 寻找~ seek support/ 生活有~ have one's livelihood assured

【依赖】 yīlài rely on; be dependent on: ~别人 be dependent on others

【依恋】 yīliàn be reluctant to leave; feel regret at parting from

【依凭】 yīpíng rely on; depend on

【依然】 yīrán still; as before: ~有效 still hold good; remain valid

【依然故我】 yīrán gù wǒ ① one's circumstances haven't changed much ② one is still one's same old self

【依然如故】 yīrán rú gù remain as before; remain unchanged (或 the same)

【依顺】 yīshùn be obedient: 百依百顺 be all obedience

【依托】 yītuō ① rely on; depend on ② support; prop; backing

【依稀】 yīxī vaguely; dimly: ~记得 vaguely remember/ ~可见 faintly (或 dimly) visible

【依样葫芦】 yī yàng huà hú lu copy mechanically

【依依】 yīyī reluctant to part: ~不舍 be reluctant to part; cannot bear to part

【依仗】 yīzhàng count on; rely on: ~权势 rely on one's power and position; count on one's powerful connections

【依照】 yīzhào according to; in the light of: ~情况而定 decide as circumstances require

咿

【咿呀】 yīyā ① 〈象〉 squeak; creak: ~的桨声 the squeak of oars in oarlocks/ 咿咿呀呀的提琴声 squeaky notes of a violin ② prattle; babble

猗

yī 〈书〉〈助〉〔多用于句末,相当于"啊"〕: 河水清且涟~。 The clear river ripples on.

揖

yī (make a) bow with hands clasped

壹

yī one (used as the numeral 一 on cheques, banknotes, etc. to avoid mistakes or alterations)

漪

yī 〈书〉 ripples

噫

yī 〈叹〉 alas

yí

仪*

yí ① appearance; bearing: 威~ dignified bearing ② ceremony; rite: 司~ master of ceremonies ③ present; gift: 贺~ present for wedding, birthday, etc. ④ apparatus; instrument: 地震~ seismograph

【仪表】 yíbiǎo ① appearance; bearing: ~堂堂 noble and dignified/ ~大方 poised and graceful ② meter

【仪器】 yíqì instrument; apparatus: 精密~ precision instrument

【仪容】 yíróng looks; appearance

【仪式】 yíshì ceremony; rite; function: 协定签字~ a ceremony for signing an agreement/ 宗教~ religious rites

【仪态】 yítài 〈书〉 bearing; deportment: ~万方 (of a beauty) appear in all her glory

【仪仗队】 yízhàngduì guard of honour; honour guard: 陆海空三军~ a guard of honour of the three services

夷

yí 〈书〉 ① smooth; safe: 化险为~ turn danger into safety; head off a disaster ② raze: ~为平地 level to the ground; raze ③ exterminate; wipe out: ~族 extermination of an entire family (a punishment in ancient times)

诒

yí 见"贻" yí

宜*

yí ① suitable; appropriate; fitting: 适~ appropriate; fitting and proper/ 老幼咸~ suitable (或 good) for both young and old ② should; ought to: 不~操之过急 You should not act in haste.

【宜人】 yírén pleasant; delightful: 气候~ pleasant (或 delightful) weather/ 景物~ attractive (或 charming) scenery

怡

yí 〈书〉 happy; joyful; cheerful: 心旷神~ feel relaxed and happy

【怡然】 yírán happy; contented: ~自得 happy and pleased with oneself

迤

yí 见"逶迤" wēiyí
另见 yǐ

饴

yí maltose: 甘之如~ enjoy sth. bitter as if it were sweet as malt sugar — gladly endure hardships

迻

yí 见"移" yí

【迻录】 yílù 〈书〉 write down; transcribe

【迻译】 yíyì 〈书〉 translate

贻

yí 〈书〉 ① make a gift of sth.; present ② bequeath; leave behind: ~患 sow seeds of disaster

【贻害】 yíhài leave a legacy of trouble: ~无穷 entail untold troubles

【贻人口实】 yí rén kǒushí give occasion for talk; give people grounds for ridicule; be a source of ridicule

【贻误】 yíwù affect adversely; bungle: ~工作 affect the work adversely

【贻笑大方】 yíxiào dàfāng make a laughingstock of oneself before experts; incur the ridicule of experts

咦

yí 〈叹〉〔表示惊异〕well; why: ~,你怎么又来了？ Why, you're here again!/ ~,这是怎么回事？ Hey, what's all this about?

姨*

yí ① one's mother's sister; aunt ② one's wife's sister; sister-in-law: 大~子 one's wife's elder sister/ 小~子 one's wife's younger sister

【姨表】 yíbiǎo maternal cousin: ~兄弟 male maternal cousins/ ~姐妹 female maternal cousins

【姨夫】 yífu the husband of one's maternal aunt; uncle 又作"姨父"

【姨妈】 yímā 〈口〉 (married) maternal aunt; aunt

【姨母】 yímǔ maternal aunt; aunt

【姨太太】 yítàitai 〈口〉 concubine

胰

yí 〈生理〉 pancreas

痍

yí 〈书〉 wound; trauma: 满目疮~。 Everywhere a scene of desolation meets the eye.

移*

yí ① move; remove; shift: ~走 move away/ ~沙造田 create farmland by removing sand drifts

【移动】 yídòng move; shift: 冷气团正向南~。 A cold air mass is moving southward./ 把靶位向左~两米。 Shift the target two metres to the left.

【移风易俗】yífēng-yìsú change prevailing habits and customs; transform social traditions

【移花接木】yíhuā-jiēmù ① graft one twig on another; graft ② stealthily substitute one thing for another

【移交】yíjiāo ① turn over; transfer; deliver into sb.'s custody: 这批仪器已经～给研究所了。These instruments have been turned over to the research institute. ② hand over one's job to a successor: 他临走前把工作～给我了。Before he left he handed over his job to me.

【移居】yíjū move one's residence; migrate

【移民】yímín ① migrate; (移出) emigrate; (移入) immigrate ② (移出) emigrant; (移入) immigrant

【移山倒海】yíshān-dǎohǎi remove mountains and drain seas — transform nature

【移栽】yízāi transplant

【移植】yízhí ① transplant: ～秧苗 transplant seedlings ② 〈医〉transplanting; grafting

【移樽就教】yí zūn jiùjiào take one's wine cup to another person's table to seek his advice — go to sb. for advice

蛇

yí 见"委蛇" wēiyí

另见 shé

遗*

yí ① lose: ～失 lose ② something lost: 路不拾～ No one pockets anything found on the road. ③ omit: ～忘 forget/ 补～ addendum ④ leave behind; keep back; not give: 不～余力 spare no efforts ⑤ leave behind at one's death; bequeath; hand down: ～风 customs handed down from past generations/ ～作 posthumous work (of an author, etc.)/ ～骨 remains (of the dead) ⑥ involuntary discharge of urine, etc.: 梦～ nocturnal emission

另见 wèi

【遗产】yíchǎn legacy; inheritance; heritage: 留下(继承)～ bequeath (inherit) a legacy/ 历史～ a legacy of history/ 文化～ cultural heritage ◇ 承受人 legatee/ ～税 inheritance tax; succession duty

【遗臭万年】yíchòu wànnián leave a stink for ten thousand years — go down in history as a byword of infamy

【遗传】yíchuán 〈生〉heredity; inheritance

【遗毒】yídú evil legacy; harmful tradition; pernicious influence

【遗腹子】yífùzǐ posthumous child

【遗稿】yígǎo a manuscript left unpublished by the author at his death; posthumous manuscript

【遗孤】yígū orphan

【遗骸】yíhái remains (of the dead)

【遗憾】yíhàn regret; pity: 对此表示～ express regret over the matter/ 一点不感到～ have no regrets/ 非常～,我不能接受你的邀请。I am very sorry I will not be able to accept your invitation./ 今晚的音乐会你不能来,实在～。It's really a pity that you can't come to the concert this evening.

【遗恨】yíhèn eternal regret

【遗迹】yíjī historical remains; vestige; traces: 古代人类的～ traces of ancient man/ 古代村落的～ sites of ancient villages

【遗老】yílǎo ① surviving adherent of a former dynasty; old fogy; old diehard ② 〈书〉old people who have witnessed big social changes

【遗留】yíliú leave over; hand down: 历史上～下来的边界问题 boundary questions left over by history/ 草案中仍然～几个问题。There are still a few points to clear up in the draft.

【遗漏】yílòu omit; leave out: 重要～ an important omission/ 名单上有～。There are some names missing from the list.

【遗民】yímín ① adherents of a former dynasty ② survivors of a great upheaval

【遗弃】yíqì abandon; forsake; cast off: ～妻儿 forsake one's wife and children

【遗缺】yíquē vacancy

【遗容】yíróng ① remains (of the deceased): 瞻仰～ pay one's respects to the remains of sb. ② a portrait of the deceased

【遗失】yíshī lose: 他的借书证～了。He has lost his library card./ ～声明 lost property notice

【遗事】yíshì ① incidents of past ages ② deeds of those now dead

【遗书】yíshū ① 〔多用做书名〕posthumous papers; writings of an author now dead ② a letter or note left by one immediately before death

【遗孀】yíshuāng widow; relict

【遗体】yítǐ remains (of the dead): 向～告别 pay one's last respects to the remains

【遗忘】yíwàng forget

【遗物】yíwù things left behind by the deceased

【遗像】yíxiàng a portrait of the deceased

【遗训】yíxùn teachings of the deceased

【遗言】yíyán words of the deceased; (a person's) last words

【遗址】yízhǐ ruins; relics: 古城～ the ruins of an ancient city

【遗志】yízhì unfulfilled wish; behest; work bequeathed by the deceased: 继承先烈～ carry out the behest of the martyrs; continue the work left by the martyrs

【遗嘱】yízhǔ testament; will; dying words

【遗著】yízhù posthumous work (of an author)

颐

yí 〈书〉① cheek: 支～ cheek in palm ② keep fit; take care of oneself

【颐养】yíyǎng 〈书〉keep fit; take care of oneself

【颐指气使】yízhǐ-qìshǐ order people about by gesture; be insufferably arrogant

疑*

yí ① doubt; disbelieve; suspect: 坚信不～ firmly believe; not have the slightest doubt/ 无可置～ beyond doubt; undoubtedly/ 释～ remove doubts; dispel suspicion ② doubtful; uncertain: ～点 doubtful (或 questionable) point: 存～ leave the question open

【疑案】yí'àn doubtful (或 disputed) case; open question; mystery

【疑兵】yíbīng troops deployed to mislead the enemy; deceptive deployment

【疑点】yídiǎn doubtful (或questionable) point: 这个案件还有几个～。There are still a few questionable points in the case.

【疑窦】yídòu cause for suspicion; suspicion: 顿生～ suddenly feel suspicious/ 启人～ arouse (或 awaken, raise) sb.'s suspicions

【疑惑】yíhuò feel uncertain; not be convinced: ～不解 feel puzzled; have doubts

【疑惧】yíjù apprehensions; misgivings

【疑虑】yílǜ misgivings; doubt: 消除心中的～ clear one's mind of doubt; free sb. from doubts and misgivings

【疑难】yínán difficult; knotty: ～问题 a knotty problem

【疑神疑鬼】yíshén-yíguǐ be terribly suspicious; be even afraid of one's own shadow

【疑团】yítuán doubts and suspicions: 满腹～ be full of doubts and suspicions/ ～顿释。The suspicions were cleared up at once.

【疑问】yíwèn query; question; doubt: 毫无～ doubtless; without a doubt; without question ◇ ～句 interrogative sentence

【疑心】yíxīn suspicion: 起～ become suspicious/ ～生暗鬼。Suspicions create imaginary fears./ 一看村里整个儿变了样,我真～自己走错了路。Finding the village completely changed, I really began to wonder whether I had come to the right place.

【疑心病】yíxīnbìng a suspicious frame of mind: 犯～ be oversuspicious (或 paranoiac)

【疑义】yíyì doubt; doubtful point: 毫无～ no doubt/ 对这一点准道还有什么～吗? Can there be any doubt about it?

【疑云】yíyún misgivings or suspicion clouding one's mind: ～消散。The misgivings were dispelled.

【疑阵】yízhèn deceptive battle array to mislead the enemy; stratagem

彝

yí 〈考古〉wine vessel: ～器 sacrificial vessel

yǐ

乙 * yǐ ① the second of the ten Heavenly Stems ② second: ~等 the second grade; grade B

已 * yǐ ① stop; cease; end: 争论不~ argue endlessly; be bogged down in endless argument ② already: 问题~解决。The problem has already been solved./ 雨季~过。The rainy season is over./ 为时~晚。It's too late./ ~成定局 be a foregone conclusion ③ 〈书〉thereafter; afterwards: ~而 later on; shortly afterwards ④ 〈书〉too: 不为~甚 refrain from going to extremes in meting out punishment, etc.

【已故】yǐgù deceased; late: ~地质学家 the late geologist

【已经】yǐjīng already: 天~黑了。It's already dark./ 这样~不错了。It's good enough as it is./ 这点前面~说过了。This has been dealt with above.

【已然】yǐrán be already so; have already become a fact: 与其补救于~, 不如防患于未然。To forestall is better than to amend. 或 Prevention is better than cure.

【已往】yǐwǎng before; previously; in the past

以 * yǐ ① use; take: ~其人之道, 还治其人之身。Deal with a man as he deals with you. 或 Pay somebody back in his own coin. ② according to: ~时启闭 open and close according to schedule/ ~到达先后为序 in order of arrival ③ because of: 不~人废言 not reject a saying because the speaker is what or who he is/ 不~失败自馁, 不~成功自满 not lose heart because of failure nor feel conceited because of success/ 何~知之? How do you know? ④ in order to; so as to: ~示区别 in order to distinguish this from other cases/ ~应急需 in order to answer an urgent need ⑤ 〈书〉at (a certain time); on (a fixed date): 余~三月一日返。I returned on March the first. ⑥ 〈书〉〈连〉〔跟"而"用法相同〕and; as well as: 淅沥~潇飒 raindrops pattering and wind rustling/ 城高~厚。The city wall is high and thick. ⑦ 〔放在方位词前表明时间、地位、方向或数量的界限〕: 十年~前 ten years ago or earlier/ 五千~内 less than five thousand

【以暴易暴】yǐ bào yì bào replace one tyranny by another

【以便】yǐbiàn so that; in order to; so as to; with the aim of; for the purpose of: 集中兵力包围敌人, ~聚而歼之 encircle the enemy with a concentrated force with the aim of annihilating him/ 今晚作好准备, ~明天一早动身 make preparations today for an early start tomorrow

【以次】yǐcì ① in proper order: 主人~给来宾斟酒。The host filled the guests' glasses in turn. ② the following: ~各章 the following chapters

【以德报怨】yǐ dé bào yuàn return good for evil; requite ingratitude with kindness

【以毒攻毒】yǐ dú gōng dú combat poison with poison; use poison as an antidote for poison

【以讹传讹】yǐ é chuán é incorrectly relay an erroneous message (so that it becomes increasingly distorted)

【以耳代目】yǐ ěr dài mù rely upon hearsay instead of seeing for oneself

【以攻为守】yǐ gōng wéi shǒu use attack as a means of defence; attack in order to defend

【以古非今】yǐ gǔ fēi jīn disparage the present by extolling the past

【以寡敌众】yǐ guǎ dí zhòng pit the few against the many; fight against heavy odds

【以观后效】yǐ guān hòu xiào (lighten a punishment and) see how the offender behaves

【以后】yǐhòu after; afterwards; later; hereafter: 会议今天开始, 大概一星期~结束。The conference begins today and will probably close in a week's time./ 别着急, ~你会有机会去的。Don't worry. You'll have a chance to go.

【以及】yǐjí as well as; along with; and

【以己度人】yǐ jǐ duó rén judge others by oneself; measure others' corn by one's own bushel

【以假乱真】yǐ jiǎ luàn zhēn mix the spurious with the genuine

【以儆效尤】yǐ jǐng xiào yóu to warn others against following a bad example; as a warning to others

【以来】yǐlái since: 长期~ for a long time past/ 三年~ in the past three years

【以礼相待】yǐ lǐ xiāng dài treat sb. with due respect

【以理服人】yǐ lǐ fú rén convince people by reasoning

【以卵投石】yǐ luǎn tóu shí throw an egg against a rock — court defeat by fighting against overwhelming odds 又作"以卵击石"

【以貌取人】yǐ mào qǔ rén judge people solely by their appearance

【以免】yǐmiǎn in order to avoid; so as not to; lest: 仔细检查~出错 check carefully to avoid mistakes/ 自行车要放在存车处, ~影响交通。Bicycles should be left at parking lots so as not to block the traffic.

【以内】yǐnèi within; less than: 本年度~ within this year/ 五十人~ less than fifty people

【以前】yǐqián before; formerly; previously: 我~的同事 a former colleague of mine/ ~各版 all the preceding (或 previous) editions/ 在明朝~ prior to the Ming Dynasty/ 我~没看过这个戏。I've never seen this opera before./ ~他当理发员。He used to be a barber.

【以求】yǐqiú in order to; in an attempt to: ~一逞 in the hope of realizing one's ambition; in a bid for success/ ~全胜 so as to achieve complete victory

【以上】yǐshàng ① more than; over; above: 五十人~ over (或 more than) fifty people/ 十岁~的孩子 children of ten and over ② the above; the foregoing; the above-mentioned: ~是我的几点建议。Those are a few of my suggestions./ 我完全同意~几位代表的发言。I fully agree with the delegates who have already spoken.

【以身试法】yǐ shēn shì fǎ defy the law

【以身殉职】yǐ shēn xùnzhí die at one's post

【以身作则】yǐ shēn zuò zé set an example

【以退为进】yǐ tuì wéi jìn retreat in order to advance; make concessions in order to gain advantages

【以外】yǐwài beyond; outside; other than; except: 长城~ beyond the Great Wall/ 除了这间~, 所有的屋子都打扫了。All the rooms have been cleaned except this one./ 除此~, 还有一件事要麻烦你。There's another thing I have to trouble you about.

【以往】yǐwǎng before; formerly; in the past: 今年的收成比~哪年都好。This year's harvest is better than any previous year's./ 这里~是一片荒野。This place used to be a vast expanse of wasteland.

【以为】yǐwéi think; believe; consider: 我还~是她呢。I thought it was her.

【以…为…】yǐ…wéi… take… as…; regard… as…: 工业以钢为纲。Steel must be taken as the key link in industry./ 以我为主 take ourselves (或 our side, our way, etc.) as the dominant factor; keep the initiative in our own hands

【以下】yǐxià ① below; under: 零度~ sub-zero/ 三岁儿童 children under three/ 俘获敌师长~三千人。3,000 of the enemy, from their divisional commander down, were taken prisoner. ② the following: ~是代表名单。The following is a list of the delegates./ ~就来谈谈具体办法。Now I'm coming to the concrete measures.

【以眼还眼, 以牙还牙】yǐ yǎn huán yǎn, yǐ yá huán yá an eye for an eye and a tooth for a tooth

【以一当十】yǐ yī dāng shí pit one against ten

【以逸待劳】yǐ yì dài láo wait at one's ease for an exhausted enemy or opponent

【以怨报德】yǐ yuàn bào dé return evil for good; requite kindness with ingratitude

【以正视听】yǐ zhèng shì-tīng in order to ensure a correct understanding of the facts

【以至】yǐzhì ① down to; up to: ② to such an extent as to…; so…that…: 他工作非常专心, ~连饭都忘了吃了。He was so absorbed in his work that he forgot his meals. 又作"以至于"

【以致】yǐzhì 〔多用来指不好的结果〕so that; with the result that; consequently; as a result: 小王平时训练不刻苦, ~射击考核没有及格。Xiao Wang didn't practise hard, so he failed the marksmanship test.

【以资】 yǐzī as a means of: ~证明 in testimony thereof; this is to certify that/ ~弥补 to make up the deficit; to make up a shortage/ ~鼓励 as an encouragement

【以子之矛,攻子之盾】 yǐ zǐ zhī máo, gōng zǐ zhī dùn set your own spear against your own shield — refute sb. with his own argument

矣 yǐ 〔古汉语助词〕①〔用在句末,跟"了"相同〕: 悔之晚~。It's too late for regrets. ②〔表示感叹〕: 毒~哉! Diabolical! 或 How ruthless!

迤 yǐ go (或 extend) towards
另见 yí

蚁* yǐ ant: 兵~ soldier ant; dinergate/ 工~ ergate; worker ant/ 雄~ aner/ 雌~ gyne
【蚁巢】 yǐcháo ant nest
【蚁丘】 yǐqiū ant hill

倚 yǐ ①lean on or against; rest on or against: ~栏 远眺 lean on the parapet and gaze into the distance ②rely on; count on: ~势欺人 take advantage of one's position to bully people ③<书> biased; partial: 不偏不~ unbiased; impartial
【倚靠】 yǐkào ①lean on or against; rest on or against ②见"依靠" yīkào
【倚老卖老】 yǐ lǎo mài lǎo take advantage of one's seniority or old age (to ignore manners, regulations, etc.); flaunt one's seniority
【倚仗】 yǐzhàng rely on; count on: ~权势 rely on one's power and position; count on one's powerful connections
【倚重】 yǐzhòng rely heavily on sb.'s service

椅* yǐ chair
【椅子】 yǐzi chair

旖 yǐ
【旖旎】 yǐnǐ <书> charming and gentle

yì

弋 yì <书> a retrievable arrow with a string attached to it

义* yì ①justice; righteousness: 见~勇为 be ready to take up the cudgels for a just cause/ 大~灭亲 sacrifice ties of blood to righteousness ②righteous; equitable; just: ~战 just war/ ~行 righteous deed ③human ties; relationship: 情~ ties of friendship, comradeship, etc. ④meaning; significance: 词~ the meaning of a word/ 一词 多~ polysemy ⑤adopted; adoptive: ~女 adopted daughter/ ~母 adoptive mother ⑥artificial; false: ~发 false hair
【义不容辞】 yì bùróng cí be duty-bound; have an unshirkable duty
【义愤】 yìfèn righteous indignation; moral indignation: 激 于~ be roused to righteous indignation
【义愤填膺】 yìfèn tián yīng be filled with (righteous) indignation
【义举】 yìjǔ a magnanimous act undertaken for the public good
【义理】 yìlǐ argumentation (of a speech or essay)
【义卖】 yìmài a sale of goods (usu. at high prices) for charity or other worthy causes; charity bazaar
【义旗】 yìqí the banner of an army fighting a just war; banner of righteousness: 举~ raise the banner of righteousness; rise against injustice
【义气】 yìqì code of brotherhood; personal loyalty: 讲~ be loyal (to one's friends)
【义师】 yìshī an army fighting a just war; righteous army
【义士】 yìshì a high-minded or chivalrous person; a person who upholds justice; righteous man
【义无反顾】 yì wú fǎngù honour permits no turning back;

be duty-bound not to turn back
【义务】 yìwù ①duty; obligation: 公民的基本权利与~ the fundamental rights and duties of citizens/ 条约规定的~ treaty obligations/ 履行所承担的~ carry out commitments ②volunteer; voluntary: 我是来尽~的。I've come to do voluntary service.
【义演】 yìyǎn benefit performance
【义勇军】 yìyǒngjūn army of volunteers; volunteers
【义正词严】 yìzhèng-cíyán speak sternly out of a sense of justice; speak with the force of justice
【义肢】 yìzhī <医> artificial limb

亿 yì a hundred million
【亿万】 yìwàn hundreds of millions; millions upon millions: ~人民 hundreds of millions of people; the people in their hundreds of millions ◇ ~富翁 billionaire

忆* yì recall; recollect

艺 yì ①skill: 球~ skill in a ball game/ ~高人胆大。 Boldness of execution stems from superb skill. ②art: 文 ~ literature and art
【艺龄】 yìlíng length of sb.'s artistic career: 他有三十多年 ~。He's been on the stage for over thirty years.
【艺名】 yìmíng stage name (of an actor or actress)
【艺人】 yìrén ①actor or artist (in local drama, storytelling, acrobatics, etc.) ②artisan; handicraftsman
【艺术】 yìshù ①art ②skill; art; craft: 领导~ art of leadership ③conforming to good taste: 这个房间布置得很~。 The room is tastefully furnished.
◇ ~标准 artistic criterion/ ~风格 artistic style/ ~技巧 artistry; craftsmanship/ ~家 artist/ ~界 art circles/ ~品 work of art/ ~团 art ensemble; troupe of musicians and artists/ ~形式 artistic form; forms of art/ ~性 artistic quality; artistry/ ~造诣 artistic attainments
【艺苑】 yìyuàn the realm of art and literature; art and literary circles: ~奇葩 exquisite works of art

刈 yì mow; cut down
【刈草机】 yìcǎojī mowing machine; mower

艾 yì 见"怨艾" yuànyì
另见 ài

议* yì ①opinion; view: 异~ disagreement; dissident view; 提~ propose; move ②discuss; exchange views on; talk over: ~而不决 discuss sth. without reaching a decision/ 我们对各种方案都~了一。We exchanged views on each of the different proposals.
【议案】 yì'àn proposal; motion
【议程】 yìchéng agenda: 列入~ place on the agenda; include in the agenda/ 第二项~ the second item on the agenda
【议和】 yìhé negotiate peace
【议会】 yìhuì parliament; legislative assembly: 召开(解散) ~ convene (dissolve) parliament
【议价】 yìjià ①negotiate a price ②negotiated price
【议决】 yìjué resolve after deliberation; pass a resolution
【议论】 yìlùn comment; talk; discuss: 大发~ speak at great length/ ~不休 carry on endless discussions/ 人们 对这件事~纷纷。Everybody is talking about the matter.
【议事】 yìshì discuss official business ◇ ~规则 rules of procedure; rules of debate/ ~日程 agenda; order of the day
【议席】 yìxí seat in a legislative assembly
【议员】 yìyuán member of a legislative assembly; (英) Member of Parliament (MP); (美) Congressman or Congresswoman
【议院】 yìyuàn legislative assembly; parliament; congress
【议长】 yìzhǎng speaker (of a legislative body); president

亦 yì <书> also; too: 反之~然 and the reverse is also true; and vice versa/ ~工~农 be both worker and peasant

【亦步亦趋】 yìbù-yìqū ape sb. at every step; imitate sb.'s every move; blindly follow suit

【亦即】 yìjí that is; i.e.; namely; viz.

屹 yì 〈书〉 towering like a mountain peak

【屹立】 yìlì stand towering like a giant; stand erect

【屹然】 yìrán towering; majestic: ～不动 stand firm and erect

异* yì ① different: 大同小～ identical on major issues though with minor differences; essentially the same though differing on minor points/ ～父(母)兄弟 half brothers/ ～词 dissenting words; disagreement ② strange; unusual; extraordinary: ～兆 strange omen/ ～香 extraordinary fragrance/ 奇才～能 extraordinary talents and abilities ③ surprise: 深以为～ it strikes one as very strange ④ other; another: ～日 some other day/ ～地 a strange land ⑤ separate: 离～ divorce

【异彩】 yìcǎi extraordinary (或 radiant) splendour

【异常】 yìcháng ① unusual; abnormal: ～现象 abnormal phenomena/ 神色～ not be one's usual self ② extremely; exceedingly; particularly: ～危险 extremely dangerous/ ～丰富 exceedingly rich/ ～需要 particularly necessary

【异端】 yìduān heterodoxy; heresy: ～邪说 heretical beliefs; unorthodox opinions

【异国】 yìguó foreign country (或 land): ～情调 an exotic atmosphere

【异乎寻常】 yì hū xúncháng unusual; extraordinary: ～地热心 unusually enthusiastic

【异己】 yìjǐ dissident; alien: 排除～ discriminate against those who hold different views; get rid of dissidents

【异教】 yìjiào paganism; heathenism ◇ ～徒 pagan; heathen

【异军突起】 yìjūn tūqǐ a new force suddenly coming to the fore

【异口同声】 yìkǒu-tóngshēng with one voice; in unison: 大家一地称赞她献身教育事业的精神。 Everybody spoke in praise of her devotion to the cause of education.

【异曲同工】 yìqǔ-tónggōng different tunes rendered with equal skill — different in approach but equally satisfactory in result

【异同】 yì-tóng similarities and differences

【异味】 yìwèi ① rare delicacy ② peculiar smell

【异乡】 yìxiāng foreign land; strange land

【异想天开】 yì xiǎng tiān kāi indulge in the wildest fantasy; have a very fantastic idea

【异心】 yìxīn infidelity; disloyalty

【异性】 yìxìng ① the opposite sex ② different in nature: ～的电互相吸引。 Unlike electric charges attract each other.

【异言】 yìyán 〈书〉 dissenting words: 并无～ raise no objection

【异样】 yìyàng ① difference: 多年没见了,看不出他有什么～。 We haven't seen each other for many years, but he doesn't look any different. ② unusual; peculiar: ～服装 peculiar dress/ 人们都用～的眼光打量他。 Everyone sized him up with curious eyes.

【异议】 yìyì objection; dissent: 提出～ raise an objection; take exception to; challenge/ 独持～ be the only one to dissent/ 如果没有～,提案就算通过了。 If there are no objections, we shall consider the resolution adopted.

【异族】 yìzú different race or nation: ～通婚 mixed marriages

译 yì translate; interpret: 笔～ written translation/ 口～ oral interpretation/ ～成英语 translate into English/ ～码 decode/ ～成电码 coding/ ～成密码 enciphering

【译本】 yìběn translation: 《石头记》的英～ an English translation of The Story of the Stone

【译笔】 yìbǐ the quality or style of a translation: ～流畅。 The translation reads smoothly.

【译码】 yìmǎ decode; decipher ◇ ～器 decoder; decipherer

【译名】 yìmíng translated term or name

【译述】 yìshù translate (或 render) freely

【译文】 yìwén translated text; translation

【译音】 yìyīn transliteration

【译员】 yìyuán interpreter

【译者】 yìzhě translator

【译制】 yìzhì dub ◇ ～片 dubbed film

抑 yì ① restrain; repress; curb: ～价 keep down the price/ ～强扶弱 curb the violent and assist the weak ② 〈书〉〈连〉 or

【抑扬】 yìyáng (of sound) rise and fall; modulate: ～顿挫 cadence; modulation in tone

【抑郁】 yìyù depressed; despondent; gloomy: ～不平 feel disgruntled ◇ ～症〈医〉 depression

【抑止】 yìzhǐ restrain; check

【抑制】 yìzhì restrain; control; check: ～自己的愤怒 restrain one's anger/ ～自己的感情 control one's emotion/ 眼泪～不住直往下流 can't hold back one's tears

呓 yì talk in one's sleep

【呓语】 yìyǔ ① talk in one's sleep ② crazy talk; ravings: 狂人～ ravings of a madman

邑 yì ① city: 通都大～ big city; metropolis ② county

佚 yì 见 "逸" yì

役 yì ① labour; service: 劳～ corvée; forced labour/ 兵～ military service ② use as servant: 奴～ enslave ③ servant: 仆～ servant; flunkey/ 衙～ yamen runner ④ battle; campaign

【役使】 yìshǐ work (an animal); use

诣 yì ① call on (sb. one respects); visit ② (academic or technical) attainments: 学术造～ scholarly attainments

易* yì ① easy: 不～解决 not easy to solve/ ～患感冒 catch cold easily; be susceptible to colds/ ～涝地区 areas liable to waterlogging ② amiable: 平～近人 amiable and easy of access ③ change: ～手 change hands ④ exchange: 以物～物 barter

【易燃物】 yìránwù combustibles; inflammables

【易如反掌】 yì rú fǎnzhǎng as easy as turning one's hand over; as easy as falling off a log

驿 yì post

【驿站】 yìzhàn post (where formerly couriers changed horses or rested)

绎 yì 〈书〉 unravel; sort out: 演～ deduction

奕 yì

【奕奕】 yìyì radiating power and vitality: 神采～ glowing with health and radiating vitality

弈 yì 〈书〉 play chess

疫 yì epidemic disease; pestilence: 鼠～ the plague/时～ epidemic disease/ 防～ epidemic prevention

【疫病】 yìbìng epidemic disease

【疫苗】 yìmiáo 〈医〉 vaccine

【疫情】 yìqíng information about and appraisal of an epidemic; epidemic situation

轶 yì 见 "逸" yì ③④

【轶事】 yìshì anecdote

益* yì ① benefit; profit; advantage: 受～良多 derive (或 receive) much benefit ② beneficial ③ increase: 延年～寿 prolong life ④ all the more; increasingly: ～发困难 increasingly difficult/ 多多～善 the more the better

【益虫】 yìchóng beneficial insect

【益处】 yìchu benefit; profit; good

【益鸟】 yìniǎo beneficial bird

【益友】 yìyǒu friend and mentor: 良师～ good teacher and helpful friend

谊* yì friendship: 深情厚～ profound friendship

恤 yì 〈书〉 sad; worried: ～～不乐 feel depressed; mope

逸 yì ① ease; leisure: 有劳有～ alternate work with rest ② escape; flee: 逃～ escape ③ be lost: ～书 ancient works no longer extant ④ excel: ～群 excel all others
【逸乐】 yìlè comfort and pleasure
【逸事】 yìshì anecdote (esp. about a famous person)
【逸闻】 yìwén anecdote

翌 yì 〈书〉 immediately following in time; next: ～日 next day/ ～年 next year

溢 yì ① overflow; spill: 河水四～. The river overflowed. ② excessive: ～美 undeserved praise; compliment
【溢出】 yìchū spill over; overflow

意* yì ① meaning; idea: 词不达～. The words fail to convey the meaning. ② wish; desire; intention: 好～ a good intention ③ anticipate; expect: 不～ contrary to expectation; unexpectedly ④ suggestion; hint; trace: 颇有秋～ make one feel that autumn has set in
【意表】 yìbiǎo what one does not expect: 出人～ beyond one's expectation; unexpectedly
【意会】 yìhuì sense: 只可～,不可言传 can be sensed, but not explained in words
【意见】 yìjiàn ① idea; view; opinion; suggestion: 交换～ exchange ideas (或 views); compare notes/ ～一致 have identical views; be of one mind/ ～分歧 have a difference (或 divergence) of opinion; disagree ② objection; differing opinion; complaint: 我对这种办法很有～. I strongly object to this method. 或 I take vigorous exception to this approach./ 大家对你～很大。 People have a lot of complaints about you./ 有～要拿到桌面上来。 Those who differ should air their views openly. ◇ ～簿 visitors' book; customers' book/ ～箱 suggestion box
【意境】 yìjìng artistic conception: 这幅油画～深远. This painting is magnificently conceived.
【意料】 yìliào anticipate; expect: 这是～中的事. That's to be expected./ 出乎～ unexpected; unforeseen; surprising
【意念】 yìniàn idea; thought: 这时每人脑子里都只有一个～: "胜利!" At that moment victory was the one idea that occupied everyone's mind. 或 Then, everybody had only one thought in mind: victory.
【意气】 yìqì ① will and spirit: ～高昂 high-spirited ② temperament: ～相投 be alike in temperament; be congenial with each other ③ personal feelings (或 prejudice): ～用事 be swayed by personal feelings/ ～之争 a dispute caused by personal feelings
【意气风发】 yìqì fēngfā high-spirited and vigorous; daring and energetic
【意趣】 yìqù interest and charm
【意识】 yìshí ① 〈哲〉 consciousness ② 〔常与"到"字连用〕 be conscious (或 aware) of; awake to; realize: ～到自己的责任 be conscious of one's responsibilities
【意思】 yìsi ① meaning; idea: 我不明白你的～. I don't understand what you mean./ 你这是什么～? What do you mean by that?/ 文章的中心～ the central idea of an article ② opinion; wish; desire: 我的～是走着去. In my opinion, (或 I think) we should walk./ 你是不是有～跟她见见面? Do you wish to meet her? ③ a token of affection, appreciation, gratitude, etc.: 这不过是我的一点儿～,请收下吧. Please accept this little gift as a token of my appreciation. ④ suggestion; hint; trace: 天有点要下雨的～. It looks like rain. ⑤ interest; fun: 他觉得年画展览很有～. He found the exhibition of New Year pictures very interesting./ 打乒乓球很有～. Ping-pong is a lot of fun.
【意图】 yìtú intention; intent: 领会上级～ understand the intentions of the higher organization
【意外】 yìwài ① unexpected; unforeseen: 感到～ be surprised; be taken by surprise ② accident; mishap: 以免发生～ so as to avoid accidents

【意味】 yìwèi ① meaning; significance; implication: ～深长的一笑 a meaning smile/ 他的话～深长, 值得玩味. What he said is significant and worth pondering. ② interest; overtone; flavour: 这首诗～无穷. This is a poem of unlimited interest./ 带有文学～的新闻报道 a news report with a literary flavour
【意味着】 yìwèizhe signify; mean; imply: 这一数字～生产提高了两倍. This figure means a twofold increase in production.
【意想】 yìxiǎng imagine; expect: ～不到的效果 unexpected results
【意向】 yìxiàng intention; purpose: 敌军～不明. The enemy's intentions are not clear.
【意象】 yìxiàng image; imagery
【意兴】 yìxìng interest; enthusiasm: ～索然 have not the least interest/ ～勃勃 be highly enthusiastic
【意义】 yìyì meaning; sense; significance: 在某种～上 in a sense/ 具有重大历史～的事件 an event of historic significance/ 一部富有教育～的影片 a very instructive film/ 这样做没有～. There's no point in doing that./ 这个词有三个～. This word has three distinct meanings.
【意译】 yìyì free translation
【意愿】 yìyuàn wish; desire; aspiration: 表达了人民的～ express the wishes of the people
【意在言外】 yì zài yán wài the meaning is implied
【意旨】 yìzhǐ intention; wish; will: 秉承某人的～ in compliance with sb.'s wish
【意志】 yìzhì will: 钢铁～ iron will; iron determination/ 坚强～ strong-willed/ ～消沉 demoralized; despondent/ 锻炼～ temper one's willpower
【意中人】 yìzhōngrén the person one is in love with; person of one's heart

裔 yì 〈书〉 ① descendants; posterity: 华～美国人 an American of Chinese descent ② borderland; distant land

肄 yì study
【肄业】 yìyè study in school or at college: 他曾在大学～二年。 He was in college for two years.

缢 yì 〈书〉 hang: 自～ hang oneself

蜴 yì 见"蜥蜴" xīyì

毅 yì firm; resolute: 刚～ fortitude
【毅力】 yìlì willpower; will; stamina: 惊人的～ amazing willpower/ 百折不回的～ indomitable will/ 以无比的～跟疾病作斗争 battle against illness with matchless stamina/ 完成这项工作需要坚强的～. It'll require great willpower to accomplish the task.
【毅然】 yìrán resolutely; firmly; determinedly

薏 yì
【薏米】 yìmǐ 〈中药〉 the seed of Job's tears 又作"薏仁米"

臆 yì ① chest ② subjectively
【臆测】 yìcè conjecture; surmise; guess
【臆断】 yìduàn assume; suppose
【臆说】 yìshuō assumption; supposition
【臆造】 yìzào fabricate (a story, reason, etc.); concoct

翼 yì ① the wing of a bird, aeroplane, etc.: 从左右两～夹攻敌人 attack the enemy on both flanks/ 主楼的两～ the two wings of the main building ② 〈书〉 assist (a ruler); aid: ～助 render assistance (to a ruler)
【翼侧】 yìcè 〈军〉 flank ◇ ～攻击 flank attack/ ～迂回 outflank
【翼翼】 yìyì cautiously: 小心～ with exceptional caution; very carefully

癔 yì
【癔病】 yìbìng 〈医〉 hysteria ◇ ～患者 hysteriac

懿 yì 〈书〉 exemplary: ～行 exemplary conduct

yīn

因 * yīn ① 〈书〉 follow; carry on: 陈陈相～ follow a set routine; stay in the same old groove ② 〈书〉 on the basis of; in accordance with; in the light of: 疗效～人而异。The curative effect varies from person to person. ③ cause; reason: 外～ external cause/ 近～ immediate cause/ 事出有～。There is good reason for it. 或 It is by no means accidental. ④ because of; as a result of: ～病请假 ask for sick leave/ ～公牺牲 die while on duty; die at one's post/ 会议～故改期。The meeting has been postponed for some reason.

【因材施教】 yīn cái shī jiào teach students in accordance with their aptitude

【因此】 yīncǐ therefore; for this reason; consequently

【因地制宜】 yīn dì zhì yí suit measures to local conditions: ～地进行密植 carry out close planting in line with local conditions

【因而】 yīn'ér thus; as a result; with the result that: 他们农业机械化搞得好，～大大提高了生产率。Their success in mechanizing farm work greatly raised their productivity.

【因果】 yīnguǒ ① cause and effect ② 〈佛教〉 karma; pre-ordained fate ◇ ～关系 causality

【因陋就简】 yīn lòu jiù jiǎn make do with whatever is available; do things simply and thriftily

【因人成事】 yīn rén chéng shì rely on others for success in work

【因势利导】 yīn shì lì dǎo adroitly guide action according to circumstances: ～，夺取胜利 make the best use of the situation and guide the struggle to victory

【因素】 yīnsù factor; element: 积极～ positive factors/ 人的～ the human factor

【因为】 yīnwei because; for; on account of

【因袭】 yīnxí follow (old customs, methods, rules, etc.); copy: ～陈规 follow outmoded rules/ ～前人 follow in the footsteps of one's predecessors

【因小失大】 yīn xiǎo shī dà try to save a little only to lose a lot

【因循】 yīnxún ① follow (old customs, etc.); continue in the same old rut: ～守旧 stick to old ways; follow the beaten path ② procrastinate: ～坐误 sit back and allow the situation to deteriorate; procrastinate until it is too late

【因噎废食】 yīn yē fèi shí give up eating for fear of choking — refrain from doing sth. necessary for fear of a slight risk

【因由】 yīnyóu reason; cause; origin

【因缘】 yīnyuán ① 〈佛教〉 principal and subsidiary causes; cause ② predestined relationship

阴 * yīn ① (in Chinese philosophy, medicine, etc.) *yin*, the feminine or negative principle in nature ② the moon: ～历 lunar calendar ③ 〈气〉 overcast: 天～了。The sky is overcast. ④ shade: 树～ the shade of a tree ⑤ north of a hill or south of a river: 华～ Huayin (a county situated on the north side of Huashan Mountain)/ 江～ Jiangyin (a county situated on the south side of the Changjiang River) ⑥ back: 碑～ the back of a stone tablet ⑦ in intaglio: ～文 characters cut in intaglio ⑧ hidden; secret; sinister: ～一套，阳一套 act one way in public and another in private; be engaged in double-dealing/ ～谋 sinister plot ⑨ of the nether world ⑩ 〈物〉 negative: ～离子 negative ion; anion ⑪ private parts (esp. of the female)

【阴暗】 yīn'àn dark; gloomy: ～的角落 a dark corner (where plots are hatched)/ ～的脸色 a glum face/ ～的心理 mentality marked by antipathy and gloom/ ～面 the dark (或 seamy) side of things

【阴部】 yīnbù 〈生理〉 private parts; pudenda

【阴沉】 yīnchén cloudy; overcast; gloomy; sombre: 一早上天都是～的。The sky was cloudy (或 grey) all morning./ 脸色～ have a sombre countenance; look glum

【阴错阳差】 yīncuò-yángchā (a mistake or error due to) a strange combination of circumstances 又作"阴差阳错"

【阴道】 yīndào 〈生理〉 vagina ◇ ～炎 vaginitis

【阴德】 yīndé a good deed to the doer's credit in the next world

【阴电】 yīndiàn negative electricity

【阴毒】 yīndú insidious; sinister

【阴沟】 yīngōu sewer

【阴魂】 yīnhún soul; spirit: ～不散。The soul (或 spirit) refuses to leave.

【阴间】 yīnjiān the nether world

【阴茎】 yīnjīng 〈生理〉 penis

【阴冷】 yīnlěng ① (of weather) gloomy and cold; raw ② (of a person's look) sombre; glum

【阴历】 yīnlì lunar calendar: ～正月 the first month of the lunar year

【阴凉】 yīnliáng ① shady and cool: 此药宜置于～处。The medicine should be kept in a cool, dark place. ② cool place; shade: 找个～儿歇歇。Let's have a rest in the shade.

【阴毛】 yīnmáo 〈生理〉 pubes

【阴门】 yīnmén 〈生理〉 vaginal orifice 又作"阴户"

【阴谋】 yīnmóu plot; scheme; conspiracy: ～诡计 schemes and intrigues/ ～破坏 plot sabotage/ ～复辟 plot to restore the old order/ ～篡权 scheme to usurp power/ ～手段 conspiratorial means ◇ ～集团 conspiratorial clique (或 group)/ ～家 schemer; intriguer; conspirator

【阴平】 yīnpíng high and level tone, the first of the four tones in modern standard Chinese pronunciation

【阴森】 yīnsēn gloomy; gruesome; ghastly: ～的树林 a deep, dark forest/ ～可怕 ghastly and bloodcurdling

【阴私】 yīnsī shameful secret

【阴天】 yīntiān overcast sky; cloudy day

【阴险】 yīnxiǎn sinister; insidious; treacherous: ～毒辣 sinister and ruthless

【阴性】 yīnxìng ① 〈医〉 negative: ～反应 negative reaction ② 〈语〉 feminine gender

【阴虚】 yīnxū 〈中医〉 deficiency of *yin* (insufficiency of body fluid), with irritability, thirst, constipation, etc. as symptoms

【阴阳】 yīn-yáng (in Chinese philosophy, medicine, etc.) *yin* and *yang*, the two opposing principles in nature, the former feminine and negative, the latter masculine and positive

【阴阳怪气】 yīnyáng guàiqì ① (of one's manner of speaking) mystifying; enigmatic; deliberately ambiguous ② eccentric; queer; cynical: 他这个人～的。He's a queer chap.

【阴阳先生】 yīnyáng xiānsheng geomancer (usu. employed as a funeral adviser)

【阴影】 yīnyǐng shadow: 树木的～ shadows of trees/ 肺部有～ have a shadow on one's lungs

【阴雨】 yīnyǔ overcast and rainy: ～连绵 cloudy and drizzly for days on end; an unbroken spell of wet weather

【阴郁】 yīnyù gloomy; dismal; depressed: 天色～。The weather is gloomy./ 心情～ feel gloomy (或 depressed)

【阴云】 yīnyún dark clouds: ～密布。The sky is overcast. 或 The sky is covered with dark clouds.

音 * yīn ① sound: 乐～ musical sound/ 噪～ noise/ 说话的口～很重 speak with a strong accent ② news; tidings: 佳～ welcome news; glad tidings ③ 〈物〉 tone: 复～ complex tone/ 纯～ pure tone; simple tone

【音标】 yīnbiāo 〈语〉 phonetic symbol; phonetic transcription

【音波】 yīnbō 〈物〉 sound wave

【音调】 yīndiào tone

【音符】 yīnfú 〈乐〉 note

【音节】 yīnjié 〈语〉 syllable ◇ ～文字 syllabic language 又作"音缀"

【音量】 yīnliàng volume (of sound) ◇ ～控制 volume control

【音容】 yīnróng 〈书〉 the likeness of the deceased: ～宛在 as if the person were in the flesh

【音色】 yīnsè tone colour; timbre

【音速】 yīnsù 〈物〉velocity (或 speed) of sound: 超～ supersonic/ 高超～ hypersonic

【音响】 yīnxiǎng sound; acoustics ◇ ～水雷〈军〉sonic (或 sound, acoustic) mine/ ～效果 sound effects; acoustics

【音信】 yīnxìn mail; message; news: 互通～ communicate with each other; be in correspondence with each other/ 他走后杳无～。 We have not heard from him since he left. 又作"音讯"

【音译】 yīnyì transliteration

【音乐】 yīnyuè music ◇ ～会 concert/ ～家 musician/ ～片 musical (film)/ ～厅 concert hall

【音质】 yīnzhì ① tone quality ② acoustic fidelity

茵 yīn mattress: 绿草如～ a carpet of green grass

洇 yīn (of ink) spread and sink in: 这种纸写字容易～。 Ink blots on this paper.

姻 yīn ① marriage: 联～ connect by marriage ② relation by marriage: ～兄弟 brothers-in-law

【姻亲】 yīnqīn relation by marriage: ～关系 relationship by marriage; affinity

【姻缘】 yīnyuán the happy fate which brings lovers together: 美满～ a happy marriage; conjugal felicity

荫 yīn shade
另见 yìn

【荫蔽】 yīnbì ① be shaded or hidden by foliage: 野战医院～在树林中。 The field hospital lies hidden among the trees. ② cover; conceal: ～集结 concentrate under cover

氤 yīn

【氤氲】 yīnyūn 〈书〉(of smoke or mist) dense; thick; enshrouding: 云烟～ enshrouding mist

殷 yīn 〈书〉① abundant; rich ② eager; ardent: 期望甚～ cherish high hopes ③ hospitable: 招待甚～ offer cordial hospitality ④ (Yīn) the Yin Dynasty, the later period of the Shang (商) Dynasty
另见 yān

【殷鉴】 yīnjiàn 〈书〉setback which serves as a warning to others: ～不远。 One need not look far for a lesson.

【殷切】 yīnqiè ardent; eager: ～的期望 ardent expectations

【殷勤】 yīnqín eagerly attentive; solicitous: 受到～接待 be accorded solicitous hospitality/ 献～ do everything to please; pay one's addresses to

【殷实】 yīnshí well-off; substantial: ～人家 well-off families/ ～的商号 a substantial firm

喑 yīn 〈书〉silent; mute: ～哑 mute; dumb

yín

吟* yín ① chant; recite: ～诗 recite or compose poetry ② song (as a type of classical poetry): 《秦妇～》 Song of a Qin Lady ③ the cry of certain animals: 龙～虎啸 the roar of dragons and tigers

【吟风弄月】 yínfēng-nòngyuè sing of the moon and the wind — write sentimental verse

【吟诵】 yínsòng chant; recite

【吟味】 yínwèi recite with relish; recite with appreciation: 反复～ recite again and again in appreciation

【吟咏】 yínyǒng recite (poetry) with a cadence; chant

垠 yín 〈书〉boundary; limit: 一望无～ stretch as far as the eye can see; stretch beyond the horizon

狺 yín

【狺狺】 yínyín 〈书〉yap; yelp: ～狂吠 bark frenziedly

淫 yín ① excessive: ～雨 excessive rains ② loose; wan-ton: 骄奢～逸 lordly, luxurious, loose and idle; wallowing in luxury and pleasure ③ licentious; lewd; lascivious ④ obscene; pornographic: ～书 pornographic book/ ～画 obscene picture

【淫荡】 yíndàng loose in morals; lascivious; licentious; lewd

【淫秽】 yínhuì obscene; salacious; bawdy

【淫乱】 yínluàn (sexually) promiscuous; licentious

【淫威】 yínwēi abuse of power; despotic power

【淫猥】 yínwěi obscene

寅 yín the third of the twelve Earthly Branches

【寅吃卯粮】 yín chī mǎo liáng eat next year's food; eat one's corn in the blade; anticipate one's income

【寅时】 yínshí the period of the day from 3 a.m. to 5 a.m.

银* yín ① silver (Ag) ② relating to currency or money: ～行 bank ③ silver-coloured: ～发 silver hair/ ～色 silvery

【银白】 yínbái silvery white

【银杯】 yínbēi silver cup

【银币】 yínbì silver coin

【银锭】 yíndìng silver ingot

【银根】 yíngēn 〈经〉money market; money: ～紧 tight/ ～松 easy

【银汉】 yínhàn 〈书〉the Milky Way

【银行】 yínháng bank: ～存款 bank deposit ◇ ～存折 bankbook; passbook/ ～家 banker/ ～信贷 bank credit

【银河】 yínhé 〈天〉the Milky Way ◇ ～系 the Milky Way system; the Galaxy

【银婚】 yínhūn silver wedding

【银匠】 yínjiàng silversmith

【银两】 yínliǎng silver (used as currency)

【银幕】 yínmù (motion-picture) screen

【银牌】 yínpái silver medal

【银器】 yínqì silverware

【银样镴枪头】 yín yàng làqiāngtóu a pewter spearhead that shines like silver — an impressive-looking but useless person

【银子】 yínzi silver

龈 yín gum

夤 yín 〈书〉① hold sb. in respectful awe ② deep: ～夜 in the depth of the night; at the dead of night

【夤缘】 yínyuán 〈书〉make use of one's connections to climb up; try to advance one's career by currying favour with important people

yǐn

尹 yǐn an ancient official title: 府～ prefect

引* yǐn ① draw; stretch: ～弓 draw a bow ② lead; guide: ～路 lead the way/ 把长江水～到黄河 divert water from the Changjiang River to the Huanghe River ③ leave: ～避 keep (或 stay, steer) clear of; make way for ④ lure; attract: ～入圈套 lure into a trap; ensnare/ 抛砖～玉 cast a brick to attract jade/ ～火 kindle a fire ⑤ cause; make: 他这一句话～得大家笑起来。 His remark set everybody laughing. ⑥ quote; cite: ～某人的话 quote sb./ ～以为荣 cite sth. as an honour; take it as an honour/ ～文 quoted passage; quotation

【引爆】 yǐnbào ignite; detonate

【引出】 yǐnchū draw forth; lead to: ～正确的结论 draw correct conclusions

【引导】 yǐndǎo guide; lead: 主人～贵宾们参观了车间。 The hosts showed the distinguished guests around the workshops.

【引逗】 yǐndòu ① tantalize; tease ② lure; entice

【引渡】 yǐndù 〈法〉extradite

【引吭高歌】 yǐn háng gāo gē sing joyfully in a loud voice; sing heartily

【引航】 yǐnháng 〈航海〉pilotage

【引号】 yǐnhào quotation marks (" "): 双～ double quotation marks (" ")/ 单～ single quotation marks (' ')

【引火烧身】 yǐn huǒ shāo shēn draw fire against oneself — make self-criticism to encourage criticism from others

【引见】 yǐnjiàn introduce; present

【引荐】 yǐnjiàn recommend

【引进】 yǐnjìn ① recommend ② introduce from elsewhere: ～新的小麦品种 introduce new varieties of wheat/ ～技术装备 import technology and equipment

【引经据典】 yǐnjīng-jùdiǎn quote the classics; copiously quote authoritative works

【引咎】 yǐnjiù 〈书〉 hold oneself responsible for a serious mistake; take the blame: ～辞职 take the blame and resign

【引狼入室】 yǐn láng rù shì invite a wolf into the house — open the door to a dangerous foe

【引力】 yǐnlì 〈物〉 gravitation; gravitational force; attraction: 核～ nuclear attraction/ 万有～ universal gravitation

【引起】 yǐnqǐ give rise to; lead to; set off; touch off; cause; arouse: ～严重后果 lead to grave consequences/ ～连锁反应 set off a chain reaction/ ～公愤 arouse (或 touch off) public indignation/ ～强烈的反响 cause strong repercussions/ ～怀疑 arouse suspicion/ ～注意 bring to sb.'s attention/ ～一场热烈的讨论 evoke a heated discussion

【引擎】 yǐnqíng 〈机〉 engine ◇ ～盖 bonnet; hood

【引人入胜】 yǐn rén rù shèng (of scenery, literary works, etc.) fascinating; enchanting; bewitching: 把报纸办得～ make the newspaper interesting and absorbing

【引人注目】 yǐn rén zhùmù noticeable; conspicuous; spectacular: ～的横幅标语 an eye-catching slogan on a banner/ ～的特点 conspicuous features/ ～的变化 spectacular changes

【引入】 yǐnrù lead into; draw into: ～歧途 lead sb. onto a wrong path; lead sb. astray

【引申】 yǐnshēn extend (the meaning of a word, etc.) ◇ ～义 extended meaning

【引水】 yǐnshuǐ ① pilot a ship into harbour ② draw or channel water: ～灌田 channel water into the fields/ ～上山 draw water up a hill

【引退】 yǐntuì retire from office; resign

【引文】 yǐnwén quoted passage; quotation

【引线】 yǐnxiàn ① 〈方〉 needle ② 〈电〉 lead (wire) ③ go-between ④ catalyst

【引言】 yǐnyán foreword; introduction

【引以为戒】 yǐn yǐ wéi jiè learn a lesson (from a previous error, etc.); take warning 又作"引为鉴戒"

【引用】 yǐnyòng ① quote; cite ② recommend; appoint

【引诱】 yǐnyòu lure; seduce: ～敌人进入伏击圈 lure the enemy into a trap/ 企图用金钱和美女来～意志薄弱的人 try to lure the weak-willed with money and women

【引证】 yǐnzhèng quote or cite as proof or evidence

【引子】 yǐnzi ① 〈剧〉 an actor's opening words ② 〈乐〉 introductory music ③ introductory remarks; introduction

饮* yǐn ① drink: ～茶 drink tea/ 冷～ cold drinks ② keep in the heart; nurse: ～恨 nurse a grievance

【饮弹】 yǐndàn 〈书〉 be hit by a bullet: ～身亡 be killed by a bullet

【饮恨】 yǐnhèn 〈书〉 nurse a grievance: ～而终 die with a grievance in one's heart

【饮料】 yǐnliào drink; beverage

【饮泣】 yǐnqì 〈书〉 weep in silence: ～吞声 swallow one's tears; weep silent tears

【饮食】 yǐnshí food and drink; diet: 给病人规定～ put a patient on a diet

【饮水思源】 yǐn shuǐ sī yuán when you drink water, think of its source — never forget where one's happiness comes from

【饮用水】 yǐnyòngshuǐ drinking water; potable water

【饮鸩止渴】 yǐn zhèn zhǐ kě drink poison to quench thirst — seek temporary relief regardless of the consequences

蚓* yǐn 见"蚯蚓" qiūyǐn

隐 yǐn ① hidden from view; concealed: ～瞒 conceal; hide ② latent; dormant; lurking: ～患 hidden danger

【隐蔽】 yǐnbì conceal; take cover: 公开的和～的活动 overt and covert activities

【隐藏】 yǐncáng hide; conceal; remain under cover

【隐恶扬善】 yǐn'è yáng shàn cover up sb.'s faults and publicize his merits; hide sb.'s wrongdoing and praise his good deeds

【隐伏】 yǐnfú lie concealed (或 hidden); lie low

【隐患】 yǐnhuàn hidden trouble; hidden danger; snake in the grass: 消除～ remove a hidden peril

【隐讳】 yǐnhuì avoid mentioning; cover up: 不要～自己的缺点。 One should not gloss over one's shortcomings.

【隐晦】 yǐnhuì obscure; veiled: 文字写得很～ be couched in ambiguous terms

【隐疾】 yǐnjí unmentionable disease (e.g. V.D.)

【隐居】 yǐnjū live in seclusion; withdraw from society and live in solitude; be a hermit

【隐瞒】 yǐnmán conceal; hide; hold back: ～错误 conceal one's mistakes/ ～事实 withhold the truth; hide (或 hold back) the facts

【隐秘】 yǐnmì ① conceal; hide: ～不说 not disclose a secret/ 地道的出口开在～的地方。 The exit of the tunnel is concealed. ② secret: 刺探～ pry into sb.'s secrets

【隐匿】 yǐnnì 〈书〉 hide; go into hiding; lie low

【隐情】 yǐnqíng facts one wishes to hide

【隐忍】 yǐnrěn bear patiently; forbear: ～不言 forbear from speaking

【隐射】 yǐnshè insinuate; hint; throw out innuendoes

【隐士】 yǐnshì recluse; hermit

【隐私】 yǐnsī one's secrets; private matters one wants to hide

【隐痛】 yǐntòng secret anguish

【隐退】 yǐntuì go and live in seclusion; retire from political life

【隐显墨水】 yǐnxiǎn mòshuǐ invisible ink

【隐姓埋名】 yǐnxìng-máimíng conceal one's identity; keep one's identity hidden; live incognito

【隐隐】 yǐnyǐn indistinct; faint: ～的雷声 a distant roll of thunder/ ～可见 faintly visible/ 感到～作痛 feel a dull pain

【隐忧】 yǐnyōu secret worry

【隐语】 yǐnyǔ enigmatic language; insinuating language

【隐喻】 yǐnyù 〈语〉 metaphor

【隐约】 yǐnyuē indistinct; faint: ～可以听到远处传来的歌声。 We could faintly hear singing in the distance./ 晨雾中一座座井架～可见。 Derricks could be seen dimly in the morning mist./ ～其词 use ambiguous language; speak in equivocal terms

【隐衷】 yǐnzhōng feelings or troubles one wishes to keep to oneself

瘾 yǐn ① addiction; habitual craving: 吸毒上～ be addicted to drugs; be a drug addict/ 发烟～ have an urge to smoke; crave a cigarette/ 过～ satisfy a craving ② strong interest (in a sport or pastime): 有球～ have a passion for ball games/ 他看小说看上～了。 He's crazy about novels.

印* yìn ① seal; stamp; chop: 盖～ affix one's seal; stamp a seal ② print; mark: 脚～ footprint/ 手～ fingerprint ③ print; engrave: ～书 print books/ 这照片～得不清楚。 This photo is not well printed./ 深深～在脑子里 be engraved on one's mind ④ tally; conform: ～证 verify

【印花】 yìnhuā ① 〈纺〉 printing: ～丝绸 printed silk ② revenue stamp; stamp

【印鉴】 yìnjiàn a specimen seal impression for checking when making payments

【印泥】 yìnní red ink paste used for seals

【印谱】 yìnpǔ a collection of impressions of seals by famous seal-engravers; a book of ancient seals

【印染】 yìnrǎn printing and dyeing (of textiles) ◇ ～厂 printing and dyeing mill

【印数】 yìnshù 〈印〉 printing; impression: ～八万册 an impression of 80,000 copies

【印刷】 yìnshuā　printing: 这本书正在～中。The book is in the press./ 第一次～ first impression (或 printing) ◇ ～厂 printing house; press/ ～错误 misprint; typographic error

【印刷机】 yìnshuājī 〈印〉 printing machine; press

【印台】 yìntái　ink pad; stamp pad

【印象】 yìnxiàng　impression: 我对他～很好。I have a good impression of him./ 这个城市给外宾们留下了深刻的～。The city left a deep impression on foreign visitors. ◇ ～派 impressionist school; impressionist/ ～主义 impressionism

【印信】 yìnxìn　official seal

【印行】 yìnxíng　print and distribute; publish

【印章】 yìnzhāng　seal; signet; stamp

【印证】 yìnzhèng　confirm; corroborate; verify: 有待～ yet to be confirmed

荫 yìn ① shady; damp and chilly ② (of a feudal ruler) confer privileges on sb.'s descendants in consideration of his distinguised service ③ 见"荫庇"
另见 yīn

【荫庇】 yìnbì 〈旧〉 protection by one's elders or ancestors

【荫凉】 yìnliáng　shady and cool

yīng

应* yīng ① answer; respond: 喊他他不～。I called him, but he didn't answer. ② agree (to do sth.); promise; accept: 这事是我～下来的，由我负责吧。I'm the one who took on the job, so let me take care of it. ③ should; ought to: ～享受的权利 a right to which one is entitled/ ～尽的义务 one's bounden duty/ ～予考虑 merit consideration/ 发现错误～立即纠正。When a mistake is discovered, it should be corrected at once.
另见 yìng

【应当】 yīngdāng　should; ought to

【应得】 yīngdé　(well) deserved; due: 罪有～。One deserves one's punishment. 或 The punishment fits the crime./ ～的一份 a due share

【应分】 yīngfèn　part of one's job: 帮助顾客选购商品是我们售货员～的事。It's part of our job as shop assistants to help customers choose what they want to buy.

【应该】 yīnggāi　should; ought to; must

【应届毕业生】 yīngjiè bìyèshēng　graduating students or pupils; this year's graduates

【应有】 yīngyǒu　due; proper; deserved: 发挥它～的作用 play its proper role/ 做出～的贡献 make a due contribution/ 遭到～的回击 receive a deserved rebuff

【应有尽有】 yīngyǒu-jìnyǒu　have everything that one expects to find: 这家商店日用品～。This general store has just about everything you'd expect to find.

【应允】 yīngyǔn　assent; consent: 点头～ nod assent (或 approval)

英* yīng ① 〈书〉 flower: 落～缤纷 petals falling in riotous profusion ② hero; outstanding person: 群～会 a gathering of heroes; a conference of outstanding workers

【英镑】 yīngbàng　pound sterling

【英才】 yīngcái　person of outstanding ability

【英豪】 yīngháo　heroes; outstanding figures 又作"英杰"

【英俊】 yīngjùn ① eminently talented; brilliant ② handsome and spirited; smart: 一个～的小伙子 a handsome young chap

【英灵】 yīnglíng　spirit of the brave departed; spirit of a martyr 又作"英魂"

【英名】 yīngmíng　illustrious name

【英明】 yīngmíng　wise; brilliant: ～领袖 wise leader/ ～的论断 brilliant thesis/ ～远见 wisdom and foresight; sagacity (或 acumen) and farsightedness

【英亩】 yīngmǔ　acre

【英气】 yīngqì　heroic spirit

【英文】 Yīngwén　English (language)

【英武】 yīngwǔ　of soldierly (或 martial) bearing

【英雄】 yīngxióng　hero: 女～ heroine/ ～本色 the true quality of a hero/ ～气概 heroic spirit; mettle/ ～所见略同。Great minds think alike.

【英雄无用武之地】 yīngxióng wú yòngwǔ zhī dì　a hero with no place to display his prowess — no scope to exercise one's abilities

【英勇】 yīngyǒng　heroic; valiant; brave; gallant: ～奋斗 fight heroically/ ～善战 brave and skilful in battle

【英语】 Yīngyǔ　English (language)

【英姿】 yīngzī　heroic bearing: 飒爽～ valiant and heroic in bearing; bright and brave

莺 yīng　warbler; oriole

【莺歌燕舞】 yīnggē-yànwǔ　orioles sing and swallows dart — the joy of spring; a scene of prosperity

婴 yīng　baby; infant

【婴儿】 yīng'ér　baby; infant ◇ ～车 perambulator; baby carriage 又作"婴孩"

罂 yīng 〈书〉 small-mouthed jar

【罂粟】 yīngsù 〈植〉 opium poppy ◇ ～花 poppy flower

嘤 yīng 〈象〉 chirp: ～其鸣矣，求其友声。A bird sings to call forth a friend's response.

缨 yīng ① tassel: 红～枪 red-tasselled spear ② sth. shaped like a tassel: 萝卜～子 radish leaves ③ ribbon

樱 yīng ① cherry ② oriental cherry

【樱花】 yīnghuā　oriental cherry: 日本～ Japanese flowering cherry

【樱桃】 yīngtáo　cherry

鹦 yīng

【鹦哥】 yīnggē　parrot

【鹦鹉】 yīngwǔ　parrot: 长尾～ parakeet

【鹦鹉学舌】 yīngwǔ xuéshé　repeat the words of others like a parrot; parrot

膺 yīng 〈书〉 ① breast: 义愤填～ be filled with righteous indignation ② bear; receive: 荣～勋章 receive a decoration/ ～此重任 hold a post of great responsibility

【膺选】 yīngxuǎn 〈书〉 be elected

鹰* yīng　hawk; eagle

【鹰鼻鹞眼】 yīngbí-yàoyǎn　hawk-nosed and vulture-eyed — sinister and fierce-looking

【鹰钩鼻子】 yīnggōubízi　aquiline nose

【鹰犬】 yīngquǎn　falcons and hounds — lackeys; hired thugs

【鹰隼】 yīngsǔn 〈书〉 hawks and falcons — brutal or fierce people

yíng

迎* yíng ① go to meet; greet; welcome; receive: ～上前去同客人握手 step forward to greet the guest and shake hands with him/ 喜～新春 joyously see in the lunar New Year ② move towards; meet face to face: ～着困难上 meet difficulties head-on

【迎风】 yíngfēng ① facing (或 against) the wind: ～飞翔 fly against the wind ② down the wind; with the wind: 彩旗～招展。Coloured flags fluttered in the breeze.

【迎合】 yínghé　cater to; pander to: ～对方心理 go along with the other side/ ～低级趣味 pander to low tastes

【迎候】 yínghòu　await the arrival of: 在宾馆门口～贵宾 await the arrival of the distinguished guest at the entrance of the guest house

【迎击】 yíngjī meet (an approaching enemy) head-on

【迎接】 yíngjiē meet; welcome; greet: 到火车站～贵宾 meet a distinguished guest at the railway station

【迎面】 yíngmiàn head-on; in one's face: ～走上去同他们打招呼 step forward to greet them/ 微风～吹来 a breeze blowing in one's face

【迎刃而解】 yíng rèn ér jiě (of a bamboo) split all the way down once it's been chopped open — (of a problem) be readily solved

【迎头】 yíngtóu head-on; directly: 给侵略者以～痛击 deal head-on blows to the invaders

【迎头赶上】 yíngtóu gǎnshàng try hard to catch up

【迎新】 yíngxīn ① see the New Year in: 送旧～ ring out the Old Year and ring in the New ② welcome new arrivals: ～晚会 an evening party to welcome newcomers

【迎迓】 yíngyà 〈书〉 meet; welcome

【迎战】 yíngzhàn meet (an approaching enemy) head-on

盈 yíng ① be full of; be filled with: 热泪～眶 one's eyes brimming with tears ② have a surplus of

【盈亏】 yíng-kuī ① profit and loss: 自负～ (of an enterprise) assume sole responsibility for its own profits or losses ② the waxing and waning of the moon

【盈利】 yínglì profit; gain

【盈余】 yíngyú surplus; profit

荧 yíng 〈书〉 ① glimmering: 一灯～然。A light is glimmering. ② dazzled; perplexed: ～惑 bewilder

【荧光】 yíngguāng 〈物〉 fluorescence; fluorescent light ◇ ～灯 fluorescent lamp/ ～屏 fluorescent screen

莹 yíng 〈书〉 ① jade-like stone ② lustrous and transparent

营* yíng ① seek: ～利 seek profits ② operate; run: 国～ state-operated; state-run ③ camp; barracks: 安～ pitch a camp ④ battalion: ～部 battalion headquarters

【营地】 yíngdì campsite; camping ground

【营房】 yíngfáng barracks

【营火】 yínghuǒ campfire ◇ ～会 campfire party

【营建】 yíngjiàn construct; build

【营救】 yíngjiù succour; rescue

【营生】 yíngshēng earn (或 make) a living: 靠打铁～ earn a living as a blacksmith

【营私】 yíngsī seek private gain; feather one's nest: ～舞弊 engage in malpractices for selfish ends; practise graft/ ～结党 form a clique (或 band together) for selfish purposes

【营养】 yíngyǎng nutrition; nourishment: 富于～ nourishing; nutritious
◇ ～不良 malnutrition; undernourishment/ ～价值 nutritive value/ ～品 nutriment/ ～素 nutrient/ ～学 nutriology

【营业】 yíngyè do business: 暂停～ business temporarily suspended/ 照常～ business as usual/ 商店上午九时开始～。The shops open at nine in the morning.
◇ ～报告 business report/ ～额 turnover; volume of business/ ～时间 business hours; （银行） banking hours/

【营帐】 yíngzhàng tent

萤 yíng firefly; glowworm

【萤火虫】 yínghuǒchóng firefly; glowworm

萦 yíng 〈书〉 entangle; encompass: 琐事～身 be preoccupied with trivialities; get bogged down in petty matters

【萦怀】 yínghuái occupy one's mind

【萦回】 yínghuí hover; linger: ～脑际 linger in one's mind

【萦绕】 yíngrǎo hover; linger

滢 yíng 〈书〉 crystal clear

楹 yíng principal columns of a hall

【楹联】 yínglián couplet written on scrolls and hung on the pillars of a hall

潆 yíng

【潆洄】 yínghuí swirl

蝇* yíng fly

【蝇拍】 yíngpāi flyswatter; flyflap

【蝇头】 yíngtóu small as the head of a fly; tiny: ～小楷 very small (hand-written) characters/ ～小利 petty profits

赢 Yíng a surname

赢* yíng ① win; beat: 这场比赛谁～了? Who won the game?/ 我象棋下不～他。I can't beat him at Chinese chess. ② gain (profit)

【赢得】 yíngdé win; gain: ～独立 win (或 attain) independence/ ～长时间的掌声 draw prolonged applause/ ～群众的赞扬 win praise from the masses

【赢利】 yínglì profit; gain

【赢余】 yíngyú surplus; profit: 略有～ with a small favourable balance

瀛 yíng 〈书〉 sea; ocean

yǐng

颖 yǐng 〈书〉 ① glume; grain husk ② tip (as of a writing brush); point ③ clever

【颖慧】 yǐnghuì 〈书〉 (of a teen-ager) clever; bright; intelligent

【颖悟】 yǐngwù 〈书〉 (of a teen-ager) clever; bright

影* yǐng ① shadow; reflection; image: 树～ shadow of a tree/ 湖光塔～ a lake with the reflection of a pagoda in it/ 倒～ inverted image ② trace; vague impression: 他早就忘得没～儿了。He's clean forgotten it. ③ photograph; picture: 合～ group photo (或 picture) ④ motion picture; film; movie: ～迷 film (或 movie) fan

【影集】 yǐngjí photograph (或 picture, photo) album

【影片】 yǐngpiàn film; movie

【影评】 yǐngpíng film review

【影射】 yǐngshè allude to; hint obliquely at; insinuate: ～攻击 attack by innuendo

【影响】 yǐngxiǎng ① influence; effect: 产生巨大～ exert a tremendous influence; produce a great impact/ 消除天灾的～ fight off the effects of natural calamities/ 这样做～不好。This would create a bad impression. ② affect; influence: 不受气候或温度～ not affected by weather or temperature changes/ ～质量 impair the quality/ ～威信 lower one's prestige/ ～工程进度 hold up the project

【影印】 yǐngyìn 〈印〉 photomechanical printing; photo-offset process: ～珍本书籍 photolithograph rare books

【影子】 yǐngzi ① shadow; reflection ② trace; sign; vague impression: 找了他半天,连个～也没见。I looked for him a long time but never even caught a glimpse of him./ 事情已经过了好多年,我脑子里连点～都没有了。It happened so long ago that I haven't the vaguest recollection of it. ◇ ～内阁 shadow cabinet

yìng

应* yìng ① answer; respond; echo: 山鸣谷～。The valleys echo the sounds of the mountains. ② comply with; grant: 有求必～ grant whatever is requested/ 以～急需 in order to fill an urgent need/ 为～广大读者需要 to meet the needs of the broad reading public ③ suit; respond to: ～景 do sth. for the occasion ④ deal with; cope with: 从容～敌 meet the enemy calmly
另见 yīng

【应变】 yìngbiàn meet an emergency (或 contingency)

【应承】 yìngchéng agree (to do sth.); promise; consent: 这件事他一口～下来了。He agreed to do it without hesitation.

【应酬】 yìngchou ① have social intercourse with; treat with

courtesy: 不善~ socially inept/ ~几句 exchange a few polite words ② <旧> dinner party: 今天晚上有个~。I've been invited to dinner this evening. ◇ ~信件 courtesy letter

【应答】 yìngdá reply; answer: ~如流 reply readily and fluently

【应对】 yìngduì reply; answer: 善于~ good at repartee

【应付】 yìngfu ① deal with; cope with; handle: ~复杂局面 deal with complicated situations/ 准备~可能的突然事变 be prepared against possible emergencies/ ~自如 handle a situation with ease; be equal to the occasion ② do sth. perfunctorily; do sth. after a fashion: 干儿 go through the motions/ 采取~的态度 take a perfunctory attitude ③ make do: 我这双凉鞋今年夏天还可以~过去 I'll make do with these sandals for this summer.

【应急】 yìngjí meet an urgent need; meet an emergency (或 contingency) ◇ ~措施 emergency measure/ ~计划 contingency plan; crash programme

【应接不暇】 yìngjiē bù xiá have more visitors or business than one can attend to: 顾客很多, 售货员~。There were so many customers that the shop assistants couldn't attend to them all.

【应景】 yìngjǐng do sth. for the occasion ◇ ~诗 occasional verses

【应考】 yìngkǎo take (或 sit for) an examination: ~的人很多。Many sat for the examination.

【应募】 yìngmù respond to a call for recruits; enlist; join up

【应诺】 yìngnuò agree (to do sth.); promise; undertake

【应声】 yìngshēng happen right at the sound of sth.: 鸟枪一响, 野鸭~而落。The wild duck fell at the report of the shotgun.

【应声虫】 yìngshēngchóng yesman; echo

【应时】 yìngshí seasonable; in season: ~货品 seasonable goods/ ~瓜果 fruits of the season

【应验】 yìngyàn come true; be confirmed; be fulfilled: 他的话~了。What he said has come true.

【应邀】 yìngyāo at sb.'s invitation; on invitation: ~派代表团参加庆祝活动 send a delegation to attend the celebrations at sb.'s invitation

【应用】 yìngyòng apply; use: 把理论~于实践 apply theory to practice/ 防御和进攻的交替~ the alternate use of defence and attack ◇ ~化学 applied chemistry/ ~科学 applied science

【应用文】 yìngyòngwén practical writing (as in official documents, notices, receipts, etc.)

【应运而生】 yìngyùn ér shēng arise at the historic moment; emerge as the times require

【应战】 yìngzhàn ① meet an enemy attack: 沉着~ meet the attack calmly ② accept (或 take up) a challenge ◇ ~书 letter accepting a challenge

【应诊】 yìngzhěn (of a doctor) see patients

【应征】 yìngzhēng ① be recruited: ~入伍 be recruited into the army ② respond to a call for contributions (to a publication): ~的稿件 contributions to a periodical, etc. at the editor's public invitation

映* yìng reflect; mirror; shine: 朝霞~在湖面上。The glory of the dawn is mirrored on the lake./ 他的脸被炉火~得通红。His cheeks shone red before the glowing oven.

【映衬】 yìngchèn set off: 红墙碧瓦,互相~。The red walls and green tiles set each other off beautifully.

【映射】 yìngshè shine upon; cast light upon: 阳光~在江面上。The sun shines upon the river.

【映象】 yìngxiàng image

【映照】 yìngzhào shine upon; cast light upon

硬 yìng ① hard; stiff; tough: ~铅笔 hard pencil/ ~领 stiff collar/ ~刷子 stiff brush ② strong; firm; tough; obstinate: 心肠~ hardhearted/ 话说得很~ express oneself in strong terms/ ~不承认错误 obstinately refuse to admit one's error/ ~的不行来软的。When hard tactics failed, soft methods were used. ③ manage to do sth. with difficulty: ~充好汉 act the hero/ ~撑着干 force oneself to

work hard/ ~压住心头怒火 choke down one's anger/ ~搬别人的经验 copy other people's experience mechanically ④ good (quality); able (person): 货色~ goods of high quality/ ~手 a good hand

【硬邦邦】 yìngbāngbāng very hard; very stiff

【硬币】 yìngbì coin; specie

【硬度】 yìngdù <物> hardness

【硬功夫】 yìnggōngfu great proficiency; masterly skill: 练就一身~ acquire masterly skill through intensive training

【硬骨头】 yìnggútou hard bone — a dauntless, unyielding person

【硬汉】 yìnghàn a dauntless, unyielding man; a man of iron 又作"硬汉子"

【硬化】 yìnghuà harden: 经久~

【硬碰硬】 yìng pèng yìng ① confront the tough with toughness ② (of a job) demanding solid, painstaking work or real skill: 改山造田可是~的事。To transform hills into fields is an extremely tough job.

【硬拼】 yìngpīn fight recklessly

【硬水】 yìngshuǐ hard water

【硬说】 yìngshuō stubbornly insist; assert; allege: 他~他做得对。He obstinately asserted that he had done the right thing./ 她~她不累。She insisted that she wasn't tired.

【硬挺】 yìngtǐng endure with all one's will; hold out with all one's might: 你牙疼别~着,快去治治吧。Don't just try to put up with your toothache. Go and see the dentist./ 那小伙子受了伤, 还~着把活干完。In spite of his injuries, the young man stuck it out.

【硬性】 yìngxìng rigid; stiff; inflexible: 至于具体做法,不作~规定。As for the details of the procedure, we won't lay down any hard and fast (或 rigid) rules.

【硬仗】 yìngzhàng tough (或 hard-fought) battle; formidable task: 一支能打~的石油钻井队 a drilling crew equal to the most formidable tasks

【硬着头皮】 yìngzhe tóupí toughen one's scalp — brace oneself; force oneself to do sth. against one's will: ~顶住 brace oneself and bear with it; hold out tenaciously/ 我~把这碗苦药喝了下去。I forced myself to gulp down the bowl of bitter medicine.

【硬纸板】 yìngzhǐbǎn hardboard; cardboard

媵 yìng <书> ① maid accompanying a bride to her new home ② concubine

yō

哟 yō <叹> 〔表示轻微的惊异〕: ~,你踩我的脚了。Oh! You've stepped on my foot. 另见 yo

唷 yō 见"喔唷" ōyō

yo

哟 yo <助> 〔用在句尾表示祈使语气〕: 用力拉~! Heave ho! 另见 yō

yōng

佣* yōng ① hire (a labourer) ② servant: 女~ woman servant; maid 另见 yòng

【佣工】 yōnggōng <旧> hired labourer; servant

拥* yōng ① hold in one's arms; embrace; hug: 把孩子紧紧~在怀里 hug the child tightly ② gather around: 一群青年~着一个老教师走出来。An old teacher came out, surrounded by a group of young people./ 病人~被而坐。The patient sat wrapped in a quilt. ③ crowd; throng; swarm: 一~而入 swarm in ④ support ⑤ have; possess:

~兵十万 have an army of 100,000

【拥抱】yōngbào　embrace; hug; hold in one's arms: 两国选手热烈~,互致问候。The players of the two countries warmly embraced and greeted each other.

【拥戴】yōngdài　support (sb. as leader): 受到全国人民的~ enjoy the support of the whole nation

【拥护】yōnghù　support; uphold; endorse

【拥挤】yōngjǐ　crowd; push and squeeze: 上下班时间, 公共汽车特别~。The buses are especially crowded during the rush hours./ 不要~! Don't push!

【拥塞】yōngsè　jam; congest: 街道~ streets jammed with traffic

【拥有】yōngyǒu　possess; have; own: ~核武器 possess nuclear weapons/ ~丰富的矿藏 have rich mineral resources/ 广大的人力资源 command vast reserves of manpower/ 一个~十万人口的新城市 a new town of 100,000 people

庸
yōng　① commonplace; mediocre: ~言~行 commonplace words and deeds ② inferior; second-rate ③〈书〉〔用于否定式〕need: 无~细述。This needn't be related in detail. 或 There is no need to go into details. ④〈书〉〔表示反问〕~可弃乎? How could this possibly be relinquished?

【庸才】yōngcái　〈书〉mediocre person; mediocrity

【庸碌】yōnglù　mediocre and unambitious: ~无能 mediocre and incompetent

【庸人】yōngrén　mediocre person

【庸人自扰】yōngrén zì rǎo　worry about troubles of one's own imagining

【庸俗】yōngsú　vulgar; philistine; low: 相互吹捧的~作风 the vulgar ways of logrolling

【庸医】yōngyī　quack; charlatan

【庸中佼佼】yōng zhōng jiǎojiǎo　a giant among dwarfs

雍
yōng　〈书〉harmony

【雍容】yōngróng　natural, graceful and poised: ~华贵 elegant and poised; distingué/ 态度~ have a dignified bearing

慵
yōng　〈书〉weary; lethargic; languid: ~困 tired and sleepy

墉
yōng　〈书〉city wall; high wall

壅
yōng　① stop up; obstruct ② heap soil or fertilizer over and around the roots (of plants and trees): ~土 hilling/ ~肥 heap fertilizer around the roots

【壅塞】yōngsè　clogged up; jammed; congested: 水道~。The waterway is blocked up.

臃
yōng

【臃肿】yōngzhǒng　① too fat to move: 穿得太~ be cumbersomely dressed; be encumbered by too much clothing ② overstaffed: ~的机构 overstaffed organizations

yǒng

永
yǒng　perpetually; forever; always

【永别】yǒngbié　part never to meet again; part forever; be parted by death

【永垂不朽】yǒng chuí bù xiǔ　be immortal

【永恒】yǒnghéng　eternal; perpetual: ~的友谊 eternal friendship/ ~的真理 eternal truth

【永久】yǒngjiǔ　permanent; perpetual; everlasting; forever; for good (and all)

【永诀】yǒngjué　〈书〉part forever; be separated by death

【永生】yǒngshēng　①〈宗〉eternal life ② immortal: ~的战士 immortal fighter/ ~永世 for ever and ever

【永世】yǒngshì　forever: ~难忘 will never forget it for the rest of one's life/ ~长存 live for ever and ever

【永远】yǒngyuǎn　〈副〉always; forever; ever

【永志不忘】yǒng zhì bù wàng　will always bear in mind; will always cherish the memory of sb. or sth.

甬
Yǒng

【甬道】yǒngdào　① paved road leading to a main hall or a tomb ② corridor

泳
yǒng　swim: 仰~ backstroke/ 蛙~ breaststroke

咏
yǒng　① chant; intone: 吟~ recite (a poem) ② express or narrate in poetic form: 《~梅》Ode to the Plum Blossom

【咏叹】yǒngtàn　intone; chant; sing

【咏赞】yǒngzàn　sing the praises of; praise

俑
yǒng　wooden or earthen human figure buried with the dead in ancient times; tomb figure; figurine: 陶~ pottery figurine/ 武士~ warrior figure

勇
yǒng　brave; valiant; courageous: ~冠三军 distinguish oneself by peerless valour in battle/ 越战越~ one's courage mounts as the battle progresses/ 智~双全 have both wisdom and courage

【勇敢】yǒnggǎn　brave; courageous: 勤劳~的人民 a brave and industrious people/ ~善战 courageous and skilful in battle

【勇猛】yǒngměng　bold and powerful; full of valour and vigour: ~前进 march boldly forward

【勇气】yǒngqì　courage; nerve: 鼓起~ pluck up (或 muster up) one's courage

【勇士】yǒngshì　a brave and strong man; warrior

【勇往直前】yǒng wǎng zhí qián　march forward courageously; advance bravely

【勇武】yǒngwǔ　valiant: ~过人 surpass others in valour; be surpassingly valorous

【勇于】yǒngyú　be brave in; be bold in; have the courage to: ~负责 be brave in shouldering responsibilities/ ~承认错误 have the courage to admit one's mistakes/ ~创新 be bold in making innovations

涌
yǒng　① gush; well; pour; surge: 泪如泉~ tears well up in one's eyes/ 石油喷~而出 Oil gushed out./ 大家都向外~。The crowd was pouring out. ② rise; surge; emerge: 风啸浪~。The wind howls; the waves rise./ 一排排巨浪向石滩~来。Huge waves surged over the rocks./ 多少往事~上心头。Memories of the past welled up in my mind./ 东方~出一轮红日。A red sun rose in the east.

【涌现】yǒngxiàn　emerge in large numbers; spring up; come to the fore: 新人新事不断~。New people and new things are constantly emerging.

恿
yǒng　见"怂恿" sǒngyǒng

蛹
yǒng　pupa: 蝶~ chrysalis/ 蚕~ silkworm chrysalis

踊
yǒng　leap up; jump up

【踊跃】yǒngyuè　① leap; jump: ~欢呼 leap and cheer ② vying with one another; eagerly; enthusiastically: ~响应号召 respond to a call enthusiastically/ 今晚的晚会大家肯定会~参加的。I'm sure everybody will be eager to come to this evening's party.

yòng

用
yòng　① use; employ; apply: ~手分开 break with one's hands/ ~火烤 bake over the fire/ ~水煮 boil in water/ ~针刺麻醉做外科手术 employ acupuncture anaesthesia in surgery/ ~严格的科学态度从事研究 do research with a strictly scientific attitude ② expenses; outlay: 家~ family expenses/ 零~钱 pocket money; spending money ③ usefulness; use: 有~ useful/ 没~ useless; worthless/ 有点~ be of some use ④〔多用于否定〕need: 不~开灯。There's no need to turn on the light./ 不~担心。Don't worry. ⑤〈敬〉eat; drink: 请~茶。Won't you have some tea, please. ⑥〈书〉hence; therefore: ~特函达。Hence this letter.

【用兵】yòngbīng　use military forces; resort to arms: 不得已而~ have no alternative but to resort to arms/ 善于~ well versed in the art of war/ 如神 direct military operations with miraculous skill; work miracles in manoeuvring troops; be a superb military commander

【用不着】 yòngbuzháo ① not need; have no use for: 把~的书放回书架。Put back the books you are not using on the shelves. ② there is no need to; it is not worth while to: ~为这些小事争论不休。There's no need to keep arguing about such triflings.

【用场】 yòngchǎng use: 有~ be useful/ 派大~ be turned to good account/ 派新~ be put to new uses

【用处】 yòngchu use; good: 这两样东西,各有各的~。Each of the two things has its own use./ 抱怨有什么~? What's the use (或 good) of complaining?/ 不要扔掉,将来会有~。Don't throw it away; it may come in handy.

【用得着】 yòngdezháo ① find sth. useful; need: 别看这台机器旧,我们目前正~。Although the machine is old, it serves our purpose at present./ 这里可能~古代希腊的一段寓言。Here it might be useful to quote an ancient Greek fable./ 没多少活儿了,还~那么多人吗? There isn't much work left. Do we still need so many people? ② there is need to; it is necessary to: it is worth while to: ~派车去接他们吗? Is it necessary to send a car for them?

【用度】 yòngdù expenditure; expense; outlay: 他家人口多,~大。He has a big family and many expenses.

【用法】 yòngfǎ use; usage: ~说明 directions (for use)/《英语~词典》A Dictionary of English Usage

【用费】 yòngfèi expense; cost

【用功】 yònggōng hardworking; diligent; studious: ~读书 be studious; study diligently; be diligent in one's studies

【用户】 yònghù consumer; user: 征求~意见 ask for consumers' opinions/ 电话~ telephone subscriber ◇ ~电报 telex

【用劲】 yòngjìn exert oneself (physically); put forth one's strength: 大家一齐~ 把大石头搬开了。We all heaved together and removed the boulder.

【用具】 yòngjù utensil; apparatus; appliance: 炊事~ kitchen (或 cooking) utensils/ 消防~ fire-fighting apparatus/ 救生~ lifesaving equipment/ 打猎~ hunting gear

【用力】 yònglì exert oneself (physically); put forth one's strength: ~把门推了一下 give the door a hard push

【用品】 yòngpǐn articles for use: 生活~ articles for daily use; daily necessities/ 办公~ things for office use; stationery

【用人】 yòngrén ① choose a person for a job; make use of personnel: 善于~ know how to choose the right person for the right job; know how to make proper use of personnel/ ~不当 not choose the right person for the job ② need hands: 现在正是~的时候。Now's the time when we are in need of personnel.

【用事】 yòngshì ① act: 意气~ be swayed by one's feelings and act rashly/ 感情~ act impetuously ② 〈书〉 be in power

【用途】 yòngtú use: 橡胶的~很广。Rubber has many uses.

【用武】 yòngwǔ use force; display one's abilities or talents: 大有~之地。There's ample scope for one's abilities.

【用心】 yòngxīn ① diligently; attentively; with concentrated attention: ~学习 concentrate on one's studies; study diligently/ ~听讲 listen attentively to a lecture/ ~思索 think hard ② motive; intention: 别有~ have ulterior motives/ ~何其毒也! How vicious his intentions are!/ ~良苦 have really given much thought to the matter

【用以】 yòng yǐ in order to; so as to: 略举数例,~说明这一原理。Here are a few examples to illustrate this principle.

【用意】 yòngyì intention; purpose: ~很好 with good intentions/ 你这是什么~? Just what are you up to? 或 What's your game?

【用语】 yòngyǔ ① choice of words; wording: ~不当 inappropriate choice of words; incorrect wording ② phraseology; term: 商业~ commercial phraseology

佣* yòng commission
另见 yōng

【佣金】 yòngjīn commission; brokerage; middleman's fee

yōu

优* yōu ① excellent: 品学兼~ be a good student of good character ② 〈旧〉 actor or actress: 名~ a famous actor or actress

【优待】 yōudài give preferential (或 special) treatment: ~军属 give favoured treatment to servicemen's families/ ~外宾 give special consideration to foreign guests ◇ ~券 complimentary ticket

【优等】 yōuděng high-class; first-rate; excellent ◇ ~品 high-class (或 first-rate) product/ ~生 top student

【优点】 yōudiǎn merit; strong (或 good) point; advantage; virtue: ~和缺点 merits and demerits; virtues and defects; strong and weak points/ 这个办法有很多~。This method has many advantages.

【优厚】 yōuhòu munificent; liberal; favourable: 待遇~ excellent pay and conditions; liberal wages and benefits

【优惠】 yōuhuì 〈经〉 preferential; favourable: 按~条件提供的经济援助 economic assistance given on liberal (或 favourable) terms ◇ ~贷款 loan on favourable terms/ ~待遇 preferential treatment/ ~关税协定 preferential tariff agreements/ ~价格 preferential prices/ ~权 preferential rights

【优良】 yōuliáng fine; good: 成绩~ get good marks; make a good showing/ 艰苦朴素的~作风 fine style of hard work and plain living/ 推广水稻~品种 popularize fine (或 good) varieties of rice

【优伶】 yōulíng 〈旧〉 actor or actress

【优美】 yōuměi graceful; fine; exquisite: 风景~ fine scenery/ ~的舞蹈动作 graceful dance movements/ ~的民间艺术 exquisite folk arts

【优柔寡断】 yōuróu guǎduàn irresolute and hesitant; indecisive: 他是个~的人。He's indecisive.

【优胜】 yōushèng winning; superior ◇ ~者 winner; champion

【优势】 yōushì superiority; preponderance; dominant position: 军事~ military superiority/ 兵力~ superior force/ 占~ occupy a dominant position; gain the upper hand

【优渥】 yōuwò 〈书〉 liberal; munificent; favourable

【优先】 yōuxiān have priority; take precedence: ~发展基础工业 give priority to the development of the basic industries/ 必须~考虑的一个问题 a question which claims precedence over all others; a first (或 top) priority ◇ ~权 priority; preference

【优秀】 yōuxiù outstanding; excellent; splendid; fine: ~作品 (literary or artistic) works of excellence/ ~电影 highly rated films

【优异】 yōuyì excellent; outstanding; exceedingly good: 考试成绩~ do exceedingly well in an examination

【优游】 yōuyóu 〈书〉 leisurely and carefree: ~自在 leisurely and carefree/ ~岁月 pass one's days in carefree leisure

【优遇】 yōuyù give special treatment: 格外~ exceptionally good treatment

【优裕】 yōuyù affluent; abundant: 生活~ be well-off; be well-to-do; live in affluence

【优越】 yōuyuè superior; advantageous: 处于~的地位 be in an advantageous position/ ~条件 favourable conditions ◇ ~感 sense of superiority; superiority complex

【优越性】 yōuyuèxìng superiority; advantage

【优哉游哉】 yōuzāi-yóuzāi 〈书〉 living a life of ease and leisure; leisurely and carefree; leisurely and unhurried

【优质】 yōuzhì high (或 top) quality; high grade: 开展~高产运动 launch a campaign for good quality and high output ◇ ~钢 high-quality steel

忧* yōu ① worry; be worried: ~国~民 be concerned about one's country and one's people ② sorrow; anxiety; concern; care: 无~无虑 carefree; free from all anxieties

【忧愁】 yōuchóu sad; worried; depressed: 面容~ look worried

【忧愤】 yōufèn worried and indignant

【忧患】 yōuhuàn suffering; misery; hardship: 饱经~ have gone through a good deal

【忧惧】 yōujù worried and apprehensive

【忧虑】 yōulǜ worried; anxious; concerned: 深感~ feel extremely anxious; be very worried/ 他的~不是没有根据的。His anxiety is not uncalled-for.

【忧闷】 yōumèn depressed; feeling low; weighed down with

cares

【忧伤】yōushāng distressed; weighed down with sorrow; laden with grief

【忧心】yōuxīn 〈书〉worry; anxiety: ～忡忡 heavyhearted; care-laden; laden with anxieties/ ～如焚 burning with anxiety; extremely worried

【忧郁】yōuyù melancholy; heavyhearted; dejected

攸 yōu 〈书〉〔常用于〕: 性命～关 a matter of life and death/ 责有～归。The responsibility should lie where it belongs.

呦 yōu 〈叹〉〔表示惊异〕: ～! 你怎么也来了? Hey! Fancy seeing you here.

幽 yōu ① deep and remote; secluded; dim: ～林 a secluded wood ② secret; hidden: ～怨 bitterness hidden in one's heart/ ～居 live in seclusion ③ quiet; tranquil; serene: ～深 deep and quiet ④ imprison: ～囚 imprison; place in confinement ⑤ of the nether world: ～魂 ghost

【幽暗】yōu'àn dim; gloomy
【幽愤】yōufèn hidden resentment
【幽谷】yōugǔ a deep and secluded valley
【幽会】yōuhuì a secret meeting of lovers; a lovers' rendezvous; tryst
【幽魂】yōuhún ghost
【幽寂】yōujì secluded and lonely
【幽禁】yōujìn put under house arrest; imprison
【幽静】yōujìng quiet and secluded; peaceful: 这里环境很～。It's rather peaceful and secluded around here.
【幽灵】yōulíng ghost; spectre; spirit
【幽冥】yōumíng the nether world
【幽默】yōumò humorous ◇ ～感 sense of humour
【幽情】yōuqíng exquisite feelings: 发思古之～ muse over things of the remote past
【幽趣】yōuqù the delightful serenity of seclusion
【幽深】yōushēn (of forests, palaces, etc.) deep and serene; deep and quiet: ～的峡谷 a deep gorge
【幽思】yōusī ① ponder; meditate ② thoughts on things remote
【幽闲】yōuxián ① (of a woman) gentle and serene ② 见"悠闲" yōuxián 又作"幽娴"
【幽香】yōuxiāng a delicate (或 faint) fragrance
【幽雅】yōuyǎ (of a place) quiet and tastefully laid out
【幽咽】yōuyè 〈书〉① whimpering: ～的哭泣 low sobs; whimpers ② murmuring: 泉水～ a murmuring spring
【幽暗】yōuyōu ① (of light or sound) faint: ～啜泣 sob quietly/ ～的路灯 dim street lamps ② 〈书〉looming in the distance
【幽怨】yōuyuàn hidden bitterness (of a young woman thwarted in love)

悠 yōu ① long-drawn-out; remote in time or space ② leisurely

【悠长】yōucháng long; long-drawn-out: ～的岁月 long years/ ～的汽笛声 the drawn-out sound of a siren
【悠荡】yōudàng swing (to and fro); sway (back and forth)
【悠忽】yōuhū lazy and idle
【悠久】yōujiǔ long; long-standing; age-old: 历史～ have a long history/ ～的文化 a civilization (或 culture) of long standing/ ～的传统 an age-old tradition
【悠然】yōurán ① carefree and leisurely: ～自得 be carefree and content ② long; distant; far away: ～神往 one's thoughts turn to things distant
【悠闲】yōuxián leisurely and carefree: ～自在 leisurely and carefree
【悠扬】yōuyáng (of music, etc.) rising and falling; melodious: ～的歌声 melodious singing
【悠悠】yōuyōu ① long; long-drawn-out; remote: ～长夜 The night seemed to drag. ② leisurely; unhurried: ～自得 carefree and content
【悠悠荡荡】yōuyōudàngdàng floating about
【悠悠忽忽】yōuyōuhūhū ① loiter ② be in a trance
【悠远】yōuyuǎn ① a long time ago; long ago; distant: ～

的往事 events of the distant past ② far off (或 away); remote; distant: 山川～ mountains and rivers far, far away

yóu

尤* yóu ① outstanding: 择～ pick out the best/ 无耻之～ have absolutely no sense of shame; brazen in the extreme ② particularly; especially: 这一点～为重要。This is even more important./ 此地盛产水果,～以梨桃著称。The place abounds with fruit, especially pears and peaches. ③ fault; wrongdoing: 效～ knowingly follow the example of a wrongdoer ④ have a grudge against; blame: 怨天～人 blame god and man — blame everyone and everything but oneself

【尤其】yóuqí 〈副〉especially; particularly: 大家干得都很猛,～是小王。Everyone was working energetically, especially Xiao Wang./ 讲话的第一部分～重要。The first part of the speech is particularly important.

由* yóu ① cause; reason: 原～ cause/ 理～ reason ② because of; due to: ～粗心大意造成的错误 mistakes due to carelessness/ 咎～自取 have only oneself to blame ③ by; through: ～边门出去。Exit by the side door./ ～此入内。This way in. 或 Entrance./ ～经理推荐 be recommended by the manager/ ～民主协商选举产生 be elected after democratic consultation ④ follow; obey: 事不～己。Things are beyond one's control. 或 Things are getting out of hand./ ～她去吧。Let her do as she pleases. ⑤ 〈介〉〔表示某事归某人去做〕: 这件事～他处理。Leave it to him./ 须～入党支部大会通过 be subject to acceptance by a general meeting of the party branch ⑥ 〈介〉〔表示凭借〕: 水～氢与氧化合而成。Water is composed of hydrogen and oxygen. ⑦ 〈介〉〔表示起点〕from: ～银川出发 set off from Yinchuan/ ～点到面 spread over a whole area from one point/ ～浅入深 proceed from the easy to the difficult/ ～下而上 from bottom to top; from the lower level upward; from below

【由不得】yóubude ① not be up to sb. to decide; be beyond the control of: 这件事～我。It's not up to him./ 事到如今就～你了。You have no choice in the matter at this late hour. ② cannot help: ～笑了起来 can't help laughing
【由此】yóucǐ from this; therefrom; thus: ～前进 go forward from here/ ～看来 judging from this; in view of this/ ～产生的一切后果 all consequences arising therefrom/ ～弄出许多错误 make many mistakes as a consequence
【由此可见】yóu cǐ kě jiàn it can be seen; this shows; that proves: ～,多数人是赞成这个计划的。Thus it can be seen that the majority are in favour of the plan.
【由来】yóulái origin: 分歧的～ origin of differences
【由来已久】yóulái yǐ jiǔ long-standing; time-honoured: 争论～。The dispute is of long-standing./ 这种风俗～。This is a time-honoured custom.
【由于】yóuyú 〈介〉owing to; thanks to; as a result of; due to; in virtue of: ～健康关系 on health grounds
【由衷】yóuzhōng from the bottom of one's heart; sincere; heartfelt: ～之言 words which come from the bottom of one's heart; sincere words/ 表示～的感激 extend one's heartfelt thanks/ 对于你的进步,我感到～的高兴。I heartily rejoice at the progress you've made.

邮* yóu ① post; mail: 信～了吗? Has the letter been posted (或 mailed)? ② postal; mail: ～路 postal (或 mail) route

【邮包】yóubāo postal parcel; parcel ◇ ～保险 parcel post insurance
【邮差】yóuchāi postman
【邮船】yóuchuán ocean liner; liner; packet ship
【邮戳】yóuchuō postmark
【邮袋】yóudài mailbag; postbag; (mail) pouch
【邮递】yóudì ① send by post (或 mail) ② postal (或 mail) delivery ◇ ～员 postman; mailman
【邮电】yóudiàn post and telecommunications
【邮费】yóufèi postage: ～免收 post-free

【邮购】yóugòu mail-order ◇ ~部 mail-order department

【邮汇】yóuhuì remit by post

【邮寄】yóujì send by post; post

【邮件】yóujiàn postal matter; post; mail: 挂号~ registered post/ 航空~ air mail/ 小包~ a postal packet

【邮局】yóujú post office

【邮票】yóupiào postage stamp; stamp: 一套纪念~ a set of commemorative stamps

【邮筒】yóutǒng pillar-box; postbox; mailbox

【邮箱】yóuxiāng postbox; mailbox

【邮政】yóuzhèng postal service ◇ ~编码 postcode; zip code/ ~代办所 postal agency/ ~汇票 postal money order; postal order/ ~局 post office/ ~局长 postmaster/ ~网 postal network/ ~信箱 post-office box (P. O. B.)

【邮资】yóuzī postage: 国内~ postage paid for inland mail/ 国外~ postage paid for overseas mail/ ~已付 postage paid; postpaid

犹 yóu 〈书〉① just as; like: 虽死~生 live on in spirit ② still: 记忆~新 be still fresh in one's memory

【犹如】yóurú just as; like; as if: 灯火辉煌,~白昼。The place was lit up as bright as day.

【犹太教】Yóutàijiào Judaism ◇ ~教士 rabbi/ ~堂 synagogue

【犹疑】yóuyí hesitate

【犹豫】yóuyù hesitate; be irresolute: ~不决 hesitate; remain undecided/ 毫不~ without the least hesitation/ 犹犹豫豫 shilly-shally

油 yóu ① oil; fat; grease: 植物~ vegetable oil/ 猪~ pork fat; lard ② apply tung oil or paint: ~饰一新 freshly varnished (或 painted) ~门窗 paint the doors and windows/ ③ be stained with oil or grease: 衣服~了。The coat has got oil stains on it. ④ oily; glib: 这家伙嘴~得很。The fellow has a very glib tongue.

【油饼】yóubǐng deep-fried dough cake

【油布】yóubù oilcloth; oilskin; tarpaulin

【油彩】yóucǎi greasepaint; paint

【油藏】yóucáng 〈石油〉 oil deposit; oil pool

【油船】yóuchuán (oil) tanker; oil carrier

【油灯】yóudēng oil lamp

【油管】yóuguǎn 〈石油〉 ① oil pipe: 铺设~ lay oil pipes ② oil tube: 未下~的井 untubed well

【油光】yóuguāng glossy; shiny; varnished: 把车子擦得~锃亮 put a good shine on the car

【油滑】yóuhuá slippery; foxy

【油画】yóuhuà oil painting: 画~ paint in oils

【油迹】yóujī oil stains; grease spots: ~斑斑 covered with grease spots

【油井】yóujǐng oil well: 钻一口~ drill (或 bore) a well

【油库】yóukù oil depot; tank farm: 转运~ oil terminal

【油矿】yóukuàng ① oil deposit ② oil field

【油轮】yóulún (oil) tanker

【油码头】yóumǎtóu oil jetty; oil wharf; tanker (loading) terminal

【油门】yóumén 〈机〉 ① throttle ② 〈口〉 accelerator: 踩~ step on the accelerator

【油墨】yóumò printing ink: 快干~ quicksetting ink

【油腻】yóunì ① greasy; oily: 不爱吃~的东西 not care for greasy (或 oily) food ② greasy food; oily food

【油漆】yóuqī ① paint: 一层~ a coat of paint/ ~未干: Wet paint! 或 Fresh paint! ② cover with paint; paint: 把大门~一下 have the gate painted ◇ ~工人 painter

【油腔滑调】yóuqiāng-huádiào glib; unctuous: 说起话来~ speak glibly; have a glib tongue

【油然】yóurán ① spontaneously; involuntarily: 敬慕之心,~而生。Admiration wells up in one's heart. ② densely; profusely: ~作云 clouds beginning to gather

【油水】yóushuǐ ① grease: 这个菜~太大。This dish is too greasy. ② profit: ~不大 not very profitable/ 捞得一点~ pick up a few crumbs; make a profit

【油酥】yóusū short; crisp; flaky: ~点心 short pastry

【油田】yóutián oil field: ~开发 oil field development (或 exploitation)/ 多层~ multi-pay oil field

【油条】yóutiáo deep-fried twisted dough sticks

【油桶】yóutǒng oil drum

【油头粉面】yóutóu-fěnmiàn sleek-haired and creamy-faced — coquettish or dandified in appearance

【油头滑脑】yóutóu-huánǎo slick; flippant

【油汪汪】yóuwāngwāng ① dripping with oil; full of grease ② glossy; shiny

【油污】yóuwū greasy dirt

【油箱】yóuxiāng fuel tank: 副~ auxiliary fuel tank; anxiliary tank

【油印】yóuyìn mimeograph: ~一百份 mimeograph a hundred copies ◇ ~机 mimeograph/ ~蜡纸 stencil; stencil paper

【油渣】yóuzhā ① dregs of fat ② 〈石油〉 oil residue

【油脂】yóuzhī oil; fat: 植物~ vegetable fat or oil/ 动物~ animal fat or oil; tallow; grease

【油棕】yóuzōng 〈植〉 oil palm

【油嘴】yóuzuǐ 〈植〉 glib; glib talker

【油嘴滑舌】yóuzuǐ-huáshé glib-tongued

柚 yóu

另见 yòu

【柚木】yóumù 〈植〉 teak

铀 yóu 〈化〉 uranium

游 yóu ① swim ② rove around; wander; travel; tour: 周~世界 travel round the world; go on a world tour/ 山水水 travel from place to place enjoying the beauties of nature; go on trips to different scenic spots ③ roving; itinerant: ~民 vagrant ④ 〈书〉 associate with: 交~甚广 have a wide circle of acquaintances ⑤ part of a river; reach: 上~ the upper reaches (of a river)

【游伴】yóubàn travel companion

【游船】yóuchuán pleasure-boat

【游荡】yóudàng loaf about; loiter; wander

【游动】yóudòng move about; go from place to place ◇ ~哨 a roving sentry; a patrol

【游逛】yóuguàng go sight-seeing; stroll about

【游击】yóujī guerrilla warfare: 打~ fight as a guerrilla; conduct guerrilla warfare

【游记】yóujì travel notes; travels

【游街】yóujiē parade sb. through the streets: ~示众 parade sb. through the streets to expose him before the public

【游客】yóukè visitor (to a park, etc.); tourist; excursionist; sightseer

【游览】yóulǎn go sight-seeing; tour; visit: ~西湖 go sight-seeing on the West Lake/ ~长城 visit the Great Wall ◇ ~车 tourist coach/ ~地 place for sight-seeing; excursion centre/ ~图 tourist map

【游离】yóulí dissociate; drift away: ~分子 one who quits the group

【游历】yóulì travel for pleasure; travel; tour: ~过很多地方 have travelled extensively

【游民】yóumín vagrant; vagabond: 无业~ vagrant

【游牧】yóumù move about in search of pasture; rove around as a nomad ◇ ~部落 nomadic tribe/ ~生活 nomadic life; nomadism

【游憩】yóuqì stroll about or have a rest

【游人】yóurén visitor (to a park, etc.); sightseer; tourist

【游刃有余】yóu rèn yǒu yú handle a butcher's cleaver skilfully — do a job with skill and ease; be more than equal to a task

【游手好闲】yóushǒu-hàoxián idle about; loaf: ~,不务正业 idle about and do no decent work

【游水】yóushuǐ swim

【游说】yóushuì go about selling an idea; go about drumming up support for an idea; go canvassing

【游艇】yóutǐng yacht; pleasure-boat

【游玩】yóuwán ① amuse oneself; play: 孩子们经常去海滨~。The children often go to the beach to play. ② go sight-seeing; stroll about

【游戏】yóuxì ① recreation; game: 做~ play games ② play: 孩子们在公园里~。The children are playing in the

游泳

蛙式

仰泳

自由式

蝴蝶式

park.

【游行】 yóuxíng parade; march; demonstration: 节日～ gala parade/ 举行～示威 hold a demonstration ◇ ～队伍 contingents of paraders or marchers; procession

【游兴】 yóuxìng interest in going on an excursion or sightseeing

【游移】 yóuyí (of attitude, policy, etc.) waver; vacillate; wobble: ～不定 keep on vacillating/ ～于两者之间 waver between the two/ 一点～的余地也没有了。 There is no wavering.

【游弋】 yóuyì cruise: 在海上～ cruise on the sea

【游艺】 yóuyì entertainment; recreation ◇ ～节目 programme (of musical and other performances)/ ～室 recreation room

【游泳】 yóuyǒng swim: 去～ go for a swim; go swimming/ 在～中学习～ learn to swim by swimming ◇ ～比赛 swimming contest/ ～池 swimming pool/ ～馆 natatorium/ ～裤 bathing (或 swimming) trunks/ ～帽 bathing (或 swimming) cap/ ～衣 swimsuit; swimming suit (或 costume); bathing suit (或 costume)

【游资】 yóuzī idle fund; idle money; floating capital

【游子】 yóuzǐ 〈书〉 man travelling or residing in a place far away from home

【游子】 yóuzi decoy

鱿 yóu

【鱿鱼】 yóuyú squid

yǒu

友* yǒu ①friend: 好～ close friend ②friendly

【友爱】 yǒu'ài friendly affection; fraternal love: 团结～ fraternal unity

【友邦】 yǒubāng friendly nation (或 country)

【友好】 yǒuhǎo ①close friend; friend: 生前～ friends of the deceased ②friendly; amicable: ～访问 friendly visit/

会谈在～的气氛中进行。 The talks proceeded in a friendly atmosphere./ 发表热情～的讲话 make a warm and friendly speech

【友情】 yǒuqíng friendly sentiments; friendship

【友人】 yǒurén friend: 国际～ foreign friend

【友善】 yǒushàn 〈书〉 friendly; amicable

【友谊】 yǒuyì friendship: 深厚的～ profound friendship/ 建立～ build (或 forge) ties of friendship ◇ ～赛 friendly match

有* yǒu ①have; possess: 我～一个弟弟。 I have a younger brother./ 她～热情，～朝气。 She is full of vigour and enthusiasm./ 属于全民所～ belong to the whole people/ ～百利而无一弊 have every advantage and no drawback ②there is; exist: 屋里～人吗？ Is there anyone in the room?/ 这座位～人吗？ Is this seat taken?/ 还～许多工作要做。 Much still remains to be done. ③〔表示估量或比较〕: 水～三米多深。 The water is more than 3 metres deep./ 他～你这么高。 He is as tall as you./ 问题～那么严重吗？ Is the problem that serious? ④〔表示发生或出现〕: 一～问题就去解决 deal with a problem as soon as it crops up/ 在朋友的帮助下，他～了很大进步。 With the help of his friends, he has made great progress. ⑤〔表示多，大〕: ～经验 be experienced/ ～了年纪 be getting on in years ⑥〔用于泛指，跟"某"的作用相近〕: 一天我在街上碰见了他。 One day I ran into him in the street./ ～些事还需要商量。 Certain things are still open to discussion. ⑦〔用在"人""时候""地方"前面，表示一部分〕: ～人说可以，～人说不可以。 Some say yes, some say no./ 这里～时候也能热到三十九度。 The temperature here sometimes goes up to thirty-nine degrees centigrade./ 这个措施～地方适用， ～地方不适用。 This measure is suited to some localities, but not to others. ⑧〔用在某些动词的前面组成套语，表示客气〕: ～劳远迎 。 I deeply appreciate your kindness in coming so far to meet me.

另见 yòu

【有碍】 yǒu'ài be a hindrance to; get in the way of; obstruct: ~交通 hinder traffic/ ~观瞻 be repugnant to the eye; be an eyesore

【有案可稽】 yǒu àn kě jī be a matter of record; be on record; be documented 又作"有案可查"

【有备无患】 yǒubèi-wúhuàn where there is precaution, there is no danger; preparedness averts peril

【有鼻子有眼儿】 yǒubízi-yǒuyǎnr with every detail vividly described: 她说得~,就象真有那么一回事。She described the whole thing in such vivid detail that it sounded quite real.

【有待】 yǒudài remain (to be done); await: ~解决 remain to be solved/ ~证明 have yet to be proved/ ~上级作出最后决定 await final decision by the higher level/ ~进一步讨论 pending further discussion

【有的】 yǒude some: ~这样说,~那样说。Some say one thing, some say another.

【有的是】 yǒudeshì have plenty of; there's no lack of: 她~时间。She has all the time in the world./ 这种草药山上~。There are plenty of these herbs in the hills.

【有的放矢】 yǒu dì fàng shǐ shoot the arrow at the target — have a definite object in view

【有点儿】 yǒudiǎnr ① some; a little: 水壶里还~水。There's still some water in the kettle./ 看来~希望 look a bit hopeful ② 〈副〉 somewhat; rather; a bit: ~反感 feel a bit resentful; have a touch of resentment/ ~不好意思 be somewhat embarrassed

【有方】 yǒufāng with the proper method; in the right way: 领导~ exercise able leadership

【有福同享,有祸同当】 yǒu fú tóng xiǎng, yǒu huò tóng dāng share joys and sorrows; share weal and woe; stick together through thick and thin

【有功】 yǒugōng have rendered great service; have performed meritorious service

【有关】 yǒuguān have something to do with; have a bearing on; relate to; concern: 这件事与他~。He has something to do with the matter./ 这些问题都跟哲学~。All these questions relate to philosophy./ 阅读~的文件 read the relevant documents/ 保证~国家的合法权利 safeguard the legitimate rights of such countries as may be affected ◇ ~部门 the department concerned/ ~当局 the authorities concerned; the proper authorities/ ~方面 the parties concerned/ ~组织 related organization

【有鬼】 yǒuguǐ there's something fishy: 这里面~。There's something fishy about it. 或 One smells a rat here./ 他心里~。He's got a guilty conscience.

【有过之无不及】 yǒu guò zhī wú bùjí 〔多用于坏的方面〕go even farther than; outdo

【有害】 yǒuhài harmful; pernicious; detrimental: 对健康~ harmful (或 detrimental) to one's health/ ~的影响 pernicious effects

【有恒】 yǒuhéng persevering

【有机】 yǒujī ①〈化〉organic ② organic: ~的整体 an organic whole

【有机可乘】 yǒu jī kě chéng there's an opportunity to take advantage of; there's a loophole that can be used

【有计划】 yǒu jìhuà in a planned way; according to plan

【有救】 yǒujiù can be saved (或 cured, remedied): 好了,这病~了!Thank goodness, we've found a cure for the disease.

【有口皆碑】 yǒu kǒu jiē bēi win universal praise; be universally acclaimed

【有口难分】 yǒu kǒu nán fēn find it hard to vindicate oneself 又作"有口难辩"

【有口难言】 yǒu kǒu nán yán cannot bring oneself to mention sth.; find it hard or embarrassing to bring up a matter

【有口无心】 yǒukǒu-wúxīn be sharp-tongued but not malicious: 他是~,你别见怪。He didn't really mean what he said, so don't take it to heart.

【有赖】 yǒulài depend on; rest on: 要实现这项改革~于大家共同努力。The success of the innovation depends on our concerted efforts.

【有理】 yǒulǐ reasonable; justified; in the right: 你讲的~。What you say is quite reasonable./ ~走遍天下,无理寸步难行。With justice on your side, you can go anywhere; without it, you can't take a step.

【有力】 yǒulì strong; powerful; forceful; energetic; vigorous: 提供~的证据 provide strong evidence; furnish convincing proof/ 作出~的回答 give a forceful answer/ ~地打击了歪风邪气 hit hard at evil trends

【有利】 yǒulì advantageous; beneficial; favourable: 形势对我们~。The situation is to our advantage. ◇ ~地形 〈军〉favourable terrain/ ~时机 opportune time/ ~条件 favourable condition

【有利可图】 yǒu lì kě tú have good prospects of gain; stand to gain; be profitable

【有两下子】 yǒu liǎng xiàzi 〈口〉have real skill; know one's stuff: 他干活又快又好,真~。He works fast and well; he obviously knows his stuff.

【有门儿】 yǒuménr 〈口〉① find the beginning of a solution; be hopeful (of success): 听他的口气,这事看来~了。Judging by the way he spoke, he might get the matter off the ground now. ② get the hang: 这活儿他干了几次,现在有点门儿了。After several trials, he began to get the hang of the work.

【有名】 yǒumíng well-known; famous; celebrated: ~的乒乓球运动员 a famous (或 well-known) table tennis player/ ~的科学家 a celebrated scientist

【有名无实】 yǒumíng-wúshí in name but not in reality; merely nominal; titular

【有目共睹】 yǒu mù gòng dǔ be there for all to see; be obvious to all

【有目共赏】 yǒu mù gòng shǎng have a universal appeal

【有奶便是娘】 yǒu nǎi biàn shì niáng whoever suckles me is my mother; submit oneself to anyone who feeds one; lick the hand of anyone who throws a few crumbs

【有年】 yǒunián 〈书〉for years

【有期徒刑】 yǒuqī túxíng 〈法〉set term of imprisonment: 判~七年 be sentenced to seven years' imprisonment

【有其父,必有其子】 yǒu qí fù, bì yǒu qí zǐ like father, like son

【有钱】 yǒuqián rich; wealthy: ~能使鬼推磨。With money you can make the devil turn the millstone. 或 Money makes the mare to go. ◇ ~人 the rich; the wealthy

【有求必应】 yǒu qiú bì yìng respond to every plea; grant whatever is requested

【有趣】 yǒuqù interesting; fascinating; amusing: ~的故事 an interesting story/ ~的游戏 a fascinating game; an exciting game

【有色】 yǒusè coloured: 戴着~眼镜看事情 look at things through coloured spectacles — take a distorted view ◇ ~金属 nonferrous metal/ ~人种 coloured race (或 people)

【有神论】 yǒushénlùn theism ◇ ~者 theist

【有生以来】 yǒu shēng yǐlái ever since one's birth: ~第一次 the first time in one's life (或 in all one's born days)

【有声有色】 yǒushēng-yǒusè full of sound and colour — vivid and dramatic: 故事讲得~ tell a story dramatically

【有识之士】 yǒu shí zhī shì a person with breadth of vision; a man of insight

【有时】 yǒushí sometimes; at times; now and then: 他~也写几句诗。Sometimes he writes a few lines of poetry.

【有史以来】 yǒu shǐ yǐlái since the beginning (或 dawn) of history; throughout history: ~最大的陨石雨 the biggest meteorite shower in history

【有始无终】 yǒushǐ-wúzhōng start sth. but fail to carry it through

【有始有终】 yǒushǐ-yǒuzhōng carry sth. through to the end

【有事】 yǒushì ① when problems crop up; if sth. happens: 做好准备,一旦~,马上出动。Get prepared so that you can set off immediately if something happens. ② occupied; busy: 你今晚~吗?Have you anything on this evening?/ 我现在~。I'm busy now.

【有恃无恐】 yǒushì-wúkǒng secure in the knowledge that one has strong backing

【有数】 yǒushù ① know exactly how things stand; have a definite idea of what one's doing: 进行调查研究,做到心中~ make investigations so as to be sure how things stand/ 这样一摸底,大家心里就~了。With this stocktaking, we know where we are./ 你放心,怎么做我心里~。Don't worry. I know what I'm doing. ② not many; only a few:

只剩下~的几天了，得加把劲儿。There are only a few days left. We must get a move on.

【有所】 yǒusuǒ to some extent; somewhat: 两国关系~改善。The relations between the two countries have improved to some extent./ 销售价格~降低。There's been some reduction in the selling prices./ 我对这一决议，~保留。I have my reservations about this resolution./ 人类总得不断地总结经验，~发现，~发明，~创造，~前进。Man has constantly to sum up his experience and go on discovering, inventing, creating and advancing.

【有条不紊】 yǒutiáo-bùwěn in an orderly way; methodically; systematically: 他做起事来~。He works methodically./ ~地进行生产 carry on production in a systematic fashion

【有望】 yǒuwàng hopeful: 丰收~。There's hope of a bumper harvest.

【有为】 yǒuwéi promising: ~的青年 a promising young person/ 年轻~ young and promising

【有…无…】 yǒu…wú… ①〔表示只有前者而没有后者〕: 有职无权 hold the post but not the power; be a figurehead/ 有眼无珠 have eyes but see not/ 有气无力 feeble ②〔表示强调有前者而没有后者〕: 有害无益 not helpful but harmful/ 有增无减 increase steadily/ 有去无还 gone never to return ③〔表示有了前者就可以没有后者〕: 有备无患。Preparedness averts peril. ④〔表示似有似无〕: 有意无意 wittingly or unwittingly; consciously or unconsciously; by accident or design

【有喜】 yǒuxǐ <口> be pregnant; be expecting

【有隙可乘】 yǒu xì kě chéng there is a crack to squeeze through -- there is a loophole to exploit

【有限】 yǒuxiàn limited in number; finite: 为数~ limited in number; not many/ 文化水平~ have had little schooling/ 对情况了解~ have a limited knowledge of the situation
◇ ~公司 limited company; limited-liability company

【有线】 yǒuxiàn wired
◇ ~传真 wirephoto/ ~电报学 wire telegraphy/ ~广播 wire (或 wired) broadcasting; rediffusion on wire/ ~广播网 wire-broadcasting network; wired broadcast network/ ~广播站 wired broadcast station; rediffusion station/ ~通讯 wire communication

【有效】 yǒuxiào efficacious; effective; valid: 采取~步骤 take effective steps/ 这药治哮喘病很~。This is an efficacious (或 effective) drug for asthma./ 这张车票三日内~。This train ticket is good (或 valid) for three days./ 这个指示仍然~。The directive still holds good./ 两种文本同样~。Both texts are equally authentic.

【有效期】 yǒuxiàoqī term (或 period) of validity; time of efficacy: 延长合同的~ prolong the contract's period of validity/ 本条约~为三十年。The present treaty shall be valid for 30 years./ 这个胶卷已过了~。This film has passed its expiry date.

【有些】 yǒuxiē ① some: ~人在看书，~人在谈天。Some people were reading, some were talking./ 旧机器还能用。Some of the old machines are still serviceable. ② somewhat; rather: ~不满意 somewhat dissatisfied/ ~失望 be rather disappointed

【有心】 yǒuxīn ① have a mind to; set one's mind on: 我~去看看他，又怕打扰他。I'd like to go and see him, but I don't want to disturb him. ② intentionally; purposely: 他是~说给你听的。What he said was intended for you.

【有心人】 yǒuxīnrén ① a person who sets his mind on doing sth. useful; a person with high aspirations and determination: 世上无难事，只怕~。Nothing in the world is difficult for one who sets his mind on it. ② an observant and conscientious person

【有形】 yǒuxíng tangible; visible

【有血有肉】 yǒuxuè-yǒuròu (of descriptions in literary works, etc.) true to life; vivid: 这个人物写得~。The portrayal of the character is lifelike./ 这篇报道是~。This news report is full of vivid details.

【有言在先】 yǒu yán zài xiān make clear beforehand; forewarn: 不是~，迟时不候吗？Wasn't it clearly understood that we wouldn't wait for anyone who was late?

【有眼不识泰山】 yǒu yǎn bù shí Tàishān have eyes but fail to see Taishan Mountain; entertain an angel unawares

【有益】 yǒuyì profitable; beneficial; useful: ~的格言 good popular maxims/ 作出~的贡献 make valuable contributions/ ~于健康 good for one's health/ 做一个~于人民的人 be a person who is of value to the people/ 世界上所有国家的~的东西,我们都要学。We should learn what is useful from every country in the world.

【有意】 yǒuyì ① have a mind to; be inclined (或 disposed) to: ~帮忙 be disposed to help ② intentionally; deliberately; purposely: ~歪曲 deliberately distort/ ~刁难 make things difficult for sb. on purpose/ 这书是他~留给我们看的。He has left this book here especially for us to read.

【有意识】 yǒuyìshí consciously: ~地克服自己的缺点 make conscious efforts to overcome one's weaknesses

【有意思】 yǒu yìsi ① significant; meaningful: 他说的话很~。What he said was significant. ② interesting; enjoyable: 今天的晚会很~。The performance this evening was most enjoyable.

【有勇无谋】 yǒuyǒng-wúmóu have valour but lack strategy; be brave but not resourceful; be foolhardy

【有…有…】 yǒu…yǒu… ①〔分别用在意思相反或相对的两个词前,表示兼而有之〕: 有利有弊 have both advantages and disadvantages/ 有来有往 give-and-take; reciprocal/ 有赏有罚 mete out punishments or rewards as the case demands ②〔分别用在意思相同或相近的两个词前,表示强调〕: 有职有权 hold both the post and the power; have authority commensurate with one's post; exercise the power that goes with one's post/ 有条有理 methodical; systematic; orderly/ 有说有笑 talking and laughing/ 有凭有据 fully substantiated; well-documented/ 有名有姓 identifiable by both given name and surname — of verifiable identity

【有余】 yǒuyú ① have a surplus; have enough and to spare: 粮食自给~ have grain enough and to spare/ 绰绰~ more than enough; enough and to spare ② odd: 二十~ twenty odd

【有则改之,无则加勉】 yǒu zé gǎi zhī, wú zé jiā miǎn correct mistakes if you have made any and guard against them if you have not

【有朝一日】 yǒuzhāo-yīrì some day; one day

【有志者事竟成】 yǒuzhìzhě shì jìng chéng where there's a will there's a way

【有志之士】 yǒu zhì zhī shì a person of noble aspirations; a person with lofty ideals

【有助于】 yǒuzhùyú contribute to; be conducive to; conduce to: 这次访问~增进我们两国人民的相互了解。This visit has contributed to a better understanding between the peoples of our two countries./ 体育锻炼~增强体质。Exercise is conducive to good health.

酉 yǒu the tenth of the twelve Earthly Branches
【酉时】 yǒushí the period of the day from 5 p.m. to 7 p.m.

莠 yǒu ① green bristlegrass ② bad people: 良~不齐。The good and the bad are intermingled.

牖 yǒu <书> window

黝 yǒu black; dark
【黝黑】 yǒuhēi dark; swarthy: 胳膊晒得~ with sunburnt arms

yòu

又 yòu <副> ① 〔表示重复或继续〕: 读了~读 read again and again/ 一年~一年 year after year ② 〔表示几种情况或性质同时存在〕: ~惊~喜 be pleasantly surprised/ ~便宜~好 cheap but good/ 她~想去,~不想去,拿不定主意。She couldn't make up her mind whether to go or not./ 你不能~要马儿跑得好,~要马儿不吃草。You can't expect the horse to run fast when you don't let it graze. ③ 〔表示意思上更进一层或在某个范围之外有所补充〕: 天很

黑，～下着雨，路更难走了。On top of it being dark it rained, which made the going even tougher./ 除了拖拉机，我们～添了一台插秧机。In addition to the tractor, we have acquired a new rice transplanter. ④〔表示整数之外再加零数〕: 一～二分之一 one and a half ⑤〔表示转折〕: 我想去，怕没时间。I'd like to go, but I'm not sure if I can find the time. ⑥〔用在否定句或反问句里，加强语气〕: 这活儿～不重，我一个人顶得下来。That's not a hard job. I'm sure I can manage it myself.

【又及】 yòují　postscript (PS)

右* yòu ①the right side; the right: 靠～走 keep to the right ② west ③the right side as the side of precedence: 无出其～ second to none ④ the Right: ～倾观点 views of a Rightist tendency/ 思想太～ too far to the Right in thinking

【右边】 yòubiān　the right (或 right-hand) side; right
【右面】 yòumiàn　the right (或 right-hand) side
【右派】 yòupài　the Right; the right wing
【右倾】 yòuqīng　Right deviation
【右手】 yòushǒu　①the right hand ②见"右首"
【右首】 yòushǒu　the right-hand side; the right: 他～坐着一位老妇人。An old woman was seated on his right.
【右翼】 yòuyì　① 〈军〉 right wing; right flank ② the Right; the right wing ◇ ～分子 right-winger; member of the Right

幼* yòu ①young; under age: 年～无知 young and ignorant/ ～畜 young animal; young stock ② children; the young: 扶老携～ bringing along the old and the young

【幼虫】 yòuchóng　〈动〉 larva
【幼儿】 yòu'ér　child; infant ◇ ～教育 preschool education/ ～园 kindergarten; nursery school; infant school
【幼苗】 yòumiáo　seedling
【幼年】 yòunián　childhood; infancy
【幼小】 yòuxiǎo　immature
【幼芽】 yòuyá　young shoot; bud
【幼稚】 yòuzhì　①young ②childish; puerile; naive: ～可笑 ridiculously childish/ ～的想法 naive ideas
【幼子】 yòuzǐ　the youngest son

有 yòu　〈书〉〔表示整数之外再加零数〕: 三十～八年 thirty-eight years
另见 yǒu

佑 yòu　help; protect; bless

侑 yòu　〈书〉 press (sb. to eat or drink); urge

宥 yòu　〈书〉 excuse; forgive: 尚希见～。 Please accept my apologies.

柚 yòu　〈植〉 shaddock; pomelo
另见 yóu
【柚子】 yòuzi　shaddock; pomelo

囿 yòu　〈书〉①animal farm; enclosure; park: 鹿～ deer farm/ 鹿～ deer park ②limited; hampered: ～于成见 blinded by prejudice/ ～于习俗 constrained by custom/ ～见闻 handicapped by lack of knowledge and experience

诱 yòu ①guide; lead; induce: 循循善～ be good at giving systematic guidance; teach with patience and skill ②lure; seduce; entice: ～敌深入 lure the enemy in deep/ ～人的景色 captivating scenery

【诱导】 yòudǎo　guide; lead; induce: 这些问题可以～大家去思考。 These are thought-provoking questions.
【诱饵】 yòu'ěr　bait
【诱发】 yòufā　bring out (sth. potential or latent); induce; cause to happen: 把麻疹～出来 bring out the rash of measles (by administering medicine)
【诱供】 yòugòng　trap a person into a confession; induce a person to make a confession: 既不～也不逼供。Neither trickery nor coercion is used to secure confessions.

【诱拐】 yòuguǎi　abduct; carry off (a woman) by fraud; kidnap (a child)
【诱惑】 yòuhuò　①entice; tempt; seduce; lure ②attract; allure: 窗外是一片～人的景色。The window commands a charming view.
【诱奸】 yòujiān　entice into unlawful sexual intercourse; seduce
【诱骗】 yòupiàn　inveigle; cajole; trap; trick
【诱降】 yòuxiáng　lure into surrender
【诱致】 yòuzhì　lead to; cause: ～堕落 lead to one's degeneration

釉 yòu　glaze: 青～瓷器 blue glazed porcelain/ ～里红 underglaze red

【釉工】 yòugōng　glazer
【釉面砖】 yòumiànzhuān　〈建〉 glazed tile
【釉陶】 yòutáo　glazed pottery
【釉子】 yòuzi　glaze

鼬 yòu　〈动〉 weasel

yū

迂 yū　①circuitous; winding; roundabout: ～道访问 make a detour to call on sb. ②clinging to outworn rules and ideas; pedantic: ～论 pedantic talk/ 这人有点～。He's a bit of a pedant.

【迂夫子】 yūfūzǐ　pedant
【迂腐】 yūfǔ　stubborn adherence to outworn rules and ideas; pedantry: ～的见解 pedantic ideas
【迂缓】 yūhuǎn　slow in movement; dilatory
【迂回】 yūhuí　①circuitous; tortuous; roundabout: 历史的发展是曲折的，～的。History moves in zigzags and by roundabout ways./ ～曲折 full of twists and turns; circuitous; tortuous/ ～前进 advance by a roundabout route ②〈军〉 outflank: 向敌人左侧～ outflank the enemy on the left ◇ ～战术 outflanking tactics
【迂阔】 yūkuò　high-sounding and impracticable: ～之论 impractical views
【迂曲】 yūqū　tortuous; circuitous: ～的山路 a tortuous mountain path
【迂拙】 yūzhuō　impractical and foolish

淤 yū　①become silted up: 水渠里～了很多泥沙。The channel is almost choked with silt. ②silt: 引～肥田 fertilize the soil with silt/ 河～ sludge from a riverbed ③ stasis (of blood)

【淤积】 yūjī　silt up; deposit: 洪水过后，地里～了一层泥浆。When the flood subsided, it left a layer of mud in the fields.
【淤泥】 yūní　silt; sludge; ooze
【淤塞】 yūsè　silt up; be choked with silt: 航道～。The waterway is silted up.
【淤血】 yūxuè　extravasated blood
【淤滞】 yūzhì　(of the flow of a river, etc.) be retarded by silt; silt up

yú

于* yú　〈介〉①〔表示时间、处所、范围等〕: 第一次世界大战爆发～一九一四年。The First World War broke out in 1914./ 运动正处～高潮。The movement is at its high tide./ 闻名～世界 famous all over the world; of world renown ②〔表示动作的方向〕: 求助～人 ask people for help ③〔用在动词后面，表示交与，付出等〕: 这项光荣归～我们大家。The credit goes to the everyone of us ④〔引进对象或事物的关系者〕: 忠～祖国 be loyal to one's country/ 有利～提高产量 conducive to higher yields/ 这样～你自己不利。It won't do you any good. ⑤〔表示起点或出发点〕: 出～自愿 of one's own free will; of one's own accord/ 出～无知 out of ignorance ⑥〔表示比较〕: 人固有

一死，或重～泰山，或轻～鸿毛。Though death befalls all men alike, it may be weightier than Mount Tai or lighter than a feather. ⑦〔表示被动〕见笑～人 be laughed at

【于今】yújīn ①up to the present; since ②nowadays; today; now: 这城市建设得真快，～已看不出它原来的面貌了。The city has been built up really fast; it's changed beyond recognition.

【于是】yúshì〈连〉thereupon; hence; consequently; as a result

予 yú〈书〉Ⅰ
另见 yǔ

【予取予求】yúqǔ-yúqiú〈书〉take from me as sb. pleases — make unlimited demands

余 yú ①surplus; spare; remaining: ～钱 spare money (或 cash)/ 下～部分 the remaining part; the remainder; the rest/ 落日～辉 afterglow ②more than; odd; over: 五十～年 fifty odd years ③beyond; after: 工作之～ after working hours; after work

【余波】yúbō repercussions: 这场纠纷～未平。The trouble hasn't ended; there are still repercussions.

【余存】yúcún balance; remainder: 核对销售数量和～数量 check the amount of sales and stock/ 取出一百元，～五十元。The balance is $50 after the withdrawal of $100.

【余党】yúdǎng remnants of an overthrown clique (或 gang); remaining confederates

【余地】yúdì leeway; margin; room; latitude: 有足够的回旋～。There is plenty of room for manoeuvre./ 还有改进的～。There is still room for improvement./ 订计划要留有～。When drawing up a plan, one should leave some margin.

【余毒】yúdú residual poison; pernicious vestige; pernicious influence

【余额】yú'é ①vacancies yet to be filled ②remaining sum

【余悸】yújì lingering fear: 心有～ have a lingering fear

【余烬】yújìn ashes; embers: 劫后～ a devastated waste of smouldering embers

【余可类推】yú kě lèituī the rest may be inferred by analogy

【余粮】yúliáng surplus grain

【余年】yúnián one's remaining years

【余孽】yúniè remaining evil element; leftover evil; surviving supporter of an evil cause

【余生】yúshēng ①the remainder of one's life; one's remaining years ②survival (after a disaster): 虎口～ a person snatched from the jaws of death

【余剩】yúshèng surplus; remainder

【余数】yúshù〈数〉remainder: 八减五，～为三。Take 5 from 8 and the remainder is 3.

【余威】yúwēi remaining prestige or influence

【余味】yúwèi agreeable aftertaste; pleasant impression: ～无穷 leave a lasting and pleasant impression or aftertaste

【余暇】yúxiá spare time; leisure time; leisure 又作"余闲"

【余下】yúxià remaining

【余兴】yúxìng ①lingering interest; a wish to prolong a pleasant diversion ②entertainment after a meeting or a dinner party

【余音】yúyīn lingering sound: ～缭绕。The music lingered in the air.

【余裕】yúyù enough and to spare; ample: ～的时间 time to spare

欤 yú〈书〉〈助〉〔表示疑问、感叹〕: 可不慎～! How could one fail to exercise caution?

盂 yú a broad-mouthed receptacle for holding liquid; jar: 痰～ spittoon

臾 yú 见"须臾" xūyú

鱼* yú fish: 两条～ two fish

【鱼鳔】yúbiào air bladder (of fish)

【鱼翅】yúchì shark's fin

【鱼刺】yúcì fishbone: 剔掉～ bone a fish

【鱼肚白】yúdùbái the whitish colour of a fish's belly — grey dawn: 东方已露出～。The sky is turning bright in the east. 或 Day is breaking.

【鱼饵】yú'ěr (fish) bait

【鱼肝油】yúgānyóu cod-liver oil

【鱼竿】yúgān fishing rod

【鱼钩】yúgōu fishhook

【鱼贯】yúguàn one following the other; in single file: ～而入 enter in single file; file in

【鱼鳞】yúlín fish scale; scale: 刮去～ scrape the scales off a fish; scale a fish

【鱼龙混杂】yú-lóng hùnzá dragons and fish jumbled together — good and bad people mixed up

【鱼米之乡】yú-mǐ zhī xiāng a land of fish and rice — a land of plenty

【鱼目混珠】yúmù hùn zhū pass off fish eyes as pearls — pass off the sham as the genuine

【鱼群】yúqún shoal of fish

【鱼肉】yúròu ①the flesh of fish ②fish and meat: 人为刀俎，我为～ be meat on sb.'s chopping block — be at sb.'s mercy ③cut up like fish and meat — cruelly oppress

【鱼网】yúwǎng fishnet; fishing net

【鱼鲜】yúxiān fish and shellfish as food; seafood

【鱼油】yúyóu fish oil

俞 Yú a surname

竽 yú〈乐〉an ancient wind instrument

谀 yú〈书〉flatter: 阿～ flatter and toady/ ～辞 flattering words; flattery

娱* yú ①give pleasure to; amuse: 聊以自～ just to amuse oneself ②joy; pleasure; amusement: 耳目之～ pleasures of the senses

【娱乐】yúlè amusement; entertainment; recreation ◇ ～场所 public place of entertainment/ ～活动 recreational activities; recreation/ ～室 recreation room

隅 yú ①corner; nook: 城～ the corner of a city wall ②outlying place; border: 海～ seaboard

喁 yú

【喁喁】yúyú〈书〉whisper: ～私语 talk in whispers

渔* yú ①fishing: ～船 fishing boat/ ～村 fishing village ②take sth. one is not entitled to: ～利 reap unfair gains

【渔产】yúchǎn aquatic products

【渔场】yúchǎng fishing ground; fishery

【渔港】yúgǎng fishing port (或 harbour)

【渔歌】·yúgē fisherman's song

【渔鼓】yúgǔ ①a percussion instrument made of bamboo, used to accompany the chanting of folk tales ②chanting of folk tales to the accompaniment of such an instrument

【渔火】yúhuǒ lights on fishing boats

【渔获量】yúhuòliàng catch

【渔具】yújù fishing tackle (或 gear)

【渔利】yúlì ①reap unfair gains; profit at others' expense: 从中～ take advantage of a situation to benefit oneself; cash in on other people's efforts ②easy gains; spoils: 坐收～ effortlessly reap the spoils of a contest fought by others; profit from others' conflict

【渔猎】yúliè fishing and hunting

【渔轮】yúlún fishing vessel

【渔民】yúmín fisherman; fisherfolk

【渔业】yúyè fishery

渝 yú (of one's attitude or feeling) change: 始终不～ unswerving; consistent

腴 yú ①fat; plump: 丰～ plump; well rounded out ②fertile: 膏～ fertile

愉* yú pleased; happy; joyful; cheerful: 面有不～之色

wear an annoyed expression; look displeased

【愉快】 yúkuài happy; joyful; cheerful: ～的微笑 a happy smile/ ～的事 something pleasant; a joyful event/ 心情～ be in a cheerful frame of mind

【愉悦】 yúyuè joyful; cheerful; delighted

逾 yú ①exceed; go beyond: ～额 exceed the allowed amount/ 情～骨肉 dearer than one's own flesh and blood/ ～常 out of the ordinary; unusual/ 这位老人已年～七十。 The old man is over seventy.

【逾期】 yúqī exceed the time limit; be overdue

【逾越】 yúyuè exceed; go beyond: ～权限 overstep one's authority/ ～界限 go beyond the limits; go out of bounds/ ～常规 depart from the usual practice/ 不可～的鸿沟 an impassable gulf; an insurmountable barrier

揄 yú 〈书〉①draw ②raise

【揄扬】 yúyáng praise

愚* yú ①foolish; stupid: ～不可及 couldn't be more foolish; be hopelessly stupid ②make a fool of; fool: 为人所～ be fooled (或 duped) by sb. ③〈谦〉I: ～见 my humble opinion

【愚笨】 yúbèn foolish; stupid; clumsy

【愚蠢】 yúchǔn foolish; foolish; silly

【愚钝】 yúdùn slow-witted; stupid

【愚公移山】 Yúgōng yí shān the Foolish Old Man removed the mountains

【愚昧】 yúmèi ignorant; benighted: ～落后 ignorant and backward/ ～无知 benighted

【愚民政策】 yúmín zhèngcè policy of keeping the people in ignorance; obscurantist policy; obscurantism

【愚弄】 yúnòng deceive; hoodwink; make a fool of; dupe

【愚顽】 yúwán ignorant and stubborn

【愚妄】 yúwàng ignorant but self-important; stupid but conceited

【愚者千虑，必有一得】 yúzhě qiān lù, bì yǒu yī dé even a fool occasionally hits on a good idea

【愚拙】 yúzhuō stupid and clumsy

瑜 yú ①fine jade; gem ②lustre of gems — virtues; good points: 瑕不掩～。The defects do not obscure the virtues.

榆 yú

【榆树】 yúshù elm

觎 yú 见"觊觎" jìyú

虞 yú 〈书〉①supposition; prediction: 以备不～ be prepared for any contingency ②anxiety; worry: 兴修水利,水旱无～ build irrigation works so as to have no worries about drought or flood/ 无冻馁之～ be secure against hunger and cold ③deceive; cheat; fool: 尔～我诈 each trying to cheat the other

舆 yú ①〈书〉carriage; chariot: 舍～登舟 change from a carriage to a boat ②〈书〉sedan chair: 彩～ decorated sedan chair ③area; territory: ～地 territory ④public; popular: ～论 public opinion

【舆论】 yúlùn public opinion: 作～准备 prepare public opinion/ 国际～ world opinion ◇ ～工具 mass media; the media/ ～界 the media; press circles

【舆情】 yúqíng public sentiment; popular feelings: 洞察～ know public sentiment well

【舆图】 yútú 〈书〉map

yǔ

与* yǔ ①give; offer; grant: ～人方便 give help to others; make things easy for others/ 信件已交～本人。The letter has been given to the person concerned. ②get along with; be on good terms with: 此人易～。He is easy to get along with. 或 He is not difficult to approach./ ～国 friendly country; allied state ③help; support: ～人为善的批评 criticism aimed at helping those criticized ④〈介〉［引进动作的对象］: ～困难作斗争 strive to overcome difficulties/ ～人民为敌 be hostile to the people; set oneself against the people ⑤〈连〉and; together with: 工业～农业 industry and agriculture/ ～友人同往 go together with a friend

另见 yù

【与虎谋皮】 yǔ hǔ móu pí ask a tiger for its skin — request sb. (usu. an evil person) to act against his own interests

【与其】 yǔqí 〈连〉［比较两件事的利害得失而决定取舍的时候,用在放弃的一面,后常用"不如"或"毋宁"呼应］: 你～坐车,不如坐船。It's better for you to go by boat than by train./ ～说是粗心大意,不如说是不负责任。It's not so much carelessness as irresponsibility.

【与日俱增】 yǔ rì jù zēng grow with each passing day; be steadily on the increase

【与世长辞】 yǔ shì chángcí depart from the world for ever; pass away

【与世无争】 yǔ shì wú zhēng hold oneself aloof from the world; stand aloof from worldly success

【与众不同】 yǔ zhòng bù tóng out of the ordinary

予 yǔ give; grant; bestow: 授～奖状 award sb. a citation of merit/ 免～处分 exempt sb. from punishment/ ～以表扬 commend sb./ ～人口实 give people a handle

另见 yú

宇 yǔ ①eaves ②house: 庙～ temple ③space; universe; world: ～内 in the world

【宇宙】 yǔzhòu universe; cosmos

【宇宙航行】 yǔzhòu hángxíng astronavigation; space navigation ◇ ～员 astronaut; spaceman; cosmonaut

屿 yǔ small island; islet: 岛～ islands and islets; islands

羽 yǔ feather; plume

【羽毛】 yǔmáo feather; plume: 美丽的～ beautiful plumage/ ～丰满 become full-fledged

【羽毛球】 yǔmáoqiú ①badminton ②shuttlecock

【羽毛扇】 yǔmáoshàn feather fan: 摇～的 the man with a feather fan —— the mastermind behind an intrigue

【羽毛未丰】 yǔmáo wèi fēng unfledged; young and immature

【羽翼】 yǔyì ①wing ②assistant

伛 yǔ

【伛偻】 yǔlǚ 〈书〉with one's back bent

雨* yǔ rain: 大～ a heavy rain/ 毛毛～ drizzle/ 大～倾盆。The rain is pelting down.

【雨暴】 yǔbào 〈气〉rainstorm

【雨点】 yǔdiǎn raindrop

【雨过天晴】 yǔ guò tiān qíng the sun shines again after the rain

【雨后春笋】 yǔ hòu chūnsǔn (spring up like) bamboo shoots after a spring rain

【雨季】 yǔjì rainy season

【雨量】 yǔliàng 〈气〉rainfall

【雨露】 yǔlù ①rain and dew ②favour; grace; bounty

【雨帽】 yǔmào ①rain cap ②hood

【雨伞】 yǔsǎn umbrella

【雨水】 yǔshuǐ rainwater; rainfall; rain: ～足 adequate rainfall/ ～调和。The rainfall is just right.

【雨衣】 yǔyī raincoat; waterproof

【雨意】 yǔyì signs of approaching rain: 颇有～。It looks like rain.

语* yǔ ①language; tongue; words: 汉～ the Chinese language/ 本族～ mother tongue/ 甜言蜜～ honeyed words ②speak; say: 低～ speak in a low voice; whisper/ 不言

不～ not say a word; keep silent ③ set phrase; proverb; saying: ～云，"将欲取之，必先与之。" As the saying goes, "Give in order to take." ④ nonlinguistic means of communicating ideas; sign; signal: 旗～ flagsignal; semaphore/ 手～ dactylology; sign language
另见 yù

【语病】 yǔbìng faulty wording or formulation
【语词】 yǔcí words and phrases
【语调】 yǔdiào 〈语〉 intonation
【语法】 yǔfǎ grammar
【语汇】 yǔhuì vocabulary
【语句】 yǔjù sentence
【语录】 yǔlù recorded utterance; quotation
【语气】 yǔqì ① tone; manner of speaking: ～友好 a friendly tone/ 用婉转的一说 speak in a tactful manner/ 听他的～，这事大概有点不妙。 From the way he spoke about the matter, I gathered something had gone wrong. ②〈语〉 mood: 祈使～ imperative mood
【语体】 yǔtǐ 〈语〉 type of writing; style: 口语～ colloquialism/ 科学～ scientific style of writing
【语体文】 yǔtǐwén prose written in the vernacular
【语文】 yǔwén ① Chinese (as a subject of study or a means of communication): 他的～程度怎么样？ How good is his Chinese? ②〈简〉（语言和文学）language and literature
【语无伦次】 yǔ wú lúncì speak incoherently
【语焉不详】 yǔ yān bù xiáng not speak in detail; not elaborate
【语言】 yǔyán language: ～隔阂 language barrier/ ～与文字 spoken and written language
【语音】 yǔyīn ① speech sounds ② pronunciation: 她的～好。 She has good pronunciation.
【语重心长】 yǔzhòng-xīncháng sincere words and earnest wishes: ～的劝告 earnest advice

禹 Yǔ the reputed founder of the Xia Dynasty (c. 21st — 16th century B.C.)

圄 yǔ 见"囹圄" língyǔ

庾 yǔ 〈书〉 an enclosure for storing grain

瘐 yǔ
【瘐死】 yǔsǐ 〈书〉 (of a prisoner) die of hunger or disease

齬 yǔ 见"龃龉" jǔyǔ

窳 yǔ 〈书〉 corrupt; bad: ～败 corrupt/ ～劣 of inferior quality

yù

与 yù take part in; participate in
另见 yǔ
【与会】 yùhuì participate in a conference ◇ ～国 countries attending a conference; participating countries/ ～者 conferee; participant
【与闻】 yùwén have a participant's knowledge of; be let into (a secret, etc.): ～其事 have a participant's knowledge of a matter; be in the know/ 不能让这样的人一国家机密。 We mustn't allow such a person access to confidential matters of the state.

玉* yù ① jade ②〈书〉 (of a person, esp. a woman) pure; fair; handsome; beautiful: 亭亭～立 fair, slim and graceful ③〈敬〉 your: ～照 your photograph
【玉帛】 yùbó 〈书〉 jade objects and silk fabrics, used as state gifts in ancient China: 化干戈为～ turn hostility into friendship
【玉成】 yùchéng 〈敬〉 kindly help secure the success of sth.: 深望～此事。 It is earnestly hoped that you will accomplish the matter.
【玉带】 yùdài jade belt

【玉雕】 yùdiāo jade carving; jade sculpture
【玉皇大帝】 Yùhuáng Dàdì the Jade Emperor (the Supreme Deity of Taoism)
【玉洁冰清】 yùjié-bīngqīng as pure as jade and as clean as ice; pure and noble
【玉米】 yùmǐ ① maize; Indian corn; corn ② ear of maize (或 corn)
【玉器】 yùqì jade article; jade object; jadeware ◇ ～工厂 jade workshop
【玉色】 yùsè jade green; light bluish green
【玉石】 yùshí jade
【玉石俱焚】 yù-shí jù fén jade and stone burned together — destruction of good and bad alike
【玉蜀黍】 yùshǔshǔ maize; corn
【玉碎】 yùsuì 见"宁为～，不为瓦全" nìng wéi yù suì, bù wéi wǎ quán
【玉玺】 yùxǐ imperial jade seal
【玉簪】 yùzān jade hairpin

驭 yù drive (a carriage)
【驭手】 yùshǒu soldier in charge of pack animals; driver of a military pack train: 炮车～ gun-carriage driver

芋 yù ①〈植〉 taro ②〈植〉 tuber crops: 洋～ potato/ 山～ sweet potato
【芋头】 yùtou 〈植〉 ① taro ②〈方〉 sweet potato

吁 yù appeal; plead: 呼～ appeal/ ～请 implore; plead; petition
另见 xū

妪 yù 〈书〉 old woman

育* yù ① give birth to: 生儿～女 give birth to children; have children ② rear; raise; bring up: ～秧 raise rice seedlings ③ educate: 德～ moral education

郁 yù ① strongly fragrant: 馥～ full of fragrance ② luxuriant; lush ③ gloomy; depressed: 忧～ sad and depressed
【郁闭】 yùbì 〈林〉 closing: 林冠～ canopy closure
【郁积】 yùjī pent-up: ～的愤怒 pent-up fury/ 仇恨～在心头 hatred smouldering in one's bosom
【郁闷】 yùmèn gloomy; depressed: ～之感 a feeling of oppression
【郁郁】 yùyù 〈书〉 ① lush; luxuriant: 苍松翠柏～葱葱。 Green and luxuriant are the pines and cypresses. ② gloomy; melancholy; depressed: ～不乐 depressed; melancholy; joyless ③ strongly fragrant ④ elegant; refined: 文采～ displaying literary elegance

语 yù 〈书〉 tell; inform: 不以～人 not to be divulged
另见 yǔ

昱 yù 〈书〉 ① sunlight; sunshine ② shine; illuminate

狱 yù ① prison; jail: 入～ be imprisoned; be put in prison/ 越～ escape from prison ② lawsuit; case: 断～ hear and pass judgment on a case
【狱吏】 yùlì 〈旧〉 warder; prison officer; jailer
【狱卒】 yùzú 〈旧〉 prison guard; turnkey

浴* yù bath; bathe: 淋～ shower bath/ 日光～ sun-bath/ 海水～ sea bathing
【浴场】 yùchǎng outdoor bathing place: 海滨～ bathing beach
【浴池】 yùchí ① common bathing pool (in a public bathhouse) ② public bathhouse; public baths
【浴巾】 yùjīn bath towel
【浴盆】 yùpén bathtub
【浴室】 yùshì bathroom; shower room
【浴血】 yùxuè bathed in blood; bloody: ～奋战 fight a bloody battle
【浴衣】 yùyī bathrobe

预* yù in advance; beforehand: ～付 pay in advance/ ～祝成功 wish sb. success/ 勿谓言之不～。Do not say that we haven't warned you.

【预报】 yùbào forecast: 天气～ weather forecast/ 地震～ earthquake forecast; earthquake prediction

【预备】 yùbèi prepare; get ready: ～功课 prepare lessons/ 你们～好了吗? Are you all ready?/ 各就位,～,跑! Ready! Set! Go! 或 On your mark! Get set! Go!

【预卜】 yùbǔ augur; foretell: ～吉凶 try to predict good or bad fortune/ 结果如何尚难～. The result is hard to foretell.

【预测】 yùcè calculate; forecast: ～日蚀 calculate an eclipse of the sun/ ～台风 detect a typhoon

【预订】 yùdìng subscribe; book; place an order: ～杂志 subscribe to a magazine/ ～火车票 book a train ticket/ ～一本书 place an order for a book/ 座位已经～一空。All seats are booked.

【预定】 yùdìng fix in advance; predetermine; schedule: 在 ～时间 at the fixed time/ 在～地点着陆 make a landing in a predetermined area/ 这项工程～在明年完成。The project is scheduled for completion next year.

【预断】 yùduàn prejudge

【预防】 yùfáng prevent; take precautions against; guard against: 采取～措施 take preventive measures

【预感】 yùgǎn ① premonition; presentiment: 不祥的～ an ominous presentiment ② have a premonition

【预告】 yùgào ① announce in advance; herald ② advance notice: 新书～ notice on forthcoming books; books in preparation

【预购】 yùgòu purchase in advance

【预计】 yùjì calculate in advance; estimate: 大楼～十个月可以完工。It is estimated that the building will be completed in ten months.

【预见】 yùjiàn ① foresee; predict: ～不到的困难 unforeseen difficulties/ 这是可以～到的。This can be predicted. ② foresight; prevision: 英明的～ brilliant foresight ◇ ～性 foresight; farsightedness

【预科】 yùkē preparatory course (in a college)

【预料】 yùliào expect; predict; anticipate: 和我们的～相反 contrary to our expectations/ 今年的收成比人们～的要好得多。This year's harvest was much better than expected (或 anticipated).

【预谋】 yùmóu premeditate; plan beforehand

【预期】 yùqī expect; anticipate: 达到～的效果 achieve the desired (或 hoped-for) results/ 结果和～的相反。The results are contrary to expectations.

【预赛】 yùsài 〈体〉 preliminary contest; preliminary heats; preliminary; trial match

【预示】 yùshì betoken; indicate; presage; forebode: 灿烂的晚霞～明天又是好天气。The splendid evening glow in the sky means another fine day tomorrow.

【预算】 yùsuàn budget

【预先】 yùxiān in advance; beforehand: ～通知 notify in advance/ ～声明 state explicitly beforehand/ ～警告 forewarn/ ～感谢 thank sb. in anticipation

【预想】 yùxiǎng anticipate; expect: 得到～的结果 obtain the anticipated results

【预言】 yùyán ① prophesy; predict; foretell ② prophecy; prediction ◇ ～家 prophet

【预演】 yùyǎn preview (of a performance or motion picture)

【预展】 yùzhǎn preview (of an exhibition)

【预兆】 yùzhào omen; presage; sign; harbinger: 吉祥的～ an auspicious omen/ 胜利的～ a harbinger of victory/ 下雨的～ a sign of coming rain

【预制】 yùzhì prefabricate ◇ ～构件 〈建〉 prefabricated components/ ～装配式房屋 prefabricated house; prefab

欲 yù ① desire; longing; wish: 食～ a desire for food; appetite/ 求知～ thirst for knowledge ② wish; want; desire: 畅所～言 pour out all that one wishes to say; speak one's mind freely/ 为所～为 do whatever one likes; act wilfully ③ about to; just going to; on the point of: 摇摇～坠 on the verge of collapse; crumbling; tottering

【欲罢不能】 yù bà bùnéng be unable to stop even though one wants to; cannot help carrying on

【欲盖弥彰】 yù gài mí zhāng the more one tries to hide, the more one is exposed; try to hide a mistake, only to make it more conspicuous

【欲加之罪,何患无词】 yù jiā zhī zuì, hé huàn wú cí if you are out to condemn sb., you can always trump up a charge

【欲擒故纵】 yù qín gù zòng leave sb. at large the better to apprehend him; allow sb. more latitude first to keep a tighter rein on him afterwards

【欲取姑与】 yù qǔ gū yǔ give in order to take; make concessions for the sake of future gains

【欲速则不达】 yù sù zé bù dá more haste, less speed; haste makes waste

【欲望】 yùwàng desire; wish; lust

域 yù land within certain boundaries; territory; region: 领～ territory; domain; field; realm/ 异～ foreign lands/ 绝～ inaccessible remote areas

谕 yù 〈书〉〔旧时用于上级对下级或长辈对晚辈〕 instruct; tell: 面～ tell sb. in person/ 上～ imperial edict/ 顷奉手～。I have just received your instructions.

尉 yù
另见 wèi
【尉迟】 Yùchí a surname

寓 yù ① reside; live: 暂～友人处 be staying with a friend ② residence; abode: 公～ apartment house; block of flats ③ imply; contain: 这个故事～有深意。This story contains a profound lesson. 或 The moral of the story is profound.

【寓居】 yùjū make one's home in (a place other than one's native place)

【寓所】 yùsuǒ residence; abode; dwelling place

【寓言】 yùyán fable; allegory; parable

【寓意】 yùyì implied meaning; moral; message; import: ～深刻 be pregnant with meaning

裕* yù ① abundant; plentiful: 富～ abundant; affluent; well-to-do; well-off ② 〈书〉 make (a country or people) rich

【裕如】 yùrú effortlessly; with ease: 应付～ handle with ease

遇* yù ① meet: 不期而～ meet by chance; chance encounter/ ～雨 be caught in a rain ② treat; receive: 优～ treat sb. with special consideration ③ chance; opportunity: 机～ favourable circumstances; opportunity

【遇刺】 yùcì be attacked by an assassin: ～身死 be assassinated

【遇到】 yùdào run into; encounter; come across: 在路上～一个老同学 run into an old schoolmate on the way/ ～意外的问题 come across unforeseen problems/ ～埋伏 run into an ambush

【遇害】 yùhài be murdered

【遇见】 yùjiàn meet; come across: ～一位朋友 meet a friend

【遇救】 yùjiù be rescued; be saved

【遇难】 yùnàn ① die (或 be killed) in an accident ② be murdered

【遇事】 yùshì when anything crops (或 comes) up: ～不慌 be unruffled whatever happens

【遇险】 yùxiǎn meet with a mishap; be in danger; be in distress: ～船只 ship in distress ◇ ～信号 distress signal; SOS

喻 yù ① explain; make clear; inform: 晓～ give explicit instructions; explain clearly; tell explicitly/ ～之以理 reason with sb.; try to make sb. see reason ② understand; know: 家～户晓 known to every household; widely known ③ analogy: 比～ analogy; metaphor

御 yù ① drive (a carriage): ～者 carriage driver ② of an emperor; imperial: ～花园 imperial garden/ 告～状

bring an accusation against sb. before the emperor/ ～林军 palace guards ③ resist; keep out; ward off: ～敌 resist the enemy/ ～寒 keep out the cold

【御侮】 yùwǔ resist foreign aggression

【御用】 yùyòng ① for the use of an emperor ② serve as a tool; be in the pay of

誉 yù ① reputation; fame: ～满全球 of world renown; famed the world over ② praise; eulogize: 毁～参半 be as much censured as praised; get both praise and censure

煜 yù 〈书〉 illuminate; shine

愈 yù ① heal; recover; become well: 病～ recover from an illness/ 伤口尚未痊~。The wound is not yet healed. ② better: 彼～于此。That one is better than this one. ③ 〔叠用，表示程度随着条件的发展而发展〕: ～多～好 the more the better/ 山路～走～陡。The mountain path becomes steeper and steeper as you go up./ 真理～辩～明。Truth becomes clearer through debate.

【愈加】 yùjiā all the more; even more; further: 变得～模糊 become even more indistinct

蜮 yù 见 “鬼蜮” guǐyù

豫 yù 〈书〉① pleased: 面有不～之色 look displeased ② comfort: 逸～亡身。Overindulgence leads to ruin. ③ (Yù) another name for Henan Province: ～剧 Henan opera

鹬 yù sandpiper; snipe

【鹬蚌相争，渔人得利】 yù bàng xiāng zhēng, yúrén dé lì when the snipe and the clam grapple, the fisherman profits — it's the third party that benefits from the tussle

鬻 yù 〈书〉 sell; vend: ～文为生 make a living with one's pen/ 卖官～爵 sell official posts and titles/ 卖儿～女 sell one's children

yuān

鸢 yuān 〈动〉 kite

【鸢尾】 yuānwěi 〈植〉 iris

冤 yuān ① wrong; injustice: 不白之～ unrighted wrong; unredressed injustice/ ～有头，债有主。Every injustice has its perpetrator, every debt has its debtor. ② feeling of bitterness; hatred; enmity: ～仇 rancour; enmity ③ bad luck; loss; disadvantage: 白跑一趟，真～! What bad luck, nothing came of my trip.

【冤仇】 yuānchóu rancour; enmity

【冤家】 yuānjiā ① enemy; foe: ～对头 opponent and foe ② 〔多用于旧时戏曲民歌中〕 one's destined love; sweetheart; lover: 不是～不聚头。Enemies and lovers are destined to meet.

【冤家路窄】 yuānjiā lù zhǎi enemies are bound to meet on a narrow road — one can't avoid one's enemy (much as ohe wants to)

【冤屈】 yuānqū ① wrong; treat unjustly ② wrongful treatment; injustice: 受～ be wronged; suffer an injustice

【冤枉】 yuānwang ① wrong; treat unjustly: ～好人 wrong an innocent person ② not worthwhile; not repaying the effort: 在这件小事上，花那么多时间，真～。It wasn't worthwhile to spend so much time on such a trifle./ 花～钱 waste money; not get one's money's worth/ 走～路 go the long way

【冤狱】 yuānyù an unjust charge or verdict a miscarriage of justice; frame-up: 平反～ reverse an unjust verdict

鸳 yuān

【鸳鸯】 yuānyang ① mandarin duck ② an affectionate couple

渊 yuān ① deep pool: 深～ a deep pool; abyss ② deep:

～泉 a deep spring

【渊博】 yuānbó broad and profound; erudite: 学识～ erudite; learned

【渊深】 yuānshēn profound; deep; erudite

【渊薮】 yuānsǒu a gathering place of fish or beasts; den; haunt: 盗贼的～ a den (或 haunt) of bandits and thieves/ 罪恶的～ a hotbed (或 breeding ground) of crime; a sink of iniquity

【渊源】 yuānyuán origin; source: 历史～ historical origins

yuán

元* yuán ① first; primary: ～月 the first month of the year; January ② chief; principal: ～戎 〈书〉 supreme commander ③ basic; fundamental: ～素 element ④ unit; component: 第一单～ unit one/ 一～化领导 unified (或 centralized) leadership

【元宝】 yuánbǎo a shoe-shaped gold or silver ingot used as money in feudal China

【元旦】 Yuándàn New Year's Day

【元老】 yuánlǎo senior statesman; founding member (of a political organization, etc.)

【元年】 yuánnián the first year of an era or the reign of an emperor

【元配】 yuánpèi 〈旧〉 first wife

【元气】 yuánqì vitality; vigour: ～旺盛 full of vitality/ 大伤～ undermine one's constitution; sap one's vitality/ 恢复～ regain one's strength (或 health, vigour)

【元首】 yuánshǒu head of state

【元帅】 yuánshuài ① marshal; (英陆军) Field Marshal; (英空军) Marshal of the Royal Air Force; (英海军) Admiral of the Fleet ② supreme commander (in ancient times)

【元素】 yuánsù ① element ② 〈数〉〈化〉 element: 稀有～ rare element

【元宵】 yuánxiāo ① the night of the 15th of the 1st lunar month ② sweet dumplings made of glutinous rice flour (for the Lantern Festival) ◇ ～节 the Lantern Festival (15th of the 1st lunar month)

【元凶】 yuánxiōng prime culprit; arch-criminal

【元勋】 yuánxūn a man of great merit; founding father: 革命～ a veteran revolutionary of great distinction/ 开国～ founders of a state

【元音】 yuányīn 〈语〉 vowel

园* yuán ① an area of land for growing plants: 果～ orchard/ 葡萄～ vineyard ② a place for public recreation: 动物～ zoological garden; zoo/ 植物～ botanical garden

【园地】 yuándì ① garden plot ② field; scope: 扩大文学创作的～ broaden the scope of literary creation/ 为科学家开辟广阔的～ open up vast fields of activity for scientists

【园丁】 yuándīng gardener

【园林】 yuánlín gardens; park

【园圃】 yuánpǔ garden; ground used for growing vegetables, flowers or fruit

【园田】 yuántián vegetable garden: 耕作～化 garden-style cultivation of farmland

【园艺】 yuányì horticulture; gardening ◇ ～家 horticulturist/ ～学 horticulture; gardening

员* yuán ① a person engaged in some field of activity: 人～ personnel/ 售货～ shop assistant ② member: 工会～ member of a trade union/ ③ 〈量〉〔用于武将〕: 一～大将 an able general

【员工】 yuángōng staff; personnel: 师生～ teachers, students, administrative personnel and workers

垣 yuán 〈书〉 wall: 城～ city wall

爰 yuán 〈书〉① whence; from what place ② hence; thereupon; consequently

原* yuán ① primary; original; former: ～计划 original plan/ ～义 original (或 primary) meaning/ ～单位 the organization (或 unit) one formerly belonged to/ ～职 former post/ ～班人马 the old cast; the former staff ② unprocessed; raw: ～矿石 raw ore/ ～油 crude oil ③ excuse; pardon: 情有可～ excusable; pardonable ④ level, open country; plain: 华北平～ the North China Plain

【原版】 yuánbǎn original edition (of a book, etc.)

【原本】 yuánběn ① original manuscript; master copy ② the original (from which a translation is made) ③ originally; formerly

【原动力】 yuándònglì motive power (或 force); motivity

【原封】 yuánfēng with the seal unbroken; intact: ～退回 return to the sender a parcel or letter unopened/ ～不动 be left intact

【原稿】 yuángǎo original manuscript; master copy

【原告】 yuángào 〈法〉(民事) plaintiff; (刑事) prosecutor

【原籍】 yuánjí ancestral home: 他～广东。His ancestral home is in Guangdong Province.

【原来】 yuánlái ① original; former: ～的想法 original idea/ 他还住在～的地方。He still lives in the same place. ②〈表示发现真实情况〉: ～如此! So that's how it is! 或 Oh, I see./ ～是你呀! So it's you./ 这～是个骗局。It turned out to be a fraud.

【原理】 yuánlǐ principle; tenet: 根本的～ a cardinal principle/ 数学的基本～ fundamentals of mathematics

【原谅】 yuánliàng excuse; forgive; pardon: 我来晚了,请～。Please excuse me for being late.

【原料】 yuánliào raw material

【原配】 yuánpèi 〈旧〉first wife

【原色】 yuánsè 〈物〉primary colours

【原始】 yuánshǐ ① original; firsthand: ～记录 original record/ ～资料 firsthand information (或 data); source material ② primeval; primitive

【原委】 yuánwěi how a thing happened from beginning to end; the whole story; all the details: 不明～,妄加评论 make presumptuous comments out of ignorance

【原文】 yuánwén original text; the original: 我没看过这本书的～。I have not read the book in the original./ 引用要加引号。Put quoted passages in quotation marks./ ～如此 sic/ 把抄件跟～核对一下 check the copy against the original

【原先】 yuánxiān former; original: 照～的计划做 act according to the original plan/ 他～是个海员,现在已经成了一位作家。He used to be a sailor, but now he's become a writer./ 我～以为他不会同意,没想到他居然答应了。I thought that he would not agree, but to my surprise he said "Yes".

【原形】 yuánxíng original shape; the true shape under the disguise: ～毕露 be revealed for what one is; show one's true colours

【原野】 yuányě open country; champaign

【原意】 yuányì meaning; original intention: 曲解～ distort the meaning/ 这不是我们的～。This was not our original intention. 或 This is not what we meant.

【原因】 yuányīn cause; reason: ～和结果 cause and effect/ 成功的～ reasons for the success/ 产生这种现象有两方面的～。Two things account for the occurrence.

【原油】 yuányóu crude oil; crude

【原宥】 yuányòu pardon; forgive

【原原本本】 yuányuánběnběn from beginning to end: 我把这件事一讲给他们听了。I told them the whole story exactly as it happened.

【原则】 yuánzé principle: ～问题 a matter of principle/ ～分歧 differences in principle/ ～上同意 agree in principle/ 具有高度的～性 be highly principled; have a strong sense of principle

【原址】 yuánzhǐ former address

【原主】 yuánzhǔ original owner (或 proprietor): 物归～ return sth. to its (rightful) owner

【原著】 yuánzhù original work; original

【原状】 yuánzhuàng original state; previous condition; *status quo ante*: 恢复～ restore the *status quo ante*; restore to the former state

【原子】 yuánzǐ atom: 标记～ labelled atom ◇ ～尘 fallout/ ～弹 atom bomb; atomic bomb; A-bomb/ ～动力船 atomic-powered ship/ ～反应堆 atomic reactor/ ～核 atomic nucleus/ ～能 atomic energy/ ～武器 atomic weapon

【原作】 yuánzuò original work; original: 译文保持了～的风格。The translation reproduces the style of the original.

袁 Yuán a surname

圆* yuán ① round; circular; spherical: ～孔 a round hole/ ～锉 round file/ 月～了。The moon is full. ②〈数〉circle ③ tactful; satisfactory: 他这话说得不～。What he said was not very tactful. ④ make plausible; justify: 自～其说 make one's statement consistent; justify oneself/ ～谎 patch up a lie

【圆场】 yuánchǎng mediate; help to effect a compromise: 打～ mediate a dispute; smooth things over

【圆成】 yuánchéng help sb. to attain his aim

【圆顶】 yuándǐng 〈天〉dome

【圆规】 yuánguī compasses: 一个～ a pair of compasses/ 制图～ drawing compasses/ 长杆～ beam compasses

【圆滑】 yuánhuá smooth and evasive; slick and sly

【圆括号】 yuánkuòhào parentheses; curves (( ))

【圆满】 yuánmǎn satisfactory: ～成功 complete success/ ～的答案 a satisfactory answer/ 问题～地解决了。The problem has been solved satisfactorily./ 邀请赛在友好团结的气氛中～结束。The invitational tournament was rounded off in an atmosphere of friendship and solidarity.

【圆盘】 yuánpán disc

【圆圈】 yuánquān circle; ring

【圆润】 yuánrùn mellow and full: ～的噪音 a sweet, mellow voice

【圆熟】 yuánshú skilful; proficient; dexterous

【圆通】 yuántōng flexible; accommodating

【圆舞曲】 yuánwǔqǔ 〈乐〉waltz

【圆形】 yuánxíng circular; round ◇ ～建筑 round building; rotunda

【圆周】 yuánzhōu circumference

【圆珠笔】 yuánzhūbǐ ball-point pen; ball-pen

【圆锥】 yuánzhuī circular cone; taper

【圆桌】 yuánzhuō round table ◇ ～会议 round-table conference

【圆子】 yuánzi ① dumpling (made of glutinous rice flour) ②〈方〉(meat, fish, etc.) ball

援* yuán ① pull by hand; hold: 攀～ climb up by holding on to sth./ ～笔疾书 take up a pen and write quickly ② quote; cite: 有例可～。There's a precedent to quote. ③ help; aid; rescue: 求～ ask for help; appeal for aid; request reinforcements/ 围点打～ encircle an enemy post in order to attack reinforcements coming to its aid

【援救】 yuánjiù rescue; save; deliver from danger

【援军】 yuánjūn reinforcements; relief troops

【援例】 yuánlì cite (或 quote) a precedent

【援手】 yuánshǒu 〈书〉aid; save; rescue

【援外】 yuánwài foreign aid: ～物资 materials in aid of a foreign country

【援引】 yuányǐn ① quote; cite: ～例证 cite an example/ ～法律条文 invoke a legal provision ② recommend or appoint one's friends or favourites

【援用】 yuányòng quote; cite; invoke: ～成例 cite a precedent/ ～条约 invoke a treaty

【援助】 yuánzhù help; support; aid: 国际～ international support/, 给他们一切可能的～ give them every possible help/ 不附带条件的～ aid with no strings attached/ 技术～ technical assistance

源* yuán ① source (of a river); fountainhead: 饮水思～ when drinking water think of its source — remember where one's happiness comes from/ 木有本,水有～。Every tree has its roots and every river has its source. ② source; cause: 财～ source of income/ 病～ cause of a disease

【源流】 yuánliú source and course (of a river, etc.); origin

and development

【源泉】 yuánquán source; fountainhead: 生活是文艺创作的
～。Life is the source of literary and artistic creation.

【源头】 yuántóu fountainhead; source

【源源】 yuányuán in a steady stream; continuously: 运往
市场的蔬菜～不绝。There is a steady flow of vegetables to
the market.

【源源本本】 yuányuánběnběn 见"原原本本" yuányuánběnběn

【源远流长】 yuán yuǎn liú cháng a distant source and a long
stream — of long standing and well established: 我们两国
人民的友谊～。The friendship between our two peoples
goes back to ancient times.

猿 yuán ape: 类人～ anthropoid ape/
从～到人 from ape to man

【猿猴】 yuánhóu apes and monkeys

【猿人】 yuánrén ape-man: 北京～
Peking man (Sinanthropus pekinensis)

缘 yuán ① reason: 无～无故 without rhyme or reason; for no reason at all/ 何～由此？What's your reason
for coming here? ② edge; fringe; brink: 外～ outer fringe
(或 edge)/ 这个城市处于沙漠南～。This city is located
on the southern fringe of the desert. ③ along: ～溪行
walk along the stream ④ predestined relationship: 姻～
predestined marriage/ 有一面之～ happen to have met
once

【缘分】 yuánfèn lot or luck by which people are brought
together: 我俩又在一起了，真是有～。So we're together
again. It must be fate./ 烟,酒跟我没有～。Smoking and
drinking don't appeal to me.

【缘故】 yuángù cause; reason

【缘木求鱼】 yuán mù qiú yú climb a tree to catch fish — a
fruitless approach

【缘起】 yuánqǐ ① genesis; origin ② an account of the
founding of an institution or the beginning of a project

【缘由】 yuányóu reason; cause

辕 yuán ① shafts of a cart or carriage ② the outer
gate of a government office in ancient times ③ a government office in ancient times

【辕马】 yuánmǎ horse in the shafts; shaft-horse

yuǎn

远 yuǎn far; distant; remote: ～不及 far inferior
to/ ～～超过 far exceed/ 敬而～之 stay at a respectful
distance from sb./ ～隔重洋 be separated by vast oceans/
十三陵水库离这里多～？How far is the Ming Tombs Reservoir from here?/ ～在公元十一世纪, 中国已使用火药。
Gunpowder was used in China as far back as the 11th
century.

【远程】 yuǎnchéng long-range; long-distance: ～火箭 long-
range rocket/ ～航行 long voyage

【远大】 yuǎndà long-range; broad; ambitious: 眼光～ be
farsighted; have a broad vision/ 前途～ (of a person) have
a bright future/ ～的计划 a long-range plan; an ambitious
plan/ ～的理想 lofty ideals

【远道】 yuǎndào a long way: ～而来 come a long way;
come from afar

【远东】 Yuǎndōng the Far East

【远方】 yuǎnfāng distant place: ～的来客 a guest from afar

【远房】 yuǎnfáng distantly related: ～亲戚 a distant relative; remote kinsfolk

【远古】 yuǎngǔ remote antiquity: 在～时代 in remote anti-
quity/ 从～流传下来的故事 a legend from ancient times

【远见】 yuǎnjiàn foresight; vision: ～卓识 foresight and
sagacity

【远交近攻】 yuǎnjiāo-jìngōng befriend distant states while
attacking those nearby

【远郊】 yuǎnjiāo outer suburbs

【远近】 yuǎnjìn ① far and near: ～闻名 be known far and
wide ② distance: 不论～我都去。I'll go no matter how
far it is./ 这两条路～差不多。The distance is about the
same by either road.

【远景】 yuǎnjǐng distant view; long-range perspective;
prospect: ～规划 a long-range plan

【远距离操纵】 yuǎnjùlí cāozòng remote control; telecontrol

【远虑】 yuǎnlǜ foresight; long view: 深谋～ think deeply
and plan carefully; be circumspect and farsighted

【远期】 yuǎnqī at a specified future date; forward: ～汇价
forward rate/ ～外汇 forward exchange

【远亲】 yuǎnqīn distant relative (或 relation); remote kinsfolk: 常言说,～不如近邻。As the saying goes, neighbours
are dearer than distant relatives.

【远视】 yuǎnshì 〈医〉 long sight; farsightedness; hyperopia;
hypermetropia ◇ ～眼镜 spectacles for long sight; spectacles for the farsighted

【远水不解近渴】 yuǎnshuǐ bù jiě jìnkě distant water cannot
quench present thirst — the aid is too slow in coming to
be of any help

【远水救不了近火】 yuǎnshuǐ jiùbuliǎo jìnhuǒ distant water
won't put out a fire close at hand — a slow remedy
cannot meet an urgency

【远行】 yuǎnxíng go on a long journey

【远洋】 yuǎnyáng ① ocean ② of the open sea beyond the
littoral zone; oceanic ◇ ～航行 oceangoing voyage/
～货轮 oceangoing freighter/ ～渔业 deep-sea (或 pelagic) fishing

【远因】 yuǎnyīn remote cause

【远征】 yuǎnzhēng expedition ◇ ～军 expeditionary army
(或 force)

【远志】 yuǎnzhì great and far-reaching ambition; high
aspiration

【远走高飞】 yuǎnzǒu-gāofēi fly far and high; be off to
distant parts

【远足】 yuǎnzú pleasure trip on foot; hike; walking tour

【远祖】 yuǎnzǔ remote ancestor

yuàn

苑 yuàn 〈书〉 ① enclosed ground for growing trees,
keeping animals, etc.; gardens: 御～ imperial gardens/ 鹿
～ deer park ② centre (of art and literature, etc.): 艺～
a centre of the arts; the art world

怨* yuàn ① resentment; enmity: 结～ arouse sb.'s enmity; incur ill will/ ～色 a resentful (或 discontented)
look/ 不计较个人恩～ give no thought to personal grievances ② blame; complain: 不要老是抱～。Don't always
complain./ 这件事～我。I am to blame for this.

【怨不得】 yuànbude ① cannot blame: 这件事～老李, 都怪
我。Lao Li is not to blame for this. It's all my fault.
② no wonder: 班车坏了, ～他们迟到了。The bus broke
down. No wonder they were late.

【怨愤】 yuànfèn discontent and indignation

【怨恨】 yuànhèn ① have a grudge against sb.; hate ② resentment; grudge; enmity

【怨偶】 yuàn'ǒu 〈书〉 an unhappy couple

【怨气】 yuànqì grievance; complaint; resentment: 出～
air one's grievances; vent one's resentment/ 一肚子～ be
full of complaints (或 grievances)

【怨声载道】 yuànshēng zài dào cries of discontent rise all
round; complaints are heard everywhere

【怨天尤人】 yuàntiān-yóurén blame god and man — blame
everyone and everything but oneself

【怨言】 yuànyán complaint; grumble: 从未发过一句～ never
utter a word of complaint

【怨艾】 yuànyì 〈书〉 resentment; grudge

院* yuàn ① courtyard; yard; compound: 前~ front yard ② a designation for certain government offices and public places: 法~ law court/ 科学~ the academy of sciences/ 疗养~ sanatorium/ 电影~ cinema
【院士】 yuànshì academician
【院子】 yuànzi courtyard; yard; compound

愿* yuàn ① hope; wish; desire: 如~以偿 have one's wishes fulfilled; obtain what one desires/ 平生之~ a lifelong wish ② be willing; be ready ③ vow (made before Buddha or a god): 还~ redeem a vow ④ 〈书〉honest and cautious
【愿望】 yuànwàng desire; wish; aspiration: 从团结的~出发 start from the desire for unity
【愿意】 yuànyì ① be willing; be ready: ~作出任何牺牲 be willing to make any sacrifice ② wish; like; want: 他们~你留在这里。 They want you to remain here.

yuē

曰 yuē 〈书〉① say: 孙子~: "知彼知己,百战不殆。" Sun Wu Zi said, "Know the enemy and know yourself, and you can fight a hundred battles with no danger of defeat." ② call; name: 美其名~ describe sth. euphemistically as; give sth. the fine-sounding name of

约* yuē ① make an appointment; arrange: 我想跟王经理~个时间谈谈。 I'd like to make an appointment with Mr. Wang, the manager./ 我们~好下星期一碰头。 We agreed to meet next Monday. ② ask or invite in advance: 请~他来。 Please ask him to come./ 我已~了王先生。 I've invited Mr Wang. ③ pact; agreement; appointment: 立~ make a pact; come to an agreement/ 商~ commercial treaty/ 践~ keep an appointment ④ restrict; restrain: ~束 restrain; bind ⑤ economical; frugal: 节~ economize/ 自奉甚~ live economically; lead a frugal life ⑥ simple; brief: 言之~ in brief; in a word ⑦ about; around; approximately: ~五十人 about fifty people ⑧ 〈数〉reduction of a fraction: 十分之五可以~成二分之一。 Five over ten can be reduced to one over two.
【约定】 yuēdìng agree on; appoint; arrange: ~会晤地点 agree on a meeting place/ 在~的时间 at the appointed time
【约法】 yuēfǎ provisional constitution
【约法三章】 yuē fǎ sān zhāng agree on a three-point law — make a few simple rules to be observed by all concerned
【约会】 yuēhuì appointment; engagement; date: 订个~ make an appointment/ 我今天晚上有个~。 I have an engagement this evening.
【约计】 yuējì count roughly; come roughly to
【约略】 yuēlüè rough; approximate: ~的估计 a rough (或 approximate) estimate/ 这件事我~知道一些。 I know something about the matter.
【约莫】 yuēmo about; roughly: 现在~有十点钟。 It is about ten now./ 我们等了~有一个小时的光景。 We waited for an hour or so.
【约期】 yuēqī fix a date; appoint a time: ~会谈 fix a date to hold talks/ 误了~ fail to keep the appointment
【约请】 yuēqǐng invite; ask
【约束】 yuēshù keep within bounds; restrain; bind
【约言】 yuēyán promise; word; pledge: 遵守~ keep one's promise (或 word)/ 违背~ break one's promise; go back on one's word/ 实行~ redeem one's pledge

yuè

月* yuè ① the moon: 新~ a new moon; crescent ② month: ~底 the end of the month/ ~工 a labourer hired by the month/ ~产量 monthly output ③ full-moon-shaped; round
【月半】 yuèbàn the 15th day of a month
【月报】 yuèbào ① monthly magazine; monthly ② monthly report
【月饼】 yuèbǐng moon cake (esp. for the Mid-Autumn Festival)
【月度】 yuèdù monthly: ~计划 a monthly plan
【月份】 yuèfèn month: 上~ last month/ 八~的产量比七~提高了百分之五。 In August output was 5% higher than in July.
【月份牌】 yuèfènpái 〈口〉calendar
【月宫】 yuègōng the palace of the moon — the moon
【月光】 yuèguāng moonlight; moonbeam
【月经】 yuèjīng menses; menstruation; period
【月刊】 yuèkān monthly magazine; monthly
【月历】 yuèlì monthly calendar
【月利】 yuèlì monthly interest
【月亮】 yuèliang the moon
【月末】 yuèmò 〈书〉the end of the month
【月票】 yuèpiào monthly ticket
【月球】 yuèqiú 〈天〉the moon ◇ ~火箭 〈字航〉moon rocket
【月色】 yuèsè moonlight
【月食】 yuèshí 〈天〉lunar eclipse: 月全食 total lunar eclipse/ 月偏食 partial lunar eclipse 又作"月蚀"
【月台】 yuètái railway platform
【月息】 yuèxī monthly interest
【月下老人】 yuèxià lǎorén the old man under the moon — the god who unites persons in marriage; matchmaker
【月薪】 yuèxīn monthly pay
【月夜】 yuèyè moonlit (或 moonlight) night
【月晕】 yuèyùn lunar halo
【月中】 yuèzhōng the middle of a month
【月子】 yuèzi ① month of confinement after giving birth to a child: 坐~ be in confinement ② time of childbirth; confinement

乐* yuè ① music: 奏~ play music/ 器~ instrumental music/ 声~ vocal music
另见 lè
【乐队】 yuèduì orchestra; band: 交响~ symphony (或 philharmonic) orchestra/ 军~ military band ◇ ~指挥 conductor; bandmaster
【乐谱】 yuèpǔ music score; music ◇ ~架 music stand
【乐器】 yuèqì musical instrument; instrument: 管~ wind instrument/ 弦~ stringed instrument/ 打击~ percussion instrument
【乐曲】 yuèqǔ musical composition; composition; music
【乐团】 yuètuán ① philharmonic society ② philharmonic orchestra

刖 yuè cutting off the feet (a form of punishment in ancient China)

岳 yuè ① high mountain: 五~ the Five Mountains ② wife's parents: ~家 family of one's wife's parents
【岳父】 yuèfù wife's father; father-in-law 又作"岳丈"
【岳母】 yuèmǔ wife's mother; mother-in-law

钥 yuè key
另见 yào

悦 yuè ① happy; pleased; delighted: 不~ displeased/ 和颜~色 a kindly countenance; a genial look ② please; delight: 取~于人 try to please sb.
【悦耳】 yuè'ěr pleasing to the ear; sweet-sounding: ~的音乐 sweet (或 melodious) music/ 歌声~。 The singing is pleasant.
【悦服】 yuèfú heartily admire
【悦目】 yuèmù pleasing to the eye; good-looking

阅* yuè ① read; go over: ~报 read newspapers/ ~卷 go over examination papers ② review; inspect: ~兵 review troops ③ experience; pass through: 试行已~三月。 Three months have passed since we started to try this out.
【阅兵】 yuèbīng review troops ◇ ~场 parade ground/ ~典礼 dress parade/ ~式 mili-

tary review; parade

【阅读】 yuèdú read: ～杂志 read magazines

【阅览】 yuèlǎn read ◇ ～室 reading room

【阅历】 yuèlì ① see, hear or do for oneself: ～过很多事 have seen much of the world ② experience: ～浅 having little experience; inexperienced

【阅世】 yuèshì 〈书〉 see the world: ～渐深 gain more and more experience of life

跃 yuè leap; jump: ～上马背 leap onto a horse/ 一～而起 get up with a jump; jump up all of a sudden/ ～居世界首位 leap to first place in the world

【跃进】 yuèjìn make (或 take) a leap; leap forward: 整个工业出现了～的局面。The whole industrial front is developing by leaps and bounds.

【跃然】 yuèrán appear vividly: 义愤之情～纸上。The author shows his righteous indignation in his writing.

【跃跃欲试】 yuèyuè yù shì be eager to have a try; itch to have a go

越 * yuè ① get over; jump over: ～墙而逃 escape by climbing over the wall/ 翻山～岭 cross over mountain after mountain ② exceed; overstep: ～出范围 overstep the bounds; exceed the limits/ ～出政策界限 go beyond the bounds of policy ③ (of one's voice or emotion) be at a high pitch: 歌声清～ sing in a clarion voice/ 激～ intense; vehement; loud and strong

【越发】 yuèfā ① all the more; even more ② 〔跟上文 "越" 或 "越是" 呼应，作用跟 "越…越…" 相同〕: 越是性急，～容易出差错。The more impatient you are, the more mistakes you'll make.

【越轨】 yuèguǐ exceed the bounds; transgress: ～行为 impermissible behaviour; transgression

【越过】 yuèguò cross; surmount; negotiate: ～戈壁沙漠 cross the Gobi Desert/ ～障碍 surmount obstacles/ ～激流险滩 negotiate turbulent rivers and treacherous shoals

【越级】 yuèjí ① bypass the immediate leadership: ～提出申诉 bypass the immediate leadership and present one's appeals and complaints to higher levels ② (of personnel promotion) skip a grade or rank: ～提升 promote sb. more than one grade at a time

【越界】 yuèjiè overstep the boundary; cross the border

【越境】 yuèjìng cross the boundary illegally; sneak in or out of a country

【越来越…】 yuèlái yuè… 〔表示程度随着时间发展〕more and more: 越来越好 get better and better/ 发挥越来越大的作用 play an increasingly important role

【越权】 yuèquán exceed (或 overstep) one's power or authority; *ultra vires*

【越野】 yuèyě cross-country ◇ ～汽车 cross-country (motor) vehicle/ ～赛跑 cross-country race

【越狱】 yuèyù escape from prison; break prison ◇ ～犯 prison breaker

【越…越…】 yuè… yuè… 〔表示程度随着条件的发展而发展〕the more…the more…: 越多越好 the more the better/ 越战越强 grow stronger with the fighting

【越组代庖】 yuè zǔ dài páo exceed one's functions and meddle in others' affairs; take sb. else's job into one's own hands

粤 Yuè another name for Guangdong Province

【粤剧】 yuèjù Guangdong opera

yūn

晕 yūn ① dizzy; giddy: 有点头～ feel a bit dizzy (或 giddy) ② swoon; faint: ～了过去 lose consciousness; faint; swoon
另见 yùn

【晕倒】 yūndǎo fall in a faint; pass out

【晕厥】 yūnjué 〈医〉 syncope; faint

【晕晕忽忽】 yūnyunhūhū ① dizzy; giddy ② muddleheaded

yún

云 * yún ① 〈书〉 say: 人～亦～ repeat what others say; parrot ② cloud

【云彩】 yúncai 〈口〉 cloud

【云层】 yúncéng cloud layer: 在～上面飞行 fly above the clouds

【云端】 yúnduān high in the clouds

【云海】 yúnhǎi a sea of clouds

【云汉】 yúnhàn 〈书〉 the Milky Way

【云集】 yúnjí come together in crowds; gather; converge: 各地代表～首都。Representatives from all over the country gathered in the capital.

【云梯】 yúntī scaling ladder

【云雾】 yúnwù cloud and mist; mist: 拨开～见青天 scatter the clouds and see the blue sky

【云霞】 yúnxiá rosy clouds

【云消雾散】 yúnxiāo-wùsàn the clouds melt and the mists disperse — vanish into thin air

【云霄】 yúnxiāo the skies: 锣鼓声响彻～。The beating of gongs and drums resounded to the skies.

【云烟】 yúnyān cloud and mist: 过眼～ as transient as a fleeting cloud

【云游】 yúnyóu (of a Buddhist monk or a Taoist priest) roam; wander

【云雨】 yúnyǔ 〈书〉 sexual intercourse; making love

【云云】 yúnyún 〈书〉〔引用文句或谈话时，表示结束或有所省略〕他来信说读了不少新书，颇有心得。He wrote to say that he had read several new books and profited greatly from them.

匀 yún ① even: 颜色涂得不～。The colour is not evenly spread./ 麦苗出得很～。The wheat sprouts are growing very evenly. ② even up; divide evenly: 这两份多少不均，再一一～吧。These two shares are not equal. Please even them up. ③ spare: 我们种子比较多，可以～给你们一些。We've got more seeds than we need. We can spare you some.

【匀称】 yúnchèn well-proportioned; well-balanced; symmetrical: 身材～ of proportional build

【匀整】 yúnzhěng neat and well spaced; even and orderly: 他的字写得很～。His handwriting is very neat.

芸 yún

【芸芸众生】 yúnyún zhòngshēng 〈佛教〉 all living things; all mortal beings

纭 yún

【纭纭】 yúnyún numerous and disorderly; diverse and confused

昀 yún sunlight; sunshine

耘 yún weed: ～田 weed the fields/ 春耕夏～ spring ploughing and summer weeding

yǔn

允 yǔn ① permit; allow; consent: 应～ consent/ ～从 comply ② fair; just: 公～ fair; equitable

【允当】 yǔndàng proper; suitable

【允诺】 yǔnnuò promise; consent; undertake: 欣然～ readily consent

【允许】 yǔnxǔ permit; allow: 不～任何破坏纪律的现象存在 permit no breach of discipline/ 请～我代表全厂职工向你们致谢。Allow me to thank you on behalf of our factory.

陨 yǔn fall from the sky or outer space

【陨落】 yǔnluò (of a meteorite, etc.) fall from the sky or outer space

【陨灭】 yǔnmiè ① fall from outer space and burn up ②

〈书〉meet one's death; perish
【陨石】yǔnshí 〈天〉aerolite; stony meteorite
【陨星】yǔnxīng 〈天〉meteorite

殒
yǔn perish; die
【殒灭】yǔnmiè 〈书〉meet one's death; perish
【殒命】yǔnmìng 〈书〉meet one's death; perish

yùn

孕 *
yùn pregnant: 怀~ be pregnant; be conceived/ 避~ contraception
【孕妇】yùnfù pregnant woman
【孕期】yùnqī 〈医〉pregnancy; gestation
【孕育】yùnyù be pregnant with; breed: ~着危险 be fraught with danger

运 *
yùn ① motion; movement ② carry; transport: ~往河边 carry to the riverside/ 货~ freight transport/ 空~ air transport; airlift ③ use; wield; utilize: ~笔 wield the pen/ ~思 exercise one's mind ④ fortune; luck; fate: 好~ good luck/ 不走~ be out of luck; have no luck
【运筹帷幄】yùnchóu wéiwò devise strategies within a command tent: ~之中，决胜千里之外 sit within a command tent and devise strategies that will assure victory a thousand *li* away
【运动】yùndòng ① motion; movement: 直线~ rectilinear motion/ 行星的~ the movement of a planet/ ~是物质的存在方式。 Motion is the mode of existence of matter./ 乘敌~之际，打击敌人。 Attack the enemy while he is on the move. ② sports; athletics; exercise: 室外~ outdoor sports/ 游泳是我喜爱的~。 Swimming is my favourite sport./ 散步也是一种~。 Walking is also a form of exercise. ③ (political) movement; campaign; drive ◇ ~场 sports (或 athletic) ground; playground/ ~服装 sportswear/ ~员 sportsman or sportswoman; athlete; player
【运动】yùndong 〈旧〉arrange things through pull
【运动会】yùndònghuì sports meet; athletic meeting; games: 全国~ national games
【运费】yùnfèi transportation expenses; freight; carriage: 到付~ freight payable at destination
【运河】yùnhé canal: 大~ the Grand Canal ◇ ~税 canal dues
【运气】yùnqì (the art of) directing one's strength, through concentration, to a part of the body
【运气】yùnqi fortune; luck: 碰~ try one's luck; take one's chance/ 唉，~老是不好。 Just my luck!/ 这回可来了~了。 This time my luck's in.
【运输】yùnshū transport; carriage; conveyance: 陆上(水路)~ land (water) transport; transport by land (water)
【运送】yùnsòng transport; ship; convey: ~物资 ship (或 transport) goods and materials
【运算】yùnsuàn 〈数〉operation: 四则~ the four fundamental operations of arithmetic
【运销】yùnxiāo (commodity) transportation and sale
【运行】yùnxíng move; be in motion: 在轨道上~ move in orbit/ 地球绕太阳~。 The earth revolves round the sun./ 列车~时，请勿打开车门。 Don't open the door while the train is in motion.
【运用】yùnyòng utilize; wield; apply; put to use
【运载工具】yùnzài gōngjù means of delivery: 战略~ strategic vehicles
【运转】yùnzhuǎn ① revolve; turn round: 行星绕着太阳~。 The planets revolve round the sun. ② work; operate: 机器~正常。 The machine is running well.

晕
yùn ① dizzy; giddy; faint: 头~目眩 have a dizzy spell; be afflicted with vertigo ② 〈气〉halo: 日~ solar halo/ 月~ lunar halo
另见 yūn
【晕车】yùnchē carsickness: 好~ be liable to carsickness
【晕船】yùnchuán seasickness
【晕机】yùnjī airsickness

酝
yùn
【酝酿】yùnniàng ① brew; ferment: 这场大辩论~已久。 This great debate has been brewing for a long time. ② have a preliminary informal discussion; deliberate on: ~候选人名单 consider and talk over the list of candidates/ 大家先~一下。 Let's have an exchange of views first./ 经过反复~协商，选举了出席大会的代表。 Delegates to the congress were elected after repeated deliberations and consultations.

愠
yùn 〈书〉angry; irritated: 面有~色 look irritated
【愠怒】yùnnù be inwardly angry

韵
yùn ① musical (或 agreeable) sound: 琴~悠扬 Sweet music was being played on the lute. ② rhyme: 押~ be in rhyme/ ~书 rhyming dictionary ③ charm: 风~ personal charm; graceful bearing
【韵律】yùnlǜ ① metre (in verse) ② rules of rhyming; rhyme scheme
【韵母】yùnmǔ 〈语〉simple or compound vowel (of a Chinese syllable), sometimes with a terminal n or ng
【韵尾】yùnwěi tail vowel, the terminal sound (vowel or nasal consonant) of certain compound vowels, as o in ao, ng in iang
【韵味】yùnwèi lingering charm; lasting appeal: 她的唱腔很有~。 Her singing has a special pleasing quality about it.
【韵文】yùnwén literary composition in rhyme; verse

熨
yùn iron; press: ~衣服 iron (或 press) clothes
【熨斗】yùndǒu flatiron; iron: 电~ electric iron

蕴
yùn 〈书〉accumulate; hold in store; contain
【蕴藏】yùncáng hold in store; contain: 中国地下~着丰富的矿物资源。 China is rich in mineral resources. ◇ ~量 reserves; deposits
【蕴涵】yùnhán 〈书〉contain
【蕴藉】yùnjiè 〈书〉temperate and refined; cultured and restrained: 风流~ graceful but not showy; urbanely charming
【蕴蓄】yùnxù lie hidden and undeveloped; be latent

Z

zā

扎 * ¹zā tie; bind: ~小辫儿 tie up one's plaits; plait one's hair; wear one's hair in plaits/ ~一根红头绳 tie one's plait with a piece of red yarn/ ~彩 hang up festoons
另见 zhā; zhá

匝 zā 〈书〉① circle; circumference: 绕树三~ circle a tree three times ② dense; full: 密密~~ dense; thick

咂 zā ① sip; suck: ~一口酒 take a sip of wine ② make clicks (of admiration, praise, etc.) ③ taste (或 savour) carefully
【咂嘴】 zāzuǐ make clicks (of admiration, praise, etc.)

zá

杂 * zá ① miscellaneous; sundry; mixed: ~事儿 miscellaneous affairs/ ~而不乱 mixed but not confused/ ~七八的东西 odds and ends; a medley ② mix; mingle: 夹~ be mixed up with; be mingled with/ 这片苹果树中有几棵梨树。 There are a few pear trees scattered among these apple trees.
【杂拌儿】 zábànr ① assorted preserved fruits; mixed sweetmeats ② mixture; miscellany; medley; hotchpotch
【杂草】 zácǎo weeds; rank grass: ~丛生 be overgrown with weeds
【杂凑】 zácòu knock together
【杂费】 záfèi ① incidental (或 miscellaneous) expenses; incidentals ② sundry fees (或 charges); extras
【杂感】 zágǎn ① random (或 stray) thoughts ② a type of literature recording such thoughts
【杂烩】 záhuì ① a stew of various ingredients; mixed stew; hotchpotch ② mixture; miscellany; medley; hotchpotch
【杂货】 záhuò sundry goods; groceries: 日用~ various household supplies ◇ ~店 grocery
【杂记】 zájì ① jottings; notes ② miscellanies (as a type of literature)
【杂技】 zájì acrobatics ◇ ~团 acrobatic troupe/ ~演员 acrobat
【杂居】 zájū (of two or more nationalities) live together: 少数民族~地区 an area inhabited by several minority nationalities
【杂粮】 záliáng food grains other than wheat and rice
【杂乱】 záluàn mixed and disorderly; in a jumble; in a muddle: 抽屉里的东西很~。 The things in the drawer were all in a jumble.
【杂乱无章】 záluàn wú zhāng disorderly and unsystematic; disorganized
【杂念】 zániàn distracting thoughts
【杂品】 zápǐn sundry goods; groceries
【杂糅】 záróu mix; mingle; blend: 古今~ a blending of the ancient and the modern
【杂色】 zásè variegated; parti-coloured; motley
【杂税】 záshuì miscellaneous levies
【杂碎】 zásui chopped cooked entrails of sheep or oxen
【杂沓】 zátà numerous and disorderly: ~的脚步声 the clatter of footsteps
【杂文】 záwén essay
【杂务】 záwù odd jobs; sundry duties
【杂音】 záyīn noise
【杂志】 zázhì ① magazine ②〔多用作书名〕records; notes ◇ ~架 magazine rack
【杂质】 zázhì ① impurity ②〈化〉foreign matter (或 substance)

【杂种】 zázhǒng ①〈生〉hybrid; crossbreed ②〈骂〉bastard; son of a bitch

砸 zá ① pound; tamp: 把地基~实 tamp the foundations solid/ ~了脚 have one's foot squashed ② break; smash: 碗~了。The bowl is broken./ ~核桃 crack walnuts/ ~碎锁链 smash the shackles/ 把门~开 smash (或 ram) the door open ③〈方〉fail; fall through; be bungled: 事儿办~了。The job was bungled.

zāi

灾 * zāi ① calamity; disaster: 天~ natural disaster/ 水~ flood/ 旱~ drought/ 虫~ plague of insects ② personal misfortune; adversity: 没病没~ good health and good luck; with one's health all right and luck not bad
【灾害】 zāihài calamity; disaster: 自然~ natural calamity
【灾患】 zāihuàn 〈书〉calamity; disaster: 屡经~ suffer calamity after calamity
【灾荒】 zāihuāng famine due to crop failures
【灾祸】 zāihuò disaster; calamity; catastrophe: ~临头。A great disaster is befalling (或 imminent).
【灾民】 zāimín victims of a natural calamity
【灾难】 zāinàn suffering; calamity; disaster; catastrophe: ~深重 disaster-ridden/ ~性的后果 disastrous consequences/ 避免一场大~ avert a catastrophe
【灾情】 zāiqíng the condition of a disaster: ~严重。The losses caused by the disaster were serious./ 这场雨减轻了~。The rain reduced the effects of the drought.
【灾区】 zāiqū disaster area: 地震~ earthquake-stricken area/ 旱~ drought-stricken area/ 水~ flooded area/ 重~ severely afflicted area
【灾殃】 zāiyāng suffering; calamity; disaster

哉 zāi 〈书〉〈助〉①〔表示感叹〕呜呼～哀～! Alas!/ 诚～斯言! How true that is! ②〔与疑问词合用表示疑问或反诘〕: 胡为乎来～? Why has it come?/ 何～? Why? 或 Wherefore?/ 有何难～? What's so difficult about it?

栽 * zāi ① plant; grow: ~树 plant trees/ ~花 grow flowers/ ~秧 transplant seedlings (as of tomatoes or eggplants) ② stick in; insert; plant: ~电线杆子 erect a wire pole ③ force sth. on sb.; impose: ~上罪名 frame sb.; fabricate a charge against sb. ④ tumble; fall: ~倒 fall down
【栽跟头】 zāi gēntou ① tumble; fall ② suffer a setback; come a cropper
【栽培】 zāipéi ① cultivate; grow: 先进的~技术 advanced cultivation techniques/ 棉花~ the culture of cotton/ ~野生植物 domesticate wild plants ② foster; train; educate ③〈旧〉help advance sb.'s career; patronize
【栽植】 zāizhí plant; transplant
【栽种】 zāizhòng plant; grow

zǎi

仔 zǎi 〈方〉① son ② young animal; whelp
另见 zǐ

宰 zǎi ① slaughter; butcher: ~猪 butcher pigs ② govern; rule: 主~ dominate; dictate
【宰割】 zǎigē invade, oppress and exploit: 任人~ allow oneself to be trampled upon
【宰杀】 zǎishā slaughter; butcher
【宰相】 zǎixiàng prime minister

载 zǎi ① year: 一年半～ six to twelve months; six months to a year ② put down in writing; record: ～入记录 record in the minutes; place on record/ ～入史册 go down in history/ 刊～ publish (in a newspaper or magazine); carry/ 据报～ according to press reports/ 条约中～明 be clearly stated in the treaty
另见 zài

崽 zǎi 〈方〉① son ② young animal; whelp
【崽子】zǎizi 〔多用作骂人的话〕whelp; bastard: 兔～ brat/ 狗～ son of a bitch

zài

再 zài 〈副〉① another time; again; once more: ～试一次 try again; have another try/ 一而～,～而三 again and again; repeatedly/ ～创新纪录 set another record/ 我不能～喝了。I can't drink any more./ ～来一个! Encore! ② 〔表示更加〕: 还有～大点儿的吗? Have you got a bigger one?/ ～好不过了。It couldn't be better./ 声音～大一点。Still louder, please./ ～冷的天我也不怕。I can stand colder weather than this. ③〔表示如果继续怎样〕: ～过几年, 山村就要整个变样了。A few more years and there will be a complete change in the mountain village./ ～不走我们就赶不上火车了。We'll miss the train if we delay any longer. ④〔表示一个动作发生在另一个动作结束之后〕: 先到张家,～到李家。First go to the Zhangs', and then to the Lis'./ 你做完了功课～出去。Finish your homework before you go out. ⑤〔表示另外有所补充〕: ～则 moreover; furthermore; besides/ ～不然 if not; or else; otherwise ⑥ come back; return: 青春无～。One's youth never returns./ 良机难～。Opportunity knocks but once.
【再版】zàibǎn ① second edition ②〈旧〉reprint; second impression
【再不】zàibu 〈口〉or else; or: 派老王去,～小李也行。Send Lao Wang, or else Xiao Li.
【再次】zàicì once more; a second time; once again: ～感谢你们的帮助。Thank you once again for your help./ 防止类似事件～发生 prevent the occurrence of similar incidents
【再度】zàidù once more; a second time; once again: ～访问贵国 visit your country a second time/ ～当选 reelected
【再会】zàihuì 〈套〉good-bye; see you again
【再婚】zàihūn remarry; marry again
【再加】zàijiā in addition; besides; on top of that: 下着大雨,～道儿不熟,所以他迟到了。What with the heavy rain and his not knowing the way, he was late.
【再嫁】zàijià (of a woman) remarry
【再见】zàijiàn 〈套〉good-bye; see you again
【再接再厉】zàijiē-zàilì make persistent efforts; continue to exert oneself; work ceaselessly and unremittingly
【再起】zàiqǐ recurrence; resurgence; revival: 防止边境冲突～ prevent the recurrence of border clashes
【再三】zàisān over and over again; time and again; again and again; repeatedly: ～考虑 consider over and over again/ ～嘱咐 bid or tell again and again
【再审】zàishěn ① review ②〈法〉retrial
【再生】zàishēng be a second so-and-so (a well-known figure already dead): 他手艺真巧, 简直是鲁班～。His carpentry is really exquisite. He's another Lu Ban.
【再生父母】zàishēng fùmǔ one's great benefactor (usu. one's saviour)
【再说】zàishuō ① put off until some time later: 这事先搁两天～。Let's put the matter aside for a couple of days. ②〈连〉what's more; besides: 现在去找他太晚了,～我路也不熟。It's too late to go and see him now; besides, I don't quite know the way.
【再现】zàixiàn (of a past event) reappear; be reproduced: ～在眼前 reappear before one's eyes
【再造】zàizào give sb. a new lease on life: 恩同～ a favour tantamount to giving sb. a new lease on life

【再者】zàizhě 〈书〉moreover; furthermore; besides

在 zài ① exist; be living: 这问题还～,并没有解决。The problem still exists. It's not solved yet. ②〔表示人或物的位置〕: 我父母～农村。My parents are in the countryside./ 你的钢笔～桌子上呢。Your pen is on the table. ③ join or belong to an organization; be a member of an organization ④〈介〉〔表示时间、地点、情形、范围等〕: 事情发生～去年。It happened last year./ ～研究所工作 work in a research institute/ ～会上发言 speak at a meeting/ ～我看来 in my opinion; as I see it/ ～这种情况下 under these circumstances/ ～这方面 in this respect ⑤〈副〉〔表示动作正在进行〕: 她～游泳。She is swimming. ⑥ rest with; depend on: 学习好,主要～自己努力。Getting good results in one's studies depends mainly on one's own efforts./ 事～人为。Human effort is the decisive factor.
【在案】zài'àn be on record: 记录～ be put on record; be a matter of record
【在场】zàichǎng be on the scene; be on the spot; be present: 当时我没～。I wasn't there at the time.
【在朝】zàicháo hold office at court
【在行】zàiháng be expert at sth.; know a job, trade, etc. well: 这方面我不～。I'm no expert at that.
【在乎】zàihu ① care about; mind; take to heart: 满不～ not care a bit/ 只要能学会,少睡点觉倒不～。As long as I can learn it, I don't mind if I have to cut down on my sleep. ② 见"在于"
【在即】zàijí near at hand; shortly; soon: 完工～ will soon be completed; be nearing completion
【在家】zàijiā ① be at home; be in: 你爸～吗? Is your father in?/ 我们让她～好好休息。We told her to stay home and have a good rest. ②〈宗〉remain a layman
【在世】zàishì be living: 他～的时候 in his lifetime/ 他妈要是还～,看到这样的好光景,该有多高兴啊! If his mother were alive, how happy she would be to see such good times.
【在所不辞】zài suǒ bù cí will not refuse under any circumstances; will not hesitate to
【在所不惜】zài suǒ bù xī will not grudge; will never balk at
【在所难免】zài suǒ nánmiǎn can hardly be avoided; be unavoidable: 工作没有经验,出点差错～。Slips are unavoidable when you are new to your work.
【在逃】zàitáo 〈法〉has escaped; be at large ◇ ～犯 escaped criminal; criminal at large
【在望】zàiwàng ① be visible; be in sight; be in view: 山头隐隐～。The mountain top was dimly visible. ② will soon materialize; be in sight; be in the offing: 胜利～。Victory is in sight.
【在位】zàiwèi 〈旧〉be on the throne; reign
【在握】zàiwò be in one's hands; be within one's grasp; be under one's control: 大权～ with power in one's hands/ 胜利～。Victory is within grasp.
【在下】zàixià 〈旧〉〈谦〉I
【在先】zàixiān formerly; in the past; before
【在心】zàixīn feel concerned; mind; be attentive: 别看他大大咧咧的,什么事他都～。He appears unconcerned, but nothing escapes his attention./ 这事儿请您在点儿心。Please keep an eye on the matter.
【在押】zàiyā 〈法〉be under detention; be in custody; be in prison ◇ ～犯 criminal in custody; prisoner
【在野】zàiyě not be in office; be out of office ◇ ～党 a party not in office
【在意】zàiyì 〔多用于否定式〕take notice of; care about; mind; take to heart: 他只顾看信,别人对他说的话,他都没～。He was poring over the letter and didn't take any notice of what people were saying to him./ 这些小事他是不会～的。He won't take such trifles to heart.
【在于】zàiyú ① lie in; rest with: 我们的力量～人民。Our strength lies in the people. ② be determined by; depend on: 有收无收～水,多收少收～肥。Water determines whether or not we have a harvest, and fertilizer determines whether the harvest is big or small.

【在在】 zàizài 〈书〉 everywhere; in all aspects: ~皆是 can be seen everywhere

【在职】 zàizhí be on the job; be at one's post: ~训练 in-service training/ ~期间 during one's tenure of office

【在座】 zàizuò be present (at a meeting, banquet, etc.): 有客人~,她没好意思说。 She was too embarrassed to bring it up in front of the guest.

载 * zài ① carry; hold; be loaded with: ~客 carry passengers/ 卡车上满～着化肥。 The truck was fully loaded with chemical fertilizer. ② all over the road; everywhere along the way: 风雪~途。 Whirling snow swept over the road. ③ 〈书〉 and; as well as; at the same time: ~笑~言 talking and laughing at the same time
另见 zǎi

【载歌载舞】 zàigē-zàiwǔ festively singing and dancing: 人们～热烈欢迎贵宾。 Singing and dancing, people gave the distinguished guests a warm welcome.

【载荷】 zàihè load

【载货】 zàihuò carry cargo (或 freight)

【载运】 zàiyùn convey by vehicles, ships, etc.; transport; carry: 本市公共汽车每天～乘客十万左右。 The city buses carry about 100,000 passengers a day.

【载重】 zàizhòng load; carrying capacity: 这辆卡车~多少? What's the carrying capacity of this truck?

zān

簪 zān ① hairpin: 碧玉~ emerald hairpin ② wear in one's hair: ~花 wear flowers in one's hair

【簪子】 zānzi hair clasp

zán

咱 zán ① we (including both the speaker and the person or persons spoken to) ② 〈方〉 I

【咱们】 zánmen we (including both the speaker and the person or persons spoken to)

zǎn

攒 zǎn accumulate; hoard; save: ~钱 save (或 scrape) up money/ 他把~的钱都买了书。 He spent all his savings on books.

zàn

暂 zàn ① of short duration: 短~ of short duration; brief ② temporary; for the time being; for the moment: ~别 temporary separation/ ~不答复 put off replying/ ~代 act for sb./ ~住 stay temporarily (at a place) /~停营业 business suspended

【暂定】 zàndìng arranged for the time being; tentative; provisional: ~议程 tentative agenda/ ~办法 provisional measures/ 学习期限～两年。 The term of study is tentatively fixed at two years.

【暂缓】 zànhuǎn postpone; put off; defer: ~作出决定 put off (或 defer) making a decision

【暂且】 zànqiě for the time being; for the moment: 讨论~告一段落吧。 Let's stop the discussion for the time being./ 这是后话,~不提。 But I'm anticipating.

【暂缺】 zànquē ① (of a post) be left vacant for the time being ② (of a commodity) be out of stock at the moment

【暂时】 zànshí temporary; transient: ~的需要 transient needs/ ~现象 transient phenomenon/ 比赛的胜负是~的,而友谊是长久的。 The results of contests are transient, but friendship is lasting./ 这事～就这样定了吧。 Let's make it a tentative decision./ 他～来不了。 He can't come right away./ ~停刊 (of a periodical, etc.) temporarily suspend publication

【暂停】 zàntíng ① suspend: ~付款 suspend payment/ 会议～,明天继续举行。 The meeting is adjourned till tomorrow. ② 〈体〉 time-out: 要求~ ask for time-out

【暂行】 zànxíng provisional; temporary: ~条例 provisional regulations/ ~规定 temporary provisions

錾 zàn ① engrave on gold or silver; carve; chisel: ~字 engrave characters/ ~花 carve flowers or patterns ② engraving tool; chisel

赞 * zàn ① support; favour; assist: ~助 support; assistance ② praise; commend: 盛~ highly praise ③ eulogy: 像~ an inscription eulogizing the subject of a portrait

【赞不绝口】 zàn bù jué kǒu be profuse in praise; be full of praise

【赞成】 zànchéng approve of; favour; agree with; endorse: 我们明天去郊游,你~吗? How about going on an outing tomorrow?/ 我完全~。 I'm all for it./ 他最不~你们这样搞。 He doesn't like the way you do it at all./ 六票~,三票反对 six votes for and three against/ ~意见 assenting views/ ~的请举手。 Those in favour please raise their hands. ◇ ~票 affirmative vote

【赞歌】 zàngē song of praise; paean

【赞美】 zànměi praise; eulogize ◇ ~诗 〈基督教〉 hymn

【赞佩】 zànpèi esteem; admire

【赞赏】 zànshǎng appreciate; admire: 对这一友好行动表示~ express appreciation for this friendly act/ 他们非常~这些精美的工艺品。 They greatly admired the exquisite handicrafts.

【赞颂】 zànsòng extol; eulogize; sing the praises of

【赞叹】 zàntàn gasp in admiration; highly praise: 演员们的高超演技令人~。 People gasped with admiration at the superb skill of the performers.

【赞同】 zàntóng approve of; agree with; endorse: 这一主张得到普遍的~。 This proposition met with general approval (或 acceptance)./ 我们~这项决议。 We subscribe to the resolution.

【赞许】 zànxǔ speak favourably of; praise; commend: 得到很多人的~ win the approval of many/ 值得~ deserve commendation; be commendable; be worthy of praise

【赞扬】 zànyáng speak highly of; praise; commend: ~声中找差距 seek out one's shortcomings amidst a shower of praise/ 这种一心为公的精神值得~。 This spirit of selflessness deserves commendation./ 热烈~两国人民之间的友谊 pay warm tribute to the friendship between the two peoples/ 他们的良好体育作风博得广泛的~。 Their fine sportsmanship won widespread acclaim.

【赞语】 zànyǔ words of praise; praise

【赞助】 zànzhù support; assistance

zāng

赃 zāng ① stolen goods; booty; spoils: 分~ share the booty; divide the spoils ② bribes: 贪~ take bribes; practise graft

【赃官】 zāngguān corrupt official

【赃款】 zāngkuǎn money stolen, embezzled or received in bribes; illicit money

【赃物】 zāngwù ① stolen goods; booty; spoils ② bribes

脏 * zāng dirty; filthy: ~衣服 dirty (或 soiled) clothes; dirty linen/ ~水 filthy water; slops; sewage/ 别把桌布弄~了。 Don't dirty the tablecloth.
另见 zàng

臧 zāng 〈书〉 good; right

zàng

脏 zàng internal organs of the body, usu. referring to the heart, liver, spleen, lungs and kidneys; viscera: 心~

heart/ 肾～ kidneys
另见 zāng
【脏腑】 zàngfǔ ＜中医＞ internal organs including the heart, liver, spleen, lungs, kidneys, stomach, gall, intestines and bladder; viscera

葬＊ zàng bury; inter: 海～ sea-burial/ 火～ cremation
【葬礼】 zànglǐ funeral (或 burial) rites; funeral
【葬身】 zàngshēn be buried: ～鱼腹 become fish food; be swept to a watery grave; be drowned/ 死无～之地 die without a burial place — come to a bad end
【葬送】 zàngsòng ruin; spell an end to

藏＊ zàng ① storing place; depository: 宝～ precious (mineral) deposits ② Buddhist or Taoist scriptures: 道～ Taoist scriptures
另见 cáng

zāo

遭 zāo ① meet with (disaster, misfortune, etc.); suffer: ～难 meet with misfortune; suffer disaster/ 几～挫折 suffer repeated setbacks/ ～灾 be hit by a natural calamity/ 险～不测 have a near (或 narrow) escape ② ＜量＞ round: 用绳子绕两～ wind the string around twice/ 走一～ make a trip ③ ＜量＞ time; turn: 在这么多人面前讲话,我还是头一～。 This is the first time I have ever spoken to such a big audience./ 一～生,两～熟。 Strangers at first meeting become familiar at the next.
【遭到】 zāodào suffer; meet with; encounter: ～失败 suffer (或 meet with) defeat/ ～拒绝 meet with refusal; be turned down/ ～困难 encounter (或 run up against) difficulties/ 这个工厂在地震中～严重破坏。 This factory was seriously damaged during the earthquake.
【遭逢】 zāoféng meet with; come across; encounter: ～盛世 live in prosperous times/ ～不幸 suffer misfortune
【遭际】 zāojì circumstances; lot
【遭劫】 zāojié meet with catastrophe
【遭受】 zāoshòu suffer; be subjected to; sustain: ～损失 sustain losses/ ～水灾 be hit by floods
【遭殃】 zāoyāng suffer disaster; suffer
【遭遇】 zāoyù ① meet with; encounter; run up against: ～不幸 meet with misfortune; have hard luck/ 先头部队与敌人～了。 The advance unit encountered (或 ran into) the enemy. ② (bitter) experience; (hard) lot: 我们有着共同的历史。～ We have shared the same historical experiences. 或 他后来的～我就不知道了。 I don't know what became of him later.

糟 zāo ① distillers' grains; grains ② be pickled with grains or in wine: ～鱼 fish pickled with grains or in wine; pickled fish ③ rotten; poor: 这案板～了。 The chopping board is rotten./ 他身体很～。 He is in very poor health. ④ in a wretched (或 terrible) state; in a mess: 把事情搞～了 make a mess of sth./ ～了,饭糊啦! Damn it! The rice is burning!
【糟糕】 zāogāo ＜口＞ how terrible; what bad luck; too bad: ～,我把钥匙锁在屋里了。 Oh, no, I've locked the key in the room!/ 真～,误了火车啦。 What bad luck! We've missed the train./ 更～的是,他把介绍信丢了。 To make things worse, he lost the letter of introduction.
【糟糠】 zāokāng distillers grains, husks, chaff, etc. foodstuffs for the poor ◇ ～之妻 wife who has shared her husband's hard lot
【糟粕】 zāopò waste matter; dross; dregs: 剔除～,吸取精华 reject the dross and assimilate the essence
【糟蹋】 zāota ① waste; ruin; spoil: ～粮食 waste grain/ 剪裁时要小心,别让料子～。 Cut the material carefully, don't spoil it. ② insult; trample on; ravage: 侵略军把这个村子～得不成样子。 The invading troops left the village in a terrible state./ 说话可不要这样～人。 You shouldn't talk about anyone like that. ③ violate (a woman) 又作"糟踏"

zǎo

凿 záo ① chisel ② cut a hole; chisel or dig: ～一个窟窿 bore a hole/ ～山劈岭 tunnel through mountains and cut across ridges/ ～冰 make a hole in the ice/ 把船～沉 scuttle the ship
另见 zuò
【凿井】 záojǐng dig (或 sink, bore) a well
【凿子】 záozi chisel

zǎo

早＊ zǎo ① (early) morning: 从～到晚 from morning till night/ 清～ early in the morning ② long ago; as early as; for a long time: 我～知道了。 I knew that long ago. 或 That's no news to me./ 我～就想来看你了。 I've been wanting to see you for a long time./ ～在二十世纪初 as early as the beginning of the twentieth century ③ early; in advance; beforehand: 你～点儿来。 Come early./ ～作准备 get prepared in advance; make timely preparations/ ～知如此,我就不回去了。 If I'd known this beforehand I would not have gone back./ 电影离开演还～哩。 It's still quite a while before the film starts. ④ ＜套＞ good morning
【早安】 zǎo'ān good morning
【早班】 zǎobān morning shift
【早餐】 zǎocān breakfast
【早操】 zǎocāo morning (setting-up) exercises
【早产】 zǎochǎn ＜医＞ premature delivery
【早场】 zǎochǎng morning show (at a cinema, theatre, etc.)
【早车】 zǎochē morning train or coach
【早晨】 zǎochén (early) morning
【早点】 zǎodiǎn (light) breakfast
【早婚】 zǎohūn marrying too early: ～妨碍工作和学习。 Marrying too early hinders one's work and study.
【早年】 zǎonián one's early years
【早期】 zǎoqī early stage; early phase: ～作品 sb.s early works; the works of sb.'s earlier period
【早日】 zǎorì at an early date; early; soon: 请～答复。 Your early reply is requested. 或 Please reply at your earliest convenience / 祝你～恢复健康。 I hope you'll get well soon. 或 I wish you a speedy recovery./ ～完工 complete the project as soon as possible
【早上】 zǎoshang (early) morning
【早熟】 zǎoshú ① ＜生理＞ precocity: ～的孩子 a precocious child ② early-maturing; early-ripe
【早退】 zǎotuì leave earlier than one should; leave early
【早晚】 zǎowǎn ① morning and evening: ～各服一丸 take one pill in the morning and one in the evening ② sooner or later: 他迟早要去那儿演还～哩。 He'll have to go there sooner or later. ③ time: 他一清早就走了,这～多半已经到家了。 He left early in the morning and should be home by now.
【早先】 zǎoxiān previously; in the past: 这儿～是臭水塘,现在成了工人新村了。 There used to be a stagnant pond here; now there are workers' flats.
【早已】 zǎoyǐ long ago; for a long time: 他～打定主意了。 He made up his mind long ago.

枣 zǎo jujube; (Chinese) date; tsao

蚤 zǎo flea: 沙～ beach flea/ 水～ water flea

澡 zǎo bath: 洗～ take a bath; bathe
【澡盆】 zǎopén bathtub
【澡堂】 zǎotáng public baths; bathhouse

藻 zǎo ① algae ② aquatic plants ③ literary embellishment: 辞～ ornate diction
【藻饰】 zǎoshì ＜书＞ embellishments in writing

zào

灶 zào   kitchen range; cooking stove ② kitchen; mess; canteen
【灶神】 Zàoshén kitchen god 又作"灶君"; "灶王爷"

皂* zào ① black ② *yamen* runner ③ soap: 香～ toilet soap/ 药～ medicated soap
【皂白】 zào-bái black and white — right and wrong: ～不分 make no distinction between right and wrong

造* zào ① make; build; create: ～房子 build a house/ ～舆论 create (或 prepare) public opinion/ ～预算 make (或 draw up) a budget/ ～表 draw up a form or list/ ～册 compile a register ② invent; cook up; concoct: 捏～ fabricate; concoct/ ～假帐 cook accounts ③ train; educate: 深～ pursue advanced studies/ 可～之才 a person suitable for training; a promising (或 hopeful) young person ④ 〈书〉 go to; arrive at: ～府 call at your house ⑤ one of the two parties in a legal agreement or a lawsuit: 两～ both parties ⑥ 〈方〉 crop: 早～ early crops/ 一年三～ three crops a year
【造币厂】 zàobìchǎng a mint
【造成】 zàochéng create; cause; give rise to; bring about: ～巨大损失 cause enormous losses
【造船】 zàochuán shipbuilding ◇ ～厂 shipyard; dockyard/ ～工业 shipbuilding industry
【造次】 zàocì 〈书〉 ① hurried; hasty: ～之间 in one's hurry; in a moment of haste ② rash; impetuous: ～行事 act rashly
【造反】 zàofǎn rise in rebellion; rebel; revolt
【造访】 zàofǎng 〈书〉 pay a visit (或 call); call on: 登门～ call at sb.'s house; pay sb. a visit
【造福】 zàofú bring benefit to; benefit: ～于人类 bring benefit to mankind/ 为后代～ benefit future generations
【造化】 zàohuà 〈书〉 the Creator; Nature
【造化】 zàohua good fortune; good luck: 有～ be born under a lucky star; be lucky
【造就】 zàojiù ① bring up; train: ～一代新人 bring up a new generation ② achievements; attainments (usu. of young people)
【造孽】 zàoniè 〈佛教〉 do evil; commit a sin
【造物】 zàowù the divine force that created the universe; Nature ◇ ～主〈基督教〉 God; the Creator
【造像】 zàoxiàng 〈美术〉 statue
【造型】 zàoxíng ① modelling; mould-making: 这些古代工艺品～优美。 These ancient art objects are beautifully shaped. ② model; mould
【造谣】 zàoyáo cook up a story and spread it around; start a rumour: ～生事 start a rumour to create trouble; stir up trouble by rumourmongering
【造诣】 zàoyì (academic or artistic) attainments: ～很高 of great attainments
【造纸】 zàozhǐ papermaking ◇ ～厂 paper mill/ ～机 paper machine
【造作】 zàozuò make; manufacture
【造作】 zàozuo affected; artificial

噪 zào ① (of birds, insects, etc.) chirp: 蝉～ the chirping of cicadas ② a confusion of voices: 鼓～ make an uproar; clamour/ 名～一时 be a celebrity for a time
【噪音】 zàoyīn noise

燥 zào dry: ～热 hot and dry

躁 zào rash; impetuous; restless: 戒骄戒～ guard against arrogance and rashness (或 impetuosity)/ 性子～ quick-tempered; hot-tempered/ ～动 move restlessly
【躁急】 zàojí restless; uneasy

zé

则* zé ① standard; norm; criterion: 准～ criterion; standard/ 以身作～ set an example by one's own conduct ② rule; regulation: 章～ rules and regulations/ 法～ law; rule ③ 〈书〉 imitate; follow: ～先烈之言行 follow the example of the martyrs in word and deed ④ 〈量〉〔用于分项或自成段落的文字的条数〕: 新闻一～ an item of news/ 寓言四～ four fables ⑤ 〈书〉〈连〉ⓐ〔表示因果、条件等〕: 物体热～涨,冷～缩。Objects expand when heated and contract when cooled./ 有～改之,无～加勉。Correct mistakes if you have made any and guard against them if you have not./ 不战～已,战～必胜。Fight no battle unless victory is sure./ 少～几年,多～几十年 several years at least and several decades at most; between several years and several decades ⓑ〔表示转折、对比等〕: 好～好,只是太贵。It's good but too expensive./ 今～不然。However, things are quite different today. ⑥ 〈书〉〔用于"一、二(再)、三"等后面 列举原因或理由〕: 这篇课文 不合适,一～太长,二～太难。This text is unsuitable. For one thing it's too long, for another it's too difficult.
【则声】 zéshēng make a sound; utter a word: 不～ keep silent

责* zé ① duty; responsibility: 爱护公物,人人有～。It is everybody's duty to take good care of public property. ② demand; require: 严以～己,宽以待人 be strict with oneself and broad-minded towards others/ 求全～备 demand perfection; nitpick ③ question closely; call sb. to account ④ reproach; blame; reprove: 自～ reprove oneself/ 斥～ reprimand; rebuke; denounce/ 痛～ rebuke severely; castigate ⑤ punish: 答～ punish by flogging
【责备】 zébèi reproach; blame; reprove; take sb. to task: ～的眼光 a look of reproach/ 受到良心的～ feel a prick of conscience
【责成】 zéchéng instruct (sb. to fulfil a task); charge (sb. with a task); enjoin (sb. to do sth.): ～小组委员会提出报告 instruct the subcommittee to submit a report
【责罚】 zéfá punish
【责怪】 zéguài blame: 这事不应该～他。He should not be blamed for this.
【责令】 zélìng order; instruct; charge: ～主管部门采取有力措施 instruct the department in charge to take effective measures
【责骂】 zémà scold; rebuke; dress down
【责难】 zénàn censure; blame: 受到各方面的～ incur censure from various quarters
【责任】 zérèn ① duty; responsibility: ～重大 have a grave responsibility/ 先进的有～帮助后进的。The advanced are duty-bound to help those lagging behind./ 我不过是尽了自己的～罢了。I've done no more than my duty./ 负起～来。Shoulder your responsibility. ② responsibility for a fault or wrong; blame: 追究～ ascertain where the responsibility lies/ 你不应该把～推到别人身上。You shouldn't shift the blame onto others./ 这事如果搞不好,你要负～。If anything goes wrong, you'll have to answer for it. ◇ ～感 sense of responsibility (或 duty)/ ～心 sense of responsibility (或 duty)
【责问】 zéwèn call (或 bring) sb. to account
【责无旁贷】 zé wú páng dài there is no shirking the responsibility; be duty-bound

泽 zé ① pool; pond: 沼～ marsh; swamp/ 湖～ lakes ② damp; moist: 润～ moist; wet ③ lustre (of metals, pearls, etc.): 光～ lustre; gloss; sheen/ 色～ colour and lustre ④ 〈书〉 favour; beneficence
【泽国】 zéguó 〈书〉 ① a land that abounds in rivers and lakes ② inundated area: 尽成～ a whole area became submerged

择* zé select; choose; pick: ～友 choose friends/ 二者

任~其一 choose either of the two/ ~日起程 fix a departure date/ 不~手段 by hook or by crook; unscrupulously

【择吉】 zéjí pick an auspicious day (for a marriage, funeral, etc.)

【择交】 zéjiāo choose friends: 慎重~ choose friends with care

【择善而从】 zé shàn ér cóng choose and follow what is good

啧 zé ① compete for a chance to speak; dispute ② click of the tongue

【啧有烦言】 zé yǒu fán yán there are a lot of complaints

【啧啧】 zézé ① click of the tongue: ~称羡 click the tongue in admiration/ ~叹赏 be profuse in one's praise ② 〔形容说话声〕: 人言~。 There is a good deal of unfavourable comment.

zè

仄 zè ① narrow: 逼~ narrow; cramped ② 〈语〉见"仄声"

【仄声】 zèshēng 〈语〉oblique tones, i.e., the falling-rising tone (上声), the falling tone (去声) and the entering tone (入声), as distinct from the level tone (平声) in classical Chinese pronunciation

zéi

贼* zéi ① thief ② traitor; enemy: 卖国~ traitor (to one's country)/ 工~ scab; blackleg ③ crooked; wicked; evil; furtive: ~眼 shifty eyes; furtive glance ④ crafty; sly; cunning; deceitful: 老鼠真~。 Rats are really cunning. ⑤〈书〉injure; harm; murder: ~害 murder

【贼船】 zéichuán pirate ship: 上~ board the pirate ship—join a reactionary faction

【贼喊捉贼】 zéi hǎn zhuō zéi a thief crying "Stop thief"

【贼眉鼠眼】 zéiméi-shǔyǎn shifty-eyed; thievish-looking

【贼去关门】 zéi qù guānmén lock the door after the thief has gone 又作"贼走关门"

【贼头贼脑】 zéitóu-zéinǎo behaving stealthily like a thief; stealthy; furtive

【贼心】 zéixīn wicked heart; evil designs; evil intentions: ~不死 refuse to give up one's evil designs

【贼赃】 zéizāng stolen goods; booty; spoils

鲗 zéi cuttlefish

zěn

怎* zěn 〈方〉why; how: 你~不早说呀? Why didn't you say so earlier?

【怎的】 zěndi 〈方〉what; why; how: 他就是不去,我能~? He just won't go. What can I do about it? 又作"怎地"

【怎么】 zěnme ①〔询问性质、状况、方式、原因等〕: 这是~回事? What's all this about?/ ~办? What's to be done?/ 你~啦? What's the matter with you? 或 Why, is anything the matter?/ 你~没去看电影? Why didn't you go to the film?/ 我~没听说过这事儿? How come I never heard of it?/ 你~搞的? See what you've done!/ 这个词~拼? How do you spell the word? ②〔泛指性质、状况或方式〕: 该~办就~办/你想~做就~做。 I'll do as you say./ ~强调也不过分 cannot be emphasized too strongly; cannot be overemphasized ③〔用于否定式,表示程度不够〕: 这地方我不~熟悉。 I don't know much about the place./ 这首歌我还没~学会。 I haven't quite learnt the song yet.

【怎么得了】 zěnme déliǎo where will it all end; what a terrible thing it would be; this is one hell of a mess

【怎么样】 zěnmeyàng ①〔询问性质、状况、方式等〕: 骑车去~? What (或 How) about going by bike?/ 后来这孩子~了? What became of the child?/ 演出的情况~? How was the performance? ②〔委婉说法,用于否定式〕: 这把扳子不~。 This spanner isn't up to much./ 她唱歌不~。 She's not much of a singer./ 他一时不小心,我们也不好把他~。 We couldn't be too hard on him, he was just being careless.

【怎么着】 zěnmezhe ①〔询问动作或情况〕: 看完戏我就回家,你打算~? I'm going straight home after the play. What about you?/ 下午干什么? 是小组讨论还是~? What's on this afternoon, group discussion or what? ②〔泛指动作或情况〕: ~也得把试验进行下去。 The experiment must be carried on whatever happens.

【怎样】 zěnyàng ①〔询问性质、状况、方式等〕: 这件事你~解释? How do you explain it?/ 步兵和炮兵~配合作战? How do the infantry and the artillery coordinate with each other? ②〔泛指性质、状况或方式〕: 想想从前~,再看看现在~ think of the past and look at the present

zèn

谮 zèn 〈书〉falsely charge; slander; calumniate: ~言 slander; calumny

zēng

曾 zēng relationship between great-grandchildren and great-grandparents 另见 céng

【曾孙】 zēngsūn great-grandson

【曾孙女】 zēngsūnnǚ great-granddaughter

【曾祖】 zēngzǔ (paternal) great-grandfather

【曾祖母】 zēngzǔmǔ (paternal) great-grandmother

憎 zēng hate; detest; abhor: 爱~分明 be clear about what to love and what to hate/ 面目可~ repulsive in appearance

【憎恨】 zēnghèn hate; detest

【憎恶】 zēngwù abhor; loathe; abominate

增* zēng increase; gain; add: 产量猛~。 Output increased sharply./ 与日俱~ grow with each passing day; be on the increase/ ~高温室的温度 raise the temperature of a hothouse/ ~拨资金 allocate more funds/ ~兵 throw in more troops; augment one's forces; reinforce

【增补】 zēngbǔ augment; supplement: 人员略有~。 The staff has been slightly augmented./ 该书内容有所~。 The book has been supplemented with new material. ◇ ~本 enlarged edition

【增产】 zēngchǎn increase production: ~节约 increase production and practise economy/ ~不增人 increase production without increasing the work force

【增订】 zēngdìng revise and enlarge (a book) ◇ ~本 revised and enlarged edition

【增多】 zēngduō grow in number or quantity; increase

【增光】 zēngguāng add lustre to; do credit to; add to the prestige of: 为国~ do credit to one's country

【增加】 zēngjiā increase; raise; add: ~积累 increase accumulation/ ~收入 increase income/ ~工资 get a raise in pay/ ~困难 add to the difficulties; multiply the difficulties/ ~复种面积 extend the area of double or triple cropping; enlarge the multiple-cropping area/ ~体重 put on weight/ ~抵抗力 build up one's resistance to disease/ 产量比去年~一倍。 Output is double that of last year./ 报名人数由三千~到五千。 The number of applicants has gone up from 3,000 to 5,000.

【增进】 zēngjìn enhance; promote; further: ~各国人民的相互了解和友谊 promote (或 further) mutual understanding and friendship between the peoples of all countries/ ~健康 improve one's health/ ~食欲 whet one's appetite

【增刊】 zēngkān supplement (to a newspaper or periodical); supplementary issue

【增强】 zēngqiáng strengthen; heighten; enhance: ~战斗力 strengthen fighting capacity; increase combat effectiveness/ ~信心 heighten one's confidence/ ~斗志 raise (或 heighten, boost) one's morale

【增删】 zēng-shān additions and deletions

【增添】 zēngtiān add; increase: ~设备 get additional equipment/ ~力量和信心 gain strength and confidence/ 新出土的文物为研究古代史~了资料。The new archaeological finds provide fresh material for the study of ancient history.

【增援】 zēngyuán 〈军〉 reinforce ◇ ~部队 reinforcements; reinforcing units

【增长】 zēngzhǎng increase; rise; grow: 平均~百分之四十 register an average increase of 40%/ 有计划地控制人口的 ~ control population growth in a planned way/ ~才干 enhance (或 develop) one's abilities/ ~知识 broaden (或 enrich) one's knowledge

【增值】 zēngzhí 〈经〉 rise (或 increase) in value; appreciation; increment

zèng

赠* zèng give as a present; present as a gift: ~书 present sb. with a book/ 某某敬~ with the compliments of so-and-so

【赠答】 zèngdá present each other with gifts, poems, etc.

【赠品】 zèngpǐn (complimentary) gift; giveaway

【赠送】 zèngsòng give as a present; present as a gift: 向演员~花篮 present a basket of flowers to the performers ◇ ~仪式 presentation ceremony

【赠言】 zèngyán words of advice or encouragement given to a friend at parting: 临别~ parting words of advice or encouragement

【赠阅】 zèngyuè (of a book, periodical, etc.) given free by the publisher ◇ ~本 complimentary copy

zhā

扎* zhā prick; run or stick (a needle, etc.) into: 手指上~了一根刺 prick one's finger on a thorn; have a splinter in one's finger/ ~一刀 stab with a knife
另见 zā; zhá

【扎实】 zhāshi ①sturdy; strong ②solid; sound; down-to-earth: 工作很~ do a solid job

【扎手】 zhāshǒu ①prick the hand: 树上有刺,留神。The tree is thorny. Mind you don't prick your hands. ②difficult to handle; thorny: 这事真~。This is really a hard nut to crack.

【扎眼】 zhāyǎn ①dazzling; offending to the eye; loud; garish: 这块布的颜色太~。This cloth is too dazzling./ 她穿得很~。She's loudly dressed. ②offensively conspicuous

渣 zhā ①dregs; sediment; residue: 豆腐~ soya-bean residue (after making bean curd)/ 蔗~ bagasse/ 猪油~儿 cracklings/ 炉~ slag; cinder ②broken bits: 面包~儿 (bread) crumbs

【渣滓】 zhāzǐ dregs; sediment; residue: 溶液的~ dregs of a solution/ 社会~ dregs of society

喳 zhā 〈象〉喜鹊的~~声 the chatter of magpies
另见 chā

揸 zhā 〈方〉①pick up sth. with the fingers ②spread one's fingers

zhá

扎* zhá pitch (a tent, etc.)
另见 zā; zhā

【扎营】 zháyíng pitch a tent or camp; encamp

札 zhá ①thin pieces of wood used for writing on in ancient China ②〈书〉 letter: 适奉大~。I have just received your esteemed letter.

【札记】 zhájì reading notes

轧 zhá roll (steel)
另见 yà

闸 zhá ①floodgate; sluice gate ②dam up water ③brake: 气~ air (或 pneumatic) brake/ 踩~ step on the brake/ 捏~ apply the hand brake/ 紧急~ emergency brake/ 制动~ damper brake ④〈口〉switch: 扳~ operate a switch; switch on or off

【闸门】 zhámén ①(水闸) sluice gate; gate; (船闸) lock gate ②〈机〉 throttle valve

炸* zhá fry in deep fat or oil; deep-fry: ~豆腐 deep-fried bean curd/ ~糕 fried cake
另见 zhà

铡 zhá ①hand hay cutter; fodder chopper ②cut up with a hay cutter: ~猪草 chop fodder for pigs

【铡草机】 zhácǎojī hay cutter; chaffcutter

【铡刀】 zhádāo hand hay (或 straw) cutter; fodder chopper

zhǎ

眨 zhǎ blink; wink: 眼睛一~ blink (one's eyes)/ 他向我~了~眼。He winked at me.

【眨巴】 zhǎba 〈方〉blink: 这孩子的眼睛直~,想是困了。The child is blinking his eyes. He must be sleepy.

【眨眼】 zhǎyǎn very short time; wink; twinkle: 一~的工夫 in the twinkling of an eye

zhà

乍 zhà ①first; for the first time: ~一听 at first hearing/ ~看起来 at first glance/ 新来~到 be a newcomer; be a new arrival ②suddenly; abruptly: ~暖还寒。After suddenly getting warmer, the weather has turned cold again. 天气~冷~热。The temperature changes abruptly. ③spread; extend: ~翅 spread wings

诈 zhà ①cheat; swindle: 尔虞我~ each trying to cheat or outwit the other/ ~人钱财 swindle people out of their money; get money by fraud ②pretend; feign: ~死 feign (或 fake) death; play dead/ ~败 feign defeat ③bluff sb. into giving information: 他是拿话~我。He was trying to draw me out.

【诈骗】 zhàpiàn defraud; swindle ◇ ~犯 swindler

【诈降】 zhàxiáng pretend to surrender; feign surrender

【诈语】 zhàyǔ lie; falsehood; fabrication

咋 zhà 〈书〉 bite

【咋舌】 zhàshé be left speechless or breathless (with wonder or fear): 杂技演员的惊险动作使观众为之~。The acrobat's feat took the audience's breath away.

咤 zhà 见"叱咤风云" chìzhà fēngyún

炸* zhà ①explode; burst: 暖瓶~了。The thermos flask has burst. ②blow up; blast; bomb: ~桥 blow up a bridge/ ~毁 blow up; blast to pieces; demolish/ 把障碍物~掉 blast away the barriers/ ~平 bomb flat/ ~沉 bomb and sink ③〈口〉fly into a rage; flare up: 肺都气~了 flare up; explode with rage
另见 zhá

【炸弹】 zhàdàn bomb: 爆破~ demolition bomb/ 定时~ time bomb

【炸药】 zhàyào explosive (charges); dynamite: 烈性~ high explosive

栅 zhà railings; paling; bars: 木～ paling; palisade/ 铁～ iron railings; metal rails; iron bars/ 炉～ grate
【栅栏】 zhàlan railings; paling; bars

蚱 zhà
【蚱蜢】 zhàměng grasshopper

榨 zhà ① press; extract: ～甘蔗 press sugar cane/ ～油 extract oil/ ～干血汗 wring every ounce of sweat and blood out of sb. ② a press for extracting juice, oil, etc.
【榨取】 zhàqǔ squeeze; extort
【榨油机】 zhàyóujī oil press

zhāi

斋 zhāi ① 见"斋戒" ② vegetarian diet adopted for religious reasons: 吃～ practise abstinence from meat (as a religious exercise); be a vegetarian for religious reasons ③ give alms (to a monk) ④ room or building: 书～ study
【斋戒】 zhāijiè abstain from meat, wine, etc. (when offering sacrifices to gods or ancestors); fast
【斋期】 zhāiqī fast days; fast
【斋月】 zhāiyuè 〈伊斯兰教〉 Ramadan; the month of fast

摘 zhāi ① pick; pluck; take off: ～棉花(苹果) pick cotton (apples)/ ～花 pluck flowers/ 把眼镜～下来 take off one's glasses/ ～帽子 take off one's hat or cap/ 把灯泡～下来 remove the bulb ② select; make extracts from: ～译 translation of selected passages ③ borrow money when in urgent need
【摘抄】 zhāichāo ① take passages; make extracts; extract; excerpt ② extracts; excerpts
【摘除】 zhāichú 〈医〉 excise: ～腹部肿瘤 excise an abdominal tumour
【摘记】 zhāijì ① take notes: 报告很长,我只～了要点。The report was rather long. I just jotted down the main points. ② extracts; excerpts
【摘录】 zhāilù ① take passages; make extracts; extract; excerpt ② extracts; excerpts: 文件～ extracts from a document
【摘要】 zhāiyào ① make a summary: ～发表 publish excerpts (或 extracts) of sth. ② summary; abstract; précis: 社论～ the summary of an editorial
【摘引】 zhāiyǐn quote

zhái

宅 zhái residence; house: 赵～ the Zhaos' residence
翟 Zhái a surname

zhǎi

窄 zhǎi ① narrow: ～道 narrow path ② petty; narrow: 心眼儿～ petty; oversensitive ③ hard up; badly off

zhài

债 zhài debt: 欠～ get (或 go) into debt; be in debt/ 还～ pay (或 repay, pay back) one's debt/ 借～ borrow money
【债户】 zhàihù debtor
【债款】 zhàikuǎn loan
【债权】 zhàiquán 〈法〉 creditor's rights ◇ ～国 creditor nation/ ～人 creditor
【债券】 zhàiquàn bond; debenture ◇ ～持有者 bondholder
【债台高筑】 zhàitái gāo zhù be heavily in debt; be up to one's ears in debt; be debt-ridden
【债务】 zhàiwù debt; liabilities ◇ ～国 debtor nation/ ～

人 debtor
【债主】 zhàizhǔ creditor

寨 zhài ① stockade ② stockaded village ③ camp: 营～ military camp/ 安营扎～ pitch a camp; encamp ④ mountain stronghold

zhān

占 zhān practise divination
另见 zhàn
【占卜】 zhānbǔ practise divination; divine
【占卦】 zhānguà divine by means of the Eight Diagrams (八卦)
【占课】 zhānkè divine by tossing coins
【占梦】 zhānmèng divine by interpreting dreams
【占星】 zhānxīng divine by astrology; cast a horoscope ◇ ～术 astrology

沾 zhān ① moisten; wet; soak: 泪～襟 tears wet the front of one's jacket ② be stained with: ～水 get wet ③ touch: 他跑得真快,脚不～地似的。He ran so fast that his feet seemed hardly to touch the ground./ 一～枕头就着 fall asleep as soon as one's head hits the pillow/ 烟酒不～ touch neither tobacco nor alcohol ④ get sth. out of association with sb. or sth.: ～点便宜 get a bargain
【沾光】 zhānguāng benefit from association with sb. or sth.: 我们工厂每周放电影,附近小孩儿都~。 Kids in the neighbourhood enjoy the chance of seeing our factory's weekly film.
【沾亲带故】 zhānqīn-dàigù have ties of kinship or friendship
【沾染】 zhānrǎn be infected with; be contaminated by; be tainted with: 伤口～了细菌。The wound was infected with germs.
【沾手】 zhānshǒu ① touch with one's hand: 雪花一～就化。Snowflakes melt as they fall on one's hand. ② have a hand in: 看来这事他沾了手。It seems that he has a hand in the matter./ 这活儿她一～就会了。She got the hang of the job the moment she started it.
【沾沾自喜】 zhānzhān zì xǐ feel complacent; be pleased with oneself: 不要～于一得之功。Don't be complacent over occasional success.

毡 zhān felt: ～帽 felt hat
【毡子】 zhānzi felt; felt rug; felt blanket

粘 zhān glue; stick; paste: 把两块木片～在一起 glue the two chips of wood together/ 把信封～上 seal (up) an envelope/ 这糖不～牙。This candy doesn't stick to your teeth.
另见 nián
【粘贴】 zhāntiē paste; stick: 在墙上～标语 paste slogans on the wall

詹 Zhān a surname

谵 zhān rave; be delirious
【谵语】 zhānyǔ 〈书〉 delirious speech; wild talk; ravings

瞻 zhān look up or forward
【瞻顾】 zhāngù 〈书〉 look ahead and behind
【瞻念】 zhānniàn look to; think of: ～前途 think of the future
【瞻前顾后】 zhānqián-gùhòu look ahead and behind — be overcautious and indecisive
【瞻望】 zhānwàng look forward; look far ahead: ～未来 look to the future
【瞻仰】 zhānyǎng look at with reverence

zhǎn

斩 zhǎn ① chop; cut: ～断侵略者的魔爪 chop off the

claws of the invaders/ 快刀～乱麻 cut the Gordian knot ②
behead; decapitate: ～尽杀绝 kill all; wipe out the whole lot
【斩草除根】 zhǎncǎo-chúgēn cut the weeds and dig up the
roots — destroy root and branch; stamp out the source
of trouble
【斩钉截铁】 zhǎndīng-jiétiě resolute and decisive; categorical: ～地拒绝 give a categorical rebuff/ 他说得～。He
spoke with curt finality.
【斩首】 zhǎnshǒu behead: decapitate

展 * zhǎn ① open up; spread out; unfold; unfurl: ～卷
opea a book/ 风～旗子。 The flags are fluttering in the
wind./ 舒眉～眼 beam with joy ② put to good use; give
free play to: ～技 give full play to one's skill/ 立大志,～
宏图 cherish high aspirations and carry out a great plan
③ postpone; extend; prolong: ～限 extend a time limit
④ exhibition: 画～ painting exhibition/ 预～ preview
【展翅】 zhǎnchì spread the wings; get ready for flight: ～
高飞 soar to great heights
【展出】 zhǎnchū put on display; be on show (或 view); exhibit: 展览会上～了各种各样的机床。A good variety of
machine tools are on display at the exhibition.
【展缓】 zhǎnhuǎn postpone; extend; prolong: 行期一再～。
The date for departure was postponed again and again./
限期不得～。The time limit is not to be extended.
【展开】 zhǎnkāi ① spread out; unfold; open up: 把地图～
unfold the map/ 把队伍～ deploy the forces ② launch;
unfold; develop; carry out: ～攻势 unfold an offensive/
～热烈的讨论 set off an animated discussion/ 运动会的各
项比赛已全面～。The sports meet is now in full swing.
【展览】 zhǎnlǎn put on display; exhibit; show: 工业～
industrial exhibition/ 菊花～ chrysanthemum show
◇ ～馆 exhibition centre (或 hall)/ ～会 exhibition/ ～品
exhibit; item on display/ ～室 exhibition room; showroom
【展品】 zhǎnpǐn exhibit; item on display: 请勿抚摸。
Please do not touch the exhibits.
【展期】 zhǎnqī ① extend a time limit; postpone: 会议～举
行。The meeting has been postponed./ 交易会～两天结束。
The fair will be extended for another two days. ② duration
of an exhibition; exhibition period
【展示】 zhǎnshì open up before one's eyes; reveal; show;
lay bare: ～人物的内心世界 reveal a character's inner world/
这场辩论～了问题的实质。The debate laid bare the essence
of the issue.
【展望】 zhǎnwàng ① look into the distance: 登上山顶向四
周～ climb to the top of the mountain and get a view of
the surrounding country ② look into the future; look
ahead: ～未来 look forward to the future/ ～前程,信心百
倍。Looking ahead, we are filled with boundless confidence.
③ forecast; prospect: 八十年代～ prospects for the 1980's;
1980's in prospect
【展现】 zhǎnxiàn unfold before one's eyes; emerge; develop: 到了工地,一派繁忙的景象～在我们眼前。As we
reached the construction site, a scene of bustling activity
presented itself before our eyes.

盏 zhǎn ① small cup: 酒～ small wine cup ②〈量〉〔用
于灯〕:一～电灯 an electric lamp

崭 zhǎn ①〈书〉towering (over) ②〈方〉fine; swell
【崭新】 zhǎnxīn brand-new; completely new: 穿一身～的制
服 wear a brand-new tunic suit/ ～的阶段 a completely
new stage/ 文艺界呈现出一派～的气象。An entirely new
atmosphere prevails in artistic and literary circles.

搌 zhǎn wipe or dab (with a soft dry object) to sop up
liquid: 纸上落了一滴墨水,快拿吸墨纸～一～吧。A drop of
ink has fallen on the paper; blot it up quickly.

辗 zhǎn
【辗转】 zhǎnzhuǎn ① pass through many hands or places:
～流传 spread from place to place; pass through many
places ② toss about (in bed): ～不能成眠 toss and turn (in
bed); unable to go to sleep

【辗转反侧】 zhǎnzhuǎn fǎncè toss about (in bed); toss and
turn restlessly

黵 zhǎn 〈方〉make dirty; dirty; soil: 深色布禁 (jīn)～。
Dark cloth doesn't show the dirt.

zhàn

占 * zhàn ① occupy; seize; take: 霸～ forcibly occupy;
seize/ 多吃多～ take more than one is entitled to; grab
more than one's share/ ～用不少时间 take up much
time ② constitute; hold; make up; account for: ～多(少)
数 constitute the majority (minority)/ ～统治地位 hold (或
occupy) a dominant position/ ～世界第一位 rank first in
the world/ ～总产值的百分之四十 make up (或 account for,
amount to) 40 per cent of the total output value/ 光明面
～优势,黑暗面～劣势。The bright side predominates over
the dark./ 海洋几乎～地球表面四分之三。The sea covers
nearly three-fourths of the earth's surface.
另见 zhān
【占据】 zhànjù occupy; hold: ～重要的战略地位 occupy a
position of strategic importance
【占领】 zhànlǐng capture; occupy; seize: ～要塞 capture a
fort ◇ ～军 occupation army/ ～区 occupied area
【占便宜】 zhàn piányi ① gain extra advantage by unfair
means; profit at other people's expense: 占小便宜 gain
petty advantages ② advantageous; favourable: 你个子高,
打篮球～。A tall fellow like you has an advantage in playing basketball.
【占先】 zhànxiān take precedence; take the lead; get ahead
of: 上个月劳动竞赛,第一组～了。The first team led all the
others in last month's emulation drive.
【占有】 zhànyǒu ① own; possess; have: ～生产资料 own
the means of production/ ～第一手资料 have firsthand
data ② occupy; hold: 商业在国民经济中～重要地位。Com-
merce occupies an important place in the national economy.
【占着茅坑不拉屎】 zhànzhe máokēng bù lāshǐ neither shit
nor get off the pot — hold on to a post without doing
any work and not let anyone else take over; be a dog in
the manger

战 * zhàn ① war; warfare; battle; fight: 持久～ protracted war/ 运动～ mobile warfare/ 夜～ night fighting ②
fight: ～而胜之 fight and defeat the enemy/ 为保卫祖国而
～ fight to defend one's motherland ③ shiver; tremble;
shudder: 冷得打～ shiver with cold
【战败】 zhànbài ① be defeated; be vanquished; suffer a defeat; lose (a battle or war) ② defeat; vanquish; beat
◇ ～国 vanquished (或 defeated) nation
【战报】 zhànbào war communiqué; battlefield report
【战备】 zhànbèi war preparedness; combat readiness: 加
强～ step up combat readiness
【战场】 zhànchǎng battlefield; battleground; battlefront: 开
辟新～ open another front
【战刀】 zhàndāo sabre
【战地】 zhàndì battlefield; battleground; combat zone
◇ ～记者 war correspondent/ ～指挥部 field headquarters
【战抖】 zhàndǒu tremble; shiver; shudder
【战斗】 zhàndòu ① fight; battle; combat; action: 英勇～ put
up a heroic fight/ 进行了数十次～ have fought scores of
battles/ 作好～准备 get ready for action; be combat ready/
投入～ go into battle/ 在～中牺牲 be killed in action/ 每
一次胜利都是经过激烈～赢得的。Each victory was won
through fierce struggle. ② militant; fighting: 满怀～
豪情 be filled with militant pride
◇ ～部队 combat forces/ ～部署 tactical disposition/
～队 fighting force/ ～队形 battle formation/ ～轰炸机
fighter-bomber/ ～机 lighter plane; fighter/ ～舰艇
combat vessels
【战斗力】 zhàndòulì combat effectiveness (或 strength, capability); fighting capacity: ～强(弱) high (low) combat
effectiveness/ 有～ combat-worthy

【战端】zhànduān　the beginning of a war: 重启～。War broke out again.

【战犯】zhànfàn　war criminal

【战费】zhànfèi　war expenses

【战俘】zhànfú　prisoner of war (P.O.W.)

【战功】zhàngōng　meritorious military service; outstanding military exploit; battle achievement: 立～ distinguish oneself in action/ 赫赫～ brilliant achievements in war

【战鼓】zhàngǔ　war drum; battle drum

【战果】zhànguǒ　results of battle; combat success; victory: 取得辉煌～ achieve splendid results on the battlefield/ 扩大～ exploit the victory (或 success)

【战壕】zhànháo　trench; entrenchment

【战后】zhànhòu　postwar: ～时期 postwar period

【战火】zhànhuǒ　flames of war: 在那～纷飞的岁月里 in those war-ridden years

【战祸】zhànhuò　disaster of war

【战绩】zhànjī　military successes (或 exploits, feats); combat gains

【战舰】zhànjiàn　warship

【战局】zhànjú　war situation

【战况】zhànkuàng　situation on the battlefield; progress of a battle

【战利品】zhànlìpǐn　spoils of war; captured equipment; war trophies (或 booty)

【战例】zhànlì　a specific example of a battle (in military science): 有名的～ a famous battle

【战栗】zhànlì　tremble; shiver; shudder: 吓得全身～ tremble all over with fear

【战乱】zhànluàn　chaos caused by war

【战略】zhànlüè　strategy: 全球～ global strategy ◇ ～部署 strategic plan (或 deployment, disposition)/ ～储备 strategic reserves (或 stockpiles)/ ～反攻 strategic counteroffensive/ ～核武器 strategic nuclear weapons/ ～家 strategist

【战马】zhànmǎ　battle steed; war-horse

【战前】zhànqián　prewar: ～时期 prewar period/ ～动员 mobilization before a battle

【战区】zhànqū　war zone; theatre of operations

【战胜】zhànshèng　defeat; triumph over; vanquish; overcome: ～敌人 defeat (或 vanquish) the enemy/ ～困难 overcome (或 surmount) difficulties/ ～自然灾害 conquer natural disasters

【战时】zhànshí　wartime ◇ ～内阁 wartime cabinet

【战士】zhànshì　① soldier; man ② champion; warrior; fighter: 国际主义～ champion of internationalism

【战事】zhànshì　war; hostilities: ～结束 conclusion of the war; termination of hostilities

【战书】zhànshū　written challenge to war; letter of challenge

【战术】zhànshù　(military) tactics

【战无不胜】zhàn wú bù shèng　invincible; ever-victorious; all-conquering

【战线】zhànxiàn　battle line; battlefront; front: ～太长 overextended battle line; far-flung battlefront/ 思想～ the ideological front/ 在各条～上 on every front of endeavour; on all fronts

【战役】zhànyì　campaign; battle

【战友】zhànyǒu　comrade-in-arms; battle companion: ～的情谊 comradeship-in-arms/ 亲密～ close comrades-in-arms

【战云】zhànyún　war cloud: ～密布 gathering war clouds

【战战兢兢】zhànzhànjīngjīng　① trembling with fear; with fear and trepidation: 敌军怕遭埋伏状,～地向前移动。Fearing an ambush, the enemy troops advanced with trepidation. ② with caution; gingerly

【战争】zhànzhēng　war; warfare: ～的双方 the two sides in a war; both belligerents

栈 zhàn　① warehouse: 货～ warehouse; storehouse ② inn: 客～ inn ③ shed; pen: 羊～ sheep pen ④ 见"栈道"

【栈道】zhàndào　a plank road built along the face of a cliff

【栈房】zhànfáng　① warehouse; storehouse ② 〈方〉inn

站* zhàn　① stand; be on one's feet; take a stand: ～起来 stand up; rise to one's feet/ 往后～～! Stand back!/ 别象椅子了,就～着看吧。Don't bother to get chairs. Let's just stand and watch./ 我都～了一天了。I've been on my feet all day./ ～得高,看得远 stand on a high plane and see far ahead; have vision; be farsighted ② stop; halt: 这车中途不～。This bus makes no stops along the way./ 不怕慢,只怕～。It's better to go slowly than just to mark time. ③ station; stop: 火车～ railway station/ 公共汽车～ bus stop/ 长途汽车～ bus station/ 终点～ terminal; terminus ④ station or centre for rendering certain services: 服务～ service station (或 centre)

【站岗】zhàngǎng　stand (或 mount) guard; be on sentry duty; stand sentry: 今天晚上我～。I'm on sentry duty tonight./ 站好最后一班岗 (of one who is about to leave his job) continue working hard till the last minute

【站稳】zhànwěn　① come to a stop: 等车～了再下。Don't get out until the car stops. ② stand firm; take a firm stand: ～脚跟 get a firm foothold; stand firm

【站住】zhànzhù　① stop; halt: 他听到有人叫他～。He heard someone calling to him to stop./ ～,要不就开枪了! Halt, or I fire!/ 谁？～! Who's that? Don't move! ② stand firmly on one's feet; keep one's feet: 风刮得人都站不住了。The wind was so strong that one could hardly keep one's feet. ③ stand (或 hold) one's ground; consolidate one's position ④ hold water; be tenable: 他的说法站不住。His opinion doesn't hold water.

【站住脚】zhànzhùjiǎo　① stop; halt: 他跑得太快,一下子站不住脚。He was running too fast to stop suddenly. ② stand (或 hold) one's ground; consolidate one's position: 我们向敌人猛烈攻击,打得他们站不住脚。We attacked the enemy so fiercely that they couldn't hold their ground. ③ stay put: 忙得站不住脚 be so busy one can't stand still ④ hold water; be tenable: 这些论点没有一个是站得住脚的。None of these arguments are tenable.

绽 zhàn　split; burst: 衣裳～线了。The seam has split (或 burst)./ 鞋开～了。The shoe has split open.

湛 zhàn　① profound; deep: 精～ consummate; exquisite ② crystal clear

颤 zhàn　tremble; shiver; shudder: 她打了一个寒～。A cold shiver ran down her spine.
另见 chàn

【颤栗】zhànlì　tremble; shiver; shudder

蘸 zhàn　dip in (ink, sauce, etc.): ～墨水 dip in ink/ 大葱～酱 scallions dipped in thick sauce

zhāng

张* zhāng　① open; spread; stretch: ～开手 open one's hand/ ～翅膀 spread the wings/ ～网 spread a net/ ～开双臂 stretch out both arms/ ～弓 draw a bow/ ～帆 make sail; hoist sail ② set out; display: 大～筵席 lay on a feast ③ magnify; exaggerate: 夸～ exaggerate; overstate ④ look: 东～西望 gaze (或 peer) around ⑤ opening of a new shop: 开～ open a business; begin doing business ⑥ 〈量〉一～桌子 a table/ 两～床 two beds/ 一～纸 a piece (或 sheet) of paper/ 一～弓 a bow/ 你这～嘴啊! What a tongue you've got!

【张大】zhāngdà　magnify; exaggerate; publicize widely: ～其词 exaggerate/ ～其事 publicize the matter widely

【张灯结彩】zhāngdēng-jiécǎi　be decorated with lanterns and coloured streamers

【张挂】zhāngguà　hang up (a picture, curtain, etc.)

【张冠李戴】Zhāng guān Lǐ dài　put Zhang's hat on Li's head — attribute sth. to the wrong person or confuse one thing with another

【张皇】zhānghuáng　〈书〉① alarmed; scared; flurried; flustered: ～失措 be in a flurry of alarm; lose one's head; get into a panic ② magnify; exaggerate

【张家长，李家短】 Zhāng jiā cháng, Lǐ jiā duǎn the virtues of the Zhangs and the defects of the Lǐs — gossip

【张口结舌】 zhāngkǒu-jiéshé be agape and tongue-tied; be at a loss for words: 他被问得～，半天说不出话来。He was stumped by the questions and remained tongue-tied for a good while.

【张狂】 zhāngkuáng flippant and impudent; insolent

【张三李四】 Zhāng Sān Lǐ Sì Zhang, Li or anybody; any Tom, Dick or Harry

【张贴】 zhāngtiē put up (a notice, poster, etc.): ～海报 put up posters/ ～通告 post a notice/ 禁止～。Post no bills.

【张望】 zhāngwàng ① peep (through a crack, etc.) ② look around: 探头～ crane one's neck and look around .

【张牙舞爪】 zhāngyá-wǔzhǎo bare fangs and brandish claws — make threatening gestures; engage in sabre rattling

【张扬】 zhāngyáng make widely known; make public; publicize: 四处～ publicize everywhere; spread (a story) all over the place/ 这事还没定下来，先别～出去。The final decision hasn't been made yet, so don't spread this around.

【张嘴】 zhāngzuǐ ① open one's mouth (to say sth.): 他正要～，一个年轻妇女抢先说了。He was on the point of saying something when a young woman started to speak. ② ask for a loan or a favour: 我想找他帮忙，又不好意思～。I would have liked him to give me a hand, but found it embarrassing to ask.

章 zhāng ① chapter; section: 全书共二十～。The book has twenty chapters./ 乐～ movement (of a symphony, etc.) ② order: 杂乱无～ disorderly and unsystematic ③ rules; regulations; constitution: 规～ rules and regulations ④ seal; stamp: 盖～ affix one's seal; seal; stamp ⑤ badge; medal: 领～ collar badge (或 insignia)/ 奖～ medal; decoration

【章程】 zhāngchéng rules; regulations; constitution

【章法】 zhāngfǎ ① presentation of ideas in a piece of writing; art of composition: 文章结构严谨,很有～。The article is well organized and the ideas are skilfully presented. ② orderly ways; methodicalness: 他办事很有～。He is quite methodical in his work./ 碰到这样意外的事,他乱了～。He was thrown off balance by such an unexpected turn of events.

【章回小说】 zhānghuí xiǎoshuō a type of traditional Chinese novel with each chapter headed by a couplet giving the gist of its content

【章节】 zhāngjié chapters and sections

【章句】 zhāngjù ① chapters, sections, sentences and phrases in ancient writings ② syntactic and semantic analysis of ancient writings

【章鱼】 zhāngyú octopus

【章则】 zhāngzé rules and regulations

彰 zhāng clear; evident; conspicuous: ～～若是 as clear (或 obvious) as that/ ～～在人耳目 be clear for all to see

【彰明较著】 zhāngmíng jiào zhù very obvious; easily seen

獐 zhāng river deer

【獐头鼠目】 zhāngtóu-shǔmù with the head of a buck and the eyes of a rat — repulsively ugly and sly-looking

璋 zhāng a jade tablet

樟 zhāng camphor tree

【樟木】 zhāngmù camphorwood

【樟脑】 zhāngnǎo camphor ◇ ～丸 camphor ball; mothball/ ～油 camphor oil

【樟树】 zhāngshù camphor tree

蟑 zhāng

【蟑螂】 zhānglá ng cockroach; roach

zhǎng

长 zhǎng ① older; elder; senior: 比他年～ older than him/ 他比我～一辈。He belongs to my father's generation. ② eldest; oldest: ～兄 eldest brother/ ～女 eldest daughter ③ chief; head: 科～ section chief/ 代表团～ head of a delegation ④ grow; develop: 青年时期是～身体的时期。Youth is the time of physical growth./ 庄稼～得很旺。The crops are growing very well./ 这孩子光～个儿,不～肉。The child keeps growing taller but doesn't fill out. ⑤ come into being; begin to grow; form: ～疮 have a boil/ ～癌 get cancer/ ～锈 get rusty/ 孩子～牙了。The baby is teething./ ～叶子了。The leaves are coming out./ 桃树～虫了。The peach tree is wormy. ⑥ acquire; enhance; increase: ～见识 increase one's knowledge; gain experience/ ～自己的志气,灭敌人的威风 boost our morale and dampen the enemy's spirit
另见 cháng

【长辈】 zhǎngbèi elder member of a family; elder; senior

【长大】 zhǎngdà grow up; be brought up

【长官】 zhǎngguān 〈旧〉 senior officer or official; commanding officer

【长进】 zhǎngjìn progress: 在学习上很有～ make good progress in one's studies

【长老】 zhǎnglǎo ① elder ② elder of a Buddhist monastery

【长孙】 zhǎngsūn ① son's eldest son; eldest grandson ② (Zhǎngsūn) a surname

【长相】 zhǎngxiàng 〈口〉 looks; features; appearance: ～好 be good-looking/ 看她们的～好象是姐儿俩。They look like sisters.

【长者】 zhǎngzhě ① elder; senior ② venerable elder

【长子】 zhǎngzǐ eldest son

涨 zhǎng (of water, prices, etc.) rise; go up: 河水暴～。The river suddenly rose. 或 The river was in spate.
另见 zhàng

【涨潮】 zhǎngcháo rising tide; flood tide: 正在～。The tide is at the flood.

【涨风】 zhǎngfēng upward trend of prices

【涨价】 zhǎngjià rise in price

【涨落】 zhǎng-luò (of water, prices, etc.) rise and fall; fluctuate: 潮水的～ ebb and flow of the tide/ 价格的～ fluctuations of prices

掌 zhǎng ① palm: 击～为号 signal by clapping hands ② strike with the palm of the hand; slap: ～嘴 slap sb. on the face ③ hold in one's hand; be in charge of; control; wield: ～兵权 wield military power; have command of the armed forces ④ the bottom of certain animals' feet; pad; sole: 脚～ sole (of a human foot)/ 鸭～ duck's foot/ 熊～ bear's paw ⑤ shoe sole or heel: 鞋子打前后～ have a shoe soled and heeled

【掌灯】 zhǎngdēng ① hold a lamp in one's hand ② light an oil lamp

【掌舵】 zhǎngduò be at the helm; operate the rudder; take the tiller; steer a boat ◇ ～人 helmsman; steersman

【掌故】 zhǎnggù anecdotes: 文坛～ literary anecdotes/ 他熟悉这座城市的～。He knows a lot of historical anecdotes about this city.

【掌管】 zhǎngguǎn be in charge of; administer: ～财政 administer finances/ ～一个部门 be in charge of a department/ 各项事务都有专人～。Everything is taken care of by specially assigned people.

【掌柜】 zhǎngguì shopkeeper; manager (of a shop)

【掌权】 zhǎngquán be in power; wield power; exercise control

【掌上明珠】 zhǎngshàng míngzhū a pearl in the palm — a beloved daughter

【掌声】 zhǎngshēng clapping; applause: 经久不息的～ prolonged applause/ 全场～雷动。The audience burst into thunderous applause.

【掌握】 zhǎngwò ① grasp; master; know well ② have in hand; take into one's hands; control: ～办公室的钥匙 keep the key to the office/ ～局势 have the situation well in hand; have the situation under control/ ～主动权 have the initiative in one's hands/ ～自己的命运 take one's destiny into one's own hands; be master of one's own destiny/ ～国家的经济命脉 control the economic lifelines of the country

【掌心】 zhǎngxīn the centre (或 hollow) of the palm: 孙悟空跳不出如来佛的～。The Monkey King cannot jump out of Buddha's palm. — be unable to escape.

【掌印】 zhǎngyìn keep the seal — be in power

zhàng

丈 zhàng ① *zhang*, a unit of length ($=3^1/_3$ metres) ② measure (land): 清～ make an exact measurement of the land ③ a form of address for certain male relatives by marriage: 岳～ wife's father; father-in-law/ 姐～ elder sister's husband; brother-in-law/ 姑～ the husband of one's father's sister; uncle

【丈夫】 zhàngfū man: ～气概 manliness
【丈夫】 zhàngfu husband
【丈母娘】 zhàngmuniang wife's mother; mother-in-law 又作 "丈母"
【丈人】 zhàngren wife's father; father-in-law

仗 zhàng ① 〈书〉 weaponry; weapons: 仪～ flags, weapons, etc. carried by a guard of honour/ 明火执～ carry torches and weapons in a robbery — conduct evil activities openly ② hold (a weapon): ～剑 hold a sword ③ rely on; depend on: 这事我一人干不了,全～大家帮忙。I can't manage it on my own. I must rely on all of you for help. ④ battle; war: 打～ go to war; be at war/ 硬～ hard-fought battle; tough fight/ 打了一个漂亮～ won a brilliant victory

【仗势欺人】 zhàng shì qī rén take advantage of one's or sb. else's power to bully people; bully others on the strength of one's powerful connections or position
【仗恃】 zhàngshì rely on (an advantage)
【仗义疏财】 zhàng yì shū cái be generous in aiding needy people
【仗义执言】 zhàng yì zhí yán speak out from a sense of justice

杖 zhàng ① cane; stick: 扶～而行 walk with a cane/ 手～ (walking) stick ② rod or staff used for a specific purpose ③ flogging with a stick (a punishment in ancient China)

帐 zhàng ① curtain; canopy: 营～ tent/ 蚊～ mosquito net ② account: 记～ keep accounts/ 结～ settle (或 square) accounts ③ account book ④ debt; credit: 还～ repay a debt/ 赊～ buy or sell on credit

【帐簿】 zhàngbù account book 又作"帐本"
【帐单】 zhàngdān bill; check
【帐房】 zhàngfáng 〈旧〉① accountant's office ② accountant
【帐户】 zhànghù account
【帐款】 zhàngkuǎn funds on account; credit
【帐目】 zhàngmù items of an account; accounts: 清理～ square accounts/ 定期公布～ publish the accounts regularly/ ～公开 accounts open to public inspection/ ～不清。The accounts (或 books) are not in order.
【帐幕】 zhàngmù tent
【帐篷】 zhàngpeng tent: 搭(拆)～ pitch (strike) a tent
【帐子】 zhàngzi ① bed-curtain ② mosquito net

胀 zhàng ① expand; distend: 热～冷缩 expand when heated and contract when cooled ② swell; be bloated: 肿～ swollen/ 吃多了,感到肚子有点发～ feel bloated after overeating

涨 zhàng ① swell after absorbing water, etc.: 豆子泡～了。The beans swelled up after being soaked. ② (of the head) be swelled by a rush of blood: 气得～红了脸 redden (或 flush) with anger/ 头昏脑～ feel one's head swimming
另见 zhǎng

障 zhàng ① hinder; obstruct ② barrier; block: 路～ roadblock; barricade

【障碍】 zhàng'ài ① hinder; obstruct ② obstacle; obstruction; barrier; impediment: 扫清～ clear away obstacles/ 制造～ erect barriers; create obstacles
◇ ～赛跑 steeplechase; obstacle race/ ～物 obstacle; barrier; entanglement
【障蔽】 zhàngbì block; obstruct; shut out: ～视线 obstruct one's view
【障眼法】 zhàngyǎnfǎ cover-up; camouflage: 玩弄～ throw dust into people's eyes
【障子】 zhàngzi a barrier made of reeds, sorghum stalks or closely planted shrubs; hedge

幛 zhàng a large, oblong sheet of silk with an appropriate message attached, presented at a wedding, birthday or funeral

嶂 zhàng a screen-like mountain peak: 层峦叠～ peaks rising one higher than another

瘴 zhàng miasma
【瘴疠】 zhànglì communicable subtropical diseases, such as pernicious malaria, etc.
【瘴气】 zhàngqì miasma

zhāo

钊 zhāo 〈书〉 encourage; spur; exhort

招 zhāo ① beckon: 他把手一～,要我跟上。He beckoned me to follow. ② recruit; enlist; enrol: ～工 recruit workers ③ attract; incur; court: ～苍蝇 attract flies/ ～灾 court disaster; invite calamity/ ～人嫌 incur odium/ ～人喜欢的孩子 a charming (或 lovable) child ④ provoke; tease: 别～这孩子。Don't tease the child. ⑤ confess; own up: 不打自～ confess without being pressed ⑥ 〈方〉 infect; be contagious: 这病～人。This disease is catching. ⑦ trick; device; move: 你这一～可真高。That was really a brilliant stroke (或 move, idea) of yours.

【招安】 zhāo'ān (of feudal rulers) offer amnesty and enlistment to rebels: 受～ (of former rebels) accept amnesty and serve the ruler
【招标】 zhāobiāo invite tenders (或 bids, public bidding)
【招兵】 zhāobīng recruit soldiers; raise troops
【招兵买马】 zhāobīng-mǎimǎ recruit men and buy horses — raise or enlarge an army; recruit followers
【招待】 zhāodài receive (guests); entertain; serve (customers): 设宴～外宾 give a dinner for (或 in honour of) foreign guests/ ～客人 entertain guests/ 谢谢你们的热情～。Thank you for your kind hospitality.
【招待会】 zhāodàihuì reception: 冷餐～ buffet reception/ 记者～ press conference/ 举行～ give (或 hold) a reception
【招风】 zhāofēng catch the wind — attract too much attention and invite trouble
【招供】 zhāogòng make a confession of one's crime; confess
【招股】 zhāogǔ raise capital by floating shares
【招呼】 zhāohu ① call: 那边有人～你。Someone over there is calling you. ② hail; greet; say hello to: 热情地打～

greet warmly ③ notify; tell: ~他赶快来开会。 Tell him to come to the meeting at once./ 你要是不去,事先打个~。 Let me know beforehand if you won't be going. ④ take care of: ~老人 take care of old people

【招魂】 zhāohún call back the spirit of the dead

【招架】 zhāojià ward off blows; hold one's own: ~不住 unable to hold one's own; unable to withstand/ 只有~之功,没有还手之力 can only parry sb.'s blows without being able to hit back

【招考】 zhāokǎo give public notice of entrance examination; admit (students, applicants, etc.) by examination

【招徕】 zhāolái solicit (customers or business); canvass: ~顾客 solicit customers/ 以广~ so as to have more customers

【招揽】 zhāolǎn solicit (customers or business); canvass: ~主顾 solicit customers/ ~生意 canvass business orders; drum up trade

【招领】 zhāolǐng announce the finding of lost property: 失物~(布告标题) Found/ 拾物~处 Lost and Found

【招募】 zhāomù recruit; enlist

【招女婿】 zhāo nǚxu have the groom move into one's house after the marriage

【招牌】 zhāopai shop sign; signboard: 据说这~是一位名书法家写的。 This signboard is said to have been written by a famous calligrapher.

【招聘】 zhāopìn give public notice of a vacancy to be filled; invite applications for a job: ~技术工人 advertise for skilled workers

【招亲】 zhāoqīn ① 见"招女婿" ② marry into and live with one's bride's family

【招惹】 zhāore ① provoke; incur; court: ~是非 bring trouble on oneself ② ⟨方⟩[多用于否定式] tease; provoke: 这人~不得。 You'd better not provoke that fellow.

【招认】 zhāorèn confess one's crime; plead guilty

【招生】 zhāoshēng enrol new students; recruit students

【招收】 zhāoshōu recruit; take in: ~工人 recruit workers/ ~大学生 enrol new students in universities and colleges

【招手】 zhāoshǒu beckon; wave: 他~要我进去。 He beckoned me in./ ~致意 wave one's greetings; wave back in acknowledgement

【招贴】 zhāotiē poster; placard; bill

【招降】 zhāoxiáng summon sb. to surrender

【招摇】 zhāoyáo act ostentatiously

【招摇过市】 zhāoyáo guò shì swagger through the streets — blatantly seek publicity

【招摇撞骗】 zhāoyáo-zhuàngpiàn swindle and bluff

【招引】 zhāoyǐn attract; induce: 灯光~蛾子。 Lights attract moths.

【招灾惹祸】 zhāozāi-rěhuò court disaster; invite trouble: 这孩子老给大人~。 This child is always making trouble for his parents.

【招展】 zhāozhǎn flutter; wave

【招致】 zhāozhì ① recruit (followers); scout about for (talents, etc.) ② incur; bring about; lead to: ~意外的损失 incur unexpected losses/ ~失败 cause defeat/ ~无穷后患 lead to endless trouble

昭
zhāo clear; obvious

【昭然若揭】 zhāorán ruò jiē abundantly clear; all too clear

【昭示】 zhāoshì make clear to all; declare publicly: ~全国 declare to the whole nation

【昭雪】 zhāoxuě exonerate; rehabilitate: 冤案得到了~。 The wrong has been righted. 或 The person wronged has been rehabilitated.

【昭彰】 zhāozhāng clear; manifest; evident: 罪恶~ have committed flagrant crimes

【昭著】 zhāozhù clear; evident; obvious: 成绩~ have achieved signal successes

着
zhāo ① a move in chess: 高~儿 a clever move/ 走错一~ make a false move; take a wrong step ② trick; device; move: 这一~厉害。 That's a shrewd move./ 他没~儿了。 He's at the end of his tether.
另见 zháo; zhe; zhuó

朝
zhāo ① early morning; morning: ~阳 morning sun ② day: 一~有事 should anything happen some day/ 今~ today; the present
另见 cháo

【朝不保夕】 zhāo bù bǎo xī not know in the morning what may happen in the evening; be in a precarious state

【朝不谋夕】 zhāo bù móu xī be unable to plan out one's day; be preoccupied with the current crisis 又作"朝不虑夕"

【朝发夕至】 zhāo fā xī zhì start at dawn and arrive at dusk — a short journey

【朝晖】 zhāohuī morning sunlight

【朝令夕改】 zhāo lìng xī gǎi issue an order in the morning and rescind it in the evening; make unpredictable changes in policy

【朝露】 zhāolù ⟨书⟩ morning dew — ephemeral; transitory

【朝气】 zhāoqì youthful spirit; vigour; vitality: 有~ be full of vigour

【朝气蓬勃】 zhāoqì péngbó full of youthful spirit; full of vigour and vitality; imbued with vitality: ~的青年 spirited young people

【朝秦暮楚】 zhāo Qín mù Chǔ serve the State of Qin in the morning and the State of Chu in the evening — quick to switch sides; fickle; inconstant

【朝三暮四】 zhāosān-mùsì blow hot and cold; play fast and loose; chop and change

【朝思暮想】 zhāosī-mùxiǎng yearn day and night

【朝夕】 zhāoxī ① morning and evening; from morning to night; day and night; daily: ~相处 be together from morning to night; be closely associated ② any short time: 只争~ seize the day, seize the hour; seize every minute

【朝霞】 zhāoxiá rosy clouds of dawn; rosy dawn

【朝阳】 zhāoyáng the rising sun; the morning sun

zháo

着
zháo ① touch: 上不~天,下不~地 touch neither the sky nor the ground; be suspended in midair/ 说话不~边际 not speak to the point ② feel; be affected by (cold, etc.): ~风 become unwell through being in a draught ③ burn: 炉子~得很旺。 The fire is burning briskly in the stove./ 灯都~了。 The lights are all on. ④〔用在动词后,表示已经达到目的或有了结果〕: 猜~了 have guessed right/ 打~了 have hit the mark/ 你见~他了吗? Did you get to see him? ⑤ ⟨方⟩ fall asleep: 他躺下就~了。 He fell asleep as soon as he lay down.
另见 zhāo; zhe; zhuó

【着慌】 zháohuāng get alarmed; become flustered (或 jittery); be thrown into a panic: 这下子他可~了。 At that point he panicked.

【着火】 zháohuǒ catch fire; be on fire: ~啦! Fire!

【着急】 zháojí worry; feel anxious: 别~,安心养病。 Just take care of yourself and don't worry./ 着什么急。 There's nothing to worry about./ 等得~了 become impatient with waiting/ 冷静点,别~。 Keep calm. Don't get excited.

【着凉】 zháoliáng catch cold; catch a chill: 外面有点冷,当心~。 It's chilly outside; be careful not to catch cold.

【着迷】 zháomí be fascinated; be captivated: 观众越看越~。 The audience watched the performance with growing fascination./ 孩子们听故事都听得着了迷。 The children were spellbound by the story.

【着魔】 zháomó be bewitched; be possessed: 他这几天练乒乓球象着了魔似的。 He's been practising ping-pong like crazy these few days.

zhǎo

爪
zhǎo claw; talon
另见 zhuǎ

【爪牙】 zhǎoyá talons and fangs — lackeys; underlings

找* zhǎo ① look for; try to find; seek: 他到处在~你。He's been looking for you all over the place./ ~矿 look for mineral deposits/ ~到油田 discover an oil field/ ~出地震的规律 discover the laws of earthquakes/ ~答案 try to find the answer ② want to see; call on; approach; ask for: 有人~你。Someone wants to see you./ 有人来~过我吗？Did anyone ask for me?/ 明天再来~你。I'll call on you again tomorrow./ 干吗不去~老杨帮忙？Why not go and ask Lao Yang for help?/ ~我有什么事？What can I do for you? 或 What do you want to see me about?/ 出了问题可得~你。If anything goes wrong we'll hold you responsible. ③ give change: 他~我两块钱。He gave me two dollar change.

【找对象】 zhǎo duìxiàng 〈方〉look for a partner in marriage

【找麻烦】 zhǎo máfan ① look for trouble: 自~ ask for trouble; ask for it ② cause sb. trouble: 对不起，给你们～了。I'm sorry to have caused you so much trouble.

【找钱】 zhǎoqián give change

【找事】 zhǎoshì ① look (或 hunt) for a job ② pick a quarrel

【找死】 zhǎosǐ court death

【找寻】 zhǎoxún look for; seek

沼 zhǎo natural pond

【沼气】 zhǎoqì marsh gas; firedamp; methane ◇ ~池 methane-generating pit

【沼泽】 zhǎozé marsh; swamp; bog ◇ ~地 marshland/ ~土 bog soil

zhào

召 zhào call together; convene; summon

【召唤】 zhàohuàn call; summon

【召回】 zhàohuí recall: ~大使 recall an ambassador

【召祸】 zhàohuò 〈书〉court disaster

【召集】 zhàojí call together; convene: ~会议 call (或 convene) a conference ◇ ~人 convener

【召见】 zhàojiàn ① call in (a subordinate) ② 〈外〉summon (an envoy) to an interview

【召开】 zhàokāi convene; convoke: ~一次国际会议 convene an international conference

【召之即来】 zhào zhī jí lái come as soon as called

兆 zhào ① sign; omen; portent: 不祥之~ an ill (或 evil) omen ② portend; foretell: 瑞雪~丰年。A timely snow promises a good harvest. ③ million; mega- ④ a million millions; billion

【兆头】 zhàotou sign; omen; portent

诏 zhào 〈书〉① instruct ② imperial edict

【诏书】 zhàoshū imperial edict

赵 Zhào a surname

棹 zhào 〈方〉① oar ② row (a boat)

照* zhào ① shine; illuminate; light up: 拿手电~路 light the way with a torch ② reflect; mirror: ~镜子 look in the mirror ③ take a picture (或 photograph); photograph; film; shoot: 我想~一张相。I want to have a picture taken./ 这镜头可不容易~。This scene is by no means easy to shoot. ④ photograph; picture: 剧~ stage photo; still ⑤ licence; permit: 禁止无~行车。It is forbidden to drive without a licence. ⑥ take care of; look after: ~看 look after; attend to; keep an eye on ⑦ notify; inform: 知~ notify; inform ⑧ contrast: 对~ contrast; check against ⑨ understand: 心~不宣 have a tacit understanding ⑩ in the direction of; towards: ~这个方向走。Go in this direction. ⑪ according to; in accordance with: ~他们的说法 according to what they say/ ~规章办事 act in accordance

with the regulations

【照搬】 zhàobān indiscriminately imitate; copy: 全盘~人家的经验 copy indiscriminately the experience of others

【照办】 zhàobàn act accordingly; act in accordance with; act upon; comply with; follow: 你说得对，我们就照你的办。If what you propose is right, we will act upon it./ 你们提出的要求我们尽量~。We'll try our best to comply with your request.

【照常】 zhàocháng as usual: ~营业 business as usual

【照抄】 zhàochāo ① copy word for word: 这个材料请你~一份。Please make a copy of this material. ② 见"照搬"

【照发】 zhàofā ① issue as before: 女工产假期间工资~。Women workers are entitled to maternity leave with full pay. 或 Women workers receive full pay during maternity leave. ② 〔文件批语〕approved for distribution

【照拂】 zhàofú 〈书〉look after; care for; attend to: 请惠予~。Please be so kind as to take good care of him.

【照顾】 zhàogu ① give consideration to; show consideration for; make allowance(s) for: ~到两国的友好关系 out of consideration for the friendship of the two countries/ ~全局 take the whole into account; consider the situation as a whole/ ~多数 make allowance for the majority; think in terms of the majority/ ~实际需要 consider actual needs/ ~他的困难 take his difficulties into account/ 给予适当~ give appropriate preferential treatment ② look after; care for; attend to: ~伤员 look after the wounded

【照管】 zhàoguǎn look after; tend; be in charge of: ~孩子 look after a child; mind a child/ ~机器 tend a machine/ ~仓库 be in charge of a storehouse

【照护】 zhàohù look after (patients, the wounded, etc.)

【照会】 zhàohuì ① present (或 deliver, address) a note to (a government) ② note: 提出~ present (或 deliver, address) a note/ 交换~ exchange notes

【照价】 zhàojià according to the set (或 arranged) price: ~付款 pay according to the arranged price/ 如有损坏，~赔偿 pay the full price for anything damaged

【照旧】 zhàojiù as before; as usual; as of old: 程序~。The procedure remains unchanged./ 参观改期，入场券~有效。Visit postponed. Tickets remain valid.

【照例】 zhàolì as a rule; as usual; usually

【照料】 zhàoliào take care of; attend to: 她把小女儿托给一位老太太~。She left her baby daughter in the care of an old woman

【照临】 zhàolín shine on; illuminate; light up: 曙光~大地。The early sun bathes the land in light.

【照明】 zhàomíng illumination; lighting: 舞台~ stage illumination

【照片】 zhàopiàn photograph; picture: 彩色~ colour photograph/ 加印~ print off copies from a negative; make copies of a print

【照射】 zhàoshè shine; illuminate; light up; irradiate: 用紫外线~ irradiate with ultraviolet rays

【照说】 zhàoshuō ordinarily; as a rule: ~这时候该热了。As a rule, it should be warm by now./ ~我们早就应当通知你的。We ought to have told you much earlier.

【照相】 zhàoxiàng take a picture (或 photograph); photograph: 我们星期天~去。Let's go and take photographs this Sunday./ 宾主在一起照了相。Guests and host were photographed together.

【照相机】 zhàoxiàngjī camera: 反光式~ reflex camera

【照样】 zhàoyàng ① after a pattern or model: 照着样儿画 draw after a model/ 照这个样儿做 do it this way ② in the same old way; all the same; as before: ~办理 act in the same way; follow suit 他们在不利条件下~完成了任务。Despite adverse circumstances, they fulfilled their task just the same.

【照妖镜】 zhàoyāojìng monster-revealing mirror; demon-detector

【照耀】 zhàoyào shine; illuminate

【照应】 zhàoyìng coordinate; correlate: 文章要前后~。A composition must be well organized.

【照应】 zhàoying look after; take care of: 火车上乘务员对旅客~得很好。The attendants on the train take good care of the passengers.

罩 zhào ① cover; overspread; ·wrap: 工人们下班时都细心地把仪器~好。The workers carefully covered all the instruments before they went off work. / 山坡上~着一层薄雾。The mountain slope was wrapped in a thin mist. ② cover; shade; hood; casing: 玻璃~ glass cover/ 灯~ lampshade

【罩衫】 zhàoshān overall; dustcoat
【罩衣】 zhàoyī dustcoat; overall
【罩子】 zhàozi cover; shade; hood; casing

肇 zhào 〈书〉① start; commence; initiate ② cause (trouble, etc.)
【肇端】 zhàoduān 〈书〉beginning
【肇祸】 zhàohuò cause trouble; cause an accident
【肇始】 zhàoshǐ 〈书〉start; commence; initiate
【肇事】 zhàoshì cause trouble; create a disturbance ◇ ~者 a person who has created a disturbance; troublemaker

zhē

蜇 zhē sting: 当心别给马蜂~了。Mind the wasps don't sting you.
另见 zhé

遮 zhē ① hide from view; cover; screen: 月亮给云彩~住了。The moon was hidden by clouds./ 拿塑料布把脱粒机~起来 spread a plastic sheet over the thresher/ 乌鸦的翅膀~不住太阳的光辉。A crow's wings can never shut out the sunlight. ② block; obstruct; impede: ~道 block the way ③ keep out: ~风挡雨 keep out wind and rain
【遮蔽】 zhēbì ① hide from view; cover; screen ② obstruct; block: ~视线 obstruct the view
【遮藏】 zhēcáng hide; conceal; cover up
【遮丑】 zhēchǒu gloss over one's blemishes; hide one's shame; cover up one's defect
【遮挡】 zhēdǎng shelter from; keep out: ~寒风 keep out the cold wind/ 用帘子把窗户~起来 cover the window with a curtain
【遮盖】 zhēgài ① cover; overspread: 山路全给大雪~住了。The mountain paths were all covered by snow. ② hide; conceal; cover up: 错误总是~不住的。Mistakes can never be hidden.
【遮拦】 zhēlán block; obstruct; impede
【遮羞】 zhēxiū hush up a scandal; cover up one's embarrassment
【遮掩】 zhēyǎn ① cover; overspread; envelop: 远山被云雾~着。The distant hills were enveloped in clouds and mist. ② cover up; hide; conceal: 大胆承认错误，不要遮遮掩掩 Admit your mistakes courageously. Don't try to cover them up.
【遮眼法】 zhēyǎnfǎ cover-up; camouflage

zhé

折 zhé ① break; snap: ~断一根树枝 break off a branch/ ~断腿 fracture (或 break) one's leg ② suffer the loss of; lose: 损兵~将 suffer heavy casualties ③ bend; twist: 曲~ twists and turns ④ turn back; change direction: 边界由此~向西南。From here the boundary turns southwestward./ 他刚走出去不远又~了回来。He hadn't gone very far when he turned back. ⑤ be convinced; be filled with admiration: 心~ be deeply convinced; be filled with heartfelt admiration ⑥ convert into; amount to: 把市斤~成公斤 convert (或 change) jin into kilograms ⑦ discount; rebate: 打八~ give 20% discount; charge 80% of the original price ⑧ fold: 把信~好 fold the letter/ 把纸对~起来 fold the sheet of paper in two ⑨ booklet in accordion forum with a slipcase, used for keeping accounts, etc.; folder: 存~ deposit book; bankbook

另见 shé

【折半】 zhébàn reduce (a price) by half; give 50% discount: 按原价~出售 sell at 50% discount; sell at half price
【折冲樽俎】 zhéchōng zūnzǔ outmanoeuvre the enemy over glasses of wine; win by diplomacy; engage in diplomatic negotiations
【折叠】 zhédié fold: 把报纸~好 fold up the newspaper ◇ ~床(椅) folding bed (chair)/ ~翼飞机 folding-wing aircraft
【折兑】 zhéduì exchange (gold or silver) for money; convert
【折服】 zhéfú ① subdue; bring into submission: 艰难困苦~不了为正义事业而奋斗的人。No hardship can subdue people fighting for a just cause. ② be convinced; be filled with admiration: 令人~ compel admiration
【折合】 zhéhé convert into; amount to: 把美元~成瑞士法郎 convert dollars into Swiss francs
【折回】 zhéhuí turn back (halfway)
【折价】 zhéjià convert into money; evaluate in terms of money: ~退赔 pay compensation at the market price
【折扣】 zhékòu discount; rebate: 这价钱已经打了~了。This is the discounted price.
【折磨】 zhémo cause physical or mental suffering; torment: 受疾病的~ suffer severely from a lingering illness/ 受尽~ suffer a lot
【折辱】 zhérǔ 〈书〉humiliate
【折扇】 zhéshàn folding fan
【折射】 zhéshè 〈物〉refraction
【折实】 zhéshí ① reckon the actual amount after a discount ② adjust payment in accordance with the price index of certain commodities
【折算】 zhésuàn convert ◇ ~率 conversion rate
【折腰】 zhéyāo 〈书〉bow: 江山如此多娇，引无数英雄竞This land so rich in beauty Has made countless heroes bow in homage.
【折纸】 zhézhǐ paper folding
【折中】 zhézhōng compromise: ~方案 a compromise proposal ◇ ~主义 eclecticism 又作"折衷"

哲 zhé ① wise; sagacious ② wise man; sage: 先~ the sages of old
【哲理】 zhélǐ philosophic theory; philosophy
【哲人】 zhérén 〈书〉sage; philosopher
【哲学】 zhéxué philosophy ◇ ~家 philosopher

辄 zhé 〈书〉① always; often: 所言~听 always heed sb.'s advice/ 动~得咎 be frequently taken to task; be blamed for whatever one does ② then: 饮少~醉 get drunk after a few sips

蛰 zhé 〈书〉hibernate
【蛰伏】 zhéfú ① 〈动〉dormancy; hibernation ② 见"蛰居"
【蛰居】 zhéjū live in seclusion: ~书斋 cloister oneself in one's study

蜇 zhé 见"海蜇" hǎizhé
另见 zhē

谪 zhé 〈书〉① relegate a high official to a minor post in an outlying district (as a form of punishment in feudal times); banish; exile ② (of fairies, etc.) be banished from Heaven ③ censure; blame: 众口交~ be censured by everybody

辙 zhé ① the track of a wheel; rut ② rhyme (of a song, poetic drama, etc.): 合~ in rhyme ③ 〈方〉〔多用在"有""没"后面〕way; idea: 没~ can find no way out; be at the end of one's rope

zhě

者 zhě 〈助〉〔用在形容词或动词后面，或带有形容词或动词的词组后面，代替人或事物〕老~ old man/ 大~ the big.

one/ 前(后)~ the former (latter)/ 贫(富)~ the poor (rich)/ 读~ reader/ 出版~ publisher/ 胜利~ victor/ 符合标准~ those which are up to standard ②〈助〉〔用在"工作"和"主义"后面，表示从事某项工作或信仰某个主义的人〕医务工作~ medical worker ③〈书〉〈助〉〔用在"二""三""数"等词后面，指上文所说的几件事物〕：二~必居其一。It must be one or the other./ 两~缺一不可。 Neither is dispensable. ④〈书〉〈助〉〔用在词，词组、分句后面表示停顿〕：风~，空气流动而成。 Wind is air in motion.

褶 zhě pleat; crease: 百~裙 pleated skirt; accordion-pleated skirt/ 把衬衫上的~儿熨平 iron the wrinkles out of the shirt

zhè

这* zhè ① this: ~地方 this place/ ~一回 this time/ ~究竟是怎么回事? What's all this about?/ ~都是我们厂的新产品。 These are new products from our plant./ ~才是好孩子! That's a good boy (girl)! 或 That's a dear!/ ~消息我知道了。 I've heard that news already. 或 Yes, so I've heard./ ~就对了。 Now, you're on the right track. 或 Now, that's better. ② now: 他~才知道锻炼身体的好处。 Only now does he see the good of taking exercise./ 我~就走。 I'm leaving right now.
另见 zhèi
【这般】 zhèbān such; so; like this: ~仔细 so careful/ 大小~ this size; this big/ 如此~ thus and thus; thus and so
【这边】 zhèbiān this side; here: 风景~独好。 The landscape here is beyond compare./ 正义在我们~。 Justice is on our side./ 到~来。 Come over here.
【这次】 zhècì this time; present; current: ~会议 the present session/ ~运动 the current movement (或 campaign)/ ~我们提前三天完成了任务。 This time we fulfilled our task three days ahead of schedule.
【这个】 zhège ① this one; this: ~比那个沉。 This one is heavier than that one./ 他为了~忙了好几天。 He's been busy with this for quite a few days. ②〈口〉〔用在动词、形容词之前，表示夸张〕so; such: 看见大象吹口琴，孩子们~乐啊！ When they saw the elephant blowing the mouth organ, the children roared with laughter.
【这会儿】 zhèhuìr 〈口〉now; at the moment; at present: 你~又上哪儿去呀? Where are you going now?/ ~电话占线。 The line's busy at the moment. 又作"这会子"
【这里】 zhèlǐ here: 我们~一年种两季稻子。 We grow two crops of rice a year here.
【这么】 zhème so; such; this way; like this: 他就是~个人。 That's just like him./ 那个句子应该~译。 The sentence should be translated this way./ 大家都~说。 So they say./ 往~挪一挪。 Move over this way a little bit. 又作"这末"
【这么点儿】 zhèmediǎnr such a little bit: ~水，怕不够喝。 I'm afraid so little water won't be enough to drink.
【这么些】 zhèmexiē so much; so many: ~活儿，得有个人帮帮你吗? Surely you need some help with so much work?/ ~人，坐得开吗? Is there seating for that many people?
【这儿】 zhèr 〈口〉① here ②〔只用在"打""从""由"后面〕now; then: 打~起我就要天天学英语了。 From now on I'm going to study English every day./ 从~以后我再也没见着他。 Since then I haven't seen him again.
【这山望着那山高】 zhè shān wàngzhe nà shān gāo it's always the other mountain that looks higher; always think the grass is greener on the other side; never happy where one is
【这些】 zhèxiē these: ~日子我们特别忙。 We've been particularly busy these days. 又作"这些个"
【这样】 zhèyàng so; such; like this; this way: 别走~快。 Don't walk so fast./ ~的文学作品很受群众欢迎。 Literary works of this kind are well received by the masses./ 他怎么病成~了? How did he get so ill?/ 如果你们觉得可以~办，就~办。 If you people feel this is the right thing to do, then do it./ ~那样的问题 various problems; one question or another; all sorts of problems/ 一会儿~，一会儿那样 now one way, now another/ 情况就是~。

That's how it is.

浙 Zhè short for Zhejiang Province

蔗* zhè sugarcane
【蔗糖】 zhètáng ①〈化〉sucrose ② cane sugar

zhe

着* zhe 〈助〉①〔表示动作或状态的持续〕: 他们正谈~话呢。 They are having a talk./ 别站~，坐下吧。 Don't just stand there; sit down./ 大门敞~。 The gate is wide open./ 山顶覆盖~积雪。 The mountaintop is covered with snow./ 茶几上放~一瓶花。 A vase of flowers stands on the tea table. ②〔加强命令或嘱咐的语气〕你听~。 You just listen./ 快~点儿。 Be quick./ 脚步轻~点儿。 Walk more quietly. ③〔加在某些动词后面，使变成介词〕沿~ along/ 挨~ next to/ 朝~ towards
另见 zhāo; zháo; zhuó

zhèi

这 zhèi 〔常用在量词或数量词前〕this: ~本词典 this dictionary/ ~三架飞机 these three planes
另见 zhè

zhēn

贞 zhēn ① loyal; faithful: 坚~ staunch and faithful ② (of women) chastity or virginity ③ divination (in ancient times)
【贞操】 zhēncāo ① chastity or virginity ② loyalty; moral integrity
【贞节】 zhēnjié chastity or virginity, i.e. remaining chaste and faithful to one's husband or betrothed, even after his death, as demanded by the Confucian moral code
【贞洁】 zhēnjié chaste and undefiled
【贞烈】 zhēnliè ready to die to preserve one's chastity

针* zhēn ① needle: 绣花~ embroidery needle/ 毛线~ knitting needle ② stitch: 在袜子上缝两~ sew (或 put) a couple of stitches in a sock/ 织漏一~ drop a stitch/ 伤口缝了四~。 The wound was closed with four stitches. ③ anything like a needle: 松~ pine needle/ 大头~ pin/ 时 (分)~ hour (minute) hand ④ injection; shot: 打~ give or have an injection ⑤ acupuncture
【针砭】 zhēnbiān ① an ancient form of acupuncture ② point out sb.'s errors and offer salutary advice
【针对】 zhēnduì ① be directed against; be aimed at; counter: 这个条约不~任何第三国。 The treaty is not directed against any third country./ 这个讲话~性很强。 There was no mistaking what the talk was aimed at./ ~这种倾向，我们需要加强自然科学的基础理论的研究。 To counter this tendency, we must strengthen research in the basic theories of natural science. ② in the light of; in accordance with; in connection with: ~儿童的特点进行教育 educate children in accordance with their special characteristics/ ~这种情况 in view of this situation
【针锋相对】 zhēnfēng xiāng duì give tit for tat; be diametrically opposed to
【针尖】 zhēnjiān the point of a needle; pinpoint
【针灸】 zhēnjiǔ acupuncture and moxibustion
【针线】 zhēnxiàn needlework ◇ ~包 sewing kit/ ~活 needlework; stitching; sewing
【针眼】 zhēnyǎn ① the eye of a needle ② pinprick
【针织】 zhēnzhī knitting: ~外衣 knitted (或 knit) coat ◇ ~厂 knitting mill; knit goods mill/ ~机 knitting machine/ ~品 knit goods; knitwear; hosiery

侦 zhēn detect; scout; investigate
【侦查】 zhēnchá 〈法〉investigate (a crime)

【侦察】 zhēnchá 〈军〉 reconnoitre; scout: 敌后～ reconnoitre the enemy rear/ 进行～活动 conduct reconnaissance/ 火力～ reconnaissance by fire/ ～敌情 gather intelligence about the enemy

【侦缉】 zhēnjī track down and arrest

【侦探】 zhēntàn ① do detective work ② detective; spy ◇ ～小说 detective story

【侦听】 zhēntīng 〈军〉 intercept (enemy radio communications); monitor ◇ ～器 detectaphone/ ～台 intercept station

珍* zhēn ① treasure: 奇～异宝 rare treasures ② precious; valuable; rare: ～禽异兽 rare birds and animals ③ value highly; treasure: ～赏 treasure and delight in (curios, etc.); highly value and appreciate

【珍爱】 zhēn'ài treasure; love dearly; be very fond of

【珍宝】 zhēnbǎo jewellery; treasure

【珍本】 zhēnběn rare edition; rare book

【珍藏】 zhēncáng collect (rare books, art treasures, etc.)

【珍贵】 zhēnguì valuable; precious: ～药材 valuable ingredients of traditional Chinese medicine/ ～的历史文物 precious historical relics/ ～的纪念品 precious mementos

【珍品】 zhēnpǐn treasure: 艺术～ art treasure

【珍奇】 zhēnqí rare: ～的动物 rare animals

【珍视】 zhēnshì value; prize; cherish; treasure: 教育青年人～今天的美好生活 teach young people to prize the happy life they lead today/ ～我们两国人民之间的友谊 treasure the friendship between the peoples of our two countries

【珍玩】 zhēnwán rare curios

【珍闻】 zhēnwén news titbits; fillers: 世界～ world briefs (或 miscellany)

【珍惜】 zhēnxī treasure; value; cherish/ ～时间 value one's time

【珍馐】 zhēnxiū delicacies; dainties 又作"珍羞"

【珍异】 zhēnyì rare

【珍重】 zhēnzhòng ① highly value; treasure; set great store by ② take good care of yourself: 两人紧紧握手，互道～ They clasped hands, each asking the other to take good care of himself.

【珍珠】 zhēnzhū pearl ◇ ～贝 pearl shell; pearl oyster

祯 zhēn 〈书〉 auspicious; propitious

桢 zhēn ① hardwood ② terminal posts used in building a wall in ancient times

真* zhēn ① true; real; genuine: 去伪存～ eliminate the false and retain the true/ ～丝 real silk/ 这幅宋人的画是～的。This is a genuine Song painting. ② really; truly; indeed: 我～不知道。I really don't know./ 他～信了。He actually believed it./ ～感激 be truly grateful/ ～有你的！You're a smart fellow, you are!/ 演～精采。The performance was just splendid./ 时间过得～快！How time flies! ③ clearly; unmistakably: 你看得～么？Can you see clearly?/ 字音咬得～ pronounce words distinctly

【真才实学】 zhēncái-shíxué real ability and learning; genuine talent: 有～的科技人员 well-trained scientific and technical workers

【真诚】 zhēnchéng sincere; genuine; true: ～的愿望 a sincere wish (或 desire)/ ～的友谊 true friendship/ ～过悔 sincerely (或 genuinely) repent/ ～合作 sincerely cooperate

【真刀真枪】 zhēndāo-zhēnqiāng real swords and spears — the real thing: ～地干起来 start a shooting war; start in real earnest

【真谛】 zhēndì true essence; true meaning: 人生的～ the true meaning of life

【真迹】 zhēnjī authentic work (of painting or calligraphy)

【真假】 zhēn-jiǎ true and false; genuine and sham: 辨别～ tell the true from the false/ 真真假假 the true mingled with the false; a mixture of truth and falsehood

【真金不怕火炼】 zhēnjīn bù pà huǒ liàn true gold fears no fire — a person of integrity can stand severe tests

【真空】 zhēnkōng 〈物〉 vacuum

【真理】 zhēnlǐ truth

【真面目】 zhēnmiànmù true features; true colours: 不识庐山～，只缘身在此山中。I see not the true face of Lushan because I am in the mountains./ 认清其～ see sb.'s true colours; know sb. for what he is

【真名实姓】 zhēnmíng-shíxìng real name

【真凭实据】 zhēnpíng-shíjù conclusive evidence; hard evidence

【真枪实弹】 zhēnqiāng-shídàn real guns and bullets; live ammunition: 进行～的演习 conduct exercises (或 manoeuvres) with live ammunition

【真切】 zhēnqiè vivid; clear; distinct: 这篇通讯写得～感人。The report is vividly written and very moving./ 看得～ see clearly

【真情】 zhēnqíng ① the real (或 true) situation; the facts; the actual state of affairs; truth ② true feelings; real sentiments: ～的流露 a revelation of one's true feelings

【真确】 zhēnquè ① true; real; authentic: ～的消息 authentic (或 reliable) news ② clear; distinct

【真人真事】 zhēnrén-zhēnshì real people and real events; actual persons and events

【真善美】 zhēn-shàn-měi the true, the good and the beautiful

【真实】 zhēnshí true; real; authentic: ～的感情 true feelings; real sentiments/ ～情况 the real (或 true) situation; how things actually stand/ ～记录 authentic records ◇ ～感 sense of reality/ ～性 truthfulness; authenticity

【真是】 zhēnshi 〔表示不满意的情绪〕: 他把一支新笔丢了，～。It's too bad he's lost his new pen./ 下点雨就不让我们去，～。Just because of a bit of rain we're not allowed to go. The idea!/ 你也～，连灯也不关，就走了。Look at this! You didn't even turn off the light when you left.

【真率】 zhēnshuài sincere; unaffected; straightforward

【真相】 zhēnxiàng the real (或 true) situation; the real (或 actual) facts; the actual state of affairs; truth: 掩盖～ cover up the facts/ 弄清事情的～ clarify the truth of the matter/ ～大白。The whole truth has come out./ 给人以假象，而将～荫蔽着 conceal one's true features and give a false impression/ 这就是事情的～。This is the actual state of affairs. 又作"真象"

【真心】 zhēnxīn wholehearted; heartfelt; sincere: ～拥护 give wholehearted support to/ ～话 sincere words/ 说～话 speak from the bottom of one's heart/ ～悔改 sincerely repent and earnestly reform oneself

【真心实意】 zhēnxīn-shíyì genuinely and sincerely; truly and wholeheartedly; wholeheartedly; sincerely: ～地为人民谋福利 sincerely and wholeheartedly work for the well-being of the people/ ～地支持 wholeheartedly support

【真正】 zhēnzhèng genuine; true; real: ～的吉林人参 genuine Jilin ginseng/ ～的朋友 a true friend

【真知】 zhēnzhī genuine (或 real) knowledge: 实践出～。Real knowledge comes from practice.

【真知灼见】 zhēnzhī-zhuójiàn real knowledge and deep insight; penetrating judgment

【真挚】 zhēnzhì sincere; cordial: ～的友谊 sincere friendship

【真珠】 zhēnzhū pearl

【真主】 Zhēnzhǔ 〈伊斯兰教〉 Allah

砧 zhēn hammering block; anvil: ～台 〈机〉 bench anvil/ 镫～〈机〉 smith anvil

【砧板】 zhēnbǎn chopping block

【砧子】 zhēnzi 〈口〉 hammering block; anvil

斟 zhēn pour (tea or wine): 给她～一杯酒。Pour her a glass of wine.

【斟酌】 zhēnzhuó consider; deliberate: 再三～ consider carefully again and again/ ～词句 weigh one's words/ ～办理 act at one's discretion; act as one sees fit/ ～情况作适当调整 make appropriate adjustments according to circumstances

甄 zhēn 〈书〉 discriminate; distinguish; examine: ～

选 select
【甄拔】 zhēnbá select: ～人才 select people of talent
【甄别】 zhēnbié ① examine and distinguish; screen; discriminate ② reexamine a case

箴 zhēn 〈书〉 ① admonish; exhort ② a type of didactic literary composition
【箴言】 zhēnyán admonition; exhortation; maxim

臻 zhēn 〈书〉 attain (a high level): 交通日～便利。Transportation and communications are becoming easier day by day./ 方法日～完善。The methods are being perfected.

zhěn

诊* zhěn examine (a patient)
【诊病】 zhěnbìng diagnose a disease
【诊察】 zhěnchá examine (a patient)
【诊断】 zhěnduàn diagnose
【诊疗】 zhěnliáo make a diagnosis and give treatment ◇ ～所 clinic; dispensary
【诊脉】 zhěnmài feel the pulse
【诊视】 zhěnshì examine (a patient)
【诊所】 zhěnsuǒ clinic
【诊治】 zhěnzhì make a diagnosis and give treatment

枕* zhěn ① pillow ② rest the head on: ～着胳臂睡觉 sleep with one's head resting on one's arm
【枕戈待旦】 zhěn gē dài dàn lie with one's head pillowed on a spear, waiting for day to break; be ready for battle; maintain combat readiness
【枕巾】 zhěnjīn a towel used to cover a pillow
【枕木】 zhěnmù 〈铁道〉 sleeper; tie
【枕套】 zhěntào pillowcase; pillowslip
【枕头】 zhěntou pillow
【枕席】 zhěnxí ① a mat used to cover a pillow; pillow mat ② bed

轸 zhěn 〈书〉 ① the cross board at the rear of an ancient carriage ② carriage ③ sorrowful; distressed
【轸念】 zhěnniàn 〈书〉 sorrowfully cherish the memory of sb.; think anxiously about: 殊深～ express great solicitude for sb.

疹 zhěn rash: 荨麻～ nettle rash
【疹子】 zhěnzi 〈口〉 measles

畛 zhěn 〈书〉 raised paths between fields
【畛域】 zhěnyù 〈书〉 boundary: 不分～ make no distinctions

缜 zhěn
【缜密】 zhěnmì careful; meticulous; deliberate: ～的计划 a deliberate (或 carefully thought-out) plan/ ～的分析 a careful (或 minute) analysis/ ～的研究 a meticulous study

zhèn

阵* zhèn ① battle array (或 formation): 长蛇～ single-line battle formation ② position; front: 上～杀敌 go to the front to fight the enemy ③ a period of time: 病了一～儿 be ill for some time/ 那～儿 in those days; then/ 这～儿 these days; recently ④ 〈量〉[表示事情或动作经过的段落]: 一～雨 a spatter of rain/ 一～风 a gust (或 blast) of wind/ 一～寒潮 a cold spell/ 一～咳嗽 a fit (或 spasm) of coughing/ 一～热烈的掌声 a burst of warm applause
【阵地】 zhèndì position; front: 进入～ get into position/ 人在～在 fight to the death in defence of one's position; hold one's position at all costs
【阵脚】 zhènjiǎo ① front line ② position; situation; circumstances: 稳住～ secure one's position/ 乱了～ be thrown into confusion
【阵容】 zhènróng ① battle array (或 formation) ② lineup: ～强大 have a strong lineup/ 演员～整齐 a well-balanced cast
【阵势】 zhènshì ① battle array (或 formation); a disposition of combat forces: 摆开～ deploy the ranks in battle array/ 敌人的～全给打乱了。The enemy formations were completely broken up. ② situation; condition; circumstances
【阵痛】 zhèntòng 〈医〉 labour pains; throes (of childbirth)
【阵亡】 zhènwáng be killed in action; fall in battle
【阵线】 zhènxiàn front; ranks; alignment
【阵营】 zhènyíng a group of people who pursue a common interest; camp
【阵雨】 zhènyǔ shower

鸩 zhèn ① a legendary bird with poisonous feathers ② 〈书〉 poisoned wine ③ 〈书〉 kill sb. with poisoned wine
【鸩毒】 zhèndú poisoned wine

振* zhèn ① shake; flap: ～翅 flap the wings; flutter/ ～笔直书 wield the pen furiously ② rise with force and spirit; brace up: 食欲不～ lose one's appetite; have a jaded appetite/ 精神为之一～ feel one's spirits buoyed up/ 我军士气大～。The morale of our troops was greatly boosted.
【振拔】 zhènbá 〈书〉 extricate oneself from a predicament and brace oneself up to action
【振臂】 zhènbì raise one's arm
【振荡】 zhèndàng 〈物〉 vibration
【振动】 zhèndòng 〈物〉 vibration
【振奋】 zhènfèn ① rouse oneself; rise with force and spirit; be inspired with enthusiasm: 人人～，个个当先 everyone full of vigour, each one forging ahead ② inspire; stimulate: ～人心 inspire people; fill people with enthusiasm/ ～士气 boost (或 raise) the morale (of the troops)
【振聋发聩】 zhènlóng-fākuì rouse the deaf and awaken the unhearing; awaken the deaf; enlighten the benighted
【振兴】 zhènxīng develop vigorously; promote: ～教育事业 vitalize education/ ～工业 vigorously develop industry
【振振有辞】 zhènzhèn yǒu cí speak plausibly and at length
【振作】 zhènzuò bestir (或 exert) oneself; display vigour: ～精神 bestir oneself; brace (或 cheer) up/ ～起来！Brace up! 或 Pull yourself together!

朕 zhèn ① I, the sovereign; we (used by a royal person in proclamations instead of I) ② 〈书〉 sign; omen
【朕兆】 zhènzhào sign; omen; portent: 有～可寻。There are signs for us to read.

赈 zhèn relieve; aid: 以工代～ provide work as a form of relief
【赈济】 zhènjì relieve; aid: ～灾民 relieve the people in stricken areas; aid the victims of natural calamities
【赈款】 zhènkuǎn relief fund
【赈灾】 zhènzāi relieve the people in stricken areas

震 zhèn ① shake; shock; vibrate; quake: 地～ earthquake/ 他捶了一下桌子，杯子被～得跳起来。He gave the table a thump which shook the cups. ② greatly excited; deeply astonished; shocked: ～骇 shocked; stunned; astounded
【震波】 zhènbō 〈地〉 seismic wave; earthquake wave
【震颤】 zhènchàn tremble; quiver
【震荡】 zhèndàng shake; shock; vibrate; quake
【震动】 zhèndòng shake; shock; vibrate; quake: 春雷～山谷。Spring thunder shook the valley./ 火车～了一下，开走了。The train pulled out with a jerk./ ～全国 reverberate through the whole country
【震耳欲聋】 zhèn ěr yù lóng deafening: ～的鞭炮声 the deafening noise of firecrackers
【震古烁今】 zhèngǔ-shuòjīn surpassing the ancients and amazing the contemporaries — earthshaking
【震撼】 zhènhàn shake; shock; vibrate: ～天地的英雄气概

earthshaking heroism

【震惊】 zhènjīng shock; amaze; astonish: ～中外 shock the country and the whole world

【震怒】 zhènnù be enraged; be furious

【震慑】 zhènshè awe; frighten

【震源】 zhènyuán ‹地›focus (of an earthquake)

镇*
zhèn ① press down; keep down; ease: ～痛 ease pain ② calm; tranquil; at ease: ～静 calm ③ guard; garrison: 坐～ assume personal command (of a garrison, etc.) ④ garrison post: 军事重～ strategic post ⑤ town ⑥ cool with cold water or ice: 冰～啤酒 iced beer/ 把西瓜放在冷水里一～ put the watermelon in cold water for a while to chill it

【镇定】 zhèndìng calm; cool; composed; unruffled: 神色～ be calm and collected; show composure and presence of mind/ 保持～ keep cool; remain calm; keep one's head

【镇静】 zhènjìng calm; cool; composed; unruffled: 遇到紧急情况要～。 Keep calm in an emergency./ 努力～下来 compose oneself with an effort

【镇守】 zhènshǒu guard (a strategically important place); garrison

【镇压】 zhènyā suppress; repress; put down: ～叛乱 put down a rebellion

zhēng

正*
zhēng the first month of the lunar year; the first moon
另见 zhèng

【正月】 zhēngyuè the first month of the lunar year; the first moon: ～初一 the lunar New Year's Day

争*
zhēng ① contend; vie; strive: ～领导权 contend for leadership/ 不～一日之短长 not strive for only temporary superiority/ 不～一城一地的得失 not contend for a city or a piece of ground (in mobile warfare)/ ～名～利 strive (或 scramble) for fame and gain/ ～挑重担 rush to carry the heaviest load; vie with each other for the hardest job/ ～分夺秒 race (或 work) against time; make every minute and second count ② argue; dispute: 你们在～什么 What are you arguing about?/ ～长论短 squabble; argue

【争霸】 zhēngbà contend (或 struggle) for hegemony; scramble (或 strive) for supremacy

【争辩】 zhēngbiàn argue; debate; contend: 无休止的～ an endless debate/ 无可～ indisputable; incontestable/ 真理不怕～。 Truth does not fear contention.

【争吵】 zhēngchǎo quarrel; wrangle; squabble: 无谓的～ a pointless quarrel/ 激烈的～ fierce (或 bitter) wrangling/ ～不休 bicker (或 squabble) endlessly

【争持】 zhēngchí refuse to give in; stick to one's guns

【争斗】 zhēngdòu fight; struggle; strife

【争端】 zhēngduān controversial issue; dispute; conflict: 国际～ an international dispute/ 边界～ a border dispute/ ～当事国 parties to a dispute (between nations)/ 调解两国～ act as mediator in a conflict between two countries

【争夺】 zhēngduó fight (或 contend, scramble) for; enter into rivalry with sb. over sth.; vie with sb. for sth.: ～制高点 fight (或 contend) for possession of a commanding height/～市场 scramble for markets/ ～势力范围 scramble for spheres of influence

【争光】 zhēngguāng win honour (或 glory) for

【争衡】 zhēnghéng scramble for supremacy; strive for mastery; be in rivalry with

【争论】 zhēnglùn controversy; dispute; debate; contention: 不同意见的～ controversies over differing opinions/ 激烈的～ a heated dispute/ ～不休 an endless debate/ ～的双方 the two contending sides/ ～之点 the point at issue/ 科学上不同学派的自由～ free contention among different schools in science

【争鸣】 zhēngmíng contend: 百家～。 A hundred schools of thought contend.

【争气】 zhēngqì try to make a good showing; try to win credit for; try to bring credit to: 有人说这活儿妇女干不了，我们偏要争这口气。 Some people say women can't do this job, but we'll show them.

【争取】 zhēngqǔ strive for; fight for; win over: ～时间 race (或 work) against time/ ～主动 take the initiative

【争权夺利】 zhēngquán-duólì scramble for power and profit

【争先】 zhēngxiān try to be the first to do sth.: 大家～发言。 Everyone tried to get the floor./ 人人跃进，个个～。 All took part in the leap forward, each trying to outdo the others.

【争先恐后】 zhēngxiān-kǒnghòu strive to be the first and fear to lag behind; vie with each other in doing sth.

【争议】 zhēngyì dispute; controversy: 有～的地区 a disputed area/ 有～的条款 a contentious clause

【争执】 zhēngzhí disagree; dispute; stick to one's position (或 guns): ～不下。 Each sticks to his own stand (或 to his guns).

怔
zhēng seized with terror; terrified; panic-stricken

征*
zhēng ① go on a journey: ～帆 a ship on a long journey ② go on an expedition (或 a campaign): 出～ go on an expedition/ 南～北战 fighting north and south; campaigning up and down the country/ ～马 battle steed ③ levy (troops); call up; draft: 应～入伍 be drafted ④ levy (taxes); collect; impose: ～粮 impose grain levies; collect grain taxes ⑤ ask for; solicit: ～稿 solicit contributions (to a journal, etc.) ⑥ evidence; proof: 有实物可～。 There is solid evidence./ 无～之言 an unfounded assertion ⑦ sign; portent

【征兵】 zhēngbīng conscription; draft; call-up

【征调】 zhēngdiào requisition; call up: ～物资和人员 requisition supplies and draft personnel

【征伐】 zhēngfá go on a punitive expedition

【征服】 zhēngfú conquer; subjugate: 用武力～ conquer by force of arms/ ～自然 conquer nature/ ～黄河 tame the Huanghe River

【征购】 zhēnggòu requisition by purchase: 粮食～ grain purchases by the state/ ～任务 state purchase quotas

【征集】 zhēngjí ① collect: ～签名 collect signatures (for an appeal)/ ～军粮 collect grain for the army/ ～物资 the acquisition of supplies ② draft; call up; recruit: ～新兵 recruitment/ 战时～ wartime draft

【征募】 zhēngmù enlist; recruit

【征聘】 zhēngpìn give public notice of vacancies to be filled; invite applications for jobs; advertise for (a secretary, teacher, etc.)

【征求】 zhēngqiú solicit; seek; ask for: ～意见 solicit (或 seek) opinions; ask for criticisms

【征收】 zhēngshōu levy; collect; impose: ～赋税 levy (或 collect) taxes/ ～进口税 impose import duties/ ～烟草税 put a tax on tobacco

【征税】 zhēngshuì levy (或 collect) taxes; taxation ◇ ～货物 dutiable goods

【征讨】 zhēngtǎo go on a punitive expedition

【征途】 zhēngtú journey: 艰险的～ a perilous journey

【征文】 zhēngwén solicit articles or essays ◇ ～启事 a notice soliciting contributions for a special issue, etc.

【征象】 zhēngxiàng sign; symptom

【征询】 zhēngxún seek the opinion of; consult

【征引】 zhēngyǐn quote; cite

【征用】 zhēngyòng take over for use; commandeer; requisition: ～人力、物力、财力 requisition manpower, material or funds

【征战】 zhēngzhàn go on an expedition (或 a campaign)

【征召】 zhēngzhào ① call up; enlist; draft; conscript: ～入伍 enlist in the army ② ‹书› appoint to an official position

【征兆】 zhēngzhào sign; omen; portent

挣*
zhēng
另见 zhèng

【挣扎】 zhēngzhá struggle: ～着坐起来 struggle to a sitting position／ 进行垂死的～ put up a last-ditch struggle／ 在死亡线上 struggle for existence on the brink of death; struggle for a bare subsistence

峥 zhēng

【峥嵘】 zhēngróng ① lofty and steep; towering ② outstanding; extraordinary: 头角～ (of youth) outstanding; very promising; brilliant／ ～岁月 eventful years

狰 zhēng

【狰狞】 zhēngníng ferocious; savage; hideous: ～面目 ferocious features; a vile visage

症 zhēng
另见

【症结】 zhēngjié crux; crucial reason: 这就是问题的～所在。Therein lies the crux of the problem.

睁 *
zhēng open (the eyes): ～一只眼，闭一只眼 turn a blind eye to sth.／ ～着眼睛说瞎话 tell a bare-faced (或 out-and-out) lie

【睁眼瞎子】 zhēngyǎn xiāzi illiterate person

铮 zhēng

【铮铮】 zhēngzhēng ＜象＞ clank; clang

筝 *
zhēng ① zheng, a 21- or 25-stringed plucked instrument in some ways similar to the zither ② 见"风筝" fēngzheng

蒸 *
zhēng ① evaporate ② steam: ～饭 steam rice／ 菜凉了，～一～。The food is cold. Let's warm it up in the steamer.

【蒸发】 zhēngfā evaporate

【蒸馏】 zhēngliú ＜物＞ distillation: 拔顶～＜化＞ topping distillation／ 常压～＜化＞ atmospheric distillation／ 真空～＜化＞ vacuum distillation
◇ ～器 distiller; retort／ ～水 distilled water／ ～塔 distilling tower

【蒸笼】 zhēnglóng food steamer (usu. made of bamboo)

【蒸气】 zhēngqì vapour

【蒸汽】 zhēngqì steam
◇ ～锅炉 steam·boiler／～机 steam engine／～浴 steam bath

【蒸腾】 zhēngténg (of steam) rising: 热气～ steaming ◇ ～作用＜植＞ transpiration

【蒸蒸日上】 zhēngzhēng rì shàng becoming more prosperous every day; flourishing; thriving: 一派～、欣欣向荣的景象 a scene of prosperity

zhěng

拯 zhěng save; rescue; deliver

【拯救】 zhěngjiù save; rescue; deliver

整 *
zhěng ① whole; complete; full; entire: ～砖 a whole (或 an unbroken) brick／ ～夜 the whole night; all night long／～～页 a full page／ 十二点～ twelve o'clock sharp／ 恰好～一年。It's a year to the day. ② in good order; neat; tidy: 仪容不～ untidy in one's appearance／ 衣冠不～ slovenly in one's dress; not properly dressed ③ put in order; rectify: ～改 rectify and reform ④ repair; mend; renovate: ～修 renovate／ ～旧如新 repair sth. old and make it as good as new ⑤ make sb. suffer; punish; fix: 挨～ be the target of criticism or attack

【整备】 zhěngbèi reorganize and outfit (troops)

【整编】 zhěngbiān reorganize (troops)

【整饬】 zhěngchì ① put in order; strengthen: ～纪律 strengthen discipline ② in good order; neat; tidy: 服装～ neatly dressed

【整队】 zhěngduì dress the ranks; get (或 bring) the ranks into orderly alignment; line up: ～出发 get the ranks in good order and set out; set out in orderly formation／ ～入场 file into the arena, auditorium, etc.

【整顿】 zhěngdùn rectify; consolidate; reorganize: ～文风 rectify the style of writing／ ～纪律 strengthen discipline／ ～组织 overhaul and consolidate an organization

【整风】 zhěngfēng rectification of incorrect styles of work ◇ ～运动 rectification movement

【整个】 zhěnggè whole; entire: ～上午 the whole morning／ ～会场响起热烈的掌声。The whole hall resounded with applause.／ 国民经济的～ the whole national economy／ ～社会 the whole of society／ ～国际形势 the entire international situation／ ～说来 (taken) as a whole; on the whole; by and large

【整洁】 zhěngjié clean and tidy; neat; trim: 房间收拾得很～。The room is kept clean and tidy (或 spick-and-span).／ 衣着～ neatly dressed

【整理】 zhěnglǐ put in order; straighten out; arrange; sort out: ～房间 put a room in order; tidy a room／ ～桌上东西 straighten out the things on the table／ ～书架上的书 rearrange the books on the shelves／ ～资料 sort out the data

【整齐】 zhěngqí ① in good order; neat; tidy: 保持队伍～ keep the ranks in good order／ 字写得清楚～ clear and neat handwriting／ 服装～ neatly dressed／～划一 uniform／ 被子叠得整整齐齐的。The quilts were rolled up tidily. ② even; regular: 出苗～ an even emergence of seedlings／ ～的牙齿 regular teeth

【整容】 zhěngróng ① tidy oneself up (i.e. have a haircut, a shave, etc.) ② face-lifting

【整数】 zhěngshù ① ＜数＞ integer; whole number ② round number (或 figure)

【整套】 zhěngtào a complete (或 whole) set of: ～设备 a complete set of equipment／ 这就是他们的～观点。This is the sum total of their views.／ 对这个问题他有一～看法。He has a lot of views of his own on this matter.

【整体】 zhěngtǐ whole; entirety: 从～上看形势 view the situation as a whole／ ～的一个组成部分 an integral part of the whole／ 为了～的利益牺牲局部的利益 give up individual or local interests for the sake of the whole

【整天】 zhěngtiān the whole day; all day; all day long: 干～三 work for three whole days

【整形】 zhěngxíng ＜医＞ plastic ◇ ～手术 plastic operation／～外科 plastic surgery; plastics

【整修】 zhěngxiū rebuild; renovate; recondition: ～水利工程 rebuild water conservancy projects／ ～梯田 reinforce terraced fields／ ～房子 renovate a house

【整训】 zhěngxùn train and consolidate (troops)

【整整】 zhěngzhěng whole; full: ～半小时 a whole half hour／ ～两天 two whole days／ ～一小时 a full (或 good) hour／ ～六公里 a good six kilometres／ ～五十年 fully fifty years／ ～一个月 a solid month

【整治】 zhěngzhì ① renovate; repair; dredge (a river, etc.): ～房屋 renovate a house／ ～机器 repair a machine／ ～航道 dredge waterways／ ～河道 the realignment of a river ② punish; fix: 这坏蛋得～一下。That scoundrel needs to be punished.

【整装】 zhěngzhuāng get one's things ready (for a journey, etc.): ～待发 ready and waiting／ ～待命 be ready for orders

zhèng

正 *
zhèng ① straight; upright: 这画挂得不～。This picture is not straight.／ 把柱子扶～ set the post upright／～北 (南、西、东) due north (south, west, east) ② situated in the middle; main: ～门 main entrance／ ～厅 main hall ③ (of time) punctually; sharp: 九点～ at nine o'clock sharp ④ obverse; right: 布的～面 the right side of the cloth ⑤ honest; upright: 为人～ upright; righteous ⑥ correct; right: ～路 the correct path; the right way／ ～论 a correct and sensible view ⑦ (of colour or flavour) pure; right: ～黄 pure yellow／ 味儿不～ not the right flavour ⑧ principal;

chief: ~副班长 squad leader and deputy squad leader/ ~驾驶员 first pilot/ ~税和附加税 regular tax and surtax ⑨ (of figures, designs, etc.) regular: ~八边形 regular octagon/ ~多面体 regular polyhedron ⑩ 〈物〉 positive; plus: ~晶体 positive crystal/ ~离子 positive ion; cation ⑪ 〈数〉 positive: ~号 positive sign; plus sign ⑫ rectify; correct; set right: ~帽子 put one's cap straight/ ~音 correct one's pronunciation ⑬ just; right; precisely; exactly: ~如你所说的 just as you say/ 大小~合适 just the right size/ ~中奸计 fall right into the villain's trap/ 因为如此 precisely because of this/ 我~要谈这个问题。 I'm just coming to that point./ 这~是我们需要的东西。This is exactly what we need. 或 This is just the thing we need./ ~是这些人创造了这样伟大的奇迹。They are the very people who worked such wonders. ⑭〔表示动作的进行、状态的持续〕: ~下着雨呢。It's raining./ 时钟~打十二点。The clock was striking twelve.
另见 zhēng

【正本】 zhèngběn ① original (of a document): 将~送存档案库 deposit the original in the archives ② reserved copy (of a library book)

【正常】 zhèngcháng normal; regular: 在~情况下 under normal conditions/ 发动机运转~。The engine is functioning normally./ 恢复~ return to normal/ 脉搏~ have a normal pulse/ 两国关系~化 normalization of the relations between the two countries

【正大】 zhèngdà upright; honest; aboveboard: ~光明 open and aboveboard; just and honourable

【正当】 zhèngdāng just when; just the time for: ~春耕之时 just the time for spring ploughing/ ~人手少的时候,他们来了。They came to help just when we were short of hands.

【正当中】 zhèngdāngzhōng right in the middle (或 centre)

【正当】 zhèngdàng proper; appropriate; legitimate: 通过~途径 in proper ways; by appropriate means; through proper channels/ 他们的要求是完全~的。Their demand is entirely justified.

【正道】 zhèngdào the right way (或 course); the correct path: 走~ follow the correct path/ 这才是~。That's the correct thing to do.

【正殿】 zhèngdiàn main hall (in a palace or temple)

【正法】 zhèngfǎ execute (a criminal): 就地~ execute (a criminal) on the spot

【正反】 zhèng-fǎn positive and negative: 总结~两方面的经验 sum up both positive and negative experience/ ~两方面的看法 the pros and cons

【正方】 zhèngfāng square: ~盒子 a square box ◇ ~形 square

【正告】 zhènggào earnestly admonish; warn sternly

【正规】 zhèngguī regular; standard ◇ ~部队 regular troops; regulars/ ~化 regularize; standardize; be put on a regular basis/ ~军 regular army/ ~学校 regular school/ ~战争 regular warfare

【正轨】 zhèngguǐ the right (或 correct) path: 纳人~ lead onto the correct path; put on the right track

【正好】 zhènghǎo ① just in time; just right; just enough: 你来得~。You've come just in time./ 这双鞋我穿~。This pair of shoes fits me nicely./ 这~证明我们的作法是对的。That only goes to prove that our approach is correct. ② happen to; chance to; as it happens: 小王~从那儿路过。Xiao Wang happened (或 chanced) to be passing by.

【正号】 zhènghào positive sign; plus sign

【正教】 Zhèngjiào the Orthodox Church

【正襟危坐】 zhèngjīn-wēizuò 〈书〉 straighten one's clothes and sit properly; be all seriousness

【正经】 zhèngjing ① decent; respectable; honest: ~人 a decent person ② serious: 钱必须用在~地方。Money must be put to right uses./ ~事儿 serious affairs/ 谈~事 talk business ③ standard: ~货 standard goods

【正楷】 zhèngkǎi (in Chinese calligraphy) regular script 又作"正书"

【正理】 zhènglǐ correct principle; valid reason (或 argu-

ment); the right thing to do

【正门】 zhèngmén front door (或 gate); main entrance

【正面】 zhèngmiàn ① front; frontage; facade: 房屋的~ front (或 facade) of a house/ ~进攻 frontal attack/ ~冲突 head-on confrontation (或 clash) ② the obverse side; the right side: 牛皮纸的~ the right side of kraft paper/ 硬币的~ the obverse side of a coin/ 皮革的~ the grain side of leather/ ~和反面 the obverse and the reverse sides of a thing; both sides ③ positive: ~教育 educate by positive measures or examples; positive education/ ~阐明自己的观点 state one's views in a positive way ④ directly; openly: 有问题请~提出来。Please ask your question directly.

【正派】 zhèngpài upright; honest; decent: ~人 a decent person/ 作风~ honest and upright in one's ways

【正品】 zhèngpǐn certified products (或 goods); quality products (或 goods)

【正气】 zhèngqì healthy atmosphere (或 tendency): 发扬~ encourage healthy trends; encourage standing up for what is right

【正巧】 zhèngqiǎo ① happen to; chance to; as it happens: 他们~带有仪器。They happened (或 chanced) to have their instruments with them. ② just in time; in the nick of time; just at the right time: 你~来得,我们马上就要出发了。You've come just in time. We're leaving immediately.

【正确】 zhèngquè correct; right; proper: ~的立场 a correct stand/ 你这样做是~的。What you are doing is right. ◇ ~性 correctness; soundness; validity

【正人君子】 zhèngrén-jūnzǐ 〈旧〉 a man of honour; gentleman: 打扮成~ masquerade as a gentleman

【正史】 zhèngshǐ history books written in biographical style

【正式】 zhèngshì formal; official; regular: ~列入记录 be officially placed on record/ 代表团的~成员 a regular (或 full) member of the delegation/ 大会于八月二十四日~开幕。The conference formally opened on August 24.

【正视】 zhèngshì face squarely; face up to; look squarely at: ~困难 face difficulties squarely; face up to difficulties/ ~现实 look reality in the face/ ~缺点 acknowledge one's shortcomings

【正事】 zhèngshì one's proper business: 现在我们谈~。Now let's talk business.

【正数】 zhèngshù 〈数〉 positive number

【正题】 zhèngtí subject (或 topic) of a talk or essay: 转入~ come to the subject/ 离开~ wander (或 digress) from the subject/ 不离~ stick to one's text

【正厅】 zhèngtīng ① main hall (in the middle) ② stalls (in a theatre)

【正统】 zhèngtǒng ① legitimism ② orthodox: ~观念 orthodox ideas ◇ ~派 orthodox party or school

【正文】 zhèngwén main body (of a book, etc.); text: 书的~ the text of a book/ 词典~ the main body of a dictionary; the dictionary proper

【正午】 zhèngwǔ high noon

【正误】 zhèngwù correct (typographical) errors ◇ ~表 errata; corrigenda

【正颜厉色】 zhèngyán-lìsè look serious and severe; put on a stern countenance

【正业】 zhèngyè regular occupation; proper duties: 不务~ not attend to one's proper duties; not engage in honest work

【正义】 zhèngyì ① justice: 主持~ uphold justice/ 为~而战 fight for justice/ ~之师 an army dedicated to a just cause ② just; righteous: ~立场 a just stand/ ~的事业 a just cause ◇ ~感 sense of justice (或 righteousness); sense of what is right

【正音】 zhèngyīn ① correct one's pronunciation ② standard pronunciation

【正在】 zhèngzài 〈副〉〔表示动作在进行中〕in process of; in course of: 他们~聊天。They're having a chat./ 许多问题~讨论。Many questions are under discussion./ ~修建一条新铁路。A new railway is under construction./ ~进行

磋商。Consultations are under way.

【正直】 zhèngzhí honest; upright; fair-minded: ～的人 an honest person; a person of integrity

【正中】 zhèngzhōng middle; centre: 把茶具放在桌子的～。Put the tea-things right in the middle (或 centre) of the table.

【正中下怀】 zhèng zhòng xiàhuái be just what one hopes for; fit in exactly with one's wishes

【正宗】 zhèngzōng orthodox school

证* zhèng ① prove; demonstrate: 求～ seek to prove/ ～几何定理 demonstrate (或 prove) a geometric theorem ② evidence; proof; testimony: 作～ give evidence; bear testimony/ 确～ proof positive; conclusive evidence/ 物～ material evidence ③ certificate; card: 出生～ birth certificate/ 许可～ permit ④ disease; illness

证婚人 zhènghūnrén chief witness at a wedding ceremony

【证件】 zhèngjiàn credentials; papers; certificate: 请出示～。Please show your credentials (或 papers).

【证据】 zhèngjù evidence; proof; testimony: 搜集～ collect evidence/ 提出～ offer testimony

【证明】 zhèngmíng ① prove; testify; bear out: 充分～ fully prove/ 雄辩地～ give (或 be) eloquent proof of/ 无数事实已～了这一点。Countless facts have proved this point. ② certificate; identification; testimonial: 医生～ medical certificate ◇ ～文件 certificate; testimonial; papers

【证明书】 zhèngmíngshū certificate; testimonial: 质量～ certificate of quality/ 产地～ certificate of origin/ 健康～ health certificate

【证券】 zhèngquàn negotiable securities ◇ ～交易所 stock exchange

【证人】 zhèngren witness ◇ ～席 witness-box; witness stand

【证实】 zhèngshí confirm; verify: 有待～ remain to be confirmed/ ～一个科学上的假设 verify a scientific hypothesis

【证书】 zhèngshū certificate; credentials: 结婚～ marriage certificate; marriage lines/ 毕业～ diploma

【证物】 zhèngwù 〈法〉 exhibit (produced in court as evidence)

【证验】 zhèngyàn ① verify ② real results; efficacy

【证章】 zhèngzhāng badge

诤 zhèng 〈书〉 criticize sb.'s faults frankly; admonish; expostulate

郑 Zhèng

【郑重】 zhèngzhòng serious; solemn; earnest: 态度～ be serious in one's attitude/ ～表示 earnestly declare; solemnly state/ ～声明 solemnly declare/ ～其事 seriously; in earnest

政* zhèng ① politics; political affairs: 议～ discuss political affairs ② certain administrative aspects of government: 民～ civil administration/ 邮～ postal service/ 财～ (public) finance ③ 〈旧〉 affairs of a family or an organization: 家～ household management/ 校～ school administration

【政变】 zhèngbiàn coup d'état; coup: 发动～ stage a coup d'état

【政策】 zhèngcè policy: ～教育 education in policy/ 提高～水平 enhance the understanding of policy/ 划清～界限 draw clear lines of demarcation in applying a policy

【政党】 zhèngdǎng political party

【政敌】 zhèngdí political opponent

【政府】 zhèngfǔ government ◇ ～部门 government departments/ ～机构 government apparatus/ ～机关 government bodies (或 organizations)/ ～人士 government circles/ ～首脑 head of government

【政纲】 zhènggāng political programme; platform

【政绩】 zhèngjì achievements in one's official career

【政见】 zhèngjiàn political view

【政教分离】 zhèng-jiào fēnlí separation of religion from politics; separation of the church from the state

【政界】 zhèngjiè political circles; government circles: 退出～ withdraw from political life

【政局】 zhèngjú political situation; political scene

【政客】 zhèngkè politician

【政令】 zhènglìng government decree (或 order)

【政论】 zhènglùn political comment ◇ ～家 political commentator; political writer/ ～文 political essay

【政权】 zhèngquán political (或 state) power; regime: 夺取～和巩固～ seize and consolidate political power/ 国家～ state power

【政事】 zhèngshì government affairs

【政体】 zhèngtǐ system (或 form) of government

【政务】 zhèngwù government affairs; government administration

【政治】 zhèngzhì politics; political affairs ◇ ～避难 (political) asylum/ ～家 statesman/ ～派别 political grouping or faction

挣* zhèng ① struggle to get free; try to throw off: ～脱枷锁 throw off the shackles ② earn; make: ～饭吃 earn a living 另见 zhēng

【挣揣】 zhèngchuài 〈书〉 struggle; strive hard

【挣命】 zhèngmìng struggle to save one's life

【挣钱】 zhèngqián earn (或 make) money: ～养家 earn money to support one's family

帧 zhèng 〈量〉〔用于字画〕: 一～油画 an oil painting

症 zhèng disease; illness: 不治之～ incurable disease/ 急～ acute disease 另见 zhēng

【症候】 zhènghou ① disease ② symptom

【症状】 zhèngzhuàng symptom: 前驱～ premonitory (或 signal) symptoms/ 早期～ early (或 incipient) symptoms

zhī

之* zhī 〈书〉 ①〔代替人或事物，限于做宾语〕: 取而代～ replace (或 supersede) someone/ 偶一为～ do something once in a while/ 将如～何？ What is to be done? ②〔虚用，无所指〕: 总～ to sum up; in short; in a word/ 久而久～ with the lapse of time; as time passes/ 手之舞～,足之蹈～ with joy ③ this: ～子于归, The maiden goes to her future home. ④ 〈助〉〔用在定语和中心词之间，表示领属关系或一般的修饰关系〕钟鼓～声 the sound of drums and bells' 原因～一 one of the reasons/ 无价～宝 a priceless treasure/ 一水～隔 be separated only by a river/ 以我～长, 攻敌～短 utilize our strong points to attack the enemy at his weak points ⑤〈助〉〔用在主谓结构之间，取消它的独立性，使变成偏正结构〕: 皮～不存，毛将焉附!/ With the skin gone, to what can the hair attach itself?/ 如因势利导，则如水～就下，极为自然。If we guide the matter along its course of development, it will proceed as naturally as water flows downwards. ⑥ go; leave: 君将何～? Where are you bound for?

【之后】 zhīhòu later; after; afterwards: 三天～ three days later/ 这次大会～ following this conference/ 从那～她没来过。She hasn't been here since then./ ～他又给我写了两封信。Afterwards he wrote to me twice.

【之乎者也】 zhī-hū-zhě-yě pedantic terms; literary jargon; archaisms: 老学究满口～,教人半懂不懂 The old pedant used so many archaisms that half of what he said was unintelligible.

【之前】 zhīqián before; prior to; ago: 在她动身～ prior to her departure/ 这药在睡觉～吃。Take the medicine before bedtime./ 两星期～他还在这儿。He was here until two weeks ago.

【之字路】 zhīzìlù zigzag course; S curve in a road

支 zhī ① prop up; put up: ～帐篷 put up a tent/ 用两张凳子把木板～起来 prop up the board with two stools/ 两手～着头 rest one's head in both hands ② protrude;

raise: ~着耳朵听 prick up one's ears ③ support; sustain; bear: ~前 support the front/ 乐不可~ overwhelmed with joy; overjoyed/ 孩子疼得~不住了。The child couldn't bear the pain. ④ send away; put sb. off: 把他们~开 put them off with excuses; send them away upon some pretext/ 这事甭~别人了，你自个儿去吧。Don't send anyone else; better go yourself. ⑤ pay or draw (money): ~拨 pay a sum of money or transfer a sum of money in payment/ 上银行~款 go to the bank to draw money/ 收~ income and expenses; revenue and expenditure/ 预~一百块钱 get an advance of 100 dollars ⑥ branch; offshoot: ~店 branch store ⑦〈量〉用于队伍、歌曲、电灯光度等]: 三~队伍 three contingents of troops/ 一~新歌 a new song/ 一~钢笔 a pen/ 一个六十~光的灯泡 a 60-watt bulb ⑧ the twelve Earthly Branches

【支部】 zhībù branch

【支撑】 zhīcheng ① prop up; sustain; support: 病人~着坐了起来。The patient propped himself up into a sitting position.

【支持】 zhīchí ① sustain; hold out; bear: 他冻得~不住了。He was so cold he couldn't hold out any longer. ② support; back; stand by: 我完全~这个建议。I am all for this proposal.

【支出】 zhīchū ① pay (money); expend; disburse ② expenses; expenditure; outlay; disbursement: 追加~ supplementary expenditure/ 国防~ expenditure on national defence/ 收入与~相抵。The income balances the expenditure.

【支绌】 zhīchù (of funds) not enough; insufficient: 由于经费~ due to insufficient funds

【支付】 zhīfù pay (money); defray: ~水电费 pay for electricity and water/ 立即~ immediate payment

【支架】 zhījià support; stand; trestle: 自行车~ prop stand of a bicycle

【支解】 zhījiě dismemberment

【支离】 zhīlí ① fragmented; broken; disorganized ② (of writing) trivial and jumbled; incoherent

【支离破碎】 zhīlí-pòsuì torn to pieces; broken up; fragmented

【支流】 zhīliú ① tributary; affluent: 珠江的一条~ a tributary of the Zhujiang River ② minor aspects; nonessentials: 看问题时，不要把~当作主流。In considering a problem, one mustn't mistake the nonessentials for the essentials.

【支脉】 zhīmài offshoot (of a mountain range); branch range: 天山的~ a branch range of the Tianshan Mountains

【支派】 zhīpài branch; sect; offshoot

【支派】 zhīpài order; send; dispatch

【支配】 zhīpèi ① arrange; allocate; budget: 善于~自己的时间 be good at budgeting one's time ② control; dominate; govern: 受人~ be controlled by others/ 受自然规律的~ be subject to the laws of nature

【支票】 zhīpiào cheque; check: 开~ write a cheque/ 划线~ crossed cheque/ 空白~ blank cheque/ 空头~ rubber cheque/ 旅行~ traveller's cheque ◇ ~簿 cheque book/ ~票根 stub of a cheque; counterfoil

【支气管】 zhīqìguǎn bronchus

【支取】 zhīqǔ draw (money): ~存款 draw one's deposit (from a bank)

【支使】 zhīshi ① order about ② send away; put sb. off

【支吾】 zhīwu prevaricate; equivocate; hum and haw: ~其词 speak evasively; hum and haw

【支线】 zhīxiàn branch line; feeder (line): 铁路~ feeder railway/ 公路~ feeder highway

【支援】 zhīyuán support; assist; help

【支柱】 zhīzhù pillar; prop; mainstay

汁* zhī juice: 橘子~ orange juice/ 牛肉~ beef extract/ 乳~ milk/ 椰子~ coconut milk/ 墨~ prepared Chinese ink

【汁液】 zhīyè juice

只* zhī ① single; one only: ~字不提 not say a single

word (about sth.) ②〈量〉: 两~手 two hands/ 一~鸡 a chicken/ 三~箱子 three suitcases/ 一~小船 a boat 另见 zhǐ

【只身】 zhīshēn alone; by oneself: ~独往 go there alone/ ~在外 be away from home all by oneself

【只言片语】 zhīyán-piànyǔ a word or two; a few isolated words and phrases: 只听见~ catch (或 overhear) only a word or two/ 未留下~ leave behind not even a single word

芝 zhī

【芝兰】 zhīlán irises and orchids (symbolic of noble character, true friendship, or beautiful surroundings): 如入~之室 like going into a room full of fragrant orchids — benefit from associating with people of a noble character

【芝麻】 zhīma ① sesame: ~开花节节高。A sesame stalk puts forth blossoms notch by notch, higher and higher. ② sesame seed: 拣了~，丢了西瓜 pick up the sesame seeds but overlook the watermelons — concentrate on minor matters to the neglect of major ones ◇ ~酱 sesame paste/ ~油 sesame-seed oil; sesame oil

吱 zhī 〈象〉: 门~地一声开了。The door creaked open. 另见 zī

枝* zhī ① branch; twig: 柳~ willow branches ②〈量〉: 一~步枪 a rifle/ 一~蜡烛 a candle/ 一~梅花 a spray of plum blossoms

【枝杈】 zhīchà branch; twig

【枝接】 zhījiē 〈农〉 scion grafting

【枝节】 zhījié ① branches and knots — minor matters: ~问题 a minor problem; a side issue/ 不要过多地注意那些枝枝节节。Don't pay too much attention to the minor issues. ② complication; unexpected difficulty: 横生~ raise unexpected difficulties; deliberately complicate an issue; create side issues

【枝解】 zhījiě dismemberment

【枝条】 zhītiáo branch; twig

【枝桠】 zhīyā branch; twig 又作“枝丫”

【枝叶】 zhīyè ① branches and leaves: 那棵大樟树~茂盛。That big camphor tree is a mass of branches and leaves. ② nonessentials; minor details

【枝子】 zhīzi branch; twig

知* zhī ① know; realize; be aware of: 强不~以为~ pretend to know what one doesn't know/ ~过必改 always correct an error when one becomes aware of it/ ~其然并求其~其所以然 know the how and endeavour to know the why ② inform; notify; tell: 通~ inform; notify ③ knowledge: 求~欲 thirst for knowledge/ 经过努力学习，可以由无~转化为有~，由~之不多转化为~之甚多。By assiduous study, ignorance can be transformed into knowledge and scanty knowledge into substantial knowledge.

【知彼知己，百战不殆】 zhī bǐ zhī jǐ, bǎi zhàn bù dài know the enemy and know yourself, and you can fight a hundred battles with no danger of defeat

【知道】 zhīdoo know; realize; be aware of: 我不~这事儿。I know nothing about it./ 你的意思我~。I know what you mean. 或 I see your point./ 他们~问题的严重性。They realize how serious the problem is./ 我们~在前进的路上还会有困难。We are aware that on our way forward there will still be difficulties.

【知底】 zhīdǐ know the inside story; be in the know

【知法犯法】 zhī fǎ fàn fǎ knowingly violate the law; deliberately break the law

【知己】 zhījǐ ① intimate; understanding: ~的朋友 bosom (或 intimate) friend/ 和他很~ be on intimate terms with him/ ~话 intimate words; heart-to-heart talk ② bosom (或 intimate) friend

【知交】 zhījiāo bosom (或 intimate) friend: 他和我父亲是~。He is an intimate friend of my father's.

【知觉】 zhījué ① consciousness: 失去~ lose consciousness; pass out/ 恢复~ recover consciousness; come to ②〈心〉 perception

【知名】 zhīmíng well-known; noted; celebrated; famous: ～人士 well-known (或 noted) personage; public figure; celebrity/ 海内～ be known throughout the country

【知难而进】 zhī nán ér jìn press forward in the face of difficulties; advance despite difficulties

【知难而退】 zhī nán ér tuì beat a retreat in the face of difficulties; shrink back from difficulties

【知其一,不知其二】 zhī qí yī, bù zhī qí èr know only one aspect of a thing; have only a one-sided view: 总之,事物都有两点而不是一点,说只有一点,叫。 In short, there are two aspects to everything, not just one. To say there is only one is to be aware of one aspect and be ignorant of the other.

【知情】 zhīqíng know the facts of a case or the details of an incident; be in the know: ～不报 conceal what one knows of a case

【知情达理】 zhīqíng-dálǐ reasonable; sensible

【知趣】 zhīqù know how to behave in a delicate situation; be sensible; be tactful

【知人善任】 zhī rén shàn rèn (of a leader) know one's subordinates well enough to assign them jobs commensurate with their abilities

【知人之明】 zhī rén zhī míng ability to appreciate a person's character and capability; a keen insight into a person's character

【知人知面不知心】 zhī rén zhī miàn bù zhī xīn you may know a person's face but not his heart; one may know a person for a long time without understanding his true nature

【知识】 zhīshi ① knowledge: ～渊博 have a wide range of knowledge; be erudite; be learned/ 技术～ technical know-how/ 书本～ book learning ② pertaining to learning or culture; intellectual ◇ ～界 intellectual circles; the intelligentsia

【知识分子】 zhīshifènzǐ intellectual; the intelligentsia

【知无不言,言无不尽】 zhī wú bù yán, yán wú bù jìn say all you know and say it without reserve

【知悉】 zhīxī know; learn; be informed of: 业已～ have already learned of the matter

【知晓】 zhīxiǎo know; be aware of; understand

【知心】 zhīxīn intimate; understanding: ～朋友 intimate (或 bosom) friend/ ～话 intimate words; heart-to-heart talk

【知音】 zhīyīn a friend keenly appreciative of one's talents; bosom friend

【知足】 zhīzú be content with one's lot

肢 zhī limb: 四～ the four limbs (of the human body)

【肢解】 zhījiě dismemberment

【肢体】 zhītǐ ① limbs ② limbs and trunk

织* zhī ① weave: 纺～ spinning and weaving/ ～席 weave (或 make) a mat ② knit: ～毛衣 knit a sweater

【织补】 zhībǔ darning; invisible mending

【织布】 zhībù weaving cotton cloth; weaving ◇ ～工 weaver

【织锦】 zhījǐn ① brocade ② picture-weaving in silk: 风景～ landscape woven in silk ◇ ～厂 brocade mill

【织女】 zhīnǚ ① woman weaver ② (织女) the Girl Weaver in the legend "The Cowherd and the Girl Weaver"

【织物】 zhīwù fabric: 机织～ woven fabric

指* zhī
另见 zhǐ; zhì

【指甲】 zhījia nail: 手～ fingernail/ 脚～ toenail ◇ ～刀 nail clippers/ ～油 nail polish

祇 zhī <书> venerate; respect

胝 zhī 见"胼胝" piánzhī

脂 zhī ① fat; grease; tallow: 油～ fat; grease/ 含～羊毛 wool in the grease ② rouge: 胭～ rouge

【脂肪】 zhīfáng fat: 动物～ animal fat /植物～ vegetable fat

【脂粉】 zhīfěn rouge and powder; cosmetics

【脂膏】 zhīgāo ① fat; grease ② fruits of the people's labour; wealth of the people

掷 zhī throw; cast: ～色子 throw dice; play dice
另见 zhì

蜘* zhī

【蜘蛛】 zhīzhū spider: 海～ sea spider ◇ ～丝 the thread of a spider web; cobweb/ ～网 spider (或 spider's) web; cobweb

zhí

执 zhí ① hold; grasp ② take charge of; direct; manage: ～教 be a teacher; teach ③ stick to (one's views, etc.); persist: 各～己见。 Each sticks to his own view. ④ carry out; observe: ～礼甚恭 punctiliously observe etiquette; treat sb. with great respect ⑤ catch; capture: 战败被～ be captured after being defeated in battle

【执笔】 zhíbǐ write; do the actual writing

【执法】 zhífǎ enforce (或 execute) the law: ～如山 enforce the law strictly

【执绋】 zhífú take part in a funeral procession

【执迷不悟】 zhí mí bù wù obstinately stick to a wrong course; be perverse; refuse to come to one's senses

【执牛耳】 zhí niú'ěr (of an ancient prince presiding over a ceremony marking the conclusion of an alliance) hold the plate on which the ears of a sacrificial bull lie — be the acknowledged leader; occupy a leading position; rule the roost

【执拗】 zhíniù stubborn; pigheaded; wilful

【执行】 zhíxíng carry out; execute; implement: ～任务 carry out a task; perform a mission/ ～命令 execute an order ◇ ～机构 executive body/ ～机关 executive organ/ ～秘书 executive secretary/ ～委员会 executive committee

【执意】 zhíyì insist on; be determined to; be bent on: 他～要走。 He insisted on leaving./ 她～不收彩礼 She firmly refused to accept betrothal presents from her fiancé's family.

【执掌】 zhízhǎng wield; be in control of: ～兵权 wield military power

【执照】 zhízhào license; permit: 驾驶～ driver's license

【执政】 zhízhèng be in power; be in office; be at the helm of the state ◇ ～党 the party in power (或 in office); the ruling (或 governing) party

【执着】 zhízhuó inflexible; rigid; punctilious

直 zhí ① straight: 街道又宽又～。 The streets are wide and straight./ 把铁丝拉～ straighten a piece of wire ② straighten: ～起腰来 straighten one's back; stand up straight ③ vertical; perpendicular: ～行的文字 characters written from top to bottom/ ～上云霄 soar straight up into the sky; 这屋子～里有六米,横里有三米。 The room is 6 metres in length and 3 in width. ④ just; upright: 正～ upright; fair-minded/ 是非曲～ rights and wrongs; truth and falsehood ⑤ frank; straightforward: 心～口快 plain-spoken and straightforward; frank and outspoken/ ～认不讳 admit frankly; own up readily. 我就～说了。 I'll speak very frankly. ⑥ stiff; numb: 天太冷,手指都冻～了。 It was so cold that my fingers were frozen stiff. ⑦ vertical stroke (in Chinese characters) ⑧ directly; straight: ～走 go straight ahead ⑨ continuously: 新井～往外喷油。 Oil gushed continuously from the new well./ 他冻得～哆嗦。 He was so cold that he kept shivering./ 这个故事逗得她～乐。 The story tickled her fancy. ⑩ just; simply: 我待他～如兄弟 treat him just like a brother/ 疼得～像针扎一样 feel a piercing pain

【直达】 zhídá through; nonstop

【直到】 zhídào ① until: 我们～昨晚才接到通知。 We didn't get the notice until last night. ② up to: ～现在我们还没

有接到正式通知。We've received no official information about it up to now.

【直角】zhíjiǎo 〈数〉 right angle ◇ ~尺 square/ ~三角形 right (或 right-angled) triangle

【直接】zhíjiē direct; immediate: ~原因 immediate cause; direct cause/ ~会晤 meet sb. in person

【直截了当】zhíjié-liǎodàng straightforward; blunt; point-blank: ~的回答 a point-blank answer/ ~地说吧。Let's put it bluntly. 或 Come straight to the point./ ~地拒绝对方的无理要求 flatly reject the other side's unreasonable demands

【直径】zhíjìng 〈数〉 diameter

【直觉】zhíjué 〈心〉 intuition

【直眉瞪眼】zhíméi-dèngyǎn ① stare in anger; fume ② stare blankly; be in a daze; be stupefied: 他~地站在那里, 也不说话。He stood there staring blankly, saying nothing.

【直升飞机】zhíshēng fēijī helicopter; copter ◇ ~机场 heliport/ ~母舰 helicopter carrier/ ~运载 helilift

【直抒己见】zhí shū jǐ jiàn state one's views frankly; be plainspoken

【直属】zhíshǔ directly under; directly subordinate (或 affiliated) to

【直率】zhíshuài frank; candid; straightforward: 你~地告诉我吧。Now tell me frankly./ 她说话很~。She is very straightforward in what she says.

【直爽】zhíshuǎng frank; candid; straightforward; forthright: 性格~ forthright in character

【直挺挺】zhítǐngtǐng straight; stiff; bolt upright: ~地站着 stand ramrod straight/ ~地坐着 sit bolt upright

【直系亲属】zhíxì qīnshǔ directly-related members of one's family — parents, spouse and children

【直辖】zhíxiá directly under the jurisdiction of: 文化部~机构 organizations directly under the Ministry of Culture

【直线】zhíxiàn ① straight line ② steep; sharp (rise or fall): 捕鱼量~上升。The total catch of fish has shot up.

【直性子】zhíxìngzi ① straightforward; downright; forthright ② straightforward person: 他是个~, 有什么说什么。He's a straightforward chap, always ready to say what's on his mind.

【直言】zhíyán speak bluntly; state outright: 恕我~。Excuse me for speaking bluntly.

【直言不讳】zhíyán bù huì speak without reservation; not mince words; call a spade a spade: 他~地指出我们工作中的缺点。He pointed out the shortcomings in our work without mincing words.

【直译】zhíyì literal translation; word-for-word translation

【直至】zhízhì ① till; until: 继续战斗, ~胜利。Keep on fighting till victory is assured. ② up to: ~此时 up to this moment

侄* zhí brother's son; nephew

【侄女】zhínǚ brother's daughter; niece

【侄孙】zhísūn brother's grandson; grandnephew

【侄孙女】zhísūnnǚ brother's granddaughter; grandniece

【侄子】zhízi brother's son; nephew 又作"侄儿"

指* zhí
另见 zhǐ; zhì

【指头】zhítou ① finger ② toe

值* zhí ① value: 币~ currency value ② be worth: 这~多少钱? How much (或 What) is this worth?/ 不~一提 not worth mentioning/ 跑这一趟不~。The trip is not worthwhile. ③ happen to: 你上次来访, 正~我外出。I happened to be out when you called./ ~此贵国三十周年国庆之际 on the occasion of the 30th anniversary of your National Day ④ be on duty; take one's turn at sth.: ~夜 be on night duty; be on the night shift/ 轮~ work in shifts ⑤ 〈数〉 value

【值班】zhíbān be on duty: 今天谁~? Who's on duty today?/ 他值夜班。He's on night duty. 或 He's on the night shift. ◇ ~员 person on duty

【值得】zhíde be worth; merit; deserve: ~买 be worth buying/ ~赞许 deserve commendation; be praiseworthy/ ~怀疑 be open to doubt/ ~仔细考虑 warrant careful consideration/ 历史的经验~注意。Historical experience merits attention./ 李贺的诗很~一读。Li He's poems are well worth reading.

【值钱】zhíqián costly; valuable

【值勤】zhíqín (of armymen, policemen, etc.) be on duty; be on point duty

【值日】zhírì be on duty for the day; be one's turn to be on duty: 今天谁~打扫教室? Whose turn is it to clean the classroom today? ◇ ~表 rota; duty roster/ ~生 student on duty

职* zhí ① duty; job: 尽~ fulfil one's duty/ 本~工作 one's own job ② post; office: 调~ be transferred to another post/ 撤~ be removed (或 dismissed) from office/ 就~ take office; assume office

【职别】zhíbié official rank

【职称】zhíchēng the title of a technical or professional post (such as engineer, professor, lecturer, academician, etc.)

【职分】zhífèn ① duty ② official post; position

【职工】zhígōng ① staff and workers; workers and staff members ② 〈旧〉 workers; labour ◇ ~运动 labour movement; trade union movement

【职权】zhíquán powers or authority of office: 行使~ exercise one's functions and powers/ 超越~ overstep one's authority; exceed one's powers

【职权范围】zhíquán fànwéi limits (或 scope) of one's functions and powers; terms of reference: 在自己的~内 within one's functions and powers

【职守】zhíshǒu post; duty: 擅离~ leave one's post without permission/ 忠于~ be faithful in the discharge of one's duties

【职位】zhíwèi position; post

【职务】zhíwù duties; job: 履行~ do (或 perform) one's duties

【职衔】zhíxián post and rank

【职业】zhíyè occupation; profession; vocation: 从事各种~的人 people of all occupations/ 这里填上你的姓名、~等等。Put down your name, occupation, etc. here./ 他的~是医生。He is a doctor by profession./ 我们的~有保障。Our jobs are secure. ◇ ~病 occupational disease/ ~团体 professional organization/ ~外交官 career diplomat/ ~学校 vocational school/ ~运动员 professional athlete; professional

【职员】zhíyuán office worker; staff member; functionary

【职责】zhízé duty; obligation; responsibility: 应尽的~ bounden duty/ 神圣~ sacred duty/ 分清~ define the duties incumbent on each person or post

【职掌】zhízhǎng 〈书〉 ① be in charge of: ~财务 be in charge of financial affairs ② duty; charge

【职志】zhízhì 〈书〉 lifework; mission: 以教育为~ take education as one's lifework

植* zhí ① plant; grow: ~树 plant trees/ 移~ transplant ② set up; establish: ~党营私 set up a clique for one's own selfish interests

【植树】zhíshù 〈林〉 tree planting: ~造林 afforestation

【植物】zhíwù plant; flora

殖 zhí breed; multiply: 生~ breed; reproduce/ 繁~ multiply; propagate

【殖民】zhímín establish a colony; colonize: 非~化 decolonize; decolonization ◇ ~国家 colonialist power/ ~扩张 colonial expansion/ ~战争 colonialist war

【殖民地】zhímíndì colony: 沦为~ be reduced to a colony ◇ ~国家 colonial country/ ~人民 people under colonial rule; colonial people

【殖民主义】zhímínzhǔyì colonialism: ~祸害 the scourge of colonialism/ 新~ new colonialism; neocolonialism

◇~者 colonialist

摭 zhí 〈书〉pick up
【摭拾】 zhíshí 〈书〉pick; gather; collect: ~群言 collect views from various sources

蹢 zhí
【蹢躅】 zhízhú 〈书〉walk to and fro; loiter around: ~街头 tramp the streets

蹠 zhí ①〈生理〉metatarsus ②〈书〉sole of the foot ③〈书〉tread
【蹠骨】 zhígǔ 〈生理〉metatarsal bones

zhǐ

止 zhǐ ① stop: 中~ stop halfway; discontinue; suspend/ 不达目的不~ refuse to give up without attaining one's aim/ ~痒 stop the itching/ ~渴 quench one's thirst ② to; till: 到目前为~ to date; till now/ 从本月十号起到十六号~ from the 10th to the 16th of this month ③ only; 不~一次 not just once; more than once
【止步】 zhǐbù halt; stop; go no further: ~不前 halt; stand still/ 如果就此~，就会前功尽弃。If we stop where we are, all our previous efforts will be wasted./ 游人~ no visitors out of bounds
【止付】 zhǐfù 〈经〉stop payment ◇ ~通知书 stop-payment notice
【止境】 zhǐjìng end; limit: 学无~。There is no end to learning./ 科学的发展是没有~的。There is no limit to the development of science.
【止咳】 zhǐké relieve a cough ◇ ~糖浆 cough syrup
【止痛】 zhǐtòng relieve pain; stop pain ◇ ~药 anodyne; analgesic; pain-killer
【止息】 zhǐxī cease; stop
【止泻药】 zhǐxièyào antidiarrheal
【止血】 zhǐxuè stop bleeding; stanch bleeding

只 zhǐ 〈副〉only; merely: ~剩一个了。There is only one left./ 我~想问一个问题。I have just one question.
另见 zhī
【只不过】 zhǐ bùguò only; just; merely: 这~是一种猜测。It's just (或 nothing but) a guess./ 别害怕，他~是吓唬你。Don't be afraid. He was only trying to frighten you.
【只得】 zhǐdé have no alternative but to; be obliged to; have to: 他们~把会议延期。They had no alternative but to put the meeting off./ 没有桥，我们~涉水过去。As there was no bridge, we were obliged to wade across.
【只顾】 zhǐgù ① be absorbed in: 他~干他的事。He was entirely absorbed in his work. ②〈副〉merely; simply
【只管】 zhǐguǎn ①〈副〉by all means: 有意见~提出来。Don't hesitate to put forward your suggestions if you have any./ 你~干下去。Go ahead by all means. ② merely; simply
【只好】 zhǐhǎo have to; be forced to: ~作罢 be forced to give up/ ~另想办法 cannot but seek other means/ 末班车过去了，我们~走回家。As the last bus had gone, we had to walk home.
【只是】 zhǐshì ① merely; only; just: 我今天进城，~去看看朋友，没有什么要紧的事儿。Today I'm going to town just to see friends, not on business./ 这~个时间问题。It is merely a question of time. ② simply: 大家问他是什么事，他~笑，不回答。When people asked him what had happened, he simply laughed without replying. ③ however; but then: 这架电视机不错，~小了点。This TV set is quite good, only it's a bit too small.
【只许州官放火，不许百姓点灯】 zhǐ xǔ zhōuguān fànghuǒ, bù xǔ bǎixìng diǎndēng the magistrates are free to burn down houses, while the common people are forbidden even to light lamps; one may steal a horse while another may not look over the hedge
【只要】 zhǐyào 〈连〉so long as; provided: ~虚心，就会进步。Provided you are modest, you'll surely make progress

【只要功夫深，铁杵磨成针】 zhǐyào gōngfu shēn, tiěchǔ mó-chéng zhēn constant grinding can turn an iron rod into a needle — perseverance spells success
【只有】 zhǐyǒu 〈连〉only; alone: ~他知道这事的内情。He alone knows the inside story./ 这样~好处，没有坏处。This is all to the good and no harm can come of it.
【只争朝夕】 zhǐ zhēng zhāo-xī seize the day, seize the hour; seize every minute; race against time

旨 zhǐ ① purport; purpose; aim: 主~ purport; main purpose/ 宗~ purpose; aim/ ~在加快工程进度的措施 measures aimed at speeding up the project ② decree: 圣~ imperial decree
【旨趣】 zhǐqù 〈书〉purport; objective
【旨意】 zhǐyì decree; order: 你这样做是奉谁的~? On whose orders did you do this?

址 zhǐ location; site: 厂~ factory site/ 地~ address

纸 zhǐ ① paper: 一张白~ a blank sheet of paper ②〈量〉〈书信、文件的张数〉: 一~空文 a mere scrap of paper
【纸板】 zhǐbǎn paperboard; cardboard: 波纹~ corrugated cardboard ◇ ~盒(箱) cardboard case or box; carton
【纸版】 zhǐbǎn 〈印〉paper mould; paper matrix
【纸包不住火】 zhǐ bāobuzhù huǒ you can't wrap fire in paper — there is no concealing the truth; truth will be out
【纸币】 zhǐbì paper money; paper currency; note: 发行~ issue (bank) notes/ 不兑现~ fiat money
【纸花】 zhǐhuā paper flower
【纸浆】 zhǐjiāng paper pulp; pulp
【纸老虎】 zhǐlǎohǔ paper tiger
【纸牌】 zhǐpái playing cards
【纸钱】 zhǐqián paper made to resemble money and burned as an offering to the dead
【纸上谈兵】 zhǐshàng tán bīng fight only on paper; be an armchair strategist; engage in idle theorizing
【纸烟】 zhǐyān cigarette
【纸鸢】 zhǐyuān kite
【纸张】 zhǐzhāng paper
【纸醉金迷】 zhǐzuì-jīnmí (a life of) luxury and dissipation

祉 zhǐ 〈书〉happiness; blessedness

指 zhǐ ① finger: 屈~可数 can be counted on one's fingers — very few/ 天黑得伸手不见五~。It was so dark that you couldn't see your own fingers (或 couldn't see your hand in front of your face). ② fingerbreadth; digit: 两~宽的纸条 a strip of paper two fingerbreadths wide/ 下了四~雨。We had about three inches of rain. ③ point at; point to: 时针~向十二点。The hour hand points to twelve./ 千人所~，无病而死。When a thousand people point accusing fingers at a man he will die even though not ill — it is dangerous to incur public wrath. ④ indicate; point out; refer to: ~出缺点 point out sb.'s shortcomings/ 他的话不是~你说的。His remarks were not directed at you. ⑤ depend on; count on: 他们就~着你帮忙呢。They're counting on your help.
另见 zhī; zhí
【指标】 zhǐbiāo target; quota; norm; index: 完成国家计划规定的~ attain the targets (或 fulfil the norms) set in the state plan/ 生产~ production target/ 质量~ quality index
【指不胜屈】 zhǐ bù shèng qū too numerous to be counted on the fingers; a great many
【指斥】 zhǐchì reprove; reprimand; denounce
【指导】 zhǐdǎo guide; direct
【指点】 zhǐdiǎn give directions (或 pointers, advice); show how (to do sth.): 教练耐心地~他们。The coach patiently instructs them./ 请~我们如何去做。Please show us how to do it./ 经他一~，我就全明白了。A few pointers from him made it all clear to me.
【指定】 zhǐdìng appoint; assign: ~谈判代表 appoint representatives to the negotiations/ 在~地点见面 meet at the

designated place

【指环】zhǐhuán (finger) ring

【指挥】zhǐhuī ①command; direct; conduct: ~一个连 command a company; be in command of a company/ ~交通 direct traffic/ ~乐队 conduct an orchestra/ ~若定 direct (work, etc.) with perfect ease; give highly competent leadership ②commander; director ③〈乐〉conductor ◇ ~棒〈乐〉baton

【指教】zhǐjiào 〈套〉give advice or comments: 请多多~。Kindly give us your advice./ 望不吝~。1 hope you won't spare your comments.

【指靠】zhǐkào depend on (for one's livelihood); look to (for help); count on: 这件事我们就~你了。We'll count on you for this.

【指控】zhǐkòng accuse; charge: 有人~他纳贿。He's been accused of taking bribes.

【指令】zhǐlìng ①instruct; order; direct ②instructions; order; directive ③〈计算机〉instruction ◇ 遥控~ remote control command

【指鹿为马】zhǐ lù wéi mǎ call a stag a horse — deliberately misrepresent

【指路明灯】zhǐlù míngdēng beacon light; beacon

【指名】zhǐmíng mention by name; name: ~攻击 assail sb. by name/ ~道姓 name names

【指明】zhǐmíng show clearly; demonstrate; point out: ~两者之间的差别 show clearly the difference between the two/ ~出路 point the way out

【指南】zhǐnán guide; guidebook

【指南车】zhǐnánchē an ancient Chinese vehicle with a wooden figure always pointing to the south

【指南针】zhǐnánzhēn compass: 十二世纪初中国航海已普遍使用~。By the early twelfth century the compass was already in general use among Chinese navigators.

【指派】zhǐpài appoint; name; designate: ~代表出席会议 name delegates to the conference

【指日可待】zhǐ rì kě dài can be expected soon; be just round the corner: 胜利~。Victory is just round the corner.

【指桑骂槐】zhǐ sāng mà huái point at the mulberry and abuse the locust — point at one but abuse another; make oblique accusations

【指使】zhǐshǐ instigate; incite; put sb. up to sth.: ~少数坏人进行破坏 incite a handful of bad elements to engage in sabotage/ 受别人~ act on sb.'s instigation/ 揭露幕后~者 expose the person behind the scenes; unmask the hidden instigator

【指示】zhǐshì ①indicate; point out: ~前进的方向 indicate the direction of advance ②instruct: ~部队立即出发 instruct the troops to set out at once ③directive; instructions: 下达~ give instructions

【指手划脚】zhǐshǒu-huàjiǎo ①make gestures; gesticulate: ~地高谈阔论 talk volubly with animated gestures ②make indiscreet remarks or criticisms

【指数】zhǐshù index number; index: 综合~ composite index/ 物价~ price index/ 生活费~ cost of living index

【指望】zhǐwàng ①look to; count on: ~有一天能实现这个计划 look forward to the day when this plan will be put in practice ②prospect; hope 这病还有~吗? Is there still hope of his recovery?

【指纹】zhǐwén ①loops and whorls on a finger ②fingerprint ◇ ~学 dactylography

【指引】zhǐyǐn point (the way); guide; show

【指印】zhǐyìn fingerprint; finger mark: 按~ make a fingerprint

【指责】zhǐzé censure; criticize; find fault with: 横加~ make unwarranted charges/ 受到舆论的~ be subjected to the censure of public opinion/ 用事实回击他们的~ answer their attacks with facts/ 我们怎能~这种现实事求是的态度呢? How can we find fault with this realistic approach?

【指摘】zhǐzhāi pick faults and criticize; censure

【指针】zhǐzhēn ①indicator; pointer; needle ②guiding principle; guide: 作为今后工作的~ as a guide for future

【指正】zhǐzhèng ①point out mistakes so that they can be corrected ②〈套〉make a comment or criticism: 请惠予~。Please oblige me with your valuable comments. 或 Be kind enough to give me your opinion.

咫 zhǐ an ancient measure of length, equal to 8 cun
（寸）

【咫尺】zhǐchǐ 〈书〉very close: 近在~ close at hand

【咫尺天涯】zhǐchǐ-tiānyá a short distance away, and yet poles apart — see little of each other though living nearby

趾 zhǐ ①toe ②foot

【趾高气扬】zhǐgāo-qìyáng strut about and give oneself airs; be swollen with arrogance

【趾甲】zhǐjiǎ toenail

黹 zhǐ 〈书〉needlework; embroidery: 针~ needlework

zhì

至 zhì ①to; until: 从左~右 from left to right/ 截~上月底为止 up to the end of last month ②〈书〉extremely; most: 感人~深 deeply moving; extremely moving/ 是为~盼。That is our sincerest hope./ ~嘱。See that you act accordingly.

【至宝】zhìbǎo most valuable treasure: 如获~ feel as if one had found a priceless treasure

【至诚】zhìchéng complete sincerity: 出于~ in all sincerity; from the bottom of one's heart

【至诚】zhìchéng sincere; straightforward: ~的朋友 a sincere friend

【至迟】zhìchí at (the) latest: 这条铁路~五月通车。This railway will be opened to traffic in May at the latest.

【至多】zhìduō 〈副〉at (the) most: 这张画~两个星期就能画好。It'll take two weeks at most to finish the painting.

【至高无上】zhìgāo-wúshàng most lofty; paramount; supreme: ~的事业 most lofty undertaking/ ~的权力 absolute power

【至交】zhìjiāo most intimate friend; best friend

【至今】zhìjīn up to now; to this day; so far: ~没有人提出过反对意见。Up to now no one has raised any objections./ 我~未得到他的答复。So far I've had no reply from him.

【至理名言】zhìlǐ-míngyán famous dictum; maxim; axiom; golden saying

【至亲】zhìqīn very close relative; close kin: ~好友 close relatives and good friends

【至上】zhìshàng supreme; the highest

【至少】zhìshǎo 〈副〉at (the) least: ~有一万人参加了大会。At least ten thousand people attended the rally./ 他并不了解我,~是了解得不全面。He doesn't understand me, or at any rate not fully./ ~可以说,这样处理不妥。This is not the proper way to handle the matter, to say the least.

【至死】zhìsǐ unto death; till death: ~不屈 not yield even unto death/ ~不悟 incorrigibly stubborn

【至于】zhìyú ①as for; as to: ~其他问题,以后再说。As for other matters, we'll take them up later. ②go so far as to: 他不~不来开会吧? He wouldn't go so far as to refuse to come to the meeting, would he?

识 zhì 〈书〉①remember; commit to memory: 博闻强~ have wide learning and a retentive memory; have encyclopaedic knowledge ②mark; sign: 款~ inscriptions (on bronzes, etc.)
另见 shí

志* zhì ①will; aspiration; ideal: ~坚如钢 have an iron will; have a will of steel/ 胸怀大~ cherish high ideals; have lofty aspirations/ 立~当优秀的科学家 be determined to become a first-rate scientist ②keep in mind;

永～不忘 forever bear in mind ③ records; annals: 县～ annals of a county/ 《三国～》 *History of the Three Kingdoms* ④ mark; sign: 标～ mark

【志哀】 zhì'āi indicate mourning: 下半旗～ fly a flag at half-mast as a sign of mourning

【志大才疏】 zhì dà cái shū have great ambition but little talent; have high aspirations but little ability

【志气】 zhìqì aspiration; ambition: 有～ have high aspirations

【志趣】 zhìqù aspiration and interest; inclination; bent

【志士】 zhìshì person of ideals and integrity: 仁人～ people with lofty ideals/ 爱国～ noble-minded patriot

【志同道合】 zhìtóng-dàohé cherish the same ideals and follow the same path; have a common goal

【志向】 zhìxiàng aspiration; ideal; ambition: 青年人应有远大的～。 Young people should have lofty aspirations.

【志愿】 zhìyuàn ① aspiration; wish; ideal ② do sth. of one's own free will; volunteer ◇ ～兵 volunteer (soldier)

【志愿军】 zhìyuànjūn people who volunteer to fight in another country; volunteers

治* zhì ① rule; govern; administer; manage: ～国 administer a country/ ～家 manage a household/ 自～ self-government; autonomy ② order; peace: 达到天下大～ achieve great order across the land ③ 〈旧〉 seat of a local government: 县～ county seat/ 省～ provincial capital ④ treat (a disease); cure: ～好战争创伤 heal the wounds of war/ 他的病不久就～好了。 He was soon cured of his illness. ⑤ control; harness (a river); wipe out: ～沙 sand-control/ ～山～水 transform mountains and tame rivers/～蝗 eliminate locusts ⑥ punish: 惩～ punish ⑦ study; research: 专～宋史 specialize in the history of the Song Dynasty

【治安】 zhì'ān public order; public security: 维持～ maintain public order

【治本】 zhìběn effect a permanent cure; get at the root (of a problem, etc.); take radical measures: 河流的～工程 project for the permanent control of a river

【治标】 zhìbiāo merely alleviate the symptoms of an illness; bring about a temporary solution (of a problem, etc.); take stopgap measures

【治病救人】 zhìbìng-jiùrén cure the sickness to save the patient

【治国】 zhìguó administer (或 run) a country; manage state affairs: ～安民 run the country well and give the people peace and security

【治理】 zhìlǐ ① administer; govern: ～国家 administer a country; run a state ② harness; bring under control; put in order: ～河流 harness a river; bring a river under control

【治疗】 zhìliáo treat; cure: 住院～ be hospitalized/ ～效果 therapeutic effect/ 她还在医院～。 She is still under treatment in hospital.

【治丧】 zhìsāng make funeral arrangements ◇ ～委员会 funeral committee

【治世】 zhìshì times of peace and prosperity

【治水】 zhìshuǐ regulate rivers and watercourses; prevent floods by water control

【治罪】 zhìzuì punish sb. (for a crime)

帜 zhì 〈书〉 flag; banner: 独树一～ fly one's own colours — develop a school of one's own

炙 zhì ① broil; roast ② 〈书〉 roast meat

【炙手可热】 zhì shǒu kě rè if you stretch out your hand you feel the heat — the supreme arrogance of a person with great power

质* zhì ① nature; character: 性～ nature; character/ 本～ innate character; essence ② quality: 按～分等 grade according to quality/ ～的飞跃 a qualitative leap/ 优～钢 high-quality (或 high-grade) steel ③ matter; substance: 流～食物 liquid food/ 木～纤维 wood fibre ④ simple; plain: ～直 upright; straightforward/ ～言之 to put it

bluntly ⑤ question: ～疑 call in question ⑥ 〈书〉 pawn: 典～ pawn; mortgage ⑦ 〈书〉 pledge: 以此为～ with this as a pledge/ 人～ hostage

【质地】 zhìdì ① quality of a material; texture; grain: ～细密 of close texture; fine-grained ② character; disposition

【质量】 zhìliàng ① quality: ～好 of high quality/ ～不高 of low quality; inferior/ 提高～ improve the quality ② 〈物〉 mass

【质料】 zhìliào material: 这套衣服的～很好。 This suit is made of very good material.

【质朴】 zhìpǔ simple and unadorned; unaffected; plain: 文字～ written in a simple style/ 为人忠厚～ be simple and honest; be unsophisticated

【质问】 zhìwèn question; interrogate; call to account: 提出～ bring sb. to account

【质询】 zhìxún address inquiries to; ask for an explanation

【质疑】 zhìyí call in question; query: 对他的说法提出～ query (或 question) the validity of his statement

【质疑问难】 zhìyí-wènnàn raise doubts and difficult questions for discussion

制* zhì ① make; manufacture: 中国～ made in China/ 机～ machine-made/ 精～糖 refined sugar ② work out; formulate: 因地～宜 work out measures to suit local conditions ③ restrict; control: 限～ restrict/ 控～ control/ ～敌于死命 have the enemy by the throat; spell death to the enemy ④ system: 公～ the metric system

【制裁】 zhìcái sanction; punish: 实行～ apply sanctions (against); impose sanctions (upon)/ 受到法律～ be punished according to law/ 给以严厉～ mete out severe punishment to sb.

【制成品】 zhìchéngpǐn finished products; manufactured goods; manufactures

【制订】 zhìdìng work (或 map) out; formulate: ～《汉语拼音方案》 work out *The Scheme for the Chinese Phonetic Alphabet*

【制定】 zhìdìng lay down; draw up; formulate; draft: ～操作规程 lay down operating rules/ ～宪法 draw up a constitution/ ～政策 formulate a policy/ ～计划 work out a plan/ ～法律 make laws/ ～法令 enact decrees

【制度】 zhìdù system; institution: 规章～ rules and regulations

【制伏】 zhìfú check; subdue; bring under control: ～风沙 check wind and sand/ ～敌人 subdue the enemy/ 这条河给～了。 The river was brought under control.

【制服】 zhìfú uniform

【制品】 zhìpǐn products; goods: 奶～ dairy products/ 黄麻～ jute goods/ 竹～ articles made of bamboo; bamboo articles

【制胜】 zhìshèng get the upper hand of; subdue: ～敌人 subdue the enemy/ 出奇～ defeat one's opponent by a surprise move

【制图】 zhìtú ① 〈地〉 charting; map-making ② 〈机〉〈建〉 drafting ◇ ～学 cartography/ ～仪器 drawing (或 drafting) instrument/ ～员 〈地〉 cartographer; 〈机〉〈建〉 draftsman

【制药】 zhìyào pharmacy ◇ ～厂 pharmaceutical factory/ ～学 pharmaceutics

【制造】 zhìzào ① make; manufacture: 日本～的飞机 Japan-made aircraft/ 这设备是我们自己～的。 The equipment is of our own manufacture. ② engineer; create; fabricate: ～纠纷 create trouble; sow dissension/ ～紧张局势 create tension/ ～分裂 foment splits/ ～谣言 fabricate rumours (或 lies)/ ～假象 put up a false front/ ～重重障碍 raise one obstacle after another/ ～烟幕 spread a smoke screen/ ～内乱 stir up internal strife/ ～舆论 mould public opinion ◇ ～商 manufacturer/ ～业 manufacturing industry

【制止】 zhìzhǐ check; curb; prevent; stop: ～流沙 curb shifting sand/ ～通货膨胀 check (或 halt) inflation/ ～派别活动 put an end to factional activities/ 我做了一个手势，～他再说下去。 I made a gesture to stop him from saying any more.

【制作】 zhìzuò make; manufacture: ～家具 make furniture/

精心～的银器 elaborately wrought silverware

栉 zhì <书> comb

【栉比】 zhìbǐ <书> placed closely side by side (like the teeth of a comb)

【栉风沐雨】 zhìfēng-mùyǔ be combed by the wind and washed by the rain — travel or work despite wind and rain

峙 zhì <书> stand erect; tower: 对～ stand up against each other; confront each other/ ～立 stand towering

桎 zhì <书> fetters

【桎梏】 zhìgù <书> fetters and handcuffs; shackles: 打碎精神上的～ smash spiritual shackles

轾 zhì 见"轩轾" xuān-zhì

致 zhì ① send; extend; deliver: ～电 send a telegram/ ～贺 extend one's congratulations ② devote (one's efforts, etc.): 专心～志 be wholeheartedly devoted to; be wholly absorbed in ③ incur; result in; cause: 招～失败 cause defeat/ 学以～用 learn sth. in order to use it; gear one's study to practical use ④ manner or style that engages attention or arouses interest: 别～ original in style; unique ⑤ fine; delicate: 工作细～ be meticulous in one's work/ 精～ exquisite

【致辞】 zhìcí make (或 deliver) a speech: 请来宾向大会～ call upon a guest to address the conference/ 新年～ New Year message 又作"致词"

【致敬】 zhìjìng salute; pay one's respects to; pay tribute to: 鸣礼炮二十一响 fire a 21-gun salute

【致力】 zhìlì devote oneself to; work for: ～于中医学的研究 devote (或 dedicate) oneself to the study of traditional Chinese medical science

【致命】 zhìmìng causing death; fatal; mortal; deadly: ～的打击 a fatal (或 mortal, vital) wound/ ～的弱点 fatal weakness

【致使】 zhìshǐ cause; result in: 由于地址字迹不清，～信件无法投递。It is impossible to deliver this letter because the address is illegible.

【致死】 zhìsǐ causing death; lethal; deadly: ～原因 cause of death

【致谢】 zhìxiè express one's thanks (或 gratitude); extend thanks to: 谨此～。We hereby express our thanks.

【致意】 zhìyì give one's regards (或 best wishes); present one's compliments; send one's greetings: 请向边防战士们～。Please give our best wishes to the frontier guards./ 点头(挥手)～ nod (wave) a greeting

秩 zhì <书> ① order: ～然不紊 orderly; shipshape ② <书> decade: 七～寿辰 seventieth birthday

【秩序】 zhìxù order; sequence: 工作～ sequence of work/ 维持社会～ maintain public order/ 紧张而有～的工作 intense but orderly work

挚 zhì <书> sincere; earnest: 诚～ sincere/ 真～的友谊 true friendship

【挚友】 zhìyǒu intimate friend; bosom friend

贽 zhì <书> gift presented to a senior at one's first visit as a mark of esteem

掷 zhì throw; cast: 投～ throw; fling/ 弃～ cast aside; throw away/ 孤注一～ risk everything on a single throw; stake all one has
另见 zhì

【掷还】 zhìhuán <书> please return (to the writer, etc.): 前请审阅之件,请早日～为荷。Please return at your earliest convenience the manuscript (或 draft, material) submitted to you for approval.

窒 zhì <书> stop up; obstruct: ～塞 stop up; block

【窒碍】 zhì'ài <书> have obstacles; be obstructed

【窒闷】 zhìmèn close; stuffy

【窒息】 zhìxī stifle; suffocate: 浓烟几乎使他～。The dense smoke almost suffocated him.

鸷 zhì <书> ferocious; violent: ～鸟 birds of prey

痔 zhì haemorrhoids; piles

【痔疮】 zhìchuāng haemorrhoids; piles

滞 zhì stagnant; sluggish

【滞碍】 zhì'ài block (up); obstruct

【滞留】 zhìliú be detained; be held up

【滞销】 zhìxiāo unsalable; unmarketable ◇ ～货 unsalable (或 slow-selling) goods; a drug on the market

痣 zhì nevus; mole: 色～ pigmented mole (或 nevus)/ 胎～ birthmark

蛭 zhì leech

智 zhì wisdom; resourcefulness; wit: 足～多谋 wise and resourceful/ ～穷才尽 at the end of one's wits (或 resources)/ 斗～ a battle of wits

【智多星】 zhìduōxīng nickname for Wu Yong, the resourceful strategist of the peasant army in the Water Margin (《水浒传》); resourceful person; mastermind

【智慧】 zhìhuì wisdom; intelligence

【智力】 zhìlì intelligence; intellect ◇ ～测验 intelligence test

【智略】 zhìlüè wisdom and resourcefulness

【智谋】 zhìmóu resourcefulness: 靠勇敢也靠～ rely on both courage and resourcefulness/ 人多～高。More people mean more ideas.

【智囊】 zhìnáng brain truster ◇ ～团 brain trust

【智取】 zhìqǔ take (a fort, town, etc.) by strategy: 只可～,不可强攻。The only way to take the enemy position is by strategy, not by forceful attack.

【智术】 zhìshù trickery; stratagem

【智勇双全】 zhì-yǒng shuāng quán both intelligent and courageous; both brave and resourceful

【智育】 zhìyù intellectual education; intellectual development: 使学生在德育、～、体育几方面都得到发展 enable the students to develop morally, intellectually and physically

【智者千虑,必有一失】 zhìzhě qiān lǜ, bì yǒu yī shī even the wise are not always free from error

彘 zhì <书> pig; swine

置 zhì ① place; put: 安～ find a place for; help sb. settle down/ 搁～ put aside; shelve; pigeonhole ② set up; establish; install: 设～新课程 establish new courses/ 装～配电盘 install a switchboard/ ～酒款待 give a feast to entertain sb. ③ buy: ～一身衣服 buy a suit or have one made to order/ ～添一些家具 buy some furniture

【置办】 zhìbàn buy (durables); purchase: ～家具 buy furniture/ ～图书仪器 procure books and instruments

【置备】 zhìbèi purchase (equipment, furniture, etc.)

【置辩】 zhìbiàn <书> 〔多用于否定〕 argue (in self-defence): 不屑～ disdain to argue/ 不容～ indisputable

【置若罔闻】 zhì ruò wǎng wén turn a deaf ear to; pay no heed to: 我多次劝告,他都～。I cautioned him many times but he paid no heed.

【置身】 zhìshēn place oneself; stay: ～事外 stay aloof from the affair; keep out of the business; refuse to be drawn into the matter

【置信】 zhìxìn 〔多用于否定〕 believe: 难以～ hard to believe; unbelievable; incredible

【置疑】 zhìyí 〔多用于否定〕 doubt: 不容～ allow of no doubt; not be open to doubt

【置之不理】 zhì zhī bù lǐ ignore; brush aside; pay no attention to: 对于这种挑衅,我们不能～。We cannot ignore such provocations.

【置之度外】 zhì zhī dù wài give no thought to; have no regard for: 他为了抢救落水儿童，把个人安危~。 He went to the rescue of a drowning child regardless of his personal safety. 或 He ventured his life to save a child from drowning.

【置之脑后】 zhì zhī nǎo hòu banish from one's mind; ignore and forget

【置之死地而后快】 zhì zhī sǐdì érhòu kuài will be content with nothing less than sb.'s destruction

雉 zhì pheasant

稚* zhì young; childish: 幼~ childish
【稚气】 zhìqì childishness
【稚子】 zhìzi (innocent) child

踬 zhì 〈书〉① trip; stumble: 颠~ trip over sth. ② suffer a setback: 屡试屡~ fail at each trial

zhōng

中* zhōng ① centre; middle: 居~ in the centre ② in; among; amidst: 记在心~ keep in mind ③ middle; mid: 月~ in the middle of a month/ ~年 middle age ④ medium; intermediate: ~号 medium-sized ⑤mean; halfway between two extremes: 适~ moderate ⑥intermediary: 作~ act as an intermediary; be a middleman ⑦ in the process of: 在修建~ being built; under construction/ 发展~国家 developing country ⑧fit for; good for: 不~用 good for nothing
另见 zhòng

【中饱】 zhōngbǎo batten on money entrusted to one's care; line one's pockets with public funds or other people's money; embezzle
【中保】 zhōng-bǎo middleman and guarantor
【中部】 zhōngbù central section; middle part: 根据地~ the central section of the base area/ 在高原~ in the middle part of the plateau
【中餐】 zhōngcān Chinese meal; Chinese food
【中策】 zhōngcè the second best plan
【中层】 zhōngcéng middle-level
【中程】 zhōngchéng intermediate range; medium range ◇ ~导弹 intermediate-range missile; medium-range missile/ ~轰炸机 medium bomber
【中辍】 zhōngchuò stop (doing sth.) halfway; give up halfway
【中等】 zhōngděng ① medium; moderate; middling: ~个儿 of medium height/ ~城市 medium-sized city ② secondary: ~教育 secondary school education/ ~专科学校 technical secondary school; polytechnic school
【中点】 zhōngdiǎn 〈数〉 midpoint
【中断】 zhōngduàn suspend; break off; discontinue: ~谈判 break off the negotiations (或 talks)/ 两国关系~了好多年。 Relations between the two countries were suspended for many years./ 交通~了几小时。 Traffic was held up for a few hours.
【中饭】 zhōngfàn midday meal; lunch
【中锋】 zhōngfēng ①〈足球〉〈水球〉 centre forward ②〈篮球〉 centre
【中古】 zhōnggǔ ① the middle ancient times (in Chinese history, from the 3rd to the 9th century) ② medieval times; Middle Ages ◇ ~史 medieval history
【中和】 zhōnghé 〈化〉 neutralization ◇ ~剂 neutralizer
【中华】 Zhōnghuá China
【中级】 zhōngjí middle rank; intermediate
【中坚】 zhōngjiān nucleus; hard core; backbone: ~分子 backbone elements
【中间】 zhōngjiān ① among; between: 坐在他们两人~ sit between the two of them/ 她是我们三人~最年轻的。 She is the youngest of us three. ② centre; middle: ~突破 make a breakthrough at the centre (或 in the middle)/ 从我家到工厂，~要换车。 I have to change buses on the way from home to the factory.

【中将】 zhōngjiàng 〈军〉(英美陆军,美空军) lieutenant general; (英空军) air marshal; (英美海军) vice admiral
【中看】 zhōngkàn be pleasant to the eye: ~不中吃 look nice but not taste nice; be pleasant to the eye but not agreeable to the palate
【中立】 zhōnglì neutrality: 守~ observe neutrality/ 保持~ remain neutral/ 永久~ permanent neutrality ◇ ~地带 neutral zone/ ~法 law of neutrality; neutrality law/ ~国 neutral state/ ~政策 policy of neutrality/ ~主义 neutralism
【中流】 zhōngliú midstream
【中流砥柱】 zhōngliú dǐzhù firm rock in midstream; mainstay
【中落】 zhōngluò (of family fortunes) decline; ebb
【中年】 zhōngnián middle age ◇ ~人 a middle-aged person
【中篇小说】 zhōngpiān xiǎoshuō medium-length novel; novelette
【中秋节】 Zhōngqiūjié the Mid-autumn Festival (15th day of the 8th lunar month)
【中人】 zhōngrén middleman; go-between; mediator; intermediary
【中山狼】 zhōngshānláng the Zhongshan wolf in the fable — a person who repays good with evil
【中世纪】 zhōngshìjì Middle Ages
【中枢】 zhōngshū centre: 领导~ leading centre/ 电讯~ telecommunications centre/ 神经~ nerve centre ◇ ~神经系统 〈生理〉 central nervous system
【中听】 zhōngtīng pleasant to the ear; agreeable to the hearer
【中途】 zhōngtú halfway; midway: ~停留 stop halfway; stop over/ ~下汽车 get off the car midway/ 这趟公共汽车~不停。 This is a nonstop bus./ 他原是学建筑的，~改行搞地质了。 At first he studied architecture, but later he switched to geology./ 开会不要~退场。 Don't leave before the meeting is over. 或 Don't leave when the meeting is in progress.
【中外】 Zhōng-wài China and foreign countries: 驰名~ well known both in China and abroad/ 古今~ both ancient and modern, Chinese and foreign; at all times and in all countries
【中文】 Zhōngwén the Chinese language; Chinese: ~书刊 books and magazines in Chinese
【中午】 zhōngwǔ noon; midday
【中西】 Zhōng-Xī Chinese and Western: ~医结合 combine traditional Chinese and Western medicine
【中校】 zhōngxiào (英美陆军,美空军) lieutenant colonel; (英美海军) commander; (英空军) wing commander
【中心】 zhōngxīn centre; heart; core; hub: 在广场~ at the centre of the square/ 抓住问题的~ get to the heart of the matter/ 商业(贸易)~ business (trade) centre/ 陆路交通的~ hub of overland communications ◇ ~思想 central idea; gist/ ~问题 central issue; crucial question
【中兴】 zhōngxīng resurgence (usu. of a nation)
【中型】 zhōngxíng medium-sized; middle-sized: ~词典 a medium-sized dictionary
【中性】 zhōngxìng 〈化〉 neutral: ~反应 neutral reaction
【中学】 zhōngxué middle school: 初(高)级~ junior (senior) middle school
【中旬】 zhōngxún the middle ten days of a month: 四月~ the middle ten days of April
【中央】 zhōngyāng ① centre; middle: 湖的~有一座亭子。 At the centre of the lake, there is a pavilion. ② central authorities (of a state, party, etc.)
【中央集权】 zhōngyāng jíquán centralization (of authority): ~的国家 centralized state power
【中药】 zhōngyào traditional Chinese medicine ◇ ~铺 shop (或 store) of traditional Chinese medicines; Chinese pharmacy/ ~学 traditional Chinese pharmacology
【中叶】 zhōngyè middle period: 十九世纪~ the mid-1800s; the middle of the 19th century

【中医】 zhōngyī ① traditional Chinese medical science ② doctor of traditional Chinese medicine; practitioner of Chinese medicine

【中庸】 zhōngyōng the golden mean (of the Confucian school): ～之道 the doctrine of the mean

【中用】 zhōngyòng 〔多用于否定〕 of use; useful: 不～ be of no use

【中游】 zhōngyóu ① middle reaches (of a river) ② the state of being middling: 甘居～ be resigned to the middling state; be content to stay middling

【中止】 zhōngzhǐ discontinue; suspend; break off: ～谈判 suspend (或 break off) negotiations

【中指】 zhōngzhǐ middle finger

忠* zhōng loyal; devoted; honest

【忠臣】 zhōngchén official loyal to his sovereign

【忠诚】 zhōngchéng loyal; faithful; staunch

【忠告】 zhōnggào ① sincerely advise; admonish ② sincere advice; advice

【忠厚】 zhōnghòu honest and tolerant; sincere and kindly

【忠实】 zhōngshí true; faithful: ～于原文 true (或 faithful) to the original/ ～的信徒 faithful disciple

【忠顺】 zhōngshùn loyal and obedient

【忠心】 zhōngxīn loyalty; devotion: 赤胆～ ardent loyalty; wholehearted devotion; utter devotion

【忠心耿耿】 zhōngxīn gěnggěng loyal and devoted; most faithful and true

【忠言】 zhōngyán sincere advice; earnest advice

【忠言逆耳】 zhōngyán nì ěr good advice jars on the ear: ～利于行。 Honest advice, though unpleasant to the ear, induces good conduct.

【忠于】 zhōngyú true to; loyal to; faithful to; devoted to: ～祖国、～人民 be loyal to one's country and people/ ～职守 be devoted to one's duty

【忠贞】 zhōngzhēn loyal and steadfast: ～不渝 unswerving in one's loyalty/ ～不屈 staunch and indomitable

终* zhōng ① end; finish: 年～ end of the year/ 自始至～ from beginning to end; from start to finish/ 善始善～ start well and end well; see sth. through ② death; end: 临～ on one's deathbed; just before one dies ③ eventually; after all; in the end: ～非良策。 It's not a good plan after all. ④ whole; entire; all: ～岁 the whole year; throughout the year/ ～日 all day long; all day

【终场】 zhōngchǎng ① end of a performance or show ② 〈旧〉 final session in an examination

【终点】 zhōngdiǎn terminal point; destination: 旅行的～ destination of a journey

【终归】 zhōngguī eventually; in the end; after all: 要两面派～不会有好下场。 Double-dealers will come to no good end./ 他～还是个新手。 After all he is still a new hand./ 孩子～是孩子。 Children will be children.

【终极】 zhōngjí ultimate: ～目标 ultimate aim

【终结】 zhōngjié end; final stage: 这不是故事的～, 而只是开始。 This is just the beginning, not the end, of the story.

【终究】 zhōngjiū eventually; in the end; after all: 一个人的力量～有限。 The strength of the individual is limited after all./ 你～会明白的。 In the end you'll understand.

【终局】 zhōngjú end; outcome: 战争的～ the outcome of a war

【终了】 zhōngliǎo end (of a period): 学期～ the end of the (school) term

【终南捷径】 Zhōngnán jiéjìng ① shortcut to high office; royal road to fame ② shortcut to success

【终年】 zhōngnián ① (all) the year round; throughout the year: ～积雪的高山 mountains perennially covered with snow ② the age at which one dies: 他～七十八岁。 He died at the age of seventy-eight.

【终身】 zhōngshēn lifelong; all one's life: ～伴侣 lifelong companion (referring to one's husband or wife)/ ～事业 one's lifework/ ～大事 an important event in one's life (usu. marriage)

【终生】 zhōngshēng all one's life: ～难忘的教训 a lesson for life

【终于】 zhōngyú at (long) last; in the end; finally: 他们～赢得了独立。 At long last they won their independence.

【终止】 zhōngzhǐ ① stop; end: 要求～这种不正常状态 demand an end to this abnormal state of affairs/ ～日期 closing date ② termination; annulment; abrogation: ～条约通知书 notice of termination of a treaty; notice of denunciation

盅 zhōng handleless cup: 茶～ teacup/ 酒～ winecup

钟* zhōng ① bell: 撞～ toll (或 ring) a bell ② clock: 电～ electric clock ③ time as measured in hours and minutes: 六点～ six o'clock/ 十分～ ten minutes ④ concentrate (one's affections, etc.) ⑤ handleless cup

【钟爱】 zhōng'ài dote on (a child); cherish

【钟摆】 zhōngbǎi pendulum

【钟表】 zhōngbiǎo clocks and watches; timepiece ◇ ～店 watchmaker's shop/ ～油 watchmaker's oil

【钟点】 zhōngdiǎn 〈口〉 ① a time for sth. to be done or to happen: 到～儿了, 我们快走吧! It's time; let's be off. ② hour

【钟楼】 zhōnglóu ① bell tower; belfry ② clock tower

【钟情】 zhōngqíng be deeply in love: 一见～ fall in love at first sight

【钟乳石】 zhōngrǔshí 〈地〉 stalactite

【钟头】 zhōngtóu 〈口〉 hour

衷 zhōng inner feelings; heart: 由～之言 words spoken from the bottom of one's heart

【衷情】 zhōngqíng 〈书〉 heartfelt emotion; inner feelings: 久别重逢, 互诉～。 Meeting again after a long separation, they opened their hearts to each other.

【衷心】 zhōngxīn heartfelt; wholehearted; cordial: 表示～的感激 express one's heartfelt gratitude/ ～拥护 give wholehearted support/ 表示～的祝贺 extend cordial greetings/ ～感谢你的帮助。 I thank you for your help from the bottom of my heart.

zhǒng

肿* zhǒng swelling; swollen: 我的腿～了。 My legs are swollen./ ～消了一点。 The swelling has gone down a little.

【肿瘤】 zhǒngliú 〈医〉 tumour: 良 (恶) 性～ benign (malignant) tumour

【肿胀】 zhǒngzhàng swelling

种* zhǒng ① 〈生〉 species: 本地～ endemic species/ 亚～ subspecies/ 外地～ exotic species ② race: 黄～人 the yellow race ③ seed; strain; breed: 麦～ wheat seeds/ 良～牛 good breed of cattle ④ guts; grit: 有～的站出来! Let anyone who has guts step forward! ⑤ kind; sort; type: 各～仪器 all kinds of instruments/ 这～论调 this sort of argument/ 四十～钢材 forty types of rolled steel 另见 zhòng

【种类】 zhǒnglèi kind; type; variety: 不同～的刀具 cutters of different kinds/ ～繁多 a great variety

【种种】 zhǒngzhǒng all sorts (或 kinds) of; a variety of: 设置了～障碍 put up all sorts of obstacles/ 由于～原因 for a variety of reasons/ 用～手段 by hook or by crook; resort to every means (或 trick)/ 凡此～, 不一而足。 Such instances are legion.

【种子】 zhǒngzǐ seed

【种族】 zhǒngzú race: ～平等 racial equality ◇ ～隔离 racial segregation; (南非) apartheid/ ～灭绝 genocide/ ～歧视 racial discrimination/ ～主义 racism; racialism/ ～主义者 racist

冢 zhǒng tomb; grave: 古～ ancient tomb

踵 zhǒng 〈书〉 ① heel: 接～ follow on sb.'s heels ②

call in person: ~门道谢 call in person to express one's thanks ③ follow close behind

zhòng

中* zhòng ① hit; fit exactly: 射~靶心 hit the bull's eye/ 击~要害 hit the most vulnerable point; hit home/ 猜~ guess right/ 你说~了。 You've hit it. 或 That's right. ② be hit by; fall into; be affected by; suffer: 腿上~了一枪 be shot in the leg/ ~计 be taken in; fall into a trap/ ~埋伏 fall into an ambush/ ~煤气 be gassed 另见 zhōng

【中的】 zhòngdì hit the mark; hit the nail on the head: 批驳有力,语语~。 The refutation is forceful and every word hits home.

【中毒】 zhòngdú poisoning; toxicosis: 食物~ food poisoning/ 酒精~ alcoholism/ 煤气~ gas poisoning

【中风】 zhòngfēng apoplexy

【中奖】 zhòngjiǎng draw a prizewinning ticket (或 win a prize) in a lottery; get the winning number in a bond

【中肯】 zhòngkěn ① apropos; pertinent; to the point: ~的评语 pertinent remarks/ 回答简短而~。 The reply was brief and to the point./ 作出~的分析 make a sound analysis ② <物> critical

【中伤】 zhòngshāng slander; malign; vilify: 造谣~ spread slanderous rumours/ 恶语~ malign sb. viciously

【中暑】 zhòngshǔ ① suffer heatstroke (或 sunstroke); be affected by the heat ② heatstroke; sunstroke

【中选】 zhòngxuǎn be chosen; be selected

【中意】 zhòngyì be to one's liking; catch the fancy of: 这些暖瓶,我一个都不~。 None of these thermosflasks is to my liking.

众* zhòng ① many; numerous: 寡不敌~ be hopelessly outnumbered; fight against hopeless odds ② crowd; multitude: 大~ the multitude; the masses/ 观~ spectators; audience/ 听~ audience; listeners

【众多】 zhòngduō multitudinous; numerous.

【众寡悬殊】 zhòng-guǎ xuánshū a great disparity in numerical strength

【众口一词】 zhòng kǒu yī cí with one voice; unanimously

【众目睽睽】 zhòng mù kuíkuí the eyes of the masses are fixed on sb. or sth.: ~之下 in the public eye; in the public gaze

【众目昭彰】 zhòng mù zhāozhāng the masses are sharp-eyed

【众怒难犯】 zhòng nù nán fàn you cannot afford to incur public wrath; it is dangerous to incur the anger of the masses

【众叛亲离】 zhòngpàn-qīnlí the masses are in rebellion and one's friends are deserting; be opposed by the masses and deserted by one's followers; be utterly isolated

【众擎易举】 zhòng qíng yì jǔ many hands make light work

【众人】 zhòngrén everybody: ~拾柴火焰高。 When everybody adds fuel the flames rise high.

【众生】 zhòngshēng <佛教> all living creatures

【众说纷纭】 zhòng shuō fēnyún opinions vary: ~,莫衷一是。 As opinions vary, no unanimous conclusion can be drawn.

【众所周知】 zhòng suǒ zhōu zhī as everyone knows; as is known to all; it is common knowledge that

【众望】 zhòngwàng people's expectations; popular confidence: 不孚~ fall short of people's expectations/ ~所归 enjoy popular confidence

【众议院】 zhòngyìyuàn （美、澳、日等） House of Representatives; （意、墨、智等） Chamber of Deputies

【众志成城】 zhòng zhì chéng chéng unity of will is an impregnable stronghold; unity is strength

仲 zhòng ① (of the three months in a season) second: ~春 second month of spring ② (of brothers) second in order of birth: ~兄 the second eldest brother ③ middle; intermediate

【仲裁】 zhòngcái arbitrate: 对争端进行~ arbitrate a dispute ◇ ~法庭 arbitration tribunal; court of arbitration/ ~人 arbitrator

【仲夏】 zhòngxià second month of summer; midsummer

种* zhòng grow; plant; cultivate: ~水稻 grow rice/ ~庄稼 plant crops 另见 zhǒng

【种地】 zhòngdì till (或 cultivate) land; go in for farming

【种痘】 zhòngdòu vaccination (against smallpox): 这孩子~了吗? Has the baby been vaccinated? 又作"种牛痘"

【种瓜得瓜,种豆得豆】 zhòng guā dé guā, zhòng dòu dé dòu plant melons and you get melons, sow beans and you get beans — as you sow, so will you reap

【种花】 zhònghuā ① cultivate (或 grow) flowers ② <方> vaccination (against smallpox)

【种田】 zhòngtián till the land; farm

【种植】 zhòngzhí plant; grow: 油菜~面积 rape-growing areas; areas sown to rape ◇ ~园 plantation/ ~园主 plantation owner; planter

重* zhòng ① weight: 举~ weight lifting/ 毛(净)~ gross (net) weight/ 这条鱼有三斤~。 This fish weighs three jin. ② heavy; weighty; important: 工作很~ have a heavy work load/ ~税 heavy (或 oppressive) taxation/ 以友谊为~ set store by friendship ③ considerable in amount or value: ~赏 a handsome reward/ 金购买 pay a high price for ④ deep; heavy; serious: 情意~ deep affection/ 私心很~ extremely selfish; grow ~ be seriously ill/ 受了~伤 be `severely injured ⑤ lay stress on; attach importance to: ~调查研究 lay stress on investigation and study/ ~男轻女的封建思想 the feudal idea of regarding men as superior to women ⑥ discreet: 自~ self-respect/ 慎~ careful; cautious 另见 chóng

【重办】 zhòngbàn severely punish (a criminal)

【重兵】 zhòngbīng a large number of troops; massive forces: 派驻~ station massive forces/ 有~把守 be heavily guarded

【重创】 zhòngchuāng inflict heavy losses (或 casualties) on; maul (heavily)

【重大】 zhòngdà great; weighty; major; significant: 具有~的现实意义 be of great immediate significance/ ~的原则分歧 a major difference of principle/ ~成就 significant (或 tremendous) achievements/ ~胜利 a signal victory/ ~问题 vital problem; major issue/ ~损失 heavy losses

【重担】 zhòngdàn heavy burden; difficult task

【重地】 zhòngdì important place (usually not open to the public): 施工~,闲人免进。 Construction Site. No Admittance.

【重点】 zhòngdiǎn focal point; stress; emphasis: 突出~ make the focal (或 key) points stand out/ ~工程 major (或 priority) project

【重负】 zhòngfù heavy burden; heavy load: 如释~ feel as if relieved of a heavy load

【重工业】 zhònggōngyè heavy industry

【重活】 zhònghuó heavy work

【重价】 zhòngjià high price: ~收购古物 offer high prices for antiques

【重力】 zhònglì <物> gravity; gravitational force

【重利】 zhònglì ① high interest: ~盘剥 practise usury ② huge profit

【重量】 zhòngliàng weight

【重任】 zhòngrèn important task; heavy responsibility: 身负~ be charged with important tasks

【重商主义】 zhòngshāngzhǔyì mercantilism

【重视】 zhòngshì attach importance to; pay attention to; think highly of; take sth. seriously; value

【重听】 zhòngtīng hard of hearing

【重托】 zhòngtuō great trust

【重武器】 zhòngwǔqì heavy weapons

【重心】 zhòngxīn ① <物> centre of gravity ② heart; core;

focus: 问题的～ the heart of a matter

【重要】 zhòngyào important; significant; major: ～人物 important figure; prominent personage; VIP/ ～关头 critical juncture/ ～任务 vital task; important mission/ ～原则 cardinal principle/ ～政策 major policy/ ～因素 key factor ◇ ～性 importance; significance

【重用】 zhòngyòng put sb. in an important position

【重镇】 zhòngzhèn place of strategic importance

zhōu

州 * zhōu ① 〈旧〉 an administrative division ② (autonomous) prefecture

舟 * zhōu 〈书〉 boat: 轻～ a light boat/ 泛～ go boating

【舟车】 zhōuchē 〈书〉 ① vessel and vehicle ② journey: ～劳顿 fatigued by a long journey; travel-worn

【舟楫】 zhōují 〈书〉 vessels: 江河湖泽给我们以～和灌溉之利。 Rivers and lakes provide us with water transport and irrigation.

【舟子】 zhōuzǐ 〈书〉 boatman

诌 zhōu fabricate (tales, etc.); make up: 别胡～了。 Stop making up wild stories.

周 * zhōu ① circumference; periphery; circuit: 圆～ circumference (of a circle)/ 运动员绕场一～。 The athletes made a circuit of the arena. /在村子四～植树 plant trees round the village ② make a circuit; move in a circular course ③ all; whole; all over; all around: 众所～知 as is known to all/ ～身 the whole body ④ thoughtful; attentive: 丁宁～至 give thoughtful advice/ 计划不～ not well planned; not planned carefully enough/ 招待不～ not be attentive enough to guests ⑤ week: 上～ last week

【周报】 zhōubào weekly publication; weekly

【周遍】 zhōubiàn all round; all over

【周到】 zhōudào attentive and satisfactory; thoughtful; considerate: 服务～ offer good service/ 想得很～ be very thoughtful (或 considerate)/ 安排得很～ be satisfactorily arranged; be carefully worked out

【周而复始】 zhōu ér fù shǐ go round and begin again; go round and round; move in cycles

【周济】 zhōují help out (the needy); relieve

【周刊】 zhōukān weekly publication (或 magazine); weekly

【周密】 zhōumì careful; thorough: ～思考 think over carefully/ 进行～的调查 carry out a thorough investigation/ ～的分析 a detailed analysis/ ～的计划 a well-conceived plan

【周末】 zhōumò weekend

【周年】 zhōunián anniversary: 建厂十五～ the 15th anniversary of the founding of the factory/ 一百～ centenary

【周期】 zhōuqī period; cycle: 工作～ 〈机〉 action cycle ◇ ～表 〈化〉 periodic table/ ～律 〈化〉 periodic law

【周期性】 zhōuqīxìng periodicity; cyclicity: ～循环 periodic return/ ～经济危机 periodic (或 cyclical) economic crises/ 疟疾～发作 periodic attacks of malaria

【周全】 zhōuquán ① thorough; comprehensive ② 〈旧〉 help sb. attain his aim

【周身】 zhōushēn the whole body; all over the body: ～疼痛 ache all over

【周岁】 zhōusuì one full year of life: 今天孩子满～。 Today is the child's first birthday./ 他三十二～。 He is thirty-two years old.

【周围】 zhōuwéi around; round; about: 环顾～ look about; look around/ ～环境 surroundings; environment

【周详】 zhōuxiáng comprehensive; complete; careful: 考虑～ give careful consideration to

【周旋】 zhōuxuán ① mix with other people; socialize: ～于达官贵人之间 move in high society ② deal with; contend with

【周游】 zhōuyóu travel round; journey round: ～世界 travel round the world/ ～各国 travel to many countries;

travel far and wide

【周章】 zhōuzhāng 〈书〉 ① be scared: 狼狈～ be scared out of one's wits; be panic-stricken ② trouble; effort: 煞费～ take great pains; spare no effort

【周折】 zhōuzhé twists and turns; setbacks: 这事恐怕要费一番～。 I'm afraid this business will cause us a good deal of bother./ 几经～，才告成功。 Only after many setbacks was success achieved.

【周转】 zhōuzhuǎn 〈经〉 turnover: 加速资本～ speed up capital turnover

洲 * zhōu ① continent ② islet in a river; sand bar

【洲际】 zhōujì intercontinental ◇ ～弹道导弹 intercontinental ballistic missile/ ～导弹 intercontinental missile

啁 zhōu

【啁啾】 zhōujiū 〈书〉〈象〉 (of birds) twitter; chirp; warble

粥 zhōu gruel (made of rice, millet, etc.); porridge; congee: 小米～ millet gruel

【粥少僧多】 zhōu shǎo sēng duō the gruel is meagre and the monks are many — not enough to go round

zhóu

妯 zhóu

【妯娌】 zhóuli wives of brothers; sisters-in-law

轴 zhóu ① axle; shaft: 车～ car axle; axle/ 曲～ crank shaft/ 心～ spindle ② axis: 地～ the earth's axis/ 椭圆的长(短)～ the major (minor) axis of an ellipse ③ spool; rod: 线～儿 spool (for thread)/ 画～ roller for a scroll of Chinese painting ④ 〈量〉 一～线 a spool of thread/ 一～山水画 a scroll painting of scenery

另见 zhòu

【轴心】 zhóuxīn ① 〈机〉 axle centre ② axis ◇ ～国 Axis powers; the Axis

zhǒu

肘 zhǒu elbow

帚 zhǒu broom

zhòu

纣 Zhòu name of the last ruler of the Shang Dynasty (c. 16th — 11th century B.C.), reputedly a tyrant

宙 zhòu time (conceived as past, present and future) 参见"宇宙" yǔzhòu

咒 zhòu ① incantation: 念～ chant incantations ② curse; damn: 诅～ curse

【咒骂】 zhòumà curse; swear; abuse; revile

【咒语】 zhòuyǔ incantation

胄 zhòu ① helmet: 甲～ armour and helmet ② descendants; offspring: 贵～ descendants of feudal rulers or aristocrats

昼 zhòu daytime; daylight; day: ～伏夜出 hide by day and come out at night

【昼夜】 zhòu-yè day and night; round the clock: ～看守 keep watch round the clock/ ～警戒 be on a round-the-clock alert/ 他们英勇地战斗了七～。 They battled heroically for seven days and nights.

轴 zhòu 见"压轴子" yāzhòuzi

另见 zhóu

皱 zhòu wrinkle; crease: 这种料子不起～。 This material won't crease./ 注意别把地图弄~了。Mind you don't crumple the map.

【皱眉头】zhòu méitóu knit (或 contract) one's brows; frown

【皱纹】zhòuwén wrinkles; lines: 满脸~ have a wrinkly face/ 眼角的 ~ crow's-feet

【皱褶】zhòuzhě fold

骤 zhòu ① (of a horse) trot: 驰~ gallop ② sudden; abrupt: 一阵~雨 a passing heavy shower/ 天气 ~ 变。There was a sudden change of weather./ 狂风~起。A sudden gale struck.

【骤然】zhòurán suddenly; abruptly: ~离去 leave abruptly/ ~响起雷鸣般的掌声。Stormy applause broke forth suddenly.

籀 zhòu 〈书〉① read aloud; recite ② 见"籀文"

【籀文】zhòuwén a style of calligraphy, current in the Zhou Dynasty (c. 11th century – 256 B.C.)

zhū

朱* zhū ① vermilion; bright red ② cinnabar

【朱笔】zhūbǐ writing brush dipped in red ink (formerly used in marking students' papers or writing comments on official documents)

【朱红】zhūhóng vermilion; bright red

【朱门】zhūmén vermilion gates — red-lacquered doors of wealthy homes: ~酒肉臭,路有冻死骨。Behind the vermilion gates meat and wine go to waste while out on the road lie the bones of those frozen to death.

【朱批】zhūpī comments or remarks written in red with a brush

【朱漆】zhūqī red paint; red lacquer: ~大门 vermilion gates/ ~木箱 red-lacquered chest

【朱砂】zhūshā cinnabar

【朱文】zhūwén characters on a seal carved in relief

诛 zhū 〈书〉① put (a criminal) to death: 伏~ be executed/ ~锄异己 wipe out dissenters ② punish: 卖国贼人人得而~之。Everybody has the right to punish traitors.

【诛戮】zhūlù 〈书〉kill; put to death

【诛心之论】zhūxīn zhī lùn penetrating criticism; exposure of sb.'s ulterior motives

侏 zhū 〈书〉dwarf

【侏儒】zhūrú dwarf; midget; pygmy

珠 zhū ① pearl: 明~ bright pearl; jewel ② bead: 露~ beads of dew; dewdrops/ 算盘~ beads on an abacus/ 泪~儿 teardrop

【珠宝】zhūbǎo pearls and jewels; jewelry ◇ ~店 a jeweller's (shop)/ ~商 jeweller

【珠玑】zhūjī 〈书〉pearl; gem: 字字~ each word a gem

【珠联璧合】zhūlián-bìhé strings of pearls and girdles of jade — a perfect pair; a happy combination

【珠算】zhūsuàn reckoning by the abacus; calculation with an abacus

【珠圆玉润】zhūyuán-yùrùn round as pearls and smooth as jade — excellent singing or polished writing

【珠子】zhūzi ① pearl ② bead

株* zhū ① trunk of a tree; stem of a plant ② individual plant; plant: 幼~ young plant; sapling ③〈量〉:两~梨树 two pear trees

【株连】zhūlián involve (others) in a criminal case; implicate

【株守】zhūshǒu hold on stubbornly to (a silly idea, etc.) 参见"守株待兔" shǒu zhū dài tù

诸* zhū ① all; various: 自然科学~部门 the various branches of natural science ②〈书〉〔"之于"或"之乎"的合

音〕: 付~实施 put into practice; bring into effect/ 有~? Is there (such a thing)?

【诸多】zhūduō 〈书〉〔用于抽象事物〕a good deal; a lot of: ~不便 a lot of trouble: great inconvenience

【诸侯】zhūhóu dukes or princes under an emperor

【诸如】zhūrú such as

【诸如此类】zhūrú cǐ lèi things like that; such; and so on and so forth: ~的科学发明,都大大提高了劳动生产率。Scientific inventions such as these have raised labour productivity by a big margin./ ~的事例太多,不胜枚举。Such instances are too numerous to mention.

【诸位】zhūwèi 〈敬〉〔总称所指的若干人〕: ~有什么意见,欢迎提出来。You are welcome to put forward your views./ ~女士,~先生！Ladies and Gentlemen!

【诸子百家】zhūzǐ bǎijiā the various schools of thought and their exponents during the period from pre-Qin times to the early years of the Han Dynasty

猪* zhū pig; hog; swine: 小~ pigling; piglet/ 母~ sow/ 公~ boar

【猪肝】zhūgān pork liver

【猪猡】zhūluó 〈方〉pig: swine

【猪排】zhūpái pork chop

【猪皮】zhūpí pigskin; hogskin

【猪肉】zhūròu pork

【猪食】zhūshí pig feed: pigwash; swill ◇ ~缸 (pig) trough

【猪瘟】zhūwēn swine fever; hog cholera

【猪油】zhūyóu lard

铢 zhū an ancient unit of weight, equal to 1/24 liang (两)

【铢积寸累】zhūjī-cùnlěi accumulate little by little; build up bit by bit

【铢两悉称】zhū-liǎng xī chèn exactly equal in weight; have the same weight

蛛* zhū spider

【蛛丝马迹】zhūsī-mǎjī thread of a spider and trail of a horse — clues; traces

【蛛网】zhūwǎng spider web: cobweb

【蛛蛛】zhūzhu spider

zhú

竹* zhú bamboo: ~篓 bamboo crate (或 basket)/ ~林 bamboo forest; groves of bamboo

【竹板】zhúbǎn bamboo clappers

【竹帛】zhúbó bamboo slips and silk (used for writing on during ancient times); ancient books

【竹竿】zhúgān bamboo pole; bamboo

【竹简】zhújiǎn bamboo slip (used for writing on during ancient times)

【竹笋】zhúsǔn bamboo shoots

【竹子】zhúzi bamboo

竺 Zhú a surname

烛* zhú ① candle: 蜡~ (wax) candle/ ~心 candlewick ②〈书〉illuminate; light up: 火光~天。Leaping flames lit up the sky. ③ watt: 二十五~灯泡 a 25-watt bulb

【烛光】zhúguāng 〈物〉candlepower; candle

【烛花】zhúhuā snuff: 剪~ trim off the snuff (of a candle); snuff

【烛台】zhútái candlestick

【烛照】zhúzhào 〈书〉illuminate; light up

逐 zhú ① pursue; chase: 追~ pursue; chase/ ~水草而居 move from place to place in search of water and grass ② drive out; expel: ~出门外 drive out of the door ③ one by one: ~项 item by item/ ~月 month by month/ ~条加以说明 explain point by point

【逐步】zhúbù step by step; progressively: ~加以解决 settle

sth. step by step/ ～降低生产成本 progressively reduce the production cost

【逐个】 zhúgè one by one: 我们得～研究这些问题。We must look into these matters one by one.

【逐渐】 zhújiàn gradually; by degrees: 他对情况～熟悉起来了。He's gradually getting better acquainted with the situation./ 天～暗下来了。It's getting darker and darker.

【逐客令】 zhúkèlìng order for guests to leave: 下～ show sb. the door

【逐鹿】 zhúlù 〈书〉 chase the deer — fight for the throne; bid for state power: ～中原 fight among rivals for the throne/ 群雄～ feudal lords vying for the throne; powerful politicians fighting for supremacy

【逐年】 zhúnián year by year; year after year: 产量～增加。Production has been increasing year after year.

【逐日】 zhúrì day by day; every day: 病情～好转。The patient's condition is improving day by day.

【逐一】 zhúyī one by one: 对这些规定～加以说明 explain all these provisions one by one

【逐字】 zhúzì word for word; verbatim: ～记录 verbatim record

【逐字逐句】 zhú zì zhú jù word by word and sentence by sentence; word for word: ～地宣读文件 read the document word by word and sentence by sentence/ ～的翻译 word-for-word (或 literal) translation

舳 zhú stern (of a ship, etc.)

蠋 zhú larva of a butterfly or moth

躅 zhú 〈书〉 footprint; footmark

zhǔ

主* zhǔ ① host: 宾～ host and guest ② owner; master: 奴隶～ slave owner/ 企业～ proprietor of an enterprise/ 当家作～ be master in one's own house ③ person or party concerned: 买～ buyer/ 卖～ seller ④ 〈基督教〉 God; Lord ⑤ 〈伊斯兰教〉 Allah ⑥ main; primary: ～航道 main (或 principal) channel/ 预防为～ put prevention first ⑦ manage; direct; be in charge of: ～其事 be in charge of the business; manage the affairs ⑧ indicate; signify: 早霞～雨, 晚霞～晴。Rosy morning clouds indicate rain, and a rosy sunset means fine weather. ⑨ hold a definite view about sth.; advocate: ～和 advocate peace; be for a peaceful settlement/ 我一时心里没～。For a moment I just didn't know what to do.

【主办】 zhǔbàn direct; sponsor: 展览会将由外贸部～。The exhibition will be sponsored by (或 held under the auspices of) the Ministry of Foreign Trade.

【主笔】 zhǔbǐ 〈旧〉 ① editor in chief ② chief commentator

【主编】 zhǔbiān ① chief editor (或 compiler); editor in chief (supervise the publication of (a newspaper, magazine, etc.); edit

【主持】 zhǔchí ① take charge (或 care) of; manage; direct: ～日常事务 take care of routine matters ② preside over; chair: ～讨论 chair a discussion/ ～今晚的宴会 host this evening's banquet ③ uphold; stand for: ～正义 uphold justice

【主次】 zhǔcì primary and secondary: 我们干工作要分清～。In our work we must differentiate what is primary from what is secondary.

【主从】 zhǔcóng principal and subordinate: ～关系 the relationship between the principal and the subordinate

【主导】 zhǔdǎo leading; dominant; guiding: 起～作用 play a leading role

【主动】 zhǔdòng initiative: 争取～ try to gain the initiative; contend for the initiative/ ～帮助人 help others of one's own accord/ 我们应～派人去支援。We ought to send people to help on our own initiative.

【主队】 zhǔduì 〈体〉 home team; host team

【主犯】 zhǔfàn 〈法〉 prime culprit; principal criminal (或 offender); principal: ～和从犯 principal and accessories in a crime

【主峰】 zhǔfēng the highest peak in a mountain range

【主妇】 zhǔfù housewife; hostess

【主干】 zhǔgàn ① 〈植〉 trunk ② main force; mainstay

【主顾】 zhǔgù customer; client

【主观】 zhǔguān subjective

【主管】 zhǔguǎn ① be responsible for; be in charge of: 谁～这项工作？Who is in charge of this job? ② person in charge ◇ ～部门 department responsible for the work/ ～机关 competent authorities; responsible institution

【主婚】 zhǔhūn (usu. of the parents of the bride and the bridegroom) preside over a wedding ceremony

【主祭】 zhǔjì officiate at funeral or sacrificial rites

【主见】 zhǔjiàn ideas or thoughts of one's own; one's own judgment; definite view: 没有～ have no definite views of one's own/ 她这人很有～。She knows her own mind.

【主讲】 zhǔjiǎng be the speaker; give a lecture

【主将】 zhǔjiàng chief commander; commanding general

【主教】 zhǔjiào 〈宗〉 bishop: 大～ archbishop/ 红衣～ cardinal

【主角】 zhǔjué leading role; lead; protagonist: 在该片中演～ play the lead in the film/ 女～ a leading lady

【主考】 zhǔkǎo ① be in charge of an examination ② chief examiner (in a school, etc.)

【主力】 zhǔlì main force; main strength of an army

【主力军】 zhǔlìjūn main (或 principal) force

【主流】 zhǔliú ① main stream; main current; mother current ② essential or main aspect; main trend: ～和支流 principal and secondary aspects

【主谋】 zhǔmóu ① head a conspiracy; be the chief plotter ② 〈法〉 chief instigator

【主脑】 zhǔnǎo ① control centre; centre of operation ② leader; chief

【主权】 zhǔquán sovereign rights; sovereignty: 领土～ territorial sovereignty ◇ ～国家 a sovereign state

【主人】 zhǔrén ① master ② host: 女～ hostess ③ owner: 房子的～ owner of the house

【主人公】 zhǔréngōng leading character in a novel, etc.; hero or heroine; protagonist

【主人翁】 zhǔrénwēng ① master: 新社会的～ masters of the new society/ 有一种～感 have a sense of being the master of one's own affairs ② 见 "主人公"

【主任】 zhǔrèn director; head; chairman

【主使】 zhǔshǐ instigate; incite; abet

【主题】 zhǔtí theme; subject; motif; leitmotiv: 诗的～ the subject of a poem/ 作品的～思想 the theme of a literary work ◇ ～歌 〈电影〉 theme song

【主体】 zhǔtǐ ① main body; main part; principal part

【主席】 zhǔxí ① chairman (of a meeting): 当～ be in the chair; preside over a meeting ② chairman or president (of an organization or a state) ◇ ～台 rostrum; platform/ ～团 presidium

【主修】 zhǔxiū ① specialize (in a subject); major: 她～原子物理。She majors in atomic physics. ② be responsible for the repair or overhaul (of a machine) ◇ ～科目 major subjects

【主演】 zhǔyǎn act the leading role (in a play or film)

【主要】 zhǔyào main; chief; principal; major: ～敌人 chief enemy/ ～目的 major objective

【主义】 zhǔyì doctrine; -ism: 个人～ individualism/ 资本～ capitalism

【主意】 zhǔyì ① idea; plan: 好～ a good idea ② decision; definite view: 打定～ make a decision; make up one's mind/ 改变～ change one's mind/ 拿不定～ be in two minds (about sth.)/ 我一时没了～。I was quite at a loss, then.

【主语】 zhǔyǔ 〈语〉 subject

【主宰】 zhǔzǎi dominate; dictate; decide: ～自己的命运 decide one's own destiny; be master of one's own fate

【主张】 zhǔzhāng ① advocate; stand for; maintain; hold: ～自力更生 advocate self-reliance/～改革 favour reforms ② view; position; stand; proposition: 这是我们一贯的～。That has been our consistent stand./ 听起来两种～都有理

由。Both propositions sound reasonable.

【主旨】zhǔzhǐ purport; substance; gist: 文章的～ the gist of the article

【主子】zhǔzi master; boss: ～和奴才 the boss and his flunkey; master and servant

渚 zhǔ ‹书› small piece of land surrounded by water; islet: 江～ islet in a river

属 zhǔ ‹书› ① join; combine: ～文 compose a piece of prose writing/ 前后相～ (of two parts) join together ② fix (one's mind) on; centre (one's attention, etc.) upon: ～望 centre one's hope on; look forward to
另见 shǔ

【属意】zhǔyì ‹书› fix one's mind on sb. (as one's choice, favourite, etc.)

【属垣有耳】zhǔ yuán yǒu ěr walls have ears; someone has his ear to the wall

煮 * zhǔ boil; cook: ～鸡蛋 boil eggs/ ～饭 cook rice

【煮豆燃萁】zhǔ dòu rán qí burn beanstalks to cook beans — fratricidal strife

嘱 zhǔ enjoin; advise; urge

【嘱咐】zhǔfu enjoin; tell; exhort: 再三～ exhort again and again; din sth. into sb./ ～他保守秘密 enjoin him to secrecy/ 临终～ death-bed injunction/ 大夫～他好好休息。The doctor told him to take a good rest.

【嘱托】zhǔtuō entrust: 她～我办这件事。She entrusted me with the task.

瞩 zhǔ gaze; look steadily: 高瞻远～ stand high and see far; take a broad and long-term view; show great foresight

【瞩目】zhǔmù ‹书› fix one's eyes upon; focus one's attention upon: 举世～ be the focus of world attention

【瞩望】zhǔwàng ‹书› ① look forward to: ～已久 have been eagerly looking forward to it for a long time ② gaze at; look long and steadily upon

zhù

伫 zhù ‹书› stand for a long while

【伫候】zhùhòu ‹书› stand waiting: ～佳音 look forward to hearing good news from you

【伫立】zhùlì ‹书› stand still for a long while

助 * zhù help; assist; aid: 互～ help each other/ ～消化 aid digestion/ ～一臂之力 lend sb. a helping hand/ ～人为乐 find it a pleasure to help others

【助词】zhùcí ‹语› auxiliary word, an unstressed form word which performs the grammatical functions of structure (as 的,地,得,所), of tense (as 了,着,过) or of mood (as 呢,吗,吧,啊)

【助动词】zhùdòngcí ‹语› auxiliary verb

【助教】zhùjiào assistant (of a college faculty)

【助桀为虐】zhù Jié wéi nüè aid King Jie in his tyrannical rule; help a tyrant to do evil

【助理】zhùlǐ assistant: 部长～ assistant minister

【助手】zhùshǒu assistant; helper; aide

【助听器】zhùtīngqì audiphone; hearing aid; deaf-aid

【助威】zhùwēi boost the morale of; cheer (for): 给我们的篮球队～ cheer for our basketball team

【助兴】zhùxìng liven things up; add to the fun

【助学金】zhùxuéjīn stipend; grant-in-aid: 领～的学生 grant-aided student

【助长】zhùzhǎng ‹贬› encourage; abet; foster; foment: ～侵略者的野心 whet the ambitions of the aggressors

【助纣为虐】zhù Zhòu wéi nüè aid King Zhou in his tyrannical rule; help a tyrant to do evil

住 * zhù ① live; reside; stay: ～城外 live outside the city/ ～旅馆 stay at a hotel/ ～上新房 move into a new house ② stop; cease: 雨～了。The rain has stopped. ③ 〔做动词的补语, 表示牢固、稳当、停顿、静止等〕: 站～! Halt!/ 愣～了 be struck dumb; be left speechless/ 支持不～ cannot withstand/ 扣～一封信 stop a letter/ 记～ bear in mind; remember

【住持】zhùchí ‹宗› (Buddhist or Taoist) abbot

【住处】zhùchù residence; dwelling (place); lodging; quarters: 找到～没有? Have you found accommodation?/ 我不知道他的～。I don't know where he lives.

【住房】zhùfáng housing; lodgings: ～问题 the housing problem; accommodation

【住户】zhùhù household; resident: 院内有三家～。There are three households in the compound./ 这儿有姓马的～吗? Is there anyone named Ma living here?

【住家】zhùjiā (of one's family) live; reside in: 他在郊区～。He lives with his family in the suburbs.

【住口】zhùkǒu shut up; stop talking: 你给我～! Hold your tongue!

【住手】zhùshǒu stay one's hand; stop: 他不做完不肯～。He won't stop until he finishes the job.

【住宿】zhùsù stay; put up; get accommodation: 他今晚在旅店～。He will put up at an inn for the night./ 给客人安排～ find lodgings (或 arrange accommodation) for the visitors/ 大学生大部分在校～。Most college students are boarders.

【住所】zhùsuǒ dwelling place; residence; domicile: 固定～ permanent dwelling place; domicile

【住院】zhùyuàn be in hospital; be hospitalized: ～期间 during one's hospitalization; while in hospital ◇ ～病人 inpatient/ 医生 resident (physician)

【住宅】zhùzhái residence; dwelling ◇ ～区 residential quarters (或 district)

【住址】zhùzhǐ address

注 * zhù ① pour: 大雨如～。The rain poured down. ② concentrate; fix: 全神贯～ concentrate on; be engrossed in; be preoccupied with ③ stakes (in gambling): 孤～一郑 stake everything on a single throw ④ annotate; explain with notes ⑤ provide critical and explanatory notes for; annotate ⑤ notes: 附～ annotations/ 脚～ footnote ⑥ record; register

【注册】zhùcè register ◇ ～处 registration office; registrar's office/ ～商标 registered trademark

【注定】zhùdìng be doomed; be destined: ～要失败 be doomed to failure/ 命中～ decreed by fate; predestined

【注脚】zhùjiǎo footnote

【注解】zhùjiě ① annotate; explain with notes ② (explanatory) note; annotation

【注明】zhùmíng give clear indication of: ～出处 give sources (of quotations, etc.)/ 该表未～日期。That form is undated.

【注目】zhùmù gaze at; fix one's eyes on: 引人～ spectacular/ 行～礼 salute with eyes

【注入】zhùrù pour into; empty into: 长江～东海。The Changjiang River empties into the East China Sea.

【注射】zhùshè ‹医› inject

【注视】zhùshì look attentively at; gaze at: 久久～着陌生人的脸 look fixedly at the stranger's face for a long time/ 密切～会议的进展 closely follow the progress of the conference/ 雷达兵目不转睛地～着荧光屏。The radarman's eyes were glued to the screen.

【注释】zhùshì explanatory note; annotation ◇ ～读物 annotated readings

【注疏】zhùshū ‹书› notes and commentaries

【注销】zhùxiāo cancel; write off: 把借条～ cancel a written acknowledgment of a loan; cancel an I.O.U./ 账已～。The account has been written off.

【注意】zhùyì pay attention to; take note (或 notice) of: ～工作方法 pay attention to methods of work/ 必须～团结一切可以团结的人。Care must be taken to unite with all those that can be united with./ 我没～他什么时候走的。I didn't notice when he left./ ～, 马上就要点炮啦! Look out! We're ready to blast./ ～别摔倒。Mind you don't fall.

【注音】zhùyīn 〈语〉 phonetic notation: 课文有～吗? Is the text marked with phonetic symbols?

【注音字母】zhùyīn zìmǔ the national phonetic alphabet (in use before the publication of the Scheme for the Chinese Phonetic Alphabet) 又作"注音符号"

【注重】zhùzhòng lay stress on; pay attention to; attach importance to: ～基本功的训练 lay stress on basic training

贮 zhù store; save; lay aside: ～蓄 save up/ ～粮备荒 store grain against a lean year

【贮备】zhùbèi store up; have in reserve; lay aside

【贮藏】zhùcáng store up; lay in: ～过冬的大白菜 lay in cabbages for the winter/ 这一带地下～着丰富的矿产。This place is rich in mineral deposits.

【贮存】zhùcún store; keep in storage

驻 zhù ① halt; stay: ～足 make a temporary stay/ 敌～我扰。When the enemy halts, we harass him. ② be stationed: 我国～英大使 our ambassador to Britain

【驻地】zhùdì ① place where troops, etc. are stationed: 边防军～ frontier guard station/ 地质勘探队的～ encampment of a geological prospecting team ② seat (of a local administrative organ)

【驻防】zhùfáng be on garrison duty; garrison

【驻守】zhùshǒu garrison; defend

【驻屯】zhùtún (of troops) be stationed; be quartered

【驻扎】zhùzhá (of troops) be stationed; be quartered: ～重兵 station a huge force

炷 zhù 〈书〉① wick (of an oil lamp) ② burn: ～香 burn a joss stick ③〈量〉: 一～香 a burning joss stick

祝 zhù express good wishes; wish: ～你健康。I wish you the best of health./ ～你旅途愉快。Have a pleasant journey. 或 *Bon voyage*!/ ～我们两国人民的友谊万古长青! May the friendship between our two peoples be everlasting!

【祝词】zhùcí ① congratulatory speech (at a ceremony, etc.); congratulations ② prayers at sacrificial rites in ancient times

【祝福】zhùfú ① blessing; benediction ② new year's sacrifice (an old custom in certain parts of Zhejiang Province)

【祝贺】zhùhè congratulate: ～演出成功 congratulate the artists on their successful performance/ 向你～! Congratulations!/ ～两国建交 acclaim the establishment of diplomatic relations between the two countries/ 致以兄弟般的～ extend fraternal greetings

【祝捷】zhùjié celebrate a victory ◇ ～大会 victory celebration (meeting)

【祝酒】zhùjiǔ drink a toast; toast: 向来宾们～ toast the guests/ 致～辞 propose a toast/ 答谢～ respond (或 reply) to a toast

【祝寿】zhùshòu congratulate (an elderly person) on his or her birthday

【祝颂】zhùsòng express good wishes

【祝愿】zhùyuàn wish: 致以良好的～ with best wishes/ ～贵国日益繁荣昌盛。We wish your country ever growing prosperity.

柱 zhù ① post; upright; pillar; column: 门～ doorposts/ 房～ pillars of a house; upright/ 圆～ column ② sth. shaped like a column: 水～ water column/ 水银～ mercury column

【柱石】zhùshí pillar; mainstay

【柱子】zhùzi post; pillar

著 zhù ① marked; outstanding: 卓～ outstanding; distinguished/ 臭名昭～ notorious ② show; prove: 颇～成效 prove rather effective ③ write: ～书 write books/ ～录 put down in writing; record ④ book; work: 名～ a celebrated piece of writing; a famous work/ 新～ sb.'s latest work/ 译～ a translation

【著称】zhùchēng 〈书〉celebrated; famous: 以风景优美～ be celebrated for its scenic beauty

【著名】zhùmíng famous; celebrated; well-known: ～论断 a celebrated (或 well-known) thesis/ 李时珍是明代～的药物学家。Li Shizhen was a famous pharmacologist of the Ming Dynasty.

【著述】zhùshù ① write; compile: 从事～ be engaged in writing or compiling scholarly works ② book

【著者】zhùzhě author; writer

【著作】zhùzuò ① work; book; writings: 古代医学～ ancient books on medicine; ancient medical literature ② write: 他一生～甚多。He wrote many books during his lifetime. 或 He was a prolific author. ◇ ～权 copyright

蛀 zhù ① moth or any other insect that eats books, clothes, wood, etc. ② (of moths, etc.) eat; bore through: 这件呢大衣给虫子～了。This woollen coat is moth-eaten.

【蛀齿】zhùchǐ decayed tooth; dental caries

【蛀虫】zhùchóng insect that eats books, clothes or wood; moth; borer

筑 zhù build; construct: ～路 construct a road/ ～堤 build a dyke

铸 zhù casting; founding: ～钟 cast a bell/ ～钱 coin (或 mint) money/ ～成大错 make a gross error

【铸币】zhùbì coin; specie ◇ ～权 mintage

【铸工】zhùgōng 〈冶〉① foundry work ② foundry worker; founder

【铸造】zhùzào casting; founding

【铸字】zhùzì 〈印〉typefounding; typecasting

箸 zhù chopsticks

zhuā

抓 zhuā ① grab; seize; clutch: ～权 grab power/ ～机会 seize an opportunity/ 他～起帽子就往外走。He snatched up his cap and made for the door. ② scratch: ～痒痒 scratch an itch/ 猫把孩子的手～了。The cat scratched the child's hand. ③ arrest; catch; press-gang: ～特务 catch an enemy agent/ ～壮丁 press-gang able-bodied men ④ stress; pay special attention to: ～重点 stress the essentials

【抓耳挠腮】zhuā'ěr-náosāi tweak one's ears and scratch one's cheeks (as a sign of anxiety or delight); scratch one's head

【抓紧】zhuājǐn firmly grasp; pay close attention to: ～时机 seize the opportunity/ ～时间 make the best use of one's time

【抓药】zhuāyào ① make up (或 fill) a prescription of Chinese herbal medicine ② have a prescription of Chinese herbal medicine made up (或 filled)

【抓住】zhuāzhù ① catch (或 seize) hold of; grip: ～她的胳膊 catch hold of her arm/ ～一点小事做文章 seize on a trifle and make an issue of it; make a fuss about something trivial ② catch; capture: ～个小偷 catch a thief ③ grip sb.'s attention: 这出戏一开场就～了观众。The play gripped the attention of the audience from the moment the curtain rose.

zhuǎ

爪 zhuǎ claw; talon 另见 zhǎo

【爪子】zhuǎzi 〈口〉claw; paw; talon: 猫～ a cat's paws/ 鹰～ an eagle's talons

zhuāi

拽 zhuāi 〈方〉fling; throw; hurl: 把皮球～出去 fling the ball out

另见 zhuài

zhuài

拽* zhuài ⟨方⟩ pull; drag; haul: 生拉硬~ drag sb. along against his will/ 一把~住不放 catch hold of sb. or sth. and not let go
另见 zhuāi

zhuān

专* zhuān ① for a particular person, occasion, purpose, etc.; focussed on one thing; special: 心不~ not concentrate (on any one thing)/ ~车 special train or car/ 奎宁~治疟疾。Quinine is a specific for malaria./ ~找重活干。He made a point of picking the heaviest jobs for himself. ② expert ③ monopolize: ~权 monopolize power

【专长】 zhuāncháng speciality; special skill or knowledge: 学有~ have specialized knowledge of a subject; be expert in a special field of study/ 制图是她的~。Cartography is her speciality.

【专诚】 zhuānchéng for a particular purpose; specially: ~拜访 pay a special visit to sb.

【专程】 zhuānchéng special trip

【专电】 zhuāndiàn special dispatch (或 telegram)

【专攻】 zhuāngōng specialize in: 他~空间技术。He specializes in space technology.

【专横】 zhuānhèng imperious; peremptory; domineering: ~跋扈 imperious and despotic

【专机】 zhuānjī ① special plane ② private plane

【专家】 zhuānjiā expert; specialist: 水稻~ expert in rice-growing/ 眼科~ ophthalmologist; eye specialist

【专刊】 zhuānkān ① special issue or column ② monograph

【专科学校】 zhuānkē xuéxiào college for professional training; training school

【专栏】 zhuānlán special column: 书评~ book review column ◇ ~作家 columnist

【专利】 zhuānlì patent ◇ ~品 patent; patented article/ ~权 patent right; patent

【专卖】 zhuānmài monopoly; exclusive possession of the trade in some commodity

【专门】 zhuānmén special; specialized: ~研究化学 specialize in chemistry/ ~为儿童写的故事 stories specially written for children/ 从今以后你就~搞会计工作好了。From now on you'll concentrate on accounting alone.

【专名】 zhuānmíng ⟨语⟩ proper noun

【专区】 zhuānqū prefecture; subprovincial administrative region

【专人】 zhuānrén person specially assigned for a task or job: 这项工作一定要有~负责。Someone must be put in charge of the work./ 这个文件是~送来的。The document was brought by a special messenger.

【专任】 zhuānrèn full-time; regular: ~教员 full-time teacher

【专使】 zhuānshǐ special envoy

【专题】 zhuāntí special subject; special topic

【专心】 zhuānxīn concentrate one's attention; be absorbed: ~致志 wholly absorbed; with single-hearted devotion/ 学习必须~。Study requires undivided attention.

【专修】 zhuānxiū specialize in: ~数学 specialize in mathematics ◇ ~科 special (training) course

【专业】 zhuānyè ① special field of study; specialized subject; speciality; discipline: 这个系有八个~。This department offers eight specialities. ② specialized trade or profession; special line

【专业化】 zhuānyèhuà specialization

【专一】 zhuānyī single-minded; concentrated: 心思~ with concentrated attention/ 爱情~ be constant in love

【专用】 zhuānyòng for a special purpose

【专员】 zhuānyuán ① (assistant director; (administrative) commissioner: 礼宾司~ an assistant director of the Protocol Department/ 商务~ commercial attaché ② person specially assigned for a job

【专责】 zhuānzé specific responsibility: 分工明确,各有~。The division of labour is clear-cut, each one being charged with specific responsibilities.

【专政】 zhuānzhèng dictatorship

【专职】 zhuānzhí ① sole duty; specific duty ② full-time: 他是工会的~干部。He is a full-time cadre of the trade union.

【专制】 zhuānzhì ① autocracy ② autocratic; despotic: ~帝王 autocratic monarch; despotic emperor/ 君主~ autocratic (或 absolute) monarchy ◇ ~君主 autocrat/ ~政府 autocratic government/ ~体 autocracy

【专注】 zhuānzhù concentrate one's attention on; be absorbed in; devote one's mind to

【专著】 zhuānzhù monograph; treatise

砖* zhuān brick: 砌~ lay bricks/ ~房 brick house/ ~墙 brick wall

【砖厂】 zhuānchǎng brickfield; brickyard

【砖头】 zhuāntou ⟨方⟩ brick

zhuǎn

转* zhuǎn ① turn; shift; change: 好~ take a turn for the better/ ~败为胜 turn defeat into victory/ ~弱为强 transform (或 grow) from weak to strong/ 晴~多云 change from fine to cloudy/ 她~过头来和我说话。She spoke to me over her shoulder. ② pass on; transfer: 这封信请你~给他。Please pass the letter on to him./ 把她的邮件~寄到她的新地址 forward her mail to her new address
另见 zhuàn

【转变】 zhuǎnbiàn change; transform: ~立场 change one's stand; shift one's ground/ 世界观的~ change in one's world outlook/ 把一种能~为另一种能 transform one form of energy into another

【转播】 zhuǎnbō relay (a radio or TV broadcast) ◇ ~台 relay station

【转车】 zhuǎnchē change trains or buses; transfer to another train or bus

【转船】 zhuǎnchuán change to another ship; transship

【转达】 zhuǎndá pass on; convey; communicate: 请向他~我的问候。Please give him my regards.

【转道】 zhuǎndào make a detour; go by way of

【转动】 zhuǎndòng turn; move; turn round: ~手腕子 flex one's wrist/ ~门把手 turn the door knob/ 水龙头转不动。The tap's stuck.
另见 zhuàndòng

【转发】 zhuǎnfā transmit: 此件~全国。This document is to be transmitted throughout the country.

【转告】 zhuǎngào pass on (word); communicate; transmit: 他把这消息~了他的姐姐。He passed on the news to his sister.

【转化】 zhuǎnhuà ⟨哲⟩ change; transform: 向反面~ transform oneself into one's opposite; change into the reverse

【转换】 zhuǎnhuàn change; transform: ~方向 change direction/ ~话题 change the subject of conversation; switch the conversation to another subject ◇ ~开关 change-over switch

【转机】 zhuǎnjī a favourable turn; a turn for the better: 他的病有了~。The patient has taken a turn for the better. 或 His condition is improving.

【转嫁】 zhuǎnjià ① (of women) marry again; remarry ② shift; transfer: 把责任~给他人 shift off one's responsibility; put the blame on someone else/ 向别国~金融危机 shift a financial crisis on to other countries

【转交】 zhuǎnjiāo pass on; transmit

【转角】 zhuǎnjiǎo street corner; corner

【转口】 zhuǎnkǒu transit ◇ ~货物 transit goods/ ~贸易 entrepôt trade

【转脸】 zhuǎnliǎn ① turn one's face ② in no time; in the twinkling of an eye: 他刚才还在这儿,怎么一~就不见了?He was here just now. How come he disappeared in a wink?

【转捩点】 zhuǎnlièdiǎn　turning point
【转卖】 zhuǎnmài　resell
【转念】 zhuǎnniàn　reconsider and give up an idea; think better of: 他刚想开口,但一~,又不说了。He was just going to speak when he thought better of it.
【转让】 zhuǎnràng　transfer the possession of; make over
【转入】 zhuǎnrù　change over to; shift to; switch to: ~正常 return to normal/ ~下一个项目 move on to the next item/ 由进攻~防御 switch (或 shift) from the offensive to the defensive
【转身】 zhuǎnshēn　(of a person) turn round; face about
【转生】 zhuǎnshēng　〈佛教〉reincarnation; transmigration
【转手】 zhuǎnshǒu　① pass on: 你就直接交给他,不必要我一了。Give it directly to him; there is no need to do it through me. ② sell what one has bought
【转述】 zhuǎnshù　report; relate sth. as told by another: 我只是~他的话。I am merely reporting what he said.
【转瞬】 zhuǎnshùn　in a twinkle; in a flash
【转送】 zhuǎnsòng　① pass on; transmit on ② make a present of what one has been given
【转托】 zhuǎntuō　ask someone else to do what is asked of one: 你让我办的事,我已一老张了。I've asked Lao Zhang to take care of the matter you spoke to me about.
【转弯】 zhuǎnwān　turn a corner; make a turn: 邮局一~儿就是。The post office is just round (或 right around) the corner./ 来一个一百八十度的大~ make a 180-degree turn; do an about-face/ 他是个直性子,说话从来不会~儿。He's straightforward; he never minces his words./ 右~走! (横队) Right wheel! (纵队) Right turn march! 或 Column right march!/ 给他们一个~的余地 give them some leeway
【转弯抹角】 zhuǎnwān-mòjiǎo　① full of twists and turns: 我们一地走了好一会才找到那个地方。We had to take a tortuous route before we got to the place./ 这条路一的,可难走了。This road is full of twists and turns, which makes the going hard. ② beat about the bush; speak in a roundabout way
【转危为安】 zhuǎn wēi wéi ān　take a turn for the better and be out of danger; pull through
【转向】 zhuǎnxiàng　① change direction ② change one's political stand
【转学】 zhuǎnxué　(of a student) transfer to another school
【转眼】 zhuǎnyǎn　in the twinkling of an eye; in an instant; in a flash: 这孩子一~就不见了。The child disappeared in the twinkling of an eye./ ~间,一个月就过去了。A month passed before we knew it.
【转移】 zhuǎnyí　① shift; transfer; divert: ~兵力 shift forces; transfer troops/ ~视线 divert sb.'s attention/ ~目标 distract people's attention from sth. or sb. ② change; transform: ~社会风气 change prevalent social customs
【转运】 zhuǎnyùn　① transport; transfer; transship ② have a change of luck; luck turns in one's favour ◇ ~公司 transport company; forwarding agency/ ~站 transfer post
【转载】 zhuǎnzǎi　reprint sth. that has been published elsewhere; reprint: 各报都一了这篇报道。The report was reprinted in all the newspapers.
【转赠】 zhuǎnzèng　make a present of sth. given to one
【转折】 zhuǎnzhé　① a turn in the course of events: 世界历史上的急剧~ an abrupt turn in world history ② transition (of an essay) ◇ ~点 turning point
【转租】 zhuǎnzū　sublet; sublease

zhuàn

传* zhuàn　① commentaries on classics: 经~ Confucian classics and commentaries on them ② biography: 外~ unauthorized biography/ 别~ supplementary biography/ 小~ biographical sketch; profile ③ a novel or story written in historical style: 《水浒~》 Water Margin
另见 chuán
【传记】 zhuànjì　biography
【传略】 zhuànlüè　brief biography; biographical sketch

转 zhuàn　① turn; revolve; rotate: 地球绕着太阳~。The earth revolves round the sun./ 你在这儿~来~去干什么? What are you hanging around here for? ② 〈量〉revolution: 每分钟二千~ 2,000 revolutions per minute; 2,000 r.p.m.
另见 zhuǎn
【转动】 zhuàndòng　turn; revolve; rotate: ~辘轳把 turn the crank of a windlass/ 这个电厂的涡轮全是用核动力~的。All the turbines of this power plant are driven by nuclear energy./ 经过修理,机器又一起来了。The machine started working again after being put right.
另见 zhuǎndòng
【转向】 zhuànxiàng　lose one's bearings; get lost: 晕头~ get confused and lose one's bearings; feel one's head reeling
另见 zhuǎnxiàng
【转椅】 zhuànyǐ　swivel chair; revolving chair

啭 zhuàn　〈书〉(of birds) twitter; sing

赚* zhuàn　① make a profit; gain: ~钱 make money; make a profit/ ~钱生意 a profitable business; a paying proposition (或 concern) ② 〈方〉profit ③ 〈方〉earn

馔 zhuàn　〈书〉food: 盛~ sumptuous dinner

撰 zhuàn　write; compose: 为报纸~稿 write articles for a newspaper
【撰著】 zhuànzhù　write; compose

篆 zhuàn　① 见"篆书" ② seal
【篆刻】 zhuànkè　seal cutting
【篆书】 zhuànshū　seal character (a style of Chinese calligraphy, often used on seals)

zhuāng

妆 zhuāng　① apply makeup; make up: 梳~ dress one's hair and apply makeup ② woman's personal adornments ③ trousseau
【妆奁】 zhuānglián　trousseau
【妆饰】 zhuāngshì　adorn; dress up; deck out

庄 zhuāng　① village: 王家~ Wangjiazhuang Village ② manor ③ a place of business: 钱~ old-fashioned Chinese private bank/ 饭~ restaurant ④ banker (in a gambling game) ⑤ serious; grave: 亦~亦谐 serious and facetious at the same time; seriocomic
【庄家】 zhuāngjia　banker (in a gambling game)
【庄稼】 zhuāngjia　crops: 种~ grow crops
【庄严】 zhuāngyán　solemn; dignified; stately: ~地声明 solemnly declare/ 态度~ dignified in manner/ 追悼会会场~肃穆。The mourning hall was filled with a solemn silence.
【庄园】 zhuāngyuán　manor
【庄重】 zhuāngzhòng　serious; grave; solemn

桩 zhuāng　① stake; pile: 打~ drive piles ② 〈量〉: 一~大事 an important matter / 一~买卖 a business transaction

装* zhuāng　① dress up; attire; deck; play the part (或 role) of; act: 她~老太太真像。She acted an old woman and really looked the part. ② outfit; clothing: 春~ a spring outfit/ 学生~ students' uniform/ 童~ children's wear (或 clothing) ③ stage makeup and costume: 上~ dress and put on makeup (for a theatrical performance)/ 卸~ remove stage makeup and costume ④ pretend; feign; make believe: ~病 pretend sickness; malinger/ ~死 feign death; sham dead/ ~傻 pretend to be naive or stupid/ ~出一副可怜相 assume a pitiable look/ 不要不懂~懂。Don't pretend to know what you don't know. ⑤ load; pack; hold: ~车 load a truck (或 cart)/ ~箱 pack a box; put sth. in a crate; crate/ ~料 feed (a machine)/ ~烟袋 fill one's pipe/ 这书包~不下这么多东西。This satchel won't hold so many things. ⑥ install; fit; assemble: 给门~上锁 fit a lock on the door

【装扮】 zhuāngbàn ① dress up; attire; deck out ② disguise; masquerade: ~成朋友的敌人是最危险的。 The most dangerous enemy is one who disguises himself as a friend.

【装备】 zhuāngbèi ① equip; fit out: ~新式武器 be equipped with modern weapons ② equipment; outfit: 军事~ military equipment/ 登山运动员的~ a mountaineer's outfit

【装裱】 zhuāngbiǎo mount (a picture, etc.)

【装点】 zhuāngdiǎn decorate; dress; deck: 大厅里~着花彩。 The hall was decorated with festoons.

【装订】 zhuāngdìng binding; bookbinding: 布面~ cloth-bound/ 皮面~ bound in leather/ 硬面~ hardbound

【装疯卖傻】 zhuāngfēng-màishǎ feign madness and act like an idiot; play the fool

【装糊涂】 zhuāng hútu pretend not to know; feign ignorance

【装潢】 zhuānghuáng ① mount (a picture, etc.); decorate; dress ② decoration; mounting; packaging: ~讲究的茅台酒 tastefully packaged bottles of *maotai* 又作"装璜"

【装甲】 zhuāngjiǎ ① plate armour ② armoured ◇ ~兵 armoured force (或 troops)/ ~车 armoured car/ ~列车 armoured train/ ~师 armoured division/ ~输送车 armoured carrier

【装假】 zhuāngjiǎ pretend; feign; make believe

【装殓】 zhuāngliàn dress and lay a corpse in a coffin

【装聋作哑】 zhuānglóng-zuòyǎ pretend to be deaf and dumb; pretend to be ignorant of sth.

【装门面】 zhuāng ménmiàn put up a front; maintain an outward show; keep up appearances

【装模作样】 zhuāngmú-zuòyàng be affected; attitudinize; put on an act

【装配】 zhuāngpèi assemble; fit together: ~机器 assemble a machine ◇ ~件 assembly parts/ ~线 assembly line

【装腔】 zhuāngqiāng behave affectedly; be artificial: ~作势 be affected or pretentious; strike a pose

【装饰】 zhuāngshì decorate; adorn; ornament; deck: 彩旗和鲜花把公园~得十分绚丽。 The park was gaily decorated with bunting and flowers. ◇ ~品 ornament

【装束】 zhuāngshù dress; attire: 看他的~，可能是藏族。 Judging from his dress, he's probably a Tibetan.

【装蒜】 zhuāngsuàn 〈口〉 pretend not to know; feign ignorance: 你比谁都明白，别~了！ Don't pretend; you know better than anybody else.

【装卸】 zhuāngxiè ① load and unload: ~货物 load and unload a truck, ship, etc.; load and unload goods ② assemble and disassemble: 他会~自行车。 He can take a bicycle apart and put it back again.

【装修】 zhuāngxiū fit up (a house, etc.): ~门面 fit up the front of a shop

【装样子】 zhuāng yàngzi put on an act; do sth. for appearance sake

【装运】 zhuāngyùn load and transport; ship

【装载】 zhuāngzài loading ◇ ~量 loading capacity

【装置】 zhuāngzhì ① install; fit: 仪器已经~好了。 The instrument has been installed. ② installation; unit; device; plant: 雷达~ radar installation

zhuǎng

奘 zhuǎng 〈方〉 big and thick; stout; robust

zhuàng

壮* zhuàng ① strong; robust: ~苗 strong sprout/ 他身体很~。 He is sturdy. 或 He has a strong physique. ② magnificent; grand: 雄~ magnificent; full of grandeur ③ strengthen; make better: ~声势 to lend impetus and strength; to make it appear more vigorous and impressive/ 以~观瞻 (deck out a place) to make it more sightly

【壮大】 zhuàngdà grow in strength; expand; strengthen

【壮胆】 zhuàngdǎn embolden; boost sb.'s courage

【壮丁】 zhuàngdīng 〈旧〉 able-bodied man (subject to conscription)

【壮观】 zhuàngguān grand (或 magnificent) sight

【壮举】 zhuàngjǔ magnificent feat; heroic undertaking: 史无前例的~ an unparalleled feat

【壮阔】 zhuàngkuò vast; grand; magnificent; grandiose: 波澜~ surging forward with great momentum; unfolding on a magnificent scale

【壮丽】 zhuànglì majestic; magnificent; glorious: ~的景色 magnificent scenery; majestic view/ 一篇~的史诗 a magnificent (或 glorious) epic

【壮烈】 zhuàngliè heroic; brave: ~牺牲 heroically give one's life; die a hero's death

【壮年】 zhuàngnián the more robust years of a person's life (between thirty and fifty); prime of life

【壮士】 zhuàngshì heroic man; hero; warrior

【壮实】 zhuàngshi sturdy; robust: 一个~的小伙子 a sturdy young chap

【壮志】 zhuàngzhì great aspiration; lofty ideal: ~凌云 with soaring aspirations/ ~未酬 with one's lofty aspirations unrealized

状* zhuàng ① form; shape: 其~不一 of different forms/ 奇形怪~ of grotesque shapes ② state; condition: 现~ present state of affairs; status quo ③ describe: 不可名~ indescribable; nondescript; beyond description ④ account; record: 功~ an account of sb.'s meritorious service ⑤ written complaint; plaint: 告~ lodge a complaint (或 an accusation); file a suit (against sb.) ⑥ certificate: 奖~ certificate of commendation/ 委任~ certificate of appointment; commission

【状况】 zhuàngkuàng condition; state; state of affairs: 健康~ state of health; health/ 改善这种~ remedy this state of affairs/ 经济~ (a person's) financial situation; (a country's) economic situation

【状貌】 zhuàngmào appearance; form

【状态】 zhuàngtài state; condition; state of affairs: 心理~ psychology; state of mind/ 无组织~ disorganized state of affairs/ 战争~ state of war

【状元】 zhuàngyuan ① Number One Scholar, title conferred on the one who came first in the highest imperial examination ② the very best (in any field): 行行出~。 Every profession produces its own leading authority.

撞* zhuàng ① bump against; run into; strike; collide: ~车 collision of vehicles/ ~墙 bump against a wall/ ~了个满怀 bump into sb./ ~钟 toll (或 strike) a bell/ 一辆卡车~坏了我们的汽车。 A lorry ran into our car and damaged it./ 被卡车~倒了 be knocked down by a truck/ 两船在雾中相~。 Two ships collided in the fog. ② meet by chance; bump into; run into: 我不想见他，偏~上他了。 I tried to avoid him, but it was just my luck to bump into him. ③ rush; dash; barge: 横冲直~ barge around; dash about madly

【撞击】 zhuàngjī ram; dash against; strike: 波浪~着岩石。 The breakers dashed on the rocks.

【撞见】 zhuàngjiàn meet or discover by chance; run across; catch sb. in the act

【撞骗】 zhuàngpiàn look about for a chance to swindle; swindle

幢 zhuàng 〈方〉〈量〉: 一~三层楼房 a three-storeyed building 另见 chuáng

戆 zhuàng

【戆直】 zhuàngzhí 〈书〉 blunt and tactless; simple and honest

zhuī

追* zhuī ① chase (或 run) after; pursue: ~兵 pursuing

troops/ ～上他 catch up with him/ 紧～不舍 be in hot pursuit; be hot on sb.'s trail/ 把比分～到十比十一 close the margin to 10-11; catch up and bring the score to 10-11 ② trace; look into; get to the bottom of: ～穷根 trace the root cause of one's poverty ③ seek; go after: ～名逐利 seek fame and wealth ④ recall; reminisce: ～念往事 reminisce about the past; recall early days/ 托今～昔 recall the past and compare it with the present ⑤ retroactively; posthumously

【追本溯源】 zhuīběn-sùyuán trace to its source; get at the root of the matter

【追逼】 zhuībī ① pursue closely (a fleeing enemy) ② press for (repayment); extort (a confession)

【追捕】 zhuībǔ pursue and capture

【追查】 zhuīchá investigate; trace; find out: ～事故原因 investigate the causes of an accident/ ～谣言 trace a rumour to its source

【追悼】 zhuīdào ◇mourn over a person's death ◇ ～会 memorial meeting

【追赶】 zhuīgǎn quicken one's pace to catch up; run after; pursue: 他已走远,你～不上了。You won't be able to catch him now — he's too far away.

【追根】 zhuīgēn get to the bottom of sth.: 这件事一定得～究底。We must get to the root of the matter.

【追回】 zhuīhuí recover: ～赃物 recover stolen property

【追悔】 zhuīhuǐ repent; regret: ～莫及 too late to repent

【追击】 zhuījī pursue and attack; follow up: ～敌人 pursue and attack the enemy/ 战略～ strategic pursuit

【追记】 zhuījì ① write down afterwards or from memory ② cite (或 award) posthumously: ～特等功 be posthumously awarded a Special-Class Merit citation

【追加】 zhuījiā add to (the original amount): ～支出 make an additional expenditure/ ～预算 supplement a budget; make a supplementary budget

【追剿】 zhuījiǎo pursue and wipe out ◇ ～队 pursuit detachment

【追究】 zhuījiū look into; find out; investigate: ～事故的责任 investigate and affix the responsibility for an accident; find out who is to blame for an accident

【追求】 zhuīqiú ① seek; pursue: ～真理 seek truth; be in pursuit of truth/ ～名誉地位 be after fame and position ② woo; court; chase; run after

【追认】 zhuīrèn ① subsequently confirm or endorse; recognize retroactively: ～一项法令 subsequently endorse a decree ② admit or confer posthumously

【追溯】 zhuīsù trace back to; date from: 这个传说可以～到遥远的过去。The legend goes (或 can be traced) back to remote antiquity.

【追随】 zhuīsuí follow: ～不舍 follow sb. closely/ ～错误路线 follow an erroneous line ◇ ～者 follower; adherent; following

【追问】 zhuīwèn question closely; make a detailed inquiry; examine minutely: ～事实真相 make detailed inquiries about the facts/ 我们～他渔船失踪的原因。We questioned him trying to find out how the fishing boat got lost.

【追想】 zhuīxiǎng recall; reminisce

【追叙】 zhuīxù ① tell about the past; relate; recount ② narration of earlier episodes; flashback

【追寻】 zhuīxún pursue; search; track down

【追忆】 zhuīyì recollect; recall; look back: ～往事,历历在目。As I look back, scenes of the past leap before my eyes./ 年代太久,难以～。It happened ages ago and I can't call it to mind.

【追赃】 zhuīzāng order the return of stolen money or goods; recover stolen money or goods; make sb. disgorge the spoils

【追赠】 zhuīzèng confer posthumously (a title)

【追逐】 zhuīzhú ① pursue; chase ② seek; quest: ～高额利润 seek exorbitant profits

【追踪】 zhuīzōng follow the trail of; track; trace

椎 zhuī vertebra: 颈～ cervical vertebra/ 胸～ thoracic vertebra

【椎骨】 zhuīgǔ 〈生理〉 vertebra

锥 zhuī ① awl ② anything shaped like an awl ③ bore; drill: ～孔 make a hole with an awl

zhuì

坠 zhuì ① fall; drop: ～马 fall off a horse/ 飞机～入海中。The plane crashed into the sea. ② weigh down: 苹果把树枝～得弯弯的。The branches were bending down with the weight of the apples. 或 The apples weighed the branches down. ③ weight; a hanging object: 铅～ plummet/ 扇～儿 pendant of a fan

【坠地】 zhuìdì 〈书〉 (of a child) be born

【坠毁】 zhuìhuǐ (of a plane, etc.) fall and break; crash

【坠落】 zhuìluò fall; drop

缀 zhuì ① sew; stitch: 补～ mend; patch/ 你的袖子扯破了,我给你～上两针。Your sleeves's torn. I'll put in a few stitches for you. ② put words together correctly; compose: ～文 compose an essay; write a composition ③ embellish; decorate: 点～ embellish; adorn/ 天上～满了星星。The sky was studded with twinkling stars.

惴 zhuì

【惴惴不安】 zhuìzhuì bù ān 〈书〉 be anxious and fearful; be alarmed and on tenterhooks

赘 zhuì ① superfluous; redundant: 不待～言 It would be superfluous to dwell on the matter any more. ② (of a man) go to live in the household of one's in-laws on getting married; (of the bride's parents) gain a son-in-law in such a manner ③ 〈方〉 be burdensome; be cumbersome: 孩子多了真～人。It's really burdensome to have many children.

【赘述】 zhuìshù give unnecessary details; say more than is needed: 不必一一～。It is unnecessary to go into details.

【赘婿】 zhuìxù a son-in-law who lives in the home of his wife's parents

zhūn

肫 zhūn ① gizzard (of a fowl): 鸭～ duck gizzard ② 〈书〉 sincere; genuine

谆 zhūn

【谆谆】 zhūnzhūn earnestly and tirelessly: ～教导 earnestly instruct/ ～告诫 repeatedly admonish

zhǔn

准* zhǔn ① allow; grant; permit: 获～ obtain permission/ ～假两周 grant sb. two weeks' leave/ 不～吸烟。No smoking. ② in accordance with; follow: ～前例处理 to be settled by following precedent ③ standard; norm; criterion: 以此为～ take this as the standard (或 criterion)/ 标～ standard; criterion/ ～则 norm; standard; criterion ④ accurate; exact: 投篮不～ inaccurate shooting (in basketball)/ 这表走得～。The watch keeps good time. ⑤ definitely; certainly: 我明天～去。I'll certainly be there tomorrow. ⑥ quasi-; para-: ～军事组织 paramilitary organization/ ～单色光 〈物〉 quasi-monochromatic light

【准保】 zhǔnbǎo 〈副〉 certainly; for sure: 你现在给他打电话,他～会来。He will certainly come if you ring him up now./ 我检查了两遍,～没错儿。I've checked twice. You can be sure there's no mistake.

【准备】 zhǔnbèi ① prepare; get ready: 为会议～文件 prepare documents for a meeting/ 作最坏的～ prepare for the worst/ 随时～歼灭入侵之敌 be prepared at all times to wipe out any invader ② intend; plan: 今年暑假我～回老家看看。I intend to visit my native place this summer vacation./ 我们～下星期一开始试验。We plan to start the experiment next Monday.

【准将】 zhǔnjiàng （英陆军）brigadier；（英空军）air commodore；（海军）commodore；（美陆、空军）brigadier general

【准确】 zhǔnquè accurate；exact；precise： ～而有力地打击敌人 deal accurate and powerful blows at the enemy/ ～地说明 explain in precise terms ◇ ～度 degree of accuracy；accuracy/ ～性 accuracy

【准绳】 zhǔnshéng criterion；yardstick

【准时】 zhǔnshí punctual；on time；on schedule： ～起飞 take off at the scheduled time/ 请～出席。Please be punctual. 或 You are requested to come on time.

【准许】 zhǔnxǔ permit；allow

【准予】 zhǔnyǔ grant；approve；permit： ～入境 allow sb. to enter the country/ ～休假 grant a leave

【准则】 zhǔnzé norm；standard；criterion： 行为 ～ code of conduct/ 外交 ～ diplomatic norms/ 国际法的起码～ elementary requirements of international law

zhuō

拙 zhuō ①clumsy；awkward；dull： 手～ be all thumbs/ ～于言词 be inarticulate；be clumsy in expressing oneself ②〈谦〉my： ～著 my writing

【拙笨】 zhuōbèn clumsy；dull；unskilful

【拙见】 zhuōjiàn 〈谦〉my humble opinion

【拙劣】 zhuōliè clumsy；inferior： ～表演 a clumsy performance；a bad show/ ～手法 inferior tactics；clumsy trick

卓 zhuó ①tall and erect： ～立 stand upright ②eminent；outstanding： 成绩～然 achieve outstanding results

【卓见】 zhuójiàn excellent opinion；brilliant idea

【卓绝】 zhuójué unsurpassed；extreme；of the highest degree： 英勇～ extremely brave/ 艰苦～ extreme hardships and difficulties

【卓识】 zhuóshí judicious judgment；sagacity： 远见～ foresight and sagacity

【卓有成效】 zhuó yǒu chéngxiào fruitful；highly effective： 进行～的努力 have made fruitful efforts/ 几年来绿化荒山已～。In the past few years good results have been attained in afforesting the barren hills.

【卓越】 zhuóyuè outstanding；brilliant；remarkable： ～的成就 remarkable achievements/ ～的科学家 a brilliant scientist/ 作出～的贡献 make outstanding contributions

【卓著】 zhuózhù distinguished；outstanding；eminent： 该省农业机械化的工作成效～。That province has achieved outstanding results in farm mechanization.

捉 zhuō ①clutch；hold；grasp： ～笔 hold a pen/ ～住不放 seize hold of sb. or sth. and not let go ②catch；capture： 活～ capture sb. alive/ 贼喊～贼 a thief crying "stop thief"

【捉刀】 zhuōdāo write (an article, etc.) for someone else；ghostwrite ◇ ～人 ghostwriter

【捉襟见肘】 zhuōjīn-jiànzhǒu pull down one's jacket to conceal the raggedness, only to expose one's elbows — have too many difficulties to cope with；have too many problems to tackle

【捉迷藏】 zhuō mícáng ①hide-and-seek；blindman's buff ②be tricky and evasive；play hide-and-seek： 你就直说吧，不要跟我～了。Get straight to the point. Don't beat about the bush.

【捉摸】 zhuōmō 〔多用于否定〕fathom；ascertain： ～不定 difficult to ascertain；unpredictable；elusive

【捉拿】 zhuōná arrest；catch： ～逃犯 arrest an escaped prisoner/ ～归案 bring sb. to justice

【捉弄】 zhuōnòng tease；make fun of；embarrass

桌* zhuō ①table；desk： 餐～ dining table/ 书～ writing desk/ ～椅板凳 tables, chairs and benches — ordinary household furniture ②〈量〉： 三～客人 three tables of guests (at a dinner party)

【桌布】 zhuōbù tablecloth

【桌灯】 zhuōdēng desk lamp

【桌面】 zhuōmiàn top of a table；tabletop

【桌面儿上】 zhuōmiànrshang on the table；aboveboard；in public： ～的话 polite and unimpeachable remarks/ 把问题摆到～来 place problems on the table；bring problems out into the open

【桌子】 zhuōzi table；desk

zhuó

灼 zhuó ①burn；scorch： ～伤 burn ②bright；luminous

【灼见】 zhuójiàn profound view；penetrating view： 真知～ profound knowledge and penetrating insight

【灼热】 zhuórè scorching hot

【灼灼】 zhuózhuó 〈书〉shining；brilliant： 目光～ with keen, sparkling eyes

茁 zhuó

【茁壮】 zhuózhuàng healthy and strong；sturdy： 小麦长得很～。The wheat has grown sturdy.

浊 zhuó ①turbid；muddy： ～水 turbid water/ ～流 muddy stream/ 污～ dirty；filthy ②deep and thick： ～声～气 in a deep, raucous voice ③chaotic；confused；corrupted

【浊世】 zhuóshì ①〈书〉the corrupted world；chaotic times ②〈佛教〉the mortal world

斫 zhuó hack (with an axe or sword)

酌 zhuó ①pour out (wine)；drink： 对～ (two people) have a drink together/ 独～ drink alone ②a meal with wine： 便～ informal dinner ③consider；think over；use one's discretion： ～办 act according to one's judgment；do as one thinks fit/ 请～加修改。Make any alterations as you may think fit./ 以上几点意见是否可行，请～定。Please weigh the above points and see if they are practicable.

【酌量】 zhuóliàng consider；deliberate；use one's judgment

【酌情】 zhuóqíng take into consideration the circumstances；use one's discretion： ～处理 settle a matter as one sees fit；act at one's discretion

着 zhuó ①wear (clothes)：穿～整齐 be neatly dressed/ 吃～不尽 have as much food and clothing as one wants ②touch；come into contact with： 附～ adhere to ③apply；use： 再～一把力 make one more effort/ ～墨不多 sketchily painted or described ④whereabouts： 寻找无～ whereabouts unknown；nowhere to be found/ 经费无～ no funds available ⑤send： 请～人前来领取。Please send someone here for it.

另见 zhāo；zháo；zhe

【着笔】 zhuóbǐ put (或 set) pen to paper；begin to write or paint： 不知如何～ not know how to begin the writing or the painting

【着力】 zhuólì put forth effort；exert oneself： ～描写 concentrate one's efforts on depicting sb. or sth.；take great pains to describe/ 无从～ fail to see where to direct one's efforts

【着陆】 zhuólù land；touch down： 飞机就要～了。The plane is about to land. 或 The plane is going to touch down.

【着落】 zhuóluò ①whereabouts： 遗失的行李已经有～了。The missing luggage has been found. ②assured source： 这笔经费还没有～。We still don't know where to get the funds from.

【着色】 zhuósè put colour on；colour

【着实】 zhuóshí ①really；indeed： 这台播种机～不错。This seeder is very good indeed./ 为了改装这台机器，他们～花了些功夫。They really put in a good deal of time refitting the machine. ②severely： ～说了他一顿 give him a good talking-to；lecture him severely

【着手】 zhuóshǒu put one's hand to；set about： ～一项工作 set about a job/ ～编制计划 start drawing up plans/ 从调查研究～ start with investigation and study

【着想】 zhuóxiǎng　consider (the interests of sb. or sth.): 为人民的利益～ think about the interests of the people/ 他是为你～才劝你不要去的。It was for your good that he advised you not to go.

【着眼】 zhuóyǎn　have sth. in mind; see (或 view) from the angle of: ～于人民 have the people in mind/ ～于未来 have one's eyes on the future ◇ ～点 starting point; focus of attention; object in mind

【着意】 zhuóyì　act with care and effort; take pains: ～经营 manage with diligent care

【着重】 zhuózhòng　stress; emphasize: ～指出 emphatically point out/ ～说明问题的重要性 stress the importance of the matter/ 我想～地讲一讲这个问题。Here I would like to go into one question in particular. ◇ ～号 mark of emphasis (as in "正是他本人")

啄 zhuó　peck: 小鸡～米。The chicks are pecking at the rice.
【啄木鸟】 zhuómùniǎo　woodpecker

琢 zhuó　chisel; carve: 翡翠～成的小茶壶 a small carved jadeite teapot
另见 zuó
【琢磨】 zhuómó　① carve and polish (jade) ② improve (literary works); polish; refine
另见 zuómo

斲 zhuó　<书> chop; hack
【斲轮老手】 zhuó lún lǎoshǒu　expert wheelwright; old hand

濯 zhuó　<书> wash: ～足 wash one's feet
【濯濯】 zhuózhuó　<书> (of mountains) bare; bald: 童山～ treeless hills

擢 zhuó　<书> ① pull out; extract ② raise (in rank); promote
【擢升】 zhuóshēng　<书> promote; advance (to a higher position or rank)
【擢用】 zhuóyòng　<书> promote to a post

镯 zhuó　bracelet: 玉～ jade bracelet

zī

吱 zī　<象> ① (of mice) squeak ② (of small birds) chirp; peep
另见 zhī
【吱声】 zīshēng　<方> utter sth.; make a sound: 我们问他几遍，他都没～。We asked him several times, but couldn't get a peep out of him.

孜 zī
【孜孜】 zīzī　diligent; industrious; hardworking: ～以求 diligently strive after; assiduously seek
【孜孜不倦】 zīzī bù juàn　diligently; assiduously; indefatigably

咨 zī　consult; take counsel
【咨文】 zīwén　① <旧> official communication (between government offices of equal rank) ② report delivered by the head of a government on affairs of state: 国情～ (美) State of the Union Message
【咨询】 zīxún　seek advice from; hold counsel with; consult ◇ ～机关 advisory body/ ～委员会 consultative (或 advisory) committee

姿* zī　① looks; appearance: ～色 (of a woman) good looks ② gesture; carriage; posture: 舞～ a dancer's posture and movements
【姿容】 zīróng　looks; appearance: ～秀美 good-looking; pretty
【姿色】 zīsè　(of a woman) good looks: 略有几分～ be rather good-looking

【姿势】 zīshì　posture; gesture: 直立的～ an erect posture/ ～优美 have a graceful carriage
【姿态】 zītài　① posture; carriage: 各种不同的泥塑 figures in various postures ② attitude; pose: 以一个普通劳动者的～出现 (of a senior cadre) appear among the masses as an ordinary worker

兹 zī　<书> ① this: ～事体大。This is indeed a serious matter. ② now; at present: ～将新到书籍开列如下。Below is a list of books recently received. ③ year: 今～ this year/ 来～ the coming year

资 zī　① money; expenses: 投～ put money in; invest/ 川～ travelling expenses/ 劳～双方 labour and capital ② subsidize; support: ～敌 give supplies to the enemy; support the enemy ③ provide; supply: 可～对比 provide a contrast/ 广泛报道，以～鼓励 give wide publicity by way of encouragement/ 以～补救 to serve as a remedy ④ endowment; natural ability: 天～ natural endowments; aptitude ⑤ qualifications; record of service: 年～ years of service; seniority
【资本】 zīběn　① capital ② what is capitalized on; sth. used to one's own advantage
【资本家】 zīběnjiā　capitalist
【资本主义】 zīběnzhǔyì　capitalism
【资产】 zīchǎn　① property ② capital fund; capital ③ <经> assets: 固定(流动)～ fixed (liquid) assets/ ～冻结 freezing of assets
【资方】 zīfāng　those representing capital; capital
【资格】 zīge　① qualifications: 具备必要的～ have the requisite qualifications; be qualified/ 取消比赛～ be disqualified from the contest ② seniority: 摆老～ flaunt one's seniority
【资金】 zījīn　fund: 建设～ funds for construction/ 发展工业的～ funds for developing industry
【资力】 zīlì　financial strength: ～雄厚 have a large capital; be financially powerful
【资历】 zīlì　qualifications and record of service
【资料】 zīliào　① means: 生产～ means of production; capital goods/ 生活～ means of livelihood (或 subsistence); consumer goods ② data; material: 参考～ reference material/ 搜集～ gather material; collect data/ ～处理 data processing ◇ ～室 reference room
【资望】 zīwàng　seniority and prestige
【资源】 zīyuán　natural resources; resources: ～丰富 abound (或 be rich) in natural resources/ 开发 (或 exploit) natural resources
【资助】 zīzhù　aid financially; subsidize

赀 zī　① estimate: 所费不～ incur a considerable or great expense ② 见 "资" zī ①

缁 zī　<书> black

滋 zī　① grow; multiply: ～蔓 grow and spread/ ～事 create (或 stir up) trouble/ ～繁 multiply profusely ② more: 为害～甚 cause greater havoc than ever ③ <方> spurt; burst: 水管裂缝了，直往外～水。Water is spurting from the crack in the pipe./ 电线～火。Sparks are spurting out from the electric wire.
【滋补】 zībǔ　nourishing; nutritious: ～食品 nourishing food; nourishment
【滋蔓】 zīmàn　<书> grow and spread; grow vigorously: 湖中水藻～。Algae grow and spread quickly in the lake.
【滋润】 zīrùn　① moist: ～的土地 moist soil ② moisten: 雨露～禾苗壮。Moistened by rain and dew, young crops grow strong.
【滋生】 zīshēng　① multiply; breed; propagate: 防止蚊蝇～ prevent the breeding of flies and mosquitoes ② cause; create; provoke: ～事端 cause trouble; create a disturbance
【滋味】 zīwèi　taste; flavour: 这个菜真有～。This dish tastes good./ 尝尝艰苦生活的～ have a taste of hard life

【滋养】zīyǎng ①nourish: ～身体 be nourishing ②nutriment; nourishment: 丰富的～ rich nutriment ◇ ～品 nourishing food; nutriment; nourishment

【滋长】zīzhǎng grow; develop: 防止～骄傲自满情绪 guard against arrogance and conceit

孳 zī multiply; propagate
【孳生】zīshēng multiply; breed; propagate
【孳孳】zīzī 见"孜孜" zīzī

辎 zī an ancient covered wagon
【辎重】zīzhòng 〈军〉impedimenta; supplies and gear of an army; baggage

锱 zī an ancient unit of weight, equal to one fourth of a *liang* (两)
【锱铢必较】zī-zhū bì jiào haggle over every penny; dispute over every detail

龇 zī 〈口〉bare; show: ～着牙 bare one's teeth
【龇牙咧嘴】zīyá-liězuǐ ①show one's teeth; look fierce ②contort one's face in agony; grimace in pain

髭 zī moustache

zǐ

子* zǐ ①son; child ②person: 男～ male person; man/ 女～ female person; woman ③ancient title of respect for a learned or virtuous man: 荀～ Master Xun (313 ?-238 B.C.) ④seed: 瓜～儿 melon seed/ 结～儿 bear seed; go to seed ⑤egg: 鸡～儿 hen's egg/ 鱼～ roe ⑥young; tender; small: ～鸡 chick/ ～姜 tender ginger ⑦something small and hard: 棋～儿 chessman; piece/ 枪～儿 bullet/ 算盘～儿 abacus bead/ 石头～儿 small stone; pebble ⑧the first of the twelve Earthly Branches

子* zi ①〔名词后缀〕帽～ cap; hat/ 旗～ flag/ 胖～ fat person, fatty/ 推～ hair-clippers; barber's clippers 〔个别量词后缀〕: 这档～事 this matter; this business/ 我一下～想不起他的名字。I just can't recall his name. 或 His name escapes me for the moment.

【子弹】zǐdàn bullet; cartridge: 步枪～ rifle bullet/ 汽枪～ air-gun pellet/ 练习～ dummy cartridge

【子弟】zǐdì sons and younger brothers; juniors; children: 纨袴～ profligate sons of the rich/ 职工～ children of the workers and staff (of a factory, etc.)

【子宫】zǐgōng 〈生理〉uterus; womb

【子爵】zǐjué viscount ◇ ～夫人 viscountess

【子女】zǐnǚ sons and daughters; children

【子时】zǐshí the period of the day from 11 p.m. to 1 a.m.

【子嗣】zǐsì son; male offspring

【子孙】zǐsūn children and grandchildren; descendants: ～后代 descendants; posterity; coming generations

【子虚】zǐxū 〈书〉fictitious; unreal: 事属～。It is sheer fiction.

【子夜】zǐyè midnight

仔* zǐ (of domestic animals or fowls) young: ～猪 piglet; pigling/ ～鸡 chick 另见 zǎi

【仔细】zǐxì ①careful; attentive: ～分析 analyse carefully/ ～地研究文件 pore over a document/ 上课～听讲 listen attentively in class/ 她做事很～。She's very careful in everything she does. ②be careful; look out: 路很滑，～点儿。Watch your step! The road is very slippery. ③〈方〉frugal; economical: 日子过得～ be frugal of one's expenses

姊 zǐ elder sister; sister
【姊妹】zǐmèi elder and younger sisters; sisters

籽 zǐ seed: 菜～儿 vegetable seed/ 棉～儿 cotton seed

梓 zǐ ①〈植〉Chinese catalpa (*Catalpa ovata*) ②cut blocks for printing: 付～ send to the printers
【梓里】zǐlǐ 〈书〉native place; home town

紫* zǐ purple; violet
【紫外线】zǐwàixiàn 〈物〉ultraviolet ray

滓 zǐ 见"渣滓" zhāzǐ

訾 zǐ 〈书〉slander; calumniate
【訾议】zǐyì 〈书〉discuss the failings of others; criticize; impeach: 无可～ above criticism; unimpeachable

zì

字* zì ①word; character: ～义 meaning of a word/ 汉～ Chinese character ②pronunciation (of a word or character): 咬～清楚 pronounce every word clearly; have clear articulation ③form of a written or printed character; style of handwriting; printing type: 篆～ seal character/ 黑体～ boldface; boldface type/ 柳～ style of calligraphy of Liu Gongquan (柳公权, 778-865 A.D.)/ 他写得一手好～。He writes a good hand. 或 He has good handwriting. ④scripts; writings: 专藏～，不藏画 only collect scripts (或 writings), not paintings ⑤receipt; written pledge: 立～为凭 give a written pledge/ 收到钱了，写个～儿给他。Write him a receipt when you get the money from him. ⑥a style (或 name) taken at the age of twenty, by which a man is sometimes called: 诸葛亮～孔明。Zhuge Liang styled himself Kongming. ⑦〈旧〉(of a girl) be betrothed: 待～闺中 not be betrothed yet

【字典】zìdiǎn dictionary: 查～ consult a dictionary

【字号】zìhào the name of a shop

【字画】zìhuà calligraphy and painting

【字汇】zìhuì glossary; wordbook; lexicon

【字迹】zìjī handwriting; writing: ～工整 neat writing/ ～模糊 illegible handwriting

【字句】zìjù words and expressions; writing: ～通顺 coherent and smooth writing

【字据】zìjù written pledge (e.g. receipt, IOU, contract, etc.)

【字里行间】zìlǐ-hángjiān between the lines: 他的信～流露出畏难情绪。His letter reveals, between the lines, a certain fear of difficulty.

【字谜】zìmí a riddle about a character or word

【字面】zìmiàn literal: ～上的意思 literal meaning/ 从～上看 taken literally

【字模】zìmú 〈印〉(type) matrix

【字母】zìmǔ letters of an alphabet; letter: 汉语拼音～ the Chinese phonetic alphabet/ 英语～ the English alphabet/ 大写～ a capital letter/ 按～顺序排列 be arranged in alphabetical order; be arranged alphabetically ◇ ～表 alphabet

【字幕】zìmù captions (of motion pictures, etc.); subtitles: 中文～ Chinese subtitles (或 captions)

【字书】zìshū wordbook; lexicon; dictionary

【字体】zìtǐ ①form of a written or printed character; script; typeface ②style of calligraphy

【字条儿】zìtiáor brief note

【字帖】zìtiè copybook (for calligraphy)

【字眼】zìyǎn wording; diction: 玩弄～ play with words/ 挑～儿 cavil at sb.'s choice of words; quibble

【字样】zìyàng ①model of written characters ②printed or written words (which succinctly inform, instruct, warn, etc.): 封面上有"初稿"～。On the cover are the words "First Draft"

【字斟句酌】zìzhēn-jùzhuó choose one's words with great care; weigh every word

【字纸】zìzhǐ wastepaper with characters written or printed on it ◇ ～篓 wastepaper basket

自 zì ①self; oneself; one's own: ～画像 self-portrait

~不自量力 overestimate one's strength or oneself; not know one's own limitations/ ~打耳光 slap one's own face; contradict oneself ② certainly; of course: ~当努力 will certainly do one's best/ ~不待言 it goes without saying; be self-evident ③ from; since: ~即日起生效 become effective (as) from this date; with effect from (w.e.f.)/ ~古以来 since ancient times; from time immemorial/ ~幼 since childhood

【自爱】 zì'ài regard for oneself; self-respect

【自拔】 zìbá free oneself (from pain or evildoing); extricate oneself: 不能~ unable to extricate oneself

【自白】 zìbái make clear one's meaning or position; vindicate oneself

【自暴自弃】 zìbào-zìqì be backward and have no urge to make progress; be resigned to one's backwardness; give oneself up as hopeless

【自卑】 zìbēi feel oneself inferior; be self-abased ◇ ~感 inferiority complex; sense of inferiority

【自备】 zìbèi provide for oneself

【自便】 zìbiàn at one's convenience; as one pleases: 听其~。Let him do as he pleases./ 请~。Please do as you like.

【自惭形秽】 zì cán xíng huì feel unworthy (of others' company); have a sense of inferiority or inadequacy

【自称】 zìchēng call oneself; claim to be; profess: ~内行 call oneself an expert; claim to be an old hand/ ~不知情 profess ignorance

【自成一家】 zì chéng yī jiā (in calligraphy, painting, sculpture, etc.) have a style of one's own; be unique in one's style

【自持】 zìchí control oneself; restrain oneself; exercise self-restraint

【自吹自擂】 zìchuī-zìléi blow one's own trumpet; crack oneself up

【自从】 zìcóng since: ~去年秋天到现在 from last autumn till now; since last fall

【自大】 zìdà self-important; arrogant ◇ ~狂 megalomania

【自得】 zìdé contented; self-satisfied: 怡然~ contentedly take one's ease; act in a leisurely, contented manner/ 洋洋~ complacent; smug

【自得其乐】 zì dé qí lè be content with one's lot

【自动】 zìdòng ① voluntarily; of one's own accord: ~参加 participate voluntarily ② automatic: ~延长 (of a lease, etc.) be automatically extended

【自动化】 zìdònghuà automation: 工艺过程~ process automation/ 铁路编组站~ automation of a railway marshalling yard

【自渎】 zìdú 〈书〉 self-abuse; masturbation

【自发】 zìfā spontaneous ◇ ~性 spontaneity

【自肥】 zìféi fatten oneself; enrich oneself by misappropriating funds or material; feather one's nest

【自费】 zìfèi at one's own expense: ~旅行 travel at one's own expense

【自封】 zìfēng ① proclaim (或 style) oneself: ~为诗人 proclaim oneself a poet ② confine oneself; isolate oneself: 故步~ stand still and refuse to make progress; be complacent and conservative

【自负】 zìfù ① be responsible for one's own action, etc.: 文责~。The author takes sole responsibility for his views. ② think highly of oneself; be conceited: 这个人很~。This person is rather conceited.

【自负盈亏】 zì fù yíng-kuī (of an enterprise) assume sole responsibility for its profits or losses

【自甘堕落】 zì gān duòluò wallow in degeneration; abandon oneself to vice

【自高自大】 zìgāo-zìdà self-important; conceited; arrogant

【自告奋勇】 zì gào fènyǒng offer to undertake (a difficult or dangerous task); volunteer (to do sth. difficult)

【自个儿】 zìgěr 〈方〉 oneself; by oneself: 我很忙，你~去，好吗？I'm busy. Would you go there by yourself?

【自供】 zìgòng confess ◇ ~状 confession

【自顾不暇】 zì gù bù xiá be unable even to fend for oneself (much less look after others); be busy enough with one's own affairs

【自豪】 zìháo have a proper sense of pride or dignity; be proud of sth. ◇ ~感 sense of pride

【自毁】 zìhuǐ 〈军〉 self-destruction: 导弹~ missile self-destruction

【自己】 zìjǐ ① oneself: 生~的气 be angry with oneself/ 动手 use one's own hands/ 打击别人，抬高~ sling mud at others so as to boost oneself/ 你~看看去! Go and see for yourself!/ 瓶子不会一倒下来，准是有人碰了它。The bottle couldn't have fallen down of itself. Someone must have knocked it over. ② closely related; own: ~弟兄 one's own brothers

【自己人】 zìjǐrén people on one's own side; one of us: 他是~。He's one of us./ 都是~，你别客气了。You're among friends, so make yourself at home.

【自给】 zìjǐ self-sufficient; self-supporting: 粮食~有余 be more than self-sufficient in grain

【自给自足】 zìjǐ-zìzú self-sufficiency; autarky

【自家】 zìjiā 〈方〉 oneself

【自荐】 zìjiàn recommend oneself (for a job); offer one's services

【自尽】 zìjìn commit suicide; take one's own life

【自咎】 zìjiù blame oneself; rebuke oneself

【自救】 zìjiù save oneself; provide for and help oneself: 团结~ get united for one's own salvation/ 生产~ provide for and help oneself by engaging in production

【自居】 zìjū consider oneself to be; pose as: 以功臣~ pose as one who has rendered great service; give oneself the airs of a hero

【自决】 zìjué self-determination: 民族~ national self-determination ◇ ~权 right to self-determination

【自觉】 zìjué conscious; aware: 这种病初起时，患者每不~。Those suffering from the disease are often unaware of it in the early stages.

【自觉自愿】 zìjué-zìyuàn voluntarily; willingly; of one's own free will

【自绝】 zìjué alienate oneself: ~于人民 alienate oneself from the people

【自掘坟墓】 zì jué fénmù dig one's own grave; work for one's own destruction

【自夸】 zìkuā sing one's own praises; crack oneself up

【自拉自唱】 zìlā-zìchàng ① accompany one's own singing ② hold forth all alone in defence of one's own views or proposals; second one's own motion

【自来】 zìlái from the beginning; in the first place; originally

【自来水】 zìláishuǐ running water; tap water ◇ ~厂 waterworks

【自来水笔】 zìláishuǐbǐ fountain pen

【自理】 zìlǐ take care of or provide for oneself: 伙食~ make one's own eating arrangements/ 旅费~ pay one's own travelling expenses

【自立】 zìlì stand on one's own feet; support oneself; earn one's own living

【自力更生】 zìlì gēngshēng regeneration (或 reconstruction) through one's own efforts; self-reliance: ~重建家园 rebuild one's homeland through self-reliance (或 one's own efforts)/ 我们是主张~的。We stand for self-reliance.

【自量】 zìliàng estimate one's own ability or strength: 不知~ overrate one's abilities

【自流】 zìliú ① (of water, etc.) flow automatically; flow by itself ② (of a thing) take its natural course; (of a person) do as one pleases: 听其~ let things drift along; let people act freely without leadership

【自留地】 zìliúdì plot of land for personal needs; family plot; private plot

【自卖自夸】 zìmài-zìkuā praise the goods one sells; indulge in self-glorification; blow one's own trumpet

【自满】 zìmǎn complacent; self-satisfied: ~情绪 complacency; self-satisfaction/ 要认真学习一点东西，必须从不~开始。We cannot really learn anything until we rid ourselves of complacency.

【自明】 zìmíng self-evident; self-explanatory; obvious: 共理~。The principle involved is obvious./ 含义~，无须多说。

This point is self-evident and needs no elaboration

【自鸣得意】 zì míng déyì show self-satisfaction; be very pleased with oneself; preen oneself

【自鸣钟】 zìmíngzhōng striking clock; chime clock

【自命】 zìmìng consider oneself; regard oneself as: ～为历史学家 consider oneself a historian; profess to be a historian

【自命不凡】 zìmìng bù fán consider oneself no ordinary being; have an unduly high opinion of oneself; think no end of oneself

【自馁】 zìněi lose confidence; be discouraged

【自欺欺人】 zì qī qī rén deceive oneself as well as others

【自遣】 zìqiǎn divert oneself from melancholy, etc.; cheer oneself up: 无以～ have no way to cheer oneself up (或 amuse oneself); have nothing to divert oneself with

【自戕】 zìqiāng 〈书〉 commit suicide; take one's own life

【自强不息】 zìqiáng bù xī make unremitting (或 unceasing) efforts to improve oneself; constantly strive to become stronger

【自轻自贱】 zìqīng-zìjiàn belittle oneself; lack self-confidence or self-respect

【自取灭亡】 zì qǔ mièwáng court (或 invite) destruction; take the road to one's doom

【自取其咎】 zì qǔ qí jiù bring blame on oneself; have only oneself to blame: 你这是～。 You asked for it.

【自然】 zìrán ① natural world; nature: 改造～ transform nature/ 与～作斗争 struggle with nature; battle the elements/ ～条件 natural conditions ② naturally; in the ordinary nary course of events: ～地归于消灭 die out naturally/ 功到～成。 Constant effort yields sure success./ 这病只要吃药，休息一两天～会好的。 No medicine is necessary for this illness. With a couple of days of rest you'll be all right./ 你先别问，到时候～明白。 Don't ask now. You'll understand in due course. ③ of course; naturally: 你第一次登台感到紧张是很～的。 Naturally, you were keyed up when you went on the stage for the first time./ 只要努力，～会取得好成绩。 If you work hard, you're bound to get good results.

【自然】 zìran at ease; natural; free from affectation: 态度非常～ be quite at ease/ 她虽是初次演出，但是演得很～。 Her acting was very natural although it was the first time she appeared on the stage./ 他不～地笑了一笑。 He forced a smile.

【自然而然】 zìrán'érrán naturally; automatically; spontaneously; of oneself

【自认晦气】 zì rèn huìqì accept bad luck without complaint; grin and bear it

【自如】 zìrú 〈书〉 freely; smoothly; with facility: 操纵～ operate with facility/ 旋转～ rotate or revolve freely/ 运用～ handle and use (a tool) with skill; wield skilfully

【自若】 zìruò 〈书〉 self-possessed; composed; calm and at ease: 神态～ appear calm and at ease; appear composed/ 临危不惧,谈笑～ talk and laugh imperturbably in face of danger

【自杀】 zìshā commit suicide; take one's own life

【自上而下】 zì shàng ér xià from above to below; from top to bottom: 军队中～的统一指挥 unified command from above in the army

【自身】 zìshēn self; oneself: ～难保 be unable even to fend for oneself

【自生自灭】 zìshēng-zìmiè (of a thing) emerge of itself and perish of itself; run its course

【自食其果】 zì shí qí guǒ eat one's own bitter fruit; reap what one has sown

【自食其力】 zì shí qí lì support oneself by one's own labour; earn one's own living

【自始至终】 zì shǐ zhì zhōng from start to finish; from beginning to end

【自视】 zìshì consider (或 think, imagine) oneself: ～甚高 think highly of oneself; be self-important

【自信】 zìxìn be self-assured for having sth. or sb. to rely on; count on; capitalize on: ～有功 capitalize on one's achievements/ ～有靠山 count on sb.'s backing

【自是】 zìshì naturally; of course: 久别重逢，～高兴。 It was of course a delight for them to meet again after such a long separation.

【自首】 zìshǒu ① (of a criminal) voluntarily surrender oneself; confess one's crime; give oneself up: 投案～ surrender oneself to the police or judicial department ② make a political recantation; surrender to the enemy: ～变节 recant and turn traitor ◇ ～书 confession

【自赎】 zìshú redeem oneself; atone for one's crime: 立功～ perform meritorious services to atone for one's crime

【自述】 zìshù an account in one's own words

【自私】 zìsī selfish; self-centred: ～自利是可鄙的。 Selfishness is contemptible./ 毫无～自利之心的精神 the spirit of absolute selflessness

【自讨苦吃】 zì tǎo kǔ chī ask for trouble

【自投罗网】 zì tóu luówǎng hurl oneself willingly into the net; bite the hook

【自卫】 zìwèi ① defend oneself: ～能力 the capacity to defend oneself ② self-defence: ～反击 fight (或 strike) back in self-defence

【自慰】 zìwèi console oneself: 聊以～ just to console oneself

【自刎】 zìwěn commit suicide by cutting one's throat; cut one's throat

【自问】 zìwèn ① ask oneself; examine oneself: 反躬～ examine one's conscience ② reach a conclusion after weighing a matter: 我～是花过不少力气的。 I flatter myself that I have spared no pains./ 我～没有什么对不起他的地方。 I don't remember ever doing him wrong.

【自我】 zìwǒ 〔用在双音动词前面，表示这个动作由自己发出，同时又以自己为对象〕 self; oneself: ～介绍 introduce oneself

【自下而上】 zì xià ér shàng from bottom to top; from below: ～的监督 supervision from below

【自相残杀】 zì xiāng cánshā (of persons within a group, party, etc.) kill each other; cause death to one another

【自相惊扰】 zì xiāng jīngrǎo alarm one's own group, etc.; create disturbance within one's ranks; raise false alarms

【自相矛盾】 zì xiāng máodùn contradict oneself; be self-contradictory: 他的话～。 What he says is self-contradictory./ 你这不是～吗？ Aren't you contradicting yourself?

【自新】 zìxīn turn over a new leaf; make a fresh start: 改过～ correct one's errors and make a fresh start; turn over a new leaf

【自信】 zìxìn self-confident: 有～心 have self-confidence; be sure of oneself/ 我～能够完成这项任务。 I'm sure I can fulfil the task.

【自行】 zìxíng ① by oneself: ～解决 settle (a problem) by oneself/ ～安排 arrange by oneself/ ～设计 make designs of one's own ② of oneself; of one's own accord; voluntarily: ～到来 come of itself

【自行车】 zìxíngchē bicycle; bike: 骑～ ride a bicycle

【自行其是】 zì xíng qí shì act as one thinks fit; go one's own way

【自修】 zìxiū ① (of students) study by oneself; have self-study ② study on one's own; study independently: ～法语 teach oneself French

【自诩】 zìxǔ 〈书〉 praise oneself; crack oneself up; brag

【自序】 zìxù ① author's preface; preface ② autobiographic note; brief account of oneself 又作"自叙"

【自学】 zìxué study on one's own; study independently; teach oneself: 培养～能力 cultivate (或 foster) one's ability to study independently ◇ ～课本 teach-yourself books

【自寻死路】 zì xún sǐlù bring about one's own destruction

【自言自语】 zìyán-zìyǔ talk to oneself; think aloud; soliloquize

【自以为是】 zì yǐwéi shì consider oneself (always) in the right; regard oneself as infallible; be opinionated

【自缢】 zìyì 〈书〉 hang oneself

【自用】 zìyòng ① obstinately holding to one's own views; opinionated; self-willed: 刚愎～ obstinate; self-opinionated/ 愚而好～ ignorant and self-willed ② for private use; personal: ～物品 personal effects; personal belongings

【自由】 zìyóu ① freedom; liberty ② 〈哲〉 freedom: ～和必

然 freedom and necessity ③ free; unrestrained: ～ 讨论 have a free exchange of views/～选择 be free to choose; have a free choice/ ～行动 act on one's own/. ～发表意见 express one's views unreservedly

【自由放任】 zìyóu fàngrèn allowing unrestrained freedom; laissez-faire ◇ ～主义 laissez-faire

【自由散漫】 zìyóu-sǎnmàn slack; lax in discipline: ～现象 slackness (in discipline)

【自由主义】 zìyóuzhǔyì liberalism: ～的倾向 liberal tendencies ◇ ～者 liberal

【自由自在】 zìyóu-zìzài leisurely and carefree; free and unrestrained

【自圆其说】 zì yuán qí shuō make one's statement consistent; justify oneself: 这样解释能～吗 Is this a plausible explanation?/ 不能～ cannot offer a tenable argument; cannot justify oneself

【自怨自艾】 zìyuàn-zìyì ① repent and redress one's errors ② be full of remorse

【自愿】 zìyuàn voluntary; of one's own accord; of one's own free will: 出于～ on a voluntary basis; of one's free will

【自在】 zìzài free; unrestrained: 逍遥～ leisurely and carefree; free from trammels; at liberty to enjoy oneself

【自在】 zìzai comfortable; at ease: 主人太客气了,反而使他们有些不～。 The host's assiduous attentions made them feel rather ill at ease./ 身体有点不～ feel a little out of sorts; not be quite oneself

【自找】 zìzhǎo suffer from one's own actions; ask for it: 这是你～的嘛 You asked for it./ 麻烦 be looking for trouble

【自知之明】 zìzhī zhī míng self-knowledge: 无～ lack of self-knowledge/ 人贵有～。 It is important to know one's own limitations. 或 Self-knowledge is wisdom.

【自治】 zìzhì autonomy; self-government: jurisdiction ◇ ～区 autonomous region/ ～权 autonomy

【自制】 zìzhì ① made by oneself: 这台铣床是我们厂～的。 This milling machine was made in our own plant. ② self-control; self-restraint: 失去～ lose self-control

【自重】 zìzhòng ① conduct oneself with dignity; be self-possessed. ② dead weight: 车皮～ the dead weight of a wagon

【自主】 zìzhǔ act on one's own; decide for oneself; keep the initiative in one's own hands: 独立～ independently and with the initiative in one's own hands/ 不由～ cannot help (it); involuntarily/ 男女婚姻～。 Men and women shall marry the partners of their choice.

【自传】 zìzhuàn autobiography

【自转】 zìzhuàn 〈天〉 rotation: 地球的～ the rotation of the earth ◇ ～轴 〈天〉 axis of rotation

【自尊】 zìzūn self-respect; self-esteem; proper pride: 伤了他的～心 injure his self-esteem; wound his pride ◇ ～感 sense of self-respect

【自作自受】 zìzuò-zìshòu suffer from one's own actions; as a man sows. so shall he reap: 这是你～。 As you make your bed, so you must lie on it.

【自作聪明】 zì zuò cōngmíng think oneself clever (in making suggestions, etc.)

【自作主张】 zì zuò zhǔzhāng act on one's own; decide for oneself: 这件事我们得请示领导,不能～。 We can't decide this matter for ourselves; we must ask the leadership for instructions.

恣 zì throw off restraint; do as one pleases: 得以自～ be able to do as one likes (或 indulge oneself)

【恣肆】 zìsì 〈书〉 ① unrestrained; self-indulgent; wanton ② (of writing style) forceful and unrestrained; free and natural

【恣睢】 zìsuī 〈书〉 reckless; unbridled

【恣行无忌】 zì xíng wú jì act wilfully and unscrupulously; behave recklessly

【恣意】 zìyì unscrupulous; reckless; unbridled; wilful: ～妄为 behave unscrupulously/ ～践踏 wilfully trample on/ ～掠夺别国的资源 indulge in unbridled plunder of the resources of other countries

渍 zì ① steep; soak; ret: ～麻 ret flax, jute, etc./ 白衬衫被汗水～黄了。 The white shirt has yellowed with sweat. ② floodwater on low-lying land: 防洪排～ prevention of floods and drainage of floodwater ③ be soiled (with grease, etc.): 她每天擦机器,不让～一点油泥。 She polishes the machine every day so that there's not a speck of dirt on it./ 烟斗里～了很多油子。 The pipe is caked with tar. ④ 〈方〉 stain; sludge: 油～ oil sludge/茶～ tea stains

眦 zì corner of the eye;

zōng

宗* zōng ① ancestor: 列祖列～ successive generations of ancestors ② clan: 同～ of the same clan ③ sect; faction; school: 正～ orthodox school ④ principal aim; purpose: 开～明义 make clear the purpose and main theme from the very beginning ⑤ (in academic or artistic work) take as one's model ⑥ model; great master: 一代诗～ an outstanding figure among the poets of the time ⑦ 〈量〉: 一～心事 a matter that worries one/ 大～款项 a large sum of money/ 大～货物 a large quantity of goods

【宗祠】 zōngcí ancestral hall (或 temple)

【宗法】 zōngfǎ patriarchal clan system ◇ ～社会 patriarchal society

【宗匠】 zōngjiàng 〈旧〉 great master (in academic or artistic work)

【宗教】 zōngjiào religion

【宗庙】 zōngmiào ancestral temple (或 shrine) of a ruling house

【宗派】 zōngpài faction; sect ◇ ～斗争 factional strife

【宗师】 zōngshī 〈旧〉 master of great learning and integrity

【宗旨】 zōngzhǐ aim; purpose

【宗主国】 zōngzhǔguó suzerain (state); metropolitan state

【宗主权】 zōngzhǔquán suzerainty

【宗族】 zōngzú ① patriarchal clan ② clansman

综 zōng put together; sum up: ～上所述 to sum up

【综观】 zōngguān make a comprehensive survey

【综合】 zōnghé ① synthesize: ～群众的意见 synthesize (或 sum up) the opinions of the masses ② synthetical; comprehensive; multiple; composite: ～的研究 a synthetical (或 comprehensive) study ◇ ～报导 comprehensive (或 composite) dispatch; news roundup/ ～报告 comprehensive report; summing-up report

【综括】 zōngkuò sum up: ～起来 to sum up; to state succinctly

【综述】 zōngshù summarize; sum up: 来稿～ a summary of readers' contributions

棕* zōng ① palm ② palm fibre; coir: ～绳 coir rope

【棕榈】 zōnglǘ palm ◇ ～油 palm oil; palm butter

【棕色】 zōngsè brown

【棕树】 zōngshù palm

踪* zōng footprint; track; trace: 跟～ follow the tracks of; trail

【踪迹】 zōngjī trace; track: 不留～ not leave a trace

【踪影】 zōngyǐng 〔多用于否定式〕 trace; sign: 毫无～ leaving without a trace

鬃 zōng hair on the neck of a pig, horse, etc.: 马～ horse's mane/ 猪～ pig's bristles/ ～刷 bristle brush

zǒng

总* zǒng ① assemble; put together; sum up: 汇～ assemble; collect; gather together/ ～起来说 to sum up/ 其成 assume overall command of a project and bring it to completion/ 把两笔帐～到一块算 settle the two accounts together ② general; overall; total: ～产量 total output/

~趋势 general trend/ ~危机 general crisis/ ~开关 master switch/ ~根源 root cause/ 抓~ assume overall responsibility/ ~的说来 generally speaking; by and large/ 开会结会,算~帐 hold summing-up meetings for a general check-up ③ chief; head; general: ~编辑 editor in chief/ ~工程师 chief engineer/ ~店 head office (of a firm)/ ~部 general headquarters/ ~书记 secretary-general; general secretary/ ~头目 chief boss; chieftain ④ always; invariably ⑤ anyway; after all; inevitably; sooner or later: 问题~是要解决的。The problem will be settled sooner or later.

【总参谋长】zǒngcānmóuzhǎng chief of the general staff
【总得】zǒngděi must; have to; be bound to: ~想个办法 have got to find a way out/ 他今天~来一趟。He's bound to come today.
【总动员】zǒngdòngyuán general (或 total) mobilization
【总督】zǒngdū governor-general; governor; viceroy
【总额】zǒng'é total: 存款~ total deposits/ 工资~ total wages
【总而言之】zǒng ér yán zhī in short; in a word; in brief; to make a long story short
【总方针】zǒngfāngzhēn general policy; general principle: 经济工作的~ the general policy guiding economic work/ 外交政策~ general principles of foreign policy
【总纲】zǒnggāng general programme; general principles
【总共】zǒnggòng in all; altogether; in the aggregate: ~约五千人 about five thousand people in all/ 这个地区~有二百二十家工厂。There are altogether 220 factories in this area.
【总管】zǒngguǎn manager
【总归】zǒngguī anyhow; eventually; after all: 困难~是可以克服的。Difficulties can after all be overcome./ 事实~是事实。After all, facts are facts.
【总和】zǒnghé sum; total; sum total
【总汇】zǒnghuì ① (of streams) come or flow together: ~入海 flow into the sea together ② confluence; concourse; aggregate
【总机】zǒngjī switchboard; telephone exchange
【总计】zǒngjì ① <数> grand total ② amount to; add up to; total/ 观众~有十万人。The audience totalled 100,000. 或 There were 100,000 spectators in all.
【总价】zǒngjià total (price)
【总监】zǒngjiān inspector general; chief inspector
【总结】zǒngjié ① sum up; summarize: ~经验 sum up one's experience/ ~工作 summarize one's work ② summary; summing-up: 作~ make a summary
【总括】zǒngkuò sum up: ~起来 to sum up; to state succinctly
【总揽】zǒnglǎn assume overall responsibility; take on everything: ~大权 have overall authority; assume a dominant role
【总理】zǒnglǐ premier; prime minister
【总领事】zǒnglǐngshì consul general ◇ ~馆 consulate general
【总目】zǒngmù comprehensive table of contents
【总评】zǒngpíng general comment; overall appraisal
【总数】zǒngshù total; sum total
【总司令】zǒngsīlìng commander in chief
【总算】zǒngsuàn <副> ① at long last; finally: 会议一再延期,现在~开成了。After several postponements the meeting has been held at last./ 他想来想去,最后~想出了一个好主意。He thought it over and over and finally hit upon a good idea. ② considering everything; all things considered; on the whole: 小孩子的字能写成这样,~不错了。For a child's handwriting, it's quite good.
【总体】zǒngtǐ overall; total ◇ ~规划 overall plan/ ~战 general war; total warfare
【总统】zǒngtǒng president (of a republic) ◇ ~府 presidential palace; the residence and/ or office of a president/ ~选举 presidential election/ ~制 presidential government
【总务】zǒngwù ① general affairs ② person in charge of general affairs

【总之】zǒngzhī in a word; in short; in brief
【总值】zǒngzhí total value: 生产~ total output value/ 进(出)口~ gross import (export) value/ 国民生产~ gross national product (GNP)
【总指挥】zǒngzhǐhuī ① commander in chief ② general director

zòng

纵 zòng ① from north to south: 大运河~贯河北、山东、江苏、浙江四省。The Grand Canal flows southwards through the four provinces of Hebei, Shandong, Jiangsu and Zhejiang. ② vertical; longitudinal; lengthwise: ~剖面 vertical section ③ release; set free: ~擒七~ capture and release seven times ④ indulge; let loose; let oneself go: 放~ let sb. have his way; indulge/ 娇~ pamper (a child)/ ~声大笑 have a hearty laugh ⑤ jump up; jump into the air: 他向前一~,就把球接住了。He leaped forward and caught the ball. ⑥ <书> even if; though; even though: ~有千难万险,也挡不住英勇的勘探队员。Even though there are myriad hardships and hazards, they can't stop the dauntless prospectors.
【纵步】zòngbù ① stride: ~向前走去 stride forward ② jump; bound: 他一个~跳过了小河。He crossed the brook in one big jump.
【纵队】zòngduì column; file: ~队形 column formation
【纵横】zòng-héng ① in length and breadth; vertically and horizontally: ~数百里的山区 a mountainous area several hundred li in length and breadth/ ~交错的水渠 a crisscross network of irrigation channels ② with great ease; freely: 笔意~ write with great ease
【纵横捭阖】zònghéng-bǎihé manoeuvre among various political groupings
【纵横驰骋】zònghéng chíchěng (of an army) move about freely and quickly; sweep through the length and breadth of
【纵虎归山】zòng hǔ guī shān let the tiger return to the mountain — cause calamity for the future
【纵火】zònghuǒ set on fire; commit arson ◇ ~犯 arsonist
【纵酒】zòngjiǔ drink to excess
【纵览】zònglǎn look far and wide; scan: ~群书 read extensively
【纵目】zòngmù look as far as one's eyes can see: ~四望 look far into the distance in all directions
【纵情】zòngqíng to one's heart's content; as much as one likes: ~歌唱 sing to one's heart's content; sing heartily
【纵然】zòngrán even if; even though: ~成功的希望不大,我们也要试试。We will try even if there isn't much hope of success.
【纵容】zòngróng connive; wink at: 在某人~下 with the connivance of sb./ 受到~和庇护 be winked at and shielded
【纵身】zòngshēn jump; leap: ~一跳 jump into the air; jump up/ ~上马 leap onto a horse
【纵使】zòngshǐ even if; even though
【纵谈】zòngtán talk freely
【纵欲】zòngyù give way to one's carnal desires; indulge in sensual pleasures

粽* zòng 见"粽子"
【粽子】zòngzi a pyramid-shaped dumpling made of glutinous rice wrapped in bamboo or reed leaves (eaten during the Dragon Boat Festival)

zǒu

走* zǒu ① walk; go: 一直往前~ go straight ahead/ ~很远的路 walk a long distance/ ~遍全国 travel the length and breadth of the whole country/ ~前人没有~过的道路 break new paths; take paths never trodden before/ ~回头路 turn back; retrace one's steps/ ~弯路 take a roundabout route; make a detour/ ~一步看一步 take one step and look around before taking another — proceed without a plan, or with caution/ 孩子还不会~。 The baby cannot walk yet./ 这船一小时~十五海里。 The ship makes 15 knots. ② run; move: 奔~ run; rush about/ 钟不~了。 The clock has stopped./ 这个表~得很准。 This watch keeps good time./打得赢就打,打不赢就~。Fight when you can win, move away when you can't./ 你这步棋~坏了。 You've made a bad move. ③ leave; go away: ~开! Get away! 或 Clear off!/ 我们该~了。 It's time for us to leave. 或 We must be off now./ 他已经把蓝图拿~了。 He's taken the blueprint away. ④ visit; call on: ~亲戚 call on relatives/ ~娘家 (of a married woman) visit her parents' home/ 他们两家~得很近。The two families often visit each other. ⑤ through; from: 我们~这个门进去吧。 Let's go in through this door. ⑥ leak; let out; escape: ~气了。 The gas is leaking. 或 The air is escaping./ 说~了嘴 make a slip of the tongue; blurt something out ⑦ depart from the original; lose the original shape, flavour, etc.: 把原来的意思讲~了 fail to get across the original meaning/ 说话~题儿 speak beside the point; wander from the subject

【走道】 zǒudào ① pavement; sidewalk ② path; walk; footpath

【走动】 zǒudòng ① walk about; stretch one's legs: 坐了一整天了,出去~~吧。 We've been sitting all day long. Let's go out for a stroll./ 病人能~了。 The invalid is able to get about now. ② (of relatives and friends) visit each other: 他们两家关系不错,常常~。 The two families are on good terms and often visit each other.

【走访】 zǒufǎng ① interview; have an interview with: 本报记者~了几位著名的小说家。 Our reporter interviewed several famous novelists. ② pay a visit to; go and see

【走风】 zǒufēng let out a secret; leak out

【走狗】 zǒugǒu running dog; lackey; flunkey; stooge; servile follower

【走后门】 zǒu hòumén get in by the back door; secure advantages through pull or influence: 纠正"~"之类的不正之风 overcome such unhealthy tendencies as "entering by the back door"

【走火】 zǒuhuǒ ① <电> sparking ② (of firearms) discharge accidentally: 他一时不慎,枪~了。 He wasn't careful and his rifle went off accidentally. ③ go too far in what one says; put sth. too strongly; overstate

【走江湖】 zǒu jiānghu wander from place to place and earn a living by juggling, fortune-telling, etc.; become a vagrant

【走廊】 zǒuláng corridor; passage; passageway

【走漏】 zǒulòu ① leak out; divulge: ~风声 divulge a secret; leak information ② smuggling and tax evasion

【走路】 zǒulù walk; go on foot: 你们是坐车去还是~去? Will you go there by bus or on foot?

【走马】 zǒumǎ gallop or trot along on horseback

【走马灯】 zǒumǎdēng a lantern with papercut figures of men, animals, etc. made to revolve when the lantern is lit: 人员不断更换,就象~似的。 Personnel were shifted about as often as if they were on a merry-go-round.

【走马看花】 zǒu mǎ kàn huā look at flowers while riding on horseback — gain a superficial understanding through cursory observation 又作"走马观花"

【走内线】 zǒu nèixiàn seek sb.'s favour by approaching his family members (esp. wife) or confidant; use private influence to achieve one's end; go through private channels

【走失】 zǒushī wander away; be lost; be missing: 一只羊~了。 A sheep has wandered away from the flock./ 我们一起出去的,半路上他~了。 We went out together and he got lost on the way.

【走兽】 zǒushòu beast; quadruped; four-footed animal

【走私】 zǒusī smuggle: ~的货物 smuggled goods

【走投无路】 zǒu-tóu-wú-lù have no way out; be in an impasse; come to the end of one's tether: 逼得~ be driven (或 pushed) to the wall

【走向】 zǒuxiàng ① run; trend; alignment: 矿脉的~ the run of the ore vein/ 海岸线~ the trend of the coastline/ 确定两国边线的全部~ determine the entire alignment of

the boundary line between the two countries/ 横断山脉是南北~的山脉。 The Hengduan Mountains run from south to north. ② move towards; head for; be on the way to· ~大治 move towards great order/~胜利 advance towards victory; march to victory

【走样】 zǒuyàng lose shape; go out of form; be different from what is expected or intended: 放上鞋楦免得鞋~。 Use shoe trees to keep your shoes from losing shape./ 这事让他给说~了。 His account presented a distorted picture of the matter.

【走运】 zǒuyùn be in luck; have good luck: 不~ have bad luck (或 fortune)/ 我们真~! We're really in luck.

【走着瞧】 zǒuzheqiáo wait and see: 我们~! We'll see (who's right).

【走卒】 zǒuzú pawn; cat's-paw; lackey; stooge

【走嘴】 zǒuzuǐ make a slip of the tongue; let slip an inadvertent remark

zòu

奏* zòu ① play (music); perform (on a musical instrument): ~国歌 play the national anthem/ 独~ (instrumental) solo/ 伴~ accompaniment/ 当贵宾进入宴会厅时,乐队开始~迎宾曲。 The band struck up a tune of welcome when the distinguished guests entered the banquet hall. ② achieve; produce: ~功 achieve success ③ present a memorial to an emperor

【奏捷】 zòujié win a battle; score a success

【奏凯】 zòukǎi win victory; be victorious; triumph

【奏效】 zòuxiào prove effective; be successful; get the desired result: 这药服了马上~。 This medicine will have immediate efficacy./ 这个办法能~吗? Will this method work?

【奏乐】 zòuyuè play music; strike up a tune

揍 zòu <口> beat; hit; strike: 把他~一顿 beat him up/ 挨~ get a thrashing

zū

租* zū ① rent; hire; charter: ~三间房 rent three rooms/ ~一条小船 hire a boat/ ~一架飞机 charter a plane ② rent out; let out; lease: 这块地已经~给人了。 This piece of land has been leased out./ 此屋招~。 Room to let./ 出~连环画 lend picture-story books (for a small fee) ③ rent: 房~ house rent/ 地~ land rent (to a landlord)/ 收~ collect rent ④ land tax

【租船】 zūchuán chartering

【租户】 zūhù ① tenant (of a building or part of it); lessee; leaseholder ② hirer (of a thing)

【租借】 zūjiè rent; hire; lease ◇ ~地 leased territory; leasehold/ ~人 leaseholder; lessee; tenant; hirer

【租金】 zūjīn rent; rental

【租赁】 zūlìn rent; lease; hire: ~服装和道具 rent costumes and stage properties

【租钱】 zūqián <口> rent; rental

【租用】 zūyòng rent; hire; take on lease: ~家具 rent furniture/ ~礼堂 hire a hall ◇ ~人 leaseholder; tenant; lessee; hirer

【租约】 zūyuē lease: ~什么时候到期? When does the lease expire?

zú

足* zú ① foot; leg: 赤~ barefoot/ 鼎~而立 standing like a tripod — a tripartite balance of forces ② sufficient; enough; ample: 富~ plentiful; abundant; wealthy/ 丰衣~食 have ample food and clothing; be well-fed and well-clothed ③ full; as much as: 路上~走了两个钟头。 The journey took fully two hours. ④ 〔多用于否定式〕 enough; sufficient: 微不~道 not worth mentioning

【足够】 zúgòu enough; ample; sufficient: ～用十个月的燃料 sufficient fuel to last ten months/ 有～的时间吗？ Is there enough time?/ 我们对困难要有～的估计。We must take full account of our difficulties.

【足迹】 zújì footmark; footprint; track: 雪地上的～ footprints (或 tracks) in the snow

【足见】 zújiàn it serves to show; one can well perceive: 他的发言内容丰富，～他是作了认真准备的。His speech is substantial, which shows he took great pains to prepare it.

【足金】 zújīn pure gold; solid gold

【足球】 zúqiú ① soccer; football: 踢～ play soccer (或 football)/ 美国式～ American football/ 英国式～ soccer; association football ② football (the ball used in playing either soccer or American football) ◇ ～队 football team; eleven/ ～运动员 footballer

【足下】 zúxià a polite form of address between friends (used mostly in letters): ～以为如何？ I wonder what you think of this.

【足以】 zúyǐ enough; sufficient: 你的话不～说服她。What you say isn't enough to convince her.

【足月】 zúyuè (of a foetus) born after the normal period of gestation; mature

【足智多谋】 zúzhì-duōmóu wise and full of stratagems; resourceful

卒 zú ① soldier; private: 士～ soldiers; the rank and file/ 小～ private; a mere pawn ② servant: 走～ underling; lackey ③ finish; end: ～其事 finish the job; wind up the business/ 聊以～岁 just to tide over the year ④ finally; at last: ～底于成 finally achieve success ⑤ die: 病～ die of illness/ 生～年月 dates of birth and death ⑥ pawn, one of the pieces in Chinese chess

【卒业】 zúyè ＜书＞ graduate; finish a course of study

族* zú ① clan: 合～ all the members of a clan; the whole clan ② a death penalty in ancient China, imposed on an offender and his whole family, or even the families of his mother and wife ③ race; nationality: 汉～ the Han nationality ④ a class or group of things with common features: 水～ aquatic animals/ 语～ a family of languages/ 猫～ the cat tribe

【族权】 zúquán clan authority; clan power

【族人】 zúrén clansman

【族长】 zúzhǎng clan elder; the head of a clan

镞 zú ＜书＞ arrowhead

zǔ

阻 zǔ hinder; block; obstruct: 拦～ block; hold back/ 劝～ dissuade sb. from; advise sb. against/ 通行无～ go through without hindrance/ 道路险～。The road is dangerous and difficult.

【阻碍】 zǔ'ài hinder; block; impede: ～交通 block the traffic/ 遇到～ meet with obstruction/ ～生产力的发展 hinder the development of the productive forces

【阻挡】 zǔdǎng stop; stem; resist; obstruct

【阻遏】 zǔ'è check; stem; stop

【阻隔】 zǔgé separate; cut off: 山川～ be separated by mountains and rivers

【阻击】 zǔjī ＜军＞ block; check

【阻拦】 zǔlán stop; obstruct; bar the way: 他决心要走，我们也不好～。As he was determined to go, we thought it better not to stop him.

【阻力】 zǔlì ① obstruction; resistance: 减少前进的～ reduce resistance to forward movement/ 冲破各种～ break through all kinds of obstructions ② ＜物＞ resistance; drag: 空气～ air resistance/ 迎面～ frontal resistance/ 摩擦～ friction drag

【阻挠】 zǔnáo obstruct; thwart; stand in the way; put a spoke in sb.'s wheel: 条约的履行受到了～。The execution of the treaty was obstructed./ ～两国关系正常化 stand in the way of the normalization of relations between the two countries

【阻塞】 zǔsè block; obstruct; clog: 交通～。The traffic is held up. 或 There's a traffic jam./ 脏东西把管子～了。The pipe is clogged with dirt.

【阻止】 zǔzhǐ prevent; stop; hold back: ～事态的恶化 prevent the situation from deteriorating

诅 zǔ

【诅咒】 zǔzhòu curse; swear; wish sb. evil; imprecate

组* zǔ ① organize; form: 改～ reorganize; reshuffle ② group: 读报～ a newspaper-reading group ③ ＜量＞ set; series; battery: 两～发电机 two generators/ 一～邮票 a set of stamps

【组成】 zǔchéng form; make up; compose: ～部分 component part; component/ 每五个人～一组。Every five persons constitute a group.

【组阁】 zǔgé form (或 set up, organize) a cabinet

【组合】 zǔhé ① make up; compose; constitute: 这本集子是由诗、散文和短篇小说三部分～而成的。This collection is made up of three parts: poems, essays and short stories./ 各种政治力量的重新～ a realignment of various political forces ② association; combination

【组织】 zǔzhī ① organize; form: ～劳力 organize a labour force; organize labour power/ ～一个登山队 form a mountaineering team/ ～一次座谈 organize a discussion/ ～一次演出 get up a performance/ 这篇文章～得很好。This article is well-organized. ② organization; organized system

祖* zǔ ① grandfather: 外～ maternal grandfather ② ancestor: 远～ remote ancestors ③ founder (of a craft, religious sect, etc.); originator: 鼻～ the earliest ancestor; originator (of a tradition, school of thought, etc.) ④ (Zǔ) a surname

【祖辈】 zǔbèi ancestors; forefathers; ancestry

【祖传】 zǔchuán handed down from one's ancestors: ～秘方 a secret prescription handed down in the family from generation to generation

【祖坟】 zǔfén ancestral grave

【祖父】 zǔfù (paternal) grandfather

【祖国】 zǔguó one's country; homeland; native land; motherland; fatherland

【祖籍】 zǔjí original family home; ancestral home; the land of one's ancestors

【祖母】 zǔmǔ (paternal) grandmother

【祖上】 zǔshàng ancestors; forefathers; forbears

【祖师】 zǔshī ① the founder of a school of learning, a craft, etc. ② the founder of a sect of Buddhism or Taoism

【祖孙】 zǔ-sūn grandparent and grandchild: ～三代 three generations

【祖先】 zǔxiān ancestry; ancestors; forbears; forefathers

【祖宗】 zǔzōng forefathers; ancestry; forbears ◇ ～崇拜 ancestor (或 ancestral) worship

【祖祖辈辈】 zǔzǔbèibèi for generations; from generation to generation: 我家～都是种地的。Our family have been farmers for generations.

俎 zǔ ① an ancient sacrificial utensil ② a kind of chopping block used in ancient times

【俎上肉】 zǔshàngròu ＜书＞ meat on the chopping block — a helpless victim

zuān

钻* zuān ① drill; bore: ～孔 drill a hole/ ～木取火 drill wood to make fire ② get into; go through; make one's way into: ～进密林深处 go deep into a forest/ 火车走这条线路～许多山洞。The train has to pass through quite a few tunnels on this railway line./ 月亮从云缝里～了出来。The moon broke through the clouds. ③ study inten-

sively; dig into: ~书本 dig into books/ ~故纸堆 bury oneself in outdated writings/ ~业务 dig into one's job or a subject; work hard to perfect oneself professionally/ 有许多人~进去了，就有一点内行的味道了。Quite a few have studied their trade and become quite professional.
另见 zuàn

【钻牛角尖】zuān niújiǎojiān ① take unnecessary pains to study an insignificant or insoluble problem; split hairs ② get into a dead end (或 a blind alley)

【钻探】zuāntàn (exploration) drilling: 海底~ offshore drilling/ ~设备 drilling equipment ◇ ~工 driller/ ~机 drilling machine

【钻研】zuānyán study intensively; dig into: 努力 ~业务 endeavour to gain professional proficiency

【钻营】zuānyíng curry favour with sb. in authority for personal gain; secure personal gain

蹿 zuān ① jump up ② dash forward: 燕子~天儿。The swallow dashed (或 shot) through the air.

zuǎn

纂 zuǎn 〈书〉 compile; edit: ~修 compile; edit/ 编 ~字典 compile a dictionary

zuàn

钻* zuàn ① drill; auger: 手摇~ hand drill; drill/ 风~ pneumatic drill ② diamond; jewel: ~戒 diamond ring/ 十九~的手表 a 19-jewel watch ③ bore; drill: 在木头上~个眼 bore a hole in wood
另见 zuān

【钻井】zuànjǐng well drilling

【钻石】zuànshí ① diamond ② jewel (used in a watch)

zuǐ

嘴* zuǐ ① mouth: 闭~ keep one's mouth shut/ ~上说说而已 pay lip service ② anything shaped or functioning like a mouth: 茶壶~ the spout of a teapot/ 瓶~儿 the mouth of a bottle/ 烟~儿 cigarette holder

【嘴巴】zuǐba ①〈方〉 mouth: 张开~。Open your mouth. ②〔口〕〔多用于〕: 打~ slap sb. in the face; box sb.'s ears/ 挨了个~ get a slap in the face

【嘴笨】zuǐbèn inarticulate; clumsy of speech

【嘴馋】zuǐchán fond of good food

【嘴唇】zuǐchún lip: 上(下)~ the upper (lower) lip/ 咬着~ bite one's lips

【嘴尖】zuǐjiān sharp-tongued; cutting in speech: 他这个人~,说的话真刺耳。He's sharp-tongued and what he says is often very biting.

【嘴角】zuǐjiǎo corners of the mouth

【嘴紧】zuǐjǐn tight-lipped; closemouthed; secretive

【嘴快】zuǐkuài have a loose tongue

【嘴脸】zuǐliǎn 〈贬〉 look; features; countenance/ 他那副~真难看。He had a very nasty look on his face./ 社会上各种人物的~被区别得清清楚楚。All sorts of people in society have been clearly shown up for what they are.

【嘴甜】zuǐtián ingratiating in speech; smooth-tongued; honeymouthed

【嘴硬】zuǐyìng stubborn and reluctant to admit mistakes or defeats: 知道错了,就别~。You know you're wrong, so don't stubbornly insist that you aren't.

zuì

最* zuì 〈副〉〔表示某种属性超过所有同类的人或事物〕: ~小 the smallest; the tiniest/ ~为积极 be the most active/ 速度~快 the fastest/ 政治上~有远见 be the most farsighted

politically/ ~大的幸福 supreme happiness/ ~基本的条件 fundamental prerequisites

【最初】zuìchū initial; first: ~阶段 the initial stage/ ~的印象 first impressions/ ~的计划 the original plan; the first and earliest plan/ ~她不想来,后来改变了主意。At first she didn't want to come, but later she changed her mind.

【最低】zuìdī lowest; minimum

【最多】zuìduō at most; maximum: 屋里~不过十个人。There were at most ten people in the room./ ~能容纳一千人。This hall can hold a maximum of one thousand people./ 这所学校学生~的时候有三千人。The school's enrolment at its height reached 3,000./ 我~只能等半个小时。I can wait half an hour at the longest.

【最高】zuìgāo highest; supreme; tallest: ~国家权力机关 the highest organ of state power/ 达到~峰 reach the climax (或 peak); reach a culminating point/ 创造历史上~纪录 hit an all-time high ◇ ~权力 supreme power/ ~速度 maximum speed/ ~统帅 supreme commander/ ~限额 ceiling

【最高级】zuìgāojí ① highest; summit: ~会谈 top-level talks; summit talks/ ~会议 summit conference ②〈语〉 the superlative degree

【最好】zuìhǎo ① best; first-rate: ~的办法 the best way ② had better; it would be best: 你~今天把它搞完。You'd better finish it today.

【最后】zuìhòu final; last; ultimate: ~胜利 final victory/ ~解决问题 bring the issue to a final solution; settle the question once and for all/ 作~挣扎 make a last-ditch struggle/ 坐在~一排 sit in the last row/ 他们的建议~被采纳了。Their suggestion was eventually accepted

【最后通牒】zuìhòu tōngdié ultimatum

【最惠国】zuìhuìguó most-favoured-nation: 给以~待遇 accord (a country) most-favoured-nation treatment

【最佳】zuìjiā 〈物〉 optimum ◇ ~数 optimum number

【最近】zuìjìn ① recently; lately; of late: 我~很忙。I've been very busy recently./ 几天 in the last few days/ ~的消息 the latest news; recent news ② in the near future; soon: ~要上演许多新电影。Many new films will be released soon.

【最终】zuìzhōng final; ultimate: ~结果 the final outcome

罪 zuì ① crime; guilt: 有~ guilty of a crime; guilty/ 轻~ misdemeanour/ 重~ felony/ 判~ condemn; pass sentence/ ~上加~ be doubly guilty/ 宣告无~ acquit sb. (of a crime); declare sb. innocent/ ~有应得 deserve the punishment ② fault; blame: 归~于人 lay the blame on others ③ suffering; pain; hardship: 受~ endure suffering; be in pain; have a hard time ④ put the blame on: ~己 bear the blame oneself; take the blame on oneself

【罪案】zuì'àn details of a criminal case; case

【罪不容诛】zuì bùróng zhū even death cannot atone for the offence; be guilty of crimes for which even death is insufficient punishment

【罪大恶极】zuìdà-èjí be guilty of the most heinous crimes

【罪恶】zuì'è crime; evil: ~多端 be guilty of all kinds of evil/ ~滔天 be guilty of monstrous crimes

【罪犯】zuìfàn criminal; offender; culprit

【罪该万死】zuì gāi wàn sǐ be guilty of a crime for which one deserves to die ten thousand deaths; be guilty of a crime for which even death cannot atone

【罪过】zuìguò ① fault; offence; sin: 这是我的。It's my fault./ 他有什么~要受这样的苦? What sin has he committed to deserve all this? ②〈谦〉 thanks, but this is really more than I deserve

【罪魁】zuìkuí chief criminal (或 culprit, offender); arch-criminal

【罪名】zuìmíng charge; accusation: 偷窃的~ a charge of theft/ 罗织~ frame a case against sb.

【罪孽】zuìniè wrongdoing that brings retribution; sin: ~深重 sinful

【罪人】zuìrén guilty person; offender; sinner: 历史~ a person condemned by history

【罪行】 zuìxíng crime; guilt; offence: 他的~较轻。His offence is a minor one.

【罪责】 zuìzé responsibility for an offence: ~难逃 cannot escape the responsibility for the offence; cannot get away with it

【罪证】 zuìzhèng evidence of a crime; proof of one's guilt

【罪状】 zuìzhuàng facts about a crime; charges in an indictment

醉* zuì ① drunk; intoxicated; tipsy: 烂~ be dead drunk/ 他喝~了。He's tipsy. 或 He's had a drop too much. ② (of some kinds of food) liquor-saturated; steeped in liquor: ~蟹 liquor-saturated crab

【醉鬼】 zuìguǐ drunkard; sot; inebriate

【醉汉】 zuìhàn drunkard; drunken man

【醉生梦死】 zuìshēng-mèngsǐ live as if intoxicated or dreaming; lead a befuddled life

【醉态】 zuìtài the state of being drunk; drunkenness

【醉翁之意不在酒】 zuìwēng zhī yì bù zài jiǔ the drinker's heart is not in the cup — have ulterior motives

【醉心】 zuìxīn be bent on; be wrapped up in: 他~于数学的研究。He's deeply engrossed in mathematical research./ ~名利 be infatuated with fame and gain

【醉醺醺】 zuìxūnxūn sottish; drunk; tipsy

【醉眼】 zuìyǎn <书> eyes showing the effects of drink: ~朦胧 drunken and bleary-eyed

【醉意】 zuìyì signs or feeling of getting drunk: 他已经有几分~了。He is a bit tipsy.

zūn

尊* zūn ① senior; of a senior generation: ~长 elders ② respect; venerate; honour: ~师爱生 respect the teacher and love the student ③ <敬> 〔旧时称跟对方有关的人或事物〕: ~夫人 your wife/ ~府 your residence/ ~姓大名? May I know your name? ④ <量>: 一~佛像 a statue of a Buddha/ 五十~大炮 fifty artillery pieces ⑤ a kind of wine vessel used in ancient times

【尊称】 zūnchēng ① a respectful form of address; honorific title ② address sb. respectfully: 人们~他为郭老。People respectfully called him the venerable Guo.

【尊崇】 zūnchóng worship; revere; venerate

【尊贵】 zūnguì honourable; respectable; respected: ~的客人 an honoured guest

【尊敬】 zūnjìng ① respect; honour; esteem: 非常~他 have the greatest esteem for him ② 见"尊贵"

【尊严】 zūnyán dignity; honour: 国家~ national dignity/ 维护法律的~ guard the sanctity of the law

【尊长】 zūnzhǎng elders and betters: 目无~ with no regard for one's elders and betters

【尊重】 zūnzhòng respect; value; esteem: 互相~ respect each other/ ~少数民族的风俗习惯 respect the habits and customs of the minority nationalities

遵* zūn abide by; obey; observe; follow: ~纪爱民 observe discipline and cherish the people/ ~医嘱 follow the doctor's advice

【遵从】 zūncóng defer to; comply with; follow: ~上级的指示 in compliance with the directives of the leadership/ ~老师的教导 follow the teacher's advice

【遵命】 zūnmìng <敬> comply with your wish; obey your command: ~办理 act in compliance with instructions

【遵守】 zūnshǒu observe; abide by; comply with: ~劳动纪律 observe labour discipline/ ~公共秩序 observe public order/ ~时间 be on time; be punctual/ ~法律 abide by the law/ ~并执行协议 comply with and carry out the agreement

【遵行】 zūnxíng act on; follow: ~一贯的原则 act according to one's consistent principles

【遵循】 zūnxún follow; abide by; adhere to: 制定一个章程, 使大家有所~ work out a set of rules so that people will have something to go by

【遵照】 zūnzhào obey; conform to; comply with; act in accordance with

樽 zūn a kind of wine vessel used in ancient times

鳟 zūn trout: 虹~ rainbow trout

zǔn

撙 zǔn save: 每月~下一些钱 save some money every month

【撙节】 zǔnjié retrench; practise economy: ~开支 retrench; cut down expenses

zuō

作* zuō ① 〔限用于某些词语〕do: 自~自受 suffer through one's own misdeeds; stew in one's own juice; lie in the bed one has made ② workshop: 木工~ carpenters' workshop/ 洗衣~ laundry
另见 zuó; zuò

【作弄】 zuōnòng tease; make a fool of; play a trick on; poke fun at

【作死】 zuōsǐ seek death; take the road to ruin; look for trouble: 天这么冷不穿棉衣, 你~呀! Are you tired of life that you don't wear padded clothes in such cold weather?

【作揖】 zuōyī make a bow with hands folded in front

嘬 zuō <口> suck: 小孩儿~奶。The baby is sucking its mother's breast.

zuó

作 zuó 〔限用于下列词语〕
另见 zuō; zuò

【作践】 zuójian <口> ① spoil; waste: ~东西 spoil things ② run sb. down; disparage: 他这不是故意~人吗? Didn't he say that just to run me down? ③ humiliate; insult

昨* zuó yesterday: ~晚 yesterday evening; last night

【昨儿】 zuór <口> yesterday 又作"昨儿个"

【昨天】 zuótiān yesterday

琢 zuó
另见 zhuó

【琢磨】 zuómo turn sth. over in one's mind; ponder: ~问题 turn a problem over in one's mind/ ~出个办法 figure out a way (to do sth.)/ 这件事她~了很久。She pondered over the matter for a long time.
另见 zhuómó

zuǒ

左* zuǒ ① the left side; the left: ~上方 the upper left/ 向~转 turn to the left; turn left ② east: 山~ areas east of the Mountains ③ the Left: 思想极~ be ultra-left in one's thinking ④ queer; unorthodox; heretical: ~脾气 have a queer temperament ⑤ wrong; incorrect: 你想~了。You're not thinking in the right way. 或 You've got a wrong idea. ⑥ different; contrary; opposite: 意见相~ hold different views; be at variance

【左边】 zuǒbian the left; the left (或 left-hand) side: 房子~有一棵榆树。There's an elm tree on the left of the house.

【左顾右盼】 zuǒgù-yòupàn glance right and left: 他~, 象是在找人。Casting his glances about, he seemed to be looking for somebody.

【左近】 zuǒjìn in the vicinity (或 neighbourhood); nearby: ~有邮局吗? Is there a post office in the vicinity?/ 他就在~。He lives nearby.

【左轮】zuǒlún revolver

【左面】zuǒmiàn the left side; the left-hand side

【左派】zuǒpài ① the Left; the left wing ② Leftist ◇ ~势力 Left forces; forces of the Left

【左倾】zuǒqīng left-leaning; progressive; inclined towards the revolution

【左手】zuǒshǒu ① the left hand ② 见"左首"

【左首】zuǒshǒu the left-hand side: 坐在我的~ sit on my left

【左翼】zuǒyì ① <军> left wing; left flank ② the left wing; the Left ◇ ~分子 Leftist; Left-winger

【左右】zuǒyòu ① the left and right sides: 主席台~，旗子迎风飘扬. Flags are fluttering on both sides of the rostrum./ ~摇摆 vacillate now to the left and now to the right ② 〔用在数目字后面表示概数〕: 八点钟~ around eight o'clock/ 一个月~ a month or so/ 价值十元~. It's worth about $10. ③ master; control; influence: ~局势 be master of the situation/ 为人所~ be controlled by sb.; fall under sb.'s influence ④ those in close attendance; retinue: 屏退~ order one's attendants to clear out ⑤ anyway; anyhow; in any case: 我~闲着没事，就陪你走一趟吧. Anyway I'm free now. Let me go with you.

【左右逢源】zuǒ-yòu féng yuán ① be able to achieve success one way or another ② gain advantage from both sides

【左右开弓】zuǒ-yòu kāi gōng shoot first with one hand, then with the other; shoot first to one side, then to the other; use first one hand and then the other in quick succession

【左右手】zuǒyòushǒu right-hand man; valuable assistant

【左右为难】zuǒ-yòu wéinán in a dilemma; in an awkward predicament

【左…右…】zuǒ…yòu… 〔强调同类行为的反复〕: 左思右想 think from different angles; turn sth. over in one's mind/ 左劝右劝 try again and again to persuade sb./ 左一条清规，右一条戒律 one taboo after another/ 左一趟右一趟地去请他 go several times to invite him

【左证】zuǒzhèng evidence; proof

【左支右绌】zuǒzhī-yòuchù not have enough money to cover the expenses; be unable to cope with a situation; be in straitened circumstances

佐 zuǒ ① assist: ~理 assist sb. with a task ② assistant

【佐餐】zuǒcān be eaten together with rice or bread; go with rice or bread

【佐证】zuǒzhèng evidence; proof

撮 zuǒ <量>〔用于成丛的毛发〕: 一~儿黑毛 a tuft of black hair
另见 cuō

zuò

坐* zuò ① sit; take a seat: 请~! Please sit down. 或 Please be seated./ 进来~. Come in and sit down for a while./ 我们一听说有新任务，就~不住了. When we learnt that we'd been given a new task, we just couldn't sit still any longer. ② travel by (a plane, etc.): ~飞机去法国 go to France by plane ③ (of a building) have its back towards: 这所房子~北朝南. This house faces south. ④ put (a pan, pot, kettle, etc.) on a fire: 把壶~上 put the kettle on (the fire) ⑤ 见"座" zuò① ⑥ (of a building) sink; subside: 这个房子向后~了. This house is beginning to slope backwards. ⑦ (of rifles, guns, etc.) recoil; kick back: 这枝步枪的~劲儿不小. This rifle has a terrible kick.

【坐禅】zuòchán <佛教> sit in meditation

【坐吃山空】zuò chī shān kōng sit idle and eat, and in time your whole fortune will be used up

【坐待】zuòdài sit back and wait

【坐等】zuòděng sit back and wait: ~胜利 sit back waiting for victory with folded arms

【坐地分赃】zuò dì fēn zāng (of a ringleader, criminal, booty harbourer, etc.) take a share of the spoils without participating personally in the robbery

【坐垫】zuòdiàn cushion

【坐观成败】zuò guān chéng-bài wait to see what will come of another's venture; look on coldly; be a mere onlooker

【坐井观天】zuò jǐng guān tiān look at the sky from the bottom of a well — have a very narrow view

【坐具】zuòjù a thing to sit on; seat

【坐牢】zuòláo be in jail; be imprisoned

【坐冷板凳】zuò lěngbǎndèng hold a title without any obligations of office; be kept waiting long for an assignment or an audience with a VIP

【坐立不安】zuò-lì bù ān feel uneasy whether sitting or standing; be fidgety; be on tenterhooks

【坐落】zuòluò (of a building) be situated; be located: 我们工厂~在山脚下. Our factory is located at the foot of a hill.

【坐山观虎斗】zuò shān guān hǔ dòu sit on top of the mountain to watch the tigers fight — watch in safety while others fight, then reap the spoils when both sides are exhausted

【坐失良机】zuò shī liángjī let slip a golden opportunity

【坐视】zuòshì sit by and watch; sit tight and look on: ~不理 sit by idly and remain indifferent/ ~不救 sit back and watch without going to the rescue

【坐收渔利】zuò shōu yúlì reap the spoils of victory without lifting a finger; profit from others' conflict; reap third party profit 又作"坐收渔人之利"

【坐位】zuòwei ① a place to sit; seat: 留几个~ reserve some seats/ 排~ make seating arrangements/ 回到你的~上去. Go back to your place. ② a thing to sit on; seat: 给我搬个~儿来. Get (或 Fetch, Bring) me a seat.

【坐卧不宁】zuò-wò bù níng be unable to sit down or sleep at ease; feel restless; be on tenterhooks 又作"坐卧不安"

【坐席】zuòxí ① take one's seat at a banquet table ② attend a banquet

【坐享其成】zuò xiǎng qí chéng sit idle and enjoy the fruits of others' work; reap where one has not sown

【坐以待毙】zuò yǐ dài bì sit still waiting for death; await one's doom; resign oneself to death

【坐以待旦】zuò yǐ dài dàn sit up and wait for daybreak; remain awake till dawn

【坐月子】zuò yuèzi <口> confinement in childbirth; lying-in

【坐镇】zuòzhèn (of a commander) personally attend to garrison duty; assume personal command

作* zuò ① do; make: ~功课 do one's homework/ ~报告 make a report; deliver a speech/ ~长期打算 plan on a long-term basis ② rise; get up: 日出而~ get up at sunrise/ 枪声大~. Heavy firing broke out. ③ write; compose: ~诗 compose a poem/ ~书一封 write a letter/ ~画 paint a picture ④ writings; work: 遗~ a posthumous work/ 新~ a new work ⑤ pretend; affect: 装模~样 put on an act; behave in an affected way/ 故~怒容 pretend to be angry ⑥ regard as; take sb. or sth. for: 认贼~父 take the foe for one's father/ 把他看~英雄 regard him as a hero ⑦ feel; have: ~冷 feel a chill/ ~痒 have an itch ⑧ act as; be; become: ~口译 act as interpreter
另见 zuō; zuó

【作案】zuò'àn commit a crime or an offence: ~时被捕 be caught in the act; be caught red-handed

【作罢】zuòbà drop; relinquish; give up: 双方意见不一，事情只好~. Since the two sides couldn't agree, the matter had to be dropped.

【作保】zuòbǎo be sb.'s guarantor; go bail for sb.; sponsor sb.

【作弊】zuòbì practise fraud; cheat; indulge in corrupt practices

【作壁上观】zuò bìshàngguān stay behind the breastworks and watch others fight; be an onlooker; sit by and watch

【作别】zuòbié <书> bid farewell; take one's leave: 与亲友~ take leave of one's relatives and friends

【作词】zuòcí write words (for a song): 李红~ words by

Li Hong

【作对】 zuòduì set oneself against; oppose: 他没有理由和你 ~。 He has no reason to oppose you.

【作恶】 zuò'è do evil: ~多端 do all kinds of evil; be steeped in iniquity

【作法】 zuòfǎ ① way of doing things; course of action; practice: 这种~已经很普遍了。 This has become a common practice./ 他现在的~是行不通的。 His present course of action will get him nowhere./ 文章~ technique of writing; art of composition ② 〈旧〉 resort to magic arts

【作法自毙】 zuò fǎ zì bì make a law only to fall foul of it oneself; be hoist with or by one's own petard; get caught in one's own trap

【作废】 zuòfèi become invalid: 宣布~ declare invalid/ 过期~ become invalid after a specified date/ 宣布条约~ declare a treaty null and void

【作风】 zuòfēng style; style of work; way: 工作~ style of work/ ~正派 be honest and upright; have moral integrity

【作梗】 zuògěng obstruct; hinder; create difficulties: 这一定是有人从中~。 Somebody must have been creating difficulties.

【作古】 zuògǔ 〈书〉 〈婉〉 die; pass away

【作怪】 zuòguài do mischief; make trouble: 保守思想在他们头脑中~。 Conservative ideas are doing mischief in their minds.

【作家】 zuòjiā writer ◇ ~协会 the Writers' Union

【作假】 zuòjiǎ ① counterfeit; falsify ② cheat; play tricks ③ behave affectedly

【作奸犯科】 zuòjiān-fànkē violate the law and commit crimes; commit offences against law and discipline

【作茧自缚】 zuò jiǎn zì fù spin a cocoon around oneself — get enmeshed in a web of one's own spinning

【作客】 zuòkè 〈书〉 sojourn: ~他乡 sojourn in a strange land ◇ ~思想 feeling of not belonging; guest mentality

【作乐】 zuòlè make merry; enjoy oneself; have a good time: 寻欢~ seek pleasure and make merry

【作乱】 zuòluàn stage an armed rebellion

【作美】 zuòměi 〔多用于否定〕 (of weather, etc.) help; cooperate; make things easy for sb.: 我们正想去郊游,天公不~,下起雨来了。 We were just thinking of going on an outing when, as Heaven wasn't cooperative, it began to rain.

【作难】 zuònán ① feel embarrassed; feel awkward ② make things difficult for sb.

【作孽】 zuòniè 〈佛家〉 do evil; commit a sin

【作呕】 zuò'ǒu feel sick; feel like vomiting; be overcome by nausea: 令人~的气味 a sickening smell/ 令人~地吹捧 nauseatingly extol

【作陪】 zuòpéi help entertain the guest of honour; be invited along with the chief guest

【作品】 zuòpǐn works (of literature and art)

【作畦】 zuòqí 〈农〉 bedding ◇ ~机 bedder

【作曲】 zuòqǔ write music; compose: 王芳~ music by Wang Fang ◇ ~家 composer

【作势】 zuòshì assume a posture; attitudinize

【作数】 zuòshù count; be valid: 怎么昨天说的, 今天就不~了! How is it that what you said yesterday no longer counts today?/ 那条旧规定不~了。 That old rule doesn't hold any longer.

【作祟】 zuòsuì ① (of ghosts, spirits, etc.) haunt ② make mischief; cause trouble; exercise evil influence: 这都是利己主义~。 All this trouble is caused by selfishness.

【作态】 zuòtài pose; affect; strike an attitude: 我讨厌她的忸怩~。 Her affectations annoy me.

【作威作福】 zuòwēi-zuòfú tyrannically abuse one's power; ride roughshod over others; act like a tyrant: 骑在人民头上~ ride roughshod over the people; lord it over the people

【作为】 zuòwéi ① conduct; deed; action: 从他的~可以看出他的态度。 From his deeds we can discern his attitude. ② accomplish; do sth. worthwhile: 无所~ attempt nothing and accomplish nothing ③ regard; look on as; take for: ~借口 use sth. as an excuse/ ~靠山 look upon sb.

as one's prop ④ as

【作伪】 zuòwěi fake (works of art, cultural relics, etc.); make an imitation; forge

【作文】 zuòwén ① (of students) write a composition ② composition

【作物】 zuòwù crop: 高产~ high-yield crops

【作业】 zuòyè ① school assignment: 做~ do one's assignment/ 家庭~ homework/ 改~ correct students' papers ② work; task; operation; production: 水下~ underwater operation/ 野外~ field work

【作用】 zuòyòng ① act on; affect: 外界事物~于我们的感官, 在我们的头脑中形成印象。 External things act on our sense organs and give rise to impressions in our brains. ② action; function: 化学~ chemical action/ 反~ reaction/ 心脏的~ the function of the heart ③ effect: 惯性~ inertial effect/ 副~ side effect/ 积极~ positive role/ 起带头~ play a vanguard role ④ intention; motive: 他那样说是有他的~的。 He had an axe to grind when he said that. ◇ ~范围 sphere of action/ ~力 effort; applied force

【作战】 zuòzhàn fight; conduct operations; do battle: 英勇~ fight heroically/ 大规模~ conduct large-scale operations ◇ ~部队 combat (或 fighting) troops/ ~部署 operational preparations

【作者】 zuòzhě author; writer: ~不详 by an anonymous author; authorship unknown

【作证】 zuòzhèng testify; give evidence; bear witness: 在法庭上~ bear witness in a lawcourt

【作主】 zuòzhǔ ① decide; take the responsibility for a decision: 我作不了主。 I am not in a position to decide./ 这件事是他自己~办的。 He did it on his own responsibility./ 只能作一半主 have only half the say ② back up; support

【作准】 zuòzhǔn ① 见"作数" ② valid; authentic ◇ ~文本 authentic text

座* zuò ① seat; place: 就~ take one's seat/ 满~ full house/ 请入~。 Please be seated./ 剧场内~无虚席。 The theatre had a full house. ② stand; pedestal; base: 花瓶儿 vase stand/ 塑像~儿 pedestal for a statue ③ 〈天〉 constellation: 大熊~ the Great Bear ④ 〈量〉 〔多用于较大或固定的物体〕: 一~山 a mountain/ 一~桥 a bridge/ 一~铜像 a bronze statue

【座次】 zuòcì order of seats; seating arrangements

【座上客】 zuòshàngkè guest of honour; honoured guest

【座谈】 zuòtán have an informal discussion

【座谈会】 zuòtánhuì forum; symposium; informal discussion: 文艺~ forum on literature and art

【座位】 zuòwèi seat; place: 这个体育馆有一万八千个~。 The stadium seats 18,000.

【座右铭】 zuòyòumíng motto; maxim: "为人民服务"是我们的~。 "Serve the people" is our motto.

【座钟】 zuòzhōng desk clock

做* zuò ① make; produce; manufacture: ~衣服 make clothes/ 这种糖是甜菜~的。 This sugar is made from beets./ 这是你自己~的吗? Did you make this yourself? ② cook; prepare: ~饭 do the cooking; prepare a meal/ ~菜 cook a dish ③ do; act; engage in: ~好事 do good; do a good deed/ ~生意 do business; carry on trade/ ~好本职工作 do one's best at one's own job/ 从点滴的事情~起 start with little things/ 大事~不来,小事又不~ be unable to do big jobs and look down on small ones/ 照正确的意见去~ act upon correct views/ 我们正在~我们的前人从来没有~过的极其光荣伟大的事业。 We are now engaged in a great and most glorious cause, never undertaken by our forefathers. ④ be; become: ~演员 become an actor or actress; go on the stage/ 今天开会由你~主席。 You'll be the chairman at today's meeting. ⑤ write; compose: ~一首诗 write a poem ⑥ hold a family (或 home) celebration: ~生日 celebrate sb.'s birthday ⑦ be used as: 这篇文章可以~教材。 This article may be used as teaching material. ⑧ form or contract a relationship: ~朋友 make friends with/ ~亲 (of two families) become relatives by marriage/ ～对头 set oneself against sb.

【做伴】 zuòbàn keep sb. company

【做到】 zuòdào accomplish; achieve: 说到～ be as good as one's word; abide by one's promise/ 我们应当～增产不增人。 We should manage to increase production without taking on new hands.

【做东】 zuòdōng play the host; host sb.; act as host to sb.

【做法】 zuòfǎ way of doing or making a thing; method of work; practice: 惯常的～ the usual practice; the usual way of doing sth.

【做工】 zuògōng ① do manual work; work: 她在纺织厂～。 She works in a textile mill. ② charge for the making of sth.: 这套衣服～一五十块钱。 The charge for the tailoring of this suit was $50. ③ workmanship: ～精美 of excellent workmanship

【做官】 zuòguān be an official; secure an official position: ～当老爷 act like high officials and overbearing bureaucrats; act as bureaucrats and overlords

【做鬼】 zuòguǐ play tricks; play an underhand game; get up to mischief

【做活儿】 zuòhuór work; do manual labour: 他们一块儿在地里～。 They worked together in the fields.

【做客】 zuòkè be a guest: 我昨天到一个老朋友家里去～。 I was a guest at an old friend's yesterday.

【做礼拜】 zuò lǐbài 〈基督教〉 go to church; be at church

【做媒】 zuòméi be a matchmaker (或 go-between)

【做梦】 zuòmèng ① have a dream; dream: 做恶梦 dream a bad dream; have a nightmare/ 我们～也没有想到有今天。 We never dreamt that we would be as we are today. ② have a pipe dream; daydream: 做美梦 cherish fond hopes/ 他岂不是在～吗? Isn't he just daydreaming?

【做人】 zuòrén ① conduct oneself; behave: 懂得如何～处世 know how to conduct oneself in society ② be an upright person: 重新～ turn over a new leaf

【做声】 zuòshēng make a sound (as when speaking, coughing, etc.): 别～! Keep quiet!

【做事】 zuòshì ① handle affairs; do a deed; act: ② work; have a job: 他在钢铁厂～。 He works in an iron and steel mill.

【做寿】 zuòshòu celebrate the birthday (usu. of elderly people); hold a birthday party

【做文章】 zuò wénzhāng ① write an essay ② make an issue of: 他想抓住这件事情～。 He tried to seize upon the matter and make an issue of it.

【做戏】 zuòxì ① act in a play ② put on a show; playact

【做一天和尚撞一天钟】 zuò yī tiān héshang zhuàng yī tiān zhōng go on tolling the bell as long as one is a monk — do the least that is expected of one; take a passive attitude towards one's work

【做贼心虚】 zuò zéi xīnxū have a guilty conscience: 他们推三阻四,正好暴露了他们～。 In making so many excuses, they revealed their own guilty conscience.

【做主】 zuòzhǔ 见"作主" zuòzhǔ

【做作】 zuòzuo affected; artificial: 他老是那么～。 He's always affected. 或 He's never natural./ 她唱得还可以,就是演得太～。 Her singing is all right, but her acting is overdone.

酢 zuò 见"醋酢" chóuzuò

凿 zuò ① 〈书〉 certain; authentic; irrefutable: 确～ authentic; conclusive ② mortise
另见 zháo

【凿空】 zuòkōng 〈书〉 forced; farfetched: ～之论 farfetched argument

【凿凿】 zuòzuò 〈书〉 true; certain; verified: 言之～ say sth. with certainty/ ～有据 with irrefutable evidence

附　录

汉语拼音方案

Scheme for the Chinese Phonetic Alphabet

一　字母表

字母:	A a	B b	C c	D d	E e	F f	G g
名称:	ㄚ	ㄅㄝ	ㄘㄝ	ㄉㄝ	ㄜ	ㄝㄈ	ㄍㄝ

H h	I i	J j	K k	L l	M m	N n
ㄏㄚ	ㄧ	ㄐㄧㄝ	ㄎㄝ	ㄝㄌ	ㄝㄇ	ㄋㄝ

O o	P p	Q q	R r	S s	T t
ㄛ	ㄆㄝ	ㄑㄧㄡ	ㄚㄦ	ㄝㄙ	ㄊㄝ

U u	V v	W w	X x	Y y	Z z
ㄨ	ㄪㄝ	ㄨㄚ	ㄒㄧ	ㄧㄚ	ㄗㄝ

ｖ只用来拼写外来语、少数民族语言和方言。字母的手写体依照拉丁字母的一般书写习惯。

二　声母表

b	p	m	f		d	t	n	l
ㄅ玻	ㄆ坡	ㄇ摸	ㄈ佛		ㄉ得	ㄊ特	ㄋ讷	ㄌ勒

g	k	h		j	q	x
ㄍ哥	ㄎ科	ㄏ喝		ㄐ基	ㄑ欺	ㄒ希

zh	ch	sh	r		z	c	s
ㄓ知	ㄔ蚩	ㄕ诗	ㄖ日		ㄗ资	ㄘ雌	ㄙ思

在给汉字注音的时候，为了使拼式简短，zh ch sh 可以省作 ẑ ĉ ŝ。

三　韵母表

		i ㄧ 衣	u ㄨ 乌	ü ㄩ 迂
a	ㄚ 啊	ia ㄧㄚ 呀	ua ㄨㄚ 蛙	
o	ㄛ 喔		uo ㄨㄛ 窝	
e	ㄜ 鹅	ie ㄧㄝ 耶		üe ㄩㄝ 约
ai	ㄞ 哀		uai ㄨㄞ 歪	
ei	ㄟ 欸		uei ㄨㄟ 威	
ao	ㄠ 熬	iao ㄧㄠ 腰		

ou ㄡ 欧	iou ㄧㄡ 忧		
an ㄢ 安	ian ㄧㄢ 烟	uan ㄨㄢ 弯	üan ㄩㄢ 冤
en ㄣ 恩	in ㄧㄣ 因	uen ㄨㄣ 温	ün ㄩㄣ 晕
ang ㄤ 昂	iang ㄧㄤ 央	uang ㄨㄤ 汪	
eng ㄥ 亨的韵母	ing ㄧㄥ 英	ueng ㄨㄥ 翁	
ong (ㄨㄥ)轰的韵母	iong ㄩㄥ 雍		

（1）"知、蚩、诗、日、资、雌、思"等七个音节的韵母用 i，即：知、蚩、诗、日、资、雌、思等字拼作 zhi, chi, shi, ri, zi, ci, si。

（2）韵母ㄦ写成 er，用做韵尾的时候写成 r。例如："儿童"拼作 ertong，"花儿"拼作 huar。

（3）韵母ㄝ单用的时候写成 ê。

（4）i 行的韵母，前面没有声母的时候，写成：yi（衣），ya（呀），ye（耶），yao（腰），you（忧），yan（烟），yin（因），yang（央），ying（英），yong（雍）。

u 行的韵母，前面没有声母的时候，写成：wu（乌），wa（蛙），wo（窝），wai（歪），wei（威），wan（弯），wen（温），wang（汪），weng（翁）。

ü 行的韵母，前面没有声母的时候，写成：yu（迂），yue（约），yuan（冤），yun（晕）；ü 上两点省略。

ü 行的韵母跟声母 j, q, x 拼的时候，写成：ju（居），qu（区），xu（虚），ü 上两点也省略；但是跟声母 n, l 拼的时候，仍然写成：nü（女），lü（吕）。

（5）iou, uei, uen 前面加声母的时候，写成：iu, ui, un。例如 niu（牛），gui（归），lun（论）。

（6）在给汉字注音的时候，为了使拼式简短，ng 可以省作 ŋ。

四　声调符号

阴平	阳平	上声	去声
－	／	∨	＼

声调符号标在音节的主要母音上，轻声不标。例如：

妈 mā	麻 má	马 mǎ	骂 mà	吗 ma
（阴平）	（阳平）	（上声）	（去声）	（轻声）

五　隔音符号

a, o, e 开头的音节连接在其他音节后面的时候，如果音节的界限发生混淆，用隔音符号（'）隔开，例如：pi'ao（皮袄）。

汉语拼音和威妥玛式拼法音节对照表

Chinese Phonetic Alphabet and Wade System

汉语拼音	威妥玛拼法	汉语拼音	威妥玛拼法	汉语拼音	威妥玛拼法
a	a	chuang	ch'uang	fo	fo
ai	ai	chui	ch'ui	fou	fou
an	an	chun	ch'un	fu	fu
ang	ang	chuo	ch'o	ga	ka
ao	ao	ci	tz'ŭ(ts'ŭ)	gai	kai
ba	pa	cong	ts'ung	gan	kan
bai	pai	cou	ts'ou	gang	kang
ban	pan	cu	ts'u	gao	kao
bang	pang	cuan	ts'uan	ge	kê,ko
bao	pao	cui	ts'ui	gei	kei
bei	pei	cun	ts'un	gen	kên
ben	pên	cuo	ts'o	geng	kêng
beng	pêng	da	ta	gong	kung
bi	pi	dai	tai	gou	kou
bian	pien	dan	tan	gu	ku
biao	piao	dang	tang	gua	kua
bie	pieh	dao	tao	guai	kuai
bin	pin	de	tê	guan	kuan
bing	ping	deng	têng	guang	kuang
bo	po	di	ti	gui	kui
bu	pu	dian	tien	gun	kun
ca	ts'a	diao	tiao	guo	kuo
cai	ts'ai	die	tieh	ha	ha
can	ts'an	ding	ting	hai	hai
cang	ts'ang	diu	tiu	han	han
cao	ts'ao	dong	tung	hang	hang
ce	ts'ê	dou	tou	hao	hao
cen	ts'ên	du	tu	he	hê,ho
ceng	ts'êng	duan	tuan	hei	hei
cha	ch'a	dui	tui	hen	hên
chai	ch'ai	dun	tun	heng	hêng
chan	ch'an	duo	to	hong	hung
chang	ch'ang	e	ê	hou	hou
chao	ch'ao	ê	ê	hu	hu
che	ch'ê	ei	ei	hua	hua
chen	ch'ên	en	ên	huai	huai
cheng	ch'êng	eng	êng	huan	huan
chi	ch'ih	er	êrh	huang	huang
chong	ch'ung	fa	fa	hui	hui
chou	ch'ou	fan	fan	hun	hun
chu	ch'u	fang	fang	huo	huo
chua	ch'ua	fei	fei	ji	chi
chuai	ch'uai	fen	fên	jia	chia
chuan	ch'uan	feng	fêng	jian	chien

汉语拼音	威妥玛拼法
jiang	chiang
jiao	chiao
jie	chieh
jin	chin
jing	ching
jiong	chiung
jiu	chiu
ju	chü
juan	chüan
jue	chüeh, chüo
jun	chün
ka	k'a
kai	k'ai
kan	k'an
kang	k'ang
kao	k'ao
ke	k'ê, k'o
ken	k'ên
keng	k'êng
kong	k'ung
kou	k'ou
ku	k'u
kua	k'ua
kuai	k'uai
kuan	k'uan
kuang	k'uang
kui	k'ui
kun	k'un
kuo	k'uo
la	la
lai	lai
lan	lan
lang	lang
lao	lao
le	lê, lo
lei	lei
leng	lêng
li	li
lia	lia
lian	lien
liang	liang
liao	liao
lie	lieh
lin	lin
ling	ling
liu	liu
long	lung
lou	lou
lu	lu
lü	lü
luan	luan
lüe	lüeh
	lüo
	lio

汉语拼音	威妥玛拼法
lun	lun
luo	luo
ma	ma
mai	mai
man	man
mang	mang
mao	mao
me	me
mei	mei
men	mên
meng	mêng
mi	mi
mian	mien
miao	miao
mie	mieh
min	min
ming	ming
miu	miu
mo	mo
mou	mou
mu	mu
na	na
nai	nai
nan	nan
nang	nang
nao	nao
ne	nê
nei	nei
nen	nên
neng	nêng
ni	ni
nian	nien
niang	niang
niao	niao
nie	nieh
nin	nin
ning	ning
niu	niu
nong	nung
nou	nou
nu	nu
nü	nü
nuan	nuan
nüe	nüeh
	nüo
	nio
nuo	no
o	o
ou	ou
pa	p'a
pai	p'ai
pan	p'an
pang	p'ang
pao	p'ao

汉语拼音	威妥玛拼法
pei	p'ei
pen	p'ên
peng	p'êng
pi	p'i
pian	p'ien
piao	p'iao
pie	p'ieh
pin	p'in
ping	p'ing
po	p'o
pou	p'ou
pu	p'u
qi	ch'i
qia	ch'ia
qian	ch'ien
qiang	ch'iang
qiao	ch'iao
qie	ch'ieh
qin	ch'in
qing	ch'ing
qiong	ch'iung
qiu	ch'iu
qu	ch'ü
quan	ch'üan
que	ch'üeh
	ch'üo
qun	ch'ün
ran	jan
rang	jang
rao	jao
re	jê
ren	jên
reng	jêng
ri	jih
rong	jung
rou	jou
ru	ju
ruan	juan
rui	jui
run	jun
ruo	jo
sa	sa
sai	sai
san	san
sang	sang
sao	sao
se	sê
sen	sên
seng	sêng
sha	sha
shai	shai
shan	shan
shang	shang
shao	shao

汉语拼音	威妥玛拼法	汉语拼音	威妥玛拼法	汉语拼音	威妥玛拼法
she	shê	tun	t'un	yun	yün
shei	shei	tuo	t'o	za	tsa
shen	shên	wa	wa	zai	tsai
sheng	shêng	wai	wai	zan	tsan
shi	shih	wan	wan	zang	tsang
shou	shou	wang	wang	zao	tsao
shu	shu	wei	wei	ze	tse
shua	shua	wen	wên	zei	tsei
shuai	shuai	weng	wêng	zen	tsên
shuan	shuan	wo	wo	zeng	tsêng
shuang	shuang	wu	wu	zha	cha
shui	shui	xi	hsi	zhai	chai
shun	shun	xia	hsia	zhan	chan
shuo	sho	xian	hsien	zhang	chang
si	sǔ, szǔ, ssǔ	xiang	hsiang	zhao	chao
song	sung	xiao	hsiao	zhe	chê
sou	sou	xie	hsieh	zhei	chei
su	su	xin	hsin	zhen	chên
suan	suan	xing	hsing	zheng	chêng
sui	sui	xiong	hsiung	zhi	chih
sun	sun	xiu	hsiu	zhong	chung
suo	so	xu	hsü	zhou	chou
ta	t'a	xuan	hsüan	zhu	chu
tai	t'ai	xue	hsüeh, hsüo	zhua	chua
tan	t'an	xun	hsün	zhuai	chuai
tang	t'ang	ya	ya	zhuan	chuan
tao	t'ao	yan	yen	zhuang	chuang
te	t'ê	yang	yang	zhui	chui
teng	t'êng	yao	yao	zhun	chun
ti	t'i	ye	yeh	zhuo	cho
tian	t'ien	yi	yi	zi	tzǔ(tsǔ)
tiao	t'iao	yin	yin	zong	tsung
tie	t'ieh	ying	ying	zou	tsou
ting	t'ing	yo	yo	zu	tsu
tong	t'ung	yong	yung	zuan	tsuan
tou	t'ou	you	yu	zui	tsui
tu	t'u	yu	yü	zun	tsun
tuan	t'uan	yuan	yüen	zuo	tso
tui	t'ui	yue	yüeh		

化 学 元 素 表
A Table of Chemical Elements

元 素 名 称			符 号	原子序数	元 素 名 称			符 号	原子序数
中 文	汉语拼音	英 文			中 文	汉语拼音	英 文		
锕	ā	actinium	Ac	89	硅	guī	silicon	Si	14
锿	āi	einsteinium	Es	99	铪	hā	hafnium	Hf	72
砹	ài	astatine	At	85	氦	hài	helium	He	2
钯	bǎ	palladium	Pd	46	(𬭩)	hǎn	hahnium	Ha	105
钡	bèi	barium	Ba	56	钬	huǒ	holmium	Ho	67
铋	bì	bismuth	Bi	83	镓	jiā	gallium	Ga	31
铂	bó	platinum	Pt	78	钾	jiǎ	potassium	K	19
钚	bù	plutonium	Pu	94	金	jīn	gold	Au	79
氮	dàn	nitrogen	N	7	锔	jú	curium	Cm	96
锝	dé	technetium	Tc	43	锎	kāi	californium	Cf	98
镝	dī	dysprosium	Dy	66	钪	kàng	scandium	Sc	21
碲	dì	tellurium	Te	52	氪	kè	krypton	Kr	36
碘	diǎn	iodine	I	53	铼	lái	rhenium	Re	75
铥	diū	thulium	Tm	69	镧	lán	lanthanum	La	57
氡	dōng	radon	Rn	86	铹	láo	lawrencium	Lw	103
锇	é	osmium	Os	76	铑	lǎo	rhodium	Rh	45
铒	ěr	erbium	Er	68	镭	léi	radium	Ra	88
钒	fán	vanadium	V	23	锂	lǐ	lithium	Li	3
钫	fāng	francium	Fr	87	钌	liǎo	ruthenium	Ru	44
镄	fèi	fermium	Fm	100	磷	lín	phosphorus	P	15
氟	fú	fluorine	F	9	硫	liú	sulphur	S	16
钆	gá	gadolinium	Gd	64	(𬬻)	lú	rutherfordium	Rf	104
钙	gài	calcium	Ca	20	镥	lǔ	lutetium	Lu	71
锆	gào	zirconium	Zr	40	铝	lǚ	aluminium	Al	13
镉	gé	cadmium	Cd	48	氯	lù	chlorine	Cl	17
铬	gè	chromium	Cr	24	镅	méi	americium	Am	95
汞	gǒng	mercury	Hg	80	镁	měi	magnesium	Mg	12
钴	gǔ	cobalt	Co	27	钔	mén	mendelevium	Md	101

元　素　名　称			符号	原子序数	元　素　名　称			符号	原子序数
中文	汉语拼音	英　文			中文	汉语拼音	英　文		
锰	měng	manganese	Mn	25	钛	tài	titanium	Ti	22
钼	mù	molybdenum	Mo	42	钽	tǎn	tantalum	Ta	73
镎	ná	neptunium	Np	93	碳	tàn	carbon	C	6
钠	nà	sodium	Na	11	铽	tè	terbium	Tb	65
氖	nǎi	neon	Ne	10	锑	tī	antimony	Sb	51
铌	ní	niobium	Nb	41	铁	tiě	iron	Fe	26
镍	niè	nickel	Ni	28	铜	tóng	copper	Cu	29
钕	nǚ	neodymium	Nd	60	钍	tǔ	thorium	Th	90
锘	nuò	nobelium	No	102	钨	wū	tungsten	W	74
锫	péi	berkelium	Bk	97	硒	xī	selenium	Se	34
硼	péng	boron	B	5	锡	xī	tin	Sn	50
铍	pí	beryllium	Be	4	氙	xiān	xenon	Xe	54
钋	pō	polonium	Po	84	锌	xīn	zinc	Zn	30
钷	pǒ	promethium	Pm	61	溴	xiù	bromine	Br	35
镤	pú	protactinium	Pa	91	氩	yà	argon	Ar	18
镨	pǔ	praseodymium	Pr	59	氧	yǎng	oxygen	O	8
铅	qiān	lead	Pb	82	铱	yī	iridium	Ir	77
氢	qīng	hydrogen	H	1	钇	yǐ	yttrium	Y	39
铷	rú	rubidium	Rb	37	镱	yì	ytterbium	Yb	70
铯	sè	cesium	Cs	55	铟	yīn	indium	In	49
钐	shān	samarium	Sm	62	银	yín	silver	Ag	47
砷	shēn	arsenic	As	33	铀	yóu	uranium	U	92
铈	shì	cerium	Ce	58	铕	yǒu	europium	Eu	63
锶	sī	strontium	Sr	38	锗	zhě	germanium	Ge	32
铊	tā	thallium	Tl	81					

度 量 衡 单 位 简 表

Units of Weights and Measures

市 制 及 进 位 法 Market System	折 合 米 制 Converted to Metric System	折 合 英 制 Converted to British System
长 度 **Length**		
1 分(10 厘)		
1 寸(10 分)	3.3333 厘米 (cm)	1.3123 英寸 (in)
1 尺(10 寸)	0.3333 米 (m)	1.0936 英尺 (ft)
1 丈(10 尺)	3.3333 米 (m)	3.6454 码 (yd)
1 里(150 丈)	500 米 (m)	0.3107 英里 (mi)
面积和地积 **Area**		
1 平方尺(100 平方寸)	0.1111 平方米 (m²)	1.1960 平方英尺 (ft²)
1 平方丈(100 平方尺)	11.1111 平方米 (m²)	13.2888 平方码 (yd²)
1 平方里(22500 平方丈)	0.2500 平方公里 (km²)	0.0965 平方英里 (mi²)
1 分(6 平方丈)	66.6666 平方米 (m²)	79.7328 平方码 (yd²)
1 亩(10 分)	6.6666 公亩 (a)	0.1647 英亩 (ac)
1 顷(100 亩)	6.6666 公顷 (ha)	16.4737 英亩 (ac)
体积和容量 **Volume and Capacity**		
1 立方尺(1000 立方寸)	0.0370 立方米 (m³)	1.3080 立方英尺 (ft³)
1 立方丈(1000 立方尺)	37.0370 立方米 (m³)	1308 立方英尺 (ft³)
1 合	1 分升 (dl)	0.1760 品脱 (pt)
1 升(10 合)	1 升 (l)	0.2200 加仑 (gal)
1 斗(10 升)	10 升 (l)	2.1997 加仑 (gal)
1 石(10 斗)	100 升 (l)	2.7497 蒲式耳 (bu)
质 量 **(重量)** **Mass** **(weight)**		
1 钱	5 克 (g)	0.1764 盎司(常衡) (oz) (av)
1 两(10 钱)	50 克 (g)	1.7637 盎司(常衡) (oz) (av)
1 斤(10 两)	0.5 千克(公斤) (kg)	1.1023 磅(常衡) (lb) (av)
1 担(100 斤)	0.5 公担 (q)	110.2310 磅(常衡) (lb) (av)

天 干 地 支
The Heavenly Stems and Earthly Branches

天干　The Heavenly Stems
甲　the first of the ten Heavenly Stems
乙　the second of the ten Heavenly Stems
丙　the third of the ten Heavenly Stems
丁　the fourth of the ten Heavenly Stems
戊　the fifth of the ten Heavenly Stems
己　the sixth of the ten Heavenly Stems
庚　the seventh of the ten Heavenly Stems
辛　the eighth of the ten Heavenly Stems
壬　the ninth of the ten Heavenly Stems
癸　the last of the ten Heavenly Stems

地支　The Earthly Branches
子　the first of the twelve Earthly Branches
丑　the second of the twelve Earthly Branches
寅　the third of the twelve Earthly Branches
卯　the fourth of the twelve Earthly Branches
辰　the fifth of the twelve Earthly Branches
巳　the sixth of the twelve Earthly Branches
午　the seventh of the twelve Earthly Branches
未　the eighth of the twelve Earthly Branches
申　the ninth of the twelve Earthly Branches
酉　the tenth of the twelve Earthly Branches
戌　the eleventh of the twelve Earthly Branches
亥　the last of the twelve Earthly Branches

二 十 四 节 气
The Twenty-four Solar Terms

立春　the Beginning of Spring (1st solar term)
雨水　Rain Water (2nd solar term)
惊蛰　the Waking of Insects (3rd solar term)
春分　the Spring Equinox (4th solar term)
清明　Pure Brightness (5th solar term)
谷雨　Grain Rain (6th solar term)
立夏　the Beginning of Summer (7th solar term)
小满　Grain Full (8th solar term)
芒种　Grain in Ear (9th solar term)
夏至　the Summer Solstice (10th solar term)
小暑　Slight Heat (11th solar term)
大暑　Great Heat (12th solar term)

立秋　the Beginning of Autumn (13th solar term)
处暑　the Limit of Heat (14th solar term)
白露　White Dew (15th solar term)
秋分　the Autumnal Equinox (16th solar term)
寒露　Cold Dew (17th solar term)
霜降　Frost's Descent (18th solar term)
立冬　the Beginning of Winter (19th solar term)
小雪　Slight Snow (20th solar term)
大雪　Great Snow (21st solar term)
冬至　the Winter Solstice (22nd solar term)
小寒　Slight Cold (23rd solar term)
大寒　Great Cold (24th solar term)